Proceedings
of the
Thirtieth
International Conference
on
Very Large Data Bases
Toronto, Canada
August 31 - September 3, 2004

Editors:
Mario A. Nascimento
M. Tamer Özsu
Donald Kossmann
Renée J. Miller
José A. Blakeley
Berni Schiefer

Ordering Information

Morgan Kaufmann Publishers is the exclusive worldwide distributor for the VLDB proceedings volumes listed below:

	ISBN
2004 Toronto, Canada	0-12-088469-0
2003 Berlin, Germany	0-12-722442-4
2002 Hong Kong, China	1-55860-869-9
1990 Brisbane, Australia	1-55860-149-X
1989 Amsterdam, The Netherlands	1-55860-101-5
1988 Los Angeles, USA	0-934613-75-3
1985 Stockholm, Sweden	0-934613-17-6
1984 Singapore	0-934613-16-8
1983 Florence, Italy	0-934613-15-X

Prices are $50.00 per copy for the 2000 - 2004 volumes, $40.00 per copy for all other volumes.

Shipping is free from Morgan Kaufmann within the U.S on prepaid orders. International shipping costs are $7 per volume via DHL/regular mail combination, or $20.00 per volume via international overnight courier. Morgan Kaufmann accepts credit card payments: the buyer should provide card number, expiration date, and name as it appears on the card for Visa, MasterCard, or American Express credit cards. Morgan Kaufmann also accepts cheque payments in U.S. dollars only; cheques must be drawn on a U.S. bank.

Order from Morgan Kaufmann Publishers

By Mail: Morgan Kaufmann Publishers/Elsevier Science
            Attention: Order Fulfillment Department
            11830 Westline Industrial Drive
            St. Louis, MO 63146-9938

By Phone: 1-800-545-2522 (from within US & Canada) and 1-314-453-7010 (International)
By Fax: 1-800-535-9935 or 1-314-453-7095 (International)
By Email: custserv.mkp@elsevier.com
By Web: http://www.mkp.com

VLDB 2004   ISBN 0-12-722442-4
             ISSN 0730-9317

Copyright © 2004 VLDB Endowment

Conference Officers

General Chair
  John Mylopoulos, University of Toronto, Canada

VLDB Endowment Liaison
  Kyu-Young Whang, KAIST, Korea
Area Coordinator, North America
  Philip Bernstein, Microsoft Research, USA
Area Coordinator, South America
  Alberto Laender, Federal University of Minas Gerais, Brazil
Area Coordinator, Europe, Mideast & Africa
  Avigdor Gal, Technion, Israel
Area Coordinator, Far East & Australia
  Hongjun Lu, Hong Kong University of Science and Technology, China
Publicity and Publications Chair
  Mariano Consens, University of Toronto, Canada
Web Coordinator
  Manuel Kolp, Catholic University of Louvain, Belgium

Technical Program

Technical Program Chair
  M. Tamer Özsu, University of Waterloo, Canada
Core Database Technology Program Chair
  Donald Kossmann, University of Heidelberg, Germany
Infrastructure for Information Systems Program Chair
  Renée J. Miller, University of Toronto, Canada
Industrial and Applications Program Co-Chairs
  José A. Blakeley, Microsoft Corporation, USA
  Berni Schiefer, IBM Laboratories, Canada
Tutorial Program Co-Chairs
  Raymond Ng, University of British Columbia, Canada
  Matthias Jarke, RWTH Aachen, Germany
Panel Program Co-Chairs
  Jarek Gryz, York University, Canada
  Fred Lochovsky, HKUST, Hong Kong
Demonstrations Co-Chairs
  Bettina Kemme, McGill University, Canada
  David Toman, University of Waterloo, Canada
Proceedings Editor
  Mario A. Nascimento, University of Alberta, Canada
eProceedings Editor
  Patricia Rodriguez-Gianolli, University of Toronto, Canada
Workshops Co-Chairs
  Alberto Mendelzon, University of Toronto, Canada
  S. Sudarshan, Indian Institute of Technology, Bombay, India

Local Organization

Local Arrangements Chair
  Nick Koudas, AT&T Labs Research, USA
Exhibits Chair
  H.-Arno Jacobsen, University of Toronto, Canada
Treasurer
  Kenneth Barker, University of Calgary, Canada
Fund Raising Chair
  Victor DiCiccio, University of Waterloo, Canada
Registration Chair
  Grant Weddell, University of Waterloo, Canada

Program Committee Members

Core Database Technology

Karl Aberer, EPFL, Switzerland
Anastassia Ailamaki, CMU, USA
Demet Aksoy, UC Davis, USA
Paul Aoki, PARC, USA
Walid Aref, Purdue University, USA
Remzi Arpaci-Dusseau, University of Wisconsin, USA
Philip Bohannon, Bell Labs, USA
Christian Böhm, University of Munich, Germany
Philippe Bonnet, University of Copenhagen, Denmark
Stephane Bressan, National University of Singapore, Singapore
Mike Carey, BEA Systems, USA
Stefano Ceri, Politecnico Milan, Italy
Surajit Chaudhuri, Microsoft Research, USA
Arbee Chen, National Dong Hwa University, Taiwan
Bobby Cochrane, IBM Almaden, USA
Laurent Daynes, Sun Microsystems, France
Alin Deutsch, UC San Diego, USA
Klaus Dittrich, University of Zurich, USA
Wenfei Fan, Bell Labs, USA
Mary Fernandez, ATT Research, USA
Elena Ferrari, University of Milano, Italy
Daniela Florescu, BEA Systems, USA
Mike Franklin, UC Berkeley, USA
Johann-Christoph Freytag, Humboldt-Universität zu Berlin, Germany
Johannes Gehrke, Cornell University, USA
Goetz Graefe, Microsoft, USA
Ralf Güting, Fernuni Hagen, Germany
Peter Haas, IBM Almaden, USA
Alon Halevy, University of Washington, USA
Sven Helmer University of Mannheim, Germany
Alexander Hinneburg, University of Halle, Germany
Wie Hong, Intel Research Lab, USA
H.V. Jagadish, University of Michigan, USA
Christian S. Jensen, Aalborg University, Denmark
Björn Þór Jónsson, Reykjavík University, Iceland
Alfons Kemper, University of Passau, Germany
Martin Kersten, CWI, Netherlands
Masaru Kitsuregawa, Kitsuregawa Lab, Japan
George Kollios, Boston University, USA
Hank Korth, Lehigh University, USA
Alexandros Labrinidis, University of Pittsburgh, USA
Paul Larson, Microsoft Research, USA
David Lomet, Microsoft Research, USA
Hongjun Lu, HKUST, China
Ioana Manolescu, INRIA Futurs, France
Volker Markl, IBM Almaden, USA
Guido Moerkotte, University of Mannheim, Germany
Mario Nascimento, University of Alberta, Canada
Chris Olston, Carnegie Mellon University, USA
Fatma Ozcan, IBM Almaden, USA
Dimitris Papadias, HKUST, China
Yannis Papakonstantinou, UC San Diego, USA
Krithi Ramamritham, IIT Bombay, India
Tore Risch, Uppsala University, Sweden
Michael Rys, Microsoft, USA
Ken Salem, University of Waterloo, Canada
Sunita Sarawagi, IIT Bombay, India
Oded Shmueli, Technion, Israel
Ioana Stanoi, IBM Almaden, USA
S. Sudarshan, IIT Bombay, India
Kian-Lee Tan, National University of Singapore, Singapore
Dirk van Gucht, University of Indiana, USA
Jun Yang, Duke University, USA
Clement Yu, University of Illinois, USA
Masatoshi Yoshikawa, Nagoya University, Japan
Carlo Zaniolo, UCLA, USA
Justin Zobel, RMIT, Australia

Infrastructure for information Systems

Sihem Amer-Yahia, AT&T Labs Research, USA
Paolo Atzeni, Università di Roma Tre, Italy
Phil Bernstein, Microsoft Research, USA
Leo Bertossi, Carleton University, Canada
Peter Buneman, University of Edinburgh, UK
Tiziana Catarci, Università di Roma La Sapienza, Italy
Soumen Chakrabarti, Indian Institute of Technology, Bombay, India
Mitch Cherniack, Brandeis University, USA
Panos Chrysanthis, University of Pittsburgh, USA
Mariano Consens, University of Waterloo, Canada
Isabel Cruz, University of Illinois at Chicago, USA
Tamraparni Dasu, AT&T Labs-Research, USA
Asuman Dogac, Middle East Tech Univ., Turkey
Lise Getoor, University of Maryland, USA
Dimitrios Gunopulos, University of California, Riverside, USA
Laura Haas, IBM Silicon Valley Lab, USA
Jayant Haritsa, Indian Institute of Science, Bangalore, India
Wynne Hsu, National University of Singapore, Singapore
Carlos Hurtado, Universidad de Chile, Santiago, Chile
Chris Jermaine, University of Florida, USA
Christoph Koch, University of Edinburgh, UK
Nick Koudas, AT&T Labs Research, USA
Hans-Peter Kriegel, University of Munich, Germany
Mong Li Lee, National University of Singapore, Singapore
Maurizio Lenzerini, Università di Roma, La Sapienza, Italy
Qiong Luo, Hong Kong Univ. Science & Tech., Hong Kong, China
Pat Martin, Queens University, Canada
David Maier, Oregon Health & Science University, USA
Alberto Mendelzon, University of Toronto, Canada
Tova Milo, Tel Aviv University, Israel
Jeff Naughton, University of Wisconsin, USA
Raymond Ng, UBC, Canada
Joann Ordille, Avaya, USA
Themis Palpanas, University of California, Riverside, USA
Jignesh Patel, University of Michigan, USA
Lucian Popa, IBM Almaden Research Center, USA
Alexandra Poulovassilis, Univ. of London, UK
Davood Rafiei, University of Alberta, Canada
Raghu Ramakrishnan, University of Wisconsin, USA
Rajeev Rastogi, Bell Labs, USA
Prasan Roy, Indian Institute of Technology, Bombay, India
Elke Rundensteiner, Worcester Polytechnic Institute, USA
Timos Sellis, National Technical Univ. of Athens, Greece
Dennis Shasha, New York University, USA
Kyuseok Shim, Seoul National Univ., South Korea
Eric Simon, Inria Rocquencourt, France
Avi Silberschatz, Yale University, USA
Divesh Srivastava, AT&T Labs Research, USA
Wang-Chiew Tan, University of California, Santa Cruz, USA
David Toman, University of Waterloo, Canada
Alejandro Vaisman, Universidad de Buenos Aires, Argentina
Victor Vianu, Univ. California, San Diego, USA
Limsoon Wong, Institute for Infocomm Research, Singapore

Industrial and Applications Program

Achim Kraiss, SAP, Germany
Alejandro P. Buchmann, Darmstadt University of Technology, Germany
Anand Deshpande, Persistent Systems, India
Anil K. Nori, Microsoft Corporation, USA
Erhard Rahm, Universität Leipzig, Germany
Francois J. Raab, TPC Certified Auditor, USA
Glenn Paulley, iAnywhere Solutions, Canada
Guy M. Lohman, IBM Almaden Research Center, USA
Jacob Slonim, Dalhousie University, Canada
Joseph M. Hellerstein, University of California, Berkeley, USA
Josep-L. Larriba-Pey, Universitat Politècnica de Catalunya, Spain
Michael L. Brodie, Verizon, USA
Srinivasan Seshadri, Strand Genomics, India
Seckin Unlu, Intel Corporation, USA
Sophie Cluet, INRIA, France
Umeshwar Dayal, Hewlett-Packard Laboratories, USA
Vishu Krishnamurthy, Oracle Corporation, USA

Workshop Selection

Nicolas Bruno, Microsoft, USA
Gianni Mecca, Universita della Basilicata, Italy
Alberto Mendelzon, University of Toronto, Canada (co-chair)
Beng Chin Ooi, National University of Singapore
S. Sudarshan, IIT Bombay, India (co-chair)
Janet Wiener, Hewlett-Packard, USA
Peter Wood, Birkbeck College, UK
Calisto Zuzarte, IBM Toronto, Canada

Additional Reviewers

Ashraf Aboulnaga
Shipra Agrawal
Josep Aguilar
Bugrahan Akcay
Juan M. Ale
Mehmet Altinel
Toshiyuki Amagasa
Bernd Amann
Cristiana Amza
Periklis Andritsos
Subramanian Arumugam
Ricardo Baeza-Yates
Dirk Balfanz
Denilson Barbosa
Jonathan L. Beaver
Srikanta Bedathur
Michael Benedikt
Omar Benjelloun
Daniela Berardi
Enrico Bertini
Kevin Beyer
Bodo Billerbeck
Peter Boncz
Roque Bonilla
Ivan T. Bowman
Paul Brown
Luca Cabibbo
Andrea Calì
Diego Calvanese
Adam Cannane
Mario Cannataro
Carlos Castillo
Barbara Catania
Ugur Cetintemel
Chee Yong Chan
Shyamal S. Chandra
Adriane Chapman
Yun Chen
Jin Chen
Krishna Chitrapura
Gregory Cobena
Alex Coman
Valter Crescenzi
Istvan Cseri
Susan Davidson
Giuseppe De Giacomo
Amol Deshpande
Christian Digout
Jens-Peter Dittrich
Alin Dobra

Georges Dupret
Tanmoy Dutta
Takeharu Eda
Said Elnaffar
Maged El-Sayed
Mehmet Erkanar
Mauricio Minnuto Espil
Martin Ester
Daniel J. Farrar
Gabriela Flores
Kei Fujimoto
Michael Gillmann
Jordi Gomez
Sergio Gomez
Zeus Gomez
Ozgür Gülderen
Yavuz Gürcan
Claudio Gutierrez
Marios Hadjieleftheriou
Maria Halkidi
Richard A. Hankins
Lilian Harada
Kenji Hatano
Katia Hayati
Bingsheng He
Marti Hearst
Mauricio Hernandez
Tim Hoad
Vagelis Hristidis
Jen-Chieh Huang
Yoshiharu Ishikawa
Anoop Jain
Dani Jimenez
Shantanu Joshi
Yildirak Kabak
Panagiotis Kalnis
Ibrahim Kamel
Nikos Karayannidis
Norio Katayama
Stefan Katzenbeisser
Dao Dinh Kha
Jerry Kiernan
Stephen Kimani
Hiroyuki Kitagawa
Johannes Klein
Yannis Kotidis
Sailesh Krishnamurthy
A. Kumaran
Zoe Lacroix
Gökce Banu Laleci
Philip Levis
Jessica Lin
Bertram Ludaescher

Richard Chang Luo
Stefan Manegold
Ulrich Marquard
Anurag Maskey
Sergey Melnik
Paolo Merialdo
Laurent Mignet
Gerome Miklau
Diego Milano
Paolo Missier
Jun Miyazaki
Yasuhiro Mori
Andreea E. Munteanu
Victor Muntes
Jussi Myllymaki
Benjamin Nguyen
Andrew Nierman
Baoning Niu
William O'Connell
Tadashi Ohmori
Beng Chin Ooi
Pietro Pala
HweeHwa Pang
Spiros Papadimitriou
Dimitris Papadopoulos
Cris Pedregal-Martin
Michalis Petropoulos
Abhijit Pol
Mercel Pons
Vishy Poosala
Rachel Pottinger
Wendy Powley
Vikram Pudi
Huiming Qu
Mukund Raghavachari
Vijayshankar Raman
Pradeep Ravikumar
Fred Reiss
Flavio Rizzolo
Marie-Christine Rousset
Esther Ryvkina
Yasushi Sakurai
Simonas Saltenis
Parag Sarda
Monica Scannapieco
Ken Sevcik
Mehul Shah
Mohamed A. Sharaf
Christian Shelton
Reza Sherkat
Toshiyuki Shimizu
Siyamed Sinir

Markus Sinnwell
Zhexuan Song
Jessica Staddon
Jan Steffan
Uta Störl
Liying Sui
Sandeep Tata
Igor Tatarinov
Yannis Theodoridis
Wenhu Tian
Mehmet Nuri Tike
Leonardo Tininini
Riccardo Torlone
Panayiotis Tsaparas
Anthony Tung
Alexandra Uitdenbogerd
Seda Ünal
Peter van Oosterom
Alexander Vaschillo
Panos Vassiliadis
Jeroen Vermeulen
Antonino Virgilito
Florian Waas
Jason Wang
Xiaoyu Wang
Amol Wanjari
Leejay Wu
Tzu-Chiang Wu
Vilas Wuwongse
Ping Xia
Yu Xu
Wenwei Xue
John Yiannis
Ali Yildiz
Haruo Yokota
Masatoshi Yoshikawa
Xiaohui Yu
Murat Yükselen
Markos Zaharioudakis
Jenny Zhang
Wei Zhang
Dyce Jing Zhao
Farhana Zulkernine

Premier Sponsor

Platinum Sponsors

ORACLE

Gold Sponsors

Silver Sponsors

Academic Sponsors

University of Waterloo   University of Toronto

VLDB Endowment Board of Trustees

The Very Large Data Base Endowment Inc. (VLDB Endowment) is a non-profit organization incorporated in the USA for the sole purpose of promoting and exchanging scholarly work in database system research and related fields throughout the world. The VLDB Endowment Board of Trustees has 21 members. The election procedure is documented elsewhere. The Board elects an Executive of 4 from among its members (see below). Some of the Trustees have specific responsibilities (as indicated below). All give their time freely to the management of the Endowment and to serving on special sub-committees for specific (time-limited) purposes.

The VLDB Endowment trustees are the legal guardians of its activities and charters. The trustees are elected among internationally distinguished researchers and professionals in the database field who have contributed to the objectives of the Endowment with dedication and distinction, and who are willing to commit their own time and resources. Trustees are elected for a six-year period, with one third up for election by the trustees every two years. The Endowment makes it a policy to spread the composition of the trustees across all continents. The Endowment does not have individuals as its members, nor does it have as members national computer societies; however, it closely co-operates with many international and national computer societies and other organizations.

President
Gerhard Weikum

Vice-President
Laura M. Haas

Secretary
Hongjun Lu

Treasurer
Michael J. Franklin

Members

Amr El Abbadi
Peter M. G. Apers
Paolo Atzeni
Philip A. Bernstein
Elisa Bertino
Peter Buneman
Sophie Cluet
Umeshwar Dayal
Johann Christoph Freytag

H. V. Jagadish
Christian S. Jensen
Renée J. Miller
Shojiro Nishio
Krithi Ramamritham
Raghu Ramakrishnan
Hans-Jörg Schek
Stanley B. Zdonik

Further information on the VLDB Endowment, its role and its activities is available on the World Wide Web at http://www.vldb.org.

Welcome to VLDB'04

The international conference series on Very Large Data Bases (VLDB) was launched in 1975 in Framingham MA, about 20 miles from Boston. The conference was a huge success for its time, attracting almost 100 papers and more than 150 participants.

We have come a long way since then! VLDB conferences attract today hundreds of submissions and participants. Thanks to the efforts of programme committees, authors, and the VLDB Endowment over the years, VLDB conferences constitute today a prestigious scientific forum for the presentation and exchange of research results and practical experiences among members of the international Databases community.

VLDB conference regulars are familiar with Canada. This is the third time the conference is visiting, after Montreal (1980) and Vancouver (1992.) In all three occasions, the Canadian Databases community served as backbone for the organizing and the programme committees. At the same time, as with other years, the committees that put together this conference were international, with participation from all regions of the globe. We are grateful to all members of these committees for their time and efforts. Special thanks to Tamer Özsu, the general programme chair of this year's conference; also Kyu-Young Whang, who served as the VLDB Endowment liaison. Their spirit of cooperation throughout was invaluable.

Of course, the technical programme is not the only attraction of this year's conference. The conference hotel is located in the core downtown area of Toronto, within walking distance of museums, parks, shopping areas and tourist attractions such as the CN tower, the Harbourfront or Lake Ontario. Toronto has been called the most multicultural city in the world and while here, you will have the opportunity to visit neighborhoods that have the distinctive ethnic flavour of parts of the Far East and Europe. More than that, Toronto is a well-run, safe city that visitors enjoy visiting and revisiting.

Welcome to VLDB'04 and Toronto. We hope that you enjoy both the technical programme and the city!!

John Mylopoulos
General Chair, VLDB'04

Foreword from the Program Chairs

Welcome to the 30th International Conference on Very Large Databases (VLDB'04). VLDB Conferences are among the premier database meetings for dissemination of research results and for the exchange of latest ideas in the development and practice of database technology. The program includes two keynote talks, a 10-year award presentation, 81 research papers, 26 industrial papers (9 of which are invited), 5 tutorials, 2 panels and 34 demonstrations. It is a very rich program indeed.

This year we witnessed a significant jump of submissions. There were 504 research and industrial paper submissions, accounting for about 10% increase over last year and about 7% increase over 2002. Consequently the competition was fierce with an acceptance rate of 16.1% for research papers and about 40% for industrial papers.

The first keynote talk is by David Yach, who is the Senior Vice President of Software at Research in Motion (RIM). RIM is a leading designer, manufacturer and marketer of innovative wireless solutions for the worldwide mobile communications market. Their best-known product is the Blackberry line of wireless handhelds. David oversees and manages the development of all lines of software at RIM. In his talk entitled "Databases in a Wireless World", David addresses the emerging environment where "information is stored not only in these central databases, but on a myriad of computers and computer-based devices in addition to the central storage. These range from desktop and laptop computers to PDA's and wireless devices such as cellular phones and BlackBerry's. The combination of large centralized databases with a large number and variety of associated edge databases effectively form a large distributed database, but one where many of the traditional rules and assumptions for distributed databases are no longer true." His talk discusses some of the new and challenging attributes of this new environment, particularly focusing on the challenges of wireless and occasionally connected devices.

Alon Halevy of the University of Washington gives the second keynote talk. His talk is entitled "Structures, Semantics and Statistics" and addresses the issues in integrating data from multiple sources. This is a problem that has occupied our community for a long time and has gained renewed importance with the emergence of the World Wide Web and the very many (and diverse) data sources that have become available on the Web. Alon's talk begins by "highlighting some of the significant recent achievements in the field of data integration, both in research and in industry." He then focuses on the main challenge going forward, namely, large-scale reconciliation of semantic heterogeneity, and on-the-fly information integration.

The ten-year best paper award this year goes to and Ramakrishan Srikant for their paper entitled "Fast Algorithms for Mining Association Rules in Large Databases" that appeared in the 1994 VLDB Conference Proceedings. The Awards Committee (consisting of Masaru Kitsuregawa, Johann-Christoph Freytag, Raghu Ramakrishnan, Anastassia Ailamaki, Paolo Atzeni, and Limsoon Wong and chaired by Tamer Özsu) considered this to be one of the seminal papers in data mining. The paper identifies association rule mining and they discover a very nice property (a priori) that helps in pruning candidates in association rule mining. Rakesh and Ramakrishnan present a talk at this year's conference that focuses on the future of data mining.

The same committee has selected the paper "Model-Driven Data Acquisition in Sensor Networks" by Amol Deshpande, Carlos Guestrin, Samuel R. Madden, Joseph M. Hellerstein, and Wei Hong as the best paper.

The five tutorials that are scheduled cover a wide range of topics including core database topics as well as emerging issues in data management. The tutorials are the following:

- Database Architectures for New Hardware by Anastassia Ailamaki of Carnegie Mellon University
- Security of Shared Data in Large Systems by Arnon Rosenthal of Mitre Corporation and Marianne Winslett of University of Illinois at Urbana Champaign
- Self-Managing Technology in Database Management Systems by Surajit Chaudhuri of Microsoft Research, Benoit Dageville of Oracle, and Guy Lohman of IBM Almaden Research Lab.
- Architectures and Algorithms for Internet-Scale (P2P) Data Management by Joseph M. Hellerstein of University of California, Berkeley and Intel Research Berkeley
- The Continued Saga of DB-IR Integration by Ricardo Baeza-Yates of University of Chile and Mariano Consens of University of Toronto

There are two panels scheduled at this year's conference. The first panel is moderated by Thodoros Topaloglou of MDS Proteomics and is on "Biological Data Management: Research, Practice and Opportunities". The panel focuses on the data management problems that arise in the field of biological research. The panelists (Susan B. Davidson, H. V. Jagadish, Victor M. Markowitz, Evan W. Steeg, and Mike Tyers) discuss the ways in which database researchers can better serve the needs of biomedical research.

The second panel is entitled "Where is Business Intelligence taking today's database systems" and is moderated by William O'Connell of IBM Canada. The panelists are Andy Witkowski, Ramesh Bhashyam, Surajit Chauduri, Nigel Campbell. The panel addresses issues that arise in the production level deployment of business intelligence solutions (e.g., data mining, OLAP) over relational systems.

The technical program is the result of efforts by a large group of people. Three Program Committees were formed along themes (core database, infrastructure for information systems, and industrial and applications) consisting of 137 colleagues, each of whom reviewed about 13 papers. Raymond Ng and Matthias Jarke handled the tutorials, Jarek Gryz and Fred Lochovsky selected the panels, Bettina Kemme and David Toman assembled the demonstrations program. We thank them all for helping us put together an exciting program. We also thank Mario Nascimento for the excellent work he has done in putting together these Proceedings. We, along with Mario, also want to extend our thanks to DCC/UFAM in Brazil for the local support they have provided during the compilation of these proceedings while he was in Brazil.

M. Tamer Özsu
Donald Kossmann
Renée J. Miller
José A. Blakeley
Berni Schiefer

CONTENTS

KEYNOTES

Databases in a Wireless World 3
David Yach (Research in Motion)

Structures, Semantics and Statistics 4
Alon Halevy (Univ. of Washington)

TEN YEAR BEST PAPER AWARD

Whither Data Mining? 9
Rakesh Agrawal and Ramakrishnan Srikant (IBM Almaden)

RESEARCH SESSIONS

Research Session 1: Compression & Indexing

Compressing Large Boolean Matrices using Reordering Techniques 13
David S. Johnson, Shankar Krishnan (AT&T Labs-Research), Jatin Chhugani, Subodh Kumar (John Hopkins Univ.), Suresh Venkatasubramanian (AT&T Labs-Research)

On the Performance of Bitmap Indices for High Cardinality Attributes 24
Kesheng Wu, Ekow Otoo, Arie Shoshani (Lawrence Berkeley National Laboratory)

Practical Suffix Tree Construction 36
Sandeep Tata, Richard A. Hankins, Jignesh M. Patel (Univ. of Michigan)

Research Session 2: XML Views and Schemas

Answering XPath Queries over Networks by Sending Minimal Views 48
Keishi Tajima, Yoshiki Fukui (JAIST)

A Framework for Using Materialized XPath Views in XML Query Processing 60
Andrey Balmin, Fatma Özcan, Kevin Beyer, Roberta Cochrane, Hamid Pirahesh (IBM Almaden)

Schema-Free XQuery 72
Yunyao Li, Cong Yu, H. V. Jagadish (Univ. of Michigan)

Research Session 3: Controlling Access

Client-Based Access Control Management for XML Documents 84
Luc Bouganim (INRIA Rocquencourt), François Dang Ngoc, Philippe Pucheral (PRiSM Laboratory)

Secure XML Publishing without Information Leakage in the Presence of Data Inference 96
Xiaochun Yang (Northeastern Univ.), Chen Li (Univ. of California, Irvine)

Limiting Disclosure in Hippocratic Databases 108
Kristen LeFevre (IBM Almaden and Univ. of Wisconsin-Madison), Rakesh Agrawal (IBM Almaden), Vuk Ercegovac, Raghu Ramakrishnan (Univ. of Wisconsin-Madison), Yirong Xu (IBM Almaden), David DeWitt (Univ. of Wisconsin-Madison)

Research Session 4: XML (I)

On Testing Satisfiability of Tree Pattern Queries 120
Laks V.S. Lakshmanan, Ganesh Ramesh, Hui (Wendy) Wang, Zheng (Jessica) Zhao (Univ. of British Columbia)

Containment of Nested XML Queries 132
Xin Dong, Alon Halevy, Igor Tatarinov (Univ. of Washington)

Efficient XML-to-SQL Query Translation: Where to Add the Intelligence? 144
Rajasekar Krishnamurthy (IBM Almaden), Raghav Kaushik (Microsoft Research), Jeffrey Naughton (Univ. of Wisconsin-Madison)

Taming XPath Queries by Minimizing Wildcard Steps 156
Chee-Yong Chan (National Univ. of Singapore), Wenfei Fan (Univ. of Edinburgh & Bell Laboratories), Yiming Zeng (National Univ. of Singapore)

The NEXT Framework for Logical XQuery Optimization 168
Alin Deutsch, Yannis Papakonstantinou, Yu Xu (Univ. of California, San Diego)

Research Session 5: Stream Mining

Detecting Change in Data Streams 180
Daniel Kifer, Shai Ben-David, Johannes Gehrke (Cornell Univ.)

Stochastic Consistency, and Scalable Pull-Based Caching for Erratic Data Stream Sources 192
Shanzhong Zhu, Chinya V. Ravishankar (Univ. of California, Riverside)

False Positive or False Negative: Mining Frequent Itemsets from High Speed Transactional Data Streams 204
Jeffrey Xu Yu (The Chinese Univ. of Hong Kong), Zhihong Chong (Fudan Univ.), Hongjun Lu (The Hong Kong Univ. of Science and Technology), Aoying Zhou (Fudan Univ.)

Research Session 6: XML (II)

Indexing Temporal XML Documents 216
Alberto Mendelzon, Flavio Rizzolo (Univ. of Toronto), Alejandro Vaisman (Univ. of Buenos Aires)

Schema-based Scheduling of Event Processors and Buffer Minimization for Queries on Structured Data Streams 228
Christoph Koch, Stefanie Scherzinger (Technische Univ. Wien), Nicole Schweikardt (Humboldt Univ. Berlin), Bernhard Stegmaier (Technische Univ. München)

Bloom Histogram: Path Selectivity Estimation for XML Data with Updates 240
Wei Wang (Univ. of NSW), Haifeng Jiang, Hongjun Lu (Hong Kong Univ. of Science and Technology), Jeffrey Xu Yu (The Chinese Univ. of Hong Kong)

Research Session 7: XML and Relations

XQuery on SQL Hosts 252
  Torsten Grust, Sherif Sakr, Jens Teubner (Univ. of Konstanz)

ROX: Relational Over XML 264
  Alan Halverson (Univ. of Wisconsin-Madison), Vanja Josifovski, Guy Lohman, Hamid Pirahesh (IBM Almaden), Mathias Mörschel

From XML View Updates to Relational View Updates: Old Solutions to a New Problem 276
  Vanessa Braganholo (Universidade Federal do Rio Grande do Sul), Susan Davidson (Univ. of Pennsylvania and INRIA-FUTURS), Carlos Heuser (Universidade Federal do Rio Grande do Sul)

Research Session 8: Stream Mining (II)

XWAVE: Optimal and Approximate Extended Wavelets for Streaming Data 288
  Sudipto Guha (Univ. of Pennsylvania), Chulyun Kim, Kyuseok Shim (Seoul National Univ.)

REHIST: Relative Error Histogram Construction Algorithms 300
  Sudipto Guha (Univ. of Pennsylvania), Kyuseok Shim, Jungchul Woo (Seoul National Univ.)

Distributed Set-Expression Cardinality Estimation 312
  Abhinandan Das (Cornell Univ.), Sumit Ganguly (IIT Kanpur), Minos Garofalakis, Rajeev Rastogi (Bell Labs, Lucent Technologies)

Research Session 9: Stream Query Processing

Memory-Limited Execution of Windowed Stream Joins 324
  Utkarsh Srivastava, Jennifer Widom (Stanford Univ.)

Resource Sharing in Continuous Sliding-Window Aggregates 336
  Arvind Arasu, Jennifer Widom (Stanford Univ.)

Remembrance of Streams Past: Overload-Sensitive Management of Archived Streams 348
  Sirish Chandrasekaran, Michael J. Franklin (UC Berkeley)

WIC: A General-Purpose Algorithm for Monitoring Web Information Sources 360
  Sandeep Pandey, Kedar Dhamdhere, Christopher Olston (Carnegie Mellon Univ.)

Research Session 10: Managing Web Information Sources

Similarity Search for Web Services 372
  Xin Dong, Alon Halevy, Jayant Madhavan, Ema Nemes, Jun Zhang (Univ. of Washington)

AWESOME: A Data Warehouse-based System for Adaptive Website Recommendations 384
  Andreas Thor, Erhard Rahm (Univ. of Leipzig)

Accurate and Efficient Crawling for Relevant Websites 396
   Martin Ester (Simon Fraser Univ.), Hans-Peter Kriegel, Matthias Schubert (Univ. of Munich)

Instance-based Schema Matching for Web Databases by Domain-specific Query Probing 408
   Jiying Wang (Hong Kong Univ. of Science and Technology), Ji-Rong Wen (Microsoft Research Asia), Fred Lochovsky (Hong Kong Univ. of Science and Technology), Wei-Ying Ma (Microsoft Research Asia)

Research Session 11: Distributed Search and Query Processing

Computing PageRank in a Distributed Internet Search System 420
   Yuan Wang, David DeWitt (Univ. of Wisconsin-Madison)

Enhancing P2P File-Sharing with an Internet-Scale Query Processor 432
   Boon Thau Loo (UC Berkeley), Joseph M. Hellerstein (UC Berkeley and Intel Research Berkeley), Ryan Huebsch (UC Berkeley), Scott Shenker (UC Berkeley and International Computer Science Institute), Ion Stoica (UC Berkeley)

Online Balancing of Range-Partitioned Data with Applications to Peer-to-Peer Systems 444
   Prasanna Ganesan, Mayank Bawa, Hector Garcia-Molina (Stanford Univ.)

Network-Aware Query Processing for Stream-based Applications 456
   Yanif Ahmad, Uğur Çetintemel (Brown Univ.)

Data Sharing Through Query Translation in Autonomous Sources 468
   Anastasios Kementsietsidis, Marcelo Arenas (Univ. of Toronto)

Research Session 12: Stream Data Management Systems

Linear Road: A Stream Data Management Benchmark 480
   Arvind Arasu (Stanford Univ.), Mitch Cherniack, Eduardo Galvez (Brandeis Univ.), David Maier (Oregon Health & Science Univ.), Anurag Maskey, Esther Ryvkina (Brandeis Univ.), Michael Stonebraker, Richard Tibbetts (MIT)

Query Languages and Data Models for Database Sequences and Data Streams 492
   Yan-Nei Law (UCLA), Haixun Wang (IBM T. J. Watson Res. Ctr.), Carlo Zaniolo (UCLA)

Research Session 13: Auditing

Tamper Detection in Audit Logs 504
   Richard Snodgrass, Shilong Stanley Yao, Christian Collberg (Univ. of Arizona)

Auditing Compliance with a Hippocratic Database 516
   Rakesh Agrawal, Roberto Bayardo, Christos Faloutsos, Jerry Kiernan, Ralf Rantzau, Ramakrishnan Srikant (IBM Almaden)

Research Session 14: Data Warehousing

High-Dimensional OLAP: A Minimal Cubing Approach 528
   Xiaolei Li, Jiawei Han, Hector Gonzalez (Univ. of Illinois at Urbana-Champaign)

The Polynomial Complexity of Fully Materialized Coalesced Cubes 540
    Yannis Sismanis, Nick Roussopoulos (Univ. of Maryland at College Park)

Research Session 15: Link Analysis

Relational Link-based Ranking 552
    Floris Geerts (Univ. of Edinburgh), Heikki Mannila, Evimaria Terzi (Univ. of Helsinki)

ObjectRank: Authority-Based Keyword Search in Databases 564
    Andrey Balmin (IBM Almaden), Vagelis Hristidis (Florida International Univ.), Yannis Papakonstantinou (UC San Diego)

Combating Web Spam with TrustRank 576
    Zoltan Gyöngyi, Hector Garcia-Molina (Stanford Univ.), Jan Pedersen (Yahoo! Inc.)

Research Session 16: Sensors, Grid, Pub/Sub

Model-Driven Data Acquisition in Sensor Networks 588
    Amol Deshpande (UC Berkeley), Carlos Guestrin (Intel Research Berkeley), Samuel Madden (MIT and Intel Research Berkeley), Joseph M. Hellerstein (UC Berkeley and Intel Research Berkeley), Wei Hong (Intel Research Berkeley)

GridDB: A Data-Centric Overlay for Scientific Grids 600
    David Liu, Michael J. Franklin (UC Berkeley)

Towards an Internet-Scale XML Dissemination Service 612
    Yanlei Diao, Shariq Rizvi, Michael J. Franklin (UC Berkeley)

Research Session 17: Top-K Ranking

Efficiency-Quality Tradeoffs for Vector Score Aggregation 624
    Pavan Kumar C. Singitham, Mahathi Mahabhashyam (Stanford Univ.), Prabhakar Raghavan (Verity Inc.)

Merging the Results of Approximate Match Operations 636
    Sudipto Guha (Univ. of Pennsylvania), Nick Koudas, Amit Marathe, Divesh Srivastava (AT&T Labs-Research)

Top-k Query Evaluation with Probabilistic Guarantees 648
    Martin Theobald, Gerhard Weikum, Ralf Schenkel (Max-Planck Institute of Computer Science)

Research Session 18: DBMS Architecture and Performance

STEPS Towards Cache-resident Transaction Processing 660
    Stavros Harizopoulos, Anastassia Ailamaki (Carnegie Mellon Univ.)

Write-Optimized B-Trees 672
    Goetz Graefe (Microsoft Corp.)

Cache-Conscious Radix-Decluster Projections 684
    Stefan Manegold, Peter Boncz, Niels Nes, Martin Kersten (CWI)

Clotho: Decoupling Memory Page Layout from Storage Organization 696
    Minglong Shao, Jiri Schindler, Steven Schlosser, Anastassia Ailamaki, Gregory R. Ganger (Carnegie Mellon Univ.)

Research Session 19: Privacy

Vision Paper: Enabling Privacy for the Paranoids 708
Gagan Aggarwal, Mayank Bawa, Prasanna Ganesan, Hector Garcia-Molina, Krishnaram Kenthapadi, Nina Mishra, Rajeev Motwani, Utkarsh Srivastava, Dilys Thomas, Jennifer Widom, Ying Xu (Stanford Univ.)

A Privacy-Preserving Index for Range Queries 720
Bijit Hore, Sharad Mehrotra, Gene Tsudik (Univ. of California, Irvine)

Resilient Rights Protection for Sensor Streams 732
Radu Sion, Mikhail Atallah, Sunil Prabhakar (Purdue Univ.)

Research Session 20: Nearest Neighbor Search

Reverse kNN Search in Arbitrary Dimensionality 744
Yufei Tao (City Univ. of Hong Kong), Dimitris Papadias, Xiang Lian (Hong Kong Univ. of Science and Technology)

GORDER: An Efficient Method for KNN Join Processing 756
Chenyi Xia (National Univ. of Singapore), Hongjun Lu (Hong Kong Univ. of Science and Technology), Beng Chin Ooi, Jing Hu (National Univ. of Singapore)

Query and Update Efficient B+-Tree Based Indexing of Moving Objects 768
Christian S. Jensen (Aalborg Univ.), Dan Lin, Beng Chin Ooi (National Univ. of Singapore)

Research Session 21: Similarity Search and Applications

Indexing Large Human-Motion Databases... 780
Eamonn Keogh, Themistoklis Palpanas, Victor B. Zordan, Dimitrios Gunopulos (Univ. of California, Riverside), Marc Cardle (Univ. of Cambridge)

On The Marriage of Lp-norms and Edit Distance 792
Lei Chen (Univ. of Waterloo), Raymond Ng (Univ. of British Columbia)

Approximate NN queries on Streams with Guaranteed Error/performance Bounds 804
Nick Koudas (AT&T Labs-Research), Beng Chin Ooi, Kian-Lee Tan, Rui Zhang (National Univ. of Singapore)

Object Fusion in Geographic Information Systems 816
Catriel Beeri, Yaron Kanza, Eliyahu Safra, Yehoshua Sagiv (The Hebrew Univ.)

Maintenance of Spatial Semijoin Queries on Moving Points 828
Glenn Iwerks, Hanan Samet (Univ. of Maryland at College Park), Kenneth Smith (MITRE Corp.)

Voronoi-Based K Nearest Neighbor Search for Spatial Network Databases 840
Mohammad R. Kolahdouzan, Cyrus Shahabi (Univ. of Southern California)

A Framework for Projected Clustering of High Dimensional Data Streams 852
Charu Aggarwal (T.J. Watson Res. Ctr.), Jiawei Han, Jianyong Wang (Univ. of Illinois at Urbana-Champaign), Philip Yu (T.J. Watson Res. Ctr.)

Research Session 22: Query Processing

Efficient Query Evaluation on Probabilistic Databases 864
    Nilesh Dalvi, Dan Suciu (Univ. of Washington)

Efficient Indexing Methods for Probabilistic Threshold Queries over Uncertain Data 876
    Reynold Cheng, Yuni Xia, Sunil Prabhakar, Rahul Shah, Jeffrey S. Vitter (Purdue Univ.)

Probabilistic Ranking of Database Query Results 888
    Surajit Chaudhuri, Gautam Das (Microsoft Research), Vagelis Hristidis (Florida International Univ.), Gerhard Weikum (MPI Informatik)

Research Session 23: Novel Models

An Annotation Management System for Relational Databases 900
    Deepavali Bhagwat, Laura Chiticariu, Wang-Chiew Tan, Gaurav Vijayvargiya (Univ. of California, Santa Cruz)

Symmetric Relations and Cardinality-Bounded Multisets in Database Systems 912
    Kenneth Ross, Julia Stoyanovich (Columbia Univ.)

Algebraic Manipulation of Scientific Datasets 924
    Bill Howe, David Maier (Oregon Health & Science Univ.)

Research Session 24: Query Processing and Optimization

Multi-objective Query Processing for Database Systems 936
    Wolf-Tilo Balke (Univ. of California, Berkeley), Ulrich Güntzer (Univ. of Tübingen)

Lifting the Burden of History from Adaptive Query Processing 948
    Amol Deshpande (Univ. of California, Berkeley), Joseph M. Hellerstein (Univ. of California, Berkeley and Intel Research, Berkeley)

A Combined Framework for Grouping and Order Optimization 960
    Thomas Neumann, Guido Moerkotte (Univ. of Mannheim)

The Case for Precision Sharing 972
    Sailesh Krishnamurthy, Michael J. Franklin (UC Berkeley), Joseph M. Hellerstein (UC Berkeley and Intel Research Berkeley), Garrett Jacobson (UC Berkeley)

INDUSTRIAL AND APPLICATIONS SESSIONS

Industrial Session 1: Novel SQL Extensions

Returning Modified Rows - SELECT Statements with Side Effects 987
    Andreas Behm, Serge Rielau, Richard Swagerman (IBM Toronto Lab)

PIVOT and UNPIVOT: Optimization and Execution Strategies in an RDBMS 998
    Conor Cunningham, Cesar Galindo-Legaria, Goetz Graefe (Microsoft Corp.)

A Multi-Purpose Implementation of Mandatory Access Control in Relational Database Management Systems 1010
    Walid Rjaibi, Paul Bird (IBM Toronto Lab)

Industrial Session 2: New DBMS Architectures and Performance

Hardware Acceleration in Commercial Databases: A Case Study of Spatial Operations 1021
  Nagender Bandi (Univ. of California, Santa Barbara), Chengyu Sun (California State Univ., Los Angeles), Divyakant Agrawal, Amr El Abbadi (Univ. of California, Santa Barbara)

P*TIME: Highly Scalable OLTP DBMS for Managing Update-Intensive Stream Workload 1033
  Sang K. Cha (Transact In Memory, Inc.), Changbin Song (Seoul National Univ.)

Generating Thousand Benchmark Queries in Seconds 1045
  Meikel Poess (Oracle Corp.), John M. Stephens, Jr. (Gradient Systems)

Industrial Session 3: Semantic Query Approaches

Supporting Ontology-based Semantic Matching in RDBMS 1054
  Souripriya Das, Eugene Chong, George Eadon, Jagannathan Srinivasan (Oracle Corp.)

BioPatentMiner: An Information Retrieval System for BioMedical Patents 1066
  Sougata Mukherjea, Bhuvan Bamba (IBM India Research Lab)

Flexible String Matching Against Large Databases in Practice 1078
  Nick Koudas, Amit Marathe, Divesh Srivastava (AT&T Labs–Research)

Industrial Session 4: Automatic Tuning in Commercial DBMSs

DB2 Design Advisor: Integrated Automatic Physical Database Design 1087
  Daniel Zilio (IBM Toronto Lab), Jun Rao (IBM Almaden), Sam Lightstone (IBM Toronto Lab), Guy Lohman (IBM Almaden), Adam Storm, Christian Garcia-Arellano (IBM Toronto Lab), Scott Fadden (IBM Portland)

Automatic SQL Tuning in Oracle 10g 1098
  Benoit Dageville, Dinesh Das, Karl Dias, Khaled Yagoub, Mohamed Zait, Mohamed Ziauddin (Oracle Corp.)

Database Tuning Advisor for Microsoft SQL Server 2005 1110
  Sanjay Agrawal, Surajit Chaudhuri, Lubor Kollar, Arun Marathe, Vivek Narasayya, Manoj Syamala (Microsoft Corp.)

Industrial Session 5: XML Implementations, Automatic Physical Design and Indexing

Query Rewrite for XML in Oracle XML DB 1122
  Muralidhar Krishnaprasad, Zhen Hua Liu, Anand Manikutty, James W. Warner, Vikas Arora, Susan Kotsovolos (Oracle Corp.)

Indexing XML Data Stored in a Relational Database 1134
  Shankar Pal, Istvan Cseri, Oliver Seeliger, Gideon Schaller, Leo Giakoumakis, Vasili Zolotov (Microsoft Corp.)

Automated Statistics Collection in DB2 UDB 1146
> *Ashraf Aboulnaga, Peter Haas (IBM Almaden), Mokhtar Kandil, Sam Lightstone (IBM Toronto Lab), Guy Lohman, Volker Markl (IBM Almaden), Ivan Popivanov (IBM Toronto Lab), Vijayshankar Raman (IBM Almaden)*

High Performance Index Build Algorithms for Intranet Search Engines 1158
> *Marcus Fontoura, Eugene Shekita, Jason Zien, Sridhar Rajagopalan, Andreas Neumann (IBM Almaden)*

Automated Design of Multi-Dimensional Clustering Tables in Relational Databases 1170
> *Sam Lightstone (IBM Toronto Laboratory), Bishwaranjan Bhattacharjee (IBM T.J. Watson Res. Ctr.)*

Industrial Session 6: Data Management with RFIDs and Ease of Use

Integrating Automatic Data Acquisition with Business Processes - Experiences with SAP's Auto-ID Infrastructure (invited) 1182
> *Christof Bornhövd, Tao Lin, Stephan Haller, Joachim Schaper (SAP Research)*

Managing RFID Data (invited)... 1189
> *Sudarshan S. Chawathe (Univ. of Maryland), Venkat Krishnamurthy, Sridhar Ramachandran (OAT Systems), and Sanjay Sarma (MIT)*

Production Database Systems: Making Them Easy is Hard Work (invited) 1196
> *David Campbell (Microsoft Corp.)*

Industrial Session 7: Data Management Challenges in Life Sciences and Email Systems

Managing Data from High-Throughput Genomic Processing: A Case Study (invited) 1198
> *Toby Bloom, Ted Sharpe (Broad Institute of MIT and Harvard)*

Database Challenges in the Integration of Biomedical Data Sets (invited) 1202
> *Rakesh Nagarajan (Washington Univ.), Mushtaq Ahmed, Aditya Phatak (Persistent Systems Pvt. Ltd.)*

The Bloomba Personal Content Database (invited).. 1214
> *Raymie Stata (Stata Labs and UC Santa Cruz), Patrick Hunt (Stata Labs), Thiruvalluvan M. G. (iSoftTech Ltd.)*

Industrial Session 8: Issues in Data Warehousing

Trends in Data Warehousing: A Practitioner's View (invited).. 1224
> *William O'Connell (IBM Toronto Lab)*

Technology Challenges in a Data Warehouse (invited).. 1225
> *Ramesh Bhashyam (NCR Corporation)*

Sybase IQ Multiplex - Designed For Analytics (invited) 1227
> *Roger MacNicol, Blaine French (Sybase Inc.)*

PANEL SESSIONS

Biological Data Management: Research, Practice and Opportunities 1233
Moderator: Thodoros Topaloglou (MDS Proteomics). Panelists: Susan B. Davidson (Univ. of Pennsylvania), H. V. Jagadish (Univ. of Michigan), Victor M. Markowitz (Lawrence Berkeley National Laboratory), and Evan W. Steeg (Consultant), Mike Tyers (Univ. of Toronto).

Where is Business Intelligence taking today's Database Systems? 1237
Moderator: William O'Connell (IBM Toronto Lab). Panelists: Andy Witkowski (Oracle Corp.), Ramesh Bhashyam (NCR – Teradata), Surajit Chauduri (Microsoft Corp.)

TUTORIAL SESSIONS

Database Architecture for New Hardware.. 1241
Anastassia Ailamaki (Carnegie Mellon Univ.)

Security of Shared Data in Large Systems: State of the Art and Research Directions 1242
Arnon Rosenthal (MITRE Corp.), Marianne Winslett (Univ. of Illinois at Urbana-Champaign)

Self-Managing Technology in Database Management Systems 1243
Surajit Chaudhuri (Microsoft Research), Benoit Dageville (Oracle Corp.), Guy Lohman (IBM Almaden)

Architectures and Algorithms for Internet-Scale (P2P) Data Management........................ 1244
Joseph M. Hellerstein (UC Berkeley and Intel Research Berkeley)

The Continued Saga of DB-IR Integration 1245
Ricardo Baeza-Yates (Univ. of Chile) and Mariano Consens (Univ. of Toronto)

DEMONSTRATIONS

GPX: Interactive Mining of Gene Expression Data 1249
Daxin Jiang, Jian Pei, Aidong Zhang (State Univ. of New York at Buffalo)

Computing Frequent Itemsets Inside Oracle 10G... 1253
Wei Li, Ari Mozes (Oracle Corp)

StreamMiner: A Classifier Ensemble-based Engine to Mine Concept-drifting Data Streams.. 1257
Wei Fan (IBM T.J. Watson Res. Ctr.)

Semantic Mining and Analysis of Gene Expression Data 1261
Xin Xu, Gao Cong, Beng Chin Ooi, Kian-Lee Tan, Anthony K.H.Tung (National Univ. of Singapore)

HOS-Miner: A System for Detecting Outlying Subspaces of High-dimensional Data 1265
Ji Zhang, Meng Lou (Univ. of Toronto), Tok Wang Ling (National Univ. of Singapore), Hai Wang (Univ. of Toronto)

VizTree: a Tool for Visually Mining and Monitoring Massive Time Series Databases 1269
   Jessica Lin, Eamonn Keogh, Stefano Lonardi (Univ. of California, Riverside), Jeffrey P. Lankford, Daonna M. Nystrom (The Aerospace Corporation)

An Electronic Patient Record "on Steroids": Distributed, Peer-to-Peer, Secure and Privacy-conscious 1273
   Serge Abiteboul (INRIA), Bogdan Alexe (Bell Labs, Lucent Technologies), Omar Benjelloun, Bogdan Cautis (INRIA), Irini Fundulaki (Bell Labs, Lucent Technologies), Tova Milo (INRIA, France, and Tel-Aviv Univ.), Arnaud Sahuguet (Tel-Aviv Univ.)

Queries and Updates in the coDB Peer to Peer Database System 1277
   Enrico Franconi (Free Univ. of Bozen-Bolzano), Gabriel Kuper (Univ. of Trento), Andrei Lopatenko (Free Univ. of Bozen-Bolzano and Univ. of Manchester), Ilya Zaihrayeu (Univ. of Trento)

A-ToPSS: A Publish/Subscribe System Supporting Imperfect Information Processing 1281
   Haifeng Liu, Hans-Arno Jacobsen (Univ. of Toronto)

Efficient Constraint Processing for Highly Personalized Location Based Services 1285
   Zhengdao Xu, Hans-Arno Jacobsen (Univ. of Toronto)

LH*RS: A Highly Available Distributed Data Storage 1289
   Witold Litwin, Rim Moussa (Université Paris Dauphine), Thomas Schwarz (Santa Clara Univ.)

Semantic Query Optimization in an Automata-Algebra Combined XQuery Engine over XML Streams 1293
   Hong Su, Elke A. Rundensteiner, Murali Mani (Worcester Polytechnic Institute)

ShreX: Managing XML Documents in Relational Databases 1297
   Fang Du (Oregon Health & Science Univ), Sihem Amer-Yahia (AT&T Labs-Research), Juliana Freire (Oregon Health & Science Univ)

A Uniform System for Publishing and Maintaining XML Data 1301
   Byron Choi (Univ. of Pennsylvania), Wenfei Fan (Univ. of Edinburgh and Bell Laboratories), Xibei Jia (Univ. of Edinburgh), Arek Kasprzyk (European Bioinformatics Institute)

An Injection of Tree Awareness: Adding Staircase Join to PostgreSQL 1305
   Sabine Mayer, Torsten Grust (Univ. of Konstanz), Maurice van Keulen (Univ. of Twente), Jens Teubner (Univ. of Konstanz)

FluXQuery: An Optimizing XQuery Processor for Streaming XML Data 1309
   Christoph Koch, Stephanie Scherzinger (Technische Univ. Wien), Nicole Schweikardt (Humboldt Univ. Berlin), Bernhard Stegmaier (Technische Univ. München)

COMPASS: A Concept-based Web Search Engine for HTML, XML, and Deep Web Data 1313
   Jens Graupmann, Michael Biwer, Christian Zimmer, Patrick Zimmer, Matthias Bender, Martin Theobald, Gerhard Weikum (Max-Planck Institute for Computer Science)

Discovering and Ranking Semantic Associations over a Large RDF Metabase 1317
  Chris Halaschek, Boanerges Aleman-Meza, I. Budak Arpinar, Amit P. Sheth (Univ. of Georgia)

An Automatic Data Grabber for Large Web Sites 1321
  Valter Crescenzi (Univ. of Roma), Giansalvatore Mecca (Univ. of Potenza), Paolo Merialdo , Paolo Missier (Univ. of Roma)

WS-CatalogNet: An Infrastructure for Creating, Peering, and Querying e-Catalog Communities 1325
  Karim Baina, Boualem Benatallah, Hye-young Paik (Univ. of New South Wales), Farouk Toumani, Christophe Rey (ISIMA), Agnieszka Rutkowska, Bryan Harianto (Univ. of New South Wales)

Trust-Serv: A Lightweight Trust Negotiation Service 1329
  Halvard Skogsrud, Boualem Benatallah (Univ. of New South Wales), Fabio Casati (Hewlett-Packard Labs), Manh Q. Dinh (Univ. of New South Wales)

Green Query Optimization: Taming Query Optimization Overheads through Plan Recycling 1333
  Parag Sarda, Jayant R. Haritsa (Indian Institute of Science)

Progressive Optimization in Action 1337
  Vijayshankar Raman, Volker Markl, David Simmen, Guy Lohman, Hamid Pirahesh (IBM Almaden)

CORDS: Automatic Generation of Correlation Statistics in DB2....................................... 1341
  Ihab F. Ilyas (Univ. of Waterloo), Volker Markl, Peter J. Haas, Paul G. Brown, Ashraf Aboulnaga (IBM Almaden)

CHICAGO: A Test and Evaluation Environment for Coarse-Grained Optimization 1345
  Tobias Kraft, Holger Schwarz (Univ. of Stuttgart)

SVT: Schema Validation Tool for Microsoft SQL-Server 1349
  Ernest Teniente, Carles Farré, Toni Urpí, Carlos Beltrán, David Gañán (Univ. of Catalunya)

CAPE: Continuous Query Engine with Heterogeneous-Grained Adaptivity......................... 1353
  Elke A. Rundensteiner, Luping Ding, Timothy Sutherland, Yali Zhu, Brad Pielech, Nishant Mehta (Worcester Institute of Technology)

HiFi: A Unified Architecture for High Fan-in Systems 1357
  Owen Cooper, Anil Edakkunni, Michael J. Franklin (UC Berkeley), Wei Hong (Intel Research Berkeley), Shawn R. Jeffery, Sailesh Krishnamurthy, Fredrick Reiss, Shariq Rizvi, Eugene Wu (UC Berkeley)

An Integration Framework for Sensor Networks and Data Stream Management Systems 1361
  Daniel J. Abadi, Wolfgang Lindner, Samuel Madden (MIT), Jörg Schuler (Tufts Univ.)

QStream: Deterministic Querying of Data Streams 1365
  Sven Schmidt, Henrike Berthold, Wolfgang Lehner (Dresden Univ. of Technology)

AIDA: an Adaptive Immersive Data Analyzer 1369
Mehdi Sharifzadeh, Cyrus Shahabi, Bahareh Navai, Farid Parvini, Albert A. Rizzo (Univ. of Southern California)

BilVideo Video Database Management System 1373
Özgür Ulusoy, Uğur Güdükbay, Mehmet Emin Dönderler, Ediz Şaykol, Cemil Alper (Bilkent Univ.)

PLACE: A Query Processor for Handling Real-time Spatio-temporal Data Streams 1377
Mohamed F. Mokbel, Xiaopeng Xiong, Walid G. Aref, Susanne E. Hambrusch, Sunil Prabhakar, Moustafa A. Hammad (Purdue Univ.)

KEYNOTES

Databases in a Wireless World

David Yach

Research in Motion
Waterloo, Ontario
Canada N2L 3W8

Abstract

The traditional view of distributed databases is based on a number of database servers with regular communication. Today information is stored not only in these central databases, but on a myriad of computers and computer-based devices in addition to the central storage. These range from desktop and laptop computers to PDA's and wireless devices such as cellular phones and BlackBerry's. The combination of large centralized databases with a large number and variety of associated edge databases effectively form a large distributed database, but one where many of the traditional rules and assumptions for distributed databases are no longer true.

This keynote will discuss some of the new and challenging attributes of this new environment, particularly focusing on the challenges of wireless and occasionally connected devices. It will look at the new constraints, how these impact the traditional distributed database model, the techniques and heuristics being used to work within these constraints, and identify the potential areas where future research might help tackle these difficult issues.

Permission to copy without fee all or part of this material is granted provided that the copies are not made or distributed for direct commercial advantage, the VLDB copyright notice and the title of the publication and its date appear, and notice is given that copying is by permission of the Very Large Data Base Endowment. To copy otherwise, or to republish, requires a fee and/or special permission from the Endowment.

Proceedings of the 30th VLDB Conference, Toronto, Canada, 2004

Structures, Semantics and Statistics

Alon Y. Halevy
University of Washington, Seattle
alon@cs.washington.edu

Abstract

At a fundamental level, the key challenge in data integration is to reconcile the semantics of disparate data sets, each expressed with a different database structure. I argue that computing statistics over a large number of structures offers a powerful methodology for producing *semantic mappings*, the expressions that specify such reconciliation. In essence, the statistics offer hints about the semantics of the symbols in the structures, thereby enabling the detection of semantically similar concepts. The same methodology can be applied to several other data management tasks that involve search in a space of complex structures and in enabling the next-generation *on-the-fly* data integration systems.

Data Integration

Data integration is a pervasive challenge faced in data management applications that need to query across *multiple* data sources. Data integration is crucial in large enterprises that own a multitude of data sources, for progress in large-scale scientific projects, where data sets are being produced independently by multiple researchers, for better cooperation among government agencies, each with their own data sources, and in searching the *deep web*, the part of the web that is hidden behind web forms. The emergence of XML and web services as technologies for sharing data and for accessing remote data sources have further fueled the desire of organizations to share data. The many applications of data integration have led to a very fruitful line of research in the Database and Artificial Intelligence Communities, and recently to a budding industry, known as Enterprise Information Integration (EII) [1].

Permission to copy without fee all or part of this material is granted provided that the copies are not made or distributed for direct commercial advantage, the VLDB copyright notice and the title of the publication and its date appear, and notice is given that copying is by permission of the Very Large Data Base Endowment. To copy otherwise, or to republish, requires a fee and/or special permission from the Endowment.

**Proceedings of the 30th VLDB Conference,
Toronto, Canada, 2004**

Structures and Semantics

There are many factors that make data integration a hard problem, not all of which are purely technical. Some of these include query processing across multiple autonomous systems, processing XML documents (and other semi-structured data) streaming from the network, managing data ownership and privacy across organizational boundaries, and in some cases, even capturing or locating the data needed for particular applications, or transforming it into machine processable form. However, the most notable and unique challenge in data integration is reconciling the semantic heterogeneity of the sources being integrated.

The fundamental reason that makes semantic heterogeneity so hard is that the data sets were developed independently, and therefore varying structures were used to represent the same or overlapping concepts. By structures, I mean both the choice of data model (relational, XML, object-oriented, ontology formalism) and the particular choices made in designing the schema (naming of relations, attributes or tags, choices of data types, decomposition, and nesting structure). The presence of a variety of structures is unavoidable both because humans think differently from one another and because the applications these data sets were designed for have different needs. Efforts to circumvent this problem by imposing standardized schemas have met limited success at best.

As a first step toward reconciling semantic heterogeneity, researchers developed languages for describing *semantic mappings*, expressions that relate the semantics of data expressed in different structures [6, 9, 15]. These languages typically relate different structures with a variety of query and constraint expressions. With these languages, researchers have developed algorithms for *query reformulation*, which translate a query posed over one schema into a set of queries over other schemas. More generally, recent research on *model management* investigates a general algebra for manipulating structures (called models) and mappings between them [2, 13]. The algebra includes operations such as merging and applying transformations on models, and for composing and inverting mappings.

Structures and Statistics

Given the languages for expressing semantic mappings between disparate structures, the bottleneck is to *create* and *maintain* these mappings. Writing these mappings is very tedious and error prone, and often very repetitive. In fact, in many integration projects, more than half of the resources are spent on these tasks. Clearly, completely automating the creation of semantic mappings is unlikely. Hence, the focus of research has been on reducing the human effort needed in the process (see [14] for a recent survey).

This is where statistics come into play. A powerful approach for discovering semantic mappings is based on analyzing a large number of structures and mappings in a particular domain. The intuition behind this approach is that statistics computed over large number of structures can be used to provide *hints* about the semantics of the symbols used in these structures. Therefore, these statistics can be leveraged to predict when two symbols, from disparate structures, are meant to represent the same domain concept.

In a sense, the goal of this approach is to mirror the success of statistical analysis of large corpora of texts in the field of Information Retrieval (IR) and of the recent significant advances made in the field of Natural Language Processing by analyzing large corpora of annotated sentences [12]. However, the analogy to these fields also highlights the unique challenges we face here.

In the IR context, text documents typically contain a significant amount of information and high level of redundancy. Hence, IR techniques can be effective by abstracting a document as a bag of words. By contrast, in our context, schema descriptions are very terse and the underlying semantics are very rich. Hence, the bag of words abstraction does not suffice.

As a consequence, to exploit a corpus of schemas and mappings, we need statistics that provide hints about deeper domain concepts and at a finer granularity. The following are a few examples:

- **Domain concepts and their representational variations:** As a first step, we can analyze a corpus to identify the main concepts in the domain. For example, in a corpus of book inventory schemas, we may identify the concept of book and warehouse and a cluster of price-related elements. Even more importantly, we will discover *variations* on how these concepts are represented. The variations may differ on naming of schema elements, grouping attributes into tables or the granularity of modeling a particular concept. Knowledge of these variations will be leveraged when we match two schemas in the domain.

- **Relationships between concepts:** Given a set of concepts, we can discover relationships between them, and the ways in which these relationships are manifested in the representation. For example, we can find that the Books table typically includes an ISBN column and a foreign key into an Availability table, but that ISBN never appears in a Warehouse table. These relationships are useful in order to prune candidate schema matches that appear less likely. They can also be used to build a system that provides advice in *designing* new schemas.

- **Domain constraints:** We can leverage a corpus to find integrity constraints on the domain and its representations. For example, we can observe that ISBN is a foreign key into multiple tables involving books, and hence possibly an identifier for books, or discover likely data types for certain fields (e.g., address, price). Constraints may have to do with *ordering* of attributes. For example, in a corpus of web forms about cars for sale, we may discover that the make attribute is always placed before the model and price attribute, but occurs after the new/used attribute.

  Typically, constraints we discover in this way are *soft constraints*, in the sense that they are sometimes violated, but can still be taken as rules of thumb about the domain. Therefore, they are extremely useful in resolving ambiguous situations, such as selecting among several candidate schema matches [3, 11].

It is important to note that in all of these examples there is a close interplay between properties of the underlying domain (e.g., books, warehouses and their properties) and of the representations of the domain (e.g., the particular relational structures in schemas). In fact, this interplay is the reason this technique is so powerful.

Several works have already applied this approach in various contexts [3, 5, 7, 8, 10]. Doan et al. [3] address the problem of matching schemas of data sources to a single mediated schema. [3] uses Machine Learning techniques to compute models of the elements in the mediated schema from a set of manually provided mappings. These models are then used to recognize the mediated schema elements in the schemas of unmapped data sources. He and Chang [7] generate a mediated schema for a domain based on analyzing a corpus of web forms in that domain. Madhavan et al. [11] leverage a corpus of schemas and mappings to match between two *unseen* schemas. In doing so, [11] learns from the corpus models for elements of the domain and constraints on the domain.

Another application of this paradigm is search for web services [4]: locating web services (or operations within them) that are relevant to a particular need. Simple keyword search does not suffice in this context because keywords (or parameter names) do not capture the underlying semantics of the web service. Dong et al.[4] show how to analyze a corpus of web services and cluster parameter names into semantically meaningful concepts. These concepts are used to predict when two web service operations have similar functionality.

Searching for web services is an instance of a general class of search problems, where the objects being searched have rich semantics, but the descriptions of these objects (e.g., schema definitions or WSDL descriptions) are terse and do not fully capture their semantics. Other examples of such search problems are in trying to locate web forms that are relevant to a particular information need, or locating relevant data sources within an enterprise. In all of these examples, simple keyword search does not suffice. Analyzing a corpus of such objects, and using the statistics to glean hints about the semantics of the objects offers a powerful supplement to keyword search. I now outline a major challenge for the field of data integration which will benefit significantly from this general approach.

A Data Integration Challenge

Despite the immense progress, building a data integration application is still a major undertaking that requires significant resources, upfront effort and technical expertise. As a result, data integration systems have two major drawbacks. First, evolving the system as the requirements in the organization change is hard. Second, many smaller-scale and more transient information integration tasks that we face on a daily basis are not supported.

Hence, a challenge to our community is to fundamentally change the cost-benefit equation associated with integrating data sources. Our goal should be to enable *on-the-fly* data integration, thereby facilitating the evolution of data integration applications and enabling individuals to easily integrate information for their personal, possibly transient, needs.

To achieve this goal, I believe a data integration environment should incorporate the following two principles. First, as data integration tasks are performed, the system should accumulate and analyze them, and then leverage prior tasks when facing a new task. Second, the data integration environment should be a natural extension of the user's *personal* information space, i.e., the information one stores on the desktop. In that way, a user can extend her personal data space with public data sources, and seamlessly integrate personal information (e.g., spreadsheets, contacts lists, personal databases) with organizational resources. Achieving these goals will substantially increase the perception of data management systems and their impact on our daily lives.

Acknowledgements

The ideas espoused in this paper have benefited from many discussions and hard work by my colleagues and students. I'd like to thank Phil Bernstein, AnHai Doan, Pedro Domingos, Luna Dong, Oren Etzioni, Zack Ives, Jayant Madhavan, Luke McDowell, Peter Mork, Rachel Pottinger, Dan Suciu, Peter Tarczy-Hornoch and Igor Tatarinov. The work has been supported by NSF ITR grant IIS-0205635, NSF CAREER Grant IIS-9985114 and a gift from Microsoft Research.

References

[1] Aberdeen Group. Enterprise information integration – the new way to leverage e-information. Aberdeen Group, Boston, Mass., 2003.

[2] P. A. Bernstein. Applying Model Management to Classical Meta Data Problems. In *Proceedings of the Conference on Innovative Data Systems Research (CIDR)*, 2003.

[3] A. Doan, P. Domingos, and A. Y. Halevy. Reconciling Schemas of Disparate Data Sources: A Machine Learning Approach. In *Proceedings of the ACM SIGMOD Conference*, 2001.

[4] X. L. Dong, A. Y. Halevy, J. Madhavan, E. Nemes, and J. Zhang. Similarity search for web services. In *Proc. of VLDB*, 2004.

[5] A. Halevy, O. Etzioni, A. Doan, Z. Ives, J. Madhavan, L. McDowell, and I. Tatarinov. Crossing the structure chasm. In *Proceedings of the First Biennial Conference on Innovative Data Systems Research (CIDR)*, 2003.

[6] A. Y. Halevy. Answering Queries Using Views: A Survey. *VLDB Journal*, 10(4), 2001.

[7] B. He and K. C.-C. Chang. Statistical Schema Matching across Web Query Interfaces. In *Proceedings of the ACM SIGMOD Conference*, 2003.

[8] A. Hess and N. Kushmerick. Learning to Attach Semantic Metadata to Web Services. In *Proceedings of the International Semantic Web Conference*, 2003.

[9] M. Lenzerini. Data Integration: A Theoretical Perspective. In *In Proceedings of PODS*, 2002.

[10] J. Madhavan, P. Bernstein, K. Chen, A. Halevy, and P. Shenoy. Matching schemas by learning from others. In *Working notes of the IJCAI-03 workshop on Data Integration on the Web*, 2003.

[11] J. Madhavan, P. Bernstein, A. Doan, and A. Halevy. Corpus-based schema matching. Technical Report 2004-06-04, University of Washington, 2004.

[12] C. Manning and H. Schutze. *Foundations of Statistical Natural Language Processing*. MIT Press, 1999.

[13] S. Melnik, E. Rahm, and P. Bernstein. Rondo: A programming platform for generic model management. In *Proc. of SIGMOD*, 2003.

[14] E. Rahm and P. A. Bernstein. A survey of approaches to automatic schema matching. *VLDB Journal*, 10(4):334–350, 2001.

[15] J. D. Ullman. Information Integration using Logical Views. In *Proceedings of the International Conference on Database Theory (ICDT)*, 1997.

TEN YEAR BEST PAPER AWARD

Whither Data Mining?

Rakesh Agrawal   Ramakrishnan Srikant

IBM Almaden Research Center
650 Harry Road, San Jose, CA 95120

Abstract

The last decade has witnessed tremendous advances in data mining. We take a retrospective look at these developments, focusing on association rules discovery, and discuss the challenges and opportunities ahead.

The full version of the paper will be made available at http://www.almaden.ibm.com/software/quest.

RESEARCH PAPERS

Compressing Large Boolean Matrices Using Reordering Techniques

David Johnson
AT&T Labs – Research
dsj@research.att.com

Shankar Krishnan
AT&T Labs – Research
krishnas@research.att.com

Jatin Chhugani
Johns Hopkins University
jatinch@cs.jhu.edu

Subodh Kumar
Johns Hopkins University
subodh@cs.jhu.edu

Suresh Venkatasubramanian
AT&T Labs – Research
suresh@research.att.com

Abstract

Large boolean matrices are a basic representational unit in a variety of applications, with some notable examples being interactive visualization systems, mining large graph structures, and association rule mining. Designing space and time efficient scalable storage and query mechanisms for such large matrices is a challenging problem.

We present a lossless compression strategy to store and access such large matrices efficiently on disk. Our approach is based on viewing the columns of the matrix as points in a very high dimensional Hamming space, and then formulating an appropriate optimization problem that reduces to solving an instance of the Traveling Salesman Problem on this space.

Finding good solutions to large TSP's in high dimensional Hamming spaces is itself a challenging and little-explored problem – we cannot readily exploit geometry to avoid the need to examine all N^2 inter-city distances and instances can be too large for standard TSP codes to run in main memory. Our multi-faceted approach adapts classical TSP heuristics by means of instance-partitioning and sampling, and may be of independent interest. For instances derived from interactive visualization and telephone call data we obtain significant improvement in access time over standard techniques, and for the visualization application we also make significant improvements in compression.

1 Introduction

Consider the following three problems:

- You are visualizing a large and complex three-dimensional geometric model and you would like to have a real-time walkthrough ($\geq$ 20 frames/s update). In order to do this, you need to determine quickly what parts of the model can be seen from a region of space (cell) bounding your current location.

- You work for a major phone company, and you have access to data that tells you which numbers call which numbers. You would like to manage this data to develop graph models of *communities of interest*.

- You have large volumes of data describing various purchases that people make, and you'd like to infer *association rules* from this very large database.

In all of the above problems, the basic unit of data is a large, disk-resident matrix of ones and zeros. In the first case, rows correspond to transitions between view cells, and columns are the primitives (typically collections of triangles) that become visible in moving from one cell to the next. These matrices are very large, having of the order of hundreds of thousands of rows and columns. Representing them and querying them efficiently is a non-trivial problem. In the second case, rows and columns are individual customers, and each entry of the matrix represents a call made from

Permission to copy without fee all or part of this material is granted provided that the copies are not made or distributed for direct commercial advantage, the VLDB copyright notice and the title of the publication and its date appear, and notice is given that copying is by permission of the Very Large Data Base Endowment. To copy otherwise, or to republish, requires a fee and/or special permission from the Endowment.

**Proceedings of the 30th VLDB Conference,
Toronto, Canada, 2004**

one person to another. In the third case, rows are customers and columns are products.

In general, our problem is to store the data so that we can efficiently access the information corresponding to a row:

Problem. *Given two sets R, C and a binary relation $M \subseteq R \times C$, store M efficiently such that for any $r \in R$, the set $M(r) = \{c \mid (r, c) \in M\}$ can be retrieved efficiently.*

If M (viewed as a matrix) is sufficiently dense, then representing M as an adjacency matrix is plausible. However, this does not scale well at all; for $|R|, |C| \geq 10^5$, this is already an impractical solution.

A more reasonable option, given that in applications of interest M tends to be sparse, is to use a sparse graph representation. For each $r \in R$, we maintain a list of elements of $M(r)$. This can be done in two ways; we either explicitly enumerate the elements of C, or maintain pointers into a data structure for C. Note that given the scales involved, both approaches will require using offline storage; in one application each element of C can be 10KB, and each $M(r)$ can be on average of size 1000, yielding over 100 GB of needed storage with the first approach and nearly 1 GB of storage with the second (assuming 10^5 rows).

There are tradeoffs between the two approaches; explicit enumeration is wasteful in space due to the replication of data elements, which means that updates to C can be hard. However, the second approach may require making many seeks into a list, in comparison with the first approach where access to $M(r)$ is relatively efficient.

1.1 Paper Organization

Our proposed solution exploits both the superior access time of the first approach and the efficient space usage of the second. We describe it using a simple example in Section 2 and go into more detail in Sections 3 and 4. We survey related work in Section 5. A detailed experimental study follows in Section 6.

2 Problem Formulation

We start with a brief example to illustrate our approach. Consider the relation M depicted in Table 1. This relation is defined between the sets $R = \{A, B, C, D\}$ and $C = [1..16]$. If we wished to retrieve $M(D)$ from disk, we can either make three distinct seeks into C to extract the entries $\{4, 5, 10, 15, 16\}$, or we can perform one seek and scan the entire list, retaining only the relevant entries (we assume that rows are laid out sequentially on disk).

Suppose however we were able to reorder the IDs of C, so that the relation looked like Table 2. Note now that for each row, all the relevant entries are clustered together; in fact $M(B)$ and $M(C)$ can each be retrieved in a single seek and scan with no wasted disk access.

Definition 2.1. *A* run *in a row of a matrix M is a maximal sequence of non-zero entries.*

Going back to Table 1, row C has 3 runs ($\{2, 3\}$, $\{6\}$ and $\{9\}$). However, after reordering (see Table 2), it has only 1 run. Since each run requires a single seek, we can now define a cost measure for a given relation.

Definition 2.2. *The cost* $\mathrm{runs}(M)$ *of a matrix M is the sum of the number of runs in each of its rows.*

The *reordering problem* can now be stated as:

Problem 2.1 (Matrix Reordering). *Given a binary matrix M, find a matrix M' obtained by permuting the columns of M that minimizes* $\mathrm{runs}(M')$.

Note that minimizing $\mathrm{runs}(M')$ not only speeds up access time – as we shall see later in this paper, it may also significantly decrease the space needed to store the matrix.

One special case of the Matrix Reordering problem can be solved efficiently: the question of whether the optimum value for $\mathrm{runs}(M')$ equals the number of rows of M that contain non-zeros. This is equivalent to asking whether the matrix has the following well-studied property.

Definition 2.3 (Consecutive-ones Property). *A matrix M is said to have the* consecutive-ones *property if its columns can be permuted such that in the resulting matrix M', all nonzero elements in each row appear consecutively.*

Booth and Lueker [4] showed in 1976 that for a given matrix M, there is a linear time algorithm that determines whether M has the consecutive-ones property and produces the desired permutation if so. Thus, if the relation has the consecutive-ones property, we can reorder the columns on disk so that the elements of each row can be accessed in a single seek. However, this will in general not be possible and minimizing the number of runs when a matrix does not have the consecutive-ones property is hard:

Theorem 2.1. *Matrix Reordering is NP-hard.*

Proof. We demonstrate a reduction from Hamiltonian Path [14, GT39]. Given an undirected graph $G(V, E)$, construct the boolean matrix M whose rows are edges, columns are vertices, and an entry is 1 if the corresponding vertex and edge are adjacent.

Each row has exactly two 1s in it. Consider an edge $e = (u, v)$. If u and v are adjacent in the column order, e contributes a cost of 1 to the total run cost, else it contributes two. Thus each pair of consecutive vertices that share an edge reduce one unit from the maximum run cost $2|E|$.

	1	2	3	4	5	6	7	8	9	10	11	12	13	14	15	16
A	*		*		*		*	*			*	*	*		*	
B				*			*			*			*			*
C		*	*			*			*							
D				*	*					*					*	*

Table 1: An example relation M between the sets $\{A, B, C, D\}$ and [1..16].

	12	15	5	7	13	16	10	4	14	8	1	11	3	2	6	9
A	*	*	*	*	*					*	*	*	*			
B				*	*	*	*	*								
C													*	*	*	*
D		*	*			*	*	*								

Table 2: The same relation M after reordering the columns

If G has a Hamiltonian path, then there exists a reordering of the columns of M yielding a matrix M' such that $runs(M') = 2|E| - n + 1$. If not, then any reordering must have cost at least $2|E| - n + 2$. Setting $K = 2|E| - n + 1$, the theorem holds. □

Matrix reordering can be related to the Traveling Salesman Problem in the following manner. Recall that a *Hamming space* is a vector space over binary vectors where the sum of two vectors is their component-wise sum, taken over GF(2) (i.e $0 + 1 = 1 + 0 = 1$, $1 + 1 = 0 + 0 = 0$). This space has a norm $\|\cdot\|$, defined as $\|v\| = \sum_i v_i$, and the corresponding *Hamming metric* $d_H(v_1, v_2) = \|v_1 - v_2\|$. A *tour* in a Hamming (or any distance) space is an order in which points are visited, and the cost of the tour is the sum of distances between adjacent points in the tour. For a given space, let T denote the cost of the shortest tour that visits all points.

Now if we view each column of M as a point in a Hamming space, it is easy to relate $runs(M)$ and the cost of a minimum tour.

Theorem 2.2.

$$0.5T \leq \text{runs}(M) \leq T$$

Proof Sketch. Note that each run contributes at most two units to a tour; one $0 \rightarrow 1$ transition at the beginning, and one $1 \rightarrow 0$ transition at the end. Runs at the beginning or end of a row contribute only one unit. Thus if we sum up the contributions to the tour for any particular dimension (row), we obtain a quantity that is at least equal to, and is at most twice, the number of runs in that row. □

3 Traveling Salesman Heuristics

The traveling salesman problem is NP-hard even for instances with metric distance functions. The best polynomial-time approximation guarantee known for such instances is 1.5, proved for the $O(N^3)$ Christofides algorithm [10]. Such a running time is infeasible for our applications, but many significantly faster heuristics are known to perform well in practice, typically getting much closer to optimal than promised by the above bound [17]. Four commonly considered such heuristics are

NN: Starting at an arbitrary point, move to its nearest neighbor and repeat. If at any point the nearest neighbor of the current point is in the tour, pick the next nearest neighbor.

2-OPT: Start with NN tour. Pick any two edges (u, v) and (w, x), and delete them, reconnecting with edges (u, x) and (w, v) if the resulting tour has lower cost. Repeat.

3-OPT: Similar to 2-OPT, except that three edges are broken, and the tour is reconstructed in one of two different ways.

Lin-Kernighan: This is a sophisticated algorithm that can perform k-OPT moves for arbitrarily large k, but in a highly structured way that keeps the worst-case running time polynomial.

For random Euclidean instances as studied in [17], NN typically gets within 25% of optimal and the implementations of 2-OPT, 3-OPT, and Lin-Kernighan described therein get within 5%, 3%, and 2% respectively. For the instances we study here, Lin-Kernighan performed too many distance calculations to be run effectively, so it and still-more-sophisticated heuristics were ruled out. On the other hand, results from the other three heuristics were much closer together than for Euclidean instances. 3-OPT was never more than 7% better than NN and, where we could test it, Lin-Kernighan offered little further improvement. Thus restricting ourselves to the first three algorithms should allow us to quantify a realistic range of running-time/solution-quality tradeoffs.

The reason that distance calculations play such a key role in running time here (as opposed to the case of Euclidean instances for example) is that they can be much more expensive. In a high-dimensional Hamming space where each vector can have thousands of non-zero entries, computing the distance between two points will require thousands of operations, compared to just 6 for the Euclidean distance in two dimensions, and even though the latter may be individually more expensive (involving multiplications and square roots), the former can still add up to much more work. Even high-dimensional Euclidean spaces can be projected to a smaller number of dimensions using standard embedding methods; as we will discuss in more detail later, this is not likely to help for Hamming spaces.

Our implementations of 2- and 3-OPT mitigate this somewhat by first computing a list of 50 nearest neighbors for each city and caching the distances to them. This data structure is also used to guide the search for improving moves, as first suggested by Lin and Kernighan [20], and once constructed can also speed the computation of the NN tour.

Unfortunately, we know of no way to construct the data structure without looking at all $N(N-1)/2$ inter-city distances, which is prohibitively expensive for large N. Another problem with large N is that the data structure or the instance itself may not fit in main memory, which would result in substantial additional costs in terms of disk I/O. We thus must resort to a classic technique for dealing with large TSP's.

3.1 Splitting The Tour

Given a TSP instance, instead of computing a tour on the entire input we can partition the cities into two sets, compute a tour for each part, and concatenate the two partial tours. Since neighbor-list construction is at least quadratic in the input size, this approach will speed up the TSP computation process, presumably at the cost of a decrease in the quality of the combined tour. In general, we can break up the input into k pieces, solve the TSP on each piece, and then glue the pieces together. In addition to speeding up the individual TSP calculations, this approach, by reducing the size of each instance, makes it feasible to run each partial input completely in-core, thus allowing us to ignore disk access issues.

The quality of the tours generated by this approach will depend not just on the number k of pieces, but also how the partition is constructed. Ideally one would like cities that are close to each other to be in the same sets of the partition. For geometric instances, a standard approach is to partition the space in which the cities are located in contiguous regions (rectangles in the 2-dimensional case), This can be done efficiently and can be quite effective, leading to only a slight worsening of overall tour quality as k increases. There is unfortunately no obvious way to similarly exploit the geometry of high-dimensional Hamming-space instances. What structure the instances have that might be exploitable is implicit rather than explicit.

That such structure exists can be seen from experiments we report later for the **POWER** instance, where simply partitioning the instance based on the input order of the cities (the first n/k going into the first set, etc.) yields substantially better results than a random partition. This is because the instance is based on a visualization application, and was constructed based on walkthroughs of the model and thus the initial ordering of the cities to a certain extent reflects the implicit geometry of that model.

In general, however, we may not be given an instance in a form that already reflects such implicit structure, so it would be useful to have a generic partitioning procedure that can find at least some of the structure when it exists, and can run relatively quickly even when the instance does not fit in memory. To that end, we have devised the following scheme, which has enabled us essentially to match the effectiveness of the "original order" partition. Other methods are possible, but a full study of the alternatives is beyond the scope of this paper.

Our approach reduces the problem to one of finding a good ordering of the cities and then, as above, partitioning into k contiguous blocks of size roughly n/k. This reordering problem is then in turn solved by a combination of clustering and the solution of another (much smaller) TSP. (Using classical clustering algorithms to generate a partition directly doesn't work because those algorithms can yield clusters of widely varying size.) The overall schema of our approach looks like this:

1. Compute K centers from the input (K can be bigger than k).

2. Determine an order among the centers (a TSP).

3. For each center, reorder points in the associated cluster to form a tour, taking into account the identity of the clusters on either side.

4. Concatenate the tours.

Step 1 can be performed in one pass over the input, as can Step 3. Step 4 can be performed either via a sorting phase, or (if K is small) by a grouping algorithm that employs K passes.

Step 1: Computing the centers

Most clustering algorithms are designed to work on points in ℓ_2 spaces, rather than Hamming spaces. In addition, the size of our instances requires the use of *streaming* clustering methods. Various methods are possible, such as BIRCH [24] or the streaming K-median algorithm of Guha *et al.* [16]. We take the following related approach that computes K-centers:

Pick a uniform random sample of K points from the input data (all subsets of K points are equally likely). Then assign each point p to the sample point $s(p)$ it is closest to. Also determine p's l closest neighbors, and construct a bit vector v_p of length p where $v_p[i] = 1$ if center $i \neq s(p)$ is one of p's l closest neighbors. Later, we will also use $\tilde{v}_p = v_p/\|v_p\|_1$, where $\|v\|_r$ denotes the ℓ_r-norm $\|v\|_r = (\sum_i v_i^r)^{1/r}$. We will abuse notation and use s to refer both to a sample point and the cluster of all points assigned to it. For each center s, let $v_s = \sum_{i \in s} v_p$. Normalize v_s so that $\|v_s\|_1 = 1 - \alpha$, and set $v_s[s] = \alpha$.

Intuitively, the vector v_s is a *signature* of this cluster, representing how other clusters appear when viewed from s. If two clusters are close together, then they will "see" all other clusters the same way, and so should be placed close to each other. Notice that if we dropped the restriction $i \neq s(p)$, then a large cluster could swamp v_s when normalized, rendering the neighbourhood information useless. The parameter α is a way of compromising, by fixing a contribution to this signature from s itself, but not making it too large.

In our implementation, we fix $l = 5$ and $\alpha = 0.2$ arbitrarily. The parameter K is set to 100.

Step 2: Determining an order among centers

Define $d(s_1, s_2) = \|v_{s_1} - v_{s_2}\|_1$. Compute a tour using this metric. For this we use the best of multiple runs of Iterated Lin-Kernighan (a variant of Lin-Kernighan [17]). .

Step 3: Reordering points in a cluster

Let s_l, s, s_r be three adjacent points in the tour generated in Step 2. Consider a point $p \in s$. If p's second nearest neighbour is s_l, then we place p in the set $L(s)$. If p's second nearest neighbour is s_r, then we place p in set $R(s)$. If neither case holds, we place p in set $L(s)$ or $M(s)$ depending on which of $d(\tilde{v}_p, v_{s_l})$ and $d(\tilde{v}_p, v_{s_r})$ is smaller.

All points in $L(s)$ are then sorted with respect to the measure $d(\tilde{v}_p, v_{s_l})$, and all points in $R(s)$ are sorted with respect to $d(\tilde{v}_p, v_{s_r})$. The output order for cluster s is then $L(s) \cdot s \cdot R(s)$.

The intuition here is that points more similar to s_l should appear closer in the order to s_l than to s_r and vice versa.

4 Sampling to Reduce Instance Size

One drawback of any partitioning scheme is that even if we divide into parts that can fit in main memory, it still may be the case that N is too large for us to do the required nearest neighbor computation or even simply to construct a true **NN** tour. Thus we will either have to partition the problem further, incurring additional penalties in tour length, or constrain our codes in some other way.

Since the basic issue is that there are too many potential distances that need to be computed, an appealing approach would be to discard a large proportion of the $N(N-1)/2$ edges as unimportant, and only concentrate on a sample of KN supposedly "good" edges.

Our implementations of NN, 2-OPT, and 3-OPT can all take a "sparse graph" input consisting of a list of (edge,true distance) pairs and a default length for the distance between any pair of cities not represented in the list. They then find good tours with respect to this revised distance metric, which, depending on the quality of the sparse graph, will be fairly good tours for the original instance. The default length we typically use is $1,000,000$, meaning that the algorithms will work hard to use few "non-edges" and, subject to that, use as short a tour as possible.

Note that this approach introduces a second trade-off: for a fixed memory size, choosing a smaller value of N means we have room for more edges per city, and hence possibly better tours. Tour quality will also depend on the quality of the sparse graph we construct. We obviously would like the edges included in this graph to connect relatively near cities.

A standard approach for computing such "near neighbors" in large high-dimensional data sets is to perform an embedding into a "nice" space like ℓ_2 and then reduce the dimension via projections or other means. The resulting set of points will approximately preserve the distances in the original set, and near neighbor calculations can then be performed efficiently.

There are a few problems with this approach. Hamming spaces are much harder to approximate than Euclidean spaces. Kushilevitz, Ostrovsky and Rabani present an algorithm [19] for computing approximate nearest neighbors in Hamming spaces; their algorithm requires space that is polynomial in n and d, and is thus impractical. Also, a result of Brinkman and Charikar [5] suggests that like ℓ_1, the Hamming metric is not amenable to embedding in ℓ_2 without undergoing severe distortion. Furthermore, as noted in [3], dimensionality reduction and the associated distortion in distance measurements are useful only if distances are *well-separated*; informally, the difference between a point's nearest neighbor and its farthest neighbor is large. For high-dimensional data sets, this is often not the case, and Table 4 demonstrates this for three example data sets that we use.

To resolve this issue, we exploit the "distance compression" that causes such a hindrance to approximate methods. Define $B_m(p)$ to be the ball of radius r, where r is m times the distance from p to its nearest neighbor. Assume there exists an $1 > \alpha > 0$ such that for any point p, an α-fraction of the points in the space lie in the ball $B_2(p)$. Intuitively, the larger α is, the less separated points are.

Fix a point p. If we now sample $1/\alpha$ points from P, with a constant probability one of these points lies in $B(p, r)$. The probability of success can be amplified further by sampling $\log n/\alpha$ points instead. This can be repeated, and so if we wish to compute k near neighbors (points that are at most twice the nearest neighbour distance away from p), we merely sample $k \log n/\alpha$ points and take k points from this sample closest to p. The algorithm we use is sketched below. We use c as a boosting parameter to increase the probability of finding true near neighbors. The algorithm runs in two passes over the input.

Input: Set of points P, distance metric d, and parameters K, $\alpha > 0$, $c > 1$.
Output: For each point $p \in P$, set of K near neighbors.

    for each p in a scan over P **do**
        Sample uniformly a set S of $s = cK$ points.
        Find K closest points in S to p and output p and this set.
    end for

Algorithm 1: Algorithm

Note that under this scheme we sample c potential neighbors for each near neighbor we want to retain in the end. This preserves a certain standard of quality for the neighbor set as the number K of neighbors increases. It also keeps the time to construct a sparse subproblem fixed independent of the number k of such subproblems. However, it also means that the total time to construct all k subproblems in a k-way partition grows linearly with k, adding another tradeoff to our mix. We will discuss other options when we cover directions for further research at the end of the paper. In practice, we use a factor $c = 16$.

5 Related Work

The most well-known example of using reordering to improve compression is the Burrows-Wheeler transform [8]. Buchsbaum et al. [6] use the idea of column reordering to improve table compression. In a separate paper, Buchsbaum et al. [7] also use reorderings based on computing TSPs. Their TSP's also had an expensive-to-compute distance function – the distance between two columns reflects the improvement in compression achieved by gzip or another compression routine when the two columns were compressed together rather than separately. The TSP's arising in their application were however much smaller than ours (less than 1,000 cities), and so did not raise the running time and memory constraint issues that are our chief concern here.

The connection between TSP's and the number of runs was also made by Alizadeh*et al.* [2] in the context of reconstructing DNA sequences from probes, although their tests involved even smaller instances ($N = 100$).

Variants of the consecutive-ones property have been used in data mining [15] to identify interesting patterns in market-basket data. There is a vast body of research into mining based on association rules represented in terms of a boolean matrix; an extensive survey is beyond the scope of this paper. The paper by Cohen et al. [11] examines the problem of computing approximate near neighbors in a large Hamming space under a different measure (the so-called 'intersection over union' metric).

Managing large amounts of disk-resident data efficiently for real-time walkthroughs of three-dimensional geometric and radiosizited databases is a well studied problem in computer graphics [13, 23, 1, 22]. Some preliminary work on reordering was done by Chhugani et al. [9]. That paper mentions the TSP heuristics we describe here, but focuses mainly on the data management and visualization aspects of the large-scale walkthrough problem.

Cortes et al. [12] proposed and developed the use of graph structures to determine *communities of interest* in order to detect patterns of calls among groups of customers; such patterns are also of interest in detecting fraud in telephone service.

6 Experiments

We now present a detailed experimental evaluation of our reordering strategy. We start with the experimental framework.

Data

POWER: Rows consist of transitions between visibility regions and columns are objects. An entry in the matrix is 1 if the object is in one of the regions defined by the transition and not in the other. The data comes from a 3D model of a power plant used for the walkthrough system developed by Chhugani et al. [9].

CITY: A similar data set obtained from a 3D model of the city of Atlanta.

PHONE: This data set consists of a sampling of call data from a major telecommunications company; rows correspond to callers and columns to callees (all data is anonymized).

Table 3 summarizes the basic properties of each data set.

	Rows	Columns	Sparsity (avg. entries/row)
POWER	47064	385828	8938
CITY	554455	789502	2000
PHONE	470728	543549	2

Table 3: Statistics for the data sets.

Data Characteristics

We demonstrate the *distance compression* that we discussed in Section 4. We sampled points at random from the three data sets and computing their complete list of distances to other points in the set, and then calculated the size of $B_2(p)$ and $B_3(p)$ as a fraction of the number of points in the site. In Table 4, we record the average values.

	$B_2(p)$	$B_3(p)$
POWER	13.5%	24.6%
CITY	27.8%	36.2%
PHONE	35.4%	62.4%

Table 4: Aggregate Data Distribution statistics: For each data set, the first column indicates the fraction of points (on average) that lie in a ball of radius twice the nearest neighbour distance for a given point; the second column does the same for three times this value.

Platform

All experiments were run on a 32 CPU SGI with R12000 400 Mhz processors and 28 GB of main memory. The code for the sampling was written in C and compiled using CC/gcc. Auxiliary scripts for managing the data were written in ksh/perl/awk. For computing tours, we used the Johnson-McGeoch implementation from their survey of local search methods for the TSP [17].

Validation

The primary measure of quality we will use is $runs(M)$, the number of runs on the reordered matrix. We will report the cost reduction achieved as a fraction of the identity ordering.

As mentioned earlier, a secondary benefit of reordering is the improvement in compression it yields (because long runs of 1s get placed together). To test this claim, we will use the well known *ExpGol* [21] compression scheme, studied by Johnson [18] in his 1999 review of methods for compressing bitmaps. We will use the codecs that he designed. For more details on how *ExpGol* works, we refer the reader to the paper by Moffat and Zobel [21].

Compression schemes like *ExpGol* are designed to compress sequences of integers, and work well when the integers are small. In a sparse representation, each row of the boolean matrix is a sequence of column IDs; however these are not small. Consider such a sequence $x_1, x_2, \ldots x_n$. *Offset mapping* (*Offset*) will convert this sequence to the form $x_1, x_2 - x_1, x_3 - x_2, \ldots, x_n - x_{n-1}$. A run of k 1s starting at column ID x in the matrix will thus be represented as $(x, 1, 1, 1, ...k-1$ times), A more efficient method is the well known *run-length encoding* that would represent the run by the pair (x, k).

A slightly better method called *two-sided run length encoding* (*2SidedRLE*) exploits the fact that runs of 0s and 1s can be encoded simultaneously. Each sequence of integers is represented as the sequence $\mathbf{0}_1, \mathbf{1}_1, \mathbf{0}_2, \ldots$, where $\mathbf{0}_i$ is the length of the ith sequence of 0s and $\mathbf{1}_j$ is the length of the jth sequence of 1s[1]. The advantage of this approach is that if intervals of 1s and 0s are interspersed, then there are no large numbers in the resulting sequence.

We will evaluate our algorithms by first using *Offset* or *2SidedRLE* to transform each row, and then using *ExpGol* to compress the row. The total compressed size will be the sum of compressed sizes for each row. It will often happen that the best compression scheme for the original input is different from the best scheme after reordering. In all cases, we use the best results to determine compression ratios.

Table 5 summarizes the cost of the input data under these three measures.

	$runs(M)$	$Offset$ $+ExpGol$	$2SidedRLE$ $+ExpGol$
POWER	251689169	235460917	245255311
CITY	807562396	823185832	906690088
PHONE	826766	4029710	4665946

Table 5: Three different cost measures for the data.

Reporting: In all the results below, we report the *relative improvement* achieved with respect to the identity ordering. For many situations, we will have tours generated using sampling to compute smaller instances, and tours generated from a full instance (typically only when the pieces are small). We will use the term *sample* to refer to tours generated by sampling, and *full* to refer to tours generated by exact distance computations. All times are reported in seconds.

6.1 Overall performance of the algorithm

We start with a start-to-finish evaluation of our schemes on the three data sets. Results reported in this section reflect the best choice of parameters at various stages in the computation pipeline, independent of running time; the goal is to verify that the *null hypothesis*, that reordering has no effect, is false.

Table 6 summarizes the results achieved.

	$runs(M)$	Compression
POWER	58%	38%
CITY	34%	25%
PHONE	35%	15%

Table 6: Relative improvement of **REORDER** with respect to the identity ordering.

In all cases, we get a substantial improvement after reordering the data. It is worth mentioning that in the case of **PHONE**, the compression achieved is small (we reduce the input by 15%) because the data set itself is extremely sparse, having an average of two entries per row.

---
[1]This scheme can be interpreted as performing run length encoding, and then doing further run length encoding on the start IDs of each tuple.

For all the data sets, the best approach (independent of time) is obtained by splitting the data set into the fewest number of subproblems that can individually fit in memory, and then computing full tours i.e tours based on looking at the entire subproblem. In general, the best tours are obtained using **3-OPT**, although there are occasional situations where this is not true.

For **POWER**, the best split comes at $k = 16$, and for city at $k = 32$. The data set **PHONE** is small enough to fit entirely in memory.

6.2 A Closer Look At The Approach

We now undertake a more detailed study of how various parameter choices in our reordering strategy affect the running time and the resulting cost.

6.2.1 Number Of Subproblems And Sampling

The number of subproblems the input is split into prior to tour computation is constrained by the TSP algorithm. In order to run in-core, it needs to be able to fit either the sampled sparse graph or the entire subproblem into main memory. Thus, the number of neighbours computed for each point in a subproblem will be inversely related to the size of the piece.

We first illustrate how the performance of the tours varies with the number of pieces. Table 8 illustrates the improvement in $runs(M)$ achieved, in all cases using **3-OPT** as the tour construction algorithm. Notice that in all cases, sampling yields better results as the number of subproblems increases, because this allows us to sample more "edges" in the sparse graph for each input point.

		\multicolumn{4}{c}{Number of Subproblems (k)}
		4	8	16	32
POWER	sample	21%	35%	48%	54%
POWER	full	–	–	57%	–
CITY	sample	–	7%	16%	26%
CITY	full	–	–	–	34%
PHONE	sample	1%	2%	3%	–
PHONE	full	18%	14%	11%	–

Table 8: Relative Improvement in $runs(M)$ as number of subproblems increases. For each data set, a *full* tour was computed for the value of k such that each subproblem fits in memory.

However, partitioning and computing a tour based on the full instance is always better. Table 8 also illustrates that it is important to partition into the *fewest* number of subproblems that allow each subproblem to fit in memory. In the case of **PHONE**, where the entire input fits in memory, partitioning only degrades the performance.

When time is no object, the best strategy is clearly to compute *full* tours on as few subproblems as possible. However, this is significantly slower than sampling, because of the quadratic distance computations. Table 7 compares running times of sampling and full instance-based approaches; notice that once sampling is performed, the TSP cost itself is very small.

6.2.2 Tour Algorithms

We use three algorithms to compute tours; **NN**, **2-OPT** and **3-OPT**. As we described in Section 3, **2-OPT** and **3-OPT** perform local refinements on a tour generated by **NN**, so in general for full instances **3-OPT** achieves better compression than **2-OPT**, which in turns improves upon **NN**. However there is a trade-off between the time spent optimizing, and the improvement obtained. Table 9 summarizes the relative improvement (and the time needed for these improvements) for the three algorithms. The numbers reflect the best-case settings for the other parameters, and only show time for computing the TSP.

What the table indicates is that unlike the case of Euclidean TSPs, even an **NN**-based tour is a good approximation to the best answer we can achieve. The times reported here for **NN** are overestimates, because they include time spent constructing neighbour lists for the **2-OPT** and **3-OPT** phases of the tour construction.

Interestingly, when we construct tours from sampled instances, it is not always the case that **2-OPT** and **3-OPT** are better than **NN**. For reasons discussed in Section 4, the tour construction algorithm have to deal with the occasional "infinite" edge in the sparse graph. As a result, **NN** can sometimes give the best cost solution. One such example is the 8-way partition for **CITY**. In this instance, the improvement achieved by **NN** is 7% in comparison to 5% achieved by **2-OPT** and **3-OPT**

6.3 Finding A Good Starting Order

Finding a good starting order can be a crucial component of a successful reordering. We start with Table 10, comparing the cost of a random reordering to the cost achieved by **REORDER**. Once again, we use best-case settings for all the data sets.

	Random	Identity	**REORDER**
POWER	+52%	–	-58%
PHONE	+0.4%	–	-35%
CITY	+36%	–	-34%

Table 10: Why the initial ordering matters: Random orderings are bad.

This table suggests that the initial orderings given to us in the case of **POWER** and **PHONE** were quite good. For **PHONE**, the initial ordering is close to random. This is not a coincidence; there is strong spatial structure in the way the elements of **POWER** and

	POWER				CITY				PHONE			
	sampling			*full*	*sampling*			*full*	*sampling*			*full*
	Sampling	TSP	Total	−	Sampling	TSP	Total		Sampling	TSP	Total	
4	37429	3736	41165	−	−	−	−		2723	4903	7626	11802
8	106748	3618	110366	−	112020	6166	118186		5644	4482	10126	5606
16	149388	2842	152230	202252	216159	5676	221835		5287	3585	8872	2925
32	330719	3792	334511		375940	6089	382029	823052	−	−	−	

Table 7: Time taken (in seconds) by **REORDER** as the number of tour pieces varies

	POWER		PHONE		CITY	
	Time	*runs*(M)	Time	*runs*(M)	Time	*runs*(M)
NN	192520	55.8%	43308	30.4%	772745	32.6%
2-OPT	192878	57.0%	−	−	774292	33.5%
3-OPT	202252	57.4%	43688	35.2%	823052	34.1%

Table 9: Relative performance of the three TSP heuristics (in seconds). The running times do not include sampling time. The times measured are cumulative, since **3-OPT** takes the output of **NN** as its input. We did not measure the **2-OPT** time for **PHONE** because running **3-OPT** (with its better quality solution) takes only a few seconds more than running **2-OPT**.

PHONE were generated. Note that since **PHONE** can be run entirely in main memory and thus does not need to be partitioned, no prior reordering will have an effect on the outcome. Thus, in the sequel, we only present results for **POWER** and **CITY**.

Our next experiment checks the overall efficacy of clustering alone. We evaluate the quality of the reordering computed using the clustering strategy of Section 3.1. Since our clustering strategy is independent of the input, all comparisons will be made with respect to a random ordering. Observe that the reordered input is slightly better than the original input we were given.

	Identity	Clustering
POWER	34%	43%
CITY	26%	27%

Table 11: The improvement in quality of the ordering generated by clustering, relative to a random ordering

Finally, we use the new order generated via clustering to partition the input as before, and compute tours in the manner described above. Once again, we present results for the optimal combination of settings. Table 12 presents these results, in comparison to the results obtained without clustering for the same parameter settings.

	Reordering based on given order	Reordering based on clustering
POWER	72.0%	71.1%
CITY	51.7%	51.4%

Table 12: Evaluation of improvement due to clustering and reordering phase, relative to a random ordering

It is important to note that the clustering strategy is *oblivious of the input ordering*. In other words, merely by clustering the data, we were able to recreate (mostly) all the locality-preserving properties of the original input. Thus, for an arbitrary input set, an initial clustering phase to generate an initial order can greatly improve the effectiveness of tour computation in the next phase of the reordering process.

As a final experiment, we randomly reordered **POWER** and used this random ordering as the starting order for **REORDER**. The run reduction we obtain, again using the best possible settings of a 16-way split and **3-OPT**, is 57.4%, which is less than the 71.1% improvement obtained using clustering. This further demonstrates the value of a good starting order.

6.4 Discussion

We conclude this section with a review of the major findings. Overall, the use of a TSP for reordering yields significant benefits, both in terms of access cost (measured by *runs*(M)), and in terms of compression. If the input is too large to fit entirely in main memory, an effective strategy is to break it into pieces small enough to fit in memory, and compute tours for each piece, using **3-OPT**.

If time is a constraint, and memory is limited, sampling is a good way to generate tours that are reasonably good in a small amount of time. Again, the best strategy is to use smaller pieces and pick more neighbours.

The improvement achieved via partitioning and/or sampling is a function of how well-ordered the original input is. The better the input ordering, the better the output. Therefore an initial clustering step that tries to group points in clusters if they are near each other is very effective in creating a good starting order to partition.

The type of algorithm used to compute the tour matters somewhat less than has been traditionally observed for TSPs. **NN**-based tours are close to, but worse than tours based on **2-OPT** and **3-OPT**, and so a choice of which method to use can be based on the amount of time one is willing to spend.

7 Directions for Further Research

As in most papers concerned with how to handle out-of-memory problems, we have concentrated here on just a few instances and applications. In future work we hope to confirm the wider applicability of our approach.

For example, much larger instances from the **PHONE** application exist and would provide new challenges – the total number of phone-numbers is in the 100's of millions, not 100's of thousands as studied here. We would also like to study instancs from "association rule" applications, for example data sets in which the rows correspond to documents and the columns to key words (or vice versa).

In addition, several algorithmic questions are worthy of further study. One of our conclusions here was that the best results were obtained by partitioning down to the largest subproblems for which it was feasible to run 3-OPT on the full subproblems and then doing so. Is this true in general? If we need to partition into 1024 subproblems to get them small enough for 3-OPT, might not the subdivision penalty be so severe that it would be better to solve sparse versions of the subproblems in a 32-way partition?

Another question has to do with the quality of the sampled subproblems. Here we allowed a fixed sampling time to create a subproblem, independent of its size. What if we only allowed a fixed amount of time overall to create all the sparse subproblems? This would mean even though the sparse subproblems have more edges when k is large, they would be of lower average quality, so the improvement in results as k grows might be lessened (or disappear).

Finally, for particular applications, are there application-specific sampling techniques that might generate better sparse graphs? For example, in the **PHONE** application, one might exploit the "community of interest" ideas of Cortes *et al.* [12], and get neighbors for a given column by preferentially sampling columns corresponding to phone numbers that call or are called by the given column's number, and columns that correspond to numbers that *those* numbers call.

8 Acknowledgements

We thank Ted Johnson for providing us with his code for *ExpGol* compression and Lyle McGeoch for modifications to the TSP codes to handle Hamming metrics. We also would like to thank Divesh Srivastava for useful discussions and pointers to related work.

References

[1] ALIAGA, D., COHEN, J., WILSON, A., ZHANG, H., ERIKSON, C., HOFF, K., HUDSON, T., STUERZLINGER, W., BAKER, E., BASTOS, R., WHITTON, M., BROOKS, F., AND MANOCHA, D. Mmr: An integrated massive model rendering system using geometric and image-based acceleration. In *Proc. of ACM Symposium on Interactive 3D Graphics* (1999), pp. 199–206.

[2] ALIZADEH, F., KARP, R. M., NEWBERG, L. A., AND WEISSER, D. K. Physical mapping of chromosomes: A combinatorial problem in molecular biology. In *Proc. 3rd ACM-SIAM Symp. Discrete Algorithms* (1993), pp. 371–381.

[3] BEYER, K., GOLDSTEIN, J., RAMAKRISHNAN, R., AND SHAFT, U. When is "nearest neighbor" meaningful? *Lecture Notes in Computer Science 1540* (1999), 217–235.

[4] BOOTH, K. S., AND LUEKER, G. S. Testing for the consecutive ones property, interval graphs, and graph planarity using P-Q tree algorithms. *J. of Comp. and Syst. Sci. 13* (1976), 335–379.

[5] BRINKMAN, B., AND CHARIKAR, M. On the impossibility of dimension reduction in l_1. In *Proc. 44th IEEE Symp. Foundations of Computer Science* (2003), pp. 514–523.

[6] BUCHSBAUM, A. L., CALDWELL, D. F., CHURCH, K. W., FOWLER, G. S., AND MUTHUKRISHNAN, S. Engineering the compression of massive tables: an experimental approach. In *Proc. 10th ACM-SIAM Symp. Discrete Algorithms* (2000), Society for Industrial and Applied Mathematics, pp. 175–184.

[7] BUCHSBAUM, A. L., FOWLER, G. S., AND GIANCARLO, R. Improving table compression with combinatorial optimization. *J. ACM 50*, 6 (2003), 825–851.

[8] BURROWS, M., AND WHEELER, D. J. A block-sorting lossless data compression system. Tech. Rep. 124, DEC SRC, 1994.

[9] CHHUGANI, J., PURNOMO, B., KRISHNAN, S., COHEN, J., VENKATASUBRAMANIAN, S., JOHNSON, D., AND KUMAR, S. vLOD: High-fidelity walkthrough of large virtual environments. Submitted., 2003.

[10] CHRISTOFIDES, N. Worst-case analysis of a new heuristic for the travelling salesman problem. Tech. Rep. 388, Graduate School of Industrial Administration, CMU, 1976.

[11] COHEN, E., DATAR, M., FUJIWARA, S., GIONIS, A., INDYK, P., MOTWANI, R., ULLMAN, J. D., AND YANG, C. Finding interesting associations without support pruning. *Knowledge and Data Engineering 13*, 1 (2001), 64–78.

[12] CORTES, C., PREGIBON, D., AND VOLINSKY, C. Computational methods for dynamic graphs. *Journal of Computational and Graphical Statistics 12* (2003), 950–970.

[13] FUNKHOUSER, T. A., SEQUIN, C. H., AND TELLER, S. J. Management of large amounts of data in interactive building walkthroughs. In *Computer Graphics (1992 Symposium on Interactive 3D Graphics)* (Mar. 1992), D. Zeltzer, Ed., vol. 25, pp. 11–20.

[14] GAREY, M. R., AND JOHNSON, D. S. *Computers and Intractability*. W. H. Freeman, 1979.

[15] GIONIS, A., KUJALA, T., AND MANNILA, H. Fragments of order. In *Proc. 9th ACM Conf. Knowledge Discovery and Data Mining* (2003).

[16] GUHA, S., MEYERSON, A., MISHRA, N., MOTWANI, R., AND O'CALLAGHAN, L. Clustering data streams: Theory and practice. *IEEE Trans. Knowl. Data Eng 15*, 3 (2003), 515–528.

[17] JOHNSON, D. S., AND MCGEOCH, L. A. *The Traveling Salesman Problem: A Case Study in Local Optimization*. John Wiley and Sons, 1997, ch. 8.

[18] JOHNSON, T. Performance measurements of compressed bitmap indices. In *Proc. 25th Intnl. Conf. Very Large Databases (VLDB)* (1999).

[19] KUSHILEVITZ, E., OSTROVSKY, R., AND RABANI, Y. Efficient search for approximate nearest neighbor in high dimensional spaces. In *Proc. 30th ACM Symp. Theory of Computing* (1998), pp. 614–623.

[20] LIN, S., AND KERNIGHAN, B. An effective heuristic algorithm for the traveling-salesman proble m. *Operations Research 21* (1973), 498–516.

[21] MOFFAT, A., AND ZOBEL, J. Parameterised compression for sparse bitmaps. In *Research and Development in Information Retrieval* (1992), pp. 274–285.

[22] SHOU, L., CHIONH, J., HUANG, Z., RUAN, Y., AND TAN, K.-L. Walking through a very large virtual environment in real-time. In *Proc. 27th Intnl. Conf. Very Large Databases (VLDB)* (2001).

[23] TELLER, S., FOWLER, C., FUNKHOUSER, T., AND HANRAHAN, P. Partitioning and ordering large radiosity computations. In *Proceedings of SIGGRAPH '94 (Orlando, Florida, July 24–29, 1994)* (July 1994), A. Glassner, Ed., Computer Graphics Proceedings, Annual Conference Series, ACM SIGGRAPH, ACM Press, pp. 443–450. ISBN 0-89791-667-0.

[24] ZHANG, T., RAMAKRISHNAN, R., AND LIVNY, M. Birch: an efficient data clustering method for very large databases. In *Proceedings of the 1996 ACM SIGMOD international conference on Management of data* (1996), ACM Press, pp. 103–114.

On the Performance of Bitmap Indices for High Cardinality Attributes*

Kesheng Wu and Ekow Otoo and Arie Shoshani

Lawrence Berkeley National Laboratory, Berkeley, CA 94720
Email: {KWu, EJOtoo, AShoshani}@lbl.gov

Abstract

It is well established that bitmap indices are efficient for read-only attributes with low attribute cardinalities. For an attribute with a high cardinality, the size of the bitmap index can be very large. To overcome this size problem, specialized compression schemes are used. Even though there are empirical evidences that some of these compression schemes work well, there has not been any systematic analysis of their effectiveness. In this paper, we systematically analyze the two most efficient bitmap compression techniques, the Byte-aligned Bitmap Code (BBC) and the Word-Aligned Hybrid (WAH) code. Our analyses show that both compression schemes can be optimal. We propose a novel strategy to select the appropriate algorithms so that this optimality is achieved in practice. In addition, our analyses and tests show that the compressed indices are relatively small compared with commonly used indices such as B-trees. Given these facts, we conclude that bitmap index is efficient on attributes of low cardinalities as well as on those of high cardinalities.

---

*The authors gratefully acknowledge the help received from Dr. Kurt Stockinger for review a draft of this paper. This work was supported by the Director, Office of Science, Office of Laboratory Policy and Infrastructure Management, of the U.S. Department of Energy under Contract No. DE-AC03-76SF00098. This research used resources of the National Energy Research Scientific Computing Center, which is supported by the Office of Science of the U.S. Department of Energy.

Permission to copy without fee all or part of this material is granted provided that the copies are not made or distributed for direct commercial advantage, the VLDB copyright notice and the title of the publication and its date appear, and notice is given that copying is by permission of the Very Large Data Base Endowment. To copy otherwise, or to republish, requires a fee and/or special permission from the Endowment.

**Proceedings of the 30th VLDB Conference,
Toronto, Canada, 2004**

1 Introduction

Bitmap indexing scheme of one kind or another have appeared in all major commercial database systems. This is a strong indication that the bitmap index technology is indeed efficient and practical [9]. The basic bitmap index scheme builds one bitmap for each distinct value of the attribute indexed, and each bitmap has as many bits as the number of tuples. The size of this index can be very large for a high cardinality attribute where there are thousands or even millions of distinct values. Many strategies have been devised to reduce the index sizes, such as, more compact encoding strategies [5, 6, 10, 13], binning [11, 12, 14, 19], and compression [2, 3, 16, 17]. In this paper, we study how compression schemes improve the bitmap indices. A number of empirical studies have shown that some compression schemes can reduce the index sizes as well as the query response time [8, 16, 17]. In this paper, we present analyses and performance tests on two of the most efficient compression schemes, and show that the compressed bitmap indices are efficient for attributes of any cardinality.

Let N denote the number of tuples in a relation, the basic bitmap index for any attribute of the relation has N bits in each bitmap; one corresponding to each tuple. If an attribute has c distinct values, where c is a short hand for its cardinality, then there are c bitmaps with N bits each. For example, in the bitmap index for an integer attribute in the range of $0 \ldots (c-1)$, the ith bit of the jth bitmap is 1 if the attribute's value in the ith tuple equals to j. Without compression, this bitmap index requires $cN/8$ bytes to store. If the attribute values are 4-byte integers, a typical B-tree index from a commercial database system is observed to use $10N$ to $15N$ bytes which is about 3 to 4 times the original data. If the cardinality is high, the bitmap index can be much larger than the B-tree index and the original data. One effective way to overcome this size problem is to compress the bitmaps.

There are many general-purpose text compression schemes, such as LZ77 [4, 8, 20], that can compress bitmaps. However these schemes are not efficient for answering queries[8, 16]. To answer a query, the most common operations on the bitmaps are bitwise logical operations, such as AND, OR and NOT. For example, for an integer attribute "I" with values ranging from 0 to 99, to answer a query for the form "I < 50", 50 of the bitmaps corresponding to values from 0 to 49 will be ORed together. Bitwise logical operations on bitmaps compressed with a typical text compression algorithm are generally much slower than the same operations on the uncompressed bitmaps [8, 16]. To improve the speed of operations, a number of specialized bitmap compression schemes have been developed. Two of the most efficient schemes are the Byte-aligned Bitmap Code (BBC) [2] and the Word-Aligned Hybrid code (WAH) [17]. Both are based on the run-length encoding. They represent a long sequence of 0s or 1s using a counter, and represent a mixture of 0s and 1s literally.

There are a number of empirical studies that indicate that these two compression schemes are efficient [1, 8, 16, 17]. In this paper, we systematically analyze the performance of answering range queries using compressed bitmap indices. The first result of the analyses is that the sizes of the compressed bitmap indices are relatively small compared with the typical B-tree indices. This is true even for attributes with very high cardinalities. The second result is that the time and space required to perform a bitwise logical operation on two compressed bitmaps are at worst proportional to the total size of the two. Furthermore we show that bitwise OR operations on a large number of bitmaps can be performed in time linear in the total size by using an in-place algorithm. This is optimal because it has the same complexity as reading the same bitmaps once. For a searching algorithm, one stringent definition of optimality is that its time complexity is linear in the number of hits. Using this definition, the compressed bitmap index is optimal for high cardinality attributes because the total size of the bitmaps involved in answering a query is proportional to the number of hits.

Depending on the number of bitmaps involving in answering a query, different algorithms achieve the optimal performance. Guided by the above analyses, we developed a simple yet effective strategy to select the appropriate algorithms to ensure the best performance in practice. Tests show that the bitmap indices, compressed with both WAH and BBC, scale linearly with the total size of bitmaps involved as predicted by the analyses. In the tests reported in this paper, a WAH compressed index typically uses about half the time required by a BBC compressed index to answer the same query. When querying high-dimensional datasets, the projection index is often the best option [10]. In out tests, a WAH compressed index always outperforms the projection index, a BBC compressed index may take more time than the projection index.

The rest of this paper is organized as follows. Sections 2 and 3 contain our analyses of the worst case sizes with WAH and BBC compression. Section 4 has a discussion on the time complexity of bitwise logical operations on two bitmaps. We discuss the options to operate on a large number of bitmaps in Section 5, and show that the in-place OR algorithm is a linear algorithm. A number of measurements are shown in these sections to verify the analyses. However, the bulk of performance measurements are shown in Section 6, where we also discuss how to select the best options to perform logical operations on many bitmaps. Finally, a short summary is given in Section 7.

2 Sizes of WAH Compressed Bitmap Indices

The Word-Aligned Hybrid (WAH) code is much simpler than the Byte-aligned Bitmap Code (BBC) and much easier to analyze. For this reason, we start with WAH. WAH is a hybrid of the run-length encoding and the literal bitmap [16, 17]. It contains two types of code words, *literal words* for storing literal bits and *fill words* for storing fills. In general, a *fill* is a consecutive group of bits of the same value. A group of 0s is a *0-fill* and a group of 1s is a *1-fill*. Both WAH and BBC require their fills to be of specific lengths. This causes short groups of bits with mixed 0s and 1s to be left out. Both schemes store these left out bits literally. We say a bitmap is *uncompressible* if all of the bits have to be stored literally. A bitmap is *uncompressed* if all bits are stored literally.

Since there are two types of words in WAH, one bit is required to distinguish them. In a literal word, the remaining bits are used to store raw bit values. To improve operational efficiency, WAH requires each fill to contain an integer multiple of bits stored in a literal word. For example, on a machine that uses 32-bit words, a literal word can store 31 bits from the bitmap, therefore each fill must contain a multiple of 31 bits. The length of a fill is recorded as the multiple of literal word size. For example, a fill with 93 bits would be recorded as length 3. In a fill word, one bit is used to distinguish it from a literal word, one bit is needed to record the bit value of the fill, and the remaining bits are used to store the fill length. On a 32-bit machine, the maximum fill length is $2^{30} - 1$, which represents a fill with $31 \times (2^{30} - 1)$ bits.

In an implementation of the bitmap index, the index is typically segmented. In this case, a bitmap index can be viewed as having a number of smaller indices each for a subset of the tuples of the relation indexed. This is necessary to reduce the size of each bitmap, improve the flexibility of the index generation process, and reduce possible access conflicts during update. Under this arrangement, a bitmap might contain only a few thousand bits or a few million bits. The maximum fill length is usually much smaller than 2^{30}. With this observation, we can safely assume that a fill of any length can be represented in one fill word. This significantly simplifies the analysis of WAH compressed bitmaps.

Using WAH to compress a bitmap, we first divide the input bits into groups that fit in literal words. If there are two or more consecutive groups with only 0s (or 1s), these groups form one fill and can be represented in one fill word. All remaining groups are represented literally. Let us call a fill followed by a group of literal bits a *run* and call the literal bits in a run the *tail*, see Figure 1 for an example. A run takes at most two words to represent; one fill word for the leading fill and one literal word for the tail. The only run that might not have a tail must be the last run of a bitmap. Typically, the last few bits of a bitmap do not use up a literal word, however a whole word has to be used to store them. Even though the last run might not have a tail, we always need at least a literal word. All together, the number of words in a WAH compressed bitmap is at most twice the number of runs, which proves the following theorem.

Theorem 1 *Let r denote the number of runs in a bitmap, the WAH compressed version of it requires at most $2r$ words.*

A bit with value 1 is also known as a *set bit*. All runs of a bitmap, except the last one, must contain at least one set bit. If a bitmap has n set bits, then it can have at most $n+1$ runs. Using the above theorem, the WAH compressed bitmap would use at most $2n+2$ words.

The number of 1s in any particular bitmap depends on the characteristics of the attribute. However, the total number of 1s of the entire bitmap index must equal the number of tuples N. Because of this, the maximum total size of all bitmaps is $2N+2b$, where b is the number of bitmaps used. This proves the following theorem.

Theorem 2 *Let N be the number of tuples in a relation, and let b denote the number of bitmaps used in the basic bitmap index for an attribute, using WAH compression, the maximum number of words required by the compressed bitmap index is $2N + 2b$.*

In the extreme case where every value of the attribute is distinct, the number of bitmaps is the number of tuples, i.e., $b = N$. In this case, a total of $4N$ words are required for the bitmap index. This extreme value is close to the typical size of a B-tree index. Therefore, with WAH compression, even in the most extreme case the bitmap index size is no larger than the commonly used B-tree index. As long as the attribute cardinality is much smaller than N, the bitmap index size is about half of that of a B-tree.

When a bitmap index is segmented, more bitmaps are used than the unsegemented index. This will increase the total size of the index. However, this increase is straightforward to account for. To ease the

type	fill	tail	encoding
1	short	normal	header, tail
2	short	special	header
3	long	normal	header, counter, tail
4	long	special	header, counter

Figure 2: The four types of BBC runs. The special tail is one byte long and has only one bit that is different from the fill just before it. A normal tail may have up to 15 bytes of any value. A fill is considered short if it has no more than three or seven bytes, see footnote 1.

analyses and comparisons, we concentrate on unsegmented indices from now on.

3 Sizes of BBC Compressed Bitmap Indices

In this section, we derive an upper bound for the sizes of BBC compressed bitmap indices. To do this, we first outline the BBC compression scheme, then compute the maximum number of runs required to index a high cardinality attribute and the average size of the runs.

3.1 Outline of the BBC Compression

The Byte-aligned Bitmap Code (BBC) was developed by Antoshenkov and is used in a commercial database product [2]. There are two main variants of this scheme. One is designed primarily to compress 0-fills and the other to compress both 0-fills and 1-fills. The former is known as the 1-sided BBC and the later the 2-sided BBC. For sparse bitmaps, the 1-sided variant compresses slightly better than the 2-sided variant.

The BBC compression scheme breaks a bitmap into bytes. A BBC *fill* is a consecutive group of bytes that contains the same bits. In BBC, a *run* contains a fill followed a number of literal bytes. BBC encodes a bitmap one run at a time. A header byte is always used for each run. The length of a fill is recorded in the number of bytes. For short fills[1], its length is recorded in the header byte. For a longer run, a multi-byte counter is used to record the fill length. Each byte of the counter reserves one bit to indicate whether there are more bytes in the counter, and the remaining seven bits are concatenated in the order of their appearance to form a binary integer. This integer plus an offset[2] δ, is the actual number of bytes in the fill. Each byte of the multi-byte counter is basically a digit of a base 128 integer. For a fill with f bytes ($f \geq \delta$), the multi-byte counter uses $1 + log_{128}(f - \delta)$ bytes[3]. In the example shown in Figure 1, using the 2-sided BBC, the first two runs have short fills and the rest have long fills. The counters for runs 3 and 4 are one-byte long with value 8 indicating the fills have 12 bytes and 96 bits. The

---
[1]For a 1-sided variant, a short fill can have up to seven bytes; for a 2-sided variant, a short fill can have up to three bytes.
[2]For a 1-sided variant, the offset δ is eight; for a 2-sided variant, the offset δ is four.
[3]When $f = \delta$, one byte is used.

	sample bits	30*1, 1*1, 8*0, 9*1, 100*0, 100*1, 1060*0, ...				
WAH		run 1 30*0,1*1; 4 bytes	run 2 8*0,9*1,14*0; 4 bytes	run 3 62*0; 24*0,7*1; 8 bytes	run 4 93*1; 4 bytes	run 5 1054*0, ... 4+ bytes
BBC		run 1 30*0,1*1,1*0; type 2 1 byte	run 2 7*0,9*1; type 1 3 bytes	run 3 96*0,4*0,4*1; type 3 3 bytes	run 4 96*1; type 3 2 bytes	run 5 1060*0,... type 3/4 3+ bytes

Figure 1: A sample bitmap

fill in run 5 has 132 bytes, which requires a two-byte counter. The counter records the value of 128, which is 1 0 in base 128 integer.

BBC also identifies a special tail. This special tail is one byte long and has only one bit different from the majority. The majority of the bits are the same as the preceding fill. This special byte is not explicitly stored. Instead three bits of the header byte are used to store the position of the bit that is different. Clearly, this special byte is very common in sparse bitmaps. In its simplest form, a BBC compression scheme divides runs into four types as illustrated in Figure 2 [2, 8].

3.2 Number of Runs

In this paper, we only analyze sparse bitmaps. Let N denote the number of bit in a bitmap and n denote the number of set bits. A *sparse bitmap* satisfies the relation $n < N/100$. As with WAH compression, a run must have at least one set bit, except the last run which might not have any set bit. The worst case size of BBC can be computed by assuming that all BBC runs, except the last one in each bitmap, contain exactly one set bit. This leads to a maximum of $N + b$ runs in the entire index.

The key to compute an upper bound of the index size is to show that having the maximum number of runs indeed requires more space. This basic idea is formalized in the following theorem.

Theorem 3 *For sparse bitmaps ($n < N/100$), the maximum size of a BBC compressed bitmap is achieved when each each run has at most one set bit and the last run has no set bit.*

Proof. We prove this theorem by contradiction, i.e., by showing that merging set bits together would not increase the storage required.

Let runs A and B be two arbitrary runs of a sparse bitmap, and let C be the run immediately following B. Runs A and C may be the same. If the set bit in B is moved to the tail byte of run A, then run A changes from type 4 to type 3 or from type 2 to type 1, because the tail byte is no longer a special byte. This causes the tail byte of A to be explicitly stored and the new run A requires one more byte than before.

To see what happens to the runs B and C, we first assume both of them are type 4 runs. After removing the set bit from run B, runs B and C will merge to form a longer fill. Let f_B and f_C denote the fill lengths of B and C before merging. The length of the combined fill is $f_B + f_C + 1$, since the tail byte of B is now part of the fill. The multi-byte counter for run B has $(1 + \lfloor \log_{128}(f_B - \delta) \rfloor)$ bytes, and the multi-byte counter for run C has $(1 + \lfloor \log_{128}(f_C - \delta) \rfloor)$ bytes. In most cases, the length of the combined fill can be represented using the same number of bytes as the larger of these two counters. In these cases, the space used to store the shorter of B and C is removed. This removes at least two bytes. Since only one extra byte is used by run A, moving the set bit from B to A reduces the total size by one or more bytes.

If the set bit is moved from another run to run A again, the size of A will not change, and the total size will definitely decrease. In general, if a run has multiple set bits, the total size of the compressed bitmap would be smaller than if all the runs have only one set bit.

The above is for the normal cases where combining B and C does not increase the size of the counter. Next, we examine the special cases where the combined fill takes more bytes to represent. An important observation is that the combined fill needs at most one more byte than the larger one of the two old counters. This can happen when both f_B and f_C are smaller than an integer power of 128, but $f_B + f_C + 1 - \delta$ is not. For example, with the 2-sided BBC, when $f_B = 66$ and $f_C = 65$, counters for both runs are one-byte long, but the combined fill has 132 bytes which requires a two-byte counter. In this case, moving the set bit from B to A may reduce the total size of the compressed bitmap if the shorter one of B and C takes more than two bytes. It does not change the total size if the shorter one of B and C takes exactly two bytes.

If either B or C has only a short fill, i.e., the run requires only one byte to represent, then removing the set bit of B actually increases the total size of the compressed bitmap by one byte. Let us assume C has a short fill, in order for the combined fill to use one more byte than that of B, the fill length of B

must be fairly close to an integer power of 128. In this case, some fill bytes can be moved from B to C to make run C a long fill, this increases the total storage required. Therefore, the sparse bitmap that has the maximum compressed size must not have any short fills. Similarly, if B is the last run of the bitmap and C does not exist, the total size of the compressed bitmap can be increased by moving some fill bytes from B to C. Therefore the last run of a compressed bitmap with the maximum size should have no set bit. ■

In a bitmap index, there is always a few bitmaps whose last run contain set bits. These bitmaps will be slightly smaller than the maximum computed here.

3.3 Average Size of a Run

If the set bit from B were moved to the middle of A's fill, run A would be split in two. This does not change the number of runs, but changes the distribution of 0-fills. Next we construct a way to rearrange the 0-fills of an infinite bitmap to maximize the average number of bytes required to represent each run.

If a multi-byte counter is m-byte long, the minimum fill length[4] it represents is $128^{m-1} + \delta$. If each fill is the minimum length for the counter, then the number of bytes required by the counters would be maximized. This is the core idea behind the following construction.

If f is the average number of bytes in a fill, the size of the multi-byte counter is $m = 1 + \lfloor \log_{128}(f - \delta) \rfloor$. To use the same size counter, the minimal fill length is $\underline{f} = 128^{m-1} + \delta$. We can take away $f - \underline{f}$ bytes from each fill without decreasing the size of the counter used, and these bytes can be added to some fills to increase the sizes of their counters. The number of bytes required to make an average fill use $(m+1)$ byte is $\overline{f} = 128^m + \delta$, which needs $\overline{f} - f$ new bytes. We need to take the excess bytes from γ ($\equiv (\overline{f} - f)/(f - \underline{f})$) runs in order to make one run have a larger counter. After this redistribution, we have γ runs with $(1+m)$ bytes for every run with $(2+m)$ bytes. The average number of bytes needed to represent a run is

$$(\gamma(1+m) + 2 + m)/(\gamma + 1).$$

It easy to see that there is no fill that takes m or less bytes, because some bytes can be taken away from a run with $2+m$ bytes and make many shorter ones with $1+m$ bytes.

In the above construction, we assume that the bitmap has infinite number of bits, otherwise there may not be enough 0-fills to increase the bytes used by any counter. This indicates that the average number of bytes used by an infinite bitmap is an upper bound for a finite bitmap.

3.4 Size of a Compress Bitmap

---
[4]For $m = 1$, the minimum fill length is δ, not $1 + \delta$ as the formula shown. This will cause the average fill size computed to be less accurate for denser bitmaps, particularly those with $n \sim N/100$.

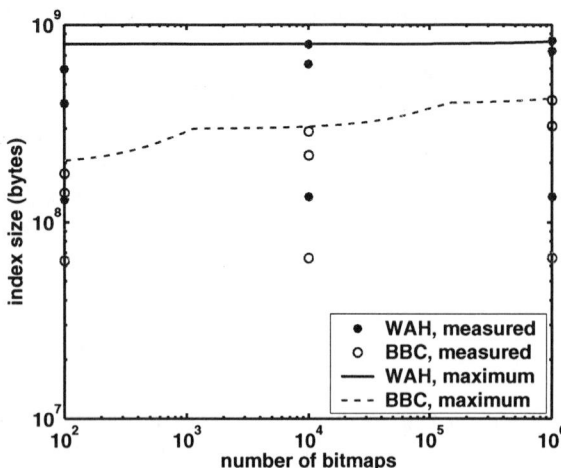

Figure 3: Sizes of compressed bitmap indices on a synthetic dataset ($N = 10^8$).

For ease of estimation, let us assume the index is not segmented. Thus the number of bitmaps b is the attribute cardinality c. The total number of bits in the entire bitmap index is Nc, the total number of runs is $N + c$, and the average number of bits in a run is about $Nc/(N + c)$. Plugging in the formula for the average number of bytes per run, we have the following theorem for the maximum size of a compressed index.

Theorem 4 *Let N denote the number of tuples in a relation, and let c denote the cardinality of the attribute indexed ($c > 100$), then the maximum number of bytes in a BBC compressed bitmap index is approximately*

$$(N + c)(\gamma(1 + m) + 2 + m)/(\gamma + 1),$$

where $\gamma = (\overline{f} - f)/(f - \underline{f})$, $\underline{f} = 128^{m-1} + \delta$, $\overline{f} = 128^m + \delta$, $m = 1 + \lfloor \log_{128}(f - \delta) \rfloor$, $f = \frac{Nc}{8(N+c)} - 1$.

When $f = \underline{f}$, the maximum size is $(N + c)(1 + m)$.

To verify the above formulas, we show the sizes of actual bitmap indices against the maximum values given by Theorems 2 and 4. The results are shown in Figures 3 and 4. Figure 3 shows the index sizes on some synthetic data and Figure 4 shows the index sizes on a set of real application data. The solid lines are based on the formula given in Theorem 2 and the dashed lines are based on the formula given in Theorem 4. These predicted maximum sizes are achieved with bitmap indices on uniform random attributes. Indices for other attributes are smaller than the predicted maximum.

4 Logical Operation on Two Bitmaps

It was observed that the time complexity of a bitwise logical operation is proportional to the total size of two compressed operands [16, 17]. It is straightforward to count the number of operations required by

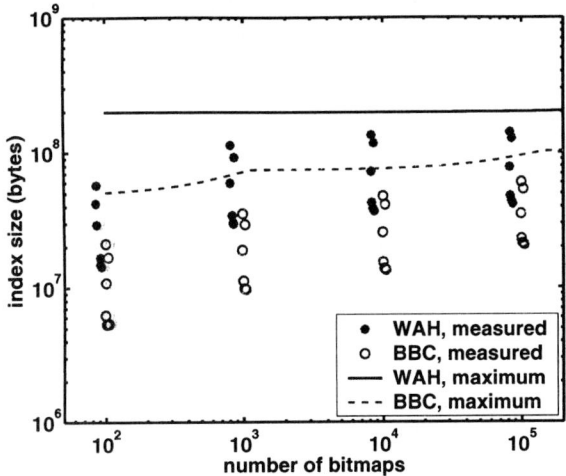

Figure 4: Sizes of compressed bitmap indices on a combustion dataset ($N = 2.5 \times 10^7$).

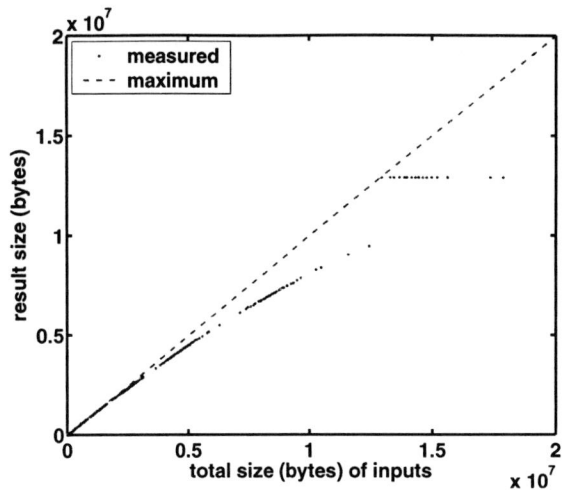

Figure 5: The result size of a logical operation plotted against the total size of two operands ($N = 10^8$).

examining the algorithms used to perform these operations. However, due to space limitation we would not discuss the details. Instead, we describe the major steps performed in these operations and provide the upper bound for the time and space complexities of the algorithms.

With either WAH or BBC, a bitwise logical operation on two sparse bitmaps basically need to decode the compressed bitmaps, determine the result bitmap one piece at a time, and put the pieces together to form the compressed result. It is easy to see the time required to decode the operands is proportional to the size of input bitmaps. With an appropriate algorithm, the pieces produced at each step should be as large as possible. For sparse bitmaps, the result contains at most the same number of runs as the total number of runs in the two input bitmaps. Therefore, the size of the result, and the time required to compute and compress the result are also proportional to the total size of the input bitmaps. Overall, both the time and space complexity of a bitwise logical operation is linear in the total size of the input bitmaps. This is optimal because an arbitrary logical operation has to at least examine every byte of the input operands.

We have measured the result sizes of many bitwise OR operations. The results are displayed in Figure 5. In this plot, the dashed line along the diagonal shows that the result size is exactly equal to the total size of the two input bitmaps. Each dot is a test case on two random bitmaps. For sparse bitmaps, i.e., those with small total sizes, the result size is very close to the total size of input bitmaps. As the sizes of the input bitmaps become larger, the size of the result becomes less than the total size of the input bitmaps. Larger bitmaps have more runs, therefore more literal tails. This increases the likelihood of two literal bits from the input bitmaps being located close enough to each other to produce tails that contain multiple 1s. This reduces the number of runs, and consequently reduces

the size of the resulting bitmap. The result with the maximum size is an uncompressed bitmap. In this case, its size is about 13 MB. When the total size of two input bitmaps are larger than 13 MB, the result is always 13 MB.

The above shows the worst case behavior of binary logical operations. Though these worst cases are often achieved, an actual operation may be a lot faster. For example, when performing an AND operation, if one of the operands is a single 0-fill, then the result is also a single 0-fill no matter what the other operand is.

5 Algorithms for Many Bitmaps

For a high cardinality attribute, the basic bitmap index contains many bitmaps. To answer a query such as "find all records with attribute I less than 100", one may need to OR a large number of bitmaps. Without compression, the execution time could be much longer than scanning the projection of the attribute I. We propose that the compressed bitmap index is efficient in this case. One evidence supporting this proposition is that the total size of a compressed bitmap is relatively small. With WAH compression, the compressed index sizes is about $2N$ words for high cardinality attributes where $c \ll N$. The size of a BBC compressed bitmap index is even smaller. In any series of OR operations, at most half of the bitmaps are involved. If more than a half of the bitmaps are required, it is easy to use the remaining bitmaps to compute the complement of the solution. Using WAH compressed index, we need to access no more than N words. In many data warehousing applications, the projection index[5] is considered the most efficient scheme when the attribute cardinality is high [10]. For an attribute whose values take one word each to store, the projection index requires N words. Using the projection index one

---

[5]The projection index is typically implemented as a sequential scan of a materialized view of a projection.

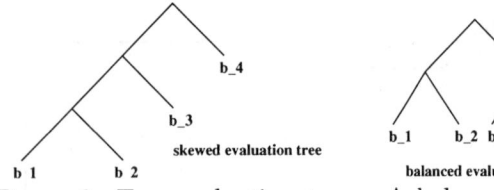

Figure 6: Two evaluation trees. A balanced tree is shorter and reduces the evaluation cost.

always accesses all N words, but using a compressed bitmap index one accesses N words only in the worst cases.

Previously we discussed operations on two compressed bitmaps. Next we discuss five different strategies to perform OR operations on many compressed bitmaps. The goal is to find a strategy that performs the best.

Let us denote the bitmaps $b_1, b_2, \ldots, b_k$, and denote their sizes in bytes as $s_1, s_2, \ldots, s_k$. The first option is a simple application of the binary logical OR operator, which can be expressed as a simple `for` loop, where the variable r denotes the result and the operator $|=$ denotes a bitwise OR operation that stores the result back to the variable on the left hand side.

$r = b_1$;
for $i = 2$ to k, do $r \mathrel{|}= b_i$.

To see the worst case behavior of this approach, we assume the result of a bitwise OR operation always has the maximum size. In addition, we assume that the time required to perform a bitwise OR operation is exactly proportional to the total size of the two input bitmaps. Let C_c be the proportional constant. The total time required to complete $k-1$ logical operations is

$$\begin{aligned} t_1 &= C_c(s_1 + s_2) + C_c(s_1 + s_2 + s_3) + \ldots \\ &= -C_c s_1 + C_c \sum_{i=1}^{k}(k+1-i)s_i. \end{aligned} \quad (1)$$

If all the compressed bitmaps have exactly the same size s, then the above equation simplifies to

$$t_1 = C_c s(k+2)(k-1)/2.$$

This option is very easy to implement and requires the minimal number of bitmaps in memory. In the following tests, we refer to this as option 1.

Since the multiplier in front s_i decreases gradually, we can order the bitmaps so that the smaller ones are in the front to decrease the overall cost. This approach of sorting the bitmaps according their sizes is referred to as option 2 in the following tests. Clearly, sorting the bitmaps does not change the worst case complexity, which is still quadratic in k.

Pictorially, the evaluation process of options 1 and 2 can be depicted as a skewed binary tree, which we call the *evaluation tree*. It is easy to see that balancing the evaluation tree will reduce the multipliers in front of the variables s_i in the expression for the total time. If all the bitmaps have the same size s, and $k = 2^h$, where h is an integer, the total time required using a balanced evaluation tree would be

$$t_3 = C_c s k \log_2(k). \quad (2)$$

As k becomes large, this approach clearly is better than the two previous options. For our implementation, we use a priority queue to hold all input bitmaps and intermediate results. The priority queue puts the smallest bitmap on the top. Every binary OR operation is then performed on two bitmaps from the top of the queue. This ensures that the cheapest operations are performed first. It effectively implements the balanced evaluation tree without explicitly maintaining a tree. We refer to this as option 3.

Both option 2 and 3 require the sizes of all input bitmaps before any operation can be carried out. Typically, this means the input bitmaps have to be read into memory. Therefore, these options require more memory than option 1. If these input bitmaps are held in memory during the whole process, a maximum of three times the total size of the input bitmaps may be required near the end of the process. If we free the input bitmaps immediately after they are used, the factor goes down from three to two. This amount of space is required to store the last two intermediate results and the final result.

All previous approaches use compressed bitmaps as the result of bitwise logical operations, which requires bitmaps to be generated and destroyed for each intermediate result. The cost of which may become a significant portion of the total execution time. One way to avoid this is to use an uncompressed bitmap to store the result. In fact, one uncompressed bitmap can be used for all intermediate results and the final result. Since the uncompressed bitmap is not deleted or allocated repeatedly, it might reduce the overall cost of the operations especially for a large number of bitmaps. We have implemented two variations of this approach, which we call option 4 and 5. Option 4 decompresses the first input bitmap, and option 5 decompresses the largest input bitmap. Normally, in any compressed bitmap, fills are stored in a compact form. The decompression procedure explicitly forces all fills to be stored literally, therefore turns a compressed bitmap into an uncompressed one.

In our implementations of options 4 and 5, we use the same data structure for both compressed and uncompressed bitmaps. Since we use compressed data structures to store uncompressed bitmaps, we pay a small percentage of storage overhead. However, this allows us to efficiently operate between uncompressed and compressed bitmaps. When the left-hand side of the operator $|=$ is an uncompressed bitmap, it always writes back the result into the uncompressed bitmap without allocating any new storage. In later discussions, we refer to this as the *in-place OR operation* or the in-place operation.

The in-place OR operation can be implemented very efficiently. In tests, we observed that the time required for these functions are linear in the total size of the compressed bitmaps. A detailed analysis is beyond the scope of this paper, here we give the key ideas that support the observations. The in-place OR operation can be viewed as a function that modifies the uncompressed bitmap to add more 1s. These new 1s are from the compressed operand. With either BBC or WAH, it is straightforward to determine the position of these 1s and the cost of determining these positions is proportional to the size of the compressed bitmaps. The number of words or bytes that need to be modified is determined by the number of runs in the compressed operand. If there are lots of bitmaps to be ORed, each bitmap must be very sparse. For sparse bitmaps, it is very rear to have 1-fills. For each run in the compressed bitmap, only one word or a small number of bytes of the uncompressed bitmap need to be modified. The number of runs in a compressed bitmap is proportional to its size. Overall, the time required to modify an uncompressed bitmap with a compressed bitmap is linear in the size of the compressed bitmaps. The constant term in the linear expression comes from the initial time required to generate an uncompressed bitmap with only 0s. Since this initial cost depends on N, it does not qualify to be a constant in the strictest sense. However, because this initial cost is so small compared with others, when a large number bitmaps is involved, this initial cost is negligible, and the total execution time is indeed proportional to the total size of the input bitmaps.

We can express the time required by option 4 as

$$t_4 = C_d + C_i \sum_{i=1}^{k} s_i, \qquad (3)$$

where C_d is the constant time required to generate a uncompressed bitmap and C_i is the per byte cost of performing the in-place logical operation. For option 5, there is an extra cost of finding the largest bitmap, which should be relative small. Since it is also proportional to k, it does not change the theoretical complexity.

Figure 7 contains a summary of the five options discussed. Clearly, for a large number of bitmaps, the best option is either option 4 or 5, and for a small number of bitmaps, one of the first three options might be better. In next section, we examine their relative performance and determine a way to combine them to always achieve the best performance. In the rest of this section, we briefly compare these algorithm against a theoretical optimal one.

Without considering the setup cost, the minimal cost of any searching algorithm is proportional to the size of the search result, because it needs to enumerate the result. Let h denote the number of hits, a hypothetical optimal search algorithm would have both time and space complexity of $\mathcal{O}(h)$. Using the basic bitmap index to answer a range query, the number of hits is the number of set bits in all bitmaps involved. In the worst case, with both BBC and WAH compression, the sizes of the bitmaps are proportion to the number of set bits, $sk \propto h$. This shows that all complexity expressions of the form $\mathcal{O}(sk)$ are optimal. More specifically, the space complexities of options 1, 2 and 3 are optimal and the time complexities of options 4 and 5 are optimal.

6 Selecting the Best Algorithm

From analyses, we know that different algorithms have different performance characteristics, to achieve the best performance in practice, we need to dynamically select the best algorithm for answering a particular query. To address this issue, we start by measuring the performance of all five options. By analyzing their relative performances, we come to a simple combined strategy for ensuring the best overall performances.

For measuring the performance of the five different options outlined in the previous section, we tested a large number of range queries on two sets of data, a set of random integers with various distributions and a set from a combustion simulation [7, 15]. Most of the tests are performed on the random data set because their bitmap indices are closer to the predicted worst case sizes. The real application data show significant skewness which makes the bitmap indices much smaller, see Figure 4.

The timing tests are conducted on a Linux machine with 2.8 GHz Pentium IV Xeon processor and a small hardware RAID with two SCSI disks. The machine has 1 GB RAM and the maximum reading speed of the disk system is about 80 MB/s. For sequential scan of large amounts of data, it actually sustains a read speed of about 40 MB/s. To scan 100 million records of a projection index, 400 MB in size, it takes about 10.3 seconds. This is the performance of projection index, which we use as the yard stick to measure the performance of other indices.

The random data set contains 100 million tuples of discrete random attributes some following a uniform distribution and other following different Zipf distributions. Their sizes are shown in Figure 3. The attributes with the uniform distribution have the largest bitmap indices compared with other attributes of the same cardinalities. Timing results from bitmap indices on these attributes also follow the formulas more closely.

We have generated bitmap indices with both WAH and BBC compression. The time used to perform bitwise OR on different number of bitmaps are shown in Figures 8 and 9. Each point in the plots shows one

option	description	memory		time
1	unordered bitmaps, compressed result	three compressed bitmaps	$\mathcal{O}(sk)$	$\mathcal{O}(sk^2)$
2	ordered bitmap, compressed result	all input bitmaps plus two intermediate results	$\mathcal{O}(sk)$	$\mathcal{O}(sk^2)$
3	priority queue, compressed result	all input bitmaps plus many intermediate results	$\mathcal{O}(sk)$	$\mathcal{O}(sk \log_2(k))$
4	decompressed first bitmap, uncompressed result	one uncompressed bitmap plus one compressed	$\mathcal{O}(N)$	$\mathcal{O}(sk)$
5	decompressed largest bitmap, uncompressed result	one uncompressed bitmap plus one compressed	$\mathcal{O}(N)$	$\mathcal{O}(sk)$

Figure 7: Summary of the five options used to OR many compressed bitmaps, where N is the number of bits in a bitmap, s is the average size (bytes) of the bitmaps involved and k is the number of bitmaps.

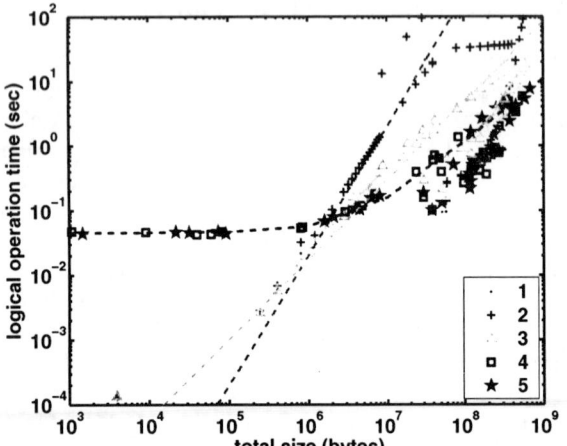

Figure 8: Time to OR many bitmaps compressed with WAH. Dashed trend lines are defined by formulas given in Figure 7.

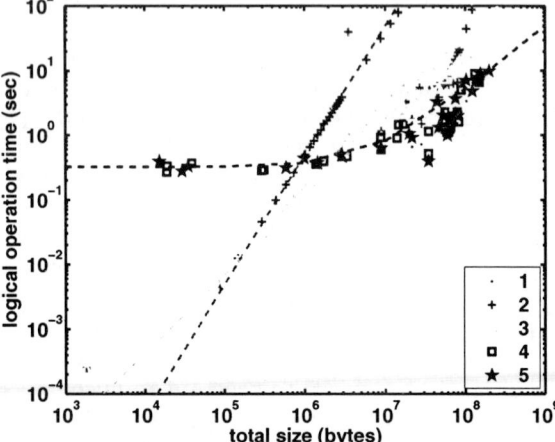

Figure 9: Time to OR many bitmaps compressed with BBC. Dashed trend lines are defined by formulas given in Figure 7.

timing measurement. The total size of the bitmaps is used as the horizontal axis. Assuming the bitmaps are the same size, the time required for the various options should follow the complexity formulas given in Figure 7. The dashed lines in the figures are the *trend lines* defined by these complexity formulas. The bitmaps from the indices for the uniform random attributes are about the same size. The time required to operate on these bitmaps basically follow the trend lines.

Of the five options, options 1 and 2 use about the same amount of time in many cases; options 4 and 5 take about the same amount of time in every case. This suggests that option 4 should be used since option 5 needs to find the largest bitmap. The cost to decompress a bitmap dominates the execution time when the total size of the input bitmaps is small. To decompress 100 million bits, it takes about 0.05 seconds with WAH compression and 0.33 seconds with BBC compression. Let S denote the total size (bytes) of the input bitmaps, the trend line for options 4 and 5 drawn in Figure 8 is $t = 0.05 + 1.1 \times 10^{-8}S$, and the same trend line in Figure 9 is $t = 0.33 + 5.1 \times 10^{-8}S$.

We also notice that there is a significant number of test cases that are far from the trend lines. This is largely because the trend lines are established for the worst cases.

To find out which option to use for a particular set of bitmaps, we plot the best options for the sets of bitmaps tested. Figure 10 shows the best options for WAH compressed bitmaps and Figure 11 shows the best options for BBC compressed bitmaps. As expected, option 3 is better for a small number of bitmaps and bitmaps with small sizes, but options 4 and 5 are better for a large number of bitmaps and bitmaps with large sizes. In each plot, we have drawn a dashed line to separate the region dominated by option 3 from the rest. The dashed lines separate the regions fairly cleanly. However, there are some cases with a small number of bitmaps, where option 1 is the best. We have examined these cases and found the performance differences between option 1 and option 3 to be very small. For ease of implementation, we will only use option 3 in these cases.

Option 1 also showed up in many test cases with very large bitmaps. In these cases, the first few bitmaps are relatively large and the intermediate results produced from operating on these bitmaps

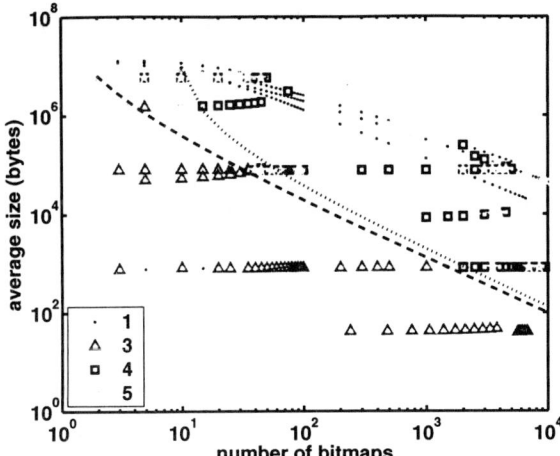

Figure 10: The best option to perform bitwise OR on WAH compressed bitmaps.

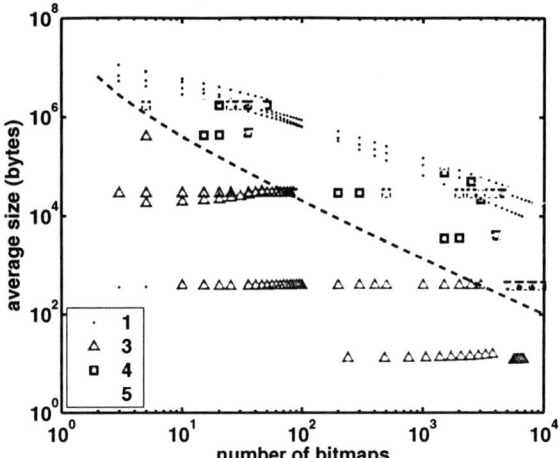

Figure 11: The best option to perform bitwise OR on BBC compressed bitmaps.

quickly become uncompressible. This effectively turns option 1 into option 4 because the same operator |= is used in the implementation of both options. This suggests that if the total size of first two bitmaps is larger or equal to the size of an uncompressed bitmap, option 1 should be used to avoid explicitly decompressing any bitmap.

In cases where option 1 works well, we expected option 2 to do even better. This turns out not to be the case because option 2 delays the generation of the uncompressible results and increase the time spent in generating intermediate results.

To perform operations on a small number of bitmaps, say two or three, clearly, it is best to use option 1. In cases where the first two bitmaps are very large we should also use option 1. Outside of these cases, the two primary options to consider are option 3 and option 4. The dashed lines shown in Figures 10 and 11 suggest a way to choose between the two. All cases above the lines should use option 4 and all those below the lines should use option 3. Next, we explain how we draw the lines.

Since we have derived the estimated time for all options, one way to decide whether to use option 3 or option 4 is to compare their expected time t_3 and t_4, and use the one with a smaller expected execution time. In this case, the divider would be defined by equation $t_3 = t_4$. Let s denote the average size of the bitmaps and let k denote the number of bitmaps. The dividing line is given by the following equation.

$$s = \frac{C_d}{k(C_c \log_2(k) - C_i)}. \quad (4)$$

To use this equation, we need to estimate three parameters, C_c, C_d and C_i. We have computed C_c as the average of $t_3/(nk \log_2(k))$ for all the test cases, and used a linear regression to compute the parameters C_d and C_i from the measured results. The line for WAH is plotted as the dotted line in Figure 10.

It is easy to see that the dotted line does not divide the points cleanly. This is because Equations 2 and 3 are derived for the worst case scenarios. More importantly, to use Equation 4, we have to estimate three parameters. For this reason, our actual implementation uses the following equation to decide whether to use option 3 or option 4.

$$sk \log_2(k) = C, \quad (5)$$

where C is the size of one uncompressed bitmap. We use this equation to define the divider because it works well for both compression schemes and there is no parameter to estimate.

There is a small number of cases where the triangles representing option 3 fall on the wrong side of the line defined by Equation 5. However, the difference between using option 3 and 4 is relatively small in these cases. For example, for the triangle that is above the line in Figure 10 with 5 bitmaps (total size about 7.4 MB), the time spent using option 3 is 0.11 seconds and using option 4 is 0.12 second. In these cases, using either option 3 or option 4 gives reasonable performance.

When performing a bitwise logical operation on two bitmaps, we have found that if the total size is greater than that of one uncompressed bitmap, it is faster to decompress one operand and use the in-place operation to produce an uncompressed result [18]. This indicates that with two bitmaps the dividing line between option 3 or 4 is $s_1 + s_2 = C$. Equation 5 can be viewed as an extension of this observation based on the expected execution time, see Equation 2.

Analyses show that the time required to answer a query using the compressed bitmap indices is proportional to the total size of bitmaps involved and to the size of the search result. Figure 12 plots the time measurements against the number of hits in the synthetic dataset. In this figure, the total time refers to the total query processing time, including the time to operate

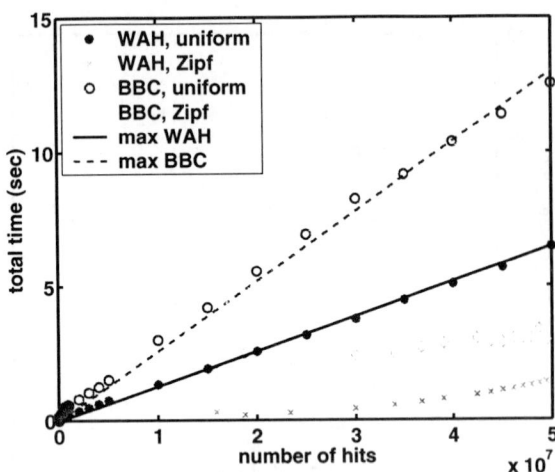

Figure 12: The total query processing time plotted against the number of hits for two type of random attributes, uniform and Zipf($1/x$).

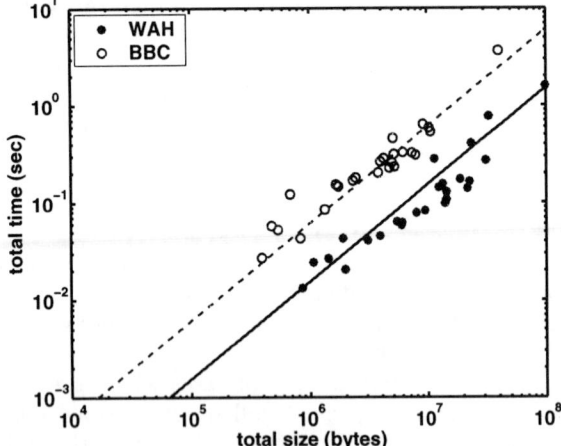

Figure 13: The total query processing time plotted against the total size of bitmaps used for the combustion dataset.

on the bitmaps and the time to read the bitmaps from disk. The total time shown here is measured using the combined option for operating on many bitmaps. The linear relation between the total time and the number of hits is clearly evident from this plot. Because of the use of the complement when more than half of the bitmaps are involved, the query processing time for uniform random attributes actually decreases when more than half of the records are hits. The time required using WAH compressed indices is about half of that using BBC compressed indices.

Figure 13 shows the timing results on the combustion dataset against the total size of the bitmaps involved. The total time is measured using the combined option and also includes time for all IO operations. The solid line and the dashed line shown are the average cases assuming the total time is proportional the total size of the bitmaps involved. Even though linearity is only expected for some cases, we see that the

random, $N = 10^8$		
	average	max
projection	10.3	10.3
WAH	1.2	6.8
BBC	2.8	12.5

combustion, $N = 2.5 \times 10^7$		
	average	max
projection	2.6	2.6
WAH	0.2	2.7
BBC	0.4	3.9

Figure 14: The average and worst case time (seconds) used by various searching schemes.

timing results follow the linear relation fairly closely.

Figure 14 shows how the bitmap indexing schemes compare with the projection index. On the average, both types of compressed bitmap indices are significantly faster than the projection index. In the worst cases, the WAH compressed bitmap indices are no worse than the projection index, but the BBC compressed indices may take longer because operations on BBC compressed bitmaps are slower.

The relative performance difference between WAH and BBC compressed bitmap indices in these tests is at the low end of the performance differences measured in previous tests [17]. This is consistent with the fact that most of the bitmaps used in these tests are very sparse. On denser bitmaps, the performance difference can be much larger.

7 Summary

The effectiveness of the bitmap indexing scheme for low cardinality attributes is well accepted. There are also evidences that compressed bitmap indices can work well for high cardinality attributes [16, 17]. To fully understand their effectiveness for high cardinality attributes, we analyze the space and time complexities of WAH and BBC compressed bitmap indices for answering one-dimensional range queries. The analyses show that the total sizes of the compressed bitmap indices are fairly modest even for attributes with very high cardinalities. For most high cardinality attributes, where $c \ll N$, the WAH compressed indices use about $2N$ words, which is about half the size of a typical B-tree index. The BBC compressed indices are even smaller. We also develop a strategy to select the best algorithm to operate on a large number of bitmaps. This strategy is important for us to achieve predicted optimal speed in practice. Timing measurements confirm this optimality because the query response time is indeed linear in the number of hits for uniform random attributes. The query response time on other types of attributes is much lower than that for uniform random attributes.

Event though bitmap indices compressed with both BBC and WAH are theoretically optimal. On the average, WAH compressed bitmap indices are about twice as fast as BBC compressed indices in our tests. Because the projection index is often the best option for searching high dimensional datasets, we also measured its performance. On the average, bitmap indices compressed with both BBC and WAH can significantly outperform the projection index. In the worst cases, the WAH compressed indices take no more time than the projection index, but the BBC compressed indices may take longer because they require more CPU time.

We currently have a prototype software that can use both WAH and BBC compressions. In the future, we plan to implement a more robust version based solely on WAH compression. The software would include segmented indices mentioned earlier. The prototype implementation currently makes a number of decisions based on the number of bitmaps involved rather than on the total size of the bitmaps involved. For example, on attributes with non-uniform distributions, this may lead to wrong decisions on when to compute the complement of the query conditions. According to the analyses presented in this paper, the decision of when to use the complement should be based on the total size of the bitmaps involved.

References

[1] S. Amer-Yahia and T. Johnson. Optimizing queries on compressed bitmaps. In *VLDB 2000*, pages 329–338. Morgan Kaufmann, 2000.

[2] G. Antoshenkov. Byte-aligned bitmap compression. Technical report, Oracle Corp., 1994. U.S. Patent number 5,363,098.

[3] G. Antoshenkov and M. Ziauddin. Query processing and optimization in ORACLE RDB. *VLDB Journal*, 5:229–237, 1996.

[4] T. C. Bell, I. H. Witten, and J. Cleary. *Text Compression*. Prentice Hall, 1989.

[5] C.-Y. Chan and Y. E. Ioannidis. Bitmap index design and evaluation. In *SIGMOD 1998*, pages 355–366. ACM press, 1998.

[6] C. Y. Chan and Y. E. Ioannidis. An efficient bitmap encoding scheme for selection queries. In *SIGMOD 1999*, pages 215–226. ACM Press, 1999.

[7] H. G. Im, J. H. Chen, and C. K. Law. Ignition of hydrogen/air mixing layer in turbulent flows. In *Twenty-Seventh Symposium (International) on Combustion, The Combustion Institute*, pages 1047–1056, 1998.

[8] T. Johnson. Performance measurements of compressed bitmap indices. In M*VLDB 1999*, pages 278–289. Morgan Kaufmann, 1999.

[9] P. O'Neil. Model 204 architecture and performance. In *2nd International Workshop in High Performance Transaction Systems, Asilomar, CA*, volume 359 of *Lecture Notes in Computer Science*, pages 40–59, September 1987.

[10] P. O'Neil and D. Quass. Improved query performance with variant indices. In *SIGMOD 1997*, pages 38–49. ACM Press, 1997.

[11] A. Shoshani, L. M. Bernardo, H. Nordberg, D. Rotem, and A. Sim. Multidimensional indexing and query coordination for tertiary storage management. In *SSDBM 1999*, pages 214–225. IEEE Computer Society, 1999.

[12] K. Stockinger. Bitmap indices for speeding up high-dimensional data analysis. In *DEXA 2002*. Springer-Verlag, 2002.

[13] H. K. T. Wong, H.-F. Liu, F. Olken, D. Rotem, and L. Wong. Bit transposed files. In *VLDB 1985*, pages 448–457, 1985.

[14] K.-L. Wu and P. Yu. Range-based bitmap indexing for high cardinality attributes with skew. Technical Report RC 20449, IBM Watson Research Division, Yorktown Heights, New York, May 1996.

[15] K. Wu, W. Koegler, J. Chen, and A. Shoshani. Using bitmap index for interactive exploration of large datasets. In *SSDBM 2003*, pages 65–74, 2003.

[16] K. Wu, E. J. Otoo, and A. Shoshani. A performance comparison of bitmap indexes. In *Proceedings of the 2001 ACM CIKM International Conference on Information and Knowledge Management, Atlanta, Georgia, USA, November 5-10, 2001*, pages 559–561. ACM, 2001.

[17] K. Wu, E. J. Otoo, and A. Shoshani. Compressing bitmap indexes for faster search operations. In *SSDBM'02*, pages 99–108, 2002. LBNL-49627.

[18] K. Wu, E. J. Otoo, A. Shoshani, and H. Nordberg. Notes on design and implementation of compressed bit vectors. Technical Report LBNL/PUB-3161, Lawrence Berkeley National Laboratory, Berkeley, CA, 2001.

[19] M.-C. Wu and A. P. Buchmann. Encoded bitmap indexing for data warehouses. In *ICDE 1998*, pages 220–230. IEEE Computer Society, 1998.

[20] J. Ziv and A. Lempel. A universal algorithm for sequential data compression. *IEEE Transactions on Information Theory*, 23(3):337–343, 1977.

Practical Suffix Tree Construction

Sandeep Tata   Richard A. Hankins   Jignesh M. Patel

University of Michigan
1301 Beal Avenue; Ann Arbor, MI 48109-2122; USA
{tatas,hankinsr,jignesh}@eecs.umich.edu

Abstract

Large string datasets are common in a number of emerging text and biological database applications. Common queries over such datasets include both exact and approximate string matches. These queries can be evaluated very efficiently by using a suffix tree index on the string dataset. Although suffix trees can be constructed quickly in memory for small input datasets, constructing persistent trees for large datasets has been challenging. In this paper, we explore suffix tree construction algorithms over a wide spectrum of data sources and sizes. First, we show that on modern processors, a cache-efficient algorithm with $O(n^2)$ complexity outperforms the popular $O(n)$ Ukkonen algorithm, even for in-memory construction. For larger datasets, the disk I/O requirement quickly becomes the bottleneck in each algorithm's performance. To address this problem, we present a buffer management strategy for the $O(n^2)$ algorithm, creating a new disk-based construction algorithm that scales to sizes much larger than have been previously described in the literature. Our approach far outperforms the best known disk-based construction algorithms.

1 Introduction

Querying large string datasets is becoming increasingly important in a number of emerging text and life sciences applications. Life science researchers are often interested in explorative querying of large biological sequence databases, such as genomes and large sets of protein sequences. Many of these biological datasets are growing at exponential rates — for example, the sizes of the sequence datasets in GenBank have been doubling every six-teen months [31]. Consequently, methods for *efficiently* querying large string datasets are critical to the success of these emerging database applications.

Suffix trees are versatile data structures that can help execute such queries very efficiently. In fact, suffix trees are useful for solving a wide variety of string based problems [17]. For instance, the exact substring matching problem can be solved in time proportional to the length of the query, once the suffix tree is built on the database string. Suffix trees can also be used to solve approximate string matching problems efficiently. Some bioinformatics applications such as MUMmer [10, 11, 22], REPuter [23], and OASIS [25] exploit suffix trees to efficiently evaluate queries on biological sequence datasets. However, suffix trees are not widely used because of their high cost of construction. As we show in this paper, building a suffix tree on moderately sized datasets, such as a single chromosome of the human genome, takes over 1.5 hours with the best known existing disk-based construction technique [18]. In contrast, the techniques that we develop in this paper reduce the construction time by a factor of 5 on inputs of the same size.

Even though suffix trees are currently not in widespread use, there is a rich history of algorithms for constructing suffix trees. A large focus of previous research has been on linear-time suffix tree construction algorithms [24, 32, 33]. These algorithms are well suited for small input strings where the tree can be constructed entirely in main memory. The growing size of input datasets, however, requires that we construct suffix trees efficiently on disk. The algorithms proposed in [24, 32, 33] cannot be used for disk-based construction as they have poor locality of reference. This poor locality causes a large amount of random disk I/O once the data structures no longer fit in main memory. If we naively use these main-memory algorithms for on-disk suffix tree construction, the process may take well over a day for a single human chromosome.

Large (and rapidly growing) size of many string datasets underscores the need for fast *disk-based* suffix tree construction algorithms. A few recent research efforts have also considered this problem [4, 18], though neither of these approaches scales well for large datasets (such as a large chromosome, or an entire eukaryotic genome).

In this paper, we present a new approach to *efficiently*

Permission to copy without fee all or part of this material is granted provided that the copies are not made or distributed for direct commercial advantage, the VLDB copyright notice and the title of the publication and its date appear, and notice is given that copying is by permission of the Very Large Data Base Endowment. To copy otherwise, or to republish, requires a fee and/or special permission from the Endowment.

**Proceedings of the 30th VLDB Conference,
Toronto, Canada, 2004**

construct suffix trees on disk. We use a philosophy similar to the one in [18]. We forgo the use of suffix links in return for a much better memory reference pattern, which translates to better scalability and performance for large trees.

The main contributions of this paper are as follows:

1. We introduce the "Top Down Disk-based" (TDD) approach to building suffix trees efficiently for a wide range of sizes and input types. This technique, includes a suffix tree construction algorithm called PWOTD, and a sophisticated buffer management strategy.

2. We compare the performance of TDD with the popular Ukkonen's algorithm [32] for the in-memory case, where all the data structures needed for building the suffix trees are memory resident (i.e. the datasets are "small"). Interestingly, we show that even though Ukkonen has a better worst case *theoretical* complexity, TDD outperforms Ukkonen on modern cached processors, since TDD incurs significantly fewer processor cache misses.

3. We systematically explore the space of data sizes and types, and highlight the advantages and disadvantages of TDD with respect to other construction algorithms.

4. We experimentally demonstrate that TDD scales gracefully with increasing input size. Using the TDD process, we are able to construct a suffix tree on the *entire human genome in 30 hours* (on a single processor machine)! To our knowledge, suffix tree construction on an input string of this size (3 billion symbols approx.) has yet to be reported in literature.

The remainder of this paper is organized as follows: Section 2 discusses related work. The TDD technique is described in Section 3, and we analyze the behavior of this algorithm in Section 4. Section 5, presents the experimental results, and Section 6 presents our conclusions.

2 Related Work

Linear time algorithms for constructing suffix trees have been described by Weiner [33], McCreight [24], and Ukkonen [32]. Ukkonen's is a popular algorithm because it is easier to implement than the other algorithms. It is an $O(n)$, in-memory construction algorithm based on the clever observation that constructing the suffix tree can be performed by iteratively expanding the leaves of a partially constructed suffix tree. Through the use of *suffix links*, which provide a mechanism for quickly traversing across sub-trees, the suffix tree can be expanded by simply adding the $i+1$ character to the leaves of the suffix tree built on the previous i characters. The algorithm thus relies on suffix links to traverse through all of the sub-trees in the main tree, expanding the outer edges for each input character. However, they have poor locality of reference since they traverse the suffix tree nodes in a random fashion. This leads to poor performance on cached architectures and when used to construct on-disk suffix trees.

Recently, Bedathur et al. developed a buffering strategy, called TOP-Q, which improves the performance of the Ukkonen's algorithm (which uses suffix links) when constructing on-disk suffix trees [4]. A different approach was suggested by Hunt et al. [18] where the authors drop the use of suffix links and use an $O(n^2)$ algorithm with a better locality of reference. In one pass over the string, they index all suffixes with the same prefix by inserting them into an on-disk subtree managed by PJama [3], a Java based object store. Construction of each independent subtree requires a full pass over the string.

Several $O(n^2)$ and $O(n \log n)$ algorithms for constructing suffix trees are described in [17]. A top-down approach has been suggested in [1, 14, 16]. In [15], the authors explore the benefits of using a lazy implementation of suffix trees. In this approach, the authors argue that one can avoid paying the full construction cost by constructing the subtree only when it is accessed for the first time. This approach is useful only when a small number of queries are posed against a string dataset. When executing a large number of queries, most of the tree must be materialized, and in this case, this approach will perform poorly.

Previous research has also produced theoretical results on understanding the average sizes of suffix trees [5, 30], and theoretical complexity of using sorting to build suffix trees for different computational models such as RAM, PRAM, and various other external memory models [12].

Suffix arrays have also been used as an alternative to suffix trees for specific string matching tasks [8, 9, 26]. However, in general, suffix trees are more versatile data structures. The focus of this paper is only on suffix trees.

Our solution uses a simple partitioning strategy. However, a more sophisticated partitioning method has been proposed recently [6], which can complement our existing partitioning method.

3 The TDD Technique

Most suffix tree construction algorithms do not scale due to the prohibitive disk I/O requirements. The high per-character overhead quickly causes the data structures to outgrow main memory and the poor locality of reference makes efficient buffer management difficult.

We now present a new disk-based construction technique called the "Top-Down Disk-based" technique, hereafter referred to simply as TDD. TDD scales much more gracefully than existing techniques by reducing the main-memory requirements through strategic buffering of the largest data structures. The TDD technique consists of a suffix tree construction algorithm, called PWOTD, and the related buffer management strategy described in the following sections.

3.1 PWOTD Algorithm

The first component of the TDD technique is our suffix tree construction algorithm, called PWOTD (Partition and Write Only Top Down). This algorithm is based on the *wotdeager* algorithm suggested by Kurtz [15]. We improve on

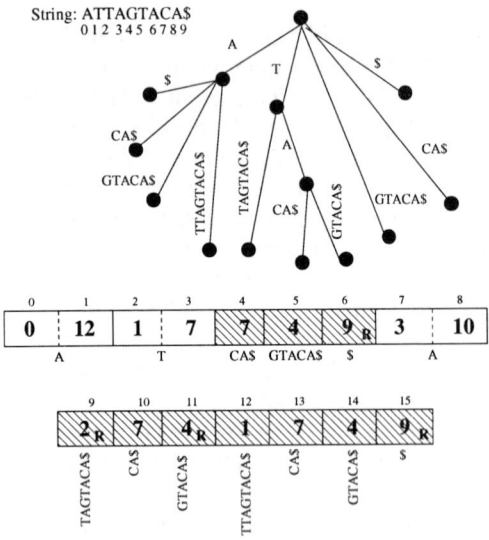

Figure 1: Suffix Tree Representation

Algorithm PWOTD(*String,prefixlen*)
Phase1:
Scan the *String* and partition *Suffixes* based on the first *prefixlen* symbols of each suffix
Phase2: Do for each partition:
1. START BuildSuffixTree
2. Populate *Suffixes* from current partition
3. Sort *Suffixes* on first symbol using *Temp*
4. Output branching and leaf nodes to the *Tree*
5. Push the nodes pointing to an unevaluated range onto the *Stack*
While *Stack* is not empty
  6. Pop a node
  7. Find the Longest Common Prefix (LCP) of all the suffixes in this range by checking the *String*
  8. Sort the range in *Suffixes* on the first symbol using *Temp*
  9. Write out branching nodes or leaf nodes to *Tree*
  10. Push the nodes pointing to an unevaluated range onto the *Stack*
11. END

Figure 2: The TDD Algorithm

this algorithm by using a partitioning phase which allows one to immediately build larger, independent sub-trees in memory. Before we explain the details of the algorithm, we briefly discuss the representation of the suffix tree.

The suffix tree is represented by a linear array, as in *wotdeager*. This is a compact representation using an average of 8.5 bytes per symbol indexed. Figure 1 illustrates a suffix tree on the string ATTAGTACA$ and the tree's corresponding array representation in memory. Shaded entries in the array represent leaf nodes, with all other entries representing non-leaf nodes. An *R* in the lower right-hand corner of an entry denotes a rightmost child. A branching node is represented by two integers. The first is an index into the input string; the character at that index is the starting character of the incoming edge's label. The length of the label can be deduced by examining the children of the current node. The second entry points to the first child. Note that the leaf nodes do not have a second entry. The leaf node requires only the starting index of the label; the end of the label is the string's terminating character. See [15] for a more detailed explanation.

The PWOTD algorithm consists of two phases. In phase one, we partition the suffixes of the input string into $|A|^{prefixlen}$ partitions, where $|A|$ is the alphabet size of the string and *prefixlen* is the depth of the partitioning. The partitioning step is executed as follows. The input string is scanned from left to right. At each index position i the *prefixlen* subsequent characters are used to determine one of the $|A|^{prefixlen}$ partitions. This index i is then written to the calculated partition's buffer. At the end of the scan, each partition will contain the suffix pointers for suffixes that all have the same prefix of size *prefixlen*.

To further illustrate the partition step, consider the following example. Partitioning the string ATTAGTACA$ using a *prefixlen* of 1 would create four partitions of suffixes, one for each symbol in the alphabet. (We ignore the final partition consisting of just the string terminator symbol $.) The suffix partition for the character A would be {0,3,6,8}, representing the suffixes {ATTAGTACA$, AGTACA$, ACA$, A$}. The suffix partition for the character T would be {1,2,5} representing the suffixes {TTAGTACA$, TAGTACA$, TACA$}. In phase two, we use the *wotdeager* algorithm to build the suffix tree on each partition using a top down construction.

The pseudo-code for the PWOTD algorithm is shown in Figure 2. While the partitioning in phase one of PWOTD is simple enough, the algorithm for *wotdeager* in phase two warrants further discussion. We now illustrate the *wotdeager* algorithm using an example.

3.1.1 Example Illustrating the *wotdeager* Algorithm

The PWOTD algorithm requires four data structures for constructing suffix trees: an input string array, a suffix array, a temporary array, and the suffix tree. For the discussion that follows, we name each of these structures *String*, *Suffixes*, *Temp*, and *Tree*, respectively.

The Suffixes array is first populated with suffixes from a partition after discarding the first *prefixlen* characters. Using the same example string as before, ATTAGTACA$, consider the construction of the Suffixes array for the T-partition. The suffixes in this partition are at positions 1, 2, and 5. Since all these suffixes share the same prefix, T, we add one to each offset to produce the new Suffix array {2,3,6}. The next step involves sorting this array of suffixes based on the first character. The first characters of each suffix are {T, A, A}. The sorting is done using an efficient algorithm called *count-sort* in linear time (for a constant alphabet size). In a single pass, for each character

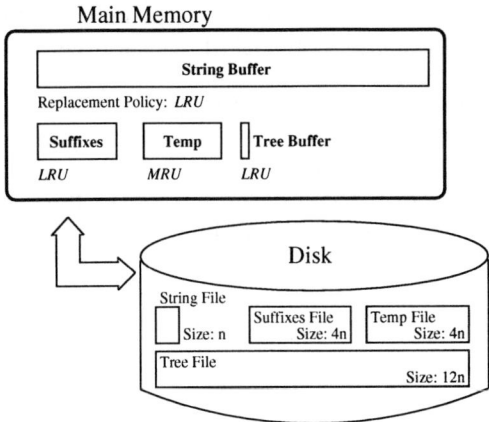

Figure 3: Buffer Management Schema

in the alphabet, we count the number of occurrences of that character in the first character of each suffix, and copy the suffix pointers into the Temp array. We see that the count for A is 2 and the count for T is 1; the counts for G, C, and $ are 0. We can use these counts to determine the character group boundaries: group A will start at position 0 with two entries, and group T will start at position 2 with 1 entry. We make a single pass through the Temp array and produce the Suffixes array sorted on the first character. The Suffixes array is now {3, 6, 2}. The A-group has two members and is therefore a branching node. These two suffixes completely determine the sub-tree below this node. Space is reserved in the Tree to write this non-leaf node once it is expanded, then the node is pushed onto the stack. Since the T-group has only one member, it is a leaf node and will be immediately written to the Tree. Since no other children need to be processed, no additional entries are added to the stack, and this node will be popped off first.

Once the node is popped off the stack, we find the longest common prefix (LCP) of all the nodes in the group {3, 6}. We examine position 4 (G) and position 7 (C) to determine that the LCP is 1. Each suffix pointer is incremented by the LCP, and the result is processed as before. The computation proceeds until all nodes have been expanded and the stack is empty. Figure 1 shows the complete suffix tree and its array representation.

3.1.2 Discussion of the PWOTD Algorithm

Observe that phase 2 of PWOTD operates on subsets of the suffixes of the string. In *wotdeager*, for a string of n symbols, the size of the Suffixes array and the Temp array needed to be $4 \times n$ bytes (assuming 4 byte integers are used as pointers). By partitioning in Phase 1, the amount of memory needed by the suffix arrays in each run is just $\frac{4 \times n}{|A|^{prefixlen}}$. This is an important point: partitioning decreases the main-memory requirements for suffix tree construction, allowing independent sub-tree to be built entirely in main memory. Suppose we are partitioning a 100 million symbol string over an alphabet of size 4. Using a $prefixlen = 2$ will decrease the space requirement of the Suffixes and Temp arrays from 400 MB to 25 MB each, and the Tree array from 1200 MB to 75 MB. Unfortunately, this savings is not entirely free. The cost to partition increases linearly with *prefixlen*. For small input strings where we have sufficient main memory for all the structures, we can skip the partitioning phase entirely. It is not necessary to continue partitioning once the Suffixes and Temp arrays fit into memory. For even very large datasets, such as the human genome, partitioning beyond 7 levels is not beneficial.

3.2 Buffer Management

Since suffix trees are an order of magnitude larger in size than the input data string, suffix tree construction algorithms require large amounts of memory, which may exceed the amount of main memory that is available. For such large data sets, efficient disk-based construction methods are needed that can scale well for large input sizes. One strength of TDD is that it transitions the data structures gracefully to disk as necessary, and uses individual buffer management polices for each structure. As a result, TDD can scale gracefully to handle large input sizes.

Recall that the PWOTD algorithm requires four data structures for constructing suffix trees: *String*, *Suffixes*, *Temp*, and *Tree*. Figure 3 shows each of these structures as separate, in-memory buffer caches. By appropriately allocating memory and by using the right buffer replacement policy for each structure, the TDD approach is able to build suffix trees on extremely large inputs. The buffer management policies are summarized in Figure 3 and are discussed in detail below.

The largest data structure is the Tree buffer. This array stores the suffix tree during its intermediate stages as well as the final computed result. The Tree data structure is typically 8-12 times the size of the input string. The reference pattern to Tree consists mainly of sequential writes when the children of a node are being recorded. Occasionally, pages are revisited when an unexpanded node is popped off the stack. This access pattern displays very good temporal and spatial locality. Clearly, the majority of this structure can be placed on disk and managed efficiently with a simple LRU (*Least Recently Used*) replacement policy.

The next largest data structures are the Suffixes and the Temp arrays. The Suffixes array is accessed as follows: first a sequential scan is used to copy the values into the Temp array. The sort operation following the scan causes random writes from the Temp array back into the Suffixes array. However, there is some locality in the pattern of writes, since the writes start at each character-group boundary and proceed sequentially to the right. Based on the (limited) locality of reference, one expects LRU to perform reasonably well.

During the sort, the Temp array is referenced in two linear scans: the first to copy all of the suffixes in the Suffixes array, and the second to copy all of them back into the Suffixes array in sorted order. For this reference pattern, replacing the most recently used page (MRU) works best.

The String array has the smallest main-memory requirement of all the data structures, but the worst locality of ac-

39

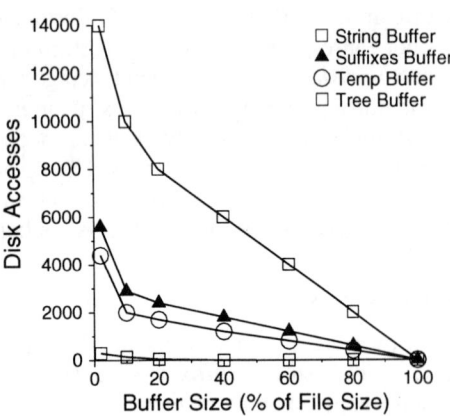

Figure 4: Sample Page Miss Curves

cess. The String array is referenced when performing the count-sort and to find the longest common prefix in each sorted group. During the count-sort all of the portions of the string referenced by the suffix pointers are accessed. Though these positions could be anywhere in the string, they are always accessed in left to right order. In the function to find the longest common prefix of a group, a similar pattern of reference is observed. In the case of the find-LCP function, each iteration will access the characters in the string, one symbol to the right of those previously referenced. In the case of the count-sort operation, the next set of suffixes to be sorted will be a subset of the current set. Based on these observations, one can conclude that the LRU policy would be the best management policy.

We summarize the choice of buffer management policies for each of the structures in Figure 3. As shown in the figure, the String, Suffixes, and Tree arrays should use the LRU replacement policy; the Temp array should use an MRU replacement policy. Based on experiments in Section 5.3, we confirm that these are indeed good choices.

3.3 Buffer Size Determination

To obtain the maximum benefit from buffer management policy, it is important to divide the available memory between the data structures appropriately. A careful apportioning of the available memory between these data structures can affect the overall execution time dramatically. In the rest of this section, we describe a technique to divide the available memory among the buffers.

If we know the access pattern for each of the data structures, we can devise an algorithm to partition the memory to minimize the overall number of buffer cache misses. Note that we only need an access pattern on a string representative of each class, such as DNA sequences, protein sequences, etc. In fact, we have found experimentally that these access patterns are similar across a wide-range of datasets (we discuss these results in detail in Section 5.3.) An illustrative graph of the buffer cache miss pattern for each data structure is shown in Figure 4. In this figure, the X-axis represents the number of pages allocated to the buffer as a percentage of the total size of the data structure.

The Y-axis shows the number of cache misses. This figure is representative of biological sequences derived from actual experiments in Section 5.3.

As we will see at the end of section 3.3.1, our buffer allocation strategy only needs to estimate the relative magnitudes of the slopes of each curve, and the position of the "knee" towards the start of the curve. The full curve as shown in Figure 4 is not needed for the algorithm. However, it is useful to facilitate the following discussion.

3.3.1 TDD Heuristic for Allocating Buffers

We know from Figure 4 that the cache miss behavior for each buffer is approximately linear once the memory is allocated beyond a minimum point. Once we identify these points, we can allocate the minimum buffer size necessary for each structure. The remaining memory is then allocated in order of decreasing slopes of the buffer miss curves.

We know from arguments in Section 3.2 that references to the String have poor locality. One can infer that the String data structure is likely to require the most buffer space. We also know that the references to the Tree array have very good locality, so the buffer space it needs is likely to be a very small fraction of its full size. Between Suffixes and Temp, we know that the Temp array has more locality than the Suffixes array, and will therefore require less memory. Both Suffixes and Temp require a smaller fraction of their pages to be resident in the buffer cache when compared to the String. We exploit this behavior to design a heuristic for memory allotment.

We suggest the minimum number of pages allocated to the Temp and Suffixes arrays to be $|A|$. During the sort phase, we know that the Suffixes array will be accessed at $|A|$ different positions which correspond to the character group boundaries. The incremental benefit of adding a page will be very high until $|A|$ pages, and then one can expect to see a change in the slope at this point. By allocating at least $|A|$ pages, we avoid the penalty of operating in the initial high miss-rate region. The TDD heuristic chooses to allocate a minimum of $|A|$ pages to Suffixes and Temp first.

We suggest allocating two pages to the Tree array. Two pages allow a parent node, possibly written to a previous page and then pushed onto the stack for later processing, to be accessed without replacing the current active page. This saves a large amount of I/O over choosing a buffer size of only one page.

The remaining pages are allocated to the String array. If any pages are left over, they are allocated to Suffixes, Temp, and Tree, in that order.

The reasoning behind this heuristic is borne out by the graphs in Figure 4. The String, which has the least locality of reference, has the highest slope and the largest magnitude. Suffixes and Temp have a lower magnitude and a more gradual slope, indicating that the improvement with each additional page allocated is smaller. Finally, the Tree, which has excellent locality of reference, is nearly zero. All curves have a knee at the initial point which we estimate by choosing minimum allocations.

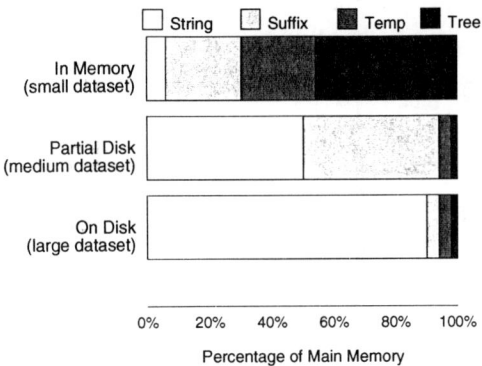

Figure 5: Scaling Buffer Allocation

3.3.2 An Example Allocation

The following example demonstrates how to allocate the main memory to the buffer caches. Assume that your system has 100 buffer pages available for use and that you are building a suffix tree on a small string that requires 6 pages. Further assume that the alphabet size is 4 and that 4 byte integers are used. Assuming that no partitioning is done, the Suffixes array will need 24 pages (one integer for each character in the String), the Temp array will need 24 pages, and the Tree will need at most 72 pages. First we allocate 4 pages each to Suffixes and Temp. We allocate 2 pages to Tree. We are now left with 90 pages. Of these, we allocate 6 pages to the String, thereby fitting it entirely in memory. From the remaining 84 pages, Suffixes and Temp are allocated 20 and fit into memory, and the final 44 pages are all given to Tree. This allocation is shown pictorially in the first row of Figure 5.

Similarly, the second row in Figure 5 is an allocation for a medium sized input of 50 pages. First, the heuristic allocates 4 pages each to Suffixes and Temp, and 2 pages to Tree. The String is given 50 pages. The remaining 40 pages are given to Suffixes, producing the second allocation in Figure 5. The third allocation corresponds to a large string of 120 pages. Here, Suffixes, Temp, and Tree are allocated their minimums of 4, 4, and 2 respectively, and the rest of the memory (90 pages) is given to String. Note that the entire string does not fit in memory now, and portions will be swapped into memory from disk when they are needed.

It is interesting to observe how the above heuristic allocates the memory as the size of the input string increases. This trend is indicated in Figure 5. When the input is small and all the structures fit into memory, most of the space is occupied by the largest data structure: the Tree. As the input size increases, the Tree is pushed out to disk. For very large strings that do not fit into memory, everything but the String is pushed out to disk, and the String is given nearly all of the memory. By first pushing the structures with better locality of reference onto disk, TDD is able to scale gracefully to very large input sizes.

Note that our heuristic does not need the actual utility curves to calculate the allotments. It estimates the "knee" of each curve using the algorithm, and assumes that the curve is linear for the rest of the region.

4 Analysis

In this section, we analyze the advantages and the disadvantages of using the TDD technique for various types and sizes of string data. We also describe how the design choices we have made in TDD overcome the performance bottlenecks present in other proposed techniques.

4.1 I/O Benefits

Unlike the approach of [4] where the authors use the best in-memory $O(n)$ algorithm (Ukkonen) as the basis for their disk-based algorithm, we use the theoretically less efficient $O(n^2)$ *wotdeager* algorithm [15]. A major difference between the two algorithms is that the Ukkonen algorithm sequentially accesses the string data and then updates the suffix tree through random traversals, while our TDD approach accesses the input string randomly and then writes the tree sequentially. For disk based construction algorithms, random access is the performance bottleneck as on each access an entire page will potentially have to be read from disk; therefore, efficient caching of the randomly accessed disk pages is critical.

On first appearance, it may seem that we are simply trading random disk I/Os for more random disk I/Os, but the input string is the smallest structure in the construction algorithm, while the suffix tree is the largest structure. TDD can place the suffix tree in very small buffer cache as the writes are almost entirely sequential, which leaves the remaining memory free to buffer the randomly accessed, but much smaller, input string. Therefore, our algorithm requires a much smaller buffer cache to contain the randomly accessed data. Conversely, for the same amount of buffer cache, we can cache much more of the randomly accessed pages, allowing us to construct suffix trees on much larger input strings.

4.2 Main-Memory Analysis

When we build suffix trees on small strings, where data structures fit in memory, no disk I/O is incurred. For the case of in-memory construction, one would expect that a linear time algorithm such as Ukkonen would perform better than the TDD approach which has an average case complexity of $O(nlog_{|A|}n)$. However, one must consider more than just the computational complexity to understand the execution time of the algorithms.

Traditionally, all accesses to main memory were considered equally good, as the disk I/O was the performance bottleneck. But, for programs that require little disk I/O, the performance bottleneck shifts into the main-memory hierarchy. Modern processors typically employ one or more data caches for improving access times to memory when there is a lot of spatial and/or temporal locality in the access patterns. The processor cache is analogous to a database's buffer cache, the primary difference being that the user does not have control over the replacement policy. Reading data from the processor's data cache is an order of magnitude faster than reading data from the main memory. And as the speed of the processor increases, so does the main-memory latency; as a result, the latency of random memory accesses will only grow with future processors.

Linear time algorithms such as Ukkonen require a large number of random memory accesses due to linked list traversals through the tree structure. A majority of cache misses occur after traversing a suffix link to a new sub-tree and then examining each child of the new parent. The traversal of the suffix link to the sibling sub-tree and the subsequent search of the destination node's children require random accesses to memory over a large address space. Because this span of memory is too large to fit in the processor cache, each access has a very high probability of incurring the full main-memory latency. Using an array based representation [21], where the pointers to the children are stored in an array with an element for each symbol in the alphabet, can reduce the number of cache misses. However, this representation uses up a lot more space and could therefore lead to a higher run time anyway.

Observe that as the alphabet size of the input string grows, the number of children for each non-leaf node will increase proportionately. As more children are examined to find the right position to insert the next character, the more cache misses will be incurred. Therefore, the Ukkonen method will incur an increasing number of processor cache misses with an increase in alphabet size.

For TDD, the alphabet size has the opposite effect. As the branching factor increases, the working set of the Suffixes and Temp arrays quickly decreases, and can fit into the processor cache sooner. The majority of read misses in the TDD algorithm occur when calculating the size of each character group (in Line 8 of Figure 2). This is because the beginning character of each suffix must be read, and there is little spatial locality in the reads. While both algorithms must perform random accesses to main memory which incur very expensive cache misses, there are three properties about the TDD algorithm that make it more suited for in-memory performance: (a) the access pattern is sequential through memory, (b) each random memory access is independent of the others accesses, and (c) the accesses are known a priori. Because the accesses to the input data string are sequential through the memory address space, hardware-based data prefetchers may be able to identify opportunities for prefetching the cache lines [19]. In addition, recently proposed techniques for overlapping execution with main-memory latency, such as software pipelining [7], can easily be incorporated in TDD.

4.3 Effect of Alphabet Size and Data Skew

There are two properties of the input string that can affect the execution time of suffix tree construction techniques: the size of the alphabet and the skew in the string. The average case running time for constructing a suffix tree on uniformly random input strings is $O(n \log_{|A|} n)$, where $|A|$ is the size of the input alphabet and n is the length of the input string. The intuition behind this average case time is as follows. There are $\log_{|A|} n$ levels in the tree, and at

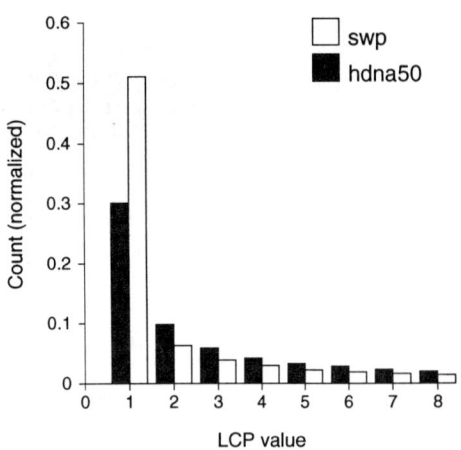

Figure 6: LCP Histogram

each level i the suffixes array is divided into $i^{|A|}$ parts. On each part, the count-sort and the find-LCP functions have to be run. The running time of count-sort is linear. To find the longest common prefix for a set of suffixes from a uniformly distributed string, the expected number of suffixes compared before a mismatch is slightly over 1. Therefore, the find-LCP function would return after just one or two comparisons most of the time. In some cases, the actual LCP is more than 1 and a scan of all suffixes is required. Therefore, in the case of uniformly distributed data, the find-LCP function is expected to run in constant time. This gives rise to the overall running time of $O(n \log_{|A|} n)$.

Interestingly, the longest common prefix is actually the label on the incoming edge for the node that corresponds to this range of suffixes. The average of all the LCPs computed while building a tree is equal to the average length of the labels on each edge ending in a non-leaf node.

Real datasets, such as DNA strings, have a skew that is particular to them. By nature, DNA often consists of large repeating sequences; different symbols occur with more or less the same frequency and certain patterns occur more frequently than others. As a result, the average LCP is higher than that for uniformly distributed data. Figure 6 shows a histogram for the longest common prefixes generated while constructing suffix trees on the SwissProt [2] and a 50 MB Human DNA sequence [13]. Notice that both sequences have a high probability that the LCP will be greater than 1. Even among biological datasets, the differences can be quite dramatic. From the figure, the DNA sequence is much more likely to have LCPs greater than 1 compared with the protein sequence (70% versus 50%). It is important to note that the LCP histograms for the DNA and protein sequences shown in the figure do not represent all strings, but these particular results do highlight the differences one can expect between input sets.

For data with a lot of repeating sequences, the find-LCP function will not be able to complete in a constant amount of time. It will have to scan at least the first l characters of all the suffixes in the range, where l is the actual LCP. In this case, the cost of find-LCP becomes $O(l \times r)$ where l is the actual LCP, and r is the number of suffixes in the range that the function is examining. As a result, the PWOTD algorithm will take longer to complete. However, note that the average case complexity remains $O(n \log_{|A|} n)$.

Inputs with a lot of repeated sequences, such as DNA, decrease the performance of TDD but may perform well for algorithms similar to Ukkonen's. Ukkonen's algorithm can exploit the repeated subsequences by terminating an insert phase when the duplicate suffix is already in the tree. This will happen more frequently in the case of input string like DNA which often have long repeating sequences, thereby providing a computational savings to the Ukkonen algorithm. Unfortunately, this advantage is offset by the random reference pattern which makes it a poor choice for larger input string on cached architectures.

The size of the input alphabet also has an important effect. Larger input alphabets are an advantage for TDD because the running time is $O(n \log_{|A|} n)$, where $|A|$ is the size of the alphabet. A larger input alphabet implies a larger branching factor for the suffix tree. This in turn implies that the working size of the Suffixes and Temp arrays shrinks more rapidly - and could fit into the cache entirely at a lower depth. For Ukkonen, a larger branching factor would imply that on an average, more siblings will have to be examined while searching for the right place to insert. This leads to a longer running time for Ukkonen. There are hash-based and array based approaches that alleviate this problem [21], but at the cost of consuming much more space for the tree. A larger representation naturally implies that we are limited to building trees on smaller strings. We experimentally demonstrate these effects in Section 5.

Note that the case where Ukkonen will have an advantage over TDD is for short input strings over a small alphabet with high skew (repeat sequences). TDD is a better bet in all other cases.

4.4 Summary of the Analysis

In this section, we discussed why the $O(n^2)$ construction algorithm used in the TDD technique is more amenable to disk-based suffix tree construction than the $O(n)$ algorithm of Ukkonen. Because the PWOTD algorithm trades random accesses into the input string (of size n) for sequential accesses into the Tree data structure (of size $12n$), we can manage the Tree structure with only a fraction of the main memory required by other techniques. This property provides a fundamental advantage over other disk-based approaches since our disk I/O performance is primarily dependent on the smallest data structure, instead of being dependent on the largest data structure as is the case with other techniques.

We also argued that even for small strings where all the structures fit into main memory, using an $O(n)$ algorithm like Ukkonen might not be the best choice. The behavior of the algorithm with respect to the processor caches is also important, and as we show later in Section 5, TDD outperforms existing methods even for the in-memory case.

Finally, we explored the effects of alphabet size and the skew in the input string on TDD. We argue that TDD performs better on larger alphabet sizes, and is disadvantaged by skew in the string. Algorithms like Ukkonen on the other hand are poor for larger alphabet sizes and have an advantage for skewed data. Again, we point to Section 5 for an experimental verification of these claims.

5 Experimental Evaluation

In this section, we present the results of an extensive experimental evaluation of the different suffix tree construction techniques. In addition to TDD, we compare Ukkonen's algorithm [32] for in-memory construction performance, and Hunt's algorithm [18] for disk-based construction performance. Ukkonen's and Hunt's algorithms are considered the best known suffix tree construction algorithms for the in-memory case and the disk based case respectively.

5.1 Experimental Implementation

Our TDD algorithm uses separate buffer caches for the four main structures: the string, the suffixes array, the temporary working space for the count sort, and the suffix tree. We use fixed-size pages of 8K for reading and writing to disk. Buffer allocation for TDD is done using the method described in Section 3.3. If the amount of memory required is less than the size of the buffer cache, then that structure is loaded into the cache, with accesses to the data bypassing the buffer cache logic. TDD was written in C++ and compiled with GNU's g++ compiler version 3.2.2 with full optimizations activated.

For an implementation of the Ukkonen's algorithm, we use the version from [34]. It is a textbook implementation of Ukkonen's algorithm based on Gusfield's description [17] and written in C. The algorithm operates entirely in main memory, and there is no persistence. The representation uses 32 bytes per node.

Our implementation of Hunt's algorithm is from the OASIS search tool [25], which is part of the Periscope project [27]. The OASIS implementation uses a shared buffer cache instead of the persistent Java object store, PJama [3], described in the original proposal [18]. The buffer manager employs the CLOCK replacement policy. The OASIS implementation performed better than the implementation described in [18]. This is not surprising since PJama incurs the overhead of running through the Java Virtual Machine.

For the disk based experiments that follow, unless stated otherwise, all I/O is to raw devices; i.e., there is no buffering of I/O by the operating system and all reads and writes to disk are synchronous (blocking). This provides an unbiased accounting of the performance for disk based construction as operating system buffering will not (positively) affect the performance. Therefore, our results present the worst case performance of disk based construction. Using asynchronous writes is expected to improve the performance of our algorithm over the results presented. Each raw device accesses a single partition on one Maxtor Atlas

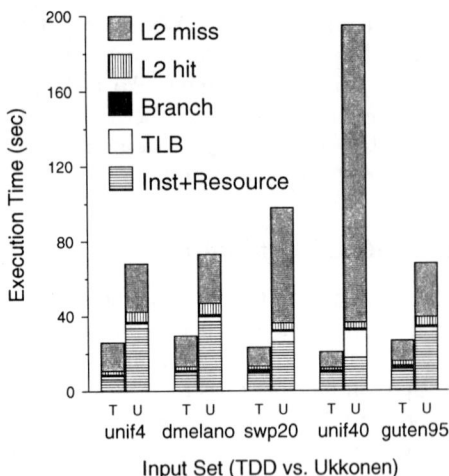

Figure 7: Execution Time Breakdown

Data Source	Description	Symbols (10^6)
dmelano	D.Melanogaster Chr. 2 (DNA)	20
guten95	Gutenberg Project, Year 1995 (English Text)	20
swp20	Slice of SwissProt (Protein)	20
unif4	4-char alphabet, uniform distrib.	20
unif40	40-char alphabet, uniform distrib.	20

Table 1: Main Memory Data Sources

10K IV drive. The disk drive controller is an LSI 53C1030, Ultra 320 SCSI controller.

The experiments were performed on an Intel Pentium 4 processor with 2.8 GHz clock speed and 2 GB of main memory. This processor includes a two level cache hierarchy. There are two first level caches, named L1-I and L1-D, that cache instructions and data respectively. There is also a single L2 cache that stores both instructions and data. The L1 data cache is an 8 KB, 4-way set-associative cache with a 64 byte line size. The L1 instruction cache is a 12 K trace cache, 4-way set associative. The L2 cache is a 512 KB, 8-way, set-associative cache, also with a 128 byte line size. The operating system was Linux, kernel version 2.4.20.

The Pentium 4 processor includes 18 event counters that are available for recording micro-architectural events, such as the number of instructions executed [20]. To access the event counters, the *perfctr* library was used [28]. The events measured include: clock cycles executed, instructions and micro-operations executed, L2 cache accesses and misses, TLB misses, and branch mispredictions.

5.2 Comparison of In-Memory Algorithms

To evaluate the performance of the TDD technique for in-memory construction, we chose to compare with the performance of the $O(n)$ time Ukkonen's algorithm. We do not evaluate Hunt's algorithm in this section as it was not designed as an in-memory technique. For this experiment, we used five different data sources : chromosome 2 of Drosophila Melanogaster from GenBank [13], a slice of the SwissProt dataset [2] having 20 million symbols, and the text from the 1995 collection from project Gutenberg [29]. We also chose two strings that contain uniformly distributed symbols from an alphabet of size four and forty. This data is summarized in Table 1.

Figure 7 shows the execution time breakdown for both algorithms, grouped by data source with TDD performance on the left and Ukkonen performance on the right. Note that since this is the in-memory case, TDD reduces to just the PWOTD algorithm. In these experiments, all data structures fit into memory. The total execution time is decomposed into the time executing the following micro-architectural events (from bottom to top): instructions executed plus resource related stalls, TLB misses, branch mispredictions, L2 cache hits, and L2 cache misses (or main-memory reads).

From Figure 7, the L2 cache miss component is a large contributor to the execution time for both algorithms. Both algorithms show a similar breakdown for the small alphabet sizes of DNA data (unif4 and dmelano). When the alphabet size increases from 4 symbols to 20 symbols for SwissProt and to 40 symbols for unif40, the cache miss component of Ukkonen's algorithm increases dramatically while the cache miss component for the TDD algorithm remains low. The reason for this, as discussed in Section 4.2, is that Ukkonen's algorithm incurs a lot of cache misses while following the suffix link to a new portion of the tree, and traversing all the children when trying to find the right position to insert the new entry.

We observe that for each dataset, TDD outperforms Ukkonen's algorithm and the performance difference increases with alphabet size. This was expected based on discussions in Section 4.3. For instance, on the DNA dataset of *dmelano* ($|A| = 4$), TDD is faster than Ukkonen by a factor of 2.5. For the *swp20* protein dataset ($|A| = 20$), TDD is faster by a factor of 4.5. Finally, for the *unif40* ($|A| = 40$), TDD is faster by a factor of 10! These results demonstrate that, despite having a $O(n^2)$ time complexity, the TDD technique significantly outperforms Ukkonen's algorithm on cached architectures.

5.3 Buffer Management with TDD

In this section we evaluate the effectiveness of various buffer management policies . For each data structure used in the TDD algorithm, we analyze the performance of the LRU, MRU, RANDOM, and CLOCK page replacement polices over a wide range of buffer cache sizes. To facilitate this analysis over the wide range of variables, we employed a buffer cache simulator. The simulator takes as input a trace of the address requests into the buffer cache and the page size. The simulator outputs the disk I/O statistics for the desired replacement policy. For all data shown here except the Temp array, MRU performs the worst by far and is not shown in the figures that we present in this section.

To generate the traces of address requests, we built suffix

Data Structure	SwissProt (size in pages)	Human DNA (size in pages)
String	6,250	6,250
Suffixes	1,250	6,250
Temp	1,250	6,250
Tree	4,100	16,200

Table 2: Array Sizes

trees on the *SwissProt* database [2] and a 50 Mbps slice of the *Human Chromosome*-1 database [13]. A *prefixlen* of 1 was used for partitioning in the first phase. The size of each of the arrays for these datasets is summarized in Table 2.

5.3.1 Page Size

In order to determine the page size to use for the buffers, we conducted several experiments. We observed that larger page sizes produced fewer page misses when the alphabet size was large (protein datasets, for instance). Smaller page sizes seemed to have a slight advantage in the case of input sets with smaller alphabets (like DNA sequences). We observed that a page size of 8192 bytes performed well for a wide range of alphabet sizes. In the interest of space, we omit the details of our page-size study. For all the experiments described in this section we use a page size of 8KB.

5.3.2 Buffer Replacement Policy

The results showing the effect of the various buffer replacement policies for the four data structures are shown in Figures 8 to 11. In these figures, the x-axis is the buffer size (shown as a percentage of the original input string size), and the y-axis is the number of buffer misses that are incurred by various replacement policies.

From Figure 8, we observe that for the String buffer LRU, RANDOM, and CLOCK all perform similarly. In fact, RANDOM has a very small advantage over the other two because there is very limited locality in the reference pattern in the string. Of all the arrays, when the buffer size is a fixed fraction of the total size of the structure, the String incurs the largest number of page misses. This is not surprising since this structure is accessed the most and in a random fashion.

In the case of the Suffixes buffer (shown in Figure 9), all three policies perform similarly for small buffer sizes. In the case of the Temp buffer, the reference pattern consists of one linear scan from left to right to copy the suffixes from the Suffixes array, and then another scan from left to right to copy the suffixes back into the Suffixes array in the sorted order. Clearly, MRU is the best policy in this case as shown by the results in Figure 10. It is interesting to observe that the space required by the Temp buffer is much smaller than the space required by the Suffixes buffer to keep the number of misses down to the same level, though the array sizes are the same.

For the Tree buffer (see Figure 11), with very small buffer sizes, LRU and CLOCK outperform RANDOM. However, this advantage is lost for even moderate buffer sizes. The most important fact here is that despite being the largest data structure, it requires the smallest amount of buffer space, and takes a relatively insignificant number of misses for any policy. Therefore for the Tree buffer, we can choose to implement the cheapest policy - the random replacement policy.

Data Source	Description	Symbols (10^6)
swp	Entire UniProt/SwissProt (Protein)	53
H.Chr1-50	50 Mbps slice of Human Chromosome-1 (DNA)	50
guten03	2003 Directory of Gutenberg Project (English Text)	58
trembl	TrEMBL (Protein)	338
H.Chr1	Entire Human Chromosome-1 (DNA)	227
guten	Entire Gutenberg Collection (English Text)	407
HG	Entire Human Genome (DNA)	3,000

Table 3: On-Disk Data Sources

Data Source	Symbols (10^6)	Hunt (min)	TDD (min)	Speedup
swp	53	13.95	2.78	5.0
H.Chr1-50	50	11.47	2.02	5.7
guten03	58	22.5	6.03	3.7
trembl	338	236.7	32.00	7.4
H.Chr1	227	97.50	17.83	5.5
guten	407	463.3	46.67	9.9
HG	3,000	—	30hrs	—

Table 4: Performance Comparison

5.4 Comparison of Disk-based Algorithms

In this section we first compare the performance of our technique with the technique proposed by Hunt et al. [18], which is currently considered the best disk-based suffix tree construction algorithm. For this experiment, we used seven datasets which are described in Table 3. The suffix tree construction times for the two algorithms are shown in Table 4.

From this table, we see that in each case TDD performs significantly better than Hunt's algorithm. For example, on the TrEMBL database, ($|A| = 20$), TDD is faster by a factor of 7.4. For Human Chromosome-1 ($|A| = 4$), TDD is faster by a factor of 5.5. For a large text dataset like the Gutenberg Collection ($|A| = 60$), TDD is nearly ten times faster! For the largest dataset, the human genome, Hunt's algorithm did not complete in a reasonable amount of time. The reason why TDD performs better is that Hunt's algorithm traverses the on-disk tree during construction, while TDD does not. During construction, a given node in the tree is written over at most once. By careful management of the buffer sizes, and the buffer replacement policies, the disk I/O in TDD is brought down further.

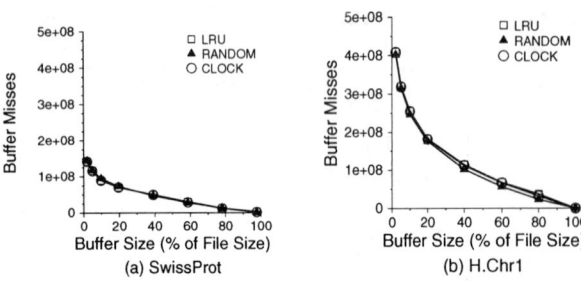

Figure 8: String Buffer

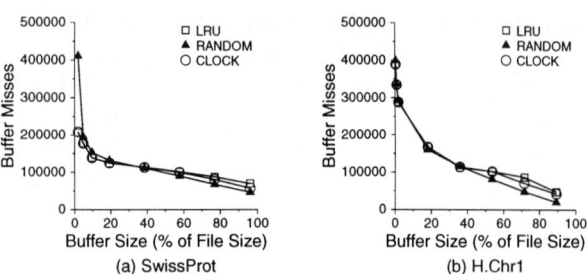

Figure 9: Suffix Buffer

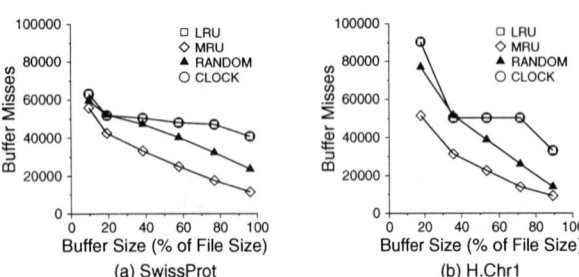

Figure 10: Temp Buffer

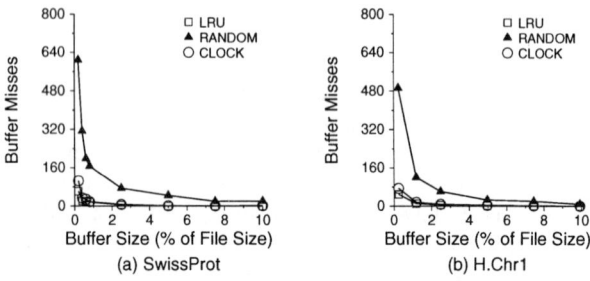

Figure 11: Tree Buffer

Comparison of TDD with TOP-Q

Very recently, Bedathur and Haritsa have proposed the TOP-Q technique for constructing suffix trees [4]. TOP-Q is a new low overhead buffer management method which can be used with Ukkonen's construction algorithm. The goal of these researchers is to invent a buffer management technique that does not require modifying an existing in-memory construction algorithm. In contrast, TDD and Hunt's algorithm [18] take the approach of modifying existing suffix tree construction algorithms to produce a new disk-based suffix tree construction algorithm. Even though the research focus of TOP-Q is different from TDD and Hunt's algorithm, it is natural to ask how the TOP-Q method compares to these other approaches.

To compare TDD with TOP-Q, we obtained a copy of the TOP-Q code from the authors. This version of the code only supports building suffix tree indices on DNA sequences. As per the recommendation in [4], we used a buffer pool of 880M for the internal nodes and 800M for the leaf nodes (this was the maximum memory allocation possible with the TOP-Q code). On 50Mbp of Human Chromosome-1, TOP-Q took about 78 minutes. By contrast, under the same conditions, TDD took about 2.1 minutes: faster by a factor of 37. On the entire Human Chromosome-1, TOP-Q took 5800 minutes, while our approach takes around 18 minutes. In this case, TDD is faster by two orders of magnitude!

6 Conclusions and Future Work

Suffix tree construction on large character sequences has been virtually intractable. Existing approaches have excessive memory requirements and poor locality of reference and therefore do not scale well for even moderately sized datasets.

To address these problems and unlock the potential of this powerful indexing structure, we have introduced the "Top Down Disk-based" (TDD) technique for disk-based suffix tree construction. The TDD technique includes a suffix tree construction algorithm (PWOTD), and an accompanying buffer cache management strategy. We demonstrate that PWOTD has an advantage over Ukkonen's algorithm by a factor of 2.5 to 10 for in-memory datasets.

Extensive experimental evaluations show that TDD scales gracefully as the dataset size increases. The TDD approach lets us build suffix trees on large frequently used sequence datasets such as UniProt/TrEMBL [2] in a few minutes. Algorithms to construct suffix trees on this scale (to our knowledge) have not been mentioned in literature before. The TDD approach outperforms a popular disk-based suffix tree construction method (the Hunt's algorithm) by a factor of 5 to 10. In fact, to demonstrate the strength of TDD, we show that using slightly more main-memory than the input string, a suffix tree can be constructed on the *entire Human Genome in 30 hours on a single processor machine!* These input sizes are one or two orders of magnitude larger than the datasets that have been used in previously published approaches.

Others researchers have proposed buffer management strategies for on-disk suffix tree construction, but our method is unique in that the larger data structures that are required during the suffix tree construction can be accessed efficiently even with a small number of buffer pages. This behavior leads to the highly scalable aspect of TDD.

As part of our future work, we plan on making TDD more amenable to parallel execution. We believe that the

TDD technique is extremely parallelizable due to the partitioning phase that it employs. Each partition is the source for an independent subtree of the complete suffix tree. Since the partitions are independent, multiple processors can simultaneously construct the sub-trees.

7 Acknowledgements

This research was supported by the National Science Foundation under grant IIS-0093059, and by research gift donations from IBM and Microsoft. We would like to thank the reviewers of VLDB and Ela Hunt for their valuable comments on earlier drafts of this paper. We would also like to thank Srikanta J. Bedathur and Jayant Haritsa for providing us a copy of their TOP-Q code.

References

[1] A. Andersson and S. Nilsson. Efficient Implementation of Suffix Trees. *Software–Practice and Experience (SPE)*, 25(2):129–141, 1995.

[2] R. Apweiler, A. Bairoch, C. H. Wu, W. Barker, B. Boeckmann, S. Ferro, E. Gasteiger, H. Huang, R. Lopez, M. Magrane, M. J. Martin, D. Natale, A. C. O'Donovan, N. Redaschi, and L. L. Yeh. UniProt: the Universal Protein Knowledgebase. *Nucleic Acids Research*, 32(D):115–119, 2004.

[3] M. Atkinson and M. Jordan. Providing Orthogonal Persistence for Java. In *European Conference on Object-Oriented Programming (ECOOP)*, 1998.

[4] S. J. Bedathur and J. R. Haritsa. Engineering a Fast Online Persistent Suffix Tree Construction. In *ICDE*, 2004.

[5] A. Blumer, A. Ehrenfeucht, and D. Haussler. Average Sizes of Suffix Trees and DAWGs. *Discrete Applied Mathematics*, 24(1):37–45, 1989.

[6] A. Carvalho, A. Freitas, A. Oliveira, and M.-F. Sagot. A Parallel Algorithm for the Extraction of Structured Motifs. In *ACM Symposium on Applied Computing*, 2004.

[7] S. Chen, A. Ailamaki, P. Gibbons, and T. Mowry. Improving Hash Join Performance through Prefetching. In *ICDE*, 2004.

[8] L.-L. Cheng, D. Cheung, and S.-M. Yiu. Approximate String Matching in DNA Sequences. In *Proceeings of the Eighth International Conference on Database Systems for Advanced Applications*, pages 303–310, 2003.

[9] A. Crauser and P. Ferragina. A Theoretical and Experimental Study on the Construction of Suffix Arrays in External Memory and its Applications. *Algorithmica*, 32(1):1–35, 2002.

[10] A. Delcher, S. Kasif, R. Fleischmann, J. Peterson, O. White, and S. Salzberg. Alignment of Whole Genomes. *Nucleic Acids Research*, 27(11):2369–2376, 1999.

[11] A. Delcher, A. Phillippy, J. Carlton, and S. Salzberg. Fast Algorithms for Large-scale Genome Alignment and Comparision. *Nucleic Acids Research*, 30(11):2478–2483, 2002.

[12] M. Farach-Colton, P. Ferragina, and S. Muthukrishnan. On the Sorting-complexity of Suffix tree Construction. *J. ACM*, 47(6):987–1011, 2000.

[13] GenBank, NCBI, 2004. www.ncbi.nlm.nih.gov/GenBank.

[14] R. Giegerich and S. Kurtz. From Ukkonen to McCreight and Weiner: A Unifying View of Linear-time Suffix Tree Construction. *Algorithmica*, 19(3):331–353, 1997.

[15] R. Giegerich, S. Kurtz, and J. Stoye. Efficient Implementation of Lazy Suffix Trees. In *Proceedings of the Third Workshop on Algorithm Engineering (WAE'99)*, 1999.

[16] D. Gusfield. An "Increment-by-one" Approach to Suffix Arrays and Trees. *Technical Report CSE-90-39, Computer Science Division, University of California, Davis*, 1990.

[17] D. Gusfield. *Algorithms on Strings, Trees and Sequences: Computer Science and Computational Biology*. Cambridge University Press, 1997.

[18] E. Hunt, M. P. Atkinson, and R. W. Irving. A Database Index to Large Biological Sequences. *The VLDB J.*, 7(3):139–148, 2001.

[19] Intel Corporation. *The IA-32 Intel Architecture Optimization Reference Manual*. Intel (Order Number 248966), 2004.

[20] Intel Corporation. *The IA-32 Intel Architecture Software Developer's Manual, Volume 3: System Programming Guide*. Intel (Order Number 253668), 2004.

[21] S. Kurtz. Reducing Space Requirement of Suffix Trees. *Software Practice and Experience*, 29(13):1149–1171, 1999.

[22] S. Kurtz, A. Phillippy, A. Delcher, M. Smoot, M. Shumway, C. Antonescu, and S. Salzberg. Versatile and Open Software for Comparing Large Genomes. *Genome Biology*, 5(R12), 2004.

[23] S. Kurtz and C. Schleiermacher. REPuter: Fast Computation of Maximal Repeats in Complete Genomes. *Bioinformatics*, 15(5):426–427, 1999.

[24] E. M. McCreight. A Space-economical Suffix Tree Construction Algorithm. *J. ACM*, 23(2):262–272, 1976.

[25] C. Meek, J. M. Patel, and S. Kasetty. OASIS: An Online and Accurate Technique for Local-alignment Searches on Biological Sequences. In *VLDB*, 2003.

[26] G. Navarro, R. Baeza-Yates, and J. Tariho. Indexing Methods for Approximate String Matching. *IEEE Data Engineering Bulletin*, 24(4):19–27, 2001.

[27] J. M. Patel. The Role of Declarative Querying in Bioinformatics. *OMICS*, 7(1):89–92, 2003.

[28] M. Pettersson. Perfctr: Linux Performance Montioring Counters Driver, user.it.uu.se/~mikpe/linux/perfctr.

[29] Project Gutenberg, www.gutenberg.net.

[30] W. Szpankowski. *Average-Case Analysis of Algorithms on Sequences*. John Wiley and Sons, 2001.

[31] The Growth of GenBank, NCBI, 2004. www.ncbi.nlm.nih.gov/genbank/genbankstats.html.

[32] E. Ukkonen. Constructing Suffix-trees On-Line in Linear Time. *Algorithms, Software, Architecture: Information Processing*, 1(92):484–92, 1992.

[33] P. Weiner. Linear Pattern Matching Algorithms. In *Proceedings of the 14th Annual Symposium on Switching and Automata Theory*, 1973.

[34] S. Yona and D. Tsadok. ANSI C Implementation of a Suffix Tree, cs.haifa.ac.il/~shlomo/suffix_tree.

Answering XPath Queries over Networks by Sending Minimal Views

Keishi Tajima   Yoshiki Fukui

Japan Advanced Institute of Science and Technology (JAIST)
Asahidai, Tatsunokuchi, Ishikawa 923-1292 Japan, {tajima, y-fukui}@jaist.ac.jp

Abstract

When a client submits a set of XPath queries to a XML database on a network, the set of answer sets sent back by the database may include redundancy in two ways: some elements may appear in more than one answer set, and some elements in some answer sets may be subelements of other elements in other (or the same) answer sets. Even when a client submits a single query, the answer can be self-redundant because some elements may be subelements of other elements in that answer. Therefore, sending those answers as they are is not optimal with respect to communication costs. In this paper, we propose a method of minimizing communication costs in XPath processing over networks. Given a single or a set of queries, we compute a minimal-size view set that can answer all the original queries. The database sends this view set to the client, and the client produces answers from it. We show algorithms for computing such a minimal view set for given queries. This view set is optimal; it only includes elements that appear in some of the final answers, and each element appears only once.

1 Introduction

Recently, XML has become a standard data format for information exchange and dissemination over the Internet. There have been many researches on various styles of XML information services on networks, such as on-line XML databases that provide interactive querying interfaces over the Internet, continuous query systems [21, 9, 2], and XML streaming systems [22, 5, 17, 25]. A continuous query system is a push-based information service, in which the users

Permission to copy without fee all or part of this material is granted provided that the copies are not made or distributed for direct commercial advantage, the VLDB copyright notice and the title of the publication and its date appear, and notice is given that copying is by permission of the Very Large Data Base Endowment. To copy otherwise, or to republish, requires a fee and/or special permission from the Endowment.

**Proceedings of the 30th VLDB Conference,
Toronto, Canada, 2004**

first register their queries to the system. Then, the system monitors the changes in its data, and when data matching the user queries become available, it is delivered to the corresponding users. In XML streaming systems, a server transmits a XML stream to the clients, and the clients monitor the stream to detect the data of interest to them.

Most of those systems use some kind of query language. Some of them use their own languages, but recently a language called XPath [12, 13] has become very popular. Although it was originally designed as a component of other standards, it is now also used as a stand-alone query language for many XML information systems because of its simplicity and yet enough expressive power [2, 8, 17, 25]. XML data is essentially a tree with node labels, and XPath is a tree pattern language, which extracts from a XML data a set of subtrees rooted by nodes that match the tree pattern. XPath can only extract a whole subtree rooted by some element; it never adds or trims edges, nor modifies labels.

XML information services can be classified into two categories: those that process queries on the server side, such as on-line XML databases and continuous query systems, and those that process queries on the client side, such as XML streaming systems. In the former, only necessary information is sent over networks from the server to the clients, and therefore, they are more efficient with respect to communication costs.

Even in the server-side approach, however, the communication cost is not always optimal. For example, if a client submits two queries to a database on a network, and the two answer sets to them have some data in common, sending those two answer sets separately to the client is not optimal in the sense that some data are sent twice. For example, suppose a client submits two queries asking:

- abstracts of papers including "XML" in their titles

- entire papers including both "XML" and "XPath" in their titles

to an on-line digital library or a continuous query system. If some paper includes "XML" and "XPath" in its title, its abstract appears in the answer sets twice, once as an answer to the first query, and once as a subelement of an answer to the second query. Hence, sending the two answer sets to the client over the network is not optimal with respect to the communication cost.

Even when a client submits a single XPath query, the answer can be self-redundant, i.e., some elements in the answer set may be subelements of other elements in that answer set. For example, suppose a client issues the query:

- retrieve chapters, sections, or subsections that have the word "XML" in their headings.

Then, if a book has a section with the heading "XML" and its subsection with the heading "XML queries", that subsection is sent to the client twice, once as an answer and once as a subelement of another answer. Answers to XPath queries are self-redundant very often. Notice that the same situation also occurs if a user issues a single query asking the union of the two queries in the previous example.

In the worst case, if a client submits a query "retrieve any subtree of the database tree," the result sent to the client can be far larger than the database itself. Self-redundancy of answers comes from the characteristic of XPath queries in which an answer to a query is a set of subtrees of the database tree, and a member of an answer set may be a subtree of another member of the same answer set. (However, a similar phenomenon can occur in other databases as well because it is quite usual that a query language can create an answer that is bigger than the database itself. For example, in relational databases, one can query the product of all the relations in the database [11].)

If the server and the client agree on some encoding or protocol, we can avoid such redundancy in query answers in various ways, e.g., embedding "pointers" in the answers. In this research, however, we assume the server is a service on the Internet provided by someone else, and all we can do is to submit XPath queries and get answers.

Even in such an environment, it is possible to minimize the size of the data sent over the network in the examples above. In the first example, we can minimize it by submitting the following two queries instead of the original ones:

- retrieve abstracts of papers including the word "XML" in their titles, but not "XPath", and

- retrieve entire papers including the words "XML" and "XPath" in their titles.

The server sends the answers to those queries, and then, the client can produce the answers to the original queries from those two results. In this scenario, the data sent over the network is optimal because it only includes data that appears in either (or both) of the final answers without duplication. In the same way, in the second example, the client should submit the following query:

- retrieve chapters, sections, or subsections that have "XML" in their headings, but have no ancestor with "XML" in its heading.

Then, the client can extract all the answers to the original query from the answers to this query. The data sent over the network in this example is again optimal.

In this way, we can sometimes optimize the communication cost by leaving a part of the query evaluation to the client, rather than fully evaluating queries at the server. By generalizing these examples, we study the following problem in this paper: *Given a single or a set of XPath queries, we compute another set of queries such that:*

- *we can produce the answers to the original queries from their answers, and*

- *the total size of their answers is minimal.*

In other words, we compute a minimal view set that can answer all the original queries. In this paper, we show algorithms for computing such a view set. Notice that a view set that includes all the information in the final answers does not necessarily guarantee we can correctly extract them. This is because some context in the database may be lost in the views. We will show some examples later.

If the server supports a full-fledged query language like XQuery, we can write queries that embed markers in views so that the client can easily extract the answers to the original queries. XPath, however, can only extract a set of subtrees of the database tree without modification, thus making the problem non-trivial; nevertheless, it is also this property that makes XPath efficiently processable, and it is the reason why many researches on large-scale information services adopt XPath [2, 8, 17, 25].

The techniques shown in this paper can be used in several ways. One way is to embed them in an intelligent querying agent, which resides at the client site. The agent transforms the user queries before submitting them, and extracts the answers from the views received from the server. Another approach is to embed them in a proxy server which resides between a continuous query server on the Internet and its users on the local network. Those users register queries to the proxy server, and the proxy server registers transformed queries to the server. By this, if many users register queries with overlapping answers, we can optimize the communication cost over the Internet.

In the next section, we explain the fragment of XPath we use in this paper. Next, we show some examples to clarify the problem and its inherent difficulties, and then, we formulate the problem. In the following three sections, we show our algorithm in three steps. We begin with an algorithm for non-recursive queries. (The meaning of non-recursive/recursive queries is explained later.) Second, we show an algorithm for a single recursive query, and finally we show an algorithm for the general case. Then, we discuss related work. The final section summarizes the paper and briefly discusses the practicality of our method.

2 XPath

As mentioned above, XPath is evaluated on a XML tree, and returns a set of subtrees rooted by nodes matching the pattern. Here, we assume that a query answer is given in the form of a XML tree rooted by a node labeled Ans that has all the matching subtrees as its children (as in some

XPath processors, e.g., Xalan [27]). For example, when a query answer is the following set of three subtrees:

$$\{\langle a\rangle\ldots\langle/a\rangle,\ \langle b\rangle\ldots\langle/b\rangle,\ \langle b\rangle\ldots\langle/b\rangle\}$$

it is given as an XML tree in a form:

$$\langle Ans\rangle\ \langle a\rangle\ldots\langle/a\rangle\ \langle b\rangle\ldots\langle/b\rangle\ \langle b\rangle\ldots\langle/b\rangle\ \langle/Ans\rangle.$$

In this paper, we use a fragment of XPath language that only includes its main features. The syntax of the language is defined as follows:

$$q ::= /p \mid //p \mid q \cup q \mid q - q$$
$$p ::= a \mid \overline{\{a_1,\ldots,a_n\}} \mid * \mid p/p \mid p//p \mid p[p] \mid p[\overline{p}]$$

A query q is either an absolute location path (in XPath terminology) of the form $/p$ or $//p$, the union of two queries $q \cup q$, or the difference of two queries $q - q$. An absolute location path $/p$ matches nodes which are reachable from the root through paths matching a relative location path (in XPath terminology) p. On the other hand, $//p$ matches nodes which are reachable through paths matching p starting from any nodes. $q \cup q$ and $q - q$ are the ordinary set union and the ordinary set difference.

A relative location path p is composed of the following constructs. a is a label test that matches nodes with a label a, and a negative label test $\overline{\{a_1,\ldots,a_n\}}$ matches nodes with a label other than $a_1,\ldots,a_n$. $*$ is a wild card that matches nodes with any labels. p/p is a concatenation of two location paths. For example, /a/* matches nodes with any label which are children of the "a" node at the root of the database tree. $p_1//p_2$ is also a concatenation, but it does not require a path matching p_2 appears immediately beneath a path matching p_1. For example, /a/*//b matches any "b" nodes which are descendants of the nodes matching the previous query /a/*. // represents a restricted form of recursion, and we call queries with // (without //) recursive queries (non-recursive queries, respectively).

$p_1[p_2]$ is called a predicate expression, and it matches nodes which are reachable through paths matching p_1, and also have at least one path matching p_2 beneath them. For example, //a[b/c] matches "a" nodes at any depth that has a child node "b" which, in turn, has a child node "c". Similarly, //a[b][c] matches "a" nodes at any depth that have both "b" children and "c" children. $p_1[\overline{p_2}]$ is a negative predicate and it matches nodes that are reachable through paths matching p_1 but have no path matching p_2 beneath them.

The definition above does not include the intersection operation $q_1 \cap q_2$, but it can be computed by $q_1 - (q_1 - q_2)$. Complementation of q can also be computed by $//* - q$. If we assume a finite set of labels, $\overline{\{a_1,\ldots,a_n\}}$ and $*$ add no expressive power to the language, but here we assume an infinite set of labels. Notice that $\overline{\{a_1,\ldots,a_n\}}$ has more power than the combination of $\overline{\{a\}}$ and $\cap$. For example, $//\overline{\{a,b\}}//c$ is not equivalent to $(//\overline{\{a\}}//c) \cap (//\overline{\{b\}}//c)$.

$q - q$ is supported in XPath 2.0 [13]. In XPath 1.0 [12], it is not directly supported, but we can express it by using a negative eq-join with identity-equality. Negative eq-join can be expressed by absolute location paths in negative predicates, and identity-equality can be expressed by using built-in count function as shown in [24]. Similarly, $\overline{\{a_1,\ldots,a_n\}}$ is not directly supported in XPath standard, but we can express it by *[not(self::a_1)]...[not(self::a_n)]. Negative predicates are expressed by $p[\text{not}(p)]$. For more details of the XPath standards, please refer to [12, 13].

3 Problem Analysis

In this section, we show some motivating examples in order to clarify what is the problem in XPath processing over a network, and what are the difficulties in it.

3.1 Examples with Non-recursive Queries

First, we consider examples that only include non-recursive queries. Below are two simple examples of a set of XPath queries that cause redundancy in their answers:

$$\begin{cases} Q_1: & \text{/a/*} \\ Q_2: & \text{/a/b} \end{cases} \qquad \begin{cases} Q_3: & \text{/a/b[c]} \\ Q_4: & \text{/a/b[d]} \end{cases}$$

In the example on the left side, the answer to Q_2 is a subset of Q_1, and therefore, sending the answers to Q_1 and Q_2 separately is not optimal with respect to communication costs. In this case, a simple solution is that we submit only Q_1 to the server, and produce the answer to Q_2 at the client side by extracting only b elements from the answer to Q_1. Because we assume that the answer to a query is given in a form of a XML tree rooted by Ans node whose children are answer elements, we can do that by evaluating a query /Ans/b against the answer to Q_1. In the rest of the paper, we write this in the following syntax:

$$Q_2 \leftarrow (Q_1, \text{/Ans/b})$$

On the other hand, in the case of Q_3 and Q_4, their answers overlap only partially. In this case, we can submit the query below instead of Q_3 and Q_4:

$$\{\ Q_{3\cup4}: \quad \text{/a/b[c]} \cup \text{/a/b[d]}$$

and we can extract the answer to Q_3 and Q_4 at the client in the following way:

$$\begin{array}{rl} Q_3 \leftarrow & (Q_{3\cup4}, \text{/Ans/b[c]}) \\ Q_4 \leftarrow & (Q_{3\cup4}, \text{/Ans/b[d]}) \end{array}$$

Similar situations are caused by union, difference, and negative label tests, such as:

$$\begin{cases} Q_5: & \text{/a/b} \cup \text{/a/c} \\ Q_6: & \text{/a/b} \end{cases} \qquad \begin{cases} Q_7: & \text{/a/}\overline{\{b\}} \\ Q_8: & \text{/a/}\overline{\{c\}} \end{cases}$$

Those two cases can be handled in the same way as the two examples above, respectively.

In some cases, however, we cannot extract the answer to some query from the answer to another query even if the former is a subset of the latter. For example, suppose we have two queries below:

$$\begin{cases} Q_9: & \text{/a/*/c} \\ Q_{10}: & \text{/a/b/c} \end{cases}$$

The answer to Q_9 is a superset of the answer to Q_{10}. In this case, however, only given the answer to Q_9 of the form:

$$\langle \mathsf{Ans} \rangle \quad \langle \mathsf{c} \rangle ... \langle \mathsf{/c} \rangle \quad ... \quad \langle \mathsf{c} \rangle ... \langle \mathsf{/c} \rangle \quad \langle \mathsf{/Ans} \rangle$$

we cannot tell which c elements in this answer are to be included in the answer to Q_{10} because we cannot know the labels of their parents in the original database tree. In this way, some context information in the database may be lost in query answers. In this case, we can minimize the communication cost, i.e., the total size of the data sent over the network, by submitting the following two queries:

$$\begin{cases} Q_{9-10}: & /\mathsf{a}/\overline{\{\mathsf{b}\}}/\mathsf{c} \\ Q_{10}: & /\mathsf{a}/\mathsf{b}/\mathsf{c} \end{cases}$$

The answer to Q_9 can be produced at the client side by taking union of the answers to Q_{9-10} and Q_{10} as follows:

$$Q_9 \leftarrow (Q_{9-10}, /\mathsf{Ans}/*)$$
$$Q_9 \leftarrow (Q_{10}, /\mathsf{Ans}/*)$$

The pair of Q_{9-10} and Q_{10} is optimal with respect to the communication cost because their answers only include data that appear in the final answers without duplication.

Similarly, if given two intersecting queries below:

$$\begin{cases} Q_{11}: & /\mathsf{a}/\overline{\{\mathsf{b}\}}/\mathsf{d} \\ Q_{12}: & /\mathsf{a}/\overline{\{\mathsf{c}\}}/\mathsf{d} \end{cases}$$

then, we should submit the following queries:

$$\begin{cases} Q_{11-12}: & /\mathsf{a}/\mathsf{c}/\mathsf{d} \\ Q_{11 \cap 12}: & /\mathsf{a}/\overline{\{\mathsf{b},\mathsf{c}\}}/\mathsf{d} \\ Q_{12-11}: & /\mathsf{a}/\mathsf{b}/\mathsf{d} \end{cases}$$

and produce the final answers in the following way:

$$Q_{11} \leftarrow (Q_{11-12}, /\mathsf{Ans}/*)$$
$$Q_{11} \leftarrow (Q_{11 \cap 12}, /\mathsf{Ans}/*)$$
$$Q_{12} \leftarrow (Q_{11 \cap 12}, /\mathsf{Ans}/*)$$
$$Q_{12} \leftarrow (Q_{12-11}, /\mathsf{Ans}/*)$$

This is more efficient with respect to the communication cost than submitting Q_{11} and Q_{12}, which results in sending elements in their intersection twice.

In the example above, the source of the redundancy are elements matching more than one query. Redundancy also arises when some answers also appear as subelements of other answers. Shown below are two simple examples:

$$\begin{cases} Q_{13}: & /\mathsf{a}/* \\ Q_{14}: & /\mathsf{a}/\mathsf{b}/\mathsf{c} \end{cases} \quad \{ Q_{15}: \quad /\mathsf{a}/* \cup /\mathsf{a}/\mathsf{b}/\mathsf{c}$$

In the case of Q_{15}, its answer can be self-redundant, i.e., some elements in its answer set may also appear as subelements of other elements in the answer set. In these cases, we should submit the following queries, respectively:

$$\{ Q_{13}: \quad /\mathsf{a}/* \quad \quad \{ Q_{15}^\top: \quad /\mathsf{a}/*$$

and extract the final answers in the following way:

$$Q_{14} \leftarrow (Q_{13}, /\mathsf{Ans}/\mathsf{b}/\mathsf{c}) \quad \quad Q_{15} \leftarrow (Q_{15}^\top, /\mathsf{Ans}/*)$$
$$Q_{15} \leftarrow (Q_{15}^\top, /\mathsf{Ans}/\mathsf{b}/\mathsf{c})$$

In the examples above, we can extract elements matching /a/b/c from the answer to /a/* because the answer to /a/* includes enough context information for /a/b/c. In general, however, some context information may be lost in query answers as explained before, and we may need to submit up to three queries, as shown in the example below:

$$\begin{cases} Q_{16}: & /\mathsf{a}/*/\mathsf{c} \\ Q_{17}: & /\mathsf{a}/\mathsf{b}/\mathsf{c}/\mathsf{d} \end{cases} \quad \begin{cases} Q_{18}: & /\mathsf{a}/\overline{\{\mathsf{b}\}}/\mathsf{d} \\ Q_{19}: & /\mathsf{a}/\overline{\{\mathsf{c}\}}/\mathsf{d}/\mathsf{e} \end{cases}$$

Here, we should submit the following set of queries:

$$\begin{cases} Q_{16-17}: & /\mathsf{a}/\overline{\{\mathsf{b}\}}/\mathsf{c} \\ Q_{16 \cap 17}: & /\mathsf{a}/\mathsf{b}/\mathsf{c} \end{cases} \quad \begin{cases} Q_{18-19}: & /\mathsf{a}/\mathsf{c}/\mathsf{d} \\ Q_{18 \cap 19}: & /\mathsf{a}/\overline{\{\mathsf{b},\mathsf{c}\}}/\mathsf{d} \\ Q_{19-18}: & /\mathsf{a}/\mathsf{b}/\mathsf{d}/\mathsf{e} \end{cases}$$

and produce the final answers in the following way:

$$Q_{16} \leftarrow (Q_{16-17}, /\mathsf{Ans}/*) \quad Q_{18} \leftarrow (Q_{18-19}, /\mathsf{Ans}/*)$$
$$Q_{16} \leftarrow (Q_{16 \cap 17}, /\mathsf{Ans}/*) \quad Q_{18} \leftarrow (Q_{18 \cap 19}, /\mathsf{Ans}/*)$$
$$Q_{17} \leftarrow (Q_{16 \cap 17}, /\mathsf{Ans}/*/\mathsf{d}) \quad Q_{19} \leftarrow (Q_{18 \cap 19}, /\mathsf{Ans}/*/\mathsf{e})$$
$$Q_{19} \leftarrow (Q_{19-18}, /\mathsf{Ans}/*)$$

If we want to make the number of submitted queries as small as possible, in the example of Q_{18} and Q_{19}, we can merge Q_{18-19} with Q_{19-18} into a query (/a/c/d)∪(/a/b/d/e) because we can extract the answers to Q_{18-19} and Q_{19-18} from its answer by /Ans/e and /Ans/d. It is also possible to merge $Q_{18 \cap 19}$ and Q_{19-18} instead. Although it is not difficult to detect such cases, in this paper, because of space limitations, we only consider the elimination of data redundancy, and do not discuss the minimization of the number of queries. Therefore, even in the previous example of Q_{13} and Q_{14}, where we need to submit only Q_{13}, the algorithm we show later produces two queries.

3.2 Examples with Recursive Queries

The examples shown so far included only non-recursive queries, i.e., queries without //. When queries include // or union operator ∪, the redundancy in the answers occurs even when a user submits a single query. We have already shown an example with ∪. Below is an example with //:

$$\{ Q_{20}: //\mathsf{a}$$

This query retrieves all the subtrees rooted by "a" nodes in the database tree. Therefore, if some "a" nodes occur as descendants of other "a" nodes, the subtrees rooted by those descendant "a" are sent more than once over the network. In this way, answer sets to recursive XPath queries are self-redundant by nature because of the nested structure of XML.

In this case, we can minimize the size of the data sent over the network by submitting the query below to the server:

$$\{ Q_{20}^\top: //\mathsf{a} - //\mathsf{a}//*$$

This query retrieves "a" nodes that occur as the first "a" node in each path from the root. Then, we can produce the answer to the original query in the following way:

$$Q_{20} \leftarrow (Q_{20}^\top, /Ans//a)$$

Extraction of answers that are descendant of other answers can be more complicated. Suppose we have a query:

$$\{ Q_{21} : //a/b/a/b$$

Then, we should submit the query below:

$$\{ Q_{21}^\top : //a/b/a/b - //a/b/a/b//*$$

$-//a/b/a/b//*$ at the tail eliminates the self-redundancy in the answer. In order to extract all the answers to Q_{21} from the answer to $Q_{21}^\top$, we need three queries shown below:

$$Q_{21} \leftarrow (Q_{21}^\top, /Ans/b)$$
$$Q_{21} \leftarrow (Q_{21}^\top, /Ans/b/a/b)$$
$$Q_{21} \leftarrow (Q_{21}^\top, /Ans//a/b/a/b)$$

Because a b element in the answer to $Q_{21}^\top$ is an element that has matched //a/b/a/b, if it has a path a/b beneath it, that grandchild b node was also matched //a/b/a/b in the database. Therefore, we need /Ans/b/a/b shown above. The computation of how to extract descendant answers is similar to the computation of the prefix function in the classic Knuth-Morris-Pratt algorithm for substring search [19].

For recursive queries, we sometimes need more than one query even when a client submits a single union-free query. For example, suppose we have the query below:

$$\{ Q_{22} : //a/*/*$$

which retrieves grandchildren of "a" nodes occurring at any level in the database tree. In this case, the single query and two procedure below are not sufficient:

$$\{Q_{22}^\top : //a/*/* - //a/*/*//* \quad \begin{array}{l} Q_{22} \leftarrow (Q_{22}^\top, /Ans/*) \\ Q_{22} \leftarrow (Q_{22}^\top, /Ans//a/*/*) \end{array}$$

because these two procedures cannot extract answers that are children of some answers to $Q_{22}^\top$. For example, if there is a path /a/a/b/c in the database tree, both the node b and the node c match Q_{22}, and only b is included in the answer to $Q_{22}^\top$. Only from the path /Ans/b/c in the answer to $Q_{22}^\top$, however, we cannot know the labels of the parent of b, and therefore, we cannot tell if we should extract the c node.

In this case, we can correctly extract the answer to Q_{22} while minimizing the communication cost by submitting the following two queries:

$$\begin{cases} Q_{\mathbf{a}}^\top : & //a/a/* - //a/*/*//* \\ Q_{\overline{\{a\}}}^\top : & //a/\overline{\{a\}}/* - //a/*/*//* \end{cases}$$

and by extracting the answer to Q_{22} in the following way:

$$Q_{22} \leftarrow (Q_{\mathbf{a}}^\top, /Ans/*)$$
$$Q_{22} \leftarrow (Q_{\mathbf{a}}^\top, /Ans/*/*)$$
$$Q_{22} \leftarrow (Q_{\mathbf{a}}^\top, /Ans//a/*/*)$$
$$Q_{22} \leftarrow (Q_{\overline{\{a\}}}^\top, /Ans/*)$$
$$Q_{22} \leftarrow (Q_{\overline{\{a\}}}^\top, /Ans//a/*/*)$$

4 Problem Formulation

Now we formulate the problem we study in this paper. First, when an XML element e_1 is a descendant of another XML element e_2, we write $e_1 \prec e_2$. We also write $e_1 \preceq e_2$ to mean $e_1 \prec e_2$ or $e_1 = e_2$. Next, for a bag B of elements (we use a bag because data sent over a network may include the same element more than once), we define $\mathcal{E}(B)$, the subelement-enumeration of B, as follows:

$$\mathcal{E}(B) \equiv \bigcup_{e \in B}^{b} \{s \mid s \preceq e\}$$

where $\bigcup_{e \in B}^{b}$ is the iteration of the bag union operation $\cup^b$ for all the elements in B including multi-occurrences. Using $\mathcal{E}(B)$, we define a partial order $\subseteq_\mathcal{E}$ as follows:

$$B_1 \subseteq_\mathcal{E} B_2 \equiv \mathcal{E}(B_1) \subseteq^b \mathcal{E}(B_2)$$

where $\subseteq^b$ is the bag inclusion. Next, $Q(t)$ denotes the result of the evaluation of a query Q against an XML tree t. Then, we say a set of queries $\{V_1, \ldots, V_m\}$ is a view set that can answer a query Q iff:

$$(\exists q_1, \ldots, q_m)(\forall t) Q(t) = q_1(V_1(t)) \cup \ldots \cup q_m(V_m(t))$$

Now, we formulate the problem as follows:

Minimal View Selection Problem: Given a set of XPath queries $\{Q_1, \ldots, Q_n\}$, we compute a view set (i.e., another set of XPath queries) $\mathcal{V} = \{V_1, \ldots, V_m\}$, such that:

1. $\mathcal{V}$ can answer all of $Q_1, \ldots, Q_n$, and

2. among those satisfying 1, $V_1(t) \cup^b \ldots \cup^b V_m(t)$ is minimal under $\subseteq_\mathcal{E}$ for any t. □

In the following three sections, we show algorithms to compute such minimal view sets. We begin with an algorithm for an arbitrary number of non-recursive queries, then show an algorithm for a single recursive query, and finally explain an algorithm for the general case, i.e., for an arbitrary number of recursive queries. In this paper, for the sake of brevity, we restrict the input of our algorithms to a language without union ($q \cup q$) and difference ($q - q$). We can, however, extend our algorithms for the language including them. Although we forbid those operations in the input, we use them in the output when we have recursive queries as shown in the later sections.

5 Algorithm for Non-Recursive Queries

This section explains an algorithm that computes a minimal view set for a given set of non-recursive XPath queries.

5.1 Intuition behind the Algorithm

First, we explain the intuition behind our algorithm, and show a simpler algorithm only for two queries.

Suppose we are given a set of non-recursive queries $Q_1, \ldots, Q_n$. In the simplest case, if all of them have the same length, i.e., the same number of /, then an element in the answer to some Q_i cannot be a subelement of elements in the answers to the other queries. In that case, the problem is rather easy. The following set of queries is a minimal view that can answer to $Q_1, \ldots, Q_n$:

$$\{V(S) \mid S \neq \emptyset, S \subseteq \{1, \ldots, n\}\}$$

where

$$V(S) = \bigcap_{i \in S} Q_i - \bigcup_{i \in \{1, \ldots, n\} - S} Q_i$$

From this view set, we can extract answers by executing:

$$Q_j \leftarrow (V(S), \text{/Ans/*})$$

for every j, S s.t. $j \in S$. For example, if $n = 2$, the minimal view is:

$$\{Q_1 - Q_2, Q_1 \cap Q_2, Q_2 - Q_1\}$$

and we can extract the answers to Q_1 and Q_2 by

$$\begin{aligned}
Q_1 &\leftarrow (Q_1 - Q_2, \text{/Ans/*}) \\
Q_1 &\leftarrow (Q_1 \cap Q_2, \text{/Ans/*}) \\
Q_2 &\leftarrow (Q_1 \cap Q_2, \text{/Ans/*}) \\
Q_2 &\leftarrow (Q_2 - Q_1, \text{/Ans/*})
\end{aligned}$$

In general, however, the length of $Q_1, \ldots, Q_n$ are not the same, and some element in one answer may be a subelement of elements in other answers. To deal with it, we define four set operations, generalized upper intersection $\cap_\succ$, generalized lower intersection $\cap_\prec$, generalized difference $-_\preceq$, and self-redundancy elimination $^\top$, as follows:

$$\begin{aligned}
S_1 \cap_\succ S_2 &\equiv \{e_1 \in S_1 \mid (\exists e_2 \in S_2)\, e_1 \succ e_2\} \\
S_1 \cap_\prec S_2 &\equiv \{e_1 \in S_1 \mid (\exists e_2 \in S_2)\, e_1 \prec e_2\} \\
S_1 -_\preceq S_2 &\equiv \{e_1 \in S_1 \mid (\forall e_2 \in S_2)\, e_1 \not\preceq e_2 \wedge e_2 \not\preceq e_1\} \\
S^\top &\equiv \{e \mid e \text{ is maximal in } S \text{ under } \preceq\}
\end{aligned}$$

If we substitute $=$ for $\prec, \succ$ in those definitions, $\cap_\succ, \cap_\prec, -_\preceq$ fall back into the ordinary intersection and difference. Notice that $\cap_\succ, \cap_\prec$ are not symmetric. (They are actually instances of "filter" operator in [1], while $-_\preceq$ is an instance of generalized difference in [1].) If $S^\top \neq S$, we say S is self-redundant. Then, the following properties hold.

Proposition 1 *The following equation holds:*
$S_1 = (S_1 -_\preceq S_2) \cup (S_1 \cap_\succ S_2) \cup (S_1 \cap S_2) \cup (S_1 \cap_\prec S_2)$

Proof: l.h.s.$\supseteq$r.h.s. is obvious from the definition of $-_\preceq$, $\cap_\succ, \cap, \cap_\prec$. l.h.s.$\subseteq$r.h.s. is also obvious because every $e_1 \in S_1$ appears at least one of the four sets in r.h.s. $\square$

Proposition 2 *If S_1, S_2 are not self-redundant, seven sets: $S_1 -_\preceq S_2$, $S_1 \cap_\succ S_2$, $S_1 \cap_\prec S_2$, $S_1 \cap S_2$, $S_2 \cap_\prec S_1$, $S_2 \cap_\succ S_1$, $S_2 -_\preceq S_1$ are disjoint with one another.*

Proposition 3 *If S_1, S_2 are not self-redundant, the seven sets above are also pairwise disjoint in the sense of $\cap_\succ$ and $\cap_\prec$ except for the four cases below:*

$$\begin{aligned}
(S_1 \cap_\succ S_2) \cap_\succ (S_2 \cap_\prec S_1) &= (S_1 \cap_\succ S_2) \\
(S_1 \cap_\prec S_2) \cap_\prec (S_2 \cap_\succ S_1) &= (S_1 \cap_\prec S_2) \\
(S_2 \cap_\succ S_1) \cap_\succ (S_1 \cap_\prec S_2) &= (S_2 \cap_\succ S_1) \\
(S_2 \cap_\prec S_1) \cap_\prec (S_1 \cap_\succ S_2) &= (S_2 \cap_\prec S_1)
\end{aligned}$$

Proof Outline of Proposition 2, 3: It is easy to show that if any two of the seven sets have other intersections, it implies that either S_1 or S_2 is self-redundant. $\square$

We also define those operations for queries, such as:

$$\begin{aligned}
Q_1 \cap_\succ Q_2 &\equiv \{Q \mid (\forall t) Q(t) = Q_1(t) \cap_\succ Q_2(t)\} \\
Q_1 \cap_\prec Q_2 &\equiv \{Q \mid (\forall t) Q(t) = Q_1(t) \cap_\prec Q_2(t)\} \\
Q_1 -_\preceq Q_2 &\equiv \{Q \mid (\forall t) Q(t) = Q_1(t) -_\preceq Q_2(t)\} \\
Q_1^\top &\equiv \{Q \mid (\forall t) Q(t) = Q_1(t)^\top\}
\end{aligned}$$

They are defined by the set of equivalent queries, but we also use those notations to denote some representative queries for those equivalent classes in the rest of the paper. We also say Q is self-redundant if $(\exists t) Q(t) \neq Q^\top(t)$. Then, the following proposition holds for $Q^\top$.

Proposition 4 *Non-recursive union-free queries are never self-redundant.*

Proof: All the elements in the answer to a non-recursive union-free query appear at the same level in the database tree corresponding to the length of the query. Therefore, no element can be a subelement of the other. $\square$

Therefore, Proposition 2 and 3 apply to the answers to non-recursive union-free queries. Then, the following property holds:

Proposition 5 *When given two non-recursive union-free queries Q_1 and Q_2, we can retrieve all the necessary elements for their answers without duplication by five queries $Q_1 -_\preceq Q_2$, $Q_1 \cap_\succ Q_2$, $Q_1 \cap Q_2$, $Q_2 \cap_\succ Q_1$, and $Q_2 -_\preceq Q_1$.*

Proof: Let S_1 and S_2 be the answers to Q_1 and Q_2. By Proposition 1, those five sets include all the elements in $S_1 \cup S_2$ except for those in $S_1 \cap_\prec S_2$ and $S_2 \cap_\prec S_1$. Elements in $S_1 \cap_\prec S_2$ and $S_2 \cap_\prec S_1$ are, however, included in $S_2 \cap_\succ S_1$ and $S_1 \cap_\succ S_2$ as subelements because of Proposition 3. In addition, by Proposition 2 and 3, those five sets include no duplication even in the sense of $\cap_\prec$ or $\cap_\succ$. $\square$

This property suggests that the set of those five sets may work as a minimal view that can answer Q_1 and Q_2 (although this proposition just guarantees that all the necessary elements are included in those five sets, and does not guarantee that $S_1 \cap_\prec S_2$ and $S_2 \cap_\prec S_1$ can correctly be extracted from $S_2 \cap_\succ S_1$ and $S_1 \cap_\succ S_2$).

Following this observation, we can develop a simple algorithm for computing a minimal view set for two non-recursive union-free queries. Let Q_1 be $/p_1^1/\ldots/p_1^n$ and Q_2 be $/p_2^1/\ldots/p_2^m$ where p_i^j are expressions that do not include / nor //. We can assume $n \leq m$ w.l.o.g. We can compute the minimal view for Q_1 and Q_2 in the following way.

If $n = m$, $Q_1 \cap_\succ Q_2$, $Q_1 \cap_\prec Q_2$, $Q_2 \cap_\succ Q_1$, and $Q_2 \cap_\prec Q_1$ are empty queries, and the following three queries constitute a minimal view:

$$\begin{aligned}
Q_1 -_\preceq Q_2 &: \quad /p_1^1/\ldots/p_1^n - /p_2^1/\ldots/p_2^m \\
Q_1 \cap Q_2 &: \quad /p_1^1/\ldots/p_1^n \cap /p_2^1/\ldots/p_2^m \\
Q_2 -_\preceq Q_1 &: \quad /p_2^1/\ldots/p_2^m - /p_1^1/\ldots/p_1^n
\end{aligned}$$

and we can extract the final answers as follows:

$$\begin{aligned}
Q_1 &\leftarrow (Q_1 -_{\preceq} Q_2, /\text{Ans}/*) \\
Q_1 &\leftarrow (Q_1 \cap_{\succ} Q_2, /\text{Ans}/*) \\
Q_2 &\leftarrow (Q_1 \cap_{\succ} Q_2, /\text{Ans}/*) \\
Q_2 &\leftarrow (Q_2 -_{\preceq} Q_1, /\text{Ans}/*)
\end{aligned}$$

If $n < m$, $Q_1 \cap_{\preceq} Q_2$, $Q_1 \cap_{\succ} Q_2$, and $Q_2 \cap_{\succ} Q_1$ are empty, and the three queries below constitute a minimal view:

$$\begin{aligned}
Q_1 -_{\preceq} Q_2 &: /p_1^1/\ldots/p_1^n - /p_2^1/\ldots/p_2^n[p_2^{n+1}/\ldots/p_2^m] \\
Q_1 \cap_{\succ} Q_2 &: /p_1^1/\ldots/p_1^n \cap /p_2^1/\ldots/p_2^n[p_2^{n+1}/\ldots/p_2^m] \\
Q_2 -_{\preceq} Q_1 &: /p_2^1/\ldots/p_2^m - /p_1^1/\ldots/p_1^n//*
\end{aligned}$$

and we can extract the final answers as follows:

$$\begin{aligned}
Q_1 &\leftarrow (Q_1 -_{\preceq} Q_2, /\text{Ans}/*) \\
Q_1 &\leftarrow (Q_1 \cap_{\succ} Q_2, /\text{Ans}/*) \\
Q_2 &\leftarrow (Q_1 \cap_{\succ} Q_2, /\text{Ans}/*/p_2^{n+1}/\ldots/p_2^m) \\
Q_2 &\leftarrow (Q_2 -_{\preceq} Q_1, /\text{Ans}/*)
\end{aligned}$$

The third line above corresponds to the extraction of $Q_2 \cap_{\preceq} Q_1$ from $Q_1 \cap_{\succ} Q_2$. This solution is directly following the observation explained above, but we can slightly simplify the view set above to the one shown below:

$$\begin{aligned}
Q_{1-2} &: /p_1^1/\ldots/p_1^n - /p_2^1/\ldots/p_2^n \\
Q_{1 \cap 2} &: /p_1^1/\ldots/p_1^n \cap /p_2^1/\ldots/p_2^n \\
Q_2 -_{\preceq} Q_1 &: /p_2^1/\ldots/p_2^m - /p_1^1/\ldots/p_1^n//*
\end{aligned}$$

From this view set, we can extract the answer to Q_1 and Q_2 in exactly the same procedure as above with substituting $Q_1 -_{\preceq} Q_2$ and $Q_1 \cap_{\succ} Q_2$ with Q_{1-2} and $Q_{1 \cap 2}$, respectively.
Proof: It is easy to show $(Q_1 -_{\preceq} Q_2) \cup (Q_1 \cap_{\succ} Q_2) = Q_{1-2} \cup Q_{1 \cap 2}$. It is also easy to show that the result of both $(Q_1 \cap_{\succ} Q_2, /\text{Ans}/p_2^n/\ldots/p_2^m)$ and $(Q_{1 \cap 2}, /\text{Ans}/p_2^n/\ldots/p_2^m)$ are equal to the answer to $Q_1// * \cap Q_2$. □

For example, let Q_1 be /a/b and Q_2 be /a/*/c. Then, $Q_1 -_{\preceq} Q_2$ is /a/b − /a/*[c], and $Q_1 \cap_{\succ} Q_2$ is /a/b ∩ /a/*[c], but we can also extract the answers to Q_1 and Q_2 from /a/b − /a/* and /a/b ∩ /a/* in the same procedure.

5.2 Algorithm

In the previous subsection, we explained the intuition behind our algorithm, and showed a simple algorithm for two queries. In this subsection, we show a complete algorithm for an arbitrary number of non-recursive union-free queries. In the simple algorithm, we computed $-_{\preceq}$ and $\cap_{\succ}$ of queries by using − and ∩ constructs for queries, and it may create unnecessary views which are always empty. On the other hand, the algorithm shown in this subsection produces simpler queries that do not include − and ∩, and does not produce unnecessary empty views.

The main part of the algorithm is translation of queries into automata, and construction of their product automaton. When given a set of non-recursive union-free XPath queries, we first translate them to a deterministic finite automata on a alphabet of symbols sym defined as below:

$$sym ::= a \mid \overline{\{a_1, \ldots, a_n\}} \mid * \mid sym[p] \mid sym\overline{[p]}$$

$$Q_1 : s_1^0 \xrightarrow{a} s_1^1 \xrightarrow{b} e_1$$
$$Q_2 : s_2^0 \xrightarrow{a} s_2^1 \xrightarrow{\overline{\{c\}}[c]} e_2$$
$$Q_3 : s_3^0 \xrightarrow{a} s_3^1 \xrightarrow{*} s_3^2 \xrightarrow{c} e_3$$

Figure 1: Automata for Queries Q_1, Q_2, Q_3

$$Q_2 : s_2^0 \xrightarrow{a} s_2^1 \xrightarrow{\overline{\{c\}}[c]} e_2$$

Figure 2: Automaton for Q_2 with a fail state

where a or $a_1, \ldots, a_n$ are any label, and p is a relative location path defined before.

Because input queries do not include //, a query is translated into an automaton of the form of a simple sequence. For example, suppose we have the following set of queries: Q_1: /a/b, Q_2: /a/$\overline{\{c\}}$[c], Q_3: /a/*/c. Those queries are translated into the three automata shown in Figure 1.

Then, we explicitly add a "fail state" to each automaton. For example, Figure 2 shows the automaton for Q_2 with the fail state. To add fail states, we need to compute the complementation of symbols. Complementation of symbols sym, denoted by $(sym)^-$, is defined by the following rules corresponding to the syntax definition of sym above:

$$\begin{aligned}
(a)^- &= \{\overline{\{a\}}\} \\
(\overline{\{a_1, \ldots, a_n\}})^- &= \{a_1, \ldots, a_n\} \\
(*)^- &= \emptyset \\
(sym[p])^- &= (sym)^- \cup \{sym\overline{[p]}\}
\end{aligned}$$

Notice that the complementation of a symbol is represented by a set of symbols. Because of that, we may need many transition rules from each state to the fail state.

Then, we construct the product of all those automata in the standard way. The only difference from the standard product construction is that we need to compute the intersection and the difference between symbols. Intersection of two symbols, $\cap(sym, sym)$ is also defined by the rules corresponding to the syntax definition above. Here, we list only part of the rules:

$$\begin{aligned}
\cap(a, \overline{\{a_1, \ldots\}}) &= a \quad \text{if } a \notin \{a_1, \ldots\} \\
&\quad \underline{undefined} \text{ otherwise} \\
\cap(\overline{\{a_1, \ldots\}}, \overline{\{b_1, \ldots\}}) &= \overline{\{a_1, \ldots, b_1, \ldots\}} \\
\cap(sym, sym[p]) &= \cap(sym, sym)[p] \\
\cap(sym, sym\overline{[p]}) &= \cap(sym, sym)\overline{[p]}
\end{aligned}$$

Notice that intersection of two symbols can always be represented by a single symbol while complementation of a symbol can be a set of symbols. The difference of two symbols, $-(sym_1, sym_2)$, are computed by the rule below:

$$-(sym_1, sym_2) = \cap(sym_1, (sym_2)^-)$$

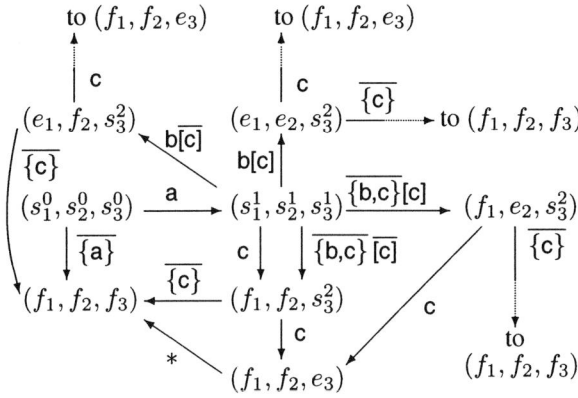

Figure 3: Product Automaton for Q_1, Q_2, Q_3

By using intersection and difference defined above, we construct a product of all the automata for the given queries. The product automaton for Q_1, Q_2, Q_3 is shown in Figure 3. Notice that automata for queries with the fail states forms DAG, and their product also forms DAG.

A product automaton constructed in this way may include paths that are never followed. For example, in the automaton shown in Figure 3, the transition with a label c from (e_1, f_2, s_3^2) to (f_1, f_2, e_3) is never followed because of b$\overline{[c]}$ on the only transition into (e_1, f_2, s_3^2). The path $\overline{\{b,c\}}\ \overline{[c]}$/c from (s_1^1, s_2^1, s_3^1) to (f_1, f_2, e_3) is also never followed (although each of $\overline{\{b,c\}}\ \overline{[c]}$ and c are used in other paths). There may also exist unsatisfiable symbols produced in the computation of intersection or difference. In addition, even the original queries submitted by the users may include some unsatisfiable conditions by mistake.

We can determine satisfiability of a path by testing the satisfiability of the set of predicates:

$$\{[pp_1], \ldots, [pp_n], \overline{[np_1]}, \ldots, \overline{[np_m]}, [p]\}$$

for each symbol $sym[pp_1]\ldots[pp_n]\overline{[np_1]}\ldots\overline{[np_m]}$ in the path and the suffix p of the path following that symbol (or $\{[pp_1], \ldots, [pp_n], \overline{[np_1]}, \ldots, \overline{[np_m]}\}$ if the suffix p does not exists). For example, the satisfiability of the path a[b]$\overline{[b/c]}$/b/c/d is determined by testing the satisfiability of $\{[b], \overline{[b/c]}, [b/c/d]\}$, which is unsatisfiable because of $\overline{[b/c]}$ and [b/c/d]. Therefore, this path is unsatisfiable.

We test satisfiability of a set of predicates as follows:

Proposition 6 $\{[pp_1], \ldots, [pp_n], \overline{[np_1]}, \ldots, \overline{[np_m]}\}$ *is not satisfiable iff some prefix of some pp_i is contained (in the ordinary sense of query containment) by some np_j.*

Proof: If no prefix of pp_i is contained by any of np_j, we can create a path that matches pp_i but not any of np_j. Then, an element with n children each of which satisfies one of $pp_1, \ldots, pp_n$ but not any np_j satisfies all the predicates. □

We can determine if any prefix of some pp_i is contained by some np_j by constructing a product automaton for $/pp_i$ and $/np_j$ as explained below.

By using the product automaton for $Q_1, \ldots, Q_n$, we can compute the following relations and operations on queries:

Proposition 7 Q_i *is contained by Q_j iff there is no satisfiable path from* $(s_1, \ldots, s_n)$ *to any states of the form* $(\ldots, e_i, \ldots, s_j^k, \ldots)$ *where $s_j^k \neq e_j$.*

Proposition 8 *Intersection of Q_i and Q_j, $Q_i \cap Q_j$, is a union of queries corresponding to all satisfiable paths from* $(s_1, \ldots, s_n)$ *to any states of the form* $(\ldots, e_i, \ldots, e_j, \ldots)$.

Proposition 9 *Difference of Q_i and Q_j, $Q_i - Q_j$, is a union of queries corresponding to all satisfiable paths from* $(s_1, \ldots, s_n)$ *to any states of the form* $(\ldots, e_i, \ldots, s_j^k, \ldots)$ *where $s_j^k \neq e_j$.*

Therefore, we can express the intersection and the difference of two queries without using $-$. In other words, the language without recursion and $-$ is closed under intersection and difference. The proofs of those propositions are easy and omitted here. The computation of containment is used to test the satisfiability of predicates as explained above, and the computation of intersection or difference will be used in the next section.

Now we show the algorithm.

Algorithm for Non-recursive Queries
Input: n non-recursive queries $Q_1, \ldots, Q_n$.
Output: a set of queries $\{V_1, \ldots, V_m\}$ corresponding to the minimal view set, and a list of triplets $Q_i \leftarrow (V_j, q_i^j)$ showing how to extract answers to $Q_1, \ldots, Q_n$ from them.
begin

1. Translate $Q_1, \ldots, Q_n$ into automata, add fail states explicitly, and construct a product automaton.

2. For each satisfiable path X from $(s_1, \ldots, s_n)$ to a state T of the form $(\ldots, e_{i_1}, \ldots, e_{i_2}, \ldots, e_{i_a}, \ldots)$ that does not go through any other states of the form $(\ldots, e_j, \ldots)$:

    (a) add X to the view set, and add $Q_i \leftarrow (X, /\text{Ans}/*)$ to the triplet list for each $i \in \{i_1, \ldots, i_a\}$.

    (b) for each path Y from the state T to any state of the form $(\ldots, e_j, \ldots)$, if X/Y is satisfiable, add a triplet $Q_j \leftarrow (X, /\text{Ans}/*/Y)$ to the list.

end □

For example, from the product automaton shown in Figure 3, the algorithm above produces a view set:

$$\{/a/b\overline{[c]},\ /a/b[c],\ /a/\overline{\{b,c\}}[c],\ /a/c/c\}$$

and the following triplets:

$$\begin{array}{ll}
Q_1 \leftarrow (/a/b\overline{[c]}, /\text{Ans}/*) & Q_1 \leftarrow (/a/b[c], /\text{Ans}/*) \\
Q_2 \leftarrow (/a/b[c], /\text{Ans}/*) & Q_2 \leftarrow (/a/\overline{\{b,c\}}[c], /\text{Ans}/*) \\
Q_3 \leftarrow (/a/c/c, /\text{Ans}/*) & Q_3 \leftarrow (/a/b[c], /\text{Ans}/*/c) \\
Q_3 \leftarrow (/a/\overline{\{b,c\}}[c], /\text{Ans}/*/c) &
\end{array}$$

Please examine that we can correctly extract the answers to Q_1, Q_2, Q_3 by these procedures. Notice that the view set includes /a/c/c instead of /a/c/c∪/a/$\overline{\{b,c\}}\ \overline{[c]}$/c because /a/$\overline{\{b,c\}}\ \overline{[c]}$/c is unsatisfiable. Similarly, $Q_3 \leftarrow (/a/b\overline{[c]}, /\text{Ans}/*/c)$ was not included in the triplet list because /a/b$\overline{[c]}$/c is unsatisfiable.

Theorem 1 *The algorithm above is correct.*

Proof Outline: Each query added to the view set in the step 2(a) in the algorithm above corresponds to a simplified version (explained at the end of the previous subsection) of $Q_{i_1} \cap \ldots \cap Q_{i_a} \cap_\succ Q_{j_1} \ldots \cap_\succ Q_{j_b} -_\preceq Q_{k_1} \ldots -_\preceq Q_{k_c}$ for some disjoint sets $\{j_1, \ldots, j_b\}$ and $\{k_1, \ldots, k_c\}$ s.t. $\{i_1, \ldots, i_a, j_1, \ldots, j_b, k_1, \ldots, k_c\} = \{1, \ldots, n\}$. From this view, we can extract part of answers to $Q_{i_1}, \ldots, Q_{i_a}$ by /Ans/*, and part of answers to $Q_{j_1}, \ldots, Q_{j_b}$ by /Ans/*/Y. In addition, the queries added to the view set do not include duplication under $\cap$ and even under $\cap_\prec$ or $\cap_\succ$. □

It is also easy to prove the following proposition on the number of queries to be evaluated on servers and on clients.

Theorem 2 *When given non-recursive union-free queries $Q_1, \ldots, Q_n$, we need to submit up to $2^n - 1$ queries to the server, and need up to $n * 2^{n-1}$ queries on the client.*

Proof: As an upper bound, the number of views cannot be larger than $2^n - 1$ because there cannot be larger number of the states of the form $(\ldots, e_{i_1}, \ldots, e_{i_2}, \ldots, e_{i_a}, \ldots)$ in the product automaton. We need to extract the answer to Q_i from up to $(2^x - 1) + 2^y$ views where x is the number of queries which are shorter than Q_i and y is the number of queries which have the same length as Q_i. It takes its maximum value 2^{n-1} when $\{x, y\} = \{n-1, 0\}$. Therefore, $n * 2^{n-1}$ is an upper bound for the number of queries evaluated on the client. As the lower bound, we actually need $2^n - 1$ views and $n * 2^{n-1}$ client queries if $Q_1, \ldots, Q_n$ are /a/b[c_1]/d, ..., /a/b[c_n]/d for some distinct $c_1, \ldots, c_n$. □

If we want to minimize the number of queries in the view set, we can merge two views V_1 and V_2 *iff* the intersection of two symbols on the transitions to the states corresponding to V_1 and V_2 is undefined or unsatisfiable. This is because only information that can be used to distinguish elements in the answer to $V_1 \cup V_2$ is the information represented by those two symbols. If they have intersection, and if the answer to $V_1 \cup V_2$ includes some element that matches that intersection, we cannot tell whether that element was belonging to V_1 or V_2 (or both). In this paper, however, we do not discuss this issue in more detail as mentioned in Section 4.

6 Algorithm for One Recursive Query

In this section, we show an algorithm that computes a minimal view set that can answer one given recursive query. Even though we restrict the input language of our algorithms to a language without $\cup$ and $-$ operations, the output language of the algorithms for recursive queries includes them. This is partly because the language with recursion but without $-$ operations is not closed under difference or complementation. For example, //a$-$//a//a cannot be expressed without $-$. (In XPath standard, it can be expressed by using an "ancestor axis," which we do not explain here. In this paper, we assume a language without an ancestor axis.) As shown in [6], most XPath fragments used in recent researches are closed under intersection but not closed under difference or complementation.

Suppose we are given a recursive query of the form:

$$Q : /p_1//p_2//\ldots//p_n \quad \text{or} \quad Q : //p_1//p_2//\ldots//p_n$$

where $p_1, \ldots, p_n$ are relative location paths that do not include //. Because whether the query starts with / or // does not matter in the following discussion, here we assume /.

As shown in the examples in Section 3, the redundancy in the answer to this query occurs in two ways:

- there are elements that match /p_1//...//p_n//p_n
- there are elements that match /p_1//...//p_n/p where p is some suffix of p_n s.t. the remaining prefix of p_n matches the suffix of p_n. Please refer to the example of //a/b/a/b in Section 3.

If we have only the former kind of redundancy, we can simply submit a view query:

$$(/p_1//\ldots//p_n) - (/p_1//\ldots//p_n//*)$$

and produce the final answer by applying /Ans/* and /Ans//p_n to the view. To also remove the latter kind of redundancy, we consider a set of relative location paths:

$$S = \{*/p_n^{(1,k-1)}, \ */*/p_n^{(1,k-2)}, \ \ldots, \ */\ldots/*/p_n^{(1,2)}\}$$

where k is the length of p_n, and $p_n^{(i,j)}$ is the subsequence of p_n from the position i to the position j. Then, the algorithm computes the following views:

$$V(T) : (/p_1//\ldots//(p_n \cap \bigcap_{p \in T} p - \bigcup_{p \in S-T} p)) - /p_1//\ldots//p_n//*$$

for every $T \subseteq S$. Here, we use ordinary $\cap$ and $-$ because p_n and every $p \in S$ have the same length k, that is, their answers cannot be subelements of other answers. The algorithm computes $\cap$ and $-$ of paths by using the product automaton explained in the previous section. If the result of $p_n \cap \bigcap p - \bigcup p$ is empty for some T, $V(T)$ is discarded. Then, for each survived view $V(T)$, the algorithm produces the following triplets:

$$(Q, V(T), /\text{Ans}/*)$$
$$(Q, V(T), /\text{Ans}//p_n)$$
$$(Q, V(T), /\text{Ans}/*/p_n^{(i+1,k)}) \text{ for each } */\ldots/*/p_n^{(1,i)} \in T$$

When the length of p_n is 1, the first one can be omitted because the second one contains the first one.

For example, suppose we are given a query $Q =$ /a//b/c/*/$\overline{\{d\}}$. Then $S = \{p_3' : */b/c/*, \ p_2' : */*/b/c\}$, and the algorithm examines the following four views:

$$V_1 : /\text{a}// \ (\text{b/c}/*/\overline{\{d\}} \ \cap \ p_3' \ \cap \ p_2') - /\text{a/b/c}/*/\overline{\{d\}}//*$$
$$V_2 : /\text{a}// \ (\text{b/c}/*/\overline{\{d\}} \ \cap \ p_3' \ - \ p_2') - /\text{a/b/c}/*/\overline{\{d\}}//*$$
$$V_3 : /\text{a}// \ (\text{b/c}/*/\overline{\{d\}} \ \cap \ p_2' \ - \ p_3') - /\text{a/b/c}/*/\overline{\{d\}}//*$$
$$V_4 : /\text{a}// \ (\text{b/c}/*/\overline{\{d\}} \ - \ p_3' \ - \ p_2') - /\text{a/b/c}/*/\overline{\{d\}}//*$$

By computing $\cup$ and $-$ with the product automaton, the algorithm find V_1 and V_2 are empty, and finally produces a view set consisting of the following two views:

V_3 : /a//b/c/b/c $-$ /a//b/c/*/$\overline{\{d\}}$//*
V_4 : (/a//b/c/$\overline{\{b\}}$/$\overline{\{d\}}$ $\cup$ /a//b/c/b/$\overline{\{c,d\}}$) $-$ /a//b/c/*/$\overline{\{d\}}$//*

The algorithm also produces the following triplets:

$$\begin{aligned}
Q &\leftarrow (V_3, \text{/Ans/*}) \\
Q &\leftarrow (V_3, \text{/Ans/b/c/*/}\overline{\{d\}}) \\
Q &\leftarrow (V_3, \text{/Ans/*/*/}\overline{\{d\}}) \\
Q &\leftarrow (V_4, \text{/Ans/*}) \\
Q &\leftarrow (V_4, \text{/Ans/b/c/*/}\overline{\{d\}})
\end{aligned}$$

Theorem 3 *The algorithm above is correct.*

Proof Outline: The view set above does not include self-redundancy because of $-(\text{//}p_1\text{//} \ldots \text{//}p_n\text{//*})$ at the tail of each view. Next, we show that the triplets above extract all the answers. Answers that appear as the first answers in the paths from the root are extracted by /Ans/*. We call those answers "top-most answers". Answers that appear as children of top-most answers are extracted by /Ans/*/$p_n^{(k,k)}$, answers that appear as grandchildren are extracted by /Ans/*/*/$p_n^{(k-1,k)}$, ..., and so on, and finally answers that appear k or more levels deeper than the top-most answers are extracted by /Ans//p_n. □

Theorem 4 *When given one recursive query, we need up to 2^{k-2} (or 1 when $k = 1$) queries to the server where k is the length of the longest non-recursive suffix of the query (i.e., p_n above). On the client, we need to evaluate up to $2^{k-1} + (k-2) * 2^{k-3}$ (or 2 when $k = 1$) queries.*

Proof: The algorithm above creates up to 2^{k-2} views. On the client, we may need to execute two queries /Ans/* and /Ans//p_n for all of 2^{k-2} views, which amounts to 2^{k-1} queries, and also need to evaluate each /Ans/*/$p_n^{(i,k)}$ ($3 \leq i \leq k$) on up to 2^{k-3} views, and it amounts to $(k-2) * 2^{k-3}$. As the lower bound, we actually need those number of views and client queries when we have a query of the form /a//$\overline{\{b_1\}}$/.../$\overline{\{b_k\}}$ for some distinct $b_1, \ldots, b_k$. □

7 Algorithm for Recursive Queries

By combining the intuition shown in 5.1 and the algorithm in the previous section, we develop an algorithm that computes a minimal view set in general case, i.e., when given the following set of recursive queries:

$$Q_1 : /_1^1 p_1^1 /_1^2 p_1^2 \ldots /_1^{l_1} p_1^{l_1}$$
$$\vdots$$
$$Q_n : /_n^1 p_n^1 /_n^2 p_n^2 \ldots /_n^{l_n} p_n^{l_n}$$

where p_i^j is an expression that includes neither / nor //, and each $/_i^j$ represents either / or //. We define prefix paths pp_i^j ($1 \leq i \leq n, 0 \leq j \leq l_i - 1$) as follows:

$$pp_i^j \equiv \begin{cases} /_i^1 p_i^1 \ldots /_i^j p_i^j & \text{if } /_i^{j+1} = / \\ (/_i^1 p_i^1 \ldots /_i^j p_i^j) \cup (/_i^1 p_i^1 \ldots /_i^j p_i^j \text{//*}) & \text{if } /_i^{j+1} = \text{//} \\ \emptyset & \text{if } j = 0, /_i^1 = / \\ \text{//*} & \text{if } j = 0, /_i^1 = \text{//} \end{cases}$$

where $\emptyset$ is the empty path that matches no elements.

Then, we create views defined as below for any S, T s.t. $S \subseteq \{1, \ldots, n\}, S \neq \emptyset, T \subseteq \{(i,j) \mid 1 \leq i \leq n, 0 \leq j \leq l_i - 1\}$:

$$(\bigcap_{i \in S} Q_i - \bigcup_{i \notin S} Q_i) \cap (\bigcap_{(i,j) \in T} pp_i^j - \bigcup_{(i,j) \notin T} pp_i^j) - \bigcup_{1 \leq i \leq n} Q_i\text{//*}$$

Let $V(S,T)$ denote a view defined with S, T. Then, for each $V(S,T)$, we produce the following triplets:

$Q_i \leftarrow (V(S,T), \text{/Ans/*})$ for $i \in S$
$Q_i \leftarrow (V(S,T), \text{/Ans/*/}_i^{j+1} p_i^{j+1} \ldots /_i^{l_i} p_i^{l_i})$ for $(i,j) \in T$

For example, suppose we are given two queries:

$$\begin{cases} Q_1 : \text{//a} \\ Q_2 : \text{/b//}\overline{\{c\}} \end{cases}$$

Then, $pp_1^0 = \text{//*}, pp_2^0 = \emptyset$, and $pp_2^1 = \text{/b} \cup \text{/b//*}$ are defined for Q_1 and Q_2. We can consider three sets for S and eight sets for T. For T, however, we only need to consider those including pp_1^0 and not including pp_2^0 because views created by other T are empty. In addition, $\cap pp_1^0$ and $-pp_2^0$ in the view queries can be omitted because they do not change the semantics of the entire query. As a result, we create the following views:

$V_1 : (Q_1 \cap Q_2) \cap pp_2^1 - (Q_1\text{//*} \cup Q_2\text{//*})$
$V_2 : (Q_1 \cap Q_2) - pp_2^1 - (Q_1\text{//*} \cup Q_2\text{//*})$
$V_3 : (Q_1 - Q_2) \cap pp_2^1 - (Q_1\text{//*} \cup Q_2\text{//*})$
$V_4 : (Q_1 - Q_2) - pp_2^1 - (Q_1\text{//*} \cup Q_2\text{//*})$
$V_5 : (Q_2 - Q_1) \cap pp_2^1 - (Q_1\text{//*} \cup Q_2\text{//*})$
$V_6 : (Q_2 - Q_1) - pp_2^1 - (Q_1\text{//*} \cup Q_2\text{//*})$

We also produce the following triplets:

$Q_1 \leftarrow (V_i, \text{//Ans/*})$ where $i \in \{1,2,3,4\}$
$Q_2 \leftarrow (V_i, \text{//Ans/*})$ where $i \in \{1,2,5,6\}$
$Q_1 \leftarrow (V_i, \text{//Ans/*//a})$ where $i \in \{1,2,3,4,5,6\}$
$Q_2 \leftarrow (V_i, \text{//Ans/*//}\overline{\{c\}})$ where $i \in \{1,3,5\}$

Theorem 5 *The algorithm above is correct.*

Proof Outline: Because of $-\bigcup Q_i\text{//*}$ at the tail of every view query, this view set only includes top-most answers to $Q_1, \ldots, Q_n$. Each top-most answer e appear exactly once in the view set; e appears only in $V(S,T)$ s.t. $S = \{i \mid e \in Q_i(t)\}$ and $T = \{(i,j) \mid e \in pp_i^j(t)\}$ where t is the database tree. Therefore, the view set includes all the necessary elements without redundancy. From this view set, we can correctly extract all the answers. It is intuitively because what the algorithm does is to classify all the topmost answers based on how their subelements should be extracted as other answers. □

This algorithm may create many empty views. For example, $V_1, \ldots, V_6$ shown above can be simplified into the following queries:

$$V_1 : /b//a - //a//* - /b//\overline{\{c\}}//*$$
$$V_4 : //a - /b//* - //a//*$$
$$V_5 : /b//\overline{\{a,c\}} - //a//* - /b//\overline{\{c\}}//*$$
$$V_2, V_3, V_6 : \emptyset$$

Therefore, V_2, V_3, V_6 can be discarded. For such query simplification and empty view elimination, we need to solve the containment problem of XPath queries including //. We could use the techniques shown in the past researches, such as [3, 23], but that is out of the scope of this paper.

Theorem 6 *When given n recursive queries whose total length is l, we need up to $(2^n - 1) * 2^{l-n}$ queries to the server, and we need up to $n * 2^{n-1} * 2^{l-n} + (l-n) * (2^n - 1) * 2^{l-n-1} + n * (2^n - 1) * 2^{l-n}$ queries on the client.*

Proof Outline: We have $2^n - 1$ different S and 2^l different T, but as explained above, for each pp_i^0, we need to consider only T including or not including pp_i^0, thus only 2^{l-n} different T. We need $2^{n-1} * 2^{l-n}$ queries of the form /Ans/* for each Q_i, $(2^n - 1) * 2^{l-n-1}$ queries for each $pp_i^j (j \leq 1)$, and $(2^n - 1) * 2^{l-n}$ queries for each pp_i^0. As the lower bound, we actually need those number of views and client queries when we have queries $Q_1, \ldots, Q_n$ of the form $Q_i : //\overline{\{a_i^1\}}/\ldots/\overline{\{a_i^{l_i}\}}$ for some distinct a_i^j. □

8 Related Work

There have been a large number of researches on the view selection problem [18]. The main goal of the traditional view selection problem is to choose a set of views that minimizes the cost of answering queries within a limited resource for storing views, and also within a limited cost for maintaining them. On the other hand, the goal of our research is to minimize the size of the data sent between servers and clients over networks, which may actually increase computation costs both on servers and clients.

A similar idea of computing minimal views to reduce communication costs has been discussed in [11]. In that paper, the authors discuss the problem of minimal views in the context of relational databases, conjunctive queries, and the redundancy caused by join operations. In this paper, we discuss the minimal view problem in the context of XML (or any data with nested structure), XPath queries (or any language for nested data structure), and the redundancy caused by the nested structure in the data.

In the context of client-server database architecture, the concepts of semantic caching and remainder queries have been proposed in [14], and they have also been studied in the context of XML data in [10]. In semantic caching, the client caches the answers to previous queries together with the query expressions. When a user on the client issues a new query whose answer partially overlaps with answers to some previous queries, the client computes and submits a "remainder query" that only retrieves data that are not available in the cached answers. In general, however, some context information may not be available in the cached answers nor in their query expressions, and therefore, it is not always possible to correctly extract part of answers to new queries from the cached data only by looking at the expressions and the answers of the cached queries. For example if we submit Q_9 in Section 3 first, and submit Q_{10} later, we cannot extract the answers to Q_{10} from the cached answer to Q_9. On the other hand, in our problem setting, first we are given a set of queries. For that, we can divide given queries into smaller queries before submitting them so that we can extract answers to overlapping queries. In addition, [14] and [10] does not consider the duplication caused by answers appearing as substructure of other answers.

The optimization of communication costs in query processing over a network has also been studied in the context of distributed databases [4], where distributed data servers cooperate. In this paper, however, we assumed an environment where all clients can do is to submit queries, and they cannot use special encodings or protocols.

The view minimization problem has also been studied in [20]. Their goal is to minimize given views without losing the power to answer queries, while our goal is to compute a minimal view that can answer a given set of queries.

There also have been researches on answering queries on tree or graph structured data using views [7, 15]. Their goal is, however, to answer queries with a given view set, not to compute minimal view set for a given set of queries.

9 Discussion and Conclusion

In this paper, we studied a problem in XML database systems on networks, which has recently become very important both in the academy and in the industry. The problem is the redundancy in the answers to XPath queries sent over the network, which wastes network resources. A similar problem can occur in other data models and query languages, but this problem occurs especially frequently in the context of XML and XPath. Even when a user submits a single, quite ordinary XPath query, the answer to it may include significant redundancy. This problem comes from the characteristics of XML and XPath: the data have a nested structure and the language retrieves substructures appearing at arbitrary levels. Therefore, although this paper discussed the problem in the context of XML and XPath, similar problems occur in any nested data structure and query languages that retrieves substructure at arbitrary level.

To solve this problem, we proposed the minimal view approach. Given a set of queries, we compute a minimal view set that can answer all the given queries, and submit the queries asking for that view set to the database. Then, the database sends that view set to the client, and the client uses it to produce the answers to the original queries. We showed algorithms that compute such a minimal view set.

Because view sets we compute are minimal in size, we can optimize communication costs between database servers and the clients.

One problem in this approach is that the queries for a minimal view set are usually more complex than its original queries, and it may increase the computation cost on the server. To verify that this problem is not too serious for our approach to be practical, we conducted experiments to examine how much our approach improves communication costs for practical queries, and how it affects computation costs on the servers. Here, due to space limitations, we only briefly summarize the result of our experiments. The detail of the experiments will be reported in another publication.

As test data, we generated 233MB of artificial auction data by XMark [26]. We ran experiments in two settings. First, we stored XML data in a plain file, and evaluated XPath using a DOM-based in-memory XPath processor Xalan [27]. Second, we stored the data in a RDBMS, Oracle 9i, using a standard relational encoding scheme of XML used in many researches, such as [16], and evaluated XPath by transforming them into SQL. We tested various practical queries, and for non-recursive queries, we could even reduce the computation cost on the server in many cases. For example, we tested the queries below:

Q_1 : /site/region/namerica/item
Q_2 : /site/region/europe/item
Q_3 : /site/region/*/item/description

which asks for complete information on auction items in North America and Europe, and also asks for descriptions of auction items in any region. Our algorithm computes the view set consisting of Q_1 and Q_2 above, and $\overline{q_3}$ below:

q_3 : /site/region/$\overline{\{namerica,europe\}}$/item/description

Then, the total size of the query results, i.e., the size of the data to be sent over the network was reduced by more than 60%. It is not surprising, but a more surprising result is even the computation cost was reduced slightly in the DOM setting, and by more than 25% in the relational encoding setting. This is because the evaluation cost includes some factors which are proportional to the answer size, and view queries are more complicated but have smaller answers.

For recursive queries, if we evaluate $-Q_i$//* directly, its computation cost was very high. However, by expanding // into a union of many queries, we could reduce the computation cost in many cases. The detail of such optimization of the queries produced by our algorithm shown in this paper is an important future work.

It is also interesting to investigate the interaction between our approach and the compression approach, which compresses the data before sending, and decompresses it on the client. Because compression removes redundancy, it may offset the difference of the size of the original answers and our minimal views. It is another important future work.

References

[1] M. Cherniack, S. B. Zdonik, M. H. Nodine: To Form a More Perfect Union (Intersection, Difference). In *DBPL*, 1995

[2] M. Altinel and M. J. Franklin. Efficient filtering of XML documents for selective dissemination of information. In *VLDB*, pp. 53–64, 2000.

[3] S. Amer-Yahia, *et al*. Minimization of tree pattern queries. In *SIGMOD*, pp. 497–508, 2001.

[4] P. M. G. Apers. Data allocation in distributed database systems. *TODS*, 13(3):263–304, 1988.

[5] C. Barton, *et al*. Streaming XPath processing with forward and backward axes. In *ICDE*, pp. 455–466, 2003.

[6] M. Benedikt, W. Fan, G. M. Kuper. Structural properties of XPath fragments. In *ICDT*, pp. 79–95, 2003.

[7] D. Calvanese, *et al*. Answering regular path queries using views. In *ICDE*, pp. 389–398, 2000.

[8] C.-Y. Chan, *et al*. Efficient filtering of XML documents with XPath expressions. In *ICDE*, pp. 235–244, 2002.

[9] J. Chen, *et al*. NiagaraCQ: A scalable continuous query system for internet databases. In *SIGMOD*, pp. 379–390, 2000.

[10] L. Chen and E. A. Rundensteiner. ACE-XQ: A CachE-aware XQuery answering system. In *WebDB*, pp. 31–36, 2002

[11] R. Chirkova and C. Li. Materializing views with minimal size to answer queries. In *PODS*, pp. 38–48, 2003.

[12] J. Clark and S. DeRose, eds. *XML Path Language (XPath) Version 1.0 – W3C Recommendation*, 1999.

[13] J. Clark and S. DeRose, eds. *XML Path Language (XPath) Version 2.0 – W3C Working Draft*, 2003.

[14] S. Dar, *et al*. Semantic Data Caching and Replacement. In *VLDB*, pp. 330–341, 1996.

[15] G. Grahne and A. Thomo. Query containment and rewriting using views for regular path queries under constraints. In *PODS*, pp. 111–122, 2003.

[16] T. Grust. Accelerating XPath location steps. In *SIGMOD*, pp. 109–120, 2002.

[17] A. K. Gupta and D. Suciu. Stream processing of XPath queries with predicates. In *SIGMOD*, pp. 419–430, 2003.

[18] A. Y. Halevy. Answering queries using views: A survey. *VLDB Journal*, 10(4):270–294, 2001.

[19] D. E. Knuth, J. H. Morris, and V. B. Pratt. Fast pattern matching in strings. *SIAM Journal of Computing*, 6:323–350, 1977.

[20] C. Li, M. Bawa, J. D. Ullman. Minimizing view sets without losing query-answering power. In *ICDT*, pp. 99–113, 2001.

[21] L. Liu, C. Pu, W. Tang. Continual queries for internet scale event-drive information delivery. *TKDE*, 11(4):610–628, 1999.

[22] B. Ludäscher, P. Mukhopadhyay, Y. Papakonstantinou. A transducer-based XML query processor. In *VLDB*, pp. 227–238, 2002.

[23] G. Miklau and D. Suciu. Containment and equivalence for an XPath fragment. In *PODS*, pp. 65–76, 2002.

[24] D. Olteanu, *et al*. XPath: looking forward. In *XMLDM*, pp. 109–127, 2002.

[25] F. Peng and S. S. Chawathe. XPath queries on streaming data. In *SIGMOD*, pp. 431–442, 2003.

[26] A. Schmidt, *et al*. XMark: A benchmark for XML data management. In *VLDB*, pp. 974–985, 2002.

[27] Xalan. http://xml.apache.org/xalan-j/.

A Framework for Using Materialized XPath Views in XML Query Processing

Andrey Balmin   Fatma Özcan   Kevin S. Beyer   Roberta J. Cochrane
Hamid Pirahesh

IBM Almaden Research Center, San Jose CA 95120
{abalmin, fozcan, kbeyer, bobbiec, pirahesh}@us.ibm.com

Abstract

XML languages, such as XQuery, XSLT and SQL/XML, employ XPath as the search and extraction language. XPath expressions often define complicated navigation, resulting in expensive query processing, especially when executed over large collections of documents. In this paper, we propose a framework for exploiting materialized XPath views to expedite processing of XML queries. We explore a class of materialized XPath views, which may contain XML fragments, typed data values, full paths, node references or any combination thereof. We develop an XPath matching algorithm to determine when such views can be used to answer a user query containing XPath expressions. We use the match information to identify the portion of an XPath expression in the user query which is not covered by the XPath view. Finally, we construct, possibly multiple, compensation expressions which need to be applied to the view to produce the query result. Experimental evaluation, using our prototype implementation, shows that the matching algorithm is very efficient and usually accounts for a small fraction of the total query compilation time.

1 Introduction

With large amounts of data represented and exchanged as XML documents, there is a pressing need to persistently store and efficiently query large XML collections. To address this requirement, W3C has proposed an XML query language, *XQuery* [17]. At the same time, ANSI and ISO has defined SQL/XML [1] (XML-Related Specifications), a new part of SQL standard which extends SQL to handle XML data.

XPath [16] is the W3C recommendation for navigating XML documents, which is designed to be embedded in a host language such as XQuery, XSLT or SQL/XML[1]. It is a reference based language; hence, subsequent expressions on the results an XPath expression may traverse the document in both forward and reverse directions.

XPath expressions often define complicated navigation, resulting in expensive query processing, especially when executed over large collections of documents. As a result, optimization of XPath expressions is vital to efficiently process XML queries.

In this paper we propose a framework for exploiting materialized XPath views to expedite processing of XML queries. The views may contain copies of XML fragments, or node references which point into the original document. The framework also considers value and structure indexes built on top of the views to efficiently locate information within them. We do not propose any particular structure to assist query processing, but rather a general framework for exploiting a large class of such structures.

Our framework addresses rewriting of XPath expressions that are embedded in XQuery. Consider the following XQuery:

Q1 : *for* $i in collection('URI')//order
  where $i//@price > 100
  return <order> {$i//lineitem} </order>

This query contains three XPath expressions, and all three return different types of values. In the *for binding*, the XPath expression //order returns node references to *order* nodes. In the *where clause*, the comparison $i//@price > 10 requires the typed value

---

[1]The latest draft of SQL/XML embeds XQuery which includes XPath

Permission to copy without fee all or part of this material is granted provided that the copies are not made or distributed for direct commercial advantage, the VLDB copyright notice and the title of the publication and its date appear, and notice is given that copying is by permission of the Very Large Data Base Endowment. To copy otherwise, or to republish, requires a fee and/or special permission from the Endowment.

**Proceedings of the 30th VLDB Conference,
Toronto, Canada, 2004**

of the price attributes, and finally within the element constructor copied subtrees rooted at *lineitem* nodes are needed.

As the above example illustrates, it is worthwhile to store additional "values" with the results of XPath expressions. In this paper, we explore XPath views containing XML fragments, typed data values, node references, full paths and a combination thereof.

The problem of rewriting queries using materialized views becomes even more relevant in the world of XML query processing, since XML indexes also can be modeled as materialized views. Indeed, most of the recently proposed XML indexing schemes (e.g., [14, 9, 3, 5, 11, 7]), can be viewed as materialized views that contain a value and a node reference for every element in the collection. Similarly relational indexes can be viewed as very limited materialized views that contain column values and row IDs. The materialized view model is especially accurate for *partial* XML indexes, which contain only nodes that satisfy a certain XPath expression. An index does not have to contain all elements in the collection. After all, relational indexes are rarely defined for all columns of all tables in the database. A partial XML index is likely to improve access time and reduce index maintenance costs. We envision such indexes to be very useful for XML query processing.

Consider a query $Q = collection('uri1')//order[date > "Jan 1, 2004" and price > 100]$, which asks for recent expensive orders. First, let us consider a view $V_1 = collection('uri1')//*$ which contains data values and node references of all elements in a collection. We model this view as a table with attributes *value* and *reference*. One way to execute the query using this view is to find all elements with values greater than 100, then follow the node references to the original documents and select only *price* elements that have *order* parent with $date > "Jan 1, 2004"$.

Now let's assume that, in addition to values and node references, V_1 also contains elements' full path, i.e., a list of all ancestor tags. This enables us to specifically locate *price* elements with *order* parents and then follow node references to execute the expression $..[date > "Jan 1, 2004"]$.

Of course not all materialized XPath views can be used to answer a query. For example, it is not beneficial to use the view $V_2 = collection('uri1')//order[date > "Feb 1, 2004"]/price$, since it does not contain January orders. The document collection needs to be scanned anyway to locate January orders.

The above examples illustrate two main problems associated with answering XML queries using materialized XPath views. First, an XPath query containment is required to make sure that a view can be used to answer a query. Second, a *compensation* expression needs to be constructed, that would compute the query result using the information available from the view.

We address the XPath query containment problem with an XPath matching algorithm. The containment problem was shown to be co-NP complete for a restricted subset of XPath by [10]. We propose an efficient polynomial-time matching algorithm which is sound and works in most practical cases.

The algorithm is based on the observation made in [10] that a total node mapping from view nodes to query nodes implies containment for conjunctive XPath expressions. We build on the same observation, but extend it to a more functional subset of XPath that includes value predicates, disjunction and the six axes allowed in XQuery.

The mappings produced by the algorithm are used to construct the compensation expression. A mapping between view and query trees is not necessarily unique. Multiple mappings imply that the view can answer different predicates and/or fragments of the query. In those cases the compensation needs to combine information from multiple instances of the view.

To enable the best compensation expression, the matching algorithm produces all possible mappings. The number of tree mappings may be exponential, but we are able to encode them in a polynomial size structure. The running time of the matching algorithm is also polynomial.

The rest of the paper is organized as follows. In Section 2 we describe the XPath materialized views supported by our framework. We present our XPath query matching algorithm in Section 3. In Section 4 we discuss the framework that uses the matching algorithm to decide when and how to use the materialized views to answer a query. We present experimental evaluation of the matching algorithm in Section 5. Finally, we discuss related work in Section 6 and conclude in Section 7.

2 Materialized XPath Views

In relational databases, indexes and materialized views are two well-known techniques to accelerate processing of expensive SQL queries. In this section, we explore a class of materialized XPath views to speed-up processing of XQuery or SQL/XML queries. We consider XPath views containing XML fragments, typed data values, node references, full paths and a combination thereof.

One class of XPath views may contain only typed data values of nodes. Storing typed values facilitates computation of value based comparison predicates. B^+-tree indexes on typed values further expedites query processing. For example, if an XPath view contains the typed values of $/lineitem/@price$, then it can be used to answer the comparison predicate $/lineitem/@price > 1000$.

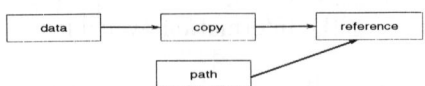

Figure 1: Extraction Type Hierarchy

Note that this type of XPath views can also be considered as a regular value index. However, there is one important restriction of such XPath views: The XPath expression in the comparison has to be exactly the same as the view XPath expression. Because the XPath view does not contain enough information if the query XPath expression does not exactly match. Consider the query /lineitem/@price < 100. An XPath view $V = //lineitem/@price$ cannot be used to evaluate this comparison predicate, because there is no way to determine from the view that lineitem nodes are top-level element nodes.

To remedy this problem, one may also store full paths in an XPath view. A full path of a node is defined as a list of ancestor tags. Such paths can be computed when XML data is processed and inserted into the view results. These full paths can be very useful if the defining XPath expression of the view contains descendant axes and/or wildcard name tests. For example, we can use the XPath view $V = //@*$ to evaluate comparison predicates /lineitem/@price > 100, /lineitem/order/@quantity < 10, /lineitem/*/@amount = 1000, and etc.

Storing typed values is only helpful to evaluate comparison predicates, whether in where clause of a FLWOR expression, or in a predicate of an XPath step expression. However as shown in **Q1** in the Introduction, XPath expressions are also used in other contexts. To evaluate those queries, it is often required to apply further navigation to the results of an XPath view. In such scenarios, we need to store node references in the materialized XPath view.

Consider the query **Q1** and the XPath view $V = //order$. If V only contains typed values of orders, we cannot use it to process **Q1**. However, if V contains references to order nodes, then we can use this view, as we can execute the XPath expressions $i//@price and $i//lineitem, by using the results of V.

Sometimes it is also beneficial to store actual copies of XML fragments in an XPath view. For example, it might be sufficient to store copies to answer value-based expressions of SQL/XML. Furthermore, concurrency control is easier in the case of copy semantics. Note that copy semantics loses the parent property as well as node identity. This implies that XPath views containing copies can only be used to answer XQueries when subsequent operations on the results of the view do not require to navigate to the parent or ancestors, or require node identity, such as node comparisons, and sequence operations of XQuery.

One can think of different kinds of materialized XPath views which contain a combination of node references, full paths, typed data values and copied XML fragments. We refer to node references simply as *references*, typed data values as *data*, copied XML fragments as *copy* and full paths simply as *paths* in the rest of this paper. A view definition language to create these different kinds of materialized XPath views is beyond the scope of this paper. Here, we assume that views are relations with the schema *(reference, copy, data, path)* and are defined with XPath expressions where view extraction point is marked with copy, data, path and reference extraction types. Figure 1 summarizes the relationships between these extraction types in terms of the information they represent. We explain how these different extraction points are used in Section 4.

3 XPath Matching Algorithm

In this section, we present an algorithm to decide if a given XPath view can be utilized in a user query. The algorithm finds tree mappings between the view and the query expression trees, and records them in a match structure. If a mapping exists then the view can potentially be used to evaluate the XPath expression in the user query. However, further computation may be necessary. We use the match structure produced by the algorithm to derive the *compensation*, which is an expression applied to the contents of the view to compute the query result.

In the remainder of this section, we first introduce our XPath representation. We then describe the basic algorithm, which concentrates on "structure-only" XPath queries, followed by an extension to handle comparison predicates.

3.1 XPath Representation

We represent XPath expressions as labeled binary trees, called *XPS trees*. An XPS node is labeled with its *axis* and *test*, where *axis* is either the special "root", or one of the 6 axes allowed in XQuery [17]: "child", "descendant", "self", "attribute", "descendant-or-self", or "parent". The *test* is either a name test, a wildcard test, or a kind test, such as node() or text(). The first child of an XPS node is called *predicate*, and it can be a conjunction (and), a disjunction (or), a comparison operator ($<, \leq, \geq, >, =, \neq, eq, ne, lt, le, gt, ge$), a constant, or an XPath Step (XPS) node. The second child, called *next*, points to the next step, and is always an XPS node. *Next* and *predicate* are optional. We use "null" nodes to denote missing children. An XPS node which does not have a next step, and is reachable from the root of the XPS tree by visiting only *next* children, is called the *extraction point*, since this node represents the result of the XPath expression. Example XPS trees can be found in Figure 2.

3.2 Basic Matching Algorithm

The algorithm described in this section traverses both the view and the query expression trees and computes

1	$matchStep(v, q)$	
1.1	if $(q = q_1 \wedge q_2)$	$matchStep(v, q) \to matchStep(v, q_1) \vee matchStep(v, q_2)$
1.2	else if $(q = q_1 \vee q_2)$	$matchStep(v, q) \to matchStep(v, q_1) \wedge matchStep(v, q_2)$
1.3	else if $(v_{axis} = $ "descendant"$)$	$matchStep(v, q) \to \bigvee \{matchChildren(v, c), \forall c \in \{$ preorder traversal of $q\}$, such that $c_{axis} \neq$ "attribute", unless $v_{test} = $ node()$\}$
1.4	else if $(v_{axis} = q_{axis})$	$matchStep(v, q) \to matchChildren(v, q)$
1.5	else	$matchStep(v, q) \to False$
2	$matchChildren(v, q)$	
2.1	if $(v_{test} = $ "*"$) \vee (v_{test} = q_{test})$	$matchChildren(v, q) \to matchPred(v_{pred}, q) \wedge matchNext(v_{next}, q))$
2.2	else	$matchChildren(v, q) \to False$
3	$matchPred(v_{pred}, q)$	
3.1	if $(v_{pred} = $ null$)$	$matchPred(v_{pred}, q) \to True$
3.2	else if $(q = $ null$)$	$matchPred(v_{pred}, q) \to False$
3.3	else if $(v_{pred} = v_1 \wedge v_2)$	$matchPred(v_{pred}, q) \to matchPred(v_1, q) \wedge matchPred(v_2, q)$
3.4	else if $(v_{pred} = v_1 \vee v_2)$	$matchPred(v_{pred}, q) \to matchPred(v_1, q) \vee matchPred(v_2, q)$
3.5	else	$matchPred(v_{pred}, q) \to matchStep(v_{pred}, q_{pred}) \vee matchStep(v_{pred}, q_{next})$
4	$matchNext(v_{next}, q)$	
4.1	if $(v_{next} = $ null$)$	$matchNext(v_{next}, q) \to True$
4.2	else if $(q = $ null$)$	$matchNext(v_{next}, q) \to False$
4.3	else	$matchNext(v_{next}, q) \to matchStep(v_{next}, q_{pred}) \vee matchStep(v_{next}, q_{next})$

Table 1: Rules for finding containment mappings between expression trees

all possible mappings from XPS nodes of the view to XPS nodes of the query expression, in a single top-down pass of the view tree. For the ease of readability, we denote the XPath expression defining the view with V, and the XPath expression in the user query with Q.

In the basic algorithm we restrict the view and query XPS trees to contain only AND, OR nodes and XPS nodes with child, attribute, or descendant axis.

Table 1 summarizes the basic algorithm in terms of the four functions used. Every function of the table evaluates to Boolean. The algorithm is invoked by the initial call $matchStep(v\_root, q\_root)$, and there exists a match if this call evaluates to $true$. The first rule whose condition is satisfied is fired for each function.

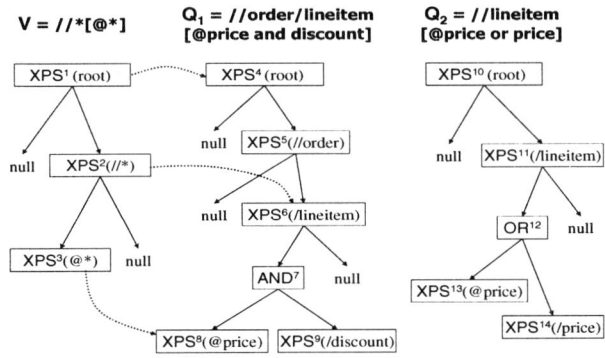

Figure 2: Example view definition, matching and non-matching query expressions

Rule 1.1 handles the situation where the query expression can be more restrictive than the view definition. It is sufficient for one of the conjuncts of q_{pred} to be mapped by a node of V. For example, the view $V = //*[@*]$, which contains all XML element nodes which have an attribute, can be used to evaluate $Q_1 = //order/lineitem[@price\ and\ discount]$ as shown in Figure 2. Dotted lines denote the mapping.

Rule 1.2 says that if one disjunct of q_{pred} is mapped by a node $v \in V$, then v also has to map to some node in the other disjunct of Q. For example, the same V of Figure 2 cannot be used to evaluate the expression $Q_2 = //order/lineitem[@price\ or\ price]$, which asks for lineitem nodes, which have either a price attribute or a price element.

When the view node contains a "descendant" axis, we need to keep looking for matches down in the tree, even if the current query expression node matches (rules 1.3). For example, in Figure 2, we will try to map $XPS^2(//*)$ to XPS^5 (//order), XPS^6(/lineitem), and XPS^9(/discount). We do not include rules that handle "self" and "descendent-or-self" due to lack of space. "Parent" axis is handled by rewriting the expression into an equivalent XPS tree that uses forward axes only. The rewriting is done using transformations similar to the ones proposed in [13]. If the axes match, we try to match the predicate and next children of the view node (rule 1.4). If there is no match (rule 1.5), the algorithm returns $false$.

When matching children, if the tests match, then we try to match the predicate and the next step of v (rule 2.1). If v does not have a predicate then the step trivially matches (rule 3.1). Recall that the view expression can not be more restrictive than the query. Hence, if v has a predicate and q does not, then the match fails (rule 3.2). The next children of XPS nodes are matched in the same fashion.

The rule 3.3 states that if there is a conjunction

in V, then both conjuncts has to map to some node in Q. However, it is sufficient for one disjunct in V to participate in the mapping (rule 3.4). For example, the view $V = //order[@price\ or\ lineitem/@price]$ can be used to evaluate Q_1 of Figure 2.

The rules of $matchNext()$ are similar to those of $matchPred()$.

As the predicate of an XPath step may contain a nested XPath expression, we try to match v_{pred} both to q_{pred} and q_{next} (rule 3.5), and match v_{next} to both q_{pred} and q_{next} (rule 4.3). For example, a view expression $V = //a[b/c]$ matches the XPath expression $Q = //a/b[c]$.

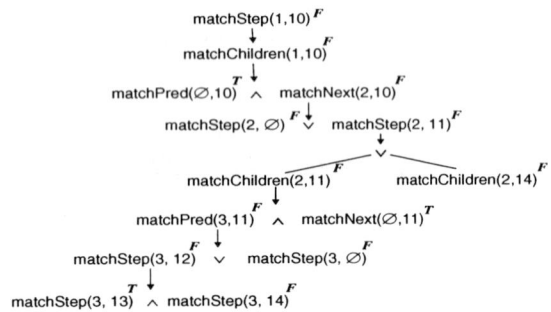

Figure 3: Execution of the matching algorithm for V and Q_2 of Figure 2

Figure 3 shows the execution of the algorithm as the rules fire, and return *false*. There is no match because there is no XPS node in the view that maps to $XPS^{14}(/price)$. That is, the view does not contain `lineitem` elements with a `price` sub-element, but no attribute.

3.3 Recording the Match

We need to preserve information about all tree mappings found by the algorithm to fully take advantage of data stored in the view, when constructing the compensation expression. We keep track of all mappings in a *match matrix* structure, which also facilitates matching intradocument joins (discussed in Section 3.5), and reduces time complexity of the algorithm by eliminating redundant computation.

The basic matching algorithm may generate exponential (in the number of XPS nodes) number of tree mappings. For example, consider a view that consists of n nodes $//a//a\dots//a$ and a query expression that consists of m nodes $/a/a\dots/a$, where $m > n$. Any view node v can map to any query expression node q such that v's parent maps to some ancestor of q. Thus for any subset of n query nodes, there is exactly one mapping from the nodes of the view to these query expression nodes. Hence, there are C_n^m distinct tree mappings of the view to the query expression. However, a lot of information in these mappings is redundant, since the space of mapping options for a node v depends only on the mapping of v's parent (which we will refer to as *mapping context*) and is independent of all other view node mappings. In other words, $matchStep()$ function of our algorithm may be called multiple times with the same parameters v and q, which is wasteful, since it is guaranteed to return the same result, due to the top-down nature of the algorithm.

Match matrix allows us to encode an exponential number of tree mappings in a polynomial size structure, by recording all possible contexts for each node mapping. It also reduces running time of the algorithm to polynomial, by eliminating redundant computation.

Intuitively, each cell of the match matrix corresponds to a pair of view and query XPS tree nodes. Result of each $matchStep()$ call is cached in the corresponding cell of the matrix. Before executing each $matchStep()$ the matrix is checked, and if the same pair of nodes has already been matched, we return the result stored in the matrix instead of running the $matchStep()$ again. More precisely, each row of the matrix corresponds to an XPS node of the view tree, and each column corresponds to an XPS node of the query expression. Each cell of the matrix may contain one of three possible values: "empty", "true" or "false". All cells are initialized as "empty".

In addition to the cell values, we also record directed edges between cells to represent the context in which the mapping was detected for a pair of nodes. An edge $(i, j) \rightarrow (k, l)$ means that (a successful) $matchStep(v_k, q_l)$ was called (possibly through other functions) from $matchStep(v_i, q_j)$. Recall that matching proceeds in a top-down traversal of the view tree, which means that v_i is a guaranteed to be an ancestor of v_k. Thus the edges form a directed acyclic graph (DAG) of matrix cells.

The $matchStep()$ function of the algorithm of Table 1 is modified as follows: Before executing a call $matchStep(v_i, q_j)$, cell (i, j) of the matrix is checked. If the cell is empty, the function is executed. Otherwise the function returns the content of the cell. After a call $matchStep(v_i, q_j)$ is executed and returns *true* or *false*, we store this value in the matrix cell (i, j). If the result was *true*, we also create the edge $(k, l) \rightarrow (i, j)$ to the structure, where $matchStep(v_k, q_l)$ is the first $matchStep()$ function on the call stack. This edge signifies that node v_i matches q_j in the context of the match of v_k to q_l.

EXAMPLE 3.1 Consider a hierarchy of employees, where each employee element has salary and bonus attributes, and zero or more employee sub-elements. Consider a view that contains all attributes in a subtree of any employee, and an XPath expression that asks for the salary of employees who, together with their direct managers, have bonuses. The XPS trees for these view and query are shown in Figure 4. Note that according to XPath standard $//@*$ is translated into $/descendent-or-self :: node()/@*$. The result-

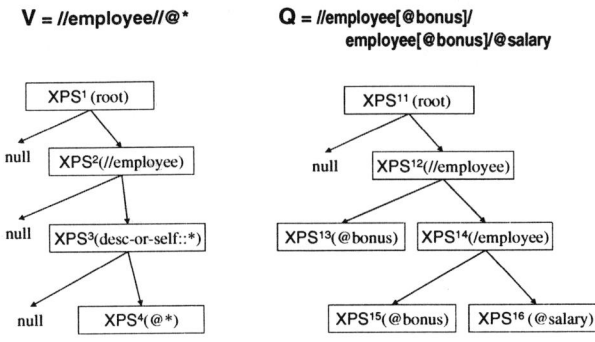

Figure 4: Example view and query expression trees.

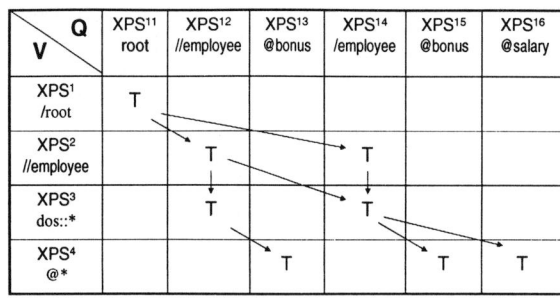

Figure 5: Match matrix for view and query expression trees of Figure 4.

ing match matrix for these view and query expression is shown in Figure 5. For clarity we only show "true" cells.

The matching starts by calling *matchStep*() on root nodes XPS^1 and XPS^{11}, which in turn tries to match $XPS^2(//employee)$ to all XPS nodes of the query[2]. Two of these match attempts will succeed. Let us consider them one at a time.

First, $matchStep(XPS^2, XPS^{12})$ calls $matchStep(XPS^3, XPS^{12})$, which in turn calls $matchStep(XPS^4, XPS^{13})$. The later returns *true*, which is recorded in cell (4,13) of the matrix. At this point the first edge $(3,12) \to (4,13)$ is added to the structure. $matchStep(XPS^3, XPS^{12})$ also returns *true*, so we set $(3,12) = true$ and add edge from (2,12) to (3,12). Similarly we find matches (3,14), (4,15) and add edges $(2,12) \to (3,14)$ and $(3,14) \to (4,15)$.

Now consider execution of the call $matchStep(XPS^2, XPS^{14})$. It starts by calling $matchStep(XPS^3, XPS^{14})$. However, cell (3,14) is not empty – it has already been set to *True*, so we immediately return *true*, without re-executing the call. We also add an edge from (2,14) to (3,14), since the same match has been found in a new context. Finally, we set $(3,12) = true$ and add edge $(1,11) \to (2,14)$ to complete the structure.

Notice that this structure encodes five distinct mappings of the view tree into the query. □

3.4 Handling Comparison Predicates

In this section, we extend our matching algorithm to handle comparison predicates, i.e., expressions of the form L *op* R, where *op* is one of XQuery general or value comparison operators, and L and R are either an XPS node or a constant.

Needless to say, predicate conditions complicate the matching algorithm. For example, consider the view $V = //order/*[@price > 60]$ that matches the query expression $Q = //order[lineitem/@price > 100]$.

---
[2]For simplicity we omit intermediate *matchChildren*(), *matchPred*(), and *matchNext*() calls in this example.

Their XPS trees are shown in the upper part of Figure 6. Notice that view XPS node $XPS^2(/*)$ should match query expression node $XPS^5(/lineitem)$. However, in the view tree ">" appears under $XPS^2(/*)$, while in the query ">" is above $XPS^5(/lineitem)$.

To enable matching in the presence of comparison nodes, we normalize the expression trees by extracting the predicate conditions from the expression trees as a pre-process of the matching algorithm. For example, we create the trees V' and Q' shown in the lower half of Figure 6.

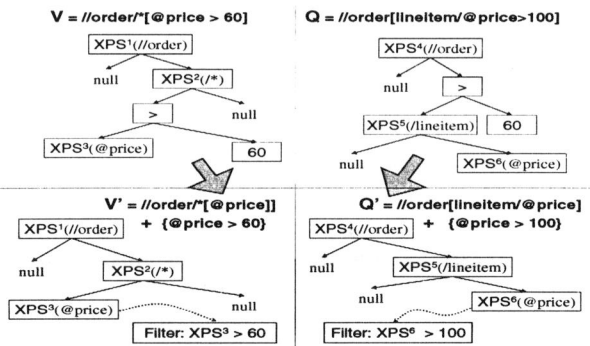

Figure 6: Normalizing the expression trees by extracting predicate conditions.

Both trees are traversed bottom-up and all comparison predicates are moved into a *filter list*. Each filter in the list is associated with the XPS node(s) it includes.

There are two types of filters: *local predicates* f_n of the form n *op const*, where n is an XPS node, and *intradocument join filters* f_{nm} of the form n *op* m, where both n and m are XPS nodes. During normalization, for each local predicate f_n, we replace its comparison operator node, with the subtree rooted at n, and associate f_n with n's extraction point n_e, which is an XPS node obtained by starting at n and following next children. For each intradocument join filter f_{nm}, we replace the comparison operator with an *AND* node, and associate f_{nm} with extraction points of both n and m.

EXAMPLE 3.2 Consider an XPath expression $//order[date = lineitem[@price > 100]/shipdate]$. It contains one local predicate and one intradocument join filter. Its normal form is $//order[date\ AND\ lineitem[@price]/shipdate]$ with two filters:

1. $price > 100$, associated with $@price$ XPS node

2. $date = shipdate$, associated with $/date$ and $/shipdate$ XPS nodes. $/shipdate$ is an extraction point, obtained by following the next step of the $/lineitem$ XPS node.

□

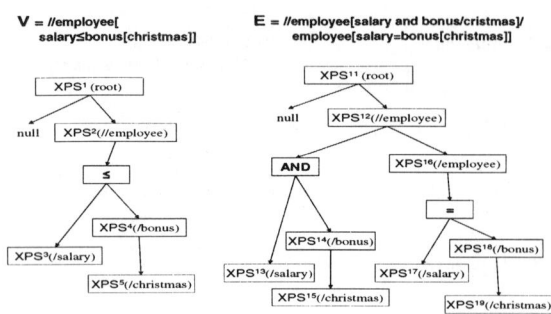

Figure 7: View and query expression trees with intradocument joins.

We extend the basic algorithm to match local predicates in the view during a single pass of the view tree. While the matching algorithm builds the mapping of view nodes to query expression nodes, it also checks whether for every local predicate f_v, that is associated with the current XPS node $v \in V$, there exists a predicate f_q associated with node $q \in Q$, such that v maps to q and f_q implies f_v ($f_q \rightarrow f_v$). Note that for local predicates implication can be detected in polynomial time, by examining the comparison operators and the constants in the predicates. Disjunction and conjunctions are handled as part of the matching algorithm.

EXAMPLE 3.3 The matching of V and Q of Figure 6 proceeds as follows. First, we extract the predicates, by replacing the > nodes with their XPS children, producing trees V' and Q'. The extracted view predicate is associated with the $XPS^3(@price)$ node of the view. The query expression predicate is connected to $XPS^6(@price)$. Next, the algorithm of Table 1 proceeds by matching view node XPS^1 to query node XPS^4, which requires matching XPS^2 to XPS^5, which in turn attempts to match the view node $XPS^3(@price)$, to the query expression node $XPS^6(@price)$. At this point we find out that a view predicate $XPS^3 > 60$ is associated with node XPS^3, so we look for query expression predicates associated with the XPS^6 node. We find the predicate $XPS^6 > 100$, which is more restrictive than the view predicate. As a result, the algorithm matches XPS^3 to XPS^6. □

Notice that query expression predicates do not require any additional matching, since the query expression can be more restrictive than the view.

To match intradocument join filters in views requires matching both sides of the join predicate first. Hence, intradocument join filters are matched in a post processing step which is described next.

3.5 Matching Intradocument Joins

Recall that *intradocument join* filters represent joins that occur inside a single document. For example, the expression $//employee[@bonus > @salary]/name$ contains an intradocument join filter $@bonus > @salary$. To match a view predicate f_v of the form $v_1\ op\ v_2$, we first need to find mappings for both XPS nodes v_1 and v_2. Given a match matrix that contains all node mappings for v_1 and v_2, we may need to prune some of these mappings if there is no query expression filter that implies f_v. In other words, the query has to contain a matching filter that is at least as restrictive.

Once we construct the match matrix, we analyze each intradocument join filter $f_v = v_1\ op\ v_2$ in the view.

If there is no query predicate $f_q = q_1\ op\ q_2$ that implies f_v, such that v_1 maps to q_1 and v_2 maps to q_2, we prune (i.e. set matrix cell to $false$) all node mappings that involve v_1 or v_2.

Finally, we clean-up the matrix, by repeating the following steps until no more modifications can be made.

- Remove all dangling edges for which either source or target matrix cell is not set to *true*.

- Remove orphan node matches, i.e., matrix cells with value *true* that do not have at least one incoming edge, are set to $false$.

We test that the resulting matrix is valid (i.e. encodes at least one tree mapping) by a single bottom up traversal of the view tree. An XPS node is valid, if its row in the matrix contains at least one $true$ cell, and all its children are valid. An OR node is valid if at least one of its children is valid. An AND node is valid if all its children are valid. A matrix is valid, if the root of the view tree is valid.

EXAMPLE 3.4 Consider a view that lists all employees with Christmas bonuses no less than their salaries: $V = //employee[salary \leq bonus[christmas]]$, and an XPath expression that asks for employees that have salaries, Christmas bonuses and are managers of employees whose Christmas bonuses are equal to their salaries: $Q = //employee[salary\ and\ bonus/cristmas]/employee$

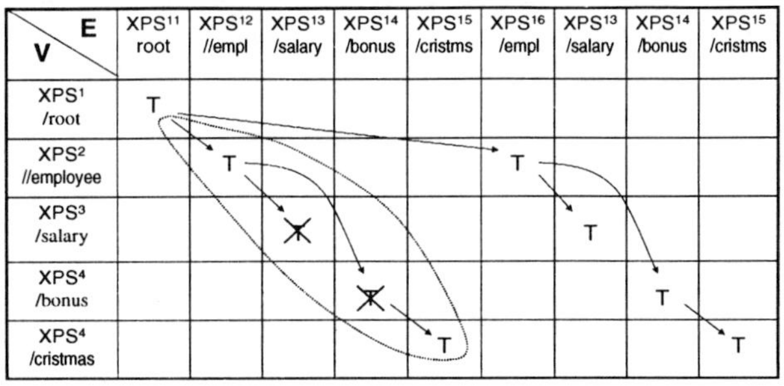

E V	XPS¹¹ root	XPS¹² //empl	XPS¹³ /salary	XPS¹⁴ /bonus	XPS¹⁵ /cristms	XPS¹⁶ /empl	XPS¹³ /salary	XPS¹⁴ /bonus	XPS¹⁵ /cristms
XPS¹ /root	T								
XPS² //employee		T				T			
XPS³ /salary			✗				T		
XPS⁴ /bonus				✗				T	
XPS⁴ /cristmas					T				T

Figure 8: Match matrix for XPS trees of Figure 7 and its pruning.

$[salary = bonus[christmas]]$. The XPS trees of these expressions are shown in Figure 7.

Intuitively, *employee* node in the view can map to either of the two *employee* nodes in the query. However, the first mapping $(XPS^2(//employee) \to XPS^{12}(//employee))$ is not valid because the intradocument join $[salary^3 \leq bonus^4]$ is not implied by any query filter (there is no filter involving $XPS^{13}(/salary)$ and $XPS^{14}(/bonus)$). Thus, node mappings $(XPS^3(/salary), XPS^{13}(/salary))$ and $(XPS^4(/bonus), XPS^{14}(/bonus))$ are pruned from the matrix. The node mappings $(XPS^2(//employee), XPS^{12}(//employee))$ and $(XPS^5(/cristmas), XPS^{15}(/cristmas))$ are removed from the matrix by the clean-up phase that eliminates dangling DAG edges.

The second mapping $(XPS^2(//employee) \to XPS^{12}(//employee))$ is valid, because the query predicate $bonus = salary$ is more restrictive than $salary \leq bonus$, and hence implies the view predicate.

Figure 8 shows match matrix for this example. Node mappings removed by pruning are crossed with an "X". Circled portion of the match is removed by the clean-up phase. □

3.6 Complexity of the Algorithm

Let us, first, consider space complexity of the algorithm. The size of the match matrix is $O(|V| * |Q|)$, where $|V|$ and $|Q|$ are the number of XPS nodes in the view and query expressions respectively. Each matrix cell can have at most $|Q|$ incoming edges (by construction an edge $(i, j) \to (l, k)$ may exist only if v_i is the parent of v_l). Thus the number of edges in the DAG is $O(|V| * |Q|^2)$.

The cost of constructing the matrix is also polynomial. The *matchStep* function has only $|V| * |Q|$ distinct sets of parameters. By definition of a match matrix, the same pair of nodes cannot be matched more than once. In the worst case (rule 1.3) a function call may expand into $|Q|$ function calls. Thus the algorithm runs in $O(|V| * |Q|^2)$ time.

The cost of pruning the matrix is a product of size of the matrix and the number of predicates extracted from V and Q, which is $O(|V|^2 * |Q|^3)$. Note that predicate subsumption ($f_q \to f_v$) can be checked in constant time, since f_q and f_v can only contain comparison operators: Disjunction or conjunction are handled by normalization and the matching algorithm, and no negation is allowed.

4 Matching Framework

The previous section defines matching of XPS view and query trees. In this section we exploit the resulting matches in a framework for rewriting XPath expressions using materialized XPath views.

When a view does not contain the exact results of an XPath query, we need to compensate, by applying some computation to the content of the view. This extra computation, called *compensation*, depends on what information is stored in the view.

Recall that a view expression extraction point is marked with one or more of four types: *reference*, *copy*, *path* and *data*. Thus a view is a relation with one attribute for each extraction type. To express compensation we use a variant of a relational algebra which consists of "select", "project" and "intersection" operators. These operators are extended to handle XML type. The select operator allows any XML comparison on *data* extraction type, any XPath expression on *reference* and *copy* extractions, and a new *match_path* operation, denoted ∼, on *path* extractions. We do not elaborate on the details of the algebra due to lack of space.

We construct compensation expressions by a two step process. First, we take a copy of the query XPS tree and *relax* it, i.e., eliminate conditions that are guaranteed to be satisfied given the view definition. For example, given $V = //a[@b]$ and $Q = //a[@b \wedge @c]$, the relaxed expression doesn't need to include a $[@b]$ predicate, since it is implied by the view. Second, we *optimize* the relaxed XPS tree and produce a compensation algebraic expression that fully utilizes information stored in the view. Since different extraction types may have the same information there may be multiple equivalent compensation expressions. We must chose amongst the alternatives.

In Sections 4.1 and 4.2 we describe compensation construction for a single mapping case. I.e. a single view whose extraction point maps to exactly one query node. We'll generalize the compensation for the case of multiple views and mappings in Section 4.3.

4.1 Eliminating unnecessary conditions

At this stage, a copy of the query XPS tree is *relaxed*, i.e. made less restrictive. We consider three possible types of XPS tree relaxation: removing a filter, replacing a name test with a *, and eliminating a step. The relaxed query produces the same result as the original query, when applied to the result of the view expression.

Notice that a relaxed query is always simpler than the original. We do not consider relaxations that complicate query processing, e.g. replacing child axis with descendant.

First, we identify a *compensation root node*, i.e., an XPS node in the query tree, that was mapped by the view extraction point. In this section we assume that the compensation root is unique. We will relax this assumption in Section 4.3.

The relaxation starts by constructing a Q' expression that is equivalent to the query Q, but starts at the compensation root. This is achieved by moving all XPS ancestors of the compensation root into it's predicate and reversing their axes. I.e. a "child" axis becomes "parent" and "descendant" axis is changed into "ancestor". For example, consider a query $Q = //a[b]/c[d]//e[f]/g$. If node e is the compensation root, we transform the query into:
$Q' = self :: e[f \land ancestor :: c[d \land parent :: a[b]]]/g$. If the compensation root is inside an intradocument join predicate, the new path expression starts with an upward traversal to the first XPS node outside of all such predicates, and then continues as if that node was the compensation root. For example, $Q = //a[b = c[d]]/e$, where d is the compensation root, translates into $Q' = self :: d/parent :: c/parent :: a[b = c[d]]/e$. This Q' start with upward traversal to the a node, which is the first XPS node outside the equality predicate.

While constructing the Q' expression we also transform the predicate of the new root node. All next steps inside the predicate are converted into an equivalent predicate step. E.g. $a[b[c]/d]$ is normalized into $a[b[c \land d]]$.

Next, we construct a V' expression that is equivalent to the view V, but starts at the view extraction point. This process is identical to Q' construction, further simplified by the fact that the extraction point, by definition, cannot occur in a predicate.

A "relaxed" query Q^r is obtained from Q' by the algorithm of Figure 9. The algorithm compares root node predicates of Q' and V' and eliminates all conjuncts of the Q' predicate, such that there is exactly the same conjunct in the predicate of V'. If the root of Q' or V' is not an *AND* node, we say that the entire predicate is a single conjunct.

4.2 Compensation Optimization

The result of query relaxation, Q^r, could be used as a compensation expression if *reference* extraction type is available. However, following the reference to the data storage may be significantly more expensive than using data stored directly with the view. Thus, it is desirable to use other extraction types in the compensation expression. We decompose Q^r into one or more expressions, one per available extraction type, using the following rules.

1. If *data* extraction is available, it is used to answer

```
RelaxQuery(q,v)
  copy Q^r = Q';
  call RelaxQueryRec(Q^r.root, V'.root);
  return Q^r;

RelaxQueryRec(q,v)
  if (q.axis ≠ v.axis) ∨
     (q.axis = "descendant" ∧ q.name ≠ v.name)
    exit;
  if (q.axis = "parent" ∧ q.name = v.name)
    set q.name = "*";
  foreach q_c in conjuncts of q.pred do
    foreach v_c in conjuncts of v.pred do
      call RelaxQueryReq(q_c, v_c);
  // If the recursive calls removed the entire predicate,
  // and there is no next step, this step can be
  removed
  if (q.pred==null ∧ q.next==null)
    remove q from Q^r;
```

Figure 9: Algorithm to eliminate unnecessary query conditions.

any local predicate on the compensation root.

2. If *path* is available, it provides information about labels of ancestors of the compensation root.

3. If *copy* is available, use it if it can answer the portion of Q^r, not covered by *data* and *path*.

4. If *reference* is available, it is used to answer all query conditions not covered by other extractions.

The compensation construction algorithm applies each rule in turn and marks nodes of the Q^r XPS tree that were covered by each extraction. Rules 3 and 4 construct an expression from all unmarked nodes in Q^r and execute it against the view or data storage respectively.

EXAMPLE 4.1 A view $V = //a$ with *copy*, *data*, and *path* extractions can answer a query $Q = /b/a[. > 0]/c$ utilizing only information stored in the view, without accessing the data storage. The relaxed query in this case is $Q^r = self :: *[. > 0 \land parent :: b[parent :: root]]/c$. A $[. > 0]$ filter on the compensation root is answered using *data* extraction. Labels of the compensation root's parent and grandparent are checked using *path*. The rest of the query ($/c$) is answered using the *copy* information. Hence, Q_C is:
$$\pi_{copy/self::*/c}(\sigma_{data>0 \land path \sim /b/*}(V))$$

Symbol $\sim$ stands for *match_path* operation that applies regular pattern matching between a linear XPath expression derived from Q^r and *path* extraction. Note that we inverted $parent :: b[parent :: root]$ into $/b/*$. □

If a view does not contain a *reference* extraction, the compensation may not exist, even if the matching algorithm was successful. The compensation construction algorithm detects these cases. If a *reference* extraction is not available, every node in the Q^r has to be marked by the first 3 rules. Otherwise, the compensation cannot be built, which means that the query cannot be answered using the view.

EXAMPLE 4.2 The view $V = //a[b]/c$ with extraction *copy* cannot be used to answer query $Q = //a[b/d]/c/e$. Even though there is an obvious match, the view only contains copies of "c" nodes without their original context. So we cannot check weather sibling node "b" had a "d" child.

Our algorithm will detect this by constructing $Q^r = self::*[parent::*[b/d]]/e$. According to rule 3 *copy* extraction can answer $self::*/e$ part of Q^r, so nodes $self::*$ and $/e$ of the Q^r are marked as covered by the compensation. Nodes $/b$ and d remain unmarked. Since Q^r contains unmarked nodes, the compensation cannot be constructed, and the view is not usable. □

4.3 Utilizing Multiple Views

Up to now we only considered using a single view and a single compensation root to construct compensation. However, a query can benefit from using multiple views. Similarly the same view could potentially be used multiple times, if the view extraction point mapped to multiple query nodes.

We construct a compensation plan using the following four-step algorithm, which takes as input a set of compensation roots produced by matching one or more views into the query.

1. Find an XPS node in the query tree, that is a lowest common ancestor (LCA) of all compensation roots.

2. For each compensation root q_i, construct an XPath expression Q_i that starts at the compensation root and traverses upward to the LCA node. The Q_i includes local predicates of q_i if the corresponding view contains *data* extraction.

3. Optimize each Q_i, as if it was a compensation, using the algorithm of Section 4.2; construct an intersection of all Q_i expressions.

4. Construct the compensation expression with $\bigcap Q_i$ as the view and LCA as the compensation root.

Note that every view involved in the plan, has to store node references to facilitate upward traversal from the compensation roots to the LCA node.

EXAMPLE 4.3 Consider $Q = //order[@date > "Jan 1, 2004" \text{ and } lineitem/@price > 100]/number$, and a view $V = //@*$ with *data*, *path*, and *reference*

extractions. The view maps into the query in two different ways. The two compensation roots are $@date$ and $@price$. Thus the LCA node is $//order$.

In the second step we construct expressions Q_1 and Q_2 which start at the compensation roots and navigate to $//order$. $Q_1 = self :: attribute(date)[. > "Jan 1, 2004"]/parent :: order$. $Q_2 = self :: attribute(price)[. > 100]/parent :: lineitem/parent :: order$. Both Q_1 and Q_2 contain local predicates on the compensation roots, because V can answer these predicates directly using the *data* extraction.

The Q_1 and Q_2 are optimized into the expressions P_1 and P_2, shown below, using the three types of extractions stored in the view.

$$P_1 = \pi_{reference/parent::*}($$
$$\sigma_{data>"Jan 1,2004" \land path \sim //order/@date}(V))$$
$$P_2 = \pi_{reference/parent::*/parent::*}($$
$$\sigma_{data>100 \land path \sim //order/lineitem/@price}(V))$$

Finally, the compensation expression is computed using $//order$ (LCA) as the compensation root and $Q_1 \cap Q_2$ as the view. The resulting plan is:

$$\pi_{self::*/number}(P_1 \cap P_2)$$ □

Note that the above algorithm provides only one of many ways to construct compensation from multiple materialized views. For some queries and some datasets it might make sense to apply a portion of the compensation before the structural join on the LCA. We are currently investigating cost-based optimization of compensation expressions.

5 Experiments

We implemented the matching framework in the context of XML database research prototype that is under development at IBM Almaden Research Center.

In this section we report on the experimental evaluation of the matching algorithm. We investigated scalability of the algorithm for different classes of queries and view definitions. We do not report compensation construction time, since our algorithm always heuristically picks one compensation to construct, which is relatively cheap. We are currently considering a cost based algorithm, that would construct and estimate costs of various compensations.

Figure 10 shows the performance of the matching algorithm for queries of the following structure: $Q_n = /a[@a_1 = 1 \text{ and } @a_2 = 2 \text{ and} \ldots \text{and } @a_n = n]$. The query was matched against a view $V = //@*$ resulting in n matches. We varied the value of n from 4 to 64. The bars show the relative[3] time it took to do predicate normalization and matrix construction (matching) steps.

Both predicate normalization and matrix construction time grows linearly with the size of the query. The

---
[3]The matching and predicate normalization time is reported relative to matching time for the query and view of size one

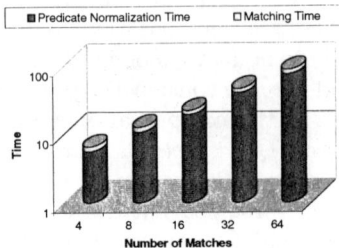

Figure 10: Matching algorithm performance for different sized queries with a single view.

normalization step takes more time since it requires memory allocation to create filter lists and other supporting structures.

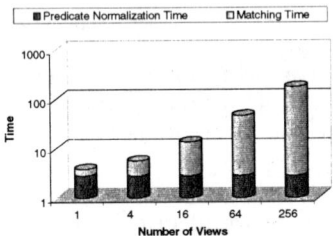

Figure 11: Matching algorithm performance for the same query with a different number of views.

Figure 11 shows that (relative) matching time is a linear function of the number of views defined on the collection of documents that is being queried. For this experiment we used the smallest query expression of the previous experiment: $Q_4 = /a[@a_1 = 1\ and\ @a_2 = 2\ and\ @a_3 = 3\ and\ @a_4 = 4]$. The view definitions where of the form $//@a_k$, where $1 \leq k \leq 4$, so that there was exactly one mapping from each view into the query. Notice that the normalization time plays a much smaller role now, since we normalize the query expression only once.

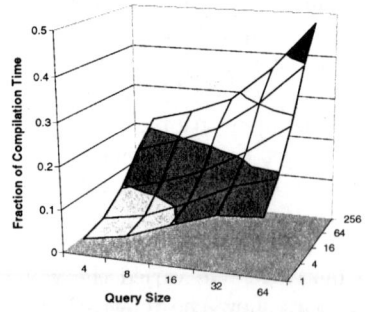

Figure 12: The sum of predicate normalization and matching time as a fraction of total compilation time under various query sizes and number of views.

Figure 12 shows matching time (including predicate normalization), as a fraction of the total query compilation time. The matching time grows linearly in the size of the query and number of views, while the total compiler time grows slower. As a result, the share of the matching algorithm in the total query compilation time increases from 4% in the lower left corner to 48% in the upper right. Note that 64 local predicates may be unrealistically large for a query. It is also unlikely that 256 views are defined over a single document collection. However, some applications do require a large number of views. To address this situation, we are currently exploring pre-filtering techniques that would avoid matching irrelevant views.

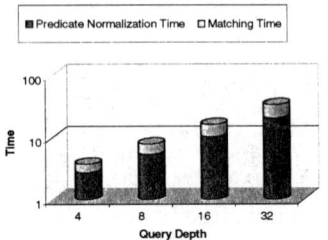

Figure 13: Matching time in case of an exponential number of mappings.

Figure 13 reports the matching algorithm performance for the combinatorial case discussed in Section 3.3, where the match matrix encodes an exponential number of tree mappings. For this experiment the view definition was $V = //a//a//@*$ and the queries were of the form $Q_m = /a[@a_1 = 1]/a[@a_2 = 2]/\ldots/a[@a_m = m]$ resulting in $2 * C_4^m$ possible tree mappings. Our matching algorithm constructs a single match matrix that encodes all of these mappings. The matching time depends almost linearly on the parameter m.

In summary, the overhead of matching for typical queries is not significant. The matching time grows linearly with the number of views defined on a collection. Both predicate normalization and matching time grows almost linearly with the size of the query.

6 Related Work

The problem of rewriting queries using materialized views has been studied extensively in the relational setting [2, 8, 6, 18]. Our XPath matching and compensation algorithms complement this previous work with support for XPath queries.

XPath query containment is a necessary condition for using materialized views, and has recently been studied in [4, 10, 12]. Miklau and Suciu [10] showed that for a subset of XPath containing descendant edges, wildcard tests, and branching, denoted $XP^{\{//,*,[]\}}$, query containment is co-NP complete. Neven and Schwentick [12] showed that adding disjunction to the problem of XPath containment does not increase computational complexity, but did not provide any algorithms for deciding the containment. They also proved that even with a very simple form of negation, the problem becomes undecidable.

Miklau and Suciu [10] outline an incomplete, but sound and efficient algorithm based on tree mappings, which is able to find containment in vast majority of cases. Our matching algorithm is also based on tree mappings, but considers a richer subset of XPath, including comparison predicates, disjunction, and a full set of axes. They also do not distinguish between next steps and predicates in their XPath representation, as they do not consider disjunctions or comparison predicates.

To the best of our knowledge, the problem of computing compensation to enable rewriting queries using materialized XPath views is not addressed in the literature.

7 Conclusion

We presented a framework for utilizing materialized XPath view in XML Query processing. Our techniques are also applicable in the context of materialized SQL/XML views which contain XML querying functions, such as XMLQuery and XMLExists [15]. The problem of rewriting XML queries using materialized XPath views can be vital for efficient XML query processing, as XML indexes can also be modeled as materialized views.

We addressed two main problems to exploit materialized XPath views: XPath query matching and compensation construction. Our matching algorithm handles a rich subset of XPath, including disjunctions and value-based comparisons. We believe that value based comparison predicates are vital to accelerate processing of XML queries. This is based on the fact that value based comparison predicates are in general more selective than existential structural tests, and a B^+-tree index on typed data values might be exploited to further speed up evaluation of such predicates. The matching algorithm records all mappings which are later used to construct compensation.

The algorithm has polynomial time complexity in the size of the view and query. Moreover, the experimental study shows that in most cases matching time is actually linear in the size of the input.

We also provided algorithms to compute compensation. We investigated exploiting different kinds of extractions in compensation expressions and described heuristics to exploit these extraction types.

In the future, we plan to investigate a cost-based compensation construction, that will produce a number of compensation plans and chose the one based on a cost estimate. Using this cost model, we also plan to investigate algorithms to choose the most effective set of materialized XPath views given a query workload.

We also plan to employ this framework in a larger scope of rewriting XQuery using materialized XQuery views.

References

[1] ISO/IEC 9075-14:2003. Information technology – database languages – sql – part 14: Xml-related specifications (sql/xml).

[2] S. Chaudhuri, R. Krishnamurthy, S. Potamianos, and K. Shim. Optimizing queries with materialized views. In *Proceedings of ICDE*, pages 190–200, 1995.

[3] B. F. Cooper, N. Sample, M. J. Franklin, G. R. Hjaltason, and M. Shadmon. A fast index for semistructured data. In *Proceedings of VLDB*, pages 341–350, Roma, Italy, 2001.

[4] A. Deutsch and V. Tannen. Containment and integrity constraints for xpath. In *Proceedings of KRDB*, 2001.

[5] R. Goldman and J. Widom. Dataguides:enabling query formulation and optimization in semistructured databases. In *Proceedings of VLDB*, pages 436–445, 1997.

[6] J. Goldstein and P. Larson. Optimizing queries using materialized views: A practical, scalable solution. In *Proceedings of SIGMOD*, Santa Barbara, CA, 2001.

[7] R. Kaushik, P. Bohannon, J. F. Naughton, and H. F. Korth. Covering indexes for branching path queries. In *Proceedings of SIGMOD*, 2002.

[8] A. Y. Levy, A. O. Mendelzon, Y. Sagiv, and D. Srivastava. Answering queries using views. In *Proceedings of PODS*, pages 95–104, 1995.

[9] Quanzhong Li and Bongki Moon. Indexing and querying xml data for regular path expressions. In *Proceedings of the 27th International Conference on Very Large Databases (VLDB)*, pages 361–370, Roma, Italy, September 2001.

[10] G. Miklau and D. Suciu. Containment and equivalence for an xpath fragment. In *Proceedings of PODS*, pages 65–76, 2002.

[11] S. Nestorov, J. D. Ullman, J. L. Wiener, and S. S. Chawathe. Representative objects: Concise representations of semistructured, hierarchial data. In *Proceedings of ICDE*, pages 79–90, 1997.

[12] F. Neven and T. Schwentick. Xpath containment in the presence of disjunction, dtds and variables. In *Proceedings of ICDT*, 2003.

[13] D. Olteanu, H. Meuss, T. Furche, and F. Bry. Xpath: Looking forward. In *Workshop on XML-Based Data Management*, 2002.

[14] F. Rizzolo and A. O. Mendelzon. Indexing xml data with toxi. In *Proceedings of WebDB*, pages 49–54, 2001.

[15] SQL/XML. See http://www.sqlx.org.

[16] *XML Path Language (XPath) Version 2.0*, November 2003. W3C Working Draft, See http://www.w3.org/TR/xpath20.

[17] *XQuery 1.0: An XML Query Language*, November 2003. W3C Working Draft, See http://www.w3.org/TR/xquery.

[18] M. Zaharioudakis, R. Cochrane, G. Lapis, H. Pirahesh, and M. Urata. Answering complex sql queries using automatic summary tables. In *Proceedings of SIGMOD*, pages 105–116, 2000.

Schema-Free XQuery

Yunyao Li*   Cong Yu*   H. V. Jagadish*

Department of EECS, University of Michigan
Ann Arbor, MI 48109, USA
{yunyaol, congy, jag}@eecs.umich.edu

Abstract

The widespread adoption of XML holds out the promise that document structure can be exploited to specify precise database queries. However, the user may have only a limited knowledge of the XML structure, and hence may be unable to produce a correct XQuery, especially in the context of a heterogeneous information collection. The default is to use keyword-based search and we are all too familiar with how difficult it is to obtain precise answers by these means. We seek to address these problems by introducing the notion of Meaningful Lowest Common Ancestor Structure (MLCAS) for finding related nodes within an XML document. By automatically computing MLCAS and expanding ambiguous tag names, we add new functionality to XQuery and enable users to take full advantage of XQuery in querying XML data precisely and efficiently without requiring (perfect) knowledge of the document structure. Such a Schema-Free XQuery is potentially of value not just to casual users with partial knowledge of schema, but also to experts working in a data integration or data evolution context. In such a context, a schema-free query, once written, can be applied universally to multiple data sources that supply similar content under different schemas, and applied "forever" as these schemas evolve. Our experimental evaluation found that it was possible to express a wide variety of queries in a schema-free manner and have them return correct results over a broad diversity of schemas. Furthermore, the evaluation of a schema-free query is not expensive using a novel stack-based algorithm we develop for computing MLCAS: from 1 to 4 times the execution time of an equivalent schema-aware query.

1 Introduction

XML is gradually becoming the standard in exchanging and representing data. Not surprisingly, effective and efficient querying of XML data has become an increasingly important issue. Traditionally, research work in this area has been following one of the two paths: the structured query approach and the keyword-based approach. XQuery [9] is the generally acknowledged standard of the former, while the latter class has several recent suggestions, including XKeyword [17] and XSEarch [11]. Both approaches have their advantages and disadvantages. Fully structured query (e.g., XQuery) works effectively with the structure, can convey complex semantic meaning in the query, and therefore can retrieve precisely the desired results. However, if the user does not know the (full) structure, it is difficult to write the right query. Even if the user does know the schemas, when data is to be amalgamated from multiple sources with different schemas, it typically will not be possible to write a single query applicable to all sources; rather, multiple queries will have to be written (or at least generated through translation), a process that is complex and error-prone. Keyword-based query can overcome the problems with unknown schema or multiple schemas because knowledge of structure is not required for the query. However, this absence of structure leads to two serious drawbacks. First, it is often difficult and sometimes impossible to convey semantic knowledge in pure keyword queries. Second, the user cannot specify exactly how much of the database should be included in the result.

Consider the example in Figure 1 showing the same bibliography data arranged in two different formats: A organizes publications based on the year of publication and B organizes publications according to their type (*book* or *article*). Let's first look at Query 1, which is a simple query asking for some information (*title* and *year*) on a publication given a certain condition (*author* is "Mary"). To construct an XQuery to represent this simple query, the user faces two challenges: first, she has to know that "publication" in the schema is actually presented as *book* and *article* in both schemas; second, she has to know that *title* and *author* are the child elements of "publication", while *year* could be either a

---

*Supported in part by NSF under grant number IIS 0219513, by NIH under grant number LM08106-01, and by a gift from Microsoft.

Permission to copy without fee all or part of this material is granted provided that the copies are not made or distributed for direct commercial advantage, the VLDB copyright notice and the title of the publication and its date appear, and notice is given that copying is by permission of the Very Large Data Base Endowment. To copy otherwise, or to republish, requires a fee and/or special permission from the Endowment.

**Proceedings of the 30th VLDB Conference,
Toronto, Canada, 2004**

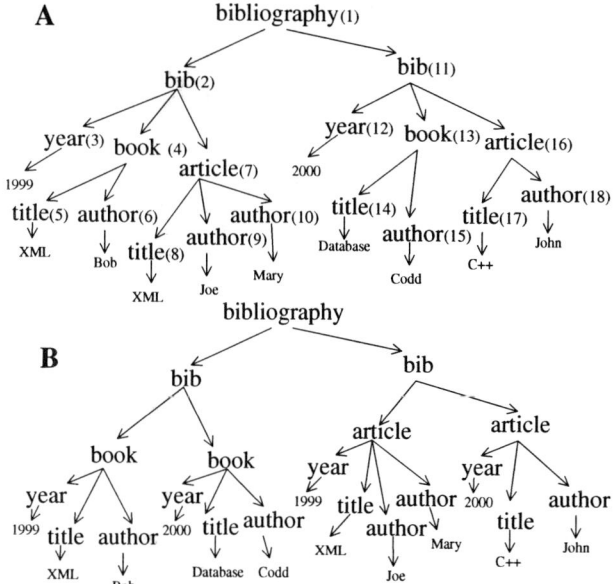

Query 1: Find title and year of the publications, of which Mary is an author.

Query 2: Find additional author of the publications, of which Mary is an author.

Query 3: Find year and author of the publications with similar titles to a publication of which Mary is an author.

Figure 1: Querying XML data with multiple schemas.

child or a sibling. Depending on the schema, the resulting XQuery expression is non-trivial even for this simple query in this very small example. The keyword based approach, on the other hand, often returns results that include too many irrelevant answers. Query 1 (with the underlined keywords) on data in A may return the *bib* node **2**, which contains not just the desired *article* node **7**, but also the unwanted *book* node **4**. Queries 2 and 3 pose even greater challenges for the keyword-based approach. Keywords cannot distinguish the two different *author*s in Query 2 and will simply return node **10** whose content is "Mary". Query 3 involves two logical structures linked together through a value join–it even shares the same set of keywords with Query 1! Therefore it is hard to imagine how the limited semantic capacity of a keyword search specification could capture user intent.

In this paper, we developed a framework that enables users to query XML data exploiting whatever partial knowledge of the schema they have. If they know the full schema, they can write regular XQuery. If they do not know the schema at all, they can just specify keywords. Most importantly, they can be somewhere in between, in which case the system will respect whatever specifications are given.

The notion of Lowest Common Ancestor (LCA) (of individual term/tag matches) has been suggested (e.g. Meet [22]) as an effective mechanism to identify segments of the database of interest to a pure keyword query. While this intuition is reasonable, we show that LCA can frequently be too inclusive. We refine LCA and define the concept of a *Meaningful Lowest Common Ancestor Structure* (MLCAS). Each MLCAS is an XML fragment that meaningfully relates together the nodes corresponding to the relevant variables in the XQuery expression. In Section 2, we show how this structure, and its root node, can be referenced and manipulated in an XQuery expression with embedded **mlcas** functions.

An **mlcas** function precisely specifies a particular non-trivial computation. We may prefer to hide this from a novice user. Furthermore, users may lack knowledge not only about the structure, but also about the specific tag names in the structure. In Section 3, we propose Schema-Free XQuery to address these two issues. Ordinary users are thus able to write simplistic XQuery expressions, specifying keywords and/or tag names and/or structural restrictions, ranging all the way from an open-ended IR-style keyword specification to a completely specified full-fledged XQuery expression.

MLCAS computation is a core part of Schema-Free XQuery evaluation. In Section 4, we show how to accomplish this using standard XQuery evaluation operators. We then introduce a novel stack-based algorithm to compute MLCAS more efficiently, in a manner reminiscent of containment join.

In Section 5, we present an experimental evaluation of our proposal, in terms of both the quality of the results produced and the time taken to produce them. Over both XMark, a standard XML Benchmark, and a wide variety of autonomously created schemas in a well-circumscribed domain (publication lists) we found that Schema-Free XQuery almost always produced exactly the desired results. Moreover, the time taken to do so was only somewhat greater than an equivalent schema-specific query would require.

Finally, we discuss related work in Section 6 and conclude in Section 7.

2 MLCAS

In this section, we describe the concept of MLCAS and present the **mlcas** function as an addition to standard XQuery. The resulting **mlcas**-embedded XQuery gives a user the full expressive power of XQuery while forgiving incompleteness in schema specification.

We begin first with a description of the XML data model that we employ. An XML document is a rooted, ordered, and labeled tree. Nodes in this rooted tree correspond to elements in the XML document.

Definition 2.1 (Descendant-Or-Self) *Tree node n_d is said to have a descendant-or-self relationship with n_a if it is a descendant of n_a or is equal to n_a, denoted as descendant-or-self(n_d, n_a) = true.*

Definition 2.2 (LCA) *Let the set of nodes in an XML document be N. For $d_1, d_2 \in N$, $a \in N$ is the LCA of d_1 and d_2 if and only if:*

- *descendant-or-self(d_1, a) = true, and*
- *descendant-or-self(d_2, a) = true, and*
- *$\forall\ a' \in N$, if descendant-or-self(d_1, a') = true and descendant-or-self(d_2, a') = true, then descendant-or-self(a, a') = true.*

a is denoted as $LCA(d_1, d_2)$.

2.1 Motivation for MLCAS

An XML query typically involves one or more sets of structurally related XML elements that are the processing context used by the query (either to evaluate conditions or to return results). If a user knows the document structure, she can write a meaningful query in XQuery specifying exactly how the nodes involved in the query are structurally related with each other. Without knowledge of the structural relationships, as long as the user knows the element tag names, she can still write an XQuery specifying only the tag names of elements involved in the query. Figure 2 shows one such expansion for Query 1 in Figure 1. A literal evaluation of this expansion will retrieve many meaningless results because the default context is too general (i.e., all of *bib.xml*).

Given the structured nature of XML, it is natural to find the LCA of the set of nodes specified, and treat the subtree rooted at this node as the context for query evaluation. In fact, this idea has been employed in several previously proposed systems [11, 17] and works well in certain cases. For example, consider nodes **8** (*title*) and **10** (*author*) in Figure 1. The LCA of these two nodes is node **7** (*article*) and the subtree rooted at node **7** does make a good context: the *title*, *author*, and *article* nodes form a logical entity together. However, blindly computing the LCA can bring together unrelated nodes. For example, consider a different pair of nodes in Figure 1: nodes **5** (*title*) and **10** (*author*). Their LCA is node **2** (*bib*), whose subtree contains many *book*s and *article*s and is clearly not an appropriate context for the query evaluation. We address this problem by introducing the notion of MLCAS, and using it as the refined context for query evaluation.

2.2 MLCA

A node in an XML document, along with its entire subtree, typically represents a real-world entity. The tag name usually identifies the type of the entity (called *entity type* to distinguish it from the data type used by XML Schema [25]).

Definition 2.3 (ENTITY TYPE) *An entity type (or simply type) of a node n in an XML tree is defined as the tag name (label) of n. Two nodes n_1 and n_2 are of the same entity type $\mathcal{T}$ if and only if they have the same tag name.*

In the presence of ontology (i.e. type hierarchy), nodes with different tag names may still be regarded as of the same type. For example, *book* and *article* nodes can be deemed as of the same super-type $\mathcal{P}$ (*Publication*). For the simplicity of presentation, we do not consider ontology-guided type matching here.

We now describe, through the diagrams in Figure 3, what it means intuitively when we say two nodes are meaningfully related to each other. Let node n_1 represent an entity of type $\mathcal{A}$, and node n_2 represent an entity of type $\mathcal{B}$. First, suppose that n_1 is an ancestor node of n_2 (shown in Figure 3(a)), we believe n_1 and n_2 are meaningfully related to each other. Second, consider the situation where two nodes have no hierarchical relationship with each other. Suppose the LCA of n_1 and n_2 is n (shown in Figure 3(b)), we can regard both entities represented by n_1 and n_2, respectively, belong to the entity represented by n. Therefore, nodes n_1 and n_2, regardless of their types, are related to each other by belonging to the same entity represented by n, which is regarded as the *Meaningful Lowest Common Ancestor*(MLCA) of n_1 and n_2. However, there is an exception to this second case. As demonstrated by Figure 3(c), let there be a node n'_2 of the same type as node n_2, and the LCA of n_1 and n'_2 be n'. If n is an ancestor node of n', we should then conclude that nodes n_1 and n_2 are not meaningfully related to each other because node n'_2, which is of the same type as n_2, is more related to n_1 under the node n', which is actually the MLCA of n'_2 and n_1.

Consider the previously mentioned example of nodes **5** and **10** in Figure 1, their LCA is node **2**. However, it is not their MLCA, because it is an ancestor of node **7**, which is an MLCA of nodes **8** and **10**, and node **8** is of the same type as node **5** (both are *titles*). In fact, the entities *title* and *article* are related to each other by belonging to the same "publication" (*book* or *article*). Nodes **5** and **10** are not related (i.e., not in the same MLCAS) because they belong to different publications.

We now formalize this idea. First of all, given two sets of nodes, where nodes within each set are of the same type, we define how to find pairs of nodes that are meaningfully related to each other from these two sets.

Definition 2.4 (MLCA of two nodes) *Let the set of nodes in an XML document be N. Given $A, B \subseteq N$, where A is comprised of nodes of type $\mathcal{A}$, and B is comprised of nodes of type $\mathcal{B}$, the Meaningful Lowest Common Ancestors Set $C \subseteq N$ of A and B satisfies the following conditions:*

- $\forall c_k \in C$, $\exists a_i \in A$, $b_j \in B$, such that $c_k = LCA(a_i, b_j)$. c_k is denoted as $MLCA(a_i, b_j)$.
- $\forall a_i \in A$, $b_j \in B$, if $d_{ij} = LCA(a_i, b_j)$ and $d_{ij} \notin C$, then $\exists c_k \in C$, $descendant(c_k, d_{ij}) = true$.

The set C is denoted as $MLCASET(A, B)$.

A pair of nodes (a, b), where a is of type $\mathcal{A}$ in set A and b is of type $\mathcal{B}$ in set B, are regarded as meaningfully related to each other if and only if c, the LCA of a and

```
for   $a in doc("bib.xml")//author,
      $b in doc("bib.xml")//title,
      $c in doc("bib.xml")//year
where $a/text() = "Mary"
return <result> { $b, $c } </result>
```

Figure 2: Query 1 in XQuery within no structural knowledge

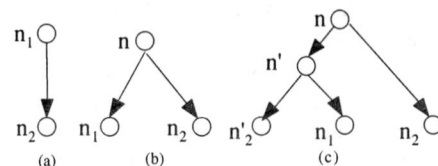

Figure 3: Structural relationships among nodes

b, belongs to C, where C is MLCASET(A, B). This restriction ensures that only the most specific results are returned. If an element's subelement is returned, then the element would not be returned, because its subelement has a closer relationship between the entities represented by nodes in A and B respectively. Given multiple sets of nodes, where nodes within each set are of the same type, we can easily extend Definition 2.4 to define the MLCA of multiple nodes:

Definition 2.5 (MLCA of multiple nodes) *Let the set of nodes in an XML document be N. Given $A_1, A_2, \ldots, A_m \subseteq N$, where $\forall j, a_{ij} \in A_i$ is of type $\mathcal{A}_i$ ($i \in [1, \ldots, m]$), a Meaningful Lowest Common Ancestor $c = MLCA(a_1, \ldots, a_m)$, where $a_i \in A_i$ ($i \in [1, \ldots, m]$), satisfies the following conditions:*

- $\forall j, k \in [1, \ldots, m]$ $(j \neq k)$, $\exists$ $m = MLCA(a_j, a_k)$, $m \neq$ null *and descendant-or-self(m, c) = true.*
- $\exists j, k \in [1, \ldots, m]$ $(j \neq k)$, $c = MLCA(a_j, a_k)$.

2.3 MLCAS

We have seen above how to find MLCA for multiple nodes. However, this in itself is not enough since the same node could be the meaningful lowest common ancestor to many different sets of nodes. For instance, given a *book* with two *authors*, the same *book* node can be the MLCA for the *title* node and each of the *author* nodes, separately. Consider the query in Figure 2 against the data in schema A in Figure 1. Simply computing the MLCA of nodes (*author,title,year*) involved in the query will regard the subtrees rooted at nodes **2** and **11** as the context for query evaluation. Although they do contain the desired result, they often include too much irrelevant information. A user must read the results returned and manually discover the desired answer. This could require a significant amount of work in a large database. Even worse, the system may return additional (incorrect) answers. In this particular example, the user requests the nodes *year* and *title*, answers (**3**,**5**) and (**3**,**8**) will be returned. The former is a wrong answer because only the latter *title* is the desired result. We resolve this ambiguity by identifying not just the MLCA itself, but rather an entire structure, MLCAS, for each such established relationship.

Definition 2.6 (MLCAS) *Let the set of nodes in an XML document be N. Given $A_1, A_2, \ldots, A_m \subseteq N$, where $\forall i, a_{ij} \in A_j$ is of type $\mathcal{A}_j$ ($j \in [1, \ldots, m]$), the Meaningful Lowest Common Ancestor Structure Set $S = \{(r, a_1, \ldots, a_m) \mid r \in N, a_i \in A_i$ ($i \in [1, \ldots, m]$), $r = MLCA(a_1, \ldots, a_m)\}$. Each element of this set is denoted as $MLCAS(a_1, \ldots, a_m)$, with r as its root.*

Each MLCAS is a refined context for query evaluation, and contains only the nodes that are meaningfully related to one another. If an MLCAS satisfies the search conditions, it is unlikely to contain a wrong answer. For example, for the running example Query 1 in Figure 1, expressed as shown in Figure 2, we obtain several MLCASs, including (**2**,**10**,**8**,**3**) and (**11**,**15**,**14**,**12**). The only MLCAS satisfying the original search condition

$a/text() =$"Mary" is (**2**,**10**,**8**,**3**). Hence, the result is (*title*="XML", *year*="1999"), which is exactly the desired result.

Finally, we would like to point out the differences between the concept of MLCAS and the concept of interconnected nodes employed by the XSEarch system [11]. Both concepts are designed to capture the meaningful substructure of the XML document based on both the tag names and the keywords provided in a query. Interconnected nodes are the set of connected nodes with a root node, where no two internal nodes are of the same type (i.e., having the same tag name) and the root node is the LCA of leaf nodes. This concept works well for simple XML data where logically equivalent entities always have the same tag name. However, it does not recognize meaningful structure when those entities (e.g., *book* and *article* in the previous example) have different tag names. In addition, it does not work well on XML data with more than one logical hierarchy. Consider evaluating running example Query 1 against the data in Figure 4, the unrelated *title:Streaming* will be returned by XSEarch. Due to the fact that no two nodes have the same tag name along the path, XSEarch fails to recognize that this title is actually more meaningfully associated with *author:John* under *ref*. Search based on MLCAS, on the other hand, can easily recognize this fact and therefore avoid returning the incorrect result.

2.4 Adding mlcas Function to XQuery

In this section, we introduce a new language construct, **mlcas** function, to the standard XQuery language:

Definition 2.7 (mlcas Function) *$mlcas(a_1, \ldots, a_n)$ is a function that returns (i) root node of $MLCAS(a_1, \ldots, a_n)$, if it exists, (ii)* null *otherwise.*

Figure 5 shows how each of the three running queries presented in Figure 1 can be expressed in the XQuery enriched with the **mlcas** function. Each query will retrieve precisely the desired result, when executed against either example schema in the figure.

Query 1 is the most straightforward. Given the tag names of individual nodes, the condition <u>exists</u> *mlcas($a, $b, $c)* defines the context for evaluation to be the MLCAS of those nodes and filters out any node that cannot be part of any MLCAS. The query is flexible since it does not require user to know the exact

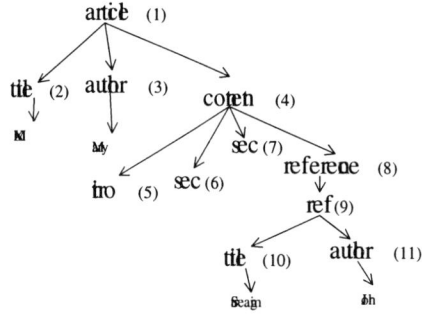

Figure 4: XML data with multiple hierarchies

Query 1:
```
for  $a in doc("bib.xml")//author,
     $b in doc("bib.xml")//title,
     $c in doc("bib.xml")//year
where $a/text() = "Mary"
      and exists mlcas($a,$b,$c)
return <result> {$b, $c} </result>
```

Query 2:
```
for  $a in doc("bib.xml")//author,
     $b in doc("bib.xml")//author,
where $a/text() = "Mary" and $a != $b
      and exists mlcas($a,$b)
return $b
```

Query 3:
```
for  $y in doc("bib.xml")//year,
     $a1 in doc("bib.xml")//author,
     $t1 in doc("bib.xml")//title,
     $t2 in {
         for  $a in doc("bib.xml")//author,
              $t in doc("doc.xml")//title
         where $a/text() = "Mary"
               and exists mlcas($a,$t)
         return $t }
let $m := mlcas($y,$a1,$t1)
where $t1 ≈ $t2 and exists $m
return <result> {$y, $a1} </result>
```

Figure 5: Example XQueries with **mlcas** function

relationships between nodes of the three types. Query 2 shows another aspect of the flexibility in the **mlcas** function: the individual nodes do not have to be of different types. By combining the conditions $a! = $b and exists mlcas($a, $b), the only MLCASs retained are publications with at least two different *authors*. Query 3 shows a more complex example. It contains two contexts for evaluation: one in the outer query, which contains *year*, *author*, and *title*; the other in the inner query, which contains *author* and *title*. The two contexts are linked together through the similarity join $t1 ≈ $t2. This query is difficult to express in any keyword based approach simply because the keyword to be used to match the content of title is only known during the runtime. Although the binding of the result of **mlcas** function to a variable $m is not necessary, it is shown here to illustrate that the root of the MLCAS can be manipulated just like any other regular elements in the XML document. If we evaluate this query against data in schema A of Figure 1, the only MLCAS satisfying the conditions in the inner query will be (**7,10,8**), and the only *title* to be returned is "XML". The outer query, without considering the similarity join, will have several MLCASs, including (**2,3,6,5**), (**2,3,9,8**), (**2,3,10,8**), (**11,12,15,14**), and (**11,12,18,17**). Only the first three have *title* similar to "XML" and are the final MLCASs when we consider the similarity join. The final results to be returned are therefore (*year* = "1999", *author* = "Bob"), (*year* = "1999", *author* = "Joe"), and (*year* = "1999", *author* = "Mary").

3 Schema-Free XQuery

To achieve true flexibility in the query (i.e., Schema-Free XQuery), one first needs to address the issue of *structure ambiguity*, where the relationship among elements is unclear. While the use of **mlcas** function inside XQuery, as described in Section 2.4, effectively deals with the *structure ambiguity*, adding one more language construct to the already complex XQuery will likely prevent ordinary users from adopting it: we would like to allow users to write XQuery using the standard syntax as much as possible and have the system automatically figure out what to do. We present our solution to this through the use of mlcas keyword in Section 3.1. The second issue is *tag name ambiguity*, where the exact tag name of a particular element is unknown (although the user should have a rough idea what the tag name is in general) and we address this issue in Section 3.2. As we will show in this section, a Schema-Free XQuery is underspecified: our task is to derive a completely specified query that best captures the user's intent.

3.1 MLCAS Transformation

Toward the goal of allowing user to take advantage of **mlcas**-embedded XQuery while maintaining the simplicity of XQuery, we propose adding a simple mlcas keyword to the standard XQuery. The keyword is used to ask the system to transform the original simplistic XQuery into an XQuery with **mlcas** function, which then resolves the structure ambiguity automatically. The following query illustrates a simple mlcas-enhanced XQuery representing Query 1 in Figure 1.

```
for  $a in mlcas doc("bib.xml")//author,
     $b in mlcas doc("bib.xml")//title,
     $c in mlcas doc("bib.xml")//year
where $a/text() = "Mary"
return <result> { $b, $c } </result>
```

This query can be automatically transformed into Query 1 in Figure 5 through a simple transformation algorithm, which will be briefly discussed later. One restriction we put on the semantics of the mlcas-enhanced XQuery is to have all mlcas marked variables within one FLWOR block belonging to the same MLCAS: we believe this is the intention for most queries and it simplifies the construction of the query for the user. However, nested queries will have separate MLCASs. For example:

```
for  $y in mlcas doc("bib.xml")//year,
     $a1 in mlcas doc("bib.xml")//author,
     $t1 in mlcas doc("bib.xml")//title,
     $t2 in {
         for  $a in mlcas doc("bib.xml")//author,
              $t in mlcas doc("bib.xml")//title
         where $a/text() = "Mary"
         return $t
     }
where $t1 ≈ $t2
return <result>{$y, $a1}</result>
```

As shown in this example, the MLCAS is designed to have a scope that is local to the query. Hence, the MLCAS formed from the mlcas marked variables in the subquery is different from the MLCAS formed from the mlcas marked variables in the parent query. The two MLCASs are linked together by a similarity value join and our system will transform this query into Query 3 in Figure 5. Furthermore, the mlcas marked variables do not always have to represent descendant elements with respect to the document root. If the user has a better understanding of the document structure, she can explicitly specify the part that she knows and leaves the part that she doesn't know to the system. Consider the query:

> for $r in doc("bib.xml")//bib[1],
> $a in mlcas $r//author,
> $b in mlcas $r//author
> where $a/text() = "Mary" and $a != $b
> return $b

The user here explicitly wants the two *author*s to be within the first *bib* element, she does so by associating the first *bib* element with the variable $r, and marking the relationship between $r and the two *author*s with mlcas. The system will then take all *author*s that are descendants of the first *bib* element and try to compute MLCASs from those nodes only. The transformed query is not shown, and is similar to Query 2 in Figure 5: it is slightly different on account of the additional $r binding.

Transformation algorithm: Here we describe the algorithm that accomplishes the above transformations in a brief outline, not the complete presentation, due to the space limitation. The algorithm begins by taking an arbitrary expression (XQuery, XPath, binary condition, etc.) as its input. If the expression does not have any XQuery (i.e. FLWOR block) inside, it is simply returned as it is. Otherwise, the algorithm extracts all mlcas marked variables within the XQuery at the current nesting level into a **mlcas** function in the where clause of the mlcas-embedded XQuery to be returned. The procedure repeats for each nested XQuery it recursively extracts from the input expression. As a result, each nested query with mlcas keyword will have one and at most one single **mlcas** condition, which is consistent with our intention that all mlcas marked variables in a single query block belong to the same MLCAS.

3.2 Term Expansion

While mlcas-enhanced XQuery addresses the issue of structure ambiguity, it still relies on the correctness of element tag names in a given query. For example, in the queries shown in Section 3.1, if the document being queried upon uses *au* instead of *author* to denote the concept of author, none of the queries will be able to generate the correct results. In an *ad hoc* information retrieval task, a casual user is as unlikely to have perfect knowledge of those tag names as to have the perfect knowledge of the structure relationships. We call this issue *tag name ambiguity*: the discrepancy between a query term and its actual tag name counterpart in the document. According to [14], less than 20% of people choose the same term for a single well-known object. Although the statistics with regard to the tag name usage in XML data is not available, we expect the same issue will be common. In fact, in the real data we collected from the web, people use different names–"paper", "publication", "pub"–to mean the same concept. Apparently, mlcas-enhanced XQuery is still not schema-free. To resolve this problem, we propose to add a simple function **expand** to standard XQuery, indicating the user's lack of knowledge of the exact tag name. The system will then expand the particular tag name to match its equivalents in the XML document based on a domain-specific thesaurus[1]. For example,

> for $a in mlcas doc("bib.xml")//expand(author),
> $b in mlcas doc("bib.xml")//title
> where $a/text() = "Mary"
> return $b

The tag name *author* in the query is indicated by the **expand** function as not exact, and can be matched to *au* by the system if *au* is recognized as the synonym of *author* based on the domain-specific thesaurus. The tag name *title*, however, is not marked (the user is sure of the exact spelling) and will not be expanded. This reflects the principle of Schema-Free XQuery: helping the user construct meaningful query when the knowledge of schema (in terms of both structure and tag name ambiguity) is missing, while giving the user power to express the exact meaning when the knowledge of the schema is present. In addition to domain-specific synonyms, an ontology-driven hierarchical thesaurus can be applied. For example, in Figure 1, both *book* and *article* can be regarded as a kind of *publication*. Therefore, a query tag name of *publication* can be expanded to match both *book* and *article* even though they are not considered as the same concept. Incorporating this ontology-driven term expansion into our framework raises some interesting issues (e.g., how to efficiently determine one term is contained in another) and is the subject of our future work. In the next paragraph, we describe our approach of implementing domain-specific synonym expansion.

Given the thesaurus, a naive implementation of term expansion is to issue multiple queries, each with the to-be-expanded tag name replaced by one of its synonyms in the thesaurus. However, the time cost is proportional to the total number of synonyms of all the expand marked tag names in the query. This is very expensive especially when the query evaluation cost is high. Here, we propose a more efficient approach using term normalization. For each set of synonyms within the thesaurus, one of them is designated as the standard (or normalized) form. When building tag name index on the XML document, two indices are built: one is the regular tag name index with the tag name as it is in the document as the key; the other is the normalized tag name index, where only the normalized form is used as the key. Whenever an element with a non-standard tag name is to be added to the normalized index, the standard tag name is fetched and the element is added to the position keyed by the standard tag name. At query time, if a tag name marked with the

---

[1] If the actual schema for the document(s) is available, the thesaurus can be derived from the actual schema. Otherwise, such a domain-specific thesaurus can be developed either by domain experts or through some standard information retrieval techniques like bootstrapping. In the worst case, a universal thesaurus like WordNet [2] can be used.

Figure 6: Data structure of stack node

expand function in the query is non-standard, the standard name will be fetched and used as the key to the normalized tag name index. Using this approach, with some space overhead of storing the normalized tag name index (the index is built only once when the document is loaded and updated independent of queries, therefore its time cost has no impact on the query time), only one user query (with all expand marked tag names normalized) needs to be evaluated, the result is a faster query response time. We note that term expansion works only when query terms that are semantically close to the tag names in the XML data are provided: we expect this to be a reasonable assumption.

3.3 Summary

Marking structurally ambiguous elements with mlcas keyword and ambiguous tag names with expand function enables a user to query XML documents without perfect knowledge of either the structural relationship among the elements or their tag names. XQuery equipped with these two features has effectively become schema-free: the user only needs minimal knowledge of the schema to issue a query that is far more meaningful than a keyword query and far more flexible than the standard XQuery.

4 Computing MLCAS

MLCAS computation is central to Schema-Free XQuery evaluation. In Section 4.1, we show how MLCAS can be evaluated as a composition of standard access methods likely to be available in most XQuery engines. In Section 4.2, we present a more efficient algorithm for computing MLCAS directly.

In the ensuing discussion, for a Schema-Free XQuery with an embedded function $\text{mlcas}(e_1, e_2, \ldots, e_m)$, where e_i are the elements involved in the MLCAS, we use $IList[i] = \{a_{11}, a_{12}, \ldots, a_{1n_i}\} \subseteq N$, to represent a list of nodes matching e_i $(1 \leq i \leq m)$ in the XML data.

4.1 Basic Implementation

Computing MLCAS can easily be implemented using the existing query standard operators. The basic idea is to find all the ancestors for each node in the ILists, and join nodes sharing common ancestors into trees such that the "leaf level" contains exactly one node from each IList, and each leaf node has descendant-or-self relationship with the root. For any pair of trees, we eliminate the one whose root is an ancestor (in the database tree) of the root of the other, as it conflicts with the definition of MLCAS (Definition 2.6). The remaining trees are returned as the MLCASs.

Theorem 4.1 *The time complexity of the straightforward implementation is $O(h^m \prod_{i=1}^{m} n_i)$, where h is the height of the XML data tree.*

```
MLCAS (I₁, I₂, ..., Iₘ):
0.  let the set of input nodes from I₁, I₂, ..., Iₘ be I
1.  while (unprocessed input or stack is not empty)
2.    let t_min (from I_index) be the node with smallest StartPos in I
3.    while (stack is not empty &&
4.           t_min is not a descendant of current stack top)
5.      /* pop the top element in the stack */
6.      popped = stack→Pop(), top = stack→Top()
7.      if (popped and its Elists contain MLCASs)
8.        output popped /*no more MLCAS on current stack*/
9.        while (stack is not Empty) stack→Pop()
10.       /* popped will not be a root of any MLCAS*/
11.     else if (popped→head is a child of top→head)
12.       mark all the non-empty Elists of popped as Related
13.       /* if popped qualified to be part of an MLCAS */
14.       if (for any i, popped→Elist[i] or top→Elist[i] is empty)
15.         top→AppendLists(popped→GetLists())
16.       else if(for any i,j(i≠j), if top→ElistsRelated(i,j)=true
17.         then popped→ElistsRelated(i,j) = true
18.         if(exists i,j(i≠j) that top→ElistsRelated(i,j)=false
19.             && popped→ElistsRelated(i,j)=true)
20.           /*delete nodes unqualified to be in an MLCAS*/
21.           delete all nodes from top→Elist[i], top→Elist[j]
22.         top→AppendLists(popped→GetLists())
23.     else let pt = popped→head→GetParent()
24.       mark all the non-empty Elists of popped as Related
25.       popped→ReplaceHead(pt) /*replace with parent*/
26.       stack→Push(popped)
27.   if (stack is empty)
28.     stack→Push(t_min), top = stack→Top()
29.     top→SetMaxID(0)
30.     /*set min of newnode be 0*/
31.     newnode=NewListNode(t_min, 0)
32.     top→Elist[index]→AppendNode(newnode)
33.   else
34.     oldtop = stack→Top(), stack→Push(t_min)
35.     top = stack→Top()
36.     top→SetMaxID(oldtop→GetMaxID())
37.     /*assign min to distinguish nodes of different MLCASs*/
38.     if (oldtop→Elist[index] is empty)
39.       newnode=NewListNode(t_min, oldtop→GetMaxID())
40.     else if(oldtop→Elist[index] not Related with other Elists)
41.       newnode=NewListNode(t_min,oldtop→GetMaxID())
42.     else
43.       top→SetMaxID(oldtop→GetMaxID()+1)
44.       newnode=NewListNode(t_min,top→GetMaxID())
45.     top→Elist[index]→AppendNode(newnode)
46.   read I for the next t_min
```

Figure 7: Algorithm MLCAS: it finds all MLCASs for the input nodes, and returns the root node for each MLCAS. Each input list I_k $(1 \leq k \leq m)$ is a set of nodes of the same entity type, sorted by StartPos.

The maximum number of ancestors each input node may have is $h - 1$; the number of combination possible of one node from each Ilist is $\prod_{i=1}^{m} n_i$. During the node merging process, for each node (a node from an IList or one of its ancestors), we attempt to join it with all the nodes from other ILists and their ancestors; for each such merge, one pass is made over the entire set of nodes and ancestors, excluding other nodes from the same IList and their ancestors. The time complexity for the merge process thus is $O(h^m \prod_{i=1}^{m} n_i)$. The remaining operations are in proportion to the number of trees generated from the merge process, which is $O(h^m \prod_{i=1}^{m} n_i)$. Hence, the total time complexity of this approach is $O(h^m \prod_{i=1}^{m} n_i)$.

4.2 Efficiently Computing MLCAS

Computing MLCAS using the standard operators, as described above, is simple, but expensive. To efficiently compute MLCASs, we developed a new operator specifically for this purpose, and an evaluation method tailored for it. Our algorithm is inspired by the stack-based family of algorithms for structural join [6, 7, 8, 10], and is limited to XQuery implementations that can support stack-based structural joins.

Let the position of a node in the XML tree be represented as (DocID, StartPos, EndPos, Level)[2], and let each *IList* be sorted by (DocID, StartPos). The basic idea is to perform one single merge pass over the nodes in *ILists*, in the order of their (start) position in the database tree, and conceptually merge them into rooted trees containing MLCASs. Within each such tree, the root is an MLCA of the inputs, and the leaf level contains all the nodes from different MLCASs sharing the same root. Identification numbers are then used to distinguish nodes from different MLCASs. Each node may have many ancestors: they are not looked up until required. Furthermore, a node is retrieved only once even if it is an ancestor of multiple nodes in the *ILists*.

The main data structure of the algorithm is a stack, with the head of each stack node being a descendant of the head of the stack node below it. Details of the data structure of the stack node are shown in Figure 6. Each stack node is also associated with lists of elements (*Elists*); each element from *Elist*[i] comes from the corresponding input list *Ilist*[i] ($1 \leq i \leq m$), and has *descendant-or-self* relationship with the head. Some *Elists* may be marked as *Related* with each other, indicating that the MLCA(s) of nodes from these lists are descendant of the head[3]. Intuitively, one may view a stack node as a tree, with the head being the root, and the elements in the *Elists* being the leaf nodes.

The full algorithm is shown Figure 7. Here, we walk through it using an example. Consider the XML document in schema A in Figure 1 and Query 3 in Figure 5. For the function **mlcas**($\$y$, $\$a1$, $\$t1$), the input lists are *IList*[1]={**3,12**}, *IList*[2]={**6,9,10,15,18**}, and *IList*[3]={**5,8,14,17**}, matching elements *year*, *author*, and *title*, respectively (we ignore term expansion here for the simplicity of illustration). Inputs (nodes) are fetched in ascending order of their StartPos and the first input being read is element **3** (a *year*), which is simply pushed onto the empty stack (lines 27-32) (Figure 8(a)).

The algorithm then reads in the next element with smallest StartPos, **5** (a *title*), which is not a descendant of the stack top. The current stack top **3** is therefore replaced with its parent **2** (lines 23-26) and added to the *ELists* of **2**. **5** is now a descendant of the new stack top **2**, and is pushed onto the stack (Figure 8(b)). Similarly, when **6** is read in, we replace **5** with its parent **4**, and then push **6** onto the stack (Figure 8(c)). Note that this is a subtle, yet important, optimization to the algorithm: we access an ancestor node only when it is needed to compute MLCASs.

Element **8** is read in next and it is again not a descendant of the stack top **6**. However, at this time, each stack node is a child (not just descendant) of the stack

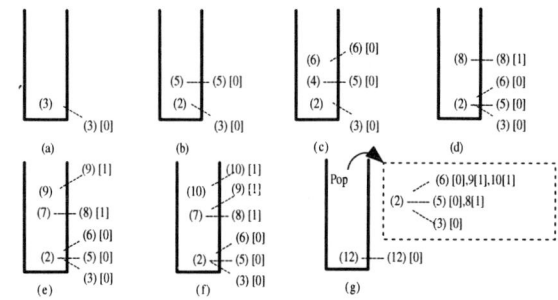

Figure 8: State of stack during evaluation of **mlcas**($\$y$, $\$a1$, $\$t1$). Each square bracket contains the *min* value used to distinguish nodes from different MLCASs.

node below it. The stack top and its *Elists* are therefore recursively appended to the stack node below it (lines 11-22)[4]. Note that a node is retrieved only once even if it is an ancestor of multiple nodes. Such optimization reduces unnecessary index access and contributes to computational saving. With **2** now being the stack top, **8** is pushed onto the stack (Figure 8(d)). Note that the *min* value assigned to **8** is different from that of **5**. The meaning and usage of *min* will be discussed later.

The process of adding **9** and **10** is similar to that of adding **5** and **6** (Figure 8(e) and (f)). When **12** is read in, as what happens with **8**, the stack top and the associated *Elists* are recursively appended to the node below it. Finally, stack top **2** is found to contain no empty *Elists* (indicating that it contains MLCASs), and popped as output. It is guaranteed that all the MLCASs sharing **2** as the root have been found (in the *Elists*). We then push **12** onto the empty stack (Figure 8(g)). The algorithm continues until there is no input element and the stack is empty.

Identification numbers [*min*, *max*] are used to distinguish different MLCASs. *min* is assigned for each input element when it is added to the stack (lines 34-45), while *max* equals $min(nextMin - 1, \infty)$, where *nextMin* refers to the *min* value of the next element in the same list. Elements from *Related Elists* with compatible identification numbers, i.e., the intersection of their identification numbers is non-empty, belong to the same MLCAS(s), while element from not *Related Elists* may belong to the same MLCAS(s), regardless of their identification numbers. When a node is popped from the stack with associated *ELists*, such numbers are used to identify nodes (in *Elists*) belonging to the same MLCAS and construct MLCASs.

Theorem 4.2 *The time complexity of the stack-based MLCAS algorithm is $O(h \sum_{i=1}^{m} n_i + \prod_{i=1}^{m} n_i)$, where h denotes the height of the XML data tree.*

The intuition is as follows. Each input element, and its ancestors, may be pushed onto the stack at most once, and when on the stack, be popped from stack, appended to, or deleted from an *Elist* associated with another node at most once (the *ELists* are implemented as linked lists, with start and end pointers; appending or deletion can

---

[2] DocID: the identifier of the document; StartPos/EndPos: generated by counting word numbers from the beginning of the document until the start of the element and the end of the element, respectively; Level: the nesting depth of the element. Notice that a node can be identified by the pair (DocID, StartPos).

[3] Bitset array relBits is used to denote which lists are related with each other at a level lower than that of the head node. Due to space limitation, we use the simple notion of marking lists as *Related*, and will not discuss the details of how to manipulate relBits in this paper.

[4] First add **6** and its *Elists* to **4**; then add **4** and its *Elists* to **2**; finally, **4** is removed since it does not belong to any *IList*.

be performed in unit time). Since each stack operation falls into the one of those constant time operations, the time complexity is $O(h \sum_{i=1}^{m} n_i)$. Finally, the time required for merging MLCASs from the output trees is linear in the output size. In the worst case, all MLCASs share the same root and each node in a list is meaningfully related with every node from other lists. In such a case, the time required for the merge process will be $O(\prod_{i=1}^{m} n_i)$. Putting all together, we get a time complexity of $O(h \sum_{i=1}^{m} n_i + \prod_{i=1}^{m} n_i)$ for our stack-based algorithm. Clearly, no competing algorithm that has the same input lists, and is required to compute the same output, could have better asymptotic complexity, since each input has to be read and each output has to be computed.

5 Experimental Evaluation

We implemented Schema-Free XQuery using the Timber native XML database [1, 19] and evaluated the system on two aspects: 1) search quality, which is evaluated using both a standard XML benchmark (Section 5.1) and a heterogeneous data collection (Section 5.2); 2) search performance, where we measure the overhead caused by evaluating schema-free query versus the schema-aware query (Section 5.3).

Throughout this section, the quality of a search technique was measured in terms of accuracy and completeness using standard precision and recall metrics, where the correct results are the answers returned by the corresponding schema-aware XQuery. Precision measures accuracy, indicating the fraction of results in the approximate answer that are correct, while recall measures completeness, indicating the fraction of all correct results actually captured in the approximate answer.

We note here that information retrieval systems can usually trade off precision against recall by choosing a different threshold value for a scoring function used to evaluate candidate results. A high threshold will return results only with a high score, giving good precision at the expense of recall. A low threshold will have the opposite effect. Evaluation of IR systems usually includes a precision-recall curve representing this tradeoff. Schema-free XQuery is still a database query language, and does not use any scoring functions in its evaluation. As such, there is no possibility of returning more or fewer results, and so no possibility of establishing a precision-recall curve.

5.1 Search Quality: XMark

XMark: XMark is a popular benchmark and its queries pose a wide range of challenges: from stressing the textual content of the document to ad-hoc data analysis [3]. We generated the XMark data set using a factor of 0.45, which had 1.45 millions of nodes and occupied 179 MB when loaded into our database. Indices with a total size of 106MB were also built.

To evaluate the relative strength of Schema-Free XQuery, we compared it with two techniques that support search over XML documents without knowledge of

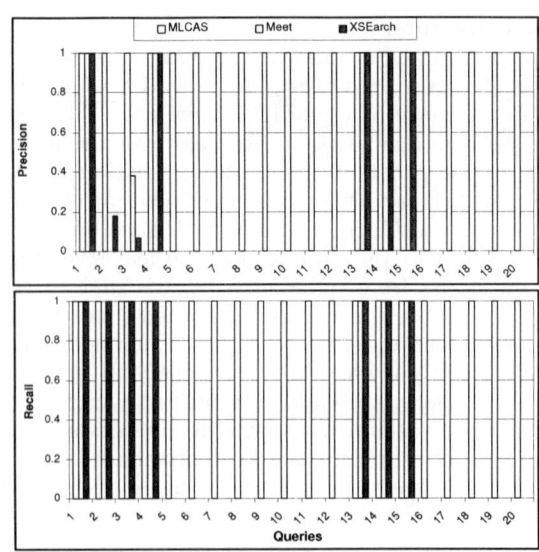

Figure 9: Precision and recall of different search strategies on XMark. Missing bars indicate a value of zero.

XML schema: Meet [22] and XSEarch [11]. Meet proposes to find the LCA for the set of keywords given in the query and return the subtree rooted at the LCA as the answer to the query. XSEarch is considered superior to a pure keyword based approach as it distinguishes tag names from textual content and has a better way of determining meaningful relationships among nodes based on the document structure (for our comparison, we adopted the all-pairs strategy of XSEarch, which is more competitive in search quality).

We expanded each original natural language query into a keyword search query, an XSEarch query, and a Schema-Free XQuery. We also wrote a schema-aware XQuery for each query and each XML document (different documents have different schema and a schema-aware XQuery has to be constructed for each of them). We obtained the correct answers by running the schema-aware XQuery and additionally verified correctness manually.

Result: Figure 9 presents the precision and recall of the three techniques for XMark. Schema-free XQuery (MLCAS) achieved perfect precision and recall for all the queries (i.e., all the results returned by **mlcas**-embedded XQuery were correct and all the possible correct results were returned). In contrast, Meet and XSEarch performed poorly on many of the queries, especially those with dynamic search conditions, or requiring complex manipulations such as ordering or grouping (Queries 5, 6, etc.). In particular, the root of the structure returned by Meet is on average 3 levels higher than the root of the correct structure: this observation indicates that a simple subtree rooted at LCA of the keywords, although usually covers the correct segments of interest, too often includes much irrelevant information, and cannot be easily manipulated to generate correct answers. Even for queries with simple constant search conditions and requiring no further manipulation (Queries 1, 4, etc.), Meet and XSEarch often produce results that are correct but too inclusive (we have counted those as correct answers in the Figure 9): unrelated elements are returned along with the meaningful ones.

5.2 Search Quality: Publication Collection

In working with XMark, we certainly knew its schema. We tried not to let this influence our specification of Schema-Free XQuery, and believe that we were successful in this. Nevertheless, a skeptic may have reason to be suspicious of our results. One way to address this concern is to work with heterogenous schema. But now we face the problem that there is no standard heterogeneous XML benchmark, so we decided to focus on a set of meaningful queries and search for a collection of heterogeneous data set to accommodate them. Queries from XMark were considered first, but unfortunately, real-world auction data required by XMark were not publicly available. We noticed, however, that "XMP," a comprehensive set of queries from XQuery use case [24], were largely based on bibliography documents, which were relatively easy to collect from the web. We therefore decided to use the 11 queries[5] from "XMP," plus an example query (also based on bibliography data) from XSEarch [11] for this part of evaluation.

Publication collection: We manually collected personal publication lists from 300 faculty personal homepages in a large research university[6] to serve as the data set for the "XMP" queries. Those publication lists, while obtained from the real world, are semantically close enough to the bibliography data such that our "XMP" query set can be applied with only minor changes (e.g., tag name *year* is used to replace *price*, which is not in the data set but has similar characteristics). These publication lists, despite the similarity in their semantics, vary greatly in terms of structure and normalization rules. In fact, if we rewrite them into XML documents, a total of 72 distinct schemas are found. However, many of these schemas either have equivalent structures or only differ from each other in minor details (e.g., a few include abstracts while most do not). If we group the lists based on their structural similarity, the union of the schemas of the lists within each group can then be used to represent all the lists in the same group. We refer to each group as a *schema family*. Schemas within a schema family are similar and therefore tend to have similar effects on the search quality for different search techniques. We identified six schema families for the 300 personal publication lists collected, and present results for one representative document from each.

Result: Figure 10 shows the average[7] precision and recall of the three techniques over the set of "XMP" queries against the publication collection. For all the queries, Schema-Free XQuery achieved perfect precision and recall, while Meet and XSEarch had poor precision and recall for many queries. This result demonstrates the robustness of Schema-Free XQuery against changes in document schema, considering that for each original

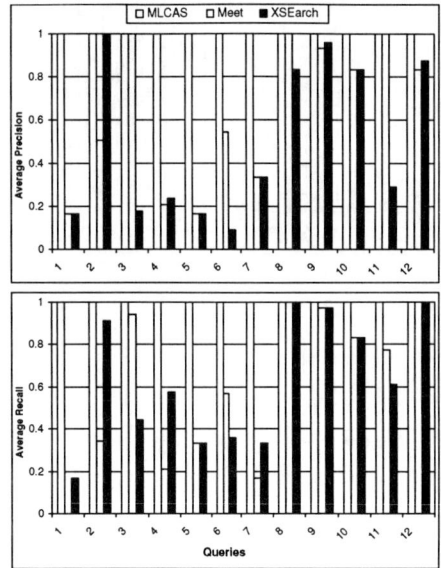

Figure 10: Average precision/recall of different search strategies for publication collection with term expansion. Missing bars indicate a value of zero.

natural language query, we ran exactly the same schema-free query on all the publication lists.

Although Schema-Free XQuery achieved 100% precision and recall for all of our queries, it does not imply that Schema-Free XQuery guarantees such perfect search quality for any dataset and/or any query. For instance, if we change the XML document shown in Figure 1(A) such that *author* node **6** and *title* node **8** are removed, for Query 1 in Figure 1, Schema-Free XQuery will return (**5,3**) as the result, while the correct answer should be (empty,**3**). Our extensive experimental evaluation suggests that such instances are uncommon.

Term expansion was employed for all the three strategies investigated in this comparison. The absence of term expansion reduced the average precision and recall of about half of the queries for all three strategies (Figure 11). It is not a surprise to see that a mismatch on even one single tag name could reduce the search quality significantly. If no nodes with the correct tag name can be found, one can obviously not find MLCAS, all-pair R answer, or LCA.

5.3 Search Performance

We measure the performance of Schema-Free XQuery in terms of simplicity and efficiency. To evaluate simplicity, we compare the number of operators in the evaluation plan generated for the **mlcas**-embedded XQuery and the corresponding XQuery, with **mlcas** computation being considered a single operator. To evaluate efficiency, we compare the time cost of evaluating an **mlcas**-embedded XQuery, with both the basic and the stack-based implementation of MLCAS computation, with that of evaluating a schema-aware, fully specified XQuery. For these experiments, the XMark data set worked fine, but the heterogeneous publication collection was too small to be interesting. Instead, we used the DBLP data set [20], which was of sufficient size to show non-trivial running

---
[5] Q12 is not included since set comparison is not yet supported in Timber.
[6] This includes all the personal homepages from four departments (123 in all), and a few randomly chosen personal homepages from 21 other departments (177 in all).
[7] Over the six representative documents

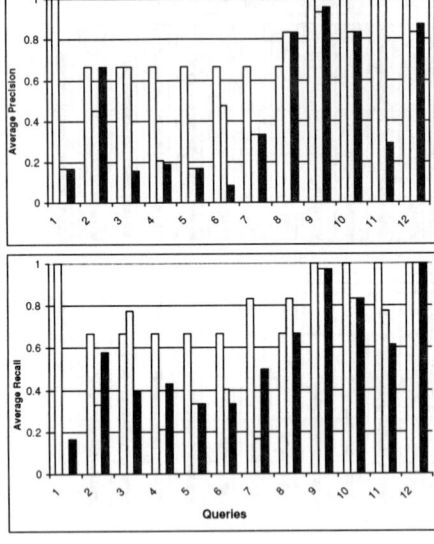

Figure 11: Average precision/recall of different search techniques for publication collection without term expansion.

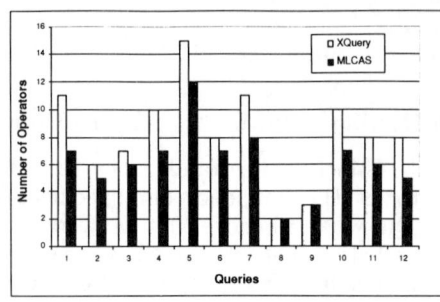

Figure 12: Average number of operators in evaluation plans generated by schema-aware XQuery (XQuery) and **mlcas**-embedded XQuery (MLCAS) for "XMP" queries on DBLP.

Query	XQuery	MLCAS	COMPOSE
1	530	1533	25621
2	290	1173	DNF
3	527	1421	DNF
4	479	1665	26591
5	1132	2518	DNF
6	371	1116	DNF
7	552	1469	24590
8	240	243	241
9	237	240	240
10	367	1456	24536
11	511	1321	DNF
12	473	1088	DNF

Table 1: Performance (seconds) of XQuery, MLCAS, and COMPOSE for the "XMP" queries on DBLP.

time while still within the bibliography domain such that the queries evaluated in the experiments above could apply. This data set comprised nearly 86 millions nodes, and occupied 957 MB for the data and 437 MB for the indices when loaded into our database.

The experiments were carried out on a Pentium III PC machine (800 MHz CPU, 512MB RAM, 120GB hard drive) running Windows 2000 Professional. The Timber buffer size was set to 64KB. We excluded the time for query parsing and evaluation plan generation in all the cases. Each query was run five times for each XML document with a cold operating system cache. The average running time was used in the performance evaluation. Note that for COMPOSE (the basic implementation for computing MLCAS previously discussed in Section 4.1), the execution time for some queries is marked as DNF, which means that the execution was killed when it did not finish within 7 hours.

Results: Figure 12 shows that evaluation plans generated by **mlcas**-embedded XQuery for the "XMP" queries on DBLP data are usually simpler than those of XQuery, with 2 fewer operators on average, an approximately 25% savings in plan generation. Furthermore, unlike the schema-aware XQuery, the same evaluation plan can be generated once and used over multiple documents with different schemas.

Table 1 reports the actual execution time of **mlcas**-embedded XQuery, both the stack-based algorithm (MLCAS) and the basic algorithm (COMPOSE), and schema-aware XQuery (XQuery) for the "XMP" queries on DBLP data. Our stack-based MLCAS algorithm speeds up the processing of **mlcas**-embedded XQuery by approximately 16 times, often reducing the execution time from more than 7 hours to less than 30 minutes. The capability of Schema-Free XQuery does not require expensive cost in performance. The overhead of **mlcas**-embedded XQuery using MLCAS algorithm is between 100% and 300%, with the exception of Q8 and Q9. There is no overhead for these two because they involve only one tag name, and thus no computation of MLCASs is needed. The existence of such overhead is expected. **mlcas**-embedded XQuery usually has to process more data than its schema-aware counterpart: the filtering of results according to the search conditions is done after the computation of MLCASs, while in schema-aware XQuery, most such filtering is done at data fetching time. In our future work, we will exploit optimization techniques to reduce such overhead.

Results for XMark are similar: over 20 different query types, the geometric mean of the running time of **mlcas**-embedded XQuery is 26.2 seconds, while that of schema-aware XQuery is 12.3 seconds. We cannot compute the geometric mean of the running time for COMPOSE, as 11 out of 20 queries failed to finish within 7 hours. The overhead for **mlcas**-embedded XQuery, compared to schema-aware XQuery varied from 0% to 250%.

6 Related Work

Extensive research has been done on structured declarative queries as well as on keyword based text search. In recent years, there has been interests in techniques that merge the two. BANKS [4], DBXplorer [5], and DISCOVER [18] attempt to apply keyword search on relational database. In those studies, a database is viewed as a graph with objects/tuples as nodes and relationship as edges, and sub-graphs of the database are returned as answers to the original keyword query. Similar approach has also been taken to apply keyword search in XML documents (e.g., XKeyword [17] and XRANK [15]). Ranking mechanisms have been applied to the search results such that results with perceived higher relevance are returned to the user first. All such keyword search approaches suffer from two drawbacks: (1) they do not distinguish tag name from textual content; (2) they cannot express complex query semantics.

A number of attempts have also been made to support information retrieval style search by expanding XQuery [9] or other structured query languages (e.g., XXL [23], XIRQL [13], and [12]). These approaches require a user to learn the query semantics and in cases where a user is unaware of the document structure, they do not exploit any document structure. Other approaches (e.g., LOREL [21] and Meet [22]) created query languages to enable keyword search in XML documents and exploit some structural information that is not specified in the query. The differences between those approaches and ours are that we eliminate any requirement for path expressions, and we exploit the document structure better to identify results that are more meaningful.

A recent closely related work is XSEarch [11], which attempts to return meaningful results based on query as well as document structure using a heuristic called *interconnection* relationship. In XSEarch, two nodes are considered to be semantically related if and only if there are no two distinct nodes with the same tag name on the path between these two nodes (excluding the two nodes themselves). Queries are allowed to specify tag names and attribute value pairs. However, *interconnection* does not work when two unrelated entities are present in entities of different types. For example, two *author* nodes may be considered as interconnected, even though one of them belongs to an *article* node and the other belongs to a *book* node. Moreover, due to the simple query semantics used, XSEarch suffers from drawbacks similar to keyword search methods: difficulty to express complex knowledge semantics. The MLCAS operator, on the other hand, takes full advantage of well-defined XQuery, and enables the user to take more control of the search results without knowing the document structure.

Finally, the REVERE system allows query answering across schemas by deploying schema mapping and query rewriting techniques [16]. Users are still required to have extensive knowledge of at least one schema to pose queries. No experimental evaluation on the effectiveness of the system has been reported.

7 Conclusion

The main contribution of this paper is to show that a simple, novel XML document search technique, namely Schema-Free XQuery, can enable users to take full advantage of XQuery in querying XML data precisely and efficiently without requiring full knowledge of the document schema. At the same time, any partial knowledge available to the user can be exploited to advantage. We have shown that it is possible to express a wide variety of queries in a schema-free manner and have them return correct results over a broad diversity of schema. Given its robustness against schema changes, Schema-Free XQuery is potentially of value in a data integration or data evolution context where one would like a query written once to apply "universally" and "forever". We also devised a stack-based algorithm for the MLCAS computation at the heart of schema-free query. Experiments showed that this algorithm was up to 16 times faster than a basic MLCAS computation using standard operators. Schema-free queries evaluated with this stack-based algorithm incurred an overhead no more than 3 times the execution time of an equivalent schema-aware query. Future directions for research include ontology-driven term expansion and further optimization of query processing by exploiting possibilities of pushing MLCAS calculation further down in the evaluation plan. We also intend to investigate techniques for applying MLCAS to queries involving attributes and references. Finally, we intend to use more sophisticated IR techniques where appropriate in schema-free queries.

References

[1] TIMBER: http://www.eecs.umich.edu/db/timber.

[2] WordNet: http://www.cogsci.princeton.edu/~wn/.

[3] XMark: http://monetdb.cwi.nl/xml/index.html.

[4] B. Aditya et al. BANKS: Browsing and keyword searching in relational databases. In *VLDB*, 2002.

[5] S. Agrawal et al. DBXplorer: a system for keyword-based search over relational databases. In *ICDE*, 2002.

[6] S. Al-Khalifa et al. Structural joins: A primitive for efficient XML query pattern matching. In *ICDE*, 2001.

[7] S. Al-Khalifa et al. Querying structured text in an XML database. In *SIGMOD*, 2003.

[8] N. Bruno et al. Holistic twig joins: Optimal XML pattern matching. In *SIGMOD*, 2002.

[9] D. Chamberlin. XQuery: An XML query language. *IBM System Journal*, 41:597–615, 2003.

[10] S.-Y. Chien et al. Efficient structural joins on indexed XML documents. In *VLDB*, 2002.

[11] S. Cohen et al. XSEarch: A semantic search engine for XML. In *VLDB*, 2003.

[12] D. Florescu et al. Integrating keyword search into XML query processing. *Computer Networks*, 33:119–135, 2000.

[13] N. Fuhr and K. Großjohann. XIRQL: An extension of XQL for information retrieval. In *SIGIR*, 2000.

[14] G. W. Furnas et al. The vocabulary problem in human-system communication. *CACM*, 30(11):964–971, 1987.

[15] L. Guo et al. XRANK: Ranked keyword search over XML documents. In *SIGMOD*, 2003.

[16] A. Halevy et al. Crossing the structure chasm, 2003.

[17] V. Hristidis et al. Keyword proximity search on XML graphs. In *ICDE*, 2003.

[18] V. Hristidis and Y. Papakonstantinou. Discover: Keyword search in relational databases. In *VLDB*, 2002.

[19] H. V. Jagadish et al. Timber: A native xml database. *The VLDB Journal*, 11(4):274–291, 2002.

[20] M. Ley. DBLP bibliography, 2003.

[21] D. Quass et al. Querying semistructured heterogeneous information. In *DOOD*, 1995.

[22] A. Schmidt et al. Querying XML documents made easy: Nearest concept queries. In *ICDE*, 2001.

[23] A. Theobald and G. Weikum. The index-based XXL search engine for querying XML data with relevance ranking. In *EDBT*, 2002.

[24] W3C. XML query use cases, 2003.

[25] W3C. XML schema, 2003.

Client-Based Access Control Management for XML documents

Luc Bouganim[*]   François Dang Ngoc[*,**]   Philippe Pucheral[*,**]

[*]INRIA Rocquencourt
Domaine de Voluceau
78153 Le Chesnay - France
Firstname.Lastname@inria.fr

[**]PRiSM Laboratory
45, avenue des Etats-Unis
78035 Versailles - France
Firstname.Lastname@prism.uvsq.fr

Abstract

The erosion of trust put in traditional database servers and in Database Service Providers, the growing interest for different forms of data dissemination and the concern for protecting children from suspicious Internet content are different factors that lead to move the access control from servers to clients. Several encryption schemes can be used to serve this purpose but all suffer from a static way of sharing data. With the emergence of hardware and software security elements on client devices, more dynamic client-based access control schemes can be devised. This paper proposes an efficient client-based evaluator of access control rules for regulating access to XML documents. This evaluator takes benefit from a dedicated index to quickly converge towards the authorized parts of a – potentially streaming – document. Additional security mecanisms guarantee that prohibited data can never be disclosed during the processing and that the input document is protected from any form of tampering. Experiments on synthetic and real datasets demonstrate the effectiveness of the approach.

1. Introduction

Access control management is one of the foundation stone of database systems and is traditionally performed by the servers, the place where the trust is. This situation, however, is rapidly evolving due to very different factors: the suspicion about Database Service Providers (DSP) regarding data confidentiality preservation [HIL02, BoP02], the increasing vulnerability of database servers facing external and internal attacks [FBI03], the emergence of decentralized ways to share and process data thanks to peer-to-peer databases [NOT03] or license-based distribution systems [XrM] and the ever-increasing concern of parents and teachers to protect children by controlling and filtering out what they access on the Internet [PIC].

Permission to copy without fee all or part of this material is granted provided that the copies are not made or distributed for direct commercial advantage, the VLDB copyright notice and the title of the publication and its date appear, and notice is given that copying is by permission of the Very Large Data Base Endowment. To copy otherwise, or to republish, requires a fee and/or special permission from the Endowment

**Proceedings of the 30th VLDB Conference,
Toronto, Canada, 2004**

The common consequence of these orthogonal factors is to move access control from servers to clients. Due to the intrinsic untrustworthiness of client devices, all client-based access control solutions rely on data encryption. The data are kept encrypted at the server and a client is granted access to subparts of them according to the decryption keys in its possession. Sophisticated variations of this basic model have been designed in different context, such as DSP [HIL02], database server security [HeW01], non-profit and for-profit publishing [MiS03, BCF01, Med] and multilevel databases [AkT82, BZN01, RRN02]. These models differ in several ways: data access model (pulled vs. pushed), access right model (DAC, RBAC, MAC), encryption scheme, key delivery mechanism and granularity of sharing. However these models have in common to minimize the trust required on the client at the price of a static way of sharing data. Indeed, whatever the granularity of sharing, the dataset is split in subsets reflecting a current sharing situation, each encrypted with a different key, or composition of keys. Thus, access control rules intersections are precompiled by the encryption. Once the dataset is encrypted, changes in the access control rules definition may impact the subset boundaries, hence incurring a partial re-encryption of the dataset and a potential redistribution of keys.

Unfortunately, there are many situations where access control rules are user specific, dynamic and then difficult to predict. Let us consider a community of users (family, friends, research team) sharing data via a DSP or in a peer-to-peer fashion (agendas, address books, profiles, research experiments, working drafts, etc.). It is likely that the sharing policies change as the initial situation evolves (relationship between users, new partners, new projects with diverging interest, etc.). The exchange of medical information is traditionally ruled by strict sharing policies to protect the patient's privacy but these rules may suffer exceptions in particular situations (e.g., in case of emergency) [ABM03], may evolve over time (e.g., depending on the patient's treatment) and may be subject to provisional authorizations [KmS00]. In the same way, there is no particular reason for a corporate database hosted by a DSP to have more static access control rules than its home-administered counterpart [BoP02][1] . Regarding parental

---

[1] In [BoP02], we identified the need for separating the concern between encryption and access right management and we proposed a solution to protect a relational database server from internal attacks conducted by a

control, neither Web site nor Internet Service Provider can predict the diversity of access control rules that parents with different sensibility are willing to enforce. Finally, the diversity of publishing models (non-profit or lucrative) leads to the definition of sophisticated access control languages like XrML or ODRL [XrM, ODR]. The access control rules being more complex, the encrypted content and the licenses are managed through different channels, allowing different privileges to be exercised by different users on the same encrypted content.

In the meantime, software and hardware architectures are rapidly evolving to integrate elements of trust in client devices. Windows Media9 [Med] is an example of software solution securing published digital assets on PC and consumer electronics. Secure tokens and smart cards plugged or embedded into different devices (e.g., PC, PDA, cellular phone, set-top-box) are hardware solutions exploited in a growing variety of applications (certification, authentication, electronic voting, e-payment, healthcare, digital right management, etc.). Finally, TCPA [TCP] is a hybrid solution where a secured chip is used to certify the software's installed on a given platform, preventing them from hacking[2]. Thus, Secure Operating Environments (SOE) become a reality on client devices [Vin02]. SOE guarantee a high tamper-resistance, generally on limited resources (e.g., a small portion of stable storage and RAM is protected to preserve secrets like encryption keys and sensitive data structures).

The objective of this paper is to exploit these new elements of trust in order to devise smarter client-based access control managers. The goal pursued is being able to evaluate dynamic and personalized access control rules on a ciphered input document, with the benefit of dissociating access rights from encryption. The considered input documents are XML documents, the de-facto standard for data exchange. Authorization models proposed for regulating access to XML documents use XPath expressions to delineate the scope of each access control rule [BCF01, GaB01, DDP02]. Having this context in mind, the problem addressed in this paper can be stated as follows.

Problem statement

- *To propose an efficient streaming access control rules evaluator*
  The streaming requirement is twofold. First, the evaluator must adapt to the memory constrained SOE, thereby precluding materialization (e.g., building a DOM representation of the document). Second, some target applications mentioned above are likely to consume streaming documents. Efficiency is, as usual, an important concern.

- *To guarantee that prohibited information is never disclosed*
  The access control being realized on the client device, no clear-text data but the authorized ones must be made accessible to the untrusted part of this client device.

- *To protect the input document from any form of tampering*
  Under the assumption that the SOE is secure, the only way to mislead the access control rule evaluator is to tamper the input document, for example by substituting or modifying encrypted blocks.

Contributions

To tackle this problem, this paper makes the following contributions:

1. Accurate streaming access control rules evaluator
We propose a streaming evaluator of XML access control rules, supporting a robust subset of the XPath language. At first glance, one may consider that evaluating a set of XPath-based access control rules and a set of XPath queries over a streaming document are equivalent problems [DF03, GMO03, CFG02]. However, access control rules are not independent. They may generate conflicts or become redundant on given parts of the document. The proposed evaluator detects accurately these situations and exploits them to stop eagerly rules becoming irrelevant.

2. Skip index
We design a streaming and compact index structure allowing to quickly converge towards the authorized parts of the input document, while skipping the others, and to compute the intersection with a potential query expressed on this document (in a pull context). Indexing is of utmost importance considering the two limiting factors of the target architecture: the cost of decryption in the SOE and the cost of communication between the SOE, the client and the server. This second contribution complements the first one to match the performance objective.

Combined together, these two contributions form the core of our client-based XML access control solution. Additional mechanisms are however required to guarantee that prohibited data can never be disclosed during the processing and that the input document is protected from any form of tampering. For the sake of conciseness, these mechanisms are mentioned below but are not discussed further in the paper. The reader interested by these aspects is referred to [BDP04]:

- *Pending predicates management*
  Pending predicates (i.e., a predicate P conditioning the delivery of a subtree S but encountered after S while parsing the document) are difficult to manage in a streaming fashion. We propose a strategy to detect eagerly the pending parts of the document, to skip them at parsing time and to reassemble afterwards the relevant pending parts at the right place in the final

---

[1] Database Administrator.
[2] Architectures like TCPA are controversial today. Our objective is not to fuel this debate. But, clearly, secured client-based architectures are on the way and considering them to design new security models, new ways to protect data confidentiality and privacy is undoubtedly an important challenge. The real danger would be to leave a single actor or consortium decide about a unique security model that imposes to everyone.

result. The way pending predicates are managed guarantees that prohibited data can never be disclosed on the client device.

- *Random integrity checking*
  We combine hashing (Merkle hash tree [Mer90]) and encryption (Cypher Block Chaining [Sch96]) techniques to make the integrity of the document verifiable in a streaming way, despite the forward and backward random accesses generated by the use of the skip index and by the management of pending predicates.

The paper is organized as follows. Section 2 introduces the XML access control model we consider and illustrates it on a motivating example. Sections 3 and 4 detail the two main contributions mentioned above. Section 5 presents experimental results based on both synthetic and real datasets. Section 6 concludes. Related works are addressed throughout each section.

2. Access control model

Access control model semantics

Several authorization models have been recently proposed for regulating access to XML documents. Most of these models follow the well-established Discretionary Access Control (DAC) model [BCF01, GaB01, DDP02], even though RBAC and MAC models have also been considered [Cha00, CAL02]. We introduce below a simplified access control model for XML, inspired by Bertino's model [BCF01] and Samarati's model [DDP02] that roughly share the same foundation. Subtleties of these models are ignored for the sake of simplicity.

In this simplified model, access control rules, or access rules for short, take the form of a 3-uple <*sign, subject, object*>. *Sign* denotes either a permission (positive rule) or a prohibition (negative rule) for the read operation. *Subject* is self-explanatory. *Object* corresponds to elements or subtrees in the XML document, identified by an XPath expression. The expressive power of the access control model, and then the granularity of sharing, is directly bounded by the supported subset of the XPath language. In this paper, we consider a rather robust subset of XPath denoted by $XP^{\{[], *, //\}}$ [MiS02]. This subset, widely used in practice, consists of node tests, the child axis (/), the descendant axis (//), wildcards (*) and predicates or branches [...]. Attributes are handled in the model similarly to elements and are not further discussed.

The cascading propagation of rules is implicit in the model, meaning that a rule propagates from an object to all its descendants in the XML hierarchy. Due to this propagation mechanism and to the multiplicity of rules for a same user, a conflict resolution principle is required. Conflicts are resolved using two policies: *Denial-Takes-Precedence* and *Most-Specific-Object-Takes-Precedence*. Let assume two rules R1 and R2 of opposite sign. These rules may conflict either because they are defined on the same object, or because they are defined respectively on two different objects O1 and O2, linked by an ancestor/descendant relationship (i.e., O1 is ancestor of O2). In the former situation, the *Denial-Takes-Precedence* policy favors the negative rule. In the latter situation, the *Most-Specific-Object-Takes-Precedence* policy favors the rule that applies directly to an object against the inherited one (i.e., R2 takes precedence over R1 on O2). Finally, if a subject is granted access to an object, the path from the document root to this object is granted too (names of denied elements in this path can be replaced by a dummy value). This *Structural* rule keeps the document structure consistent with respect to the original one.

The set of rules attached to a given subject on a given document is called an *access control policy*. This policy defines an authorized view of this document and, depending on the application context, this view may be queried. We consider that queries are expressed with the same XPath fragment as access rules, namely $XP^{\{[], *, //\}}$. Semantically, the result of a query is computed from the authorized view of the queried document (e.g., predicates cannot be expressed on denied elements even if these elements do not appear in the query result). However, access rules predicates can apply on any part of the initial document.

Motivating example

We use an XML document representing medical folders to illustrate the semantics of the access control model and to serve as motivating example. A sample of this document is pictured in Figure 1, along with the access control policies associated to three profiles of users: secretaries, doctors and medical researchers. A secretary is granted access only to the patient's administrative subfolders. A doctor is granted access to the patient's administrative subfolders and to all medical acts and analysis of her patients, except the details for acts she didn't carry out herself. Finally, a researcher is granted access only to the laboratory results and the age of patients who have subscribed to a protocol test of type G3, provided the measurement for the element Cholesterol does not exceed 250mg/dL.

Medical applications exemplify the need for dynamic access rules. For example, a researcher may be granted an exceptional and time-limited access to a fragment of all medical folders where the rate of Cholesterol exceeds 300mg/dL (a rather rare situation). A patient having subscribed to a protocol to test the effectiveness of a new treatment may revoke this protocol at any time due to a degradation of her state of health or for any other personal reasons. Models compiling access control policies in the data encryption cannot tackle this dynamicity. However, the reasons to encrypt the data and delegate the access control to the clients are manifold: exchanging data among medical research teams in a protected peer-to-peer fashion, protect the data from external attacks as well as from internal attacks. The latter aspect is particularly important in the medical domain due to the very high level of confidentiality attached to the data and to the very high level of decentralization of the information system (e.g., small clinics and general practitioners are prompted to subcontract the management of their information system).

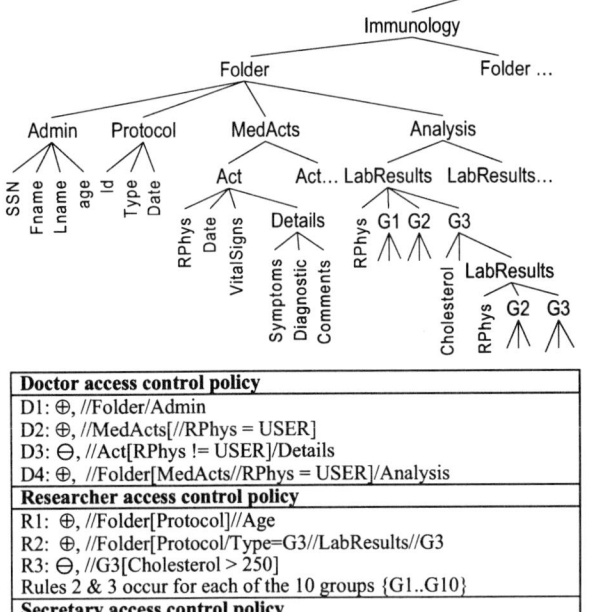

Figure 1: *Hospital XML document*

Target architectures

Figure 2 pictures an abstract representation of the target architecture for the motivating example as well as for the applications mentioned in the introduction. The access control being evaluated on the client, the client device has to be made tamper resistant thanks to a Secure Operating Environment (SOE). As discussed in the introduction, this SOE can rely on software or hardware solutions or on a mix of them. In the sequel of this paper, and up to the performance evaluation section, we make no assumption on the SOE, except the traditional ones: 1) the code executed by the SOE cannot be corrupted, 2) the SOE has at least a small quantity of secure stable storage (to store secrets like encryption keys, 3) the SOE has at least a small quantity of secure working memory (to protect sensitive data structures at processing time). In our context, the SOE is in charge of decrypting the input document, checking its integrity and evaluating the access control policy corresponding to a given (document, subject) pair. This access control policy as well as the key(s) required to decrypt the document can be permanently hosted by the SOE, refreshed or downloaded via a secure channel from different sources (trusted third party, security server, parent or teacher, etc).

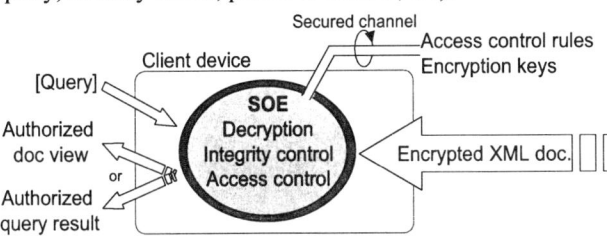

Figure 2: *Abstract target architecture*

3. Streaming the access control

While several access control models for XML have been proposed recently, few papers address the enforcement of these models and, to the best of our knowledge, no one considers access control in a streaming fashion. At first glance, streaming access control resembles the well-known problem of XPath processing on streaming documents. There is a large body of work on this latter problem in the context of XML filtering [DF03, GMO03, CFG02]. These studies consider a very large number of XPath expressions (typically tens of thousands). The primary goal here is to select the subset of queries matching a given document (the query result is not a concern) and the focus is on indexing and/or combining a large amount of queries. One of the first works addressing the precise evaluation of complex XPath expressions over streaming documents is due to [PfC03] which proposes a solution to deliver parts of a document matching a single XPath. While access rules are expressed in XPath, the nature of our problem differs significantly from the preceding ones. Indeed, the rule propagation principle along with its associated conflict resolution policies (see section 2) makes access rules not independent. The interference between rules introduces two new important issues:

- *Access rules evaluation:* for each node of the input document, the evaluator must be capable of determining the set of rules that applies to it and for each rule determining if it applies directly or is inherited. The nesting of the access rules scopes determines the authorization outcome for that node. This problem is made more complex by the fact that some rules are evaluated lazily due to pending predicates.

- *Access control optimization:* the nesting of rule scopes associated with the conflict resolution policies inhibits the effect of some rules. The rule evaluator must take advantage of this inhibition to suspend the evaluation of these rules and even to suspend the evaluation of all rules if a global decision can be reached for a given subtree.

3.1 Access rules evaluation

As streaming documents are considered, we make the assumption that the evaluator is fed by an event-based parser (e.g., SAX [SAX]) raising *open*, *value* and *close* events respectively for each opening, text and closing tag in the input document.

We represent each access rule (i.e., XPath expression) by a non-deterministic finite automaton (NFA) [HjU79]. Figure 3.b pictures the Access Rules Automata (*ARA*) corresponding to two rather simple access rules expressed on an abstract XML document. This abstract example, used in place of the motivating example introduced in Section 2, gives us the opportunity to study several situations (including the trickiest ones) on a simple document. In our ARA representation, a circle denotes a state and a double circle a final state, both identified by a unique *StateId*. Directed edges represent transitions, triggered by *open* events matching the edge label (either an element name or *). Thus, directed edges represent the child (/) XPath axis or a wildcard depending on the label. To model the descendant axis (//), we add a self-transition with a label * matched by any *open* event. An ARA includes one *navigational path* and optionally one or several *predicate paths* (in grey in the figure). To manage the set of ARA representing a given access control policy, we introduce the following data structures:

- *Tokens and Token Stack:* we distinguish between *navigational tokens* (NT) and *predicate tokens* (PT) depending on the ARA path they are involved in. To model the traversal of an ARA by a given token, we actually create a token proxy each time a transition is triggered and we label it with the destination StateId. The terms token and token proxy are used interchangeably in the rest of the paper. The navigation progress in all ARA is memorized thanks to a unique stack-based data structure called *Token Stack*. The top of the stack contains all active NT and PT tokens, i.e. tokens that can trigger a new transition at the next incoming event. Tokens created by a triggered transition are pushed in the stack. The stack is popped at each close event. The goal of Token Stack is twofold: allowing a straightforward backtracking in all ARA and reducing the number of tokens to be checked at each event (only the active ones, at the top of the stack, are considered).

- *Rule status and Authorization Stack:* Let assume for the moment that access rule expressions do not exploit the descendant axis (no //). In this case, a rule is said to be *active*, – meaning that its scope covers the current node and its subtree – if all final states of its ARA contain a token. A rule is said *pending* if the final state of its navigational path contains a token while the final state of some predicate path has not yet been reached. The *Authorization Stack* registers the NT tokens having reached the final state of a navigational path, at a given depth in the document. The scope of the corresponding rule is bounded by the time the NT token remains in the stack. This stack is used to solve conflicts between rules. The status of a rule present in the stack can be fourfold: *positive-active* (denoted by $\oplus$), *positive-pending* (denoted by $\oplus^?$), *negative-active* (denoted by $\ominus$), *negative-pending* (denoted by $\ominus^?$). By convention, the bottom of the stack contains an implicit *negative-active* rule materializing a closed access control policy (i.e., by default, the set of objects the user is granted access to is empty).

- *Rule instances materialization:* Taking into account the descendant axis (//) in the access rules expressions makes things more complex to manage. Indeed, the same element names can be encountered at different depths in the same document, leading several tokens to reach the final state of a navigational path and predicate paths in the same ARA, without being related together[3]. To tackle this situation, we label navigational and predicate token proxies with the *depth* at which the original predicate token has been created, materializing their participation in the same *rule instance*[4].

- Consequently, a token (proxy) must hold the following information: RuleId (denoted by R, S, ...), Navigational/Predicate status (denoted by n or p), StateId and Depth[5]. For example, $Rn2_2$ and $Rp4_2$ (also noted 2_2, 4_2 to simplify the figures) denotes the navigational and predicate tokens created in Rule R's ARA at the time element b is encountered at depth 2 in the document. If the transition between states 4 and 5 of this ARA is triggered, a token proxy $Rp5_2$ will be created and will represent the progress of the original token $Rp4_2$ in the ARA. All these tokens refer to the same rule instance since they are labeled by the same depth. A rule instance is said *active* or *pending* under the same condition as before, taking into account only the tokens related to this instance.

- *Predicate Set:* this set registers the PT tokens having reached the final state of a predicate path. A PT token, representing a predicate instance, is discarded from this set at the time the current depth in the document becomes less than its own depth.

Stack-based data structures are well adapted to the traversal of a hierarchical document. However, we need a direct access to any stack level to update pending information and to allow some optimizations detailed below. Figure 3.c represents an execution snapshot based on these data structures. This snapshot being almost self-explanatory, we detail only a small subset of steps.

- Step 2: the *open* event b generates two tokens $Rn2_2$ and $Rp4_2$, participating in the same rule instance.
- Step 3: the ARA of the negative rule S reaches its final state and an active instance of S is pushed in the Authorization Stack. The current authorization remains negative. Token $Rp5_2$ enters the Predicate Set. The corresponding predicate will be considered true until level 2 of the Token Stack is popped (i.e., until event /b is produced at step 9). Thus, there is no need to continue to evaluate this predicate in this subtree and token $Rp4_2$ can be discarded from the Token Stack.
- Step 5: An active instance of the positive rule R is pushed in the Authorization Stack. The current authorization becomes positive, allowing the delivery of element d.

---

[3] The complexity of this problem has been highlighted in [PfC03].

[4] To illustrate this, let us consider the rule R and the right subtree of the document presented in Figure 3. The predicate path final state *5* (expressing //b[c]) can be reached from two different instances of b, respectively located at depth 2 and 3 in the document, while the navigational path final state *3* (expressing //b/d) can be reached only from b located at depth 3. Thus, a single rule instance is valid here, materialized by navigational and predicate tokens proxies labeled with the same depth 3.

[5] If a same ARA contains different predicate paths starting at different levels of the navigational path, a NT token will have in addition to register all PT tokens related to it.

- Step 16: A new instance of R is pushed in the Authorization Stack, represented by token $Rn3_3$. This instance is pending since the token $Rp5_2$ pushed in the Predicate Set at step 12 (event c) does not participate in the same rule instance.
- Step 18: Token $Rp5_3$ enters the Predicate Set, changing the status of the associated rule instance to *positive-active*.

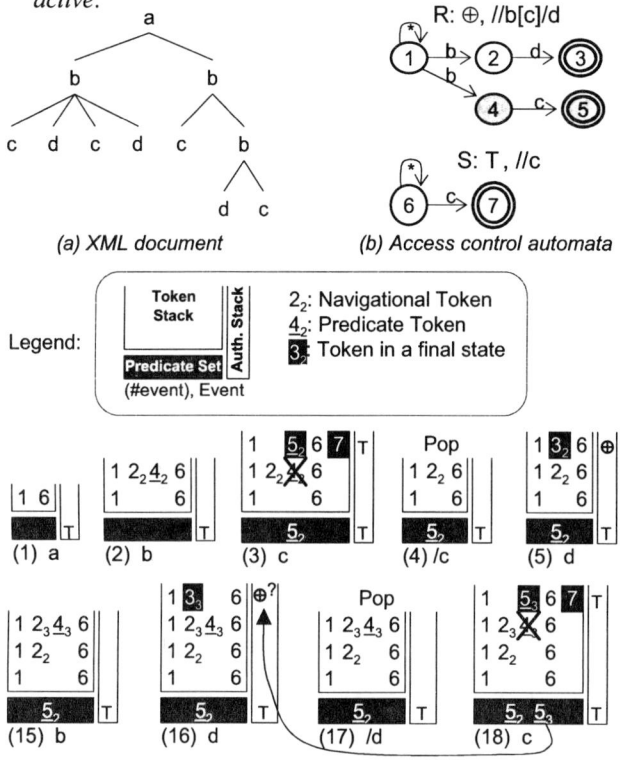

(a) XML document   (b) Access control automata

(c) Snapshots of the stack structure

Figure 3: *Execution Snapshot*

3.2 Conflict Resolution

From the information kept in the Authorization Stack, the outcome of the current document node can be easily determined. The conflict resolution algorithm presented in Figure 4 integrates the closed access control policy (line 1), the *Denial-Takes-Precedence* (line 2) and *Most-Specific-Object-Takes-Precedence* (lines 5 and 7) policies to reach a decision. In the algorithm, AS denotes the Authorization Stack and AS[i].RuleStatus denotes the set of status of all rules registered at level *i* in this stack. In the first call of this recursive algorithm, depth corresponds to the top of AS. Recursion captures the fact that a decision may be reached even if the rules at the top of the stack are pending, depending on the rule status found in the lower stack levels. Note, however, that the decision can remain pending if a pending rule at the top of the stack conflicts with other rules. In that case, the current node has to be buffered, waiting for a delivery condition. This issue is tackled in [BDP04]. The rest of the algorithm is self-explanatory and examples of conflict resolutions are given in the figure.

The DecideNode algorithm presented below considers only the access rules. Things are slightly more complex if queries are considered too. Queries are expressed in XPath and are translated in a non-deterministic finite automaton in a way similar to access rules. However, a query cannot be regarded as an access rule at conflict resolution time. The delivery condition for the current node of a document becomes twofold: (1) the delivery decision must be true and (2) the query must be interested in this node. The first condition is the outcome of the DecideNode algorithm. The second condition is matched if the query is *active*, that is if all final states of the query ARA contain a token, meaning that the current node is part of the query scope.

DecideNode(depth) → Decision ∈ {⊕, ⊖, ?}

1: If depth = 0 then return '⊖'
2:   elseif '⊖'∈ AS[depth].RuleStatus then return '⊖'
3:   elseif '⊕' ∈ AS[depth].RuleStatus and
4:     '⊖?' ∉ AS[depth].RuleStatus then return '⊕'
5:   elseif DecideNode(depth -1) = '⊖' and
6:     ∀t∈ {'⊕?','⊕'} t∉ AS[depth].RuleStatus then return '⊖'
7:   elseif DecideNode(depth -1) = '⊕' and
8:     '⊖?' ∉ AS[depth] RuleStatus then return '⊕'
9:   else return '?'

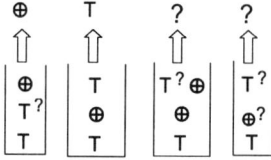

Examples of conflict resolution

Figure 4: *Conflict resolution algorithm*

3.3 Optimization issues

The first optimization that can be devised is doing a static analysis of the system of rules composing an access control policy. Query containment property can be exploited to decrease the complexity of this system of rules. Let us denote by ⊆ the containment relation between rules R, S ...T. If S⊆R ∧ (R.Sign=S.Sign), the elimination of S could be envisioned. However, this elimination is precluded if, for example, ∃T / T⊆R ∧ (T.Sign≠R.Sign) ∧ (S⊆T). Thus, rules cannot be pairwise examined and the problem turns to check whether some partial order among rules can be defined wrt. the containment relation, e.g., $\{T_i, ...T_k\} \subset \{S_i, ...S_k\} \subseteq \{R_i, ...R_k\} \land \forall i$, $(R_i.Sign=S_i.Sign \land S_i.Sign \neq T_i.Sign) \Rightarrow \{S_i, ...S_k\}$ can be eliminated. Note that this strong elimination condition is sufficient but not necessary. For instance, let R and S be two positive rules respectively expressed by /a and /a/b[P1] and T be a negative rule expressed by /a/b[P2]/c. S can still be eliminated while T⊄S, because the containment holds for each subtree where the two rules are active together. The problem is particularly complex considering that the query containment problem itself has been shown co-NP complete for the class of XPath expressions of interest, that is $XP^{\{[],//,*\}}$ [MiS02]. This issue could be further investigated since more favorable results have been found for subclasses of $XP^{\{[],//,*\}}$ [ACL01], but this work is outside the scope of this paper.

A second form of optimization is to suspend dynamically the evaluation of ARA that become irrelevant or useless inside a subtree. The knowledge gathered in the Token Stack, Authorization Stack and Predicate Set can be exploited to this end. The first optimization is to suspend the evaluation of a predicate in a subtree as soon as an instance of this predicate has been evaluated to true in this subtree. This optimization has been illustrated by Step 3 of Figure 3.c. The second optimization is to evaluate dynamically the containment relation between active and pending rules and take benefit of the elimination condition mentioned above. From the Authorization Stack, we can detect situations where the following local condition holds: $(T \subset S \subseteq R) \land (R.Sign=S.Sign \land S.Sign \neq T.Sign)$, the stack levels reflecting the containment relation inside the current subtree. S can be inhibited in this subtree. If stopping the evaluation of some ARA is beneficial, one must keep in mind that the two limiting factors of our architecture are the decryption cost and the communication cost. Therefore, the real challenge is being able to take a common decision for complete subtrees, a necessary condition to detect and skip prohibited subtrees, thereby saving both decryption and communication costs.

Without any additional information on the input document, a common decision can be taken for a complete subtree rooted at node n iff: (1) the DecideNode algorithm can deliver a decision D (either $\oplus$ or $\ominus$) for n itself and (2) a rule R whose sign contradicts D cannot become active inside this subtree (meaning that all its final states, of navigational path and potential predicate paths, cannot be reached altogether). These two conditions are compiled in the algorithm presented in Figure 5. In this algorithm, AS denotes the Authorization Stack, TS the Token Stack, TS[i].NT (resp. TS[i].PT) the set of NT (resp. PT) tokens registered at level i in this stack and top is the level of the top of a stack. In addition, t.RuleInst denotes the rule instance associated with a given token, Rule.Sign the sign of this rule and Rule.Pred a boolean indicating if this rule includes predicates in its definition.

```
DecideSubtree() → Decision ∈ {⊕, ⊖,?}
1:   D = DecideNode(AS.top)
2:   if D = '?' then return '?'
3:   if not (∃ nt ∈TS[top].NT / nt.Rule.Sign ≠ D
4:            and (not nt.Rule.Pred
5:            or (∃ pt ∈TS[top].PT / pt.RuleInst = nt.RuleInst))
6:   then TS[top].NT = ∅; return (D)
7:   else return '?'
```

Figure 5: *Decision on a complete subtree*

The immediate benefit of this algorithm is to stop the evaluation for any active NT tokens and the main expected benefit is to skip the complete subtree if this decision is $\ominus$. Note however that only NT tokens are removed from the stack at line 6. The reason for this is that active PT tokens must still be considered, otherwise pending predicates could remain pending forever. As a conclusion, a subtree rooted at n can be actually skipped iff: (1) the decision for n is $\ominus$, (2) the DecideSubtree algorithm decides $\ominus$ and (3) there are no PT token at the top of the Token Stack (which turns to be empty). Unfortunately, these conditions are rarely met together, especially when the descendant axis appears in the expression of rules and predicates. The next section introduces a Skip index structure that gives useful information about the forthcoming content of the input document. The goal of this index is to detect a priori rules and predicates that will become irrelevant, thereby increasing the probability to meet the aforementioned conditions.

When queries are considered, any subtree not contained in the query scope is candidate to a skip. This situation holds as soon as the NT token of the query (or NT tokens when several instances of the same query can co-exist) becomes inactive (i.e., is no longer element of TS[top].NT). This token can be removed from the Token Stack but potential PT tokens related to the query must still be considered, again to prevent pending predicate to remain pending forever. As before, the subtree will be actually skipped if the Token Stack becomes empty.

4. Skip index

This section introduces a new form of indexation structure, called *Skip Index*, designed to detect and skip the unauthorized fragments (wrt. an access control policy) and the irrelevant fragments (wrt. a potential query) of an XML document, while satisfying the constraints introduced by the target architecture (streaming encrypted document, scarce SOE storage capacity).

The first distinguishing feature of the required index is the necessity to keep it encrypted outside of the SOE to guarantee the absence of information disclosure. The second distinguishing feature (related to the first one and to the SOE storage capacity) is that the SOE must manage the index in a streaming fashion, similarly to the document itself. These two features lead to design a very compact index (its decryption and transmission overhead must not exceed its own benefit), embedded in the document in a way compatible with streaming. For these reasons, we concentrate on indexing the structure of the document, pushing aside the indexation of its content. Structural summaries [ABC04] or XML skeleton [BGK03] could be considered as candidate for this index. Beside the fact that they may conflict with the size and streaming requirements, these approaches do not capture the irregularity of XML documents (e.g., medical folders are likely to differ from one instance to another while sharing the same general structure).

In the following, we propose a highly compact structural index, encoded recursively into the XML document to allow streaming. An interesting side effect of the proposed indexation scheme is to provide new means to further compress the structural part of the document.

4.1 Skip Index encoding scheme

The primary objective of the index is to detect rules and queries that cannot apply inside a given subtree, with the expected benefit to skip this subtree if the conditions stated in section 3.3 are met. Keeping the compactness requirement in mind, the minimal structural information required to achieve this goal is the set of element tags, or tags for short, that appear in each subtree. While this metadata does not capture the tags nesting, it reveals oneself as a very effective way to filter out irrelevant XPath expressions. We propose below data structures encoding this metadata in a highly compact way. These data structures are illustrated in Figure 7.a on an abstract XML document.

- *Encoding the set of descendant tags*: The size of the input document being a concern, we make the rather classic assumption that the document structure is compressed thanks to a dictionary of tags [ABC04, TpH02][6]. The set of tags that appear in the subtree rooted by an element e, named $DescTag_e$, can be encoded by a bit array, named $TagArray_e$, of length N_t, where N_t is the number of entries of the tag dictionary. A recursive encoding can further reduce the size of this metadata. Let us call $DescTag(e)$ the bijective function that maps $TagArray_e$ into the tag dictionary to compute $DescTag_e$. We can trade storage overhead for computation complexity by reducing the image of $DescTag(e)$ to $DescTag_{parent(e)}$ in place of the tag dictionary. The length of the $TagArray$ structure decreases while descending into the document hierarchy at the price of making the $DescTag()$ function recursive. Since the number of element generally increases with the depth of the document, the gain is substantial. To distinguish between intermediate nodes and leaves (that do not need the TagArray metadata), an additional bit is added to each node.
- *Encoding the element tags:* In a dictionary-based compression, the tag of each element e in the document is replaced by a reference to the corresponding entry in the dictionary. $Log_2(N_t)$ bits are necessary to encode this reference. The recursive encoding of the set of descendant tags can be exploited as well to compress further the encoding of tags themselves. Using this scheme, $Log_2(DescTag_{parent(e)})$ bits suffice to encode the tag of an element e.
- *Encoding the size of a subtree:* Encoding the size of each subtree is mandatory to implement the skip operation. At first glance, $log_2(size(document))$ bits are necessary to encode $SubtreeSize_e$, the size of the subtree rooted by an element e. Again, a recursive scheme allows to reduce the encoding of this size to $log_2(SubtreeSize_{parent(e)})$ bits. Storing the SubtreeSize for each element makes closing tags unnecessary.

- *Decoding the document structure*: The decoding of the document structure must be done by the SOE, efficiently, in a streaming fashion and without consuming much memory. To this end, the SOE stores the tag dictionary and uses an internal *SkipStack* to record the DescTag and SubtreeSize of the current element. When decoding an element e, $DescTag_{parent(e)}$ and $SubtreeSize_{parent(e)}$ are retrieved from this stack and used to decode in turn $TagArray_e$, $SubtreeSize_e$ and the encoded tag of e.
- *Updating the document:* In the worst case, updating an element e induces an update of the SubtreeSize, the TagArray and the encoded tag of each e ancestors and of their direct children. In the best case, only the SubtreeSize of e ancestors need be updated. The worst case occurs in two rather infrequent situations. The SubtreeSize of e ancestor's children have to be updated if the size of e father grows (resp. shrinks) and jumps a power of 2. The TagArray and the encoded tag of e ancestor's children have to be updated if the update of e generates an insertion or deletion in the tag dictionary.

4.2 Skip index usage

As said before, the primary objective of the Skip index is to detect rules and queries that cannot apply inside a given subtree. This means that any active token that cannot reach a final state in its ARA can be removed from the top of the Token Stack. Let us call *RemainingLabels(t)* the function that determines the set of transition labels encountered in the path separating the current state of a token t from the final state of its ARA, and let us call e the current element in the document. A token t, either navigational or predicate, will be unable to reach a final state in its ARA if RemainingLabels(t) $\not\subset$ $DescTag_e$. Note that this condition is sufficient but not necessary since the Skip index does not capture the element tags nesting.

SkipSubtree () → Decision ∈ {true,false}
1: For each token t ∈ TS[top].NT ∪ TS[top].PT
2:   if RemainingLabels(t) $\not\subset$ DescTag_e then remove t from TS[top]
3: if DecideSubTree() ∈ {'⊖', '?'} and (TS[top].NT = ∅) and
4:   (TS[top].PT = ∅) then return true
5: else return false

Figure 6: *Skipping decision*

Once this token filtering has been done, the probability for the DecideSubtree algorithm to reach a global decision about the subtree rooted by the current element e is greatly increased since many irrelevant rules have been filtered. If this decision is negative (⊖) or pending (?), a skip of the subtree can be envisioned. This skip is actually possible if there are no more active tokens, either navigational or predicate, at the top of the Token Stack. The algorithm SkipSubtree given in Figure 6 decides whether the skip is possible or not. Let us remark that this algorithm should be triggered both on open and close events. Indeed, each

---
[6] Considering the compression of the document content itself is out of the scope of this paper. Anyway, value compression does not interfere with our proposal as far as the compression scheme remains compatible with the SOE resources.

element may change the decision delivered by the algorithm DecideNode, then DecideSubtree and finally SkipSubtree with the benefit of being able to skip a bigger subtree at the next step.

Figure 7 shows an illustrative XML document and its encoding, a set of access rules and the skips done while analyzing the document. The information in grey is presented to ease the understanding of the indexing scheme but is not stored in the document.

Let us consider the document analysis (for clarity, we use below the real element tags instead of their encoding). At the time element b (leftmost subtree) is reached, all the active rules are stopped thanks to $TagArray_b$ and the complete subtree can be skipped (the decision is $\ominus$ due to the closed access control policy). When element c is reached, Rule R becomes pending. However, the analysis of the subtree continues since $TagArray_c$ does not allow more filtering. When element e is reached, $TagArray_e$ filters out rules R, T and U. Rule S becomes negative-active when the value '3' is encountered below element m. On the closing event, SkipSubtree decides to skip the e subtree. This situation illustrate the benefit to trigger the SkipSubtree at each opening and closing events. The analysis continues following the same principle and leads to deliver the elements underlined in Figure 7.c.

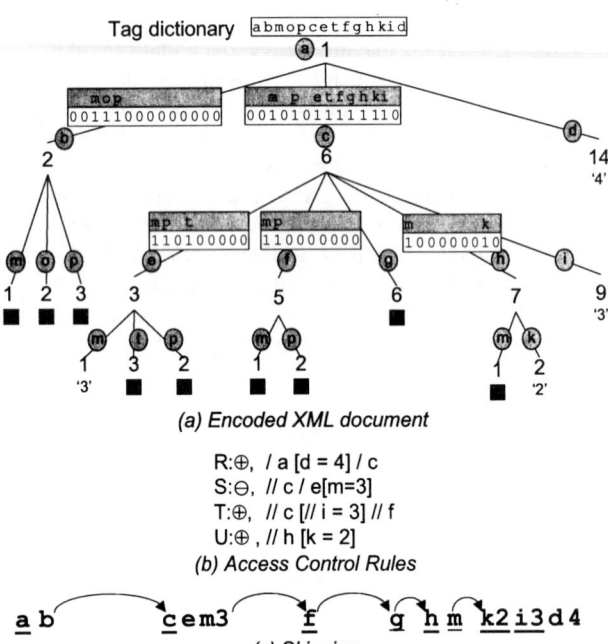

Figure 7: *Skip Index example*

5. Experimental results

This section presents experimental results obtained from both synthetic and real datasets. We first give details about the experimentation platform. Then, we analyze the storage overhead incurred by the Skip index and compare it with possible variants. Next, we study the performance of access control management and query evaluation. Finally, the global performance of the proposed solution is assessed on four datasets that exhibit different characteristics.

Experimentation platform

The abstract target architecture presented in Section 2 can be instantiated in many different ways. In this experimentation, we consider that the SOE is embedded in an advanced smart card platform. While existing smart cards are already powerful (32 bits CPU running at 30Mhz, 4 KB of RAM, 128KB of EEPROM), they are still too limited to support our architecture, especially in terms of communication bandwidth (9.6Kbps). Our industrial partner, Axalto (the Schlumberger's smart card subsidiary), announces by the end of this year a more powerful smart card equipped with a 32 bits CPU running at 40Mhz, 8KB of RAM, 1MB of Flash and supporting an USB protocol at 1MBps. Axalto provided us with a hardware cycle-accurate simulator for this forthcoming smart card. Our prototype has been developed in C and has been measured using this simulator. Cycle-accuracy guarantees an exact prediction of the performance that will be obtained with the target hardware platform.

As this section will make clear, our solution is strongly bounded by the decryption and the communication costs. The numbers given in Table 1 allow projecting the performance results given in this section on different target architectures. The number given for the smart card communication bandwidth corresponds to a worst case where each data entering the SOE takes part in the result. The decryption cost corresponds to the 3DES algorithm, hardwired in the smart card (line 1) and measured on a PC at 1Ghz (lines 2 and 3).

Context	Communication	Decryption
Hardware based (e.g., future smartcards)	0.5 MB/s	**0.15 MB/s**
Software based - Internet connection	**0.1 MB/s**	1.2 MB/s
Software based - LAN connection	10 MB/s	1.2 MB/s

Table 1: *Communication and decryption costs*

In the experiment, we consider three real datasets: *WSU* corresponding to university courses, *Sigmod records* containing index of articles and *Tree Bank* containing English sentences tagged with parts of speech [UWX]. In addition, we generate a synthetic content for the Hospital document depicted in Section 2 (real datasets are very difficult to obtain in this area), thanks to the ToXgene generator [ToX]. The characteristics of interest of these documents are summarized in Table 2.

	WSU	**Sigmod**	**Treebank**	**Hospital**
Size	1.3 MB	350KB	59MB	3.6 MB
Text size	210KB	146KB	33MB	2,1 MB
Maximum depth	4	6	36	8
Average depth	3.1	5.1	7.8	6.8
# distinct tags	20	11	250	89
# text nodes	48820	8383	1391845	98310
# elements	74557	11526	2437666	117795

Table 2: *Documents characteristics*

92

Index storage overhead

The Skip index is an aggregation of three techniques for encoding respectively tags, lists of descendant tags and subtree sizes. Variants of the Skip index could be devised by combining these techniques differently (e.g., encoding the tags and the subtree sizes without encoding the lists of descendant tags makes sense). Thus, to evaluate the overhead ascribed to each of these metadata, we compare the following techniques. NC corresponds to the original Non Compressed document. TC is a rather classic Tag Compression method and will serve as reference. In TC, each tag is encoded by a number expressed with $log_2(\#distinct\ tags)$ bits. We denote by TCS (Tag Compressed and Subtree size) the method storing the subtree size to allow subtrees to be skipped. The subtree size is encoded with $log_2(compressed\ document\ size)$ bits. In TCS, the closing tag is useless and can be removed. TCSB complements TCS with a bitmap of descendant tags encoded with $\#dictinct\ tags$ bits for each element. Finally, TCSBR is the recursive variant of TCSB and corresponds actually to the Skip Index detailed in Section 4. In all these methods, the metadata need be aligned on a byte frontier. Figure 8 compares these five methods on the datasets introduced formerly. These datasets having different characteristics, the Y-axis is expressed in terms of the ratio *structure/(text length)*.

Clearly, TC drastically reduces the size of the structure in all datasets. Adding the subtree size to nodes (TCS) increases the structure size by 50%, up to 150% (big documents require an encoding of about 5 bytes for both the subtree size and the tag element while smaller documents need only 3 bytes). The bitmap of descendant tags (TCSB) is even more expensive, especially in the case of the Bank document which contains 250 distinct tags. TCSBR drastically reduces this overhead and brings back the size of the structure near the TC one. The reason is that the subtree size generally decreases rapidly, as well as the number of distinct tags inside each subtree. For the Sigmod document, TCSBR becomes even more compact than TC.

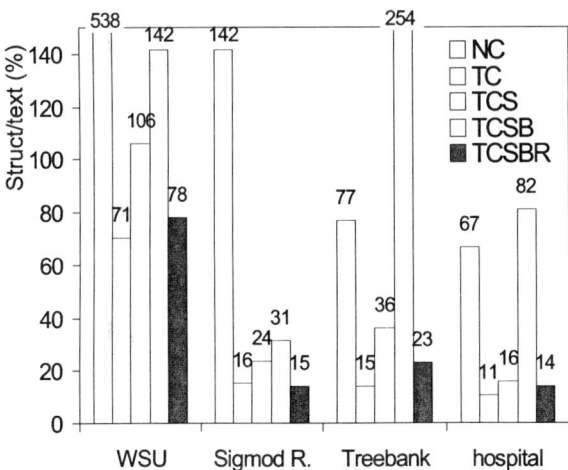

Figure 8: *Index storage overhead*

Access control overhead

To assess the efficiency of our strategy (based on TCSBR), we compare it with: (i) a Brute-Force strategy (BF) filtering the document without any index and (ii) a time lower bound LWB. LWB cannot be reached by any practical strategy. It corresponds to the time required by an oracle to read only the authorized fragments of a document and decrypt it. Obviously, a genuine oracle will be able to predict the outcome of all predicates – pending or not – without checking them and to guess where the relevant data are in the document.

Figure 9 shows the execution time required to evaluate the authorized view of the three profiles (Secretary, Doctor and Researcher) introduced in Section 2 on the Hospital document. Integrity checking is not taken into account here. The size of the compressed document is 2.5MB and the evaluation of the authorized view returns 135KB for the Secretary, 575KB for the Doctor and 95 KB for the Researcher. In order to compare the three profiles despite this size discrepancy, the Y-axis represents the ratio between each execution time and its respective LWB. The real execution time in seconds is mentioned on each histogram. To measure the impact of a rather complex access control policy, we consider that the Researcher is granted access to 10 medical protocols instead of a single one, each expressed by one positive and one negative rule, as in Section 2.

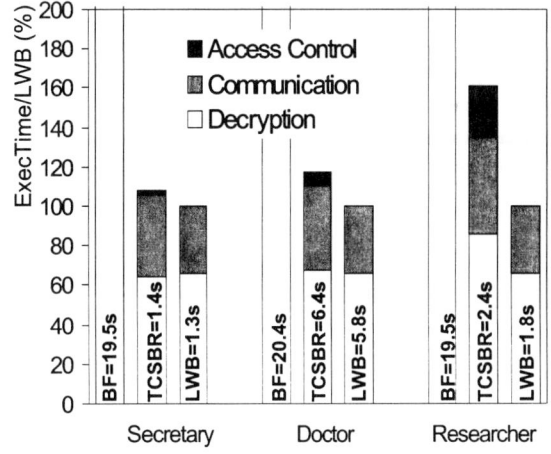

Figure 9: Access control overhead

The conclusions that can be drawn from this figure are threefold. First, the Brute-Force strategy exhibits dramatic performance, explained by the fact that the smart card has to read and decrypt the whole document in order to analyze it. Second, the performance of our TCSBR strategy is generally very close to the LWB (let us recall that LWB is a theoretical and unreachable lower bound), exemplifying the importance of minimizing the input flow entering the SOE. The more important overhead noticed for the Researcher profile compared to LWB is due to the predicate expressed on the protocol element that can remain pending until the end of each folder. Indeed, if this predicate is evaluated to false, the access rule evaluator will continue – needlessly in the current case – to look at another instance of this predicate. Third, the cost of access control (from 2% to 15%) is largely dominated by the decryption cost (from 53% to 60%) and by the communication cost (from 30% to 38%). The cost of access control is determined by the number of active tokens that are to be managed at the same time. This number depends on the number of ARA in the access control policy and the number of descendant transitions (//) and predicates inside each ARA. This explain the larger cost of evaluating the Researcher access control policy.

Impact of queries

To measure accurately the impact of a query in the global performance, we consider the query //Folder[//Age>v] (v allows us to vary the query selectivity), executed over five different views built from the preceding profiles and corresponding to: a secretary (S), a part-time doctor (PTD) having in charge few patients, a full-time doctor (FTD) having in charge many patients, a junior researcher (JR) being granted access to few analysis results and a senior researcher (SR) being granted access to several analysis results. Figure 10 plots the query execution time (including the access control) as a function of the query result size. The execution time decreases linearly as the query and view selectivity's increase, showing the accuracy of TCSBR. Even if the query result is empty, the execution time is not null since parts of the document have to be analysed before being skipped. The parts of the document that need be analysed depends on the view and on the query. The embedded figure shows the same linearity for larger values of the query result size.

Performance on real datasets

To assess the robustness of our approach when different document structures are faced, we measured the performance of our prototype on the three real datasets WSU, Sigmod and Bank. For these documents we generated random access rules (including // and predicates). Each document exhibits interesting characteristics. The Sigmod document is well-structured, non-recursive, of medium depth and the generated access control policy was simple and not much selective (50% of the document was returned). The WSU document is rather flat and contains a large amount of very small elements (its structure represents 78% of the document size after TCSBR indexation). The Bank document is very large, contains a large amount of tags that appear recursively in the document and the generated access control policy was complex (8 rules). Figure 11 reports the results. We added in the figure the measures obtained with the Hospital document to serve as a basis for comparisons. The figure plots the execution time in terms of throughput for our method and for LWB, both with and without integrity checking. Although integrity checking is not discussed in this paper (see [BDP04] for details), taking its cost into account is mandatory to fully assess our solution. We show that our method tackles well very different situations and produces a throughput ranging from 55KBps to 85KBps depending on the document and the access control policy. These preliminary results as encouraging when compared with xDSL Internet bandwidth available nowadays (ranging from 16KBps to 128KBps).

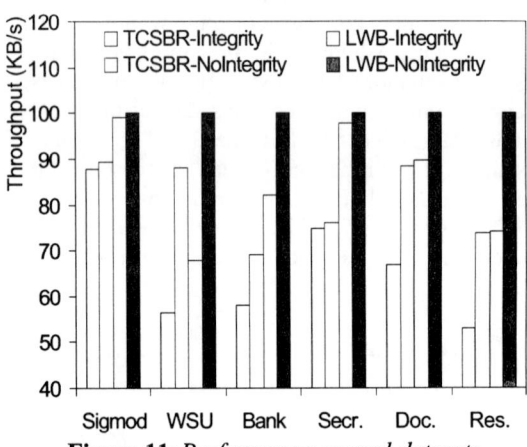

Figure 11: *Performance on real datasets*

6. Conclusion

Important factors motivate today the access control to be delegated to client devices. By compiling the access control policies into the data encryption, existing client-based access control solutions minimize the trust required on the client at the price of a rather static way of sharing data. Our objective is to take advantage of new elements of trust in client devices to propose a client-based access control manager capable of evaluating dynamic access rules on a ciphered XML document.

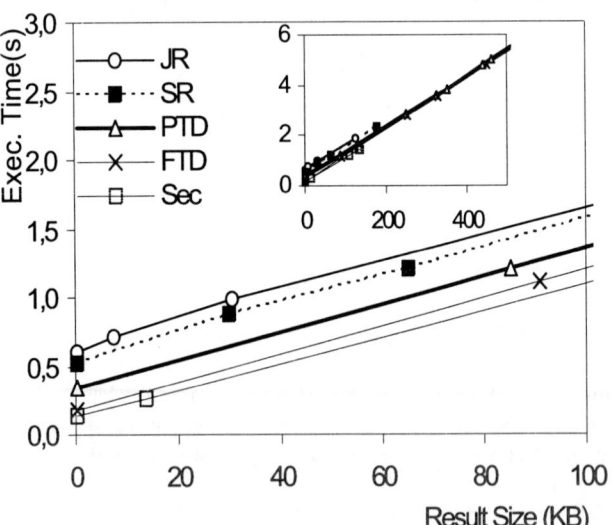

Figure 10: *Impact of queries*

The contribution of this paper is twofold. First, we proposed a streaming evaluator of access control rules supporting a rather robust fragment of the XPath language. To the best of our knowledge, this is the first paper dealing with XML access control in a streaming fashion. Second, we designed a streaming index structure allowing skipping the irrelevant parts of the input document, with respect to the access control policy and to a potential query. This index is essential to circumvent the inherent bottlenecks of the target architecture, namely the decryption cost and the communication cost. Combined together, these two mechanisms form the core of our client-based XML access control solution. Pending predicate management and random integrity checking complement this solution [BDP04].

Our experimental results have been obtained from a C prototype running on a hardware cycle-accurate smart card simulator provided by Axalto. The global throughput measured is around 70KBps and the relative cost of the access control is less than 20% of the total cost. These first measurements are promising and demonstrate the applicability of the solution. A JavaCard prototype is currently developed and will be submitted to the e-gate'04 software contest organized by SUN and Axalto.

Open issues concern the better use of query containment techniques to improve the optimization before and during the access rules evaluation as well as the definition of more accurate streaming indexation techniques. More generally, client-based security solutions deserve a special attention for the new research perspectives they broaden and for their foreseeable impact on a growing scale of applications.

Acknowledgments

Special thanks are due to Anaenza Maresca, physician at the Tenon hospital (Paris), for her contribution to the definition of the motivating example, inspired by a real-life experience.

References

[ABC04] A. Arion, A. Bonifati, G. Costa, S. D'Aguanno, I. Manolescu, A. Puglies, "Efficient Query Evaluation over Compressed Data", EDBT, 2004.

[ABM03] A. El Kalam, S. Benferhat, A. Miege, R. Baida, F. Cuppens, C. Saurel, P. Balbiani, Y. Deswarte, G. Trouessin, "Organization based access control", IEEE 4th International Workshop on Policies for Distributed Systems and Networks, 2003.

[AkT82] S. Akl and P. Taylor, "Cryptographic solution to a problem of access control in a hierarchy". ACM TOCS, 1983.

[ACL01] S. Amer-Yahia, S. Cho, L. Lakshmanan, and D. Srivastava, "Minimization of tree pattern queries", ACM SIGMOD, 2001.

[BCF00] E.Bertino, S.Castano, E.Ferrari, M.Mesiti, "Specifying and Enforcing Access Control Policies for XML Document Sources", WWW Journal, vol.3, n.3, 2000.

[BCF01] E. Bertino, S. Castano, E. Ferrari, "Securing XML documents with Author-X", IEEE Internet Computing, 2001.

[BDP04] L. Bouganim, F. Dang Ngoc, P. Pucheral, "Client-Based Access Control Management for XML Documents", INRIA internal report, june 2004. www-smis.inria.fr/~bouganim/Publis/BDP04.pdf

[BGK03] P. Buneman, M. Grobe, C. Koch, "Path Queries on Compressed XML", VLDB, 2003

[BoP02] L. Bouganim, P. Pucheral, "Chip-Secured Data Access: Confidential Data on Untrusted Servers", VLDB, 2002.

[BZN01] J.-C. Birget, X. Zou, G. Noubir, B. Ramamurthy, "Hierarchy-Based Access Control in Distributed Environments", IEEE ICC, 2001.

[CAL02] S. Cho, S. Amer-Yahia, L. Lakshmanan, D. Srivastava, "Optimizing the secure evaluation of twig queries", VLDB, 2002.

[CFG02] C Chan, P. Felber, M. Garofalakis, R. Rastogi, "Efficient Filtering of XML Documents with Xpath Expressions", ICDE, 2002.

[Cha00] R.Chandramouli, "Application of XML Tools for Enterprise-Wide RBAC Implementation Tasks", 5th ACM workshop on Role-based Access Control, 2000.

[DDP02] E. Damiani, S. De Capitani di Vimercati, S. Paraboschi, P. Samarati, "A Fine-Grained Access Control System for XML Documents", ACM TISSEC, vol. 5, n. 2, 2002.

[DF03] Y. Diao, M. Franklin, "High-Performance XML Filtering: An Overview of YFilter", ICDE, 2003.

[FBI03] Computer Security Institute, "CSI/FBI Computer Crime and Security Survey", www.gocsi.com/forms/fbi/pdf.html

[GaB01] A. Gabillon and E. Bruno, "Regulating access to XML documents. IFIP Working Conference on Database and Application Security, 2001.

[GMO03] T. Green, G. Micklau, M. Onizuka, D. Suciu, "Processing XML streams with Deterministic Automata", ICDT, 2003.

[HeW01] J. He, M. Wang, "Cryptography and Relational Database Management Systems", IDEAS, 2001.

[HIL02] H. Hacigumus, B. Iyer, C. Li, S. Mehrotra, "Executing SQL over encrypted data in the database-service-provider model", ACM SIGMOD, 2002.

[HjU79] J. Hopcroft, J. Ullman, "Introduction to Automata Theory, Languages and Computation", Addison-Wesley, 1979.

[KmS00] M. Kudo, S. Hada, "XML document security based on provisional authorization", ACM CCS, 2000.

[Med] Windows Microsoft Windows Media 9, http://www.microsoft.com/windows/windowsmedia/.

[Mer90] R. Merkle, "A Certified Digital Signature", Advances in Cryptology--Crypto'89, 1989.

[MiS02] G. Miklau and D. Suciu, "Containment and equivalence for an XPath fragment", ACM PODS, 2002.

[MiS03] G. Micklau, D. Suciu, "Controlling Access to Published Data Using Cryptography", VLDB, 2003.

[NOT03] W. Ng, B. Ooi, K. Tan, A. Zhou, "Peerdb: A p2p-based system for distributed data sharing", ICDE, 2003.

[ODR] The Open Digital Rights Language Initiative, http://odrl.net/.

[PfC03] F. Peng, S. Chawathe, "XPath Queries on Streaming Data", ACM SIGMOD, 2003.

[PIC] W3C consortium, "PICS: Platform for Internet Content Selection", http://www.w3.org/PICS.

[RRN02] I. Ray, I. Ray, N. Narasimhamurthi, "A Cryptographic Solution to Implement Access Control in a Hierarchy and More", ACM SACMAT, 2002.

[SAX] Simple API for XML, http://www.saxproject.org/.

[Sch96] B. Schneier, "Applied Cryptography", 2nd Edition, John Wiley & Sons, 1996.

[TCP] Trusted Computing Platform Alliance, http://www.trustedcomputing.org/.

[ToX] ToXgene - the ToX XML Data Generator, http://www.cs.toronto.edu/tox/toxgene/.

[TpH02] P. Tolani, J. Haritsa, "XGRIND: A Query-Friendly XML Compressor", ICDE, 2002.

[UWX] UW XML Data Repository, www.cs.washington.edu/research/xmldatasets/.

[Vin02] R. Vingralek, "GnatDb: A Small-Footprint, Secure Database System", VLDB, 2002.

[XrM] XrML eXtendible rights Markup Language, www.xrml.org/

Secure XML Publishing without Information Leakage in the Presence of Data Inference

Xiaochun Yang [*]

Department of Computer Science
Northeastern University, Liaoning 110004, China
yangxc@mail.neu.edu.cn

Chen Li [†]

School of Information and Computer Sciences
University of California, Irvine, CA 92697, USA
chenli@ics.uci.edu

Abstract

Recent applications are seeing an increasing need that publishing XML documents should meet precise security requirements. In this paper, we consider data-publishing applications where the publisher specifies what information is sensitive and should be protected. We show that if a partial document is published carelessly, users can use common knowledge (e.g., "all patients in the same ward have the same disease") to infer more data, which can cause leakage of sensitive information. The goal is to protect such information in the presence of data inference with common knowledge. We consider common knowledge represented as semantic XML constraints. We formulate the process how users can infer data using three types of common XML constraints. Interestingly, no matter what sequences users follow to infer data, there is a unique, maximal document that contains all possible inferred documents. We develop algorithms for finding a partial document of a given XML document without causing information leakage, while allowing publishing as much data as possible. Our experiments on real data sets show that effect of inference on data security, and how the proposed techniques can prevent such leakage from happening.

---

[*] Work partially done during a visit to UC Irvine and partially supported by NSF China No. 60173051.
[†] Supported by NSF CAREER Award No. IIS-0238586.

Permission to copy without fee all or part of this material is granted provided that the copies are not made or distributed for direct commercial advantage, the VLDB copyright notice and the title of the publication and its date appear, and notice is given that copying is by permission of the Very Large Data Base Endowment. To copy otherwise, or to republish, requires a fee and/or special permission from the Endowment.

**Proceedings of the 30th VLDB Conference,
Toronto, Canada, 2004**

1 Introduction

With the fast development of the Internet, there is an increasing amount of data published on the Web. Meanwhile, recent database applications see the emerging need to support data sharing and dissemination in peer-based environments [2, 12, 17, 20, 24], in which autonomous sources share data with each other. In these applications, the owner of a data source needs to publish data to others such as public users on the Web or collaborative peers. Often the data owner may have sensitive information that needs to be protected. As illustrated by the following example, if we publish data carelessly, users can use common knowledge to infer more information from the published data, causing leakage of sensitive information.

A hospital at a medical school has XML documents about its patients and physicians. Fig. 1 shows part of such an XML document represented as a tree. Each patient has a name (represented as a `pname` element), suffers from a disease (a `disease` element), and lives in a ward. Each physician has a name (`phname`), and treats patients identified by their names. For instance, physician Smith is treating patient Cathy, who has a leukemia and lives in ward W305. (We add a superscript to each node for later references.)

The hospital plans to provide the data to another department at the same school to conduct related research. Some data is sensitive and should not be released. In particular, the hospital does not want the department to know the disease of patient Alice (leukemia) for some reason. One simple way is to hide the shaded *leukemia*[1] subtree of Alice. But if it is well known that patients in the same ward have the same disease, then this common knowledge can be used by the department users to infer from the seen document that Alice has a leukemia. It is because Alice and Betty live in the same ward W305, and Betty has a leukemia. The users can do the similar inference using the information about patient Cathy, who also lives in ward W305. As a consequence, hiding the shaded *leukemia*[1] branch cannot protect the sensitive infor-

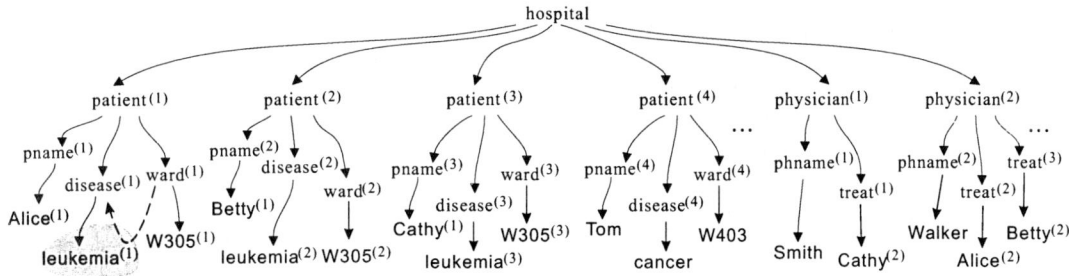

Figure 1: An XML document of hospital data. The shaded subtree is sensitive data. The dashed line shows a functional-dependency link.

mation due to this common knowledge.

One solution to this information-leakage problem is that, in addition to hiding the *leukemia*[(1)] branch of Alice, we also hide the *Alice*[(1)] branch, so that users do not know the name of this patient. Another solution is to hide the ward number $W305^{(1)}$ of patient Alice, or the ward branches of both Betty and Cathy, so that the users cannot infer the disease of Alice. A third option is to hide the disease branches of both Betty and Cathy. There are other solutions as well.

In general, publishing XML data with security requirements faces a multitude of challenges when users can infer data using common knowledge. First, how do we model data inference using common knowledge in XML documents? Such common knowledge can be represented as *semantic constraints*, which specify relationships that must be satisfied by the nodes. For instance, the common knowledge in the hospital example can be represented as a functional dependency from the ward elements to their corresponding disease elements. We thus need to understand the data-inference effects of different constraints. Some effect could be very subtle, e.g., we show in Section 3 that users could infer the existence of a new branch, even though its exact position is unknown. Such a branch could still contain sensitive information.

A second problem is: how do we compute all possible inferable data? Since users can apply constraints in arbitrary sequences to infer different documents, it is not clear what inferred documents we should consider to test if sensitive information is leaked.

A third problem is: how do we compute a partial document to be published without leaking sensitive information, even if users can do inference? As there are many possible partial documents that do not cause information leakage (a trivial one is the empty document), it is natural to publish as much data as possible without leaking sensitive information. Meanwhile, there are various kinds of constraints, and the inference result of one constraint could satisfy the conditions of another. Thus it is challenging to decide which nodes in the document should be published.

In this paper, we study these problems and make the following contributions.

- We formulate the process of data inference using common knowledge represented as semantic XML constraints. We show that there is a unique, maximal document users can infer using the constraints, which contains all possible inferred documents. We also develop a validation algorithm for testing if a partial document can leak sensitive information.

- We propose algorithms for computing a partial document to be published without leaking information, while to release as much data as possible.

- We conducted experiments using real data sets to evaluate our proposed techniques.

The rest of the paper is organized as follows. Section 2 gives the preliminaries on data security in XML publishing. In Section 3 we consider three kinds of common XML constraints, and show how each constraint can be used to infer data. Section 4 studies what data can be inferred by users using multiple constraints. We formally define information leakage, and give an algorithm for testing if a partial document is secure. In Section 5 we develop algorithms for calculating a valid partial document. Section 6 provides our experimental results on two real data sets. We conclude in Section 7.

1.1 Related Work

Recently there has been a large amount of work on data security and privacy. Miklau and Suciu [18] show a good diagram (shown in Fig. 2) to classify different settings for related studies based on trust domains. In Scenario A with a single trust domain, there are no main security issues. For client-server access control in Scenario B, the data is owned by the server. A lot of work in this setting has focused on how to respond to user queries without revealing protected data [4, 5, 15, 26]. Scenario C assumes that the client (data owner) does not trust the server, and a main problem is how to allow the server to answer clients' queries without knowing the exact data [11, 13].

In the data-publishing case (Scenario D), we mainly focus on how to publish data without leaking sensitive information. Several data-dependent approaches have been proposed [6, 7, 16]. Some existing approaches specify sensitive data by marking positive and/or negative authorizations on single data items.

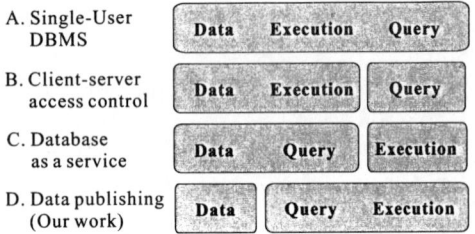

Figure 2: Different scenarios of database security based on trust domains [18].

These approaches consider each sensitive node individually. One limitation of this way of defining sensitive data is that it is not expressive to define some sensitive data such as "Alice's disease" that is independent from the specific position of the data. Another related work is [28], which shows how to compress documents to support efficient access control of sensitive XML data. Recently, Miklau and Suciu [18] study XML publishing, and develop an encryption-based approach to access control on publishing XML documents. They use an extension of XQuery to define sensitive data in a published document.

There have been works on inference control in relational databases [5, 8, 14, 23]. There are also studies on XML security control (e.g., [3, 10, 15, 28]), and they do not formally consider the effect of XML constraints. Our work formulates the process that users can infer data in XML publishing, and formally studies what additional data should be hidden in order to prevent information leakage. Notice that when we say "hide a branch in a document," we could either remove the branch from the document, or encrypt the branch and provide a key to the users who are allowed to access the branch. Therefore, our approach is orthogonal to whether encryption techniques are used to hide sensitive information [18].

2 Data Security in XML Publishing

We review basic concepts of data security in XML publishing. We view an XML document as a tree. An interior node represents either an ELEMENT or an ATTRIBUTE. A leaf node is of the string type, represented as a system-reserved symbol S, which corresponds to PCDATA for an ELEMENT parent node or CDATA for an ATTRIBUTE parent node. We do not consider the sibling order in the tree.

When publishing an XML document tree D, some nodes are *sensitive* and should be hidden from users. In our running example, the disease name of patient Alice is sensitive and should be protected. We assume such a sensitive node is specified by an XQuery, called a *regulating query*. For simplicity, we represent an XQuery as a tree pattern [1], with two types of edges: (1) a single edge represents an immediate-subelement relationship between a parent and a child (called a "c-child"); (2) a double edge represents a relationship between a node and a descendant (called a "d-child"). The tree pattern specifies the *conditions* to be satisfied when matching with the document. It has one special *sensitive node*, whose entire subtree should not be published. The sensitive node is marked with a symbol "*" in the regulating query. We make this single-sensitive-node assumption for the sake of simplicity. In general, we could allow multiple sensitive nodes in a regulating query. Such a query could be translated to multiple queries, each of which defines a single sensitive node.

A *mapping* μ from the nodes in a regulating-query tree A to the nodes in the document tree D is defined as follows: (1) if a leaf node n in A has a type or a value, then so does the corresponding node $\mu(n)$ in D; (2) if a node n is a c-child (resp., d-child) of another node v in A, then $\mu(n)$ is a child (resp., descendant) of $\mu(v)$ in D. Under mapping μ, the target subtree of the sensitive node in A is called the *excluded subtree* of A under μ. All the excluded subtrees of A under different mappings in the document are denoted as $A(D)$. According to regulating query A, all these excluded subtrees $A(D)$ should not be published.

A set of regulating queries $\mathcal{A} = \{A_1, \ldots, A_m\}$ define a partial document that can be published. Such a document is calculated by removing every subtree in each $A_i(D)$. Formally, we define the set of excluded subtrees $\mathcal{A}(D) = \cup_{i=1}^{m} A_i(D)$, which represent the sensitive items in the XML tree that should not be published. The *remaining document* of document D under these regulating queries $\mathcal{A}$, denoted by $D_r(D, \mathcal{A})$, is the remaining subtree after those subtrees in $\mathcal{A}(D)$ are removed, i.e., $D_r(D, \mathcal{A}) = D - \mathcal{A}(D)$.

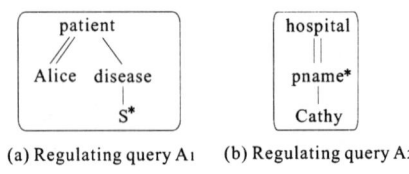

(a) Regulating query A_1 (b) Regulating query A_2

Figure 3: Example regulating queries.

For instance, the sensitive information "Alice's disease" in the hospital example can be specified by the regulating query A_1 in Fig. 3(a). The shaded subtree $leukemia^{(1)}$ in Fig. 1 is the corresponding excluded subtree. Suppose we have another regulating query A_2 as shown in Fig. 3(b), which specifies that the subtree of $pname^{(3)}$ of Cathy is sensitive. Given the set $\mathcal{A} = \{A_1, A_2\}$ of the two regulating queries, the corresponding remaining subtree $D - \mathcal{A}(D)$ should exclude both subtree $leukemia^{(1)}$ and subtree $pname^{(3)}$.

3 Data Inference Using Single XML Constraints

We consider the case where users can do data inference using common knowledge represented as XML constraints. Such constraints for an XML document specify relationships that must be satisfied by the nodes in the document. XML constraints can be defined using XML schema languages, such as XML DTD, XML Schema [25], and UCM [9]. In this section, we formulate three common constraints, and show how they can be used individually to infer data.

3.1 XML Constraints

An XML constraint can be represented in the form "*conditions* → *facts*." It means that if the *conditions* on an XML document are satisfied, then those *facts* must also be true for the document. We focus on the following three types of common constraints.

- A *child constraint*, represented as $\tau \to \tau/\tau'$, means every node of type τ must have a child of type τ'.
- A *descendant constraint*, represented as $\tau \to \tau//\tau'$, means that every node of type τ must have a descendant of type τ'.
- A *functional dependency*, represented as $p/p_1 \to p/p_2$, where p, p_1, and p_2 are finite non-empty subsets of paths conforming to the document. It means that for any two subtrees t_1 and t_2 matching path p/p_1, if they have equal values in their p_1 paths, then (1) both of them have non-null, (value) equal subtrees that match p/p_2; or (2) neither of them has a subtree that matches p/p_2.[1]

Fig. 4 shows a few constraints for the hospital document. The child constraint C_1 says that each `patient` element must have a child of type `pname`. The descendant constraint C_2 says that each `patient` element must have a descendant of type `disease`. The functional dependency C_3 says that if two subtrees have the same //patient/ward value, then they must have the same //patient/disease value, i.e., patients in the same ward must have the same disease.

C_1:	//patient → //patient/pname
C_2:	//patient → //patient//disease
C_3:	//patient/ward → //patient/disease

Figure 4: Example constraints.

3.2 Data Inference Using a Single Constraint

Given a partial document P of the original document D and a constraint C, if P does not satisfy C, then users can use the condition in C to match the partial document. Whenever there is a match, users may infer more data in the document that is supposed to exist. Let $C(P)$ denote the inferred document after applying constraint C on the partial document P. We study the inference effect of different constraints.

A child constraint can be used to expand a partial document by adding one more branch. In this case,

---

[1] Personal communication with Marcelo Arenas and Leonid Libkin.

users know the exact location of the new branch. For instance, suppose the partial document in Fig. 5(a) is published to users. From the child constraint C_1, users know that there must be a `pname` branch, and they know the exact location of this branch, which is under the *patient*[(2)] element. Fig. 5(b) shows the new document $C_1(P)$.

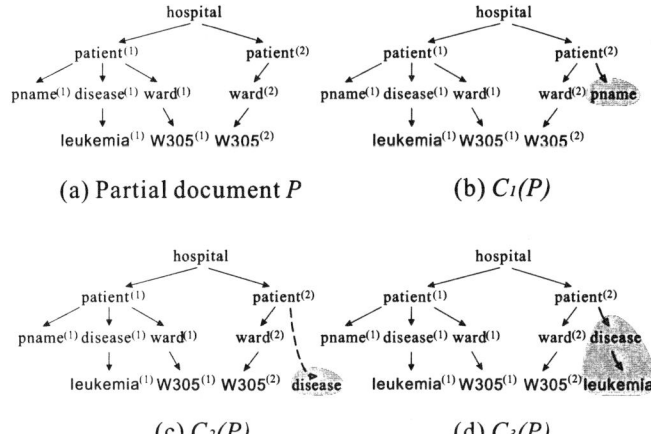

(a) Partial document P (b) $C_1(P)$

(c) $C_2(P)$ (d) $C_3(P)$

Figure 5: Inferred documents using constraints. The shaded areas represent inferred branches. The dotted edge in $C_2(P)$ represents a floating branch.

A descendant constraint can also be used to expand a partial document by adding a branch. In this case, however, users may not know the exact location of the new branch. Consider again the partial document in Fig. 5(a) and the descendant constraint C_2. With this constraint, users know there exists a `disease` branch, but they do not know its exact location under node *patient*[(2)]. Users can thus add the branch to node *patient*[(2)], and let it "float" in the tree, as shown in Fig. 5(c). Such an inferred branch is called a *floating branch*, represented using a dotted edge.[2]

To allow floating branches in XML documents, we need to relax the definition of XML well-formedness by allowing dotted edges between elements to represent floating branches. Correspondingly, we define a mapping from a tree-pattern regulating query to an XML document (possibly with floating branches) in a straightforward way, similarly to the definition of "mapping" from an XQuery tree to a standard XML document. The only subtlety here is that the XML document could have a floating (descendant) edge, which can be the mapping image of another descendant edge in the query.

A functional dependency can also help users expand a tree. For a functional dependency $p/p_1 \to p/p_2$, if there are two branches t_1 and t_2 that match p/p_1, then users can use the subtree p_2 of t_1 to expand

---

[2] A floating edge is similar to a descendant edge in XQuery. Here we use the word "floating" to emphasize the fact that the location of the subtree in the XML document is unknown.

t_2, i.e., users can copy the subtree p_2 of t_1 as a subtree of t_2. (Some branches of the subtree may have already existed.) Fig. 5(d) shows the resulting document after applying the constraint C_3 to infer data.

4 Data Inference Using Multiple XML Constraints

Now we study how users can use multiple constraints to infer data, which could potentially leak sensitive information. Formally, we consider a partial document P of the original document D, a set of regulating queries $\mathcal{A}$, and a set of constraints $\mathcal{C}$ known by users.

4.1 Equivalent Documents of Different Inference Sequences

Since users can do data inference with arbitrary sequences of constraints, different users could infer different results. For instance, consider the partial document in Fig. 5(a) and the two constraints C_2 and C_3 above. Fig. 6(a) shows the document after applying the sequence $\langle C_3, C_2 \rangle$ on the document. In particular, after applying C_3 first, we cannot use C_2 to infer any new branch, since the current document already satisfies C_2. The sequence $\langle C_2, C_3 \rangle$ expands the document P to the one shown in Fig. 6(b). Specifically, after applying C_2 to infer the floating branch, constraint C_3 can still be used to infer the disease subtree of node $patient^{(2)}$. Even though these two resulting documents look different, essentially they have the same amount of information. Intuitively, the floating branch in Fig. 6(b) says that there exists a disease somewhere under node $patient^{(2)}$. Since the document already has a disease element under the $patient^{(2)}$ node, this floating branch does not carry any additional information.

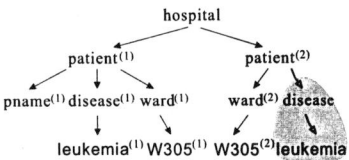

(a) Result of sequence $<C_3, C_2>$

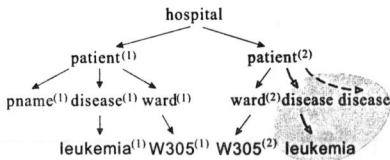

(b) Result of sequence $<C_2, C_3>$

Figure 6: Inferred documents using different constraint sequences.

To formulate this notion of equivalence (or more generally, containment) between XML documents with floating (descendant) branches, we define the following concepts. (Notice this containment relationship is different from the subtree relationship.)

Definition 1 *Let D_1 and D_2 be two XML documents with possibly floating edges. We say D_1 is m-contained in D_2 if the following is true. If D_1 is treated as an XQuery, there is a mapping from query D_1 to document D_2. Such a mapping is called a* document mapping. *The two documents are called "m-equivalent" if they are m-contained in each other.*

The "m" in "m-containment" represents "mapping." Clearly any subtree of a document is m-contained in the document. The document in Fig. 5(c) is m-contained in that of Fig. 5(d). The two documents in Fig. 6 are m-equivalent. In particular, there is a document mapping from Fig. 5(b) to Fig. 5(a), which maps the floating edge to the edge from the $patient^{(2)}$ node to its $disease$ child. Intuitively, a containing document D_2 has at least the same amount of information as the contained document D_1. Since floating branches in D_1 can be mapped to the branches in D_2, they do not really represent additional information, and could be eliminated to make the document more concise.

Even though different sequences of applying the constraints to do data inference can result in different documents, there is a unique, maximal document that m-contains all these documents.

Theorem 1 *Given a partial document P of an XML document D and a set of constraints $\mathcal{C} = \{C_1, \ldots, C_k\}$, there is a document $\mathcal{M}$ that can be inferred from P using a sequence of constraints, such that for any sequence of the constraints, its resulting document is m-contained in $\mathcal{M}$. Such a document $\mathcal{M}$ is unique under m-containment.*

The document $\mathcal{M}$ is called the *maximal inferred document* of P using $\mathcal{C}$. The proof is in the full version of this paper [27]. Its main idea is to show the following algorithm, called CHASE, can compute a sequence of constraints that produces a document $\mathcal{M}$. This document m-contains any possible inferred document. The CHASE algorithm iteratively picks a constraint to apply on the current document. If the resulting document is not m-equivalent to the old one (e.g., new information has been inferred), the algorithm continues to apply the constraints. The algorithm terminates when no constraint can be applied to get a document that is not m-equivalent to the old document.

4.2 Information Leakage

Since users could use arbitrary sequences of constraints to do data inference, we need to prepare for the worst scenario, where a user could get the maximal inferred document. Now we formally define information leakage. Given a set of regulating queries $\mathcal{A} =$

$\{A_1, \ldots, A_n\}$, a set of constraints $\mathcal{C} = \{C_1, \ldots, C_k\}$, and a partial document P of the original document D, consider the maximal inferred document $\mathcal{M}$. If there is a regulating query A_i, such that $\mathcal{M}$ can produce a nonempty answer to the query, then we say that this partial document causes *information leakage*. A partial document is called *valid* if it does not cause information leakage. To be consistent with the definition of "remaining document" $D_r(D, \mathcal{A}) = D - \mathcal{A}(D)$ in Section 2 in the case without constraints, we require that a valid document must be a subtree of $D_r(D, \mathcal{A})$.

For instance, consider the XML document in Fig. 1 and the regulating query A_1 in Fig. 3. The remaining document excludes subtree *leukemia*[1]. Suppose users know all the constraints in Fig. 4. Then removing the *Alice*[1] node from the remaining document can yield a valid partial document. Alternatively, we can remove node $W305$[1] node of patient Alice, or remove the W305 nodes of both Betty and Cathy. Then users cannot use the functional dependency C_3 to infer the leukemia value of Alice.

5 Computing a Valid Partial Document

Given a document with sensitive data specified by regulating queries, in the presence of constraints, we need to decide a valid partial document to be published. There are many such valid partial documents, e.g., the empty document is a trivial one. Often we want to publish as much data as possible without leaking information. In this section, we study how to compute such a valid partial document. Since there are multiple partial valid documents, when in deciding what partial document should be published, we also need to consider application-specific requirements. For instance, if the application requires certain information (e.g., "Betty's ward number") to be published, then among the valid documents, we should publish one that did not remove this node. Here we mainly focus on finding one valid document assuming no such restriction. In case the application does require certain information be published, our solutions can be modified to take this requirement into consideration.

For simplicity, we mainly focus on the case of a single regulating query A, and the results can be extended to the case of multiple regulating queries. Fig. 7 shows the main idea of our approach. We first get the remaining document $D_r = D - A(D)$ by removing the sensitive elements $A(D)$ that match the sensitive node specified in A, possibly under different mappings. These sensitive elements are shown as shaded triangles in $A(D)$. Then we compute the maximal inferred document $\mathcal{M}$ using the CHASE algorithm in Section 4.1, and check if this document leaks any sensitive data (Fig. 7(a)). If not, we do not need to do anything, since D_r is already a valid document with maximum amount of information. Otherwise, we need to remove more nodes. As shown in Fig. 7(b), we consider each leaf node in the tree pattern A, and try to remove its target in $\mathcal{M}$ under a mapping, so that the mapping becomes "broken" after this removal. If some of the image nodes are inferred using the constraints, when removing such a node, we also need to "chase" back the data-inference process, and remove other branches to prevent such an inference (Fig. 7(c)). During the chase-back process, we find the subtree that matches the condition of the utilized constraint, and decide the branches that need to be removed.

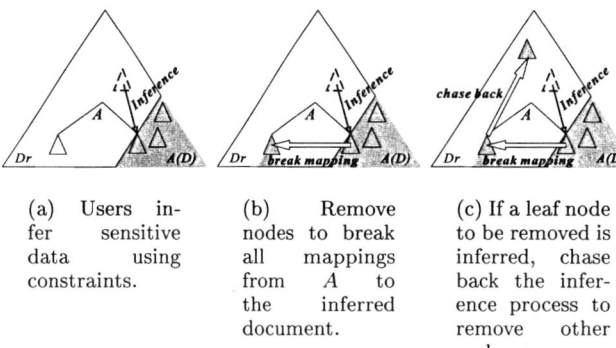

(a) Users infer sensitive data using constraints.

(b) Remove nodes to break all mappings from A to the inferred document.

(c) If a leaf node to be removed is inferred, chase back the inference process to remove other nodes.

Figure 7: Computing a valid partial document.

One key challenge is deciding how to break mappings from the regulating query to the inferred document, and how to chase back the inference steps. In this section we present an algorithm for finding a valid partial document by constructing an *AND/OR graph* [21]. We first use an example to explain AND/OR graphs. We then discuss how the algorithm constructs such a graph, and uses the graph to find a valid partial document.

5.1 AND/OR Graphs

An AND/OR graph is a structure representing how a goal can be reached by solving subproblems. In our case, such a graph shows how to compute a valid partial document to satisfy the regulating query A. We use the following example to explain such a graph. Consider the hospital document in Fig. 1, the regulating query A_1 in Fig. 3(a), and the constraint C_3 : $//patient/ward \rightarrow //patient/disease$. The shaded part in Fig. 1 should be hidden from users. Fig. 8 shows part of the corresponding AND/OR graph for the problem of finding a valid partial document.

The graph has a special node called **START**, which represents the goal of computing a valid partial document. The graph has nodes corresponding to nodes in the maximal inferred document $\mathcal{M}$. Such a node in the graph represents the subproblem of *hiding* its corresponding node n in $\mathcal{M}$; that is, this node n should be removed from $\mathcal{M}$, and it cannot be inferred using the constraints and other nodes in $\mathcal{M}$. For example,

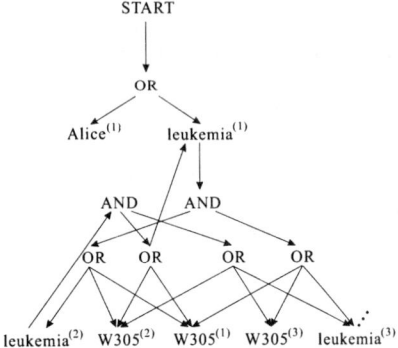

Figure 8: AND/OR graph.

the node $leukemia^{(1)}$ in Fig. 8 represents the subproblem of completely hiding the node $leukemia^{(1)}$ in $\mathcal{M}$; that is, we need to not only remove this node from the XML tree, but also make sure this node cannot be inferred using the constraint.

An AND/OR graph contains hyperlinks, called *connectors*, which connect a parent with a set of successors (nodes or connectors). (To avoid confusions, we use "nodes" in the AND/OR graph to refer to the START state and other vertices corresponding to some elements in the document $\mathcal{M}$, while we use "connectors" to refer to those vertices representing AND/OR relationships between a parent and its successors.) There are two types of connectors. An *OR connector* from a parent p to successors $s_1, \ldots, s_k$ represents the fact that, in order to solve problem p, we need to solve one of the subproblems $s_1, \ldots, s_k$. For instance, the OR connector below the START node in Fig. 8 shows that, in order to achieve the goal, we can either hide node $Alice^{(1)}$ or hide node $leukemia^{(1)}$. An *AND connector* from a node p to successors $s_1, \ldots, s_k$ represents the fact that solving problem p requires solving *all* the subproblems $s_1, \ldots, s_k$. For instance, the AND connector below the $leukemia^{(1)}$ represents the fact that hiding node $leukemia^{(1)}$ requires solving two subproblems. The first one, represented as an OR connector, is to hide one of the nodes $W305^{(1)}$, $W305^{(2)}$, and $leukemia^{(2)}$. This subproblem is due to the fact that, with the constraint C_3, users can use these three nodes to infer $leukemia^{(1)}$ (from Betty's information). Similarly, the second subproblem, also represented as an OR connector, is to hide one of the nodes $W305^{(1)}$, $W305^{(3)}$, and $leukemia^{(3)}$. Both nodes $leukemia^{(2)}$ and $leukemia^{(3)}$ have an AND connector similar to that of $leukemia^{(1)}$. For simplicity we do not draw the AND-connector structure of node $leukemia^{(3)}$.

To compute a valid partial document, we first search in the graph for a *solution graph*, which has the following properties: (1) It is a connected subgraph including the START node. (2) For each node in the subgraph, its successor connectors are also in the subgraph. (3) If it contains an OR connector, it must also contain one of the connector's successors. (4) If it contains an AND connector, it must also contain all the successors of the connector. After computing a solution graph G, for each non-connector node in G, we remove the corresponding node in the XML tree $\mathcal{M}$. In addition, we remove the nodes in $A(D)$, due to the assumption that these nodes must be removed (see Section 4.2). The final tree is a valid partial document.

Fig. 9 shows two solution graphs for the hospital AND/OR graph. The first one corresponds to a valid partial document that excludes the $Alice^{(1)}$ node. The second one corresponds to a valid partial document that excludes nodes $leukemia^{(1)}$, $W305^{(2)}$, and $W305^{(3)}$. By default, the corresponding partial documents do not include the node $leukemia^{(1)}$ due to assumption that this sensitive node must be removed.

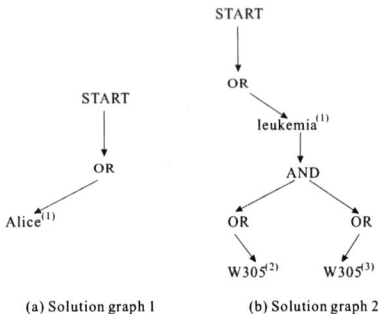

Figure 9: Solutions graphs for the hospital example.

In the rest of the section we give details of how to construct such an AND/OR graph, and how to find a valid partial document by using a solution graph.

5.2 Constructing an AND/OR Graph

Consider a document D, a set of constraints $\mathcal{C}$, and a regulating query A. Let $\mathcal{M}$ be the maximal inferred document that causes information leakage, i.e., there is at least one mapping from A to $\mathcal{M}$. We construct an AND/OR graph in three steps.

Step 1: To avoid information leakage, we need to break all the mappings from A to $\mathcal{M}$. If there is only one such mapping μ, as illustrated by the example in Fig. 8, we introduce an OR connector from the START node to a set of nodes, each of which corresponds to the image node (under μ) of a leaf node in A. (We choose leaf nodes of A in order to remove as few nodes as possible.) If there are more than one such mapping, for each of them we introduce an OR connector to its successor nodes in a similar manner. We then add an AND connector from the START node to these OR connectors, representing the fact that we must break all these mappings.

Step 2: For a node n in the AND/OR graph, its corresponding node in $\mathcal{M}$ could be inferred due to the constraints. In this step, we chase back these data inferences, and add nodes to the AND/OR graph to show how to break such an inference. Now we give the detail of how to break the inference of each type of constraint.

Child constraint: If node n can be inferred using a child constraint $\tau \to \tau/\tau'$, then n must be of type τ', and its parent p node in $\mathcal{M}$ must be of type τ. In order to break this inference, we need to remove the parent node p. Therefore, in the AND/OR graph we add an AND connector from node n to a new node p. (If an AND connector connects a node a to only one node b, for simplicity we can replace this connector with a single edge from a to b.)

Descendant constraint: If node n can be inferred using a descendant constraint $\tau \to \tau//\tau'$, then n must be of type τ', and it must be a floating branch in the inferred document $\mathcal{M}$ from a node a of type τ. In order to break this inference, we need to remove the node a. Therefore, in the AND/OR graph we add an AND connector from node n to a new node a.

Functional dependency: Consider the case where node n can be inferred by a functional dependency $p/t_1 \to p/t_2$. That is, node n is of type p/t_1 in the inferred document $\mathcal{M}$, and there exist nodes n_2, n', and n_2' of types p/t_2, p/t_1, and p/t_2, respectively, such that n_2 is equal to n_2' (as values) and n is equal to n' (as values). In this case, in order to break this inference, we need to remove one of n_2, n', and n_2'. Thus we add an OR connector from node n in the AND/OR graph to new nodes of n_2, n', and n_2'. Notice that the functional dependency can be used to infer node n with different sets of n_2, n', and n_2'. In this case, as illustrated by the example in Fig. 8, we introduce an AND connector from the node n to the corresponding OR connectors, each of which corresponds to such a set.

In the process of breaking the inferences, we may need to add new nodes (and connectors) to the AND/OR graph. If the nodes are already in the AND/OR graph, we can just add the necessary links to these existing nodes. In addition, for each newly added node, we still need to check if it can be inferred using constraints. If so, we need to repeat this process by adding necessary nodes and connectors. This step will repeat until each node in the graph either cannot be inferred, or have the necessary successors to break possible inferences for this node.

Step 3: In this step, we consider the fact that removing a node from the inferred document $\mathcal{M}$ also requires removing all its descendants. Thus we identify the ancestor-descendant relationships among all the nodes in the AND/OR graph, add an AND connector from each node to its descendant nodes (if any).

We use another example to show how to construct an AND/OR graph. Consider the document shown in Fig. 10(a), the regulating query in Fig. 10(b), and the following constraints.

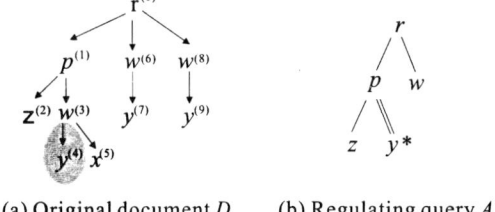

(a) Original document D (b) Regulating query A

Figure 10: A document and a regulating query.

C_1: $//w \to //w/y$;
C_2: $//p \to //p//y$;
C_3: $//p \to //p/z$.

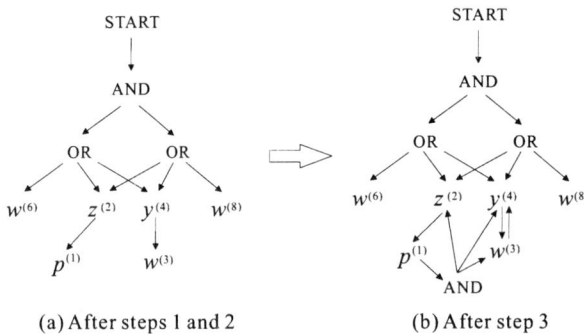

(a) After steps 1 and 2   (b) After step 3

Figure 11: AND/OR graph for Fig. 10.

The corresponding AND/OR graph after steps 1 and 2 is shown Fig. 11(a). In particular, in step 1, we consider the two mappings from A to the maximal inferred document (i.e., the whole document in this example). The images of leaf nodes in A under the two mappings are $\{z^{(2)}, y^{(4)}, w^{(6)}\}$ and $\{z^{(2)}, y^{(4)}, w^{(8)}\}$, respectively. Thus we add one AND connector and two OR connectors to show the need to break both mappings. In step 2, we consider all constraints that can infer these nodes. Constraint C_3 can be used to infer node $z^{(2)}$ from $p^{(1)}$. Thus we add an AND connector (simplified as a single edge) from node $z^{(2)}$ to $p^{(1)}$ in the graph. Similarly, we add an AND connector from node $y^{(4)}$ to $w^{(3)}$ due to constraint C_1. Notice that node $y^{(4)}$ cannot be inferred from $p^{(1)}$ using constraint C_2, since this constraint can only infer a floating branch of $y^{(4)}$ from $p^{(1)}$, and this branch has already been merged with the path from $p^{(1)}$ to $y^{(4)}$.

In step 3, we add those ancestor-descendant links, and the final graph is shown in Fig. 11(b). In particular, node $p^{(1)}$ is an ancestor of nodes $z^{(2)}$, $w^{(3)}$, and $y^{(4)}$, and we add an AND connector from this ancestor to these descendants. Node $w^{(3)}$ is a parent node of $y^{(4)}$, so we add an edge from $w^{(3)}$ to $y^{(4)}$.

5.3 Computing a Valid Partial Document Using the AND/OR Graph

We search within the constructed AND/OR graph for a solution graph, which can be used to produce a valid partial document. We want to remove as few nodes as possible. If it is computationally expensive to find a solution graph with the minimum number of nodes to remove, we can use heuristics to search for a solution graph. For instance, we can adopt the depth-first search strategy as follows. Initially we add the START node to the solution graph G. We mark it SOLVED and add it to a stack. In each iteration, we remove the top element e from the stack. There are four cases: (1) e is a node without any successors. Then we do nothing. (2) e is a node with successors. We add these successors and the corresponding edges to the solution graph G. For each of the successors that is not marked SOLVED, we mark it SOLVED and add it to the stack. (3) e is an AND connector. We add all its successors and the corresponding edges to G. For each of its successors that is not marked SOLVED, we mark it SOLVED and add it to the stack. (4) e is an OR connector. Then we choose one of its successors, add this successor and the corresponding edge to G. If the successor is not marked SOLVED, we then mark it SOLVED and add it to the stack. We repeat the process until the stack becomes empty.

After finding a solution graph, for each of its nodes, we remove the corresponding node in the maximal inferred document $\mathcal{M}$. We also remove the nodes in $A(D)$, and the final document is a valid partial document. For example, Fig. 12 shows a solution graph for the AND/OR graph in Fig. 11(b).

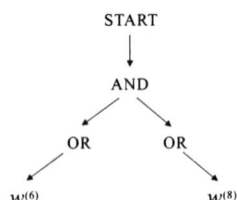

Figure 12: A solution graph.

Remarks: So far we have described how to construct a *complete* AND/OR graph and then search for a solution graph. Often we only need to find just one solution graph. Thus we can find a such solution graph without constructing the complete AND/OR graph. That is, we search for a solution graph as we construct the AND/OR graph "on the fly." There has been a lot of work on heuristic searches in AND/OR graphs [21, 22], such as GBF, GBF*, AO, AO*, and etc. These heuristics can be adopted for efficiently finding a solution graph.

6 Experiments

We conducted experiments to evaluate the effect of data inference on security and the effectiveness of our proposed techniques. In this section we report the experimental results.

6.1 Setting

Data sets: We used two real XML data sets. The first one was from the University of Illinois.[3] It had a file "course_washington.xml" with course information. It contained 3,904 course elements with 162,102 nodes including elements and text nodes. The second data set is from DBLP.[4] It contained more than 427,000 publications (at the time of the experiments), represented as an XML file with about 8,728,000 nodes, including elements, attributes, and their text nodes.

XML Constraints: In general, constraints known to users are defined according to common knowledge [19] or the possible schema of the application domain. We analyzed the two data sets, and found that many constraints were valid. In the experiments, we used the constraints shown in Fig. 13 as examples. They were assumed to be common knowledge known to users. For instance, in data set 1, each course must have a title, represented as the constraint "//course → //course/title." In data set 2, two papers with the same title should have the same authors. (Some conference papers were also published as journal articles with the same title and authors.) Such a fact could be represented as a functional dependency "//dblp/pub/title → //dblp/pub/author," when we treated different types of publications as a single type called "pub."

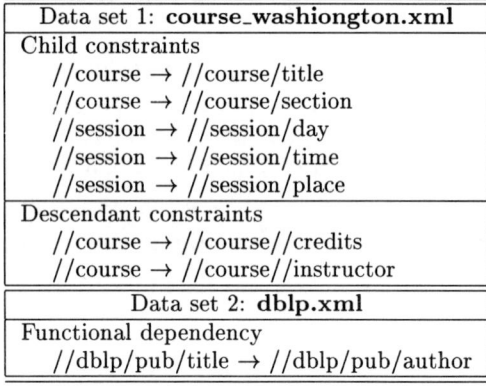

Figure 13: Sample constraints.

Which part of an XML document is sensitive depends on the application. In our experiments, we considered sensitive information defined by two types of regulating queries. The first type of regulating queries ("Type 1") were manually defined as XQuery expressions after we analyzed the semantics of different nodes. The following are two examples.

- A_1: In course_washington.xml, hide codes of all courses.
- A_2: In dblp.xml, hide authors who published papers in 2001.

---
[3] anhai.cs.uiuc.edu/archive/data/courses/washington/
[4] www.informatik.uni-trier.de/~ley/db/

The second type of regulating queries ("Type 2") were generated by randomly marking a set of nodes in the document as sensitive data. The goal is to see the relationship between the percentage of sensitive nodes and the amount of leaked information.

6.2 Amount of Leaked Information Defined by Regulating Queries of Type 1

We first evaluated how much sensitive information was leaked due to constraints. The information was defined using regulating queries of type 1. We measured the number of sensitive nodes defined by each regulating query of type 1, and the number of leaked nodes after the user does data inference. For example, in the course_washington.xml document, 3,904 `code` elements were defined as sensitive. However, using the given constraints, no information can be inferred because no constraint can be used to infer any `code` element. In the dblp.xml document, there were 63,653 authors who published papers in 2001, and their names were defined as sensitive by regulating query A_2. If we just published the document by removing these sensitive names, users could use the functional dependency "//dblp/pub/title → //dblp/pub/author" to infer 977 such author names. In particular, the corresponding publications of these inferred authors have been published in year 2001, whereas there exist some other (journal) publications that have the same title of these publications, but they were published in other years. Using the functional dependency, users can infer some of these hidden author names.

6.3 Amount of Leaked Information Defined by Regulating Queries of Type 2

We let the percentage of sensitive nodes specified by regulating queries $\mathcal{A}$ of type 2 vary from 0 to 100%. We assumed that users know the constraints in Fig. 13. We measured how much information can be leaked if the system just published the document $D - \mathcal{A}(D)$ by removing the sensitive nodes $\mathcal{A}(D)$ (their subtrees). We used the validation approach discussed in Section 4 to compute the number of leaked sensitive nodes. We considered different factors that can affect the amount, such as the types of constraints, the number of constraints, and the number of nodes that satisfy the conditions in the constraints. The percentage of leaked nodes is calculated as

$$\frac{\text{number of leaked sensitive nodes}}{\text{number of nodes in the whole document}}.$$

Effect of Different Constraints

Fig. 14 shows the relationship between the number of leaked nodes and the number of sensitive nodes for different types of constraints.

Child and descendant constraints: Fig. 14(a) shows the results for the child and descendants in Fig. 13 for

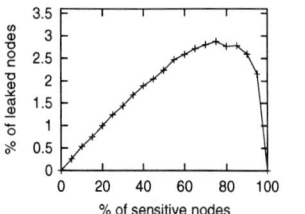 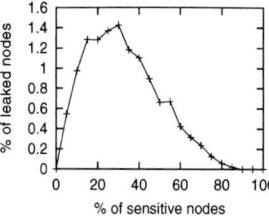

(a) Child and descendant constraints in course_washington.xml

(b) Functional dependencies in dblp.xml

Figure 14: Effect of different kinds of constraints.

document course_washington.xml. As the percentage of sensitive nodes increased, the percentage of leaked nodes increased to a peak (about 2.8%), when the percentage of sensitive nodes was around 82%. The reason for this increase is that more nodes inferred by users could be sensitive. If the number of sensitive nodes further increased, then the number of leaked nodes started to drop. The result is not surprising, since there were fewer nodes in the remaining document, and it became less likely for users to do data inference, causing less information to be leaked.

Functional dependencies: We used dblp.xml to test the effect of the functional dependency shown in Fig. 13. Since the number of nodes satisfying the functional dependency was relatively small compared to the document size, we chose a subdocument by using a subset of the represented publications, such that the subdocument had 8% of its publications satisfying the functional dependency. We then varied the number of sensitive nodes in the subdocument. The result is shown in Fig. 14(b). Similarly to the previous case, as the percentage of sensitive nodes increased, the percentage of leaked nodes increased quickly to a peak value of 1.4%, when the corresponding percentage of sensitive nodes was around 26%. The number of leaked nodes also started to drop as we increased the percentage of sensitive nodes, for the similar reason as in the case of child/descendant constraints. Notice that in this case, the percentage of sensitive nodes that yielded the peak value was smaller than that of the previous case. The main reason is that functional dependencies often need more nodes to be satisfied than child/descendant constraints.

Effect of Number of Constraints

We then evaluated the effect of the number of constraints (corresponding to the amount of common knowledge) on data inference. We chose different numbers of constraints and tested how they affected the number of leaked elements. We considered two cases for the document course_washington.xml.

105

- Using 4 constraints: We assumed that users know the first three child constraints and the first one descendant constraint in Fig. 13.
- Using 7 constraints: We assumed that users know the five child constraints and the two descendant constraints in Fig. 13.

The results in Fig. 15 are consistent with our intuition. As the number of constraints increases, there is more common knowledge known by users. Then they can infer more data, causing more information to be leaked. For both cases, as the percentage of sensitive nodes increased, the percentage of leaked nodes increased to reach a peak before it started to drop.

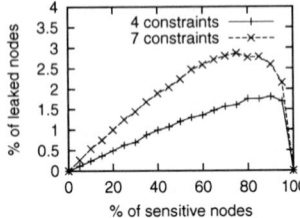

Figure 15: Different numbers (4 and 7) of constraints in course_washington.xml.

Effect of Nodes Satisfying Constraints

Different partial documents could have different numbers of nodes that satisfy the conditions in the constraints. We studied the effect of this number on data inference and information leakage. In the experiments, we chose a subdocument of the dblp.xml document with about $800,000$ nodes as a test document. We adjusted the number of nodes satisfying the condition in the functional dependency in Fig. 13. We adjusted this number to about $40,000$, $64,000$, and $80,000$, by removing some of the represented publications. Fig. 16 shows the results, where V is the number of nodes satisfying the condition in the functional dependency. Not surprisingly, as we increased V, the percentage of leaked nodes increased, since more such nodes can help users infer more sensitive nodes.

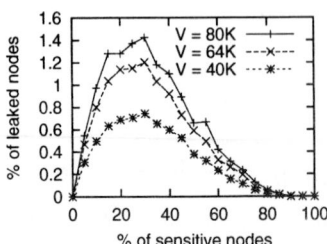

Figure 16: Effect of number of nodes satisfying the condition in the functional dependency.

6.4 Removing Nodes to Prevent Leakage

We used the method described in Section 5 to compute a valid partial document without information leakage. In this experiment we measured how many nodes the algorithm decided to remove to compute a valid partial document. Based on the analysis in Section 6.2, we know that the nodes that need to be removed highly depend on the regulating queries. If there are many ways the conditions in the regulating queries can be mapped to the document, then many nodes are sensitive and should be hidden. Whereas, if the conditions are very selective, few nodes satisfying these conditions, and few nodes need to be hidden. Furthermore, different kinds of constraints have different effects on what nodes should be removed.

We considered the constraints in Fig. 13. We considered regulating queries that have a condition that is either a single element (the element is sensitive) or a path (the root of the path is sensitive). We randomly chose certain percentage of the nodes as sensitive nodes, and applied our algorithm to decide what nodes should be removed to avoid information leakage. We could choose a node in a mapping image of the regulating query to remove, or we could chase back the process from an inferred sensitive node and remove other nodes as well. In the case there were different ways to remove nodes, we randomly selected one solution. For each solution, we measured how many nodes needed to be removed. We ran 10 rounds to compute the average percentage of nodes that can be removed. When we removed an interior node, we also counted its descendants in the number of nodes.

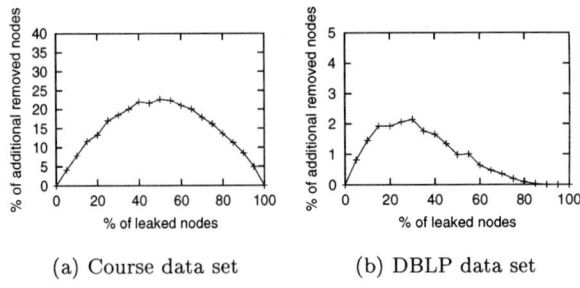

(a) Course data set   (b) DBLP data set

Figure 17: Additional removed nodes to get a valid partial document.

Fig. 17 shows the results for both data sets. The document course_washington.xml with child and descendant constraints required relatively more nodes to be removed compared to that of document dblp.xml with a functional dependency. The reason is the following. For the child/descendant constraints, when we chased back their inference process, we had to choose a parent or ancestor to remove, which can remove a lot of child/descendant nodes. On the other hand, for the functional dependency, when we chose a node to break the inference process, we could often find a leaf node (or a node close to leaf nodes) to remove, thus the total number of removed nodes was smaller.

Summary: Our experiments show that sensitive information could be leaked during XML publishing if common knowledge (constraints) is not considered carefully. The amount of leaked information depends on the number and type of regulating queries, the number and type of constraints, and the number of nodes satisfying the conditions in the constraints. Our proposed techniques can measure how much sensitive data is leaked, and can also compute a valid partial document without information leakage.

7 Conclusions

In this paper, we studied the effect of data inference using common knowledge (represented as XML constraints) on data security in XML publishing. We formulated the process how users can infer data using three types of common XML constraints. We showed that there is a unique, maximal document that contains all possible inferred documents. We developed algorithms for finding a partial document of a given XML document without causing information leakage. Our experiments on real data sets showed that effect of inference on data security, and how the proposed techniques can avoid such leakage.

Acknowledgments: We thank Marcelo Arenas and Leonid Libkin for clarifying the definition of XML functional dependencies. We thank Lei Shi and Ge Yu for their discussions and help on the implementation.

References

[1] S. Amer-Yahia, S. Cho, L. V. S. Lakshmanan, and D. Srivastava. Minimization of Tree Pattern Queries. In *SIGMOD Conference*, 2001.

[2] P. A. Bernstein et al. Data management for peer-to-peer computing: A vision. In *WebDB*, 2002.

[3] E. Bertino, B. Carminati, and E. Ferrari. A Secure Publishing Service for Digital Libraries of XML Documents. In *ISC*, pages 347–362, 2001.

[4] J. Biskup and P. Bonatti. Controlled Query Evaluation for Known Policies by Combining Lying and Refusal. In *Foundations of Information and Knowledge Systems*, pages 49–66, 2002. LNCS 2284.

[5] A. Brodskyand, C. Farkas, and S. Jajodia. Secure Databases: Constraints, Inference Channels, and Monitoring Disclosures. *TKDE*, 12(6):900–919, 2000.

[6] E. Damiani, S. D. C. D. Vimercati, S. Paraboschi, and P. Samarati. Design and Implementation of an Access Control Processor for XML Documents. *Computer Networks*, 33(1-6):59–75, June 2000.

[7] E. Damiani, S. D. C. D. Vimercati, S. Paraboschi, and P. Samarati. A Fine-Grained Access Control System for XML Documents. *ACM Transaction on Information and System Security*, 5(2):169–202, 2001.

[8] S. Dawson, S. D. C. D. Vimercati, P. Lincoln, and P. Samarati. Minimal Data Upgrading to Prevent Inference and Association Attacks. In *PODS*, 1999.

[9] W. Fan, G. M. Kuper, and J. Siméon. A Unified Constraint Model for XML. *Computer Networks*, 39(5):489–505, 2002.

[10] A. Gabillon and E. Bruno. Regulating Access to XML Documents. In *Proceedings of the 15th Annual IFIP WG 11.3 conference on Database Security*, July 2001.

[11] H. Hacigumus, B. R. Iyer, C. Li, and S. Mehrotra. Executing SQL over Encrypted Data in the Database Service Provider Model. In *SIGMOD*, 2002.

[12] A. Y. Halevy et al. Schema mediation in peer data management systems. In *ICDE*, 2003.

[13] B. Hore, S. Mehrotra, and G. Tsudik. A privacy preserving index for range queries. In *VLDB*, 2004.

[14] S. Jajodia and C. Meadows. Inference Problems in Multilevel Secure Database Management Systems. In *Inofrmation Security: An Integrated Collection of Essays*, pages 570–584, 1995.

[15] S. Jajodia, P. Samarati, M. L. Sapino, and V. S. Subrahmanian. Flexible Support for Multiple Access Control Policies. *ACM Transaction on Database Systems*, 26(2):241–286, 2001.

[16] M. Kudoh, Y. Hirayama, S. Hada, and A. Vollschwitz. Access Control Specification Based on Policy Evaluation and Enforcement Model and Specification Language. In *Symposium on Cryptograpy and Information Security (SCIS)*, 2000.

[17] C. Li, J. Li, and Q. Zhong. RACCOON: A peer-based system for data integration and sharing. In *ICDE*, 2004.

[18] G. Miklau and D. Suciu. Controlling Access to Published Data using Cryptography. In *VLDB*, 2003.

[19] G. Miklau and D. Suciu. A Formal Analysis of Information Disclosure in Data Exchange. In *SIGMOD*, 2004.

[20] W. S. Ng et al. PeerDB: A P2P-based system for distributed data sharing. In *ICDE*, 2003.

[21] N. J. Nilsson. *Principles of Artificial Intelligence*. Morgan Kaufmann, 1994.

[22] J. Pearl. *Heuristics: intelligent search strategies for computer problem solving*. Addison-Wesley Longman Publishing Co., Inc., 1984.

[23] X. Qian and T. Lunt. A Semantic Framework of the Multilevel Secure Relational Model. *IEEE Transactions on Knowledge and Data Engineering*, 9(2):292–301, 1997.

[24] The Hyperion Project. Computer Science Dept., University of Toronto.

[25] H. S. Thompson, D. Beech, M. Maloney, and N. Mendelsohn. XML Schema Part 1: Structures. W3C. http://www.w3.org/TR/xmlschema-1, 2000.

[26] M. G. W. Fan, C.-Y. Chan. Secure XML Querying with Security Views. In *SIGMOD*, 2004.

[27] X. Yang and C. Li. Secure XML Publishing without Information Leakage in the Presence of Data Inference (Full Version). Technical report, UC Irvine, 2004.

[28] T. Yu, D. Srivastava, L. V. S. Lakshmanan, and H. V. Jagadish. Compressed Accessibility Map: Efficient Access Control for XML. In *VLDB*, pages 478–489, 2002.

Limiting Disclosure in Hippocratic Databases

Kristen LeFevre[†*] Rakesh Agrawal[†] Vuk Ercegovac[*] Raghu Ramakrishnan[*]
Yirong Xu[†] David DeWitt[*]

[†]IBM Almaden Research Center, San Jose, CA 95120
[*]University of Wisconsin, Madison, WI 53706

Abstract

We present a practical and efficient approach to incorporating privacy policy enforcement into an existing application and database environment, and we explore some of the semantic tradeoffs introduced by enforcing these privacy policy rules at cell-level granularity. Through a comprehensive set of performance experiments, we show that the cost of privacy enforcement is small, and scalable to large databases.

1 Introduction

The Lowell database research self-assessment of June 2003 points to data privacy as an important area for future research [4]. One of the defining principles of data privacy, *limited disclosure* [6], is based on the premise that data subjects[1] have control over who is allowed to see their personal information and for what purpose. For example, a patient entering a hospital provides some information at the time of registration with the understanding that this information may only be used under certain circumstances; for example, the billing office may use the patient's address information to process insurance claims, but the hospital may not give patient address information to charities for the purpose of solicitation without consent [1].

Increasingly, organizations want the ability to define a *privacy policy* that describes such agreements with data subjects and to ensure that the policy is enforced with respect to all data access. Essentially, a privacy policy is comprised of a set of rules that describe to whom the data may be disclosed (the *recipients*) and how the data may be used (the *purposes*). Additional *conditions* may be specified to govern disclosure. For instance, a policy may specify that a particular data item may be disclosed, but only with "opt-in" consent from the data subject, or that the data item will be disclosed unless the subject has specifically "opted out" of this default. The policy may also specify more complex conditions; for example, a patient's medical history may only be seen by nurses assigned to the same floor. While there is recent work on defining languages for specifying privacy policies (e.g. P3P [12], EPAL [7]), database mechanisms for enforcing such policies have not been investigated.

An approach often taken is to enforce privacy policies at the application level [8]: First, the application issues the query to the database and retrieves the result. Then, the application scans the resulting records and filters prohibited information (for example, by setting it to *null*). However, this approach leads to privacy leaks when applied at the cell level. Consider a query involving a predicate over a privacy-sensitive field: `SELECT Name, Disease FROM Patients WHERE Disease = "Hepatitis"`, and Bob, who has hepatitis, and chose to disclose his name but not his disease history. The query result contains Bob's record with the `Disease` value filtered out. Unfortunately, this allows anyone looking at the results to conclude that Bob has hepatitis.[2]

1.1 Requirements for Limited Disclosure Mechanisms

A solution to the limited disclosure problem should ideally protect information according to the appropri-

---

[1] We use the term *data subject* to mean the individual whose private information is stored and managed by the database system.

[2] An alternative might retrieve all of the patient records, not just those with a particular disease, and apply the privacy-sensitive predicate in the application. However, this approach leads to significant performance problems as much data must be unnecessarily fetched from the database. Query execution is more difficult yet when we consider more complicated queries, such as those involving aggregates or joins, because we must extract a significant amount of data from the database, and then perform a large amount of the query processing at the application level.

Permission to copy without fee all or part of this material is granted provided that the copies are not made or distributed for direct commercial advantage, the VLDB copyright notice and the title of the publication and its date appear, and notice is given that copying is by permission of the Very Large Data Base Endowment. To copy otherwise, or to republish, requires a fee and/or special permission from the Endowment.

Proceedings of the 30th VLDB Conference, Toronto, Canada, 2004

ate policies with minimal privacy-checking overhead. Further, given the time and expense required to modify existing application code, such a solution should require minimal change to existing applications and little reorganization of existing data.

It is particularly important that we manage disclosure at a very fine granularity because privacy policies can refer to "data items" at the level of an individual cell in a relational table. Traditional databases provide access control at the table level and use the view mechanism to restrict access to certain columns or rows of a table. Some systems [19] now provide access control at the row level, but this is still inadequate. Consider Alice, who has opted to allow the hospital to release her email address but not her phone number to charities. Bob might choose to provide his phone number, but not his address. Row-level enforcement must either filter information that should be permitted, or disclose prohibited information.

1.2 Contributions and Paper Organization

Our principal contribution is a database mechanism, introduced in Section 2, for enforcing privacy policies, with the following features:

- Privacy policies can be stored and managed in the database.
- A broad range of privacy policies expressible in high-level privacy specification languages (e.g. the privacy rules expressible in P3P, including opt-in and opt-out choices, and more complex conditions as seen in EPAL) can be enforced.
- Enforcing privacy policies does not require any modification to existing database applications.

The power of our approach is based on two technical properties: first, it supports cell-level enforcement; second, it allows full use of SQL query capabilities to express conditions. In more detail, our contributions are:

- We investigate the alternative semantics for limited disclosure in relational databases and present two models of cell-level limited disclosure: *table semantics* and *query semantics*, weighing the relative semantic and performance tradeoffs implicit in the two models. (Section 3)
- We provide techniques for enforcing a broad class of privacy policies by automatically modifying all queries that access the database in a way that ensures the desired disclosure semantics. Rather than viewing the disclosure control problem as one of checking against a list of privileges, we transform it into a query modification problem. Thus, our implementation automatically benefits from years of experience in database query processing, including parallelism. We examine several implementation issues, including privacy meta-data storage, query modification algorithms, and structures for storing conditions and individual choices. (Section 4)

- An experimental evaluation of our techniques shows that our approach has low overhead and frequently speeds up queries by using privacy-related restrictions as additional selection conditions. The conventional wisdom has been that cell-level access control is prohibitively expensive. We provide extensive experiments comparing the implementation alternatives that we present and demonstrate that our implementation is scalable to large databases. (Section 5)

Although the work presented here has been done in the Hippocratic database setting [6], it has much wider application. A growing range of applications in content management, customer support, financial analysis, and e-commerce require cell-level access control. In fact, many such applications might use privacy policies in the dual role of *access control policies*.

1.3 Related Work

The work in database access control can largely be grouped into the areas of discretionary and mandatory [21]. Discretionary access control allows a database administrator to grant and revoke access privileges, which typically refer to entire tables or views; optionally, the DBA may specify that others are authorized to grant and revoke privileges [14]. Role-based access control is an additional refinement which allows this type of privilege to be granted not to an individual user, but to the user's group, or role [23].

The mandatory access control model involves a single set of rules governing access to the entire system. A well-known model of mandatory access control, the Bell-LaPadula multilevel secure database, defines permissions in terms of objects, subjects, and classes [9]. Each object is a member of some class, for example "Top Secret" or "Unclassified," which typically form a hierarchy. The model also allows for the possibility of polyinstantiation [18]. These formalizations are further refined by [15, 16], and a schema decomposition allowing cell-level classification to be expressed as row-level classification is described in [20].

To our knowledge, the only cell-level implementation of multi-level security was done by SRI in the SeaView system [18], but its performance was never published [3]. The idea of modifying queries for access control was introduced in [24], and the idea of "reformulating" queries for security was also alluded to by [25]. A query rewrite mechanism to control access to federated XML user-profile data was used by [22]. Oracle's Virtual Private Database product allows for the definition of access control functions, which may be data-driven, and which operate at the row level through addition of predicates [19]. Some content-management applications have enforced fine-grained security by introducing an application layer that modifies queries with conditions that enforce access control policies, e.g. [2, 17], but they are application-specific in their design and do not extend a DBMS for general use.

There has been extensive research in the area of statistical databases motivated by the desire to provide statistical information (sum, count, etc.) without compromising individual information (see surveys in [5, 26]). It was also shown that we cannot provide high quality statistics and, at the same time, prevent partial disclosure of individual data. Our goal in this paper is to provide database support that allows individual queries to respect privacy policy rules and individual subject choices, and we assume that additional mechanisms such as query admission control and audit trails [5] are in place to guard against the inference problem. This paper also does not purport to address the use of covert channels to leak information[3], but assumes that the appropriate security mechanisms are in place to control such leaks [10].

2 System Overview

We have developed a database architecture for enforcing limited disclosure as expressed by privacy policies. The basic components are the following:

- **Policy definition:** Privacy policies are expressed electronically and stored in the database where they can be used to enforce limited disclosure. Our prototype provides a policy "meta-language" for defining privacy policy rules. Privacy policies defined using P3P [12] or EPAL [7] may be translated into this meta-language and then stored in the database, making our architecture policy-language independent.

- **Privacy meta-data:** The rules and conditions prescribed by the privacy policy are stored as privacy meta-data tables in the database. The structures for storing this information are described in Section 4.1.

- **Application context:** Each query must be associated with a purpose and recipient. In our system, this information is inferred based on the context of the application issuing the query, which is similar to the approach described in [19]. The query interceptor infers the purpose and recipient of the query based on context information stored in an additional meta-data table.[4]

- **Query modifier:** SQL queries issued to the database are intercepted and augmented to reflect the privacy policy rules regarding the purpose and recipient issuing the query. The results

---
[3]For example, error messages generated during the evaluation of privacy rules could become a *covert channel* for leaks.

[4]An alternative would extend the syntax of a SQL query to include purpose and recipient information, for example SELECT * FROM Patients FOR PURPOSE Solicitation RECIPIENT External_Charity. Because this method requires extensions to the query language and modification to existing applications, we elect to use application contexts, though the rest of our implementation is compatible with either alternative.

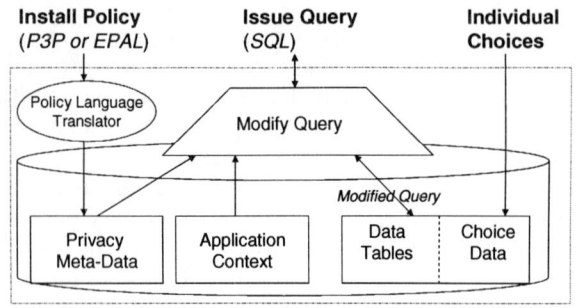

Figure 1: Implementation architecture overview

of this new query are returned to the issuer. Several query modification algorithms are detailed in Section 4.2.

- **Disclosure model:** The result of executing a privacy-modified query will reflect one of two cell-level limited disclosure models, as described in Section 3.

2.1 Policy Meta-Language, Rules and Conditions

A privacy policy will be considered to be a set of rules of the form <*data, purpose-recipient pair, condition*>. An example of such a rule is <*address, solicitation-charity, optin = yes*>, meaning that a data subject's address can be released to a charity organization for the purpose of solicitation, provided the subject has explicitly consented to this disclosure. A *condition* is any boolean predicate that is expressible in SQL. Electronic privacy policies are programatically translated into this policy "meta-language" before being deployed.

A conditional predicate may refer to the data table T, in addition to any other data tables. By joining T with other tables on primary key $T.key$, these conditions can be made to depend on any attributes of the "current" T row, and by referring to the context environment variable (which we denote $USERID) that identifies the user issuing the current request, the conditions can be made specific with respect to the current user. For example, suppose we were to define a condition to govern the disclosure of patient data to hospital nurses such that, for treatment, nurses may only see the medical histories of patients assigned to the same floor. This condition can be expressed using the following predicate:

```
EXISTS (SELECT NurseID
   FROM Nurses
   WHERE Patients.floor = Nurses.floor
   AND $USERID = Nurses.NurseID)
```

Another example of data-driven conditions arises when we consider defining disclosure based on application-defined user groups. In this scenario, the application owns some database table $D(key, a_1, a_2, ...)$ storing application data. The application also maintains a list of users $U(uid)$ and groups $G(gid)$, a table mapping users to groups, M(uid, gid), and an access control list $A(key, a_i, gid)$ associating each record in D with a list of groups that have access to attribute a_i. Suppose one of the privacy policy rules allows disclosure of data attribute $D.a_i$ to purpose P and recipient R only when the current user belongs to a group which has been granted access to $D.a_i$. Such a condition is specified as a simple SQL predicate joining tables M and A:

```
EXISTS
   (SELECT gid
   FROM M, A
   WHERE M.gid = A.gid AND M.uid = $USERID
   AND A.key = D.key AND A.a_i)
```

A potential source of difficulty in translating from a high-level policy specification into our meta specifications could be the gap in vocabulary. Policy specifications are written in terms of an information model that might use entity names that need translation into the column and table names used in the meta specification. However, the necessary mapping can be specified using a GUI tool and then used in the translator from the high-level specification into meta specification.

Another difficulty could be the difference in the expressive power of the the two condition languages and the difference in the execution models. We investigated this problem by experimenting with translating conditions from P3P and EPAL into our condition language. Writing the translator for P3P was straightforward. We could also translate most of EPAL, although this translation was more challenging. The EPAL engine evaluates rules sequentially, in the order they appear in the policy. Our policy language is set-oriented, so we had to modify the execution semantics of EPAL so that if two or more rules qualify, they are all fired to allow access to data. Similarly, EPAL conditions support some operators and data types for which there is no corresponding analog in SQL. However, not supporting these constructs does not appear to be a limitation in practice; we looked at several EPAL policies and found easy translations for them into our policy meta-language.

3 Limited Disclosure Models

We introduce two models of cell-level limited disclosure enforcement: *table semantics* and *query semantics*. The table semantics model conceptually defines a view of each data table for each purpose-recipient pair, based on the disclosure constraints specified in the privacy policy. These views combine to produce a coherent relational database for each purpose-recipient pair, independent of any queries, and queries are evaluated against this database. In contrast, the query semantics model takes the query into account when enforcing disclosure. Both models mask prohibited values using SQL's *null* value.

Let a privacy policy consist of statements that involve m purpose-recipient pairs $P = <P_1, P_2, ..., P_m>$.

In order to define the semantics of the limited disclosure model, every data table T with n columns will be (conceptually) extended with $m * n$ columns that record disclosure conditions for the corresponding cell for a given purpose-recipient pair.

We use the notation $T[i]$, $1 \leq i \leq n$, to refer to the data columns of T. We use $t[i,j], 1 \leq i \leq n, 1 \leq j \leq m$, to refer to the column containing the disclosure condition for data column i and purpose-recipient pair j. For any set of columns S in a table T, "$t[S]$ nonenull" denotes that every column in S is non-null in tuple t. We use $eval(t[i,j])$ to denote the boolean result of evaluating the (predicate expressing the) condition that controls disclosure of data column i in the current row of T to purpose-recipient pair j. We say that the cell in column i of the current row is *prohibited* to purpose-recipient j (or simply *prohibited*) if the value of $eval(t[i,j])$ is $false$.

3.1 Table Semantics Model

In the table semantics model, each purpose-recipient pair Pj is assigned a view over each table in the database, and prohibited cells are replaced with null values. Also, if any column in the primary key of a row is prohibited, then the entire row is prohibited.[5] This model is formally defined as follows:

Definition 1: (Table Semantics) Let T be a table with n data columns, and let K be the set of columns that constitute the primary key of T. For a given purpose-recipient pair Pj, the table T, seen as T_{Pj}, is defined as follows:

$$\{r | \exists t \in T \quad \wedge \forall i, 1 \leq i \leq n \\ (r[i] = t[i] \; if \; eval(t[i,j]) = true, \\ r[i] = null \; otherwise) \\ \wedge \; r[K] \; nonenull\}$$

Consider a table containing patient information, as shown in Figure 2. The hospital allows patients to choose on an opt-in basis if they want these categories of information to be released to charities (recipient) for solicitation (purpose). Figure 3 shows the choices made by the patients. The resulting privacy-enforced table of patients according to table semantics is shown in Figure 4, assuming that P# is the primary key.

3.2 Query Semantics Model

With query semantics, prohibited data is removed from a query's result set based on the purpose-recipient pair and the query itself. Here, we do not aim to define a version of the underlying table for each

---

[5] A simpler cell-level enforcement model can be obtained by dropping the null-restriction on the primary key, but the privacy-enforced data tables will no longer be consistent with the relational data model, which requires primary keys to be non-null. We call this alternative *strict cell-level* semantics, but we do not consider it further.

P#	Name	Age	Address	Phone
1	Alice Adams	10	1 April Ave.	111-1111
2	Bob Blaney	20	2 Brooks Blvd.	222-2222
3	Carl Carson	30	3 Cricket Ct.	333-3333
4	David Daniels	40	4 Dogwood Dr.	444-4444

Figure 2: Full data table of patient information.

P#	P#	Name	Age	Address	Phone
1	✓	✓	✓	✓	✓
2	✗	✗	✗	✗	✗
3	✓	✗	✗	✓	✓
4	✓	✓	✗	✗	✗

Figure 3: Patient choices for disclosure of information to charities for solicitation.

P#	Name	Age	Address	Phone
1	Alice Adams	10	1 April Ave.	111-1111
3	-	-	3 Cricket Ct.	333-3333
4	David Daniels	-	-	-

Figure 4: Privacy-enforced table of patient information, using table semantics.

Name	Age
Alice Adams	10
-	-
David Daniels	-

Name	Age
Alice Adams	10
David Daniels	-

Figure 5: Comparing Table Semantics and Query Semantics for a simple projection

purpose and recipient, so a row in the query result set may include a null value for a column that is part of the primary key in the underlying schema. The query semantics model is defined as follows:

Definition 2: (Query Semantics) Consider a query Q that is issued on behalf of some purpose-recipient pair Pj and that refers to table T. Query Semantics is enforced as follows:

1. Every table T in the FROM clause is replaced by T_{Pj}, defined as follows:

$$\{r | \exists t \in T \;\; \wedge \;\; \forall i, 1 \leq i \leq n$$
$$(r[i] = t[i] \; if \; eval(t[i,j]) = true,$$
$$r[i] = null \; otherwise)\}$$

2. Result tuples that are null in all columns of Q are discarded.

For example, suppose we were to project the Name and Age columns from the Patients table. Using query semantics, the result of this query would be the table on the right of Figure 5; using table semantics, we would obtain the table on the left.

Note that in the query semantics model, different project lists in otherwise identical queries might yield different numbers of rows depending on the column(s) projected. This slight departure from the norms of conventional SQL may result in substantial performance gains, but the semantic tradeoff should nonetheless be carefully considered.

3.3 Representing a Prohibited Value as Null

In SQL, null is a special value meant to denote "no value" [11]. For this reason, it is intuitive to use null to represent a prohibited value. Adopting the semantics of SQL queries run against null values for prohibited values is desirable for several reasons:

- Predicates applied to null values, such as X > null, do not evaluate to true. Similarly, null values do not join with other null values. Predicates applied to privacy-enforced tables will thus behave as though the prohibited cells were not present.

- Null values do not affect computation of aggregates, so an aggregate is actually computed based only on the values available to the purpose and recipient.

- Many applications are written to withstand nulls in the query results. Such applications can be privacy-enabled without requiring expensive rewriting.

However, we also carry over the well-known semantic anomalies inherent in the use of null values [11]. For example, the SQL expression AVG(Age) is not necessarily equal to the expression SUM(Age)/COUNT(*). One might expect that an expression such as SELECT * FROM Patients WHERE Age > 50 OR Age <= 50 will return all tuples in Patients, but it might not do so in the presence of nulls.

Replacing prohibited values with nulls also makes some practical assumptions. While it is not its intended use, null may sometimes be used with application-specific semantics. For example, an application may treat a null value in the Phone column as an indication that a patient has no phone; the use of null for prohibited fields might conflict with such usage. The alternative to using nulls is to introduce a new special data value, *prohibited*, carrying special semantics with regard to SQL queries, but such an approach would require substantial augmentation to the query processing engine and add new semantic complexities.

4 Implementation

This section details the implementation of the architecture introduced in Section 2. We first describe the mechanisms used to store privacy meta-data, including rules and conditions as implemented using the policy meta-language. We then describe two algorithms for modifying queries to incorporate privacy enforcement. Finally, we describe an optimized implementation for enforcing opt-in and opt-out choices.

4.1 Privacy Meta-Data: Rules and Conditions

The disclosure rules from an electronic privacy policy are stored inside the database as the *privacy meta-data*. These tables capture the purpose and recipient information (Figure 6), as well as disclosure conditions (Figure 7). When a purpose P, recipient R, and data column D of table T appear in a row of the policy

RuleID	Policy	Purpose	Recipient	Table	Column	CondID
R1	P1	Insurance	Billing Office	Patients	Phone	-
R2	P1	Solicitation	External Charity	Patients	Name	C5
R3	P1	Solicitation	External Charity	Patients	Phone	C3
R4	P1	Treatment	Hospital Nurses	Patients	Disease	C1
R5	P1	Treatment	Hospital Nurses	LabResults	Diagnosis	C2
R6	P1	Solicitation	External Charity	Patients	P#	C4
R7	P2	Insurance	Billing Office	Patients	Address	-
R8	P2	Insurance	Billing Office	Patients	Phone	-

Figure 6: Policy Rules Table

CondID	Predicate
C1	"EXISTS (SELECT NurseID FROM Nurses WHERE Patients.floor = Nurses.floor AND \$USERID = Nurses.NurseID)"
C2	"EXISTS (SELECT NurseID FROM Nurses, Patients WHERE Patients.floor = Nurses.floor AND Patient.P# = LabResults.P# AND \$USERID = Nurses.NurseID)"
C3	"EXISTS (SELECT Phone_Choice FROM PatientChoices WHERE Patients.P# = PatientChoices.P# AND PatientChoices.Phone_Choice = 1)"
C4	"EXISTS (SELECT ID_Choice FROM PatientChoices WHERE Patients.P# = PatientChoices.P# AND PatientChoices.ID_Choice = 1)"
C5	"EXISTS (SELECT Name_Choice FROM PatientChoices WHERE Patients.P# = PatientChoices.P# AND PatientChoices.Name_Choice = 1)"

Figure 7: Conditions table

table, this denotes a rule, which indicates that D is available to recipient R for purpose P. If this row contains a condition, it means that (P, R) has access to D, but with restrictions as indicated by the condition. For example, the rules described in Figure 6 indicate that, under policy *P1*, `Phone` information is always provided to the billing office for the purpose of processing insurance claims (Rule R1), but it is provided to external charities for solicitation only conditionally, on an opt-in or opt-out basis (Rule R3)

4.2 Query Modification

We have two algorithms for query modification that are described in this section, one using case-statements, and the other using outer-joins.

4.2.1 Case-Statement Modification

The first query modification algorithm augments incoming queries with case statements to enforce the rules and conditions expressed in the privacy meta-data. Consider, for example, a data table `Patients`, containing an attribute `Phone`. Under the privacy policy that is in place, the `Phone` attribute is made available to charities for the purpose of solicitation on an opt-in basis, as is the primary key, `P#`. Suppose the query `SELECT Phone FROM Patients` is issued for this recipient and purpose. Using the table semantics model, this query can be rewritten to resolve the condition as follows, where the choice condition on `Phone` is used to perform cell-level enforcement, and the condition on `P#` is used for record filtering:

```
SELECT
CASE WHEN EXISTS
    (SELECT Phone_Choice
    FROM PatientChoices
    WHERE Patients.P# = PatientChoices.P#
    AND PatientChoices.Phone_Choice = 1)
THEN Phone ELSE null END
FROM Patients
```

```
WHERE EXISTS
    (SELECT ID_Choice
    FROM PatientChoices
    WHERE Patients.P# = PatientChoices.P#
    AND PatientChoices.ID_Choice = 1)
```

The basic modification algorithm is given in Figure 8.[6] Through a series of simple lookup queries to the privacy meta-data tables, the algorithm resolves the appropriate rules, and modifies the query appropriately. The given algorithm filters records in accordance with the table semantics model, but the filtering method for query semantics applies predicates similarly.

An optimization not reflected in the above pseudo-code is available when the original query includes a predicate on an indexed column. Consider for example the query `SELECT Phone, Name FROM Patients WHERE Phone = 222-2222` over a data table in which there is an index on `Phone` and `Name` is non-indexed. For simplicity, in this and subsequent query modification examples we refer to the predicate implementing condition "C3" for table `Patients` as C3, etc. We also disregard row filtering and translate the query to:

```
SELECT Phone, Name
FROM (SELECT CASE WHEN C3
    THEN Phone ELSE null END,
    CASE WHEN C5
    THEN Name ELSE null END
    FROM Patients) AS q1(Phone, Name)
WHERE q1.Phone = 222-2222
```

This query cannot use the index on `Phone` because the reference to `Phone` is embedded inside a case-statement. We fix this problem by pulling the indexed data attribute and the corresponding choice out to the predicate, where the index can more easily be used,

---

[6]The query translation techniques are described to simplify exposition, not in their optimized form. We assume that the queries are further rewritten by the query optimizer.

> **Modify_Query**
> **Input**: Query string Q to be modified, unique policy identifier PID, Purpose P, Recipient R
> **Output**: Query string Q', reflecting the privacy semantics of P and R under policy PID
> **Method**: For each table t referenced by query Q, (1) replace the reference to t with a sub-query that reconciles the semantics associated with each column in the table based on the policy and conditions, and (2) add a predicate that filters rows where at least one attribute of the primary key is forbidden. *GetPolicy* and *GetCondition* are functions of PID, P, R, t, and column c that query the privacy meta-data tables. *GetPolicy* resolves the privacy semantics of a column for the given purpose and recipient, and returns a value of "allowed", "prohibited", or "condition." *GetCondition* retrieves the appropriate conditional predicate. $Eval(condition, row)$ is a boolean function that evaluates a particular condition predicate over an individual row. We use bracket $<>$ notation to distinguish commands executed at query runtime from those executed at query modification time.
>
> $Q' = Q$
> **for all** Tables t referenced by Q **do**
> $C[\,] \leftarrow$ column list of t
>   **for** $i = 0$ to length of C **do**
>   **if** $GetPolicy(PID, P, R, t, C[i]) =$ allowed **then**
> $C'[i] \leftarrow C[i]$
>   **else if** $GetPolicy(PID, P, R, t, C[i]) =$ prohibited **then**
> $C'[i] \leftarrow null$
>   **else**
>   /* Replace with a column function that resolves the condition on a per-row basis */
> $condition \leftarrow GetCondition(PID, P, R, t, C[i])$
> $C'[i] \leftarrow$ $<$**if** $Eval(condition, row)$ **then** $C[i]$
>   **else** $null$ **endif**$>$
>   **end if**
>   **end for**
> $K[\,] \leftarrow$ the primary key columns of t
>   /* Define a predicate function *predicate* to filter individual rows based on the semantics of the primary key attributes */
> $predicate \leftarrow$ $<\neg(\exists k \in K$ such that $Policy(PID, P, R, t, k)$ is forbidden$) \land$
> $\neg(\exists k \in K$ such that $\neg Eval(GetCondition(PID, P, R, t, k), row))>$
>   Create selection subquery t' with projection list C'; Append predicate function *predicate* to t'
>   Replace reference to t in Q' with t'
> **end for**
> **return** Q'

Figure 8: Basic algorithm for modifying queries for privacy enforcement using table semantics.

but the meaning of the query is still consistent with the desired semantics[7]:

```
SELECT Phone, Name
FROM (SELECT Phone,
        CASE WHEN C5 THEN Name ELSE null END,
     FROM Patients) AS q1(Phone, Name)
WHERE q1.Phone = 222-2222 AND C3
```

4.2.2 Outer Join Modification

An alternative modification mechanism implements the Table Semantics and Query Semantics enforcement models using the left outer join and full outer join operators, respectively. Consider the query `SELECT Phone FROM Patients` from the previous section. This query can be rewritten as follows to reflect the table semantics enforcement model:

```
SELECT Phone FROM
(SELECT P# FROM Patients WHERE C4) AS t1(P#)
LEFT OUTER JOIN
    (SELECT P#, Phone
     FROM Patients
     WHERE C3) AS t2(P#, Phone)
ON t1.P# = t2.P#
```

---

[7]Thank you to Jerry Kiernan and Ramakrishnan Srikant for pointing out this fix. Note that this optimization also requires modification of the correlated sub-query in condition predicate C3, and it necessitates a dynamic rewriting mechanism which cannot be applied if we simply define a view for each purpose-recipient pair.

The modification algorithm for table semantics is a SQL implementation of the following relational algebra expression; we omit pseudo-code. Consider some query Q. Each table T referenced by Q contains some columns, $a_1 \ldots a_n$. Let k represent the primary key of T, and for simplicity assume that the primary key is comprised of just one column. We replace Q's reference to T with the following, where "⋈" denotes the left outer join operator:

$$[\sigma_{k=\text{``Allowed''}}(\Pi_k(T))] \bowtie_{\$1=\$1} [\sigma_{a_1=\text{``Allowed''}}(\Pi_{k,a_1}(T))]$$
$$\bowtie_{\$1=\$1} \ldots \bowtie_{\$1=\$1} [\sigma_{a_n=\text{``Allowed''}}(\Pi_{k,a_n}(T))]$$

We have a similar algorithm for query semantics. Consider a query Q which projects a set of columns from some set of tables. For each such table T, let $p_1 \ldots p_n$ denote the columns of T projected by Q, and let k be the primary key of T. Again assume the primary key contains just one column. We replace the reference to T by Q with the following, where "×" denotes the full outer join operator:

$$[\sigma_{p_1=\text{``Allowed''}}(\Pi_{k,p_1}(T))] \times_{\$1=\$1} [\sigma_{p_2=\text{``Allowed''}}(\Pi_{k,p_2}(T))]$$
$$\times_{\$1=\$1 \lor \$3=\$1} \ldots \times_{\$1=\$1 \lor \$3=\$1 \lor \ldots} [\sigma_{a_n=\text{``Allowed''}}(\Pi_{k,a_n}(T))]$$

The SeaView system took a similar approach in constructing cell-level access control, recovering multilevel relations from the underlying relations using the left outer join and union operators [18].

4.3 Optimized Implementation of Opt-In/Opt-Out Conditions

We have described how query modification can be used to handle general data-driven conditions. In this section, we describe how the database can provide high-performance support for the important special class of conditions that are expressed as simple opt-in or opt-out choices.

There are several possible approaches to storing choice values. The simplest approach, termed the *internal* design, appends additional columns to the data table (one per choice), where it stores the binary choices (1 denotes consent). While this approach may be satisfactory in some cases, it is preferable to avoid schema modification when adding privacy support to an existing database environment. For this reason, we explore options for storing choice values *externally*, in tables separate from the data tables.

The *external multiple table* design uses one table per choice. The schema of each external choice table consists of a foreign key that references table T. The table C_i corresponding to choice i contains one row for each row of T for which the data subject provided consent for the ith choice. Thus, if the data table T were extended with n choices to yield the table T', table $C_i = \pi_{key}(\sigma_{choice_i=1}(T'))$ for choice i.

These external choice tables can be used to enforce limited disclosure using either the table semantics or query semantics enforcement model. We describe in detail only the implementation of table semantics, but query semantics follows handily. Let V_C refer to a view of the choice tables corresponding to the columns in table T. Let *key* choices refer to those that involve a key column in T, and let *non-key* choices refer to those that do not. A row of T is not visible unless the subject has opted in for all key choices; therefore, the corresponding choice tables are combined using joins to produce the view V_C. A non-key choice determines whether the corresponding column is visible (assuming that the row is visible according to the key choices). This is enforced by using left-outer join to add each non-key choice table to V_C. V_C is then joined with T, and the following condition is tested by the modified query (using either modification algorithm): If the choice field (generated from the outer join of the corresponding external table) has a value other than *null*, then the condition is satisfied and the data returned; otherwise the data is forbidden and replaced with *null*.

The definition of view V_C is illustrated below for an example data table T with a key column K, a choice (C_0) on this column, and choice C_1 on non-key column A. For the multiple external table design, V_C is defined as:

```
SELECT C_0.key, C_1.key
FROM C_0 LEFT OUTER JOIN C_1 ON C_0.key = C_1.key
```

Alternatively, the *external single table* design replaces the multiple external tables with a single table C_C. This design essentially stores the choice columns described for the internal design in a separate table which can be joined with the data table. The schema contains the key for data table T and n choice columns. The basic query modification algorithm is similar to that of the internal design, though the data and choice tables must first be joined.

5 Performance Evaluation

We describe here the results of experiments studying the performance of our architecture and of query modification as a method of enforcing limited disclosure. The primary focus of these experiments is to measure the performance of enforcing unconditional policy rules and those containing opt-in and opt-out conditions, as these are by and large the most common cases. Our experiments are intended to address the following key questions:

- **Overhead of Privacy Enforcement** What is the overhead cost introduced by privacy checking? We address this question through an experiment that factors out the impact of choice selectivity, incurring the cost of checking privacy semantics, but gaining nothing from filtering prohibited tuples from the result set.
- **Scalability** We test the scalability of our modification mechanism in terms of database size and application selectivity. We vary both the percentage of users who elect to share their data for a particular purpose and recipient (*choice selectivity*)[8], and the percentage of the records selected by an issued query (*application selectivity*).
- **Impact of Filtering** In both the table and query semantics models, there are cases where tuples are filtered entirely from the result set of a query. We perform an experiment to show the performance gain due to this filtering.
- **Choice Storage** We compare the performance of the internal, external single, and external multiple choice table designs for storing choices.
- **Enforcement Model** We describe the performance implications of choosing between Table Semantics and Query Semantics models.
- **Modification Algorithm** We compare the performance of the case-statement and outer join modification algorithms for different opt-in and opt-out scenarios.

There are several distinct sources of performance cost in our architecture. There is some cost incurred by rewriting queries, but this cost is small, and constant in the number of columns. Moreover, this step is likely

---

[8] Except where otherwise noted, our experiments use cell-level enforcement, but make the simplifying assumption that access to all columns in the data table is based on a single opt-in/opt-out choice. This means that every record is either fully visible or fully invisible; however, for the case-statement rewrite mechanism we still perform cell-level enforcement by evaluating a case statement over each column.

Column	Description
Unique2 (int)	Primary key, Sequential order
Unique1 (int)	Candidate key, random order
Onepercent (int)	Values 0-99, random order
Tenpercent (int)	Values 0-9, random order
Twentypercent (int)	Values 0-4, random order
Fiftypercent (int)	Values 0-1, random order
stringu1 (32-byte str)	Unique character string
stringu2 (32-byte str)	Unique character string
Choice_0 (int)	Values 0-1 (1% = 1), indexed
Choice_1 (int)	Values 0-1 (10% = 1), indexed
Choice_2 (int)	Values 0-1 (50% = 1), indexed
Choice_3 (int)	Values 0-1 (90% = 1), indexed
Choice_4 (int)	Values 0-1 (100% = 1), indexed

Figure 9: Benchmark dataset and choice columns.

circumvented altogether for pre-compiled queries. For these reasons, we focus on the cost of query execution.

5.1 Experimental Setup

We evaluate performance using the synthetically-generated dataset described in Figure 9, which is based on the Wisconsin Benchmark [13]. All experiments were run using DB2 UDB 8.1. The operating system was Microsoft Windows 2000 Server, Service Pack 4. The hardware consisted of a dual-processor 1.8Ghz AMD machine with two GB of memory and four 80 GB IDE Western Digital hard drives. The data was spread across two of the disks. The buffer pool size was set to 50MB, the pre-fetch size was set to 64KB, and the level of optimization was set to 5. All other DB2 default settings were used.

To measure the cost of executing queries, we used the DB2batch utility. Each query was run 6 to 11 times, flushing the buffer pool, query cache, and system memory between unique queries. The results below give the average warm performance numbers for each query. With 95% confidence, the margin of error for the reported numbers is less than ±5%.

5.2 Experimental Results and Analysis

5.2.1 Overhead and Scalability

Our first set of experiments measures the overhead cost of performing privacy enforcement and the scalability of our algorithms to large databases. To measure this cost, we consider simple queries that select all records from the data table. We report the results for our table semantics enforcement model, but the trends are similar for query semantics. We consider the worst case scenario, where the choice selectivity is 100%. Here we incur all the cost of privacy processing, but we do not see the performance gains of filtering. The application selectivity was kept fixed at 100%.

Figure 10 shows the overhead cost of executing queries modified for privacy enforcement over tables containing 1, 5, 10, and 15 million records. The graph shows the total execution time for unmodified "SELECT *" queries, as well as queries modified to incorporate choices stored using the internal and external multiple approaches. The queries incorporating internal choices

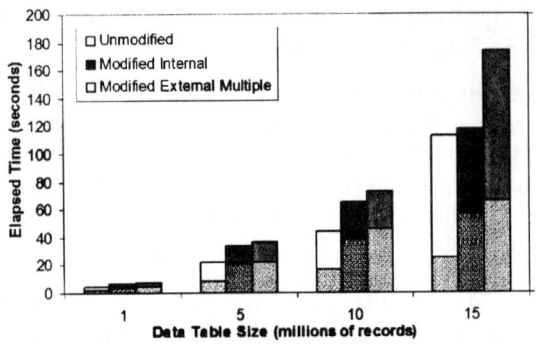

Figure 10: Scalability and performance of modified and unmodified queries, choice selectivity = 100% and application selectivity = 100%. CPU time is the bottom portion of each bar, and the full bar represents the total query execution time.

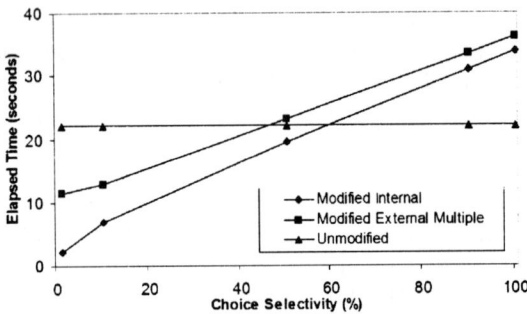

Figure 11: Comparing original and modified queries (5 million records, application selectivity = 100%)

incur the overhead of processing the additional case statement for each cell, and the external also incurs the cost of joining with the choice table. Note that the join is performed quickly as both the data and choice tables are clustered on the join key.

Because the figures show the warm numbers, the queries over the smaller tables can largely be processed from the buffer pool and system memory. In the case of the 15 million-record table, however, the query processing becomes I/O-bound. Thus, in the case of the former, the cost is dominated by the CPU time spent processing the case statements, whereas in the latter, the cost is dominated by I/O. Here the relative cost of performing privacy checking is reduced as the database size grows. We observe an increase in elapsed time for the external strategy and the 15 million-record table because of the extra I/O cost of reading the indexes on the data and choice tables.

Overall, the overhead cost of privacy-checking is small, particularly for the internal choice storage design. Because the cost of privacy-checking is largely CPU-based, privacy enforcement scales well to larger queries in which I/O dominates the cost.

5.2.2 Impact of Record Filtering

In cases with choice selectivity less than 100%, queries modified to reflect the table semantics or query se-

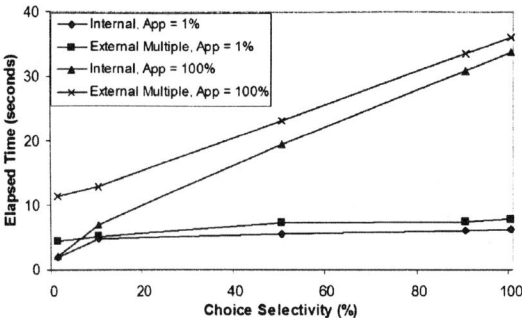

Figure 12: Comparing the internal and external multiple strategies (5 million records table)

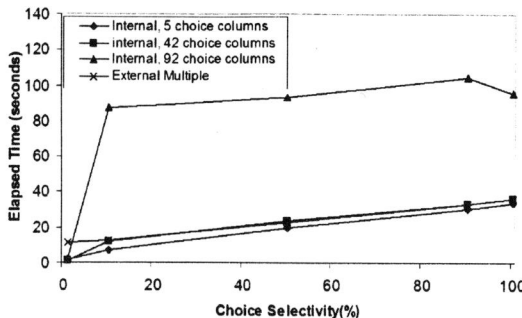

Figure 13: Comparing storage strategies for varying number of choice columns (5 million records, application selectivity = 100%)

mantics enforcement model perform significantly better that the original queries. Because the choice values are indexed, these queries avoid reading tuples that are filtered from the result set. Figure 11 compares the performance of original and rewritten queries over a table containing five million records. In our experiment, the queries with choice selectivity 1% and 10% used the index on the choice column; the others did not. The performance gain is considerable when the choice selectivity is 1% or 10%.

5.2.3 Comparing Choice Storage Methods

There are a number of performance issues to consider when choosing a choice storage design. In particular, when using an external design, it is necessary to join the data table with the choice table when processing a query. Using our original experimental dataset, we found that the internal approach performed better than the external multiple approach (Figure 12). However, on further investigation, we found that the cost of performing this join may be offset when the number of choice columns stored internally is large. In addition to database design considerations, this performance trade-off should be considered when choosing a choice storage design.

To measure this performance trade-off, we ran experiments varying the number of choices *stored*. The number of choices stored is distinct from the number of choices *enforced* because choices might be stored for a number of different purpose-recipient pairs, but all of these choices are not necessarily enforced for each query. Figure 13 compares the performance of queries enforcing a single choice modified using the internal and external multiple storage strategies. The application selectivity was held constant at 100%. In the case where the total number of stored choices is small, the internal strategy performs slightly better than the external strategy. However, as the number of stored choices grows, the internal strategy widens the data table, causing performance to suffer. The external approach performs similarly to an internal table of width 50. (This is equivalent to our standard benchmark data table, plus 42 choice columns appended internally.) For the tables of one hundred columns and with

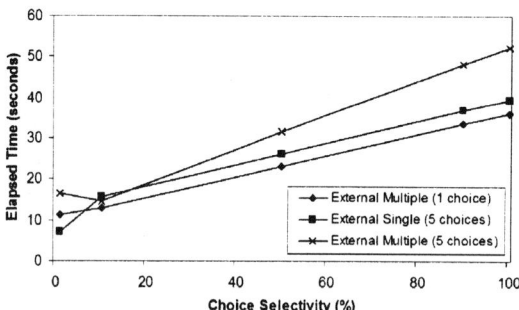

Figure 14: Comparing external multiple and external single for multiple choices (5 million records, application selectivity = 100%)

the internal strategy the queries become I/O bound and perform poorly in comparison.[9]

As the number of choices stored increases, performance of the internal strategy deteriorates. On the other hand, as the number of choices enforced increases, the number of joins required for the external multiple strategy grows, causing performance to suffer. In this case, we can substitute the external single strategy to obtain better performance. Figure 14 shows the results of an experiment varying the number of choices enforced; the number of stored choices was held constant at five. This represents a tradeoff because the choice table will likely contain more records than a single choice table from the external multiple design, and like the internal design, the single external table could potentially be wide. To partially address this concern, it is possible to create several external choice tables, grouped by choice values.

5.2.4 Performance Differences Among Enforcement Models

As we saw in Section 5.2.2, record filtering can have a significant impact on performance. For this reason, there is a clear performance distinction between

---

[9] It is also possible to encode choices as a bit vector in one (or a small number of) columns. We do not consider this option because in our implementation the necessary bitwise operations precluded the use of an index on the choice values.

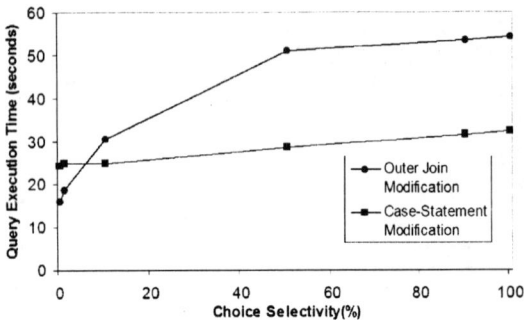

Figure 15: Comparing modification algorithms for a "sparse" choice space (internal choice storage, 5 million records, application selectivity = 100%)

the table semantics and query semantics enforcement models. In the table semantics model, a tuple is not filtered from the result set if the primary key is not prohibited, although all of the non-key columns might have been prohibited. Assume that the key columns of a table have independent privacy rules and that the primary key columns are allowed if any of the non-key columns of the record is allowed. In this case, it is convenient to think of the independent choice selectivities for all of the columns in the table combining to form the *effective choice selectivity*. If the table contains x columns, the effective selectivity can be determined by $1 - \prod_{i=1}^{x}(1-s_i)$, where s_i is the choice selectivity corresponding to column i. Thus fewer rows are filtered as the number of columns in the table increases.

In the query semantics model, the effective choice selectivity is determined by the selectivities of only those columns projected by the query. In many situations, therefore, using the query semantics model will likely lead to substantial performance gain.

5.2.5 Comparing Modification Algorithms

In most situations, our case-statement modification algorithm outperforms the outer-join algorithm. However, there are some situations where outer join does better, particularly when the space of choice values is "sparse", meaning few data subjects have provided consent for a particular column, but many of the records must still be fetched because of other data columns. In this case, the outer join algorithm is able to make use of the index over the "sparse" choice column. Thus, it avoids processing a case-statement over each of these cells.

Figure 15 shows the performance of the outer join algorithm compared to case-statements over a table with the following privacy semantics: `Unique2` can be unconditionally disclosed, but the rest of the columns are provided based on some choice, the selectivities of which are shown in the graph.

5.2.6 Summary of Performance Results

Through our experiments, we found that in general the cost of privacy checking is small and CPU intensive. For large I/O bound queries, the relative cost is minimal, so the cost of privacy enforcement scales well. Both semantic models, Table Semantics and Query Semantics, filter records from the result set in addition to performing cell-level enforcement. This filtering leads to substantial performance gains when the choice selectivity is small. We expect that in many situations, the query semantics model would filter more records than would the table semantics model, and for this reason, we expect that it would generally show superior performance.

There is a performance tradeoff to be considered when choosing between the internal, external multiple, and external single choice storage designs. When the number of stored choices is high, the performance of the internal design suffers because of an increase in I/O due to the increase in the width of the records. When the number of choices enforced is high, the performance of external multiple suffers because of the number of required joins. Frequently, the external single design serves as an effective compromise.

Finally, the case-statement modification algorithm almost always outperforms the outer-join mechanism, except in certain cases, such as sparse choice spaces.

6 Conclusion and Future Work

Limited disclosure is a vital component of a data privacy management system. We proposed a scalable architecture for enforcing limited disclosure rules and conditions at the database level, and we presented several models for cell-level limited disclosure enforcement in a relational database. Application-level solutions are unable to process arbitrary SQL queries efficiently. By pushing the enforcement down to the database, we gain improved performance and query power. This mechanism can be deployed without modifying legacy application code or existing database schemas. We showed that the performance overhead of database-level privacy enforcement is small, and often times the overhead is more than offset by the performance gains obtained through record filtering.

The work reported here has broader applicability than the Hippocratic databases. Specifically, our techniques can be used in any application requiring policy-driven fine-grained access and disclosure control.

There are several important extensions to this architecture that are areas of ongoing and future work. One such extension would allow us to assign versions to privacy policies. In this case, personal data would be permanently associated with the policy in place at the time of collection. The database would then be responsible for enforcing these multiple policies as queries are issued. Another such extension would provide granular privacy enforcement for data modification commands.

7 Acknowledgements

Our thanks to Jerry Kiernan for his invaluable help in implementing query modification and discussions about EPAL and cell-level enforcement semantics, to Ramakrishnan Srikant for discussions about choice storage and query modification, and to Ameet Kini and Diana Zhou for their work on the prototype implementation.

References

[1] US Department of Health and Human Services. http://www.hhs.gov/ocr/hipaa.

[2] Vignette Corportation. www.vignette.com.

[3] Nov. 2003. Personal communications with Sushil Jajodia.

[4] The Lowell database research self assessment, June 2003.

[5] N. Adam and J. Wortman. Security-control methods for statistical databases. *ACM Computing Surveys*, 21(4):515–556, Dec. 1989.

[6] R. Agrawal, J. Kiernan, R. Srikant, and Y. Xu. Hippocratic databases. In *VLDB*, Hong Kong, China, August 2002.

[7] P. Ashley, S. Hada, G. Karjoth, C. Powers, and M. Schunter. Enterprise privacy authorization language 1.2 (EPAL 1.2). W3C Member Submission, November 2003.

[8] P. Ashley and D. Moore. Enforcing privacy within an enterprise using IBM Tivoli Privacy Manager for e-business, May 2003.

[9] D. Bell and L. LaPadula. Secure computer systems: Unified exposition and multics interpretation. Technical Report ESD-TR-75-306, MITRE Corp., Bedford, Mass., March 1976.

[10] S. Castano, M. Fugini, G. Martella, and P. Samarati. *Database Security*. Addison Wesley, 1995.

[11] D. Chamberlin. *A Complete Guide to DB2 Universal Database*. Morgan Kauffmann, San Francisco, California, USA, 1998.

[12] L. Cranor, M. Langheinrich, M. Marchiori, M. Pressler-Marshall, and J. Reagle. The platform for privacy preferences 1.0 (P3P1.0) specification. W3C Recommendation, April 2002.

[13] D. DeWitt. The Wisconsin benchmark: Past, present, and future. In J. Gray, editor, *The Benchmark Handbook*. Morgan Kaufmann, 1993.

[14] P. Griffiths and B. Wade. An authorization mechanism for a relational database system. In *SIGMOD*, Washington, DC, June 1976.

[15] S. Jajodia and R. Sandhu. Polyinstantiation integrity in multilevel relations. In *IEEE Symposium on Security and Privacy*, May 1990.

[16] S. Jajodia and R. Sandhu. A novel decomposition of multilevel relations into single-level relations. In *IEEE Symposium on Security and Privacy*, Oakland, California, USA, May 1991.

[17] N. Kabra, R. Ramakrishan, and V. Ercegovac. The QUIQ Engine: A hybrid IR-DB system. In *ICDE*, Bangalore, India, March 2003.

[18] T. Lunt, D. Denning, R. Schell, M. Heckman, and W. Shockley. The SeaView security model. *IEEE Transactions on Software Eng.*, 16(6):593–607, June 1990.

[19] A. Nanda and D. Burleson. *Oracle Privacy Security Auditing*. Rampant, 2003.

[20] X. Qian and T. Lunt. Tuple-level vs. element-level classification. In *Database Security, VI: Status and Prospects. Results of the IFIP WG 11.3 Workshop on Database Security*, Vancouver, Canada, August 1992.

[21] R. Ramakrishnan and J. Gehrke. *Database Management Systems*. McGraw-Hill, 3rd edition, 2003.

[22] A. Sahuguet, R. Hull, D. Lieuwen, and M. Xiong. Enter once, share everywhere: User profile management in converged networks. In *CIDR*, Asilomar, CA, January 2003.

[23] R. Sandhu, E. Coyne, H. Feinstein, and C. Youman. Role-based access control models. *IEEE Computer*, 29(2):38–47, Feb. 1996.

[24] M. Stonebraker and E. Wong. Access control in a relational data base management system by query modification. In *ACM/CSC-ER*, 1974.

[25] G. Wiederhold, M. Bilello, V. Sarathy, and X. Qian. A security mediator for healthcare information. In *AMIA Conference*, Washington, DC, Oct. 1996.

[26] L. Willenborg and T. deWaal. *Elements of Statistical Disclosure Control*. Springer Verlag, 2000.

On Testing Satisfiability of Tree Pattern Queries

**Laks V.S. Lakshmanan, Ganesh Ramesh,
Hui (wendy) Wang, Zheng (Jessica) Zhao**
Department of Computer Science
University of British Columbia
{laks,ramesh,hwang,zzhao}@cs.ubc.ca

Abstract

XPath and XQuery (which includes XPath as a sublanguage) are the major query languages for XML. An important issue arising in efficient evaluation of queries expressed in these languages is *satisfiability*, i.e., whether there exists a database, consistent with the schema if one is available, on which the query has a non-empty answer. Our experience shows satisfiability check can effect substantial savings in query evaluation.

We systematically study satisfiability of tree pattern queries (which capture a useful fragment of XPath) together with additional constraints, with or without a schema. We identify cases in which this problem can be solved in polynomial time and develop novel efficient algorithms for this purpose. We also show that in several cases, the problem is NP-complete. We ran a comprehensive set of experiments to verify the utility of satisfiability check as a preprocessing step in query processing. Our results show that this check takes a negligible fraction of the time needed for processing the query while often yielding substantial savings.

1 Introduction

With XML becoming the standard for data exchange, substantial work has been done on XML storage, and query processing and optimization [17, 6, 19, 7, 15, 1, 18, 12, 23, 13]. However, relatively little work has been done on detecting whether a given query is *satisfiable*, i.e., whether there is any database satisfying the query. This is an important problem for the following reasons. (1) Formulating queries against XML databases can be more challenging than for relational databases. As a preview, we will show by example, how *very similar queries can greatly vary in terms of satisfiability*. Indeed, even in the context of relational databases, Levy et al. [8] studied satisfiability for various fragments of the datalog query language and established complexity and decidability results. Hidders [5] is the only work on XPath satisfiability we are aware of. A detailed comparison with our work appears in Section 6. (2) XML is intended to cater for situations where no a priori schema is available for data. Querying an XML database in the absence of any schema knowledge can be tricky. The interaction between various structural constraints, that restrict structural relationships among elements, and value-based constraints, that constrain the contents of elements or their attribute values, can be intricate. (3) Even when a schema is known, getting the query right can still be non-trivial for the user. For, the schema imposes structural constraints on its own which tend to interact with structural and value-based constraints in the query in subtle ways and may make the query unsatisfiable. Our experience shows that checking satisfiability of queries can pay substantial dividends in saving considerable time in query evaluation, while adding a negligible overhead to the overall query evaluation. Besides, given the considerable similarity between a satisfiable query and an unsatisfiable one, it would be useful to have the system assist the user in getting their queries right. Satisfiability testing is a necessary first step in building any such tool. This was the motivation behind our work. Next, we shall illustrate these points with examples.

XQuery [3] is the de facto standard query language for XML and includes XPath [3] as a sublanguage. Both these languages are based on a basic paradigm of finding bindings of variables by matching tree patterns against a database. Benedikt et al. [9] study the expressive power of tree pattern queries in relation to XPath and existential first-order logic. E.g., consider the XPath expression //a[/b//d = /c//d]. It corresponds to the tree pattern query (TPQ) Q_4 in Figure 1 (ignore dashed lines for now). Single (double) lines represent parent-child (ancestor-descendant) relationship between nodes.[1] As another example, consider the XQuery statement:

```
FOR    $a IN document(``doc.xml'')//a,
```

Permission to copy without fee all or part of this material is granted provided that the copies are not made or distributed for direct commercial advantage, the VLDB copyright notice and the title of the publication and its date appear, and notice is given that copying is by permission of the Very Large Data Base Endowment. To copy otherwise, or to republish, requires a fee and/or special permission from the Endowment.

**Proceedings of the 30th VLDB Conference,
Toronto, Canada, 2004**

[1]TPQs are formally defined in Section 2.

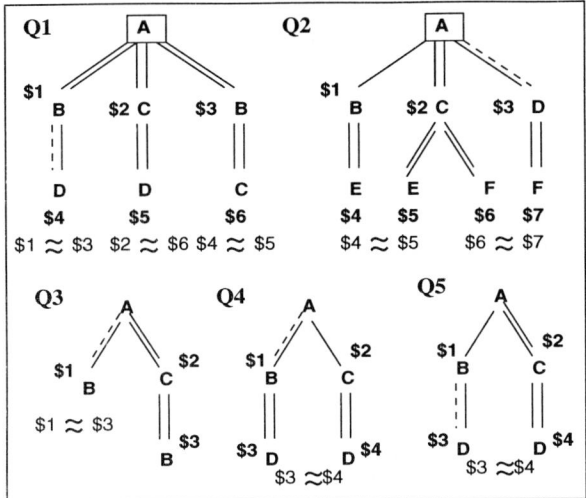

Figure 1: Examples in the Absence of Schema

```
      $e IN $a/b//e, $f IN $a/d//f,
      $c IN $a//c, $e1 IN $c//e, $f1 IN $c//f
WHERE $e = $e1 AND $f = $f1
RETURN{$a}
```

This corresponds to the TPQ Q_2 in Figure 1. Indeed, each TPQ in the figure corresponds to an XPath expression, or an XQuery query. Each query is unsatisfiable, but when the dashed lines are added (i.e., when certain parent-child relationships are relaxed to ancestor-descendant), the queries become satisfiable. We explain this below.

First, consider Q_3. It asks for A nodes that have a node B that is both a child and is a descendant via an intermediate node C. This is clearly unsatisfiable in any tree. However, relaxing the child to descendant makes it satisfiable. Next, consider Q_4, which asks for A nodes which have a descendant D via a B child as well as via a C child. Since each element has a unique tag, this is unsatisfiable. Again, relaxing one of the child constraints to descendant renders the query satisfiable. Q_5 is unsatisfiable, but for a subtler reason. If the two D nodes are the same, the C descendant of A must be a descendant of the B child. The descendant D of the C node must thus be at a distance 3 or more whereas the D child of B is at a distance 2 from A, which is impossible. Once again, relaxing any of the child constraints to descendant renders the query satisfiable.

Next, consider Q_2. The constraint that the two E leaves must be identical requires nodes A, B, C and the two E nodes to lie on the same (root-to-leaf) path. Similarly, the identity of the two F nodes requires nodes A, B, C and the two F nodes to lie on the same path. This is impossible, since C, having a different tag than the two children of A, is forced to be a descendant of both, whereas B and D cannot lie on the same path. Relaxing the child constraint on A, D, e.g., to descendant makes the query satisfiable. Finally, consider Q_1. All edges except on B, D are descendant constraints. The query is unsatisfiable because the two B nodes are the same node, say v, and v has a child D, which is a descendant of a descendant C node of v. A contradiction arises because of the inconsistency in the required distance between v and the D node. Again, relaxing the only child constraint in the query to descendant renders it satisfiable. A general remark about all queries is instead of relaxing a child constraint, dropping any other constraint in the query (e.g., identity of two nodes) also renders it satisfiable.

The examples show that reasoning about satisfiability is interesting and non-trivial. We make the following contributions in this paper.

- Reasoning about satisfiability can be reduced to making inferences about relationships between nodes and/or their contents or attribute values. We develop inference rules for deducing additional structural relationships between query nodes from those stated in the query (Sections 3 and 4).

- We propose a *constraint graph* for a tree pattern query. It consists of a structural part that captures structural constraints in the query and a value-based part that captures value-based constraints. Using our inference rules, we develop a *chase procedure* for closing the constraint graph w.r.t. all constraints implied by given ones. We show the chase is complete when the query contains no wildcards: a query is satisfiable iff its constraint graph, when chased, does not result in any violations, in a precisely defined sense. Our inference rules and chase are developed for both when no schema is known and when a schema is given (Sections 3 and 4).

- We identify conditions under which testing satisfiability is NP-complete (Sections 3.3 and 4.2.1) and when it can be done in polynomial time. For the latter cases, we develop efficient algorithms for satisfiability testing (Sections 3.2 and 4.2).

- Finally, we ran a comprehensive set of experiments on a synthetically generated data set on several well-known DTDs including `auction.dtd` and `protein.dtd`, tested various kinds of satisfiable and unsatisfiable queries, and measured both the additional overhead incurred on satisfiable queries and the amount of savings on unsatisfiable queries. While the savings are more than an order of magnitude, our results show that the overhead is a small fraction of overall query evaluation time (Section 5).

Some basic definitions and a problem statement are given in Section 2. Related work appears in Section 6, while Section 7 summarizes the paper and discusses future work.

2 Background and Problems Studied

A(n XML) *database* is a finite rooted ordered tree $D = (\mathcal{N}, \mathcal{E}, r, \lambda)$, where $\mathcal{N}$ represents element nodes, $\mathcal{E}$ represents parent-child relationship, λ, the labeling function, assigns a tag with each node, and r is the root. Associated with each node is a set of attribute-value pairs. In this paper, we do not consider order any further. Fig. 2(a) shows an example database D.

Tree pattern queries, introduced in [1], capture a useful fragment of XPath. A *tree pattern query* (TPQ) is a triple Q = (V, E, F), where (V, E) is a rooted tree, with nodes V labeled by variables, and with E = $E_c \cup E_d$ consisting of two kinds of edges, called pc-(E_c) and ad-edges (E_d), corresponding to the child and descendant axes of XPath. A distinguished node in V (shown boxed in Figure 1)[2] corresponds to the answer element. F is a conjunction of tag constraints (TCs), value-based constraints (VBCs), and node identity constraints (NICs). TCs are of the form $x.tag = t$, where t is a tag name. VBCs include selection constraints $x.val$ relop c, $x.attr$ relop c, and join constraints $x.attr$ relop $y.attr'$, and $x.val$ relop $y.val$, where relop $\in \{=, \neq, >, \leq, \geq, <\}$, attr, attr' are attributes, val represents content, and c is a constant. With a few clearly identified exceptions, we assume no disjunctions appear in VBCs, throughout the paper. When we do allow disjunctions, they are confined to selection conditions. NICs are x idop y, where idop $\in \{\approx, \not\approx\}$.[3] We adopt the term structural constraints to refer to NICs and predicates of the form $pc(\$x, \$y)$, $ad(\$x, \$y)$, representing pc- and ad-edges. Figure 2(b) shows an example TPQ Q. An example use of disjunction in selection constraints is the constraint $3.type = $'paperback'$\lor$ $3.type = $'spiralbound' on node $3 in place of the existing constraint there.

Answers for TPQs are formalized using matchings. A *matching* of a TPQ Q to a database D is a function h : Q→D that maps nodes of Q to nodes of D such that: (i) structural relationships are preserved – whenever $(x, y) \in E_c$ $h(y)$ is a child of $h(x)$ in D and whenever $(x, y) \in E_d$, there is a path from $h(x)$ to $h(y)$ in D; and (ii) the formula F is satisfied. We say that a database D *satisfies* a query Q provided there is a matching h : Q→D. A matching of the query Q in Figure 2(b) to the database D of Figure 2(a) is schematically illustrated with numbers besides database nodes. A query Q is *satisfiable* provided there is a database D that satisfies Q.

For readability, whenever the tag constraint $x.tag = t$ appears in a TPQ Q = (V, E, F), we drop that constraint from the formula part F, and write t right next to node $x in Q. If node $x is not tagged, we associate a wildcard '*' next to node $x in Q. This is illustrated for query Q in Figure 2(b)-(c). This corresponds to the XPath expression /bib[//*/text()='Raymond Smullyan']/*[@type=paperback]/author[text()='B.Russel']. If the constraint $3.type $\neq$ paperback were replaced by $3.type = paperback in Q, database D in Figure 2(a) wouldn't satisfy it, as no matching

---
[2] Since distinguished nodes do not play any role in satisfiability, we do not consider them further.
[3] The constraints $x \approx $y and $x \not\approx $y say nodes $x and $y are (not) the same.

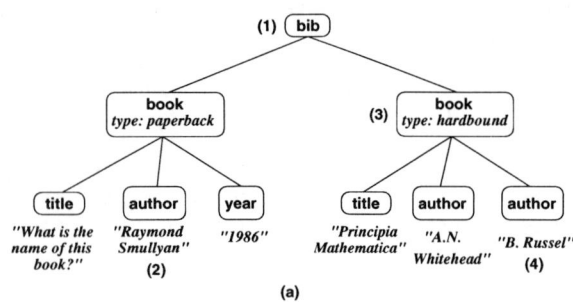

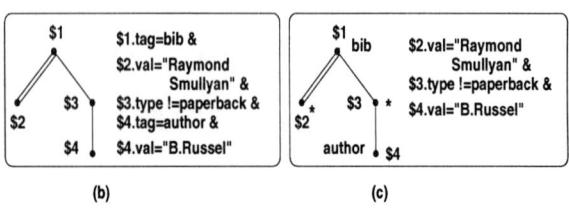

Figure 2: An example: (a) database D and: (b) TPQ Q, (c) Q made more readable.

is possible. In the sequel, we write element tags or wildcards next to query nodes as appropriate. Thus, a query Q is said to have wildcards if one or more nodes do not have their tags constrained by a TC. Otherwise it *wildcard-free*. Q is *join-free* if it contains no join constraints and no NICs.

We abstract the schema of a database (in our paper, we only consider DTDs) as a graph with nodes corresponding to tags and edges labeled by one of the quantifiers '?, 1, *, +' with their standard meaning of 'optional', 'one', 'zero or more', and 'one or more' respectively. An example of a schema graph appears in Figure 8. It says, e.g., that categories consists of category elements, each of which has a unique description.

Problems Studied: We consider testing satisfiability of various classes of TPQs (with/without VBCs, with/without disjunction in VBCs, with/without join and node identity constraints, with/without wildcards) both in the absence of a schema and in the presence of a schema without disjunction (i.e., choice) and cycles.

3 Satisfiability without Schema

Given a TPQ Q, determining whether Q is satisfiable in the absence of a schema, solely depends on the structural constraints and any VBCs present in Q. In addition, it may be necessary to consider disjunctions and wildcards in the query, if present. We systematically study the problem for various TPQ classes.

3.1 Join-free TPQs with Wildcards

Recall that join-free TPQs do not contain join or node identity constraints. Note that Q may still involve value-based selection constraints. In the special case that Q has no VBCs, it is always satisfiable. Indeed, a satisfying instance D for Q can be constructed as follows. D is a tree isomorphic to the query tree Q except all edges are pc-edges. For every query node that is tagged, the corresponding node in D has the same tag; if the query node is a wildcard, the corresponding node in D may have an arbitrary tag. It is easy to see that D always satisfies Q.

Suppose $Q = (V, E, F)$ does contain VBCs. Since it does not contain any join constraints, every VBC constrains a unique node in Q. Let F_x be the maximal subformula of F that constrains node x. To verify that Q is satisfiable, it then suffices to verify if F_x is satisfiable for each node x. The following proposition summarizes the situation for join-free TPQs.

Proposition 3.1 *For a join-free tree pattern query Q, possibly containing wildcards, the following holds:*

1. *If Q contains no VBCs associated with any node, then Q is satisfiable.*

2. *If Q contains value-based selection constraints (but is join-free), then Q is satisfiable iff for every node, the associated set of VBCs is consistent.* ∎

The complexity of verifying satisfiability thus depends on the kinds of formulas F_x constraining each node x. If no disjunction occurs, consistency of F_x and hence of F can be verified in polynomial time using the sound and complete axiom system given in [21]. If VBCs F_x associated with a node x can involve arbitrary disjunctions, testing consistency of F_x becomes equivalent to SAT and hence is NP-complete. If F_x is a disjunction of conjunctions, then the method proposed in [21] can be easily extended to yield a polynomial time test for satisfiability of Q.

3.2 Wildcard-free TPQs with Joins

Let Q be a TPQ containing join and/or node identity constraints, but no wildcards and no disjunction. We relax the latter restrictions in Section 3.3. The presence of join and node identity constraints interacts in an intricate way with the structural constraints. E.g., the constraint $x \approx y$ implies any ancestors of x and y in the query Q must lie on the same path in a satisfying database. Below, we separate the reasoning into structure and value-based parts and pin down exactly how they handshake.

3.2.1 Reasoning about Structure

In this section, we consider queries with just NICs. The effect of VBCs of the form $x.val$ relop $y.val$ etc. are addressed in Section 3.2.2. Some issues involved in reasoning about satisfiability are illustrated by the following example.

Example 3.1 [Structural reasoning]
Consider the query in Figure 3, which is identical to query Q2 in Figure 1. As discussed in the introduction, it is unsatisfiable. The reasoning involves inferring that node pairs $2 and $4 must lie on the same root-to-leaf path as well as that they must be cousins of each other, leading to a contradiction. ∎

The example illustrates several points. **1.** Testing satisfiability involves inferring relationships between pairs of nodes based on structural constraints stated in the query. Thus, we need inference rules. **2.** Some of the intermediate relationships inferred above cannot be directly represented in the language of TPQs (e.g., "x and y must lie on the same path"). Thus, the language is not "closed" w.r.t. satisfiability reasoning. We could represent the new relationships by permitting disjunction in structure. E.g., x and y lie on the same path iff $(x \approx y \vee ad(x,y) \vee ad(y,x))$. However, permitting arbitrary disjunctions can lead to high complexity. We show that all we need to do is add the following predicates: $sad(x,y)$ meaning $x \approx y$ or $ad(x,y)$, $OTSP(x,y)$ meaning $sad(x,y)$ or $ad(y,x)$, $COUS(x,y)$ meaning $\neg OTSP(x,y)$. Note that the predicates $OTSP, COUS, \approx, \not\approx$ are symmetric while pc, ad, sad are not. This expanded set of predicates is indeed closed w.r.t. satisfiability reasoning.

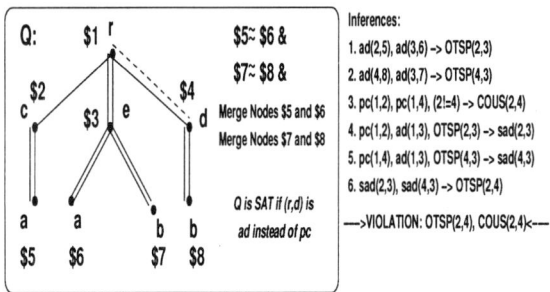

Figure 3: Inferring Structural Predicates

Determining satisfiability of a query works as follows. First, we use inference rules to obtain the closure of structural predicates. Then, we check the resulting set of predicates for violations (defined below). The query is satisfiable iff the set of predicates is violation-free (consistent).

Structural Constraint Graph: In order to efficiently implement a procedure for satisfiability checking, we construct a *(structural) constraint graph* G_Q for the query Q as follows. G_Q contains one node for each query node. For each predicate $\phi(x,y)$ in Q, G_Q contains a directed edge labeled ϕ from x to y. For symmetric predicates, the edge is bidirected.

Inference Rules and Chase: New structural predicates are inferred from existing ones in the query by using a set of *inference rules*. An inference rule is of the form $P_1, \ldots P_k \to R$ and says "if predicates $P_1, \ldots, P_k$ are true, then R is true". Inference rules are used for achieving closure of structural predicates and thus for catching inconsistencies caused by conflicting pairs of predicates. For the structural predicates, we have developed a total of 22 inference rules.[4] For brevity, we show only some interesting rules in Figure 4 and explain some selected ones. The complete details can be found in [11]. We explain three of the rules. Rule **2** says whenever x lies on the same path as each of a pair of cousins y and z, then x must be their ancestor[5]. Rule **3** says two unequal nodes x, y at an equal distance from a node z must be cousins. The equal distance implies the paths from z to x and y must involve only pc-edges. Rule **7** says whenever x and y are on the same path, x is a child of an ancestor of y, then y must be a self or descendant of x, i.e., $sad(x,y)$. The *chase procedure* is to simply apply the inference rules until no new inferences are possible. If a violation, defined next, is detected at any point, we can exit from chase early. We will discuss a more efficient implementation of chase shortly.

1. $sad(x,z), sad(y,z) \rightarrow OTSP(x,y)$
2. $OTSP(x,y), OTSP(x,z), COUS(y,z) \rightarrow ad(x,y)$
3. $x \not\approx y \rightarrow COUS(x,y)$, whenever x, y are at the same distance from their least common query ancestor z.
4. $pc(x,z), pc(y,z) \rightarrow x \approx y$.
5. $pc(z,x), pc(z,y), OTSP(x,y) \rightarrow x \approx y$.
6. $ad(x,z), pc(y,z) \rightarrow sad(x,y)$.
7. $pc(z,x), ad(z,y), OTSP(x,y) \rightarrow sad(x,y)$.

Figure 4: Selected Inference Rules (no schema).

Violations: A *violation* is a pair of conflicting predicates between a pair of nodes. Examples of conflicting pairs of predicates are $x \approx y, x \not\approx y$; $ad(x,y), sad(y,x)$; and $OTSP(x,y), COUS(x,y)$. Indeed, these three pairs capture all possible violations, since other violations are subsumed by them. For instance, $pc(x,y)$ conflicts with $COUS(x,y)$. But since $pc(x,y)$ implies $OTSP(x,y)$ this conflict is covered by the pair $OTSP(x,y), COUS(x,y)$. Violations make the query unsatisfiable.

Figure 3 demonstrates the chase as logical inferences. At the end of step 6, we find a violation because of the conflicting predicates OTSP() and COUS(). To implement the chase more efficiently, we employ the constraint graph. Specifically, given a TPQ Q, we initialize its constraint graph CG_Q. For every pair of nodes i, j, whenever their tags are different, we add a bidirected edge labeled $\not\approx$ between i and j. We apply the inference rules repeatedly. Whenever predicate p(i, j) is derived, add a (directed) edge from i to j labeled p if p is one of ad, sad and make it bidirected if p is one of $\not\approx$, OTSP, COUS. When $i \approx j$ is derived, we merge nodes i and j. We repeat until no new inferences are made or a violation is detected. A constraint graph, with chase applied on it, is a *chased* constraint graph. Here is an example. The query of Figure 3 becomes satisfiable if the pc-edge from $1 to $4 is changed to an ad-edge (shown dotted in the figure). Figure 5(a) shows the constraint graph

[4]Including "trivial" ones such as $pc(x,y) \rightarrow ad(x,y)$.
[5]Note that the rule is symmetric

for this query and Figure 5(c) shows the chased constraint graph. Figure 5(b) shows a satisfying instance of the query.

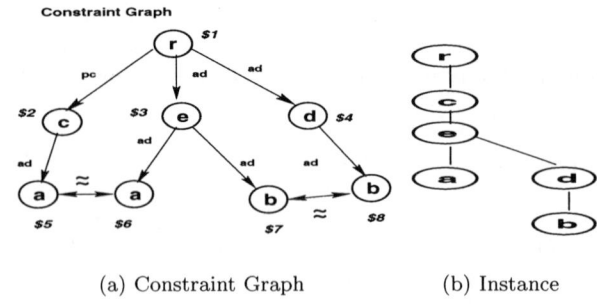

(a) Constraint Graph   (b) Instance

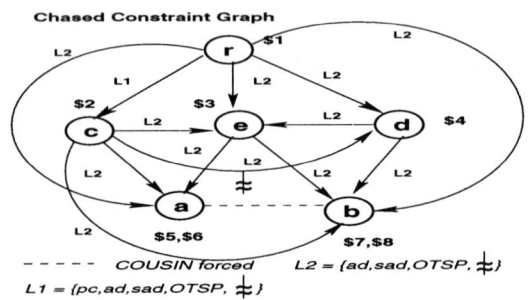

(c) Chased Constraint Graph

Figure 5: Determining Satisfiability

The main result of this section is the following:

Theorem 3.1 (Completeness of Chase): Let Q be a tree pattern query containing node identity constraints but no wildcards. It is satisfiable iff the chased constraint graph of Q is violation-free. ∎

We refer the reader to [11] for the proof. Here, we give the key intuition. The "If" direction is easy to see since every inference rule is sound and therefore preserves satisfiability. For the "Only If" direction, suppose G is the chased constraint graph of query Q and G is violation-free. We construct a satisfying tree instance as follows.

```
Procedure FastChase(CGraph CG)
   find all ≈-classes of nodes;
   for each equivalence class E, find the maximal
      OTSP set as ⋃_{x∈E} pred(x)
      in G, where pred(x) is the set of
      predecessors of x in G;
   for all x,y s.t. x≉y ∈ G, apply the
      distance rule (#3) to derive COUS(x,y);
      propagate COUS() downward using inference rules;
      if COUS(x,y) is derived, add x≉y to G;
      if a violation is found return ''unsatisfiable'';
      if x≈y is derived, merge x and y;
   while there is no change {
      apply rules for inferring ≈, ad, sad;
      if nodes are equated, merge them;
      if a violation is found return ''unsatisfiable''; }
   return true;
```

Figure 6: Apply Chase in CGraph

Call a set S of nodes in Q an OTSP set provided $\forall x, y \in S: OTSP(x, y) \in G$. OTSP sets are upward closed, i.e., when $x \in S$, and $sad(y, x) \in G$, then $y \in S$. Henceforth, we consider maximal OTSP sets, i.e., OTSP sets whose proper supersets are not OTSP sets. The idea is to force relationships between pairs of nodes until G becomes a complete set, i.e., $\forall$ nodes $x, y \in G$ and for any predicate p, either $p(x, y)$ or $\neg p(x, y)$ holds in G. In particular, all nodes in a maximal OTSP sets are totally ordered using a topological sort. Different maximal OTSP sets are incorporated in different branches of the tree.

We next briefly comment on an efficient implementation of the chase. A naive implementation would take time $O(n^5)$, where n is the number of nodes in the query. This is because each rule involves 3 nodes and there are $O(n^2)$ iterations possible in the worst case before no new inferences are made. A more efficient implementation is suggested in Figure 6. The idea is to exploit the upward closure (downward closure) of OTSP (COUS) predicate. It can be shown that maximal OTSP sets can be computed "statically" based on the constraints given in the query. Similarly, we can infer COUS edges efficiently. Inference rules for the remaining predicates need to be applied repeatedly until either a violation is found or no new inferences are possible. The worst-case complexity of this algorithm remains the same. However, in practice it is much better than the naive algorithm.

3.2.2 Interaction with VBCs

Up to this point, we have not considered VBCs. Even when a query is satisfiable w.r.t. its structural constraints, the VBCs may render it unsatisfiable. As mentioned earlier, consistency of a conjunction of VBCs can be checked in polynomial time using the sound and complete axiom system provided in [21]. The checking algorithm can be implemented efficiently using a separate *value-based constraint graph* using ideas similar to the structural constraint graph. The details are similar and are omitted. What about interactions between structural constraints and VBCs? It can be shown that the interaction happens via two main links: (i) The structural constraints may imply $x \approx y$ for nodes x, y. All VBCs applicable to x are applicable to y. This is automatically captured by merging x and y. (ii) VBCs can imply $x \not\approx y$ for nodes x, y. This can in turn trigger inferences of structural predicates.

The procedure for testing satisfiability of a query Q with structural constraints and VBCs is then as follows: (i) Chase the VBCs (using a separate value-based constraint graph); if any violation is found return "unsatisfiable". (ii) Construct the (structural) constraint graph G of Q; propagate all constraints $x \not\approx y$ derived from VBC chase to G and chase it; (iii) Q is satisfiable iff the chase terminates with no violation.

We can show:

Theorem 3.2 (TPQs with VBCs): Let Q be a tree pattern query with structural constraints and

Disjunction	NICs/join constraints	Wildcards	Complexity
		X	PTIME
	X		PTIME
X	X		NP-Complete
	X	X	NP-complete

Figure 7: Complexity of checking Satisfiability without Schema

VBCs and no wildcards. Then testing satisfiability of Q can be done in polynomial time using the procedure above. ∎

3.3 TPQs with Wildcards, Joins, and Disjunction

We relax the restrictions on TPQs w.r.t. wildcards and disjunctions in this section. The first observation is that when wildcards are allowed, satisfiability testing becomes NP-complete, even when there is no disjunction. This follows from the following result, proved by Hidders [5].

Theorem 3.3 ([5]): Suppose Q is a tree pattern query with wildcards and only $\approx$ constraints, where the query uses only pc- and sad-edges. Then testing whether Q is satisfiable is NP-complete. ∎

While Hidders' result is couched in terms of a syntactically different language, the fragment for which this result applies corresponds to tree pattern queries with wildcards and $\approx$ constraints, where the entire query reduces to a single maximal OTSP set. It is trivial to adapt his proof for tree pattern queries with regular pc- and ad-edges.

Next, what if we disallow wildcards but allow disjunction in VBCs. The problem again becomes NP-complete.

Theorem 3.4 (TPQs with disjunction): Let Q be a tree pattern query containing VBCs, with disjunction allowed in selection constraints associated with nodes. Then testing satisfiability of Q is NP-complete. ∎

The proof is by reduction from 3SAT, and only makes use of pc-edges, disjunctive value-based selection constraints, and $\not\approx$ constraints. It continues to hold when $\not\approx$ constraints are replaced by join constraints.

The complexity results for the schemaless case are summarized in Figure 7.

4 Satisfiability in the Presence of Acyclic Schema

A schema provides additional knowledge for inferring structural predicates in a query. E.g, consider the schema and query Q4 in Figure 8. It is not satisfiable. The query Q4 asks for *text* which is both a child of *description* and a descendent of *parlist*, but the schema does not permit this. However, if *text* is changed to be a descendent of *parlist*, Q4 becomes satisfiable. Suppose Q4 is accordingly changed. In the absence of schema, the best we can conclude about *description* and *text* then is that they must lie *on the same path* but using the schema, we can conclude that *description* is the *ancestor of text*. A schema (auction.dtd) together with a set of unsatisfiable queries as well as minor variants which are satisfiable are given in Figure 8. The reader is encouraged to reason about their satisfiability.

In the rest of this section, we consider acyclic (DAG) schema. Extensions to cyclic schemas will appear in the full paper.

4.1 TPQs without VBCs

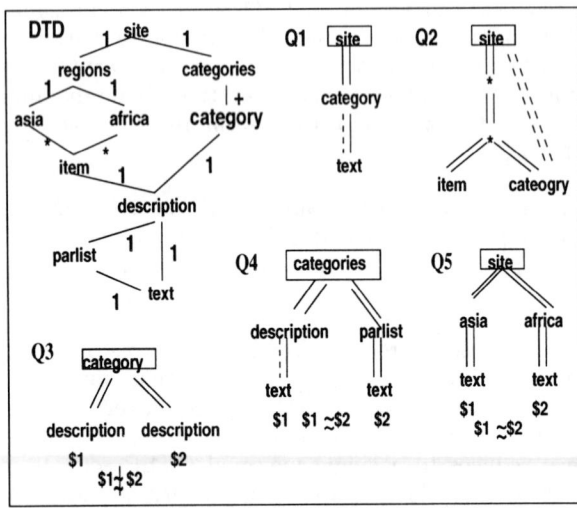

Figure 8: Examples in the Presence of Schema

When no VBCs are present, for a query to be satisfiable with respect to a schema, its structural constraints need to be consistent with the schema. An *embedding* of a query into a schema, defined below, precisely captures this consistency.

Definition 4.1 [Embedding] An *embedding* of a query Q into a schema Δ is a function $f : Q \to \Delta$ satisfying the following conditions: (i) f maps each tagged node to a node with the same tag; (ii) whenever (x,y) is a pc-edge (ad-edge) in Q, there is an edge (path) from $f(x)$ to $f(y)$ in Δ. ∎

Consider query Q4 in Figure 8, but without the join condition. The reader can verify the existence of an embedding into the schema in Figure 8. In the absence of wildcards, the testing the existence of an embedding reduces to testing for each edge (x,y) in Q with $tag(x) = a, tag(y) = b$ (say), whether an edge or path from a to b exists in Δ, which can be easily tested.

The following result is straightforward:

Proposition 4.1 *Let Δ be a schema and let Q be a tree pattern query with no wildcards or VBCs. Then Q is satisfiable with respect to Δ iff there is an embedding f from Q into Δ.* ∎

4.1.1 With Wildcards

Consider the examples in Figure 9. Query Q1 is not satisfiable because no valid instance of the schema can have a path from a to e of length 2. On the other hand, query Q2 is satisfiable because there exists a valid instance of the schema which has a path of length at least 2 from a to e. For each of the queries, the possible schema nodes it could embed to are illustrated as a set, right next to the node in Figure 9. For the node $3 in query Q1, the set of schema nodes it can embed to is empty. Note that if the query contains *only* wildcard nodes, checking satisfiability trivially reduces to checking if the schema is of a given depth.

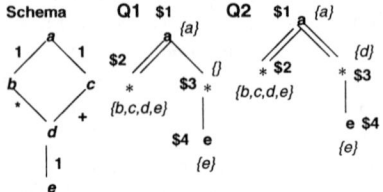

Figure 9: Queries with Wildcards

When wildcards are present, semantically we can assign any tags to the wildcards and check for the existence of an embedding. This approach takes exponential time. What we need is merely confirm the existence of an embedding. This can be accomplished by associating with each query node x a label set L(x). For each tagged node x, we initialize L(x) to be the unique schema node with that tag. For a wildcard node x, we initialize L(x) to be the set of all tags in the schema Δ. We next prune L(x) as follows. First, in a bottom-up phase, we mark all leaves. Whenever all children $y_1, ..., y_k$ of a node x are marked, we delete a tag t from L(x) provided for some y_i, $r(x, y_i)$ holds according to the query Q, where r is pc or ad, but there is no tag $u \in L(y_i)$ such that Δ contains an edge or path to verify $r(t, u)$. Then mark node x. If at any stage any label set becomes empty, we know the query is unsatisfiable. Once the root is marked, we do a top-down sweep as follows. First unmark the root. For any node x whose parent y is unmarked, delete from L(x) any tag t if there is no tag $u \in L(y)$ such that $r(y, x)$ according to Q, and Δ contains an edge or path verifying this. Then unmark x. The procedure terminates when an empty label set is detected or when all nodes are unmarked. The pseudocode for this algorithm is shown in Figure 10. We can show:

Theorem 4.1 (Labeling) : Let Q be a TPQ containing wildcards but no VBCs and no NICs. Then Q is satisfiable with respect to a schema Δ iff for each $x \in Q$, $L(x) \neq \emptyset$, where L(x) is the set of schema labels computed by the procedure in Figure 10. ∎

By precomputing reachability on Δ, given t, t', we can test if Δ verifies $r(t, t')$, where $r \in \{pc, ad\}$, in constant time. We visit each query node and each query edge at most twice. During each visit, we may

```
CheckLabel(Q,△)
For each node x tagged t in Q, L(x) = {t}
For each wildcard leaf l in Q, L(l) = {tags of △}
Mark all leaf nodes.   Let r ∈ {pc, ad}
Repeat { // Bottom-up Phase
  ∀ nodes x ∈ Q whose children y_1,...y_k are all marked
    For each child y_i of x {
      Initialize S_i = {};
      For each u ∈ L(y_i) {
        S_i = S_i ∪ {t' | r(t', u) ∈ △}; }
      L(x) = ∩_{i=1}^{k} S_i; }
    Mark x;
    If L(x) is empty, return(Q is not SAT); }
Until all nodes are marked.
Unmark the root;
Repeat { // Top-down Phase
  For each x whose query parent y is unmarked {
    For each u ∈ L(x) {
      If ∄t' ∈ L(y) s.t.  r(t', u) ∈ △
        remove u from L(x); }
    Unmark x; if L(x) is empty, return(Q is not SAT); }
Until all nodes are unmarked.
return(Q is SAT)
```

Figure 10: Check Wildcard Embedding

need to compare all pairs of tags in the label sets of the two nodes in the edge. Thus, the worst-case time complexity is $O(m^3 + n \times m^2)$, where m is the number of nodes in $\triangle$ and n is the number of nodes in Q.

4.2 Reasoning in the presence of Node Identity Constraints

Let us consider the class of TPQs that contain no wildcards but may contain NICs ($\approx, \not\approx$), and VBCs (without disjunctions). Apart from the interaction between structural predicates and VBCs, there is interaction between schema and the structural constraints imposed by the query.

Example 4.1 [Impact of Schema]
Consider the examples in Figure 11. Query Q1 is satisfiable with respect to the schema. The reasoning behind this is as follows. Since nodes $4 and $5 are identical, nodes $2 and $3 must lie on the same path. From the schema, we can then conclude that $2 is an ancestor of $3. Indeed, an instance can be obtained from the chased constraint graph that satisfies the query.

Query Q2 is not satisfiable with respect to the schema. Here is why. From the schema, every occurrence of d necessarily has a grandchild f, which is unique. The query asks for two distinct descendents of d tagged f, one as a grandchild and one as any descendent. However, from the schema, we can conclude that nodes $4 and $5 are identical i.e., $4≈$5 which contradicts the query constraint 4\not\approx$$5.

The example illustrates several points. **1.** The query contains no wildcards. Thus, for two nodes if either sad or OTSP predicate holds, then from the schema, it is possible to conclude a strict pc or ad relationship between them. Hence, the predicates sad and OTSP which we used in the absence of schema, now become redundant. **2.** We can use the schema to determine when two query nodes are identical. In the schema of Figure 11, there is a *unique path* from node d to f, with all edge labels either '1' or '?'. Hence any two descendents f of a d in the instance should be identical. **3.** Following the same argument, using the schema it is also possible to infer that two nodes must be *cousins*, by determining when the nodes lie on distinct paths.

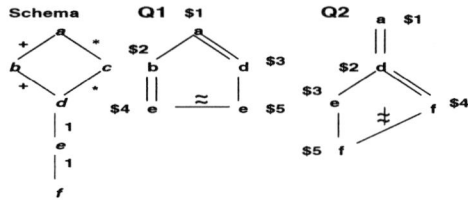

Figure 11: Inference from Schema

Determining satisfiability of a query works as follows. We use the schema to infer structural predicates between any pair of query nodes (which are tagged). We use inference rules to compute the closure of structural predicates and check the resulting set for violations. The query is satisfiable iff the resulting set is violation-free. As before, we use a constraint graph and a set of inference rules to compute the closure, with some differences in the inference rules used.

Inference Rules and Chase: The set of inference rules are adapted from those developed for the schema-less case. Rules involving sad or OTSP are dropped, since the schema allows us to derive an unambiguous ad relationship whenever sad or OTSP holds. Additionally, we need to infer relationships between element types from the schema. The schema can tell us that two tags t, t' are related by a pc-/ad-relationship, or that two query nodes must be identical or that they must be cousins. This static analysis of the schema can be performed using the rules shown in Figure 12, explained next. The complete set of inference rules can be found in [11].

Rule 1 corresponds to "disjoint" nodes. Let x, y be any nodes in a query Q and suppose z is their least common ancestor in Q. Let $\triangle$ be a given schema. Suppose $(z, u_1, ..., u_k, x)$ and $(z, v_1, ..., v_m, y)$ are the paths in Q from z to x and y respectively. We call these paths the query context of x and y. Note that all nodes are tagged in Q. For simplicity, denote the tag of each node by its primed version, i.e., node x has tag x'. Suppose *there is no path in $\triangle$ that passes through all the nodes $z', u_1', ..., u_k', v_1', ..., v_m', x', y'$ and in an order compatible with the query contexts above, which respects any pc-relationships present in the query contexts.* Then we can conclude that x and y must be cousins in every valid instance of $\triangle$, which satisfies Q. When this condition holds, we say x' and y' are *disjoint*.

As an example, consider query Q4 in Figure 8, *without* the dashed line added. Then query nodes $1 and $2 (with tag text) are necessarily cousins. This is because there is no path in the schema that passes through categories, description, parlist, and text in any compatible order, such that there is

> 1. whenever x, y are disjoint, infer COUS(x,y).
> 2. whenever z is lca(x,y), x and y are unique w.r.t. z, the path from z' to x' that satisfies the query context of x is identical to the path from z' to y' that satisfies the query context of y, tag(x) = tag(y), infer ≈(x,y)
> 3. whenever z is the lca(x,y), x and y are unique w.r.t. z, the unique path from z' to y' that satisfies the query of x and y contains edge (x',y'), tag(x) ≠ tag(y), infer pc(x,y)
> 4. whenever ad(x,z), ad(y,z), △: exactly one path from x' to y' and that path is an edge, infer pc(x,y)

Figure 12: Selected Inference Rules(with Schema)

a direct edge from description to text, so $1' and $2' are disjoint. However, if the edge is relaxed to an ad-edge (i.e., dashed line is added), such a path exists in the schema, so $1' and $2' are not disjoint, hence $1 and $2 are not necessarily cousins. Disjointness can be checked efficiently using a variant of merge sort and in time linear in the sum of sizes of the two query contexts.

Rules 2-3 correspond to "unique" nodes. Let Q be a query and x and y be the nodes in Q, such that $ad(y,x) \in G$. Let △ be a schema. Then x is *unique* with regard to y whenever △ has exactly one path from y' to x' satisfying the query context of x and y, and no edge on this path is labeled * or +. The intuition behind rule 2 is that the query paths from z to x as well as from z to y will both be mapped necessarily to one path in every valid instance of △. So, if x and y have the same tag, they must map to the same instance node. Rule 3 has a similar intuition.

Rule 4 says whenever $ad(x,z), ad(y,z)$ holds, clearly one of x,y must be a parent/ancestor of the other (when x and y have different tags). This is determined by the schema.

Finally, the chase procedure for TPQs (with NICs but no wildcards) in the presence of a schema is as follows.

- First, construct the constraint graph G of Q as for the schemaless case.

- Next, using static analysis of the schema, infer all COUS, ≈, pc, ad relationships and add them to G.

- Chase G using the inference rules identified above until saturation or violation detection.

We can show:

Theorem 4.2 (Chase Completeness with Schema): Let △ be an acylic schema without choice and Q a tree pattern query with NICs but no wildcards. Then Q is satisfiable w.r.t. △ iff there is an embedding of Q into △ and no violation is detected when the constraint graph of Q is chased. ∎

To understand the implications of Theorem 4.2 for the complexity of checking satisfiability of a tree pattern query w.r.t. a given acyclic schema without choice, we consider this problem at two levels. Firstly, let △ be any schema. Then we define the language SAT$_△$={Q | Q is a query & Q is satisfiable w.r.t. △}. We call the complexity of checking this membership *query complexity*, by analogy with the notion of data complexity in [22]. Secondly, we define the language SAT to be SAT={(△, Q) | △ is a schema & Q is a query & Q is satisfiable w.r.t △}. We call the complexity of checking this membership the *combined complexity* of satisfiability checking, by analogy to the well-known notion of combined complexity[22].

We have the following results.

Theorem 4.3 (Query Complexity): The query complexity of satisfiability checking in the presence of acyclic schema without choice is PTIME.

The idea is that we can apply the inference rules to saturation or until a violation is detected, which is a process that takes polynomial time in the size of query. We can also test whether there is an embedding from the query to the schema in PTIME. This yields a polynomial time algorithm for testing satisfiability in the presence of schema. Efficient implementation, similar to that discussed in Section 3.2.1, is possible. The details are omitted. A final note is that VBCs can be easily incorporated in the same way they were for the schemaless case. Thus, we can test satisfiability in polynomial time in the presence of schema and VBCs.

Theorem 4.4 (Combined Complexity): The combined complexity of satisfiability in the presence of acylic schema without choice is co-NP-complete.

The complexity comes not directly from the chase, but from violation checking. Figure 13 illustrates the violation checking procedure.

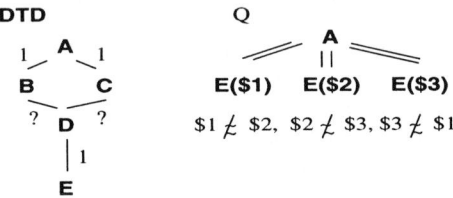

Figure 13: Violation Detection Example

The query Q in Figure 13 is not satisfiable because it asserts there must exist at least three different Es under A. However, there are only two paths from A to E in the DTD, all of whose edges are labeled 1/?. Thus there exist at most two Es under A in any valid instance.

The proof of Theorem 4.4 is by reduction from Maximal Clique. The details can be found in [11]. While the combined complexity is high, in practice, we will often want to check the satisfiability of many queries against a fixed schema, illustrating the significance of query complexity and of Theorem 4.3.

4.2.1 Node Identity Constraints and Wildcards

In the presence of a schema, testing satisfiability of a tree pattern query with wildcards and NICs is NP-complete. Similarly, when there are no wildcards but the query contains value-based disjunctive selection constraints, again the problem is NP-complete.

Theorem 4.5 (Hardness results): Let $\triangle$ be a schema and Q tree pattern query. Then satisfiability of Q w.r.t. $\triangle$ is NP-complete in the following cases:
(1) Q contains wildcards and NICs.
(2) Q contains disjunctive VBCs (and no NICs).

The first result is by reduction of 3-colorability and the proof only uses $\neq$ constraints. The second result is by reduction of 3SAT. Both proofs only make use of tree schemas and only pc-edges in Q.

The complexity results for the schema case are summarized in Figure 14. All results shown correspond to query complexity.

Disjunction	NICs/join constraints	Wildcards	Complexity
		X	PTIME
	X		PTIME
	X	X	NP-complete
X			NP-complete

Figure 14: Complexity of checking Satisfiability with schema.

5 Experimental Results

To study the effectiveness of testing satisfiability, we systematically ran a range of experiments to measure the impact of various parameters. In addition to measuring savings and overhead, we also measured how satisfiability checking time varies as a function of the number and kinds of constraints.

We ran our experiments on the **XMark** benchmark dataset [24] and **Biomedical** dataset [25] from the National Biomedical Research Foundation. For each dataset we constructed the documents of various size using the IBM XMLGenerator [26].

We used *Wutka DTDparser* [27] to parse the DTD, which is needed for static analysis of schema. For query evaluation, we used an XQuery engine *XQEngine* [28] for convenience and flexibility. Both tools are open source, developed in Java. We implemented our satisfiability tests in Java.

Setup: We ran our experiments on a *sparc* workstation running SunOS version 5.9 with 8 processors each having a speed of 900MHz and 32GB of RAM. All values reported are the average of 5 trials after dropping the maximum and minimum, observed during different workloads.

Query Set: All queries chosen for experimentation correspond to classes of tree pattern queries studied in this paper. Please note that when multiple node equalities are present in a TPQ, we need to use XQuery for its implementation.

For satisfiability testing without schema and with schema cases, we used Q1-Q3 in Figure 8. Although

```
Q1:
1  for $A in doc(''auction.xml'')//category,
2       $B1 in $A//description,
3       $C in $A//parlist,
4       $B2 in $A//description
5  where $B1//text is $C//text and $B2//parlist is $C
6  return $A
Q2:
7  for $A in doc(''auction.xml'')//description,
8       $B in $A//parlist,
9       $C in $A//listitem,
10      $D in $A//text
11 where $B//bold is $C//bold and $D//keyword is $C//keyword
12 return $A
Q3:
13 for $A in doc(''auction.xml'')//categories
14 where $A/description/text is $A//parlist//text
15 return $A
```

Figure 15: Examples for Schemaless case

we use the same set of queries, we use different analysis for "no schema" mode and "schema" mode seperately.

We also experimentsed with the **Biomedical** dataset but we did not include the details for space limitations. The details can be found in the full version of this paper.

Saving&Overhead Ratio: Let c be the time taken to determine the satisfiability of a query Q and let e be the time it takes to evaluate the query over the document (without using satisfiability check). The *savings ratio* S_Q obtained by using satisfiability check on unsatisfiable queries is defined as $S_Q = \frac{e-c}{e}$ and the *overhead ratio* incurred by doing satisfiability check on satisfiable queries is defined as $O_Q = \frac{c+e}{e}$. Intuitively, the closer to 1 the two ratios are the better.

Saving Ratio: Not surprisingly, on unsatisfiable queries, satisfiability check leads to phenomenal savings. Our saving ratio is close to 1 (usually between about 0.8 and 0.9) whether the schema is present or not. We omit these results for brevity.

Overhead Ratio: Figures 16 and 17 show the variation of savings ratio with document size for the three satisfiable queries Q1 − Q3 in Figure 8 (with schema) and Q1 − Q3 in Figure 15 (without schema). We expect the overhead ratio to decrease as the document size increases.

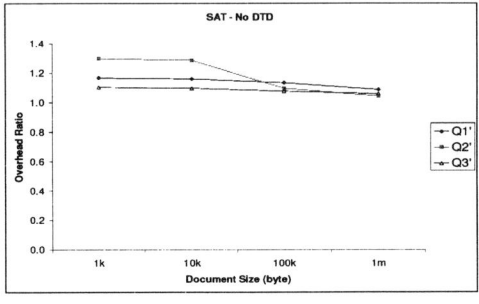

Figure 16: Overhead Ratio - Without Schema

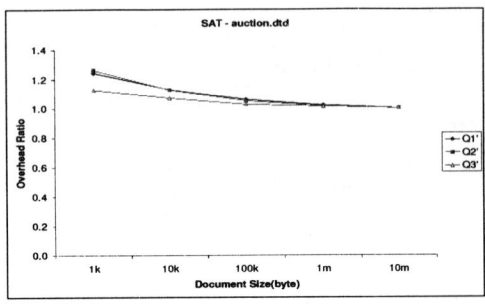

Figure 17: Overhead Ratio - With Schema

Indeed, this behavior can be observed from the figures. Overall, our results show that the overhead is a negligible fraction of the evaluation time.

In addition, we also tested the impact of number of constraints on satisfiability check time. For satisfiable queries, as expected the time increases, while for unsatisfiable queries, it decreases as violations are found faster. We also varied the structure of resulting OTSP sets by adding constraints and studied their effect on satisfiability check time. We found a few large OTSP sets increase the testing time more than several small OTSP sets.

The same conclusions were also obtained from the experiments on the **Biomedical** dataset.

6 Related Work

Containment: There has been much work on query processsing, containment and minimization of various XPath fragments [18, 7, 15, 12, 13, 1, 23]. Kuper et al. [9] study expressive power and closure properties of various XPath fragments and tree pattern queries. Levy et al. [8] studied query equivalence and satisfiability for datalog extensions. Satisfiability can be reduced to containment: query Q is unsatisfiable iff Q is contained in a (fixed) unsatisfiable query Q'. However, our results on satisfiability in this paper cannot be obtained from known results on containment. Specifically, we showed satisfiability can be tested in polynomial time for the following classes of tree pattern queries queries: (i) $TP^{/,//,[],*}$ and (ii) $TP^{/,//,[],NIC}$, both in the absence of a schema and in the presence of an acyclic DTD without disjunction. In the absence of a schema, containment for the former class is co-NP-complete [12] while for the latter it is Π_2^p-complete [18]. While [18] considered containment in the presence of integrity constraints, as pointed out by the authors, they do not capture a DTD completely. Containment for $TP^{/,//,[],*}$ w.r.t. a DTD was shown to be EXP-TIME complete [13], but it should be noted that the DTD is allowed to contain choice and cycles. Complexity of containment when the DTD is acyclic and/or choice-free is open. Finally, complexity of containment for $TP^{/,//,[],NIC}$ w.r.t. a DTD is open, although [13] showed that containment for $TP^{/,[]}$ and $TP^{//,[]}$ w.r.t. a DTD is co-NP-hard, when the DTD is allowed to contain choice and cycles. In sum, our PTIME results for satisfiability cannot be obtained from known results on containment.

Containment can be reduced to satisfiability: given queries Q, Q', Q is contained in Q' iff $Q - Q'$ is unsatisfiable. But this cannot be used to derive the hardness results in this paper since $Q - Q'$ does not belong to the class of tree pattern queries studied in this paper.

Satisfiability: The closest work is Hidders [5], where he considers the complexity of satisfiability testing for XPath fragments in the absence of schema. However, there are important differences in the contributions of the two papers, as we explain in detail below. The main contribution of [5] was showing that testing satisfiability of XPath expressions is NP-complete for various XPath fragments: (i) XPath with child and self-or-descendant and intersection, (ii) parent, union, and branching, (iii) root, branching, child, parent, self-or-ancestor. All these results depend on wildcard being present in the query. Secondly, he showed that when only branching (and all forward and backward axes as well as order) are present, satisfiability can be tested in polynomial time. For this, he uses a "tree description graph", which is similar to our constraint graph, except VBCs are not considered. The procedure he adopts for satisfiability testing has a flavor similar to our chase, but the "inference rules" are considerably simpler. The main reason is when set operations (union, intersection) are absent, one cannot express equality. In this case, the inferences become much simpler. He also showed that when all the axes and root are present, but none of the set operations or branching are allowed, again satisfiabilty can be tested in polynomial time. A similar comment applies to inferences in this case.

By contrast, all our PTIME results allow branching. In particular, when the query contains no wildcards but contains VBCs and NICs, we give an efficient polynomial time test for satisfiability. This result does not follow from the results of [5]. Besides, we have extended the techniques and results for testing satisfiability in the presence of schema. To the best of our knowledge, this has not been addressed before. Finally, our NP-completeness results are orthogonal to those in [5]. One exception is Theorem 3.3, which as we mentioned, is an easy corollary of a result in [5].

Testing satisfiability of tree descriptions, based on partial tree descriptions is of considerable interest in computational linguistics [10, 2, 16]. Constraint graphs are one kind of partial tree description. Kutz and Brodirsky [10] recently presented an efficient algorithm that checks the satisfiability of *pure dominance constraints*, which describe unlabeled rooted trees using a partial order. For arbitrary pairs of nodes they specify sets of admissible relative positions in a tree. However, the (pure) dominance constraints are a subset of the structure constraints studied in this paper. Besides, relationships such as OTSP and COUS are not considered there, nor is reasoning in the presence of a schema.

There are also other work related to satisfiability problem. Papakonstantinou et al.[14] studied the inference of DTDs for views of XML data. This paper proposed two extensions that enhance DTD's descriptive power. It mentioned that satisifiability for the views produced by the selective queries in the context of the extended DTD can be checked in PTIME. However, the selective queries are only a subset of the TPQs we discussed in our paper; they didn't allow either wildcards or node equality. Thus the problem of checking the satisfiability of selective queries is equivalent of finding the embedding of the query in our paper.

7 Summary

While there has been considerable work on containment and minimization for various XPath and tree pattern query fragments, the related problem of satisfiability has been largely ignored. We developed a method for testing satisfiability of various classes of tree pattern queries, which are known to be closely related to XPath and XQuery and to be of fundamental importance [9]. We study this problem both with and without a schema (acyclic and choic-free) and identify cases in which it is NP-complete and when it is PTIME. For the latter case, we developed efficient algorithms based on a chase procedure. We complemented our analytical results with an extensive set of experiments. While satisfiability checking can effect substantial savings in query evaluation, our results demonstrate that it incurs negligible overhead over satisfiable queries.

Satisfiability, for larger query classes, in the presence of cycles and/or choice are interesting problems. Satisfiability in the presence of XML schema is an important problem. Results on some of these problems will appear in the full version of this paper.

References

[1] Sihem Amer-Yahia et al. Minimization of tree pattern queries. In *ACM SIGMOD Conference*, 2001.

[2] T. Cornell. On determining the consistency of partial descriptions of trees. In *32nd ACL Conference*, 1994.

[3] D. Draper et. al. Xquery 1.0 and xpath 2.0 formal semantics. Technical report, W3C, 2002.

[4] M. F. Fernandez et. al. Xquery 1.0 and xpath 2.0 data model. Technical report, W3C, 2002.

[5] J. Hidders. Satisfiability of xpath expressions. In *DBPL* 2003.

[6] H. V. Jagadish et. al. Timber: A native xml database. *VLDB Journal*, 2002.

[7] C. Koch and G. Gottlob. Xpath query processing. In *9th International Workshop on Database Programming Languages (DBPL)*, Potsdam, Germany, September 2003.

[8] A.Y. Levy et. al. Equivalence, query-reachability, and satisfiability in datalog extensions. In *ACM PODS Conference*, 1993.

[9] G. M. Kuper et al. Structural properties of xpath fragments. In *ICDT* 2003.

[10] M. Kutz and M. Brodirsky. Pure dominance constraints. In *STACS* 2002.

[11] Laks V.S. Lakshmanan et al. On Testing Satisfiability of Tree Pattern Queries. Tech. Report, Dept. of Computer Science, UBC, March 2004. Available from http://www.cs.ubc.ca/~laks/papers.html.

[12] G. Miklau and D. Suciu. Containment and equivalent for an xpath fragment. In *PODS* 2002.

[13] F. Neven and T. Sch. Xpath containment in the presence of disjunction, dtds and variables. ICDT 2003.

[14] Yannis Papakonstantinou et al. DTD Inferencefor Views of XML Data In *ACM PODS Conference* 2000.

[15] R. Pichler et al. The complexity of xpath query evaluation. In *ACM PODS Conference*, 2003.

[16] J. Rogers and K. Vijay-Shanker. Reasoning with descriptions of trees. In *ACL Conference*, 1992.

[17] J. Shanmugasundaram et.al. Relational databases for querying xml documents: Limitations and opportunities. In *VLDB Conference*, 1999.

[18] V. Tannen and A. Deutsch. Containment and integrity constraints for xpath fragments. In *8th KRDB*, 2001.

[19] I.Tatarinov et. al. Storing and querying ordered xml using a relational database system. In *ACM SIGMOD Conference*, 2002.

[20] R. Treinen et al. Dominance constraints: Algorithms and complexity. In *3rd conference on Logical Aspects of Computational Linguistics*, 2001.

[21] Jeffrey D. Ullman. *Principles of Database and Knowledge-base Systems Volume II: The New Technologies*. Computer Science Press, 1989.

[22] Moshe Vardi. The complexity of relational query languages. In *ACM STOC*, 1982,pp 137-146.

[23] Peter T. Wood. Containment for xpath fragments under dtd constraints. icdt 2003.

[24] XMark: http://monetdb.cwi.nl/xml/.

[25] Biomedical database: http://www.cs.washington.edu/research/xmldatasets/www/repository.html.

[26] IBM XML generator: http://www.alphaworks.ibm.com/tech/xmlgenertor.

[27] Wutka DTD parser:http://www.wutka.com/dtdparser.html.

[28] XQuery: http://xqengine.sourceforge.net.

Containment of Nested XML Queries

Xin Dong   Alon Y. Halevy   Igor Tatarinov

{lunadong,alon,igor}@cs.washington.edu
University of Washington, Seattle

Abstract

Query containment is the most fundamental relationship between a pair of database queries: a query Q is said to be contained in a query Q' if the answer for Q is always a subset of the answer for Q', independent of the current state of the database. Query containment is an important problem in a wide variety of data management applications, including verification of integrity constraints, reasoning about contents of data sources in data integration, semantic caching, verification of knowledge bases, determining queries independent of updates, and most recently, in query reformulation for peer data management systems. Query containment has been studied extensively in the relational context and for XPath queries, but not for XML queries with nesting.

We consider the theoretical aspects of the problem of query containment for XML queries with nesting. We begin by considering conjunctive XML queries (c-XQueries), and show that containment is in polynomial time if we restrict the fanout (number of sibling sub-blocks) to be 1. We prove that for arbitrary fanout, containment is coNP-hard already for queries with nesting depth 2, even if the query does not include variables in the return clauses. We then show that for queries with fixed nesting depth, containment is coNP-complete.

Next, we establish the computational complexity of query containment for several practical extensions of c-XQueries, including queries with union and arithmetic comparisons, and queries where the XPath expressions may include descendant edges and negation. Finally, we describe a few heuristics for speeding up query containment checking in practice by exploiting properties of the queries and the underlying schema.

1 Introduction

Query containment is a fundamental relationship between a pair of database queries: in the relational context, a query Q is said to be contained in a query Q' if the answer for Q is always a subset of the answer for Q', independent of the current state of the database. In the context of XML queries with nesting (or more generally, queries over complex objects), where answers are trees, we require the answer of Q be embedded in the answer of Q'. This paper considers the formal aspects of determining query containment for XML queries with nesting. We begin by describing the many motivations for studying query containment.

1.1 Motivation

Originally, query containment was studied for optimization of relational queries [9, 33]. Removing redundant parts of a query reduces the number of joins performed by the query processor. Determining that a minimized query is equivalent to the original one requires a containment test.

More recently, query containment has found several applications in systems that need to reason about contents of data sources, such as data integration and peer-data management systems. As an illustration, consider the problem of query answering in a peer-data management system (PDMS) [21, 35, 32, 23, 4].

A PDMS offers a decentralized architecture for sharing data among *peers*, removing the need for a mediated schema that is required in data integration systems. Each peer has an associated schema that represents its domain of interest. In addition, a peer can contribute actual data. Semantic relationships between peers are described locally by mappings between pairs (or small sets) of peers. Note that a PDMS offers a data-sharing architecture that is a strict generalization of data integra-

Permission to copy without fee all or part of this material is granted provided that the copies are not made or distributed for direct commercial advantage, the VLDB copyright notice and the title of the publication and its date appear, and notice is given that copying is by permission of the Very Large Data Base Endowment. To copy otherwise, or to republish, requires a fee and/or special permission from the Endowment.

**Proceedings of the 30th VLDB Conference,
Toronto, Canada, 2004**

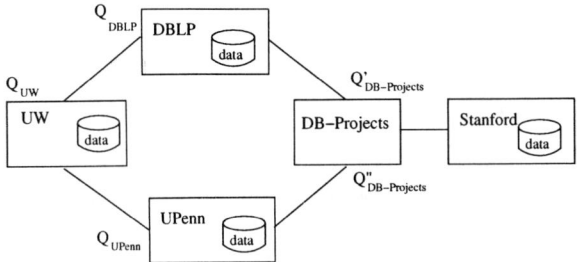

Figure 1: A PDMS for the database research domain. Query containment is needed in order to reformulate a query on a peer onto its neighbor (e.g., from UW to DBLP), and to prune redundant reformulations (e.g., one of the two paths from UW to DB-Projects may result in a redundant query.)

tion systems [36, 8, 18]. Figure 1 shows a PDMS for supporting sharing of database-research related data.

The semantic mappings between peer schemas enable *reformulating* a query over a peer to queries over its neighbors. Given a query at a peer, the query processor applies reformulation iteratively to explore all possible semantic paths in the PDMS, until it reaches every relevant peer. In Figure 1, the user has posed a query over the UW peer. The PDMS has reformulated the input query over the UPenn, DBLP, and DB-Projects peers. This is the first place where query containment is needed: query reformulation algorithms, typically based on algorithms for answering queries using views [20, 25, 21], require checking query containment.

Continuing with the example, because there are two paths from UW to DB-Projects, two reformulated queries over DB-Projects have been obtained: $Q'_{DB-Projects}$ and $Q''_{DB-Projects}$. Next, the PDMS will reformulate these two queries over the Stanford peer. However, one of these two queries may be redundant in the sense that all the answers it produces are guaranteed to be produced by the other query. In recent experiments on the XML-based Piazza PDMS [35], we showed that pruning such redundant queries significantly speeds up query reformulation in a PDMS. Detecting that a reformulated query is redundant reduces to the problem of query containment.

Furthermore, it turns out that it is also crucial to minimize reformulated queries after every reformulation step [35, 16]. As already described, query minimization involves query containment.

Query containment is also important for *semantic caching*, which is a current need in several recent data integration products [14, 1]. Intuitively, checking whether an answer to a new query is already in the cache amounts to a containment check between the new query and the cache.

It is important to note that XML is increasingly being used in the kinds of middleware and data-sharing applications mentioned above. Therefore it is important to develop query containment techniques for XML queries. Finally, we note that query containment has also been used in maintenance of integrity constraints [19, 15] and knowledge-base verification [26].

1.2 Related Work

Query containment has been studied in depth for the relational model, beginning with conjunctive queries [9, 2], then acyclic queries [38], queries with union [33], negation [27], arithmetic comparisons [24, 37, 27, 39, 19], recursive queries [34, 10] and queries over bags [11, 22].

Query containment for XML poses two challenges: the use of XPath expressions to specify patterns on the input data, and the nesting structure of the resulting tree. Several recent works considered query containment for XPath in isolation. In [30] it is shown that for a simple fragment of XPath that contains descendant axis($//$), wildcards($*$), and qualifiers (or branching, denoted $[...]$), but without either tag variables or disjunctions, query containment is coNP-complete. If we drop any one of the constructs $*$, $//$, and $[...]$ in the above case, query containment is in PTIME [3, 31]. In [12] the authors studied XPath containment under a limited use of tag variables and equality testing, and showed the problem is Π_2^p-complete in general and NP-complete if no disjunction or wildcards are allowed. Finally, [17] showed that containment of queries with regular path expressions on general cyclic graphs is PSPACE-hard. In [35] we describe a practically-motivated algorithm for containment of XQuery queries with nesting, but that algorithm is complete only for queries *without* nesting.

Containment of queries returning nested structures has been considered for only the general case of queries over complex objects [28]. The study shows that the containment problem can be reduced to the problem of *query simulation*; however, the proposed reduction is not accurate. As we demonstrate, the algorithm of [28] considers only a *subset* of the simulations that a sound algorithm should check. Furthermore, from a practical perspective, we consider several extensions not addressed in [28], and we show how the complexity depends on restrictions such as the nesting depth and fanout in the queries.

1.3 Example

Example 1.1: Figure 2 shows an example of two XQuery queries, where containment cannot be determined solely based on comparing their respective

```
Q: for $group in /group                              Q': for $group in /group
   where $group/gname/text() = "database"               return
   return                                                < area > {
    < area > {                                            for $person in $group/person
      for $person in $group/person                        return
      return                                               < person >
       < person >                                           < name > {$person/text()} < /name >
         < name > {$person/text()} < /name >                < group > {$group/gname/text()} < /group >
         {for $paper in $group/paper                        {for $paper in $group/paper
         where $paper/author/text() = $person/text()        where $paper/author/text() = $person/text()
         return                                             return
          < paper > {$paper/title/text()} < /paper > }       < paper > {$paper/title/text()} < /paper > }
       < /person > }                                      < /person > }
    < /area >                                          < /area >
```

Figure 2: The query on the left, Q, is contained in the query on the right, Q', but not the other way around. We note that checking XPath containment on this example is not sufficient to establish nested XML query containment.

XPath components. The two queries, Q and Q', take an input document consisting of paper and person elements where a person element contains a person name and a paper element contains a title and author subelements. In the output, the person elements have a name and paper subelements instead. Clearly, checking containment of XPath fragments in every block is not sufficient to establish that Q is contained in Q'. In addition, one must consider the structure of the queries, the predicates and returned values that appear in each block and how the XPath expressions are spread across the query blocks.

1.4 Our Contributions

We begin by considering a fragment of XML queries, called *conjunctive XML Queries (c-XQueries)*, which covers many queries used in practice (analogous to select-project-join queries in SQL). We show that query containment for this fragment can be checked in polynomial time if we restrict the fanout (number of sibling sub-blocks) in the query to be 1. However, if we allow arbitrary fanout, then query containment is coNP-hard even for queries with nesting depth 2 and even if the query does not include variables in the return clauses. Since XPath expressions in c-XQueries can be modeled as acyclic conjunctive queries, and containment of unnested acyclic queries is in PTIME, our result isolates the exact effect of nesting on the complexity of query containment.

Next, we show that query containment for c-XQueries with arbitrary fanout but *fixed* nesting depth is coNP-complete. Our technique is based on considering a finite number of *canonical databases* (a technique also used in [24, 17]). Here, the appropriate set of canonical databases is obtained by inspecting a set of *canonical answers* to the query, each representing a possible structure for the answer tree. We note that without restricting the nesting depth of the query, the number of canonical databases that need to be inspected can be super-exponential, and the exact complexity for this case remains open.

Last, we consider several extensions of c-XQueries that are important in practice. In particular, we consider queries with union, negation, and queries where the XPath expressions may include descendant edges (besides wildcards and branching). In each of these cases we show that even with fanout 1, query containment is coNP-complete, and that query containment for queries with fixed nesting depth is still coNP-complete. We also consider nested queries with equality predicates on tag variables, and show that containment is NP-complete for queries with fanout 1 and Π_2^p-complete for queries with arbitrary fanout but fixed nesting depth. Then, we show that for queries with arithmetic comparisons on tag variables, containment is Π_2^p-complete both for queries with fanout 1 and for queries with arbitrary fanout but fixed nesting depth. Finally, we describe a few heuristics for speeding up query containment checking in practice by exploiting properties such as cardinality knowledge gleaned from the query and the schema of the underlying XML data. In particular, these heuristics significantly reduce the number of canonical databases that actually need to be considered.

We note that there are two aspects of XQueries that we do not consider: bag semantics and order. Our results entail necessary conditions for query containment in these cases – if containment does not hold for sets, it certainly does not hold for ordered lists or bags. Although order is part of the semantics of XQuery, it is less important in data management applications of XML. In fact, query containment with ordered lists has not been addressed even for XPath. Our focus here is on the additional challenges that arise from adding nesting to XML queries.

The paper is organized as follows. Section 2 for-

```
<project>
    <title>Piazza</title>
    <member>Alice</member>
</project>
<project>
    <title>Tukwila</project>
    <member>Bob</member>
</project>
```

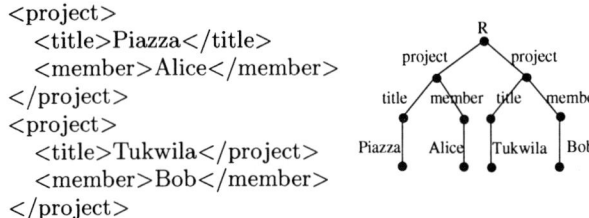

Figure 3: An XML instance and corresponding tree.

mally defines the problem. Section 3 considers cc-XQueries, and Section 4 extends the results to c-XQueries. Section 5 describes our results for extensions of c-XQueries, and Section 6 concludes.

2 Preliminaries

We begin by defining XML instances and the different query language fragments we consider. We then define containment on instances and on queries.

2.1 XML Instances and XML Trees

In our discussion we model XML instances and elements as unordered edge-labeled trees. Nodes in the tree represent XML (sub)elements, and have identifiers from a domain $\mathcal{N}$, which is disjoint from the domain of tag constants, $\mathcal{T}$. Edges between nodes represent nesting relationships, and the labels on the edges (taken from $\mathcal{T}$) represent XML tags. The identifier of the root is $\Re$. Note that in the tree representation, labels on edges leading to leaf nodes correspond to *text values* in the XML document, while internal edge labels correspond to *XML element tags*. We use edge labeling instead of node labeling to distinguish tag and node variables. All of our results also hold in the node-labeled representation.

Example 2.1: Figure 3 shows an XML instance and its corresponding tree that include information about projects in a research group. □

In the rest of the paper, we use the terms *XML instance* and *XML tree* interchangeably.

2.2 Conjunctive XML Queries

We start by considering a subset of XML queries, called *conjunctive XML queries (c-XQueries)*. c-XQueries are similar in spirit to select-project-join queries in SQL, and therefore already form useful subset of XQuery.

Syntax: c-XQueries satisfy the following restrictions:

- In a c-XQuery, the returned variables are bound to tag names or text values only. Note that if an XML query has a variable bound to an XML

```
Q: for $x in /project return
   < group > {
     for $s in $x/title/text() return
       < projtitle >{$s}< /projtitle > } {
     for $t in $x/member/text() return
       < name >{$t}< /name > }
   < /group >
```

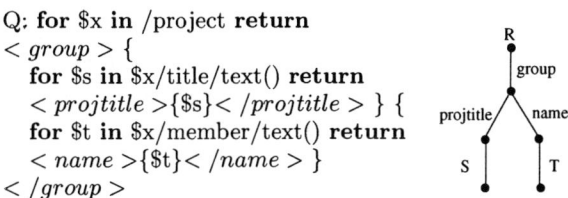

Figure 4: An example c-XQuery and its head tree.

element, we can easily expand the RETURN clause according to the schema and transform the query to a c-XQuery. Henceforth, the term *tag variable* will refer to a variable that can be bound to either a text value or an element tag (i.e., both types of labels on tree edges).

- XPath expressions in a c-XQuery contain only child axis (/), wildcards (∗) and branching ([...]). In Section 5 we extend our results to decide query containment for more general XML queries, where there are descendant axis (//) or negations in XPath expressions, or there are unions or comparisons in XPath expressions or WHERE-clause conditions.

- To exclude disjunction, we require that sibling blocks always return *distinct* tag constants. Consequently, a block can return a tag variable only when it has no siblings. Section 5 discusses containment of disjunctive queries.

A c-XQuery consists of nested *query blocks*. A query block may have a set of sub-blocks. The *fanout* of a query block is the number of its immediate sub-blocks. A query with no sub-blocks has a *nesting depth* of 1. The nesting depth of a query is 1 plus the maximal nesting depth of its sub-blocks. The nesting depth of the query is the depth of its outer-most block. In the example c-XQuery Q shown in Figure 4, the outer-most query block has fanout 2 and the nesting depth is 3.

The structure of an XML query and its answers can be described using the notion of a query *head tree*. The nodes of the head tree of Q are the query blocks of Q, and there is an edge between the node corresponding to a query block and the node corresponding to its parent block. The label of the incoming edge of a node n in the head tree is the returned tag of the block corresponding to n in Q (which can also be a variable). Note that we consider an expression {$s} a query block with empty for and where clauses and with a return tag of $s; such nodes will appear as leaves of the head tree. Figure 4 also shows the head tree of the example c-XQuery. Note that a head tree is also an XML instance if its variables are substituted with actual values.

For our analysis in Section 3 we define a smaller fragment of c-XQueries, called *constant conjunctive XML queries (cc-XQueries)*. A cc-XQuery is a c-XQuery that does not return tag variables. The head tree of a cc-XQuery has constant labels only.

Semantics: The semantics of a c-XQuery is an extension of the semantics of an un-nested conjunctive query. Specifically, each node n in the answer is *generated* by a query block with the same depth as n. Note that since c-XQuery does not allow disjunction, each node has a unique generator. For every valid variable substitution in a query block, we generate an output element with the corresponding tag. When there is at least one satisfying substitution, we evaluate the block's sub-blocks. Note that a variable substitution of a sub-block is an extension of that for its parent block. The output element of the outer-most block of an c-XQuery is the answer to the query.

We note that a c-XQuery can be evaluated on an input XML instance in polynomial data complexity and exponential query complexity.

2.3 Containment of Instances and Queries

An XML tree is a special case of a complex object, where each record is binary. Hence, we follow the definition of containment given in [28]. Specifically, we base XML instance containment on tree homomorphism (not necessarily injective). Following [30], we define an *embedding* as follows:

Definition 2.2 (Tree embedding). *Given two trees, a node mapping ψ from t_1 to t_2 is said to be an embedding from t_1 to t_2 if*

- ψ *maps the root of t_1 to the root of t_2,*

- *if node n_2 is a child of node n_1 in t_1, then $\psi(n_2)$ is a child of $\psi(n_1)$, and the edge between n_1 and n_2 has the same label as the edge between $\psi(n_1)$ and $\psi(n_2)$.* □

Definition 2.3 (XML Instance Containment). *Let e and e' be two XML instances. e is contained in e', denoted as $e \sqsubseteq e'$, if the tree of e can be embedded in the tree of e'.* □

This definition of XML tree containment has several desirable properties. First, containment is reflexive and transitive. Second, it is the smallest order relation for XML trees which is a congruence, i.e., $e_1 \sqsubseteq e'_1 \wedge \cdots \wedge e_n \sqsubseteq e'_n$ implies $<t>e_1,\ldots,e_n</t> \sqsubseteq <t>e'_1,\ldots,e'_n</t>$ where $<t>e_1,\ldots,e_n</t>$ is an XML instance constructed by adding a common parent $<t>$ element over $e_1,\ldots,e_n$. Third, our containment definition is consistent with set semantics. An XML instance

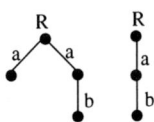

Figure 5: Two XML instances that contain each other but are not equivalent.

with multiple copies of its subelement is contained in the XML instance that has just one copy of each subelement. From a theoretical perspective, there are additional justifications for this definition. This notion of containment has also been used previously for partial information [7] and or-sets [29], and it coincides with the simulation relation between complex objects represented as graphs [5, 6].

Note that this definition of containment is not antisymmetric: $e \sqsubseteq e'$ and $e' \sqsubseteq e$ do not imply $e = e'$. As an example, consider the two XML instances in Figure 5. They contain each other, but are not equivalent.

The following sections make use of *minimal XML instances* that we define as follows:

Definition 2.4 (Minimal XML Instance). *An XML instance e is said to be minimal if the XML tree of e does not contain a pair of sibling subtrees (sub-instances) e' and e'' anywhere in e such that $e' \sqsubseteq e''$.* □

Based on the definition of XML tree containment, we define XML query containment as follows:

Definition 2.5 (XML Query Containment). *Let Q and Q' be two XML queries. Q is contained in Q', denoted as $Q \sqsubseteq Q'$, if for every input XML instance D, $Q(D) \sqsubseteq Q'(D)$.* □

3 Containment of cc-XQueries

We begin by considering query containment for cc-XQueries. A cc-XQuery does not return tag variables, and thus can be viewed as a generalization of a boolean conjunctive query (i.e, a conjunctive query with an empty head). Nevertheless, unlike boolean conjunctive queries, cc-XQueries can return one of *several* tree structures, rather than only true or false. Although cc-XQueries are rarely useful in practice, we study them for two reasons: first, they already show some of the important lower bounds on query containment; and second, they help us obtain insights on the techniques we use to establish containment, which later carry over to c-XQueries.

Intuitively, given a pair of queries Q and Q', we cannot check that for *every* possible XML input D, $Q(D) \sqsubseteq Q'(D)$. Hence, our goal is to find a finite set of representative inputs, called *canonical databases*, which have the property that $Q \sqsubseteq Q'$ if and only

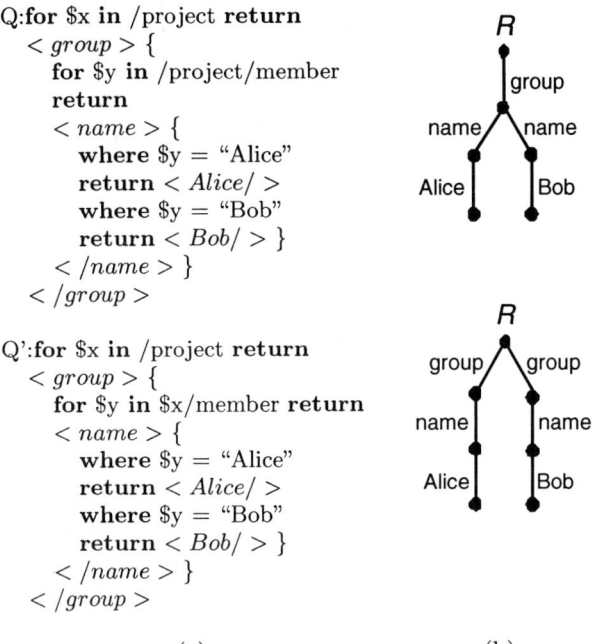

Figure 6: Example 3.1: (a) Q and Q'; (b) the answers to Q and Q' on the input XML instance in Figure 3.

if $Q(DB) \sqsubseteq Q'(DB)$ for every canonical database DB.

Our approach is based on considering the different *canonical answers* that can be generated for Q, and creating a canonical database for each canonical answer. One could conjecture that it suffices to consider all the answers corresponding to *prefix subtrees* (the subtrees that contain the root) of Q's head tree. However, the following example refutes this conjecture.[1]

Example 3.1: Consider the two cc-XQueries, Q and Q', in Figure 6(a). The query Q checks whether Alice and Bob are in the research group, and groups them together regardless of their projects. The query Q' also checks whether Alice and Bob are in the research group, but in contrast, groups them according to whether they are working on the same project. Figure 6(b) shows the results of Q and Q' on the XML instance D of Example 2.1. $Q(D) \not\sqsubseteq Q'(D)$, and thus $Q \not\sqsubseteq Q'$. In contrast, containment *does* hold for canonical databases generated for all prefix subtrees of the head tree. □

3.1 Canonical Answers and Databases

The observation leading to our first result is that it suffices to consider canonical answers that are minimal XML instances and are *contained* in the head tree (which is different from being prefix subtrees of the head tree).

Definition 3.2 (Canonical Answer of a cc-XQuery). Let Q be a cc-XQuery and H be its head tree. A canonical answer of Q is a minimal XML instance CA, such that $CA \sqsubseteq H$. □

For each canonical answer we define a canonical database as follows.

Definition 3.3 (Canonical Database of a cc-XQuery). Let Q be a cc-XQuery, and CA be a canonical answer of Q. Q's canonical database for CA, denoted as DB_{CA}, is an XML instance, s.t. for each node N of CA where N's generator query block is $\hat{q}_n$, the following holds: Let $p_0/p_1/\ldots/p_n$ be a path expression in $\hat{q}_n$, where p_0 is an optional node variable from an ancestor query block. For each $p_i, i \in [1, n]$, there is a distinct node, labeled p_i, that is a child of the node for p_{i-1}. If p_0 is absent, then p_1 is a child of DB_{CA}'s root. □

The number of canonical databases for a cc-XQuery is the same as the number of canonical answers. The size of a canonical database is polynomial in the size of its corresponding canonical answer.

For example, Figure 7(a) shows six canonical answers for Q in Example 3.1. Figure 7(b) shows the corresponding canonical databases. (Note that tag names are abbreviated.)

3.2 Query Containment Algorithm

Our first result shows that to test query containment, it suffices to consider only canonical databases constructed from the canonical answers. In the following theorem, DB_{CA} (DB'_{CA}) refers to the canonical database of $Q(Q')$ corresponding to the canonical answer CA. The following theorem gives several equivalent characterizations of query containment. For complete proofs of the theorems in this paper, see [13].

Theorem 3.4 (Containment of cc-XQueries). Let Q and Q' be two cc-XQueries. The following three conditions are equivalent:

1. $Q \sqsubseteq Q'$;
2. for every canonical database DB of Q, $Q(DB) \sqsubseteq Q'(DB)$;
3. for every canonical answer CA of Q, (a) CA is a canonical answer of Q'; and (b) $DB'_{CA} \sqsubseteq DB_{CA}$. □

The proof of the above theorem is based on two important properties of canonical answers and canonical databases.

---

[1] Furthermore, since the result in [28] considers only these subtrees, this example entails that the algorithm of [28] offers only a necessary condition for query containment, but not a sufficient one.

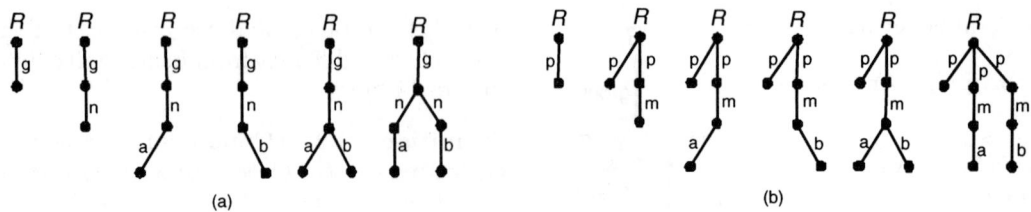

Figure 7: Example 3.1: (a) Q's canonical answers; (b) Q's canonical databases.

Lemma 3.5. *Let Q be a cc-XQuery and D be an XML instance. There exists a unique canonical answer CA of Q, such that $Q(D) \sqsubseteq CA$ and $CA \sqsubseteq Q(D)$.* □

Lemma 3.6. *Let Q be a cc-XQuery, CA be a canonical answer of Q, DB_{CA} be the canonical database for CA of Q, and D be an XML instance. $CA \sqsubseteq Q(D)$ if and only if $DB_{CA} \sqsubseteq D$.* □

Proof sketch for Theorem 3.4:
(1) ⇒ (2): Follows from the definition.

(2) ⇒ (3): Consider a canonical answer CA and its canonical database, DB_{CA}. According to Lemma 3.6, $CA \sqsubseteq Q(DB_{CA})$. Since condition (2) holds, $Q(DB_{CA}) \sqsubseteq Q'(DB_{CA})$. Putting the above two containments together, we have $CA \sqsubseteq Q'(DB_{CA})$. This implies that (a) holds. Applying Lemma 3.6 again gives $DB'_{CA} \sqsubseteq DB_{CA}$. Hence, (b) holds.

(3) ⇒ (1): To show $Q \sqsubseteq Q'$, we need to show for every XML instance D, $Q(D) \sqsubseteq Q'(D)$. According to Lemma 3.5, there exists a unique canonical answer CA of Q, such that $Q(D) \sqsubseteq CA$ and $CA \sqsubseteq Q(D)$. According to Lemma 3.6, $DB_{CA} \sqsubseteq D$. Since conditions (a) and (b) hold, $DB'_{CA} \sqsubseteq DB_{CA}$. So $DB'_{CA} \sqsubseteq D$. Applying Lemma 3.6 again gives $CA \sqsubseteq Q'(D)$. Based on containment transitivity, $Q(D) \sqsubseteq Q'(D)$. □

The third condition of Theorem 3.4 is of practical importance, and will become useful in the complexity analysis. The condition states that we do not actually have to evaluate the two queries on each of the canonical databases. Instead, it suffices to check tree embedding on each pair of canonical databases, which can be done in polynomial time in the size of the canonical databases.

However, as the following analysis shows, the number and sizes of canonical databases, determined by the number and sizes of canonical answers, are quite large. Let m be the largest fanout of a query block in Q, and let d be the nesting depth of Q. We can show that the maximal size of Q's canonical answers is $\Theta\left(m \cdot 2^{m \cdot \left(2^{\cdot^{\cdot^{\cdot^{m \cdot (2^m)}}}}\right)}\right)$ (which is a tower of exponents with $d-1$ levels), while the number of canonical answers is similar, but d levels tall. However, this is only a temporary setback. We will show that there is no need to consider so many canonical answers.

3.3 Effect of the Fanout

In this section, we show that the fanout of the queries has a significant impact on the complexity of query containment. A cc-XQuery is said to be *linear* if the fanout of each query block is at most 1. We show the following:

Theorem 3.7 (Containment for linear cc-XQueries). *Let Q and Q' be cc-XQueries. If either of them is linear, testing $Q \sqsubseteq Q'$ is in PTIME.* □

We note that this is the only case in which nesting does not add to the complexity of containment in comparison to similar queries without nesting. As we will soon see, the restriction on the fanout is crucial for obtaining polynomial-time complexity.

Proof sketch: The proof of Theorem 3.7 is based on the following observations. First, to check that $Q \sqsubseteq Q'$, where Q is a linear cc-XQuery, the number of canonical answers we need to consider is equal to the nesting depth of Q, denoted as d, and the sizes of canonical answers are bounded by d. Second, as entailed by the third part of Theorem 3.4, for each such canonical answer we need to perform an embedding test on the corresponding canonical databases, which can be done in polynomial time in the sizes of the canonical databases, bounded by the sizes of the queries. Specifically, the time complexity is $O(d \cdot |Q| \cdot |Q'|)$. □

The following theorem shows that the restriction on the fanout is critical. The following lower bound is proved by a reduction from the complement of 3SAT.

Theorem 3.8 (coNP-Hardness). *Testing containment of cc-XQueries with nesting depth 2 and arbitrary fanout is coNP-hard.* □

3.4 cc-XQueries with Fixed Nesting Depth

In this section we show that for cc-XQueries with *any* fixed nesting depth, query containment is in coNP. Hence, we obtain the following result:

Theorem 3.9 (coNP-Completeness). *Let Q and Q' be cc-XQueries. If either of them has a fixed nesting depth, testing $Q \sqsubseteq Q'$ is coNP-complete.* □

The key observation behind Theorem 3.9 is to further reduce the number of canonical answers (and hence of canonical databases) we need to consider. As we show below, it suffices to consider *kernel canonical answers*.

Definition 3.10 (Kernel Canonical Answer). *Let Q be a cc-XQuery. Let d be the nesting depth of Q and c be the maximum number of path steps in a query block of Q. A canonical answer CA of Q is called a* kernel canonical answer *if the following hold: (1) the root node has a single child, and (2) suppose N is a node in CA and p is a path from N to a leaf; at most $cd-1$ siblings of N are roots of paths that are the same as p.* □

In the following lemma, DB_{KCA} (DB'_{KCA}) refers to the canonical database of $Q(Q')$ corresponding to the canonical answer KCA.

Lemma 3.11. *Let Q and Q' be two cc-XQueries. The containment $Q \sqsubseteq Q'$ holds if and only if for each kernel canonical answer KCA of Q, (1) KCA is a canonical answer of Q'; and (2) $DB'_{KCA} \sqsubseteq DB_{KCA}$.* □

Proof sketch: Let CA be the canonical answer with the minimal size that violates $DB'_{CA} \sqsubseteq DB_{CA}$. We show CA must be a kernel canonical answer. First, the root of CA must has a single child. Otherwise, we split it and obtain a set of subtrees, each of which is a canonical answer. At least one of them also violates $DB'_{CA} \sqsubseteq DB_{CA}$, contradicting that CA has the minimal size.

Second, for every node in CA, each conjunct in its generator query block introduces no more than one distinct node to the canonical database. Thus, the size of DB_{CA} is bounded by the size of CA times the maximum number of conjuncts in a query block of Q. On the other hand, considering that CA is minimal, DB_{CA} needs to be at least a certain size in order to guarantee that $DB'_{CA} \not\sqsubseteq DB_{CA}$, and for all canonical answers with a smaller size, denoted as $\widetilde{CA}$, $DB'_{\widetilde{CA}} \sqsubseteq DB_{\widetilde{CA}}$. This size of DB_{CA} is determined by the fanout of CA. Considering the upper bound and the minimum requisite for the size of DB_{CA}, we show that the fanout of CA is bounded, and CA is a kernel canonical answer. □

Now we examine the time complexity of the algorithm derived from Theorem 3.4(3), by analyzing the number and sizes of kernel canonical answers. Let m be the maximum fanout, and b be the number of query blocks in Q. In a kernel canonical answer, the fanout of each node is no more than bcd, since there are no more than cd outgoing edges containing a common path pattern, and there are at most b different path patterns in the query. Hence the size of the canonical answer is in $O((bcd)^d)$. Consider a specific node N in the canonical answer. There are no more than m candidate labels for the edge leading to N. So the number of kernel canonical answers is in $O(m^{(bcd)^d})$. Hence, the time complexity of the algorithm is in $O(m^{(bcd)^d})$.

Corollary 3.12. *Testing containment for cc-XQueries with fixed nesting depth is in coNP. Testing containment for cc-XQueries with arbitrary nesting depth is in coNEXPTIME.* □

Proof sketch: Given two cc-XQueries Q and Q', to check $Q \not\sqsubseteq Q'$, we need to guess a kernel canonical answer of Q, denoted as KCA; construct Q' and Q's canonical databases for KCA, denoted as DB' and DB; and check whether $DB' \not\sqsubseteq DB$. When the nesting depth is fixed, the size of a kernel canonical answer is polynomial in the size of Q. Thus, constructing canonical databases and checking containment both take polynomial time. Hence, query containment is in coNP. When the nesting depth is arbitrary, the size of a kernel canonical answer is exponential in the nesting depth, thus query containment is in coNEXPTIME. □

From Corollary 3.12 and Theorem 3.8 we obtain Theorem 3.9.

Finally, we note that the complexity of query containment for cc-XQueries with arbitrary nesting depth remains an open problem.

4 Containment of c-XQueries

We now consider general c-XQueries, which may return tag variables. A tag variable can be set to any value in $\mathcal{T}$, and therefore the number of candidate answers to a given query is infinite. Consequently, the algorithms for cc-XQueries do not apply directly.

There are two key points underlying our algorithm for checking containment of c-XQueries. First, we consider canonical answers that may contain variables. As we will see, the number of such canonical answers is the same as we had in Section 3. Second, we check query containment by applying a more elaborate procedure for each canonical answer. Specifically, we apply a condition called *query simulation* [28] to a pair of *indexed conjunctive queries* that we create for each canonical answer. Since query simulation, albeit more elaborate, is also in polynomial time, we are able to show that the complexity results for c-XQueries are, for the most part, the same as for cc-XQueries.

4.1 Simulation of Indexed Queries

We begin by explaining indexed conjunctive queries and the condition of query simulation, both from [28]. We represent indexed conjunctive queries using a datalog-like notation, as follows.

$$Q(\bar{I}_1;\ldots;\bar{I}_m;\bar{V}) :- X_1R_1Y_1,\ldots,X_nR_nY_n$$

The body of the indexed conjunctive query is similar to that of an ordinary conjunctive query (except that we write XRY instead of $R(X,Y)$), but the head has a set of tuples of *index* variables, $\bar{I}_1,\ldots,\bar{I}_m$, in addition to the head variables $\bar{V}$. An indexed conjunctive query produces a nested structure: the tuples $\bar{V}$ of the answer are grouped first by the index variables $\bar{I}_1$, then by $\bar{I}_2$, etc., and finally by $\bar{I}_m$.

Example 4.1: Consider query Q in Figure 4. Given the head tree shown in the same figure as the canonical answer CA, the indexed conjunctive query for CA is the following (note that XPath tag names are abbreviated):

$$IQ_{CA}(X;W,Y;S,T) :- \Re pX, XtW, WSV,\\ XmY, YTZ$$

Note that the last XML instance shown in Figure 7(a), denoted as CA', is also a canonical answer of Q by applying variable isomorphism. The indexed conjunctive query for CA' is the following:

$$IQ_{CA'}(X;Y_1,Y_2;\emptyset) :- \Re pX, XmY_1, XmY_2,\\ Y_1aZ_1, Y_2bZ_2$$

By applying Theorem 4.4, which we will describe shortly, we can justify that the query Q' in Example 3.1 is contained in the above query Q, but not the other way around. □

Query simulation is a generalization of query containment for indexed conjunctive queries. Simulation reduces to query containment when the queries contain no index variables. Formally, simulation is defined as follows.

Definition 4.2 (Query Simulation). *Let Q and Q' be two indexed conjunctive queries, each with m sets of index variables. We say that Q' simulates Q to depth m, denoted by $Q \preceq_m Q'$, if for any database the following holds:*

$$\forall \bar{I}_1.\exists \bar{I}'_1 \ldots \forall \bar{I}_m.\exists \bar{I}'_m.[\forall \bar{V}.\\ (Q(\bar{I}_1;\ldots;\bar{I}_m;\bar{V}) \Rightarrow Q'(\bar{I}'_1;\ldots;\bar{I}'_m;\bar{V}'))]$$

□

In [28] it is shown that query simulation can be checked by establishing a *simulation mapping* between Q and Q'. In our context, where the body of the conjunctive query is acyclic, finding a simulation mapping can be translated into a tree embedding problem, where the sizes of trees are polynomial in the sizes of the queries. Thus, checking simulation is PTIME in the size of the indexed conjunctive queries.

4.2 Query Containment Algorithm

In general, a c-XQuery may have an infinite number of candidate answers, given all the possible substitutions to the tag variables. Recall that a head tree of a c-XQuery may contain tag variables. When creating canonical answers, we treat the variables as constants. Hence, we can still represent all candidate answers with a finite number of canonical answers.

Given a canonical answer CA, we create an indexed conjunctive query, which is a generalization of the canonical database, as defined below.

Definition 4.3 (Indexed conjunctive query for a canonical answer). *Let Q be a c-XQuery and CA be a canonical answer with depth d. Q's indexed conjunctive query for CA, denoted as IQ_{CA}, has the form*

$$IQ_{CA}(\bar{I}_1;\ldots;\bar{I}_{d-1};V) :- X_1R_1Y_1,\ldots,X_nR_nY_n,$$

and is constructed in two steps. Let N be a node of CA on level k, $k \in [1,d]$, and let $\hat{q}_n$ be N's generator query block in Q. First, if there exists any node M, which may be N's ancestor, descendant, or N itself, where the incoming edge of M is labeled by a tag constant c from $\mathcal{T}$, the generator query block of M returns a tag variable T, and T also occurs in $\hat{q}_n$, we substitute T with c in $\hat{q}_n$. Second, we compose IQ_{CA} as follows:

- *If $k < d$, then $\bar{I}_k$ includes every fresh node variable and tag variable of $\hat{q}_n$.*
- *If $k = d$, then $\bar{V}$ includes the returned tag variable in $\hat{q}_n$, if any.*
- *Let $p_0/p_1/\ldots/p_n$ be a path expression in $\hat{q}_n$, where p_0 is an optional node variable from ancestor query blocks. The body of IQ_{CA} contains $X_0p_1X_1, X_1p_2X_2,\ldots,X_{n-1}p_nX_n$, where $X_k, k \in [1,n]$ are distinct node variables, X_0 is an inherited node variable for p_0, or $\Re$ if p_0 is absent.*

We can now show how to test query containment for c-XQueries. The following theorem shows that it suffices to check query simulation on pairs of indexed conjunctive queries generated from the canonical answers. In the theorem, IQ_{CA} (IQ'_{CA}) refers to Q's (Q''s) indexed conjunctive query for CA.

Theorem 4.4. *Let Q and Q' be two c-XQueries. The containment $Q \sqsubseteq Q'$ holds if and only if for every canonical answer CA of Q, (1) CA is a canonical answer of Q' (modulo tag variable isomorphism); and (2) $IQ_{CA} \preceq IQ'_{CA}$.* □

Together with the insights into kernel canonical answers from Section 3, we obtain the following complexity results, which show that the introduction of output tag variables does not make the containment problem harder. (Note that the first bullet has a slightly stronger condition than in Theorem 3.7. Here, we require that Q has fanout 1, rather than *either Q or Q'* does.)

Theorem 4.5. *Let Q and Q' be c-XQueries.*

- *If Q has a maximal fanout 1, then query containment is in PTIME.*
- *For arbitrary fanout, if either Q or Q' has fixed nesting depth, then containment is coNP-complete.*
- *Otherwise, containment is in coNEXPTIME.* □

4.3 Containment Checking in Practice

Containment checking for general nested queries is hard; however, as query sizes in practice tend to be relatively small, query containment can be employed in application. Furthermore, we can drastically reduce the number of canonical answers for containment checking by analyzing the cardinality of elements in the query answer. In this section, we illustrate the effectiveness of this technique based on the example query in Section 1. Our discussion here is meant to suggest possible optimizations that we have found promising. The effect of these techniques still needs to be verified by a thorough experimental evaluation. We also note that the techniques do not decrease the upper bound of the computational complexity.

The intuition behind our technique is that given the query structure and the underlying XML database schema, we can infer the cardinality of elements in the query answer. Canonical answers violating the cardinality constraints do not need to be considered by our algorithm. Specifically, we prune the canonical answers for containment checking according to the following three rules. Suppose we are testing whether Q is contained in Q'. Let $\hat{p}$ be a query block in Q and t be its tag name.

1. (= 1): If the schema implies that the variables in the FOR clause of $\hat{p}$ will have exactly one binding, then we only need to consider those canonical answers where t occurs *exactly* once within its parent element. This observation also applies if the FOR and WHERE clauses of $\hat{p}$ are empty. Consider the two queries in Figure 2 for example; to test $Q' \sqsubseteq Q$, we only need to check those canonical answers in which every person element contains exactly one name subelement.

2. ($\geq$ 1): A schema can imply that t will occur *at least once* under its parent element. In the above example, if the schema indicates that every group has one or more person subelements, we only need to check those canonical answers in which every area contains at least one person subelement.

3. ($\leq$ 1): If the schema indicates a certain element occurs *at most once* under its parent element, the set of canonical answers can be constrained similarly to the previous case.

Applying all three techniques to the example in Figure 2 demonstrates the effect of pruning. Testing whether $Q' \sqsubseteq Q$ without applying the above techniques requires considering 71 canonical answers. The first rule prunes 68 of them, and the second rule prunes one more, leaving us with only two canonical answers to be considered.

5 Extensions to c-XQuery

The previous section established the basic complexity results on query containment for conjunctive XML queries with nesting. This section discusses several extensions of c-XQueries that occur frequently in applications.

Union and Disjunction: Union can be introduced into XML queries when two sibling query blocks return XML objects with the same tag. This happens when either two sibling query blocks return the same tag constant, or when at least one of the siblings returns a tag variable, which may be instantiated to the same value returned by the other sibling. This form of union does not affect the complexity of the problem.

Disjunctions in the query's XPath expression or WHERE-clause is another way of expressing certain types of unions. This case can be translated into the above cases, but with an exponential blowup in the size of the resulting queries. We refer to queries with disjunctions as *d-XQueries*. We prove the following result.

Theorem 5.1. *Let Q and Q' be d-XQueries. Query containment is coNP-complete in each of the following cases:*

- *Q has nesting depth of 1,*
- *Q has maximal fanout of 1, and*
- *Q has a fixed nesting depth.*

If Q is a c-XQuery, then the complexity results of Theorem 4.5 still apply. □

Table 1: **Complexity Results for Containment of Nested XML Queries**

Nesting Type	cc-XQueries	c-XQueries	With Union	With Negation	With Descendant Edges (//)	With Equi-join on Tags	With Arithmetic Comparisons
Fanout=1 Arbitrary Depth	PTIME	PTIME	coNP complete	coNP complete	coNP complete	NP complete	Π_2^p complete
Arbitrary Fanout Fixed Depth	coNP complete	coNP complete	coNP complete	coNP complete	coNP complete	Π_2^p complete	Π_2^p complete
General	in coNEXPTIME						

Recall that without union, containment is in polynomial time for the first two cases above. This result is analogous to the relational case, where containment for conjunctive queries and containment for queries with unions are both NP-complete, while containment for disjunctive queries (when union can occur anywhere in the query) is Π_2^p complete. The complexity of the first two cases also increases when we consider negation and descendant edges.

Negation: We consider XQueries where predicates in XPath expressions can contain the "not" operator (e.g. *person[not paper]*). This type of negation is similar in spirit to "NOT EXISTS" in SQL. We refer to such queries as *c-XQueries*$^\neg$. We show the following result:

Theorem 5.2. *Let Q and Q' be c-XQueries*$^\neg$. *Query containment is coNP-complete in each of the following cases:*

- *Q has nesting depth of 1,*
- *Q has maximal fanout of 1, and*
- *Q has a fixed nesting depth.* □

Descendant Edges: We refer to c-XQueries in which the XPath expressions contain the descendant axis (//) as *c-XQueries*$^{//}$. Recall that wildcards(*) and branching([...]) are already allowed in c-XQueries. In [30] it is shown that containment of XPath expressions with //,* and [...] is coNP-complete. The following theorem shows that nesting with fixed depth does not increase the complexity of containment.

Theorem 5.3. *Let Q and Q' be c-XQueries*$^{//}$. *Query containment is coNP-complete in each of the following cases:*

- *Q has maximal fanout of 1, and*
- *Q has a fixed nesting depth.*

If the number of // in Q is fixed, then the complexity results of Theorem 4.5 still apply. □

Equi-join Predicates: We consider equi-join predicates on tag variables. They result in cyclic queries, where simulation mapping becomes NP-complete [28]. We refer to c-XQueries with equi-join predicates on tag variables as *c-XQueries*$^=$.

Theorem 5.4. *Testing containment of c-XQueries*$^=$ *with maximal fanout 1 is NP-complete. Testing containment of c-XQueries*$^=$ *with arbitrary fanout but a fixed nesting depth is* Π_2^p-*complete.* □

Arithmetic Comparisons: We consider arithmetic comparisons on tag variables. We assume the comparison predicates are interpreted over an ordered and dense domain, and we consider the predicates $<$ and $\leq$. We refer to queries with arithmetic comparisons as *c-XQueries*$^\leq$. In [37] it is shown that containment of cyclic queries with arithmetic comparisons is Π_2^p-complete. We show the following.

Theorem 5.5. *Let Q and Q' be c-XQueries*$^\leq$. *Query containment is* Π_2^p-*complete in each of the following cases:*

- *Q has maximal fanout of 1, and*
- *Q has a fixed nesting depth.* □

6 Conclusions

XML data is being increasingly used in applications that require integration and sharing of multiple data sources. At several levels, these applications need to reason about the relationship between pairs of queries, either for query reformulation, semantic caching, or various optimization methods. Thus far, in the context of XML, query containment has only been considered for queries expressed as XPath expressions. However, in practice, XQueries are common, and they contain multiple levels of nesting. This paper fills this important gap, by establishing the theoretical underpinnings for XML queries with nesting.

Our results are summarized in Table 1. Our main result is that query containment is coNP-complete for queries with bounded nesting depth, under a variety of conditions. If we consider queries with maximal fanout of 1, then we are able to obtain polynomial-time results in some cases. We have also considered several important practical extensions of the basic conjunctive query language. The main open gap in the complexity analysis is the case of queries with arbitrary nesting depth. In future work, we are interested in extending our containment algorithms to algorithms for answering queries using views. In addition, we would like to perform an empirical evaluation of our containment algorithms and to develop optimizations for common cases.

Acknowledgments

We would like to thank Zack Ives, Richard Ladner, Gerome Miklau, Rachel Pottinger, Dan Suciu, and the reviewers of this paper for their insightful comments and suggestions. This work was supported by NSF ITR grant IIS-0205635 and NSF CAREER grant IIS-9985114.

References

[1] Bea liquid data for weblogic. www.bea.com/liquiddata.

[2] A. Aho, Y. Sagiv, and J. D. Ullman. Equivalence of relational expressions. *SIAM Journal of computing*, (8)2:218–246, 1979.

[3] S. Amer-Yahia, S. Cho, L.V.S.Lakshmanan, and D.Srivastava. Minimization of tree pattern queries. In *Proc. of SIGMOD*, 2001.

[4] P. Bernstein, F. Giunchiglia, A. Kementsietsidis, J. Mylopoulos, L. Serafini, and I. Zaihrayeu. Data management for peer-to-peer computing : A vision. In *Proceedings of the WebDB Workshop*, 2002.

[5] P. Buneman, S. Davidson, G. Hillebrand, and D. Suciu. A query language and optimization techniques for unstructured data. In *Proc. of SIGMOD*, 1996.

[6] P. Buneman, S. Davidson, G. Hillebrand, and D. Suciu. Adding structures to unstructured data. In *Proc. of ICDT*, 1997.

[7] P. Buneman, A. Ohori, and A. Jung. Using powerdomains to generalize relational databases. *Theoretical Computer Science*, 91:23–55, 1991.

[8] D. Calvanese, G. D. Giacomo, M. Lenzerini, D. Nardi, and R. Rosati. Description logic framework for information integration. In *Proceedings of KR*, 1998.

[9] A. K. Chandra and P. M. Merlin. Optimal implementation of conjunctive queries in relational databases. In *Proc. of STOC*, 1977.

[10] S. Chaudhuri and M. Vardi. On the equivalence of recursive and nonrecursive datalog programs. In *Proc. of PODS*, pages 55–66, San Diego, CA., 1992.

[11] S. Chaudhuri and M. Vardi. Optimizing real conjunctive queries. In *Proc. of PODS*, 1993.

[12] A. Deutsch and V. Tannen. Containment and integrity constraints for xpath. In *KRDB*, 2001.

[13] X. Dong, A. Halevy, and I. Tatarinov. Containment of nested xml queries. Technical Report UW-CSE-03-12-05, Univ. of Washington, 2003.

[14] D. Draper, A. Y. Halevy, and D. S. Weld. The nimble integration system. In *Proc. of SIGMOD*, 2001.

[15] M. Fernandez, D. Florescu, A. Levy, and D. Suciu. Verifying integrity constraints on web-sites. In *IJCAI*, 1999.

[16] M. Fernandez, W.-C. Tan, and D. Suciu. Silkroute: Trading between relations and xml. In *WWW*, 1999.

[17] D. Florescu, A. Levy, and D. Suciu. Query containment for conjunctive queries with regular expressions. In *Proc. of PODS*, Seattle,WA, 1998.

[18] M. Friedman, A. Levy, and T. Millstein. Navigational plans for data integration. In *Proceedings of AAAI*, 1999.

[19] A. Gupta, Y. Sagiv, J. D. Ullman, and J. Widom. Constraint checking with partial information. In *Proc. of PODS*, pages 45–55, Minneapolis, Minnesota, 1994.

[20] A. Y. Halevy. Answering queries using views: A survey. *VLDB Journal*, 10(4), 2001.

[21] A. Y. Halevy, Z. G. Ives, D. Suciu, and I. Tatarinov. Schema mediation in peer data management systems. In *Proc. of ICDE*, 2003.

[22] Y. E. Ioannidis and R. Ramakrishnan. Containment of conjunctive queries: Beyond relations as sets. *ACM Transactions on Database Systems*, 20(3):288–324, 1995.

[23] A. Kementsietsidis, M. Arenas, and R. J. Miller. Mapping data in peer-to-peer systems: Semantics and algorithmic issues. In *Proc. of SIGMOD*, 2003.

[24] A. Klug. On conjunctive queries containing in-equalities. *Journal of the ACM*, 35(1):146–160, 1988.

[25] M. Lenzerini. Data integration: A theoretical perspective. In *Proc. of PODS*, 2002.

[26] A. Y. Levy and M.-C. Rousset. Verification of knowledge bases using containment checking. In *Proceedings of AAAI*, 1996.

[27] A. Y. Levy and Y. Sagiv. Queries independent of updates. In *Proc. of VLDB*, 1993.

[28] A. Y. Levy and D. Suciu. Deciding containment for queries with complex objects and aggregations. In *Proc. of PODS*, Tucson, Arizona., 1997.

[29] L. Libkin and L. Wong. Semantic representations and query languages for orsets. In *Proc. of PODS*, 1993.

[30] G. Miklau and D. Suciu. Containtment and equivalence for an xpath fragment. In *Proc. of PODS*, 2002.

[31] T. Milo and D. Suciu. Index structures for path expressions. In *Proc. of ICDT*, pages 277–295, 1999.

[32] W. S. Ng, B. C. Ooi, K.-L. Tan, and A. Zhou. Peerdb: A p2p-based system for distributed data sharing. In *ICDE*, Bangalore, India, 2003.

[33] Y. Sagiv and M. Yannakakis. Equivalence among relational expressions with the union and difference operators. *Journal of the ACM*, 27(4):633–655, 1980.

[34] O. Shmueli. Equivalence of datalog queries is undecidable. *Journal of Logic Programming*, 15:231–241, 1993.

[35] I. Tatarinov and A. Halevy. Efficient query reformulation in peer data management systems. In *SIGMOD (to appear)*, 2004.

[36] J. D. Ullman. Information integration using logical views. In *ICDT*, 1997.

[37] R. van der Meyden. The complexity of querying indefinite data about linearly ordered domains. In *Proc. of PODS*, pages 331–345, San Diego, CA., 1992.

[38] M. Yannakakis. Algorithms for acyclic database schemes. In *Proc. of VLDB*, pages 82–94, 1981.

[39] X. Zhang and M. Z. Ozsoyoglu. On efficient reasoning with implication constraints. In *Proc. of DOOD*, 1993.

Efficient XML-to-SQL Query Translation: Where to Add the Intelligence?

Rajasekar Krishnamurthy *

IBM Almaden Research Center
sekar@cs.wisc.edu

Raghav Kaushik *

Microsoft Research
skaushi@microsoft.com

Jeffrey F Naughton

University of Wisconsin-Madison
naughton@cs.wisc.edu

Abstract

We consider the efficiency of queries generated by XML to SQL translation. We first show that published XML-to-SQL query translation algorithms are suboptimal in that they often translate simple path expressions into complex SQL queries even when much simpler equivalent SQL queries exist. There are two logical ways to deal with this problem. One could generate suboptimal SQL queries using a fairly naive translation algorithm, and then attempt to optimize the resulting SQL; or one could use a more intelligent translation algorithm with the hopes of generating efficient SQL directly. We show that optimizing the SQL after it is generated is problematic, becoming intractable even in simple scenarios; by contrast, designing a translation algorithm that exploits information readily available at translation time is a promising alternative. To support this claim, we present a translation algorithm that exploits translation time information to generate efficient SQL for path expression queries over tree schemas.

1 Introduction

Exporting XML views of relational data gives rise to the problem of translating XML queries into SQL. To date, the focus of most of the work in the published literature [10, 16, 21] has been on mechanisms for correctly translating complex XML queries into SQL queries, with less emphasis on evaluating the quality of the resulting SQL queries. The efficiency of the SQL queries generated by the translation process is the focus in this paper.

* Work done while the authors were students at the University of Wisconsin-Madison.

Permission to copy without fee all or part of this material is granted provided that the copies are not made or distributed for direct commercial advantage, the VLDB copyright notice and the title of the publication and its date appear, and notice is given that copying is by permission of the Very Large Data Base Endowment. To copy otherwise, or to republish, requires a fee and/or special permission from the Endowment.

**Proceedings of the 30th VLDB Conference,
Toronto, Canada, 2004**

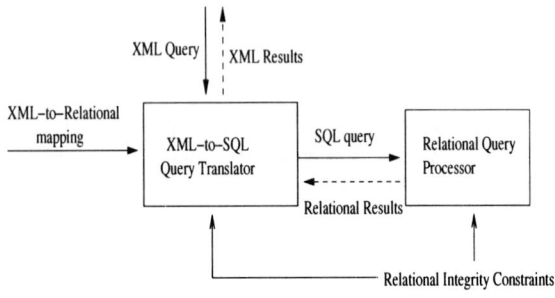

Figure 1: Stages in using an RDBMS to evaluate an XML query

Translating XML queries to SQL involves translating queries over hierarchical schemas into queries over flat relational schemas. This turns out to be problematic — a closer look at the queries generated by the published translation algorithms shows that the hierarchical nature of the exported XML schema is often blindly reflected in the generated SQL query, even when this is clearly not necessary. As a result, in many cases even simple path expression queries result in unnecessarily complex SQL queries. This problem is aggravated when the input XML query includes a traversal of the descendant axis (//), because it does not have a simple equivalent in SQL.

A natural question to ask next is whether the phenomenon of large, complex SQL queries arising from simple XML queries is avoidable, or if it is intrinsic due to the mismatch in data models. We show by example in Section 2.1 that complex SQL is not necessary in many cases — while the SQL generated by published translation algorithms is complex, usually there is a much simpler equivalent SQL query. This observation motivated us to search for techniques that make use of readily available semantic information to improve the quality of the generated SQL.

To understand the alternatives for how we can do this, consider the different stages in the translation process as shown in Figure 1. Given an XML-to-Relational mapping, some relational integrity constraints, and an XML query, the XML-to-SQL query translator generates an equivalent SQL query and hands it over to the relational query processor. The relational query processor optimizes and executes the query, and returns the results to the query translator, which adds the appropriate XML tags to the results and returns them to the user. There are two important points to note here: (i) As the XML-to-Relational mapping and relational integrity constraints are valid across multiple query invocations, they are shown separately, and (ii) We have made no assumptions about whether the XML-to-SQL query translator is inside an RDBMS or in middleware. This is the reason for using the term Relational Query Processor instead of RDBMS for the box on the right.

There are two logical extremes in approaches toward obtaining efficient SQL queries for XML workloads. One could generate suboptimal SQL queries using a fairly naive translation algorithm, and then optimize the resulting SQL queries (SQL Optimization); or one could use a more intelligent query translation algorithm and attempt to generate efficient SQL queries directly (Intelligent Query Translation).

In Section 4, we will show that if we take the SQL Optimization approach, then in order to obtain efficient SQL queries we have to solve the relational query minimization problem under bag semantics. The techniques for query minimization in the published literature rely on algorithms for query containment or query equivalence. Unfortunately, these problems become intractable in even simple scenarios, making the SQL Optimization approach impractical. In view of this problem, we need to find a way to generate good SQL queries that does not require the solution of these intractable problems during actual query translation.

In response to this goal, we propose that Intelligent Query Translation should be used instead of SQL Optimization, and propose a translation approach that relies upon three main ideas. First, we identify a class of tree XML-to-relational mappings called *bijective* mappings. Bijective mappings cover a large class of the mappings we have encountered in print, and they have the desirable property that they can be optimized using containment and equivalence algorithms under set semantics instead of multiset semantics.

Second, we observe that for a given XML schema over a given relational schema, the SQL queries generated from XML queries are not arbitrary. That is, the XML-to-Relational mapping determines the class of SQL queries that are likely to be output by the XML-to-SQL query translation algorithm, which in turn fixes the class of queries that need to be minimized. Since the XML-to-Relational mapping and the underlying relational integrity constraints are independent of the query being optimized, we can use them to precompute some useful information, and then use this information during the runtime query translation. This way, we can move the potentially expensive task of reasoning about integrity constraints to the precomputation phase, keeping the run time overhead small.

Third, the conjunctive queries produced by XML to SQL translation are mainly *chain* queries of the form

$$R(x_n) := R_1(x_1, x_2), R_2(x_2, x_3), \ldots, R_{n-1}(x_{n-1}, x_n)$$

As we will show, in the XML to SQL translation domain, exploiting integrity constraints enables the minimization of such queries by removing a prefix of the relational predicates. We refer to this as *prefix elimination*. This turns out to be more tractable than general conjunctive query minimization.

We show that by exploiting the above three ideas, the XML-to-SQL query translation problem can be solved in polynomial time for path expression queries over bijective tree mappings. Our proof works by presenting a query translation algorithm that solves the problem with the required efficiency. Our algorithm works correctly even over non-bijective mappings; it identifies the bijective portions of the mapping and performs more efficient query translation in those parts. This translation algorithm produces SQL queries that in many cases are far more efficient than those produced by previously published translation algorithms.

The rest of the paper is organized as follows. In Section 2.1, we present an example scenario to illustrate the problems with published XML-to-Relational translation algorithms. Next we define the query translation problem in Section 3. Then, in Section 4, we present some of the known complexity results we bump into if we attempt to minimize the SQL queries after generating them. We describe our strategy for more intelligent query translation in Section 5. A more formal description of the various components of this approach is presented in Section 6.

1.1 Related Work

Translating XML queries into SQL in an XML Publishing context has been addressed in [9, 10, 12, 16, 17, 20]. Excepting MARS [9], the main focus has been on translating complex XML queries into SQL, and not on the quality of the final SQL query. A more detailed description of the existing published work on XML-to-SQL query translation is given in [15].

In MARS [9], a technique for translating XQuery queries into SQL is given, when both Global-As-View (GAV) and Local-As-View (LAV) views are present. The system achieves the combined effect of rewriting-with-views, composition-with-views, and query minimization under integrity constraints. While this technique has its own advantages, it does not produce efficient SQL queries for simple XML queries that contain the descendant axis (//) (like the example in Section 2.1). The technique in MARS [9] can be viewed as a SQL Optimization technique since the main optimization occurs after the SQL query is generated from the XML query. In our work, we assume a simpler setting of only GAV-style views and show how one can obtain efficient SQL queries by placing the intelligence in the translation process.

2 Motivation

2.1 Translation example

In this section, we present an example recursive query (with the descendant axis //) over a tree XML schema to illustrate that even simple XML queries can give rise to fairly complex SQL queries if we use published translation algorithms.

Part of a sample relational schema for an auction database is shown in Figure 2. The figure also shows one way of exporting this data as XML. The example XML schema is part of the XMark benchmark [23] schema. The associated view definition is easy to construct and is omitted. Each node in the XML schema is annotated with a table name, to indicate the relational table that corresponds to the element represented by the node. Each leaf node has a column name next to it, which indicates the column in which the value of corresponding element is stored.

Consider the evaluation of the following query Q_1, which finds the number of items in a given category:

```
count(/Site/Regions//Item/InCategory[
            @Category = 'cat1'])
```

Consider the following simple algorithm for handling queries with the descendant axis (//) [12]: Identify all paths in the schema that satisfy the query. For each path, generate a relational query by joining all relations appearing in this path. The final query is the union of the queries over all satisfying paths (six paths for Q_1). This algorithm will result in the following SQL query SQ_1.

```
select count(*)
from   Site S, Item I, InCat C
where  S.id = I.siteid and I.id = C.itemid and
       C.category='cat1' and I.continent='africa'
union all ... (6 queries)
```

Suppose furthermore that the underlying relational schema has the following domain integrity constraint (in addition to the key and foreign key constraints shown in the figure): the column *Item.continent* has only six potential values {asia, africa, australia, europe, namerica, samerica }.

For the above query, we have found through experimentation that the optimizers in current relational systems will use foreign key constraints to eliminate some redundant joins. For instance, the join between Site and Item can be removed. Though the join between Item and InCat is a key-foreign key join, it cannot be removed due to the condition on Item.continent. Thus the query as rewritten by a relational optimizer becomes the new query SQ_1^1:

```
select count(*)
from   Item I, InCat C
where  I.id = C.itemid and C.category='cat1'
       and I.continent = 'africa'
union all ... (6 queries)
```

We have seen that existing commercial RDBMS optimizers convert SQ_1 to SQ_1^1. A reasonable question is whether the XML to SQL translation routines proposed in SilkRoute [10] and Xperanto [21] do better. We find that by merging common subexpressions, they generate a better initial query than SQ_1. But, interestingly, if you feed the queries that they generate to a relational optimizer, the resulting final query is once again SQ_1^1. So, no matter whether we use a naive XML to relational translation, or these more sophisticated translation schemes, in the end the RDBMS will evaluate SQ_1^1.

Another valid question to ask at this point is whether the algorithms for minimizing XML queries, such as in [3, 18], will help in this context. These algorithms remove parts of the XML query that are made redundant by other parts of the query. Notice that the XML query Q_1 has no redundant parts in it, and so XML query minimization will not help in this case.

Unfortunately, SQ_1^1 is far from optimal, since all of these queries are equivalent to the even simpler OQ_1 given below:

```
select count(*)
from   InCat
where  category = 'cat1'
```

The equivalence between the queries SQ_1, SQ_1^1 and OQ_1 holds under the key, foreign key and domain constraints mentioned above. Notice how we are able to replace a query SQ_1^1, which was the union of six queries each with a join, by a single scan query OQ_1.

2.2 Experimental Study

The previous example showed that while published algorithms translate the example XML query into a fairly complex SQL query, there is an equivalent query that looks much simpler. An important question to answer at this point is whether the associated performance gains are substantial. In order to demonstrate that this improvement can be sizable in practice, we performed an experimental study using two datasets: a synthetic ADEX dataset conforming to a standard advertisement schema [1] and a dataset from the XMark Benchmark [23].

The ADEX dataset conforms to the standard DTD being developed by the Newspaper Association of America Classified Advertising Standards Task Force [1]. This standard is intended to pave the way for the aggregation of classified ads among publishers on the Internet, as well as to enhance the development of classified processing systems. We generated synthetic data conforming to the ADEX schema. This generated data consists of 100K advertisements and 200 publications, and is approximately 150 MB. The XMark Benchmark [23] schema contains information about an auction database and we used the standard 100 MB dataset defined in the benchmark. For both scenarios, we built indexes on all columns that appeared in a query. We ran the experiments using the

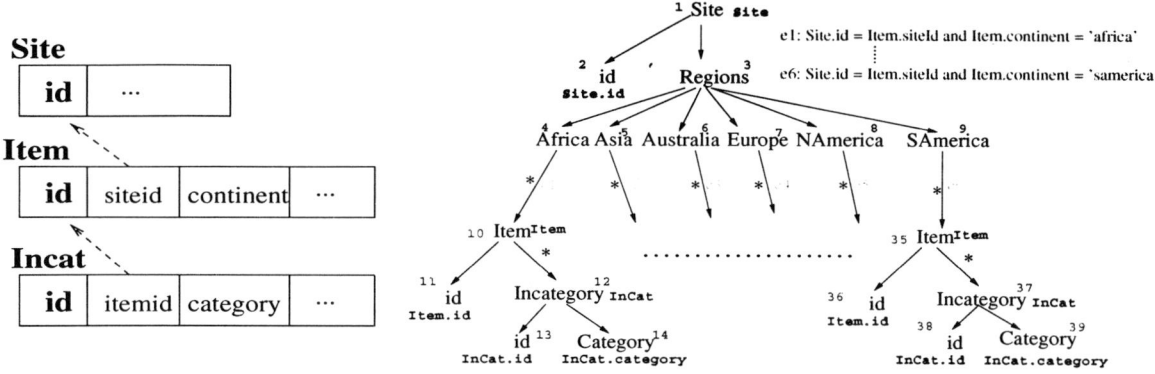

Figure 2: Sample relational schema and corresponding XML view

	Queries	Speedup (Cold buffer)	Speedup (Warm buffer)
A1	Get the number of open-house ads in the campus area	1.22	1.15
A2	Get the number of real-estate ads in the campus area	2.73	3.25
A3	Get the addresses of ads in the campus area	27.05	31.1
A4	For each geographic area, get the number of ads in that area	51.34	92.96
A5	For each person, get the number of times (s)he is a reference	12.82	29.79
A6	For each job category, get the number of people interested in that category	6.11	34.13
X1	Get the number of items in a particular category	2.69	5.56
X2	For a particular person, get categories of items for which (s)he made a bid	5.35	13.20
X3	For each category, get the number of items in that category	6.40	7.63

Table 1: **Relative performance improvement obtained by using constraint information**

IBM DB2 database on a Linux workstation with an Intel 800 MHZ Pentium processor and 256 MB of main memory. The buffer pool was set to 32 MB. A complete description of the experimental setup is given in [14].

We compare the execution times we measured for the queries in Table 1. The queries labeled Ai are on the advertisement dataset, while those labeled Xi are on the XMark dataset. Note that query X1 in this table is the example query we considered in the previous section. For each XML query, we generated relational queries using several prior published algorithms and used the best timing for comparison with our approach, where we use the constraint information as well. The speedups obtained in execution times are given in the table.

The relative improvement in performance ranges from 1.15 to 93. In general, by using the constraint information we do no worse than any of the prior strategies; so the relative performance is always greater than or equal to 1. We found that the actual performance improvement depends on two main factors: (i) number of satisfying paths that can be merged together due to the fact that they have the same relation sequence and (ii) the length of the prefix that can be eliminated.

For example, the wild card in query A1 had two satisfying paths, while that in A2 and A3 had seven and twenty satisfying paths respectively. The response times show that as the number of satisfying paths for a wild card increases, the benefit obtained by our approach also increases considerably. The above three queries have a selection condition on the geographic area of an advertisement. Queries A4, A5 and A6 compute information across all areas. For example, A4 gets the number of ads for each area. Even for these queries, we observed significant speedups when constraint information was used to generate optimized SQL queries.

Similarly, queries X1, X2 and X3 on the XMark dataset also had significant speedups ranging from a factor of 2.7 to a factor of 13.2. The speedup was smaller in these cases relative to the ADEX dataset as the maximum number of satisfying paths for a wild card is only six for the XMark schema.

2.3 Observations

The above experimental results show that by using constraint information it is possible to obtain significant speedups in SQL query execution times in a number of cases. This improvement is markedly higher when the XML query has wild cards in it and the constraints on the data allow several of these branches to be merged. Opportunities for such optimizations occur when we build a hierarchy in the XML view from flat relational data. For example, in the XMark schema in Figure 2 a hierarchy was created by partitioning items based on the continents to which they belong to.

In the rest of the paper, we look at two different ways of attempting to automatically generate these better queries: SQL Optimization, and Intelligent Query Translation. In the former approach, SQL queries are generated in a straightforward fashion and then optimized using the relational integrity constraints. In the latter approach, we use the constraint information during the XML-to-SQL query translation process itself.

3 Problem Definition

In this section, we present a formal description of the XML-to-SQL query translation problem.

For concreteness, we need to provide some mechanism for representing how an XML schema is mapped to a relational schema. In this paper, we use the simple approach of defining an XML view with annotations on the XML schema nodes and edges. A non-leaf node is annotated with a relation name, while a leaf node is annotated with the name of a relational column. Each edge $e = (u \rightarrow v)$ is annotated with a conjunctive query, where the relations allowed in the query are the relational annotations of nodes on the path from the root of the graph to node v. A *simple* XML view is one in which each of the edge annotations involves at most one join condition.

We illustrate this approach to defining views with an example[1]. Consider the relational schema and the corresponding XML view definition in Figure 2. Consider a top-down traversal of this schema, which illustrates how an XML document can be constructed from underlying relational data. The Site element is the root of the document and it has an id child whose value is the value of Site.id attribute. A Regions child element is created within the Site element and six subelements are created within Regions, one for each continent. Within each continent element, the information about the items in that continent are exported. For example, consider the element Africa. The annotation on the outgoing edge (4, 10) indicates that for each tuple in the Item relation corresponding to this continent and satisfying the join condition, an Item subelement is created. For each such item, its id is exported as an id child element and the categories to which the item belongs is represented as incategory subelements. The annotation on edge (10, 12) is a join condition Item.id = InCategory.itemId (not shown in figure). This view definition is an example of a *simple* view definition as each edge annotation has at most one join condition.

In this paper we focus on a simple but useful class of queries: simple path expressions. A simple path expression can be denoted as "$s_1\ l_1\ s_2\ l_2 \ldots s_k\ l_k$," where each of the l_i is a tag name and each of the s_i is either / (denoting a parent-child traversal) or // (denoting an ancestor-descendant traversal).

For a path expression query over a tree XML view, the equivalent relational query output by published translation algorithms can be viewed as the union of several conjunctive queries. So, we consider this class of queries with a simple extension: a disjunction of selection conditions is allowed for each conjunctive query.

---
[1] See [14] for a formal description of the view definition

For concreteness, we need to define what is meant by a translation of an XML query to a SQL query. That is, we need to define when a SQL query is considered a correct translation for a given path expression query Q under a mapping $\mathcal{T}$. Our approach to defining these semantics is to present a straightforward translation algorithm that returns the query $baseline(Q)$. Any SQL query SQ that is equivalent to $baseline(Q)$ under the given relational integrity constraints is a correct SQL translation for the XML query Q.

For a leaf node n in the schema, we define the root-to-leaf query $rtol(n)$ as the SQL query obtained by (conjunctively) combining the annotations on the edges of the root-to-leaf path of n and projecting the annotation of node n. For example, $rtol(14)$ is the query

```
select C.category
from   Site S, Item I, InCat C
where  S.id = I.siteid and I.id = C.itemid
       and I.continent='africa'
```

Given a tree XML-to-Relational mapping $\mathcal{T}$ and a simple path expression query Q, let $S = \{n_1, n_2, \ldots, n_k\}$ denote the set of nodes in $\mathcal{T}$ that match the query Q. Then a *baseline* query translation algorithm is to return the SQL query $\bigcup_{n \in S} rtol(n)$. Let $baseline(Q)$ denote this query.

Finally, we are able to define what we mean by the XML-to-SQL translation problem: Given an XML-to-Relational mapping $\mathcal{T}$, a simple path expression query Q and integrity constraints on the underlying relational schema, find the equivalent SQL query with minimum cost.

The above definition is precise modulo the interpretation of the phrase "minimum cost." Different problems will result with different cost metrics. A reasonable cost metric is the traditional metric for conjunctive query minimization — that is, the cost of a query is the number of relational conjuncts. Let us denote this metric *RelCount*.

4 The SQL Optimization approach

The scenario we presented in Section 2.1 showed that query minimization is a core issue in generating efficient SQL queries for XML workloads. For the class of path expression queries over a tree XML-to-Relational mapping, recall that $baseline(Q)$ is a union of conjunctive queries. Hence, we need to minimize a union of conjunctive queries under multiset semantics in the presence of relational integrity constraints. In this section, we first discuss prior work on relational query minimization and then discuss the impact on the SQL Optimization approach.

4.1 Previous work on Relational Query Minimization

Most, if not all, techniques in the published literature for minimizing relational queries are based on algorithms for query containment or query equivalence.

We next present some known results about the complexity of these problems.

- The containment, equivalence and minimization problems for conjunctive queries under set semantics are NP-complete [2, 5].
- The containment problem for conjunctive queries under multiset semantics is π_2^P-hard [6].
- The equivalence problem for conjunctive queries under multiset semantics is same as graph isomorphism [6].
- The containment and equivalence problems for monotonic relational expressions under set semantics is π_2^P-complete [19].
- The containment problem for union of conjunctive queries is undecidable under multiset semantics [11].

There has also been a lot of work on the use of constraints in query optimization of relational queries [7, 13, 25]. In [13], the query containment problem under functional dependencies and inclusion dependencies is studied. In [22], a scheme for utilizing semantic integrity constraints in query optimization, using a graph theoretic approach, is presented. In [24], a necessary and sufficient condition for the IC-RFT problem (does a conjunctive query always produce an empty result under a given set of implication constraints) is presented and in [25] the results are extended when referential constraints are also allowed. Polynomial equivalence to other problems like the query containment problem are also proved.

More recently, the chase and backchase algorithm (c&b) was introduced in [7] motivated by logical redundancy and physical independence in mediator-like components. This approach brings together use of indexes, use of materialized views, semantic optimization and join/scan minimization and allows non-trivial use of indexes and materialized views through the use of semantic constraints. In [8], the authors present a generalization of the classical chase algorithm for embedded dependencies [4] to a richer class of constraints known as Disjunctive Embedded Dependencies (DEDs).

4.2 Impact on the SQL Optimization approach

While a lot of research has been done on relational query optimization in the presence of constraints, there are some mismatches with what we need in the XML-to-SQL query translation scenario.

- Most of the prior work is on reasoning under set semantics. On the other hand, we need to optimize relational queries under multi-set semantics. We are not aware of any published algorithm for minimizing union of conjunctive queries under multi-set semantics (both in the absence and presence of integrity constraints).

- Even under set semantics, the running time of these algorithms are exponential in the size of the input (relational schema, constraints and query). Incurring this overhead on a per-query basis may be expensive in practice.

- The class of constraints handled by different approaches vary considerably and no single technique dominates the others.

By a simple reduction, we have the following result.

PROPOSITION 1 *Solving the XML-to-SQL Query Translation problem using the SQL Optimization approach for a simple tree XML view under the metric RelCount is at least as hard as minimizing a union of conjunctive queries under multiset semantics.*

5 Intelligent Query Translation

In this section, we present our approach to generating SQL queries that are often more efficient than those generated by existing translation algorithms. We are able to do so by focusing on a tractable yet important subpart of the problem space. This section is somewhat complex; we begin with an overview of our approach and then explain the main components of our approach. A more formal description is presented in the following section (Section 6).

5.1 Outline of our approach

As we saw in the previous section, the SQL Optimization approach has three main problems: (i) lack of techniques for query minimization under multi-set semantics, (ii) high overhead for reasoning using constraints even under set semantics and (iii) variety of techniques for different class of constraints. In the Intelligent Query Translation approach, we circumvent each of these problems in the following fashion.

While reasoning about query minimization under multi-set semantics can be a lot different from reasoning under set semantics, there are scenarios where the two notions are similar. In our approach, we identify a class of views that, informally speaking, have the property that the target relational data is exported *exactly* once in the XML view. We refer to such views as *bijective*, and describe this concept in more detail in Section 5.2. Such mappings have the desirable property that they can be optimized using containment and equivalence algorithms under set semantics instead of multiset semantics. In our approach, we identify parts of the mapping that are bijective and apply our optimizations to those parts.

In order to address problems (ii) and (iii), we adopt the following strategy. By observing that the XML-to-Relational mapping and the underlying relational integrity constraints remain constant across multiple query invocations, we compute some summary information in a precomputation phase. In this precomputation phase, we make use of an algorithm for reasoning about conjunctive query containment under set

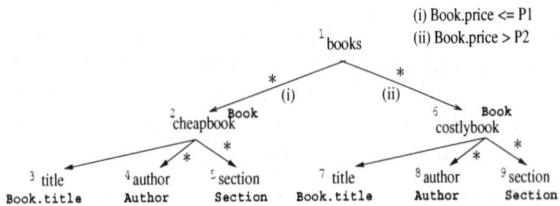

Figure 3: Sample mapping

semantics (say $\mathcal{A}$). Then, when we need to translate an XML query into SQL, we use this summary information in the run-time query translation phase. This way, the potentially expensive part of reasoning using integrity constraints is moved to a (offline) phase and the run-time overhead is kept small. In addition, we can make use of different algorithms for $\mathcal{A}$ that work for varying classes of relational integrity constraints. This is especially useful as we can choose algorithm $\mathcal{A}$ based on the class of relational integrity constraints that are applicable for the current relational schema.

Since, we are going to use some summary information during the run-time query translation process, we need to relax the optimality metric that we hope to achieve. As we have seen in Section 2.1, optimizing SQL generated by XML to SQL translation frequently involves eliminating unnecessary prefixes in the SQL queries. Motivated by this observation, we define a different notion of minimality for generated SQL queries — one where we would like to maximize the length of the prefix eliminated for each matching path in the schema. We define this metric, *PrefixMetric* in Section 5.3.

Using the above techniques, we developed a *constraint-aware* approach to efficiently translate path expression queries into SQL. We describe the main components of our approach informally in the following subsections. A more formal description of our approach is presented in Section 6.

5.2 Bijective mappings

Consider the XML schema shown in Figure 3, which represents information about a collection of books. The XML view has created a simple hierarchy, partitioning the books into cheap and costly books by the relationship of their prices to two constants P_1 and P_2.

Let us now consider three possible scenarios: $P_1 = P_2$, $P_1 < P_2$ and $P_1 > P_2$. If $P_1 = P_2$, then the XML view has information about all the books exactly once, while if $P_1 < P_2$ the XML view has information about only certain books. On the other hand, when $P_1 > P_2$, the XML view has information about the books in the price range $\{P_2 - P_1\}$ twice.

The scenario when $P_1 = P_2$ corresponds to an interesting and common class of mappings, one in which there is a one-to-one correspondence between the XML view data and the underlying relational data. We refer to this class of mappings as *bijective*. These mappings have the property that the query results of two root-to-leaf path queries do not have any common results, so

the corresponding SQL queries can be merged without worrying about preserving counts of duplicates.

For example, the *rtol* queries for nodes 3 and 7 returning the titles of cheapbooks and costlybooks will not have any common results when the mapping is bijective. This simple observation makes the query minimization process a lot simpler as we can use algorithms for query minimization under set semantics instead of multiset semantics.

Notice that whether an XML view definition is *bijective* or not is a property of the view, and that one cannot determine if an XML view definition is bijective by simply examining the relational schema without the mapping. So, while one can easily use this information during the query translation process (where we know about the XML view), in order to perform similar optimizations after the SQL query has been generated, the appropriate module (be it the relational optimizer or some other module) needs to know about properties of the XML view. This means that if existing relational optimizers are to be extended to handle optimizations based upon bijective views, they need to be extended to understand XML views, which is not very attractive.

5.3 Prefix Elimination Optimality

We define the cost metric $PrefixMetric(SQ, \mathcal{T})$ to be the number of nodes in the XML-to-Relational mapping $\mathcal{T}$ that correspond to the SQL query SQ. For example, consider the query SQ_1 in Section 2.1. The fragment of this query identifying items in Africa corresponds to the sequence of nodes $<1,3,4,10,12,14>$, and so the cost is six. Since there are six such fragments in SQ_1, the total cost $PrefixMetric(SQ_1, \mathcal{T})$ is 36. Similarly, the cost for each fragment of query SQ_1^1 is four and the total cost $PrefixMetric(SQ_1^1, \mathcal{T})$ is 24. For query OQ_1, the total cost $PrefixMetric(OQ_1, \mathcal{T})$ is six.

By definition, the cost of any SQL query that does not correspond to a path in the mapping is undefined.

Notice that the definition of the *PrefixMetric* metric restricts the class of equivalent SQL queries considered. For example, we are only interested in finding equivalent queries that are in some sense "syntactically" contained in some conjunctive query fragment in *baseline* (Q). While this misses opportunities to find equivalent queries that involve materialized views or cached query results or eliminating intermediate relations in the conjunctive query, it is still general enough to cover a large number of interesting scenarios.

5.4 The query translation algorithm

In this section, we briefly explain the main components of our query translation algorithm using examples. The algorithm has two parts: an (offline) pre-computation phase, in which summary information is computed; and a run time phase when the actual query translation occurs.

5.4.1 Precomputation Phase

Here, we make use of the fact that the XML-to-Relational mapping and the relational integrity constraints are valid across multiple queries and use them to precompute some summary information. The information that we precompute is related to properties of the root-to-leaf queries we discussed in connection with the semantics of translation in Section 3.

For a given node in the XML schema, it may be possible to eliminate a prefix of its corresponding root to leaf query. The actual prefix that can be eliminated for a leaf node varies depending on the subset of schema nodes selected by the query. We define the notion of **L**east **D**istinguishing **A**ncestors (LDAs) to capture this. For each pair of leaf nodes (u, v), we compute $LDA(u, v) = w$. Intuitively, w is the lowest ancestor of u such that if node u matches a given XML query, it is sufficient to issue the query from $w - u$ (instead of the root to leaf query for u) without returning any results corresponding to node v. In order to create the query for a node u, it suffices to pick the highest ancestor among $LDA(u, v)$ over all leaf nodes v not matching the query.

For example, for the schema in Figure 2, $LDA(14, 39) = 4$ and $LDA(39, 14) = 9$. In other words, if node 14 matches a query and node 39 does not, then it suffices to issue the query corresponding to the path $\{4, 10, 12, 14\}$ in order to return the results corresponding to node 14. This query is shown below.

```
select IC.category
from Item I, Incat IC
where I.id = IC.itemid and I.continent = 'africa'
```

In our precomputation phase, for every pair of non-leaf nodes u, v that have the same annotation, we compute $LDA(u, v)$. In addition, we identify the parts of the XML view definition that are bijective. In our running example, the entire XML view is bijective.

5.4.2 Run-time Query Translation

We use the following query on the mapping schema in Figure 2 to illustrate the translation algorithm.

Q: //Item/InCategory/Category

We first execute Q on the schema graph and identify the satisfying nodes: $S = \{14, 19, 24, 29, 34, 39\}$. For each node $n \in S$, issuing $rtol(n)$ is a correct translation. Our goal is to find the smallest suffix of each such query. Consider the leaf node $n_1 = 14$. We need to identify the lowest ancestor a_1 of n_1 such that it suffices to output the query for the path $<a_1, ..., n_1>$. In order to find a_1, we look at the other nodes with the same annotation, namely $C = \{19, 24, 29, 34, 39\}$ and compute $LDA(14, x), \forall x \in (C - S)$. The highest node among these corresponds to a_1. In this particular case, $(C - S)$ is empty, so we do not have to look at the LDA values. As a result, for node 14 it suffices to issue the scan query corresponding to the leaf node. We obtain a similar scan query for the other five schema nodes in S. Since the six scan queries are on the same relation, we merge them and issue a single query OQ given below:

```
select C.eid from InCat C
```

On the other hand, using existing algorithms we would have obtained a relational query SQ that is the union of six queries, each with two joins (similar to the example query SQ_1 in Section 2.1).

5.5 Analysis

The proofs of the theorems in this section are omitted due to lack of space and are presented in [14].

THEOREM 1 *Given a tree XML-to-Relational mapping $\mathcal{T}$ along with the integrity constraints that hold on the underlying relational schema, and a path expression query P, the constraint-aware algorithm outputs a correct equivalent SQL query in polynomial time.*

We would like to point out that our algorithm performs XML-to-SQL query translation correctly even when part of the mapping is not bijective or when the conjunctive query containment algorithm $\mathcal{A}$ is sound but not complete for the class of relational constraints that are applicable. Note that the running time of algorithm $\mathcal{A}$ does not impact the complexity of the translation algorithm, since $\mathcal{A}$ is run once as a precomputation step, not on a per-query basis during translation.

Let Q_1 be a conjunctive query and Q_2 be a union of conjunctive queries. Let UQC denote the problem: is $Q_1 \subseteq Q_2$ under set semantics? and DUP denote the problem: Are the results of Q_1 duplicate-free?

Suppose $\mathcal{C}$ is the class of integrity constraints that hold on the relational schema and $\mathcal{A}$ and $\mathcal{A}'$ are sound and complete algorithms for the UQC and DUP problems over this class of constraints. Examples of such algorithms and a description of the corresponding class of integrity constraints can be found in [7, 25]. In such cases, our algorithm actually outputs the optimal query under metric *PrefixMetric*.

THEOREM 2 *Given sound and complete algorithms $\mathcal{A}$ and $\mathcal{A}'$ for the UQC and DUP problems over the class $\mathcal{C}$, the XML-to-SQL Query Translation problem for a bijective tree XML view under metric PrefixMetric can be solved in polynomial time.*

6 The *constraint-aware* approach

In this section, we formally describe the various components of our approach. We start by describing some terminology used in the formalization followed by the actual description of the two main components: precomputation phase and run-time query translation phase.

6.1 Terminology

Most of the properties we talk about address leaf nodes in the schema that are annotated with the same relational column. We define $nodes(R.C)$ to be the set of leaf nodes annotated with $R.C$. We call two leaf nodes *column-compatible* if they are annotated with the same relational column. We refer to the annotation of node n as $annot(n)$.

Recall that we defined $rtol(n)$ to be the root-to-leaf query for a node n. We generalize this notion to an arbitrary sequence of nodes as follows. A *node sequence* $NS = <n_1, n_2, \ldots, n_k>$ is a sequence of nodes in the schema graph that corresponds to a path starting from the node $n_1 = NS.first$ and terminating in the leaf node $n_k = NS.last$. The relational query $Query(NS)$ is obtained by combining the conditions on the edges of the sequence and projecting $annot(n_k)$. The relational query $keyQuery(NS)$ is the same as $Query(NS)$, except that the key column(s) of $Rel(n_k)$ is (are) also projected. $Query(NS)$ and $keyQuery(NS)$ are always conjunctive queries. Just like $Query(NS)$ corresponds to $rtol(n)$, we refer to $keyQuery(NS)$ as $keyrtol(n)$.

Let $RelSeq(NS)$ denote the sequence of relations joined in $Query(NS)$, in a bottom-up order. For example, for $NS = <1, 3, 4, 10, 12>$, $RelSeq(NS) = $ <InCat,Item,Site>.

Two node sequences NS_1 and NS_2 are said to be *combinable* if the corresponding relation sequences $RelSeq(NS_1)$ and $RelSeq(NS_2)$ are the same, the join conditions are on the same set of columns for each pair of relations, and $NS_1.last$ and $NS_2.last$ are column-compatible. In other words, the two relation sequences are identical modulo the selection conditions.

6.2 Precomputation Phase

Recall that, in the precomputation phase we identify the parts of the XML-to-Relational mapping that are bijective and also compute LDA information. We formally define these two notions in the next two subsections and then describe how we compute this information.

6.2.1 Bijective column mappings

For a relational column $R.C$, let $KeyProject(R.C)$ denote the query "select R.key, R.C from R" and $NodeKeyProject(R.C)$ denote the query $\bigcup_{n \in nodes(R.C)} keyrtol(n)$. Here, $R.key$ denotes the key column(s) of R. We will make use of the following definitions:

DEFINITION 1 *For a relational column $R.C$,*

- *If $KeyProject(R.C) \subseteq NodeKeyProject(R.C)$, then $R.C$ is At-least-once mapped*

- *If $KeyProject(R.C) \supseteq NodeKeyProject(R.C)$, then $R.C$ is At-most-once mapped*

- *If $KeyProject(R.C) = NodeKeyProject(R.C)$, then $R.C$ is bijectively mapped*

In the preceding definition, the containment operations are under multi-set semantics.

Informally, if all the values in the column $R.C$ appear in the XML view "exactly once", then the relational column is bijectively mapped. In order to check this under multi-set semantics, we use the key field(s) of the relation R.

An XML-to-Relational mapping $\mathcal{T}$ is bijectively mapped if each of the relational columns annotating some leaf node in $\mathcal{T}$ is bijectively mapped.

6.2.2 Lowest Distinguishing Ancestor

Let u and v be two column-compatible leaf nodes in the schema. Let node sequence $NS = <n_1, n_2, \ldots, n_k>$, where $n_1 = root(\mathcal{T})$ and $n_k = u$, represent the root-to-leaf path in to u.

DEFINITION 2 *The node n_j is a distinguishing ancestor for u with respect to v if the intersection of the results of the two queries, $keyQuery(<n_j, \ldots, n_k>)$ and $keyrtol(v)$, is empty.*

If n_j is a *distinguishing ancestor* for u with respect to v, then we write $u \mid^{n_j} v$. Thus, for the above example, 4 is a distinguishing ancestor of 14 with respect to every other *column-compatible* node. In other words, issuing the query from 4 to 14, we will obtain all the results corresponding to node 14 and no result corresponding to any other column-compatible node (such as node 39).

Observe that the *distinguishing ancestor* relation is not a symmetric relation. For example, in the annotated schema graph shown in Figure 2, consider schema nodes 14 and 39, which are column-compatible. Now, $14 \mid^4 39$ is true. Notice that node 4 is an ancestor of node 14 but not an ancestor of node 39. So, $39 \mid^4 14$ is false.

DEFINITION 3 *The lowest distinguishing ancestor for u with respect to v, $u \parallel v$, is the lowest ancestor w of u such that $u \mid^w v$.*

We represent this as $w = lda(u, v)$ or $w = u \parallel v$. The lda relation is not symmetric. For example, $14 \parallel 39 = 4 \neq 39 \parallel 14$.

Using these definitions, and our previously defined notion of a a bijective column mapping, we have the following lemma that aids in the identification of lowest distinguishing ancestors:

LEMMA 1 *Let u and v be two column-compatible nodes in the schema graph $\mathcal{T}$, where $annot(u) = annot(v) = R.C$ and $R.C$ is bijectively mapped. Then $u \mid^{root(\mathcal{T})} v$ holds.*

6.2.3 Computing Summary Information from the Constraints

Given an XML-to-Relational mapping $\mathcal{T}$ and the integrity constraints that hold on the underlying relational schema, we precompute the following information

- For each relational column $R.C$, is $R.C$ bijective?
- For every pair of column-compatible nodes (u,v), $u \parallel v$ and $v \parallel u$.

In this computation, we use procedures for solving the following problems on conjunctive queries in the presence of constraints.

UQC: Given a conjunctive query Q_1 and a union of conjunctive queries Q_2, is $Q_1 \subseteq Q_2$ under set semantics?

EQI: Is the intersection of two given conjunctive queries empty?

DUP: Are the results of a given conjunctive query duplicate-free?

We have developed procedures for these three problems by adapting the chase and query containment algorithms proposed in [8]. We have also designed an alternate solution using the algorithm proposed in [25]. In general, any algorithm for conjunctive query containment under set semantics can be used to develop procedures for the above three problems. The details of the above procedures and how we use them to pre-compute the required summary information are omitted due to lack of space. These details can be found in [14].

6.3 Run-Time Query Translation Algorithm

The run-time query translation algorithm is outlined in Figure 4. Given a path expression query Q, we first identify the parts of the schema that match the query. Let S denote the set of matching schema nodes. For purposes of exposition, we assume that S consists only of leaf nodes, leaving the handling of non-leaf nodes to Section 6.4.1.

We then partition the set S into two sets based on whether the corresponding relational column is bijectively mapped. For the set S_{nonbij}, we construct the root-to-leaf queries just like prior algorithms. On the other hand, for the set S_{bij} we utilize the summary information to eliminate parts of the query that are redundant. This is a two stage process: first we find the longest prefix that can be eliminated for each node $n \in S_{bij}$ (*Prefix-Elimination*); then we construct the SQL query using the prefix-eliminated set of nodes (*SQLGen*). Finally, we union the queries corresponding to the bijective and non-bijective nodes.

We next describe the prefix-elimination and *SQL-Gen* stages.

6.3.1 Eliminating Redundant Prefixes

The *Prefix-Elimination* algorithm is given in Figure 5. We use the pre-computed information about least distinguishing ancestors in this computation. Instead of taking the naive approach of issuing the full query for each of these nodes and taking their union, we wish, at the very least, to be able to issue a smaller query

procedure *constraint-aware*(Q)
begin
    Let $S \leftarrow NodeId(Q)$
    Partition S into S_{bij} and S_{nonbij}
        based on whether $annot(n)$ is *bijective*
    $SQL_{nonbij} = \bigcup_{n \in S_{nonbij}} rtol(n)$
    Prefix-Elimination(S_{bij})
    $SQL_{bij} = SQLGen(S_{bij})$
    Return $SQL_{bij} \bigcup SQL_{nonbij}$
end

Figure 4: *constraint-aware* **query translation algorithm for path expression queries**

procedure Prefix-Elimination(S)
begin
    for each node $n \in S$ do
        Let $Schema(n)$ denote the set of schema nodes
        mapped to the same column as n
        Let $Conflict(n) \leftarrow Schema(n) - S$
        Let LDA_Set(n) denote set of $n \parallel x$ for
        every node x in Conflict(n)
        C_lda(n) = highest node in LDA_Set(n)
    While true do
        If $(\exists n, n_1 \in S)$, such that
        RelSeq(C_lda(n),n) and RelSeq(C_lda(n_1),n_1)
        are not combinable **and**
        $n \parallel n_1$ is a strict ancestor of C_lda(n)
    Then
        C_lda(n) = $n \parallel n_1$
    Else
        Break
end

Figure 5: **Prefix-Elimination phase**

for each node $n \in S$. Thus, we want to find the lowest ancestor a such that $Query(<a,\ldots,n>)$ returns the correct answer, that is, where the prefix of $rtol(n)$ from $root(\mathcal{T})$ to a can be safely eliminated. There are two conditions to check here:

- a must distinguish n from all column-compatible nodes not in S. This computation corresponds to the *for* loop in Figure 5.
- For each column-compatible node $n_1 \in S$, either the two queries are combinable or a distinguishes n from n_1. This corresponds to the *while* loop in Figure 5.

The *while* loop is an iterative process that will terminate in at most $(k*d)$ iterations, where $k = |S|$ and d is the maximum depth (in the XML schema) among all nodes in S. At the end of this process we have the prefix eliminated node sequence for every node in S.

6.3.2 *SQLGen* Stage

We next construct the optimized SQL query by taking the prefix-eliminated set of nodes and grouping multiple paths that involve the same sequence of relations.

Let $\mathcal{NS} = \{<C\_lda(n),\ldots,n>: n \in \textit{NodeId}(Q)\}$. Notice that combinability of node sequences is an equivalence relation. We partition $\mathcal{NS}$ based on combinability and construct a SQL query for each equivalence class created. The final SQL query is the union of the queries across all equivalence classes. Notice that all the queries in an equivalence class have the same relation sequence and differ only in the selection conditions. This operation is correct under multi-set semantics because it is only applied to columns that are bijectively mapped.

6.4 Extensions to More General Cases

In this section, we discuss how the methods discussed to up to this point extend to more general situations. Note that our optimization techniques will never generate an incorrect query — they will either not apply (in which case we will generate the naive query) or they will apply and will generate a query expected to be more efficient than the naive query. Hence the discussion here outlines techniques that allow us to apply optimizations to more queries.

6.4.1 Path Expression Queries Involving Non-Leaf Nodes

In our discussion in Section 6.3 on translating path expression queries, we assumed that the query matches a set of leaf nodes in the schema. If the result includes non-leaf nodes as well, then there are two alternative ways of returning the resulting XML elements corresponding to the non-leaf nodes.

1. For each non-leaf element, we can return an identifier or representative subelement. In this case, each non-leaf node n in the schema is associated with a child leaf node n_c. If n appears in a query result, then the corresponding n_c elements are returned instead. For example, we can associate the key field(s) of the corresponding relations with each non-leaf node.

2. For each non-leaf element, we can return the entire subtree rooted at this element. The problem of efficiently constructing entire subtrees of XML documents has been considered in [10, 21]. We leave the interesting problem of combining our algorithm with one of these algorithms for future work.

6.4.2 Beyond Path Expressions

Our techniques can be extended in a straightforward way to handle branching path expression queries (as we show in [14]); because that extension does not provide any additional insight, and due to space constraints, we do not discuss that extension here.

We now briefly describe how to extend *constraint-aware* translation to more general queries. A path expression query corresponds to a single For clause in XQuery. Consider an XQuery that has several of these For clauses and (optional) Where clauses. A natural way of applying our techniques is to perform *constraint-aware* translation for each of the individual path expressions, and then combine the resulting queries with appropriate join conditions. For example, consider a query XQ involving two path expressions p_1 and p_2 with a join condition between them. We apply our *constraint-aware* translation on p_1 and p_2 individually to obtain relational queries Q_1 and Q_2 respectively. Note that Q_1 and Q_2 are the union of k_1 and k_2 queries respectively. We generate the query $Q = Q_1 \bowtie Q_2$ as the SQL query corresponding to XQ. If $k_1 > 1$ or $k_2 > 1$, then we could have generated the final SQL query in a number of other ways. For example, we could have distributed the unions over the join and generated the query Q' that is the union of $k_1 * k_2$ queries. Choosing the best query from amongst these (possibly exponential) alternatives is also an interesting area for future work.

6.4.3 Beyond Bijective Mappings

Recall that our technique optimizes the SQL query corresponding to bijective parts of the mapping. It constructs the *baseline* query for the non-bijective parts of the mapping. While we expect bijectively mapped columns to be common, we have extended our algorithm to perform efficient XML to SQL query translation when either the At-least-once or the At-most-once condition is satisfied. We outline the main ideas here with an example and omit the details due to lack of space.

Let us look at the scenario when a relational column $R.C$ satisfies the At-most-once condition but violates the At-least-once condition. For example, consider the example in Figure 2. While the XMark XML schema contains information about items in six continents, in reality, there is actually a seventh continent (Antarctica). So, it is reasonable to assume that the relational schema has an integrity constraint on *Item.continent* allowing seven potential values. In this case, parts of the relational data are not present in the XML view, namely the items corresponding to Antarctica. Now while SQ_1 and SQ_1^1 are correct SQL queries for Q_1, OQ_1 is not. The best query in this scenario will be a variation of SQ_1^1 that combines all the six queries into one, since they are on the same sequence of relations. This query is given below.

```
select  count(*)
from    Item I, InCat C
where   I.id = C.itemid and C.category='cat1'
        and I.continent IN {'africa',...,'samerica'}
```

Notice how we were able to group together the six paths corresponding to different continents. This was possible due to the fact that InCat.category satisfied the At-most-Once condition. As a result, the rtol queries corresponding to any two column-compatible schema nodes mapped to InCat.category will not have any common results. So, we can translate the unions to a disjunction. In other words, we can perform the *SQLGen* phase without any change.

On the other hand, we need to be careful in the prefix-elimination stage. We cannot eliminate any prefix below the continent nodes due to one missing continent in the XML schema. To account for this fact, we have to augment the prefix-elimination stage. We do this as follows: $S = nodes(InCat.category) = \{14, 19, 24, 29, 34, 39\}$. For each schema node $n \in S$, we compute the lowest schema node below which the prefix cannot be eliminated (since the column is not completely exported). Let us call this *lowest required ancestor* (lra(n)). For example, lra(14) = 4 and lra(39) = 9. This ensures that the selection condition on Item.continent is always present in the query.

The lra computation is another summary information that we precompute for schema nodes corresponding to relational columns that violate the At-least-once condition.

7 Conclusion

We have considered the problem of generating efficient SQL queries for XML workloads and showed that published translation algorithms can generate SQL queries that are suboptimal. We consider the problem of where to add the intelligence in order to obtain optimized SQL queries using integrity constraint information. Our results argue that the quality of the resulting SQL should be a concern of the translation algorithm itself, rather being left in the hands of a traditional relational optimizer. This is because many "easy" opportunities for optimization are apparent only when the XML view definition and relational integrity constraints are considered simultaneously. These opportunities vanish by the time the relational optimizer is presented with SQL.

A number of directions for future research exist. Extending our approach to a more general class of XML-to-Relational mappings (including recursive mappings) is an interesting problem. Similarly, looking at a larger class of input XML queries gives rise to other interesting problems. In a different direction, the XML-to-SQL query translation problem also arises in another context: XML Storage, where data that was originally XML is to be stored and queried in an RDBMS (as opposed to the case considered here, where data that was originally relational is to be viewed and queried as XML.) The class of XML-to-Relational mappings produced by existing techniques for XML storage are bijective and there may be alternative ways of computing the summary information without even resorting to relational integrity constraints. Exploring this variant of the problem is another open problem.

Acknowledgement: This work was supported in part by NSF grant ITR-0086002.

References

[1] Naa classified advertising standards task force. http://www.naa.org/technology/clsstdtf/.

[2] A. Aho, Y. Sagiv, and J. Ullman. Equivalence among relational expressions. *SIAM J. Comput.*, 8(2), 1979.

[3] S. Amer-Yahia, S. Cho, L. V. S. Lakshmanan, and D. Srivastava. Minimization of tree pattern queries. In *SIGMOD*, 2001.

[4] C. Beeri and M. Vardi. A proof procedure for data dependencies. *Journal of the ACM*, 31(4), 1984.

[5] A. K. Chandra and P. M. Merlin. Optimal implementation of conjunctive queries in relational data bases. In *ACM STOC*, 1977.

[6] S. Chaudhuri and M. Y. Vardi. Optimization of real conjunctive queries. In *PODS*, 1993.

[7] A. Deutsch, L. Popa, and V. Tannen. Physical data independence, constraints and optimization with universal plans. In *VLDB*, 1999.

[8] A. Deutsch and V. Tannen. Containment and Integrity Constraints for XPath Fragments. In *KRDB*, 2001.

[9] A. Deutsch and V. Tannen. MARS: A System for Publishing XML from Mixed and Redundant Storage. In *VLDB*, 2003.

[10] M. Fernandez, A. Morishima, and D. Suciu. Efficient Evaluation of XML Middle-ware Queries. In *SIGMOD*, 2002.

[11] Y. E. Ioannidis and R. Ramakrishnan. Containment of conjunctive queries: beyond relations as sets. *ACM TODS*, 20(3), 1995.

[12] S. Jain, R. Mahajan, and D. Suciu. Translating XSLT Programs to Efficient SQL Queries. In *WWW*, 2002.

[13] D. S. Johnson and A. C. Klug. Testing containment of conjunctive queries under functional and inclusion dependencies. In *PODS*, 1982.

[14] R. Krishnamurthy, R. Kaushik, and J. F. Naughton. Efficient XML-to-SQL Query Translation: Where to Add the Intelligence? (full version). http://www.cs.wisc.edu/sekar/publications.html.

[15] R. Krishnamurthy, R. Kaushik, and J. F. Naughton. XML-SQL Query Translation Literature: The State of the Art and Open Problems. In *XML Database Symposium*, 2003.

[16] C. Li, P. Bohannon, H. Korth, and P.P.S. Narayan. Composing XSL Transformations with XML Publishing Views. In *SIGMOD*, 2003.

[17] I. Manolescu, D. Florescu, and D. Kossman. Answering XML queries over heterogeneous data sources. In *VLDB*, 2001.

[18] P. Ramanan. Efficient algorithms for minimizing tree pattern queries. In *SIGMOD*, 2002.

[19] Y. Sagiv and M. Yannakakis. Equivalences among relational expressions with the union and difference operators. *Journal of the ACM (JACM)*, 27(4), 1980.

[20] J. Shanmugasundaram, J. Kiernan, E. J. Shekita, C. Fan, and J. Funderburk. Querying XML Views of Relational Data. In *VLDB*, 2001.

[21] J. Shanmugasundaram, E. Shekita, R. Barr, M. Carey, B. Lindsay, H. Pirahesh, and B. Reinwald. Efficiently Publishing Relational Data as XML Documents. In *VLDB*, 2000.

[22] S. T. Shenoy and Z. M. Ozsoyoglu. A system for semantic query optimization. In *SIGMOD*, 1987.

[23] Xmark: The xml benchmark project. http://monetdb.cwi.nl/xml/index.html.

[24] X. Zhang and Z. M. Ozsoyoglu. On efficient reasoning with implication constraints. In *DOOD*, 1993.

[25] X. Zhang and Z. M. Ozsoyoglu. Implication and referential constraints: A new formal reasoning. *TKDE*, 9(6), 1997.

Taming XPath Queries by Minimizing Wildcard Steps

Chee-Yong Chan[*]
National University of Singapore
chancy@comp.nus.edu.sg

Wenfei Fan
University of Edinburgh & Bell Laboratories
wenfei@inf.ed.ac.uk

Yiming Zeng
National University of Singapore
zengyimi@comp.nus.edu.sg

Abstract

This paper presents a novel and complementary technique to optimize an XPath query by minimizing its wildcard steps. Our approach is based on using a general composite axis called the *layer axis*, to rewrite a sequence of XPath steps (all of which are wildcard steps except for possibly the last) into a single layer-axis step. We describe an efficient implementation of the layer axis and present a novel and efficient rewriting algorithm to minimize both non-branching as well as branching wildcard steps in XPath queries. We also demonstrate the usefulness of wildcard-step elimination by proposing an optimized evaluation strategy for wildcard-free XPath queries that enables selective loading of only the relevant input XML data for query evaluation. Our experimental results not only validate the scalability and efficiency of our optimized evaluation strategy, but also demonstrate the effectiveness of our rewriting algorithm for minimizing wildcard steps in XPath queries. To the best of our knowledge, this is the first effort that addresses this new optimization problem.

1 Introduction

XPath [15] is a widely-used language for XML data, and it is a core component of several important XML languages including XSLT [6] and XQuery [4]. While there has been a host of work on the efficient evaluation of XPath queries

---

[*]Supported in part by NUS grants R-252-000-164-112/101.

Permission to copy without fee all or part of this material is granted provided that the copies are not made or distributed for direct commercial advantage, the VLDB copyright notice and the title of the publication and its date appear, and notice is given that copying is by permission of the Very Large Data Base Endowment. To copy otherwise, or to republish, requires a fee and/or special permission from the Endowment.

**Proceedings of the 30th VLDB Conference,
Toronto, Canada, 2004**

(e.g., structural join algorithms [1, 5, 11], specialized indexing techniques [16, 14]), research on the optimization of XPath queries itself has only begun to attract more attention. Since the size of an XPath query (in terms of the number of steps) is a key determinant of its evaluation complexity (e.g., [8]), an obvious optimization that has been explored is to minimize the size of a XPath query by eliminating redundant steps [17, 2, 13]. More recent work has shifted to understanding the properties of XPath expressions to identify useful rewriting rules [3], eliminating reverse axes in queries to facilitate their evaluation on streaming data [12], and to transforming queries to algebraic form for efficient evaluation [10].

In this paper, we present a novel and complementary approach to optimizing XPath queries by minimizing (non-redundant) wildcard steps. A *wildcard step* refers to an XPath step with the wildcard nodetest; examples include *child::** and *ancestor::**. Wildcard steps are commonly used when the element names are unknown or do not matter. For example, wildcard steps are common when querying against some secured XML views in the form of DTDs where some element labels have been intentionally replaced with wildcard-equivalent labels to hide their original labels [7]. Wildcard steps are also useful as shorthand notation to represent a set of element names. For example, if a publication element has either a journal or conference subelement, then the query /child::publication/child::journal/child::title union /child::publication/child::conference/child::title can be expressed more succinctly using the wildcard-based path expression /child::publication/child::*/child::title. Furthermore, queries generated from certain optimization techniques (e.g., rewriting techniques to eliminate reverse axes [12]) may also contain wildcard steps. Thus, wildcard steps are very convenient and useful in XPath queries.

However, wildcard steps can be rather expensive to evaluate; for example, evaluating desc::* would require accessing all the descendant nodes of a context node. Thus removing/reducing wildcard steps in a query q is an important optimization issue. The basic idea of our approach is to rewrite a sequence of two steps s_1 and s_2, where s_1

is a wildcard step and either s_2 is the next step following s_1 in q (i.e., $s_1[\ldots]\ldots[\ldots]/s_2$) or s_2 is the first step in some qualifier expression of s_1 (i.e., $s_1[\ldots]\ldots[s_2\ldots]$), into an equivalent *single, composite step*. Removing wildcard steps leads to performance improvement on query-evaluation not only by reducing query size, but also by allowing selective loading of only the relevant input XML data. To enable this query rewriting approach, we introduce a new axis, called the *layer axis*, which is a natural generalization of XPath's "vertical" navigation axes (i.e., self, child, descendant, parent, and ancestor).

To give an idea of how the wildcard steps in a query can be eliminated via rewriting with the layer axis, consider the following XPath query $q = desc::a/desc::*[par::b/child::c][anc::d/child::e][child::f]/desc::g$, which is depicted as a rooted tree in Figure 4(a). Observe that there is a single wildcard step $desc::*$ in q which happens to be also a "branching" step in the sense that it has more than one child steps in Figure 4(a) comprising of the next step after itself and the first step of each of its qualifier expressions. The wildcard step $desc::*$ in q can be eliminated by transforming q into an equivalent query q''' (shown in Figure 4(d)) which contains three instances of the layer axis represented by L^X. Note that our rewriting approach does not require knowledge of the data schema, and the size of the rewritten query (in terms of the number of steps) is no more than that of the input query.

In this paper, we make the following contributions:

- We introduce a novel and complementary approach to optimizing an XPath query by minimizing its wildcard steps. Our approach is based on using a new composite axis, called the layer axis, to facilitate efficient query rewriting to eliminate wildcard steps.

- We develop a novel and efficient query rewriting algorithm to minimize wildcard steps based on the layer axis.

- We propose an efficient and scalable evaluation algorithm for wildcard-free XPath queries, capitalizing on a selective loading strategy.

- We also experimentally demonstrate the benefits of our rewriting and evaluation optimizations for processing XPath queries.

Organization. The rest of this paper is organized as follows. Section 2 presents some definitions and notations. In Section 3, we define a new navigation axis called the layer axis. Section 4 presents rewriting techniques using the layer axis to eliminate wildcard steps in XPath expressions. In Section 5, we present an efficient and scalable approach to evaluate wildcard-free XPath queries. We review related work in Section 6, and present our experimental performance results in Section 7. Finally, we conclude with some future research directions in Section 8.

2 Preliminaries

In this paper, we consider the class of XPath queries that are formed using only the following axes: self, child, descendant, parent, and ancestor (which are abbreviated to *self*, *child*, *desc*, *par*, and *anc*, respectively). We refer to these five axes as *vertical axes*[1], and refer to a step with axis χ as a *χ-axis step*. This fragment of XPath is syntactically defined as follows:

$$q \ ::= \ \chi :: l \ | \ \chi :: * \ | \ q/q \ | \ q[q],$$

where l is an XML tag, $*$ is the wildcard, and '/' and '[.]' denote concatenation and qualifier, respectively. This fragment does not contain the union, negation, and the logical *or* operator. Observe that logical *and* is implicitly supported: $q[q_1 \ and \ q_2]$ is equivalent to $q[q_1][q_2]$.

We consider the two common semantics of XPath query evaluation that are used in practice: the first returns only the selected nodes without their subtrees, while the second returns both the selected nodes and subtrees. Based on the type of query evaluation being considered, we shall refer to an XPath query as a *node-selecting* XPath query if it is the first case; and as a *standard* query, otherwise.

Given an XPath query q, one can represent q by an unordered rooted tree, denoted by $Tree(q)$, where each step s_i in q is represented by a node v_i in $Tree(q)$ such that there is an edge (v_i, v_j) in $Tree(q)$ if steps s_i and s_j are "consecutive" steps in q of the form s_i/s_j or $s_i[s_j]$. Observe that there could be zero or more qualifier expressions between s_i and s_j (or $[s_j]$) in q. Given two steps s_i and s_j in q, we say that s_j is a *child step* of s_i (or equivalently, s_i is a *parent step* of s_j)[2] if v_j is a child node of v_i in $Tree(q)$. A step s_i in q is said to be a *branching step* if its corresponding node v_i in $Tree(q)$ has out-degree of at least 2. Furthermore, if the branching step is also a wildcard step (i.e., its nodetest is *), then we refer to it as a *branching wildcard step*, abbreviated as B*-step. A wildcard step that is not a B*-step is abbreviated as NB*-step (for non-branching wildcard step). In the tree representation of the XPath query q, nodes that are underlined indicate the selected nodes to be returned as the query result.

Example 2.1 Figure 1 shows the tree representation of the XPath query */desc::a[child::*[child::b][desc::c]/anc::d /desc::*/child::e*, which has two wildcard steps: a B*-step *child::** and a NB*-step *desc::**. □

Consider a data node v in an XML data tree. We define the *level of* v, denoted by $level(v)$, as follows: $level(v) = 0$ if v is the root node; otherwise, $level(v) = level(v') + 1$, where v' is the parent node of v. We use $\delta(x, y)$ to denote the difference in levels between nodes x and y; i.e., $\delta(x, y) = level(x) - level(y)$. We define the *height of* v, denoted by $ht(v)$, as $ht(v) = \max_{v' \in V}\{level(v')\} - level(v)\}$, where V is the set of descendant leaf nodes of

---
[1] For simplicity and without loss of generality, we omit the descendant-or-self and ancestor-or-self axes.
[2] A child (parent) step is not to be confused with a child-axis (parent-axis) step!

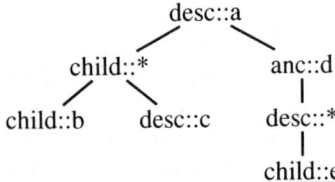

Figure 1: Tree representation $Tree(q)$ of query q

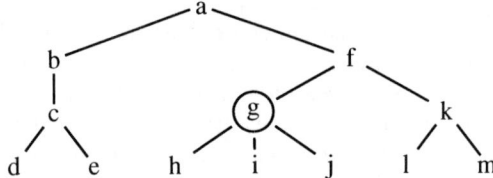

Figure 2: Example XML Data Tree

v. Thus, $level(v)$ and $ht(v)$ represent the maximum vertical distances between v and respectively, the top-most and bottom-most nodes reachable from v. More generally, for a given set of nodes V, we define the *height of* V, denoted by $ht(V)$, as $ht(V) = \max_{v \in V}\{ht(v)\}$.

We use v_c to denote the context node, and η (or η_i for some value i) to denote a nodetest that is either an element label or the wildcard $*$.

3 Layer Axis

In this section, we introduce a new navigation axis, called the *layer axis*, which is a natural generalization of the basic vertical axes (i.e., self, child, descendant, parent, and ancestor). We show that the layer axis is capable of expressing all the vertical axes, and thus XPath queries in our fragment can be rewritten into an intermediate form in terms of the layer axis. Furthermore, the layer axis can be implemented very efficiently. In the next section we shall present an algorithm for minimizing wildcard steps by capitalizing on the layer axis, followed by an efficient selective loading strategy for evaluating wildcard-free XPath queries in Section 5.

3.1 Basic Layer Axis

The basic form of the layer axis, denoted by L^i, selects the "layer" of nodes that are exactly i levels away from the context node v_c either below the context node if i is positive; or above the context node if i is negative. More formally, L^i (where i is an integer) can be defined inductively in terms of the self, child, and parent axes as follows:

- L^0 is defined to be *self*;
- $L^{i+1} = L^i.child$ if $i > 0$ (downward);
- $L^{i-1} = L^i.par$ otherwise (upward).

For example, when the root is v_c, the sequence of three steps /child::*/child::*/child::η is equivalent to the single step /L^3::η.

More generally, it is often convenient to refer to consecutive layers of data nodes that are located at a certain number of levels away from the context node. For example, the sequence of steps child::*/child::*/child::*/anc::η will select a "subtree" of nodes (with nodetest η) starting from the root layer to two layers below the layer containing the context node. The layer axis L^i can be easily extended to support such navigations in terms of $L^{\geq i}$ and $L^{\leq i}$ as follows:

$$L^{\geq i} = \begin{cases} \emptyset & \text{if } i > ht(v_c) \\ L^i \cup L^{\geq i+1} & \text{otherwise} \end{cases}$$

$$L^{\leq i} = \begin{cases} \emptyset & \text{if } i < -level(v_c) \\ L^i \cup L^{\leq i-1} & \text{otherwise} \end{cases}$$

Clearly, both the descendant and ancestor axes are special cases of $L^{\geq i}$ and $L^{\leq -i}$, respectively, with $i = 1$. For example, L^{-3}::*/anc::* can be expressed as $L^{\leq -4}$::η.

For notational convenience, we define $L^{[i,j]}$, with $i \leq j$, as follows:

$$L^{[i,j]} = L^{\geq i} \cap L^{\leq j}$$

Observe that $L^{\geq i}$ and $L^{\leq i}$ can be expressed as $L^{[i,ht(v_c)]}$ and $L^{[-level(v_c),i]}$, respectively. As a special case, $L^i = L^{[i,i]}$. Thus in the sequel we shall focus on the general form $L^{[i,j]}$ of the layer axis.

We sometimes also use the layer axis with respect to an explicit context node v, which is expressed as $L^{[i,j]}(v)$. Thus, $L^{[i,j]}$ refers to $L^{[i,j]}(v_c)$.

Example 3.1 Consider the XML data tree in Figure 2. If g is the context node, then L^1::* = \{h,i,j\}, L^{-2}::* = \{a\}, $L^{\leq 1}$::* = \{a,f,g,h,i,j\}, and $L^{\geq -1}$::* = \{f,g,h,i,j\}. □

The layer axis provides a concise specification for a sequence of XPath steps $s_1/s_2/\cdots/s_n$, where all the steps, except for possibly the last step s_n, are wildcard steps. For example, the query $q_1 = \underbrace{child::*/\cdots/child::*}_{i-1}/child::\eta_1$, is equivalent to L^i::η_1.

3.2 Height Constraints

In many cases, it is necessary to augment the layer-axis specification with additional constraints on the height of the selected nodes to preserve equivalence. For example, the query $q_2 = L^i$::*/par::η_2, where $i \geq 1$, is equivalent to

$$\{v \in L^{i-1}::\eta_2 \mid ht(v) \geq 1\}$$

Here, the additional constraint on the height of the selected nodes indicates that the selected nodes must not be leaf nodes. Clearly, $q_2 \not\equiv L^{i-1}::\eta_2$.

More generally, there is a need to be able to specify constraints on the height of both the selected nodes as well as their ancestors. For example, the query $q_3 = L^i$::*/par::*/par::*/child::η_3, where $i \geq 2$, is equivalent to

$$\{v \in L^{i-1}::\eta_3 \mid ht(L^{-1}(v)) \geq 2\}$$

Here, each selected node needs to satisfy the constraint that its parent node can reach some descendant node that is at least 2 levels below the parent node. Observe that the constraint on $L^{-1}(v)$ is not equivalent to the following height constraint on v: $ht(v) \geq 1$. Thus, supporting height constraints on ancestors of selected nodes is necessary. However, note that height constraints on descendants of selected nodes can be rewritten to equivalent constraints on the selected nodes themselves. For example, $L^i::*/par::*/par::* \equiv \{v \in L^{i-2}::* \mid ht(L^1(v)) \geq 1\}$, and the constraint on $L^1(v)$ can be rewritten as a constraint on v: $ht(v) \geq 2$.

As a final example, let us consider the query $q_4 = \{v \in L^{[i,j]}::* \mid ht(v) \geq h\} / desc::\eta_4$. This query is equivalent to

$$\{v \in L^{\geq i+1}::\eta_4 \mid \exists\, r \in [\delta(v,v_c) - j, \delta(v,v_c) - i],$$
$$ht(L^{-r}(v)) \geq h\}$$

Here, we have a height constraint that specifies that each selected node v must have some ancestor node w that is r levels above v (i.e., w is in $L^{[i,j]}$) such that the height of w is at least h.

More formally, height constraints can be defined as follows. Let $cexp$ denote an integer expression defined in terms of integer constants as well as '+' and '−'. Let exp_1 and exp_2 denote integer expressions defined in terms of $level(v)$, $level(v_c)$, integer constants, as well as '+' and '−'. Then a height constraint ϕ on a selected node v can be specified as one of the following two forms:

(F1) $ht(L^{cexp}(v)) \geq exp_1$; or

(F2) $\exists\, i \in I\, \phi$, where $I = [exp_1, exp_2]$ (with $exp_1 \leq exp_2$) is a range of consecutive integers, and ϕ is a height constraint of the form (F1).

Note that height constraints of the form $ht(v) \geq exp_1$ are allowed in (F1) since $ht(v) = ht(L^0(v))$.

For example, $\exists\, i \in I\, (ht(L^i(v)) \geq h)$ states that v must have some ancestor/descendant node w that is i levels above/below v, where i is some value from a set of consecutive integers I, such that the height of w is at least h.

Putting these together, the layer axis is typically associated with a set of height constraints, and is thus denoted as $L^X(S)::\eta$, where X is a set of consecutive integers (of the form i, $\leq i$, $\geq i$, or $[i,j]$), and S is a (possibly empty) set of height constraints as defined above; it extracts nodes that are reachable via the layer axis and satisfies every height constraint in S.

Example 3.2 Using the new notation $L^X(S)::\eta$, the example queries q_3 and q_4 given above can be specified as $L^{i-1}(\{ht(L^{-1}(v)) \geq 2\})::\eta_3$ and $L^{\geq i+1}(\{\exists\, r \in [\delta(v,v_c) - j, \delta(v,v_c) - i](ht(L^{-r}(v)) \geq h)\})::\eta_4$, respectively. □

As a final remark, the vertical axes in XPath can be specified in terms of the layer axis as follows: $self \equiv L^0(\emptyset)$, $child \equiv L^1(\emptyset)$, $desc \equiv L^{\geq 1}(\emptyset)$, $par \equiv L^{-1}(\emptyset)$, and $anc \equiv L^{\leq -1}(\emptyset)$.

3.3 Implementation of Layer Axis

In order for a rewriting-based approach using the layer axis to be effective, it is critical that the layer axis be implemented efficiently. In this section, we describe how the layer axis can be efficiently supported by precomputing certain additional information as the input XML document is parsed and loaded into main memory for query evaluation.

There are essentially two key operations that need to be efficiently supported in a layer-axis step evaluation. Specifically, to determine if a data node v is selected by a layer axis $L^{[i,j]}(S)$, we need to (1) check if v is in $L^{[i,j]}(v_c)$; and (2) check if v satisfies each height constraint in S. These two checkings can be efficiently supported by precomputing $level(v)$ and $ht(v)$ for each data v. With these precomputed values, v is in $L^{[i,j]}(v_c)$ if $\delta(v,v_c) = level(v) - level(v_c)$ is in $[i,j]$; and v satisfies the height constraint "$ht(L^k(v)) \geq h$" if $ht(v) \geq h + k$ (for non-negative k values), and if $ht(u) \geq h$ (for negative k values), where u is the ancestor node of v that is k levels above v.

The $level(.)$ and $ht(.)$ information can be easily precomputed by a single parse of the input XML data file as it is loaded into main memory, by using a stack of size H (where H is the height of the input XML data tree T) to store information about the current path of data nodes being parsed. In particular, $ht(v)$ is computed by using the property that $ht(v) = \max_w\{ht(w)+1\}$, where w is a child node of v in T. Note that the height H of an XML data tree T is usually a small value (independent of the size of T).

Thus, an efficient implementation of the layer axis can be easily supported by precomputing some information during the parsing of the input XML data file.

3.4 Extended Layer Axis

Recall that the motivation for the layer axis is to have a general composite axis (that can be efficiently implemented) to be used for eliminating wildcard steps. Specifically, the goal is to be able to rewrite any sequence of XPath steps that consists of all wildcard steps (except for possibly the last step) into a single layer-axis step. However, even with the most general form of the layer axis presented in Section 3.2, there are certain sequences of steps that can not be expressed using a single layer-axis step. For example, consider the query $q = L^{-i}(\emptyset)::*/child::\eta$, where $i > 0$. Note that $q \not\equiv L^{-i+1}(\emptyset)::\eta$. This is because $L^{-i+1}(\emptyset)::*$ will select at most one single node, which is the ancestor node of the context node v_c that is $i - 1$ levels above v_c, instead of a set of child nodes as intended. Thus, q can not be rewritten using a single layer-axis step.

This limitation arises whenever a sequence of steps first navigates upwards to some ancestor node of the current context node v_c, and is then followed by a downward navigation. In this case, some of the nodes selected by the downward navigation are neither ancestors nor descendants of v_c, which means that they can not be be captured using a single layer-axis step (which is defined with respect to v_c).

159

To overcome this restriction, we propose a simple extension of the layer axis of the form $L^{X/Y}(S)$, where for some non-negative integer i, X (which is of the form $-i$ or $\leq -i$) specifies an upward navigation; Y (which is of the form i or $\geq i$) specifies a downward navigation; and S is a set of height constraints. More formally, the extended variant of the layer axis $L^{X/Y}(S)$ is defined as follows:

$$L^{X/Y}(S)::\eta \equiv L^X(\emptyset)::* / L^Y(S)::\eta \quad (1)$$

We refer to the two variants of the layer axis as *basic layer axis* and *extended layer axis*. Thus, using the extended layer axis, q can now be rewritten as $L^{-i/1}(\emptyset)::\eta$.

Supporting the extended variant is, however, more involved. Checking whether or not two data nodes v_1 and v_2 are related by the axis $L^{-i/j}$, for example, is equivalent to checking if v_1 and v_2 have a common ancestor node that is i and j levels above them, respectively. Clearly, there is a need to balance the tradeoff between the generality of the layer axis and the efficiency of its implementation. Intuitively, a more general layer specification should be able to eliminate wildcard steps for a larger class of queries, but its implementation cost is likely to be higher. In this paper, for practical reasons, we will focus on the basic layer axis together with a special case of the extended variant of the form $L^{-1/Y}(S)$, which can be efficiently implemented by additionally storing a pointer to the parent node for each data node. We intend to explore the tradeoffs of more general variants as part of future work.

4 Minimizing Wildcard Steps

The basic idea of our rewriting algorithm is to iteratively eliminate one wildcard step at a time until either all the wildcard steps have been eliminated or none of the remaining wildcard steps can be eliminated. Each iteration therefore merges a sequence of two steps s_1 and s_2, either of the form s_1/s_2 or of the form $s_1[s_2]$ (at least one of which is a wildcard step) into a single layer-axis step.

We first discuss the simpler case of minimizing NB*-steps in Section 4.1 and then extend our techniques to handle B*-steps in Section 4.2. Finally, we combine these techniques to present an algorithm to minimize wildcard steps in Section 4.3.

4.1 Non-branching Wildcard Steps

In this section, we consider the elimination of wildcard steps that appear in "linear" path expressions (without qualifier expressions) of the form s_1/s_2, where s_1 is a wildcard step; i.e., s_1 is of the form $L^{[i,j]}(S)::*$ with $i \leq j$. Step s_2 is of the form $\chi::\eta$, where χ is any vertical XPath axis and η is either an element name or a wildcard.

Our goal is to rewrite a two-step path expression of the form

$$p = L^{[i,j]}(S)::* / \chi::\eta$$

into an equivalent layer-axis step:

Algorithm `Rewrite-NB*-step` (s_1, s_2)
Input: A NB*-step $s_1 = L^{[i,j]}(S)::*$
A step $s_2 = \chi::\eta$
Output: A step $s' = L^{[i',j']}(S')::\eta$ (equivalent to s_1/s_2) if s_1 can be removed; or s_1/s_2 otherwise

1) **if** $(i < 0)$ **and** $(\chi \in \{child, desc\})$ **then**
2)   **return** s_1/s_2;
3) Apply appropriate rule from (R1) to (R4) to rewrite $L^{[i,j]}(\emptyset)::*/\chi::\eta$ to $L^{[i',j']}(S_{new})::\eta$;
4) $S_{update} = \emptyset$;
5) **for each** $\phi \in S$ **do**
6)   rewrite ϕ to ϕ' as described in Section 4.1.1;
7) $S_{update} = S_{update} \cup \{\phi'\}$;
8) **return** $L^{[i',j']}(S_{new} \cup S_{update})::\eta$;

Figure 3: Algorithm to remove NB*-steps

$$p' = L^{[i',j']}(S')::\eta$$

to eliminate the wildcard step $L^{[i,j]}(S)::*$.

Note that if step s_1 was of the form $L^{-1/[i,j]}(S)$, then p' is simply replaced with $L^{-1/[i',j']}(S')::\eta$. Thus, the rewritings involving the basic layer axis can be easily extended over to the extended variant; therefore, for simplicity and with loss of generality, we will focus our discussion on the basic layer axis.

Our rewriting algorithm to eliminate a NB*-step is shown in Figure 3. We explain the rewriting rules in terms of two cases, depending on whether or not $i \geq 0$.

4.1.1 Case 1: $i \geq 0$

We first consider the case where the set of constraints S in p is empty and then extend the results to the general case where S could be non-empty.

When $i \geq 0$ and $S = \emptyset$, p can be transformed into p' using the following set of four rewriting rules[3]:

(R1) $L^{[i,j]}(\emptyset)::* / child::\eta \equiv L^{[i+1,j+1]}(\emptyset)::\eta$

(R2) $L^{[i,j]}(\emptyset)::* / desc::\eta \equiv L^{\geq i+1}(\emptyset)::\eta$

(R3) $L^{[i,j]}(\emptyset)::* / par::\eta \equiv L^{[i-1,j-1]}(S')::\eta$ where $S' = \{ht(v) \geq 1\}$

(R4) $L^{[i,j]}(\emptyset)::* / anc::\eta \equiv L^{\leq j-1}(S')::\eta$ where $S' = \{ht(v) \geq i - \delta(v, v_c), ht(v) \geq 1\}$.

The rewriting from $L^{[i,j]}$ to $L^{[i',j']}$ in each rule is self-explanatory: in (R1), for example, the transformation essentially adjusts the relative location of the selected nodes (w.r.t. v_c) down by one level from $[i,j]$ to $[i+1, j+1]$ due to the second child-axis step. Note that only rules (R3) and (R4), which have a reverse-axis for their second steps, require a height constraint to be specified to preserve equivalence. For (R3), the height constraint is necessary to select only non-leaf nodes that are in $L^{[i-1,j-1]}(S')::\eta$. For

---

[3]Note that the expression $x + 1$ is actually $\min\{x + 1, ht(v_c)\}$, and the expression $x - 1$ is actually $\max\{x - 1, -level(v_c)\}$.

(R4), a selected node v in $L^{\leq j-1}(S')::\eta$ must have a descendant node w in $L^{[i,j]}$. Clearly, v is a non-leaf node, and so its height must be at least one. Furthermore, if v is in $L^{\leq i-1}(S')::\eta$, then v must be able to reach some descendant node w in L^i, and so the height of v must be at least $i - \delta(v, v_c)$. Combining these two constraints, we have $ht(v) \geq \max\{i - \delta(v, v_c), 1\}$, which is shorthand for the set of two constraints given above for (R4).

We now explain how the above results can be extended to the scenario where S is non-empty. The rewriting rules (R1) to (R4) are still applicable except that the set of existing constraints in S need to be updated. Thus the set of height constraints S' can be represented as $S' = S_{update} \cup S_{new}$; where S_{update} denotes the set of updated constraints in S, and S_{new} is the set of new constraints as defined by the above rules. Note that the updating of S to S_{update} is independent of the generation of any new height constraint in S_{new}. Moreover, each constraint in S is updated independently of the other updates.

To simplify the discussion, let us consider $p = L^{[i,j]}(S)::* / \chi::\eta$ where $S = \{ht(L^{-k}(v)) \geq h\}$, k and h are non-negative integers[4]. The constraint S is updated by incorporating the distance between the old selected nodes and the new selected nodes as follows.

1. If χ = *child*, then $S_{update} = \{ht(L^{-(k+1)}(v)) \geq h\}$.

2. If χ = *par*, then $S_{update} = \{ht(L^{-(k-1)}(v)) \geq h\}$.

3. If χ = *desc*, then
$$S_{update} = \{\exists r \in [\delta(v, v_c) - j, \delta(v, v_c) - i]$$
$$(ht(L^{-(r+k)}(v)) \geq h)\}.$$

   That is, v has an ancestor w in $L^{[i,j]}$ such that $ht(L^{-k}(w)) \geq h$.

4. If χ = *anc*, then
$$S_{update} = \{\exists r \in [i - \delta(v, v_c), j - \delta(v, v_c)]$$
$$(ht(L^{r-k}(v)) \geq h)\}.$$

   That is, v has a descendant w in $L^{[i,j]}$ such that $ht(L^{-k}(w)) \geq h$.

In general, height constraints may involve $level(v)$, which can occur on the left hand side of "$\geq$" (in $[exp_1, exp_2]$ of the form (F2)) or on the right hand side of "$\geq$" (in exp_1 of the form (F1)).

As an example of the first case, consider $L^{[i,j]}(S)::*$ / *desc*::η, where $S = \{\exists r \in [\delta(v, v_c) - a, \delta(v, v_c) - b](ht(L^{r-k}(v)) \geq h)\}$ for some integer constant expressions a, b, and k. The updated constraint S_{update} is to assert that a new selected node v has an ancestor w in $L^{[i,j]}$ such that there exists $r \in [\delta(w, v_c) - a, \delta(w, v_c) - b]$ with $ht(L^{r-k}(w)) \geq h$. This requires adjustment to the range

[4] Recall that if $k < 0$, then the constraint $ht(L^{-k}(v)) \geq h$ can be rewritten as $ht(v) \geq h - k$.

of r by incorporating $\delta(v, w)$. In a nutshell, this is done by capitalizing on the following relations:

$$\delta(v, w) + \delta(w, v_c) = \delta(v, v_c)$$
$$\delta(w, v_c) \leq j$$
$$\delta(w, v_c) \geq i$$

It is easy to verify that the height constraint S is updated to $S_{update} = \{\exists r \in [\delta(v, v_c) - j - a, \delta(v, v_c) - i - b](ht(L^{r-k}(v)) \geq h)\}$.

As an example of the second case, consider $L^{[i,j]}(S)::*$ / *desc*::η, where $S = \{ht(L^k(v)) \geq \delta(v, v_c) + h\}$ for some integer constant expressions k and h. By similar reasoning as in the example for the first case, it can be verified that the height constraint S is updated to $S_{update} = \{\exists r \in [\delta(v, v_c) - j, \delta(v, v_c) - i](ht(L^{k-r}(v)) \geq \delta(v, v_c) + h - r)\}$.

Due to the lack of space we omit updating of height constraints of other forms, which can be derived by a straightforward structural induction. We should remark that the new and updated constraints can be checked efficiently with the implementation strategy described in Section 3.3.

4.1.2 Case 2: $i < 0$

When $i < 0$, the rules (R3) and (R4) remain intact and are applicable. However, rules (R1) and (R2) no longer hold when $i < 0$ because the sequence s_1/s_2 now corresponds to an upward navigation followed by a downward navigation, which can not be handled by the basic layer axis as explained in Section 3.4. Thus, for such cases, the wildcard step s_2 can not be eliminated. However, if the upward navigation is restricted only to a single level, then the extended layer axis variant $L^{-1/[i,j]}(S)$ can be applied.

Similarly, when it comes to updating existing height constraints, the rules for *par* and *anc* given above remain unchanged when $i < 0$, whereas those for *child* and *desc* do not apply here.

4.2 Branching Wildcard Steps

In this section, we extend the techniques for eliminating NB*-steps to eliminate B*-steps. Our algorithm (shown in Figure 5) to eliminate a B*-step s in an XPath query consists of two rewriting steps:

PullUpChildStep The first rewriting step tries to transform s into a NB*-step by "pulling up" some of the child steps of s to become above s. The goal is try to reduce the problem of eliminating a B*-step to the simpler case of eliminating a NB*-step.

MergeChildStep If s still remains a B*-step after the *PullUpChildStep*, the second rewriting step then tries to merge s with one of its child steps to eliminate s.

Example 4.1 Consider the XPath query q, where $Tree(q)$ is shown in Figure 4(a). To eliminate the B*-step *desc*::*, PullUpChildStep first transforms $Tree(q)$ into $Tree(q')$ (shown in Figure 4(b)) by pulling up the

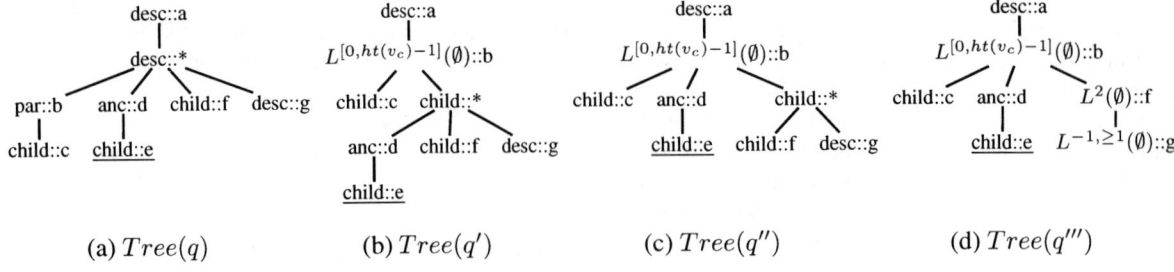

(a) $Tree(q)$ (b) $Tree(q')$ (c) $Tree(q'')$ (d) $Tree(q''')$

Figure 4: Example of branching wildcard step elimination

Algorithm `Rewrite-B*-step` (q, s)
Input: An XPath query q with a B*-step s.
Output: An equivalent query q',
where s may be removed
1) **if** (s has a *par*-axis child step s_{par}) **then**
2)   Pull up step s_{par} in q;
3) **for each** *anc*-axis child step s_{anc} of s **do**
4)   Pull up step s_{anc} in q;
5) **if** (s is now a NB*-step in q) **then**
6)   let s_{child} be the child step of s in q;
7) s' = `Rewrite-NB*-step` (s, s_{child});
8)   Modify q by replacing s/s_{child} with s';
9) **else**
10)   **if** (s has some *child*-axis child step s_{child}) **then**
11)   Merge s with s_{child} in q;
12) **return** q;

Figure 5: Algorithm to remove a B*-step

---

subtree rooted at *par::b* to become above *desc::**; the axes of these two steps are updated to $L^{[0,ht(v_c)-1]}(\emptyset)::b$ and *child::**. Next, $Tree(q')$ is transformed into $Tree(q'')$ (shown in Figure 4(c)) by pulling up the subtree rooted at *anc::d* to become a child subtree of $L^{[0,ht(v_c)-1]}(\emptyset)::b$. Note that the transformed wildcard step *child::** in $Tree(q'')$ is still a B*-step with two child steps.

The second rewriting step MergeChildStep then transforms $Tree(q'')$ into $Tree(q''')$ (shown in Figure 4(d)) by the following two changes: (1) the step *child::** is merged with its child step *child::f* into $L^2(\emptyset)::f$; and (2) the axis of *desc::g* is changed to $L^{-1,\geq 1}(\emptyset)$. □

We now elaborate on the two rewriting steps in the following subsections.

4.2.1 Pulling Up Child Steps

To eliminate a B*-step s_1 in an XPath query q, our algorithm first tries to transform s_1 into a NB*-step (which can then be eliminated by algorithm `Rewrite-NB*-step` described in the preceding section) by "pulling up" all the child steps of s_1 that have reverse axes (i.e., *par* or *anc*) to become above step s_1 in $Tree(q)$.

This transformation is best explained with a diagram as shown in Figure 6 to eliminate the B*-step s_1 in query q. Here, the par-axis child step s_2 in Figure 6(a) is pulled up to become above step s_1 in Figure 6(b); and the axes for steps s_1 and s_2 are updated accordingly to obtain an equivalent query q'. Note that the set of height constraints S associated with the B*-step s_1 is not affected by the transformation of $Tree(q)$ to $Tree(q')$.

More formally, given an XPath query of the form $s_0/s_1[s_2\ T_2][s_3\ T_3]\cdots$, where $s_1 = L^{[x,y]}(S)::\ast$ is a B*-step that has a *par*-axis child step $s_2 = par::\eta_2$, the rewrite rule for pulling up s_2 above s_1 can be stated as follows:

$$s_0/s_1[s_2\ T_2][s_3\ T_3]\cdots \equiv s_0/s'_2[T_2]/s'_1[s_3\ T_3]\cdots$$

where s_2 is rewritten to $s'_2 = L^{[x-1,y-1]}(\emptyset)::\eta_2$, and s_1 is rewritten to $s'_1 = L^1(S)::\ast$.

Once a par-axis child step[5] has been pulled up above the B*-step s_1, each of the anc-axis child steps of s_1 (if any) can also be pulled up to transform q' to q'' as illustrated in Figure 6(c). Specifically, the subtree rooted at step s_3 in Figure 6(b) is pulled up to become a child subtree of step s'_2, and its axis is changed from *anc* to *anc-or-self* to preserve equivalence. Note that if both the nodetests η_2 and η_3 in Figure 6(c) have distinct element labels, then the axis of s'_3 can be simplified from *anc-or-self* to *anc*, as illustrated by the step *anc::d* in Figure 4(c). Here again, the transformation of $Tree(q')$ to $Tree(q'')$ does not affect the set of height constraints S associated with the B*-step s_1.

Note that if the B*-step $s_1 = L^{[x,y]}(S)::\ast$ does not have any par-axis child steps, then it is only possible to pull up any of its anc-axis child steps provided if s_1 is a child-axis step (i.e., $x = 1$ and $y = 1$).

4.2.2 Merging With Child Step

The second *MergeChildStep* rewriting step is used to eliminate a B*-step s_1 that could not be transformed into a NB*-step by the *PullUpChildStep* rewriting. As its name suggests, the idea of this second rewriting is to try to merge s_1 with one of its child steps to transform s_1 into a non-wildcard step. Note that, after applying the *PullUpChildStep* rewriting, s_1 does not have any *par*-axis child step (i.e., each child step of s_1 must be either a *child-*, *desc-*, or *anc*-axis step).

The simplest way to perform the merging is to merge the B*-step with a child-axis child step as illustrated in Figure 7, which shows the elimination of a B*-step $s_1 =$

---

[5] In the event that s_1 has multiple par-axis child steps, the collection of par-axis child steps can be first combined and optimized to remove redundancies (e.g., [13]). Such issues are, however, orthogonal to the techniques described here and are beyond the scope of this paper.

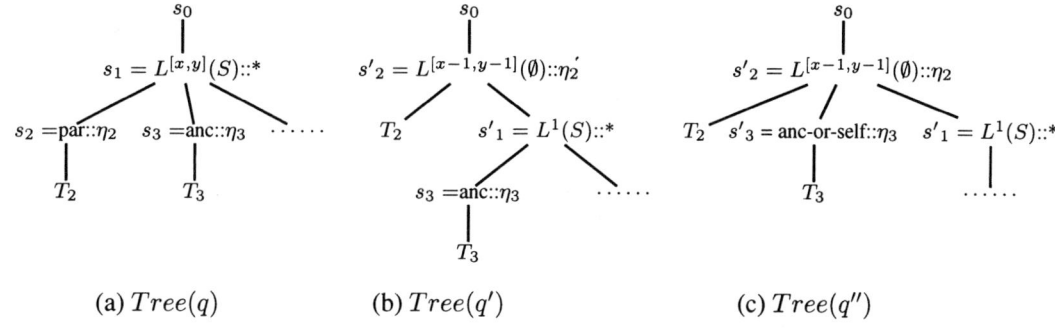

(a) $Tree(q)$ (b) $Tree(q')$ (c) $Tree(q'')$

Figure 6: Pulling up *par*-axis and *anc*-axis steps

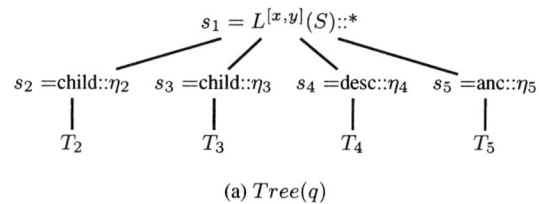

(a) $Tree(q)$

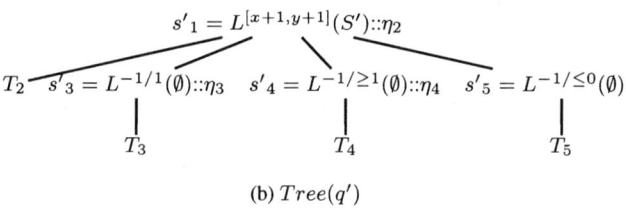

(b) $Tree(q')$

Figure 7: Merging a B*-step with a *child*-axis child step

$L^{[x,y]}(S)::*$ in a query $q = s_1[s_2\ T_2][s_3\ T_3]\cdots$. Here, $Tree(q)$ in Figure 7(a) is transformed into $Tree(q')$ in Figure 7(b) by merging s_1 with its child step $s_2 = child::\eta_2$, which can be viewed as eliminating the NB*-step s_1 in a "linear" expression s_1/s_2. Thus, by rule (R1) in Section 4.1, s_2 becomes rewritten into $s'_2 = L^{[x+1,y+1]}(S')::\eta_2$; note that S is updated to S' using the updating rules as discussed in Section 4.1. Other child steps s_j (or $[s_j]$) of s_1 are updated accordingly to cope with the merging, as follows:

- $child::\eta$ is changed to $L^{-1/1}(\emptyset)::\eta$, namely, moving upward one level and then moving one level down;
- $desc::\eta$ now becomes $L^{-1/\geq 1}(\emptyset)::\eta$; and
- $anc::\eta$ is changed to $L^{-1/\leq 0}(\emptyset)::\eta$.

For a concrete illustration of the *MergeChildStep* rewriting, the reader can refer to Figure 4(c) again, where the B*-step $child::*$ is eliminated by merging with its child step $child::f$ to transform q'' to q''' as shown Figure 4(d).

Observe that the transformed query produced by the *MergeChildStep* rewriting step is not unique as it depends on the choice of the child step selected for merging with the B*-step. Referring again to the example in Figure 7, note that if the child step s_3 had been selected (instead of s_2) for merging with the B*-step s_1, the transformed query tree in Figure 7(b) would have been different with T_2 and η_2 being swapped with T_3 and η_3, respectively.

4.3 Rewriting Algorithm

In this section, we combine the techniques developed in the preceding sections to present a rewriting-based approach (shown in Figure 9) to minimize wildcard steps in an input XPath query.

The algorithm consists of two stages: the first stage (lines 1 to 4) calls `Rewrite-NB*-step` to remove NB*-steps, and the second stage (lines 5 to 8) calls `Rewrite-B*-step` to remove B*-steps.

In both stages, the algorithm traverses the tree in a top-down manner to search for wildcard steps; this is important to guarantee that a wildcard step s_1 is rewritten before its descendant wildcard step s_2 of the same type (i.e., both B*-steps or NB*-steps). The purpose of this requirement is to maximize the number of wildcard steps that can be eliminated. For NB*-steps, recall that the rewriting rules for them are of the form $L^{[i,j]}(S)::* / \chi::\eta \equiv L^{[i',j']}(S')::\eta$, with the wildcard-based layer axis "on top" and a basic vertical axis "below". Thus, rewriting a "lower" NB*-step first before its "upper" NB*-step could deprive the latter from being eliminated. A similar reasoning also applies to B*-steps, which is why a top-down traversal is preferred over an arbitrary traversal for both stages.

Furthermore, the reason for eliminating NB*-steps first before B*-steps is also for the purpose of maximizing the number of wildcard step eliminations. For example, consider the query q in Figure 8(a) containing two wildcard steps s_0 and s_1. If the B*-step s_0 is first rewritten, then q is transformed to q' in Figure 8(b), and the B*-step s'_0 in q' can not be eliminated by Algorithm `Rewrite-B*-step`. On the other hand, if the NB*-step s_1 is first rewritten, then q is transformed to q'' in Figure 8(c), and the remaining B*-step can still be eliminated using Algorithm `Rewrite-NB*-step`. Thus, to maximize the number of wildcard step eliminations, NB*-steps are eliminated first before B*-steps.

The algorithm takes at most quadratic time in the size of the input XPath query q. The overhead is negligible since q is typically small in practice. Note that since the output of the *MergeChildStep* rewriting is not unique, it follows that the output of the rewrite algorithm is also not unique.

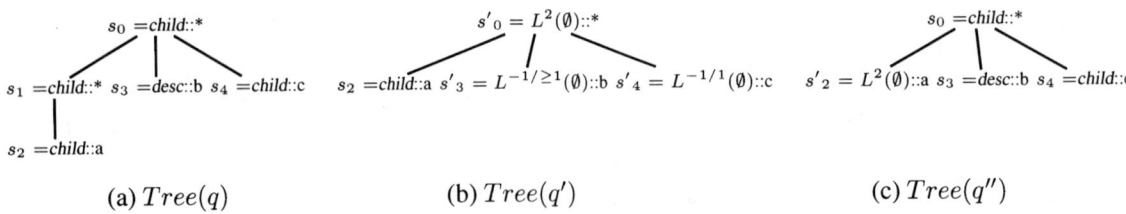

(a) $Tree(q)$ (b) $Tree(q')$ (c) $Tree(q'')$

Figure 8: Example showing the advantage of eliminating NB*-steps before B*-steps

---

Algorithm Rewrite(q)
Input: An XPath query q.
Output: An equivalent query to q that has the minimal number of wildcard steps.
1) Traverse $Tree(q)$ top-down:
2)   **for each** step s visited **do**
3)   **if** (s is a NB*-step in s/s') **then**
4)   Rewrite-NB*-step (s, s');
5) Traverse $Tree(q)$ top-down:
6)   **for each** step s visited **do**
7)   **if** (s is a B*-step) **then**
8)   Rewrite-B*-step (q, s);
9) **return** q;

Figure 9: Rewrite Algorithm

5 Optimized Evaluation of Wildcard-free Queries

In this section, we demonstrate the usefulness of wildcard step elimination by presenting a simple and yet effective optimized evaluation strategy for XPath queries that are free of wildcard steps.

One limitation of XPath query evaluators that rely on a main-memory representation of the input XML data (e.g., DOM-based implementations) is that they can not scale to process large input XML data due to their large space requirement. An obvious idea to alleviate this problem is to selectively load only the necessary portion of the input data into main memory to evaluate the input query. However, determining the necessary portion of the data to load seems to be a difficult problem itself when the input XPath query contains wildcard steps since a *desc*-axis wildcard step in a query can potentially refer to the entire data. However, if the input query is wildcard-free or if its wildcard steps can be completely eliminated, then it becomes possible to employ a selective data-loading strategy to improve both the scalability as well as the efficiency of query evaluation.

In this section, we present an optimized evaluation strategy for wildcard-free XPath queries that is based on the simple idea of selectively loading only a portion of the data nodes into main memory based on the set of element labels that appear in the input query. We first explain the idea for evaluating node-selecting XPath queries and then discuss how this strategy can also be applied (to some extent) to standard XPath queries.

5.1 Node-selecting XPath Queries

To illustrate the basic idea, let us consider a simple node-selecting XPath query q =/child::a/desc::*/child::b. Instead of loading the entire input data into main memory to evaluate q, a more efficient approach is to first rewrite q into an equivalent wildcard-free query q' =/child::a/$L^{\geq 2}(\emptyset)$::b. Then, by exploiting the absence of wildcard steps in q', it is now possible to selectively load only the data nodes whose labels are explicitly referenced in the query (i.e., data nodes that are labeled a or b).

More specifically, as the input data file is parsed, the necessary node information is precomputed as described in Section 3.3. If an input data node's label is referenced in the rewritten query q', this data node is cached in main memory (to be used for evaluating the query); otherwise, this node is "irrelevant" for the query evaluation and it is only cached temporarily in the stack (described in Section 3.3) for the purpose of precomputing the $ht(.)$ and $level(.)$ information. Once the input data has been completely parsed and selectively loaded, the query can now be processed using the loaded relevant data.

However, note that even though an irrelevant node v itself is not needed for query evaluation, its precomputed $ht(v)$ value might still be needed for checking the height constraints for some other relevant data node. This can be solved by storing the precomputed height information of all ancestors of each relevant data node v (including v itself) in an array $Ht_v[0, ..., H]$ (where H is the height of the data tree) such that $Ht_v[i] = ht(L^{i-level(v)}(v))$ for $i \leq level(v)$. Clearly, the storage of the collection of arrays Ht_v for the relevant data nodes can be optimized given that there are overlapping entries in them.

Since the set of element labels that are explicitly referenced in the input query (in the earlier example, only $\{a, b\}$) is generally a small subset of the set of element labels that appear in the input XML data, this selective-loading strategy can lead to significant reduction in the data that need to be loaded for query evaluation, thereby improving its scalability. Furthermore, since the data size (more accurately, the size of the loaded data) is a key determinant of the time-complexity of XPath query evaluation (e.g., [8]), the query processing can also be significantly improved using this optimized evaluation strategy.

As a final remark on the implementation of the optimized evaluation, we note that it is necessary to precompute the array $Ht_v[0, ..., H]$ only for data nodes v (with element label η) if there is some layer axis $L^X(S)::\eta$ in the rewritten query with $S \neq \emptyset$. For the example query

q', since the only layer-axis there does not have any height constraints, the array $Ht_v[0, ..., H]$ need not be precomputed at all.

5.2 Standard XPath Queries

The above optimized evaluation strategy can also be applied to standard XPath queries, but the portion of input data that needs to be loaded is likely to be larger (compared to node-selecting queries). This is due to the semantics of standard XPath queries which require returning not only the selected target nodes but also the subtrees rooted under them. Consequently, data nodes that are descendants of potential target nodes must also be cached in main memory (in addition to the data nodes whose element labels are explicitly referenced in the query) for evaluation.

6 Related Work

To the best of our knowledge, this is the first paper that addresses the problem of reducing the size of XPath queries by minimizing wildcard steps. Our proposed rewriting optimizations are different from but complementary to existing XPath query rewriting techniques.

In contrast to the research on minimizing redundant XPath steps [17, 2, 13] which relies on integrity constraints of the data schema, our rewriting techniques are designed for minimizing non-redundant wildcard steps and do not require knowledge of the data schema. Another difference from these work is that our techniques apply to a larger fragment of XPath queries beyond the child and descendant axes considered for twig queries there.

Our work also differs from the recent research on eliminating reverse axes in XPath queries [12]; indeed, the rewriting techniques there can actually introduce additional wildcard steps into the transformed queries.

7 Performance Study

To verify the effectiveness of our rewriting algorithms and optimized evaluation strategy for XPath queries, we conducted a performance study using the XMark benchmark data [18]. Our results indicate that our proposed optimizations achieve a significant performance improvement over traditional evaluation methods for XPath queries, with our selective data loading evaluation strategy (based on wildcard step elimination) outperforming a conventional evaluation method by a factor ranging from 2 to 4.

7.1 Experimental Testbed and Methodology

Data Sets: We used the XMark benchmark data [18] for our experiments and generated four data files of size 70MB, 175MB, 260MB, and 340MB. The number of element nodes contained in these files are, respectively, about 1.1 million, 2.5 million, 3.8 million, and 5 million.

Queries: We generated node-selecting XPath queries using the XMark benchmark schema by varying three parameters: the number of non-consecutive NB*-steps (denoted by N_{nc}), the number of consecutive NB*-steps (denoted by N_c), and the number of B*-steps (denoted by N_b). N_{nc} is varied from 0 to 3, where the query with $N_{nc} = 3$ consists of a single step followed by three predicates (each of which contains a wildcard step) as follows: "/desc::mailbox [anc::*/anc::site] [desc::*/desc::from] [desc::*/desc::to]". Queries with $N_{nc} < 3$ are generated from this query by removing the appropriate number of predicates. N_c is varied from 0 to 3, where the query with $N_c = 3$ is of the form "/desc::site/desc::*/desc::*/desc::*/child::keyword", and queries with $N_c < 3$ are generated from this query by removing the appropriate number of wildcard steps. Finally, N_b is varied from 0 to 3 as follows. The query with no B*-steps is /desc::bidder [par::openauction] [anc::regions] /anc::site, and the query with a single B*-step is q_1 = /desc::personref /anc::* [par::openauction] [anc::regions] /anc::site. A query with n B*-steps, $n > 1$, is generated by concatenating n copies of q_1.

Algorithms: We compared the performance of three different methods for evaluating XPath queries. The first method ("`eval`") corresponds to an unoptimized approach where the wildcard steps in the input query are not eliminated, and the query is evaluated by first constructing a main-memory representation of the entire input XML data before query evaluation. We implemented this evaluation method based on [9]. The second method ("`layer+eval`") is an enhancement of the first method that optimizes the input query by eliminating its wildcard steps using the layer axis. Finally, the third method ("`layer+optEval`") is a further improvement of the second method which is based on our proposed optimized evaluation strategy using selective loading together with wildcard step elimination.

We compared the evaluation methods in terms of the total evaluation time that includes two components: the parsing time as well as the querying time. The *parsing time* includes the time to parse and load the data into main memory (either partially or entirely) as well as the time to perform any precomputations (e.g., both the `layer+eval` and `layer+optEval` methods might need to precompute $level(.)$ and $ht(.)$ values). The *querying time* refers to the actual time required to evaluate the input query using the loaded data and any precomputed information to compute the query's result. Our experiments were conducted on a 2.6 GHz Intel Pentium IV machine with 1 GB of main memory running Windows XP; and all algorithms were implemented using Java.

7.2 Experimental Results

Figures 10(a), (b), and (c), compare the performance results of the three evaluation algorithms on the 70MB data file by varying the parameters N_{nc}, N_c, and N_b, respectively. Figure 10(d) compares the performance of evaluating the single NB*-step query with $N_c = 1$ by varying the size of the XML data file. Our results demonstrate that both the wildcard-step elimination strategy (i.e., `layer+eval`) as well as the selective-loading evaluation strategy (i.e., `layer+optEval`) consistently outper-

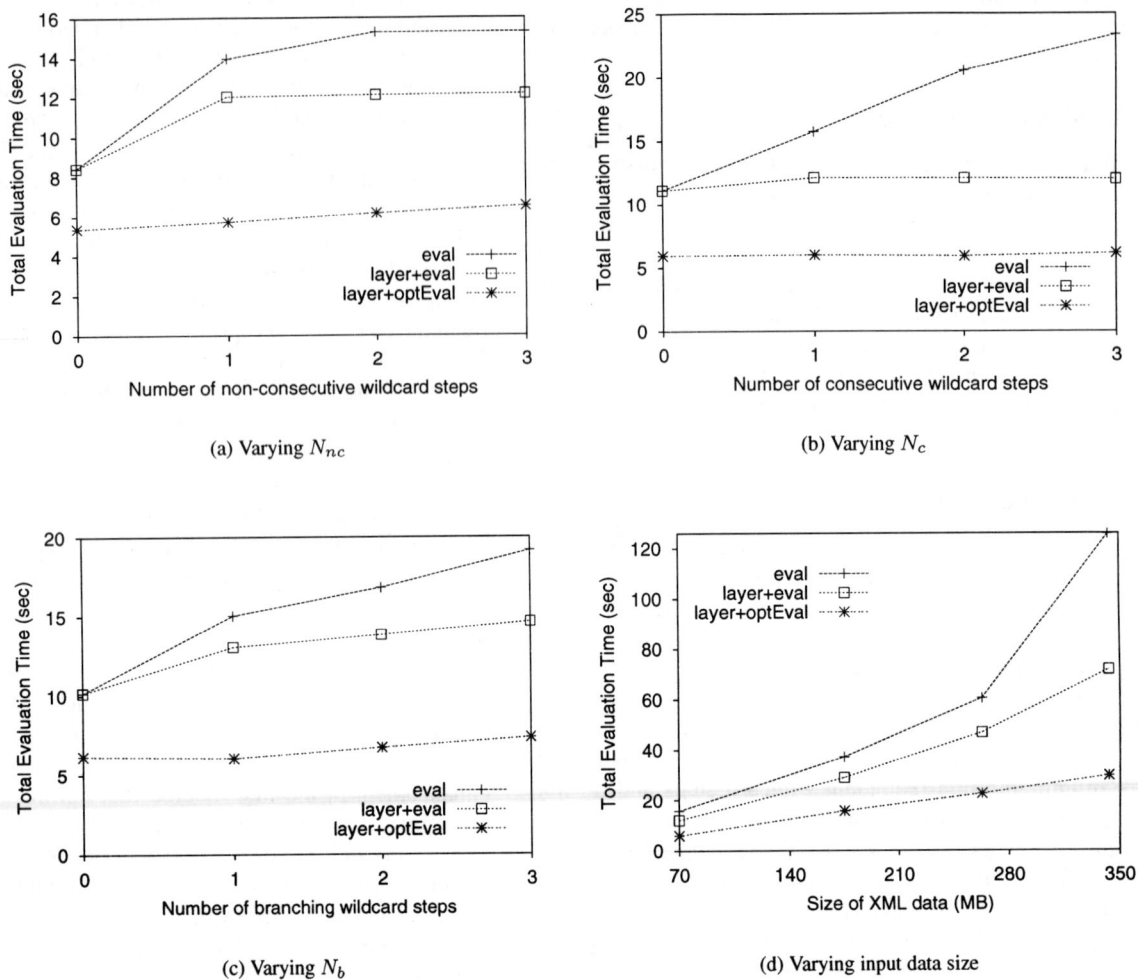

Figure 10: Evaluation of Node-selecting XPath Queries.

form the traditional evaluation method (i.e., eval), with layer+optEval giving the best performance. Specifically, layer+eval improves eval by a factor of up to 2.3, and layer+optEval improves eval by a factor of up to 4.2.

Figure 10(a) shows that as a query's complexity increases (with a larger number of non-consecutive wildcard steps), its total evaluation time also increases as expected; and generally, the performance gain of our proposed optimizations over eval also increases. Note that when the query has no wildcard steps (i.e., $N_{nc} = 0$), both eval and layer+eval are essentially the same and they have the same evaluation cost.

The parsing time turns out to be the dominant component of the total evaluation cost for all three methods. In particular, for both layer+eval and layer+optEval, the parsing time constitutes over 90% of the total evaluation cost. For eval, while the parsing time is about 90% of the total cost when $N_{nc} = 0$, this reduces to about 55% when $N_{nc} > 0$ due to the higher querying cost for queries with wildcard steps. Among the three methods, the parsing time for layer+eval is the highest, while layer+optEval incurs the lowest parsing cost. The reason for the latter is due to the effectiveness of selective data loading. layer+eval is more costly than eval in terms of parsing because layer+eval incurs the additional overhead of precomputation without the benefit of selective loading; however, the overall evaluation cost of layer+eval is still lower than that of eval due to the significant performance benefit with wildcard step elimination.

In terms of querying time, layer+eval is more efficient than eval because the wildcard steps in the queries are eliminated by layer+eval which results in faster query evaluations. The querying performance of layer+eval is further improved by layer+optEval which significantly reduces the data nodes loaded for evaluation; indeed, the proportion of data nodes being loaded by layer+optEval ranges from 1.3% to 3.8% as N_{nc} increases from 0 to 3.

Similar trends are also observed for the performance comparisons with varying number of consecutive non-branching wildcard steps N_c and varying number of branching wildcard steps N_b in Figures 10(b) and (c), respectively. In particular, the performance improvement of both `layer+eval` and `layer+optEval` over `eval` is greater as the query's complexity increases.

Finally, Figure 10(d) compares the performance of evaluating the single NB*-step query with $N_c = 1$ as a function of the size of the XML data file. The results indicate that the performance benefits of both `layer+eval` and `layer+optEval` over `eval` become more significant as the data size increases.

8 Conclusions

In this paper, we have proposed a new and complementary approach to optimize XPath queries by minimizing their wildcard steps. Our approach is based on using a general, composite axis called the layer axis, to rewrite a sequence of XPath steps into a single layer-axis step. We have described an efficient implementation of the layer axis and presented a novel and efficient rewriting algorithm to minimize both non-branching as well as branching wildcard steps in XPath queries. We have also demonstrated the usefulness of wildcard-step elimination by proposing an optimized evaluation strategy that capitalizes on the absence (or reduction) of wildcard steps in XPath queries. Our experimental results show that both the rewriting techniques and optimized evaluation strategy can result in significant performance improvement for XPath query evaluation. To the best of our knowledge, this is the first paper that addresses this new optimization problem.

As part of our future work, we intend to investigate the optimality and completeness of our rewriting algorithm, and also examine the possibility of extending the layer axis to handle the "horizontal" axes (i.e., preceding, following, and sibling-related axes) as well.

References

[1] S. Al-Khalifa, H. V. Jagadish, J. M. Patel, Y. Wu, N. Koudas, and D. Srivastava. Structural joins: a primitive for efficient XML query pattern matching. In *ICDE*, pages 141–152, 2002.

[2] S. Amer-Yahia, S. Cho, L. V. S. Lakshmanan, and D. Srivastava. Minimization of tree pattern queries. In *SIGMOD*, pages 497–508, March 2001.

[3] M. Benedikt, W. Fan, and G. M. Kuper. Structural properties of XPath fragments. In *ICDT*, pages 79–95, 2003.

[4] S. Boag, D. Chamberlin, M. Fernandez, D. Florescu, J. Robie, and J. Simeon. *XQuery 1.0: An XML query language.* "http://www.w3.org/TR/xquery", November 2003.

[5] N. Bruno, N. Koudas, and D. Srivastava. Holistic twig joins: optimal xml pattern matching. In *SIGMOD*, pages 310–321, 2002.

[6] J. Clark. *XSL Transformations (XSLT) 1.0.* "http://www.w3.org/TR/xslt", November 1999.

[7] W. Fan, C.-Y. Chan, and M. Garofalakis. Secure XML querying with security views. In *SIGMOD*, 2004.

[8] G. Gottlob, C. Koch, and R. Pichler. Efficient algorithms for processing XPath queries. In *VLDB*, pages 95–106, 2002.

[9] G. Gottlob, C. Koch, and R. Pichler. XPath query evaluation: improving time and space efficiency. In *ICDE*, pages 379–390, 2003.

[10] S. Helmer, C.-C. Kanne, and G. Moerkotte. Optimized translation of XPath into algebraic expressions parameterized by programs containing navigational primitives. In *WISE*, pages 215–224, 2002.

[11] H. Jiang, W. Wang, H. Lu, and J. X. Yu. Holistic twig joins on indexed XML documents. In *VLDB*, pages 273–284, 2003.

[12] D. Olteanu, H. Meuss, T. Furche, and F. Bry. XPath: looking forward. In *Workshop on XML-based Data Management*, pages 109–127, March 2002.

[13] P. Ramanan. Efficient algorithms for minimizing tree pattern queries. In *SIGMOD*, pages 299–309, 2002.

[14] P. Rao and B. Moon. PRIX: indexing and querying XML using Prufer sequences. In *ICDE*, pages 288–300, 2004.

[15] W3C. *XML Path Language (XPath) 1.0.* "http://www.w3.org/TR/xpath", 1999.

[16] H. Wang, S. Park, W. Fan, and P. S. Yu. ViST: a dynamic index method for querying XML data by tree structures. In *SIGMOD*, pages 110–121, 2003.

[17] P. T. Wood. Minimising simple XPath expressions. In *WebDB*, pages 13–18, 2001.

[18] XMark Project. *XMark – an XML benchmark project.* "http://www.xml-benchmark.org", 2001.

The NEXT Framework for Logical XQuery Optimization *

Alin Deutsch   Yannis Papakonstantinou   Yu Xu

University of California, San Diego
{deutsch,yannis,yxu}@cs.ucsd.edu

Abstract

Classical logical optimization techniques rely on a logical semantics of the query language. The adaptation of these techniques to XQuery is precluded by its definition as a functional language with operational semantics. We introduce Nested XML Tableaux which enable a logical foundation for XQuery semantics and provide the logical plan optimization framework of our XQuery processor. As a proof of concept, we develop and evaluate a minimization algorithm for removing redundant navigation within and across nested subqueries. The rich XQuery features create key challenges that fundamentally extend the prior work on the problems of minimizing conjunctive and tree pattern queries.

1 Introduction

The direct applicability of logical optimization techniques (such as rewriting queries using views, semantic optimization and minimization) to XQuery is precluded by XQuery's definition as a functional language [30]. The normalization module of the NEXT XQuery processor enables logical optimization of XQueries by reducing them to *NEsted Xml Tableaux (NEXT)*, which are based on logical semantics. NEXT extend tree patterns [3, 21] (which have been used in XPath minimization and answering XPath queries using XPath views) with nested subqueries, joins, and arbitrary mixing of set and bag semantics.

As a proof-of-concept of NEXT's applicability to XQuery logical optimization, but also for its own importance in improving query performance, we developed and evaluated a query minimization algorithm that removes redundant navigation within and across nested subqueries.

---

* Work supported by NSF ITR 313384

Permission to copy without fee all or part of this material is granted provided that the copies are not made or distributed for direct commercial advantage, the VLDB copyright notice and the title of the publication and its date appear, and notice is given that copying is by permission of the Very Large Data Base Endowment. To copy otherwise, or to republish, requires a fee and/or special permission from the Endowment.

Proceedings of the 30th VLDB Conference,
Toronto, Canada, 2004

Minimization is particularly valuable in an XQuery context, since redundant XML navigation arises naturally and unavoidably in *nested* queries, where the subqueries perform navigation that is redundant relative to the query they are nested in. A common case is that of queries that perform grouping in order to restructure or aggregate the source data. The grouping is typically expressed using a combination of self-join and nesting, in which the navigation in the nested, inner subquery completely duplicates the navigation of the outer query (see Examples 1.1 and 1.2). Another typical scenario pertains to mediator settings, where queries resulting from unfolding the views [20, 17, 25] in the original client queries contain nested and often redundant subqueries (when the navigation in two view definitions overlaps). Finally query generation tools tend to generate non-minimal queries [31].

EXAMPLE 1.1 Consider the following query that groups books by authors (it is a minor variation of query Q9 from W3C's XMP use case [27]). The **distinct-values** function eliminates duplicates, comparing elements by value-based equality [30].

let $doc := **document**("input.xml")
for $a **in** **distinct-values**($doc//book/author)
return ⟨result⟩ { $a,   (X1)
    for $b **in** $doc//book
    where some $ba **in** $b/author **satisfies** $ba **eq** $a
    return $b }
⟨/result⟩

Notice that the **for** loop binding $a (from now on called the $a loop) has *set* semantics, all others have *bag* semantics i.e., duplicates are not removed.[1]

The straightforward nested-loop execution of this query is wasteful since the nested loops (the $b **for** loop and the $ba **some** loop) are redundant: the $a loop has already navigated to the corresponding book and author elements. In this case, we say that the redundant navigation appears *across* nested subqueries, where nesting is w.r.t. the **return** clause. The NEXT XQuery processor performs a more

---

[1] The query can be expressed in a shorter form by replacing its **where** clause with "**where** $a = $b/author" or by replacing the inner **for** with "$doc//book[author = $a]". It is well known [19] how to reduce such syntactic sugar (use of "=" or use of predicates in paths) to the basic XQuery constructs we use (see Figure 3).

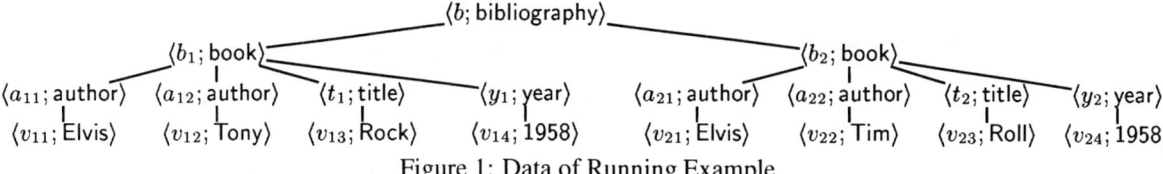

Figure 1: Data of Running Example

efficient execution (inspired by the OQL groupby operator [8]): eliminate the redundant navigation by scanning books and authors just once and then apply a group-by operation. ◊

It turns out that, when attempting to perform grouping by more than one variable, the resulting XQueries contain redundant navigation both across and within subqueries.

EXAMPLE 1.2 The following nested XQuery groups on two variables: book titles are grouped by author and year of publication.

for $a in distinct-values($doc//book/author)   (X2)
    $y in distinct-values($doc//book/year)
where some $b_3 in $doc//book,$a_3 in $b_3/author,
            $y_3 in $b_3/year
    satisfies $a eq $a_3 and $y eq $y_3
return ⟨result⟩ {$a, $y,
    for $b' in $doc//book
    where some $a' in $b'/author, $y' in $b'/year
        satisfies $a' eq $a and $y' eq $y
    return $b'/title}
⟨/result⟩

The $doc variable is defined as in the first line of (X1) and its definition will be omitted from now on. Notice the use of join equality conditions on *author* and *year* in the **some** of the $b' loop. Once again, the navigation of the outermost subquery (the $a and $y loops) is duplicated by the nested subquery. In addition, redundant navigation occurs also within the outermost subquery: the **some** loop binding $b_3 navigates to *book*, *author* and *year* elements, all of whom are also visited by the $a and $y loops. ◊

The combined effect of the normalization and minimization modules of the NEXT XQuery processor removes the redundant navigation from the above examples. This minimization is beneficial regardless of the query execution model. In many XQuery processors, including our own, the matching of paths and equality conditions is performed by joins that outperform brute force loops. Minimization reduces the number of joins in such cases.

Section 2 describes the system architecture and NEXT and highlights NEXT's key logical optimization enabling feature: NEXT consolidate all navigation of the original query in the XTableaux tree pattern structure, regardless of whether navigation originally appeared in the **where** clause, within non-path expressions in the **in** clause, or even within subqueries that are within a **distinct-values** and hence follow set semantics.

Section 3 describes the normalization algorithm that reduces a wide set of XQueries, called OptXQuery, to NEXT.

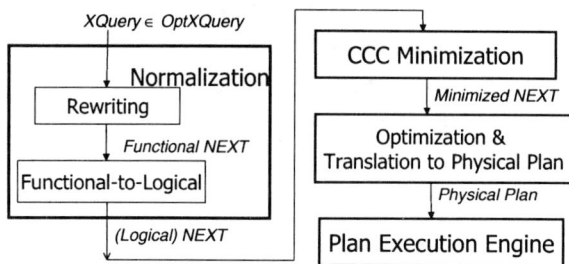

Figure 2: The NEXT XQuery Processor Architecture

All example XQueries appearing in this paper fall in this class. Due to space limitations we only discuss in the full paper [9] the processing of non-OptXQuery XQueries.

Section 4 describes a minimization algorithm that, given a NEXT, fully removes redundant navigation, in a formally defined sense. The expressiveness of OptXQuery raises the following novel challenges that fundamentally change the nature of the minimization problem, such that previous algorithms for the minimization of conjunctive queries [5, 2] and XPath queries [3, 23, 11], do not apply:

1. OptXQueries are nested (as opposed to conjunctive queries and tree patterns).

2. OptXQueries perform arbitrary joins (in contrast to tree patterns, which correspond to acyclic joins [12]).

3. OptXQueries freely mix bag and set semantics (as opposed to allowing either pure bag or pure set semantics in relational queries, and only set semantics in tree patterns).

Section 5 discusses the implementation of the minimization algorithm. Though the problem is NP-hard, as is the case for minimization of relational queries, the implementation reduces the exponentiality to an approximation of the query tree width [12] and results in fast minimization even for very large queries, as proven by our experimental results. We summarize the contributions of this work and provide future directions in Section 6. Related work is described in Section 7.

2 Framework and Architecture

XML We model an XML document D as a labeled tree of nodes N_{XML}, edges E_{XML}, a function $\lambda : N_{XML} \to Constants$ that assigns a label to each node, and a function $id : N_{XML} \to IDs$ that assigns a unique id to each node. We ignore node order. The tree of Figure 1 serves as our running example.

OptXQuery The paper focuses on the OptXQuery subset of XQuery, which follows the syntax of Figure 3 and also

$$
\begin{aligned}
XQ \;::=\; & \langle n\rangle\{XQ_1,\ldots,XQ_m\}\langle/n\rangle \\
\mid\; & XQ_1, XQ_2 \\
\mid\; & \textbf{for } (V \textbf{ in } XQ)+ \; (\textbf{where } CList)? \\
& \textbf{return } XQ \\
\mid\; & (\textbf{document }(\text{``}constant\text{''})|Var) \\
& ((/|//)Constant)* \\
\mid\; & Constant \\
\mid\; & \textbf{distinct-values}(XQ) \\
CList \;::=\; & Cond \; (\textbf{and } Cond)* \\
Cond \;::=\; & Var_1 \textbf{ eq } (Var_2|Constant) \\
\mid\; & \textbf{some } (V \textbf{ in } XQ)+ \textbf{ satisfies } CList
\end{aligned}
$$

Figure 3: OptXQuery

satisfies the constraints described below. Notice that OptXQuery allows navigation along the children (/) and descendant (//) axes of XPath, existential quantification using **some**, arbitrary conjunctive conditions (as opposed to acyclic conditions only [12]), element creation that may include nested queries (as opposed to tree conditions that return a single element or tuples of variable bindings, and duplicate elimination using the **distinct-values** function (which allows both bags and sets). The grammar can be trivially extended with additional constructs that have an obvious reduction to OptXQuery, such as predicates in path expressions.

OptXQuery's constraints rule out (i) queries that directly or indirectly test the equality of constructed sets (ii) implicit disjunctive conditions (aside from the explicit absence of **or**). The full paper [9] provides sufficient conditions for ruling out (i) and (ii). We limited the syntax and included the first constraint in order to be able to guarantee full minimization, as explained in Section 4, since it is well known from both relational and object-oriented query processing that minimization and containment problems become undecidable once set equality, negation and universal quantification are allowed. On the contrary, there is no theoretical reason against disjunctions and we can extend NEXT to incorporate them, but for simplicity we focus on purely conjunctive queries. Though only OptXQueries are guaranteed to be fully minimized, the processor may also input arbitrary XQueries and optimize them using minimization, as discussed in the full paper [9]. The main body of the paper assumes that the input query is in OptXQuery.

Normalization and NEXT The normalization module of the NEXT processor (see Figure 2) inputs an OptXQuery, applies a series of rewriting rules, discussed in Section 3, and produces a *functional NEXT*, whose syntax (see Figure 4) extends a subset of OptXQuery with an OQL-inspired group-by construct [4].

Functional NEXT The functional NEXT syntax allows only path expressions in the **for** clause, while OptXQuery also allowed nested subqueries. Also, NEXT allows only variables in the condition, while OptXQuery also allowed **some**, which include existential navigation. It is the use

$$
\begin{aligned}
XQ \;::=\; & \langle n\rangle\{XQ_1,\ldots,XQ_m\}\langle/n\rangle & \text{(P1)} \\
\mid\; & V & \text{(P2)} \\
\mid\; & \textbf{for } V_1 \textbf{ in } Path_1,\ldots,V_n \textbf{ in } Path_n & \text{(P3)} \\
& (\textbf{where } CList)? \\
& \textbf{groupby } (V_1'|[V_1'])\ldots(V_k'|[V_k'])(\textbf{into } P)? \\
& \textbf{return } XQ_1 \\
Path \;::=\; & (\textbf{document }(\text{``}Constant\text{''})|Var) \\
& (/|//)Constant & \text{(P4)} \\
CList ::=\; & Cond \; (\textbf{and } Cond)* & \text{(P5)} \\
Cond ::=\; & V_1 \textbf{ eq } (V_2|Constant) & \text{(P6)}
\end{aligned}
$$

Figure 4: Functional NEXT Syntax

of group-by that has enabled us to move all navigation to the path expressions of the **in** clauses. The *Functional-to-Logical* module performs a straightforward translation of its input into a *logical NEXT*, whose syntax extends tree patterns [21, 3, 23] to capture nesting, cyclic joins, and mixed set and bag semantics. There is an 1-1 correspondence between functional and logical NEXT expressions.

Group-By The arguments of group-by are a list of *groupby variables* $G_1,\ldots,G_k$, the name of an optional *partition variable* P, and the result expression. A group-by inputs the tuples of variable bindings produced by the **for** and **where** clauses and outputs a tuple set that has exactly one tuple for every set of tuples that have equal groupby variable bindings. Equality is identity-based if the groupby variable appears as $[G_i]$ or value-based if the variable appears as G_i. In OQL fashion, a new variable binding is created for the variable P and binds to a table that has the tuples that belong to this group. However, in order to stay within the XML data model, we emulate the nested table with a special **partition** element that contains tuple elements, which in turn contain elements named after the names of the aggregated variables, excluding $.

For example, consider the functional NEXT (X3), which groups book titles by author and year (indeed, it is the minimized form of XQuery (X2), and the corresponding logical NEXT will be seen in Figure 8(c)).

for $\$b_3$ **in** $\$doc//book, $\$a_1$ **in** $\$b_3$/author, $\$y_1$ **in** $\$b_3$/year
groupby $\$a_1, \$y_1$ **into** $L **return** (X3)
⟨result⟩{ $\$a_1, \$y_1$
    for $\$b'$ **in** $L/tuple/b_3$ **groupby** $[\$b']$ **return**
        for $\$t$ **in** $\$b'/title$ **groupby** $[\$t]$ **return** $\$t$ }
⟨/result⟩

The first table below illustrates the tuples generated by the outermost **for** clauses of (X3) when run on the data of Figure 1 and the next table illustrates the output of its first group-by. For illustration purposes, the bindings of the partition variable are also shown in nested table format. The notation (x) stands for the tree rooted at the node with id x. Notice that grouping by value results into creating copies for the bindings of the group-by variables in the result. For example, notice that the first binding

a_1	y_1	b_3
(a_{11})	(y_1)	(b_1)
(a_{12})	(y_1)	(b_1)
(a_{21})	(y_2)	(b_2)
(a_{22})	(y_2)	(b_2)

of $\$a_1$ is neither (a_{11}) nor (a_{21}) but is a new object (n_1) that has equal value with (a_{11}) and (a_{21}). Efficient implementations of group-by can avoid to physically produce copies.

Logical Next The Functional-to-Logical module creates the logical NEXT that corresponds to its input. Figure 5 illustrates the functional and the logical NEXT that correspond to query (X2).

Logical NEXT reflect the nesting of group-by expressions using a *groupby tree* (see tree on the left side of the logical NEXT of Figure 5). Each node of the groupby tree corresponds to a **for** expression of the functional NEXT and the immediate nesting of two **for** expressions is represented by an edge between their nodes. We label a node N with $N(\mathbf{X}; G_i; G_v; \mathbf{f})$ (for example, $N_1(X_1; ; \$a_1, \$y_1; f_1(\$a_1, \$y_1, N_2)))$, where:

$\Rightarrow$ the *XTableau* $\mathbf{X} = (F, EQ_{val}, EQ_{id})$ consists of a forest F of tree patterns, which captures navigation, a set of value-based equality conditions EQ_{val} (represented by bubble-ended dotted lines) and a set of id-based equalities EQ_{id} (represented by arrow-ended dotted lines). The three shaded sections of the pattern in Figure 5 correspond to the Xtableaux of N_1, N_2, N_3. The formal XTableau semantics extend the tree pattern semantics of [21] to account for the equality conditions and specify the set of bindings for the variables of the tree pattern $\mathbf{X}$. An alternate (and shorter) route towards specifying the bindings of the variables of the XTableaux is based on the 1-1 correspondence between logical and functional NEXT: Each node in the XTableau of group-by tree node N corresponds to a variable in the **for** expression that corresponds to N. Each edge corresponds to a navigation step to a child (graphically represented by a single edge) or a descendant (represented by a double edge). Nodes are labeled with the corresponding tag name tests, or $*$ if no such test is performed. Similarly, the equality conditions in the **where** clause correspond to the equalities of the XTableau. The set of variable bindings delivered by the XTableau is the set of bindings delivered for the variables of the corresponding **for** expression in the functional NEXT. In addition to prior tree pattern formalisms, we accommodate free and bound variables: since the nested queries may refer to variables bound in outer queries. For example, variable $\$b'$ is bound in N_2 and free in N_3. Tree patterns of a groupby node may be rooted at variable nodes bound in the tree pattern of an ancestor groupby node. Similarly, equalities may involve variables that are bound at ancestor groupby nodes. The equality $\$a_1$ **eq** $\$a'$ belongs to X_2 despite $\$a_1$ being free in X_2. Also, $\$b'$ belongs to X_2 (where it is bound), and it is free in X_3.

$\Rightarrow$ G_i and G_v are the vectors of groupby-id variables and groupby-value variables. For example, N_1 has an empty groupby-id list and its groupby-value variable list "$\$a_1, \$y_1$" specifies that the result expression f_1 will be invoked once for each unique pair of values of $\$a_1, \$y_1$, where uniqueness is based on value comparison. The variable list corresponds to the groupby list of the functional NEXT.

$\Rightarrow$ the *result* function **f** inputs the group-by variables' bindings and the results of the nested queries and outputs an XML tree. The result function may be the identity function or it may involve concatenation and/or new element creation. The function f_1 creates an element named **result** that contains $\$a_1, \$y_1$ and the result of N_2 (in this order). The function f_2 returns the result of N_3 and f_3 returns $\$t$. The specifics of the function are unimportant for minimization purposes, since it cannot be minimized; hence in the rest of the paper we refer to the result functions as $f_1, f_2, \ldots$.

Normalization Benefit Normalization reduces queries into the NEXT form, where all selections and navigations are consolidated in the XTableaux, regardless of whether navigation initially appeared in **some** loops, within **distinct-values** functions, or within subqueries nested in the **in** clause (see following example). This consolidation enables minimization to detect the opportunities for eliminating redundant navigation, regardless of the context in which navigation originally appeared. Normalization is crucial for maximizing the minimization opportunities and guaranteeing full minimization for the queries of OptXQuery. Example 2.1 below illustrates the need for the consolidation achieved through normalization. It shows a query that is semantically equivalent to (X2) but involves a more complex **in** clause. The combined action of normalization and minimization reduces it to the same minimal form with (X2). We will see how this query is normalized in Section 3.

EXAMPLE 2.1 While apparently more complicated than the query (X2), query (X5) below is what an XQuery expert would write, since it results in a more efficient execution plan, that avoids redundant navigation within the same subquery. In fact this is the most efficient way to perform grouping by multiple variables in XQuery.

```
for $p in distinct-values(
    for $b_1 in $doc//book,
        $a_1 in $b_1/author, $y_1 in $b_1/year
    return ⟨pair⟩⟨a⟩{$a_1}⟨/a⟩⟨y⟩{$y_1}⟨/y⟩⟨/pair⟩),
  $a in $p/a/author, $y in $p/y/year                    (X5)
return ⟨result⟩ {$a}{$y}
         { for $b' in $doc//book
             where some  $a' in $b'/author,
                         $y' in $b'/year
             satisfies $a' eq $a and $y' eq $y
             return $b'/title}
       ⟨/result⟩
```

$$N_1 \begin{cases} \textbf{for } \$b_1 \textbf{ in } \$doc//book, \$a_1 \textbf{ in } \$b_1/author, \\ \quad \$b_2 \textbf{ in } \$doc//book, \$y_1 \textbf{ in } \$b_2/year, \\ \quad \$b_3 \textbf{ in } \$doc//book, \$a_3 \textbf{ in } \$b_3/author, \$y_3 \textbf{ in } \$b_3/year \\ \textbf{where } \$a_1 \textbf{ eq } \$a_3 \textbf{ and } \$y_1 \textbf{ eq } \$y_3 \\ \textbf{groupby } \$a_1, \$y_1 \textbf{ return} \\ \langle result \rangle \{ \$a_1, \$y_1, \\ N_2 \begin{cases} \textbf{for } \$b' \textbf{ in } \$doc//book, \$a' \textbf{ in } \$b'/author, \\ \quad \$y' \textbf{ in } \$b'/year \quad\quad\quad\quad (X4) \\ \textbf{where } \$a_1 \textbf{ eq } \$a' \textbf{ and } \$y_1 \textbf{ eq } \$y' \\ \textbf{groupby } [\$b'] \textbf{return} \\ N_3 \begin{cases} \textbf{for } \$t \textbf{ in } \$b'/title \\ \textbf{groupby } [\$t] \textbf{ return } \$t \end{cases} \end{cases} \\ \}\langle /result \rangle \end{cases}$$

Figure 5: Logical and Functional NEXT corresponding to query (X2)

The outermost **for** binds the variable $\$p$ to distinct pairs of *author* and *year* subelements of *book* elements. For each pair, the nested $\$b'$ loop retrieves the corresponding book elements. This loop is the unavoidable redundant navigation across subqueries. ◇

Minimization Module Normalization does not solve the minimization problem by itself, as we still have to identify *which* navigations are reusable. The CCC algorithm minimizes the redundant navigation in a given NEXT query and provably finds the minimal equivalent XTableaux of its input NEXT. This requires detecting and eliminating redundant navigation *within* and *across* nested XTableaux.

For example, the NEXT of Figure 8(c) and its corresponding functional NEXT (X3) are the minimized form of XQueries (X2) and (X5). We navigate to books just once and the inner subqueries utilize the navigation of the outer level. Notice that the minimized NEXT of Figure 8(c) has fewer nodes and edges than the original NEXT of Figure 5(b). Indeed it is the minimum possible number of nodes and edges.

Executing NEXT Finally, the minimized NEXT is reduced to a physical plan, similar to the algebraic plans of [14, 15] and is executed. Our logical optimization steps can be easily incorporated in other implementations of XQuery as well by attaching a groupby clause to FLWR, i.e., by having the ability to execute the groupby of the functional NEXT. One can improve performance by removing trivial **groupby**'s, such as those of the inner **for** loops of (X3), and keeping only the essential ones, such as only the outermost **groupby** of (X3).

3 Normalization into NEXT

Figure 6 presents a set of rewrite rules which provably normalize any OptXQuery to a NEXT query (as shown by Theorem 3.1 below). Some of these rules are known simplification rules of XQuery; they are used extensively both in reducing XQuery to its formal core [29] as well as in query optimization [19]. We focus the presentation on the rules that are particular to **groupby**, such as Rules (G1), (G3), (G4) and (G5) and leave out the trivial standard normalization rules. Notice that, for simplicity of presentation, all rules are shown using **for** and **some** expressions

that define exactly one variable. The extension to multiple variables is obvious.

The normalization process is stratified in two stages. First, all standard XQuery rewriting rules are applied in any order. Next, the **groupby**-specific rules are used. Rule (RG1) may be applied in both stages. In the extended version of this paper [9], we prove:

Theorem 3.1 *The rewriting of any XQuery Q with the rules in Figure 6 terminates regardless of the order in which rules are applied, i.e. we reach a query T for which no more rewrite rule applies. If Q is an OptXQuery, then T is guaranteed to be a NEXT query.* ◇

EXAMPLE 3.1 Recall query (X2) from Example 1.2. In the first phase of the normalization of (X2), Rules (R1), (R11), (R12) and (R6) apply, yielding the query (X6).

```
for $a in distinct-values(                               (X6)
    for $b_1 in $doc//book return for $a_1 in $b_1/author
    return $a_1)
return for $y in distinct-values(
  for $b_2 in $doc//book return
    for $y_1 in $b_2/year return $y_1)
where some $b_3 in $doc//book satisfies
      some $a_3 in $b_3/author satisfies
      some $y_3 in $b_3/year
      satisfies $a eq $a_3 and $y eq $y_3
return ⟨result⟩ {$a, $y,
    for $b' in $doc//book
    where some $a' in $b'/author satisfies
          some $y' in $b'/year satisfies
          $a' eq $a and $y' eq $y
    return for $t in $b'/title return $t}
⟨/result⟩
```

The second phase of the normalization applies **groupby** rewriting rules to (X6). A rewrite step with Rule (G1) applied to the outermost **for** replaces the **distinct-values** function with a **groupby** clause which groups by the value of variable $\$a$. Similarly, Rule (G3) turns the inner **for** expression, which does not involve **distinct-values**, into a **for** expression that involves grouping by identity. By applying Rule (G4) the **some** structures are eliminated. Notice that the variables defined in **some** do not participate in the groupby variable lists.

Standard XQuery Rewriting Rules

(R1)   **for** V_1 **in** $E_1, \ldots,$ V_n **in** E_n **return** $E \mapsto$ **for** V_1 **in** E_1**return for** V_2 **in** E_2 **return** $\ldots$ **for** V_n **in** E_n **return** E

(R2)   **for** V **in** (**for** V_1 **in** E_1 **return** E_2) **return** $E_3 \mapsto$ **for** V_1 **in** E_1 **return for** V **in** E_2 **return** E_3

(R3)   **for** V **in** $\langle e \rangle E_1 \langle /e \rangle$ **return** $E_2 \mapsto \theta_{\$V \mapsto \langle e \rangle E_1 \langle /e \rangle}(E_2)$ (* $\theta_{\$V \mapsto E_1}(E_2)$ substitutes E_1 for V in E_2 *)

(R4)   **for** V_1 **in** V_2 **return** $E \mapsto \theta_{\$V_1 \mapsto \$V_2}(E)$ (*if V_2 is not defined by **let** *)

(R5)   **for** V **in** (E_1, E_2) **return** $E_3 \mapsto$ (**for** V **in** E_1 **return** E_3), (**for** V **in** E_2 **return** E_3)

(R6)   **some** V_1 **in** $E_1, \ldots,$ V_n **in** E_n **satisfies** C
     $\mapsto$ **some** V_1 **in** E_1 **satisfies some** V_2 **in** E_2 **satisfies** $\ldots$ **some** V_n **in** E_n **satisfies** C

(R7)   **some** V **in** (**for** V_1 **in** E_1 **return** E_2) **satisfies** $C \mapsto$ **some** V_1 **in** E_1 **satisfies some** V **in** E_2 **satisfies** C

(R8)   **some** V **in** $\langle e \rangle E_1 \langle /e \rangle$ **satisfies** $C \mapsto \theta_{\$V \mapsto \langle e \rangle E_1 \langle /e \rangle}(C)$

(R9)   **some** V_1 **in** V_2 **satisfies** $C \mapsto \theta_{\$V_1 \mapsto \$V_2}(C)$ (* if V_2 is not defined by **let** *)

(R10)   **some** V **in** **distinct-values**(E) **satisfies** $C \mapsto$ **some** V **in** E **satisfies** C

(R11) $V(/|//)C \mapsto$ **for** V_1 **in** $V(/|//)C$ **return** V_1 (* if V/C does not appear in "X **in** V/C"*)

(R12) $V(/|//)C_1\ldots(/|//)C_n \mapsto$ **for** V_1 **in** $V(/|//)C_1$ **return** $\ldots$ **for** V_n **in** $V_{n-1}(/|//)C_n$ **return** V_n (* for $n \geq 2$ *)

(R13)   **distinct-values**$(\$V|\langle e \rangle E_1 \langle /e \rangle|\textbf{distinct-values}(E)) \mapsto \$V|\langle e \rangle E_1 \langle /e \rangle|\textbf{distinct-values}(E)$
     (*if V is not defined by **let** *)

(RG1) $\langle e \rangle E_1, \ldots, E_n \langle /e \rangle/c \mapsto \sigma_c(E_1), \ldots, \sigma_c(E_n)$
     $\sigma_c(\langle c \rangle E \langle /c \rangle) \mapsto \langle c \rangle E \langle /c \rangle$ $\sigma_c(\langle a \rangle E \langle /a \rangle) \; (*a \neq c*) \mapsto ()$
     $\sigma_c(\$V) \mapsto \$V$ (*if $(tagName(\$V) = c)$*)   ()   (*else*) $\sigma_c(E(/|//)a) \mapsto ()(*a \neq c*)$
     $\sigma_c(\textbf{for } \$V_1 \textbf{ in } E_1 \textbf{ return } E_2) \mapsto \textbf{for } \$V_1 \textbf{ in } E_1 \textbf{ return } \sigma_c(E_2)$ $\sigma_c(E(/|//)c) \mapsto E(/|//)c$
     $\sigma_c(E_1, E_2) \mapsto \sigma_c(E_1), \sigma_c(E_2)$ $\sigma_c(\textbf{distinct-values}(E)) \mapsto \textbf{distinct-values}(\sigma_c(E))$

Group-By Rewriting Rules

(G1)   **for** V **in** **distinct-values**(E_1) **return** $E_2 \mapsto$ **for** V **in** E_1 **groupby** V **return** E_2

(G2)   **distinct-values**$(E_1) \mapsto$ **for** V **in** E_1 **groupby** V **return** V
     (*for **distinct-values**(E_1) which does not appear in "X **in** **distinct-values**(E_1)"*)

(G3)   **for** V **in** E_1 **return** $E_2 \mapsto$ **for** V **in** E_1 **groupby** $[V]$ **return** E_2

(G4)   **for** V_1 **in** E_1 **where some** V_2 **in** E_2 **satisfies** C **groupby** G **return** E_3
     $\mapsto$ **for** V_1 **in** E_1, V_2 **in** E_2 **where** C **groupby** G **return** E_3

(G5)   **for** V_2 **in** (**for** V_1 **in** E_1 **groupby** G_1 **return** E_2) **groupby** V_2 **return** E_3
     $\mapsto$ **for** V_1 **in** E_1, V_2 **in** E_2 **groupby** V_2 **return** E_3

(G6)   **for** X **in** $(X' \mid \langle c \rangle E \langle /c \rangle)$ **groupby** G **return** $E_r \mapsto \theta_{X \mapsto (X' \mid \langle c \rangle E \langle /c \rangle)}(E_r)$
     $\mapsto \theta_{X \mapsto (X' \mid \langle c \rangle E_2 \langle /c \rangle)}(\textbf{for } V \textbf{ in } E \textbf{ where } C \textbf{ groupby } G_1 \textbf{ return } E_r)$

(G7)   **for** V_1 **in** E_1, X **in** $(X' \mid \langle c \rangle E \langle /c \rangle)$ **groupby** G **return** $E_r \mapsto \theta_{X \mapsto (X' \mid \langle c \rangle E \langle /c \rangle)}(\textbf{for } V_1 \textbf{ in } E_1 \textbf{ groupby } G \textbf{ return } E_r)$

(G8)   **for** V_1 **in** $E_1, \ldots, V_n$ **in** E_n **groupby** G_1 **return for** V'_1 **in** $E'_1, \ldots, V'_k$ **in** E'_k **groupby** G_2 **return** E_r
     $\mapsto$ **for** V_1 **in** $E_1, \ldots, V_n$ **in** E_n, V'_1 **in** $E'_1, \ldots, V'_k$ **in** E'_k **groupby** G_1, G_2 **return** E_r
     (*if G_1 and G_2 only contain grouping by value variables*)

(G9)   **groupby** $E \mapsto$ **groupby** $strip(E)$
     $strip(\langle tag \rangle E \langle /tag \rangle) \mapsto strip(E)$ $strip(E_1, E_2) \mapsto strip(E_1), strip(E_2)$
     $strip([E]) \mapsto [strip(E)]$ $strip(\$V, \$V) \mapsto strip(\$V) \mapsto \$V$

Figure 6: Rules for rewriting OptXQuery into NEXT

Rule (G5) removes nested subqueries from generator expressions. Rule (G6) substitutes a_1 for a and y_1 for y. Rule (G8) collapses **groupby**'s. The transformations reduce the query (X2) to the NEXT (X4). ◇

Example 3.2 illustrates the normalization of (X5), which is the efficient variant of query (X2).

EXAMPLE 3.2 Recall from Section 1 (X5), the expert's choice of writing query (X2). Standard XQuery normalization rules (R1),(R11), (R12), (R6) and (R2) are applied. Then **groupby**-specific rules (G1,G3, G4, G5, G6, G7, G9) and RG1 are applied and the final result is the NEXT query shown below.

for b_1 **in** $doc//book, a_1 **in** $b_1/author, y_1 **in** $b_1/year
groupby $a_1, y_1 **return**
   $\langle result \rangle \{\$a_1, \$y_1,$
   for b' **in** $doc//book, a' **in** $b'/author,$y'$ **in** $b'/year
   where a' **eq** a_1**and** y' **eq** y_1
     groupby [b'] **return**
       for t **in** $b'/title **groupby** [$t] **return** $t $\}$
   $\langle /result \rangle$
◇

4 Minimization of NEXT Queries

The minimization algorithm focuses on the Xtableaux, which describe the navigation part of NEXT queries, in order to eliminate redundant navigation. The algorithm we present here does not incorporate knowledge about the semantics of the result functions, treating them as uninterpreted symbols.[2] It is easy to see that under this assumption, two equivalent NEXT queries must have isomorphic group-by trees, where the corresponding (according to the isomorphism) nodes of the two group-by trees have identical (up to variable renaming) groupby lists and result func-

---

[2] Which means that $f_1(x, y)$ is equal to $f_2(u, v)$ iff f_1 and f_2 are the same function symbol and $x = u$ and $y = v$. Exploiting the semantics of the result functions in minimization is a future work direction.

tions. However, this does not constrain the Xtableaux associated with the corresponding group-by nodes in any other way than having to deliver the same set of bindings for their variables.

We say that NEXT query Q is *minimal*, if for any other NEXT query Q_o equivalent to Q, and for any group-by node N of Q, the node N_o of Q_o corresponding to N via the isomorphism has at least as many variable nodes in its Xtableau. Clearly, minimality rules out redundant navigation: if NEXT query Q performs redundant navigation, this can be removed, yielding an equivalent query with strictly less navigation steps, hence strictly less variables, so Q is not minimal.

Theorem 4.1 *Any NEXT query with uninterpreted result functions has a unique minimal form (up to variable renaming).*[3] ◇

We present the *Collapse and Check Containment (CCC)* algorithm, which searches for this minimal form and is guaranteed to find it. Note that Theorem 4.1 implies that no other algorithm can further minimize CCC's output without manipulating the result functions. As a matter of fact, we conjecture that in the absence of any schema information, no manipulation of the result function can generate additional minimization opportunities. This conjecture and Theorem 4.1 imply that the CCC algorithm fully minimizes any NEXT query, regardless of its result function.

The CCC algorithm is shown in Figure 7. It minimizes a NEXT query Q by invoking min_query on the empty context and Q. min_query visits the group-by tree of Q in a top-down fashion. Let T be a subtree of Q's groupb-by tree and denote with N the root of T. T may have free variables whose bindings are provided by the *context* C, where C is the list of N's ancestors in Q's group-by tree. min_query(C, T) returns a minimized equivalent of T in context C as follows. First, the Xtableau X of N is minimized in context C by the min_tableau function (described shortly), which returns a minimized Xtableau X^{min} and a variable mapping θ. θ maps eliminated variables of X into retained variables – potentially variables provided by ancestor groupby nodes. This variable mapping is applied to the groupby lists and the arguments of the result function of N, yielding a new group-by tree node N'. The children of N' are set to the result of recursively applying min_query to each child of N under the appropriate context. Finally, the new group-by tree rooted at N' is returned.

Tableau Minimization The tableau minimization algorithm min_tableau is based on two key operations: collapsing variable nodes, and checking that this rewriting preserves equivalence.

---
[3]Contrast this with the uniqueness problem for nested OQL queries, which is open, as a consequence of the open problem of deciding their equivalence [18]. We have developed a decision procedure for equivalence of NEXT queries with arbitrary nesting depth and uninterpreted result functions. This procedure is not needed in minimization, but its existence is crucial for the proof of minimal form uniqueness. Checking equivalence of NEXT queries is of independent interest for their optimization.

CCC(Q: NEXT query) := min_query(*empty context*, Q)

min_query (*Context*: group-by tree,
$$N(X; G_i; G_v; f) \atop T_1 \ \ldots \ T_n \quad : \text{group-by tree})$$
returns group-by tree

$(X^{min}, \theta) \leftarrow$ min_tableau(*Context*, X, G_i, G_v)
if *Context* is empty
   NewCtxt $\leftarrow N'(X^{min}; \theta(G_i); \theta(G_v); \theta(f))$
else /* *Context* is of the form $N_1^a(\ldots) - \ldots - N_m^a(\ldots)$ */
$$NewCtxt \leftarrow \begin{array}{c} Context \\ | \\ N'(X^{min}; \theta(G_i); \theta(G_v); \theta(f)) \end{array}$$
return
$$N'(X^{min}; \theta(G_i); \theta(G_v); \theta(f)) \atop \text{min\_query}(NewCtxt, \theta(T_1)) \ldots \text{min\_query}(NewCtxt, \theta(T_n))$$

Figure 7: The CCC Minimization Algorithm

The collapse step. Consider two variables x, y in the input tableau X. Assume that x is bound in X, while y may be either bound or free. Then *collapsing x into y* means substituting y for x in X. Notice that after a sequence of collapse steps, we may end up with two /-edges between the same pair of variable nodes. In this case, we remove one /-edge. We also remove any //-edge $e = (s, t)$ such that there exists a path from s to t in X which does not include e. Clearly, the removed edges correspond to redundant navigation steps.

EXAMPLE 4.1 We illustrate the minimization of the NEXT of Figure 5. First we apply min_tableau to tableau X_1 of the root N_1 of the groupby tree. Since there is no ancestor context, it collapses only variables bound in X_1: $\$b_1$ into $\$b_3$, $\$b_2$ into $\$b_3$, then $\$y_3$ into $\$y_1$ and finally $\$a_3$ into $\$a_1$, to obtain the minimized groupby node N_1' in Figure 8 (a). Using the algorithm described later, min_tableau verifies that X_1 and X_1' (the Xtableau of N_1') are equivalent. Coincidentally, the variable mapping $\theta_1 = [\$b_1 \mapsto \$b_3, \$b_2 \mapsto \$b_3, \$y_3 \mapsto \$y_1, \$a_3 \mapsto \$a_1]$ does not affect the groupby lists and result function of N_1.

Next, N_2 is minimized under the context of N_1'. Now we can also collapse nodes across Xtableaux: we map $\$b'$ (from N_2) into $\$b_3$ (from N_1') to get the temporary Xtableau X_2' shown in Figure 8 (b). We continue collapsing $\$y'$ into $\$y_1$ and $\$a'$ into $\$a_1$ to obtain the groupby node N_2'' shown in Figure 8 (c). Notice that N_2'' has the empty Xtableau X_2'', which means that it performs no new navigation. Instead, it reuses the navigation in N_1' to get the bindings of $\$b_3$, on whose identity it then groups. It turns out that the above collapse steps are equivalence preserving, i.e., X_2 is equivalent to X_2'' in the context of N_1'.

The minimization of N_3 results in an identical N_3'. The overall effect is that the NEXT query (X4) has been optimized into the NEXT query of Figure 8 (c). ◇

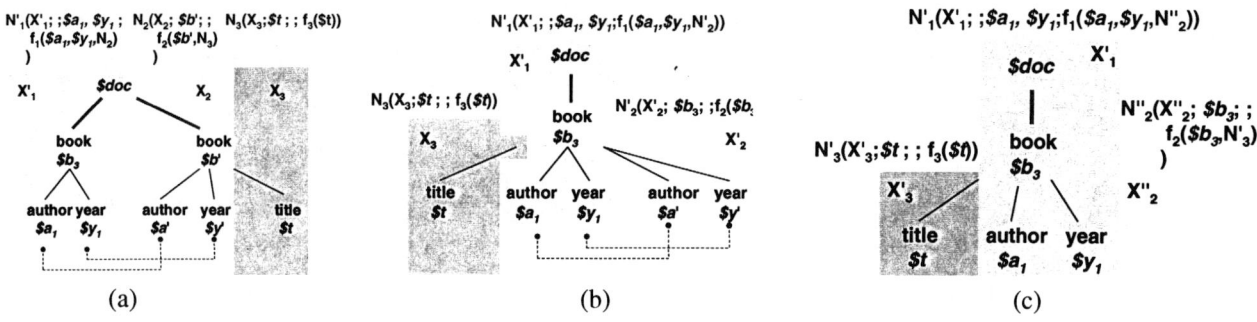

Figure 8: (a) after minimization of Q_1 (b) after collapsing $\$b'$, $\$b_3$ in Q_2 (c) the minimal form

While not needed in the above example, there is one more case in which we try to collapse pairs of variables x, y, namely when they are both free in the Xtableau X. Collapsing them in X means adding the id-based equality x **is** y to X. The reason we consider such collapse steps on free variables is subtle. The fact that X has a non-empty set of bindings may say something about the structure of the XML document which in turn may render the bindings of variable x reusable to obtain those of y. However, for documents where X has no bindings, the bindings of x and y may be unrelated. Therefore we need a way to say that x and y have related bindings *provided* X has bindings. The solution is to add the equality x **is** y to X (see Example 4.4).

Equivalence of group-by nodes in a context. After a collapse step of min_tableau has reduced the Xtableau X of a groupby node $N(X; G_i; G_v; f)$ into an Xtableau X' by deriving a mapping θ, it checks the equivalence of $N(X; G_i; G_v; f)$ to $N'(X'; \theta(G_i); \theta(G_v); \theta(f))$ in the context C provided by the ancestors of N. This means verifying that X and X' produce the same sets of bindings for the variables of the groupby lists when the bindings of their free variables are provided by the context C. The function min_tableau reduces the problem to checking containment of nodes without free variables (i.e., to equivalence of nodes in the absence of any context) and then solves the latter.

The reduction proceeds as follows: Let the context C be the list $N_1^a, \ldots, N_m^a$ of N's ancestors. Let $N_{C,N}$ be a new groupby node. Its groupby-id and groupby-value variables are the list of all group-by variables of $N_1^a, \ldots, N_m^a, N$. Its result function is the same as N's. Its Xtableau is obtained by merging the Xtableaux of $N_1^a, \ldots, N_m^a, N$ (put together all nodes and edges). Analogously, define $N_{C,N'}$. Then the following holds:

Proposition 1 *Group-by nodes N and N' are equivalent in context C if and only if the sets of bindings of the groupby variables of $N_{C,N}$ and $N_{C,N'}$ are contained in one another.*

EXAMPLE 4.2 By Proposition 1, the correctness of the collapse step of $\$b'$ into $\$b_3$ in Example 4.1 reduces to the equivalence of groupby nodes $N_{N'_1,N_2}(N'_1 \# N_2; \$b'; \$a_1, \$y_1; f_2(\$b', N_3))$ and $N_{N'_1,N'_2}(N'_1 \# N'_2; \$b_3; \$a_1, \$y_1; f_2(\$b_3, N_3))$. Here N'_1, N_2, N'_2 refer to Figure 8, and $X \# Y$ denotes the Xtableau obtained by merging Xtableaux X and Y. ◇

While the reducibility of equivalence to containment is self-understood for conjunctive queries and tree patterns, it is a pleasant surprise for NEXT queries, as this is not true in general for nested OQL queries [18].[4]

Containment Mappings. Next we show how to check the containment of $N_{C,N}$ in $N_{C,N'}$ and vice versa. We will show in Proposition 2 below that containment is equivalent to finding a *containment mapping*, defined as follows. Let N, N' be two groupby nodes with identical result functions, with associated Xtableaux X, X', groupby-id variable lists G_i, G'_i and groupby-value variable lists G_v, G'_v. We omit the result functions from the discussion since they are identical (modulo variable renaming). A containment mapping from N to N' is a mapping h from the pattern nodes and constants of X to those of X' such that

1. h is the identity on constant values.

2. for any node n in X, n's tag is the same as that of $h(n)$.

3. for any /-edge $n \to m$ in X, there is a /-edge $u \to v$ in X' such that the conditions in X' imply the value-based equality of $h(n)$ with u and of $h(m)$ with v (by reflexivity, symmetry, transitivity, and the fact that id-equality implies value-equality). [5]

4. for any //-edge $n \to m$ in X, there are edges (regardless of their type) $s_1 \to t_1, \ldots, s_n \to t_n$ in X', such that the conditions in X' imply the value-based equality of t_i with s_{i+1} (for all $1 \leq i \leq n-1$), of s_1 with $h(n)$, and of t_n with $h(m)$.

5. for each equality condition x **eq** y in X (x, y are variables or constants) $h(x)$ **eq** $h(y)$ is implied by the conditions of X'. Analogously for x **is** y.

---

[4][18] does show however that equivalence reduces to containment for nested OQL queries whose output is a VERSO relation [1]. It turns out that there is a close relationship between VERSO relations and NEXT queries: If we neglect the result functions of the groupby nodes and simply output tuples of bindings, the resulting nested relation is a VERSO relation.

[5]Checking that a certain equality is implied by the conditions in X' can be done in PTIME. It simply involves checking the membership of the equality in the reflexive, transitive closure of the equalities in X' (which is PTIME-computable).

6. the value-based equality of vectors $h(G_v)$ and G'_v is implied by the conditions in X'.

7. the id-based equality of vectors $h(G_i)$ and G'_i is implied by the conditions in X'.

The difference between the tree pattern containment mappings from [21] and the ones defined in this work is that the latter were designed to help reasoning about equality conditions, which are not allowed in tree patterns. For example, the intuition behind clauses 3. and 4. is that whenever two XML nodes are equal (by value or id), so are the subtrees T_1, T_2 rooted at them, so any path in T_1 has a correspondent in T_2.

EXAMPLE 4.3 Continuing Example 4.2, the mapping defined as $h = \{\$b_3 \mapsto \$b', \$a_1 \mapsto \$a', \$y_1 \mapsto \$y', \$a' \mapsto \$a', \$y' \mapsto \$y'\}$ is a containment mapping from $N_{N'_1,N'_2}(N'_1 \# N'_2; \$b_3; \$a_1, \$y_1; f_2(\$b_3, N_3))$ into $N_{N'_1,N_2}(N'_1 \# N_2; \$b'; \$a_1, \$y_1; f_2(\$b', N_3))$. Here the equality $h(\$a_1)$ **eq** $h(\$a')$ becomes $\$a'$ **eq** $\$a'$, which is trivially implied by the reflexivity of equality. ⋄

Proposition 2 $N_{C,N}$ is contained in $N_{C,N'}$ if and only if there is a containment mapping from $N_{C,N'}$ to $N_{C,N}$.

By Propositions 1 and 2, all the CCC algorithm has to do to check the equivalence of nodes N and N' in context C is to find containment mappings in both directions between $N_{C,N}$ and $N_{C,N'}$. In fact, the nature of the collapse operation guarantees the existence of a containment mapping from $N_{C,N}$ to $N_{C,N'}$. Hence only the opposite mapping must be checked.

In the extended version [9], we prove:

Theorem 4.2 Let Q be a NEXT query. Then (a) the CCC algorithm finds the minimal form M, and (b) M is reached regardless of the order of collapse steps. ⋄

Remarks. 1. Note that collapse steps are quite different and more complex than the basic step used in tree pattern minimization, namely simply removing a variable node. This complexity is unavoidable: see Example 4.4 for a non-minimal NEXT query for which, if instead of collapsing nodes we only try removing them, no removal is equivalence preserving and we cannot modify the original query at all. Moreover, for the same query, if we do not collapse variables that are both free in a groupby node, confining ourselves to pairs with at most one free variable, we cannot reach the minimal form, and for two distinct sequences of collapse steps, we obtain two distinct, non-minimal queries.

EXAMPLE 4.4 Consider the NEXT query in Figure 9 (a), where N_2 is a child of N_1 in the groupby tree. The navigation in N_2 binding variable $\$b_3$ can reuse from N_1 either the navigation for $\$b_2$ or that for $\$b_1$. We thus have a choice of collapsing $\$b_3$ into $\$b_2$ and then $\$y_3$ into $\$y_2$ and $\$p_3$ into $\$p_2$, obtaining the NEXT in Figure 9(b). Alternatively, we can collapse $\$b_3$ into $\$b_1$ and then $\$a_3$ into $\$a_1$ and $\$y_3$ into $\$y_1$, obtaining the NEXT query in Figure 9(c). In both cases, there are no more equivalence preserving collapse steps that involve at least one free variable, and we get "stuck" with either of the NEXT queries, depending on the initial collapse choice. However, note that we can continue by collapsing $\$b_1$ into $\$b_2$ in both versions of N'_2. Since in both versions these variables are free in N'_2, this means adding the id-based equality $\$b_1$ **is** $\$b_2$ to N'_2. This step in turn enables the collapse of all remaining nodes from N'_2 into nodes from N_1, leading in both cases to the same minimal NEXT query having a node N''_2 with an empty Xtableau. ⋄

2. The CCC minimization algorithm applies directly also to queries Q containing $*$-labeled pattern nodes or id-based equality conditions. However, Theorem 4.2 fails in this case, i.e. the algorithm may not fully minimize Q, leaving some residual redundant navigation. But so will any other NP algorithm, unless $\Pi_2^p = NP$, for the following reason. The complexity of checking for the containment mapping is NP-complete in the number of variable nodes in the Xtableau. [10] shows that even for XQueries without nesting, but allowing either navigation to descendants and children of unspecified tag name, or id-based equality checks, equivalence is Π_2^p-complete. It follows that even if $N_{C,G}, N_{C,G'}$ are equivalent, the existence of the containment mapping is not necessary, i.e. the *only if* part of Proposition 2 fails. Consequently, the CCC algorithm might wrongly conclude that the collapse step leading to Q' is not equivalence preserving, and discard it.

From Logical NEXT to Functional NEXT. Notice that the translation of the logical NEXT output by the minimization algorithm into a functional NEXT must deal with a subtlety that minimization may have introduced: the translation of a groupby node N with a free variable $\$r$. Two cases may arise. First, $\$r$ may be among the groupby variables of some ancestor groupby node N^a (e.g. in the NEXT query from Figure 8 (c), $\$b_3$ appears in the groupby list of N''_2, and free in N'_3). Then in the translation of N we simply refer to $\$r$, using it as a free variable. Second, $\$r$ may not be in any groupby variable list (e.g. variable $\$b_3$ is free in N''_2 and not in any groupby list for the query in Figure 8 (c)). Then denote with N^a the groupby node in which $\$r$ is bound (N'_1 for $\$b_3$ in our example). The individual bindings for $\$r$ are collected in the nested relations created by N^a's groupby operation. To access these bindings, we add to the groupby construct in the translation of N^a the clause **into** $\$L$, with $\$L$ a fresh variable binding to the list of bindings of $\$r$. Now in the translation of N we add the loop **for** $\$r$ **in** $\$L/tuple/r$. The query in Figure 8 (c) translates to (X3).

5 Minimization Implementation Issues

The implementation of the minimization module sheds light on the cost of applying minimization and on the benefits of minimization in XQuery processing. The former was not a priori clear, since the CCC algorithm is based on

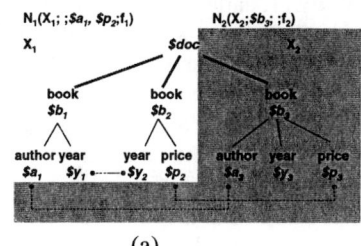 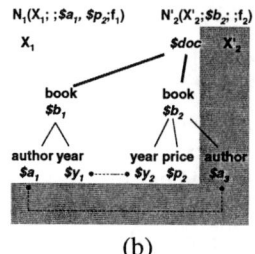 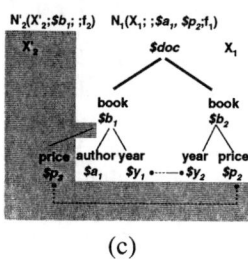

Figure 9: Query with two distinct partial minimized forms

Figure 10: $N_2(X_2;;\$a_2;f_2)$ Figure 11: $N_1(X_1;;\$a_1;f_1)$

repeatedly finding containment mappings, a step that is NP-complete in the general case. Notice that, in special cases when there are no equality conditions and no wildcard child navigation is allowed, the pattern of a NEXT query degenerates to the simple tree patterns of [3] for which containment is in PTIME.

We came up with an algorithm that behaves optimally on every input. The algorithm is based on the key observation that finding a containment mapping from groupby node N_1 to groupby node N_2 can be reduced to evaluating a boolean *relational* query obtained from N_1 on a small database computed from N_2. This allows us to exploit standard relational optimization techniques. In particular, the relational query corresponding to a simple tree pattern is *acyclic*. This class of queries can be evaluated in PTIME in the size of both N_1 and N_2 according to Yannakakis' algorithm [12]. We illustrate the reduction on an example.

EXAMPLE 5.1 Consider two NEXT queries Q_1, Q_2 whose groupby trees consist of one node each, N_1 respectively N_2 shown in Figures 11 and 10. We do not specify the result functions f_1, f_2 as they are ignored when checking for containment mappings. We represent N_2 internally as the relational "frozen" database D_{N_2} below, constructed in the spirit of [26]: we create a special constant $\overline{v}$ representing the equivalence class of variable $\$v$ with respect to the value-based equality conditions in N_2.

Child$_{N_2}$	sourceNode	targetNodeTag	targetNode
	$\overline{b_2}$	author	$\overline{a_2}$
	$\overline{b_2}$	year	$\overline{y_2}$

Desc$_{N_2}$	sourceNode	targetNodeTag	targetNode
	$\overline{doc}$	book	$\overline{b_2}$

We also add relation RTC$_{N_2}$ containing the reflexive, transitive closure of the union of Child$_{N_2}$ and Desc$_{N_2}$. We translate N_1 to the query

$M_{N_1}() \leftarrow \text{RTC}_{N_2}(\overline{\$doc}, \text{book}, \overline{\$b_1}), \text{Child}_{N_2}(\overline{\$b_1}, \text{author}, \overline{a_2})$

Clearly, there is a containment mapping from N_1 into N_2 if and only if M_{N_1} returns a non-empty answer on D_{N_2}. ◊

We emphasize that M_{N_1} in the above example is shown for brevity in conjunctive query syntax but it is implemented as an operator tree, in which selections and projections are pushed and joins are implemented as hash joins. Most importantly, the join ordering and pushing of projections are chosen according to Yannakakis' algorithm applied to the acyclic conjunctive query obtained if we ignore equality conditions in N_1 [12]. This approach results in a running time of $O(|N_2|^2 \times |N_1|)$ if there are no equality conditions in N_1 (where $|N|$ denotes the number of pattern nodes in the Xtableau of N)[6]. Moreover, it performs very well in practice in the general case. Our experimental evaluation shows that queries with up to 15 nesting levels and 271 path expressions are minimized in less than 100ms. Our experimental evaluation shows that such added optimization cost is clearly less than the benefit we obtain in query execution.

Note that in the CCC algorithm, the roles of N_1, N_2 are played by the queries $N_{C,N}$, respectively $N_{C,N'}$ from Proposition 1, which change at every iteration, so D_{N_2} and M_{N_1} must be repeatedly recomputed. The most expensive operations are those of recomputing the equivalence classes of variables, and the transitive closure RTC$_{N_2}$. Fortunately, this does not have to be done from scratch if we recall that at every iteration, the Xtableau is changed by a simple collapse operation. We chose the following data structures which are easy to incrementally maintain with respect to collapse operations. For every Xtableau, we keep the equivalence classes of variables in a union-find data structure, so whenever node n is collapsed into m, we simply union the class of n with that of m in constant time. RTC$_N$ is represented as an adjacency matrix in which RTC$_N[x][y] = 1$ if and only if y is a descendant of x in the tree pattern of N. When n is collapsed into m, we set RTC$_N[n][m] = $ RTC$_N[m][n] = 1$ and recompute the transitive closure by multiplying RTC$_N$ with itself until we reach a fixpoint (guaranteed to occur in at most $\log |N|$ iterations, but much earlier in practice because of the small incremental change).

---

[6]We make the standard assumption of $O(1)$ for indexing into the hash table when joining. Otherwise, an additional $\log |N_2|$ factor must be counted for sort-merge join.

6 Conclusions and Future Work

We described the NEXT generalization of tree patterns, which enables logical optimization of XQuery and demonstrated its value by developing an effective technique for minimization of nested XQueries, which removes redundancy across and within subqueries. A key ingredient of NEXT is the **groupby** operation, which reduces mixed (bag and set) semantics to pure set semantics that provides the typical framework for logical optimization such as minimization. Furthermore, it enables consolidation of all navigation in the XTableaux. The provided rewriting rules reduce any query from the OptXQuery subset of XQuery into a NEXT.

The minimization algorithm also capitalizes on the **groupby** of NEXT, which allows the navigation performed on a nesting level to reuse the navigation performed on higher levels. In addition, our minimization algorithm went fundamentally beyond prior minimization algorithms for tree patterns and conjunctive queries by introducing a new type of minimization step, called *collapsing*. The collapse step *adds* to a subquery identity-based equality conditions between its variables to state that their bindings are the same. Prior algorithms only *remove* variables [3, 23]. The removal step alone turns out to be insufficient for nested XQueries, as removal-based techniques not only fail to find a minimal form, but depending on the application order, they yield several distinct queries, each non-minimal. Indeed, we prove the existence of a unique minimal form for any NEXT query and show that our algorithm is guaranteed to find it regardless of the order in which it applies collapse steps (Theorem 4.2).

Minimization of queries from our XQuery subset is NP-complete, which is no surprise since even in the absence of XQuery's nesting, arbitrary (cyclic) joins, which one can write using XPath predicates, increase the complexity of minimizing XPath expressions described by tree patterns from PTIME [3, 23] to NP-hard [10]. Our minimization algorithm behaves optimally on every input: it runs in PTIME if the tree patterns have no cyclic joins and in NP in the presence of cyclic joins. As shown by our experimental evaluation, even in the NP-complete case optimization time is low (below 100ms for queries with up to 15 nesting levels and up to 271 path expressions, as explained in the full paper [9]) thanks to a careful implementation which reduces the exponential to an approximation of the tree width of the query [12] (small in practice), as opposed to the number of navigation steps (may by very large in practice). We incorporated minimization in our NEXT XQuery processor and provided experimental data points that prove the beneficial effect of minimization on the total execution time. Due to space constraints, the experimental evaluation is reported in the full paper, and included in Appendix 5 for the reviewer's convenience.

NEXT normalization and minimization can be used in any XQuery processor, regardless of its underlying execution model, as long as it supports an OQL-style **groupby** operator.

An extension of NEXT, called NEXT+, allows the normalization of arbitrary XQueries, which may be outside the OptXQuery set, into NEXT+ queries. Guaranteeing full minimization for NEXT+ is either impossible (e.g., it is straightforward to show that no algorithm can guarantee the full minimization of XQueries involving negation) or requires various extensions to NEXT and the minimization algorithm (e.g., extra minimization can be achieved by algorithms that understand the semantics of aggregation functions.) Nevertheless, the minimization algorithm can be applied to the NEXT subexpressions of NEXT+ queries and guarantee their full minimization (which, as said, does not imply the full minimization of the NEXT+ query). Space constraints relegate this discussion to the full paper [9].

Looking beyond minimization, we plan to employ the NEXT notation to address , in the context of our mediator efforts (which include the Local-As-View approach), an answering-queries-using-views algorithm for XQuery.

7 Related Work

There is an extensive body of work on nested query optimization, for relational (SQL) and object-oriented (OQL [4]) queries. See [6], respectively [8] and the references within. For both OQL and SQL, the main effort is that of unnesting nested queries (merging query blocks), not their minimization. The group-by operation is crucially exploited to this end, by evaluating a nested query using an outerjoin followed by a group-by operation. See [16, 13] for the relational query evaluation, [8] for the object-oriented case, and [20, 24] for XML query evaluation. Such rewrites have only limited applicability when bag and set semantics are mixed [22] or the nesting occurs in the select clause. Our techniques succeed in these situations. One of our rewrite rules introduces group-by operations with every **for** loop, exploiting the well-known fact that the **distinct-values** operation is a special case of group-by [6]. Another common fact we exploit was recognized in [22], namely that quantifiers are not affected by duplicates. There is an interesting duality between our technique and the generalization of predicate pushdown [26] to nested (SQL) queries in [17]. The latter pushes conditions from the **where** clause of a query into its nested subqueries. Our technique pulls **for** loops up from nested queries. Existing algorithms for the minimization of tree patterns consider no nesting, no arbitrary joins, and only set semantics [3, 23]. Group-by detection is particularly important in XQuery, where surface syntax does not include a group-by construct. [24] uses algebraic rewriting for nested queries that perform grouping. Our algorithm solves this problem as a special case of minimization. [7] is the first work that introduces *Generalized Tree Patterns (GTPs)* that model nested queries and reduce the problem of evaluating a nested query into one of finding matches for its GTP. In addition, [7] shows a translation of GTPs to a physical plan algebra, which we have adopted, with minor modifications. There is an interesting correspondence as well as subtle differences between GTPs and NEXTs and the corresponding modules, stemming from NEXT's orientation towards problems such as minimization and answering queries using views. First, we make a distinction between optXQuery/NEXT and full XQuery/NEXT+. OptXQuery scopes the area where minimization (and, we conjecture, answering queries using views) is guaranteed to find optimal plans. OptXQuery/NEXT omits XQuery features that make minimization undecidable (e.g., negation and universal quantification) or too complex (e.g., aggregate functions). Such features are allowed in NEXT+, where we do not guarantee optimality of the resulting plan. Finally, note we have introduced a distinction between grouping-by-id and grouping-by-value since we find multiple aggregation examples in mediation. (A similar extension for [7] is possible.)

[25] addresses minimization of nested XQueries in the context of Peer-to-Peer systems, where scalability is an acute problem. They develop a PTIME algorithm, trading completeness of minimization for scalability. The algorithm is incomparable to ours: on one hand, it changes the structure of the group-by tree, which we do not do, as we treat result functions as uninterpreted. On the other hand, it only minimizes the nested subqueries in the context of their ancestor subqueries, but it does not attempt to reuse the navigation of the ancestors. No grouping is used, and the only step considered is removal of variables, which leaves even the simple XQuery from Example 1.1 unchanged. The key to our technique's success is precisely the sophisticated collapse step which goes beyond node removal, as well as the essential use of grouping.

References

[1] S. Abiteboul, R. Hull, and V. Vianu. *Foundations of Databases*. Addison-Wesley, 1995.

[2] A. V. Aho, Y. Sagiv, and J. D. Ullman. Efficient optimization of a class of relational expressions (abstract). In *SIGMOD*, 1978.

[3] S. Amer-Yahia, S. Cho, L. V. S. Lakshmanan, and D. Srivastava. Minimization of tree pattern queries. In *SIGMOD*, 2001.

[4] R. G. G. Cattell, editor. *The Object Database Standard: ODMG-93*. Morgan Kaufmann, San Mateo, California, 1996.

[5] Ashok Chandra and Philip Merlin. Optimal implementation of conjunctive queries in relational data bases. In *STOC*, 1977.

[6] S. Chaudhuri. An overview of query optimization in relational systems. In *PODS*, 1998.

[7] Z. Chen, H. V. Jagadish, L.Lakshmanan, and S. Paparizos. From Tree Patterns to Generalized Tree Patterns: On Efficient Evaluation of XQuery. In *VLDB*, 2003.

[8] S. Cluet and G. Moerkotte. Nested queries in object bases. In *DBPL*, 1993.

[9] A. Deutsch, Y. Papakonstantinou, and Y. Xu. The NEXT Framework for Logical Query Optimization (Extended Version). In *http://www.db.ucsd.edu/People/alin/papers/vldb-2004-full.ps*.

[10] A. Deutsch and V. Tannen. Containment and integrity constraints for xpath fragments. In *KRDB*, 2001.

[11] S. Flesca, F. Furfaro, and E. Masciari. On the minimization of XPath queries. In *VLDB*, 2003.

[12] J. Flum, M. Frick, and M. Grohe. Query evaluation via tree-decompositions. In Jan Van den Bussche and Victor Vianu, editors, *ICDT*, 2001.

[13] R. A. Ganski and H. K. T. Wong. Optimization of nested SQL queries revisited. In *SIGMOD*, 1987.

[14] H.V.Jagadish, S.Al-Khalifa, A.Chapman, L.V.S.Lakshmanan, A.Nierman, S.Paparizos, J.Patel, D.Srivastava, N.Wiwatwattana, Y.Wu, and C.Yu. Timber:a native xml database. *VLDB Journal*, 11(4), 2002.

[15] H. V. Jagadish, Laks V. S. Lakshmanan, D. Srivastava, and k.Thompson. Tax: A tree algebra for XML. In *DBPL*, 2001.

[16] W. Kim. On optimizing an sql-like nested query. *TODS*, 7(3):443–469, 1982.

[17] A. Y. Levy, I. S. Mumick, and Y. Sagiv. Query optimization by predicate move-around. In *VLDB*, 1994.

[18] A. Y. Levy and D. Suciu. Deciding containment for queries with complex objects. In *PODS*, 1997.

[19] I. Manolescu, D. Florescu, and D. Kossman. Answering XML Queries on Heterogeneous Data Sources. In *VLDB*, 2001.

[20] M.Carey, J. Kiernan, J. Shanmugasundaram, E. Shekita, and S. Subramanian. XPERANTO: Middleware For Publishing Object-Relational Data as XML Documents. In *VLDB*, 2000.

[21] G. Miklau and D. Suciu. Containment and equivalence for an xpath fragment. In *PODS*, 2002.

[22] H. Pirahesh, J. M. Hellerstein, and W. Hasan. Extensible/rule based query rewrite optimization in starburst. In *SIGMOD*, 1992.

[23] P. Ramanan. Efficient algorithms for minimizing tree pattern queries. In *SIGMOD*, 2002.

[24] S.Paparizos, S. Al-Khalifa, H.V. Jagadish, L. Lakshmanan, A. Nierman, D.Srivastava, and Y. Wu. Grouping in XML. In *EDBT Workshop on XML Data Management (XMLDM'02)*, 2002.

[25] I. Tatarinov and A. Y. Halevy. Efficient query reformulation in peer-data management systems. In *SIGMOD*, 2004.

[26] J. D. Ullman. *Principles of Database and Knowledge-Base Systems*, volume 2. Computer Science Press, 1989.

[27] W3C. XML Query Use Cases . W3C Working Draft 15 November 2002. Available from http://www.w3.org/TR/xmlquery-use-cases/.

[28] W3C. XQuery 1.0 and XPath 2.0 Functions and Operators. W3C Working Draft 12 November 2003. Available from http://www.w3.org/TR/xpath-functions.

[29] W3C. XQuery 1.0 Formal Semantics. W3C Working Draft 07 June 2001. Available from http://www.w3.org/TR/query-semantics/.

[30] W3C. XQuery: A Query Language for XML. W3C Working Draft 12 November 2003. Available from http://www.w3.org/TR/xquery.

[31] Y.Papakonstantinou, M. Petropoulos, and V.Vassalos. QURSED: querying and reporting semistructured data. In *SIGMOD*, 2002.

Detecting Change in Data Streams

Daniel Kifer, Shai Ben-David, Johannes Gehrke

Department of Computer Science
Cornell University

Abstract

Detecting changes in a data stream is an important area of research with many applications. In this paper, we present a novel method for the detection *and* estimation of change. In addition to providing statistical guarantees on the reliability of detected changes, our method also provides meaningful descriptions and quantification of these changes. Our approach assumes that the points in the stream are independently generated, but otherwise makes no assumptions on the nature of the generating distribution. Thus our techniques work for both continuous and discrete data. In an experimental study we demonstrate the power of our techniques.

1 Introduction

In many applications, data is not static but arrives in data streams. Besides the algorithmic difference between processing data streams and static data, there is another significant difference. For static datasets, it is reasonable to assume that the data was generated by a fixed process, for example, the data is a sample from a static distribution. But a data stream has necessarily a temporal dimension, and the underlying process that generates the data stream can change over time [17, 1, 23]. The quantification and detection of such change is one of the fundamental challenges in data stream settings.

Change has far-reaching impact on any data processing algorithm. For example, when constructing data stream mining models [17, 1], data that arrived before a change can bias the models towards characteristics that no longer hold. If we process queries over data streams, we may want to give separate answers for each time interval where the underlying data distribution is stable. Most existing work has concentrated on algorithms that adapt to changing distributions either by discarding old data or giving it less weight [17]. However, to the best of our knowledge, previous work does not contain a formal definition of change and thus existing algorithms cannot specify precisely *when and how* the underlying distribution changes.

In this paper we make a first step towards formalizing the detection and quantification of change in a data stream. We assume that the data points are generated sequentially and independently by some underlying probability distribution. Our goal is to detect when this distribution changes, and to quantify and describe this change.

It is unrealistic to allow data stream processing algorithms enough memory capacity to store the full history of the stream. Therefore we base our change-detection algorithm on a two-window paradigm. The algorithm compares the data in some "reference window" to the data in a current window. Both widows contain a fixed number of successive data points. The current window slides forward with each incoming data point, and the reference window is updated whenever a change is detected. We analyze this paradigm and develop algorithms (or *tests*) that can be supported by proven guarantees on their sensitivity to change, their robustness against raising false alarms, and their running time. Furthermore, we aim to obtain not only reliable change detection, but also a *comprehensible description* of the nature of the detected change.

1.1 Applications

A change detection test with the above properties has many interesting applications:

Quality Control. A factory manufactures beams made from a metal alloy. The strengths of a sample of the beams can be measured during quality testing. Estimating the amount of defective beams and determining the statistical significance of this number are well-studied problems in the statistics community [5]. However, even if the number of defective beams does not change, the factory can still benefit by analyzing

Permission to copy without fee all or part of this material is granted provided that the copies are not made or distributed for direct commercial advantage, the VLDB copyright notice and the title of the publication and its date appear, and notice is given that copying is by permission of the Very Large Data Base Endowment. To copy otherwise, or to republish, requires a fee and/or special permission from the Endowment.

**Proceedings of the 30th VLDB Conference,
Toronto, Canada, 2004**

the distribution of beam strengths over time. Changes in this distribution can signal the development of a problem or give evidence that a new manufacturing technique is creating an improvement. Information that describes the change could also help in analysis of the technique.

Data Mining. Suppose a data stream mining algorithm is creating a data mining model that describes certain aspects of the data stream. The data mining model does not need to change as long as the underlying data distribution is stable. However, for sufficiently large changes in the distribution that generates the data stream, the model will become inaccurate. In this case it is better to completely remove the contributions of old data (which arrived before the change) from the model rather than to wait for enough new data to come in and outweigh the stale data. Further information about where the change has occurred could help the user avoid rebuilding the entire model – if the change is localized, it may only be necessary to rebuild part of the model.

1.2 Statistical Requirements

Recall that our basic approach to change detection in data streams uses two sliding windows over the data stream. This reduces the problem of detecting change over a data stream to the problem of testing whether the two samples in the windows were generated by different distributions. Consequently, we start by considering the case of detecting a difference in distribution between two input samples. Assume that two datasets S_1 and S_2 where generated by two probability distributions, P_1, P_2. A natural question to ask is: Can we infer from S_1 and S_2 whether they were generated by the same distribution $P_1 = P_2$, or is it the case that $P_1 \neq P_2$? To answer this question, we need to design a "test" that can tell us whether P_1 and P_2 are different. Assuming that we take this approach, what are our requirements on such a test?

Our first requirement is that the test should have two-way guarantees: We want the guarantee that our test detects true changes with high probability, i.e., it should have few false negatives. But we also want the test to notify us only if a true change has occurred, i.e., it should have few false positives. Furthermore we need to be able to extend those guarantees from the two-sample problem to the data stream.

There are also practical considerations that affect our choice of test. If we know that the distribution of the data has a certain parametric form (for example, it is a normal distribution), then we can draw upon decades of research in the statistics community where powerful tests have been developed.Unfortunately, real data is rarely that well-behaved in practice; it does not follow "nice" parametric distributions. Thus we need a *non-parametric* test that makes no assumptions on the form of the distribution.

Our last requirement is motivated by the users of our test. A user not only wants to be notified that the underlying distribution has changed, but she also wants to know *how* it has changed. Thus we want a test that does not only detects changes, but also describes the change in a user-understandable way.

In summary, we want a change detection test with these four properties: the rate of spurious detections (false positives) and the rate of missed detections (false negatives) can be controlled, it is non-parametric, and it provides a description of the detected change.

1.3 An Informal Motivation of our Approach

Let us start by discussing briefly how our work relates to the most common non-parametric statistical test for change detection, the Wilcoxon test [24]. (Recall that parametric tests are unsuitable as we do not want to restrict the applicability of our work to data that follows certain parametric distributions.)

The Wilcoxon test is a statistical test that measures the tendency of one sample to contain values that are larger than those in the other sample. We can control the probability that the Wilcoxon test raises a false alarm. However, this test only permits the detection of certain limited kinds of changes, such as a change in the mean of a normal distribution. Furthermore, it does not give a meaningful description of the changes it detects.

We address the issue of two-way guarantees by using a *distance function* (between distributions) to help describe the change. Given a distance function, our test provides guarantees of the form: "to detect a distance $> \epsilon$ between two distributions P_1 and P_2, we will need samples of at most n points from the each of P_1 and P_2."

Let us start by considering possible distance functions. One possibility is to use powerful information theoretic distances, such as the Jensen-Shannon Divergence (JSD) [19]. However, to use these measures we need discrete distributions and it may also be hard to explain the idea of entropy to the average end-user. There exist many other common measures of distance between distributions, but they are either too insensitive or too sensitive. For example, the commonly used L^1 distance is too sensitive and can require arbitrarily large samples to determine if two distributions have L^1 distance $> \epsilon$ [4]. At the other extreme, L^p norms (for $p > 1$) are far too insensitive: two distributions D_1 and D_2 can be close in the L^p norm and yet can have this undesirable property: all events with nonzero probability under D_1 have 0 probability under D_2. Based on these shortcomings of existing work, we introduce in Section 3 a new distance metric that is specifically tailored to find distribution changes while providing strong statistical guarantees with small sample sizes.

In addition, users are usually not interested in arbitrary change, but rather in change that has a succinct, representation that they can understand. Thus we restrict our notion of change to showing the hyper-rectangle (or, in the special case of one attribute, the interval) in the attribute space that is most greatly affected by the change in distribution. We formally introduce this notion of change in Section 3.

1.4 Our Contributions

In this paper we give the first formal treatment of change detection in data streams. Our techniques assume that data points are generated independently but otherwise make no assumptions about the generating distribution (i.e. the techniques are nonparametric). They give provable guarantees that the change that is detected is not noise but statistically significant, and they allow us to describe the change to a user in a succinct way. To the best of our knowledge, there is no previous work that addresses all of these requirements.

In particular, we address three aspects of the problem: (1) We introduce a novel family of distance measures between distributions; (2) we design an algorithmic set up for change detection in data streams; and (3) we provide both analytic and numerical performance guarantees on the accuracy of change detection.

The remainder of this paper is organized as follows. After a description of our meta-algorithm in Section 2, we introduce novel metrics over the space of distributions and show that they avoid statistical problems common to previously known distance functions (Section 3). We then show how to apply these metric to detect changes in the data stream setting, and we give strong statistical guarantees on the types of changes that are detected (Section 4). In Section 5 we develop algorithms that efficiently find the areas where change has occurred, and we evaluate our techniques in a thorough experimental analysis in Section 6.

2 A Meta-Algorithm For Change Detection

In this section we describe our meta-algorithm for change detection in streaming data. The meta-algorithm reduces the problem from the streaming data scenario to the problem of comparing two (static) sample sets. We consider a datastream S to be a sequence $<s_1, s_2, \cdots>$ where each item s_i is generated by some distribution P_i and each s_i is independent of the items that came before it. We say that a change has occurred if $P_i \neq P_{i+1}$, and we call time $i+1$ a *change point*[1]. We also assume that only a bounded amount of memory is available, and that in general the size of the data stream is much larger than the amount of available memory.

---

[1] It is not hard to realize that no algorithm can be guaranteed to detect any such change point. We shall therefore require the detection of change only when the difference between P_i and P_{i+1} is above some threshold. We elaborate on this issue in section 3.

Algorithm 1 : FIND_CHANGE

1: **for** $i = 1 \ldots k$ **do**
2:    $c_0 \leftarrow 0$
3:    Window$_{1,i} \leftarrow$ first $m_{1,i}$ points from time c_0
4:    Window$_{2,i} \leftarrow$ next $m_{2,i}$ points in stream
5: **end for**
6: **while** not at end of stream **do**
7:    **for** $i = 1 \ldots k$ **do**
8:      Slide Window$_{2,i}$ by 1 point
9:      **if** $d(\text{Window}_{1,i}, \text{Window}_{2,i}) > \alpha_i$ **then**
10:        $c_0 \leftarrow$ current time
11:        Report change at time c_0
12:        Clear all windows and GOTO step 1
13:      **end if**
14:    **end for**
15: **end while**

Note that the meta-algorithm above is actually running k independent algorithms in parallel - one for each parameter triplet $(m_{1,i}, m_{2,i}, \alpha_i)$. The meta-algorithm requires a function d, which measures the discrepancy between two samples, and a set of triples $\{(m_{1,1}, m_{2,1}, \alpha_1), \ldots, (m_{1,k}, m_{2,k}, \alpha_k)\}$. The numbers $m_{1,i}$ and $m_{2,i}$ specify the sizes of the ith pair of windows (X_i, Y_i). The window X_i is a 'baseline' window and contains the first $m_{1,i}$ points of the stream that occurred after the last detected change. Each window Y_i is a sliding window that contains the latest $m_{2,i}$ items in the data stream. Immediately after a change has been detected, it contains the $m_{2,i}$ points of the stream that follow the window X_i. We slide the window Y_i one step forward whenever a new item appears on the stream. At each such update, we check if $d(X_i, Y_i) > \alpha_i$. Whenever the distance is $> \alpha_i$, we report a change and then repeat the entire procedure with X_i containing the first $m_{1,i}$ points after the change, etc. The meta-algorithm is shown in Figure 1.

It is crucial to keep the window X_i fixed while sliding the window Y_i, so that we always maintain a reference to the original distribution. We use several pairs of windows because small windows can detect sudden, large changes while large windows can detect smaller changes that last over longer periods of time.

The key to our scheme is the intelligent choice of distance function d and the constants α_i. The function d must truly quantify an intuitive notion of change so that the change can be explained to a non-technical user. The choice of such a d is discussed in Section 3. The parameter α_i defines our balance between sensitivity and robustness of the detection. The smaller α_i is, the more likely we are to detect small changes in the distribution, but the larger is our risk of false alarm.

We wish to provide statistical guarantees about the accuracy of the change report. Providing such guarantees is highly non-trivial because of two reasons: we have no prior knowledge about the distributions and the changes, and the repeated testing of $d(X_i, Y_i)$ necessarily exhibits the multiple testing problem - the more times you run a random experiment, the more likely you are to see non-representative samples. We deal with these issues in section 3 and section 4, respectively.

3 Distance Measures for Distribution Change

In this section we focus on the basic, two-sample, comparison. Our goal is to design algorithms that examine samples drawn from two probability distributions and decide whether these distributions are different. Furthermore, we wish to have two-sided performance guarantees for our algorithms (or tests). Namely, results showing that if the algorithm accesses sufficiently large samples then, on one hand, if the samples come from the same distributions then the probability that the algorithm will output "CHANGE" is small, and on the other hand, if the samples were generated by different distributions, our algorithm will output 'CHANGE" with high probability. It is not hard to realize that no matter what the algorithm does, for every finite sample size there exist a pair of distinct distributions such that, with high probability, samples of that size will not suffice for the algorithm to detect that they are coming from different distributions. The best type of guarantee that one can conceivably hope to prove is therefore of the type: "If the distributions generating the input samples are sufficiently different, then sample sizes of a certain bounded size will suffice to detect that these distributions are distinct". However, to make such a statement precise, one needs a way to measure the degree of difference between two given probability distributions. Therefore, before we go on with our analysis of distribution change detection, we have to define the type of changes we wish to detect. This section addresses this issue by examining several notions of distance between probability distributions.

The most natural notion of distance (or similarity) between distributions is the *total variation* or the L^1 norm. Given two probability distributions, P_1, P_2 over the same measure space $(X, \mathcal{E})$ (where X is some domain set and $\mathcal{E}$ is a collection of subsets of X - the measurable subsets), the total variation distance between these distributions is defined as $TV(P_1, P_2) = 2 \sup_{E \in \mathcal{E}} |P_1(E) - P_2(E)|$ (or, equivalently, when the distributions have density functions, f_1, f_2, respectively, the L^1 distance between the distributions is defined by $\int |f_1(x) - f_2(x)| dx$). Note that the total variation takes values in the interval $[0, 1]$.

However, for practical purposes the total variation is an overly sensitive notion of distance. First, $TV(P_1, P_2)$ may be quite large for distributions that should be considered as similar for all practical purposes (for example, it is easy to construct two distributions that differ, say, only on real numbers whose 9th decimal point is 5, and yet their total variation distance is 0.2). The second, related, argument against the use of the total variation distance, is that it may be infeasibly difficult to detect the difference between two distributions from the samples they generate. Batu et al [4] prove that, over discrete domains of size n, for every sample-based change detection algorithm, there are pairs of distribution that have total variation distance $\geq 1/3$ and yet, if the sample sizes are below $O(n^{2/3})$, it is highly unlikely that the algorithm will detect a difference between the distributions. In particular, this means that over infinite domains (like the real line) any sample based change detection algorithm is bound to require arbitrarily large samples to detect the change even between distributions whose total variation distance is large.

We wish to employ a notion of distance that, on one hand captures 'practically significant' distribution differences, and yet, on the other hand, allows the existence of finite sample based change detection algorithms with proven detection guarantees.

Our solution is based upon the idea of focusing on a family of significant domain subsets.

Definition 1. Fix a measure space and let $\mathcal{A}$ be a collection of measurable sets. Let P and P' be probability distributions over this space.

- The $\mathcal{A}$-*distance* between P and P' is defined as
$$d_{\mathcal{A}}(P, P') = 2 \sup_{A \in \mathcal{A}} |P(A) - P'(A)|$$

We say that P, P' are ϵ-*close with respect to* $\mathcal{A}$ if $d_{\mathcal{A}}(P, P') \leq \epsilon$.

- For a finite domain subset S and a set $A \in \mathcal{A}$, let the *empirical weight* of A w.r.t. S be
$$S(A) = \frac{|S \cap A|}{|S|}$$

- For finite domain subsets, S_1 and S_2, we define the *empirical distance* to be
$$d_{\mathcal{A}}(S_1, S_2) = 2 \sup_{A \in \mathcal{A}} |S_1(A) - S_2(A)|$$

The intuitive meaning of $\mathcal{A}$-distance is that it is the largest change in probability of a set that the user cares about. In particular, if we consider the scenario of monitoring environmental changes spread over some geographical area, one may assume that the changes that are of interest will be noticeable in some local regions and thus be noticeable by monitoring spatial rectangles or circles. Clearly, this notion of $\mathcal{A}$-distance is a relaxation of the total variation distance.

It is not hard to see that $\mathcal{A}$-distance is always $\leq$ the total variation and therefore is less restrictive. This point helps get around the statistical difficulties associated with the L^1 norm. If $\mathcal{A}$ is not too complex[2], then there exists a test t that can distinguish (with high probability) if two distributions are ϵ-close (with respect to $\mathcal{A}$) using a sample size that is independent of the domain size.

For the case where the domain set is the real line, the Kolmogorov-Smirnov statistics considers $\sup_x |F_1(x) - F_2(x)|$ as the measure of difference between two distributions (where $F_i(x) = P_i(\{y : y \leq x\})$). By setting $\mathcal{A}$ to be the set of all the one-sided intervals $(-\infty, x)$ the $\mathcal{A}$ distance becomes the Kolmogorov-Smirnov statistic. Thus our notion of distance, $d_\mathcal{A}$ can be viewed as a generalization of this classical statistics. By picking $\mathcal{A}$ to be a family of intervals (or, a family of convex sets for higher dimensional data), the $\mathcal{A}$-distance reflects the relevance of locally centered changes.

Having adopted the concept of determining distance by focusing on a family of relevant subsets, there are different ways of quantifying such a change. The $\mathcal{A}$ measure defined above is additive - the significance of a change is measured by the *difference* of the weights of a subset between the two distributions. Alternatively, one could argue that changing the probability weight of a set from 0.5 to 0.4 is less significant than the change of a set that has probability weight of 0.1 under P_1 and weight 0 under P_2.

Next, we develop a variation of notion of the $\mathcal{A}$ distance, called *relativized discrepancy*, that takes the relative magnitude of a change into account.

As we have clarified above, our aim is to not only define sensitive measures of the discrepancy between distributions, but also to provide statistical guarantees that the differences that these measures evaluate are detectable from bounded size samples. Consequently, in developing variations of the basic $d_\mathcal{A}$ measure, we have to take into account the statistical tool kit available for proving convergence of sample based estimates to true probabilities. In the next paragraph we outline the considerations that led us to the choice of our 'relativized discrepancy' measures.

Let P be some probability distribution and choose any $A \in \mathcal{A}$, let p be such that $P(A) = p$. Let S be a sample with generated by P and let n denote its size. Then $nS(A)$ behaves like the sum $S_n = X_1 + \cdots + X_n$ of $|S|$ independent binomial random variables with $P(X_i = 1) = p$ and $P(X_i = 0) = 1 - p$. We can use Chernoff bounds [16] to approximate that tails of the distribution of S_n:

$$P[S_n/n \geq (1+\epsilon)p] \leq e^{-\epsilon^2 np/3} \quad (1)$$
$$P[S_n/n \leq (1-\epsilon)p] \leq e^{-\epsilon^2 np/2} \quad (2)$$

Our goal is to find an expression for ϵ as a func-

---
[2]there is a formal notion of this complexity - the VC-dimension. We discuss it further in Section 3.

tion $\omega(p)$ so that the rate of convergence is approximately the same for all p. Reasoning informally, $P(p - S_n/n \geq p\omega(p)) \approx e^{-\omega(p)^2 np/2}$ and the right hand side is constant if $\omega(p) = 1/\sqrt{p}$. Thus

$$P\left[(p - S_n/n)/\sqrt{p} > \epsilon\right]$$

should converge at approximately the same rate for all p. If we look at the random variables $X_1^*, \ldots, X_n^*$ (where $X_i^* = 1 - X_i$) we see that $S_n^* = \sum X_i^* = n - S_n$ is a binomial random variable with parameter $1 - p$. Therefore the rate of convergence should be the same for p and $1 - p$. To make the above probability symmetric in p and $1 - p$, we can either change the denominator to $\sqrt{\min(p, 1-p)}$ or $\sqrt{p(1-p)}$. The first way is more faithful to the Chernoff bound. The second approach approximates the first approach when p is far from $1/2$. However, the second approach gives more relative weight to the case when p is close to $1/2$.

Substituting $S(A)$ for S_n/n, $P(A)$ for p, we get that $(P(A) - S(A))/\sqrt{\min(P(A), 1 - P(A))}$ converges at approximately the same rate for all A such that $0 < P(A) < 1$ and $(P(A) - S(A))/\sqrt{P(A)(1 - P(A))}$ converges at approximately the same rate for all A (when $0 < P(A) < 1$). We can modify it to the two sample case by approximating $P(A)$ in the numerator by $S'(A)$. In the denominator, for reasons of symmetry, we approximate $P(A)$ by $(S'(A) + S(A))/2$. Taking the absolute values and the sup over all $A \in \mathcal{A}$, we propose the following measures of distribution distance, and empirical statistics for estimating it:

Definition 2 (Relativized Discrepancy). Let P_1, P_2 be two probability distributions over the same measure space, let $\mathcal{A}$ denote a family of measurable subsets of that space, and A a set in $\mathcal{A}$.

- Define $\phi_\mathcal{A}(P_1, P_2)$ as

$$\sup_{A \in \mathcal{A}} \frac{|P_1(A) - P_2(A)|}{\sqrt{\min\{\frac{P_1(A) + P_2(A)}{2}, (1 - \frac{P_1(A) + P_2(A)}{2})\}}}$$

- For finite samples S_1, S_2, we define $\phi_\mathcal{A}(S_1, S_2)$ similarly, by replacing $P_i(A)$ in the above definition by the empirical measure $S_i(A) = |S_i \cap A|/|S_i|$.

- Define $\Xi_\mathcal{A}(P_1, P_2)$ as

$$\sup_{A \in \mathcal{A}} \frac{|P_1(A) - P_2(A)|}{\sqrt{\frac{P_1(A) + P_2(A)}{2}\left(1 - \frac{P_1(A) + P_2(A)}{2}\right)}}$$

- Similarly, for finite samples S_1, S_2, we define $\Xi_\mathcal{A}(S_1, S_2)$ by replacing $P_i(A)$ in the above definition by the empirical measure $S_i(A)$.

Our experiments show that indeed these statistics tend to do better than the $d_\mathcal{A}$ statistic because they use the data more efficiently - a smaller change in an area of low probability is more likely to be detected by these statistics than by the $D_\mathcal{A}$ (or the KS) statistic.

These statistics have several nice properties. The $d_\mathcal{A}$ distance is obviously a metric over the space of probability distributions. So is the relativized discrepancy $|\phi_\mathcal{A}|$ (as long as for each pair of distribution P_1 and P_2 there exists a $A \in \mathcal{A}$ such that F_1 and $P_1(A) \neq P_2(A)$). The proof is omitted due to space limitations. We conjecture that $|\Xi_\mathcal{A}|$ is also a metric.

However, the major benefit of the $d_\mathcal{A}$, $\phi_\mathcal{A}$, and $\Xi_\mathcal{A}$ statistics is that in addition to detecting change, they can describe it. All sets A which cause the relevant equations to be $> \epsilon$ are statistically significant. Thus the change can be described to a lay-person: the increase or decrease (from the first sample to the second sample) in the number of points that falls in A is too much to be accounted for by pure chance and therefore it is likely that the probability of A has increased (or decreased).

3.1 Technical preliminaries

Our basic tool for sample based estimation of the $\mathcal{A}$ distance between probability distributions is based on the Vapnik-Chervonenkis theory.

Let $\mathcal{A}$ denote a family of subsets of some domain set X. We define a function $\Pi_\mathcal{A} : \mathbb{N} \mapsto \mathbb{N}$ by

$$\Pi_\mathcal{A}(n) = \max\{|\{A \cap B : A \in \mathcal{A}\}| : B \subseteq X \text{ and } |B| = n\}$$

Clearly, for all n, $\Pi_\mathcal{A} \leq 2^n$. For example, if $\mathcal{A}$ is the family of all intervals over the real line, then $\Pi_\mathcal{A}(n) = O(n^2)$, ($0.5n^2 + 1.5n$, to be precise).

Definition 3 (VC-Dimension). The Vapnik-Chervonenkis dimension of a collection $\mathcal{A}$ of sets is

$$\text{VC-dim}(\mathcal{A}) = \sup\{n : \Pi_\mathcal{A}(n) = 2^n\}$$

The following combinatorial fact, known as Sauer's Lemma, is a basic useful property of the function $\Pi_\mathcal{A}$.

Lemma 3.1 (Sauer, Shelah). If $\mathcal{A}$ has a finite VC-dimension, d, then for all n, $\Pi_\mathcal{A}(n) \leq \Sigma_{i=0}^{d} \binom{n}{i}$

It follows that for any such $\mathcal{A}$, $Pi_\mathcal{A}(n) < n^d$. In particular, for $\mathcal{A}$ being the family of intervals or rays on the real line, we get $Pi_\mathcal{A}(n) < n^2$.

3.2 Statistical Guarantees for our Change Detection Estimators

We consider the following scenario: P_1, P_2 are two probability distributions over the same domain X, and $\mathcal{A}$ is a family of subsets of that domain. Given two finite sets S_1, S_2 that are i.i.d. samples of P_1, P_2 respectively, we wish to estimate the $\mathcal{A}$ distance between the two distributions, $d_\mathcal{A}(P_1, P_2)$. Recall that, for any subset A of the domain set, and a finite sample S, we define the S- empirical weight of A by $S(A) = \frac{|S \cap A|}{|S|}$.

The following theorem follows by applying the classic Vapnik-Chervonenkis analysis [22], to our setting.

Theorem 3.1. Let P_1, P_2 be any probability distributions over some domain X and let $\mathcal{A}$ be a family of subsets of X and $\epsilon \in (0,1)$. If S_1, S_2 are i.i.d m samples drawn by P_1, P_2 respectively, then,

$$P[\exists A \in \mathcal{A} ||P_1(A) - P_2(A)| - |S_1(A) - S_2(A)|| \geq \epsilon]$$

$$< \Pi_\mathcal{A}(2m) 4e^{-m\epsilon^2/4}$$

It follows that

$$P[|d_\mathcal{A}(P_1, P_2) - d_\mathcal{A}(S_1, S_2)| \geq \epsilon] < \Pi_\mathcal{A}(2m) 4e^{-m\epsilon^2/4}$$

Where P in the above inequalities is the probability over the pairs of samples (S_1, S_2) induced by the sample generating distributions (P_1, P_2).

One should note that if $\mathcal{A}$ has a finite VC-dimension, d, then by Sauer's Lemma, $\Pi_\mathcal{A}(n) < n^d$ for all n.

We thus have bounds on the probabilities of both missed detections and false alarms of our change detection tests.

The rate of growth of the needed sample sizes as a function of the sensitivity of the test can be further improved by using the *relativized discrepancy* statistics. We can get results similar to Theorem 3.1 for the distance measures $\phi_\mathcal{A}(P_1, P_2)$ and $\Xi_\mathcal{A}(P_1, P_2)$. We start with the following consequence of a result of Anthony and Shawe-Taylor [2].

Theorem 3.2. Let $\mathcal{A}$ be a collection of subsets of a finite VC-dimension d. Let S be a sample of size n each, drawn i.i.d. by a probability distribution, P (over X), then

$$P^n(\phi_\mathcal{A}(S, P) > \epsilon) \leq (2n)^d e^{-n\epsilon^2/4}$$

(Where P^n is the n'th power of P - the probability that P induces over the choice of samples).

Similarly, we obtain the following bound on the probability of false alarm for the $\phi_\mathcal{A}(S_1, S_2)$ test.

Theorem 3.3. Let $\mathcal{A}$ be a collection of subsets of a finite VC-dimension d. If S_1 and S_2 are samples of size n each, drawn i.i.d. by the same distribution, P (over X), then

$$P^{2n}(\phi_\mathcal{A}(S_1, S_2) > \epsilon) \leq (2n)^d e^{-n\epsilon^2/4}$$

(Where P^{2n} is the $2n$'th power of P - the probability that P induces over the choice of samples).

To obtain analogous guarantees for the probabilities of missed detection of change, we employ the fact that $\phi_{\mathcal{A}}$ is a metric.

Claim 3.1. For finite samples, S_1, S_2, and a pair of probability distributions P_1, P_2 (all over the same domain set),

$$|\phi_{\mathcal{A}}(P_1, P_2) - \phi_{\mathcal{A}}(S_1, S_2)| \leq \phi_{\mathcal{A}}(P_1, S_1) + \phi_{\mathcal{A}}(P_2, S_2)$$

We can now apply Theorem 3.2 to obtain

Theorem 3.4. Let $\mathcal{A}$ be a collection of subsets of some domain measure space, and assume that the VC-dimension is some finite d. Let P_1 and P_2 be probability distributions over that domain and S_1, S_2 finite samples of sizes m_1, m_2 drawn i.i.d. according to P_1, P_2 respectively. Then

$$P^{m_1+m_2}\left[|\phi_{\mathcal{A}}(S_1, S_2) - \phi_{\mathcal{A}}(P_1, P_2)| > \epsilon\right]$$
$$\leq (2m_1)^d e^{-m_1\epsilon^2/16} + (2m_2)^d e^{-m_2\epsilon^2/16}$$

(Where $P^{m_1+m_2}$ is the $m_1 + m_2$'th power of P - the probability that P induces over the choice of samples).

Finally, note that, it is always the case that

$$\phi_{\mathcal{A}}(P_1, P_2) \leq \Xi_{\mathcal{A}}(P_1, P_2) \leq 2\phi_{\mathcal{A}}(P_1, P_2)$$

It therefore follows that guarantees against both false-positive and missed-detection errors similar to Theorems 3.3 and 3.4, hold for the $\Xi_{\mathcal{A}}$ statistics as well.

To appreciate the potential benefits of using this relative discrepancy approach, consider the case where $\mathcal{A}$ is the collection of all real intervals. It is easy to verify that the VC-dimension of this family $\mathcal{A}$ is 2. Let us estimate what sample sizes are needed to be 99% sure that an interval I, that changed from having no readings to having η fraction of the detected readings in this interval, indicate a real change in the measured field. Note that for such an interval, $\frac{S_1(I) - S_2(I)}{\sqrt{0.5(S_1(I)+S_2(I))}} = \sqrt{2\eta}$. We can now apply Theorem 3.3 to see that $m = 30/\eta$ should suffice. Note that if we used the $d_{\mathcal{A}}$ measure and Theorem 3.1, the bound we could guarantee would be in the order of $1/\eta^2$.

4 Tight Bounds for Streaming Real Data

Traditional statistical hypothesis testing consists of three parts: the null hypothesis, a test statistic, and a critical region. The null hypothesis is a statement about the distributions that generate the data. A statistic is a function that is computed over the sampled data. For example, it could be the average, or the Wilcoxon statistic, or the number of heads in a series of coin tossings. A critical region (or rejection region) is a subset of the range of the statistic. If the value of the statistic falls in the critical region, we reject the null hypothesis. Critical regions are designed so that if the null hypothesis were true, the probability that the test statistic will take a value in the critical region is less than some user-specified constant.

This framework does not fare very well when dealing with a data stream. For example, suppose a datastream is generated in the following way: an adversary has two coins, one of them is a fair coin, having probability 1/2 of landing heads, and the other is a coin that always falls heads. At each time unit, the adversary flips a coin and reports its results. The adversary can secretly switch coins at any time.

Even if the adversary never switches coins, any pattern of heads and tails will eventually show up in the stream, and thus for any test statistic of bounded memory (that cannot keep track of the length of the sequence) and non-trivial critical region, we will eventually get a value that causes us to falsely reject the null hypothesis (that only the fair coin is being used).

Since there is no way to avoid mistakes all together, we direct our efforts to limiting the rate of mistakes. We propose the following measure of statistical guarantee against false positive errors, in the spirit of the error rate:

Definition 4 (size). A statistical test over data streams is a $size(n, p)$ test if, on data that satisfies the null hypothesis, the probability of rejecting the null hypothesis after observing n points is at most p.

In the rest of this section we will show how to construct a critical region (given n and p) for the Wilcoxon, Kolmogorov-Smirnov, $\phi_{\mathcal{A}}$, and $\Xi_{\mathcal{A}}$ tests. Proofs are omitted due to space limitations. The critical region will have the form $\{x : x \geq \alpha\}$. In other words, we reject the null hypothesis for inordinately large values of the test statistic.

For the rest of this section, we will assume that the points of a stream $S = <s_1, s_2, \cdots >$ are real-valued and that the collection $\mathcal{A}$ is either a collection of all initial segments $(-\infty, x)$ or the collection of all intervals (a, b).

4.1 Continuous Generating Distribution

In order to construct the critical regions, we must study the distributions of the test statistics under the null hypothesis (all n points have the same generating distribution).

Our change-detection scheme can use the Wilcoxon, Kolmogorov-Smirnov, $\phi_{\mathcal{A}}$ and $\Xi_{\mathcal{A}}$ statistics as well as any other statistic for testing if two samples have the same generating distribution. Let K represent the statistic being used. Pick one window pair and let m_1 be the size of its first window and m_2 be the size of its second window. Over the first n points of the stream S, our change-detection scheme computes the values: $K(<s_1, \ldots, s_{m_1}>, <s_{i+m_1}, \ldots, s_{i+m_1+m_2}>)$

for $i = 1 \ldots n - m_1 - m_2$. Let $F_{K,m_1,m_2,n}(S)$ be the maximum of these values (over all window locations i). We reject the null hypothesis if $F_{K,m_1,m_2,n}(S) \geq \alpha$. That is, we conclude that there was a change if, for some i, the i'th Y window revealed a sample which is significantly different than the sample in the reference X window. It turns out that when the n points are generated independently by the same continuous generating distribution G then $F_{K,m_1,m_2,n}$ is a random variable whose distribution does not depend on G. Namely,

Theorem 4.1. If $s_1, \ldots, s_n$, are generated independently by any fixed continuous probability distribution, G, and the statistic K is either the Wilcoxon, Kolmogorov-Smirnov, $\phi_\mathcal{A}$ or $\Xi_\mathcal{A}$, then the distribution of $F_{K,m_1,m_2,n}$ does not depend on G.

When $n = m_1 + m_2$ this is the same as testing if two samples have the same continuous generating distribution. In this case, this result for the Wilcoxon and Kolmogorov-Smirnov statistics is well-known. We can provide a concrete description of the distribution of F. Consider the stream $< 1, 2, \ldots, n >$. Given a statistic K, parameters m_1, m_2, and c, and a permutation, $\pi = < \pi_1, \ldots, \pi_n >$ of $< 1, 2, \ldots, n >$, we say that π is *odd* if, when we apply our change detection scheme to that sequence of numbers, we get $F_{K,m_1,m_2,n} > c$.

Theorem 4.2. Under the hypothesis of 4.1, for any c, $P(F_{K,m_1,m_2,n} > c)$ is $1/n!$ times the number of odd permutations of the stream $< 1, 2, \ldots, n >$.

In light of Theorems 4.1 and 4.2 the only component we are still missing, to construct a size (n, p) test for continuous distributions, is determining the value α (that, in turn, defines our test's critical region). We consider three ways to can compute α:

1. Direct Computation: generate all $n!$ permutations of $< 1, 2, \ldots, n >$ and compute $F_{K,m_1,m_2,n}$. Set α to be the $1 - p$ percentile of the computed values.

2. Simulation: since the distribution of $F_{K,m_1,m_2,n}$ does not depend on the generating distribution of the stream, choose any continuous distribution, generate ℓ samples of n points each, compute $F_{K,m_1,m_2,n}$ for each sample and take the $1-p$ quantile. We will show how to choose ℓ in Subsection 4.2.

3. Sampling: since simulation essentially gives us ℓ permutations of $< 1, 2, \ldots, n >$, we can generate ℓ permutations directly, compute $F_{K,m_1,m_2,n}$ and take the $1-p$ quantile. This uses less random bits than the simulation approach since we don't need to generate random variables with many significant digits.

Next we consider the case of non-continuous probability distributions. If we are dealing with discrete distributions and use the Kolmogorov-Smirnov, $\phi_\mathcal{A}$ or $\Xi_\mathcal{A}$ statistics, then Theorem 4.3 assures us that we can construct the critical region as above and the probability of falsely rejecting the null hypothesis is $\leq p$.

Theorem 4.3. Let G be any distribution function and let H be a continuous distribution function. If K is either the Kolmogorov-Smirnov, $\phi_\mathcal{A}$ or $\Xi_\mathcal{A}$ statistic, then for any $c \geq 0$, $P_G(F_{K,m_1,m_2,n} > c) \leq P_H(F_{K,m_1,m_2,n} > c)$

4.2 Choosing ℓ

In this section we discuss how to choose ℓ (the number of simulation runs we need to compute the $(1 - p)$ quantile). We have an unknown distribution G from which we sample ℓ many n-size sequences of points. For each sequence of size n, we compute the $F_{K,m_1,m_2,n}$ statistic to get a set of ℓ values. We use the element that falls in the $(1 - p)$ quantile as an estimate of the true $1 - p$ quantile of the distribution for $F_{K,m_1,m_2,n}$. If the $1 - p$ quantile is unattainable, then we actually compute an estimate of the $1-p^*$ quantile where $1-p^*$ is the smallest attainable quantile $\geq 1 - p$. Note that by Theorem 4.1, the distribution of $F_{K,m_1,m_2,n}$ does not depend on G in any way. Thus estimating the $1-p$ quantile presents a one-time cost. This value can then be reused for any stream.

So given constants L^* and U^* (where $L^* < 1 - p < U^*$), and δ, we want to choose ℓ so that our estimate of the of the $1-p$ quantile is between L^* and U^* with probability $1 - \delta$. Let L to be the largest attainable quantile $\leq L^*$ and choose x_L such that $P_G(X \leq x_L) = L$. Similarly, let U be the smallest attainable quantile $\geq U^*$ and choose x_U such that $P_G(X \leq x_U) = U$.

Now let $X_1, \ldots, X_n$ be random variables with distribution G. Define the random variables $Y_1, \ldots, Y_n$ such that $Y_i = 1$ if $X_i \leq x_L$ and 0 otherwise. Define $Z_1, \ldots, Z_n$ so that $Z_i = 1$ if $X_i \leq x_U$ and 0 otherwise. Note that $P(Y_i = 1) = L$ and $P(Z_i = 1) = U$.

Suppose v is the element that falls in the $1 - p$ quantile of the X_i and let $\mu_v = P_G(X \leq v)$ be the true quantile of v. If $\mu_v < L$ then at least $n(1 - p)$ of the Y_i are 1 and if $\mu_v > U$ then at most $n(1 - p)$ of the Z_i are 1. Thus

$$P(\mu_v \notin [L, U]) \leq P\left(\sum_{i=1}^n Y_i \geq n(1 - p)\right)$$
$$+ P\left(\sum_{i=1}^n Z_i \leq n(1 - p)\right) \quad (3)$$

Now, if $W_1, \ldots, W_n$ are i.i.d $0 - 1$ random variables with $P(W_i = 1) = \theta$ and $S_n = W_1 + \cdots + W_n$ then the following holds [10]:

$P(S_n \leq k) = (n - k)\binom{n}{k} \int_0^{1-\theta} t^{n-k-1}(1 - t)^k \, dt$

This integral is known as the incomplete beta function $I_x(a, b)$ where $x = 1 - \theta$, $a = n - k$ and $b = k + 1$.

[21] shows how to numerically evaluate the incomplete beta function. Once this integral is evaluated, we use a binary search to find a value of n such that the right hand side of Equation 3 is $\leq \delta$.

5 Algorithms

In this section we will assume that the stream $S = <s_1, s_2, \cdots>$ consists of real-valued points and that $\mathcal{A}$ is either the collection of initial segments or intervals. Algorithms and suitable choices of $\mathcal{A}$ for higher dimensions is an open problem. Our algorithms use the following data structure:

Definition 5 (KS structure). We say that A is a KS structure if

- It is a finite array $<a_1, \ldots, a_m>$ of elements in $\mathbb{R}^2$ where the first coordinate is called the "value" and the second coordinate is called the "weight". The value is referred to as $v(a_i)$. The weight is referred to as $w(a_i)$.
- The array is sorted in increasing order by value.
- The length of the array is referred to as $|A|$.

For each integer k, we can define $G_A(k) = \sum_{i=1}^{k} w(A_i)$

Let (X, Y) be a window pair where X is the rear window and Y is the front window, $|X| = m_1$ and $|Y| = m_2$. We sort all the elements and create a KS-structure $Z = <z_1, z_2, \ldots, z_{m_1+m_2}>$ where $w(z_i) = -1/m_1$ if z_i came from x and $w(z_i) = 1/m_2$ if z_i came from Y. Z can be maintained throughout the life of the stream with incremental cost $O(\log(m_1 + m_2))$ by using a balanced tree.

Using this data structure, the Wilcoxon can be recomputed in time $O(m_1 + m_2)$. The same thing holds for $\phi_\mathcal{A}$ and $\Xi_\mathcal{A}$ when $\mathcal{A}$ is the set of initial segments. If $\mathcal{A}$ is the set of all intervals then the recomputation time for $\phi_\mathcal{A}$ and $\Xi_\mathcal{A}$ is $O([m_1 + m_2]^2)$. It is an open question whether it is possible to incrementally recompute those statistics faster.

In the rest of this section, we show how to recompute the Kolmogorov-Smirnov statistic over intervals and initial segments in $O(\log(m_1 + m_2))$ time. For intervals, this is the same as finding the a, b (with $a < b$) that maximize $|G_Z(b) - G_Z(a)|$. For initial segments we need to maximize $|G_Z(a)|$.

Lemma 5.1. Let Z be a KS-structure. Then $\max_{a<b} |G_Z(b) - G_Z(a)| = \max_c G_Z(c) - \min_d G_Z(d)$

Thus it is sufficient to compute $\max_c G_Z(c)$ and $\min_d G_Z(d)$. The quantities of interest are $\max_c G_Z(c) - \min_d G_Z(d)$ (for intervals) and $\max\{\max_c G_Z(c), |\min_d G_Z(d)|\}$ (for initial segments). The next lemma forms the basis of the incremental algorithm.

Lemma 5.2. Let A and B be KS structures. Furthermore, $v(a) \leq v(b)$ for all $a \in A$, $b \in B$. Let M_A maximize G_A and m_A minimize G_A. Similarly let M_B maximize G_B and m_B minimize G_B. Let Z be the KS structure formed from the elements of a and b. Then either M_A or $M_B + |A|$ maximizes G_Z and either m_A or $m_B + |A|$ minimizes G_Z.

Algorithm 2 : START(X,Y)

1: For each $x \in X$ set weight$(x) = 1/|X|$
2: For each $y \in Y$ set weight$(y) = -1/|Y|$
3: Create the KS structure Z from X and Y (Z is sorted by value)
4: Create a binary tree B where the elements of Z are the leaves.
5: DESCEND(B.root)
6: Return B.root.VMax-B.root.vmin

Thus we can create a divide-and-conquer algorithm that maintains KS structures at every level and uses Lemma 5.2 to combine them. The algorithm sorts the elements in the windows X and Y into an array Z and builds a binary tree over it (where the elements of X and Y are contained in the leaves). For every node n, the set of leaves descended from n, referred to as $J(n)$, forms a consecutive subset of Z (we refer to this as a subarray). Thus if n_1 and n_2 are siblings then $J(n_1)$ and $J(n_2)$ are disjoint and the concatenation of $J(n_1)$ and $J(n_2)$ is a subarray of Z. Furthermore, each $J(n)$ is a KS structure. Each node n has the following 5 fields:

1. **sum**= sum of the weights of elements of $J(n)$.
2. **imin** = the integer that minimizes $G_{J(n)}$
3. **IMax** = the integer that maximizes $G_{J(n)}$
4. **vmin** = $G_{J(n)}(imin)$
5. **VMax** = $G_{J(n)}(IMax)$

The algorithm starts at the root. The general step is as follows: if we are examining node n and one of its children c does not have any values for its fields then we recurse down that child. Otherwise if both children have values for those fields, we use Lemma 5.2 to compute these values for n. Algorithms 2 and 3 show how this is done.

The algorithm performs one $O(|X| + |Y|)$ sorting step. Building a blank binary try over these elements can be done in $O(|X| + |Y|)$ time since there are $O(|X| + |Y|)$ nodes and for each node it computes the values of its fields in constant time. Therefore, after the sorting step, the algorithm runs in linear time.

To make this incremental, we note that when a new element arrives in the stream, we remove one element from the front window Y and then add this new element and the weights of the elements in X and Y do not change. Thus we just need to maintain the tree structure of the algorithm in $O(\log(|X| + |Y|))$ time under insertions and deletions. To do this, we replace

Algorithm 3 : DESCEND(n)
1: **if** n is a leaf **then**
2:     $a \leftarrow$ the element of Z contained in n
3:     n.sum$\leftarrow$ weight(a).
4:     **if** weight(a) > 0 **then**
5:        n.imin$\leftarrow$ 1; n.IMax$\leftarrow$ 1
6:        n.vmin$\leftarrow$ 0; n.VMax$\leftarrow$ a
7:     **else**
8:        n.imin$\leftarrow$ 1; n.IMax$\leftarrow$ 1
9:        n.vmin$\leftarrow$ a; n.VMax$\leftarrow$ 0
10:    **end if**
11:    return
12: **end if**
13: $lc \leftarrow$ left_child(n); $rc \leftarrow$ right_child(n)
14: DESCEND(lc);   DESCEND(rc)
15: n.sum$\leftarrow$ lc.sum + rc.sum
16: **if** lc.VMax $\geq$ lc.sum+rc.VMax **then**
17:     n.VMax$\leftarrow$ lc.VMax; n.IMax$\leftarrow$ lc.IMax
18: **else**
19:     n.VMax$\leftarrow$ lc.sum + rc.VMax
20:     n.IMax$\leftarrow$ rc.IMax + $|J(lc)|$
21: **end if**
22: **if** lc.vmin $\leq$ lc.sum+rc.vmin **then**
23:     n.vmin$\leftarrow$ lc.vmin; n.imin$\leftarrow$ lc.imin
24: **else**
25:     n.vmin$\leftarrow$ lc.sum + rc.vmin
26:     n.imin$\leftarrow$ rc.imin + $|J(lc)|$
27: **end if**
28: return

the binary tree with a balanced tree, such as a B* tree. Now when a new element is inserted or deleted, we can follow the path this element takes from the root to a leaf. Only the nodes along this path are affected and so we can recursively recompute the fields values for those nodes in constant time per node (in a way similar to procedure DESCEND, shown in Algorithm 3). Since the both path length and insert/delete costs are $O(\log(|X| + |Y|))$ the incremental algorithm runs in time $O(\log(|X| + |Y|))$.

6 Experimental Results

In order to compare the various statistics for nonparametric change detection, it is necessary to use simulated data so that the changes in generating distributions are known. In each experiment, we generate a stream of 2,000,000 points and change the distribution every 20,000 points. Note that the time at which a change is detected is a random variable depending on the old and new distributions. Thus the time between changes is intentionally long so that it would be easier to distinguish between late detections of change and false detections of change. Furthermore, in order to estimate the expected number of false detections, we run the change-detection scheme on 5 control streams with 2 million points each and no distribution change. Figure 1 reports the average number of errors per 2

Figure 1: Average number of errors in 2,000,000 points

size(n,p)	W	KS	KS (Int)	ϕ	Ξ
$\mathcal{S}(20k, .05)$	8	8	9.8	3.6	7.2
$\mathcal{S}(50k, .05)$	1.4	0.6	1.8	1.6	1.8

million points.

In the experiments, our scheme uses 4 window pairs where both windows in a pair have the same size. The sizes are 200, 400, 800, 1600 points. We evaluate our scheme using the Kolmogorov-Smirnov statistic over initial segments "KS", the Kolmogorov-Smirnov statistic over intervals "KSI", the Wilcoxon statistic "W", and the $\phi_\mathcal{A}$ and $\Xi_\mathcal{A}$ statistics (where $\mathcal{A}$ is the set of initial segments). We have two version of each experiment, each using a different critical region. The critical regions correspond to size (50000, .05) and (20000, .05). These are referred to as $\mathcal{S}(50k, .05)$ and $\mathcal{S}(20k, .05)$, respectively. The critical regions for each window were constructed by taking the .95 quantile over 500 simulation runs (using the uniform distribution between 0 and 1).

When some window detects a change, it is considered *not* late if the real change point is within the window or if the change point was contained in the window at most M time units ago (where M is the size of the window). Otherwise the change is considered late.

Distribution changes are created as follows: each stream starts with some distribution F with parameters $p_1, \ldots, p_n$ and rate of drift r. When it is time for a change, we choose a (continuous) uniform random variable R_i in $[-r, r]$ and add it to p_i, for all i.

The rest of the experiments deal with streams where the generating distribution changes (there are 99 true changes in each stream and a change occurs every 20,000 points). The numbers are reported as a/b where a is the number of change reports considered to be *not* late and b represents the number of change reports which are late or wrong. Note the average number of false reports should be around the same as in the control files.

The first group of experiments show what happens when changes occur primarily in areas with small probabilities. In Figure 2, the initial distribution is uniform on $[-p, p]$ and p varies at every change point. The changes are symmetric, and as expected, the Wilcoxon statistic performs the worst with almost no change detection. The Kolmogorov-Smirnov test primarily looks at probability changes that are located near the median and doesn't do very well although it clearly outperforms the median. In this case, performing the Kolmogorov-Smirnov test over intervals is clearly superior to initial segments. Clearly the best performance is obtained by the ϕ and Ξ statistics. For example, using the $\mathcal{S}(50k, .05)$ test for ϕ there are 86 on-time detections and 13 late detections. Since its error rate is about 1.6, it is very likely that this test

Figure 2: Uniform on $[-p,p]$ ($p=5$) with drift= 1

St.	$\mathcal{S}(20k,.05)$	$\mathcal{S}(50k,.05)$
W	0/5	0/4
KS	31/30	25/15
KSI	60/34	52/27
ϕ	92/20	86/13
Ξ	86/19	85/9

Figure 3: Mixture of Standard Normal and Uniform[-7,7] ($p=0.9$) with drift= 0.05

St.	$\mathcal{S}(20k,.05)$	$\mathcal{S}(50k,.05)$
W	0/2	0/0
KS	0/15	0/7
KSI	4/32	2/9
ϕ	16/33	12/27
Ξ	13/36	12/18

Figure 4: Normal ($\mu=50$, $\sigma=5$) with drift= 0.6

St.	$\mathcal{S}(20k,.05)$	$\mathcal{S}(50k,.05)$
W	10/27	6/16
KS	17/30	9/27
KSI	16/47	10/26
ϕ	16/38	11/31
Ξ	17/43	16/22

truly detected all changes.

Figure 3 shows a more subtle change. The starting distribution is a mixture of a Standard Normal distribution with some Uniform noise (uniform over $[-7,7]$). With probability p we sample from the Normal and with probability $1-p$ we sample from the Uniform. A change in generating distribution is obtained by varying p. Initially $p=.9$, meaning that the distribution is close to Normal. Here we have similar results. The Wilcoxon does not detect any changes and is clearly inferior to the Kolmogorov-Smirnov statistic. Once again, change detection improves when we consider intervals instead of initial segments. The ϕ and Ξ statistics again perform the best (with ϕ being slightly better than Ξ).

The next group of experiments investigates the effects of changing parameters of commonly used distributions. Figures 4 and 5 show results for Normal and Exponential distributions. The performance of the tests is similar, given the error rate for $\mathcal{S}(20k,.05)$ tests and so the $\mathcal{S}(50k,0.5)$ tests are more informative. Overall, the Kolmogorov-Smirnov test does better, suggesting that such parametrized changes primarily affect areas near the median.

Finally, we show results discrete distributions. For all tests but the Wilcoxon, we showed that the error bounds from the continuous case are upper bounds on the error in the discrete case. Thus the results can indicate that some tests perform better in the discrete setting or that for some tests, bounds for discrete distributions are closer to the bounds for continuous distributions. However, it is not possible to distinguish between these two cases without more theoretical analysis. In the case of the Wilcoxon test, we do not know if the bounds for continuous distributions are upper bounds for discrete distributions. However, if we assume the same error rate as in Figure 1 we could compare the results. Figures 6 and 7 show our results for Binomial and Poisson distributions. The Wilcoxon appears to perform the best, both in early detection and total detection of change. However, it is difficult to judge the significance of this result. Among the other tests, the Kolmogorov-Smirnov test appears to be best.

7 Related Work

There is much related work on this topic. Some of the standard background includes statistical hypothesis testing and the multiple testing problem [5]. There has been much work on change point analysis in the statistics literature [6], However, most of the tests are parametric in nature (except the tests discussed in Section 1), and thus their assumptions are rarely satisfied for real data. Furthermore, the tests are run only once - after all of the data has been collected. The most related work from the statistics literature is the area of scan statistics [14, 15]. However, work on scan statistics does not work in the data stream model: the algorithms require that all the data can be stored in-memory, and that the tests are preformed only once after all the data is gathered. Neill and Moore improve the efficiency of Kulldorff's spatial scan statistics using a hierarchical tree structure [20].

In the database and data mining literature there is a plethora of work on processing data streams (see [3] for a recent survey). However, none of this work addresses the problem of change in a data stream. There is some work on evolving data [11, 12, 13, 7], mining evolving data streams [7, 17], and change detection in semistructured data [9, 8]. The focus of that work, however, is detection of specialized types of change and not general definitions of detection of change in the underlying distribution. There has been recent work on frameworks for diagnosing changes in evolving data streams based on velocity density estimation [1] with the emphasis on heuristics to find trends, rather than formal statistical definitions of change and when change is statistically meaningful, the approach taken in this paper.

The work closest to ours is work by Kleinberg on the detection of word bursts in data stream, but his work is tightly coupled with the assumption of discrete distributions (such as the existence of words), and does not apply to continuous distributions [18].

8 Conclusions and Future Work

We believe that our work is a promising first step towards non-parametric change detection. Our experiments confirm a fact that is well known in the statistics community: there is no test that is "best" in all situ-

Figure 5: Exponential ($\lambda = 1$) with drift= 0.1

St.	$\mathcal{S}(20k,.05)$	$\mathcal{S}(50k,.05)$
W	12/38	6/34
KS	11/38	9/26
KSI	7/22	4/14
ϕ	7/29	5/18
Ξ	11/46	4/20

Figure 6: Binomial ($p = 0.1$, $n = 2000$) with drift= 0.001

St.	$\mathcal{S}(20k,.05)$	$\mathcal{S}(50k,.05)$
W	36/42	25/30
KS	24/38	20/26
KSI	17/22	13/15
ϕ	12/32	11/18
Ξ	23/33	15/23

Figure 7: Poisson ($\lambda = 50$) with drift $= 1$

St.	$\mathcal{S}(20k,.05)$	$\mathcal{S}(50k,.05)$
W	36/35	31/26
KS	23/30	16/27
KSI	14/25	10/18
ϕ	14/21	9/17
Ξ	23/22	17/11

ations. However, the $\phi_{\mathcal{A}}$ and $\Xi_{\mathcal{A}}$ statistics do not perform much worse than the other statistics we tested, and in some cases they were vastly superior.

Our work is only the first step towards an understanding of change in data streams. We would like to formally characterize the relative strengths and weaknesses of various non-parametric tests and to study the types of changes that occur in real data. Other interesting directions for future work are relaxing the assumption that points in the stream are generated independently, improving bounds for discrete distributions, designing fast algorithms (especially for statistics computed over intervals), determining which classes of sets $\mathcal{A}$ are useful in higher dimensions, and better estimation of the point in time at which the change occurred.

Acknowledgments. Dan Kifer was supported by an NSF Fellowship. The authors are supported by NSF grants 0084762, 0121175, 0133481, 0205452, and 0330201, and by a gift from Microsoft. Any opinions, findings, conclusions, or recommendations expressed in this paper are those of the authors and do not necessarily reflect the views of the sponsors.

References

[1] C. Aggarwal, J. Han, J. Wang, and P. S. Yu. A framework for clustering evolving data streams. In *VLDB 2003*.

[2] M. Anthony and J. Shawe-Taylor. A result of vapnik with applications. *Discrete Applied Mathematics*, 47(2):207–217, 1993.

[3] B. Babcock, S. Babu, M. Datar, R. Motwani, and J. Widom. Models and issues in data stream systems. In *PODS 2002*.

[4] T. Batu, L. Fortnow, R. Rubinfeld, W. D. Smith, and P. White. Testing that distributions are close. In *FOCS 2000*.

[5] P. J. Bickel and K. Doksum. *Mathematical Statistics: Basic Ideas and Selected Topics*. Holden-Day, Inc., 1977.

[6] E. Carlstein, H.-G. Müller, and D. Siegmund, editors. *Change-point problems*. Institute of Mathematical Statistics, Hayward, California, 1994.

[7] S. Chakrabarti, S. Sarawagi, and B. Dom. Mining surprising patterns using temporal description length. In *VLDB 1998*.

[8] S. S. Chawathe, S. Abiteboul, and J. Widom. Representing and querying changes in semistructured data. In *ICDE 1998*.

[9] S. S. Chawathe and H. Garcia-Molina. Meaningful change detection in structured data. In *SIGMOD 1997*.

[10] W. Feller. *An Introduction to Probability Theory and its Applications*, volume 1. John Wiley & Sons, inc., 3rd edition, 1970.

[11] V. Ganti, J. Gehrke, and R. Ramakrishnan. Demon: Mining and monitoring evolving data. *IEEE Transactions on Knowledge and Data Engineering (TKDE)*, 13(1):50–63, 2001.

[12] V. Ganti, J. Gehrke, and R. Ramakrishnan. Mining data streams under block evolution. *SIGKDD Explorations*, 3(2):1–10, 2002.

[13] V. Ganti, J. Gehrke, R. Ramakrishnan, and W.-Y. Loh. A framework for measuring differences in data characteristics. *Journal of Computer and System Sciences (JCSS)*, 64(3):542–578, 2002.

[14] J. Glaz and N. Balakrishnan, editors. *Scan statistics and applications*. Birkhäuser Boston, 1999.

[15] J. Glaz, J. Naus, and S. Wallenstein. *Scan statistics*. Springer New York, 2001.

[16] T. Hagerup and C. Rub. A guided tour of chernoff bounds. *Information Processing Letters*, 33:305–308, 1990.

[17] G. Hulten, L. Spencer, and P. Domingos. Mining time-changing data streams. In *KDD 2001*.

[18] J. M. Kleinberg. Bursty and hierarchical structure in streams. In *KDD 2002*.

[19] J. Lin. Divergence measures based on the shannon entropy. *IEEE Transactions on Information Theory*, 37(1):145–151, 1991.

[20] D. Neill and A. Moore. A fast multi-resolution method for detection of significant spatial overdensities. Carnegie Mellon CSD Technical Report, June 2003.

[21] W. H. Press, B. P. Flannery, S. A. Teukolsky, and W. T. Vetterling. *Numerical Recipes in C*. Cambridge University Press, 1992.

[22] V. N. Vapnik. *Statistical Learning Theory*. John Wiley & Sons, 1998.

[23] G. Widmer and M. Kubat. Learning in the presence of concept drift and hidden contexts. *Machine Learning*, 23(1):69–101, 1996.

[24] F. Wilcoxon. Individual comparisons by ranking methods. *Biometrics Bulletin*, 1:80–83, 1945.

Stochastic Consistency, and Scalable Pull-Based Caching for Erratic Data Stream Sources [*]

Shanzhong Zhu   Chinya V. Ravishankar

Department of Computer Science and Engineering
University of California, Riverside
Riverside, CA 92521
{szhu, ravi}@cs.ucr.edu

Abstract

We introduce the notion of stochastic consistency, and propose a novel approach to achieving it for caches of highly erratic data. Erratic data sources, such as stock prices, sensor data, are common and important in practice. However, their erratic patterns of change make caching hard. Stochastic consistency guarantees that errors in cached values of erratic data remain within a user-specified bound, with a user-specified probability. We use a Brownian motion model to capture the behavior of data changes, and use its underlying theory to predict when caches should initiate pulls to refresh cached copies to maintain stochastic consistency. Our approach allows servers to remain totally stateless, thus achieving excellent scalability and reliability. We also discuss a new real-time scheduling approach for servicing pull requests at the server. Our scheduler delivers prompt response whenever possible, and minimizes the aggregate cache-source deviation due to delays during server overload. We conduct extensive experiments to validate our model on real-life datasets, and show that our scheme outperforms current schemes.

1 Introduction

Many applications must confront the challenge of efficient delivery of erratically changing data to a large population of clients. Caching is widely used to reduce latency, client-server bandwidth, and server load, but it is difficult to guarantee cache consistency for erratic data. We propose a novel approach to this problem.

Erratic data are numerical data that change frequently and unpredictably, usually in response to uncontrollable environmental factors or other random influences in real systems. Erratic data have been recognized as common in streaming applications [11], and examples include sensor streams [23], stock prices [5], and network statistics.

Source-cache consistency for content delivery [27] is typically maintained under the *push* or the *pull* model. The push method [7, 10, 28, 33] monitors all data changes at the server, and disseminates updates to the client caches whenever data changes beyond user-specified error tolerance. Push is easy to implement, but suffers from several drawbacks.

First, push is not scalable, since the server must provide most of the required resources, such as processing power, sockets, and memory, and monitor data changes and manage communications with clients. Second, it is less reliable, since state information about connections with clients is lost when the server fails, and is hard to restore upon reboot. Finally, it is not power-efficient when clients are wireless and battery-powered, since clients must remain in listen mode, in anticipation of push updates.

1.1 The Pull Model

In the pull method [17, 19, 30], in contrast, clients decide when to refresh local copies. While the effectiveness of a pull scheme depends on the client's ability to initiate pulls at proper times, it is better than push in many real-world situations, especially with erratic and streaming data sources. Servers remains stateless, so the method is scalable and resilient to server failure. Wireless clients can sleep between scheduled pulls, saving power.

For example, in environmental monitoring systems, such as in [4], sensors are deployed at remote ocean lo-

---

[*] This work was supported by a grant from Tata Consultancy Services, Inc.

Permission to copy without fee all or part of this material is granted provided that the copies are not made or distributed for direct commercial advantage, the VLDB copyright notice and the title of the publication and its date appear, and notice is given that copying is by permission of the Very Large Data Base Endowment. To copy otherwise, or to republish, requires a fee and/or special permission from the Endowment.

**Proceedings of the 30th VLDB Conference,
Toronto, Canada, 2004**

cations at various depths to collect data. Such systems must be wireless and battery-powered because their locations may be hard to access. Research vessels are charged with collecting data updates with a certain accuracy, but frequently move out of wireless range of sensors to perform other functions. Since broadcasting takes much more power than to listen [6], it would be wasteful for the sensors to initiate data pushes, since there may be no vessels listening. We show in Section 4 how vessels can schedule visits to the area to pull data as appropriate to ensure monitoring accuracy constraints.

A similar problem arises when clients (such as PDAs or laptops) are power-limited. The push model would force the clients to remain in listen mode in anticipation of data. This is unacceptable, since the listen power is still significant, albeit less than in transmit mode. Our model allows clients to "sleep" most of the time, and change mode at pull times.

Finally, consider a system which manages stock portfolios for hundreds of thousands of clients, each with a local cache, for which the cache-source error must be less than some predetermined value. A model in which the server pushes updates to each client whenever the its cache error exceeds its threshold would simply not scale. The server would need to dedicate an enormous number of connections to this task.

Combinations of push and pull have also been proposed [8, 16] to achieve better performance. The success of such combined schemes also depends on the pull strategy at the client.

1.2 Stochastic Consistency for Erratic Data

We propose a novel pull-based synchronization scheme for maintaining *stochastic consistency* (see Section 4) of erratic data, applicable when users are willing to tolerate some error.

Our notion of stochastic consistency guarantees that cache-source deviation remains within user-specified error tolerance with a certain probability level. In many applications, slightly out-of-sync values are satisfactory, if they are within specified error bounds. For example, a stock holder may want to track stock price changes higher than $0.1, and a system administrator may only care when machine loads change by more than 10%.

In such cases, strict consistency between cache and source is unnecessary. It suffices to adaptively synchronize cached copies with the source guided by user-defined error tolerances. Also, because of the erratic nature of such data, it is desirable to associate a confidence metric with the cache-source error. For example, a stock holder may be satisfied with a quote if it is within $0.1 of its true value, with confidence 90%. In this paper, we show how to achieve stochastic consistency by modeling the evolution of erratic data as Brownian motions [29].

The success of pull schemes depends largely on effective modeling of source data evolution. Some recent work examines stochastic modeling of web page content evolution. Cho et al. [13, 14] verify the modeling of web page updates as Poisson process, by experiments on more than half a million web pages over four months, and use the model to synchronize local copies of web data with their remote sources. A formal discussion of stochastic modeling of content evolution in relational database appears in [18]. The authors use compound nonhomogeneous Poisson processes to model the behavior of record insertion and deletion, and Markov chains to model attribute modification. However, none of these models are suitable for erratic data, since erratic sources are typically numeric data, and changes to them are much more frequent than those due to web page or relational database evolution. We need a new model for such erratic data, which can dynamically capture source data characteristics.

1.3 Our Contributions

We make several contributions in this paper. First, we introduce the notion of stochastic consistency, and demonstrate that it is a reasonable consistency model for many practically important classes of erratic data.

Second, we show how to model source data evolution as Brownian motions. We verify many real-life datasets can be modeled as Brownian motions by experiments. Proxies, which cache data on behalf of clients, can schedule pulls adaptively, using this model to determine when the expected error in the cached copy exceeds user-specified error tolerance. Although we present a pure pull scheme, it can be applied seamlessly to other push-and-pull schemes, say, as in [16].

Third, we solve a novel real-time scheduling problem for processing pull requests at the server. When the number of proxies is large, the server may be overwhelmed by bursts of pull requests, resulting in poor response. Our scheduling method aims to minimize cache-source disparities caused by such delays overall. As far as we are aware, this problem formulation has not appeared in the literature before.

Finally, we study the performance of our approach to real-life data by experiments. We examine stock traces, system load data collected from university servers and real-time sensor data sampled from distributed ocean buoys, showing that all of them can achieve good *fidelity* (see Section 5). We compare the performance of our Brownian motion based pull scheme with the *Adaptive TTL Scheme* proposed in [30]. We also simulate our scheduling algorithm and compare it with the simple FCFS scheme.

The rest of this paper is organized as follows: Section 2 reviews some previous work on consistency models and data synchronization techniques. We briefly review the Brownian motion model in Section 3, and verify our datasets conform to the model well. In Sec-

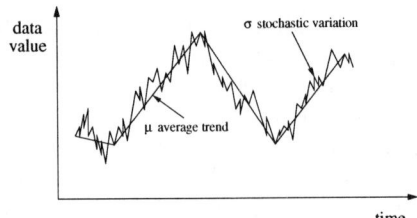

Figure 1: Brownian motion with drift

Symbol	Company Name	β (Volatility)
NOVL	Novell	2.33
BRCM	Broadcom	3.91
SEBL	Siebel Systems	3.06
YHOO	Yahoo Inc	3.88
QCOM	Qualcomm	2.05
SUNW	Sun Micro	2.23
CSCO	Cisco	1.98
XLNX	Xilinx	2.07

Table 1: Stock traces used in our simulation

tion 4, we discuss how to apply Brownian motion to maintain stochastic consistency, and give the adaptive pull algorithm. Simulation results are given in Section 5. We discuss how to schedule pull requests at the server to minimize overall cache-source deviation in Section 6. Section 7 concludes this paper.

2 Related Work

Data synchronization in replicated systems has been widely studied. Since strong consistency incurs high overheads and poor scalability, weak consistency is frequently preferred [10, 22, 26]. Techniques such as lazy replication [22], epsilon-serializability [26], and anti-entropy [20] have been proposed.

Alonso et al. [10] introduce the concept of *quasi-caching*, which allows the cached value to deviate from the true value in a controlled way. Several coherency conditions are proposed, including the *delay* condition, which states by how much time a cached image may lag its source value, and the *arithmetic* condition, which gives the allowable difference between the true values and cached image. A pull-based synchronization technique, *implicit invalidation*, is proposed, which forces refreshing by invalidating the cached copy after a certain time. However the authors have not discussed how to set the invalidation time, based on the update pattern of the source object.

The concept of *probabilistic consistency* is introduced in [37], which guarantees the value returned by the system is temporally consistent with the newest copy with a probability p. However, this approach does not consider the important related issue of bounding the errors in cached values.

Maintaining temporal consistency of erratic, frequently changing (dynamic) data is studied in [16, 28, 30, 34]. In [28], pure push is used to disseminate updates through a tree of cooperating repositories. In [30], various schemes are discussed for clients to calculate the time to refresh cached copies, so that temporal coherency is maintained. If $U(t)$ and $S(t)$ denote the cached and source values at time t, respectively, and c is the desired error bound, then the goal is to maintain the constraint $|U(t) - S(t)| < c$. They experimentally show that the *adaptive TTL scheme* has the best temporal consistency properties among various TTL schemes proposed in the paper. However, the adaptive TTL scheme uses a simple linear model to model the evolution of a erratic source, which fails to capture the frequent fluctuations associated with the data. In Section 5, we show by experiments that our Brownian motion based pull scheme outperforms *adaptive TTL scheme*. Deolasee et al. [16] propose an adaptive *PaP* algorithm, which combines push and pull. In the algorithm, the performance of the client side pull is very crucial to the overall performance.

Yu et al. [34] study bounding numerical errors among replicated servers, where every server can store and accept updates. In their approaches, each server has to keep state information of other servers, which is not possible for our system with potentially large number of proxies.

Wolfson et al. [32] study how to represent and update the locations of moving objects in spatial database. Their goal, which is to seek balance between location precisions and the update frequency, is similar to ours. Yet the nature of erratic data demands a different approach.

3 Using Brownian Motion Models

The Brownian motion [29], is widely used to model fluctuating data in finance, engineering, communications, physics, and so on. It models increments in random data as independent normal samples. We first describe the model and demonstrate that it models many practical erratic datasets well.

3.1 The Brownian Motion Model

A continuous-time stochastic process $W(t)$, which varies as a function of time t, is called a *Standard Brownian motion (SBM)* [29] if it satisfies three conditions: (1) $W(0) = 0$, (2) $W(t) - W(s)$ is normally distributed with mean 0 and variance $t - s$ ($t \geq s$), and (3) $W(t) - W(s)$ is independent of $W(v) - W(u)$ if (s, t) and (u, v) are non-overlapping time intervals. Property (2) says every increment of SBM is a normal deviate. In general, SBM is a Martingale process [29], meaning loosely that the best estimate for its future value is its current value.

Drifting Brownian Motion (DBM) $S(t)$ is similar, but includes a secular drift in the expectation of the process. Its behavior can be captured by the following equation:

$$dS(t) = \mu(t)\,dt + \sigma(t)\,dW(t), \qquad (1)$$

time interval	stock datasets			*temp* datasets			system load dataset
	BRCM	*QCOM*	*SEBL*	*0N/140W/36M*	*0N/140W/47M*	*0N/140W/70M*	
10 min	75.50%	80.28%	75.50%	75.21%	72.96%	79.58%	76.00%
15 min	71.80%	75.67%	76.17%	72.38%	75.90%	79.44%	75.23%
20 min	72.14%	70.88%	76.11%	73.45%	73.55%	77.20%	75.41%
30 min	70.92%	65.23%	72.14%	71.47%	66.13%	62.21%	70.59%

Table 2: Average *p*-values of *W-S* test for various datasets and time intervals, confidence interval: 95%. *0N/140W/36M* trace is sampled at longitude 0N, latitude 140W, sea depth 36M.

$\mu(t)$ and $\sigma(t)$ are the time-dependent *drift* and *diffusion* parameters, respectively. Using finite differences for differentials for simplicity, $\Delta W(t)$ represents the increment of the SBM, $\Delta W(t) \sim N(0, \Delta t)$. Intuitively, $\mu(t)$ models a secular upward or downward trend in the erratic data, while $\sigma(t)$ models the randomness associated with the data, as shown in Figure 1. Fundamentally, DBM is a combination of a predictable linear trend and a Brownian motion process. The term $\mu(t)\Delta t$ represents the non-stochastic part of the process, and characterizes the current moving trend. The term $\sigma(t)\Delta W(t)$ is the stochastic or Brownian motion part, and represents the randomness in the data. At time t, the process increment $\Delta S(t)$ follows the normal distribution $(\mu(t)\Delta t, \sigma^2(t)\Delta t)$.

3.2 Applicability of Brownian Motion

A key property of Brownian motions is that data increments are modeled as independent normal distributions $(\mu(t)\Delta t, \sigma^2(t)\Delta t)$. We expect the drift and diffusion parameters $\mu(t)$ and $\sigma(t)$ to be relatively constant in the short term. To show that this model is useful in modeling real-world datasets, it suffices to show that increments for small, non-overlapping, and equal-length time intervals are samples from normal distributions in the short term.

Normality testing [15, 31] has been extensively studied in the statistical literature, because of the great importance of the normal distribution. Various tests exist [15, 31], including the Kolmogorov-Smirnov (*K-S*) test, the Chi-Square (χ^2) test, the Wilk-Shapiro (*W-S*) test, and the Anderson-Darling (*A-D*) test. Each normality test is formulated as a *hypothesis test* in which the *null hypothesis* is that samples are normal. Some of these tests are general *goodness-of-fit* tests, such as the *K-S* test and χ^2 tests, while others are specifically designed for testing normality, such as the *W-S* test. Generally speaking, the tests specific to normality are more powerful in detecting non-normality than the general goodness-of-fit tests [31]. We chose to apply the *W-S* test for testing normality, as it has high *power* [31], given no prior knowledge about the possible alternatives.

We tested the applicability of the Brownian motion model to a variety of real-life streaming data sources. We selected datasets from three classes of real-life data, namely, stock prices, sensor data, and system load data, and tested whether their increments were normal. The stock streams we chose are listed in Table 1 with values arriving every minute for the entire year 06/2001–06/2002. Each stream contained about 10^5 data values. Our sensor time series were taken from the TAO project [4] at the Pacific Marine Environmental Laboratory (PMEL), and comprised a year's measurements (11/1991–11/1992) of temperature (*temp*) at various ocean depths. Each *temp* stream contained about 10^4 values, sampled every 1 minute. Our system load data comprised 1-minute averages of system loads collected every five seconds for two days on our main server.

We deliberately chose data streams with high volatility. Such data show high uncertainty of movement, and display large fluctuations even over short intervals. Highly erratic data are more challenging for our adaptive pull model. The β value [36] shown in Table 1 is a measure of the relative volatility of a stock to the market. Generally, symbols with $\beta \in [1, 4]$ are considered to have high volatility.

Table 2 shows the average *p-values* [31] of the *W-S* test evaluated on increment samples taken over various time intervals. For each time interval, we repeatedly applied the *W-S* test on samples over the intervals through the entire data series, and record the average results (*p*-values). The *p*-value measures the probability that the *W-S* test statistic will take on a value that is at least as extreme as the observed value when the null hypothesis is true. In our context, the larger the *p*-value, the stronger the confidence with which we may accept the samples as normal. The *significance level* (α) of our test is 0.05. Any sample with *p*-value lower than α can be flagged as non-normal with high confidence. The *p*-values for our datasets are far higher than α, indicating that we can have high confidence in modeling the increments as normal samples. Not surprisingly, for longer time intervals, the *p*-value drops somewhat, suggesting the model may evolve during longer intervals (see Section 5.1).

4 The Stochastic Consistency Model

Figure 2 depicts our system model. There are three major components in our system: a central server or erratic data source, proxies with caches (only one proxy is shown), and clients. The server maintains N data objects $\{o_1, o_2, \ldots, o_N\}$, whose values are updated frequently, say, by incoming update streams. Users request object values through proxies. At each

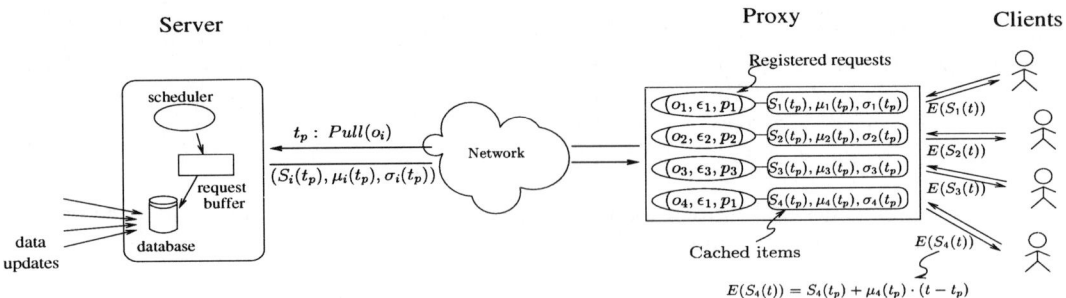

Figure 2: System architecture

proxy, users register tuples (o_i, ϵ_j, p_j) specifying that the user is interested in object o_i, and can tolerate error ϵ_j with probability confidence p_j. Proxies adaptively pull object values on behalf of users, at intervals designed to maintain stochastic consistency with the server. The server responses have the form $(S_i(t_p), \mu_i(t_p), \sigma_i(t_p))$, where $S_i(t_p)$ denotes the value of o_i at pull time t_p, $\mu_i(t_p)$ and $\sigma_i(t_p)$ are the estimates of o_i's drift and diffusion parameters, respectively (see Section 4.3). When a user requests o_i's value from the proxy at some time t, the current estimate of o_i's value, based on last pulled object value and parameters, is returned.

As pull requests arrive at the server, a real-time scheduler dynamically schedules these requests for service (see Section 6), to ensure prompt responses.

In what follows, we introduce the stochastic consistency model in Section 4.1. In Section 4.2, we show how proxies can determine their pull times under the DBM model, to maintain stochastic consistency. The *drift* and *diffusion* parameters, which capture data characteristics on the fly, are estimated for each data object periodically at the server. The issue of parameter estimation is discussed in Section 4.3. In 4.4, we describe our adaptive pull algorithm.

4.1 Stochastic Consistency

In our approach, proxies cache and serve data objects under a stochastic consistency model. A client is satisfied if the value returned by the proxy for object o_i is within ϵ of its true value with probability at least p. Let $S_i(t)$ and $U_i(t)$ be the true and cached values of object o_i at time t. Let ϵ be the user-specified error tolerance and p be the confidence expressed as a probability. The cache is stochastically consistent if

$$\Pr\left[\,|(S_i(t) - U_i(t))| \leq \epsilon\,\right] \geq p, \quad \text{at all times } t. \quad (2)$$

A proxy must frequently refresh cached copies to maintain stochastic consistency. To reduce communication overhead and server loads, we need a mechanism to adaptively decide when the cache-source deviation is likely to exceed ϵ, and refresh the cached copy only at such times.

Let the proxy have pulled object o_i's values from the server at times $t_1, t_2, \ldots, t_k$. At time t_k, the proxy must determine the next time $t_{k+1} = t_k + \Delta t_k$ the data must be pulled. During the interval $[t_k, t_{k+1}]$, the proxy returns to the user an estimate for o_i's value, based on the last pulled value $S_i(t_k)$. Consider the probability function:

$$F_i(t, \Delta t) = \Pr[|S_i(t + \Delta t) - E[S_i(t + \Delta t)]| \leq \epsilon] \quad (3)$$

$F_i(t, \Delta t)$ is the probability that the cache-source deviation of o_i's value is within ϵ at time $t + \Delta t$, given the last proxy-pulled value is $S_i(t)$. $S_i(t+\Delta t)$ is the actual source value, and $E[S_i(t + \Delta t)]$ is the estimated value at the proxy. How the proxy determines $E[S_i(t+\Delta t)]$ depends on the source data evolution model, which will be discussed shortly.

The cached value is stochastically consistent at time $t_k + \Delta t_k$ if $F_i(t_k, \Delta t_k) \geq p$. Clearly, to maintain stochastic consistency, the proxy must pull to refresh the local value before $F_i(t_k, \Delta t_k)$ drops below p. Thus, at time t_k, the next pull time $t_{k+1} = t_k + \Delta t_k$ for object o_i is determined by the smallest Δt_k for which $F_i(t_k, \Delta t_k) \leq p$.

4.2 Determining the Next Pull Time

After justifying the appropriateness of the DBM model in Section 3.2, we model the increment of source object o_i, $\Delta S_i(t, \Delta t) = S_i(t + \Delta t) - S_i(t)$, as follows:

$$\Delta S_i(t, \Delta t) = \mu_i(t) \cdot \Delta t + \sigma_i(t) \cdot \Delta W(t), \quad (4)$$

$\mu_i(t)$ and $\sigma_i(t)$ are the time varying drift and diffusion parameters, respectively. $W(t)$ is a SBM. It's not difficult to see $\Delta S_i(t, \Delta t)$ follows a normal distribution:

$$\Delta S_i(t, \Delta t) \sim N(\mu_i(t)\Delta t, \ \sigma_i^2(t)\Delta t). \quad (5)$$

Let $E[S_i(t + \Delta t)] = S_i(t) + \mu_i(t)\Delta t$, we obtain:

$$S_i(t + \Delta t) - E(S_i(t + \Delta t)) \sim N(0, \ \sigma_i^2(t)\Delta t). \quad (6)$$

In Equation 6, $E[S_i(t + \Delta t)]$ is the expected value of $S_i(t + \Delta t)$ at time $t + \Delta t$. Thus $E[S_i(t + \Delta t)]$ can serve as the best estimate of $S_i(t + \Delta t)$ at such time. Suppose $S_i(t)$ and $\mu_i(t)$ are pulled by the proxy at time t, $E[S_i(t+\Delta t)]$ will be returned to users upon requests before $S_i(t)$ expires. We also need to find such Δt_ϵ that the probability the cache-source error remains within ϵ at time $t + \Delta t_\epsilon$, as defined in Equation 3, starts dropping below p.

Equations 3 and 6 indicate that $F_i(t, \Delta t)$ is a decreasing function of Δt. Thus, it suffices to find Δt_ϵ

for which $\Pr[|I_i(t, \Delta t_\epsilon)| \leq \epsilon] = p$. One must solve the following equation to obtain Δt_ϵ:

$$\frac{1}{\sqrt{2\pi}} \int_{-\hat{\epsilon}}^{\hat{\epsilon}} \exp\left(-\frac{x^2}{2}\right) dx = p, \qquad (7)$$

where $\hat{\epsilon} = \frac{\epsilon}{\sigma_i(t)\sqrt{\Delta t_\epsilon}}$. We note that this integral is simply the well-known error function [1], and since it is evaluated at the proxies and not at the server, our model remains scalable. Using Equation 7, proxies can obtain $t + \Delta t_\epsilon$, the next due time to refresh the local copy so that the expected error remains within user-specified tolerance.

We have thus far treated error tolerances as absolute values. However, one might be also interested in relative error tolerance. For example, a user may need to know the value of a stock portfolio within a given percentage bound. If we denote the relative error tolerance as $\epsilon_r\%$, we need to find Δt_{ϵ_r} such that:

$$\Pr[|S_i(t + \Delta t_{\epsilon_r}) - E[S_i(t + \Delta t_{\epsilon_r})]| \leq \epsilon_r\% \cdot |S_i(t)|] = p \qquad (8)$$

Now we can similarly calculate the next pull time as the case of absolute error tolerance described before.

4.3 Updating the Model

Proxies need the current drift parameter $\mu_i(t)$ to calculate the expected object value $E(S_i(t))$, and the diffusion parameter $\sigma_i(t)$ to calculate Δt_ϵ. Both parameters reflect the current characteristics of o_i, and should be estimated on a regular basis at the server.

The server maintains a buffer B_i containing the k most recent data values for each object o_i, sampled at regular intervals, h. When a new sampled value comes in to a full buffer, the oldest value in the buffer is simply discarded. Parameters $\mu_i(t)$ and $\sigma_i(t)$ are estimated using the current contents of B_i. According to the DBM model, increments follow normal distribution $N(\mu_i(t)\Delta t, \sigma_i^2(t)\Delta t)$. Given a fixed Δt, such as h, over short term, estimating $\mu_i(t)$ and $\sigma_i(t)$ is equivalent to estimating the mean and variance of increments over Δt. The issue of estimating mean and variance has been extensively studied, and sample mean and sample variance are typically used as estimators [29]. We show in our experiments, that for the short time horizons we will be concerned with, simpler methods work quite well. Let $\hat{\mu}_i(t)$ represent the estimated value of $\mu_i(t)$, we have:

$$\hat{\mu}_i(t) = \frac{1}{(k-1)h} \sum_{j=0}^{k-2} (B_i[j+1] - B_i[j]) \qquad (9)$$

The estimated value of $\sigma_i(t)$ is:

$$\hat{\sigma}_i^2(t) = \frac{1}{(k-2)h} \sum_{j=0}^{k-2} (B_i[j+1] - B_i[j] - \hat{\mu}_i(t)h)^2 \qquad (10)$$

$\hat{\mu}_i(t)$ and $\hat{\sigma}_i^2(t)$ are both unbiased and easy to compute. Since h is comparatively small, the estimated values are quite accurate.

Algorithm 1 Adaptive Pull Algorithm

Proxy side (o_i, ϵ, p):
loop
  if $t_{curr} == t_{pull}(o_i)$ **then**
    /* time to pull new value of object o_i */
    Send a pull request $pull(o_i)$ to the server, and wait;
    On receiving server response, proxy obtains (S_i, μ_i, σ_i);
    Update local copy with new value S_i;
    Calculate Δt_ϵ based on obtained μ_i and σ_i;
    $t_{last}(o_i) = t_{pull}(o_i)$, $\quad t_{pull}(o_i) = t_{curr} + \Delta t_\epsilon$;
  end if

  if proxy receive a user request $req(o_i)$ **then**
    /* the proxy receives a user request for object o_i */
    $E(t_{curr}) = S_i + \mu_i(t_{curr} - t_{last})$;
    Return $E(t_{curr})$ to the user;
  end if
end loop

Server side:
loop
  if server receive a pull request $pull(o_i)$ **then**
    Process the request, retrieve current value of object o_i, S_i;
    Retrieve latest evaluated μ_i and σ_i;
    Send (S_i, μ_i, σ_i) back to the proxy;
  end if
end loop

The parameter estimation process for each object must be carried out repeatedly at the server. On processing a pull request, the latest estimates of μ_i and σ_i are returned with the object values to the proxy (see Figure 2), which will use them to calculate expected object value and decide the next pull time.

4.4 Adaptive Pull Algorithm

Algorithm 1 outlines our adaptive pull algorithm. t_{curr} is the current system time at the proxy. $t_{pull}(o_i)$ is the calculated next pull time for object o_i, and $t_{last}(o_i)$ is the last time the cached copy of o_i is updated. On receiving response (S_i, μ_i, σ_i) from the server, the proxy calculates Δt_ϵ based on σ_i as well as ϵ and p. On receiving user request at time t_{curr}, the proxy returns its best estimated value $E(t_{curr})$ based on current cached value S_i and μ_i. Our server is totally stateless, guaranteeing good scalability. For simplicity, we assume the pulled value is immediately available at the proxy after it sends the pull request, which may not be true in the real world. We will tackle this problem in section 6.

It should be possible to extend our model to hierarchical proxying schemes. As user requests (o_i, ϵ, p) propagate up the hierarchy, each non-leaf node picks the most conservative values of ϵ and p for each object cached in the subtree, and propagate them upwards. Root nodes communicate with the server using our pull scheme. Updates are pushed down the hierarchy according to ϵ value at each node.

5 Adaptive Pull Performance

We conducted a series of experiments to demonstrate the performance of our scheme on real-life erratic data

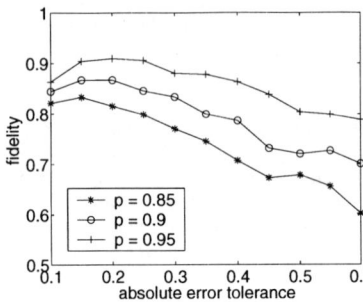

Figure 3: Fidelity for stock trace BRCM

sources, such as stock prices, sensor data, and system loads. We showed in Section 3.2 that it is appropriate to model these datasets as Brownian motions. Here we show that our approach outperforms previous approaches in terms of accuracy and efficiency. We simulated our approach using the csim simulation package [3] on an Intel Pentium 4 at 1.70GHz.

We first introduce the *fidelity* metric [30], which measures how often our predictions of pull times meet the user-specified error tolerance. Fidelity characterizes the confidence we may place in our model, and is defined as:

$$fidelity(o_i) = \frac{\text{time cache-source errors are } \leq \epsilon \ (\epsilon_r \%)}{\text{total simulation time}}$$

5.1 Adjusting σ_i On-line

As in Section 3.2, we deliberately chose highly erratic datasets, since they represent greater challenges for our method than do ordinary datasets. In particular, we must confront a paradox in the case of such highly erratic data—the *fidelity* of our approach actually degrades as we increase the error tolerance, due to rapid changes in data characteristics. Not only is σ_i high in this case, but the values of σ_i and μ_i are themselves likely to change rapidly. This effect leads to poor predictions of pull times, since the data evolution model will likely have changed significantly even before the current Δt_ϵ has expired.

Figure 3 illustrates this paradox on the highly erratic stock trace BRCM, since its fidelity drops off as we increase the error tolerance. BRCM has the extremely high β value of 3.91 (see Table 1), so its σ_i is also likely to change rapidly. As we increase the error tolerance, the interval between pulls increases. Unfortunately, the proxies can only obtain the updates of σ_i at those pull times, and the value of σ_i is likely outdated quite early in this interval, so that our predictions of next pull time is likely to be wrong.

The changing behaviour of σ_i, also known as *stochastic volatility*, has been extensively studied in Econometrics [12]. Typically, various stochastic process models are applied to $\sigma(t)$. We choose the *Hull-White (H-W)* model [12], since it is one of the simplest and very widely used. H-W models $\sigma_i^2(t)$ as a geomet-

ric Brownian motion [29]:

$$d\sigma_i^2(t) = \alpha(t)\sigma_i^2(t)\,dt + \beta(t)\sigma_i^2(t)\,dW_\sigma(t),$$

where $\alpha(t)$ and $\beta(t)$ are both time dependent coefficients, $W_\sigma(t)$ is a SBM uncorrelated with the $W(t)$ driving $S_i(t)$ (see Equation 4).

Let the proxy pull values $S_i(t_k), \mu_i(t_k), \sigma_i(t_k)$ from the server at time t_k. $\sigma_i^2(t_k)$ is a reasonable estimate of the current volatility, but will change in the next interval. We use the H-W model to estimate the expected volatility $\hat{\sigma}_i^2(t_{k+1})$ in the next interval. Using finite differences for differentials, we get

$$\hat{\sigma}_i^2(t_{k+1}) = \sigma_i^2(t_k) \cdot (\alpha(t_k)\Delta t_k + 1). \quad (11)$$

Coefficient $\alpha(t_k)$ can be estimated from the previous obtained volatilities $\sigma_i^2(t_k)$ and $\sigma_i^2(t_{k-1})$ as follows:

$$\alpha(t_k) = \frac{\sigma_i^2(t_k) - \sigma_i^2(t_{k-1})}{\sigma_i^2(t_{k-1})\Delta t_{k-1}}, \quad (12)$$

where $\Delta t_{k-1} = t_k - t_{k-1}$. Taking $\Delta t_{k-1}/\Delta t_k \approx 1$, we obtain $\hat{\sigma}_i(t_{k+1}) = \frac{\sigma_i^2(t_k)}{\sigma_i(t_{k-1})}$ from Equation 11 and 12. Now, We can calculate Δt_k as before, using the adjusted diffusion parameter $\hat{\sigma}_i(t_{k+1})$ instead of $\sigma_i(t_k)$.

5.2 Performance of Our Approach

Equipped with the σ adjustment method discussed above, we first demonstrate the *fidelity* of our approach on the three classes of streaming data with both absolute (ϵ) and relative error tolerance ($\epsilon_r\%$). We simulate each data stream as an erratic data object, and only one proxy is simulated in this experiment.

Each point in Figure 4 is the averaged fidelity over five datasets belonging to the same class of data. The fidelity achieved by our model closely matches the prespecified confidence p. For example, the average fidelity at 90% level is 89.4% for stock data ($\epsilon_r\%$), 88.4% for *temp* data (ϵ), and 89.1% for system load data ($\epsilon_r\%$). Such results suggest that our approach captures source data change patterns well, and predicts pull times well. Not surprisingly, a higher p value achieves higher fidelity, but incurs larger communication overhead, as explained below.

Figure 5 demonstrates the communication overhead incurred for maintaining stochastic consistency for different datasets. The communication overhead is measured as the number of pulls generated during the entire simulation period, and varies across the datasets, depending on the dataset's trends and fluctuation patterns. A higher p triggers more pulls, while a looser $\epsilon(\epsilon_r\%)$ triggers fewer pulls. The *total updates* curve shows the total number of data updates in the stream. The *optimal* curve shows the minimum number of pulls needed for a certain error tolerance, obtained from an off-line calculation. These two curves represent the number of pulls for a naive scheme and the optimal scheme respectively. As can be seen, the communication overhead incurred by our scheme is far less than

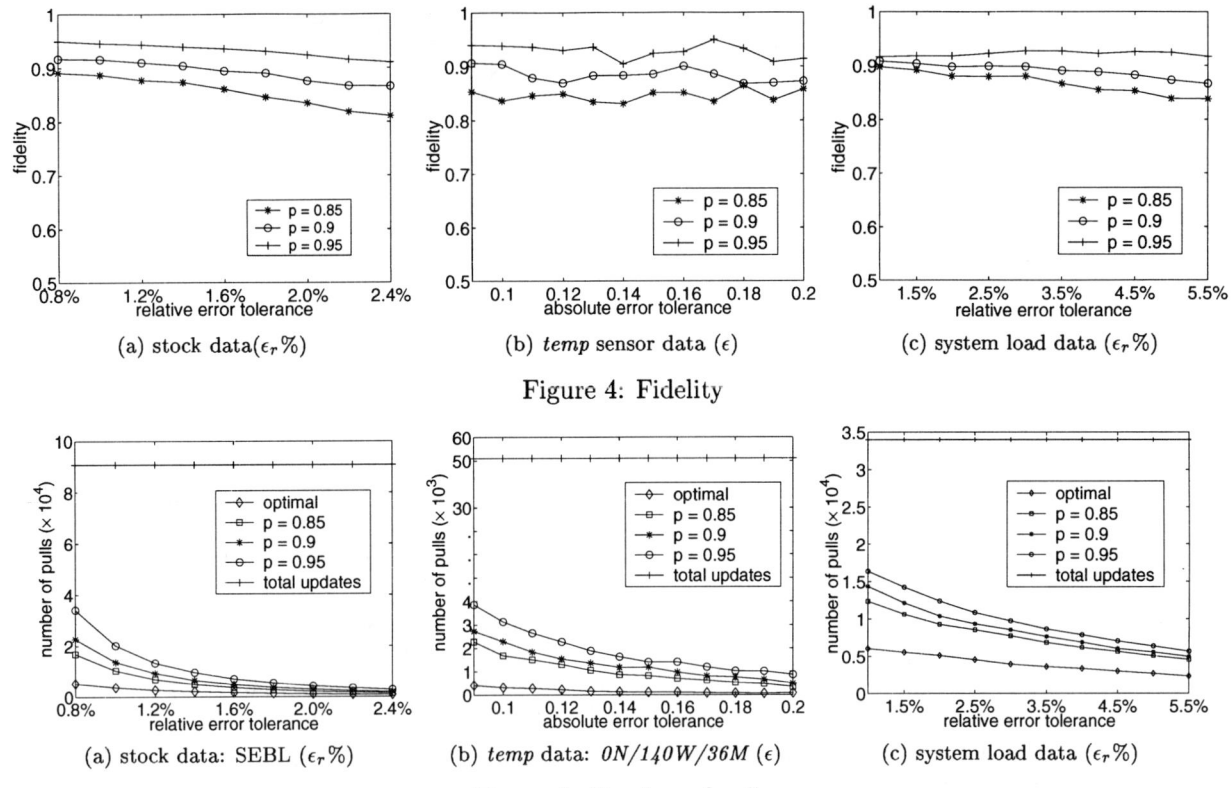

(a) stock data(ϵ_r%) (b) *temp* sensor data (ϵ) (c) system load data (ϵ_r%)

Figure 4: Fidelity

(a) stock data: SEBL (ϵ_r%) (b) *temp* data: 0N/140W/36M (ϵ) (c) system load data (ϵ_r%)

Figure 5: Number of pulls

the naive scheme and close to the optimal scheme.

5.3 Comparison with Adaptive TTL Scheme

A linear adaptive pull scheme (*Adaptive TTL*) with user-provided temporal coherency requirement was introduced in [16, 30]. Their notion of *temporal coherency requirement* is equivalent to our *error tolerance*. *TTL* (time-to-live) denotes the time interval before the current local copy is invalidated, i.e, the time before next pull. The scheme applies a linear change model on source objects. Proxies estimate the linear coefficients based on their last retrieved values and the latest calculated TTL (T_l). The next TTL is determined by a weighted combination of estimated TTL (T_{est}), the latest TTL, and the most conservative TTL thus far (T_{mr}) [16].
$T = \max(T_{min}, \min(T_{max}, a \cdot T_{mr} + (1-a) \cdot T_{dyn}))$, where $T_{dyn} = w \cdot T_{est} + (1-w) \cdot T_l$, $T_{est} = (T_l/|D_{latest} - D_{penultimate}|) \cdot \epsilon$, and $[T_{min}, T_{max}]$ denotes a static bound for the next TTL value. In [30], the authors compare *Adaptive TTL* with other pull schemes by experiments, and conclude that *Adaptive TTL* outperforms all other schemes.

We compare our scheme with *Adaptive TTL* on various stock traces, in Figure 6. An ideal scheme is such one that can achieve high fidelity with minimum number of pulls. We record the number of pulls needed by each scheme to achieve the same fidelity, and show the results for three individual stock traces (BRCM, SEBL, and QCOM). The parameters for *Adaptive TTL* are as follows: $w = 0.5$, $TTR_{min} = 0.3$, $TTR_{max} = 500$. The coefficient a is dynamically adjusted to match the fidelity achieved by our approach. Clearly, for all traces we show, to achieve the same fidelity, *Adaptive TTL* scheme requires far more pulls than our scheme, which suggests that our Brownian motion model can capture the source data characteristics much better than *Adaptive TTL*'s linear model.

6 Pull Request Scheduling at Server

Server scalability is one of our major goals, since we want to maximize the number of proxies that a server can handle. If σ_i is high, the request rate for o_i at the server will be high (see Equation 7) as well as bursty. Proxies may then experience long delays, or even receive no replies at all, if the server queue overflows. Thus, we need a scheduler which can intelligently schedule pull requests at the server, so that it guarantees prompt responses whenever possible, and minimizes the total cache-source errors across the proxies when the server is overloaded.

Paradoxically, it is as bad for the server to respond early as it is to respond late. To see this, consider a wireless client which has scheduled the next response from the server to arrive at time t_d. To save power, the client will turn off its wireless receiver, turning it on just before t_d. At time t_d, the client expects the server's response to be "fresh", that is, to contain $S(t_d), \mu(t_d)$, and $\sigma(t_d)$. If the server responds at time

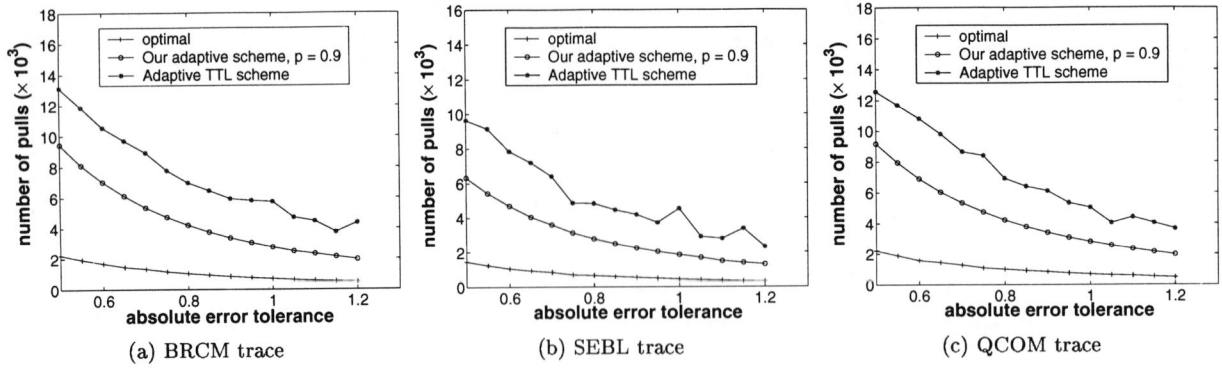

Figure 6: Comparing our approach with *Adaptive TTL* scheme on stock traces.

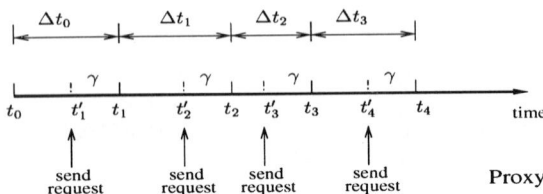

Figure 7: Our scheduling model

$t_a < t_d$, two problems arise. First, the receiver will still be off at t_a, so that this response will be missed entirely. Second, even if we assume that the response can be delivered to the client after it wakes up at t_d, the values $S(t_a), \mu(t_a)$, and $\sigma(t_a)$ will be stale, since the client requires $S(t_d), \mu(t_d)$, and $\sigma(t_d)$. The values $S(t_a)$ and $S(t_d)$ will differ by an amount determined by the DBM model. Early responses by the server cause stale values of S_i, μ_i and σ_i to be delivered at the due times, while late processing will cause cache-source errors to exceed the user-specified bound.

In this section, we introduce a novel variant of *Just-In-Time (JIT)* scheduling, in which a request must complete before its due time, *but as close to it as possible* [21]. We propose a penalty function in Section 6.2, and aim to minimize the overall penalties at any time at the server.

6.1 Scheduling Model Options

Figure 7 shows the scheduling of pull requests for object o_i from the proxy. $t_1, t_2, \cdots, t_k$ are the times the proxy is supposed to refresh the cached value. Missing these times may cause the cache-source deviation exceeds the user tolerance.

In a naive scheme, the proxy would send the $(k+1)$-th request to the server at time $t_{k+1} = t_k + \Delta t_k$, the point when the data is needed. The server processes incoming requests on FCFS basis. However, this strategy gives the server very little leeway, since it must respond hastily to each request.

Another approach would be for the proxy to notify the server as soon as it computes Δt_k, so that the server has the maximum latitude in scheduling requests. However, we have observed, the server must not respond too soon, and must effectively deliver the current value of o_i, μ_i and σ_i at time t_{k+1}. The server must keep also track of the Δt_k for a potentially large number of proxies, and can no longer be called stateless, which violates the spirit of the pull model.

Our strategy represents a good compromise. Proxies issue pull requests γ time units before they are really needed, so that the the $(k+1)$-th pull request is made at time $t_{k+1} - \gamma$ (see Figure 7). The scheduler at the server now has more flexibility in deciding when to process each request, and it retains no proxy-specific state. We show how to derive γ in section 6.4.

Request processing at the server may involve retrieval of the current object value, σ_i, and μ_i from the database, assembling *HTML* pages or *XML* documents, encrypting data, and so on. In fact, different proxies may interact with different server applications, so even for the same o_i, requests from different proxies may require different processing times. For simplicity, we assume constant network delays. Using more complex network models will be our future work.

6.2 Real-Time Scheduling Model

Each pull request, $pull(o_i)$, arriving at the server can be treated a real-time task, parametrized as $T_j(o_i, p_j, d_j)$, where p_j is T_j's processing time; d_j is its due time, $d_j = t + \gamma - \delta$, ($t$ is server's current time, and δ is the proxy-server round-trip network delay. Since the request is sent at time $t_{k+1} - \gamma$, only $\gamma - \delta$ time units are available for server processing.)

As explained before, we must start processing the request as close as possible to the due time d_j, that is, at $d_j - p_j$, to provide the proxy the latest object value and μ_i, σ_i. Such scheduling is called *Just-In-Time (JIT)* scheduling [21, 24, 25], and penalizes *earliness*, as well as *tardiness*. Tasks finish exactly on their due dates is an ideal *JIT* schedule.

We must first define a penalty function which properly penalizes both tardiness and earliness. If the server's response is tardy, arriving after t_{k+1}, the proxy must continue to estimate the object's value beyond t_{k+1} using the old drift parameter value $\mu_i(t_k)$, although the actual drift and diffusion parameters will have changed to $\mu_i(t_{k+1})$ and $\sigma_i(t_{k+1})$ by t_{k+1}.

200

Beyond time t_{k+1}, the actual data values change as $S_i(t_{k+1} + \Delta t) = S_i(t_{k+1}) + \mu_i(t_{k+1})\Delta t + \sigma_i(t_{k+1})\Delta W(t)$. However, the proxy has to continue to use $S_i(t_k)$ and $\mu_i(t_k)$ to first estimate $E[S_i(t_{k+1})]$ and then the additional change in this value during the interval Δt as $\mu_i(t_k)\Delta t$. Since t_{k+1} was chosen to make $|S_i(t_{k+1}) - E[S_i(t_{k+1})]| \leq \epsilon$, the extra cache-source value deviation will consist of two parts: a drift-induced component, $|\mu_i(t_{k+1}) - \mu_i(t_k)|\Delta t$, and a diffusion-induced component, $\sigma_i \Delta W(t)$. Since $\Delta W(t)$ is $N(0, \Delta t)$, changes in it can be expressed in terms of its standard deviation $\sqrt{\Delta t}$. Thus, if the due time and the completion time for task T_j are d_j and C_j respectively, the extra error is $|\mu_i(t_{k+1}) - \mu_i(t_k)|(C_j - d_j) + \sigma_i(t_{k+1})\sqrt{C_j - d_j}$.

On the other hand, if the server responds early, at $C_j < d_j$, the proxy receives the values $S_i(C_j), \mu_i(C_j), \sigma_i(C_j)$ at d_j. Consequently, these values are out of date by $d_j - C_j$ time units, resulting in error $\mu_i(C_j) \cdot (d_j - C_j) + \sigma_i(C_j) \cdot \sqrt{d_j - C_j}$.

If the penalty is taken to be proportional to the additional error, The following function penalizes both earliness and tardiness, and accounts for both the drift and diffusion terms. Let μ_j and σ_j are the current drift and diffusion parameters when the pull request T_j arrives the server, and μ'_j is the old drift parameter at the proxy.

$$P_j = \mu_j \max(0, d_j - C_j) + \tilde{\mu}_j \max(0, C_j - d_j) + \sigma_j \sqrt{|C_j - d_j|}, \quad (13)$$

where $\tilde{\mu}_j = |\mu_j - \mu'_j|$. The penalty is zero only when $C_j = d_j$. As C_j deviates more from d_j, more penalty will be incurred. Our goal is to minimize $\sum_j P_j$, the total penalties, at any time at the server. Since the server scheduler needs to know the old drift parameter μ'_j of each pulling proxy, the value of μ'_j should be sent to the server along with each pull request.

JIT scheduling has been well studied, and Baker et al. [21] review the literature on scheduling n tasks on single machine to minimize total earliness and tardiness penalty. Most work to date uses linear penalty functions, such as: $h_j \max(0, d_j - C_j) + w_j \max(0, C_j - d_j)$, where h_j is the early cost rate, and w_j is the tardy cost rate. It is known that minimizing an aggregate linear penalty function is NP-hard [25]. Since our version is a combination of a linear penalty and a square root penalty, it is more general, and clearly, also NP-hard. We seek heuristics to solve our problem.

6.3 An Off-Line LINSQT-ET Heuristic

Our scheduling algorithm must be efficient and on-line, since scheduling decisions have to be made as pull requests arrive. We start with the heuristic *LIN-ET* proposed for off-line scheduling with linear penalties [25].

Theorem 1. *Given n tasks, let the objective be to minimize $\sum_{j=1}^{n}(h_j \max(0, d_j - C_j) + w_j \max(0, C_j - d_j))$.*

Any adjacent pairs of tasks in the optimal sequence must satisfy

$$w_x p_y - \Omega_{xy}(w_x + h_x) \geq w_y p_x - \Omega_{yx}(w_y + h_y),$$

where task x immediately precedes task y, and Ω_{xy} and Ω_{yx} are defined as:

$$\Omega_{uv} = \begin{cases} 0 & \text{if } s_u \leq 0, \\ s_u & \text{if } 0 < s_u < p_v, \\ p_v & \text{otherwise}. \end{cases} \quad (14)$$

Here $s_u = d_u - t - p_u$ is the slack of task u, p_u is its processing time, and t is the current system time.

Proof: See [25]. □

Theorem 1 offers a necessary condition for an optimal schedule, from which the *LIN-ET* heuristic [25] is derived as follows: given n tasks at time t, they are sequenced in order of priority R_j, calculated as follows:

$$R_j(s_j) = \begin{cases} W_j & \text{if } s_j \leq 0, \\ W_j - s_j(W_j + H_j)/k\bar{p} & \text{if } 0 < s_j < k\bar{p}, \\ -H_j & \text{if } s_j \geq k\bar{p}. \end{cases} \quad (15)$$

where $W_j = w_j/p_j$, $H_j = h_j/p_j$, and $\bar{p}$ is the average processing time of n tasks, and k is called *lookahead parameter*, used to extend the scope of optimality beyond two adjacent tasks. In practice, as discussed in [25], a low k ($k = 2$, or $k = 3$) may be adequate.

LIN-ET performs quite well under various settings [25], and is computing efficient, so it is a good candidate for an on-line heuristic. Before designing the heuristic for our problem, which we will call *LINSQT-ET*, we must first reconcile our non-linear penalty function (Equation 13) with the priority representation (Equation 15) as follows.

Theorem 2. *Given n tasks, let the objective be to minimize $\sum_{j=1}^{n}(\mu_j \max(0, d_j - C_j) + \tilde{\mu}_j \max(0, C_j - d_j) + \sigma_j \sqrt{|C_j - d_j|})$. All adjacent pairs of tasks in the optimal sequence must satisfy*

$$w_x p_y - \Omega_{xy}(w_x + h_x) \geq w_y p_x - \Omega_{yx}(w_y + h_y)$$

where

$$w_x = \tilde{\mu}_x + \frac{\sigma_x}{\sqrt{|s_x|} + \sqrt{|s_x - p_y|}},$$

$$h_x = \mu_x + \frac{\sigma_x}{\sqrt{|s_x|} + \sqrt{|s_x - p_y|}}. \quad (16)$$

The other notations are as in Theorem 1.

We proved Theorem 2 in [35]. Now our scheduling problem can be mapped to the linear penalty case (Theorem 1) with weights w_x and h_x defined in Equation 16. Our heuristic *LINSQT-ET* sequences tasks in order of priority R_j defined in Equation 15, using w_j and h_j as in Equation 16.

6.4 An On-line LINSQT-ET Heuristic

The heuristic LINSQT-ET we have just described is off-line, but Algorithm 2 outlines an on-line version.

Algorithm 2 On-line LINSQT-ET heuristic

PRIO-LIST: List of tasks with $s_j < k\bar{p}$, in priority order.

On Arrival of Task T_j:
/* calculate priority of T_j: W_j is as in Equation 16 */
$T_j \cdot priority = W_j - s_j(W_j + H_j)/k\bar{p}$;
insert T_j into *PRIO-LIST*;

Task Execution:
/* when one task done, pick next task in PRIO-LIST */
loop
  if *PRIO-LIST* is not empty then
    update priorities of top h tasks in *PRIO-LIST*, and re-order them;
    T_k = *PRIO-LIST*(0);
    dequeue T_k from *PRIO-LIST*, and execute;
  else
    /* if PRIO-LIST is empty, wait for time ω. */
    $wait(\omega)$;
  end if

  for every l time units do
    /* update the whole PRIO-LIST regularly */
    update all priorities in *PRIO-LIST*;
  end for
end loop

According to Equation 15, tasks whose slack times exceed $k\bar{p}$ have the lowest priorities ($-H_j$), and are unlikely to be scheduled in the immediate future. In other words, if a task has slack time $k\bar{p}$ when it arrives, there is little danger of it having arrived later. Consequently, if δ is the network round-trip delay, a proxy needs to initiate a pull no earlier than $k\bar{p} + p_j + \delta$ time units ahead of its due time. So we can derive $\gamma = k\bar{p} + p_j + \delta$ in Figure 7.

In Algorithm 2, pending tasks are ordered by their priorities in *PRIO-LIST*. Task priority is a function of the slack time (Equation 16), and changes with time. However, updating priority values and reordering *PRIO-LIST* requires $O(n \log n)$ time. This is too expensive to perform before every scheduling decision, especially when n is large. Instead, we schedule after updating and reordering only the top h tasks in *PRIO-LIST*. However, we do update and reorder all of *PRIO-LIST* every l time units. In our experiments, we set $h = 10$ and $l = 10$ sec.

6.5 Experimental Results

We simulate our on-line *LINSQT-ET* scheduling algorithm on stock traces, and compare its performance with the FCFS-based scheduling under various workloads. FCFS scheduling is widely used in current systems, such as Apache [2]. We set the constant lookahead parameter $k = 3$. To calculate γ, proxies obtain the value of k, $\bar{p}$, and p_j the first time they contact the server. We assume each proxy caches one data object, the value of ϵ is randomly chosen from range $0.1 - 0.5$. The request processing time for each proxy is randomly drawn from the range 25ms-40ms [9].

Figure 8(a) compares FCFS and *LINSQT-ET* with respect to the fraction of time the server is overloaded, which is calculated as the percentage of total simulation time that at least one task misses its due time. As the figure shows, the server gets more overloaded as the number of proxies increases in both schemes. However, *LINSQT-ET* remains far more scalable than FCFS throughout the wide range considered. Figure 8(b) compares the two schemes with respect to the average penalties during overload. As can be seen, *LINSQT-ET* scheduling incurs significantly less penalty, and consequently less cache-source deviation than FCFS.

Figure 8(c) compares the penalties incurred by the two schemes relative to the optimal, given a certain number of pending tasks to schedule. The optimal schedule is the sequence of tasks with minimum penalties, which is computed through an off-line exhaustive search. Generally, the deviation between *LINSQT-ET* and optimal is quite low, while the deviation between FCFS and optimal becomes much larger as the number of pending tasks increases.

7 Conclusions

We have proposed *stochastic consistency*, a new model of consistency appropriate for situations when users can tolerate some error. We have also presented a novel pull-based scheme for maintaining stochastic consistency for caches holding erratic and volatile data. Our approach models changes in source data as Brownian motions, and schedules pulls from the proxy to keep errors in the cached data within user-specified error tolerance. Pulls are initiated at times determined by user error tolerance, probability confidence and data characteristics.

To guarantee high scalability and prevent the server from becoming a bottleneck, the server schedules pull requests using a new variant of *JIT* scheduling. Our variant uses a non-linear penalty function, which has not been addressed previously in the literature.

We show through simulations that our Brownian motion based scheme achieves high fidelity on stock traces, sensor data and system load data, while keeping the communication overhead low. We also compare our adaptive scheme with the *adaptive TTL* scheme in [30], and find that to achieve the same fidelity, our scheme requires much fewer pulls. We simulate the server scheduling algorithm under various workloads, and demonstrate that it far outperforms naive FCFS scheme both in scalability and overload penalties.

References

[1] http://mathworld.wolfram.com/erf.html.
[2] http://www.apache.org.
[3] http://www.mesquite.com/htmls/guides.htm.
[4] http://www.pmel.noaa.gov/tao/index.shtml.
[5] http://www.traderbot.com.
[6] Mpr/mib mote sensor hardware users manual. http://www.xbow.com/Support/Support_pdf_files/MPR-MIB_Series_User_Manual_7430-0021-05_A.pdf. Crossbow Inc.

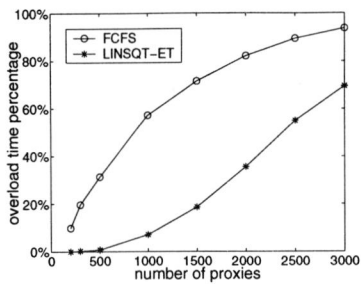 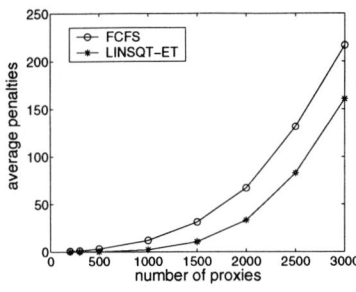 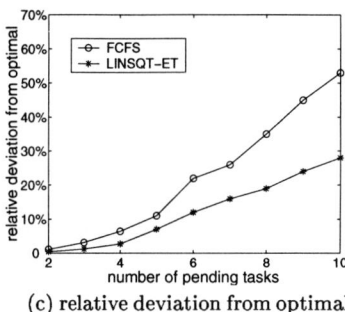

(a) fraction of time server is overloaded (b) average penalties during overload (c) relative deviation from optimal

Figure 8: Performance comparison between FCFS and *LINSQT-ET* heuristic ($p = 0.9$, $\epsilon \in [0.1, 0.5]$)

[7] S. Acharya, M. Franklin, and S. Zdonik. Disseminating updates on broadcast disks. In *Proc. of the 22nd VLDB Conf*, Mumbai, India, September 1996.

[8] S. Acharya, M. Franklin, and S. Zdonik. Balancing push and pull for data broadcast. In *Proc. of the 1997 ACM-SIGMOD Conf*, Tucson, May 1997.

[9] J. Almeida, V. Almeida, and D. Yates. Measuring the behavior of a world-wide web server. Technical Report 1996-025, 29, 1996.

[10] R. Alonso, D. Barbara, and H. G. Molina. Data caching issues in an information retrieval system. In *ACM Trans. Database Systems*, page 15(3). 1990.

[11] B. Babcock, S. Babu, M. Datar, R. Motwani, and J. Widom. Models and issues in data stream systems. In *Proc. 21th ACM SIGACT-SIGMOD-SIGART Symp. on Principle of Database Systems*, Madison, May 2002.

[12] J. Y. Campbell, A. W. Lo, and A. C. MacKinlay. *The Econometrics of Financial Markets*. Princeton University Press, 1997.

[13] J. Cho and H. C. Molina. Synchronizing a database to improve freshness. In *Proc. of the 2000 ACM-SIGMOD conference*, Dallas, May 2000.

[14] J. Cho and H. G. Molina. The evolution of the web and implications for an incremental crawler. In *Proc. of the 26th International Conference on Very Large Databases*, Cairo, Egypt, September 2000.

[15] R. B. D'Agostino and M. A. Atephens. *Goodness-of-fit Techniques*. Marcel Dekker, Inc., 1986.

[16] P. Deolasee, A. Katkar, A. Panchbudhe, K. Ramamritham, and P. Shenoy. Adaptive push-pull: Disseminating dynamic web data. In *The 10th WWW Conference*, Hong Kong, May 2001.

[17] V. Duvvuri, P. Shenoy, and R. Tewari. Adaptive leases: A strong consistency mechanism for the world wide web. In *The 19th INFOCOM Conf.*, Tel Aviv, Israel, March 2000.

[18] A. Gal and J. Eckstein. Managing periodically updated data in relational databases: A stochastic modeling approach. In *Technical Report, Rutgers University Center for Operations Research*, 2001.

[19] J. Gettys, J. Mogul, et al. Hypertext transfer protocol – http/1.1. In *RFC 2616*. 1999.

[20] R. A. Golding. *Weak-Consistency Group Communication and Membership*. PhD thesis, 1992.

[21] K.R.Baker and G.D.Scudder. Sequencing with earliness and tardiness penalties: A review. In *Operations Research*, page 38(1). 1990.

[22] R. Ladin, B. Liskov, L. Shrira, and S. Ghemawat. Providing high availability using lazy replication. *ACM Transactions on Computer Systems*, 10(4), 1992.

[23] S. Madden and M. J. Franklin. Fjording the stream: An architecture for queries over streaming sensor data. In *Proc. of the 18th ICDE Conf*, San Jose, 2002.

[24] M.R.Garey, R.E.Tarjan, and G.T.Wilfong. One-processor scheduling with symmetric earliness and tardiness penalties. In *Mathematics of Operations Research*, page 13(2). 1988.

[25] P.S.Ow and T.E.Morton. The single machine early/tardy problem. In *Management Science*, page 35(2). 1989.

[26] C. Pu and A. Leff. Replica control in distributed systems: An asynchronous approach. In *SIGMOD Conference*, 1991.

[27] S. Saroiu, K. P. Gummadi, R. Dunn, S. D. Gribble, and H. M. Levy. An analysis of internet content delivery systems. In *Proc. of the 5th OSDI Conf*, Boston, MA, December 2002.

[28] S. Shah, K. Ramamritham, and P. Shenoy. Maintaining coherency of dynamic data in cooperating repositories. In *Proc. of the 28th VLDB Conf*, Hong Kong, 2002.

[29] S.Karlin and H.M.Taylor. *A First Course in Stochastic Processes, 2nd Edition*. Academic Press, 1975.

[30] R. Srinivasan, C. Liang, and K. Ramamritham. Maintaining temporal coherency of virtual data warehouses. In *The 19th IEEE Real-Time Systems Symposium*, Madrid, Spain, December 1998.

[31] H. C. Thode. *Testing for Normality*. Marcel Dekker, Inc., 2002.

[32] O. Wolfson, S. Chamberlain, S. Dao, L. Jiang, and G. Mendez. Cost and imprecision in modeling the position of moving objects. In *Proc. of the 14th ICDE Conf*, Orlando, Florida, 1998.

[33] J. Yin, L. Alvisi, M. Dahlin, and A. Lyengar. Engineering server-driven consistency for large scale dynamic web services. In *Proc. of the 10th WWW Conf*, Hong Kong, May 2001.

[34] H. Yu and A. Vahdat. Efficient numerical error bounding for replicated network services. In *The VLDB Journal*, 2000.

[35] S. Zhu and C. Ravishankar. Stochastic consistency, and scalable pull-based caching for erratic data sources. Technical Report UCR-CS-03-85, Univ. of California, Riverside, Nov 2003. http://www.cs.ucr.edu/~szhu/stochpull.pdf.

[36] Y. Zhu and D. Shasha. Statstream: Statistical monitoring of thousands of datastreams in real time. In *Proc. of the 28th VLDB Conf*, Hong Kong, 2002.

[37] H. Zou, N. Soparkar, and F. Jahanian. Probabilistic data consistency for wide-area applications. In *Proc. of the 16th ICDE Conf*, San Diego, February 2000.

False Positive or False Negative: Mining Frequent Itemsets from High Speed Transactional Data Streams

Jeffrey Xu Yu[1], Zhihong Chong[2], Hongjun Lu[3], Aoying Zhou[2]

[1] The Chinese University of Hong Kong, Hong Kong, China, yu@se.cuhk.edu.hk
[2] Fudan University, Shanghai, China, {zhchong,ayzhou}@fudan.edu.cn
[3] The Hong Kong University of Science and Technology, Hong Kong, China, luhj@cs.ust.hk

Abstract

The problem of finding frequent items has been recently studied over high speed data streams. However, mining frequent itemsets from transactional data streams has not been well addressed yet in terms of its bounds of memory consumption. The main difficulty is due to the nature of the exponential explosion of itemsets. Given a domain of I unique items, the possible number of itemsets can be up to $2^I - 1$. When the length of data streams approaches to a very large number N, the possibility of an itemset to be frequent becomes larger and difficult to track with limited memory. However, the real killer of effective frequent itemset mining is that most of existing algorithms are false-positive oriented. That is, they control memory consumption in the counting processes by an error parameter ϵ, and allow items with support below the specified minimum support s but above $s - \epsilon$ counted as frequent ones. Such false-positive items increase the number of false-positive frequent itemsets exponentially, which may make the problem computationally intractable with bounded memory consumption. In this paper, we developed algorithms that can effectively mine frequent item(set)s from high speed transactional data streams with a bound of memory consumption. While our algorithms are false-negative oriented, that is, certain frequent itemsets may not appear in the results, the number of false-negative itemsets can be controlled by a predefined parameter so that desired recall rate of frequent itemsets can be guaranteed. We developed algorithms based on Chernoff bound. Our extensive experimental studies show that the proposed algorithms have high accuracy, require less memory, and consume less CPU time. They significantly outperform the existing false-positive algorithms.

1 Introduction

Recently, data streams emerged as a new data type that attracted great attention from both researchers and practitioners. A data stream is essentially a virtually unbounded sequence of data items arriving at a rapid rate. Since data items arrive continuously, it is only feasible to store certain form of synopsis (in memory or disk) rather than the raw data for analysis or information extraction. It is also infeasible to multiple scan the original data to build such synopsis because of the massive volume as well as the rapid arrival rate. Research work related to data streams boils down to the problem of finding the right form of synopsis and related construction algorithms so that the required statistics or patterns can be obtained with a bounded error for unbounded input data items with limited memory. A large amount of work has been reported for various statistics and patterns, including simple aggregates and statistics such as maximum, minimum, average, median values and quantiles as well as complex patterns such as decision trees, clusters, and frequent itemsets.

In this paper we study the problem of mining frequent item(set)s (or pattern) from high speed *transactional data streams*. Manku and Motwani gave an excellent review of wide range applications for the problem of frequent data stream pattern mining [12]. The problem can be stated as follows. Let $I = \{x_1, x_2, \cdots, x_n\}$ be a set of items. An itemset is a subset of items I. A transactional data stream, $\mathcal{D}$, is a sequence of incoming transactions, $(t_1, t_2, \cdots, t_N)$, where a transaction t_i is an itemset and N is a unknown large number of transactions that will arrive. The number of transactions in $\mathcal{D}$ that contain X is called the support of X, denoted as $sup(X)$. An itemset X is a frequent pattern, if and only if $sup(X) \geq sN$, where $s = sup(X)/N$ is a threshold called a minimum support such that $s \in (0, 1)$. The *frequent data stream pattern mining*, denoted FDPM, is to find an *approximate* set of frequent patterns (itemsets) in $\mathcal{D}$ with respect to a given support threshold, s. The approximation is controlled by two parameters, ϵ and δ, where ϵ ($\in (0,1)$) controls errors and δ ($\in (0,1)$) controls reliability. We call it (ϵ, δ) approximation scheme.

Permission to copy without fee all or part of this material is granted provided that the copies are not made or distributed for direct commercial advantage, the VLDB copyright notice and the title of the publication and its date appear, and notice is given that copying is by permission of the Very Large Data Base Endowment. To copy otherwise, or to republish, requires a fee and/or special permission from the Endowment.

Proceedings of the 30th VLDB Conference, Toronto, Canada, 2004

The challenge is to devise algorithms to support (ϵ, δ) approximation for the FDPM problem with a bound regarding space complexity. The main difficulty is the nature of the exponential explosion of frequent patterns mining. For data streams, the incoming transactions will not be stored, and we can only scan them once. If counts are required for each itemsets, an application with m distinct items will require $2^m - 1$ counts. Even with a moderate set of items, for example $m = 1,000$. The total number of itemsets is $2^m - 1 = 2^{1000} - 1$, which is obviously intractable.

A simple version of FDPM problem, that is, mining frequent items but not itemsets, has been recently widely studied in data stream environments with bounded memory [2, 3, 5, 6, 7, 9, 10, 12]. After a careful study of these published work, we observed that, while the detailed algorithms are different, almost all of them are *false-positive* oriented approaches. That is, given a minimum support s, they control memory consumption in the counting processes by an error parameter ϵ, and allow items with support below the specified minimum support s but above $s - \epsilon$ counted as frequent ones.

In this paper, we argue that since frequent item mining is the first step in frequent itemsets mining, even a small number of false-positive items, resulted from the false-positive oriented item counting, could lead to a large number of false-positive itemsets, which makes efficient and effective frequent itemsets mining infeasible. This motivated us to develop a false-negative oriented approach for frequent items mining. In addition, to further address the problem caused by explosion of frequent itemsets, we explored a tight bound to control the counting process for frequent item(set)s mining. As a summary, our contribution can be summarized as follows.

- While most existing work follows the approach of false-positive oriented frequent item counting, we show that false-negative oriented approach that allows a controlled number of frequent itemsets missing from the output is a more promising solution for mining frequent itemsets from high speed transactional data streams.

- We developed the first set of one-scan false-negative oriented algorithms which significantly outperform the existing false-positive oriented approaches for frequent itemsets mining as well as frequent items mining. We also derived memory bounds for both cases.

- Most existing approaches use the error parameter for two purposes which are conflict: quality control (ϵ) and memory size control ($1/\epsilon$ or $1/\epsilon^2$), which leads to a dilemma: a little increase of ϵ will make the number of false-positive items large, and a little decrease of ϵ will make memory consumption large. Our algorithms adopt a (ϵ, δ) approximation scheme with $\epsilon = 0, \delta > 0$ that decouples the two interrelated but conflict purposes and makes the parameter setting of the mining process easier.

The remainder of the paper is organized as follows. Section 2 analyzes the false-positive and false-negative approaches in frequent item(set)s mining. Section 3 and 4 present our frequent items mining algorithm, and the results of performance study. Section 5 and 6 present our frequent itemsets mining algorithm, and the results of performance study. Section 7 concludes the paper.

2 False-Positive versus False-Negative

Due to the little space allowed to mine frequent data stream patterns, the key point becomes how to prune those potentially infrequent patterns and how to maintain potentially frequent patterns with probabilistic guarantees [11]. Approximate mining frequent patterns with probabilistic guarantee can take two possible approaches, namely, false-positive oriented and false-negative oriented. The former includes some infrequent patterns in the final result, whereas the latter misses some frequent patterns.

There are a large number of publications on the false-positive oriented approaches [2, 3, 5, 6, 7, 9, 10, 12], and there is no reported study on one-scan false-negative oriented approach. All false-positive oriented approaches focused on frequent items mining, rather than frequent itemsets mining. In [12], as the first attempt, Manku and Motwani also studied false-positive oriented frequent itemsets mining in a less theoretical nature and with a focus on system-level issues.

2.1 Deficiency of False-Positive Oriented Approaches

Because the focus of this paper is on frequent itemsets mining, we concentrate ourselves on frequent itemsets mining, and we mainly address it in comparison with the algorithms proposed by Manku and Motwani [12].

In [12], Manku and Motwani developed two false-positive oriented algorithms for frequent items counting, Sticky-Sampling and Lossy-Counting. The Sticky-Sampling uses $O(\frac{1}{\epsilon} \log(s^{-1}\delta^{-1}))$ expected number of entries, and Lossy-Counting uses $O(\frac{1}{\epsilon} \log(\epsilon N))$ entries. In theory, Sticking-Sampling requires constant space, while Lossy-Counting requires space that grows logarithmically with N. In practice, as shown in [12], Sticky-Sampling performs worse because of its tendency to remember unique items sampled. Lossy-Counting can prune low frequency items quickly and keep only high frequent items. Based on this fact, Manku and Motwani give a Lossy-Counting based three module system (Buffer-Trie-SetGen) for mining frequent itemsets in a less theoretical nature. The main features of their algorithms include (1) All item(set)s whose true frequency exceeds sN are output, (2) no item(set)s whose true frequency is less than $(s - \epsilon)N$ is output, and (3) estimated frequencies are less than the true frequencies by at most ϵ.

In the following, without loss of generality, we address our false-negative approach in comparison with the Lossy-Counting algorithm and the Buffer-Trie-SetGen approach.

Remark 1 *Like Sticky-Sampling, Lossy-Counting is false-positive oriented and is ϵ-deficient. The parameter ϵ is coupled with two conflict goals. First, let f_ϵ be the number of items in $[s-\epsilon, s]$. Then $f_\epsilon \geq f_{\epsilon'}$ if $\epsilon > \epsilon'$. The smaller ϵ is, a less number of false-positive items are included in the result set. Second, because the memory consumption is a factor of $1/\epsilon$, the memory consumption increases reciprocally in terms of ϵ.*

The Remark 1 states the dilemma of false-positive oriented approaches (ϵ-deficient). The memory consumption increases reciprocally in terms of ϵ where ϵ controls the error bound. It is difficult to decouple the two functions, memory consumption control and error control, from the error bound ϵ. In Sticky-Sampling, ϵ is used to determine a sampling rate, and in Lossy-Counting, ϵ is used to determine the bucket width. Changing their ways of dealing with ϵ means to change the worst case space-complexity analysis.

The impacts of parameter ϵ will be even great when frequent itemsets mining is concerned, which is in fact related to the fundamental issue on application of Apriori property [1]. The Apriori property states: if any length k pattern is not frequent in a dataset, its length (k+1)-th super-patterns can never be frequent. In other words, the Apriori property suggests to use possibly smallest k-th frequent itemsets to generate the (k+1)-th candidate itemsets, and then mine the (k+1)-th candidate itemsets. The false-positive oriented approaches allow 1-itemsets with support below s but above $s-\epsilon$ counted as frequent. Consequently, when there are some false-positive 1-itemsets in $[s-\epsilon, s]$, the nature of the exponential explosion makes the number of potential frequent itemsets be very large and makes false-positive oriented approaches difficult to manage it.

2.2 Our False-Negative Oriented Approach: ϵ-Decoupling

False-positive oriented approaches have their limit to support frequent item(set)s mining. One of the main difficulties is caused by the conflicts of the error parameter ϵ as stated in Remark 1. In this paper, we decouple the two conflict functions of the error parameter ϵ as follows.

- **Error Control and Pruning**: We use an effective ϵ to control error bound, which is *changeable* and is not fixed. The effective value of ϵ becomes smaller while more data items are received from a data stream. In brief, we compute the effective value of ϵ using minimum support s (user given), reliability δ (user given), and the number of observations n (variable), where ϵ is reciprocal to n. The effective value of ϵ approaches to zero when the number of observations increases. Therefore, the frequent item(set)s mining becomes more accurate. It is important to note that we use ϵ to prune data but do not use it to control memory.

- **Memory Control**: We use the reliability δ instead of ϵ to control memory consumption. Different from false-positive oriented approaches whose memory consumption is determined by $1/\epsilon$, the memory consumption in our algorithms is related to $\ln(1/\delta)$. Consider the same memory space using either ϵ or δ, we have $1/\epsilon = \ln(1/\delta)$. For getting the same memory space, when $\epsilon = 0.1$, $\delta = 0.00005$; when $\epsilon = 0.01$, $\delta = 3.7 \times 10^{-44}$. Because in practice, $\delta = 0.0001$, our approach can significantly reduce the memory consumption and processing cost for frequent item(set)s mining, while achieving high accuracy. We will discuss bounds for frequent item(set)s mining later.

Our approach does not allow 1-itemsets with support below s counted as frequent, and therefore is a false-negative oriented approach. We will give the details of our approach, and show that the possibility of missing frequent item(set)s is considerably small later in this paper.

Our one-scan false-negative oriented approach is different from Toivonen's two-scan false-negative oriented approach [13]. In brief, Toivonen's algorithm is to pick a random sample and find all association rules using this sample that probably hold in the whole dataset in one pass, and to verify the results with the rest of the dataset. It allows false-negative with probabilistic guarantees, and the sample size can be at least $O((\frac{c}{\epsilon^2}\log(\delta^{-1})))$. One of the problem of the Toivonen's algorithm is that, because the error parameter ϵ can be very small, the memory consumption using Toivonen's algorithm can be very large ($1/\epsilon^2$). We summarized some bounds in Table 1 for comparison. Note, in Table 1, as a false-positive approach, GroupTest does not rely on ϵ. But it requests the knowledge of the domain of a data stream, which is difficult to obtain beforehand.

2.3 Frequent Itemsets Mining: A Comparison

To verify our analysis, we conducted experiments to study the impacts of a large number of itemsets in the range of $[s-\epsilon, s+\epsilon]$ on frequent itemsets mining. We report here one of the experiments. We generated a data stream of length 1,000K which has an average transaction size 15 and maximal potentially frequent itemset size 6, with 10K unique items. We implemented the Lossy-Counting based frequent itemset mining approach, denoted as BTS (Buffer-Trie-SetGen) [12]. With $\epsilon = \frac{s}{10}$ and $\delta = 0.1$, we obtained results as shown in Table 2. To measure the quality, we use two metrics, recall and precision, that are defined as follows. Given a set of true frequent itemsets A and a set of obtained frequent itemsets B, the recall is $\frac{|A \cap B|}{|A|}$ and the precision is $\frac{|A \cap B|}{|B|}$.

s (%)	True Size	Mined Size	Recall	Precision
0.08	21,361	126,307	1.00	0.17
0.10	12,252	68,275	1.00	0.18
0.20	2,359	23,154	1.00	0.16

Table 2: Impact of false positives in BTS

In Table 2, the first column is the minimum support (s), and the second is the true size of frequent

Algorithm	Type	Space
Charikar et al [3]	False-Positive	$O(\frac{k}{\epsilon^2}\log(n/\delta))$
Sticky-Sampling [12]	False-Positive	$O(\frac{1}{\epsilon}\log(s^{-1}\delta^{-1}))$
Lossy-Counting [12]	False-Positive	$O(\frac{1}{\epsilon}\log(\epsilon N))$
GroupTest [6]	False-Positive	$O(k(\log(k)+\log(\delta^{-1}))\log(M))$
Toivonen [13]	False-Negative	$O((\frac{c}{\epsilon^2}\log(\delta^{-1}))$
FDPM-1 (this paper)	False-Negative	$O((2+2\ln(2/\delta))/s)$

Table 1: Theoretical Memory Bounds

itemsets($|A|$). The next three columns are a summary for the quality of BTS using minimum support s. The first of the three columns is the result size ($|B|$). The second and third columns of the three columns are its recall and precision. It can be seen that the sizes of obtained results are about 10 times larger than the true size. All the three recalls are 1, which means that the obtained results contain all the true frequent itemsets. All the three precisions are less than 0.2, which means that the obtained results contain a large number of itemsets below s but above $s - \epsilon$. The number of false positive is large, and its impact is significant in two ways: i) the quality of mining result is low, and ii) the memory needed at run time is even larger accordingly.

Astute readers may suggest to turn a false-positive algorithm into a false-negative one for frequent itemset mining. That is, for user given s and ϵ, we can deliberately use $s + \epsilon$ as the minimum support to mine the frequent itemset so that the output will contain only those frequent itemsets with support greater than s but some of frequent itemsets between s and $s + \epsilon$ may not be in the output, which makes the algorithm false-negative. We implemented such idea and obtained results as shown in Table 3. Note, the true frequent itemsets in Table 2 and Table 3 are the same. We can see that, in Table 3, the precisions become 1.0 as there are no false-positive. However, the recall rate drops 15-26% that seems unsatisfactory low.

s (%)	True Size	Mined Size	Recall	Precision
0.08	21,361	18,351	0.86	1.00
0.10	12,252	10,411	0.85	1.00
0.20	2,359	1,739	0.74	1.00

Table 3: Impact of false negatives: BTS($s+\epsilon$) where $\epsilon = s/10$.

We tested our false-negative oriented approach. For the same minimum support (s) in Table 2, with $\epsilon = s/10$ and $\delta = 0.1$, we achieve 0.99 recall and 1.0 precision in all the setting. Recall: BTS does not perform well, because there are many itemsets in $[s-\epsilon, s+\epsilon]$ (Table 2). In order to test whether our false-negative oriented approach misses itemsets, we used the same setting as Table 2 but set minimum support to be $s - \epsilon$ instead, and tested if we miss many itemsets in $[s-\epsilon, s+\epsilon]$. We found that we can still achieve 0.99 recall and 1.0 precision in all the setting.

As a conclusion, we believe that contrary to most existing approaches, the false-negative oriented approach is more promising to solve the FDPM problem.

3 Mining Frequent Items from a Data Stream

In this section, we focus on frequent items mining, and discuss Chernoff bound [4], our basic approach and algorithm. We will discuss frequent itemsets mining in Section 5.

3.1 Chernoff Bound

Suppose there is a sequence of observations, $o_1, o_2, \cdots, o_n, o_{n+1}, \cdots$. Chernoff bound gives us certain probabilistic guarantees on the estimation of statistics about the underlying data, that generates these observations, based on the n observations obtained so far. Consider the sequence of observations, $o_1, o_2, \cdots, o_n$, as n independent Bernoulli trails (coin flips) such that $Pr[o_i = 1] = p, Pr[o_i = 0] = 1 - p$ for a probability p. Let r be the number of heads in the n coin flips. The expectation of r is np. Chernoff bound states, for any $\gamma > 0$,

$$Pr\{|r - np| \geq np\gamma\} \leq 2e^{\frac{-np\gamma^2}{2}}$$

Let $\bar{r}$ be r/n, and consider the minimum support s as the probability p. The above equation becomes

$$Pr\{|\bar{r} - s| \geq s\gamma\} \leq 2e^{\frac{-ns\gamma^2}{2}}$$

Further, we replace $s\gamma$ with ϵ.

$$Pr\{|\bar{r} - s| \geq \epsilon\} \leq 2e^{\frac{-n\epsilon^2}{2s}} \qquad (1)$$

Let the right side of Equation (1) be δ. We see that, with probability $\leq \delta$, the running average $\bar{r}$ is beyond $\pm\epsilon$ of s, where

$$\epsilon = \sqrt{\frac{2s\ln(2/\delta)}{n}} \qquad (2)$$

FDPM can be considered as an application of Chernoff bound as follows. Given a sequence of 1-item transactions, $\mathcal{D} = t_1, t_2, \cdots, t_n, t_{n+1}, \cdots, t_N$, where n is the number of first n transactions being observed such as $n \ll N$. For a pattern X, its running support up to n is $\overline{sup}(X)$ and its true support up to N is $sup(X)$. By replacing $\bar{r}$ with $\overline{sup}(X)/n$ and r with $s (= sup(X)/N)$, respectively, we can make the following statement. For a pattern X, when n observations have been made, the running support of X is beyond $\pm\epsilon$ of s with probability $\leq \delta$. In other words, the running support of X is within $\pm\epsilon$ of s with probability

$\geq 1 - \delta$.

Consider $s = 0.1$, $\delta = 0.1$ and $\epsilon = 0.01$. With Chernoff bound, $n \approx 5,991$ (Equation (2)). This implies the following for a pattern X. If we have about 5,991 observations, its true value $sup(X)/N$ is in the range of $(\overline{sup}(X)/n - 0.01, \overline{sup}(X)/n + 0.01)$ with high probability 0.9.

3.2 The Basic Approach

Based on the Chernoff bound, we group arrival items into two groups, namely potentially infrequent patterns and potentially frequent patterns. They are defined as follows.

Definition 1 *Given n observations, a running error ϵ_n in term of n can be obtained (Eq. (2)). A pattern X is potential infrequent if $\overline{sup}(X)/n < s - \epsilon_n$ in terms of n. A pattern X is potential frequent if it is not potential infrequent in terms of n.*

The conditions for determining potential infrequent pattern can be represented alternatively as $\overline{sup}(X) < (s - \epsilon_n)n$ for a given n observations. A pattern X is potential frequent if $\overline{sup}(X) \geq (s - \epsilon_n)n$.

It is important to note that ϵ_n is not the user-specified parameter ϵ but a running variable. The running error ϵ_n decreases, while the number of observations n increases. When n becomes a very large number N, $\epsilon_n \approx 0$. Therefore, $\overline{sup}(X) \approx sN$.

Remark 2 *Our algorithm is false-negative oriented and is a $(0, \delta)$ approximate scheme.*

Remark 3 *For a given minimum support s and reliability δ. The memory consumption is bounded in terms of the number of observations, and is much less than the number of observations in practice.*

The Remark 3 states the fact that the same transactions may appear many times in a transactional data stream. As discussed later, our bound does not rely on the user-specified error ϵ, but on a running error ϵ_n which decreases while the number of observations n increases.

3.3 Mining Frequent Items

Our algorithm for mining frequent items from a data stream, denoted FDPM-1, is outlined in Algorithm 1, which takes s and δ as inputs. Note that we do not take ϵ as input. Algorithm 1 makes use of the Chernoff bound. In line 1, n_0 is the required number of observations, which is given below.

$$n_0 = \frac{2 + 2\ln(2/\delta)}{s} \quad (3)$$

We will show how we determine n_0 later, which in fact is the memory bound. Now, when we receive a transaction t from a 1-itemset transactional data stream, we check whether it exists in the pool of P. If it exits, we increase its count by 1 (line 4-5). Otherwise, we insert t into P if the number of entries in P is less

---

Algorithm 1 FDPM-1(s, δ)

1: let n_0 be the required number of observations (Eq. (3));
2: $n \leftarrow 0, P \leftarrow \emptyset$;
3: **while** a new transaction t arrives **do**
4:   **if** $t \in P$ **then**
5:     increase t's count by 1;
6:   **else**
7:     **if** $|P| > n_0$ **then**
8:       calculate the running ϵ_n for the n observations;
9:       delete all entries in P that are potentially infrequent;
10:     **end if**
11:     insert t with an initial count 1 into P;
12:   **end if**
13:   $n \leftarrow n + 1$;
14:   output P on demand;
15: **end while**

---

than n_0. When P becomes full ($P \geq n_0$) (line 7), we prune potential infrequent patterns X in P based on Definition 1.

We output the mining results (P) only when there is such a demand at line 14. Note: we do not initially allocate memory for keeping n_0 entries in P. We increase the size of P incrementally.

Theorem 1 *Algorithm 1 finds frequent 1-itemsets in a data stream, with two parameters s and δ. Algorithm 1 ensures the followings, when data is independent.*

(a) All items whose true frequency exceeds sN are output with probability of at least $1 - \delta$.

(b) No items whose true frequency is less than sN are output.

(c) The probability of the estimated support that equals the true support is no less than $1 - \delta$.

(d) The bound on memory space is $(2 + 2\ln(2/\delta))/s$ when the Chernoff bound is used.

The proof of Theorem 1 is sketched below.

First, the first three properties (a), (b) and (c) can be directly derived from the Chernoff bound. When n transactions have been received, the true support of a pattern X, $sup(X)/N$, for $N \gg n$, is within $\pm \epsilon_n$ of the running support $\overline{sup}(X)/n$ when the Chernoff bound is used. Recall ϵ_n approaches 0 when the number of observations n increases. Because we prune potential infrequent patterns whose true support is not in the given range with probability δ, the probability of pruning a frequent pattern is at most δ. Therefore, the probability of the estimated support that equals the true support is no less than $1 - \delta$.

Second, we show the proof for the property (d) when the Chernoff bound is concerned. As shown in Algorithm 1, P always keeps all potential frequent patterns

X such that $\overline{sup}(X) \geq (s - \epsilon_n)n$, when n transactions have been received. Therefore, $|P| \leq 1/(s - \epsilon_n)$, when $s - \epsilon_n > 0$, otherwise $|P| \cdot (s - \epsilon_n)n > n$, which is impossible. let $|P| = n = 1/(s - \epsilon_n)$. We have the following equation.

$$n = \frac{1}{s - \epsilon_n} = \frac{1}{s - \sqrt{\frac{2s\ln(2/\delta)}{n}}} \qquad (4)$$

Solve the equation, we get

$$n = \frac{2 + 2\ln(2/\delta)}{s} \qquad (5)$$

as the proof of the last property (d) of Theorem 1.

The last property of Theorem 1 is proved for the minimum number of observations. As an example, suppose $s = 0.001$, $\epsilon = s/10$ and $\delta = 0.1$. The memory bound is $n_0 = 7,991$. Consider ϵ_n as follows. When $n \leq n_0$, $\epsilon_n = 0$, because all items can be kept in the pool. When $n = 7,992 (= n_0 + 1)$, $\epsilon_n = 0.000866$ (the largest possible error). When $n = 100,000$, $\epsilon_n = 0.000245$. When $n = 1,000,000$, $\epsilon_n = 0.000077$.

We discuss the time complexity regarding Algorithm 1 in brief. In Algorithm 1, the cost for inserting a new item is $O(1)$. The cost for one pruning is $O(1)$ because we only maintain n_0 items. The maximum number of pruning is at most N/n_0 where N is the length of the data stream.

Algorithm 1 is designed on top of the Chernoff bound which assumes data independent. In reality, data in a data stream is highly possible to be dependent. When data is dependent in a transactional data stream, the quality of Algorithm 1 cannot be guaranteed. Several approaches can be taken to handle data dependent data streams. One is to conduct random sampling with a reservoir [14], as indicated in [12]. The technique of random sampling with a reservoir is, in one sequential pass, to select a random sample of n records without replacement from a pool of N records where N is unknown [14]. With this technique, we can handle a data dependent data stream as a data independent data stream. In [8], a probabilistic-inplace algorithm was introduced to handle different distributions. Given m counters, the probabilistic-inplace algorithm reserves $m/2$ to store the current best candidates, and uses the unreserved $m/2$ to monitor network traffic. For every run, the probabilistic-inplace algorithm replaces the $m/2$ reserved counters with the top out of all m counters. With this technique, we can divide a transactional data stream into segments and apply Algorithm 1 to segments one-by-one continuously. The length of each segment is $k \cdot n_0$ where k is a positive number and n_0 is the smallest number of observations. The memory required is $2n_0$ – one for reserving potentially frequent patterns and the other for monitoring a segment.

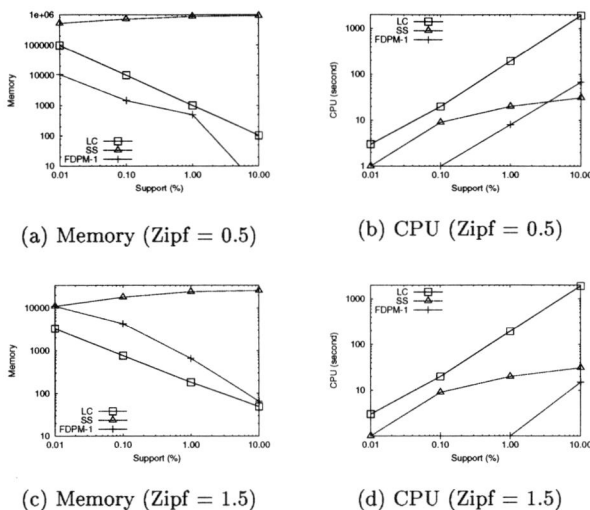

(a) Memory (Zipf = 0.5)   (b) CPU (Zipf = 0.5)

(c) Memory (Zipf = 1.5)   (d) CPU (Zipf = 1.5)

Figure 1: The effectiveness of s ($\epsilon = s/10$, $\delta = 0.1$)

4 Performance Study I: Mining Frequent Items

We report our experimental results for frequent items mining in this section. For frequent items mining, we implemented our false-negative oriented algorithm FDPM-1 (Algorithm 1). We also implemented false-positive oriented algorithms, Lossy-Counting [12] and Sticky Sampling [12], and denote them as LC and SS, respectively. For testing frequent items mining, we generate 1-itemset transactional data streams using Zipf distribution.

We implemented all the frequent item(set)s mining algorithms using Microsoft Visual C++ Version 6.0. We used the same data structures and subroutines in all implementations, in order to minimize any performance differences caused by minor differences in implementation. We conducted all testings (Section 4 and Section 6) on a 1.7GHz CPU Dell PC with 1GB memory. Because the memory size is 1GB, there were no I/Os in all our testings. We report our results in terms of memory consumption (the number of counters) and CPU time (seconds), as well as the recall and precision.

4.1 Data Distribution

We first test two data sets of length 1000K using two Zipf factors, 0.5 and 1.5. We compare the three algorithms: CL, SS, and FDPM-1, by varying s, where $\epsilon = s/10$ and $\delta = 0.1$. The memory and CPU are shown in Figure 1. In both cases, SS consumes the largest memory for different s. Different from SS, the memory consumption of both LC and FDPM-1 decreases while s increases. It is interesting to note that when Zipf = 0.5, FDPM-1 outperforms LC in terms of memory consumption. On the other hand, when Zipf = 1.5, LC outperforms FDPM-1 in terms of memory consumption. In terms of CPU time, FDPM-1 outperforms LC in all the cases.

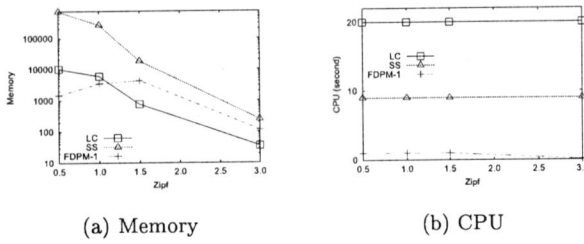

(a) Memory (b) CPU

Figure 2: Effectiveness of Zipf factors

Some explanations can be made below. When Zipf = 0.5, the data distribution is near uniform. Because of uniform distribution, there are only a small number of items whose support is greater than the minimum support s. LC and SS need more memory to maintain items in a rather sparse data stream. FDPM-1 prunes items using the running error ϵ_n. While n increases, ϵ_n approaches zero, and it allows us to track those near s items with less memory consumption. When Zipf = 1.5, data is more skewed, and the number of unique items is less. FDPM-1 cannot prune as it does when Zipf = 0.5. LC can effectively prune items whose support is less than $s - \epsilon$. The recall and precision for Zipf = 1.5 are given in Table 4. FDPM-1 achieves 100% recall and 100% precision. SS and LC ensure recall to be 100%, but allow precision to be down to (91%, 92%), despite the fact that the patterns are skewed.

s (%)	LC R	LC P	SS R	SS P	FDPM-1 R	FDPM-1 P
0.01	1	0.91	1	0.91	1	1
0.1	1	0.96	1	0.96	1	1
1	1	0.92	1	0.92	1	1
10	1	1	1	1	1	1

Table 4: Varying s (Zipf = 1.5)

In order to investigate the effectiveness of Zipf distribution, we fix $s = 0.1\%$, $\epsilon = s/10$, and $\delta = 0.1$, and test different Zipf factors. The results are shown in Figure 2 in which there is turn over when Zipf is about 1.25 (Figure 2 (a)). When Zipf is less than 1.25, FDPM-1 consumes less memory than LC. FDPM-1 performs best in terms of CPU cost. The recall and precision are shown in Table 5. When Zipf = 0.5, $s = 0.1\%$, no frequent items can be found. When Zipf = 1.0, the precisions of LC and SS are even down to 0.87. FDPM-1 ensures high recall and precision.

Zipf	LC R	LC P	SS R	SS P	FDPM-1 R	FDPM-1 P
0.5	-	-	-	-	-	-
1.0	1	0.87	1	0.87	0.99	1
1.5	1	0.96	1	0.96	1	1
3.0	1	1	1	1	1	1

Table 5: Varying Zipf factors

s (%)	LC R	LC P	SS R	SS P	FDPM-1 R	FDPM-1 P
0.010	1	0.79	1	0.79	1	1
0.009	1	0.73	1	0.73	1	1
0.008	1	0.79	1	0.79	1	1
0.007	1	0.80	1	0.80	1	1
0.006	1	0.82	1	0.82	1	1
0.005	1	0.80	1	0.80	1	1
0.004	1	0.78	1	0.78	1	1

Table 6: Sliding Window (Zipf = 0.5)

s (%)	LC R	LC P	SS R	SS P	FDPM-1 R	FDPM-1 P
0.010	1	0.91	1	0.91	1	1
0.009	1	0.95	1	0.95	1	1
0.008	1	0.92	1	0.92	1	1
0.007	1	0.96	1	0.96	1	1
0.006	1	0.93	1	0.93	1	1
0.005	1	0.93	1	0.93	1	1
0.004	1	0.93	1	0.93	1	1

Table 7: Sliding Window (Zipf = 1.5)

4.2 Critical Region Testing

In this section, we further conduct several testing to test a critical region of $[s - \epsilon, s]$. Suppose that many frequent items reside in the critical region. LC and SS may suffer if they use s and ϵ to mine, because it is most likely to include many false-positive and affect the precision. On the other hand, FDPM-1 may suffer if it uses $s - \epsilon$ to mine, because it is most likely to miss items.

First, with a window size $\epsilon = 0.00001$, we slide the minimum support starting from $s = 0.01\%$ to $s - i \cdot \epsilon$ where $i = 1, 2, \cdots, 6$, and test two data streams with Zipf = 0.5 and Zipf = 1.5. The recall and precision are shown in Table 6 and Table 7. Both LC and SS perform in a similar way. When data is not skewed (Zipf = 0.5), LC and SS are easier to include false-positives. FDPM-1 reaches 100% recall and 100% precision in all the cases.

Second, we identify a region with $[s - \epsilon, s]$ using the data stream of Zipf = 1.5 where LC and SS perform well. We artificially move frequent items from $(s, 1]$ to $[s - \epsilon, s]$. where $s = 0.1\%$ and $\epsilon = s/10$. We test LC and SS using s as the minimum support, and test FDPM-1 using $s - \epsilon$ as the minimum support. The recall and precision are shown in Table 8. As expected, the precision of LC and SS decreases while more items reside in $[s - \epsilon, s]$. But, FDPM-1 is insensitive to the number of items in the critical region.

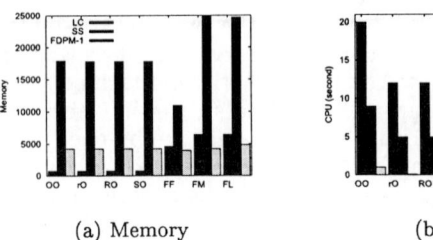

(a) Memory (b) CPU

Figure 3: Effectiveness of data arrival order

210

$[s-\epsilon, s]$	$(s, 1]$	LC		SS		FDPM-1
		R	P	R	P	R	P
25	247	1	0.91	1	0.91	1	1
73	200	1	0.74	1	0.74	1	1
123	150	1	0.55	1	0.55	1	1
173	100	1	0.36	1	0.36	1	1
223	50	1	0.17	1	0.17	1	1

Table 8: Critical Region: Test LC/SS with $s = 0.1\%$, and test FDPM-1 with $s = 0.09\%$ where $\epsilon = s/10$, $\delta = 0.1$, Zipf $= 1.5$

Data	LC		SS		FDPM-1	
	R	P	R	P	R	P
OO	1	0.96	1	0.96	1	1
rO	1	0.96	1	0.96	1	1
RO	1	1	1	1	1	1
SO	1	1	1	1	1	1
FF	1	0.95	1	0.95	1	1
FM	1	0.95	1	0.95	1	1
FL	1	0.95	1	0.95	1	1

Table 9: Data arrival order

4.3 The Impacts of Data Arrival Order

We test data arrival orders, in order to ensure whether our approaches are order sensitive. Let $s = 0.1\%$, $\epsilon = s/10$, $\delta = 0.1$, and Zipf $= 1.5$. Several data arriving orders are tested: OO (Original Order), rO (reverse Order), RO (Random Order), SO (segment-based random order[1], FF (Frequent First), FM (Frequent Middle), FL (Frequent Last). FDPM-1 is shown to be insensitive to data arrival order. The results are shown in Figure 3 and Table 9. It achieves 100% recall and 100% precision. It outperforms the others in terms of CPU. The memory consumption is not influenced by the data arrival order. LC and SS are rather sensitive to the data arrival order. For example, when frequent items arrive late (FM or FL), both LC and SS consume more than FDPM-1.

Algorithm 2 FDPM(s, δ)

1: let n_0 be the required number of observations (Eq. (3));
2: $n_1 \leftarrow k \cdot n_0$;
3: $n \leftarrow 0$, $\mathcal{F} \leftarrow \emptyset$, $\mathcal{P} \leftarrow \emptyset$;
4: **for** every n_1 transactions **do**
5:    keep potential frequent patterns in $\mathcal{P}$ in terms of n_1;
6:    $\mathcal{F} \leftarrow \mathcal{P} \cup \mathcal{F}$;
7:    prune potential infrequent patterns from $\mathcal{F}$ further if $|\mathcal{F}| > c_u \cdot n_0$;
8:    $\mathcal{P} \leftarrow \emptyset$;
9:    $n \leftarrow n + n_1$;
10: **end for**
11: output the patterns in $\mathcal{F}$ whose count $\geq sn$ on-demand;

---

[1]We randomly reorder data in a unit of segment (1,000 items)

5 Mining Frequent Itemsets from a Data Stream

We show our frequent data stream pattern (itemsets) mining algorithm in Algorithm 2. In line 1, we obtain n_0 based on the Chernoff bound. Here n_0 is the number of transactions. We divide a transactional data stream into segments. The length of segment is $n_1 = k \cdot n_0$ (line 2). The parameter k controls the size of transactions we process in each run in a similar way like the probabilistic-inplace algorithm in [8]. We maintain potential frequent patterns in $\mathcal{F}$, and use $\mathcal{P}$ for each segment in a run. Both are initialized in line 3. We will discuss the size of $\mathcal{P}$ and $\mathcal{F}$ in detail later. In a for loop statement (line 4-10), we deal with every segment of length of n_1 transactions as an individual data stream repeatedly. For each segment, first, we prune potential infrequent patterns (line 5), using the same techniques given in Algorithm 1. A pattern X is potential infrequent if $\overline{sup}(X) < (s - \epsilon_n)n$ where n increases from 0 to n_1 and ϵ_n is computed in terms of n (Definition 1). Second, we merge the potential frequent patterns in $\mathcal{P}$ with $\mathcal{F}$. That is for every pattern $X \in \mathcal{P}$ with a count c, we increase the count of the same pattern X by c if we can find it in $\mathcal{F}$. Otherwise, we create X in $\mathcal{F}$ with an initial count of c. Third, we further prune potential infrequent patterns in $\mathcal{F}$, when $|\mathcal{F}| > c_u \cdot n_0$ using an existing association rule mining algorithm. We will discuss c_u in detail next.

In Algorithm 2, the k controls the size of segment ($k \cdot n_0$) in a run. If k is small, Algorithm 2 will prune potential infrequent patterns frequently, which leads to less memory but more CPU time. On the other hand, a large k may lead to more memory but less CPU time. Regarding data dependent, we found in our extensive testing that a small k does not necessarily decrease the quality of frequent itemsets mining, because the number of combinations is large, in comparison with frequent items mining.

Theorem 2 *Algorithm 2 finds frequent itemsets in a data stream, with two parameters s and δ. Algorithm 2 ensures the same properties.*

(a) All itemsets whose true frequency exceeds sN are output with probability of at least $1 - \delta$.

(b) No itemsets whose true frequency is less than sN are output.

(c) The probability of the estimated support that equals the true support is no less than $1 - \delta$.

Theorem 2 can be directly derived from the Chernoff bound. Below, we concentrate ourselves on bounds of Algorithm 2.

In Algorithm 2, $\mathcal{P}$ keeps potential frequent itemsets in a segment of n_1 transactions, and $\mathcal{F}$ keeps potential frequent itemsets in all n transactions received so far. At run time, some potential infrequent itemsets may exist in $\mathcal{P}$ ($\mathcal{F}$). An itemset in $\mathcal{P}$ ($\mathcal{F}$) is an entry (a pair of itemset and count). We discuss the size of $\mathcal{P}$ ($\mathcal{F}$) in terms of the number of entries, denoted $|\mathcal{P}|$

($|\mathcal{F}|$). Obviously, $|\mathcal{P}| \leq |\mathcal{F}|$. The size $|\mathcal{P}|$ ($|\mathcal{F}|$) can be possibly larger than n_1 (n). For example, suppose that we receive 2 transactions, $\cdots, t_1, t_2, \cdots$, where $t_1 = \{1, 2\}$ and $t_2 = \{2, 3\}$. The possible potential frequent itemsets can be $\{1\}, \{2\}, \{3\}, \{1,2\}, \{1,3\}, \{2,3\}$, and $\{1, 2, 3\}$. Because $\mathcal{P}$ ($\mathcal{F}$) may contain potential infrequent patterns, the theoretical upper bound of $\mathcal{P}$ ($\mathcal{F}$) is difficult to be determined due to the nature of the exponential explosion of itemsets.

In this paper, we address an empirical upper bound of $|\mathcal{F}|$ ($|\mathcal{P}| \leq |\mathcal{F}|$) using the Chernoff bound. We show that the empirical upper bound of $|\mathcal{F}|$, u_F, can be determined as a factor of n_0, that is,

$$u_F = c_u \cdot n_0$$

such as $|\mathcal{F}| \leq u_F$. Here, n_0 is determined by the Chernoff bound (Eq. (3)). The empirical upper bound (u_F) is determined as follows.

First, let $\mathcal{F}_{max}$ denote the largest $|\mathcal{F}|$ for a given minimum support s in the process of frequent itemsets mining. Here, $\mathcal{F}_{max}$ is the number of entries used for processing transactions up to the current n transactions ($n \geq n_1$). We obtained different $\mathcal{F}_{max}$ values using T10.I4.D1000K and T15.I6.D1000K, by varying s and δ. In Table 10, due to the space limit, we only show the results with $\delta = 0.1$. We find that $c_{max} = \mathcal{F}_{max}/s^{-3}$ is about the same for different minimum support values (s), for a data stream with a given δ. The c_{max} value obtained from T15.I6.D1000K is larger than the c_{max} value obtained from T10.I4.D1000K, because the average of transaction size and the maximal potentially frequent itemsets of T15.I6.D1000K are larger than those of T10.I4.D1000K. Note: when δ decreases (higher reliability), c_{max} increases a little. For example, when $s = 0.1\%$ and $\delta = 0.01$, $c_{max} = 0.0001$ and $c_{max} = 0.00072$ for T10.I4.D1000K and T15.I6.D1000K, respectively.

Second, based on our finding, consider $F_{max} = b_{max} \cdot n_0$ for a given minimum support s, then, we have

$$b_{max} = \mathcal{F}_{max}/n_0 = (c_{max}/s^3)/n_0.$$

Some b_{max} values are shown in Table 11 for different minimum supports. Several points can be made: i) b_{max} increases while the minimum support s decreases. ii) b_{max} can be greater than, equal to, or less than 1.

Third, for determining the empirical upper bound of $|\mathcal{F}|$ for different data streams, $\mathcal{D}_1, \mathcal{D}_2, \cdots$, the above finding suggests that we can select the largest c_{max}, $\bar{c}_{max}$, to determine the largest b_{max} value using a *representative* data stream $\mathcal{D}_r$. For example, T15.I6.D1000K is the representative in comparison with T10.I4.D1000K, because T15.I6.D1000K has a larger transaction size and a larger maximal potentially frequent itemsets than T10.I4.D1000K. As future work, we will further study the issues related to the representative data streams. In Table 10, $\bar{c}_{max} = 0.00045$. Alternatively, we can determine $\bar{c}_{max}$ based on a regression line among c_{max} values. Consequently, we can determine the largest b_{max} value, $\bar{b}_{max}$, for a transactional data stream ($\mathcal{D}_i$), that is represented by

s (%)	n_0	T10.I4.D1000K		T15.I6.D1000K	
		$\mathcal{F}_{max}$	c_{max}	$\mathcal{F}_{max}$	c_{max}
0.1	7,991	59,385	0.00006	454,092	0.00045
0.2	3,996	6,874	0.00005	19,690	0.00015
0.4	1,998	875	0.00006	1,722	0.00011
0.6	1,332	233	0.00005	660	0.00014
0.8	999	71	0.00004	245	0.00012
1.0	799	20	0.00002	102	0.00010

Table 10: The c_{max} for $|\mathcal{F}|$

s (%)	n_0	b_{max} (T10.I4)	b_{max} (T15.I6)
0.1	7,991	7.43	56.82
0.2	3,996	1.72	4.93
0.4	1,998	0.44	0.86
0.6	1,332	0.17	0.50
0.8	999	0.07	0.25
1.0	799	0.03	0.13

Table 11: The b_{max} for Table 10

the representative data stream ($\mathcal{D}_r$), with an arbitrary minimum support s.

$$\bar{b}_{max} = (\bar{c}_{max}/s^3)/n_0.$$

Finally, we identify $c_u = \bar{b}_{max}$.

Remark 4 *For mining frequent patterns from a transactional data stream, the number of entries in $\mathcal{F}$ can empirically be bounded by $c_u \cdot n_0$ where c_u is selected using a representative data stream.*

Remark 4 is important because it states that in fact the number of potential frequent itemsets can be possibly bounded by $c_u \cdot n_0$. In addition, c_u is a considerably small constant, and is not necessarily related with the domain of I unique items. Recall the number of potential frequent itemsets can be up to 2^I for a transactional data stream in a domain of I unique items. In other words, it states that the memory required for $|\mathcal{F}|$ is possible to be multiplication of n_0 (linearity).

The value c_u is used as a way to determine pruning (line 7) in Algorithm 2. In addition, we are able to do *eager* pruning. There are patterns that we can possibly prune if the running error $\epsilon_n > s$ in terms of n observations. It is based on Definition 1. A pattern X is potential infrequent if $\overline{sup}(X)/n < s - \epsilon_n$. Because $\overline{sup}(X) \geq 0$, $\epsilon_n < s$ means no patterns can be pruned.

Remark 5 *Based on Algorithm 2, the empirical upper bound for transactional data streams is $O(1/s^3)$ if c_u is selected from a representative data stream with a fixed δ.*

The Remark 5 is based on $u_F = c_u \cdot n_0$ where n_0 is a denominator of c_u. Note: the bound, $(2 + 2\ln(2/\delta))/s$, for Algorithm 1 is an exact bound.

6 Performance Study II: Mining Frequent Itemsets

We report our experimental results for frequent itemsets mining. For frequent itemsets mining, we implemented our false-negative oriented algorithm FDPM

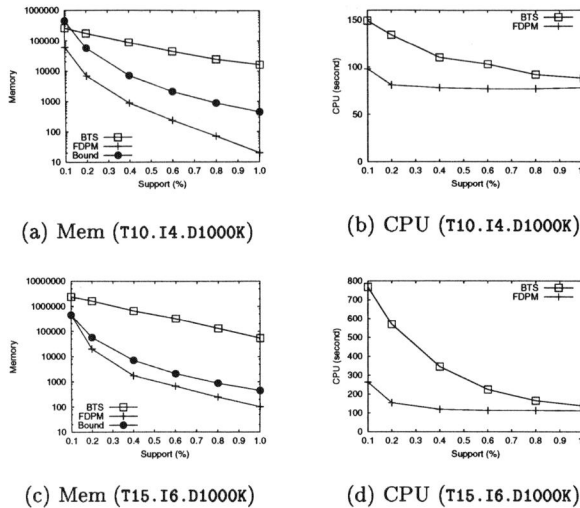

(a) Mem (T10.I4.D1000K) (b) CPU (T10.I4.D1000K)

(c) Mem (T15.I6.D1000K) (d) CPU (T15.I6.D1000K)

Figure 4: Varying s ($\epsilon = s/10$, $\delta = 0.1$)

(Algorithm 2). The idea of probabilistic-inplace is also used in Algorithm 2. For comparison purposes, we implemented Manku and Motwani's false-positive oriented three module system BTS (Buffer-Trie-SetGen). The Apriori implementation we used is available from, http://fuzzy.cs.uni-magdeburg.de/~borgelt/software.html#assoc, which is used in many commercial data mining tools. Its version is 4.07.

For testing frequent itemsets mining, we generate transactional data streams using IBM data generator [12]. We mainly use two datasets, T10.I4.D1000K and T15.I6.D1000K with 10K unique items (as default). We process transactional data in batches. The size of a batch is 50,000 transactions. The parameter k used in FDPM and β used in BTS are adjusted accordingly.

6.1 Effect of Minimum Support

We fix $\epsilon = s/10$ and $\delta = 0.1$, and vary s from 0.1% to 1.0%. Figure 4 (a) and (b) show memory consumption and CPU for T10.I4.D1000K, and Figure 4 (c) and (d) show memory consumption and CPU for T15.I6.D1000K. Recall memory consumption is the number of counters. In addition to BTS and FDPM, we show our empirical bounds (Bound) of FDPM, which is computed by $c_u \cdot n_0$ and c_u is computed using $\bar{c}_{max} = 0.00045$.

As shown in Figure 4, FDPM significantly outperforms BTS. In the worst case, when $s = 0.1\%$, FDPM only consumes 59,385 entries for T10.I4.D1000K and 454,092 entries for T15.I6.D1000K, whereas BTS consumes 259,581 and 2,373,968, accordingly. In the best case, when $s = 1.0\%$, FDPM consumes only 20 entries for T10.I4.D1000K and 102 entries for T15.I6.D1000K, whereas BTS consumes 16,218 and 53,767, accordingly. FDPM significantly outperforms BTS for both memory consumption and CPU cost. Figure 4 (a) and (c) show that the memory consumption is bounded by our empirical bound $c_u \cdot n_0$.

s (%)	BTS R	BTS P	FDPM R	FDPM P
0.1	1	0.85	1	1
0.2	1	0.84	1	1
0.4	1	0.70	0.99	1
0.6	1	0.68	0.99	1
0.8	1	0.46	1	1
1.0	1	0.55	1	1

Table 12: Varying s (T10.I4.D1000K, $\epsilon = s/10$, $\delta = 0.1$)

s (%)	BTS R	BTS P	FDPM R	FDPM P
0.1	1	0.72	1	1
0.2	1	0.91	1	1
0.4	1	0.80	0.99	1
0.6	1	0.72	0.99	1
0.8	1	0.64	0.99	1
1.0	1	0.58	0.95	1

Table 13: Varying s (T15.I6.D1000K, $\epsilon = s/10$, $\delta = 0.1$)

Table 12 and Table 13 show the recall and precision for Figure 4. Here, FDPM achieves high recall (at least 95%) and ensures 100% precision.

6.2 Effect of Error Control

We fix $s = 0.1\%$ and $\delta = 0.1$, and vary ϵ. Figure 5 (a) and (b) show memory consumption and CPU for T10.I4.D1000K, and Figure 5 (c) and (d) show memory consumption and CPU for T15.I6.D1000K. The recall and precision are shown in in Table 14 and Table 15.

As shown in Figure 5, our false-negative oriented algorithm FDPM is not influenced by ϵ. Both memory consumption and CPU are constant while varying ϵ. FDPM only needs 59,385 and 454,092 entries for T10.I4.D1000K and T15.I6.D1000K, respectively. However, ϵ has great impacts on the false-positive oriented approach BTS. Its memory consumption increases while ϵ decreases. When $\epsilon = 0.005\%$, BTS needs large memory to keep 360,476 entries for T10.I4.D1000K, and 3,196,445 entries for T15.I6.D1000K, and achieves 93% and 85% precision, respectively. When $\epsilon = 0.04\%$, BTS needs small memory to keep 86,537 entries for T10.I4.D1000K, and 659,233 entries for T15.I6.D1000K. But, BTS can only have 32% precision, and 16% precision for T10.I4.D1000K and T15.I6.D1000K, respectively. In sequent, BTS faces a dilemma: a little increase of ϵ will make the number of false-positive items large, and a little decrease of ϵ will make memory consumption large.

ϵ (%)	BTS R	BTS P	FDPM R	FDPM P
0.040	1	0.32	1	1
0.030	1	0.42	1	1
0.020	1	0.58	1	1
0.010	1	0.85	1	1
0.005	1	0.93	1	1

Table 14: Varying ϵ (T10.I4.D1000K, $s = 0.1\%$, $\delta = 0.1$)

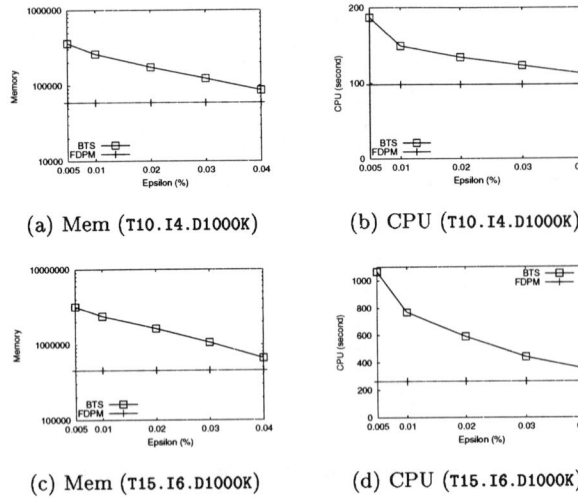

(a) Mem (T10.I4.D1000K)

(b) CPU (T10.I4.D1000K)

(c) Mem (T15.I6.D1000K)

(d) CPU (T15.I6.D1000K)

Figure 5: Varying ϵ ($s = 0.1\%$, $\delta = 0.1$)

ϵ (%)	BTS R	BTS P	FDPM R	FDPM P
0.040	1	0.16	1	1
0.030	1	0.27	1	1
0.020	1	0.48	1	1
0.010	1	0.72	1	1
0.005	1	0.85	1	1

Table 15: Varying ϵ (T15.I6.D1000K, $s = 0.1\%$, $\delta = 0.1$)

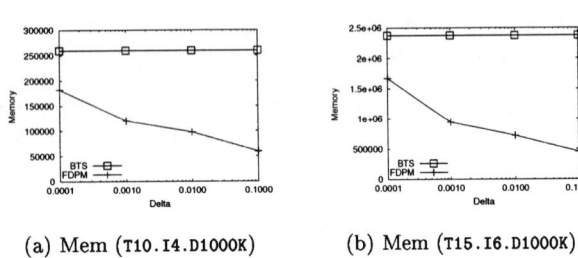

(a) Mem (T10.I4.D1000K)

(b) Mem (T15.I6.D1000K)

Figure 6: Varying δ

δ	BTS R	BTS P	FDPM R	FDPM P
0.1	1	0.85	1	1
0.01	1	0.85	1	1
0.001	1	0.85	1	1
0.0001	1	0.85	1	1

Table 16: Varying δ (T10.I4.D1000K)

$|\mathcal{D}|$	BTS R	BTS P	FDPM R	FDPM P
1000K	1	0.72	0.99	1
3000K	1	0.72	0.99	1
6000K	1	0.72	0.99	1
9000K	1	0.72	1	1

Table 17: Varying length (T15.I6.D1000K)

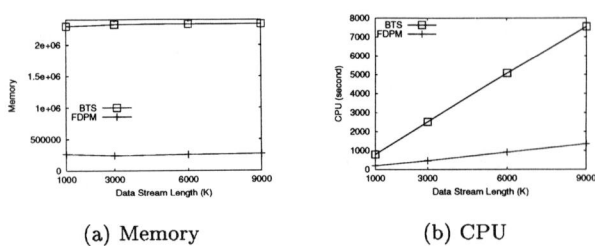

(a) Memory

(b) CPU

Figure 7: Varying length (T15.I6.D1000K)

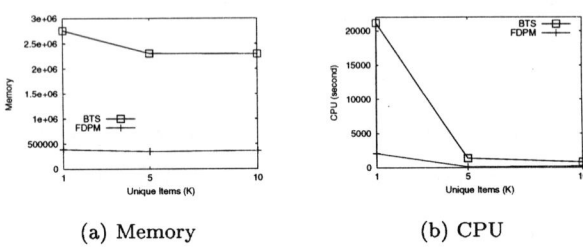

(a) Memory

(b) CPU

Figure 8: Varying domain (T15.I6.D1000K)

6.3 Effect of Reliability Control

We fix $s = 0.1\%$ and $\epsilon = s/10$, and vary δ. We compare FDPM with BTS, and show results in Figure 6. As expected, varying δ does not affect BTS, because it treats $\delta = 0$. As shown in Figure 6, while the reliability increases (smaller δ), the memory consumption of FDPM increases, because it uses δ to approximate the memory consumption. Even when $\delta = 0.0001$, the memory consumption of FDPM is much smaller than the memory consumption of BTS. As shown in Table 16, FDPM achieves 100% recall and 100% precision, even with $\delta = 0.1$, while BTS achieves 100% recall and 85% precision. FDPM outperforms BTS.

6.4 The Impacts of Data Stream Length

We test the impacts of the data stream length on FDPM. We fix $s = 0.1\%$ ($\epsilon = s/10$, $\delta = 0.1$), and vary the length of T15.I6.D1000K from 1000K to 9000K. The memory consumption and CPU cost are shown in Figure 7. FDPM significantly outperforms BTS. When dealing with a 9000K data stream, BTS consumes 2,333,510 entries, while as FDPM consumes only about its 10%, 269,126. Also, BTS requires 7,545 seconds to process it, whereas FDPM only needs 1,355 seconds. As shown in Table 17, FDPM guarantees high recall and precision (almost 100%). The precision of BTS is only 72%.

$|\mathcal{I}|$	BTS R	BTS P	FDPM R	FDPM P
1K	1	0.76	0.99	1
5K	1	0.71	0.99	1
10K	1	0.72	0.99	1

Table 18: Varying domain (T15.I6.D1000K)

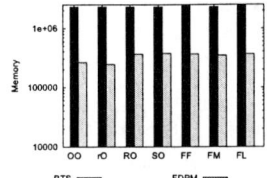
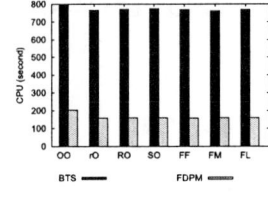

(a) Memory (b) CPU

Figure 9: Impacts of data arrival order

Data	BTS R	BTS P	FDPM R	FDPM P
OO	1	0.72	0.99	1
rO	1	0.72	0.99	1
RO	1	0.72	0.97	1
SO	1	0.72	0.99	1
FF	1	0.72	0.99	1
FM	1	0.72	0.99	1
FL	1	0.72	0.96	1

Table 19: Impacts of data arrival order

6.5 The Impacts of Unique Items

We test the impacts of the domain sizes, 1K, 5K and 10K, using T15.I6.D1000K, where $s = 0.1\%$, $\epsilon = s/10$ and $\delta = 0.1$. The results are shown in Figure 8 and Table 18. When the data is dense (1K), there are many patterns. BTS needs 10 times of CPU than FDPM. Also, as shown in Table 18, FDPM ensures 100% precision and high recall (99%). BTS can only achieve about 71% precision.

6.6 The Impacts of Data Arrival Order

We test several data arrival orders using T15.I6.D1000K: OO (Original Order), rO (reverse Order), RO (Random Order), SO (segment-based random order, FF (Frequent First), FM (Frequent Middle), FL (Frequent Last) where $s = 0.1\%$, $\epsilon = s/10$, and $\delta = 0.1$. As shown in Figure 9 and Table 19. FDPM and BTS are insensitive to data arrival orders regarding frequent itemsets mining. FDPM achieves high recall (almost all 99% only one 97%) and ensures 100% precision. The precision of BTS is low (72%). In addition, FDPM outperforms BTS in terms of CPU and memory consumption.

7 Conclusion

In this paper, we study the problem of mining frequent patterns from transactional data streams, the problem of FDPM. While most existing algorithms in mining frequent items for data streams using false-positive oriented approaches to control the error on the estimated frequency of mined patterns and memory requirement, we explored a new paradigm in FDPM, the false-negative oriented approach. That is, we control the data mining process by limiting the probability of a frequent pattern that misses in the result, but all mined patterns are frequent. We developed both frequent item and itemset mining algorithms using the Chernoff bound. The bound enables us pruning infrequent patterns from the continuously arriving transactions with the guarantee of the required recall rate of frequent patterns. The performance study demonstrated the effectiveness and efficiency of our false-negative oriented approach which uses a running error, ϵ_n, to prune infrequent item(set)s, and uses δ to control memory space.

The Chernoff bound assumes some underlying property of the underlying distributions of the data. Although the current performance study indicated that even the data does not follow strictly the assumptions, the bound is surprisingly effective. One of our immediate future work is to further study the data distribution issues and explore possible theoretical bounds for frequent data stream pattern mining.

Acknowledgment

The authors would like to thank Zhenjie Zhang for his contribution to this project. The work described in this paper was supported by grant from the Research Grants Council of the Hong Kong SAR, China (CUHK4229/01E).

References

[1] R. Agrawal and R. Srikant. Fast algorithms for mining association rules. In *Proc. of 20th Intl. Conf. on Very Large Data Bases*, pages 487 – 499, 1994.

[2] N. Alon, Y. Matias, and M. Szegedy. The space complexity of approximating the frequency moments. In *Proc. of ACM STOC*, 1996.

[3] M. Charikar, K. Chen, and M. Farach-Colton. Finding frequent items in data streams. In *Proc. of the Intl. Colloquium on Automata, Languages and Programming (ICALP)*, pages 693 – 703, 2002.

[4] H. Chernoff. A measure of asymptotic efficiency for tests of a hypothesis based on the sum of observations. *The Annals of mathematical Statistics*, 23(4):493–507, 1952.

[5] S. Cohen and Y. Matias. Spectral bloom filter. In *Proc. of ACM SIGMOD*, 2003.

[6] G. Cormode and S.Muthukrishnan. What's hot and what's not: Tracking most frequent items dynamically. In *Proc. of 22nd ACM Symposium on Principles of Database Systems (PODS)*, pages 296 – 306, 2003.

[7] M. Datar, A. Gionis, P. Indyk, and R. Motwani. Maintaining stream statistics over sliding windows. In *13th Annual ACM-SIAM Symp. on Discrete Algorithms*, 2002.

[8] E. Demaine, A. López-Ortiz, and J. I. Munro. Frequency estimation of internet packet streams with limited space. In *Proc. of 10th Annual European Symposium on Algorithms*, pages 348 – 360, 2002.

[9] J. Feigenbaum and S. Kannan. An approximate l1-difference algorithm for massive data streams. In *IEEE Symposium on Foundations of Computer Science*, 1999.

[10] P. Flajolet and G. N. Martin. Probabilistic counting algorithms. *J. of Comp. and Sys. Sci*, (31):182–209, 1985.

[11] M. Garofalakis, J. Gehrke, and R. Rastogi. Querying and mining data streams: You only get one look. In *Tutorial in 28th Intl. Conf. on Very Large Data Bases*, 2002.

[12] G. S. Manku and R. Motwani. Approximate frequency counts over data streams. In *Proc. of 28th Intl. Conf. on Very Large Data Bases*, pages 346 – 357, 2002.

[13] H. Toivonen. Sampling large databases for association rules. In *Proc. of 22nd Intl. Conf. on Very Large Data Bases*, pages 134 – 145, 1996.

[14] J. S. Vitter. Random sampling with a reservoir. *ACM Transactions on Mathematical Software (TOMS)*, 11(1):37–57, 1985.

Indexing Temporal XML Documents

Alberto O. Mendelzon
University of Toronto
Department of Computer Science
mendel@cs.toronto.edu

Flavio Rizzolo
University of Toronto
Department of Computer Science
flavio@cs.toronto.edu

Alejandro Vaisman
Universidad de Buenos Aires
Departamento de Computación
avaisman@dc.uba.ar

Abstract

Different models have been proposed recently for representing temporal data, tracking historical information, and recovering the state of the document as of any given time, in XML documents. We address the problem of indexing temporal XML documents. In particular we show that by indexing *continuous paths*, *i.e.* paths that are valid continuously during a certain interval in a temporal XML graph, we can dramatically increase query performance. We describe in detail the indexing scheme, denoted TempIndex, and compare its performance against both a system based on a non-temporal path index, and one based on DOM.

1 Introduction

The topic of representing, querying and updating temporal information in XML documents has been receiving increasing attention from the database community, leading to proposals aimed at defining, querying and managing temporal XML documents, *i.e.* XML documents that can be navigated across time.

In a separate paper [23], we propose a model for temporal documents and a query language called TX-Path. TXPath extends XPath [25] for supporting temporal queries (*i.e.* queries over temporal XML documents.) This abstract data model represents the temporal document as a data graph which has time interval information on its paths. Navigating this temporal data graph is a key part of the TXPath query evaluation. However, simply scanning the whole document in search of those paths that satisfy a given temporal query is highly expensive.

Permission to copy without fee all or part of this material is granted provided that the copies are not made or distributed for direct commercial advantage, the VLDB copyright notice and the title of the publication and its date appear, and notice is given that copying is by permission of the Very Large Data Base Endowment. To copy otherwise, or to republish, requires a fee and/or special permission from the Endowment.

**Proceedings of the 30th VLDB Conference,
Toronto, Canada, 2004**

Several index structures have been proposed in order to optimize path query evaluation over non-temporal data graphs. Some of the more recent works on path indexing in the XML context include [12, 18, 7, 17, 14]. Most of these indexing schemes keep record of the paths in the XML data by summarizing label path information. Although indexing label paths on temporal documents helps reduce the search space, our experiments show that computing paths within a given time interval is quite expensive even in the presence of traditional path indexes. One possible solution is to integrate the temporal dimension into the indexing scheme in order to obtain better performance. Our proposal, denoted TempIndex, accomplishes this integration by summarizing label paths together with temporal intervals and *continuous paths* (*i.e.* paths that are valid continuously during a certain interval.)

1.1 Temporal XML documents

In Section 3 we review the temporal XML model that we use. We give an example here. The graph depicted in Figure 1 is an abstract representation of a temporal XML document for a portion of the NBA[1] database. The league is composed of franchises, which maintain teams, such that each team has a set of players that may change over time. Some franchises may have players directly associated to them, not included in teams. The database also records some statistics for each player. For instance, in this database, node 16 represents a player (McGrady), playing for the Toronto Raptors between instants '0' and '20'. After that, he played for the Orlando Magic (represented by node 2), from instant '21' to the present time (note the edge between nodes 2 and 16.) Notice that in spite of the change of franchise, there is only one node for McGrady. Thus, regardless of the franchise he played for, the graph shows that he scored eleven goals between instants '0' and '30', and twelve goals from instant '31' to the present time. This information is encapsulated

---
[1]National Basketball Association, a professional basketball league

216

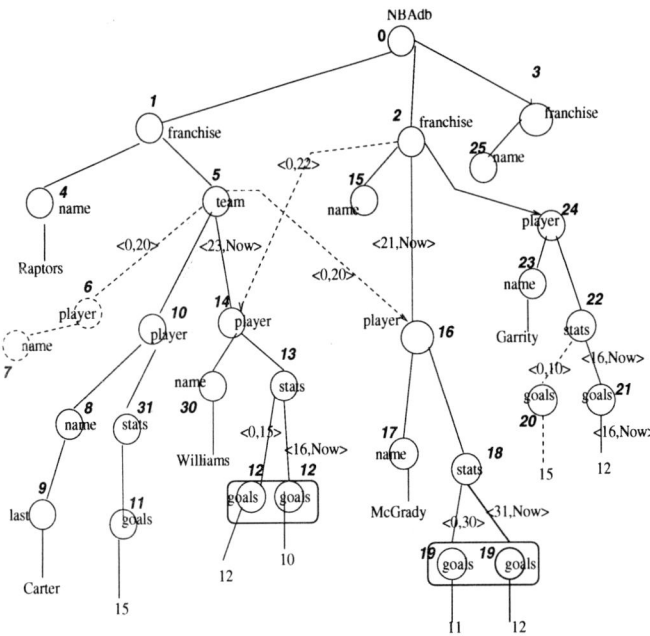

Figure 1: Example database

in a sequence that we denote *versioned* node (see Section 3), represented by the box enclosing the two nodes labeled '19'.

1.2 Contributions

In this paper we describe in detail the TempIndex indexing scheme. In addition, we present the results of our experiments, which show that an index summarizing temporal intervals and continuous paths clearly outperforms traditional path indexes on temporal query evaluation.

The remainder of the paper is organized as follows: in Section 2 we comment on previous efforts in XML path indexing and temporal XML. In Section 3 we review the main features of the data model and the TXPath query language. In Section 4 we present the details of the proposed indexing scheme while in Section 5 we show how a TXPath query is processed using TempIndex. Finally, Section 6 discusses the results of our experiments. We conclude in Section 7.

2 Related Work

Index structures for XML data have been proposed in recent years in order to optimize path query evaluation. Most of these indexing schemes keep record of the paths in the XML data by summarizing path information in different ways. Examples of such index structures are dataguides [12], 1-indexes and T-indexes [18], and more recently, Index Fabric [7], XISS [17], ToXin [20], F&B-Index and F+B-Index [14], and A(k)-index [16]. On a different vein, *adaptive indexes* are based on query workloads that may change over time, such as APEX [6] and D(k)-index [19]. Finally,

Kaushik *et al* [15] discuss fast updating of structure indexes.

Dataguides are a summary of the path structure of the database in which every label path starting at the root appears exactly once. The nodes in the data graph are grouped into sets according to the label paths they belong to (each node may appear more than once in the index). The 1-index, T-index, F&B-Index and F+B-Index, on the other hand, partition the data graph nodes into equivalence classes so that each node appears only once. The partition is computed in different ways: based on the label paths that reach the nodes (1-index) or further refined into smaller classes according to the label paths of any length (F&B-Index) or of a fixed length (F+B-Index) that leave from the nodes. The size of the index can also be reduced by indexing only the class of paths specified by a given path template (T-index), or making the index approximate for paths longer than a given k (A(k)-index). All these indexes either store a limited class of paths or the number of equivalence classes grows to a point in which evaluating generic XPath queries is no longer efficient. Other two approaches (XISS and ToXin) use separate structures for storing nodes. Both implement different join algorithms to efficiently reconstruct paths of any length. In addition to that, ToXin keeps a dynamic schema of the document for query optimization. Index Fabric, in a completely different approach, summarizes paths and data values together, and encodes them as strings.

In the temporal XML field, many efforts [1, 8, 3, 4] have proposed data models and query languages for representing the histories of XML documents. Most of them create a new physical version each time an update occurs, leading to large overheads when processing temporal queries that span multiple versions. A *version index* for managing multiple versions of XML documents was proposed by Chien *et al* [5]. The TX-Path temporal data model, on the other hand, maintains a single temporal document from which versions can be extracted when needed. Gergatsoulis and Stavrakas [11] introduced a model for representing changes using an extension to XML denoted MXML (Multidimensional XML), where dimensions are applied to elements and attributes.

Closer to TXPath ideas, Gao *et al* [9, 10] introduced an extension to XQuery, called τXQuery, that supports valid time while maintaining the data model unchanged. Queries are translated into XQuery, and evaluated by an XQuery engine. Even for simple temporal queries, this approach results in long XQuery programs. Moreover, translating a temporal query into a non-temporal one makes it more difficult to apply query optimization and indexing techniques particularly suited for temporal XML documents.

In this work we will take advantage of the structure of the temporal XML document, showing that it is possible to index temporal continuous paths rather than nodes, enhancing query performance dramatically.

3 Temporal XML

A *temporal XML document* is a directed labeled graph with different kinds of nodes: the *root* of the document, denoted r, such that r has no incoming edges; *Value nodes*, representing text or numeric values; *Attribute nodes*, labeled with the name of an attribute, plus possibly one of the 'ID' or 'REF' annotations; and *Element nodes*, labeled with an element tag, and containing outgoing links to attribute nodes, value nodes, and other element nodes. Each node is uniquely identified by an integer, the *node number*, and is described by a string, the *node label*. Edges in the document graph can be either *containment edges* or *reference edges*. Containment edges connect element, attribute or value nodes, while reference edges represent IDREF to ID references. Each edge e is labeled by a time interval T_e that represents the *valid* time of the edge, *i.e.* the interval during which the edge was valid. Time is discrete, with instants represented by positive integers. The *lifespan* of a node is the union of all the containment edges incoming to the node. If an edge e is labeled with a temporal label T_e, we will use $T_e.TO$ and $T_e.FROM$ to refer to the endpoints of the interval T_e. Temporal XML documents also support the concept of *versioned nodes*, which encapsulate a sequence of *consecutive* element or attribute nodes (of type other than ID or REF).

A temporal XML document must verify some consistency conditions. The key ones are: the union of the temporal labels of the containment edges outgoing from a node is contained in the lifespan of the node; the temporal labels of the containment edges incoming to a node must be consecutive; and, for any time instant t, the sub-graph composed of all the containment edges e such that $t \in T_e$ is either empty or a tree with root r (we call such a subgraph a *snapshot* of the document at time t.)

Example 1 *In Figure 1 the fact that McGrady played for the Orlando Magic from instant '21' to the current time, is represented by the containment edge $e(2, 16)$. The lifespan of node '16' is the union of the elements [0,20] (the temporal label of the incoming node edge from node 5) and [21,Now] (the label of the containment edge incoming from node 2). The boxes in bold line represent versioned nodes, composed in this case by two nodes of type goals, associated with the element nodes Stats. To simplify the figures, we omit all temporal labels of the form $[t_0, Now]$, and represent containment edges currently valid by solid lines; other containment edges are represented by dashed lines.*

There are different ways of mapping the abstract graph to an XML document [23]. For the rest of this paper, except for the experimental results, it does not matter which representation is used. We sketch below the representation we used for the experiments. A node n is physically nested within its "oldest" parent. If n was contained in some other parent p during interval T, an element with the same tag as n, annotated with T, and pointing to the ID for node n, is nested within node p. Below, we show a portion of the XML document resulting from mapping the graph in Figure 1:

```
<NBAdb>
  <franchise ID='1'[0,Now]>
    <name[0,Now]>Raptors</name>
    <team[0,Now] ID = '5' >
      <player[23,Now] IN = '14'/>
      ...
      <player[0,20] ID='16'>
        <name[0,Now]>Tracy McGrady</name>
        <stats[0,Now]>
          <SEQUENCE>
            <goals[0,30]>11</goals>
            <goals[31,Now]>12</goals>
          </SEQUENCE>
        </stats>
      </player>
```

The inclusion of the element <player [23,Now] IN = '14'/> within node 5 means that the player represented by node 14, whose oldest parent is node 2, was contained in node 5 between 23 and Now. For the sake of clarity we use a simplified syntax for the XML documents. For example, <franchise ID = '1' [0, Now]> would actually read <franchise ID='1' Time:FROM = '1999-01-01' Time:TO = 'Now'>.

TXPath Overview

The TXPath query language extends XPath 2.0 [25] with temporal features. In non-temporal XPath 2.0, the meaning of a path expression is the sequence of nodes at the end of each path that matches the expression. In TXPath, the meaning is a sequence of (node,interval) pairs such that the node has been continuously at the end of a matching path during that interval. To make this precise, we define the notion of *continuous path*, which we will be using throughout the paper, and *maximal continuous path*.

Definition 1 (Continuous Path) *A continuous path with interval T from node n_1 to node n_k in a temporal document graph is a sequence $(n_1, \ldots, n_k, T)$ of k nodes and an interval T such that there is a sequence of containment edges of the form $e_1(n_1, n_2, T_1)$, $e_2(n_2, n_3, T_2)$, ..., $e_k(n_{k-1}, n_k, T_k)$, such that $T = \bigcap_{i=1,k} T_i$. We say there is a maximal continuous path (mcp) with interval T from node n_1 to node n_k if T is the union of a maximal set of*

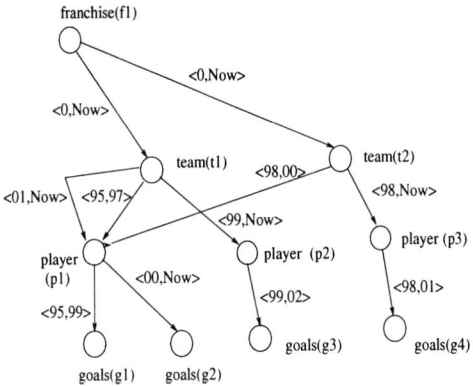

Figure 2: Maximal Continuous Path

consecutive intervals T_i such that there is a continuous path from n_1 to n_k with interval T_i.

Example 2 *Consider Figure 2. There is only one mcp from node team(t1) to goals(g3), with interval [99, 02]. There are 2 mcp's from node team(t1) to player(p1), with intervals [01, Now] and [95, 97]. There are 3 continuous paths from the root to player(p1), with intervals [95, 97], [98, 00], and [01, Now]; since these are consecutive, they produce a single mcp with interval [95, Now].*

Figure 3 shows the semantics of the most common TXPath constructs, adapting the formal XPath semantics introduced by Wadler [24]. The meaning of a TXPath expression is specified with respect to a *context pair* (node,interval). We define three semantic functions: $\mathcal{S}, \mathcal{Q}$ and $\mathcal{Q}_T$ such that $\mathcal{S}[\![p]\!]x$ denotes the sequence of pairs (node,interval) (or values, as we will see below) selected by pattern p when x is the context pair. The boolean expression $\mathcal{Q}[\![q]\!]x$ denotes whether the qualifier q is satisfied when the context pair is x. Finally, another boolean expression $\mathcal{Q}_T[\![q_T]\!]x$ denotes whether a temporal condition q_T is satisfied.

In order to give the flavor of the language, let us show the query *"Player nodes for players with the Toronto Raptors on October 10th, 2001"* in TXPath:

```
NBAdb/franchise[name='Raptors']//players
[@from ≥ '10/10/01' and @to ≤ '10/10/01']
```

Assuming that the date October 10th, 2001 is represented by instant 15, the result is the sequence $\{6, [0, 20]; 10[0, Now]; 16, [0, 20]\}$. Note that the order of the answer corresponds to the *document* order at the time asked for in the query. If the query had not asked for a particular instant, the result would have been listed in arbitrary order.

Document order

In a non-temporal XML document, there is a total order between the nodes. A temporal document does not

$\mathcal{S}$
$\mathcal{S}[\![/p]\!]x = \mathcal{S}[\![p]\!]root(x)$;
$\mathcal{S}[\![//p]\!]x = \{x_2 \mid x_1 \in subnodes(root(x)), x_2 \in \mathcal{S}[\![p]\!]x_1\}$;
$\mathcal{S}[\![p_1/p_2]\!]x = \{(v_2, I_1 \cap I_2) \mid (v_1, I_1) \in \mathcal{S}[\![p_1]\!]x,$
$\qquad (v_2, I_2) \in \mathcal{S}[\![p_2]\!](v_1, I_1)\}$;
$\mathcal{S}[\![p_1//p_2]\!]x = \{x_2 \mid x_1 \in subnodes(x), x_2 \in \mathcal{S}[\![p]\!]x_1\}$;
$\mathcal{S}[\![p[q]]\!]x = \{(v, I) \mid (v, I) \in \mathcal{S}[\![p]\!]x, \mathcal{Q}[\![q]\!](v, I)\}$;
$\mathcal{S}[\![n]\!]x = \{(v, I) \mid isElement(v), child(x) = (v, I),$
$\qquad name(v) = n\}$;
$\mathcal{S}[\![@n]\!]x = \{(v, I) \mid isAttribute(v), child(x) = (v, I),$
$\qquad name(v) = n\}$;
$\mathcal{S}[\![@from]\!]x = \{f \mid (v, I) \in \mathcal{S}[\![p]\!]x, I = [f, t]\}$;
$\mathcal{S}[\![@to]\!]x = \{t \mid (v, I) \in \mathcal{S}[\![p]\!]x, I = [f, t]\}$;
$\mathcal{S}[\![p[q_T]]\!]x = \{(v, I) \mid (v, I) \in \mathcal{S}[\![p]\!]x, \mathcal{Q}_T[\![p]\!](v, I)\}$;

$\mathcal{Q}$
$\mathcal{Q}[\![p = s]\!]x = \{(v, I) \mid (v, I) \in \mathcal{S}[\![p]\!]x, value(v) = s\} \neq \emptyset$;
$\mathcal{Q}[\![p]\!]x = \{x_1 \mid x_1 \in \mathcal{S}[\![p]\!]x\} \neq \emptyset$;

$\mathcal{Q}_T$
$\mathcal{Q}_T[\![d \text{ IN } (\text{@from},\text{@to})]\!]x = \{x \mid x = (v, [\text{@from}, \text{@to}]),$
$\qquad d \geq \text{@from}, d \leq \text{@to}\} \neq \emptyset$;
$\mathcal{Q}_T[\![\text{@from op } d]\!]x = \{x \mid r \in \mathcal{S}[\![\text{@from}]\!]x,$
$\qquad r \text{ op } d\} \neq \emptyset$;
$\mathcal{Q}_T[\![\text{@to op } d]\!]x = \{x \mid r \in \mathcal{S}[\![\text{@to}]\!]x,$
$\qquad r \text{ op } d\} \neq \emptyset$;

$subnodes(y) = \{(v, I) \mid \exists$ an mcp from y to v with interval $I\}$;
$root(x)$ is the $(root, interval)$ pair of the tree in which x is a $(node, interval)$ pair;
$child(x) = \{(v, I) \mid$ there exists an mcp of length 1 from x to v with interval $I\}$.

Figure 3: Formal semantics of TXPath

necessarily impose a total order among its nodes, but for any instant t there must be a total order, denoted $<_t$, among the nodes of each snapshot $D(t)$ of document D at time t. In general, for any pair of nodes n_1 and n_2, we may have $n_1 <_{t_1} n_2$, and $n_2 <_{t_2} n_1$, in two different instants t_1 and t_2. However, we can show that there is an interval during which the relative order between n_1 and n_2 does not change. If I_1 is the interval on a continuous path from the root to n_1, and similarly I_2 for n_2, then the ordering between n_1 and n_2 is the same for any instant t in the interval $I_1 \cap I_2$. This is formalized in the following proposition.

Proposition 1 *Let D be a temporal XML document; n_1 and n_2 two nodes in D; $p_1 = (r, \ldots, n_1, I_1)$ and $p_2 = (r, \ldots, n_2, I_2)$ two continuous paths to n_1 and n_2 with intervals I_1 and I_2, respectively; then, either $n_1 <_t n_2$ for every $t \in I_1 \cap I_2$, or $n_2 <_t n_1$ in every such t.*

4 Temporal Indexing Scheme

As we mentioned in Section 1, efficiently querying temporal XML documents requires the ability to find the paths in the graph that were valid at a given time (*i.e.* the *continuous paths* in the document.) This ability is not provided by traditional path indexes. Our proposal adds the time dimension to path indexing by indexing *continuous paths* to element or value nodes.

The standard notion of label paths can be easily extended to continuous paths. Let $p = (n_1, \ldots, n_k, T)$ be a continuous path with interval T. The *label path of p*, denoted $\lambda(p)$ is the concatenation of the labels of the n_i in p.

Traditional path indices [12, 18] often define equivalence classes of nodes that are reachable from the root by a path with the same label. In TempIndex, we define equivalence classes of pairs $\langle node, interval \rangle$ such that for all the pairs $\langle n, I \rangle$ in a class, there is a continuous path from the root to n, with interval I and the same label. This classes are stored in tables called *cp* and *cp+value*, which we will define next.

Definition 2 (CP and CP+Value Tables)
Consider the set of all labels $\lambda(p)$ such that p is a continuous path from the root of document d to some node in d. For each string l in this set, let [l] be the equivalence class of all pairs $\langle n, I \rangle$ such that n is a node in d, I is an interval, and there is a continuous path from the root of d to n with interval I and label l. For each class [l] in d there is a cp table in which each tuple t has attributes `parent`, `child`, `from` *and* `to` *such that there is a continuous path from the root of d to* `t.child` *with interval* [`t.from`, `t.to`] *via* `t.parent`*. When* `t.child` *has a value* `v` *associated to it, the cp table is called* cp+value table *and has an extra attribute named* `value`*, where* `t.value=v`*. Tuples in the cp and cp + value tables are sorted by* `child`*.*

In other words, each *cp* and *cp+value* table corresponds to a path label l and encodes the last edge of all the continuous paths in d labeled by l. The parent-child relationship contained in each tuple is used during query evaluation to traverse continuous paths with a given label and interval (see Subseccion 5 for more details). Figure 4 shows the *cp* table for the path */NBA/franchise/player/stats* and 5 shows the *cp+value table* for the path *NBA/franchise/player/name*.

Indexing intervals

Since cp's in the *cp* and *cp+value* tables are clustered by label and sorted by the `child` attribute, we need additional structures to index the intervals and to capture the node ordering at any given instant (as defined in Proposition 1). There are many proposals in the literature for indexing temporal intervals. Some of them are based on the methods proposed by Bozkaya *et al* [2] and Salzberg *et al* [21], where a B+ tree indexes the `FROM` value in the intervals being indexed, and each internal node is augmented with the information of the maximum `TO` value in an interval of the corresponding subtree. We propose a different scheme, embodied in

Parent	Child	From	To
14	13	0	22
16	18	21	Now
24	22	0	Now

Figure 4: *cp* table NBA/franchise/player/stats

Parent	Child	From	To	Value
16	17	21	Now	McGrady
24	23	0	Now	Garrity
14	30	0	22	Williams

Figure 5: *cp+value* table NBA/franchise/player/name

a set of tables called δ_k tables, that are based on the notion of *temporal depth*.

Definition 3 (Temporal Depth) *For each node n in d such that there exists a continuous path $cp = (r, \ldots, n, I)$ in d, $\delta(n, I) = length(cp)$ is a function called the* temporal depth *of n during the interval I. (Note that, due to the consistency conditions of Section 3, there is at most one continuous path with interval I from the root to each node n).*

For each temporal depth k, we define the nodes that are valid at that depth during an interval I as follows.

Definition 4 (Node Validity) *A node n is* valid at temporal depth k in an interval I *iff there exists an interval I' such that $\delta(n, I') = k$ and $I \subseteq I'$.*

Thus, $\delta(n, I)$ defines an equivalence relation between the nodes in the temporal XML graph where for each pair $\langle n, I \rangle$ in a class the length of the continuous path from the root to n is the same. For each temporal depth k, we will define a table called δ_k table, listing the nodes that are valid at certain intervals and their relative order. These intervals are obtained by taking all the intervals that label some continuous path of length k and partitioning them as needed to obtain a set of pairwise-disjoint intervals. This is formalized with the notion of *interval partition*.

Definition 5 (Interval Partition) *The interval partition P of a set of intervals $I_1 \ldots I_n$ is the smallest set of intervals $\mathcal{P} = P_1 \ldots P_m$ such that all the P_i's in $\mathcal{P}$ are pairwise disjoint and $\mathcal{P}$ contains a partition of every interval I_j.*

Definition 6 (δ_k Tables) *For each temporal depth k in a document d there is a table called δ_k table. Each tuple* `t` *in a δ_k table has two temporal attributes,* `from`, `to`, *and a list-valued attribute* `valid`*. Let $I_1 \ldots I_n$ be all the intervals such that there is a cp of length k labeled by one of the I_j's, and $P_1 \ldots P_m$ be the interval partition of $I_1 \ldots I_n$. Each P_k is represented by a tuple* `t` *in δ_k. The* `t.valid` *attribute contains the*

From	To	Valid
0	19	{9, 11, 19}
20	22	{9, 11}
23	Now	{9, 11, 12}

Figure 6: δ_5 table

list of all nodes at temporal depth k that are valid in the interval [t.from, t.to). The nodes in t.valid are ordered by the order relation defined in the interval [t.from, t.to]. (Note that, according to Proposition 1, this order relation is always defined for all nodes in [t.from, t.to]). Tuples in the δ_k tables are indexed by from and to.

For example, Figure 6 shows the δ_5 table for the running example.

The δ_k tables can be used for computing snapshots efficiently. When creating a snapshot at time i we simply have to find the tuple t in the δ_k tables such that i is contained in t's interval. In addition, the δ_k tables support efficient retrieval of all nodes that are valid during a given interval. In the next section we will explain query processing using the cp, cp+value and δ_k tables in detail.

Space Requirements

The size of the index is proportional to the number of cp's. Our experiments in Section 6 show that, for the NBA database, the number of cp's is about three times the number of nodes in the temporal graph. We support three types of updates, insertion, deletion and modification. When the XML graph is a tree, i.e. before any update is performed, for each edge in the temporal graph there is one tuple in the cp/cp+value tables. Furthermore, since there is only one interval of relevance, [0, Now], there is only one tuple t in each δ_k and the list of its valid nodes contains all nodes at temporal depth k. As updates are performed, the number of cp's in the document – and consequently the number of tuples in the tables – increases. The tables affected by an update are those that index descendants of a node at the update point, so the closer the update is to the root, the larger the increase in the index size. Occasionally, an update may also create a new partition in a δ_k table, in which case the nodes from the last partition that are still valid in the new partition have to be replicated.

There are several ways to reduce the space requirements for the index. In many applications, we expect most updates to occur close to the leaves, so that the size of the index will grow linearly in the size of the document. Our experiments so far confirm that expectation: the main-memory representation of TempIndex has a size comparable to that of the DOM representation (see Section 6) for both document sizes tested.

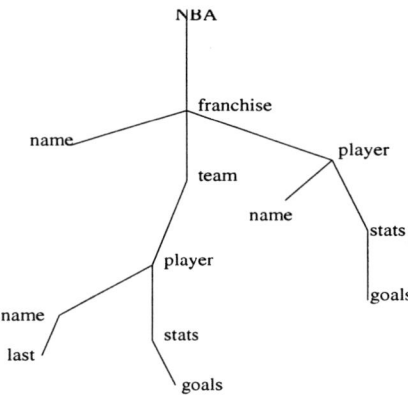

Figure 7: Temporal Schema

Another typical property of temporal applications is that there is a great deal of skew in the distribution of queries, with recent instants being accessed more frequently than older ones. In a space-constrained situation we could exploit this property by limiting how far the temporal window extends back in time, and periodically reindexing to take this into account.

Finally, there is a lot of room for compression in the main memory TempIndex structures. For example, the Java `date` datatype that we are currently using consumes a lot more space than a typical application would need. We have made no attempt yet to optimize space usage by the index.

5 Query processing in TXPath

In this section we will introduce the query evaluation algorithms. The evaluation of a TXPath query is divided into stages based on its *filter sections*. The filter sections of a TXPath query (also called *filters*) are the expressions that appear between brackets in the query. A filter is a predicate which is applied to the pairs (node, interval) that are at the end of the cp's that match the path expression before it. For simplicity, we consider in this section TXPath expressions without nested filters. After each filter section, the evaluation of the rest of the query continues only for those pairs (node, interval) that satisfy the filter.

Before giving the query evaluation algorithms we will need the notion of *temporal schema*.

Definition 7 (Temporal Schema) *Consider the [l] classes from Definition 2. The* temporal schema $S(d)$ *is a tree with a node for each class [l]. The root of the tree corresponds to the class for the root label. There is an edge from $[l_1]$ to $[l_2]$ in $S(d)$ iff there is an element name e in the document such that $l_2 = l_1.e$ (where "." is the concatenation symbol). Each node n in $S(d)$ has either a* cp *or a* cp+value *tables associated to it.*

We decompose each TXPath query into a sequence of calls to evaluation procedures called `navigate()`, `pathFilter()` and `tempFilter()`. Each procedure receives as a parameter a set of temporal schema nodes N and a list of pairs (child, interval) from the cp/cp+value tables associated to the nodes in N. In addition, procedure `pathFilter()` receives a path expression and a value selection, `tempFilter()` a temporal predicate and `navigate()` a path expression between filters. All procedures return a set M of temporal schema nodes and a list of pairs (child, interval) from the cp/cp+value tables associated to the nodes in M. For simplicity, we consider in this discussion only filters that contain either path/value selections or temporal predicates, but not both. Based on these procedures, a query of the form:

PathExp1[PathExp2=Val][TempPred]...PathExpn

Will be decomposed as follows:

```
list.add(graph root, interval);
set.add(schema root);
navigate(set, list, PathExp1);
pathFilter(set, list, PathExp2, Val);
tempFilter(set, list, TempPred);
...
navigate(set, list, PathExpn);
```

Next, we will give the algorithms for `navigate()` and `pathFilter()`; the one for `tempFilter()` is similar.

5.1 Query Evaluation

Algorithm 1 (navigate) *Input/Output: nodeSet, pairList. Input: PathExpr, Value.*

1. *Compute the NFA P corresponding to PathExpr.*

2. *Determine the cp and cp+value tables that participate in the evaluation and navigate among them as follows:*

    2.1. We view the temporal schema as an automaton T whose states correspond to the schema nodes. Each of T's transitions corresponds to an edge in the schema, and is labeled by the label of the edge's target node. An auxiliary node with the root as its only child provides the start state of T. All states of T, except the start state, are final. Let X be the product of the P and T automata. Each schema node and cp/cp+value table is therefore associated to a transition in X.

    2.2. Navigate the product automaton X and follow the parent-child reference chains in the cp/cp+value tables associated to the transitions.

3. *When visiting a final state of X via a transition s in the navigation, add to pairList all pairs $(t.child, [t.from, t.to])$ such that t is a tuple in a cp/cp+value table associated to s and $t.child$ is at the end of some parent-child reference chain.*

Parent	Child	From	To	Value
1	4	0	Now	Raptors
2	15	0	Now	Magic
3	25	0	Now	San Antonio

Figure 8: $cp + value$ table NBA/franchise/name

4. *When visiting a final state of X via a transition s in the navigation, assign to nodeSet the schema nodes associated to s.*

Algorithm 2 (pathFilter) *Input/Output: nodeSet, pairList. Input: PathExpr, Value.*

1. *Perform steps 1 and 2 from algorithm 1.*

2. *When visiting a final state of X via a transition s in the navigation, add to pairList all pairs (n, I) such that there is a tuple t in a cp+value table associated to s, where t.child is at the end of some reference chain starting at n, and t.value=Value.*

3. *Assign to nodeSet all schema nodes with a cp/cp+value table T such that there is a tuple t in T and a pair $p = (n, I)$ in pairList such that $t.child = n$.*

We now present an example of how a TXPath query can be processed using TempIndex and the document in Figure 1. Consider the query "name of the players playing for the Toronto Raptors, and the corresponding seasons". This is written in TXPath as:

//franchise[name='Raptors']//player/name

The evaluation process begins following the path NBA/franchise/name in the temporal schema. From the $cp + value$ table of Figure 8, we obtain that node 4, with parent 1, between 0 and Now satisfies the condition (note that in Figure 1 the names of the last two teams have been omitted for clarity reasons.) Thus, we must look in the franchise with node 1, and find its players. In the $cp + value$ table in Figure 9 we find the team corresponding to franchise in node 1 (node 5). However, according to the temporal schema, we must also look for node 4 in the cp table for NBA/franchise/player, depicted in Figure 10 (node 4 is not present in this table). Finally, we join the table NBA/franchise/team, with the tables NBA/franchise/team/player (cp table) and NBA/franchise/team/player/name ($cp + value$ table), in this order (Figures 11 and 12, respectively), taking into account the time intervals. Note that player 'Carter' is not included in the table of Figure 12, because it is the value of an element *last*, rather than *name*. Also notice that the value for the player in node 7 in Figure 1 (not shown in that figure) is 'Oakley'.

Parent	Child	From	To
1	5	0	Now

Figure 9: *cp* table NBA/franchise/team

Parent	Child	From	To
2	14	0	20
2	16	21	Now
2	24	0	Now

Figure 10: *cp* table NBA/franchise/player

Now, consider the query "name of the players playing in the NBA in 2002". This is written in TXPath as:

//player[@from ≤ 2002 and @to ≥ 2002]/name

Navigating the temporal schema, we find that the players are in two different *cp + value* tables. The process is analogous to the one described above. However, as there is a temporal condition, we will use the δ_2 and δ_3 tables to obtain the players that were active in 2002.

5.2 Ancestor-Descendant encoding for temporal XML documents

So far we have used *node numbers* for identifying nodes in the XML graph. However, we will show that we can encode nodes in order to improve the performance of some queries in TXPath when using the TempIndex indexing scheme. We devised the *temporal interval encoding*, which is an ancestor-descendant encoding inspired by the interval scheme first presented by Santoro and Khatib [22]. In this scheme, the leaves of a tree are numbered from left to right and each internal node is labeled with a pair of numbers corresponding to its smallest and largest leaf descendants. All known ancestor-descendant encoding schemes (see [13] for a recent survey) are variations of Santoro and Khatib's interval scheme. The average label length of these class of schemes has an upper bound of $2 \log n$, n being the number of nodes in the XML graph. In our index, the integration of the encoding with other index structures allows us to encode the ancestor-descendant relationship using only one number instead of two (the end of each interval is implicitly stored in the order of the δ_k tables).

The main idea for the *temporal interval encoding* is based on taking advantage of three facts: (a) again, we are indexing continuous paths, not just nodes; (b) the intervals of all the continuous paths in which a node n participates are disjoint; (c) the graph representing a snapshot of a temporal XML document is acyclic. Thus, we can encode the nodes in a way such that each node has as many encodings as continuous paths it is part of.

Parent	Child	From	To
5	6	0	20
5	10	0	Now
5	14	23	Now
5	16	0	20

Figure 11: *cp* table NBA/franchise/team/player

Parent	Child	From	To	Value
6	7	0	20	Oakley
14	30	23	Now	Williams
16	17	0	20	McGrady

Figure 12: *cp + value* table NBA/franchise/team/player/name

In order to formally define the temporal interval encoding, we need to define first a total order relation among the continuous paths in the data graph.

Definition 8 *Let $p_1 = (root, \ldots, v, T_1)$ and $p_2 = (root, \ldots, w, T_2)$ be continuous paths in d. The total order relation $\prec$ is defined as follows:*

1. *If p_i is a proper subpath of p_j, then $p_i \prec p_j$*

2. *Otherwise, let $q_1 = (root, \ldots, n, T_1')$ be the shortest subpath of p_1 that is not a subpath of p_2 and let $q_2 = (root, \ldots, m, T_2')$ be the shortest subpath of p_2 that is not a subpath of p_1.*

   (a) *If $T_1' \cap T_2' = \emptyset$ then $p_1 \prec p_2$ iff $T_1'.FROM < T_2'.FROM$.*

   (b) *If $T_1' \cap T_2' \neq \emptyset$ then $p_1 \prec p_2$ iff $n < m$, where $<$ is the order relation defined in Proposition 1 in $T_1' \cap T_2'$.*

Definition 9 (Temporal Interval Encoding)
Let $\prec$ be the order relation from Definition 8, $succ_\prec$ be the successor function in $\prec$, and gap be a function assigning an integer to each continuous path starting at the root. The temporal interval encoding function τ is defined over pairs $\langle node, cp \rangle$ by $\tau(n, p) = \tau(m, q) + gap(q)$ if there is a q such that $succ_\prec(q) = p$, $\tau(n, p) = 0$ otherwise.

Using the temporal interval encoding, Algorithm 1 can be optimized so that it does not need to follow the parent-child reference chains, but instead, given a node-interval pair (m, I), it computes the successor of m, m', and retrieves from the product automaton all the tuples t associated with final state transitions such that $t.child$ is between m and m'.

Example 3 *Consider for instance Figure 13. The player node corresponding to 'Williams' has initially been encoded as '67'. This number encodes the node*

223

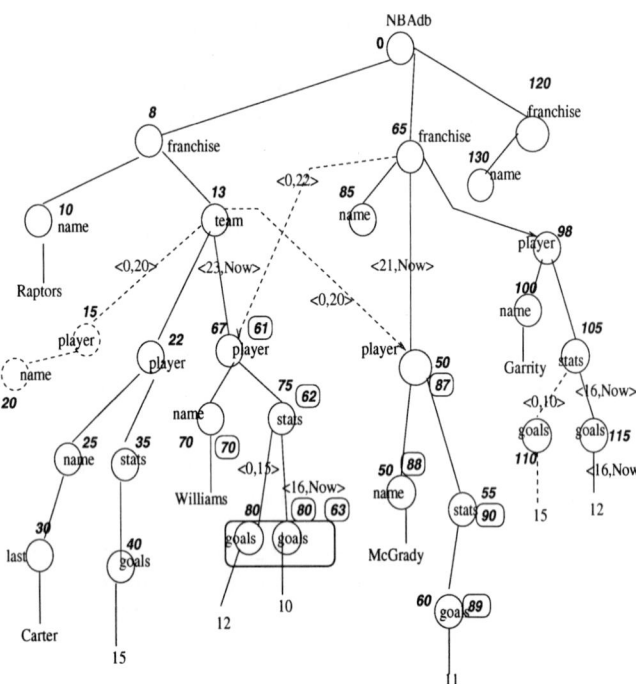

Figure 13: Indexing intervals with *temporal interval encoding*

in the interval $[0, 22]$. For the interval $[23, Now]$, the node's number is '61', because it became a descendant of '13', and must have a number less than '65'. In other words, there are two continuous paths (with disjoint intervals) from the root to the node. For each one of them, we use a different encoding for the same node. Note that these different node numbers do not imply a larger number of tuples in the cp tables, because there is always one tuple for each cp, as in the encoding used so far. For example, a portion of the *NBA-franchise-player* cp table using the encoding of Figure 13 is shown below:

Child	From	To
87	21	Now
67	0	22
61	23	Now
	...	
98	0	Now

Note that the temporal interval encoding does not require explicitly representing the parent of the target node. Thus, we only keep the attribute 'child' in the cp and cp + value tables.

Now, suppose we are asked for the goals scored by players in the Toronto Raptors. The TXPath expression will be:

//franchise[name='Raptors']//goals/text()

Answering this query just requires finding node '8' in the NBA-franchise table, checking that the succesor at any interval is node 65, and looking up in the value table for the path NBA/franchise/player/team/stats/goals the nodes with numbers between 8 and 65.

6 Experiments

In this section we will show how indexing temporal intervals and continuous paths improves TXPath query evaluation. We compare TempIndex with two other systems: one index-based and the other DOM-based. We chose ToXin [20] as a representative of the non-temporal XML index class. We choose this particular scheme for convenience, since it is easily available to us; but we believe the results would not be substantially different using any of the other path indexing schemes discussed in Section 2. The second comparison will be against a DOM representation of the base data without any indexing.

Although using a non-temporal index reduces the search space for TXPath queries – compared to the DOM approach – it still does not help with the temporal part of query evaluation. Both ToXin and DOM materialize paths rather than continuous paths; therefore, these two non-temporal backends have to compute the continuous paths involved in a query on-the-fly during query evaluation time. Our experiments will show how important indexing the temporal structure of the data base is for TXPath queries.

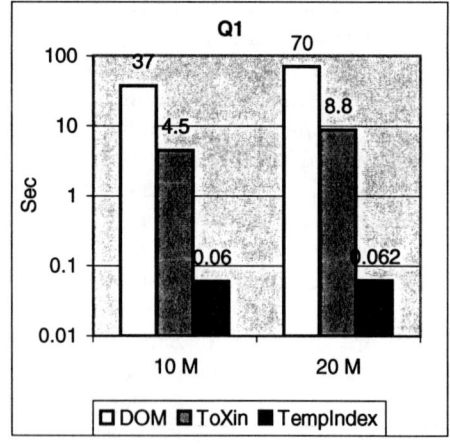

Figure 14: Query Q1 – log scale

For all our experiments we use query processing time as the performance metric. We evaluate the performance of the three systems on a set of five queries, as shown in Table 24. Queries Q1 to Q4 are TXPath retrieval queries, Q5 and Q6 are TXPath update queries, and SN is a document snapshot.

For inserting a node (Query Q5), we specify a time instant t, the new node n' to be inserted, and a current node n (i.e. a node with an incoming containment edge where $T_{e_c}.TO = Now$). When deleting a node n at time t_d, (Query Q6) 'Now' is replaced by t_d

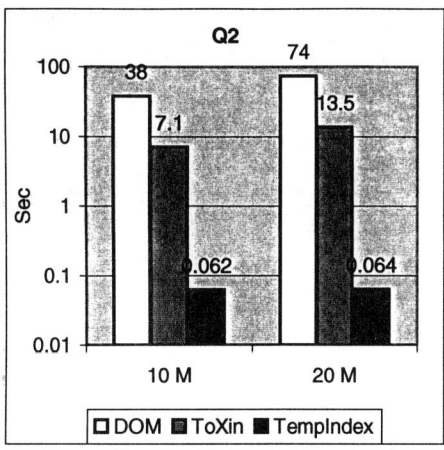

Figure 15: Query Q2 – log scale

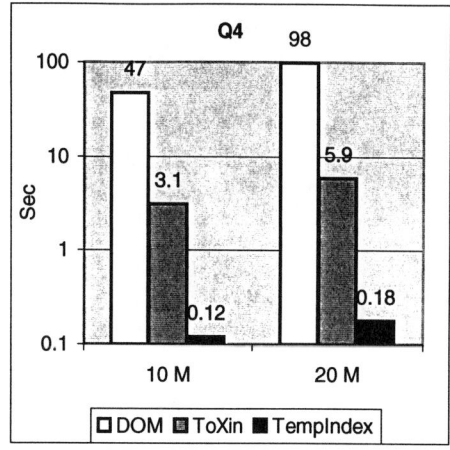

Figure 17: Query Q4 – log scale

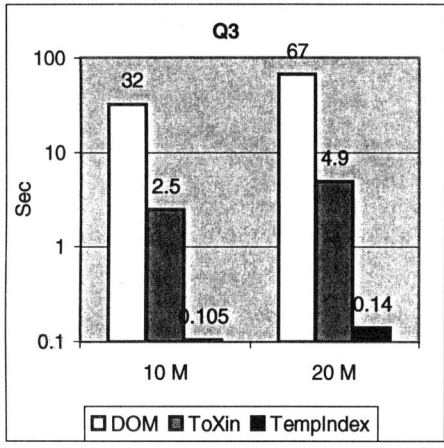

Figure 16: Query Q3 – log scale

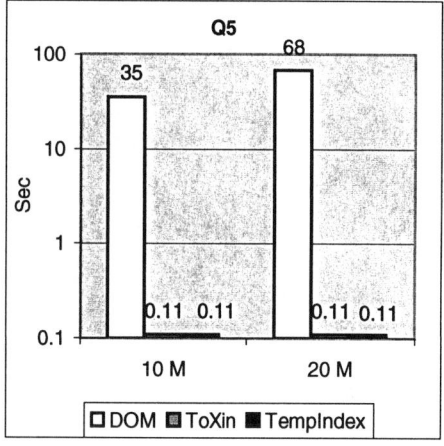

Figure 18: Query Q5: Insert – log scale

in $T_{e_c}.TO$. The same occurs with all the containment edges in the current subtree (the subtree with root n where all the edges e_c have $T_{e_c}.TO = Now$). Reference edges are deleted by setting $T_{e_r}.TO = t_d$ in the temporal label of the edge.

Queries that contain value and interval selections (Q3 through Q6) were performed with ten different combinations of values and intervals. For those four queries we report the average results. We run the queries over the NBA database, which we consider to be a representative example of temporal data. We loaded the data from the NBA web site (www.nba.com) into a relational database (Microsoft SQL Server 2000.) From this database we produced two documents of 10 and 20 Megabytes. We ran all queries over the two documents and the results are reported in Figures 14 to 20. For the experiments we used a Pentium 4 PC at 2Ghz with 1GB of RAM memory and a 60 GB hard drive.

In all retrieval queries TempIndex performed faster than ToXin. The TempIndex speed-up against ToXin ranged from a minimum of nine times (Snapshot–10MB) to a maximum of 210 times (Q2–20MB). Since both systems index label paths and values, the difference in performance can be mostly attributed to the indexing of continuous paths.

Q2 is one of the fastest in TempIndex but one of the slowest in ToXin. The reason for that is that the answer to Q2 is a whole class of continuous paths in the temporal index, which is very easy to find and retrieve using the TempIndex schema. Although in ToXin we can narrow the search by following only those label paths that match the regular expression in the query, we still have to compute all continuous paths over them.

The snapshot, in contrast, requires heavy computation even for TempIndex. We can still narrow the search considerably by using the interval index to locate the classes corresponding to the instant in time we are looking for. However, once these classes are

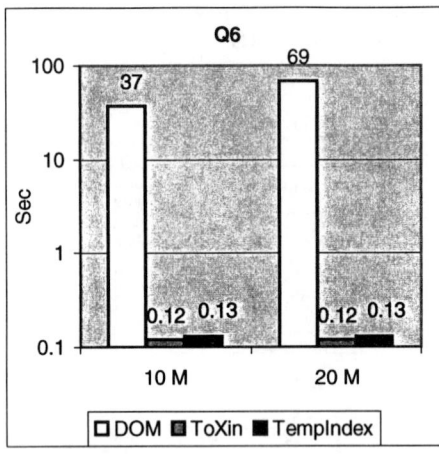

Figure 19: Query Q6: Delete – log scale

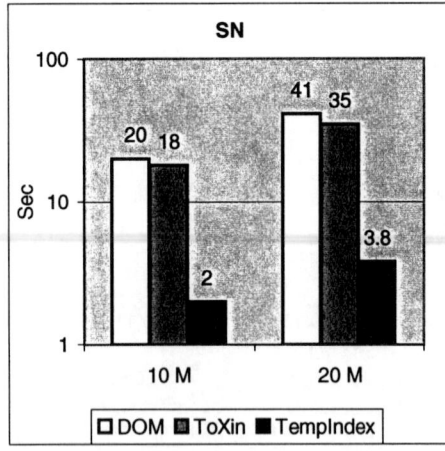

Figure 20: Snapshot – log scale

found we have to reconstruct a whole document navigating back and forth over them. That being said, TempIndex still is almost one order of magnitude faster than ToXin and DOM. Since a path index is not very efficient for document reconstruction operations, the snapshot computation performance of ToXin and DOM are quite similar.

Queries Q1 and Q2 do not contain either interval or value selection predicates and have relatively large answer sets. The answer set of Q1 is closer to the root and smaller than that of Q2. This affects the query processing time in ToXin because the continuous paths to be computed are fewer and much shorter in Q1 than in Q2, with the consequent impact on query evaluation (Q2 takes almost twice the time than Q1). In contrast, since the DOM implementation is not aware of the label path structure of the data graph, it requires the traversal of the whole temporal graph in order to match the regular expression on both Q1 and Q2. Consequently, the difference in query processing

Document size	data graph nodes	*cp*'s	temporal index nodes
10 MB	270150	847005	94
20 MB	540300	1694010	94

Figure 21: Data sets and index parameters

Doc. size	TempToxin size	DOM size
10 MB	105 MB	165 MB
20 MB	205 MB	330 MB

Figure 22: Main-memory structure sizes

time between Q1 and Q2 is minimal in DOM.

Queries Q3 and Q4 require the additional computation of value and interval selection, which is reflected in the TempIndex results. In contrast, the size of the answer set and the length of the continuous paths seems to have a bigger impact on ToXin performance than the selection operations, and almost no impact at all in DOM. The reason for that seems to be that ToXin spends most of the query processing time on continuous path computations, while DOM does it on data graph traversal.

Update queries Q5 (insert) and Q6 (delete) require label path traversal in order to locate the update point. Since no continuous path computation is involved, the difference between ToXin and TempIndex is minimal and can be mostly attributed to the extra time needed to update the *cp* and *cp+value* tables. In contrast, the DOM implementation has to traverse the whole temporal graph in order to locate the update point, with the consequent time difference against both ToXin and TempIndex.

7 Conclusion and Future Work

We studied the problem of indexing temporal XML documents. We formally described an indexing scheme, denoted TempIndex, composed of three kinds of structures: the temporal schema, the temporal depth tables, and the *cp* and *cp + value* tables. We showed that materializing *continuous paths* instead of paths increases query performance by several orders of magnitude when compared against index-based and DOM-based implementations of TXPath, the temporal query language that we used. Even snapshots perform one order of magnitude faster, on the average. This performance is due to the fact that the non-temporal backends have to compute on-the-fly the continuous paths involved in a query during query evaluation time.

Our future work includes extending the indexing scheme presented here, in order to support a temporal version of XQuery, and developing a disk-based index for temporal XML documents supporting larger documents.

Doc. size	Answer size				
	Q1	Q2	Q3	Q4	Snapshot
10 MB	3009	7890	450	1300	15400
20 MB	6018	15780	900	2600	30800

Figure 23: Answer sizes of retrieval queries

Query	TXPath template
Q1	//Player/Name
Q2	//APG
Q3	//Div[Name='X']/Player[Interval='I']
Q4	//SEQUENCE[APG$\geq$'n' and Interval='I']/ancestor::Player/Name
Q5	for $p in //Player[Name='X'] INSERT newNode $p//APG VALUE 'V'
Q6	for $p in //Player[Name='X'] DELETE node $p//stats
SN	Snapshot

Figure 24: Benchmark queries

Acknowledgments

This work was supported by the Institute for Robotics and Intelligent Systems and the Natural Sciences and Engineering Research Council of Canada.

References

[1] T. Amagasa, M. Yoshikawa, and S. Uemura. A temporal data model for XML documents. In *DEXA*, pages 334–344, 2000.

[2] T. Bozkaya and M. Ozsoyoglu. Indexing valid time intervals. In *DEXA*, pages 541–550, 1998.

[3] S. Chien, V. Tsotras, and C. Zaniolo. Version management of XML documents. In *WebDB*, pages 75–80, Dallas, TX, 2000.

[4] S. Chien, V. Tsotras, and C. Zaniolo. Efficient management of multiversion documents by object referencing. In *VLDB*, pages 291–300, Rome, Italy, 2001.

[5] S. Chien, V. Tsotras, C. Zaniolo, and D. Zhang. Efficient complex query support for multiversion XML documents. In *EDBT*, pages 161–178, Prague, Czech Republic, 2002.

[6] C. Chung, J. Min, and K. Shim. Apex: An adaptive path index for XML data. In *ACM SIGMOD*, pages 121–132, Madison, Wisconsin, 2002.

[7] B. Cooper, N. Sample, M.J. Franklin, G.R Hjaltason, and M. Shadmon. A fast index for semistructured data. In *VLDB*, pages 341–350, Rome, Italy, 2001.

[8] C.E. Dyreson. Observing transaction-time semantics with TTXPath. In *WISE*, pages 193–202, 2001.

[9] C. Gao and R. Snodgrass. Syntax, semantics and query evaluation in the τXQuery temporal XML query language. *Time Center Technical Report TR-72*, 2003.

[10] C. Gao and R. Snodgrass. Temporal slicing in the evaluation of XML queries. In *VLDB*, pages 632–643, Berlin, Germany, 2003.

[11] M. Gergatsoulis and Y. Stavrakas. Representing changes in XML documents using dimensions. In *XSym*, pages 208–222, Berlin, Germany, 2003.

[12] R. Goldman and J. Jennifer Widom. Dataguides: Enabling query formulation and optimization in semistructured databases. In *VLDB*, pages 436–445, Athens, Greece, 1997.

[13] H. Kaplan, T. Milo, and R. Shabo. A comparison of labeling schemes for ancestor queries. In *ACM-SIAM SODA*, pages 954–963, 2002.

[14] R. Kaushik, P. Bohannon, J.F. Naughton, and H. Korth. Covering indexes for branching path queries. In *ACM SIGMOD*, pages 133–144, Wisconsin, Madison, 2002.

[15] R. Kaushik, P. Bohannon, J.F. Naughton, and P. Shenoy. Updates for structure indexes. In *VLDB*, pages 239–250, Hong Kong, China, 2002.

[16] R. Kaushik, P. Shenoy, P. Bohannon, and E. Gudes. Exploiting local similarity for indexing paths in graph-structured data. In *IEEE/ICDE*, pages 129–140, San Jose, California, 2002.

[17] Q. Li and B. Moon. Indexing and querying XML data for regular path expressions. In *VLDB*, pages 361–370, Rome, Italy, 2001.

[18] T. Milo and D. Dan Suciu. Index structures for path expressions. In *ICDT*, pages 277–295, Jerusalem, Israel, 1999.

[19] C. Qun, A. Lim, and K. W. Ong. D(k)-index: An adaptive structural summary for graph-structured data. In *ACM SIGMOD*, pages 134–144, San Diego, California, USA, 2003.

[20] F. Rizzolo and A.O. Mendelzon. Indexing XML data with ToXin. In *WebDB*, pages 49–54, Santa Barbara, CA, 2001.

[21] B. Salzberg and V. Tsotras. Comparison of access methods for time-evolving data. *ACM Computing Surveys, vol. 31, no. 2, pp 158-221*, 1999.

[22] N. Santoro and R. Khatib. Labelling and implicit routing in networks. *The Computer Journal (28)*, pages 5–8, 1985.

[23] A. Vaisman, A.O. Mendelzon, E. Molinari, and P. Tome. Temporal XML: Data model, query language and implementation. http://www.cs.toronto.edu/~avaisman/papers.html, 2004.

[24] P. Wadler. A formal semantics of patterns in XSLT. In *Markup Technologies*, pages 183–202, Philadelphia, 1999.

[25] World Wide Web Consortium. *XML Path Language XPath 2.0*, 2003. http://www.w3.org/TR/2003/WD-xpath20-20030502.

Schema-based Scheduling of Event Processors and Buffer Minimization for Queries on Structured Data Streams

Christoph Koch[†,*]   Stefanie Scherzinger[‡]   Nicole Schweikardt[♮]   Bernhard Stegmaier[♯]

[†]: Technische Universität Wien, Vienna, Austria, Email: `koch@dbai.tuwien.ac.at`
[‡]: Technische Universität Wien, Vienna, Austria, Email: `scherzinger@wit.tuwien.ac.at`
[♮]: Humboldt Universität zu Berlin, Berlin, Germany, Email: `schweikardt@informatik.hu-berlin.de`
[♯]: Technische Universität München, Munich, Germany, Email: `bernhard.stegmaier@in.tum.de`

Abstract

We introduce an extension of the XQuery language, FluX, that supports event-based query processing and the conscious handling of main memory buffers. Purely event-based queries of this language can be executed on streaming XML data in a very direct way. We then develop an algorithm that allows to efficiently rewrite XQueries into the event-based FluX language. This algorithm uses order constraints from a DTD to schedule event handlers and to thus minimize the amount of buffering required for evaluating a query. We discuss the various technical aspects of query optimization and query evaluation within our framework. This is complemented with an experimental evaluation of our approach.

1 Introduction

XML is the preeminent data exchange format on the Internet. Stream processing naturally bears relevance in the data exchange context (e.g., in e-commerce). An increasingly important data management scenario is the processing of XQueries on streams of exchanged XML data. While the weaknesses of XML as a semistructured data model have been observed time and again (cf. e.g. [1]), XQuery on XML streams can be seen as the prototypical instance of the problem of queries on *structured* (vs. flat tuple) *data streams*.

Query engines for processing streams are naturally main-memory-based. Conversely, in some efforts towards developing main-memory XQuery engines whose original emphasis was *not* on stream processing (e.g., BEA's XQRL [9]), it was observed that it is worthwhile to build such systems using stream processing operators.

The often excessive need for buffers in current main memory query engines causes a scalability issue that has been identified as a significant research challenge [14, 13, 16, 7, 4]. While the efficient evaluation of XPath queries on streams has been worked on extensively in the past (here, state-of-the-art techniques use very little main memory) [2, 5, 10, 11], not much work has been done on efficiently processing XQuery on streams. The nature of XQuery, as a *data-transformation* query language entirely different from *node-selecting* XPath, requires new techniques for dealing with (and reducing) main memory buffers. State-of-the-art XQuery engines consume main memory in large multiples of the actual size of input XML documents [14].

Several recent projects have addressed XQuery on streams using transducer networks [13, 16]. Automata-based techniques are usually quite elegant but are hard to compare or integrate with other approaches and usually do not generalize to real-world query languages such as (full) XQuery with their great expressive power and all their odd features and artifacts of the standardization process. One approach [14] towards addressing the problem of reducing main memory consumption in an engine for full XQuery aims at reducing the amount of data buffered in main memory by pre-filtering the data read from the stream with the paths occurring in the query. However, for real-world XQueries, the need for substantial main memory buffers cannot be avoided in general.

An important goal is thus to devise a well-principled machinery for processing XQuery that is parsimonious with resources and allows to minimize the amount of buffering. Such machinery needs to be based on intermediate representations of queries that are syntactically close to XQuery and has to allow for an algebraic approach to query optimization, with buffering

---

*Work support by project Z29-N04 of the Austrian Science Fund (FWF).

Permission to copy without fee all or part of this material is granted provided that the copies are not made or distributed for direct commercial advantage, the VLDB copyright notice and the title of the publication and its date appear, and notice is given that copying is by permission of the Very Large Data Base Endowment. To copy otherwise, or to republish, requires a fee and/or special permission from the Endowment.

**Proceedings of the 30th VLDB Conference,
Toronto, Canada, 2004**

as an optimization target. This is necessary to allow for both extensibility and the leverage of a large body of related earlier work done by the database research community. However, to our knowledge, no principled work exists on query optimization in the framework of XQuery (rather than automata) for *structured data streams* (such as XML, but unlike flat tuple streams) which honors the special features of stream processing. Moreover, no framework for optimizing queries on structured data streams exists that captures the spirit of stream processing and allows for query optimization using schema information. (However, there are XQuery algebras meant for conventional query processing [17, 8], and there is work on applying them in the streaming context [7]. Moreover, the problem of optimizing XQueries using a set of constraints holding in the XML data model – rather than a schema – was addressed in [6].)

In this paper, we attempt to improve on this situation. We introduce a query language, *FluX*, which extends XQuery by a new construct for event-based query processing called `process-stream`. FluX motivates a very direct mode of query evaluation on data streams (similar to query evaluation in XQRL [9]), and provides a strong intuition for what main memory buffers are needed in which queries. This allows for a strongly "buffer-conscious" mode of query optimization. The main focus of this paper is on automatically rewriting XQueries into event-based FluX queries and at the same time optimizing (reducing) the use of buffers using schema information from a DTD.

Consider the following XQuery Q in a bibliography domain, taken from the XML Query Use Cases [18] (XMP Q3):

```
<results>
{ for $b in $ROOT/bib/book return
    <result> { $b/title } { $b/author } </result> }
</results>
```

For each book in the bibliography, this query lists its title(s) and authors, grouped inside a "result" element. Note that the XQuery language requires that, within each book, all titles are output before all authors.

The DTD

```
<!ELEMENT bib  (book)*>
<!ELEMENT book (title|author)*>
```

specifies that each `book` node may have several `title` and several `author` children. A priori, no order among these items is inferable from the given DTD. To implement this query, we may output the `title` children inside a `book` node as soon as they arrive on the stream. However, the output of the `author` children needs to be delayed (using a memory buffer) until we reach the closing tag of the `book` node (at that time, no further `title` nodes may be encountered). Then we may flush the buffer of `author` nodes, empty it, and later refill it with the `author` nodes from the next book.

We thus only need to buffer the `author` children of one `book` node at a time, but not the titles. Current main memory query engines do not exploit this fact, and rather buffer either the entire book nodes or, as an optimization [14], all `title` and all `author` nodes of `book`. Previous frameworks for evaluating or optimizing XQuery do not provide any means of making this seeming subtlety explicit and reasoning about it.

The `process-stream` construct of FluX allows to express precisely the mode of query execution just described. XQuery Q is then phrased as a FluX query as follows:

```
<results>
{ process-stream $ROOT: on bib as $bib return
    { process-stream $bib: on book as $book return
      <result>
      { process-stream $book:
          on title as $t return {$t};
          on-first past(title,author) return
            { for $a in $book/author return {$a} } }
      </result> } }
</results>
```

A `process-stream $x` expression consists of a number of *handlers* which process the children of the XML tree node bound by variable `$x` from left to right. An "on a" handler fires on each child labeled "a" visited during such a traversal, executing the associated query expression. In the `process-stream $book` expression above, the `on-first past(title,author)` handler fires exactly once as soon as the DTD implies for the first time that no further `author` or `title` node can be encountered among the children of `$book`. (As observed above, in the given, very weak DTD, this is the case only as soon as the last child of `$book` has been seen.) In the query associated with the `on-first past(title,author)` handler, we may freely use paths of the form `$book/author` or `$book/title`, because such paths cannot be encountered anymore and we may assume that the query engine has already buffered all matches of these paths for us. It is a feasible task for the query engine to buffer only those paths that the query actually employs (see also [14]).

We call a query *safe* for a given DTD if, informally, it is guaranteed that XQuery subexpressions (such as the for-loop in the query above) do not refer to paths that may still be encountered in the stream. The above FluX query is safe: The for-expression employs the `$book/author` path, but is part of an on-first handler that cannot fire before all `author` nodes relative to `$book` have been seen.

If the path `$book/author` was replaced by, say, `$book/price` and the DTD production for `book` were

```
<!ELEMENT book ((title|author)*,price)>
```

then the FluX query above would not be safe. In that case, on the firing of `on-first past(title,author)`, the buffer for `$book/price` items would still be empty and the query result would be incorrect.

Query Q can be processed more efficiently with the schema used in the XML Query Use Cases,

```
<!ELEMENT bib   (book)*>
<!ELEMENT book (title,(author+|editor+),
                        publisher,price)>
```

Here, no buffering is required to execute our query because the DTD asserts that for each book, the title occurs strictly before the authors (we denote this as $Ord_{book}(\text{title}, \text{author})$, called an *order constraint*). We may phrase our query in FluX so as to directly copy titles and authors to the output as they arrive on the input stream. No data items need to be buffered.

```
<results>
{ process-stream $ROOT: on bib as $bib return
   { process-stream $bib: on book as $book return
      <result>
      { process-stream $book:
         on title  as $t return {$t};
         on author as $a return {$a} }
      </result> } }
</results>
```

The contributions of this paper are as follows.

- We introduce the FluX query language, which extends XQuery by the natural stream processing construct discussed above.

- We define the *safe* FluX queries (under a given DTD), which are those FluX queries in which XQuery subexpressions have the usual semantics (i.e., are never executed before the data items referred to have been fully read from the stream and may be assumed available in main memory buffers).

- We present an algorithm that schedules XQueries on streams using DTDs and transforms them into optimized FluX queries.

- We discuss the realization of query engines for FluX and the runtime buffer management.

- We have built a prototype FluX query engine which we evaluate by means of a number of experiments.

This is, to our knowledge, the first work on optimizing XQuery using schema constraints derived from DTDs[1]. A main strength of the approach taken in this paper is its extensibility, and even though space limitations require us to restrict our discussion to a (powerful) *fragment* of XQuery, our results can be generalized to even larger fragments. In our discussion at the end of the paper, we will also lay the foundations for algebraic optimization of queries using further information from the schema.

This paper is structured as follows. We start with basics on DTDs and regular languages in Section 2. Section 3 defines the query languages considered in this paper: Section 3.1 specifies an XQuery fragment. Based on this, Section 3.2 defines the FluX language, and Section 3.3 singles out the safe FluX queries. Section 4 presents our algorithms for translating XQuery

---
[1]To simplify presentation we restrict ourselves to DTDs, but the required information could also be derived from XML Schemata.

into a particular normal form (Section 4.1) and for transforming this normal form into FluX (Section 4.2). Some examples of this transformation are given in Section 4.3. In Section 5 we discuss the implementation of our prototype system and the actual handling of buffers during query evaluation. In Section 6, we present our experiments, and we conclude with a discussion in Section 7.

2 Preliminaries

For simplicity of exposition, we consider the fragment of XML without attributes as our data model. Note that this is no substantial restriction, since attributes can be handled in the same way as subelements.

We focus on *valid* documents, i.e. documents conforming to a given *document type definition* (DTD).

Let Σ be a set of symbols (or tag names). A DTD is an extended context free grammar over Σ. DTDs are *local* tree grammars [15], i.e. without competing nonterminals to the left-hand sides of productions, so each production in a DTD is unambiguously identified by a tag name in Σ.

Let ρ be a regular expression and let $symb(\rho)$ be the set of atomic symbols that occur in ρ. By $L(\rho)$ we denote the language defined by ρ, i.e., the set of words over $symb(\rho)$ that are recognizable by ρ. Given a word w, let w_i denote its i-th symbol. We define a binary relation $Ord_\rho \subseteq \Sigma \times \Sigma$ such that for $a, b \in \Sigma$,

$$Ord_\rho(a,b) :\Leftrightarrow \not\exists w \in L(\rho) : w_i = b \wedge w_j = a \wedge i < j.$$

That is, $Ord_\rho(a,b)$ holds if there is no word in $L(\rho)$ in which a symbol a is preceded by a symbol b. (All a symbols occur before all b symbols.) We refer to a constraint of the form $Ord_\rho(a,b)$ as an *order constraint*.

Example 2.1 Let $\rho = (a^*.b.c^*.(d|e^*).a^*)$. Then, $Ord_\rho(b,c)$, $Ord_\rho(c,d)$, and $Ord_\rho(c,e)$, but $\neg Ord_\rho(a,c)$. Ord_ρ is transitive, so we also have e.g. $Ord_\rho(b,d)$. □

DTDs have the nice property that regular expressions appearing in the right-hand sides of productions are *one-unambiguous*. This guarantees that an equivalent *deterministic* finite automaton can be computed in polynomial – even quadratic – time [3]. One can show the following [12]:

Proposition 2.2 *Given a regular expression ρ from a DTD, Ord_ρ can be computed in time $O(|\rho|^2)$.*

Let ρ be a regular expression and let $S \subseteq \Sigma$. Then, for each word $u = u_1 \ldots u_n \in symb(\rho)^*$,

$Past_{\rho,S}(u) :\Leftrightarrow$
$\quad \forall w \in symb(\rho)^* : uw \in L(\rho) \rightarrow \not\exists i : w_i \in S,$
$first\text{-}past_{\rho,S}(u) :\Leftrightarrow$
$\quad Past_{\rho,S}(u) \wedge \bigl(n > 0 \rightarrow \neg Past_{\rho,S}(u_1 \ldots u_{n-1})\bigr).$

Intuitively, when processing a word $uw \in L(\rho)$ from left to right, if $first\text{-}past_{\rho,S}(u)$ holds, then the reading of the last symbol of u is the earliest possible time at which we know that none of the symbols in S can be seen anymore until the end of the word uw.

3 Query Language

In this section, we define the syntax and semantics of the FluX query language, which extends an XQuery fragment, denoted as XQuery$^-$, by a construct for event-based query processing.

Before defining FluX and XQuery$^-$, we need some more notation. We write $\$x$, $\$y$, $\$z$, ... to denote variables that range over XML trees. In the following, we overload the meaning of variable $\$x$ bound to an XML tree whose root is labeled a, by writing $\$x$ when we actually mean the DTD production unambiguously identified by the element a. For example, if the DTD contains the rule `<!ELEMENT a `ρ^a`>` for a regular expression ρ^a, we write $Ord_{\$x}(c,d)$ instead of $Ord_{\rho^a}(c,d)$, and we write $symb(\$x)$ instead of $symb(\rho^a)$.

A *fixed path* is a sequence $a_1/\ldots/a_n$, where the a_i are symbols from the DTD and $n \geq 1$. XPath expressions such as $a/*/b$, or $a//b$ or $a[b]$ are excluded.

An *atomic condition* is either of the form $\$x/\pi$ *RelOp* s, exists $\$x/\pi$, or $\$x/\pi$ *RelOp* $\$y/\pi'$, where s is a string, π and π' are fixed paths, and $RelOp \in \{=, <, \leq, >, \geq\}$. A *condition* is a Boolean combination (using "and", "or", "not", and "true") of atomic conditions.

3.1 An XQuery Fragment: XQuery$^-$

Definition 3.1 (XQuery$^-$) The XQuery fragment XQuery$^-$ is the smallest set consisting of expressions

1. ϵ (the empty query)
2. s (output of a fixed string)
3. $\alpha\,\beta$ (sequence)
4. `{ for `$\$x$` in `$\$y/\pi$` return `$\alpha$` }` (for-loop)
5. `{ for `$\$x$` in `$\$y/\pi$` where `$\chi$` return `$\alpha$` }` (conditional for-loop)
6. `{ `$\$x/\pi$` }` (output of subtrees reachable from node $\$x$ through path π)
7. `{ `$\$x$` }` (output of subtree of node $\$x$)
8. `{ if `χ` then `α` }` (conditional)

where π is a fixed path, s a fixed string, χ a condition, and α and β are XQuery$^-$ expressions.

Indeed, XQuery$^-$ is very similar to (a fragment of) standard XQuery [17], but differs in how we treat fixed strings inside queries. For example, the string `<hello>` is valid in XQuery$^-$, but not in standard XQuery. The query

```
<result> { $ROOT/bib/book } </result>
```

is understood in standard XQuery as a "result" node with an embedded query to produce its children. In the present paper, the same query is read as a sequence of three queries which write the string `<result>`, the /bib/book subtrees, and finally the string `</result>` to the output.

This, however, is only a subtlety which, on the one hand, is very convenient for obtaining our main results in Section 4 and which, on the other hand, as the following Proposition 3.2 shows, does not cause any problems. The alternative semantics of XQuery$^-$ is the basis of optimizations used *internally* by the query engine. Users formulate input queries in standard XQuery and may assume the usual semantics.

Let $[\![Q]\!]_{XQuery^-}(D)$ (resp., $[\![Q]\!]_{XQuery}(D)$) denote the XML document stream produced by evaluating query Q on document D under our XQuery$^-$ semantics (resp., under the standard XQuery semantics [17]).

Proposition 3.2 *Let Q be an XQuery that parses as an XQuery$^-$ query. Then, for any input document D, $[\![Q]\!]_{XQuery^-}(D) = [\![Q]\!]_{XQuery}(D)$.*

3.2 Syntax and Semantics of FluX

A *simple expression* is an XQuery$^-$ expression of the form $\alpha\,\beta\,\gamma$ where

- α and γ are possibly empty sequences of strings and of expressions of the form "`{if `χ` then `s`}`", where χ is a condition and s is a string.
- β is either empty, "`{`$\$u$`}`", or "`{if `$\chi$` then {`$\$u$`} }`", for some variable $\$u$ and some condition χ.
- if β is of the form "`{`$\$u$`}`", or "`{if `$\chi$` then {`$\$u$`} }`", then no atomic condition that occurs in $\alpha\,\beta$ contains the variable $\$u$.

For instance,

`<a>{`$\$x$`}</a> {if `$\$x$`/b=5 then <b>5</b>}`

is a simple expression, but `{`$\$x$`}{`$\$y$`}` is not.

Definition 3.3 (FluX) The class of FluX expressions is the smallest set of expressions that are either *simple* or of the form

$$s\ \{\ \texttt{process-stream}\ \$y\colon\ \zeta\ \}\ s'$$

where s and s' are possibly empty strings, $\$y$ is a variable, and ζ is a list (where entries are separated by semicolons ";") of one or more *event handlers*. Each event handler is of one of the following two types:

1. (so-called "on-first" handler)

   `on-first past(`S`) return `α

   where $S \subseteq symb(\$y)$ and α is an XQuery$^-$ expression

2. (so-called "on" handler)

   `on `a` as `$\$x$` return `$Q$

   where $\$x$ is a variable, a is an element name in $symb(\$y)$, and Q is a FluX expression.

We will use `ps` as a shortcut for `process-stream`, `on-first past(*)` as an abbreviation for `on-first past(`$symb(\$y)$`)`, and furthermore `on-first past()` in place of `on-first past(`$\emptyset$`)`.

Some examples of FluX expressions, as well as an informal description of the FluX semantics, were already given in Section 1; further examples can be found in Section 4.3. In general, we evaluate an expression

$$\{ \texttt{process-stream}\ \$y\colon \zeta\ \}$$

as follows: An event-handling statement considers the children of the node currently bound by variable $\$y$ as a list (or stream) of nodes and processes this list one node at a time. On processing a node v with children $t_1, \ldots, t_n$, with the labels of t_i denoted as $label(t_i)$, we proceed as follows. For each i from 0 to $n+1$ (i.e., $n+2$ times), we scan the list of event handlers $\zeta = \zeta_1; \ldots; \zeta_m$ once from the beginning to the end. In doing so, we test for each event handler ζ_j whether its event condition is satisfied, in which case the event handler ζ_j "fires" and the corresponding query expression is executed:

- A handler "on a as $\$x$ return Q" fires if $1 \leq i \leq n$ and $label(t_i) = a$.

- A handler "on-first past(S) return α" fires if $0 \leq i \leq n$ and $\textit{first-past}_{\$y,S}(label(t_1)\ldots label(t_i))$ is true (i.e., for the first time while processing the children of $\$y$, no symbol of S can be encountered anymore) or if $i = n+1$ and this event handler has not fired in any of the previous ($n+1$) scans.

In summary, it is well possible that several events fire for a single node, in which case they are processed in the order in which the handlers occur in ζ. During the run on $t_1, \ldots, t_n$, each "on" handler may fire zero up to several times, while each "on-first" handler is executed exactly once.

For a FluX or XQuery$^-$ expression Q, let $free(Q)$ be the set of all *free variables* in Q, defined analogously to the free variables of a formula in first-order logic. That is, $free(\{\$x/\pi\}) = \{\$x\}$, and $free(\{\texttt{if}\ \chi\ \texttt{then}\ \alpha\})$ consists of $free(\alpha)$ and the variables that appear in χ. Further, $free(\{\texttt{for}\ \$x\ \texttt{in}\ \$y/\pi\ \texttt{return}\ \alpha\})$ contains the variable $\$y$ and the variables in $free(\alpha) \setminus \{\$x\}$. Finally, $free(\{\texttt{process-stream}\ \$y\colon \zeta\})$ consists of the variable $\$y$, for each event handler in ζ of the form "on-first past(S) return α" also of the variables in $free(\alpha)$, and likewise for each event handler in ζ of the form "on a as $\$x$ return Q" of the variables in $free(Q)\setminus\{\$x\}$.

Note that expressions of the form "{for $\$x$ in $\$y/a$ return α}" and event handlers of the form "on a as $\$x$ return Q" *bind* the variable $\$x$, i.e., remove it from the free variables of the superexpressions.

A FluX *query* is a FluX expression in which all free variables except for the special variable $\texttt{\$ROOT}$ corresponding to (the root of) the document are bound. That is, for a *query* Q in FluX (resp., α in XQuery$^-$) we require that $free(Q) \subseteq \{\texttt{\$ROOT}\}$ (resp., $free(\alpha) \subseteq \{\texttt{\$ROOT}\}$).

As the following example shows, every XQuery$^-$ query can be transformed into a FluX query in a straightforward way.

Example 3.4 Every XQuery$^-$ query α is equivalent to the FluX query

$$\{ \texttt{ps \$ROOT:}\ \texttt{on-first past(*) return}\ \alpha\ \}$$

In Section 4 below we will show how, depending on a given DTD, this FluX query can be transformed into an equivalent FluX query that can be evaluated more efficiently. □

By the *size* of an expression Q, denoted $|Q|$, we refer to the size of its string representation.

By the *parent variable* of (FluX or XQuery$^-$) expression α in FluX query Q, denoted $parentVar(\alpha)$, we refer to the variable bound by the nearest superexpression of α, or $\texttt{\$ROOT}$ if no such variable exists.

By the *condition paths* in α, we refer to the set of paths $\$x/\pi$ in a condition χ that occurs in α.

For FluX or XQuery$^-$ expressions α and β we write $\alpha \preceq \beta$ (resp., $\alpha \prec \beta$) to denote that α is a subexpression (resp., proper subexpression) of β. An XQuery$^-$ subexpression α of a FluX expression Q is called *maximal* if there is no XQuery$^-$ expression β with $\alpha \prec \beta \preceq Q$. Note that a FluX query may contain several such maximal expressions.

Example 3.5 The maximal XQuery$^-$ subexpressions of the first FluX query from Section 1 are "{$\$t$}" and "{ for $\$a$ in $\$book/author$ return {$\$a$} }". □

3.3 Safe Queries

We next define the notion of *safety* for FluX queries. Informally, a query is called *safe* for a given DTD if it is guaranteed that XQuery$^-$ subexpressions do not refer to paths that might still be encountered in an input stream compliant with the given DTD. For the precise definition we need the following notion.

The set of *dependencies* w.r.t. variable $\$y$ in a FluX or XQuery$^-$ expression α is defined as

$dependencies(\$y, \alpha) :=$
$\{a \mid \text{ex. a condition path }\$y/a \text{ or } \$y/a/\pi \text{ in } \alpha\} \cup$
$\{b \mid \text{ex. }\$u, \pi, Q \text{ s.t. }\pi \text{ starts with symbol } b \text{ and}$
$\quad \text{"\{for }\$u\text{ in }\$y/\pi\text{ return }Q\text{\}"} \preceq \alpha\}.$

Definition 3.6 (safe queries) A FluX query Q is called *safe* w.r.t. a given DTD if, and only if, for each subexpression "{ps $\$y$: ζ }" of Q, the following two conditions are satisfied:

1. For each handler "on-first past(S) return α" in the list ζ, the following is true:

   - $\forall\ b \in dependencies(\$y, \alpha)$ we have: $b \in S$ or ex. $a \in S$ s.t. $Ord_{\$y}(b, a)$.
   - $\forall\ \$z \in free(\alpha)$ s.t. $\{\$z\} \preceq \alpha$ or $\{\$z/\pi\} \preceq \alpha$ (for some π) we have: $\$z = \$y$ and $\forall\ b \in symb(\$y)$: $b \in S$ or ex. $a \in S$ s.t. $Ord_{\$y}(b, a)$.

$$\frac{\{\ \text{for}\ \$x\ \text{in}\ \$y/\pi\ \text{where}\ \chi\ \text{return}\ \beta\ \}}{\{\ \text{for}\ \$x\ \text{in}\ \$y/\pi\ \text{return}\ \{\ \text{if}\ \chi\ \text{then}\ \beta\ \}\ \}}$$

$$\frac{\{\ \$y/\pi\ \}}{\{\ \text{for}\ \$x\ \text{in}\ \$y/\pi\ \text{return}\ \{\$x\}\ \}}$$

$$\frac{\{\ \text{for}\ \$x\ \text{in}\ \$y/a/\pi\ \text{return}\ \beta\ \}}{\{\ \text{for}\ \$x_0\ \text{in}\ \$y/a\ \text{return}\ \{\ \text{for}\ \$x\ \text{in}\ \$x_0/\pi\ \text{return}\ \beta\ \}\ \}} \quad (\$x_0\ \text{new})$$

$$\frac{\{\ \text{if}\ \chi\ \text{then}\ \{\ \text{for}\ \$x\ \text{in}\ \$y/\pi\ \text{return}\ \alpha\ \}\ \}}{\{\ \text{for}\ \$x\ \text{in}\ \$y/\pi\ \text{return}\ \{\ \text{if}\ \chi\ \text{then}\ \alpha\ \}\ \}}$$

$$\frac{\{\ \text{if}\ \chi\ \text{then}\ \alpha\ \beta\ \}}{\{\ \text{if}\ \chi\ \text{then}\ \alpha\ \}\ \{\ \text{if}\ \chi\ \text{then}\ \beta\ \}}$$

$$\frac{\{\ \text{if}\ \chi\ \text{then}\ \{\ \text{if}\ \psi\ \text{then}\ \alpha\ \}\ \}}{\{\ \text{if}\ (\chi\ \text{and}\ \psi)\ \text{then}\ \alpha\ \}}$$

Figure 1: Normal form rewrite rules. Each rule is always applied downwards, i.e., the expression above the line is replaced by the expression below the line.

2. For each handler "on a as $\$x$ return $\tilde{Q}$" in the list ζ, and for each maximal XQuery$^-$ subexpression α of $\tilde{Q}$, the following is true:

- $\forall\, b \in \textit{dependencies}(\$y, \alpha)$ we have: $\textit{Ord}_{\$y}(b, a)$
- if $\alpha = \tilde{Q}$ (note that according to Definition 3.3 α must then be *simple*), then for all $\$u$ s.t. $\{\$u\} \preceq \alpha$ we have: $\$u = \$x$.

It can be shown that this notion of *safety* is sufficient to ensure that main memory buffers are fully populated when they are accessed by a query, i.e., that a FluX query can be evaluated in a straightforward way on input streams compliant with the given DTD.

Examples of safe FluX queries can be found in Sections 1 and 4. (To be precise, all FluX queries occurring in this paper are safe.)

4 Translating XQuery into FluX

In this section we address the problem of rewriting a query of our XQuery fragment into an equivalent FluX query that employs as little buffering as possible. This rewriting proceeds in two steps: First, we transform the given XQuery$^-$ query into an equivalent query in XQuery$^-$ *normal form* (Section 4.1). Afterwards, depending on a given DTD, this normalized query is rewritten into an equivalent safe FluX query (Section 4.2). The FluX extensions manage the event based, streaming execution of the query. All subqueries exclusively working on buffered data are XQuery$^-$ expressions.

4.1 A Normal Form for XQuery$^-$

An XQuery$^-$ expression is transformed into *normal form* by rewriting (subexpressions of) it using the rules in Figure 1 until no further changes are possible.

In an XQuery$^-$ expression in normal form, the following three properties hold: (1) All paths except those inside conditionals are simple-step paths, i.e. of the form $\$x/a$. (2) An expression in normal form does not contain any *conditional* for-loops, as the normalization process pushes conditionals inside the innermost for-loops. (3) For each subexpression of the form "$\{\text{if}\ \chi\ \text{then}\ \alpha\}$", α is either a fixed string or of the form "$\{\$x\}$" for some variable $\$x$.

Theorem 4.1 *The rule applications of Figure 1 can be implemented in such a way that the rewriting terminates for an input XQuery$^-$ expression Q after $O(|Q|)$ rule applications with a unique result, the so-called normalization of Q, which is equivalent to Q.*

Example 4.2 ([18], XMP, Q1) Consider the following XQuery Q_1 for books published by Addison-Wesley after 1991, including their year and title.

```
<bib>
{ for $b in $ROOT/bib/book
    where $b/publisher = "Addison-Wesley" and
          $b/year > 1991
    return <book> {$b/year} {$b/title} </book> }
</bib>
```

We abbreviate the where-condition in the above query as χ. Then Q_1 has the following normalization Q'_1:

```
<bib>
{ for $bib in $ROOT/bib return
    { for $b in $bib/book return
        { if χ then <book> }
        { for $year in $b/year return
            { if χ then {$year} } }
        { for $title in $b/title return
            { if χ then {$title} } }
        { if χ then </book> } } }
</bib>
```
□

4.2 Rewriting normalized XQuery$^-$ into FluX

To formulate our main rewrite algorithm for transforming normalized XQuery$^-$ queries into equivalent, safe FluX queries, we need some further notation.

Let Σ be the set of tag names occurring in the given DTD. Let $\bot$ denote the empty list. For a list ζ of event handlers, we inductively define the set $\textit{hsymb}(\zeta)$ of handler symbols for which an "on" handler or an "on-first" handler exists in ζ:

$$\textit{hsymb}(\bot) := \emptyset$$
$$\textit{hsymb}(\zeta; \text{on}\ a\ \text{as}\ \$x\ \text{return}\ \alpha) := \textit{hsymb}(\zeta) \cup \{a\}$$
$$\textit{hsymb}(\zeta; \text{on-first}\ \text{past}(S)\ \text{return}\ \alpha) :=$$
$$\textit{hsymb}(\zeta) \cup S$$

Our algorithm for recursively rewriting normalized XQuery$^-$ expressions into FluX is shown in Figure 2. Note that this algorithm uses order constraints and hence depends on the underlying DTD. Given

```
 1 function rewrite(Variable parentVar, Set⟨Σ⟩ H,
 2                  XQuery⁻ β) returns FluXQuery
 3 begin
 4   let $x = parentVar;
 5   if {$x} ⪯ β then
 6   begin
 7     if β is simple and dependencies($x,β) = ∅ then
 8       return β
 9     else
10       return { ps $x: on-first past(*) return β }
11   end
12   else /* {$x} ⋠ β */
13   begin
14     if β = β₁ β₂ then
15     begin
16       β'₁ := rewrite(parentVar, H, β₁);
17       match ζ₁ such that β'₁ = { ps $x: ζ₁ };
18       β'₂ := rewrite(parentVar, H ∪ hsymb(ζ₁), β₂);
19       match ζ₂ such that β'₂ = { ps $x: ζ₂ };
20       return { ps $x: ζ₁; ζ₂ }
21     end
22     else if β is simple then
23       /* β is either of the form s or { if χ then s } */
24       return { ps $x:
25                  on-first past(dependencies($x,β) ∪ H)
26                  return β }
27     else if β is of the form
28          { for $y in $z/a return α } then
29     begin
30       X := {b ∈ dependencies($x,α) ∪ H | ¬Ord_{$x}(b,a)};
31       if $z ≠ $x then
32         return { ps $x: on-first past(X) return β }
33       else if X ≠ ∅ then
34         return { ps $x: on-first past(X ∪ {a}) return β }
35       else
36       begin
37         α' := rewrite($y, ∅, α);
38         return { ps $x: on a as $y return α' }
39       end
40     end /* if β is for-expression */
41   end /* else {$x} ⋠ β */
42 end
```

Figure 2: Algorithm for rewriting XQuery⁻ into FluX.

query Q, we obtain the corresponding FluX query as "rewrite($ROOT, ∅, Q)". Some example runs of this algorithm are given in Section 4.3 below. The goals in the design of the algorithm were to produce a FluX query which (1) is safe w.r.t. the given DTD, (2) is equivalent to the input XQuery, and (3) minimizes the amount of buffering needed for evaluating the query in an XML document.

To meet goals (1) and (2), e.g. the particular order of the if-statements in the algorithm (lines 5, 14, 22, 27) is crucial. Also, a set H of handler symbols must be passed on in recursive calls of the algorithm, because otherwise the resulting FluX query would not be safe. One important construct for meeting goal (3) is the case distinction in lines 31–39, where an "on" handler is created provided that this is *safe*, and an "on-first" handler is created otherwise.

Theorem 4.3 *Given a DTD D and a normalized XQuery⁻ query Q, "rewrite($ROOT, ∅, Q)" runs in time $O(|D|^3 + |Q|^2)$ and produces a safe FluX query that is equivalent to Q on all XML documents compliant with the given DTD.*

Our algorithm performs only a single traversal of the query tree. Runtime $O(|Q|^2)$ is mainly caused by the need to compute *dependencies*. Note that the resulting FluX query is in normal form.

4.3 Examples

We now discuss the effect of our rewrite algorithm on sample queries from the XQuery Use Cases [18].[2]

Example 4.4 ([18], XMP, Q2) Let us consider the XQuery Q_2 from the XQuery Use Cases [18], which creates a flat list of all the title–author pairs, with each pair enclosed in a `result` element. Due to space limitations we omit Q_2 here and only give its normalization Q'_2 (which is very similar to the original XQuery Q_2):

```
1 <results>
2 { for $bib in $ROOT/bib return
3   { for $b in $bib/book return
4     { for $t in $b/title return
5       { for $a in $b/author return
6         <result> {$t} {$a} </result> } } }
7 </results>
```

When given a DTD that does not impose any order constraints on `title` and `author`, e.g., the first DTD from Section 1, then "rewrite($ROOT,∅,$Q'_2$)" proceeds as follows: First, Q'_2 is decomposed into two subexpressions $β_1$, consisting of line 1, and $β_2$, consisting of lines 2–7. Then, the rewrite algorithm is recursively called for $β_1$ and for $β_2$. As $β_1$ is *simple*, the call for $β_1$ produces the result

{ps $ROOT: on-first past() return <results> }

The call for $β_2$ decomposes $β_2$ into two subexpressions $β_{21}$, consisting of lines 2–6, and $β_{22}$, consisting of line 7 of Q'_2. The recursive call "rewrite($ROOT,∅,$β_{21}$)" then executes lines 36–39 of the algorithm in Figure 2, because $β_{21}$ is a for-loop with parent variable $ROOT and associated set $X = X_{β_{21}} = ∅$. That is, the result

{ps $ROOT: on bib as $bib return $α'_1$ }

is produced, where $α'_1$ is the result produced by the recursive function call "rewrite($bib,∅,$α_1$)", for the subquery $α_1$ of Q'_2 in lines 3–6. This recursive call for $α_1$ again executes lines 36–39 of the algorithm, producing the expression $α'_1 =$

{ps $bib: on book as $b return $α'_2$ }

where $α'_2$ is the result of "rewrite($b,∅,$α_2$)" for the subquery $α_2$ of Q'_2 in lines 4–6. As $α_2$ is a

---
[2]We rewrite the queries to work without attributes.

for-loop with parent variable $\$b$ and associated set $X = X_{\alpha_2} = \{\texttt{author}\}$, in this call line 34 of the algorithm is executed, producing the expression $\alpha_2' =$

```
{ps $b: on-first past(author,title) return α₂ }
```

All in all, "rewrite($\$\texttt{ROOT},\emptyset,Q_2'$)" returns the following FluX query F_2:

```
1 {ps $ROOT:
2  on-first past() return <results>;
3  on bib as $bib return
4    {ps $bib: on book as $b return
5      {ps $b: on-first past(author,title) return
6        { for $t in $b/title return
7          { for $a in $b/author return
8            <result> {$t} {$a} </result> } } };
9  on-first past(bib) return </results> }
```

We will refer to the "$\{\texttt{ps }\$b\cdots\}$"-expression in lines 5–8 of F_2 as α_2'. When evaluating the query F_2 on an XML document, the XQuery inside α_2' will be evaluated once *all* author and *all* title nodes have been encountered and buffered.

Let us now consider the case where we are given a DTD with the production

```
<!ELEMENT book (author*,title*)>
```

where the order constraint $Ord_{\text{book}}(\texttt{author},\texttt{title})$ is met. While running "rewrite($\$\texttt{ROOT},\emptyset,Q_2'$)" we now encounter the situation where $X = X_{\alpha_2} = \emptyset$ (rather than $\{\texttt{author}\}$, as with the previous DTD). Therefore, when processing the recursive call "rewrite($\$b,\emptyset,\alpha_2$)", now lines 36–39 of the algorithm are executed, eventually producing the following result $\alpha_2'' =$

```
{ps $b: on title as $t return
  {ps $t: on-first past(*) return
    { for $a in $b/author return
      <result> {$t} {$a} </result> } } }
```

Now, "rewrite($\$\texttt{ROOT},\emptyset,Q_2'$)" yields query F_2' differing from F_2 in the lines 5–8, which must be replaced by the above expression α_2''.

When evaluating F_2' on an XML document compliant with the second DTD, all author nodes arrive before title nodes and are buffered. Encountering a title node in the input stream invokes the following actions: The value of that particular node is buffered, i.e., "on-first past(*)" delays the execution until the complete title node has been seen. Then, we iterate over the buffer containing all collected author nodes, each time writing the buffered title and the current author to the output. In contrast to the worst-case scenario above, we only buffer one title at a time in addition to the list of all authors. If there is more than one title, this strategy is clearly preferable. □

We next demonstrate that conditional for-loops are optimized correspondingly.

Example 4.5 ([18], XMP, Q1) Let us consider the query Q_1 and its normalization Q_1' from Example 4.2.

Given a DTD that does not impose any order constraints, e.g., the DTD

```
<!ELEMENT bib   (book)*>
<!ELEMENT book  (title|publisher|year)*>
```

the function call "rewrite($\$\texttt{ROOT},\emptyset,Q_1'$)" rewrites Q_1' into the following FluX query F_1:

```
1 {ps $ROOT:
2  on-first past() return <bib>;
3  on bib as $bib return
4    {ps $bib: on book as $b return
5      {ps $b:
6       on-first past(publisher,year) return
7         { if χ then <book> };
8       on-first past(publisher,year) return
9         { for $year in $b/year return
10          { if χ then {$year} } };
11       on-first past(publisher,year,title) return
12          { for $title in $b/title return
13           { if χ then {$title} } };
14       on-first past(publisher,year,title) return
15           { if χ then </book> } };
16  on-first past(bib) return </bib> }
```

The "on-first" handler in lines 11–13 delays query execution until all title nodes have been buffered and all publisher and year nodes have been seen.

When given a different DTD, ensuring that both $Ord_{\text{book}}(\texttt{year},\texttt{title})$ and $Ord_{\text{book}}(\texttt{publisher},\texttt{title})$ hold, the title nodes can be processed in the streaming fashion. The query F_1' produced by "rewrite($\$\texttt{ROOT},\emptyset,Q_1'$)" with this new DTD differs from the above query F_1 in the subexpression in lines 11–13 which must be replaced by

```
on title as $title return
  { if χ then {$title} }
```

Consequently, titles will not be buffered at all during evaluation of this query. □

Our rewrite algorithm is well capable of optimizing joins over two or more join predicates, as is demonstrated in the following example which is not part of the XQuery Use Cases.

Example 4.6 We remain in the bibliography domain and consider documents compliant with the DTD

```
<!ELEMENT bib   (book|article)*>
<!ELEMENT book  (title,(author+|editor+),publisher)>
<!ELEMENT article (title,author+,journal)>
```

The following XQuery Q_3 retrieves those authors of articles which are coauthored by people who have also edited books:

```
<results>
{ for $bib in $ROOT/bib return
  { for $article in $bib/article return
    { for $book in $bib/book
        where $article/author = $book/editor return
        { <result> {$article/author} </result> } }}
</results>
```

For the remainder of this example, we abbreviate the join-condition comparing the authors of articles with the editors of books by χ. Normalization yields the following query Q'_3:

```
1 <results>
2 { for $bib in $ROOT/bib return
3   { for $article in $bib/article return
4     { for $book in $bib/book return
5       { if χ then <result> }
6       { for $author in $article/author return
7         { if χ then {$author} } }
8       { if χ then </result> } } } }
9 </results>
```

When executing "rewrite($ROOT,∅,$Q'_3$)" with the DTD above, a recursive call "rewrite($bib,∅,β)" is eventually invoked for the subexpression $β$ of Q'_3 in lines 3–8. As $β$ is a for-loop with parent variable $bib and associated set $X = X_β = \{book\} \neq ∅$, line 34 of the algorithm is executed, returning an expression of the form {ps $bib: on-first past(book,article) ··· }. That is, as no order constraint between article and book holds, an on-first handler ensures that all articles and books will be buffered.

Altogether, "rewrite($ROOT,∅,$Q'_3$)" produces the following FluX query F_3, where $α$ is used as abbreviation for the for-loop over books in lines 4–8 of Q'_3:

```
1 {ps $ROOT:
2   on-first past() return <results>;
3   on bib as $bib return
4     {ps $bib: on-first past(book,article) return
5       { for $article in $bib/article return α } };
6   on-first past(bib) return </results> }
```

When given a different DTD which imposes an order on books and articles, e.g. by the following production

<!ELEMENT bib (book*,article*)>

we can evaluate Q'_3 by buffering only book nodes but processing article nodes in a streaming fashion.

Indeed, when executing "rewrite($ROOT,∅,$Q'_3$)" with this new DTD, we eventually encounter the situation where set $X = X_β = ∅$, and therefore, lines 36–39 (rather than line 34, as with the previous DTD) are executed. Altogether, the FluX query F'_3 produced now, differs from the above query F_3 in the subexpression in lines 4–5, which must be replaced by

```
4 {ps $bib: on article as $article return
5   {ps $article: on-first past(author) return α }};
```

As all book nodes will have arrived before an article node can be encountered, data from books is available in buffers once the first article node is being read. When processing the children of an article node, we first buffer all author nodes before the query can be evaluated for the current article.

During the evaluation of F'_3, we therefore only buffer the authors of a single article in addition to the data already stored on books, whereas the evaluation of F_3 requires the authors of *all* articles to be buffered. □

5 Implementation

In this section, we discuss our implementation of a query engine for evaluating FluX queries obtained from XQuery$^-$ by the rewriting algorithm of the previous section.

We focus on the allocation of buffers and their use during query evaluation. Given a FluX query, we statically infer the buffers which are actually necessary in order to avoid superfluous buffering. Our prefiltering techniques generalize those of [14] to the scenario where certain parts of the input do not need to be buffered – even though they are used by the query – because they can be processed on-the-fly.

Buffers are implemented as lists of SAX events. The events stored in a buffer represent well-formed XML in the sense that start-element events and end-element events are properly nested within each other. This renders data read from (a stream replayed from) a buffer indistinguishable from data read from the input stream. In our implementation, we employ the same set of operators for handling both events originating from streams and from buffers.[3]

In the following, we say that a FluX query is in normal form if all of its (maximal) XQuery$^-$ subexpressions are in normal form.

Let Q be a safe FluX query in normal form. The FluX query engine identifies all nodes that must be stored in buffers, i.e. all nodes compared in join conditions, the roots of buffered subtrees that are output, and buffered nodes over which for-loops iterate.

More formally, let $α$ be an XQuery$^-$ subexpression of Q. We define $\Pi(\$r, α)$, the set of all buffered paths in $α$ starting with variable $r, as $\Pi(\$r, \epsilon) = \Pi(\$r, s) = ∅$, $\Pi(\$r, \{\$r\}) = \{\$r\}$, $\Pi(\$r, αβ) = \Pi(\$r, α) \cup \Pi(\$r, β)$,

$$\Pi(\$r, \{\text{for } \$x \text{ in } \$y/a \text{ return } α\}) =$$
$$\Pi(\$r, α) \cup \{\$r/a \mid \$y = \$r \text{ and } \Pi(\$x, α) = ∅\}$$
$$\cup \{\$r/a/w \mid \$y = \$r \text{ and } \$x/w \in \Pi(\$x, α)\},$$

and $\Pi(\$r, \{\text{if } \chi \text{ then } α\}) = \Pi(\$r, α) \cup \{\$r/π \mid \chi \text{ contains an atomic condition } \$r/π \text{ RelOp } \$y/π'$ or $\$y/π' \text{ RelOp } \$r/π\}$.

For a variable $r and a safe FluX query Q in normal form, we now define $\Pi(\$r)$ as the union of all $\Pi(\$r, α)$ s.t. $α$ is a maximal XQuery$^-$ subexpression of Q.

Let $\mathcal{T}(\$r)$ be the prefix tree constructed by merging all paths from $\Pi(\$r)$. Intuitively, the prefix tree defines a projection of the input document, as it describes which parts of the input tree will be buffered.

We optimize the prefix tree in order to restrict the amount of data being buffered. Let $\mathcal{T}^m(\$r)$ be the tree obtained from $\mathcal{T}(\$r)$ by marking each node v if v either occurs in a join condition or the entire subtree rooted at node v is output and must therefore be buffered. For unmarked nodes in $\mathcal{T}^m(\$r)$, we merely store the SAX events for the opening and the closing tag.

---
[3]Thus, physical query evaluation proceeds in a way similar to that followed in XQRL [9].

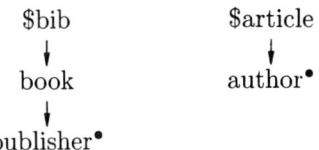

Figure 3: Buffer trees of variables $bib and $article.

Clearly, if a node is marked and we buffer it together with its subtree, we also buffer the subtrees of any descendant nodes at the same time. Thus we only buffer the data of the topmost marked nodes in $\mathcal{T}^m(\$r)$. For example, if we need to buffer two subtrees reachable by paths π and π' respectively, where π is a prefix of π', we restrict ourselves to buffering the subtree identified by π. Let $\mathcal{T}^p(\$r)$ be the pruned prefix tree obtained from $\mathcal{T}^m(\$r)$ by successively removing a subtree rooted at node v' if an ancestor node v is marked. We refer to $\mathcal{T}^p(\$r)$ as a *buffer tree*.

W.l.o.g., below we will assume that variables in queries are used uniquely, i.e., each variable name is bound at most at one place in the query. For a safe FluX query Q in normal form, let X be the set of variables that are free in maximal XQuery$^-$ subexpressions of Q. The variables in X are precisely those for which we will later define buffers.

Example 5.1 The following FluX query selects all book publishers whose CEO has published articles.

```
{ ps $ROOT: on bib as $bib return
  { ps $bib: on article as $article return
    { ps $article: on-first past(author) return
      { for $book in $bib/book return
        { for $p in $book/publisher return
          { if $article/author = $book/publisher/ceo
            then {$p} } } } } }
```

Here, $X = \{\$bib, \$article\}$ and we compute the sets of buffer paths for each variable in X:

$$\begin{aligned}\Pi(\$bib) &= \{\$bib/book/publisher/ceo,\\ &\quad \$bib/book/publisher\}\\ \Pi(\$article) &= \{\$article/author\}\end{aligned}$$

We construct a buffer tree for each variable in X with a nonempty set of buffer paths. Here, we obtain the trees shown in Figure 3 (the bullet denotes a marked node). Note that the leaf node ceo has been pruned off the buffer tree of variable $bib. □

We evaluate a safe FluX query Q in normal form as follows. We compute X and construct the buffer tree $\mathcal{T}^p(\$r, Q)$ for each variable $\$r \in X$.

We further associate an evaluator function with each variable $\$r$ in X. When variable $\$r$ is bound to a node v of the incoming XML tree, then the evaluator Eval_$r is responsible for handling all events generated while processing the children of v.

We define a buffer buffer_$r for variable $\$r$ in the evaluator which calls Eval_$r. This buffer is initialized on entering the scope of $\$r$ and freed on re-entering it.

The buffer tree of $\$r$ can be considered a schema for all events stored in buffer buffer_$r. At the same time, the buffer tree determines how the set of evaluators is to be extended such that all buffers are correctly filled.

For a node v in buffer tree $\mathcal{T}^p(\$r)$, reachable by path $\$r/a_1/\ldots/a_n$, we implement the corresponding buffering strategy in a set of evaluators. Starting with Eval_$r and a_1, we successively extend the evaluators responsible for handling the children of a node labeled a_i such that the events for the opening and closing tag of the respective node will be added to buffer_$r. In cases where no such evaluator exists, we introduce new variables and evaluators accordingly. As there is at most one case statement in an evaluator for an "on a" event under a given node label "a", it is clear where corresponding commands are to be introduced. In case a_n is marked, we insert the respective code for adding all events corresponding to node a_n and its subtree to buffer_$r.

Example 5.2 Consider query F_3' of Example 4.6. The set of buffer trees for this query is as in Figure 3 with the publisher node replaced by an editor node. Its FluX evaluation strategy is as follows.

```
for each event e of Eval_$ROOT, switch(e) {
  case(ofp()):    { output "<results>"; }
  case(on bib):   { initialize(buffer_$bib);
                    Eval_$bib(node(e)); }
  case(ofp(bib)): { output "</results>"; } }

for each event of Eval_$bib, switch(e) {
  case(on book):    { buffer_$bib.add(<book>);
                      Eval_$book(node(e));
                      buffer_$bib.add(</book>); }
  case(on article): { initialize(buffer_$article);
                      Eval_$article(node(e)); } }

for each event of Eval_$book, switch(e) {
  case(on editor):  { buffer_$bib.add(node(e));} }

for each event of Eval_$article, switch(e) {
  case(on author):
          { buffer_$article.add(node(e)); }
  case(ofp(author)): { execute_subquery(α); } }
```

At the beginning of the stream, the evaluator of variable $ROOT handles the event on-first past(), denoted ofp() above, by writing the opening tag to the output. Correspondingly, the event ofp(bib) signals the end of the stream and the closing tag is output.

Yet when processing the SAX event for the opening tag of root node bib, the buffer associated with variable $bib is initialized and the evaluator for $bib takes over to handle all events generated while parsing the children of bib.

Book nodes arriving on the stream are stored in the buffer of variable $bib, while editor nodes are buffered by the evaluator for variable $book together with their complete subtrees. As with all safe FluX queries, we may rely on the fact that buffer

237

		FluX	Galax	AnonX
Q_1	5M	2.1s/0	13.4s/37M	3.4s
	10M	2.8s/0	29.8s/83M	6.7s
	50M	7.8s/0	- / >500M	38.3s
	100M	14.0s/0	- / >500M	-
Q_8	5M	6.8s/1.54M	296.9s/50M	143.8s
	10M	17.2s/3.16M	1498.3s/100M	534.8s
	50M	357.8s/16.00M	- / >500M	-
	100M	11566.9s/32.25M	- / >500M	-
Q_{11}	5M	5.6s/374k	277.0s/50M	n/a
	10M	11.4s/741k	1663.7s/100M	n/a
	50M	170.8s/3.64M	- / >500M	n/a
	100M	626.8s/7.27M	- / >500M	n/a
Q_{13}	5M	2.2s/0	12.8s/38M	3.0s
	10M	3.1s/0	27.2s/73M	5.2s
	50M	7.9s/0	230.1s/344M	88.0s
	100M	13.9s/0	- / >500M	-
Q_{20}	5M	2.8s/4.66k	13.2s/36M	2.5s
	10M	3.4s/5.18k	29.7s/80M	6.2s
	50M	8.7s/7.01k	- / >500M	151.9s
	100M	15.4s/7.02k	- / >500M	-

Figure 4: Benchmark results.

buffer_$bib is filled by the time we encounter the first article node. The buffer is not freed until the complete subtree under the node bound to variable $bib has been parsed.

Processing the children of an article node, any authors are first buffered in buffer_$article until the event ofp(author) guarantees that the subquery α of F_3' can be executed correctly. □

Join conditions are handled similarly, by buffering both constituent paths of the condition. Simple conditions comparing a path with a constant can be evaluated on the fly while reading the paths, so only a Boolean flag is required, which has to be appropriately initialized upon entering the relevant variable scope.

6 Experiments

In order to assess the merits of the approach presented in this paper, we have experimentally evaluated our prototype query engine implemented in JAVA using a number of queries on data obtained using the XMark benchmark generator.

Our implementation supports the XQuery⁻ fragment as defined in Section 3. We took selected queries of the XMark benchmark and, as XQuery⁻ does not include certain features that are used in these queries, adapted them correspondingly. In detail, attributes were converted into subelements of their parent element in our tests (the XMark DTD was adjusted accordingly). Occurrences of the XPath step text() were replaced by {$x} expressions that print the whole element instead. We eliminated the count($x) aggregations by again outputting $x instead. XMark queries 1, 8, 11, and 13 were adjusted as sketched above. We extracted the last FLWR subexpression of original query 20 (which computes persons whose income is not available) for our novel query 20. The queries thus obtained can be found in full in [12].

We used data generated by the XMark xmlgen data generation tool (V. 0.96) of the sizes 5MB, 10MB, 50MB, and 100MB as input data. All tests were performed with the SUN JDK 1.4.2_03 and the built-in SAX parser on an AMD Athlon XP 2000+ (1.67GHz) with 512MB RAM running Linux (gentoo linux using kernel 2.6). Our query engine was implemented precisely as described in this paper. As a reference implementation the Galax query engine (V. 0.3.1) was employed with projection turned on [14]. The performance of query evaluation was studied by measuring the execution time[4] (in seconds) and maximum memory consumption (in bytes) of each engine. The memory and CPU usage of both query engines were measured by internal monitoring functions (excluding the fixed memory consumption of the Java Virtual Machine).

To give a broader overview over the performance of our approach we evaluated our queries additionally with a commercial XQuery system of a major company that has to remain anonymous and will be called AnonX below. Unfortunately, we could not determine the exact memory consumption for this system. Hence, we only state its execution time. As AnonX was not able to parse Query 11, we are not able to list the execution time.

Figure 4 shows the results of our experiments. To evaluate most queries with input greater than 10MB, Galax needed more than 500MB of main memory after running for a few minutes (which caused the system to start swapping). These runs were aborted. Obviously, our prototype engine clearly outperforms Galax with respect to both execution time and memory consumption. Queries 1 and 13 are evaluated on-the-fly without any buffering because of the order constraints imposed by the DTD. Query 20 has to buffer only a single element at a time, which leads to very low memory consumption in comparison to the traditional approach. Queries 8 and 11 perform a join on two subtrees (i.e. of people and closed_auction resp. open_auction) and therefore inevitably have to buffer elements. Nevertheless, due to our effective projection scheme only a small fraction of the original data is buffered. The rapid increase in execution time is due to the fact that we compute joins by naive nested loops at the moment. (We will work on this orthogonal but vital issue in the future.)

The comparison of the execution times to AnonX again shows the competitiveness of our query engine. AnonX ran out of memory processing queries marked by "-" (the maximum heap size of the Java VM was set to 512MB in both cases) and hence did not give any results in this case.

Altogether, our optimization approach seems to perform very well with respect to execution time, max-

---

[4]The times taken for query rewriting were negligible and are not reported separately in our experiments.

imum memory consumption, and the maximum size of XML documents that can be processed.

7 Discussion and Conclusions

Main memory is probably the most critical resource in (streamed) query processing. Keeping main memory consumption low is vital to scalability and has – indirectly – a great impact on query engine performance in terms of running time.

The main contribution of this paper is the FluX language together with an algorithm for automatically translating a significant fragment of XQuery into equivalent FluX queries. FluX – while intended as an internal representation format for queries rather than a language for end-users – provides a strong intuition for buffer-conscious query processing on structured data streams. The algorithm uses schema information to schedule FluX queries so as to reduce the use of buffers.

As evidenced by our experiments, our approach indeed dramatically increases the scalability of main memory XQuery engines, even though we think we are not yet close to exhausting this approach, neither with respect to run-time buffer management and query processing nor query optimization.

In particular, further constraints such as cardinality constraints derived from the DTD, telling, e.g., that a `book` node has at most one `publisher` child (let this be denoted by $\texttt{publisher} \in \|_{\texttt{book}}^{\leq 1}$), could be used to simplify XQueries before they are rewritten into FluX using rewrite rules such as

$$\frac{\{\ \texttt{for}\ \$x\ \texttt{in}\ \$r/a\ \texttt{return}\ \alpha\ \}\quad \{\ \texttt{for}\ \$x\ \texttt{in}\ \$r/a\ \texttt{return}\ \beta\ \}}{\{\ \texttt{for}\ \$x\ \texttt{in}\ \$r/a\ \texttt{return}\ \alpha\ \beta\ \}}\ \left(a \in \|_{\$r}^{\leq 1}\right)$$

which can form the basis of algebraic query optimization for buffer minimization.

Sequences of for-loops iterating over singletons are a natural product of the normalization process that we have described. For example, the query

```
{ for $b in $ROOT/book return
    {$b/publisher/name} {$b/publisher/address} }
```

uses a sequence of two loops over `publisher` in its normal form, which can be rewritten into one using the rule above. By first merging for-loops, it is often possible to obtain FluX queries that require no buffering at all, while two subsequent loops over the same path generally cause that path to be buffered.

Another important optimization is to push `if`-expressions – which we have moved down the query tree to obtain our normal form – back "up" the expression tree as soon as the other simplifications have been realized.

References

[1] S. Abiteboul, P. Buneman, and D. Suciu. *Data on the Web*. Morgan Kaufmann Publishers, 2000.

[2] M. Altinel and M. Franklin. "Efficient Filtering of XML Documents for Selective Dissemination of Information". In *Proc. VLDB 2000*, pages 53–64, Cairo, Egypt, 2000.

[3] A. Brüggemann-Klein and D. Wood. "One-Unambiguous Regular Languages". *Information and Computation*, 142(2):182–206, 1998.

[4] P. Buneman, M. Grohe, and C. Koch. "Path Queries on Compressed XML". In *Proc. VLDB 2003*, pages 141–152, 2003.

[5] C. Y. Chan, P. Felber, M. N. Garofalakis, and R. Rastogi. "Efficient Filtering of XML Documents with XPath Expressions". In *Proc. ICDE 2002*, San Jose, California, USA, February 26–March 1 2002.

[6] A. Deutsch and V. Tannen. "Reformulation of XML Queries and Constraints". In *Proc. ICDT'03*, 2003.

[7] L. Fegaras, D. Levine, S. Bose, and V. Chaluvadi. "Query Processing of Streamed XML Data". In *Proc. CIKM 2002*, pages 126–133, 2002.

[8] M. Fernandez, J. Siméon, and P. Wadler. "A Semimonad for Semi-structured Data". In *Proc. ICDT'01*, pages 263–300, 2001.

[9] D. Florescu, C. Hillery, D. Kossmann, P. Lucas, F. Riccardi, T. Westmann, M. J. Carey, A. Sundararajan, and G. Agrawal. "The BEA/XQRL Streaming XQuery Processor". In *Proc. VLDB 2003*, pages 997–1008, 2003.

[10] T. J. Green, G. Miklau, M. Onizuka, and D. Suciu. "Processing XML Streams with Deterministic Automata". In *Proc. ICDT'03*, 2003.

[11] A. K. Gupta and D. Suciu. "Stream Processing of XPath Queries with Predicates". In *SIGMOD Conference*, pages 419–430, 2003.

[12] C. Koch, S. Scherzinger, N. Schweikardt, and B. Stegmaier. "Schema-based Scheduling of Event Processors and Buffer Minimization for Queries on Structured Data Streams". Technical Report cs.DB/0406016, CoRR, 2004. http://arxiv.org/abs/cs.DB/0406016.

[13] B. Ludäscher, P. Mukhopadhyay, and Y. Papakonstantinou. "A Transducer-Based XML Query Processor". In *Proc. VLDB 2002*, pages 227–238, 2002.

[14] A. Marian and J. Siméon. "Projecting XML Documents". In *Proc. VLDB 2003*, pages 213–224, 2003.

[15] M. Murata, D. Lee, and M. Mani. "Taxonomy of XML Schema Languages using Formal Language Theory". In *Extreme Markup Languages*, Montreal, Canada, Aug. 2001.

[16] D. Olteanu, T. Kiesling, and F. Bry. "An Evaluation of Regular Path Expressions with Qualifiers against XML Streams". In *Proc. ICDE 2003*, Bangalore, Mar. 2003. Poster Session.

[17] World Wide Web Consortium. "XQuery 1.0 and XPath 2.0 Formal Semantics. W3C Working Draft (Aug. 16th 2002), 2002. http://www.w3.org/TR/query-algebra/.

[18] "XML Query Use Cases. W3C Working Draft 02 May 2003", 2003. http://www.w3.org/TR/xmlquery-use-cases/.

Bloom Histogram: Path Selectivity Estimation for XML Data with Updates[*]

Wei Wang

School of Computer Science
and Engineering
University of NSW, Australia
and
NICTA, Australia
weiw@cse.unsw.edu.au

Haifeng Jiang   Hongjun Lu

Dept. of Computer Science
Hong Kong Univ. of Sci. & Tech.
Hong Kong, China

{jianghf, luhj}@cs.ust.hk

Jeffrey Xu Yu

Department of System Engineering
and Engineering Management
The Chinese Univ. of Hong Kong
Hong Kong, China

yu@se.cuhk.edu.hk

Abstract

Cost-based XML query optimization calls for accurate estimation of the selectivity of *path expressions*. Some other interactive and internet applications can also benefit from such estimations. While there are a number of estimation techniques proposed in the literature, almost none of them has any guarantee on the estimation accuracy within a given space limit. In addition, most of them assume that the XML data are more or less static, i.e., with few updates. In this paper, we present a framework for XML path selectivity estimation in a dynamic context. Specifically, we propose a novel data structure, *bloom histogram*, to approximate XML path frequency distribution within a small space budget and to estimate the path selectivity accurately with the bloom histogram. We obtain the upper bound of its estimation error and discuss the trade-offs between the accuracy and the space limit. To support updates of bloom histograms efficiently when underlying XML data change, a *dynamic summary* layer is used to keep exact or more detailed XML path information. We demonstrate through our extensive experiments that the new solution can achieve significantly higher accuracy with an even smaller space than the previous methods in both static and dynamic environments.

1 Introduction

Both the amount of XML data and the number of XML applications have exploded in recent years as XML becomes the *de facto* standard for information representation and exchange. Consequently, there is a great demand for efficient XML data management systems for managing complex queries over large volumes of local and Internet-based XML data.

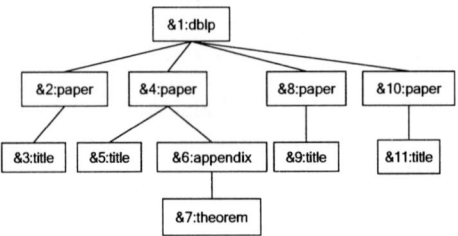

Figure 1: A sample XML data tree (Each node is labeled with a unique ID and its tag)

Efficient query processing requires accurate selectivity estimation of *path expressions*, which are commonly used in XML query languages to locate a subset of XML data. A query optimizer needs such estimation to judiciously select the most efficient query execution plan among alternative ones. For example, given the sample XML data in Figure 1, the following XPath query selects titles of all the papers that have at least one theorem appearing in their appendix: /dblp/paper[appendix/theorem]/title. According to the data, it might be most efficient to retrieve the paper that has a theorem in its appendix first, and then, for the only one qualified paper, retrieve its title. In other words, as is widely adopted in relational query processing, we

---

[*]This work is partially supported by the Research Grant Council of the Hong Kong Special Administrative Region, China (grant AoE/E-01/99).

Permission to copy without fee all or part of this material is granted provided that the copies are not made or distributed for direct commercial advantage, the VLDB copyright notice and the title of the publication and its date appear, and notice is given that copying is by permission of the Very Large Data Base Endowment. To copy otherwise, or to republish, requires a fee and/or special permission from the Endowment.

**Proceedings of the 30th VLDB Conference,
Toronto, Canada, 2004**

should process the most *selective* (path) predicates first—/dblp/paper/appendix/theorem in our example. With a path selectivity estimator, we can retrieve such selectivity information effectively without referring to the source data. In addition, accurate path selectivity estimation is desirable in interactive and internet applications as well. The system could warn the user that his/her query is so coarse that either the amount of results will be overwhelming for manual processing or the query will consume a large amount of system resources. Another important application is approximate query answering. The estimated value could be returned as an approximate answer to aggregate queries using the COUNT function.

Desiderata of any data structure that is capable of estimating the selectivity of path expressions can be summarized as follows:

- The estimate should be highly accurate. A bad estimate may mislead the query optimizer to choose a bad plan, whose cost could be orders of magnitude higher. Ideally, the estimation error should be upper bounded. This is particularly important for approximate query answering.

- The estimator should be space efficient. When the data structure is to be loaded into main memory during the query optimization phase, it must be small in size. In addition, a smaller size often implies less estimation time, which in turn helps reduce the query optimization time. Finally, if we consider internet-scale applications, both the storage and scalability of the system are dependent on the size of the estimator.

Summarizing the distribution of XML path selectivities is a substantially different problem from most statistics estimation problems considered in the relational context. Therefore, the traditional techniques designed for flat relational data cannot be directly applied to tree-structured XML data. Some work has recently appeared in the XML literature [6, 1, 14, 9, 17, 18]. However, all the work is *ad hoc* in the sense that no theoretical guarantee on the accuracy of the proposed methods is given and the trade-offs between accuracy and space limit are unknown. Another crucial drawback is that most of them consider only the case where data are static.

In this paper, we propose a two-layer solution that is capable of estimating the selectivity of XML path expressions for dynamic data. At the heart of our new solution is a *bloom histogram*, a compact yet high accurate estimator for XML path expressions. A bloom histogram provides better approximation for the original value-frequency distribution by sorting on the frequencies and using bloom filters to record values within each bucket. Several encouraging results are obtained about the bloom histogram: it occupies much less space than that is required by the previous methods, and its estimation error is small and can be bounded probabilistically. We also present optimal construction algorithms for the bloom histogram. To handle data updates, we employ in our solution a dynamic summary, which keeps an exact or approximate description of the necessary information for histogram updates. The dynamic summary is typically larger than the bloom histogram, yet it is still much smaller than the XML data and is easily maintainable. New histograms can thus be recomputed from the dynamic summary, without the costly process of accessing the huge XML data itself.

Our contributions can be summarized as follows:

- We propose a compact yet highly accurate estimator, the bloom histogram, which has theoretical upper bound on its estimation error. Furthermore, we analyze the trade-offs between accuracy and space requirement for the bloom histogram so that it becomes possible to set appropriate space limits based on specific estimation accuracy requirements in real applications. We note that the bloom histogram is an interesting data structure in its own right and might find applications in other domains.

- We consider the problem of maintaining the bloom histogram when underlying data change and propose to use the dynamic summary with a controllable size to track approximate or exact changes of path selectivities. The bloom histogram can then be rebuilt without the costly process of accessing the source XML data. This solution can be generalized to work with previously proposed estimators as well.

- We complement our analytical results with an extensive experimental study. Our results indicate that the new method can indeed estimate the selectivity of XML path expressions accurately within a small space in both static and dynamic environments.

The remainder of the paper is organized as follows. We define formally the path-expression selectivity estimation problem in Section 2. We also provide an overview of our proposed solution. Sections 3 and 4 discuss the two major components of our system: the estimator and the dynamic summary, respectively. Specifically, *bloom histogram*, a new data structure and method to accurately estimate path selectivity for XML data is presented in Section 3, and Section 4 discusses two solutions to dealing with data updates. Section 5 presents our experimental results. Related work is presented in Section 6. Section 7 concludes the paper.

2 Problem definition and overview of our solution

In this section, we first define the problem and then present an overview of our solution. More technical details of our solution will be presented in Sections 3 and 4.

2.1 Problem definition

XML documents are usually modeled as a node-labeled, rooted tree, such as the one shown in Figure 1. In XQuery data model[1], seven types of nodes are defined: document, element, attribute, text, namespace, processing instruction, and comment nodes. In this paper, we only consider element nodes and attribute nodes. Text nodes are treated as the values of their parent element nodes. For any element or attribute node, the tags on its root-to-node path form its *label path*. For example, in Figure 1, the label path for the node &6 is `/dblp/paper/appendix`.

XPath is a common query language for locating a subset of nodes in an XML data tree. In this paper, we only deal with *simple path expressions* in the form of $/t_1/t_2/\ldots/t_n$ and $//t_1/t_2/\ldots/t_n$, where t_i is a tag (i.e., element or attribute) name. We will focus on the former type of simple path expressions in this paper for the ease of illustration. Nonetheless, our method can be extended to handle the latter type of simple path expressions.

Given a simple path expression p, it may match with a set of label paths lp_i ($1 \leq i \leq k$). Let $c(lp_i)$ be the number of nodes whose label paths are lp_i and N be the total number of nodes in the XML data tree, then the selectivity of p is defined as: $sel(p) = \frac{1}{N} \sum_{1 \leq i \leq k} c(lp_i)$. Since N can be easily maintained, we only need to estimate the $c(lp_i)$ values. Therefore, the static path-expression selectivity problem is to build a data structure within a space limit and support estimating the selectivity of path expression queries accurately. The dynamic version of the same problem studies the case when the underlying XML data are dynamic due to updates.

2.2 Overview of the solution

Figure 2 illustrates our proposed solution for XML path selectivity estimation in a dynamic environment. There are three components in the system: the data file, the dynamic summary and the estimator. The latter two components form our two-layer solution. Data files are typically large, in the magnitude of megabytes or gigabytes. The estimator is responsible for accurately and efficiently estimating the selectivity of path expression queries. Typically, the estimator is of several kilobytes in size. The dynamic summary component is designed to keep necessary information about the changing data so that the estimator can be updated *without* the need to access the data file.

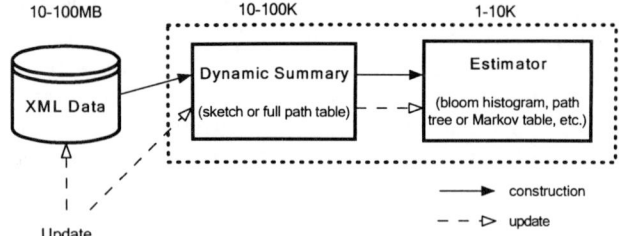

Figure 2: System overview

There are two types of activities in the system: *construction* and *updating*. In the construction phase, dynamic summaries are built from source XML data files and used to create the estimators (corresponding to data files). During *updating*, updates to XML data files are delegated to the dynamic summaries to reflect the latest data distribution. The estimators will be recomputed either periodically or on demand from the dynamic summaries.

In this paper, we focus on a new estimator, the bloom histogram. However, previous methods, such as Path Tree and Markov Table, can be used in our system as well.

3 The bloom histogram

In this section, we propose the bloom histogram, a new estimator for selectivity estimation. Compared to other alternatives, such as Path Tree and Markov Table, it is of smaller size yet offers superior accuracy. We present the basic structure of a bloom histogram, and the algorithms to estimate the selectivity of XML path expressions using bloom histograms. The algorithm for constructing a bloom histogram with minimum estimation error is also presented.

3.1 The basic bloom histogram

The bloom histogram keeps counting statistics for paths in XML data. The design objective of the bloom histogram, like all other histograms, is small size yet high estimation accuracy.

Given an XML document D, it is always possible to construct a *path-count table* $T(path, count)$ such that for each path $path_i$ in D, there is a tuple t_i in T with $t_i.path = path_i$ and $t_i.count = count_i$, where $count_i$ is the number of occurrences (also referred to as *frequency*) of $path_i$ in D. Given a path p, we can then use T to obtain the selectivity of p. A histogram is a commonly used data structure to approximate data distribution of a given attribute—or, the *target attribute*. In the context of XML path selectivity estimation, the target attribute is the *path* attribute of T. A histogram H for D is therefore a two-column table $H(paths, v)$ where *paths* represents a *set* of paths in D

---

[1] http://www.w3.org/TR/xpath-datamodel

and v is a representative value for the frequency values of all $path_i$ in $paths$. Given a path p, we can find from H a tuple H_i with $p \in H_i.paths$ and return $H_i.v$ as an estimation of the frequency of p in D. Different from the path-count table T, the table H usually contains a fixed number, b, of tuples (often referred as *buckets*). To design a good histogram, we need to choose an appropriate b and the way in which the value range of the target attribute is divided into the given b buckets so that both the size of H and the accuracy of estimation are acceptable. When we construct a histogram for XML paths, a new issue arises. That is, how to represent paths so that the bucket that contains the count for a given path can be quickly identified.

Path	Count
/a	10
/a/f	10
/a/e	499
/a/c	501
/a/b	999
/a/d	1001

Bloom Filter	Count
BF(/a, /a/f)	10
BF(/a/c, /a/e)	500
BF(/a/d, /a/b)	1000

Figure 3: An example path-count table and its bloom histogram. BF(P) is a bloom filter for a set of paths.

To provide an elegant solution to all the above design issues, we adopt a new type of histograms, *bloom histogram*, to maintain approximate counts for XML paths. The bloom histogram has two novel features:

1. Instead of dividing the value range of the target attribute into buckets, we sort the frequency values and then group paths with similar frequency values into buckets so that the estimation errors can be reduced; and

2. Bloom filters are used to represent the set of paths in each bucket so that, for a given path, the bucket containing the frequency of the path can be quickly located.

Figure 3 shows an example path table and a corresponding bloom histogram. There are 6 distinct paths in the path table. In the bloom histogram, they are grouped into 3 buckets based on their frequencies. The first column of the histogram contains bloom filters, $BF(P)$, where P is a set of paths.

A bloom filter is a succinct data structure that represents a set and supports approximate *set membership* queries [2]. Specifically, given a set $P = \{p_1, p_2, \ldots, p_n\}$, a bloom filter is a bit array of length m with k independent hash functions $h_1, h_2, \ldots, h_k$; and the hash functions are assumed to be able to hash x_i into a random number uniformly over range $[1, m]$. The bit array is initially set to 0. To insert a data element p to a bloom filter, k hash functions are applied to the value of p and the bit at position $h_i(p)$ is set to 1. To test whether a query element q is in the set represented by a bloom filter, the same k hash functions are applied to the value of q. The result is true only if every bit in the bloom filter at position $h_i(q)$ is set to 1, for all $1 \leq i \leq k$.

A good feature of a bloom filter is that it only has *false positive* error, i.e., errors due to incorrectly identifying that an element y belongs to the set S while it does not. In addition, the probability of its false positive error (denoted as ϵ) can be controlled by the parameters k and m:

$$\epsilon = \left(1 - \left(1 - \frac{1}{m}\right)^{kn}\right)^k \approx \left(1 - e^{-kn/m}\right)^k$$

Since the approximation is very accurate, we will use it to represent the actual error in our study. Further analysis also shows that ϵ is minimized by choosing $k = \ln 2 \cdot \frac{m}{n}$. Let $l = \frac{m}{n}$ be the *load factor*. The optimal ϵ is 0.6185^l.

In the next, we first discuss how to use a bloom histogram to estimate the selectivity of a path expression and the possible estimation errors. We then discuss the construction of an optimal bloom histogram.

3.2 Selectivity estimation using bloom histograms

In this section, we first give the algorithm that searches a bloom histogram to return the frequency of a given path from which the path selectivity can be estimated. We then analyze the estimation errors.

3.2.1 Selectivity estimation

Algorithm 1 QueryBloomHistogram(BH, p)

1: $count = 0; k = 0;$
2: **for** $i = 1$ to b **do**
3:    **if** IsMember(p, $BH.BF[i]$) **then**
4:       $count+ = BH.count[i];$
5:       $k++;$
6:    **end if**
7: **end for**
8: **if** $k > 0$ **then**
9:    **return** $count/k$;
10: **else**
11:    **return** 0;
12: **end if**

With a bloom histogram BH, we can obtain the approximate frequency for a given path p. The algorithm is outlined in Algorithm 1. In line 3 of the algorithm, function IsMember(p, BF) takes a path and a bloom filter for a set of paths as input, and returns TRUE if p is in the set of paths. As mentioned previously, this can be done by applying k hash functions to check whether all bits corresponding to $h_i(p), 1 \leq i \leq k$ are set. Although a path should be a member of the path set of at most one bucket, multiple bloom filters may report that the path belongs to them. In such cases, the frequency returned is the average frequency of those sets (lines 7-8). Note that, this is one type of error introduced by the bloom filters, and the probability that a path belongs to more than one set is very low and bounded by $b\epsilon$. The error can be further minimized by our optimization techniques discussed later.

Algorithm 1 needs to calculate $b \cdot k$ hash functions. As $k = O(\log \frac{1}{\epsilon})$, the time complexity of the algorithm is $O(b \log \frac{1}{\epsilon})$.

3.2.2 Errors in selectivity estimation

We now analyze the errors in selectivity estimation using bloom histograms. We use *absolute error* as the error metric. The absolute error e_X of an estimate X is the absolute difference between the estimated value and the real value $\hat{X}$, i.e., $e_X = |X - \hat{X}|$. The absolute-error metric has been used in previous XML path selectivity work as well. The main reasons are (a) the relative error is meaningless for queries which have an empty result set; and (b) the relative error with sanity bound is sensitive to the value of the sanity bound parameter.

During our analysis, we assume the full path-count table has n entries; and the bloom histogram has b buckets and the bloom filter error rate is ϵ. The count values in the bloom histogram are within $(0, M]$, for some constant M; and the count value in bucket i is V_i, $1 < V_i \leq M$. Let V be the actual frequency of a path. Query workload on selectivity can be divided into two types according to V of the query path. Those queries with $V = 0$ are referred as *negative query workload*, and those with $V > 0$ are referred as *positive query workload*. We assume queries in the workload are distinct and have the same frequency. It is easy to generalize our method for skewed workload.

Estimation error for negative query workload

For negative query workload, the estimation error comes from one or more buckets incorrectly reporting that the given query belongs to them. Let e_k denote the absolute error when k buckets report that a query path with frequency V belongs to them. We have $e_k = \left|\frac{1}{k}\sum_{i=1}^{k} V_i - V\right|$ where V_i is the count value in bucket i (and $V = 0$ for negative query workload). It is obvious that $0 \leq e_k \leq M$. Then, the expected error for negative queries can be calculated by summing over all possible errors when k buckets incorrectly report that the given query belongs to them, for $0 \leq k \leq b$.

$$\begin{aligned}E[e] &= 0 + \sum_{i=1}^{b}\binom{b}{i}\epsilon^i(1-\epsilon)^{b-i} \cdot E[e_i] \\ &< b\epsilon \cdot M\end{aligned} \quad (1)$$

By *Markov Inequality*, for any given $\gamma \geq 0$:

$$Pr[e \geq \gamma] \leq \frac{b\epsilon \cdot M}{\gamma}$$

Therefore, we have the following theorem that bounds the error of a bloom histogram for negative queries.

Theorem 3.1. *For any given γ and δ, there exists a bloom histogram such that with probability at least $1-\delta$, the estimation error of the bloom histogram for the negative queries is within γ, i.e., $Pr[|X - \hat{X}| \leq \gamma] \geq 1 - \delta$ holds.*

Estimation Error for Positive Query Workload

For positive queries, the expected estimation error is

$$\begin{aligned}E[e] &= (1-\epsilon)^{b-1} \cdot E[|V - V_*|] \\ &+ \sum_{i=1}^{b-1}\binom{b-1}{i}\epsilon^i(1-\epsilon)^{b-1-i}e_{i+1}\end{aligned}$$

where V and V_* are the actual and returned frequency values of the query, respectively. In the above equation, the first term is the error due to histogram approximation when the correct bucket is located; and the second term is the error due to the conflict resolution method when a query is reported to belong to multiple buckets. Again, since e_i is bounded by M, we have

$$E[e] < (1-\epsilon)^{b-1} \cdot E[|V - V_*|] + (b-1)\epsilon \cdot M \quad (2)$$

Similarly, by Markov Inequality, we have the following theorem that bounds the error of a bloom histogram for positive queries.

Theorem 3.2. *For any given γ and δ, there exists a bloom histogram such that with probability at least $1-\delta$, the estimation error of the bloom histogram for the positive queries is within γ, i.e., $Pr[|X - \hat{X}| \leq \gamma] \geq 1 - \delta$ holds.*

With those relationships established, we are ready to discuss our optimal histogram construction algorithm, which directly minimizes the error for positive queries.

3.3 Optimal histogram construction

Given a bloom histogram with b and ϵ parameters, in order to minimize the expected error for the positive workload, we need to minimize $E[|V - V_*|]$ in Equation 2. This is the goal of our optimal histogram construction algorithm.

We assume that all the paths and their counts are stored in a table sorted in the non-decreasing order on their counts, as shown in Figure 3; otherwise an additional sorting is required. For simplicity, we use

$count[k]$, $1 \leq k \leq n$, to denote the count of the kth path with $count[1] \leq count[2] \leq \ldots count[n]$. We note that:

$$E[|V - V_*|] = \frac{1}{n} \sum_{i=1}^{b} \left(\sum_{j=s[i]}^{e[i]} (|count[j] - V_i|) \right)$$

where $s[i]$ and $e[i]$ are the start and end indexes of the path table for the set of paths in the ith bucket, respectively.

Because this error metric is different from that in traditional histograms, such as the sum of square error in V-optimal histogram [13], we cannot directly apply previous algorithms. However, we can follow the same spirit in [13] when devising our optimal histogram construction algorithm. There are two main tasks: (1) to determine the optimal bucket boundaries efficiently; and (2) to select appropriate count values for each bucket.

We first address the second issue, i.e., to select appropriate V_i values for the buckets after the bucket boundaries have been fixed. To minimize $E[|V - V_*|]$, we only need to choose V_i to be the smaller median value in each bucket, based on the following observation: the median value of the data points in a bucket minimizes the function $\sum_{j=s[i]}^{e[i]}(|count[j] - V_i|)$.

Next, we investigate how to determine the optimal bucket boundaries efficiently. We leverage the dynamic programming paradigm, due to the following observation:

$$OPT[n, b] = \min_{i=b-1}^{n-1} \{OPT[i, b-1] + f(i+1, n)\} \quad (3)$$

where $OPT[x, b]$ denotes the sum of errors when b buckets are used to approximate the first x data points in an optimal way. $f(x, y)$ is the error of a single bucket comprising of data points within the index range $[x, y]$. The naïve computation of $f(x, y)$ takes $O(y - x + 1)$ time and will increase the running time of the dynamic programming algorithm. We observe that

$$f(x, y) = PSUM[y] + PSUM[x-1] \\ -2PSUM[t] + (2t - x - y + 1)count[t]$$

where $PSUM[]$ is the prefix sum array and t is the index of the median value. Hence we can compute $f(x, y)$ in constant time by building the prefix sum array for all the data points.

Algorithm 2 shows the optimal histogram-construction algorithm based on dynamic programming. Lines 1–4 initialize the $PSUM[]$ array, which helps to compute $f(x, y)$ function in constant time. Lines 5–7 initialize the $OPT[]$ for the special case of 1 bucket. Lines 8–15 are the dynamic programming part: We compute $OPT[j, b]$ according to the recurrence equation (Equation 3). Optimal bucket boundary can be reported by additional bookkeeping,

Algorithm 2 BuildHistogram($x[]$, n, b)
1: $PSUM[1] = x[1]$
2: **for** $i = 2$ to n **do**
3: $\quad PSUM[i] = PSUM[i-1] + x[i]$
4: **end for**
5: **for** $i = 1$ to n **do**
6: $\quad OPT[i, 1] = f(1, i)$
7: **end for**
8: **for** $k = 2$ to b **do**
9: $\quad$ **for** $j = 1$ to n **do**
10: $\quad\quad OPT[j, k] = +\infty$
11: $\quad\quad$ **for** $i = k - 1$ to $j - 1$ **do**
12: $\quad\quad\quad OPT[j, k] = \min(OPT[j, k], OPT[i, k-1]+f(i+1, j))$
13: $\quad\quad$ **end for**
14: $\quad$ **end for**
15: **end for**
16: **return** $OPT[n, b]$

which is omitted in the algorithm. The total errors of the optimal histogram, $OPT[n, b]$, are returned.

The time complexity of the algorithm is $O(bn^2)$. The space complexity is $O(n)$.

We note that $E[|V - V_*|]$ is exactly $\frac{1}{n} \cdot OPT[n, b]$, thus it can be computed after the building of the histogram. Therefore, given a dataset, the expected error for both positive and negative queries can be determined once the parameters b, ϵ and M are fixed.

3.4 Space bounded bloom histograms

In this subsection, we analyze the space requirement of our bloom histogram and discuss how to construct a bloom histogram within a space limit. The relationship between the space limit and the expected error of the resulting bloom histogram is also discussed.

The size of a bloom histogram is the sum of the sizes of b bloom filters for n paths and b approximate count values. The total size of b bloom filters is $l * (\sum_{1 \leq i \leq b} n_i) \approx 0.2602 \cdot \ln \frac{1}{\epsilon} \cdot n$, where l is the load factor defined in Section 3.1 and each bucket contains n_i values. Therefore, the total size of a bloom histogram is $0.2602 \cdot \ln \frac{1}{\epsilon} \cdot n + 4b$.

The minimum size of a bloom filter with a fixed ϵ parameter is therefore $S_{\min} = 0.2602 \cdot \ln \frac{1}{\epsilon} \cdot n + 4$, if we use only one bucket. Since the maximum number of buckets needed is upper bounded by the number of distinct values of path counts, the maximum size of a bloom filter, $S_{\max}$, is in turn bounded by $0.2602 \cdot \ln \frac{1}{\epsilon} \cdot n + 4n$.

Given a space limit S,

- If $S > S_{\max}$, we can either use less space by setting b to the number of distinct path counts, or choosing a smaller ϵ to utilize the additional space and reduce the estimation error.

- If $S \in [S_{\min}, S_{\max}]$, we fix the number b of buckets to $\frac{S - S_{\min}}{4}$.

- If $S < S_{\min}$, we need to increase ϵ. Another possible solution is to prune paths with the smallest count values, thus reducing n. This is similar to the No-* pruning strategy used in [1].

Therefore, by replacing the parameter b with the function of space limit S in Equations 1 and 2, we can establish the association between the space a bloom histogram uses and the expected estimation errors. This is a desirable feature and enables users to have a better understanding of the trade-offs.

We note that in practice, we do not always choose the largest possible b under a given budget. The rationale is that, although a larger b can reduce the error due to value distributions within each bucket, it will increase the errors by misclassifying a path into multiple buckets (see, Equation 2). This is reflected in our experiments, especially when ϵ is not small enough. Since the term $E[|V - V_*|]$ cannot be explicitly expressed as a function on b, currently we can only find the optimal b value empirically by considering all possible b values.

Compared to the previous Path Tree estimator [1], the space requirement of a bloom histogram is extremely small. Assume there are n distinct paths. A full path tree will occupy at least $16n + 16$ bytes. This translates to the following statement: a full path tree is always larger than the worst-case bloom histogram unless $\epsilon < 9 \times 10^{-21}$.

4 Dynamic summary

In this section, we discuss the dynamic summary component, which enables us to maintain the histogram under updates. Two alternative solutions are proposed and compared.

4.1 Overview

The dynamic summary component is an intermediate, small-sized data structure from which the bloom histogram can be recomputed periodically or upon request. The component can be described as follows:

- When updates arrive, we update not only the XML data, but also the dynamic summary. Specifically, all the paths are extracted from the updates and then grouped. In general, the dynamic summary takes as input a sequence of primitive update operations denoted as $U_i(p_i, \Delta_i)$, where Δ_i is the amount of *relative* change of the frequency of path p_i. Note that such primitive update operations can express both insertion and deletion.

- The dynamic summary processes the sequence of primitive update operations. Depending on the actual data structure of the dynamic summary, either approximate or exact value distribution can be maintained.

- The dynamic summary supports a *rebuild* operation to recompute a new bloom histogram from an approximate or exact path-count table maintained by the dynamic summary.

Next, we discuss some of the technical details that are related to the implementation of the above operations.

4.2 Two candidate data structures

Here, we consider two alternative data structures that implement the dynamic summary interface: the *Count-Min Sketch* based method and the *Full Label-Path Table* based method.

Count-min sketch based method

Our count-min sketch based method comprises of two parts:

1. A list of *hashID*s, in the domain of $[0, N]$.
2. A count-min sketch built for a length-N array of values.

The count-min sketch is proposed recently as an efficient and versatile synopsis structure for an array of n values [8]. Given parameters ε and δ, it employs $d = \lceil \log \frac{1}{\delta} \rceil$ pair-wise independent hash functions. Each hash function can map an incoming value into a random position within an array of $\lceil \frac{2}{\varepsilon} \rceil$ integers. With probability at least $1 - \delta$, point query, range query and inner product of two arrays can all be well approximated by the sketch. Its advantages over previous proposals (e.g., backing sample [10] or other sketches [11]) are (a) it supports deletion; and (b) the size requirement of count-min sketch is smaller than other synopses both in theory and in practice. The size of a count-min sketch is exactly $4\lceil \frac{e}{\varepsilon} \rceil \lceil \ln \frac{1}{\delta} \rceil + 8\lceil \ln \frac{1}{\delta} \rceil$ bytes, while other sketches use space linear to $\frac{1}{\varepsilon^2}$ with some constant hidden in the $O()$ notation.

The update and rebuilding operations can be supported as follows:

- To process the update operation $U_i(p_i, \Delta_i)$, we first obtain an integer ID_i by hashing the path p_i; and then invoke the standard update procedure of the count-min sketch that accepts an (ID_i, Δ_i) pair. We add ID_i into the hashID list if it does not exist in the current hashID list.

- An approximate path-count table can be reconstructed to rebuild the bloom histogram: we iterate through the hashID list and issue a point query to retrieve the approximate count value for each hashID.

We note that the rationale to use the hashID list is to save space. A naïve solution without using hashing would need to store the entire list of paths, which is usually much larger. One subtle thing is that those hashIDs should be treated as "paths" when building

Table 1: Statistics of datasets

Dataset	Size	#Path	M	| Path Table |	|Path Tree|	| MT ($m=2$) |	Comment
DBLP	184M	155	666920	3069	3100	1384	Regular
XMark	111M	548	59486	14578	10860	1584	Irregular
MathML	110K	734	23	49393	14680	1248	Extremely Irregular

the bloom filters for the bloom histogram and the same hash function needs to be applied when querying the resulting bloom histogram with a real path.

Update and rebuilding overhead: The update overhead for the count-min sketch based method can be shown to be $O(\ln \frac{1}{\delta})$. Let $R(n,b)$ be the cost of the bloom histogram construction algorithm (exclusive of the sorting cost). The cost of rebuilding is $O(n \ln \frac{1}{\delta} + n \log n + R(n,b))$. The rebuilding cost can be further reduced by computing on samples only.

Full label-path table based method

A full label-path table records the count values for all distinctive label paths in the XML data tree. Therefore, both the update and rebuilding operations can be supported in an exact manner:

- To process the update operation $U_i(p_i, \Delta_i)$, we simply use a hash lookup to locate and then update the corresponding entry in the full label-path table.
- The full label-path table is exactly the path-count table that can be fed into the bloom histogram construction algorithm.

Update and rebuilding overhead: The update overhead for the full label-path based solution is $O(1)$. Let $R(n,b)$ be the rebuilding cost of the bloom histogram construction algorithm (exclusive of the sorting cost). The total rebuilding cost is $O(n \log n + R(n,b))$.

4.2.1 Discussions

The two methods mainly differ in the update overhead, the size, and the quality of the resulting bloom histogram. In terms of size, the count-min sketch based solution takes $4 \lceil \frac{e}{\varepsilon} \rceil \lceil \ln \frac{1}{\delta} \rceil + 8 \lceil \ln \frac{1}{\delta} \rceil + 4n$ space, while the full label-path table based solution takes $(4+k)n$ space, where k is the average length of the paths. Therefore, the count-min sketch based method will take less space when n or k is large. An empirical comparison of the two methods is included in the experiment section.

5 Experiment

We describe in this section the result of extensive experiments we have conducted to compare our method to previous ones. We first describe the experiment setup and then present results that address different aspects of the proposed solution.

5.1 Experiment setup

We implemented our dynamic XML path selectivity system in C++. The hardware is a PC with AMD Atholon 900MHz CPU, 512M memory and 30G hard disk. The operating system is Windows XP Professional. We implemented the proposed two-layer solution. For the estimator component, we implemented the bloom histogram, Path Tree (with sibling-* pruning strategy) and Markov Table algorithms (with suffix-* pruning strategy). They are abbreviated as **BH**, **PT** and **MT**, respectively. For the dynamic summary component, we implemented the CM-Sketch based approach and the Full Label-Path Table based approach. They are abbreviated as **CM** and **LP**, respectively.

The performance metric used in the experiment is the *average* absolute error, defined as $\frac{1}{n} \sum_i^n |X_i - \hat{X}_i|$, where X_i is the real selectivity of the i-th query in the workload and $\hat{X}_i$ is its estimated selectivity. For the BH method, we take the average of its average absolute errors over 10 runs.

Both synthetic and real-world datasets were used in our experiments. In this paper, we present results on DBLP, XMark and MathML datasets. DBLP is a real-world dataset describing computer science bibliography information. The structure of the DBLP dataset is relatively shallow and non-recursive. XMark is a commonly used XML benchmark dataset, simulating an auction database. The structure of the XMark dataset is relatively deep and recursive. Another real-world dataset, the MathML dataset[2], is deliberately chosen as an extreme dataset, because its structure is very deep and highly recursive. Some statistics about the datasets are listed in Table 1, including the size of the dataset, number of paths, the maximum path-count value, size of the Path Table, size of the Path Tree, size of the Markov Table.

We generated both the positive and negative workloads as follows. For the positive workload, we randomly chose 1000 paths from the label-path table. For the negative workload, we chose random tags from the set of distinctive tags and concatenated them into a path. We controlled the distribution of the length of the generated paths to follow a zipf distribution of $\alpha = 0.4$, with the lengths varying from 2 to 4. A generated path was discarded if its selectivity was not 0. We will describe the generation of the update workload in Section 5.4.

---
[2] Available from http://support.sciencedirect.com/tectext_sgml.shtml.

We chose the load factor l of the bloom histogram to be a multiple of 8, so that the resulting bloom histograms are aligned at the byte boundary. Table 2 gives the corresponding error probability ϵ for different choices of load factors. The space budgets are always chosen to be between S_{min} and S_{max} (see, Section 3.4).

Table 2: Load factor vs. error probability

l	$\epsilon = 0.6185^l$
16	4.59×10^{-4}
24	9.82×10^{-6}
32	2.10×10^{-7}

5.2 Accuracy

In this set of experiments, we study and compare the accuracy of different estimators. Figures 4(a)—(c) show the accuracy of three estimators for the positive queries on the DBLP, XMark and MathML datasets. Figures 4(d)—(f) show the accuracy of three estimators for the negative queries on the three datasets. We fix the load factor parameter l to 24, thus the bloom filter error rate ϵ is fixed at 9.82×10^{-6}. We vary the space limit and plot the estimation errors. In all the figures, X-axis is the space limit and Y-axis is the error metric (in *logarithm* scale).

The range of the size limit is chosen to be starting from slightly greater than the minimum size of the bloom histogram to a size much larger than the maximum size of the bloom histogram. For example, in DBLP dataset, the minimum size of the bloom histogram is 469 and the maximum size of the bloom histogram is 801. Our current BH implementation does not use the extra space beyond its current maximum size.

For all the datasets, the accuracy of BH is almost always better than the other two estimators for all the positive queries. The main reasons are as follows.

- BH method is space efficient. Thus, for a given space limit, other methods need to perform significant amount of pruning which sacrifices their accuracy.

- On the other hand, our BH method is guaranteed to find the best grouping of all the paths and this directly minimizes the estimation error. The pruning methods of PT and MT, however, are *ad hoc* in nature.

For the negative queries, BH outperforms PT and MT on DBLP and MathML datasets. It also achieves reasonably good accuracy on the XMark dataset, as its errors are almost always below 10.

There are two interesting findings here:

- Comparatively speaking, the BH method has greater accuracy advantages than PT and MT on DBLP and MathML datasets. This is because the number of paths in DBLP is smaller, thus we only need to use a smaller number of buckets (i.e., b is small); and the maximum value of the MathML dataset is very small (i.e., M is small). According to the formulae for the errors of BH, these all lead to a smaller estimation error.

- There are some spikes and fluctuations on the curves. This is because when space budget increases, the number of buckets b also increases. As discussed in Section 3.4, the misclassification error due to a large b value will increase. This part of error is probabilistic in nature and leads to the fluctuations. On the other hand, such error is scaled by M, the maximum path-count value. As a result, fluctuations are more significant on DBLP and XMark datasets than those in the MathML dataset.

5.3 Effect of the bloom filter error (ϵ)

In this subsection, we investigate the effect of the bloom filter error ϵ on the accuracy of the BH method. Figure 5 shows the accuracy of both the positive and negative queries for the DBLP datasets, with different ϵ values ranging from 0.6185^{32} to 0.6185^{16}. As our estimator error formulae predict, the smaller the ϵ value is, the smaller the estimation error will be. Our experiment results agree with this prediction well. For the largest $\epsilon = 0.6185^{16}$, BH does not have significant advantages over the other estimators for both the positive and negative queries. Furthermore, the accuracy of BH fluctuates a lot. If we decrease the ϵ to 0.6185^{24}, BH clearly outperforms other estimators for the positive queries. The accuracy for the negative queries is greatly enhanced as well, with infrequent spikes and fluctuations. If we take $\epsilon = 0.6185^{32}$, BH is then the consistent winner for both query workloads. In terms of storage space, we note that the additional increase in space consumption due to the decrease of ϵ is moderate: the ranges of the bloom histograms for the three cases are $[314, 646]$, $[469, 801]$ and $[624, 956]$, respectively.

5.4 Handling dynamic data

In order to test our proposed methods for dynamic data, we designed an update workload to simulate the process of populating an initially empty XML database in k batch updates. The estimator is rebuilt k times from the dynamic summary. Specifically, we generate the update and querying workloads as follows. We start with a final XML data file: for each distinctive path p_i, its count value is denoted as $count_i$. We randomly pick $k-1$ integers as cut points within the range $[0, count_i]$. After sorting the $k-1$ cut points (denoted as v_{i_j} and specify $v_{i_0} = 0$), we can generate the k updates for this path p_i as $U(p_i, v_{i_j} - v_{i_{j-1}})$. We repeat this process for all paths and thus generate k batch

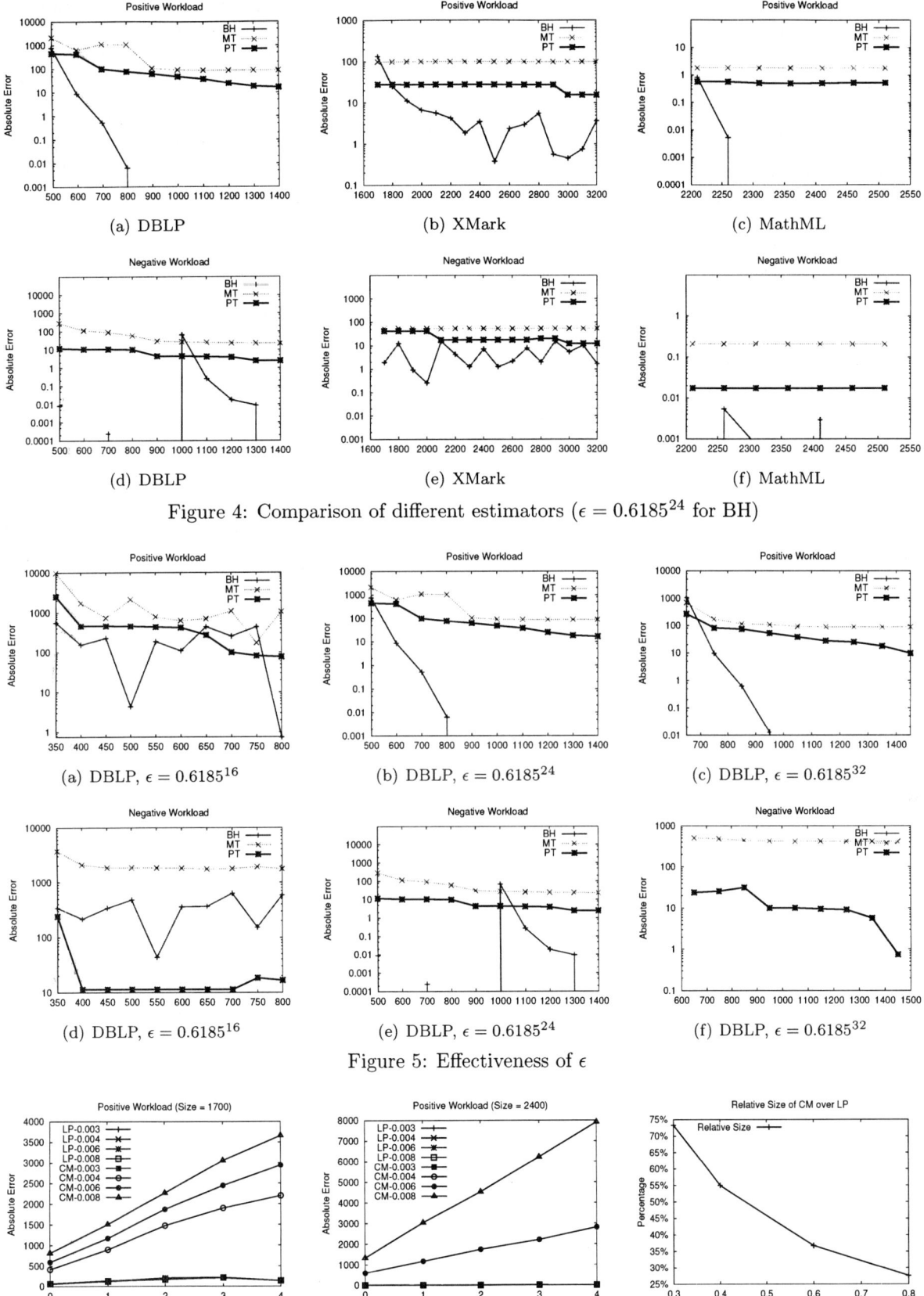

Figure 4: Comparison of different estimators ($\epsilon = 0.6185^{24}$ for BH)

Figure 5: Effectiveness of ϵ

Figure 6: LP vs. CM for dynamic data

updates. The generation of both the positive and the negative query workloads is the same as previous experiments.

We compared the following two experimental configurations: LP + BH and CM + BH. Notice that CM is only an approximation of the real path-count distribution, while LP records the exact distribution. In the interest of space, Figure 6 only shows the result of the positive queries. We used five batch updates and fixed the δ parameter for the CM to be 0.013. Figures 6(a) and (b) are obtained by fixing the space limit of the BH estimator to 1700 and 2400 bytes, respectively. For each case, we vary the other parameter of CM, ε, from 0.003 to 0.008. Therefore, the X-axis in Figures 6(a) and (b) is the ε value, and the Y-axis is the estimation error. As we can see from both figures, CM's error is very sensitive to the ε parameter, which determines how well the CM-Sketch approximates the original data distribution. In Figure 6(a), for $\varepsilon = 0.003$, CM can achieve almost the same accuracy as LP, which is optimal as the exact path-count distribution is preserved. However, for $\varepsilon > 0.003$, the estimation errors of CM are significantly larger. Similar observation can be made for the case when the size limit is set to 2400. This time, the cut point of the ε parameter is 0.004 instead. We note that for all the cases, CM occupies less space than LP. This is shown in Figure 6(c). Specifically, the relative sizes of CM over LP with ε equal to 0.003 and 0.004 are about 73% and 55%, respectively.

In summary, the experiment results indicate that

- The bloom histogram is the most accurate estimation method under small space budgets.

- Reasonable accuracy for dynamic XML data can be achieved by choosing an appropriate dynamic summary and building bloom histograms periodically.

6 Related work

6.1 Statistics estimation for XML data

There has been some recent work to estimate the selectivity of path expressions for XML data. Most existing approaches solve the problem in a *top-down* manner, by capturing the full structure of the XML data tree (or graph) with a small-sized synopsis structure and pruning it until a given space constraint is satisfied. [1] proposed two techniques, namely path trees and Markov tables. The path tree approach starts with a trie of all sub-paths and their associated counts; The Markov table approach starts with the full path-selectivity table of paths length up to m. A set of greedy pruning rules are proposed, and they differ mainly in the amount of information preserved in the pruning process. XPathLearner [14] used the Markov Histogram, an variant of Markov table which additionally captures value distribution. Their focus is on the learning methods of the Markov Histogram though. XSKETCH [17] exploited localized graph stability in a graph-synopsis model to approximate path and branching distributions in an XML data graph. Its successor, XSKETCHes [18], integrates support for value constraints as well, by using multidimensional synopsis to capture value correlations. For tree structured data, XSKETCH synopsis is just a path tree in [1]. [9] proposed StatiX, which takes advantage of XML schema types and builds both structural and value histograms as statistical summaries. However, the effectiveness of StatiX is highly dependent on the quality of system-generated OIDs. [6] proposed correlated subpath tree (CST), which is a pruned suffix tree with set hashing signatures that help to determine the correlation between branching paths when estimating the selectivity of twig queries. CST is usually large in size and has been outperformed by [1] for simple path expressions.

6.2 Traditional statistics estimation methods

Histogram is one of the most important statistics estimation data structure in relational DBMSs. [12] offers a latest, comprehensive survey on this subject. In particular, V-optimal histogram was proposed as the optimal histogram under the *sum of square error* metric [13]. Its optimal construction algorithms were also presented.

Maintaining histogram for dynamic data is a hard task. For one-dimensional histograms, [5] proposed to recompute the histogram periodically or under request by using samples from the base relation. [10] and [11] proposed to maintain a secondary data structure, *backing sample*, and a sketch, respectively, from which histograms can be recomputed. Similar approaches are adopted for maintaining multidimensional histograms, as in [20]. Another fundamentally different approach to construct and maintain histograms for dynamic data is to build histograms solely from query feedback, without looking at the data [4, 19, 15]. They are usually termed dynamic histograms or self-tuning histograms.

6.3 Bloom filter

Bloom filter was first proposed in [2] as a space efficient data structure for answering approximate membership queries over a given set. It was used in Bloom Join in [16]. [3] is a recent survey of various applications of bloom filters in the network domain. Most recently, a spectral bloom filter was proposed that generalize the original bloom filter to answer queries regarding the multiplicity of an element for a multiset [7]. Our bloom histogram can be viewed as a further compressed spectral bloom filter, which occupies even much smaller space.

7 Conclusion

In this paper, we studied the problem of dynamically estimating the selectivity for XML path expressions. We proposed a two-layer solution consisting of an estimator component and a dynamic summary component. A novel *bloom histogram* was proposed as a compact yet highly accurate estimator for XML path expressions. One unique feature is that the estimation error can be theoretically bounded by its size. We investigated both approximate and exact forms of the dynamic summary and discussed how they assist in updating the bloom histogram. Our extensive experiment results demonstrated the effectiveness of our proposed solution compared to the previous methods under both static and dynamic environments.

This paper presents our first endeavor towards solving the selectivity estimation problem for general XML queries. Some future work can be pursued hereafter. We are investigating the appropriate way to generalize our method to support other types of path expressions (e.g., with value predicates and branching subexpressions). On the other hand, we are also seeking opportunities to apply the bloom histogram method in other database applications.

References

[1] A. Aboulnaga, A. R. Alameldeen, and J. F. Naughton. Estimating the selectivity of XML path expressions for Internet scale applications. In *Proceedings of the 27th International Conference on Very Large Data Bases (VLDB 2001)*, pages 591–600, 2001.

[2] B. H. Bloom. Space/time trade-offs in hash coding with allowable errors. *Commun. ACM*, 13(7):422–426, 1970.

[3] A. Broder and M. Mitzenmacher. Network applications of bloom filters: A survey. In *Proceeding of Allerton Conference*, 2002.

[4] N. Bruno, S. Chaudhuri, and L. Gravano. STHoles: A multidimensional workload-aware histogram. In *Proceedings of the 2001 ACM SIGMOD International Conference on Management of Data (SIGMOD 2001)*.

[5] S. Chaudhuri, R. Motwani, and V. R. Narasayya. Random sampling for histogram construction: How much is enough? In *Proceedings ACM SIGMOD International Conference on Management of Data (SIGMOD 1998)*, pages 436–447.

[6] Z. Chen, H. V. Jagadish, F. Korn, N. Koudas, S. Muthukrishnan, R. T. Ng, and D. Srivastava. Counting twig matches in a tree. In *Proceedings of the 17th International Conference on Data Engineering (ICDE 2001)*, pages 595–604, 2001.

[7] S. Cohen and Y. Matias. Spectral bloom filters. In *Proceedings of the 2003 ACM SIGMOD International Conference on Management of Data (SIGMOD 2003)*, pages 241–252.

[8] G. Cormode and S. Muthukrishnan. Improved data stream summaries: The count-min sketch and its applications (extended abstract). In *Latin American Theoretical Informatics 2004 (LATIN 2004)*, 2004.

[9] J. Freire, J. R. Haritsa, M. Ramanath, P. Roy, and J. Siméon. Statix: making XML count. In *Proceedings of the 2002 ACM SIGMOD International Conference on Management of Data (SIGMOD 2002)*, pages 181–191, 2002.

[10] P. B. Gibbons, Y. Matias, and V. Poosala. Fast incremental maintenance of approximate histograms. In *Proceedings of 23rd International Conference on Very Large Data Bases (VLDB 1997)*.

[11] A. C. Gilbert, S. Guha, P. Indyk, Y. Kotidis, S. Muthukrishnan, and M. Strauss. Fast, small-space algorithms for approximate histogram maintenance. In *Proceedings on 34th Annual ACM Symposium on Theory of Computing (STOC 2002)*.

[12] Y. E. Ioannidis. The history of histograms (abridged). In *Proceedings of 29th International Conference on Very Large Data Bases (VLDB 2003)*, pages 19–30.

[13] H. V. Jagadish, N. Koudas, S. Muthukrishnan, V. Poosala, K. C. Sevcik, and T. Suel. Optimal histograms with quality guarantees. In *Proceedings of 24rd International Conference on Very Large Data Bases (VLDB 1998)*, pages 275–286.

[14] L. Lim, M. Wang, S. Padmanabhan, J. S. Vitter, and R. Parr. XPathLearner: An on-line self-tuning Markov histogram for XML path selectivity estimation. In *Proceedings of 28th International Conference on Very Large Data Bases (VLDB 2002)*, pages 442–453, 2002.

[15] L. Lim, M. Wang, and J. S. Vitter. SASH: A self-adaptive histogram set for dynamically changing workloads. In *Proceedings of 29th International Conference on Very Large Data Bases, September 9-12, 2003 (VLDB 2003)*.

[16] L. F. Mackert and G. M. Lohman. R* optimizer validation and performance evaluation for local queries. In *Proceedings of the 1986 ACM SIGMOD International Conference on Management of Data (SIGMOD 1986)*, pages 84–95, 1986.

[17] N. Polyzotis and M. N. Garofalakis. Statistical synopses for graph-structured XML databases. In *Proceedings of the 2002 ACM SIGMOD International Conference on Management of Data (SIGMOD 2002)*, pages 358–369, 2002.

[18] N. Polyzotis and M. N. Garofalakis. Structure and value synopses for XML data graphs. In *Proceedings of 28th International Conference on Very Large Data Bases (VLDB 2002)*, pages 466–477, 2002.

[19] L. Qiao, D. Agrawal, and A. E. Abbadi. RHist: adaptive summarization over continuous data streams. In *Proceedings of the 2002 ACM CIKM International Conference on Information and Knowledge Management (CIKM 2002)*.

[20] N. Thaper, S. Guha, P. Indyk, and N. Koudas. Dynamic multidimensional histograms. In *Proceedings of the 2002 ACM SIGMOD International Conference on Management of Data (SIGMOD 2002)*.

XQuery on SQL Hosts

Torsten Grust   Sherif Sakr   Jens Teubner

University of Konstanz
Department of Computer and Information Science
P.O. Box D 188, 78457 Konstanz, Germany
{grust,sakr,teubner}@inf.uni-konstanz.de

Abstract

Relational database systems may be turned into efficient XML and XPath processors if the system is provided with a suitable relational tree encoding. This paper extends this relational XML processing stack and shows that an RDBMS can also serve as a highly efficient XQuery runtime environment. Our approach is purely relational: XQuery expressions are compiled into SQL code which operates on the tree encoding. The core of the compilation procedure trades XQuery's notions of variable scopes and nested iteration (FLWOR blocks) for equi-joins.

The resulting relational XQuery processor closely adheres to the language semantics, *e.g.*, it obeys node identity as well as document and sequence order, and can support XQuery's *full axis* feature. The system exhibits quite promising performance figures in experiments. Somewhat unexpectedly, we will also see that the XQuery compiler can make good use of SQL's OLAP functionality.

1 Introduction

It is a virtue of the relational database model that its canonical physical representation, *tables of tuples*, is simple and thus efficient to implement. Typical operations on tables, *e.g.*, sequential scans, receive excellent support from current computing hardware in terms of prefetching CPU caches and read-ahead in disk-based secondary memory. If linear access is not viable, the regular table structure is sufficiently simple to allow for the definition of efficient *indexes*.

Permission to copy without fee all or part of this material is granted provided that the copies are not made or distributed for direct commercial advantage, the VLDB copyright notice and the title of the publication and its date appear, and notice is given that copying is by permission of the Very Large Data Base Endowment. To copy otherwise, or to republish, requires a fee and/or special permission from the Endowment.

**Proceedings of the 30th VLDB Conference,
Toronto, Canada, 2004**

At the same time, the table proves to be a generic data structure: it is often straightforward to map other data types onto tables. Among others, such encodings have been described for *ordered, unranked trees*, the data type that forms the backbone of the XML data model. These mappings turn RDBMSs into *relational XML processors*. Furthermore, if the tree encoding is designed such that core operations on trees—XPath axis traversals—lead to efficient table operations, this can result in high-performance *relational XPath* implementations. In [9, 10] we developed a tree encoding with this property: axis traversals lead to sequential table scans.

This work extends the relational XML processing stack: we devise a compilation procedure that transforms XQuery [2] expressions into SQL code. The compilation itself does not involve interaction with the database back-end. Once shipped to the DBMS, the emitted SQL code evaluates the input XQuery expression by means of a single SQL query. The result is a sequence of atomic values and node identifiers which may then be serialized by a post-processing step [11].

We assume a minimalistic encoding of both, trees and ordered sequences of atomic values and nodes. Several existing XML mapping techniques [3, 15] provide these assumptions, and our compiler can easily be modified to target any such scheme.

We exercise special care in translating the XQuery FLWOR construct. There is some tension between XQuery's concept of iterating the evaluation of an expression e_2 for successive bindings of a variable $v (\texttt{for } \$v \texttt{ in } e_1 \texttt{ return } e_2)$ and the set- or table-oriented processing model of SQL. In a nutshell, we thus map for-bound variables like v into tables containing all bindings and translate expressions in dependence of the variable scopes in which they appear. The resulting SQL code implements iteration via equi-joins, a table operation which RDBMS engines know how to execute most efficiently.

The compiler emits an SQL query with uncorrelated subqueries and does not depend on particularly advanced or "exotic" language features. It is interesting to observe, however, how the compiler can take advantage of widely available SQL/OLAP functions to speed up the evaluation of a number of XQuery constructs, *e.g.*, sequence and element construction as well as `for` expressions.

The paper proceeds as follows. Section 2 discusses relational encodings of trees and sequences, both simple by design. Support for nested variable scopes and efficient iteration affects the overall compilation process and is introduced in Section 3. Section 4 presents a compositional compilation procedure for a subset of XQuery Core in terms of inference rules. We will also see what is to be gained if OLAP ranking functionality is available. Compiler extensions and optimizations are the topic of Section 5: we will discuss bundling of XPath axis steps and how to exploit disjointness properties of tree fragments to evaluate element constructors. Section 6 reports on experiments in which IBM DB2 runs XQuery benchmarks before a review of related work summarizes (Sections 7, 8).

2 Encoding Trees and Sequences

The dynamic evaluation phase of XQuery operates with data of two principal types: *nodes* and *atomic values* (collectively referred to as `item`-typed data). Nodes may be assembled into *ordered, unranked trees*, *i.e.*, instances of XML documents or fragments thereof. Nodes and atomic values may form *ordered, finite sequences*. We will now briefly review minimalistic relational encodings of trees as well as sequences. Both encodings exhibit just those properties necessary to support a semantically correct and efficient XQuery to SQL compilation.

2.1 Trees and XPath Support

We assemble the components of the relational tree encoding piece by piece. Two basic concepts of the XQuery tree data model are *node identity* and *document order* (the latter orders nodes according to the order of their opening tags in the serialized tree instance). To represent both concepts, we assign to each node v its unique *preorder traversal rank* [9] in the tree, $v.pre$. The XQuery node comparison operators `is` and `<<` then compile into comparisons of ranks.

XQuery embeds XPath as a sublanguage to navigate tree structures. Given a sequence of context nodes e, an XPath *axis step* e/α returns the sequence of nodes which are reachable from e via axis α. If we extend the tree encoding for node v by (1) $v.size$, the number of nodes in the subtree below v, and (2) $v.level$, the length of the path from the tree root to v, we can express the semantics of all 13 XPath axes—and thus support XQuery's *full axis* feature—via simple conjunctive predicates. To illustrate, for the `ancestor` axis and two nodes v and c, we have that

$$v \in c/\texttt{ancestor} \Leftrightarrow$$
$$v.pre < c.pre \text{ AND } c.pre \leqslant v.pre + v.size \ .$$

Axis α	Predicate $axis(c, v, \alpha)$: $v \stackrel{?}{\in} c/\alpha$
`descendant`	$v.pre > c.pre$ AND $v.pre \leqslant c.pre + c.size$
`child`	$axis(c, v, \texttt{descendant})$ AND $v.level = c.level + 1$
`following`	$v.pre > c.pre + c.size$
`preceding`	$v.pre + v.size < c.pre$

Table 1: Predicate $axis()$ represents XPath axes semantics (selected axes).

Further axes are listed in Table 1. Note that we do not require $v.size$ to be exact: as long as the XPath axis semantics (Table 1) are obeyed, $v.size$ may overestimate the actual number of nodes below v. Via the *pre* property we can ensure that the node sequence resulting from an axis step is free of duplicates and in document order as required by the XPath semantics.

Support for XPath *name* and *kind tests* is added by means of two further node properties, $v.prop$ and $v.kind \in \{\texttt{"elem"}, \texttt{"text"}\}$.[1] For an element node v with tag name `t`, we have $v.prop = \texttt{"t"}$, for a text node v' with content `c`, $v'.prop = \texttt{"c"}$.

XQuery is not limited to query single XML documents. In general, query evaluation involves nodes from multiple documents or fragments thereof, possibly created at runtime via XQuery's element constructors. The query

```
(element a { element b { () }}, element c { () })
```

creates three element nodes in two independent fragments, for example. We thus record the unique fragment identity for each constructed fragment in the node property *frag*.

The database system maintains a table `doc` of *live nodes* (*i.e.*, nodes of persistent XML documents as well as nodes constructed at runtime) and their properties. Figure 1 depicts two XML fragments as well as their relational encoding. Note that the document order of two nodes v, v' in separate fragments is consistent with the XQuery semantics: if v precedes v' ($v \ll v' \equiv v.pre < v'.pre$), the same is true for any pair of nodes taken from these two fragments.

Any XML encoding which provides the above properties or allows for their derivation may be plugged into the compilation procedure. One example of such an encoding is the *XPath accelerator* [9], others include [3, 15].

2.2 Sequences

XQuery expressions evaluate to ordered, finite sequences of `items`. Since sequences are flat and cannot be nested, a sequence may be represented by a single relation in which each tuple encodes a sequence item i. We preserve *sequence order* by means of a

---
[1] We omit the discussion of further XML node kinds for space reasons.

253

```
<a>
  <b><c/></b>
  <d/>
  <e/>
</a>
```

```
<f>
  s<g/>t
</f>
```

(a) Two XML fragments.

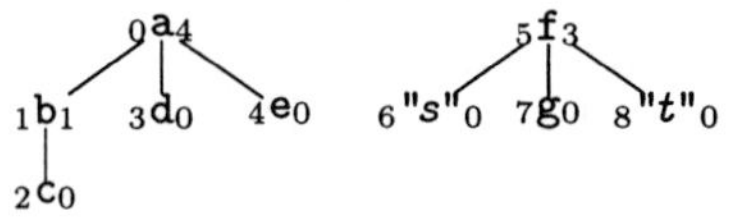

(b) Fragment trees.

pre	*size*	*level*	*kind*	*prop*	*frag*
0	4	0	"elem"	"a"	0
1	1	1	"elem"	"b"	0
2	0	2	"elem"	"c"	0
3	0	1	"elem"	"d"	0
4	0	1	"elem"	"e"	0
5	3	0	"elem"	"f"	1
6	0	1	"text"	"s"	1
7	0	1	"elem"	"g"	1
8	0	1	"text"	"t"	1

(c) Tree encoding (table doc).

Figure 1: Relational encoding of two XML fragments. Nodes in the fragment trees (b) have been annotated with their *pre* and *size* properties. Both trees are encoded as independent fragments 0 and 1 in (c).

property $i.pos \geqslant 1$. In sequences, nodes are represented by their unique preorder rank (property *i.pre*) while atomic values, *i.e.*, values of type `xs:float`, `xs:string`, *etc.*, are recorded with their lexical representation *i.val* as defined by XML Schema [1]. The relational representation of the sequence `(1.0,"x",`v`,`v'`)` where v and v' denote the root nodes of the two XML fragments of Figure 1 is shown in Figure 2. The empty relation encodes the empty sequence `()`. A single item i and the singleton sequence (i) are represented identically, which coincides with the XQuery semantics. Note that XQuery's positional predicates e`[`p`]`, $p \geqslant 1$, are easily evaluated if the *pos* column is populated *densely* starting at 1 as is the case in Figure 2.

pos	*pre*	*val*
1	NULL	"1.0"
2	NULL	"x"
3	0	NULL
4	5	NULL

Figure 2: Relational sequence encoding.

3 Relational FLWORs: Turning Variable Scopes and Iteration into Joins

The core of the XQuery language, with syntactic sugar like path expressions, quantifiers, or sequence comparison operators removed, has been designed around an *iteration* primitive, the `for-return` construct. A `for`-expression evaluates the body e of the return clause for successive bindings of the `for`-bound variable $\$v$:

$$\texttt{for } \$v \texttt{ in } (x_1, x_2, \ldots, x_n) \texttt{ return } e \equiv (e[x_1/\$v], e[x_2/\$v], \ldots, e[x_n/\$v])$$

where $e[x/\$v]$ denotes the consistent replacement of all free occurrences of $\$v$ in e by x. XQuery provides a functional style of iteration: it is semantically sound to evaluate e for all n bindings of $\$v$ in parallel.

3.1 Loop Lifting for Constant Subexpressions

This property of XQuery inspires our loop compilation strategy:

(1) A loop of n iterations is represented by a relation loop with a single column *iter* of n values $0, 1, \ldots, n-1$.

(2) If a constant subexpression c occurs inside a loop body e, the relational representation of c is *lifted* (intuitively, this accounts for the n independent evaluations of e).

For a constant atomic value c, lifting with respect to a given loop relation is performed as follows:

```
SELECT iter, 1 AS pos, NULL AS pre, c AS val
  FROM loop .
```

Figure 3(a) exemplifies how the constant subexpression `10` is lifted with respect to the loop

```
for $v0 in (1,2,3) return 10 .
```

If, for example, `10` is replaced by the sequence `(10,20)` in this loop, we require the lifting result to be the relation of Figure 3(b) instead.

Generally, a tuple $(i, p, \texttt{NULL}, v)$ in a loop-lifted relation for subexpression e may be read as the assertion that, during the ith iteration, the item at position p in e has value v—an analogous interpretation applies for a tuple $(i, p, n, \texttt{NULL})$ which represents a node with preorder rank n (Section 2.1). With this in mind, suppose we rewrite the `for`-loop as

$$\texttt{for } \$v_0 \texttt{ in (1,2,3) return (10,}\$v_0\texttt{)} . \qquad (Q_1)$$

Consistent with the loop lifting scheme, the database system will represent variable $\$v_0$ as the relation shown in Figure 3(c). We will shortly see how we can derive this representation of a variable from the representation of its domain (in this case the sequence `(1,2,3)`).

Finally, to evaluate the query Q_1, the system solely operates with the loop-lifted relations to compute the result shown in Figure 3(d). The upcoming discussion of nested variable scopes and Section 4 will fill in the missing details.

3.2 Nested Scopes

In XQuery, `for`-loops nest arbitrarily and we will now generalize the loop lifting idea to support nesting.

iter		pos	pre	val
0		1	NULL	"10"
1				
2				

$\underbrace{}_{\text{loop}}$ $\underbrace{}_{\text{encoding of 10}}$

iter	pos	pre	val
0	1	NULL	"10"
1	1	NULL	"10"
2	1	NULL	"10"

lifted encoding of 10

iter	pos	pre	val
0	1	NULL	"10"
0	2	NULL	"20"
1	1	NULL	"10"
1	2	NULL	"20"
2	1	NULL	"10"
2	2	NULL	"20"

iter	pos	pre	val
0	1	NULL	"1"
1	1	NULL	"2"
2	1	NULL	"3"

iter	pos	pre	val
0	1	NULL	"10"
0	2	NULL	"1"
0	3	NULL	"10"
0	4	NULL	"2"
0	5	NULL	"10"
0	6	NULL	"3"

(a) Lifting the constant 10. (b) Loop-lifted sequence. (c) Encoding of variable $\$v_0$. (d) Result of query Q_1.

Figure 3: Loop lifting.

Assume an expression with three nested for-loops as shown here:

$$s \begin{cases} (\text{ for } \$v_0 \text{ in } e_0 \text{ return} \\ \quad s_0 \{\ e'_0\ , \\ \text{ for } \$v_1 \text{ in } e_1 \text{ return} \\ \quad s_1 \begin{cases} \text{for } \$v_{10} \text{ in } e_{10} \text{ return} \\ \quad s_{10} \{\ e'_{10} \end{cases} \\ ) \end{cases}$$

The curly braces visualize the *variable scopes* in this query: variable $\$v_0$ is visible in scope s_0, variable $\$v_1$ is visible in scopes s_1 and s_{10}, while variable $\$v_{10}$ is accessible in scope s_{10} only. No variables are bound in top-level scope s. (In the context of this section, only for expressions are considered to open a new scope; let expressions are treated in Section 4.)

Note that the compositionality and scoping rules of XQuery, in general, lead to a tree-shaped hierarchy of scopes. For the above query, we obtain

$$\begin{array}{c} s \\ s_0 \quad s_1 \\ \quad \quad | \\ \quad \quad s_{10} \end{array}$$

In the following, we write $s_{x \cdot y}$, $x \in \{0, 1, \dots\}^*, y \in \{0, 1, \dots\}$ to identify the yth child scope of scope s_x. Furthermore, let $q_x(e)$ denote the representation of expression e in scope s_x.

Bound variables. Consider a for-loop in its directly enclosing scope s_x:

$$s_x \begin{cases} \vdots \\ \text{for } \$v_{x \cdot y} \text{ in } e_{x \cdot y} \text{ return} \\ \quad s_{x \cdot y} \{\ e'_{x \cdot y} \\ \vdots \end{cases}$$

According to the XQuery semantics, $e_{x \cdot y}$ is evaluated in scope s_x. Variable $\$v_{x \cdot y}$ is then successively bound to each single item in the resulting sequence; these bindings are used in the evaluation of $e'_{x \cdot y}$ in scope $s_{x \cdot y}$. A suitable representation for $\$v_{x \cdot y}$ in scope $s_{x \cdot y}$ is thus given by[2]

$q_{x \cdot y}(\$v_{x \cdot y}) = $ SELECT $row()$ AS $iter, 1$ AS pos, pre, val
FROM $q_x(e_{x \cdot y})$
ORDER BY $iter, pos$.

---
[2]We assume the presence of a builtin function $row()$ which densely numbers the tuples of an ordered table starting from 0. Section 4 discusses two possible implementations of $row()$.

This is exactly how we obtained the representation of variable $\$v_0$ in query Q_1 (see Figure 3(c)):

$q_0(\$v_0) = $ SELECT $row()$ AS $iter, 1$ AS pos, pre, val
FROM $q((1,2,3))$
ORDER BY $iter, pos$

where $q((1,2,3))$ simply is the relational encoding of the sequence $(1,2,3)$ as introduced in Section 2.2.

Constants. The compilation of an atomic constant c requires loop lifting (Section 3.1). If c occurs in scope s_x:

for $\$v_x$ in e_x return
$s_x \{\ \cdots c \cdots$

we compile c into

SELECT $iter, 1$ AS $pos,$ NULL AS pre, c AS val
FROM loop_x

in which

$\text{loop}_x = $ SELECT $iter$
FROM $q_x(\$v_x)$.

represents the iterations of the surrounding for-loop. The loop relation associated with the top-level scope s is $\text{loop} = \frac{iter}{0}$.

Free variables. In XQuery, an expression e may refer to variables which have been bound in an enclosing scope: a variable bound in scope s_x is also visible in any scope $s_{x \cdot x'}$, $x' \in \{0, 1, \dots\}^+$. If scope $s_{x \cdot x'}$ is viewed in isolation, such variables appear to be free.

We will derive the compiled representation of a free variable in scope $s_{x \cdot y}$ from its representation in the directly enclosing scope s_x (if the variable is also free in s_x, we repeat the process). To understand the derivation, consider the evaluation of two nested for-loops (note the reference to $\$v_0$ in the inner scope $s_{0 \cdot 0}$):

$$s \begin{cases} \text{for } \$v_0 \text{ in } (1,2) \text{ return} \\ s_0 \begin{cases} (\ \$v_0, \\ \text{for } \$v_{0 \cdot 0} \text{ in } (10,20) \text{ return} \\ \quad s_{0 \cdot 0} \{\ (\$v_0, \$v_{0 \cdot 0}) \\ ) \end{cases} \end{cases} \quad (Q_2)$$

In the zeroth outer iteration, $\$v_0$ is bound to 1. With this binding, two evaluations of the innermost loop body occur, each with a new binding for $\$v_{0 \cdot 0}$. Then, during the next outer iteration, two further evaluations of the innermost loop body occur with $\$v_0$ bound to 2.

255

iter	pos	·	val
0	1	·	"1"
1	1	·	"2"

iter	pos	·	val
0	1	·	"1"
1	1	·	"1"
2	1	·	"2"
3	1	·	"2"

iter	pos	·	val
0	1	·	"10"
1	1	·	"20"
2	1	·	"10"
3	1	·	"20"

(a) $q_0(\$v_0)$ (b) $q_{0\cdot 0}(\$v_0)$ (c) $q_{0\cdot 0}(\$v_{0\cdot 0})$

Figure 5: Q_2: Scope-dependent representation of variables (entries in the omitted *pre* column are all NULL).

outer	inner
0	0
0	1
1	2
1	3

Figure 4: $\mathsf{map}_{(0,0\cdot 0)}$.

iter	pos	·	val
0	1	·	"1"
0	2	·	"10"
1	1	·	"1"
1	2	·	"20"
2	1	·	"2"
2	2	·	"10"
3	1	·	"2"
3	2	·	"20"

iter	pos	·	val
0	1	·	"1"
0	2	·	"10"
0	3	·	"1"
0	4	·	"20"
1	1	·	"2"
1	2	·	"10"
1	3	·	"2"
1	4	·	"20"

iter	pos	·	val
0	1	·	"1"
0	2	·	"1"
0	3	·	"10"
0	4	·	"1"
0	5	·	"20"
0	6	·	"2"
0	7	·	"2"
0	8	·	"10"
0	9	·	"2"
0	10	·	"20"

(a) Intermediate result in $s_{0\cdot 0}$. (b) Intermediate result in s_0. (c) Final result in top-level scope.

Figure 6: Q_2: Intermediate and final results.

The semantics of this nested iteration may be captured by a relation $\mathsf{map}_{(0,0\cdot 0)}$ shown in Figure 4 ($\mathsf{map}_{(x,x\cdot y)}$ will be used to map representations between scopes s_x and $s_{x\cdot y}$). A tuple (o,i) in this relation indicates that, during the ith iteration of the inner loop body in scope $s_{0\cdot 0}$, the outer loop body in scope s_0 is in its oth iteration. This is the connection we need to derive the representation of a free variable $\$v_x$ in scope $s_{x\cdot y}$ via the following equi-join:

$$q_{x\cdot y}(\$v_x) = \text{SELECT } inner \text{ AS } iter, pos, pre, val$$
$$\text{FROM } \mathsf{map}_{(x,x\cdot y)}, q_x(\$v_x)$$
$$\text{WHERE } outer = iter \;.$$

Note that relation $\mathsf{map}_{(x,x\cdot y)}$ is easily derived from the representation of the domain $e_{x\cdot y}$ of variable $\$v_{x\cdot y}$ (much like the representation of $\$v_{x\cdot y}$ itself):

$$\mathsf{map}_{(x,x\cdot y)} = \text{SELECT } iter \text{ AS } outer, \text{row}() \text{ AS } inner$$
$$\text{FROM } q_x(e_{x\cdot y})$$
$$\text{ORDER BY } iter, pos \;.$$

Figure 5 contains a line-up of the relational variable representations involved in evaluating query Q_2. Note how the relations in Figures 5(b) and 5(c) represent the fact that, for example, in iteration 2 of the inner loop body variable $\$v_0$ is bound to 2 while $\$v_{0\cdot 0}$ is bound to 10, as desired.

The intermediate result computed by the inner loop is shown in Figure 6(a). To use this result in scope s_0 (as is required due to the sequence construction in line 2 of Q_2), we need to map its representation back into s_0. This back-mapping from scope $s_{x\cdot y}$ into the parent scope s_x may, again, be achieved via an equi-join with $\mathsf{map}_{(x,x\cdot y)}$. The FOR compilation rule in Section 4 emits the required SQL code to achieve this back-mapping. Figure 6(b) depicts the inner loop body result after it has been mapped back into scope s_0. Sequence construction (Rule SEQ, Section 4) and a second back-mapping step (from scope s_0 into the top-level scope s via $\mathsf{map}_{(\cdot,0)}$) produces the final result of Q_2 (Figure 6(c)).

Other expression types. The compilation procedure ensures that the correct loop relation and variable representations are available when an expression is compiled. Section 4 describes in which way (if any)

$$
\begin{aligned}
e ::= \;& c & \text{atomic constants} \\
| \;& \$v & \text{variables} \\
| \;& (e,e) & \text{sequence construction} \\
| \;& e/\alpha :: n & \text{loc. step (axis } \alpha, \text{ node test } n) \\
| \;& \texttt{element } t \, \{ e \} & \text{element constructor (tag } t) \\
| \;& \texttt{for } \$v \texttt{ in } e \texttt{ return } e & \text{iteration} \\
| \;& \texttt{let } \$v := e \texttt{ return } e & \text{let binding}
\end{aligned}
$$

Figure 7: Syntax of XQuery Core subset.

other expression types, e.g., sequence construction, element constructors, or path expressions, are affected by variable scoping and iteration.

4 XQuery on SQL Hosts

The core of the XQuery to SQL compiler is defined in terms of a set of inference rules (Figure 8). In these rules, a judgment of the form

$$\Gamma; \mathsf{loop}; \mathsf{doc} \vdash e \mapsto (q, \mathsf{doc}')$$

indicates that, given
(1) Γ (an *environment* mapping XQuery variables to their relational representation, *i.e.*, an SQL query),
(2) the current loop relation, and
(3) doc (the table of currently live nodes),
the XQuery expression e compiles into the SQL query q with a new table of live nodes doc′. New live nodes are created by XQuery's element constructors only, otherwise we have doc = doc′.

Compilation starts with the top-level expression, an empty environment[3] $\Gamma = \emptyset$, the singleton loop relation associated with the top-level scope (Section 3.2), and a table doc populated with all persistent XML document instances maintained by the RDBMS; in particular, doc may be empty. All inference rules pass Γ, loop, and doc top-down, while the emitted SQL code is synthesized bottom-up. The compiler produces a single SQL query that operates on the tree and sequence encodings of Section 2.

This paper contains inference rules to compile a subset of XQuery Core defined by the grammar in Figure 7. This subset, plus a few extensions, suffices to

---
[3]The initial environment Γ may already contain bindings if external variables have been defined in the input query.

256

iter	pos	·	val
0	1	·	"1"
1	1	·	"10"
1	2	·	"20"

iter	pos	·	val
0	1	·	"2"
1	1	·	"30"

iter	pos	·	val
0	1	·	"1"
0	3	·	"2"
1	1	·	"10"
1	2	·	"20"
1	3	·	"30"

(a) Encoding q_1 of e_1. (b) Encoding q_2 of e_2. (c) Encoded result of (e_1, e_2).

Figure 9: Sequence construction. The dashed lines separate the represented iterations (*iter* partitions).

express the XMark benchmark query set [18], for example. We will sketch a few extensions in the sequel.[4]

Rule CONST implements loop lifting for constant atomic values as introduced in Section 3.1. The variable environment Γ is updated and accessed in Rules LET and VAR in a standard fashion: to compile let $\$v := e_1$ return e_2, translate e_1 in environment Γ to yield the SQL query q_1, then compile e_2 in the enriched environment $\Gamma + \{\$v \mapsto q_1\}$. A reference to $\$v$ in e_2 then yields q_1 via Rule VAR.

Essentially, Rule SEQ compiles the sequence construction (e_1, e_2) into an SQL UNION ALL of the relational encodings q_1 and q_2 of e_1 and e_2. Note that this evaluates the sequence construction for *all* iterations encoded in q_1, q_2 at once. Figure 9 exemplifies the operation of the compiled code. Relation q_1 encodes two sequences: (1) in iteration 0 and (10,20) in iteration 1, while q_2 encodes (2) in iteration 0 and (30) in iteration 1. The SQL code generated by Rule SEQ computes the result in Figure 9(c): the sequence construction evaluates to (1,2) in iteration 0 and (10,20,30) in iteration 1, as expected.

Exploiting OLAP functionality. In Figure 9(c), note that the resulting *pos* column, in general, is not densely populated for each iteration (*i.e.*, in each *iter* partition). While this is neither a problem for the sequence encoding nor for the compilation process *per se*, we can use an alternative SQL implementation—based on the SQL/OLAP amendment defined for SQL:1999 [17]—which will generate a dense *pos* column, ascending from 1 in each *iter* partition (ordering by columns *ord,pos* ensures that sequence order is obeyed: items encoded in q_1 will appear before items encoded in q_2):

```
SELECT iter,
       DENSE_RANK() OVER
         (PARTITON BY iter ORDER BY ord, pos) AS pos,
       pre, val
  FROM (SELECT *, 0 AS ord FROM q₁
        UNION ALL
        SELECT *, 1 AS ord FROM q₂) .
```

[4] In fact, the subset may be extended to embrace the complete XQuery Core language. Support for dynamic typing and validation, however, requires extensions to the minimalistic tree and sequence encoding discussed here.

Node test n	Predicate $test(v, n)$
*	$v.kind =$ "elem"
t (tag name)	$v.kind =$ "elem" AND $v.prop = "t"$
text()	$v.kind =$ "text"
node()	TRUE

Table 2: Predicate *test()* represents XPath node tests.

This variant (1) executes substantially faster in our experimental setup (Section 6), (2) avoids early INTEGER overflow in the *pos* column, and (3) works correctly in case relation q_1 is empty (the original SQL code in Rule SEQ requires a slight adaption to ensure this).

Rule STEP compiles an XPath location step $\alpha::n$. The SQL code yields a node sequence that obeys the XPath semantics: while the DISTINCT clause removes duplicate nodes, we use the nodes' preorder rank—which reflects document order—to order the sequence (*d.pre* AS *pos*). Property *frag* is tested to avoid that step evaluation escapes the document fragment of the current context node e'.

Rule STEP uses region queries as described in [9] to evaluate XPath axis steps. For some common location steps we listed predicate *axis()* in Table 1 to evaluate axis α, predicate *test()* encodes the associated node (name or kind) test (Table 2).

Rule FOR essentially implements the compilation procedure for for-loops as introduced in Section 3.2. Note how the rule makes use of the map relation to map all variables $\$v_i$ in the environment into the scope opened by the for expression. The SQL code emitted by Rule FOR implements the back-mapping step explained in Section 3.2.

In this context, the OLAP function DENSE_RANK() may serve as an efficient implementation of the hypothetical *row()* function introduced in Section 3.2. If DENSE_RANK() (or equivalent functionality, *e.g.*, ROW_NUMBER) is not provided by the SQL dialect of the target RDBMS, we can rephrase the definition of map as follows:

```
SELECT iter AS outer,
       iter * m.pos + e₁.pos AS inner
  FROM q₁ AS e₁, (SELECT MAX(pos) AS pos FROM q₁) AS m
```

(q_v may be rewritten accordingly). To illustrate, given the *iter* and *pos* columns of relation q_1 as shown in Figure 10(a), this SQL query computes the map relation of Figure 10(b)—which performs inferior to the OLAP variant but is good enough to ensure correct compilation.

Rule ELEM emits SQL code for the evaluation of an XQuery element constructor element $t\{e\}$ in which subexpression e is required to evaluate to a sequence of nodes $(v_1, v_2, \ldots, v_n)$: (1) a new element node

$$\Gamma; \text{loop}; \text{doc} \vdash c \Mapsto \begin{pmatrix} \text{SELECT } l.iter, 1 \text{ AS } pos, \\ \text{NULL AS } pre, c \text{ AS } val \quad , \text{doc} \\ \text{FROM loop AS } l \end{pmatrix} \quad (\text{Const}) \qquad \overline{\{\ldots, \$v \mapsto q_v, \ldots\}; \text{loop}; \text{doc} \vdash \$v \Mapsto (q_v, \text{doc})} \quad (\text{Var})$$

$$\frac{\Gamma; \text{loop}; \text{doc} \vdash e_1 \Mapsto (q_1, \text{doc}') \qquad \Gamma + \{\$v \mapsto q_1\}; \text{loop}; \text{doc}' \vdash e_2 \Mapsto (q_2, \text{doc}'')}{\Gamma; \text{loop}; \text{doc} \vdash \texttt{let } \$v := e_1 \texttt{ return } e_2 \Mapsto (q_2, \text{doc}'')} \quad (\text{Let})$$

$$\frac{\Gamma; \text{loop}; \text{doc} \vdash e_1 \Mapsto (q_1, \text{doc}') \qquad \Gamma; \text{loop}; \text{doc}' \vdash e_2 \Mapsto (q_2, \text{doc}'')}{\Gamma; \text{loop}; \text{doc} \vdash (e_1, e_2) \Mapsto \left(q_1 \text{ UNION ALL} \begin{array}{l} \text{SELECT } iter, e_2.pos + m.pos \text{ AS } pos, pre, val \\ \text{FROM } q_2 \text{ AS } e_2, \\ (\text{SELECT MAX}(pos) \text{ AS } pos \text{ FROM } q_1) \text{ AS } m \end{array}, \text{doc}''\right)} \quad (\text{Seq})$$

$$\frac{\Gamma; \text{loop}; \text{doc} \vdash e \Mapsto (q_e, \text{doc}')}{\Gamma; \text{loop}; \text{doc} \vdash e/\alpha::n \Mapsto \begin{pmatrix} \text{SELECT DISTINCT } e.iter, d.pre \text{ AS } pos, d.pre, \text{NULL AS } val \\ \text{FROM } q_e \text{ AS } e, \text{doc}' \text{ AS } e', \text{doc}' \text{ AS } d \\ \text{WHERE } e'.pre = e.pre \\ \text{AND } e'.frag = d.frag \\ \text{AND } axis(e', d, \alpha) \text{ AND } test(d, n) \end{pmatrix}, \text{doc}'} \quad (\text{Step})$$

$$\{\ldots, \$v_i \mapsto q_{v_i}, \ldots\}; \text{loop}; \text{doc} \vdash e_1 \Mapsto (q_1, \text{doc}') \qquad \text{loop}' \equiv (\text{SELECT } iter \text{ FROM } q_v)$$

$$q_v \equiv \begin{pmatrix} \text{SELECT } row() \text{ AS } iter, 1 \text{ AS } pos, pre, val \\ \text{FROM } q_1 \\ \text{ORDER BY } iter, pos \end{pmatrix} \qquad \text{map} \equiv \begin{pmatrix} \text{SELECT } iter \text{ AS } outer, row() \text{ AS } inner \\ \text{FROM } q_1 \\ \text{ORDER BY } iter, pos \end{pmatrix}$$

$$\frac{\left\{\ldots, \$v_i \mapsto \begin{pmatrix} \text{SELECT } inner \text{ AS } iter, pos, pre, val \\ \text{FROM map}, q_{v_i} \\ \text{WHERE } outer = iter \end{pmatrix}, \ldots\right\} + \{\$v \mapsto q_v\}; \text{loop}'; \text{doc}' \vdash e_2 \Mapsto (q_2, \text{doc}'')}{\{\ldots, \$v_i \mapsto q_{v_i}, \ldots\}; \text{loop}; \text{doc} \vdash \texttt{for } \$v \texttt{ in } e_1 \texttt{ return } e_2 \Mapsto \begin{pmatrix} \text{SELECT } outer \text{ AS } iter, \\ e_2.iter * m.pos + e_2.pos \text{ AS } pos, \\ e_2.pre, e_2.val \\ \text{FROM map}, q_2 \text{ AS } e_2, \\ (\text{SELECT MAX}(pos) \text{ AS } pos \\ \text{FROM } q_2) \text{ AS } m \\ \text{WHERE } inner = e_2.iter \end{pmatrix}, \text{doc}''} \quad (\text{For})$$

$\Gamma; \text{loop}; \text{doc} \vdash e \Mapsto (q_e, \text{doc}')$

$$\textit{subtree-copies} \equiv \begin{pmatrix} \text{SELECT } d.pre - e'.pre + m_d.pre + 2 + (e.iter * m_e.pos + e.pos) * m_d.size \text{ AS } pre, d.size, \\ d.level - e'.level + 1 \text{ AS } level, d.kind, d.prop, m_d.frag + 1 + e.iter \text{ AS } frag \\ \text{FROM } q_e \text{ AS } e, \text{doc}' \text{ AS } e', \text{doc}' \text{ AS } d, \\ (\text{SELECT MAX}(pos) \text{ AS } pos \text{ FROM } q_e) \text{ AS } m_e, \\ (\text{SELECT MAX}(pre + size) \text{ AS } pre, \text{MAX}(size) + 1 \text{ AS } size, \text{MAX}(frag) \text{ AS } frag \\ \text{FROM doc}') \text{ AS } m_d \\ \text{WHERE } e'.pre = e.pre \text{ AND } e'.frag = d.frag \text{ AND } axis(e', d, \texttt{descendant-or-self}) \end{pmatrix}$$

$$\textit{new-roots} \equiv \begin{pmatrix} \text{SELECT } l.iter, l.iter * m_e.pos * m_d.size + m_d.pre + 1 \text{ AS } pre, \\ m_e.pos * m_d.size \text{ AS } size, 0 \text{ AS } level, \texttt{"elem" AS } kind, \\ t \text{ AS } prop, m_d.frag + 1 + l.iter \text{ AS } frag \\ \text{FROM loop AS } l, (\text{SELECT MAX}(pos) \text{ AS } pos \text{ FROM } q_e) \text{ AS } m_e, \\ (\text{SELECT MAX}(pre + size) \text{ AS } pre, \text{MAX}(size) + 1 \text{ AS } size, \text{MAX}(frag) \text{ AS } frag \\ \text{FROM doc}') \text{ AS } m_d \end{pmatrix}$$

$$\Gamma; \text{loop}; \text{doc} \vdash \texttt{element } t \text{ } \{e\} \Mapsto \begin{pmatrix} \text{SELECT } iter, 1 \text{ AS } pos, & \text{doc}' \\ pre, \text{NULL AS } val &, \text{UNION ALL} \\ \text{FROM } \textit{new-roots} & \textit{subtree-copies} \\ & \text{UNION ALL} \\ & \text{SELECT } pre, size, level, kind, prop, frag \\ & \text{FROM } \textit{new-roots} \end{pmatrix} \quad (\text{Elem})$$

Figure 8: XQuery to SQL compilation procedure.

iter	pos	·	·
0	1	·	·
0	2	·	·
1	1	·	·
1	2	·	·
1	3	·	·

outer	inner
0	1
0	2
1	4
1	5
1	6

(a) Encoding q_1.   (b) Resulting map.

Figure 10: Computing map without OLAP extensions.

r with tag name t is appended to the table doc of live nodes, (2) the n subtrees rooted at the nodes v_i are extracted (the code effectively evaluates the location step v_i/descendant-or-self::node()) and then appended to doc, and (3) r is made the common new root of the subtree copies.

Consider the query

```
let $v := e//b return element r { $v }
```

in which we assume that e evaluates to the singleton sequence containing the root element node a of the tree depicted in Figure 11(a).[5] After XPath step evaluation, v will be bound to the sequence containing the two element nodes with tag b (preorder ranks 1, 4). Figure 11(b) shows the newly constructed tree fragment: the copies of the subtrees rooted at the two b nodes now share the newly constructed root node r. The latter also constitutes the result of the overall expression.

Figure 11(c) illustrates how the new fragment is appended to the doc table:
(1) the new root node r is appended and assigned the next available preorder rank $\text{MAX}(pre + size) + 1$,
(2) the nodes in the affected subtrees are appended to doc (with $pre \geq \text{MAX}(pre + size) + 2$) with their size, kind, and prop properties unchanged, and their level property updated.

To simplify the generated SQL code, we overestimate the size of the copied subtrees to be the size of the largest subtree. In general, this leads to gaps in the pre column and an overestimation of the size property of the new root node: in Figure 11(c), root r is recorded with size 4 while the actual number of nodes below r is 3. Again, this does not affect correctness (see Section 2.1) and can be fully remedied if OLAP functionality is available.

5 Extensions and Optimizations

The compilation procedure could be extended to embrace a significantly larger subset of XQuery Core than presented here.

Consistent with our sequence encoding and with the XQuery semantics we can, for example, define the *effective boolean value* [2] of a sequence in different iterations via the absence or presence of *iter* values in its encoding (Figures 12(a) and 12(b)). This enables the compilation of XQuery's *conditional expression* if e_1 then e_2 else e_3 as shown in Figure 12(c).

With the conditional available, the language subset may be further extended by (1) *predicates* $e[e]$, (2) the existential and universal *quantifiers* (some, every), (3) the *general comparison operators* for sequences, and (4) the XQuery where e clause which is an optional part of the syntactical FLWOR construct.

5.1 Exploiting the Disjointness of Fragments During Element Construction

Recall that the evaluation of an element constructor places both, the newly created element node and the subtree copies in a new separate fragment in table doc. The new current table of live nodes, computed in Rule ELEM via SQL's UNION ALL operator, may thus be written as the *disjoint union*

$$\text{doc} \,\dot\cup\, \Delta$$

where doc is the table of persistent XML nodes and Δ denotes the transient nodes in the new fragment.

Now consider the evaluation of a second element constructor element t { e } with $e \subseteq \text{doc} \,\dot\cup\, \Delta$. Rule ELEM performs the XPath location step

$$e/\texttt{descendant-or-self::node()}$$

to extract the subtrees which need to be copied into the new fragment. Since the evaluation of an XPath location step never escapes the fragment of its context node, the following would be an equivalent way to compute the nodes in the subtrees:

$$(e \cap \text{doc})/\texttt{descendant-or-self::node()}$$
$$\dot\cup$$
$$(e \cap \Delta)/\texttt{descendant-or-self::node()}$$

Although more complex at first sight, this variant performs the bulk of the work[6] on the persistent doc table and thus can fully benefit from the presence of indexes (Section 6). The former variant, on the other hand, has to evaluate the descendant-or-self axis step on the derived table doc UNION ALL Δ which lacks index support.

After evaluation of the second element constructor, the new table of live nodes is

$$(\text{doc} \,\dot\cup\, \Delta) \,\dot\cup\, \Delta' = \text{doc} \,\dot\cup\, (\Delta \,\dot\cup\, \Delta')$$

such that this optimization remains applicable after an arbitrary number of element constructor evaluations. More importantly, note that XPath step evaluation in general can benefit from this disjointness of fragments.

---

[5]Here, for ease of presentation, we assume that e encodes a node sequence in a single iteration. The SQL code in Rule ELEM handles the general case.

[6]Typically, $|\Delta| \ll |\text{doc}|$.

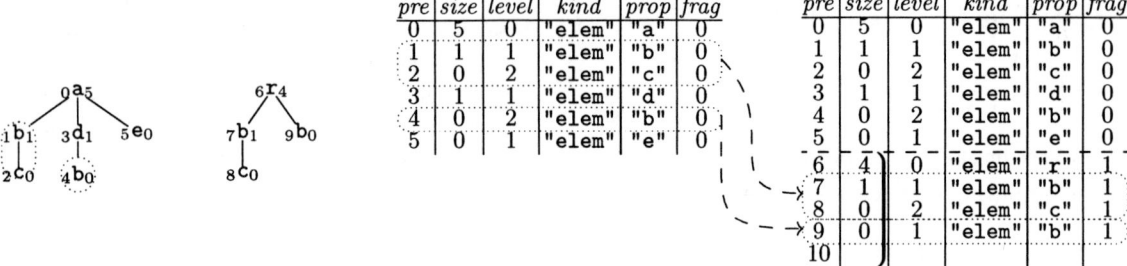

(a) Original tree. (b) New tree fragment. (c) Table doc before (left) and after element construction. The size of node r has been overestimated.

Figure 11: Element construction and the resulting extension of table doc.

(a) Current loop. (b) Encoded sequence. (c) Evaluation of a conditional expression (q_i encodes expression e_i).

Figure 12: The effective boolean value of the encoded sequence (b) in the current loop is *true* in iterations 0 and 2, and *false* (*i.e.*, the empty sequence) in iteration 1. SQL code generated for if e_1 then e_2 else e_3 in (c).

5.2 Bundling XPath Steps

Even if a query addresses nodes in only moderately complex XML documents, XPath path expressions are usually comprised of *multiple*, say $k > 1$, location steps (let e denote a sequence of context nodes):

$$e/\alpha_1::n_1/\alpha_2::n_2/\cdots/\alpha_k::n_k \ . \qquad (Q_3)$$

Operator / associates to the left such that the above is seen by the compiler as

$$(\cdots((e/\alpha_1::n_1)/\alpha_2::n_2)/\cdots)/\alpha_k::n_k$$

which also suggests the evaluation mode of such a multi-step path. Proceeding from left to right, the ith location step computes the context node sequence (in document order and with duplicates removed) for step $i+1$. For $k=2$, the normalized XQuery Core [5] equivalent reads (slightly simplified):

```
distinct-doc-order(
  for $v_1 in e return
    distinct-doc-order(
      for $v_2 in $v_1/α_1::n_1 return
        $v_2/α_2::n_2))
```

Note that Rule STEP already improves on this naive evaluation scheme: while the above iterates the step evaluation for each context node, the compiler emits SQL code that applies a location step to a *whole context node sequence*. In a sense, Rule STEP implements the above iteration implicitly via the self-join of table doc.

Nevertheless, the compilation of a k-step path, and thus the k-fold application of Rule STEP, leads to an SQL query that is nested to depth k. The nesting is not a problem *per se* for the RDBMS—in the terminology of Kim [13], Rule STEP generates uncorrelated *type N* nested queries. However, at each nesting level, *i.e.*, k times, the system

(1) joins the current context node sequence with doc to retrieve the necessary context node properties (only the preorder rank property *pre* is available in the sequence encoding),

(2) performs the doc self-join to evaluate the XPath axis and node test, and finally

(3) removes duplicate nodes generated in step (2).

Especially the latter proves to be quite expensive [12].

Since we target a relational database backend, we can do better: the tree encoding of Section 2.1 allows us to evaluate a multi-step path *as a whole* [9, 10]. In a modified compiler, Rule STEP is replaced by a new Rule STEPS which is applicable to queries of the general form Q_3. For a k-step path, the new rule emits a flat k-way self-join of table doc (plus a single join with the initial context node sequence e). This, in turn, enables the RDBMS to choose and optimize join order. In our experiments (Section 6) we observed that the system decided to evaluate certain paths in a "backward" fashion. Furthermore, duplicate removal is now required only once. If the RDBMS kernel includes a tree-aware join operator, *e.g.*, *staircase join* [10], duplicate removal may even become obsolete.

6 Experiments: DB2 Runs XQuery

An RDBMS can be an efficient host to XQuery. To support this claim and in order to assess the viability and performance of our approach, we ran a number of queries from the XMark benchmark series [18] on the IBM DB2 UDB V8.1 database system. The database was hosted on a dual 2.2 GHz Pentium 4 Xeon system with 2 GB RAM, running a version 2.4 Linux kernel. The experiment was the only client connected to the database. No other processes were active besides a small number of system daemons.

We used the XML generator XMLgen from the XMark project to create XML document instances with sizes ranging from 110 KB to 1.1 GB (5,000 to 50 million nodes). An instance of the doc table was created for each document size and then populated with the encoded XMark XML documents as described in Section 2. The database resided on a single SCSI disk, with the buffer pool size set to 200,000 pages.

To make the point that an RDBMS can indeed be an efficient host to XQuery, we presented the result of the compilation process to the system's workload analysis tools. The DB2 *index advisor* db2advis was used to recommend a set of indexes to optimally support our workload. The recommendations included indexes on the *pre* column of the doc table to support queries on the XML tree structure, and indexes on the *prop* column to support node tests.

We created the recommended indexes and issued DB2's reorg command to optimize the physical data placement on secondary storage. No other "wizardry" was applied. Experiments were run with a "warm" database buffer cache, each query was run multiple times with timings averaged.

6.1 Impact of OLAP Availability and XPath Step Bundling

Sections 4 and 5 described the use of SQL OLAP functions as well as the bundling of successive XPath steps as two promising optimization hooks. To verify the effectiveness of these techniques, we repeatedly executed query XMark 1 on a 110 KB XML document with and without these optimizations applied. The effects are substantial: execution times are reduced by orders of magnitude (Table 3).

It turns out, that our choice of sequence encoding and representation of iteration, *i.e.*, a *single* relation encodes the sequence value for *all* iterations of a for-loop, is a perfect match for the SQL/OLAP ranking and partitioning functionality. The compiler can repeatedly make use of the idiom

DENSE_RANK() (PARTITION BY *iter* ORDER BY *iter*, *pos*)

Optimization	exec. time [s]	# tbl. acc.
no optimization	5995	196
use of OLAP functions	0.14	43
bundled XPath steps	0.02	24
OLAP and bundled XPath	0.002	13

Table 3: Effectiveness of optimizations. Execution times and number of accesses to the doc relation for XMark 1 run on a 110 KB document with different optimizations applied.

to compute dense sequence positions (property *pos*) inside an iteration, *i.e.*, inside an *iter* partition. Likewise, the compiler may emit

DENSE_RANK() (ORDER BY *iter*, *pos*)

to densely populate *iter* columns, *e.g.*, during the computation of map (Section 3.2).

Furthermore, most XMark queries feature multi-step path expressions—typical path lengths are 3 or 4 steps—such that these queries are also subject to the XPath step bundling optimization (Section 5.2). Taken together, both optimizations reduced the number of accesses to the persistent doc relation by a factor of 15.

6.2 Disjointness of Fragments

Remember that the construction of new element nodes essentially leads to a UNION ALL operation that extends the persistent doc relation by a disjoint transient set of nodes.

XMark 13 features two successive element constructors[7] and thus is a typical candidate for the disjoint fragments optimization of Section 5.1:

```
for $i in fn:doc("auction.xml")/site
                /regions/australia/item
return
  element item { (element name { $i/name/text() },
        $i/description) }
```

Document "auction.xml" resided in the persistent doc table and thus received full index support.

To evaluate the query, the system eventually created the name element nodes and subtree copies and extended the doc table accordingly. Note that the situation in XMark 13 perfectly matches the scenario of Section 5.1: when the item element nodes are created, their child nodes are taken from both, the persistent document ($i/description) and the transient live nodes (the name element nodes).

With the optimization applied, access without index support was only required for the relatively few transient name nodes. Without this optimization, *all*

---

[7]In the original XMark 13 query, the inner constructor creates an attribute node. Our discussion is not affected by this adaptation.

Optimization	execution time [s] 1.1 MB	11 MB	55 MB
no optimization	1.1	48.7	1088
fragment disjointness	0.31	2.9	14.7

Table 4: XMark 13 on various XML document sizes with and without exploitation of fragment disjointness.

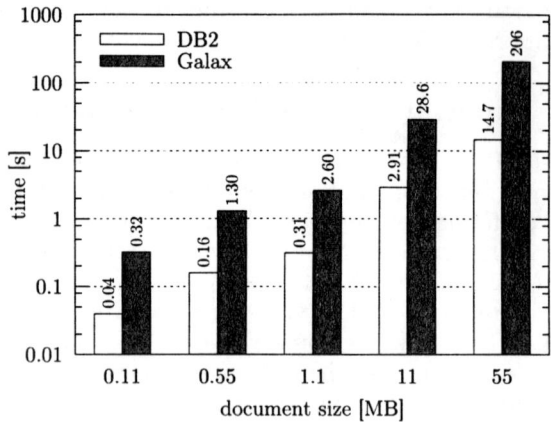

Figure 14: XMark 13: DB2 and Galax 0.3.5 compared.

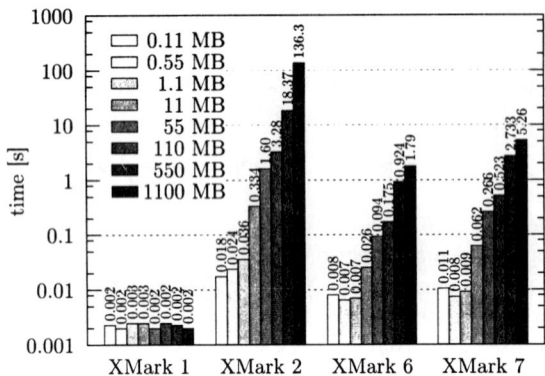

Figure 13: XMark queries run on documents of various sizes.

child nodes of the newly created `item` elements resided in a derived table with no persistent index support at all. We ran both variants on our test database and observed the execution times documented in Table 4. The experiment clearly indicates the potential of this optimization technique.

6.3 XMark on DB2

Finally, to evaluate our compilation procedure on a range of document sizes, we chose a set of queries from the XMark benchmark. The set comprises the XQuery constructs which have been discussed in the foregoing, namely `FLWOR` and XPath expressions (all queries), and element construction (XMark 2). XMark 6 and 7 further contain XQuery aggregate functions (`fn:count`) and can benefit from the efficient implementation of their SQL counterparts in the relational system.

All queries were compiled with optimizations applied. The results are depicted in Figure 13 and confirm the scalability of our approach with respect to the document size. Execution times are reasonable even for the 1 GB XMark document instance. The milli-second range timings for XMark 1 stem from the fact that this query essentially measures XPath performance. We have observed similar figures in earlier work [9, 10].

7 Related Research and Systems

As of today, we are not aware of any other published work which succeeded in hosting XQuery *efficiently* on an SQL-based RDBMS. A recent survey paper suggests the same [14]. The compilation procedure described here (1) is compositional, (2) does *not* depend on the presence of XML Schema or DTD knowledge (the compiler is *schema-oblivious* unlike [16, 19]), and, (3) is *purely relational* in the sense that the compiler translates XQuery into standard SQL:1999 plus OLAP extensions: there is no need to invade or extend the database kernel to make the approach perform well (although we may benefit from such extensions [10]).

Evidence for the latter is also provided by experiments in which we compared the relational XQuery host and the XQuery processor Galax [6]. Galax operates on an in-memory representation of XML documents and implements the XQuery Formal Semantics specification quite literally, *i.e.*, nested `for`-loops are evaluated in a nested-loops fashion, XPath path expressions are evaluated step-by-step, *etc.* We thus expected the strengths of relational technology to come in useful especially with increasing document sizes—this is exactly what the measured execution times for XMark 13 indicate (Figure 14).

The work described in [4] comes closest to what we have developed here. Based on a dynamic interval encoding for XML instances, the paper presents a compositional translation from a subset of XQuery Core into a set of SQL view definitions. The translation scheme falls short, however, of preserving fundamental semantic properties of XQuery: the omission of a backmapping step in the translation of `for`-expressions prevents arbitrary expression nesting and, lacking an explicit treatment of sequence positions, the encoding cannot distinguish between sequence and document order.

We feel that the most important drawback, however, is the complexity and execution cost of the SQL view definitions generated in [4]. The compilation of path expressions, for example, leads to nested *correlated* queries—the RDBMS falls back to nested-loops plans, which renders the relational backend a poor

XQuery runtime environment. To achieve acceptable performance, the authors indeed proposed modifications to the relational engine specifically geared to support the dynamic interval encoding (SQL-based timings were never published).

8 Conclusions and Work in Flux

The XQuery compiler described in this paper targets SQL-based relational database backends and thus extends the relational XML processing stack, which was already known to be capable of providing XML mass storage as well as efficient XPath support. The compilation procedure is largely based on a specific encoding of sequences (the principal data structure in the XQuery data model apart from trees) which allows for the set-oriented evaluation of nested `for`-loops (the principal query building block in XQuery). Operations on this encoding receive excellent support from widely available OLAP extensions to the SQL:1999 standard.

Our XQuery to SQL compiler offers a variety of interesting hooks for extension and optimization, many of which we were not able to present here. Current work in flux is related to a considerable generalization of the *disjoint fragments* observation of Section 5.1. Since the early days of the development of XQuery Core, it has been observed that certain language constructs, in particular `FLWOR` expressions, enjoy homomorphic properties—in [7] this was shown by reducing `FLWOR` expressions to list (or sequence) comprehensions. This may open the door for compiler optimizations [8] that minimize those parts of a query which need to operate on transient live nodes.

References

[1] P.V. Biron and A. Malhotra. XML Schema Part 2: Datatypes. World Wide Web Consortium, May 2001. http://www.w3.org/TR/xmlschema-2/.

[2] S. Boag, D. Chamberlin, M.F. Fernández, D. Florescu, J. Robie, and J. Simeon. XQuery 1.0: An XML Query Language. World Wide Web Consortium, November 2003. W3C Working Draft http://www.w3.org/TR/xquery/.

[3] S. Chien, Z. Vagena, D. Zhang, V.J. Tsotras, and C. Zaniolo. Efficient Structural Joins on Indexed XML Documents. In *Proc. of the 28th Int'l Conference on Very Large Databases (VLDB)*, pages 263–274, Hong Kong, China, August 2002.

[4] D. DeHaan, D. Toman, M.P. Consens, and M.T. Özsu. A Comprehensive XQuery to SQL Translation using Dynamic Interval Encoding. In *Proc. of the 22nd Int'l ACM SIGMOD Conference on Management of Data*, pages 623–634, San Diego, California, USA, June 2003.

[5] D. Draper, P. Fankhauser, M.F. Fernández, A. Malhotra, K. Rose, M. Rys, J. Simeon, and P. Wadler. XQuery 1.0 and XPath 2.0 Formal Semantics. World Wide Web Consortium, February 2004. W3C Working Draft http://www.w3.org/TR/xquery-semantics/.

[6] M.F. Fernández, J. Simeon, B. Choi, A. Marian, and G. Sur. Implementing XQuery 1.0: The Galax Experience. In *Proc. of the 29th Int'l Conference on Very Large Data Bases (VLDB)*, pages 1077–1080, Berlin, Germany, September 2003.

[7] M.F. Fernández, J. Simeon, and P. Wadler. A Semimonad for Semi-structured Data. In *Proc. of the 8th Int'l Conference on Database Theory (ICDT)*, pages 263–300, London, UK, January 2001.

[8] D. Gluche, T. Grust, C. Mainberger, and M.H. Scholl. Incremental Updates for Materialized OQL Views. In *Proc. of the 5th Int'l Conference on Deductive and Object-Oriented Databases (DOOD)*, pages 52–66, Montreux, Switzerland, December 1997.

[9] T. Grust. Accelerating XPath Location Steps. In *Proc. of the 21st Int'l ACM SIGMOD Conference on Management of Data*, pages 109–120, Madison, Wisconsin, USA, June 2002.

[10] T. Grust, M. van Keulen, and J. Teubner. Staircase Join: Teach a Relational DBMS to Watch its Axis Steps. In *Proc. of the 29th Int'l Conference on Very Large Databases (VLDB)*, Berlin, Germany, September 2003.

[11] T. Grust, M. van Keulen, and J. Teubner. Accelerating XPath Evaluation in Any RDBMS. *ACM Transactions on Database Systems*, 29(1):91–131, March 2004.

[12] J. Hidders and P. Michiels. Avoiding Unnecessary Ordering Operations in XPath. In *Proc. of the 9th Int'l Workshop on Database Programming Languages (DBPL)*, Potsdam, Germany, September 2003.

[13] W. Kim. On Optimizing an SQL-like Nested Query. *ACM Transactions on Database Systems*, 7(3):443–469, September 1982.

[14] R. Krishnamurthy, R. Kaushik, and J. Naughton. XML-to-SQL Query Translation Literature: The State of the Art and Open Problems. In *Proc. of the 1st Int'l XML Database Symposium (XSym)*, pages 1–18, Berlin, Germany, September 2003.

[15] Q. Li and B. Moon. Indexing and Querying XML Data for Regular Path Expressions. In *Proc. of the 27th Int'l Conference on Very Large Databases (VLDB)*, pages 361–370, Rome, Italy, September 2001.

[16] I. Manolescu, D. Florescu, and D. Kossmann. Answering XML Queries over Heterogeneous Data Sources. In *Proc. of the 27th Int'l Conference on Very Large Databases (VLDB)*, Rome, Italy, September 2001.

[17] J. Melton. *Advanced SQL:1999: Understanding Object-Relational and Other Advanced Features*. Morgan Kaufmann Publishers, Amsterdam, 2003.

[18] A. Schmidt, F. Waas, M. Kersten, M.J. Carey, I. Manolescu, and R. Busse. XMark: A Benchmark for XML Data Management. In *Proc. of the 28th Int'l Conference on Very Large Databases (VLDB)*, pages 974–985, Hong Kong, China, August 2002.

[19] J. Shanmugasundaram, J. Kiernan, E.J. Shekita, C. Fan, and J. Funderburk. Querying XML Views of Relational Data. In *Proc. of the 27th Int'l Conference on Very Large Databases (VLDB)*, pages 261–270, Rome, Italy, September 2001.

ROX: Relational Over XML

Alan Halverson[†], Vanja Josifovski[*], Guy Lohman[*], Hamid Pirahesh[*], Mathias Mörschel[+]

alanh@cs.wisc.edu, vanja@us.ibm.com, lohman@almaden.ibm.com, pirahesh@almaden.ibm.com,
M.Moerschel@web.de

[†]University of Wisconsin-Madison, 1210 W. Dayton St., Madison, WI 53706
[*]IBM Almaden Research Center, 650 Harry Road, San Jose, CA 95120
[+]Am Rederwald 9, D-66954 Pirmasens, Germany

Abstract

An increasing percentage of the data needed by business applications is being generated in XML format. Storing the XML in its native format will facilitate new applications that exchange business objects in XML format and query portions of XML documents using XQuery. This paper explores the feasibility of accessing natively-stored XML data through traditional SQL interfaces, called Relational Over XML (ROX), in order to avoid the costly conversion of legacy applications to XQuery. It describes the forces that are driving the industry to evolve toward the ROX scenario as well as some of the issues raised by ROX. The impact of denormalization of data in XML documents is discussed both from a semantic and performance perspective. We also weigh the implications of ROX for manageability and query optimization. We experimentally compared the performance of a prototype of the ROX scenario to today's SQL engines, and found that good performance can be achieved through a combination of utilizing XML's hierarchical storage to store relations "pre-joined" as well as creating indices over the remaining join columns. We have developed an experimental framework using DB2 8.1 for Linux, Unix and Windows, and have gathered initial performance results that validate this approach.

Permission to copy without fee all or part of this material is granted provided that the copies are not made or distributed for direct commercial advantage, the VLDB copyright notice and the title of the publication and its date appear, and notice is given that copying is by permission of the Very Large Data Base Endowment. To copy otherwise, or to republish, requires a fee and/or special permission from the Endowment

**Proceedings of the 30th VLDB Conference,
Toronto, Canada, 2004**

1. Introduction

After two decades of commercially-available products, relational database systems (RDBMSs) supporting the SQL query language standard are an unqualified commercial success, with a huge industry-wide investment in applications such as Enterprise Resource Planning (ERP) [SAP04, PSW04, ORC04] and Customer Relationship Management [SIB04, ORC04] that query an RDBMS with SQL. As the acceptance and sources of XML documents have proliferated, many commercial relational database systems have adapted by developing techniques for storing XML documents in relational systems by shredding documents into relations [EDO01, SB00, SQX04] and/or by storing each document as an unstructured, large object (LOB) [EDO01]. However, shredding and recomposing all documents, many of which will never be retrieved, is unduly expensive. Alternatively, searching XML documents stored as LOBs is prohibitively slow. As more enterprises exchange business objects, such as purchase orders, in XML format, applications will increasingly need to efficiently query portions of XML documents via the emerging XQuery standard [BCF03]. This will lead to storing the data in some native XML format that efficiently supports XQuery.

Legacy relational interfaces and native XML storage appear to be on a collision course that raises many interesting questions. Can the relational and XML data be treated separately, storing each in the appropriate type of repository? In other words, will data from relational sources be queried exclusively by SQL, and XML data exclusively by XQuery? Or will databases of the future have to be hybrids, storing both relational and XML? Or will we just convert relations into XML objects and store everything in XML format? Regardless, what is to become of the "legacy" applications written in "good old" SQL that need access to data that increasingly originates as XML data? Do they need to be re-written, or can XML repositories support both XQuery and SQL? Will there be evolution, or a revolution?

We are convinced that XML adoption must necessarily be an evolution – that existing relational applications are too big and complicated to convert them all rapidly or inexpensively from SQL to XQuery. We also project that the data accessed by these SQL applications will increasingly come from XML sources and need to also be accessible via XQuery, and hence will be stored in native XML format.

This paper therefore explores how to efficiently support Relational Over XML (ROX), i.e. the existing SQL interface to a native XML store. We postulate a database containing a blend of both tables and XML documents, with an increasing percentage of XML documents over time. The ROX scenario limits our consideration to SQL queries as input that return rows as output, in order to support legacy applications, even though the system is very likely to also support XQuery interfaces to the same database.

The ROX scenario alone raises many important issues. Perhaps the most important is whether ROX can perform as well as today's SQL engines. What is the impact of the obvious expansion of data caused by tags and other structuring information? How much should XML documents be normalized, and does the denormalization supported by XML help or hinder performance? Or is normalization of data obsolete with the advent of XML?

The remainder of this paper is organized as follows. The next section summarizes the evolution of XML data management. Section 3 discusses issues involving query semantics of SQL and XQuery, tradeoffs for selecting an

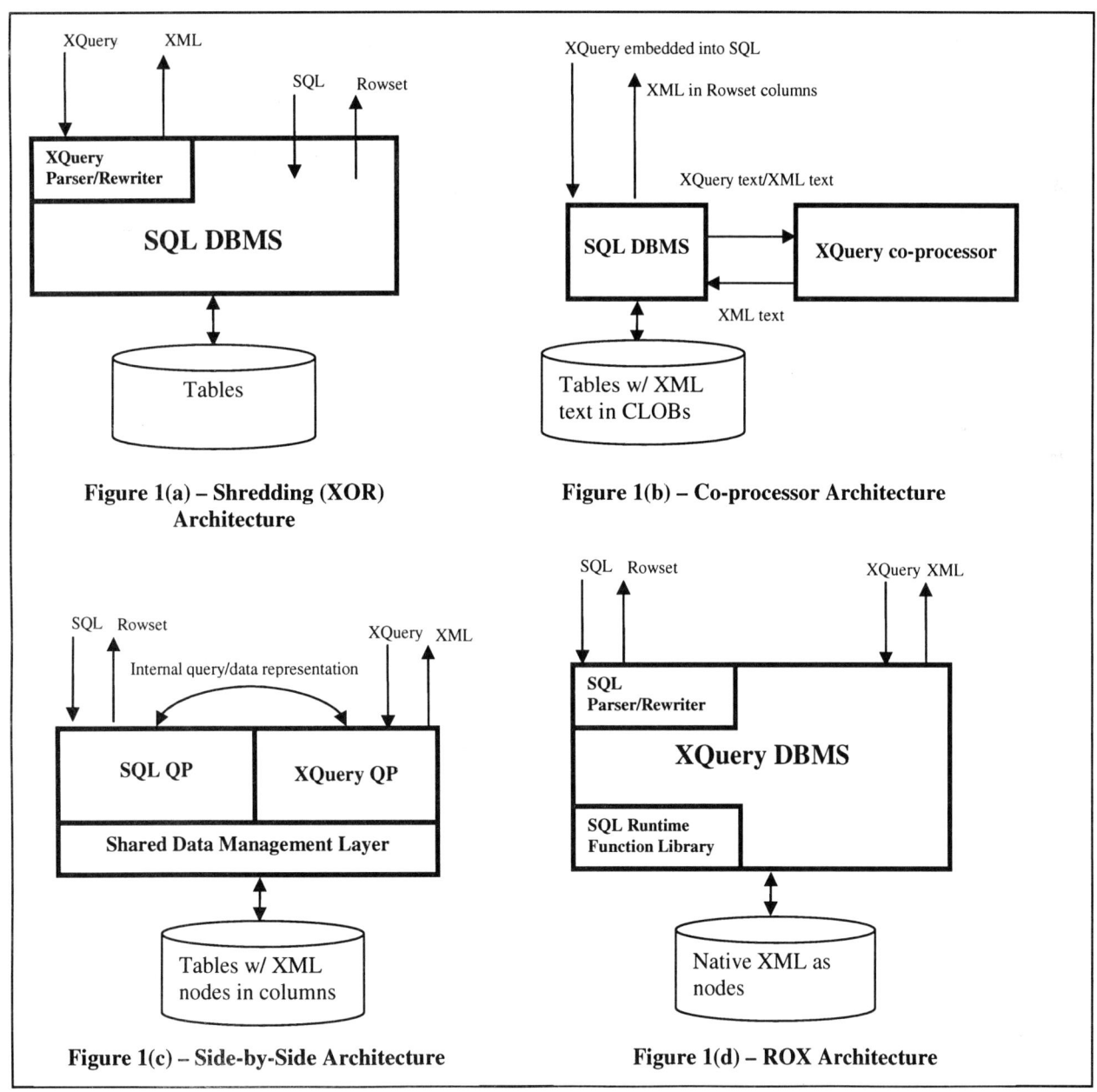

Figure 1 - Architecture choices for mixed SQL and XQuery systems

appropriate XML schema, and performance concerns. We present our ROX experimental design in Section 4, and the results of those experiments in Section 5. Our conclusions and directions for future research comprise the last section.

2. The Evolution of XML Data Management Systems

Storing and processing XML data have been a focus of the database research community for much of the last decade. Several XML data management systems have been proposed, most based on various degrees of adaptation and reuse of relational technology. There are two main reasons for reuse of relational technology. First, adaptation is presumably less expensive and allows faster time to market than development from scratch. The other reason is that such hybrid systems are capable of storing both relational (structured) and XML (semi-structured) data. As most applications are likely to operate over both types of data, the new generation of databases will need to support both allowing the application to access a single data repository.

Several different architectures have been proposed for building a hybrid XML-relational database, as illustrated in Figure 1. Chronologically, the first attempts were based on reusing the whole RDBMS stack when processing XQuery queries: from the SQL query language to the relational data storage. In this XML-Over-Relational (XOR) approach, the XML documents are shredded into atomic values that are then stored in relational tables. XQuery queries are translated into SQL queries to be evaluated by the existing query processor. Several research prototypes have explored this scheme, such as LegoDB [BFH00], and XPeranto [SKS01], and several products offer different shredding and XPath querying capabilities based on this approach [EDO01, MSF00]. The advantage of this architecture is that it requires almost no modification of existing database engines. As such, an XQuery implementation can easily be adapted to several different DBMS systems. However, as the XQuery language has evolved into an elaborate and complex standard, it has become clear that translating XQuery queries into SQL queries is a daunting task. While shred-and-query systems claim compatibility with a subset of the language, none has managed to produce a fully compliant XQuery implementation.

Next in the timeline were systems that are on the other side of the architectural spectrum, named Co-processor Architecture in Figure 1(b). Here, XML is stored as unparsed text in VARCHAR or LOB columns of relational tables. The XML data is opaque to the RDBMS and only the storage layer is re-used. The XML data is queried using an XQuery processor that is external to the database and invoked much like a user-defined function. The communication between the two processors is using textual or equivalent format. The SQL and the XQuery processors can be developed separately and interchanged. This solution is attractive for its relative simplicity and modularity.

Most of today's commercial systems support this type of XML manipulation using stored procedures to invoke an external XQuery processor [EDO01, MSF00], in conjunction with XOR support. However, due to the loose coupling of the query processors, usually the entire XML document is brought into memory before processing, severely limiting the size of the data and optimization possibilities

Several systems have been reported that support only XQuery. Systems such as Niagara [NDM01] and Timber [JAK02] break the XML document into nodes and store the node information in a B+-tree, with all document nodes stored in order at the leaf level. This allows for efficient document or sub-tree reconstruction by a simple scan of the leaf pages of the tree. In Niagara, additional inverted list indexes are created to enable efficient structural join algorithms for ancestor/descendant paths. However, these systems do not support SQL or relational storage.

More recently more native storage of XML documents has been proposed in [KM99] and [ZKO04]. In our work we take a similar approach where the XML data is stored as in a native tree format in which document nodes are in most cases clustered together on a page. Bulk processing is performed using indexes, while the storage is optimized for fast navigation to evaluate the non-index portions of the query. Parent-child traversal does not require a join between different tables. Since most XPath expressions require parent-child traversal, this scheme allows for efficient access to the data. The details of the storage are beyond the scope of this paper. We use this model as an example to explore the consequences of representing relational data with hierarchical trees.

At this point we consider where will the system architecture move beyond today's state of the art? Can we project the direction of the path based on the evolution so far? Is the current situation similar to the introduction of the relational database systems compared to IMS? We try to analyze the issues from several angles and answer to these questions.

One probable direction in the short term is the side-by-side architecture, as shown in Figure 1(c). In this architecture there is a tighter coupling between the query processors than in the architecture based on shredding. Query fragments can be translated from one language to the other and exchanged using internal data structures that may not adhere to the language semantics. Such a mechanism improves the efficiency of the translation and allows more degrees of freedom in the evaluation. For example, when returning values from XQuery to SQL, as required when evaluating SQL/XML, queries might require that an element is constructed by an embedded XQuery query and then shredded by an SQL table function. Instead, the optimizer can re-write such queries so that rows of values are returned from the XQuery processor directly into the SQL processor, although rows are not part of the Query Data Model.

While more efficient than the first two architectures, the side-by-side architecture introduces many complexities. It requires that various system components have compatible definitions on both sides of the system. For example, the catalogue description of internal objects such as indexes and materialized view definitions need to be matched to both the SQL and XQuery queries. While these issues pose interesting research challenges, we view this architecture only as a partial solution that will be simplified and eventually morph into the Relational over XML architecture shown in Figure 1(d) where the primary processing is performed by an XQuery engine with native XML storage model. In its engine all transformations are governed by the XQuery language specification and the Query Data Model. The SQL support is divided between a thin parse-and-rewrite layer and a library for support of the SQL functions and operators that cannot be mapped to the XQuery functions and operators.

The ROX architecture is at the opposite extreme of the solution space when compared to the first XQuery query processor designs, in which the XQuery processor was a thin layer over SQL database systems. The obvious question is what makes this architecture viable if the opposite solution has not been implemented in any of the major database products? Furthermore, in terms of development cost, this architecture requires a complete XQuery engine that is adapted to run SQL queries, seemingly a much more demanding path than the opposite route.

As XQuery and the QDM data model conceptually subsume the SQL language and the relational model, implementing SQL on top of an XQuery engine poses significantly lesser challenge than the opposite. We also believe that this architecture will not be achieved by developing an XQuery engine from scratch. Existing relational engines will be morphed into this architecture possibly through the intermediate stages represented by the other architectures depicted in Figure 1. It seems to us that, beyond the initial releases of the commercial database products for XML data management, the main forces in the database engine evolution will be to increase the performance and reduce the complexity of the relational-XML engines. These two forces will be the major factors in the appearance of the ROX architecture, shown in Figure 1(d).

3. ROX Model Issues

While unable to implement a complete ROX architecture, we single out three issues that are crucial to demonstrate the viability of the infrastructure and explore in more details each. We first overview the language semantics issues and how the semantics differences between SQL and XQuery impact the ROX architecture. Then we turn our attention to the data layout and normalization related issues as posed by the nested XML data model. Finally we consider the performance impact of an XML native format, query optimization issues, and XML data manageability.

3.1. Language Semantics

The main difficulty in running SQL queries over an XQuery implementation is providing semantically correct answers to the queries. Although SQL and XQuery have similarities, there is an abundance of differences. First of all, the languages are defined over different data models. The SQL language is defined over the relational model [SQL98], while the XQuery language is based on the Query Data Model [FMM03] that represents XML data as typed trees. SQL queries operate over column values, while XQuery manipulates ordered, heterogeneous sequences of values and node references. While a detailed description of the differences is beyond the scope of this discussion, in general, QDM is much more elaborate than the relational data model. This is the core reason why XQuery-to-SQL translation is unsuitable as a basis for a fully functional XQuery system.

The languages also differ in their operational semantics. The most quoted difference is the document order preservation of XQuery vs. unordered semantics of SQL. Furthermore, each language standard contains precise descriptions of the language operators. These specifications seldom match. For example, the comparison operators in SQL use 3-value logic, operating over Boolean operands and returning true, false or NULL. The same XQuery operators (general comparison) operate over sequences of nodes or values and return true and false. There is no NULL value defined in the XQuery data model. Another discrepancy stems from the different definitions of the basic data types as decimals and date-time. As many of the built-in functions operate over such values, they might potentially return different results.

Despite these differences, XQuery is designed to be able to manipulate structured data along with unstructured [CFF03]. Therefore, there is an overlap in the functionality of SQL and XQuery. While different in data model and semantics, when constrained over structured data, many XQuery operations have semantics close to that of SQL, and under certain cardinality constraints match the SQL semantics. For example both XQuery and SQL numeric operations are based on the IEEE standard and seem to be reconcilable. Furthermore the XQuery arithmetic operators treat empty sequences in the same manner as SQL operators treat the NULL values. This is also true for the XQuery value comparison operators (eq, gt, neq, etc.) which have 3-value logic (returning empty sequence if any of the operators is an empty sequence) as the comparison operators of SQL. Translating the SQL comparison operators into XQuery value comparison operators, we can achieve the same semantics as in SQL. This allows pushdown of simple arithmetic and comparison predicates from SQL to XQuery. While the XQuery Boolean operators operate using 2-value logic, it is simple to implement 3-valued Boolean operators in XQuery that have same semantics as the SQL operators. With such a small implementation effort, a large class of SQL predicates over numeric types and strings can be translated into equivalent XQuery predicates. However, based on the current standards proposal for XQuery, it seems that it will not be possible to translate all SQL functions to existing XQuery functions. We envision this necessary for SQL datatypes that are not subsumed into XQuery datatypes, such as types representing date-time and timestamps [SQX04].

3.2. Normalization

One of the key benefits of a native XML store is not having to normalize the elements that make up a business object by shredding them into tables. For example, consider a common business object -- a purchase order, which might contain some customer elements and one or more line items describing each object being purchased:

```
<order>
  <date>12 July 2003</date>
  <customer>
   <ID>43839</ID>
   <name>Slaghorn Bolts</name>
   <contact>Joyce Smith</contact>
   <address>
    53495 N. First St.
    Cleveland, OH 45678
   </address>
   <order_discount>
    0.10
   </order_discount>
  </customer>
  <line_item>
   <part_ID>RYZ04856-8945</part_ID>
   <quantity>33</quantity>
   <discount>0.12</discount>
  </line_item>
  <line_item>
   <part_ID>KFE389745-2248</part_ID>
   <quantity>15</quantity>
   <discount>0.05</discount>
  </line_item>
  <line_item>
   <part_ID>OI230988-2833</part_ID>
   <quantity>100</quantity>
   <discount>0.21</discount>
  </line_item>
</order>
```

Figure 2 – Purchase order in XML format

Since the purchase order arrives in XML format, it is tempting to store the entire document as it comes into the system, to minimize any processing. But is that the right thing to do? Does the nesting of XML documents make normalization of objects in databases obsolete? And if not, what elements should be normalized and which should not?

The answer is that normalization is still needed in XML databases, for the same reason it was needed in relational databases: redundancy of data and update anomalies [DAT03]. In the above example, the line items nested within an order are wholly owned by that order, so they cannot suffer the update anomalies of shared sub-objects. However, the customer information is a bit more subtle. It is likely to be shared by many other orders, so keeping it with each purchase order would both be unnecessarily redundant and risk update anomalies. For example, the customer address is on the purchase order, but it's probably the same address as on hundreds of other orders from the same customer. But if it suddenly changed, this order might be sent to the address that was in effect at the time the order was made, rather than the address in effect when the order is shipped. Similarly for other attributes of the customer. So pretty clearly the customer information should be normalized. However, some elements of the customer are really elements of the interaction of the customer and this order. For example, the order_discount element might depend upon the size of the overall order and how valued this customer is. Hence it cannot be normalized out of the purchase order.

The good news is that native storage of XML documents permits denormalization when it makes sense semantically (sub-objects are not shared), while still retaining the option to normalize data, i.e. when sub-objects may be shared and hence risk update anomalies. The database designer is thus free to do what best models the data, rather than forcing the design into a large number of overly-normalized, homogeneous tables. And, as we shall see later, denormalization can also have performance benefits by obviating the need for some joins when the data is queried.

Today's relational engines use data redundancy in form of pre-joined relations to speed up evaluation of queries [HAL01]. Materialized view techniques will also be important in XML databases in general and with the ROX model in particular. In section 5.3, we show that data nesting that matches the query structure allow for much better evaluation times. As opposed to relational systems in which the materialized, pre-joined views are flat tables, an XML engine allows these to be in non-first normal form, similar to the proposal of [SPS87].

3.3. Performance

To achieve good query performance for the ROX model, we must consider several issues. The storage of the XML tree could be sorted in either depth-first (document) or breadth-first order. The depth-first order is advantageous when the goal is efficient reconstruction of the XML. However, if our XML documents have several levels of hierarchy, queries referencing only data at the top levels of the document will suffer.

Another concern is the overhead of storing the structure of the document inline with the data being represented. Although it is possible that the stored XML document conformed to a stated XML schema, in general our storage format must allow for XML documents which lack a predefined schema. This storage overhead forces a native XML store to consume more space for representing a certain dataset than the relational storage. The absence of an XML schema also forces data in the document to be stored as text, which also adds storage overhead.

To facilitate efficient selection and value-based joins between XML documents, an XML index is required. As with relational systems, such an index will allow us to find documents which contain a certain value in a certain location. Many indexing strategies for XML have been proposed, such as inverted lists of elements for structural joins and path indexes.

3.4 Optimization

Compiling SQL queries on XML documents presents new challenges for query optimization. Although denormalized data in the form of materialized views and join indexes is already widely exploited by relational query optimizers, both the query and the denormalized data are defined in relational terms, usually SQL. In ROX, the optimizer must now match joins and predicates in the SQL query to XPath expressions that define the schema of XML documents (presumably the XML documents manipulated by ROX will have a schema with sufficient homogeneity to permit a tabular view of them). Join predicates between documents must also be folded into predicates at various points of an XPath expression, depending upon the join order. In our experiments, discussed below, we performed this mapping manually to avoid the challenge of automating it. Having documents with various schemas – or even no schema at all! – mixed together in the same repository, called "schema chaos", negates the homogeneity that simplified the cost model and the database statistics on which relational optimization depended. And though the denormalization of XML documents reveals correlations among objects, it is not at all clear what database statistics are needed to summarize those correlations and how those statistics can be exploited to accurately estimate the number of documents satisfying a particular SQL query. And this doesn't even consider the considerable challenges of optimizing XQuery queries!

3.5 Manageability

Will a database of XML documents be easier or more difficult to manage than relational tables?

Some would argue that management of XML repositories should be child's play. Since real-world objects no longer need to be normalized into homogeneous collections of rows (tables), the XML repository can be reduced to a single, virtualized heap of heterogeneous objects (documents), creating the relational equivalent of the Universal Relation [MUV84]. In lieu of perhaps tens of thousands of normalized tables, there would be only one collection of documents to configure, backup, recover, reorganize, collect statistics on, etc. Database design would be trivial, normalization would be unnecessary, and one index over this entire collection would suffice to find any object in the database -- the "Google model" applied to databases!

On the other hand, management of modern databases entails far more than just deciding what tables and indexes to create. As argued in Section 3.2 above, some normalization will still be required to avoid update anomalies, so logical database design may be less constrained but certainly not obviated. Eventually, XML systems will permit the definition of the XML equivalent of materialized views, and deciding which to create will surely be no easier than it is now for relational systems. Even if all documents are in one monolithic collection, administrators will probably have to define arbitrary boundaries within that collection for administration purposes, so that pieces can be maintained while the rest of the database is available for querying and updating, much as the rows of large tables are usually divided into ranges for administrative purposes [IBM01]. And given the increased challenges posed by optimizing queries against these heterogeneous collections (see previous section), it is likely that the database statistics required for optimization will be far more extensive than for relational systems. For performance reasons, we might still want to cluster related documents together to exploit the larger pre-fetching chunks that relatively slower disk arms necessitate, or possibly de-cluster them to spread access among multiple arms for greater I/O parallelism, rather than simply append each new document to the end of the heap.

4. Design for Experimentation

In Section 2, we described a number of architectural alternatives for a mixed SQL and XQuery system, including the ROX model. We now provide a description of the implementation we chose for our experimental framework.

A full implementation of the ROX architecture would require a fully-functional XQuery DBMS, upon which a thin SQL-to-XQuery translation layer would sit. However, building a system like this would take a significant number of person-years to implement. Instead, we took advantage of a prototype XML store available to us and implemented a much simpler mapping layer. This experimental architecture is described in detail in the following sections.

4.1 SQL to XQuery translation using the XML Wrapper

For our experiments, we modified an existing product called the XML Wrapper, which is part of the IBM DB2 Information Integrator, version 8.1. The unmodified XML Wrapper provides a mechanism for presenting relational views of XML data stored as text files on disk. Each relational view defined over an XML document is called a nickname, and utilizes syntax similar to the CREATE TABLE statement.

```
CREATE NICKNAME REGION(
  R_REGIONKEY int
    OPTIONS(XPATH 'R_REGIONKEY/text()'),
  R_NAME char(25)
    OPTIONS(XPATH 'R_NAME/text()'),
  R_COMMENT varchar(152)
    OPTIONS(XPATH 'R_COMMENT/text()'))
FOR SERVER xml_server
OPTIONS(XPATH '/REGION');
```

Figure 3 - Nickname definition

```
<REGION>
  <R_REGIONKEY>2</R_REGIONKEY>
  <R_NAME>ASIA</R_NAME>
  <R_COMMENT>sladfkj weoiu sdflkj
  </R_COMMENT>
</REGION>
```

Figure 4 - Sample XML document

In Figure 3 we show a possible CREATE NICKNAME statement that DB2 would use in conjunction with the XML Wrapper to query the XML document shown in Figure 4. The product version of the XML Wrapper uses the Xerces [XER03] XML parser and the Xalan [XAL03] XPath evaluator to find data in the XML document(s). Both Xerces and Xalan are subprojects of the Apache XML project [APX04]. The wrapper queries the XML and creates relational rows conforming to the CREATE NICKNAME statement to hand back to the database engine.

Because XML allows hierarchical nesting of elements, entities may be stored physically together in the same document. For example, you might store a Customer with all of the Orders he has placed as child elements of the Customer. To exploit this, the XML wrapper allows special columns to be specified as the PRIMARY_KEY or FOREIGN_KEY for a nickname. For example, a column 'fk' in a nickname for ORDERS may be defined as the FOREIGN_KEY of the PRIMARY_KEY column 'pk' in a nickname for CUSTOMER. When a SQL query references these two nicknames with an equality join predicate between fk and pk, the wrapper knows that any Order information returned will be found as sub-elements of the Customer in the XML document. Any paths specified by the ORDERS nickname must be relative to the XPATH specified for the CUSTOMER nickname. The value for the pk column is simply a serialization of a Xerces element reference.

For our experiments, we modified the existing XML Wrapper to be an interface to a prototype XML store. Since our data had been previously parsed and stored in this native XML store, we removed the Xerces code. Also, the Xalan XPath evaluator could not be used, since it operates over in-memory DOM trees only. In its place, we used a custom XPath evaluation engine that evaluates paths over the prototype XML store. To implement the PRIMARY_KEY column option, we used an internally generated XML node identifier. We present an overview of our experimental architecture in Figure 5.

One of the primary advantages of a native XML store is that we have an opportunity to create one or more indices over the loaded data. The prototype XML store contains a path-based XML indexing module, but lacks automatic XML index selection in the query optimizer. To enable using each XML index created, we wrote custom parameterized table functions that take a key value as input and return relational rows that are the inner join result for that key value. This works because the XML index stores the same XML node reference value that the XPath evaluator uses. This idea also allows us to hand-optimize the join order for queries that refer to more than two nicknames by using a column from the result of one table function call as the input for another. For example, if we want to force a scan of the CUSTOMER nickname to be the outer entity in an index nested-loops join with ORDERS, we would write the following SQL query:

```
SELECT O.O_ORDERDATE
FROM CUSTOMER C, tfORDERS(C.C_CUSTKEY) O;
```

In this example, tfORDERS() is a user-defined table function that takes as input a customer key and returns columns from the ORDERS nickname from rows that contain a matching O_CUSTKEY value. The XML documents that match are found by performing a lookup in the XML index to find all documents which contain the path /ORDERS/O_CUSTKEY/text() = [C_CUSTKEY], where C_CUSTKEY is the value passed to the table function.

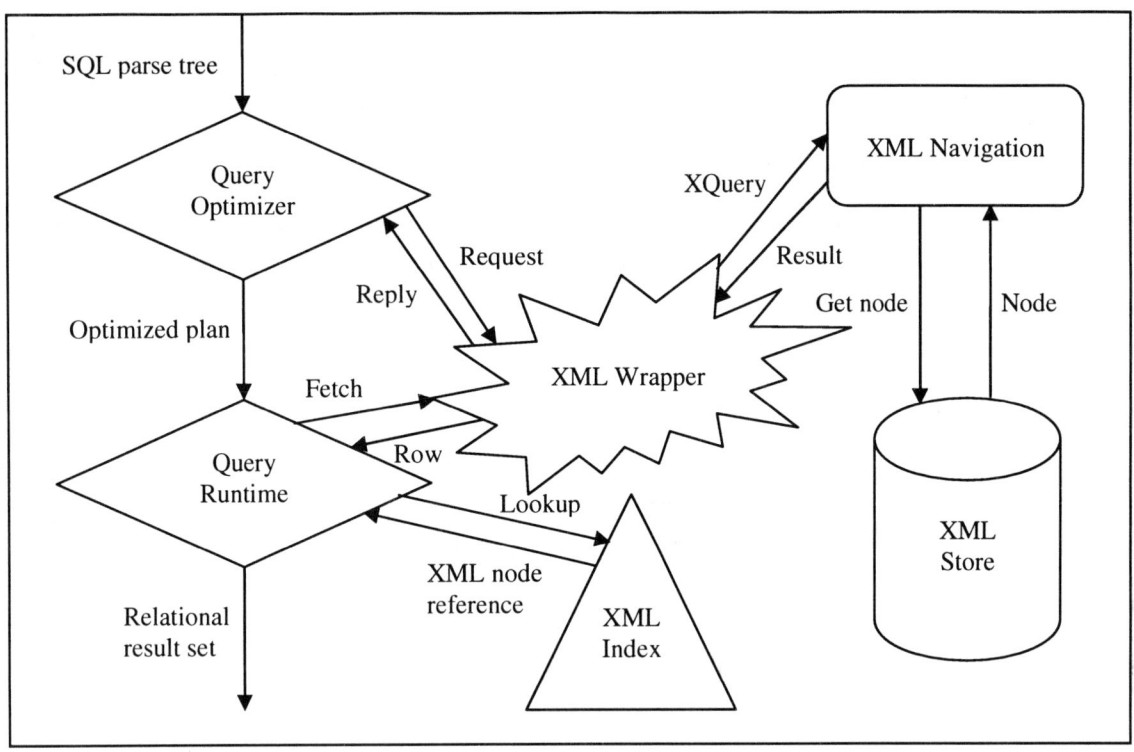

Figure 5 - Experimental Architecture

4.2. Prototype Walkthrough

To illustrate the prototype ROX architecture, we will describe how the following SQL query is executed:

```
SELECT r_name,
   COUNT(n_nationkey) AS n_count
FROM region, nation
WHERE r_regionkey = n_regionkey
GROUP BY r_name;
```

Logically, the input to the query optimizer is a SQL parse tree. For our example query, it will contain references to our nickname definitions for REGION and NATION, as well as the R_REGIONKEY = N_REGIONKEY predicate. Since DB2 only knows about the definition, it must consult the server specified by the CREATE NICKNAME statement, and therefore our modified XML wrapper, to create alternate execution plans and cost estimates. Plans enumerated include plans for: REGION only, NATION only, a plan that pushes the equality predicate into the wrapper and returns rows containing both REGION and NATION columns, and a plan for NATION which takes as input a context R_REGIONKEY and returns rows with an equal N_REGIONKEY column. We would accept this last plan only if R_REGIONKEY was defined with the PRIMARY_KEY option in the REGION nickname, and N_REGIONKEY defined with the FOREIGN_KEY option and referencing the REGION nickname. With a full cost model in the wrapper, we could tell the optimizer that one or more of these plans would provide the best performance. For each plan the wrapper can accept, we create a structure containing everything necessary to execute the plan later at runtime, and return control back to the optimizer. In the prototype, the structure would contain an XQuery to be executed at runtime. For example, we would create the following XQuery when asked to scan the REGION nickname:

```
for $a in /REGION, $b in $a/R_NAME
return $a, $b;
```

Once the optimizer chooses a final query plan, the query runtime takes control and begins to execute the plan. Any operator in the plan containing a packed structure created by the wrapper during optimization now calls back into the wrapper requesting to open a cursor based on the information contained in that structure. For our example query, the first request might be to do a table scan on the REGION nickname.

For each row returned from the wrapper for that scan, a second cursor would be opened over the NATION nickname, with an additional parameter containing the value of the R_REGIONKEY column for the current REGION row. Recall that the value of the R_REGIONKEY column would be the internal XML node identifier for the REGION element parenting the NATION information to return. The XML navigation would begin with the node identifier passed in, rather than from the document root. If the XML nodes are stored on disk in document order, we likely have the relevant NATION elements already in memory.

The prototype expects DB2 to perform the calculation of the N_COUNT output column and to handle the GROUP BY R_NAME clause. Note that better performance could be achieved for this query by pushing the aggregate down into the XML Wrapper, but the prototype did not do so.

4.3. Experimental Dataset

We chose the TPC-H [TPC02] dataset for our experiments. This dataset is well known throughout both the industrial and academic research communities, and is representative of a normalized relational schema that can be adapted to the ROX model. The schema consists of eight entities, namely REGION, NATION, SUPPLIER, PART, PARTSUPP, CUSTOMER, ORDERS, and LINEITEM. The PARTSUPP entity exists to allow a many-to-many relationship between PART and SUPPLIER.

For the corresponding XML schema of this dataset, we have quite a few choices. As with the relational schema, we discard any choice which results in data duplication. Please refer to section 3.2 for our discussion of data normalization. We compare three XML schemas for our experiments, named Unnest, Nest2, and Nest3.

Our Unnest schema consists of one XML document per relational row per relational table. The root element of each document is the name of the relation from which it came, each sub-element the name of a column from that relation, and the text contained in each sub-element is a value from the row that we used to generate the document. Figure 4 shows an example XML document created from one row of the REGION table. Our Nest2 schema stores LINEITEM elements nested within the correct ORDERS element, and PARTSUPP within PART, but leaves the remaining data as in the Unnest schema. Finally, the Nest3 schema stores LINEITEM elements within ORDERS elements, which in turn are nested within the correct CUSTOMER element, with all other data as in the Unnest schema. With the TPC-H schema, it is not possible to create a semantically meaningful, properly normalized document with four levels of nesting.

5. Experiments and Results

This section presents the experimental results we gathered to validate the feasibility and performance of the ROX model.

All experiments were executed on a quad processor PowerPC-based machine running AIX 5.1, equipped with 16GB of main memory and SCSI disks. Data and indices were loaded into separate DB2-managed tablespaces striped across 22 5GB SCSI disks. All timings reported in this section are an average of 5 runs. We calculated that all timings for each average are within 1% of the average value with 95% confidence.

All experiments are run using data generated at TPC-H Scale Factor 0.1. This means our largest entity, LINEITEM, has approximately 600,000 rows. The raw data is nearly 100 MB on disk.

5.1. Storage Comparison

In this section, we examine the storage requirements of both the relational and XML versions of the TPC-H data set. The number of disk pages required to store the data has a direct impact on the cost of any sequential scan. For this experiment, we loaded several of the TPC-H relations into both standard DB2 tables and our native XML storage engine, and present the disk storage requirements in Table 1.

Table 1 - Relational and XML Storage Requirements for selected TPC-H relations, in KB

Relation(s)	Relational	XML
CUSTOMER	2656	13312
ORDERS->LINEITEM	100960	888832
PART->PARTSUPP	15904	66560

It is clear that a generic XML store generates significant storage overhead when compared to the same data stored relationally. These overheads are due mostly to three factors. All text data is stored in Unicode format in the prototype XML store. Although DB2 allows tables to store Unicode data, it does not do so unless explicitly asked to by the user. This is a factor of two size increase for any text data in the TPC-H tables. Secondly, a generic XML store must duplicate the document structure for every relational record converted to XML format. For XML documents with a high structure-to-data ratio, this overhead is high. Finally, our XML storage engine currently stores all XML data in text format. For any numeric data, this adds significant storage overhead. Storage for the element tags does not require significant overhead, however. Each unique element and attribute name is entered into a mapping table, which allows us to store an integer tag ID for each document node.

5.2. Bufferpool Effects

As discussed in section 5.1, the storage required for the XML schemas under test is significantly more than for the relational load of the data into DB2. It therefore makes sense to consider the effects of varying the size of DB2's bufferpool on query performance. We chose to run each series of queries using four different bufferpool sizes. The sizes were chosen to be 10%, 25%, 50%, and 100% of the total storage (data and indices) required for the schema. Using this definition implies that the 10% case for the relational schema is a much smaller number of pages than for the 10% XML schema case. Please refer to Table 2 for the specific bufferpool sizes tested.

It may seem unfair to use different bufferpool sizes for the tests. After all, when 100% of the relational data and indices fit in memory, only 11% of the XML data and indices fit. Further, given a specific memory budget, the relational data has a size advantage and should benefit from it. However, if the scale factor of the data increased, we would not have a choice but to choose a bufferpool size < 10% in both cases.

Table 2 - Tested bufferpool sizes (in number of 32K pages)

Size	Relational	XML
10%	450	4000
25%	1125	10000
50%	2250	20000
100%	4500	40000

We present a graph in Figure 6 which illustrates the effects that the bufferpool size has on the performance of TPC-H query 10. The results presented are normalized to the execution time when the 100% bufferpool size is used. For the relational schema, additional memory directly contributes to decreased query execution time. However, additional memory does not give an advantage for queries executed using the XML schemas. The additional CPU cost of navigating through the XML schema and converting the retrieved text to the correct column datatype may be to blame, but additional experiments are necessary. Similar results were obtained for the other queries we tested.

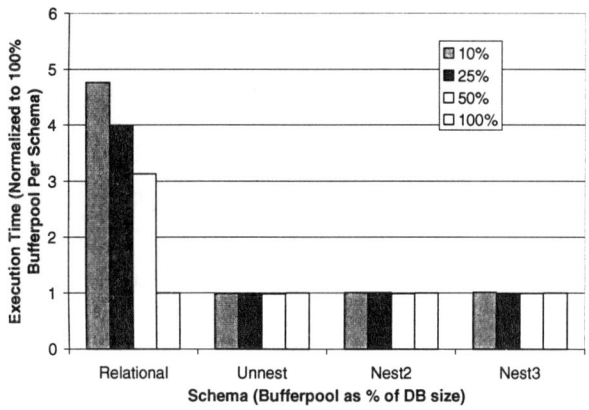

Figure 6 - TPC-H Q10 bufferpool effects. For each schema, the execution times are normalized to the 100% bufferpool execution time. The percentages listed are relative to the total size of the data and indicies being tested.

When the number of bufferpool pages are roughly the same for the relational and XML schemas, the relational schema appears to be the clear winner. In Figure 7, we present the results of two queries executed over all schemas. The relational schema was tested at the 100% bufferpool level of 4500 pages, while the XML schemas used their 10% level of 4000 pages. For Q10, the best XML schema is still a factor of about 19x slower than the relational schema. For Q22, we see that the Unnest and Nest2 schemas are about a factor of 5 slower.

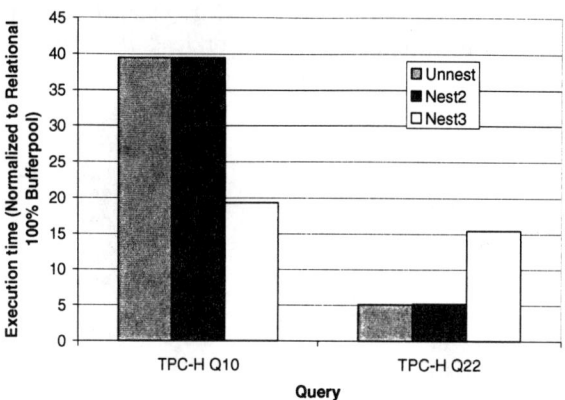

Figure 7 - Bufferpool effects when all queries are executed with approximately the same number of bufferpool pages

5.3. Schema Variations

In this section, we discuss the measured effects of varying the nesting of the XML schema. All experiments discussed in this section assume a 10% bufferpool size.

As the level of nesting in each XML document is increased, we encounter mixed performance results. Consider the graph in Figure 8, which shows the normalized execution times for two TPC-H queries for our three XML schemas. TPC-H Q10 is called the Returned Item Reporting Query. This query is basically a four-way join between NATION, CUSTOMER, ORDERS, and LINEITEM. This query fits our Nest3 schema extremely well, and the results show that this query is about twice as fast with Nest3 as with either the Nest2 or Unnest schemas. One obvious question, though, is why we don't see any benefit from the Nest2 schema, which has LINEITEM nested in ORDERS. The answer lies in the fact that we are utilizing the XML index to join CUSTOMER to ORDERS in both cases, and also for ORDERS to LINEITEM in the Unnest case. As we will see in the next section, the XML index performs very well and brings Unnest's performance in line with Nest2.

Although Nest3 was the clear favorite for Q10, it suffers for other queries such as Q22. This query scans CUSTOMER looking for customers in specific countries who have never placed an order but have a good account balance. The country selection predicate is reasonably selective, and so the join to ORDERS can be avoided for most customers. The Nest3 schema performs very poorly for this query due to the storage of each CUSTOMER's ORDERS and LINEITEM information – the very attribute that made it much better for Q10. Since this query does not use the ORDERS information very often and never uses the LINEITEM information, we needlessly pay to load them from disk. CUSTOMER information packs much better in the Unnest and Nest2 schemas, as both utilize the CUSTOMER-only XML document format.

These results suggest that the XML schema chosen should factor in the expected query workload, if known.

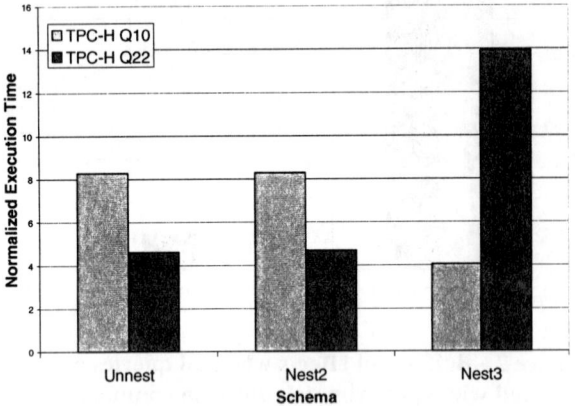

Figure 8 - Schema Effects for two TPC-H queries, normalized to the Relational time for each query

5.4. XML Index Exploitation

We now consider the benefits of utilizing the XML index to aid in joining across documents. In all of our chosen XML schemas, we maintain some normalization. For example, all of our schemas keep PART and LINEITEM unnested. To find the name of a part given a specific lineitem, we must do a standard join. In this section, we compare two types of joins – index nested loops join using the XML index, and DB2's hash join. In Figure 9, we show results for TPC-H query 5 – the Local Supplier Volume Query. This query joins six of the eight tables using a total of six equijoin predicates. The extra join ensures that the supplier and customer are from the same nation. Here, we have normalized the results to the execution time for the Relational schema. For this query, utilizing the XML index provides a very tangible benefit. The Unnest schema shows a much larger improvement over the hash join plan than the Nest2 schema, with both schemas at about 3 times the relational query time when the XML index is used. In the Hash Join case, the Unnest2 performs better because the plan executed still takes advantage of the nesting of LINEITEM in ORDERS, thereby obviating a very expensive join.

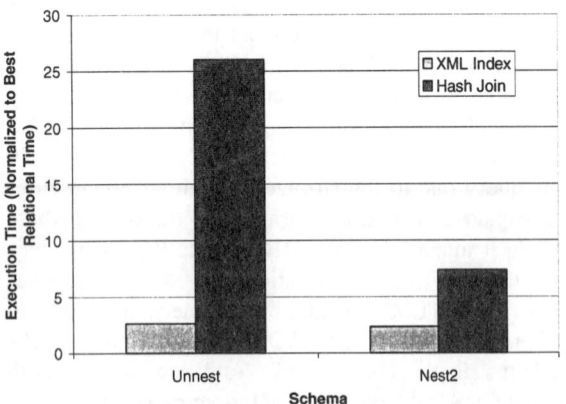

Figure 9 - TPC-H Q5: Local Supplier Volume Query

These results show that our immature ROX prototype can achieve performance within a factor of three of a mature relational database system for an important category of queries. With proper tuning and optimization of the storage format, XML navigation, and XML index utilization, even better results could be obtained.

6. Conclusions/Future Work

In this paper, we have discussed an alternate solution to the problem of integrating relational and XML data sources to support both new XQuery and legacy SQL queries. We called this solution the ROX model, and described the architectural tradeoffs involved. Our solution allows existing SQL applications to continue to run unmodified, and allows a gradual transition of some or all data to the XML storage format. We created a prototype to compare the performance of the ROX model to the standard relational model, and found that it can compete for an important class of queries. We found that the choice of the XML schema to represent the relational data can have a profound impact on performance. Also, by utilizing an index over the XML storage, we could achieve performance within a factor of three of a mature relational DBMS for queries with many joins.

Many research questions remain open for future work. Updates in a native XML storage system can pose problems such as document order anomalies and subtree locking issues. Further, an XML update standard (or even a candidate specification) does not yet exist. It would be interesting to consider the ROX model as the XML update standard is created.

Storage overheads associated with general native XML stores are a significant source of performance problems when using the ROX model to perform sequential scans. Identifying ways to store XML compactly and exploring tree storage alternatives based on document access patterns are interesting areas for future research.

For a given query workload and XML schema, we could utilize the query optimizer to create alternate plans that would be possible if a different XML schema was available, and use this information to automatically suggest a better XML schema for that query workload, much as was done in DB2's Index Advisor [VZZ00] and Design Advisor [ZIL04].

Resolving these questions will bring us closer to the time when XQuery and SQL queries can both be processed efficiently against both structured and semi-structured databases.

Acknowledgement: In order to assemble the prototype, we relied on components built by many contributors, including Bert van der Linden, Brian Vickery, Tuong Truong, Bob Lyle, George Lapis, Bobbie Cochrane, Chun Zhang and others. We would also like to thank Kevin Beyer and Matthias Nicola for useful discussions and support provided while performing the experimental evaluation.

7. References

[APX04] The Apache XML Project: http://xml.apache.org/

[BCF03] Boag, Scott D. Chamberlin, M. Fernandez, D. Florescu, J. Robie, J. Simeon: *XQuery 1.0: An XML Query Language (Working Draft)*. November 2003. http://www.w3.org/TR/xquery

[BFH00] P. Bohannon, J. Freire, J. Haritsa, M. Ramanath, P. Roy, J. Simeon, *LegoDB: Customizing Relational Storage for XML Documents*, In Proc of VLDB 2000, Septermber 2000

[CFF03] D. Chamberlin, P. Fankhauser, D. Florescu, M. Marchiori, J. Robie: *XML Query Use Cases*, W3C Working Draft, November 2003, http://www.w3.org/TR/xquery-use-cases/

[DAT03] C. Date: *An Introduction to Database Systems, Eighth Edition*, Pearson Addison Wesley, 2003.

[EDO01] L. Ennser, C. Delporte, M. Oba, K. Sunil: *Integrating XML with DB2 XML Extender and DB2 Text Extender*, IBM Redbooks, 2001, http://www.redbooks.ibm.com/pubs/pdfs/redbooks/sg246130.pdf

[FMM03] M. Fernandez, A. Malhorta, J. Marsh, M. Nagy: *XQuery and XPath 2.0 Data Model*, W3C Working Draft, November 2003, http://www.w3.org/TR/xpath-datamodel

[HAL01] A. Y. Halevy: *Answering queries using views: A survey*. The VLDB Journal 10(4), 2001.

[IBM01] *DB2 for z/OS and OS/390 Version 7 Using the Utilities Suite*, IBM Red Book, http://publib-b.boulder.ibm.com/Redbooks.nsf/0/03b3f70ce5666bec85256a5300663f26?OpenDocument

[JAC02] H. V. Jagadish, S. Al-Khalifa, A. Chapman, L. V. S. Lakshmanan, A. Nierman, S. Paparizos, J. Patel, D. Srivastava, N. Wiwatwattanan, Y. Wu, C. Yu: *Timber: A Native XML Database*, In Proc of VLDB 2002, September 2002

[JS03] V Josifovski, P. Schwarz: Querying *XML data sources in DB2: the XML Wrapper*. In Proc of ICDE 2003, Banglore India, 2003.

[JFB04] V. Josifovski, M. Fontoura, A. Barta: Querying *XML Streams*, to appear in the VLDB Journal, 2004

[KM99] C. Kanne, G. Moerkotte: *Efficient Storage of XML Data*, In proc of ICDE 1999, 1999

[MUV84] David Maier, Jeffrey D. Ullman, Moshe Y. Vardi: *On the Foundations of the Universal Relation Model*. ACM Trans. Database Syst. 9(2): 283-308 (1984)

[MSF00] *Microsoft SQL Server 2000 SDK Documentation*, Microsoft 2000, http://www.microsoft.com

[NDM01] J. Naughton, D. DeWitt, D, Meier et al.: *The Niagara Internet Query System*, IEEE Data Engineering Bulletin, volume 24, number 2, June 2001, pp. 27-33.

[ORC04] Oracle: http://www.oracle.com/solutions/

[PSW04] Peoplesoft: http://www.peoplesoft.com/corp/en/products/ent/index.jsp

[SAP04] SAP: http://www.sap.com/solutions/erp/

[SB00] M. Scardinia, S. Banerjee: *XML Support in Oracle 9i*, Oracle Corporation, December 2000.

[SIB04] Siebel: http://siebel.com/products/index.shtm

[SKS01] J. Shanmugasundraram, J. Kiernan, E. Shekita, C. Fan, J. Funderburk: *Querying XML Views of Relational Data*. In proc of VLDB 2001, September 2001.

[SPS87] M. Scholl, H.-B. Paul, H.-J. Schek: *Supporting Flat Relations by a Nested Relational Kernel*. In proc of VLDB 1987, September 1987.

[SQL98] *Database Language SQL – Part 2: Foundations (SQL/Foundations)*, ISO Final Draft International Standard, ISO 1998.

[SQX04] A. Eisenberg, J. Melton: *SQL/XML is Making Good Progress*. SIGMOD Record 31(2), 2002.

[TPC02] *TPC Benchmark H*, Transaction Processing Performance Council, San Jose, CA 2002. http://www.tpc.org/tpch/spec/tpch2.1.0.pdf

[VZZ00] G. Valentin, M. Zuliani, D. Zilio, G. Lohman, A. Skelley: *DB2 Advisor: An Optimzer Smart Enough to Recommend its Own Indexes*, In proc of ICDE 2000, San Diego, CA, 2000.

[XAL03] *Xalan an XSL Processor*,The Apache XML project,http://xml.apache.org/xalan-c/index.html

[XER03] *Xerces: a validating XML Parser*, The Apache XML project, http://xml.apache.org/xerces-c/index.html

[ZIL04] D. Zilio et al.: *Recommending Materialized Views and Indexes with IBM's DB2 Design Advisor*, To appear in proc of ICAC 2004.

[ZKO04] N. Zhang, V. Kacholia,, M. T. Özsu: *A Succinct Physical Storage Scheme for Efficient Evaluation of Path Queries in XML*, In proc of ICDE 2004, Boston, MA, March 2004.

From XML view updates to relational view updates: old solutions to a new problem *

Vanessa P. Braganholo[1]
vanessa@inf.ufrgs.br

Susan B. Davidson[2]
susan@cis.upenn.edu

Carlos A. Heuser[1]
heuser@inf.ufrgs.br

[1]Instituto de Informática
Universidade Federal do Rio Grande do Sul - UFRGS
Brazil

[2]Department of Computer and Information Science
University of Pennsylvania, USA &
INRIA-FUTURS, France

Abstract

This paper addresses the question of updating relational databases through XML views. Using *query trees* to capture the notions of selection, projection, nesting, grouping, and heterogeneous sets found throughout most XML query languages, we show how XML views expressed using query trees can be mapped to a set of corresponding relational views. We then show how updates on the XML view are mapped to updates on the corresponding relational views. Existing work on updating relational views can then be leveraged to determine whether or not the relational views are updatable with respect to the relational updates, and if so, to translate the updates to the underlying relational database.

1 Introduction

XML is frequently used as an interface to relational databases. In this scenario, XML documents (or views) are exported from relational databases and published, exchanged, or used as the internal representation in user applications. This fact has stimulated much research in exporting and querying relational data as XML views [15, 23, 22, 8]. However, the problem of updating a relational database through an XML view has not received as much attention: Given an update on an XML view of a relational database, how should it be translated to updates on the relational database? Since the problem of updates through relational views has been studied for more than 20 years by the

*Research partially supported by CNPq and Capes (Brazil) as well as NSF DBI-9975206 (USA).

Permission to copy without fee all or part of this material is granted provided that the copies are not made or distributed for direct commercial advantage, the VLDB copyright notice and the title of the publication and its date appear, and notice is given that copying is by permission of the Very Large Data Base Endowment. To copy otherwise, or to republish, requires a fee and/or special permission from the Endowment.

**Proceedings of the 30th VLDB Conference,
Toronto, Canada, 2004**

Vendor(<u>vendorId</u>, vendorName, url, state, country)
Book(<u>isbn</u>, title, publisher, year)
DVD(<u>asin</u>, title, genre, nrDisks)
Sell-Book(<u>vendorId</u>, <u>isbn</u>, price)
— foreign key(vendorId) references Vendor
— foreign key(isbn) references Book
Sell-DVD(<u>vendorId</u>, <u>asin</u>, price)
— foreign key(vendorId) references Vendor
— foreign key(asin) references DVD

Figure 1: Sample database

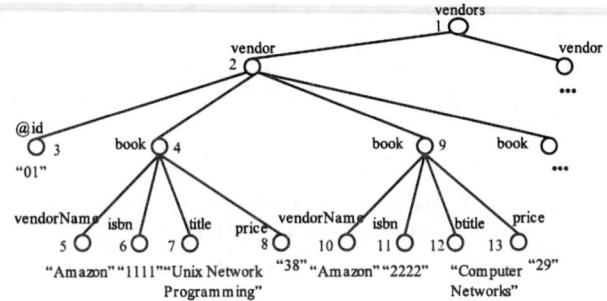

Figure 3: View 1: books and vendors

database community, it would be good to use all that work to solve the new problem of updates though XML views. Specifically, is there a way to leverage existing work on updating through relational views to map view updates to the underlying relational database?

In the relational case, attention has focused on updates through select-project-join views since they represent a common form of view that can be easily reasoned about using key and foreign key information. Similarly, we focus on a common form of XML views that allows nesting, composed attributes, heterogeneous sets and repeated elements. An example of such a view is shown in figure 2, which was defined over the database of figure 1. In this XML view, *books* are nested under the *products* node, and the *address* node composes attributes in a nested record format. The *products* node is composed of tuples of two different types, *book* and *dvd*.

We represent XML view expressions as *query trees*. Query trees can be thought of as the intermediate represen-

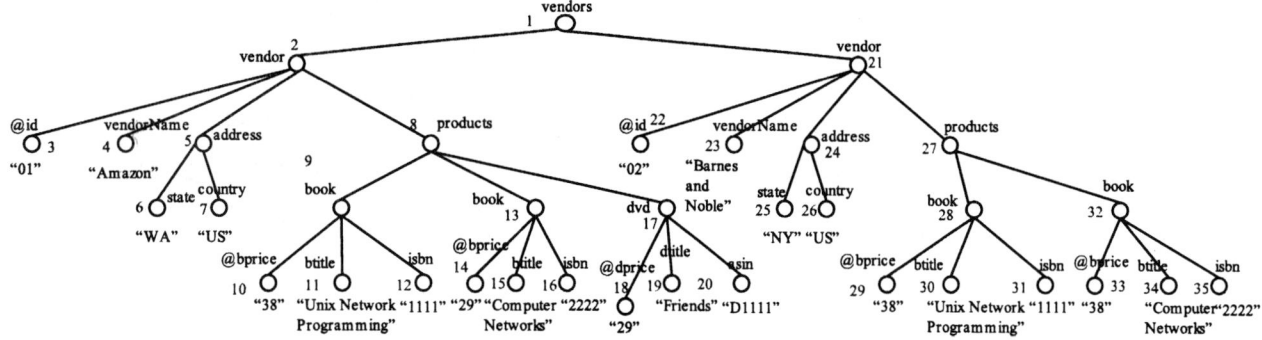

Figure 2: View 2: vendors, books and dvds

tation of a query expressed by some high-level XML query language, and provide a language independent framework in which to study how to map updates to an underlying relational database. They are expressive enough to capture the XML views that we have encountered in practice, yet are simple to understand and manipulate. Their expressive power is equivalent to that of DB2 DAD files [9]. Throughout the paper, we will use the term "XML view" to mean those produced by query trees.

The strategy we adopt is to map an XML view to a set of underlying relational views. Similarly, we map an update against the XML view to a set of updates against the underlying relational views. It is then possible to use any existing technique on updates through relational views to both translate the updates to the underlying relational database and to answer the question of whether or not the XML view is updatable with respect to the update.

This strategy is similar to that adopted in [5] for XML views constructed using the nested relational algebra (NRA), however, our view and update language are far more general. In particular, nested relations cannot handle heterogeneity. Thus, the NRA is capable of representing the XML view of Figure 3 but not that of Figure 2, and maps an XML view to exactly one underlying relational view.

The outline and contributions of this paper are as follows:

- Section 2 defines query trees, their abstract types, and the resulting XML view DTD.
- Section 3 presents the algorithm for mapping an XML view to a set of underlying relational views, and proves its correctness.
- Section 4.1 defines a simple XML update language and algorithms to detect whether or not an update is correct with respect to the XML view DTD.
- Section 4.2 gives an algorithm for mapping insertions, modifications and deletions on XML views to updates on the underlying relational views, and Section 4.3 proves its correctness.
- Section 4.4 illustrates our approach by showing how to use the techniques of [13] to detect if an XML view is updatable with respect to a given update.
- Section 5 discusses the expressive power of our language, and evaluates our technique with respect to existing proposals on extracting XML views of relational databases.

Related work can be found in Section 6. We conclude in Section 7 with a discussion of future work.

2 Query Trees

Query trees are used as a representation of the XML view extraction query. We use this abstract representation rather than an XML query language syntax for several reasons: First, reasoning about updates and the updatability of an XML view is performed at this level. Second, they are easy to understand yet expressive enough to capture several important aspects of XQuery such as nesting, composed attributes, and heterogeneous sets.[1] They can therefore be thought of as the intermediate processing form for a subset of many different XML query languages. For example, we have developed an implementation of our technique which uses a subset of XQuery as the top-level language [6].

After defining query trees, we introduce a notion which will be used to describe the mapping to relational queries, the abstract type of a query tree node. We use this notion of typing to define the semantics of query trees, and then present their result type DTD.

2.1 Query Trees Defined

An example of a query tree can be found in Figure 4, which retrieves books that are sold for prices greater than $30. The query tree resembles the structure of the resulting XML view. The root of the tree corresponds to the root element of the result. Leaf nodes correspond to attributes of relational tables, and interior nodes whose incoming edges are starred capture repeating elements. The result of this query is also presented in Figure 4.

Query trees are very similar to the *view forests* of [15] and *schema-tree queries* presented in [3]. The difference is that, instead of annotating all nodes with the relational queries that are used to build the content model of a given node, we annotate interior nodes in the tree using only the selection criteria (not the entire relational query). An annotation can be a *source* annotation or a *where* annotation. Source annotations bind variables to relational tables, and *where* annotations impose restrictions on the relational tables making use of the variables that were bound to the tables.

---
[1]They can also capture grouping, but for simplicity we omit that [7].

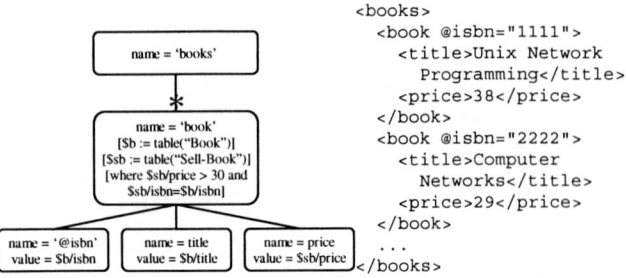

```
<books>
    <book @isbn="1111">
        <title>Unix Network
            Programming</title>
        <price>38</price>
    </book>
    <book @isbn="2222">
        <title>Computer
            Networks</title>
        <price>29</price>
    </book>
    ...
</books>
```

Figure 4: Example of query tree and its resulting XML view

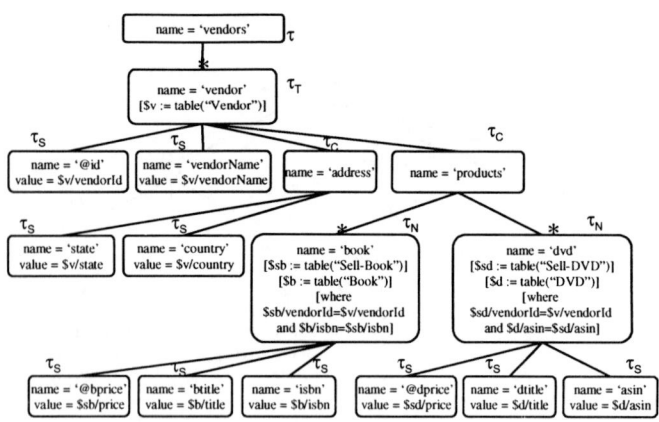

Figure 5: Query tree for View 2

In the definitions that follow, we assume that $\mathcal{D}$ is a relational database over which the XML view is being defined. $\mathbb{T}$ is the set of table names of $\mathcal{D}$. $\mathbb{A}_T$ is the set of attributes of a given table $T \in \mathbb{T}$.

Definition 2.1 *A query tree defined over a database $\mathcal{D}$ is a tree with a set of nodes $\mathbb{N}$ and a set of edges $\mathbb{E}$ in which:* **Edges** *are simple or starred ("*-edge"). An edge is simple if, in the corresponding XML instance, the child node appears exactly once in the context of the parent node, and starred otherwise.* **Nodes** *are as follows:*

1. *All nodes have a name that represents the tag name of the XML element associated with this node in the resulting XML view.*
2. *Leaf nodes have a value (to be defined). Names of leaf nodes that start with "@" are considered to be XML attributes.*
3. *Starred nodes (nodes whose incoming edge is starred) may have one or more source annotations and zero or more where annotations (to be defined).*

Since we map XML views to relational views, nodes with the same name in the query tree may cause ambiguities in the mapping. This problem can easily be solved by associating with each node name a number corresponding to its position in the query tree, and using it internally in the mapping. For simplicity, in this paper we will ignore this problem and use unique names for nodes in the query trees.

Returning to the example in Figure 4, there is a *-edge from the root (named *books*) to its child named *book*, indicating that in the corresponding XML instance there may be several *book* subelements of *books*. There is a simple edge from the node named *book* to the node named *title*, indicating that there is a single *title* subelement of *book*. The node named *@isbn* will be mapped to an XML attribute instead of an element.

Before giving an example of how values are associated with nodes, we define *source* and *where* annotations on nodes of a query tree.

Definition 2.2 *A source annotation s within a starred node n is of the form [$x := table(T)$], where x denotes a variable and $T \in \mathbb{T}$ is a relational table. We say that x is bound to T by s.*

Definition 2.3 *A where annotation on a starred node n is of the form [where x_1/A_1 op Z_1 AND ... AND x_k/A_k op Z_k], $k \geq 1$, where $A_i \in \mathbb{A}_{T_i}$ and x_i is bound to T_i by a source annotation on n or some ancestor of n. The operator op is a comparison operator $\{=, \neq, >, <, \leq, \geq\}$. Z_i is either a literal (integer, string, etc.) or an expression of the form y/B, where $B \in \mathbb{A}_T$ and y is bound to T by a source annotation on n or some ancestor of n.*

Definition 2.4 *The value of a node n is of form x/A, where $A \in \mathbb{A}_T$ and x is bound to table T by a source annotation on n or some ancestor of n.*

In Figure 4, the node *book* has source annotations and where annotations. The source annotations bind variable b to the relational table *Book*, and variable sb to the relational table *Sell-Book*. The where annotations restrict the books that appear in the view to those with price greater than $30, and specify the join condition of tables *Book* and *Sell-Book*. The value of the node *@isbn* is specified as $b/isbn$, indicating that the content of the XML view attribute *isbn* will be generated using attribute *isbn* of the table *Book*.

A more complex example of a query tree can be found in Figure 5 (ignore for now the types τ associated with nodes). This query tree retrieves *vendors*, and for each *vendor*, its *@id*, *vendorName*, *address* and a set of *books* and *dvds* within *products*. The root *vendors* has a set of *vendor* child nodes (*-edge). The *vendor* node is annotated with a binding for v (to table Vendor), and has several children at the end of simple edges (*@id*, *vendorName*, and *address*). The value of its *id* attribute is specified by the path $v/vendorId$, and that of *vendorName* is specified by the path $v/vendorName$. The node *address* is more complex, and is composed of *state* and *country* subelements. The node *products* has two *-edge children, *book* and *dvd*. Source annotations of the *book* node include bindings for b (Book) and sb (Sell-Book) and its where annotations connect tuples in Sell-Book to tuples in Book, and tuples in Sell-Book with tuples in Vendor (join conditions). Node *dvd* has source annotations for d (DVD) and sd (Sell-DVD). Its where annotation connects tuples in Sell-DVD to tuples in DVD and tuples in Sell-DVD with tuples in Vendor. The result of this query tree is View 2, shown in Figure 2.

From now on, we assume that a query tree is *non-empty*, i.e. that it consists of more than a root node.

2.2 Abstract Types

In our mapping strategy, it will be important to recognize nodes that play certain roles in a query tree. In particular, we identify five abstract types of nodes: τ, τ_T, τ_N, τ_C and τ_S. We call them *abstract types* to distinguish them from the type or DTD of the XML view elements.

Nodes in the query tree are assigned abstract types as follows:

1. The root has abstract type τ.
2. Each leaf has abstract type τ_S (Simple).
3. Each non-leaf node with an incoming simple edge has abstract type τ_C (Complex).
4. Each starred node which is either a leaf node or whose subtree has only simple edges has an abstract type of τ_N (Nested).
5. All other starred nodes have abstract type τ_T (Tree).

Note that each node has exactly one type unless it is a starred leaf node, in which case it has types τ_S and τ_N.

As an example of this abstract typing, consider the query tree in Figure 5, which shows the type of each of its nodes. Since *book* and *dvd* are repeating nodes whose descendants are non-repeating nodes, their types are τ_N rather than τ_T.

We call the XML views produced by query trees and their associated abstract types *well-behaved* because, as we will show in the next section, they can be easily mapped to a set of corresponding relational views. However, before turning to the mapping we prove two facts about query trees that will be used throughout the paper.

Proposition 2.1 *There is at least one τ_N node in the abstract type of a query tree qt.*

Proof: Since query trees are assumed to be non-empty, qt must have at least one leaf. This means that qt must have at least one starred node n, since the leaf node has a value which involves at least one variable which must be defined in some source annotation attached to a starred node. Since the tree is finite, at least one of these starred nodes is either a leaf node or has a subtree of simple edges, i.e. the starred node is a τ_N node. ∎

Proposition 2.2 *There is at most one τ_N node along any path from a leaf to the root in the abstract type of a query tree qt.*

Proof: Suppose there are two τ_N nodes, n_1 and n_2, along the path from some leaf to the root of qt. Without loss of generality, assume that n_1 is the ancestor of n_2. By definition of τ_N, n_2 must be a starred node. Therefore n_1 has a *-edge in its subtree, a contradiction. ∎

We will refer to the abstract type of an element by the abstract type that was used to generate it followed by the element name. As an example, the abstract type of the element *dvd* in Figure 5 is referred to as $\tau_N(dvd)$, and its type (DTD) is *<!ELEMENT dvd (dtitle, asin)>*.

2.3 Semantics of Query Trees

The semantics of a query tree follows the abstract type of its nodes, and can be found in algorithm 1. The algorithm

```
eval(qt, d) {qt is the root of the query tree, d the database instance}
{qt is the query tree and d is the database instance}
evaluate(root(qt), d)

evaluate(n, d)
{Assume a node type has functions abstract_type(n), name(n), value(n),
children(n), sources(n), and where(n) (with the obvious meanings).}
Let bindings{} be a hash array of bindings of variable attributes to values, initially
empty.
case abstract_type(n)
    τ|τ_C: buildElement(n)
    τ_T|τ_N: table(n)
    τ_S: print "<name(n)>value(n)</name(n)>"
end case

buildElement(n)
let tag = "name(n)"
for each attribute c in children(n) do
    add "name(c) = value(c)" to tag
end for
print "< tag >"
for each non-attribute c in children(n) do
    evaluate(c)
end for
print "</name(n)>"

table(n)
let w be a list of conditions in sources(n)
for each w[i] do
    if w[i] involves a variable v in bindings{} then
        substitute the value binding{v} for v
    end if
end for
calculate the set B of all bindings for variables in sources(n) that makes the con-
junction of the modified w[i]'s true, using d
for each b in B do
    add b to bindings{}
    buildElement(n)
    remove b from bindings{}
end for
```

Algorithm 1: Eval algorithm

constructs the XML view resulting from a query tree recursively, and starts with n being the root of the query tree. The basic idea is that the source and where annotations in each starred node n are evaluated in the database instance d, producing a set of tuples. The algorithm then iterates over these tuples, generating one element corresponding to n in the output for each of these tuples and evaluating the children of n once for each tuple.

The *bindings{}* hash array stores the current values of variables, taken from the underlying relational database. We assume that values in *bindings{}* are represented as *$x/A = 1, $x/B = 2*, where *$x* is a variable bound to a relational table T, A and B are the attributes of T and 1 and 2 are the values of attributes A and B in the current tuple of T.

2.4 DTD of a Query Tree

Query tree views defined over a relational database have a well-defined schema (DTD) that is easily derived from the tree. Given a query tree, its DTD is generated as follows:

1. For each attribute leaf node named @A with parent named E, create an attribute declaration
   <!ATTLIST E @A CDATA #REQUIRED>
2. For each non-attribute leaf node named E, create an element declaration *<!ELEMENT E (#PCDATA)>*
3. For each non-leaf node named E, create an element declaration *<!ELEMENT E (E_1, ..., E_k, E_{k+1}*, ..., E_n*)>*, where $E_1, ..., E_k$ are non-attribute child nodes

of E connected by a simple edge, and $E_{k+1}*, ..., E_n*$ are child nodes of E connected by a *-edge. In case $n = 0$, then create an element declaration <!ELEMENT E EMPTY>

As an example, the DTD of the view produced by the query tree shown in Figure 5 is:

```
<!ELEMENT vendors (vendor*)>
<!ELEMENT vendor (vendorName, address, products)>
<!ATTLIST vendor id CDATA #REQUIRED>
<!ELEMENT vendorName (#PCDATA)>
<!ELEMENT address (state, country)>
<!ELEMENT state (#PCDATA)>
<!ELEMENT country (#PCDATA)>
<!ELEMENT products (book*,dvd*)>
<!ELEMENT book (btitle, isbn)>
<!ATTLIST book bprice CDATA #REQUIRED>
<!ELEMENT btitle (#PCDATA)>
<!ELEMENT isbn (#PCDATA)>
<!ELEMENT dvd (dtitle, asin)>
<!ATTLIST dvd dprice CDATA #REQUIRED>
<!ELEMENT asin (#PCDATA)>
<!ELEMENT dtitle (#PCDATA)>
```

Note that all (#PCDATA) elements are required. When the value of a relational attribute is null, we produce an element with a distinguished null value.

3 Mapping to Relational Views

In our approach, updates over an XML view are translated to SQL update statements on a set of corresponding relational view expressions. Existing techniques such as [13, 17, 20, 2, 27] can then be used to accept, reject or modify the proposed SQL updates. In this section, we discuss how an XML view constructed by a query tree is mapped to a set of corresponding relational view expressions.

Map. Given a query tree qt with only one τ_N node, the corresponding SQL view statement is generated as follows. Join together all tables found in source annotations (called *source tables*) in a given node n in qt, using the where annotations that correspond to joins on source tables in n as inner join conditions. If no such join condition is found then use "true" (e.g. 1=1) as the join condition, resulting in a cartesian product. Call these expressions *source join expressions*. Use the hierarchy implied by the query tree to left outer join source join expressions in an ancestor-descendant direction, so that nodes with no children still appear in the view. The conditions for the outer joins are captured as follows: If node a is an ancestor of n and a where annotation in n specifies a join condition on a table in n with a table in a, then use this annotation as the join condition for the outer join. Similar to inner joins, if no condition for the outer join is found, then use "true" as the join condition so that if the inner relation is empty, the tuples of the outer will still appear. Use the remaining where annotations (the ones that were not used as inner or outer join conditions) in an SQL where-clause and project the values of leaf nodes. The resulting SQL view statement represents an unnested version of the XML view.

For example, the relational view corresponding to the query tree in Figure 4 is:

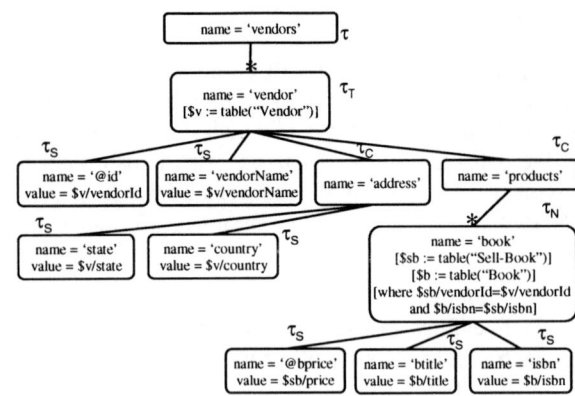

Figure 6: Partitioned query tree for $\tau_N(book)$

```
SELECT b.isbn AS isbn, b.title AS title, sb.price AS price
FROM (Book AS b INNER JOIN Sell-Book AS sb
      ON sb.isbn=b.isbn) WHERE sb.price > 30
```

Split. For a query tree with more than one τ_N node, this process is incorrect. As an example, consider the query tree of Figure 5 which has two τ_N nodes (*book* and *dvd*). If we follow the mapping process described above, the tables DVD and Book will be joined, resulting in a cartesian product. In this expression, a book is repeated for each DVD, violating the semantics of the query tree. We must therefore split a query tree into sub-query trees containing exactly one τ_N node each before generating the corresponding relational views. After the splitting process, each sub-query tree produced is mapped to a relational view as explained above.

The splitting process consists in isolating a node n of type τ_N in the query tree qt, and taking its subtree as well as its ancestors and their non-repeating descendants (types τ_C and τ_S) to form a new tree qt_i. Recall that qt must have at least one τ_N node by Proposition 2.1.

The first step to generate qt_i is to copy qt to qt_i. Then, delete from qt_i all subtrees rooted at nodes of type τ_N, except for the subtree rooted at n. Observe that deleting a subtree r may change the abstract type of the ancestors of r. Specifically, if r has an ancestor a with type τ_T, and r is a's only starred descendant, the type of a becomes τ_N after the deletion of r. Continue to delete subtrees rooted at nodes of type τ_N in qt_i and retype ancestors until n is the only node of type τ_N in qt_i. The process is repeated for every node of type τ_N in qt and results in exactly one τ_N node per split tree (algorithms *map* and *split* are available in [7]).

The result of this process for the query tree of Figure 5 is shown in Figures 6 and 7. Using these split trees, the corresponding relational views *ViewBook* and *ViewDVD* are (we name these views so we can refer to them in the examples of Section 4):

```
CREATE VIEW VIEWBOOK AS
SELECT v.vendorId AS id, v.vendorName AS vendorName,
  v.state AS state, v.country AS country,
  sb.price AS bprice, b.isbn AS isbn, b.title AS btitle
FROM (Vendor AS v LEFT JOIN (Sell-Book AS sb INNER JOIN
Book AS B ON b.isbn=sb.isbn) ON v.vendorId=sb.vendorId);
CREATE VIEW VIEWDVD AS
SELECT v.vendorId AS id, v.vendorName AS vendorName,
  v.state AS state, v.country AS country,
  sd.price AS dprice, d.asin AS asin, d.title AS dtitle
FROM (Vendor AS v LEFT JOIN (Sell-DVD AS sd INNER JOIN
DVD AS d ON d.asin=sd.asin) ON v.vendorId=sd.vendorId)
```

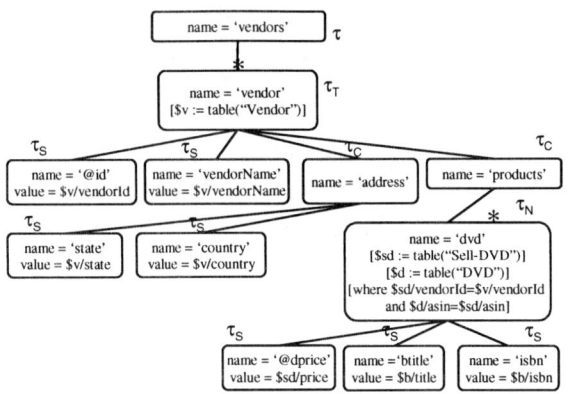

Figure 7: Partitioned query tree for $\tau_N(dvd)$

As described above, *split* takes as input the original query tree qt and produces as output a set of query trees $\{qt_1, ..., qt_n\}$, each of which has one τ_N node; *map* takes $\{qt_1, ..., qt_n\}$ as input and produces a set of relational view expressions $\{V_1, ..., V_n\}$, where each V_i is produced from qt_i as described above. It follows directly from these algorithms that:

Proposition 3.1 *The number of relational view expressions in* map(split(qt)) *is the number of τ_N nodes in qt.*

The correctness of the set of relational view expressions resulting from *map* and *split* can be understood in the following sense: Each tuple in the bindings relations for the XML view is in one or more instances of the corresponding relational views. To be more precise, we define the following:

Definition 3.1 *The* evaluation schema S *of a query tree qt is the set of all names of leaf nodes in qt.*

Definition 3.2 *Let x be an XML instance of a query tree qt with evaluation schema S, in which the instance nodes are annotated by the query tree type from which they were generated. Let n be the deepest τ_N or τ_T instance nodes for some root to leaf path in x. Let p be the set of nodes in the path from n to the root of x. An* evaluation tuple *of x is created from n by associating the value of each leaf node l that is a descendant of n or of some node in p with the attribute in S corresponding to the name of l, and leaving the value of all other attributes in S null.*

The multi-set of all evaluation tuples of x is called its evaluation relation *and is denoted* evalRel(x).

For example, Table 1 shows the result of *evalRel(x)* for the query tree of Figure 5.

Definition 3.3 *Let $\{V_1, ..., V_n\}$ be defined over a relational schema $\mathcal{D}$, and d be an instance of $\mathcal{D}$. Then* relOuterUnion($\{V_1, ..., V_n\}, d$) *denotes the set of relational instances that result from taking the outer union of the evaluation of each V_i over d:* relOuterUnion($\{V_1, ..., V_n\}, d$) $= evalV(V_1, d) \bigcup ... \bigcup evalV(V_n, d)$*, where $\bigcup$ denotes outer union, and* evalV(V, d) *instantiates V over d.*

For example, *relOuterUnion({ViewBook, ViewDVD}, d)* is the outer union of *evalV(ViewBook, d)* and *evalV(ViewDVD, d)*, whose result is shown in Table 2.

The correctness of the set of relational views resulting from *map* and *split* can now be understood in the following sense:

Theorem 3.1 *Given a query tree qt defined over a database $\mathcal{D}$ and an instance d of $\mathcal{D}$, then* evalRel(eval(qt, d)) $\subseteq$ relOuterUnion(map(split(qt)), d).

(Proofs for all the theorems of this papers are available in [7].)

Furthermore, the tuples in *relOuterUnion(map(split(qt)), d) − evalRel(eval(qt, d))* represent starred nodes with an empty evaluation (which we call "stubbed" nodes). More precisely:

Definition 3.4 *Let x be an XML instance of a query tree qt with evaluation schema S, and n be a τ_N or τ_T instance node in x. A* stubbed tuple *of x is created from n by associating the value of each leaf node l that is an ancestor of n with the attribute in S corresponding to the name of l, and leaving the value of all other attributes in S null.*

The set of all stubbed tuples of x is denoted stubs(x).

As an illustration of a stubbed tuple, consider tuple t_6 in table 2. Since the XML instance of Figure 2 does not have any dvd sold by vendor *Barnes and Noble*, there is a tuple [2, Barnes and Noble, NY, US, null, null, null] in *ViewDVD* which was added by the LEFT join. This is correct, since *vendor* is in a common part of the view, so its information appears both in *ViewBook* and *ViewDVD*. However, t_6 is not in table 1, since when the entire view is evaluated, this vendor joins with a book.

Theorem 3.2 *Given a query tree qt defined over a database $\mathcal{D}$ and an instance d of $\mathcal{D}$, then every tuple t in* relOuterUnion(map(split(qt)), d) − evalRel(eval(qt, d)) $\subseteq$ stubs(x).

Note that the statement of correctness is *not* that the XML view can be constructed from instances of the underlying relational views. The reason is that we do not know whether or not keys of relations along the path from τ_N nodes to the root are preserved, and therefore do not have enough information to group tuples from different relational view instances together to reconstruct the XML view. When keys at all levels *are* preserved, then the query tree can be modified to a form in which the variables iterate over the underlying relational views instead of base tables, and used to reconstruct the XML view. Details of this algorithm (*replace*) can be found in [7].

4 Updates

Given an update against a well-behaved view, we translate it to a set of SQL update statements against the corresponding relational view expressions, so existing work on updates through relational views can be used to translate the updates to the underlying relational database. In this section, we start by defining XML updates and then describe the translation. We also summarize how to determine whether or not an update is side-effect free.

Although no standard has been established for an XML update language, several proposals have appeared [1, 25, 4,

281

	id	vendorName	state	country	bprice	btitle	isbn	dprice	dtitle	asin
t_1	1	Amazon	WA	US	38	Unix Network Programming	1111	NULL	NULL	NULL
t_2	1	Amazon	WA	US	29	Computer Networks	2222	NULL	NULL	NULL
t_3	1	Amazon	WA	US	NULL	NULL	NULL	29	Friends	D1111
t_4	2	Barnes and Noble	NY	US	38	Unix Network Programming	1111	NULL	NULL	NULL
t_5	2	Barnes and Noble	NY	US	38	Computer Networks	2222	NULL	NULL	NULL

Table 1: Tuples resulting from *evalRel(eval(qt, d))* for the query tree of Figure 5

	id	vendorName	state	country	bprice	btitle	isbn	dprice	dtitle	asin
t_1	1	Amazon	WA	US	38	Unix Network Programming	1111	NULL	NULL	NULL
t_2	1	Amazon	WA	US	29	Computer Networks	2222	NULL	NULL	NULL
t_3	2	Barnes and Noble	NY	US	38	Unix Network Programming	1111	NULL	NULL	NULL
t_4	2	Barnes and Noble	NY	US	38	Computer Networks	2222	NULL	NULL	NULL
t_5	1	Amazon	WA	US	NULL	NULL	NULL	29	Friends	D1111
t_6	2	Barnes and Noble	NY	US	NULL	NULL	NULL	NULL	NULL	NULL

Table 2: Tuples resulting from *relOuterUnion({ViewBook, ViewDVD}, d)*

19]. The language described below is much simpler than any of these proposals, and in some sense can be thought of as an internal form for one of these richer languages (assuming a static translation of updates [4]). The simplicity of the language allows us to focus on the key problem we are addressing.

4.1 Update language

Updates are specified using path expressions to point to a set of target nodes in the XML tree at which the update is to be performed. For insertions and modifications, the update must also specify a Δ containing the new values.

Definition 4.1 *An update operation u is a triple <t,Δ,ref>, where t is the type of operation (insert, delete, modify); Δ is the XML tree to be inserted, or (in case of a modification) an atomic value; and ref is a simple path expression in XPath [10] which indicates where the update is to occur.*

The path expression *ref* is evaluated from the root of the tree and may yield a set of nodes which we call *update points*. In the case of modify, it must evaluate to a set of leaf nodes. We restrict the filters used in *ref* to conjunctions of comparisons of attributes or child elements with atomic values, and call the expression resulting from removing filters in *ref* the *unqualified portion* of *ref*. For example, the unqualified portion of */vendors/vendor[@id="01"]* is */vendors/vendor*.

Definition 4.2 *An update path ref is valid with respect to a query tree qt iff the unqualified portion of ref is non-empty when evaluated on qt.*

For example, */vendors/vendor[@id="01"]/vendorName* is a valid path expression with respect to the query tree of Figure 5, since the path */vendors/vendor/vendorName* is non-empty when evaluated on that query tree.

The semantics of insert is that Δ is inserted as a child of the nodes indicated by *ref*; the semantics of modify is that the atomic value Δ overwrites the values of the leaf nodes indicated by *ref*; and the semantics of a delete is that the subtrees rooted at nodes indicated by *ref* are deleted.

The following examples refer to Figure 2:

Example 4.1 *To insert a new book selling for $38 under the vendor with id="01" we specify:* t = insert, ref = /vendors/vendor[@id="01"]/ products,

Δ = {<book bprice = "38">
<btitle>New Book</btitle><isbn>9999</isbn>
</book>}.

Example 4.2 *To change the* vendorName *of the vendor with id = "01" to* Amazon.com *we specify:* t = modify, ref = /vendors/vendor[@id = "01"]/vendorName, Δ = {Amazon.com}.

Example 4.3 *To delete all books with title "Computer Networks" we specify:* t= delete, ref = /vendors/vendor/products/book[btitle="Computer Networks"].

Note that not all insertions and deletions make sense since the resulting XML view may not conform to the DTD of the query tree (see Section 2.4). For example, the deletion specified by the path */vendors/vendor/vendorName* would not conform to the DTD of Figure 5 since *vendorName* is a required subelement of *vendor*. We must also check that Δ's inserted and subtrees deleted are correct.

Definition 4.3 *An update <t,Δ,ref> against an XML view specified by a query tree qt is correct iff*

- *ref is valid with respect to qt;*
- *if t is a modification, then the unqualified portion of ref evaluated on qt arrives at a node whose abstract type is τ_S;*
- *if t is an insertion (deletion), then the unqualified portion of ref + the root of Δ (ref) evaluated on qt arrives at a node whose incoming edge is starred (equivalently, its abstract type is τ_T or τ_N);*
- *if nonempty, then Δ conforms to the DTD of the element arrived at by ref.*

For example, the deletion of example 4.3 is correct since *book* is a starred subelement of *products*. However, the deletion specified by the update path */vendors/vendor/vendorName* is not correct since *vendorName* is of abstract type τ_S, as is the deletion specified by the invalid update path */vendors/vendor/dvd*.

4.2 Mapping XML updates to relational views

We now discuss how correct updates to an XML view are translated to SQL updates on the corresponding relational views produced in the previous section.

Throughout this section, we will use the XML view 2 of Figure 2 as an example. The relational views *ViewBook* and

ViewDVD corresponding to this XML view were presented in Section 3.

The translation algorithm for insertions, deletions and modifications, *translateUpdate*, is given in [7].

4.2.1 Insertions

To translate an insert operation on the XML view to the underlying relational views we do the following: First, the unqualified portion of the update path *ref* is used to locate the node in the query tree under which the insertion is to take place. Together with Δ, this will be used to determine which underlying relational views are affected. Second, *ref* is used to query the XML instance and identify the update points. Third, SQL insert statements are generated for each underlying relational view affected using information in Δ as well as information about the labels and values in subtrees rooted along the path from each update point to the root of the XML instance.

Observe that by proposition 2.2, there is at most one node of type τ_N along the path from any node to the root of the query tree and that insertions can never occur below a τ_N node, since all nodes below a τ_N node are of type τ_S or τ_C by definition.

For example, to translate the insertion of example 4.1, we use the unqualified update path */vendors/vendor/products* on the query tree of Figure 5, and find that the type of the update point is $\tau_C(products)$. Continuing from $\tau_C(products)$ using the structure of Δ, we discover that the only τ_N node in Δ is its root, which is of type $\tau_N(book)$. The underlying view affected will therefore be *ViewBook*. We then use the update path *ref= /vendors/vendor[@id="01"]/ products* to identify update points in the XML document. In this case, there is one node (8). Therefore, a single SQL insert statement against view *ViewBook* will be generated.

To generate the SQL insert statement, we must find values for all attributes in the view. Some of these attribute-value pairs are found in Δ, and others must be taken from the XML instance by traversing the path from each update point to the root and collecting attribute-value pairs from the leaves of trees rooted along this path. In example 4.1, Δ specifies *bprice="38"*, *btitle="New Book"* and *isbn="9999"*. Along the path from the node 8 to the root in the XML instance of Figure 2, we find *id="01"*, *vendorName="Amazon"*, *state="WA"* and *country="US"*. Combining this information, we generate the following SQL insert statement:

```
INSERT INTO VIEWBOOK (id, vendorName, state, country,
   bprice, isbn, btitle)
VALUES ("01","Amazon","WA","US",38,"9999","New Book")
```

As another example, consider the following insertion against the view 2: *t = insert, ref = /vendors,*

```
Δ={<vendor id="03">
      <vendorName>New Vendor</vendorName>
      <address>
         <state>PA</state>
         <country>US</country>
      </address>
      <products>
         <book bprice="30">
            <btitle>Book 1</btitle><isbn>9111</isbn></book>
         <book bprice="30">
            <btitle>Book 2</btitle><isbn>9222</isbn></book>
         <dvd dprice="30">
            <dtitle>DVD 1</dtitle><asin>D9333</asin></dvd>
      </products>
   </vendor>}.
```

The unqualified update path *ref* evaluated against the query tree of Figure 5 yields a node $\tau(vendors)$, which is the root. Continuing from here using labels in Δ, we discover two nodes of type τ_N: $\tau_N(book)$ and $\tau_N(dvd)$. We will therefore generate SQL insert statements to *ViewBook* and as well as *ViewDVD*.

Evaluating *ref* against the XML instance of Figure 2 yields one update point, node 1. Traversing the path from this update point to the root yields no label-value pairs (since the update point is the root itself). We then identify each node of type τ_N in Δ, and generate one insertion for each of them. As an example, traversing the path from the first $\tau_N(book)$ node in Δ yields label-value pairs *bprice = "30"*, *btitle = "Book 1"*, and *isbn = "9111"*. Going up to the root of Δ, we have *id = "03"*, *vendorName = "New Vendor"*, *state = "PA"* and *country = "US"*. This information is therefore combined to generate the following SQL insert statement:

```
INSERT INTO VIEWBOOK (id, vendorName, state, country,
   bprice, isbn, btitle)
VALUES ("03","New Vendor","PA","US",30,"9111","Book 1");
```

In a similar way, information is collected from the remaining two τ_N nodes in Δ to generate:

```
INSERT INTO VIEWBOOK (id, vendorName,  state, country,
   bprice, isbn, btitle)
VALUES ("03","New Vendor","PA","US",30,"9222","Book 2");
INSERT INTO VIEWDVD (id, vendorName, state, country,
   dprice, asin, dtitle)
VALUES ("03","New Vendor","PA","US",30,"D9333","DVD 1");
```

4.2.2 Modifications

By definition, modifications can only occur at leaf nodes. To process a modification, we do the following: First, we use the unqualified *ref* against the query tree to determine which relational views are to be updated. This is done by looking at the first ancestor of the node specified by *ref* which has type τ_T or τ_N, and finding all nodes of type τ_N in its subtree. (At least one τ_N node must exist, by definition.) If the leaf node that is being modified is of type τ_N itself, then it is guaranteed that the update will be mapped only to the relational view corresponding to this node.

Second, we generate the SQL modify statements. The qualifications in *ref* are combined with the terminal label of *ref* and value specified by Δ to generate an SQL update statement against the view.

For example, consider the update in example 4.2. The unqualified *ref* is */vendors/vendor/vendorName*. The τ_N nodes in the subtree rooted at *vendor* (the first τ_T or τ_N ancestor of *vendorName*) are $\tau_N(book)$ and $\tau_N(dvd)$, and we will therefore generate SQL update statements for both *ViewBook* and *ViewDVD*. We then use the qualification *id = "01"* from *ref = /vendors/vendor[@id = "01"]/vendorName* together with the new value in Δ, to yield the following SQL modify statements:

```
UPDATE VIEWBOOK SET vendorName="Amazon.com" WHERE id="01";
UPDATE VIEWDVD SET vendorName="Amazon.com" WHERE id="01"
```

4.2.3 Deletions

Deletions are very simple to process. First, the unqualified portion of the update path *ref* is used to locate the node in the query tree at which the deletion is to be performed. This is then used to determine which underlying relational views are affected by finding all τ_N nodes in its subtree. Second, SQL delete statements are generated for each underlying relational view affected using the qualifications in *ref*.

As an example, consider the deletion in example 4.3. The unqualified update path is */vendors/vendor/products/book*. The only τ_N node in the subtree indicated by this path in the query tree is $\tau_N(book)$. This means that the deletion will be performed in *ViewBook*. Examining the update path */vendors/vendor/products/book[btitle="Computer Networks"]* yields the label-value pair *btitle="Computer Networks"*. Thus the deletion on the XML view is translated to an SQL delete statement as:

`DELETE FROM VIEWBOOK WHERE btitle="Computer Networks"`

It is important to notice that if a tuple t in one relation "owns" a set of tuples in another relation via a foreign key constraint (e.g. a vendor "owns" a set of books), then deletions must cascade in the underlying relational schema in order for the deletion of t specified through the XML view to be allowed by the underlying relational system.

4.3 Correctness

Since we are not focusing on how updates over relational views are mapped to the underlying relational database, our notion of correctness of the update mappings is their effect on each relational view *treated as a base table*.

Let $x = eval(qt, d)$ be the initial XML instance, u be the update as specified in Definition 4.1, and $apply(x, u)$ be the updated XML instance resulting from applying u to x. The function *translateUpdate(x, qt, u)* (shown in [7] and summarized in Section 4.2) translates u to a set of SQL update statements $\{U_{11}, ..., U_{1m_1}, ..., U_{n1}, ..., U_{nm_n}\}$, where each U_{ij} is an update on the underlying view instance $v_i = evalV(V_i, d)$ generated by *map(split(qt))*.

We use the notation $v'_i = applyR(v_i, \{U_{i1}, ..., U_{im_i}\})$ to denote the application of $\{U_{i1}, ..., U_{im_i}\}$ to v_i, resulting in the updated view v'_i. If the set of updates for a given v_i is empty, then $v'_i = v_i$.

Theorem 4.1 *Given a query tree qt defined over database $\mathcal{D}$, then for any instance d of $\mathcal{D}$ and correct update u over qt, $evalRel(apply(x, u)) \subseteq v'_1 \bigcup ... \bigcup v'_n$, where $\bigcup$ denotes outer union.*

Theorem 4.2 *Given a query tree qt defined over a database $\mathcal{D}$ and an instance d of $\mathcal{D}$, then $v'_1 \bigcup ... \bigcup v'_n - evalRel(apply(x, u)) \subseteq stubs(apply(x, u))$.*

Note that a correctness definition like $apply(eval(qt, d), u) \equiv eval(qt, d')$, where d' is the updated relational database state resulting from the application of the translated view updates $\{U_{11}, ..., U_{1m_1}, ..., U_{n1}, ..., U_{nm_n}\}$ to updates on d, does not make sense due to the fact that we do not control the translation of view updates. Therefore we cannot claim that they are side-effect free.

In the next subsection, we discuss a scenario in which this claim can be made.

4.4 Updatability

There are several choices of techniques that could be used to translate from updates on relational views to updates on the underlying relational database. Some consider a translation to be correct if it does not affect any part of the database that is outside the view [2, 20]. Others consider a translation to be correct as long as it corresponds exactly to the specified update, and does not affect anything else in the view [13]. Still others use additional information to build specific translators for each view [18, 21, 27]. Here, we choose [13] to illustrate how reasoning about *side-effect free* relational view updates can be extended to XML views.

In [5], we define conditions under which XML views constructed by "nest-last" nested relational algebra (NRA) expressions are updatable. Since nest-last NRA expressions perform nests over a relational algebra expression, our results are based on the ability to unnest the NRA expression to obtain a (single) corresponding relational view, and then build on the results of [13] to detect updatability. Since query trees also express nesting and are mapped to a *set* of corresponding relational views, we can use these results to reason about the updatability of XML views constructed by query trees. We assume the underlying relational database is in BCNF (as required by [13]), and impose three restrictions on the query tree and update: (1) each table must be bound to at most one variable; (2) each value in a leaf node must be unique, that is, if the value of n is specified as $\$x/A$, then this value specification does not appear on any other node in the query tree; (3) comparisons in the filters of *ref* must be equalities. These restrictions are imposed so that the resulting relational views do not include joins of the same tables and projections of the same attribute (as required by [13]). The restriction to equalities in conditions is also required by [13].

Theorem 4.3 *A correct update u to an XML view defined by a query tree qt is side-effect free if for all (U_i, V_i), where V_i is the corresponding relational view of qt_i and U_i is the translation of u over V_i, U_i is side-effect free in V_i.*

Based on Theorem 4.3, we can now answer a more general question: Is there a class of query tree views for which all possible updates are side-effect free? To answer this question, we summarize the results of [5] and [13] for conditions under which NRA views are updatable, and generalize them for XML views constructed by query trees.

Insertions. An insertion over an NRA view is side-effect free when the corresponding relational view V is a select-project-join view, the primary and foreign keys of the source relations of V are in the view and joins are made only through foreign keys. In terms of query trees, this means that the primary keys of the source relations of qt_i must appear as values in leaf nodes of qt_i and the *where* annotations in qt_i specifies joins using foreign keys, for all split trees qt_i corresponding to a query tree qt.

Deletions and modifications. Deletions and modifications over an NRA view V are side-effect free when the above conditions for insertions are met and V is *well-nested* [5]. By *well-nested*, we mean that the source relations in V must be nested according to key-foreign key constraints in the underlying relations. We rephrase this condition in terms of query trees as follows:

Definition 4.4 *A query tree qt is* well-nested *if for any two source relations R and S in qt, if S is related to R by a foreign key constraint then the source annotation for R occurs in an ancestor of the node s containing the source annotation for S. Additionally, attributes of R must not appear as values in the descendants of s.*

The results above identify three classes of updatable XML views: one that is updatable for all possible insertions; one that is updatable for all possible insertions, deletions and modifications; and a general one whose updatability with respect to a given update can be reasoned about using Theorem 4.3. Furthermore, we can now prove the following:

Theorem 4.4 *Given a query tree qt with the restrictions mentioned above and defined over a BCNF database $\mathcal{D}$, then for any instance d of $\mathcal{D}$ and correct update u over qt:* apply(eval(qt,d), u) $\equiv$ eval(qt, d'), *where d' is the updated relational database state resulting from the application of the translated view updates $\{U_{11}, ..., U_{1m_1}, ..., U_{n1}, ..., U_{nm_n}\}$ using the techniques of [13].*

We leave the study of updatability using other existing relational techniques for future work.

5 Evaluation

For purposes of presentation, the query tree language presented in this paper was kept simple to highlight how the mapping of the query tree and updates are performed.

Query trees can be extended in a number of ways, for example to deal with grouping, aggregates, function applications and so on. As an example of such extension, in [7] we allow *grouped values* which allow tuples that agree on a given value to be clustered together, as well as leaf nodes with attributes. With such an extension, *books* and *dvds* that agree on a given price could be grouped under a common *products* ancestor. In this case, the node *products* would be a starred node with a child *@price*. The node *products* would repeat for every distinct value of *price* on tables Sell-Book and Sell-DVD. This extension affects the mapping algorithm only superficially and does not affect the results of this paper.

However, another consideration that must be kept in mind when extending the language is whether or not the relational views resulting from the XML view are updatable. The language presented in this paper, with suitable restrictions on the way in which joins and nesting are performed with respect to keys and foreign keys in the underlying relational database, presents a subset of XQuery in which *side-effect free* updates can be defined as discussed in the previous section. While grouped values and leaf nodes with attributes do not affect these results, the addition of functions and aggregates would. Analogous to work on updating views in relational databases which restricts views to select-project-join queries, we have therefore initially decided against considering a richer language (although we plan to do so in future work).

The EBNF for the subset of XQuery corresponding to our language (with grouped values) can be found in [7].

To evaluate our language, we first discuss the restrictions in our form of queries, and what query trees can or cannot express. Second, we examine the power of expression of query trees, and compare it with existing proposals in literature. We have also analyzed the "practicality" of XML views constructed by query trees by collecting examples of real XML views extracted from relational databases and evaluating whether or not query trees can capture them. For these real XML views, query trees were sufficiently expressive. Details can be found in [7].

5.1 Limitations of Query Trees

Although query trees are quite expressive, there are some restrictions.

Values must come from the relational database. We do not allow constants to be introduced as values in leaves, nor do we allow functions to calculate new values from values in the database. Allowing constant values in leaves is potentially useful (for example, to add a version number to the view), but they are not interesting from the perspective of updates to the relational database nor can they themselves be updated since they are not part of the database schema. Calculating a value from a set of values (e.g. taking the average of a relational column) creates a one to many mapping which cannot be updated; research on relational views also disallows this case. However, calculating a new value from a single value in the database (e.g. translating length in centimeters to length in inches) could be allowed as long the reverse function was also specified.

Queries are trees rather than graphs. This restriction disallows recursive queries, which are also disallowed in SilkRoute [15]. For example, suppose the relational database contained a relation Patriarchs(PName, CName) with instance {(John, Marc), (John, Chris), (Justin, John)}. An XML view of this that one might wish to construct would be:

```
<Patriarch>
 <Name>Justin</Name>
 <Children>
    <Name>John</Name>
    <Children> <Name>Marc</Name>
               <Name>Chris</Name>
    </Children>
 </Children>
</Patriarch>
```

Since recursive queries cannot be mapped to select-project-join queries, our technique would have to be extended significantly to reason about them.

On the other hand, query trees are flexible enough to represent heterogeneous structures (e.g. the view in Figure 5).

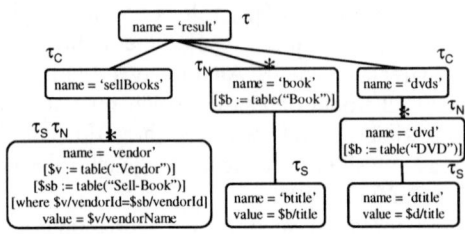

Figure 8: Example of query tree

It can also represent query trees with a repeating leaf node, as shown in Figure 8 (note that *vendor* is labeled with τ_N and τ_S). The XML view resulting from this query tree is as follows:

```
<result>
  <sellBooks>
    <vendor>Amazon</vendor>
    <vendor>Barnes and Nobel</vendor>
  </sellBooks>
  <book><btitle>Unix Network Programming</btitle></book>
  <book><btitle>Computer Networks</btitle></book>
  ...
  <dvds>
    <dvd><dtitle>Friends</dtitle></dvd>
    ...
  </dvds>
</result>
```

It turns out that XML views with heterogeneous content and repeating leaves arise frequently in practice, but that recursive views are not common. We therefore believe that the above restrictions do not limit the usefulness of our approach.

5.2 Power of Expression

We now compare the expressive power of query trees with SilkRoute's *view forests* [15], XPERANTO [22], and DB2 DAD files [9].

XPERANTO [22] can express all queries in XQuery. View forests [15] are capable of expressing any query in the XQueryCore that does not refer to element order, use recursive functions or use is/is not operators. Query trees present the same limitations as [15], and are also not capable of expressing *if/then/else* expressions; sequences of expressions (since we require that the result of the query always be an XML document); function applications; and arithmetic and set operations. Input functions are also a limitation of query trees; in contrast to SilkRoute, variables cannot be bound to the results of expressions.

DB2 XML Extender provides mappings from relations to XML through DAD files. Mappings can be done in two ways: using a single SQL statement (by using the SQL_stmt element in the DAD file), or using the RBD_node mapping. The SQL_stmt method allows only a single SQL statement, so XML views with heterogeneous structures (like the one in Figure 5) can not be constructed. The RBD_node method allows heterogeneous structures, since instead of specifying a single SQL statement for the XML extraction, the user specifies, for each XML element or attribute in the XML view, the table and attribute name from which the data must be retrieved. It is also possible to specify conditions for each XML node in the DAD file (join conditions and selection conditions). DB2 DAD files with RDB_node method are equivalent to query trees in expressive power, since all the data come directly from the relational database and functions cannot be applied over the retrieved data. This is meaningful, since DB2 DAD files represent features that are useful in practice, and because this subset can easily be mapped to relational views.

6 Related Work

There are several proposals for exporting and querying XML views of relational databases [8, 15, 22, 23]. For updates, [28] presents a round trip case study, where XML documents are stored in relational databases, reconstructed and then updated. In this case, it is always possible to translate the updates back to the underlying relational database. Our approach differs since we address updates of *legacy* databases through XML views.

Commercial relational databases offer support for extracting XML data from relations as well as restricted types of updates. In SQL Server [11], an XML view generated by an annotated XML Schema can be modified using *updategrams*. To update, the user provides a before and after image of the XML view [12]. The system computes the difference between the images and generates SQL update statements. The views supported by this approach are very restricted: joins are through keys and foreign keys, and nesting is controlled to avoid redundancy. This corresponds to our well-nested query trees, which are therefore provably updatable with respect to all insertions, deletions and modifications. Oracle [14] offers the specification of an annotated XML Schema, but the only possible update is to insert an XML document that agrees with the schema. IBM DB2 XML Extender [9] requires that updates be issued directly in the relational tables.

Native XML databases also support updates [26, 16, 24]. The goal of all these systems differs from ours since they do not update through views.

7 Conclusions

In this paper, we present a technique for updating relational databases through XML views. The views are constructed using query trees, which allow nesting as well as heterogeneous sets of tuples, and can be used to capture mixed content, grouping, as well as repeating text elements and text elements with attributes.

The main contributions of this paper are the mapping of the XML view to a set of underlying relational views, and the mapping of updates on an XML view instance to a set of updates on the underlying relational views. By providing these mappings, the XML update problem is reduced to the relational view update problem and existing techniques on updates through views [13, 17, 2, 20] can be leveraged. As an example, we show how to use the approach of [13] to produce side-effect free updates on the underlying relational database.

Another benefit of our approach is that query trees are agnostic with respect to a query language. Query trees represent an intermediate query form, and any (subset of an) XML query language that can be mapped to this form could be used as the top level language. In particular, we have implemented our approach in a system called *Pataxó* that uses a subset of XQuery to build the XML views and translates XQuery expressions into query trees as an intermediate representation [6]. Similarly, our update language represents an intermediate form that could be mapped into from a number of high-level XML update languages (using a static evaluation of which updates are to be performed). In our implementation, we use a graphical user interface which allows users to click on the update point or (in the case of a set oriented update) specify the path in a separate window and see what portions of the tree are affected.

In future work, we plan to study the updatability of XML views using other proposals of updates through relational views in the literature. We also plan to extend the language to include other features such as aggregates, and to extend the model to include order.

References

[1] S. Abiteboul, D. Quass, J. McHugh, J. Widom, and J. Wiener. The Lorel Query Language for Semistructured Data. *International Journal on Digital Libraries*, 1(1):68–88, 1997.

[2] F. Bancilhon and N. Spyratos. Update semantics of relational views. *ACM Transactions on Database Systems*, 6(4), Dec. 1981.

[3] P. Bohannon, S. Ganguly, H. Korth, P. Narayan, and P. Shenoy. Optimizing view queries in ROLEX to support navigable result trees. In *Proceedings of VLDB 2002*, Hong Kong, China, Aug. 2002.

[4] A. Bonifati, D. Braga, A. Campi, and S. Ceri. Active XQuery. In *ICDE*, San Jose, California, Feb. 2002.

[5] V. Braganholo, S. Davidson, and C. Heuser. On the updatability of XML views over relational databases. In *Proceedings of WEBDB 2003*, San Diego, CA, June 2003.

[6] V. Braganholo, S. Davidson, and C. Heuser. UXQuery: building updatable XML views over relational databases. In *Brazilian Symposium on Databases*, pages 26–40, Manaus, AM, Brazil, 2003.

[7] V. Braganholo, S. Davidson, and C. Heuser. Propagating XML View Updates to a Relational Database. Technical Report TR-341, UFRGS, Porto Alegre, RS, Brazil, Feb. 2004.

[8] S. Chaudhuri, R. Kaushik, and J. Naughton. On relational support for XML publishing: Beyond sorting and tagging. In *Proceedings of SIGMOD 2003*, San Diego, CA, June 2003.

[9] J. Cheng and J. Xu. XML and DB2. In *Proceedings of ICDE'00*, San Diego, CA, 2000.

[10] J. Clark and S. DeRose. XML Path Language (XPath) Version 1.0. W3C Recomendation, Nov. 1999.

[11] A. Conrad. A Survey of Microsoft SQL Server 2000 XML Features. MSDN Library. *http://msdn.microsoft.com/library/en-us/dnexxml/html/xml07162001.asp*. Jul 2001.

[12] A. Conrad. Interactive microsoft SQL Server & XML online tutorial. *http://www.topxml.com/tutorials/main.asp?id=sqlxml*.

[13] U. Dayal and P. A. Bernstein. On the correct translation of update operations on relational views. *ACM Transactions on Database Systems*, 8(2):381–416, Sept. 1982.

[14] A. Eisenberg and J. Melton. SQL/XML is making good progress. *SIGMOD RECORD*, 31(2), 2002.

[15] M. Fernández, Y. Kadiyska, D. Suciu, A. Morishima, and W.-C. Tan. Silkroute: A framework for publishing relational data in XML. *ACM Transactions on Database Systems (TODS)*, 27(4):438–493, Dec. 2002.

[16] H. V. Jagadish, S. Al-Khalifa, A. Chapman, L. V. Lakshmanan, A. Nierman, S. Paparizos, J. M. Patel, D. Srivastava, N. Wiwatwattana, Y. Wu, and C. Yu. TIMBER: A native XML database. *The VLDB Journal*, 11(4):274–291, 2002.

[17] A. M. Keller. Algorithms for translating view updates to database updates for views involving selections, projections, and joins. In *Proceedings of SIGMOD*, pages 154–163, Portland, Oregon, Mar. 1985. ACM.

[18] M. Keller. The role of semantics in translating view updates. *IEEE Computer*, 19(1):63–73, 1986.

[19] A. Laux and L. Martin. XUpdate WD, Sept. 2000. Working Draft. *http://www.xmldb.org/xupdate/xupdate-wd.html*.

[20] J. Lechtenbörger. The impact of the constant complement approach towards view updating. In *Proceedings of PODS 2003*, pages 49–55, San Diego, CA, June 2003.

[21] L. A. Rowe and K. A. Shoens. Data abstraction, views and updates in RIGEL. In *SIGMOD*, pages 71–81, Boston, Massachusetts, 1979.

[22] J. Shanmugasundaram, J. Kiernan, E. Shekita, C. Fan, and J. Funderburk. Querying XML views of relational data. In *Proceedings of VLDB 2001*, Roma, Italy, Sept. 2001.

[23] J. Shanmugasundaram, E. J. Shekita, R. Barr, M. J. Carey, B. G. Lindsay, H. Pirahesh, and B. Reinwald. Efficiently publishing relational data as XML documents. *The VLDB Journal*, pages 65–76, 2000.

[24] Software AG. Tamino XML Server, 2002. *http://www.softwareag.com/tamino/details.htm*.

[25] I. Tatarinov, Z. Ives, A. Halevy, and D. Weld. Updating XML. In *Proceedings of SIGMOD 2001*, Santa Barbara, CA, May 2001.

[26] The Apache Software Foundation. Apache Xindice. *http://xml.apache.org/xindice*, 2002.

[27] L. Tucherman, A. L. Furtado, and M. A. Casanova. A pragmatic approach to structured database design. In *VLDB*, pages 219–231, Florence, Italy, Oct. 1983.

[28] L. Wang, M. Mulchandani, and E. A. Rundensteiner. Updating XQuery Views Published over Relational Data: A Round-trip Case Study. In *Proc. of XML Database Symposium*, Berlin, Germany, Sept. 2003.

XWAVE: Optimal and Approximate Extended Wavelets for Streaming Data

Sudipto Guha

University of Pennsylvania
sudipto@cis.upenn.edu

Chulyun Kim

Seoul National University
cykim@kdd.snu.ac.kr

Kyuseok Shim

Seoul National University
shim@ee.snu.ac.kr

Abstract

Wavelet synopses have been found to be of interest in query optimization and approximate query answering. Recently, extended wavelets were proposed by Deligiannakis and Roussopoulos for data sets containing multiple measures. Extended wavelets optimize the storage utilization by attempting to store the same wavelet coefficient across different measures. This reduces the bookkeeping overhead and more coefficients can be stored. An optimal algorithm for minimizing the error in representation and an approximation algorithm for the complementary problem was provided.

However, both their algorithms take linear space. Synopsis structures are often used in environments where space is at a premium and the data arrives as a continuous stream which is too expensive to store. In this paper, we give algorithms for extended wavelets which are space sensitive, i.e., use space which is dependent on the size of the synopsis (and at most on the logarithm of the total data) and operates in a streaming fashion. We present better optimal algorithms based on dynamic programming and a near optimal approximate greedy algorithm. We also demonstrate the performance benefits of our algorithms compared to previous ones through experiments on real-life and synthetic data sets.

1 Introduction

Approximate query processing has recently emerged as

Permission to copy without fee all or part of this material is granted provided that the copies are not made or distributed for direct commercial advantage, the VLDB copyright notice and the title of the publication and its date appear, and notice is given that copying is by permission of the Very Large Data Base Endowment. To copy otherwise, or to republish, requires a fee and/or special permission from the Endowment.

Proceedings of the 30th VLDB Conference, Toronto, Canada, 2004

a viable solution for dealing with the huge amounts of data, the high query complexities, and the increasingly stringent response-time requirements that characterize decision support systems (DSS) applications.

Due to the exploratory nature of many DSS applications, in several scenarios such as ad-hoc mining or dealing with remote data [8, 1] approximate answers obtained from synopses suffice. In DSS applications, databases with multiple measures are common. For example, market basket database may include information on the revenue, the quantity of being sold and the profits. One natural and widely used tool for synopses with multiple measures is approximate Wavelet representation.

Traditionally, wavelet approximation methods in this multi-measure scenario used either decomposition on individual dimensions, or treated the data as a vector and applied a multidimensional decomposition. As pointed out by Deligiannakis and Roussopoulos in [3], these methods may result in suboptimal solutions. It is not hard to see that the former may store the same coordinate for more than one measure – which stores the coordinate of the coefficient multiple times and wastes space. The latter on the other hand, may be forced to store very small number of coordinate values of which only a few coefficients might help reduce significantly the error and not be effective as well. To remedy this, extended wavelets were proposed in [3]. This problem seeks to optimize the storage utilization by attempting to store the same wavelet coefficient across different measures, thereby eliminating the bookkeeping overhead for one (or possibly, more) of them. They gave an optimal algorithm for the sum of squared error between the representation of the data achieved by the synopsis and the input. They also gave a faster 2-approximation algorithm for the problem of maximizing the sum of weighted squares of the representation, termed as "benefit". The benefit and error add up to weighted sum of squares of the input coefficients and is therefore fixed, thus the problems can be thought of as"complimentary". They also demonstrated that extended wavelets achieve better estimation quality compared to multidimensional wavelets in several cases.

However, there are two problems with the proposed solutions. (i) Both their algorithms require linear space. Synopsis structures are frequently used in environments where space is at a premium and the data arrives as a continuous stream which is too expensive to store. Thus, linear space algorithms are not desirable in such scenarios. (ii) An approximation algorithm for maximizing the benefit does not give a good approximation algorithm for minimizing error, e.g., suppose the optimum solution had benefit 99 and error 1. Suppose a 2-approximation of the benefit achieved a benefit of 50 (which is more than $\frac{99}{2}$) — but the error of this solution is 50 as well, 50 times the optimum error.

1.1 Our contributions

We make the following contributions:

- To address the problem of linear space, we present optimal algorithms for extended wavelets which are space sensitive, i.e., use space which is dependent on the size of the synopsis (and at most on the logarithm of the total data size) and operates in a streaming fashion.

- For the problem of no guarantee on error by the previous approximation algorithm, we give an algorithm that has error *less than or equal* to the error of the optimum solution (therefore at least as much benefit), but relaxes the space bound to store a few extra coefficients (at most as many as the number of different measures).

- We also demonstrate how to adapt all the above algorithms to the context of streaming data (which connects to the linear space requirement of previous work), i.e., given multidimensional points as a stream we construct the coefficients on the fly as well as maintain the synopsis. This is particularly of use in modeling time series data.

- Through experiments on real-life and synthetic data sets, we demonstrate that our proposed algorithms have significant performance benefits while requiring much less space.

We would like to mention that if the space bound is indeed *strict*, we can give a different $(1 + \epsilon)$-approximation algorithm for the optimum error preserving the space bound. In this process, we show a *non-trivial connection* between extended wavelets and histograms similar to the V-Optimal objective. The complexity of the algorithm is asymptotically the same as the approximation algorithm presented here. However, due to space limitations, this connection cannot be described in this paper. It can be found in [7]. Furthermore, the algorithm that arises from the connection to histograms is somewhat theoretical and significantly complicated to implement, which we relegate to future work.

1.2 Organization

The paper is organized as follows. In the next section, we present related work. In Section 3, we introduce preliminary definitions and the problem of constructing extended wavelet on databases with multiple measures. In Section 4, we introduce improved optimal algorithms. We then present the approximation algorithm in Section 5. Section 6 discusses how to adapt the extended wavelet to stream. In Section 7, we present experimental results. Finally, we make concluding remarks in Section 8. Due to the lack of space, we are unable to present any proofs of the lemmas and theorems. They can be found in [7].

2 Related Work

Several approximation techniques using small summary have been developed for selectivity estimation and approximate query answering. These techniques include histograms [14, 15, 9, 13], wavelets [10, 2] and sampling [4, 20].

Wavelet-based approaches provide a mathematical tool for the hierarchical decomposition of functions, with a long history of successful applications in image processing [12, 16]. In [2, 10, 16], they demonstrated that wavelets can be accurate even in high-dimensional datasets. Recent studies have also demonstrated the applicability of wavelets in selectivity estimation [10], answering range-sum aggregates queries over data cubes [19, 18], approximate query processing [2] and data streams [11, 5].

3 Preliminaries

Wavelets, particularly Haar wavelets, provide useful tools for multi-resolution summarization. In context of databases they have been found to be of interest in query optimization, approximate query answering, and similarity estimation. We review the definition of wavelets before discussing our problem.

3.1 Wavelets

We consider signals indexed on $\{1, \ldots, N\}$, where N is a power of 2. Given a sequence of N numbers $\mathbf{X} = x_1, \ldots, x_N$, which can thought of belonging to the Euclidean space $\Re^N$, we can represent the sequence as a linear combination $\sum_{i=1}^{N} x_i \mathbf{u}_i$ where $\mathbf{u}_i$ is the N-dimensional vector where the i-th coordinate is set to 1 and all other coordinates are 0.

Definition 3.1 The function that equals 1 on set S and zero elsewhere is denoted by $\mathbf{\Gamma}(S)$. A (Haar) wavelet is a function $\mathbf{\Psi}$ on $[1, N]$ of one of the following forms:

- $\frac{1}{\sqrt{N}} \mathbf{\Gamma}([1, N])$

- $\dfrac{\mathbf{\Gamma}([i+1, i+2^j]) - \mathbf{\Gamma}([i+2^j+1, i+2\cdot 2^j])}{2^{(j+1)/2}}$
  where $i = 2k2^j$ for some integer k and $j \geq 0$.

The first type of wavelets is a vector with all coordinates equal to $1/\sqrt{N}$. Example wavelets of the second type are

$$(\tfrac{1}{\sqrt{2}}, -\tfrac{1}{\sqrt{2}}, 0, 0, 0, 0, \ldots, 0, 0),$$
$$(0, 0, \tfrac{1}{\sqrt{2}}, -\tfrac{1}{\sqrt{2}}, 0, 0, \ldots, 0, 0), \ldots$$
$$(\tfrac{1}{2}, \tfrac{1}{2}, -\tfrac{1}{2}, -\tfrac{1}{2}, 0, 0, 0, 0, \ldots,) \ldots$$

There are N wavelets altogether, and they form an orthonormal basis. Thus any N-dimensional vector can be decomposed uniquely as a linear combination of the wavelet vectors (Basis property). Further if $\mathbf{\Psi}, \mathbf{\Psi}'$ are two wavelets then $\langle \mathbf{\Psi}, \mathbf{\Psi}' \rangle$ is 1 if $\mathbf{\Psi} = \mathbf{\Psi}'$ and 0 otherwise (orthonormality).

Every signal can be reconstructed exactly from all its wavelet coefficients (its full *wavelet transform*, an orthonormal linear transformation), as $\mathbf{X} = \sum_i w_i \mathbf{\Psi}_i$ where $w_i = \langle \mathbf{X}, \mathbf{\Psi}_i \rangle$ is defined as the *i-th coefficient*. We will term i as the *index* of $\mathbf{\Psi}_i$. Observe that the wavelet $\tfrac{1}{\sqrt{N}}\mathbf{\Gamma}([1, N])$ will have a coefficient which is $\sqrt{N}$ times the average of all the values.

Both the transformations (to the wavelet representation and from wavelets to the original representation) can be performed in linear time. There are several ways of computing them, for more details consult [16, 10, 5].

3.2 Extended Wavelets

Given N points*, each having M "measures" we have several choices in choosing a wavelet representation. In [16], two choices were outlined – "individual", i.e., to treat each of the dimensions independently or "combined", i.e., to compute the wavelet transform of the columns (dimensions) and then perform a wavelet transform along the rows. In [3], a more flexible strategy termed as "extended wavelets" were proposed, which outperformed the earlier two strategies.

Definition 3.2 An extended wavelet coefficients of N points with M measures is a triplet $< Bit, i, V >$ consisting of:

- A bitmap Bit consisting of M bits. $Bit(j)$ indicates whether the coefficient corresponding to the j-th measure has been stored.

- The i indicates the coefficient number. The space to store Bit and i is denoted by H.

- The stored list of coefficient values V, where the r-th item in the list corresponds to the i-th coefficient of measure j if $Bit(j) = 1$ and $\sum_{j'=1}^{j} Bit(j') = r$. Each of the stored coefficients

---
*Without loss of generality, N is a power of 2.

are assumed to take space S. We denote the i-th coefficient of measure j by w_{ij}.

Extended wavelet provides a flexible storage method and bridges the gap between the two extreme approaches of individual or multi-dimensional decompositions.

Since the most common objective used as an error measure is minimizing L_2 norm of approximation, a natural extension for datasets with multiple measures is how to minimize the weighted sum of the squared error for all measures. If the error (the difference between the original data and the wavelet reconstruction) for i-th data item in j-th measure is denoted by e_{ij} then the optimization problem is the following:

Problem 1 *Given a set of NM wavelet coefficients $\{w_{ij}\}$ points in D-dimensional dataset with M measures, a storage constraint B, and a set of weights W, select the extended wavelet coefficients to be stored in order to minimize the weighted sum $\sum_{i=1}^{N} \sum_{j=1}^{M} W_j \cdot e_{ij}^2$*

Following [16], it is shown in [3] that the above is equivalent to the following:

Problem 2 *Given the NM wavelet coefficients $\{w_{ij}\}$, a storage constraint B, and a set of weights W, select the extended wavelet coefficients to be stored in order to minimize the weighted sum*

$$\sum_{i,j: w_{ij} \text{ is not stored}} W_j \cdot w_{ij}^2$$

Observe that Problem 2 is equivalent the "maximizing the benefit" where the benefit is defined as:

$$\sum_{i,j: w_{ij} \text{ is stored}} W_j \cdot w_{ij}^2$$

But a good approximation for one may not mean a good approximation for the other. A more useful problem in the DSS scenario is:

Problem 3 *Given a N data points in D-dimensions with M measures, a storage constraint B, and a set of weights W, compute and select the extended wavelet coefficients to be stored in order to minimize the error*

$$\sum_{i=1}^{n} \sum_{j=1}^{M} W_j \cdot e_{ij}^2 = \sum_{i,j: w_{ij} \text{ is not stored}} W_j w_{ij}^2$$

in a single pass over the data.

3.3 DynL2: An Optimal Algorithm for Problem 2

An optimal dynamic programming algorithm, $DynL2$, in Figure 1 was proposed in [3] to solve Problem 2.

```
Procedure DynL2(InCoeffs, B, W)
begin
1.  for u :=1 to N*M do
2.    for v :=0 to S+H-1 do {
3.      /* Nothing can be stored! */
4.      OPT[u,v].ben := FORCE[u,v].ben := 0
5.      OPT[u,v].choice := FORCE[u,v].choice := 1
6.    }
7.    for v :=S+H to B do {
8.      OPT[1,v].ben := FORCE[1,v].ben := W[1]*w²[1,1]
9.      OPT[1,v].choice := FORCE[1,v].choice := 3
10.   }
11. for u :=2 to N*M do {
12.   x := 1 + (u-1) div M (Coefficient index)
13.   y := 1 + (u-1) mod M (Measure index)
14.   for j :=S+H to B do {
15.     a := OPT[u-1,v].ben
16.     b := OPT[u-1,v-S-H].ben+W[y]*w²[x,y]
17.     c := FORCE[u-1,v-S].ben+W[y]*w²[x,y]
18.     d := FORCE[u-1,v].ben
19.     if y > 1 {
20.       OPT[u,v].ben := max(a, b, c)
21.       FORCE[u,v].ben := max(d, b, c)
22.     }
23.     else {
24.       OPT[u,v].ben := max(a, b)
25.       FORCE[u,v].ben := b
26.     }
27.     Set OPT[u,v].choice and FORCE[i,j].choice
              to the value 2, 3 or 4, appropriately.
28.     /* If ben = a or ben = d, set choice to 2 */
29.     /* If ben = b, set choice to 3 */
30.     /* If ben = c, set choice to 4 */
31.   }
32. }
33. Reconstruct optimum solution by doing a reverse
        traversal starting from the entry OPT[NM,B], and
        moving based on the choice field of the current entry.
34. return OPT[NM,B].ben (Maximum benefit)
end
```

Figure 1: The DynL2 Algorithm in [3]

Suppose the coefficients are ordered in the canonical order, i.e., w_{ij} is in position $u = i*M + j$ in an array. Let OPT$[u, b]$ the optimal solution with at most b units of space where no coefficient which occurs later than u in the order is being used. We also let FORCE$[u, b]$ be defined as the same as OPT$[u, b]$ except that the solution of the former should store some $w_{ij'}$ with $j' \leq j$ where $u = i*M + j$, i.e., at least for one of the measures the i-th coefficient is stored.

The intuition behind the algorithm is that from $u-1$ to u the algorithm tries to figure out the extra space it would have to use and the benefit derived. Thus four choices, denoted by the variables a, b, c, d in the pseudocode arise depending on w_{ij} being added or not to OPT$[u, b]$ or FORCE$[u, b]$.

The algorithm stores OPT and FORCE, and thus takes $O(NMB)$ space. Since each entry of both OPT and FORCE is evaluated in $O(1)$ time, the time complexity of DynL2 is $O(NMB)$.

In [3], a 2-approximation algorithm with $O(NM^2 \log(NM))$ time and $O(NM)$ space was also proposed for Problem 2.

4 Improved Optimum Algorithms

4.1 OptWaveI: A Simple Algorithm

We first present the definitions that will be used to describe our improved optimum algorithms.

Definition 4.1 Let NEWOPT$[i, b]$ denote the minimum error (maximum benefit) of using at most b space and no coefficient of index larger than i (irrespective of measure). To aid the presentation, we also define:

- Let ALL$[i] = \sum_{j=1}^{M} W_j w_{ij}^2$.

- Let BOTTOM$[i, j]$ be the sum of the j *smallest* items of the set of numbers $W_1 w_{i1}^2, W_2 w_{i2}^2, \ldots, W_M w_{iM}^2$.

- Let TOP$[i, j]$ be the sum of the j *largest* items in the set of numbers $W_1 w_{i1}^2, \ldots, W_M w_{iM}^2$. Naturally,

$$\text{ALL}[i] = \text{TOP}[i, j] + \text{BOTTOM}[i, M - j]$$

Lemma 4.2 *If we are storing the i-th coefficient for a subset $C \subseteq \{1, \ldots, M\}$ of the measures, the best solution is to store the $|C|$ coefficients which have the largest contribution, i.e., $W_j w_{ij}^2$. Thus* TOP$[i, p]$ *gives the best benefit over all subsets C with $|C| = p$. The minimum error of choosing to store $|C|$ coefficients is therefore* BOTTOM$[i, p]$.

Intuition: The above lemma allows us to decouple the choices of subsets C' and C for the coefficients with indexes $i - 1$ and i respectively. Thus, the choice reduces to how much space we allocate to all coefficients of index $i - 1$ versus all coefficients of index i.

As a result, we have the naive optimum algorithm *OptWaveI* shown in Figure 2. This algorithm, as we will see later in the experiments, already performs much better than the *DynL2*. Observe that, without any further improvements (which we will make later), the space required is $O(NM + NB)$. In the $O(NB)$ space, we need to maintain the choice of p for each NEWOPT$[i, b]$. Given p and i, the subset of the measures for which we store the coefficient is automatically the coefficients being in the sorted order of the contribution $W_j w_{ij}^2$. We can prove the following:

Theorem 4.3 *The algorithm OptWaveI evaluates* NEWOPT$[i, b]$ *correctly for all i and b.*

The running time of the algorithm is $O(NMB + NM \log M)$. A sorting with $O(M \log M)$ time allows us to compute all of BOTTOM$[i, M - p]$.

```
Procedure OptWaveI()
begin
1.  SUMALL := 0
2.  for b := 1 to B do
3.    NEWOPT[0,b] := 0
4.  for i := 1 to N do {
5.    for j := 1 to M do
6.      Compute BOTTOM[i,j]
7.    SUMALL := SUMALL + BOTTOM[i,M]
8.    for b := 1 to B do {
9.      if b < H + S (cannot store anything)
10.        NEWOPT[i,b] := SUMALL
11.     else {
12.        NEWOPT[i,b] := NEWOPT[i-1,b] + BOTTOM[i,M]
13.        for p := 1 to M do
14.          if b-H-S*p ≥ 0
15.            NEWOPT[i,b] := min(NEWOPT[i,b],
16.               NEWOPT[i-1,b-H-S*p]+
17.               BOTTOM[i,M-p])
18.      }
19.   }
20. }
end
```

Figure 2: The OptWaveI

The rest of the algorithm take $O(NMB)$ time.

Improved Space Requirement: Note that, to evaluate NEWOPT[i,j] for $1 \leq j \leq B$, we *only* need the array of NEWOPT[$i-1,j$] for $1 \leq j \leq B$. Since for each of NEWOPT[i,j] we need $O(B)$ space to store the information regarding chosen coefficients so far, the space required is $O(B^2)$ only. If we try to *copy* the solutions, the running time will increase due to $O(B)$ time for a single copy operation. We instead use a pointer to speed up coping operation of chosen coefficients so far. Since multiple entries of NEWOPT[i,b] table may be extended from the same NEWOPT[i',b'] with $i' < i$, the selected coefficients for the latter may be shared. Thus, when we deallocate space for NEWOPT[i',b'], we have to make sure not to delete its selected coefficients if they are still pointed by other NEWOPT[i,b]. To handle this, a counter of how many different NEWOPT[i,b] are using NEWOPT[i',b'] is maintained in each NEWOPT[i',b']. We delete all information stored for NEWOPT[i',b'] if it is not used by any NEWOPT[i,b] for $i > i'$. In this process, we will decrease the counters of earlier coefficients selected and may need to delete them. Notice that the amortized cost of all the delete is $O(NB)$ since the total number of deletions can be at most the total number of NEWOPT[i,b] being computed which is $O(NB)$. Thus, we arrive at a $O(NMB)$ time and $O(B^2)$ space algorithm.

Notice that $B \ll NM$, since otherwise there is no benefit in space by storing a synopsis, and thus we improve over *DynL2* in terms of the space bounds.

4.2 OptWaveII: A Better Optimum Algorithm

Definition 4.4 Define $L = \lfloor \frac{B}{S + \frac{H}{M}} \rfloor$. Observe that the optimum algorithm can store at most L coefficients since each coefficient w_{ij} takes up *at least* $S + \frac{H}{M}$ space on the average. The extra space H has to be shared by the coefficients – and the best case scenario is when all coefficients corresponding to an index i have been chosen.

Definition 4.5 Suppose we ordered the coordinates of i for $1 \leq i \leq N$ in a non-increasing order of TOP[i,p] (the maximum benefit of storing p coefficients) into $i_1^p, i_2^p, \ldots, i_n^p$. That is, TOP[$i_j^p, p$] $\geq$ TOP[$i_{j'}^p, p$] if $1 \leq j \leq j' \leq N$. We let BEST[p] = $\{i_j^p | j \leq L\}$. Notice that BEST[p] need not be disjoint as p varies.

Ideally, we would like to say that the subsets of coefficients with index i stored by optimum must belong to $\bigcup_{p=1}^{M}$ BEST[p] for some p, but it may be that there are several solutions with equal error. But in that case one of them will always select coordinates in $\bigcup_{p=1}^{M}$ BEST[p] only and this is captured in the following theorem:

Theorem 4.6 *There exists an optimum solution which only stores the coefficients of the coordinates from $\bigcup_{p=1}^{M}$ BEST[p].*

Intuition: The motivation behind the above theorem is to introduce a *filtering step* where we try to recognize the more useful coordinates. The idea is that given two subsets of coefficients C', all of which correspond to index i' and C which corresponds to i, if we have $|C| = |C'|$, it is better to choose the subset which has the greater contribution to the benefit. Now, the proof of the theorem is more involved, since the optimum may store coefficients with indices i and i' but $|C| \neq |C'|$.

Using the above theorem, we develop a significantly better optimal algorithm *OptWaveII*. The *OptWaveII* first invokes the *OptWavePreProcess* shown in Figure 3 to compute $\bigcup_{p=1}^{M}$ BEST[p]. It then runs the same algorithm as *OptWaveI* in Figure 2 except that the for-loop in line (4) is replaced as below:

for each i $\in \bigcup_{p'=1}^{M}$ BEST[p'] **do** {

Since we consider only $i \in \bigcup_{p'=1}^{M}$ BEST[p'], we add

NEWOPT[n,B] := NEWOPT[n,B]+TOTSUM−SUMALL

where $TOTSUM = \sum_{i=1}^{N}$ BOTTOM[i,M] at end of *OptWaveII* to compute correct value of NEWOPT[n,B]. *TOTSUM* is computed by *OptWavePreProcess*.

We maintain M min-heaps of size L for BEST[p]. The min-heaps are implemented using M arrays of

```
Procedure OptWavePreProcess()
begin
1.  for i :=1 to N do {
2.     Sort the coefficients of i-th coordinate
3.     for p :=1 to M do {
4.        Compute TOP[i,p] using TOP[i,p-1]
5.        if sizeof(BEST[p]) < L {
6.           Insert i with key TOP[i,p] to BEST[p]
7.           count[i] := count[i]+1;
8.        }
9.        else {
10.          if findmin(BEST[p]).key < TOP[i,p] {
11.             Let m be the minimum element in BEST[p]
12.             count[m] := count[m]-1;
13.             if count[m] = 0
14.                Eliminate m from hash table.
15.             Insert i with key TOP[i,p] to BEST[p]
16.             count[i] := count[i]+1;
17.          }
18.       }
19.    }
20.    If count[i] > 0
21.       Store $w_{i1},\ldots,w_{iM}$ in the hash table with $count[i]$.
22. }
end
```

Figure 3: The OptWavePreProcess()

size L. The key of element i (for heap p) is TOP[i,p]. the operations $findmin()$ costs $O(1)$ time and insert/delete costs $O(\log L)$ time. We also maintain a hash table which for the key i will store $w_{i1},\ldots,w_{iM}$ and $count_i$, the number of heaps i is currently present in.

We first compute $\bigcup_{p=1}^{M}$ BEST[p] using *OptWavePreProcess* as in Figure 3. For each i, we compute TOP[i,p] for all p in $O(M\log M)$ time, and the cost of at most M insertions is $O(M\log L)$. Thus in this phase we take $O(NM(\log M + \log L))$ time.

For the second phase, the outer for loop will be executed at most ML times, which is an upper bound on $\bigcup_{p'=1}^{M}$ BEST[p']. The inner loops take time MB.

Thus the time for the second phase is M^2LB, and in total we take $O(NM(\log M + \log L) + \frac{M^2B^2}{S+\frac{H}{M}})^{\dagger}$. The total space bound is $O(MB + B^2)$ where the two terms correspond to the two different phases.

5 An Approximation Algorithm

A natural question arises in this context – if the $O(NMB)$ worst case algorithm can be speeded up. In [3], the authors proposed a greedy 2-approximation of the "benefit" which runs in time $O(NM^2 \log(NM))$. Recall that the benefit of choosing a subset C of coefficients in $\{1,\ldots,M\}$ that is i-th coordinate is defined as $\sum_{j\in C} W_j w_{ij}^2$. The benefit quantifies the

---
†We can assume $ML \leq N$ otherwise we can use a bound of N on the set, and thus the total time is at most $O(NM(\log M + \log L) + NMB)$.

error "saved" by choosing the coefficients in C.

Our approximation at the surface is similar to the 2-approximation algorithm in that it uses benefit to space ratios. However our algorithm will take a different road. Our algorithm will *try to reduce the space subject to maintaining the same quality of solution as the optimum.*

It may appear that we are comparing apples and oranges, but these algorithms are known as *pseudo approximation algorithms* – where we find an approximate solution, but relax some constraints (in this case, space bound) slightly (by $MS + H$). But because in this case we are able to prove that the quality of our solution is at least as good as the optimum (restricted to B), the result can be viewed as approximating the space while keeping the quality fixed. Note, that we assume no knowledge of the quality of the solution beforehand.

Technically our algorithm in this section differs from the 2-approximation in [3] in the following aspects:

1. We use our previous idea of not considering all coefficients.

2. We are more cautious in selecting the subsets for which we compute benefit.

3. Unlike previous work, *our definition of the benefit-space ratio will not be uniform over all subsets.*

4. Our algorithm operates in $O(B)$ space.

5. Unlike previous algorithm, we do not consider inserting coefficients corresponding to the same index i more than once (i.e., if they are ejected).

Before describing the algorithm, we make a few important observations.

Lemma 5.1 *Let $S, H > 0$. Given a sequence $X = \{x_1, x_2, \ldots, x_M\}$ of non-negative numbers in non-increasing order, let $\hat{p}$ be the value of p that maximizes* $\max_{p=1,\ldots,M} \frac{\sum_{j=1}^{p} x_j}{S*p + H}$. *Among every subset $Y \subseteq X = \{x_1, x_2, \ldots, x_M\}$, the subset $Y = \{x_1, x_2, \ldots, x_{\hat{p}}\}$ maximizes* $\frac{\sum_{x_j \in Y} x_j}{S|Y| + H}$.

Definition 5.2 *Let us define* RATIO[i].wt *as follows:*

$$\text{RATIO}[i].wt = \max_{p=1,\ldots,M} \text{TOP}[i,p]/(S*p + H)$$

Let us also define RATIO[i].p as the smallest value p for which the maximum ratio is obtained.

Lemma 5.3 *Suppose $w_{ij_1}, w_{ij_2}, \ldots, w_{ij_M}$ are the coefficients with index i such that $W_{j_u} w_{ij_u}^2 \geq W_{j_v} w_{ij_v}^2$ whenever $u \leq v$. For all $u > $ RATIO[i].p, we have* RATIO[i].$wt \geq W_{j_u} w_{ij_u}^2 / S$. *Furthermore, for all $1 \leq u \leq $* RATIO[$i$].$p$, *we have $W_{j_u} w_{ij_u}^2 / S \geq $* RATIO[$i$].$wt$.

The algorithm: The algorithm *ApproxWave* is given in Figure 4. We will maintain a min-heap of size *at most* $B + M*S + H$. The heap will shrink and grow — but the total space required to store all the coefficients associated with the heap will not exceed $O(B)$. The min-heap will be implemented using an array as before. The elements in the heap will be tuples $(i, p, flag)$ where $flag = 1$ will indicate all the coefficients $w_{ij_1}, \ldots, w_{ij_p}$ are (which define $\text{TOP}[i, p]$) are chosen. $flag = 0$ would mean only the coefficient w_{ij_p} is chosen. We can implement $findmin()$ in $O(1)$ time and insert/delete in $O(\log B)$ time. We will maintain a hash table to store the wavelet coefficients for every tuple $(i, p, flag)$ in min-heap. It is straightforward to observe that the time complexity of the algorithm is $O(NM(\log M + \log B))$ since the size of the heap is bound by B.

Due to the lack of space we cannot prove any of the claims made, but we indicate an outline of the proof. In a very high level, we will show that if we consider the elements in our solution which are not in the optimum, they must have a better benefit to space ratio than the elements in the optimum solution which we have not included. We show the separation by bounding the former from below, and the latter from above, by the key value of the minimum element in the heap.

Observation 5.4 *If the key value of the minimum element in the heap is λ, then any item with key value at least λ must be present in the heap.*

Lemma 5.5 *In the above algorithm, once we reach the condition of $Free < 0$, we have $-(M*S + H) \leq Free < 0$ in all subsequent steps.*

The above lemma can be proved by induction and the proof is omitted due to lack of space. But the lemma implies that we exceed the space bound by *at most M* coefficients. Thus we can bound the size of the heap to be $O(B)$.

Lemma 5.6 *Let $\text{ONES} = \{i | (i, p, 1) \text{ in heap}\}$ and $\text{ZEROS} = \{i | (i, p, 0) \text{ in heap}\}$, then the condition of $\text{ONES} \supseteq \text{ZEROS}$ always holds. That is, if $(i, u, 0)$ is present in the heap at any point, so must be $(i, \text{RATIO}[i].p, 1)$.*

The next set of lemmas will be used as the critical part of the proof for the main theorem of this section that states that the benefit of our solution is *no less* than that of the optimal solution.

Lemma 5.7 *Further let $|\text{ZEROS}|$ be the number of elements of the form $(i, p, 0)$ in the heap, then*

$$B - Free = \sum_{i \in \text{ONES}} (S*\text{RATIO}[i].p + H) + S*|\text{ZEROS}|$$

Procedure ApproxWave()
begin
1. $Free := B$
2. **for** i := 1 **to** N **do** {
3.   Compute $\text{RATIO}[i]$
4.   **if** $(Free \geq 0)$ {
5.   Insert $(i, \text{RATIO}[i].p, 1)$ in heap
         with $key = \text{RATIO}[i].wt$
6. $Free \leftarrow Free - S \cdot \text{RATIO}[i].p - H$
7.   } **else if** $(findmin().key < \text{RATIO}[i].wt)$ {
8.   **while** ($(findmin().key < \text{RATIO}[i].wt)$
         and $(Free < 0)$) {
9.   Suppose the min element was $(i', m_p, flag)$.
10.   **if** $(flag = 1)$ {
11.   **if** $(Free + S(m_p - \text{RATIO}[i].p) \geq 0)$ {
12.   /* leave while loop */
13.   **break**
14.   }
15. $Free \leftarrow Free + S \cdot m_p + H$
16.   }
17.   **else**
18. $Free \leftarrow Free + S$
19.   Remove the min element in the heap.
20.   }
21.   Insert $(i, \text{RATIO}[i].p, 1)$ in heap
         with $key = \text{RATIO}[i].wt$
22. $Free \leftarrow Free - S \cdot \text{RATIO}[i].p - H$
23.   }
24.   **for** $u := \text{RATIO}[i].p + 1$ **to** M {
25.   **if** $(Free \geq 0)$ {
26.   Insert $(i, u, 0)$ with $key = \frac{W_{j_u} w_{ij_u}^2}{S}$
27. $Free \leftarrow Free - S$
28.   } **else if** $(findmin().key \geq \frac{W_{j_u} w_{ij_u}^2}{S})$ **break**
29.   **else** {
30.   Suppose the min element was $(i', m_p, flag)$
31.   **if** $flag = 0$ {
32.   Remove the min element in the heap.
33.   Set $Free \leftarrow Free + S$
34.   } **else if** $(Free + S(m_p - 1) + H < 0)$ {
35.   Remove the min element in the heap.
36.   Set $Free \leftarrow Free + S \cdot m_p + H$
37.   }
38.   Insert $(i, u, 0)$ with $key = \frac{W_{j_u} w_{ij_u}^2}{S}$
39. $Free \leftarrow Free - S$
40.   }
41.   }
42. }
43. Include all the coefficients stored in the heap.
end

Figure 4: The ApproxWave

Corollary 5.8 *The space taken by the solution is at most $B+M*S+H$, i.e., we exceed the budgeted space at most M extra coefficients.*

Before proving the quality of our solution we will have to define some notation. Suppose that λ^* is the ratio of the minimum element after all coefficients have been processed. Thus for any item in the heap and not considered by our algorithm, the key could have been at most λ^*. Suppose the optimum solution uses a set of coefficients corresponding to $S_{opt} \subseteq [1,\ldots,n]$ and we choose a set of coefficients corresponding to $S_{sol} \subseteq [1,\ldots,n]$. For each $i \in S_{opt}$ suppose that the optimal chooses $o(i)$ coefficients (it will choose the best ones) and for $i \in S_{sol}$ suppose that we chose $p(i)$ coefficients.

Lemma 5.9 *Recall that by $w_{ij_1}, w_{ij_2}, \ldots, w_{ij_M}$ we refer to the coefficients of i sorted in non-increasing order of $W_j w_{ij}^2$. The following four conditions hold.*

(P1): *If $i \in S_{opt}$ and $i \notin S_{sol}$ then*

$$\sum_{u=1}^{o(i)} W_{j_u} w_{ij_u}^2 \leq \lambda^*(So(i) + H)$$

(P2): *If $i \notin S_{opt}$ and $i \in S_{sol}$ then*

$$\sum_{u=1}^{p(i)} W_{j_u} w_{ij_u}^2 \geq \lambda^*(Sp(i) + H)$$

(P3): *If i is in both S_{opt}, S_{sol} and $p(i) < o(i)$ then for all $p(i) < u \leq o(i)$ we have $W_{j_u} w_{ij_u}^2 \leq \lambda^* S$.*

(P4): *If i is in both S_{opt}, S_{sol} and $p(i) > o(i)$ then for all $o(i) < u \leq p(i)$ we have $W_{j_u} w_{ij_u}^2 \geq \lambda^* S$.*

Observe that the above lemma shows that for all the coefficients not stored by our solution the benefit is at most λ^* times the space taken by those coefficients[‡]. Likewise, the lemma says that for the coefficients we stored and the optimal solution did not store, the benefit is at least λ^* times the space[§].

Theorem 5.10 *The benefit of our solution is no less than the benefit of the optimum solution (which takes at most B space).*

6 Adapting small space extended wavelet algorithms to streams

Formally, a data stream computation is a space bounded algorithm, where the space is sub-linear in the input. Any input items are accessed sequentially and any item not explicitly stored cannot be accessed again in the same pass. A comprehensive discussion of streaming is beyond the current scope. For our current problem, we need a small space algorithm that that makes one-pass over the data and generates the extended wavelet synopsis. In this scenario we see the data items $x_{i1}, x_{i2}, \ldots, x_{iM}$, and then we proceed to see the data items $x_{(i+1)1}, x_{(i+1)2}, \ldots, x_{(i+1)M}$ and likewise to $i+2$, etc.

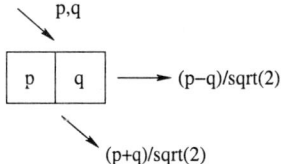

Figure 5: The algorithm A_ℓ

We will draw upon [6] for computing wavelet decompositions. Suppose we have a simple algorithm illustrated in Figure 5 which takes two numbers p, q and outputs the two wavelet coefficients $(p-q)/\sqrt{2}$ and $(p+q)/\sqrt{2}$. Now suppose we made this algorithm, say A_1, repeatedly pick pairs of items from the stream and output the two associated coefficients, but with a difference. Suppose the coefficients corresponding to the difference, e.g. $(p-q)/\sqrt{2}$ are output directly and the sums are handed to a different algorithm A_2 which does exactly the same thing.

As an example consider a single dimension with 8 data values: $8, 7, 6, 5, 4, 3, 2, 1$. A_2 will receive $(8+7)/\sqrt{2}, (6+5)/\sqrt{2}, (4+3)/\sqrt{2}$ and $(2+1)/\sqrt{2}$. From the first two numbers, A_2 will output $\left(\frac{8+7}{\sqrt{2}} - \frac{6+5}{\sqrt{2}}\right)/\sqrt{2}$ immediately and pass the corresponding sum to A_3. The number which is being output is actually $\frac{8+7-6-5}{2}$ and is the coefficient of the wavelet vector whose support is the first half of the input! Thus A_2 will output the coefficients corresponding to wavelet vectors with support 4. A_3 will receive $\frac{8+7+6+5}{2}, \frac{4+3+2+1}{2}$ and output the wavelet coefficient of the wavelet vector with support 8. A_3 will pass the coefficient corresponding to the sum of all the coefficients to A_4. On seeing the end of input A_4 will output this single number.

Observe that each A_ℓ will need only space $O(1)$ since it stores the first value it receives; on seeing a second value it outputs the difference (divided by $\sqrt{2}$), sends the other value to $A_{\ell+1}$ and forgets both the numbers. A_ℓ keeps repeating this process for every pair of answers it sees. When the end-of-input signal is seen it passes the signal to $A_{\ell+1}$.

If one $A_{\ell'}$ receives only one input and then the end of input of the original data, it just output the stored input. *Notice that the division by $\sqrt{2}$ happens at each stage recursively* and the last output is the sum of all the numbers divided by $\sqrt{N}$, or the average of all numbers multiplied by $\sqrt{N}$. Several researchers compute the coefficients differently, by computing the

---

[‡]Including the space required by the bitmaps if we did not store any coefficient for i, whereas optimum stored at least one coefficient.
[§]Once again including the space required by bitmaps.

recursive averages and multiplying by *normalization constants*. The processes are equivalent, and the process described here adapts to streams readily. Due to lack of space, we relegate further details to [7]. See also [16, 10, 5] for further details on wavelets. Summarizing all the above, we get:

Fact 6.1 *Using $O(\log n)$ space we can compute the wavelet decomposition in a single pass. The order in which the coefficients will be output will correspond to a post-order traversal of the complete binary tree defined on the input indices $\{i\}$. Note that n need not be known in advance for the process.*¶

An immediate corollary would be

Corollary 6.2 *Any one-pass algorithm for Problem 1 can be used to get a one-pass algorithm for Problem 3 with an additional space of $O(M \log N)$*

7 Experimental result

We conducted experiments on real-life as well as synthetic data sets. We implemented algorithms DynL2 and GreedyL2 proposed in [3] and compared them against the algorithms proposed in this paper. All experiments reported in this section were performed on Pentium-4 2.8 GHz machine with 512 MB of main memory, running Linux operating system. All the methods are implemented using GCC compiler of Version 2.95.3

Experimental results confirm that our optimal algorithms, optWaveI and optWaveII, are faster than DynL2. The ApproxWave is at least as accurate as GreedyL2 but much faster.

7.1 Synthetic Data Sets

For our synthetic data sets, we implemented a data generator suggested in [3, 2, 17]. The input parameters to the data generator along with their description and default values are as illustrated in Table 1. The generator begins by randomly selecting $n\_regions$ rectangular regions in a N-dimensional array. The volume of any dense region is randomly chosen between V_{min} and V_{max}. Sum_i is the summation of the values for all the cells contained in $n\_regions$ dense regions for measure i. Through the use of Zipf function with parameter Z, Sum_i is partitioned across the $n\_regions$ rectangular regions. Within each region, the values are distributed by using one of the four distributions in Table 2 with skew parameter between z_{max_i} and z_{min_i}. Note that we use the notion of the *Altered-X*∥ distribution to help create pairs of measures with

---

¶As an aside, each of the A_ℓ form a transducer and the above describes a wavelet coefficient computation using transducers.

∥X can be either one of the Center, Middle or Reverse distributions.

Parameter	Description	Default Value
N	Number of dimensions	2
M	Number of measures	30
$Card_i$	Cardinality of dimension i	512
n_regions	Number of dense regions	10
V_{min}	Minimum and maximum volume of regions	4900
V_{max}		4900
Z	Skew across regions	0.5
z_{min_i}, z_{max_i}	Minimum and maximum skew within region i	1, 1
Sum_i	Sum of values for measure i	1,000,000
spCount	Fraction of populated cells in sparse areas	0.05
$spSum_i$	Sum of values of populated cells in sparse area i	0.05

Table 1: Data Generator Input Parameters

Distribution	Description
Center	Cells with smaller L1-distance from center have larger values
Reverse	Cells with smaller L1-distance from center have smaller values
Middle	Consider a hyper-rectangle centered at the region's center, and having for each dimension, half the length of the corresponding region length. Cells with smaller L1-distance from this hyper-rectangle have larger values
Altered-X	This measure follows the same distribution as X distribution, but its values are randomly altered by up to 50%

Table 2: Data Generator Value Distributions

similar, but not identical, data distribution. The generator also populates nonzero cells outside the dense regions. The fraction of such cells is defined by spCount parameter and the total sum of the values of these cells is denoted by the $spSum_i$ parameter.

In each experiment, the parameters of the data generator were set to the default values, unless specified otherwise.

7.2 Algorithms

We conducted a comprehensive performance evaluation of the various schemes. Specifically, we show the performance figures of the following schemes:

- **DynL2:** This is our implementation of the dynamic programming algorithm DynL2 in [3]. It is an improved version of [3] using less space.
- **GreedyL2:** It is the greedy approximate algorithm in [3] which uses a heap instead of an AVL-

tree.

- **OptWaveI and OptWaveII:** It represents our optimal algorithms presented in Section 4.1 and Section 4.2 respectively.

- **ApproxWave:** It represents approximate algorithm described in Section 5.

7.3 Synthetic Data Sets
7.3.1 Behavior of All Algorithms

Figure 6 shows the results of optimum and approximate algorithms with varying the number of measures M from 2 to 6. We also varied the space constraint B from 1K to 10K bytes. The initial two measures are the ones with distributions Center and Middle, and the measures that are later added are: Reverse, Altered-Center, Altered-Reverse, Altered-Middle. We fixed $Card_i$ to 1024. Other parameters were set to default values. The execution times are shown using a log scale.

Both OptWaveI and OptWaveII are much faster than traditional optimum algorithm DynL2. The execution time for OptWaveII is again at least two orders of magnitude faster than DynL2. Our ApproxWave is also much faster than traditional GreedyL2. Furthermore, when the value of B is small (e.g. $B = 1K$ bytes), the optimum algorithm OptWaveII is actually even faster than the approximation algorithm GreedyL2. As we increase B, GreedyL2 starts to win optWaveII with larger M values and finally becomes better regardless of the value of M (e.g. $B = 4K$ bytes). In Figure 6, we present two graphs only for $B = 1K$ and $B = 4K$ bytes.

7.3.2 Behavior of Approximate Algorithms

To see the behavior of approximate algorithms, we tested synthetic data sets with both GreedyL2 and ApproxWave.

Storage Space: In Figure 7-(a) and Figure 7-(b), we present the execution time and average weighted sum squared error for approximation algorithms as the storage space is varied from 1K to 1M bytes. We set the number of measures M to 30 and the skew parameter of the data distributions within each region was set to 1.0. The errors of both GreedyL2 and ApproxWave are very close, but the error of ApproxWave is slightly better than that of GreedyL2. Furthermore, the speed of ApproxWave is much faster than that of GreedyL2.

Skew within Region: We modified the zipfian parameter controlling the skew of the measure's data distributions within each region from 0.5 to 4 and we set B to 100K bytes. The Figure 7-(c) and Figure 7-(d) presents the obtained results for the average weighted sum of squared error and execution time respectively. When the skew is small, the values of the measures are very similar and most of *detail wavelet coefficients* become zero. Thus, the error becomes very small. As the skew increases more, the measure values become different and the detail wavelet coefficients start to have non-zero values. It results in larger errors. However, as the skew parameter increases even larger (after 1.5) values, the large coefficients are restricted to a smaller area for each distribution. This produces the reduction of the weighted sum of squared error of the results, as the number of significantly influencing coefficients becomes smaller. On the other hand, the probability that coefficients from multiple measures become important simultaneously becomes smaller. This explains the shape of the average weighted sum of squared error graph in Figure 7-(d). Even though the graphs of the errors of both algorithms are close, the error of ApproxWave is slightly better that that of GreedyL2. However, regardless of skew changes, the execution times do not show any big change. It is expected since the time complexities of both algorithms are not dependent on skew in data distribution. ApproxWave is again much faster than that of GreedyL2.

Number of Measures: We present the execution time with varying the number of measures M from 5 to 50 in Figure 8. The distributions of measures are cyclically repeated in order of Center, Middle, Reverse, Altered-Center, Altered-Reverse and Altered-Middle. We set B to 100K bytes. The experiments validate our earlier analysis that the time complexities of $GreedyL2$ and $ApproxWave$ are $O(NM^2 \log(NM))$ and $O(NM(\log M + \log B))$ respectively. Furthermore, since the space requirement of GreedyL2 is much larger than that of ApproxWave, as the number of measures increases, GreedyL2 starts to suffer from some memory problem and thus its running time degrades significantly. The execution time of GreedyL2 is slower than that of ApproxWave up to in an order of magnitude.

7.4 Real-life Data Set

For our real-life data experiments, we used the Pacific Northwest weather measurement data from the state of Washington [**] The coordinates of the dataset are day and time. We selected one year dataset and used the solar irradiance, wind speed, wind peak, air temperature, dewpoint temperature and relative humidity for the station in the university of Washington. We set a weight value of 3 to the first two measure, a weight value of 2 to the next two measures and a weight value of 1 to the remaining measures. The number of tuples in the dataset is 525600. We computed the average weighted sum of squared absolute errors.

[**] It is available from http://www-k12.atmos.washington.edu/ k12/grayskies/nw_weather.html.

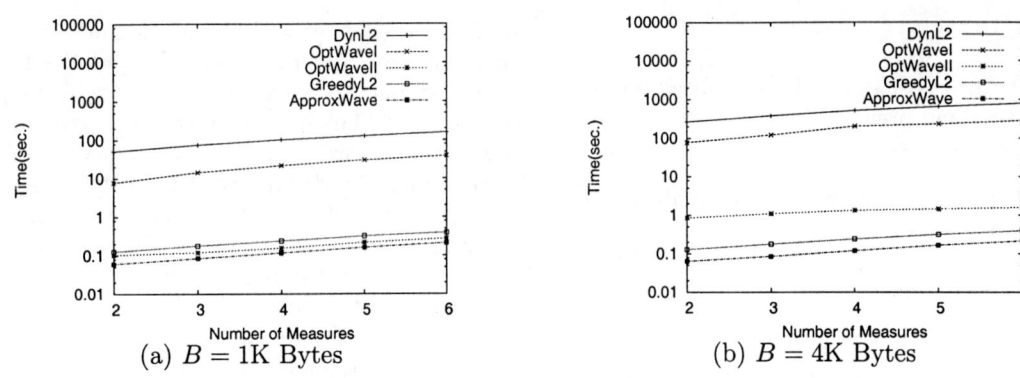

Figure 6: Execution Time with Varying M

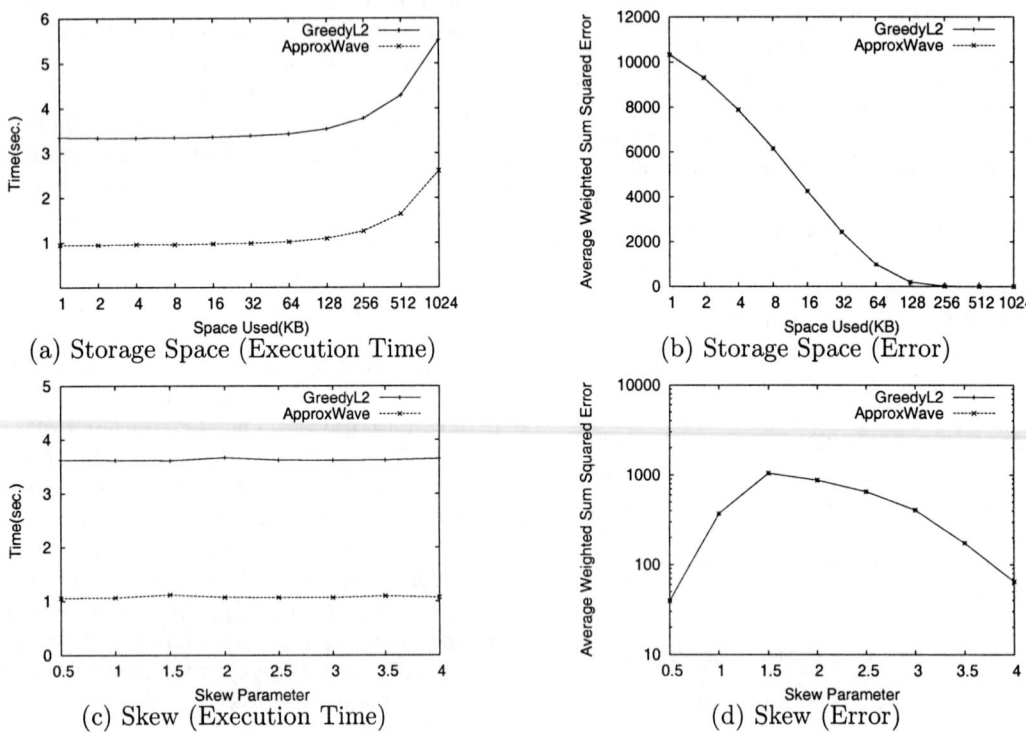

Figure 7: Approximate Algorithms

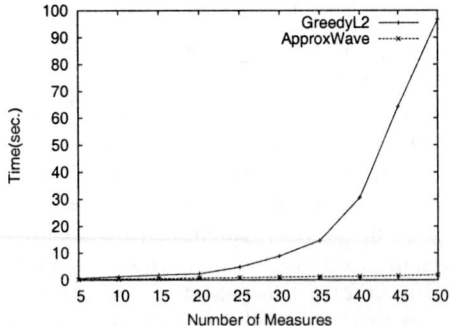

Figure 8: Execution Time with Varying M by Approximate Algorithms

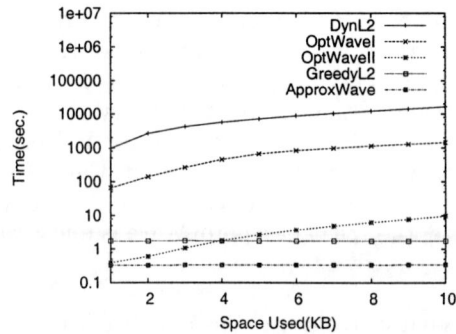

Figure 9: Execution Time for Real-life Dataset

Figure 9 presents the result for execution time, as the storage bound B was varied from 1K to 10K bytes. The execution times of the three optimum algorithms grow linearly in increasing B as the time complexities of the algorithms illustrate. The value of B affects the execution times of the approximation algorithms very little as expected. Our results show that the execution time for OptWaveII is at least two orders of magnitude better than DynL2. The execution time for ApproxWave is again much faster than GreedyL2 too. We believe that our results clearly demonstrate the significant performance gains by both OptWave and ApproxWave algorithms compared to traditional DynL2 and GreedyL2 algorithms.

8 Summary

Degligiannakis and Roussopoulos [3], pointed out that traditional wavelet approximation methods for multiple dimensions may result in suboptimal space utilization in constructing synopses, and proposed extended wavelets. They gave an optimal algorithm for the sum of squared error and a faster 2-approximation for the problem of maximizing the weighted sum of squares of the representation, termed as "benefit". This approximation algorithm however does not guarantee the error. However, both their algorithms required linear space.

To address the problem of linear space, we presented optimal algorithms for extended wavelets which are space sensitive. We gave an algorithm that has error *less than or equal* to the error of the optimum solution (therefore at least as much benefit), but relaxes the space bound to store a few extra coefficients (at most as many as the number of different measures). We also demonstrate how to adapt all the above algorithms to the context of streaming data. Through experiments on real and synthetic data sets, we demonstrated that our proposed algorithms have significant performance benefits while requiring much less space.

Acknowledgments

The authors wish to thank the referees for many useful comments which have helped in improving the presentation of the manuscript. The work was supported by the Ministry of Information and Communication in Korea through the University Information Technology Research Center (ITRC) Support Program.

References

[1] L. Amsaleg, P. Bonnet, M. J. Franklin, A. Tomasic, and T. Urhan. Improving responsiveness for wide-area data access. *IEEE Data Eng.*, 20(3):3–11, 1997.

[2] K. Chakrabarti, M. N. Garofalakis, R. Rastogi, and K. Shim. Approximate query processing using wavelets. In *VLDB Conference*, 2000.

[3] A. Deligiannakis and N. Roussopoulos. Extended wavelets for multiple measures. In *SIGMOD Conference*, 2003.

[4] P. B. Gibbons and Y. Matias. New sampling-based summary statistics for improving approximate query answers. In *SIGMOD Conference*, 1998.

[5] A. C. Gilbert, Y. Kotidis, S. Muthukrishnan, and M. Strauss. Surfing wavelets on streams: One-pass summaries for approximate aggregate queries. In *VLDB Conference*, 2001.

[6] S. Guha, P. Indyk, S. Muthukrishnan, and M. Strauss. Histogramming data streams with fast per-item processing. In *ICALP*, 2002.

[7] S. Guha, C. Kim, and K. Shim. XWAVE: Optimal and approximate extended wavelets for streaming data. Techical Report, Seoul National University, Seoul, Korea, July 2004.

[8] J. M. Hellerstein, P. J. Haas, and H. J. Wang. Online aggregation. In *SIGMOD Conference*, 1997.

[9] Y. E. Ioannidis and V. Poosala. Histogram-based approximation of set-valued query-answers. In *Proceedings of 25th International Conference on Very Large Data Bases*, Edinburgh, Scotland, September 1999.

[10] Y. Matias, J. S. Vitter, and M. Wang. Wavelet-Based Histograms for Selectivity Estimation. *SIGMOD Conference*, 1998.

[11] Y. Mattias, J. S. Vitter, and M. Wang. Dynamic Maintenance of Wavelet-Based Histograms. *VLDB Conference*, 2000.

[12] A. Natsev, R. Rastogi, and K. Shim. WALRUS: A Similarity Retrieval Algorithm for Image Databases. In *SIGMOD Conference*, 1999.

[13] V. Poosala and V. Ganti. Fast approximate answers to aggregate queries on a data cube. In *SSDBM*, 1999.

[14] V. Poosala and Y. E. Ioannidis. Selectivity estimation without the attribute value independence assumption. In *VLDB Conference*, 1997.

[15] V. Poosala, Y. E. Ioannidis, P. J. Haas, and E. J. Shekita. Improved histograms for selectivity estimation of range predicates. In *SIGMOD Conference*, 1996.

[16] E. J. Stollnitz, T. D. DeRose, and D. H. Salesin. *Wavelets for Computer Graphics - Theory and Applications*. Morgan Kaufmann, San Francisco, CA, 1996.

[17] J. Vitter and M. Wang. Approximate computation of multidimensional aggregates on sparse data u sing wavelets. *Proceedings of SIGMOD*, pages 193–204, June 1999.

[18] J. S. Vitter and M. Wang. Approximate computation of multidimensional aggregates of sparse data using wavelets. In *SIGMOD Conference*, 1999.

[19] J. S. Vitter, M. Wang, and B. R. Iyer. Data cube approximation and histograms via wavelets. In *CIKM*, 1998.

[20] Y.-L. Wu, D. Agrawal, and A. E. Abbadi. Using the golden rule of sampling for query estimation. In *SIGMOD Conference*, 2001.

REHIST: Relative Error Histogram Construction Algorithms

Sudipto Guha

University of Pennsylvania
sudipto@cis.upenn.edu

Kyuseok Shim

Seoul National University
shim@ee.snu.ac.kr

Jungchul Woo

Seoul National University
jcwoo@kdd.snu.ac.kr

Abstract

Histograms and Wavelet synopses provide useful tools in query optimization and approximate query answering. Traditional histogram construction algorithms, such as V-Optimal, optimize absolute error measures for which the error in estimating a true value of 10 by 20 has the same effect of estimating a true value of 1000 by 1010. However, several researchers have recently pointed out the drawbacks of such schemes and proposed wavelet based schemes to minimize relative error measures. None of these schemes provide satisfactory guarantees – and we provide evidence that the difficulty may lie in the choice of wavelets as the representation scheme.

In this paper, we consider histogram construction for the known relative error measures. We develop optimal as well as fast approximation algorithms. We provide a comprehensive theoretical analysis and demonstrate the effectiveness of these algorithms in providing significantly more accurate answers through synthetic and real life data sets.

1 Introduction

Motivation and Background: Histograms and Wavelet synopsis provide useful tools in query optimization [13] and approximate query answering [1]. Recently these techniques have also been used in constructing short signatures of time series data for various mining tasks [2]. In all these problems, given a sequence of data values $x_1, \ldots, x_n$, the task is to construct a suitable summary of the data which can be stored in small space (e.g. a small fixed number, say B, of the n coefficients in the Wavelet transform, or a histogram involving B buckets). In the query optimization context, the value x_i is the frequency of i and is non-negative. In the context of time-series data, [2], x_i is the value seen in the stream at time i and may be arbitrary. We make no assumptions about x_i.

Given a query that asks the value at i, a suitable "estimate" of x_i, say $\hat{x}_i$, is constructed and returned as an answer. This is known as a "point query". The error, defined as the *absolute error*, incurred in the process for the point i is $|x_i - \hat{x}_i|$. The objective of good synopsis construction algorithms is to build the summary structure restricted by B that minimizes a suitable function of these errors. Histograms are typically defined to be a piecewise constant representation[*], and are constrained to have at most B pieces or "buckets". The popular V-Optimal histogram minimizes the sum of squares of absolute errors (i.e. $\sum_i (x_i - \hat{x}_i)^2$) and was introduced in [12]. Approximation algorithms for the V-Optimal histogram were given in [14, 9, 8, 5, 7].

Authors of [16, 4] rightly point out that, the measures (e.g. sum, sum of squares, etc.) which minimize some function of the absolute errors at the data points are not the most desirable measures[†]. The drawback of these measures involving the absolute errors is that the error in approximating $x_i = 1000$ by $\hat{x}_i = 1010$ has the same effect of approximating $x_i = 10$ by $\hat{x}_i = 20$. In percentages, the first is a 0.1% error and the latter is a 100% error. Notice, if we multiply all the involved numbers by 100, the disparity in the error remains — the disparity is scale independent and arises because 10 is *relatively small* compared to 1000.

The relative error measures seek to minimize a suit-

---

[*]Quantile summaries are sometimes referred as histograms as well, but we will use histograms to denote piecewise constant representations.

[†]The discussion here is limited to point queries. For "range queries", which will be out of scope for this paper, the reader is asked to follow the pointers in [15, 6, 10].

able function of $|x_i - \hat{x}_i|/\max\{|x_i|, c\}$, where c is a sanity constant which is used to reduce excessive domination of relative error by small data values. The authors of [16] propose the use of deterministic thresholding to select the wavelet coefficients of the data value. The work in [4] introduces probabilistic thresholding and provides the first theoretical guarantees on the quality of the approximation achieved by the constructed wavelet synopsis. However their proposed solution using wavelets suffers the following drawbacks:

- **Difficulty of optimizing relative error measures.** It is observed in [4] that wavelets are not easily amenable for minimizing functions other than L_2 norms. The fundamental problem is that a change of any wavelet coefficient affects more than a single data value. In fact, in [4], convex programming (not known to be solvable in polynomial time) was used. To simplify, the authors of [4] restricted the problem to select coefficients from the wavelet representation of the data. However if the coefficients are selected from the wavelet representation, the relative error measures do not monotonically decrease as the number of selected coefficients increase.

  Consider a simple example $X = [4, 3, 2, 1]$ whose Haar wavelet transform with normalization is $[2.5, 1, 0.35, 0.35]$. If we do not choose any coefficient to store, the zero vector has 100% error for the maximum relative error (considered in [4]). However, choosing any single coefficient to store gives an error larger than 100% relative error. Interestingly, if we replace 2.5 by 1.6 and use the corresponding wavelet vector, the maximum relative error becomes 60%.

- **Expectation guarantees.** In [16], the authors do not provide any error guarantee for relative error measures with their scheme. In [4], they give expected guarantees on *both* the error and the space used. For example, if we have a solution with error 9 and space 1 (in some unit) and a second solution with error 1 and space 9; then choosing a solution with the same probability 0.5 for each solution will give a solution with expected space and expected error 5. Thus although in expectation we have a space bound of 5 and error bound 5, if we choose any one of the two solutions we will have to settle for twice the expected space or twice the expected error *irrespective* of the number of times we repeat the experiment. Expectation guarantees would have been useful if *any one* of the parameters were obeyed strictly. In fact preliminary calculations show that the variance of the space requirement of algorithms in [4] can be as large as $\Theta(B)$ implying that the space bound is likely to be overshot significantly.

The above issues clearly demonstrate the need for algorithms that minimize relative error measures optimally. Motivated by the above we consider histogram representations instead of wavelet synopses. Many researchers have the following in support of histograms: (1) Any (reasonable) error measure does not increase as the number of buckets increase (2) Histograms consider arbitrary intervals, compared to fixed wavelet boundaries. Thus, histograms offer a richer class of representations and often allow a better representation of the data[‡].

In this paper we propose histogram construction algorithms under relative error measures. We seek to design deterministic optimal and approximation algorithms that obey the space bound strictly. We can summarize our contributions as follows:

- **Optimal algorithms for relative error measures.** We provide the first optimal histogram construction algorithms for minimizing the relative error measures. For minimizing the maximum relative relative error, we give a deterministic algorithm in time required by the complicated approximation strategy in [4]. For the other measures, the running time is similar to the time required for computing the V-Optimal histogram.

- **Histogram construction for data streams.** We also provide truly linear ($O(n)$, with no hidden constants like $B, \frac{1}{\epsilon}$ in the O) approximation algorithms for most of the error measures. The linear algorithms have the special property that they examine the data only once in a left-to-right order and require small memory. Thus, they are suitable for constructing histograms for *streaming time series data* as well. For the rest, the approximation runs in time $O(n \log n)$, with no hidden terms.

- **Extensive experimentation validating our algorithms.** We demonstrate the effectiveness of our histogram construction algorithms in providing highly accurate answers using synthetic and real-life data sets. *We use the real-life data sets used in the previous work.* We compare our algorithms with those proposed in [16, 4] in both quality of answers and execution time.

The paper is organized as follows. In the next section, we present preliminary definitions and formally introduce the problem of constructing histograms with relative error measures. In Section 3 and Section 4, we introduce optimal and approximation algorithms respectively. Section 5 presents experimental results, and finally, we summarize in Section 6. Due to the lack

---

[‡]It can be shown that a B bucket wavelet synopsis can be represented *exactly* by $3B+1$ bucket histograms, but a B bucket histogram may require $O(B \log n)$ wavelet coefficients.

of space, we omit the proofs of lemmas and theorems presented in the paper. They can be found in [11].

2 Preliminaries & Related Work

2.1 Problem Statement

Let $X = x_1, \ldots, x_n$ be a finite data sequence. The general problem of histogram construction is as follows: given some space constraint B, create and store a compact representation H_B of the data sequence. H_B uses at most B storage and is optimal under some notion of error.

The representation collapses the values in a sequence of consecutive points x_i where $i \in [s_r, e_r]$ (say $s_r \leq i \leq e_r$) into a single value $\hat{x}(r)$, thus forming a bucket b_r, that is, $b_r = (s_r, e_r, \hat{x}(r))$. The histogram H_B is used to answer queries about the value at point i where $1 \leq i \leq n$. The histogram uses at most B buckets which cover the entire interval $[1, n]$, and saves space by storing only $O(B)$ numbers instead of n.

For a point query, the histogram is used to estimate the x_i, and for $s_r \leq i \leq e_r$, the estimate is $\hat{x}(r)$. Since $\hat{x}(r)$ is an estimate for the values in bucket b_r, we suffer an error.

Definition 2.1 The absolute and the relative errors for a point $i \in [s_r, e_r]$ are respectively defined as

$$|\hat{x}(r) - x_i| \quad \text{and} \quad |\hat{x}(r) - x_i| / \max\{c, |x_i|\}.$$

The error of the histogram H_B can be defined as a function of these point errors. The most popular ways are: (1) sum of errors at every point i, (2) sum of squared errors at every point i, or (3) maximum error considering every point i. Each of the choices induces a natural notion of error for a bucket. We introduce the following definitions:

Definition 2.2 Given an interval $[s_r, e_r]$, we define

- $\text{SSQERROR}(s_r, e_r) = \min_{\hat{x}(r)} \sum_{i=s_r}^{e_r} (x_i - \hat{x}(r))^2$
- $\text{ERR}_M(s_r, e_r) = \min_{\hat{x}(r)} \max_{i \in [s_r, e_r]} \frac{|x_i - \hat{x}(r)|}{\max\{c, |x_i|\}}$
- $\text{ERR}_{\text{sq}}(s_r, e_r) = \min_{\hat{x}(r)} \sum_{i=s_r}^{e_r} \frac{(x_i - \hat{x}(r))^2}{\max\{c^2, x_i^2\}}$
- $\text{ERR}_S(s_r, e_r) = \min_{\hat{x}(r)} \sum_{i=s_r}^{e_r} \frac{|x_i - \hat{x}(r)|}{\max\{c, |x_i|\}}$

Definition 2.3 Let $\text{TERR}[j, k]$ be the error of the best k bucket histogram representation for $x_1, \ldots, x_j$ under the sum of squared absolute error measure. Thus the optimum histogram construction problem under this measure is to find the histogram for $\text{TERR}[n, B]$.

Similarly, we define $\text{TERR}_M[j, k]$, $\text{TERR}_{\text{sq}}[j, k]$ and $\text{TERR}_S[j, k]$ as the errors of the best k bucket histogram representation for $x_1, \ldots, x_j$ under the maximum relative error, sum of squared relative error, and sum of relative error respectively.

There exists an efficient algorithm to determine the V-Optimal histogram given by Jagadish et. al., [14], which requires time $O(n^2 B)$ and $O(Bn)$ space. We will review their algorithm in next.

2.2 V-Optimal Histogram Construction

Two important contributions are made in [14]. First, the value of $\hat{x}(r)$ for a bucket $[s_r, e_r]$ which achieves the minimum error, $\text{SSQERROR}(s_r, e_r)$, is the mean of the values $x_{s_r}, \ldots, x_{e_r}$. Thus, we have

$$\text{SSQERROR}(i, j) = \sum_{\ell=i}^{j} x_\ell^2 - \frac{1}{j-i+1}\left(\sum_{\ell=i}^{j} x_\ell\right)^2 \quad (1)$$

Second, if the last bucket in the optimal histogram contains the data points denoted by the interval $[i+1, n]$, then the rest of the buckets must form an optimal histogram with $(B-1)$ buckets for the interval $[1, i]$[§]. The best i will minimize the sum of the two parts.

Generalizing the discussion (from B to an arbitrary number of buckets $k > 2$, and from n to an arbitrary point $j > 1$), the following dynamic programming algorithm arises immediately:

$$\text{TERR}[j, k] = \min_{1 \leq i < j} \{\text{TERR}[i, k-1] + \text{SSQERROR}(i+1, j)\} \quad (2)$$

To compute $\text{SSQERROR}(i+1, n)$ in $O(1)$ time, two arrays SUM and SQSUM are maintained,

$$\text{SUM}[1, i] = \sum_{\ell=1}^{i} x_\ell \qquad \text{SQSUM}[1, i] = \sum_{\ell=1}^{i} x_\ell^2 \quad (3)$$

The sums in Equation (1) can be replaced by $\text{SUM}[1, j] - \text{SUM}[1, i-1]$ and $\text{SQSUM}[1, j] - \text{SQSUM}[1, i-1]$ respectively. In Equation (2), the value of j can have at most n values. Since each entry of $\text{TERR}[j, k]$ requires $O(n)$ time, with $O(nB)$ entries, we can establish that the complexity of the optimal histogram construction is $O(n^2 B)$.

3 Optimal Histograms under Relative Error

In this section, we focus on developing optimum algorithms for the relative error measures. We first show that the optimum histogram under the maximum relative error criterion can be constructed in $O(nB \log^2 n)$ time. Note that the algorithm in [4] which returns an approximate wavelet decomposition has a similar running time. We subsequently investigate the sum of relative error measure and finally the sum of squares of relative error measure.

[§]Otherwise, it is easy to observe that the error of the optimal solution can be decreased by taking the optimal histogram with $(B-1)$ buckets and the last bucket defined on the points belonging to $[i+1, n]$.

Case	Representative	Error
$\max \geq \min \geq c$	$\frac{(2*\max*\min)}{(\max+\min)}$	$\frac{\max-\min}{\max+\min}$
$\min \leq \max \leq -c$	$\frac{(2*\max*\min)}{(\max+\min)}$	$\frac{\min-\max}{\max+\min}$
$-c < \min < c \leq \max$	$\frac{\max(\min+c)}{\max+c}$	$\frac{\max-\min}{\max+c}$
$\min \leq -c \leq \max \leq c$	$\frac{\min(c-\max)}{c-\min}$	$\frac{\max-\min}{c-\min}$
$-c \leq \min \leq \max \leq c$	$\frac{(\max+\min)}{2}$	$\frac{\max-\min}{2c}$
$\min \leq -c < c \leq \max$	0	1.0

Table 1: Optimal Maximum Relative Error

Procedure NaiveHistERR$_M$()
begin
1. **for** j := 1 **to** n **do** {
2. TRERR$_M$[j, 1] := ERR$_M$(1, j)
3. **for** k := 2 **to** B **do** {
4.   max := $-\infty$; min := ∞; TRERR$_M$[i, k] := ∞
5.   **for** i := j - 1 **down to** 1 **do** {
6.   If (max < x_{i+1}) then max := x_{i+1}
7.   If (min > x_{i+1}) then min := x_{i+1}
8.   TRERR$_M$[j, k] := min(TRERR$_M$[j, k], max(
         TRERR$_M$[i, k $-$ 1], ERR$_M$(i + 1, j))
9.   }
10. }
11. }
end

Figure 1: The NaiveHistERR$_M$

3.1 Maximum Relative Error

Recall that the maximum relative error of a bucket $b_r = (s_r, e_r, \hat{x})$ is defined as follows:

$$\text{ERR}_M(s_r, e_r) = \min_{\hat{x}} \max_{i \in [s_r, e_r]} \frac{|x_i - \hat{x}|}{\max\{c, |x_i|\}}$$

We can prove the following:

Lemma 3.1 *Given a set of numbers $x_1, \ldots, x_\ell$, the maximum relative error generated by minimizing maximum relative errors is defined by the minimum and the maximum over these x_i as described in Table 1.*

A Simple Algorithm: Lemma 3.1 allows us to consider a naive optimal algorithm, NaiveHistERR$_M$, with $O(n^2 B)$ running time. The NaiveHistERR$_M$ is illustrated in Figure 1. The computation of ERR$_M$ can be performed in time $O(1)$ if we are maintaining the running minimum and the maximum incrementally over the interval $[i+1, j]$ as i changes (decreases).

An Improved $O(nB \log^2 n)$ Construction: Consider line (8) of Figure 1, where TRERR$_M$[j, k] is

$$\min_i \{\max(\text{TRERR}_M[i, k-1], \text{ERR}_M(i+1, j))\}$$

Observe that TRERR$_M$[i, k$-$1] is an increasing function and ERR$_M$ is a decreasing function of i. This problem can be solved faster.

Lemma 3.2 *To compute $\min_x \{\max(F(x), G(x))\}$ where $F(x)$ and $G(x)$ are non-decreasing and non-increasing functions respectively, we can perform binary search for the value of x such that $F(x) > G(x)$ and $F(x-1) < G(x-1)$, and we can take minimum of $G(x-1)$ and $F(x)$.*

By the above Lemma, we find the smallest i such that TRERR$_M$[i, k $-$ 1] $\geq$ ERR$_M$(i + 1, j). Let the value of i found by the binary search be i^*. The minimum is achieved at either $i = i^* - 1$ or $i = i^*$. This algorithm, OptHistERR$_M$, is presented in Figure 2. We can verify that the running time of the algorithm is $O(Bn \log n)$ times of the time to compute ERR$_M$(i, j).

Procedure OptHistERR$_M$()
begin
1. **for** j := 1 **to** n **do** {
2. TRERR$_M$[j, 1] := ERR$_M$(1, j)
3. **for** k := 2 **to** B **do** {
4.   low := 1; high := j $-$ 1; TRERR$_M$[j, k] := ∞
5.   **while** (low < high) **do** {
6.   mid := (high + low + 1)/2
7.   **if** TRERR$_M$[mid, k $-$ 1] $\geq$ ERR$_M$(mid + 1, j)
8.   low := mid
9.   **else** high := mid $-$ 1
10.   }
11.   **if** (TRERR$_M$[low, k $-$ 1] < ERR$_M$(low, j))
12.   TRERR$_M$[j, k] :=
          min(TRERR$_M$[j, k], ERR$_M$(low, j))
13.   **else** TRERR$_M$[j, k] :=
          min(TRERR$_M$[j, k], TRERR$_M$[low, k $-$ 1])
14. }
15. }
end

Figure 2: The OptHistERR$_M$

To compute ERR$_M$(i, j) efficiently, we use an interval tree defined below:

Definition 3.3 *Given an interval on $[1, n]$ we construct an interval tree which is a binary tree over subintervals of $[1, n]$. The root of the tree corresponds to the entire interval $[1, n]$ and the leaf nodes corresponds to the intervals of length one, e.g. $[i, i]$. For the interval $[i, j]$ of a node in the interval tree, we store the minimum and the maximum of $x_i, \ldots, x_j$. The children of a node with the interval $[i, j]$ correspond to the two (near) half-size intervals $[i, r-1], [r, j]$ where $r = \lfloor \frac{i+j+1}{2} \rfloor$.*

It is easy to observe that an interval tree can be constructed in $O(n)$ time and will require $O(n)$ storage. Given an arbitrary interval $[i, j]$, we partition $[i, j]$ into $O(\log n)$ intervals such that each of the resulting subintervals belong to the interval tree. Using the decomposed subintervals, we find the optimal maximum relative for the bucket. It reduces the time complexity of computing the minimum (or maximum) to $O(\log n)$.

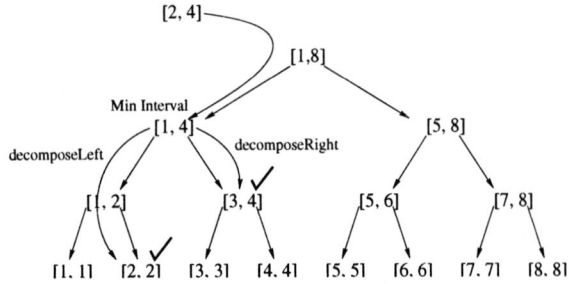

Figure 3: The Steps of Decomposing [2, 4] with an Interval Tree

Decomposing $[i, j]$ **into subintervals** For an interval $[i, j]$, we traverse the interval tree starting from the root node to find the smallest interval $[i_m, j_m]$ that contains $[i, j]$ as a subinterval. If $[i_m, j_m]$ is exactly $[i, j]$, we are done. Otherwise, let $[i_m, m_m]$ and $[m_m + 1, j_m]$ be the left and right children of $[i_m, j_m]$.

It must be that $i \leq m_m < j$, otherwise there exists an interval smaller than $[i_m, j_m]$ that contains $[i, j]$ entirely. We will recursively find a set of intervals partitioning $[i, m_m]$ and similarly $[m_m + 1, j]$.

Let us focus on $[i, m_m]$, since the other case is symmetrical. We term this interval as "active", in the sense that we seek to partition it. We start from the root of a subtree corresponding to $[i_m, m_m]$. If $[i_m, m_m]$ is the same as $[i, m_m]$ we are done. If $i \neq i_m$ then the interval $[i_m, m_m]$ has length at least 2 and let $[i_m, i'], [i' + 1, m_m]$ be its children. If $i \leq i'$, we add the interval $[i' + 1, m_m]$ to our set and set $[i, i']$ as an active interval and move to the left subtree. Otherwise if $i > i'$ the same interval remains active but we move to the right subtree. We traverse down the tree adding at most one interval in each downward move. Thus, the subintervals found for both $[i, m_m]$ and $[m_m + 1, j]$ can be at most $2 \log n$ and this decomposition takes $O(\log n)$ time.

Example 3.4 We illustrate the decomposition of $[2, 4]$ for a given interval tree in Figure 3. The interval $[2, 4]$ is decomposed into $[2, 2]$ and $[3, 4]$. ∎

Lemma 3.5 *The height of an interval tree corresponding to $[1, n]$ is at most $O(\log n)$. For any interval $[i, j]$, we can express the interval as a set of at most $O(\log n)$ non-overlapping intervals belonging to the nodes in the interval tree. This decomposition can be performed in $O(\log n)$ time. Furthermore, we can compute the maximum and the minimum over $x_i, \ldots, x_j$ in $O(\log n)$ time.*

Therefore, we conclude with the following:

Theorem 3.6 *The optimum maximum relative error for n values and B buckets can be found in time $O(Bn \log^2 n)$ and space $O(Bn)$. The $O(Bn)$ space is required to output the representative values and bucket boundaries after the optimum error has been found, the error itself can be computed in $O(n)$ space.*

3.2 Sum of Squared Relative Errors

Recall that the sum of squared relative error, ERR_{sq}, for the bucket $b_r = (s_r, e_r, \hat{x}(r))$ is defined as follows:

$$\text{ERR}_{\text{sq}}(s_r, e_r) = \min_{\hat{x}(r)} \left(\sum_{j=s_r}^{e_r} \frac{(\hat{x}(r) - x_j)^2}{\max\{c^2, x_j^2\}} \right)$$

The right hand side of the above equation can be rewritten as $\min_{\hat{x}(r)} \left(A\hat{x}(r)^2 - 2B\hat{x}(r) + C \right)$ where if we denote by $w_j = \max\{c^2, x_j^2\}$,

$$A = \sum_{j=s_r}^{e_r} \frac{1}{w_j} \quad \& \quad B = \sum_{j=s_r}^{e_r} \frac{x_j}{w_j} \quad \& \quad C = \sum_{j=s_r}^{e_r} \frac{x_j^2}{w_j}$$

Since $A > 0$, the value of $\text{ERR}_{\text{sq}}(\hat{x})$ is minimized when $\hat{x}$ is B/A, and its minimum value becomes $C - B^2/A$. The aggregated sum values of A, B and C as are stored in the arrays ASUM, BSUM and CSUM respectively to allow computing $\text{ERR}_{\text{sq}}(i+1, j)$ in $O(1)$ time. Thus, using the following recursive definition for $k > 1$,

$$\text{TRERR}_{\text{sq}}[j, k] = \min_i (\text{TRERR}_{\text{sq}}[i, k-1] + \text{ERR}_{\text{sq}}(i+1, j))$$

we can prove the following:

Theorem 3.7 *In $O(Bn^2)$ time, we can compute the optimal histogram under sum of squared relative error measure.*

3.3 Sum of Relative Errors

The sum of relative errors ERR_S for a bucket $b_r = (s_r, e_r, \hat{x}(r))$ is defined as follows:

$$\text{ERR}_S(s_r, e_r) = \min_{\hat{x}(r)} \sum_{i=s_r}^{e_r} \frac{|x_i - \hat{x}(r)|}{\max\{c, |x_i|\}} = \min_{\hat{x}(r)} g(\hat{x}(r))$$

Definition 3.8 Given $V = \{x_{s_r}, x_{s_r+1}, \ldots, x_{e_r}\}$, and $m = e_r - s_r + 1$. Let $V_s = \{v_1, v_2, \ldots v_m\}$ denote the elements of V in the sorted order. If $v_i = v_j$ then if $i < j$ we say that v_i is before v_j in the order.

To simplify the notation, since we are in the context of a particular bucket b_r we will use $\hat{x}$ to represent $\hat{x}(r)$. Using the above equation, we rewrite $g(\hat{x}) = P(\hat{x}) \cdot \hat{x} + Q(\hat{x})$.

$$P(\hat{x}) = 2 \sum_{j: v_j \leq \hat{x}} \frac{1}{max\{c, |v_j|\}} - \sum_{j=1}^{m} \frac{1}{max\{c, |v_j|\}} \quad (4)$$

$$Q(\hat{x}) = \sum_{j=1}^{m} \frac{v_j}{max\{c, |v_j|\}} - 2 \sum_{j: v_j \leq \hat{x}} \frac{v_j}{max\{c, |v_j|\}} \quad (5)$$

We can show that the minimum of ERR$_S$ is obtained at $v_k \in V_s$ such that k is the least index satisfying $P(v_k) \geq 0$, which is Theorem 3.15. The proof is involved and we provide a road map omitting the proofs of the lemmas.

Lemma 3.9 *The values of $P(\hat{x})$ and $Q(\hat{x})$ do not change with $\hat{x}$ for $v_k \leq \hat{x} < v_{k+1}$.*

Lemma 3.10 *The function $g(\hat{x})$ is continuous at every $v_j \in V_s$.*

Lemma 3.11 *When $P(v_k) < 0$ for $v_k \in V_s$, $g(\hat{x})$ is a decreasing function and we have $g(v_{k+1}) \leq g(\hat{x}) \leq g(v_k)$ for $\hat{x}$ such that $v_k \leq \hat{x} \leq v_{k+1}$.*
If $P(v_k) > 0$, $g(\hat{x})$ is an increasing function and we have $g(v_k) \leq g(\hat{x}) \leq g(v_{k+1})$ for $\hat{x}$ with $v_k \leq \hat{x} \leq v_{k+1}$.

Lemma 3.12 *For $\hat{x} \in (-\infty, v_1]$, we have $P(\hat{x}) < 0$ and $g(v_1) \leq g(\hat{x})$. Furthermore, for $\hat{x} \in [v_m, \infty)$, $P(\hat{x}) > 0$ and $g(v_m) \leq g(\hat{x})$ holds.*

Lemma 3.13 *$P(v_i)$ is an increasing function of i and $P(v_m) > 0$ holds.*

Lemma 3.14 *If $P(v_k) < 0$ for $v_k \in V_s$, the function $g(\hat{x})$ is minimum at $\hat{x} = v_{k+1}$ for $\hat{x} \in (-\infty, v_{k+1}]$. When $P(v_k) > 0$ for $v_k \in V_s$, the function $g(\hat{x})$ is minimum when $\hat{x} = v_k$ for $\hat{x} \in [v_k, \infty)$.*

Theorem 3.15 *The minimum of $g(\hat{x})$ is achieved at $v_k \in V_s$ such that k is the least index satisfying $P(v_k) \geq 0$.*

Optimal Histogram Algorithm: The algorithm presented in Figure 4 gives an optimal histogram for ERR$_S$ in $O(n^2(B + \log n))$ time. The binary tree T_B in the algorithm help us to maintain the sorted order in $O(\log n)$ time ¶.

One strategy would be to obtain the sorted ordered set V_s of $V = \{x_{i+1}, \ldots, x_j\}$, and find v_k satisfying Theorem 3.15. This would result in an $O(n^3)$ algorithm. We can improve the complexity by storing additional information in the binary tree to find v_k faster and computing ERR$_S(i,j)$ in $O(\log n)$ time. With every node t with key x_t in the tree, we keep a multiplicity field, d_t, which denotes the number of x-values seen which are equal to x_t. Let the subtree rooted at t is T. Each node is also augmented with two other fields m and vm to keep the following values:

$$m = \sum_{x \in T} \frac{1}{\max\{c, |x|\}} \quad \text{and} \quad vm = \sum_{x \in T} \frac{x}{\max\{c, |x|\}}$$

As we insert a new key x to the binary tree, the values in m and vm of the nodes in the binary search tree must be updated appropriately.

¶Under balanced tree implementations, we use AVL-trees.

Procedure OptHistERR$_S$()
begin
1. for i := 1 to n do {
2.   TRERR$_S[i,1]$:= ERR$_S(1,i)$
3.   for k := 2 to B do
4.   TRERR$_S[i,k]$:= ∞
5. T_B := $\emptyset$
6.   for j := i-1 to 1 do {
7.   // T_B contains values in $[j+2, i]$
8.   insert(T_B, x_{j+1})
9.   // T_B now contains values in $[j+1, i]$
10.   Compute ERR$_S(j+1, i)$ using T_B
11.   for k := 2 to B do {
12.   TRERR$_S[i,k]$:= min{TRERR$_S[i,k]$,
                      TRERR$_S[j, k-1]$ + ERR$_S(j+1, i)$}
13.   }
14.   }
15. }
end

Figure 4: The OptHistERR$_S$

Computation of ERR$_S(i,j)$: We will traverse down a path leading to the appropriate v_k giving the solution to ERR$_S$. Suppose we are at a node t with value x_t, and its nearest ancestor node t_n having $P(x_{t_n}) > 0$. Let the subtree rooted at t is T. We maintain the following quantities while traversing T_B:

$$\text{EX}.m = \sum_{x \notin T, x < x_t} \frac{1}{\max\{c, |x|\}} \quad \& \quad \text{EX}.vm = \sum_{x \notin T, x < x_t} \frac{x}{\max\{c, |x|\}}$$

EX has information regarding the keys in the nodes that are less than x_t and do not belong to the subtree T rooted at t. Let $P_0 = T_B.m$ and $Q_0 = T_B.vm$. We first compute

$$P^*(x_t) = 2\text{EX}.m + 2\text{LEFT}(T).m - P_0$$

where LEFT(T) is the left subtree of t in T. Note that LEFT$(T).m = 0$ if the left subtree is empty. Since the formula of $P^*(x_t)$ is the same as that of $P(x_t)$ except the contribution from $v_j = x_t$, we always have $P^*(x_t) < P(x_t)$. In each node t, we perform the following steps according to the condition below:

When $P^*(x_t) + d_t/\max\{c, |x_t|\} < 0$, we know that v_k cannot be x_t (or any of its duplicates) and we need to investigate the right subtree of T. In the recursive call to the right subtree, we pass the current t_n if we have t_n in this traversal. We update EX.m and EX.vm by adding $t.m$ and $t.vm$ respectively.

If $P^*(x_t) + d_t/\max\{c, |x_t|\} \geq 0$ and $P^*(x_t) < 0$, we have $v_k = x_t$(the condition $P() > 0$ is satisfied by some duplicate of x_t). In this case we are done.

Otherwise, we have $P^*(x_t) \geq 0$ and the value of x_t may be the solution, but we cannot be assured of it without inspecting the rest of the subtree. We replace t_n as t and investigate the left subtree LEFT(T).

By this process we recursively maintain the invariant that: *the solution v_k is contained in the current subtree or is the stored value in t_n.* If we reach a leaf node and decide to take the (empty) right path we know that the stored value in t_n must be v_k. If we attempt to take the empty left path then the stored value of the leaf node must be v_k.

To get ERR_S, we simply calculate

$$Q^*(x_t) = Q_0 - 2\text{Ex}.vm - 2\text{LEFT}(T).vm$$

and compute $P^*(x_t)x_t + Q^*(x_t)$ which is actually $P(x_t)x_t + Q(x_t)$. Thus, we can claim the following:

Lemma 3.16 *We can compute v_k, equivalently $\text{ERR}_S(i,j)$ given an AVL-tree, in time $O(\log n)$.*

Thus, we conclude with the following Theorem.

Theorem 3.17 *We can compute the optimal histogram under sum of relative error measure in time $O(n^2(B + \log n))$.*

4 Approximate Histograms for Relative Error

Due to the lack of space we relegate the discussion on previous work on approximate V-Optimal histograms to [11]. We point out why newer approximation algorithms are needed for relative error measures.

The approximation algorithm in [14] gives a factor 3 approximation (ignoring other issues) and we will be interested in $(1+\epsilon)$ approximations. The approximate algorithms in [9, 8] depend on the fact that the error for a bucket in the V-Optimal histogram depends on the mean and the sum of the values in the bucket. However, the sum of relative error ERR_S in a bucket depends on *the sorted order* of the values in the bucket and not on simple aggregate values. Thus, the algorithms in the style of [8, 9] cannot work for ERR_S without substantial modification. The algorithms in [5, 7] use properties of the L_2 norm and are too dependent on the definition of V-Optimal error to be useful in context of relative error.

For maximum relative error ERR_M, we need to maintain the maximum and minimum values in a bucket to compute the error. An algorithm similar to [9] can give a $(1+\epsilon)$ approximation — but unfortunately the running time of such an algorithm will be $O(nB^3\epsilon^{-2}\log n)$ which is greater than the time required by the optimal algorithm! An algorithm like [8] cannot maintain the minimum or maximum for an arbitrary interval since the lazy evaluation strategy does not inspect all the elements (which is necessary to find the maximum and minimum).

Based on the above facts, we need to design new approximation algorithms. We give a $(1+\epsilon)$-approximation algorithm for the maximum relative error requiring $O(n)$ time and $O(B^2\epsilon^{-1}\log n(\log\log n + \log\frac{B}{\epsilon})^3)$ space in Section 4.1. Subsequently we provide the a $(1+\epsilon)$ approximation for sum of squared relative error in $O(n)$ time but $O(B^3\epsilon^{-2}\log^2 n(\log\log n +$ $\log\frac{B}{\epsilon}))$ space. These results extend naturally to the streaming context, and are directly applicable for time series data.

For sum of relative error we give a $O(n\log n)$ time and space algorithm in Section 4.3.

4.1 ERR_M: Maximum Relative Error

The main idea behind approximate histograms in [8, 9] is the observation that an increasing function can be approximated by a step function. We will read the input in blocks of which each contains M data values.

Let δ be $\epsilon/(2B)$. We approximate the function $\text{TRERR}_M[i, k+1]$ at a subset of the points by the function $\text{APXERR}_M[i, k+1]$. We let $\text{APXERR}_M[i, 1] = \text{ERR}_M(1, i)$ and $\text{APXERR}_M[i, k]$ is defined for $k > 1$ as:

$$\max_l\{\text{APXERR}_M[e_l^k, k-1], \text{ERR}_M(e_l^k + 1, i)\}$$

We will not evaluate $\text{APXERR}_M[i, k]$ for all i, and retain the values of $\text{APXERR}_M[i, k]$ at the endpoints of several intervals $[s_l^k, e_l^k]$ only such that:

$$(1+\delta)\text{APXERR}_M[s_l^k, k] \geq \text{APXERR}_M[e_l^k, k] \quad (6)$$

with the property that the intervals $[s_l^k, e_l^k]$ are mutually disjoint for the same k and $\bigcup_l [s_l^k, e_l^k]$ is all the input we have seen so far.

Suppose we have stored a set of values $\text{APXERR}_M[i, k]$ with $1 \leq i \leq n - M$, as shown in figure 5. The dotted line corresponds to the approximate intervals stored for the interval $[1, n-M]$, and corresponds to $\text{APXERR}_M[i, k]$ (estimated or approximated $\text{TRERR}_M[i, k]$). The solid line corresponds to $\text{APXERR}_M[i, k]$ for the last M values — note that we will not even compute $\text{APXERR}_M[i, k]$ for all these points. But if we did, we would get the solid line.

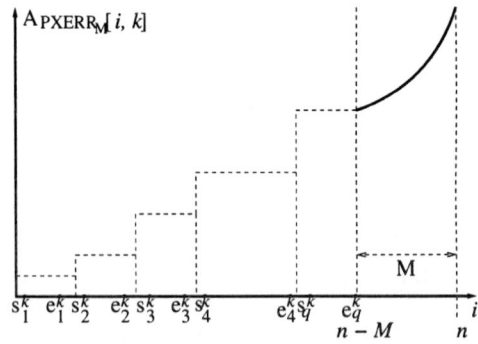

Figure 5: Extending $\text{APXERR}_M[i, k]$

We have B lists of intervals in which the k-th list stores the set of intervals corresponding to Equation (6). Intuitively, we approximate $\text{TRERR}_M[i, k]$ with $1 \leq i \leq n - M$. We will extend the B interval lists to include the approximation of $\text{TRERR}_M[i, k]$ for the last M data values. Assume that $[s_q^k, e_q^k]$ is the last interval of $[1, n-M]$ for $\text{APXERR}_M[i, k]$.

We find the *maximum* for $n - M + 1 \leq e \leq n$ such that $\text{APXERR}_M[e, k] \leq (1 + \delta)\text{APXERR}_M[s_q^k, k]$. This e defines an interval $[s_q^k, e]$ that replaces the interval $[s_q^k, e_q^k]$ in k-th interval list. We start a new interval from $e + 1$ and repeat this process to find next intervals until we run out of the last M data values. Notice we can use binary search to find e, and subsequently next e etc. To extend the k-th list by one element of APXERR_M, we require binary search with $O(\log M)$ time. Suppose n_q is the maximum number of elements in any list. The number of evaluating $\text{APXERR}_M[i, k]$ to extend k-th list is $O(n_q * \log M)$. Thus, the time complexity of extending k-th list becomes $O(n_q * \log M)$ times that of evaluating $\text{APXERR}_M[i, k]$.

Extending k-th List: Assume that we processed r blocks of data values whose interval is $[1, n - M]$ and we are about to process the $(r+1)$-th block whose size is M. With each end-point e_l^k of intervals in $[1, n-M]$, we maintain the minimum and the maximum values seen in $[e_l^k, e_q^k]$ where e_q^k is the end of the last (i.e. r-th) block. We will update these values and they will help us calculate $\text{ERR}_M(e + 1, n)$. We also build an interval tree with $O(M)$ time which is introduced in Section 3.1. We describe the algorithm at a high level only, the detailed description of the algorithm can be found in [11]. We set

$$\text{APXERR}_M[i, 1] = \text{TRERR}_M[i, 1] = \text{ERR}_M(1, i)$$

Now, $\text{APXERR}_M[i, k]$ for $k > 1$ is:

$$\min_l \{\max(\text{APXERR}_M[e_l^{k-1}, k-1], \text{ERR}_M(e_l^{k-1} + 1, i))\}$$

where e_l^{k-1} are end points of the $(k-1)$-th list. By Lemma 3.2, computation of $\text{APXERR}_M[i, k]$ can be done with binary search in $O(\log n_q)$ time.

In each step of this binary search, $\text{APXERR}_M[e_l^{k-1}, k-1]$ is already memorized, but we need to compute $\text{ERR}_M(e_l^{k-1} + 1, i)$. We find the maximum and minimum values using the interval $[e_l^{k-1} + 1, i]$. If both $e_l^{k-1} + 1$ and i are in the current block (i.e. $(r+1)$-th block), we use the interval tree and it takes $O(\log M)$ time. If $e_l^{k-1} + 1$ (therefore e_l^{k-1}) belonged to a previous block (r-th block), we already know the maximum and minimum values from $e_l^{k-1} + 1$ to end of the last (i.e. r-th) block. We can also get the minimum and maximum of the values for the current block using the interval tree in $O(\log M)$ time.

The time to compute $\text{APXERR}_M[i, k]$ for $k > 1$ with binary search is $O(\log n_q \log M)$ because binary search and evaluating $\text{ERR}_M()$ takes $O(\log n_q)$ and $O(\log M)$ respectively. Since the number of evaluations of $\text{APXERR}_M[i, k]$ needed to extend k-th list is $O(n_q * \log M)$, the total time to extend k-th list is

Procedure ApproxHistERR$_M$()
begin
1. **For** $r = 1$ **to** n/M {
2.   Read the next block of M elements
3.   Create an interval tree
      with M elements for min/max queries
4.   **For** $k = 1$ **to** $B - 1$
5.   Extend k-th List
6.   **For** $k = 1$ **to** $B - 1$
7.   Update min/max values of end-points
8. }
9. //S is a set of end-points of $(B-1)$-th queue
10. $\text{APXERR}_M(n, B) = \min_{i \in S}$
    $(\text{APXERR}_M(i, B-1) + \text{ERR}_M(i+1, n))$
end

Figure 6: Approx. Max Relative Error

$O(M + n_q(\log M)^2 (\log n_q))$ where $O(M)$ is the time to read and process a single block of data.

Lemma 4.1 *The maximum number of elements in the interval lists, n_q is $O(B\epsilon^{-1} \log n)$.*

Lemma 4.2 *The time to read the next M data values and extend all of B lists is given by:*

$$O\left(M + (B^2\epsilon^{-1} \log n)(\log^2 M)(\log \log n + \log(B/\epsilon))\right)$$

Thus, the total time of *ExtendList* is n/M times the above time to process a single block, it becomes

$$O\left(n + \frac{n}{M}(B^2\epsilon^{-1} \log n)(\log^2 M)(\log \log n + \log \frac{B}{\epsilon})\right)$$

Observe that, for our choice of M, this is $O(n)$. The following can be proved by induction on k'.

Lemma 4.3 (Proof of Correctness) *For any i for which $\text{APXERR}_M[i, k']$ is evaluated, we have*

$$\text{APXERR}_M[i, k'] \leq (1 + \delta)^{k'} \text{TRERR}_M[i, k']$$

When $\delta = \epsilon/(2B)$, by the inductive claim, we have

$$(1 + \epsilon/(2B))^B \text{TRERR}_M[n, B] \leq (1 + \epsilon)\text{TRERR}_M[n, B]$$

for $0 \leq \epsilon < 1$, where $\text{TRERR}_M[n, B]$ is the optimal error. Thus, the approximate error $\text{APXERR}_M[n, B]$ is at most $(1 + \epsilon)\text{TRERR}_M[n, B]$ and we have a $(1 + \epsilon)$-approximation of the optimal error.

The approximation algorithm, ApproxHistERR$_M$(), is presented in Figure 6. Observe that if we set $M = (B^2\epsilon^{-1} \log n)(\log^2 M)(\log \log n + \log \frac{B}{\epsilon})$, then the running time of ApproxHistERR$_M$() is $O(n)$, with relatively small space. Notice that since we would be reading block by block, we would get a streaming algorithm. Observe for this value of M, we have $\log M = O(\log \log n + \log \frac{B}{\epsilon})$. Putting everything together, we have

Theorem 4.4 *We can find a $(1+\epsilon)$ approximation to maximum relative error histogram in time $O(n)$ and space $M = \Omega(B^2 \epsilon^{-1} \log n (\log \log n + \log \frac{B}{\epsilon})^3)$. This algorithm considers the input sequence left to right and looks at every input value (block) at most once. Thus this algorithm applies to streaming data as well.*

4.2 Sum of Squared Relative Errors

In the case of ERR_{sq}, we would need to store ASUM, BSUM and CSUM for each i and k such that $\text{ERR}_{sq}[i, k]$ increases by a factor of $(1 + \epsilon/(2B))$. We apply a similar algorithm as in Figure 6 to incrementally read blocks of M points each and construct the requisite approximations. The block size determines the space requirement and will be *larger* in this case than that for ERR_M as the reason will be seen shortly. We can prove that Lemma 4.1 holds in this case as well. Notice that in this case, since we have to compute

$$\text{TRERR}_{sq}[i,k] = \min_l \{\text{TRERR}_{sq}[e_l^{k-1}, k-1] + \text{ERR}_{sq}(e_l^{k-1}+1, i)\}$$

which means we cannot use binary search and have to spend $O(n_q)$ time to evaluate the minimum. However, evaluation of $\text{ERR}_{sq}(e_l^{k-1}+1, i)$ can be performed in time $O(1)$ now using the stored ASUM, BSUM and CSUM. Thus, k-th interval list can be extended in time $O(M + (n_q)^2 \log M)$. Thus the overall time will be $O(n + \frac{n}{M}(n_q)^2 \log M)$ – therefore to achieve $o(n)$ running time, M needs to be larger in this case.

Theorem 4.5 *We can construct a $(1 + \epsilon)$-approximation for the sum of squared relative error histograms in time $O(n)$ and space $O(B^3 \epsilon^{-2} (\log^2 n)(\log \log n + \log \frac{B}{\epsilon}))$.*

4.3 Sum of Relative Errors

We propose a similar algorithm as in previously subsections. However, for sum of relative errors, computation of $\text{ERR}_S(i, j)$ does depend *not only* on some aggregate statistics at the endpoints i and j, *but also* on the entire set of values in the interval. Thus, to answer ERR_S for arbitrary intervals quickly, preprocessing step of building an interval tree is required. We can prove the following (along the same lines as the proofs of Lemma 4.1, and Lemma 4.3):

Lemma 4.6 *If the evaluation of $\text{ERR}_S(i,j)$ for any $[i,j]$ can be supported in $O(T)$ time with preprocessing $O(P)$, we can construct a $(1 + \epsilon)$ factor approximation of the optimal histogram in time $O(P + nB^3 \epsilon^{-2} T \log^3 n)$.*

Lemma 4.7 *We can evaluate ERR_S for an arbitrary interval with $P = O(n \log n)$ and $T = O(\log^3 n)$.*

From Lemma 4.6, and Lemma 4.7, we conclude:

Theorem 4.8 *In $O(n \log n + B^3 \epsilon^2 \log^6 n)$ time and $O(n \log n)$ space, we can compute a $(1 + \epsilon)$-approximation for the sum of relative errors histograms.*

5 Experimental Result

To investigate the performance gains of REHIST over existing techniques, we conducted experiments using real-life as well as synthetic data sets. The sanitary bound c is set to the 10-percent value in the data as in [3, 4]. We used our implementations of the probabilistic thresholding scheme [3, 4] and the deterministic thresholding scheme [17] as representatives of traditional summarization techniques that considers relative errors as objective function.

5.1 Synthetic Data Sets

We considered one-dimensional synthetic data distribution. The data sets were generated with Zipfian frequencies for various levels of skew controlled by the z parameter of the Zipfian. The tuple count was set to 10^6. We varied the z parameter values between 0.3 (low skew) and 2.0 (high skew), the distinct values between $128 (= 2^7)$ and $16384 (= 2^{14})$. Note that the time and space complexities are not dependent on number of tuples and thus we did not vary this parameter.

A permutation step was also applied on the produced Zipfian frequencies to decide the order of frequencies over the data domain. We experimented with four different permutation techniques that were used in [3, 4]: *NoPerm*, *Normal*, *PipeOrgan* and *Random*. Normal permutes the frequencies to resemble a bell-shaped normal distribution, with higher frequencies at the center of the domain. Due to the lack of space, we present the experimental results with Normal permutation only. The detailed description of these permutations are presented in [3, 4].

5.2 Algorithms

Since the probabilistic [4] and deterministic thresholding schemes [17] did not consider all of three relative error measures, we modified their algorithm to report these errors as well. We conducted a comprehensive performance evaluation of the various schemes. Specifically, we show the performance figures of the following schemes:

- **V-OPT:** It represents the V-Optimal histogram construction algorithm [14] presented in Section 2.2. Even though the error metric used for V-optimal histograms is different, it is interesting to see how other state-of-the-art histogram techniques compare against REHIST which minimizes relative error.

- **P-Wavelet:** This is our implementation of the probabilistic thresholding scheme of [3]. ‖ We used the same default parameter values that were used in [3]. For instance, we set the value of q to 10 and the perturbation parameter δ to $\min\{0.01, c/100\}$. As the authors in [3, 4] suggested, we performed five trials using different random seeds, and the synopsis with the least value was chosen.

- **D-Wavelet:** It is the deterministic thresholding method that was introduced in [17].

- **REHIST-OPT:** These represent optimal histogram construction algorithms presented in Section 3. Depending on the error measure used, REHIST-OPT-M, REHIST-OPT-SQ and REHIST-OPT-S represent OptHistERR_M, OptHistERR_{sq}, and OptHistERR_S respectively.

- **REHIST-APPROX:** These represent approximate histogram construction algorithms described in Section 4. REHIST-APP-M, REHIST-APP-SQ and REHIST-APP-S represent approximation algorithms using ERR_M, ERR_{sq}, and ERR_S respectively.

  Since none of the competitive suggestions consider streaming data, the comparisons are given for offline algorithms only, with blocksize as the number of distinct values.

Note: In case of all the histogram algorithms, we found that first obtaining a coarse approximation (say factor 2) and using that solution to prune the lists (not to use $\text{APXERR}_M[i, k]$ larger than this coarse value) has significant performance benefits.

All experiments reported in this section were performed on Pentium-4 2.8 GHz machine with 512 MB of main memory, running Linux. All the methods were implemented using GCC compiler of Version 2.95.3.

5.3 Experimental Results - Synthetic Data

We present some of our experimental results with synthetic data sets. For wavelet methods, each coefficient requires two numbers: the coefficient value and the coefficient index. Similarly, in histograms, starting boundary value of the next bucket is the current bucket's ending value plus one, each bucket needs two numbers: its representative value and ending boundary value. Thus, the number of buckets in histogram and the number of coefficients in wavelets methods were set to be equal and represented by B. The default value of B was set to 50. The default skew was 1.0 and the default number of distinct values was set to 2048.

‖ It is an improved version of [4] using binary search.

Number of Buckets: Figure 7-(a), (b) and (c) represent the graphs as the number of buckets B is varied. We plot the maximum relative error for ERR_M in the graph. However, for ERR_S and ERR_{sq}, we plot the average per distinct value. We notice that the accuracy of REHIST is much better than P-Wavelet, D-Wavelet and V-OPT. Typically, as we expected, V-OPT is the worst performer. For small B, the wavelet methods are bad. As expected, the relative error measures decrease with increasing the number of buckets B. The quality of histograms produced by REHIST-APP was almost the same as REHIST-OPT.

Skew Parameter: We also varied the skew parameter. The relative error measures increase with higher skew parameter value. The graphs show that REHIST results in significant improvement in quality as compared to both wavelet methods and V-OPT. The quality of REHIST-APP was very close to that of REHIST-OPT. Due to the lack of space, we can not present the graphs in this paper.

Number of Distinct Values: Figure 7-(d), (e) and (f)) were obtained by varying the number of distinct values. These graphs again show that the solutions obtained by REHIST are much more accurate than D-Wavelet, P-Wavelet and V-OPT. V-OPT is again the worst performer. We also compare execution times in Figure 7-(g), (h) and (i). D-Wavelet is the fastest. For ERR_M and ERR_{sq}, REHIST-APP was at least as fast as P-Wavelet. However, P-Wavelet is faster than REHIST-APP for ERR_S. Since increasing q value for P-Wavelet improves the quality of wavelet synopsis, we increased the value of q from 10 to 50. However, while the execution time with $q = 50$ is typically 10 times slower than that with $q = 10$, the quality with $q = 50$ was not significantly better. Thus, spending more time and increasing q does not help for P-Wavelet. In this regard, the running time of REHIST appears justifiable considering the significantly better quality of representations constructed by REHIST. Although REHIST-OPT is the slowest, for small number of distinct values, REHIST-OPT is faster than REHIST-APP. As expected, this is reversed as we increased the number of distinct values.

5.4 Experimental Results - Real-life Data Sets

We also experimented with real-life data sets. We used the *Cover Type* data set from the National Forest Service, which was downloaded from UC Irvine**. There are 581,012 tuples in the data set. Among 54 attributes, we report "hillshade3pm" (CovType-HS3) and "aspect" (CovType-A). Because these attributes have widely different distributions, they were used for performance study in [3, 4]. CovType-HS3 measures a

---

**Available at ftp://ftp.ics.uci.edu/pub/machine-learning-databases.

(a) ERR_M (b) ERR_S (c) ERR_sq

(d) ERR_M (e) ERR_S (f) ERR_sq

(g) ERR_M (h) ERR_S (i) ERR_sq

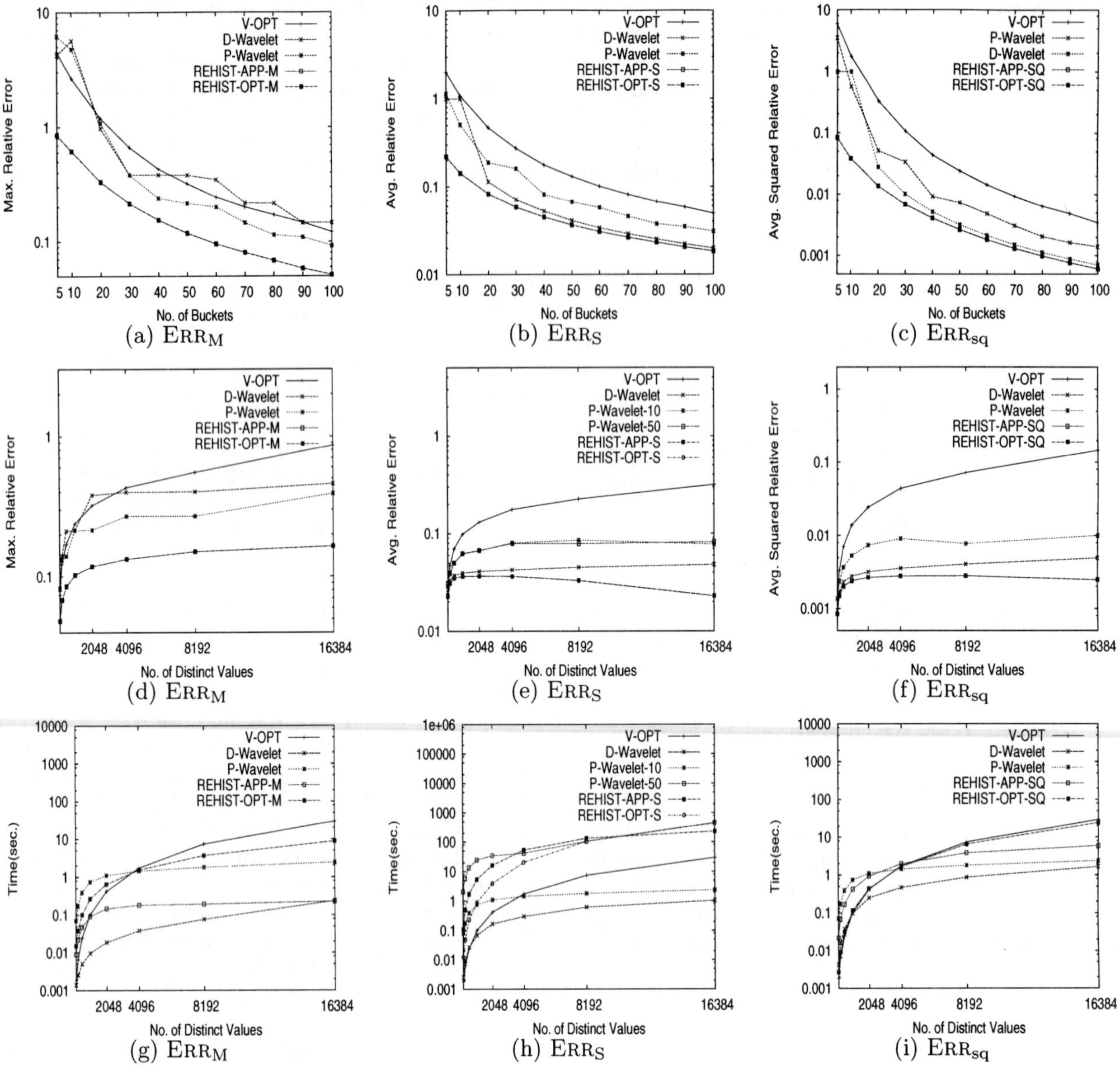

Figure 7: Approximation Error for Normal Zipfian permutation with Synthetic Data Sets

(a) ERR_M (CovType-HS3) (b) ERR_S (CovType-HS3) (c) ERR_sq (CovType-HS3)

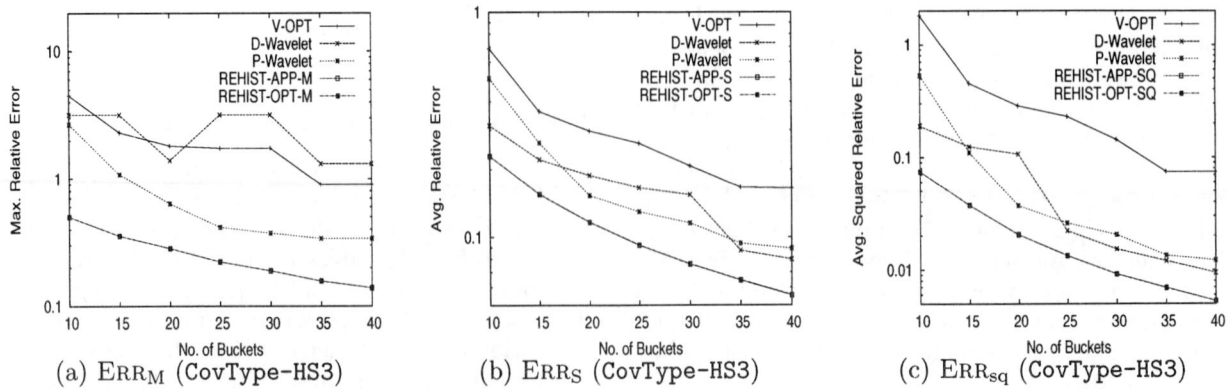

Figure 8: Approximation Error for Real-Life Data Set

hillshade index (from 0 to 255) at 3 pm on the summer solstice. Its histogram is bell-shaped and relatively smooth. `CovType-A` has uniformly spread distribution with a pipe-organ-style fluctuation and considerable peaks of noise. Due to lack of space, the quality of histograms were plotted for `CovType-HS3` only in Figure 8. Our results show that REHIST provides significantly better accuracy than D-Wavelet, P-Wavelet and V-OPT.

6 Summary

Histograms and Wavelet synopsis provide useful tools in query optimization and approximate query answering. Previous algorithms for relative error use wavelet approximation schemes with deterministic or probabilistic thresholding. The deterministic scheme suggests heuristics which are not guaranteed to minimize relative error. The probabilistic scheme proposes a complicated optimization, and proceeds to provide an approximation, which holds in expectation only. Expected guarantees are not sufficient for minimizing maximum error objective. We presented optimal as well as faster approximation algorithms with several relative error measures. We did comprehensive analysis of time and space complexities of these algorithms and, with synthetic and real-life data sets, demonstrated the effectiveness of our algorithms in providing significantly more accurate answers compared to the wavelet based methods and V-Optimal algorithm.

Acknowledgments

The authors wish to thank the referees for many useful comments which have helped in improving the presentation of the manuscript. The work was supported by the Ministry of Information and Communication in Korea through the University Information Technology Research Center (ITRC) Support Program.

References

[1] S. Acharya, P. Gibbons, V. Poosala, and S. Ramaswamy. The Aqua Approximate Query Answering System. *Proc. of ACM SIGMOD*, 1999.

[2] K. Chakrabarti, E. J. Keogh, S. Mehrotra, and M. J. Pazzani. Locally adaptive dimensionality reduction for indexing large time series databases. *ACM TODS*, 27(2):188–228, 2002.

[3] M. N. Garofalakis and P. B. Gibbons. Probabilistic wavelet synopses. *To appear in ACM TODS*.

[4] M. N. Garofalakis and P. B. Gibbons. Wavelet synopses with error guarantees. In *Proc. of ACM SIGMOD*, 2002.

[5] A. C. Gilbert, S. Guha, P. Indyk, Y. Kotidis, S. Muthukrishnan, and M. Strauss. Fast, small-space algorithms for approximate histogram maintenance. In *Proc. of ACM STOC*, 2002.

[6] A. C. Gilbert, Y. Kotidis, S. Muthukrishnan, and M. Strauss. Optimal and approximate computation of summary statistics for range aggregates. In *Proc. of ACM PODS*, 2001.

[7] S. Guha, P. Indyk, S. Muthukrishnan, and M. Strauss. Histogramming data streams with fast per-item processing. In *Proc. of ICALP*, 2002.

[8] S. Guha and N. Koudas. Approximating a Data Stream for Querying and Estimation: Algorithms and Performance Evaluation. In *Proc. of ICDE*, 2002.

[9] S. Guha, N. Koudas, and K. Shim. Data Streams and Histograms. In *Proc. of STOC*, 2001.

[10] S. Guha, N. Koudas, and D. Srivastava. Fast algorithms for hierarchical range histogram construction. In *Proc. of ACM PODS*, 2002.

[11] S. Guha, K. Shim, and J. Woo. REHIST: Relative error histogram construction algorithms. Techical Report, Seoul National University, Seoul, Korea, July 2004.

[12] Y. Ioannidis and V. Poosala. Balancing Histogram Optimality and Practicality for Query Result Size Estimation. *Proc. of ACM SIGMOD*, 1995.

[13] Y. E. Ioannidis. Universality of serial histograms. In *Proc. of the VLDB Conference*, 1993.

[14] H. V. Jagadish, N. Koudas, S. Muthukrishnan, V. Poosala, K. C. Sevcik, and T. Suel. Optimal Histograms with Quality Guarantees. In *Proc. of the VLDB Conference*, 1998.

[15] N. Koudas, S. Muthukrishnan, and D. Srivastava. Optimal histograms for hierarchical range queries. In *Proc. of ACM PODS*, 2000.

[16] Y. Matias, J. S. Vitter, and M. Wang. Wavelet-Based Histograms for Selectivity Estimation. *Proc. of ACM SIGMOD*, 1998.

[17] J. Vitter and M. Wang. Approximate computation of multidimensional aggregates on sparse data using wavelets. *Proc. of SIGMOD*, 1999.

Distributed Set-Expression Cardinality Estimation

Abhinandan Das[†][*] Sumit Ganguly[§][*] Minos Garofalakis[‡] Rajeev Rastogi[‡]

[†] Cornell University
asdas@cs.cornell.edu

[§] IIT Kanpur
sganguly@cse.iitk.ac.in

[‡] Bell Labs, Lucent Technologies
{minos,rastogi}@bell-labs.com

Abstract

We consider the problem of estimating set-expression cardinality in a *distributed streaming* environment where rapid update streams originating at remote sites are continually transmitted to a central processing system. At the core of our algorithmic solutions for answering set-expression cardinality queries are two novel techniques for lowering data communication costs without sacrificing answer precision. Our first technique exploits global knowledge of the distribution of certain frequently occurring stream elements to significantly reduce the transmission of element state information to the central site. Our second technical contribution involves a novel way of capturing the semantics of the input set expression in a boolean logic formula, and using models (of the formula) to determine whether an element state change at a remote site can affect the set expression result. Results of our experimental study with real-life as well as synthetic data sets indicate that our distributed set-expression cardinality estimation algorithms achieve substantial reductions in message traffic compared to naive approaches that provide the same accuracy guarantees.

1 Introduction

The widespread deployment of wireline and wireless networks linking together a broad range of devices has resulted in a new class of *distributed data streaming* applications. In these applications, rapid update streams originating at tens or hundreds of remote sites are continuously transmitted to a central processing system for online querying and analysis. Examples include monitoring of service provider network traffic statistics, telecommunication call detail records, Web usage logs, financial stock tickers, retail chain transactions, weather data, sensor data, and so on.

[*]Work done while visiting Bell Labs, Murray Hill, NJ.

Permission to copy without fee all or part of this material is granted provided that the copies are not made or distributed for direct commercial advantage, the VLDB copyright notice and the title of the publication and its date appear, and notice is given that copying is by permission of the Very Large Data Base Endowment. To copy otherwise, or to republish, requires a fee and/or special permission from the Endowment.

**Proceedings of the 30th VLDB Conference,
Toronto, Canada, 2004**

An important consideration in the above-mentioned monitoring applications is the communication overhead imposed by the distributed query processing architecture on the underlying network. A naive approach in which every stream update is shipped to the central site for processing can lead to inordinate amounts of message traffic, and thus have a crippling effect on the communication infrastructure as well as the central processor. For instance, monitoring flow level information within AT&T's IP backbone using Cisco's NetFlow tool [1] is known to generate in excess of 500 GBytes of data per day [4]. Clearly, transmitting every flow record to the central network operations center of a large ISP can seriously strain its processing and network resources. As another example, consider wireless sensor networks (e.g., for environmental monitoring, inventory tracking, etc.), where sensors have a very limited battery life, and radio communication is much more expensive in terms of power consumption compared to processing. In order to ensure longer lifetimes for sensor nodes, it is critical to reduce the amount of data transmitted, even if that implies additional processing at the sensor nodes [13, 12, 10].

Fortunately, for many distributed stream-oriented applications, exact answers are not required and approximations with guarantees on the amount of error suffice. Thus, it is possible to trade answer accuracy for reduced data communication costs. For example, consider the problem of detecting distributed denial-of-service (DDoS) attacks by analyzing network flow information collected from an ISP's border routers. In a typical DDoS attack scenario, hundreds of compromised "zombie" hosts flood a specific victim destination with large numbers of seemingly legitimate packets. Furthermore, in order to elude source identification, attackers typically forge, or "spoof", the IP source address of each packet they send with a randomly-chosen address [11]. Consequently, a possible approach for detecting DDoS attacks is to look for sudden spikes in the number of distinct IP source addresses observed in the flows across the ISP's border routers. Clearly, our DDoS monitoring application does not require IP source address counts to be tracked with complete precision. Approximate counts can be equally effective for the purpose of discerning DDoS activity as long as errors are small enough so as to not mask abrupt changes. Thus, depending on the accuracy requirements of the DDoS application, routers only need to transmit a subset of flow records to the central monitoring site.

As another example, consider a Web content delivery

service such as that provided by *Akamai* (www.akamai.com). In this case, Web sites are replicated at a large number of geographically distributed servers, and users accessing a Web site are automatically redirected to the geographically closest server, or the least loaded server. Here, one might often be interested in tracking (approximately) the number of (distinct) users accessing a Web site (across all servers), the number of users who visit both a Web site A and Web site B, or the number of users who visit Web site A but not B. These statistics can be useful for determining the servers at which to replicate Web sites, deciding which advertisements to display at each Web site, and so on.

The problem of counting the number of distinct IP source addresses or web-site users, as discussed above, are special cases of the more general *set-expression cardinality* estimation problem, which we tackle in this paper. In this more general problem, we are interested in estimating the number of distinct values in the result of an arbitrary set expression over distributed data streams. For example, in the DDoS scenario, we may want to employ the set difference cardinality query $|S - T|$ to detect significant traffic deviations – here, S is the IP source address set for the sliding window spanning the past week (until now) and T is the set of IP source addresses from the week prior to that (e.g., two weeks ago). Similarly, in our Web example, if S and T are the sets of users who visit Web sites A and B, respectively, then the set intersection query $|S \cap T|$ yields the number of users who access both sites A and B.

Prior Work. The tradeoff between answer accuracy and communication overhead for specific classes of continuous queries over distributed update streams was recently studied in [12, 2]. In [12], Olston et al. consider aggregation queries that compute sums and averages of dynamically changing numeric values spread over multiple sources. In their approach, each site is assigned an interval of a certain width such that the sum of site interval widths is less than the application's total error tolerance. Thus, as long as the numeric value at each site stays within the interval for the site, no messages need to be sent by the sites in order to satisfy the application's accuracy requirements. However, in case the value at a site drifts outside the site's interval, the site is required to transmit the value to the central site and make appropriate adjustments to its interval. Reference [2] focuses on the problem of continually tracking the top-k values in distributed data streams; the developed techniques ensure the continuing validity of the current top-k set (at the central site) by installing arithmetic constraints at each site.

Our work is most similar to the above two research efforts, but considers *set-expression cardinality queries* as opposed to the aggregation and top-k queries handled in [12, 2]. As we will see later in the paper, processing set-expression cardinality queries requires substantially new algorithms to be developed for effectively trading off answer accuracy and communication costs in a distributed-streams setting.

Much of the recent work on data streams has focused on developing memory-efficient one-pass algorithms for performing a wide range of computations on a single stream; examples include computing quantiles [9], estimating distinct values [7, 8], set-expression cardinality [6] and frequent stream elements [3]. An exception is [8] where randomized hash-based sampling algorithms are employed to estimate the number of distinct values in a sliding window over distributed streams. However, [8] does not address the issue of optimizing data-shipping costs when guaranteed precision estimates are required to be continually tracked at the central processing site. Our work differs from these existing proposals that are primarily concerned with exploring space-accuracy tradeoffs (mostly for single streams) rather than communication-accuracy tradeoffs in a distributed streams setting.

Our Contributions. In this paper, we focus on the problem of estimating the cardinality of arbitrary set expressions over distributed update streams. Our proposed algorithmic solutions are the *first* to provide provable guarantees on the accuracy of the final set-expression cardinality estimate, while keeping data transmission costs at a minimum. Since set-expression queries subsume the important class of distinct-value queries, our work also constitutes the first attempt at providing low-cost high-quality answers to this latter type of queries in a distributed setting. More concretely, our contributions can be summarized as follows.

- **Distributed Framework for Processing Set-Expression Cardinality Queries.** We develop our solutions in the context of a general framework for guaranteeing precision constraints for set-expression cardinality queries in a distributed setting. In our framework, each site is allocated an error budget which governs when the site communicates stream state information to the central processing site (for estimating set-expression cardinality). Basically, each remote site associates a *charge* with every stream element that is inserted or deleted since stream state was last transmitted to the central site. Only when the sum of element charges at a site exceeds the site's error budget does it communicate the current stream state information to the central site. Our framework allows for flexibility in how elements are assigned charges – methods for computing charges are only required to satisfy certain basic properties needed for correctness in terms of providing the stipulated error guarantees. Obviously, methods that return smaller charges for elements are more desirable since they result in lower communication overhead.

- **Techniques that Incorporate Global Knowledge to Reduce Communication.** In many distributed streaming environments, the frequency distribution of stream elements will be skewed with certain elements occurring more frequently than others. For example, in the flows collected from an ISP's border routers, IP addresses corresponding to popular Web sites like Yahoo, Google, Amazon, etc. will be contained in a disproportionately large number of flows. Now, if such a frequently occurring element is inserted into a stream at a site (where it does not appear previously), then we do not need to charge for it since the element must already be present at the central site, and thus the insert has no effect on the set-expression cardinality at the central site. Similarly, the charge for the deletion of a frequent element can be distributed across all the sites where the element occurs since the element would need to be deleted at all these sites to truly go away. Thus, global knowledge of frequent stream elements can lead to lower overall communication costs due to reduced element charges at each site. We propose protocols for disseminating this global information to the various sites while incurring minimal message overhead.

- **Techniques that Exploit Set-Expression Semantics to Reduce Communication.** We develop schemes that exploit the semantics of set expressions to obtain further reductions in element charges. For example, in the expression $S \cup T$, if an element e is already present in stream S, then inserts and deletes of e from T have no effect on the set-expression result, and thus we do not need to charge for them. We propose a logic-based approach where we capture the conditions for a change in the set-expression result in a boolean formula. Models for the boolean formula then represent scenarios for result changes and are used to compute element charges. Finally, in order to address the (provably required) exponential time complexity of model enumeration, we develop an efficient heuristic for computing element charges whose running time is polynomial in the number of streams.

- **Experimental Results Validating our Approach.** We present the results of an experimental study (with a real-life TCP traffic data set and multiple synthetic data sets) that demonstrate the effectiveness of our distributed algorithms for estimating set-expression cardinality. Our results indicate that, compared to obvious approaches, our estimation algorithms can lead to reductions in communication costs ranging from a factor of 2 (for the real-life data set) to more than 6 (for synthetic data sets) while guaranteeing high precision for the returned estimates.

Note that while our primary focus in this paper is on estimating set-expression *cardinality*, our techniques are quite powerful, and can also be used to approximate set expression *results* (i.e., sets of data elements) at the central site. This can be used by the coordinator to run other potentially complex queries on top of it, which could be more useful than just cardinality queries. For example, in the DDoS scenario, the results could be filtered to identify malicious *hosts*, or in the *Akamai* example, to identify *users* corresponding to certain traffic patterns.

2 System Model

In this section, we describe our distributed update-stream processing architecture and formally define the set-expression cardinality estimation problem addressed in this paper. Consider a distributed environment with $m+1$ sites and n update streams. Stream updates arrive continuously

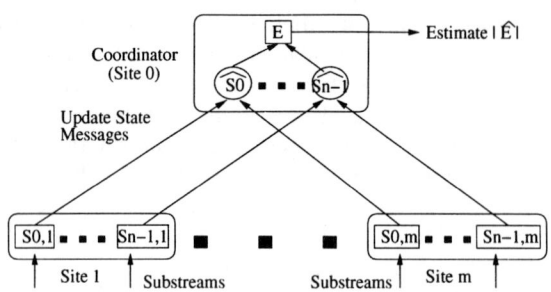

Figure 1: Distributed Stream Processing Model.

at *remote* sites $1, \ldots, m$, and site 0 is a special *coordinator* site that is responsible for generating answers to user (set-expression cardinality) queries. We adopt a similar model to [2, 12] where there is no direct communication among remote sites; instead, as illustrated in Figure 1, each remote site exchanges messages only with the coordinator, providing it with state information for streams at the site. Note that this distributed communication model is representative of a large class of real-life applications including network monitoring where a central Network Operations Center (NOC) is responsible for processing network traffic statistics collected at the switches and routers distributed across the network.

At each remote site j, the n update streams render n distinct multi-sets $S_{0,j}, \ldots, S_{n-1,j}$ of elements from the integer domain $[M] = \{0, \ldots, M-1\}$. Each stream update at remote site j is a triple of the form $<i, e, \pm v>$, where i identifies the multi-set $S_{i,j}$ being updated, $e \in [M]$ is the specific data element whose frequency changes, and $\pm v$ is the net change in the frequency of e in $S_{i,j}$, i.e., "$+v$" ("$-v$") denotes v insertions (resp., deletions) of e. We assume that all deletions in our update streams are legal; that is, an update $<i, e, -v>$ can only be issued if the net frequency of e in $S_{i,j}$ is at least v. Note that delete operations help to substantially enrich our streaming model; for example, with deletions, we can easily handle sliding window queries by simply issuing a delete operation for each expired stream update that is no longer in the window of interest. For each $i = 0, \ldots, n-1$, let $S_i = \cup_j S_{i,j}$. Thus, S_i reflects the global state of the ith update stream, while each multi-set $S_{i,j}$ captures the local state of stream i at site j. In the remainder of the paper, we will loosely refer to S_i and $S_{i,j}$ as streams even though the intended meaning is the current states of the underlying streams.

Our focus is on the problem of answering set-expression cardinality queries over the underlying collection of distributed update streams. Specifically, given a set expression E over streams $S_0, \ldots, S_{n-1}$ (with the standard set operators $\cup, \cap,$ and $-$ as connectives), we seek to estimate $|E|$, the number of distinct elements in E. For example, $|S_0 \cap S_1|$ is the number of distinct elements in the intersection of streams S_0 and S_1. If for $m = 2$ remote sites, $S_{0,1} = \{a\}, S_{0,2} = \{a, b\}, S_{1,1} = \{b\}$ and $S_{1,2} = \{c\}$, then

$S_0 = \{a, b\}$ and $S_1 = \{b, c\}$. Thus, $E = S_0 \cap S_1 = \{b\}$ and $|E| = 1$.

The problem of estimating $|E|$ at the coordinator is complicated in our setting because the substreams $S_{i,j}$ that comprise each distributed stream S_i are distributed across the remote sites. Accurately tracking $|E|$ by having remote sites continuously ship every stream update to the coordinator is clearly impractical for high data rate streams. Consequently, in order to reduce the burden on the communication infrastructure, we allow $|E|$ to be approximated, but enforce a bound on the error in the final estimate. Specifically, for a prespecified error tolerance ϵ, we seek to compute an estimate $\hat{X}$ for $X = |E|$ (at the coordinator) such that $X - \epsilon \leq \hat{X} \leq X + \epsilon$. The ϵ error parameter provides system designers with a useful knob that enables them to trade accuracy for efficiency. Essentially, the larger the error tolerance of an application, the smaller the communication overhead required to ensure that the estimate $\hat{X}$ meets the ϵ accuracy guarantee.

3 Estimating Single Stream Cardinality

We begin by describing our distributed algorithm for the case when the expression E whose cardinality we wish to estimate is a single stream S_i (which is the union of substreams $S_{i,j}$ at remote sites). Thus, we are basically looking to estimate the number of distinct elements in stream S_i. Our scheme for the distinct elements estimation problem illustrates the key concepts underlying our approach as well as the overall structure of our distributed solutions. In the next section, we will generalize our solution for a single stream to handle arbitrary set expressions.

3.1 Overview

Our objective is to be able to continuously estimate $|E|$ at the coordinator with ϵ accuracy. To achieve this, we distribute the error tolerance of ϵ among the m remote sites. We denote the error budget allocated to site j by ϵ_j; thus, $\sum_j \epsilon_j = \epsilon$. While there are multiple ways to allocate error budgets to sites [12], a simple approach is to allocate these proportional to the stream update rates at the sites. The error parameter ϵ_j essentially dictates when site j sends the current states of substreams $S_{i,j}$ at site j to the coordinator. We denote by $\hat{S}_{i,j}$ the most recent state of substream $S_{i,j}$ communicated (by site j) to the coordinator. In addition to $S_{i,j}$, site j also stores in its local memory, the transmitted states $\hat{S}_{i,j}$ for substreams at the site. For each stream S_i, the coordinator constructs the global state $\hat{S}_i$ by taking the union of all the local substream states $\hat{S}_{i,j}$ received from the remote sites. Thus, $\hat{S}_i = \cup_j \hat{S}_{i,j}$. Now let $\hat{E}$ be the result of evaluating expression E on the states $\hat{S}_i$ instead of S_i. The coordinator estimates the cardinality of set expression E as $|\hat{E}|$.

We would like to emphasize here that if remote sites have limited memory, then our scheme can be modified to store a *compact sketch synopsis* for each substream (instead of the complete substream state). Due to space constraints, we describe details of our sketch-based distributed algorithm in [5], and assume that each remote site keeps track of substream states in our current presentation.

In order to guarantee that the estimate $|\hat{E}|$ is correct, we need to ensure that $|E| - \epsilon \leq |\hat{E}| \leq |E| + \epsilon$. A simple approach (based on adapting the scheme of [12]) for ensuring this for $E = S_i$ is as follows. At each remote site j, if either of $|S_{i,j} - \hat{S}_{i,j}|$ or $|\hat{S}_{i,j} - S_{i,j}|$ exceeds ϵ_j, then site j sends the most recent state $S_{i,j}$ to the coordinator. One can easily show that this simple scheme guarantees that at all times, $|E - \hat{E}| \leq \epsilon$ and $|\hat{E} - E| \leq \epsilon$, and is thus correct. For instance, consider an element e in $E - \hat{E}$. The element must belong to $S_{i,j} - \hat{S}_{i,j}$ at some site j, and since $|S_{i,j} - \hat{S}_{i,j}| \leq \epsilon_j$, it must be counted against the error budget ϵ_j at site j. As a result, since $\sum_j \epsilon_j = \epsilon$, we get that $|E - \hat{E}| \leq \epsilon$. Further, since $|E| - |\hat{E}| \leq |E - \hat{E}|$, we obtain that $|E| - |\hat{E}| \leq \epsilon$. Similarly, it is possible to show that $|\hat{E}| - |E| \leq \epsilon$, and thus the estimate $|\hat{E}|$ is within ϵ error of $|E|$.

Intuitively, the simple scheme described above associates a charge $\phi_j(e)$ with each element e at every remote site j, and if the total of these charges exceed ϵ_j, then the remote site communicates state information to the coordinator. More formally, let $\phi_j^+(e) = 1$ if $e \in (S_{i,j} - \hat{S}_{i,j})$, $\phi_j^-(e) = 1$ if $e \in (\hat{S}_{i,j} - S_{i,j})$, and $\phi_j^+(e) = \phi_j^-(e) = 0$, otherwise. As a result, $\sum_e \phi_j^+(e) = |S_{i,j} - \hat{S}_{i,j}|$ and $\sum_e \phi_j^-(e) = |\hat{S}_{i,j} - S_{i,j}|$. Thus, there is a message exchange between site j and the coordinator if either $\sum_e \phi_j^+(e) > \epsilon_j$ or $\sum_e \phi_j^-(e) > \epsilon_j$.

In the simple scheme, element charges are computed based entirely on the local state information available at each site. We next show that by exploiting global knowledge about element e, we can reduce the charge $\phi_j(e)$ for e, and as a consequence, the overall message traffic between remote sites and the coordinator. The key observation we make is that in many stream-oriented domains, there will be a certain subset of globally "popular" elements. For instance, in an IP network monitoring scenario, destination IP addresses corresponding to popular Web sites like Yahoo, Amazon, Google etc. will frequently appear in the flow records collected from network routers. An important characteristic of each such globally popular element is that, at any given point in time, it will appear in substreams at multiple sites although the exact sites that contain the element may vary over time.

Now suppose that for a popular element e, each remote site (approximately) knows the number of substream states $\hat{S}_{i,j}$ that contain e. Specifically, for stream S_i, let $\theta_i(e) > 1$ be a lower bound on the number of sites for which e appears in the $\hat{S}_{i,j}$ states communicated to the coordinator. Then, even if element e is newly inserted into $S_{i,j}$ at site j (that is, $e \in (S_{i,j} - \hat{S}_{i,j})$), we should not charge for it since e is already in $\hat{S}_i$ and, thus, cannot possibly be in $S_i - \hat{S}_i$. Similarly, if e is deleted from $S_{i,j}$ at site j (that is, $e \in (\hat{S}_{i,j} - S_{i,j})$), then in order for e to be deleted from S_i and thus be in $\hat{S}_i - S_i$, e must be deleted from $S_{i,j}$ at least $\theta_i(e)$ sites. Thus, it suffices to charge $\phi_j^-(e) = 1/\theta_i(e)$ (instead of 1) for the local delete of e at each site j. This way, if local deletions at the $\geq \theta_i(e)$ sites cause e to be globally deleted (that is, $e \in (\hat{S}_i - S_i)$), then the cumulative charge $\sum_j \phi_j^-(e)$ for e across the sites is at least 1. As a result, since $\sum_e \phi_j^-(e) \leq \epsilon_j$ at each site j, this total charge of 1 is counted against the various ϵ_js, and correctness is not compromised.

3.2 Distributed Algorithm

We are now ready to describe the details of our distributed scheme for producing a correct cardinality estimate $|\hat{E}|$ at the coordinator. For each element $e \in \hat{S}_i$, the coordinator maintains a count $C_i(e)$ of the number of remote sites whose states $\hat{S}_{i,j}$ contain the element e. Elements whose counts $C_i(e)$ exceed a threshold τ are considered to be *frequent*, and added to a frequent element set F_i for stream S_i. The coordinator also uses the count $C_i(e)$ for each element $e \in F_i$ to compute a lower bound threshold $\theta_i(e)$ such that the invariant $C_i(e) \geq \theta_i(e)$ always holds. It continuously communicates changes in the frequent element sets F_i and the threshold values $\theta_i(e)$ to the remote sites so that these can be used to compute element charges $\phi_j(e)$ at the sites (as described in the previous subsection). Thus, in order to keep the message overhead under control, the coordinator does not send exact element counts $C_i(e)$ to remote sites, but rather disseminates the thresholds, as described in the paragraph below. Each remote site j keeps track of the sum of local element charges $\sum_e \phi_j(e)$ in variable Φ_j. Further, when Φ_j becomes greater than ϵ_j, it sends the deltas $\Delta_i^+ = S_{i,j} - \hat{S}_{i,j}$ and $\Delta_i^- = \hat{S}_{i,j} - S_{i,j}$ that capture the local state changes for substream $S_{i,j}$ since site j last transmitted state information to the coordinator. (Note that the deltas are *sets* and not multi-sets).

Coodinator Actions. Figure 2 depicts the actions performed by the coordinator when it receives the deltas Δ_i^+ and Δ_i^- for substream $S_{i,j}$ from site j. The coordinator employs the received deltas to first update element counts $C_i(e)$ and the stream state $\hat{S}_i$ stored at the coordinator. (Recall that the sets $\hat{S}_i$ are used to generate the final estimate $|\hat{E}|$.) It then uses the new counts $C_i(e)$ to adjust the frequent element set F_i, and the threshold values $\theta_i(e)$ for frequent elements. It also informs all the remote sites of changes to F_i and $\theta_i(e)$ by sending them "make frequent" and "adjust threshold" control messages, which trigger the remote sites to apply the same changes to their local copies of F_i and $\theta_i(e)$. The control messages thus ensure that the values of F_i and $\theta_i(e)$ are synchronized between the coordinator and remote sites.

The correctness of our distributed scheme hinges on the fact that for each element $e \in F_i$, the threshold value $\theta_i(e)$ is always a lower bound on the number of sites j for whom e is in the local state $\hat{S}_{i,j}$ sent to the coordinator. Thus, our scheme for modifying F_i and $\theta_i(e)$ needs to preserve

Procedure COORDINATOR($i, \Delta_i^+, \Delta_i^-$)
Input: Newly inserted (Δ_i^+) and deleted (Δ_i^-) elements for some substream $S_{i,j}$.
begin
1. **foreach** element $e \in \Delta_i^-$ **do** {
2. $C_i(e) := C_i(e) - 1$;
3.   **if** ($C_i(e) = 0$) **then** $\hat{S}_i := \hat{S}_i - \{e\}$;
4.   **if** ($e \in F_i$ **and** $C_i(e) < \tau$) {
5. $F_i := F_i - \{e\}$;
6.   Send "make infrequent" control msgs for e to all remote sites;
7.   }
8.   **else if** ($e \in F_i$ **and** $C_i(e) < \theta_i(e)$){
9. $\theta_i(e) := \theta_i(e)/2$;
10.   Send "adjust threshold" control msgs with new threshold
11. $\theta_i(e)$ for e to all remote sites;
12.   }
13. }
14. **foreach** element $e \in \Delta_i^+$ **do** {
15. $C_i(e) := C_i(e) + 1$;
16.   **if** ($C_i(e) = 1$) **then** $\hat{S}_i := \hat{S}_i \cup \{e\}$;
17.   **if** ($e \notin F_i$ **and** $C_i(e) \geq 2\tau$) {
18. $F_i := F_i \cup \{e\}$;
19. $\theta_i(e) := \tau$;
20.   Send "make frequent" control msgs for e to all remote sites;
21.   }
22.   **else if** ($e \in F_i$ **and** $C_i(e) \geq 4\theta_i(e)$){
23. $\theta_i(e) := 2\theta_i(e)$;
24.   Send "adjust threshold" control msgs with new threshold
25. $\theta_i(e)$ for e to all remote sites;
26.   }
27. }
end

Figure 2: Coordinator Actions for Processing Remote Deltas.

the invariant $C_i(e) \geq \theta_i(e)$ while controlling the number of messages between the coordinator and remote sites. Clearly, to maintain the invariant, the coordinator needs to send messages to all sites every time the count $C_i(e)$ drops below the current threshold $\theta_i(e)$ for an element $e \in F_i$. Consequently, in order to prevent minor fluctuations in the value of $C_i(e)$ from generating excessive amounts of control message traffic, our strategy is to try and keep a sufficient gap between $C_i(e)$ and $\theta_i(e)$. Thus, for instance, if $C_i(e)$ becomes less than $\theta_i(e)$, then we simply halve the value of $\theta_i(e)$. Similarly, we double the value of $\theta_i(e)$ only when $C_i(e)$ exceeds $4\theta_i(e)$, and (conservatively) consider an element to be frequent only if $C_i(e)$ exceeds 2τ.

An additional mechanism that we found to be effective for keeping the volume of control messages low (in our experimental study reported in Section 5) is to double $\theta_i(e)$ only after the count $C_i(e)$ is somewhat stable (that is, has stayed above $3\theta_i(e)$ for a certain time period after crossing $4\theta_i(e)$). Using this strategy, we found that the number of control messages is relatively insensitive to the value of the threshold parameter τ. Finally, observe that while increasing $\theta_i(e)$ is not required for preserving the invariant $C_i(e) \geq \theta_i(e)$, larger $\theta_i(e)$ values are key to reducing the charges $\phi_j(e)$ that sites incur for elements.

Procedure REMOTE(i, e, j)
Input: Update stream S_i, element e and site j.
begin
1. $old^+ := \phi_j^+(e)$;
2. $old^- := \phi_j^-(e)$;
3. $[\phi_j^+(e), \phi_j^-(e)] :=$ COMPUTECHARGE(e, j, E);
4. $\Phi_j^+ := \Phi_j^+ + (\phi_j^+(e) - old^+)$;
5. $\Phi_j^- := \Phi_j^- + (\phi_j^-(e) - old^-)$;
6.   **if** $(\Phi_j^+ > \epsilon_j \vee \Phi_j^- > \epsilon_j)$ {
7.   **for** $l := 1$ to n **do** {
8. $\Delta_l^+ := S_{l,j} - \hat{S}_{l,j}$;
9. $\Delta_l^- := \hat{S}_{l,j} - S_{l,j}$;
10. $\hat{S}_{l,j} := S_{l,j}$;
11.   }
12.   Send "update state" message with triples $<l, \Delta_l^+, \Delta_l^->$
13.   for all substreams $S_{l,j}$ to the coordinator;
14.   **foreach** element e, $\phi_j^+(e) := \phi_j^-(e) := 0$;
15. $\Phi_j^+ := \Phi_j^- := 0$;
16. }
end

Procedure COMPUTECHARGE($e, j, E = S_i$)
Input: Element e for whom to compute charge at site j, expression E.
Output: Charges $\phi_j^+(e)$ and $\phi_j^-(e)$.
begin
1. $\phi^+ := \phi^- := 0$;
2.   **if** $(e \notin F_i)$ {
3.   **if** $(e \in (S_{i,j} - \hat{S}_{i,j}))$ **then** $\phi^+ := 1$;
4.   **else if** $(e \in (\hat{S}_{i,j} - S_{i,j}))$ **then** $\phi^- := 1$;
5.   }
6.   **else**   /* $e \in F_i$ */
7.   **if** $(e \in (\hat{S}_{i,j} - S_{i,j}))$ **then** $\phi^- := 1/\theta_i(e)$;
8.   **return** $[\phi^+, \phi^-]$;
end

Figure 3: Remote Site Actions for Computing Charges.

Remote Site Actions. Figure 3 depicts the actions taken by remote site j when an element e is inserted into or deleted from $S_{i,j}$ (due to a stream update), or the frequent set F_i or threshold value $\theta_i(e)$ gets modified (due to a "make frequent" or "adjust threshold" control message for e from the coordinator). Essentially, remote site j computes new charges $\phi_j^+(e)$ and $\phi_j^-(e)$ for e, and appropriately adjusts the total site charges Φ_j^+ and Φ_j^-. Further, if either of these charges exceeds ϵ_j, the deltas for all substreams $S_{l,j}$ are sent to the coordinator; thus, $\hat{S}_{l,j} = S_{l,j}$, and consequently, all charges $\phi_j(e)$ are reset to 0. (Note that sending the deltas for all 'other' substreams to the coordinator is not required when the expression $E = S_i$ since there is only 1 substream at each site, but is needed for the more general set expressions considered in the next section.)

Procedure COMPUTECHARGE in Figure 3 is tailored for the single stream case (that is, $E = S_i$). Later in the paper, we will present alternate charge computation procedures that apply to general set expressions. In a nutshell, COMPUTECHARGE associates a charge of 1 for non-frequent elements that are newly inserted into or deleted from $S_{i,j}$ since the last message to the coordinator. For frequent elements $e \in F_i$, charge $\phi_j^+(e) = 0$ if e is newly inserted, and charge $\phi_j^-(e) = 1/\theta_i(e)$ if e is locally deleted.

Correctness Argument. For ease of exposition, in the arguments pertaining to the correctness of our distributed scheme, we assume that all message transmissions and the actions they trigger are performed instantaneously. While this is clearly not a realistic assumption, our scheme can be extended to simulate such an instantaneous execution (at a logical level) by having sites send special acknowledgements for messages once all the actions triggered by the messages have completed. Details can be found in [5].

The charges $\phi_j^+(e)$ and $\phi_j^-(e)$ computed by COMPUTECHARGE can be shown to satisfy the following two invariants:

$$\text{For each } e \in E - \hat{E}, \quad \sum_j \phi_j^+(e) \geq 1 \quad (1)$$

$$\text{For each } e \in \hat{E} - E, \quad \sum_j \phi_j^-(e) \geq 1 \quad (2)$$

Thus, our distributed scheme is correct because it can be shown (see [5]) that Equation (1) implies that $|E| - \epsilon \leq |\hat{E}|$ and Equation (2) implies that $|\hat{E}| \leq |E| + \epsilon$.

Using Sketch Synopses to Reduce Space/Communication. The space usage of our distributed algorithm can be reduced by storing a compact sketch synopsis for each substream $S_{i,j}$ instead of the entire substream state. Our scheme would then provide probabilistic as opposed to deterministic error guarantees. For instance, we can maintain a (delete-resistant) distinct sample [7] for each substream, and use the substream samples in place of the substream states in our distributed scheme. Due to lack of space, we defer the details of our distinct sample-based estimation algorithms and hash-based techniques for obtaining delete-resistant distinct stream samples to the full paper [5].

4 Estimating Cardinality of Arbitrary Set Expressions

In this section, we generalize our single stream solution (described in the previous section) to tackle the problem of estimating (to within ϵ absolute error) the cardinality of an arbitrary set expression E involving the distributed update streams $S_0, \ldots, S_{n-1}$. Our distributed scheme for general set expressions is identical to the scheme for single streams except for the charging procedure COMPUTECHARGE. Thus, as before, for each stream S_i, the coordinator maintains the states $\hat{S}_i$, the frequent sets F_i, and the threshold values $\theta_i(e)$ for the number of sites j whose shipped state $\hat{S}_{i,j}$ contains element e. The cardinality estimate at the coordinator is $|\hat{E}|$, where $\hat{E}$ is the result of evaluating expression E using $\hat{S}_i$ instead of S_i. The coordinator processes the deltas from a remote site for an arbitrary stream S_i as described in procedure COORDINATOR (see Figure 2). Similarly, site j executes the actions described in procedure REMOTE (see Figure 3) every time there is a change in the substream state $S_{i,j}$, the frequent set F_i, or the local threshold value $\theta_i(e)$.

In the charging procedure for the single stream case, we charged 1 for inserts and deletes of elements $e \notin F_i$, and if $e \in F_i$, inserts were free and deletes were charged $1/\theta_i(e)$. However, when E contains multiple streams, computing the charge $\phi_j(e)$ for an element e is more involved since e may be concurrently inserted/deleted from more than one substream $S_{i,j}$ at site j. A straightforward approach that overcomes this complication is to set the charges $\phi_j^+(e) = \phi_j^-(e) = 1$ if for any of the substreams $S_{i,j}$, either $e \in (S_{i,j} - \hat{S}_{i,j})$ or $e \in (\hat{S}_{i,j} - S_{i,j})$. However, while this straightforward scheme is obviously correct, it is too conservative, and may end up overcharging in many situations. This, in turn, could lead to frequent state transmission messages from remote sites to the coordinator.

Example 4.1 Consider distributed streams S_1, S_2 and S_3, and let expression $E = S_1 \cap (S_2 - S_3)$. For element e at site j, let $e \in \hat{S}_{3,j}$ and $e \in S_{3,j}$. Clearly, $e \in \hat{S}_3$ and $e \in S_3$, and thus $e \notin \hat{E}$ and $e \notin E$. As a result, even if $e \in (\hat{S}_{1,j} - S_{1,j})$ or $e \in (S_{2,j} - \hat{S}_{2,j})$, we should not charge for element e at site j since e cannot possibly be in either $E - \hat{E}$ or $\hat{E} - E$; thus, based on the semantics of expression E, setting the charges $\phi_j^+(e) = \phi_j^-(e) = 0$ will still ensure correctness. ∎

In the following subsections, for an arbitrary set expression E, we focus on the problem of computing the minimum possible charges $\phi_j^+(e)$ and $\phi_j^-(e)$ for a *fixed* element e at site j by leveraging the semantics of expression E. Our proposed charging schemes ensure that charges $\phi_j^+(e)$ and $\phi_j^-(e)$ satisfy Equations (1) and (2) (from Section 3.2), and thus provide an accuracy guarantee of ϵ for the final estimate $|\hat{E}|$. Our first charging method, presented in Section 4.1, is based on enumerating models for a boolean formula corresponding to expression E, and thus has an exponential time complexity. In Section 4.2, we develop a heuristic that at the expense of overcharging in some situations (described later), is able to eliminate model enumeration altogether, and bring down the time complexity so that it is polynomial in the number of streams.

In the remainder of this section, we will say that a stream S_i has a local state change at site j if either $e \in (S_{i,j} - \hat{S}_{i,j})$ or $e \in (\hat{S}_{i,j} - S_{i,j})$. Similarly, we will say that a stream S_i has a global state change if either $e \in (S_i - \hat{S}_i)$ or $e \in (\hat{S}_i - S_i)$.

4.1 A Model-Based Charging Scheme

Our charging procedure first constructs a boolean formula Ψ_j that captures the semantics of expression E and local stream constraints at each site j. It then defines the charge $\phi_j(e)$ at site j in terms of the charges for models M that satisfy Ψ_j.

4.1.1 Constructing Boolean Formula Ψ_j

For each stream S_i, let p_i and $\hat{p}_i$ be boolean variables with semantics $e \in S_i$ and $e \in \hat{S}_i$, respectively. We construct two boolean formulae Ψ_j^+ and Ψ_j^- over the variables p_i and $\hat{p}_i$. Intuitively, Ψ_j^+ and Ψ_j^- specify the conditions that stream states S_i and $\hat{S}_i$ must satisfy for $e \in (E - \hat{E})$ and $e \in (\hat{E} - E)$, respectively. The formulae also capture constraints on S_i and $\hat{S}_i$ due to local knowledge at site j of the substream states $S_{i,j}$, $\hat{S}_{i,j}$, and threshold values θ_i. For example, if $e \in S_{i,j}$, then it must be the case that $e \in S_i$ (since $S_i = \cup_j S_{i,j}$), and thus, variable p_i must be true.

The formulae Ψ_j^+ and Ψ_j^- are built using the following three formulae: (1) an *Expression* formula F_E representing the logic of expression E, (2) *State* formulae $\hat{G}_j, G_j$ that model the local knowledge that site j has about stream states S_i and $\hat{S}_i$, and (3) a *Threshold* formula H that captures the constraints due to the thresholds θ_i for each stream S_i. We describe each of them below.

Expression Formula. The expression formula F_E is constructed recursively as follows.

1. For every stream S_i in E, we replace its occurrence by the boolean variable p_i.
2. The expression $E_1 \cup E_2$ is translated as $F_{E_1} \vee F_{E_2}$.
3. The expression $E_1 \cap E_2$ is translated as $F_{E_1} \wedge E_{E_2}$.
4. The expression $E_1 - E_2$ is translated as $F_{E_1} \wedge (\neg F_{E_2})$.

For example, the set expression $E = S_1 \cap (S_2 - S_3)$ is translated into the boolean formula $F_E = p_1 \wedge (p_2 \wedge \neg p_3)$. It is easy to see that element $e \in E$ iff F_E is true for the stream states S_i. For instance, $e \in S_1 \cap (S_2 - S_3)$ iff $e \in S_1 \wedge (e \in S_2 \wedge e \notin S_3)$. Formula $\hat{F}_E$ is constructed similarly, except that variables p_i are replaced by $\hat{p}_i$.

State Formula. The state formulae G_j and $\hat{G}_j$ are conjunctions of a subset of the boolean variables p_i and $\hat{p}_i$, respectively. Essentially, if $e \in S_{i,j}$, then variable p_i is added to G_j. Thus, G_j captures the constraints on streams S_i for whom we can infer that $e \in S_i$ based on local information that $e \in S_{i,j}$ at site j. Similarly, we construct $\hat{G}_j$ by adding variable $\hat{p}_i$ to it if $e \in \hat{S}_{i,j}$. Note that G_j and $\hat{G}_j$ may be different for the various remote sites depending on the substream states at each site.

Threshold Formula. The threshold formula H only applies to boolean variables $\hat{p}_i$. Basically, if $e \in F_i$ for stream S_i, then we add variable $\hat{p}_i$ to H. Thus, H captures the constraints on stream states $\hat{S}_i$ for whom we can deduce that $e \in \hat{S}_i$ from the frequent element sets. Note that formula H is identical at all sites since F_i is the same at all sites.

We now construct the formulae Ψ_j^+ and Ψ_j^- at site j as follows.

$$\Psi_j^+ = (\neg \hat{F}_E \wedge F_E) \wedge (\hat{G}_j \wedge G_j \wedge H)$$
$$\Psi_j^- = (\hat{F}_E \wedge \neg F_E) \wedge (\hat{G}_j \wedge G_j \wedge H)$$

The formulae Ψ_j^+ and Ψ_j^- comprise two parts; the first part, involving F_E and $\hat{F}_E$, captures the conditions for one of

$e \in (E - \hat{E})$ or $e \in (\hat{E} - E)$ to hold. The second part $(\hat{G}_j \wedge G_j \wedge H)$ specifies the constraints on stream states $\hat{S}_i$ and S_i due to local knowledge at site j of substream states and frequent element sets. Thus, for the boolean formula Ψ_j^+, it follows that $e \in (E - \hat{E})$ iff Ψ_j^+ is true for stream states $\hat{S}_i, S_i$. Consequently, if Ψ_j^+ is unsatisfiable, then it is impossible that $e \in (E - \hat{E})$, and so we can set $\phi_j^+(e) = 0$. Similarly, if Ψ_j^- is unsatisfiable, then charge $\phi_j^-(e) = 0$.

Revisiting Example 4.1 where $E = S_1 \cap (S_2 - S_3)$, and element $e \in \hat{S}_{3,j}$ and $e \in S_{3,j}$, we get that

$$\Psi_j^+ = (\neg \hat{p}_1 \vee \neg \hat{p}_2 \vee \hat{p}_3) \wedge (p_1 \wedge p_2 \wedge \neg p_3) \wedge (\hat{p}_3 \wedge p_3)$$

Obviously, Ψ_j^+ is unsatisfiable (due to $\neg p_3 \wedge p_3$), and thus, charge $\phi_j^+(e) = 0$. In the following subsection, we show how models for Ψ_j can be used to compute the charges $\phi_j(e)$ when Ψ_j is satisfiable.

4.1.2 Computing Charges using Formula Ψ_j

Overview. Let us consider the problem of computing the charge $\phi_j^+(e)$. For an arbitrary boolean formula over $\hat{p}_i, p_i$, we define a *model* to be an arbitrary subset of $\cup_i \{p_i, \hat{p}_i\}$. Each model M basically assigns *truth* values to variables $p_i, \hat{p}_i$ with variable p_i ($\hat{p}_i$) being assigned *true* iff $p_i \in M$ (resp., $\hat{p}_i \in M$); otherwise, p_i (resp., $\hat{p}_i$) is assigned *false*. We say that model M satisfies a boolean formula if the formula evaluates to *true* for the truth assignment specified by M. For example, model $\{\hat{p}_1, p_2\}$ satisfies the formula $\hat{p}_1 \wedge p_2$, but the model $\{\hat{p}_1\}$ does not. Now, each model M represents a specific scenario for states $\hat{S}_i, S_i$. Essentially, $e \in S_i$ ($e \in \hat{S}_i$) iff $p_i \in M$ (resp., $\hat{p}_i \in M$). Clearly, if $e \in (E - \hat{E})$ for stream states $S_i, \hat{S}_i$, then the model corresponding to these states must satisfy Ψ_j^+. Further, every model M that satisfies Ψ_j^+ represents (from the local viewpoint of site j) a possible scenario for states $\hat{S}_i, S_i$ that is consistent with local substream states at site j, and in which $e \in (E - \hat{E})$.

Our model-based approach assigns a charge $\phi_j(M)$ to each model M that satisfies Ψ_j^+ at site j. Furthermore, since as far as site j is concerned, any of these models can potentially occur and cause $e \in (E - \hat{E})$, we set charge $\phi_j^+(e)$ as follows.

$$\phi_j^+(e) = \max\{\phi_j(M) : \text{Model } M \text{ satisfies } \Psi_j^+\} \quad (3)$$

Recall that for correctness, we require that if $e \in (E - \hat{E})$, then $\sum_j \phi_j^+(e) \geq 1$. Thus, by choosing the charge $\phi_j(M)$ for each model M such that $\sum_j \phi_j(M) \geq 1$ if M were to occur, we can ensure that $\sum_j \phi_j^+(e) \geq 1$ if $e \in (E - \hat{E})$ due to some model M that satisfies Ψ_j^+.

Now let us see how to compute the charge $\phi_j(M)$ for a model M that satisfies Ψ_j^+. Let P be the set of streams S_i such that exactly one of p_i or $\hat{p}_i$ belongs to M, i.e., either $\{p_i, \hat{p}_i\} \cap M = \{p_i\}$ or $\{p_i, \hat{p}_i\} \cap M = \{\hat{p}_i\}$. Thus, P is the set of streams that experience a global state change in model M. In our model-based scheme, site j selects a single "culprit" stream S_i from P using a selection mechanism that satisfies the following property.

UNIFORM CULPRIT SELECTION PROPERTY: Given a model M and a set P of streams with global state changes in M, every site selects the same culprit stream $S_i \in P$ for M. ∎

Later in this subsection, we will provide one specific culprit selection scheme satisfying the above property that attempts to minimize the magnitude of the charge $\phi_j^+(e)$ at site j. For the selected culprit stream S_i, let charge $\phi(S_i)$ be defined as follows.

$$\phi(S_i) = \begin{cases} 1/\theta_i(e) & \text{if } e \in F_i \\ 1 & \text{otherwise} \end{cases} \quad (4)$$

Intuitively, the reciprocal of this charge $1/\phi(S_i)$ is the minimum number of sites where stream S_i must have local state changes for it to have a global state change. For instance, if $e \in F_i$, then for e to be in $(\hat{S}_i - S_i)$, e must be in $(\hat{S}_{i,j} - S_{i,j})$ for at least $1/\phi(S_i) = \theta_i(e)$ sites. We define the charge $\phi_j(M)$ for model M in terms of the charge $\phi(S_i)$ for the culprit stream S_i.

$$\phi_j(M) = \begin{cases} \phi(S_i) & \text{if } S_i \text{ has a local state change at site } j \\ 0 & \text{otherwise} \end{cases} \quad (5)$$

Thus, we are able to ensure that if model M indeed does occur, then since the culprit stream S_i has a global state change in M, at least the $1/\phi(S_i)$ sites j at which S_i has local state changes, choose $\phi_j(M) = \phi(S_i)$ and thus, $\sum_j \phi_j(M) \geq (1/\phi(S_i))\phi(S_i) \geq 1$.

Correctness Argument. The correctness of our charging scheme follows from the lemma below.

Lemma 4.2 *Let charge $\phi_j^+(e)$ be computed as described in Equations (3), (4) and (5), and the culprit stream S_i for each model M be selected using a scheme that satisfies the uniform culprit selection property. If $e \in (E - \hat{E})$, then $\sum_j \phi_j^+(e) \geq 1$. (An analogous lemma holds for $\phi_j^-(e)$)* □

Culprit Selection. For a model M, a possible culprit selection scheme is as follows: lexicographically order streams $S_i \in P$ based on charge, index pairs $< \phi(S_i), i >$, and choose the smallest stream in the lexicographic ordering as the culprit. In other words, the culprit stream is the stream with the minimum charge $\phi(S_i)$, with ties being broken in favor of the stream with the smallest index. Clearly, since the charge $\phi(S_i)$ for stream S_i is the same across all the sites, our simple culprit selection scheme satisfies the uniform culprit selection property. Thus, due to Lemma 4.2, our charging procedure is correct. Also, observe that since our charging procedure selects the stream with the smallest charge as the culprit for model M, it minimizes the maximum charge incurred for M across the sites.

Example 4.3 Consider distributed streams S_1, S_2 and S_3, and let expression $E = S_1 \cap (S_2 - S_3)$. At some site j, let the substream states be as shown in the table below.

	$i=1$	$i=2$	$i=3$
$\hat{S}_{i,j}$		e	e
$S_{i,j}$	e	e	

Thus, element e is in all substream states except for $\hat{S}_{1,j}$ and $S_{3,j}$. Also, let $e \in F_3$, $e \notin F_1$, $e \notin F_2$ and $\theta_3(e) = 4$; the meaning here is that e is contained in at least 4 substream states for S_3 transmitted to the coordinator. It follows that $\phi(S_1) = \phi(S_2) = 1$ and $\phi(S_3) = 1/4$. Also, the formula Ψ_j^+ for E at site j is

$$(\neg \hat{p}_1 \lor \neg \hat{p}_2 \lor \hat{p}_3) \land (p_1 \land p_2 \land \neg p_3) \land (p_1 \land \hat{p}_2 \land p_2 \land \hat{p}_3)$$

Thus, for any model M that satisfies Ψ_j^+, it must be the case that $\{\hat{p}_3, \neg p_3\} \subseteq M$. As a result, $S_3 \in P$ and since the charge $\phi(S_3)$ for S_3 is the smallest, it is chosen as the culprit for all models. Consequently, since S_3 has a local state change at site j, $\phi_j(M) = \phi(S_3) = 1/4$ for all models M that satisfy Ψ_j^+, and thus, the charge $\phi_j^+(e) = 1/4$. Furthermore, since Ψ_j^- is unsatisfiable, charge $\phi_j^-(e) = 0$.

Now suppose that stream S_3 does not have a local state change at site j, that is, e is neither in $\hat{S}_{3,j}$ nor in $S_{3,j}$. Then, since $e \in F_3$, Ψ_j^+ will remain the same as before, and S_3 will still be chosen as the culprit stream for all models M that satisfy Ψ_j^+. However, since S_3 does not have a local state change at site j, $\phi_j(M)$ will be 0 for the models, and thus charge $\phi_j^+(e) = 0$. ∎

Computational Complexity. In order to determine the complexity our model-based approach, we consider the following decision problem for $\phi_j^+(e)$.

PROBLEM (MAXIMUM CHARGE MODEL): Given expression E, site j, element e, and constant k, does there exist a model M that satisfies Ψ_j^+ and for which $\phi_j(M) \geq k$? ∎

The following theorem can be proved using a reduction from 3-SAT.

Theorem 4.4 *The MAXIMUM CHARGE MODEL problem is NP-complete.* ∎

From the above theorem, it follows that since $\phi_j^+(e)$ is the maximum charge for models M that satisfy Ψ_j^+, computing $\phi_j^+(e)$ is intractable.

4.2 Heuristic for Charge Computation

Our model-based charging procedure enumerates all models M in the worst case, and thus, has a worst-case time complexity of $O(2^{2n})$. While this may be reasonable for small values of n (e.g., 3 or 4 streams), the model enumeration-based approach will clearly not scale when set expressions involve a moderately large number of streams, a scenario likely in practice. (e.g. in the *Akamai* case). In this section, we present a heuristic solution for computing the charges $\phi_j^+(e)$ and $\phi_j^-(e)$ for an element e at site j. Our heuristic procedure has a time complexity that is polynomial in the number of streams n, and computes identical charge values as the model-based approach as long as every stream appears at most once in the expression E. However, our heuristic may overcharge for element e in certain cases when there are duplicate occurrences of streams in expression E.

Overview. Our model-based charging procedure essentially computes $\phi_j^+(e)$ as the maximum stream charge $\phi(S_i)$ such that (1) S_i has a local state change at site j, and (2) S_i is the culprit stream for some model M that satisfies Ψ_j^+. (Recall that the culprit stream S_i for model M is the stream with the smallest charge, index pair $<\phi(S_i), i>$ from among streams with a global state change in M.) Thus, for a stream S_i, if we can develop a test for quickly determining if S_i is the culprit stream for some model that satisfies Ψ_j^+, then we can speed up the computation of charge $\phi_j^+(e)$. This is the key idea underlying our heuristic.

Let T denote the expression tree for E with leaves and internal nodes corresponding to streams and set operators in E, respectively. For each node V of T, let $E(V)$ be the subexpression for the subtree rooted at node V, and $\hat{F}_{E(V)}$ and $F_{E(V)}$ be the formulae for $E(V)$ as defined in Section 4.1.1. For example, in the expression tree for $E = S_1 \cap (S_2 - S_3)$, the subexpression for the subtree rooted at $V = $"$-$" is $E(V) = S_2 - S_3$, and $F_{E(V)} = p_2 \land \neg p_3$. Now, in order to quickly test if a stream S_i is the culprit stream for some model satisfying Ψ_j^+, our heuristic keeps track of culprit streams (for models) at each node of the expression tree using the notion of *charge triples*. Formally, suppose that M is a model that satisfies the local constraints $(G_j \land \hat{G}_j \land H)$ at site j. At node V in T, we define the charge triple for model M, denoted by $t(M, V)$, as the triple (a, b, x) with the following values:

- If M satisfies $\hat{F}_{E(V)}$, then bit $a = 1$; otherwise, $a = 0$. Similarly, if M satisfies $F_{E(V)}$, then bit $b = 1$; otherwise $b = 0$.

- If none of the streams in V's subtree have a global state change in model M, then $x = \infty$. (The charge, index pair $<\phi(S_\infty), \infty>$ is considered to be greater than $<\phi(S_i), i>$ for all streams S_i.) Otherwise, x is the index of the culprit stream for M in V's subtree; that is, $x = i$, where S_i is the stream with the smallest charge, index pair $<\phi(S_i), i>$ from among streams (in V's subtree) with a global state change in M.

For example, consider a model M that satisfies $\neg \hat{F}_{E(V)} \land F_{E(V)}$ (in addition to local constraints). Then, if the culprit stream S_i for M in V's subtree is defined, the charge triple $t(M, V)$ for M at node V is $(0, 1, i)$; otherwise, $t(M, V) = (0, 1, \infty)$. Our charging heuristic computes, in a bottom-up fashion, a set C of charge triples for each node V of T. Furthermore, it ensures that for every model M that satisfies $(G_j \land \hat{G}_j \land H)$, the computed set C for node V contains the triple $t(M, V)$. Here, it is important to note that the size of C (in the worst case) is linear in the number of streams n – this is because there are at most $O(n)$ distinct charge triples $t(M, V)$ (one for each combination of a, b and x).

Now, consider the charge triple set C for the root V of T. Clearly, since $E(V) = E$, if a model M satisfies $\Psi_j^+ = (\neg \hat{F}_E \wedge F_E) \wedge (\hat{G}_j \wedge G_j \wedge H)$ and has culprit stream S_i, then triple $t(M, V) = (0, 1, i)$ must be in C. Thus, we can quickly determine if a stream S_i is the culprit stream for some model satisfying Ψ_j^+ by checking if C contains the triple $(0, 1, i)$. Hence, by selecting $\phi_j^+(e)$ to be the maximum stream charge $\phi(S_i)$ such that (1) S_i has a local state change at site j, and (2) triple $(0, 1, i) \in C$, we can ensure that $\phi_j^+(e) \geq \max\{\phi_j(M) : \text{Model } M \text{ satisfies } \Psi_j^+\}$ and thus, due to Lemma 4.2, our charging heuristic is correct.

Due to lack of space, we defer the details of our bottom-up charge triple computation algorithm to [5] but illustrate its execution in the following example.

Example 4.5 Consider the distributed scenario described in Example 4.3 involving streams S_1, S_2 and S_3, and expression $E = S_1 \cap (S_2 - S_3)$. Suppose that element e is in all substream states except for $\hat{S}_{1,j}$ and $S_{3,j}$, and also $e \in F_3$ and $\theta_3(e) = 4$. Thus, $\phi(S_1) = \phi(S_2) = 1$ and $\phi(S_3) = 1/4$. The following figure illustrates the charge triple sets computed for the nodes of the expression tree for E by our charging heuristic.

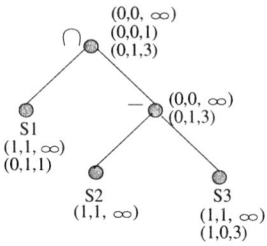

The charge triple set for each leaf S_i is first initialized to contain $t(M, S_i)$ for models M that satisfy local constraints. For example, since e is in $S_{1,j}$ but not in $\hat{S}_{1,j}$, it follows that $p_1 \in G_j$ and thus for models M that satisfy $(G_j \wedge \hat{G}_j \wedge H)$, $p_1 \in M$ but $\hat{p}_1$ may or may not be in M; so the charge triple set for S_1 contains the triples $(1, 1, \infty)$ (for models that contain $\hat{p}_1$) and $(0, 1, 1)$ (for models that do not contain $\hat{p}_1$).

Next, the charge triple (a, b, x) for each internal node V is computed by combining pairs of triples (a_1, b_1, x_1) and (a_2, b_2, x_2) from V's two children. Suppose that op is the boolean operation corresponding to the set operation for V; the boolean operations for $\cup, \cap$ and $-$ are $\vee, \wedge$ and $\wedge \neg$, respectively. Then $a = a_1 \; op \; a_2$, $b = b_1 \; op \; b_2$ and x is set to one of x_1 or x_2, whichever has the smaller charge, index pair $< \phi(S_{x_i}), x_i >$. For example, the charge triples for node "$-$" of T are generated by combining triples for nodes S_2 and S_3. Triples $(1, 1, \infty)$ and $(1, 1, \infty)$ when combined result in the triple $(0, 0, \infty)$ (since $1 \wedge \neg 1 = 0$). Similarly, combining triples $(1, 1, \infty)$ and $(1, 0, 3)$ results in the triple $(0, 1, 3)$ (since $1 \wedge \neg 0 = 1$, and $< \phi(S_3), 3 >$ is less than $< \phi(S_\infty), \infty >$). Finally, the sets for S_1 and "$-$" are combined to obtain the charge triple set C for the root node "$\cap$", which is then used by our charging heuristic to

compute the charges $\phi_j^+(e)$ and $\phi_j^-(e)$. Since C contains the triple $(0, 1, 3)$ and S_3 has a local state change at site j, charge $\phi_j^+(e) = \phi(S_3) = 1/4$. Further, since C does not contain a triple of the form $(1, 0, x)$, $\phi_j^-(e) = 0$. ∎

Correctness Argument. The following lemma establishes the correctness of our charging heuristic.

Lemma 4.6 *Consider a model M that satisfies local constraints $(G_j \wedge \hat{G}_j \wedge H)$ at site j. Then, for an arbitrary node V in T, charge triple $t(M, V)$ is in the set of charge triples for V computed by our heuristic.* ∎

Computational Complexity. The maximum size of a charge triple set for a node is $O(n)$, and thus, the worst-case time complexity of our charging heuristic can be shown to be $O(n^2 s)$, where s is the size of set expression E [5].

The following lemma implies that when E contains no duplicate streams, our heuristic returns the same charge values as the model based approach.

Lemma 4.7 *Let E be a set expression in which each stream appears at most once. For an arbitrary node V in T, charge triple t is in the set of charge triples for V computed by our heuristic if and only if $t = t(M, V)$ for some model M satisfying $(G_j \wedge \hat{G}_j \wedge H)$ at site j.* ∎

5 Experimental Study

In this section, we present the results of an empirical study of our distributed set-expression cardinality estimation algorithms with real-life as well as synthetic data sets. The main objective of this study is to gauge the effectiveness of our approximation techniques in cutting down the volume of message traffic. Our results indicate that compared to naive approaches, our estimation algorithms can lead to reductions in communication costs ranging from a factor of 2 (for real-life data sets) to more than 6 (for synthetic data).

5.1 Testbed and Methodology

Algorithms for Query Answering. We implemented our distributed algorithm from Section 3.2 where the coordinator executes the actions in procedure COORDINATOR (see Figure 2) to process substream deltas, and each remote site performs the actions in procedure REMOTE (see Figure 3) to detect error violations. In procedure COORDINATOR, we choose the threshold parameter for considering elements to be frequent as $\tau = 4$. In our experiments, we observed that the conservative policy (described in Section 3.2) of "doubling $\theta_i(e)$ only after the count $C_i(e)$ has stabilized" increases the robustness of our algorithm by making the number of control messages virtually independent of the choice of τ. Further, we employ our expression tree-based charging heuristic procedure to compute element charges at each remote site. We will refer to this implementation of our distributed scheme as *Tree-based algorithm*.

To test the efficacy of our tree-based algorithm, we compare it to a naive algorithm in which the coordinator does

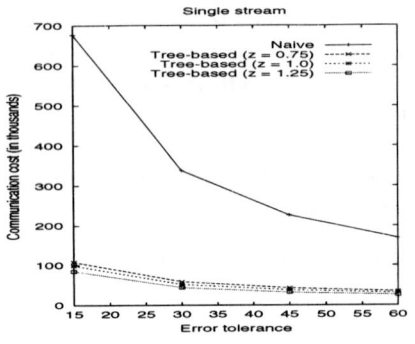
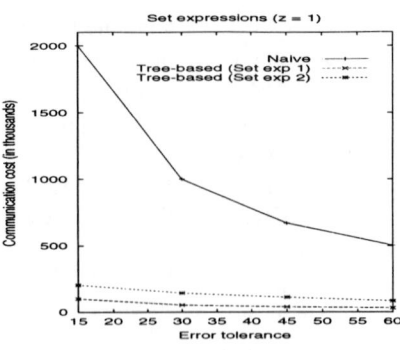
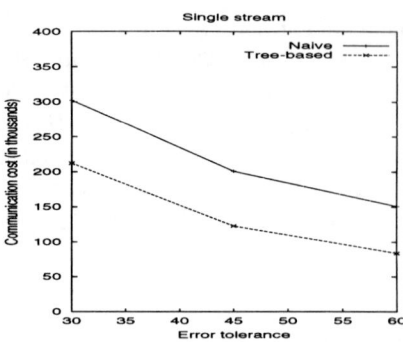

Figure 4: Distinct Values Query. Figure 5: Set Expression Query. Figure 6: Distinct Values Query.

not send any control messages to remote sites. Instead, each remote site j simply keeps track of the number of elements that have been inserted or deleted from any of the substreams $S_{i,j}$ since stream state information was last communicated to the coordinator. If this element count exceeds the error budget ϵ_j for the site, then it transmits all the substream deltas to the coordinator. Essentially, the naive algorithm adapts the scheme of [12] to our set-expression setting; it considers the charges $\phi_j^+(e)$ and $\phi_j^-(e)$ to be 1 if element e is newly inserted/deleted from any substream at site j completely oblivious of global element frequencies and set-expression semantics.

In the above two algorithms, we distributed the error tolerance budget ϵ uniformly across the m sites; thus, each $\epsilon_j = \frac{\epsilon}{m}$. Recall that ϵ represents the *absolute error* and not the relative error tolerance. For both real-life as well as synthetic data sets, we found the performance of this uniform distribution policy to be comparable to more sophisticated schemes that allocate error budgets to the various sites proportional to stream update rates.

Data Sets. We experimented with multiple synthetic data sets where we varied the frequency distribution for stream elements and one real-life data set.

•*Synthetic data sets.* Our synthetic data stream generator sequentially outputs 1 million stream updates for the n streams at 16 remote sites. For each update, it randomly selects the substream $S_{i,j}$ to be updated at one of the 16 remote sites. The element e for the update is chosen from the domain $[1000] = \{0,\ldots,999\}$ following a Zipfian distribution. Essentially, the zipf parameter z provides a knob to control the skew in the frequency with which elements in $[1000]$ are updated. If the selected element e is not present in substream $S_{i,j}$, then the update is treated as an insert operation. Otherwise, the update is either an insert or a delete with a slight bias towards deletes to ensure that elements are continuously inserted and deleted from substreams.

•*Real-life data set.* We used the LBL-TCP-3 data set[1] which is a packet trace containing two hour's worth of all wide-area TCP traffic between the Lawrence Berkeley Laboratory and the rest of the world. We considered 500,000 records from the data set, where each record includes a timestamp, source host and destination host field. Even though the trace was collected at a single site, we treat it as if it were collected in a distributed fashion at 16 sites. Thus, each record corresponds to an insert operation for a single distributed stream at one of the 16 sites and whose arrival time is given by the record timestamp. Further, we delete each record using a sliding window of 2 seconds; that is, we issue a delete for each record exactly 2 seconds after its insertion into the stream.

Performance Metrics. Similar to [2], we use the number of messages exchanged between the coordinator and the remote sites as a measure of the communication costs incurred by the tree-based and naive algorithms. The rationale for this is that in our study, we found message sizes to be generally small (≤ 200 bytes); as a result, the number of messages is an appropriate metric to compare the performance of the two algorithms.

5.2 Experimental Results
5.2.1 Synthetic Data Sets
In our experiments, we compare the message overhead of the tree-based and naive approaches as the skew z in element update rates and the error tolerance ϵ are varied. In the following, we first consider a single stream scenario where our goal is to estimate the number of distinct values in a single distributed stream. This case essentially allows us to isolate the performance improvements realized by our tree-based algorithm as a result of propagating global frequency threshold information. We then turn our attention to general set expressions to further explore the gains obtained due to exploiting set-expression semantics.

Single Stream Cardinality Estimation. In Figure 4, we plot the communication costs for the tree-based and naive algorithms as the error tolerance ϵ is varied. In Figure 4, we consider three values for z (0.75, 1 and 1.25), but only plot a single curve for the naive scheme since the message traffic does not change much as the element update skew is altered. As expected, in the graph of Figure 4, the messaging overhead for both algorithms decreases as the accuracy requirements are relaxed. Furthermore, for all the error and skew values shown in Figure 4, our tree-based algorithm outperforms the naive scheme by a factor of at least 5. The reason is that as elements are randomly inserted and deleted from the various substreams, a significant fraction of them occur at more than $\tau = 4$ sites, and are thus considered to

---
[1] Available from http://ita.ee.lbl.gov/html/contrib/LBL-TCP-3.html.

be frequent. Now, for such frequently occurring elements e, our tree-based algorithm propagates the threshold values $\theta_i(e)$ which ensure that inserts of e are 'free' and deletes are charged $1/\theta_i(e)$. In contrast, the naive algorithm charges 1 for both inserts and deletes, and thus, sends many more "update state" messages to the coordinator.

Note that there is a cost associated with disseminating the θ_i values to remote sites in our tree-based algorithm – on an average, we counted the number of such "adjust threshold" control messages sent by the coordinator to be approximately 18 thousand for the 1 million stream updates. Clearly, this is negligible compared to the savings in state transmission messages obtained due to the smaller charge values at sites. In general, control messages (whose counts have been included in all graphs shown) constituted between 20% and 50% of the total message traffic for our tree-based algorithm.

Set-Expression Cardinality Estimation. Figure 5 depicts the number of messages sent by the tree-based and naive algorithms for two set expressions as the error tolerance ϵ is varied between 15 and 60, and skew z is fixed at 1. The expressions we consider are over 3 streams S_0, S_1 and S_2, with the first being $(S_0 - S_1) \cup S_2$, and $(S_0 \cup S_1) \cap S_2$, the second. In the graph, we only plot one curve for the naive scheme since the communication cost was the same for the two set expressions. This is not surprising since the naive scheme does not really care about the structure of set expressions, and simply charges 1 for each element that is inserted/deleted from any of the streams. On the other hand, our tree-based algorithm, by exploiting the semantics of set expressions (in addition to element frequency threshold information), is able to deliver impressive reductions in the data transmission overhead. For the expression $(S_0 - S_1) \cup S_2$, our tree-based algorithm results in factors ranging from 16 (for $\epsilon = 60$) to 20 (for $\epsilon = 15$) lower communication compared to the naive scheme. For the expression $(S_0 \cup S_1) \cap S_2$, the performance improvement factors are halved (since the set-difference operator provides more opportunities to suppress communication as compared to the set-intersection operator), but still lie between 7 and 10.

5.2.2 Real-life Data Set

We compare the communication costs of the tree-based and naive algorithms for the following query over the distributed TCP trace data: How many distinct destination hosts are contained in the TCP trace records within the most recent 2 second sliding window? As shown in Figure 6, our tree-based algorithm incurs between 35% (for $\epsilon = 30$) and 50% (for $\epsilon = 60$) less communication overhead compared to the naive scheme. The reason for the comparatively modest improvement over the naive scheme in this case is the lesser stability in element counts resulting in lower thresholds valid for short durations of time. Also note that our techniques which exploit set-expression semantics did not come into play. It is interesting to note that for our tree-based algorithm, the number of control messages transmitted is actually quite low and ranges between 5% and 20% of the total message traffic.

6 Concluding Remarks

In this paper, we considered the problem of approximately answering set-expression cardinality queries over distributed streams originating at tens or hundreds of remote sites. We proposed novel algorithms for estimating set-expression cardinality with guaranteed accuracy at a central processing site, while keeping data communication costs between the remote sites and the central processor at a minimum. Our solutions exploit global knowledge of the distribution of frequent elements as well as the semantics of set expressions to reduce data transmission overhead while preserving user-specified error guarantees. We developed protocols for efficiently propagating global frequency information across sites, and devised a logic-based formulation for identifying the element state changes (at a remote site) that can affect the set expression result (at the central site). Through experiments with a real-life TCP traffic data set and multiple synthetic data sets, we demonstrated the effectiveness of our techniques in reducing the volume of message traffic compared to naive approaches that provide the same error guarantees.

References

[1] "NetFlow Services and Applications". Cisco Systems White Paper (http://www.cisco.com/), 1999.

[2] B. Babcock and C. Olston. "Distributed Top-K Monitoring". In *SIGMOD*, 2003.

[3] M. Charikar, K. Chen, and M. Farach-Colton. "Finding Frequent Items in Data Streams". In *ICALP*, 2002.

[4] C. Cranor, T. Johnson, O. Spatscheck, and V. Shkapenyuk. "Gigascope: A Stream Database for Network Applications". In *SIGMOD*, 2003.

[5] A. Das, S. Ganguly, M. Garofalakis, and R. Rastogi. "Approximating Set-Expression Cardinality over Distributed Update Streams". Bell Labs Tech. Memorandum, 2003.

[6] S. Ganguly, M. Garofalakis, and R. Rastogi. "Processing Set Expressions over Continuous Update Streams". In *SIGMOD*, 2003.

[7] P. B. Gibbons. "Distinct Sampling for Highly-Accurate Answers to Distinct Values Queries and Event Reports". In *VLDB*, 2001.

[8] P. B. Gibbons and S. Tirthapura. "Distributed Streams Algorithms for Sliding Windows". In *SPAA*, 2002.

[9] A. C. Gilbert, Y. Kotidis, S. Muthukrishnan, and M. J. Strauss. "How to Summarize the Universe: Dynamic Maintenance of Quantiles". In *VLDB*, 2002.

[10] S. Madden, M. J. Franklin, J. H. Hellerstein, and W. Hong. "The Design of an Acquisitional Query Processor for Sensor Networks". In *SIGMOD*, 2003.

[11] D. Moore, G. M. Voelker, and S. Savage. "Inferring Internet Denial-of-Service Activity". In *USENIX Security Symposium*, 2001.

[12] C. Olston, J. Jiang, and J. Widom. "Adaptive Filters for Continuous Queries over Distributed Data Streams". In *SIGMOD*, 2003.

[13] G. Pottie and W. Kaiser. "Wireless Integrated Network Sensors". *Communications of the ACM*, 43(5), 2000.

Memory-Limited Execution of Windowed Stream Joins

Utkarsh Srivastava   Jennifer Widom

Stanford University
{usriv,widom}@db.stanford.edu

Abstract

We address the problem of computing approximate answers to continuous sliding-window joins over data streams when the available memory may be insufficient to keep the entire join state. One approximation scenario is to provide a *maximum subset* of the result, with the objective of losing as few result tuples as possible. An alternative scenario is to provide a *random sample* of the join result, e.g., if the output of the join is being aggregated. We show formally that neither approximation can be addressed effectively for a sliding-window join of arbitrary input streams. Previous work has addressed only the maximum-subset problem, and has implicitly used a *frequency-based model* of stream arrival. We address the sampling problem for this model. More importantly, we point out a broad class of applications for which an *age-based* model of stream arrival is more appropriate, and we address both approximation scenarios under this new model. Finally, for the case of multiple joins being executed with an overall memory constraint, we provide an algorithm for memory allocation across the joins that optimizes a combined measure of approximation in all scenarios considered. All of our algorithms are implemented and experimental results demonstrate their effectiveness.

1 Introduction

Data stream systems [14, 18, 22] face the challenge that immediate online results often are required, but sufficient memory may not be available for the run-time state required by a workload of numerous queries over high-volume data streams [7, 13]. There are two basic solutions: provide *approximate* instead of accurate query results using memory exclusively to ensure high performance [2, 7, 9], or provide accurate results by using disk with the risk of

Permission to copy without fee all or part of this material is granted provided that the copies are not made or distributed for direct commercial advantage, the VLDB copyright notice and the title of the publication and its date appear, and notice is given that copying is by permission of the Very Large Data Base Endowment. To copy otherwise, or to republish, requires a fee and/or special permission from the Endowment.

**Proceedings of the 30th VLDB Conference,
Toronto, Canada, 2004**

failing to keep up with the input rate [7, 19]. In this paper, we address the problem of memory-limited execution of *sliding-window joins* [2] in data stream systems, focusing on providing approximate results.

Consider a continuous sliding-window join between two streams S_1 and S_2, denoted as $S_1[W_1] \bowtie_\theta S_2[W_2]$. Windows W_1 and W_2 consist of the most recent tuples on their respective streams, and may be tuple-based (e.g., the last 1000 tuples), or time-based (e.g., tuples arriving in the last 10 minutes). The output of the join contains every pair of tuples from streams S_1 and S_2 that satisfy the join predicate θ and are simultaneously present in their respective windows. In general, to perform the join accurately, the entire contents of both windows must be maintained at all times. If we have many such joins with large windows over high-volume data streams, memory may be insufficient for maintaining all windows in their entirety. If the data stream application has stringent performance requirements (to preclude the use of disk), but can tolerate an approximate join result, there are two interesting types of approximation:

1. **"Max-Subset" Results:** If the application benefits from having a maximum subset of the result, we can selectively drop tuples (sometimes referred to as *load shedding* [7, 17]) with the objective of maximizing the size of the join result produced.

2. **Sampled Results:** A random sample of the join result may often be preferable to a larger sized but arbitrary subset of the result. For example, if the join result is being aggregated, the sample can be used to provide a consistent and unbiased estimate of the true aggregate.

Previous work on memory-limited join execution [7, 13] has considered only max-subset results, and has implicitly assumed a *frequency-based* model of stream arrival. In this model, each join-attribute value has a roughly fixed frequency of occurrence on each stream. These frequencies (either known or inferred through monitoring) are used to make load-shedding decisions, i.e., which tuples to drop and which to retain, in order to maximize the size of the join result produced. However, no justification has been provided as to why this (or any other) model is required for addressing the max-subset approximation problem. Our first contribution is to show formally that if a sliding-window join over arbitrary streams is to be executed without enough memory for retaining the entire windows, neither of the above types of approximations can be carried out effectively: For the max-subset problem, any online algorithm

Model	Max-Subset	Random Sample
Age-Based	Section 3	Section 4
Frequency-Based	Addressed in [7]	

Figure 1: Problem space

can return an arbitrarily small subset as compared to the optimal (offline) algorithm [7], and for the sampling problem, no algorithm can guarantee a nonzero uniform random sample of the join result. Thus, we must have some model of stream arrival to make any headway on the problem.

There are many applications for which the frequency-based model considered in previous work is inappropriate. (One obvious case is a foreign-key join, where on one stream each value occurs at most once.) For these applications, we define an *age-based* model that is often appropriate and enables much better load-shedding decisions. In the age-based model, the expected join multiplicity of a tuple depends on the time since its arrival rather than on its join-attribute value. Examples will be given in Section 2.2.

Given the two types of approximation and the two models, we have the problem space shown in Figure 1. The max-subset problem has been addressed in [7], but only for the frequency-based model. To the best of our knowledge, the sampling problem, i.e., the problem of extracting a random sample of the join result with limited memory, has not been addressed in previous work. Our contribution is to address the max-subset problem for the age-based model, and the sampling problem for both models.

Our discussion so far assumes a single two-way sliding-window join. In reality, we expect to be executing many queries simultaneously in the system. Thus, there is an added dimension to all of the above problems: memory allocation among multiple joins. The total available memory should be allocated to the different joins such that a combined approximation measure is optimized. We provide an optimal memory allocation scheme that minimizes the maximum approximation error in any join. Our technique also extends to the weighted case, i.e., when different joins have different relative importance.

1.1 Related Work

There has been considerable work recently on data stream processing; see [11] for a survey. We discuss only the body of work related to answering queries approximately when available memory is insufficient. This work can be broadly classified into two categories. One category consists of load-shedding strategies for max-subset approximation of joins. Random load-shedding is the simplest, and has been considered in [13]. [7] primarily considers the offline load-shedding problem (one in which all future tuple arrivals are known), and provides some heuristics for the online case that implicitly assume a frequency-based model. An alternative stream model for load-shedding uses a stochastic process [20]. Although this model is more general, the primary focus in [20] is on scenarios in which the tuples arriving on one stream are independent of those that have already arrived on another stream. However, most scenarios we consider do not exhibit this independence, e.g., our age-based example in Section 2.2. Moreover, the process of inferring a general stochastic process merely by observing the stream is not clear.

The other category consists of randomized sketch-based solutions for approximately answering aggregate queries over joins, providing probabilistic error guarantees [1, 9]. These techniques do not extend to handle sliding-window joins or windowed aggregates which are required in many applications: although the techniques handle explicit deletions within streams, they cannot handle the implicit deletions generated by sliding windows.

In this paper, we only consider the stream system being memory-limited. The stream system could instead (or also) be CPU-limited, i.e., the rate of incoming tuples is higher than can be processed. Load-shedding for the CPU-limited case has been considered in [4, 17]. Sampling from a window is addressed in [3], but only for a single stream and not for a join result. Random sampling for joins has been considered in the relational context [5]. However, all sampling methods developed there require repeated access or indices on at least one of the relations, making these techniques inapplicable in the stream context.

1.2 Summary of Contributions

1. We show formally that the problem of approximating a sliding-window join with limited memory cannot be addressed effectively for arbitrary streams (Sections 3.1 and 4.1).

2. We introduce a novel *age-based model* for stream arrival that captures many applications not captured by the frequency-based model assumed in previous work (Section 2).

3. For a single two-way join with a fixed memory constraint, we provide novel algorithms for the max-subset problem under the age-based model (Section 3), and the sampling problem under both the frequency and age-based models (Section 4).

4. For multiple two-way joins with an overall memory constraint, we give an algorithm to allocate memory among the various joins so as to optimize a combined measure of approximation (Section 5).

5. We provide a thorough experimental evaluation showing the effectiveness of our techniques (Section 6).

2 Preliminaries and Models

We briefly describe our basic model of continuous query processing over data streams. Assume any discrete time domain. For a stream S_i, $i = 1, 2$, a variable number of tuples may arrive in each unit of time. However, we assume that over time, tuples on stream S_i arrive at a constant average rate of r_i tuples per unit time. $S_i[W_i]$ denotes a window on stream S_i. We consider *time-based* windows, where W_i denotes the length of the window in time units. At time t, a tuple s belongs to $S_i[W_i]$ if s has arrived on S_i in the time interval $[t - W_i, t]$. At time t, we say s is of age k if it arrived at time $t - k$. We consider time-based windows

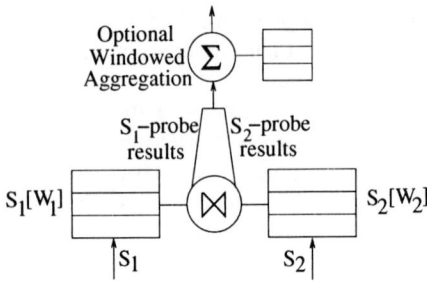

Figure 2: Sliding-window join with aggregation

for generality; tuple-based windows can also be captured by assuming that a single tuple arrives every time unit.

The basic query we consider (shown in Figure 2) is a sliding-window equijoin between two streams S_1 and S_2 over a common attribute A, denoted $S_1[W_1] \bowtie_A S_2[W_2]$. The output of the join consists of all pairs of tuples $s_1 \in S_1$, $s_2 \in S_2$, such that $s_1.A = s_2.A$ and at some time t, both $s_1 \in S_1[W_1]$ and $s_2 \in S_2[W_2]$. Conceptually, a sliding-window join is executed as shown in Figure 3, which details the steps to be followed for a newly arriving tuple on S_1. A symmetric procedure is followed for a newly arriving tuple on S_2. We also consider queries with a *windowed aggregation* operator on top of the streamed join result. Other work [8] has focused on approximate windowed aggregation in memory-limited environments. We do not consider this aspect of memory usage in our calculations, however analyzing the tradeoff between memory allocation to joins and aggregation is an interesting subject of future work.

We classify every join-result tuple as either an S_1-*probe join tuple* or an S_2-*probe join tuple*. When a new tuple s arrives on S_1 and joins with a tuple $s' \in S_2[W_2]$ (line 3 of Figure 3), s and s' are said to produce an S_2-probe join tuple. S_1-probe join tuples are defined symmetrically. A tuple $s \in S_1$ may first produce S_2-probe join tuples when it arrives. Then, before it expires from $S_1[W_1]$, it may produce S_1-probe join tuples with newly arriving tuples on S_2. We use $n_i(s)$, $i = 1, 2$, to denote the number of S_i-probe join tuples produced by a tuple $s \in S_i$ before it expires from $S_i[W_i]$.

2.1 Frequency-Based Stream Model

Continue to consider the sliding-window join $S_1[W_1] \bowtie_A S_2[W_2]$. Let $\mathcal{D}$ denote the domain of join attribute A. The frequency-based model that has been assumed in previous work [7, 13] is defined as follows:

Definition 2.1 (Frequency-Based Model). *For each value $v \in \mathcal{D}$, a fixed fraction $f_1(v)$ of the tuples arriving on S_1, and a fixed fraction $f_2(v)$ of the tuples arriving on S_2, have value v in attribute A.* □

Assuming an average rate r_2 of arrivals per unit time on S_2, the expected number of S_1-probe join tuples that a tuple $s \in S_1$ produces is given by:

$$E[n_1(s)] = r_2 \cdot W_1 \cdot f_2(s.A) \qquad (1)$$

Example Scenario: Suppose we are monitoring a sys-

1. When a new tuple s arrives on S_1
2.   Update $S_2[W_2]$ by discarding expired tuples
3.   Emit $s \bowtie_A S_2[W_2]$
4.   Add s to $S_1[W_1]$

Figure 3: Sliding-window join execution

tem with a fixed number of *components*. We have a stream of *actions* and a stream of *errors* on all components, and we want to perform a sliding-window join on component-id to look for possible correlations between actions and errors. Some components may be more heavily used than others, and some may be more error-prone than others, but each component-id may have a roughly fixed frequency of occurrence on each stream.

2.2 Age-Based Stream Model

For many applications, the frequency-based model is inappropriate. As a simple example, consider online auction monitoring [16] with the following streams:

   S_1: OpenAuction(auction-id, seller-id)
   S_2: Bid(auction-id, bid-amount)

When a seller starts an auction, a tuple arrives on S_1. When a bid is placed on an auction, a tuple arrives on S_2. Suppose we are interested in knowing, for each seller, the average number of bids received on all of his auctions in the last 5 days. This query requires a sliding-window join between S_1 and S_2 with a window on S_1 equal to the maximum lifetime of an auction, followed by an aggregation operator with a 5-day window.

Suppose memory is insufficient to retain all the tuples in S_1's window, and suppose we use the frequency-based model for making load-shedding decisions in this scenario. Auction-ids are unique, so on stream S_1 we see each auction-id only once. On stream S_2, the arriving auction-ids are the currently open auctions, so this set changes over time. Thus, no fixed frequency distribution can be inferred through monitoring. In this case, load-shedding schemes based on the frequency model [7] will simply retain new tuples and discard old ones. However, that is exactly the wrong thing to do, since most bids are received on auctions that are about to close, i.e., are relatively old. To capture such scenarios, we propose a new *age-based* model defined for the sliding-window join $S_1[W_1] \bowtie S_2[W_2]$ as follows:

Definition 2.2 (Age-Based Model). *For a tuple $s \in S_1$, the S_1-probe join tuples produced by s obey the following two conditions:*

1. *The number of S_1-probe join tuples produced by s is a constant independent of s, and is denoted by n_1.*

2. *Out of the n_1 S_1-probe join tuples of s, $p_1(k)$ are produced when s is between age $k - 1$ and k.*

A symmetric case holds for the S_2-probe join tuples produced by a tuple $s' \in S_2$. Define $C_i(k)$, $i = 1, 2$, as the cumulative number of S_i-probe join tuples that a tuple $s \in S_i$ produces by age k, i.e., $C_i(k) = \sum_{j=1}^{k} p_i(j)$. □

Thus, according to this model, the number of joins a tuple produces is independent of its join-attribute value, but is a function of the age of the tuple in the window. Assumption 1 in Definition 2.2 is not strictly necessary for our approach. However, in the scenarios we have considered, the set of join-attribute values changes over time. Thus, even if $n_i(s)$ depends on $s.A$ for a tuple $s \in S_i$, it would be difficult to infer this dependence by monitoring the stream.

Different Age Curves: Consider a curve that plots $p_i(k)$ against k; we call this the *age curve* for window $S_i[W_i]$. Intuitively, the age curve shows how likely a tuple in $S_i[W_i]$ is to produce join tuples, as it becomes older. Different applications that adhere to the age-based model may have very different age-curve shapes:

- *Increasing*: An example is the auction scenario described above. In a typical auction, relatively few bids are received in the beginning, followed by a large number of bids when the auction is about to close. Thus $p_1(k)$ is small for small k, and increases with k until the auction lifetime, after which it drops to 0.

- *Decreasing*: Consider a join between an *Orders* and a *Fulfillments* stream on `order-id`, with a window on the orders stream. Most parts of an order are fulfilled soon, but some may require backorder and are fulfilled later. Thus we expect to see a decreasing age curve.

- *Bell*: Consider a join between streams of readings from two different sensors, with a band-join condition on timestamp. This join may be used to discover correlations between readings from two different observation points taken at roughly the same time. In this case, the age curve is expected to be bell-shaped. The age k at which the peak of the age curve occurs will be determined by factors such as clock skew between the two sensors, and the difference in network latency from the sensors to the stream system. We perform an experiment of this form in Section 6.

2.3 Parameter Estimation

For using any of the models described above, the model parameters must be instantiated, i.e., we must determine the frequencies of occurrence $f_1(v)$ and $f_2(v)$ of values $v \in \mathcal{D}$ for the frequency-based model, and the age curves for the age-based model. We assume the standard technique of using the past to predict the future, so parameters are estimated by monitoring the streams. There is previous work on building histograms in an online fashion using small space [10, 12], which can be used to estimate the values of $f_1(v)$ and $f_2(v)$. For the age-based model, n_i, $i = 1, 2$, is estimated as the average number of S_i-probe join tuples that an S_i-tuple produces in its lifetime. Similarly, $p_i(k)$ is estimated as the average number of S_i-probe join tuples that an S_i-tuple produces between age $k - 1$ and k.

We do not need to collect $p_i(k)$ for each time unit k, but can use a coarser time granularity. To accurately determine $p_i(k)$, we should execute the join with the full window $S_i[W_i]$ being retained. For now, we assume that we can allocate an extra chunk of "monitoring memory" that is circulated periodically to each window in turn to monitor its parameters accurately. If this memory is not available, $p_i(k)$ can be approximately estimated by retaining a small fraction of the tuples on S_i in $S_i[W_i]$ for their entire lifetime. Alternative schemes for approximately estimating the age curve when extra memory is not available is a topic of future work.

3 Max-Subset

Recall our basic algorithm for executing join $S_1[W_1] \bowtie_A S_2[W_2]$ shown in Figure 3. If memory is limited, we need to modify the algorithm in two ways. First, in Line 2, we update $S_1[W_1]$ in addition to $S_2[W_2]$ to free up memory occupied by expired tuples. More importantly, in Line 4, memory may be insufficient to add s to $S_1[W_1]$. In this case, we need to decide whether s is to be discarded or admitted into $S_1[W_1]$, and if it is to be admitted, which of the existing tuples is to be discarded. An algorithm that makes this decision is called a *load-shedding strategy* [4, 7, 17]. Due to load-shedding, only a fraction of the true result will actually be produced. We denote the fraction of the result tuples produced as *recall*.

$$Recall(t) = \frac{\text{Number of result tuples produced up to time } t}{\text{Number of actual result tuples up to time } t}$$

Definition 3.1 (Max-Subset Problem). *Given a fixed amount of memory for a sliding-window join $S_1[W_1] \bowtie_A S_2[W_2]$, devise an online load-shedding strategy that maximizes $\lim_{t \to \infty} Recall(t)$.* □

We first state a result on the hardness of the problem for arbitrary streams (Section 3.1), then present a load-shedding strategy for the age-based model (Section 3.2), and finally discuss the max-subset problem for the frequency-based model (Section 3.3).

3.1 Hardness Result

A load-shedding strategy is *optimal* if it eventually produces the maximum recall among all strategies using the same amount of memory. For bounded streams, an *offline* strategy is one that is allowed to make its load-shedding decisions after knowing all the tuples that are going to arrive in the future. We show that for arbitrary streams, it is not possible for any online strategy to be *competitive* with the optimal offline strategy.

Let S denote a bounded sequence of tuple arrivals on the streams S_1 and S_2. Consider any online strategy. Let $R_{on}(M, S)$ denote the recall obtained at the end of executing the online strategy with memory M on the sequence S. Similarly, let $R_{off}(M, S)$ denote the recall for the optimal offline strategy. We assume M is insufficient to retain the entire windows. The online strategy is k-competitive if for any sequence S, $R_{off}(M, S)/R_{on}(M, S) \leq k$.

Theorem 3.2. *For the max-subset problem, no online strategy (even randomized) can be k-competitive for any k that is independent of the length of the input sequence.* □

A detailed proof is omitted due to space constraints. The idea is to construct an input distribution and to lower-bound the expected competitive ratio of any deterministic strategy on that input distribution. We then obtain Theorem 3.2 by applying Yao's min-max theorem [21].

This result shows that we cannot expect to find an effective load-shedding strategy that addresses the max-subset problem for arbitrary streams.

3.2 Age-Based Model

Consider the max-subset problem for a join $S_1[W_1] \bowtie S_2[W_2]$ that adheres to the age-based model. We first assume a fixed amount of memory is available for $S_1[W_1]$, and consider the problem of maximizing the number of S_1-probe join tuples produced. A symmetric procedure applies for maximizing the number of S_2-probe join tuples given a fixed memory for $S_2[W_2]$. Then we show how to allocate the overall available memory between $S_1[W_1]$ and $S_2[W_2]$ to maximize the recall of the entire join.

3.2.1 Fixed Memory for $S_1[W_1]$

Suppose the available memory for $S_1[W_1]$ is sufficient to store M_1 tuples of stream S_1. We denote the amount of memory required to store one tuple as a "cell". For now we assume $r_1 = 1$, i.e., one tuple arrives on S_1 at each time step. At the end of the section we show the easy generalization to other r_1.[1] We first give the optimal strategy for $M_1 = 1$, which forms the building block for our strategy for $M_1 > 1$. Recall that $C_1(k)$ denotes the total number of S_1-probe join tuples that a tuple $s \in S_1$ produces by age k. Let k_1^{opt} denote the k ($\leq W_1$) at which $\frac{C_1(k)}{k}$ is maximized.

Strategy 1 ($M_1 = 1$). *Retain the first tuple $s \in S_1$ in $S_1[W_1]$ for k_1^{opt} time units, discarding other tuple arrivals on S_1. After k_1^{opt} time units, discard s, retain the tuple arriving next for the next k_1^{opt} time units, and continue.* □

The relatively straightforward proof that Strategy 1 is optimal is omitted due to space constraints.

Example 3.3. *Let $r_1 = 1$ and $M_1 = 1$ as we have assumed so far. Let the window size $W_1 = 4$, and let the age curve be defined by $p_1(1) = 1, p_1(2) = 1, p_1(3) = 2, p_1(4) = 1$. $C_1(k)/k$ is maximized at $k_1^{opt} = 3$.*

Let s_i denote the tuple arriving at time i on S_1. The following diagram illustrates Strategy 1 on this example. Entries in the third row denote the number of S_1-probe join tuples produced between each time step and the next.

Time	1	2	3	4	5	6	7	8
Cell 1	s_1	s_1	s_1	s_4	s_4	s_4	s_7	...
Discard		s_2	s_3	s_1	s_5	s_6	s_4	...
# Results	1	1	2	1	1	2	1	...

Strategy 1 produces 4 join tuples every 3 time units and is optimal among all possible strategies. □

---
[1]Note that all of our optimality claims assume constant rather than average r_1, however our experiments (Section 6) show that our algorithm performs well for a distribution of arrival rates.

Now suppose $M_1 > 1$. We must consider two cases:

1. If $k_1^{opt} \geq M_1$, the optimal strategy is to run Strategy 1 "staggered", for each of the M_1 cells. For example, if $M_1 = 2$ in Example 3.3, we get:

Time	1	2	3	4	5	6	7	8
Cell 1	s_1	s_1	s_1	s_4	s_4	s_4	s_7	...
Cell 2		s_2	s_2	s_2	s_5	s_5	s_5	...
Discard			s_3	s_1	s_2	s_6	s_4	...

2. If $k_1^{opt} < M_1$, the problem becomes more complex because running a staggered Strategy 1 uses only k_1^{opt} cells, thereby underutilizing the available memory.

To address Case 2 ($k_1^{opt} < M_1$), we first define an age curve with a *minima*. The age curve $p_1(k)$ against k has a minima if there exist $k_1 < k_2 < k_3$ such that $p_1(k_1) > p_1(k_2)$ and $p_1(k_2) < p_1(k_3)$.

If the age curve has no minima, the optimal strategy is to retain every tuple for exactly M_1 time units. Once a tuple has been retained for k_1^{opt} time units, retaining it any further becomes less useful, and since the curve has no minima the tuple cannot become more useful in the future. Thus, it should be discarded as early as possible after k_1^{opt} time units. At the same time, tuples should not be discarded any earlier than M_1 time units, as that would lead to underutilization of memory.

If the age curve has a minima, retaining each tuple for exactly M_1 time units may be suboptimal. We illustrate the subtleties through an example.

Example 3.4. *Let $W_1 = 3$ and $M_1 = 2$. Let the age curve be defined by $p_1(1) = 3, p_1(2) = 0$, and $p_1(3) = 2$. Thus, the age curve has a minima at $k = 2$. We have $k_1^{opt} = 1$, so $k_1^{opt} < M_1$. The following strategy alternates between retaining every tuple for 1 and 3 time units, and by exhaustive search is seen to be optimal for this example:*

Time	1	2	3	4	5	6	7	8
Cell 1	s_1	s_1	s_1	s_4	s_5	s_5	s_5	...
Cell 2		s_2	s_3	s_3	s_3	s_6	s_7	...
Discard			s_2	s_1	s_4	s_3	s_6	...
# Results	3	3	5	3	5	3	5	...

This strategy produces an average of 4 join tuples per time unit. Note that retaining every tuple for $M_1 = 2$ time units produces only 3 join tuples per time unit. □

We do not have an optimal strategy for the general case of age curves with minima, but in practice, age curves are unlikely to have minima (e.g., none of the examples discussed in Section 2.2 have minima). However, for completeness, we give the following greedy heuristic for this case. For each tuple $s \in S_1[W_1]$, assign a *priority* that represents the fastest rate at which s can produce S_1-probe join tuples. The priority of a tuple at age i is given by:

$$Priority(i) = \max_{i < j \leq W_1} \frac{C_1(j) - C_1(i)}{j - i}$$

When a tuple needs to be discarded due to a memory constraint, the tuple with the lowest priority is discarded.

This greedy strategy leads to the optimal solution for Example 3.4. Interestingly, this strategy reduces to the optimal strategy for all the previous cases as well. In the rest of this paper, we do not consider age curves with minima.

We shall refer to the overall approach for the age-based max-subset problem presented in this section as the *AGE* algorithm. We evaluate *AGE* experimentally in Section 6.

3.2.2 Fixed Memory for $S_1[W_1] + S_2[W_2]$

So far we have addressed the problem of maximizing the number of S_i-probe join tuples, $i = 1, 2$, given a fixed amount of memory for $S_i[W_i]$. Now suppose we have a fixed amount of memory M for the entire join. To determine how to allocate the available memory between $S_1[W_1]$ and $S_2[W_2]$, we need a function that relates the memory allocation to the overall recall obtained. Let M_i be the memory allocated to $S_i[W_i]$. Let R_i denote the rate at which S_i-probe join tuples are produced. If the *AGE* algorithm from Section 3.2.1 is applied:

$$R_i = \begin{cases} M_i \frac{C_i(k_i^{opt})}{k_i^{opt}} & \text{if } M_i \leq k_i^{opt} \\ C_i(M_i) & \text{if } M_i > k_i^{opt} \end{cases} \quad (2)$$

Then the overall recall of the join is given by $\frac{R_1+R_2}{n_1+n_2}$. To determine the memory allocation between $S_1[W_1]$ and $S_2[W_2]$, we simply find M_1 and M_2 such that this expression for the recall of the join is maximized, subject to the constraint $M_1 + M_2 = M$.

Finally, so far we have assumed $r_i = 1$. If $r_i > 1$, and memory M_i is available for $S_i[W_i]$, Equation 2 becomes:

$$R_i = \begin{cases} M_i \cdot \frac{C_i(k_i^{opt})}{k_i^{opt}} & \text{if } M_i/r_i \leq k_i^{opt} \\ r_i \cdot C_i(M_i/r_i) & \text{if } M_i/r_i > k_i^{opt} \end{cases} \quad (3)$$

The recall for the entire join is then given by $\frac{R_1+R_2}{r_1n_1+r_2n_2}$.

3.3 Frequency-Based Model

We briefly consider the max-subset problem for the frequency-based model as covered in [7]. We derive the recall obtained given a fixed amount of memory for the join, This relationship between memory and recall is needed in Section 5 for overall memory allocation across joins.

Consider S_1-probe join tuples first. Recall Definition 2.1 of the frequency-based model. The following approach, called *PROB*, is suggested in [7]: Every tuple $s_1 \in S_1[W_1]$ is assigned a priority equal to $f_2(s_1.A)$. If a tuple needs to be discarded due to a memory constraint, the tuple with the lowest priority is discarded.

Without loss of generality, assume the values in $\mathcal{D}$ are $v_1, \ldots, v_n$, and for $i < j$, $f_2(v_i) \geq f_2(v_j)$. Then for $i < j$, *PROB* will prefer to retain all instances of v_i in $S_1[W_1]$ over any instance of v_j. Let M_1 be the memory allocated to $S_1[W_1]$. *PROB* will retain all instances of $v_1, v_2, \ldots, v_i$, where i is the largest number such that $r_1W_1 \sum_{j=1}^{i} f_1(v_j) \leq M_1$. (A fraction of the instances of v_{i+1} will be retained too, but our analysis is not affected significantly.) Thus, S_1-probe result tuples are produced at a rate given by $R_1 = r_1r_2W_1 \sum_{j=1}^{i} f_1(v_j)f_2(v_j)$. A symmetric expression can be derived for the rate R_2 at which the S_2-probe join tuples are produced, given memory M_2 for $S_2[W_2]$. The overall recall of the join is then given by $\frac{R_1+R_2}{r_1r_2(W_1+W_2)\sum_{v\in\mathcal{D}} f_1(v)f_2(v)}$. Thus, given a total amount of memory M for the join, we can find M_1 and M_2 such that the overall recall of the join is maximized, subject to the constraint $M_1 + M_2 = M$.

4 Random Sampling

In this section, we address the problem of extracting a random sample of the $S_1[W_1] \bowtie_A S_2[W_2]$ join result with limited memory. We first state a result on the hardness of performing uniform random sampling on the join result for arbitrary streams (Section 4.1). We then give an algorithm for uniform random sampling that applies for both the age-based and frequency-based models (Section 4.2). Finally, in Section 4.3, we consider the case when a uniform sample is not required directly by the application, but is being gathered only for estimating an aggregate over the join result. For these cases, we consider a statistically weaker form of sampling called *cluster sampling* [6], which can be performed more easily than uniform sampling, and often yields a more accurate estimate of the aggregate.

4.1 Hardness Result

For sampling over the windowed join result of arbitrary streams, we have the following negative result:

Theorem 4.1. *If the available memory is insufficient to retain the entire windows, it is not possible to guarantee a uniform random sample for any sampling fraction > 0.* □

A detailed proof is omitted due to space constraints but the basic idea is as follows. Suppose we choose to discard a tuple s in $S_1[W_1]$ because memory is full. Then we must know that all S_1-probe join tuples that s would subsequently produce are guaranteed not to be needed in our sample. However, for arbitrary streams, at any time during the lifetime of s, there is no upper bound on the number of S_1-probe join tuples that s will produce before expiry. Thus, for any sampling fraction greater than 0, it cannot be guaranteed that we can discard s but preserve the sample.

This result shows that we cannot expect to find an effective procedure that performs uniform random sampling over the join result of arbitrary streams with limited memory. However, we can compute a sample when we have a model of stream arrivals, as we show next.

4.2 Uniform Random Sampling

For random sampling we can consider the frequency-based and the age-based models together. We shall assume *Bernoulli sampling*, or sampling under the coin-flip semantics [5]: for sampling a fraction p from a set of tuples, every tuple in the set is included in the sample with probability p independent of every other tuple.

s_1 : Tuple arriving on S_1
$n_1(s_1)$: Number of S_1-probe join tuples that s_1 produces
p : Sampling fraction

DecideNextJoin(s_1):
1. pick $X \sim \mathcal{G}(p)$
2. $s_1.next = s_1.num + X$
3. **if** $(s_1.next > n_1(s_1))$
4.   discard s_1

Join(s_1, s_2):
1. $s_1.num = s_1.num + 1$
2. **if** $(s_1.num = s_1.next)$
3.   output $s_1 \bowtie_A s_2$
4.   *DecideNextJoin*(s_1)

Figure 4: Algorithm UNIFORM

4.2.1 Sampling Algorithm

Our algorithm UNIFORM for uniform random sampling over a sliding-window join with limited memory is shown in Figure 4. We only show the procedure for sampling from the S_1-probe join tuples by selectively retaining tuples in $S_1[W_1]$. The procedure for sampling from the S_2-probe join tuples is analogous. UNIFORM needs to know, for each arriving tuple $s_1 \in S_1$, the number of S_1-probe join tuples that s_1 will produce, i.e., $n_1(s_1)$. For the age-based model, $n_1(s_1) = n_1$. For the frequency-based model $n_1(s_1) = r_2 \cdot W_1 \cdot f_2(s_1.A)$ (recall Equation 1). We assume the sampling fraction p is known for now. In the next subsection, we show how p can be determined based on the amount of memory available.

When a tuple s_1 arrives on S_1, $s_1.num$ is initialized to 0, and the procedure *DecideNextJoin*(s_1) is called. *Join*(s_1, s_2) is called when a tuple s_2, that joins with s_1, arrives on S_2. $\mathcal{G}(p)$ denotes the geometric distribution with parameter p [15], and $X \sim \mathcal{G}(p)$ denotes that we pick X at random from $\mathcal{G}(p)$. When *DecideNextJoin*(s_1) is called, UNIFORM logically flips coins with bias p for deciding the next S_1-probe join tuple of s_1 that will be included in the sample. If all remaining S_1-probe join tuples of s_1 are rejected by the coin flips, s_1 is discarded.

4.2.2 Determining the Sampling Fraction p

To determine the sampling fraction p, we first obtain the expected memory usage of UNIFORM (i.e., the expected number of tuples retained) in terms of p. We then equate this expected memory usage to the amount of memory available for performing the join and solve for p. For robustness, we can also calculate the variance of the memory usage of UNIFORM and decide the sampling fraction such that the probability of the memory usage exceeding the available memory is sufficiently small. The following results about the expected memory usage follow from simple properties of the geometric distribution; proofs are omitted. Note that now the tuple size must include the space required to store the extra fields *next* and *num* (Figure 4).

Frequency-Based Model: Recall Definition 2.1. We assume that the S_1-probe join tuples of a tuple $s_1 \in S_1$ are produced uniformly throughout the lifetime of s_1 (because a uniform fixed fraction of tuples arriving on S_2 join with s_1).

Theorem 4.2. *For the frequency-based model, the expected memory usage of $S_1[W_1]$ is (let $q = 1 - p$):*

$$r_1 W_1 \sum_{v \in \mathcal{D}} f_1(v) \left(1 - \frac{q(1 - q^{r_2 W_1 f_2(v)})}{p r_2 W_1 f_2(v)}\right) \qquad \square$$

Age-Based Model: Recall Definition 2.2. Recall that $C_1(k)$ denotes the cumulative number of S_1-probe join tuples that a tuple $s_1 \in S_1$ produces by age k. Define the inverse of the C_1 function, $C_1^{-1}(m)$, as the smallest k such that $C_1(k) \geq m$. Thus, a tuple $s_1 \in S_1$ produces m S_1-probe join tuples by the time its age is $C^{-1}(m)$.

Theorem 4.3. *For the age-based model, the expected memory usage of $S_1[W_1]$ is $r_1 \sum_{i=1}^{n_1} p(1-p)^{n_1 - i} C^{-1}(i)$.* $\quad \square$

In both models, a symmetric expression holds for the expected memory usage of $S_2[W_2]$, assuming we use the same sampling fraction p for the S_2-probe join tuples. Summing these expressions gives us the total memory usage for the join $S_1[W_1] \bowtie_A S_2[W_2]$.

4.3 Cluster Sampling

The correctness of UNIFORM depends heavily on the accuracy with which $n_i(s)$ is estimated for a tuple $s \in S_i$, $i = 1, 2$. For example, for a tuple $s_1 \in S_1$, if $n_1(s_1)$ is underestimated as $n_1'(s_1)$, then all the S_1-probe join tuples of s_1 subsequent to its first $n_1'(s_1)$ join tuples will never be selected for the sample. On the other hand, if $n_1(s_1)$ is overestimated, s_1 may remain in $S_1[W_1]$ until expiry, waiting for joins that never take place, and the overall memory usage may be considerably higher than the expected value derived in Theorems 4.2 and 4.3.

If a uniform random sample of the join is not required directly by the application, but the sample is being taken only to estimate an aggregate over the join results, these difficulties can be overcome by using a statistically weaker form of sampling called *cluster sampling* [6].

In general, cluster sampling is applicable when the population to be sampled can be divided into groups, or *clusters*, such that the cost of sampling a single element of a cluster is equal to that of sampling the entire cluster. Thus, for cluster sampling, a certain number of clusters are chosen at random, and all elements of selected clusters are included in the *cluster sample*. A cluster sample is *unbiased*, i.e., each element of the population has equal probability of being included in the sample. However, it is *correlated*, i.e., the inclusion of tuples is not independent of each other as in a uniform sample. A detailed analysis of cluster sampling can be found in [6]. In the remainder of this section we assume the sample of the join is being gathered for estimating either a sum or an average aggregate, and the objective is to minimize the error in the estimated aggregate.

4.3.1 Two Approaches

Consider sampling from the S_1-probe join tuples; a symmetric procedure applies for sampling from the S_2-probe join tuples. A tuple $s_1 \in S_1$ joins with $n_1(s_1)$ tuples arriving on S_2. These join tuples form a cluster, and the entire cluster can be sampled by simply retaining s_1 in $S_1[W_1]$ until expiry. The fraction of clusters that can be sampled is determined by the number of tuples that can be retained until expiry in the memory available for $S_1[W_1]$. Thus we have the following naïve approach to cluster sampling.

Strategy 2 (EQ-CLUSTER). *Add an incoming tuple $s_1 \in S_1$ to $S_1[W_1]$ with probability p. If s_1 is added to $S_1[W_1]$, retain it until expiry and include all its S_1-probe join tuples in the sample.* □

Notice that this scheme does not depend on $n_1(s_1)$, and always produces an unbiased sample. The expected memory usage for $S_1[W_1]$ according to this scheme is $r_1 W_1 p$. Thus, p can be decided based on the amount of memory available.

EQ-CLUSTER is suitable when the clusters are roughly of equal size (e.g., as in the age-based model). However, if clusters are of unequal sizes, as in the frequency-based model, statistics literature [6] suggests that better estimates of the aggregate can be obtained by selecting a cluster with probability proportional to its size. Otherwise, if clusters are selected with equal probability, large clusters that contribute most to the aggregate may be missed altogether. We thus have the following approach:

Strategy 3 (PPS-CLUSTER). *Add an incoming tuple $s_1 \in S_1$ to $S_1[W_1]$ with probability proportional to $n_1(s_1)$. If s_1 is added to $S_1[W_1]$, retain it until expiry and include all its S_1-probe join tuples in the sample.* □

With *PPS-CLUSTER*, to get an unbiased estimate of the aggregate, we must perform weighted aggregation on the cluster sample: the contribution of each cluster to the aggregate is assigned a weight inversely proportional to the cluster size. Details can be found in [6]. Notice that even if $n_1(s_1)$ is incorrectly estimated, the same incorrect estimate is used in performing weighted aggregation. Hence, the resulting estimate of the aggregate is still unbiased.

Consider the application of *PPS-CLUSTER* for the frequency-based model. Since $n_1(s_1) \propto f_2(s_1.A)$, let s_1 be added to $S_1[W_1]$ with probability $p \cdot f_2(s_1.A)$ where p is a proportionality constant. The expected memory usage of $S_1[W_1]$ is $r_1 W_1 p \sum_{v \in \mathcal{D}} f_1(v) f_2(v)$. Thus, p can be determined according to the amount of memory available.[2]

4.3.2 Comparison of Approaches

To summarize, let us briefly consider which sampling approach is preferable in different scenarios. Recall that the objective is to minimize the error in an estimated aggregate. The relevant factors to be considered are:

- *Accuracy of model parameters*: If $n_i(s)$ is incorrectly estimated for a tuple $s \in S_i$, $i = 1, 2$, *UNIFORM* may perform poorly since it may produce a biased sample. In this case, cluster sampling should be used.

- *Inter-cluster variance*: Consider the variance in the values of the aggregate for different clusters. The lower this variance, the better the performance of cluster sampling compared to uniform sampling [6].

- *Cluster sizes*: *PPS-CLUSTER* should be used for unequal-size clusters. *PPS-CLUSTER* reduces to *EQ-CLUSTER* for equal-size clusters.

5 Memory Allocation across Multiple Joins

Now suppose our stream system is executing a number of continuous queries, each of which involves a sliding-window join. In this section, we address the problem of allocating the available memory across these multiple joins. For now, let us assume the unweighted case, i.e., all joins are equally important. The goal of our allocation scheme is to ensure that no join does "too badly" in terms of approximation error, i.e., we seek to minimize the maximum approximation error in any join. It is important to observe that different joins may differ in the accuracy of their approximation even when given the same fraction of their memory requirement. Thus, simple proportional allocation of memory among the joins is generally not optimal.

Suppose there are n sliding-window joins with an overall memory constraint M. Each join may follow either the age-based or the frequency-based model. Further, each join has a certain *approximation metric* which we denote by $\mathcal{Q}$: For the max-subset problem, $\mathcal{Q}$ is the recall of the join. For the sampling problem, $\mathcal{Q}$ is the error in an aggregate (e.g., SUM) estimated from the sample. We assume that each join uses the same approximation metric (i.e., either recall or aggregation error), otherwise the choice of a combined approximation metric is not clear. We shall focus on the case when $\mathcal{Q}$ is recall. A similar technique applies when $\mathcal{Q}$ is aggregation error.

For a particular memory allocation, let q_i be the recall obtained for the ith join. The optimal memory allocation we seek is the one that maximizes $\min_{1 \leq i \leq n} q_i$. The key to our scheme is the following observation (a similar observation is made in [4]).

Theorem 5.1. *To maximize the minimum recall, the optimal memory allocation is one that produces the same recall in all joins.*

By Theorem 5.1, in the optimal memory allocation the recall obtained in each join is the same, say q_{opt}. Let $f_i(q)$ denote the minimum amount of memory required to obtain recall q in the ith join. Then q_{opt} is the maximum q such that $\sum_{i=1}^{n} f_i(q) \leq M$. Assuming the functions f_i are known, q_{opt} can be found by an iterative binary search. The amount of memory to be allocated to the ith join is then given by $f_i(q_{opt})$.

Let us consider how the function $f_i(q)$ can be obtained for the ith join. Recall that we specified the relationship between memory available for a join and the recall obtained, both for the age-based (Section 3.2.2) and the frequency-based (Section 3.3) models. These can be used to obtain $f_i(q)$. When the metric $\mathcal{Q}$ is aggregation error, we use the

---

[2] A value of p obtained in this way can cause $p f_2(s_1.A)$ to exceed 1 for some s_1, resulting in an overestimate of memory usage. The correct value of p can be chosen by an iterative procedure; details are omitted.

relationship between memory and sampling fraction (Theorems 4.2 and 4.3). The expected aggregation error for a given sampling fraction can be derived in terms of population characteristics such as mean and variance [4]. Together, these can be used to calculate $f_i(q)$.

Finally, suppose that different joins have different relative importance. Let w_i be the weight of the ith join. Now our objective is to maximize $\min_{1 \leq i \leq n} q_i/w_i$. Our argument extends to show that the optimal solution is to allocate memory $f_i(w_i q_{opt})$ to the ith join, where q_{opt} is the maximum q such that $\sum_{i=1}^{n} f_i(w_i q) \leq M$.

We shall refer to the approach for memory allocation presented in this section as *ALLOC*, and evaluate its performance experimentally in Section 6.

6 Experiments

We now present an experimental evaluation of our techniques. Our experiments demonstrate the following:

1. In a real-life scenario that adheres to the age-based model, our algorithm *AGE* (Section 3.2.1) gives considerably higher recall than more naïve approaches.

2. Our sampling approaches *UNIFORM* and *PPS-CLUSTER* (Section 4) provide low-error estimates of windowed aggregates over the join result. Either of the two approaches may be preferable, depending on the specific scenario.

3. Our algorithm *ALLOC* for memory allocation across joins (Section 5) significantly outperforms simple proportional allocation in terms of maximizing the minimum recall.

6.1 Age-Based Experiment

For initial experimentation with the age-based model, we captured real data as follows. We set up two stream sources, ϕ_1 and ϕ_2, and a central server. Source ϕ_1 and the server run on the same physical machine, while source ϕ_2 runs on a distant machine connected over a wide-area network (WAN). Each source produces tuples at a constant rate of $r_1 = r_2 = 50$ per second. Each tuple contains a timestamp ts from the local clock at the source. All tuples are streamed to the server using a UDP channel.

Denote the streams from sources ϕ_1 and ϕ_2 as S_1 and S_2 respectively. We execute a sliding-window join whose purpose is to identify causal correlation between the two streams—to do so, it matches tuples from S_2 with tuples from S_1 that were timestamped approximately one minute earlier. The join predicate chosen is $S_2.\text{ts} - S_1.\text{ts} \in [59.9, 60.1]$ where time units are seconds. To ensure that S_1 tuples do not expire before matching S_2 tuples arrive (the network latency from source ϕ_2 to the server is high), we conservatively set the window on S_1 as $W_1 = 2$ minutes. Since joining tuples always arrive later on S_2 than on S_1, a window on S_2 need not be stored.

We generated a trace of approximately 40 minutes of tuple arrivals at the server and then used this trace for repeatability. Figure 5 shows the age curve ($p_1(k)$ vs. k)

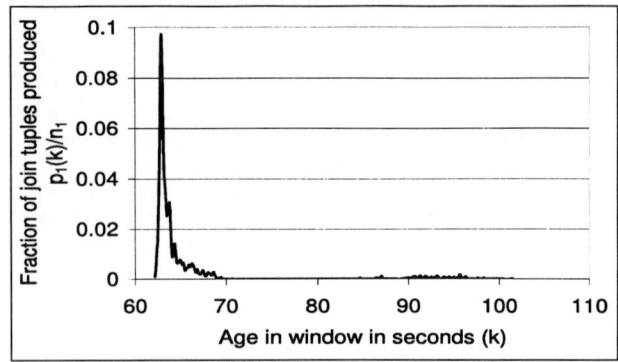

Figure 5: Age curve for WAN experiment

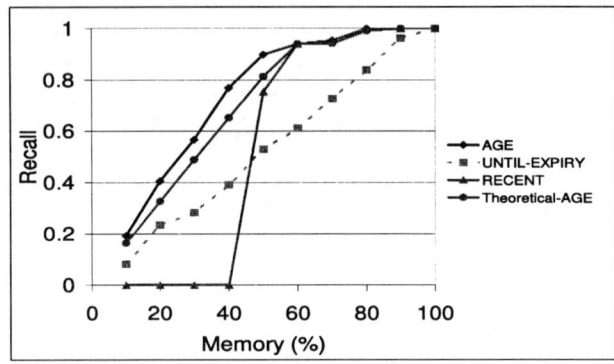

Figure 6: Recall obtained on WAN experiment

determined by an initial pass through our trace. We show $p_1(k)$ as a fraction of n_1 (recall Definition 2.2). The granularity chosen for k was 0.1 second. We see that a tuple $s \in S_1$ produces most join tuples at an age of approximately $k = 63$ seconds. Out of this, a 60 second delay is due to the join predicate, and the rest of the delay is due to clock skew between sources ϕ_1 and ϕ_2, and significantly higher network latency for tuples from ϕ_2 than from ϕ_1.

6.1.1 Results

Figure 6 shows the recall obtained on our trace by various load-shedding approaches as we vary the amount of allocated memory. Memory is shown as a percentage of the amount required to retain the entire window ($r_1 W_1$). We compare: (1) *AGE*: Section 3.2.1; (2) *UNTIL-EXPIRY*: A tuple is added to $S_1[W_1]$ only if memory is available, and then retained until expiry; (3) *RECENT*: The most recent tuples in the window are retained; and (4) *Theoretical-AGE*: The recall that should be theoretically obtained by applying the *AGE* approach, as given by Equation 3. Note that *RECENT* is the approach that we get if we simply apply the frequency-based model in this scenario.

Although in reality the age curve shown in Figure 5 has some minima, $p_1(k)$ never increases significantly after decreasing. Hence, for all practical purposes, we can apply our *AGE* approach assuming the curve has no minima. k_1^{opt} was calculated to be 68.8 seconds.

We see that *AGE* outperforms *RECENT* and *UNTIL-EXPIRY*. *RECENT* performs especially badly, producing no join tuples even when the allocated memory is as much as 40%. However, when the allocated memory is high enough so that $M_1 \geq r_1 k_1^{opt}$, *AGE* reduces to *RECENT* (see Equation 3), and hence both approaches produce the same recall. Note that if W_1 had been conservatively set to be higher, the performance of *UNTIL-EXPIRY* would degrade, whereas the performance of *AGE* would not be affected. We also see that the actual recall obtained by *AGE* closely agrees with the theoretically predicted value.

6.2 Experiments on Synthetic Data

For the next set of experiments, we synthetically generate streams S_1 and S_2 for both the age-based and the frequency-based model, and perform the sliding-window join $S_1[W_1] \bowtie S_2[W_2]$ with limited memory. For simplicity, we consider only the S_1-probe join tuples in our experimental results. For both models, tuples on streams S_i, $i = 1, 2$, are generated at an average rate of r_i tuples per unit time. This is done by choosing the inter-arrival time uniformly at random between $1/2r_i$ and $2/r_i$ time units. For all experiments we fix $r_1 = 1, r_2 = 5$, and $W_1 = 500$.

6.2.1 Age-Based Data Generation

First stream S_1 is generated. Each tuple on S_1 contains a unique `id` which serves as the join attribute, as in the examples of Section 2.2 (e.g., in the auction scenario, each tuple on S_1 has a unique `auction-id`). Next, we specify the age curve for $S_1[W_1]$ by dividing the window duration W_1 into m buckets and specifying $p_1(k)$ for the kth bucket. The first bucket consists of the newest tuples, and the mth bucket the oldest tuples. We fix $n_1 = 5$ and $m = 20$.

We then generate stream S_2 according to this age curve. Suppose a tuple is to be generated on S_2 at time t. The value of its join attribute is determined as follows. We choose one of the m buckets at random with the kth bucket being chosen with probability $p_1(k)/n_1$. Then, we choose one tuple at random from all the tuples of $S_1[W_1]$ occupying the chosen bucket at time t. The `id` of this randomly-chosen tuple is assigned as the join-attribute value of the newly generated tuple on S_2.

6.2.2 Max-Subset Problem with Age-Based Data

We experimented with three different age curves. (1) Increasing (*INC*): $p_1(k) \propto k^2$; (2) Decreasing (*DEC*): $p_1(k) \propto (m-k)^2$; and (3) Bell-shaped (*BELL*): $p_1(k) \propto k^2$ for $1 \leq k \leq m/2$ and $p_1(k) \propto (m-k)^2$ for $m/2 < k \leq m$. Figure 7 shows a comparison of the recall obtained by various approaches for different types of age curves. For the *INC* curve, *AGE* significantly outperforms *RECENT*. For the *DEC* curve, *AGE* reduces to *RECENT*, so we do not show their results separately. For the *BELL* curve, *AGE* outperforms *RECENT* until $M_1 < r_1 k_1^{opt}$ (see Equation 3). For $M_1 \geq r_1 k_1^{opt}$, *AGE* reduces to *RECENT*.

Note that for the same amount of allocated memory, the recall differs greatly depending on the shape of the age curve. This indicates that in the presence of multiple joins, in order to maximize the minimum recall, simple proportional memory allocation is not sufficient, which we verify empirically in Section 6.2.5.

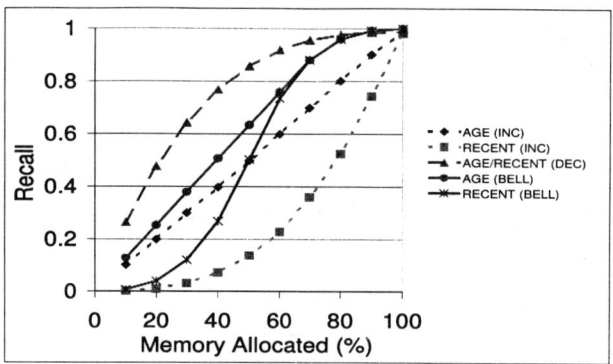

Figure 7: Recall obtained on synthetic age-based data

6.2.3 Frequency-Based Data Generation

Data generation for the frequency-based model is relatively easier than for the age-based model. We choose a domain $\mathcal{D}$. The domain size is fixed at $|\mathcal{D}| = 50$. For each stream, the join-attribute values are drawn from a Zipfian distribution of parameter Z over $\mathcal{D}$ [23]. The distribution used for both streams need not be the same. We consider three cases: (1) Directly Correlated (*DC*): The order of frequency of occurrence of values is the same for S_1 and S_2; (2) Inversely Correlated (*IC*): The order of frequency of occurrence of values for S_1 is opposite of that for S_2, i.e., the rarest value on S_1 is the most common on S_2 and vice-versa; and (3) Uncorrelated (*UC*): The order of frequency of occurrence of values for the two streams is uncorrelated.

6.2.4 Random Sampling

To evaluate our sampling approaches, we perform a windowed average over the sampled result of a join, and compare the approaches in terms of aggregation error. We report results only for the case when the join follows the frequency-based model. Results for the age-based model are similar and are omitted. The aggregation window is fixed at $W_{aggr} = 500$. The values of the aggregation attribute are drawn from a normal distribution having mean μ and variance σ. At each time step, the value of the windowed aggregate over the true result (U) and over the sampled result ($\hat{U}$) are calculated. The relative error in the aggregate is $|\hat{U} - U|/U$. We report the average of these errors over the entire run. In all experiments, while implementing *UNIFORM*, we assume a tuple size of 32 bytes. The two extra fields required (see Figure 4) are stored compactly in two bytes, thus giving a new tuple size of 34 bytes.

We first consider the case when the aggregated attribute is part of S_1. Recall that all the S_1-probe join tuples produced by a tuple $s \in S_1$ form a cluster. Thus, in this case, all tuples in a cluster have the same value in the aggregated attribute, which is the worst case for cluster sampling.

Effect of Allocated Memory: Figure 8 shows the aggregation error of the various sampling approaches as we vary the amount of allocated memory. We use the inversely correlated (*IC*) frequency-based model with $Z = 2$, and we fix $\mu = \sigma = 100$. We see that *PPS-CLUSTER* outperforms *EQ-CLUSTER*: in the *IC* case, there are a small

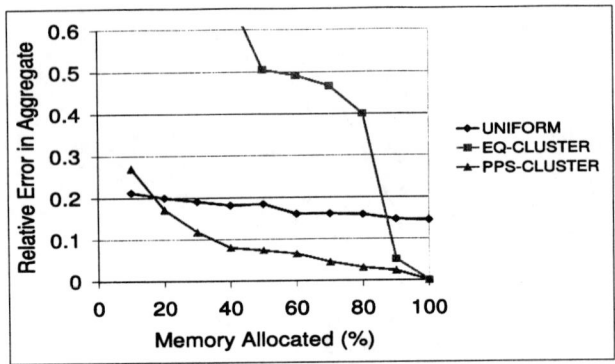

Figure 8: Aggregation error vs. memory allocated, *IC* frequency-based model, $Z = 2$, $\mu = \sigma = 100$

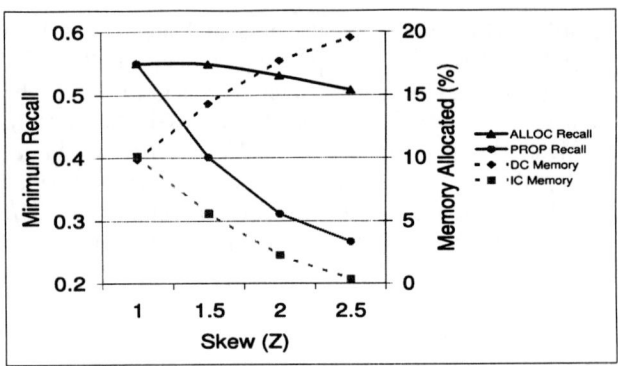

Figure 10: Memory allocation across joins: frequency-based model, Memory=20%

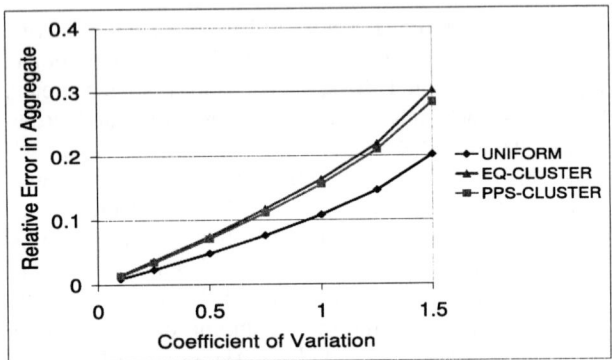

Figure 9: Aggregation error vs. population variance, *UC* frequency-based model, $Z = 2$, $\mu = 100$, Memory=10%

number of large clusters in the result which may be missed by *EQ-CLUSTER*. *UNIFORM* performs better than *PPS-CLUSTER* when the allocated memory is 10%. However, the fraction that can be sampled grows more rapidly for *PPS-CLUSTER* than for *UNIFORM*. Consequently, *PPS-CLUSTER* performs better at higher allocated memory. Note that the error of *UNIFORM* does not go down to 0 even when allocated memory is 100%. This is because even the synthetic data does not adhere perfectly to the model, as is required for the correctness of *UNIFORM* (Section 4.3).

Effect of Population Variance: Figure 9 shows the aggregation error of the various sampling approaches as the variance of the aggregated attribute is varied. We show the variance normalized by the mean, i.e., we show the coefficient of variation (σ/μ). The allocated memory is 10%, $\mu = 100$, and the model used is the uncorrelated (*UC*) frequency-based model with $Z = 2$. As the population variance increases, since all tuples in a cluster have the same value, the inter-cluster variance increases. As a result, the performance of cluster sampling approaches degrades as compared to *UNIFORM*.

If the aggregated attribute is a part of S_2, the values in a cluster are uncorrelated. Consequently, cluster sampling performs much better than *UNIFORM*. We omit the results due to lack of space. Finally, note that for comparing our sampling approaches, we have calculated the exact aggregate over the sampled result. In reality, when memory is limited, this aggregation may be approximated [8].

6.2.5 Memory Allocation across Multiple Joins

For memory allocation among multiple joins, we study the performance of our *ALLOC* scheme in comparison with simple proportional memory allocation (*PROP*). We only study the case when the approximation metric of each join is the recall obtained in that join.

Frequency-Based Model: We allocate memory across two joins that follow the frequency-based model: one follows the directly correlated (*DC*) case, and the other, the inversely correlated (*IC*) case (recall Section 6.2.3). The total available memory is 20% of that required for executing both joins accurately. The load-shedding strategy used for each join is *PROB* [7]. Figure 10 shows a comparison of the minimum recall obtained by both approaches when we vary the skew parameter (Z) of the frequency-based model. As Z increases, the minimum recall remains almost constant for *ALLOC*, but decreases sharply for *PROP*. The amount of memory allocated to each join by *ALLOC* (as a percentage of the total memory required) is shown by the dashed plots on the secondary Y-axis. Note that *PROP* always splits the available memory evenly between the two joins, i.e., 10% to each join.

To understand these results, notice that the *IC* case is "easy", i.e., a relatively higher recall can be produced using a small amount of memory: only the rare values of S_1 (which are frequent on S_2) need to be retained. In contrast, the *DC* case is "hard", i.e., more memory is required to obtain the same recall because the common values on S_1 need to be retained. Moreover, as the skew (Z) increases, the *IC* case becomes easier, and the *DC* case becomes harder. *ALLOC* is able to outperform *PROP* by allocating less memory to the *IC* case, and using this extra memory to boost the performance of the *DC* case.

Age-Based Model: We allocate memory across two joins that follow the age-based model, one with an increasing (*INC*) age curve, and another with a decreasing (*DEC*) one. The *INC* curve is chosen as $p_1(k) \propto k^p$ and the *DEC* curve as $p_1(k) \propto (m - k)^p$, where the exponent p is varied. The total available memory is 50% of that required for executing both joins accurately. The load-shedding strategy used

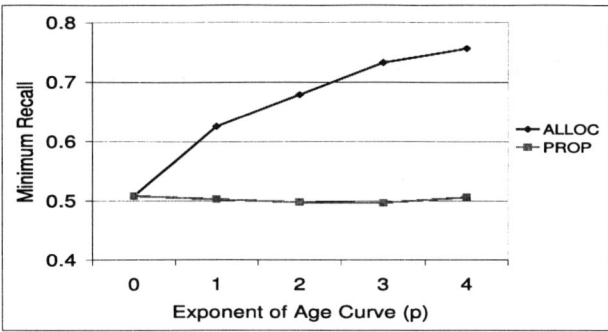

Figure 11: Memory allocation across joins: age-based model, Memory=50%

for each join is *AGE* (Section 3.2.1). Figure 11 shows a comparison of the minimum recall obtained by both approaches when we vary the exponent p. As p increases, the minimum recall increases for *ALLOC* but remains constant for *PROP*. With increase in p, the *DEC* case becomes "easier", while the *INC* case remains equally "hard" (by Equation 3). Thus *ALLOC* is able to outperform *PROP* by allocating less memory to *DEC*, and using the extra memory to boost the performance of *INC*.

More Joins: We omit the results of experimenting with a greater number of joins, but the findings were similar: As more "hard" joins are added, the gain of *ALLOC* over *PROP* decreases, while if more "easy" joins are added, the gain of *ALLOC* over *PROP* increases. Intuitively, the performance of *PROP* is always limited by the hardest join, while *ALLOC* equalizes the recall among all joins.

7 Conclusion

In this paper we addressed memory-limited approximation of sliding-window joins. We defined a novel age-based model that often enables us to address the max-subset problem more effectively than the frequency-based model used previously. We also introduced and addressed the problem of extracting a random sample of the join result with limited memory. Finally, we gave an optimal algorithm for memory allocation across joins to minimize the maximum approximation error.

One promising avenue for future work is to extend the approximation techniques developed here to address a related but distinct problem: memory-limited computation of exact answers. Now, instead of load-shedding we must offload selected data on disk. The frequency-based and age-based models may help us develop algorithms that minimize disk I/O in this setting. Another interesting direction is to generalize our techniques for a broader class of queries and plan operators such as multi-way joins. Finally, so far we have considered only the static version of the problem, where stream characteristics are assumed to be relatively stable. For volatile environments, we plan to develop adaptive versions of our algorithms.

Acknowledgements

We are grateful to Arvind Arasu, Rajeev Motwani, and the entire STREAM group at Stanford for useful discussions.

References

[1] N. Alon, P. Gibbons, Y. Matias, and M. Szegedy. Tracking join and self-join sizes in limited storage. In *Proc. of the 1999 ACM Symp. on Principles of Database Systems*, pages 10–20, 1999.

[2] B. Babcock, S. Babu, M. Datar, R. Motwani, and J. Widom. Models and issues in data stream systems. In *Proc. of the 2002 ACM Symp. on Principles of Database Systems*, pages 1–16, June 2002.

[3] B. Babcock, M. Datar, and R. Motwani. Sampling from a moving window over streaming data. In *Proc. of the 2002 Annual ACM-SIAM Symp. on Discrete Algorithms*, pages 633–634, 2002.

[4] B. Babcock, M. Datar, and R. Motwani. Load-shedding for aggregation queries over data streams. In *Proc. of the 2004 Intl. Conf. on Data Engineering*, 2004. To appear.

[5] S. Chaudhuri, R. Motwani, and V. Narasayya. On random sampling over joins. In *Proc. of the 1999 ACM SIGMOD Intl. Conf. on Management of Data*, pages 263–274, June 1999.

[6] W. G. Cochran. *Sampling Techniques*. John Wiley & Sons, 1977.

[7] A. Das, J. Gehrke, and M. Riedewald. Approximate join processing over data streams. In *Proc. of the 2003 ACM SIGMOD Intl. Conf. on Management of Data*, June 2003.

[8] M. Datar, A. Gionis, P. Indyk, and R. Motwani. Maintaining stream statistics over sliding windows. In *Proc. of the 2002 Annual ACM-SIAM Symp. on Discrete Algorithms*, pages 635–644, 2002.

[9] A. Dobra, M. Garofalakis, J. Gehrke, and R. Rastogi. Processing complex aggregate queries over data streams. In *Proc. of the 2002 ACM SIGMOD Intl. Conf. on Management of Data*, pages 61–72, 2002.

[10] A. Gilbert, S. Guha, P. Indyk, Y. Kotidis, S. Muthukrishnan, and M. Strauss. Fast, small-space algorithms for approximate histogram maintenance. In *Proc. of the 2002 Annual ACM Symp. on Theory of Computing*, 2002.

[11] L. Golab and M. Ozsu. Issues in data stream management. *SIGMOD Record*, 32(2):5–14, June 2003.

[12] S. Guha, N. Koudas, and K. Shim. Data-streams and histograms. In *Proc. of the 2001 Annual ACM Symp. on Theory of Computing*, pages 471–475, 2001.

[13] J. Kang, J. F. Naughton, and S. Viglas. Evaluating window joins over unbounded streams. In *Proc. of the 2003 Intl. Conf. on Data Engineering*, March 2003.

[14] S. Krishnamurthy et al. TelegraphCQ: An Architectural Status Report. *IEEE Data Engineering Bulletin*, 26(1):11–18, March 2003.

[15] R. Motwani and P. Raghavan. *Randomized Algorithms*. Cambridge University Press, 1995.

[16] SQR – A Stream Query Repository. http://www-db.stanford.edu/stream/sqr.

[17] N. Tatbul, U. Cetintemel, S. Zdonik, M. Cherniack, and M. Stonebraker. Load-shedding in a data stream manager. In *Proc. of the 2003 Intl. Conf. on Very Large Data Bases*, September 2003.

[18] The STREAM Group. STREAM: The Stanford Stream Data Manager. *IEEE Data Engineering Bulletin*, 26(1):19–26, March 2003.

[19] T. Urhan and M.J. Franklin. Xjoin: A reactively-scheduled pipelined join operator. *IEEE Data Engineering Bulletin*, 23(2):27–33, June 2000.

[20] J. Xie, J. Yang, and Y. Chen. On joining and caching stochastic streams. Technical report, Duke University, Durham, North Carolina, November 2003.

[21] A. C. Yao. Probabilistic computations: Towards a unified measure of complexity. In *Proc. of the 1977 Annual IEEE Symp. on Foundations of Computer Science*, pages 222–227, 1977.

[22] S. Zdonik et al. The Aurora and Medusa Projects. *IEEE Data Engineering Bulletin*, 26(1), March 2003.

[23] G. E. Zipf. *Human Behavior and the Principle of Least Effort*. Addison-Wesley Press, Inc., 1949.

Resource Sharing in Continuous Sliding-Window Aggregates

Arvind Arasu   Jennifer Widom

Stanford University
{arvinda,widom}@cs.stanford.edu

Abstract

We consider the problem of resource sharing when processing large numbers of continuous queries. We specifically address sliding-window aggregates over data streams, an important class of continuous operators for which sharing has not been addressed. We present a suite of sharing techniques that cover a wide range of possible scenarios: different classes of aggregation functions (algebraic, distributive, holistic), different window types (time-based, tuple-based, suffix, historical), and different input models (single stream, multiple substreams). We provide precise theoretical performance guarantees for our techniques, and show their practical effectiveness through experimental study.

1 Introduction

We consider *continuous-query* based applications involving a large number of concurrent queries over the same data. Examples of such applications include *publish-subscribe* systems (such as Traderbot [29]) that allow a large number of users to independently monitor *published* information of interest using *subscriptions*. Another example is intrusion detection, where a large number of *rules* are used to continuously monitor system and network activity [24, 30]. In these applications, subscriptions and rules are continuous queries.

Handling each continuous query separately is inefficient, and may be infeasible for large numbers of queries and high data rates. Queries must be handled *collectively*, by exploiting similarities and *sharing resources* such as computation, memory, and disk bandwidth among them. Numerous papers [8–10, 14, 25] have highlighted the importance of resource sharing in continuous queries.

One avenue for resource sharing is based on detecting and exploiting common subexpressions in queries, related to traditional multi-query optimization [27, 28]. However,
we are interested in more basic sharing—at the operator level. If several queries use different instances of operators belonging to a same class, it is sometimes possible to process all the operator instances more efficiently using a single generic operator. A good example of operator level sharing is processing many range predicates using a single *predicate index* [11, 16, 25]. The predicate index identifies all the indexed range predicates that a given tuple satisfies more efficiently than the naïve method that checks each predicate separately.

Previous work on operator-level sharing has focused primarily on filters, which are stateless and have simple semantics. In this paper, we address operator-level sharing for an important class of operators based on *aggregations over sliding windows*, detailed in the next subsection. The importance of these operators has been identified before [12], but the sharing problem is largely unstudied. (The problem is considered just briefly in PSoup [10]. PSoup is discussed in detail in Section 3.1.3.) We show that there exist significant opportunities for sharing in sliding-window aggregates, and by exploiting them we obtain dramatic improvements in performance over the naïve, non-sharing approaches.

1.1 Sliding-Window Aggregates

Continuous queries typically work on unbounded *data streams*, rather than static data sets. For many applications, recent elements of a stream are more important than older ones. This preference for recent data is commonly expressed using *sliding windows* over a stream [7]. The size of a window is often specified using a time interval (*time-based*), but may use number of tuples instead (*tuple-based*). The window usually ends at the current time, called a *suffix* window, but nonsuffix (*historical*) windows may also be used.

An *aggregation over a sliding window (ASW)* operator continuously applies an aggregation function over the contents of a sliding window. The aggregation value changes over time as the window slides. ASW is widely recognized as a fundamental operation over streams, and is the subject of numerous previous papers [4, 10, 12, 18].

Example 1.1 Consider a stream of stock trades, and two ASW operators. One operator asks for the "average number of shares in the last 10,000 stock trades" (a suffix, tuple-based sliding window), while the other asks for "average number of shares in trades between 1 and 2 minutes ago" (a time-based historical window). Assuming the windows may overlap, using our techniques we can share state and computation between these two operators. In practice our techniques are most important when there are hundreds or thousands of such operators, as would occur in Traderbot [29] or other publish-subscribe systems. □

Although historical windows are less frequent than suffix windows, most of our algorithms are no simpler for the suffix-only case. In those cases where suffix-only is simpler, we explicitly say so (e.g., Algorithm L-INT in Section 3.1.2).

1.1.1 Sliding-Window Aggregates on Substreams

Some streams can be partitioned logically into *substreams* [31], each identified by a *key*. For example, our stock trade stream can be partitioned into substreams based on the stock symbol (key). Similarly, a stream of network packets can be partitioned into substreams, one per *flow* [15].

With partitioning, a useful primitive is the application of an ASW operator over each substream [31]. This operation conceptually produces a dynamic relation: at any point in time, there is one tuple for each substream in the relation, containing the current answer of the ASW operator for that substream. The sharing techniques that we develop for general ASW operators are applicable for substreams as well. However, we show that when an ASW operator over substreams is followed by a range predicate over the conceptual dynamic relation—a class of operators we call *SubStream Filters (SSF)*—there are additional sharing possibilities.

Example 1.2 Consider the class of operators "find all stocks whose trading volume during a certain sliding window exceeds a certain threshold." These are SSF operators. If we have many such operators, with different thresholds and windows, our techniques let us share resources by maintaining a single index-like structure over all the different ASW operators and range predicates. □

1.1.2 Additional Examples

We briefly illustrate that realistic queries are composed of aggregations over sliding windows. The following two queries were taken directly from the Traderbot site [29].

1. **NASDAQ Short-term Downward Momentum:** Find all NASDAQ stocks between $20 and $200 that have moved down more than 2% in the last 20 minutes and there has been significant buying pressure (70% or more of the volume has traded toward the ask price) in the last 2 minutes.

2. **High Volatility with Recent Volume Surge:** Find all stocks between $20 and $200 where the spread between the high tick and the low tick over the past 30 minutes is greater than 3% of the last price and in the last 5 minutes the average volume has surged by more than 300%.

Both queries apply ASW operators over stock substreams. Query 1 uses a SUM aggregate over a 2-minute suffix sliding window. Query 2 uses MAX (high-tick), MIN (low-tick), and AVG aggregates over two different windows ("last 5 minutes" and "last 30 minutes"). Various relational operators like filters and joins are performed over the dynamic relations output by the ASW operators.

1.1.3 Output Model

We assume that an ASW or SSF operator does not actively stream its current answer, but instead produces answers only when requested. We call such a request an *answer lookup* (or simply *lookup*). We chose the lookup model over the streaming model for several reasons:

1. The lookup model is more general, i.e., it can emulate the streaming model.

2. In many cases, the current ASW result is needed at most when new stream tuples arrive, and certainly not at every time instant (e.g., correlated aggregates [17]).

3. Reference [10] cites several applications that prefer to periodically refresh continuous query answers, rather than keep them fully up-to-date.

1.2 Space-Update-Lookup Tradeoff and Our Approach

Any algorithm for processing a large number of continuous queries with the lookup model involves three *cost parameters*: the memory required to maintain state (*space*), the time to compute an answer (*lookup time*), and the time to update state when a new stream tuple arrives (*update time*). There is a tradeoff among these three costs and generally no single, optimal solution.

For example, we can make lookups efficient by maintaining up-to-date answers for all queries. However, this approach has a high update cost, since arrival of a new stream tuple potentially requires updating answers of all the queries, and a large space requirement, since current answers for all the queries need to be stored. Alternatively, we can maintain a single historical snapshot of the input that is large enough to compute the answer for any given query, but defer actual answer computation to lookup time. This approach has small update and space costs, but potentially high lookup cost.

These two approaches are appropriate only for the extreme scenarios—very high update rates compared to lookups, or vice-versa. Many applications lie between the extremes. Our techniques are designed to capture a wide range of these "in between" scenarios, by performing partial answer computation at update time and using the partial results to compute the final answer at lookup time. Furthermore, our partial answer schemes are designed specifically so that partial answers can be shared by a large number of queries.

Operator Type	Aggregation Function	Update Time	Lookup Time	Space
ASW	Algebraic, Distributive	$O(1)$	$O(\log W)$	$O(N_{max})$
ASW	Algebraic, Distributive	$O(\gamma)$	$O(1)$	$O(\gamma N_{max})$
ASW	Subtractable	$O(1)$	$O(1)$	$O(N_{max})$
ASW	Holistic: QUANTILE	$O(\log N_{max})$	$O(\log^2 W \log \log W)$	$O(N_{max} \log N_{max})$
SSF	COUNT	$O(\frac{1}{\epsilon} \log |\mathcal{K}|)$	$O(|\mathcal{K}_o|)$	$O(\frac{1}{\epsilon} \log |\mathcal{K}| \log N_{max})$
SSF	SUM	$O(\frac{1}{\epsilon} \log |\mathcal{K}| \log A_m)$	$O(|\mathcal{K}_o|)$	$O(\frac{1}{\epsilon} \log |\mathcal{K}| \log(N_{max} A_m))$
SSF	MAX, MIN	$O(\log^2 N_{max})$	$O(\log^2 N_{max} + |\mathcal{K}_o|)$	$O(N_{max} \log N_{max})$

Figure 1: Summary of results. N_{max} = Max left end of a window; W = width of lookup window; $|\mathcal{K}|$ = # substreams; $|\mathcal{K}_o|$ = output size for SSF operators; ϵ = error parameter; γ = "spread" of window widths; A_m = Max value of aggregated attribute.

1.3 Summary of Contributions

General

Our high-level contribution is that of identifying the resource sharing possibilities in sliding-window aggregations and devising a suite of algorithms to exploit them. We precisely formulate the sharing problem for this class of operators, indicate the basic tradeoffs involved, and study techniques for a wide variety of scenarios. While many of the sharing techniques are our original contributions, some are a synthesis of existing ideas from other fields such as data structures and computational geometry. The entire suite of results is summarized in Table 1.

ASW Operators

For ASW operators, we present general sharing techniques based on properties of aggregation functions. As in [20], we divide aggregation functions into *distributive*, *algebraic*, and *holistic*.

1. For distributive and algebraic aggregates, we present two techniques: one has low update and space costs, while the other has low lookup cost.

2. We identify a subclass of distributive and algebraic aggregates, which we call *subtractable*, and show that they can be handled more efficiently than the general class.

3. Since there is no common property for the class of holistic aggregates (they are defined as aggregates that are not algebraic), we cannot have a general technique. However, we present sharing techniques for the well-known holistic QUANTILE aggregate.

SSF Operators

For SSF operators, one simple approach is to use ASW sharing techniques for processing the ASW suboperators corresponding to each substream. At SSF lookup time, we perform an ASW lookup for each substream and return those substreams that satisfy the range predicate. Therefore, the SSF lookup operation depends linearly on the number of substreams. For specific aggregation functions (COUNT, SUM over positive values, MAX, MIN) and window types (suffix, time-based), we show that we can achieve a lookup cost that is sublinear in the number of substreams, without significantly increasing update cost. Our techniques for SUM and COUNT are *approximate*: they slightly relax the range predicate. However the approximation is controlled by a parameter ϵ, which can be made as small as desired at the expense of increased space and update time. Further, exact answers can be obtained by postprocessing.

1.4 Outline of Paper

Section 2 presents formal definitions and notation. Sections 3 and 4 present our algorithms for resource sharing in ASW and SSF operators, respectively. Section 6 contains a thorough experimental evaluation of the algorithms. Section 7 covers related work, and Section 8 contains our conclusions and directions for future work.

All proofs and some of the algorithms (ASW algorithms for time-based windows, SSF algorithms for MAX and MIN) have been omitted due to space constraints. These can be found in the full version of the paper [5].

2 Formal Preliminaries

Streams and Substreams

A *stream* S is a sequence of tuples arriving at a continuous query processing system. Tuples of S are timestamped on arrival using the system clock. At a given point in time, we refer to the number of tuples of S that have arrived so far as the *current length* of S.

Stream S may be partitioned into *substreams* based on a set of *key attributes*. We assume a single key attribute; generalizing is trivial. Let K denote the key attribute and $\mathcal{K}$ the domain of K. Every value $k \in \mathcal{K}$ identifies a unique substream, which we denote S_k, and k is called the *key* of S_k. All tuples of S with a value k for attribute K belong to the substream S_k, and their relative ordering within S_k is the same as their relative ordering in S.

Sliding Windows

Consider a stream S with the sequence of tuples $s_1, s_2, \ldots$ and corresponding timestamps $\tau_1, \tau_2, \ldots$. For any two non-negative integers $N_L > N_R$, $S[N_L, N_R]$ denotes a tuple-based sliding window over S: When the current length of S is r, $S[N_L, N_R]$ contains the set of tuples $\{s_i \mid \max\{r - N_L + 1, 1\} \leq i \leq (r - N_R)\}$. Similarly, for any two time periods $T_L > T_R$, $S[T_L, T_R]$ denotes a time-based sliding window over S: When the current time is τ, $S[T_L, T_R]$ contains the set of tuples $\{s_i \mid (\tau - T_L + 1) \leq \tau_i \leq (\tau - T_R)\}$. Note that we use the same notation for time-based and tuple-based windows. The type of window is usually clear from context and our different conventions for numbers (e.g., N, N_L, N_i) and time intervals (e.g., T, T_L, T_i). Whenever the window type is not important to the discussion, we abuse this naming convention further and denote a generic window over S by $S[X_L, X_R]$.

Aggregation Functions

We use the classification from [20] that divides aggregation functions into three categories: *distributive*, *algebraic*, and *holistic*. Let X, X_1, and X_2 be arbitrary bags of elements drawn from a numeric domain. An aggregation function f is *distributive* if $f(X_1 \cup X_2)$ can be computed from $f(X_1)$ and $f(X_2)$ for all X_1, X_2. An aggregation function f is *algebraic* if there exists a "synopsis function" g such that for all X, X_1, X_2: (1) $f(X)$ can be computed from $g(X)$; (2) $g(X)$ can be stored in constant memory; and (3) $g(X_1 \cup X_2)$ can be computed from $g(X_1)$ and $g(X_2)$. An aggregation function is *holistic* if it is not algebraic. Among the standard aggregates, SUM, COUNT, MAX, and MIN are distributive, AVG is algebraic, since it can be computed from a synopsis containing SUM and COUNT, and QUANTILE is holistic.

ASW and SSF Operators

An ASW operator over a stream S with window specification $[X_L, X_R]$ and aggregation function f over attribute $S.A$ is denoted $f_A(S[X_L, X_R])$. At any point in time, its current answer is obtained by applying the aggregation function f over the values of attribute A of all the tuples that are currently in the window $S[X_L, X_R]$. An SSF operator is denoted by: $\{k \in \mathcal{K} \mid f_A(S_k[X_L, X_R]) \in (v_1, v_2)\}$, where $f_A(S_k[X_L, X_R])$ denotes the ASW operator that is applied to each S_k and (v_1, v_2) denotes the predicate range.

Example 2.1 The ASW operator $\text{AVG}_A(S[120, 0])$ continuously computes the average value of attribute A over S tuples in the last 120 time units. The SSF operator $\{k \in \mathcal{K} \mid \text{SUM}_A(S_k[300, 0]) \in (1000, \infty)\}$ continuously computes all substreams for which the sum over attribute A values in the last 300 time units is greater than or equal to 1000. Using a SQL-like syntax (e.g., in CQL [3]) this SSF operation is expressed as follows:

```
Select K, SUM (A)
From S [Range 300]
Group By K
Having SUM(A) > 1000
```

3 ASW Operators

In this section, we present our algorithms for collectively processing a set of ASW operators. Sharing resources is not possible between operators over different streams, or between operators with different aggregated attributes, since their input data is completely different: there is no benefit to processing them collectively. Sharing is sometimes possible between operators with different aggregation functions (e.g., AVG and SUM) over the same input stream and aggregated attribute. However, for presentation clarity, we do not address this special case.

Therefore, our algorithms are designed for collectively processing a set of ASW operators with the same input stream, aggregation function, and aggregated attribute. The only difference between different operators is the sliding window specification. One exception is the QUANTILE aggregation function, where we allow the quantile parameter to be different; see Section 3.3.

Due to space constraints, we only present algorithms for the case where all the windows are tuple-based. Algorithms that handle time-based windows are described in the full version of the paper [5].

Notation: For the rest of this section, let $o_1, \ldots, o_n$ denote the input set of operators. Let S denote the common input stream, f the common aggregation function, and A the common aggregated attribute. For these operators, only the sequence of attribute A values are relevant, which we denote $a_1, a_2, \ldots$. We call each a_i a stream *element*. Further, let each $o_i = f_A(S[N_{Li}, N_{Ri}])$.

Intervals: The notion of an *interval* over positions of S is useful to describe our algorithms. The interval $I = (l, r)$ ($l \leq r$) denotes the positions $l, l+1, \ldots, r$ of S, and the elements $a_l, \ldots, a_r$ *belong to* interval I. For an interval I, $f(I)$ denotes the aggregation over the elements of S belonging to I.

For each algorithm, we specify: (1) the state that it maintains; (2) an operation UPDATE(a_{m+1}) that describes how the state is updated when element a_{m+1} arrives; and (3) an operator LOOKUP(I) that describes, for certain intervals I, how $f(I)$ can be computed using the current state. LOOKUP(I), as the name suggests, is used to perform answer-lookups for operators o_i: when the current size of S is m, the current answer for o_i can be obtained using LOOKUP(I) where $I = (m - N_{Li} + 1, m - N_{Ri})$. Therefore, for correctness, when the current length of S is m, we require that LOOKUP(I) correctly compute $f(I)$ for all intervals $I = (m - N_{Li} + 1, m - N_{Ri})$ ($1 \leq i \leq n$); it may or may not compute $f(I)$ correctly for other intervals.

3.1 Distributive, Algebraic Aggregates

In this section, we present two algorithms, B-INT and L-INT, for the case where f is distributive or algebraic. For presentation clarity, we assume that f is distributive; the generalization to the algebraic case is straightforward.

Both algorithms are based on a simple, but fairly general approach: For certain intervals I, precompute $f(I)$ and store it as part of the state. The basic intuition behind this step is that, since f is distributive, the precomputed aggregate values can be used to compute lookups more efficiently. For example, $f(101, 200)$ and $f(201, 300)$ can be used to compute $f(101, 300)$, and therefore, LOOKUP(101, 300). More generally, $f(I)$ can potentially help compute LOOKUP(I') for any I' that contains I.

For what intervals I should we precompute $f(I)$? Selecting more intervals for precomputation is likely to improve lookup efficiency, but at the cost of space and update time—a manifestation of the space-lookup-update tradeoff discussed in Section 1.2. Also, any precomputed aggregate $f(I)$ loses its utility eventually, once all the windows of o_i slide past I. (In fact, the answer to this question of which intervals to precompute is not very obvious even for processing a single operator, i.e., $n = 1$.)

Next we present our two algorithms, which are essentially two different schemes for dynamically selecting the intervals I to precompute, along with the details of how $f(I)$ aggregates for selected intervals are (pre)computed and used for lookups.

3.1.1 B-INT Algorithm

Our first algorithm is called B-INT (for *Base-Intervals*), since it precomputes aggregate values $f(I_b)$ for intervals I_b that belong to a special class called *base-intervals*. Intuitively, base-intervals form a "basis" for intervals: any interval can be expressed as a disjoint union of a small number of base-intervals. Using this property, any $f(I)$ can be computed using a small number of precomputed $f(I_b)$ values. At any point in time, B-INT stores $f(I_b)$ values for only recent or "active" base-intervals—only these are potentially useful for future lookups of the operators $o_1, \ldots, o_n$.

Figure 2 abstractly illustrates the state maintained by algorithm B-INT, when the current length of S is m. The active base-intervals, for which the B-INT precomputes aggregate values, are shown as solid rectangles. The base-intervals which are not active are shown using dotted rectangles. The figure also shows how the aggregate value for a lookup interval is computed using precomputed aggregates for active base-intervals.

Definition 3.1 (Base-Interval) An interval I_b is a base-interval if it is of the form $(2^\ell i + 1, 2^\ell (i+1))$ for some integer $i \geq 0$, in which case it is called a *level-ℓ base-interval*. □

For example, $(385, 512) = (2^7 \cdot 3 + 1, 2^7 \cdot 4)$ is a level-7 base-interval. A level-ℓ base-interval has a width 2^ℓ and is a disjoint union of exactly two level-$(\ell-1)$ base-intervals.

Base intervals turn out to be the same concept as *dyadic intervals*, which have been used in [19] for approximate quantile computation over updatable relations. In the context of sliding windows, in related work [4] we have used base (dyadic) intervals for computing approximate statistics over sliding windows.

The following theorem, whose proof is straightforward, formally states that any interval can be expressed as a union of a small number of base-intervals.

Theorem 3.1 *Any interval $I = (l, r)$ of width $W = (r - l + 1)$ can be expressed as a disjoint-union of $k =$*

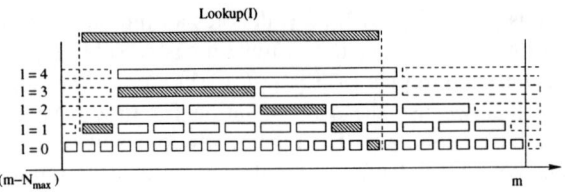

Figure 2: Base-intervals used by B-INT when current length of S is m

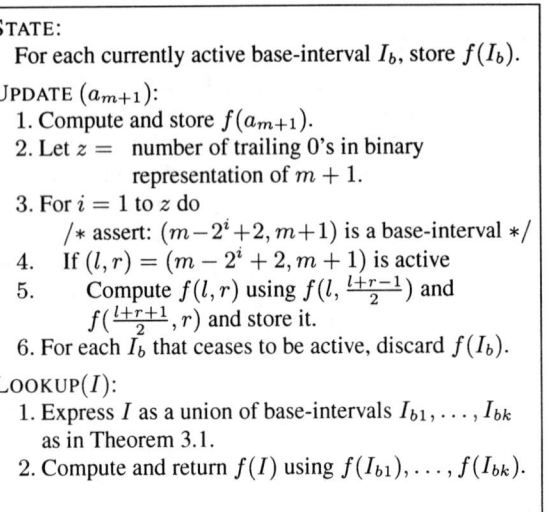

Figure 3: Algorithm B-INT

$O(\log W)$ *base-intervals of the form $I_{bi} = (l_i, r_i)$ ($1 \leq i \leq k$), where $l_1 = l$, $r_k = r$, and $r_i = l_{i+1} - 1$, ($1 \leq i < k$). Given interval I, the intervals $I_{b1}, \ldots, I_{bk}$ can be determined in $O(k) = O(\log W)$ time.*

Example 3.1 The interval $(1, 43)$ can be expressed as a union of base-intervals $(1, 2)$, $(3, 4)$, $(5, 8)$, $(9, 16)$, $(17, 32)$, $(33, 40)$, $(41, 42)$, $(43, 43)$. □

Active Intervals: Let $N_{max} = \max_i(N_{Li})$ denote the "earliest" left end of a window in $o_1, \ldots, o_n$. When the current size of S is m, we call an interval $I = (l, r)$ *active* if $(l > m - N_{max})$ and $(r \leq m)$. Intuitively, an interval is active at some point of time, if it is completely within the last N_{max} positions of the stream.

Figure 3 contains the formal description of B-INT. When the current size of S is m, LOOKUP(I) computes $f(I)$ for all intervals $I = (m - N_{Li} + 1, m - N_{Ri})$ ($1 \leq i \leq n$) that correspond to lookups of operators $o_1, \ldots, o_n$. By definition, any such interval $(m - N_{Li} + 1, m - N_{Ri})$ is active, and therefore each interval $I_{b1}, \ldots, I_{bk}$ in Step 1 of LOOKUP(I) is active as well, implying that $f(I_{bi})$ is stored as part of the state.

Conceptually, UPDATE(a_{m+1}) computes $f(I_b)$ for all base-intervals I_b that become newly active and adds it to the current state (Steps 1–5), and discards $f(I_b)$ for all intervals that cease to be active (Step 6). UPDATE(a_{m+1}) always introduces at least one new base-interval: (a_{m+1}, a_{m+1}). In general, if 2^z denotes the largest power of 2 that divides $(m + 1)$, then UPDATE(a_{m+1}) introduces $z + 1$ new base-intervals. One obvious technique for computing $f(I_b)$ is to do so from scratch, using the elements of S that belong to I_b. A more efficient technique is to compute it recursively, using aggregate values corresponding to base-intervals of the next lower-level, as shown in Step 5 of UPDATE(a_{m+1}).

Theorem 3.2 *Algorithm* B-INT *requires* $O(N_{max})$ *space, has an amortized update time complexity of* $O(1)$, *and has a worst-case lookup time complexity of* $O(\log W)$, *where* W *denotes the width of the lookup interval.*

3.1.2 L-INT Algorithm

Our second algorithm for distributive and algebraic aggregates, called L-INT (for *Landmark Intervals*), uses an interval scheme based on certain *landmarks* or specific positions of the stream. L-INT is more efficient than B-INT for lookups, but its update and space costs are higher. Further, L-INT is more input-specific: while B-INT depends only on N_{max}, L-INT, in addition to N_{max}, depends on the distribution of window widths.

We first present L-INT for a special case, where all the window widths are close to equal. Specifically, we assume that they are within a small constant factor c of each other, i.e., $W_{max}/W_{min} \leq c$, where $W_{max} = \max_i(N_{Li} - N_{Ri})$ denotes the maximum width, and $W_{min} = \min_i(N_{Li} - N_{Ri})$, the minimum width of a window. For this special case, L-INT is optimal: it uses $O(N_{max})$ space and has $O(1)$ update and lookup time. (Clearly, we cannot do better than $O(1)$ update and lookup time and $O(N_{max})$ space.) Then, we show how we can extend L-INT to handle the general case.

Definition 3.2 (Landmark Interval) Landmark intervals are defined for two width parameters $W_{min} \leq W_{max}$. A landmark interval is of the form $(\alpha W_{min}, \alpha W_{min} + d)$ or of the form $(\alpha W_{min} - d, \alpha W_{min} - 1)$, for some $\alpha \geq 0$ and $d \leq W_{max}$. □

We call stream positions of the form αW_{min} ($\alpha \geq 0$) *landmarks*. A landmark interval is one that begins at or ends just before a landmark, and has a width less than W_{max}. For example, if $W_{max} = 2000$ and $W_{min} = 1000$, intervals $(75, 999)$, $(1762, 2999)$, and $(5000, 6542)$ are landmark intervals, while $(5000, 7162)$ is not, since its width is greater than 2000. Figure 4 schematically illustrates landmark intervals that begin or end at the landmark αW_{min}.

The following theorem states that any interval with width between W_{min} and W_{max} can be expressed as a union of at most two landmark intervals.

Theorem 3.3 *Any interval* $I = (l, r)$, *such that* $W_{min} \leq (r - l + 1) \leq W_{max}$, *can be expressed as a disjoint union of at most two landmark intervals defined for parameters* W_{min} *and* W_{max}.

Example 3.2 Let $W_{max} = 2000$ and $W_{min} = 1000$. The interval $(3257, 5164)$ can be expressed as a union of landmark intervals $(3257, 3999)$ and $(4000, 5164)$. □

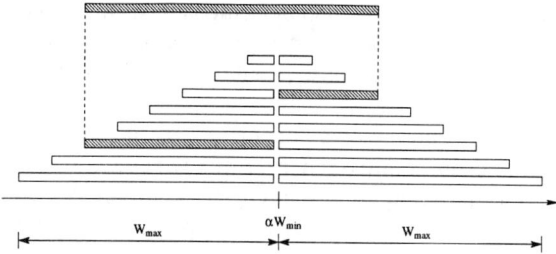

Figure 4: Landmark intervals that begin or end at the landmark αW_{min} for some $\alpha \geq 0$

STATE:
1. For each currently active landmark interval I_l, store $f(I_l)$.
2. For each currently active element a_i, store $f(a_i)$.

UPDATE (a_{m+1}):
1. Compute and store $f(a_{m+1})$.
2. If $m + 1 = \alpha W_{min}$
3.   For $d = 2$ to W_{max}
4.   Compute $f(m+1-d, m)$ from $f(m+2-d, m)$ and $f(a_{m+1-d})$ and store it.
5. For each β such that $m + 1 - W_{max} \leq \beta W_{min} \leq m$
6.   Compute $f(\beta W_{min}, m+1)$ from $f(\beta W_{min}, m)$ and $f(a_{m+1})$
7. Drop $f(I_l)$ for intervals I_l that cease being active.

LOOKUP(I):
1. Express I as a union of landmark intervals I_{l1} and I_{l2} as in Theorem 3.3
2. Compute and return $f(I)$ using $f(I_{l1})$ and $f(I_{l2})$.

Figure 5: Algorithm L-INT for $W_{max}/W_{min} \leq c$

Figure 5 contains the formal description of L-INT for the special case of $W_{max}/W_{min} \leq c$. Using a reasoning similar to that for algorithm B-INT, we can argue that algorithm L-INT is correct, i.e., it can be used to compute lookups corresponding to the operators $o_1, \ldots, o_n$. The update operation is also similar to that of B-INT: it computes $f(I_l)$ for all landmark intervals I_l that newly become active, and discards $f(I_l)$ for intervals I_l that cease to be active.

Theorem 3.4 *Algorithm* L-INT *presented in Figure 5 requires* $O(N_{max})$ *space, has an amortized update time of* $O(1)$, *and has a worst case lookup time of* $O(1)$.

Extending L-INT algorithm for the general case is straightforward: partition the set of operators $o_1, \ldots, o_n$ into γ partitions $P_1, P_2, \ldots, P_\gamma$, such that for the operators belonging to each partition, the property $W_{max}/W_{min} \leq c$ is satisfied. Use γ instances of the special-case version of the L-INT algorithm (Figure 5) to process these partitions independently. This extended algorithm requires $O(\gamma N_{max})$ space, has an update cost of $O(\gamma)$ and a lookup cost of $O(1)$.

For any set of operators $o_1, \ldots, o_n$, we can always define a partitioning scheme with $\gamma = O(\log N_{max})$. However, for many real-world applications, it seems natural to expect the window widths to be clustered around a few values. For such applications, γ could be significantly smaller than $\log N_{max}$.

Further, if all the operators $o_1, \ldots, o_n$ have suffix windows, or even "approximately" suffix windows, we can reduce the space required from $O(\gamma N_{max})$ to $O(N_{max})$. A tuple-based window $[N_L, N_R]$ is approximately suffix if $(N_L - N_R)$ is comparable in value to N_L.

3.1.3 PSoup Algorithm

PSoup [10] proposes a different algorithm for distributive and algebraic aggregates, that uses an augmented n-ary search tree. Each leaf of the search tree contains an element of the stream (only the last N_{max} elements need to be stored), and the leaves are ordered based on insertion times of the elements. Each internal node stores the value of the aggregation function computed over the descendant leaves (elements) of that node. This algorithm has an update and lookup cost of $O(\log N_{max})$. Both B-INT and L-INT algorithms perform asymptotically better than PSoup for at least one of update or lookup operations. Also, note that the lookup cost of B-INT depends only on the window size W of the operator involved in the lookup (the lookup cost is $O(\log W)$), and is independent of N_{max}. In Section 6, we compare empirically the performance of PSoup against our algorithms.

3.2 Subtractable Aggregates

An algebraic aggregation function f is *subtractable* if its synopsis function g has the following property: for any bags $X_1 \subseteq X_2$, $g(X_2 - X_1)$ is computable from $g(X_1)$ and $g(X_2)$. Among the standard algebraic aggregation functions SUM, COUNT, and AVG are subtractable, while MAX and MIN are not. For instance, SUM is subtractable since $\text{SUM}(X_2 - X_1) = \text{SUM}(X_2) - \text{SUM}(X_1)$, if $X_1 \subseteq X_2$.

For subtractable aggregates, we present a simple algorithm called R-INT (for *running intervals*) that has $O(1)$ update and lookup cost. For presentation clarity, we assume that f is subtractable and distributive, i.e., $f(X_2 - X_1)$ is computable from $f(X_2)$ and $f(X_1)$, whenever $X_1 \subseteq X_2$. Generalizing to the case where f is algebraic and subtractable is straightforward.

A *running interval* is an interval of the form $(1, r)$, whose left end is at the beginning of S. Any interval (l, r) can be expressed as a difference of two running intervals: $(1, r) - (1, l-1)$. R-INT (Figure 6) is based on this observation. R-INT stores aggregate values corresponding to currently active running intervals, and uses these to compute lookup answers. When the current length of S is m, a running interval $(1, r)$ is *active*, if $m - N_{max} \leq r \leq m$. It can be easily shown that R-INT uses $O(N_{max})$ space and has $O(1)$ update and lookup time.

3.3 Quantiles

The quantile aggregation function is specified using a parameter $\phi \in (0, 1]$ and is denoted $\text{QUANTILE}(\phi)$. The output of $\text{QUANTILE}(\phi)$ for a bag of N elements is the element

---

STATE:
1. For each currently active running interval I_r, store $f(I_r)$.

UPDATE (a_{m+1}):
1. Compute $f(1, m+1)$ using $f(1, m)$ and $f(a_{m+1})$.
2. For each I_r that is no longer active, discard $f(I_r)$.

LOOKUP$(I = (l, r))$:
1. Compute and return $f(l, r)$ using $f(1, l-1)$ and $f(1, r)$.

Figure 6: Algorithm R-INT

---

at position $\lfloor \phi \cdot N \rfloor$ in a sorted sequence of these elements.

We briefly sketch one algorithm (called B-INT-QNT) for processing ASW operators with quantiles (possibly with different parameters ϕ) that uses the base-intervals defined in Section 3.1.1: Corresponding to each active base-interval I_b store a sorted array of the elements of S that belong to I_b. To perform LOOKUP(I) for a quantile parameter ϕ, express I as a union of base-intervals $I_{b1}, \ldots, I_{bk}$, using Theorem 3.1, and compute $\text{QUANTILE}(\phi)$ using the sorted arrays corresponding to $I_{b1}, \ldots, I_{bk}$. In general, given a set of p sorted arrays of length $\leq q$, we can compute any quantile over all the elements in the sorted arrays in $O(p \log p \log q)$ time, using a greedy algorithm.

4 SSF Operators

We now consider the problem of processing a collection of SSF operators $o_1, \ldots, o_n$. As in Section 3, we assume that all operators have the same input stream S, the same aggregation function f, the same aggregated attribute A. So they differ only in their window specification and range predicate. Therefore each operator o_i has the form $\{k \in \mathcal{K} \mid f_A(S_k[X_{Li}, X_{Ri}]) \in (v_{li}, v_{hi})\}$.

A simple strategy for processing these operators is as follows: For each substream S_k, process the set of ASW suboperators $f_A(S_k[X_{Li}, X_{Ri}])$ $(1 \leq i \leq n)$ using the algorithms of Section 3. To perform a lookup for operator o_i, perform a lookup on the ASW suboperator $f_A(S_k[X_{Li}, X_{Ri}])$ for each substream S_k, and return those substreams for which the lookup output lies within (v_{li}, v_{hi}). Clearly, the SSF lookup cost for this approach depends linearly on $|\mathcal{K}|$, the number of substreams.

In this section, we present algorithms for certain combinations of aggregation functions (COUNT, SUM over positive values) and window types (suffix, time-based) that have lookup cost sublinear in $|\mathcal{K}|$. (The full version of the paper [5] contains algorithms for MAX and MIN for suffix, time-based windows.) We call our algorithms CI-COUNT and CI-SUM. CI stands for *collective index*) since, conceptually, the algorithms can be thought of as a collection of search indexes, one for each ASW suboperator.

Notation: Throughout this section, let $a_{k1}, a_{k2}, \ldots$ denote the sequence of attribute A values for substream S_k. As before, we call them *elements* of S_k. Let $\tau_{k1}, \tau_{k2}, \ldots$ denote the timestamps of these elements. As in Section 3, for each algorithm we present: (1) the state that it maintains; (2) an operation UPDATE(a_{km}, τ_{km}) that describes how the state is modified when element a_{km} with timestamp τ_{km} arrives on substream S_k; and (3) an operation LOOKUP$(\tau, T, (v_1, v_2))$ that describes how the current answer for the SSF operator $\{k \in \mathcal{K} \mid f_A(S_k[T,0]) \in (v_1, v_2)\}$ can be computed using the current state.

4.1 CI-COUNT

CI-COUNT is an approximate algorithm for processing a collection of SSF operators of the form $o_i = \{k \in \mathcal{K} \mid \text{COUNT}_A(S_k[T_i, 0]) \in R\}$, where R is a one-sided range condition of the form (v, ∞) or $(0, v)$. The approximation produced by CI-COUNT for LOOKUP(τ, T, R) is as follows. If K_{co} denotes the correct output, the output K_{ao} produced by CI-COUNT has the following guarantees:

1. The approximate output K_{ao} is a superset of the exact output K_{co}.

2. The current ASW answer for each substream in the approximate output satisfies a relaxed version of the range condition R. Specifically, if R is of the form (v, ∞), for every key $k \in K_{ao}$, $\text{COUNT}_A(S_k[T,0]) \in (v(1-\epsilon), \infty)$, for some *approximation parameter* $\epsilon \in (0, 1)$. Similarly, if R is of the form $(0, v)$, for every key $k \in K_{ao}$, $\text{COUNT}_A(S_k[T,0]) \in (0, v(1+\epsilon))$.

The approximation parameter ϵ in the above guarantees can be made as small as desired, but decreasing ϵ increases the required space and update cost: both grow linearly in $\frac{1}{\epsilon}$.

Although CI-COUNT supports only approximate lookups, it can be used along with our ASW algorithms for performing exact lookups. Specifically, we can compute the correct answer K_{co} from the approximate output K_{ao} by checking for each $k \in K_{ao}$ whether $\text{COUNT}_A(S_k[T,0]) \in R$ using an ASW-lookup.

We first present a non-parameterized version of CI-COUNT that yields a fixed $\epsilon = 0.75$, and then describe how this algorithm is modified to produce the parameterized version. Also, for clarity, we assume that the range conditions of all the operators are of the form (v, ∞). Handling range conditions of the form $(0, v)$ is a straightforward generalization. In the rest of this subsection, we abbreviate LOOKUP$(\tau, T, (v, \infty))$ as LOOKUP(τ, T, v).

4.1.1 Non-Parameterized CI-COUNT

To get an intuition for CI-COUNT, consider the LOOKUP(τ, T, v). This operation seeks all substreams S_k which have received more than v elements in the last T time units. An alternate, but equivalent, view of this operation is that it seeks all substreams S_k, for which the vth element from the end has a timestamp greater than $\tau - T$. Based on this observation, one idea for improving the efficiency of lookup is as follows: Maintain an index over the timestamp values of the vth element from the end of all the substreams. Use this index to determine, in $O(\log |\mathcal{K}|)$ time, all the substreams for which the timestamp of the vth element from the end is greater than $\tau - T$.

Since v is a parameter in LOOKUP(τ, T, v), we would need to maintain such an index for every possible v in order to use the above idea. However, doing so would dramatically increase the update cost: every new element a_{ki} of substream S_k changes the timestamp of the vth element from the end for every v, and so requires updating all the indexes.

However, if we are permitted to approximate v, i.e., use a different value v' that is close to v, we can reduce the number of different indexes that need to be maintained, since many values v can use the same approximation v'.

This observation forms the basis for algorithm CI-COUNT: CI-COUNT divides the positions from the end of a substream S_k into different *levels* (not to be confused with levels of base-intervals in Section 3.1.1). It maintains one search index for each level. The index for level-ℓ contains, for each substream S_k, the timestamp of some element that currently belongs to level-ℓ. These indexed timestamps are used for approximate answer lookups.

Definition 4.1 (Level) Let m be the current length of substream S_k. Then the current *level* of a position $p \leq m$ of S_k is defined to be $\lfloor \log_2(m - p + 1) \rfloor$. $\square$

The last position, m, of substream S_k belongs to level-0, the previous two ($m-1$ and $m-2$) to level-1, and so on. In general, 2^ℓ positions belong to level-ℓ.

Figure 7 contains the formal description of algorithm CI-COUNT. The variable TSTAMP$[k, \ell]$ contains the timestamp of the element of S_k that currently belongs to level-ℓ and whose position is a multiple of 2^ℓ. Note that, at any point of time, such an element (if it exists) is unique, since at most 2^ℓ contiguous positions belong to level-ℓ. For each level ℓ, all the TSTAMP$[k, \ell]$ values are indexed using a search tree SEARCHTREE$[\ell]$. In order to perform

---

STATE:
1. For each substream S_k
2.   For each level-ℓ with at least one element
3.   Let i be unique position of S_k such that:
4.   (a) i currently belongs to level-ℓ, and
5.   (b) i is a multiple of 2^ℓ
6.   TSTAMP$[k, \ell] = \tau_{ki}$
7. For each level-ℓ
8.   Store TSTAMP$[k, \ell]$, for all valid k, using a search tree SEARCHTREE$[\ell]$.

UPDATE(a_{km}, τ_{km}):
1. $p = 1$
2. Let z = number of trailing 0s in binary representation of $m + p$.
3. For $\ell = z$ downto 1 do:
4.   TSTAMP$[k, \ell] = $ TSTAMP$[k, \ell - 1]$
5. TSTAMP$[k, 0] = \tau_{km}$

LOOKUP(τ, T, v):
1. Let $\ell = \lfloor \log_2 v \rfloor - 1$
2. Determine $\mathcal{A} = \{k \in \mathcal{K} \mid $ TSTAMP$[k, \ell] \geq \tau - T\}$ using SEARCHTREE$[\ell]$.
3. Return $\mathcal{A}$.

Figure 7: Algorithm CI-COUNT

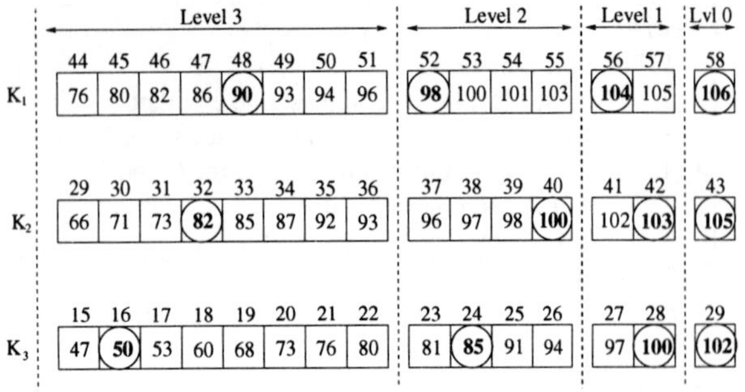

Figure 8: CI-COUNT Example

LOOKUP(τ, T, v), CI-COUNT uses SEARCHTREE$[\ell]$ for $\ell = \lfloor \log_2 v \rfloor - 1$ to determine all substreams S_k such that TSTAMP$[k, \ell] \geq (\tau - T)$.

Example 4.1 Figure 8 shows the timestamps (within boxes) and positions (above boxes) of elements belonging to three substreams. The elements themselves are not shown. The timestamps that are stored in TSTAMP$[k, \ell]$ are circled. For example, TSTAMP$[k_3, 2] = 85$. The search trees over TSTAMP$[k, \ell]$ values are not shown.

Consider LOOKUP$(106, 20, 11)$ which seeks at time 106 all substreams that have received more than 11 tuples in the last 20 time units, i.e., in the time interval $(87, 106)$. Clearly, the correct output is $\{k_1\}$. The same output can also be obtained by checking if the timestamp of the 11th tuple from the end (which is 90, 85, and 68, for S_{k_1}, S_{k_2}, and S_{k_3}, respectively) is ≥ 87.

Since $\lfloor \log_2 11 \rfloor - 1 = 2$, CI-COUNT returns those substream keys k for which TSTAMP$[k, 2] \geq 87$, which is $\{k_1, k_2\}$ for this example. In other words, for each substream, CI-COUNT uses the timestamp of a position at a distance 4–7 from the end of the substream, instead of the timestamp of the position that is at a distance 11, and checks if it is greater than 87. □

We now briefly comment the on update operation. Consider any one particular TSTAMP$[k, \ell]$ for $\ell > 1$. By definition, TSTAMP$[k, \ell]$ stores the timestamp of the element that currently belongs to level-ℓ and whose position is $i2^\ell$ for some i. Clearly, TSTAMP$[k, \ell]$ changes only when this element moves to level-$(\ell+1)$, and the element corresponding to position $(i+1)2^\ell$ enters level-ℓ. Since $(i+1)2^\ell$ is also a multiple of $2^{\ell-1}$, the timestamp of this element would previously have been stored in TSTAMP$[k, \ell-1]$. Therefore, TSTAMP$[k, \ell]$ can be updated by just copying the previous value of TSTAMP$[k, \ell-1]$ (Step 4 in UPDATE(a_{km}, τ_{km})).

Lemma 4.1 *Algorithm CI-COUNT presented in Figure 7 has approximation parameter $\epsilon = 0.75$: If $k \in \mathcal{K}$ is returned in the output of LOOKUP(τ, T, v), then* COUNT$_A(S_k[T, 0]) \in (v/4, \infty)$ *at time τ. If at time τ,* COUNT$_A(S_k[T, 0]) \in (v, \infty)$, *then k is returned in the output of LOOKUP(τ, T, v).*

Theorem 4.1 *Let T_{max} denote maximum time interval of a sliding window that CI-COUNT supports, and let N_{max}* denote the current number of elements belonging to all substreams with timestamps in the last T_{max} time-units. The CI-COUNT algorithm presented in Figure 7 requires $O(|\mathcal{K}| \log N_{max})$ space, has an amortized update time complexity of $O(\log |\mathcal{K}|)$, and a lookup time complexity of $O(|\mathcal{K}_o|)$, where $|\mathcal{K}_o|$, the number of substreams in the output of lookup. Further, the lookup has an approximation parameter $\epsilon = 3/4$.

4.1.2 Parameterized CI-COUNT

The technique that we use to parameterize CI-COUNT is well-known and has been suggested before [12]. We only present the main ideas the statement of the results. Consider a simple generalization of the non-parameterized CI-COUNT. The generalized version has p levels of size 1, p levels of size 2, and so on. As before, for each level whose size is 2^ℓ, CI-COUNT stores the timestamp of the element that belongs to the level, and whose position is a multiple of 2^ℓ. We can extend the lookup and update operations presented earlier to the general case in a straightforward manner. The update complexity is now $O(p)$, while the lookup complexity remains unchanged at $O(|K_{ao}|)$.

As we increase p, the relative error, ϵ, of the generalized version reduces. For example, we can show that relative error for the case $p = 2$ is $\epsilon = 1/2$ instead of $\epsilon = 3/4$ for $p = 1$. In general, we can prove that as p increases the relative error falls roughly as $2/p$. Therefore, by setting p to be roughly $2/\epsilon$, we can achieve any desired relative error ϵ. The results claimed in Table 1 follow directly from this relation between p and ϵ.

4.2 CI-SUM

CI-SUM is derived from CI-COUNT in a straightforward manner: Replace the SUM aggregation functions in the input operators with COUNT aggregation functions, and process a modified stream S' using algorithm CI-COUNT. Corresponding to every element a_{ki} of S_k, there are a_{ki} copies of the same element in S'_k with the same timestamp τ_{ki}. Any lookup involving the SUM aggregation function can be translated into an equivalent lookup involving COUNT aggregation function on the modified stream S', and therefore can be processed using CI-COUNT. The only problem with this approach is that naïvely performing an update for each of the a_{ki} copies of an element a_{ki} of the original stream S_k would result in an update operation whose time complexity grows linearly in a_{ki}. However, we can show that the updates corresponding to all the a_{ki} duplicate copies can be collectively performed with $O(\log a_{ki})$ multiplicative overhead.

5 Implementation Issues

We have implemented all of the algorithms in this paper, and we briefly touch on some of the more important implementation issues. All of our algorithms permit an implementation that uses simple arrays. In particular, they do not require pointer manipulations or dynamic memory management. For example, our implementation of Algorithm R-INT (Figure 6) uses an array of N_{max} values (recall that

N_{max} is the earliest left-end of a supported window). Each array location is used to store the value $f(I_r)$ for some active running interval I_r. The array is conceptually treated is a circular buffer, and values $f(1, r)$ and $f(1, r+1)$ are stored in adjacent locations of the buffer. Clearly, this organization lets us access any active $f(I_r)$ in a single memory lookup.

A similar implementation strategy is used for Algorithm B-INT: We use an array of size N_{max} for the level-0 intervals, an array of size $\frac{N_{max}}{2}$ for level-1 intervals, and so on. Further, all common operations in the B-INT algorithm, such as expressing a lookup interval as a union of base-intervals (Step 1 of the Lookup operation in Figure 3) can be implemented using low-level, highly efficient bit-level operations. Details are omitted due to space constraints.

6 Experiments

A wide variety of experiments evaluating the empirical performance of our algorithms can be conducted. Due to space limitations, here we report on three sets of experimental results that are representative of overall performance.

1. *Comparison against alternate approaches*: For SUM, we compare the performance of the R-INT and B-INT algorithms against the PSoup algorithm sketched in Section 3.1.3 and the two naïve extreme approaches discussed in Section 1. We see that our algorithms outperform the alternatives.

2. *Performance of ASW algorithms*: We present raw performance numbers for three basic ASW algorithms, showing they are capable of handling very high lookup and stream update rates (millions of events per second).

3. *Performance of* CI-COUNT: Using real stock trade data, we compare the performance of algorithm CI-COUNT against the alternative approach of processing each ASW suboperator independently as described in Section 4. We show that there exist cases where CI-COUNT provides orders of magnitude improvement in overall performance.

The first two experiments are data-independent, since the performance of none of the relevant algorithms depend on the actual data values, while the third experiment is data dependent. Therefore, we use synthetically generated data for the first two, and real financial data for the third experiment.

All experiments were performed on a 4-processor 700 Mhz. Pentium III machine running Linux with 4 GB of main memory RAM.

6.1 Comparison with alternate approaches

For the SUM aggregation function, we compared the performance of the R-INT and B-INT algorithms against PSoup, as well as against the naïve approaches discussed in Section 1: (1) Materialize the results of all operators at all times (*materialize all*); (2) Maintain the maximum required

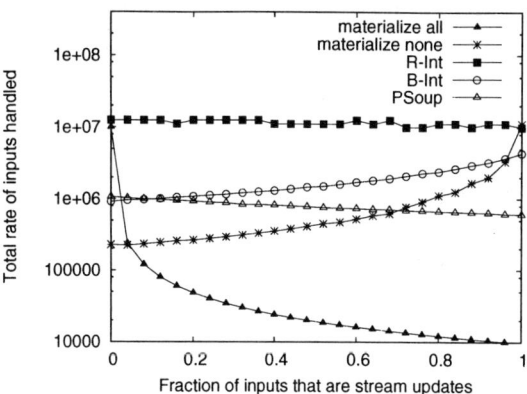

Figure 9: Comparing R-INT and B-INT against alternatives

window of the input stream and perform all answer computations only at lookup time (*materialize none*). Since PSoup [10] does not provide implementation details, we adapted *libavl* [23], a publicly available implementation of red-black (binary) search trees.

We used 1000 operators of the form $\text{SUM}_A S[N, 0]$ with tuple-based windows varying in size from $N = 0$ to $N = 999$. For each algorithm, we measured the total input rate that it was able to handle. Each input consisted of a mixture of query lookups and stream updates. We constructed different inputs by varying the ratio of updates to lookups. Lookups were picked uniformly at random from one of the 1000 operators.

Figure 9 shows the results. As expected the performance of the full materialization approach is good when update rates are low, while that of the on-demand approach is good when lookup rates are low. However, both approaches deteriorate quickly as we move away from their favorable ends. The performance of the other three algorithms remains relatively stable for all inputs. As expected, R-INT outperforms the other two. The performance of B-INT and PSoup are similar when there are no stream updates, however the performance of PSoup falls and B-INT improves as the ratio of updates in the input increases. This occurs because the actual cost of updates in PSoup is higher than the actual cost of lookups although their asymptotic costs are the same, while for B-INT updates are cheaper than lookups (asymptotically and empirically).

6.2 Performance of ASW algorithms

We present raw performance numbers for three basic algorithms: R-INT (for SUM), B-INT (for MAX), and B-INT-QNT (for QUANTILE). For each one we measured its performance handling updates and handling lookups separately. From these numbers we can easily derive the expected performance for a combined workload. Update handling was measured for different values of maximum window left-end N_{max}, and lookup handling was measured for different values of the query windows (W). For lookups, we set $N_{max} = 100,000$. Individual operator windows were distributed uniformly over the entire permitted range, i.e., we considered both suffix and historical windows.

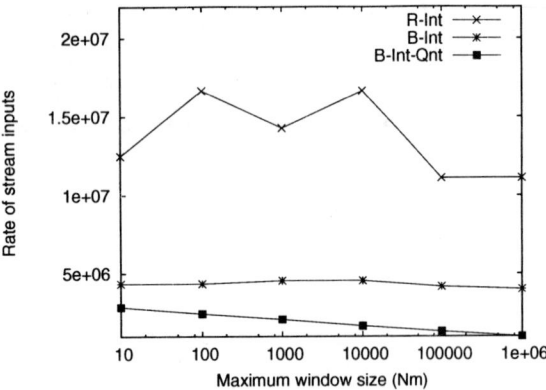

Figure 10: Stream update rates for the ASW algorithms

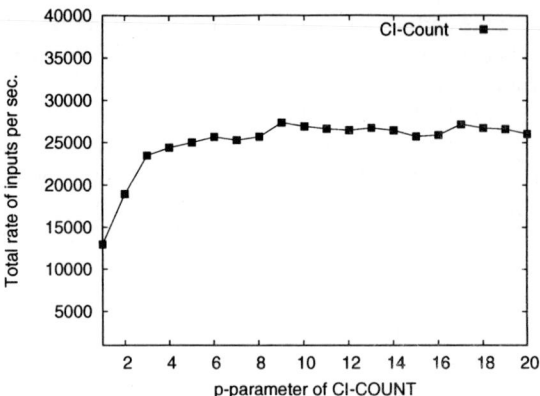

Figure 12: Performance of CI-COUNT for various values of p. The naïve approach processes 1000 inputs/second.

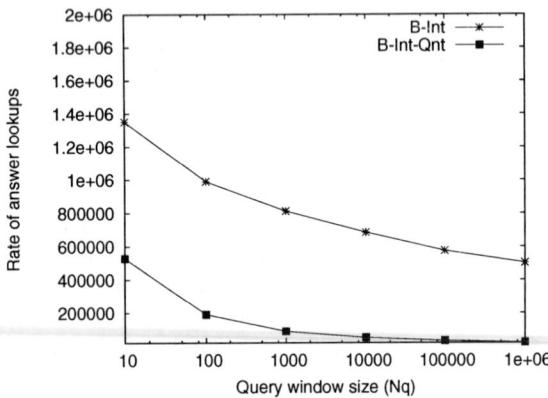

Figure 11: Maximum lookup rates for the ASW algorithms

Figures 10 and 11 present the results, showing that our algorithms handle up to millions of events per second, depending on window sizes. Note that the y-axis in these figures does not go to zero. For example, in Figure 11 B-INT-QNT handles a lookup rate of about 22,000 per second even at the maximum window size (not obvious from the graph). In Figure 11 we deleted the plot for R-INT in order to better depict those for B-INT and B-INT-QNT. The performance of R-INT is uniformly around 10^7 lookups per second. Note that all of these results are for tuple-based windows only. Time-based windows have similar performance characteristics with a slight degradation due to additional overhead.

6.3 Performance of CI-COUNT

Unlike the algorithms in our first two sets of experiments, the performance of CI-COUNT is highly dependent on actual data and operators, specifically the selectivity of range conditions and the "spread" of aggregation answers across different substreams. Further, picking the right value of ϵ represents a tradeoff between update performance and lookup performance. A detailed study of these issues is left as future work.

Here, we report on one particular experiment for CI-COUNT. We used a one-day stream of real stock trades from the TAQ database, containing approximately 5000

substreams based on ticker symbol. Our queries were synthetically generated by specifying a suffix window ranging from 15 minutes to 3 hours, monitoring stocks over the window with total trades above a given threshold. We selected the threshold to make its selectivity roughly .03–.05. Lookups and updates were equally interleaved.

We compared the performance of two approaches: (1) The naïve approach that uses algorithm R-INT to process each substream independently; (2) The approach that uses CI-COUNT in conjunction with R-INT to produce exact answers. For the second approach we varied the parameter p, which directly affects the relative error ϵ.

The naïve approach processes only about 1000 inputs (lookups and updates) per second. In Figure 12 we see that CI-COUNT with an appropriately chosen value of p (or ϵ) processes about 25,000 inputs per second. Note that the selectivity of the range condition imposes a upper bound on the relative performance of CI-COUNT when compared to the simple approach, suggesting that we can expect greater benefits for more selective range conditions.

7 Related Work

One class of techniques for resource sharing between different queries is based on detecting and exploiting common subexpressions. All of the multiquery optimization techniques for conventional one-time queries, e.g., [27, 28], belong to this class. In the context of continuous queries, similar techniques have been used in the NiagaraCQ system [11]. Recent work in the TelegraphCQ project [9, 25] suggests using the *Eddy operator* [6] for sharing, and argues that since the Eddy operator does not fix a query plan, it exposes greater sharing possibilities.

The second class of techniques, which is the focus of this paper, is sharing resources at the operator level. Most previous work on operator-level sharing has focused on filters. All traditional pub-sub systems, e.g., [1, 16, 21], and some continuous query processing systems, e.g., [11, 25], use variants of predicate indexes for resource sharing in filters. Work on resource sharing for XML-based filters, e.g., [2, 13, 22, 26], also belongs to this class. Recently, reference [14] considers the problem of sharing *sketches* for approximate join-based processing. As described in Section 3.1.3, PSoup briefly considers the problem of resource sharing and proposes an algorithm for ASW operators.

Lot of research on sliding window aggregates has focused on computing approximate aggregates (statistics) over sliding windows in limited space, e.g., [4, 12, 18]. Our goal in this paper is to compute exact aggregates. For many applications (e.g., applications over financial data) the ability to compute exact answers is crucial. Also, aggregation functions like MAX and MIN are inherently difficult to approximate [12].

8 Conclusions

We presented new techniques for scalable processing of large numbers of operators based on sliding-window aggregates. Our techniques have precise theoretical guarantees, and they perform extremely well in practice.

We have identified at least two avenues for future work. First, the techniques in this paper represent alternatives, rather than a single "optimal" solution. An optimal solution depends on the exact rates of answer requests and stream updates, and may change as these rates change. Thus, one direction is to consider adaptive techniques that factor in relative answer/update rates. A second direction is to extend the class of operators we handle to include arbitrary filters, both before and after the sliding window is applied.

Acknowledgments

We thank Mayur Datar and Gurmeet Manku for useful feedback.

References

[1] M. K. Aguilera, R. E. Strom, et al. Matching events in a content-based subscription system. In *Proc. of the 18th Annual ACM Symp. on Principles of Distributed Computing*, pages 53–61, May 1999.

[2] M. Altinel and M. J. Franklin. Efficient filtering of XML documents for selective dissemination of information. In *Proc. of the 26th Intl. Conf. on Very Large Data Bases*, pages 53–64, Sept. 2000.

[3] A. Arasu, S. Babu, and J. Widom. The CQL Continuous Query Language: Semantic Foundations and Query Execution. Technical report, Stanford University, Oct. 2003. http://dbpubs.stanford.edu/pub/2003-67.

[4] A. Arasu and G. Manku. Approximate counts and quantiles over sliding windows. In *Proc. of the 23rd ACM SIGACT-SIGMOD-SIGART Symp. on Principles of Database Systems*, June 2004.

[5] A. Arasu and J. Widom. Resource sharing in continuous sliding window aggregates. Technical Report http://dbpubs.stanford.edu/pub/2004-15, Stanford University, 2004.

[6] R. Avnur and J. M. Hellerstein. Eddies: Continuously adaptive query processing. In *Proc. of the 2000 ACM SIGMOD Intl. Conf. on Management of Data*, pages 261–272, May 2000.

[7] B. Babcock, S. Babu, et al. Models and issues in data stream systems. In *Proc. of the 21st ACM SIGACT-SIGMOD-SIGART Symp. on Principles of Database Systems*, pages 1–16, June 2002.

[8] D. Carney, U. Centintemel, et al. Monitoring streams - a new class of data management applications. In *Proc. of the 28th Intl. Conf. on Very Large Data Bases*, pages 215–226, Aug. 2002.

[9] S. Chandrasekharan, O. Cooper, et al. TelegraphCQ: Continuous dataflow processing for an uncertain world. In *Proc. of the 1st Conf. on Innovative Data Systems Research*, pages 269–280, Jan. 2003.

[10] S. Chandrasekharan and M. J. Franklin. Streaming queries over streaming data. In *Proc. of the 28th Intl. Conf. on Very Large Data Bases*, pages 203–214, Aug. 2002.

[11] J. Chen, D. J. DeWitt, F. Tian, and Y. Wang. NiagaraCQ: A scalable continuous query system for internet databases. In *Proc. of the 2000 ACM SIGMOD Intl. Conf. on Management of Data*, pages 379–390, May 2000.

[12] M. Datar, A. Gionis, P. Indyk, and R. Motwani. Maintaining stream statistics over sliding windows. In *Proc. of the 13th Annual ACM-SIAM Symp. on Discrete Algorithms*, pages 635–644, Jan. 2002.

[13] Y. Diao, P. M. Fischer, M. J. Franklin, and R. To. YFilter: Efficient and scalable filtering of XML documents. In *Proc. of the 18th Intl. Conf. on Data Engineering*, pages 341–344, Feb. 2002.

[14] A. Dobra, M. Garofalakis, J. Gehrke, and R. Rastogi. Sketch-based multi-query processing over data streams. In *Proc. of the 9th Intl. Conf. on Extending Database Technology*, Mar. 2004.

[15] C. Estan and G. Varghese. New directions in traffic measurement and accounting: Focusing on the elephants, ignoring the mice. *ACM Transactions on Computer Systems*, 21(3):270–313, Aug. 2003.

[16] F. Fabret, H. Jacobsen, et al. Filtering algorithms and implementation for very fast publish/subscribe. In *Proc. of the 2000 ACM SIGMOD Intl. Conf. on Management of Data*, pages 115–126, May 2001.

[17] J. Gehrke, F. Korn, and D. Srivastava. On computing correlated aggregates over continual data streams. In *Proc. of the 2001 ACM SIGMOD Intl. Conf. on Management of Data*, pages 13–24, May 2001.

[18] P. B. Gibbons and S. Tirthapura. Distributed streams algorithms for sliding windows. In *Proc. of the 14th Annual ACM Symp. on Parallel Algs. and Architectures*, pages 63–72, Aug. 2002.

[19] A. C. Gilbert, Y. Kotidis, et al. How to summarize the universe: Dynamic maintenance of quantiles. In *Proc. of the 28th Intl. Conf. on Very Large Data Bases*, pages 454–465, Aug. 2002.

[20] J. Gray, S. Chaudhuri, et al. Data cube: A relational aggregation operator generalizing group-by, cross-tab, and sub totals. *Data Mining and Knowledge Discovery*, 1(1):29–53, Mar. 1997.

[21] R. E. Gruber, B. Krishnamurthy, and E. Panagos. READY: A high performance event notification system. In *Proc. of the 16th Intl. Conf. on Data Engineering*, pages 668–669, Mar. 2000.

[22] A. K. Gupta and D. Suciu. Stream processing of XPath queries with predicates. In *Proc. of the 2003 ACM SIGMOD Intl. Conf. on Management of Data*, pages 419–430, June 2003.

[23] libavl: Library for balanced binary trees. Available at http://www.gnu.org/directory/GNU/libavl.html.

[24] U. Lindqvist and P. A. Porras. Detecting computer and network misuse through the production-based expert system toolset (P-BEST). In *Proc. of the IEEE Symp. on Security and Privacy*, pages 146–161, May 1999.

[25] S. Madden, M. A. Shah, J. M. Hellerstein, and V. Raman. Continuously adaptive continuous queries over streams. In *Proc. of the 2002 ACM SIGMOD Intl. Conf. on Management of Data*, pages 49–60, June 2002.

[26] F. Peng and S. S. Chawathe. XPath queries on streaming data. In *Proc. of the 2003 ACM SIGMOD Intl. Conf. on Management of Data*, pages 431–442, June 2003.

[27] P. Roy, S. Seshadri, et al. Efficient and extensible algorithms for multi query optimization. In *Proc. of the 2000 ACM SIGMOD Intl. Conf. on Management of Data*, pages 249–260, May 2000.

[28] T. K. Sellis. Multiple-query optimization. *ACM Trans. on Database Systems*, 13(1):23–52, Mar. 1988.

[29] Traderbot home page. http://www.traderbot.com, 2003.

[30] G. Vigna and R. A. Kemmerer. NetSTAT: A network-based intrusion detection approach. In *Proc. of the 14th Annual Computer Security Appln. Conf.*, pages 25–38, Dec. 1998.

[31] Y. Zhu and D. Shasha. StatStream: Statistical monitoring of thousands of data streams in real time. In *Proc. of the 28th Intl. Conf. on Very Large Data Bases*, pages 358–369, Aug. 2002.

Remembrance of Streams Past:
Overload-Sensitive Management of Archived Streams

Sirish Chandrasekaran
EECS Department, UC Berkeley
sirish@cs.berkeley.edu

Michael Franklin
EECS Department, UC Berkeley
franklin@cs.berkeley.edu

Abstract

This paper studies Data Stream Management Systems that combine real-time data streams with historical data, and hence access incoming streams and archived data simultaneously. A significant problem for these systems is the I/O cost of fetching historical data which inhibits processing of the live data streams. Our solution is to reduce the I/O cost for accessing the archive by retrieving only a reduced (summarized or sampled) version of the historical data. This paper does not propose new summarization or sampling techniques, but rather a framework in which multiple resolutions of summarization/sampling can be generated efficiently. The query engine can select the appropriate level of summarization to use depending on the resources currently available. The central research problem studied is whether to generate the multiple representations of archived data eagerly upon data-arrival, lazily at query-time, or in a hybrid fashion. Concrete techniques for each approach are presented, which are tied to a specific data reduction technique (random sampling). The tradeoffs among the three approaches are studied both analytically and experimentally.

1. Introduction

The queries that can be posed on a Data Stream Management System (DSMS) [1,3,5] can be distinguished into three classes (see Figure 1). The first consists of queries over archived disk data that is already present in the system before the query is posed. Traditional database literature has largely focused on supporting these *historical queries*. The second class consists of queries over live network data that enters the system after the query is posed. These *live queries* have been the subject of much recent research on continuous query (CQ) processing [14]. Neither CQ engines nor traditional databases, however have adequately addressed the problem of supporting queries that access a combination of disk *and* live data. This third class of *hybrid queries* is the focus of this paper. The following are representative examples of hybrid queries, based on the scenario of a freeway embedded with sensors that record information about passing cars.

Query 1 – **Load on Freeway**: This is a single-stream query that accesses a window of data that begins in history, and continues into the future: *"Perform a running count on the increase in number of cars between Ashby exit and the Bay Bridge since the beginning of rush hour. Compute this value once every fifteen minutes till the end of rush hour."*

Query 2 – **How many Commuters**: This is a join query where the the live data is combined with different portions of history: *"For the cars that have been observed to pass Ashby exit, choose those that have been seen at the same exit at the same hour every day this last week. Count the total numbers that match this condition today."*

As the number of such hybrid queries accessing different portions of the archive increases, so do the number of random disk accesses. Given the dramatic improvements in computation power and network bandwidth witnessed recently, the cost of interleaving random disk accesses with the processing of live network data has become substantial. These I/O costs can have a debilitating effect on the ability of a query processor to run multiple hybrid queries and cause it to fall increasingly behind in the processing of the live data.

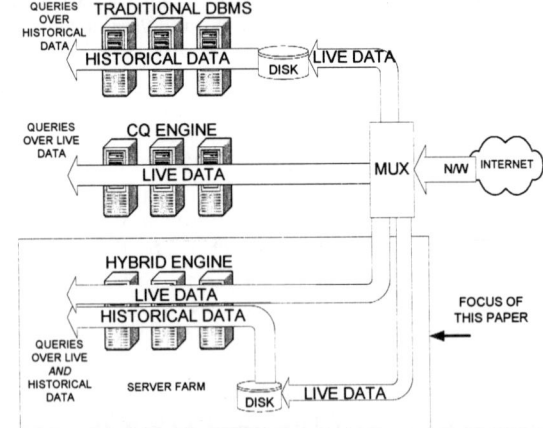

Figure 1: DSMS design following query classification

While it is tempting to reuse solutions developed in traditional DBMSs and in CQ engines to address this problem, the approaches developed in those systems to handle overload are either inapplicable or inadequate for workloads of hybrid queries. Historical queries do not typically have real time (or near real-time) requirements, allowing traditional databases the option of postponing some computation in the case of overload (e.g., data warehousing). This is, however,

---

This work was funded in part by the NSF under ITR grants IIS-0086057 and SI-0122599, by the IBM Faculty Partnership Award program, and by research funds from Intel, Microsoft, and the UC MICRO program.

Permission to copy without fee all or part of this material is granted provided that the copies are not made or distributed for direct commercial advantage, the VLDB copyright notice and the title of the publication and its date appear, and notice is given that copying is by permission of the Very Large Data Base Endowment. To copy otherwise, or to republish, requires a fee and/or special permission from the Endowment

**Proceedings of the 30th VLDB Conference,
Toronto, Canada 2004**

not possible in a hybrid engine since query processing is coupled to the arrival of live data. Suspending a query only causes it to fall even further behind the live data. Further, in 24x7 applications, there might not even be a time of sufficiently reduced load at which to execute all the postponed queries. Indexing techniques combined with batched I/O can be used to support fast simultaneous inserts and reads of historical data [15,16]. However, even if the correct index is available for use by the query, it only pushes away the point at which a system is overloaded: it does not address what happens then.

Admission control at the network (also called load-shedding), on the other hand, has been proposed for CQ engines as a way to directly deal with overload [3,4]. Dropping the network data is, however, an unsuitable solution for hybrid-query workloads for two reasons. First, disk access is a more significant bottleneck for hybrid query workloads than the processing of network data. Dropping the network data therefore does not confront the root of the problem. Second, and more importantly, the dropped network data is lost forever, and unavailable for any future hybrid queries.

The key to immediately and precisely addressing overload in a hybrid query processor is to retrieve only a reduced version of the data on disk. A wealth of literature exists in the area of data reduction (henceforth abbreviated as DR) including sampling, summarization (such as aggregates, histograms) and compression. Rather than propose a new DR method, this paper focuses on the architectural issues of allowing a DSMS to exploit a variety of these pre-existing techniques to handle overload. In particular, we concentrate our efforts on designing mechanisms within the storage system to generate multiple resolutions of data reduced through random sampling or windowed aggregation. The query engine can select the appropriate level of summarization to use depending on the resources currently available.

By focusing our solution to the architectural issues concerning the storage system, rather than the DR methods or the query engine, we allow the DSMS considerable flexibility in handling overload. For example, the query engine can employ various responses to overload ranging from constant-rate data reduction to reduction based on the attribute-values of the live data or even the age of the historical data. Further, the DSMS is free to present applications with varying degrees of information about the fidelity of results ranging from nothing to sophisticated statistical guarantees.

1.1 Our solution: the 10,000 ft. view

In this section, we present an abstraction of the design of the hybrid query processing engine, and point out the portions of the system we modify to handle overload.

Figure 2 shows the three principal components of a hybrid query engine: the *network interface*, the *executor*, and the *disk*. The network interface reads the data off the network and is responsible for both making this data directly available to the executor, as well as writing it to disk. The queries run in the executor and can access the live data directly from the network interface and the historical data from the disk. In order to handle disk overload, we make the following modifications to the system.

First, all disk accesses (reads and writes) are controlled through a special access method called the *Overload-sensitive Stream Capture and Archive Reduction* access method *(OSCAR)*. OSCAR organizes the data on disk in a fashion that makes it possible to trade-off I/Os for the quality of data scanned. For example, OSCAR might store multiple versions of the stream on disk, with each version representing a different choice in the trade-off of quality and size of data. The OSCAR access method can then scan the appropriate version at query time.

The second modification to the system has to do with informing OSCAR about the degree of data reduction desired by the query for scans of historical data. To do this, we require all queries to associate each scan module over historical data with a *reduction User-Defined-Function (r-UDFs)*. As data scanned from the disk passes through the scan module at the leaf of the query plan, this r-UDF communicates back to OSCAR the degree of data reduction that is required. OSCAR uses this feedback to control the quality of data returned by the scan.

In this paper, we focus on the design of OSCARs for handling r-UDFs based on random sampling and windowed aggregation. Supporting other classes of r-UDFs is the subject of future work and discussed in Section 7.

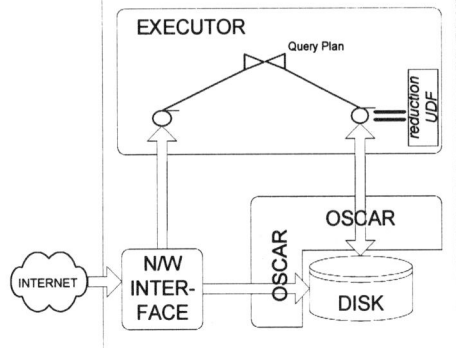

Figure 2: Our solution: the 10,000 ft. view

1.2 Contributions of this paper

In this section, we summarize the contributions of our paper.

Our first contribution is the identification of disk overload as a key problem in the support of hybrid queries that simultaneously access disk and network data, and the accompanying observation that load-shedding is an unsuitable solution to address this problem.

Second, we propose *Overload-sensitive Stream Capture and Archive Reduction* (OSCAR), an access method which can interface with a variety of user defined data reduction functions *(r-UDFs)* to retrieve reduced versions of the archive for correspondingly fewer I/Os.

Third, we present concrete OSCAR designs for r-UDFs based on random sampling and windowed aggregation. These designs differ as to when they perform most of their work generating the multiple resolutions of archived data. We describe the implementation of three OSCAR designs for r-UDFs based on random sampling in TelegraphCQ. The tradeoffs among these three designs are studied both analytically and experimentally, with an emphasis on the effects of a real file-system and operating system on the behavior of the solutions.

The rest of this paper is organized as follows. In Section 2, we discuss related work. In Section 3, we describe OSCAR, the r-UDFs, and their interaction in more detail using an example. In Section 4, we present different OSCAR designs for both r-UDFs based on sampling and windowed aggregation. In Section 5, we describe the implementation of the mechanisms for sampling-based DR schemes in TelegraphCQ. Section 6 demonstrates and compares the performance benefits of our various storage schemes. We discuss future work in Section 7, and conclude in Section 8.

2. Related Work

Data reduction, admission control, and optimized disk access are all areas that have been extensively research by the database community. In this section, we discuss some representative and relevant work in each, discussing their applicability to overload in hybrid query workloads.

We cover the related work according to how they can be applied to the problem of disk overload.

Converting random to sequential I/O: The first important area of related work is the literature on fast inserts and reads in traditional databases. Saving random I/Os has always been a key theme of database systems research, and the goal of avoiding random I/Os in favor or sequential I/O has led to the proposal of various extent-based storage systems (e.g., [9,16]). Indexes [15] also can be used very effectively to reduce random I/O if the data is clustered. While it is difficult to ensure clustered organization of data in the presence of continually growing streams, the batching of writes of live data to disk offers an approximation. Both these approaches can reduce the impact of disk accesses; however, they suffer from some shortcomings. First, these solutions require periodic reorganization of the disk in order to make the above batches coalesce into larger ones. Second, given that it is not feasible to maintain indexes over every attribute on a high-throughput stream, and also that the queries might not be known ahead of time; the indexes maintained by the system might be inefficient for the query at hand. Finally, while these approaches increase the extent to which the system can scale, they still do not address the problem of overload, they only delay the problem.

Postponing query processing to a later time of lower load: This works for situations involving historical queries which do not typically have real time (or near real-time) requirements. A traditional database therefore has the option of postponing some computation in case of overload, for example, to the end of the business day. Examples of this can be seen in data-warehousing [13]. This is however not an option for the hybrid engine where query processing is coupled to the arrival of live data. Suspending a query only causes it to fall even further behind the live data. Further, for 24x7, high data-rate applications, it is unclear if there are any periods of lower load.

Shed load at the network: In CQ engines which neither archive nor revisit stream data, admission control at the network pipe has been proposed for dealing with overload [3,4]. As stated previously, however, this solution is not well suited to hybrid query workloads for the following reasons. For workloads involving hybrid queries, disk access is a more significant bottleneck than the main memory processing of live data: dropping data on the network pipe therefore does not directly address the current cause of overload, which is disk access. Second, and more importantly, the data dropped in the network is lost for ever, and cannot be queried by future hybrid queries.

Data Reduction (DR): There is a wealth of literature proposing different DR techniques [17]. Our work aims to complement these efforts by providing a framework where these techniques can be plugged into a DSMS. Since these techniques often require the special modifications to the executor, we restrict our focus to those based on sampling and windowed aggregation. These techniques have the dual advantage of requiring simpler enhancements to the executor, while still allowing a range of application-specific responses to the problem of overload. Other previous work, such as [8] has looked at ways to store the data on disk at multiple resolutions in order to tradeoff disk I/Os and accuracy. While we share the same goals, we are attempting to define an architectural solution that can encompass a wider range of DR techniques, and by extension, queries.

3. Our solution – the 100 ft. view

In this section, we expand on the overview of the solution we presented in Section 1.1, revealing more detail about OSCAR and the *r-UDF*. Figure 3 shows our solution for a specific disk organization and r-UDF.

OSCAR: We first discuss the most important component of our solution, the *Overload-sensitive Stream Capture and Archive Reduction* access method (OSCAR). OSCAR organizes the data on disk in a fashion that allows reduced versions to be retrieved in order to save I/Os. While the data should ideally be retrievable at any reduction level between 0 and 100% with matching savings in I/Os, in practice there can only be a finite number of reduction levels for which OSCAR can provide exactly matching I/O savings. In Figure 3, these levels are 25%, 50% and 75%. The disk therefore logically appears to have three additional copies of the stream containing 75%, 50%, and 25% of the original data respectively. The actual content of the disk is invisible to the executor and as we shall show in Section 4.1 for example, this logical view can be physically implemented using one, two or more copies of the stream on disk.

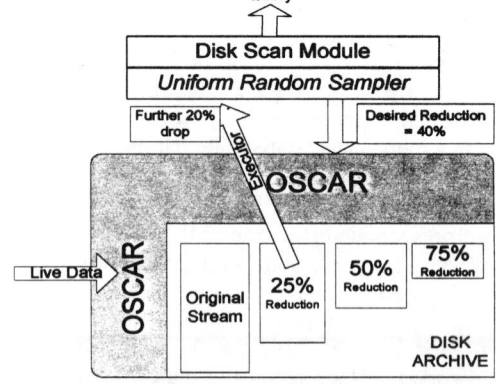

Figure 3: 100 ft. view of solution

In order to organize the data on disk and allow access at multiple levels of the reduction, OSCAR controls all disk accesses, both by the network interface and by the executor. It can therefore perform its modifications to the archive either *eagerly* when the network interface calls its insert() method to write the incoming data to disk, or *lazily* when the executor subsequently calls its *read()* method. In this paper, we present different approaches that perform most of their work either at data-arrival time or at query time, or split their work between the two phases. We also show how the approach chosen influences the physical implementation of the logical view of the disk.

The Reduction UDF: The second important part of our solution is the *r-UDFs*. Each physical scan over historical data is associated with an r-UDF that notifies OSCAR as to the degree of reduction required. The r-UDF is a piece of user code that takes in data as it is scanned from the disk and continuously returns values representing the *degree of reduction* desired in the scan. For example, an r-UDF that performs random sampling returns a value between 0 and 1 that indicates the fraction of data that can be dropped from the scan. To implement windowed aggregation, the r-UDF returns a time-interval that indicates the size of the window over which the aggregation is to be performed. The r-UDF shown in Figure 3 is a uniform random sampler that always returns 0.4; i.e., it drops 40% of the data passing through it.

The r-UDF can be considerably more sophisticated. For example, an age-based r-UDF can determine the reduction level based on the age of the tuples in the section of the archive being scanned: it can thus demand increasingly higher fidelity for more recent data as in [11]. The r-UDF can also determine the level of reduction according to the current load on the system. Finally, the r-UDF can maintain internal state on the tuples that it has seen, and perform more sophisticated statistical analyses according to the desired approximation levels of the output (as in CONTROL [18]).

Putting it all together: A hybrid live/historical query is specified by associating each archived stream in the FROM clause of the query with one of the r-UDFs registered with the system. For example, the scan module over the archived stream in Figure 3 is associated with a uniform random sampler that drops 40% of all input. This level of reduction specified by the r-UDF (0.4) does not equal any of the levels of the reduction that OSCAR can directly satisfy (0.25, 0.5 and 0.75). OSCAR does the best it can and reads from the copy with 25% reduction. Though it will not save any more I/Os, the scan module can choose to drop 20% of this data, if it wishes to achieve the original target of 40% reduction ((100 − 20)% of (100 − 25)% = (100 − 40)% of original).

4. The OSCAR access method

In this section, we present various OSCAR designs that support r-UDFs based on sampling and windowed aggregation. In Section 5, we discuss the actual implementation of different OSCARs for sampling-based r-UDFs in TelegraphCQ.

4.1 OSCAR designs for random sampling

In this section, we present three different OSCAR designs to enable a variety of sampling-based r-UDFs to reduce overload caused by disk accesses in a hybrid query engine.

As shown in Figure 4, the three solutions perform their actions at different points in the system: OnWriteReplicate is an eager data-driven mechanism, performing most of its work at data arrival. OnReadModify lazily peforms most of its work modifying the archive at query time. The RandomizeThenSort method splits its work between data-arrival and query-execution.

Figure 4: Different mechanisms for sampling-based DR

4.1.1 OnWriteReplicate: The Eager Approach

We first discuss an eager data-driven approach that exploits the fact that while random disk I/Os are expensive, disk space is not.

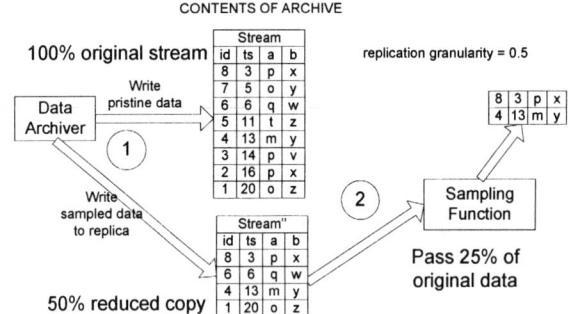

Figure 5: OnWriteReplicate in action

In this method, we always keep one pristine (non-reduced) copy of the stream on disk. This copy is referred to as the primary. In addition, there are a set of copies at increasing levels of reduction. The number and levels of reduction of these copies is specified at the time the stream is created, but can also be changed at any later time. OSCAR writes a pristine copy of the incoming data to the primary, while also randomly sampling this data at the different pre-determined levels to populate the various copies. Later, as the executor scans tuples, it continuously feeds the values returned by the r-UDF back to OSCAR. OSCAR uses these values to continuously identify (and if needed switch the scan to) the copy whose data granularity is closest to (and finer than) the desired coarseness.

Figure 5 shows an example of this technique in action. The stream has one copy (in addition to the primary) at a reduction level of 50%. At data arrival (step 1 in the figure), OSCAR populates the primary with all the incoming data, and the copy with half of this data. The r-UDF in the example specifies a uniform sample rate of 25% (i.e., a reduction level of 75%). Therefore, at query time (step 2), OSCAR reads data from the copy, rather than the primary. Note that this, however, only reduces I/Os by 50%, rather than 75%. The scan module can drop 50% of the data scanned from the copy to achieve the desired 75% reduction on the original.

4.1.2 OnReadModify: The Lazy Approach

In this section, we discuss a lazy, query-driven technique that performs most of its work at the executor.

One way to design this method is to maintain multiple copies of the stream at pre-determined levels and populate them on demand. This solution, however, is problematic. It increases the implementation complexity without offering significant new insight into the cost trade-offs with respect to the eager solution. To understand the increased implementation complexity, consider Figure 6, which shows the above approach in action for a stream with three copies. Different hybrid queries have caused the different copies to be filled arbitrarily. Each copy thus has sequences of extents of tuples followed by *holes* corresponding to the portions of the archive that have not yet been accessed by any hybrid queries.

Because of the arbitrary order in which these holes are filled, and the potentially unknown sizes of the tuples that will fill them, we can no longer use a simple heap file to store the copies; an extent-based storage structure must be used for each copy of the stream.

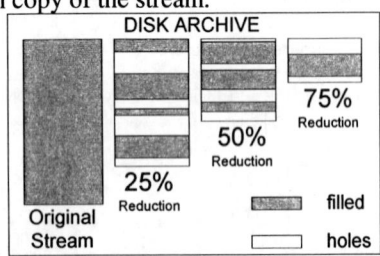

Figure 6: Effect of eager filling on pre-defined copies

A database like PostgreSQL does not have an inbuilt extent-based storage method, requiring one to be implemented from scratch. Further, the above solution would also require a managing data structure that continuously directs scan to the smallest possible copy while also filling these copies on demand. For these reasons, we have developed a solution that uses a simpler storage structure: a heap file for the original stream, and another for a reduced copy. The resulting design is different from the above mirror of the eager solution. We describe our solution below for the case of one r-UDF. In the presence of multiple r-UDFs, the solution is just repeated in parallel, with multiple copies.

In this technique, at data-arrival time, OSCAR simply streams a complete copy of the arriving data to disk. Later, at query time, OSCAR randomly marks some of the tuples that are scanned as *dead*, at the reduction rates returned by the r-UDF. These tuples do not make it to the query plan. A periodic *vacuumer* process later copies the remaining *live* tuples to a new location on disk. Future incoming tuples are written to both the original and to this copy. Subsequent disk accesses by the same or a different query using the same r-UDF are then directed to this new, smaller copy so they will incur fewer I/Os. As before, this will result in OSCAR marking some of the tuples in this copy as *dead*. Instead of moving them to yet another copy, the vacuumer just purges the tuples from this copy and compacts it in-place.

If the reduction level of any portion of this copy becomes too low for a new query using the same *r-UDF*, then the new query switches to scanning the original, with no further modifications to the archive. If the fraction of accesses that switch to the original crosses a preset threshold, then the copy can be deleted and the whole process repeated.

Figure 7 illustrates this approach. In Step 1, OSCAR writes all the data to disk. At query time (Step 2), let us assume that the sampling r-UDF requires a 50% reduction in data. These tuples are then marked dead in the original. At Step 3, the vacuumer copies the remaining live tuples to a new location on disk. A future query (shown in Step 4) uses the same r-UDF over this stream. At this time, however, the r-UDF requests a 75% reduction on the original data. This can be satisfied entirely by scanning only the copy. The vacuumer, however, had already removed 50% of the original data in constructing this copy. We therefore, only retrieve (25/50)*100 = 50% of the current copy. The remaining tuples are purged from the copy on a subsequent pass by the vacuumer.

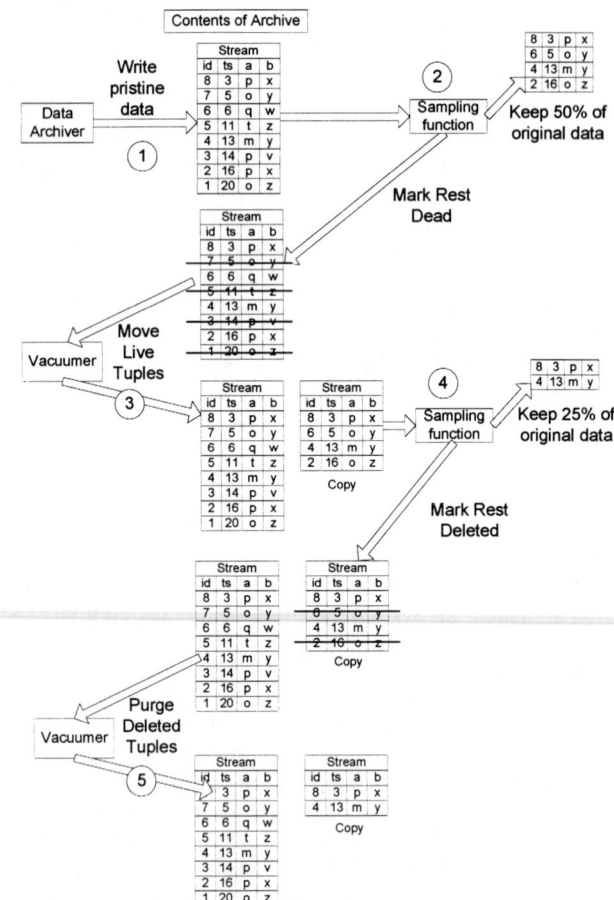

Figure 7: OnReadModify in action

4.1.3 In RandomizeThenSort: The Hybrid Approach

The solutions described in the previous sections perform significant amounts of work either at data-arrival or query-time in order to enable sampled access to disk data. Depending on the query and data workloads, they might even exacerbate the degree of overload. The method we discuss in this section fixes this problem by spreading the burden across these two phases and improving the performance of both reads and writes.

In this technique, there is a single copy of the stream on disk, which is divided into separate "runs" or batches, with each "run" corresponding to a fixed number of blocks. The data source writes the arriving tuples uniformly at random to one of the blocks in the current run. When any of the blocks in the current run fills up, the entire set of the blocks in the run is flushed to disk and a new run is created for inserting new tuples. At query time, when OSCAR begins to scan a new run of blocks, it uses the latest value returned by the r-UDF to only read from a corresponding fraction of the blocks in this new run. Since the tuples within each block are sorted by timestamp, a merge sort is employed to retrieve the original order of tuples across the different blocks in the run.

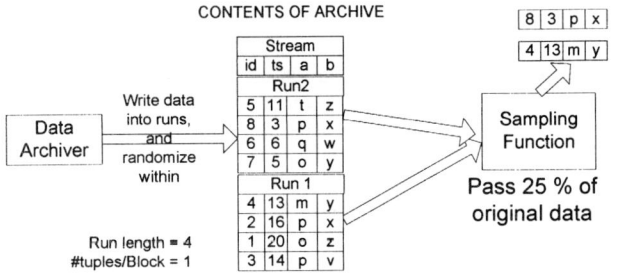

Figure 8: RandomizeThenSort in action

Figure 8 shows an example of this technique in action. The stream is defined to have runs of size 4 blocks each (In the above figure, we assume one tuple per block for ease of visualization). The r-UDF specifies a 75% level of reduction. Therefore, OSCAR reads exactly block from each run.

4.1.4 Comparison of the solutions

Having discussed our three basic algorithms, we briefly compare them analytically. In Section 6, we will compare them experimentally. Table 1 summarizes the analytically computed I/O costs of three OSCAR designs and a strawman that performs all the sampling in the executor, does not modify the archive, and saves no I/Os.

As can be seen, OnWriteReplicate, always maintains the original data, and in fact, pays a higher insertion cost by maintaining extra copies in the hope of saving I/Os at query time. It however pays a low cost on every read.

OnReadModify, on the other hand, performs most of its work on the first time it scans an archive. Both its original write costs, and subsequent read costs are restricted to the minimum possible. It does however require additional work by the vacuumer. The fact that it removes tuples from the copy can be an asset. If the solution is modified to allow the vacuumer to purge tuples from the original itself, it can be used to limit the size of the archive.

RandomizeThenSort is a hybrid solution that has both low write and read costs, with the #I/Os at write time being the same as that for the OnReadModify solution, and the #I/Os at read time very close to the minimum possible #I/Os.

4.1.5 Analytical Plots

In order to better visualize the formulae in Table 1, we use them to analytically compute and plot the write and read rates for the various OSCAR designs.

First, we parametrize the eager and hybrid OSCAR designs as follows. We assume that OnWriteReplicate has four copies in addition to the original stream at reduction levels of 20%, 40%, 60% and 80%. This determines the function $g(r)$ in the table. For the hybrid solution, we assume a run length (R) of a hundred blocks.

To determine the values of the other parameters in the analytical formulae, we ran some tests on our implementation of OSCAR in TelegraphCQ. We measured the size on disk of a stream (based on the strawman described above) containing 20 million tuples to be 108,000 blocks of 8192-bytes each. Since the size of each index entry is only 20 bytes, we approximate I/S to be zero. Therefore, B = 108,000 blocks. We also measured the time it took to populate the strawman with these tuples to be 430 seconds.

Based on the above parameters, Figure 9 displays a generated plot that shows the analytically computed time for the

Mechanism	Cost of Writes	Cost of reads
OnWrite Replicate	$\sum_{i=1}^{n} B_j(1+\frac{I}{S})$	$\sum_{i=1}^{B} g(f(i))$
OnRead Modify	No copy: $B(1+\frac{I}{S})$ 1 copy: $2*B(1+\frac{I}{S})$	1st Read: $B + \sum_{i=1}^{B}\lceil 1-f(i) \rceil$ 2nd Read: B Post Vac.: $\sum_{i=1}^{B} f(i)$
Randomize ThenSort	$B(1+\frac{I}{R*S})$	$\sum_{j=1}^{B/R}\lceil R*f'(j) \rceil$
Strawman	$B(1+\frac{I}{S})$	B

B = # blocks of stream in archive
I = size of index entry
S = size of a block
R = run-length
n = # copies of stream

$f(i)$ = 1 – min(reduction level for tuples in i^{th} block)
$f'(j)$ = 1 – min(reduction level for tuples in j^{th} run)
$g(r)$ = 1 – (reduction level amongst copies closest to r)

Table 1: I/O costs of storage mechanisms

different OSCAR designs to write the same stream. As can be seen, the hybrid solution, RandomizeThenRead, pays the same cost as the strawman, requiring very little work at data insertion time. The lazy solution takes the same time as the strawman and hybrid solution prior to vacuuming. After being vacuumed, however, it contains an additional copy that also receives all the incoming data, doubling the write cost. The eager solution is computed to take the most time, since the sum of the sizes of its copies is twice the size of the original stream. The cost of writing the stream for the eager solution is thus thrice that of the strawman.

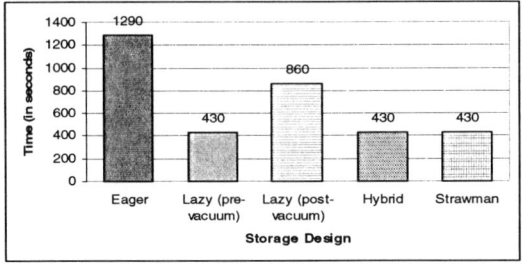

Figure 9: Time to insert 20 million tuples

Next, we ran a *count(*)* query over the entire strawman archive; this took 20 seconds. Based on this measurement, we computed the time it would take to query the data for different values of the reduction level ($f(i)$) for the different OSCAR designs. Figure 10 shows the plot for these generated values.

In the figure, the first and second reads for the lazy design are assumed to occur before the vacuuming. In order to

353

reduce the visual clutter, we group together designs that have very similar or identical performance. The performance of the strawman is independent of the reduction level. As can be seen, the first query pays a high price for OnReadModify, the lazy solution. The second query performs as well as the strawman. After vacuuming, the lazy solution matches the hybrid solution, and has the best possible performance. The cost of the eager solution is a step function, since the OnWriteReplicate solution can only offer savings commensurate to the granularities of its pre-stored copies. It has much lower cost than the pre-vacuuming lazy solution. It still has comparable, but slightly higher cost relative to the post-vacuum version of the lazy solution.

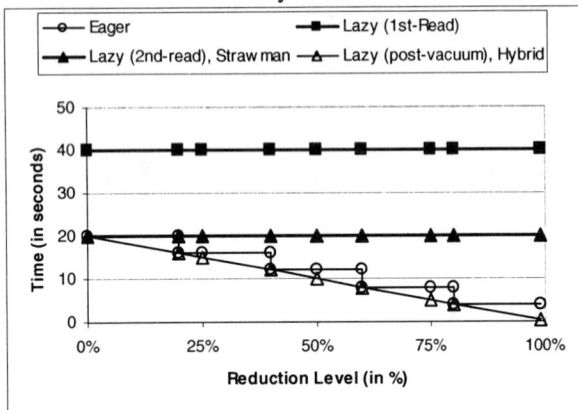

Figure 10: Time to query 20 million tuples for different reduction levels

The analysis of the performance of the system when the write and the reads occur simultaneously is as follows. Since the disk is the bottleneck, the available disk bandwidth will be parcelled out between the queries and the insertion process at the rate at which they access the disk. Therefore, the total time for insertion will increase in proportion to the number of disk accesses by the queries for a given query-completion rate. As we shall see in Section 6, however, reality is quite different: the disk elevator algorithm used in Linux (and the ext3 file system) removes contention between the writes and reads, by guaranteeing each a minimum latency. Further, the operation system unfairly schedules the write process more if it does not realize that the queries are performing sequential I/O.

In this analysis, the hybrid OSCAR design emerges as the best solution because it offers both low insert and reduces I/Os at exactly the rate demanded by the r-UDF.

4.2 OSCARs for windowed aggregation

In Section 4.1 we described storage schemes for sampling-based r-UDFs. In this section, we will discuss a mechanism for supporting *summary-based* techniques such as grouped averages.

We propose solutions here similar to the lazy (OnReadModify) and eager (OnWriteReplicate) methods described in Section 4.1. Like those other techniques, these two work by storing multiple copies of the data at different degrees of summarization. The main difference is that unlike sampling, decisions about the reduction are now made on a per-window rather than per-tuple basis. This observation leads us to our key insight in supporting windowed-aggregation:

the r-UDFs in this case can be abstracted away as a query on the window of tuples being summarized. The results of this query can then be written to the replicas.

To drive the rest of the discussion, we use the following example of an r-UDF over a stream of stock-ticker data.

Example windowed aggregation r-UDF: For each hour of data, return a tuple per distinct stock symbol containing the average value of that symbol over that hour. This r-UDF is a tumbling-window [1] grouped-average query.

4.2.1 The Eager Approach

As before, OSCAR writes one complete copy of the data on disk, and other reduced versions of the data. The number of these other versions is specified at stream creation time, as are windowed-aggregation queries that populate them. Copies can also be added and removed at a later time.

As an example, consider the stock ticker and r-UDF presented above. Let us also assume that the stream is created with two additional copies: the first (copy#1) stores the hourly averages and the other (copy#2), the daily averages of the stock data, both grouped by company symbol.

OSCAR writes the individual records to the master copy of the stream on disk. In addition, it populates these two additional copies using either triggered historical queries, or tumbling window continuous queries. The trigger approach requires one purely historical copy for each of the copies that have to be populated. Copy#1, is therefore populated by a grouped average query that is triggered every hour and executes over the previous hour of data. Copy#2, is populated by a similar query that is triggered every day. The CQ approach, on the other hand has two permanently running grouped average continuous queries, one with a window that tumbles every hour, and the other with a window that tumbles every day. In either case, a new query that uses the r-UDF described above (which requires hourly averages) can scan Copy#1 to reduce overload.

4.2.2 The Lazy Approach

As with OnReadModify, there is a single copy of the complete data on disk, and one additional reduced copy per r-UDF. At data-arrival OSCAR simply writes the complete data to disk. At query time as data is scanned from disk, it is passed to the through the tumble query in the r-UDF. The result of this DR query is passed on to the user query. These results are also written back to disk in a new temporary location on disk. Each of these tuples is also encoded with information about the time window to which it corresponds. A vacuumer process can later combine the data from the original with the tuples in this temp location to create a new copy, replacing those original tuples that were scanned through the r-UDF with the summarized version in the temp copy. Future queries can then access this new copy. As with OnReadModify, modifications to this copy are made in place. Again, as in the case of OnReadModify, the reduction level of this copy might be too low for a certain query, in which case the original must be scanned.

In summary, the design of eager and lazy OSCAR mechanisms for r-UDFs based on windowed aggregation is essentially the same as that for random-sampling. They only differ in their details, to accommodate the different properties of the input and output to these r-UDFs.

5. Implementation in TelegraphCQ

We implemented the above OSCAR designs for sampling-based r-UDFs in TelegraphCQ, the CQ extension to PostgreSQL v7.3. The implementation closely follows the description in Section 4.1; therefore we only describe our experiences that were specific to building within TelegraphCQ (and PostgreSQL). In the rest of this section, we discuss the implementation of hybrid queries in TelegraphCQ, the custom vacuumer and free space map we built for OnReadModify, the implementation of stream copies and the special tuple format used for OnReadModify.

5.1 Running hybrid queries in TelegraphCQ

We first describe the changes we make to TelegraphCQ to run hybrid queries. These include the addition of an access method that retrieves archived streams, and modifications to the symmetric join operator to allow the executor to combine network and disk data properly.

The access method underlying OSCAR consists of an append-only heap file clustered by timestamp, and a sparse BTree on the timestamp attribute. This design allows both efficient archiving and scans by hybrid queries. Most streaming systems assume that incoming streams are in timestamp-order (modulo a maximum finite skew that can be handled through a reorder buffer). The append-only timestamp-clustered heap file therefore allows for very efficient inserts. Further, hybrid queries such as those shown in Section 1 require access, in increasing timestamp order, to all tuples with timestamp greater than a certain historical value. The Btree can be used to efficiently locate the starting point, after which a sequential scan on the heap file can be used to retrieve further tuples.

The second change we made to TelegraphCQ to support hybrid queries was to its executor, which uses an eddy and SteMs[19] to implement main-memory symmetric joins. Since TelegraphCQ only supports sliding window band joins, the SteMs only maintain a limited main memory window on the each input stream. In order to extend this mechanism to disk data, we force the eddy to coordinate the rate of data access from the network and the disk for queries that access both the network and disk. This prevents the disk scan from outstripping the rate of arrival of live data during periods of low data arrival rate.

5.2 Changes to PostgreSQL

We now discuss implementation details relating to PostgreSQL components and data structures.

The vacuumer: While PostgreSQL v7.3 has two vacuum modes, both are inapplicable in the streaming scenario, and we had to implement the vacuumer for OnReadyModify from scratch.

The *full* vacuuming mode requires a lock on the entire relation. This is clearly unsuitable for unbounded streams, since it blocks read and write accesses to the stream for a potentially unbounded time. Further, the full vacuumer destroys the original ordering of the tuples during compaction of the relation heap files. While this does not matter for relations, we care about preserving the ordering of tuples in a stream according to timestamp, as described in Section 5.1.

The other vacuum mode, called *lazy*, does not compact the relation: it only removes the dead tuples in-place. The uncompacted heap file is of no use to us as it cannot be used to save any I/Os upon future scans. Also, this vacuum mode performs no index maintenance (PostgreSQL removes index entries for tuples as soon as they are marked dead in the executor). We found that index deletion operation as performed in PostgreSQL is very expensive; invoking it in the fast path during query time in the executor therefore severely impacts the performance of the system. Hence, we move all index maintenance to the vacuumer.

The Free Space Map: A key data-structure in implementing vacuuming is the free space map (FSM) which records the available space on each page. PostgreSQL has a free space map, which however, is soft-state, and even worse, possibly stale. We therefore implement our own free space map that uses fast Judy arrays [7] to record for each stream which pages have atleast one dead tuple (these need to be processed by the vacuumer), and how much free space is available on each page (to determine which pages to compact).

5.3 Miscellaneous implementation details

Stream copies: The multi-copy streams in the lazy and eager solutions are implemented in a straightforward manner. Each copy is stored in an append-only heap file, and has an index on the timestamp attribute as described in Section 5.1. Creation, destruction, write and read calls to the stream are conducted through wrapper functions that are responsible for managing the copies.

Tuple format for OnReadModify: Finally, we discuss the unique tuple attribute requirements of OnReadModify. Recall from Section 4.1.2, that the copy stream might not exist at a uniform level of reduction. Rather, different portions of the stream might be reduced to different levels, according to the run-time reduction levels demanded by the r-UDF. To allow OSCAR to decide if the copy can be used or not to satisfy a certain query, we add an implicit attribute to each tuple in the stream, called *samplerate* that indicates the level of reduction for each tuple. This overhead of 25% to the 32 byte header of a TelegraphCQ tuple can be reduced even further if we sample all the tuples in a block at the same rate and store that granularity in the disk block header.

6. Performance

In this section, we test our central thesis that reducing I/Os at the disk scans is an essential tool for hybrid engines if they wish to support high insert rates in the presence of numerous hybrid queries. We describe the setup for the experiments in Section 6.1. In Section 6.2, we examine the insertion times for the different OSCAR designs for sampling-based r-UDFs in the absence of any queries. In Section 6.3, we look at the query-times for these schemes in the absence of concurrent insertions. In Section 6.4, we study the performance of simultaneous queries and data archiving. We summarize our results in Section 6.5.

6.1 Experimental Setup

In this section, we first explain our data and query workload and then describe the hardware and software environment for our experiments.

6.1.1 Data and Query Workloads

In addition to the three OSCAR designs described in this paper for sampling-based r-UDFs, we also measure the performance of a strawman in which all the sampling takes place in the executor. We tried three variants of our hybrid RandomizeThenSort solution with run-lengths of 10, 100 and 500 blocks respectively. For the OnWriteReplicate solution, we replicated the original stream into four additional copies at reduction levels of 20%, 40%, 60% and 80%.

OnWriteReplicate, OnReadModify and RandomizeThenSort are referred to as Eager, Lazy and Hybrid in the plot legends. Suffixes are used to indicate different states or parametrizations for the eager and hybrid solutions. We now describe the tuples that populate the streams and the queries over them.

Input Data: For the strawman and for the eager and hybrid OSCAR designs the input tuples have the schema "(float8 *timestamp*, int4 *userattr*)", where *userattr* is a dummy attribute. As explained in Section 5.3, the input tuples to OnReadModify have an additional *samplerate* attribute of type float8. The value of this attribute is set to 1 on entry (indicating pristine data). The *timestamp* attribute for tuples of all streams is set by the network interface to the time of entry.

Queries: Since our experiments focus on OSCAR, and not the executor, we use very simple count(*) landmark queries (e.g. *Query 1* in Section 1) rather than hybrid join queries (e.g. *Query 2* of Section 1). As we shall see in Section 6.4, however, the behavior of the OS affects the processing of live data in a way that is also applicable to join queries.

6.1.2 Execution Environment

Machine and OS: All the experiments were run on a Linux box (kernel 2.4.18) with a 1390 MHz Pentium III processor with 512 KB cache size. The machine had 512 MB RAM and 2 GB swap space. The underlying file system was ext3. One Seagate Cheetah 36ES disk using the SCSI Ultra 160 interface was dedicated to our experiments. The response time of the disk is 5.2 ms, its peak data transfer rate is 320MBps, and it has an internal buffer of 4MB. The observed raw throughput through the file system is much lower at about 60MBps.

PostgreSQL Settings: We initialized PostgreSQL to have a buffer pool with 4096 frames. The size of each frame (and also disk pages) is 8K bytes. The buffer replacement policy is LRU. We modified our vacuumer to be invoked on demand, rather than execute periodically. This allows us to generate repeatable observations. We also disabled logging because we only had access to one disk to store our database. This is acceptable because most real systems write log records to a separate disk.

6.2 Inserting into the Archive

In this section, we present an experiment that measures the insertion-performance into streams for the three OSCAR designs and the strawman.

To perform this test, we measured the time it took to insert 20 million tuples into a stream for each OSCAR design. Data was generated online by a C program and piped to the data archiver. The total overhead generated by this data generator was less than a half second, and is negligible. At the end of the insertion of the 20 million tuples, we flush the buffer pool and sync the filesystem buffers to ensure that we measure the complete cost to write and disk the relation.

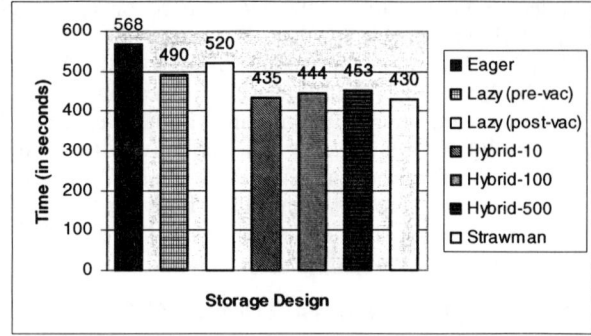

Figure 11: Insertion Times for 20M tuples

Figure 11 shows the time taken to insert the data into the various schemes. The three RandomizeThenRead solutions (marked as Hybrid in the legend) write the stream at about the same rate as the strawman. The slight differences between the three can be attributed to the different amounts of wasted space in the different runs of the streams. As the run size increases, so does the wasted space, increasing the size of the stream that must be written to disk. OnReadModify ('Lazy' in the plot) is a little slower than the strawman and hybrid solutions since the extra samplerate attribute results in increased total #I/Os. As the tuple payload increases, this overhead will disappear, and OnReadModify will approach the performance of the strawman. The cost of replication in OnWriteReplicate ('Eager') is sub-linear in the total size of the original stream and its copies. This is due to the amortization of the overhead of the processing in the wrapper clearing house. From these results, it might seem that the strawman is better than the eager and lazy OSCAR designs. As we shall see in the next section, however, the strawman performs poorly at query time under overload overload that OSCAR is intended to solve.

In terms of absolute bandwidth, the insertion rates are much lower than can be supported by the disk. It might thus seem that the network interface is the bottleneck, not the disk. As we shall see shortly, however, with multiple queries, disk accesses rapidly becomes a problem.

6.3 Querying the Archive

In this section, we present an experiment that measures the time taken for a *count(*)* query over the entire archive for the three OSCAR designs, and also the strawman. We repeat this test for different reduction levels to study the response of the different designs to overload. Figure 12 shows the results of the experiment.

The strawman uniformly takes around 20 seconds because it scans the same number of blocks irrespective of the reduction level. The size of each tuple is around 50 bytes; the strawman therefore runs near the peak 60MBps disk bandwidth available at the application level.

For each of the reduction levels, the first query on the OnReadModify stream (Lazy-1st read in plot) has the greatest cost of all the schemes. This is because it pays a write cost in addition to the read cost for all buffers it dirties. Thus, even at 99% reduction, the method continues to pay almost twice the cost of the strawman, since it dirties at least

356

one tuple in each page. On the second pass through the OnReadModify stream, the write cost does not have to be paid again, and the cost of this solution drops almost to that of the strawman. After the vacuuming has been performed, the copy is smaller than the original by a fraction equal to the reduction level. The cost of subsequent scans drop dramatically, by the same fraction.

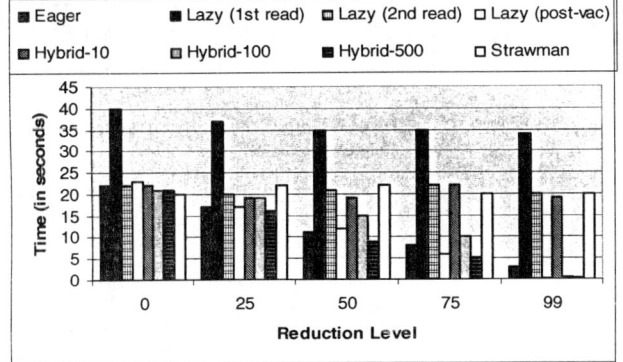

Figure 12: Query time for different reduction levels

The cost of the query for the OnWriteReplicate design drops with the reduction level. It is slightly more expensive than the post-vacuuming version of OnReadModify, since the method can only reduce I/Os according to the granularities of the pre-stored copies.

The different hybrid alternatives offer the most interesting results. Based on the earlier theoretical analysis, we would expect all the hybrid solutions to have improving query times as the reduction level increases. This improvement is, however, always realized only for the hybrid design with run-length of 500. For some of the reduction levels, Hybrid-100 also shows improvement in performance. Hybrid-10, however, is never better than the strawman. The reason for this has to do with the pre-fetching and buffering in the file system. For the hybrid design with run-length 10, and for low reduction levels for Hybrid-100, the blocks that are read are so close on disk that the file-system ends up performing a sequential read, instead of only picking exactly the required blocks. As a result, in these cases, the hybrid solution performs no better than the strawman.

6.4 Putting Insertions and Queries together

In this section, we test our central hypothesis that disk accesses have a significant impact on the insertion process in a hybrid stream query processor.

To conduct this test, we measure the time taken to insert 20 million tuples into a stream in the presence of simultaneous *count(*)* queries over N other streams which each have previously had 20 million tuples inserted into them. We then vary N to measure the effect of an increasing number of simultaneous queries. Since query rates are much higher than insertion rates (see Sections 6.2 and 6.3), the queries complete much before the insertions are completed. To maintain a constant number of simultaneous queries we start a new query on a stream, once the previous one completes.

Measuring the insertion rate by itself, however, does not tell us anything, since the insertion-performance can be artificially inflated if the queries are not scheduled at all. Therefore, for each of the above readings, we also measure the corresponding number of queries that are completed in the time it took to insert the 20 M tuples.

Figures 13 through 16 show these measurements for 25% and 75% reduction (we also measured these values for reduction levels of 0%, 50% and 99%; the trends are similar). Figures 13 and 15 show the insertion time and the total queries completed in that time for varying number of simultaneous queries, for 25% reduction. Figure 14 and 16 show the corresponding figures for 75% reduction.

Let us first analyze Figures 13 and 15. In the absence of any archived queries, the strawman can populate the stream in about 430 seconds. As we increase the number of queries, the insertion-time increases, but once we reach 3 archived queries, it stabilizes at around 1500 seconds. Looking at the corresponding numbers in Figure 15, we see that the total number of completed queries increases from 13 for a single query to about 25 for two queries, and then stabilizes at around 30. This number does not increase, or decrease significantly with increasing number of simultaneous queries.

This pattern is also observed for all the OSCAR designs. This curious phenomenon is explained by looking at the disk-elevator algorithm used by the system. The algorithm sets separate latency limits for reads and writes. This means that hybrid queries cannot affect the write process beyond a certain limit. Initially, the insertion process is not disk-bound (see Section 6.2). With increasing number of queries, however, the disk bandwidth available to the insertion process reduces, reducing its performance. However, once the disk subsystem is saturated for reads, the write process cannot be affected further. Therefore, the write throughput stays constant after a certain number of simultaneous queries. Further, since the same read bandwidth has to be shared amongst the concurrent queries, no matter how many of them there are, the total number of completed queries also stays fixed.

Figures 13 and 15, however, also suggest that for the strawman, if the total number of simultaneous queries is increased past the early-thirties, the system cannot run them at the rate of data arrival. This is because with all queries running at the same rate, no single query will actually be able to reach completion in the time it takes to insert the 20 M tuples. This therefore represents a bound on the number of simultaneous hybrid queries in system before it starts to fall behind.

The OnReadModify stream ('Lazy' in the figures) performs marginally poorer than the strawman solution prior to vacuuming, both with respect to the insertion times and the number of completed scans. This is because the sizes of the tuples are larger than in the other solutions, as explained in Section 6.1.1. The real savings with this mechanism kicks in after the stream has been vacuumed. The size of the archive is reduced by a quarter and the total number of completed scans increases correspondingly. Since the overhead of the network interface is amortized between the original and the new copy, the write performance for the lazy solution is largely unaffected from the pre-vacuum version.

The OnWriteReplicate method ('Eager') has higher insertion times than the others, as expected. But again, the cost of the extra writes is sub-linear in the size of the stream, and the increase in insertion time is not significant. The number of completed queries is almost as good as the post-

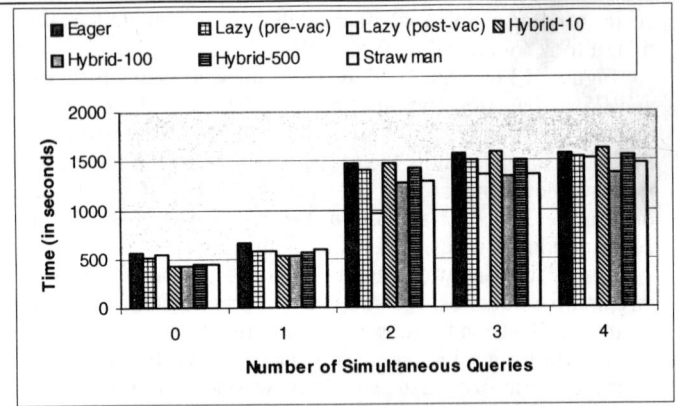

Figure 13: Insertion time for 20M tuples, 25% reduction

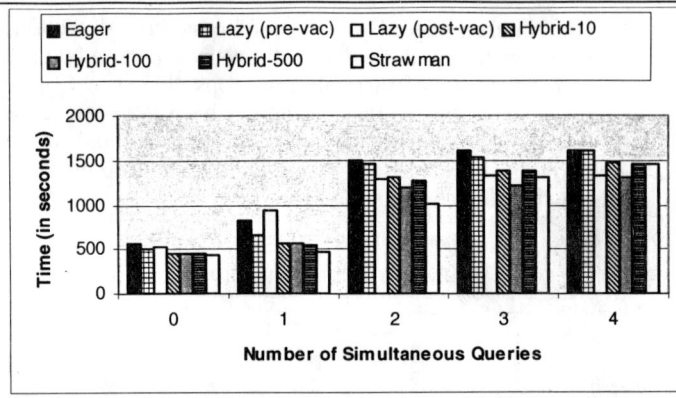

Figure 14: Insertion time for 20M tuples, 75% reduction

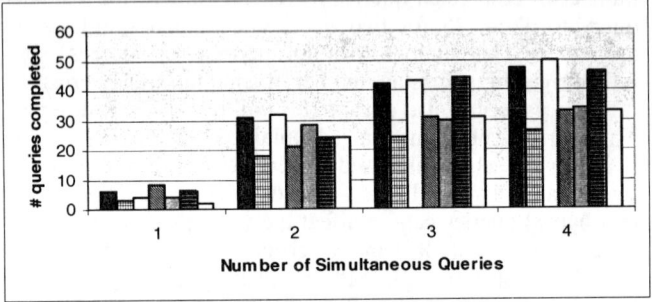

Figure 15: #queries completed within 20M tuples insertion, 25% reduction

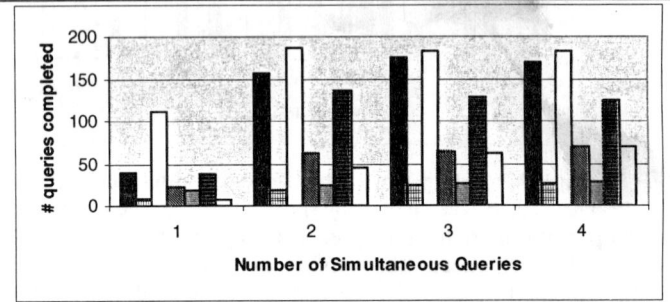

Figure 16: #queries completed within 20M tuples insertion, 75% reduction

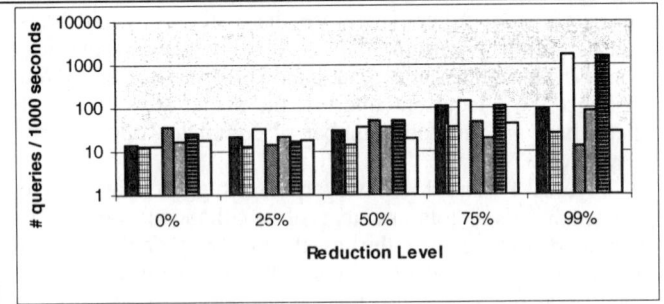

Figure 17: Queries completed/1000 sec, 2 simultaneous queries

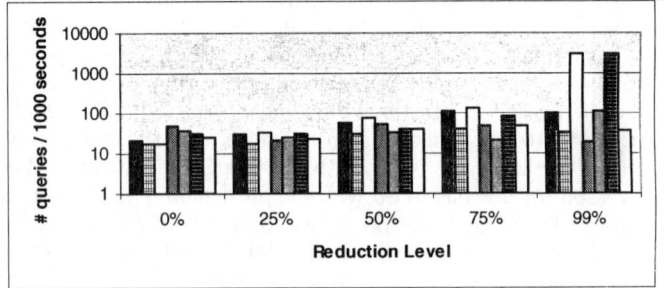

Figure 18: Queries completed/1000 sec, 4 simultaneous queries

vacuumed lazy solution. It is slightly lower, since this solution can only offer performance improvement in steps according to the reduction levels of its pre-stored copies.

All the hybrid solutions have insert performance approximately as good as the strawman. At query time, however, the hybrid solutions display interesting behavior. As explained in Section 6.3, at 25% reduction, Hybrid-10 and Hybrid-100 are essentially performing sequential scans because of pre-fetching and buffering by the file system. Their performance numbers are therefore similar to the strawman. Hybrid-500 on the other hand, does save some physical I/Os, leading to higher queries completed.

Now, let us look at Figures 14 and 16. These show the insertion-time and number of queries completed in the meanwhile, for 75% reduction. The insertion rates in Figure 14 are largely the same as in Figure 13 because of the above-mentioned effect of the disk scheduler. In Figure 16 (note that the scale is different from Figure 14), the number of completed queries increases only slightly for the straw-

man, since its actions are independent of the reduction level. The slight increase corresponds to the available bandwidth till the disk saturates. The same is true for the OnReadModify solution.

The post-vacuum version of OnReadModify, and OnWriteReplicate have significantly higher completed queries than in Figure 14 because of the greater reduction level. Of the two, the eager version is slightly better since it tracks the reduction level exactly, while the eager solution only offers reduction at preset rates.

As before, the hybrid design offers the most interesting results. At 75% reduction, the hybrid-10 continues to perform sequential scan (since it still reads 3 out of every 10 contiguous blocks). Hybrid-100 is, however, reading fewer blocks now. Instead of showing improved performance, the number of completed queries actually decreases. The reason for this lies with the OS process scheduler. When the OS guesses that a query is not performing sequential I/O (in our system this happens if two blocks that are accessed consecutively are more than 8 blocks apart), it gets scheduled less often. The number of physical I/Os saved by Hybrid-100 is not sufficient to overcome this scheduling bias. Hybrid-500, however, does save enough physical I/Os (since it skips 375 blocks at a time) and has more completed queries as compared to the 25% reduction.

We also ran the above tests for reduction levels of 0%, 50%, and 99%. Figures 17 and 18 (note the log-scale on the y-axis) give a flavor of the results, showing the number of queries completed per 1000 seconds for the different reduction levels. The eager solution stops providing improved performance once the reduction level is less than its smallest copy. The lazy solution and Hybrid-500 continue to support more queries with greater reduction levels.

6.5 Summary of Results

In this section, we summarize the results of our performance study. The behavior of the file-system prevents us from directly proving our central hypothesis that the processing of live data suffers with increasing number of hybrid live/historical queries. On the other hand, the results shown in Figures 15 through 18 demonstrate the performance benefits of the different OSCAR designs for hybrid queries in the presence of overload.

The strawman, which samples only in the executor, has excellent write performance, but does poorly when overloaded. Among the OSCAR designs, the hybrid solution offers the most benefit. It has low write costs and offers excellent I/O savings with different reduction levels provided the run-length is suitably large to prevent interference from the file-system and OS process scheduler. The lazy approach has even better response to overload than the hybrid solution, but only after it is vacuumed. The eager solution performs well as long as the desired reduction levels are close to those of the pre-stored copies.

These performance results underscore an additional important point: the OS kernel and its various policies have a tremendous effect on the benefits, or lack thereof, of storage level solutions. For example, pre-fetching and buffering in the file system and the OS process scheduler cause our hybrid OSCAR design to show widely different behavior depending on the size of the runs. On a more global level, the disk scheduling algorithm on the platform we used for our experiments limited the interference between read and write accesses to disk.

7. Future Work

There is much interesting work to be done in the area of supporting hybrid stream queries. One avenue for further work in the area of overload handling is the extension of the framework presented in this paper to include more classes of data reduction. Another is to provide overload handling for index access methods just as OSCAR does for scan-based disk access. We are currently engaged in studying a framework for making run-time decisions as to which indexes are updated on data-arrival, and handling the resulting "holes" in other indexes that do not get built. Other challenges involving hybrid query include intelligent buffer management that can exploit the predictable access patterns of long-running windowed queries. Finally, current techniques [20,21,5] for shared computation of stream queries rely on all queries processing the same tuple at the same time. This is not possible for hybrid queries that access different portions of the archive; a new soluton is therefore needed.

8. Conclusion

Random disk accesses in a DSMS that processes hybrid queries can have a detrimental effect on the performance of a system. Under sufficiently high load, the system might fall further and further behind in its processing of the stream. We therefore propose that such systems should support means to deliver reduced versions of historical data to these queries to ease the disk load on the system. In this paper we propose the *Overload-sensitive Stream Capture and Data Reduction (OSCAR)* access method to achieve this. We discuss different designs of OSCAR to handle data reduction based on random sampling and windowed aggregation. We describe its implementation in TelegraphCQ for doing this, and present experimental results validating our thesis.

9. References

[1] Carney et al., "Monitoring Streams - A New Class of Data Management Applications", In VLDB 2002

[2] Madden et al. "Continuously Adaptive Continuous Queries", In SIGMOD 2002

[3] Motwani et al. "Query Processing, Approximation, and Resource Management in a Data Stream Management System". In CIDR 2003.

[4] Tatbul et al., "Load Shedding in a Data Stream Manager", In VLDB 2003.

[5] Chandrasekaran et al. "TelegraphCQ: Continuous Dataflow Processing for an Uncertain World". In CIDR 2003.

[6] TelegraphCQ source code: http://telegraph.cs.berkeley.edu/

[7] Judy Arrays sourceforge project: http://judy.sourceforge.net/

[8] Lazaridis I. and Mehrotra, S.. "Progressive Approximate Aggregate Queries with a multi-resoltion tree structure". In SIGMOD 2001.

[9] Roesenblum et al, "The Design and Implementation of a LogStructured File System", ACM TOCS 1991

[10] Manku and Motwani, "Approximate Frequency Counts over Data Streams", In VLDB 2002.

[11] Broniamann et al, "Efficient DR Methods for On-Line Association Rule Discovery".

[12] R. Read et al. A multi-resolution relational data model. VLDB 1992

[13] S. Chaudhuri and U. Dayal: An Overview of Data Warehousing and OLAP Technology. In SIGMOD Record (1): 65-74 (1997)

[14] L. Golab and M. T. Özsu: "Issues in data stream management". SIGMOD Record(2): 5-14 (2003)

[15] P. Muth et al.. "The LHAM Log-Structured History Data Access Method". VLDB J. 8(3-4): 199-221 (2000)

[16] M. Overmars: "The design of dynamic data structures". LNCS 1983

[17] Barbara et al. "The new jersey data reduction report". Data Engineering Bulletin, September 1996

[18] J M. Hellerstein, et al. Informix under CONTROL: Online Query Processing. Data Min. Knowl. Discov. 4(4): 281-314 (2000)

[19] V. Raman et al. Using State Modules for Adaptive Query Processing. In ICDE 2003.

[20] Chen et al. NiagaraCQ: A Scalable Continuous Query System for Internet Databases. In SIGMOD 2000.

[21] S. Chandrasekaran and M. Franklin. Streaming Queries over Streaming data. In VLDB 2002

WIC: A General-Purpose Algorithm for Monitoring Web Information Sources

Sandeep Pandey, Kedar Dhamdhere,[*] Christopher Olston

Carnegie Mellon University
Pittsburgh, PA 15213
{spandey, kedar, olston}@cs.cmu.edu

Abstract

The Web is becoming a universal information dissemination medium, due to a number of factors including its support for content dynamicity. A growing number of Web information providers post near real-time updates in domains such as auctions, stock markets, bulletin boards, news, weather, roadway conditions, sports scores, etc. External parties often wish to capture this information for a wide variety of purposes ranging from online data mining to automated synthesis of information from multiple sources. There has been a great deal of work on the design of systems that can process streams of data from Web sources, but little attention has been paid to how to produce these data streams, given that Web pages generally require "pull-based" access.

In this paper we introduce a new general-purpose algorithm for monitoring Web information sources, effectively converting pull-based sources into push-based ones. Our algorithm can be used in conjunction with continuous query systems that assume information is fed into the query engine in a push-based fashion. Ideally, a Web monitoring algorithm for this purpose should achieve two objectives: (1) timeliness and (2) completeness of information captured. However, we demonstrate both analytically and empirically using real-world data that these objectives are fundamentally at odds. When resources available for Web monitoring are limited, and the number of sources to monitor is large, it may be necessary to sacrifice some timeliness to achieve better completeness, or vice versa. To take this fact into account, our algorithm is highly parameterized and targets an application-specified balance between timeliness and completeness. In this paper we formalize the problem of optimizing for a flexible combination of timeliness and completeness, and prove that our parameterized algorithm is a 2-approximation in all cases, and in certain cases is optimal.

1 Introduction

The Web is becoming a universal medium for disseminating information of all kinds, including highly dynamic information. A significant amount of valuable dynamic information is being posted to the Web, and people want to access it. In many situations, direct manual viewing of dynamic Web pages is not an adequate mode of access for one or both of the following two reasons. First, most information posted on the Web is not made available forever, and may disappear or be replaced by new information at any time [5]. This aspect presents a challenge, especially for applications in which historical information is of interest. Second, many applications require automated synthesis of information from multiple dynamic Web sources [10].

As a result, there is significant interest in systems that monitor and process updates to frequently updated Web pages automatically. These systems perform a variety of information management functions including synthesis, archiving, and continuous query processing. Web-based continuous query (CQ) processing systems proposed in the literature include CONQUER [9], Niagara [10], OpenCQ [7] and WebCQ [8].

The main focus of this work has been on language design and efficient query processing, and the crucial issue of how to capture information from dynamically changing Web pages has largely been ignored. Most work on continuous query processing assumes that data is "pushed" into the query engine in the form of *data streams*. However, generally speaking, Web data must be "pulled," *i.e.*, continuous query systems must explicitly download Web pages, check for changes, and submit any resulting new data to the query processor.

So far, only heuristics with no formal guarantees on effectiveness have been proposed for converting pull-

---

[*] Supported by NSF ITR grants CCR-0085982 and CCR-0122581.

Permission to copy without fee all or part of this material is granted provided that the copies are not made or distributed for direct commercial advantage, the VLDB copyright notice and the title of the publication and its date appear, and notice is given that copying is by permission of the Very Large Data Base Endowment. To copy otherwise, or to republish, requires a fee and/or special permission from the Endowment.

**Proceedings of the 30th VLDB Conference,
Toronto, Canada, 2004**

oriented Web sources into push-oriented data streams. The designers of Niagara [10] and other CQ systems for the Web have suggested that simple periodic polling be used for this purpose. However, periodic polling breaks down in the presence of a large number of frequently-updated Web sources, when resources become inadequate for polling all Web pages at a fast rate. The work in [13] was the first to study ways to improve upon simple periodic polling, but the algorithm proposed in [13], called CAM, has a number of serious drawbacks: (1) CAM is only suitable for a narrow range of applications in which timeliness of information captured is of utmost importance, whereas many real-life applications must balance timeliness with completeness, a serious issue we discuss shortly, (2) even for the specialized set of applications handled by CAM, there is no formal guarantee that CAM performs well at capturing information, and (3) CAM relies on a computationally intensive, offline algorithm to schedule monitoring.

In this paper we introduce a new general-purpose Web monitoring algorithm called the *Web Information Collector* (WIC), which is suitable for use in conjunction with a variety of CQ systems. WIC has the following desirable properties: (1) it handles a wide range of application scenarios, (2) it provably performs within a factor of two of the optimal offline Web monitoring algorithm in all cases, and (3) it is highly efficient and executes in an online fashion, making it practical for real-world use.

1.1 Web Monitoring Objectives

In continuous Web monitoring applications, it is usually desirable to capture as much information as possible, with as little delay as possible. Dynamic Web pages undergo updates over time, and each updated version of the page potentially contains new information of value to the application. Therefore, an ideal Web monitoring system would capture every change to each page of interest, immediately following the update that causes the change.

Unfortunately, this ideal situation is often difficult to achieve in practice. Due to the nature of Web protocols, obtaining updates to Web pages generally requires polling those pages. For applications that monitor a large number of Web pages, high-frequency polling and processing of all pages of interest can be prohibitively expensive. Typically it is not feasible or desirable to provision systems with adequate communication bandwidth and processing power to support exhaustive and rapid polling of a large number of Web pages.[1]

As a result, polling must be performed selectively, and some criteria for deciding when to poll each page must be established. Although it may not be possible to capture all changes to all pages of interest in a timely fashion due to resource limitations, it is generally desirable to come as

---

[1]While processing of unchanged pages may be avoided using fast checksum comparisons or by outfitting HTTP requests with an "if-modified-since" qualifier, such techniques are usually ineffective in the presence of frequently changing superficial content such as advertisements, counters, etc.

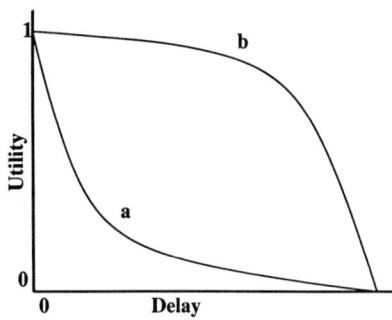

Figure 1: Urgency functions.

close as possible to that ideal. Hence, scheduling polling of pages for Web monitoring can be viewed as a constrained optimization problem with two objectives:

1. **Completeness:** Maximize the number of changes captured.

2. **Timeliness:** Minimize the delay in capturing changes.

In certain cases these two objectives are at odds with each other. We illustrate this property through a very simple example. Suppose we wish to capture changes to a single Web page that is updated in such a way that new information is always appended (thus, information is never removed from the page). Given a single opportunity to download a snapshot of this page, we are clearly faced with a tradeoff between timeliness and completeness. If we download the page early, we will only capture a few changes, but with little delay. Conversely, if we wait a long time before downloading the page, we may capture more changes, but there will be a high delay, on average, between the time at which a change occurs and the time at which it is captured.

When facing resource-constrained situations, the appropriate balance to strike between timeliness and completeness depends on the application. Applications that need to react rapidly to new information, such as stock market day-trading programs, may value timeliness over completeness when both cannot be had. On the other hand, applications whose purpose is to compile historical archives for offline querying may opt for completeness.

To accommodate a diverse variety of applications with differing requirements, we introduce a flexible method of specifying the relative importance of timeliness and completeness: application designers supply a function $urgency : \mathcal{Z}^+ \to [0, 1]$ specifying the *utility* of a captured change as a function of the delay between the occurrence of the change and the time of capture. Example urgency functions are illustrated in Figure 1. For applications in which timeliness is critical, an urgency function with steep downward slope, such as function a in Figure 1, should be used. Conversely, for applications that value completeness over timeliness, a more gradually decreasing function such as function b is more appropriate.

In this paper we formalize our notions of timeliness, completeness, and utility, and provide both analytical and empirical evidence of the existence of a tradeoff between

Changes append information Timeliness is not critical	Changes overwrite information Timeliness is not critical
Example: Creating and maintaining a searchable resume database	*Example:* Collecting "front-page" news stories for long term archival
Changes append information **Timeliness is critical**	**Changes overwrite information** **Timeliness is critical**
Example: Capturing new Internet security bulletins, health risk alerts etc. for selective automatic dissemination within an organization	*Example:* Reacting in real-time to stock market price fluctuations, or online auction maximum bid increases

Figure 2: Extreme scenarios.

timeliness and completeness. We formulate the problem of scheduling polling of remote Web pages as an optimization problem whose objective is to maximize utility under the constraint of limited resources available for polling. Our formulation is parameterized by an application-dictated urgency function, allowing the solution to be customized to the needs of specific applications. Of course, the appropriate polling schedule also depends heavily on the way in which the Web pages being monitored change over time, discussed next.

1.2 Modeling Changes to Web Pages

We define a *change* to a Web page as an update that causes information of value to the application to be added to the page. The information added during a change to a page may not remain on the page forever. For example, typical financial reporting sites only display the most recent news reports. Similarly, some online auction sites only show the most recent bids. To model this fact, we assume a certain *lifetime* of information, which may vary among pages and by application. Lifetime indicates the probability that information made available by a change at time t is removed at any future time $t + x$.

It is instructive to consider the two extreme possibilities for lifetime. First, on long-lived, append-only pages, the lifetime of information is essentially infinite. In the opposite extreme, some pages are updated such that each change overwrites the information presented by the previous change completely. In the case of complete overwrites, the lifetime of information made available due to a given change extends only to the time of the subsequent change.

Figure 2 provides examples of application scenarios that can roughly be categorized into each of these two extremes in terms of information lifetime. The applications are also categorized based on the orthogonal dimension of whether timeliness is critical (see Section 1.1), resulting in four extreme categories overall. The flexibility of our formulation

makes it suitable for a large variety of Web monitoring applications. The only previous approach we are aware of, CAM [13], only handles applications that fit into the shaded region of Figure 2.

It is important to note that our classification of applications into quadrants in Figure 2 is very rough, and variants of these applications may fit more or less well into their assigned category (which represent extremes in terms of information lifetime and criticality of delay). Our approach accommodates this fact, and can handle applications falling in between these extreme categories since our urgency and lifetime specifications are highly adjustable, as we shall see later in the paper.

1.3 Contributions

The specific contributions of this paper are as follows:

- We formalize the scheduling problem in Web monitoring as a parameterized optimization problem.

- We demonstrate that there exists a fundamental trade-off between timeliness and completeness, which makes our parameterized formulation necessary.

- We present an efficient, online Web monitoring algorithm that meets the needs of all applications encompassed by Figure 2.

- We prove that our algorithm is a 2-approximation for all cases, and is optimal for the shaded region of Figure 2.

1.4 Outline

The remainder of this paper is organized as follows. In Section 2 we formalize the scheduling problem in Web monitoring as a parameterized optimization problem. We present an efficient, online algorithm and prove that it is a 2-approximation for our Web monitoring scheduling problem in Section 3. Then, in Section 4 we show analytically that, when resources are limited, a fundamental tradeoff exists between timeliness and completeness. In Section 5 we report the results of extensive experiments on real-world data. We confirm that a tradeoff does exist between timeliness and completeness, and that our urgency parameter enables application designers to control that tradeoff.

2 Monitoring the Web: Models and Assumptions

Our models for the Web monitoring scheduling problem and the way in which Web pages change extend the framework introduced in [13, 14]. Let $\mathcal{P}$ be the set of Web pages under consideration for monitoring. Each page $P_i \in \mathcal{P}$ has an associated *importance weight* $W_i \in [0, 1]$, denoting the relative importance of capturing changes to P_i. Time is divided into discrete time instants, and monitoring is performed in epochs of N consecutive time instants. $\mathcal{T}$ denotes the sequence of time instants $T_1, T_2, \ldots, T_N$ in an epoch.

We focus on the problem of scheduling monitoring of the pages in $\mathcal{P}$ during a single epoch. Monitoring a page includes the duties of fetching the page from its remote source, determining whether it has undergone one or more changes of interest and, if so, processing the change(s) and propagating them to the target application. We assume the cost of monitoring a page to be uniform across all pages and across time. This simplification is based on the assumption that the fixed overhead for the operations required (*i.e.*, polling, downloading, and processing a page) is the dominant factor, which is consistent with the assumption made in most work on Web crawling, *e.g.*, [2, 14].

Let C denote the maximum number of pages that can be monitored in a single time instant. The value of C depends on the availability of resources for monitoring, including CPU cycles, communication bandwidth, etc. If C equals or exceeds the number of pages, $|\mathcal{P}|$, then the scheduling problem is trivial: simply monitor each page at every instant. In practice, however, we expect that C may be much less than $|\mathcal{P}|$, making careful scheduling a requirement. A legal *monitoring schedule* for an epoch is one that performs at most C monitorings of pages during each time instant $T_1, T_2, \ldots, T_N$. A monitoring schedule $S = \{s_{1,1}, s_{1,2} \ldots s_{1,N}, s_{2,1}, s_{2,2} \ldots s_{|\mathcal{P}|,N}\}$ consists of a set of Boolean variables $s_{i,j} \in \{0,1\}$, where $s_{i,j} = 1$ iff page $P_i \in \mathcal{P}$ is scheduled to be monitored at time instant T_j, and $s_{i,j} = 0$ otherwise.

For convenience, a summary of the symbols used in this paper is provided in Table 1. Some of these symbols are not introduced until later in the paper, and should be ignored for now.

2.1 Nature of Changes

A *change* to a page is defined to be an update that causes information of value to the application to be added to the page. We assume that the information presented with each change to a particular page carries equal value, or importance.[2] However, we do not assume that all pages are equally valuable to monitor. For example, in financial monitoring applications, pages providing periodic earnings reports may be of significantly higher importance for certain purposes than those displaying stock prices, even though stock prices are typically updated much more frequently. To model this fact we allow custom importance weights to be associated with each page, as stated above.

As discussed in Section 1.2, we model information posted to Web pages as having an associated lifetime. Let $life_i(j, k)$ denote the probability that information made available by a change at time T_j to page P_i remains available at time T_k. (It is assumed that $1 \leq j \leq k \leq N$.) We assume that life is a monotonically nonincreasing function of $k - j$. Our life function can be used to model a variety of common Web page update patterns ranging from ones in which changes strictly append information to ones

---
[2]While our model can be extended to enable differentiation among changes in terms of importance, we believe that even with this restriction it is adequate to capture the basic properties of most applications.

Notation	Definition
$\mathcal{P}$	Set of pages that are considered for monitoring. Variable i is used for iterating over this set.
$\mathcal{T}$	Sequence of time instants $\{T_1, T_2, \ldots, T_N\}$ in an epoch. Variables j, k, q and z are used for iterating over this set.
C	Maximum number of monitorings allowed in each time instant.
$urgency_i$	A function to model the value of information of page P_i as a function of timeliness. $urgency(0)$ is always assumed to equal 1.
$life_i$	A function to model the decay of existence of information on page P_i with time.
$\pi_{i,j}$	The estimated probability that the page P_i is updated at time instant T_j.
$s_{i,j}^x$	A decision variable, set to 1 if page P_i is monitored at time instant T_j by algorithm x (o for OPTIMAL algorithm and g for WIC algorithm), and 0 otherwise. For notational convenience, we define $s_{i,0}^x = 0$.
S^x	A monitoring schedule that consists of a set of Boolean variables $s_{i,j}^x$, where $s_{i,j}^x = 1$ iff page $P_i \in \mathcal{P}$ is scheduled to be monitored at time T_j by algorithm $x \in \{o, g\}$, and $s_{i,j}^x = 0$ otherwise.
$prev_{i,j}^x$	The most recent time instant before T_j at which page P_i was monitored by algorithm $x \in \{o, g\}$. $prev_{i,j}^x$ is 0 if the page is never monitored before time T_j by algorithm x. Mathematically, $prev_{i,j}^x = max\{j' : 1 \leq j' < j \wedge s_{i,j'}^x = 1\}$.
$seq_i^x(j, k)$	The sequence of time instants in the open interval (j, k) at which page P_i is monitored by algorithm x. Mathematically, $seq_i^x(j, k) = \{j' : j < j' < k \wedge s_{i,j'}^x = 1\}$.
seq_i^x	For convenience, we refer to $seq_i^x(0, N+1)$ as seq_i^x. We use $seq_i^x(k)$ to refer to the kth element of the sequence. $seq_i^x(0)$ is defined to be 0. Also, $seq^x = \cup_{i \in \mathcal{P}}(seq_i^x)$.

Table 1: Summary of symbols and their meanings.

in which all changes overwrite information supplied by previous changes, and covering situations in between. We supply some examples later in Section 2.3.

We assume that each page $P_i \in \mathcal{P}$ has an associated probability of change $\pi_{i,j} \in [0,1]$ at each time instant $T_j \in \mathcal{T}$ that has been estimated in advance. This so-called *quasi-deterministic* model of change probability has been shown to be appropriate for modeling frequently updated Web pages [11, 14]. The problem of assigning probabilities of change to Web pages is beyond the scope of this paper. We demonstrate in Section 5.2 that our approach is tolerant of a moderate degree of inaccuracy in the estimated change probabilities.

2.2 Web Monitoring Objective

Given a life parameter $life_i()$ and change probabilities $\pi_{i,*}$ for each page $P_i \in \mathcal{P}$, we can compute the expected number of changes captured by monitoring P_i at a particular time instant T_j. For any prior time instant T_k, $1 \leq k \leq j$, the probability that a change occurred at time T_k and can still be captured at time T_j is $\pi_{i,k} \cdot life_i(k,j)$. Suppose for the moment that the first monitoring of P_i during the epoch occurs at time T_j. Summing over all time instants in the epoch up to T_j we obtain:

$$\sum_{k=1}^{j} \left(\pi_{i,k} \cdot life_i(k,j) \right)$$

Now, consider a monitoring schedule S, which consists of a set of Boolean variables $s_{i,j}$ giving monitoring times for each of the pages in $\mathcal{P}$ during the epoch. The expected total number of changes captured by S from all pages during the epoch is given by:

$$\sum_{P_i \in \mathcal{P}} \sum_{j=1}^{N} \left(s_{i,j} \cdot \sum_{k=prev_{i,j}+1}^{j} \pi_{i,k} \cdot life_i(k,j) \right)$$

where $prev_{i,j}$ denotes the index of the most recent time instant prior to T_j at which page P_i was monitored.

Not all captured changes may be of equal value to an application. Instead, each page P_i has an associated importance weight $W_i \in [0,1]$. Furthermore, recall from Section 1.1 that an application-specific *urgency* function $urgency_i : \mathcal{Z}^+ \to [0,1]$ may be associated with each page P_i. Together, W_i and P_i specify the *utility* of a captured change in P_i as a function of the delay between the occurrence of the change and the time of capture. In particular, if a change in P_i occurs at time T_k, and is captured later at time T_j, $j > k$, then the utility of capturing that change is $W_i \cdot urgency_i(j-k)$. Note that $W_i \cdot urgency_i(j-k) \leq W_i \leq 1$. If a change is captured during the same instant in which it occurred, i.e., at time T_k, then the utility of capturing the change is $W_i \cdot urgency_i(0)$. We require that $urgency_i(0) = 1$, so the utility of capturing a change to P_i immediately is W_i.

The expected total utility U accrued by executing monitoring schedule S in the epoch is given by:

$$U = \sum_{P_i \in \mathcal{P}} \sum_{j=1}^{N} \left(s_{i,j} \sum_{k=prev_{i,j}+1}^{j} W_i \cdot urgency_i(j-k) \cdot \pi_{i,k} \cdot life_i(k,j) \right)$$

The objective when selecting a monitoring schedule is to maximize U.

2.3 Life and Urgency Parameters

Note that life and urgency are tuning parameters in the above objective function. Life is used to model different Web page change behaviors, while urgency can be tuned according to application requirements in terms of timeliness and completeness. Below are some examples of how life and urgency can be set in order to model various data and application scenarios that arise in practice.

- $life(k,j)$, for $k \leq j$:

  1. **Unbounded-Append:** All changes are of an append-only nature and information is never deleted:
  $$life_i(k,j) = 1.$$

  2. **Time-window–Append(W):** Changes append new information, and old information is removed after W time instants:
  $$life_i(k,j) = \begin{cases} 1 & \text{if } j - k \leq W \\ 0 & \text{otherwise} \end{cases}$$

  3. **Change-window–Append(Z):** Changes append new information, and old information is removed after Z subsequent changes occur. In general, it is difficult to write a concise formula for this scenario. For the special case in which the change probability for page P_i has the same value π_i at all time instants, it can be written as:
  $$life_i(k,j) = \sum_{q=0}^{Z-1} \binom{j-k}{q} \pi_i^q (1-\pi_i)^{N-1-q}$$

  4. **Overwrite:** Each change completely obliterates all information made available by previous changes:
  $$life_i(k,j) = \prod_{q=k+1}^{j} (1 - \pi_{i,q})$$

- $urgency(t)$, for $t \geq 0$:

  1. **Uniform:** Utility is independent of delay:
  $$urgency(t) = 1$$

  2. **Exponential Decay(r):** For a decay parameter $r \in [0,1]$:
  $$urgency(t) = r^t$$

  3. **Sliding Window(W):** For a window size parameter $W \geq 0$:
  $$urgency(t) = \begin{cases} 1 & \text{if } t \leq W \\ 0 & \text{otherwise} \end{cases}$$

Other decay functions may also be used to specify urgency, such as polynomial decay, polyexponential decay, and chordal decay (see [3]).

Figure 3 shows how our life and urgency parameters should be set in order to model the extreme data and application scenarios represented in Figure 2.

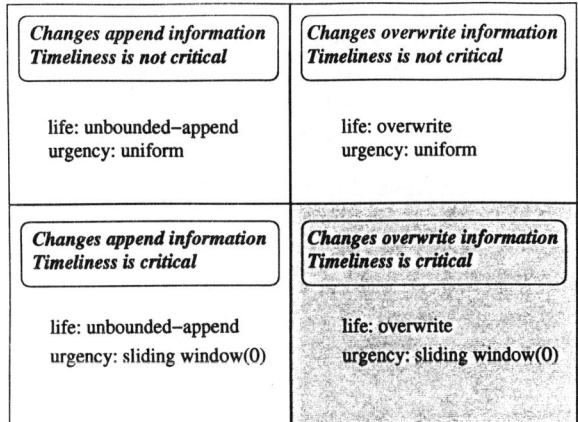

Figure 3: Life and urgency under various scenarios.

Relaxed versions of these extreme life and urgency settings, such as the windowed and exponentially decaying functions outlined above, can be used to accommodate applications falling in between these extreme scenarios. For example, some online auction sites display a sliding window of recent bids for each item, which can be modeled using Time-window–Append or Change-window–Append for *life*. Auction monitoring applications needing access to bid histories up to the last hour may specify urgency as Sliding-window(1 hour).

We note that the RIR objective presented in [13] assumes that any nonzero delay in capturing changes is unacceptable and that changes in the target pages are fully overwritten, which corresponds to the shaded region of Figure 3. Hence, by setting life and urgency to Overwrite and Sliding-window(0), respectively, our utility objective is equivalent to RIR as a special case.

3 General-Purpose Web Monitoring Algorithm

In selecting a monitoring schedule S we are faced with the optimization problem of choosing values for the boolean variables $s_{i,j}$, $P_i \in \mathcal{P}$, $T_j \in \mathcal{T}$ so that the total utility U is maximized, given a constraint C on the number of monitorings allowed at each time instant. To simplify exposition in this and subsequent sections, we define a function $g_i : \mathcal{Z}^+ \times \mathcal{Z}^+ \to \mathbb{R}$ for page P_i as:

$$g_i(j_1, j_2) = W_i \sum_{k=j_1+1}^{j_2} \left(urgency_i(j_2-k) \cdot \pi_{i,k} \cdot life_i(k, j_2) \right)$$

This quantity represents the utility accrued by monitoring page P_i at time T_{j_2}, assuming that the most recent monitoring of P_i occurred at T_{j_1}, $j_1 < j_2$.

We can express our optimization problem in terms of g_i as follows:

$$\text{maximize} \sum_{P_i \in \mathcal{P}} \sum_{j=1}^{N} s_{i,j} \cdot g_i(prev_{i,j}, j)$$

subject to the resource constraint:

$$\forall j, \sum_{P_i \in \mathcal{P}} s_{i,j} \leq C$$

where $s_{i,j} \in \{0, 1\}$.

3.1 Optimal Offline Algorithm

This problem can be formulated as a nonserial constrained optimization problem, and solved using nonserial dynamic programming [1]. The running time complexity of nonserial dynamic programs depends on the interaction among decision variables [1, 6]. It turns out that in our problem the decision variables (*i.e.*, $s_{i,j}$ variables) are highly intertwined, so the optimal dynamic programming algorithm is likely to be too expensive for large-scale applications.

We address this issue by proposing a greedy algorithm that serves as a 2-approximation and runs in time linear in the number of decision variables, *i.e.*, $O(|\mathcal{P}| \cdot |\mathcal{T}|)$.

3.2 Efficient Online Algorithm

We present the following greedy algorithm for scheduling monitoring of dynamic Web pages, which we call *WIC* for "Web Information Collector":

Algorithm 1 *(WIC)*:

1. For all pages $P_i \in \mathcal{P}$ and time instants $T_j \in \mathcal{T}$:

   Initialize $s_{i,j} \leftarrow 0$.

2. *For $j = 1$ to N:*

   For each $P_i \in \mathcal{P}$ let $u_i = g_i(prev_{i,j}, j)$.

   Let $\mathcal{L}$ contain the pages P_i with the top C values of u_i.

   For each $P_i \in \mathcal{L}$ set $s_{i,j} = 1$.

   For each P_i,
   if $P_i \in \mathcal{L}$,
       set $prev_{i,j+1} = j$
   else,
       set $prev_{i,j+1} = prev_{i,j}$

Recall that $g_i(prev_{i,j}, j)$ denotes the utility accrued by monitoring page P_i on instant T_j. Since at each instant the above algorithm monitors those pages which offer maximum current utility, it operates in a greedy manner. WIC maximizes utility locally, at each time instant, but does not necessarily maximize overall utility accrued during the entire epoch.

We now examine the running-time complexity of WIC, which depends on the nature of the life and urgency parameters. For all example settings of life and urgency outlined in Section 2.3 except for life = Change-window–Append, the value of $g_i(prev_{i,j}, j)$ can be computed in constant time from its value in the previous time instant,

$g_i(prev_{i,j-1}, j-1)$, and $\pi_{i,j}$. In those cases the running time of WIC is linear in the number of decision variables, i.e., $O(|\mathcal{P}| \cdot |\mathcal{T}|)$.

WIC can be executed in an *online* fashion, meaning that the values of decision variables $s_{*,j}$ are assigned immediately prior to time T_j. Therefore, it is compatible with algorithms for estimating change probabilities at the "last minute," i.e., ones that assign change probability estimates $\pi_{*,j}$ as late as time T_{j-1}. When executed in an online fashion, WIC requires only $O(|\mathcal{P}|)$ computations per time instant.

3.3 WIC is a 2-Approximation

We show that for monotonic urgency functions WIC is a 2-approximation algorithm for the optimization problem formulated above. Let S^g denote the schedule selected by WIC and S^o denote an optimal schedule. Our claim is that the expected total utility accrued by S^g is not less than half of that accrued by S^o. Mathematically, our claim is:

$$\sum_{P_i \in \mathcal{P}} \sum_{j=1}^{N} s_{i,j}^o \cdot g_i(prev_{i,j}^o, j) \leq$$
$$(1+a) \cdot \sum_{P_i \in \mathcal{P}} \sum_{j=1}^{N} s_{i,j}^g \cdot g_i(prev_{i,j}^g, j)$$

where the superscripts "g" and "o" denote aspects of S^g and S^o, respectively, and a depends on urgency as follows:

$$a = \max_i \max_t \left(\frac{urgency_i(t+1)}{urgency_i(t)} \right)$$

If *urgency* is a monotonically nonincreasing function, $0 \leq a \leq 1$ and this inequality implies that WIC is a 2-approximation.

Our complete formal proof is rather involved, and is given in the extended technical report version of this paper [12]. Here we present the main idea behind our proof, focusing on the special case of $C = 1$ for simplicity.

We begin by stating a simple property of WIC that follows from its construction:

$$s_{i,j}^g = 1 \implies \forall P_{i'} \in \mathcal{P}, g_i(prev_{i,j}^g, j) \geq g_{i'}(prev_{i',j}^g, j) \quad (1)$$

Suppose that at a certain time instant T_j, in the schedule selected by WIC, S^g, page $P_{i'}$ is monitored, and in S^o page $P_{i''}$ is monitored, where $P_{i'}$ and $P_{i''}$ may be the same or different. Consider two cases:

- $P_{i''}$ is not monitored in S^g at any time T_k, $1 \leq k \leq j$: In this case the WIC and optimal schedules for $P_{i''}$ are as follows (* denotes either 0 or 1):

Time Instant	T_1	T_2	.	.	.	T_{j-1}	T_j
$s_{i'',j}^o$	*	*	*	*	*	*	1
$s_{i'',j}^g$	0	0	0	0	0	0	*

$prev_{i'',j}^g = 0$, so it must be the case that $prev_{i'',j}^g \leq prev_{i'',j}^o$. By Lemma 1 in [12], this fact implies $g_{i''}(prev_{i'',j}^o, j) \leq g_{i''}(prev_{i'',j}^g, j)$. Combining this result with Equation 1, which states that $g_{i''}(prev_{i'',j}^g, j) \leq g_{i'}(prev_{i',j}^g, j)$, we obtain:

$$g_{i''}(prev_{i'',j}^o, j) \leq g_{i'}(prev_{i',j}^g, j)$$

which means that the utility accrued by S^o at time T_j is not greater than the utility accrued by S^g.

- $P_{i''}$ is monitored in S^g at some time T_k, $1 \leq k \leq j$: In this case the WIC and optimal schedules for $P_{i''}$ may look as follows, for example:

Time Instant	T_1	T_2	.	.	.	T_{j-1}	T_j
$s_{i'',j}^o$	*	*	*	*	*	*	1
$s_{i'',j}^g$	0	1	0	1	0	0	*

Here the inequality $g_{i''}(prev_{i'',j}^o, j) \leq g_{i'}(prev_{i',j}^g, j)$ does not necessarily hold. However, we prove in [12] that the difference $g_{i''}(prev_{i'',j}^o, j) - g_{i'}(prev_{i',j}^g, j)$ is bounded by a times the utility accrued in S^g for page $P_{i''}$ in the time interval $[prev_{i'',j}^g, j]$, i.e.:

$$g_{i''}(prev_{i'',j}^o, j) \leq g_{i'}(prev_{i',j}^g, j) + a \cdot \sum_{q \in seq_{i''}^g(prev_{i'',j}^g, j)} g_{i''}(prev_{i'',q}^g, q)$$

where $seq_{i''}^g(prev_{i'',j}^g, j)$ denotes the set of time instants T_q with $prev_{i'',j}^g \leq q \leq j$ and $s_{i'',q}^g = 1$.

Combining both cases and making two simple transformations, we find that for all pages $P_{i''} \in \mathcal{P}$ and all time instants $T_j \in \mathcal{T}$:

$$s_{i'',j}^o \cdot g_{i''}(prev_{i'',j}^o, j) \leq \sum_{P_{i'} \in \mathcal{P}} s_{i',j}^g \cdot g_{i'}(prev_{i',j}^g, j) + a \cdot \sum_{q \in seq_{i''}^g(prev_{i'',j}^g, j)} g_{i''}(prev_{i'',q}^g, q)$$

By summing over all $P_{i''} \in \mathcal{P}$ and all $T_j \in \mathcal{T}$ and transforming the resulting expression (see [12]) we obtain our desired result:

$$\sum_{P_i \in \mathcal{P}} \sum_{j=1}^{N} s_{i,j}^o \cdot g_i(prev_{i,j}^o, j) \leq (1+a) \cdot \sum_{P_i \in \mathcal{P}} \sum_{j=1}^{N} s_{i,j}^g \cdot g_i(prev_{i,j}^g, j)$$

Corollaries:

(i) For monotonic urgency functions, $a \leq 1$, so

$$\sum_{P_i \in \mathcal{P}} \sum_{j=1}^{N} s_{i,j}^o \cdot g_i(prev_{i,j}^o, j) \leq 2 \sum_{P_i \in \mathcal{P}} \sum_{j=1}^{N} s_{i,j}^g \cdot g_i(prev_{i,j}^g, j)$$

and WIC is a 2-approximation.

(ii) For the Sliding Window(0) setting of urgency (see Section 2.3), $a = 0$ and WIC is guaranteed to produce an optimal schedule.

4 Timeliness-Completeness Tradeoff

In this section we study the tradeoff between timeliness and completeness analytically, and show that this tradeoff can be controlled by adjusting the urgency parameter. (In Section 5 we measure this effect empirically.)

For our analysis we focus on the following simple example scenario for which optimal schedules are easy to find. (Comprehensive analytical study of the nature of the timeliness-completeness tradeoff in a wider context is left as future work.) Suppose that all changes are append-only in nature, i.e., for all pages $P_i \in \mathcal{P}$, $life_i(k,j) = 1$, independent of k and j. Further suppose that for all pages in $\mathcal{P}$ except a special page $P_{i'}$, the probability of change $\pi_{i,j}$ is uniform and equal to some constant π for all time instants $T_j, 1 \leq j \leq N$. For page $P_{i'}$, let $\pi_{i',j} = \pi'$ at each time instant T_j, where $\pi' > \pi$. Page $P_{i'}$ is more likely to change than any other page at each time instant.

Furthermore, let the number of time instants in an epoch be much larger than the number of pages under consideration for monitoring, i.e., $N \geq |\mathcal{P}| \geq 2$, and let $W_i = 1$ for all $P_i \in \mathcal{P}$. Finally, assume that at most one page can be monitored at each time instant, i.e., $C = 1$.

Now consider two extreme scenarios for urgency:

- **Timeliness-Only**: *No delay in capturing information is acceptable.* Information not captured immediately is of no value to the application. This is the Sliding Window(0) scenario for urgency described in Section 2.3, in which $urgency(0) = 1$ and $urgency(t) = 0$ for all $t > 0$. In this scenario,

$$g_i(prev_{i,j}, j) = \begin{cases} \pi & \text{if } i \neq i' \\ \pi' & \text{otherwise} \end{cases}$$

Here, the optimization problem reduces to that of maximizing the number of changes captured with zero delay. The unique optimal schedule in this case is as follows: Monitor page $P_{i'}$ at each time instant, and do not monitor any other pages. In this scenario prior changes have no bearing and overall utility is maximized by always monitoring the page with the highest probability of change in the current time instant.

- **Completeness-Only**: *Any delay in capturing the changes is acceptable.* This is the uniform scenario for urgency described in Section 2.3, in which urgency is set to $urgency(t) = 1$, independent of t. In this scenario,

$$g_i(prev_{i,j}, j) = \begin{cases} \sum_{k=prev_{i,j}+1}^{j} \pi & \text{if } i \neq i' \\ \sum_{k=prev_{i,j}+1}^{j} \pi' & \text{otherwise} \end{cases}$$

Here, the optimization problem reduces to that of maximizing the total number of changes captured, regardless of delay. One optimal schedule for this scenario is as follows: During time instants $T_1, T_2, \ldots, T_{N-|\mathcal{P}|}$ monitor page $P_{i'}$ repeatedly. Then, during time instants $T_{N-|\mathcal{P}|+1}, \ldots, T_{N-1}$ monitor each page $P_i \in \mathcal{P}$, $i \neq i'$ exactly once in some order. Finally, at the last time instant T_N monitor $P_{i'}$ again.

We now argue informally that this schedule is optimal in terms of expected total utility accrued. A formal proof is omitted for brevity. Since changes only append information and timeliness has no bearing, only the last monitoring of each page during the epoch is important. Furthermore, the last monitoring of a given page captures the most information if it is as late in the schedule as possible. Therefore, an optimal schedule for this scenario is one that monitors a different page in each of the final $|\mathcal{P}|$ time instants, in ascending order of probability of change. The monitorings scheduled for time instants between T_1 and $T_{N-|\mathcal{P}|}$ are irrelevant in terms of utility.

Below we tabulate the number of changes captured as well as the number captured with zero delay between occurrence and capture:

Urgency setting	Number of changes captured	Number captured with zero delay
Timeliness-Only	$N \cdot \pi'$	$N \cdot \pi'$
Completeness-Only	$N \cdot \pi' + [(|\mathcal{P}|-1) \cdot N - \frac{|\mathcal{P}| \cdot (|\mathcal{P}|-1)}{2}] \cdot \pi$	$\leq N \cdot \pi' - (|\mathcal{P}| - 1) \cdot (\pi' - \pi)$

In the Timeliness-Only case, all changes to $P_{i'}$ are captured, and all are captured in the same time instant in which they occur. The expected number of such changes is $N \cdot \pi'$, which represents the maximum number of changes that can be captured with zero delay under any schedule, on expectation. In the Completeness-Only case, not only are all $N \cdot \pi'$ changes to $P_{i'}$ captured, but most of the changes to the other pages are captured as well. The expected number of such changes is $[(|\mathcal{P}|-1) \cdot N - |\mathcal{P}| \cdot (|\mathcal{P}|-1)/2] \cdot \pi$. Overall, $N \cdot \pi' + [(|\mathcal{P}|-1) \cdot N - |\mathcal{P}| \cdot (|\mathcal{P}|-1)/2] \cdot \pi$ changes are captured, which represents the maximum number of changes that can be captured under any schedule, on expectation. Since we assume $N > |\mathcal{P}|/2$, the expected total number of changes captured in the Completeness-Only case is greater than in the Timeliness-Only case.

Although more changes are captured in the Completeness-Only case, the delay between the time of occurrence and time of capture of those changes tends to be longer than in the Timeliness-Only case. We quantify the difference by comparing the expected number of changes captured immediately, with zero delay, in the two cases. First observe that the particular choice of optimal schedule given above for the Completeness-Only scenario represents the best case for expected number of changes captured with zero delay. In that best case, the expected total number of zero-delay changes captured is $(N-|\mathcal{P}|) \cdot \pi' + (|\mathcal{P}|-1) \cdot \pi + \pi' = N \cdot \pi' - (|\mathcal{P}|-1) \cdot (\pi'-\pi)$. This quantity is less than the number of zero-delay changes captured in the Timeliness-Only case, $N \cdot \pi'$ (recall that $\pi' > \pi$). Hence, more changes are captured immediately after they occur in the Timeliness-Only case than in the Completeness-Only case, even though the total number of changes captured is fewer.

In this example scenario, if we maximize the expected total number of changes captured, the expected number captured with zero delay is less than maximal. Conversely, if we maximize the expected number captured with zero delay, the total number of changes we expect to capture is less than maximal. Based on our analysis of this example scenario we conclude that the following two facts appear to be true:

1. A fundamental tradeoff exists between timeliness and completeness of information captured during monitoring.

2. Our urgency parameter serves as a knob to control this tradeoff.

Extending our analysis to encompass a broader range of scenarios appears nontrivial and is left as a topic of future work. In the rest of this paper we prefer to focus on empirical measurements.

5 Experiments

To evaluate our WIC algorithm empirically, we used real-world online auction data from a major auction site. Auction bids are of significant interest to monitor for purposes of offline trend analysis as well as real-time counter-bidding.

We obtained 7550 Web pages from the site, each of which contains bidding histories for one item up for auction. Since bids have timestamps, we were able to reconstruct the past temporal behavior of these pages. Each page is updated whenever a new bid is made for the corresponding item, at which time information about the new bid (including bidder, price, time) is appended to the bidding history. However, for the sake of testing the flexibility of our approach, some of our experiments assume that each page displays only the most recent, or maximum, bid for the item, and prior bids are erased. Some auction sites only display the maximum bid.

For our experiments we treated one day as an epoch, with time instants corresponding to one-minute intervals. Hence, $N = 60 \cdot 24 = 1440$ time instants. The number of pages $|\mathcal{P}| = 7550$. We set $W_i = 1$ for all pages $P_i \in \mathcal{P}$. Change probabilities ($\pi_{*,*}$) are determined as follows: we begin with the "exact probabilities," in which each $\pi_{i,j} \in \{0, 1\}$, depending on whether page P_i undergoes a change at time instant T_j. Then, we add noise to simulate inaccuracies introduced by a change probability estimation algorithm in the following two ways:

- **False positives and false negatives**: Given an error factor $FPN \in [0, 1]$, we remove each change with probability FPN, i.e., set $\pi_{i,j} = 0$ when originally $\pi_{i,j} = 1$. Each time a change to page P_i at time instant T_j is removed, we insert a spurious change to P_i at a randomly-selected time instant $T_{j'}$, i.e., set $\pi_{i,j'} = 1$. The smaller FPN is, the more accurate the change probability estimates are.

- **Spread**: For each change to page P_i at time instant T_j, we spread the probability of change according to a Gaussian distribution parameterized by standard deviation $\sigma \geq 0$ (in units of time instants). As with FPN, the smaller σ is, the more accurate the change probability estimates are.

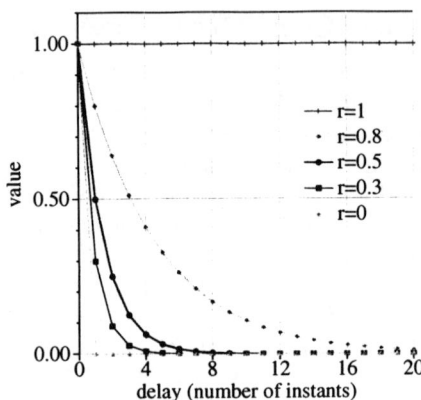

Figure 4: Urgency function for different values of r.

5.1 Metric and Parameters

We evaluate the performance of monitoring scheduling algorithms in terms of total utility accrued. To normalize our measurements in the range $[0, 1]$ we divide total utility by the total number of changes undergone by all pages at all time instants in the epoch. If a scheduling algorithm captures all changes with zero delay, the normalized utility is 1.

Recall that utility is parameterized by an urgency specification. For our experiments we used exponential decay with parameter $r \in [0, 1]$ for urgency. Figure 4 shows urgency functions for different values of r. By tuning r, the desired balance between timeliness and completeness can be specified. Using a small value for r, timeliness is preferred over completeness. In the extreme, setting $r = 0$ signals that changes not captured immediately, i.e., during the same time instant in which they occur, are of no value and do not increase utility. On the other hand, using a large value for r, completeness is preferred over timeliness. In the extreme, setting $r = 1$ signals that timeliness has no bearing and utility depends only on completeness.

5.2 Effect of Inaccuracies in Change Probability Estimation

In our first experiment we investigate how inaccuracies in change probability estimation effect the performance of our WIC algorithm (Section 3.2). First we vary the estimation accuracy by changing the value of σ (standard deviation of spread), while fixing $FPN = 0$. Figure 5 shows the result. In each graph, the x-axis plots the resource constraint

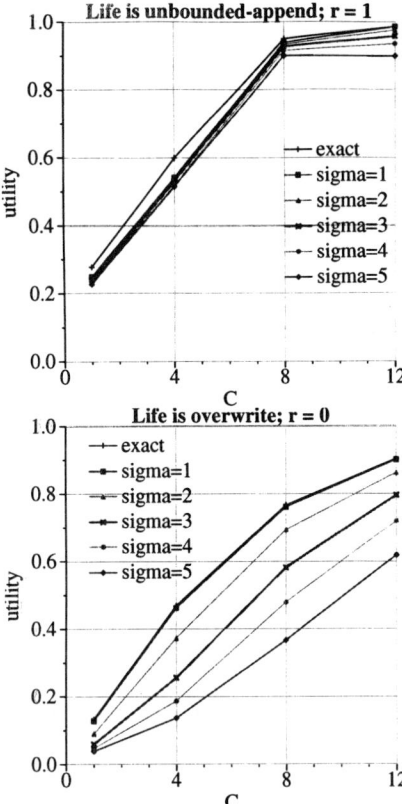

Figure 5: Effect of change probability estimation inaccuracy in terms of spread (σ) on performance.

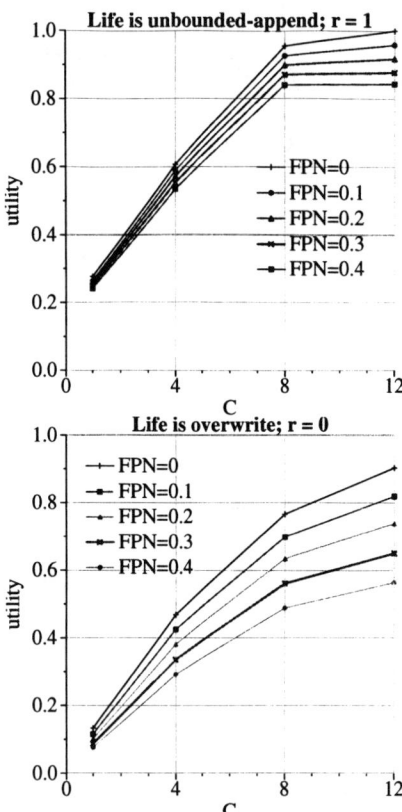

Figure 6: Effect of change probability estimation inaccuracy in terms of false positives and negatives (FPN) on performance.

C (maximum number of pages that can be monitored per time instant), and the y-axis plots utility captured. In both graphs the utility obtained decreases with increasing σ, as would be expected. The two graphs shown correspond to the best and worst cases in terms of loss in utility due to spread in change probability estimation. The graphs for other combinations of life and urgency fall in between these two extremes, so we omit them.

As we can see from Figure 5, our algorithm is fairly tolerant of a modest degree of spread on this data. When $\sigma = 4$, the height of the central peak of the distribution of change probability estimates falls at around 0.1 (it is well below 0.1 for $\sigma = 5$). In other words, with $\sigma = 4$ the estimate only indicates a 10% probability of change at the time instants in which a change does occur, yet our approach still performs reasonably well.

Next we measure the effect of introducing false positives and false negatives by varying FPN, fixing $\sigma = 0$ (no spread). Figure 6 shows the result. As before, we show the two graphs corresponding to the settings of life and urgency yielding the best and worst cases in terms of utility lost due to inaccuracy in change probability estimation. Again, our algorithm appears to be fairly intolerant of a modest degree of inaccuracy in estimation of change probability due to false positives and negatives. Furthermore, both in terms of spread and false positives and negatives, the degree to which estimation inaccuracy undermines the ability to achieve high utility is highly dependent on the life and urgency parameters. We fix $FPN = 0.1$ and $\sigma = 2$ for the rest of our experiments.

5.3 Timeliness-Completeness Tradeoff

In our next experiment we demonstrate the control provided by our urgency parameter in trading off timeliness against completeness. We fix $FPN = 0.1$ and $\sigma = 2$, and life is set to Unbounded-Append for all pages in $\mathcal{P}$ (similar results were obtained with life set to Overwrite).

In Figure 7 we show the number of changes captured by our WIC algorithm, as a fraction of the total number of changes that occurred, under different urgency functions. The resource constraint C is plotted on the $x-axis$. As we expect, in each case as C increases, more changes are captured. The number of changes captured also increases as r (the urgency parameter) increases. (Recall that increasing r increases the relative importance of completeness compared with that of timeliness.) When availability of resources is relatively low ($C \leq 12$ in this case), our algorithm captures between around 20% and 80% more changes when $r = 1$ than when $r = 0$.

We now turn to timeliness. Figure 8 plots the distribution of delay between the times of occurrence and capture of the changes captured, with $C = 8$ and for different

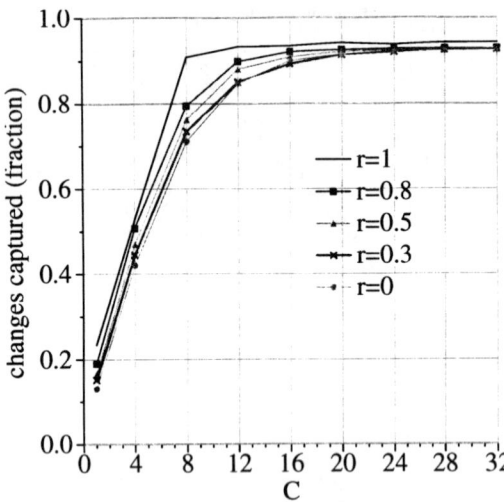

Figure 7: Number of changes captured under various exponential urgency functions (r). Life is Unbounded-Append.

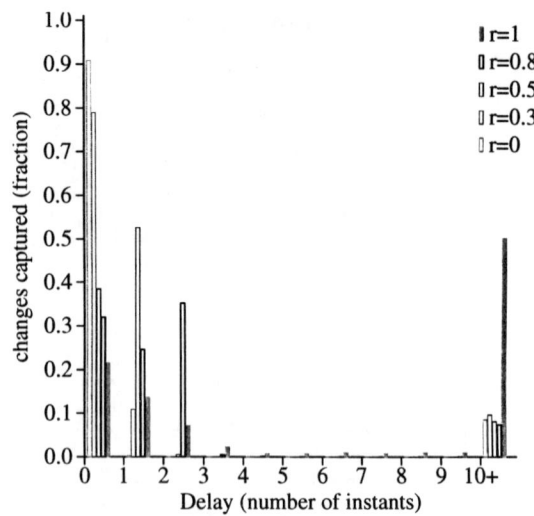

Figure 8: Distribution of delay in changes captured under various exponential urgency functions (r). Life is Unbounded-Append.

settings of r (urgency). Delay that exceeds 10 minutes is shown in the rightmost bar, labeled "10+." For $r = 0$, over 90% of the changes captured are captured with zero delay. However, this figure drops below 25% for the case of $r = 1$, in which roughly 50% of the changes captured are captured with a delay of 10 minutes or more.

These results indicate a tradeoff does indeed exist between timeliness and completeness, and it can be controlled by adjusting our urgency parameter, as our analytical results of Section 4 indicated. The tradeoff is perhaps best visualized as plotted in Figure 9. This graph shows the total number of changes captured (as a fraction of the total number of changes that occurred), as well as the total number captured with zero delay (again as a fraction of the total number that occurred), when $C = 8$, for different settings of urgency (r). It can clearly be seen that by adjusting the urgency parameter r, timeliness can be traded off against completeness.

5.4 Comparison Against Prior Approach

For our final experiment we compare our approach against the only prior work we are aware of on scheduling monitoring of dynamic Web pages, CAM [13]. Since CAM was designed to optimize for the "returned information ratio" (RIR) objective, we set our life parameter to Overwrite and $r = 0$ (equivalently, Sliding Window(0) urgency) to make utility equivalent to RIR. Note that the RIR objective strongly favors timeliness over completeness and assumes that all changes overwrite information due to previous changes. In this way our approach generalizes that of [13]. However, our approach is less general in the sense that we assume unit time to monitor a page, whereas CAM handles cases in which each pages takes a different amount of time to download. Therefore, neither approach subsumes the other.

We compared the two approaches on the scenario in

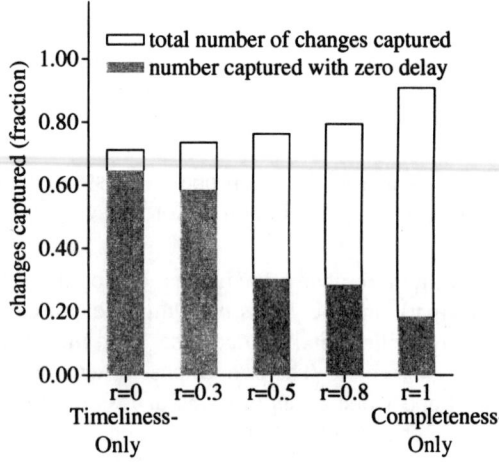

Figure 9: Tradeoff between timeliness and completeness.

which they overlap, namely: scheduling unit-time monitorings of pages that undergo changes that completely overwrite information, while optimizing for timeliness. Note that our WIC algorithm is guaranteed to find the optimal monitoring schedule in this case (Section 3.3). We measured total utility accrued for different values of C (available resources), under the two algorithms, with $FPN = 0.1$ and $\sigma = 2$. Our WIC algorithm outperformed CAM by as much as a factor of two.

6 Related Work

Web monitoring has been addressed in the context of systems that evaluate continuous queries over the Web [7–10]. The main focus of this work has been on language design and scalability of the query engine, rather than on how best to capture information from sources requiring pull-based access, like Web pages. Our work addresses this largely ignored yet important research topic.

The only prior work we are aware of that addresses this topic in a nontrivial way is [13], which introduced the CAM Web monitoring algorithm. CAM requires access to predicted change probabilities in advance (*i.e.*, it is not an online algorithm), and is geared toward maximizing an objective called "returned information ratio" (RIR). RIR strongly favors timeliness over completeness, and assumes that all changes overwrite information due to previous changes. RIR is a special case of our much broader formulation, in which the tradeoff between timeliness and completeness of information captured, as well as the way in which information is posted to Web pages, are exposed as parameters. When our algorithm parameters are set to match the RIR objective, our online algorithm (WIC) is guaranteed to find the optimal solution. In all other cases WIC is a 2-approximation. No formal guarantees about the effectiveness of CAM were provided in [13], although the CAM heuristic does handle cases in which the cost of monitoring is nonuniform across pages (WIC does not).

Work on scheduling Web crawlers, *e.g.*, [2,4,14] focuses on maximizing the current "freshness" of a local repository containing copies of Web pages. In contrast, in our work the focus is on capturing the history of changes to pages.

7 Summary

In this paper we studied the problem of scheduling polling of remote Web pages for the purpose of monitoring the dynamic Web. The goal is to use limited resources most effectively in order to maximize the overall utility of information captured. Utility is a highly application-dependent notion, and our approach is parameterized by custom specifications of (1) the relative importance of information available from individual pages under consideration and (2) the sensitivity of the application to delay in captured information. Our highly parameterized formulation makes it suitable for a wide variety of Web monitoring applications.

We formalized the scheduling problem as a parameterized optimization problem. We then presented an efficient online algorithm that we showed always achieves total utility within a factor of two of the optimal offline solution in all cases. Both analysis and experiments on real-world online auction data confirmed that a fundamental tradeoff exists between timeliness and completeness of information captured during monitoring; our urgency parameter serves as a knob to control this tradeoff.

References

[1] U. Bertele and F. Brioschi. *Nonserial Dynamic Programming*. Academic Press, New York, 1972.

[2] J. Cho and H. Garcia-Molina. Synchronizing a database to improve freshness. In *Proceedings of the 2000 ACM SIGMOD International Conference on Management of Data*, May 2000.

[3] E. Cohen and M. Strauss. Maintaining time-decaying stream aggregates. In *Proceedings of the Twenty-Second ACM SIGMOD-SIGACT-SIGART*, June 2003.

[4] J. Edwards, K. S. McCurley, and J. A. Tomlin. An adaptive model for optimizing performance of an incremental web crawler. In *Proceedings of the Tenth International World Wide Web Conference*, May 2001.

[5] D. Fetterly, M. Manasse, M. Najork, and J. Wiener. A large-scale study of the evolution of web pages. In *Proceedings of the 12th International World Wide Web Conference*, May 2003.

[6] T. Ibaraki and N. Katoh. Resource allocation problems: Algorithmic approaches. *MIT Press, Cambridge, MA*, 1988.

[7] L. Liu, C. Pu, and W. Tang. Continual queries for internet scale event-driven information delivery. *Knowledge and Data Engineering*, 11(4):610–628, 1999.

[8] L. Liu, C. Pu, and W. Tang. WebCQ: Detecting and delivering information changes on the web. In *Proceedings of International Conference on Information and Knowledge Management*, November 2000.

[9] L. Liu, C. Pu, W. Tang, and W. Han. CONQUER: A continual query system for update monitoring in the WWW. *International Journal of Computer Systems, Science and Engineering*, 1999.

[10] J. Naughton, D. DeWitt, D. Maier, A. Aboulnaga, J. Chen, L. Galanis, J. Kang, R. Krishnamurthy, Q. Luo, N. Prakash, R. Ramamurthy, J. Shanmugasundaram, F. Tian, K. Tufte, E. Viglas, Y. Wang, C. Zhang, B. Jackson, A. Gupta, and R. Chen. The Niagara internet query system. *IEEE Data Engineering Bulletin*, 24(2):27–33, 2001.

[11] V. N. Padmanabhan and L. Qui. The content and access dynamics of a busy web site: findings and implications. In *Proceedings of ACM SIGCOMM*, August, 2000.

[12] S. Pandey, K. Dhamdhere, and C. Olston. WIC: A General-Purpose Algorithm for Monitoring Web Information Sources. Technical report, June 2004. Available at: http://www.cs.cmu.edu/~olston/publications/wic.html.

[13] S. Pandey, K. Ramamritham, and S. Chakrabarti. Monitoring the dynamic web to respond to continuous queries. In *Proceedings of the Twelfth International World Wide Web Conference*, May 2003.

[14] J. Wolf, M. Squillante, P. Yu, J. Sethuraman, and L. Ozsen. Optimal crawling strategies for web search engines. In *Proceedings of the Eleventh International World Wide Web Conference*, May 2002.

Similarity Search for Web Services

Xin Dong   Alon Halevy   Jayant Madhavan   Ema Nemes   Jun Zhang

{lunadong, alon, jayant, enemes, junzhang}@cs.washington.edu
University of Washington, Seattle

Abstract

Web services are loosely coupled software components, published, located, and invoked across the web. The growing number of web services available within an organization and on the Web raises a new and challenging search problem: locating desired web services. Traditional keyword search is insufficient in this context: the specific types of queries users require are not captured, the very small text fragments in web services are unsuitable for keyword search, and the underlying structure and semantics of the web services are not exploited.

We describe the algorithms underlying the Woogle search engine for web services. Woogle supports similarity search for web services, such as finding similar web-service operations and finding operations that compose with a given one. We describe novel techniques to support these types of searches, and an experimental study on a collection of over 1500 web-service operations that shows the high recall and precision of our algorithms.

1 Introduction

Web services are loosely coupled software components, published, located, and invoked across the web. A web service comprises several operations (see examples in Figure 1). Each operation takes a SOAP package containing a list of input parameters, fulfills a certain task, and returns the result in an output SOAP package. Large enterprises are increasingly relying on web services as methodology for large-scale software development and sharing of services within an organization. If current trends continue, then in the future many applications will be built by piecing together web services published by third-party producers.

Permission to copy without fee all or part of this material is granted provided that the copies are not made or distributed for direct commercial advantage, the VLDB copyright notice and the title of the publication and its date appear, and notice is given that copying is by permission of the Very Large Data Base Endowment. To copy otherwise, or to republish, requires a fee and/or special permission from the Endowment.

**Proceedings of the 30th VLDB Conference,
Toronto, Canada, 2004**

The growing number of web services available within an organization and on the Web raises a new and challenging search problem: locating desired web services. In fact, to address this problem, several simple search engines have recently sprung up [1, 2, 3, 4]. Currently, these engines provide only simple keyword search on web service descriptions.

As one considers search for web services in more detail, it becomes apparent that the keyword search paradigm is insufficient for two reasons. First, keywords do not capture the underlying semantics of web services. Current web service search engines return a particular service if its functionality description contains the keywords in the query; such search may miss results. For example, when searching zipcode, the web services whose descriptions contain term zip or postal code but not zipcode will not be returned.

Second, keywords do not suffice for accurately specifying users' information needs. Since a web-service operation is going to be used as part of an application, users would like to specify their search criteria more precisely than by keywords. Current web-service search engines often enable a user to explore the details of a particular web-service operation, and in some cases to try it out by entering an input value. Nevertheless, investigating a single web-service operation often requires several browsing steps. Once users drill down all the way and find the operation inappropriate for some reason, they want to be able to find *similar* operations to the ones just considered, as opposed to laboriously following parallel browsing patterns. Similarly, users may want to find operations that take similar inputs (respectively, outputs), or that can *compose* with the current operation being browsed.

To address the challenges involved in searching for web services, we built Woogle[1], a web-service search engine. In addition to simple keyword searches, Woogle supports similarity search for web services. A user can ask for web-service operations similar to a given one, those that take similar inputs (or

---
[1] See http://www.cs.washington.edu/woogle

W_1: Web Service: GlobalWeather
    Operation: GetTemperature
        Input: Zip
        Output: Return
W_2: Web Service: WeatherFetcher
    Operation: GetWeather
        Input: PostCode
        Output: TemperatureF, WindChill, Humidity
W_3: Web Service: GetLocalTime
    Operation: LocalTimeByZipCode
        Input: Zipcode
        Output: LocalTimeByZipCodeResult
W_4: Web Service: PlaceLookup
    Operation1: CityStateToZipCode
        Input: City, State
        Output: ZipCode
    Operation2: ZipCodeToCityState
        Input: ZipCode
        Output: City, State

Figure 1: Several example web services (not including their textual descriptions). Note that each web service includes a set of operations, each with input and output parameters. For example, web services W_1 and W_2 provide weather information.

outputs), and those that compose with a given one. This paper describes the novel techniques we have developed to support these types of searches, and experimental evidence that shows the high accuracy of our algorithms. In particular, our contributions are the following:

1. We propose a basic set of search functionalities that an effective web-service search engine should support.

2. We describe algorithms for supporting similarity search. Our algorithms combine multiple sources of evidence in order to determine similarity between a pair of web-service operations. The key ingredient of our algorithm is a novel clustering algorithm that groups names of parameters of web-service operations into semantically meaningful concepts. These concepts are then leveraged to determine similarity of inputs (or outputs) of web-service operations.

3. We describe a detailed experimental evaluation on a set of over 1500 web-service operations. The evaluation shows that we can provide both high precision and recall for similarity search, and that our techniques substantially improve on naive keyword search.

The paper is organized as follows. Section 2 begins by placing our search problem in the context of the related work. Section 3 formally defines the similarity search problem for web services. Section 4 describes the algorithm for clustering parameter names, and Section 5 describes the similarity search algorithm. Section 6 describes our experimental evaluation. Section 7 discusses other types of search that Woogle supports, and Section 8 concludes.

2 Related Work

Finding similar web-service operations is closely related to three other matching problems: text document matching, schema matching, and software component matching.

Text document matching: Document matching and classification is a long-standing problem in information retrieval (IR). Most solutions to this problem (e.g. [10, 20, 27, 19]) are based on term frequency analysis. However, these approaches are insufficient in the web service context because text documentations for web-service operations are highly compact, and they ignore structure information that aids capturing the underlying semantics of the operations.

Schema matching: The database community has considered the problem of automatically matching schemas [24, 12, 13, 22]. The work in this area has developed several methods that try to capture clues about the semantics of the schemas, and suggest matches based on them. Such methods include linguistic analysis, structural analysis, the use of domain knowledge and previous matching experience. However, the search for *similar* web-service operations differs from schema matching in two significant ways. First, the granularity of the search is different: operation matching can be compared to finding a similar schema, while schema matching looks for similar components in two given schemas that are assumed to be related. Second, the operations in a web service are typically much more loosely related to each other than are tables in a schema, and each web service in isolation has much less information than a schema. Hence, we are unable to adapt techniques for schema matching to this context.

Software component matching: Software component matching is considered important for software reuse. [28] formally defines the problem by examining signature (data type) matching and specification (program behavior) matching. The techniques employed there require analysis of data types and post-conditions, which are not available for web services.

Some recent work (e.g., [9, 23]) has proposed annotating web services manually with additional semantic information, and then using these annotations to compose services [8, 26]. In our context, annotating the collection of web services is infeasible, and we rely on only the information provided in the WSDL file and the UDDI entry.

In [15] the authors studied the supervised classification and unsupervised clustering of web services.

Our work differs in that we are doing unsupervised matching at the operation level, rather than supervised classification at the entire web service level. Hence, we face the challenge of understanding operations in a web service from very limited amount of information.

3 Web Service Similarity Search

We begin by briefly describing the structure of web services, and then we motivate and define the search problem we address.

3.1 The Structure of Web Services

Each web service has an associated WSDL file describing its functionality and interface. A web service is typically (though not necessarily) published by registering its WSDL file and a brief description in UDDI business registries. Each web service consists of a set of operations. For each web service, we have access to the following information:

- **Name and text description**: A web service is described by a name, a text description in the WSDL file, and a description that is put in the UDDI registry.
- **Operation descriptions**: Each operation is described by a name and a text description in the WSDL file.
- **Input/Output descriptions**: Each input and output of an operation contains a set of parameters. For each parameter, the WSDL file describes the name, data type and arity (if the parameter is of array type). Parameters may be organized in a hierarchy by using complex types.

3.2 Searching for Web Services

To motivate similarity search for web services, consider the following typical scenario. Users begin a search for web services by entering keywords relevant to the search goal. They then start inspecting some of the returned web services. Since the result of the search is rather complex, the users need to drill down in several steps. They first decide which web service to explore in detail, and then consider which specific operations in that service to look at. Given a particular operation, they will look at each of its inputs and outputs, and if the engine provides a *try it* feature, they will try entering some value for the inputs.

At this point, the users may find that the web service is inappropriate for some reason, but *not* want to have to repeat the same process for each of other potentially relevant services. Hence, our goal is to provide a more direct method for searching, given that the users have already explored a web service in detail. Suppose they explored the operation GetTemperature in W_1. We identify the following important similarity search queries they may want to pose:

Similar operations: Find operations with similar functionalities. For example, the web-service operation GetWeather in W_2 is similar to the operation GetTemperature in W_1. Note that we are searching for specific *operations* that are similar, rather than similar web services. The latter type of search is typically too coarse for our needs. There is no formal definition for operation similarity, because, just like in other types of search, similarity depends on the specific goal in the user's mind. Intuitively, we consider operations to be similar if they take similar inputs, produce similar outputs, and the relationships between the inputs and outputs are similar.

Similar inputs/outputs: Find operations with similar inputs. As a motivating example for such a search, suppose our goal is to collect a variety of information about locations. While W_1 provides weather, operations LocalTimeByZipCode in W_3 and ZipCodeToCityState in W_4 provide other information about locations, and thereby may be of interest to the user.

Alternatively, we may want to search for operations with similar outputs, but different inputs. For example, we may be looking for temperature, but the operation we are considering takes zipcode as input, while we need one that takes city and state as input.

Composible operations: Find operations that can be composed with the current one. One of the key promises of building applications with web services is that one should be able to compose a set of given services to create ones that are specific to the application's needs. In our example, there are two opportunities for composition. In the first case, the output of the operation is similar to the input of the given operation, such as CityStateToZipCode in W_4. Composing CityStateToZipCode with GetWeather in W_1 offers another option for getting the weather when the zipcode is not known. In the second case, the output of the given operation may be similar to the input of another operation; e.g., one that transforms Centigrade and Fahrenheit and thereby produces results in the desired scale.

In this paper we focus on the following two problems, from which we can easily build up the above search capabilities.

Operation matching: *Given a web-service operation, return a list of similar operations.* □

Input/output matching: *Given the input (respectively, output) of a web-service operation, return a* *list of web-service operations with similar inputs (respectively, outputs).* □

We note that these two problems are also at the core of two other types of search that Woogle supports (See Section 7): *template search* and *composition search*. Template search goes beyond keyword search by specifying the functionality, input and output of a desired operation. Composition search returns not only single operations, but also compositions of operations that fulfill the user's need.

3.3 Overview of Our Approach

Similarity search for web services is challenging because neither the textual descriptions of web services and their operations nor the names of the input and output parameters completely convey the underlying semantics of the operation. Nevertheless, knowledge of the semantics is important to determining similarity between operation.

Broadly speaking, our algorithm combines multiple sources of evidences to determine similarity. In particular, it will consider similarity between the textual descriptions of the operations and of the entire web services, and similarity between the parameter names of the operations. The key ingredient of the algorithm is a technique that clusters parameter names in the collection of web services into *semantically meaningful* concepts. By comparing the concepts that input or output parameters belong to, we are able to achieve good similarity measures. Section 4 describes the clustering algorithm, and Section 5 describes how we combine the multiple sources of evidence.

4 Clustering Parameter Names

To effectively match inputs/outputs of web-service operations, it is crucial to get at their underlying semantics. However, this is hard for two reasons. First, parameter naming is dependent on the developers' whim. Parameter names tend to be highly varied given the use of synonyms, hypernyms, and different naming rules. They might even not be composed of proper English words—there may be misspellings, abbreviations, etc. Therefore, lexical references, such as *Wordnet* [5], are hard to apply. Second, inputs/outputs typically have few parameters, and the associated WSDL files rarely provide rich descriptions for parameters. Traditional IR techniques, such as TF/IDF [25] and LSI [11], rely on word frequencies to capture the underlying semantics and thus do not apply well.

A parameter name is typically a sequence of concatenated words (not necessarily proper English words), with the first letter of every word capitalized (*e.g.*, LocalTimeByZipCodeResult). Such words are referred to as *terms*. We exploit the co-occurrence of terms in web service inputs and outputs to cluster terms into meaningful concepts. As we shall see later, using these concepts, in addition to the original terms, greatly improves our ability to identify similar inputs/outputs and hence find similar web service operations.

Applying an off-the-shelf text clustering algorithm directly to our context does not perform well because the web service inputs/outputs are sparse. For example, whereas synonyms tend to occur in the same document in an IR application, they seldom occur in the same operation input/output; therefore, they will not get clustered. Our clustering algorithm is a refinement of *agglomerative* clustering. We begin by describing a particular kind of association rules that capture our notion of term co-occurrence and then describe the clustering algorithm.

4.1 Clustering Parameters by Association

We base our clustering on the following heuristic: *parameters tend to express the same concept if they occur together often.* This heuristic is validated by our experimental results. We use it to cluster parameters by exploiting their conditional probabilities of occurrence in inputs and outputs of web-service operations. Specifically, we are interested in *association rules* of the form:

$$t_1 \rightarrow t_2 \ (s, c)$$

In this rule, t_1 and t_2 are two terms. The *support*, s, is the probability that t_1 occurs in an input/output; *i.e.*, $s = P(t_1) = \frac{\|IO_{t_1}\|}{\|IO\|}$, where $\|IO\|$ is the total number of inputs and outputs of operations, and $\|IO_{t_1}\|$ is the number of inputs and outputs that contain t_1. The *confidence*, c, is the probability that t_2 occurs in an input or output, given that t_1 is known to occur in it; *i.e.*, $c = P(t_2|t_1) = \frac{\|IO_{t_1,t_2}\|}{\|IO_{t_1}\|}$, where $\|IO_{t_1,t_2}\|$ is the number of inputs and outputs that contain both t_1 and t_2. Note that the rule $t_1 \rightarrow t_2(s_{12}, c_{12})$ and the rule $t_2 \rightarrow t_1(s_{21}, c_{21})$ may have different support and confidence values. These rules can be efficiently computed using the A-Priori algorithm [7].

4.2 Criteria for Ideal Clustering

Ideally, parameter clustering results should have the following two features:

1. Frequent and rare parameters should be left unclustered; strongly connected parameters in-between are clustered into concepts. First, not clustering frequent parameters is consistent with the IR community's observation that such

technique leads to the best performance in automatic query expansion [16]. Second, leaving rare parameters unclustered avoids over-fitting.

2. The *cohesion* of a concept—the connections between parameters inside the concept—should be strong; the *correlation* between concepts—the connections between parameters in different concepts—should be weak.

Traditionally, cohesion is defined as the sum of squares of Euclidean distances from each point to the center of the cluster it belongs to; correlation is defined as the sum of squares of distances between cluster centers [14]. This definition does not apply well in our context because of "the curse of dimensionality": our feature sets are so large that a Euclidean distance measure is no longer meaningful. We hence quantify the cohesion and correlation of clusters based on our association rules.

We say that t_1 is *closely associated* to t_2 if the rule $t_1 \rightarrow t_2$ has a confidence greater than threshold t_c. The threshold t_c is chosen manually to be the value that best separates correlated and uncorrelated pairs of terms.

Given a cluster I, we define the *cohesion* of I as the percentage of closely associated term pairs over all term pairs. Formally,

$$coh_I = \frac{\| \{i,j \mid i,j \in I, i \neq j, i \rightarrow j(c > t_c)\} \|}{\|I\|(\|I\| - 1)}$$

where $i \rightarrow j(c > t_c)$ is the association rule for term i and j. As a special case, the cohesion of a single-term cluster is 1.

Given clusters I and J, we define the *correlation* between I and J as the percentage of closely associated cross-cluster term pairs. Formally,

$$cor_{IJ} = \frac{C(I,J) + C(J,I)}{2\|I\|\|J\|}$$

where $C(I,J) = \| \{i,j \mid i \in I, j \in J, i \rightarrow j(c > t_c)\} \|$.

To measure the overall quality of a clustering $\mathcal{C}$, we define the *cohesion/correlation score* as

$$score_\mathcal{C} = \frac{\frac{\sum_{I \in \mathcal{C}} coh_I}{\|\mathcal{C}\|}}{\frac{\sum_{I,J \in \mathcal{C}, I \neq J} cor_{IJ}}{\|\mathcal{C}\|(\|\mathcal{C}\|-1)/2}} = \frac{(\|\mathcal{C}\|-1)\sum_{I \in \mathcal{C}} coh_I}{2\sum_{I,J \in \mathcal{C}, I \neq J} cor_{IJ}}$$

The cohesion/correlation score captures the trade-off between having a high cohesion score and a low correlation score. Our goal is to obtain a high $score_\mathcal{C}$ that will indicate tight connections inside clusters and loose connections between clusters.

4.3 Clustering Algorithm

We can now describe our clustering algorithm as a series of refinements to the classical agglomerative clustering [18].

4.3.1 The basic agglomeration algorithm

Agglomerative clustering is a bottom-up version of hierarchical clustering. Each object is initialized to be a cluster of its own. In general, at each iteration the two most similar clusters are merged until no more clusters can be merged.

In our context, each term is initialized to be a cluster of its own; *i.e.*, there are as many clusters as terms. The algorithm proceeds in a greedy fashion. It sorts the association rules in descending order first by the confidence and then by the support. Infrequent rules with less than a minimum support t_s are discarded. At every step, the algorithm chooses the highest ranked rule that has not been considered previously. If the two terms in the rule belong to different clusters, the algorithm merges the clusters. Formally, the condition that triggers merging cluster I and J is

$$\exists i \in I, j \in J \,.\, i \rightarrow j(s > t_s, c > t_c)$$

where i and j are terms. The threshold t_s is chosen to control the clustering of terms that do not occur frequently. We note that in our experiments the results of operation and input/output matching are not sensitive on the values of t_s and t_c.

4.3.2 Increasing cluster cohesion

The basic agglomerative algorithm merges two clusters together when any two terms in the two clusters are closely associated. The merge condition is very loose and can easily result in low cohesion of clusters. To illustrate, suppose there is a concept for weather, containing **temperature** as a term, and a concept for address, containing **zip** as a term. If, when operations report temperature, they often report the area zipcode as well, then the confidence of rule **temperature** $\rightarrow$ **zip** is high. As a result, the basic algorithm will inappropriately combine the weather concept and the address concept.

The cohesion of a cluster is decided by the association of each pair of terms in the cluster. To ensure that we obtain clusters with high cohesion, we merge two clusters only if they satisfy a stricter condition, called *cohesion condition*.

Given a cluster C, a term is called a *kernel* term if it is closely associated with at least half[2] of the remaining terms in C. Our cohesion condition requires that *all the terms in the merged cluster be kernel terms*. Formally, we merge two clusters I and J only if they satisfy the cohesion condition:

$$\forall i \in I \cup J \,.\, \| \{j \mid j \in I \cup J, i \neq j, i \rightarrow j(c > t_c)\} \|$$
$$\geq \frac{1}{2}(\|I\| + \|J\| - 1)$$

---

[2] We tried different values for this fraction and found $\frac{1}{2}$ yielded the best results.

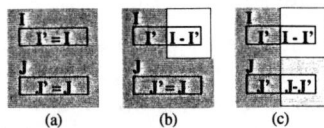

Figure 2: Splitting and merging clusters

4.3.3 Splitting and Merging

A greedy algorithm pursues local optimal solutions at each step, but usually cannot obtain the global optimal solution. In parameter clustering, an inappropriate clustering decision at an early stage may prevent subsequent appropriate clustering. Consider the case where there is a cluster for zipcode {zip, code}, formed because of the frequent occurrences of parameter ZipCode. Later we need to decide whether to merge this cluster with another cluster for address {state, city, street}. The term zip is closely associated with state, city and street, but code is not because it also occurs often in other parameters such as TeamCode and ProxyCode, which typically do not co-occur with state, city or street. Consequently, the two clusters cannot merge; the clustering result contrasts with the ideal one: {state, city, street, zip} and {code}.

The solution to this problem is to split already-formed clusters so as to obtain a better set of clusters with a higher cohesion/correlation score. Formally, given clusters I and J, we denote

$$I' = \{i \mid i \in I, \|\{j \mid j \in I \cup J, i \to j(c > t_c)\}\| \geq \frac{1}{2}(\|I\| + \|J\| - 1)$$
$$J' = \{j \mid j \in J, \|\{i \mid i \in I \cup J, j \to i(c > t_c)\}\| \geq \frac{1}{2}(\|I\| + \|J\| - 1) \quad (1)$$

Intuitively, I' (respectively, J') denotes the set of terms in I that are closely associated with terms in the union of I and J. Our algorithm makes splitting decision depending on which of the four following cases occurs:

- If $I' = I, J' = J$, then I and J can be merged directly (see Figure 2(a)).
- If $I' \neq I, J' = J$, then merging I and J directly disobeys the cohesion condition. There are two options: one is to split I into I' and $I - I'$, and then merge I' with J (see Figure 2(b)); the other is not to split or merge. We decide in two steps: the first step checks whether the merged result in the first option satisfies the cohesion condition; if so, the second step computes the cohesion/correlation score for each option, and chooses the option with a higher score. The decision is similar for the case where $J' \neq J, I' = I$.

- If $I' \neq I, J' \neq J$, then again, merging I and J directly disobeys the cohesion condition. There are two options: one is to split I into I' and $I - I'$, split J into J' and $J - J'$, and then merge I' with J' (see Figure 2(c)); the other is not to split or merge. We choose an option in two steps: the first step checks whether in the first option, the merged result satisfies the cohesion condition; if so, the second step computes the cohesion/correlation score for each option, and chooses the option with a higher score.

After the above processing, the merged cluster necessarily satisfies the cohesion condition. However, the clusters that are split from the original clusters may not. To ensure cohesion, we further split such clusters: each time, we split the cluster into two, one containing all kernel terms, and the other containing the rest. We repeat splitting until eventually all result clusters satisfy the cohesion condition. Note that applying such splitting strategy on an arbitrary cluster may generate clusters of small size. Therefore, we do not merge two clusters directly (without applying the above judgment) and then split the merged cluster.

Remark 4.1. *Our splitting-and-clustering technique is different from the dynamic modeling in the Chameleon algorithm [17], which also first splits and then merges. We do splitting and clustering at each step of the greedy algorithm. The Chameleon algorithm first considers the whole set of parameters as a big cluster and splits it into relatively small sub-clusters, and then repeatedly merges these sub-clusters.* □

4.3.4 Removing noise

Even with splitting, the results may still have terms that do not express the same concept as other terms in its cluster. We call such terms *noise terms*. To illustrate how noise terms can be formed, we continue with the zipcode example. Suppose there is a cluster for address {city, state, street, zip, code}, where code is a noise term. The cluster is formed because the rules zip → city, zip → state, and zip → street all have very high confidence, e.g., 90%; even if the rule code → zip has a lower confidence, e.g., 50%, the rules code → city, code → state, and code → street can still have high confidence.

We use the following heuristic to detect noise terms. A term is considered to be noise if in half of its occurrences there are no other terms from the same concept. After one pass of the greedy algorithm (considering all association rules above a given threshold), we scan the resulting concepts to remove noise terms. Formally, for a term t, denote $\|IO_t\|$ as the number of inputs/outputs that contain t, and

```
procedure MergeParameters(T, R) return (C)
// T is the term set, R is the association rule set
// C is the result concept set
    for (i = 1, n) C_i = {t_i}; //initiate clusters
    sort R first by the descending order of confidence,
        then by the descending order of support value;
    for each (r : t_1 → t_2(s > t_s, c > t_c) in R)
        if t_1 and t_2 are in different clusters I and J
            Compute I' and J' according to formula (1);
            if (I' = I ∧ J' = J) merge I and J;
            else if (splitting and merging satisfies the
                cohesion condition and has a higher score_C)
                split and merge;
                if (I'' = I - I' and/or J'' = J - J'
                    does not observe the cohesion condition)
                    split I'' and/or J'' iteratively;
    scan inputs/outputs and remove noise terms;
    return result clusters;
```

Figure 3: Algorithm for parameter clustering

$||SIO_t||$ as the number of inputs/outputs that contain t but no other terms in the same concept of t. We remove t from the concept if $||SIO_t|| \geq \frac{1}{2}||IO_t||$.

4.3.5 Putting it all together

Figure 3 puts all the pieces together, and shows the details of a single pass of the clustering algorithm.

The above algorithm still has two problems. First, the cohesion condition is too strict for large clusters, so it may prevent closely associated large clusters to merge. Second, early inappropriate merging may prevent later appropriate merging. Although we do splitting, the terms taken off from the original clusters may have already missed the chance to merge with other closely associated terms. We solve the problems by running the clustering algorithm iteratively. After each pass, we replace each term with its corresponding concept, re-collect association rules, and then re-run the clustering algorithm. This process continues when no more clusters can be merged.

We illustrate with an example that the iteration of clustering does not sharply loosen the clustering condition. Consider the case where {zip} is not clustered with {temperature, windchill, humidity}, because zip is closely associated with only temperature, but not the other two. Another iteration of clustering will replace each occurrence of temperature, windchill and humidity with a single concept, say weather. The term zip will be closely associated with weather; however, the term weather is not necessarily closely associated with zip, because that requires zip to occur often when any of temperature, windchill, or humidity occurs. Thus, the iteration will (correctly) keep the two clusters.

4.4 Clustering Results

We now briefly outline the results of our clustering algorithm. Our dataset, which we will describe in detail in Section 6, contains 431 web services and 3148 inputs/outputs. There are a total of 1599 terms. The clustering algorithm converges after the seventh run. It clusters 943 terms into 182 concepts. The rest 656 terms, including 387 infrequent terms (each occurs in at most 3 inputs/outputs) and 54 frequent terms (each occurs in at least 30 of the inputs/outputs) are left unclustered. There are 59 *dense* clusters, each with at least 5 terms. Some of them correspond roughly to the concepts of address, contact, geology, maps, weather, finance, commerce, statistics, and baseball, etc. The overall cohesion is 0.96, correlation is 0.003, and average cohesion for the dense clusters is 0.76. This result observes the two features of an ideal clustering.

5 Finding Similar Operations

In this section we describe how to predict similarity of inputs/outputs sets and of web-service operations. We will determine similarity by combining multiple sources of evidence. The intuition behind our matching algorithm is that the similarity of a pair of inputs (or outputs) is related to the similarity of the parameter names, that of the concepts represented by the parameter names, and that of the operations they belong to. Note that parameter name similarity compares inputs/outputs on a fine-grained level, and concept similarity compares inputs/outputs on a coarse-grained level. The similarity between two web-service operations is related to the similarity of their descriptions, that of their inputs and outputs, and that of their host web services.

Input/output similarity: We identify the input i of a web-service operation op with a vector $i = (p_i, c_i, op)$, where p_i is the set of input parameter names, and c_i is the set of concepts associated with the parameter names (as determined by the clustering algorithm described in Section 4). While comparing a pair of inputs, we determine the similarity on each of the three components separately, and then combine them. We treat op's output o as a vector $o = (p_o, c_o, op)$, and process it analogously.

Web-service operation similarity: We identify a web-service operation op with a vector $op = (w, f, i, o)$, where w is the text description of the web service to which op belongs, f is the textual description of op, and i and o denote the input and output parameters. Here too, we determine similarity by combining the similarities of the individual components of the vector.

Observe that there is a recursive relationship between the similarity of inputs/outputs and the similarity of web-service operations. Intuitively, this relationship holds because each one depends on the other, and any decision on how to break this recursive relationship would be arbitrary. In Section 5.2 we show that with sufficient care for the choice of the combination weights, we can guarantee that the recursive computation converges.

5.1 Computing Individual Similarities

We now describe how we compute similarities for each one of the components of the vectors.

Input/output parameter name similarity: We consider the terms in an input/output as a bag of words and use the TF/IDF (*Term Frequency/Inverse Document Frequency*) measure [25] to compute the similarity of two such bags.

To improve our accuracy, we pre-process the terms as follows.

1. Perform word stemming and remove stopwords. Stemming improves recall by removing term suffixes and reducing all forms of a term to a single stemmed form. Stopword removal improves precision by eliminating words with little substantive meaning.

2. Group terms with close edit distance [21] and replace terms in a group with a normalized form. This step helps normalize misspelled and abbreviated terms.

3. Remove from the output bag the terms that refer to the inputs. For example, in the output parameter LocalTimeByZipCodeResult, the term By indicates that the following terms describe inputs; thus, terms Zip and Code can be removed.

4. Extract additional information from names of web-service operations. Most operations are named after the output (*e.g.*, GetWeather), and some include input information (*e.g.*, ZipCodeToCityState). We put such terms into the corresponding input/output bag.

Input/output concept similarity: To compute the similarity of the concepts represented by the inputs/outputs, we replace each term in the bag of words described above with its corresponding concept, and then use the TF/IDF measure. Note that the clustering algorithm is applied on the input/output terms *after* preprocessing.

Operation description similarity: To compute the similarity of operation descriptions, we consider the tokenized operation name and WSDL documentation as a bag of words, and use the TF/IDF measure. Furthermore, we supplement information by adding the terms in their inputs and outputs to the bag of words.

Web service description similarity: To compute the similarity of web service descriptions, we create a bag of words from the following: the tokenized web service name, WSDL documentation and UDDI description, the tokenized names of the operations in the web service, and their input and output terms. We again apply TF/IDF on the bag of words.

5.2 Combining Individual Similarities

We use a linear combination to combine the similarity of each component of the operation. Each type of similarity is assigned a weight that is dependent on its relevance to the overall similarity. Currently we set the weights manually based on our analysis of the results from different trials. Learning these weights based on direct or indirect user feedback is a subject of future work.

As noted earlier, there is a recursive dependency between the similarity of operations and that of inputs/outputs. We prove that computing the recursive similarities ultimately converges.

Proposition 1. *Computing operation similarity and input/output similarity converges.* □

Proof (Sketch): Let S_{op}, S_i and S_o be the similarity of operations, of inputs, and of outputs. Let w_i and w_o be the weights for input similarity and output similarity in computing operation similarity, and w_{op} be the weight for operation similarity in computing input/output similarity.

We start by assigning zero to the operation similarity, and based upon it compute input/output similarity and operation similarity iteratively. We can prove that if $z = w_{op}(w_{in} + w_{out}) < 1$, the computation converges and the results are:

$$S_{op}^{(\infty)} = S_{op}^{(0)} \cdot \frac{1}{1-z}$$
$$S_i^{(\infty)} = S_i^{(0)} + S_{op}^{(0)} \cdot \frac{w_{op}}{1-z}$$
$$S_o^{(\infty)} = S_o^{(0)} + S_{op}^{(0)} \cdot \frac{w_{op}}{1-z}$$

where $s_{op}^{(0)}, s_i^{(0)}$ and $s_o^{(0)}$ are the results of the first round, and $s_{op}^{(\infty)}, s_i^{(\infty)}$ and $s_o^{(\infty)}$ are the converged results. □

6 Experimental Evaluation

We now describe a set of experiments that validate the performance of our matching algorithms. Our goal is to show that we produce high precision and recall on similarity queries and to investigate the contribution of the different components of our method.

6.1 Experimental Setup

We implemented a web-service search engine, called Woogle, that has access to 790 web services from the main authoritative UDDI repositories. The coverage of Woogle is comparable to that of the other web-service search engines [1, 2, 3, 4]. We ran our experiments on the subset of web services whose associated WSDL files are accessible from the web, so we can extract information about their functionality descriptions, inputs and outputs. This set contains 431 web services, and 1574 operations in total.

Woogle performs parameter clustering, operation matching and input/output matching offline, and stores the results in a database. TF/IDF was implemented using the publicly available *Rainbow* [6] classification tool.

Our experiments compared our method, which we refer to as WOOGLE, with a couple of naive algorithms FUNC and COMB. The FUNC method matches operations by comparing only the words in the operation names and text documentation. The COMB method considers the words mentioned in the web service names, descriptions and parameter names as well; in contrast to WOOGLE, these words are all put into a single bag of words.

Performance Measure: We measured overall performance using *recall(r)*, *precision(p)*, *R-precision(p_r)* and *Top-k precision* (p_k). Consider these measures for operation matching. Let *Rel* be the set of relevant operations, *Ret* be the set of returned operations, *Retrel* be the set of returned relevant operations, and *Retrel$_k$* be the set of relevant operations in the top k returned operations. We define

$$p = \frac{|Retrel|}{|Ret|}, \quad r = \frac{|Retrel|}{|Rel|}$$

$$p_k = \frac{|Retrel_k|}{k}, \quad p_r = p_{|Rel|} = \frac{|Retrel_{|Rel|}|}{|Rel|}$$

Among the above measures, p_r is considered to most precisely capture the precision and ranking quality of a system. We also plotted the *recall/precision curve (R-P curve)*. In an R-P curve figure, the X-axis represents recall, and the Y-axis represents precision. An ideal search engine has a horizontal curve with a high precision value; a bad search engine has a horizontal curve with a low precision value. The R-P curve is considered by the IR community as the most informative graph showing the effectiveness of a search engine.

6.2 Measuring Precision

Given a web service, Woogle generates five lists: similar operations, operations with similar inputs, operations with similar outputs, operations that com-

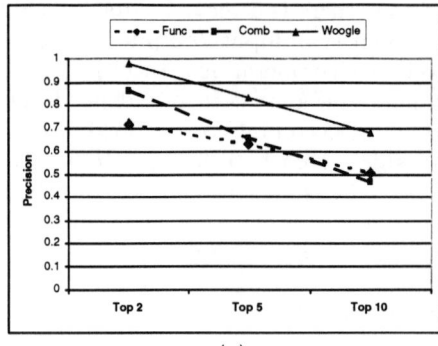

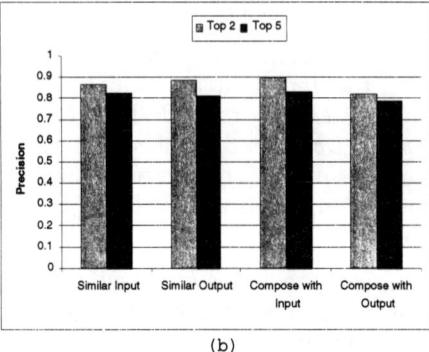

Figure 4: Top-k precision for Woogle similarity search.

pose with the output of the given operation, and operations that compose with the input of the given operation. We evaluated the precision of these returned lists, and report the average top-2, top-5 and top-10 precision.

We selected a benchmark of 25 web-service operations for which we tried to obtain similar operations from our entire collection. When selecting these, we ensured that they are from a variety of domains and that they have different input/output sizes and description sizes. To ensure the top-10 precision is meaningful, we selected only operations for which WOOGLE and COMB both returned more than 10 relevant operations. (FUNC may return less than 10 relevant operations because typically it obtains result sets of very small size.)

Figure 4(a) shows the results for top-k precision on operation matching. The top-2, top-5, and top-10 precisions of WOOGLE are 98%, 83%, 68% respectively, higher than those of the two naive methods by 10 to 30 percentage points. This demonstrates that considering different sources of evidence, and considering them separately, will increase the precision. We also observe that COMB has a higher top-2 and top-5 precision than FUNC, but its top-10 precision is lower. This demonstrates that considering more evidence by simple combination does not greatly enhance performance.

Figure 4(b) shows the precision for the four other

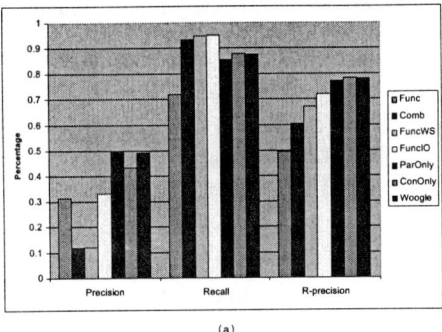

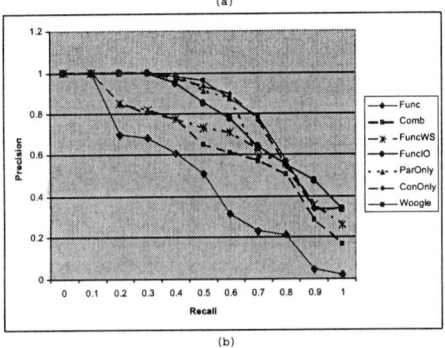

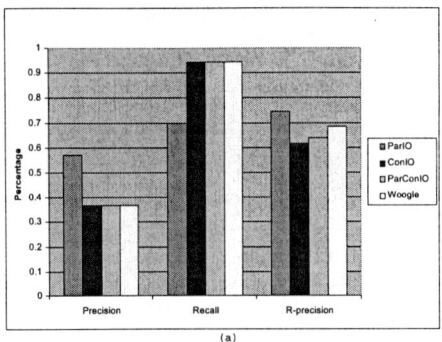

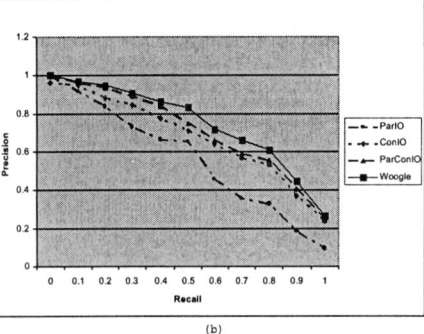

Figure 5: Performance for different operation matchers.

Figure 6: Performance of different input/output matchers

returned lists. Note that we only reported the top-2 and top-5 precision, as these lists are much smaller in size. From the 25-operation test set, we selected 20 where both input and output parameters are not empty, and the sizes of the returned lists are not too short. Figure 4(b) shows that for the majority of the four lists, the top-2 and top-5 precisions are between 80% and 90%.

6.3 Measuring Recall

In order to measure recall of similarity search, we need to know the set of all operations that are relevant to a given operation in the collection. For this purpose, we created a benchmark of 8 operations from six different domains: weather(2), address(2), stock(1), sports(1), finance(1), and time(1) (weather and address are two major domains in the web service corpus). We chose operations with different popularity: four of them have more than 30 similar operations each, and the other four each have about 10 similar operations. Among the 8 operations, one has empty input, so we have 15 inputs/outputs in total. When choosing the operations, we ensured that their inputs/outputs convey different numbers of concepts, and the concepts involved vary in popularity.

For each of the 8 operations, we hand-labeled other operations in our collection as relevant or irrelevant. We began by inspecting a set of operations that had similar web service descriptions, or similar operation descriptions, or similar inputs or outputs.

From that list we chose the set of similar operations and labeled them as relevant. The rest are labeled as irrelevant. In a similar fashion, we label relevant inputs and outputs.

In this experiment we also wanted to test the contributions of the different components of WOOGLE. To do that, we also considered the following stripped-down variations of WOOGLE:

- FUNCWS: consider only operation descriptions and web service descriptions;
- FUNCIO: consider only operation descriptions, inputs and outputs;
- PAROnly: consider all of the four components, but compare inputs/outputs based on only parameter names;
- CONOnly: consider all of the four components, but compare inputs/outputs based on only the concepts they express.

Figure 5(a) plots the average precision, recall and R-precision on the eight operations in the benchmark for each of the above matchers and also for FUNC, COMB, and WOOGLE. Figure 5(b) plots the average R-P curves. We observe the following.

First, WOOGLE generally beats all other matchers. Its recall and R-precision are 88% and 78% respectively, much higher than those of the two naive methods. Second, considering evidences from different sources by simply putting them into a big bag of words (COMB) does not help much. This strategy only beats FUNC, which considers evidence from a single source. Even FUNCWS, which discards all input and output information, has a better performance than COMB. Third, FUNCIO performs better than FUNCWS. It shows that in operation matching, the semantics of input and output provides stronger evidence than the web service description. This observation agrees with the intuition that operation similarity depends more on input and output similarity. Fourth, WOOGLE performs better than PARONLY, and also slightly better than CONONLY. PARONLY has a higher precision, but a lower recall; CONONLY has a higher recall, but a lower precision. By considering parameter matching (fine-grained matching) and concept matching (coarse-grained matching) together, WOOGLE obtains a recall as high as CONONLY, and a precision as high as PARONLY.

An interesting observation is that WOOGLE beats FUNCIO in precision up till the point when the recall reaches 80%. Also, the recall of WOOGLE is 8 percentage points lower than that of FUNCIO. This is not surprising because verbose textual descriptions of web services have two-fold effects: on the one hand, they provide additional evidence, which helps significantly in the top returned operations, where the input and output already provide strong evidence; on the other hand, they contain noise that dilutes the high-quality evidence, especially at the end of the returned list where real evidence is not very strong.

In our experiments, we also observe that compared with the benefits of our clustering technique and that of the structure-aware matching, tuning the parameters in a reasonable range and pre-processing the input/output terms improve the performance only slightly.

6.3.1 Input/output matching

We performed an additional experiment focusing on the performance of input/output matching. This experiment considered the following matchers:

- WOOGLE: matches inputs/outputs by considering parameter names, their corresponding concepts, and the operations they belong to.
- PARCONIO: considers both parameter names and concepts, but not the operations.
- CONIO: considers only concepts.
- PARIO: considers only parameter names.

Figure 6(a) shows the average recall, precision and R-precision on the fifteen inputs/outputs in the benchmark for each of the above matchers. We also plotted the average R-P curves in Figure 6(b). We observe the following. Matching inputs/outputs by comparing the expressed concepts significantly improves the performance: the three concept-aware matchers obtain a recall 25 percentage points higher than that of PARIO. Based on concept comparison, the performance of input/output matching can be further improved by considering parameter name similarity and host operation similarity.

7 Searching with Woogle

Similarity search supplements keyword search for web services. Besides, its core techniques power other search methods in the Woogle search engine, namely, template search and composition search. These two methods go beyond keyword-search by directly exploring the semantics of web-service operations. Because of lack of space, we describe them only briefly.

Template search: The user can specify the functionality, input and output of the desired web-service operation, and Woogle returns a list of operations that fulfill the requirements. It is distinguished from the keyword search in that (1) it explores the underlying structure of operations; and (2) the parameters of the returned operations are relevant to the user's requirement, but do not necessarily contain the specific words that the user uses. For example, the user can ask for operations that take zipcode of an area and return its nine-day forecast by specifying input as zipcode, output as forecast, and description as the weather in the next nine days. The inputs of the returned operation can be named zip, zipcode, or postcode. The outputs can be forecast, weather, or even temperature, humidity at the end of the list of the returned operations.

Template search is implemented by considering a user-specified template as an operation and applying the similarity search algorithm. A key challenge is to perform the operation matching efficiently on-the-fly.

Composition search: Much of the promise of web services is the ability to build complex services by composition. Composition search in Woogle returns not only single operations, but also operation compositions that achieve the desired functionality. The composition can be of any length. For example, when an operation satisfying the above search requirement is not available, it will be valuable to return a composition of an operation with zipcode as input and city and state as output, and an operation with city and state as input and nine-day forecast as output.

Based on the machinery that we have already built for matching operation inputs and outputs, we can discover compositions automatically. The challenge lies in avoiding redundancy and loop in the composition. Another challenge is to discover the compositions efficiently on-the-fly.

8 Conclusions and Future Work

As the use of web services grows, the problem of searching for relevant services and operations will get more acute. We proposed a set of similarity search primitives for web service operations, and described algorithms for effectively implementing these searches. Our algorithm exploits the structure of the web services and employ a novel clustering mechanism that groups parameter names into meaningful concepts. We implemented our algorithms in Woogle, a web service search engine, and experimented on a set of over 1500 operations. The experimental results show that our techniques significantly improve the precision and recall compared with two naive methods, and perform well overall.

In future work, we plan to expand Woogle to include automatic web-service invocation; *i.e.*, after finding the potential operations, Woogle should be able to fill in the input parameters and invoke the operations automatically for the user. This search is particularly promising because it will, in the end, be able to answer questions such as "what is the weather of an area with zipcode 98195."

While this paper focuses exclusively on searches for web services, the search strategy we have developed applies to other important domains. As a prime example, if we model web forms as web service operations, a deep-web search can be performed by first searching appropriate web forms with a desired functionality, and then automatically filling in the inputs and displaying the results. As another example, applying template search and composition search to class libraries (considering each class as a web service, and each of its methods as a web-service operation) would be a valuable tool for software component reusing.

Acknowledgments

We would like to thank Pedro Domingo, Oren Etzioni and Zack Ives for many helpful discussions, and thank the reviewers of this paper for their insightful comments. This work was supported by NSF ITR grant IIS-0205635 and NSF CAREER grant IIS-9985114.

References

[1] Binding point. http://www.bindingpoint.com/.
[2] Grand central. http://www.grandcentral.com/directory/.
[3] Salcentral. http://www.salcentral.com/.
[4] Web service list. http://www.webservicelist.com/.
[5] Wordnet. http://www.cogsci.princeton.edu/ wn/.
[6] rainbow. http://www.cs.cmu.edu/ mccallum/bow, 2003.
[7] R. Agrawal, H. Mannila, R. Srikant, H. Toivonen, and A. Verkamo. Fast discovery of association rules. *Advances in Knowledge Discovery and Data Mining*, 1996.
[8] J. Cardoso. *Quality of Service and Semantic Composition of Workflows*. PhD thesis, University of Georgia, 2002.
[9] D.-S. Coalition. Daml-s: Web service description for the semantic web. In *ISWC*, 2002.
[10] S. Cost and S. Salzberg. A weighted nearest neighbor algorithm for learning with symbolic features. *Machine Learning*, 10:57–78, 1993.
[11] S. C. Deerwester, S. T. Dumais, T. K. Landauer, G. W. Furnas, and R. A. Harshman. Indexing by latent semantic analysis. *JASIS*, 41(6):391–407, 1990.
[12] H.-H. Do and E. Rahm. COMA - A System for Flexible Combination of Schema Matching Approaches. In *Proc. of VLDB*, 2002.
[13] A. Doan, P. Domingos, and A. Halevy. Reconciling schemas of disparate data sources: a machine learning approach. In *Proc. of SIGMOD*, 2001.
[14] D. Hand, H. Mannila, and P. Smyth. *Principles of Data Mining*. The MIT Press, 2001.
[15] A. Hess and N. Kushmerick. Learning to attach semantic metadata to web services. In *ISWC*, 2003.
[16] K. S. Jones. Automatic keyword classification for information retrieval. *Archon Books*, 1971.
[17] G. Karypis, E. H. Han, and V. Kumar. Chameleon: A hierarchical clustering algorithm using dynamic modeling. *COMPUTER*, 32, 1999.
[18] L. Kaufman and P. J. Rousseeuw. *Finding Groups in Data: An Introduction to Cluster Analysis*. John Wiley & Sons, New York, 1990.
[19] L. S. Larkey. Automatic essay grading using text classification techniques. In *Proc. of ACM SIGIR*, 1998.
[20] L. S. Larkey and W. Croft. Combining classifiers in text categorization. In *Proc. of ACM SIGIR*, 1996.
[21] V. Levenshtein. Binary codes capable of correcting deletions, insertions and reversals. *Soviet Physics Daklady*, 10:707–710, 1966.
[22] S. Melnik, H. Garcia-Molina, and E. Rahm. Similarity Flooding: A Versatile Graph Matching Algorithm. In *Proc. of ICDE*, 2002.
[23] M. Paolucci, T. Kawmura, T. Payne, and K. Sycara. Semantic matching of web services capabilities. In *Proc. of International Semantic Web Conference(ISWC)*, 2002.
[24] E. Rahm and P. A. Bernstein. A survey on approaches to automatic schema matching. *VLDB Journal*, 10(4), 2001.
[25] G. Salton, editor. *The SMART Retrieval System—Experiments in Automatic Document Retrieval*. Prentice Hall Inc., Englewood Cliffs, NJ, 1971.
[26] E. Sirin, J. Hendler, and B. Parsia. Semi-automatic composition ofweb services using semantic descriptions. In *WSMAI-2003*, 2003.
[27] Y. Yang and J. Pedersen. A comparative study on feature selection in text categorization. In *International Conference on Machine Learning*, 1997.
[28] A. M. Zaremski and J. M. Wing. Specification matching of software components. *TOSEM*, 6:333–369, 1997.

AWESOME – A Data Warehouse-based System for Adaptive Website Recommendations

Andreas Thor   Erhard Rahm

University of Leipzig, Germany
{thor, rahm}@informatik.uni-leipzig.de

Abstract

Recommendations are crucial for the success of large websites. While there are many ways to determine recommendations, the relative quality of these recommenders depends on many factors and is largely unknown. We propose a new classification of recommenders and comparatively evaluate their relative quality for a sample website. The evaluation is performed with AWESOME (Adaptive website recommendations), a new data warehouse-based recommendation system capturing and evaluating user feedback on presented recommendations. Moreover, we show how AWESOME performs an automatic and adaptive closed-loop website optimization by dynamically selecting the most promising recommenders based on continuously measured recommendation feedback. We propose and evaluate several alternatives for dynamic recommender selection including a powerful machine learning approach.

1 Introduction

Recommendations are crucial for the success of large web sites to effectively guide users to relevant information. E-commerce sites offering thousands of products cannot solely rely on standard navigation and search features but need to apply recommendations to help users quickly find "interesting" products or services. With many users and products manual generation of recommendations is much too laborious and ineffective. Hence a key question becomes how should recommendations be generated automatically to optimally serve the users of a website.

There are many ways to automatically generate recommendations taking into account different types of information (e.g. product characteristics, user characteristics, or buying history) and applying different statistical or data mining approaches ([JKR02], [KDA02]). Sample approaches include recommendations of top-selling products (overall or per product category), new products, similar products, products bought together by customers, products viewed together in the same web session, or products bought by similar customers. Obviously, the relative utility of these recommendation approaches (*recommenders* for short) depends on the website, its users and other factors so that there cannot be a single best approach. Website developers thus have to decide about which approaches they should support and where and when they should be applied. Surprisingly, little information is available in the open literature on the relative quality of different recommenders. Hence, one focus of our work is an approach for comparative quantitative evaluations of different recommenders.

Advanced websites, such as Amazon [LSY03], support many recommenders but apparently are unable to select the most effective approach per user or product. They overwhelm the user with many different types of recommendations leading to huge web pages and reduced usability. While commercial websites often consider the buying behaviour for generating recommendations, the usage (navigation) behaviour on the website remains largely unexploited. We believe this a major shortcoming since the navigation behaviour contains detailed information on the users' interests not reflected in the purchase data. Moreover, the web usage behaviour contains valuable user feedback not only on products or other content but also on the presented recommendations. The utilization of this feedback to automatically and adaptively improve recommendation quality is a major goal of our work.

AWESOME (Adaptive website recommendations) is a new data warehouse-based website evaluation and recommendation system under development at the University of Leipzig. It contains an extensible library of recommender algorithms that can be comparatively evaluated for real websites based on user feedback. Moreover,

---

Permission to copy without fee all or part of this material is granted provided that the copies are not made or distributed for direct commercial advantage, the VLDB copyright notice and the title of the publication and its date appear, and notice is given that copying is by permission of the Very Large Data Base Endowment. To copy otherwise, or to republish, requires a fee and/or special permission from the Endowment

**Proceedings of the 30th VLDB Conference,
Toronto, Canada, 2004**

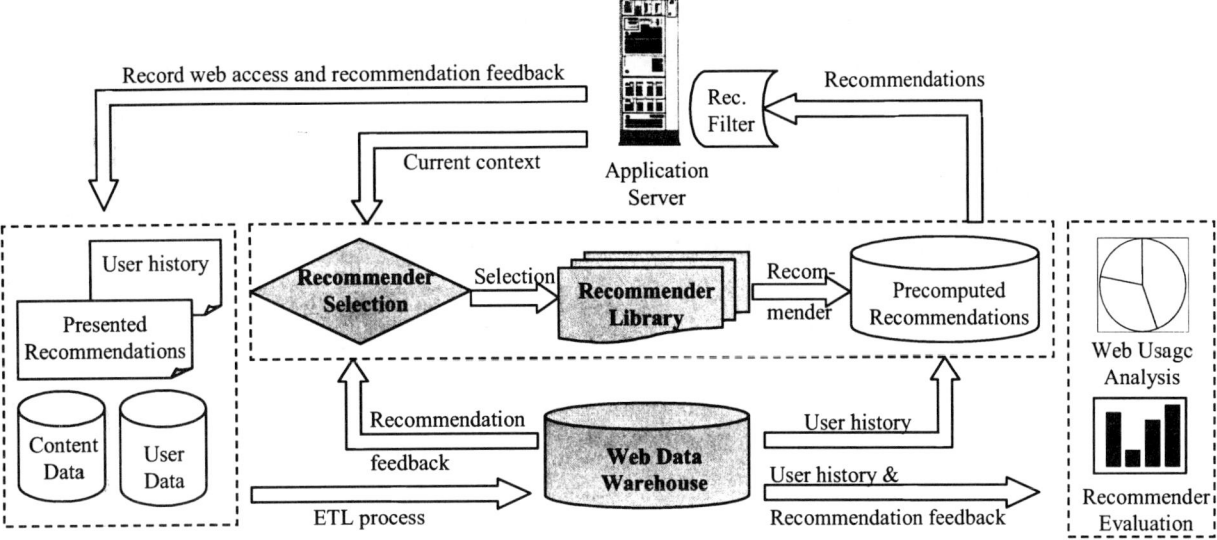

Figure 1: AWESOME architecture

AWESOME can perform an automatic closed-loop website optimization by dynamically selecting the most promising recommenders for a website access. This selection is based on the continuously measured recommendation quality of the different recommenders so that AWESOME automatically adapts to changing user interests and changing content. To support high performance and scalability, quality characteristics of recommenders and recommendations are largely precomputed. AWESOME is fully operational and in continuous use at a sample website; adoption to further sites is in preparation.

The main contributions of this paper are as follows:
- Presentation of the AWESOME architecture for warehouse-based recommender evaluation and for scaleable adaptive website recommendations
- A new classification of recommenders for websites supporting a comparison of different approaches. We show how sample approaches fit the classification and propose a new recommender for users coming from search engines.
- A comparative quantitative evaluation of several recommenders for a sample website. The considered recommenders cover a large part of our classification's design space.
- Description and comparative evaluation of several rule-based approaches for dynamic recommender selection. In particular, a machine learning approach for feedback-based recommender selection is presented.

In the next section we present the AWESOME architecture and the underlying data warehouse approach. We then outline our recommender classification and sample recommenders (Section 3). Section 4 contains the comparative evaluation of several recommenders for a non-commercial website. In Section 5 we describe and evaluate approaches for dynamic recommender selection. Related work is briefly reviewed in Section 6 before we conclude.

2 Architecture

2.1 Overview

Fig. 1 illustrates the overall architecture of AWESOME which is closely integrated with the application server running the website. AWESOME is invoked for every website access, specified by a so-called *context* including information from the current HTTP request such as URL, timestamp and user-related data. For such a context, AWESOME dynamically generates a list of recommendations which are displayed by the application server together with the requested website content. Recommendations are automatically determined by a variety of algorithms from an extensible *recommender library*. The recommenders use information on the usage history of the website and additional information maintained in a *web data warehouse*. The recommendations are subject to a final filter step to avoid the presentation of unsuitable or irrelevant recommendations (e.g., recommendation of the current page or the homepage).

Dynamic selection of recommendations is a two-step process. For a given context, AWESOME first selects the most appropriate recommender(s). This recommender selection is controlled by a moderate number of *selection rules*. For evaluation purposes, we support several selection strategies for determining and adapting these rules, in particular automatic approaches based on user feedback on previously presented recommendations. This recommendation feedback is also recorded in the web data warehouse. For the chosen recommender(s), the best recommendations for the current context are selected in the second step. For performance reasons, these recommendations are precomputed (and periodically refreshed) and can thus quickly be looked up at runtime.

Separating the selection of recommenders and recommendations makes it easy to add new recommenders. Moreover, using recommendation feedback at the level of recommenders is simpler and more stable than trying to use this feedback for individual recommendations, e.g. specific web pages or products. One problem with the latter approach is that individual pages/products are frequently added and that there is no feedback available for such new content. Conversely, removing content would result in a loss of the associated recommendation feedback.

AWESOME is based on a comprehensive web data warehouse integrating information on the website structure and content (e.g., product catalog), website users and customers, the website usage history and recommendation feedback. The application server continuously records the users' web accesses and which presented recommendations have been and which ones have NOT been followed. During an extensive ETL (extract, transform, load) process (including data cleaning, session and user identification) the usage data and recommendation feedback is added to the warehouse.

The warehouse serves several purposes. Most importantly it is the common data platform for all recommenders and keeps feedback for the dynamic recommender selection thus enabling an automatic closed-loop website optimization. However, it can also be used for extensive offline evaluations, e.g., using OLAP tools, not only for web usage analysis but also for a comparative evaluation of different recommenders and of different strategies for recommender selection. This functionality of AWESOME allows us to systematically evaluate the various approaches under a large range of conditions. It is also an important feature for website designers to fine-tune the recommendation system, e.g. to deactivate or improve less effective recommenders.

The current AWESOME implementation runs on different servers. The warehouse is on a dedicated machine running MS SQL server. The recommendation engine runs on a Unix-based application server where the precomputed recommendations and selection rules are maintained in a MySQL database. In the following, we provide some more details on the ETL process and the warehouse. More information on the recommenders and selection strategies are presented in the subsequent sections.

2.2 ETL process, data warehouse

The ETL workflow to refresh the data warehouse is executed periodically, e.g. once a day. It processes the web log files of the application server and other data sources (e.g., on the website and users). The standard log files of web servers are not sufficient for our purposes because to obtain sufficient recommendation feedback we need to record all presented recommendations and whether or not they have been followed. We thus decided to use tailored application server logging to record this information. Application server logging also enables us to apply effective approaches for session and user identification and early elimination of crawler accesses, thus supporting high data quality.

The AWESOME extensions of the application server are implemented by PHP programs and run together with standard web servers such as Apache. We use two log files: a web usage and a recommendation log file with the formats shown in Table 1. The recommendation log file records all presented recommendations and is required for our recommender evaluation. It allows us to determine positive and negative user feedback, i.e. whether or not a presented recommendation was clicked. For each presented recommendation, we also record the relative position of the recommendation on the page, the generating recommender and the used selection strategy.

The web usage log file adds two elements to the standard Common Log Format (CLF) of common web servers: session ID and user ID. The session ID is generated by the application server and stored inside a temporary cookie on the user's computer (if enabled). These cookies allow a highly reliable session reconstruction [SMB+03]. If the user does not accept temporary cookies, we use heuristic algorithms using client and referrer information for session identification [CMS99]. User IDs are stored inside permanent cookies and are used for user identification. If the user does not accept permanent cookies, user recognition is not done. About 85% of the users of our prototype website accept at least temporary cookies. Hence, cookies support a good balance between data quality and user acceptance, in contrast to client side tracking approaches requiring application of java applets or the like [SBF01].

We use several approaches to detect and eliminate web crawler requests. First, we utilize an IP address list of known crawlers (e.g., from Google) to avoid logging their

Page	requested page
Date, Time	date and time of the request
Client	IP address of the user's computer
Referrer	referring URL
Session ID	session identifier
User ID	user identifier

a) Web usage log

Pageview ID	page view where recommen-dation has been presented
Recommendation	recommended content
Position	position of this recommendation inside a recommendation list
Recommender	recommender that generated the recommendation
Strategy	strategy that selected the applied recommender

b) Recommendation log

Table 1: Log file formats

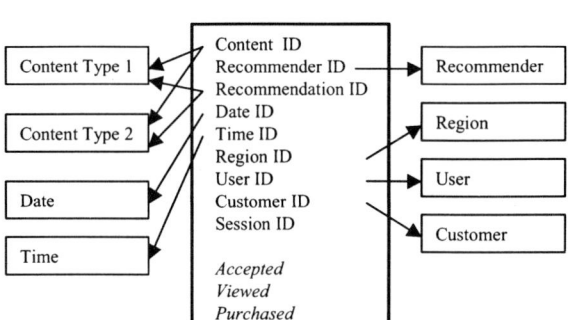

Figure 2: Schema subset for recommendations (simplified)

accesses. In addition, AWESOME eliminates all sessions containing special page views that can only be reached by following links invisible to humans. Finally, we analyze the navigation behavior and attributes like session length, average time between two requests and number of requests with blank referrer to distinguish between human user sessions and web crawler sessions [TK00].

The web data warehouse is a relational database with a "galaxy" schema consisting of several fact tables sharing several dimensions. Like in previous approaches on web usage analysis [KM00] we use separate fact tables for page views, sessions, and – for commercial sites – purchases. In addition we use a recommendation fact table as shown in Fig. 2. The details of the dimension and fact tables depend on the website, e.g. on how the content (e.g., products), users or customers are categorized. In the example of Fig. 2 there are two content dimensions for different hierarchical categorizations. Other dimensions such as user, customer, region and date are also hierarchically organized to allow evaluations at different levels of detail. The recommendation fact table represents the positive and negative user feedback on recommendations. Each record in this table refers to one presented recommendation. The ID attributes are foreign keys on the various dimension tables and identify the recommender algorithm, the recommended content, customer and details of the context (content, user, time, etc.) for which the recommendation was presented. Three Boolean measures are used to derive recommendation quality metrics (see Section 4). *Accepted* indicates whether or not the recommendation was directly accepted (clicked) by the user, while *Viewed* specifies whether the recommended content was viewed later during the respective session (i.e. the recommendation was a useful hint). *Purchased* is only used for e-commerce websites to indicate whether or not the recommended product was purchased during the current session.

The ETL process updates all affected warehouse dimension and fact tables. Moreover, the quality metrics for all recommenders as well as the rules for dynamic recommender selection are updated (see Sections 4 and 5).

3 Recommenders

A recommender generates for a given web page request, specified by a context, an ordered list of recommendations. Such recommendations link to current website content, e.g. pages describing a product or providing other information or services. Recommendations usually are presented as titled links with a short description or preview.

To calculate recommendations, recommenders can make use of the information available in the context as well as additional input, e.g. recorded purchase and web usage data. We distinguish between three types of context information relevant for determining recommendations:
- Current content, i.e. the currently viewed content (page view, product, ...) and its related information such as content categories
- Current user, e.g. identified by a cookie, and associated information, e.g. her previous purchases, previous web usage, interest preferences, or current session
- Additional information available from the HTTP request (current date and time, user's referrer, ...)

3.1 Recommender classification

Given the many possibilities to determine recommendations, there have been several attempts to classify recommenders ([Bu02], [KDA02], [SKR01], [TH01]). These classifications typically started from a given set of recommenders and tried to come up with a set of criteria covering all considered recommenders. This led to rather complex and specialized classifications with criteria that are only relevant for a subset of recommenders. Moreover, new recommenders can easily require additional criteria to keep the classification complete. For example, [SKR01] introduce a large number of specialized criteria for e-commerce recommenders such as input from target customers, community inputs, degree of personalization, etc.

To avoid these problems we propose a general top-level classification of website recommenders focusing on the usable input data, in particular the context information. This classification may be refined by taking additional aspects into account, but already leads to a distinction of major recommender types thus illustrating the design space. Moreover, the classification helps to compare different recommenders and guides us in the evaluation of different approaches.

Fig. 3 illustrates our recommender classification and indicates where sample approaches fit in. We classify recommenders based on three binary criteria, namely whether or not they use information on the current *content*, the current *user*, and recorded usage (or purchase) *history* of users. This leads to a distinction of eight types of recommenders (Fig. 3). We specify each recommender type by a three-character-code describing whether (+) or not (–) each of the three types of information is used. For instance, type [+,+,–] holds for recommenders that use

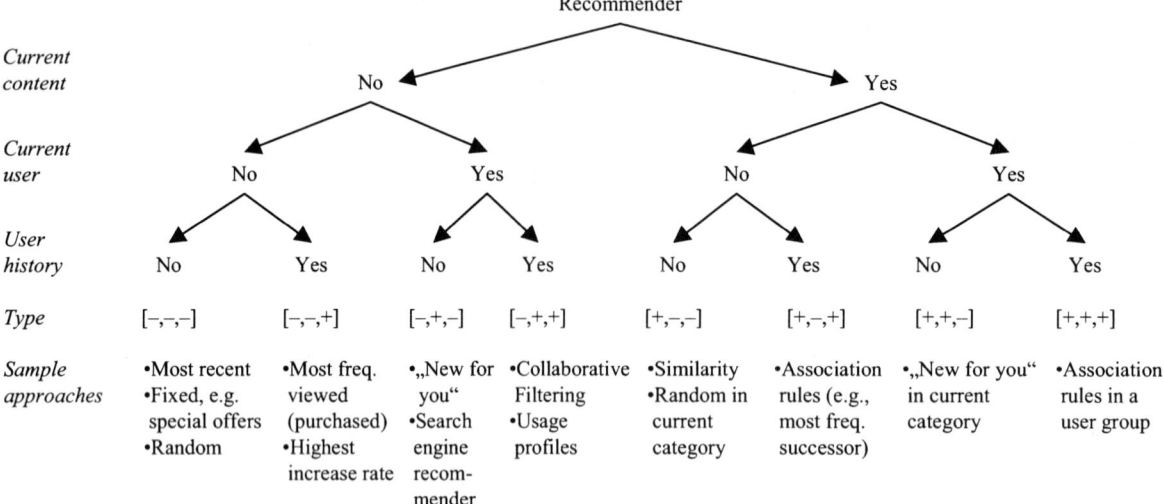

Figure 3: Top-level classification of recommenders

information on the current content and current user, but do not take into account user history.

The first classification criteria considers whether or not a recommender uses the current content, i.e. the currently requested page or product. A sample content-based approach (type [+,−,−]) is to recommend content that is most *similar* to the current content, e.g. based on text-based similarity metrics such as TF/IDF. Content-based recommenders may also use generalized information on the content category (e.g., to recommend products within the current content category). Sample content-insensitive recommenders (type [−,−,−]) are to recommend the *most recent* content, e.g. added within the last week, or to give a fixed recommendation at each page, e.g. for a special offer.

At the second level we consider whether or not a recommender utilizes information on the current user. User-based approaches could thus provide special recommendations for specific user subsets, e.g. returning users or customers, or based on personal interest profiles. Recommenders could also recommend content for individuals, e.g. new additions since a user's last visit (*"New for you"*). We developed a new recommender of type [−,+,−] for users coming from a search engine such as Google. This *search engine recommender (SER)* utilizes that the HTTP referrer information typically contains the search terms (keywords) of the user [KMT00]. SER recommends the website content (different from the current page that was reached from the search engine) that best matches these keywords. The SER implementation in AWESOME utilizes a predetermined search index of the website to quickly provide the recommendations at runtime.

With the third classification criteria we differentiate recommenders by their use of *user history* information. For commercial sites, recommenders can consider information on previous product purchases of customers. Another example is the evaluation of the previous navigation patterns of website users. Simple recommenders of type [−,−,+] recommend the *most frequently* purchased/viewed content (top-seller) or the content with the *highest* recent *increase* of interest.

While not made explicit in the classification, recommenders can utilize additional information than on current content, current user or history, e.g. the current date or time. Furthermore, additional classification criteria could be considered, such as metrics used for ranking recommendations (e.g. similarity metrics, relative or absolute access/purchase frequencies, recency, monetary metrics, etc.) or the type of analysis algorithm (simple statistics, association rules, clustering, etc.).

3.2 Additional approaches

Interesting recommenders often consider more than one of the three main types of user input. We briefly describe some examples to further illustrate the power and flexibility of our classification and to introduce approaches that are considered in our evaluation.

[+,−,+]: *Association rule* based recommenders such as "Users who bought this item also bought ...", made famous by Amazon [LSY03], consider the current content (item) and purchase history but are independent of the current user (i.e. every user sees the same recommendations for an item). Association rules can also be applied on web usage history to recommend content which is frequently viewed together within a session.

[−,+,+] Information on navigation/purchase history can be used to determine *usage profiles* [MDL+02] or groups of similar users, e.g. by *collaborative filtering* approaches. Recommenders can assign the current user to a user group (either based on previous sessions or the current session) and recommend content most popular for this group.

In our evaluation we test a *personal interests* recommender, which is applicable to returning users. It determines the most frequently accessed content categories per user as an indication of her personal interests. When the user returns to the website, the most frequently accessed content of the respective categories is recommended.

[+,+,+] A recommender of this type could use both user groups (as discussed for [–,+,+]) and association rules to recommend the current user those items that were frequently accessed (purchased) by similar users in addition to the current content.

4 Recommender evaluation

The AWESOME prototype presented in Section 2 allows us to systematically evaluate recommenders for a given website. In Section 4.2, we demonstrate this for a sample non-commercial website. Before that, we introduce several metrics for measuring recommendation quality which are needed for our evaluation of recommenders and selection strategies.

4.1 Evaluation metrics

To evaluate the quality of presented recommendations we utilize the Accepted, Viewed, and Purchased measures recorded in the recommendation fact table (Section 2.2). The first two are always applicable, while the last one only applies for commercial websites. We further differentiate between metrics at two levels of granularity, namely with respect to page views and with respect to user sessions.

Acceptance rate is a straight-forward, domain-independent metric for recommendation quality. It indicates the share of page views for which at least one presented recommendation was accepted, i.e. clicked. The definition thus is

$AcceptanceRate = |P_A| / |P|$

where P is the set of all page views containing a recommendation and P_A the subset of page views with an accepted recommendation.
Analogously we define a session-oriented quality metric

$SessionAcceptanceRate = |S_A| / |S|$

where S is the set of all user sessions and S_A the set of sessions for which at least one of the presented recommendations was accepted.

Recommendations can also be considered of good quality if the user does not directly click them but reaches the associated content later in the session (hence, the recommendation was a correct prediction of user interests). Let P_V be the set of all page views for which any of the presented recommendations was reached later in the user session. We define

$ViewRate = |P_V| / |P|$

The corresponding metric at the session level is

$SessionViewRate = |S_V| / |S|$

where S_V is the set of all user sessions with at least one pageview in P_V. Obviously, every accepted recommenda-

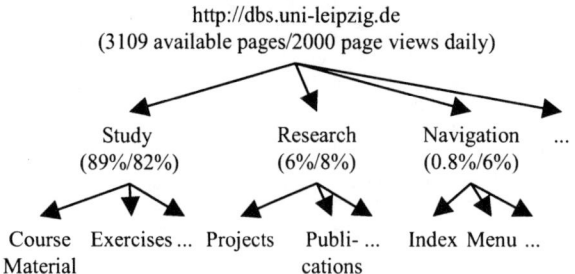

Figure 4: Example of content hierarchy

tion is also a viewed recommendation, i.e. $P_A \subseteq P_V \subseteq P$ and $S_A \subseteq S_V \subseteq S$, so that view rates are always larger than or equal to the acceptance rates.

In commercial sites, product purchases are of primary interest. Note that purchase metrics should be session-oriented because the number of page views needed to finally purchase a product is of minor interest. A useful metric for recommendation quality is the share of sessions S_{AP} containing a purchase that followed an accepted recommendation of the product. Hence, we define the following metric:

$ReommendedPurchaseRate = |S_{AP}| / |S|$

Obviously, it holds $S_{AP} \subseteq S_A \subseteq S$.

4.2 Sample evaluation

We implemented and tested the AWESOME approach for recommender evaluation for a sample website, namely the website of our database group (http://dbs.uni-leipzig.de). We use two content hierarchies and Fig. 4 shows a fragment of one of them together with some numbers on the relative size and access frequencies. The website contains more than 3100 pages and receives about 2000 human page views per day (excluding accesses from members of our database group and from crawlers). As indicated in Fig. 4, about 89% of the content is educational study material, which receives about 82% of the page views.

We changed the existing website to show two recommendations on each page so that approx. 4000 recommendations are presented every day. For each page view AWESOME dynamically selects one recommender and presents its two top recommendations (see example in Fig. 5) for the respective context as described in Section 2. We implemented and included more than 100 recommenders in our recommender library. Many of them are variations of other approaches, e.g. considering different user categories or utilizing history data for different periods of time. Due to space constraints we only present results for the six representative recommenders of different types listed in Table 2, which were already introduced in Section 3. The presented results refer to the period from December 1st, 2003 until January 31st, 2004.

Recommender		User type		
Type	Name	New users	Returning users	Σ
[−,−,−]	Most recent	(0.42%)	(0.00%)	(0.38%)
[−,−,+]	Most frequent	1.00%	0.62%	0.92%
[−,+,−]	SER	2.84%	1.95%	2.79%
[−,+,+]	Personal Interests	−	1.54%	1.54%
[+,−,−]	Similarity	1.65%	0.82%	1.56%
[+,−,+]	Association Rules	1.16%	0.68%	1.08%
	Σ	1.82%	1.09%	1.69%

Table 2: Acceptance rate vs. user type

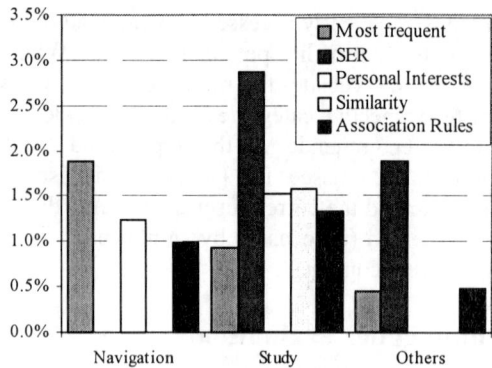

Figure 6 : Acceptance rate vs. page type

The AWESOME warehouse infrastructure allows us to aggregate and evaluate recommendation quality metrics for a huge variety of constellations (combination of dimension attributes), in particular for different recommenders. For our evaluation we primarily use (page view) acceptance rates as the most precise metric[1]. The average acceptance rate for all considered recommenders was 1.34%; the average view rate was 14.54%. For sessions containing more than one page view the average session acceptance rate was 8.16%, and the session view rate was 25.24%. These rather low acceptance rates are influenced by the fact that every single web page contains a full navigation menu with 78 links (partly nested in sub menus) and that we consciously do not highlight recommendations using big fonts or the like. Note however, that reported "click-tru" metrics are in a comparable range than our acceptance rates [CLP02]. Furthermore, the absolute values are less relevant for our evaluation than the relative differences between recommenders.

Table 2 shows the observed acceptance rates for the six recommenders differentiating between new and returning users. Fig. 6 compares the recommenders w.r.t. the current page type. As expected there are significant differences between recommenders. For our website the *search engine* recommender (SER) achieved the best average acceptance rates (2.79%), followed by the *similarity* and *personal interests* recommenders. On the other hand, simple approaches such as recommending the *most frequently* accessed or *most recent* content achieved only poor average results.

To more closely analyze the differences for different user and content types, one has to take into account that some recommenders are not always applicable. For instance, the *personal interests* recommender is only applicable for returning users (about 15% for our website). Similarly, SER can only be applied for users coming from a search engine, 95% of which turned out to be new users of the website. In Fig. 6 we only show results for recommenders with a minimum support of 5% i.e. they were applied for at least 5% of all page views of the respective page type. In Table 2 the results for the *most recent* recommender are shown in parentheses because the minimal support could not be achieved due to only few content additions during the considered time period.

Table 2 shows that new users are more likely to accept recommendations than returning users. Except for the personal interests recommender, this holds for all recommenders. An obvious explanation is that returning users (e.g., students for our website) often know where to find relevant information on the website. We also observed that the first page view of a session has a much higher acceptance rate (4.82 %) than later page views in a session (1.28 %). In the latter value, the last page view of a session is not considered, because its acceptance rate obviously equals 0^2.

Fig. 6 illustrates that the relative quality of recommenders differs for different contexts. While the SER recommender achieved the best average results for Study and Others pages, the *most frequent* recommender received the best user feedback on navigation pages. For study pages and non search engine users (when SER is not applicable), either the *personal interests* or *similarity recommender* promise the best recommendation quality.

While these observations are site-specific they illustrate that the best recommender depends on context attributes such as the current content or current user. A careful OLAP analysis may help to determine manually which recommender should be selected in which situation. However, for larger and highly dynamic websites

Figure 5: Recommendation screenshot

---

[1] The recommendations presented during a session typically come from different recommenders making the session-oriented quality metrics unsuitable for evaluating recommenders. Session acceptance rates will be used in Section 5. The Recommended-PurchaseRate does not apply for non-commercial sites.

[2] Layout aspects and other factors also influence acceptance rates. For instance, from the two recommendations shown per page the acceptance rate of the first one was about 50% higher compared to the second recommendation.

{ Usertype='new user' AND ContentCategory1='Navigation' }	➠	'Most frequent'	[0.6]
{ Referrer='search engine' }	➠	'SER'	[0.8]
{ Clienttype='university' AND Usertype='returning user' }	➠	'Personal interest'	[0.4]

Figure 7: Examples of selection rules

this is difficult and labor-intensive so that recommender selection should be automatically optimized.

5 Adaptive recommender selection

AWESOME supports a dynamic selection of recommenders for every website access. This selection is based on selection rules. Rules may either be manually defined or automatically generated. We first present the structure and use of selection rules. We then propose two approaches to automatically generate recommendation rules which utilize recommendation feedback to adapt to changing conditions. Finally we present a short evaluation to compare the different approaches for recommender selection.

5.1 Rule-based recommender selection

Recommender selection entails the dynamic selection of the most promising recommenders for a given context. Therefore selection rules have the following structure:

ContextPattern ➠ *recommender* [*weight*]

Here context pattern is a sequence of values from different context attributes (which are represented as dimension attributes in our warehouse). Typically, only a subset of attributes is specified implying that there is no value restriction for the unspecified attributes. On the right hand side of selection rules, *recommender* uniquely identifies an algorithm of the recommender library and *weight* is a real number specifying the importance of the rule. Fig. 7 shows some examples of such selection rules. In AWESOME, we maintain all rules in a single *Selection-Rules* table.

Selection rules allow a straight-forward and efficient implementation of recommender selection. It entails a *match* step to find all rules with a context pattern matching the current context. The rules with the highest weights then indicate the recommenders to be applied. The number of recommenders to choose is typically fixed. In this paper, we focus on the selection of only one recommender, i.e. we choose the rule with the highest weight. The SQL query of Fig. 8 can be used to perform the sketched selection process. Since there may be several matching rules per recommender, the ranking could also be based on the average instead of the maximal weight per recommender.

Example: Consider a new user who reaches the website from a search engine. If her current page belongs to the navigation category, only the first two rules in Fig. 7 match. We select the recommender with the highest weight – SER.

The rule-based recommender selection is highly flexible. Selection rules allow the dynamic consideration of different parts of the current context, and the weights can be used to indicate different degrees of certainty. Rules can easily be added, deleted or modified independently from other rules. Moreover, rules can be specified manually, e.g. by website editors, or be generated automatically. Another option is a hybrid strategy with automatically generated rules that are subsequently modified or extended manually, e.g. to enforce specific considerations.

5.2 Generating selection rules

We present two approaches to automatically generate selection rules, which have been implemented in AWESOME. Both approaches use the positive and negative feedback on previously presented recommendations. The first approach uses the aggregation and query functionality of the data warehouse to determine selection rules. The second approach is more complex and uses a machine learning algorithm to learn the most promising recommender for different context constellations.

5.2.1 Query-based top recommender

This approach takes advantage of the data warehouse query functionality. It generates selection rules as follows:

1. Find all relevant context patterns in the recommendation fact table, i.e. context patterns exceeding a minimal support
2. For every such context pattern *P* do
   a) Find recommender *R* with highest acceptance rate *A*
   b) Add selection rule *P* -> *R* [*A*]
3. Delete inapplicable rules

The first step ensures that only context constellations with a minimal number of occurrences are considered. This is important to avoid generalization of very rare and special situations (overfitting problem). Note that step 1 checks all possible context patterns, i.e. any of the content attributes may be unspecified, which is efficiently supported by the CUBE operator (SQL extension: GROUP BY CUBE) [GBL+95]. AWESOME is based on a commercial RDBMS providing this operator. For every such context pattern, we run a query to determine the recommender with the highest acceptance rate and produce a corresponding selection rule.

Finally, we perform a rule pruning taking into account that we only want to determine the top recommender per context. We observe that for a rule A with a more general

391

context pattern and a higher weight than rule B, the latter will never be applied (every context that matches rule B also matches rule A, but A will be selected due to its higher weight). Hence, we eliminate all such inapplicable rules in step 3 to limit the total number of rules.

5.2.2 Machine-learning approach

Recommender selection can be interpreted as a classifier selecting one recommender from a predefined set of recommenders. Hence, machine learning (classification) algorithms can be applied to generate selection rules. Our approach utilizes a well-known classification algorithm constructing a decision tree based on training instances (Weka J48 algorithm [WF00]). To apply this approach, we thus have to transform recommendation feedback into training instances. An important requirement is that the generation of training data must be completely automatic so that the periodic re-calculation of selection rules to incorporate new recommendation feedback is not delayed by the need of human intervention.

The stored recommendation feedback indicates for each presented recommendation, its associated context attributes, and the used recommender whether or not the recommendation was accepted. A naïve approach to generate training instances would simply select a random sample from the recommendation fact table (Fig. 2), e.g. in the format *(context, recommender, accepted)*. However, classifiers using such training instances would rarely predict a successful recommendation since the vast majority of the instances may represent negative feedback (> 98% for the sample website). Ignoring negative feedback is also no solution since the number of accepted recommendations is heavily influenced by the different applicability of recommenders and not only by their recommendation quality. Therefore, we propose a more sophisticated approach that determines the number of training instances according to the acceptance rates:

1. Find all relevant feedback combinations *(context, recommender)*
2. For every combination c do
   a) Determine acceptance rate for c. Scale and round it to compute integer weight n_c
   b) Add instance *(context, recommender)* n_c times to training data
3. Apply decision tree algorithm
4. Rewrite decision tree into selection rules

In Step 1, we do not evaluate context patterns (as in the previous approach), which may leave some context attributes unspecified. We only consider fully specified context attributes and select those combinations exceeding a minimal number of recommendation presentations. For each such relevant combination c *(context, recommender)*, we use its acceptance rate to determine the

```
SELECT Recommender, MAX (Weight)
FROM SelectionRules
WHERE ((RuleContextAttribute1 = CurrentContextAttribute1)
        OR (RuleContextAttribute1 IS NULL))
AND    ((RuleContextAttribute2 = CurrentContextAttribute2)
        OR (RuleContextAttribute2 IS NULL))
AND ...
GROUP BY Recommender
ORDER BY MAX(Weight) DESC
```

Figure 8: SQL query for selection strategy execution

number of training instances n_c. To determine n_c, we linearly scale the respective acceptance rate from the 0 to 1 range by multiplying it with a constant k and rounding to an integer value. For example, assume 50 page views for the combination of context ("returning user", "search engine", "Navigation", ...) and recommender "Most frequent". If there are 7 accepted recommendations for this combination (i.e. acceptance rate 0,14) and k=100, we add n_c =14 identical instances of the combination to the training data. This procedure ensures that recommenders with a high acceptance rate produce more training instances than less effective recommenders and therefore have a higher chance to be predicted.

The resulting set of training instances is the input for the classification algorithm producing a decision tree. With the help of cross-validation, all trainings instances are simultaneously used as test instances. The final decision tree can easily be rewritten into selection rules. Every path from the root to a leaf defines a context pattern where all unspecified context attributes are set to NULL. Each leaf specifies a recommender and the rule weight is set to the relative fraction of correctly classified instances provided by the classification algorithm.

5.3 Evaluation of selection rules

To evaluate the effectiveness of the two presented selection strategies we tested them with AWESOME on the sample website introduced in Section 4.2. For comparison purposes we also evaluated two sets of manually specified rules and a random recommender selection giving a total of five approaches (see Table 3). For every user session AWESOME uniformly selected one of the strategies; the chosen strategy is additionally recorded in the recommendation log file for evaluation purposes. We applied the selection strategies from January 1st until February 25th, 2004.

Table 4 shows the average number of rules per selection strategy as well as the average delay to dynamically select a recommender. Even for the two automatic approaches the number of rules is moderate (250 – 2000) and permitted very fast recommender selection of less than 20 ms on average for a Unix server (execution time for the query in Fig. 8).

Name	Description
Top-Rec	Automatic strategy of section 5.2.1 (query-based)
Decision Tree	Automatic strategy of section 5.2.2 (machine learning)
Manual 1	The most frequently viewed pages per content category are recommended. For returning users, this category is derived from previous sessions of the current user. For new users, the category of the current page is used.
Manual 2	For search engine users, the search engine recommender is applied. Otherwise the content similarity recommender (for course material pages) or association rule recommender (for other pages) is selected.
Random	Random selection of a recommender

Table 3: Tested selection strategies

Table 4 also shows the average (page view) acceptance rates and session acceptance rates for the five selection strategies. The two automatic feedback-based strategies for recommender selection (Top-Rec, Decision Tree) showed significantly better average quality than random and the first manual policy. The machine learning approach (Decision Tree) and the Manual2 policy were the best strategies. Note that the very effective strategy Manual2 utilizes background knowledge about the website structure and typical user groups (students, researchers) as well as evaluation results obtained after an extensive manual OLAP analysis (partially presented in Section 4.2), such as the effectiveness of the search engine recommender. The fact that the completely automatic machine learning algorithm achieves comparable effectiveness is thus a very positive result. It indicates the feasibility of the automatic closed-loop optimization for generating recommendations and the high value of using feedback to significantly improve recommendation quality without manual effort.

The comparison of the two automatic strategies shows that the machine learning approach performs much better than the query-based top recommender approach. The decision tree approach uses significantly fewer rules and was able to order the context attributes according to their relevance. The most significant attributes appear in the upper part of the decision tree and therefore have a big influence on the selection process. On the other hand, Top-Rec handles all context attributes equally and uses many more rules. So recommender selection was frequently based on less relevant attributes resulting in poorer acceptance rates.

The warehouse infrastructure of AWESOME allows us to analyze the recommendation quality of selection strategies for many conditions, similar to the evaluation of individual recommenders (Section 4.2). Figure 9 shows the session acceptance rates of the best two selection strategies w.r.t. user type, referrer, and entry page type, i.e. the page type of the first session page view. We observe that the manual strategy is more effective for search engine users by always applying the SER recommender to them. This helped to also get slightly better results for new users and sessions starting with an access to study material. On the other hand, the machine learning approach was significantly more effective for users not coming from search engines and returning users. These results indicate that the automatically generated selection rules help generate good recommendations in many cases without the need of extensive manual evaluations, e.g. using OLAP tools. Still, overall quality can likely be improved by adding a few manual rules (with high weight) to incorporate background knowledge. We will investigate such hybrid strategies in future work.

6 Related work

An overview of previous recommendation systems and the applied techniques can be found in [JKR02], [KDA02] and [SCD+00]. [LSY03] describes the Amazon recommendation algorithms, which are primarily content (item)-based and also heavily use precomputation to achieve scalability to many users. [Bu02] surveys and classifies so-called hybrid recommendation systems which combine several recommenders. To improve hybrid recommendation systems, [SKR02] proposes to manually assign weights to recommenders to influence recommendations. [MN03] presents a hybrid recommendation system

Strategy	Nr. of rules	Selection time	Acceptance rate	Session acceptance rate
Top-Rec	~ 2000	~ 14 ms	1.25 %	9.58 %
Decision Tree	~ 250	~ 12 ms	1.64 %	12.54 %
Manual 1	24	~ 13 ms	0.96 %	7.11 %
Manual 2	5	~ 13 ms	1.84 %	12.47 %
Random	137	~ 19 ms	0.89 %	6.51 %

Table 4: Comparison of selection strategies

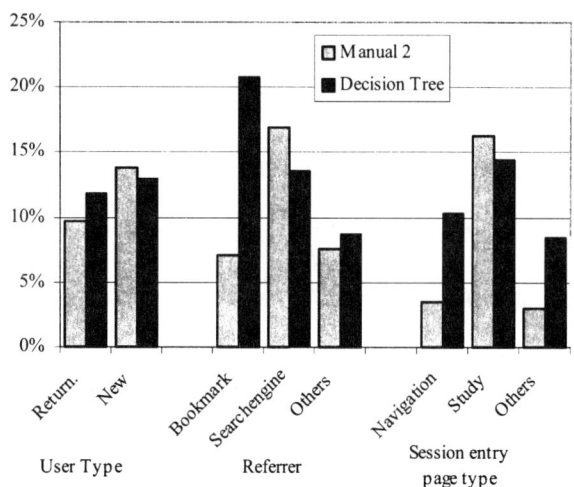

Figure 9: SessionAcceptanceRate w.r.t. user type, referrer, and session entry page type.

switching between different recommenders based on the current page's position within a website. The Yoda system [SC03] uses information on the current session of a user to dynamically select recommendations from several predefined recommendation lists. In contrast to AWESOME, these previous hybrid recommendation systems do not evaluate or use recommendation feedback.

[LK01] sketches a simple hybrid recommendation system using recommendation feedback to a limited extent. They measure which recommendations produced by three different recommenders are clicked to determine a weight per recommender (with a metric corresponding to our view rate). These weights are used to combine and rank recommendations from the individual recommenders. In contrast to AWESOME negative recommendation feedback and the current context are not considered for recommender evaluation. Moreover, there is no automatic closed-loop adaptation but the recommender weights are determined by an offline evaluation.

The evaluation of recommendation systems and quantitative comparison of recommenders has received little attention so far. [KCR02] monitored users that were told to solve certain tasks on a website, e.g. to find specific information. By splitting users in two groups (with recommendations vs. without) the influence of the recommendation system is measured. Other studies [GH02], [HC02] asked users to explicitly rate the quality of recommendations. This approach obviously is labor-intensive and cannot be applied to compare many different recommenders.

[GH02] and [SKK+00] discuss several metrics for recommendation quality, in particular the use of the information retrieval metrics precision and recall. The studies determine recommendations based on an offline evaluation of web log or purchase data; the precision metric, for instance, indicates how many of the recommendations were reached within the same session (thus corresponding to our view rate). In contrast to our evaluation, these studies are not based on really presented recommendations and measured recommendation feedback so that the predicted recommendation quality remains unverified.

In [HMA+02] a methodology is presented for evaluating two competing recommenders. It underlines the importance of such an online evaluation and discusses different evaluation aspects. Cosley et. al. developed the REFEREE framework to compare different recommenders for the CiteSeer website [CLP02]. Click metrics (e.g., how often a user followed a link or downloaded a paper), which are similar to the acceptance rates used in our study, are used to measure recommendation quality.

As an alternative to the two-level approach for selecting recommendations, we recently started to investigate how to directly determine suitable recommendations without prior selection of recommenders [GR04]. The approach requires that different recommenders produce comparable weights for individual recommendations.

Reinforcement learning approaches can be used to consider user feedback for individual recommendations. A comparative evaluation of this approach with the presented two-level scheme is subject to future work.

7 Summary

We presented AWESOME, a new data warehouse-based website evaluation and recommendation system. It allows the coordinated use of a large number of recommenders to automatically generate website recommendations. Recommendations are dynamically determined by a flexible rule-based approach selecting the most promising recommender for the respective context. AWESOME supports a completely automatic generation and optimization of selection rules to minimize website administration overhead and quickly adapt to changing situations. This optimization is based on a continuous measurement of user feedback on presented recommendations. To our knowledge, AWESOME is the first system enabling such a completely automatic closed-loop website optimization. The use of data warehouse technology and precomputation of recommendations support scalability and fast web access times.

We presented a simple but general recommender classification. It distinguishes eight types of recommenders based on whether or not they consider input information on the current content, current user and users history. To evaluate the quality of recommendations and recommenders, we proposed the use of several acceptance rate metrics based on measured recommendation feedback. We used these metrics for a detailed comparative evaluation of different recommenders and different recommender selection strategies for a sample website. Our results so far indicate that the use of machine learning is most promising for an automatic feedback-based recommendation selection. The presented policy is able to automatically determine suitable training data so that its periodic re-execution to consider new feedback does not require human intervention.

In future work, we will adopt AWESOME to additional websites, in particular e-shops, to further verify and fine-tune the presented approach. We will investigate hybrid selection strategies where automatically generated selection rules are complemented by a limited number of manually specified rules utilizing site-specific optimization criteria or specific background knowledge. Finally, we will explore specific recommendation opportunities such as selecting the best recommender for product bundling (cross-selling).

Acknowledgements

We thank Nick Golovin and Robert Lokaiczyk for fruitful discussions and help with the implementation. The first author was funded by the German Research Foundation within the Graduiertenkolleg "Knowledge Representation".

References

[Bu02] Burke, R.: *Hybrid Recommender Systems: Survey and Experiments.* User Modeling and User-Adapted Interaction 12(4), 2002

[CMS99] Cooley, R., Mobasher, B., Srivastava, J.: *Data preparation for mining world wide web browsing patterns.* Knowledge and Information Systems. 1(1), 1999

[CLP02] Cosley, D., Lawrence, S., Pennock, D. M.: *REFEREE: An open framework for practical testing of recommender systems using ResearchIndex.* Proc. 28th VLDB conf., 2002

[GBL+95] J. Gray, A. Bosworth, A. Layman, H. Pirahesh. *Data cube: A relational aggregation operator generalizing groupby, cross-tab, and sub-total.* Proc. of the 12th EEE International Conference on Data Engineering (ICDE), 1995

[GH02] Geyer-Schulz, A., Hahsler, M.: *Evaluation of Recommender Algorithms for an Internet Information Broker based on Simple Association rules and on the Repeat-Buying Theory.* Proc. of ACM WebKDD Workshop, 2002

[GR04] Golovin, N., Rahm, E.: *Reinforcement Learning Architecture for Web Recommendations.* Int. Conf. on Information Technology (ITCC), 2004

[HC02] Heer, J., Chi, E. H.: *Separating the Swarm: Categorization Methods for User Sessions on the Web.* Prof. Conf. on Human Factors in Computing Systems, 2002

[HMA+02] Hayes, C., Massa, P., Avesani, P., Cunningham, P.: *An on-line evaluation framework for recommender systems.* Proc. of Workshop on Personalization and Recommendation in E-Commerce, 2002

[JKR02] Jameson, A., Konstan, J., Riedl, J.: *AI Techniques for Personalized Recommendation.* Tutorial at 18th National Conf. on Artificial Intelligence (AAAI), 2002

[KCR02] Kim, K., Carroll, J. M., Rosson, M. B.: *An Empirical Study of Web Personalization Assistants: Supporting End-Users in Web Information Systems.* Proc. IEEE 2002 Symp. on Human Centric Computing Languages and Environments, 2002

[KDA02] Koutri, M., Daskalaki, S., Avouris, N.: *Adaptive Interaction with Web Sites: an Overview of Methods and Techniques.* Proc. 4th Int. Workshop on Computer Science and Information Technologies (CSIT), 2002

[KM00] Kimball, R., Merz, R.: *The Data Webhouse Toolkit – Building Web-Enabled Data Warehouse.* Wiley Computer Publishing, New York, 2000

[KMT00] Kushmerick, N., McKee, J., Toolan, F.: *Toward zero-input personalization: Referrer-based page recommendation.* Proc. Int. Conf. on Adaptive Hypermedia and Adaptive Web-based Systems, 2000

[LK01] Lim, M., Kim, J.: *An Adaptive Recommendation System with a Coordinator Agent.* In Proc. 1st Asia-Pacific Conference on Web Intelligence: Research and Development, 2001

[LSY03] Linden, G., Smith, B., York, J.: *Amazon.com Recommendations: Item-to-Item Collaborative Filtering.* IEEE Distributed Systems Online 4(1), 2003

[MDL+02] Mobasher, B., Dai, H., Luo, T., Nakagawa, M.: *Discovery and Evaluation of Aggregate Usage Profiles for Web Personalization.* Data Mining and Knowledge Discovery, Kluwer, 6 (1), 2002

[MN03] Mobasher, B., Nakagawa, M.: *A Hybrid Web Personalization Model Based on Site Connectivity.* Proc. ACM WebKDD Workshop, 2003

[SBF01] Shahabi, C., Banaei-Kashani, F., Faruque, J.: *A Reliable, Efficient, and Scalable System for Web Usage Data Acquisition.* Proc. ACM WebKDD Workshop, 2001

[SC03] Shahabi, C., Chen, Y.: *An Adaptive Recommendation System without Explicit Acquisition of User Relevance Feedback.* Distributed and Parallel Databases 14(2), 2003

[SCD+00] Srivastava, J., Cooley, R., Deshpande, M., Tan, P-T.: *Web Usage Mining: Discovery and Applications of Usage Patterns from Web Data.* SIGKDD Explorations, (1) 2, 2000

[SKK+00] Sarwar, B., Karypis, G., Konstan, J., Riedl, J.: *Analysis of recommendation algorithms for e-commerce.* Proc. of ACM E-Commerce, 2000

[SKR01] Schafer, J.B., Konstan, J. A., Riedl, J.: *Electronic Commerce recommender applications.* Journal of Data Mining and Knowledge Discovery, 5 (1/2), 2001

[SKR02] Schafer, J. B., Konstan, J. A., Riedl, J.: *Meta-recommendation systems: user-controlled integration of diverse recommendations.* Proc. 11th Int. Conf. on Information and Knowledge Management (CIKM), 2002

[SMB+03] Spiliopoulou, M., Mobasher, B., Berendt, B., Nakagawa, M.: *A Framework for the Evaluation of Session Reconstruction Heuristics in Web Usage Analysis.* INFORMS Journal of Computing, Special Issue on Mining Web-Based Data for E-Business Applications, 15 (2), 2003

[TH01] Terveen, L., Hill, W.: *Human-Computer Collaboration in Recommender Systems.* In: Carroll, J. (ed.): Human Computer Interaction in the New Millenium. New York: Addison-Wesley, 2001

[TK00] Tan, P., Kumar, V.: *Modeling of Web Robot Navigational Patterns.* Proc. ACM WebKDD Workshop, 2000

[WF00] Witten, I.H., Frank, E.: *Data Mining. Practical Machine Learning Tools and techniques with Java implementations.* Morgan Kaufmann. 2000

Accurate and Efficient Crawling for Relevant Websites

Martin Ester
Simon Fraser University
School of Computing Science
Burnaby BC,
Canada V5A 1S6
ester@cs.sfu.ca

Hans-Peter Kriegel
University of Munich
Institute for Computer Science
Oettingenstr. 67,
D-80538 Munich, Germany
{kriegel,schubert}@dbs.informatik.uni-muenchen.de

Matthias Schubert

Abstract

Focused web crawlers have recently emerged as an alternative to the well-established web search engines. While the well-known focused crawlers retrieve relevant webpages, there are various applications which target whole websites instead of single webpages. For example, companies are represented by websites, not by individual webpages. To answer queries targeted at websites, web directories are an established solution. In this paper, we introduce a novel focused website crawler to employ the paradigm of focused crawling for the search of relevant websites. The proposed crawler is based on a two-level architecture and corresponding crawl strategies with an explicit concept of websites. The external crawler views the web as a graph of linked websites, selects the websites to be examined next and invokes internal crawlers. Each internal crawler views the webpages of a single given website and performs focused (page) crawling within that website. Our experimental evaluation demonstrates that the proposed focused website crawler clearly outperforms previous methods of focused crawling which were adapted to retrieve websites instead of single webpages.

1. Introduction

Focused web crawlers have recently emerged as an alternative to the established web search engines like Google [12]. A focused web crawler [3] takes a set of well-selected webpages exemplifying the user interest. Searching for further relevant webpages, the focused crawler starts from a set of given pages and recursively explores the linked webpages. While the crawlers used for refreshing the indices of web search engines perform a breadth-first search of the whole web, a focused crawler explores only a small portion of the web using a best-first search guided by the user interest. Compared to web search engines, focused crawlers obtain a much higher precision and return new pages which are not yet indexed. Recently, focused web crawlers have received a lot of attention in the research areas of database systems, information retrieval and data mining [2,3,5,6,8,17].

Web search engines index individual webpages. Web directories provide a more abstract view on the web, listing relevant websites for a variety of topics. A website is a linked set of HTML-documents published by the same person or institution serving a common purpose. For several applications, the information about the topics of websites allows more accurate retrieval than the information about topics of single webpages. For example, companies are represented by entire websites, not by individual webpages. As another example, when looking for the price of a new computer, it is very helpful to search only the websites of computer retailers instead of searching the whole World Wide Web (WWW).

However, using a web directory for addressing these problems has several drawbacks. Web directories offer in most cases only a very small portion of the websites that are relevant to a given topic. The given categorization might totally lack the topic a user is interested in. Last but not least, web directory services might not be up-to-date due to manual maintenance. In this paper, we therefore extend focused crawling to the search for relevant websites offering a method to significantly increase the recall of existing web directories. Additionally, such a crawler can act as an alternative approach for searching the web for topics not yet listed in any web directory.

To adopt focused crawling for website retrieval, the simplest way is to use one of the well-established methods

Permission to copy without fee all or part of this material is granted provided that the copies are not made or distributed for direct commercial advantage, the VLDB copyright notice and the title of the publication and its date appear, and notice is given that copying is by permission of the Very Large Data Base Endowment. To copy otherwise, or to republish, requires a fee and/or special permission from the Endowment.

**Proceedings of the 30th VLDB Conference,
Toronto, Canada, 2004**

for focused webpage crawling and, in a step of post-processing, analyse the resulting webpages in order to find relevant sites. This analysis can be done by looking for relevant homepages or by applying a website classifier [11] to all pages retrieved from a given website. However, this approach is severely limited by the fact that there is no guarantee that the crawled webpages are representative of their corresponding websites.

In this paper, we argue that in order to achieve efficient and accurate website crawling the concept of websites has to be integrated into the focused crawler itself. Therefore, we introduce a novel focused crawler directly searching for relevant websites instead of single pages. The proposed focused website crawler is based on a two-level graph abstraction of the World Wide Web (WWW) representing both webpages and websites together with their links. The crawling task is divided into two major subtasks corresponding to the two different levels of abstraction:

- An *internal crawler* views the webpages of a single given website and performs focused (page) crawling within that website.
- The *external crawler* has a more abstract view of the web as a graph of linked websites. Its task is to select the websites to be examined next and to invoke internal crawlers on the selected sites.

The proposed two-level architecture allows the crawler to control the number of pages to be downloaded from each website and enables it to find a good trade-off between accurate classification and efficient crawling. Our experimental evaluation demonstrates that website classification based on the homepages is considerably less accurate than classification methods employing more than one webpage. Furthermore, we compare our prototype of a focused website crawler to a focused webpage crawler with website post-processing and show that the introduced methods of focused website crawling clearly increase the efficiency as well as the accuracy of retrieving relevant websites from the WWW. The outline of the paper is as follows. After this introduction, we briefly survey related work. In section 3, we define the task of focused website crawling and a basic solution. Section 4 presents our novel approach to focused website crawling. Section 5 reports the results of our experimental evaluation. The last section summarizes the paper and discusses several directions for future research.

2. Related Work

In this section, we discuss related work on focused crawling as well as on text and web classification. One of the first focused web crawlers was presented by [8] which introduced a best-first search strategy based on simple criteria such as keyword occurrences and anchor texts. Later, several papers such as [2] and [3] suggested to exploit measures for the importance of a webpage (such as authority and hub ranks) based on the link structure of the world-wide-web to order the crawl frontier. These measures, which are very successfully used to rank result lists of web search engines, also proved to be very effective in focusing a crawler on the topic of interest of a user.

Recently, more sophisticated focused crawlers such as [5], [9] and [17] incorporate more knowledge gained during the process of focused crawling. [9] introduced the concept of context graphs to represent typical paths leading to relevant webpages. These context graphs are used to predict the link distance to a relevant page and, consequently, are applied to order the crawl frontier. [17] explored a reinforcement learning approach, considering the successful paths observed, to weight the links at the crawl frontier based on the expected number of relevant pages reachable. [5] extends the architecture of a focused crawler by a so-called apprentice which learns from the crawler's successes and failures and is later consulted by the crawler to improve the ratio of relevant pages visited. Like a human user, the apprentice analyses the HTML structure of a webpage to judge the relevance of the outlinks of this page. To the best of our knowledge, all focused crawlers presented in the literature search for individual webpages and not for whole websites. The only site-oriented features of established page crawlers are the measures to prevent so-called spider traps and the prevention of host-to-host reinforcement proposed by Bharat and Henzinger [1]. A spider trap is an infinite loop within the WWW that dynamically produces new pages trapping a web crawler within this loop. A common approach to avoid most spider traps limits the maximum number of pages to be downloaded from a given website in order to escape the trapping situation [6]. However, these crawlers do not have any means to control the search within a website.

Most text classification algorithms rely on the so-called vector-space model. In this model, each text document is represented by a vector of frequencies of the most relevant terms. Due to the typically high dimensionality of the vector space, most frequencies are zero for any single document and many of the standard classification methods perform poorly. However, methods that do not suffer so much from high dimensionalities have been very successful in text classification, such as naive Bayes [19], support vector machines [14,19] or centroid based text classification [13]. An increasing number of publications especially deal with the classification of webpages. In particular, several methods have been proposed to exploit the hyperlinks for improving the classification accuracy. [7] introduces several methods of relational learning considering the existence of links to webpages of specific classes. [4] presents techniques for using the class labels and the text of neighboring webpages.

Most existing methods aim at classifying single webpages, not complete websites. [11] introduced the problem of website classification and presented several methods based on the representation of a website as a labeled website tree where the labels are drawn from a set of page classes. However, all methods require that the user defines an appropriate (for the task of website classification) set of page classes and provides sufficient numbers of training webpages for each of these classes. We argue that this large overhead is a major obstacle for practical applications. Furthermore, [11] only deals with the classification of given websites, but does not present a focused website crawler. While it suggests a simple search strategy for exploring a given website, this strategy is not suitable as an "internal crawl strategy". Furthermore, there is no "external crawl strategy" and no discussion of the interaction between these components. Though the approach described in [15] overcomes the first problem of defining page classes it does not treat any aspects of focused web crawling.

3. The Task of Focused Website Crawling

3.1. A Graph-Oriented View of the WWW

We identify a webpage p by its URL. Then, $content(p) \to \sigma \in \Sigma^*$ denotes the string we receive when trying to download p. Furthermore, we assume a function $f: \Sigma^* \to T \cong N^d$ which transforms a string (for example, the contents of a webpage) into a d-dimensional feature vector. Let $\Lambda(p)$ be the set of all links (p,q_1), (p,q_2), ..., (p,q_m), from p to $q_i \neq p$. The link (p,q) points from the *source page p* to the *destination page q*. Links within the same webpage are ignored. We define the *webpage graph* as a directed graph $G=(V,E)$ with V being the set of all existing webpages (extended by a special element which is needed to represent broken links) and E being the union of $\Lambda(p)$ for all $p \in V$.

The goal of focused *website* crawling is to retrieve new relevant websites from the WWW. A website is a linked set of webpages that is published by the same person, group or institution and usually serves a common purpose, e.g. to present a whole organization or company. Unfortunately, this intuitive definition is not well suited for automatic retrieval. Since there is no reliable way to find out who really published a webpage and for what purpose, there is no exact method to determine the webpages belonging to a certain site. Nonetheless, no-one would deny the existence of websites and thus, in order to retrieve relevant sites it is necessary to find a pragmatic definition that is suitable for the majority of cases. In this paper, we take advantage of the characteristic that a very large percentage of all websites is published under one dedicated domain or subdomain. For the cases that a website is spread over several domains/subdomains, we do not loose any results, but may have some duplicates in the result set. However, if large websites are classified more than once, their chance of being part of the result increases as well. The other problem of our definition is

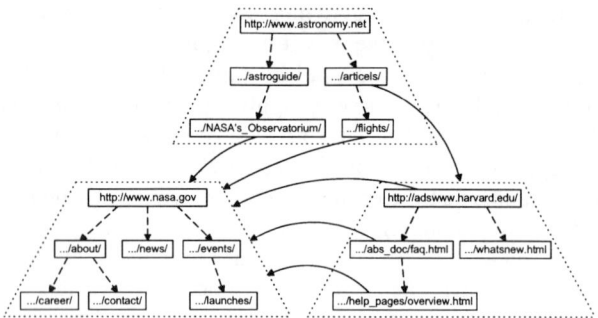

Figure 1: Sample portion of the website graph.

the case that one domain hosts several websites. Thus, websites without a domain of there own are not discovered. However, websites without a domain of there own are important in rare cases only and there is no search system on the WWW that can claim to achieve 100% recall.

Formally, for each page p, $host(p)$ returns the domain or subdomain of p, i.e. the substring of the URL of p between the protocol and the file section. We define a *website W* as a subgraph $W=(V',E')$ of the webpage graph with the following properties:

$$\forall u,v \in V': host(u) = host(v)$$
$$\forall u \in V', v \notin V': host(u) \neq host(v)$$
$$\forall e \in E': source(e) \in V' \wedge destination(e) \in V'.$$

We define the homepage as the webpage that is referenced by the URL consisting of the domain name only (e.g. http://www.cs.sfu.ca). Thus, each website has a unique homepage that can be accessed knowing the website name only. Compared to the webpage graph, the website graph (which is the conceptual view of our website crawler onto the WWW), has several important differences: We distinguish two different types of nodes at different levels of abstraction, page nodes and site nodes. We distinguish two different types of edges, representing inter-site links and intra-site links. Edges for intra-site links point to page nodes, but edges representing inter-site links point to site nodes. These differences are due to the fact that a focused website crawler searches for whole websites and visits one website after another starting the exploration of a new website from its home page. For a more formal definition, let $G=(V,E)$ be the webpage graph. We distinguish between *intrinsic links* (p,q) with $host(p) = host(q)$ and *transversal links* with $host(p) \neq host(q)$. Let U denote the union of V and let W be the set of all existing websites. We define the *website graph* as a directed graph $WG=(U,D)$ with the set of edges D given as follows:

$$\forall (p,q) \in E : host(p) = host(q) \Rightarrow (p,q) \in D$$
$$\forall (p,q) \in E : host(p) \neq host(q) \Rightarrow (p,host(q)) \in D$$

Figure 1 depicts a small sample portion of the website graph consisting of three websites. Intrinsic links are represented by dashed arrows, transversal links by solid arrows.

3.2. Retrieving Websites with Focused Crawling

A focused webpage crawler [3] takes a set of well-selected webpages exemplifying the user interest. Searching for further relevant webpages, the focused crawler starts from the given pages and recursively explores the linked webpages. The conceptual view of the WWW of a focused page crawler is the *webpage graph*. The crawl frontier consists of all hyperlinks (or the referenced webpages) from downloaded pages pointing to not yet visited pages. The performance of the crawler strongly depends on the crawling strategy, i.e. the way the frontier is ordered.

There are several ways of post-processing the results of focused *page* crawlers to adapt them for the task of retrieving relevant *websites*. The simplest way is to select all homepages of websites found within the relevant pages of a crawl and to conclude that all corresponding websites are relevant. However, the classification of websites based on the homepage alone is not as accurate as more sophisticated methods of website classification. A homepage might consist of structural information only, e.g. frame tags or provide not much text. Thus, homepages often do not contain a meaningful description of the purpose of a website. As a consequence this approach to extract relevant websites from the results of a focused webpage crawl suffers from inaccurate results. Furthermore, since the webpage crawler does not prefer homepages over other webpages, the rate of newly discovered websites tends to be rather low.

Another approach of post-processing is to group the resulting webpages by their website (i.e. domain) and apply a website classifier like [15] to each set of webpages. Though this approach promises better classification accuracy, it still has drawbacks. Since the set of webpages downloaded for each site is controlled by the page crawler which is not conscious of websites at all, this selection of pages might not be well suited for representing the website. Thus, the crawler does not guarantee that enough webpages per site are downloaded. In our experiments, it turned out that usually more than 50% of the websites that were classified as relevant by this method, were represented by one webpage only. On the other hand, the efficiency suffers from the effect that very relevant websites might be scanned completely due to the high relevance scores of most of their pages. In addition to the number, also the selection of webpages of a conventional focused crawler causes a problem. Since a focused crawler prefers relevant pages, a website might be represented by the pages closest to the relevant topic. But this selection is not a good representation for websites that are irrelevant. Thus, websites containing some pages with relevant information, belonging, however, to the other class are misclassified. For example, a university might be classified as relevant for skiing because there are some student pages referring to this topic. We argue that in order to achieve high classification accuracy and to control the number of pages to be downloaded, a focused website crawler requires an explicit concept of websites and corresponding crawl strategies.

3.3. Focused Website Crawling

Website crawling can be considered as the process of successively transforming a subgraph G_0 of the website graph WG with $V_0=\{W_1,...,W_n\}$, $n \geq 1$, where W_i is a website, $1 \leq i \leq n$, into a sequence of subgraphs $G_1,...,G_m$ such that in each step exactly one website node from WG is added to G_i to obtain G_{i+1}. V_0 is called the set of *start websites*. In the context of *focused* website crawling, we assume two classes of websites, a class of relevant sites (the target class) and a class of irrelevant sites (the "other"-class) with respect to some user interest. The set of start sites V_0 should (mainly) consist of relevant sites. To distinguish between relevant and irrelevant websites, some (automatic) classifier is required which predicts the class of a website (V',E') based on the feature vectors $f(p)$ of the pages $p \in V'$. The *website classifier* is a function that takes a website from W and a website class from the set of classes C and returns a numerical confidence value for this website w.r.t. the given class.

$$confidence: W \times C \rightarrow [0..1]$$

A website is called *relevant*, if its confidence for the target class C_{target} exceeds its confidence for the "other" class.

$$relevance: W \rightarrow \{true, false\}$$

The website classifier is trained using the start websites that can be provided either explicitly by the user (if available) or implicitly by selecting some subtrees (and the corresponding websites listed in these subtrees) of a directory service like [10,12,18].

Based on the website classifier and the notion of relevant websites, we introduce the following performance measure for focused website crawlers. The *pages per relevant site rate (pprs-rate)* of the website crawler after step s is defined by the ratio of the number of downloaded webpages to the number of relevant websites found, i.e

$$pprs(G_s) = \frac{\sum_{W \in (G_s \setminus G_{s-w})} |pages(W)|}{|\{W \in (G_s \setminus G_{s-w}) \mid relevance(W) = true\}|}$$

where $pages(W) = \{p \in W \cap (G_s \setminus G_{s-w})\}$ denotes the set of pages in W that were visited so far and w is the beginning of the time interval that is observed. The pprs-rate thus measures the average effort to retrieve one additional *relevant* website. It depends on two factors: (1) the number of pages that have to be downloaded within a relevant website (to be controlled by an internal crawler) and (2) the number of pages downloaded from irrelevant websites that were examined before finding the relevant website (to be controlled by the external crawler).

The task of a *focused website crawler* is to find as many relevant sites as possible, while downloading as few webpages as possible. A website crawl terminates if the wanted number of relevant sites is found or the pprs-rate

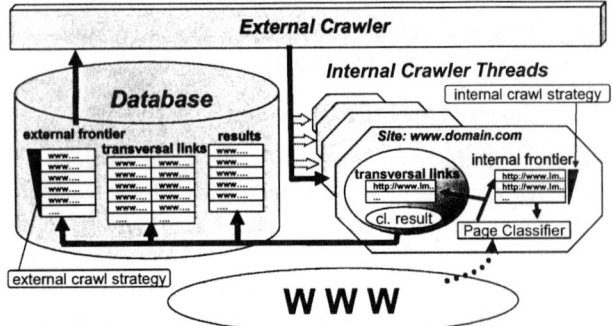

Figure 2: Architecture of the focused website crawler.

decreases significantly. In the next section, we will introduce our architecture of a focused website crawler.

4. A Focused Website Crawler

4.1. The Architecture

Focused website crawling is performed on two levels. The external or website level traverses the first level of the website graph. The external crawl orders the (hyperlinks to) yet unknown websites and invokes internal crawls on the top-ranked ones. Since there are much less domains than webpages, the external crawl frontier is rather small compared to the crawl frontier of an ordinary focused crawler. Thus, even for large crawls ranking can be done on-the-fly and sophisticated ranking algorithms can be applied. The second level is the internal or webpage level. It examines the current website to identify its purpose and extracts links to other websites while downloading as few webpages as possible. Since the webpages within the internal crawl frontier are needed for a limited time only and their number is usually small, it can be stored in main memory. Thus, expensive I/O operations are avoided and the crawl frontier can be accessed and updated very fast. Let us note that several internal crawlers examine different websites simultaneously. Thus, it is guaranteed that the data is drawn from several remote hosts at the same time which ensures a high overall download rate. Furthermore, controlling the number of pages visited from each website helps to keep the additional load at each website as low as possible, helping to increase the acceptance of the focused crawler within the webmaster community.

Figure 2 shows our architecture for a focused website crawler. The *external crawler* stores the external frontier consisting of websites only. To decide which website has to be examined next, it ranks the external frontier. To expand the frontier and to decide, if a chosen site is relevant, the external crawler invokes an internal crawler. The *internal crawler* traverses the website building an internal crawl frontier that is restricted to the pages of this site. During this traversal it examines the webpages to determine the site class. Furthermore, it collects all transversal links to other unexplored websites together with the confidence w.r.t. the target class of their source pages. As a result, the internal crawler returns information about the website class and the set of transversal links from the domain to new unexplored domains. Note that these transversal links are not real hyperlinks, but an aggregation of all hyperlinks that are found within the website directing to pages located within an other website. Thus, the number of transversal links from one site to another website is limited to one.

4.2. The External Crawler

The task of the external crawler is to order the external crawl frontier (consisting of links to not yet visited websites) and to decide which site has to be examined next by an internal crawler. The external crawler starts its traversal of the website level from the user-specified start websites and expands the graph by incorporating the newly found websites. Since the task of the external crawler is similar to the task of a focused crawler for webpages, most of the methods mentioned in section 2 are applicable to order the external frontier. The major difference is that distillation takes place at another more abstract level. Thus, the relevance scores attached to nodes and edges may be determined in a different way in order to achieve good results.

During a crawl, we distinguish two different sets of nodes of the website graph: Nodes corresponding to already examined websites are elements of V_{ex} and so-called border nodes that have not yet been examined, are elements of V_{bd}. The task of the crawler is to rank the elements of V_{bd} with respect to the information gained while examining the elements of V_{ex}. Each website $W \in V_{bd}$ is reachable by at least one link contained in some website $V_i \in V_{ex}$.

The (external) crawling strategy employed in this paper is simple but effective and is very similar to the basic crawler proposed in [5]. Note that most of the established crawling strategies [2,3,5,6,8,17] are applicable as well. For every node $W \in V_{bd}$, a *ranking score* is calculated as follows:

$$rank(W) = \frac{\sum_{V_i \in L_{ex}(W)} weight(V_i, W)}{|L_{ex}(W)|}$$

where $L_{ex}(W) = \{ V \mid V \in V_{ex} \land \exists\ edge(V,W) \}$ and $edge(V_i, W)$ denotes that there is at least one link from node V_i to node W. Furthermore, $weight(V,W)$ is a function that determines the confidence for each edge that its destination is relevant to the topic. In other words, an unknown website is judged by the average weight of the known edges referencing it. Thus, the website W with the highest $rank(W)$ should be crawled first. The edges do not directly correspond to the hyperlinks, but represent an aggregate of all hyperlinks leading from one website to another. Let us note that this method solves the same problem as the host-to-host cleaning improvement suggested in [1], i.e. it avoids that strongly connected

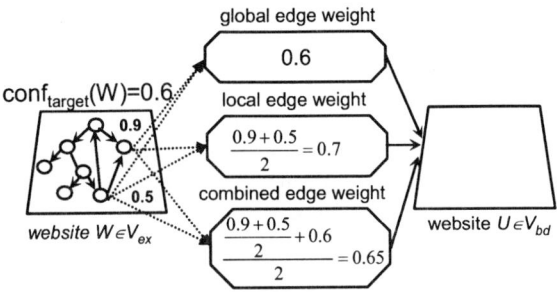

Figure 3: The three variants of edge weights for two sample websites W and U. The confidence of W w.r.t. the target class is 0.6. There are two pages in W referencing pages in U, one page with confidence (w.r.t. the target class) 0.9 and the other with confidence 0.5.

domains are overemphasized. The remaining task is how to determine the weights for the edges. To answer this question, we investigated the following three approaches:

- *Global edge weights:* Each edge is weighted by the confidence w.r.t. the target class of the *website* the edge is contained in:

$$weight_{global}(W,V) = confidence(W, C_{target})$$

where $confidence(W, C_{target})$ denotes the confidence value for website W w.r.t. the target class.

- *Local edge weights*: Each edge is weighted by the *average* confidence w.r.t. the target class of the *webpages* containing links pointing to the given website:

$$weight_{local}(W,V) = \frac{\sum_{p \in \{p | p \in W \land \exists\ (q \in V \land (p,q))\}} \Pr[target | p]}{|\{p | p \in W \land \exists\ [q \in V \land (p,q)]\}|}$$

where *Pr[target|p]* is the confidence of page *p* being contained in a target class website. These confidences for single webpages are also collected within the website classifier, but do not correspond to the complete set of webpages downloaded for classification.

- *Combined edge weights*: This is a combination of both methods integrating both scores to combine local and global aspects by taking the average weight of both methods.

$$weight_{combined}(W,V) = \frac{weight_{local}(W,V) + weight_{global}(W,V)}{2}$$

The advantage of local edge weights is that they distinguish the transversal links according to the relevance of the source pages of a link. Thus, transversal links found on irrelevant pages are weighted less than those found on highly relevant webpages. On the other hand, local edge weights might consider the links from source pages containing sparse text only as irrelevant since the page itself can be classified only poorly. This shows the strength of global edge weights. Since global edge weights consider the relevance of the complete site, they transfer relevance from other relevant pages to the link pages which do not provide enough content for proper classification. Combined edge weights incorporate both aspects. The links found in pages containing not enough text for reliable classification are at least judged by the relevance of the website and relevant pages transfer more importance to the links than irrelevant ones. Figure 3 displays an example for all three methods of edge weighting.

The performance of the external crawler influences one important aspect of the pprs-rate: the number of relevant sites that are examined compared to all websites that are crawled by an internal crawler. We will refer to this ratio as the *website harvest rate*. However, this aspect is not the only influence on the pprs-rate. Even an optimal external crawler will achieve very bad pprs-rates, if the internal crawler explores large numbers of webpages per site.

4.3. The Internal Crawler

The internal crawler is responsible for the main advantage of a dedicated website crawler namely that the results are more reliable due to better classification accuracy. On the other hand, the efficiency strongly depends on the ability of the internal crawler to restrict the number of downloaded webpages per site to as few pages as possible. Furthermore, additional goals have to be fulfilled like the avoidance of spider traps and the retrieval of new promising transversal links.

The main task of the internal crawler is to select a representative sample set of webpages from a website W and determine for each page p_i the likelihood (called *confidence* in this context) of p_i appearing in website class C_k. To determine this probability $Pr[w_i|\ w_i \in W \land W \in C_k]$, we employ a text classifier. To choose the sample set, we employ focused crawling using a so-called internal crawl strategy. To determine the class of an entire website W, for each class C_k we calculate the probability that W was generated by the process corresponding to class C_k.

Additionally, there are several other side goals of the internal crawler like collecting new transversal links and avoiding spider traps.

4.3.1 The Webpage Classifier

The task of the webpage classifier is to decide how likely it is that a certain webpage p_i appears in a website W of Class C_k. The task of this classifier is slightly different from the task of the classifier in an ordinary focused crawler. A webpage that is likely to appear in a typical website does not necessarily have to be relevant for the user interest. The page classifier should be capable to handle multi-modal classes, i.e. classes that are strongly fractioned into an unknown number of subclasses. This feature is important because the webpages found in websites of a common class provide several pageclasses, e.g. contact-pages, directory pages etc.. For our crawler, we employed a centroid based *k*-nearest neighbor (kNN) classifier as described in [13]. This variant of kNN classification constructs the centroid of the training word vectors for each class. The class is now determined by choosing that class belonging to the closest centroid. In order to achieve multi-modality, we adopted an idea mentioned in the summary of [13]. We clustered each training set using the *k*-means algorithm and represented a class as the set of centroids of the resulting clusters. Let us note that we started our prototype by using naive Bayes classification, but changed to this classifier due to its better accuracy.

Formally, each class C_k of our classifier is represented by a set of centroids CS_k. Let $d_{min}(p, CS_k)$ denote the distance of the word vector p of a given webpage to the closest element of CS_k. Then we estimate the confidence value for p belonging to C_k as follows:

$$\Pr[p \mid C_k] = \frac{\ln[d_{min}(p,c_k)]}{\sum_{c_j \in CS_k} \ln[d_{min}(p,c_j)]}.$$

In other words, we use the logarithm of the distance to the closest centroid in CS_k and normalize over all classes. Let us note that we use the logarithm to weight close distances higher than far distances. If a page has a large distance to the centroids of all classes, the confidence values are very similar for all classes. The closer the distance to a centroid is, the more sensitively the distance is measured. The resulting confidences are used by the local and combined edge weights for determining the weights of the transversal links.

To train the classifier, we first select a set of relevant websites. The websites in our experiments, for example, were taken from common directory services [10,12,18]. To represent the "other"-class, we choose several websites belonging to a variety of other non-relevant topics. Since we need to learn which kinds of webpages might occur in a relevant site and which not, we have to draw a representative sample of webpages from each training website. The pages downloaded during the process of classification of a website are limited to a small set around the homepage, since these pages are most likely connected to the purpose of the site. Thus, we should use these pages for training as well. We restrict the training pages to the first *k* pages when traversing the website using breadth first search. This simple method worked out well in our experiments.

4.3.2 The Internal Crawl Strategy

The internal crawl strategy determines the sample of pages downloaded from the website to be classified. Each internal crawl is started at the homepage. As mentioned before, the information about the purpose of a website is usually located around the homepage since most publishers want to tell the user what a website is about, before providing more specific information.

Analogously to a focused page crawler, the internal crawler traverses the web using a best-first search strategy. However, the internal crawl is restricted to the webpages of the examined site. The goal is to find a set of webpages reflecting the site's purpose in a best possible way. This is a major difference to focused page crawlers which try to find as many relevant pages as possible. However, looking for relevant pages is only appropriate for site classification, if the examined website belongs to the target class. If the given website belongs to the other class, the crawler should prefer pages that typically occur in non-relevant websites in order to find a good representation. Thus, the internal crawler should rank the pages by their confidences for any class compared to the average confidences over all classes.

To solve this problem, our internal crawling strategy works as follows. Like in the external crawler, we again build the crawling strategy similar to the basic crawler in [5]. The ranking score of a webpage p is defined as the average weight of the links referencing p:

$$rank(p) = \frac{\sum_{q_i \in L_{in}(p)} weight((q_i, p))}{|L_{in}(p)|}$$

where L_{in} is the set of pages read so far that link to p. To represent the contribution of a page for the decision in favor of either class, we determine the weight of link (q_i, p) as:

$$weight(q_i, p) = \mathrm{var}(\Pr[q_i \mid target])$$

where $\Pr[q_i|target]$ is the confidence of q_i w.r.t. the target class obtained by the page classifier. The internal frontier is sorted in decreasing order of these confidence values.

4.3.3. The Website Classifier

The combination of the page classifier and the internal crawl strategy produces a sequence of webpages downloaded from the site. Furthermore, each webpage is classified and is associated with a confidence w.r.t. the target class.

The following statistical model incrementally (i.e. after each download of a new page) aggregates these page confidences to calculate an overall confidence (w.r.t. the target class) for the entire website. In our model, each website class defines a statistical process that can generate any webpage with a certain probability. A website W belonging to that class C_k is a set of webpages generated by drawing pages from the corresponding probability distribution. In the following, we present a maximum-likelihood classifier that assigns a website to the class with the highest probability of having generated the observed website W.

Let W_t denote the sample of site W that the internal crawler has retrieved by time t. The probability that the class C_k has generated W_t is given by

$$\Pr[W_t \mid C_k] = \prod_{p_i \in W} \Pr[p_i \mid C_k].$$

Applying Bayes theorem, the desired probability is:

$$\Pr[C_k \mid W_t] = \frac{\Pr[C_k] \cdot P[W_t \mid C_k]}{\sum_{i \in C} \Pr[C_i] \cdot P[W_t \mid C_i]}.$$

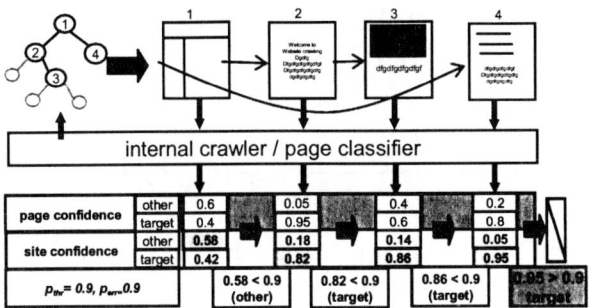

Figure 4: Illustration of website classification during an internal crawl

Unfortunately, this formalization suffers from two practical limitations:

- The apriori probabilities $Pr[C_k]$ are unknown for the WWW. However, the application of focused crawling enables us to make a suitable estimate. Since the focused website crawler focuses to relevant sites, the probability distribution within the whole web is expected to be very different from the probability distribution within relevant sites close to the frontier. Thus, we can use the rate of relevant sites found so far as an estimate for $Pr[C_k]$.

- Since there is no classifier guaranteeing 100 % accurate class predictions, the confidence values are not always realistic as well. The class prediction values generated by the classifier always suffer from a certain classification error. Thus, the combination of these results should consider this inaccuracy.

To incorporate the possibility of classification errors, we extend our model by integrating the classification error observed on the training data into the model. Thus, we obtain an error corrected probability for the occurrence of page p in a website of class C_k and the classification error p_{err}:

$$\Pr[p \mid C_k \wedge p_{err}] = \Pr[(p \mid C_k) \cdot (1 - p_{err}) + \Pr[p \mid C_{other}] \cdot p_{err}$$

The idea is that the probability that the prediction is made correctly is the confidence value multiplied with the probability that the classifier is correct. Additionally, we have to consider the case that the classifier made a wrong prediction. Thus, we have to add the confidence value of the "other"-class multiplied with the error probability perr. To estimate perr, we calculate the accuracy of the page classifier on the set of webpages in the training websites using 10-fold cross validation.

Using the error corrected probabilities avoids the effect that the influence of a single page is overestimated during classification. Even if the classifier outputs are 1.0 and 0.0, our process does not automatically overestimate the impact of a single page. Thus, the calculated value for $Pr[W_t \mid C_k]$ will usually produce meaningful values after some pages have been considered.

To stop classification, we define a certain confidence threshold $p_{threshold}$ and the internal crawl stops classification as soon as this confidence level is reached. By choosing $p_{threshold}$ the internal classifier can be adjusted to find an appropriate trade-off between accuracy and efficiency. However, if its value is chosen too high, the crawler will require too many pages with respect to a website's purpose. This is problematic, because the performance suffers significantly and the reservoir of characteristic pages within one website is limited. To conclude, after the confidence for W_t reaches $p_{threshold}$, we assume that the class of W is identical to the class of W_t and we denote:

$$confidence(W, C_{target}) = \Pr[C_{target} \mid W_t] \text{ and}$$
$$relevance(W) = (\Pr[C_{target} \mid W_t] > \Pr[C_{other} \mid W_t]).$$

Figure 4 illustrates the complete process of website classification. The displayed example describes the common case that a website starts with a frame page and, thus, the prediction of the class based only on the homepage would be wrong.

4.3.4. Retrieving Transversal Links and Terminating the Internal Crawler

Besides the primary goal to achieve accurate classification of the examined website, the internal crawler has a secondary objective of retrieving enough transversal links for extending the external crawl frontier. Therefore, the internal crawler collects all transversal links, i.e. the links leading to new unexplored websites. Additionally, the crawler stores the confidence values $Pr[p \mid C_{target}]$ of the source pages of the link. These values are used to calculate local and combined edge weights.

Since, according to the above stop condition, classification might be finished after a few pages only, it is possible that the internal crawler has not yet found enough interesting transversal links. In such cases we want to continue the crawl until a reasonable number of transversal links has been extracted. To decide if enough links have been found within a website, we define the *linkWeight* as a measure for the contribution of page p to the set of relevant transversal links found within the site:

$$linkWeight(p) = (\Pr[p \mid C_{target}] \cdot |LT_p| + c)$$

where LT_p is the set of transversal links found in p and $c \geq 1$ is an constant. Furthermore, we define the *LinkRank* for the set of webpages W_t as :

$$LinkRank(W_t) = \sum_{p \in W_t} linkWeight(p) \cdot \frac{1}{\Pr[C_{traget} \mid W_t]}$$

To employ the *LinkRank* for ensuring that enough relevant links are found, we continue the internal crawl even after classification has finished until it reaches a certain level $l_{threshold}$. The idea of this heuristic is that each webpage contributes its *linkWeight* to the *LinkRank* of the website. The more links are contained in p and the more relevant p is, the more will p contribute to the *LinkRank*. The constant c is added to ensure that the *linkWeight* has

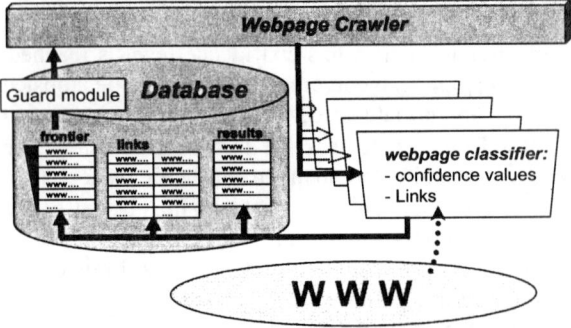

Figure 5: Architecture of our focused webpage crawler.

at least some value and thus the *LinkRank* grows constantly until $l_{threshold}$ is reached. The *LinkRank* increases slower for relevant websites and faster for irrelevant ones. Thus, an internal crawl of a relevant website will encompass more webpages than an internal crawl of an irrelevant site, which usually terminates after classification. This way relevant websites add more new links to the external frontier than irrelevant ones.

Let us note that we continue the crawl to reach $l_{threshold}$ by employing the mentioned internal crawling strategy. We argue that if a website is relevant, the crawling strategy is targeted to find new relevant pages which are most likely to contain relevant links. For websites classified to the other class, $l_{threshold}$ is reached rather fast anyway and switching the crawl strategy is not necessary.

An additional benefit of the internal crawler is that it makes the website crawler robust against spider traps. Since the number of webpages retrieved from one website is explicitly controlled, the crawler might run into a spider trap only in those rare cases where a site consists mostly of pages without any meaning to the classifier. To ensure termination in such cases, it is sufficient to restrict the number of pages downloaded from one domain. Unlike in page crawlers, no additional database table is needed to store websites containing a spider trap. This is not necessary within the focused website crawler since the crawler will not visit a website more than once.

5. EXPERIMENTAL EVALUATION

5.1. The Test Environment

We performed our experiments for the topics listed in table 1. For each topic, we first acquired a sample set of relevant websites taken from a category in [10,12,18]. Additionally, we selected a random mixture of websites to represent all other topics on the web. For each category, table 1 provides the number of training websites, and the directory service the websites were taken from. We stored the websites in a training database, to have a stable test environment consisting of 20,793 HTML-documents from 335 websites.

We implemented 2 focused crawlers. The first is our prototype of a focused website crawler. The second is a focused webpage crawler that crawls the internet by using only one frontier of webpages. To provide a fair comparison, both crawlers are based on the same algorithm for page classification and ranking. The design of our focused webpage crawler is illustrated in Figure 5. The system starts its crawl on a defined set of webpages (in our case the homepages of the websites found in a directory service). Each new unexplored webpage is stored in the crawling frontier. The page classifier generates confidence values for each webpage that is explored. Within the frontier, each unexplored webpage is measured by the average confidence value for the target class of the webpages linking it. The webpage providing the highest average confidence value within the frontier is examined next. In order to prevent spider traps and to keep the load for each website at an acceptable level, we implemented a guard module as described in [6]. This guard module prevents the page crawler from accessing webpages in websites that already contributed an extraordinarily high number of webpages to the already explored part of the web graph. To test the crawlers, we performed various crawls on the WWW. This test bed seemed to be suited best, although it is not guaranteed that the web stays the same between two crawls. However, due to the more stable character of the website graph, we argue that the influence to the results is negligible. Let us note that we performed some of the experiments again after several weeks and achieved almost identical results. On the other hand, downloading a representative section of the website graph to provide a static test environment is difficult. Since the part of the WWW visited by a website crawler tends to be spread over several thousands hosts, it is difficult to find a closed section that allows a realistic behaviour of the tested crawlers.

Our experiments were run on a workstation that is equipped with two 2.8 Ghz Xeon processors and 4 Gb main memory. As a database system we used an ORACLE 9i database server hosted on the same machine. Both crawlers were implemented in Java 1.4, with the exception of the ranking algorithms and the guard module which were partly implemented in PL/SQL to improve the runtime performance.

Table 1: Overview of the training database.

topic	number of websites in db	websites provided by
horses	32	YAHOO
astronomy	39	YAHOO
sailing	39	Google
mountain biking	34	DMOZ
skate boarding	35	DMOZ
boxing	33	DMOZ
other	132	All

Table 2: Classification results using 10-fold cross validation within the training database for the internal crawler and the homepage classifier.

topic	p_{err}	$p_{threshold}$	pages per site	prec. int crw.	rec. int crw	f-meas. int. crw.	prec homep.	rec. homep.	f-measure homepage	f-measure improve.
horses	0.85	0.9	6.9	0.84	0.97	**0.90**	0.49	0.88	**0.63**	0.27
astronomy	0.90	0.9	6.3	1.00	0.90	**0.95**	0.86	0.79	**0.83**	0.12
sailing	0.88	0.9	6.3	0.90	0.97	**0.94**	0.77	0.92	**0.84**	0.10
mountain biking	0.86	0.8	6.3	0.81	0.97	**0.88**	0.76	0.83	**0.79**	0.11
skate boarding	0.88	0.8	3.2	0.76	1.00	**0.86**	0.74	0.89	**0.81**	0.05
boxing	0.88	0.9	7.4	0.79	0.79	**0.79**	0.74	0.72	**0.73**	0.05

5.2. Evaluation of Website Classification

Our first experiment demonstrates the higher accuracy that can be achieved for website classification by using the internal crawler compared to a homepage classifier.

The homepage classifier uses the same centroid based kNN-classifier as the internal crawler, but is trained and tested on homepages only. The internal crawler used in these experiments terminates its crawl after a confidence threshold of $p_{threshold}$ is reached and does not continue the crawl to find interesting links. Since this test needs labelled test data, we performed 10-fold cross-validation on the topics stored in the training database (table 1). Table 2 displays the precision, recall and f-measure (as trade off between precision and recall) for the tested topics when employing the website classifier and the homepage classifier. Additionally, the table reports the classification error p_{err} and the average number of webpages that the website classifier downloaded per website. For the training of the page classifier of the internal crawler, we used the first 25 webpages of each training website when applying a breadth-first traversal.

For all of the tested topics, the internal crawler obtained significantly higher f-measures than the homepage classifier. For the topic horses, it even increased the f-measure from 0.63 to 0.9, i.e. by 0.27. Thus, by classifying the websites by more than one page, the classification accuracy was substantially increased. Let us note that a manual analysis of the crawled websites confirmed the hypothesis that especially commercial websites often do not provide a meaningful homepage. The average number of pages used for classification was between 3.2 and 7.4 indicating that website classification does not require large numbers of webpages per site for making more accurate predictions.

5.3 Evaluation of the Crawling Performance

To demonstrate the performance of the complete focused website crawler, we performed numerous crawls. Since we retrieved a total number of approximately 50,000 potentially relevant websites, we could manually verify only samples from each crawl. Table 3 displays a sample of relevant websites retrieved for the topic horses. The

Table 3: Example websites returned for the topic horses.

website	# visited pages	confidence
www.tbart.net	4	0.65
www.socalequine.com	6	0.59
www.thehalterhorse.com	4	0.65
www.thejudgeschoice.com	4	0.75
www.thehorsesource.com	3	0.68
...		
www.laceysarabians.com	5	0.71
www.baroquehorses.com	5	0.60
www.knightmagicfarms.com	4	0.67
www.pccha.com	7	0.64
www.danddhorsetransport.com	4	0.70

first five domains were retrieved after approximately 250 websites were visited, the last five at the end of the crawl after about 2500 relevant websites had been retrieved. This example illustrates that the crawler started to discover relevant websites early and kept his good accuracy until the end of the crawl.

Our first crawling experiment compares the three different weightings introduced in section 4.2 for ranking the external frontier. Therefore, we started each crawler using the parameters achieving maximum accuracy for the internal crawler and stopped the crawler after approximately 2500 relevant websites were found. To compare the effect of each of the weightings, we compared the website harvest rate, i.e. the ratio of relevant websites to all websites that were screened. Figure 6 displays the average website harvest rate aggregated over the last 1000 pages. For the topics horses and astronomy all three weightings performed very similar, although the global edge weights achieved a small advantage, especially at the beginning of the crawl. However, for the topic sailing the combined edge weights were able to compensate some of the weaknesses of both underlying methods. The experiments for the topic mountain biking displayed a strong advantage for the local edge weights. However, the combined edge weights were still able to compensate some of the weaknesses of global edge weights. Though our experiments did not reveal that one of the mentioned weightings showed superior results, we advise to employ the combined edge

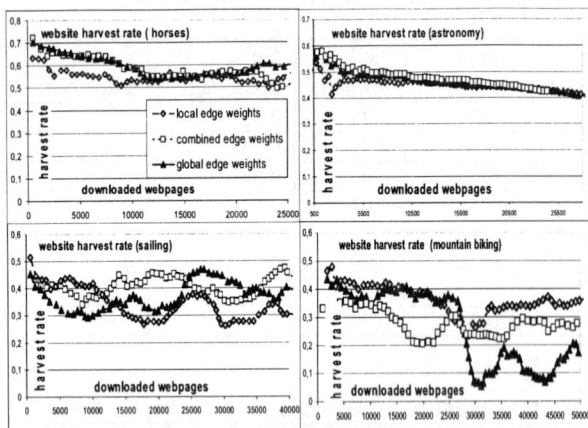

Figure 6: Website harvest rates (average of last 1000 pages) for each topic and each weighting.

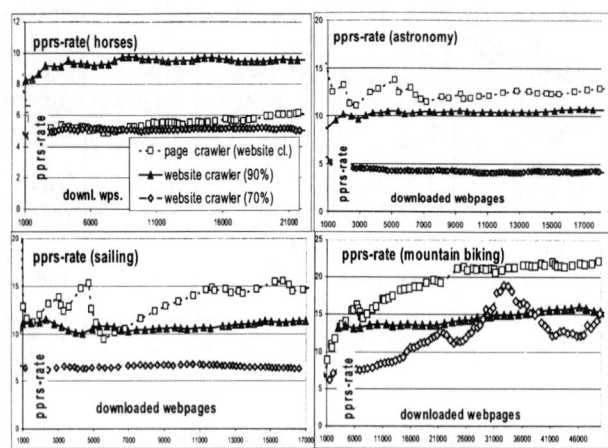

Figure 7: pprs-rates (average of last 5000 pages) for each topic and each crawler.

weights function, since it was always at least the second best and sometimes outperformed the other methods.

The next series of experiments was conducted to back up our claim that common focused (webpage) crawlers are unsuitable for retrieving websites and that the proposed focused website crawler overcomes the problems of page crawlers providing a more efficient and accurate retrieval of relevant websites.

In our first experiment, we have already demonstrated that the accuracy of the internal crawler is superior to the accuracy achieved by the homepage classifier. Thus, the post-processing counting relevant homepages is unlikely to produce the same quality of results either. To show that applying a website classifier like [15] is not sufficient for providing comparable accuracy, we determined the percentage of websites that were classified by one single webpage. For all four examples approximately 50 % of the resulting websites where classified by using one page only. Thus, in half of the cases applying a more sophisticated website classifier to the websites being aggregated from the results of a page crawl cannot perform any better than the homepage classifier.

This behaviour of the page crawler can be explained as follows. Most transversal links referencing a new site are directed at one special entry page (usually the homepage) and most other webpages found within this website are linked via internal links only. A page crawler examining a website visits this entry page first and classifies it. The ranking score of the other webpages within the website now strongly depend on the confidence value of the entry page. If the confidence w.r.t. the target class is rather high, then additional pages are examined also. If the classification result is rather uncertain, however, the ranking scores tends to be rather low and it is likely that the additional pages won't be visited during the crawl. For the task of website retrieval this behaviour is unsuitable. If the relevance of the entry page is hard to decide, it would make sense to examine additional pages from the site in order to achieve more reliable classification. On the other hand, if the relevance of the entry page is very certain, it is wasteful to proceed crawling to discover the obvious. Our proposed website crawler handles candidate sites that cannot reliably be classified based on the entry page more carefully than those where a certain classification can immediately be obtained.

To demonstrate this difference, we ran the focused webpage crawler for each of the first 4 topics listed in table 1 and applied a website classifier to the results. Additionally, we performed two different website crawls to demonstrate the capability of the website crawler to find a suitable trade-off between accuracy and efficiency by adjusting the confidence threshold. The first one uses again the parameter setting providing maximum accuracy ($p_{threshold} \approx 90\%$). Thus, we can judge the overhead for the additional accuracy. The second crawl used a confidence value of 70%. Due to this rather soft breaking condition, the second crawl usually visited very few pages per website, but provided less reliable results.

Figure 7 displays the average pprs-rate over the last 5000 webpages for the first four topics displayed in table 1. Recall that the pprs-rate measures the average number of additional webpages that are downloaded until a new relevant website is discovered. Let us note that the crawls vary in length, since we terminated crawling after reaching at least 2500 relevant websites regardless of how many webpages where downloaded.

For three out of four topics, even the website crawler aiming at more accurate results ($p_{threshold} \approx 90\%$) achieved a lower pprs-rate than the page crawler. For the topic mountain biking, e.g., it needed approximately 7 pages less than the page crawler to find an additional relevant domain at the end of the crawl. Thus, even when returning more reliable results, the website crawler in most cases gained an efficiency advantage compared to the page crawler.

For all topics, the website crawler with a 70 % confidence threshold clearly outperformed the two comparison partners with respect to efficiency. For the topic astronomy, e.g., it visited only about five additional webpages until it retrieved another relevant site. Due to the large number of results, we could not verify the entire result set, but a manual analysis of a sample supported our claim of more reliable results even for the 70% website crawler. To conclude, our experimental evaluation demonstrates that a focused website crawler is, for similar accuracy requirements, clearly more efficient for retrieving relevant websites than a focused webpage crawler with website post-processing. In an alternative scenario, when achieving a comparable pprs-rate, the focused website crawler returns more accurate results.

6. CONCLUSIONS

When searching the web, there are many applications targeting whole websites rather than single webpages. For that purpose, we introduced a focused crawler directly searching for relevant websites instead of webpages. The proposed two-level architecture allows us to control the number of pages to be downloaded from each website and to find a good trade-off between accurate classification and efficient crawling. The external crawler views the web as a graph of linked websites, selects the websites to be examined next and invokes internal crawlers. An internal crawler views the webpages of a single given website and performs focused page crawling within that website. In our experimental evaluation we demonstrated that reliable website classification requires to visit more than one but less than all pages of a given site. Furthermore, we compared our proposed crawler to a focused webpage crawler that handles the concept of websites in a corresponding step of post-processing. For the same efficiency (measured by the number of pages downloaded per relevant site), the website crawler achieved significantly higher classification accuracy than its comparison partner. For comparable accuracy, the website crawler needed a considerably smaller rate of pages visited per relevant site. These results support our claim that in order to achieve high classification accuracy and efficiency of crawling, a focused website crawler requires a two-level architecture and corresponding crawl strategies with an explicit concept of websites.

For future work, we plan to develop more specific internal and external crawling strategies. Furthermore, we will investigate the crawling of commercial websites that are not strongly linked to each other due to their competitive nature. In these cases, spotting hub pages seems to be more important than for crawling broad topics on the web. Another highly interesting direction is the use of website crawling to provide a filter for crawling highly specific content from the web. The idea is to first spot websites that are likely to contain the specific information. Afterwards these websites can be scanned for a webpage containing the specific information.

REFERENCES

[1] Bharat K., Henziger M.R.: "Improved Algorithms for Topic Distillation in a Hyperlinked Environment", Proceedings of SIGIR-98, 1998.

[2] Chakrabarti S., van den Berg M., Dom B.: "Distributed Hypertext Resource Discovery Through Examples", Proceedings VLDB 99.

[3] Chakrabarti S., van den Berg M., Dom B.: "Focused Crawling: a new Approach to Topic-Specific Web Resource Discovery", Proceedings WWW 1999.

[4] Chakrabarti S., Dom B. and Indyk P.: "Enhanced hypertext categorization using hyperlinks", Proceedings ACM SIGMOD, 1998.

[5] Chakrabarti S., Punera K., Subramanyam M.: "Accelerated Focused Crawling through Online Relevance Feedback", Proceedings WWW 2002.

[6] Chakrabarti S. :" Mining the Web", (pp. 17-43), Morgan Kaufmann Publishers, 2003.

[7] Craven M., DiPasquo D., Freitag D., McCallum A., Mitchell T., Nigam K., and Slattery S.: "Learning to Construct Knowledge Bases from the World Wide Web", Artificial Intelligence, Elsevier, 1999.

[8] Cho J., Garcia-Molina H., Page L.: "Efficient Crawling Through URL Ordering", Proceedings WWW 1998.

[9] Diligenti M., Coetzee F., Lawrence S., Giles C.L., Gori M.: "Focused Crawling Using Context Graphs", Proceedings VLDB 2000.

[10] DMOZ open directory project, http://dmoz.org

[11] Ester M., Kriegel H.-P., Schubert M.: "Website Mining : A new way to spot Competitors, Customers and Suppliers in the World Wide Web", Proceedings ACM SIGKDD 02.

[12] Google Search Engine, http://www.google.com

[13] E.-H. Han and G. Karypis. "Centroid-Based Document Classification: Analysis and Experimental Results". In Proc. PKDD'00, 2000.

[14] Joachims T.: "Text Categorization with Support Vector Machines: Learning with Many Relevant Features", Proceedings European Conference on Machine Learning, 1998.

[15] Kriegel H.-P., Schubert M.: „Classification of websites as sets of feature vectors", Proc. IASTED DBA 2004.

[16] Kleinberg J.: "Authoritative sources in a hyperlinked environment", Proc. ACM-SIAM, 1998.

[17] Rennie J., McCallum A.: "Using Reinforcement Learning to Spider the Web Efficiently", Proceedings ICML 99.

[18] Yahoo! Directory Service, http://www.yahoo.com

[19] Yang Y., Liu X.: "A Re-Examination of Text Categorization Methods", Proceedings ACM SIGIR 1999.

Instance-based Schema Matching for Web Databases by Domain-specific Query Probing

Jiying Wang*	Ji-Rong Wen	Fred Lochovsky	Wei-Ying Ma
Computer Science Department Hong Kong Univ. of Science and Technology Hong Kong	Information Management & System Group Microsoft Research Asia Beijing, China	Computer Science Department Hong Kong Univ. of Science and Technology Hong Kong	Information Management & System Group Microsoft Research Asia Beijing, China
cswangjy@cs.ust.hk	jrwen@microsoft.com	fred@cs.ust.hk	wyma@microsoft.com

Abstract

In a Web database that dynamically provides information in response to user queries, two distinct schemas, interface schema (the schema users can query) and result schema (the schema users can browse), are presented to users. Each partially reflects the actual schema of the Web database. Most previous work only studied the problem of schema matching across query interfaces of Web databases. In this paper, we propose a novel schema model that distinguishes the interface and the result schema of a Web database in a specific domain. In this model, we address two significant Web database schema-matching problems: intra-site and inter-site. The first problem is crucial in automatically extracting data from Web databases, while the second problem plays a significant role in meta-retrieving and integrating data from different Web databases. We also investigate a unified solution to the two problems based on query probing and instance-based schema matching techniques. Using the model, a cross validation technique is also proposed to improve the accuracy of the schema matching. Our experiments on real Web databases demonstrate that the two problems can be solved simultaneously with high precision and recall.

1. Introduction

Besides web pages crawlable by specific URLs, the Web also contains a vast amount of non-crawlable content. This *hidden* part of the Web is comprised of a large number of online *Web databases* consisting of a searchable interface (usually an HTML form) and a backend database, which dynamically provides information in response to user queries [5] [13]. As compared to the static surface Web, the hidden Web contains a much larger amount of high-quality (often structured) information [8].

In the hidden Web, it is usually difficult or even impossible to directly obtain the schemas of the Web databases without cooperation from the web sites. Instead, the web sites present two other distinct schemas, *interface* and *result schema*, to users (Figure 1). The interface schema presents the query interface, which exposes attributes that can be queried in the Web database. The result schema presents the query results, which exposes attributes that are shown to users. The interface schema is useful for applications, such as mediators, that query multiple Web databases, since they need complete knowledge about the query interface of each database. The result schema is critical for applications, such as data extraction, which extract instances from the query results. In addition to the importance of the interface and result schemas themselves, attribute matching[1] across different schemas is also important. First, matching between *different* interface and result schemas (i.e., *inter-site schema matching*) is critical for meta-searching and data-integration among related Web databases. Second, matching between the interface and result schema of a *single* Web database (i.e., *intra-site schema matching*) enables automatic data annotation and database content crawling. Therefore, in this paper we focus on automatically discovering both the interface and result

---

Permission to copy without fee all or part of this material is granted provided that the copies are not made or distributed for direct commercial advantage, the VLDB copyright notice and the title of the publication and its date appear, and notice is given that copying is by permission of the Very Large Data Base Endowment. To copy otherwise, or to republish, requires a fee and/or special permission from the Endowment

Proceedings of the 30th VLDB Conference, Toronto, Canada, 2004

* This work was carried out when the author was visiting at Microsoft Research Asia.

[1] Attribute matching is the process of determining the semantic correspondences among the attributes of two schemas.

schemas of Web databases and matching semantically-related attributes between them.

Previous approaches [16], [17], [21] to Web database schema matching primarily focus on matching query interfaces (i.e., on inter-site interface schema matching). The basic idea is to identify attribute labels from the descriptive text surrounding interface elements and then find *synonym relationships* between the identified labels. The performance of these approaches may be affected when no attribute description can be identified or the identified description is not informative (e.g., "Search" in the homepage of Amazon.com). In contrast, in this paper we propose a novel instance-based schema matching approach, motivated by the necessity to identify the result schemas of Web databases that often lack available attribute names or labels and the goal of simultaneously solving inter-site and intra-site schema matching.

Our approach is mainly based on three observations about Web databases. First, improper[2] queries often cause search failure or no returned results. Second, the keywords of proper queries that return results very likely reappear in the returned results' corresponding attributes. Third, there is an underlying *global schema*[3] for related Web databases in the same domain (proposed and verified in [16]). Accordingly, we introduce a query probing technique that first exhaustively sends query keywords residing in a domain-specific global schema, whose semantics are known in advance, then analyzes the re-occurrences of submitted query keywords in the returned result data, and finally identifies the semantically corresponding attributes from both the interface and result schemas based on the previous analysis.

Using a domain-specific global schema, we present a combined schema model that can describe five kinds of schema matching for Web databases in the same domain: global-interface, global-result, interface-result, interface-interface, and result-result. The model not only describes the matching relationships among different schemas of Web databases in a specific domain, but, more importantly, also provides a global view about how to reinforce the matching accuracy by conducting multiple kinds of schema matching simultaneously. Using the model, we also present a cross validation technique that improves the accuracy of the schema matching results.

The main contributions of this paper are:
- Introduction of a novel schema model of a single Web database that distinguishes what information users can query and what information users can browse.
- Introduction of a generative view that includes five kinds of schema matching for related Web databases in a specific domain.
- Introduction of an instance-based method based on domain-specific query probing, along with mutual information and vector similarity analysis, to automatically match various schemas of Web databases (intra-site and inter-site).
- Benefiting from the above generative view, introduction of a cross validation technique based on an approximate solution of the graph partitioning problem to improve the accuracy of different kinds of schema matching.

The rest of this paper is organized as follows. In section 2, we present our model with five schema matchings for Web databases. In section 3, the domain-specific query probing technique is introduced. We propose, in section 4, an instance-based schema matching approach with a cross validation technique, to solve both the intra-site and inter-site schema matching problems at the same time. Section 5 presents the experimental results of testing our approaches on real Web databases. Section 6 reviews existing work on the schema matching problem and how it correlates with our approach. Finally, we give our conclusions and future work in section 7.

2. Combined Schema Model

A Web database is usually comprised of a query interface and a backend database. When a user query is submitted through the query interface, the site accesses its backend database for relevant data and returns the results to the user. Specifically, the query interface of the Web database usually contains multiple input elements, each of which may be associated with a schema attribute of the backend database. Data objects that the Web database returns to users are usually *semi-structured*, as their attribute values are encoded into HTML tags. Therefore, both the Web database interface and the returned results partially reflect the schema of the backend database, but in different ways.

For instance, Figure 1 shows an example of an online bookstore[4]. The part labelled *Data Attributes* shows a possible schema of the backend database consisting of six[5] attributes {Title, Author, Publisher, ISBN, Format, Publication Date}. The part labelled *Interface* shows the query interface, which contains five input elements with surrounding text describing their semantics. When the keyword query "Harry Potter" is submitted through the "Title" element in the interface, a result page is returned by the web site containing its answer to the query (labelled *Result* in Figure 1 and containing three book instances with associated attribute values).

From this example we can clearly see the difference between the attribute information contained in the query interface and that contained in the result pages. Although the site may provide an element in the interface for users to search on a particular data attribute (e.g., "ISBN"

---

[2] "Proper" means that the semantics of the query keywords match the semantics of the input element.

[3] The global schema is a view capturing common attributes of data in the specific domain.

[4] http://www.mysimon.com/

[5] The exact number is not known.

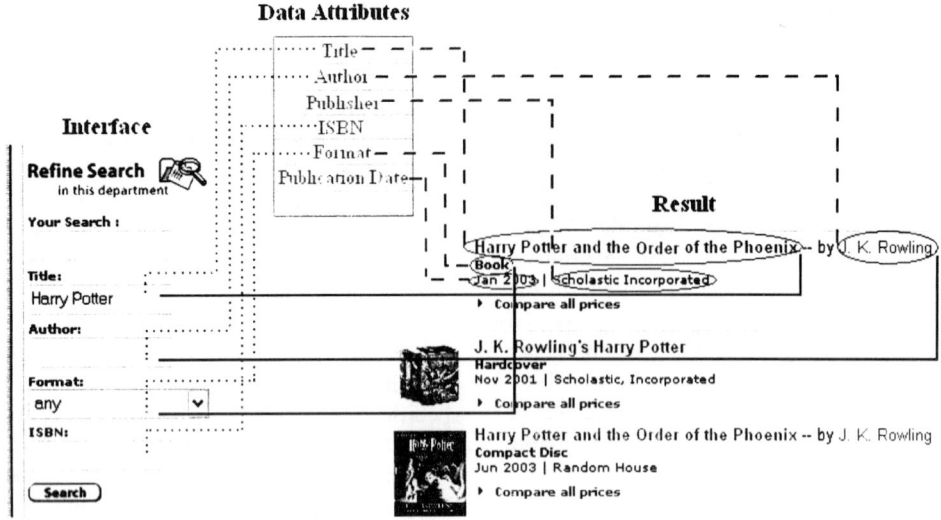

Figure 1. An example of a Web database with its search interface and result page.

element), this attribute's data values may not appear in the result pages. Likewise, the returned results may have attributes that users cannot query in the interface (e.g., Publisher attribute). Furthermore, Figure 1 shows three kinds of semantic correspondence represented by different line styles (dotted, dashed and solid). They are respectively, the correspondence between data attributes of the primary schema and elements in the query interface, the correspondence between the data attributes of the primary schema and instance values in the result pages, and the correspondence between elements in the query interface and instance values in the result pages.

In the deep Web, the primary schema of a Web database is hard to obtain directly as it is hidden behind query interfaces. However, previous work [16] makes the significant observation that, by examining the query interfaces of Web databases, an underlying generative global schema can be discovered for related Web databases in a specific domain. Thus, we introduce a global schema (i.e., a view capturing common attributes of data in the specific domain.) to substitute for the primary schema of the Web database and propose a combined 3-layer schema model for matching the schemas of Web databases. Besides its availability, another advantage of introducing a global schema is that it simplifies the process of matching schemas of different Web databases in the same domain as they share the same global schema.

Formally, we define a *schema* as a set of attributes, each of which corresponds to some unique meaning. In our model, the Web databases can be categorized into a number of domains, where Web databases in the same domain provide information about the same type of product (e.g., Book or Used-car) or on the same topic (e.g., Job). In each specific domain, there exists a unified *global schema* (**GS**) representing the common knowledge about the domain. In addition, each Web database in this model consists of two different schemas, the *interface schema* (**IS**) and the *result schema* (**RS**) (illustrated in Figure 2 as nodes). In particular, the global schema consists of the representative attributes of the data objects in this domain. The interface schema of an individual Web database consists of data attributes over which users can query, while the result schema consists of data attributes that users can browse. The three schemas of a Web database all partially represent the data objects contained in the backend database, varying only on the number of attributes and attribute names.

A *matching* between two schemas S_1 and S_2 determines that certain attributes of schema S_1 semantically correspond to certain attributes of schema S_2. For an individual Web database, there exist three kinds of *intra-site schema matching*, between GS and IS, between GS and RS, and between IS and RS (illustrated in Figure 2 as edges between heterogeneous nodes of each single site). Furthermore, given multiple Web databases in the same domain, the interface schemas of different Web databases can also be pair-wise matched (between IS and IS), as can the result schemas of different Web databases (between RS and RS). Such *inter-site schema matching* is illustrated in Figure 2 as dashed edges between homogenous nodes of different sites.

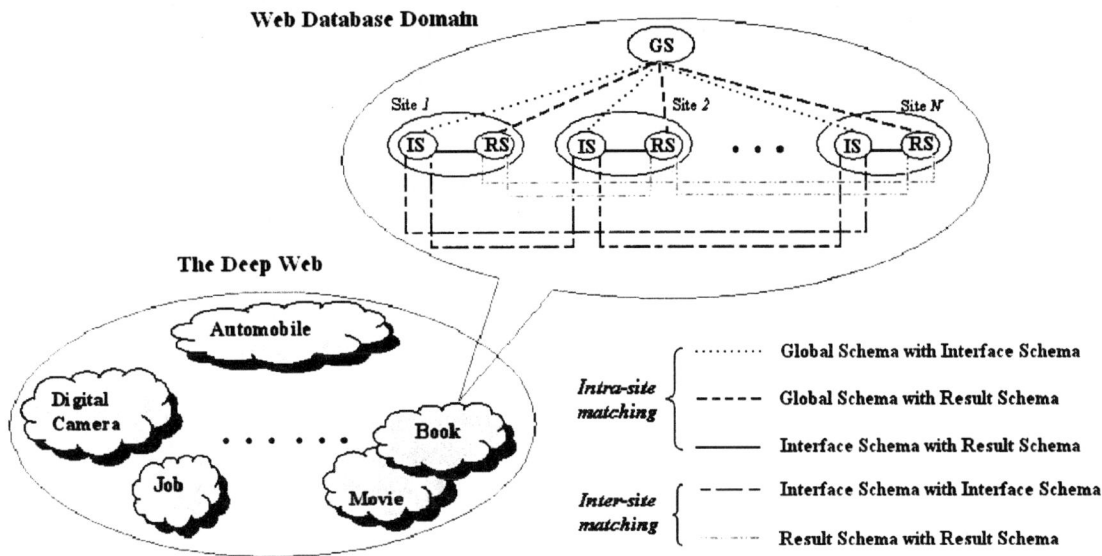

Figure 2. Global view of the Deep Web and combined schema model of Web databases.

The benefits of such a model are that it allows us to:
- **Automatically understand the semantics of schema attributes.** If the attribute semantics of one particular schema are accurately identified or known beforehand, then the attribute semantics of other schemas can also be discovered as long as they are correctly matched to an identified one. Even if the semantics of one particular schema are somehow wrongly identified in a matching with another schema, there is still opportunity for correction when it is matched to other schemas.
- **Automatically extract relevant content from Web databases.** Crawling the massive information hidden behind the query interfaces of Web databases is a major problem for the Web search community. Automatic understanding of interface schemas can make it possible for crawlers to intelligently submit "appropriate" queries into the right input elements. Furthermore, automatic understanding of result schemas can make it possible for crawlers to intelligently obtain valid query results according to their semantics (i.e., to automatically extract relevant Web database content).
- **Meta-search multiple Web databases.** In this model, related Web databases are categorized by their domain. With a meta-search interface built for each domain, users can simultaneously search multiple Web databases of the domain. Given a user query, first some promising Web databases that may contain relevant information are picked and then queries are sent to these Web databases according to the identified semantics of their query interfaces. Finally, their query results are integrated and displayed to users according to the match among their result schemas.

3. Domain-specific Query Probing

Database schema matching is the task of finding mappings between attributes of two schemas that semantically correspond to each other [3]. Previous approaches to schema matching can be categorized into two classes, *label-based* and *instance-based*, according to the different information on which they rely (see [22] for a survey). Label-based methods only consider the similarity between schema definitions or attribute labels of two databases. Instance-based methods, such as [12] and [18], depend on the content overlap or statistical properties, such as data range and pattern, to determine the similarity of two attributes.

Recent work ([16], [17], and [21]) on matching query interfaces of Web databases fall into the first category, based on identifying the descriptive text surrounding interface elements as the attribute labels and finding *synonym relationships* between the labels. Such methods are not stable and robust in the Web context as no description may exist or the identified description may not be informative. On the other hand, instance-based schema matching has seldom been employed in the deep Web scenario because of the difficulty of automatically acquiring database contents hidden behind query interfaces. Paradoxically, a key prerequisite for automatic data acquisition from the deep Web is to understand the semantics of query elements.

Different from the previous work, our goal is to understand and match not only interface schemas but also result schemas of Web databases. Consequently, the label-based matching approach is insufficient and even inapplicable due to the frequent lack of explicit attribute labels and descriptions in result pages. Therefore, we propose an instance-based solution to this problem. We first submit semantically pre-identified query keywords through query interfaces (section 3.2). After obtaining returned result data, we then analyze the results to understand the semantics of both the query interfaces and data attributes, as well as to match the homogeneous schemas of different Web databases (section 4).

3.1 Observations

During the interaction with Web databases, we observe two interesting phenomena.

On the one hand, when an improper query is submitted to a Web database there are often few results or even no results returned. Improperness here means the query keywords submitted into a particular element are not applicable values of the database attribute to which the element is associated. Taking the Web database shown in Figure 1 as an example, the site reports only 4 matches for the query "Harry Potter" when submitted through the "Author" element, while it reports 228 matches for the same query when submitted through the "Title" element. On the other hand, we observe that when a proper query that returns a result web page is submitted through the input elements of a Web database, then the query keywords very likely reappear in the returned result's corresponding attributes. For example, in Figure 1, when we submit query "Harry Potter" through the "Title" element, the three returned book instances all contain the query keywords (i.e., "Harry Potter") in their Title attribute.

Generally, how many times the keywords for a query re-appear in the result pages and where they appear tell us important information about both the interface schema and the result schema. Specifically, if we employ the values of some semantically pre-identified data attributes as queries to submit into a Web database, we can accomplish two tasks. First, the re-occurrence of the query keywords in the returned results can be used as an indicator of which query submission is appropriate (i.e., to discover semantically associated elements in the interface schema). Second, the position or location of the submitted query keywords in the result pages can be used to identify the semantically associated attributes in the result schema.

3.2 Query Probing

Given some target Web databases in a specific domain, our query probing process aims to send domain-specific queries to these target Web databases and collect their returned results for later analysis.

To accomplish this task, we make two assumptions about the query probing process. First, a global schema for the specific domain is pre-defined or pre-generated. Second, a number of sample data objects under the domain global schema are also available. In fact, global schema generation over information sources to conceptualize the underlying domain is an interesting problem. Proposed approaches rely on either the names of the schema elements and the structure of the schema ([7] and [16]) or formal ontologies ([4] and [15]). We consider this problem as a separate research direction and do not deal with it in this paper. In our experiments, we manually define the global schema and collect sample instances. In future work, we plan to implement one of the previously proposed approaches to automatically generate a global schema over a sample set of Web databases and then map new Web databases to the generated global schema.

3.2.1 Workflow

We show in Figure 3 the workflow of an automatic probing process. Given the Web database with its query interface, an element identification component first locates qualified input elements in the query interface. Equipped with instances under a global schema, a query submission component then exhaustively submits the attribute values of pre-known instances into those identified input elements. After collecting the returned results for all submitted queries, a wrapper induction component induces a regular-expression wrapper composed of HTML-tags. Next, a data extraction component employs the induced wrapper to extract structured data objects from query result pages and arrange them into a data table. Finally, the re-occurrences of submitted queries in the columns of this table are counted and stored into a *query occurrence cube*, which will be introduced in the next subsection.

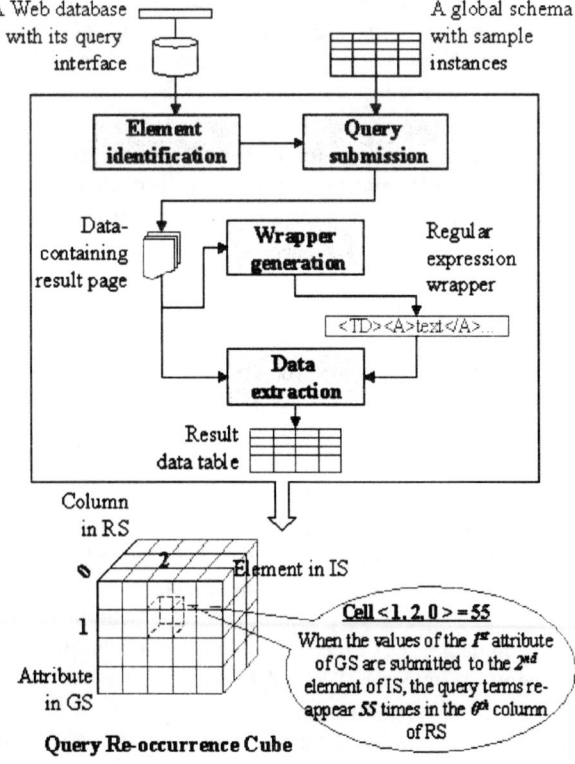

Figure 3. Flow of the query probing process and the query occurrence cube.

Given a Web database, the first task is to identify input elements in its query interface, which can be done by searching for the input-related tags [6] in a HTML searchable form. In the HTTP protocol, a query submission is carried out by sending a query request to the server containing the names of input elements and their corresponding query keywords. In this paper, we only submit one value to one element each time while keeping the default values for the other elements. We will consider the complex submission of querying multiple elements at one time in future work.

For each TEXTBOX element in HTML forms, as we do not know its value domain, we exhaustively try all the attribute values from the given sample instances. For each SELECT element, its domain values are limited to its OPTION elements (i.e., we can only choose one or more of its OPTION values as the query keywords). Thus, for each attribute value of the given instances, we try to find and submit an option "similar"[7] to the value. For other elements like CHECKBOX and RADIOBOX, the process is similar. As a consequence, the maximum submission time will be the product of the number of attributes in the global schema, the number of provided sample instances and the number of interface elements considered.

After sending queries to the identified interface elements and collecting returned result pages from the Web database, the next task is to extract structured data from the pages. While dealing with hundreds or possibly thousands of Web databases in one domain, each of which encloses its data in the result pages according to some specific HTML-tag structures, how to automatically extract data objects from the pages is a very challenging problem that has attracted increasing research interest. Recently, attempts have been made to develop fully automatic approaches for inducing wrappers to extract embedded semi-structured data content from dynamic template-generated HTML pages [1], [9], [10], [23]. Discussion of these approaches is beyond the scope of this paper and interested readers are referred to the above papers for further information.

In this paper, we choose our previous work [23] to induce a regular-expression wrapper based on nested repeated-pattern discovery in HTML pages. We also employ the data extraction module of [23] to extract the enclosed data objects into a table so that each column of the result table corresponds to one attribute of the returned result (i.e., of the result schema).

3.2.2 Query Occurrence Cube

After counting the re-appearance of each submitted value in the query results, a *Query Occurrence Cube (QOCube)* is constructed for the target Web database, as shown in Figure 3. The cube height represents the number of attributes in the given global schema. The cube width represents the number of interface elements considered (i.e., attributes of the interface schema). The cube depth is the number of columns in the result table (i.e., attributes of the result schema). Moreover, each cell in this cube stores an occurrence count associated with the three dimensions. For example, in Figure 3, *cell<1, 2, 0>* equal to *55* means that when all given values for the 1st attribute of GS are submitted to the 2nd element of IS, the query keywords re-appear *55* times in the 0th column of RS.

Conveniently, the constructed QOCube provides a unified solution to match the 3 pairs of Web database schemas. The 3-dimensional cube can be easily projected onto three *Query Occurrence Matrices* (front, top and left), which exactly reflect the relationship between pairs of the three schemas (i.e., IS and GS, IS and RS, and GS and RS). Suppose the number of attributes in the global schema is N, the number of elements in the interface schema is M, and the number of columns in the result table is L. Once a projection function is selected, say *sum*, the 3-dimensional cube $QOC_{N \times M \times L}$ can be projected into three 2-dimensional *occurrence matrices*, $OM^{IG}_{M \times N}$ for IS and GS, $OM^{IR}_{M \times L}$ for IS and RS, and $OM^{GR}_{N \times L}$ for GS and RS. The main research issue now becomes how to find the correspondence between a pair of schemas in the projection matrices.

4. Instance-based Schema Matching

4.1 Intra-site Schema Matching

In this section, we focus on how to match the attributes between IS and GS, IS and RS, and GS and RS based on the obtained matrices: $OM^{IG}_{M \times N}$, $OM^{IR}_{M \times L}$, and $OM^{GR}_{N \times L}$.

An example[8] of $OM^{IG}_{5 \times 4}$ is shown in Example 1 with the correct matching in the gray rectangles, when GS = {$Title_{GS}$, $Author_{GS}$, $Publisher_{GS}$, $ISBN_{GS}$} and IS = {$Author_{IS}$, $Title_{IS}$, $Publisher_{IS}$, $Keyword_{IS}$, $ISBN_{IS}$}.

EXAMPLE 1:

	$Title_{GS}$	$Author_{GS}$	$Publisher_{GS}$	$ISBN_{GS}$
$Author_{IS}$	93	498	534	0
$Title_{IS}$	451	345	501	0
$Publisher_{IS}$	62	184	468	2
$Keyword_{IS}$	120	248	143	275
$ISBN_{IS}$	0	0	0	258

$_{5 \times 4}$

In fact, there are some properties of the occurrence matrix to consider when searching for the correspondence

---

[6] Please refer to the HTML specification [24].

[7] The attribute value and the option value (two text strings) are similar as long as they contain at least one common keyword.

[8] All examples in this section are obtained from real Web databases in our experiments.

or correlation between its rows and columns that represent the attributes of the two schemas. First, an absolute high occurrence may not represent a correct matching. For example, the matrix element for Author$_{IS}$ and Publisher$_{GS}$ (534) has the highest value in the matrix while Author$_{IS}$ and Publisher$_{GS}$ do not semantically correspond to each other. Second, given a particular matrix element m_{ij}, its relative value (magnitude) among all elements for its row i and column j is more important than its absolute value. For example, for Keyword$_{IS}$, which is in fact not a real attribute for book objects, its similar performance on all columns indicates that it may not be a good match for any one of the columns. The matrix element for Publisher$_{IS}$ and Publisher$_{GS}$ (468) does not have the highest value among the elements for Publisher$_{GS}$. However, it is relatively larger than the values of other matrix elements in the row for Publisher$_{IS}$.

Interestingly, we can view the schema-matching problem as follows. By sending sample queries, a part of the database content relevant to the queries is fetched from the Web database. For any two schemas, S_1 and S_2, of one Web database, the obtained database content can be partitioned according to the attributes of S_1 and S_2, respectively. Suppose the partitions by the attributes of S_1 are $A_1, A_2, \ldots A_n$ and the partitions by the attributes of S_2 are $B_1, B_2, \ldots B_m$. The element m_{ij} in the occurrence matrix for S_1 and S_2 actually indicates the content overlap between partitions A_i and B_j with respect to the occurrences of submitted values re-appearing in the two partitions. The schema-matching problem now becomes that of finding the pair of partitions that belong to two schemas (e.g., A_i and B_j) such that their overlap with each other is more than their overlap with other partitions belonging to the opposite schema (e.g., A_i and B_k or A_k and B_j).

To help solve this problem, we employ the concept of *mutual information*, which interprets the overlap between two partitions X and Y of a random event set as the "information about X contained in Y" or the "information about Y contained in X" [20].

DEFINITION 1: Suppose X and Y are two partitions over a collection of events, and x_i and y_j are partition elements of X and Y with joint probability $p(x_i, y_j)$ and respective marginal probability $p(x_i)$ and $p(y_j)$. The *mutual information* of the partition X and Y is

$$I(X;Y) = \sum_i \sum_j p(x_i, y_j) \log \frac{p(x_i, y_j)}{p(x_i)p(y_j)}$$

Accordingly, we can estimate the mutual information between a pair of attributes from two schemas using the following definition.

DEFINITION 2: Given a query occurrence matrix $OM^{S_1 S_2}{}_{I \times J}$ of two schemas S_1 and S_2, the *estimated mutual information (EMI)* between the ith attribute of S_1 (say A_i) and the jth attribute of S_2 (say B_j) is

$$EMI(A_i, B_j) = \frac{m_{ij}}{M} \log \frac{\frac{m_{ij}}{M}}{\frac{m_{i+}}{M} * \frac{m_{+j}}{M}}$$

with M being $\sum_{i,j} m_{ij}$, m_{i+} being $\sum_j m_{ij}$ and m_{+j} being $\sum_i m_{ij}$. Note that if m_{ij} equals to 0, EMI is assumed to be 0 as well.

Thus, the occurrence matrix in Example 1 can induce the *EMI* matrix shown in Example 2, with each matrix element being the estimated mutual information value for the corresponding schema attributes.

EXAMPLE 2:

	Title$_{GS}$	Author$_{GS}$	Publisher$_{GS}$	ISBN$_{GS}$
Author$_{IS}$	−0.007	**0.019**	0.010	0
Title$_{IS}$	**0.033**	−0.005	−0.001	0
Publisher$_{IS}$	−0.004	−0.003	**0.025**	−0.001
Keyword$_{IS}$	−0.002	0.001	−0.011	0.029
ISBN$_{IS}$	0	0	0	**0.055**

$_{5 \times 4}$

To find a 1-1 attribute matching of the two schemas is easy in the *EMI* matrix. If one matrix element is larger than the other elements in the same row and also larger than the other elements in the same column, its related attributes will have a larger overlap between each other than their overlap with other attributes of the other schema, as shown by the gray rectangles. For example, *EMI*(Author$_{IS}$, Author$_{GS}$) = 0.019 is the largest value in both its row and its column and it is a correct match. Therefore, we propose the following definition to quantify the intra-site schema matching.

DEFINITION 3: Assume two schemas S_1 and S_2 with the corresponding *EMI* matrix $[e_{ij}]$. The ith attribute of S_1 *matches* with the jth attribute of S_2 if $e_{ij} \geq e_{ik} \mid k \neq j$ and $e_{ij} \geq e_{kj} \mid k \neq i$.

4.2 Inter-site Schema Matching

In this section, we focus on how to find the corresponding attributes for homogeneous schemas, namely, IS and IS, and RS and RS, of different Web databases.

Borrowing the idea of *vector similarity* used in the *Vector Space Model* of Information Retrieval [2], we propose an approach to match interface/result schemas of different Web databases by computing their vector similarity. In the vector space model, documents are represented as vectors in a multi-dimensional space. In this space, each dimension represents a term or concept found in a document and the values are the corresponding frequencies of the terms in the document. Similarity between two vectors is measured by the cosine of the angle between their two vectors, which is computed as the inner product of the two vectors, normalized by the products of the vector lengths.

If we consider each attribute of an individual interface/result schema as a "document" and each attribute of the global schema as a "concept", then each row in the occurrence matrix represents a corresponding document vector. Therefore, we can calculate the similarity (i.e., semantic correspondence) between attributes from different schemas by measuring their vector similarity. The following definition quantifies the inter-site schema matching between two Web databases.

DEFINITION 4: Given two query occurrence matrices of two Web databases' interface/result schemas $OM^{S_1,G} = [a_{ij}]_{n \times m}$ and $OM^{S_2,G} = [b_{ij}]_{l \times m}$ with respect to the same global schema, the *estimated vector similarity (EVS)* between the ith attribute of S_1 (say A_i) and the jth attribute of S_2 (say B_j) is

$$EVS(A_i, B_j) = \frac{\sum_k a_{ik} b_{jk}}{\sqrt{\sum_k a_{ik}^2} * \sqrt{\sum_k b_{jk}^2}}$$

To find a 1-1 attribute matching of two schemas in the *EVS* matrix is the same as in the *EMI* matrix (Definition 3). A matrix element whose value is the largest both in its row and column represents a match. For instance, Example 3 shows two occurrence matrices of two interface schemas with respect to a global schema GS = {Title, Author, Publisher, ISBN}, where IS$_1$ = {Author$_1$, Title$_1$, Publisher$_1$, Keyword$_1$, ISBN$_1$}, IS$_2$ = {Title$_2$, Author$_2$, ISBN$_2$}. The grey rectangles depict the largest similarity values among rows and columns, which is also the correct matching. Interestingly, although the second attribute of IS$_2$, Author$_2$, is wrongly matched to Publisher$_2$ of GS in the previous intra-site schema matching (underlined element in EMI matrix of S_2), our method still can find the right inter-site matching.

EXAMPLE 3:

Occurrence Matrix of S_1

$$\begin{array}{c|cccc} & T_G & A_G & P_G & I_G \\ \hline A_1 & 93 & 498 & 534 & 0 \\ T_1 & 451 & 345 & 501 & 0 \\ P_1 & 62 & 184 & 468 & 2 \\ K_1 & 120 & 248 & 143 & 275 \\ I_1 & 0 & 0 & 0 & 258 \end{array}_{5 \times 4}$$

Occurrence Matrix Of S_2

$$\begin{array}{c|cccc} & T_G & A_G & P_G & I_G \\ \hline T_2 & 166 & 177 & 118 & 0 \\ A_2 & 39 & 331 & 406 & 0 \\ I_2 & 0 & 0 & 0 & 18 \end{array}_{3 \times 4}$$

EMI Matrix Of S_2

$$\begin{bmatrix} 0.045 & -0.003 & -0.020 & 0 \\ -0.016 & 0.006 & \underline{0.032} & 0 \\ 0 & 0 & 0 & 18 \end{bmatrix}_{3 \times 4}$$

Vector Similarity Matrix of S_1 and S_2

$$\begin{array}{c|ccc} & T_2 & A_2 & I_2 \\ \hline A_1 & 0.839 & \boxed{0.996} & 0 \\ T_1 & \boxed{0.955} & 0.843 & 0 \\ P_1 & 0.717 & 0.952 & 0.004 \\ K_1 & 0.721 & 0.665 & 0.663 \\ I_1 & 0 & 0 & \boxed{1.000} \end{array}_{5 \times 3}$$

4.3 Cross Validation

Given multiple Web databases in the same domain, we can employ the techniques proposed in sections 4.1 and 4.2 to identify the matching attributes belonging to schemas of an individual Web database and the matching attributes belonging to schemas of different Web databases. Consequently, we can employ the five types of matching results (i.e., GS-IS, GS-RS, IS-RS, IS-IS and RS-RS) to cross validate each other (i.e., to recognize which matching is correct and which is not). In this section, we focus on how to cross validate different matching results produced from both inter-site and intra-site matching. Note that in this step, we do not limit how the schemas are previously matched (i.e., we can employ any applicable label-based or instance-based method) as long as the matching results are provided.

Given all the attributes from the interface schemas (or result schemas) of the target Web databases, we can categorize the IS (or RS) attributes into multiple clusters with respect to the GS attributes to which they have been matched. For example, the attributes, which are previously matched to the attribute A$_G$ of the global schema, are categorized into one cluster, while the attributes, which are previously matched to the attribute P$_G$ of the global schema, are categorized into another cluster. Recall that attributes are also matched to each other in inter-site schema matching. In the ideal case, an attribute in one cluster only matches with attributes in the same cluster. When a matching across clusters does exist (i.e., two attributes in two different clusters have a match) there must be a mismatch. The possible reason for the mismatch could be either that one of the two attributes was put into the wrong cluster or that the matching between these two attributes is wrong.

Interestingly, if we consider the attributes as vertices and matching between attributes as edges, we can convert the problem of deciding which matching is incorrect into a *graph partitioning problem*: given a set of vertices and edges, divide the vertices into N partitions such that the edge-cut is minimized. The *edge-cut* is the sum of the weights (1 in this case) of all the edges between the partitions. This *graph partitioning problem* is known to be NP-hard [14]. Therefore, we can only expect approximate solutions in general.

In our case, where there is already an initial partition of the vertices (according to the matching results with respect to GS), a simple approximate approach is to move vertices over partitions as long as the number of cuts decreases. Accordingly, a vertex v is moved to the partition in which most of its "neighbours" reside. Since a vertex v needs to be moved if many of its neighbours jump, multiple passes are likely to be needed before the process converges on a local optimum. When the process stops, we resolve the cross cluster matching between attributes A_i of site S_1 and B_j of site S_2 contained in two clusters C_1 and C_2 by first discarding it and then re-matching A_i to attribute B_k of site S_2 clustered into C_l or vice versa.

EXAMPLE 4:

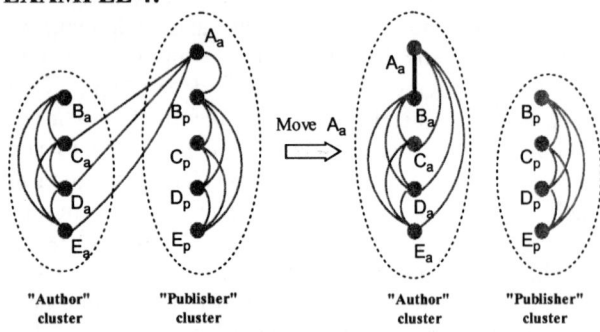

Example 4 illustrates one pass of such an approximate approach. For simplicity, suppose that the global schema only contains two attributes {Author, Publisher} and there are five Web databases with the IS attributes $IS_1 = \{A_a\}$, $IS_2 = \{B_a, B_p\}$, $IS_3 = \{C_a, C_p\}$, $IS_4 = \{D_a, D_p\}$ and $IS_5 = \{E_a, E_p\}$. The two ellipses on the left depict how the attributes are primarily clustered according to which GS attribute they are matched (by intra-site schema matching), and the edges between two attributes show whether they are matched or not (by inter-site schema matching). In the initial state, A_a is wrongly matched to the Publisher attribute of GS and also wrongly matched to B_p while it has been correctly matched to three other attributes in the Author cluster. Therefore, A_a is moved to decrease the number of edges across clusters from 3 to 1, as shown in Example 4. By such a "moving" process, we correct the matching attribute of A_a from the Publisher to the Author attribute of GS. After the move, the edge between A_a and B_p is replaced by a new edge between A_a and B_a (the attribute of site 2 that is matched to the global attribute Author).

Due to space limitations, we omit the detailed algorithm for the above cross-validation technique and only show the experimental results in the next section to verify its effectiveness.

5. Experiments

We performed a comprehensive evaluation of the proposed instance-based schema matching approaches on thirty complex Web databases over two domains: Book and Used-car. The main goal was to investigate the feasibility of a unified and accurate solution to matching schemas both in a single site and from different sites. We first describe the Web databases employed for the testing. Then we present the results for intra-site schema matching and inter-site schema matching, and the improvement achieved by cross validating the matching results.

5.1 Test Web Databases

For our evaluation, we used 20 Web databases for purchasing books online and 10 Web databases for searching for used-cars online. The global schema for the two domains are manually defined as Book = {Title, Author, Publisher, ISBN} and Used-car = {Make, Model, Postal-zip, State, Price, Mileage, Year}. We also manually collected 20 book instances and 10 car instances (details can be found in [25]) and took their attribute values as sample queries to be used to probe the test Web databases. After obtaining the query result pages from each Web database, we employed our previous work [23] on wrapper induction to automatically extract the result records according to their specific structures and re-arrange them into a result table.

Table 1. Characteristics of test Web databases.

	#Interface Elements	#TS	%SS	#Result Columns	#Extracted Data
Book	4.2	343.3	32%	6.25	1322.9
Car	6.0	123.1	72%	5	995.3

The columns #TS and %SS of Table 1 represent, respectively, the number of total submissions made to the test Web databases and the corresponding success rate[9]. The reason that the Used-car domain has a lower number of submissions and a higher success rate than the Book domain is because SELECT and TEXTBOX input elements were treated differently when submitting the queries. We exhaustively tried all the attributes of the pre-known instances for a TEXTBOX element, while we only submitted the OPTION values of a SELECT element if they were found to be similar to one or more attribute values of the pre-known instances (see section 3.2.1). In our experiments, most of the Web databases in the Book domain only contain TEXTBOX elements. Therefore, this domain has a higher number of submissions, but a lower success rate.

5.2 Matching Results

In this subsection, we report and discuss the experimental results for both intra-site and inter-site schema matching of the two domains. The intra-site schema matching results are listed in Table 2. To verify the effectiveness of our proposed instance-based matching approach (EMI) derived from mutual information analysis, we implemented a simple method as our baseline (MAX). The baseline method works as follows: in the query value occurrence matrix, the matrix element with the largest value both among the elements in the same column and among the elements in the same row is identified as an attribute matching.

In our evaluation, precision and recall originating from the information retrieval area are used as the metrics. Precision is measured as the ratio of the number of correctly identified matching attribute-pairs to the total number of attribute-pairs identified by the methods.

---

[9] A query submission is successful if the induced wrapper can extract at least one instance from the query result page.

Recall is measured as the ratio of the number of correctly identified matching attribute-pairs to the total number of matching pairs in the two schemas. Suppose the number of correctly identified matching attribute-pairs is C, the number of wrongly identified matching attribute-pairs is W and the number of correct matching attribute-pairs but somehow missed in the approach is M, then the precision of the approach is $\frac{C}{C+W}$ and its recall is $\frac{C}{C+M}$.

Table 2. Intra-site schema matching results.

		IS–GS P	IS–GS R	RS–GS P	RS–GS R	IS–RS P	IS–RS R
Book	MAX	68%	50%	91%	81%	90%	84%
	EMI	80%	71%	95%	88%	93%	87%
Car	MAX	97%	63%	96%	57%	100%	67%
	EMI	97%	64%	93%	63%	100%	73%

In Table 2, we can see that our *EMI-based* method significantly outperforms the baseline method. In the Book domain, both the *EMI-based* and *Max-based* methods produce the worst results on IS-GS schema matching. The reason is that Web databases of this domain tend to include a "Keyword" input element in the interface schema for the convenience of end-users who may want to use keyword search. Using the "Keyword" element often returns results for any query no matter to which global attribute the query belongs. Since there is no "noisy" keyword attribute in the global schemas and the result schemas, our matching approach can achieve a higher accuracy in GS-RS matching. In the Used-car domain, both MAX-based and EMI-based methods have a relatively low recall. The reason is that our matching techniques are based on counting the re-appearance of submitted queries in the result data, which is more suitable for database attributes accepting the "equal" select operator. When handling numeric-field attributes that accept "less than" or "greater than" select operators, such as Price and Mileage, the returned results sometimes may not include the exact query keyword, such as "$10,000".

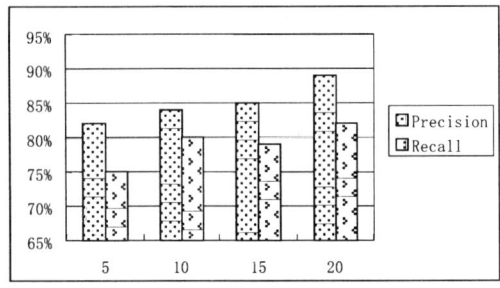

Figure 4. Result achieved by different number of sample instances.

We show in Figure 4 how the achieved results vary when the number of sample instances is increased. The columns in Figure 4 are achieved average precision and recall of the intra-site schema matching results of the Book domain, when the number of instances is set to 5, 10, 15 and 20. From the figure, we can see that the achieved results generally increase as the number of sample instances increases. However, more sample instances mean more query submissions to the Web database. Since we do not want to overburden the target Web databases, an interesting future research direction might be to find a trade-off between the number of submissions and the achieved results.

Table 3. Inter-site schema matching results.

		IS-IS P	IS-IS R	RS-RS P	RS-RS R
Book	Label-based	90%	87%	95%	14%
	EVS	91%	71%	94%	86%
Car	Label-based	89%	88%	98%	25%
	EVS	92%	72%	89%	66%

In Table 3 we compare the inter-site schema matching results achieved by our proposed approach (EVS) based on *vector similarity* analysis to the matching results achieved by label-based approaches. Label-based approaches are mainly based on finding the synonym relationship between attribute labels. In matching interface schemas, we manually identified the surrounding text of input elements as their labels [16], [17], [21]. In matching result schemas, we manually found either explicit author-supplied column headers in the result pages or the text strings commonly shared by all extracted instances as the attribute labels. Table 3 shows that the performance of the *EVS-based* method is close to that of label-based methods in IS-IS matching, while it performs much better in RS-RS matching since attribute labels are often unavailable in result pages. In addition, our approach does not require intelligent layout analysis to precisely identify the correct attribute labels.

Table 4. Effectiveness of cross validation.

		Before CV P	Before CV R	After CV P	After CV R
Book	IS–GS	80%	70%	96%	83%
	RS–GS	95%	88%	98%	91%
	IS–RS	93%	87%	97%	90%
	IS–IS	91%	71%	94%	74%
	RS–RS	94%	86%	99%	87%
Car	IS–GS	97%	64%	97%	72%
	RS–GS	93%	63%	97%	70%
	IS–RS	100%	73%	100%	75%
	IS–IS	92%	72%	95%	77%
	RS–RS	89%	66%	92%	69%

We present in Table 4 the effectiveness of the proposed cross validation approach in improving the overall accuracy. Table 4 shows that the cross validation method does improve the overall matching accuracy, especially in the Book domain. It is notable that we cannot achieve as high a recall as we can precision (over 90%). We believe that the cause is not due to the ineffectiveness of the cross validation, but is due to the nature of the probing-based approach itself.

5.3 Discussion

In our experiments, we observed some issues that need further consideration.

The performance of our instance-based matching approaches to some extent depends on the selection of the sample instances. More specifically, two properties of the sample instances could influence the matching process: the topics that they cover and their attribute-distinguishing capability. Take the Book domain as an example. Some Web databases may only contain books about computer programming while others only have novels. Therefore, to ensure that result data can be extracted from the Web databases' answers to the sample queries, various topics are required to be covered in the sample instances. At the same time, the attribute-distinguishing capability of the sample instances may also influence the matching results. For example, the name of a famous person usually frequently appears both in the Author attribute of the books he/she wrote and the Title attribute of his/her biographies, such as "Jane Austen" in our chosen sample instances.

We also notice that, as Web databases vary in their designs, some of them might generate result pages with different formats for different queries. For example, when answering a Title query, a Web database returns a list of qualified book instances and each of the instances is described by some text. However, when answering an ISBN query, the same Web database returns only one unique book instance with its detailed information shown in the result page. It is obvious that these two kinds of results are generated by two different templates. To deal with this issue, an intelligent result analysis method is needed to first extract results with different formats and then combine them into one uniform result table.

6. Related Work

Schema matching is a basic problem in database research with numerous techniques proposed to address the problem (see [11] and [22] for surveys). Existing work that addresses the problem of automatic schema matching for Web databases adopts the prior techniques on matching schemas of traditional databases. [16] presented a statistical approach to integrate the interface schemas of Web databases in the same domain. It hypothesizes that given Web databases in the same domain, the aggregate vocabulary describing the interface input elements tends to have a relatively small size. Furthermore, there exists a unified hidden schema underlying these interfaces. A statistical probability model is employed to find the hidden schema by the co-appearance of attribute names. The schema matching methods employed are label-based.

[17] introduced a tool, WISE-Integrator, that performs automatic integration of Web search interfaces in a product domain. WISE-Integrator employs comprehensive meta-data, such as element labels and default value of the elements, to automatically identify matching attributes from different search interfaces.

[19] investigated algorithms for generic schema matching, outside of any particular data model or application. An algorithm called Cupid was proposed to discover mappings between schema elements based on their names, data types, constraints, and schema structure.

[18] used a classifier to categorize attributes according to their field specifications and data values, and then train a neural network to recognize similar attributes. However, this method may not be applicable for Web databases since both field specifications and data values are incomplete in many cases.

[11] developed the COMA schema-matching system as a platform to combine multiple matchers in a flexible way. While their approach may seem similar to our cross validation method, it is fundamentally different since the goal of our method is the reinforcement of multiple matchers, not the straightforward combination of the matchers.

[21] presented HiWe, a prototype deep-web crawler that can extract the labels of interface elements and automatically submit queries through the elements. Interface elements with the same/similar labels are matched in order to obtain each other's domain values for automatic query submission.

The main difference between our work and previous work is that we aim to provide a general framework for schema matching of Web databases. To the best of our knowledge, no previous work has presented such a framework, especially the combined schema model. Moreover, the instance-based schema-matching method is seldom used for schema matching in the Web database context since it is hard to get instances from Web databases. Supplied with a set of sample instances, our work proves that instance-based methods can also be very effective for Web database schema matching.

7. Conclusion

In this paper, we investigate the problem of schema matching for Web databases. We propose a combined schema model to describe the various schemas associated with a Web database and a generative view to include five kinds of schema matching of related Web databases in a specific domain.

In the combined schema model, we address two significant schema-matching problems for Web databases, intra-site schema matching and inter-site schema matching. We then investigate a unified solution to the two problems based on domain-specific query probing and attribute content overlap. Our instance-based approaches, which adopt the mutual information concept and vector similarity analysis, are quite powerful for precisely identifying the matching relationships among attributes of Web databases' interface and result schemas. Benefiting from our general framework, a cross validation technique, converted to a graph-partitioning problem, is introduced and shown to improve the matching performance.

Currently our approach needs some human involvement to provide a precise global schema and instance samples. One direction to extend this work is to adopt automatic global schema generation techniques to make the whole system fully automatic. Another direction of improvement is to combine our work with previous label-based approaches to build a more robust matching system. In addition, we plan to extend this work to handle not only 1:1 mappings but also 1:N mappings over Web database schema attributes.

Acknowledgements

This work was partially supported by the UGC Research Grants Council of Hong Kong under the Areas of Excellence—Information Technology program.

References

[1] A. Arasu, and H. Garcia-Molina. *Extracting structured data from Web pages*. Proc. ACM SIGMOD Conf., 2003.

[2] R. Baeza-Yates, and B. Ribeiro-Neto. *Modern Information Retrieval*. ACM Press, New York, 1999.

[3] C. Batini, M. Lenzerini, and S. B. Navathe. *A comparative analysis of methodologies for database schema integration*. ACM Computing Surveys, **18**(4), 323-364, 1986.

[4] D. Beneventano, S, Bergamaschi, F. Guerra and M. Vincini. *Synthesizing an integrated ontology*. Internet Computing, vol. 7, no. 5, 2003.

[5] BrightPlanet Corp. *The deep web: surfacing hidden value*. http://www.completeplanet.com/Tutorials/DeepWeb/

[6] J. Callan, M. Connell and A. Du. *Automatic discovery of language models for text databases*. Proc. ACM SIGMOD Conf., 1999.

[7] S. Castano, V. Antonellis, and S. Vimercati. *Global viewing of heterogeneous data sources*. IEEE Trans. Data and Knowledge Eng., vol. 13, no. 2, 2001.

[8] C.H. Chang, B. He, C. Li, and Z. Zhang: *Structured Databases on the Web: Observations and Implications discovery*. Technical Report UIUCCDCS-R-2003-2321. CS Department, University of Illinois at Urbana-Champaign. February, 2003.

[9] C.H. Chang, and S.C. Lui. *IEPAD: information extraction based on pattern discovery*. Proc. 10th World Wide Web Conf., 681-688, 2001.

[10] V. Crescenzi, G. Mecca and P. Merialdo. *ROADRUNNER: towards automatic data extraction from large web sites*. Proc. 27th VLDB. Conf., 109-118, 2001.

[11] H. Do and E. Rahm. *COMA: a system for flexible combination of schema matching approaches*. Proc. 28th VLDB Conf., 2002.

[12] A. Doan, P. Domingos and A. Halevy. *Reconciling schemas of disparate data sources: a machine-learning approach*. Proc. ACM SIGMOD, 2001.

[13] D. Florescu, A.Y. Levy, and A.O. Mendelzon. *Database techniques for the world-wide web: a survey*. SIGMOD Record **27**(3), 59-74, 1998.

[14] M. R. Garey and D. S. Johnson, *Computers and Intractability: A Guide to the Theory of NP-Completeness*. Freeman, New York, 1979.

[15] F. Hakimpour, and A. Geppert. *Global schema generation using formal ontologies*. Proc. 21st Conf. on Conceptual Modeling, 2002.

[16] B. He, and C.C. Chang. *Statistical schema matching across Web query interfaces*. Proc. ACM SIGMOD Conf., 2003.

[17] H. He, W. Meng, C. Yu and Z. Wu. *WISE-Integrator: an automatic integrator of Web search interfaces for E-commerce*. Proc. 29th VLDB Conf., 2003.

[18] W. Li and C. Clifton. *Semantic integration in heterogeneous databases using neural networks*. Proc 20th VLDB Conf, 1994.

[19] J. Madhavan, P.A. Bernsstein and E. Rahm. *Generic schema matching with Cupid*. Proc. 27th VLDB Conf., 2001.

[20] A. Papoulis. *Probability, Random Variables, and Stochastic Processes*. McGraw-Hill, 1984.

[21] S. Raghavan and H. Garcia-Molina. *Crawling the hidden web*. Proc. 27th VLDB Conf., 129-138, 2001.

[22] E. Rahm and P.A. Bernstein. *A survey of approaches to automatic schema matching*. VLDB Journal, **10**(4), 334-350, 2001.

[23] J. Wang and F. Lochovsky. *Data extraction and label assignment for web databases*. Proc. 12th World Wide Web Conf., 187-196, 2003.

[24] World Wide Web Consortium. *HTML 4.01 Specification*, 1999.

[25] http://www.cs.ust.hk/~cswangjy/vldb04_exp.htm/

Computing PageRank in a Distributed Internet Search System

Yuan Wang   David J. DeWitt

Computer Sciences Department, University of Wisconsin - Madison
1210 W. Dayton St.
Madison, WI 53706
USA
{yuanwang, dewitt}@cs.wisc.edu

Abstract

Existing Internet search engines use web crawlers to download data from the Web. Page quality is measured on central servers, where user queries are also processed. This paper argues that using crawlers has a list of disadvantages. Most importantly, crawlers do not scale. Even Google, the leading search engine, indexes less than 1% of the entire Web. This paper proposes a distributed search engine framework, in which every web server answers queries over its own data. Results from multiple web servers will be merged to generate a ranked hyperlink list on the submitting server. This paper presents a series of algorithms that compute *PageRank* in such framework. The preliminary experiments on a real data set demonstrate that the system achieves comparable accuracy on *PageRank* vectors to Google's well-known *PageRank* algorithm and, therefore, high quality of query results.

1. Introduction

Internet search engines, such as Google™, use web crawlers (also called web robots, spiders, or wanderers) to download data from the Web [3]. The crawled data is stored on centralized servers, where it is parsed and indexed. Most search engines employ certain connectivity-based algorithms to measure the quality of each individual page so that users will receive a ranked page list for their queries. For instance, Google computes *PageRank* [22] to evaluate the importance of pages. Thus, the size of the crawled web data repository has two impacts on the results of a query. First, more qualified results may be found in a larger data set. Second, more web pages will provide a bigger link graph which, in turn, will result in a more accurate *PageRank* computation.

However, there are several limitations of using web crawlers to collect data for search engines:

- *Not Scalable.* According to a survey [21] released by Netcraft.com in February 2004, there are more than 47 million web servers hosting the contents in the Internet. Based on another study [19] released by Lyman et al. in 2003, it was estimated that the Web consisted of 8.9 billion pages in the "surface web" (public available static pages) and about 4,900 billion pages in the "deep web" (specialized Web-accessible databases and dynamic web sites) in year 2002[1]! The numbers have been growing even faster since. In comparison, Google indexes "only" 4.3 billion pages[2]. Even with a distributed crawling system [3], it is still impossible to consider downloading a large portion of the Web.

- *Slow Update.* Web crawlers are not capable of providing up-to-date information in the Web scale. For instance, it is estimated that Google refreshes its data set once every two to four weeks, with the exception of Google™ News, which covers "only" 4,500 sources.

- *Hidden (Deep) Web.* It is very difficult, if not impossible, for web crawlers to retrieve data that is stored in a database system of a web site that presents users with dynamically generated html pages.

- *Robot Exclusion Rule.* Web crawlers are expected to observe the robot exclusion protocol [18], which advises crawlers not to visit certain

---

Permission to copy without fee all or part of this material is granted provided that the copies are not made or distributed for direct commercial advantage, the VLDB copyright notice and the title of the publication and its date appear, and notice is given that copying is by permission of the Very Large Data Base Endowment. To copy otherwise, or to republish, requires a fee and/or special permission from the Endowment.
**Proceedings of the 30th VLDB Conference,
Toronto, Canada, 2004**

[1] 167 TB in surface web, 91,850 TB in deep web, 18.7 KB per page [19].
[2] Claimed on http://www.google.com as of June 2004.

directories or pages on a web server to avoid heavy traffic. Nevertheless, the protocol does not affect human beings surfing on the Internet. Thus, the crawled data set is not "complete" and conflicts with those connectivity-based page quality measures, such as *PageRank*, which is based on the "Random Surfer Model" [22]. Thus, an incomplete data set may result in a loss of accuracy in the *PageRank* computation.

- **High Maintenance**. It is difficult to write efficient and robust web crawlers. It also requires significant resources to test and maintain them [3].

In fact, besides web crawlers, centralized Internet search engine systems also face other challenges. A successful search engine system requires a large data cache with tens of thousands of processors to create inverted text indices, to measure page quality, and to execute user queries. Also, centralized systems are vulnerable to point failures and network problems, and thus must be replicated. For example, Google employs a cluster of more than 15,000 PCs and replicates each of its internal services across multiple machines and multiple geographically distributed sites [1].

This paper proposes a distributed Internet search engine framework that addresses the above problems. With such a framework, there are no dedicated centralized servers. Instead, every web server participates as an individual search engine over its own (local) data so that crawlers are no longer needed. User queries are processed at related web servers and results will be merged at the client side.

Since Google is by far the most utilized search engine, The framework presented in this paper is based on Google's *PageRank* algorithm. This paper introduces a series of variants of this algorithm that are used in the system. The goal of this paper is to present an efficient strategy to compute *PageRank* in a distributed environment without having all pages at a single location. The approach employs of the following steps,

1. *Local PageRank* vectors are computed on each web server individually in a distributed fashion.
2. The relative importance of different web servers is measured by computing the *ServerRank* vector.
3. The *Local PageRank* vectors are then refined using the *ServerRank* vector. Query results on a web server are rated by its *Local PageRank* vector.

This approach avoids computing the complete global *PageRank* vector. (Consider the 4.3 billion pages indexed by Google, the *PageRank* vector itself is 17 GB in size, even without including the size of the web link graph.) When a user query is executed by a web server, the result is ranked by the server's *Local PageRank* vector. As results from multiple servers are received by the server to which the query was originally submitted, they are merged and ranked by their *Local PageRank* values and *ServerRank* values to produce the final result list.

A real web data set was collected and used to evaluate the different *PageRank* algorithms. The preliminary experiments demonstrate that the *Local PageRank* vectors are very "close" to their corresponding segments in the global *PageRank* vector computed using Google's *PageRank* algorithm. They also show that the query results achieved are comparable in quality to those obtained using the centralized Google Algorithm.

The remainder of the paper is organized as follows. Section 2 describes the data set that is used throughout the paper for *PageRank* computation and query execution. The collection of algorithms is formulated in Section 3, along with experiments for each step and evaluation of Local PageRank and ServerRank vectors against the "true global" PageRank vector computed using the standard Google's *PageRank* algorithm. Section 4 presents more query results and evaluation. Section 5 summarizes the conclusions and discusses future research directions.

2. Experimental Setup

The following sections use some real web data to evaluate the proposed distributed search engine scheme. Since the authors do not have control over the web servers from which the pages were collected, a local copy of the data had to be made.

Since the scope of Internet search engines, such as Google, is the entire Web, ideally, the experiments would be conducted using all the data on the Web. This is obviously impossible. What is needed is a relatively small subset that resembles the Web as a whole. For the experiments described in this paper, the authors crawled over the Stanford.edu domain. The major characteristics of the data set are:

- The crawl was performed in October 2003, starting from "http://www.stanford.edu", in the breadth-first fashion as described by Najork and Wiener [20], in an effort to obtain high-quality pages.

- The crawl is limited to the stanford.edu domain and all out-of-domain hyperlinks are removed.

- If the data set is viewed as a breadth-first search tree, it has 8 levels of pages and thus, 9 levels of URLs[3].

- In the raw data set (15.8 GB), there are 1,168,140 unique pages. Since the experiments only performed PageRank computation and title search queries (explained in Section 4) over the dataset, only those pages of "text/html" type, all 1,168,140

---

[3] It was not an exhaustive crawl because it was asked to stop when it just finished downloading 8 levels of pages.

of them, were obtained from the crawl. Other pages, such as PDF files, images, etc., only appear as hyperlinks in the data set.

- The crawler visited 1,506 different logical domains that are hosted by 630 unique web servers (identified by their IP addresses) within the Stanford.edu domain.
- The crawler did not observe the robot rule in an effort to try to get the complete page set of the domain.

In order to create an accurate web link graph, certain data cleaning procedures were applied to the raw data set. For example, URLs that are literally different but lead to the same page were identified[4]. For such URLs, only one is retained throughout the data set in order to avoid duplicates. Also, URL redirections had to be recognized so that corresponding URLs could be corrected.

The cleaned data set consists of 630 hosts (i.e. web servers), 1,049,901 pages, and 4,979,587 unique hyperlinks. Figure 1 shows the distribution of the size (number of pages and number of hyperlinks) of these web servers[5]. For instance, 0.5% of servers host more than 100,000 pages and 4.6% of servers host more than 100,000 URLs.

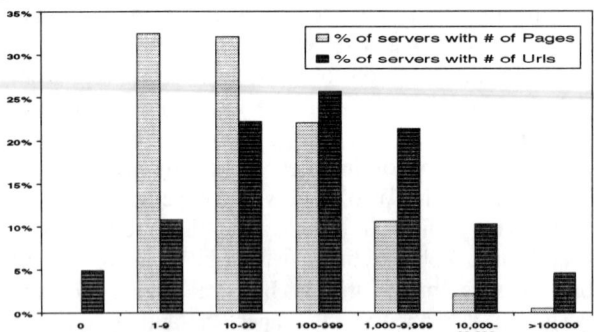

Figure 1: Histogram of Distribution over server size. The *x*-axis gives the magnitude of the number of pages or urls hosted by a web server, and the *y*-axis shows the fraction of web servers of the size.

3. The Framework

The goal is to distribute the search engine workload to every web server in the Internet, while still obtaining high-quality query results compared to those that a centralized search engine system obtain. This goal would be achieved by installing a shrunk version of the Google search engine on every web server which only answers queries against the data stored locally. Results from different web servers are merged locally to produce a ranked hyperlink list. Ideally this list would be identical to the result returned by a centralized system for the same data set.

---

[4] E.g., "www.stanford.edu", "www.stanford.edu/" and "www.stanford.edu/index.html" represent the same page.
[5] Based on the crawled data set.

It takes three steps to process a user query, namely query routing, local query execution, and result fusion.

Query Routing. In the distributed search engine scenario, every web server is equipped with a search engine, so users can submit their queries to any web server. For example, a Stanford computer science graduate student might submit his query on www.cs.stanford.edu, which, in turn, sends the query to other web servers that host the relevant pages.

(Local) Query Execution. When a web server receives a query that has been relayed from another web server, it processes the query over its local data and sends the result, a ranked URL list, back to the submitting web server.

Result Fusion. Once results from other web servers have been obtained, they are merged into a single ranked URL list to be presented to the user.

This paper focuses on how queries are executed on each web server and how to generate a ranked result list. Later in this section, related issues will be briefly discussed, which include typical routing strategies and how to improve them in order to obtain top-*k* results faster.

Section 3.1 briefly reviews the original *PageRank* algorithm. Section 3.2 explores the web link structure and explains the data locality feature that enables the distributed execution of search engine queries. A new *PageRank* computation strategy is introduced in Section 3.3 and Section 3.4 describes the metrics that are used to evaluate the algorithms. In the following sections, 3.5 through 3.8, a series of modified *PageRank* algorithms are proposed, accompanied by experiments for evaluation. Section 3.9 discusses a few other issues in the framework, such as query routing and data updates.

3.1 PageRank Review

Google uses *PageRank*, to measure the importance of web pages, which is based on the linking structure of the Web. Page and Brin [3][22] consider the basis of *PageRank* a model of user behavior, the "Random Surfer Model", where a web surfer clicks on links at random with no regard towards content. The random surfer visits a web page with a certain probability which is derived from the page's *PageRank*.

In fact, the *PageRank* value of a page is defined by the *PageRank* values of all pages, $T_1, ..., T_n$, that link to it, and a damping factor[6], d, that simulates a user randomly jumping to another page without following any hyperlinks [3], where $C(T_i)$ is the number of outgoing links of page T_i.

$$PR(A) = (1-d) + d(\frac{PR(T_1)}{C(T_1)} + ... + \frac{PR(T_n)}{C(T_n)})$$

The *PageRank* algorithm is formally defined in

---

[6] The value of *d* was taken to be 0.85 in [22]. We use this value in all experiments in this paper.

[14][15] as follows,

Function **pageRank** $\left(G, \vec{x}^{(0)}, \vec{v}\right)$ {

Construct P from G: $P_{ji} = 1/\deg(j)$;

repeat

$\vec{x}^{(k+1)} = dP^T \vec{x}^{(k)}$;

$w = \left\|\vec{x}^{(k)}\right\|_1 - \left\|\vec{x}^{(k+1)}\right\|_1$;

$\vec{x}^{(k+1)} = \vec{x}^{(k+1)} + w\vec{v}$;

$\delta = \left\|\vec{x}^{(k+1)} - \vec{x}^{(k)}\right\|_1$;

until $\delta < \varepsilon$;

return $\vec{x}^{(k+1)}$;

}

Figure 2: The PageRank Algorithm.

G is the directed web link graph of n pages (i.e. n URLs), where every vertex represents a unique URL in the Web. Let $i \rightarrow j$ denote the existence of a link from page i to page j, i.e. URL j appears on page i. Then, P is the $n \times n$ stochastic transition matrix describing the transition from page i to page j, where P_{ij}, defined as $1/\deg(i)$, is the possibility of jumping from page i to page j. Let $\vec{v}$ be the n-dimensional column vector representing a uniform probability distribution over all pages:

$$\vec{v} = \left[\frac{1}{n}\right]_{n \times 1}$$

The standard *PageRank* algorithm starts with the uniform distribution, i.e., $\vec{x}^{(0)} = \vec{v}$. The algorithm uses the power method to converge, when the L_1 residual, δ, of vectors of two consecutive runs is less than a preset value ε[7]. The result vector is the principal eigenvector of a matrix derived from P (see details in [15]). Let $\vec{\gamma}_g$ denote the global *PageRank* vector computed over G, the global web link graph. $\vec{\gamma}_g$ is also referred as the "true global" *PageRank* vector in this paper.

Note that *PageRank* is not the only factor in determining the relevance of a page to a query. Google considers other factors, including the number of occurrences of a term on a page, if terms in the query appear in the page title, or anchor text, if the terms are in large font, etc., to produce an IR score for the page. Then, the IR score for a page is combined with its *PageRank* value to produce the final rank value for the page. The algorithm for computing the IR scores is a secret. Since it is orthogonal to the *PageRank* problem, it will not be discussed in this paper.

3.2 The Server Linkage Structure

Intuitively, it would seem that all pages within a domain (e.g. www.cs.stanford.edu) have a stronger connection with each other through their intra-domain hyperlinks

---

[7] It is set to be 0.0001 in all experiments in this paper.

than their connections with pages out of their domain. Bharat et al. [2] investigated the topology of the Web link graph, focusing on the linkage between web sites. They introduced a notion of "hostgraph" to study connectivity properties of hosts and domains over time. Kamvar et al. [14] studied the block structure of the Web. They found that there are clearly nested blocks corresponding to domains, where the individual blocks are much smaller than the entire Web.

Out of the 1,049,271 pages in our test data set, 865,765 (82.5%) pages contain intra-server hyperlinks and only 255,856 (24.4%) pages contain inter-server hyperlinks. 96.6% (26,127,126) of the links are intra-server while 3.4% (908,788) are inter-server. After removing duplicates, there are 21,604,663 (96.3%) intra-server links and 833,010 (3.7%) inter-server links. Figure 3 shows that most servers have very few inter-server links while servers with large numbers of intra-server links are very common.

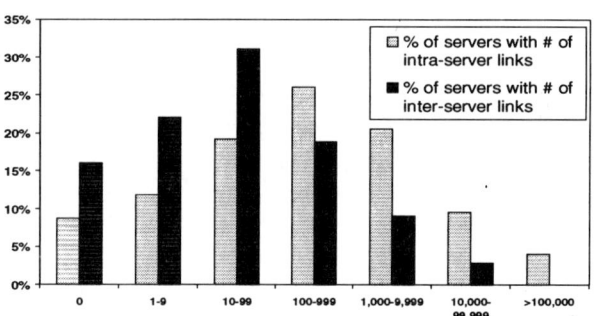

Figure 3: Histogram of Distribution over server hyperlinks. The *x*-axis gives the magnitude of the number of intra-server and inter-server hyperlinks hosted by a web server, and the *y*-axis shows the fraction of web servers of that size.

Notice that an inter-server hyperlink often points to the top page (or entry point page) of a domain, such as http://www.cs.stanford.edu. Among the 908,788 inter-server links, there are 222, 393 (24.5%) top-page links, or 187,261 (22.5%) links after removing the duplicates. Such inter-server links do not affect the relative importance of pages within a web site.

It is possible for a web server to host multiple independent web sites that do not interlink each other to a significant extent. For instance, one server in the data set, "proxy-service.lb-a.stanford.edu", hosts as many as 285 web sites. Such case is treated as a single server to avoid an explosion in the number of servers when doing *Server-Rank* calculation. Notice that it will generate more accurate result if those web sites are treated individually.

3.3 Overview of Distributed PageRank Algorithms

The topology of the web linkage structure suggests that connectivity-based page importance measures can be computed at individual web servers, i.e., every web server can independently compute a "*Local PageRank*" vector over its local pages. Since the majority of links in the web link graph are intra-server links, the relative rankings between most pages within a server are determined by the intra-server links. So the result of local query execution is likely comparable to its corresponding sublist of the result obtained using the global *PageRank* algorithm.

The inter-server links can be used to compute "*ServerRank*", which measures the relative importance of the different web servers. Both *Local PageRank* and *ServerRank* are used in combination to merge query results from multiple sites into a single, ranked hyperlink list.

The outline of the algorithm follows:

1. Each web server constructs a web link graph based on its own pages to compute its "*Local PageRank*" vector (Section 3.5).
2. Web servers exchange their inter-server hyperlink information with each other and compute a "*ServerRank*" vector (Section 3.6).
3. Web servers use the "*ServerRank*" vector to refine their "*Local PageRank*" vectors, which are actually used for local query execution (Section 3.7).
4. After receiving the results of a query from multiple sites, the submitting server uses the "*ServerRank*" vector and the "*Local PageRank*" values that are associated with the results to generate the final result list (Section 3.8).

Each step is described in detail in the following sections. Notice, that for static data sets, both the *Local PageRank* vectors and the *ServerRank* vector need to be only computed once. As shown later, all algorithms are efficient and can be exercised frequently in case of updates.

3.4 Evaluation Metrics

The goal is to apply the *PageRank* algorithm in a distributed Internet search engine system, where it should be able to provide users the same quality results as what the original algorithm does, without incurring the cost of a centralized search system. Judging the search quality of Google is not the focus of this paper; rather *PageRank* vectors and query results, generated by the algorithms presented in this paper, can be compared against those computed using the Google algorithm. Basically, given the same data set, the distributed search engine system is expected to return a very similar, if not identical, ranked page list to the results obtained in a centralized fashion using the Google *PageRank* algorithm. In this section, several metrics are described, which can be used to compare two ranked lists.

Suppose a *PageRank* vector $\vec{\gamma}$ is computed over a page set (domain) D, and p is the corresponding ranked page list, which is a permutation from D. Let $p(i)$ denote the position (or rank) of page i in p, and page i is "ahead" of page j in p if $p(i) < p(j)$. $P_D = \{\{i, j\} | i \neq j \text{ and } i, j \in D\}$ is also defined to be the set of unordered pairs of all distinct pages in the domain D.

Given two *PageRank* vectors $\vec{\gamma}_1$ and $\vec{\gamma}_2$ on D, and their respective ranked page lists, p_1 and p_2, Kendall's τ metric [16] is then defined as:

$$K(p_1, p_2) = \sum_{\{i,j\} \in P_D} K_{\{i,j\}}(p_1, p_2),$$

where $K_{\{i,j\}}(p_1, p_2) = 1$ if i and j are in different order in p_1 and p_2; otherwise, $K_{\{i,j\}}(p_1, p_2) = 0$.

To measure the similarity between p_1 and p_2, Kendall's τ–distance [9][16] is defined as follows:

$$KDist(p_1, p_2) = \frac{K(p_1, p_2)}{|D| \times (|D| - 1) / 2}$$

Notice the maximum value of $KDist(p_1, p_2)$ is 1 when p_2 is the reverse of p_1.

In practice, people are usually more interested in the top-k results of a search query. Kendall's τ–distance, however, cannot be computed directly between two top-k ranked page lists because they are unlikely to have the same set of elements. In [9], Fagin et al. generalize the Kendall's τ–distance to be able to handle this case.

Suppose $p_1^{(k)}$ and $p_2^{(k)}$ are the top-k lists of p_1 and p_2. The minimizing Kendall's τ metric is defined as:

$$K_{\min}(p_1^{(k)}, p_2^{(k)}) = \sum_{\{i,j\} \in P_D} K_{\{i,j\}}^{\min}(p_1^{(k)}, p_2^{(k)})$$

where $K_{\{i,j\}}^{\min}(p_1^{(k)}, p_2^{(k)}) = 0$ if both i and j appear in one top-k list but neither of them appears on the other list[8]; otherwise, $K_{\{i,j\}}^{\min}(p_1^{(k)}, p_2^{(k)}) = K_{\{i,j\}}(p_1, p_2)$.

Then, the minimizing Kendall's τ–distance [9] is defined as:

$$K_{\min}^{(k)} Dist(p_1, p_2) = \frac{K_{\min}(p_1^{(k)}, p_2^{(k)})}{k \times (k-1)/2}.$$

Another useful metric is the L_1 distance between two *PageRank* vectors, $\|\vec{\gamma}_1 - \vec{\gamma}_2\|_1$, which measures the absolute error between them.

3.5 Local PageRank

Since the majority of hyperlinks within a web site are intra-server links, intuitively, the *PageRank* vector calculated over the site's local page set may resemble its corresponding segment of the true global *PageRank* vector.

A straightforward way to compute a *Local PageRank* vector on a web server is to apply the *PageRank* algorithm on its page set after removing all inter-server hyper-

---

[8] This is the only case that there's not enough information to compare the ordering of i and j in p_1 and p_2. $K_{\min}$ is the optimistic choice.

links [14]. Given server-m that hosts n_m pages, $G_{(m)}$ ($n_m \times n_m$), the web link graph of server-m, is first constructed from the global web link graph G_g, where for every link $i \rightarrow j$ in G_g, it is also in $G_{(m)}$ if and only if both i and j are pages in server-m. That is, $G_{(m)}$ contains intra-server links only. Then, a *Local PageRank* vector of server-m is computed as follows:

$$\vec{\gamma}_{l(m)} = pageRank(G_{(m)}, \vec{v}_{n_m}, \vec{v}_{n_m}) \qquad \textbf{(LPR-1)}$$

where $\vec{v}_{n_m}$ is the n_m-dimensional uniform column vector as defined in Figure 2.

To evaluate the accuracy of *Local PageRank*, the *Local PageRank* vectors $\vec{\gamma}_{l(m)}$ of each of the web servers in the data set are computed. The true global *PageRank* vector $\vec{\gamma}_g$ is also computed on the entire data set. Let $p_{l(m)}$ be the corresponding ranked page list of $\vec{\gamma}_{l(m)}$, and p_g the global ranked page list. For every server-m, the elements corresponding to all of its pages from $\vec{\gamma}_g$ are taken to form $\vec{\gamma}_{g(m)}$, the corresponding vector of $\vec{\gamma}_{l(m)}$. Note that, in order to compare with $\vec{\gamma}_{l(m)}$, $\vec{\gamma}_{g(m)}$ is normalized so that its L_1 norm (the sum of all element values) is 1. Let $p_{g(m)}$ be the according ranked page list of $\vec{\gamma}_{g(m)}$.

First, the average L_1 distance between $\vec{\gamma}_{l(m)}$ and $\vec{\gamma}_{g(m)}$, $\|\vec{\gamma}_{l(m)} - \vec{\gamma}_{g(m)}\|_1$, is 0.0602. In comparison, the average L_1 distance between $\vec{v}_{n_m}$, the uniform vector, and $\vec{\gamma}_{g(m)}$ is 0.3755.

Second, the average[9] Kendall's τ–distance, $KDist(p_{l(m)}, p_{g(m)})$, is 0.00134, which is a short distance. If a server hosts 40 pages, it means that there is only 1 pair of pages mis-ordered in the *Local PageRank* list, where they are next to each other.

Finally, the average minimizing Kendall's τ–distance, $K_{\min}^{(k)} Dist(p_{l(m)}, p_{g(m)})$, is measured, which is shown in Figure 4.

The accuracy between top-k page lists seems worse than the accuracy between two full lists, though the distance declines quickly as k increases. On the one hand, because of the small size of the top-k lists, even one mis-ordered pair has a big impact on the distance, e.g., a Kendall's τ–distance of 0.022 corresponds to only 1 mis-order in a top-10 list. On the other hand, the most important pages in a web site usually have more incoming and outgoing inter-server links with other domains which are not considered by *LPR-1*. These links, in turn, affect the accuracy. Table 1 lists the average number of incoming and outgoing inter-server links on the lists of the top-10 and top-100 pages, compare to the number of all pages in the data set. The relatively large number of incoming links indicates that the true *PageRank* value of a top-k page is significantly affected by the number of out-of-domain pages that link to it.

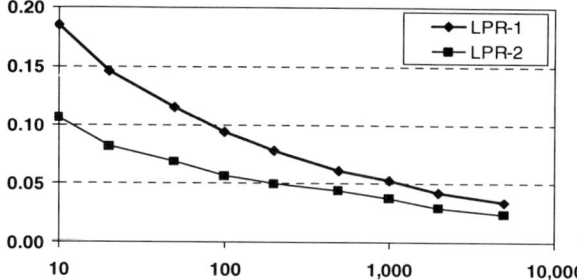

Figure 4: The minimizing Kendall's τ-distance for top-k page lists between $p_{l(m)}$ and $p_{g(m)}$ ($k = 10$ to 5,000) of algorithms *LPR-1* and *LPR-2*.

	Top-10	Top-100	All
Outgoing links	2.10	1.58	0.17
Incoming links	70.72	13.30	0.17

Table 1 Average number of inter-server links that involve top-k pages.

To improve the accuracy of the *Local PageRank* vectors, the authors present a slightly more complicated algorithm. As described in the next section, web servers need to exchange information about their inter-server hyperlinks to compute the *ServerRank* vector. The link information can also be used to compute more accurate *Local PageRank* vectors.

Given server-m, this algorithm introduces an artificial page, ξ, to its page set, which represents all out-of-domain pages. First, a local link graph, $G'_{(m)}$ (($n_m+1) \times (n_m+1)$), is constructed from the global web link graph G_g, where for every link $i \rightarrow j$, it turns into (1) $i \rightarrow j$ if both i and j are local pages; or (2) $i \rightarrow \xi$ if i is a local page but j is not; or (3) $\xi \rightarrow j$ if j is a local page but i is not. Second, a *PageRank* vector $\vec{\gamma}'_{(m)}$ is calculated as follows,

$$\vec{\gamma}'_{l(m)} = pageRank(G'_{(m)}, \vec{v}_{n_m+1}, \vec{v}_{n_m+1}) \qquad \textbf{(LPR-2)}$$

Then, the *Local PageRank* vector $\vec{\gamma}_{l(m)}$ is derived by removing ξ from $\vec{\gamma}'_{l(m)}$ and normalizing it.

For *LPR-2*, the average L_1 distance between $\vec{\gamma}_{l(m)}$ and $\vec{\gamma}_{g(m)}$ is only 0.0347, less than half that of algorithm *LPR-1*. The average Kendal's τ–distance, $KDist(p_{l(m)}, p_{g(m)})$, is also reduced to 0.00081, approximately 1 mis-ordering in 50 pages. Figure 4 also shows the improvement on the accuracy of the top-k page lists.

In order to construct $G'_{(m)}$, servers need to inform each other of their inter-server hyperlinks. For instance, server-m has to send a message to server-n that there are x links from m to n. Within the data set of 630 web servers,

---

[9] Weighted by server size.

on the average a server has outgoing links to 10.0 others, which means it needs to send 10 point-to-point messages. More details of the associated communication cost are discussed in the following sections.

3.6 ServerRank

It is encouraging that the accuracy of the *Local PageRank* vectors is improved significantly by the inclusion of some simple inter-server link information. This section presents algorithms to compute *ServerRank* that measure the relative importance of different servers. *ServerRank* is useful in two ways, refining *Local PageRank* vectors and weighing the importance of the result pages from different servers.

Similar to how the relative importance of different pages is measured by their connections with each other, *ServerRank* can be computed on the inter-server links between servers. However, unlike the *Local PageRank* computation, which can be performed individually by each server without contacting others (algorithm *LPR-1*), to calculate the *ServerRank*, servers must exchange their inter-server hyperlink information. The communication cost will be discussed after the algorithms are presented.

First, the server link graph, G_s, is constructed, in which there are n_s servers and every server is denoted by a vertex. Given servers m and n, $m \rightarrow n$ denotes the existence of a hyperlink from a page on m to a page on n. Then, a *ServerRank* vector can be simply computed as if it were a *PageRank* vector,

$$\bar{\gamma}_s = pageRank(G_s, \bar{v}_{n_s}, \bar{v}_{n_s}) \quad \textbf{(SR-1)}$$

Let p_s be the corresponding ranked server list of $\bar{\gamma}_s$.

Since there is no such "*ServerRank*" concept in Google's search engine scheme and it is an intermediate step in the framework, there are no direct ways to measure its accuracy. Intuitively, the importance of a server should correlate with the importance of the pages it hosts. Here the authors suggest to construct two "benchmark" lists to approximately check the *ServerRank* vector $\bar{\gamma}_s$ against the true global *PageRank* vector $\bar{\gamma}_g$.

- *Top_Page* server list, $Top(p_s)$. Servers are ranked by the *PageRank* value of the most important page that they host, i.e. the page with the highest *PageRank* value in $\bar{\gamma}_g$.

- *PR_Sum* server list, $Sum(p_s)$. Servers are ranked by the sum of the *RageRank* values of all pages that they host.

Both server lists are constructed using the global *PageRank* vector $\bar{\gamma}_g$. Table 2 shows p_s is near both of them and closer to $Top(p_s)$. Notice, that the Kendall's τ–distance between $Top(p_s)$ and $Sum(p_s)$ is 0.025.

Algorithm *SR-1* does not distinguish the inter-server hyperlinks when constructing the server link graph. Since an outgoing hyperlink carries a certain portion of the importance (i.e. *PageRank* value) of the source page to the destination page, in turn, it also transfers some importance to the hosting server, which means that a link from a more important page likely contributes more to the destination server. In fact, the *ServerRank* vector can be computed using the *PageRank* information of the source pages of the inter-server links. Notice, that at this phase, the *Local PageRank* value of a page is the best measure of its "true" importance within its own domain, so it can be used to weight inter-server links [14].

	$KDist(p_s, Top(p_s))$	$KDist(p_s, Sum(p_s))$
SR-1	0.035	0.053
SR-2	0.022	0.041

Table 2: The Kendall's τ-distance between the ranked server lists.

The construction of the stochastic transition matrix P, in Figure 2 can be modified to accommodate any available *Local PageRank* information into the *ServerRank* computation. Given a link $m \rightarrow n$ in the server link graph G_s, its weight, denoted by $w_{m \rightarrow n}$, is defined as the sum of the *Local PageRank* values of all source pages in server-m,

$$w_{m \rightarrow n} = \sum_{i \in D_m, j \in D_n} lp_i, \quad \forall i \rightarrow j \in G_g$$

where lp_i is the *Local PageRank* value of page i. Then P is constructed as,

$$P_{mn} = \frac{w_{m \rightarrow n}}{\sum_k w_{m \rightarrow k}} \text{ if } m \rightarrow n \in G_s; \text{ or } P_{mn} = 0, \text{ otherwise.}$$

and P is still a stochastic transition matrix. Then the rest of the algorithm is applied to compute the *ServerRank* vector,

$$\bar{\gamma}_s = pageRank'(G_s, \bar{v}_{n_s}, \bar{v}_{n_s}) \quad \textbf{(SR-2)}$$

The result ranked server list is also compared against $Top(p_s)$ and $Sum(p_s)$ in Table 2. It is clearly closer to those two lists than the list generated by *SR-1*.

Notice, that it is not necessary to share all inter-server hyperlinks explicitly across servers (and related *Local PageRank* values in *SR-2*) to compute the *ServerRank* vector. In fact, each server just needs to compose its row of the stochastic transition matrix P, which means that it sends only one message out. Suppose on average every server connects with c other servers through inter-server links (10.0 in the data set). In a message of algorithm *SR-1*, a server just needs to identify the c servers to which it connects with. In *SR-2*, the size of the message is a little bigger, which is a row in P as described above.

Since every server needs a copy of the *ServerRank* vector to refine its *Local PageRank* vector in the next step. One way to compute it is to let every server broadcast their messages to all other servers and compute the vector by themselves. A more efficient strategy is to elect a few capable servers to compute the vector and broadcast the result so most servers will not have to receive and process n messages to construct the corresponding server link graph.

3.7 Local PageRank Refinement

In this section, the *ServerRank* vector is used to refine the *Local PageRank* vectors on every web server.

The difference between a *Local PageRank* vector and its corresponding (normalized) sub-vector in the true global *PageRank* vector is caused by the lack of inter-server link information. The *ServerRank* vector indicates the relative importance of a server within the network. More inter-server hyperlink information can be added to it in order to make the *Local PageRank* vectors more accurate.

The smallest amount of information that server-n must share with server-m is the number of links from n to m, and which pages on m the links lead to. Then, the *Local PageRank* vector of server-m can be adjusted in the following way. Assuming that out of l_n inter-server hyperlinks hosted by server-n there are $l_{n(m_i)}$ links that lead to page i on server-m. The *Local PageRank* value of page i, $\gamma_{l(m)_i}$, is adjusted by transferring a portion of *PageRank* values of the links from server-n,

$$\gamma_{l(m)_i} = \gamma_{l(m)_i} + \frac{\gamma_{s_n}}{\gamma_{s_m}} \times \frac{l_{n(m_i)}}{l_n}$$

where γ_{s_n} and γ_{s_n} are the *ServerRank* values of m and n respectively. Then the updated *Local PageRank* vector is normalized, denoted by $\vec{\gamma}'_{l(m)}$, so that other pages will also be affected. Thus, the same web link graph $G_{(m)}$ of algorithm *LPR-1* can be used to further distribute the linkage information. Unfortunately, the loop operation in the *PageRank* algorithm (shown in Figure 2) cannot be performed here as $\vec{\gamma}'_{l(m)}$ will eventually converge to the old *Local PageRank* vector no matter what the initial input vector is because the *PageRank* vector is the principal eigenvector of a matrix, which is constructed over the web link graphs [15]. To avoid this problem, the *PageRank* algorithm can be performed for only one iteration, denoted by *pageRank_single*,

$$\vec{\gamma}_{l(m)} = pageRank\_single(G_{(m)}, \vec{\gamma}'_{l(m)}, \vec{v}_{n_m}) \quad (\textbf{LPR-Ref-1})$$

Results from both algorithms *LPR-1* and *LPR-2* at the *Local PageRank* computation step and *ServerRank* vectors from both *SR-1* and *SR-2* are used to evaluate the refinement algorithms. Table 3 demonstrates that the accuracy of the *Local PageRank* vectors is improved, especially these vectors resulting from *LPR-1* because they do not have any inter-server link information. Only a small gain orcurs the *LPR-2/SR-1* combination because only a small amount of additional information is added by algorithm *SR-1* to the vectors from *LPR-2*. The improvement in vectors from algorithm *LPR-1* is greater because no inter-server link information is applied in the algorithm. Figure 5 demonstrates the improvement on the accuracy of the top-k page lists. Notice, that the ranking of the few most important pages improves significantly because they are usually affected by the inter-server links much more than other pages.

Local PageRank & ServerRank	$\|\vec{\gamma}_{l(m)} - \vec{\gamma}_{g(m)}\|_1$	$KDist(p_{l(m)}, p_{g(m)})$
LPR-1/SR-1	0.0391 (35%)	0.00093 (31%)
LPR-1/SR-2	0.0284 (53%)	0.00069 (49%)
LPR-2/SR-1	0.0303 (13%)	0.00071 (12%)
LPR-2/SR-2	0.0245 (29%)	0.00055 (32%)

Table 3: The Average L_1 distance and Kendall's τ–distance of *Local PageRank* vectors after being refined by algorithm **LPR-Ref-1**. (Percentage of improvement in parentheses).

If server-n is willing to share more information with server-m, more specifically, the *Local PageRank* value of the individual pages that have hyperlinks to pages on m, it can help server-m understand better the relative importance of the incoming links. In this case, server-m's *Local PageRank* vector can be adjusted as the end page of an inter-server link receives a certain amount of the *Local PageRank* value of the starting page. Specifically,

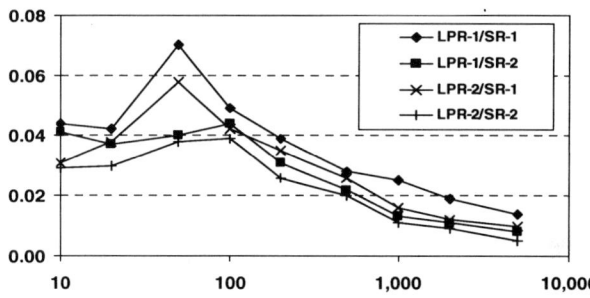

Figure 5: The minimizing Kendall's τ-distance for top-k page lists between refined $p_{l(m)}$ and $p_{g(m)}$ ($k = 10$ to 5,000), Algorithm *LPR-Ref-1*.

$$\gamma_{l(m)_i} = \gamma_{l(m)_i} + \frac{\gamma_{s_n}}{\gamma_{s_m}} \times \sum_{j \in D_n, j \to i \in G_g} \left(\gamma_{l(n)_j} \times \frac{1}{\deg(j)} \right)$$

where $\gamma_{l(n)_j}$ is the *Local PageRank* value of page j, which is on server-n and has a URL link to page i, which is on server-m. $\deg(j)$ is page j's outgoing degree in the global link graph. Similarly, the new vector can be normalized, denoted by $\vec{\gamma}''_{l(m)}$ and applied through the single-iteration *PageRank* algorithm,

$$\vec{\gamma}_{l(m)} = pageRank\_single(G_{(m)}, \vec{\gamma}''_{l(m)}, \vec{v}_{n_m}) \quad (\textbf{LPR-Ref-2})$$

Table 4 and Figure 6 show that with more link source information algorithm *LPR-Ref-2* significantly improves the accuracy of the *Local PageRank* vectors when compared with the results obtained using *LPR-Ref-1*.

In algorithm *LPR-Ref-1*, each server needs to send one message to every server to which it is connected with one or more hyperlinks. For instance, the message from server-*n* to server-*m* consists of all unique URLs hosted by *m* that occur on pages stored at *n*, along with the count of each link, and the count of all inter-server links on server-*n*. In the data set, it translates into an average 10 messages per server and the average message (uncompressed) size is 940 bytes. Because many URLs in a message share the same domain name, it is easy to reduce the size of each message using some prefix compression techniques. Algorithm *LPR-Ref-2* needs the same number of messages but requires more detailed information about the source page of each inter-server link, specifically the *Local PageRank* value of the source page of every link. In this case, the average message size increases to 2.1 Kbytes before compression. In both cases, the small message size means that the bandwidth requirement of the distributed *PageRank* algorithms is low. When scaled to the size of the Internet, the total number of messages will increase significantly due to the large number of web servers but the number of messages sent per server and the average message size will not increase significantly.

Local PageRank & ServerRank	$\|\vec{\gamma}_{l(m)} - \vec{\gamma}_{g(m)}\|_1$	$KDist(p_{l(m)}, p_{g(m)})$
LPR-1/SR-1	0.0282 (53%)	0.00061 (54%)
LPR-1/SR-2	0.0197 (67%)	0.00039 (71%)
LPR-2/SR-1	0.0205 (41%)	0.00049 (40%)
LPR-2/SR-2	0.0163 (53%)	0.00027 (67%)

Table 4: The Average L₁ distance and Kendall's τ–distance of *Local PageRank* vectors after being refined by algorithm *LPR-Ref-2*. (Percentage of improvement in parentheses).

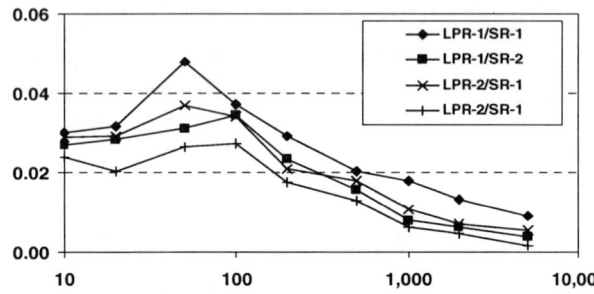

Figure 6: The minimizing Kendall's τ-distance for top-*k* page lists between refined $p_{l(m)}$ and $p_{g(m)}$ (k = 10 to 5,000), Algorithm *LPR-Ref-2*.

Since the computation of the *ServerRank* vector in algorithm *SR-2* is dependant on the *Local PageRank* vectors, the updated *Local PageRank* vectors can be used to further refine the *ServerRank* vector, etc. Multiple rounds of refinement can be applied in a relatively static environment, where hyperlinks on pages are not changed frequently.

3.8 Result Fusion

When a search query is submitted to a web server, it is forwarded to some other web servers that have relevant pages. On each receiving server, the query is executed using the server's *Local PageRank* vector, and the result, a ranked URL list, is sent back to the server to which the query was initially submitted. Then, the server performs *Result Fusion* (*RF*), which merges all the result lists into a single ranked URL list that is as close to the "true global" result list as possible, i.e. as if the query had been executed by a centralized search engine over the same data set.

Given a query q, let q_m, a ranked URL list, denote the result returned by server-*m*, where in general *m* ranges from 1 to n_s, which is the number of servers in the system. q_m is a sublist of *m*'s ranked page list, $p_{l(m)}$, and it is empty if there are no relevant pages on server-*m*. In q_m, every URL is associated with its *Local PageRank* value. Let $\vec{\gamma}_{q(m)}$ be the corresponding *Local PageRank* vector of q_m, which is also a sub vector of $\vec{\gamma}_{l(m)}$, the *Local PageRank* vector of server-*m*. The result lists from every server can be simply weighted by the *ServerRank* vector and merged together,

$$\vec{\gamma}_{q_{lg}} = \begin{bmatrix} \gamma_{s1}\vec{\gamma}_{q(1)} \\ \vdots \\ \gamma_{sm}\vec{\gamma}_{q(m)} \\ \vdots \\ \gamma_{sn_s}\vec{\gamma}_{q(n_s)} \end{bmatrix} \quad (RF)$$

where γ_{sm} is *ServerRank* value of *m*. Then, the result page list, denoted by q_{lg}, is sorted according to the values in $\vec{\gamma}_{q_{lg}}$.

If the entire *Local PageRank* vector of every server is applied in *RF*, the result, p_{lg}, will be the sorted list of all pages in the system. Obviously, q_{lg} is a sub list of p_{lg}, i.e., for any page *i* and *j* in q_{lg}, if *i* is ahead of *j* in q_{lg}, then *i* is also ahead of *j* in p_{lg}. Let q_g denote the corresponding result list obtained using the centralized *PageRank* algorithm, it is also a sub list of p_g, the complete sorted page list based on the true global *PageRank* vector $\vec{\gamma}_g$.

Notice, that the number of mis-ordered pairs between p_{lg} and p_g is the upper bound of that between q_{lg} and q_g. Also, that p_{lg} and p_g are identical is a sufficient condition of q_{lg} being identical to q_g. Thus, the algorithm RF can be evaluated by comparing p_g and p_{lg}, or $\vec{\gamma}_g$ and $\vec{\gamma}_{lg}$, the result of *RF* after normalization. The evaluation of actual queries will be shown in Section 4.

The set of *Local PageRank* vectors used in the following experiments were generated using algorithm *LPR-2*, refined by *LPR-Ref-2* using the *ServerRank* vector produced with *SR-2*. The L₁ distance between $\vec{\gamma}_{lg}$ and $\vec{\gamma}_g$ is 0.0198. The Kendal's τ–distance between p_{lg} and p_g is 0.00105, similar accuracy to the Local PageRank page lists. Figure 7 shows the minimizing Kendall's τ–distance between the top-*k* lists of p_{lg} and p_g, which illustrates a good match between two lists on the ranking of the most important pages.

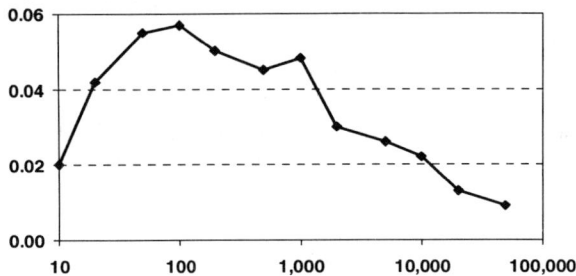

Figure 7: The minimizing Kendall's τ-distance for top-k page lists between p_{lg} and p_g (k = 10 to 50,000).

3.9 Query Routing and Data Updates

In this section, the query routing and data updates issues are briefly discussed.

In general, search engine queries are multi-term boolean text queries that request ranked results. On the one hand, more results are desired for purpose of completeness. On the other hand, the most important results need to be on the top of the result list. In the previous sections, this paper focuses on the ranking problem, assuming that queries are sent to and executed at all relevant web servers.

Recently there have been many studies on indexing techniques to help route queries in Peer-to-Peer systems. Several of these approaches could be applied to the search engine framework, such as Chord [25], one of a number of DHT-based indexing methods that have been proposed recently. Chord was designed to associate a key with each shared file in a P2P system, in which all keys are hashed into a common space and every participating peer is responsible for a portion of the key-space. DHT mechanisms like Chord can be adapted for use in a distributed search engine, where every keyword can be paired with a list of server ids that indicate which servers host pages containing that keyword. Thus, given a user's search query, the submitting server first retrieves the server lists of all query terms from the system. Second, it performs an intersection operation on the server lists to determine what servers host relevant pages. Then, it sends out the user's search query to the servers and waits for the results. This strategy guarantees the complete result if the query ends up being executed on every submitted server.

It may be expensive to send a query to all relevant web servers if the query contains some popular keywords that can be found on many websites. Furthermore, in most cases, people are more likely to be interested in the top-k results of a query, which requires only that the top-k lists are accurate. Intuitively, the query should not be sent to a server that cannot return pages whose PageRank value is not high enough to make the top-k list. Thus, a more efficient strategy can be used once the submitting server has the list of all relevant servers, denoted by S_q, as shown in Figure 8.

Set result list p_q = ();
Sort S_q by their ServerRank values, with the highest one on the top;
While (S_q is not empty)
{
  Pop s servers out of S_q and forward the search query q to them;
  Wait for results;
  Perform RF and merge the results into p_q.
  If (p_q has at least k pages)
  {
    Find the PageRank value of the k-th page, γ_{qk};
    Remove all servers in S_q whose ServerRank value is lower than γ_{qk};
  }
}
Return p_q.

Figure 8: The Query Routing Algorithm.

The submitting server can also stop forwarding the query when the user is satisfied with the top-k result list. Furthermore, it can attach the current threshold PageRank value to the query so that the receiving servers do not need to return less relevant results.

Since most search queries contain more than one term, whose corresponding indices are likely to be distributed into multiple servers using DHT-based approaches. *Direct peer indices* and *indirect peer indices*, proposed in the GALANX system [26], can be also applied in the framework, which tend to group indices of frequently co-occurring terms together so that fewer server contacts need to be made to discover the relevant server list,

To handle data updates, such as pages added/deleted on a server, or hyperlinks added/deleted on a page, every web server can periodically update their *Local PageRank* vector based on the frequency and extent of the changes. Updated inter-server link information can also be exchanged in the same fashion for the *ServerRank* computation.

4. Query Evaluation

In the previous section, the true global *PageRank* vector is used to evaluate the accuracy of the *Local PageRank* vectors in the different steps and the merged *PageRank* vector in the final fusion phase. In this section, queries are used to investigate the performance of the proposed algorithms.

As mentioned in Section 3.1, where Google's *PageRank* algorithm was reviewed, there are a few other factors in ranking search results in Google besides *PageRank*, including some standard IR measures, the appearance of query terms in page titles and anchor text, and text font size, etc. For each page, an IR score is computed for a given query and combined with its *PageRank* value to form its final page ranking value. Although the formula of the IR score is not publicly known, it is orthogonal to the *PageRank* computation. Thus, title search queries [22] can be used to further evaluate the algorithms presented in this paper. The results of a title search query are all web pages whose titles contain all the query words. So every word in the query can be treated equally and the result list is sorted by *PageRank* only.

In the over one million pages in the data set, there are about 150,000 unique terms in their <title> section. a set of 100 queries is selected, which include "Stanford University", "engineering", "research overview", "news", etc. On average, the complete result list of each query has about 3,450 pages from 11 web servers. The combination of algorithms *LPR-2*, *SR-2*, and *LPR-Ref-2* are used to construct and refine *Local PageRank* vectors on each server.

In the first experiment, the complete result list is returned for every query and it is compared against the result list produced using the true global *PageRank* vector. The average Kendal's τ–distance between two result lists is 0.00047, which corresponds to approximately 2,800 mis-ordered pairs (out of a possible total of 6 million) between two 3,450-page lists. Figure 9 shows the accuracy of the top-k result lists. Notice that the important pages are in good order – The minimizing Kendall's τ–distance between the top-10 list and its counterpart generated using the true global *PageRank* vector is 0.27, or only 1.2 mis-ordering pairs out of 45 possible pairs.

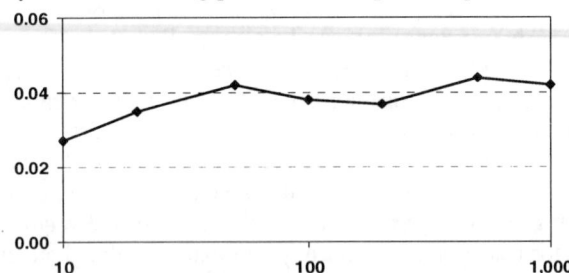

Figure 9: The minimizing Kendall's τ-distance for top-k query result quality measures (k = 10 to 1,000).

If only the top-k result lists are wanted, the progressive routing approach described in Section 3.9 can be applied. The second experiment asks for top 100 page URLs for every query in the same query set. In each round, a query will be forwarded to 3 servers. As a result, on average, each query is executed on only 7 servers out of possible 11 servers, and only about 1,500 page URLs (of 3,450 potential results) are received.

5. Related Work

Among the existing Internet search engines, Google is the most frequently used, accounting for more than 35% of searches done by US web surfers[10]. Google employs the *PageRank* algorithm, designed by Page and Brin [3][22], to measure the importance of web pages. There are also a few other hyperlink connectivity based algorithms, such as the HITS algorithm by Kleinberg et al. [17][4] used by the IBM CLEVER Searching project [6].

Several other authors have considered the computation of *PageRank* vectors. Haveliwala [10] presents a block-based strategy for efficiently compute *PageRank* on computers with limited memory. Kamvar et al. [15] propose a power extrapolation algorithm to accelerate the convergence in computing *PageRank* vectors. Haveliwala [11] and Jeh et al. [13] discuss approaches to compute topic-sensitive or personalized *PageRank*. Bharat et al. [2] and Kamar et al. [14] observed the nested block structure of the Web. Kamar et al. [14] proposed *Local PageRank* and *BlockRank* algorithms (listed as algorithms *LPR-1* and *SR-2* in Section 3) to accelerate the computation of *PageRank* vectors.

While related, the main thrust of this work is orthogonal to these earlier efforts whose primary goal is to compute the *global PageRank* vector more efficiently. Specifically, the objective is to avoid computing the *global PageRank* vector altogether while still being able to provide quality ranking functions and quality results in a distributed search environment.

Web crawling is a critical part of Internet search engines. Cho et al. [3] defined ordering schemes to direct crawling, and evaluation metrics to measure their efficiency. Najork et al. [20] studied different crawling strategies and their impact on page quality. They found that crawling in a breadth-first search order tends to discover high-quality pages early on in the crawl, which was applied when the authors downloaded the experimental data set. Raghavan et al. [23] propose a layout-based information extraction technique to extract semantic information from web search forms and result pages in an effort to crawl the "hidden" web, the database-backed automatically generated web pages.

In early Peer-to-Peer file sharing systems, query routing is fairly simple. For instance, Gnutella [12] does not have any object indices. A query is simply relayed to all neighbor peers if it cannot be answered. In contrast to the flooding-based routing approaches, several research systems such as CAN [24], Chord [25], Pastry [8], and Tapestry [27], proposed independently, construct a distributed hash table (DHT) over the peer network in an effort to provide efficient query routing. In a DHT-based system, every shared file is associated with a key, either its name or a system id. All keys are hashed to a common key-space. Every peer is responsible for a portion of the key-space and stores the files whose keys fall into that key-space. Thus, every file request can be forwarded to the specific peer that corresponds to the file's key.

6. Conclusions and Future Work

Existing Internet search engines use web crawlers to download data to their central servers to process queries. This paper describes and evaluates an alternative distributed approach in which every web server acts as an indi-

---

[10] Measured by the comScore Media Metrix gSearch service in November 2003, www.searchenginewatch.com.

vidual search engine on its own pages, eliminating the need for crawlers and centralized servers. In such a system, a query is taken by a web server of the user's choice, and then forwarded to related web servers. It is executed on those servers and results are returned to the submitting server where they are merged into a single ranked list.

Measuring the importance of web pages and ranking results are critical parts of a search engine. This paper focuses on how to apply ranking algorithms, more specifically Google's *PageRank* algorithm, in a distributed environment. The authors propose a series of *PageRank* variants, including *Local PageRank*, *ServerRank*, *Local PageRank Refinement*, and *Result Fusion*. A real web data set is used in the experiments, which shows a distributed approach can produce *PageRank* vectors that are comparable to the results of the centralized *PageRank* algorithm. Although it is premature to apply such distributed approach to the Internet scale which involves many other complicated research and engineering problems, the experiments, using a real-world domain of data, demonstrate it is promising to be adapted in an enterprise intranet environment.

Apart from improving the ranking algorithms, the authors plan to implement the framework in a real system in order to further investigate query routing issues and system performance such as query response time.

7. Acknowledgement

We would thank the anonymous reviewers for their valuable comments. The authors are supported by the NSF under grant number ITR-0086002.

8. References

[1] L. A. Barroso, J. Dean, U. Hölzle. "Web Search for a Planet: The Google Cluster Architecture", *IEEE Micro*, 23(2): 22-28, March/April, 2003.

[2] K. Bharat, B.-W. Chang, M. R. Henzinger, M. Ruhl. "Who Links to Whom: Mining linkage between Web Sites", in *Proceedings of the 2001 IEEE International Conference on Data Mining (ICDM'01)*, 2001.

[3] S. Brin, L. Page, "The Anatomy of a Large-Scale Hypertextual Web Search Engine", in *Proceedings of the 7th International World Wide Web Conference (WWW7)*, 1998.

[4] S. Chakrabarti, B. Dom, D. Gibson, S.R. Kumar, P. Raghavan, S. Rajagopalan and A. Tomkins. "Spectral Filtering for Resource Discovery", *ACM SIGIR workshop on Hypertext Information Retrieval on the Web*, 1998.

[5] J. Cho, H. Garcia-Molina, L. Page. "Efficient Crawling Through URL ordering", in *Proceedings of the 7th International World Wide Web Conference (WWW7)*, 1998.

[6] The IBM CLEVER Searching project. Available at http://www.almaden.ibm.com/cs/k53/clever.html.

[7] P. Diaconis. "Group Representation in Probability and Statistics", Number 11 in IMS Lecture Series. Institute of Mathematical Statistics, 1998.

[8] P. Druschel, A. Rowstron. "Pastry: Scalable, distributed object location and routing for large-scale peer-to-peer systems", in *Proceedings of the 18th IFIP/ACM International Conference on Distributed Systems Platforms (Middleware 2001)*, 2001.

[9] R. Fagin, R. Kumar, D. Sivakumar, "Comparing top k lists", SIAM J. Discrete Mathematics 17, 1 (2003), pp. 134 – 160.

[10] T. H. Haveliwala. "Efficient Computation of PageRank", *Stanford University Technical Report*, 1999.

[11] T. H. Haveliwala. "Topic-Sensitive PageRank", in *Proceedings of the 11th International World Wide Web Conference (WWW11)*, 2002.

[12] The Gnutella website, http://www.gnutella.com.

[13] G. Jeh, J. Widom. "Scaling Personalized Web Search", in *Proceedings of the 12th International World Wide Web Conference (WWW12)*, 2003.

[14] S. D. Kamvar, T. H. Haveliwala, C. D. Manning, G. H. Golub. "Exploiting the Block Structure of the Web for Computing PageRank", *Stanford University Technical Report*, 2003.

[15] S. D. Kamvar, T. H. Haveliwala, C. D. Manning, G. H. Golub. "Extrapolation Methods for Accelerating PageRank Computations", in *Proceedings of the 12th International World Wide Web Conference (WWW12)*, 2003.

[16] M. G. Kendall, J. D. Gibbons. "Rank Correlation Methods", *Edward Arnold*, London, 1990.

[17] J. Kleinberg. "Authoritative Sources in a Hyperlinked Environment", in *Proceedings of the ACM-SIAM Symposium on Discrete Algorithms*, 1998.

[18] M. Koster, "A Standard for Robot Exclusion", available at http://www.robotstxt.org/wc/norobots.html.

[19] P. Lyman, H. R. Varian, K. Swearingen, P. Charles, N. Good, L.L. Jordan, J. Pal, "How Much Information 2003?", School of Information Management and Systems, University of California at Berkeley, 2003. Available at *http://www.sims.berkeley.edu/how-much-info-2003*.

[20] M. Najork, J. L. Wiener. "Breath-First Search Crawling Yields High-Quality Pages", in *Proceedings of the 10th International World Wide Web Conference (WWW10)*, 2001.

[21] Netcraft Ltd. "Web Server Survey", Available at *http://news.netcraft.com/archives/web_server_survey.html*.

[22] L. Page, S. Brin, R. Motwani, T. Winograd. "The PageRank Citation Ranking: Bringing Order to the Web", *Stanford Digital Libraries Working Paper*, 1998.

[23] S. Raghavan, H. Garcia-Molina. "Crawling the Hidden Web", in *Proceedings of the 27th International Conference on Very Large Dta Bases (VLDB'01)*, 2001.

[24] S. Ratnasamy, P. Francis, M. Handley, R. M. Karp, S. Shenker. "A Scalable Content-Addressable Network", in *Proceedings of the ACM SIGCOMM 2001 Conference on Applications, Technologies, Architectures, and Protocols for Computer Communication (SIGCOMM'01)*, 2001.

[25] I. Stoica, R. Morris, D. Karger, M. F. Kaashoek, H. Balakrishnan. "Chord: A Scalable Peer-to-peer Lookup Service for Internet Applications", in *Proceedings of the ACM SIGCOMM 2001 Conference on Applications, Technologies, Architectures, and Protocols for Computer Communication (SIGCOMM'01)*, 2001.

[26] Y. Wang, L. Galanis, D. J. DeWitt. "Galanx: An Efficient Peer-to-Peer Search Engine System", Available at http://www.cs.wisc.edu/~yuanwang.

[27] B. Y. Zhao, J. D. Kubiatowicz, A. D. Joseph. "Tapestry: An Infrastructure for Fault-Tolerant Wide-Area Location and Routing", *UC Berkeley Computer Science Division Report No. UCB/CSD 01/1141*, 2001.

Enhancing P2P File-Sharing with an Internet-Scale Query Processor

Boon Thau Loo*   Joseph M. Hellerstein*[†]   Ryan Huebsch*   Scott Shenker*[‡]   Ion Stoica*

*UC Berkeley, [†]Intel Research Berkeley and [‡]International Computer Science Institute
{boonloo,jmh,huebsch,shenker,istoica}@cs.berkeley.edu

Abstract

In this paper, we address the problem of designing a scalable, accurate query processor for peer-to-peer filesharing and similar distributed keyword search systems. Using a globally-distributed monitoring infrastructure, we perform an extensive study of the Gnutella filesharing network, characterizing its topology, data and query workloads. We observe that Gnutella's query processing approach performs well for popular content, but quite poorly for rare items with few replicas. We then consider an alternate approach based on Distributed Hash Tables (DHTs). We describe our implementation of PIERSearch, a DHT-based system, and propose a hybrid system where Gnutella is used to locate popular items, and PIERSearch for handling rare items. We develop an analytical model of the two approaches, and use it in concert with our Gnutella traces to study the trade-off between query recall and system overhead of the hybrid system. We evaluate a variety of localized schemes for identifying items that are rare and worth handling via the DHT. Lastly, we show in a live deployment on fifty nodes on two continents that it nicely complements Gnutella in its ability to handle rare items.

1 Introduction

Distributed query processing has been a topic of database research since the late 1970's. In recent years, the problem has been revisited in the setting of peer-to-peer (P2P) filesharing systems, which have focused on a point in the design space that is quite different from traditional database research. P2P filesharing applications demand extreme scalability and federation, involving orders of magnitude more machines than even the most ambitious goals of distributed database systems proposed in the literature. P2P filesharing networks knit together hundreds of thousands of unmanaged computers across the globe into a unified query system. The data in filesharing consists of simple files stored at the end-hosts; the names of the files are queried *in situ* without transmitting them to any centralized repository. A P2P filesharing network typically runs thousands of concurrent keyword queries over the names of the files in the network. Separately, it supports point-to-point downloads of actual file content between peers.

Popular P2P filesharing systems like Gnutella [7] and Kazaa [13] are based on very simple designs, and there is controversy over their effectiveness. These systems connect peer machines into an ad-hoc, *unstructured* network. Query processing proceeds in a very simple fashion known as "flooding": a node transmits a keyword query to its P2P network neighbors, who forward the query on recursively for a finite number of hops known as the "time-to-live" (TTL) of the query. Any node with a matching filename reports back to the query source, which displays a list of matching file locations and properties. Given the scale of these networks, flooding-based schemes are not exhaustive; a given query will visit only a small fraction of nodes in the network. As a result, these networks provide no guarantees on query recall, and often fail to return matches that actually exist in the network.

Recently, researchers have been focusing significant attention on alternative *structured* P2P networks that can support content-based routing. These networks are able to ensure that all messages labeled with a given "key" are routed to a particular machine. This allows the network to coordinate global agreement on the location of particular items[1] to be queried: keyed items are routed by the network to a particular node, and key-based lookups are routed to that same node. This functionality is provided without any need for centralized state, and works even as machines join and leave the P2P network. Content-based routing is akin to the "put()/get()" interface of hash tables, and these networks have thus been dubbed Distributed Hash Tables (DHTs). DHTs have matured rapidly in recent years via both theoretical results and system prototypes [2]. Unlike the popular unstructured P2P networks, DHTs can in principle provide

---

Permission to copy without fee all or part of this material is granted provided that the copies are not made or distributed for direct commercial advantage, the VLDB copyright notice and the title of the publication and its date appear, and notice is given that copying is by permission of the Very Large Data Base Endowment. To copy otherwise, or to republish, requires a fee and/or special permission from the Endowment.

**Proceedings of the 30th VLDB Conference,
Toronto, Canada, 2004**

[1] In this paper, we will use the terms "files" and "items" interchangeably

full recall from a network of connected peers.

To date, there has been little agreement on the best design for query processing in P2P filesharing systems. In this paper we attempt to address the question on a number of fronts. First, we highlight the strengths and weaknesses of unstructured P2P networks via an extensive empirical analysis of the Gnutella network. We performed live, distributed monitoring of the Gnutella network via multiple machines spread across the two continents in the PlanetLab testbed [19]. We gathered extensive traces of the network's graph structure, its query workload, and its file contents. One of our key observations is that replication of files in the network follows a long-tailed distribution with a moderate number of "popular" files containing many replicas in the network, and a long tail of many "rare" files containing few replicas. Given that observation, we observe that the flooding-based approach in unstructured networks is an efficient, simple solution for finding copies of popular files, but has poor latency and result quality for queries that focus on rare items.

Second, we describe *PIERSearch*, our implementation of DHT-based keyword querying. PIERSearch is an application built on top of PIER [12], a DHT-based Internet-scale relational query engine we have built in our group. The DHT-based approach does provide better answers in terms of query recall, but can require more network overhead to "publish" files by keyword into the DHT, and to perform distributed joins of keyword lists at query processing time.

Based on our analysis of the workload and solutions, we propose a simple hybrid approach for high-quality P2P search, in which PIERSearch is used to build a partial index [23] over only the rare items in the Gnutella network. Queries are handled in a hybrid manner: popular items are found via the native Gnutella protocol, and rare items are found via PIERSearch.

We provide an analytical model to study the potential benefits of a universal deployment of PIERSearch bundled with Gnutella. Using this model together with our Gnutella traces, we study the trade-off between query recall and system overhead of the hybrid system. In addition, we propose and compare a variety of techniques for one of the key challenges in the hybrid solution: correctly identifying the "rare" files that should be indexed in the DHT.

Finally, we implemented this solution by modifying the open-source LimeWire Gnutella software, combining it with PIERSearch. We ran our implementation on fifty PlanetLab nodes across two continents, participating live in the Gnutella network; the addition of PIERSearch alongside Gnutella – even on a limited subset of Gnutella nodes – demonstrates notable benefits in both latency and recall for queries that focus on rare items.

2 Background: DHTs and PlanetLab

There have been many proposals for DHT designs in the last few years; we briefly describe their salient features here. An overview of DHT research appears in [2]. As its name implies, a DHT provides a hash table abstraction over multiple distributed compute nodes. Each node in a DHT can store data items, and each item is indexed via a lookup key. At the heart of the DHT is an overlay routing scheme that delivers requests for a given key to the node currently responsible for the key. This is done without global knowledge or permanent assignment of the mappings of keys to machines. Routing proceeds in a multi-hop fashion; each node keeps track of a small set of neighbors, and routes messages to the neighbor that is in some sense "nearest" to the correct destination. Most DHTs guarantee that routing completes in $O(\log N)$ P2P message hops for a network of N nodes. The DHT automatically adjusts the mapping of keys and neighbor tables when the set of nodes changes.

The DHT forms the basis for communication in PIER. With the exception of query answers, all messages are sent via the DHT routing layer. PIER also stores all temporary tuples generated during query processing in the DHT. The DHT provides PIER with a scalable, robust messaging substrate even when the set of nodes is dynamic.

Realistic assessments of peer-to-peer systems can be difficult to achieve without machines spread around the world. In our work, we made heavy use of the PlanetLab testbed [19], both to analyze Gnutella from multiple vantage points, and to test our implementation of PIERSearch in a truly distributed setting. PlanetLab is an open, globally distributed platform for developing, deploying and accessing planetary-scale network services. PlanetLab today consists of over 350 machines located at 148 sites in five continents. In our experiments, we utilized machines from different parts of North America (including Canada) and Europe.

PlanetLab enabled us to achieve serious experimental results: as we report later, we injected 63,000 queries into Gnutella, we crawled 100,000 Gnutella nodes in only 45 minutes, and we deployed the PIERSearch engine on fifty sites distributed on two continents. In fact, one of our challenges with PlanetLab was to use its power carefully: early on, our experiments raised warning flags among system administrators because they resembled malicious network behavior.

3 Overview of PIERSearch

PIERSearch is a DHT-based search engine implemented using PIER. Figure 1 shows the design of PIERSearch on a single node. PIERSearch supports a class of queries based on *keyword search*, which enables us to query for all items containing a given set of keywords (or terms). Items with filenames that contain all search terms will satisfy the query. PIERSearch consists of two main components: the *Publisher* and *Search Engine*, described in detail below.

3.1 Publisher

To support these queries, PIERSearch maintains an inverted file, which is an index structure that enables fast retrieval of all items that contain a search term. For each term, the index maintains an *inverted list* or *posting list* of all file identifiers (fileIDs) of items that contain the indexed term. In order to quickly find the inverted list for a search term, all possible query terms are organized in an index structure such as a B+ tree or hash index. In the case of PIERSearch, the indexing

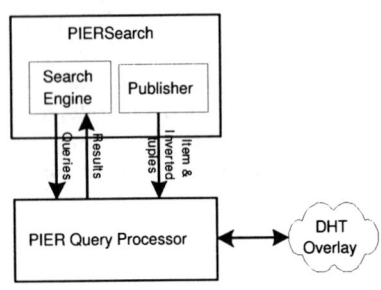

Figure 1: *PIERSearch on a single node.*

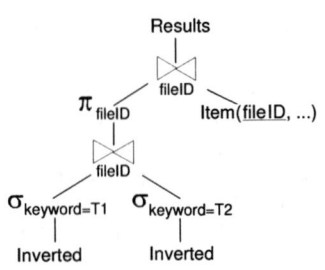

Figure 2: *Relational query plan for a two-term keyword query* "T1 AND T2".

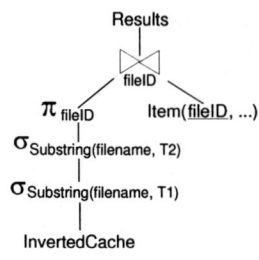

Figure 3: *Query Plan of Inverted-Cache Option for a two-term query* "T1 AND T2". *The corresponding filename is cached on every Inverted tuple.*

mechanism is provided by the DHT itself. In summary, for each item, the *Publisher* generates tuples conforming to the following schema (primary keys are underlined):

- **Item(fileID, filename, filesize, ipAddress, port)**. The *Item* table contains a tuple for each item that is being shared. It stores the filename, filesize, the location (IP Address and port) of the host sharing the file and any other additional fields describing the item. The *fileID* is a unique file identifier of the item, generated by applying a hash on the other fields, and is used as the publishing (index) key for the DHT.

- **Inverted(keyword, fileID)**. Each item has a set of keywords that describes itself. Typically in file-sharing, this comprises the terms in the filename. Stop-words such as "MP3" and "the" are usually not considered. For each keyword, we generate an *Inverted* tuple, which contains the keyword and the fileID of the item. The fields *keyword* and *fileID* form the primary key, but only the *keyword* field is used as the publishing (index) key for the DHT. This ensures that *Inverted* tuples with the same keyword are hosted by the same node.

3.2 Search Engine

For a given search query, the *Search Engine* forms a query which its local PIER engine executes on its behalf. Figure 2 shows an example query plan for a two-term query T_1, T_2. Conceptually, the query plan retrieves two sets of *Inverted* tuples, one for $keyword = T_1$ and another for $keyword = T_2$, and executes a join of the two sets of tuples by fileIDs. *Item* tuples with the resulting fileIDs form the answer set. This query plan can be extended for queries with more than two search terms simply by adding an extra self-join with the *Inverted* relation for each additional keyword.

When this query is executed, PIER routes the query plan via the DHT to all sites that host a keyword in the query, and executes a distributed join of the posting list entries of matching *Inverted* tuples. Using our example query plan, the node that hosts the first keyword (T_1) in the query plan will send (rehash) the matching *Inverted* tuples to the node that hosts for the next keyword (T_2). The receiving node will perform a *symmetric hash join (SHJ)* between the incoming tuples and its local matching tuples, and send the results to the next node (if there are more keywords). On the node hosting the last keyword in the query plan, the matching fileIDs are streamed back to the query node, which fetches the *Item* tuples from the DHT based on the incoming fileIDs.

In addition to this distributed join algorithm, PIERSearch also provides an alternative approach that we call the *InvertedCache* option. In the InvertedCache option, the schema is modified, replacing the *Inverted* table with a new table **InvertedCache(keyword, fileID, fulltext)**. This table stores the *full text* (i.e. the filename) redundantly with each (keyword, fileID) pair. Figure 3 shows the query plan. The InvertedCache option essentially "caches" the file text with each inverted file entry. Consequently, the matching fileIDs for the search query can be resolved without distributed joins: the query can be sent to a single node hosting *any one* of the search terms (T_1 in the example), and the remaining search terms are filtered locally using substring selection operators. Hence, the communication cost of computing the matching fileIDs is greatly reduced since no *Inverted* tuples need to be shipped. However, this technique incurs extra publishing overheads, which are prohibitive for typical full text document search, but tolerable for indexing short filenames. We quantify this overhead experimentally for typical filenames in Section 7.

4 Gnutella Measurements

In order to motivate the need for PIERSearch to enhance existing unstructured networks, we first analyze Gnutella, a file-sharing network based on an unstructured network design. Unlike a DHT-based search scheme, data need not be published in an unstructured network. Each node that joins the network shares its local files, and queries are flooded in the network. Whenever a node receives a query, it checks its local files and returns a query response containing information on any matches in its local files.

The current Gnutella network uses several optimizations to improve the performance over the original "flat" flooding design described above. Some of the most notable optimizations include the use of *ultrapeers* [10] and *dynamic querying* techniques [8]. We describe these informally here;

a more thorough description of the Gnutella protocol today is available in the Gnutella 0.6 protocol specification [1].

When a node starts up a Gnutella client it joins as a "leaf" node of the Gnutella network: it can issue queries to the network, but will not answer or forward query requests for any other nodes. Upon joining the network, the leaf node selects a small number of nodes that have been elected "ultrapeers", and then it publishes its file list to those ultrapeers. Ultrapeers perform query processing on the behalf of their leaf nodes. A query from a leaf node is sent to an ultrapeer, which floods the query to its ultrapeer neighbors, recursing up to the query TTL. Nodes regularly determine whether they are eligible to become ultrapeers ("ultrapeer capable") by looking at their uptime, operating system and bandwidth. Once nodes decide they are ultrapeer capable, they express their capabilities to other connecting hosts via the Gnutella connection headers.

Dynamic querying is a search technique whereby queries that return few results are re-flooded deeper into the network. While this scheme is used in Gnutella today, we will have more to say about the efficacy of "deep flooding" for small results in Section 4.3.

To analyze the Gnutella network, we modified the popular LimeWire client software [15]. Our modified client can participate in the Gnutella network either as an ultrapeer or leaf node, and can log all incoming and outgoing Gnutella messages. In addition, our client has the ability to inject queries into the network and gather the incoming results. The client software was deployed on multiple PlanetLab nodes, and participated directly in the Gnutella network.

4.1 Gnutella Topology

To estimate the size of the Gnutella network and confirm Gnutella's topology, we began our study by performing a "crawl" of the Gnutella network graph; to do this we recursively invoke a Gnutella API call that returns a node's current list of neighbors. A P2P network like Gnutella is subject to noticeable "churn" of nodes joining and leaving, so an elongated crawling process does not provide an accurate "snapshot". To increase the accuracy of our estimation, we performed a distributed, parallel crawl, starting from 30 ultrapeers running on PlanetLab for about 45 minutes on 11 Oct 2003. Based on these measurements, the network size of Gnutella during the crawl was around 100,000 nodes, and there were roughly 20 million files in the system. Note that the size of the network is a lower bound since not all nodes respond to our crawler.

Our crawl also revealed that most ultrapeers today support either 30 or 75 leaf nodes. This is confirmed by the development history of the LimeWire software: newer LimeWire ultrapeers support 30 leaf nodes and maintain 32 ultrapeer neighbors, while the older ultrapeers support 75 leaf nodes and 6 ultrapeer neighbors[2].

---
[2]As a side note, in newer versions of the LimeWire client, leaf nodes publish Bloom filters of the keywords in their files to ultrapeers [9, 8]. There have also been proposals to cache these Bloom filters at neighboring nodes. Bloom filters reduce publishing and searching costs in Gnutella, but preclude substring and wildcard searching (which are similarly unsupported in DHT-based search schemes.).

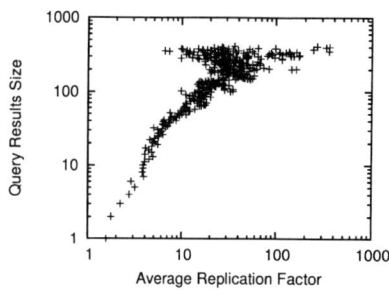

Figure 4: *Correlating Query Results Size vs. Average Replication Factor.*

4.2 Gnutella Search Quality

Next, we turn our attention to analyzing the search quality of Gnutella, both in terms of *recall* and *response time*. There are two possible definitions of recall that we will use.

- **Query Recall (QR)** is defined as the percentage of available results in the network returned. In this case, each replica of a file is counted as a distinct result. Results can be distinguished by filename, host, and filesize.

- **Query Distinct Recall (QDR)** is defined as the percentage of available *distinct* results in the network returned. In this case, there is no gain from having multiple replicas of a file within a result set. For simplicity in defining this metric, we assume that files are uniquely distinguished by their filename; files are grouped by filename in many Gnutella clients as well.

In order to measure recall accurately, we would need to know about all files in the network at the time of our experiments. Given the difficulty of taking an accurate snapshot of all files, we approximate the total number of query results available in the system by issuing the query simultaneously from all 30 PlanetLab ultrapeers, and taking the union of the results. We justify our *Union-of-30* approach to approximating the true contents of the network in two ways. First, we experimentally verified that as we increased the number of PlanetLab ultrapeers beyond 15, we found little increase in the total number of results (see Figure 6). This suggests that the number of results returned by all 30 ultrapeers a reasonable approximation of the total number of results available in the network. Second, because this approximation underestimates the number of total results in the network, the recall values that we compute for Gnutella's search strategy are at worst *overestimates* of the actual values.

We deployed our modified LimeWire ultrapeers on PlanetLab nodes on two continents to obtain real Gnutella query traces. We chose 700 distinct queries from these traces to replay at each of the PlanetLab ultrapeers. To factor out the effects of workload fluctuations, we replayed queries at three different times. In total, we injected 63,000 queries into Gnutella (700 × 30 × 3). We make three observations based on the results returned by these queries.

First, as expected, there is a strong correlation between the number of results returned for a given query, and the number of replicas in the network for each item in the query

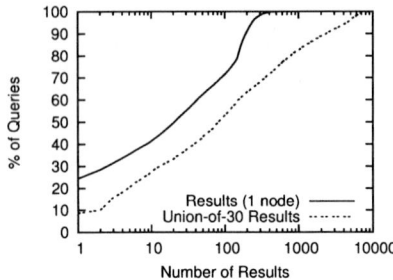
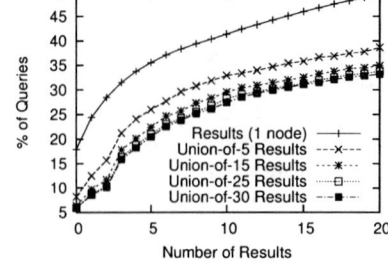
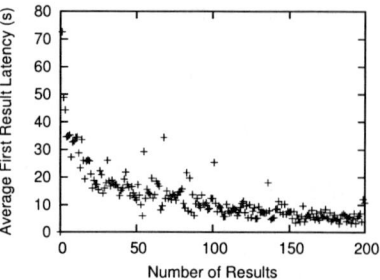

Figure 5: *Result size CDF of Queries; note the log scale on the x-axis.*

Figure 6: *Result size CDF for Queries ≤ 20 results.*

Figure 7: *Correlating Result Size vs. First Result Latency.*

result set. The *replication factor* of an item is defined as the total number of identical copies of the item in the network. Again, to approximate this number, we count the number of items with the same filename in the union of the query results obtained by the 30 ultrapeers for the same query. We then compute the average replication factor of a query by averaging the replication factors across all distinct filenames in the query result set. Figure 4 summarizes our results, where the Y-axis shows query results set size, and the X-axis shows the average replication factor averaged across all queries for each results set size. In general, queries with small result sets return mostly rare items, while queries with large result sets return both rare and popular items, with the bias towards popular items.

Second, our results demonstrate the effectiveness of Gnutella in finding highly replicated content. We present our analysis for the QR metric here; since the QDR results are similar, we omit them. Figure 5 plots the Cumulative Distribution Function (CDF) of the number of results returned by all queries (the *Results* curve), and the "Union-of-30" results, which provide a lower bound on the total number of matching items in the network. Note that there are queries returning as many as 1,500 results to a single client, which would seem more than sufficient for most file-sharing uses. In addition, Figure 7 shows that the queries with large result sets also have good response times. For queries that return more than 150 results, we obtain the first result in 6 seconds on average.

Third, our results show the *ineffectiveness* of Gnutella in locating rare items. Figure 7 shows that the average response time of queries that return few results is poor. For queries that return a single result, 73 seconds elapsed on average before receiving the first result.

An important point to note is that queries that return few items are quite prevalent. Figure 6 shows the results of the same experiment as Figure 5, limited to queries that return at most 20 results, for unions of 5, 15 and 25 ultrapeers. Note that 41% of the standard (single-node) queries receive 10 or fewer results, and 18% of standard queries receive *no* results. For a large fraction of queries that receive no results, matching results are in fact available in the network at the time of the query. By comparison, the Union-of-30 results are considerably better: only 27% of queries receive 10 or fewer results, and only 6% of queries receive no results. This means that there is an opportunity to reduce the percentage of queries that receive no results from 18% to at most 6%, or equivalently to reduce the number of queries that receive no results by at least 66%. We say "at least" because the Union-of-30 results are an underestimation of the total number of results available in the network.

When we switch to the QDR metric, while 14% of queries receive more than 100 distinct results, and 2% of queries receive more than 200 distinct results, as many as 48% of queries receive 10 or fewer distinct results. This percentage is reduced from 48% to 33% when we look at the Union-of-30 results. The improvements for empty query results remain the same for the QDR metric, since the emptyset has no duplicates. The QDR graphs are omitted for brevity.

4.3 Increase the Search Horizon?

An obvious technique to locate more rare items in Gnutella would be to increase the search horizon by using larger TTLs. While this would not help search latency, it could improve query recall. As the search horizon increases, the number of query messages sent will increase substantially, with decreasing payoffs. Figure 8 shows the the number of query messages sent on average to reach a number of ultrapeers in the network. This is based on analyzing the crawl topology obtained in Section 4.1. As the search horizon increases, even when we suppress duplicate messages received at each node, there is diminishing returns in reaching more ultrapeers as the number of messages increases. E.g., 48K messages are required to reach 9,000 ultrapeers, but to reach the next 9,000 ultrapeers, an extra 94K messages are required. Hence, even when the search horizon increases by a single hop, the number of nodes contacted does not increase at the same rate as the messaging overheads. The diminishing returns with increasing search horizon is due to nodes receiving duplicate messages from more than one neighbor node. The duplicate messages are a result of redundant paths in the network. I.e., a node that has received a query message may receive the same query message later from another neighbor as the search horizon increases. To address this problem, there has been recent proposals in the research literature [3] for flooding Gnutella nodes via a DHT overlay that would eliminate redundant paths.

Given that queries that return few results are fairly common, such aggressive flooding to locate rare items is unlikely to scale. In future work, we plan to quantify the im-

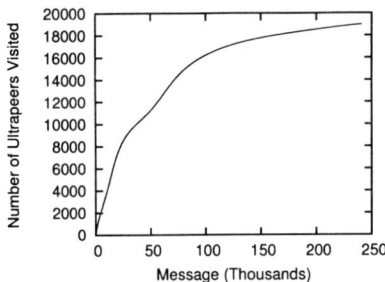

Figure 8: *Gnutella Flooding Overhead*

pact of increasing the search horizon on the overall system load.

4.4 Summary

Our Gnutella measurements reveal the following findings:

- Gnutella is highly effective for locating popular items. Not only are these items retrieved in large quantities, the queries also have good response times.

- Gnutella is less effective for locating rare items: 41% of all queries receive 10 or fewer results, and 18% of queries receive *no* results. Furthermore, the results have poor response times. For queries that return a single result, the first result arrives after 73 seconds on average. For queries that return 10 or fewer results, 50 seconds elapsed on average before receiving the first result.

- There is a significant opportunity to increase the query recall for locating rare items. For instance, the number of queries that return no results can be reduced from 18% to at least 6%.

5 Hybrid Search Infrastructure

In the view of the shortcomings of a flooding-based unstructured network, we explore the feasibility of using PIERSearch as an alternative for supporting file-sharing networks. PIERSearch utilizes DHTs; various research efforts have proposed DHT-based search engines as an alternative to unstructured networks like Gnutella, arguing that the use of DHTs can improve query performance.

While PIERSearch provides perfect recall in the absence of network failures, a full-fledged implementation where all nodes run PIERSearch has its own drawbacks. The content publishing phase can consume large amounts of bandwidth compared to queries that retrieve sufficient results via flooding in an unstructured network. Consider the query "Britney Spears" that requests all songs from this popular artist. "Britney" and "Spears" are popular keywords with large posting lists. The publishing costs of building the inverted indexes for these two keywords are high. A "Britney Spears" query also requires shipping large posting lists to perform the distributed join. Recent back-of-the-envelope calculations [14] suggest that shipping large posting lists over DHTs is bandwidth-expensive. While compression techniques and Bloom filters would reduce the bandwidth requirements of publishing, a flooding scheme that does not incur any publishing overheads is both simpler and more efficient for such queries.

On the other hand, queries over rare items are less bandwidth-intensive to compute, since fewer posting list entries are involved. To validate the latter claim, we replayed 70,000 Gnutella queries over a sample of 700,000 files[3] using the SHJ algorithm (optimized to compute smaller posting lists first) described in Section 3. We observed that on average, queries that return 10 or fewer results require shipping 7 times fewer posting list entries compared to the average across all queries. This motivates a *hybrid search infrastructure*, where the PIERSearch builds a *partial index* for locating rare items, and flooding techniques are used for searching highly replicated items.

The hybrid search infrastructure utilizes *selective publishing* techniques that identify and publish only rare items into the DHT. This hybrid infrastructure can easily be implemented if all the ultrapeers are organized into the DHT overlay and run the PIERSearch client. In this *full deployment* scenario, each ultrapeer is responsible for identifying and publishing rare files from its leaf nodes. Search is first performed via conventional flooding techniques of the overlay neighbors. If not enough results are returned within a predefined time, the query is reissued using PIERSearch.

A key challenge for the hybrid system is in identifying rare items for publishing into the DHT. The schemes should be as localized as possible, minimizing communication between nodes. Our proposed schemes are listed below. We will revisit the comparison of these schemes in Section 6.3.

- **Query Results Size (QRS).** Based on our initial observation in Section 4.2, rare files are those that are seen in small result sets. A parameter *Results Size Threshold* is used to determine what query results needs to be cached. Query results from queries with a results set size smaller than the threshold are published. In essence, the DHT is used to cache elements of small result sets. This scheme is simple, but suffers from the fact that many rare items may not have been previously queried and found, and hence will not be published via a caching scheme.

- **Term Frequency (TF).** Each hybrid node gathers term statistics of filenames over a period of time by monitoring filenames from the search results traffic. We use a parameter *Term Frequency Threshold* to determine whether an item is rare. Items with *at least one* term below the threshold are considered rare items. Based on our measurements of Gnutella ultrapeers, each ultrapeer sees an average of 30,000 query results per hour. Hence, by observing for days, an ultrapeer can easily identify millions of filenames. While this is not exhaustive, it is feasible if term frequencies remain fairly constant over a short period of time.

- **Term Pair Frequency (TPF).** Individual terms may be subjected to skews in popularity. For example, a rare item may have a popular keyword. An alternative scheme considers term pair frequencies instead. Here,

---
[3]These queries and files were collected from 30 ultrapeers as described in Section 4.2.

Parameter	Value
N	Number of nodes in the system.
$N_{horizon}$	Number of distinct nodes contacted when a query is flooded over the Gnutella network. The horizon includes the query node itself.
R_i	Number of replicas for item i.
T_i	Lifetime of item i in the network.
Q_i	Frequency that item i is queried per time unit.

Table 1: System Parameters for Hybrid System

items with *at least one* term pair below the *Term Pair Frequency Threshold* is considered rare. Since generating all possible term pairs is memory consuming, we will only consider ordered term pairs that are adjacent to each other in the filename.

- **Sampling (SAM).** This scheme samples neighboring nodes and compute a lower bound estimate on the number of replicas for each item. A parameter *Sample Threshold* is then used by each node to select only its local items whose lower bound estimate based on the sample is below the threshold for publishing. Ideally, the sampling is done on-line every time a hybrid node joins the system. Since this may incur high overhead, a less accurate but less bandwidth consuming alternative is to gather replica counts of filenames over a period of time.

6 Modeling and Evaluating Hybrid Search

In this section, we describe a simple analytical model to quantify the benefits of the hybrid system, and to better understand the trade-off between the query recall and the system overhead. In addition, we use the model to quantify the quality of the query results obtained by using the publishing schemes described in Section 5. For this purpose we use trace driven simulations (see Section 6.3).

6.1 Model

We consider a hybrid system consisting of a Gnutella network and a PIERSearch system that share a common set of N nodes. Here we assume a Gnutella network, although the model applies to any flooding-based unstructured network. Let I be the set of items (including duplicate items) shared by all the nodes, and $i \in I$ be an arbitrary item in the network. Tables 1 and 2 summarize the notations used to describe our system. We make the following simplifying assumptions:

- All nodes are involved in query processing.
- No new items and nodes are added or removed from the network, and files are not replicated after being queried.
- Replicas are randomly distributed in the network, and no identical replicas reside on the same node. The links between nodes are random. Hence, querying an item in Gnutella is equivalent to querying a *random* sub-set of nodes in the network.
- All costs of the system are dominated by the communication overhead, which is measured in terms of transmitted messages.
- The search horizon is fixed for all queries, regardless of the number of results returned[4]
- Flooding is implemented using an efficient broadcast mechanism. Thus, it takes $n - 1$ messages to flood n nodes. Note that this overhead is within a constant factor (i.e., the average node degree) of the overhead incurred by Gnutella.

In the hybrid system, a query for item i is first issued to Gnutella. If Gnutella does not return any results, the query is re-issued to the DHT. Thus, the probability $PF_{i,hybrid}$ that an item i is found in the hybrid system is simply:

$$PF_{i,hybrid} = PF_{i,Gnutella} + PNF_{i,Gnutella} \times PF_{i,DHT} \quad (1)$$

If a query for item i in Gnutella visits $N_{horizon}$ nodes, the probability that item i is not found (and thus the query has to be re-issued in the DHT) is

$$PF_{i,Gnutella} = 1 - \prod_{j=0}^{j=N_{horizon}-1} \left(1 - \frac{R_i}{N-j}\right), \quad (2)$$

where R_i represents the number of replicas of item i in the system. Note that $(1 - R_i/N)$ represents the probability that no replica of item i is found at the first node (visited by the query), $(1 - R_i/(N-1))$ represents the probability that no replica of item i is found at the second node, and so on.

Next, we compute the overheads incurred by the query and the publishing operations. Let Q_i be the query frequency of item i, i.e., the number of queries for item i per time unit. The cost per time unit of querying item i in the hybrid system is then

$$CS_{i,hybrid} = Q_i \times ((N_{horizon} - 1) + PNF_{i,Gnutella} \times CS_{i,DHT}) \quad (3)$$

where $N_{horizon} - 1$ represents the cost of querying the item using Gnutella, and $CS_{i,DHT}$ represents the cost of querying the item in the DHT. In a typical DHT system, $CS_{i,DHT}$ is $\log N$ messages [20, 22, 24, 28] (with the *InvertedCache* option).

Further, let T_i be the life-time of node i in the system[5], and let $CP_{i,DHT}$ be the cost of publishing item i into the DHT. Then the total cost per time unit of maintaining and querying item i is

$$CO_{i,hybrid} = CS_{i,hybrid} + \left(PF_{i,DHT} \times \frac{CP_{i,DHT}}{T_i}\right) \quad (4)$$

---
[4]While several optimizations such as dynamic flooding have been proposed to improve the query performance, we do not consider such optimizations in our model.

[5]Typically, the life-time of an item is equal to the interval of time the node is in the system.

Variable	Value
$PF_{i,Gnutella}$	Probability that item i is found in Gnutella network.
$PNF_{i,Gnutella}$	Probability that item i is *not* found in Gnutella network. This is set to $(1 - PF_{i,Gnutella})$.
$PF_{i,DHT}$	Probability that item i is published into the DHT.
$PF_{i,hybrid}$	Probability that item i is found in the hybrid system.
$CS_{i,hybrid}$	Cost per time unit of searching for item i in the hybrid system.
$CS_{i,DHT}$	Cost of searching for item i in the DHT.
$CP_{i,DHT}$	Cost of publishing item i and its posting list entries into the DHT.
$CO_{i,hybrid}$	Overall cost per time unit of supporting item i as a result of the hybrid system.
$CP_{all,hybrid}$	Total publishing cost of the hybrid system.

Table 2: Search Capabilities and Cost Variables of the Hybrid System

Finally, the total cost of publishing rare items into the DHT is

$$CP_{all,hybrid} = \sum_{i \in I}(PF_{i,DHT} \times CP_{i,DHT}) \quad (5)$$

The goal of the system is to maximize the probability $PF_{i,hybrid}$ that each item i is found, while minimizing the overall publishing overhead $CP_{all,hybrid}$. Maximizing the probability that an item is found in the hybrid system directly translates into improvements of the query recall.

6.2 Query Recall with Complete Knowledge

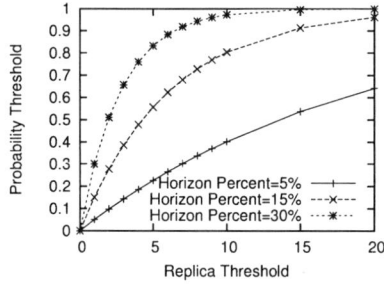

Figure 9: $PF_{threshold}$ vs Replica Threshold.

In this section, we quantify the search quality and the publishing overhead in the hybrid system as a function of the *replica threshold*. We assume that every node in the system has complete knowledge of the number of replicas for each item. Each node selects items whose number of replicas are smaller or equal to the replica threshold for publishing into the DHT. We derive the replica distribution of the items in the system from one of the experiments described in Section 4.2. In particular, we consider the results returned by 350 distinct queries issued from 30 ultrapeers. These results consists of 315,546 files stored at 75,129 nodes.

Figure 9 plots the probability threshold $PF_{threshold}$ versus the *replica threshold*, where $PF_{threshold}$ determines the lower bound on the probability $PF_{i,hybrid}$ that any item i is found in the hybrid system. The figure clearly shows a diminishing increase of $PF_{threshold}$ as more and more popular items are published into the DHT.

Figure 10 shows the publishing overhead (measured as the percentage of items being published) versus the replica threshold. Note that the percentage of items published is proportional to the total publishing cost $CP_{all,hybrid}$. When replica threshold is set to one, 23% of items are published. As the replica threshold increases, the increase of the publishing overhead diminishes.

Figure 11 plots the average *query recall* (QR) of queries in our trace versus the replica threshold for different values of the percentage of nodes in the search horizon. The search horizon represents the total number of nodes in the system that are involved in a Gnutella query. As defined in Section 4.2, QR is computed by taking a ratio of the number of results returned by the hybrid network to the total number of results in the entire network. As expected, when no items are published into the DHT (i.e., the replica threshold is zero), the average query recall is equal to the percentage of nodes in the search horizon. As the replica threshold increases, the query recall increases sharply. For a replica threshold of one, the average query recall increases to 47%, 52%, and 61%, respectively. When the replica threshold is two, the average query recall exceeds 64% in all cases.

Similarly, Figure 12 plots the *query distinct recall* (QDR) versus the replica threshold. QDR of a query is defined as the percentage of all *distinct* results in the network returned for the query. This definition naturally leads to higher recall values since replicas of the same item within the results set are ignored. Conversely, publishing multiple copies of the same item does not benefit this metric. Note that average QDR is exactly $PF_{i,hybrid}$ as computed by Equation (1).

In summary, both Figures 11 and 12 show that there is a diminishing return in the increase of the query recall as the replica threshold becomes larger. Thus, there is little benefit in publishing items that are already popular. In addition, these plots suggest that the hybrid system works well even when only the very rare items are published. For example, publishing only items with one or two replicas, raises the average QR and average QDR to 68% and 93%, respectively, for a horizon percentage of 15%.

6.3 Rare Items Schemes

In the previous section we have assumed that *all* items with a number of replicas smaller or equal to the *replica threshold* are published into the DHT. This represents the best one can do in terms of query recall subject to publishing cost constraints. For this reason, we refer to this scheme as the

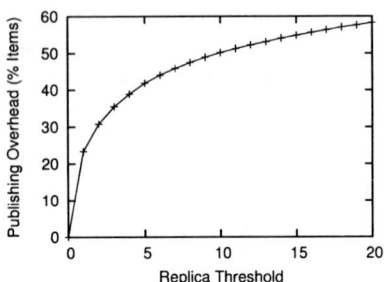
Figure 10: *Publishing Overhead (% of items published) vs Replica Threshold.*

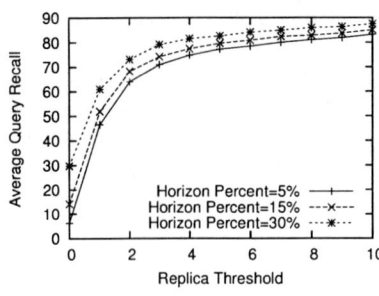
Figure 11: *Average Query Recall vs Replica Threshold*

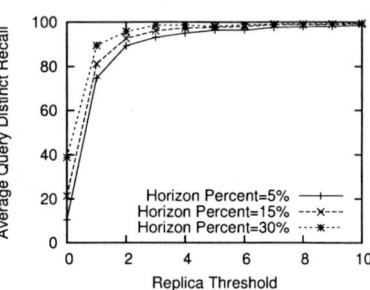
Figure 12: *Average Query Distinct Recall vs Replica Threshold*

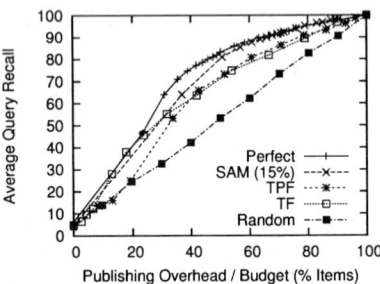
Figure 13: *Compare Schemes based on Average Query Recall for different Publishing Overhead (% of items published).*

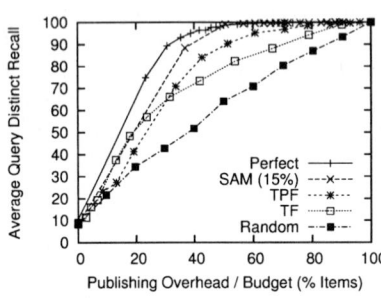
Figure 14: *Compare Schemes based on Average Query Distinct Recall for different Publishing Overhead (% of items published).*

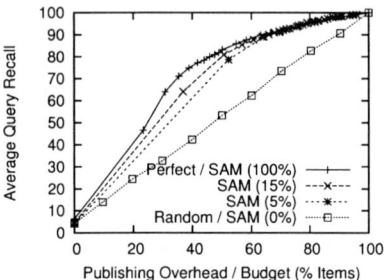
Figure 15: *Compare Sampling Sizes for SAM scheme based on Average Query Recall for different Publishing Overhead (% of items published).*

Perfect publishing scheme. Unfortunately, this scheme is not practical, as it requires knowledge of all replicas stored in the system. In this section, we evaluate the publishing schemes described in Section 5: Term Frequency (TF), Term Pair Frequency (TPF) and Sampling (SAM)[6]. In addition the *Perfect* scheme, we consider a *Random* publishing scheme, where each item is randomly published into the DHT irrespective of its number of replicas. We use the *Perfect* publishing scheme as an upper bound, and the *Random* publishing scheme as a lower bound for evaluating our publishing schemes.

Figure 13 shows the average QR achieved for each scheme, given the publishing overhead (percentage of items published) for a search horizon of 5%. The publishing overhead is the "publishing budget" available to the hybrid system. For a given budget, a good scheme that avoids false positives and false negatives will identify a set of least replicated items to be published. To vary the publishing budget in this experiment, we adjusted the *Replica Threshold*, *Term Frequency Threshold*, *Term Pair Frequency Threshold* and *Sample Threshold* for the respective schemes. We assume that SAM samples 15% random nodes, and we denoted it by SAM (15%).

As expected, the average recalls of all schemes lie between *Perfect* (best) and *Random* (worst) recalls. SAM (15%) has the highest average query recall among all schemes, achieving nearly the same average query recall as the *Perfect* recall when the publishing overhead exceeds 50%. TP and TPF perform similarly for large publishing overheads (> 50%). For low publishing overheads (50%), TP performs better than TPF. Both TP and TFP provide a noticeable improvement over *Random*. For example, when the publishing overhead is 50%, the average query recall of both schemes is 70%, which represents a 40% improvement over *Random*.

Figure 14 shows the same experiment as above, but measuring average QDR instead the average query recall. The results are similar. For large publishing overheads (i.e., > 50%), SAM (15%) preforms as well as *Perfect*. Similarly, TPF performs worse than TF for a low publishing overheads (< 30%), and better than TF for publishing overheads larger than 30%.

We summarize our observations below:

- Term Frequency schemes work relatively well, and are attractive due to modest storage requirements to keep term statistics. In our traces, there were 38,900 distinct terms and 193,104 distinct adjacent term pairs. A typical PC can easily accommodate data sets that are one or even two order of magnitude higher than what we observed. To further reduce storage requirements one could use Bloom filters [17] to encode these sets. TPF is more effective than TF, except for low publishing overheads, where a large number of term pairs with low counts leads to poorer accuracy when the *Term Pair Frequency Threshold* is small.

---

[6]Due to the lack of sufficient queries to train the Query Results Size (QRS) scheme, we omitted evaluating the scheme.

- SAM has the best query recall, but this comes at the expense of non-trivial sampling overhead. For example, in a 100,000 node network, SAM (15%) needs to sample about 15,000 nodes. There are three solutions to alleviate this problem. First, we can reduce the number of nodes that are sampled. Figure 15 suggests that this is a good approach. SAM performs only marginally worse when reducing the percentage of nodes sampled from 15% to 5%. Second, the sampling can be aggregated using ultrapeers, where each ultrapeer aggregates the file information of its leaf nodes, and is responsible for sampling other nodes through their ultrapeers. This technique would reduce the sampling overheads by a factor k, where k is the average number of leaf nodes supported by an ultrapeer. Third, the sampling can be done over a long period of time by monitoring the files via the Gnutella traffic, at the expense of being less accurate.

7 Implementation and Deployment

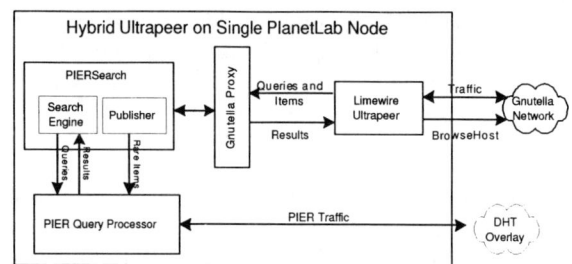

Figure 17: *Hybrid Client Implementation on a Single PlanetLab node.*

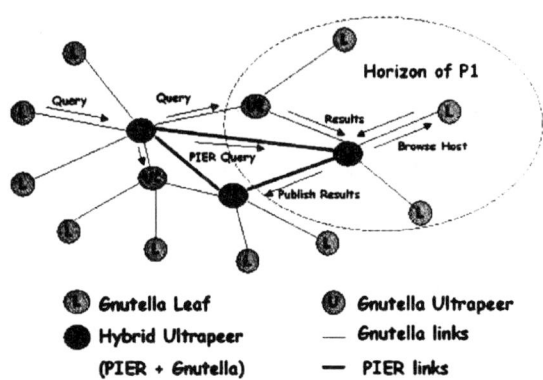

Figure 16: *Strawman Deployment on a selected set of Ultrapeers*

In this section we report on our initial deployment of the hybrid design we motivated above. Our goal in deploying a real implementation were to ensure that PIERSearch worked on live Gnutella queries at a non-trivial scale, and to get initial validation of our hypotheses about the benefits of the design. To evaluate the hybrid design, we deployed fifty hybrid LimeWire/PIERSearch clients on PlanetLab, which participate on the Gnutella network as ultrapeers. Figure 16 shows the *partial deployment* used in our experiments on PlanetLab. Unlike a *full deployment* scenario where all nodes in the system must be upgraded to run our hybrid ultrapeer, our deployment was feasible (given PlanetLab) and backward-compatible with the installed Gnutella base. Though our deployment is modest compared to Gnutella in the large, we will see that it provides significant benefits. Each hybrid ultrapeer that we deployed consists of the following main components (Figure 17):

- **Gnutella Ultrapeer.** The Gnutella Ultrapeer is based on our modified LimeWire Ultrapeer (Section 4). It participates in the Gnutella network, and from the perspective of other Gnutella nodes in the network, the hybrid ultrapeer behaves like an ordinary Gnutella ultrapeer. Our modified Limewire ultrapeer forwards both file information and queries to the *Gnutella proxy* described below. The file information is gathered via a number of mechanisms: we fetch the list of local files, fetch lists of files at neighboring nodes (accessible via Gnutella's *BrowseHost* API), and snoop file information that the LimeWire ultrapeer sees in the responses to queries it forwards on behalf of the Gnutella network[7]. The queries are also snooped from the Gnutella traffic, and can be queries issued by the leaf nodes of the local ultrapeer, or queries forwarded by the ultrapeer on behalf of neighboring ultrapeers.

- **Gnutella Proxy.** The proxy accepts queries and file information from the Gnutella ultrapeer. The file information is filtered for rare items, which are sent to the PIERSearch client. Queries are also selectively sent by the proxy to be reissued via the PIERSearch client.

- **PIERSearch client.** The PIERSearch client receives rare items from the Gnutella proxy, and constructs the *Item* and *Inverted* tuples which are published into the DHT. Similarly, it receives queries from the proxy, formulates the query described in Section 3, which it then sends to PIER for execution.

- **PIER client.** Our DHT-based query engine, PIER utilizes the Bamboo [21] DHT. Hence, the hybrid client participates in two separate networks: the Gnutella network and the Bamboo DHT overlay.

In our deployment, each LimeWire ultrapeer monitors query results from its regular Gnutella traffic. These query results are responses to queries forwarded by the ultrapeer. Query results that belong to queries with fewer than 20 results are identified as rare items, and sent to PIERSearch for publishing. This scheme is based on the QRS rare item scheme (Section 5), which we chose because it is easy to implement in the *partial deployment* model.

We begin by describing the behavior of PIERSearch publishing in our experiments. The publishing rate we observed was approximately one file per 2-3 seconds per node. Each published file and corresponding posting list entries incurred a bandwidth overhead of 3.5 KB per file. We also

---
[7]In a full-deployment scenario, forwarded query results would not need to be sent to the proxy as each ultrapeer would be only responsible for indexing files for itself and its leaves.

441

tested the *InvertedCache* option, which increased the publishing overhead to 4 KB per file. A large part of the bandwidth consumption in PIERSearch publishing today is due to the overheads of Java serialization and self-describing tuples in PIER, both of which could in principle be eliminated.

Next, we consider the latency benefits that PIERSearch brought to Gnutella in our deployment. We tested the hybrid search technique in PlanetLab on 1739 leaf queries of the hybrid ultrapeers. In our implementation, leaf queries that return no results within 30 seconds via Gnutella are considered to have "timed-out", and are re-queried by PIERSearch. In our experiments, PIER executed the query and returned the first result within 10 seconds with the *InvertedCache* option, and 12 seconds without. While decreasing the timeout to invoke PIER would improve the aggregate latency, this would also increase the likelihood of issuing queries in PIER. As part of our future work, we plan to study the tradeoffs between the timeout and query workload.

Note that the average latency for these queries to return their first result in Gnutella is 65 seconds (see Figure 7). Hence, the hybrid approach with a 30-second timeout would reduce the latency by about 25 seconds.

We also measured the bandwidth overheads of querying with PIERSearch. Using the *InvertedCache* option, each query needs to be sent to only one node. The cost of each query is hence dominated by shipping the PIER query itself, which is approximately 850 bytes. The distributed join algorithm incurs an average of 20 KB overhead for each query. Considering these numbers as well as the publishing costs and latencies reported above, the benefits of reducing per-query bandwidth seem to outweigh the publishing overheads of storing the filename redundantly, making *InvertedCache* a more attractive option for our scenario.

Finally, we consider the benefits in answer quality that resulted from our partial deployment. Our experiments show that the hybrid solution reduced the number of queries that receive no results in Gnutella by 18%. This reduction serves as a lower bound of the potential benefits of the hybrid system. The reason why this value is significantly lower than the potential 66% reduction in the number of queries that receive no results is twofold:

- Unlike the Gnutella measurements reported in Section 4.2 where queries are proactively flooded from many ultrapeers, in our experiment, we consider only the files that are returned as results to previous queries. Thus, this scheme will not return the rare items that were not queried during our experiments. Employing other schemes for identifying rare items described in Section 5 in conjunction with peers proactively publishing their list of rare items should considerably boost the benefits of the hybrid infrastructure.

- As the number of clients that implement our scheme increase, we expect the coverage to improve as well. The coverage would be even better in a full-fledged implementation in which each ultrapeer would be responsible for a set of leaf nodes from which they would identify and publish rare items.

8 Related Work

A survey of distributed database research can be found in [18]. To our knowledge, the distributed database system that targeted the largest number of nodes was Mariposa, which envisioned scaling to "1,000 sites or more" [25]. Of course the distributed database literature typically targets much broader functionality than what is offered in peer-to-peer filesharing, including flexible schemas, general SQL queries, and transactional storage.

A goal of our work on PIER is to study the challenges in scaling to many more nodes, while relaxing some of the design requirements of traditional distributed databases [11, 12]. Our current incarnation of PIER uses the Bamboo DHT [21], not the CAN DHT described in earlier papers. The simple join algorithm we describe in Section 3 of this paper is also not discussed in our earlier papers; it arose naturally in the context of filesharing workloads.

The seeds of this paper were presented in a recent workshop [16], including some of the Gnutella measurements we present here in Section 4. The workshop paper focused largely on the case for building a hybrid search infrastructure. In this paper, we expand upon the workshop paper significantly by presenting the architecture, implementation and deployment results for our PIER-based hybrid ultrapeers. This paper proposes and analyzes solutions to identifying rare items, a problem that was left unsolved in the earlier paper. The Gnutella results we present here also flesh out some issues that were unclear in the workshop paper, including the separation of the QR and QDR metrics, and results for the QDR metric.

A recent study [4] has shown that most file downloads are for highly-replicated items. One might think that their findings contradict our analysis in Section 4.2 that shows that queries for rare items are substantial. However, the two studies both correctly reflect different aspects of the Zipfian distributions. Their study shows the *head* of the Zipfian popularity distribution, and hence they measure the download requests based on the items that match the top 50 query requests seen. In contrast, our study focuses on the long *tail* of the distribution as well. While individual rare items in the tail may not be requested frequently, they represent a substantial fraction of the query workload, and are therefore worth optimizing.

There have been other recent proposals for P2P text search over DHTs [26, 6]. A feasibility study on DHT-based P2P web search [14] focuses on the more demanding web corpus (3 billion documents) and a larger query rate (1000 queries per second). There has also been work done on optimizing search performance in unstructured networks [4, 27, 5], mostly to address the shortcomings of flooding. Our hybrid infrastructure offers a simple alternative to either optimizing searching in structured or unstructured networks, by combining the strengths from both networks.

As an alternative to our hybrid infrastructure, there is a proposal [3] to build a Gnutella-like network where nodes are organized using a structured overlay. The authors argue that building Gnutella using structured overlays lead to improved performance of floods and random walks, and also can be used to reduce maintenance overheads.

9 Conclusion

In this paper, we have presented PIERSearch, a P2P search engine that utilizes PIER, a DHT-based query processor. We proposed a hybrid search infrastructure that utilizes flooding for popular items and PIERSearch for indexing and querying rare items. To support our case, we performed live measurements of the Gnutella workload from different vantage points in the Internet. We found that Gnutella is highly effective for querying popular content, but ineffective for querying rare items. A substantial fraction of queries returned very few or no results at all, despite the fact that the results were available in the network.

A key challenge for the hybrid search infrastructure is in identify rare items for publishing. Using a model for hybrid search and Gnutella traces, we study the tradeoffs of improving query recall and publishing overheads introduced by the hybrid infrastructure. Our experiments show that building a partial index over the least replicated items can improve query recall dramatically, especially when the query does not require multiple copies of the same item within its results set. On top of that, there are diminishing returns for indexing more popular items in the DHT that can already be found via flooding.

Based on our model and Gnutella traces, we also compare different schemes for identifying rare files for selective publishing by the hybrid nodes into the DHT. Our evaluation shows that the localized schemes that we proposed for identifying rare items compare favorably to a perfect baseline that assumes global knowledge of the system. Our deployment of fifty hybrid ultrapeers on Gnutella shows that our hybrid scheme has the potential to improve the recall and response times when searching for rare items, while incurring low bandwidth overheads.

10 Acknowledgements

The authors would like to thank all members of the PIER project group and Berkeley Database research group for their insights and suggestions. We thank the anonymous reviewers for their comments. This research was funded by NSF grants ANI-0225660 and IIS-0209108.

References

[1] Gnutella Protocol v0.6 protocol specification. http://groups.yahoo.com/group/the_gdf/files/Development/.
[2] H. Balakrishnan, M. F. Kaashoek, D. Karger, R. Morris, and I. Stoica. Looking Up Data in P2P Systems. *Communications of the ACM, Vol. 46, No. 2*, Feb. 2003.
[3] M. Castro, M. Costa, and A. Rowston. Should we build Gnutella on a structured Overlay? In *HOTNETS 2003*.
[4] Y. Chawathe, S. Ratnasamy, L. Breslau, N. Lanham, and S. Shenker. Making Gnutella-like P2P Systems Scalable. In *Proceedings of ACM SIGCOMM 2003*.
[5] A. Crespo and H. Garcia-Monila. Routing Indices for Peer-to-Peer Systems. In *ICDCS*, 2002.
[6] O. D. Gnawali. A Keyword Set Search System for Peer-to-Peer Networks. Master's thesis, Massachusetts Institute of Technology, June 2002.
[7] Gnutella. http://gnutella.wego.com.
[8] Gnutella Proposals for Dynamic Querying. http://www9.limewire.com/developer/dynamic_query.html.
[9] Query Routing for the Gnutella Network. http://www.limewire.com/developer/query_routing/keyword\'routing.htm/.
[10] Gnutella Ultrapeers. http://rfc-gnutella.sourceforge.net/Proposals/Ultrapeer/Ultrapeers.htm.
[11] M. Harren, J. M. Hellerstein, R. Huebsch, B. T. Loo, S. Shenker, and I. Stoica. Complex Queries in DHT-based Peer-to-Peer Networks. In *1st International Workshop on Peer-to-Peer Systems (IPTPS'02)*, March 2002.
[12] R. Huebsch, J. M. Hellerstein, N. Lanham, B. T. Loo, S. Shenker, and I. Stoica. Querying the Internet with PIER. In *Proceedings of 19th International Conference on Very Large Databases (VLDB)*, Sep 2003.
[13] Kazaa. http://www.kazaa.com.
[14] J. Li, B. T. Loo, J. Hellerstein, F. Kaashoek, D. Karger, and R. Morris. On the Feasibility of Peer-to-Peer Web Indexing and Search. In *IPTPS 2003*.
[15] Limewire.org. http://www.limewire.org/.
[16] B. T. Loo, R. Huebsch, I. Stoica, and J. Hellerstein. The Case for a Hyrid P2P Search Infrastructure. In *IPTPS 2004*.
[17] M. Mitzenmacher. Compressed Bloom Filters. In *Twentieth ACM Symposium on Principles of Distributed Computing*, August 2001.
[18] M. T. Ozsu and P. Valduriez. *Principles of Distributed Database Systems, Second Edition*. Prentice Hall, 1999.
[19] PlanetLab. http://www.planet-lab.org/.
[20] S. Ratnasamy, P. Francis, M. Handley, R. Karp, and S. Shenker. A scalable content addressable network. In *Proceedings of ACM SIGCOMM 2001*, 2001.
[21] S. Rhea, D. Geels, T. Roscoe, and J. Kubiatowicz. Handling Churn in a DHT. *UC Berkeley Technical Report UCB//CSD-03-1299*, Dec 2003. Revised version to appear in 2004 USENIX Annual Technical Conference, June-July, 2004.
[22] A. Rowstron and P. Druschel. Pastry: Scalable, decentralized object location, and routing for large-scale peer-to-peer systems. *Lecture Notes in Computer Science*, 2218:329–350, 2001.
[23] P. Seshadri and A. N. Swami. Generalized partial indexes. In *ICDE*, pages 420–427, 1995.
[24] I. Stoica, R. Morris, D. Karger, M. F. Kaashoek, and H. Balakrishnan. Chord: A scalable peer-to-peer lookup service for internet applications. In *Proceedings of ACM SIGCOMM 2001*, pages 149–160. ACM Press, 2001.
[25] M. Stonebraker, P. M. Aoki, W. Litwin, A. Pfeffer, A. Sah, J. Sidell, C. Staelin, and A. Yu. Mariposa: A wide-area distributed database system. *VLDB J.*, 5(1):48–63, 1996.
[26] C. Tang, Z. Xu, and M. Mahalingam. pSearch: Information retrieval in structured overlays. In *ACM HotNets-I*, October 2002.
[27] B. Yang and H. Garcia-Molina. Efficient Search in Peer-to-Peer Networks. In *ICDCS*, 2002.
[28] B. Y. Zhao, J. D. Kubiatowicz, and A. D. Joseph. Tapestry: An infrastructure for fault-tolerant wide-area location and routing. Technical Report UCB/CSD-01-1141, UC Berkeley, Apr. 2001.

Online Balancing of Range-Partitioned Data with Applications to Peer-to-Peer Systems

Prasanna Ganesan   Mayank Bawa   Hector Garcia-Molina

Stanford University
Stanford, CA 94305
{prasannag, bawa, hector}@cs.stanford.edu

Abstract

We consider the problem of horizontally partitioning a dynamic relation across a large number of disks/nodes by the use of range partitioning. Such partitioning is often desirable in large-scale parallel databases, as well as in peer-to-peer (P2P) systems. As tuples are inserted and deleted, the partitions may need to be adjusted, and data moved, in order to achieve storage balance across the participant disks/nodes. We propose efficient, asymptotically optimal algorithms that ensure storage balance at all times, even against an adversarial insertion and deletion of tuples. We combine the above algorithms with distributed routing structures to architect a P2P system that supports efficient range queries, while simultaneously guaranteeing storage balance.

1 Introduction

The problem of partitioning a relation across multiple disks has been studied for a number of years in the context of parallel databases. Many shared-nothing parallel database systems use range partitioning to decluster a relation across the available disks for performance gains [8, 10, 28]. For example, transactions in OLTP systems often access tuples associatively, i.e., all tuples with a specific attribute value, or a small range of values. Range partitioning ensures that a transaction requires data only from a single disk (most of the time), thus enabling inter-query parallelism and near-linear speed-up [11].

A well-known concern in range partitioning is *skew*, where only a few partitions (disks/nodes) are involved in the execution of most queries. Skew can be classified into (a) *data skew*, where data may be unequally distributed across the partitions, and (b) *execution skew*, where data accesses may not be uniform across the partitions [11]. As the relation evolves over time, or as workloads change, both data and execution skew pose a serious problem.

Today's database systems put the onus on administrators to monitor performance and re-partition data whenever the skew becomes "too large", an approach fraught with difficulties. In contrast, we consider *online load-balancing* solutions, which dynamically move data across nodes and avoid skew *at all times*. Online load-balancing promises three major advantages over periodic manual re-partitions: (a) a consistently efficient 24/7 operation by eliminating performance degradation between, and system hiccups during, manual re-partitions; (b) a simplified control panel by eliminating partition configuration from the administrator's list of chores; and (c) a smaller cost especially in systems with a high degree of parallelism, where even a few inserts/deletes may cause a large skew.

Skew can be characterized by the *imbalance ratio* σ defined as the ratio of the loads of the largest and smallest partitions in the system. In order to ensure that σ is small, data may have to be moved from one disk/node to another as the relation grows or shrinks. Thus a key requirement for a load balancing algorithm is to minimize the number of tuples moved in order to achieve a desired σ.

Summary of Results In this paper, we focus on algorithms for eliminating data skew to achieve storage balance, although our algorithms can be generalized to handle execution skew as well. Our load-balancing algorithms guarantee that σ is always bounded by a *small constant* c. The bound c is, in fact, a tunable parameter that can be set to values as low as 4.24. Moreover, each insert or delete of a tuple is guaranteed to require just an (amortized) *constant* number of tuple movements, even against an *adversarial* sequence of inserts and deletes. Thus, our algorithms offer storage balance at all times, against all data distributions, while ensuring that the overhead is asymptotically optimal, and often much less than that of periodic repartitioning.

Permission to copy without fee all or part of this material is granted provided that the copies are not made or distributed for direct commercial advantage, the VLDB copyright notice and the title of the publication and its date appear, and notice is given that copying is by permission of the Very Large Data Base Endowment. To copy otherwise, or to republish, requires a fee and/or special permission from the Endowment.

Proceedings of the 30th VLDB Conference,
Toronto, Canada, 2004

Application to P2P Systems Our online load balancing algorithms are motivated by a new application domain for range partitioning: peer-to-peer (P2P) systems. P2P systems store a relation over a large and dynamic set of nodes, and support queries over this relation. Many current systems, known as Distributed Hash Tables (DHTs) [22, 23, 27], use *hash partitioning* to ensure storage balance, and support point queries over the relation.

There has been considerable recent interest in developing P2P systems that can support efficient range queries [3, 4, 25]. For example, a P2P multi-player game might query for all objects located in an area in a virtual 2-D space. In a P2P web cache, a node may request (pre-fetch) all pages with a specific URL prefix. It is well-known [5] that hash partitioning (and hence a DHT) is inefficient for answering such *ad hoc* range queries, motivating a search for new networks that allow range partitioning while still maintaining the storage balance offered by normal DHTs.

The P2P domain throws up its own challenges for range-partitioning and load balancing. Nodes in a P2P system may arrive and depart at will; we therefore require load balance over such a dynamic set of nodes. In addition, P2P systems are decentralized, necessitating the design of distributed data structures for maintaining partition information. We show how to enhance our online load-balancing algorithm with overlay-network structures to architect a new P2P system whose performance is asymptotically identical to that of DHTs, but with the advantage of enabling efficient range queries.

Organization We define the online load-balancing problem for parallel databases in Section 2. We present our load-balancing algorithm and analyze it in Section 3. We adapt our algorithm to a P2P setting in Section 4. We experimentally evaluate our algorithms in Section 5. We discuss related work in Section 6.

2 Problem Setup and Basic Operations

We will now define a simple abstraction of a parallel database, discuss a cost model for load balancing in this context, and define two basic operations used by load-balancing algorithms. We defer a discussion of P2P systems to Section 4.

2.1 Setup

We consider a relation divided into n range partitions on the basis of a key attribute, with partition boundaries at $R_0 \leq R_1 \leq \ldots \leq R_n$. Node N_i manages the range $[R_{i-1}, R_i)$, for all $0 < i \leq n$. When $R_{i-1} = R_i$, N_i is said to manage the *empty* partition $[R_{i-1}, R_i)$. Nodes managing adjacent ranges are said to be *neighbors*. We let $L(N_i)$ denote the *load* at N_i, defined to be the number of tuples stored by N_i. We assume a central site has access to the range-partition information $[R_0, R_1, \ldots, R_n]$ and directs each query, insert and delete to the appropriate node(s).

Each insert or delete of a tuple is followed by an execution of the load-balancing algorithm which may possibly move data across nodes. The load-balancing algorithms we consider are *local* in that the algorithm executes only on the node at which the insert or delete occurs. For now, we ignore concurrency control issues (see Section 3.4), and consider only the equivalent serial schedule of inserts and deletes, interleaved with the executions of the load-balancing algorithm.

Imbalance Ratio A load-balancing algorithm guarantees an imbalance ratio σ if, after the completion of every insert or delete operation and its corresponding load-balancing step, $\max_i L(N_i) \leq \sigma \min_i L(N_i) + c_0$, for some fixed constant c_0. As is conventional, we have defined σ as the *asymptotic* ratio between the largest and smallest loads.

2.2 Costs of Load Balancing

Data Movement All load-balancing algorithms will need to move data from one node to another in order to achieve balance. We use a simple linear cost model, where moving one tuple from any node to any other node costs one unit. Such a model reasonably captures both the network-communication cost of transferring data, as well as the cost of modifying local data structures at the nodes.

Partition Change Data movement is accompanied by a change in the partition boundaries. The central site needs to be informed to enable it to correct its partition information $[R_0, R_1, \ldots, R_n]$. Notice that the movement of a tuple may cause a change in at most *one* partition boundary, resulting in at most one update message to the central site. We can thus absorb this cost into the data movement cost itself.

Load Information Finally, the load-balancing algorithm that executes locally at a node may require non-local information about the load at other nodes. For now, we assume that the central site keeps track of the load at each node, thus requiring each node to inform the site after a successful insert, delete or data movement. A node that needs load information can simply contact the central site at any time to obtain it. We can thus absorb this cost into the cost of tuple insert, delete and movement as well.

In summary, we measure the cost of a load-balancing algorithm simply as the number of tuples moved by the algorithm per insert or delete. Our interest is in the *amortized* cost per insert or delete, for *adversarial* (worst-case) sequences of insertions and deletions. The amortized cost of an insert or delete is said to be c if, for *any* sequence of t tuple inserts and deletes, the total number of tuples moved is at most tc.

Problem Statement Develop a load balancing algorithm which guarantees a constant imbalance ratio σ with low amortized cost per tuple insert and delete.

We will show that it is possible to achieve a constant σ while ensuring that the amortized cost per insert and delete is also a constant. Such an algorithm is asymptotically optimal since, for any load-balancing algorithm, there exist sequences of t operations that require $\Omega(t)$ tuple movements to ensure load balance.

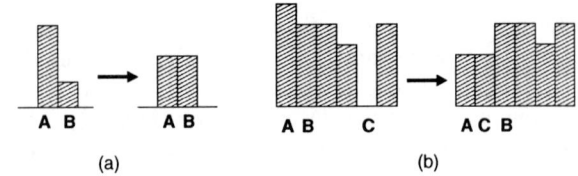

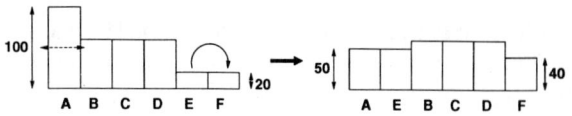

Figure 1: (a) NBRADJUST involving A and B and (b) REORDER involving A and C. The height of a bar represents the load of the corresponding node.

Figure 2: The cost of load balancing using REORDER is 70 while using successive NBRADJUST operations costs 250.

2.3 "Universal" Load-Balancing Operations

What operations can be used to perform load balancing? An intuitive operation is as follows: when a node becomes responsible for too much data, it can move a portion of its data to its neighbor and thus attempt to balance out the load. We call such an operation NBRADJUST which is illustrated in Figure 1(a) and defined below.

NBRADJUST *A pair of neighboring nodes N_i and N_{i+1} may alter the boundary R_i between their ranges by transferring data from one node to the other.*[1]

A load-balancing algorithm can be devised based on just this operation, e.g. [12, 18]. However, such an algorithm is provably expensive as we show in the following theorem.[2]

Theorem 1. *Any load-balancing algorithm, deterministic or randomized, that uses only NBRADJUST and guarantees a constant imbalance ratio σ, has amortized cost $\Omega(n)$ per insert and delete.*

The above theorem shows that any algorithm that uses only NBRADJUST would incur a cost per insert that is at least *linear* in the number of nodes. In contrast, our goal is to achieve a *constant* cost per insert. The key to efficient load balancing lies in a second operation, REORDER, illustrated in Figure 1(b) and defined below.

REORDER *A node N_i with an empty range $[R_i, R_i)$ changes its position and splits the range $[R_j, R_{j+1})$ managed by a node N_j: N_j now manages range $[R_j, X)$ while N_i takes over $[X, R_{j+1})$ for some value of X, $R_j \leq X \leq R_{j+1}$. The nodes are re-labeled appropriately.*

EXAMPLE 2.1. *Consider the scenario shown in Figure 2, where node A has 100 tuples, the next three nodes (B, C, D) have 60 tuples each, while the last two (E, F) have 20 tuples each. The least expensive scheme to improve load balance while preserving key ordering is to transfer all 20 tuples from E to F, and then use REORDER to split the load of A between A and E. The cost of such a scheme is 70 tuple movements; in contrast, a NBRADJUST-based balancing requires 250 tuple movements.* ∎

It turns out that the REORDER operation is not only necessary, but also sufficient for efficient load balancing. In fact, we show below that the operations NBRADJUST and REORDER are *universal* in that they can together be used to efficiently implement any load-balancing algorithm.

Theorem 2. *Given a load-balancing algorithm A, it is possible to construct a new algorithm $\widehat{A}$ that uses only the NBRADJUST and REORDER operations such that, for any sequence of t inserts and deletes,*
(a) Both A and $\widehat{A}$ achieve identical load distribution.
(b) The cost of $\widehat{A}$ is at most the cost of A.

3 Algorithms for Load Balancing

Consider the following approach for load balancing: a node attempts to shed its load whenever its load increases by a factor δ, and attempts to gain load when it drops by the same factor. Formally, we consider an infinite, increasing geometric sequence of thresholds $T_i = \lfloor c\delta^i \rfloor$, for all $i \geq 1$ and some constant c. When a node's load crosses a threshold T_j, the node initiates a load-balancing procedure. We call such an approach the *Threshold Algorithm*.

3.1 The Doubling Algorithm

We start with the special case $\delta = 2$, and the thresholds $T_i = 2^{i-1}$. We begin by considering tuple insertions. Every time a node's load[3] increases to a value $T_i + 1$, the node initiates ADJUSTLOAD specified in Procedure 1.

The load-balancing procedure ADJUSTLOAD is quite simple. When node N_i's load increases beyond a threshold, it first (lines 3-6) attempts to perform NBRADJUST with its lightly-loaded neighbor, say N_{i+1}, by averaging out its load with N_{i+1}. If both neighbors have high load (more than half that of N_i), N_i attempts to perform REORDER with the globally least-loaded node N_k (lines 8-12). If N_k's load is small enough (less than a quarter of N_i), N_k sheds all its data to $N_{k\pm1}$, and takes over half the load of N_i. If N_i is unable to perform either NBRADJUST or REORDER, N_i concludes that the system load is indeed balanced and performs no data movement.

Note that when N_i initiates either a NBRADJUST or REORDER, there is a corresponding recursive invocation of ADJUSTLOAD at node N_{i+1} or $N_{k\pm1}$ respectively. Frequently, these recursive invocations do not necessitate any further data movement; even if data movement is necessary, we can show that such data movement would utilize only NBRADJUST. Similarly, there is also a recursive invocation

---
[1] In the extreme case when N_i takes over the entire range, $[R_{i-1}, R_{i+1})$, N_{i+1} is assigned the empty range $[R_{i+1}, R_{i+1})$.
[2] Proofs omitted in this paper are available in a technical report [13].
[3] For technical reasons, we define $L'(N) = T_1 + L(N)$, and use L' as the node load. Note that the same guarantees on σ hold when using either L or L'; for notational convenience, we let L denote this new definition of load.

of ADJUSTLOAD at node N_i itself (line 6); this invocation is necessary only in one special case – when ADJUSTLOAD is being executed at $N_{k\pm1}$ after a REORDER – and is also guaranteed to utilize only NBRADJUST.

Procedure 1 ADJUSTLOAD(Node N_i) {On Tuple Insert}
1: Let $L(N_i) = x \in (T_m, T_{m+1}]$.
2: Let N_j be the lighter loaded of N_{i-1} and N_{i+1}.
3: **if** $L(N_j) \leq T_{m-1}$ **then** {Do NBRADJUST}
4:    Move tuples from N_i to N_j to equalize load.
5:    ADJUSTLOAD(N_j)
6:    ADJUSTLOAD(N_i)
7: **else**
8:    Find the least-loaded node N_k.
9:    **if** $L(N_k) \leq T_{m-2}$ **then** {Do REORDER}
10:      Transfer all data from N_k to $N = N_{k\pm1}$.
11:      Transfer data from N_i to N_k, s.t. $L(N_i) = \lceil x/2 \rceil$ and $L(N_k) = \lfloor x/2 \rfloor$.
12:      ADJUSTLOAD(N)
13:      {Rename nodes appropriately after REORDER.}
14:    **end if**
15: **end if**

Deletions are handled in a symmetric fashion. When a node's load drops to a threshold $T_j = 2^j$, it first attempts NBRADJUST with a neighbor, if the neighbor's load is larger than $T_{j+1} = 2^{j+1}$. Otherwise, it attempts to REORDER itself and split the highest-loaded node N_k in the system, if N_k's load is more than T_{j+2}.

We will show later that the Doubling Algorithm ensures that $\sigma = 8$, while the amortized cost of tuple insert and and delete is constant. However, it is possible to reduce σ further by generalizing this Doubling Algorithm.

3.2 The General Threshold Algorithm

The Doubling Algorithm set $\delta = 2$ and triggered load balancing when a node's load changed by a factor 2 to obtain $\sigma = 8$. A natural question, then, is to ask whether the algorithm generalizes to other values of δ, and whether it is possible to obtain a better σ by using a smaller δ value.

The Doubling algorithm generalizes to allow δ to be any real number greater than or equal to the golden ratio $\phi = (\sqrt{5}+1)/2 \simeq 1.62$. For any real number $\delta \geq \phi$, we may define a general *Threshold Algorithm* as follows: We define a threshold sequence of $T_i = \lfloor c\delta^i \rfloor$, for an appropriately chosen constant $c > 0$. Each node is required to execute Procedure ADJUSTLOAD, every time its load crosses a threshold. This Threshold Algorithm guarantees $\sigma = \delta^3$ with a constant cost per tuple insert and delete.

The Fibbing Algorithm: An extreme of the general Threshold Algorithm arises when $\delta = \phi$, for which we may define a variant called the *Fibbing Algorithm*. This algorithm defines the set of thresholds T_i to be the Fibonacci numbers (with $T_1 = 1$ and $T_2 = 2$). As we prove in Section 3.3, the Fibbing Algorithm guarantees an imbalance ratio of $\phi^3 \simeq 4.24$.

3.3 Analysis

We now present an analysis of the Threshold algorithm (and the Fibbing algorithm), both in terms of the guaranteed imbalance ratio, and in terms of the cost of insert and delete. Our analysis relies on seven properties of the threshold sequence that is satisfied both by Fibonacci numbers, and by threshold sequences of the form $T_i = \lfloor c\delta^i \rfloor$, allowing the same analysis to apply to both the Threshold algorithm and the Fibbing algorithm. We summarize these properties in the following lemma.

Lemma 1. *If $T_i = \lfloor c\delta^i \rfloor$, for a suitably large c and $\delta \geq \phi$, the following properties hold for all $r \geq 1$. The same properties hold if T_i is the ith Fibonacci number ($T_i = \lfloor c\delta^i \rfloor$, with $c = \phi/\sqrt{5}$ and $\delta = \phi$).*
(a) $\lfloor (T_r + T_{r+2})/2 \rfloor \geq T_{r+1}$
(b) $\lceil (T_r + T_{r+1} + 1)/2 \rceil \leq T_{r+1}$
(c) $T_r + T_{r+1} \leq T_{r+2}$
(d) $\lceil (T_r + 1)/2 \rceil \leq T_r$
(e) $\lfloor (T_{r+2} + 1)/2 \rfloor > T_r$
(f) $T_{r+k} + 1 \geq \delta^k T_r \geq T_{r+k} - C$, where $C = 1$ if T_i is the ith Fibonacci number, and $C = \delta^k$ otherwise, for all integers $k > 0$.
(g) $\lfloor (T_1 + T_2 + 1)/2 \rfloor > T_1$

Definition 3.1. *For any node N, define $I(N) = r$ if and only if $L(N) \in (T_{r-1}, T_r]$, i.e., N's load is in the rth geometric interval.*

Theorem 3. *The following invariants hold after any sequence of inserts and deletes for the Threshold (and Fibbing) algorithm:*
(a) NBRBALANCE: *For any pair of neighbors N_i and N_{i+1}, $I(N_i) \leq I(N_{i+1}) + 1$.*
(b) GLOBALBALANCE: *For any pair of nodes N_i and N_j, $I(N_i) \leq I(N_j) + 2$.*

Before proving the above theorem, we first establish some lemmas on the properties of the NBRADJUST and REORDER, as well as the execution of ADJUSTLOAD.

Lemma 2. *If $I(N_i) = r + 2$ and $I(N_{i+1}) = r$, then NBRADJUST between N_i and N_{i+1} ensures that $I(N_i) = I(N_{i+1}) \geq r + 1$.*

Lemma 3. *Consider a state of the system where both NBRBALANCE and GLOBALBALANCE invariants hold. If a tuple insert now causes a violation of NBRBALANCE, the consequent execution of ADJUSTLOAD will ensure both NBRBALANCE and GLOBALBALANCE.*

Proof. Consider a tuple insert at node N_i. By definition, no NBRBALANCE violation arises unless $L(N_i)$ crosses a threshold. Say $L(N_i)$ crosses threshold T_x. There may then be a violation of NBRBALANCE between N_i and either or both of its neighbors. (There may also be a GLOBALBALANCE violation involving N_i.) In this case, N_i executes a NBRADJUST by Procedure ADJUSTLOAD.

W.l.o.g., say N_i performs NBRADJUST with N_{i+1}. First, observe that there are no GLOBALBALANCE violations after this NBRADJUST, by Lemma 1(b). After this NBRADJUST, ADJUSTLOAD is recursively invoked on N_{i+1}, which may cause N_{i+1} to perform NBRADJUST with N_{i+2}, and trigger N_{i+2} into executing ADJUSTLOAD. This process continues until we reach a node N_{i+k} that does not perform a NBRADJUST, or we reach N_n.

We show that this sequence of NBRADJUST operations ensures that all NBRBALANCE conditions are satisfied. (Finally, there are recursive calls to ADJUSTLOAD in line 6, which do not perform any data movement since there are no violations of NBRBALANCE or GLOBALBALANCE.)

Let $L_j(N)$ represent the load at node N after the jth NBRADJUST operation, and $I_j(N) = I(N)$ after the jth NBRADJUST operation. (L_0 is the load before any NBRADJUST operations take place.) The jth NBRADJUST operation occurs between nodes N_{i+j-1} and N_{i+j}. Thus, the load of N_{i+j-1} remains unchanged after the jth operation.

We will show by induction that, after $j > 0$ NBRADJUST operations,
1. $I_j(N_{i+k}) \leq x$ for all $0 \leq k \leq j$.
2. The only NBRBALANCE violation may be between N_{i+j} and N_{i+j+1}.

Base Case: We show the above properties for $j = 1$. Initially, the only NBRBALANCE violations may be at (N_{i-1}, N_i) and/or (N_i, N_{i+1}). Recall that $I_0(N_i) = x+1$ and, since there is a NBRBALANCE violation, $I_0(N_{i+1}) = x-1$. From the GLOBALBALANCE invariant, we deduce $I_0(N_{i-1}) \leq x+1$.

After the first NBRADJUST operation, we know by Lemma 2 that $I_1(N_i) = I_1(N_{i+1}) \geq x$. Also, $L_1(N_{i-1}) = L_0(N_{i-1})$, thus showing that neither pair (N_{i-1}, N_i) nor (N_i, N_{i+1}) constitute a NBRBALANCE violation. Since only the loads of N_i and N_{i+1} were affected by this operation, the only possible NBRBALANCE violation is between N_{i+1} and N_{i+2}. It is also clear that $I_1(N_i) = I_1(N_{i+1}) \leq x$ (by Lemma 1(d)).

Induction Step: Assume, by induction, that after j NBRADJUST operations, $I_j(N_{i+j}) \leq x$, and the only possible NBRBALANCE violation is at (N_{i+j}, N_{i+j+1}). If there is no such violation, we are done and ADJUSTLOAD terminates. If there is a violation, a NBRADJUST takes place between N_{i+j} and N_{i+j+1}.

GLOBALBALANCE assures us that $I_0(N_{i+j+1}) = I_j(N_{i+j+1}) \geq x-2$. Since there is a NBRBALANCE violation, we may deduce $I_j(N_{i+j+1}) = x-2$ and $L_j(N_{i+j}) = x$. Invoking Lemma 2, we deduce that $I_{j+1}(N_{i+j}) = I_{j+1}(N_{i+j+1}) \geq x-1$.

Since $I_j(N_{i+j-1}) \leq x$ by the induction assumption, there is no violation between N_{i+j-1} and N_{i+j}. There is obviously no violation between N_{i+j} and N_{i+j+1}, since both loads are in the same interval. The only possible violation might be between N_{i+j+1} and N_{i+j+2}, which is permitted under the induction assumption. It is also clear that both $I_{j+1}(N_{i+j})$ and $I_{j+1}(N_{i+j+1})$ are at most x, thus completing the induction step.

The above inductive proof, combined with the fact that the procedure terminates when the last node is reached, shows that there are no NBRBALANCE violations when ADJUSTLOAD terminates. □

Lemma 4. *Consider a state of the system where both NBRBALANCE and GLOBALBALANCE invariants hold. If a tuple insert now causes a violation of GLOBALBALANCE, the consequent execution of ADJUSTLOAD will ensure both GLOBALBALANCE and NBRBALANCE.*

Proof of Theorem 3. We prove that the invariants hold by induction on the length l of the insert/delete sequence. The invariants clearly hold when $l = 0$ since all nodes contain one sentinel value.

Assume that the invariants hold for $l = r$. Let the $(r+1)^{st}$ operation be an insert. If this insert does not violate any invariants, we are done. If not, either NBRBALANCE or GLOBALBALANCE is violated. We have shown that all such violations are fixed by ADJUSTLOAD in Lemmas 3 and 4 respectively.

If the $(r+1)^{st}$ operation is a delete, it is straightforward to show that all violations are again fixed, by a proof similar to that of Lemmas 3 and 4. We have thus proved that the invariants hold after any sequence of inserts and deletes. □

Corollary 3.1. *For the Threshold algorithm, the imbalance ratio σ is δ^3 after any sequence of inserts and deletes.* ■

Corollary 3.2. *For the Fibbing algorithm, the imbalance ratio σ is ϕ^3 after any sequence of inserts and deletes.* ■

Theorem 4. *For the Threshold (and Fibbing) algorithm, the amortized cost of both inserts and deletes is constant.*

Proof. We bound the amortized costs of insert and delete by using the potential method. Let $\bar{L}$ denote the current average load. Consider the potential function $\Phi = c(\sum_{i=1}^{n} L(N_i)^2)/\bar{L}$, where c is a constant to be specified later. We will show the following: (a) the cost of NBRADJUST is bounded by the drop in potential accompanying it, (b) the cost of REORDER is bounded by the drop in potential accompanying it, and (c) the gain in potential after a tuple insert or delete, before any rebalancing actions, is bounded by a constant. The above three statements together imply that the amortized costs of tuple insert and delete are constant.

NBRADJUST: Recall that a NBRADJUST operation occurs between two nodes whose load differs by at least a factor δ. Let the loads of the two nodes involved be x and y. The drop in potential $\Delta\Phi$ from NBRADJUST is $c(x^2 + y^2 - (x+y)^2/2)/\bar{L} = c(x-y)^2/2\bar{L}$. By Lemma 1(f), $x-y > (\delta-1)y$, and y is at least $\bar{L}/\delta^3$. Therefore, $\Delta\Phi > c'(x-y)$ for some constant c'. Since the number of tuples moved is at most $(x-y)/2$, the drop in potential pays for the data movement by choosing the constant c to be sufficiently large ($> \delta^3/(\delta-1)$).

REORDER: Let a REORDER operation involve a node with load x, and a pair of neighbor nodes with loads y and z,

448

with $y \leq z$. We then have $\delta^2 y \leq x$ (for the REORDER operation to be triggered), and $\delta z \leq x$ (by NBRBALANCE between the neighbors).

The drop in potential from REORDER is given by:

$$\begin{aligned}\Delta\Phi &= c(x^2 + y^2 + z^2 - 2(x/2)^2 - (y+z)^2)/\bar{L} \\ &= c(x^2/2 - 2yz)/\bar{L} \geq c(x^2/2 - 2x^2/\delta^3)/\bar{L} \\ &\geq c'x(1 - 4/\delta^3)\end{aligned}$$

Note that $1 - 4/\delta^3$ is greater than zero for $\delta > \sqrt[3]{4} \simeq 1.587$. The data movement cost of REORDER is $\lfloor x/2 \rfloor + y < x$. Therefore, for a suitable choice of constant c ($> 2\delta^3/(\delta^3 - 4)$), the drop in potential pays for data movement.

Tuple Insert: The gain in potential, $\Delta\Phi$, from an insert at node N_i and before any rebalancing, is at most $c((L(N_i) + 1)^2 - L(N_i)^2)/\bar{L}$, where $\bar{L}$ refers to the average load before the latest insert. Therefore, $\Delta\Phi \leq c(2L(N_i) + 1)/\bar{L} \leq c(2\delta^3 + 3)$, since $L(N_i) \leq \delta^3 \bar{L} + 1$ and $\bar{L} \geq 1$. Therefore, the amortized cost of an insert is constant.

Tuple Delete: When a tuple is deleted, there may be a gain in potential due to a slight reduction in $\bar{L}$. Since $\bar{L}$ drops in value $1/n$ from a delete, the maximum gain in potential $\Delta\Phi = \frac{c(\sum L(N_i)^2)(1/n)}{\bar{L}(\bar{L}-1/n)}$. Using the facts $L(N_i) \leq \delta^3 \bar{L} + 1$, $\bar{L} \geq 1$, and $n \geq 2$, we can see that $\Delta\Phi \leq c(5\delta^3 + 3)$. Therefore, the amortized cost of a delete is constant. $\square$

We observe that the bounds on these amortized costs are quite large. When $\delta = \phi$, the cost of an insert $\simeq 412$, and the cost of a delete $\simeq 868$. We believe this to be a consequence of weak analysis stemming from our choice of potential function. We show experimentally in Section 5 that these constants are actually very close to 1. We also present variations of our algorithm next that are amenable to tighter analysis.

3.4 Discussion

Improving σ further It is possible to improve σ to arbitrarily small values larger than 1, by generalizing the Threshold algorithm, and maintaining balance over larger sets of consecutive nodes, rather than just pairs of neighbors. We do not detail this generalization in this work.

The Doubling Algorithm with Hysteresis It is possible to define a variant of the Doubling Algorithm which provides a weaker imbalance ratio ($\sigma = 32$) but has provably stronger bounds on the insertion and deletion costs. The idea is to use *hysteresis*, and require a node to lose at least half its data before it triggers load balancing for tuple deletions. We can show that this variant guarantees insertion cost of 4 and deletion cost of 29.

A Randomized Variant So far, all our algorithms attempt to find the least-loaded node (or the most-loaded node) in order to initiate the REORDER operation. In fact, the theorems we have stated hold even for a slightly weaker condition: If there are multiple nodes that violate the GLOBAL-BALANCE condition with respect to a particular node N_i executing ADJUSTLOAD, it suffices for N_i to attempt the REORDER operation with *any* of these nodes.

Such a weakening suggests an interesting randomization which avoids trying to find the least-loaded node altogether. Node N_i simply samples a set of ρ nodes at random. If one of them violates GLOBALBALANCE, N_i performs the REORDER operation using this node; otherwise, N_i simply does nothing.

If there are no data deletes, this randomized algorithm guarantees that the maximum load is at most a constant factor times the *average load* with high probability, so long as the number of nodes sampled ρ is $\Theta(\log n)$. In the presence of tuple deletes, we offer a different guarantee: If a node N_i specifies a *peak threshold* C that N_i does not want its load to exceed, the load of N_i does not exceed C with high probability, unless the average load in the system $\bar{L}$ is within a constant factor of C. It is also possible to provide guarantees on the imbalance ratio in the presence of deletes, but more caveats need to be added to the algorithm.[4]

Concurrency Control and Parallelism Until now, we have assumed that tuple inserts (and deletes) happen in sequence, and that a load-balancing step completes before the next insert. Our algorithms generalize naturally to (a) deal with parallel inserts that may happen before a load-balancing step completes, and (b) allows multiple load-balancing steps to execute in parallel.

While we do not discuss either of the above issues in detail here, we make the following observations and claims. First, the load-balancing step can be broken into multiple, smaller, atomic actions that require only simple block-level locking. Second, tuple inserts and deletes may be given higher priority, and allowed to execute even before the full load-balancing step for a previous insert/delete completes. Third, multiple load-balancing steps can execute in parallel and require very simple serialization mechanisms to ensure correctness. Finally, we note that it is possible to formalize a model of concurrency in which we can characterize the imbalance ratio under parallel insertions and deletions.

4 A P2P Network for Range Queries

There has been recent interest in developing P2P networks that can support ad-hoc queries over key ranges [3, 4, 25]. A solution is to use range partitioning of data across the peer nodes. If the data and query distributions are uniform, nodes will have equal loads. However, if the data and/or execution is skewed, the network will develop hot-spots with high query traffic for a few nodes. Load balancing thus becomes a critical requirement in such a system. The P2P environment imposes three significant challenges for developing a load-balanced, range-partitioned system:

Scale The size of the system may be extremely large, upto tens or hundreds of thousands of nodes. Our load-balancing

---
[4] Karger and Ruhl [17] offer a randomized algorithm that provides such guarantees, but require *each* node to perform such random sampling and rebalancing, whether or not any inserts or deletes are directed to that node.

algorithm deals well with scale, since its data-movement cost is *constant* and independent of the number of nodes.

Dynamism The lifetime of nodes is short (a few hours) and arbitrary (whims of the node owner). Our load-balancing algorithms need to efficiently handle dynamic arrival and departure of nodes while ensuring good load balance across the existing nodes in the system. We discuss this adaptation in Section 4.1.

Decentralization P2P systems do not have a central site that collects statistics and routes queries/inserts/deletes. We need distributed routing and data structures to enable both routing of queries/inserts/deletes, as well as to find additional load information for load balancing. Maintaining such data structures also imposes additional costs on the system, as we discuss in Section 4.2.

4.1 Handling Dynamism in the Network

Node Arrival Upon arrival, a new node N finds the most-loaded node N_h in the network. It then splits the range of N_h to take over half the load of N_h, using the NBRADJUST operation. After this split, there may be NBRBALANCE violations between two pairs of neighbors: (N_{h-1}, N_h) and (N, N_{h+1}). In response, ADJUSTLOAD is executed, first at node N_h and then at node N. It is easy to show (as in Lemma 3) that the resulting sequence of NBRADJUST operations repair all NBRBALANCE violations.

Node Departure While in the network, each node manages data for a particular range. When the node departs, the data it stored becomes unavailable to the rest of the peers. P2P networks reconcile this data loss in two ways: (a) Do nothing and let the "owners" of the data deal with its availability. The owners will frequently poll the data to detect its loss and re-insert the data into the network. (b) Maintain replicas of each range across multiple nodes. A common scheme for replication is to ensure that the partition of node N_i is replicated at the preceding r nodes (with N_n preceding N_1), for a system-specified constant r [9, 23].

First, consider the simpler data-is-lost case (a). Here, when a node N_i departs, the range boundaries between N_{i-1} and N_{i+1} must be modified. There could be a NBRBALANCE violation between the new neighbors (N_{i-1}, N_{i+1}) which can be fixed by N_{i-1} executing ADJUSTLOAD. As shown in Lemma 3, this is sufficient to restore the system invariants.

Now consider the data-is-replicated case (b). Here, when a node N_i departs the network, its preceding node N_{i-1} assumes management of N_i's partition. The node N_{i-1} already has N_i's data replicated locally. We can consider the new state as being logically equivalent to a node departure in the data-is-lost case (b), followed by a subsequent insertion of the "lost" tuples by N_{i-1}. The load-balancing algorithm is initiated whenever such insertion makes a node's load cross a threshold.

The Costs of Node Arrival and Departure The data-movement cost of a node arrival and departure is straightforward to analyze. When a new node arrives, it receives half the load of the largest node, thus requiring $\Theta(\bar{L})$ data movements, where $\bar{L}$ is the average load per node after node arrival (since all node loads are within a constant factor of each other). In addition, the average load per node decreases, leading to an increase in potential of $\Theta(\bar{L})$. Thus, the amortized cost of node insertion is still $\Theta(\bar{L})$. Note that this cost is asymptotically optimal, since it is impossible to achieve a constant imbalance ratio without the new node receiving at least $\Theta(\bar{L})$ tuples.

In the data-is-lost case, the data-movement cost of a node departure is 0, since a node departure only raises the average load, resulting in a drop in potential. All subsequent NBRADJUST operations pay for themselves, as discussed earlier. In the data-is-replicated case, the data-movement cost of a node departure is equal to the cost of "re-insertion" of the "lost" data; since the amortized cost of each insert is constant, and we re-insert only $O(\bar{L})$ tuples, the amortized cost of node departure is $O(\bar{L})$. This is again asymptotically optimal.

Note that in the replicated case, both arrival and departure of nodes requires re-creation of lost replicas, or migration of existing ones. Similarly, tuple inserts and deletes also have to be duplicated at the replica nodes. We presume that such replication is performed in the background. Observe that such replica maintenance inflates the costs of all operations only by a constant factor, if the number of replicas r is a constant.

4.2 Dealing with Decentralization

So far, we have assumed the existence of a central site that (a) maintains the global partitioning information to direct queries appropriately, and (b) maintains global load information for the load-balancing algorithm to exploit. Our next step is to devise decentralized data structures to perform both the above functions. We first describe a known data structure for efficient range queries, before discussing how to maintain load information.

Cost Model In the centralized setting of Section 2, we considered only data-movement cost, and ignored the cost of maintaining partition and load information. In the P2P setting, the lack of a central site means that we can no longer ignore this latter cost. Therefore, each operation (query, tuple insert, tuple delete, node insert, node delete) is now associated with two different costs: (a) the data-movement cost, which is measured just as earlier, and (b) communication cost, defined to be the number of *messages* that need to be exchanged between nodes (to maintain and probe the data structure) in order to perform the operation (and its corresponding load-balancing actions). Note that each message is between a pair of nodes, i.e., communication is point-to-point and broadcast is not free. (We will ignore the cost of returning query answers to the querying node.)

A Data Structure for Range Queries Our first task is the following: Any node receiving a query/insert/delete should be able to efficiently forward the operation to the appropriate node(s). One solution is to replicate the partition information across all nodes. This enables any node to directly forward a query to the relevant nodes. However, every node join/leave, or partition change, needs to be broadcast to all nodes, which is very inefficient. On the other extreme, nodes could be organized in a linked list, ordered by the partitions they manage. Updating the data structure on partition changes or node arrival/departure is efficient, but queries may have to traverse the entire linked list to reach the relevant node.

A compromise between these two costs may be achieved using a data structure known as the skip graph [6, 16]. Skip graphs are essentially circular linked lists, but each node also maintains roughly $\log n$ *skip pointers*, to enable faster list traversal. Skip pointers are randomized, and routing between any two nodes requires only $O(\log n)$ messages with high probability. Consequently, a query can be forwarded from any node to the first node in the query's range, say N_1, using $O(\log n)$ messages. If the query range is large and spans q nodes, the query is simply forwarded along on the linked list to the q successors of N_1, using a total of $O(\log n + q)$ messages. When a node arrives or departs, only $O(\log n)$ messages are required to update the data structure. Partition changes due to NBRADJUST do not require any messages at all. Thus, queries, node joins/leaves and load balancing actions are all efficient.

Maintaining Load Information Our algorithm requires that each node be able to find (a) the load of its neighbors, and (b) the most and least-loaded node in the system. Dealing with problem (a) is easy: a node already has links to its two neighbors in the skip graph, thus requiring just one message each to find their loads.

To deal with problem (b), we simply build a second, separate skip graph *on the node loads*. In other words, nodes are arranged in a sequence sorted by their current load (with ties broken arbitrarily), and a skip graph is constructed on this sequence. As node loads change, the sequence may have to be updated, but it will turn out that such updates are not expensive. As discussed earlier, this data structure enables discovery of the most and least-loaded node with just $O(\log n)$ messages, while also enabling efficient updates to the data structure.

As mentioned in Section 3.4, it is not necessary for a node to always find the most or least-loaded node, so long as it locates any node that violates GLOBALBALANCE. This property allows us to terminate searches on the skip graph even before locating the most or least-loaded node. The early termination mitigates "hot spots" created when multiple nodes simultaneously seek the most-loaded node.

The P2P Structure and its Costs: A Summary We summarize all the operations supported by the P2P system and their costs in Table 4.2. The bounds on the message costs of operations follow directly from our discussion of skip graphs above. We note that the data-movement costs are amortized, while the message costs hold with high probability. We observe that the above costs are asymptotically identical to the costs in DHTs, except for range queries where our structure is more efficient.

Operation	Messages (w.h.p)	Data Movement
Tuple Insert	$O(\log n)$	$O(1)$
Tuple Delete	$O(\log n)$	$O(1)$
Node Arrival	$O(\log n)$	$O(\bar{L})$
Node Departure	$O(\log n)$	0 or $O(\bar{L})$
Lookup Query	$O(\log n)$	0
Range Query	$O(\log n + fn)$	0

Table 1: *Cost of operations supported by the P2P network. The parameter f denotes the selectivity of the range query. The data-movement cost of Node Departure depends on the model used for data loss.*

5 Experimental Evaluation

In this section, we present results from our simulation of the Threshold algorithm on networks ranging in size from $n = 2^4$ to 2^{14}. We compare the performance of our algorithm against periodic reorganization. We also evaluate our adaptations of the algorithm on a P2P network. Our simulations show the following results:

A The Threshold Algorithm achieves the desired imbalance ratio for a range of σ values on various workloads.

B The amortized cost of load balancing is very small, decreases with increasing σ, and is much lower than the cost of periodic reorganization.

C The P2P variant achieves the desired imbalance ratio at a small cost, and scales gracefully with increasing dynamism in the network.

D The Randomized variant provides good imbalance ratios even with a small number of samples.

5.1 Simulation Model

In the parallel database setting, the simulation is designed to study load balancing as the relation evolves over time. The system is studied under three phases: (a) Growing, (b) Steady, and (c) Shrinking. At the start, all n nodes in the system are empty ("cold start"). In the Growing phase, data is loaded, one tuple at a time, using a sequence of $D = 10^6$ insert operations. In the Steady phase, inserts and deletes alternate for a total of D operations. In the following Shrinking phase, data is removed from the system, one tuple at a time, using a sequence of D delete operations.

The workload, i.e., the sequence of insertions and deletions, is set to be one of the following:

A ZIPFIAN models a static data distribution. Each tuple inserted in the Growing and Steady phases has an attribute A drawn from a Zipfian distribution (with parameter 1.0) with values in the range $[1, 10000]$. (Since our range partitioning operates on a relational key, we create a unique attribute B for each tuple, and use the sequence $\langle A, B \rangle$ as the ordering key for range partitioning.) Tuple deletion during the Steady and Shrinking phases removes one of the existing tuples uniformly at random.

B HOTSPOT models a skewed workload in which all inserts and deletes are directed to a single pre-selected ("hot") node.

C SHEARSTRESS models a dynamic workload in which

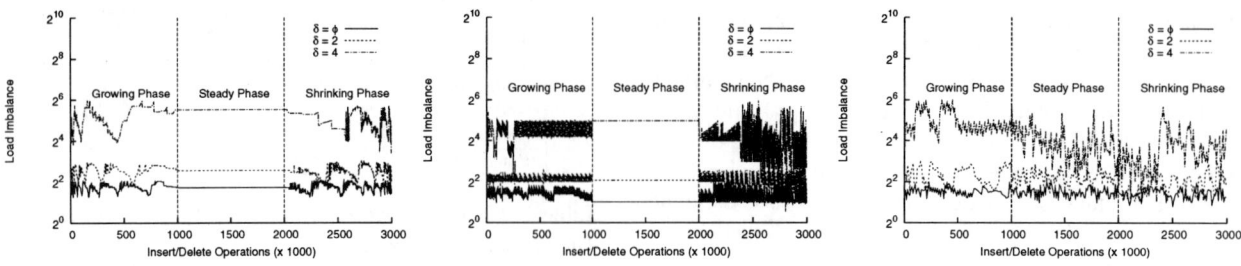

Figure 3: Imbalance ratio for (a) ZIPFIAN, (b) HOTSPOT, and (c) SHEARSTRESS when $n = 256$.

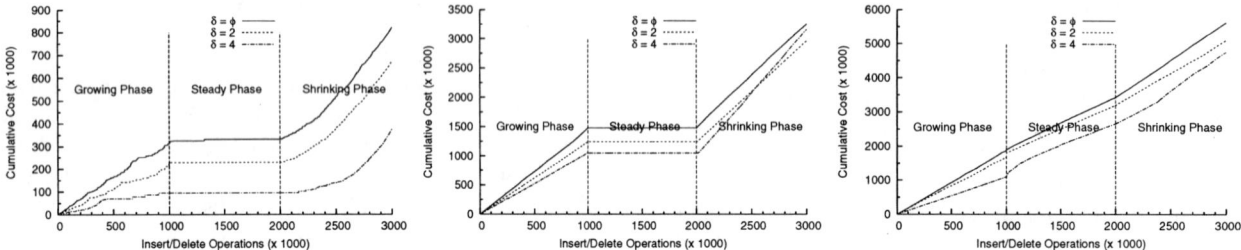

Figure 4: Data movement costs on the (a) ZIPFIAN, (b) HOTSPOT, and (c) SHEARSTRESS workload when $n = 256$.

an "adversary" inspects the load of nodes after each insert or delete of a tuple. The adversary then constructs the following insert (or delete) such that it is routed to the current most-loaded (resp. least-loaded) node.

We study the effects of network dynamism on load-balancing for a P2P network under a similar evolution model. The network starts with an initial $n = 16$ nodes, into which D tuples are inserted one by one. In the Growing phase, nodes arrive one by one and join the network, until $n = 1024$. In the following Shrinking phase, nodes depart at random until the network shrinks to $n = 16$. We use data replication to ensure that tuples are not lost on node departures. No tuples are inserted or deleted during the Growing and Shrinking phases: our goal is to isolate the costs of node arrival/departure on load balancing.

5.2 Imbalance Ratio

We start with an evaluation of imbalance ratios ensured by the Threshold Algorithm for various workloads. For the experiments, we measure the imbalance ratio at any instant as the ratio of the largest and smallest loads at that instant (with all loads being at least 1). Figure 3 shows the imbalance ratio (Y-axis) against the number of insert and delete operations (X-axis) during a run on (a) ZIPFIAN, (b) HOTSPOT, and (c) SHEARSTRESS workloads with 256 nodes. The curves are drawn for $\delta = \phi$ (Fibbing Algorithm), $\delta = 2$ (Doubling Algorithm) and $\delta = 4$.

We observe that Threshold Algorithm ensures that imbalance ratio is always less than δ^3 for all δ. Each spike in the curve corresponds to an ADJUSTLOAD step. As δ increases, the jitter introduced by the spikes gets larger and larger; this is because the algorithm allows the imbalance ratio to worsen by a *constant factor*, roughly δ, before load balancing occurs. The curves are smooth in the Steady phase for ZIPFIAN and HOTSPOT. For the former, the range partitioning "adapts" to the data distribution, ensuring that inserts and deletes are randomly sprinkled across nodes; for the latter successive inserts and deletes occurring at the same node cancel out. However, the adversary in SHEARSTRESS picks its inserts and deletes carefully to cause imbalance, leading to continuous variation in σ.

5.3 Data Movement Cost

We next study the data movement cost incurred by the Threshold Algorithm for ensuring balance in the runs discussed above. Figure 4 plots the cumulative number of tuples moved by the algorithm (Y-axis) against the number of insert and delete operations (X-axis) during a run.

We observe that costs for different δ are roughly the same (within 20% of each other) for the HOTSPOT and SHEARSTRESS workloads. Intuitively, this is because keeping the system tightly balanced causes a larger number of rebalancing operations, but each operation has lower cost due to the tight balance. We also observe that there is no data movement in the Steady phase for ZIPFIAN, indicating that the system has "adapted" to the data distribution. For the other two phases, the curves are linear confirming that the amortized cost per operation is constant, and independent of the amount of data in the system. The constants involved are also very small, with the cost per insert/delete, even in the worst phase, being roughly 0.3, 1.5 and 2 for the three workloads.

To put the above performance in perspective, we compared the data movement costs of the Fibbing Algorithm against those incurred by a periodic reorganization strategy that ensures the same imbalance ratio $\sigma = 4.2$ bound as follows: the central site continuously observes σ, and whenever $\sigma > 4.2$, a reorganization is triggered to create a perfectly balanced set of nodes. The reorganization identifies a balanced placement of tuples across nodes, and then

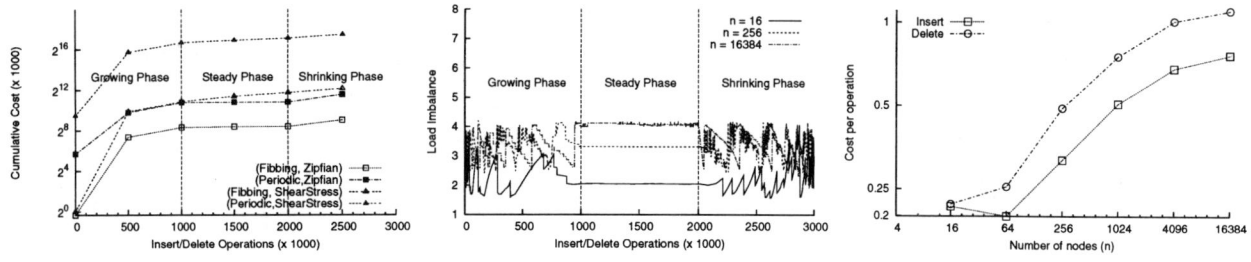

Figure 5: (a) Data movement costs for Fibbing Algorithm compared to periodic reorganization (b) Effect of n on imbalance ratios (c) Effect of n on data movement cost.

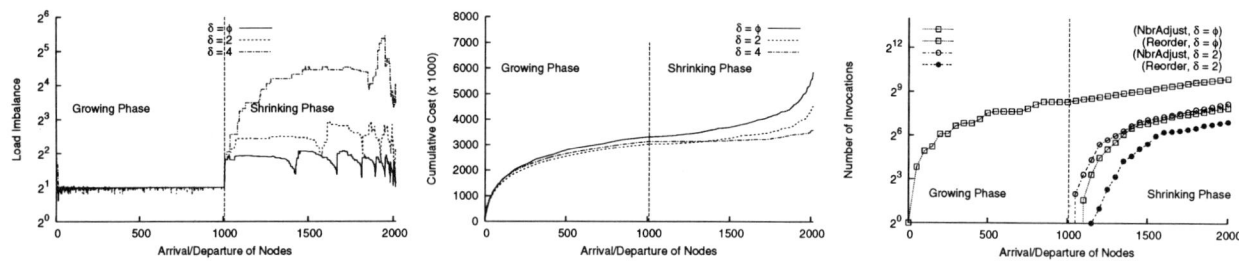

Figure 6: Performance in a P2P system: (a) imbalance ratios, (b) data movement costs, and (c) number of NBRADJUST and REORDER invocations for the Threshold Algorithm on the ZIPFIAN workload.

moves each tuple *at most once* by sending it directly to its £nal destination node. (Thus, it is more ef£cient than using only NBRADJUST operations.) Figure 5(a) plots the cumulative data movement costs on a logarithmic scale (Y-axis) against the number of operations (X-axis) in a run on 256 nodes. We observe that the periodic reorganization performs nearly 10 times *worse* for ZIPFIAN and upto 50 times worse for others. The reasons are two-fold: (a) its non-online nature allows the skew to grow requiring an expensive clean-up, and (b) its perfect balancing causes more data movement than essential to obtain the desired bounds.

5.4 The Effects of Scaling

We next study the effects of scaling in the number of nodes n on the performance of the Threshold Algorithm. Figures 5(b) and 5(c) plot load imbalance and data movement cost for the Fibbing Algorithm against a run on the ZIPFIAN workload. The network size n is varied from 16 to 16384. We observe in Figure 5(b) that the Fibbing Algorithm continues to ensure the $\sigma = \phi^3$ bound. However, as the same number of tuples are shared across more nodes, the load variance across nodes increases, leading to an increase in the imbalance ratio.

Figure 5(c) plots the data movement cost per operation (Y-axis) against the size of the network n (X-axis). Both axes are plotted on a logarithmic scale. The bottom curve plots the data movement cost per insert observed during the Growing Phase; the top curve plots the costs per delete observed during the Shrinking Phase. We observe that costs of both insert and delete operations increases with increasing n. As n increases, the load per node is smaller, making it easier to make the system unbalanced with a smaller number of inserts and deletes. Thus more load balancing steps are needed, leading to a higher cost. We also observe that the cost per operation is quite small as the curves taper off towards a value close to 1.

We had shown in Section 3.3 that the cost per insert or delete is a *constant*. The £gures here show a dependence of cost per operation on n. How can this apparent contradiction be explained? The experiments presented here evaluate the cost for a £xed workload for various n values. On the other hand, the analysis established bounds on the *worst-case* costs against all workloads.

5.5 Performance in a P2P Setting

Figure 6 shows the performance of the Threshold Algorithm adapted to a P2P system. Figures 6(a) and 6(b) plot the imbalance ratio and data-movement cost against the number of node arrivals and departures. We observe in Figure 6(a) that the system remains well-balanced through the Growing phase, because the arriving node always splits the most-loaded node. The imbalance ratio is roughly two, since the most-loaded node splits its load in half on a node arrival. On the other hand, nodes depart at random during the Shrinking phase, which leads to changes in the imbalance ratio. However, the guarantees of δ^3 are ensured.

From Figure 6(b), we see that the *incremental* data-movement cost per arrival/departure (i.e., the slope of the curve) decreases with node arrivals in the Growing phase, and increases with node departures in the Shrinking phase. This is not surprising, since the cost is proportional to the average load in the system which, in turn, is inversely proportional to the number of nodes.

NbrAdjust vs. Reorder In a P2P system, the NBRADJUST operation may turn out to be more ef£cient than REORDER,

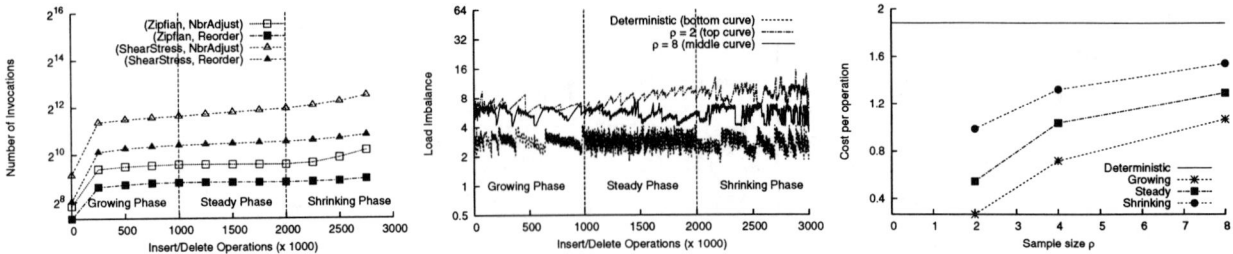

Figure 7: The Fibbing algorithm with $n = 256$. (a) The number of invocations of NBRADJUST and REORDER (b) The effect of randomization on imbalance ratio (c) The effect of randomization on data movement costs, for the SHEARSTRESS workload.

for two reasons: (a) REORDER requires the reordered node to drop its old links and set up new ones. (b) A NBRADJUST may not require immediate transfer of data to balance load, when data is replicated at neighbors; only replicas need to be updated, which can be done more lazily.

In the light of the above observations, we observed the number of invocations of the two operations to see which is used more often. Figure 6(c) shows the number of invocations of NBRADJUST and REORDER for different values of δ, as nodes are inserted and deleted. Not surprisingly, the number of invocations of both operations decreases as δ increases. We see that the number of NBRADJUST invocations is at least 4 times that of REORDER, which is reassuring given that REORDERs are more expensive.

Figure 7(a) shows the number of invocations of the two operations by the Fibbing Algorithm, on a fixed set of 256 nodes, as tuples are inserted and deleted from the three workloads. We observe that there are twice as many invocations of NBRADJUST, as compared to REORDER, which is again useful in the P2P context.

5.6 The Effects of Randomization

As discussed earlier, the REORDER operation requires global statistics and involves the least/most-loaded node in the load-balancing step. In Section 3.4, we defined a randomized variant where REORDER would sample ρ nodes at random and pick the least/most-loaded node from the *sample*. Figures 7(b) and 7(c) plot the effects of such randomization on the Fibbing Algorithm for runs of the SHEARSTRESS workload as the sample size ρ is varied. We observe in Figure 7(b) that the imbalance ratio degrades beyond the original value of ϕ^3. However, even the use of $\rho = 2$ samples provides good load balance; increasing ρ improves σ further. Correspondingly, the use of sampling reduces data movement compared to the deterministic case, for all three phases, as shown in Figure 7(c).

6 Related Work

Parallel Databases partition relations across multiple disks, using either range or hash partitioning [8, 10, 28]. Research in physical design of parallel databases can be classified into four categories: (a) Workload-driven tuning of storage for static relations, e.g. [15, 21, 26]; (b) Disk-based data structures for fast bulk insert/delete of tuples, e.g. [12, 18]; (c) Efficient data migration for load-balancing while allowing concurrent relation updates and queries, e.g. [29]; and (d) Balancing query load across disks by moving a partition from one disk to another, e.g. [24].

Work in category (a) is focused on performing workload-driven tuning of physical design, but usually does not consider a dynamic evolution of the design with relation updates. Work in category (b) is complementary to ours, in that they show *how* to efficiently update *local* disk structures when tuples move from one partition to another, while our focus is in understanding *what* tuples to move. Research in category (c) is also complementary to our work, as it helps deal with issues of concurrency control when performing online repartitioning. Finally, work in category (d) attempts to modify the *allocation* of partitions to disks, rather than change the partitions themselves. We believe such solutions could be used in combination with ours to achieve balance for dynamic query loads, but are not sufficient in themselves to guarantee storage balance for range-partitioned data.

Litwin et al. [20, 19] consider the design of scalable distributed data structures (SDDS) which share many features with the design philosophy of P2P systems, including the absence of centralization, and the ability to gracefully add or remove servers. Most work on SDDS has focused on hash partitioning, either at the tuple level [20] or at a block level [19]. Our work is complementary in that it can be utilized to enable true range partitioning for SDDS.

Range Queries in P2P Networks Recently, P2P networks supporting range queries have been proposed, that offer either storage balance or efficient queries, but not both. Ratnasamy et. al. [25] assure storage balance but at the price of data-dependent query cost and data fragmentation. Gupta et. al. [3] provide approximate answers, and do not offer any guarantees for an arbitrary range query. Others [4, 6, 16] offer exact and efficient queries, but do not offer load balance across nodes.

Aberer et al. [1, 2] develop a P2P network called P-Grid that can support efficient range queries. All nodes in this system have a fixed capacity, and content is *heuristically* replicated to fill all the nodes' capacity. However, there is no formal characterization of either the imbalance ratio guaranteed, or the data-movement cost incurred.

In a concurrent work, Karger and Ruhl [17] provide an alternative solution to the storage balance problem. The scheme is a randomized algorithm that offers a high-probability bound on the imbalance ratio, and is analyzed under a dynamic, but non-adversarial, setting. However, the best achievable bound on imbalance ratio using this algorithm appears to be more than 128, which is much higher than the load imbalance bounds we guarantee. Bharambe et al. [7] also use a load-balancing scheme similar to [17] as a heuristic to balance range partitions.

Routing in P2P Networks Most DHT interconnection networks [23, 27] require randomly chosen (uniformly spaced) partition boundaries to guarantee efficient routing. A load-balanced, range-partitioned network will not have such equi-spaced boundaries, rendering such networks unusable. Aberer [1] presents an elegant variant of Pastry which does guarantee $O(\log n)$ routing even with arbitrary partition boundaries. However, node in-degrees could become skewed, resulting in a skewed message traffic distribution. Moreover, a change of partition boundaries between neighbors necessitates a change in the network link structure. Our P2P network utilizes skip graphs and overcomes the above limitations. Bharambe et al. [7] suggest an alternative scheme involving the construction of small-world networks. However, their heuristic requires nodes to perform extensive sampling of the other nodes in the system, and provides no guarantees on routing performance. Our solution of using skip graphs is simpler and provides stronger guarantees on performance.

7 Conclusions and Future Work

Horizontal range-partitioning is commonly employed in shared-nothing parallel databases. Load balancing is necessary in such scenarios to eliminate skew. We presented asymptotically optimal online load-balancing algorithms that guarantee a constant imbalance ratio. The data-movement cost per tuple insert or delete is constant, and was shown to be close to 1 in experiments. We showed how to adapt our algorithms to dynamic P2P environments, and architected a new P2P system that can support efficient range queries.

Although our algorithms were presented in the context of balancing storage load, they generalize to balancing execution load too; all that is required is an ability to partition load evenly across two machines. Understanding the costs of load balancing for execution load is a subject of future work. We are currently exploring extensions of our algorithm to deal with node and network heterogeneity, as well as the partitioning of multi-dimensional data [14].

References

[1] K. Aberer. Scalable data access in p2p systems using unbalanced search trees. In *Proc. WDAS*, 2002.

[2] K. Aberer, A. Datta, and M. Hauswirth. The quest for balancing peer load in structured peer-to-peer systems. Technical Report IC/2003/32, EPFL, Switzerland, 2003.

[3] A.Gupta, D.Agrawal, and A. Abbadi. Approximate range selection queries in peer-to-peer systems. In *Proc. CIDR*, 2003.

[4] A. Andrzejak and Z. Xu. Scalable, efficient range queries for grid information services. In *Proc. P2P*, 2002.

[5] A.Silberschatz, H.F.Korth, and S.Sudarshan. *"Database System Concepts"*, chapter 17. McGraw-Hill, 1997.

[6] J. Aspnes and G. Shah. Skip graphs. In *Proc. SODA*, 2003.

[7] A. Bharambe, M. Agrawal, and S. Seshan. Mercury: Supporting scalable multi-attribute range queries. In *Proc. SIGCOMM*, 2004.

[8] G. Copeland, W. Alexander, E. Boughter, and T. Keller. Data placement in Bubba. In *Proc. SIGMOD*, 1988.

[9] F. Dabek, M. F. Kaashoek, D. Karger, R. Morris, and I. Stoica. Wide-area cooperative storage with CFS. In *Proc. SOSP*, 2001.

[10] D. DeWitt, R. H. Gerber, G. Graefe, M. L. Heytens, K. B. Kumar, and M. Muralikrishna. Gamma -a high performance dataflow database. In *Proc. VLDB*, 1986.

[11] D. DeWitt and J. Gray. Parallel database systems: The future of high performance database processing. *Communications of the ACM*, 36(6), 1992.

[12] H. Feelifu, M. Kitsuregawa, and B. C. Ooi. A fast convergence technique for online heat-balancing of btree indexed database over shared-nothing parallel systems. In *Proc. DEXA*, 2000.

[13] P. Ganesan, M. Bawa, and H. Garcia-Molina. Online balancing of range-partitioned data with applications to p2p systems. Technical Report http://dbpubs.stanford.edu/pubs/2004-18, Stanford U., 2004.

[14] P. Ganesan, B. Yang, and H. Garcia-Molina. One torus to rule them all: Multi-dimensional queries in p2p systems. In *WebDB*, 2004.

[15] S. Ghandeharizadeh and D. J. DeWitt. A performance analysis of alternative multi-attribute declustering strategies. In *Proc. SIGMOD*, 1992.

[16] N. J. A. Harvey, M. Jones, S. Saroiu, M. Theimer, and A. Wolman. Skipnet: A scalable overlay network with practical locality properties. In *Proc. USITS*, 2003.

[17] D. R. Karger and M. Ruhl. Simple efficient load-balancing algorithms for peer-to-peer systems. In *Proc. IPTPS*, 2004.

[18] M. L. Lee, M. Kitsuregawa, B. C. Ooi, K.-L. Tan, and A. Mondal. Towards self-tuning data placement in parallel database systems. In *Proc. SIGMOD*, 2000.

[19] W. Litwin, M.-A. Neimat, and D. A. Schneider. RP* : A family of order preserving scalable distributed data structures. In *Proc. VLDB*, 1994.

[20] W. Litwin, M.-A. Neimat, and D. A. Schneider. LH* – A scalable, distributed data structure. *ACM Transactions on Database Systems*, 21(4):480–525, 1996.

[21] J. Rao, C. Zhang, N. Megiddo, and G. Lohman. Automating physical database design in a parallel database. In *Proc. SIGMOD*, 2002.

[22] S. Ratnasamy, P. Francis, M. Handley, and R. M. Karp. A scalable Content-Addressable Network. In *Proc. SIGCOMM*, 2001.

[23] A. I. T. Rowstron and P. Druschel. Pastry: Scalable, distributed object location, and routing for large-scale peer-to-peer systems. In *Proc. Middleware*, 2001.

[24] P. Scheuermann, G. Weikum, and P. Zabback. Adaptive load balancing in disk arrays. In *Proc. FODO*, 1993.

[25] S.Ratnasamy, J.M.Hellerstein, and S.Shenker. Range queries over DHTs. Technical Report IRB-TR-03-009, Intel, 2003.

[26] T. Stohr, H. Martens, and E. Rahm. Multi-dimensional database allocation for parallel data warehouses. In *Proc. VLDB*, 2000.

[27] I. Stoica, R. Morris, D. Karger, M. F. Kaashoek, and H. Balakrishnan. Chord: A scalable peer-to-peer lookup service for internet applications. In *Proc. SIGCOMM*, 2001.

[28] Tandem Database Group. Nonstop sql, a distributed high-performance, high-reliability implementation of sql. In *Proc. HPTS*, 1987.

[29] D. C. Zilio. *Physical Database Design Decision Algorithms and Concurrent Reorganization for Parallel Database Systems*. PhD thesis, University of Toronto, 1988.

Network-Aware Query Processing for Stream-based Applications

Yanif Ahmad Uğur Çetintemel

Computer Science Department, Brown University
{yna, ugur}@cs.brown.edu

Abstract

This paper investigates the benefits of *network awareness* when processing queries in widely-distributed environments such as the Internet. We present algorithms that leverage knowledge of network characteristics (e.g., topology, bandwidth, etc.) when deciding on the network locations where the query operators are executed. Using a detailed emulation study based on realistic network models, we analyse and experimentally evaluate the proposed approaches for distributed stream processing. Our results quantify the significant benefits of the network-aware approaches and reveal the fundamental trade-off between bandwidth efficiency and result latency that arises in networked query processing.

1 Introduction

The need for widely-distributed query processing is becoming increasingly apparent with the proliferation of applications that require sophisticated processing of data generated or stored by large numbers of distributed sources (such as data streams generated by sensor networks or Internet-based data collections). Existing query processing approaches commonly address relatively small-scale systems and fail to exhibit good network scalability, a design goal that has only recently started to receive attention within the database community [8, 12] and that we believe will be central to next-generation data processing systems.

In this paper, we study the benefits of *network awareness* when processing queries in widely-distributed environments such as the Internet. We argue that exploiting knowledge of the underlying network characteristics (such as topology and link bandwidths) can significantly improve the efficiency of network-bound query processing. We present *network-aware* operator placement algorithms that utilize such characteristics to identify the network locations where the operators of a given query plan should be executed. The algorithms differ in which nodes they consider as candidates for operator placement and how they take network knowledge into account.

Specifically, we present two novel network-aware approaches for push-based continuous queries and distributed stream processing. The first approach uses heuristics that exploit pair-wise server communication latencies. The second approach extends the first one by identifying and involving in processing "well-located" servers that would otherwise not participate in the process, thereby implementing "in-network" query processing.

We describe the basic design of a distributed query processing system, built on top of a Distributed Hash Table (DHT) [22, 26], that implements the proposed placement algorithms. We have fully implemented the system and the algorithms, and use the code base to conduct a detailed emulation study under realistic network models. Our results show that, compared to representatives of traditional network-unaware approaches, the proposed approaches can significantly reduce the overall system bandwidth consumption, a key efficiency metric for large-scale networked systems. Furthermore, the algorithms can be tuned to satisfy target query-result latency bounds, typically at the expense of extra bandwidth consumption. Even though our work assumes push-based continuous queries, the results are more general and apply to pull-based pipelined queries as well.

Our work is done in the context of the *SAND* (*S*calable *A*daptive *N*etwork *D*atabases) project that strives to develop a highly-scalable and adaptive network-oriented database system and the *Borealis* project that strives to extend core data-stream processing functionality to heterogeneous distributed environments.

The rest of the paper is organized as follows: Section 2 describes the basic system and network model that we assume throughout the paper. Section 3 presents the centralized versions of the network-aware operator placement algorithms. Section 4 describes how these algorithms can be effectively implemented in a distributed manner, leveraging basic DHT primitives. Section 5 analyzes the processing and message complexity of both the centralized

---

This work has been supported in part by the National Science Foundation under the ITR grant IIS-0325838.

Permission to copy without fee all or part of this material is granted provided that the copies are not made or distributed for direct commercial advantage, the VLDB copyright notice and the title of the publication and its date appear, and notice is given that copying is by permission of the Very Large Data Base Endowment. To copy otherwise, or to republish, requires a fee and/or special permission from the Endowment.

**Proceedings of the 30th VLDB Conference,
Toronto, Canada, 2004**

and distributed approaches. Section 6 characterizes the efficiency and effectiveness of the approaches using an emulation. Section 7 summarizes prior research relevant to our work and highlights the main differences. Finally, Section 8 provides concluding remarks and directions for future research.

2 Basic System Model

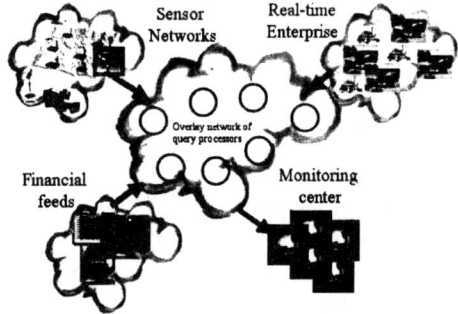

Figure 1: A widely-distributed stream processing environment.

We consider a widely-distributed query processing environment with geographically dispersed data sources that produce high-volume, fast data streams. Our target applications require sophisticated processing (e.g., fusion, aggregation, correlation) of the source data streams. Our system consists of a large number of cooperating servers, capable of executing stream-oriented query operators (e.g., [4, 5, 18]). The servers are organized into an overlay network and collectively provide processing services for multiple concurrent stream-based applications.

Figure 1 illustrates the basic application and environmental model. In the figure, the small clouds represent data sources (such as sensor networks and financial feeds) and the big cloud represents the networked stream processing system. The system transparently partitions the queries that describe the processing requirements of applications across its nodes, multiplexing its distributed resources in order to improve the overall performance, scalability, and availability.

2.1 Data and Processing Model

For our purposes, a data stream is a continuous sequence of tuples generated by a stream source (or simply *source*). Data streams are processed according to a processing network, which is a collection of (potentially overlapping) processing trees. A *processing tree* is a directed dataflow-style tree of stream-oriented operators that collectively represent a query plan. Users build such query networks either directly using a GUI, through a scripting language (e.g., [4, 12]) or indirectly through the compilation of high-level SQL-like language statements (e.g., [18]). In either case, queries are built using a standard set of operators [1, 18], which can also include user-defined functions. We assume that the specified processing tree is final and do not consider further semantic opportunities. We plan to explore this in future work. The output tuples that result from processing are delivered to an *application proxy* (or simply proxy) that is responsible for forwarding these tuples to the relevant application(s).

2.2 Server and Network Model

Our system consists of an application-level overlay network (e.g., [19, 20, 22, 26]) of geographically dispersed cooperating servers, interconnected physically by IP networks, and logically, through a DHT infrastructure. We assume that the overlay servers communicate via IP unicast.

The DHT infrastructure acts as a networking substrate, providing localized knowledge of the server space and flexibility in our routing and search operations. This flexibility is core to supporting a variety of placement mechanisms when investigating algorithmic tradeoffs in optimizing bandwidth usage. While the algorithms presented here are not reliant upon a specific DHT, we describe our system generating placement overlays on top of the Tapestry system [26].

In Tapestry, overlay servers are assigned an identifier obtained from securely hashing the servers' IP addresses. Overlay servers co-ordinate themselves into a connected network, and maintain local routing tables referring to servers whose addresses prefix match the local address, at varying lengths. Using this routing table construction, Tapestry offers a lookup mechanism designed to reach its destination in $\mathcal{O}(\log n)$ overlay hops (where n denotes the number of overlay participants), while ensuring a bound of $\mathcal{O}(n \log n)$ on the system space requirements. Furthermore, Tapestry servers' routing tables are created utilizing network locality information, making it well-suited for our purposes. Incorporating locality cues reduces the routing stretch factor, and as such, will transitively affect stretch factors in our placement overlays, and the response time for its construction.

2.3 Control Model

For improved scalability and parallelism, we use a distributed control model. For each processing tree, we create a corresponding *control tree* of coordinator nodes as follows. When a processing tree is up for execution, it is logically partitioned into a number of subtrees, called *zones*. Each zone is assigned a *coordinator* node that is responsible for the placement (and periodic dynamic re-placement) of the operators in the zone. Coordinators are also responsible for ensuring correct and highly-available execution of their zones. The application proxy is always assigned as the root coordinator and decides how many zones to create. Each zone is then assigned a *zone id*, which is used to identify the node (through the DHT) that will serve as the coordinator for the zone. Coordinators communicate among themselves and the nodes that execute the operators in their zones in order to dynamically optimize processing.

Figure 2 provides a high-level view of this basic model, illustrating a processing tree and the corresponding control amd processing networks overlayed on top of the physical IP network. The processing tree is partitioned into three zones, each assigned to a coordinator node. Each coordinator decides on the placement of the nodes in its zone using

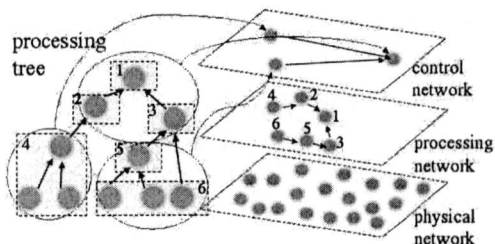

Figure 2: A processing tree and the corresponding control and processing overlay networks.

appropriate algorithms. An advantage of this approach is that zones can be optimized locally, concurrently and asynchronously.

3 Operator Placement

In this section, we first formally define the operator placement problem for processing widely-distributed data streams. We then describe three algorithms to construct processing overlay networks. The first algorithm, *Edge*, considers only source locations and the proxy for placement. Edge is an adaptation of the standard pull-based site-selection approaches to push-based streaming data. The second algorithm, called *Edge+*, is a network-aware version of Edge. Edge+ takes into account the pair-wise "network distances" (i.e., transmission latencies) between the servers. The third approach, called *In-Network*, considers a carefully selected subset of all network locations, in addition to the sources and the proxy, when making placement decisions. Finally, we describe an extension that imposes bounds on the processing delays.

In order to focus on networking-related costs, we ignore operator processing costs and other related overheads that arise during query execution. We also assume that the placement algorithms are applied periodically to dynamically adapt to changes.

3.1 Problem Statement

Consider a processing tree $T = \{O, A\}$, defined by a set of stream-oriented operators O, and their connected inputs and outputs A. Our model also consists of a network topology $G = \{V, E\}$, of peer nodes V, and their links E. A function, β, on processing tree edges yields the data-flow bandwidth between operators. In our model, β is defined as a product of the input bandwidths and selectivity (or more generally productivity) of the input operators. Our goal is to place each operator at a peer, while minimizing the bandwidth utilized in the network.

We assume that the leaves in our processing tree represent stream sources, and that a function DHT yields the sources' locations on the topology. We attempt to find a mapping function λ defined on the operators, O, yielding network locations in V. Our objective on the network edges between the resulting placements follows:

$$\min_{\lambda} \sum_{a \in A} c(a) \quad (1)$$

$$\text{s.t.} \quad \lambda(l) = DHT(l) \quad \forall l \in leaves(T) \quad (2)$$

where

$$c(a) = \begin{cases} 0 & \text{if for } a = (m, n) : \lambda(m) = \lambda(n) \\ \beta(a) & \text{otherwise} \end{cases} \quad (3)$$

In our cost function $c(a)$ above, we state that processing tree edges, $a \in A$, incur no cost if both endpoints of an edge are placed at the same location, and a cost of $\beta(a)$ otherwise. We use the terms *tree cost* and *overlay cost* to refer to the functions β and c, respectively. We regard λ as defining a query overlay, whose members are given by the range of λ, and edges are the network edges corresponding to mapped tree edges. Figure 3 provides an overview of the symbols used in this model, along with their definitions.

Symbol	Definition
o	processing tree operator.
c_i	arbitrary child of operator o.
$\beta(a)$	cost of processing tree edge a (*tree cost*)
$c(a)$	cost of mapped tree edge a (*overlay cost*)
$d(u, v)$	network distance between locations u and v
$\gamma(o, v)$	cost of operator o at location v
$\lambda(o)$	mapped location of operator o
$\phi(o)$	candidate location set of operator o

Figure 3: Model terminology.

3.2 Edge Placement

The *Edge* algorithm strives to find a good placement when the candidate locations are constrained to the sources and the proxy. Because the optimal solution of a simpler version of the problem is known to be NP-complete [16], we propose a greedy algorithm that traverses the processing tree operators in post-order, optimizing progressively larger subtrees as it proceeds.

As our algorithm encounters operators in its traversal, it places operators at the minimal cost location identified using one of three cases: placement at (1) one of its children's locations, (2) a *common* location, or (3) the proxy's location. We now describe how to compute the partial overlay's cost at each of these cases in greater detail. Note that the cost of an operator depends upon the placement of its children. We use the term *configuration* throughout the text to denote the placement and cost of an operator, and the placement of its children (and subsequently the entire subtree).

Let us consider an operator o with children $\{c_1, \ldots, c_n\}$. In case (1) above, we place the operator at a location that maximizes the total tree cost between the operator and all of its children. This configuration eliminates the maximal tree cost from our overlay cost. Formally, this is:

$$\lambda'(o) = \arg\max_{v \in \bigcup_{i=1}^{n} \lambda(c_i)} \sum_{\{c_i : \lambda(c_i) = v\}} \beta(o, c_i) \quad (4)$$

This local minimization clearly does not yield a globally optimal processing overlay. In case (2), we check for locations where we may potentially place all children of an operator. Placing an operator and its children at this common location ensures that all edges between the operator and its children incur zero overlay cost. We define cl, the set of common locations as an intersection of each child's *dl* (the set of descendant leaf locations) of an operator o:

$$dl(o) = \bigcup_{l \in leaves(o)} \lambda(l) \; , \; cl(o) = \bigcap_{i=1}^{n} dl(c_i)$$

To facilitate this heuristic, we need to compute the cost of placing an operator at a specific location:

$$\gamma(v, o) = \infty \quad \text{if } o \in leaves(T) \wedge v \neq DHT(o)$$
$$\gamma(v, o) = \sum_{\{c_i : v = \lambda(c_i)\}} \gamma(v, c_i) + \quad \text{otherwise}$$
$$\sum_{\{c_i : v \neq \lambda(c_i)\}} \min\{\gamma(\lambda(c_i), c_i) + \beta(o, c_i), \gamma(v, c_i)\} \quad (5)$$

This is γ (Equation 5), yielding the overlay cost of a subtree rooted by operator o, with o placed at v. We consider two configurations to achieve this, the minimized sum (over all children) of either (i) the existing child configuration cost and the cost of any additional edge required to place the operator at v, or (ii) the cost of placing the child at v.

In the case (3), we consider the cost of placing an operator at the proxy's location. Our motivation here is that, in placing an operator, we do not account for its outgoing tree cost. Considering this configuration helps when tree costs are higher near the root of the processing tree. In this scenario, all operator-child tree edges add to the overlay cost (assuming that the proxy is not a stream source). With a proxy location r, we now have our final mapping function, λ, for an operator o:

$$\lambda(o) = \begin{cases} DHT(o) & \text{if } o \in leaves(T) \\ \arg\min_{v \in cl \cup \{\lambda'(o), r\}} \gamma(v, o) & \text{otherwise} \end{cases} \quad (6)$$

3.3 Network-Aware Edge Placement: Edge+

The Edge algorithm does not utilize any network knowledge in making placement decisions. To better model costs on a large-scale network, we extend the original approach to include a symmetric distance function, d, that represent the network latencies between locations. In the extended algorithm, *Edge+*, this change is reflected in the cost function. Our modified overlay cost is a product of tree cost and the distance between overlay edge endpoints. We replace Equation 3 with:

$$c(m, n) = \begin{cases} 0 & \text{if } \lambda(m) = \lambda(n) \\ \beta(m, n) \cdot d(\lambda(m), \lambda(n)) & \text{otherwise} \end{cases}$$

The control flow of Edge+ is similar to that of Edge. In Edge+, we consider configurations from the three cases in Edge, and additionally examine a distance-oriented case. In this fourth case, given a child's descendant locations, we selectively enumerate location permutations that meet a distance criterion. We select permutations whose total separation is less than than the total separation of the operator configuration selected by the Edge algorithm. Formally, we choose configurations, $\{v_i \in dl(c_i)\}^n$, (of cardinality n), such that:

$$\sum_{i=1}^{n} d(v_1, v_i) \leq \sum_{i=1}^{n} d(\lambda(o), \lambda(c_i))$$

Above, we see a configuration's total separation is a sum of distances from one location to all other locations. Note we leverage our symmetry assumption here. Our intuition in selecting these configurations is to optimize for cost by reducing distances between our operator-child mappings. Providing the magnitude of this reduction is greater than any increase in the overlay cost of placing the child operators with the desired permutation, we are left with an overlay of lower total cost.

3.4 In-Network Placement

Using the techniques described above, we now describe the In-Network algorithm that considers placing operators at arbitrary network locations. In-Network extends on the previous algorithms by considering *select* configurations from a set of candidate locations other than just the sources and the proxy. A greedy, global search strategy would consider configurations from all locations. However this is computationally intractable for large topologies. We here describe a heuristic to effectively prune the configurations considered.

In-Network pursues a similar line to Edge+ in selecting configurations of small total distance. Given that configurations may include arbitrary locations, we reduce the candidate set size with the following heuristic. A location is removed from an operator's candidate set, unless its distance to all current child placements is less than all pairwise distances between child placements. Formally, operator o, with children $\{c_1, \ldots, c_n\}$ has a candidate set:

$$\phi(o) = \{v_i \in V : \forall c_i, c_j \in C.$$
$$d(v_i, \lambda(c_i)) < d(\lambda(c_i), \lambda(c_j)) \wedge$$
$$d(v_i, \lambda(c_j)) < d(\lambda(c_i), \lambda(c_j))\}$$

For intuition, the current child placements define a *convex* set of locations, and our selected configurations lie in this convex set. Hence, these configurations have a smaller total separation, in an appropriate part of the topology. However, this may still result in a large number of potential configurations, especially in scenarios where distances between stream sources are relatively large. We further rank configurations by their separations and select a number, k, of these configurations in increasing order of our ranking. Selecting a minimal cost configuration is the same as in Edge+. Once we have chosen our configuration, we place each child at a location corresponding to our configuration, and add the cost of any edges needed to connect the mapping of the operator to its children.

3.5 Latency-Constrained Placement

A desirable property of our mapping function λ would be the ability to place a path-based constraint on the sequence of locations a path in the processing tree is mapped to on the overlay network. A straightforward example is a delay constraint indicating a desired response time on the processing tree. We now abstract this into our model. Let us consider a path constraint, of value l. For a set of leaf-to-root paths P, we model the constraint as:

$$\sum_{(a,b)\in p} d(\lambda(a), \lambda(b)) \leq l \qquad \forall p \in P$$

The above inequality states that the total distance of a mapped leaf-to-root path must be bounded by the constraint value. We add this to our constraint in Equation 2, in this version of the problem. Our updated definition of λ, to meet this constraint, follows. First we define our set of valid locations, for an operator o with children $\{c_1, \ldots, c_n\}$:

$$L = \phi(c_i) - \{v_i \in \phi(c_i) : \delta(c_i) + d(v_i, \lambda(c_i)) > l\}$$

where $\delta(o) = \max_{p \in paths(subtree(o))} \sum_{(a,b) \in p} d(\lambda(a), \lambda(b))$

We now redefine our mapping function:

$$\lambda(o) = \begin{cases} DHT(o) & \text{if } o \in leaves(T) \\ \arg\min_{v \in L} \gamma(v, o) & \text{otherwise} \end{cases}$$

Here, we ensure that each member of the set L meets the delay constraint. Thus, when we come to mapping the root location, we only consider configurations meeting the constraint. Clearly, this constraint reduces the size of our search space. We assume the processing tree will meet the delay constraint when all operators, except leaves, are placed at the application proxy. If this is not the case, then we have an "infeasible" mapping, given the application proxy is unable to even access the desired sources within the given constraint. This leads to a source placement problem, which may be potentially be solved with replication techniques. This issue lies outside the scope of this paper.

4 Distributed Query Placement

It is evident that placing tree operators at arbitrary locations requires substantial network state to be fed into the mapping algorithm. This requirement significantly restricts the scalability and effectiveness of centralized approaches in the presence of a large number of highly distributed stream sources. In this section, we describe the distributed versions of Edge, Edge+, and In-Network. In the rest of the paper, unless otherwise noted, we will use these names to refer to the distributed versions of the protocols. All the distributed protocols use basic DHT primitives for improved scalability, look-up efficiency, and fault tolerance. As described before, we use the Tapestry as the underlying lookup substrate.

4.1 Overview

In the distributed version of our algorithms, we construct the processing overlay in a bottom-up manner, concurrently determining placements for siblings. We assume that each operator is assigned a globally unique identifier. As described earlier, we subdivide our processing tree into zones, and assign mapping responsibilities for each zone to a coordinator. Coordinators are chosen as the Tapestry peer whose address matches a zone's (or subtree's) identifier. For now, we assume that a subtree's identifier is that of the subtree's root. Thus, in our distributed algorithm we subdivide the optimization search space, and the collection of metadata to drive our search. Once a coordinator has placed its subtree, it communicates with its upstream coordinator (i.e., the coordinator responsible for the subtree rooted at an ancestor operator). We ensure that an operator is aware of its ancestors by appending leaf-to-root (*LR*) paths to specific messages. These paths, along with lists of operators' common locations, are precomputed at the proxy. This distributed mapping process repeats until the root of the processing tree is placed.

Deciding on the number and selection of zones is an open research issue, which should account for factors including the relevant network state, the load on the potential coordinators, and how much parallelism is feasible. Our intuition also indicates that the number of sources plays a significant role in terms of determining divisions of the workload that optimize control overhead. We here investigate one extreme of subtree assignment, a finely-grained scenario where a subtree is a single operator, leaving a more general investigation of this issue to future work.

4.1.1 Local State

Overlay peers maintain two tables, indexed by operator identifiers, to participate in the mapping protocol. The first table, known as the *boundary children* table maintains a list of children for every subtree the peer is responsible for mapping. Our definition of a subtree is one where the subtree does not necessarily extend to the leaves. Boundary children are thus defined as the children connected to subtrees created during workload assignment. The second table, the *operators mapped* table, maintains feasible operator configurations and their associated costs. We now describe how these data structures are used in our protocol. For convenience, Figure 4.1.1 summarizes the messages used in the protocols.

4.2 Edge Placement

Distributed placement is a two-phase process: (1) the application proxy distributes the mapping workload to the coordinators, and (2) the coordinators communicate to perform the mapping, instantiating an overlay.

Coordinator initialization. Workload distribution is performed in two steps. In the first step, we populate the boundary children tables of all coordinators. We traverse the processing tree at the proxy, sending an ADD_SUBTREE message to every coordinator. This message consists of a coordinator's assigned subtree, and its boundary children. In the second step, we initiate our decentralized tree mapping at the sources. Here the application proxy sends both an OPERATOR_MAPPED and a MAP message to each

Message type	Message contents
ADD_SUBTREE	subtree workload, boundary children list
OPERATOR_MAPPED	operator, min-cost configuration, alternate configurations, constraint metadata
MAP	operator, child configuration, common locations, LR path, network view, candidates, constraint metadata
INVALIDATE_MAP	operator
OPERATOR_REMAPPED	operator, configuration

Figure 4: Protocol messages and their contents.

source. The OPERATOR_MAPPED message, used to populate the operators mapped table, includes a configuration of placing the operator at the recipient, as well as a list of alternative configurations. This list is empty for sources, as they reside at fixed locations.

Iterative mapping step. The MAP message contains an operator, its present configuration, and the application proxy's address. The MAP message also contains the LR path used by coordinators for algorithm control. The MAP message triggers our placement mechanism. Mapping a subtree requires all boundary children to have already been placed in the network. Thus, an operator's last mapped boundary child completes the placement of the operator itself. Once a coordinator receives a MAP message, it computes a minimal cost placement for the operators within the subtree assigned to it, using the placement metadata. The MAP messages are sent only for subtree roots based on our workload assignment. We implicitly assume that sources are thus coordinators for leaves, and simply forward the map message based on the LR path they receive.

In the Edge algorithm, computing the least cost mapping of an operator occurs as described in Section 3. In the decentralized scenario, we may potentially have to reconfigure the mapping of the tree below this point, to ensure that our overlay is correctly built. We turn to how we perform this reconfiguration step shortly. Recall that the common location metadata was included in LR paths. Following placement, we compute the parent's cost at all common locations for each ancestor. This is a precomputation step that we utilize when placing the parent's ancestors.

Backtracked placement. We take the following steps should our subtree placement require a reconfiguration of its boundary children (e.g., if it is placed at a common location shared by its children). An OPERATOR_REMAPPED message, containing a configuration, is sent to each reconfigured child's coordinator. The coordinator verifies that the placement is valid by checking for its existence in the possible configurations for the child. The placement is then invalidated at its previous location with an INVALIDATE_MAP message, and sent to the newly mapped location via a OPERATOR_MAPPED message. We check if further reconfiguration is necessary, to enable the desired placement and cost. If so, this remapping process continues down the tree.

Final placement. The final step in subtree mapping simply involves sending OPERATOR_MAPPED messages to the locations of each operator in the newly mapped subtree. We batch our reconfigurations and placement notifications until an entire subtree is mapped by a coordinator, to improve the control efficiency. Following this, the mapping process repeats itself when we send a MAP request from the subtree root's location, to the location of the next ancestor in the LR paths received from the boundary children.

4.3 Edge+

The distributed version of Edge+ follows the same strategy as the distributed Edge, but is augmented to incorporate topology information into the protocol. The protocol employs a similar placement decision to its corresponding centralized version. The protocol is thus responsible for providing the necessary network state for every operator to our placement mechanism.

In Edge, a coordinator mapping a subtree collected an optimal configuration for each of the subtree's boundary children, in addition to the configurations for common locations. In this version of the algorithm, we extend this to include the configurations at each boundary child's descendant locations. We also aggregate each child's localised network view. The network view contains metadata on the network state, such as latencies between particular nodes. Furthermore, we collect metadata as necessary, namely pairwise distances between descendant locations. This network view is initially empty, and transported by our OPERATOR_MAPPED and MAP messages. This configuration cost and topology metadata for each descendant location is used in the Edge+ placement mechanism described in section 3.3.

Note however that this approach is not entirely equivalent to the centralized version. In the centralized version, we were able to compute an operator's cost at any of its siblings' descendant locations. Since we precompute placement costs in the decentralized algorithm to produce a two-phase protocol, we cannot precompute the cost of an operator at its siblings' descendant locations unless we know these locations a priori. This implies both a larger search space, and, more importantly, more number of rounds for our algorithm to operate, given that we would have an extra round of all pairs of siblings exchanging descendant location metadata.

4.4 In-Network Placement

We now describe the distributed version of the In-Network approach, which enables operators to be mapped and executed at arbitrary peers. Earlier, we observed that a coordinator performing a mapping requires optimization metadata containing configurations and distances between potential locations. With this information, the existing placement mechanism is sufficiently general to place an operator at any of the given locations.

The question we address involves selecting *interesting peers*: a set of locations from the topology, that are potentially good candidates upon which to place the operator, in addition to the stream sources locations. This requires performing a "walk" on the network discovering the existence of peers and tracking their distances. Our selection of such "interesting" locations is based on a shortest path tree between the application proxy and the source servers. Specifically, this is a shortest path tree on the Tapestry overlay, and is simply obtained using the routes to each source server. We collect this location information while initially distributing the workload to each source. This set of candidate locations is included in every MAP message, and is used during the placement of each operator.

4.5 Delay-Constrained Placement

We now describe protocol modifications to handle the delay-constrained placement problem. Under our modular approach to distributed optimization, we simply adapt the content of messages in our protocol, to feed additional metadata into our local heuristic to find a solution. To provide this input to our optimization mechanisms, we first modify our local state. We now require that each peer maintains constraint metadata, for each configuration in its operators mapped table. For delay bounds, this is a list of running totals of path delays, of operator-source paths in partially constructed overlays, as well as the constraint itself. In our protocol, this list of path delays is added to the OPERATOR_MAPPED and MAP messages.

In the OPERATOR_MAPPED and MAP messages sent to the sources, we start with a path delay list containing the delay between the source and the proxy. During placement, path delays are aggregated at each operator, and undergo a triangulation transformation. Specifically, we consider each delay list element in turn, and remove the path delay between the corresponding child's placement and the proxy. We then add the delay between the operator's placement and the proxy to every list element. This triangulation is performed whenever an operator is mapped to a different location than any of its children. This approach ensures that we provide correct path delays for partially built overlays of subtrees, whenever we search for valid configurations.

5 Algorithm Analysis

In this section, we briefly analyse our algorithms in order to provide approximate bounds on their (1) bandwidth efficiency (i.e., the ability to reduce the bandwidth necessary to execute a processing tree), (2) computational complexity, and (3) message complexity (in the distributed scenario).

Bandwidth efficiency. Let us consider a processing tree with maximum fanout d, and height $h + 1$. This tree has d^h leaves, and let us consider that these leaves are placed at k distinct locations in our network topology, where $0 < k \leq d^h$. We index operators in the processing tree as o_i^j, representing an operator at height j, and tree layer index i. Operators within a tree layer j are numbered left to right from $\{1, \ldots, d^j\}$. In the experimental evaluation that follows, we compare the cost of our overlays to a baseline cost. This baseline cost is viewed as the cost of evaluating the processing tree in a centralized manner, namely at the proxy itself. Our first analytical result is to quantify the probability, P_S, that our mapping algorithms are able to achieve any reduction in bandwidth over this baseline cost.

We now introduce more terminology for this analysis. We define the baseline cost as the bandwidth incurred during transfer of each source to the proxy. These costs are denoted $\{c_1^h, c_2^h, c_3^h, \ldots c_{d^h}^h\}$, and correspond to costs for operators $\{o_1^h, o_2^h, o_3^h, \ldots, o_{d^h}^h\}$. Furthermore, in the algorithms incorporating topology information, we need to distinguish between costs of operators at different locations. This is represented by a prefix subscript, $_l o_i^j$, giving the cost of operator o_i^j at location l. The baseline cost is thus, $C_B = \sum_{i=0}^{d_h} c_i^h$. We assume that the costs of sources correspond to the rates of the data streams they represent, and as such are chosen uniformly at random between two size bounds. Our mapping algorithm allows us to state that operators are mapped to a child location only if the cost at that location is less than the cost at the proxy location. Therefore we are interested in the probability that each operator at height $h + 1$ has a smaller cost at the proxy location, than at the locations of operators at height h, for the baseline cost to apply. For an arbitrary operator at height h this holds if its cost is larger at the location we are considering mapping to, than the minimum cost of any its children at this specific location, i.e $_l c_i^h > \min\{_l c_{d^i}^{h+1}, \ldots, _l c_{d^{i+1}-1}^{h+1}\}$. Furthermore, this must hold over all locations, implying

$$c_i^h > \max_l \min\{_l c_{d^i}^{h+1}, \ldots, _l c_{d^{i+1}-1}^{h+1}\}$$
$$> \max\{c_{d^i}^{h+1}, \ldots, c_{d^{i+1}-1}^{h+1}\} \quad \text{(fixed leaf locations)}$$

Above, we note that for leaves, this minimum is simply the cost of the leaf actually at the location (since we assume leaves are at fixed locations) and we drop the location prefix. For the baseline overlay to be output by our algorithm, this must additionally hold across all operators at level $h - 1$. Choosing all of these costs from a uniform random distribution, we may state the probability of the above condition as:

$$Pr(c_i^h > \max\{c_{d^i}^{h+1}, \ldots, c_{d^{i+1}-1}^{h+1}\}) = \frac{1}{d+1}$$

This yields a probability that our algorithm improves over the baseline cost of:

$$P_S = 1 - \left(\frac{1}{d+1}\right)^{d^h}$$

Note that the probability that we choose the baseline cost decreases exponentially as our processing tree size increases (in terms of width and depth). For our algorithm that is capable of mapping operators to arbitrary locations, this probability acts as a lower bound, since we may still optimize the cost of our placement even if the costs of operators at level $h - 1$ are greater than at level h, but we omit the analysis of this scenario for brevity.

Computational complexity. In the centralized algorithm, a simple greedy algorithm considering placing each operator at each leaf location has complexity $\mathcal{O}(k \times \frac{d^h-1}{d-1})$. Recall that k represents the number of unique sources our leaves are assumed to be placed at. The term $\frac{d^h-1}{d-1}$ represents the number of internal operators in our processing tree whom we must place. Our algorithm performing placements on the sources alone (without topology information) reduces this complexity as follows. When we attempt to map an operator o_i^j, we consider only the minimum cost placement for the children $\{o_{d^i}^{j+1}, \ldots, o_{d^{i+1}-1}^{j+1}\}$, and the cost at any common locations of these children if they exist. Considering minimum cost placements has complexity $\mathcal{O}(d)$ per operator. We may also bound the number of common locations an operator's children may share based on the operator's depth. Additionally, we state that the children of an operator at depth j share at most $\min(\lfloor d^{h-j} \rfloor, \frac{d^h-k}{d-1})$ common locations. The first term in this value for the number of common locations captures the number of descendant leaves, while the second captures the greatest number of common locations that may arise given k unique leaf locations. Combining these two, the computational complexity of our algorithm placing elements at sources only without topology information is:

$$\mathcal{O}((d + \min(\lfloor d^{h-j} \rfloor, \frac{d^h-k}{d-1})) \times \frac{d^h-1}{d-1})$$

Intuitively, from the analysis above, we notice that as the number of unique locations increases, we perform fewer computations of placements for common locations. In the algorithms utilising topology information, placing each internal operator also requires computing placement costs for permutations of descendant locations. For placement at arbitrary locations this is exponential in terms of the topology size, motivating the need for a heuristic in selecting our set of candidate locations. However, we omit the analysis of our heuristic for the sake of brevity.

Message complexity. We finally briefly discuss the message complexity of our distributed tree mapping algorithms. We start with the first phase, namely the workload distribution to the coordinators. We assume a coordinators are responsible for mapping subtrees of size d^{t+1}, implying mapping requires d^{h-t} coordinators. Populating the boundary children tables requires $\mathcal{O}(d^{h-t})$ ADD_SUBTREE messages. Subsequently we send MAP and OPERATOR_MAPPED messages to the sources, of whom, in the worst case, there are $\mathcal{O}(d^h)$. The two stages yield our initialization overhead of $\mathcal{O}(d^h)$ messages. We now consider a map request sent to a coordinator whose subtree depth is $j \in \{1, \ldots, \frac{h+1}{t+1}\}$. First we collect the necessary topology information, requiring $\mathcal{O}((d-1) \times d^{2(h+1-j(t+1))})$ messages. The first component represents the partitions between whom we collect pairwise distances, and the second represents the number of locations in each partition. We also incur messages to notify operators of their placements, specifically $\mathcal{O}(d^{t+1})$ OPERATOR_MAPPED messages. Finally we forward the map message, yielding a total of approximately $\mathcal{O}(d^t + (d-1)d^{2(h-jt)})$ messages per map request (relabelling our height and subtree sizes). This sums over d^{h-t} coordinators, of varying subtree depth, yielding a total complexity of mapping all internal operators of:

$$\mathcal{O}(d^h + (d-1)\sum_{j=1}^{h/t} d^{2(h-jt)}) = \mathcal{O}(d^h + d^{h(h-1)/t})$$

Intuitively, this reflects a smaller control overhead as we increase the subtree size. Note that in many cases we may utilise batching to deliver multiple messages to a single source, reducing control overhead. Analytically this is reflected above with bounds $\mathcal{O}(\min(k, d^i))$ replacing $\mathcal{O}(d^i)$ whenever we consider the number of operators at depth i. However a tighter bound analysis lies outside the scope of this paper.

6 Experimental Evaluation

6.1 Experimental Setup

We built an initial prototype system running the algorithms of Section 4 on top of Tapestry, using the OCaml language. In the experiments, we simulated the underlying network: the network topologies used were obtained from the GT-ITM [25] topology generator. We generated ten independent transit-stub topologies (14 transit domains, with 500ms of longest pair-wise path delay between stub nodes).

We generated our workload of processing trees with specific characteristics: unless stated otherwise, we considered binary trees with depths ranging from three to five. Operator selectivities were also selected uniformly at random from [0,1]. Unless otherwise specified, all results shown are averaged over ten independent runs, each mapping 100 processing trees.

In the experiments, we compare the distributed versions of Edge, Edge+, and In-Network, to a naive approach, called *baseline*. Baseline simulates an on-line warehousing model where all the streams are forwarded to the proxy (using shortest paths) for processing.

We control the placement of the data sources, to better understand the consequences of varying placements, using two metrics: *average proxy distance (APD)* and *average server distance (ASD)*. Average proxy distance represents the average distance between the application proxy and each source. Average server distance represents the average distance between a source and every other source, for all sources. Using these two metrics, we define three interesting configurations: *uniform*, *star*, and *cluster*. In uniform, as the name implies, all servers and proxies are uniformly spread (APD and ASD values to be equal to 0.4 of the length of the network diameter). In the star placement, the proxy lies near the "centroid" of the sources. In the experiments, we fix the APD to be approximately half of the ASD. In the cluster topology, the sources each has a considerably larger distance to the proxy, than between themselves. We achieve this configuration with an APD approximately twice that of the ASD. Figure 5 illustrates these source-proxy location configurations.

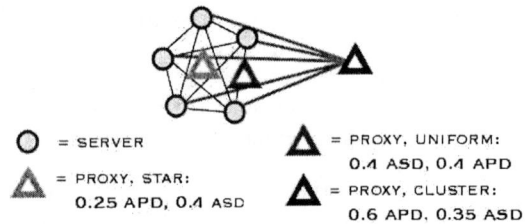

Figure 5: Source-proxy location scenarios: *star, uniform, cluster*.

As the key efficiency metric, we use *bandwidth consumption ratio*, which quantifies the ratio of the overall bandwidth consumed by a given approach to that of the baseline. To quantify the effectiveness of the system, we present results for overlay *stretch*, which is the ratio of the longest path length on the constructed overlay to the longest path length from the sources to the proxy (path lengths are specified in terms of delay). For simplicity, we ignore operator processing costs as well as operator queueing delays. As a result, stretch is an estimate of the extra latency that the system incurs (when producing result tuples) when yielding the bandwidth savings estimated by the bandwidth consumption ratio. We also investigate our algorithms' behaviours by tracking the percentages of operators placed at the proxy, at sources and inside the network. These two metrics are commonly used when evaluating large-scale networked systems.

6.2 Basic Algorithm Comparison

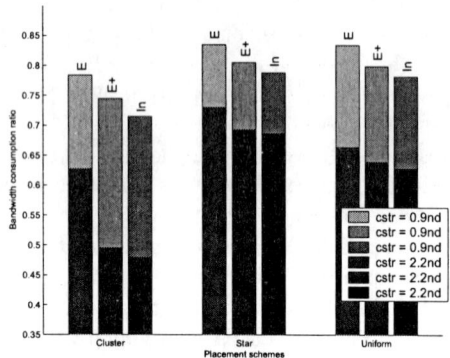

Figure 6: Bandwidth consumption ratio for various source and proxy locations.

Our first set of experiments compare the three placement algorithms described in Section 3. Figure 6 shows the bandwidth consumption ratio achieved by each mapping algorithm, for the three network configurations described above, for tight and loose delay constraints (120 and 300 ms, defined as a ratio of the average network diameter, nd). We see that the algorithms perform similarly on both the star and uniform placement schemes. In turn, the cluster scenario seems to offer greater scope for optimization. Furthermore, relaxing the delay constraint has little effect on the bandwidth consumption ratio. Both Edge+ and In-network consistently offer advantages in the bandwidth consumption ratio, over Edge, across all placement schemes. Utilizing topology information is clearly benefi-

cial, especially in the loosely constrained cluster scenario. It is difficult to differentiate Edge+ and In-network for the star and uniform scenarios. This result arises because the proxy acts as the ideal intermediate location where the streams can be pushed and executed.

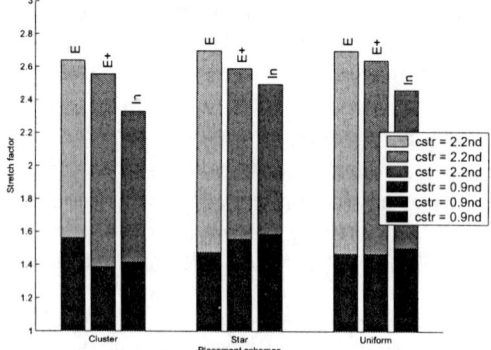

Figure 7: Latency stretch for various source and proxy locations.

In Figure 7 we investigate the effects of the three algorithms on the stretch factor. The Edge algorithm exhibits a worse stretch factor under all loosely constrained scenarios. However, Edge is comparable to Edge+ and In-network under the tightly constrained scenarios. This is a direct effect of the tightness of the constraint requiring placements similar to the baseline mapping. In the loosely constrained placement, In-network consistently outperforms Edge+. Here, In-network yields a lower stretch factor, due to the placement of operators between the cluster of sources and the proxy. Operator placement generally occurs in the "direction" of the proxy, creating a mapping of tree paths tending towards shortest network paths. Meanwhile, in Edge+, there is no such consideration of direction, implying streams may be temporarily pushed away from the direction of the proxy, lengthening the end-to-end delay. In the tightly constrained scenario, In-network tends to perform worse than Edge+, because it achieves a better optimization for bandwidth consumption. Here Edge+ is less capable of performing optimization, and has a greater tendency to simply push streams directly to the proxy, yielding a lower end-to-end delay.

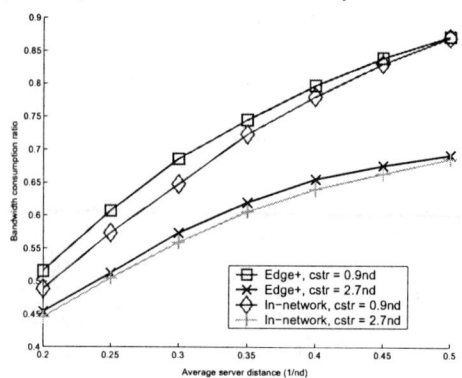

Figure 8: Source distribution effects on bandwidth.

Figure 8 shows the effects of varying the ASD (as a ratio of the network diameter) upon the bandwidth consumption

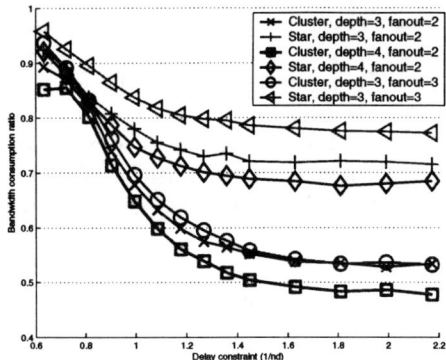

Figure 9: Impact of processing tree structure on bandwidth.

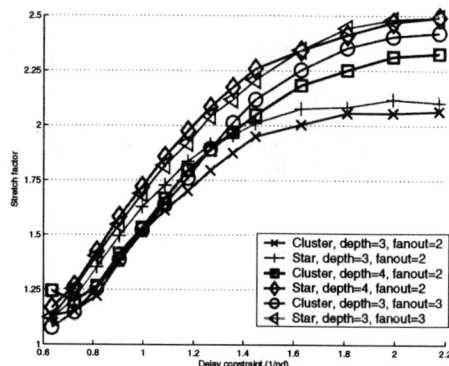

Figure 10: Impact of processing tree structure on latency.

ratio, for the cluster configuration. We see that, in general, as sources are placed further and further apart, the bandwidth consumption ratio increases. Since our cost function representing bandwidth is proportional to distance, this result is to be expected. We also observe that for tight constraints, the rate of this increase is far greater. Under tight constraints, we have little possibility of improving the cost, and so as sources are separated, we tend to the baseline approach. Under loose constraints, we may actually still perform optimizations at larger source separations, resulting in a shallower gradient for the increase in the bandwidth consumption ratio.

6.3 Varying the Processing Tree Structure

We now study the effects of the processing tree structure upon the bandwidth consumption ratio and stretch factor, when mapped by the In-network algorithm (we omit the results for Edge and Edge+ to simplify the presentation, as In-network dominates these algorithms in terms of bandwidth efficiency).

Figure 9 shows the bandwidth consumption ratio as a function of the delay constraint, for three forms of processing trees. First, as the delay constraint gets looser, the bandwidth consumption initially decreases, prior to tailing off. This occurs because the constraint becomes less and less restrictive on our feasible configurations, and stops interfering with the optimization. We witness that deeper trees result in lower bandwidth consumption, while wider trees result in a larger bandwidth consumption ratio. Deeper trees offer scope for optimization since there are a larger number of internal operators whom we may place into more elaborate configurations. Operators with higher degrees (i.e., fanout) prove more problematic to place, we directly affect data flows to a larger number of operators. Hence there is less scope for optimization, when the sources reside at a large number of unique locations.

Figure 10 plots the stretch factor as a function of delay constraint, for varying processing tree characteristics. Stretch factor behaves as a dual to the bandwidth consumption ratio. As the delay constraint is loosened, the stretch factor rises, but tails off as the constraint has less and less effect. Both deeper and wider trees result in a larger stretch factor, and a later tail-off point. In both cases the larger stretch factor is a direct effect of the increased number of operators that must be mapped.

6.4 Selectivity Impact

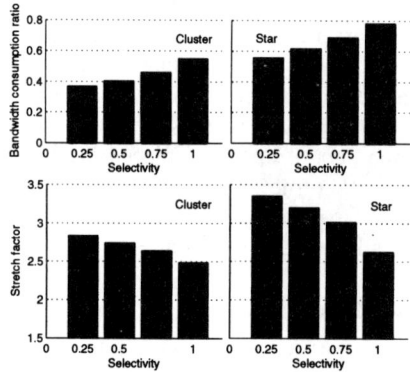

Figure 11: Impact of operator selectivities on bandwidth and latency.

We now study the impact of operator selectivities on the bandwidth consumption ratio and stretch factors. Figure 11 shows these effects for four selectivity values. Note that these selectivities are an upper bound on the actual operator selectivities, which are chosen uniformly at random from 0 to the bound. We see that as the selectivity approaches a value of 1, the bandwidth consumption ratio for both the cluster and star placement schemes increase. This is because selectivity is a direct indicator for the scope of potentially optimizing a tree; operators with selectivities close to 1 incur similar bandwidth consumption regardless of where they are placed. We also see that star placements generally have higher bandwidth consumption ratios, consistent with the results shown earlier. In terms of stretch factors, we observe that increasing selectivity results in a decreasing stretch factor. Operators with unit selectivities cannot be placed using as elaborate a configuration as operators high low selectivities. Hence the paths in our tree mappings tend to more strongly resemble the baseline mapping, since such operators are generally tightly grouped.

To provide a deeper intuition for these results, we show in Figure 12 percentages of operators that are placed at the proxy, or inside the network, for varying selectivities. Operators that are placed at neither the proxy nor inside the network are obviously placed at the sources (not ex-

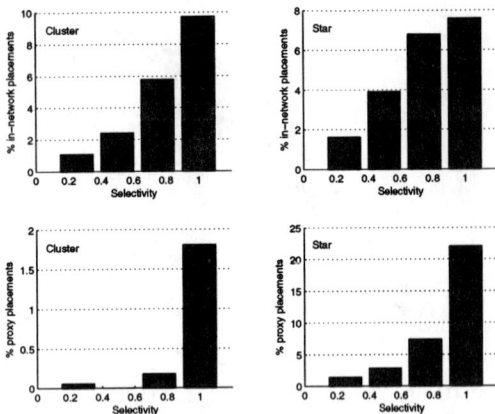

Figure 12: Operator location distributions.

plicitly shown). The algorithm generally tends to utilize in-network placements when sources are clustered moreso than when sources lie in the star formation. Furthermore, in a star placement scheme, operators are generally more likely to be placed at the proxy than at sources, when compared to a cluster placement. Examining these values per selectivity value, we see that less selective operators result in larger numbers of operators placed inside the network. This trend is also true for the operators that are placed at the proxy. As expected, highly selective operators are being pushed all the way to the sources.

7 Related Work

The work presented in this paper is related to several topics in distributed and parallel databases and systems, and networking.

Distributed query processing. Distributed query optimization and in particular the site selection problem are closely related to our work and have been explored extensively in the context of distributed and federated databases [9, 10, 15, 16, 23]. To the best of our knowledge, none of these approaches address widely-distributed processing and network awareness, and are thus well represented by the Edge approach.

More recent work addressed Internet-scale query processing and distribution scalability. IrisNet [8] focuses on querying wide-area sensor databases using XPath queries. IrisNet relies on the DNS to identify the remote databases relevant to a given query, which is then processed using XML and XPath specific optimizations. Similar to our work, PIER [12] addresses DHT-based highly-distributed query processing, although in a pull-based setting. PIER discusses how CAN [19] can be used as a hashing function on the indexes of relations, distributing tuples across a very large number of sites. While PIER and our work share many common goals, there are also some significant differences. Our algorithms attempt a finer-grained control of the placement decisions, whereas in PIER, the operations themselves are randomly distributed across peers by CAN. The semantic details of our operators are abstracted away from the placement mechanism. Instead we focus on optimizing the network positioning of operators, and as such,

operator specific optimizations such as those presented by PIER may still apply.

In-network query processing has been studied in the context of sensor databases. Recent work by Madden *et al.* [17] demonstrated the advantages of in-network data aggregation in a wireless multi-hop sensor network. In such a resource-constrained environment, potential optimizations are severely restricted and network scalability is typically not a key design goal.

Stream processing and continuous queries. Recently, there has been much work on data-stream processing (e.g., [1, 4, 5, 6, 18, 21]). Most of these efforts have commonly assumed an on-line warehousing model where all source streams are routed to a central site where they are processed. There have also been some preliminary proposals that extend the single-site model to multi-site, distributed models and environments [2, 7, 21]. Our work is also a step in this general direction.

NiagaraCQ [6] is a continuous query processing system designed for Internet-scale query processing. Babcock and Olston [2] investigated the use of adaptive filters that are executed at the stream sources based on per-query precision requirements registered at stream sources. Neither of these work investigated network-aware operator placement issues that we discuss here.

Overlay networks. Overlay networks [14, 22, 26] strive to address scalability and fault tolerance issues that arise in large-scale content distribution, using the same principles of in-network processing during message routing. Intermediate routers are envisaged as having the capability to perform certain functionality on the messages they forward. Our work can be regarded as addressing how to distribute "active networking" functionality across the overlay network servers, an issue that has not yet been addressed.

Distributed task partitioning. The parallel computing community has long studied the distribution and allocation of tasks in homogeneous distributed environments. Grid computing researchers have also developed architectures tailored to large-scale scientific applications, that perform resource allocation to servers much in the same way we map operators to locations. One common approach to allocating tasks is a multilevel graph partitioning algorithm [3, 11]. This approach partitions the computational structure of an application in an attempt to minimize the resulting data flow across partitions. The models proposed do not leverage application specific characteristics, such as selectivity, rather they are purely concerned with application structure. Furthermore, these approaches have not yet addressed wide distribution and network scalability, our main concerns in this study.

8 Conclusions and Future Work

With the proliferation of applications that involve sophisticated processing of large numbers of distributed data sources, there is a growing need for generic widely-distributed query processing services. Such systems will be fundamentally network-oriented. We believe that network scalability, which has been largely ignored by previous efforts, will be a key design goal for next-generation data processing systems. This paper addresses one of the key challenges towars achieving this goal.

We argued that widely-distributed query processing can greatly benefit from *network awareness* in terms of improved bandwidth efficiency and result latency. Previous approaches largely ignored the impact of the characteristics of the interconnecting network and the relative locations of the servers on processing. We presented network-aware operator placement algorithms and described in detail their distributed implementation, on top of a DHT infrastructure, for distributed stream processing. We analyzed the algorithms and experimentally evaluated them using a prototype implementation and realistic network models. Comparison with representative network-unaware approaches verified the benefits that can be attained through the use of network information and in-network processing.

There are several important directions for future research. One immediate direction involves exploiting opportunities for sharing among multiple queries during the mapping process. Another direction involves exploiting semantic, operator-specific optimization opportunities. Finally, we would like to integrate our prototype with Borealis (follow-on to Aurora [1]) and verify the validity of the results presented here with a real application and deployment.

This work has been done in the context of the SAND project. SAND strives to extend core data management and processing functionality to highly-distributed environments and applications. This work is an initial step in this general direction.

Acknowledgements

We are grateful to John Jannotti, Eli Upfal, Stan Zdonik, and the anonymous reviewers for valuable discussions and feedback.

References

[1] D. J. Abadi, D. Carney, U. Çetintemel, M. Cherniack, C. Convey, S. Lee, M. Stonebraker, N. Tatbul, and S. Zdonik. Aurora: A new model and architecture for data stream management. *The VLDB Journal: The International Journal on Very Large Data Bases*, 2003.

[2] B. Babcock and C. Olston. Distributed top-k monitoring. In *Proc. of the 2003 ACM SIGMOD International Conference on Management of Data*, June 2003.

[3] R. Biswas, B. Hendrickson, and G. Karypis. Graph partitioning and parallel computing. *Parallel Computing*, 26(12):1515–1517, Nov. 2000.

[4] D. Carney, U. Çetintemel, M. Cherniack, C. Convey, S. Lee, G. Seidman, M. Stonebraker, N. Tatbul, and S. Zdonik. Monitoring streams: A new class of data management applications. In *Proc. of the 28th International Conference on Very Large Data Bases (VLDB'02)*, Aug. 2002.

[5] S. Chandrasekaran, A. Deshpande, M. Franklin, and J. Hellerstein. TelegraphCQ: Continuous dataflow processing for an uncertain world. In *Proc. of the First Biennial Conference on Innovative Data Systems Research (CIDR'03)*, Jan. 2003.

[6] J. Chen, D. J. DeWitt, F. Tian, and Y. Wang. NiagaraCQ: A scalable continuous query system for Internet databases. In *Proc. of the 2000 ACM SIGMOD International Conference on Management of Data*, May 2000.

[7] M. Cherniack, H. Balakrishnan, M. Balazinska, D. Carney, U. Çetintemel, Y. Xing, and S. Zdonik. Scalable distributed stream processing. In *Proc. of the First Biennial Conference on Innovative Data Systems Research (CIDR'03)*, Jan. 2003.

[8] A. Deshpande, S. Nath, P. B. Gibbons, and S. Seshan. Cache-and-query for wide area sensor databases. In *Proc. of the 2003 ACM SIGMOD International Conference on Management of Data*, June 2003.

[9] M. J. Franklin, B. T. Jónsson, and D. Kossmann. Performance tradeoffs for client-server query processing. *SIGMOD Record (ACM Special Interest Group on Management of Data)*, 25(2):149–160, June 1996.

[10] L. M. Haas, D. Kossmann, E. L. Wimmers, and J. Yang. Optimizing queries across diverse data sources. In *Proceedings of the 23rd International Conference on Very Large Databases*, Aug. 1997.

[11] B. Hendrickson and R. Leland. A multilevel algorithm for partitioning graphs. In *Supercomputing'95*, 1995.

[12] R. Huebsch, J. M. Hellerstein, N. L. Boon, T. Loo, S. Shenker, and I. Stoica. Querying the Internet with PIER. In *Proc. of the 29th International Conference on Very Large Data Bases (VLDB'03)*, Sept. 2003.

[13] Y. E. Ioannidis and Y. Kang. Randomized algorithms for optimizing large join queries. In *Proc. of the 1990 ACM SIGMOD international conference on Management of data*, June 1990.

[14] J. Jannotti, D. K. Gifford, K. L. Johnson, M. F. Kaashoek, and J. W. O'Toole, Jr. Overcast: Reliable multicasting with an overlay network. In *Proceedings of the 2000 Fourth Symposium on Operating Systems Design and Implementation (OSDI 2000)*, San Diego, California, Oct. 2000.

[15] D. Kossmann. The state of the art in distributed query processing. *ACM Computing Surveys*, 32(4):422–469, 2000.

[16] L. F. Mackert and G. M. Lohman. R* optimizer validation and performance evaluation for local queries. In *Proc. of the 1986 ACM SIGMOD International Conference on Management of Data*, pages 84–95. ACM Press, 1986.

[17] S. Madden, M. J. Franklin, J. Hellerstein, and W. Hong. TAG: A tiny aggregation service for ad-hoc sensor networks. In *Proceedings of the 5th USENIX Symposium on Operating Systems Design and Implementation (OSDI '02)*, Boston, Massachusetts, Dec. 2002.

[18] R. Motwani, J. Widom, A. Arasu, B. Babcock, S. Babu, M. Datar, G. Manku, C. Olston, J. Rosenstein, and R. Varma. Query processing, approximation, and resource management in a data stream management system. In *Proc. of the First Biennial Conference on Innovative Data Systems Research (CIDR'03)*, Jan. 2003.

[19] S. Ratnasamy, P. Francis, M. Handley, R. Karp, and S. Schenker. A scalable content-addressable network. In *Proceedings of the ACM SIGCOMM '01 Conference*. ACM Press, 2001.

[20] A. I. T. Rowstron and P. Druschel. Pastry: Scalable, decentralized object location, and routing for large-scale peer-to-peer systems. In *Proceedings of the IFIP/ACM International Conference on Distributed Systems Platforms Heidelberg*. Springer-Verlag, 2001.

[21] M. A. Shah, J. M. Hellerstein, S. Chandrasekaran, and M. J. Franklin. Flux: An adaptive partitioning operator for continuous query systems. In *Proc. of the 19th International Conference on Data Engineering (ICDE 2003)*, Mar. 2003.

[22] I. Stoica, R. Morris, D. Karger, M. F. Kaashoek, and H. Balakrishnan. Chord: A scalable peer-to-peer lookup service for internet applications. In *Proceedings of the ACM SIGCOMM '01 Conference*. ACM Press, 2001.

[23] A. Tomasic, L. Raschid, and P. Valduriez. Scaling heterogeneous databases and the design of disco. In *Proceedings of the 16th International Conference on Distributed Computing Systems (ICDCS '96)*. IEEE Computer Society, 1996.

[24] S. Viglas and J. F. Naughton. Rate-based query optimization for streaming information sources. In *Proc. of the 2002 ACM SIGMOD International Conference on Management of Data*, June 2002.

[25] E. W. Zegura, K. L. Calvert, and S. Bhattacharjee. How to model an internetwork. In *IEEE Infocom*, volume 2, pages 594–602, San Francisco, CA, March 1996.

[26] B. Y. Zhao, L. Huang, S. C. Rhea, J. Stribling, A. D. Joseph, and J. D. Kubiatowicz. Tapestry: A global-scale overlay for rapid service deployment. *IEEE J-SAC*, 22(1):41–53, January 2004.

Data Sharing Through Query Translation in Autonomous Sources

Anastasios Kementsietsidis   Marcelo Arenas

Dept. of Computer Science
University of Toronto
{tasos,marenas}@cs.toronto.edu

Abstract

We consider the problem of data sharing between autonomous data sources in an environment where constraints cannot be placed on the shared contents of sources. Our solutions rely on the use of mapping tables which define how data from different sources are associated. In this setting, the answer to a local query, that is, a query posed against the schema of a single source, is augmented by retrieving related data from associated sources. This retrieval of data is achieved by translating, through mapping tables, the local query into a set of queries that are executed against the associated sources. We consider both sound translations (which only retrieve correct answers) and complete translations (which retrieve all correct answers, and no incorrect answers) and we present algorithms to compute such translations. Our solutions are implemented and tested experimentally and we describe here our key findings.

1 Introduction

We consider the problem of data sharing between autonomous structured data sources. Such sources may use different schemas to structure their data. Furthermore, both the data and the schemas of the sources may overlap little, if at all. Still, data residing in the different sources may be closely associated.

As an example, consider the domain of biological data sources. Different biological data sources can store inherently different data which range from data for genes or proteins to data for genetic diseases. Nevertheless, these diverse data sets are closely associated since genes *encode for* proteins and are related to genetic diseases.

How can we share data in such a setting? In the domain of biological sources, we can imagine that a biologist who queries her local source for information on a particular protein, say OPH, would like to retrieve, in addition to the local data, related information that is found in any number of networked sources including related genes that encode for protein OPH and genetic diseases related to these genes. To support such sharing of data, we must be able to translate the local query into the vocabulary of the other sources. This involves translating both the structure of the query to use the schema elements of the associated sources, but also the data itself. For example, associated sources may use synonyms of protein OPH, such as APH and AARE, or distinct identifiers for the same gene.

Notice that the related data that each source returns may be very different and it is often not possible to make this data conform to the local schema. For conformance to be possible, the local database must have anticipated the structure of all possible answers to a query. Mappings are needed to fit these structures into the local schema. Such a solution may be undesirable for several reasons. First, we may not wish to change the local schema to accommodate data for which it was not designed. In our example, the query results may be returned to users and not stored locally, so it seems onerous to insist that even virtual local structures be predefined for receiving this data. Second, if any of the networked data sources change their schemas, the local database must, somehow, become aware of this and update its mappings. Otherwise, the translated queries may not be valid on the updated sources. Again, this is an onerous requirement.

Data sharing deals with the exchange of data between heterogeneous sources whose data need not be interdependent and may represent different real world domains. In keeping with the literature, we refer to such autonomous, heterogeneous sources as peers. Data sharing between peers differs from the well-studied problems of data integration [12] and data exchange [6]. The latter two problems use schema-level mappings to express the relationships between heterogeneous schemas. In data integration, these mappings are used, at run time, to conform the data of one source to the schema of another. In data exchange, the mappings are used to populate a target schema with the data of a source schema.

In this work, we consider how to translate queries in the absence of such restrictive schema-level mappings. We make use of a form of data-level mappings called *mapping tables* which we first introduced in [11]. In brief, a mapping table contains a set of data associations between data values in two peer databases. Our previous work showed how to *automate* the management of mapping tables by checking the consistency of the associations and by inferring new associations from existing ones. Our current work focuses on how to use mapping tables during query answering. Our main contributions are:

– We introduce the semantics of query answering in an environment of autonomous peers. The semantics relies on the translation of queries between the peers through the use of mapping tables.

– We introduce the notions of sound translations (which only retrieve correct answers) and complete translations (which retrieve all correct answers, and no incorrect answers) to characterize the relationship between translated queries.

– We extend the definition of mapping tables to store not only associations between data values, but also associations between pairs of translated queries. This common representation of different types of associations permits more systematic and robust solutions for managing the associations.

– We present an algorithm for computing complete translations and an algorithm for testing if a query is a sound translation of another. We use the latter algorithm, and our ability to store past translations in mapping tables, to determine if a query can be translated (partially or in full) by means of the stored translations.

This paper is organized as follows. We motivate our solutions in Section 2, while Section 3 describes the related work. Section 4 presents the semantics of query answering and introduces the notions of sound and complete translations. Section 5 presents the algorithms for computing such translations. Section 6 discusses our implementation while Section 7 presents the experimental results. We conclude in Section 8 with a summary of the work.

2 Motivating example

In what follows, we consider two biological databases, namely MedLine and PubMed [1]. A portion of their schemas and instances can be seen in Figures 1 (a) and (b), respectively. Both databases store similar information about articles, namely, an article identifier, some keywords, which refer to protein names mentioned in the article, and date of publication (PubMed stores the month (pm) and year (py) of publication, while MedLine stores only the year). In spite of the similarities in their schemas, the databases use different vocabularies to describe articles. For one thing, the two databases use their own local identifiers. Furthermore, they often refer to the same protein by using different names. For instance, OPH in MedLine and APH in PubMed refer to the same protein. We can use mapping tables to represent how values from different vocabularies may correspond [11]. In the same figure, we show examples of such tables. Mapping table *keyword2kw* associates keywords from MedLine to keywords in the PubMed relation. Notice that not all keywords from MedLine are mapped, that is, the tables might be incomplete. Mapping table *id2id* stores the identifiers of articles that are mentioned in both databases. Finally, mapping table *year2yr* uses a variable in its single tuple to represent the identity function, i.e., that each year in the first database is mapped to itself in the second. We note that not all attributes need to be mapped through mapping tables. For example, no table involves attribute pm of the PubMed relation.

Example 1 *Assume that a user wants to retrieve all MedLine articles that mention protein OPH. Then a query such as the following may be used:*

Q_1: **select** *
    from *MedLine*
    where *keyword = "OPH"*

What if this user also wants to retrieve all PubMed articles mentioning the same protein? Given that APH and AARE are synonyms of OPH, the following query may be used:

Q_2: **select** *
    from *PubMed*
    where *(kw = "APH"* **OR** *kw = "AARE")*

Mapping tables might provide us with sufficient information to automate the process of translating a query posed against one database to a query posed

article_id	keyword	year
20185348	OPH	2000
96281126	OPH	1996
87051725	NGF receptor	1986
99455262	CRAF1	1999
99455262	TNF receptor	1999

(a) MedLine relation instance

paper_id	kw	py	pm
10719179	APH	2000	March
8724851	AARE	1996	February
9915784	p75 ICD	1999	January
10944856	Sialidase 1	2000	July

(b) PubMed relation instance

keyword	kw
OPH	APH
OPH	AARE
NGF receptor	p75 ICD
G9 sialidase	Sialidase 1

(c) Table keyword2kw

article_id	paper_id
20185348	10719179

(d) Table id2id

year	py
$\mathcal{X}$	$\mathcal{X}$

(e) Table year2py

Figure 1: Instances and Mapping tables

against another, where both queries retrieve *related* data. The details of how this is achieved, and under which circumstances such a translation is possible, is the main focus of this work.

Notice that the retrieved data do not conform to the same schema. Even in this simple scenario, where the schemas are rather homogeneous, we cannot *merge* the results due to the difference in vocabularies. In general, we will not know before-hand what data we are going to retrieve and in what format. We expect that even the types of the retrieved data may differ significantly. For example, our biological scenario includes not only information about protein articles but also data about genes and diseases. One of the objectives of this work is to deal with this heterogeneity in the retrieved results.

Example 2 *Continuing with our example, assume now that the user decides to execute query Q_3 which retrieves PubMed articles mentioning protein APH:*

Q_3: **select** *
    from PubMed
    where kw = "APH"

Intuitively, query Q_3 satisfies the initial user selection requirements since it returns PubMed articles mentioning protein OPH. However, it does not retrieve all such articles. So, query Q_3 is incomplete, compared to Q_2. Nevertheless, neither query Q_2 nor query Q_3 return any incorrect answers, i.e., articles not mentioning protein OPH.

Notions such as correctness (soundness) and completeness of query translations are formalized in the next sections. Soundness is a property that every translation must satisfy, however, executing queries that are incomplete is often sufficient. For one thing, users are often satisfied with incomplete answers if complete answers are overwhelming. We may also be able to cache the results from sound queries to deliver some answers faster. From a systems point of view, we show that significant savings in computation time can be achieved by reusing sound queries.

Our last remark concerns our representation of queries. Mapping tables allow us to store, as part of our database, the associations of values between different peers [11]. Motivated by the same rational, we offer here a similar representation for associating queries and their translations. This uniform representation allows us to develop a common set of tools to manage both data and query associations.

3 Related work

Our previous work on mapping tables focuses on the management of the tables and how these can be used for value-based lookups [11]. Thus, it does not consider structured queries. In the context of peer-to-peer systems, advanced query mechanisms have been proposed by Harren et al [8] and Huebsch et al [9]. The latter work proposes structured query answering in an architecture that can scale to accommodate a large number of peers. However, peers must agree to support a common schema. Our work does not consider scalability issues but addresses instead issues relating to the heterogeneity of peers.

In Piazza, associations between peers are expressed through either global-as-view (GAV) or local-as-view (LAV) schema-level mappings [7, 14]. Both types of mappings are considered while translating queries between different peers. Our solutions are complimentary to this work since our framework operates in the absence of schema-level mappings and the only mappings used are in the data-level and have the form of mapping tables. The main difference between the two approaches is that while their work assumes that the retrieved data can be made to conform to the schema of the peer where a query is initiated, we make no such assumption.

Ng et al [15] also deal with the translation of queries in a network of peers. Descriptive keywords are used to associate schema elements of different peers. Then, the translation of queries is performed using the associated elements. A limitation of the approach is the underlying assumption that the keywords are used consistently throughout the peer network. Thus, unlike our work, their solutions cannot handle differences in the vocabularies within the data values of the peers.

The work of Chang and Garcia-Molina [5] also deals with the translation of queries between heterogeneous sources. There, syntactic rules are used to map selection predicates from one database to that of another. At first glance, mapping tables look like *materializations* of these syntactic rules. However, the two constructs operate under different assumptions. A syntactic rule that maps MedLine article identifiers to PubMed article identifiers assumes that for any identifier of the former we can *compute* an identifier of the latter. Thus, the query translation process relies on this assumption to translate a query from the former database to one in the latter without having to deal with the intricacies of the mappings at the data level, that is, the fact that mappings are often incomplete. Our work makes no such assumptions and our translation techniques deal with exactly these circumstances. We also use a *uniform* representation both for the rules, i.e., the mappings between data values and for the queries and the mappings between translated queries.

4 Query semantics

We assume that query execution in our peer network uses a *gossiping* mechanism. The process is initiated by the execution of a user-defined query locally in a peer. Then, the user-defined query is forwarded either *as is* or in some translated form to either all or to a selected number of acquaintances of the current peer. Then, the *execute-and-forward* step is repeated in each of the forwarded peers, causing in turn the further propagation of the query. The process terminates after a fixed number of propagations of the initial user-defined query has occurred.

In accordance with the above, we assume hereafter that each query is defined, in terms of syntax, with respect to the schema of a single peer. Our thesis is that for a user to issue a query, she need only be aware of the local schema she is using. Over this schema, we assume that the user poses queries that involve only the operations of selection, projection and join. Still, this is a significant extension of the value-based lookups supported thus far. In terms of execution, queries are classified into two categories. A *local* query, much like a query in a centralized system, is executed using only the data in the local peer. On the other hand, a *global* query uses the peer network to augment locally retrieved data with data that reside in other peers. We now formalize the above notions and explain the query semantics with emphasis on the semantics of global queries.

Consider a set $P = \{P_1, P_2, \ldots, P_n\}$ of n peers. Assume that peer P_i exposes a set of attributes U_i ($1 \leq i \leq n$) and that $U_i \cap U_j = \emptyset$ ($i \neq j$, $1 \leq i, j \leq n$), and let r_i be an instance of P_i. A local query q, hereafter just called a query, over a

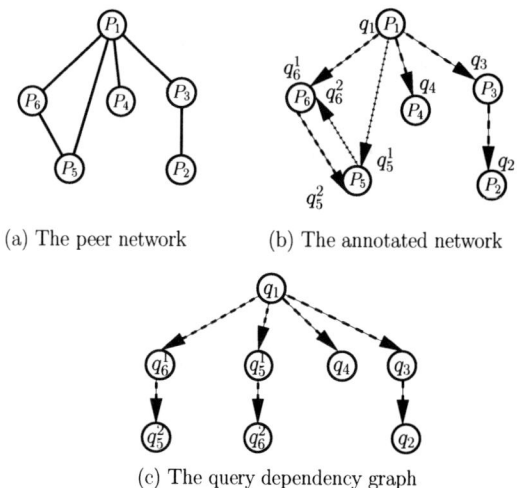

(a) The peer network (b) The annotated network

(c) The query dependency graph

Figure 2: A query dependency graph

peer P_i ($1 \leq i \leq n$) is defined with respect to the schema of P_i. The result of q is a relation over a set of attributes V_i, where $V_i \subseteq U_i$, whose content is the set of tuples $q(r_i)$. We denote by $att(q)$ the set of attributes V_i. A global query q_P over the peers in P is a set of queries $\{q_1^1, q_1^2, \ldots, q_1^{k_1}, \ldots, q_n^1, q_n^2, \ldots, q_n^{k_n}\}$, where query q_i^j ($1 \leq i \leq n$ and $1 \leq j \leq k_i$) is over the schema of peer P_i and $att(q_i^j) = att(q_i^l)$, for every $l \in [1, k_i]$. Each query in q_P is called a *component* of q_P and, conversely, q_P is said to be *comprised* of the indicated set. The result of global query q_P is a relation over the schema $R_P[V_1 \cup V_2 \cup \ldots \cup V_n]$, where $V_i = att(q_i^1) = \cdots = att(q_i^{k_i})$ ($1 \leq i \leq n$), whose content is the set of tuples in the outer-union of the union of the queries in each peer, that is, the outer-union of $\bigcup_{j=1}^{k_1} q_1^j(r_1)$, $\bigcup_{j=1}^{k_2} q_2^j(r_2)$, $\ldots$, $\bigcup_{j=1}^{k_n} q_n^j(r_n)$. Hence, we permit peers to return results with different schemas. We also propose not to merge results as merging semantics tend to be application specific. Given these definitions, each local query can be thought of as a trivial global query which is comprised of a single component query.

Example 3 *The set $\{Q_1, Q_2\}$ of queries (from Example 1) is a global query over the MedLine and PubMed peers. The execution of this global query is initiated by local query Q_1. The result of this global query is a relation with attributes $\{article\_id, keyword, year, paper\_id, kw, py, pm\}$, whose content is the outer-union of the relations obtained by applying queries Q_1 and Q_2 to the instances shown in Figures 1 (a) and (b), respectively.*

We now examine the relationship between the component queries of a global query. For this, we introduce the notion of query *dependencies*. Intuitively, as queries are propagated in the system, a

471

(directed) query dependency graph is induced. The nodes in this graph represent queries and there is an edge from query q_j to query q_k if query q_k depends on query q_j. A query q_k on peer P_k is said to depend on query q_j over peer P_j, denoted as $dep(q_k) = q_j$, if peers P_j and P_k are acquainted and query q_k has resulted from the propagation of query q_j on peer P_j to peer P_k. Special care is taken to avoid the creation of cycles in the induced graph. This happens if a query propagated by a peer P_k is re-received by the same peer through one of its acquaintances. Tagging queries with the path of peers through which they are propagated allows the detection of such situations. In Figure 2(a) there is an example of a peer network that consists of six peers, i.e., $P = \{P_1, P_2, \ldots, P_6\}$ and there is an edge between two peers if they are acquainted. In Figure 2(b), we use an intermediate representation where each peer in the network is annotated with the component queries of global query $q_P = \{q_1, q_2, q_3, q_4, q_5^1, q_5^2, q_6^1, q_6^2\}$ that it executes. The edges in this representation show the propagation of queries. Finally, Figure 2(c) shows the dependency graph of q_P. Notice that in some peers more than one query is executed. For example, in peer P_5 we have the execution of two queries, namely q_5^1 and q_5^2. Query q_5^1 results from the propagation of query q_1 from peer P_1 while query q_5^2 results from the propagation of query q_6^1 from peer P_6. We devote the next paragraphs examining how exactly the propagation, and possible translation, of queries is achieved between peers.

4.1 Mapping tables

We offer here an overview of mapping tables since they are the main vehicle used for query translation.

Consider two peers that expose relations with attributes U and V, respectively. A mapping table is a relation over the attributes $X \cup Y$, where $X \subseteq U$ and $Y \subseteq V$ are non-empty sets of attributes from the two peers. For example, a mapping table from a set of attributes $X = \{keyword\}$ to a set of attributes $Y = \{kw\}$ is shown in Figure 1(c). A vertical double line is used to separate the two attributes sets.

To represent different semantics for mapping tables and values within them, the standard convention of using variables is followed. For instance, Figure 1(e) shows a mapping table containing variables. Every valuation of these variables gives a value of *year* that can be mapped to a value of *py*. Since this mapping table contains the same variable in its two columns, every valuation is a tuple of the form (a, a), where a is a constant in the domains of *year* and *py*. Thus, in this case variables offer a compact way of representing the identity mapping.

Mapping tables restrict the way in which information may be exchanged between peers, instead of restricting their contents. Let r_1 and r_2 be instances of peers P_1 and P_2, respectively, and m be a mapping table from X to Y, where X and Y are subsets of the set of attributes exposed by P_1 and P_2, respectively. Given a valuation ρ of the variables of m, a value $x \in \pi_X(\rho(m))$ is associated with the set of values $\pi_Y(\sigma_{X=x}(\rho(m)))$ and, hence, each $t_1 \in r_1$ such that $t_1[X] = x$ can be mapped only to the tuples $t_2 \in r_2$ for which $t_2[Y] \in \pi_Y(\sigma_{X=x}(\rho(m)))$.

4.2 Sound and complete translations

We are interested in translating, through mapping tables, queries that involve the operations of projection, selection and join. In what follows, we consider how this is achieved in the presence of the latter two operators. Then, in Section 4.3 we show how to handle projections. This separation is possible since, as we show, the issues involved are orthogonal.

Consider peers P_1 and P_2 that expose attributes U_1 and U_2, respectively. To begin, we assume that a single mapping table m exists with schema $M[U_1 \cup U_2]$ that associates values of U_1 to values of U_2. We relax this assumption later. Consider two queries q_1 and q_2 over peers P_1 and P_2, respectively, such that $dep(q_2) = q_1$, that is, query q_2 resulted from the propagation and translation of query q_1. We claim that the nature of this translation should be such that q_2 retrieves from peer P_2 only the data that are related with those that could be retrieved from query q_1 in peer P_1. The exact relationship is determined by the set of mapping tables that exists between the two peers.

Definition 4 *Let q_1 and q_2 be queries over peers P_1 and P_2, respectively, such that $q_1 = \sigma_E(R_1 \bowtie \cdots \bowtie R_k)$, where E is a conjunction of equality atoms and $R_1, \ldots, R_k$ are relations in P_1. Then q_2 is a sound translation of q_1 with respect to mapping table m, denoted by $q_1 \stackrel{m}{\mapsto} q_2$, if for every relation instance r_2 of P_2 and $t_2 \in q_2(r_2)$, there exists a valuation ρ of m and a tuple $t \in \sigma_E(\rho(m))$ such that $\pi_{att(q_2)}(t) = t_2$.*

We offer a few remarks on our definition. First, observe that in the definition query q_1 operates on mapping table m, instead of operating on some instance r_1 of P_1, while query q_2 operates on an instance r_2 of P_2. This is to allow for query q_2 to retrieve data from r_2 that could be mapped to some instance r_1 of P_1 through m, but that it is not necessary for the data retrieved from q_1. Second, note that since m contains all the attributes mentioned in $R_1, \ldots, R_k$, in order to evaluate q_1 in the relation $\rho(m)$ we do not need to compute the join of $R_1, \ldots, R_k$, we just have to check the condition E.

Example 5 *Consider the mapping table ML2PM shown in Figure 3. Since all variables in the ta-*

article_id	keyword	year	paper_id	kw	py	pm
x_1	OPH	y_1	x_2	APH	y_2	z_2
x_3	OPH	y_3	x_4	AARE	y_4	z_4

Figure 3: Mapping table ML2PM.

ble are distinct, the table essentially maps protein OPH in MedLine to proteins APH and AARE in PubMed. Now, consider queries Q_1 and Q_2 from our motivating example (see Section 2). Query Q_2 is a sound translation of query Q_1 with respect to the table ML2PM. On the other hand, the following query is not a sound translation of query Q_1.

Q_4: **select** *
    from PubMed
    where kw = "APH" **OR** kw = "p75 ICD"

To see this, consider the PubMed relation instance in Figure 1(b). Its third tuple satisfies Q_4 but it cannot be associated, through ML2PM, to any MedLine article retrieved by Q_1.

Another observation is that the above definition is not symmetric. Also, note that sound translations are not unique.

Example 6 *While our previous example shows that Q_4 is not a sound translation of Q_1, notice that Q_1 is a sound translation of Q_4, with respect to table PM2ML (which is the inverse of the ML2PM). Tuples retrieved by Q_1, from every possible instance of MedLine, correspond to articles mentioning protein OPH which, through PM2ML, can be associated with PubMed articles mentioning protein APH. Concerning the uniqueness of sound translations, remember from our motivating example that both queries Q_2 and Q_3 are sound translations of query Q_1.*

Since one sound translation might retrieve more data than another, we consider next the notion of *completeness*. That is, whether there is a sound translation that retrieves from remote peers all possible sound data.

Definition 7 *Given queries q_1, q_2 over peers P_1 and P_2, respectively, we say that q_2 is a complete translation of query q_1 with respect to mapping table m, if $q_1 \stackrel{m}{\mapsto} q_2$ and for every query q'_2 over P_2 such that $q_1 \stackrel{m}{\mapsto} q'_2$ and every instance r_2 of P_2, $q_2(r_2) \supseteq q'_2(r_2)$.*

Notice that, by definition, if two queries q_2 and q'_2 are complete translations of a query q_1, then q_2 and q'_2 are equivalent.

Example 8 *Consider query Q_1 from our motivating example and its sound translations, namely, Q_2 and Q_3. We claim, without providing a formal proof, that query Q_2 is a complete translation of Q_1, with respect to mapping table ML2PM.*

We are now in a position to formally characterize the relationship between the component queries of a global query. Specifically, we require that for each pair q_i, q_j of component queries such that $dep(q_j) = q_i$, query q_j is a sound translation of query q_i.

Our definitions assume that a single mapping table maps all the attributes in the relations involved. We relax this assumption in Section 5.5. We also note that so far we have only considered the selection and join operators. We investigate the issues concerning the projection operator next.

4.3 The projection operator

Sound translations guarantee that only correct tuples are retrieved from remote peers. However, not all the attributes from the remote peers are necessarily of interest. The user has the ability, through the projection operator, to express what local attributes are of interest to her and, thus, we provide a similar mechanism for the data retrieved from remote peers.

Our solutions make use of attribute correspondences which associate attributes in different peers. Learning attribute correspondences is a main component of schema matchers [16]. An attribute correspondence for attributes requiring no data translation can be encoded by a simple mapping table with the identity mapping. This is the situation depicted in Figure 1(e). In general, a mapping table $m[X \cup Y]$ encodes, in addition to the set of data associations, an attribute correspondence between the set of attributes X and Y.

Definition 9 *Let P and P' be peers exposing set of attributes U and U', respectively, and $m[X \cup Y]$ be a mapping table such that $X \subseteq U$ and $Y \subseteq U'$. Then, m is relevant to a query q over P, if $att(q) \subseteq X$.*

Hence, when translating a query q that includes a projection on attributes $att(q)$ we make use of all the relevant mapping tables $m_1[X_1 \cup Y_1], m_2[X_2 \cup Y_2], \ldots m_k[X_k \cup Y_k]$, and the translated query returns the union of all the Y_i's in these tables.

Example 10 *Consider the query that retrieves from MedLine all the protein names mentioned in articles published in 1998:*

Q_5: **select** keyword
    from MedLine
    where year = "1998"

The complete translation of Q_5, with respect to mapping table year2py shown in Figure 1(e), is:

Q_6: **select** kw
from $PubMed$
where $py =$ "1998"

There are two points to make here. First, due to mapping table year2py, our projection is on the kw attributes of the retrieved PubMed tuples. Second, it is possible that the latter query retrieves PubMed articles that violate mapping table keyword2kw shown in Figure 1(c). However, this is consistent with our query semantics since soundness is defined here only with respect to the year2py mapping table.

5 Algorithms

In general, queries are initially expressed in a query language (e.g., relational algebra, SQL) and are later transformed in some appropriate *internal* representation. Before we discuss the issue of querying, we need to fix these two parameters, i.e., the query language and the representation used.

We focus here on queries that are expressed in $S+J$ algebra. An $S+J$ query uses the operators of selection and join. The selection formula is *positive*, i.e., it has no negation and it consists of conjunctions and disjunctions of atoms of the form $(A = B)$ and $(A = a)$, where A and B are attribute names and a is a constant. Note that projection is supported in our framework but is handled independently.

Common query representations include tableau, which is a tabular representation of a query which resembles a database instance, and query trees, which is a graph-like representation of a query [3]. In this work, the tabular representation is the preferred choice. One reason for this is uniformity. Notice that we already use a similar representation, namely, mapping tables, to address issues of heterogeneity among different peers. In the following paragraphs, we introduce T-queries which is a tabular representation of queries and we show that for each $S+J$ query we can have an equivalent T-query. Then, we show how T-queries can be used to test whether a query q' is a sound translation of query q. Finally, we show how T-queries can be used to compute sound and complete query translations.

5.1 T-queries

We start by defining T-queries over one relation. Thus, we only consider selections. We later show how our definitions are extended to consider queries over multiple relations, thus taking into account joins. The following paragraph presents the syntax and semantics of T-queries.

A T-query q_T over relation schema $R[U]$ is a table T with attributes U where each variable appears in at most one row. Intuitively, one can think of each $t \in T$ as a tableau query whose corresponding tableau only has a single tuple. Then, T represents a set of tableau queries. Given a T-query q_T over schema R and an instance r of R, the result of executing q_T on r, denoted as $q_T(r)$ is:

$$q_T(r) = \{\rho(t) \mid \rho \text{ is a valuation of } t \in T \text{ and } \rho(t) \in r\}.$$

Example 11 *Consider the following query that returns all articles from PubMed mentioning proteins APH or p75 ICD:*

Q_7: **select** $*$
from $PubMed$
where $kw =$ "APH" **OR** $kw =$ "p75 ICD"

Then, the corresponding T-query is shown below:

paper_id	kw	py	pm
$\mathcal{X}_1$	APH	$\mathcal{Y}_1$	$\mathcal{Z}_1$
$\mathcal{X}_2$	p75 ICD	$\mathcal{Y}_2$	$\mathcal{Z}_2$

Proposition 12 *For any $S+$ query q over a relation $R[U]$ there is an equivalent T-query q_T, and vice versa.*

To construct query q_T from q, first we have to transform q into an equivalent query q' of the form $\sigma_E(R)$, where E is in disjunctive normal form. T-query q_T is of size linear in the size of q', which, in turn, has a size which is exponential, in general, with respect to the size of the initial query q. However, this is not a problem in practice since large selection formulas rarely occur.

We extend the definition of T-queries over multiple relations in the following way. Let $R = \{R_1[U_1], R_2[U_2], \ldots, R_n[U_n]\}$ be a relational schema and U be $\cup_{i=1}^{n} U_i$. A T-query q_T over R is a table T with attributes U where each variable appears in at most one row. In terms of semantics, consider a T-query q_T over R and an instance $r = \{r_1, r_2, \ldots, r_n\}$ of R. Then the result of executing q_T on r, denoted by $q_T(r)$, is:

$$q_T(r) = \{\rho(t) \mid \rho \text{ is a valuation of } t \in T$$
$$\text{and } \rho(t) \in r_1 \bowtie \cdots \bowtie r_n\}.$$

Proposition 13 *For any $S+J$ query q over a relational schema R, there is an equivalent T-query q_T, and vice versa.*

We conclude this subsection by presenting the notion of *join* between T-queries. This will play a central role in all the algorithms presented in the following subsections. Let T_1 and T_2 be the tables of T-queries q_T^1 and q_T^2 with attributes U_1 and U_2, respectively. Attribute sets U_1 and U_2 are not necessarily disjoint. Then $T_1 \bowtie^{var} T_2$ is a T-query with attributes $U_1 \cup U_2$ defined as follows. Recall that a substitution is a function that maps only variables to either variables or constants. For every $t_1 \in T_1$ and $t_2 \in T_2$, find substitutions θ_1 and θ_2 for the variables of t_1 and t_2, respectively, such that $\theta_1(t_1[U_1 \cap U_2]) = \theta_2(t_2[U_1 \cap U_2])$. Furthermore, we require that for any other pair of substitutions θ'_1 and θ'_2 satisfying this condition, θ_1 is as general as θ'_1 and θ_2 is as general as θ'_2, that is, there exist substitutions γ_1 and γ_2 such that $\gamma_1 \circ \theta_1 = \theta'_1$ and $\gamma_2 \circ \theta_2 = \theta'_2$ (this corresponds to the notion of *most general unifier* used in logic programming [13]). If substitutions θ_1 and θ_2 exist, then add to $T_1 \stackrel{var}{\bowtie} T_2$ a $U_1 \cup U_2$-tuple t defined as: $t[U_1] = \theta_1(t_1)$ and $t[U_2] = \theta_2(t_2)$.

Intuitively, given relation instances r_1 and r_2 over U_1 and U_2, respectively, the join of T_1 and T_2 gives us a new T-query q_T such that:

$$q_T(r_1 \bowtie r_2) = q_T^1(r_1) \bowtie q_T^2(r_2).$$

5.2 Algorithms for sound translations

In the previous section, we introduced sound translations and we provided a definition through which we can test, given two queries q and q' over peers P and P', respectively, whether query q' is a sound translation of q with respect to a mapping table m. The definition of sound translations, however, does not provide us with a practical way to do the testing. In the next paragraphs, we show that one of the benefits of representing queries as T-queries is that we are able to perform such a test efficiently.

In brief, the proposed algorithm accepts as input two queries q and q' over peers P and P', respectively, and a mapping table m between the sets of attributes U and U' exposed by these peers. Initially, it converts both q and q' to their corresponding T-queries, say $q_T = T$ and $q'_T = T'$, respectively. Then the algorithm uses mapping table m to constrain the association of query disjunctions. Formally, given T, m and T', the algorithm constructs a T-query q_T^c with attributes $att(q')$ defined as $\pi_{att(q')}(T \stackrel{var}{\bowtie} m \stackrel{var}{\bowtie} T')$. We note that it is possible to perform this join since mapping tables and T-queries use the same syntax. In the last step, the algorithm checks whether q_T^c is *equivalent* to q'_T, that is, for every instance r' of peer P', $q_T^c(r') = q'_T(r')$. To perform such a test we use an algorithm that checks for containment of union of conjunctives queries [17]. If q_T^c is equivalent to q'_T, then the algorithm outputs *yes*.

Theorem 14 *The above algorithm outputs yes on input (q, m, q') if and only if q' is a sound translation of q with respect to mapping table m.*

The following proposition is used in the proof of this theorem. It also shows that the previous al-

article_id	keyword	year	paper_id	kw	py	pm
x_1	OPH	1998	x_2	APH	1998	y_2
x_3	OPH	1998	x_4	AARE	1998	y_4
x_5	OPH	2003	x_6	APH	2003	y_6
x_7	OPH	2003	x_8	AARE	2003	y_8

Figure 4: Storing query translations

gorithm only needs to check whether $q'_T \subseteq q_T^c$ to verify whether q' is a sound translation of q.

Proposition 15 *The queries q'_T and q_T^c computed by the above algorithm on input (q, m, q') are such that $q_T^c \subseteq q'_T$.*

Finally, we establish the exact complexity of our problem.

Theorem 16 *The problem of testing whether a query is a sound translation of another query is Π_2^p-complete.*

5.3 Computing complete translations

Here we describe an algorithm that, given a query q and a mapping table m, computes a query q' such that q' is a sound and complete translation of q with respect to mapping table m. The algorithm extends the algorithm for testing sound translations. Let P and P' be two peers that expose attributes U and U', respectively, and assume that q is a query over P and m is mapping table between the set of attributes U and U'. The algorithm begins by converting query q to its corresponding T-query $q_T = T$. Then, it considers mapping table m and computes T-query $q'_T = \pi_{U'}(T \stackrel{var}{\bowtie} m)$. Finally, the algorithm outputs the query q' represented by q'_T. The following theorem shows that q' is a sound and complete translation of query q.

Theorem 17 *Query q' computed by the above algorithm on input (q, m) is a complete translation of q.*

5.4 Composing translations

In this section, we show the benefits of using a common formalism for representing both data and query associations. In more detail, we show that the algorithms that were created for inference of mapping tables can be used to effectively perform query composition. Consider the point in time after a complete translation has been computed. This translation may be stored within a mapping table. An example is shown in Figure 4. The query on the left of the table retrieves MedLine articles that mention protein OPH and were published in 1998 or 2003.

475

The query on the right represents a complete translation on PubMed. Notice that each tuple in the mapping table pairs a query with a sound translation of the query. Such storage permits us to reuse the data association inference algorithm of our earlier work [11] to compose query translations. Consider a path $\theta = P_1, P_2, ..., P_n$ of peers with a set of mapping tables m_i storing data associations between peers P_i and P_{i+1}, for $1 \leq i \leq n-1$. Now let T_i be a mapping table containing pairs of sound query translations (that is, each tuple (q, q') in the mapping table represents a T-query q on P_i and a sound translation q' of q with respect to the mapping table m_i).

Let m denote the mapping table that results from our inference algorithm [11] over the path θ and the set of mapping tables m_i. And let T denote the mapping table that results from our inference algorithm over the path θ and the set of (query) mapping tables T_i. Then, each tuple (q, q') in T contains a T-query q' that is a sound translation of q with respect to the mapping table m.

5.5 Using multiple mapping tables

The algorithms presented in the previous sections assume the existence of a single mapping table that maps all the attributes in the relations involved. In real life, we expect that multiple mapping tables are provided and that some attributes are not mapped. In what follows, we investigate how to handle these two situations.

Assume that instead of a single mapping table m, we are given a set of mapping tables M to use during the computation of a complete translation. The exact way in which these tables are combined can be either pre-specified or it can be left to the user. Here, we propose a technique for combining multiple tables automatically. The following example illustrates that combining all available tables during the computation of translations might yield counter-intuitive translations.

Example 18 *Consider query Q_1 from our motivating example that retrieves articles from MedLine mentioning protein OPH. Assume that instead of just using mapping table keyword2kw, in Figure 1(c), we consider both mapping tables keyword2kw and id2id to compute the translation. Furthermore, assume that every retrieved tuple from PubMed must be associated with a local OPH article with respect to both mapping tables. Then, the resulting translation is equivalent to the following query:*

Q_8: **select** *
    from PubMed
    where *(kw = "APH" **OR** kw = "AARE")*
            AND *paper_id = "10719179"*

That is, by using both mapping tables, we are forced to restrict the identifiers of the retrieved articles. Since no restriction is imposed in the article_id attribute of the MedLine retrieved articles, a similar reasoning should be followed when translating this query for the PubMed articles. This reasoning supports not using mapping table id2id, in Figure 1(d), in translating this query.

The proposed technique accepts as input a query q over a peer P and a set of mapping tables M from P to a second peer P', and it uses the set M to compute a complete translation q' of q. Initially, the algorithm converts q into its equivalent disjunctive normal form. Then, it proceeds by considering each disjunct D_j of q in isolation. For each disjunct D_j, it selects a table for the translation, if this table's local attributes participate in an atom of the disjunct. Call M_j the set of selected mapping tables. If the set of attributes of D_j is contained in the set of attributes of M_j (M_j is relevant to D_j), the algorithm combines the mapping tables in M_j into a single mapping table m_j by using the $\wedge$-operator [11]. For the time being assume that m_j mentions all the attributes exposed by peers P and P'. Then, the algorithm considers D_j as a T-query T_j containing only one row and computes a sound and complete translation of T_j with respect to mapping table m_j. Then the translated T-query is converted into an equivalent relational algebra expression whose selection formula becomes a disjunct in the resulting query q'.

Example 19 *By using the algorithm described here, query Q_1 is translated to query Q_2 which is indeed its complete translation. As another example, assume that Q_9 is a query retrieving information from MedLine about articles that mention protein OPH and were published in 1999:*

Q_9: **select** *
    from MedLine
    where *keyword = "OPH" **AND** year = "1999"*

Then, our algorithm selects only mapping tables year2py and keyword2kw for the translation, resulting in the following query:

Q_{10}: **select** *
    from PubMed
    where *(kw = "APH" **OR** kw = "AARE")*
            AND *py = "1999"*

If any of the mapping tables m_j computed by the above algorithm does not mention all the attributes exposed by P and P', then it is extended to a mapping table m'_j that maps the extra attributes to *any* value. For example, mapping table *ML2PM* in Figure 3 is the extension of the following mapping table

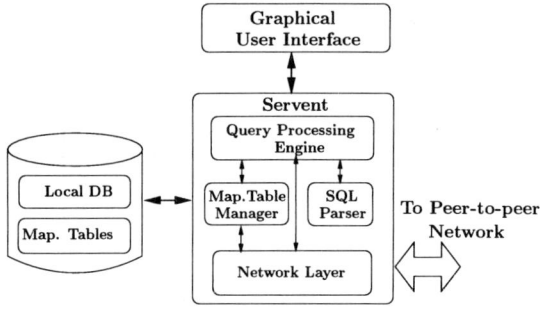

Figure 5: The architecture of a peer

keyword	kw
OPH	APH
OPH	AARE

to the set of attributes {*article_id, keyword, year, paper_id, kw, py, pm*}.

6 Implementation

We implemented our ideas over the prototype implementation of the Hyperion peer-to-peer data management system [4]. The structure of each peer in this system is shown in Figure 5. We provide a graphical user interface through which a user can set up acquaintances with new peers or pose local queries. Each peer in the system manages its own collection of data and it autonomously chooses a logical design and physical organization for the data. We use the MySQL relational DBMS to store both the peer data and any possible mapping tables that each peer might maintain.

The servent, which is the main component of this architecture, consists of four main modules. From these four modules, the query processing engine is the main focus of this work. It includes the implementation of the algorithms that convert SQL queries to their disjunctive normal form; convert SQL queries to their equivalent T-queries and back; and compute the complete translation of a query given a mapping table. Furthermore, it includes the algorithm for testing containment of T-queries and the algorithm to test whether a query is a sound translation of another one, with respect to a given mapping table. Finally, we also implemented the algorithm that, given a query q and a set of mapping tables M, selects the set of mapping tables to use in order to compute a complete translation.

We implemented a number of optimizations to improve the efficiency of our algorithms. One such optimization relies on the fact that our representation of queries as T-queries allows us to store in the database both the query itself and the relationship with its sound translations. As an example, consider again the stored translation shown in Figure 4. Assume that the calculation of this translation happened some time in the past, but the system stores this relationship between the two T-queries in the database. Now, assume that a new query is issued on MedLine asking only for articles that mention protein OPH and were published in 1998. At this point, we could run the optimized version of the algorithm for computing complete translations in order to retrieve the corresponding PubMed articles. Alternatively, one can use the algorithm for T-query containment to conclude that the correspondence between T-queries in Figure 4 can be used to compute the translation. In more detail, we test whether the T-query representation of the current query is contained in the left part of the table in the figure. Since this is the case in our running example, we treat the table in the figure as a mapping table and we use it to compute the translation of the current query. In this example, this computation will result in the selection of the right parts from the first two tuples.

An interesting application of the previous optimization relies on the observation that in peer-to-peer systems users are often satisfied with answers that are not complete, as long as they are given the guarantee that anything that is retrieved is correct. With this in mind, even a query that retrieves all articles in MedLine mentioning proteins OPH or NGF receptor can be answered satisfactorily from the PubMed peer by just retrieving articles that mention these proteins and were published in some particular time interval (for example, the last 5 years). Testing for T-query containment is also central in this approach since the stored query is contained in the query being posed.

We conclude our overview by noting that the implementation of the query processing engine was done in the C programming language and it contains approximately four thousand lines of source code.

7 Experiments

To evaluate our algorithms, we undertook two studies. The objective of our first study is to investigate the performance of our translation algorithms with respect to three problem parameters, namely, the size of the input query, the size of the output query, and the size of the mapping tables used in the translation. The second study investigates the performance of our algorithms under large query load and examines the benefits of storing and re-using past translations. Due to lack of space, our second study is only available in the extended version of the paper [10]. The data used by both studies are *real* and are extracted from publicly available sources. We use these data to create distinct peers, one per

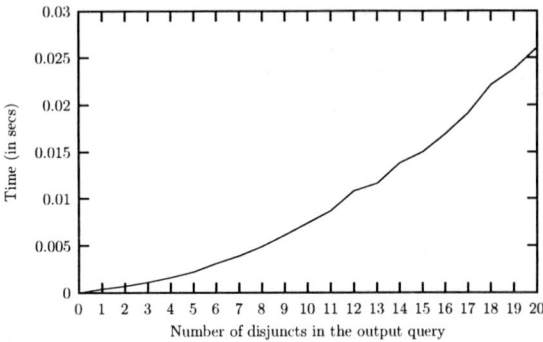

Figure 6: Generating large output queries

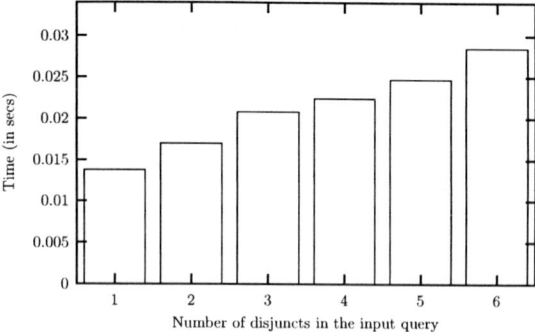

Figure 7: Translating large input queries

machine within the same LAN, and each peer has the structure shown in Figure 5.

7.1 Biological Databases

The data for this study belong to the MedLine, PubMed and SwissProt [2] databases. We populated each of the MedLine and PubMed relations with approximately 25000 tuples corresponding to protein-related articles. We assumed that MedLine articles are indexed, through the keyword attribute, by the currently approved protein name while PubMed articles are indexed by aliases of the approved names. Mapping table *id2id* had approximately 24000 tuples while mapping table *keyword2kw* had approximately 12000 tuples. The former table maps an MedLine article to at most one PubMed article while the latter table maps currently approved protein names to their corresponding aliases. Both mapping tables were retrieved from SwissProt.

Given query Q_1 and mapping table *keyword2kw*, we expect that the time to translate Q_1 is influenced by the number of values that OPH is associated with, since this number influences the number of disjuncts, and thus the size, of the output query. Thus, the objective of our first experiment is to investigate the exact relationship between the time to perform a query translation and the size, in terms of disjuncts, of the translated query. For this purpose, we select 20 distinct input queries each of which is similar, in spirit, to query Q_1, i.e., it retrieves MedLine articles for a particular keyword/protein. The queries were selected in such a manner that the first query refers to a protein with a single alias in *keyword2kw*, the second query refers to a protein with 2 aliases, and so on, while the last query refers to a protein with 20 aliases. Figure 6 shows the translation times (in seconds) for each of these queries. As we can see, the translation time scales gracefully and, even for large output queries, it is still fractions of a second.

In the previous experiment, all the input queries have only a single disjunct. In this experiment, we vary the number of disjuncts in the input query and we investigate how this influences the translation time. We start by selecting 20 distinct input queries each of which, once translated, results in an output query with 14 disjuncts. From the 20 input queries, 4 queries have 2 disjuncts, 4 have 3 disjuncts, and so on, and the last 4 queries have 6 disjuncts. We consider 4 alternative queries for the same number of disjuncts since, given the number of disjuncts in a query, there are different combinations with which these disjuncts can contribute to result in 14 output disjuncts. For example, for a query with just two disjuncts, each of the two input disjuncts can be translated to 7 output disjuncts, or alternatively, the first input disjunct can result in 10 output disjuncts while the second input disjunct can result in the remaining 4. In Figure 7, we average the translation times of input queries with the same number of disjuncts and we also report, in the first column, the translation of an input query with a single disjunct. Notice that as the number of disjuncts in the input query increases, there is a corresponding increase in the translation time of the query. Although there is a correlation between these two quantities, our next experiment shows that there is another factor that also comes into play during the translation process.

For this experiment, we use the input query that had the worst performance, in terms of time, in our previous experiment. This is the input query with 6 disjuncts, denoted with D_1 to D_6, where disjunct D_1, once translated, results in 9 output disjuncts while the remaining 5 input disjuncts all result in a single output disjunct. Notice again that the number of disjuncts in the output query is 14. During this experiment, we translate this input query 6 times and the only difference between the translations is the order with which we translated the 6 input disjuncts. In particular, in the first run, the input disjunct D_1 is considered first for translation, while in the second run, disjunct D_1 is considered second in order for translation. Continuing in this fashion, in the sixth run, the five single-output disjuncts are

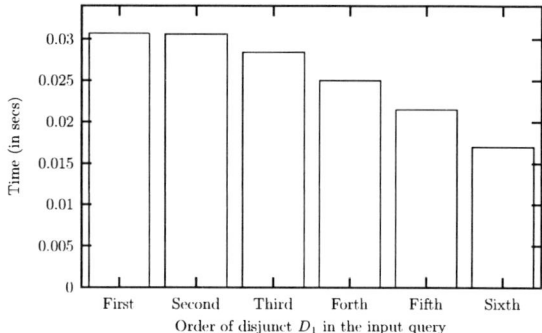

Figure 8: Translating a large input query

considered first, while disjunct D_1 is considered last. Figure 8 show the translation time for each of the six runs of the algorithm. The drop in translation time is due to the following reason. After a disjunct of the input query is translated, the algorithm checks whether any of generated output disjuncts is already part of the output query due to a previously translated input disjunct. The objective of this check is to avoid duplicate disjuncts in the output query, or pairs of disjuncts where one is contained in another. However, the check generates more comparisons, and thus more computation, if a large number of output disjuncts is generated early in the translation process. Hence, delaying the translation of a disjunct like D_1 causes reduced translation times. In general, reordering of input disjuncts seems beneficial and it can be achieved by storing frequency information about the values of a mapping table. Using these frequencies we can estimate the number of output disjuncts for each input disjunct.

We also experimented with varying the mapping table sizes. Our experiments show that this parameter does not influence the translation time. This is because we do not scan the whole table in order to locate the tuples to be used in the translation, but we use in-memory hash indexes. Our implementation of the hash indexes is customized to the semantics of mapping tables and thus takes into consideration the existence of variables in the tables.

8 Conclusions

We have considered the problem of data sharing between autonomous data sources. We used mapping tables to associate data from different sources and we have shown how the tables can be used in the translation of structured queries. We introduced the notions of sound and complete translations and we proposed algorithms to compute such translations and an algorithm to test if a query is a sound translation of another. We implemented our algorithms and we have presented experiments which show that these can be used in practice.

Our future work investigates algorithm optimizations along with support for more expressive query languages that include, for example, negation.

References

[1] PubMed/MedLine. http://www.ncbi.nlm.nig.gov/entrez/.

[2] SwissProt. http://www.ebi.ac.uk/swissprot/.

[3] S. Abiteboul, R. Hull, and V. Vianu. *Foundations of Databases*. Addison-Wesley, 1995.

[4] M. Arenas, V. Kantere, A. Kementsietsidis, I. Kiringa, R. J. Miller, and J. Mylopoulos. The Hyperion Project: From Data Integration to Data Coordination. *SIGMOD Record*, 32(3):53–58, 2003.

[5] C.-C. K. Chang and H. Garcia-Molina. Mind your vocabulary: Query mapping across heterogeneous information sources. In *SIGMOD*, pages 335–346, 1999.

[6] R. Fagin, P. Kolaitis, R. Miller, and L. Popa. Data exchange: Semantics and query answering. In *ICDT*, pages 207–224, 2003.

[7] A. Halevy, Z. Ives, D. Suciu, and I. Tatarinov. Schema Mediation in Peer Data Management Systems. In *ICDE*, 2003.

[8] M. Harren, J. M. Hellerstein, R. Huebsch, B. T. Loo, S. Shenker, and I. Stoica. Complex Queries in DHT-Based P2P Networks. In *IPTPS*, 2002.

[9] R. Huebsch, J. M. Hellerstein, N. L. Boon, T. Loo, S. Shenker, and I. Stoica. Querying the internet with pier. In *VLDB*, 2003.

[10] A. Kementsietsidis and M. Arenas. Data sharing through query translation in autonomous sources. Technical Report CSRG-491, CS Dept., University of Toronto, 2004.

[11] A. Kementsietsidis, M. Arenas, and R. J. Miller. Data mapping in p2p systems: Semantics and algorithmic issues. In *SIGMOD*, pages 325–336, 2003.

[12] M. Lenzerini. Data Integration: A Theoretical Perspective. In *PODS*, pages 233–246, 2002.

[13] J. W. Lloyd. *Foundations of logic programming*. Springer-Verlag New York, Inc., 1987.

[14] J. Madhavan and A. Y. Halevy. Composing Mappings Among Data Sources. In *VLDB*, pages 572–583, 2003.

[15] W. S. Ng, B. C. Ooi, K. L. Tan, and A. Y. Zhou. Peerdb: A p2p-based system for distributed data sharing. In *ICDE*, pages 633–644, 2003.

[16] E. Rahm and P. A. Bernstein. On Matching Schemas Automatically. *The VLDB Journal*, 10(4):334–350, Dec. 2001.

[17] Y. Sagiv and M. Yannakakis. Equivalences Among Relational Expressions with the Union and Difference Operators. *JACM*, 27(4):633–655, 1980.

Linear Road: A Stream Data Management Benchmark

Arvind Arasu*
Stanford University
arvinda@cs.stanford.edu

Mitch Cherniack[†][‡]
Brandeis University
mfc@cs.brandeis.edu

Eduardo Galvez[†]
Brandeis University
eddie@cs.brandeis.edu

David Maier[§]
OHSU/OGI
maier@cse.ogi.edu

Anurag S. Maskey[†]
Brandeis University
anurag@cs.brandeis.edu

Esther Ryvkina[‡]
Brandeis University
essie@cs.brandeis.edu

Michael Stonebraker
MIT
stonebraker@csail.mit.edu

Richard Tibbetts
MIT
tibbetts@mit.edu

Abstract

*This paper specifies the **Linear Road Benchmark** for Stream Data Management Systems (SDMS). Stream Data Management Systems process streaming data by executing continuous and historical queries while producing query results in real-time. This benchmark makes it possible to compare the performance characteristics of SDMS' relative to each other and to alternative (e.g., Relational Database) systems. Linear Road has been endorsed as an SDMS benchmark by the developers of both the Aurora [1] (out of Brandeis University, Brown University and MIT) and STREAM [8] (out of Stanford University) stream systems.*

Linear Road simulates a toll system for the motor vehicle expressways of a large metropolitan area. The tolling system uses "variable tolling" [6, 11, 9]: an increasingly prevalent tolling technique that uses such dynamic factors as traffic congestion and accident proximity to calculate toll charges. Linear Road specifies a variable tolling system for a fictional urban area including such features as accident detection and alerts, traffic congestion measurements, toll calculations and historical queries. After specifying the benchmark, we describe experimental results involving two implementations: one using a commercially available Relational Database and the other using Aurora. Our results show that a dedicated Stream Data Management System can outperform a Relational Database by at least a factor of 5 on streaming data applications.

---

* This material is based on work supported by the National Science Foundation under Grant Nos. IIS-0118173 and IIS-9817799 (*), IIS-0086057 (†), IIS-0325525 (‡) and IIS-0086002 (§).

Permission to copy without fee all or part of this material is granted provided that the copies are not made or distributed for direct commercial advantage, the VLDB copyright notice and the title of the publication and its date appear, and notice is given that copying is by permission of the Very Large Data Base Endowment. To copy otherwise, or to republish, requires a fee and/or special permission from the Endowment.

**Proceedings of the 30th VLDB Conference,
Toronto, Canada, 2004**

1 Introduction

In this paper we introduce the **Linear Road Benchmark** for Stream Data Management Systems (SDMS).

Stream data management has become a highly active research area and has inspired the development of several prototype systems including Aurora [1], STREAM [8], TelegraphCQ [4] and Niagara [5]. However, up until now there has been no way to compare the performance characteristics of these systems either to each other or to traditional data management systems configured to process streaming data (e.g., a Relational DBMS configured with triggers). Linear Road is designed to measure how well a system can meet real-time query response requirements in processing high-volume streaming and historical data. It has been endorsed by the developers of Aurora (out of Brandeis University, Brown University and MIT) and STREAM (out of Stanford University) as a basis for performance comparisons of stream processing approaches.

In this paper, we use Linear Road to compare the performance of an SDMS (Aurora) to a Relational Database configured to process stream data inputs.[1] Of course, our implementation of Linear Road over a Relational Database may not be optimal, and thus we invite others to implement Linear Road and report their numbers. Nonetheless, we believe that the results reported here show that a dedicated SDMS is far-better suited than a Relational Database for supporting streaming data applications.

Streaming data poses unique challenges to the design of a benchmark. For queries over this data to be meaningful, the input data must have *semantic validity* and not just be random. Because most stream queries are continuous, performance metrics should be based on *response time* rather than completion time. The benchmark must be *verifiable* even though results returned may vary depending on when they are generated. And the absence of a *query lan-*

---

[1] We did not get performance numbers for STREAM in time to include them in this paper. However, these numbers and a description of the STREAM implementation of Linear Road will be available on the STREAM Linear Road web page [10].

guage standard for stream queries means that the benchmark queries must be specified in a more general, though unambiguous way. Linear Road has been designed to meet each of these challenges.

Linear Road simulates an urban expressway system where tolls are determined according to such dynamic factors as congestion and accident proximity. Linear Road's traffic-based orientation is inspired by the increasing prevalence of *variable tolling* (also known as *congestion pricing*) [6, 11, 9] in urban traffic systems. Traffic congestion in major metropolitan areas is an increasing problem as expressways cannot be built fast enough to keep traffic flowing freely at peak periods. The idea behind *variable tolling* is to issue tolls that vary according to time-dependent factors such as congestion levels and accident proximity, with the motivation of charging higher tolls during peak traffic periods to discourage vehicles from using the roads and exacerbating the congestion. Variable tolling is becoming an increasingly popular option for urban planners due to its effectiveness in reducing traffic congestion and to recent advances in microsensor technology that make it feasible. Illinois, California, and Finland have pilot programs utilizing this concept. Moreover, both London and Singapore charge tolls at peak periods to let vehicles enter the downtown area using similar reasoning.

We begin in Section 2 by presenting the unique challenges that stream data introduces in designing a benchmark and describing the ways that Linear Road addresses those challenges. In Section 3, we specify the benchmark requirements. In Section 4, we describe experiments involving two implementations of the benchmark: one using a commercially available Relational Database (which we call "*System X*"), and one using Aurora. As we will show, a dedicated SDMS can outperform a Relational Database in supporting stream data applications by at least a factor of 5.

2 Challenges

Streaming data poses the following unique challenges to the design of a benchmark:

Semantically Valid Input: Input data to a stream benchmark should not be purely random but should have some semantic validity. A typical stream presents discrete measurements of a continuous activity (e.g., the movements of soldiers). The content of a stream should be consistent with this activity. For example, if the positions of a soldier are reported every 15 minutes, the positions of two consecutive reports should not differ by more than how far a soldier can travel in that time. To ensure semantic validity, input data to a stream benchmark should be produced using *simulation*.

Continuous Query (CQ) Performance Metrics: Stream queries are predominantly continuous, and therefore the typical database benchmark metric of "completion time" is inappropriate given that such queries never complete. Instead, more appropriate metrics for streams are:

- *Response Time*: What is the average or maximum difference between the time that an input arrives to an SDMS and the time when an SDMS outputs a computed response?

- *Supported Query Load*: How much input can a stream system process while still meeting specified response times and correctness constraints?

Many Correct Results: Any benchmark implementation should be validated to ensure that it produces results consistent with the benchmark specification. However, continuous queries results may depend upon evolving historical state or the arrival order tuples on a stream, and therefore several different results for the same query may be "correct". Validation should account for queries that have multiple correct answers.

No Query Language: There exists no standard query language for streaming systems, and therefore the query requirements for a stream benchmark should be language-agnostic, yet have a clear semantics.

Linear Road has been designed to meet each of the challenges listed above. The benchmark simulates an urban expressway system where toll charges are determined dynamically. Input data consists of a stream of *position reports* and *historical query requests*. Position reports specify the location of a vehicle on an expressway and are emitted by each vehicle every 30 seconds. A historical query request is issued by a vehicle with some fixed probability every time it emits a position report.

The benchmark requires processing a set of continuous and historical queries over this input stream. In processing position reports, a system must:

- maintain statistics about the number of vehicles and average speed on each segment of each expressway on a per minute basis,

- detect accidents and alert drivers of the accidents, and

- dynamically calculate toll charges based on segment statistics and proximate accidents, and notify and assess vehicles of these charges.

In processing a historical query request, a system will report an account balance, a total of all assessed tolls on a given expressway on a given day, or an estimated travel time and cost for a journey on an expressway. Each query answer must satisfy the response time and correctness requirements specified in this document, and the throughput that a system can sustain in meeting these requirements (as measured in the number of expressways, L of input it processes) constitutes the benchmark score (its **L-Rating**).

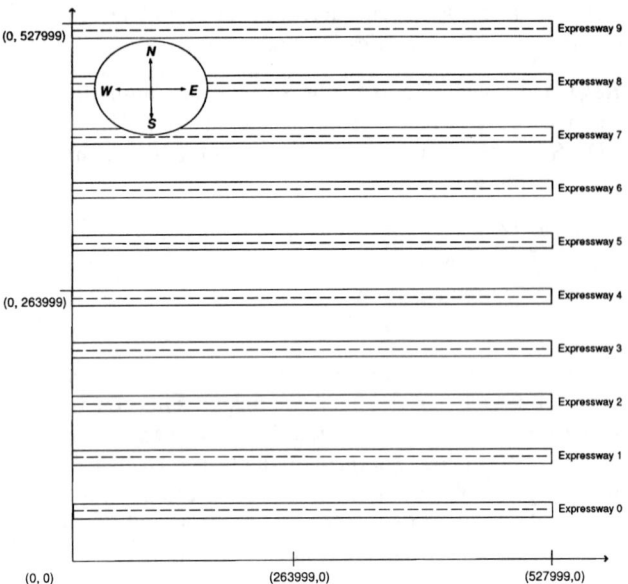

Figure 1. The Geometry of Linear City

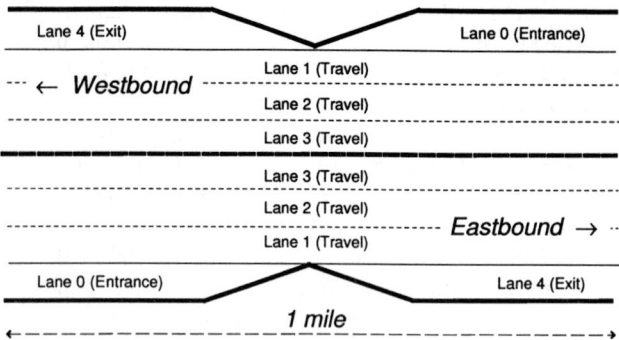

Figure 2. An Example Expressway Segment

Linear Road meets the above challenges of an SDMS benchmark:

- *Semantically Valid Input:* The input data to Linear Road is generated by the publicly available traffic simulator, MITSIM [12]. We describe the details of the simulated data in Section 3.1.1.

- *CQ Performance Metrics:* The *L-Rating* associated with Linear Road is a measure of *supported query load* in that it is a measure of the amount of input that an SDMS can process (as measured in number of expressways) while still meeting response time and correctness constraints (as specified in Section 3).

- *Many Correct Results:* For all queries that depend on some evolving state (e.g., account balance queries that depend on a table that is updated with every toll assessed), variation in response times can mean that multiple answers could be returned that are "correct". Linear Road includes two such queries, and validation for each of those considers all possible valid answers.

- *No Query Language:* All Linear Road queries are specified formally in the predicate calculus rather than a specific stream query language.

3 The Linear Road Benchmark

Linear City is a fictional metropolitan area that is the urban setting for the Linear Road benchmark. The city encompasses an area that is 100 miles wide and 100 miles long, and is divided into a grid such that the origin is the southwestern most point in the city, and coordinate (x, y) is x feet east and y feet north of the origin. Linear City contains 10 parallel expressways numbered from 0-9 and running horizontally 10 miles apart, as illustrated in Figure 1. (For simplicity, there are no expressways that run vertically.) Each expressway has four lanes in each (east and west) direction: 3 travel lanes (lanes #1-3) and one lane devoted to entrance (lane #0) and exit (lane #4) ramps. Each expressway has 100 entrance ramps and 100 exit ramps in each direction, dividing it into 100 mile-long *segments*. Figure 2 shows an example segment.

Every vehicle in Linear City is equipped with a sensor that emits a *position report* that identifies the vehicle's exact coordinates every 30 seconds. (We assume that position reports specify coordinates with 100% accuracy.) Position reports are processed to generate statistics about traffic conditions on every segment of every expressway for every minute, including average vehicle speed, number of vehicles and existence of accidents. These statistics are used to determine toll charges for variable tolling. In addition, vehicles can issue queries to find out their current account balance with the expressway system, total tolls assessed on a given day and expressway, and travel time estimates.

For simplicity, we make the following assumptions about position reports:

1. *No Clock Skew:* A global clock is assumed as the basis for position report timestamps of all vehicles.

2. *No Position Interpolation:* The position of any vehicle at any time t is assumed to be exactly the position reported by that vehicle between times $(t - 30 \text{ sec}, t]$, or *unknown* if no position report was emitted within that range.

3. *Instantaneous Delivery:* A position report with timestamp t is made available to a stream processing system exactly t seconds after the start of the simulation. This is guaranteed by the data driver.

While simplistic, we justify these assumptions by pointing out that the purpose of the benchmark suite is to serve as a stress-test of systems performing stream processing and not to accurately model traffic patterns.

3.1 Linear Road Input

Input data for the Linear Road benchmark is generated by the MIT Traffic Simulator (MITSIM) [12] and stored in flat files. A separate *data driver* is responsible for reading these files and delivering this data in a manner simulating its arrival in real-time.

3.1.1 Simulation

Position reports are generated according to the following traffic model followed by the traffic simulator. The simulator generates a set of vehicles, each of which completes at least one *vehicle trip*: a journey that begins at an entry ramp on some segment and finishes at an exit ramp on some segment on the same expressway.[2] In making a vehicle trip, a vehicle is placed on the entrance ramp and accelerates at a rate allowed by the other traffic. It then merges onto the expressway and moves towards its destination at a rate determined by the degree of traffic congestion. When the vehicle reaches its destination, it moves to the exit ramp and decelerates. For each trip, the selected source location of a vehicle is uniformly distributed over all of the possible entrance ramps on the chosen expressway. The exit ramp is normally distributed with a mean segment location in the middle of the expressway (i.e., segment #50) and with a standard deviation of 20 miles. Hence, vehicles have an affinity for exiting in the downtown area. Once on the expressway, each vehicle proceeds according to a standard traffic spacing model built into the traffic simulator.

The simulator ensures that every vehicle emits a position report every 30 seconds, staggering them so that at every second, roughly $\frac{1}{30}$ of the reports for vehicles currently on the expressway are emitted. Every position report has a timestamp, which is an integer count of seconds since the start of the simulation. A vehicle never travels faster than 100 MPH, and therefore it will emit at least one position report from every segment it travels in. Further, every vehicle is guaranteed to average 40 MPH or less when entering and exiting an expressway and therefore it will emit at least one position report from an entrance ramp and one position report from an exit ramp for every vehicle trip.

The simulator generates one *accident* in a random location on each expressway for every 20 minutes of position reports. An accident occurs when two vehicles are "stopped" at the same position at the same time. A vehicle is stopped when it reports the same position in 4 consecutive position reports. Once an accident occurs in a given segment, traffic proceeds in that segment at a reduced speed determined by the traffic spacing model. The accident takes anywhere from 10-20 minutes to be cleared once it is detected. Until the accident clears, the vehicles involved in the accident continue to emit position reports. After either of the vehicles emits a position report that reveals that it has moved from the site of the accident, the accident is assumed to be cleared.

With 1% probability, every emitted position report is accompanied by a historical query request from the same vehicle. Of historical query requests, 50% are requests for account balances, 10% are requests for total daily tolls on a given day and expressway, and 40% are requests for travel time predictions. We specify how these historical queries should be processed in Section 3.2.3.

3.1.2 Stream Data

The stream data generated by the simulator consists of four types of tuples: *Position Reports* and historical query requests for *Account Balances*, *Daily Expenditures* and *Travel Time Estimation*.

Position Reports

A position report is a tuple of the form,

(Type = 0, Time, VID, Spd, XWay, Lane, Dir, Seg, Pos)

such that Type $= 0$ identifies this tuple as a position report, Time $(0 \ldots 10799)$[3] is a timestamp identifying the time at which the position report was emitted, VID $(0 \ldots \text{MAXINT})$ is an integer *vehicle identifier* identifying the vehicle that emitted the position report, Spd $(0 \ldots 100)$ is an integer reflecting the *speed* of the vehicle (in MPH) at the time the position report is emitted, and XWay, Lane, Dir, Seg and Pos are the following functions over the vehicle's (x, y) coordinates:

- XWay $(0 \ldots L-1)$ identifies the *expressway* from which the position report is emitted

- Lane $(0 \ldots 4)$ identifies the lane of the expressway from which the position report is emitted (0 if it is an entrance ramp (ENTRY), $1 - 3$ if it is a travel lane (TRAVEL) and 4 if it is an exit ramp (EXIT)).

- Dir $(0 \ldots 1)$ indicates the direction (0 for Eastbound and 1 for Westbound) in which the vehicle is traveling when it emits its position report,

- Seg $(0 \ldots 99)$ identifies the mile-long *segment* from which the position report is emitted, and

- Pos $(0 \ldots 527999)$ identifies the horizontal *position* of the vehicle as a measure of the number of feet from the westernmost point on the expressway (i.e., Pos $= x$).[4]

---

[2]Note that some vehicles may not complete their vehicle trips by the end of the simulation period.

[3]There are 10800 seconds in a 3 hour simulation period.

[4]Strictly speaking Seg is redundant given that position reports include Pos. However, several benchmark computations depend upon a vehicle's segment number, and therefore for convenience we include it in input position reports.

Historical Query Requests

A historical query request is either:

- *Account Balance*: a request for the vehicle's current account balance,

- *Daily Expenditure*: a request for the vehicle's total tolls on a specified expressway, on a specified day in the previous 10 weeks,

- *Travel Time*: a request for an estimated toll and travel time for a journey on a given expressway on a given day of the week, at a given time.

Account balance requests are tuples of the form,

(Type = 2, Time, VID, QID)

such that Type identifies this tuple as an account balance request, Time is the time of the request, VID is the vehicle making the request, and QID is an integer *query identifier*. Daily expenditure requests are tuples of the form,

(Type = 3, Time, VID, XWay, QID, Day)

such that Type identifies this tuple as an daily expenditure request, Time is the time of the request, VID is the vehicle making the request, QID is the query identifier, and XWay and Day (1...69) identify the expressway and the day (1 is yesterday, 69 is 10 weeks ago) for which an expenditure total is desired. Travel time requests are tuples of the form,

(Type = 4, Time, VID, XWay, QID, S_{init}, S_{end}, DOW, TOD)

such that Time is the time of the request, VID is the vehicle making the request, QID is a query identifier, XWay is the expressway upon which the journey occurs (from segment S_{init} to segment S_{end}), and DOW (1...7) and TOD (1...1440) specify the day of the week and minute number in the day when the journey would take place.

To avoid the complication of unpredictable event delivery order, the four types of input tuples are multiplexed together into a single stream of tuples consisting of the union of all fields. In order, these are: Type, Time, VID, Spd, XWay, Lane, Dir, Seg, Pos, QID, S_{init}, S_{end}, DOW, TOD and Day. Linear Road implementations can use the Type field to determine which fields are relevant for a given tuple.

3.1.3 Historical Data

Historical data summarizing 10 weeks worth of tolling history must be maintained by the system to answer historical query requests that refer to data dating prior to the start of the simulation. This data includes account data for all vehicles as well as toll charges and average speeds for every segment of every expressway for every minute over the previous 10 weeks. The historical data generator constructs two flat text files of comma separated values:

- File *TollHistory* consists of tuples of the form,

(VID, Day, XWay, Tolls)

such that there is one entry for every vehicle that uses an expressway during the 3 hour simulation (VID) for every day in the previous 10 weeks (Day) and every expressway (XWay). For every (VID, Day, XWay) combination, Tolls is the total amount in tolls spent on the expressway on day Day by vehicle VID.

- File *SegmentHistory* consists of tuples of the form,

(Day, Min, XWay, Dir, Seg, Lav, Cnt, Toll)

such that there is one entry for every day, Day, minute Min, expressway, XWay, direction, Dir and segment, Seg. The values of Lav, Cnt and Toll for each such entry reflect the average speed, number of vehicles and toll charge for the given segment on the given expressway at the given time.

Implementations of Linear Road can bulk load this data into any storage system and can do so offline so that the time for bulk loading is not included in the time to run the benchmark.

3.2 Linear Road Requirements

The Linear Road benchmark requires processing a fixed set of continuous and historical queries. These queries and their response time and accuracy requirements are discussed in detail below. Queries are described informally and specified formally in the predicate calculus.

Response time checks require that every output tuple, p, include two timestamps: one that identifies the time that p was emitted (p.Emit) and one that is the timestamp of the input tuple that triggered p to be generated (p.Time). Emit requires every system implementing Linear Road to invoke a system call to get the current time immediately prior to emitting p as output. Time is the timestamp of the input resulting in p's generation. For example, for any toll notification, p, p.Time is the timestamp of the first position report from the same vehicle reporting its position in the segment for which the toll applies. This timestamp is generated by the simulator, and the data driver ensures that this timestamp is the time the tuple is made available to the stream processing system.

3.2.1 Toll Processing

Systems implementing Linear Road must calculate a toll every time a vehicle reports a position in a new segment, and notify the driver of this toll. Toll calculations are determined on the basis of the current congestion on the segment (as measured in terms of the number of vehicles and the average speed in the segment) as well as the proximity of accidents. We make a distinction between *toll notifications* and *toll assessments*, which happen at different times. Every time a vehicle issues its first position report from a segment, a toll for that segment is calculated and the vehicle is notified of that toll. Every time a position report identifies a vehicle as *crossing* from one segment into another, the toll reported for the segment being exited is assessed to the vehicle's account. Thus, a toll calculation for one segment often is concurrent with an account being debited for the previous segment. If the vehicle exits at the exit ramp of a segment, the toll for that segment is not charged.

Toll Notifications

Table 1 expresses the conditions, output, recipients and response time requirements for toll notifications. The formalization is in terms of the set, P, of all position reports, and uses the following shorthand notation:

- For any position report, $p \in P$, $\overleftarrow{p}$ identifies the position report that was emitted by the same vehicle during the same vehicle trip immediately prior to p.[5] Because every vehicle emits a position report every 30 seconds during a vehicle trip, this can be defined formally as:

$$\overleftarrow{p} = q \in P \text{ s.t.}$$
$$(q.\texttt{VID} = p.\texttt{VID} \land p.\texttt{Time} - q.\texttt{Time} = 30).$$

- Similarly for any position report $p \in P$, $\overrightarrow{p}$ identifies the position report during the same vehicle trip emitted immediately following p:

$$\overrightarrow{p} = q \in P \text{ s.t.}$$
$$(q.\texttt{VID} = p.\texttt{VID} \land q.\texttt{Time} - p.\texttt{Time} = 30).$$

- For any vehicle identifier v and time t, $Last_i(v,t)$ denotes the ith position report emitted by v prior to t:[6]

$$Last_i(v,t) = p \in P \text{ s.t.}$$
$$(p.\texttt{VID} = v \land 30(i-1) \leq t - p.\texttt{Time} < 30i).$$

For example, by the "*No Position Interpolation*" assumption, the current position of v at time t is always $Last_1(v,t)$.

- For any timestamp, t (defined as an integer number of seconds since the start of the simulation), the "minute number of t" ($M(t)$) is the minute number in which t falls. That is,

$$M(t) = \lfloor \frac{t}{60} \rfloor + 1.$$

Note that the first minute of the simulation is minute number 1.

---
[5]Obviously, this is undefined for the first position report of every vehicle trip.
[6]This function is defined for t and v provided that at time t, v was in the midst of a vehicle trip that began at least i position reports ago.

Trigger	Position report, q
Preconditions	$q.\texttt{Seg} \neq \overleftarrow{q}.\texttt{Seg}, \ l \neq \texttt{EXIT}$
Output	(Type: 0, VID: v, Time: t, Emit: t' Spd: $Lav(M(t), x, s, d)$, Toll: $Toll(M(t), x, s, d)$)
Recipient	v
Response	$t' - t \leq 5$ Sec

Table 1. Toll Notification Requirements

The trigger for a toll notification to vehicle v of a charge for traveling in segment s is a position report, $q =$

(Type: 0, Time: t, VID: v, Spd: spd,
XWay: x, Seg: s, Pos: p, Lane: l, Dir: d).

As stated in Table 1, q triggers a toll notification if it reports that v is in a new segment since the last position report, but not in an exit lane. The tuple *output* consists of fields Type $= 0$ (identifying this tuple as a toll notification), VID (identifying the vehicle being notified of the toll), Time (specifying the time that q was emitted), Emit (specifying the time the toll notification is emitted), Speed (specifying the 5-minute average speed in the segment) and Toll (specifying the calculated toll). The *recipient* of the notification is v, and the *response* time requirement is 5 seconds between the time the position report was emitted (t) and the time the toll notification is sent (t').

The values calculated for fields Spd and Toll are expressed in terms of the functions, *Lav* and *Toll* defined in Table 2. *Lav* (short for "Latest Average Velocity") computes the average speed on some expressway x, segment s and direction d by averaging vehicle speeds over the 5 minutes that precede minute $m = M(t)$. Minute averages are expressed with the function $Avgs(m, x, s, d)$ that specifies the average speed of all vehicles that emitted a position report from segment s of expressway x in direction d during minute m. Note that some vehicles might emit two position reports during this minute. This is accounted for in $Avgsv(v, m, x, s, d)$ which calculates the average speed of vehicle v according to all of the position reports it emits during minute m. Finally, $cars(m, x, s, d)$ returns the set of all vehicles that emit position reports from segment s on expressway x while traveling in direction d during minute m. Note that we use the notation, $p.(\texttt{XWay};\texttt{Seg};\texttt{Dir}) = (x;s;d)$ as shorthand for

$$p.\texttt{XWay} = x \land p.\texttt{Seg} = s \land p.\texttt{Dir} = d,$$

and use $\{\!|\ldots|\!\}$ to denote the contents of a bag.

By default, the value of Toll at time t for a segment is based on the average speed and number of vehicles reporting from the segment during minute $M(t) - 1$. Specifically, if the LAV for the time interval from minute $M(t) - 5$ to $M(t) - 1$ is greater than or equal to 40 MPH, or if the number of vehicles on the segment (*numvehicles*) was 50 or less during minute $M(t) - 1$, no toll is assessed. Otherwise,

485

the default toll is determined by the formula,

$$2 \times (numvehicles - 50)^2.$$

The basic intuition is to raise tolls when congestion is high so as to discourage drivers from contributing to worse congestion.

The toll calculation described above is issued for segment s unless an *accident* was detected 0-4 segments downstream of s as of minute $M(t)$. In this case, no toll is charged. Accident detection is discussed in Section 3.2.2.

Toll Assessments

Every time a position report identifies a vehicle as *crossing* from one segment into the next, the toll charge quoted to the vehicle when it first entered the segment that it is now leaving is assessed to the vehicle's account. Systems implementing Linear Road must keep track of all tolls assessed so that it can answer *Account Balance* queries that report the current balance of a vehicle, *Daily Expenditure* queries that report the total tolls assessed on a given expressway on a given day for a given vehicle, and *Travel Time Estimation* queries that use previous toll charges to estimate tolls for given segments on future days and times.

3.2.2 Accident Processing

Systems implementing Linear Road must detect accidents on the expressways as they occur (*detection*), and subsequently alert all vehicles in the vicinity (*notification*). As was discussed in Section 3.2.1, accident detection should also result in a reduction in tolls that are assessed within 5 segments upstream.

Accident Detection

A stream processing system should detect an *accident* on a given segment whenever two or more vehicles are *stopped* in that segment at the same lane and position. A vehicle is considered *stopped* if four consecutive position reports from this vehicle come from the same position (i.e., the same expressway, lane, position and direction). This is expressed formally in Table 3 with the predicates *Stop* and *Acc*. Predicate $Stop(v,t,x,l,p,d)$ holds if the four most recent positions reports from v as of time t are from the same location. Predicate $Acc(t,x,p,d)$ holds if there were two vehicles stopped as of time t at the same position p of expressway x in direction d.

Accident Notification

Once an accident is detected, every vehicle that enters into a segment in the vicinity of the accident must be notified so that these vehicles have the opportunity to exit the expressway and avoid the resulting congestion. The exact requirements for accident notification are summarized in Table 4.

Trigger	Position report, q
Precondition	$\exists_{s',0 \leq i \leq 4} (s' = Dn(q.\text{Seg}, d, i) \land$ $Acc\_in\_Seg(M(t)-1, x, s', d))$, $q.\text{Seg} \neq \overleftarrow{q}.\text{Seg}, l \neq \text{EXIT}$
Output	(Type: 1, Time: t, Emit: t', Seg: s')
Recipients	v
Response	$t' - t \leq 5$ Sec

Table 4. Accident Alert Requirements

The trigger for an accident notification is a position report $q =$

(Type: 0, Time: t, VID: v, Spd: spd,
XWay: x, Seg: s, Pos: p, Lane: l, Dir: d),

that identifies a vehicle entering a segment 0 to 4 segments upstream of some accident location, but only if q was emitted no earlier than the minute following the minute when the accident occurred, and no later than the minute the accident is cleared. This is expressed using the predicate

$$Acc\_in\_Seg(m, x, Dn(s, d, i))$$

that holds if there was an accident in the segment that is exactly i segments downstream of s, in expressway x and in the travel lanes for direction d during minute m.[7] The tuple *output* consists of the fields, Type = 1 (identifying this tuple as an accident alert), Time (specifying the time that q was emitted), Emit (specifying the time the notification is emitted), and Seg (specifying the segment where the accident occurred). The *response* time requirement is 5 seconds between the time that q was emitted (t) and the time the accident notification is sent (t').

Note that for a given accident, multiple accident notifications may be sent to the **same vehicle** if that vehicle does not exit the expressway and instead enters segments bringing it closer to the site of the accident. Repeated notifications are intentional, as this allows for vehicles that enter one of these segments *after* the accident occurs to be notified of the accident. Also, once a vehicle stops receiving accident notifications, it can assume that it has either passed the accident location or that the accident has been cleared.

3.2.3 Historical Query Processing

Aside from the continuous queries involving toll and accident notifications, systems implementing Linear Road must also be able to respond to historical query requests issued by vehicles. There are three types of historical queries. These are described below.

Account Balance Queries

A customer traveling on some expressway can request his account balance at any time. At the start of the simulation,

---

[7]The segment that is i segments downstream of s $Dn(s,d,i)$ is MIN $(s+i, 99)$ if the direction is eastbound ($d=0$) and MAX $(s-i, 0)$ otherwise.

$$cars\,(m,x,s,d) \;=\; \{p.\texttt{VID} \mid p \in P,\; m = M(p.\texttt{Time}),\; p.(\texttt{XWay};\texttt{Seg};\texttt{Dir}) = (x;s;d)\}$$

$$Avgsv\,(v,m,x,s,d) \;=\; \texttt{AVG}\,(\{\!|p.\texttt{Spd} \mid p \in P,\; p.\texttt{VID}=v,\; m = M(p.\texttt{Time}),\; p.(\texttt{XWay};\texttt{Seg};\texttt{Dir}) = (x;s;d)|\!\})$$

$$Avgs\,(m,x,s,d) \;=\; \texttt{AVG}\,(\{\!|Avgsv\,(v,m,x,s,d) \mid v \in cars\,(m,x,s,d)|\!\})$$

$$Lav\,(m,x,s,d) \;=\; \lfloor \texttt{AVG}\,(\{\!|Avgs\,(m-1,x,s,d),\ldots,Avgs\,(m-5,x,s,d)|\!\}) \rfloor$$

$$Toll\,(m,x,s,d) \;=\; \begin{cases} 2\cdot(|cars\,(m-1,t,x,s,d)|-50)^2 \\ \quad \text{if } Lav\,(m,x,s,d) < 40 \text{ and} \\ \quad |cars\,(m-1,x,s,d)| > 50 \text{ and} \\ \quad \forall_{0\le i\le 4}\,(\neg(Acc\_in\_Seg\,(m-1,x,Dn\,(s,d,i)))) \\ 0,\quad \text{otherwise} \end{cases}$$

Table 2. Notation Used to Define Tolls

$$Stop\,(v,t,x,l,p,d) \;\Leftrightarrow\; \forall_{1\le i\le 4}\,(Last_i\,(v,t).(\texttt{XWay};\texttt{Lane};\texttt{Pos};\texttt{Dir}) = (x;l;p;d))$$

$$Acc\,(t,x,p,d) \;\Leftrightarrow\; \exists_{v_1,v_2,l}\,(l = \texttt{TRAVEL} \wedge v_1 \ne v_2 \wedge Stop\,(v_1,t,x,l,p,d) \wedge Stop\,(v_2,t,x,l,p,d))$$

$$Acc\_in\_Seg\,(m,x,s,d) \;\Leftrightarrow\; \exists_{p,t}\,(t \in m \wedge Acc\,(t,x,p,d) \wedge \lfloor \tfrac{p}{5280} \rfloor = s)$$

Table 3. Notation Used to Define Accidents

every vehicle's account balance is zero, and thereafter the account balance at time t is the sum of all tolls assessed as of t. The requirements for account balance historical queries are summarized in Table 5. A historical query to return an account balance for a given vehicle is triggered by a request tuple $a =$

$$(\texttt{Type: 2, Time: } t,\; \texttt{VID: } v,\; \texttt{QID: } q).$$

The tuple *output* consists of the fields, Type = 2 (identifying this tuple as an account balance), Time (specifying the time that a was emitted), Emit (specifying the time the query response is emitted), QID (identifying the query that issued the request), Bal (the account balance calculated), and ResultTime (the time at which Bal was last updated). The balance is the sum of all tolls that were charged to the vehicle's account. This is expressed in terms of *tollset*: the set of all position reports that resulted in a toll charge being assessed. A subset of the position reports that generated alerts, *tollset* (v) consists of those position reports issued from some segment (s) whose subsequent position reports indicated that the vehicle did not exit the expressway from segment s. More formally,

$$tollset\,(v) \;=\; \{p \in P \mid p.\texttt{VID} = v,\; p.\texttt{Seg} \ne \vec{p}.\texttt{Seg},\; p.(\texttt{XWay};\texttt{Dir}) = (x;d)\}.$$

Function *Toll* specifies the toll calculation as described in Table 2.

That Linear Road requires answering account balance queries means that the tolls charged to each vehicle must be maintained in a timely fashion. Thus, the most substantial overhead resulting from inclusion of this historical query comes not from the cost of answering it but from the cost of maintaining the data required to answer it. The *response*

Trigger	Account balance request, a
Condition	-
Output	(Type: 2, Time: t, Emit: t', ResultTime: τ, QID: q, Bal: $\sum_{p\,\in\,tollset(v)}\,(f(p)))$ s.t. $p.\text{Time} \le \tau$, $p.\text{Seg} \ne Last_1\,(v,t).Seg$ $f(p) = Toll\,(M(p.\texttt{Time}), p.\texttt{XWay}, p.\texttt{Seg}, p.\texttt{Dir})$
Recipient	v
Response	$t' - t \le 5$ Sec
Accuracy	$\tau \ge t - 60$ Sec

Table 5. Account Balance Requirements

time requirement is 5 seconds from the time the historical query request is issued to the time a response is emitted. The *accuracy* requirement specifies that the returned balance must have been accurate at some time, τ, in the 60 seconds prior to the time when the account balance request is issued. (Given that tolls can be issued at most once per emitted position report, this means the query has up to 3 possible correct answers.) This interval gives the stream processing system some flexibility as to when to update the balance of a vehicle as a result of assessing a toll. If a query request at time t is concurrent with some toll charges that have yet to be assessed to a vehicle's account, the system might choose to process the historical query before updating the account balance (potentially producing a result that is accurate for some time $\tau < t$), or waiting until the tolls have been assessed.

Daily Expenditure Queries

A second historical query that can be issued in Linear Road is one that requests the sum of tolls spent on some express-

Trigger	Daily Expenditure request, d
Condition	-
Output	(Type: 3, Time: t, Emit: t', QID: q, Bal: $\sum_{p \in tollset(v)} (f(p)))$ s.t. $Day(p.\text{Time}) = d$, $p.\text{XWay} = x$ $f(p) = $ Toll $(M(p.\text{Time}), p.\text{XWay}, p.\text{Seg}, p.\text{Dir})))$
Recipients	v
Response	$t' - t \leq 10$ Sec

Table 6. Daily Expenditure Requirements

way on some day in the last 10 weeks (not including the current day or any day which ended within 5 minutes of t). The requirements for daily expenditure historical queries are summarized in Table 6. A historical query to return an account balance for a given vehicle is triggered by a request tuple $d =$

(Type: 3, Time: t, VID: v, QID: q, XWay: x, Day: n).

The tuple *output* consists of the fields, Type = 3 (identifying this tuple as a daily expenditure report), Time (specifying the time that d was emitted), Emit (specifying the time the query response is emitted), QID (identifying the query that issued the request), and Bal which is the account balance calculated. The value of Bal is the sum of all tolls from expressway x on day n that were charged to the vehicle's account.

To be able to respond to daily expenditure queries, systems implementing Linear Road must maintain 10 weeks worth of toll data per vehicle and expressway. Given the approximately 150,000 vehicles generated in a 3 hour simulation, this amounts to $150,000 \cdot L \cdot 70$ (roughly between 10 million and 100 million) rows.

Travel Time Estimation Queries

A historical query to return a time travel estimate is triggered by a request tuple $z =$

(Type: 4, Time: t, VID: v, QID: q,
XWay: x, S_{init}: i, S_{end}: e,
DOW: d, TOD: y)

In response, the system responds with a tuple of the form,

(Type : 4, QID : q, TravelTime : r_1, Toll : r_2)

such that r_1 and r_2 are respectively, the predicted travel time and toll charge for the vehicle journey calculated on the basis of statistics maintained over the previous 10 weeks in the manner described below.

Let z be a request for a travel time and toll charge estimate for a journey from segment i to segment e on expressway x starting on day d and time y. Now, let t_j be the *expected arrival time* at segment j ($i \leq j \leq e$). Then,

$$y_i = y, \text{ and}$$
$$y_{j+1} = y_j + tav(x, j, d, t_j) \ (i < j \leq e)$$

where $tav(Xway, Seg, DOW, TOD)$ computes the expected travel time from average vehicle speed for 10 weeks of data, for a given expressway, segment, day and time. Then, the expected travel time, $r_1 = y_e$ and the expected toll is

$$r_2 = \sum_{j=1}^{e-1} cav(x, j, d, y_j)$$

where $cav(Xway, Seg, DOW, TOD)$ computes the expected toll from average vehicle speed and number of vehicles for a given expressway, segment, day and time, using Table 2.

Systems implementing Linear Road must maintain 10 weeks worth of statistical data for each segment on the Linear Road expressways. The data that must be maintained for each of the $L \times 200$ segments includes a count of the number of vehicles in the segment and the *Lav*. Note that 10 weeks of historical data at 1 minute granularity for every segment requires maintaining $200 \cdot L \cdot 10 \cdot 7 \cdot 24 \cdot 60$ (roughly between 20 million and 200 million) rows. The response time requirement for the travel time query is 30 seconds.

3.3 Running the Benchmark

Aside from this document, the Linear Road benchmark web site [7] makes available four tools to assist researchers in the implementation of Linear Road:

- A *historical data generator* that generates a set of flat files containing historical toll data summarizing tolling activity over the 10 weeks prior to the simulation run,

- A *traffic simulator* (based on MITSIMLab [12]) that generates a set of flat files containing streaming input data for the benchmark,

- A *data driver* that delivers the data generated by the traffic simulator to a system in real-time, and

- A *validator* that verifies the correctness of query results as well as ensuring that response-time requirements are met.

The purpose of the benchmark is to determine the L-rating of a stream processing system: the maximum *scale factor* at which the system can respond to the specified set of continuous and historical queries while meeting their response time and accuracy requirements. It is assumed that the benchmark will be run with increasingly larger scale factors until one is found for which the requirements cannot be met. Once the queries are formulated in a given system, the benchmark is executed according to the steps below:

1. The *historical data generator* is run to generate flat files consisting of 10 weeks worth of historical data. Offline, this data can be loaded into the system's storage facility of choice.

2. The *traffic simulator* is run to generate L flat files, each of which consists of 3 hours of traffic data and historical query requests from vehicles reporting from a single expressway during rush hour. The *data driver* is then invoked to deliver this data in a manner simulating its arrival in real-time.

3. The system running the benchmark is configured to generate a flat file containing all output tuples (with timestamps reflecting the times of their generation and the times of the input tuples that triggered their generation) in response to the queries defined in the benchmark.

4. The *validation tool* is used to check the response times and accuracy of generated output to see if they meet the requirements of the benchmark.

A system achieves an *L-rating* for the benchmark if it meets its response time and accuracy constraints while supporting L expressways worth of input.

Systems implementing Linear Road must direct their output into a single flat file. Validation involves comparing the system's output with that generated as a reference set by the validation tool for the given input. The validation tool will read output from the flat files generated by the stream system and check the results to see if they meet the response time and accuracy requirements described previously. It is expected that most systems will produce accurate output, but will for some scale factor, be unable to continue meeting the response time constraints. When reporting its *L-rating*, a system should also specify the hardware configuration over which it ran.

4 Implementations & Experiments

In this section, we describe two implementations of the Linear Road benchmark and compare their relative performance. The first implementation is over a pre-release commercialization of Aurora [1] and is described in Section 4.1. The second implementation is over a commercially available Relational Database (System X) and is described in Section 4.2. Both systems were run on the same 3 GHz Pentium box with 2 GB RAM and running Linux. We compare the performance of these two implementations in Section 4.3 and show that a dedicated stream processing engine can outperform a Relational Database for streaming data applications (as measured in their respective scale factors) by a factor of 5.[8]

---
[8] The Aurora system we use in the benchmark is still a pre-Beta version of the commercial product, and we anticipate that this improvement factor will increase as the product matures.

Of the queries included in the benchmark, the *Travel Time Estimation* query is by far the most complex and difficult to express. Neither of the benchmark implementations described below supports this query and requests in the input for this type of query are ignored.

4.1 Linear Road in Aurora

Aurora uses a workflow-like boxes-and-arrows model for constructing queries over stream data [2]. The Aurora implementation of Linear Road consists of a *query network* of roughly 60 boxes and the following shared tables:

- *Vehicle Information:* Including, for every vehicle, such things as its last known location (expressway # + position + direction) and its account balance,

- *Stopped Cars:* Including all locations where cars are stopped and the cars involved,

- *Accidents:* Including all segments in close proximity to an accident and the time of the accident,

- *Segment Statistics:* Including for every segment of every expressway, and for every minute in the last 5 minutes, and

- *Toll History:* For every vehicle, expressway and day over the previous 10 weeks, the total tolls spent on the expressway.

Historical query requests are each handled separately from position reports, and each require 1-2 boxes to read from the appropriate tables (*Vehicle Information* for the account balance query and *Toll History* for the daily expenditure query) and process the results.

Position reports are processed by three consecutive subnetworks of the query network:

1. *Subnetwork #1* is responsible for detecting and recording when cars are stopped, and if for the ones that are, if they are in an accident. This subnetwork reads and writes the *Stopped Cars*, *Accidents* and *Vehicle Information* tables.

2. *Subnetwork #2* is responsible for maintaining statistics for every segment of every expressway with 1 minute granularity. This subnetwork reads from the *Accidents* table and writes to the *Segment Statistics* table.

3. *Subnetwork #3* is responsible for calculating and emitting tolls for those position reports that show a vehicle that has crossed into a new segment, and for emitting accident alerts for those position reports that show that the vehicle has entered a segment within 5 segments upstream of a recent accident. This subnetwork reads from the *Segment Statistics* table and emits results (toll notifications and accident alerts) to an output stream.

The subnetworks listed above are connected in sequence. Synchronization primitives between them ensure that no position report with timestamp t is processed by Subnetwork #3 before all position reports with timestamps of $t - 1$ minute or less have been processed by Subnetworks #1 and #2. The box-at-a-time scheduler of Aurora [3] is constrained only by these primitives and the availability of inputs to boxes when deciding what boxes are eligible to be scheduled.

4.2 Linear Road in System X

We built two implementations of Linear Road over System X. The first is a *trigger-based* implementation that uses the built-in trigger facility of System X to process position reports and historical query requests as they arrive. The second is a *polling-based* implementation that uses a data driver written in Perl to preload a dedicated relation with a second's worth of position reports every second and subsequently invoke a System X stored procedure. For both implementations, recovery logging was turned off. Because the polling-based implementation allows for batch processing of position reports, sensitivity analysis showed that it performed much better than the trigger-based implementation and therefore, only the polling-based implementation is presented here.

The Linear Road implementation over System X has much the same structure as the Linear Road implementation over Aurora. A stored procedure of roughly 300 lines of queries and accompanying code, this implementation also uses tables to store *vehicle information*, *stopped cars*, *accidents*, *segment statistics* and *toll history*. As well, there is an additional table to hold all input tuples delivered by the driver in the last second, and an additional table to receive the output results.

As with Aurora, historical queries are handled separately (with simple SQL queries). Position reports follow the same sequence of processing as with Aurora: first detect accidents; then generate statistics and calculate and emit toll and accident alerts. As much as possible, tuples are processed in batch mode. For example, after the arrival of a minute's worth of position reports, a query is run over these position reports to determine all segment statistics for that minute.

4.3 Results

In this section, we present experimental results from running the Aurora and System X implementations of Linear Road with varying numbers of expressways.

4.3.1 Scale Factor

Table 7 shows the L-factors achieved by Aurora and System X running Linear Road. An expressway's worth of input data consists of roughly 12 million position reports, 60,000

System X	Aurora
0.5	2.5

Table 7. L-Ratings for Linear Road

account balance query requests and 12,000 daily expenditure requests delivered in 3 hours. The corresponding output consists of roughly 2 million toll alerts and 28,000 accident alerts (as well as one historical query output for each historical query request). Therefore, on average, the System X implementation processed roughly 560 input tuples per second (delivering an average throughput of 100 tuples per second) while meeting the response time requirements of Linear Road, while Aurora processed roughly 2800 input tuples per second (delivering an average throughput of 486 tuples per second) for a factor of 5 performance gain.[9]

Table 8 shows the maximum response times for toll notifications for every run of System X and Aurora. For any given run, these numbers show the highest response time for an output toll notification such that the response time for any output q is equal to q.Emit $-$ q.Time. Note that because timestamps are in the granularity of a second, the reported response times may be off by up to a second. That is, a response time of k calculated in this way indicates that the actual response time is some time, t, such that $k - 1$ Sec $< t < k + 1$ Sec.

One can observe from this table that when either system first fails to meet the benchmark requirements for some number of expressways, it fails substantially. Aurora succeeds with 2.5 expressways but has a worst-case response time of roughly 3 minutes with 3 expressways. System X succeeds with 0.5 expressways but has a worst-case response time of roughly 33 minutes for 1.0 expressway. The degree to which a system fails depends on how early during the 3 hour run the system first starts to fall behind (i.e., the first input that fails to meet the response time requirements). When this occurs, it must be the case that input tuples are being backed up on the input queue and soon it becomes the case that response time requirements fail before processing even begins for these inputs. Aurora first fails with 3 expressways in processing an input position report with timestamp, 7931 (roughly 2.3 hours into the benchmark), and therefore tuples are only accumulating in the input queue for the last 40 min or so of the run. System X first fails with 1 expressway in processing an input position report with timestamp, 4761 (roughly 1.3 hours into the benchmark), and therefore tuples are accumulating in the input queue for the last hour and 40 minutes of the run. Because System X fails earlier in its run, its worst-case response time is much higher. Note that when run with 1.5 and 2 expressways, System X fails even sooner and with many more input tuples idling in the input queues, and reports worst-case response times of roughly 4.5 and 14.5 hours respectively.

---
[9]Because System X was unable to meet the benchmark requirements for 1 expressway, results were generated at the granularity of half of an expressway.

XWays	System X	Aurora
0.5	3	1
1.0	2031	1
1.5	16346	1
2.0	52443	2
2.5	-	2
3.0	-	196

Table 8. Max Response Times for Tolls (Sec)

4.3.2 Discussion

Our results suggest that a dedicated SDMS can outperform a Relational Database system in processing stream data by at least a factor of 5. If the response time requirements were made more strict (e.g., 3 seconds for toll alerts rather than 5 seconds), then Aurora still meets the requirements for 2.5 expressways, but System X may then fail to meet the response time requirements for 0.5 expressways. Unfortunately, the 1 second granularity of timestamps we used stopped us from confirming this result in time for the paper deadline, and thus only the factor of 5 improvement is known with certainty.

The purpose of this benchmark is to stimulate creative thought on how to meet the challenges of large scale streaming data applications. To this end, the goal of our initial experiments described above, was to see how a stream data management system that was architected for exactly these kinds of applications, would compare to a relational database system that was configured to process queries in response to pushed data. Our numbers suggest that a dedicated SDMS is far better suited for stream data applications than a relational database. We readily acknowledge that our implementation of Linear Road in a Relational Database may not be optimal, and so we invite others to implement this benchmark and report their numbers.

5 Conclusions

This paper presents *Linear Road*: a benchmark and accompanying toolkit for comparing the capabilities of systems that perform stream data management. Linear Road is inspired by the increasing prevalence of "variable tolling" in highways systems throughout the world. Based on a fictional urban area with a simple geometry, Linear Road simulates a traffic monitoring system that maintains current and historical statistics over each 1 mile segment of each expressway, detects and alerts drivers of accidents, calculates tolls based on segment statistics, accidents and frequency of use, and supports historical queries that report account balances, daily expenditures and predicted travel times and tolls.

After outlining the challenges in formulating a stream data benchmark in Section 2 and describing the benchmark itself in Section 3, we described two implementations of Linear Road: one using a commercially available Relational Database system ("System X"), and the other using a pre-release commercialization of Aurora. Our experimental results showed that Aurora has an L-factor of 2.5, whereas System X has an L-factor of 0.5, thus showing a factor of 5 performance gain resulting from using a dedicated Stream Data Management System to process stream data. In fact, the performance gain is likely higher than this, but time constraints before the paper deadline did not allow us to refine our time precision to establish this for certain.

Beyond serving as a basis for comparison, the purpose of this benchmark is to stimulate creative thought in the design of Stream Data Management Systems. We invite others to run the benchmark on their own systems and contribute to this discussion.

References

[1] D. Abadi, D. Carney, U. Cetintemel, M. Cherniack, C. Convey, S. Lee, M. Stonebraker, N. Tatbul, and S. Zdonik. Aurora: A new model and architecture for data stream management. *VLDB Journal*, 12(3), August 2003.

[2] D. Carney, U. Cetintemel, M. Cherniack, C. Convey, S. Lee, G. Seidman, M. Stonebraker, N. Tatbul, and S. B. Zdonik. Monitoring Streams - A New Class of Data Management Applications. In *Proceedings of 28th International Conference on Very Large Data Bases (VLDB '02)*, pages 215–226, Hong Kong, China, August 2002.

[3] D. Carney, U. Cetintemel, A. Rasin, S. B. Zdonik, M. Cherniack, and M. Stonebraker. Operator Scheduling in a Data Stream Manager. In *Proceedings of 29th International Conference on Very Large Data Bases (VLDB '03)*, pages 838–849, Berlin, Germany, September 2003.

[4] S. Chandrasekaran, O. Cooper, A. Deshpande, M. J. Franklin, J. M. Hellerstein, W. Hong, S. Krishnamurthy, S. R. Madden, V. Raman, F. Reiss, and M. A. Shah. Telegraphcq: Continuous dataflow processing for an uncertain world. In M. Stonebraker, J. Gray, and D. DeWitt, editors, *Proceedings of the 1st Biennial Conference on Innovative Database Research (CIDR)*, Asilomar, CA, January 2003.

[5] J. Chen, D. J. DeWitt, F. Tian, and Y. Wang. NiagaraCQ: A scalable continuous query system for internet databases. In J. N. Weidong Chen and P. Bernstein, editors, *Proceedings of the Special Interest Group on Management of Data (SIGMOD)*, Dallas, Tx, June 2000.

[6] Conjestion Pricing: A Report From Intelligent Transportation Systems (ITS, May 2002. URL: www.path.berkeley.edu/ leap/TTM/Demand_Manage/pricing.html.

[7] The Linear Road Benchmark Website, 2004. URL: http://www.cs.brandeis.edu/linearroad/.

[8] R. Motwani, J. Widom, A. Arasu, B. Babcock, S. Babu, M. Datar, G. Manku, C. Olsten, J. Rosenstein, and R. Varma. Query processing, resource management, and approximation in a data stream management system. In M. Stonebraker, J. Gray, and D. DeWitt, editors, *Proceedings of the 1st Biennial Conference on Innovative Database Research (CIDR)*, Asilomar, CA, January 2003.

[9] R. W. Poole. HOT Lanes Prompted by Federal Program, November 2002. URL: http://www.rppi.org/federalhotlanes.html.

[10] STREAM project page for Linear Road Benchmark, 2004. URL: http://www-db.stanford.edu/stream/cql-benchmark.html.

[11] A Guide for Hot Lane Development: A U.S. Department of Transportation Federal Highway Administration White Paper. , March 2003. URL: www.itsdocs.fhwa.dot.gov/JPODOCS/REPTS_TE/13668.html.

[12] Q. Yang and H. N. Koutsopoulos. A Microscopic Traffic Simulator For Evaluation of Dynamic Traffic Management Systems. *Transportation Research C*, 4(3):113–129, June 1996.

Query Languages and Data Models for Database Sequences and Data Streams

Yan-Nei Law   Haixun Wang[1]   Carlo Zaniolo

Computer Science Dept., UCLA
Los Angeles, CA 90095
{ynlaw, zaniolo}@cs.ucla.edu

IBM T. J. Watson Research[1]
Hawthorne, NY 10532
haixun@us.ibm.com

Abstract

We study the fundamental limitations of relational algebra (RA) and SQL in supporting sequence and stream queries, and present effective query language and data model enrichments to deal with them. We begin by observing the well-known limitations of SQL in application domains which are important for data streams, such as sequence queries and data mining. Then we present a formal proof that, for continuous queries on data streams, SQL suffers from additional expressive power problems. We begin by focusing on the notion of nonblocking ($\mathcal{NB}$) queries that are the only continuous queries that can be supported on data streams. We characterize the notion of nonblocking queries by showing that they are equivalent to monotonic queries. Therefore the notion of $\mathcal{NB}$-completeness for RA can be formalized as its ability to express all monotonic queries expressible in RA using only the monotonic operators of RA. We show that RA is not $\mathcal{NB}$-complete, and SQL is not more powerful than RA for monotonic queries.

To solve these problems, we propose extensions that allow SQL to support all the monotonic queries expressible by a Turing machine using only monotonic operators. We show that these extensions are (i) user-defined aggregates (UDAs) natively coded in SQL (rather than in an external language), and (ii) a generalization of the union operator to support the merging of multiple streams according to their timestamps. These query language extensions require matching extensions to basic relational data model to support sequences explicitly ordered by timestamps. Along with the formulation of very powerful queries, the proposed extensions entail more efficient expressions for many simple queries. In particular, we show that nonblocking queries are simple to characterize according to their syntactic structure.

1 Introduction

Data stream management systems represent a vibrant area of research [5, 6, 31, 10, 12, 19, 30, 17, 11, 8, 13]. The solution approach taken by most projects consists of extending database query languages and data models to support efficiently continuous queries on stream data, and is based on the sound rationale that, since many applications will span traditional databases and data streams, an unified programming environment will simplify their development. Nevertheless, database query languages were designed for persistent data residing on disks, rather than for transient data flowing through the wires: therefore their suitability to the new task need to be evaluated critically, and their limitations in this new role must be addressed. Indeed, the limitations of SQL in this new role are many and severe. For instance, the ineffectiveness of SQL to express queries on time series and sequences has been long recognized in the field and inspired much previous research [29, 27, 22, 2, 25, 24]. Since data streams are basically unbounded sequences, the inability of expressing sequence queries must be viewed as a serious limitation of SQL for continuous queries. Another well-known problem area for SQL is data mining [14, 20, 16, 26], since it is clear that SQL will be at least as ineffective at mining data streams as it is at mining persistent data. But in reality, the situation is significantly worse for data streams where additional issues arise to further impair the expressive power of

---

Permission to copy without fee all or part of this material is granted provided that the copies are not made or distributed for direct commercial advantage, the VLDB copyright notice and the title of the publication and its date appear, and notice is given that copying is by permission of the Very Large Data Base Endowment. To copy otherwise, or to republish, requires a fee and/or special permission from the Endowment.

Proceedings of the 30th VLDB Conference, Toronto, Canada, 2004

SQL. One is that queries involving traditional aggregates or constructs such as NOT IN, NOT EXISTS, ALL, EXCEPT cannot be allowed since they are blocking, i.e., they do not return their results until they have seen the whole input [5]. Only nonblocking query operators can be allowed on data streams [5], and we will prove that all monotonic queries, and only those, can be expressed using nonblocking computations—a result that was first claimed in [34].

This set the stage for one more problem (the fourth in our list) inasmuch as relational algebra (RA) and SQL are not complete for nonblocking queries, since they can only express some monotonic queries using blocking operators. The final problem follows from the fact that traditional database applications would normally be developed by embedding SQL queries in procedural languages using cursor-based interface mechanisms. Therefore, expressive-power limitations of SQL would be remedied by writing in the procedural language the part of the application that could not be readily expressed in the embedded SQL query. But the cursor-based model of embedded queries is one where the the procedural language program sees a static window onto the database and controls the movement of the cursor via get-next statements. But as data streams arrive furiously and continuously, the data stream manager cannot hold the current tuple, and all that have arrived after that, waiting for the application to issue a get-next statement. Indeed, most of current data stream management systems do not support cursor-based interfaces to programming languages.

In summary, the lack of expressive power and extensibility that were already serious problems for SQL (as per the sequence queries and data mining queries) are now made much more severe by data streams, where blocking query operators are disallowed and the remedy of embedding the SQL queries into a procedural language is also compromised. Therefore, an in-depth study of this problem and its possible solutions is sorrily needed, given that only limited studies have been proposed in the past (see next section). We will also show that the problem has interesting implications on the data model to be used for data streams: for instance, the presence of time stamps is required for query completeness.

The paper is organized as follows. In the next section, we survey several data models for sequences and streams. In Section 3, we study nonblocking query operators which we prove equivalent to monotonic operators; in Section 4 we show the incompleteness of relational query languages with respect to monotonic operators. In Section 5, we introduce a native extensibility mechanism for SQL which the data model is suitable for data stream and sequence queries. Also, this extension is Turing Complete—the result proven in Section 6. In Section 7, we prove completeness w.r.t. the functions computable by nonblocking computations. In section 8, we recap the benefits of the proposed extensions with sequence queries, data mining functions, and memory minimization.

2 Related Work

Significant projects on data streams include those described [5, 6, 31, 10, 12, 19, 30, 17, 11, 8, 13]. In this section we discuss issues such as blocking operators, data model, and query power that are most significant for this paper.

The Tapestry project was the first to model data streams as append-only databases supporting continuous queries [31]. The problem of blocking operators was also identified in [31] strategies were suggested for overcoming this problem for monotonic queries. Indeed the close relationship between monotonicity and nonblocking queries has been understood for a long time, however as far as we know, there has been no previous attempt to prove or formalize this relationship. For instance, two excellent survey papers [5, 13] clearly note the relationship, but make no statement to the fact that queries expressible by nonblocking operators are exactly the monotonic queries—more remarkably this property is not even mentioned as a 'folk theorem,' or a formal conjecture. Even the work presented in [32], these focuses on overcoming the blocking operator problem has not pursued their formal characterization. The work described in [32] presents an interesting approach for overcoming the problems of blocking operators using punctuated data streams. The data stream is modelled as an infinite sequence of finite lists of elements. Then punctuation marks can be viewed as predicates on stream elements that must evaluate to false for every element following the punctuation. Note that a punctuation is an ordered set of patterns which indicates what should be output and stored for future uses and when it should be output. Then a stream iterator is proposed that accessing the input incrementally, outputting the results as another punctuated stream and storing the state, based on the punctuation of the input elements. To achieve this, a unary stream iterator is defined as five components (inital_state, step, pass, prop, keep), where inital_state is the iterator state before any tuple arrives, step is a function that takes new tuples and a current state and output new tuples and a modified state and pass, prop, keep are three behavior functions that take punctuation marks and state as input and returns additional outputs tuples, output punctuation, and a modified state. Clearly, the structure of unary stream iterators is similar to that User-Defined Aggregates (UDAs) which we will show (i) can also deal with punctuation, (ii) are defined natively using SQL, and (iii) make the SQL's expressive power equivalent to that of a Turing machine. The use of UDAs for enhancing the power of query languages for data streams is also been advocated by the Aurora project [8], where non-SQL operators are however used to define UDAs.

While although the objective of overcoming the expressive power limitations caused by the exclusion of blocking operators provides the clear motivation for much previous work, at the best of our knowledge, there has been no attempt to characterize how much expressive power is lost without blocking query operators, or how much power is gained back with extensions such the unary stream operators [32], or the UDAs used in Aurora [8]. (In this paper, we will prove that the power loss due to blocking operators and the power gain due to UDAs are both very high.)

Although there has been no formal investigation of the limitations of SQL for data stream applications, the investigations for other application domains of interest are nearly too many to mention. Of particular significance are those focusing on sequence queries, including those presented in [29, 27, 22, 2, 25, 24]. In particular, the sequence model called $\mathcal{SEQ}$, introduced in [28], focuses on possible extensions to the relational data model and relational algebra. Therefore, many-to-many relations are defined between a set of records and a countable totally ordered domain (e.g., the integer set) to give positions for each record, along with two new classes of sequence operators, the *positional* operators and *record-oriented* operators. The expressive power entailed by these extensions, however, is not characterized.

Similar extensions to the relational model and relational algebra however have not been pursued in later studies of sequence queries [2, 25, 24] and stream queries and will not be considered in this paper. In this paper, we followed the generally accepted model of viewing data streams as bags of append-only of ordered tuples. In fact, we will show that (in Section 7) that time stamps must be added to achieve the completeness for non-blocking queries. After this necessary addition, our data stream can be modelled as an unbounded appended-only bags of elements <tuple, timestamp> as in CQL [4, 21], along the line of SQL (although CQLs *Istream*, *Dstream* and *Rstream* are not considered in this paper).

3 Nonblocking Query Operators

We can now formalize the notion of sequences as a bridge between database relations and streams. Sequences consist of ordered tuples, whereas the order is immaterial in relational tables. Streams are sequences of unbounded length, where the tuples are ordered by, and possibly time-stamped with, their arrival time. An open problem in this line of research is to find what generalizations of the relation data model, algebra, and query languages are needed to deal with sequences and streams [5]. In this section, we will characterize:

- The blocking/nonblocking properties of operators independent of the language in which they are expressed, and
- The abstract properties of stream functions expressible by blocking/nonblocking operators.

According to [5] *'A blocking query operator is a query operator that is unable to produce the first tuple of the output until it has seen the entire input.'* In an operational reading of this definition 'until it has seen the entire input' will be taken to mean 'until it has detected the end of the input'. For instance, the traditional aggregates in SQL never produce any tuple until they have seen the last input tuple: thus these are blocking operators. Since continuous queries must return answers without waiting for tuples that will arrive in the future, blocking operators are not suitable for stream processing [5]. Nonblocking operators are instead suitable for stream processing. We can now define nonblocking operators, as follows (the opposite of the statement used to define blocking operators): *'A nonblocking query operator is one that produces all the tuples of the output before it has detected the end of the input.'* Here we have discussed operators that are either blocking or nonblocking; but the case of partially blocking operators is also possible, although less frequent in practice. For instance, an online average aggregate that returns results during the computation but also the final result at the end is partially blocking. To characterize the properties of stream operators we will first formalize the notion of sequences, and computation on sequences.

Definition 1 Sequence: *Let $t_1, \ldots, t_n$ be tuples from a relation R. Then, the list $S = [t_1, \ldots, t_n]$ is called a sequence, of length n, of tuples from R. The empty sequence is denoted by $[\ ]$; $[\ ]$ has length 0.*

Observe that the tuples $t_1, \ldots, t_n$ in the sequence are not necessarily distinct. We will use the notation $t \in S$ to denote that, for some $1 \leq i \leq n$, $t_i = t$.

Definition 2 Presequence: *Let $S = [t_1, \ldots, t_n]$ be a sequence and $0 < k \leq n$. Then, $t_1, \ldots, t_k$ is the presequence of S of length k, denoted by S^k. $[\ ]$ is the zero-length presequence of S.*

Definition 3 Partial Order: *Let S and L be two sequences. Then, if for some k, $L^k = S$ we say that S is a presequence of L and write $S \sqsubseteq L$. If $k < n$, we say that S is a proper presequence of L and write $S \sqsubset L$.*

Given a relation R, $\sqsubseteq$ is a partial order (reflexive, transitive, and antisymmetric) on sequences of tuples from R. We can now consider operators that take sequences (streams) as input and return sequences (streams) as output. For instance consider an operator G that takes a sequence S as input and produces a sequence $G(S)$ as output:

$$S \longrightarrow \boxed{G} \longrightarrow G(S)$$

G operates as an incremental transducer, which for each new input tuple in S, adds zero, one, or several tuples to the output. At step j, G consumes the jth input tuple and produces any number of tuples as output. But rather than focusing on the new output produced at step j, we will concentrate on the *cumulative* output produced up to and including step j. Thus, let $G^j(S)$ be the cumulative output produced up to step j by our operator G presented with the input sequence S. $G^j(S)$ is a sequence whose content and length depend on G, j and S. Consider, for instance, a sequence of length n, i.e., $S = S^n$. If G is a traditional SQL aggregate, such as SUM or AVG, then $G^j(S)$ is the empty sequence for $j < n$, while, for $j = n$, $G^j(S)$ contains a single tuple. However, if G is the continuous count (continuous sum), defined as follows: for each new tuple, G returns the count of tuples (sum of a particular column) of the tuples seen so far—i.e., of S^j, then, by definition, $G^j(S) \sqsubseteq G^k(S)$, for $j \leq k$ — i.e., the output produced till step j is a presequence of that produced till step k. A null operator N is one where $N(S) = [\,]$ for every S. We now have the following definitions:

Definition 4 *A non-null operator G is said to be*
- blocking, *when for every sequence S of length n, $G^j(S) = [\,]$ for every $j < n$, and $G^n(S) = G(S)$*
- nonblocking, *when for every sequence S of length n, $G^j(S) = G(S^j)$, for every $j \leq n$.*

Therefore, a blocking operator is one that does not deliver any tuple in the output until the final input tuple. Instead, a nonblocking operator is one that performs the computation incrementally, i.e., the cumulative output at step $j < n$ (for an input sequence S of length n), can be computed by simply applying G to the presequence S^j. Partially blocking operators are those that do not satisfy either definition, i.e., those where, for some S and j:

$$[\,] \sqsubset G^j(S) \sqsubset G(S^j).$$

We would like now to elevate our abstraction level from that of operators and programs to that of mathematical functions. We ask the following question: what are the functions on streams that can be expressed by nonblocking operators? There is a surprisingly simple answer to this question:

Proposition 1 *A function $F(S)$ on a sequence S can be computed using a nonblocking operator, iff F is monotonic with respect to the partial ordering $\sqsubseteq$.*

Proof: Say that $S^j \sqsubseteq S^k$, i.e., S^j is a presequence of S^k, and $j \leq k$. Let G be a nonblocking computation on S. Then $G(S^j) = G^j(S^j) = G^j(S^k)$, where $G^j(S^k) \sqsubseteq G^k(S^k) = G(S^k)$. Thus 'nonblocking' implies 'monotonic'. Vice versa, say that we have a monotonic function $F(S)$ that can be computed by an operator $G(S)$. If G is nonblocking, the proof is complete. Otherwise, consider the operator $H(S)$ defined as follows: $H^j(S^n) = G^j(S^j)$. We have that $H(S) = G(S)$ and H is nonblocking. QED.

Streams are infinite sequences; thus only nonblocking operators can be used to answer queries on streams. We have now discovered that a query Q on a stream S can be implemented by a nonblocking query operator iff $Q(S)$ is monotonic with respect to $\sqsubseteq$. The traditional aggregate operators (MAX, AVG, etc.) always return a sequence of length one and they are all nonmonotonic, and therefore blocking. Continuous count and sum are monotonic and nonblocking, and thus suitable for continuous queries.

Order! In this section we have considered *physically ordered relations*, i.e., those where only the relative positions of tuples in sequence are of significance. In the next section, we will consider *unordered relations*, i.e., the traditional database relations, that we will call Codd's relations. Later, we will study *logically ordered relations*, i.e., sequences where the tuples are ordered by their timestamps or other logical keys. All three types of relations are important, since each type is needed in different applications and they have complementary properties.

For instance, the OLAP functions of SQL:1999 can compute the average of the last 100 tuples in the sequence (physical window). Besides OLAP functions, aggregates, such as continuous sum, and online average [15], are dependent on the physical order of relations. The physical order model is conducive to great expressive power, but cannot support binary operators as naturally as it does for unary ones. For instance, in SQL the union of two tables T1 and T2 is normally implemented by first returning all the tuples in T1 and then all the tuples in T2. The resulting operator, is not suitable for continuous queries, since it is partially blocking (and nonmonotonic) with respect to its first argument T1 (since tuples from T2 cannot be returned until we have seen the last tuple from T1). These issues can either be resolved by using Codd's relations (next section) or logically ordered relations, discussed in Section 7.

4 Unordered Relations, RA & SQL

Codd's relational model views relations as sets of tuples where the order is immaterial (commutativity property). In these relations duplicates are disallowed via candidate keys (or, duplicates can be simply disregarded as via the idempotence property). Thus relations are sets ordered by set containment, $\subseteq$. For Codd's relations the notions $\subseteq$ and $\sqsubseteq$ coincide. (Indeed $\sqsubseteq$ always implies $\subseteq$; moreover, if $R_1 \subseteq R_2$, then R_2 can be arranged as a presequence identical to R_1 followed by the remaining tuples in $R_2 - R_1$, if any.) Therefore we have the following theorem:

Proposition 2 *A unary query operator on Codd's relations is nonblocking iff it is monotonic w.r.t.* $\subseteq$.

Since we are only interested in deterministic queries, the only operators that are legal on Codd's relations are those that deliver the same results for any order in which the tuples are arranged in the table—also independent of duplicates if these are present. (Of course, 'same results' here means results that are equal in terms of set equality.) For instance, the select and project operators of relational algebra, traditional aggregates and continuous count are legal operators on Codd's relations, since their results do not depend on the order of tuples. However, continuous sum, or continuous averages, is not a valid operator on a Codd's relation since it produces results that depend on the order in which the tuples are arranged (if they are not identical).

Union and Cartesian product are monotonic with respect to set containment and amenable to nonblocking implementations. Set difference $R - S$ is instead antimonotonic and blocking with respect to its second argument. In fact no result can be returned for $R - S$ until the last tuple of S is known. Therefore, query operators such as $R - S$ should be avoided in expressing continuous queries on a data streams S. We explore the crippling effects of this limitation in the next section.

4.1 Relational Algebra

A complete set of operators for relational algebra consists of the following operators: $RA = \{\cup, \bowtie, \sigma, \Pi, -\}$. The monotonic (i.e., nonblocking) operators of relational algebra will be denoted $\mathcal{NB}$-RA, where $\mathcal{NB}$-RA $= \{\cup, \bowtie, \sigma, \Pi\}$.

The class of queries expressible by RA (and many equivalent query languages) is called *FO* queries [3]. Let $\mathcal{NB}$-*FO* denote the monotonic queries in *FO*. But some monotonic functions in *FO* are expressed using set difference, an operator not in $\mathcal{NB}$-RA. For instance, the intersection of two relations R_1 and R_2, a monotonic operation, can be expressed as: $R_1 \cap R_2 = R_1 - (R_1 - R_2)$. On the other hand intersection is in $\mathcal{NB}$-RA, since it can also be expressed as the natural join of its operands. But the conclusion is different for the coalesce and until queries discussed next.

Coalesce and Until We have a temporal domain, closed to the left and open to the right, which we will represent using nonnegative integers, originating at zero. (While examples are simpler with integers, any totally ordered temporal domain will do as well.) We use predicate p(I, J), with I < J, to denote that the property p holds from point I, included, till point J, excluded. Thus, we use intervals closed to the left and open to the right. Our database consists of an arbitrary number of p facts, and of some q facts that use a similar interval-based representation. Then, the temporal-logic query p $\mathcal{U}ntil$ q is true when there exists a q(I, J) where p holds for every point before I. This query can be expressed in several ways [7, 9, 23]. Example 1 expresses it using non-recursive Datalog rules, that first coalesce the p intervals and then check if there is any interval that spans from 0 to the beginning of some q (second rule).

The bottom rule in Example 1 defines cep(K) to hold for the 'covered end points' of intervals: i.e., when K is the endpoint of some interval that is contained in some other interval p(I, J). The next rule from the bottom defines broken intervals as follows: broken(I1, J2) holds true if (i) I1 is the start-point of some interval, (ii) J2 is the endpoint of an interval to its right, and (iii) there is a break point between the two in the form of the endpoint K that is not covered, i.e., ¬cep(K). This break excludes (I1, J2) from the coalesced intervals. Indeed, the third rule from the bottom defines coalesced intervals as those that satisfy conditions (i) and (ii), but are not broken.

Example 1 *Until* (pUq) *& Coalesce (*coalscp*)*

```
pUq(yes)    ←    q(0, J).
pUq(yes)    ←    coalscp(0, I), q(J, _), I ≥ J.
coalscp(I1, J2) ←  p(I1, J1), p(I2, J2), J1 < J2,
                   ¬broken(I1, J2).
broken(I1, J2) ←  p(I1, J1), p(I2, J2), p(_, K),
                   J1 ≤ K, K < I2, ¬cep(K).
cep(K)      ←    p(_, K), p(I, J), I ≤ K, K < J.
```

The safe non-recursive Datalog program of Example 1 can be translated into an RA expression on the two relations P and Q, representing, respectively, the p facts and the q facts. The resulting RA expression uses set difference to implement negation. This program and its RA equivalent defines the two queries pUq and coalscp, the first on P and Q and the second on P only. We will refer to them as the coalesce query and the until query, and observe that they are monotonic. Indeed, as we add new intervals to P, we obtain all the old intervals in coalscp and possibly some new ones. For pUq, as we add new intervals to P and/or Q, the answer could change from an empty set to a singleton set containing 'yes' but never the other way around.

However, while the coalesce query and the until queries are in $\mathcal{NB}$-*FO*, they cannot be expressed in $\mathcal{NB}$-RA:

Proposition 3 *The coalesce and until queries cannot be expressed in* $\mathcal{NB}$-RA.

Proof Sketch: Let P be the table containing the intervals to be coalesced. By selection and projection on the Cartesian product of P with itself $n-1$ times, we can express the coalescing of up to n intervals from P. But P can contain an arbitrary number of intervals. □

Meanwhile, we observe that this problem can be solved using $\mathcal{NB}$-RA with recursion. Here is a solution:

```
pUq(yes)    ←   q(0, J).
pUq(yes)    ←   coalscp(0, I), q(J, _), I ≥ J.
coalscp(I, J) ← p(I, J).
coalscp(I1, J2) ← coalscp(I1, J1), coalscp(I2, J2),
                  J1 ≥ I2.
```

SQL-$\mathcal{NB}$ We next consider $\mathcal{NB}$-SQL, i.e., the nonblocking subset of SQL-2 that can be used for writing queries on data streams. We need to exclude nonmonotonic constructs, such as EXCEPT, NOT EXIST, NOT IN and ALL. Moreover all the standard SQL-2 aggregates, must be left out because they are blocking. The surprising conclusion is that expressive power of $\mathcal{NB}$-SQL is the same as $\mathcal{NB}$-RA, although SQL can express more monotonic queries than RA. In fact, some queries expressed using aggregates are monotonic. For instance, Example 2, below, computes from empl(EmpNo, Sal, DeptNo) all the departments where the sum of employee salaries exceeds a given constant C.

Example 2 *Departments where the sum of employee salaries exceeds C. Assume Sal > 0.*

```
SELECT DeptNo
FROM empl
GROUP BY DeptNo
    HAVING SUM(empl.Sal) > C
```

This is obviously a monotonic query, insofar as the introduction of a new empl can only expand the set of departments that satisfy this query; however this sum query cannot be expressed without the use of aggregates. The problem of the blocking SQL queries has long been recognized by data stream researchers, who have proposed the use of devices such as punctuation [32] and windows [21] to address this problem. While these approaches deal effectively with important aspects of the problem, they do not solve the expressivity problems discussed so far. For instance, punctuation and windows cannot be used to implement queries of Example 1 or Example 2 unless some external constraints can be used to turn these blocking queries into nonblocking queries (such as, bounds on the maximum number of employees in a department).

One approach to remedy these problems consists in allowing the programmer to use nonmonotonic constructs but exclusively to write monotonic queries. Then, the queries of Example 1 or Example 2 will be allowed and the loss of expressive power is avoided. Unfortunately, this approach is practically attractive only if the compiler/optimizer is capable of recognizing monotonic queries, and thus warning the user when a certain query is blocking and thus cannot be used as a continuous query. Unfortunately, deciding whether a query is monotonic can be computationally intractable and can also depend on information, such as **empl.Sal >0**, which is obvious to the user but not the optimizer.

A better approach is to introduce new monotonic operators to extend the $\mathcal{NB}$-power of the query language. For instance, a natural extensions could be to add least fixpoint (LFP) operators to relational algebra, or equivalently, recursion constructs could be used in SQL [3]. LFP operators and recursive constructs are monotonic and they extend the power of RA or SQL to enable the expression of all DB-PTime queries [3]. However, it is not clear whether $\mathcal{NB}$-RA+LFP, or $\mathcal{NB}$-SQL with recursion, are $\mathcal{NB}$-DB-PTime complete— i.e. capable of expressing all monotonic queries in DB-PTime. Although the coalesce and until query can be easily expressed in $\mathcal{NB}$-RA+LFP, we do not have a general answer for this interesting theoretical question. We will leave this question for later investigations, since it is not of urgent practical importance, given that, in the past, recursive SQL queries have not proven very useful for sequence queries and mining queries. In this paper, we instead champion a very practical approach based of monotonic user-defined aggregates that deliver much higher levels of expressive power, not only in theory, but also in practice, as demonstrated in applications such as punctuated data streams, sequence queries, and mining queries.

5 User-Defined Aggregates

User Defined Aggregates (UDAs) are important for decision support, stream queries and other advanced database applications [8, 18, 12]. ATLAS [33] and ESL [18] adopt from SQL-3 the idea of specifying a new UDA by an INITIALIZE, an ITERATE, and a TERMINATE computation; however, ATLAS and ESL let users express these three computations by a single procedure written in SQL—rather than by three procedures coded in procedural languages as prescribed by SQL-3[1]. Example 3 defines an aggregate equivalent to the standard AVG aggregate in SQL. The second line in Example 3 declares a local table, **state**, where the sum and count of the values processed so far are kept. Furthermore, while in this particular example, **state** contains only one tuple, it is in fact a table that can be queried and updated using SQL statements and can contain any number of tuples. These SQL statements are grouped into the three blocks labeled, respectively, INITIALIZE, ITERATE, and TERMINATE. Thus, INITIALIZE inserts the value taken from the input stream and

---

[1] Although UDAs have been left out of SQL:1999 specifications, they were part of early SQL-3 proposals, and supported by some commercial DBMS.

sets the count to 1. The ITERATE statement updates the tuple in **state** by adding the new input value to the sum and 1 to the count. The TERMINATE statement returns the ratio between the sum and the count as the final result of the computation by the INSERT INTO RETURN statement[2]. Thus, the TERMINATE statements are processed just after all the input tuples have been exhausted.

Example 3 *Defining the standard* AVG

```
AGGREGATE myavg(Next Int) : Real
{   TABLE state(tsum Int, cnt Int);
    INITIALIZE : {
        INSERT INTO state VALUES (Next, 1);
    }
    ITERATE : {
        UPDATE state
            SET tsum=tsum+Next, cnt=cnt+1;
    }
    TERMINATE : {
        INSERT INTO RETURN
            SELECT tsum/cnt FROM state;
    }
}
```

Observe that the SQL statements in the INITIALIZE, ITERATE, and TERMINATE blocks play the same role as the external functions in SQL-3 aggregates. But here, we have assembled the three functions under one procedure, thus supporting the declaration of their shared tables (the **state** table in this example). This table is allocated just before the INITIALIZE statement is executed and deallocated just after the TERMINATE statement is completed. This approach to aggregate definition is very general. For instance, say that we want to support tumbling windows of 200 tuples [8]. Then we can write the UDA of Example 4, where the RETURN statements appear in ITERATE instead of TERMINATE. The UDA **tumble_avg**, so obtained, takes a stream of values as input and returns a stream of values as output (one every 200 tuples). While each execution of the RETURN statement produces here only one tuple, in general, the UDA can return several tuples. Also observe that UDAs are allowed to declare local tables and apply arbitrary select and update actions on these tables, including the use of built-in and user-defined aggregates (possibly in a recursive fashion) [1, 18].

Thus UDAs operate as general stream transformers. Observe that the UDA in Example 3 is blocking, while that of Example 4 is nonblocking. Thus, nonblocking UDAs are easily and clearly identified by the fact that *their* TERMINATE *clauses are either empty or absent*. The typical default implementation for SQL aggregates is that the data are first sorted according to the GROUP-BY attributes: thus the very first operation in the computation is a blocking operation.

---

[2]To conform to SQL syntax, RETURN is treated as a virtual table; however, it is not a stored table and cannot be used in any other role.

Instead, ESL uses a (nonblocking) hash-based implementation for the GROUP-BY (or PARTITION-BY) calls of the UDAs [18]. The semantics of UDAs therefore is based on sequential execution whereby the input sequence or stream is pipelined through the operations specified in the INITIALIZE and ITERATE clauses: the only blocking operations (if any) are those specified in TERMINATE, and these only take place at the end of the computation.

Example 4 AVG *on a Tumble of 200 Tuples*

```
AGGREGATE tumble_avg(Next Int) : Real
{   TABLE state(tsum Int, cnt Int);
    INITIALIZE : {
        INSERT INTO state VALUES (Next, 1)}
    ITERATE: {
        UPDATE state
            SET tsum=tsum+Next, cnt=cnt+1;
        INSERT INTO RETURN
            SELECT tsum/cnt FROM state
            WHERE cnt % 200 = 0;
        UPDATE state SET tsum=0, cnt=0
            WHERE cnt % 200 = 0
    }
    TERMINATE : {  }
}
```

UDAs can be called and used in the same way as any other built-in aggregate. For instance, say that we are given a stored sequence (or an incoming stream) of purchase actions:

webevents(CustomerID, Event, Amount, Time)

Since UDAs process tuples one-at-a-time (as the cursor mechanism used by programming languages to interface with SQL) they dovetail with the physically-ordered sequence model, and can also express well the search for pattern in sequences. Say for instance that we want to find the situation where users, immediately after placing an order, ask for a rebate and then cancel the order. Finding this pattern in SQL requires two selfjoins to be computed on the incoming stream of webevents. In general recognizing the pattern of n events would require $n-1$ joins and queries involving the joins of many streams can be complex to express in SQL, and also inefficient to execute. Also the notion that a tuple must immediately follow another tuple is complex to formulate in SQL. UDAs can be used to solve these problems. For instance, say that we want to detect the pattern of an order, followed a rebate, and then, immediately after that a cancellation. Then the following nonblocking UDA can be used to return the string 'pattern123' with the CustomerID whose events have just matched the pattern (the aggregate will be called with the group-by clause on CustomerID). This UDA models a finite state machine, where 0 denotes the failure state, which is set whenever the right combination of current-state and input is not observed. Otherwise, the state is first set to 1 and then advanced till 3, where 'pattern123' is returned, and the computation continues.

Example 5 *First the order, then the rebate and finally the cancellation*

```
AGGREGATE pattern(Next Char) : Char
{   TABLE state(sno Int);
    INITIALIZE : {
      INSERT INTO state VALUES(0);
      UPDATE state SET sno = 1
        WHEN Next='order';}
    ITERATE: {
      UPDATE state SET sno = 0
        WHERE NOT(sno = 1 AND
                  Next = 'rebate')
        AND NOT(sno = 2 AND Next = 'cancel')
        AND Next <> 'order'
      UPDATE state SET sno = 1
        WHERE Next='order';
      UPDATE state SET sno = sno+1
        WHERE (sno = 1 AND Next = 'rebate')
        OR(sno = 2 AND Next = 'cancel')
      INSERT INTO RETURN
        SELECT 'pattern123' FROM state
        WHERE sno = 3;
    }
}
```

Very often, the input order of sequence elements is the same as their production order — this fits the design of UDAs naturally. In [28], Seshadri et al. showed an example of query that asks for the 3-day average of the close of IBM stock values when the value of DEC is greater than that of HP. In the following example, the UDA only needs to store the last three-day values for IBM and compares the values of DEC and HP to see whether the average should be output. Note that it is easy to generalize the expression using UDA to compute n-day average using **state** to store last n-day values of IBM.

Example 6 *3-day average for IBM when DEC>HP*

```
AGGREGATE 3DayAve(ibm Real,dec Real,hp Real):Real
{   TABLE state(st Int, nd Int, rd Int,tcnt Int);
    INITIALIZE : {
      INSERT INTO state VALUES (0, 0, ibm, 1)}
      INSERT INTO RETURN
        SELECT third/tcnt FROM state
        WHERE dec>hp;}
    ITERATE: {
      UPDATE state
        SET st=nd, nd=rd, rd=ibm;
      UPDATE state
        SET tcnt=tcnt+1;
        WHERE tcnt<3;
      INSERT INTO RETURN
        SELECT (st+nd+rd)/tcnt FROM state
        WHERE dec>hp;
    }
    TERMINATE : { }
}
```

UDAs are also suitable for punctuated data streams [32]. When an input arrives, the UDA needs to compute the results, store the state and output based on punctuation. In Example 7, we want to output the average stock value of each company when we receive its closing value tuple which is a punctuation indicating that no more tuple of this company will arrive. We use the table **state** to store the summary (sum and count) of each company which is the minimal amount of information that we should store for further computations. Upon detection of a punctuation mark indicating the arrival of the closing-value tuple (with condition **close**=1), we return the average for this company.

Example 7 *Output average price for each company when closing price tuple enters*

```
AGGREGATE CoSum(cid Int,price Real,close Int):Real
{   TABLE state(tcid Int, tsum Int,tcnt Int);
    INITIALIZE : {
      INSERT INTO state VALUES (cid, price, 1);}
    ITERATE: {
      UPDATE state
        SET tsum=tsum+price, tcnt=tcnt+1;
        WHERE tcid=cid;
      INSERT INTO state
        SELECT cid, price, 1 FROM state
        WHERE cid NOT IN (
          SELECT tcid FROM state);
      INSERT INTO RETURN
        SELECT tsum/tcnt FROM state
        WHERE tcid=cid AND close=1;
    }
    TERMINATE : { }
}
```

Therefore UDAs, unlike traditional SQL, are well-suited to supporting state-based reasoning and queries, as needed in sequence and data stream applications. The use of UDAs to support the mining of data streams is discussed in [18]. In the next section, we show that UDAs are able to express the ultimate state machine: a Turing machine. Readers who are primarily interested in the applications of this theoretical result to data streams can proceed directly to Section 7, where we discuss the $\mathcal{NB}$-completeness of monotonic UDAs and their benefits in data stream applications.

6 Completeness on DB Relations

Turing completeness is hard to achieve for database languages [3]. In particular, SQL is not Turing complete, and thus not capable of expressing all data-intensive applications. The power of a query language is defined as the class of functions it can express on (an input tape encoding) the database [3]. We will next show that UDAs can compute an arbitrary query function encoded as a Turing machine.

A Turing Machine is defined by a tuple $M = (Q, \Sigma, \Upsilon, \delta, q_0, !, F)$, where Q is a finite set of states, $\Sigma \subseteq \Upsilon$ is a finite set of input symbols, Υ is a finite set of tape symbols with $Q \cap \Upsilon = \phi$, $! \subseteq \Upsilon - \Sigma$ is a reserved symbol representing the blank symbol, $q_0 \subseteq Q$ is an initial state, $F \subseteq Q$ is a set of accepting or final states, $\delta : Q \times \Upsilon \to Q \times \Upsilon \times \{1, 0, -1\}$ is a transition mapping where 1,0,-1 denote motion directions.

In our implementation, a user may define a Turing Machine by giving four elements: a transition map(**E1**), accepting states(**E2**), a tape containing the input(**E3**) and an initial state(**E4**). With UDA, we put **E1** into a table called **transition**. **E2** is put into table **accept**. **E3** is put into table **tape**, which uses an attribute called **pos** to memorize the position of each symbol in the tape. Also, there is a table called **current**, which stores the current state, the current symbol and its position on the tape during each iteration. At the first iteration, the initial state (**E4**) and the leftmost symbol on the tape (**pos**=0) are put into **current**.

For each iteration, a tuple of current is passed to a UDA called **turing**. If the transition function is defined for the (state, symbol) pair, we obtain the next state, the new symbol and the motion direction for the tape head. Then, the symbol pointed by the tape head is replaced by the new symbol. We move the head to the next position, which is given by **pos** + **move**. If it is a non-existing position on the tape, a new blank symbol is inserted at that position. Then, the updated tuple is inserted into **current** which is then passed to the UDA **turing** for the next iteration. The above procedures are repeated until the transition function δ is not defined for some (state, symbol) pair. In this case, the machine halts and checks whether the current state is an accepting state or not, based on the list of accepting states in table **accept**.

The following is the implementation of a Turing Machine using UDAs.

```
TABLE current(stat Char(1), symbol Char(1), pos Int);
TABLE tape(symbol Char(1), pos Int);
TABLE transition(curstate Char(1), cursymbol Char(1),
    move int, nextstate Char(1), nextsymbol Char(1));
TABLE accept(accept Char(1));
AGGREGATE turing(stat Char(1), symbol Char(1),
                 curpos Int) : Int
{   INITIALIZE: ITERATE: {
    /*If TM halts, return 1/0(accept/reject)*/
    INSERT INTO RETURN
        SELECT R.C
        FROM (SELECT count(accept) C
              FROM accept A
              WHERE A.accept = stat) R
        WHERE NOT EXISTS (
            SELECT * FROM transition T
            WHERE stat = T.curstate
              AND symbol = T.cursymbol);
    /* write tape */
    DELETE FROM  tape
        WHERE pos = curpos;
    INSERT INTO tape
        SELECT T.nextsymbol, curpos
        FROM transition T
        WHERE T.curstate = stat
          AND T.cursymbol = symbol;
    /* add blank symbol if necessary */
    INSERT INTO tape
        SELECT '!', curpos + T.move
        FROM transition T
        WHERE T.curstate = stat
          AND T.cursymbol = symbol
          AND NOT EXISTS (
            SELECT * FROM tape
            WHERE pos = curpos + T.move);
    /* move head to the next position */
    INSERT INTO current
        SELECT T.nextstate, A.symbol, A.pos
        FROM tape A, transition T
        WHERE T.curstate = stat
          AND T.cursymbol = symbol)
          AND A.pos=curpos+T.move;}}
INSERT INTO current
    SELECT 'p', A.symbol, 0
    FROM tape A WHERE A.pos = 0;
SELECT turing(stat, symbol, pos) FROM current;
```

In the following, we implement a Turing Machine to find the maximum among the input numbers. The maximum will be stored back into the tape.

Example 8 *Turing Machine for finding the maximum*

Let $M = (Q, \{0,1\}, \{0,1,2,3,!\}, \delta, p, !, \{\})$ be a Turing Machine for finding the maximum where δ is given by Table 1. For simplicity, we assume that each number is an integer. Then we represent them in unary, i.e. $i \geq 0$ is represented by the string 0^i. These integers are placed on the input tape separated by 1's. The idea of this machine is to repeatedly compare the two left most integers in the input tape and to store the largest one back into the input tape. When the machine halts, we eliminate all symbols but 0's to extract the integer(in unary) in the input tape as the output of the query, which is the maximum number.

	0	1	2	3	!
p	$q,2,1$	$u,!,1$			$p,!,1$
q	$q,0,1$	$r,1,1$			$q,!,1$
r	$s,3,-1$	$t,1,-1$		$r,3,1$	$t,!,-1$
s	$s,0,-1$	$s,1,-1$	$p,2,1$	$s,3,-1$	$s,!,-1$
t	$w,0,-1$	$t,!,-1$	$t,0,-1$	$t,!,-1$	$t,!,1$
u	$u,0,1$	$v,1,-1$		$u,0,1$	
v	$v,0,-1$				$p,!,1$
w	$w,0,-1$		$w,o,-1$		$p,!,1$

Table 1: Transition mapping δ for finding the maximum.

In the previous section, we have shown that UDA can express any function encoded in arbitrary input tape. A simple UDA can be used to encode a given table and then, on its TERMINATE state call the UDA that performs the actual computations. For several tables we can let the various UDAs write into the same input tape, with the last UDA calling the actual computation. But such an encoding of one or more tables into an input tape is a blocking computation. For continuous queries we seek nonblocking computations on one or more data streams. These are discussed next.

7 Completeness on Data Streams

According to [13], 'queries over streams run continuously over a period of time and incrementally return new results as new data arrive.' In the following, we will show how to compute a query over streams. We will focus on monotonic functions as they are the only continuous queries supported on data streams.

Every monotonic function F on an input data stream can be computed by a UDA that uses three local tables, called IN, $TAPE$, and OUT, and performs the following operations for each new arriving tuple:

1. Append the encoded new tuple to IN,
2. Copy IN to $TAPE$, and compute $F(IN) - OUT$ as described in Section 5,
3. Return the result obtained in 2 and append it to OUT.

Since these operations are executed on each arriving new tuple, they are performed in the ITERATE state of the UDA, which is therefore nonblocking. Thus, every monotonic function on a single data stream can be computed by a nonblocking UDA.

However, the situation is more complex for multiple data streams, since these need to be merged into a single stream before UDAs can be applied. For instance, the operator used in SQL:1999 for computing the union, $R_1 \cup R_2$ of the ordered relations R_1 and R_2 while preserving duplicates cannot be used. In fact, this operator will list all the tuples in R_1 before the tuples in R_2. Thus this operator is blocking with respect to its first argument. We instead need operators that merge the two streams by assuring not only fairness, but also minimizing the delay across streams. To achieve this timestamps are needed and then the union operator can be defined that union-merges these multiple streams into one by their timestamps.

Therefore we now consider explicitly timestamped data streams and time-series sequences, where tuples are explicitly ordered by increasing values of their timestamps.[3] We begin with notion of τ-presequence defined as the sequence of tuples up to a given timestamp τ:

Definition 5 Presequence: *Let S and R be two sequences ordered by their timestamp. R^τ is defined as the set of tuples of R with timestamp less than or equal to $\tau > 0$. If $S = R^\tau$ for some τ, then S is said to be a presequence of R, denoted $S \sqsubseteq^t R$. In general, let $S_1, ..., S_n$ and $R_1, ..., R_n$ be timestamped sequences. $(S_1, ..., S_n) \sqsubseteq^t (R_1, ..., R_n)$ when $(S_1, ..., S_n) = (R_1^\tau, ..., R_n^\tau)$ for some τ.*

---
[3] Similar considerations can be made to arbitrary logically ordered sequences, where tuples are arranged and visited sequentially according to an ordering key consisting of one or more attributes.

Then the notion of monotonicity can also be defined naturally. A unary operator G is monotonic if $L_1 \sqsubseteq^t S_1$ implies $G(L_1) \sqsubseteq^t G(S_1)$. A binary operator H is monotonic when $(L_1, L_2) \sqsubseteq^t (S_1, S_2)$ implies $H(L_1, L_2) \sqsubseteq^t H(S_1, S_2)$.

In operational terms, $S \sqsubseteq^t R$ can be viewed as a statement that R was obtained from $S = R^\tau$ by appending some additional tuples with timestamps larger than those in S: for instance, S might be the stream received up to time τ, and R the stream received after waiting a little longer i.e., up to time $\tau' > \tau$.

For $\tau = 0$, $S^\tau = \emptyset$ is an empty sequence. Let $\Omega(S)$ denote the largest timestamp in S (0 if S is empty). A query operator is said to be null when it returns the empty sequence for every possible value of its argument(s).

Then, the notion of nonblocking operators on logical sequences can be defined as follows:

Definition 6 *Nonblocking.*
- *A nonnull unary operator G is said to be nonblocking, when $G^\tau(S) = G(S^\tau)$, for every τ.*
- *A nonnull binary operator G is said to be nonblocking, when, $G^\tau(L, S) = G(L^\tau, S^\tau)$, for every τ.*

We can then show that functions on logically ordered sequences can be implemented by nonblocking operators iff they are monotonic w.r.t. $\sqsubseteq^t$. It also follows that only blocking implementations are possible for an operator that computes the difference of two streams, since difference is antimonotonic on its second argument.

The previous notions lead to natural generalizations for selection, projection and union; suitable generalizations of Cartesian product and join are also available [5] but they are outside the scope of this paper (since they are not needed for the completeness of our language). For union we have:

Union. Let $\cup^\tau$ denote the stream transducer implementing union. $\cup^\tau$ returns, at any given time τ, the union of the τ-presequences of its inputs:

$$L \cup^\tau S = L^\tau \cup S^\tau$$

In the following example, we demonstrate how to express a query using Union and UDA. Consider two streams of phone-call records:

StartCall(callID, time);
Endcall(callID, time);

The stream **StartCall** is used to record a starting time of each call with its ID, while the stream **EndCall** is used to record a finishing time of each call with its ID. Given the above two streams, we are interested in finding the length of each call. Instead of joining two streams, we first union them together: **CallRecord**, which is sorted by the arrival timestamp. Moreover, we use a tag to indicate which stream does each tuple come from. Tuples are grouped by different callID group.

Example 9 *Compute the length of each call.*

```
SELECT callID, length(time, tag) AS CallLength,
FROM
    ( SELECT callID, time, 'start'
      FROM StartCall
      UNION ALL
      SELECT callID, time, 'end'
      FROM EndCall) AS
  CallRecord (callID, time, tag)
GROUP BY callID;
```

The UDA **length** is used to compute the difference between the starting time and finishing time. We design this UDA to handle all the arrival ordering. This UDA is shown below:

```
AGGREGATE length(time, tag) : (CallLength)
{    TABLE state(ttime);
     INITIALIZE: ITERATE :{
       INSERT INTO state VALUES(time);
       INSERT INTO RETURN
           SELECT time-ttime FROM state
           WHERE tag='end';
       INSERT INTO RETURN
           SELECT ttime-time FROM state
           WHERE tag='start';}}
```

We can now show the completeness of languages supporting union operators and nonblocking UDAs on data streams, in the sense that they can express every monotonic function on their input.

$\mathcal{NB}$ **UDAs:** $\mathcal{NB}$-UDAs are those where the TERMINATE state is empty or missing.

Proposition 4 $\mathcal{NB}$-*Completeness. Every computable monotonic function on timestamped data streams can be expressed using $\mathcal{NB}$-UDAs and union.*

From a formal viewpoint, these results can be extended to physically ordered data streams by simply viewing sequence numbers as time stamps (then, $\sqsubseteq$ becomes a special case of $\sqsubseteq^t$). The problem is that tuples from two streams that have the same sequence number could have arrived at very different times. Therefore most systems and users prefer the solution of merging the tuples of two streams according to the order in which they are actually processed. This is equivalent to viewing them as logically ordered streams where the time stamp is the current time at the point in which the tuples are processed for union.

8 Conclusions

Data streams require significant changes in traditional DB technology. This paper is the first to propose a formal analysis of how query languages and also data models are impacted by these changes, to propose practical solutions for the resulting problems. We studied how traditional models, where data is viewed as unordered sets of tuples, can be enriched with (physical and logical) ordering, and the notion of set containment can be generalized to the new framework. While data streams bring enrichments to data models, they bring restrictions to the query languages since they require nonblocking queries.

We characterized nonblocking queries as monotonic queries, and introduce the notion of $\mathcal{NB}$-completeness that characterize the expressive power hierarchies for continuous query languages on data streams. We thus proved that RA and SQL are no longer complete for nonblocking queries (exacerbating limitations which had already surfaced with data mining and sequence queries). To solve this problem, we proposed the use of UDAs, a native extensibility mechanism that makes SQL Turing-complete on stored data. For data streams, we introduced the notion of $\mathcal{NB}$-completeness for query languages capable of expressing all functions computable via nonblocking procedures; then we showed that any query language supporting UDAs and nonblocking union is $\mathcal{NB}$-complete. Of course, this is not to suggest that practical continuous query languages, such as the ESL language we are implementing [18], only need these two constructs. Practical data-streams languages should support SQL, and additional constructs needed for data streams, such as logical and physical windows [4]. (For instance, ESL also supports windows on UDAs [18]). But there are situations where the additional power of UDAs becomes critical: these situations include data mining functions [33], sequence queries [25], and special situations where more control is needed to minimize the use of memory [18]. The fact that the notion of UDAs is fully compatible with the syntax and semantics of existing prototypes, and they already part of some systems [8, 18], enhances the practical import of the theoretical findings summarized in this extended abstract.

Acknowledgements

This work was supported in part by a gift from Teradata, and by the National Science Foundation grant NSF-IIS 0339259.

References

[1] ATLaS user manual. http://wis.cs.ucla.edu/atlas.

[2] *SQL/LPP: A Time Series Extension of SQL Based on Limited Patience Patterns*, volume 1677 of *Lecture Notes in Computer Science*. Springer, 1999.

[3] S. Abiteboul, R. Hull, and V. Vianu. *Foundations of Databases*. Addison-Wesley, 1995.

[4] A. Arasu, S. Babu, and J. Widom. An abstract semantics and concrete language for continuous queries over streams and relations. Technical report, Stanford University, 2002.

[5] B. Babcock, S. Babu, M. Datar, R. Motwani, and J. Widom. Models and issues in data stream systems. In *PODS*, 2002.

[6] D. Barbara. The characterization of continuous queries. *Intl. Journal of Cooperative Information Systems*, 8(4):295–323, 1999.

[7] M. H. Bohlen. *The Temporal Deductive Database System ChronoLog*. PhD thesis, Department Informatick, ETH Zurich, 1994.

[8] D. Carney, U. Cetintemel, M. Cherniack, C. Convey, S. Lee, G. Seidman, M. Stonebraker, N. Tatbul, and S. Zdonik. Monitoring streams - a new class of data management applications. In *VLDB*, Hong Kong, China, 2002.

[9] J. Celko. *SQL for Smarties*, chapter Advanced SQL Programming. Morgan Kaufmann, 1995.

[10] S. Chandrasekaran and M. Franklin. Streaming queries over streaming data. In *VLDB*, 2002.

[11] J. Chen, D. J. DeWitt, F. Tian, and Y. Wang. NiagaraCQ: A scalable continuous query system for internet databases. In *SIGMOD*, pages 379–390, May 2000.

[12] C. Cranor, Y. Gao, T. Johnson, V. Shkapenyuk, and O. Spatscheck. Gigascope: A stream database for network applications. In *SIGMOD Conference*, pages 647–651. ACM Press, 2003.

[13] Lukasz Golab and M. Tamer Özsu. Issues in data stream management. *ACM SIGMOD Record*, 32(2):5–14, 2003.

[14] J. Han, Y. Fu, W. Wang, K. Koperski, and O. R. Zaiane. DMQL: A data mining query language for relational databases. In *Workshop on Research Issues on Data Mining and Knowledge Discovery (DMKD)*, pages 27–33, Montreal, Canada, June 1996.

[15] J. M. Hellerstein, P. J. Haas, and H. J. Wang. Online aggregation. In *SIGMOD*, 1997.

[16] T. Imielinski and A. Virmani. MSQL: a query language for database mining. *Data Mining and Knowledge Discovery*, 3:373–408, 1999.

[17] L. Liu, C. Pu, and W. Tang. Continual queries for internet scale event-driven information delivery. *IEEE TKDE*, 11(4):583–590, August 1999.

[18] Chang R. Luo, Haixun Wang, and Carlo Zaniolo. ESL: a data stream query language and system designed for power and extensibility. In *submitted for publication*, 2004.

[19] Sam Madden, Mehul A. Shah, Joseph M. Hellerstein, and Vijayshankar Raman. Continuously adaptive continuous queries over streams. In *SIGMOD*, pages 49–61, 2002.

[20] R. Meo, G. Psaila, and S. Ceri. A new SQL-like operator for mining association rules. In *VLDB*, pages 122–133, Bombay, India, 1996.

[21] R. Motwani, J. Widom, A. Arasu, B. Babcock, M. Datar S. Babu, G. Manku, C. Olston, J. Rosenstein, and R. Varma. Query processing, approximation, and resource management in a data stream management system. In *First CIDR 2003 Conference*, Asilomar, CA, 2003.

[22] R. Ramakrishnan, D. Donjerkovic, A. Ranganathan, K. Beyer, and M. Krishnaprasad. SRQL: Sorted relational query language, 1998.

[23] D. Rozenshtein, A. Abramovich, and E. Birger. Loop-free SQL solutions for finding continuous regions. In *SQL Forum 2(6)*, 1993.

[24] Reza Sadri, Carlo Zaniolo, and Amir M. Zarkesh and-Jafar Adibi. A sequential pattern query language for supporting instant data minining for e-services. In *VLDB*, pages 653–656, 2001.

[25] Reza Sadri, Carlo Zaniolo, Amir Zarkesh, and Jafar Adibi. Optimization of sequence queries in database systems. In *PODS*, Santa Barbara, CA, May 2001.

[26] S. Sarawagi, S. Thomas, and R. Agrawal. Integrating association rule mining with relational database systems: Alternatives and implications. In *SIGMOD*, 1998.

[27] P. Seshadri. Predator: A resource for database research. *SIGMOD Record*, 27(1):16–20, 1998.

[28] P. Seshadri, M. Livny, and R. Ramakrishnan. SEQ: A model for sequence databases. In *ICDE*, pages 232–239, Taipei, Taiwan, March 1995.

[29] Praveen Seshadri, Miron Livny, and Raghu Ramakrishnan. Sequence query processing. In *ACM SIGMOD 1994*, pages 430–441. ACM Press, 1994.

[30] M. Sullivan. Tribeca: A stream database manager for network traffic analysis. In *VLDB*, 1996.

[31] D. Terry, D. Goldberg, D. Nichols, and B. Oki. Continuous queries over append-only databases. In *SIGMOD*, pages 321–330, 6 1992.

[32] Peter A. Tucker, David Maier, Tim Sheard, and Leonidas Fegaras. Exploiting punctuation semantics in continuous data streams. *IEEE Trans. Knowl. Data Eng*, 15(3):555–568, 2003.

[33] Haixun Wang and Carlo Zaniolo. ATLaS: a native extension of SQL for data minining. In *Proceedings of Third SIAM Int. Conference on Data Mining*, pages 130–141, 2003.

[34] Carlo Zaniolo, Chang Richard Luo, Y. Law, and Haixun Wang. Incompleteness of database languages for data streams and data mining: the problem and the cure. In *Eleventh Italian Symposium on Advanced Database Systems: SEBD 2003*, June 2003.

Tamper Detection in Audit Logs

Richard T. Snodgrass, Shilong Stanley Yao and Christian Collberg

University of Arizona
Department of Computer Science
Tucson, AZ 85721-0077
USA
{rts,yao,collberg}@cs.arizona.edu

Abstract

Audit logs are considered good practice for business systems, and are required by federal regulations for secure systems, drug approval data, medical information disclosure, financial records, and electronic voting. Given the central role of audit logs, it is critical that they are correct and inalterable. It is not sufficient to say, "our data is correct, because we store all interactions in a separate audit log." The integrity of the audit log itself must also be guaranteed. This paper proposes mechanisms within a database management system (DBMS), based on cryptographically strong one-way hash functions, that prevent an intruder, including an auditor or an employee or even an unknown bug within the DBMS itself, from silently corrupting the audit log. We propose that the DBMS store additional information in the database to enable a separate *audit log validator* to examine the database along with this extra information and state conclusively whether the audit log has been compromised. We show with an implementation on a high-performance storage engine that the overhead for auditing is low and that the validator can efficiently and correctly determine if the audit log has been compromised.

1 Introduction and Motivation

OLTP (on-line transaction processing) applications maintain *audit logs* so that the correctness of the trans-

Permission to copy without fee all or part of this material is granted provided that the copies are not made or distributed for direct commercial advantage, the VLDB copyright notice and the title of the publication and its date appear, and notice is given that copying is by permission of the Very Large Data Base Endowment. To copy otherwise, or to republish, requires a fee and/or special permission from the Endowment.

**Proceedings of the 30th VLDB Conference,
Toronto, Canada, 2004**

actions can be later checked. As a simple example, every deposit to and withdrawal from a bank account generates a separate audit record, so that the current balance in the account can be checked. As one test, the sum of all deposits minus the sum of all withdrawals should equal the change in total accounts over that period. If this auditing check fails the bank looks into the discrepancy further.

A variety of federal laws (e.g., Code of Federal Regulations for the Food and Drug Administration, Sarbanes-Oxley Act, Health Insurance Portability and Accountability Act, Canada's PIPEDA) and standards (e.g., Orange Book for security) mandate audit logs. The correctness of the auditing records themselves is critical. As Peha states, "An auditor should be able to retrieve a set of records associated with a given entity and determine that those records contain the truth, the whole truth, and nothing but the truth. There should be a reasonable probability that any attempt to record incorrect, incomplete, or extra information will be detected. Thus, even though many transactions will never be scrutinized, the falsification of records is deterred." [17]

The message is clear: given the central role of audit logs in performing auditing of interactions with the data (modification, exposure) as well as of the base data itself, it is critical that audit logs be correct and inalterable. It is not sufficient to say, "our data is correct, because we store all interactions in a separate audit log." The integrity of the audit log itself is still in question.

Recent experience has shown that sometimes the (human) auditors themselves cannot be trusted. (A recent security survey states that the source of cyber-security "breaches appears fairly evenly split between those originating on the outside and those originating on the inside." [9, page 9].) In cases such as Enron and WorldCom (cases that inspired the Sarbanes-Oxley Act), supposedly independent auditing firms conspired with the company under audit to hide expenses and invent fictitious revenue streams. Just as the original databases can be manipulated to tell a story, so can the audit logs be manipulated to be consistent with this new story.

This paper proposes mechanisms within a database management system (DBMS), based on cryptographically strong one-way hash functions, that prevent an intruder, including an auditor or an employee or even an unknown bug within the DBMS itself, from silently corrupting the audit log. We propose that the DBMS transparently store the audit log as a transaction-time database, so that it is available to the application if needed. The DBMS should also store a small amount of additional information in the database to enable a separate *audit log validator* to examine the database along with this extra information and state conclusively whether the audit log has been compromised. We propose that the DBMS periodically send a short document (a hash value) to an off-site digital notarization service, to bound when changes were made to the database.

In the following, we first review existing techniques for maintaining the integrity of the audit log. We then describe the context within which we have developed our approach. In Section 4, we summarize the threat model addressed by our approach. We then present a simplified approach that enables *validatable audit logs*. Section 6 discusses a range of refinements that provide increase performance. We then summarize an initial implementation of the general algorithm on Berkeley DB [22] and evaluate the performance of this prototype, showing that supporting validatable audit logs does not represent a significant performance hit in space or time. We end with a review of related work and discussion of outstanding problems.

Our contribution is to demonstrate that, with the system model, techniques and optimizations we introduce here, tamper detection in audit logs can indeed be realized within a high-performance DBMS.

2 Existing Audit Log Techniques

The traditional way [3] to protect logging data from tampering is to write it to an append-only device, such as a Write Once Read Multiple (WORM) optical drive or a continuous-feed printer. The security of such schemes assumes, however, that the computing site will not be compromised. If this is a possible attack scenario the logging data can be sent to a remote site over the network, so called *remote logging*. *Log replication* can be used to send the data to several hosts to require the attacker to physically compromise several sites.

Schneier and Kelsey [21] describe a secure audit log system. The idea is roughly as follows. An untrusted machine $\mathcal{U}$ (on which the log is kept) initially shares a secret authentication key A_0 with a trusted machine $\mathcal{T}$. To add the j:th log entry D_j, $\mathcal{U}$ computes $K = hash(A_j)$ (an encryption key), $C = E_K(D_j)$ (the encrypted log entry), $Y_j = hash(Y_{j-1}, C)$ (the j:th entry in a chain of hashes, where $Y_{-1} = 0$), and $Z_j = MAC_{A_j}(Y_j)$ (a keyed hash (*Message Authentication Code*) of Y_j). Then the j:th entry $\langle C, Y_j, Z_j \rangle$ is written to the log, a new authentication key $A_{j+1} = hash(A_j)$ is constructed, and A_j is destroyed. An attacker who compromises $\mathcal{U}$ at time t can delete (but not read nor modify) any of the first t log entries, since he will only have access to A_{t+1} but not to any of the previous $A_0 \ldots A_t$. While there is no way to prevent the attacker from deleting some or all of the log entries (or appending his own entries), any such attempted tampering will be detected by $\mathcal{T}$ on its next interaction with $\mathcal{U}$. Furthermore, since each log entry is encrypted with a key derived from A_0 (which is only stored permanently on $\mathcal{T}$) the attacker cannot read past log entries to find out if his attack was noticed or not.

As applications require access to the database (and often read access to the audit log), these existing techniques are not applicable to tamper detection of transactional database audit logs.

3 Context

We show how a database can be protected by having the DBMS maintain the audit log in the background and by using cryptographic techniques to ensure that any alteration of prior entries in this audit log can be detected. This approach thus applies to any application that uses a DBMS.

As an example, assume that we are a pharmacological research firm that develops new drugs, providing data to the FDA for approval of those drugs. As part of this effort we have a relational table, Administer, that records what drugs were administered to which patients during a drug trial. 62 FR 13430 requires a computer-generated, time-stamped audit trail. We define the table as follows, in the MySQL DBMS [7].

```
CREATE TABLE Administer (...)
AS TRANSACTIONTIME
TYPE = BDB
AUDITABLE = 1
```

The first line—which also specifies the columns and primary and foreign key constraints for the table—is supported by the conventional MySQL release, as is the third line, which specifies that the Berkeley DB storage system be used. The second line specifies that this Administer table includes transaction-time support (this is an open-source extension that we have implemented). A transaction-time database records the history of its content [11]. All past states are retained and can be reconstituted from the information in the database. This is ensured through the *append-only* property of a transaction-time database: modifications only add information; no information is ever deleted. It is this basic property that we exploit to validate the audit log (in fact, the table *is* the audit log).

The last line specifies that this transaction-time table be *auditable*, that is, that the system take additional steps so that an audit log in maintained and so that later a separate *audit log validator* can examine the database and state conclusively whether the audit log has been compromised. These additional steps are the primary topic of this paper. We have implemented support for auditable tables and independent validation in MySQL and Berkeley DB.

It is important to emphasize that the applications that update and query this table need not be aware of the last three lines of the CREATE TABLE statement. Behind the scenes, transparently to the application, the DBMS creates an audit log and ensures auditability. This is because our approach ensures *temporal upward compatibility* [2].

A transaction-time table includes all the columns declared in the CREATE TABLE statement, along with two additional columns, which are not normally directly visible to the application: the Start and Stop columns. These latter columns are maintained by the DBMS. Specifically, the value of the Start column is the time (to a granularity of, say, a millisecond) at which that row was inserted into the table. The Stop time of a newly inserted row will be the special value "until changed," or *UC*. When a row is deleted, the deletion time is recorded in the Stop column; the row itself is retained. A modification of a row is treated as a deletion of the old value of the row and an insertion of the new value. A special form of SELECT is available for the application to see these columns and past versions of the table.

The rows that are currently relevant (that is, those that have yet to be modified or deleted) all have a Stop time of UC. These rows, along with the rest, which have an explicit Stop time, form an audit log of the table. A SELECT statement evaluated by an application will, because of temporal upward compatibility, see only current rows. A modification or deletion will only affect current rows. Again, the Start and Stop columns and the audit information are maintained behind the scenes by the DBMS.

4 Threat Model

In this work, we assume a Trusted Computing Base (TCB) consisting of correctly booted and functioning hardware and a correctly installed operating system and DBMS. More precisely, we assume that the TCB is correctly functioning until such a time t when a penetration occurs. Similarly, until time t the DBMS is created, maintained, and operated in a secure manner, and all network communication is performed through secure channels (such as SSL), ensuring the correctness of the internal state of the DBMS. Since the DBMS is a transaction-time database, all previous states can be reconstructed.

A penetration by an adversary ("Bob") can take many forms. An intruder (or an insider) who gains physical access to the DBMS server will have full freedom to corrupt any database file, including data, timestamps, and audit logs stored in tuples.

Of course, physical access is not necessary to compromise a system. Malware (such as viruses, worms, and trojans) can penetrate a machine by exploiting bugs (such as buffer overflows) in trusted software. The infection can occur over the network or through DBMS extensions (Oracle cartridge, Sybase plugin, DB2 extender). Regardless, the result is typically to allow Bob full root access to the machine and the DBMS server software. Once such access has been established, the integrity of any data or software on the machine is in question: the DBMS source code (including any audit log algorithms), the data in the database, and the audit log trails themselves could all have been compromised. (The information stored in the off-site digital notarization service is assumed to remain secure and unaltered.)

Our scheme assumes the existence of a trusted notarization service which, given a digital document, will return a unique identifier. We also assume a trusted and independent audit log validation service which, given access to (a copy of) the database, will verify the validity of the audit log. The integrity of these services is assumed to remain intact even in the event of a full DBMS compromise.

5 Basic Idea

We first outline our approach, an adaptation of Peha's "verifiable audit trails" to databases, making many assumptions and simplifications. We then remove some of these assumptions and simplifications to achieve a more practical and robust system.

Figure 1(a) illustrates the normal operation of our approach. The user application performs transactions on the database, which insert, delete, and update the rows of current state. Behind the scenes, the DBMS retains for each tuple hidden Start and Stop times, recording when each change occurred. The DBMS ensures that only the current state of the table is accessible to the application, with the rest of the table serving as the audit log. Alternatively, the table itself could be viewed by the application as the audit log. In that case, the application only makes insertions to the audited table; these insertions are associated with a monotonically increasing Start time. Our approach and implementation support both usages.

The basic idea is to store a "check field" in each tuple. This check field cannot be computed directly from the data (and timestamps) of the tuple, because then Bob could simply recompute the check field after he has altered the tuple. Indeed, if needed he could replay all of the transactions, making whatever changes he wanted to the data or the timestamps.

We use a *digital notarization service* that, when pro-

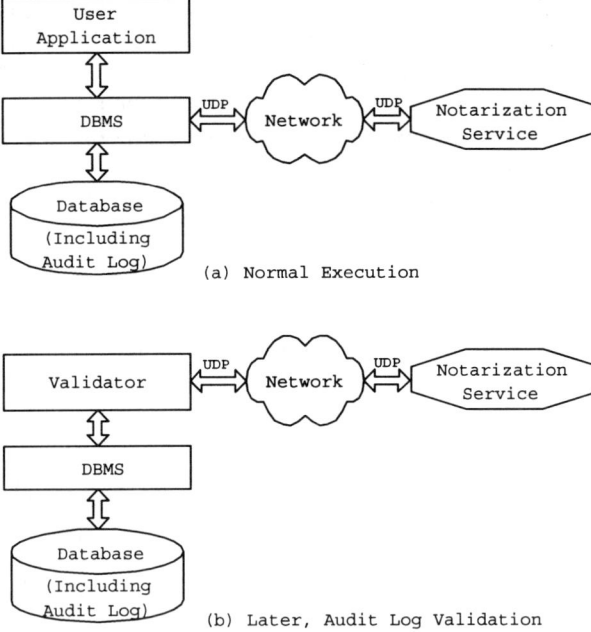

Figure 1: Normal Operation and Audit Log Validation

vided with a digital document, provides a *notary ID*[1]. Later, during audit log validation, the notarization service can ascertain, when presented with supposedly unaltered document and the notary ID, whether that document was notarized, and if so, when.

On each modification of a tuple, the DBMS obtains a timestamp, computes a *cryptographically strong one-way hash function* of the (new) data in the tuple and the timestamp, and sends that hash value, as a digital document, to the notarization service, obtaining a notary ID. The DBMS stores that ID in the tuple.

Later, Bob gets access to the database. If Bob changes the data or a timestamp, the ID will now be inconsistent with the rest of the tuple. Bob cannot manipulate the data or timestamp so that the ID remains valid, because the hash function is one-way. Note that this hold even when Bob has access to the hash function itself. Bob can instead compute a new hash value for the altered tuple, but that hash value won't match the one that was notarized.

If an independent audit log validation service was provided with the database (as illustrated in Figure 1b), that service could, for each tuple, hash the data and the timestamp, provide it with the ID to the notarization service, which will check the notarization

---

[1]Surety (www.surety.com) provides online digital notary service. Secure one-way hashing is used to generate notary IDs locking the contents and time of the notarized documents [10]. Telia's Digital Notarization Service (www.trust.telia.com) uses VeriSign's Digital Receipt and Digital Timestamping technology to create a tamper-proof digitally signed timestamp of a document, and store the records of that transaction.

time with the stored timestamp. (There is a timing issue in that the database obtains a timestamp first and later notarizes the tuple. The notarization time will be slightly later than the timestamp. Also, there will be many tuples with identical timestamps, as they were all modified within a single transaction. These details will be discussed in later sections.) The validation service would then report whether the database and the audit log are consistent. If not, either or both had been compromised.

Few assumptions are made on the threat model. The system is secure until Bob gets access, at which point he has access to everything: the DBMS, the operating system, the hardware, and the data in the database. We still assume that the notarization and validation services remain in the trusted computing base. This can be done by making them geographically and perhaps organizationally separate from the DBMS and the database.

The basic mechanism just described provides correct tamper detection. If Bob modifies even a single byte of the data or its timestamp, the independent validator will detect a mismatch with the notarized document, thereby detecting the tampering. Bob could simply re-execute the transactions, making whatever changes he wanted, and then replace the original database with his altered one. However, the notarized documents would not match in time. Avoiding tamper detection comes down to inverting the cryptographically-strong one-way hash function.

However, the basic approach exhibits unacceptable performance. Interactions with the notarization service should be infrequent, because such interactions are slow, requiring non-local network transmissions, and expensive, in that each notarized document results in a charge. Additionally, the space overhead is somewhat excessive, in that a notary ID must be stored in each tuple. Such IDs, on the order of 256 bits (32 bytes), are onerous for very small tuples.

In subsequent sections, we refine this approach to address these performance limitations. As we will see, it is challenging to achieve adequate performance while retaining the desirable properties of the basic approach. Our goal is to realize tamper detection in the context of a high-throughput transaction processing system. Existing approaches are simply inadequate in this context.

6 Minimizing Notarization Service Interactions

The basic approach just described interacts with the notarization service for each tuple that is modified. This interaction requires that a packet containing the hashed value of the tuple's data and timestamp (32 bytes) be sent to the service, which responds with another 32-byte notary ID, which is stored in the tuple. A transaction could easily modify thousands or even millions of tuples, rendering this approach impractical.

Throughout, we attempt to minimally impact the actual transaction processing and also attempt to minimize the validation time, at a cost of more work should tampering be detected. Our expectation is that an involved forensic analysis would be necessary upon detecting actual evidence of tampering. Rather, we attempt to minimize the effort to certify that the audit log has not been altered.

6.1 Opportunistic Hashing

The first step is to reduce interactions with the notarization service to one per transaction, rather than one per tuple. In this section, we first give an overview of the design and then explain the two key techniques we utilized.

As a refinement of the basic approach, we hash *all* the tuples modified by a transaction to compute a 20-byte hash value that is sent to the notarization service when the transaction commits. The notary ID returned from the notarization service is written to a separate *Notarization History Table*, which contains one tuple for each transaction. (This potential hot spot will be addressed in the next section.) Validation must also be on a per-transaction basis. The audit log validator (referred to from now on as simply the validator) scans all of the pages of the audited tables, maintaining a running hash value for each transaction, with each transaction identified by a transaction start or stop time within a tuple. After the database has been scanned, the validator has the hash value for every transaction. It can then check the notarization history table to see which transaction(s) were corrupted. This requires storing in main memory the hash value for each transaction. For high-performance systems completing hundreds or thousands of transactions a second, there may not be a sufficient amount of memory to store all of these values, and multiple passes over the database may be required. Note that if Bob changes a transaction time within a tuple, say to the transaction time of a different tuple, neither of these two transactions will match their notarized documents.

This seemingly innocuous change has wide-ranging implications. The data for the transaction may comprise many pages, which are generally not simultaneously in main memory. (Pages are written to disk when they are replaced by the buffer manager, either before or after the transaction commits [19].) One could during commit processing read in all of the pages that had been modified by the transaction and hash those tuples written by the transaction, to compute a single hash value for the entire transaction. (One could also stamp those pages, replacing the tuple ID with the commit time.) However, this imposes additional I/O on the commit, potentially doubling the I/O (if all the pages had been written out by the time the transaction committed).

Our solution is to *opportunistically hash* the transaction's data. Each tuple that is modified by a transaction is individually hashed at the time of the modification, when that tuple is present in main memory.

There are two key techniques to support the opportunistic hashing. The first technique, *incremental hashing*, is used to address the apparent contradiction of tuple-based hashing and transaction-based hash values. As an example, transaction T touches three tuples t_1, t_2 and t_3. A single hash value $H(T)$ needs to be computed from the three tuples as a whole. However, opportunistic hashing requires that each tuple t_i ($1 \leq i \leq 3$) of T is hashed independently as soon as it is processed by the auditing module. This implies that the hashing needs to be done incrementally. Whenever an unhashed tuple is encountered, it is incrementally hashed so that the hashing of that transaction progresses one more step. When the last tuple of a transaction is incrementally hashed, the hashing of that transaction is then fully accomplished and the final hash value is produced.

We utilize the well-accepted cryptographically strong hash function SHA-1 [25]. One of the advantages of SHA-1 is that its API explicitly supports incremental hashing. In SHA-1, the document to be hashed is divided into 512-bit blocks. Each block is processed in sequential order. For the first block, a 160-bit constant is used as the initial hash value. For each block, starting with the intermediate hash value from the previous block and based on the data in the current block, a new intermediate hash value is computed. If there are no subsequent blocks, the intermediate hash value of the current block is the final hash value. To leverage the SHA-1 hash function to build our incremental hash algorithm, we maintain the intermediate hash state of the SHA-1 function for each transaction. The intermediate hash state includes the intermediate hash value and the left-over data (a block). Along with a few other bookkeeping variables in the intermediate hash state (e.g., the offset of the left-over data), the total space required by a transaction to store the intermediate hash state is less than 100 bytes. This is far less than the space overhead of keeping all the tuples until the transaction commits.

The space overhead of storing the intermediate hash state can be further optimized down to 20 bytes. If we pad each tuple to the block boundary, there will never be left-over data. Thus we can eliminate the 64 bytes overhead of storing the left-over data and some bookkeeping variables.

Although the incremental hashing enables opportunistic hashing, it also introduces a new problem. In incremental hashing, the order in which tuples of a transaction are hashed is critical. Different hashing orders will result in different hash values. It has been proven that all known associative (order-independent) hash functions are cryptographically weak [18], so we have to ensure the same hashing order for the application and the validator. To enable the validator to recompute the same hash value as the one computed when the application was running, the hashing order during validation should be the same as when the application was running.

The second key technique to support opportunistic hashing is motivated by the hashing ordering problem just mentioned. In order to maintain the order consistency, a *tuple sequence number* is used to indicate the hashing order.

When the transaction is running, whenever a tuple is hashed, a sequence number, unique within the transaction and monotonically increasing, is assigned to the tuple and is stored in the tuple header. This sequence number indicates the order in which tuples were hashed during the transaction was running. We can further optimize the space allocation in the tuple header for storing sequence numbers. We can have two bits in the existing flag in the tuple header to indicate how many bytes are needed to store the sequence numbers of this tuple. For most small transactions with less than 256 tuples, only one extra byte is needed to store the sequence number.

When the validator is running, to hash the tuples of a transaction in exactly the same order as they were hashed when the transaction was running, tuples of a transaction are sorted in ascending sequence number order and are incrementally hashed in that order. Because tuples do not necessarily arrive in sequence number order while scanning the database, there will be holes (noncontinuous sequence numbers) of unseen tuples; these holes are gradually filled as the scan approaches the end of the database. To reduce the space overhead caused by storing the tuples, whenever a tuple is inserted into the sorted list we check the list to see if we can hash a subset of the consecutive tuples. Whenever there are no holes at the beginning of the queue, we can hash the leading tuples until the first hole of an unseen tuple and discard the hashed tuples so as to reclaim the memory. This sorted tuple list can be efficiently implemented with a priority queue.

At this point, only one special case is left to be explained about the opportunistic hashing. A transaction inserts a tuple. The page containing the newly inserted tuple is "stolen" by the DBMS (evicted before the transaction commits), which causes the tuple to be hashed towards the transaction hash value. Then the transaction deletes the same tuple, whose default behavior in DBMS is that the tuple is physically deleted. At the end the transaction commits. In this case, during the validation the expected transaction hash value can never be obtained, because the deleted tuple does not physically exist in the database and thus can not be hashed towards the transaction. This problem is solved by carefully handling deletions. When a tuple is deleted it is not physically deleted. Instead its start and stop time are both filled with the transaction's ID, which later is stamped with the transaction time. The tuples with identical start and stop times are regarded as transient inside the transaction. They never appear in the query results, but they participate in the hashing of the transaction twice, one is for insertion and the other for deletion.

Opportunistic hashing reduces the space overhead tremendously, as there is little per-tuple space required. (Specifically, two bits are required per tuple to indicate whether the Start and Stop times, respectively, have been hashed, two bits are needed for the sequence number size, and one to four bytes are needed for the sequence number itself.) The interaction with the notarization service is reduced to one per transaction. While the data itself remains secure, the notarization service knows for each period of time how many transactions were executed. A downside is that validator no longer can ascertain the immutability of each individual tuple. Rather, it can only check the consistency of the tuples in that transaction (identified by the transaction time stored in those tuples) with the associated hash value stored in the notarization history table, either of which may be corrupted by the attacker.

An alternative to the approach of hashing the tuples of a transaction was also considered. This alternative hashes the tuples on a page instead. Unfortunately, tuples can migrate between pages (say, because of a B-tree node split); maintaining sufficient information for the validator to determine which page a particular tuple was on when a particular hash value was computed turned out to be doable, but quite difficult. Utilizing a sequence number nicely avoids this problem.

6.2 Linked Hashing

Interacting with the notary service on each transaction is still quite expensive, especially in modern high-performance systems, which can complete thousands of transactions a second.

An attractive solution is to use *partial result authentication codes* [3] to link transactions. At database creation we get the timestamp, hash the schema and the timestamp, notarize this value, and store it in the notarization history table. Then, for each transaction, we hash the data of the transaction as before, using opportunistic hashing. At commit, we rehash a document containing this value and the previous hashed value, to obtain a new hashed value. Periodically, say at midnight, we notarize the hashed value of the most recent transaction, resulting in a notary ID. We hash the most recent hashed value with its notary ID, to compute a new value used to link subsequent transactions.

To check the validity, we repeat the hashing, in transaction-time sequence, checking the values we obtain for the transaction at midnight with the notarization service. Doing so requires a single linear scan of the database, followed by the linked hashing.

The benefit is greatly reduced interaction with the notarization service, from one per transaction to, say, one interaction per day, with a concomitant reduction of notarization history table to one tuple per day. The downsides are reduced information on attacks (we only know that the information stored on a particular day was corrupted) and an inability to do checking after an attack.

6.3 Interacting with Timestamping

The time assigned by the notarization service will be (slightly) after that assigned by the database stamp module. To address this problem we introduce the *Transaction Ordering List* (TOL). Before a transaction is committed, the user data (that is, the explicit columns, as we do not yet know the timestamp of the transaction) of the tuples modified by the transaction is hashed. When the transaction commits, the transaction time (which has just been determined) and the hash value are hashed together to get the final hash value of the transaction. Thus we do not have to delay the tuple hashing until the transaction is committed.

7 Implementation

In our implementation, the audit facility is built on top of the TUC (Temporal Upward Compatibility), CLK (Clock), and STP (Stamper) modules we previously added to the underlying Berkeley DB so that it can support transaction time. We also added several more transaction-time related commands (e.g., AS TRANSACTIONTIME) and flags in MySQL so that MySQL can support transaction time. We then added an audit (AUD) module. A notarization service requester (NSR) utility and a database validator (DBV) utility were implemented as separately running programs.

While Berkeley DB is reading or writing a disk page, or while a tuple that can be stamped is accessed, STP will scan the page to do the stamping (replacing the transaction IDs with their transaction time) and some bookkeeping. This is the perfect opportunity to piggyback the hashing of the tuples onto this STP page scan. With further analysis of the relationship of the STP and AUD modules, we found we can completely put AUD behind STP to form a clean, modularized architecture.

The auditable DBMS architecture and the AUD module internal structure are shown in Figure 2. In this figure, each process is represented by a dotted line rectangle, each piece of software is represented by a solid line rectangle and each internal module is represented by a rounded solid line rectangle. Berkeley DB serves as the storage manager for MySQL and is

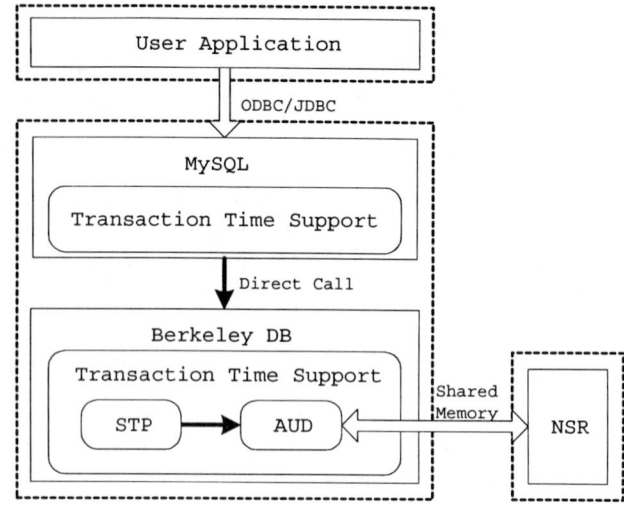

Figure 2: Auditable DBMS via MySQL+Berkeley DB

linked into the MySQL as a library. The user application running in another process interacts with MySQL through various interfaces, such as ODBC and JDBC. The NSR runs in a separate process but shares its memory region with Berkeley DB, where the database environment information is stored and shared.

AUD hashes each tuple into the transaction hash value and maintains the hash value chain across transactions. We call the last transaction on the hash chain the *tail transaction*, its transaction time the *tail time*, and its hash value the *tail hash value*. NSR is triggered every day. When triggered, it obtains the tail hash value and tail time from AUD, hashes them and sends the hash value as a document to the notarization service to be notarized. The notarization service will reply with a notary ID (NID) consisting of the notarization time and a secure timestamp computed from the document received and the time when the notarization occurred (the notarization service has its own trusted time source). The NSR hashes the NID along with the tail hash value to compute a new value to serve as the beginning of the next transaction hash chain. It also stores the (*tailtime, NID*) tuple in a notarization history table.

DBV (the audit validator) is run when a database audit is needed. It reads the entire audit log, recomputing the transaction hash values. According to the tail time information stored in the notarization history table, all the transaction hash values are grouped into hash chains, so that for each hash chain we have a corresponding tuple in the notarization history table. For each hash chain, transaction hash values are linked and the tail time and tail hash value are recomputed and sent to the notarization service. Encountering a validation that is refused by the notarization service implies something is corrupted after the beginning of the

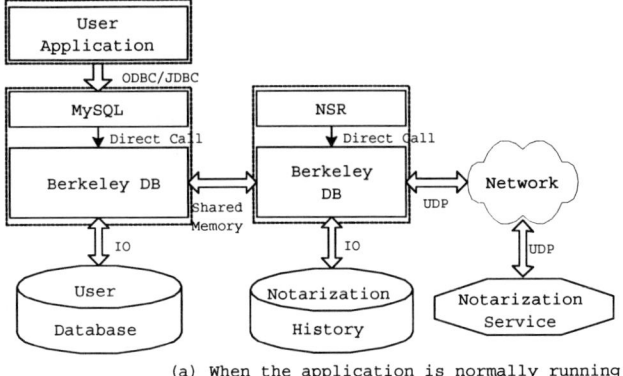

(a) When the application is normally running

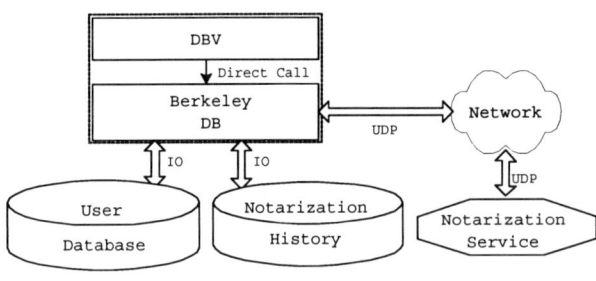

(b) When the DBV is doing the validation

Figure 3: AUD Module Architecture

transaction chain. DBV then displays the time when the invalid transaction is discovered in the database and a list of pages that are potentially involved in the unmatched hash value.

Figure 3(a) illustrates the detailed architecture of the auditing module during a normal run of the application. Figure 3(b) shows the validator validating the audit log. In the figure, each process is again represented by a dotted line rectangle. Different pieces of software are represented by solid line rectangles.

8 Performance

We studied the performance of the auditing system and the various database parameters' impact on the auditing system performance.

8.1 Opportunistic Hashing

We first compare the time and space complexity of the opportunistic hashing approach and the naive approach, during transaction processing and during validation. In the naive approach, for both phases, all tuples are kept and sorted in main memory until being hashed at transaction commit.

As far as main memory space is concerned, when the transaction is running, the naive approach has $O(n)$ (where n is the number of tuples per transaction) space overhead to store the tuples of a transaction, while the optimized approach only has constant space overhead to store the intermediate hashing state. When the validator is running, the naive approach has $O(n)$ space overhead to sort and hash the tuples, which is the same as that of the optimized approach. However the actual space overhead of the optimized approach is lower, because tuples are discarded as the validator scans the database.

As far as CPU time is concerned, when the transaction is running, the optimized approach does not sort tuples at all, while the naive approach has $O(n \lg n)$ cost to sort the tuples in a priority queue. When the validator is running, the time complexity of the sorting is the same for both naive and optimized approaches.

Since the performance improvement due to the opportunistic hashing is obvious from this analysis, we did not run experiments on it.

8.2 Notarization Service Interaction

A trivial analysis can illustrate the dramatic performance improvement due to the minimization of the notarization service interaction. If there are t transactions per day, the basic approach requires t notarization service interactions per day. However, with the opportunistic hashing and linked hashing, only one such interaction is needed. This is a dramatic reduce in the network load. If the notarization service cost is calculated based on the number of interactions, the total service cost is reduced by a factor of t. The same analysis applies to the validator. This analysis suggests that the optimization to minimize the notarization service interaction is critical.

Concerning asynchronous notarization, suppose the round trip time (from the time a request is send to the time a response is received) of a notarization is r seconds and the system throughput is t transactions per second. For each notarization, the audit system with asynchronous notarization can finish $r \cdot t$ more transactions per notarization than one without it.

8.3 Experiment Design

We now turn to a more detailed, empirical analysis of our implementation, which includes all of the optimizations just discussed. We simulated a bank account balance scenario. The database was populated with tuples inserted in random order. Each tuple represented a bank account and the key represented the unique account number. The data represents the account balance.

For all of our experiments the disk page was 8 KB. The tuple size was 250 bytes, implying 32 tuples per page. The experiments were all run on a 3.0GHz Pentium IV running Fedora 1 Linux, with the default buffer pool size of 264KB, accessing data from a local EIDE disk.

The notarization was done every five seconds. The notarization service response time was two seconds (from the DBMS sending the notarization request until receiving the notary ID back from the notarization service, a quite conservative estimate). This reflects the worst case, because in the real world application, the notarization will not be done that frequently. It would usually be around one notarization per day, which imposes much less notarization overhead than what we did here. We chose five seconds here just to accommodate the experiments, which run for a relatively short amount of time (much less than a day!). We implemented our own notarization service, rather than using one of the commercial services.

8.4 Validation Overhead

As discussed in Section 6.1, validation involves a linear scan of the audit log, which costs $O(n)$ time according to the size of the audit log. (Since an intruder could have changed any byte of the audit log, necessarily the entire audit log must be read by the validator.) As an initial experiment, we ran small transactions (inserting four tuples each), and then validated the audit log. We varied the number of transactions that were run before validation and observed the total running time, which consists of CPU time, sleep time and I/O time. Validation time was under 1% of the time required to create the audit log.

8.5 Impact of the Number of Transactions per Application

We then studied the scalability of the auditing system as the number of transactions grows. The database was initially populated with 4M tuples to simulate that many different bank accounts. implying a starting database of approximately 1GB. Then according to different experiments, insertion and/or deletion operations wrapped in transactions were applied on randomly selected tuples. In order to simulate the data access hot spots (i.e., some of the accounts are very active and represent a greater percentage of the total accesses), the access to the tuples follows a normal distribution with an average equal to half of the largest key and standard deviation equal to $\frac{1}{8}$ of the largest key.

We ran an application that performed updates on this database changing the balance of accounts to a new value (with the audit log retaining the old value in an archival tuple). Each transaction updated four tuples. We ran the application with different number of transactions, and observed the total running time and the number of I/Os with and without the auditing system.

We can see from Figure 4 that the auditing running time overhead increases proportionally to the number of transactions, at about 9% over the non-auditing database (for all the experiments in this paper, the auditing overhead was between 9% and 16%).

The auditing system introduces essentially no I/O overhead (either no or one I/O, for a slightly larger

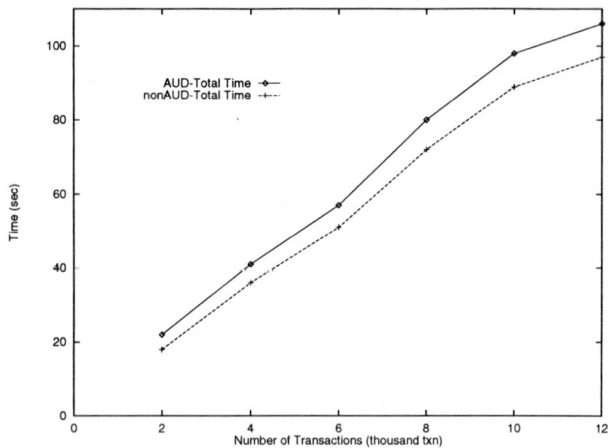

Figure 4: Performance: Changing the Number of Transactions per Application

log). For example, at 12,000 transactions, the NSR made only 44 I/O requests.

8.6 Impact of Transaction Size

We then studied the impact of transaction size (number of tuples modified per transaction) on the auditing system performance. The database configuration was identical to the above. We ran the application with 10,000 transactions, but varied the number of tuples updated per transaction, from 2 to 64. Then we observed the total running time and the number of I/Os with and without auditing system. From Figure 5, we see that the overhead of auditing is again about 11%, independent of transaction size.

8.7 Impact of Tuple Size

We then turned to the impact of the tuple size on the auditing system performance. The database configuration was identical to that above. Here each transaction modified four tuples. We fixed the data bandwidth (total bytes of data manipulated) and varied the number of transactions in inverse proportion to the tuple size, namely (10 bytes/tuple, 10,000 transactions) to (1000 bytes/tuple, 100 transactions). Note that the x-axis of Figure 6 is logarithmic.

Here the time overhead for hashing ranged from 16% in the worst case (for very small tuples) to an insignificant overhead for large tuples. From this experiment and the fact that hashing operations count for most of the auditing system overhead, we can infer that the number of hashing operations instead of the total bytes of data hashed dictates to first order the auditing system overhead.

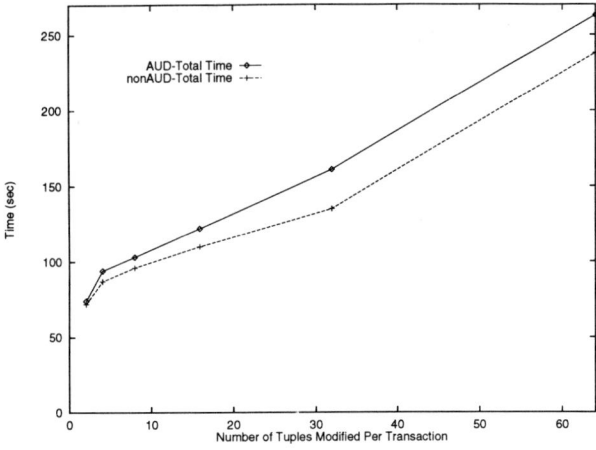

Figure 5: Performance: Changing the Transaction Size

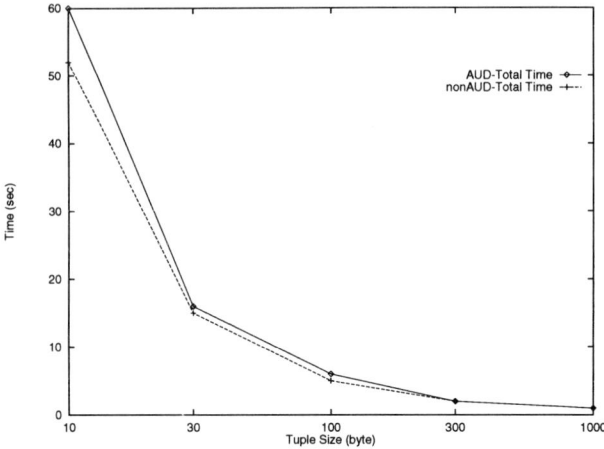

Figure 6: Performance: Changing the Tuple Size While Fixing the Data Bandwidth

8.8 Impact of the Notarization Service Response Time

In this experiment, we studied the impact of the notarization service response time on the auditing system. The "response time" is defined as the time interval from sending the notarization service request until the DBMS received the notary ID back from the notarization service. There were 10,000 transactions in this application and each updated four tuples. We ran the application with various notarization response time, namely 1, 2, 3, and 4 seconds (the system was executing about 100 transactions per second, so there are many hundreds of transactions backed up when the response time is four seconds) and observed the CPU time, total running time and number of I/Os with the auditing system.

The notarization service response time does not affect the auditing system performance. The total time was around 98 seconds, independent of the response time. When the notarization takes longer time to return the notary ID, the currently running transactions will accumulate in the TOL in the AUD module, which causes an undetectable CPU overhead to maintain the TOL data structure management.

9 Related Work

There has been related work in several fields: security, operating systems, and databases. We address each in turn.

Mercuri raises the need to audit the audit log [14]. Peha [17] uses, as we do, one-way hash functions and a "trusted" notary to hash and store every transaction. Our approach differs in that we make no assumptions about the DBMS, or even the hardware it executes on, remaining in the trusted computing base following an intrusion; Peha on the other hand advocates a "notary on a chip". Unlike Peha, we integrate hashing with stamping of tuples in the table, and we consider system issues such as the need to hash tuples and using partial result authentication codes to link transactions. Peha simply batches transactions together by hashing all the data in all the transactions, which will undoubtedly result in very poor performance, as we discussed in detail in Section 6.1. Peha goes into more detail on how customers, notarizers, validators, and auditors can use public key encryption to coordinate. Note that since we send the notarization service only hash values, no private data that is revealed to that external service. It may still be useful to encrypt the tuples that flow from the database to the validator, if that process communicates with the DBMS over non-secure channels.

As mentioned in Section 2, Schneier and Kelsey address audit logs that are used for later forensic investigations into detected intrusions [21]. Their requirements differ considerably from ours. In particular, they render the log entries impossible for the attacker to read. They use a hash linking in a similar way to our algorithm. They do not consider efficiency issues, which are critical in our situation where an online transactional database is being logged.

Merkle proposed a digital signature system based on a secure conventional encryption function over a tree of document fragments [15]. This work could be utilized within an notarization service, but is not directly applicable to our problem of hashing the data of individual transactions.

Devanbu et al. applied the Merkle Tree authentication mechanism to both relational [6] and XML [5] data. Here the model is different: queries over static data which has been previous digested are evaluated by an insecure server. The query results are sent to clients, which can independently verify, using the digest, that the result contains all the requested records and no superfluous records. While our approach also uses a hashing approach similar to Merkle and this work (though not tree-based), we focus on *modifications* made by the perhaps compromised server.

The file system equivalent of a transaction-time database is a *read-only file system*, in which new files can only be added; existing files cannot be modified [8], or a read-write system in which the files are logged, such as in the Ivy system [16]. These systems sign the data, so that programs that read a file can be assured that it has not been corrupted. They share with the present paper the need for high performance.

POSTGRES [24] and Dali [4] were two different approaches of protecting critical DBMS data structures against software errors. The former used hardware protection, while the latter used a wordcode software mechanism and also proposed a recovery algorithm for the corrupted transactions. They mainly dealt with abnormal corruptions caused by software errors instead of human hackers. And the protection was limited to the in-memory data structures instead of the whole database on disk. If Bob directly changed the data in the disk file, this intrusion would not be detected by these mechanisms.

Liu, Ammann and Jajodia propose an algorithm that rewrites the execution history backing out malicious transactions while preserving the good transactions [1, 13]. This assumes that the malicious transactions had been identified according to the application semantics; they did not deal with intrusion detection. Perhaps our detection approach could be coupled with their repair technology.

10 Summary and Future Work

Motivated by audit log requirements, we have presented a new approach to providing audit logs for transaction processing systems that can effectively and efficiently detect tampering. We based our approach on existing cryptographic techniques such as strong cryptographic hashing, partial result authentication codes, and off-site digital notarization services. Our contributions are as follows.

- We showed how a transaction-time database can be used as the basis for tamper-detecting audit logs, transparent to the application.

- To reduce the expense of interacting with the notarization service on a per-tuple basis, an opportunistic hashing algorithm was proposed to compute the data hash value of transactions, so as to enable per-transaction notarization. Incremental hashing and tuple sequence numbers are proposed to support opportunistic hashing.

- To further minimize the expense of interacting with notarization services, linked hashing of transactions was introduced, by means of partial result authentication codes.

- We used an in-memory data structure, the transaction ordering list, to handle non-monotonic assignment of transaction times that result from sophisticated timestamping algorithms as well as handling delays from the off-site notarization service.

- We designed our validator to make a single scan of the audited tables, interacting with the notarization service infrequently.

- We developed an implementation within the high-performance Berkeley DB data storage manager, and showed through experiments that the overhead never exceeds 16%, that to a first approximation the tuple size dictates the auditing system overhead, rather than the total number of bytes hashed, and that the notarization service response time minimally impacts system performance.

There is more work that can be done. We've focused in this paper on certifying in a definitive fashion that an audit log is pristine. If an audit log has been tampered with, a detailed forensic analysis would be required and would involve going back to other records, perhaps even to physical records, to document the fraud. In such circumstances, it would be helpful for the validator to provide information enabling the analysis to determine fairly precisely *who* performed the attack, *when* the attach occurred, and *which* data was compromised. To provide this information about the intrusion, various hints, such as page-level hash values, and the algorithms of inferring detailed intrusion information from these hints need to be developed. It is also possible for the DBMS and applications to log activities through additional data stored in the database. That additional data would be helpful in analyzing intrusions. Of course, such data should be stored in audited tables.

The validator should be enhanced to differentiate corruption of the hints from corruption of the data, and should be able to contend with multiple intrusions. The appropriate notarization granularity (an hour, a day?) should be investigated. And we want to look at partitioning to eliminate the need to scan all pages of audited tables.

Finally, we want to produce and evaluate mechanisms that leverage tamper detection of audit logs to produce *tamper-resistant audit logs*, which cannot be corrupted, yet are still accessible to the application, and accord with our very general threat model.

References

[1] P. Ammann, S. Jajodia, and P. Liu, "Recovery from Malicious Transactions," IEEE *Transactions on Knowledge and Data Engineering* 15(5):1167–1185, September 2002.

[2] J. Bair, M. Böhlen, C. S. Jensen, and R. T. Snodgrass, "Notions of Upward Compatibility of Temporal Query Languages," *Business Informatics (Wirtschafts Informatik)*, Vol. 39, No. 1, February, 1997, pp. 25–34.

[3] M. Bellare and B. Yee, "Forward Integrity for Secure Audit Logs," Technical Report, Computer Science and Engineering Department, University of California at San Diego, November 1997.

[4] P. Bohannon, R. Rastogi, S. Seshadri, A. Silberschatz, and S. Sudarshan, "Using Codewords to Protect Database Data from a Class of Software Errors," in *Proceedings of the IEEE International Conference on Data Engineering*, 1999, pp. 276–285.

[5] P. Devanbu, M. Gertz, A. Kwong, C. Martel, G. Nuckolls, and S. G. Stubblebine, "Flexible Authentication of XML documents," in *Proceedings of the ACM Conference on Computer and Communications Security*, Philadelphia, PA, November, 2001, pp. 136–145.

[6] P. Devanbu, M. Gertz, C. Martel and S. G. Stubblebine, "Authentic data publication over the Internet," *Journal of Computer Security* 11(3):291–314, 2003.

[7] P. DuBois, **MySQL**, Second Edition, SAMS, 2003.

[8] K. Fu, M. F. Kaashoek and D. Mazieres, "Fast and secure distributed read-only file system," in *Proceedings of the USENIX Symposium on Operating Systems Design and Implementation*, pp. 181-196, October 2000.

[9] L. A. Gordon, M. P. Loeb, W. Lucyshyn, and R. Richardson, **2004 CSI/FBI Computer Crime and Security Survey**, Computer Security Institute, 2004.

[10] S. Haber and W. S. Stornetta, "How To Time-Stamp a Digital Document," *Journal of Cryptology* 3, pp. 99–111, 1999.

[11] C. S. Jensen and C. E. Dyreson (eds), A Consensus Glossary of Temporal Database Concepts—February 1998 Version," in **Temporal Databases: Research and Practice**, O. Etzion, S. Jajodia, and S. Sripada (eds.), Springer-Verlag, pp. 367–405, 1998.

[12] C. S. Jensen and D. B. Lomet, "Transaction Timestamping in (Temporal) Databases," in *Proceedings of the International Conference on Very Large Databases*, Roma, Italy, pp. 441–450, 2001.

[13] P. Liu, P. Ammann and S. Jajodia, "Rewriting Histories: Recovering from Malicious Transactions," *Distributed and Parallel Databases Journal* (8):1:7–40, January 2000.

[14] R. T. Mercuri, "On Auditing Audit Trails," *CACM* 46(1):17–20, January 2003.

[15] R. C. Merkle, "A Certified Digital Signature," *Advances in Cryptography—Annual International Cryptography Conference*, Vol. 435, pp. 218–238, 1989.

[16] A. Muthitacharoen, R. Morris, T. M. Gil and B. Chen, "Ivy: A Read/Write Peer-to-Peer File System," in *Proceedings of USENIX Operating Systems Design and Implementation*, 2002.

[17] J.M. Peha, "Electronic commerce with verifiable audit trails," in *Proceedings of ISOC*, 1999. www.isoc.org/isoc/conferences/inet/99/-proceedings/1h/1h_1.htm, viewed on March 26, 2003.

[18] M. Rabi and A. T. Sherman, "An observation on associative one-way functions in complexity theory," in *Information Processing Letters*, Vol 64, Issue 5, pages 239-244, 1997.

[19] R. Ramakrishnan and J. Gehrke, **Database Management Systems**, Third Edition, 2003.

[20] B. Salzberg, "Timestamping After Commit," in *Proceedings of PDIS Conference*, pp. 160–167, 1994.

[21] B. Schneier and J. Kelsey, "Secure Audit Logs to Support Computer Forensics," ACM *Transactions on Information and System Security* 2(2):159–196, May 1999.

[22] Sleepycat Software Inc., **Berkeley DB**, 2001.

[23] M. Stonebraker, "The Deisgn of the POSTGRESS Storage System," in *Proceedings of the International Conference on Very Large Databases*, pp. 289–300, 1987.

[24] M. Sullivan and M. Stonebraker, "Using Write Protected Data Structures to Improve Software Fault Tolerance in Highly Available Database Management Systems," in *Proceedings of the International Conference on Very Large Dsta Bases*, pp. 171–180, 1991.

[25] National Institute of Standards and Technology, "Secure Hash Signature Standard," August 2002.

Auditing Compliance with a Hippocratic Database

Rakesh Agrawal   Roberto Bayardo   Christos Faloutsos   Jerry Kiernan   Ralf Rantzau   Ramakrishnan Srikant

IBM Almaden Research Center
650 Harry Road, San Jose, CA 95120

Abstract

We introduce an auditing framework for determining whether a database system is adhering to its data disclosure policies. Users formulate audit expressions to specify the (sensitive) data subject to disclosure review. An audit component accepts audit expressions and returns all queries (deemed "suspicious") that accessed the specified data during their execution.

The overhead of our approach on query processing is small, involving primarily the logging of each query string along with other minor annotations. Database triggers are used to capture updates in a backlog database. At the time of audit, a static analysis phase selects a subset of logged queries for further analysis. These queries are combined and transformed into an SQL audit query, which when run against the backlog database, identifies the suspicious queries efficiently and precisely.

We describe the algorithms and data structures used in a DB2-based implementation of this framework. Experimental results reinforce our design choices and show the practicality of the approach.

1 Introduction

The requirement for responsibly managing privacy sensitive data is being mandated internationally through legislations and guidelines such as the United States Fair Information Practices Act, the European Union Privacy Directive, the Canadian Standard Association's Model Code for the Protection of Personal Information, the Australian Privacy Amendment Act, the Japanese Personal Information Protection Law, and others. A vision for a Hippocratic database [2] proposes ten privacy principles for managing

Permission to copy without fee all or part of this material is granted provided that the copies are not made or distributed for direct commercial advantage, the VLDB copyright notice and the title of the publication and its date appear, and notice is given that copying is by permission of the Very Large Data Base Endowment. To copy otherwise, or to republish, requires a fee and/or special permission from the Endowment.

**Proceedings of the 30th VLDB Conference,
Toronto, Canada, 2004**

private data responsibly. A vital principle among these is compliance, which requires the database to verify that it adheres to its declared data disclosure policy.

Consider Alice who gets a blood test done at Healthco, a company whose privacy policy stipulates that it does not release patient data to external parties without the patient's consent. After some time, Alice starts receiving advertisements for an over-the-counter diabetes test. She suspects that Healthco might have released the information that she is at risk of developing diabetes. The United States Health Insurance Portability and Accountability Act (HIPAA) empowers Alice to demand from Healthco the name of every entity to whom Healthco has disclosed her information. As another example, consider Bob who consented that Healthco can provide his medical data to its affiliates for the purposes of research, provided his personally identifiable information was excluded. Later on, Bob could ask Healthco to show that they indeed did exclude his name, social security number, and address when they provided his medical record to the Cardio Institute. The demand for demonstrating compliance need not only arise from an externally initiated complaint – a company may institute periodic internal audits to proactively guard against potential exposures.

One approach to verifying that a database adheres to its disclosure policies might be to support data disclosure auditing by physically logging the results of each query. Problems with this approach include the following:

- it imposes a substantial overhead on normal query processing, particularly for queries that produce many results, and
- the actual disclosure auditing it supports is limited, since data disclosed by a query is not necessarily reflected by its output.

As an example of the limitations on disclosure auditing, consider P3P [5], which allows individuals to specify whether an enterprise can use their data in an aggregation. Verifying that database accesses have been compliant with such user preferences is not possible given only a log of aggregated results. To address this issue, one might instead consider logging the tuples "read" by a query during its execution instead of its output. However, determining which tuples accessed during query processing were actually disclosed is non-trivial. In addition, such a change dramatically increases logging overhead.

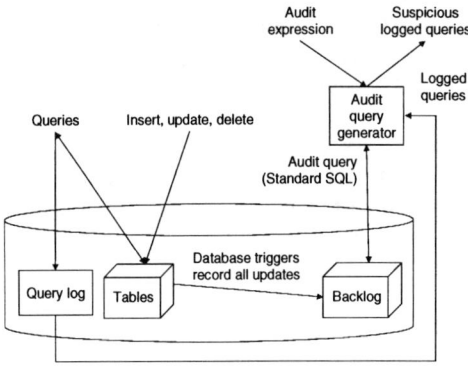

Figure 1: The system architecture

1.1 Our Contribution

We propose a system that can be used to audit whether the database system executed a query in the past that accessed the specified data. The ideal system should have the following properties:

- **Non-disruptive:** The system should put minimal burden on normal query processing.
- **Fast and precise:** The system should be able to quickly and precisely identify all the queries that accessed the specified data.
- **Fine-grained:** It should be possible to audit even a single field of a specific record.
- **Convenient:** The language for specifying data of interest should be intuitive and user friendly.

The proposed audit system satisfies the above desiderata. Figure 1 shows the overall architecture of our system. During normal operation, the text of every query processed by the database system is logged along with annotations such as the time when the query was executed, the user submitting the query, and the query's purpose. The system uses database triggers to capture and record all updates to base tables in backlog tables for recovering the state of the database at any past point in time. Read queries, which are usually predominant, do not write any tuple to the backlog database.

To perform an audit, the auditor formulates an audit expression that declaratively specifies the data of interest. Audit expressions are designed to be identical to the SQL queries, allowing audits to be performed at the level of an individual cell of a table. The audit expression is processed by the audit query generator, which first performs a static analysis of the expression to select a subset of logged queries that could potentially disclose the specified information. It then combines and transforms the selected queries into a single audit query by augmenting them with additional predicates derived from the audit expression. This audit query, expressed in standard SQL, when run against the backlog database yields the precise set of logged queries that accessed the designated data. Indices on the backlog tables make the execution of the audit query fast.

1.2 Assumptions

- There are subtle ways in which the combination of the results of a series of queries may reveal certain information. For example, the statistical database literature [1] discusses how individual information can be deduced by running several aggregate queries and the database security literature [3] shows how covert channels can be used to leak information. We limit ourselves to the problem of determining if the specified data was disclosed by a single query when that query is considered in isolation. We also assume that the queries do not use outside knowledge to deduce information without detection.
- The SQL queries we consider comprise a single **select** clause. A large class of queries (including those containing existential subqueries) can be converted into this form [12]. Specifically, we consider queries containing selection, projection (including **distinct**), relational join, and aggregation (including **having**) operations.

1.3 Paper Layout

The rest of the paper is organized as follows. Section 2 provides the syntax of an audit expression. We then propose the concept of an indispensable tuple, which in turn is used to identify suspicious queries with respect to an audit expression. Section 3 describes the system structures needed to support the proposed auditing capability. Specifically, we discuss the use of triggers to implement recovery of past database states. We also provide temporal extensions used to support the execution of an audit query, and give details of the query log. Section 4 states the algorithm for generating the audit query from an audit expression. Section 5 presents performance results, Section 6 discusses related work, and Section 7 concludes with a summary and directions for future work.

2 Definitions

We have a database D, which is a collection of base tables. We denote the scheme of table T as $T(C_0, C_1, \ldots, C_m)$ and use $t.C$ to refer to the value of the field C in tuple t. We will use the following schema in our examples:

Customer (<u>cid</u>, name, address, phone, zip, contact)
Treatment (<u>pcid, date</u>, rcid, did, disease, duration)
Doctor (<u>did</u>, name)

The primary keys have been underlined. A customer can be a patient, someone accepting financial responsibility for a patient's treatment, or an emergency *contact*. The Treatment table uses *pcid* to identify the patient receiving the treatment and uses *rcid* to identify the customer assuming financial responsibility for the treatment (who could be the same person as the patient). The *date* is the start date of the treatment and *duration* reflects the length of the treatment. Other column names are self-explanatory. To simplify exposition, we will assume that the database has referential integrity and that no field value is null.

2.1 Audit Expressions

We propose to use expressions that are very close to SQL queries to enable an auditor to conveniently specify the queries of interest, termed suspicious queries.

Specifically, the proposed syntax of an audit expression is identical to that of a select-project-join (SPJ) query without any **distinct** in the select list, except that **audit** replaces the key word **select** and the elements of the audit list are restricted to be column names:

audit *audit list*
from *table list*
where *condition list*

Let $\mathcal{U}$ be the cross product of all the base tables in the database. The audit expression marks a set of cells in the table $\mathcal{U}$. The marked cells belong to the columns in the audit list for the tuples that satisfy the predicate in the **where** clause. We are interested in finding those queries that access all the marked cells in any of the tuples in $\mathcal{U}$. These are the suspicious queries with respect to the audit expression.

Example 1 We want to audit if the disease information of anyone living in the ZIP code 95120 was disclosed. Here is the audit expression:

audit disease
from Customer c, Treatment t
where c.cid = t.pcid **and** c.zip = '95120'

This audit expression marks the cells corresponding to the disease column of those tuples in the Customer × Treatment table that have c.cid = t.pcid and c.zip = 95120. Any query that accesses the disease column of any of these tuples will be considered suspicious.

2.2 Informal Definitions

We introduce the notion of the indispensability of a tuple and then use it to define suspicious queries.

Informal Definition 1 (Indispensable Tuple - $ind(t, Q)$)
A tuple $t \in \mathcal{U}$ is indispensable in the computation of a query Q, if its omission makes a difference.

Informal Definition 2 (Candidate Query - $cand(Q, A)$)
A query Q is a candidate query with respect to an audit expression A, if Q accesses all the columns that A specifies in its audit list.

Informal Definition 3 (Suspicious Query - $susp(Q, A)$)
A candidate query Q is suspicious with respect to an audit expression A, if Q and A share an indispensable tuple.

Example 2 Consider the audit expression A given in Example 1 and the following query Q:

select address
from Customer c, Treatment t
where c.cid = t.pcid **and** t.disease = 'diabetes'

We see that Q is a candidate query with respect to A as it accesses the disease column that A is auditing. Consider the Customer × Treatment table. Clearly, tuples that match the join condition and have diabetes in the disease column are indispensable for Q. Similarly, tuples that match the join condition and have 95120 as the zip code are indispensable for A. Therefore Q will be deemed suspicious with respect to A if there was some customer who lived in the ZIP code 95120 and was also treated for diabetes.

Example 3 Consider the query Q from Example 2 and the following audit expression A:

audit address
from Customer c, Treatment t
where c.cid = t.pcid **and** t.disease = 'cancer'

Q will not be deemed suspicious with respect to A because no tuple in Customer × Treatment can simultaneously satisfy the predicates of Q and A. But how about Alice who has both cancer and diabetes? Although Q discloses Alice's address, the fact that Alice has cancer is not relevant to the query: Q only asks for people who have diabetes. In other words, anyone looking at the output of the query will not learn that Alice has cancer. Hence it is reasonable to not consider the query to be suspicious. Note that all the tuples of Customer × Treatment marked by A have cancer in the disease column and Q does not access any one of them.

2.3 Formal Definitions

Let the query Q and audit expression A be of the form:

$$Q = \ldots(\sigma_{P_Q}(\mathcal{T} \times \mathcal{R})) \quad (1)$$
$$A = \overline{\pi}_{C_{OA}}(\sigma_{P_A}(\mathcal{T} \times \mathcal{S})) \quad (2)$$

where $\mathcal{T}, \mathcal{R}, \mathcal{S}$ are *virtual* tables of the database D, that is, cross products of base tables:

$$\mathcal{T} = T_1 \times T_2 \times \ldots \times T_n$$
$$\mathcal{R} = R_1 \times R_2 \times \ldots \times R_m$$
$$\mathcal{S} = S_1 \times S_2 \times \ldots \times S_k.$$

The operator $\overline{\pi}$ is the multi-set projection operator that preserves duplicates in the output (as opposed to the relational projection operator π which eliminates duplicates). Note that $\mathcal{T}$ is common to Q and A.

We denote by C_Q the column names that appear anywhere in a query Q, and by C_{OQ} the column names appearing in the select list of Q. Similarly, C_{OA} denotes the column names present in the audit list of an audit expression A. P_Q denotes the predicate of the query and P_A is the predicate of the audit expression. We refer to the tuples of any virtual table as *virtual* tuples.

We now formalize the definition of indispensability, for all classes of queries of interest. Specifically, we discuss (a) SPJ queries, (b) queries with aggregation without **having**, and (c) queries with aggregation and **having**.

2.3.1 Indispensability - SPJ queries

Consider first a SPJ query that does not contain a **distinct** in its select list. This case is the most important case on which the rest of the cases will be based. For such queries, the form of the query of Eq. (1) is specialized to:

$$Q = \bar{\pi}_{C_{O_Q}}(\sigma_{P_Q}(\mathcal{T} \times \mathcal{R})). \quad (3)$$

We can now formalize the definition of an indispensable tuple for an SPJ query:

Definition 1 (Indispensability - SPJ) *A (virtual) tuple $v \in \mathcal{T}$ is indispensable for an SPJ query Q if the result of Q changes when we delete v:*

$$ind(v, Q) \Leftrightarrow \bar{\pi}_{C_Q}(\sigma_{P_Q}(\mathcal{T} \times \mathcal{R})) \neq \bar{\pi}_{C_Q}(\sigma_{P_Q}((\mathcal{T}-\{v\}) \times \mathcal{R})).$$

Theorem 1 *A (virtual) tuple $v \in \mathcal{T}$ of the SPJ query Q is indispensable if and only if*

$$\sigma_{P_Q}(\{v\} \times \mathcal{R}) \neq \emptyset.$$

Proof From Definition 1, we have

$$ind(v, Q) \Leftrightarrow \bar{\pi}_{C_Q}(\sigma_{P_Q}(\mathcal{T} \times \mathcal{R})) \neq \bar{\pi}_{C_Q}(\sigma_{P_Q}((\mathcal{T}-\{v\}) \times \mathcal{R})).$$

Since the projections $\bar{\pi}$ maintain the duplicates, we have

$$ind(v, Q) \Leftrightarrow \sigma_{P_Q}(\mathcal{T} \times \mathcal{R}) \neq \sigma_{P_Q}((\mathcal{T}-\{v\}) \times \mathcal{R})$$
$$\Leftrightarrow \sigma_{P_Q}(\mathcal{T} \times \mathcal{R}) \neq \sigma_{P_Q}(\mathcal{T} \times \mathcal{R}) - \sigma_{P_Q}(\{v\} \times \mathcal{R})$$
$$\Leftrightarrow \sigma_{P_Q}(\{v\} \times \mathcal{R}) \neq \emptyset. \blacksquare$$

Queries with **distinct** in the **select** clause produce a duplicate-free table. Such queries have the form $Q = \pi_{C_{O_Q}}(\sigma_{P_Q}(\mathcal{T} \times \mathcal{R}))$. Let Q' be the SPJ query obtained from the original query Q after removing **distinct** from the query text. Then, we have the following definition:

Definition 2 (Indispensability - Distinct) *A (virtual) tuple v is indispensable for $Q = \pi_{C_{O_Q}}(\sigma_{P_Q}(\mathcal{T} \times \mathcal{R}))$ if and only if it is indispensable for $Q' = \bar{\pi}_{C_{O_Q}}(\sigma_{P_Q}(\mathcal{T} \times \mathcal{R}))$.*

The motivation for this definition will become apparent after the upcoming discussion of aggregation queries. Queries with **distinct** can be viewed as a special case of aggregation, the aggregation function being the first tuple in a group.

We can state succinctly:

Observation 1 *Duplicate elimination does not change the set of indispensable tuples for an SPJ query.*

2.3.2 Indispensability - Aggregation without having

The definition of indispensability of a tuple for an aggregation query requires extra care. Consider a query that computes average salary per department. If Alice happens to have exactly the average salary of her department and her tuple is omitted, the query result will not be affected. However, it will be wrong to treat Alice's tuple as dispensable because the privacy systems such as P3P allow individuals to opt out of the use of their values in the computation of an aggregation.

The form of the query of Eq. (1) for an aggregation query without a **having** clause is specialized to:

$$Q = {}_{gby}\gamma_{agg}(\sigma_{P_Q}(\mathcal{T} \times \mathcal{R})). \quad (4)$$

where *gby* are the grouping columns and *agg* represent aggregations like **avg**(duration), **count**(disease).

Consider the query Q' that is a version of Q, but without aggregations. That is, Q' has exactly the same **from** and **where** clauses, and a **select** clause with the same columns as Q, but without the aggregation functions. Note that the columns used in *agg* (e.g. duration, disease) are included in the select list of Q'.

Definition 3 (Indispensability - Aggregation) *A (virtual) tuple v is indispensable for Q if and only if it is indispensable for the aggregate-free version Q'.*

Example 4 Consider the following query that outputs average duration of diabetes treatment by doctor:

select	name, **avg**(duration)
from	Doctor d, Treatment t
where	d.did = t.did **and** t.disease = 'diabetes'
group by	name

Indispensability of a tuple t in the the above query is determined by considering the indispensability of t in the following SPJ query:

select	name, duration
from	Doctor d, Treatment t
where	d.did = t.did **and** t.disease = 'diabetes'

We find that every Treatment tuple having diabetes in the disease field is indispensable. Thus the fact that the duration values of these tuples were used in computing the output is not lost.

The following is immediate:

Observation 2 *A tuple v is indispensable for $Q = {}_{gby}\gamma_{agg}(\sigma_{P_Q}(\mathcal{T} \times \mathcal{R}))$ if and only if it is indispensable for $Q' = \bar{\pi}_{C_Q}(\sigma_{P_Q}(\mathcal{T} \times \mathcal{R}))$.*

2.3.3 Indispensability - Aggregation with having

We will use the query in following example to help with the explanations.

Example 5 Our query is a modified version of the query given in Example 4. It outputs average duration of diabetes treatment, but only for those doctors for whom this average is greater than 100 days:

select	name, **avg**(duration)
from	Doctor d, Treatment t
where	d.did = t.did **and** t.disease = 'diabetes'
group by	name
having	**avg**(duration) > 100

The general form of an aggregation query Q that includes a **having** clause can be written as:

$$Q = \sigma_{P_H}({}_{gby}\gamma_{agg}(\sigma_{P_Q}(\mathcal{T} \times \mathcal{R}))). \quad (5)$$

Compared to Eq. (4), we now have an extra **having** predicate P_H (**avg**(duration) > 100 in Example 5). Any group that does not satisfy this predicate is not included in the result of Q, which implies that any tuple belonging to a group that gets filtered out by P_H is dispensable.

Let Q' be the **having**-free version of Q, obtained by simply removing the **having** clause from Q.

Definition 4 (Indispensability - Aggregation with having) *A (virtual) tuple v is indispensable for Q if and only if it is indispensable for Q' and it belongs to a group that satisfies the having predicate P_H.*

We will again recast indispensability in terms of an SPJ query. Define a group table G as:

$$G =_{gby} \gamma_{agg}(\sigma_{P_Q}(\mathcal{T} \times \mathcal{R})). \quad (6)$$

For our example query, G will have two columns: name and **avg**(duration). It will have as many tuples as there are doctors who treat diabetes. Every tuple will have the average duration of diabetes treatment for the corresponding doctor.

Next form the following table:

$$QG = \sigma_{P_G}((\sigma_{P_Q}(\mathcal{T} \times \mathcal{R})) \times G) \quad (7)$$

where P_G is the natural join condition on the group-by columns, gby. We have augmented the result tuples of the **having**-free version of Q with the corresponding group values. The query Q can now be computed from $\sigma_{P_H}(QG)$.

It follows then

Observation 3 *A (virtual) tuple $v \in \mathcal{T}$ is indispensable for query Q with aggregation and having if and only if v is indispensable for the SPJ query*

$$\overline{\pi}_{C_Q}(\sigma_{P_H}(\sigma_{P_G}(\sigma_{P_Q}(\mathcal{T} \times \mathcal{R} \times G)))). \quad (8)$$

2.3.4 Suspicious Queries

We first define a maximal virtual tuple for queries $Q1$ and $Q2$.

Definition 5 (Maximal Virtual Tuple) *A tuple v is a maximal virtual tuple for queries $Q1$ and $Q2$, if it belongs to the cross product of common tables in their from clauses.*

We can now formalize the definitions of *candidate* and *suspicious* queries.

Definition 6 (Candidate Query) *A query Q is a candidate query with respect to the audit expression A if and only if*

$$C_Q \supseteq C_{OA}.$$

Definition 7 (Suspicious Query) *A candidate query Q is suspicious with respect to audit expression A if they share an indispensable maximal virtual tuple v, that is:*

$$susp(Q,A) \Leftrightarrow \exists v \in \mathcal{T} \; s.t. \; ind(v,Q) \wedge ind(v,A)$$

where $\mathcal{T} = T_1 \times T_2 \times \ldots \times T_n$ is the cross product of the common tables in Q and A.

3 System Structures

We now discuss the system structures needed to handle audits in the presence of updates to the database.

3.1 Full Audit Expression

The audit expression is prepended with an additional **during** clause that specifies the time period of interest:

during *start-time* **to** *end-time*
audit *audit-list*
...

Only if a query has accessed the data of concern during the specified time period is the query deemed suspicious.

Privacy policies specify who is allowed to receive what information and for what purpose [2, 5]. An audit expression can use the **otherthan** clause to specify the purpose-recipient pairs to whom the data disclosure does not constitute non-compliance:

otherthan *purpose-recipient pairs*
during *start-time* **to** *end-time*
audit *audit-list*
...

3.2 Query Log

As shown in Figure 1, the audit system maintains a log of past queries executed over the database. The query log is used during the static analysis to limit the set of logged queries that are transformed into an audit query.

Our prototype implementation has a thin middleware that lies between the application and the database engine. This middleware has been implemented as an extension to the JDBC driver. The middleware intercepts queries and writes the query string and associated annotations to the log. We assume the isolation level of serializable [8] and log only queries of committed transactions.

The annotations include the timestamp of when the query finished, the ID of the user issuing the query, and the purpose and the recipient information extracted from the context of the application [10, 11] in which the query was embedded. The query log is maintained as a table.

Note that some database systems (e.g., DB2) provide the facility for logging incoming queries. In such cases, this capability can be extended to log additional information required for auditing.

3.3 Temporal Extensions

We determine if a candidate query Q accessed the data specified in an audit expression by selectively playing back history. We thus need to recreate the state of the database as it existed at the time Q was executed. A backlog database [9] is eminently suited for this purpose.

We describe two organizations for the backlog database: time stamped and interval stamped. In both the organizations, a backlog table T^b is created for every table T in the database. T^b records all updates to T. We will assume that every table T has a primary key column P; the system can create an internally generated key column otherwise.

3.3.1 Time stamped Organization

This organization is based on the ideas presented in [9]. Aside from all columns in T, a tuple in T^b has two additional columns: TS that stores the time when a tuple is inserted into T^b, and OP that takes one of the values from {'insert', 'delete', 'update'}. For every table, three triggers are created to capture updates. An insert trigger responds to inserts in table T by inserting a tuple with identical values into T^b and setting its OP column to 'insert'. An update trigger responds to updates to T by inserting a tuple into T^b having the after values of the tuple in T and setting its OP column to 'update'. A delete trigger responds to deletes in T by inserting into T^b the value of the tuple before the delete operation and setting its OP column to 'delete'. In all the three cases, the value of the TS column for the new tuple is set to the time of the operation.

To recover the state of T at time τ, we need to generate the "snapshot" of T at time τ. This is achieved by defining a view T^τ over the backlog table T^b:

$$T^\tau = \pi_{P,C_1,\ldots,C_m}(\{t \mid$$
$$t \in T^b \wedge t.TS \leq \tau \wedge t.OP \neq \text{'delete'} \wedge$$
$$\not\exists r \in T^b \text{ s.t. } t.P = r.P \wedge r.TS \leq \tau \wedge r.TS > t.TS\}).$$

The scheme for T^τ is identical to T. T^τ contains at most one tuple from T^b for every distinct primary key value P. Among a group of tuples in T^b having an identical primary key value, the selected tuple t is the one that was created at or before time τ, is not a deleted tuple, and there is no other tuple r having the same primary key value that was created at or before time τ but whose creation time is later than that of t.

3.3.2 Interval stamped Organization

In this organization, the end time (TE) of a tuple is explicitly stored in addition to the start time (TS). Thus, the combination of TS and TE for a tuple gives the time period during which the tuple was alive. A null value of TE is treated as current time. The operation field (OP) is no longer necessary.

When a new tuple t is inserted into T, the insert trigger also adds t to T^b, setting its TE column to null. When a tuple $t \in T$ is updated, the update trigger searches for the tuple $b \in T^b$ such that $b.P = t.P \wedge b.TE = $ null and sets $b.TE$ to the current time. Additionally, the trigger inserts a copy of t into T^b with updated values and its TE column set to null. When a tuple t is deleted from T, the delete trigger searches for $b \in T^b$ such that $b.P = t.P \wedge b.TE = $ null and sets $b.TE$ to the current time.

3.3.3 Indexing

We propose two strategies for indexing a backlog table T^b:

1. *Eager*: Index is kept fresh and updated every time T^b is updated.
2. *Lazy*: Index is created afresh at the time of audit. Otherwise, T^b is kept unindexed.

The advantage of the eager strategy is that there is no latency at the time of audit due to the time needed to build the index. However, an update during normal query processing is burdened with the additional overhead of updating the index. The trade-off is reversed in the lazy strategy.

We can also choose which columns are indexed. We can index the primary key. We can also create a composite index consisting of the primary key concatenated with the timestamp. We explore the performance trade-offs in managing backlog tables in Section 5.

4 Algorithms

The audit query is generated in two steps:

1. *Static Analysis*: Select *candidate* queries (i.e., potentially suspicious queries) from the query log. (Our use of the term "candidate query" in this section refers to a query that passes the static analysis. All such queries are also candidate queries according to the formal definition.)

2. *Audit Query Generation*: Augment every *candidate* query with information from the audit expression and combine them into an audit query that identifies the suspicious queries.

4.1 Static Analysis

For a given audit expression A, some queries will be judged as non-candidates, and excluded immediately. We use four static tests, explained next. The query log is indexed to make these tests fast.

The first is by comparing the attribute names: with audit columns C_{OA}, we simply check whether $C_Q \supseteq C_{OA}$. The second test checks whether the timestamp of query Q is out of range with respect to the audit interval in the **during** clause of A. The third test checks whether the purpose-recipient pair of Q matches any of the purpose-recipient pairs specified in the **otherthan** clause of A. Finally, we can eliminate some queries by checking for contradictions between the predicates P_Q and P_A, such as $P_Q = (age > 40)$ and $P_A = (age < 20)$. This class of tests is an instance of the constraint satisfaction problem, for which many solution techniques are available [6].

4.2 Audit Query Generation

At the end of static analysis, we have a set of candidate queries $Q = \{Q_1, \ldots, Q_n\}$ that are potentially suspicious with respect to the audit expression A. We augment every Q_i with information in A, producing another query AQ_i defined against the view of the backlog database at time τ_i, where τ_i is the timestamp of Q_i as recorded in the query log. If we were to execute these AQ_i queries, those with non-empty results will comprise the exact set of suspicious queries. However, to increase opportunities for optimization, all AQ_i are combined into one audit query AQ whose output is a set of query identifiers corresponding to those AQ_i that yield non-empty results. This audit query is the one that is executed against the backlog database.

// Q is a simple selection query over a single table T, executed at time τ.
// A is an audit expression over the same table T.

1) **create** an empty QGM for the audit query AQ
2) **add** Q to AQ
3) **add** A to AQ
4) **rewrite** A to range over the result of Q instead of T
5) **replace** A's audit list with $id(Q)$
6) **replace** T with the view T^τ

Figure 2: Audit query generation for simple selections

To simplify exposition, we will assume henceforth that $\mathcal{Q}$ has only one query Q and discuss how it is transformed into an audit query AQ. Our implementation makes use of the Query Graph Model (QGM) to manipulate Q and A to generate AQ.[1] To avoid QGM diagrams from becoming unwieldy, we will abbreviate column names. For our example schema reproduced below, the abbreviated column names used in the figures are indicated in bold letters:

Customer (**c**id, **n**ame, **a**ddress, **p**hone, **z**ip, c**o**ntact)
Treatment (**p**cid, **r**cid, **d**id, disease, duration, date)
Doctor (**d**id, name)

4.3 Simple Selections

Consider first the simple case of a candidate query Q involving a selection over a single base table T and the audit expression A over the same table. This case is a special case of the upcoming SPJ queries. However, we present it for pedagogical reasons.

Lemma 1 *Let T be a base table of our database D. Let $A = \bar{\pi}_{C_{O_A}}(\sigma_{P_A}(T))$ be an audit expression and let $Q = \bar{\pi}_{C_Q}(\sigma_{P_Q}(T))$ be a candidate query. Q is suspicious with respect to A if and only if $\sigma_{P_A}(\sigma_{P_Q}(T)) \neq \emptyset$.*

Proof From the upcoming Theorem 2, by substituting T for $\mathcal{T}$, and ignoring the non-existing $\mathcal{R}$ and $\mathcal{S}$. ∎

Thus, given that query Q has passed the static analysis, we need to check whether the combined selection $\sigma_{P_A}(\sigma_{P_Q}(T))$ is empty or not, which is what Figure 2 implements using the QGM representation. We illustrate the audit query generation algorithm using the following example.

Example 6 Candidate query Q: Retrieve all customers in ZIP code 95120.

```
select    *
from      Customer
where     zip = '95120'
```

Audit expression A: Find queries that have accessed Alice's name and address.

[1]QGM [12] is a graphical representation that captures the semantics of queries and provides convenient data structures for transforming a query into equivalent forms. QGM is composed of entities portrayed as boxes and relationships among entities portrayed as lines between boxes. Entities can be operators such as table, select, group, union, etc. Lines between operators represent quantifiers that feed an operator by ranging over the output of the other operator.

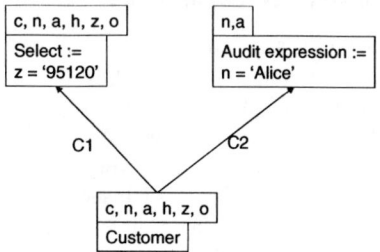

(a) After Line 3 in Figure 2

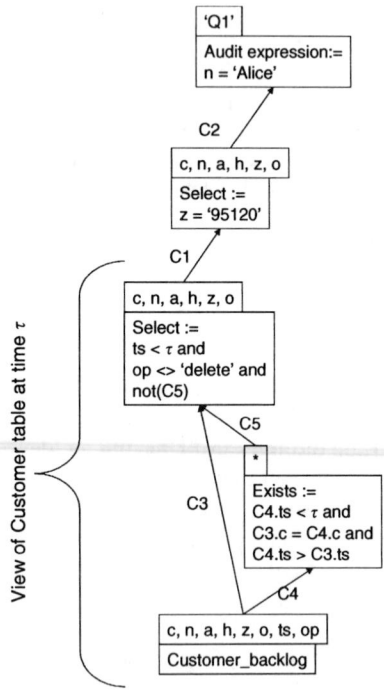

(b) After Line 6 in Figure 2

Figure 3: QGM for Example 6 (simple selection)

```
audit    name, address
from     Customer
where    name = 'Alice'
```

Figure 3(a) shows the state of the QGM graph after Line 3 (Figure 2). A new QGM structure for the audit query AQ has been created and both the candidate query Q and the audit expression A have been added to AQ. Figure 3(b) shows the state of QGM after Line 6. Line 4 has changed the audit expression's quantifier (range variable) C_2 from ranging over the Customer table to ranging over the result of the query Q. As part of this transformation, each column referenced by C_2 is changed to reference a column of Q's output. If a column referenced by C_2 is not in the output of Q, it is propagated up from the Customer table to be included in the Q's select list. Line 5 replaces the audit list with Q's id: Q1. Finally, Line 6 replaces the Customer table with a view of the Customer table at time τ when Q

1) **create** an empty QGM for the audit query AQ
2) **add** Q to AQ
3) **add** A to AQ

4) **rewrite** A to additionally range over the result of Q with quantifier x
5) **for each** quantifier r in A which is over a table T also in Q
6)   **substitute** x in place of r in A
7) **replace** A's audit list with $id(Q)$

8) **replace** every table T_i referenced in AQ with T_i^τ.

Figure 4: Audit query generation when both the candidate query and the audit expression contain joins

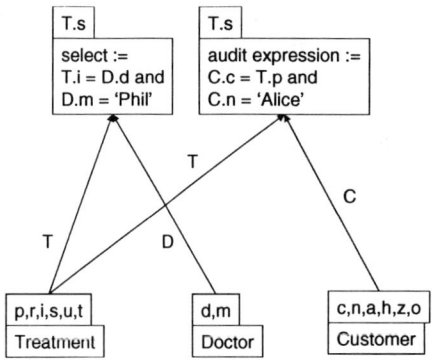

(a) After Line 3 in Figure 4

completed.

4.4 SPJ Queries

Consider now the case when the candidate query as well as the audit expression contain joins in the WHERE clauses. The audit list may contain columns from multiple tables and the join condition in the candidate query may be different from the one in the audit expression.

Theorem 2 *A candidate SPJ query $Q = \bar{\pi}_{C_Q}(\sigma_{P_Q}(\mathcal{T} \times \mathcal{R}))$ is suspicious with respect to an audit expression $A = \bar{\pi}_{C_{OA}}(\sigma_{P_A}(\mathcal{T} \times \mathcal{S}))$ if and only if*

$$\sigma_{P_A}(\sigma_{P_Q}(\mathcal{T} \times \mathcal{R} \times \mathcal{S})) \neq \emptyset.$$

Proof According to our Definition 7, we have

$$\begin{aligned}
susp(Q,A) &\Leftrightarrow \exists m \in \mathcal{T} \text{ s.t. } ind(m,Q) \wedge ind(m,A) \\
&\Leftrightarrow \exists m \in \mathcal{T}, r \in \mathcal{R}, s \in \mathcal{S} \text{ s.t.} \\
&\quad P_Q(\{m\,r\}) \wedge P_A(\{m\,s\}) \\
&\Leftrightarrow \exists m \in \mathcal{T}, r \in \mathcal{R}, s \in \mathcal{S} \text{ s.t.} \\
&\quad \{m\,r\,s\} \in \sigma_{P_A}(\sigma_{P_Q}(\mathcal{T} \times \mathcal{R} \times \mathcal{S})) \\
&\Leftrightarrow \sigma_{P_A}(\sigma_{P_Q}(\mathcal{T} \times \mathcal{R} \times \mathcal{S})) \neq \emptyset. \blacksquare
\end{aligned}$$

Figure 4 gives the algorithm. Note that an audit expression A may have multiple quantifiers, only some subset of which may range over a table that also appears in query Q. These are the only ones for which A is made to range over the result of the query (Lines 5-6). For others, A continues to range over the original tables. We illustrate the algorithm using the following example.

Example 7 Candidate query Q: Find all diseases treated by doctor Phil.

select	T.disease
from	Treatment T, Doctor D
where	T.did = D.did **and** D.name = 'Phil'

Audit expression A: Find queries that have disclosed the diseases of Alice.

audit	T.disease
from	Customer C, Treatment T
where	C.cid = T.pcid **and** C.name = 'Alice'

Figure 5(a) shows the initial QGM (after Line 3) and Figure 5(b) shows the final QGM (after Line 7). In the final QGM, the audit expression ranges over the result of the query and then joins the results with the Customer table since Customer only appears in the audit expression.

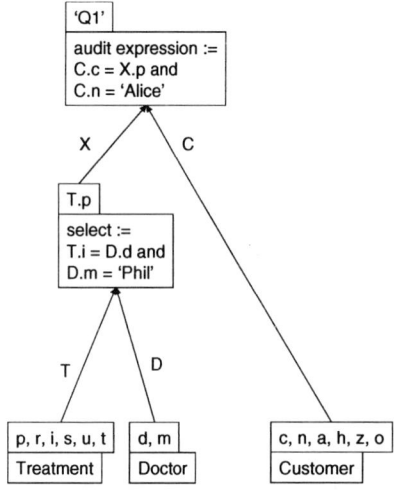

(b) After Line 7 in Figure 4

Figure 5: QGM for Example 7 (join)

4.5 Aggregation

To determine if an aggregate query without a **having** clause is suspicious, aggregate functions are simply removed along with the **group by** clause. Columns previously referenced by aggregate functions are added to the select list of the query. The resulting SPJ query is then handled using the algorithm given in Figure 4.

If the aggregate query, however, additionally contains a **having** clause, the predicate therein might have eliminated the data specified by the audit expression from the query result. Simply removing the **having** clause can thus lead to false positives. This limitation is overcome by the algorithm given in Figure 6, which is based on the upcoming theorem.

Recall that the general form of such a query is given by Eq. (5): $Q = \sigma_{P_H}(\,_{gby}\gamma_{agg}(\sigma_{P_Q}(\mathcal{T} \times \mathcal{R})))$. By Eq. (6), the group table $G = \,_{gby}\gamma_{agg}(\sigma_{P_Q}(\mathcal{T} \times \mathcal{R}))$. As always, the audit expression is $A = \bar{\pi}_{C_{OA}}(\sigma_{P_A}(\mathcal{T} \times \mathcal{S}))$.

Theorem 3 *A candidate query Q with aggregation and* **having** *is suspicious with respect to an audit expression A*

523

```
// The QGM of an aggregate query Q that
   includes having is a triplet (Q_s, Q_g, Q_h):

// Q_s is the SPJ part of Q,
// Q_g contains aggregations ranging over Q_s, and
// Q_h is a selection over Q_g representing having.

1)  create an empty QGM for the audit query AQ
2)  add Q to AQ
3)  add A to AQ
4)  rewrite A to additionally range over the result of Q_s with quantifier x

5)  for each quantifier r in A which is over a table T also in Q
6)     substitute x in place of r in A
7)  replace the audit list of A with the grouping columns of Q_g
8)  create a new empty select box B and add it to AQ
9)  add Q_h, A as inputs to B
10) join inputs of B on grouping columns from Q_h and A
11) replace Π(B) with id(Q)

12) replace every table T_i referenced in AQ
    with its backlog counterpart T_i^τ at time τ.
```

Figure 6: Audit query generation for an aggregate query containing **having**

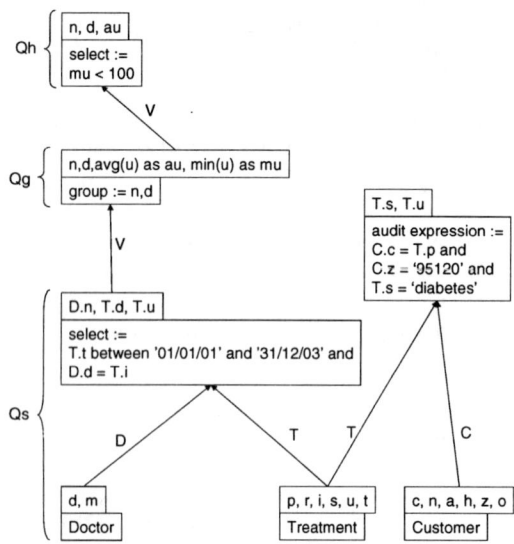

(a) After Line 3 in Figure 6

if and only if

$$\sigma_{P_A}(\sigma_{P_H}(\sigma_{P_G}(\sigma_{P_Q}(\mathcal{T} \times \mathcal{R} \times \mathcal{G} \times \mathcal{S})))) \neq \emptyset. \quad (9)$$

Proof From Observation 3, the query Q has the same indispensable tuples as the SPJ query Q' below:

$$Q' = \overline{\pi}_{C_Q}(\sigma_{P_H}(\sigma_{P_G}(\sigma_{P_Q}(\mathcal{T} \times \mathcal{R} \times \mathcal{G})))).$$

Then, from Theorem 2 we have that Q' is suspicious if and only if Eq. (9) holds. ∎

An aggregate query with a **having** clause can be viewed as consisting of three parts: Q_s, Q_g, and Q_h. The first part, Q_s, ignores grouping and aggregation and finds the tuples qualifying the WHERE clause. Grouping and aggregations are then applied to this result in Q_g. Finally, any predicates on groups are applied using a selection operator over the result of grouping and aggregation in Q_h. A new select box is created on Line 8 in Figure 6. This operator joins the tuples emanating from Q_h with those from A to ensure that these A tuples were not all filtered out by the **having** predicates in Q_h. We illustrate the algorithm with Example 8.

Example 8 Candidate query Q: Compute the average treatment duration grouped by disease and the doctor performing the treatment for treatments which were between 01/01/2001 and 31/12/2003 having a minimum duration < 100.

select	D.name, T.disease, avg(T.duration)
from	Doctor D, Treatment T
where	T.date **between** '01/01/2001' **and** '31/12/2003' and D.did = T.did
group by	D.name, T.disease
having	min (T.duration) < 100

Audit expression A: Find queries that have accessed the disease and treatment duration of patients who have diabetes and live in ZIP code 95120.

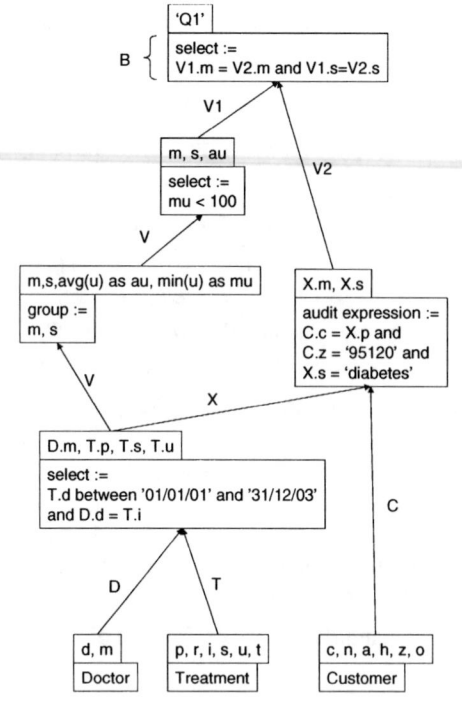

(b) After Line 11 in Figure 6

Figure 7: QGM for Example 8 (aggregation)

audit	T.disease, T.duration
from	Customer C, Treatment T
where	C.cid = T.pcid **and** C.zip = '95120' and T.disease = 'diabetes'

The QGM for the candidate query Q in Example 8 integrated with the audit expression is shown in Figure 7(a). Figure 7(b) shows the audit query. The select box B ensures that the groups formed by the grouping operator that

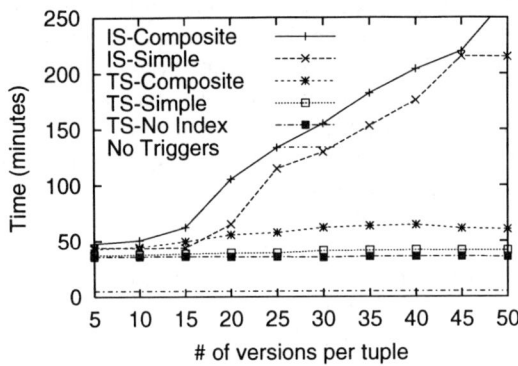

Figure 8: Cost of maintaining backlog tables.

survived the **having** predicate match the audit expression's data.

5 Performance

This section presents the results of performance experiments from a DB2 implementation of our auditing solution. Specifically, we study the overhead imposed on normal query processing, and the cost of conducting audits.

Experiments were performed on an IBM Intellistation M Pro 6868 having an 800 MHz Pentium III processor, 512 MB of memory, and a 16.9 GB disk drive, and running Windows 2000 Version 5.00.2195 service pack 4. The same machine was used to host data as well as backlog tables and to run audits. The DBMS used was DB2 UDB Version 7 with default settings. We would have liked to use real-life query logs and data tables, but no such dataset was available. We therefore performed our experiments on the Supplier table of the TPC-H database [15], using synthetic workload. The results below give the average warm performance numbers.

We report results for time stamped as well as interval stamped organizations of the backlog tables. We consider three cases: no index, simple index on the supplier key $SKEY$, and composite index on $SKEY$ and start time TS. We explore both eager and lazy strategies for updating indices.

We will write Supplier^b to refer to the Supplier backlog table.

5.1 Burden on Normal Query Processing

We performed the following experiment to study the overhead of maintaining backlog tables. The Supplier table contained 100,000 tuples and Supplier^b started with a copy of every Supplier tuple. An SQL update statement updated every Supplier tuple, resulting in the creation of a new version of every supplier in Supplier^b. Forty nine such update statements were executed, each adding 100,000 tuples to Supplier^b that finally ended up having fifty versions of every supplier and a total of 5 million tuples. Indices of Supplier^b were updated eagerly.

The update operation on the Supplier table took 5.2 minutes to complete when performed unburdened with the maintenance of Supplier^b. This time essentially consists of sequentially reading the Supplier tuples and writing them back after updating one of the values. Figure 8 shows the total time taken by the successive update operations when the additional time spent by the database system on firing the update triggers and the resultant operations on Supplier^b was also included. In the performance graphs, TS (IS) denotes the time stamped (interval stamped) organization.

With the time stamped organization, the update trigger simply adds a new tuple to Supplier^b corresponding to every updated data tuple. Therefore, when there is no index on Supplier^b, the overhead experienced by successive updates remains fairly constant. When there is an index on $SKEY$, the overhead is a bit larger due to additional index updates, and this overhead increases a little for the later updates because the size of the index grows. The composite index on $SKEY$ and TS obviously has a somewhat larger overhead than the simple index.

For equivalent operation with the interval stamped organization, the update trigger first locates the most recent version of the tuple, updates its end time, and then adds a new current tuple. Unfortunately, the cost of locating the most recent version becomes prohibitively large when there is no index; hence it is not shown in the figure. Even when there is an index on $SKEY$, all the versions of a tuple need to be brought into memory to select the most recent of them. If different versions of a supplier do not remain clustered on the same page (which we found to be the case even when we had a clustered index on $SKEY$), the number of page faults increases with the number of versions, resulting in a rapid degradation of performance. Having the additional index on TS does not help in cutting down the number of versions that are examined before the most recent one is found. On the other hand, the overhead increases somewhat due to additional index updates and a larger index.

It is substantially faster (per tuple) to sequentially update all the tuples of a table in DB2 than to update an individual tuple. Thus, updating all the tuples of the Supplier table with backlog maintenance using the time stamped organization is about 10 times slower than without maintenance. We next performed another experiment in which only one Supplier tuple was updated. Supplier^b had 25 versions of every tuple in this experiment (the average number of versions in the first experiment). The cost of an update to a single tuple with backlog maintenance was now on average 3 times the cost of the same update without maintenance when using the simple index, and 3.7 times when using the composite index.

We note that in most of the installations, there are far more read queries than update operations. Updates are often batched and performed while the system is under a light load. The read queries in our audit system do not incur any overhead beyond logging the query string (which is anyway done in many installations).

5.2 Eager vs. Lazy Indexing

It is clear from the discussion in the previous section that the lazy indexing is not a viable option for the interval stamped

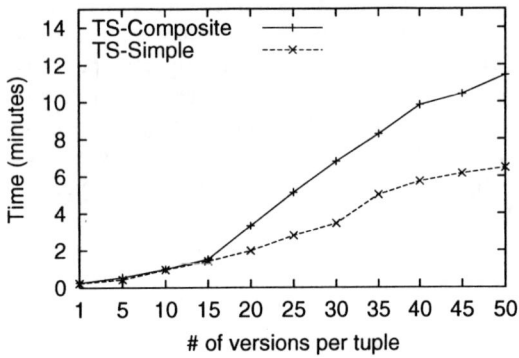

Figure 9: Cost of building indices over the backlog table.

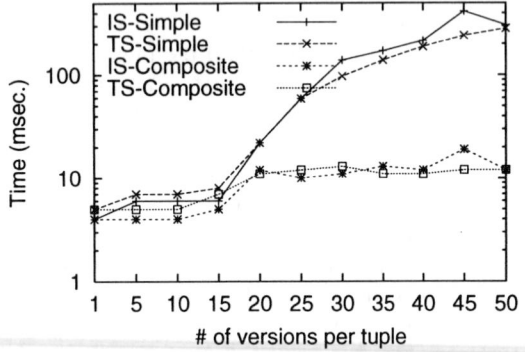

Figure 10: Execution time of an audit query

organization. However, the overhead of eagerly updating the indices can be avoided in the time stamped organization by building them as needed at the time of audit. Figure 9 shows the time needed to build indices from scratch with an initial set of 100,000 suppliers in Supplier[b], while increasing the number of versions of each supplier. The results are shown both for a simple index on *SKEY* and for a composite index on *SKEY* and *TS*.

We see that the index construction times are such that it would be acceptable to adopt the lazy strategy and strictly create indices at audit time.

5.3 Performance of Audit

We study the audit performance by measuring the execution time of simple audit queries. The audit expression is of the form:

during t_1 **to** t_2
audit   name **from** Supplier **where** skey = k

We set both t_1 and t_2 to the time when the initial versions of the Supplier tuples were created. The value of k is randomly set to one of the values of *SKEY* present in the Supplier table. We assume that static analysis has yielded one candidate query: **select** * **from** Supplier.

We consider both time stamped and interval stamped organizations, with simple as well as composite indices. Figures 10 shows the results.

Both the time stamped and interval stamped organizations benefit a great deal from the composite index on *SKEY* and *TS* as the number of versions becomes large. When there is an index only on *SKEY*, the query plan first selects all versions of a tuple with the matching supplier key and then selects the correct version amongst the matching tuples. These versions might reside on different disk pages and cause page faults as Supplier[b] becomes large. The composite index avoids this problem.

We also see that with few versions of a tuple, the interval stamped organization has a slight performance advantage, but loses this advantage as the number of versions increases. The interval stamped organization requires an extra timestamp attribute to record the end time of validity of a tuple. The larger tuple size results in more page faults as the number of versions increases, and thus the impact of the larger size outweighs the benefit of the simpler interval stamped computation over the time stamped organization that requires a join.

5.4 Takeaways

The composite index on the primary key and start time pays large dividend over an index only on the primary key at the time of audit, although it puts a slightly larger burden on updates if the indices are updated eagerly.

The interval stamped organization has a slight advantage over the time stamped organization at the time of audit if the number of versions is small. However, the lazy strategy for updating indices cannot be used with the interval stamped organization and eager updating becomes quite expensive as the number of versions increases. Overall, the use of time stamped organization along with the lazy strategy for updating indices is recommended. However, the eager strategy is also not too burdensome for the time stamped organization.

The system supports efficient auditing without substantially burdening normal query processing tasks.

6 Related Work

Closely related to compliance is the privacy principle of *limited disclosure*, which means that the database should not communicate private information outside the database for reasons other than those for which there is consent from the data subject [2, 10]. Clearly, the two are complimentary. The principle of limited disclosure comes into play at the time a query is executed against the database, whereas demonstrating compliance is post facto and is concerned with showing that usage of the database indeed observed limited disclosure in every query execution.

Oracle [11] offers a "fine-grained auditing" function where the administrator can specify that read queries are to be logged if they access specified tables. This function logs various user context data along with the query issued, the time it was issued, and other system parameters including the "system change number". Oracle also supports "flashback queries" whereby the state of the database can be reverted to the state implied by a given system change number. A logged query can then be rerun as if the database was in that state to determine what data was revealed when the query was originally run. There does not appear to be any auditing facility whereby an audit predicate can be processed to discover which queries disclosed data specified by the audit expression. Instead, Oracle seems to offer the temporal database (flashback queries) and query logging (fine-grained auditing) components largely independent of each other.

The problem of matching a query against an audit expression bears resemblance to the problem of predicate locking [7] that tests if the predicates associated with two lock requests are mutually satisfiable. Besides being expensive, this test can lead to false positives when applied to the auditing problem. Related work also includes the literature on query processing over views that contains the notion of augmenting a user query with predicates derived from the view definition [13]. Also related is the work on optimizing a group of queries (e.g. [4, 14]) that can be profitably used by our system to accelerate the execution of audit queries.

7 Summary

We identified the problem of verifying whether a database system is complying with its data disclosure policies through auditing. Given the accelerated pace at which legislations are being introduced to govern data management practices, this problem represents a significant opportunity for database research. We formalized the problem through the fundamental concepts of indispensability and suspiciousness. Additional contributions include a carefully designed and implemented system that meets the design goals enunciated in the introduction:

- **Convenient:** The audit expression language used by our system reuses the familiar SQL syntax, providing a familiar, declarative and expressive means for specifying the data whose disclosure is subject to review.

- **Fine-grained:** The audit expression language allows the auditor to specify even a single field of a record as subject for review.

- **Fast and precise audits:** Our system combines the audit expression with logged queries into an SQL audit query that examines only the specific data necessary to determine suspiciousness. Guided by our implementation and experimentation with various backlogging and indexing strategies, we proposed system structures to support efficient audit query execution.

- **Non-disruptive:** Our system imposes only a small burden on the execution of most queries. Rather than logging query results or the tuples accessed by a query, it logs the query strings. While update operations require some additional backlog database maintenance, the predominant read queries are processed without any further encumbrance.

We have considered a data disclosure model in which the querier does not possess any outside knowledge and the information gained is limited to what could be learnt from the current query. It would be interesting to see how our framework could be extended to support more adversarial disclosure scenarios. Other remaining work includes how schema evolution can be gracefully accommodated in the audit system. Finally, we feel it would be beneficial to the community to develop a set of comprehensive benchmarks for measuring and testing the effectiveness and performance of any database auditing proposal.

Acknowledgements Christos Faloutsos was on leave from Carnegie Mellon; he was partially supported by the National Science Foundation under Grants No. IIS-0083148, IIS-0209107, IIS-0205224, SENSOR-0329549, and IIS-0326322.

References

[1] N. Adam and J. Wortman. Security-control methods for statistical databases. *ACM Computing Surveys*, 21(4):515–556, Dec. 1989.

[2] R. Agrawal, J. Kiernan, R. Srikant, and Y. Xu. Hippocratic databases. In *28th Int'l Conference on Very Large Databases*, Hong Kong, China, August 2002.

[3] S. Castano, M. Fugini, G. Martella, and P. Samarati. *Database Security*. Addison Wesley, 1995.

[4] J. Chen, D. DeWitt, F. Tian, and Y. Wang. NiagaraCQ: A scalable continuous query system for internet databases. In *ACM SIGMOD Conference on Management of Data*, Dallas, Texas, 2000.

[5] L. Cranor, M. Langheinrich, M. Marchiori, M. Pressler-Marshall, and J. Reagle. The platform for privacy preferences 1.0 (P3P1.0) specification. W3C Recommendation, April 2002.

[6] R. Dechter. *Constraint Processing*. Morgan Kaufman, 2003.

[7] K. P. Eswaran, J. Gray, R. A. Lorie, and I. L. Traiger. The notions of consistency and predicate locks in a database system. *Communications of the ACM*, 19(11):624–633, 1976.

[8] J. Gray and A. Reuter. *Transaction Processing: Concepts and Techniques*. Morgan Kaufman, 1992.

[9] C. S. Jensen, L. Mark, and N. Roussopoulos. Incremental implementation model for relational databases with transaction time. *IEEE Transactions on Knowledge and Data Engineering*, 3(4):461–473, December 1991.

[10] K. LeFevre, R. Agrawal, V. Ercegovac, R. Ramakrishnan, Y. Xu, and D. DeWitt. Limiting disclosure in Hippocratic databases. In *30th Int'l Conf. on Very Large Data Bases*, Toronto, Canada, August 2004.

[11] A. Nanda and D. K. Burleson. *Oracle Privacy Security Auditing*. Rampant, 2003.

[12] H. Pirahesh, J. M. Hellerstein, and W. Hasan. Extensible/rule based query rewrite optimization in Starburst. In *ACM SIGMOD Conference on Management of Data*, San Diego, California, 1992.

[13] R. Ramakrishnan and J. Gehrke. *Database Management Systems*. McGraw-Hill, 2000.

[14] T. K. Sellis. Multiple-query optimization. *ACM Transactions on Database Systems*, 13(1):23–52, 1988.

[15] TPC-H decision support benchmark. http://www.tpc.org.

High-Dimensional OLAP: A Minimal Cubing Approach[*]

Xiaolei Li   Jiawei Han   Hector Gonzalez

University of Illinois at Urbana-Champaign, Urbana, IL 61801, USA

Abstract

Data cube has been playing an essential role in fast OLAP (online analytical processing) in many multi-dimensional data warehouses. However, there exist data sets in applications like bioinformatics, statistics, and text processing that are characterized by high dimensionality, e.g., over 100 dimensions, and moderate size, e.g., around 10^6 tuples. No feasible data cube can be constructed with such data sets. In this paper we will address the problem of developing an efficient algorithm to perform OLAP on such data sets.

Experience tells us that although data analysis tasks may involve a high dimensional space, most OLAP operations are performed only on a small number of dimensions *at a time*. Based on this observation, we propose a novel method that computes a thin layer of the data cube together with associated value-list indices. This layer, while being manageable in size, will be capable of supporting flexible and fast OLAP operations in the original high dimensional space. Through experiments we will show that the method has I/O costs that scale nicely with dimensionality. Furthermore, the costs are comparable to that of accessing an existing data cube when full materialization is possible.

1 Introduction

Since the advent of data warehousing and online analytical processing (OLAP) [9], data cube has been playing an essential role in the implementation of fast OLAP operations [10]. Materialization of a data cube is a way to precompute and store multi-dimensional aggregates so that multi-dimensional analysis can be performed on the fly. For this task, there have been many efficient cube computation algorithms proposed, such as ROLAP-based multi-dimensional aggregate computation [1], multiway array aggregation [24], BUC [7], H-cubing [11], and Star-cubing [22]. Since computing the whole data cube not only requires a substantial amount of time but also generates a huge number of cube cells, there have also been many studies on partial materialization of data cubes [12], iceberg cube computation [7, 11, 22], computation of condensed, dwarf, or quotient cubes [19, 18, 13, 14], and computation of approximate cubes [16, 5].

Besides large data warehouse applications, there are other kinds of applications like bioinformatics, survey-based statistical analysis, and text processing that need the OLAP-styled data analysis. However, data in such applications usually are high in dimensionality, e.g., over 100 or even 1000 dimensions but only medium in size, e.g., around 10^6 tuples. This kind of datasets behaves rather differently from the datasets in a traditional data warehouse which may have about 10 dimensions but more than 10^9 tuples. Since a data cube grows exponentially with the number of dimensions, it is too costly in both computation time and storage space to materialize a full high-dimensional data cube. For example, a data cube of 100 dimensions, each with 10 distinct values, may contain as many as 11^{100} aggregate cells. Although the adoption of iceberg cube, condensed cube, or approximate cube delays the explosion, it does not solve the fundamental problem.

In this paper, we propose a new method called *shell-fragment*. It vertically partitions a high dimensional dataset into a set of disjoint low dimensional datasets called *fragments*. For each fragment, we compute its local data cube. Furthermore, we register the set of tuple-ids that contribute to the non-empty cells in the fragment data cube. These tuple-ids are used to bridge the gap between various fragments and re-construct the corresponding cuboids upon request. These shell fragments are pre-computed offline and are used to compute queries in an online fashion. In other words,

---

[*]The work was supported in part by NSF IIS-02-09199. Any opinions, findings, and conclusions or recommendations expressed in this paper are those of the authors and do not necessarily reflect the views of the funding agencies.

Permission to copy without fee all or part of this material is granted provided that the copies are not made or distributed for direct commercial advantage, the VLDB copyright notice and the title of the publication and its date appear, and notice is given that copying is by permission of the Very Large Data Base Endowment. To copy otherwise, or to republish, requires a fee and/or special permission from the Endowment.

Proceedings of the 30th VLDB Conference, Toronto, Canada, 2004

data cubes in the original high dimensional space are dynamically assembled together via the fragments.

We will show that this method achieves high scalability in high dimensional space both in terms of storage space and I/O. When full materialization of the data cube is impossible, our method provides a reasonable solution. In addition, as our experiments show, the I/O costs of our method are competitive with those of the materialized data cube.

The remainder of the paper is organized as follows. In Section 2, we present the motivation of the paper. In Section 3, we introduce the shell fragment data structure and design. In Section 4, we describe how to compute OLAP queries using the fragments. Our performance study on scalability, I/O, and other cost metrics is presented in Section 5. We discuss the related work and the possible extensions in Section 6, and conclude our study in Section 7.

2 Analysis

Numerous studies have been conducted on data cubes to promote fast OLAP. However, most cubing algorithms have been confined to only low or medium dimensional data. We shall show the inherent "*curse of dimensionality*" of data cube in this section and provide motivation for our online computation model.

2.1 Curse of Dimensionality

The computation of data cubes, though valuable for low-dimensional databases, may not be so beneficial for high-dimensional ones. Typically, a high-dimensional data cube requires massive memory and disk space, and the current algorithms are unable to materialize the full cube under such conditions. Let's examine an example.

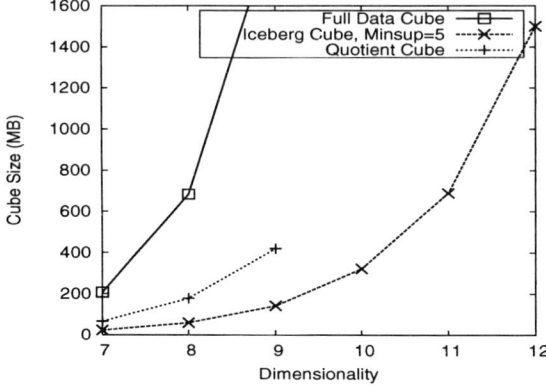

Figure 1: The curse of dimensionality on data cubes

Example 1. We generated a base database of 600,000 tuples. Each dimension had a cardinality of 100 with *zipf* equal to 2. The number of dimensions varies from 7 to 12 on the x-axis in Figure 1. The size of the data cube generated from this base cuboid grows exponentially with the number of dimensions as shown in Figure 1. The size of the full data cube reaches gigabytes when the number of dimensions reaches 9. And it climbs to well above petabytes before it reaches 20 dimensions, not to think about 100 dimensions.

Figure 1 also shows the size of an iceberg cube with minimum support of 5 for our database. It is much smaller than the full data cube because the base cuboid contains not many tuples and most high-dimensional cells fall below the support threshold. This sounds attractive because it may substantially reduce the computation time and disk usage while keeping only the "meaningful" results. However, there are several weaknesses. First, if a high-dimensional cell has the support already passing the iceberg threshold, it cannot be pruned by the iceberg condition and will still generate a huge number of cells. For example, a base-cuboid cell: "$(a_1, a_2, \ldots, a_{60})$:5" (*i.e.*, with count 5) will still generate 2^{60} iceberg cube cells. Second, it is difficult to set up an appropriate iceberg threshold. A too low threshold will still generate a huge cube, but a too high one may invalidate many useful applications. Third, an iceberg cube cannot be incrementally updated. Once an aggregate cell falls below the iceberg threshold and is pruned, incremental update will not be able to recover the original measure.

The situation is not much better for condensed, dwarf, or quotient cubes [19, 18, 13, 14]. The Dwarf cube introduced in [18] compresses the cuboid cells by exploiting sharing of prefixes and suffixes. Its size complexity was shown to be $O(T^{1+1/(\log_d C)})$ [17] where d is the number of dimensions, C is cardinality, and T is the number of tuples. In high dimensional data where d is large, $\log_d C$ could become quite small. In which case, the exponent becomes quite large and the cube size still explodes.

For quotient cubes [13, 14], compression can only be effective when the corresponding measures are the same within a local lattice structure, which has limited pruning power as shown in Figure 1.

Lastly, there is a substantial I/O overhead for accessing a full materialized data cube. Cuboids are stored on disk in some fixed order, and that order might be incompatible with a particular query. Processing such queries may need a scan of the entire corresponding cuboid.

One could avoid reading the entire cuboid if there were multi-dimensional indices constructed on all cuboids. But in a high-dimensional database with many cuboids, it might not be practical to build all these indices. Furthermore, reading via an index implies random access for each row in the cuboid, which could turn out to be more expensive than a sequential scan of the raw data.

A partial solution, which has been implemented in some commercial data warehouse systems is to compute a thin *cube shell*. For example, one might compute all cuboids with 3 dimensions or less in a 60-dimensional data cube. There are two disadvantages to this approach. First, it still needs to compute $\binom{60}{3} + \binom{60}{2} + 60 = 36050$ cuboids. Second, it does *not* support OLAP in a large portion of the high-dimensional cube space because (1) it does not support OLAP on 4 or more dimensions (the shell only offers shallow penetration of the entire data cube), and (2) it cannot support drilling along even three dimensions, such as (A_4, A_5, A_6), *on a subset of data* selected based on the constants provided in three *other* dimensions, such as (A_1, A_2, A_3). These types of operations require the computation of the corresponding 6-D cuboid, which the shell does not compute. In contrast, our model supports OLAP operations on the *entire* cube space.

2.2 Computation Model

These observations lead us to consider possibly an online computation model of data cubes. It is quite expensive to online scan a high-dimensional database, extract the relevant dimensions, and then perform on-the-spot aggregation. Instead, a *semi-online computation model with certain pre-processing* seems to be a more viable solution.

Before delving deeper into the *semi-online computation model*, we make the following observation about OLAP in high-dimensional space. Although a data cube may contain many dimensions, most OLAP operations are performed only on a small number of dimensions *at a time*. In other words, an OLAP query is likely to ignore many dimensions (*i.e.*, treating them as *irrelevant*), fix some dimensions (*e.g.*, using query constants as *instantiations*), and leave only a few to be manipulated (for drilling, pivoting, *etc.*). This is because it is not realistic for anyone to comprehend the changes of thousands of cells involving tens of dimensions *simultaneously* in a high-dimensional space at the same time. Instead, it is more natural to first locate some cuboids by certain selections and then drill along one or two dimensions to examine the changes of a few related dimensions. Most analysts only need to examine the space of a small number of dimensions once they select them.

3 Precomputation of Shell Fragments

Stemming from the above motivation, we propose a new approach, called *shell_fragment*, and two new algorithms: one for computing shell fragment cubes, and one for query processing with the fragment cubes. This new approach will be able to handle OLAP in databases of extremely high dimensionality. It explores the inverted index well-studied in information retrieval [4] and value-list index in databases [8]. The general idea is to partition the dimensions into disjoint sets called *fragments*. The base dataset is projected onto each fragment, and data cubes are fully materialized for each fragment. With the precomputed *shell fragment cubes*, one can dynamically assemble and compute cuboid cells of the original dataset online. This is made efficient by set intersection operations on the inverted indices.

3.1 Inverted Index

To illustrate the algorithm, a tiny database, Table 1, is used as a running example. Let the cube measure be `count()`. Other measures will be discussed later.

tid	A	B	C	D	E
1	a1	b1	c1	d1	e1
2	a1	b2	c1	d2	e1
3	a1	b2	c1	d1	e2
4	a2	b1	c1	d1	e2
5	a2	b1	c1	d1	e3

Table 1: The Original Database

The inverted index is constructed as follows. For each attribute value in each dimension, we register a list of tuple IDs (*tids*) associated with it. For example, attribute value a2 appears in tuples 4 and 5. The tid-list for a2 then contains exactly 2 items, namely 4 and 5. The resultant inverted indices for the 5 individual dimensions are shown in Table 2.

Attribute Value	TID List	List Size
a1	1 2 3	3
a2	4 5	2
b1	1 4 5	3
b2	2 3	2
c1	1 2 3 4 5	5
d1	1 3 4 5	4
d2	2	1
e1	1 2	2
e2	3 4	2
e3	5	1

Table 2: Inverted Indices for Individual Dimensions A, B, C, D, and E

Lemma 1 *The inverted index table uses the same amount of storage space as the original database.*

Rationale. Intuitively, we can think of Table 1 as storing the common TIDs for attributes and Table 2 as storing the common attribute values for tuples. Formally, suppose we have a database of $\mathcal{T}$ tuples and $\mathcal{D}$ dimensions. To store it as shown in Table 1 would need $\mathcal{D} \times \mathcal{T}$ integers. Now consider the inverted index. Each tuple ID is associated with $\mathcal{D}$ attributes and thus will appear $\mathcal{D}$ times in the inverted index. Since we have $\mathcal{T}$ tuple IDs in total, the entire inverted index will still only need $\mathcal{D} \times \mathcal{T}$ integers[1]. ∎

3.2 Shell Fragments

The inverted index in Table 2 can be generalized to multiple dimensions where one can store tid-lists for combinations of attribute values across different dimensions. This leads to the computation of *shell fragments* of a data cube as follows.

All the dimensions of a data set are partitioned into independent groups, called *fragments*. For each fragment, we compute the complete *local* data cube while retaining the inverted indices. For example, for a database of 60 dimensions, $A_1, A_2, \ldots, A_{60}$, we first partition the 60 dimensions into 20 fragments of size 3: $(A_1, A_2, A_3), (A_4, A_5, A_6), \ldots, (A_{58}, A_{59}, A_{60})$. For each fragment, we compute its full data cube while recording the inverted indices. For example, in fragment (A_1, A_2, A_3), we would compute seven cuboids: $A_1, A_2, A_3, A_1A_2, A_2A_3, A_1A_3, A_1A_2A_3$. An inverted index is retained for each cell in the cuboids. The sizing and grouping of the fragments are non-trivial decisions and will be discussed later in Section 4.3.

The benefit of this model can be seen by a simple calculation. For a base cuboid of 60 dimensions, there are only $7 \times 20 = 140$ cuboids to be computed according to the above *shell_fragment* partition. Comparing this to 36050 cuboids for the cube shell of size 3, the saving is enormous.

Let's return to our running example.

Example 2. Suppose we are to compute the shell fragments of size 3. We first divide the 5 dimensions into 2 fragments, namely (A, B, C) and (D, E). For each fragment, we compute the complete data cube by intersecting the tid-lists in Table 2 in a bottom-up depths-first order in the cuboid lattice (as seen in [7]). For example, to compute the cell {a1 b2 * }, we intersect the tuple ID lists of a1 and b2 to get a new list of {2, 3}. Cuboid AB is shown in Table 3.

Cell	Intersection	Tuple ID List	List Size
a1 b1	1 2 3 ∩ 1 4 5	1	1
a1 b2	1 2 3 ∩ 2 3	2 3	2
a2 b1	4 5 ∩ 1 4 5	4 5	2
a2 b2	4 5 ∩ 2 3	∅	0

Table 3: Cuboid AB

After computing cuboid AB, we can then compute cuboid ABC by intersecting all pairwise combinations between Table 3 and the row c1 in Table 2. Notice that because the entry a2 b2 is empty, it can be effectively discarded in subsequent computations based on the Apriori property [2]. The same process can be applied to computing fragment (D, E), which is completely independent from computing (A, B, C). Cuboid DE is shown in Table 4. ∎

Cell	Intersection	Tuple ID List	List Size
d1 e1	1 3 4 5 ∩ 1 2	1	1
d1 e2	1 3 4 5 ∩ 3 4	3 4	2
d1 e3	1 3 4 5 ∩ 5	5	1
d2 e1	2 ∩ 1 2	2	1

Table 4: Cuboid DE

The computed shell fragment cubes with their inverted indices will be used to facilitate online query computation. The question is how much space is needed to store them. In our analysis, we assume an array-like data structure to store the TIDs. If the cardinalities of the dimensions are small, bitmaps can be employed to save space and speed up operations. This and other techniques will be discussed in Section 6.

Lemma 2 *Given a database of $\mathcal{T}$ tuples and $\mathcal{D}$ dimensions, the amount of memory needed to store the shell fragments of size $\mathcal{F}$ is $O(\mathcal{T}(\frac{\mathcal{D}}{\mathcal{F}})(2^{\mathcal{F}} - 1))$.*

Rationale. Consider how many times each tuple ID will be stored in the shell fragments. In the 1-dimensional cuboids of the shell fragments, Lemma 1 tells us each tuple ID will appear $\mathcal{D} = \frac{\mathcal{D}}{\mathcal{F}} \binom{\mathcal{F}}{1}$ times. Now consider the 2-dimensional cuboids. Each tuple ID is associated with $\mathcal{D}$ dimensions and thus will be stored anytime a cuboid is a subset of these $\mathcal{D}$ dimensions. There are exactly $\lceil \frac{\mathcal{D}}{\mathcal{F}} \rceil \binom{\mathcal{F}}{2}$ such 2-dimensional cuboids. Sum over all cuboids (sizes 1 to $\mathcal{F}$), we see that the entire shell fragment will need $O(\mathcal{T} \sum_{i=1}^{\mathcal{F}} \left(\lceil \frac{\mathcal{D}}{\mathcal{F}} \rceil \binom{\mathcal{F}}{i} \right))$ = $O(\mathcal{T}(\frac{\mathcal{D}}{\mathcal{F}})(2^{\mathcal{F}} - 1))$ storage space. ∎

Based on Lemma 2, for our 60-dimensional base cuboid of $\mathcal{T}$ tuples, the amount of space needed to store the shell fragment of size 3 is on the order of $\mathcal{T}(\frac{60}{3})(2^3 - 1) = 140\mathcal{T}$. Suppose there are 10^6 tuples in the database and each tuple ID takes 4 bytes. The space needed to store the shell fragments of size 3 is roughly estimated as $140 \times 10^6 \times 4 = 560$ MB.

3.2.1 Computing Other Measures

For the cube with only the *tuple-counting* measure, there is no need to reference the original database for measure computation since the length of the tid-list is equivalent to *tuple-count*. "But what about other measures, such as average()?" The solution is to keep an *ID_measure* array instead of the original database. For example, to compute average(), one just needs to keep an array of three elements: (*tid, count, sum*). The measures of every aggregate cell can be computed by accessing this *ID_measure* array only. Considering a database with 10^6 tuples, each taking 4 bytes for tid and 8 bytes for two measures, the *ID_measure* array

---
[1] We assume that a TID and a value take the same unit space (*e.g.*, 4 bytes). Otherwise, the total space usage will differ proportionally to their unit space difference.

is only 12 MB, whereas the corresponding database of 60 dimensions is $(60 + 3) \times 4 \times 10^6 = 252$ MB. To illustrate the design of the *ID_measure* array, let's look at the following example.

Example 3. Suppose Table 5 shows an example database where each tuple has 2 associated values, count and sum.

tid	A	B	C	D	E	count	sum
1	a1	b1	c1	d1	e1	5	70
2	a1	b2	c1	d2	e1	3	10
3	a1	b2	c1	d1	e2	8	20
4	a2	b1	c1	d1	e2	5	40
5	a2	b1	c1	d1	e3	2	30

Table 5: A database with two measure values

tid	count	sum
1	5	70
2	3	10
3	8	20
4	5	40
5	2	30

Table 6: ID-measure array of Table 5

To compute a data cube for this database with the measure avg() (obtained by sum()/count()), we need to have a tid-list for each cell: $\{tid_1, \ldots, tid_n\}$. Because each tid is uniquely associated with a particular set of measure values, all future computations just need to fetch the measure values associated with the tuples in the list. In other words, by keeping an array of the ID-measures in memory for online processing, one can handle any complex measure computation. Table 6 shows what exactly should be kept, which is substantially smaller than the database itself. ∎

Based on the above analysis, for a base cuboid of 60 dimensions with 10^6 tuples, our precomputed *shell fragments* of size 3 will consist of 140 cuboids plus one *ID_measure* array, with the total estimated size of roughly $560 + 12 = 572$ MB in total. In comparison, a shell cube of size 3 will consist of 36050 cuboids, with estimated roughly 144 GB in size. A full 60-dimensional cube will have $2^{60} \approx 10^{18}$ cuboids, with the total cube size beyond the summation of the capacities of all storage devices. In this context, both storage space and computation time of *shell_fragment* are negligible in comparison with those of the complete data cube. Thus our high-dimensional OLAP on the precomputed *shell_fragment* can really be considered as *high-dimensional OLAP with minimal cubing*.

3.2.2 Algorithm for Shell Fragment Computation

Based on the above discussion, the algorithm for shell fragment computation can be summarized as follows.

Algorithm 1 (Frag-Shells) Computation of shell fragments on a given high-dimensional base table (*i.e.*, base cuboid).

Input: A base cuboid B of n dimensions: $(A_1, \ldots, A_n)$.

Output: (1) A set of fragment partitions $\{P_1, \ldots P_k\}$ and their corresponding (local) fragment cubes $\{S_1, \ldots, S_k\}$, where P_i represents some set of dimension(s) and $P_1 \cup \ldots \cup P_k$ are all the n dimensions, and (2) an *ID_measure* array if the measure is not *tuple-count*.

Method:

1. partition the set of dimensions $(A_1, \ldots, A_n)$ into a set of k fragments $P_1, \ldots, P_k$
2. scan base cuboid B once and do the following {
3.   insert each $\langle tid, measure \rangle$ into *ID_measure* array
4.   for each attribute value a_i of each dimension A_i
5.   build an inverted index entry: $\langle a_i, tidlist \rangle$
6. }
7. for each fragment partition P_i
8.   build a local fragment cube S_i by intersecting their corresponding tid-lists and computing their measures ∎

Note: For Line 1, Section 4.3 will discuss what kind of partitions may achieve good performance. For Line 3, if the measure is *tuple-count*, there is no need to build *ID_measure* array since the length of the tid-list is *tuple-count*; for other measures, such as avg(), the needed components should be saved in the array, such as sum() and count().

It is possible to use the above algorithm to compute the full data cube: If we let a single fragment include all the dimensions, the computed fragment cube is exactly the full data cube. The order of computation in the cuboid lattice can be bottom-up and depth-first, similar to that of [7]. This ordering also allows for Apriori pruning in the case of iceberg cubes. We name this algorithm *Frag-Cubing*.

4 Online Query Computation

Given the pre-computed shell fragments, one can perform OLAP queries on the original data space. In general, there are two types of queries: (1) *point query* and (2) *subcube query*.

A *point query* seeks a specific cuboid cell in the original data space. All the *relevant* dimensions in the query are instantiated with some particular values. In an n-dimensional data cube $(A_1, A_2, \ldots, A_n)$, a point query is in the form of $\langle a_1, a_2, \ldots, a_n : M \rangle$, where each a_i specifies a value for dimension A_i and M is the inquired measure. For dimensions that are *irrelevant* or aggregated, one can use ∗ as its value. For example, the query $\langle$a2, b1, c1, d1, ∗ : count()$\rangle$ for the database in Table 1 is a point query where the first four dimensions are instantiated to a2, b1, c1, and d1 respectively, the last dimension is irrelevant, and count() is the inquired measure.

A *subcube query* seeks a set of cuboid cells in the original data space. It is one where at least one of the *relevant* dimensions in the query is *inquired*. In an n-dimensional data cube $(A_1, A_2, \ldots, A_n)$, a subcube query is in the form of $\langle a_1, a_2, \ldots, a_n : M \rangle$, where *at least one* a_i is marked ? to denote that dimension A_i is inquired. For example, the query $\langle a2, ?, c1, *, ? : count() \rangle$ for the database in Table 1 is one where the first and third dimension values are instantiated to a2 and c1 respectively, the fourth is irrelevant, and the second and the fifth are inquired. The subcube query computes all possible value combinations of the inquired dimension(s). It essentially returns a local data cube consisting of the inquired dimensions.

Conceptually, a point query can be seen as a special case of the subcube query where the number of inquired dimensions is 0. On the other extreme, a *full-cube* query is a subcube query where the number of instantiated dimensions is 0.

4.1 Query Processing

The general query for an n-dimensional database is in the form of $\langle a_1, a_2, \ldots, a_n : M \rangle$. Each a_i has 3 possible values: (1) an instantiated value, (2) aggregate *, (3) inquire ?. The first step is to gather all the instantiated a_i's if there are any. We examine the shell fragment partitions to check which a_i's are in the same fragments. Once that is done, we retrieve the tid-lists associated with the instantiations at the highest possible aggregate level. For example, suppose a_j and a_k were in the same fragment, we would then retrieve the tid-list from the (a_j, a_k) cuboid cell. The obtained tid-lists are intersected to derive the *instantiated base table*. If the table is empty, query processing stops and returns the empty result.

If there are no inquired dimensions, we simply fetch the corresponding measures from the *ID_measure* array and finish the point query. If there is at least one inquired dimension, we continue as follows. For each inquired dimension, we retrieve all its possible values and their associated tid-lists. If two or more inquired dimensions are in the same fragment, we retrieve all their pre-computed combinations and the tid-lists. Once these tid-lists are retrieved, they are intersected with the instantiated base table to form the local base cuboid of the inquired and instantiated dimensions. Then, any cubing algorithm can be employed to compute the local data cube.

Example 4. Suppose a user wants to compute the subcube query, {a2, b1, ?, *, ? : count()}, for our database in Table 1. The shell fragments are precomputed as described in Section 3.2. We first fetch the tid-list of the instantiated dimensions by looking at cell (a2, b1) of cuboid AB. This returns (a2, b1):{4, 5}. Note that if there were no inquired dimensions in the query, we would finish the query here and report 2 as the final count.

Next, we fetch the tid-lists of the inquired dimensions: C and E. These are {(c1:{1, 2, 3, 4, 5})} and {(e1:{1, 2}), (e2:{3, 4}), (e3:{5})}. Intersect them with the instantiated base and we get {(c1:{4, 5})} and {(e2:{4}), (e3:{5})}. This corresponds to a base cuboid of two tuples: {(c1, e2), (c1, e3)}. Any cubing algorithm can take this as input and compute the 2-D data cube. ∎

4.2 Algorithm for Shell Fragment-Based Query Processing

The above discussion leads to our algorithm for processing both point query and subcube query.

Algorithm 2 (Frag-Query) Processing of point and subcube queries using shell fragments.

Input: (1) A set of precomputed shell fragments for partitions $\{P_1, \ldots, P_k\}$, where P_i represents some set of dimension(s), and $P_1 \cup \ldots \cup P_k$ are all the n dimensions; (2) an *ID_measure* array if the measure is not *tuple-count*; and (3) a query of the form $\langle a_1, a_2, \ldots, a_n : M \rangle$ where each a_i is either instantiated, aggregated, or inquired for dimension A_i. M is the measure of the query.

Output: The computed measure(s) if the query is a point query, *i.e.*, containing only instantiated dimensions. Otherwise, the data cube whose dimensions are the inquired dimensions.

Method:

1. for each P_i {
    // instantiated dimensions
2.   if $P_i \cap \{a_1, \ldots, a_n\}$ includes instantiation(s)
3. $D_i \leftarrow P_i \cap \{a_1, \ldots, a_n\}$ with instantiation(s)
4. $B_{D_i} \leftarrow$ cells in D_i with associated tid-lists
    // inquired dimensions
5.   if $P_i \cap \{a_1, \ldots, a_n\}$ includes inquire(s)
6. $Q_i \leftarrow P_i \cap \{a_1, \ldots, a_n\}$ with inquire(s)
7. $R_{Q_i} \leftarrow$ cells in Q_i with associated tid-lists
   }
8. if there exists at least one non-null B_{D_i}
9. $B_q \leftarrow merge\_base(B_{D_1}, \ldots, B_{D_k})$
10. if there exists at least one non-null R_{Q_i}
11. $C_q \leftarrow compute\_cube(B_q, R_{Q_1}, \ldots, R_{Q_k})$ ∎

Note: Function merge_base() is implemented by intersecting the corresponding tid-lists of the B_{D_i}'s. Function compute_cube() takes the merged instantiated base and the inquired dimensions as input, derive the relevant base cuboid, and use the most efficient cubing algorithm to compute the multi-dimensional cube. The *ID_measure* array will be referenced after the cube is derived in this compute_cube() function.

Algorithm 2 covers all the possible OLAP queries. In the case of point query, there exist no inquired dimensions, and Lines 6-7 and 11 are not executed. The subcube query executes all the lines of the algorithm. In the case of full-cube query, there are no instantiated dimensions, Lines 3-4 and 9 will not be executed. Additionally, B_q is instantiated to `all` and the base cuboid derived is essentially the original database.

4.3 Shell Fragment Grouping & Size

The decision of which dimensions to group into the same fragments can be made based on the semantics of the data or expectations of future OLAP queries. The goal is to have many dimensions of a query fall into the same fragments. This makes full use of the pre-computed aggregates and saves both time and I/O.

In our examples, we chose equal-sized grouping of consecutive dimensions in fragment partitioning. However, domain-specific knowledge can be used for better grouping. For example, suppose in a 60-dimensional data set, dimensions $\{A_5, A_9, A_{32}, A_{55}, A_{56}\}$ often appear together in online queries, we can group them into two fragments, such as (A_5, A_9, A_{32}) and (A_{55}, A_{56}), or even one 5-D segment, depending on the historical or expected frequent queries. Furthermore, the groupings need not to be disjoint. We could have two fragments, such as (A_5, A_9, A_{32}) and (A_9, A_{55}, A_{56}). This added redundancy may offer speed-ups in query processing. With the known (or expected) query distribution and/or constraints on dimension set, intelligent grouping can be performed to facilitate the retrieval and manipulation of relevant set of dimensions within a small number of fragments.

The decision of how many dimensions to group into the same fragment can be analyzed more carefully. Suppose each fragment contains an equal number of dimensions and let that number be $\mathcal{F}$. If $\mathcal{F}$ is too small, the space required to store the fragment cubes will be small but the time needed to compute queries online will be long. On the other hand, if $\mathcal{F}$ is big, online queries can be computed quickly but the space needed to store the fragments will be enormous.

The question is whether there exists a $\mathcal{F}$ such that there is a good balance between the amount of space allocated to store the shell fragment cubes and the cost (both time and I/O) of computing queries online.

First, we examine how space grows as a function of $\mathcal{F}$. Lemma 2 describes the exact function. It is exponential with respect to $\mathcal{F}$. However, notice that when $\mathcal{F}$ is small, the growth is actually sub-linear. The original database has size $O(\mathcal{TD})$. When $\mathcal{F} = 2$, the memory usage is $O(3/2\mathcal{TD})$, smaller than the linear growth size of $O(2\mathcal{TD})$. In fact, when $\mathcal{F} \leq 4$, the growth in space is sub-linear.

Second, we examine the implications of $\mathcal{F}$ on query performance. In general, a too small size, such as 1, may lead to fetching and processing of rather long tid-lists. Just having a $\mathcal{F}$ of 2 could greatly reduce this, because many aggregates are pre-computed. Combine this intuition with the previous paragraph, $2 \leq \mathcal{F} \leq 4$ seems like a reasonable range.

5 Performance Study

There are two major costs associated with our proposed method: (1) the cost of storing the shell fragment cubes, and (2) the cost of retrieving tid-lists and computing the queries online. In this section, we perform a thorough analysis of these costs. All algorithms were implemented using C++ and all the experiments were conducted on an Intel Pentium-4 2.6CGHz system with 1GB of PC3200 RAM. The system ran Linux with the 2.6.1 kernel and gcc 3.3.2.

As a notational convention, we use $\mathcal{D}$ to denote the number of dimensions, $\mathcal{C}$ the cardinality of each dimension, $\mathcal{T}$ the number of tuples in the database, $\mathcal{F}$ the size of the shell fragment, $\mathcal{I}$ the number of instantiated dimensions, $\mathcal{Q}$ the number of inquired dimensions, and $\mathcal{S}$ the skew or `zipf` of the data. Minimum support level is 1 in all experiments.

5.1 Dimensionality and Storage Size

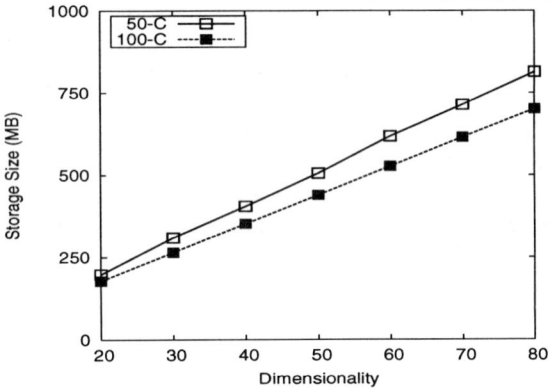

Figure 2: Storage size of shell fragments: (50-C) $\mathcal{T} = 10^6$, $\mathcal{C} = 50$, $\mathcal{S} = 0$, $\mathcal{F} = 3$. (100-C) $\mathcal{T} = 10^6$, $\mathcal{C} = 100$, $\mathcal{S} = 2$, $\mathcal{F} = 2$.

The first cost we are concerned with is the amount of space needed to store the shell-fragment cubes. Specifically, how it scales as dimensionality grows. Figure 2 shows the effect as dimensionality increases from 20 to 80. The number of tuples in both datasets were 10^6. The first dataset, 50-C, has cardinality of 50, skew of 0, and shell-fragment size 3. The second dataset, 100-C, has cardinality of 100, skew of 2, and shell-fragment size 2. The good news is that storage space grows linearly as dimensionality grows. This is expected because additional dimensions only add more fragment cubes, which are independent of the others.

5.2 Shell-Fragment Size and Storage Size

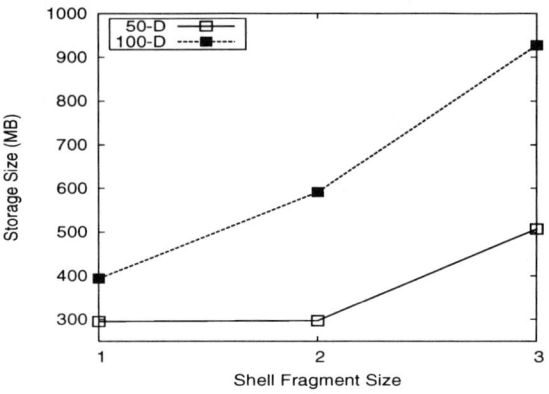

Figure 3: Storage size of shell fragments: (50-D) $\mathcal{T} = 10^6$, $\mathcal{D} = 50$, $\mathcal{C} = 50$, $\mathcal{S} = 0$. (100-D) $\mathcal{T} = 10^6$, $\mathcal{D} = 100$, $\mathcal{C} = 25$, $\mathcal{S} = 2$.

As discussed in Section 4.3, a fragment size between 2 and 4 strikes a good balance between storage space and computation time. In this and the next couple of subsections, we provide some test results to confirm that intuition.

Figure 3 shows the *storage size* of the shell fragment cubes. Figure 4 shows the *time* needed to compute them. Our experiments were conducted on two databases. The first, 50-D, has 10^6 tuples, 50 dimensions, cardinality of 50, and no skew. The second, 100-D, has 10^6 tuples, 100 dimensions, cardinality of 25, and *zipf* of 2. The shell-fragment size varies from 1 to 3.

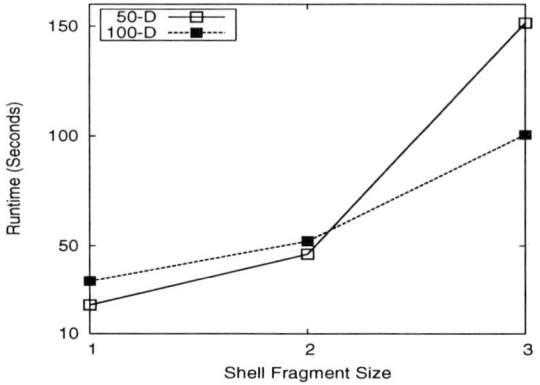

Figure 4: Time needed to compute shell fragments: (50-D) $\mathcal{T} = 10^6$, $\mathcal{D} = 50$, $\mathcal{C} = 50$, $\mathcal{S} = 0$. (100-D) $\mathcal{T} = 10^6$, $\mathcal{D} = 100$, $\mathcal{C} = 25$, $\mathcal{S} = 2$.

The sub-linear growth with respect to $\mathcal{F} \leq 3$ as mentioned in Section 4.3 is confirmed here, both in space and time. This is good news because as we will show in the next few sections, overall performance is improved as $\mathcal{F}$ increases.

5.3 Memory-Based Query Processing

As mentioned previously, the number of tuples in the databases we are dealing with is in the order of 10^6 or less. In statistics studies, it is not unusual to find datasets with thousands of dimensions but less than one thousand tuples. Thus, it is reasonable to suggest that the shell fragment cubes could fit inside main memory. Figure 3 shows with $\mathcal{F}$ equaling 3 or less, the shell fragments for 50 and 100 dimensional databases are under 1GB in size with 10^6 tuples.

In addition, recall our observation that many OLAP operations in high dimensional spaces only revolve around a few dimensions at a time. Most analysis will pin down a small set of dimensions and explore combinations within the set. Through caching of the data warehouse system, only the relevant dimensions and their shell fragments need to reside in main memory.

With the shell fragments in memory, we can perform OLAP on the database with pure in-memory processes. Note that this would be impossible had we chose to materialize the full data cube. Even with a small tuple count, a data cube with 50 or more dimensions requires petabytes and cannot possibly be stored in main memory.

In this section, we examine the implications of $\mathcal{F}$ on the speed of in-memory query processing. In this and the next subsection, we intentionally chose to have small $\mathcal{C}$ values in order to make the subcube queries meaningful. Otherwise in sparse uniform datasets, a random instantiation often leads to an empty result.

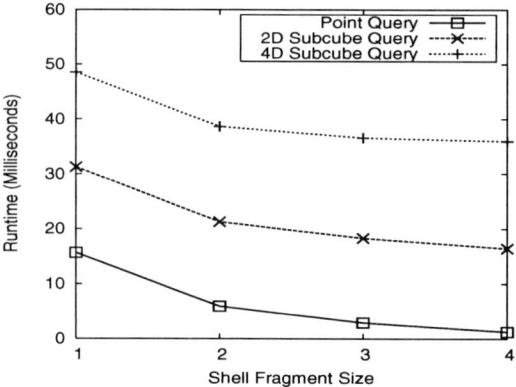

Figure 5: Average computation time per query over 1,000 trials. $\mathcal{T} = 10^6$, $\mathcal{D} = 10$, $\mathcal{C} = 10$, $\mathcal{S} = 0$, $\mathcal{I} = 4$.

Figure 5 shows the time needed to compute point and subcube queries with the shell fragments in memory. The *Frag-Cubing* algorithm is used to compute the online data cubes. The database had 10^6 tuples, 10 dimensions of cardinality 10 each, and 0 *zipf*. Each query had 4 randomly chosen instantiated dimensions, and 0 (or 2 or 4) inquired dimensions. Other dimensions are irrelevant. The times shown are *averages* of

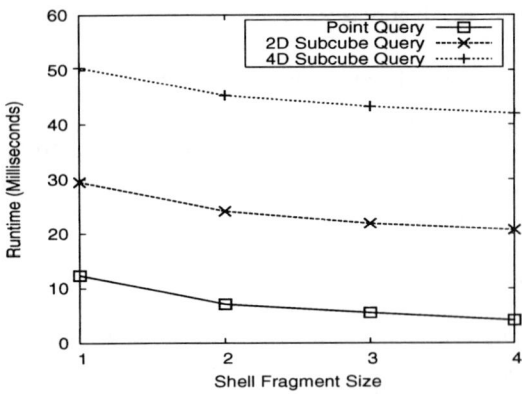

Figure 6: Average computation time per query over 1,000 trials. $\mathcal{T} = 10^6$, $\mathcal{D} = 20$, $\mathcal{C} = 10$, $\mathcal{S} = 1$, $\mathcal{I} = 3$.

1,000 such random queries. The 2D subcube queries returned a table with 84 rows on average, and the 4D subcube queries returned a table with 901 rows on average.

Figure 6 shows a similar experiment on another database. The difference is that this database had 20 dimensions and each query had 3 randomly chosen instantiated dimensions. The 2D subcube queries returned a table with 104 rows on average, and the 4D subcube queries returned a table with 2,593 rows on average.

The results show fast response time, with 50ms or less for various types of queries. They show that having $\mathcal{F} \geq 2$ results in a non-trivial speed-up during query processing over $\mathcal{F} = 1$. If any of the instantiated dimensions are in the same fragment(s), the processing of the tid-lists is much quicker due to their shorter lengths. If the inquired dimensions are in the same fragment(s), the effects are less obvious because the lengths of the tid-lists remain the same. The only difference is that they have been pre-intersected.

The speed-up of $\mathcal{F} \geq 2$ is slightly less in Figure 6 than in Figure 5, partly because there are more dimensions overall. As a result, it is less likely for the instantiated dimensions to be in the same fragment. In real world datasets where there are semantics attached to the data, the fragments will be presumably constructed so that they might be better matched to the queries.

5.4 Disk-Based Query Processing

I/O with respect to shell-fragment size: In the case that the shell fragments do not fit inside main memory, the individual tid-lists relevant to the query will have to be fetched from disk. In this section, we study the effects of $\mathcal{F}$ on these I/O costs. With a bigger $\mathcal{F}$, more relevant dimensions in a query are likely to be in the same fragment. This results in retrieval of shorter tid-lists from disk because the

multi-dimensional aggregates are already computed and stored.

Using the same two databases from the previous subsection, we measured the average number of I/Os needed to process a random query over 1,000 trials[2]. Figure 7 shows I/Os for computing point queries in the 10-D and 20-D databases. Figure 8 shows the same for 4D subcube queries. No caching of tid-lists was used between successive queries (i.e., cold-start in each query testing).

In both graphs, I/O was reduced as $\mathcal{F}$ increased from 1 to 4. This is because when instantiated dimensions were in the same fragments, their aggregated tid-lists were much shorter for retrieval. In Figure 8, the reduction was small relatively to the total I/O because there were 4 inquired dimensions. Since inquired dimensions cover all tuples in the database, shell fragment sizes do not affect the I/O cost much.

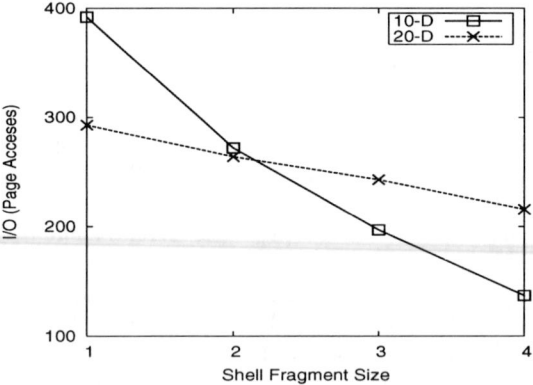

Figure 7: Average I/Os per point query over 1,000 trials. (10-D) $\mathcal{T} = 10^6$, $\mathcal{D} = 10$, $\mathcal{C} = 10$, $\mathcal{S} = 0$, $\mathcal{I} = 4$, $\mathcal{Q} = 0$; (20-D) $\mathcal{T} = 10^6$, $\mathcal{D} = 20$, $\mathcal{C} = 10$, $\mathcal{S} = 1$, $\mathcal{I} = 3$, $\mathcal{Q} = 0$.

I/O cost: shell-fragments vs. full materialized cubes: One may wonder how these I/O numbers compare to the case when full materialization of the data cube is actually possible. In general, a query has $\mathcal{I}$ instantiated dimensions and $\mathcal{Q}$ inquired dimensions. In terms of the fully materialized cube, the query seeks rows in the cuboid of all the relevant dimensions $(\mathcal{I} + \mathcal{Q})$ with certain values according to the instantiations. For example, the query {?, ?, c1, *, e3, *} seeks rows in the ABCE cuboid with certain values for dimensions C and E. These rows are used to compute all aggregates within dimensions A and B.

Because cuboid cells are stored on disk in some fixed order, they might be incompatible with the query. For example, they might happen to be sorted according to the inquired dimensions first. In the worst case, the entire cuboid of the relevant dimensions have to be retrieved. Further, it is necessary to read $(\mathcal{I} + \mathcal{Q} + 1)$ integers per row in the cuboid because we have to read

---

[2]Assuming 4K page sizes and 4 bytes per integer.

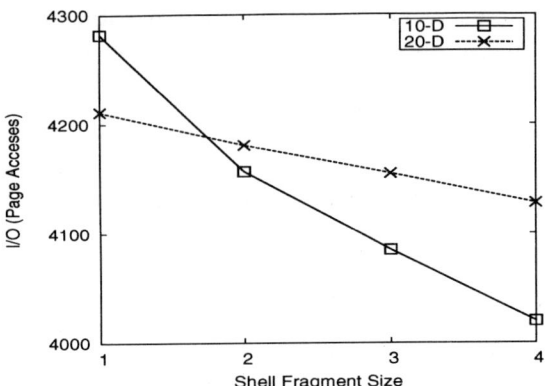
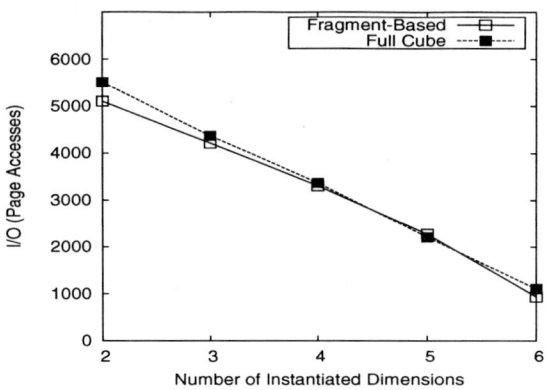

Figure 8: Average I/Os per 4D subcube query over 1,000 trials. (10-D) $\mathcal{T} = 10^6$, $\mathcal{D} = 10$, $\mathcal{C} = 10$, $\mathcal{S} = 0$, $\mathcal{I} = 4$, $\mathcal{Q} = 4$; (20-D) $\mathcal{T} = 10^6$, $\mathcal{D} = 20$, $\mathcal{C} = 10$, $\mathcal{S} = 1$, $\mathcal{I} = 3$, $\mathcal{Q} = 4$.

Figure 9: Average I/Os per query over 1,000 trials. $\mathcal{T} = 10^6$, $\mathcal{D} = 10$, $\mathcal{C} = 10$, $\mathcal{S} = 0$, $\mathcal{F} = 1$, $\mathcal{Q} = 7 - \mathcal{I}$.

the dimensional values and measure value. One may argue that the dimensional values can be skipped if there was an index on the cuboid cells. However, retrieval via an index implies random access for each row, which turns out to be much more expensive than just a plain sequential access with the dimensional values.

Figure 9 shows the average number of I/Os needed in a random query of various sizes over 1,000 trials. The number of inquired dimensions was 7 minus the number of instantiated dimensions. No caching was used, and the full data cube on disk was sorted according to the dimensional order: A, B, C, etc. Shell fragment size was set to 1. The relevant dimensions were the first 7 dimensions of the database and their materialized cuboid contained 951,483 rows.

The curves show that the shell-fragment I/O is competitive with the materialized data cube in many cases. Whenever the query had inquired dimensions before the instantiated dimensions in terms of the sort order, the materialized cuboid on disk have to pay the price of scanning useless cells. On average, these costs turn out be just as much as those in our method.

By having a shell-fragment size of 2 or more could lower I/O costs for our method. In addition, in real world applications with caching of recent queries, the I/O costs for both methods would be drastically reduced. Furthermore, had there been fewer relevant dimensions in the queries, the full data cube would have achieved lower I/O numbers due to the smaller cuboid size.

5.5 Experiments with Real-World Data Sets

Besides synthetic data, we also tested our algorithm on two real-world data sets. The first data set was the *Forest CoverType* dataset obtained from the UCI machine learning repository website (www.ics.uci.edu/~mlearn). This dataset contains 581,012 data points with 54 attributes, including 10 quantitative variables, 4 binary wilderness areas and 40 binary soil type variables. The cardinalities are (1978, 361, 67, 551, 700, 5785, 207, 185, 255, 5827, 2, 2, 2, 2, 2, 2, 2, 2, 2, 2, 2, 2, 2, 2, 2, 2, 2, 2, 2, 2, 2, 2, 2, 2, 2, 2, 2, 2, 2, 2, 2, 2, 2, 2, 2, 2, 2, 2, 2, 2, 2, 2, 2, 7). We constructed shell-fragments of size 2 using consecutive dimensions as groupings. The construction took 33 seconds and 325MB.

With the shell fragments in memory, running a point query with 1-8 instantiated dimensions took less than 10 milliseconds. This is not surprising because the number of tuples in the database is moderate. More interesting are the subcube queries. Running a 3-D subcube query with 1 instantiated dimension ranged between 67 ms (millisecond) and 1.4 second. Running a 5-D subcube query with 1 instantiated dimension ranged between 85 ms and 3.6 second. The running times were extremely sensitive to the particular dimensions inquired in the query. The high-end numbers reported were queries that included the dimension of cardinality 5827 in the inquired set. When the cardinalities of the inquired dimensions are small, subcube queries are extremely fast.

The second data set was obtained from the *Longitudinal Study of the Vocational Rehabilitation Services Program* (www.ed.gov/policy/speced/leg/rehab/eval-studies.html). It has 8818 transactions with 24 dimensions. The cardinalities are (83, 9, 2, 7, 4, 3165, 470, 131, 1511, 409, 144, 53, 21, 14, 12, 13, 27, 21, 18, 140, 130, 50, 23, 505). We constructed shell-fragments of size 3 using consecutive dimensions as the fragment groupings. The construction took 0.9 seconds and 60MB.

With the shell fragments in memory, running a point query on the dataset with 1-8 instantiated dimensions either in different fragments or the same took basically no time. Running a 3-D subcube query with no instantiations ranged between 50 ms and 1.6 second. A 3-D subcube query with 1 instantiated dimension took on average only 90 ms to compute. A 5-D subcube query with 0 instantiated dimensions ranged between 227ms and 2.6 second. We also tried a similar data set from the same collection with 6600 tuples and 96 dimensions and obtained very similar results.

6 Discussion

In this section, we discuss related work and further implementation considerations.

6.1 Related Work

There are several threads of work related to our model. First, partial materialization of data cubes has been studied previously, such as [12]. Viewing the data cube as a lattice of cuboids, some cuboids can be computed from others. Thus to save storage space, only the cuboids which are deemed most beneficial are materialized and the rest are computed online when needed. In this spirit, our approach may seem similar to theirs; however, the two models of computation are very different. In our approach, low dimensional cuboids facilitate the online construction of high dimensional cuboids via tid-lists. In [12], it is in the opposite direction: high dimensional cuboids facilitate the online construction of low dimensional cuboids by further aggregation.

Our work utilizes the construct of an *inverted index* as termed in information retrieval and *value-list index* as termed in databases. A large body of work has been devoted to this area. Inverted index has been widely used in information retrieval and Web-based information systems [4, 20]. Similar structures have been proposed and used in bitmap index of data cubes [9] and vertical format association mining [23]. Bitmaps and other compression techniques have been studied to optimize space and time usage [3, 8, 21]. In [15], projection indices and summary tables are used in OLAP query evaluations. However, all of these works have only focused on single dimensional indexing with or without aggregation. Our model studies the construction of multi-dimensional data structures (*i.e.*, 2-D, 3-D fragments) and the corresponding measure aggregation. Such structures and pre-computations not only reduce I/O costs but also speed up online computation over the single dimensional counterparts.

In [6], the authors investigated the usage of low dimensional data structures for indexing a high dimensional space. Their method, *tree-striping*, also partitions a high dimensional space into a set of disjoint low dimensional spaces. However, their data structures and algorithms were only designed to index data points, lacking the aggregations and other elements needed for data cubing.

One interesting observation made in [6] is that in trying to optimize the tradeoffs between pre-calculated result access and online computation, partitioning the original space into sets of 2 or 3 dimensions was often better than partitioning into single dimensions. Our studies from the point of view of data cubing derives a similar conclusion as they did for indexing: shell-fragment sizes between 2 and 4 achieve a good balance between storage size and online computation time.

6.2 Further Implementation Considerations

6.2.1 Incremental Update

The shell fragments and *ID_measure* array are quite adaptable to incremental updates. When a new tuple is inserted, a new $\langle tid : measure \rangle$ pair is added into the *ID_measure* array. Moreover, this new tuple is vertically partitioned according to the existing fragments and added to the corresponding inverted indices in the fragment cubes. Incremental deletion is performed similarly with the reverse process. These operations do not require the re-computation of existing data and are thus truly incremental. Furthermore, query performance with incrementally changed data is exactly the same as that of fragments re-computed from scratch.

Another interesting observation is that one can incrementally add new dimensions to the existing data. This is difficult for normal data cubes. The new dimensions $(D_i, ..., D_j)$ together with the new data form new inverted lists, still in the form of $\langle dimension\_value : tidlist \rangle$. These new dimensions can either form new fragments or be merged with the existing ones. Similarly, existing dimensions can be deleted by removing them from their respective fragments.

6.2.2 Bitmap Indexing

Throughout the paper, we have discussed I/O and computation costs with the assumption that the tid-lists are stored on disk as an array of integers. However, in data sets where cardinalities of the dimensions are small, bitmap indexing [3, 8, 15, 21] can improve space usage and speed. For example, if a column only has 2 possible values: male or female, the savings in storage space is high. Furthermore, the intersection operation can be performed much faster using the `bit-AND` operation than the standard merge-intersect operation.

6.2.3 Inverted Index Compression

Another compression method of the tid-lists come from information retrieval [4, 20]. The main observation is that the numbers in the tid-list are stored in ascending order. Thus, it would be possible to store a list of *d-gaps* instead of the actual numbers. In general, for a list of numbers $\langle d_1, d_2, ..., d_k \rangle$, the d-gap list would be $\langle d_1, d_2 - d_1, ..., d_k - d_{k-1} \rangle$. For example, suppose we have the list $\langle 7, 10, 19, 22, 45 \rangle$. The d-gaps list would be $\langle 7,3,9,3,23 \rangle$. The insight is that the largest number in the d-gap list is bounded by the difference between d_1 and d_k. Thus, it maybe possible to store them using less than the standard 32 bits of an integer. If many of the gap integers are small, the compression could be substantial. The details of compression have been exploited in information retrieval. Some of the popular techniques are unary, binary, δ, γ, and Bernoulli [20].

7 Conclusions

We have proposed a novel approach for OLAP in high-dimensional datasets with a moderate number of tuples. It partitions the high dimensional space into a set of disjoint low dimensional spaces (*i.e.*, shell fragments). Using inverted indices and pre-aggregated results, OLAP queries are computed online by dynamically constructing cuboids from the fragment data cubes. With this design, for high-dimensional OLAP-ing, the total space that needs to store such *shell fragments* is negligible in comparison with a high-dimensional cube, so is the online computation overhead. In our experiments, we showed that the storage cost grows linearly with the number dimensions. Moreover, the query I/O costs for large data sets are reasonable and are comparable with reading answers from a materialized data cube, when such a cube is available. And we also showed evidence of how different shell fragment sizes can affect query processing.

We have been performing further refinements of the proposed approach and exploring many potential applications. Traditional data warehouses have difficulties at supporting fast OLAP in high dimensional data sets, including spatial, temporal, multimedia, and text data. A systematic study of the applications of this new approach to such data could be a promising direction for future research.

References

[1] S. Agarwal, R. Agrawal, P. M. Deshpande, A. Gupta, J. F. Naughton, R. Ramakrishnan and S. Sarawagi. On the computation of multidimensional aggregates. In VLDB'96.

[2] R. Agrawal and R. Srikant. Fast algorithms for mining association rules. In VLDB'94.

[3] S. Amer-Yahia and T. Johnson. Optimizing queries on compressed bitmaps. In VLDB'00.

[4] R. Baeza-Yates and B. Ribeiro-Neto. *Modern Information Retrieval.* Addison-Wesley, 1999.

[5] D. Barbara and M. Sullivan. Quasi-cubes: Exploiting approximation in multidimensional databases. *SIGMOD Record,* 26:12–17, 1997.

[6] S. Berchtold, C. Böhm, D. A. Keim, Hans-Peter Kriegel, and Xiaowei Xu. Optimal multidimensional query processing using tree striping. In DaWaK'00.

[7] K. Beyer and R. Ramakrishnan. Bottom-up computation of sparse and iceberg cubes. In SIGMOD'99.

[8] C. Y. Chan and Y. E. Ioannidis. Bitmap index design and evaluation. In SIGMOD'98.

[9] S. Chaudhuri and U. Dayal. An overview of data warehousing and OLAP technology. *SIGMOD Record,* 26:65–74, 1997.

[10] J. Gray, S. Chaudhuri, A. Bosworth, A. Layman, D. Reichart, M. Venkatrao, F. Pellow and H. Pirahesh. Data cube: A relational aggregation operator generalizing group-by, cross-tab and subtotals. *Data Mining and Knowledge Discovery,* 1:29–54, 1997.

[11] J. Han, J. Pei, G. Dong, and K. Wang. Efficient computation of iceberg cubes with complex measures. In SIGMOD'01.

[12] V. Harinarayan, A. Rajaraman, and J. D. Ullman. Implementing data cubes efficiently. In SIGMOD'96.

[13] L. V. S. Lakshmanan, J. Pei, and J. Han. Quotient cube: How to summarize the semantics of a data cube. In VLDB'02.

[14] L. V.S. Lakshmanan, J. Pei, and Y. Zhao. Qc-trees: An efficient summary structure for semantic olap. In SIGMOD'03.

[15] P. O'Neil and D. Quass. Improved query performance with variant indexes. In SIGMOD'97.

[16] J. Shanmugasundaram, U. M. Fayyad, and P. S. Bradley. Compressed data cubes for OLAP aggregate query approximation on continuous dimensions. In KDD'99.

[17] Y. Sismanis and N. Roussopoulos. The dwarf data cube eliminates the high dimensionality curse. TR-CS4552, University of Maryland, 2003.

[18] Y. Sismanis, N. Roussopoulos, A. Deligianannakis, and Y. Kotidis. Dwarf: Shrinking the petacube. In SIGMOD'02.

[19] W. Wang, H. Lu, J. Feng, and J. X. Yu. Condensed cube: An effective approach to reducing data cube size. In ICDE'02.

[20] I. H. Witten, A. Moffat, and T. C. Bell. *Managing Gigabytes: Compressing and Indexing Documents and Images.* Morgan Kaufmann, 1999.

[21] M. C. Wu and A. P. Buchmann. Encoded bitmap indexing for data warehouses. In ICDE'98.

[22] D. Xin, J. Han, X. Li, and B. W. Wah. Star-cubing: Computing iceberg cubes by top-down and bottom-up integration. In VLDB'03.

[23] M. J. Zaki and C. J. Hsiao. CHARM: An efficient algorithm for closed itemset mining. In SDM'02.

[24] Y. Zhao, P. M. Deshpande, and J. F. Naughton. An array-based algorithm for simultaneous multidimensional aggregates. In SIGMOD'97.

The Polynomial Complexity of Fully Materialized Coalesced Cubes *

Yannis Sismanis
Dept. of Computer Science
University of Maryland
isis@cs.umd.edu

Nick Roussopoulos
Dept. of Computer Science
University of Maryland
nick@cs.umd.edu

Abstract

The data cube operator encapsulates all possible groupings of a data set and has proved to be an invaluable tool in analyzing vast amounts of data. However its apparent exponential complexity has significantly limited its applicability to low dimensional datasets. Recently the idea of the *coalesced cube* was introduced, and showed that high-dimensional coalesced cubes are orders of magnitudes smaller in size than the original data cubes even when they calculate and store every possible aggregation with 100% precision.

In this paper we present an analytical framework for estimating the size of coalesced cubes. By using this framework on uniform coalesced cubes we show that their size and the required computation time scales *polynomially* with the dimensionality of the data set and, therefore, a full data cube at 100% precision is not inherently cursed by high dimensionality. Additionally, we show that such coalesced cubes scale polynomially (and close to linearly) with the number of tuples on the dataset. We were also able to develop an efficient algorithm for estimating the size of coalesced cubes before actually computing them, based only on metadata about the cubes. Finally, we complement our analytical approach with an extensive experimental evaluation using real and synthetic data sets, and demonstrate that not only uniform but also zipfian and real coalesced cubes scale polynomially.

1 Introduction

The data cube operator is an analytical tool which provides the formulation for aggregate queries over categories, rollup/drilldown operations and cross-tabulation. Conceptually the data cube operator encapsulates all possible multidimensional groupings and it is an invaluable tool to applications that need analysis on huge amounts of data like decision support systems, business intelligence and data mining. Such applications need very fast query response on mostly ad-hoc queries that try to discover trends or patterns in the data set.

However the number of views of the data cube increases *exponentially* with the number of dimensions and most approaches are unable to compute and store but small low-dimensional data cubes. After the introduction of the data cube in [6] an abundance of research followed for dealing with its exponential complexity. The main ideas can be classified as either a cube sub-setting (partial materialization) [7, 8, 18] or storing the full cube but with less precision (approximation or lossy models) [1, 19]. However, all these techniques do not directly address the problem of exponential complexity. Furthermore, all problems associated with the data cube itself appear to be quite difficult, from computing it [2, 4, 14, 21, 3, 12], storing it [9, 5], querying and updating it[13]. Even the problem of obtaining estimates on the cube size is actually quite hard and needs exponential memory and exponential processing per tuple with respect to the dimensionality [15] in order to obtain accurate results.

Currently the most promising approaches for handling large high-dimensional cubes lie in the context of *coalesced* data cubes[17], where we demonstrate that the size and the required computation of the dwarf data cube, even when every possible aggregate is computed, stored and indexed, is orders of magnitudes smaller than expected. The coa-

---

*This material is based upon work supported by, or in part by, the U.S. Army Research Laboratory and the U.S. Army Research Office under contract/grant number DAAD19-01-1-0494. Prepared through collaborative participation in the Communications and Networks Consortium sponsored by the U. S. Army Research Laboratory under the Collaborative Technology Alliance Program, Cooperative Agreement DAAD19-01-2-0011. The U. S. Government is authorized to reproduce and distribute reprints for Government purposes notwithstanding any copyright notation thereon.

Permission to copy without fee all or part of this material is granted provided that the copies are not made or distributed for direct commercial advantage, the VLDB copyright notice and the title of the publication and its date appear, and notice is given that copying is by permission of the Very Large Data Base Endowment. To copy otherwise, or to republish, requires a fee and/or special permission from the Endowment.

**Proceedings of the 30th VLDB Conference,
Toronto, Canada, 2004**

lescing discovery [17], completely changed the perception of a data cube from a collection of distinct views into a network of interleaved groupings that eliminates both prefix and *most importantly suffix redundancies*. It is these suffix redundancies and their elimination that fuse and dramatically condense the exponential growth of high dimensional full cubes, without any loss in precision.

To help clarify the basic concepts, let us consider a cube with three dimensions. In Table 1 we present such a toy dataset for the dimensions Store, Customer, and Product with one measure Price.

Store	Customer	Product	Price
S1	C2	P2	$70
S1	C3	P1	$40
S2	C1	P1	$90
S2	C1	P2	$50

Table 1: Fact Table for Cube Sales

The size of the cube is defined as the number of the tuples it contains, which essentially corresponds to the sum of the tuples of all its views –in our case 2^3 views–. The size of the coalesced cube is defined as the total number of tuples it contains, *after* coalescing. For example, for the fact table in Table 1 and the aggregate function $f = sum$ we have a cube size of 23 tuples, while the coalesced cube size is just 9 tuples as depicted in Table 2. The redundancy of the cube is eliminated by storing the coalesced areas just once. For example, the aggregate $70 appears in total of five tuples, (S1|ALL,C2,P2|ALL) and (S1,ALL,P2), in the cube and it is coalesced in just one tuple. Although [11, 20] attempt to exploit similar suffix redundancies, they are based on a bottom-up computation[3] and require exponential computation time; only Dwarf's computation algorithm eliminates these redundancies from *both* the required storage *and* the required computation time.

no	Coalesced	f(Price)
1	(S1|ALL,C2,P2|ALL) (S1,ALL,P2)	$70
2	(S1|ALL,C3,P1|ALL) (S1,ALL,P1)	$40
3	(S1,ALL,ALL)	$110
4	(S2|ALL,C1,P1) (S2,ALL,P1)	$90
5	(S2|ALL,C1,P2) (S2,ALL,P2)	$50
6	(S2|ALL,C1,ALL)	$140
7	(ALL,ALL,P1)	$130
8	(ALL,ALL,P2)	$120
9	(ALL,ALL,ALL)	$250

Table 2: Coalesced Cube Tuples for $f = sum$

In this paper we provide a framework for estimating the size of a coalesced cube and show that for a uniform cube the expected size and computation time complexity is:

$$O\left(T\frac{d^{\log_C T+1}}{(\log_C T)!}\right) = O\left(d \cdot T^{1+1/\log_d C}\right)$$

where d is the number of dimensions, C is the cardinality of the dimensions and T is the number of tuples. This result shows that, unlike the case of non-coalesced cubes which grow -in terms of size and computation time- exponentially fast with the dimensionality, the 100% accurate and complete (in the sense that it contains all possible aggregates) coalesced representation only grows *polynomially* fast. In other words, if we keep the number of tuples in the fact table constant and increase the dimensionality of the fact table (by horizontally expanding each tuple with new attributes) then the required storage and corresponding computation time for the coalesced cube scales only polynomially. The first form of the complexity shows that the dimensionality d is raised to $\log_C T$, which does not depend on d and is actually quite small for real datasets[1].

The second form of the complexity shows that the coalesced size and corresponding computation time is polynomial w.r.t to the number of tuples of the data set T, which is raised to $1 + 1/\log_d C$ (and is very close to 1 for very large real datasets[2]). In other words, if we keep the dimensionality of the fact table constant and start appending new tuples, then the coalesced cube scales polynomially (and almost linearly). These results change the current state of the art in data-warehousing because it allows to scale up and be applicable to a much wider area of applications.

In addition we extend our analysis to cubes with varying cardinalities per dimension and we provide an efficient polynomial –w.r.t to the dimensionality– algorithm which can be used to provide close estimates for a coalesced cube size based only on these cardinalities without actually computing the cube. Such estimates are invaluable for data-warehouse/OLAP administrators who need to preallocate the storage for the cube before initiating its computation. Current approaches [15] cannot be applied to high-dimensional data cubes, not only because they require an exponential amount of work per tuple and exponential amount of memory but mostly because they cannot be extended to handle coalesced cubes.

Although our algorithm is based on uniform and independence assumptions, it provides very accurate results for both zipfian and real datasets requiring as input only basic metadata about the cube –it's dimension cardinalities–.

In particular in this paper we make the following contributions:

1. We formalize and categorize the redundancies found in the structure of the data cube into sparsity and implication redundancies.

2. We provide an analytical framework for estimating the size of the coalesced cube and show that for uniform data sets it scales only polynomially w.r.t to the number of dimensions and number of tuples.

---

[1]For example for a data set of 100 million tuples and a cardinality of 10,000, $\log_C T = 2$

[2]I.e., for a dimensionality of 30 and a cardinality of 5,000, $1 + 1/\log_d C \approx 1.4$

3. We complement our analytical contributions with an efficient algorithm and an experimental evaluation using both synthetic and real data sets and we show that our framework not only provides accurate results for zipfian distribution but most importantly that real coalesced cubes scale *even better* than polynomially due to implication redundancies.

Our work provides the *first* analytical and experimental results showing that a full (i.e. containing all possible groupings and aggregates) and 100% accurate (no approximation) data cube is *not inherently exponential both in terms of size and computation time* and that an effective coalescing data cube model can reduce it to realistic values. Therefore, we believe it has not only theoretical but also very practical value for data warehousing applications.

The remainder of the paper is organized as follows: In Section 2 we differentiate between prefix and suffix redundancies and show that suffix redundancies are by far the most dominant factor that affects coalesced cubes. Section 3 categorizes suffix redundancies based on the sparsity of the fact table or the implications between values of the dimensions. In Section 4 we introduce the basic partitioned node framework and we use it to analyze the coalesced cube structure. In Section 5 we present an algorithm that can be used to estimate the size of a coalesced cube given only the cardinalities of each dimension. The related work is presented in Section 6 and in Section 7 we show an evaluation on both synthetic and real data sets. Finally the conclusions are summarized in Section 8.

2 Redundancies

In this section we formalize the redundancies found in the structure of the cube and explain their extend and significance.

2.1 Prefix Redundancy

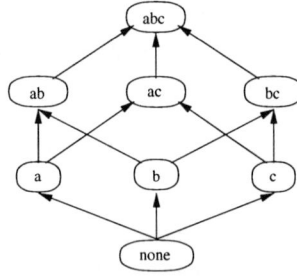

Figure 1: Lattice for the ordering a, b, c

This redundancy is the first that has been identified and can be used to build indexes over the structure of the cube. The idea is easily visualized in the lattice representation of the cube. For example, in Figure 1, one can observe that half the group-by's share the prefix a. We can exploit this by just storing the corresponding values just once and avoid replicating the same values over all views(prefix-reduction). By generalizing this to other prefixes (like for example to prefix b, which appears to one fourth of the views) we can reduce the amount of storage required to store the tuples of the cube.

Lemma 1 *The total number of tuples of the cube is not affected by prefix redundancy, only the storage required to store each tuple is reduced.*

This lemma essentially says that the prefix-reduced cube still suffers from the dimensionality curse, since we have to deal with every single tuple of the cube. The benefits of the prefix-reduction are therefore quickly rendered impractical even for medium dimensional cubes.

2.2 Suffix Redundancy

In this section we formally define the suffix redundancy and we give examples of different suffix redundancies.

DEFINITION 1 *Suffix Redundancy occurs when a set of tuples of the fact table contributes the exact same aggregates to different groupings. The operation that eliminates suffix redundancies is called **coalescing**. The resulting cube is called **coalesced cube** and we refer to its tuples as **coalesced tuples**.*

EXAMPLE 1 *Suffix redundancy can occur for just a single tuple: In the fact table of Table 1, we observe that the tuple:*

$$\langle S1\ C2\ P2\ \$70 \rangle$$

contributes the same aggregate $70 to two group-bys: (Store,Customer) and (Customer). The corresponding tuples are:

(Store,Customer)	(Customer)
⟨ S1 C1 $70 ⟩	⟨ C2 $70 ⟩

EXAMPLE 2 *We must point out that suffix redundancy does not work only on a per-tuple basis, but most importantly it extends to whole sub-cubes, for example the sub-cube that corresponds to the tuples:*

$$\langle S2\ C1\ P1\ \$90 \rangle, \langle S2\ C1\ P2\ \$50 \rangle$$

contributes the same aggregates to sub-cubes of (Store,Product), (Customer,Product), (Store), (Customer) :

(Store,Product)	(Customer,Product)
⟨ S2 P1 $90 ⟩	⟨ C1 P1 $90 ⟩
⟨ S2 P2 $50 ⟩	⟨ C1 P2 $50 ⟩

(Store)	(Customer)
⟨ S2 $140 ⟩	⟨ C1 $140 ⟩

The reason that whole sub-cubes can be coalesced is the *implication* between values of the dimensions. In our example, *C1 implies S2*, in the sense that customer *C1* only buys products from store *S2*. Dwarf is the only technique that manages to identify such whole sub-cubes as redundant and coalesce the redundancy from *both* storage and computation time, *without* calculating any redundant sub-cubes. For comparison, the condensed cube[20] can only identify redundant areas only tuple-by-tuple, and QC-Trees[11] have to compute first all possible sub-cubes and then check if coalescing can occur.

Such suffix redundancies demonstrate that there is significant overlap over the aggregates of different groupings. The number of tuples of the coalesced cube, where coalesced areas are only stored once is much smaller than the size of the cube, which replicates such areas over different groupings.

DEFINITION 2 *The size of a cube is the sum of the tuples of all its views. The size of a coalesced cube is the total number of tuples after the coalescing operation.*

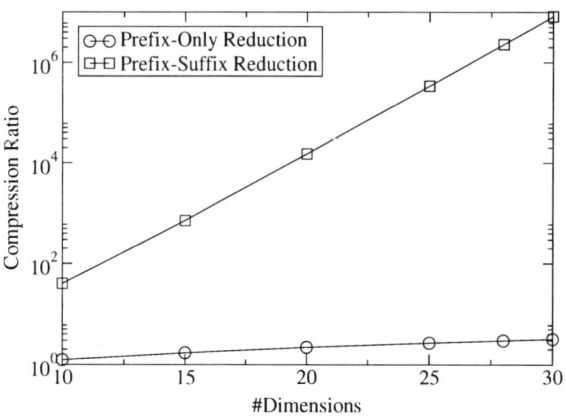

Figure 2: Compression vs. Dimensionality

Prefix redundancy works in harmony with suffix redundancy by eliminating common prefixes of coalesced areas. A comparison between these redundancies is demonstrated in Figure 2, where we depict the compression ratio achieved by storing all the tuples of a cube exploiting in the first case just the prefix redundancies and in the second both prefix and suffix redundancies w.r.t to the dimensionality of the dataset. We used a dataset with a varying number of dimensions, a cardinality of 10,000 for each dimension and a uniform fact table of 200,000 tuples. It is obvious that in high-dimensional datasets the amount of suffix redundancies is many orders of magnitudes more important the prefix redundancies.

3 Coalescing Categories

In this section we categorize suffix redundancies in *sparsity* and *implication* redundancies. We use the Dwarf model[17] in order to ease the definition and visualization of the redundancies. In the rest of the paper we will elaborate using this visualization.

3.1 Sparsity Coalescing

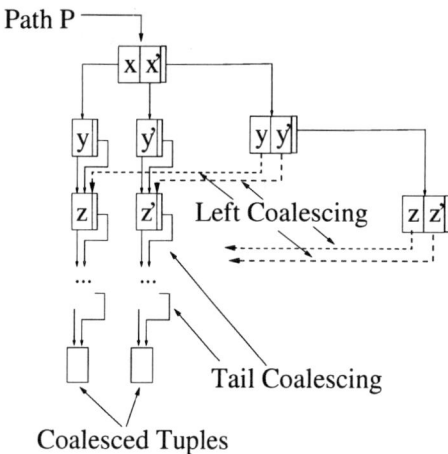

Figure 3: Sparsity Coalescings

In Figure 3 we depict two types of suffix redundancies due to the sparsity of the dataset. Lets assume that a path $\langle P \rangle$ leads to a sparse area and that for the paths $\langle P\ x \rangle$ and $\langle P\ x' \rangle$ there is only one tuple due to the sparsity of the cube. We differentiate between two different types of coalescing based on the nature of the path *P*.

DEFINITION 3 *Tail coalescing happens on all groupings that have $\langle P\ x \rangle$ as a prefix, where path $\langle P\ x \rangle$ leads to a sub-cube with only one fact tuple and path P **does not follow any ALL pointers**.*

EXAMPLE 3 *In Figure 3, since there is only one tuple in the area $\langle P\ x\ldots \rangle$ then all the group-bys that have $\langle P\ x \rangle$ as a prefix (i.e. $\langle P\ x\ ALL\ z\ldots \rangle$, $\langle P\ x\ y\ ALL\ldots \rangle$ etc.) share the same aggregate.*

DEFINITION 4 *Left coalescing occurs on all groupings with prefix $\langle P\ ALL\ y \rangle$, where path $\langle P\ ALL\ y \rangle$ leads to a sub-cube with only one tuple. In this case, P follows **at least one** ALL pointer.*

EXAMPLE 4 *Left coalescing complements tail coalescing and in Figure 3 we depict the case where $\langle P\ ALL\ y\ldots \rangle$ is redundant and corresponds to $\langle P\ x\ y\ldots \rangle$. The same is observed for $\langle P\ ALL\ ALL\ z \rangle$ and $\langle P\ ALL\ ALL\ z' \rangle$.*

Areas with just one tuple (like $\langle P\ x \rangle$ and $\langle P\ x' \rangle$) therefore produce a large number of redundancies in the structure of the cube. The difference between tail and left coalescing is two-fold:

- Paths that tail coalesce have a prefix that *does not follow* any *ALL* pointers while paths that left coalesce have a prefix that follows at least one *ALL* pointer - the one immediately above the point where coalescing happens-.

543

- Tail coalescing introduces one coalesced tuple in the coalesced cube, while left introduces no coalesced tuples.

In our analysis we consider these two types of coalescing (tail and left) and we show that their effect is so overwhelming that the exponential nature of the cube reduces into polynomial.

3.2 Implication Coalescing

The sparsity-coalescing types defined in Section 3.1 work only in sparse areas of the cube where a single tuple exists. The *implication-coalescing* complements these redundancies by coalescing *whole sub-cubes*. For example, for the fact table in Table 1 we observe that $C1$ implies $S2$ -in the sense that customer $C1$ only buys products from $S2$. This fact means that *every* grouping that involves $C1$ and $S2$ is essentially exactly the same with the groupings that involve $C1$. This redundancy can be depicted in Figure 4.

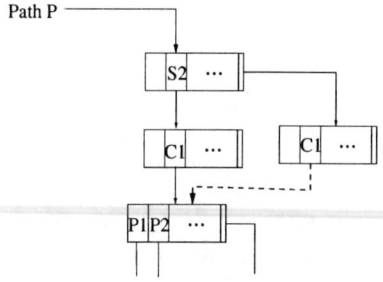

Figure 4: Implication Coalescing, where $C1 \to S2$

The implication coalescing is the generalization of left-coalescing when implications between the values of dimension occur. Such implications are very apparent in real datasets and –since we do not consider those in our analysis– they are the reason that in the experiments section we *overestimate* the size of the coalesced cube for real data sets.

4 Basic Partitioned Node Framework

In this section we formulate the coalesced cube structure by first introducing the *basic partitioned node* and then by building the rest of the coalesced cube around it –taking into account both tail and left coalescing–. Although in this paper we focus on uniform datasets our framework is applicable to more general distributions by properly adjusting the probability that is used in lemma 2.

Assume a uniform fact table with d dimensions, where each dimension has a cardinality of C and that there are $T = C$ tuples. For ease of analysis and without loss of generality we assume that: $\exists L : C = L!$. The root node of the corresponding coalesced cube is depicted in Figure 5, where the node has been partitioned[3] into L groups. We refer to such a node as the *basic partitioned node*. Group G_0

[3] for this analysis we relax the property of the dwarf, where the cells inside a node are lexicographically sorted

contains cells that get no tuples at all, group G_1 contains cells that get exactly one tuple, group G_2 contains cells that each one gets exactly two tuples, etc.

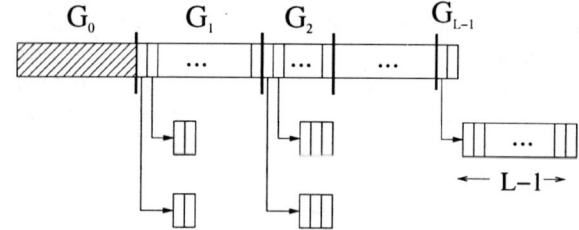

Figure 5: Node partitioned in groups where each cell in group G_z gets exactly z tuples

Lemma 2 *From a collection of C items, if we uniformly pick an item and repeat T times, then the probability that we pick one item exactly z times is:*

$$P_z(C,T) = \frac{\binom{T}{z}}{(C-1)^z} e^{-T/C}$$

[*Proof:* The probability that we will pick one item exactly z times is:

$$P_z(C,T) = \binom{T}{z} 1/C^z (1-1/C)^{T-z} =$$
$$= \binom{T}{z} 1/C^z (C-1)^{-z}/C^{-z} (1-1/C)^T$$

where the quantity $(1-1/C)^T$ can be approximated by $e^{-T/C}$ and the binomial $\binom{T}{z}$ corresponds to the number of different ways the product $1/C^z(1-1/C)^{T-z}$ can be written.]

By applying lemma 2 to the basic partitioned node we get by substituting $T = C$:

Lemma 3 *A group G_z of a basic partitioned node, where $z = 0 \ldots L-1$, contains $\approx \frac{C}{z!} e^{-1}$ cells that get exactly z tuples each*

[*Proof:* The expected number of cells inside a group G_z is:

$$C \cdot P_z(C,C) = C \frac{\binom{C}{z}}{(C-1)^z} e^{-1} \approx \frac{C}{z!} e^{-1}$$

because $z \ll C$ (z is at most $L-1$, and by definition $C = L!$) and $C - 1 \approx C$.]

Lemma 4 *The expected number of duplicate keys in a node pointed by a cell in group G_z is zero.*

[*Proof:* From lemma 3 we know that exactly z tuples are associated with each cell of group G_z and from the independence assumption we have that the probability that a key is duplicated for these tuples is $1/C^2$ with an expected number of duplicated keys z/C^2. Even for $z = L-1$, we expect $(L-1)/(L!)^2 \approx 0$ duplicate cells.]

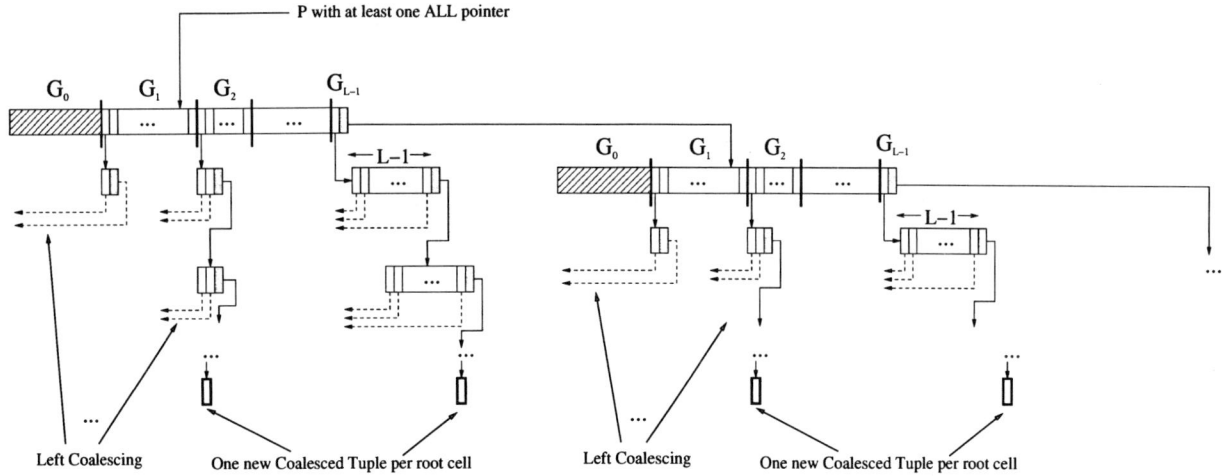

Figure 6: Left-Coalesced partitioned node with $T = C$

4.1 Left Coalesced Areas

In this section we deal with areas of the coalesced cube that are reachable through paths that follow ALL pointers. These areas have the possibility of left coalescing and as we'll show they are dominated by such redundancies.

In Figure 6 we show a basic partitioned node for a path P that follows at least one ALL pointer and corresponds to a subset of the fact table with $T = C$ tuples. We refer to the corresponding sub-cube as *left-coalesced sub-cube* and we show that it introduces a "small" number of new coalesced tuples. For the purposes of this section we refer to the root of the left-coalesced sub-cube as root. Since cells in group G_0 get no tuples, they offer no aggregates at all. Cells in group G_1, that get only a single tuple, left-coalesce to other tuples in the structure and offer no aggregation. This is the reason we differentiate between paths that follow at least one ALL pointer and paths that do not. Cells in groups $G_2, G_3, \ldots, G_{L-1}$ introduce only a single aggregate per cell.

To help clarify this, consider a cell in group G_2. Since there are two fact tuples associated with this cell (by definition) there are two paths $\langle P\ x\ \rangle$ and $\langle P\ x'\ \rangle$ that correspond to these two tuples. Additionally, the path P follows at least one ALL pointer, therefore the *exact same tuples* appear with another path Q that does not follow any ALL pointer, and paths $\langle P\ x\rangle$ and $\langle P\ x'\rangle$ coalesce to $\langle Q\ x\rangle$ and $\langle Q\ x'\rangle$. The only aggregate that this sub-cube introduces corresponds to the aggregation of these two tuples (located at the leaf nodes). The same holds for all groups $G_2, G_3, \ldots, G_{L-1}$ and the number of new coalesced tuples that a left-coalesced sub-cube with d dimensions and $T = C$ fact tuples introduces is (by using lemma 3):

$$NLeft(T = C, d, C) = a_0 \cdot C \cdot d + 1$$

where $a_0 = (e-2)/e$.

[*Proof:* As depicted in Figure 6 a left-coalesced partitioned node introduces:

$$d(C/2!e^{-1} + C/3!e^{-1} + \ldots) + 1 =$$
$$= Cd/e(1/2! + 1/3! + \ldots) + 1 =$$
$$= a_0 \cdot C \cdot d + 1$$

]

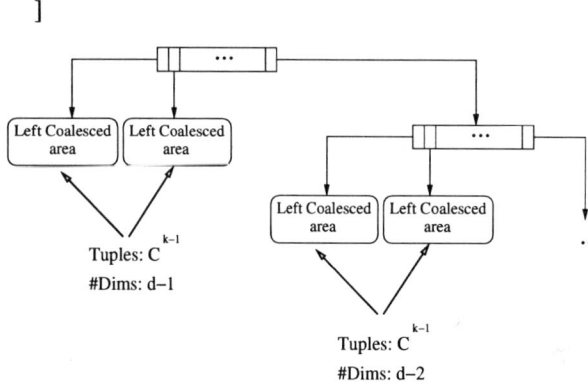

Figure 7: Left-Coalesced partitioned node with $T = C^k$

We can extend our analysis to the general case where $T = C^k$, $k = \log_C T$ in the way that is depicted in Figure 7. By induction we prove that:

Lemma 5 *The number of coalesced tuples of a left-coalesced area with $T = C^k$ tuples, dimensionality d and cardinality C is:*

$$NLeft(T = C^k, d, C) =$$
$$= C \cdot \sum_{i=1}^{d-1} NLeft(T = C^{k-1}, d-i, C) + 1 =$$
$$= a_0 C^k \binom{d}{k} + \sum_{i=1}^{k-1} C^{k-i} \binom{d}{k-i} + 1$$

where $a_0 = (e-2)/e$

4.2 Tail Coalesced Areas

In this section we deal with areas that are reachable through paths that do not follow any ALL pointers. These areas

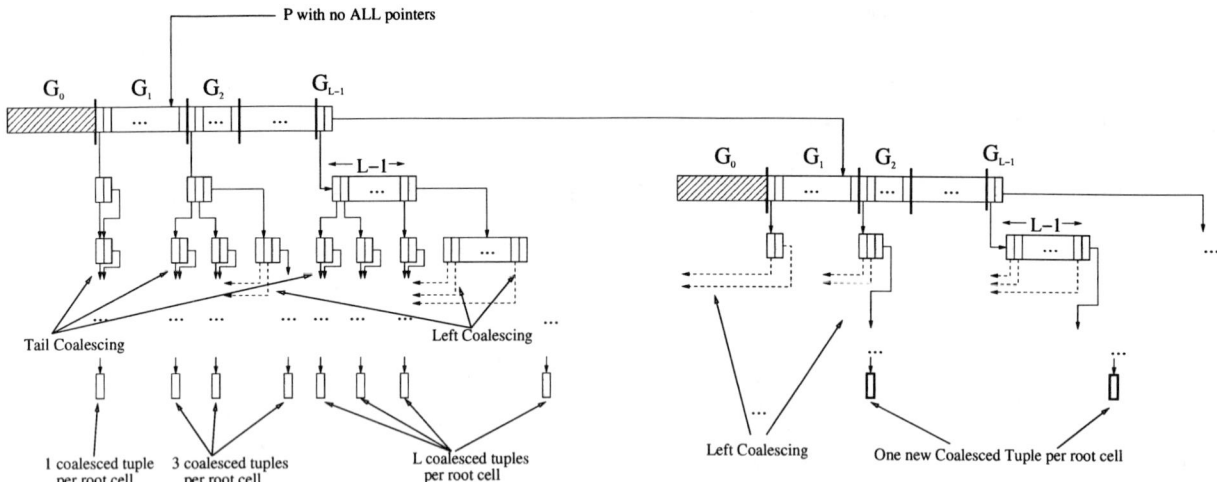

Figure 8: Tail-Coalesced partitioned node with $T = C$

have less chances for left-coalescing but as will show the amount of coalescing is still very significant.

In Figure 8 we show a basic partitioned node which corresponds to a path P that *does not* follow any ALL pointers and that it corresponds to a subset of the fact table with $T = C$ tuples. We refer to the corresponding sub-cube as *tail-coalesced sub-cube* and we count the number of coalesced tuples it introduces. As in the left-coalesced case, cells in group G_0 that get no tuples offer no tuples at all. Cells in group G_1 that get only a single tuple, offer just a single aggregate, due to tail coalescing. Cells in groups G_z, where $z = 2, \ldots, L-1$ introduce $z+1$ coalesced tuples, the z tuples of the fact table plus their aggregation. The number of coalesced tuples a tail-coalesced sub-cube with d dimensions and $T = C$ fact tuples introduces is:

$$NTail(T = C, d, C) = b_0 C + a_0 C(d-1) + 1$$

where $a_0 = (e-2)/e$ and $b_0 = (2e-2)/e$.

[Proof: The new tuples under the root tail-coalesced node (ignoring the all cell) are:

$$C/1!/e + C/3!/e + C/4!/e + \ldots = b_0 C$$

while the all cell points to a left-coalesced node with: $a_0 C(d-1) + 1$ new tuples (as explained in Section 4.1)]

We can extend our analysis to the general case where $T = C^k$, $k = \log_C T$ in the way that is depicted in Figure 9. Using induction we prove that:

Lemma 6 *The number of coalesced tuples of a tail-coalesced area with $T = C^k$ tuples, dimensionality d and cardinality C is:*

$$NTail(T = C^k, d, C) =$$
$$= C \cdot NTail(C^{k-1}, d-1, C) + \sum_{i=2}^{d-1} NLeft(C^{k-1}, d-i, C) =$$
$$= a_0 C^k \left[\binom{d}{k} - 1 \right] + \sum_{i=1}^{k} C^{k-i} \left[\binom{d}{k-i} - 1 \right] + b_0 C^k$$

where $a_0 = (e-2)/e$ and $b_0 = (2e-2)/e$

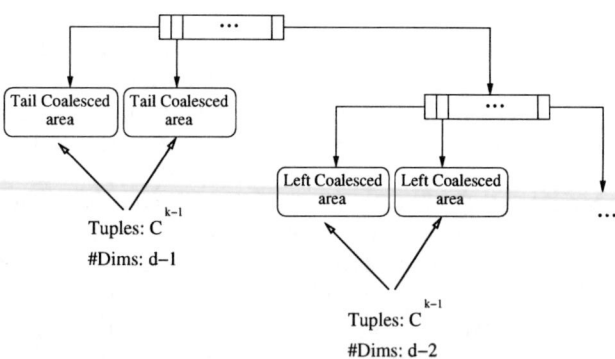

Figure 9: Tail-Coalesced partitioned node with $T = C^k$

4.3 Coalesced Size and Time Complexity

The analysis for the tail coalesced areas gives the total number of coalesced tuples for the full coalesced cube with d dimensions, cardinality C per dimension and T fact table tuples[4]. Lemma 6 gives that:

$$\#CoalescedTuples = O\left(T \frac{d^{\log_C T}}{(\log_C T)!} \right) = O\left(T^{1 + 1/\log_d C} \right)$$

with the surprising result that, even if we consider only two out the three coalesces, the size of the coalesced cube is polynomial w.r.t to the dimensionality of the fact table and polynomial (and very close to linear) w.r.t to the number of tuples in the fact table.

Additionally, if we consider the number of nodes or cells, that are introduced in the coalesced structure, the expected complexity is multiplied by d (i.e. the polynomial power increases by one), since we need *at most* d nodes

---

[4] When we start creating the root node of the coalesced cube there is no chance of left-coalescing, since nothing has been created

and cells *ignoring any prefix reduction* in order to represent each tuple. Therefore the expected complexity for the number of cells (or the full size of the structure) is:

$$\#\text{TotalCells} = O\left(T\frac{d^{\log_C T+1}}{(\log_C T)!}\right)$$

It is very important to point out that from the current algorithms that eliminate such suffix redundancies like [17, 11, 20], only the suffix coalescing algorithm of Dwarf visits the cells of the structure *just once* and therefore the time complexity for constructing dwarfs is:

$$\text{Dwarf ComputationTime} = O\left(T\frac{d^{\log_C T+1}}{(\log_C T)!}\right)$$

On the contrary, the algorithms in [11, 20] are based on a bottom-up computation[3], which requires exponential computation time on the number of dimensions.

5 Algorithm for Coalesced Cube Size Estimation

In this section we extend our analytical contribution to the general case of varying cardinalities per dimensionality. Algorithm 1 can be used to estimate the number of coalesced tuples for sparse uniform data sets given the cardinalities of each dimension.

Initially the algorithm is called with the tail coalescing flag set to 1, since there is no chance for left-coalescing (there are no tuples to coalesce to). In line 4 we check if there is just one tuple in the subcube where tail or suffix coalescing happens depending on the tail coalescing flag. In lines 12- 19 we traverse the basic partitioned node by checking iteratively how many cells get one, two, three, etc. tuples until all the available tuples for the subcube are exhausted. The quantity:

$$\frac{\binom{\text{FactT}}{x}}{(mC-1)^x} \cdot mC \cdot e^{-\text{FactT}/mC}$$

where FactT is the number of fact tuples for the current sub-dwarf and mC is the cardinality of the current dimension, returns the number of cells that get exactly x tuples.

The algorithm works in a depth-first manner over the lattice and estimates recursively the number of coalesced tuples that its sub-dwarf generates. For example, for a three-dimensional cube *abc*, the algorithm in line 21 starts the *drill-down* to all subcubes with prefix *a* and recursively it proceeds to those with prefix *ab* and finally reaches prefixes *abc*, by estimating appropriately the number of tuples that each subdwarf gets. When (lines 1-7) there are no more dimensions to drill-down (or a tail or left coalescing can be identified), the drill-down over the subdwarfs with prefixes in *abc* stops and the algorithm *rolls-up* to the subdwarfs with prefixes *ab* in line 23 by setting the nC flag to 0 -since now there is possibility of left-coalescing with the subcubes in *abc*-. The process continues recursively to all the views

Algorithm 1 NCT Algorithm - Num of Coalesced Tuples

Input: d: Number of Dimensions
Card: array of dimension cardinalities
FactT: current no of fact tuples
nc: tail coalesce flag(0 or 1)

1: **if** FactT=0 **then**
2:    return 0
3: **else if** FactT=1 **then**
4:    return nc {here tail or left-coalescing happens}
5: **else if** d=0 **then**
6:    return 1
7: **end if**
8: coalescedT ← 0
9: mC ← Card[d]
10: zeroT ← mC · $e^{-\text{FactT}/mC}$
11: oneT ← FactT/(mC − 1) · zeroT
12: **if** oneT ≥ 1 **then**
13:    x ← 1
14:    **while** there are still fact tuples **do**
15:       xT ← $\binom{\text{FactT}}{x}$/(mC − 1)^x · zeroT
16:       coalescedT += NCT(d-1,Card,xTuples,nc) {tail or left-coalescing may happen here}
17:       FactT -= xT
18:       x++
19:    **end while**
20: **else**
21:    coalescedT += NCT(d-1,Card,FactT/mC,nc) {drill-down traversal}
22: **end if**
23: coalescedT += NCT(d-1,Card,FactT,0) {roll-up traversal with left-coalescing}
24: return coalescedT

of the lattice.

The running complexity of the algorithm is derived from the basic partitioned node framework and is polynomial on the number of dimensions. It only requires $O(d)$ memory to accommodate the stack for performing a DFS to d dimensions deep.

6 Related Work

The data cube operator is introduced in [6] and its potential has generated a flurry of research on a wide-variety of topics. Its exponential complexity on almost every aspect first guided to the rediscovery of materialized views and their adaptation. For example view selection algorithms can be found in [7, 8, 18]. However the general problem is shown to be NP-Complete [10] and even greedy algorithms are polynomial on the number of views that need to consider which is actually exponential on the dimensionality of the datasets, rendering these approaches to a certain degree impractical for high-dimensional datasets.

Estimating the size of the data cube given its fact table is only addressed in [15] by using probabilistic techniques, however that approach cannot be extended to work with coalesced cubes.

The problem of just computing the data cube appears especially interesting. Various techniques that try to benefit from commonalities between partitions or sorts, partial sorts and intermediate results are proposed in [2, 4, 14]. Other techniques that use multidimensional array representations [21] suffer as well from the dimensionality curse. Techniques that try to exploit the inherent sparsity of the cube like [3, 12] seem to perform better.

Several indexing techniques have been devised for storing data cubes. Cube Forests [9], exploit prefix redundancy when storing the cube. In the Statistics Tree [5] prefix redundancy is partially exploited. Unique prefixes are stored just once, but the tree contains all possible paths (even non-existing paths) making it inappropriate for sparse datasets. Cubetrees[13] use packed R-trees to store individual views and exhibit very good update performance.

Recently compressed cubes are introduced which try to exploit the inherent redundancies in the structure of the cube. In [20] the notion of a *base single tuple* is introduced. Such a tuple is "shared" between different group-bys and is similar to the coalesced tuples discussed in this paper. However its applicability is limited since such tuples are discovered one at a time. QC-trees[11] use a bottom-up approach in discovering redundancies which checks if every grouping is redundant or not with every other grouping that it is possible to coalesce with. Both Condensed Cubes[20] and QC-Trees are based on BUC[3] and require exponential computation time.

Dwarf[17] provides a much more efficient method for the automatic discovery of all types of suffix redundancies, since whole sub-cubes can be coalesced *before any re-computation* and is therefore the only method where the computation time is also fused by the coalescing properties and is polynomial to the number of dimensions as this paper demonstrates. Dwarf additionally not only indexes the produced cube but is designed to work in secondary memory and is the only method that provides for clustering, partial materialization and hierarchies[16].

7 Experiments

In this section we provide an extensive experimental evaluation of our approach based on synthetic and real data sets. We compare the results of our analytical approach with actual results taken from our implementation of Dwarf. The experiments were executed on a Pentium 4, clocked at 1.8GHz with 1GB memory. The buffer manager of our implementation was set to 256MB.

7.1 Synthetic Datasets

In this section we use the following formalism. The graph entitled "Actual" in the legend corresponds to numbers taken from our implementation, while the graph entitled "Estim" corresponds to the estimates our analytical framework and algorithm provides. We use the symbol d to refer to the number of dimensions, C to the cardinality and a to the zipfian parameter (skewness).

7.1.1 Scalability vs dimensionality

Uniform Distributions In Figure 10 we demonstrate how the number of coalesced tuples scales w.r.t to the dimensionality, for a uniform dataset. The number of fact table tuples was set to 100,000. We used two different cardinalities of 1,000 and 10,000. We see that our analytical approach provides extremely accurate results for large cardinalities. The reason that the error decreases as the cardinality increases is the approximation in lemma 3, where we assume that $C - 1 \approx C$. The second observation has to do with the scalability w.r.t. to the dimensionality. The quantity $\log_C T$ which determines the exponent of d is much smaller in the case of $C = 10,000$ and therefore this data set scales better.

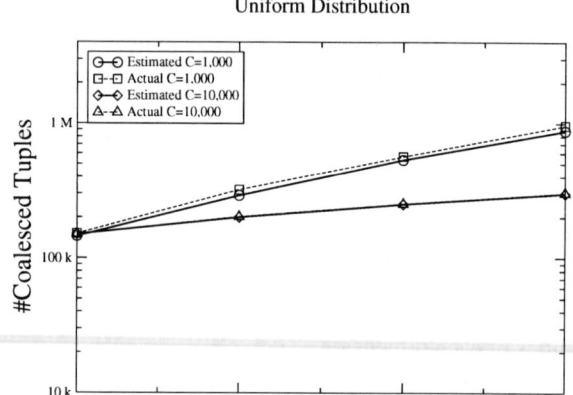

Figure 10: Size Scalability v.s. dimensionality for varying cardinalities

In Figure 11 we depict the time scalability –w.r.t to the dimensionality– required to compute and store the coalesced cubes using the Dwarf approach for the uniform datasets. We must point that the y-axis are logarithmic and that the graphs –for both #coalesced tuples and computation time– correspond to a polynomial scaling.

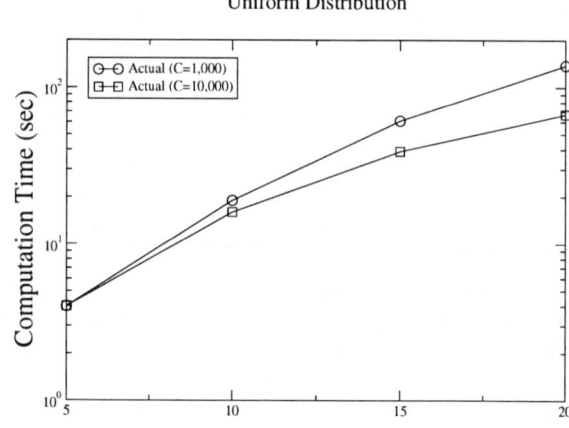

Figure 11: Computation Time Scalability v.s. dimensionality for varying cardinalities

Zipfian Distributions In Figure 12 we depict the size scalability w.r.t to the dimensionality for zipfian datasets for various values for the zipfian parameter a that controls the skew. The number of fact table tuples was set to 100,000. The cardinalities were again 1,000 and 10,000 respectively. We observe that our estimation algorithm approximates better the zipfian coalesced cube size for large values of cardinalities than it does for smaller values of cardinalities[5]. On the other side, we observe that the skew parameter affects more the dataset with $C = 1,000$ than the dataset with $C = 10,000$. The reason for these two observations is that the zipfian parameter directly affects the sparsity of the cube. For lower values of cardinalities the percentage of sparsity coalesces is significantly less than the case of higher cardinality values. However it is evident that the zipfian distribution scales polynomially and that our estimation algorithm can be used to get good estimates about zipfian coalesced cubes. We must point out that from the graphs it can be derived that the zipfian distribution affects the scalability –w.r.t to the dimensionality– in a multiplicative way. In other words, it increases the complexity factor but not the polynomial power.

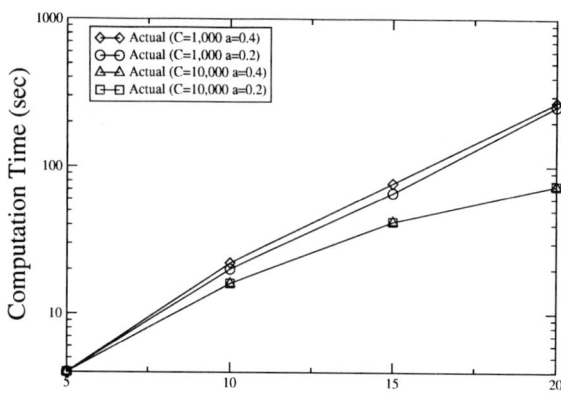

Figure 13: Computation Time Scalability v.s. dimensionality for varying cardinalities and zipf parameters

the zipfian distributions affects sparsity coalescing in a negative way and increases the corresponding coalesced cube size and computation time. For completeness we also depict the required computation time for the same cubes in Figures 14 and 15.

In this series of experiments our estimation algorithm, although based on a uniform assumption, provides very accurate results over all the range of the parameters (cardinality, number of dimensions, skewness) that we experimented on.

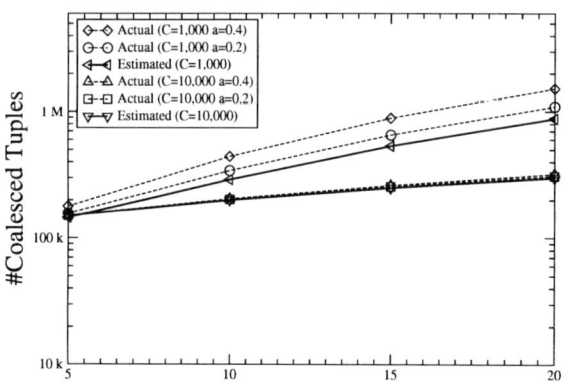

Figure 12: Size Scalability v.s. dimensionality for varying cardinalities and zipf parameters

In Figure 13 we depict that the scalability of the required computation time for varying dimensionalities, cardinalities and skew parameters is again polynomial. We observe that the skew parameter affects proportionally the computation time as it affects the coalesced cube size.

Scalability vs #Tuples In Figures 14, 15 and 16 we depict the coalesced size scalability w.r.t to the number of tuples for uniform and Zipfian datasets for a variable number of dimensions, cardinalities and skew. We observe that in all cases both the number of coalesced tuples and the computation time scale almost linearly w.r.t to the number of tuples in the fact table. We must point that a value $C = 10,000$ for the cardinality offers more chances for sparsity coalescing and therefore the required storage and time is lower than the case of $C = 1,000$. The skewness of

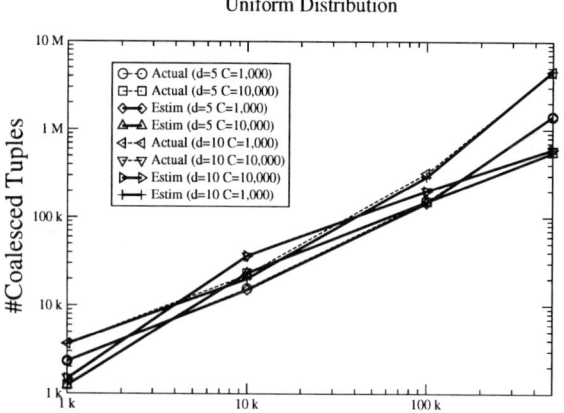

Figure 14: Size Scalability v.s. #Tuples for varying cardinalities

7.2 Real Datasets

For this experiment we use a real eight-dimensional data set given to us by an OLAP company. The data set has varying cardinalities per dimension. We used various projections on the data set in order to decrease the dimensionality and study its effect on the accuracy. For this experiment the fact table had 672,771 tuples and two measures. Table 3 summarizes the parameters of each projection. Column "Projection" denotes the name of the data set, column d the number of dimensions and column "Cardinalities" the car-

---

[5] This behavior is observed (to a lesser degree) for uniform datasets as well

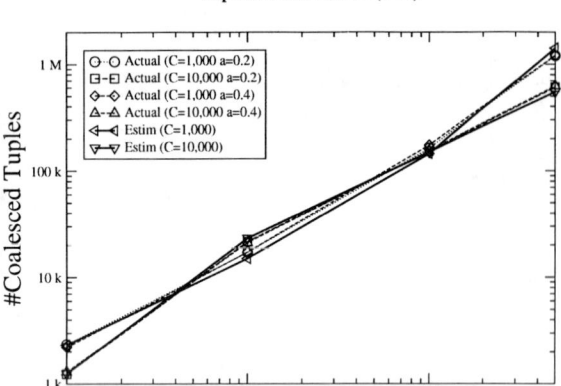

Figure 15: Size Scalability v.s. #Tuples for varying cardinalities and zipf parameters

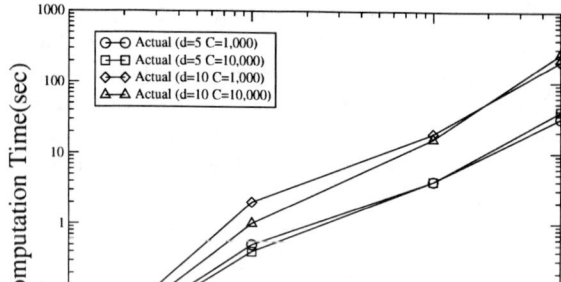

Figure 17: Computation Time Scalability v.s. #Tuples for varying cardinalities (uniform)

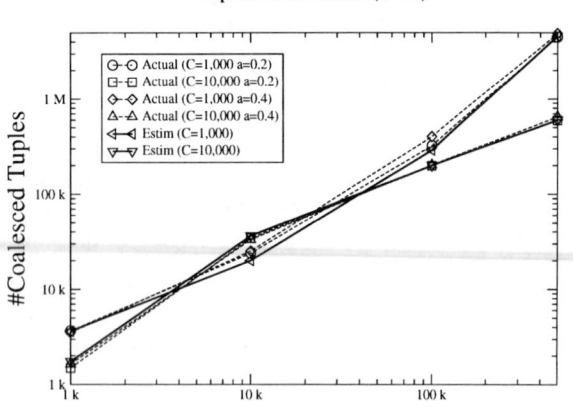

Figure 16: Size Scalability v.s. #Tuples for varying cardinalities and zipf parameters

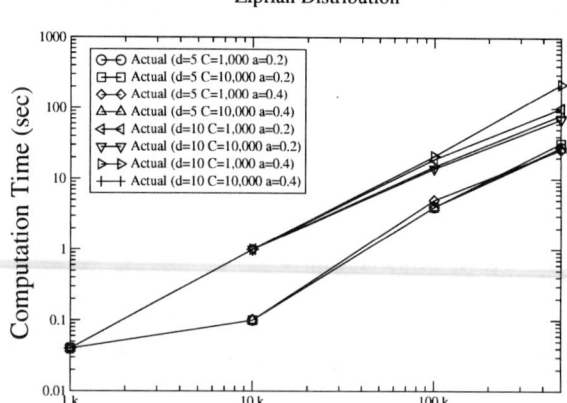

Figure 18: Computation Time Scalability v.s. #Tuples for varying cardinalities and zipf parameters

dinalities of each dimension. In Figure 19 we depict the estimates of our approach compared with the actual numbers taken, when the dwarf is computed and stored. In Figure 20 we depict –for completeness– the time scalability w.r.t the dimensionality of the real datasets.

Projection	d	Cardinalities
A	5	1300,2307,2,2,3098
B	6	1300,2307,3098,130,561,693
C	7	1300,2307,2,3098,130,561,693
D	8	1300,2307,2,2,3098,130,561,693

Table 3: Real data set parameters

We observe a very interesting pattern. As the dimensionality increases our approach *overestimates* increasingly more the coalesced size. The reason is that our approach currently handles *only sparsity coalescing* and ignores the *implication coalescing* that is very apparent in high-dimensional data sets. As the dimensionality increases such implications increase and complement the sparsity implications reducing even further the coalesced size. This observation is in contrast to what happens with zipfian datasets, which affect the sparsity of the coalesced cube in a negative way *without* creating any implications between the dimensions. However real datasets are not only skewed but present a large number of implications between values of their dimensions, that affect in a positive way the coalesced cube size.

8 Conclusions

We have presented an analytical and algorithmic framework for estimating the size of coalesced cubes, where suffix redundancies diminish the number of aggregates that need to be stored and calculated. Our analytical framework although it uses only sparsity coalescing, derives the surprising result, that a uniform coalesced cube grows –both the required storage and the computation time– polynomially w.r.t to the dimensionality. This result changes the established state that the cube is inherently exponential on the number of dimensions and extend the applicability of data warehousing methods to a much wider area. We were also able to device an efficient algorithm for estimating the size

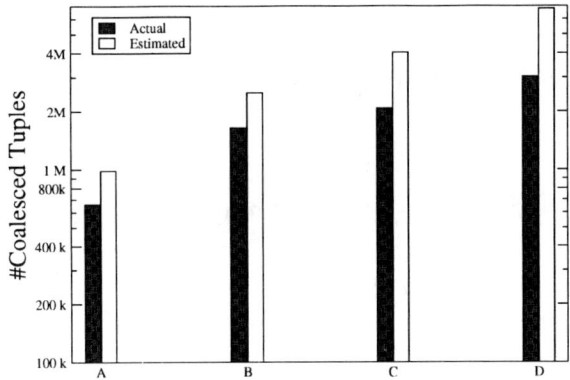

Figure 19: Size Scalability v.s. dimensionality for real data set

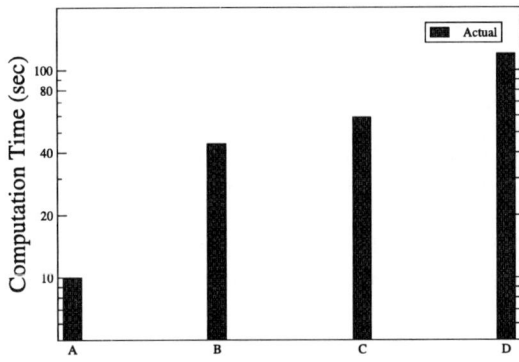

Figure 20: Time Scalability v.s. dimensionality for real data set

of a coalesced cube based only on its dimensions' cardinalities and demonstrated that it provides accurate results for a wide range of distributions. In addition we have demonstrated, using real data, that real coalesced cubes scale *even better* than our analysis derives. The reason is that the effects of implication coalescing complement the results of sparsity coalescing that we have presented here.

References

[1] S. Acharya, P. B. Gibbons, and V. Poosala. Congressional Samples for Approximate Answering of Group-By Queries. In *SIGMOD*, pages 487–498, Dallas, Texas, 2000.

[2] S. Agarwal, R. Agrawal, P. M. Deshpande, A. Gupta, J .F. Naughton, R. Ramakrishnan, and S. Sarawagi. On the computation of multidimensional aggregates. In *VLDB*, pages 506–521, 1996.

[3] K. Beyer and R. Ramakrishnan. Bottom-Up Computation of Sparse and Iceberg CUBEs. In *SIGMOD*, pages 359–370, Philadelphia, PA, USA, 1999.

[4] P.M. Deshpande, S. Agarwal, J.F. Naughton, and R. Ramakrishnan. Computation of multidimensional aggregates. Technical Report 1314, University of Wisconsin - Madison, 1996.

[5] Lixin Fu and Joachim Hammer. CUBIST: A New Algorithm for Improving the Performance of Ad-hoc OLAP Queries. In *DOLAP*, 2000.

[6] J. Gray, A. Bosworth, A. Layman, and H. Pirahesh. Data Cube: A Relational Aggregation Operator Generalizing Gro up-By, Cross-Tab, and Sub-Totals. In *ICDE*, pages 152–159, New Orleans, February 1996. IEEE.

[7] H. Gupta, V. Harinarayan, A. Rajaraman, and J. Ullman. Index Selection for OLAP. In *ICDE*, pages 208–219, Burmingham, UK, April 1997.

[8] V. Harinarayan, A. Rajaraman, and J. Ullman. Implementing Data Cubes Efficiently. In *SIGMOD*, pages 205–216, Montreal, Canada, June 1996.

[9] T. Johnson and D. Shasha. Some Approaches to Index Design for Cube Forests. *Data Engineering Bulletin*, 20(1):27–35, March 1997.

[10] H. J. Karloff and M. Mihail. On the Complexity of the View-Selection Problem. In *PODS*, pages 167–173, Philadelphia, Pennsylvania, May 1999.

[11] L. Lakshmanan, J. Pei, and Yan Zhao. QC-Trees: An Efficient Summary Structure for Semantic OLAP. In *SIGMOD*, pages 64–75, San Diego, California, 2003.

[12] K. A. Ross and D. Srivastana. Fast Computation of Sparse Datacubes. In *VLDB*, pages 116–125, Athens, Greece, 1997.

[13] N. Roussopoulos, Y. Kotidis, and M. Roussopoulos. Cubetree: Organization of and Bulk Incremental Updates on the Data Cube. In *SIGMOD*, pages 89–99, Tucson, Arizona, May 1997.

[14] S. Sarawagi, R. Agrawal, and A. Gupta. On computing the data cube. Technical Report RJ10026, IBM Almaden Research Center, San Jose, CA, 1996.

[15] A. Shukla, P. Deshpande, J. Naughton, and K. Ramasamy. Storage estimation for multidimensional aggregates in the presense of hierarchies. In *VLDB*, pages 522–531, Bombay, India, August 1996.

[16] Y. Sismanis, A. Deligiannakis, Y. Kotidis, and N. Roussopoulos. Hierarchical dwarfs for the rollup cube. In *DOLAP*, 2003.

[17] Y. Sismanis, A. Deligiannakis, N. Roussopoulos, and Y. Kotidis. Dwarf: Shrinking the PetaCube. In *SIGMOD*, pages 464–475, Madison, Wisconsin, 2002.

[18] D. Theodoratos and T. Sellis. Data Warehouse Configuration. In *VLDB*, pages 126–135, Athens, Greece, August 1997.

[19] J.S Vitter, M. Wang, and B. Iyer. Data Cube Approximation and Histograms via Wavelets. In *CIKM*, 1998.

[20] Wei Wang, Hongjun Lu, Jianlin Feng, and Jeffrey Xu Yu. Condensed Cube: An Effective Approach to Reducing Data Cube Size. In *ICDE*, 2002.

[21] Y. Zhao, P. M. Deshpande, and J. F. Naughton. An array-based algorithm for simultaneous multidimensional aggregates. In *SIGMOD*, pages 159–170, 1997.

The views and conclusions contained in this document are those of the authors and should not be interpreted as representing the official policies, either expressed or implied, of the Army Research Laboratory or the U. S. Government.

Relational link-based ranking

Floris Geerts *

Laboratory for Foundations
of Computer Science
School of Informatics
University of Edinburgh, UK
fgeerts@inf.ed.ac.uk

Heikki Mannila

Basic Research Unit
Helsinki Institute for Information Technology
Department of Computer Science
University of Helsinki, Finland
{mannila,terzi}@cs.helsinki.fi

Evimaria Terzi

Abstract

Link analysis methods show that the interconnections between web pages have lots of valuable information. The link analysis methods are, however, inherently oriented towards analyzing binary relations.

We consider the question of generalizing link analysis methods for analyzing relational databases. To this aim, we provide a generalized ranking framework and address its practical implications.

More specifically, we associate with each relational database and set of queries a unique weighted directed graph, which we call the *database graph*. We explore the properties of database graphs. In analogy to link analysis algorithms, which use the Web graph to rank web pages, we use the database graph to rank partial tuples. In this way we can, e.g., extend the PageRank link analysis algorithm to relational databases and give this extension a random querier interpretation.

Similarly, we extend the HITS link analysis algorithm to relational databases. We conclude with some preliminary experimental results.

* Work done while at the Basic Research Unit, Helsinki Institute for Information Technology, Department of Computer Science, University of Helsinki.

Permission to copy without fee all or part of this material is granted provided that the copies are not made or distributed for direct commercial advantage, the VLDB copyright notice and the title of the publication and its date appear, and notice is given that copying is by permission of the Very Large Data Base Endowment. To copy otherwise, or to republish, requires a fee and/or special permission from the Endowment.

**Proceedings of the 30th VLDB Conference,
Toronto, Canada, 2004**

1 Introduction

Methods for ranking elements have been widely discussed in a variety of settings. In the context of database systems the motivation for ranking has increased along with the size of databases. In huge databases the users that pose a query would like to see the top-k partial tuples that satisfy their query rather than thousands of tuples ordered in a completely uninformative way. Additionally, the necessity of ranking the query results goes far beyond the functionality of the existing ORDER BY operator, which sorts the results only according to the values in the specified attributes. A variety of algorithms that efficiently handle the top-k selection [15, 19] and top-k join queries [20, 24] have been proposed.

Ranking is a notion that has appeared also in the context of Web search applications. The natural need in this context is to rank the web pages returned as a result to a user query. In this case the pages are ranked such that the more relevant the page is to the query, the higher it is ranked. Furthermore, among the web pages that are equally relevant those that are more "important" should precede the less "important" ones. Many ranking algorithms for web pages have been developed ([11, 6, 22, 9, 25]) with the most popular among them being the HITS algorithm proposed by Kleinberg [22] and the PageRank algorithm proposed by Brin et.al [11]. The latter has led to the popular Google search engine.

Web pages are categorical data, and thus the problem of ranking them as such is not trivial since they do not have an intrinsic numerical value on which a ranking could be based on. However, all the ranking algorithms developed for them exploit the hyperlink information, i.e. the structure of the Web graph, in order to assign to each web page a rank value and obtain a ranking based on these values. In contrast to web pages, the assignment of rank values to categorical data in relational databases has not yet been much investigated. In this paper, we do exactly this. More specifically, *we address the problem of automated assignment of rank values to categorical partial tuples.* Based on this assignment we produce useful rankings of partial tuples. We will construct database graphs using queries and try to exploit their structure to obtain rank values.

These rank values can be used in a variety of database applications: First, one can get ranked answers to queries. Second, they can serve as input to the existing top-k algorithms mentioned above. Until now, the top-k algorithms are mainly applied to databases with non-categorical attributes and the top-k algorithms use these values as input. The rank values we obtain for categorical data can be used in a similar way. Finally, the obtained rank values can be helpful in providing ranked keyword search results in relational databases. How exactly the obtained values are going to be used is beyond the scope of this paper. Here we only consider how such rank values can be obtained.

More specifically, we present a general framework for obtaining such rank values for partial tuples of relational databases. The goal is to define those rank scores and find the algorithms to calculate them. For this we exploit information about the interconnections of the partial tuples in the database, as these can be discovered using relational algebra queries.

To obtain rankings for partial tuples we mimic the principles of link analysis algorithms. The well-studied algorithms ([11, 6, 22, 9, 25]) for the Web show that the structure of the interconnections of web pages has lots of valuable information. For example, Kleinberg's HITS algorithm [22] suggests that each page should have a separate "authority" rating (based on the links going *to* the page) and "hub" rating (based on the links going *from* the page). The intuition behind the algorithm is that important hubs have links to important authorities and important authorities are linked by important hubs. Brin's PageRank algorithm [11], on the other hand, calculates globally the PageRank of a web page by considering a random walk on the Web graph and computing its stationary distribution. The PageRank algorithm can also be seen as a model of a user's behavior where a hypothetical web surfer clicks on hyperlinks at random with no regard towards content. More specifically, when the random surfer is on a web page, the probability that he clicks on one hyperlink of the page depends solely on the number of outgoing links the latter has. However, sometimes the surfer gets bored and jumps to a random web page on the Web. The PageRank of a web page is the expected number of times the random surfer visits that page if he would click infinitely many times. Important web pages are ones which are visited very often by the random surfer.

We now rephrase the random surfer in the relational

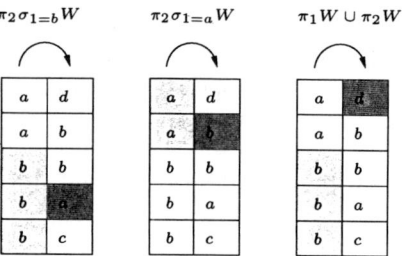

Figure 1: Random walk of random surfer using only 2 kinds of queries.

database setting. Consider the fragment of the Web shown as the binary table W in Figure 1. In the same figure we have shown the surf trail $b \to a \to b \to d$ of the random surfer. In order to walk along the partial tuples (pages) in W, the random surfer needs only two kinds of queries: The first is simply the query which returns all pages present in W. This can be expressed by the expression $\pi_1 W \cup \pi_2 W$. The second kind are queries expressed by $\pi_2 \sigma_{1=v} W$, in which v is a page present in W. In other words, these queries ask for all pages reachable from a certain page v. After the random surfer has evaluated one of these queries, he selects a random tuple out of the query result and repeats this procedure again. An important restriction is that while $\pi_1 W \cup \pi_2 W$ may be asked by the random surfer independent of the current page, $\pi_2 \sigma_{1=v} W$ may only be asked when the surfer is at page v. In Figure 1 we have shown which queries are asked in order to obtain the shown surf trail.

We use this observation to extend the random surfer model to the *random querier*, which generalizes random-walk based link analysis algorithms by providing the random surfer with a different set of queries at his disposal. Additionally, the model facilitates extensions that allow for using this model for ranking partial tuples.

Seeing the Web as a database allows us to see a hyperlink between two web pages to exist due to queries that connect the two web pages. E.g., in Figure 1 the link between page b and page a can be seen to exists due to the fact that a is in the query result $\pi_2 \sigma_{1=b} W$. This idea generalizes to arbitrary databases D and any finite set of queries $\{q_1, \ldots, q_n\}$: There exists a link between two partial tuples $\vec{s}$ and $\vec{t}$ of a database D if there exists an $i = 1, \ldots, n$ such that $\vec{t}$ is in the query result of q_i when evaluated on D and where the selection parameters of q_i are instantiated with constants in $\vec{s}$.

We augment these links with weights relative to some preference function on the queries and frequency information of tuples in the query results. In this way we obtain a weighted directed graph which we call the *database graph*. The database graph is a natural generalization of the graphs used in link analysis.

The database graph enables any graph-based link

analysis method to be used for ranking partial tuples. For example, both the PageRank and HITS algorithms can be generalized to operate on the database graph; the generalizations provide tuple ranking algorithms for relational databases.

The contributions of this paper are the following:

- We define the database graph for a given database, set of queries and preference function and explore its theoretical properties.

- We study random walks on the database graph and show that they can be interpreted as the walks of a random querier. We use the stationary distribution of the random walks to assign rank values to partial tuples.

- We show that the random querier generalizes many well-known link analysis algorithms.

- As a second application of the database graph, we extend the HITS algorithm to relational databases and use it to assign rank values as well.

- We experimentally evaluate the use of the obtained rank values to rank query results.

Related work

The problem of assigning rank values to partial tuples in the relational framework is related to the problem of ranking web pages. The latter has been extensively investigated and several link analysis algorithms have been developed for this [11, 6, 22, 9, 25]. Even some unifying frameworks for link analysis algorithms exist [12].

Interesting work on ranking elements in relational databases based on measures from Information Retrieval (IR) is described in [3], however the notion of "link" provided by the queries has not been considered there.

The representation of a database as a graph and link-based ranking appears in the context of keyword search in [5, 18, 2]. The nodes in the graph are the database tuples and the directed relationships between the nodes are induced by foreign key or other constraints. The ranking values are related to the inverse of the path distance between nodes.

Graph representations of databases and random walks on them are considered also in the context of similarity of categorical attributes. Both [26] and [21] construct a graph where the nodes are the constants in the database and two nodes are linked when they appear in the same tuple. They perform different random walks on them in order to obtain a similarity measure for the values. A related iterative approach is the idea of hyperedges connecting tuples based on values [17]. The main difference that we use partial tuples instead of tuples and that we use queries to connect them.

A random walk approach to ranking on (semi-)structured data is proposed in [4]. Although the approach to ranking is very similar to ours, the graph construction is heavily dependent on the presence of (semi-)structured data.

Organization

The rest of this paper is organized as follows. In Section 2 we define databases and query languages. In Section 3, we formally define the database graph and prove some of its properties. We then define the random walk on the database graph and the random querier in Section 4. In Section 5 we extend PageRank and HITS algorithm to relational databases using the database graph. Section 6 describes some experimental results. We conclude the paper in Section 7.

2 Preliminaries

We refer to [1, 16] for a more detailed description of basic database notions. For simplicity of exposition, we assume that the database schema S consists of a single relation name R of arity n. However, all definitions and results generalize directly to arbitrary database schemas.

Let $\mathcal{D}$ be a database instance over S. The active domain of $\mathcal{D}$, denoted by $adom(\mathcal{D})$, consists of all constants in $\mathcal{D}$. For a tuple $\vec{t} \in \mathcal{D}$ of size n, we denote the value of its i-th attribute by $t_i \in adom(\mathcal{D})$. The active domain of a tuple $\vec{t} \in \mathcal{D}$, denoted by $adom(\vec{t})$, is the set $\{t_1, \ldots, t_n\}$.

The standard query language is the relational algebra, or equivalently the relational calculus, over the database schema S. We denote this query language by RA. Relations and queries are interpreted using the bag semantics, i.e., duplicate tuples are allowed. The reason for this is that we need the notion of frequency which disappears if we do not allow for duplicates. We will not distinguish between queries and the RA expressions expressing them. We denote the query result of q on $\mathcal{D}$ by $q(\mathcal{D})$.

Let $q \in$ RA be an n-ary query and denote the set of attributes in the query result by I. We will partition I in *source attributes* $\vec{x}$ and the *target attributes* $\vec{y}$. We always assume that this partition is specified for each query q we encounter. We make this explicit by writing $q(\vec{y}|\vec{x})$ instead of simply q.

Let $\vec{s} \in adom(\mathcal{D})^k$ where $k = |\vec{x}|$ and let $\ell = |\vec{y}|$. Then we define the RA expression

$$q(\vec{y}|\vec{s}) \equiv \pi_{y_1, \ldots, y_\ell} \sigma_{x_1 = s_1, \ldots, x_k = s_k} q(\vec{y}|\vec{x}).$$

We will denote the query result of $q(\vec{y}|\vec{s})$ on $\mathcal{D}$ by $q(\mathcal{D}, \vec{s})$.

We extend the RA with the duplicate elimination operator δ for transforming bags into sets if necessary.

Given a tuple $\vec{s}$ and a query $q \in$ RA the support of $\vec{s}$ in $q(\mathcal{D})$, denoted by $supp(\vec{s}, q(\mathcal{D}))$, is the number of times $\vec{s}$ appears in $q(\mathcal{D})$. The frequency of $\vec{s}$ in $q(\mathcal{D})$ is defined as $\text{freq}(\vec{s}, q(\mathcal{D})) = \frac{\text{supp}(\vec{s}, q(\mathcal{D}))}{|q(\mathcal{D})|}$, where $|q(\mathcal{D})|$ denotes the size of $q(\mathcal{D})$.

3 The database graph

As already mentioned in the Introduction, one can consider the web as a database $\mathcal{D}$ over a binary relation W. Then following a hyperlink from a page v can be seen as first querying the database using the query $q(y|x) \equiv W(x, y)$, and then selecting a page out of $q(\mathcal{D}, v)$. Two web pages v and w are now linked by the query q iff $w \in q(\mathcal{D}, v)$. We generalize this idea to arbitrary databases and queries.

Definition 1 (Link). For a given database $\mathcal{D}$ and query language $\mathcal{L} \subseteq \text{RA}$, a tuple $\vec{s} \in adom(\mathcal{D})^k$ is $\mathcal{L}$-linked to a tuple $\vec{t} \in adom(\mathcal{D})^\ell$ iff there exists a query $q(\vec{y}|\vec{x}) \in \mathcal{L}$ such that $|\vec{x}| = k$, $|\vec{y}| = \ell$, and $\vec{t} \in q(\mathcal{D}, \vec{s})$. □

From now on we assume that $\mathcal{L}$ consists of a finite number of queries.

Let $M = \langle \mathcal{D}, \mathcal{L}, f \rangle$ where $\mathcal{D}$ is a database, $\mathcal{L} \subseteq \text{RA}$, and f is some preference function $f : \mathcal{L} \to \mathbb{Q}^+$. Here, $\mathbb{Q}^+$ denotes the set of strictly positive rational numbers.

We now define the database graph. The definition is rather technical but the intuition behind it is very natural. Indeed, the vertices of the database graph correspond to the active domain of tuples in the answers to queries in $\mathcal{L}$. The reason why we work with the active domains instead of the tuples themselves is that a constant appearing in some attribute can possibly be used in other attributes as well. So instead of storing a constant for each possible attribute separately, we store it only once. This slightly complicates the formal definition (see below) of database graph since many different tuples can correspond to the same vertex. The edge relation is based on Definition 1. Finally, we will assign weights to the edges corresponding to the preferences of the queries establishing this edge (or link) and the support of the tuples consistent with the target vertex in the query results. More formally,

Definition 2 (Database graph). Given $M = \langle \mathcal{D}, \mathcal{L}, f \rangle$ the corresponding *database graph* is the weighted directed graph $G_M = (V_M, E_M, \lambda_M)$ where,

- The set of vertices V_M is constructed as follows: For each query $q(\vec{y}|\vec{x}) \in \mathcal{L}$ we instantiate the parameters $\vec{x}$ with tuples $\vec{s} \in adom(\mathcal{D})^k$, where $k = |\vec{x}|$. For each $\vec{t} \in q(\mathcal{D}, \vec{s})$, we add the vertex $v = adom(\vec{t})$ to V_M, if not already included. Note that v is a set of constants. Thus, V_M is

$$\{adom(\vec{t}) \mid q(\vec{y} \mid \vec{x}) \in \mathcal{L}, |\vec{x}| = k$$
$$\vec{s} \in adom(\mathcal{D})^k, \vec{t} \in q(\mathcal{D}, \vec{s})\}.$$

For a vertex $v \in V_M$, we denote by v^k the set of all k-tuples formed from constants in v.

- The set of edges E_M is equal to all ordered pairs of vertices (v, w) such that there exists a tuple $\vec{s} \in v^k$ which is $\mathcal{L}$-linked to a tuple $\vec{t} \in adom(\mathcal{D})^\ell$ such that $w = adom(\vec{t})$; and

- The weight function $\lambda_M : E_M \to \mathbb{Q}^+$ is defined as $\lambda_M(v, w) =$

$$\sum_{q(\vec{y}|\vec{x}) \in \mathcal{L}} f(q) \Big(\sum_{\substack{\vec{s} \in v^k, k=|\vec{x}| \\ \vec{t} \in w^\ell, \ell=|\vec{y}|}} \text{freq}(\vec{t}, q(\mathcal{D}, \vec{s})) \Big).$$

□

We illustrate the concept of database graph by the following examples.

Example 1. Let $\mathcal{D}$ be the database given by the table in Figure 2. The language $\mathcal{L}$ consists of the queries $q_1(y|x) \equiv \pi_{1,2} R(x, y, z)$ and $q_2(y, z|x) \equiv R(x, y, z)$. Then for any constant a appearing in the first attribute $q_1(\mathcal{D}, a)$ equals $\{b \mid (a, b) \in q_1(\mathcal{D})\}$. Similarly, for any constant a, $q_2(\mathcal{D}, a)$ consists of the pairs $\{(b, c) \mid (a, b, c) \in q_2(\mathcal{D})\}$. This shows that q_1 will link the first attribute to the second one, while q_2 links the first attribute to the second and third one, as can be seen in Figure 2. We define the preference function as $f(q_1) = f(q_2) = 1$. The complete database graph is shown in Figure 2. E.g., the weight on the edge from $\{v_2\}$ to $\{t_2, v_3\}$ is equal to $f(q_2)\text{freq}((t_2, v_3), q_2(\mathcal{D}, v_2)) = 1$. □

When we disregard the weights, another example is the Gaifman graph of finite model theory [13].

Example 2. Let $\mathcal{D}$ be a database over an n-ary relation R. Consider the language $\mathcal{L}$ consisting of $q_{i,j}(x_j|x_i) \equiv \pi_{i,j} R(x_1, \ldots, x_n)$ and $f(q_{i,j}) = 1$ for all $i, j = 1, \ldots, n$. The database graph has as vertices the constants in $adom(\mathcal{D})$ and there is an edge between two constants iff they appear in the same tuple in $\mathcal{D}$. □

The database graph is a well-defined object. Indeed, we call $\langle \mathcal{D}, \mathcal{L}, f \rangle$ and $\langle \mathcal{D}', \mathcal{L}, f \rangle$ isomorphic, denoted by $\langle \mathcal{D}, \mathcal{L}, f \rangle \cong \langle \mathcal{D}', \mathcal{L}, f \rangle$, if there exists a bijection $b : adom(D) \to adom(D')$ such that for all $q(\vec{y}|\vec{x}) \in \mathcal{L}$ and $\vec{s} \in adom(\mathcal{D})^k$ for $k = |\vec{x}|$, we have for any $\vec{t} \in q(\mathcal{D}, \vec{s})$ that

$$\text{freq}(\vec{t}, q(\mathcal{D}, \vec{s})) = \text{freq}(b(\vec{t}), q(\mathcal{D}', b(\vec{s}))),$$

where b is extended to tuples $\vec{x}$ as $b(\vec{x}) = (b(x_1), \ldots, b(x_k))$.

Theorem 1. If $M = \langle \mathcal{D}, \mathcal{L}, f \rangle$ and $N = \langle \mathcal{D}', \mathcal{L}, f \rangle$ such that $M \cong N$, then G_M is isomorphic to G_N.

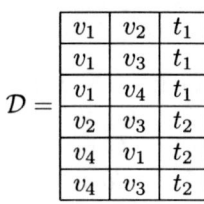 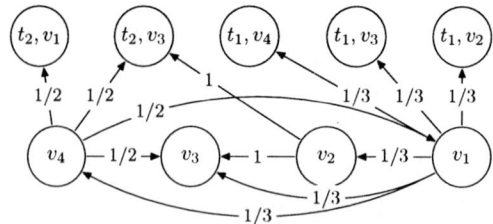

Figure 2: The database $\mathcal{D}$ (left) and the database graph G_M of $M = \langle \mathcal{D}, \mathcal{L}, f \rangle$ of Example 1 (right).

Proof. We refer for the proof to the full paper. □

We also have a monotonicity property with respect to taking sub-languages.

Theorem 2. If $M = \langle \mathcal{D}, \mathcal{L}, f \rangle$ and $N = \langle \mathcal{D}, \mathcal{L}', f' \rangle$ such that $\mathcal{L}' \subseteq \mathcal{L}$ and $f(q) = f'(q)$ for any $q \in \mathcal{L}'$, then G_N is isomorphic to a subgraph of G_M.

Proof. The proof is analogous to the proof of Theorem 1. □

In general, the reverse of Theorem 1 is not true as can be seen from the following example.

Example 3. Consider the databases $\mathcal{D}$ and $\mathcal{D}'$ shown in Figure 3. Here, different symbols denote different constants. Let $\mathcal{L}$ consist of the queries

$$q_0(x|) \equiv \pi_1 R(x, y, z, u, v),$$
$$q_1(y|x) \equiv \pi_{1,2}\sigma_{3=5} R(x, y, z, u, v),$$
$$q_2(y|x) \equiv \pi_{1,2}\sigma_{3=4} R(x, y, z, u, v),$$
$$q_3(y|x) \equiv \pi_{1,2}\sigma_{3\neq 4} R(x, y, z, u, v).$$

The preference function f assigns weight 1 to each query. It is easily verified that the graphs G_M and G_N are isomorphic and correspond to the graph shown in Figure 3. However, there is no bijection making $\langle \mathcal{D}, \mathcal{L}, f \rangle$ and $\langle \mathcal{D}', \mathcal{L}, f \rangle$ isomorphic. Indeed, from $q_1(\mathcal{D}, s)$ and $q_1(\mathcal{D}', s)$ the bijection b should map $b(t_1) = t_1$, while from $q_2(\mathcal{D}, s)$, $q_2(\mathcal{D}', s)$, $q_3(\mathcal{D}, s)$ and $q_3(\mathcal{D}', s)$ it follows that $b(t_1) = t_2$. □

The database graph is defined without taking into account any semantic relationships between attributes or additional schema constraints. However, this can be easily incorporated in the queries used in the language $\mathcal{L}$.

In the next section we define a random walk on the database graph. In order for the random walk to have nice convergence properties (see the next section), the underlying graph should be strongly connected and non-bipartite. This property turns out to be undecidable.

Theorem 3. Given a query language $\mathcal{L}$, it is undecidable whether the database graph is strongly connected and non-bipartite for all $\mathcal{D}$ and preference functions f.

Proof. First, we remark that the topology of the graph is independent of f. So, we can disregard the preference function in what follows. We use a reduction to the undecidability of satisfiability of relational algebra expressions on binary relations [8]. We construct for each $\mathbf{q}(x_1, \ldots, x_k) \in \mathrm{RA}$ the language $\mathcal{L} = \{q_1, q_2, q_3\}$ where,

$$q_1(u, z|x, y) \equiv \mathtt{if}(\exists x_1 \cdots \exists x_k \mathbf{q}(x_1, \ldots, x_k|))$$
$$\mathtt{then}$$
$$\sigma_{1\neq 2 \wedge 1=3 \wedge 2=4} R(x, y) \times R(u, z)$$
$$q_2(y|) \equiv \mathtt{if}(\exists x_1 \cdots \exists x_k \mathbf{q}(x_1, \ldots, x_k|))$$
$$\mathtt{then} \quad \pi_2 R(x, y)$$
$$q_3(z|) \equiv \mathtt{if \; not}(\exists x_1 \cdots \exists x_k \mathbf{q}(x_1, \ldots, x_k|))$$
$$\mathtt{then} \quad \pi_1 R(z, u) \cup \pi_2 R(u, z)$$

By construction, for any $\mathcal{D}$ and f, the database graph associated with $\langle \mathcal{D}, \mathcal{L}, f \rangle$ will be connected and non-bipartite iff $\mathbf{q}$ is not satisfiable.

Indeed if $\mathbf{q}$ is not satisfiable then $\mathcal{L}$ collapses to q_3. For any $\mathcal{D}$ and f, the database graph associated with $\langle \mathcal{D}, q_3, f \rangle$ is the complete graph with vertex set $adom(\mathcal{D})$. This is clearly always a strongly connected and non-bipartite graph.

For the other direction, suppose that there exists $\mathcal{D}$ and f such that the graph associated with $\langle \mathcal{D}, \mathcal{L}, f \rangle$ is disconnected or bipartite. We need to show that this implies that on $\mathcal{D}$ the query $\mathbf{q}$ is satisfiable. Therefore, we show that for any $\mathcal{D}$ and f, the database graph associated with $\langle \mathcal{D}, \{q_1, q_2\}, f \rangle$ is disconnected. W.l.o.g., we may assume that $\mathcal{D}$ only consists of tuples (s, t) such that $s \neq t$. Indeed, if $|adom(\mathcal{D})| > 1$ (The case when $|adom(\mathcal{D})| = 1$ can be disregarded), applying first the query $\pi_{14} R \times R$ ensures that $\mathcal{D}$ always contains (s, t) with $s \neq t$. We then select only those pairs (s, t) from $\mathcal{D}$ such that $s \neq t$. So, the database graph will be not connected because there is an edge in the database graph from vertex $\{s, t\}$ to vertex $\{t\}$ by q_2, but no edge exists from $\{t\}$ to $\{s, t\}$. This is because q_1 only links $\{t\}$ to vertex $\{t, t\}$, which is by construction not in $\mathcal{D}$. □

4 Random walks on databases

Let $G = (V, E, \lambda)$ be a weighted directed graph. We next define the random walk on this graph, and then show how the concept applies to database graphs.

556

$$\mathcal{D} = \begin{array}{|c|c|c|c|c|} \hline s & t_1 & \alpha & \alpha & \alpha \\ \hline s & t_1 & \alpha & \gamma & \alpha \\ \hline s & t_1 & \alpha & \gamma & \alpha \\ \hline s & t_2 & \beta & \gamma & \alpha \\ \hline s & t_2 & \beta & \beta & \alpha \\ \hline s & t_2 & \beta & \beta & \alpha \\ \hline \end{array} \qquad \mathcal{D}' = \begin{array}{|c|c|c|c|c|} \hline s & t_1 & \alpha & \alpha & \alpha \\ \hline s & t_1 & \alpha & \alpha & \alpha \\ \hline s & t_1 & \alpha & \gamma & \alpha \\ \hline s & t_2 & \beta & \gamma & \alpha \\ \hline s & t_2 & \beta & \gamma & \alpha \\ \hline s & t_2 & \beta & \beta & \alpha \\ \hline \end{array}$$

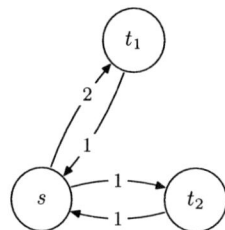

Figure 3: Two non-equivalent databases (left) giving the same database graph (right) for $\mathcal{L}$ of Example 3.

Definition 3 (RW on a graph, [7]). A simple random walk on G is the following random process: Start in a randomly selected vertex $v \in V$. Next, jump to an adjacent vertex w with probability $\lambda(v,w)/\left(\sum_{(v,w') \in E} \lambda(v,w')\right)$. This is then repeated starting from vertex w. □

A random walk on G can also be seen as a Markov chain with state space V where the transition probabilities are represented by a stochastic[1] $|V| \times |V|$-matrix $\mathbf{P}_G = (P_{vw})$, where $P_{vw} = \lambda(v,w)/\left(\sum_{(v,w') \in E} \lambda(v,w')\right)$.

Theorem (Fundamental Theorem of Markov Chains, [23]). If G is strongly connected and non-bipartite, then the Markov chain given by $\mathbf{P}_G$ has the following properties. There exists a unique stationary distribution $\vec{p}$, i.e., $\vec{p} = \vec{p}\mathbf{P}_G$ and $\sum_i p_i = 1$. Moreover, let $N(v,k)$ be the number of times the Markov chain visits v in k steps, then

$$\lim_{k \to \infty} \frac{N(v,k)}{k} = p_v.$$

□

The stationary distribution is a description of the steady-state behavior of the Markov Chain. The stationary distribution will be used to obtain rank values for partial tuples in the next section.

Definition 4 (RW on database). The random walk on $M = \langle \mathcal{D}, \mathcal{L}, f \rangle$ is the simple random walk on the database graph G_M. □

We now define the random querier. When in certain vertex of the database graph, the random querier will select a query compatible with the vertex in which he currently is. The probability of selecting such query depends on a given preference function. Once the query is asked a random tuple is selected as input parameter for the query and a random tuple is selected from the output. We make this more formal in what follows.

Let $s \subseteq adom(\mathcal{D})$. We denote by $\mathcal{L}_s$ all queries $q(\vec{y}|\vec{x}) \in \mathcal{L}$ for which there exists $\vec{s} \in s^k$ for $k = |\vec{x}|$

---
[1]A stochastic matrix is a matrix in which for each row the elements in the row sum up to one.

such that $q(\mathcal{D}, \vec{s})$ is nonempty. For a query $q(\vec{y}|\vec{x}) \in \mathcal{L}$ and $s \subseteq adom(\mathcal{D})$, let $\Gamma(q,s)$ be the set of tuples $\vec{s} \in s^k$ for $k = |\vec{x}|$ such that $q(\mathcal{D}, \vec{s})$ is nonempty. Moreover, let $\gamma(q,s) = |\Gamma(q,s)|$.

Definition 5 (Random Querier). The $(\mathcal{L}, f)$-random querier on $\mathcal{D}$ is the following random process: An initial element s is selected randomly from the set of vertices V_M from the database graph. Next, a query q is chosen from $\mathcal{L}_s$ with probability

$$\gamma(q,s)f(q)/(\sum_{q' \in \mathcal{L}_s} \gamma(q',s)f(q')),$$

and a tuple $\vec{s} \in \Gamma(q,s)$ is chosen uniformly at random. Finally, a tuple $\vec{t}$ is selected randomly from $q(\mathcal{D}, \vec{s})$. This is then repeated starting from $adom(\vec{t})$. □

Theorem 4. The random walk performed by the $(\mathcal{L}, f)$-random querier on $\mathcal{D}$ is the same random walk as the random walk on the database graph G_M of $M = \langle \mathcal{D}, \mathcal{L}, f \rangle$.

Proof. We refer for the proof to the full paper. □

Example 4. *A well-known example of a random walk is the random surfer introduced by Brin [10]. The random surfer is the same as the $(\mathcal{L}, f)$-random querier on the Web database $\mathcal{D}$, with $\mathcal{L} = \{q_1(y|x) \equiv W(x,y), q_2(x|) \equiv \delta(\pi_1 W(x,y) \cup \pi_2 W(y,x))\}$ and $f(q_1) = 1-p$ and $f(q_2) = p$. Let $V = adom(\mathcal{D})$. The transition matrix $\mathbf{P} = (P_{vw})$ of the random surfer is given by*

$$P_{vw} = \begin{cases} \frac{p}{|V|} + \frac{(1-p)}{outdeg(v)} & if (v,w) \in \mathcal{D} \\ \frac{p}{|V|} & otherwise. \end{cases}$$

In the database graph corresponding to $\langle \mathcal{D}, \mathcal{L}, f \rangle$ we have an edge (v,w) for any pair of vertices. The weight of an edge (v,w) is given by the sum of

$$f(q_2)\text{freq}(w, q_2(\mathcal{D})) = p\frac{1}{|V|},$$

and $f(q_1)\text{freq}(w, q_1(\mathcal{D}, v))$ which is equal to

$$\begin{cases} \frac{1-p}{outdeg(v)} & if (v,w) \in \mathcal{D} \\ 0 & otherwise. \end{cases}$$

Hence, the $(\mathcal{L}, f)$-random querier on $\mathcal{D}$ has the same transition matrix as the one of the random surfer.

Also other link analysis algorithms fit perfectly in the random queries framework.

Example 5 (sHITS, [6]). The stochastic HITS algorithm has as transition matrix

$$P_{vw} = \frac{|\{x \in V | (x,v) \in E \land (x,w) \in E\}|}{\sum_{y \in V} |\{x \in V | (x,v) \in E \land (x,y) \in E\}|}.$$

A simple computation shows that the $(\mathcal{L}, f)$-random querier with $\mathcal{L} = \{q(z|x) \equiv \pi_{2,4}\sigma_{1=3}W(u,x) \times W(y,z)\}$ and $f(q) = 1$ results in the same random walk.

We are primarily interested in the stationary distribution of the random walks. By the Fundamental Theorem of Markov Chains, this can be obtained by computing the matrix and solving the eigenvector problem. However, for undirected graphs we have a closed form expression for the stationary distribution.

Theorem ([23]). Let $G = (V, E)$ a connected, non-bipartite, undirected and un-weighted graph and let $m = |E|$. Then the stationary distribution $(p_v)_{v \in V}$ of the simple random walk on G is given by $\deg(v)/2m$.

We have the following result.

Theorem 5. It is decidable for a given weighted directed graph $G = (V, E, \lambda)$, whether there exists an undirected multi-graph $G_u = (V_u, E_u)$ such that the simple random walks on G and G_u have the same transition matrix. Moreover, the graph G_u can be computed, if it exists.

Proof. (Sketch) Note that weighted directed graph G can be transformed in a graph with integer weights by the multiplying for each vertex V all weights of edges starting in v with the least common multiplier (l.c.m) of the denominators of weights of the edges starting in v. So, we may assume that G has integer weights. Also note that for each node $v \in V$ we are allowed to multiply the weights of all outgoing edges by the same integer n_v without affecting the random walk. We get rid of the integer weights by replacing each edge (v, w) with integer weight k, by k edges (v, w) of weight 1. We abuse notation and call this edge set also E. So, in order to decide whether G can be replaced by an undirected multigraph we need to check whether there exist integers (n_v) with $v \in V$ such that the indegree becomes equal to the outdegree for every vertex v, or for every v,

$$\sum_{w:(v,w) \in E} n_v \lambda(v,w) = \sum_{w:(w,v) \in E} n_w \lambda(w,v). \quad (1)$$

This can be decided using standard integer programming techniques [27]. So the answer to the decision problem is yes iff there exists a solution to equation (1). In case there exists a solution, we define $G_u = (V_u, E_u)$ as $V_u = V$ and E_u contains an undirected edge (v, w) for every pair of edges (v, w) and (w, v) in E. □

The importance of the previous result is that before starting computing the stationary distribution of a random walk, one can decide whether the walk corresponds to a walk on an undirected graph. In this case the stationary distribution can be computed much more efficiently, using the Fundamental Theorem of Markov Chains.

For some languages it can be shown that there exists integers n_v such that Equation (1) holds for any $\mathcal{D}$.

Example 6. Consider the database $\mathcal{D}$ consisting of a single relation R, and let $\mathcal{L} = \{q_{i,j}(x_j|x_i) \equiv \pi_{i,j}R(x_1, \ldots, x_n) \mid 1 \leq i \leq n, 1 \leq j \leq n\}$. All queries have preference 1. Let G be the database graph. Then there exists an undirected graph G_u satisfying the property stated in Theorem 5. Indeed, for each s and each t such that $t \in q_{i,j}(\mathcal{D}, s)$ we have an edge (s, t) of weight $\text{freq}(t, q_{i,j}(\mathcal{D}, s))$. The l.c.m. of the denominators for all outgoing edges from s is $|q_{i,j}(\mathcal{D}, s)|$, so we get the integer weight

$$\begin{aligned}\lambda(s,t) &= \text{freq}(t, q_{i,j}(\mathcal{D},s))|q_{i,j}(\mathcal{D},s)| \\ &= |\{\vec{u} \in \mathcal{D} \mid u_i = s \land u_j = t\}|.\end{aligned}$$

We get the same integer weight for the edge (t, s), so $\lambda(s, t) = \lambda(t, s)$ and hence Equation (1) holds for $n_s = 1$ for all s. This reasoning is clearly independent from $\mathcal{D}$. □

5 Rank algorithms

In this section we describe two methods for obtaining rank values for partial tuples. Both are based on eigenvector computations. The first one, RELWALK, is based on the stationary distribution of a random walk on the database graph similarly to PageRank. The second, RELHITS, uses the mutual reinforcement technique of HITS. Therefore, the assignment of rank values is based on the normalized principal eigenvector of a matrix associated to a certain subgraph of the database graph. Both algorithms output rank values of partial tuples which can serve either directly as a ranking of query results, or as input for top-k selection and join algorithms.

5.1 RELWALK

The RELWALK algorithm takes as input the database $\mathcal{D}$, a language $\mathcal{L}$ and preference function f, and computes the rank values for subsets $s \subseteq adom(\mathcal{D})$. The rank value of s corresponds to the value p_s in the stationary distribution $\vec{p}$ of the random walk on the database graph G_M of $M = \langle \mathcal{D}, \mathcal{L}, f \rangle$. The Fundamental Theorem of Markov Chains says that p_s gives the probability that the $(\mathcal{L}, f)$-random querier on $\mathcal{D}$ visits s, given that he was allowed to ask the queries in $\mathcal{L}$ for infinite long time. Intuitively, frequently visited states are regarded as more important. We compute the stationary distribution $\vec{p}$ by solving the eigenvector problem $\vec{p}\mathbf{P} = \vec{p}$ where $\mathbf{P}$ is the transition matrix of the random walk.

The database graph must be strongly connected and non-bipartite in order for the stationary distribution to exist. Of course, not every database graph has this property. However, we can alter the query language such that we always end up with a strongly connected and non-bipartite database graph. Indeed, we simply add queries of the form $q(x_{i_1}, \ldots, x_{i_k}|) \equiv \pi_{i_1,\ldots,i_k} R$ where the projections are chosen such that no new vertices are introduced in the database graph. The database graph is now strongly connected since all vertices are connected to each other. It is also non-bipartite since all vertices have a self-loop. Note that the PageRank algorithm uses the same adaptation by adding the query $q_2(x|) \equiv \pi_1 R(x,y) \cup \pi_2 R(y,x)$.

5.2 RELHITS

In contrast to RELWALK, RELHITS is query dependent. Therefore, RELHITS algorithm takes as input $M = \langle \mathcal{D}, \mathcal{L}, f \rangle$ and an imposed query q. The algorithm considers the database graph G_M and selects the subgraph $G'_M = (V'_M, E'_M, \lambda'_M)$ where

$$E'_M = \{(v,w) \in E \mid w \subseteq adom(Q(q,\mathcal{D}))\},$$

and V'_M consists only of nodes connected by edges in E'_M. The weight function λ'_M is the restriction of λ_M to E'_M. From the graph G'_M we form the $m \times n$ matrix $\mathbf{Q} = (Q_{vw}) = (\lambda'_M(v,w))$, where $m = |H = \{v \in V'_M \mid \exists w \in V'_M(v,w) \in E'_M\}|$ and $n = |A = \{w \in V'_M \mid \exists v \in V'_M(v,w) \in E'_M\}|$. The elements in the sets H and A can be thought of as the hubs and the authorities in the context of the HITS algorithm and therefore RELHITS scores h_j and a_j are computed iteratively as follows.

$$\begin{cases} h_j^t & \leftarrow \sum_{(j,i) \in E'_M} \lambda'_M(j,i) h_i^{(t-1)} \\ a_j^t & \leftarrow \sum_{(i,j) \in E'_M} \lambda'_M(i,j) a_i^{(t-1)} \end{cases} \quad (2)$$

The main idea is that important hubs are related to important authorities and vice versa. Moreover, the update schema (2) converges to the principal eigenvector $\vec{h}$ of $\mathbf{QQ}^T$ for the hub scores, while the authority scores converge to the principal eigenvector $\vec{a}$ of $\mathbf{Q}^T\mathbf{Q}$ ([22]). The RELHITS normalizes these eigenvectors and outputs them.

6 Experimental evaluation

In this section we describe our implementation for constructing the database graph and obtaining rank values of partial tuples. We give the setup of our experiments and present the corresponding results.

We implemented the database graph construction on top of the Postgres relational database management system. JDBC has been used for connecting to the database system. We ran the RELWALK and the RELHITS algorithm on the bibliography database [2]. This database $\mathcal{D}$ consists of a single relation R with attributes `paper_title`, `author`, `conference`, and `year`. There are 7 677 tuples in the database, 3 062 unique paper titles and 4 203 unique authors.

The main goal of the experiments is to show that for different query languages there are different rankings obtained. These rankings are closely related to the queries used for the construction of the database graph and in all the cases have a meaningful interpretation in terms of these queries. The experiments also show the flexibility of our general framework. Any weighted set of queries can be used to construct a database graph from $\mathcal{D}$. This raises the question which queries should be used and this is a very challenging problem to explore indeed. Computing the rank values of partial tuples for a given query language is only preprocessing step. Once the rank values are computed they can be used for ranking tuples in the answer of queries imposed on the database. We illustrate this for simple query languages and queries in the next sections.

6.1 Experimental setup

For the purpose of the experiments we have constructed the database graphs and obtained partial tuple rankings using both the RELWALK and RELHITS algorithms. For each one of the algorithms we constructed the corresponding database graphs using two different query languages, namely $\mathcal{L}_1$ and $\mathcal{L}_2$ for REL-WALK and $\mathcal{L}'_1$ and $\mathcal{L}'_2$ for RELHITS. The languages were selected in such a way that $\mathcal{L}_1$ (and $\mathcal{L}_2$) is expected to show similar rankings to $\mathcal{L}'_1$ (and $\mathcal{L}'_2$).

In the sequel we show the ranked outputs (along with the rank values) we obtained when the following two queries were imposed to the database: $q(x_2|) \equiv \pi_2 R$ and $q'(x_2|) \equiv \pi_2 \sigma_{6=\text{`H. Garcia-Molina'}} \sigma_{1=5} R \times R$. Query q is a simple projection on all the authors of the database, while query q' is a projection on all the authors of the database that are co-authors of "H. Garcia-Molina". The selection of q and q' is made mainly for two reasons. First, their output consists of partial tuples already assigned a rank value from our ranking algorithms and thus we do not need to employ any other additional procedure for ranking aggregates. Second, the output of the queries demonstrates the different features of the proposed ranking algorithms.

Query languages for RELWALK

The first language used for obtaining RELWALK rankings was $\mathcal{L}_1 = \{q_1(x_j|x_i), q_2(x|)\}$ where $q_1(x_j|x_i) \equiv \pi_{i,j} R(x_1,x_2,x_3,x_4)$ with $i \neq j$ and preference $f_1 = 0.9$ and $q_2(x|) \equiv \pi_1 R \cup \pi_2 R \cup \pi_3 R \cup \pi_4 R$ with preference $f_2 = 0.1$. The intuition behind $\mathcal{L}_1$ is exactly what one

---
[2]The data set is available at `http://liinwww.ira.uka.de/bibliography/`

expects the random querier to do when he has the freedom to do a random walk on partial tuples of size one. Query q_2 makes sure that the constructed database graph is strongly connected and non-bipartite. Therefore, there is an underlying stationary distribution. Additionally, notice that for $\mathcal{L}_1$ we can apply the result of Example 6 and we can show that the degree of nodes in the corresponding undirected graph, and hence the stationary distribution, are frequency related. The database graph constructed by RELWALK when language $\mathcal{L}_1$ was considered consists of a total number of 7 294 nodes (partial tuples of size 1) and 50 434 edges (relational links taken into consideration for obtaining the ranking) when query q_1 is considered. The query q_2 makes the graph a complete graph.

The second language used for obtaining RELWALK rankings was $\mathcal{L}_2 = \{q_1(x_j|x_i), q_2(x_2|x_6), q_3(x|)\}$ where $q_1(x_j|x_i) \equiv \pi_{i,j} R(x_1, x_2, x_3, x_4)$ with $i \neq j$ and preference $f_1 = 0.45$, $q_2(x_2|x_6) \equiv \pi_{2,6}\sigma_{1=5,2\neq 6} R \times R$ with preference $f_2 = 0.45$, and finally $q_3(x|) \equiv \pi_1 R \cup \pi_2 R \cup \pi_3 R \cup \pi_4 R$ with preference $f_3 = 0.1$. For this language the results of Example 6 do not apply and thus we expect the obtained rankings to be not related to frequency. This is due to the co-author query q_2 that has been included in the language. The database graph constructed using language $\mathcal{L}_2$ has 7 294 nodes and 68 012 edges when queries q_1 and q_2 are only considered. Query q_3 again in this case makes the graph a complete graph.

Query languages for RELHITS

The two languages used for obtaining the RELHITS rankings are $\mathcal{L}'_1$ and $\mathcal{L}'_2$ and are selected such that they have similar flavor to $\mathcal{L}_1$ and $\mathcal{L}_2$ used for RELWALK. This means that they are expected to give similar rankings. Language $\mathcal{L}'_1 = \{q_1(x_2|x_3), q_2(x_2|x_4)\}$ consists of $q_1(x_2|x_3) \equiv \pi_{2,3} R(x_1, x_2, x_3, x_4)$ with preference $f_1 = 0.5$ and $q_2(x_2|x_4) \equiv \pi_{2,4} R(x_1, x_2, x_3, x_4)$ with preference $f_2 = 0.5$. The intuition behind $\mathcal{L}'_1$ is that, as in $\mathcal{L}_1$, partial tuples of size 1 and direct links between them are again included in the database graph. Language $\mathcal{L}'_2 = \{q_1(x_2|x_3, x_6)\}$ on the other hand consists of a single query $q_1(x_2|x_3, x_6) \equiv \pi_{2,3,6}\sigma_{2\neq 6, 1=5} R \times R$ with preference equal to 1. This apparently is the co-author query so that there is a relationship between $\mathcal{L}'_2$ and $\mathcal{L}_2$ and thus the comparison between the obtained rankings makes sense. For the case of RELHITS the size of the constructed database graph depends not only on the query languages ($\mathcal{L}'_1$ and $\mathcal{L}'_2$) used for the graph construction, but also on the imposed queries q and q' the results of which we want to rank. So in the case of $\mathcal{L}'_1$ and query q the constructed database graph consists of 4 232 nodes and 11 375 edges, while for the same language but for query q' the corresponding graph of RELHITS consists of only 86 nodes and 171 edges. For language $\mathcal{L}'_2$ the database graph that corresponds to q consists of 4 203 nodes and 24 620 edges while the one that corresponds to q' has only 144 nodes and 393 edges.

6.2 Experimental results

The ranked output for q when RELWALK ranking algorithm is used is shown in Tables 1 and 2 for the query languages $\mathcal{L}_1$ and $\mathcal{L}_2$ respectively. Rankings obtained by using $\mathcal{L}_1$ are related to frequency and thus are used as a baseline case. On the other hand, the effect on the co-author query in $\mathcal{L}_2$ appears in the obtained rankings. For example, "Nicolas Adiba" is included in the most highly ranked authors, though he appears to have a single paper in the database. However, he participates in a paper with 18 other co-authors among which there are "Michael J. Carey" (ranked first) with 47 entries and "Daniela Florescu" with 16 entries. The same holds for "Steve Kirsch" and "Michael Blow" who are all authors of the same 18-author paper.

The results obtained for q using the rankings of the RELHITS algorithm are shown in Tables 3 and 4 for query languages $\mathcal{L}'_1$ and $\mathcal{L}'_2$ respectively. There, we can make the similar observations as those made for the rankings obtained using the RELWALK algorithm. For example, "Eugene J. Shekita" appears to have much less entries in the database than authors ranked after him. This is due to the fact that "Michael J. Carey" (first in the ranking) appears to be among his co-authors.

A comparison plot for our rankings is shown in Figure 4. Each pair of rankings r, r' is compared by taking the first k authors of each ranking (x-axis) and forming the sets $r(k), r'(k)$. The y axis is the value of $\frac{|r(k) \cap r'(k)|}{k}$ and is used as a similarity between the two rankings. For the results of the query $q(y|) \equiv \pi_2 R(x, y)$ we use the first 200 ranked authors. In the plot the subscripts in the names of the algorithm correspond to the language used for the ranking.

We performed similar experiments for ranking the co-authors of "H. Garcia-Molina". Tables 5 and 6 for RELWALK and Tables 7 and 8 for RELHITS show highest ranked authors that are co-authors of H. "Garcia-Molina" (query $q' \equiv \pi_2 \sigma_{6=\text{'H. Garcia-Molina'}} \sigma_{1=5} R \times R$). As before the languages $\mathcal{L}_1$ ($\mathcal{L}'_1$) and $\mathcal{L}_2$ ($\mathcal{L}'_2$) were used for constructing the corresponding graphs. Phenomena analogous to the previous experiment appear here as well. For example in Table 6, "Edward Chang" has only two papers in the database but still he is ranked 5th. The same for "Svetlozar Nestorov" who is highly ranked though he has only 3 entries in the database. This is due to his co-author list which contains very highly ranked authors like S. Abiteboul, J. Widom, R. Motwani and J. Ullman.

In Figure 5 we show an overall comparison plot of the rankings for elements which are answers to the query q' The assumptions and notation are the same as those followed in the previous experiment. For the comparisons presented in Figure 5 we only used the 70 highest ranked authors (out of the 104).

RelWalk Ranking	
Language: $\mathcal{L}_1 = \{q_1(x_j\|x_i), q_2(x\|)\}$	
with: $q_1(x_j\|x_i) \equiv \pi_{i,j}R(x_1,x_2,x_3,x_4)$ with $i \neq j$ $\quad f_1 = 0.9$	
$\quad\quad q_2(x\|) \equiv \pi_1 R \cup \pi_2 R \cup \pi_3 R \cup \pi_4 R \quad f_2 = 0.1$	
H. Garcia-Molina	1.608E-4
Michael J. Carey	1.608E-4
H. V. Jagadish	1.569E-4
David J. DeWitt	1.552E-4
S. Abiteboul	1.530E-4
Rakesh Agrawal	1.513E-4
C. Faloutsos	1.508E-4
Surajit Chaudhuri	1.502E-4
Michael Stonebraker	1.502E-4
Raghu Ramakrishnan	1.497E-4
Jeffrey F. Naughton	1.497E-4
Jennifer Widom	1.491E-4
Yannis E. Ioannidis	1.486E-4
A. Levy	1.480E-4

Table 1: RelWalk ranking for all the authors in the database using $\mathcal{L}_1$.

6.3 Discussion

The experiments conducted and described in the previous subsection show that the obtained rankings are highly dependent on the query languages that are used for constructing the database graphs. For example when the co-author query was included in the language $\mathcal{L}_2$ the ranking was highly influenced by co-author relationships, meaning that authors with less papers but with more (or highly-ranked) co-authors appear high in the obtained rankings. Additionally, the second experiment gives an idea of how different RelWalk and RelHits are, since the latter is query dependent and it only considers the part of the database that is related to the imposed query. This difference although not apparent in the first experiment where the imposed query was considering all the authors in the database, it becomes obvious in the second case where only the co-authors of "H. Garcia-Molina" are to be considered. The corresponding comparison Figures 4 and 5 also imply this difference in the behavior of the two ranking algorithms for different queries.

7 Conclusions

We have shown how to associate with each database, query language, and preference function a unique database graph and explored some of its interesting properties. The database graph provides a nice framework for extending existing and creating new link analysis algorithms for the Web and relational databases. The flexibility of the framework is provided by the use of relational algebra queries. The database graph also enables us to define the random querier which performs a random walk on databases by asking queries in each step of the walk. We applied our concepts to

RelWalk Ranking	
Language: $\mathcal{L}_2 = \{q_1(x_j\|x_i), q_2(x_2\|x_6), q_3(x\|)\}$	
with: $q_1(x_j\|x_i) \equiv \pi_{i,j}R(x_1,x_2,x_3,x_4)$ with $i \neq j$ $\quad f_1 = 0.45$	
$\quad\quad q_2(x_2\|x_6) \equiv \pi_{2,6}\sigma_{1=5,2\neq 6} R \times R \quad f_2 = 0.45$	
$\quad\quad q_3(y\|) \equiv \pi_1 R \cup \pi_2 R \cup \pi_3 R \cup \pi_4 R \quad f_3 = 0.1$	
Michael J. Carey	2.695E-4
S. Abiteboul	2.142E-4
A. Cichocki	1.990E-4
V. Kashyap	1.990E-4
R. Brice	1.990E-4
J. Fowler	1.990E-4
W. Bohrer	1.990E-4
R. J. Bayardo	1.990E-4
David J. DeWitt	1.983E-4
H. Garcia-Molina	1.919E-4
Daniela Florescu	1.915E-4
Steve Kirsch	1.844E-4
Michael Blow	1.844E-4
Nicolas Adiba	1.844E-4

Table 2: RelWalk ranking for all the authors in the database using $\mathcal{L}_2$.

RelHits Ranking	
Language: $\mathcal{L}'_1 = \{q_1(x_2\|x_3), q_2(x_2\|x_4)\}$	
with: $q_1(x_2\|x_3) \equiv \pi_{2,3}R(x_1,x_2,x_3,x_4) \quad f_1 = 0.5$	
$\quad\quad q_2(x_2\|x_4) \equiv \pi_{2,4}R(x_1,x_2,x_3,x_4) \quad f_2 = 0.5$	
H. Garcia-Molina	0.007572
Michael J. Carey	0.006437
H. V. Jagadish	0.006081
Surajit Chaudhuri	0.004740
David J. DeWitt	0.004603
Rakesh Agrawal	0.004291
A. Levy	0.004283
Jennifer Widom	0.004207
S. Abiteboul	0.004179
C. Faloutsos	0.004056
Raghu Ramakrishnan	0.003795
Jeffrey F. Naughton	0.003765

Table 3: RelHits rankings for all the authors in the database using $\mathcal{L}'_1$.

obtain two algorithms that provide rank values on partial tuples. These values are interesting on their own, but can also serve as input for top-k selection and join algorithms to obtain ranking of query results.

We point out some interesting questions and open problems:

- How can the database graph be used to define measures of similarity between categorical data? Possible measures include the shortest path between tuples and the commute distance between nodes on the database graph.

- Is there a more close connection between the expressive power of $\mathcal{L}$ and the database graph and random querier? What are the properties of the random querier with memory ([14]).

- Finally, is there an objective way of selecting the query language used for defining the database graph.

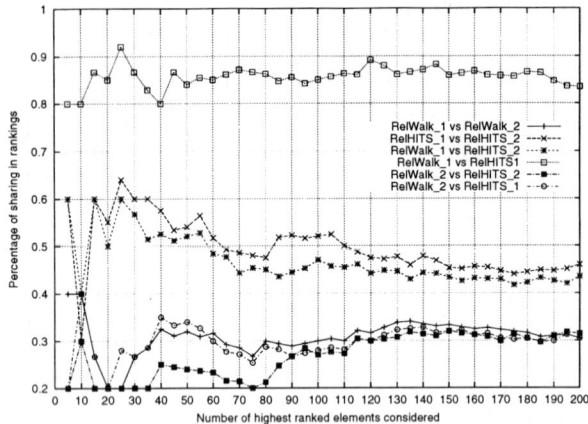

Figure 4: Comparison of rankings for all authors in the database.

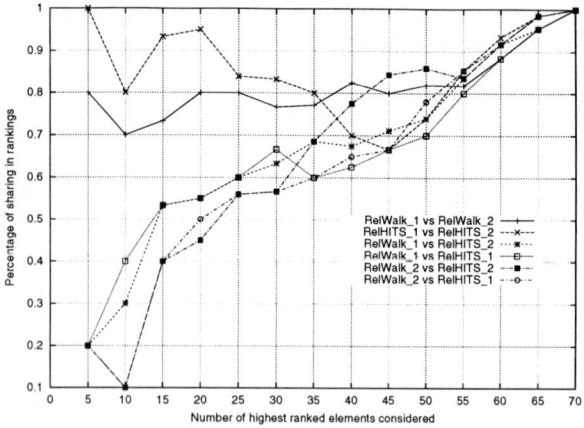

Figure 5: Comparison of rankings for all co-authors of 'H. Garcia-Molina'.

RELHITS Ranking	
Language: $\mathcal{L}'_2 = \{q_1(x_2\|x_3, x_6)\}$	
with: $q_1(x_2\|x_3, x_6) \equiv \pi_{2,3,6}\sigma_{2\neq 6, 1=5} R \times R$ $f_1 = 1.0$	
Michael J. Carey	0.55364
David J. DeWitt	0.02967
Jeffrey F. Naughton	0.02593
H. Garcia-Molina	0.02593
Yannis E. Ioannidis	0.02266
Miron Livny	0.01887
Raghu Ramakrishnan	0.01659
H. Pirahesh	0.01442
Michael J. Franklin	0.01086
Eugene J. Shekita	0.01047
Jennifer Widom	0.01042
Praveen Seshadri	0.00925

Table 4: RELHITS rankings for all the authors in the database using $\mathcal{L}'_2$.

Acknowledgment

We would like to thank Aris Gionis for helpful discussions.

References

[1] S. Abiteboul, R. Hull, and V. Vianu. *Foundations of Databases*. Addison-Wesley, 1995.

[2] S. Agrawal, S. Chaudhuri, and G. Das. DBXplorer: A system for keyword-based search over relational databases. In *ICDE*, 2002.

[3] S. Agrawal, S. Chaudhuri, G. Das, and A. Gionis. Automated ranking of database query results. In *CIDR*, 2003.

[4] A. Balmin, V. Hristidis, and Y. Papakonstantinou. ObjectRank: Authority-based keyword search in databases. In *VLDB*, 2004.

[5] G. Bhalotia, A. Hulgeri, C. Nakhe, S. Chakrabarti, and S. Sudarshan. Keyword searching and browsing in databases using BANKS. In *ICDE*, 2002.

RELWALK Ranking	
Language: $\mathcal{L}_1 = \{q_1(x_j\|x_i), q_2(x\|)\}$	
with: $q_1(x_j\|x_i) \equiv \pi_{i,j} R(x_1, x_2, x_3, x_4)$ with $i \neq j$ $f_1 = 0.9$	
$q_2(x\|) \equiv \pi_1 R \cup \pi_2 R \cup \pi_3 R \cup \pi_4 R$ $f_2 = 0.1$	
S. Abiteboul	1.530E-4
Raghu Ramakrishnan	1.497E-4
Jennifer Widom	1.491E-4
A. Silberschatz	1.480E-4
J. Ullman	1.425E-4
Rajeev Motwani	1.408E-4
Anand Rajaraman	1.391E-4
Luis Gravano	1.391E-4
Anthony Tomasic	1.375E-4
Ramana Yerneni	1.375E-4
Vasilis Vassalos	1.375E-4
Yannis Papakonstantinou	1.375E-4
Narayanan Shivakumar	1.375E-4
Sergey Brin	1.375E-4
Janet L. Wiener	1.375E-4
Kenneth Salem	1.375E-4

Table 5: RELWALK rankings for all co-authors of 'H. Garcia-Molina' using $\mathcal{L}_1$.

[6] K. Bharat and M. Henzinger. Improved algorithms for topic distillation in a hyperlinked environment. In *SIGIR*, 1998.

[7] B. Bollobás. *Modern Graph Theory*. Springer-Verlag, 1998.

[8] E. Börger, E. Grädel, and Y. Gurevich. *The Classical Decision Problem*. Springer-Verlag, 1997.

[9] A. Borodin, J. S. Rosenthal, G. O. Roberts, and P. Tsaparas. Finding authorities and hubs from link structures on the World Wide Web. In *WWW*, 2001.

[10] S. Brin, R. Motwani, L. Page, R. Motwani, and T. Winograd. What can you do with the web in your pocket? *Data Engineering Bulletin*, 1998.

[11] S. Brin and L. Page. The anatomy of a large-scale hypertextual Web search engine. *Computer Networks and ISDN Systems*, 30:107–117, 1998.

RelWalk Ranking	
Language: $\mathcal{L}_2 = \{q_1(x_j\|x_i), q_2(x_2\|x_6), q_3(x\|)\}$	
with: $q_1(x_j\|x_i) \equiv \pi_{i,j} R(x_1, x_2, x_3, x_4)$ with $i \neq j$	$f_1 = 0.45$
$q_2(x_2\|x_6) \equiv \pi_{2,6} \sigma_{1=5, 2\neq 6} R \times R$	$f_2 = 0.45$
$q_3(x\|) \equiv \pi_1 R \cup \pi_2 R \cup \pi_3 R \cup \pi_4 R$	$f_3 = 0.1$
S. Abiteboul	2.142E-4
Jennifer Widom	1.771E-4
A. Silberschatz	1.736E-4
Raghu Ramakrishnan	1.703E-4
Edward Chang	1.619E-4
J. Ullman	1.531E-4
Rajeev Motwani	1.498E-4
Roy Goldman	1.498E-4
Anand Rajaraman	1.490E-4
Svetlozar Nestorov	1.479E-4
Ramana Yerneni	1.443E-4
Yannis Papakonstantinou	1.439E-4
Luis Gravano	1.432E-4
Vasilis Vassalos	1.428E-4
Joachim Hammer	1.423E-4
Ming-Chien Shan	1.419E-4

Table 6: RelWalk rankings for all co-authors of 'H. Garcia-Molina' using $\mathcal{L}_2$.

RelHITS Ranking	
Language: $\mathcal{L}'_1 = \{q_1(x_2\|x_3), q_2(x_2\|x_4)\}$	
with: $q_1(x_2\|x_3) \equiv \pi_{2,3} R(x_1, x_2, x_3, x_4)$	$f_1 = 0.5$
$q_2(x_2\|x_4) \equiv \pi_{2,4} R(x_1, x_2, x_3, x_4)$	$f_2 = 0.5$
Jennifer Widom	0.0552
Ramana Yerneni	0.0487
Narayanan Shivakumar	0.0417
Joachim Hammer	0.0390
Luis Gravano	0.0365
Anthony Tomasic	0.0326
Chen-Chuan K. Chang	0.0298
Yannis Papakonstantinou	0.0294
Junghoo Cho	0.0291
Yue Zhuge	0.0262
Vasilis Vassalos	0.0258
Janet L. Wiener	0.0254
Sudarshan S. Chawathe	0.0245
Jeffrey Ullman	0.0238

Table 7: RelHITS rankings for all co-authors of 'H. Garcia-Molina' using $\mathcal{L}'_1$.

RelHITS Ranking	
Language: $\mathcal{L}'_2 = \{q_1(x_2\|x_3, x_6)\}$	
with: $q_1(x_2\|x_3, x_6) \equiv \pi_{2,3,6} \sigma_{2\neq 6, 1=5} R \times R$	$f_1 = 1.0$
Jennifer Widom	0.0514
Narayanan Shivakumar	0.0456
Ramana Yerneni	0.0424
Luis Gravano	0.0352
Joachim Hammer	0.0350
Yannis Papakonstantinou	0.0330
Wilburt J. Labio	0.0285
Chen-Chuan K. Chang	0.0258
Junghoo Cho	0.0254
Vasilis Vassalos	0.0249
Anthony Tomasic	0.0233
Chen Li	0.0223
Jeffrey Ullman	0.0223
Yue Zhuge	0.0203

Table 8: RelHITS rankings for all co-authors of 'H. Garcia-Molina' using $\mathcal{L}'_2$.

[12] C. Ding, X. He, P. Husbands and H. Zha, and H.D. Simon. PageRank, HITS and a unified framework for link analysis. In *SIGIR*, 2002.

[13] H. D. Ebbinghaus and J. Flum. *Finite Model Theory*. Springer-Verlag, 1995.

[14] R. Fagin, A. Karlin, J. Kleinberg, P. Raghavan, S. Rajagopalan, R. Rubinfeld, M. Sudan, and A. Tomkins. Random walks with "back buttons". *Annals of Applied Probability*, 11(3):810–862, 2001.

[15] R. Fagin, A. Lotem, and M. Naor. Optimal aggregation algorithms for middleware. In *PODS*, 2001.

[16] H. Garcia-Molina, J. Ullman, and J. Widom. *Database Systems, The Complete Book*. Prentice Hall, 2002.

[17] D. Gibson, J. Kleinberg, and P. Raghavan. Clustering categorical data: An approach based on dynamical systems. In *VLDB*, 1998.

[18] V. Hristidis and Y. Papakonstantinou. DISCOVER: Keyword search in relational databases. In *VLDB*, 2002.

[19] V. Hristidis and Y. Papakonstantinou. Algorithms and applications for answering ranked queries using ranked views. *VLDB Journal*, 2003.

[20] I. F. Ilyas, W. G. Aref, and A. K. Elmagarmid. Supporting top-k join queries in relational databases. In *VLDB*, 2003.

[21] G. Jeh and J. Widom. SimRank: a measure of structural-context similarity. In *KDD*, 2002.

[22] J. Kleinberg. Authoritative sources in a hyperlinked environment. *Journal of ACM*, 46, 1999.

[23] R. Motwani and P. Rhaghavan. *Randomized Algorithms*. MIT Press, 1995.

[24] A. Natsev, Y.-C. Chang, J.R. Smith, C.-S. Li, and J.S. Vitter. Supporting incremental join queries on ranked inputs. In *VLDB*, 2001.

[25] A. Ng, A. Zheng, and M. Jordan. Stable algorithms for link analysis. In *SIGIR*, 2001.

[26] C. R. Palmer and C. Faloutsos. Electricity based external similarity of categorical attributes. In *PAKDD*, 2003.

[27] A. Schrijver. *Theory of Linear and Integer Programming*. John Wiley & Sons, 1998.

ObjectRank: Authority-Based Keyword Search in Databases[*]

Andrey Balmin
IBM Almaden
Research Center
San Jose, CA 95120
abalmin@us.ibm.com

Vagelis Hristidis
School of Computer Science
Florida International University
Miami, FL 33199
vagelis@cs.fiu.edu

Yannis Papakonstantinou
Computer Science
UC, San Diego
La Jolla, CA 92093
yannis@cs.ucsd.edu

Abstract

The ObjectRank system applies authority-based ranking to keyword search in databases modeled as labeled graphs. Conceptually, authority originates at the nodes (objects) containing the keywords and flows to objects according to their semantic connections. Each node is ranked according to its authority with respect to the particular keywords. One can adjust the weight of global importance, the weight of each keyword of the query, the importance of a result actually containing the keywords versus being referenced by nodes containing them, and the volume of authority flow via each type of semantic connection. Novel performance challenges and opportunities are addressed. First, schemas impose constraints on the graph, which are exploited for performance purposes. Second, in order to address the issue of authority ranking with respect to the given keywords (as opposed to Google's global PageRank) we precompute single keyword ObjectRanks and combine them during run time. We conducted user surveys and a set of performance experiments on multiple real and synthetic datasets, to assess the semantic meaningfulness and performance of ObjectRank.

1 Introduction

PageRank [9] is an excellent tool to rank the global importance of the pages of the Web, proven by the success of Google [1]. However, Google uses PageRank as a tool

[*] Work supported by NSF IDM 9734548 and NSF ITR 313384.

Permission to copy without fee all or part of this material is granted provided that the copies are not made or distributed for direct commercial advantage, the VLDB copyright notice and the title of the publication and its date appear, and notice is given that copying is by permission of the Very Large Data Base Endowment. To copy otherwise, or to republish, requires a fee and/or special permission from the Endowment.

**Proceedings of the 30th VLDB Conference,
Toronto, Canada, 2004**

[1] http://www.Google.com

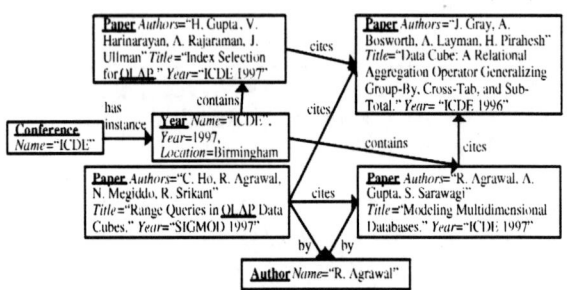

Figure 1: A subset of the DBLP graph

to measure the global importance of the pages, independently of a keyword query. (Google also uses other IR techniques to estimate the relevance of a page to a keyword query, which is then combined with the PageRank value to calculate the final score of a page.) More recent works [19, 27] apply PageRank to estimate the relevance of pages to a keyword query. We appropriately extend and modify PageRank to perform keyword search in databases for which there is a natural flow of authority between their objects (e.g.: bibliographic or complaints databases as we explain below).

Consider the example of Figure 1, which illustrates a small subset of the DBLP database in the form of a labeled graph (author, conference and year nodes except for "R. Agrawal", "ICDE" and "ICDE 1997" respectively are omitted to simplify the figure). Schema graphs, such as the one of Figure 3, describe the structure of database graphs. Given a keyword query, e.g. the single keyword query "OLAP", ObjectRank sorts the database objects by their importance with respect to the user-provided keywords. Figure 2 illustrates the top-10 "OLAP" papers in the DBLP subset (produced by our online demo at http://www.db.ucsd.edu/ObjectRank)[2] currently used by the ObjectRank prototype. Notice that many entries (the "Data Cube" and the "Modeling Multidimen-

[2] The DBLP subset currently used by ObjectRank was copied from our XKeyword [21] database (demo available at http://www.db.ucsd.edu/XKeyword) and consists of the available publications in 12 major database conferences, including SIGMOD, VLDB, PODS, ICDE, ICDT and EDBT, up to year 2001.

sional Databases" papers in Figure 1) of the top-10 list do not contain the keyword "OLAP" ("OLAP" is not even contained in their abstracts) but they clearly constitute important papers in the OLAP area, since they may be referenced by other papers of the OLAP area or may have been written by authors who have written other important "OLAP" papers.

Conceptually, the ranking is produced in the following way: Myriads of random surfers are initially found at the objects containing the keyword "OLAP" and then they traverse the database graph. In particular, at any time step a random surfer is found at a node and either (i) makes a move to an adjacent node by traversing an edge, or (ii) jumps randomly to an "OLAP" node without following any of the links. The probability that a particular traversal happens depends on multiple factors, including the type of the edge (in contrast to the Web link-based search systems [9, 19, 27]). These factors are depicted in an authority transfer schema graph. Figure 4 illustrates the authority transfer schema graph that corresponds to the setting that produced the results of Figure 2. Assuming that the probability that the surfer moves back to an "OLAP" node is 15% (damping factor [9]), the collective probability to move to a referenced paper is up to 85% × 70% (70% is the authority transfer rate of the citation edge as we explain below), the collective probability to move to an author of the paper is up to 85% × 20%, the probability to move from the paper to the forum where the paper appeared is up to 85% × 10%, and so on. As is the case with the PageRank algorithm as well, as time goes on, the expected percentage of surfers at each node v converges (Section 2) to a limit $r(v)$. Intuitively, this limit is the ObjectRank of the node.

An alternative way to conceive the intuition behind ObjectRank is to consider that authority/importance flows in the database graph in the same fashion that [25] defined authority-based search in arbitrary graphs. Initially the "OLAP" authority is found at the objects that contain the keyword "OLAP". Then authority/importance flows, following the rules in the authority transfer schema graph, until an equilibrium is established that specifies that a paper is authoritative if it is referenced by authoritative papers, is written by authority authors and appears in authority conferences. Vice versa, authors and conferences obtain their authority from their papers. Notice that the amount of authority flow from, say, paper to cited paper or from paper to author or from author to paper, is arbitrarily set by a domain expert and reflects the semantics of the domain. For example, common sense says that in the bibliography domain a paper obtains very little authority (or even none) by referring to authoritative papers. On the contrary it obtains a lot of authority by being referred by authoritative papers. Our DBLP demo offers to the user more than one authority flow settings, in order to accommodate multiple user profiles/requirements. We believe the ability to customize authority flow schemes is central to ObjectRank, since we should not assume that "one size fits all" when it comes to opinions about authority flow. For example, there is one

setting for users that primarily care for papers with high global importance and another for users that primarily care for papers that are directly or indirectly heavily referenced by papers that have the keywords. We expect that multiple settings make sense in all non-trivial ObjectRank applications.

Keyword search in databases has some unique characteristics, which make the straightforward application of the random walk model as described in previous work [9, 19, 27] inadequate. First, every database has different semantics, which we can use to improve the quality of the keyword search. In particular, unlike the Web, where all edges are hyperlinks[3], the database schema exhibits the types of edges, and the attributes of the nodes. Using the schema we specify the ways in which authority flows across the nodes of the database graph. For example, the results of Figure 2 were obtained by annotating the schema graph of Figure 3 with the authority flow information that appears in Figure 4.

Furthermore, previous work [9, 19, 27] assumes that, when calculating the global importance (in our framework we make a clear distinction between the global importance of a node and its relevance to a keyword query), the random surfer has the same probability to start from any page p of the base set (we call this probability *base ObjectRank* of p). However, this is not true for every database. For example, consider a product complaints database (Figure 14). In this case, we represent the business value of a customer by assigning to his/her node a base ObjectRank proportional to his/her total sales amount.

Another novel property of ObjectRank is adjustability, which allows for the tuning of the system according to the domain- and/or user-specific requirements. For example, for a bibliographic database, a new graduate student desires a search system that returns the best reading list around the specified keywords, whereas a senior researcher looks for papers closely related to the keywords, even if they are not of a high quality. These preference scenarios are made possible by adjusting the weight of the global importance versus the relevance to the keyword query. Changing the damping factor d offers another calibration opportunity. In particular, larger values of d favor nodes pointed by high-authority nodes, while smaller values of d favor nodes containing the actual keywords (that is, nodes in the base set). The handling of queries with multiple keywords offers more flexibility to the system as we describe in Section 3. For example, we may want to assign a higher weight to the relevance of a node to an infrequent keyword.

On the performance level, calculating the ObjectRank values in runtime is a computationally intensive operation, especially given the fact that multiple users query the system. This is resolved by precomputing an inverted index where for each keyword we have a sorted list of the nodes

---

[3]Previous works [27, 10, 8] assign weights on the edges of the data graph according to the relevance of the incident nodes' text to the keywords. In contrast, we assign authority transfer rates on the schema graph, which captures the semantics of the database, since the relevance factor is reflected in the selection of the base set.

```
41.34   Data Cube: A Relational Aggregation Operator Generalizing Group-By, Cross-Tab,
        and Sub-Total. Jim Gray. ICDE 1996
36.62   Index Selection for OLAP. Himanshu Gupta, ICDE 1997
35.11   Range Queries in OLAP Data Cubes. Ching-Tien Ho, SIGMOD 1997
31.03   Discovery-Driven Exploration of OLAP Data Cubes. Sunita Sarawagi, EDBT 1998
30.7    OLAP and Statistical Databases: Similarities and Differences. Arie Shoshani, PODS 1997
30.23   Implementing Data Cubes Efficiently. Venky Harinarayan, SIGMOD 1996
29.42   Relative Prefix Sums: An Efficient Approach for Querying Dynamic OLAP Data Cubes.
        Steven Geffner, ICDE 1999
28.49   Modeling Multidimensional Databases. Rakesh Agrawal, ICDE 1997
26.96   Summarizability in OLAP and Statistical Data Bases. Hans-J. Lenz, SSDBM 1997
26.75   Data Warehousing and OLAP for Decision Support (Tutorial). Surajit Chaudhuri, SIGMOD 1997
```

Figure 2: Top 10 papers on "OLAP" returned by ObjectRank

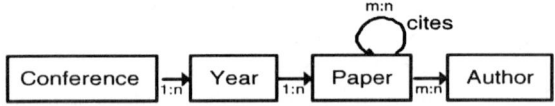

Figure 3: The DBLP schema graph.

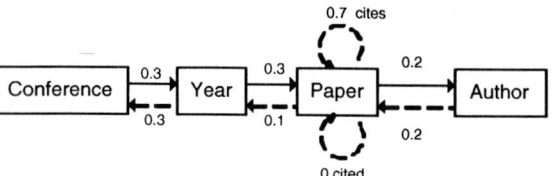

Figure 4: The DBLP authority transfer schema graph.

with non-trivial ObjectRank for this keyword. During runtime we employ the *Threshold Algorithm* [14] to efficiently combine the lists. However, our approach induces the cost of precomputing and storing the inverted index. Regarding the space requirements, notice that the number of keywords of a database is typically limited, and less than the number of users in a personalized search system [23]. Furthermore, we do not store nodes with ObjectRank below a threshold value (chosen by the system administrator), which offers a space versus precision tradeoff. In Section 7 we show that the index size is small relative to the database size for two bibliographic databases.

Regarding the index computation, we present and experimentally evaluate two classes of optimizations. First, we exploit the structural properties of the database graph. For example, if we know that the objects of a subgraph of the schema form a Directed Acyclic Graph (DAG), then given a topological sort of the DAG, there is an efficient straightforward one-pass ObjectRank evaluation. We extend the DAG case by providing an algorithm that exploits the efficient evaluation for DAGs in the case where a graph is "almost" a DAG in the sense that it contains a large DAG subgraph. In particular, given a graph G with n nodes, which is reduced to a DAG by removing a small subset of m nodes, we present an algorithm which reduces the authority calculation into a system of m equations - as opposed to the usual system of n equations. Furthermore, we present optimization techniques when the data graph has a small vertex cover, or if it can be split into a set of subgraphs and the connections between these subgraphs form a DAG.

Second, notice that the naive approach would be to calculate each keyword-specific ObjectRank separately. We have found that it is substantially more efficient to first calculate the global ObjectRank, and use these scores as initial values for the keyword-specific computations. This accelerates convergence, since in general, objects with high global ObjectRank, also have high keyword-specific ObjectRanks. Furthermore, we show how storing a prefix of the inverted lists allows the faster calculation of the ObjectRanks of all nodes.

The semantic and performance contributions of this paper are evaluated using two user surveys and a detailed experimental evaluation respectively. We have implemented a web interface, available at http://www.db.ucsd.edu/ObjectRank, to query a subset of the DBLP database using the ObjectRank technique.

The essential formal background on PageRank and authority search is presented in Section 2. Section 3 presents the semantics of ObjectRank and Section 4 describes the system's architecture. The algorithms used to calculate ObjectRank are presented in Section 5 and are experimentally evaluated in Section 7. We present the results of two user surveys in Section 6. Furthermore, related work is discussed in Section 8. Finally, conclusions and future work are discussed in Section 9.

2 Background

We describe next the essentials of PageRank and authority-based search, and the random surfer intuition. Let (V, E) be a graph, with a set of nodes $V = \{v_1, \ldots, v_n\}$ and a set of edges E. A surfer starts from a random node (web page) v_i of V and at each step, he/she follows a hyperlink with probability d or gets bored and jumps to a random node with probability $1 - d$. The PageRank value of v_i is the probability $r(v_i)$ that at a given point in time, the surfer is at v_i. If we denote by $\mathbf{r}$ the vector $[r(v_1), \ldots, r(v_i), \ldots, r(v_n)]^T$ then we have

$$\mathbf{r} = d\mathbf{A}\mathbf{r} + \frac{(1-d)}{|V|}\mathbf{e} \quad (1)$$

where $\mathbf{A}$ is a $n \times n$ matrix with $A_{ij} = \frac{1}{OutDeg(v_j)}$ if there is an edge $v_j \to v_i$ in E and 0 otherwise, where $OutDeg(v_j)$ is the outgoing degree of node v_j. Also, $\mathbf{e} = [1, \ldots, 1]^T$.

The above PageRank equation is typically precomputed before the queries arrive and provides a global, keyword-independent ranking of the pages. Instead of using the whole set of nodes V as the *base set*, i.e., the set of nodes where the surfer jumps when bored, one can use an arbitrary subset S of nodes, hence increasing the authority associated with the nodes of S and the ones most closely associated with them. In particular, we define a *base vector* $\mathbf{s} = [s_0, \ldots, s_i, \ldots, s_n]^T$ where s_i is 1 if $v_i \in S$ and 0 otherwise. The PageRank equation is then

$$\mathbf{r} = d\mathbf{A}\mathbf{r} + \frac{(1-d)}{|S|}\mathbf{s} \quad (2)$$

Regardless of whether one uses Equation 1 or Equation 2 the PageRank algorithm solves this fixpoint using a simple iterative method, where the values of the (k+1)-th execution are calculated as follows:

$$\mathbf{r}^{(k+1)} = d\mathbf{A}\mathbf{r}^{(k)} + \frac{(1-d)}{|S|}\mathbf{s} \quad (3)$$

Parameter property	Parameters
Application - specific	authority transfer rates, global ObjectRank calculation, damping factor
Combination of scores	normalization scheme, global ObjectRank weight, AND or OR semantics
Performance	epsilon, threshold

Table 1: Parameters of ObjectRank

The algorithm terminates when **r** converges, which is guaranteed to happen under very common conditions [26]. In particular, **A** needs to be irreducible (i.e., (V, E) be strongly connected) and aperiodic. The former is true due to the damping factor d, while the latter happens in practice.

The notion of the base set S was suggested in [9] as a way to do personalized rankings, by setting S to be the set of bookmarks of a user. In [19] it was used to perform topic-specific PageRank on the Web. We take it one step further and use the base set to estimate the relevance of a node to a keyword query. In particular, the base set consists of the nodes that contain the keyword as explained next.

3 ObjectRank Semantics

In this section we formally define the framework of this work, and show how ObjectRank ranks the nodes of a database with respect to a given keyword query, given a set of calibrating (adjusting) parameters (Table 1). In particular, Section 3.1 describes how the database and the authority transfer graph are modeled. Section 3.2 shows how the keyword-specific and the global ObjectRanks are calculated and combined to produce the final score of a node. Finally, Section 3.3 presents and addresses the challenges for multiple-keyword queries.

3.1 Database Graph, Schema, and Authority Transfer Graph

We view a database as a labeled graph, which is a model that easily captures both relational and XML databases. The *data graph* $D(V_D, E_D)$ is a labeled directed graph where every node v has a label $\lambda(v)$ and a set of keywords. For example, the node "ICDE 1997" of Figure 1 has label "Year" and the set of keywords {``ICDE'', ``1997'', ``Birmingham''}. Each node represents an *object* of the database and may have a sub-structure. Without loss of generality, ObjectRank assumes that each node has a tuple of attribute name/attribute value pairs. For example, the "Year" nodes of Figure 1 have name, year and location attributes. Notice that the keywords appearing in the attribute values comprise the set of keywords associated with the node. One may assume richer semantics by including the metadata of a node in the set of keywords. For example, the metadata "Forum", "Year", "Location" could be included in the keywords of a node. The specifics of modeling the data of a node are orthogonal to ObjectRank and will be neglected in the rest of the discussion.

Each edge e from u to v is labeled with its *role* $\lambda(e)$ (we overload λ) and represents a relationship between u and v. For example, every "paper" to "paper" edge of Figure 1 has the label "cites". When the role is evident and uniquely defined from the labels of u and v, we omit the edge label. For simplicity we will assume that there are no parallel edges and we will often denote an edge e from u to v as "$u \to v$".

The *schema graph* $G(V_G, E_G)$ (Figure 3) is a directed graph that describes the structure of D. Every node has an associated label. Each edge is labeled with a role, which may be omitted, as discussed above for data graph edge labels. We say that a data graph $D(V_D, E_D)$ *conforms* to a schema graph $G(V_G, E_G)$ if there is a unique assignment μ such that:

1. for every node $v \in V_D$ there is a node $\mu(v) \in V_G$ such that $\lambda(v) = \lambda(\mu(v))$;
2. for every edge $e \in E_D$ from node u to node v there is an edge $\mu(e) \in E_G$ that goes from $\mu(u)$ to $\mu(v)$ and $\lambda(e) = \lambda(\mu(e))$.

Authority Transfer Schema Graph. From the schema graph $G(V_G, E_G)$, we create the *authority transfer schema graph* $G^A(V_G, E^A)$ to reflect the authority flow through the edges of the graph. This may be either a trial and error process, until we are satisfied with the quality of the results, or a domain expert's task. In particular, for each edge $e_G = (u \to v)$ of E_G, two *authority transfer edges*, $e_G^f = (u \to v)$ and $e_G^b = (v \to u)$ are created. The two edges carry the label of the schema graph edge and, in addition, each one is annotated with a (potentially different) *authority transfer rate* - $\alpha(e_G^f)$ and $\alpha(e_G^b)$ correspondingly. We say that a data graph conforms to an authority transfer schema graph if it conforms to the corresponding schema graph. (Notice that the authority transfer schema graph has all the information of the original schema graph.)

Figure 4 shows the authority transfer schema graph that corresponds to the schema graph of Figure 3 (the edge labels are omitted). The motivation for defining two edges for each edge of the schema graph is that authority potentially flows in both directions and not only in the direction that appears in the schema. For example, a paper passes its authority to its authors and vice versa. Notice however, that the authority flow in each direction (defined by the authority transfer rate) may not be the same. For example, a paper that is cited by important papers is clearly important but citing important papers does not make a paper important.

Notice that the sum of authority transfer rates of the outgoing edges of a schema node u may be less than 1[4], if the administrator believes that the edges starting from u do not transfer much authority. For example, in Figure 4, conferences only transfer 30% of their authority.

Authority Transfer Data Graph. Given a data graph $D(V_D, E_D)$ that conforms to an authority transfer schema graph $G^A(V_G, E^A)$, ObjectRank derives an *authority*

---
[4]In terms of the random walk model, this would be equivalent to the disappearance of a surfer.

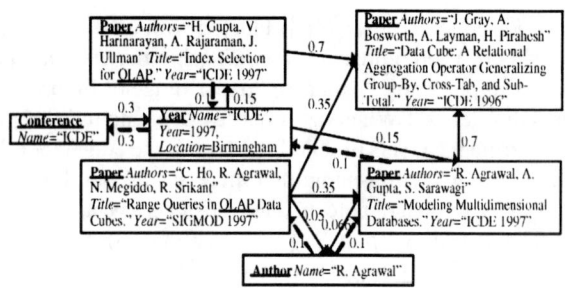

Figure 5: Authority transfer data graph

transfer data graph $D^A(V_D, E_D^A)$ (Figure 5) as follows. For every edge $e = (u \to v) \in E_D$ the authority transfer data graph has two edges $e^f = (u \to v)$ and $e^b = (v \to u)$. The edges e^f and e^b are annotated with authority transfer rates $\alpha(e^f)$ and $\alpha(e^b)$. Assuming that e^f is of type e_G^f, then

$$\alpha(e^f) = \begin{cases} \frac{\alpha(e_G^f)}{OutDeg(u, e_G^f)}, & if\ OutDeg(u, e_G^f) > 0 \\ 0, & if\ OutDeg(u, e_G^f) = 0 \end{cases} \quad (4)$$

where $OutDeg(u, e_G^f)$ is the number of outgoing edges from u, of type e_G^f. The authority transfer rate $\alpha(e^b)$ is defined similarly. Figure 5 illustrates the authority transfer data graph that corresponds to the data graph of Figure 1 and the authority schema transfer graph of Figure 4. Notice that the sum of authority transfer rates of the outgoing edges of a node u of type $\mu(u)$ may be less than the sum of authority transfer rates of the outgoing edges of $\mu(u)$ in the authority transfer schema graph, if u does not have all types of outgoing edges.

3.2 Importance vs. Relevance.

The score of a node v with respect to a keyword query w is a combination of the global ObjectRank $r^G(v)$ of v and the keyword-specific ObjectRank $r^w(v)$. We propose the following combining function, although other functions may be used as well:

$$r^{w,G}(v) = r^w(v) \cdot (r^G(v))^g \quad (5)$$

where g is the *global ObjectRank weight*, which determines how important the global ObjectRank is. Notice that g may be accessible to the users or fixed by the administrator. The calculations of the keyword-specific and the global ObjectRank are performed as follows (we assume single-keyword queries at this point).

Keyword-specific ObjectRank. Given a single keyword query w, ObjectRank finds the *keyword base set* $S(w)$ (from now on referred to simply as base set when the keyword is implied) of objects that contain the keyword w and assigns an ObjectRank $r^w(v_i)$ to every node $v_i \in V_D$ by resolving the equation

$$\mathbf{r}^w = d\mathbf{A}\mathbf{r}^w + \frac{(1-d)}{|S(w)|}\mathbf{s} \quad (6)$$

where $A_{ij} = \alpha(e)$ if there is an edge $e = (v_j \to v_i)$ in E_D^A and 0 otherwise, d controls the base set importance,

and $\mathbf{s} = [s_1, \ldots, s_n]^T$ is the base set vector for $S(w)$, i.e., $s_i = 1$ if $v_i \in S(w)$ and $s_i = 0$ otherwise.

The damping factor d determines the portion of ObjectRank that an object transfers to its neighbors as opposed to keeping to itself. It was first introduced in the original PageRank paper [9], where it was used to ensure convergence in the case of PageRank sinks. However, in addition to that, in our work it is a calibrating factor, since by decreasing d, we favor objects that actually contain the keywords (i.e., are in base set) as opposed to objects that acquire ObjectRank through the incoming edges. The value for d used by PageRank [9] is 0.85, which we also adopt when we want to balance the importance of containing the actual keywords as opposed to being pointed by nodes containing the keywords.

Global ObjectRank. The definition of global ObjectRank is different for different applications or even users of the same application. In this work, we focus on cases where the global ObjectRank is calculated applying the random surfer model, and including all nodes in the base set. The same calibrating parameters are available, as in the keyword-specific ObjectRank. Notice that this way of calculating the global ObjectRank, which is similar to the PageRank approach [9], assumes that all nodes (pages in PageRank) initially have the same value. However, there are many applications where this is not true, as we discuss in Section 9.

3.3 Multiple-Keywords Queries.

We define the semantics of a multiple-keyword query "$w_1, \ldots, w_m$" by naturally extending the random walk model. We consider m independent random surfers, where the ith surfer starts from the keyword base set $S(w_i)$. For AND semantics, the ObjectRank of an object v with respect to the m-keywords query is the probability that, at a given point in time, the m random surfers are simultaneously at v. Hence the ObjectRank $r_{AND}^{w_1,\ldots,w_m}(v)$ of the node v with respect to the m keywords is

$$r_{AND}^{w_1,\ldots,w_m}(v) = \prod_{i=1,\ldots,m} r^{w_i}(v) \quad (7)$$

where $r^{w_i}(v)$ is the ObjectRank with respect to the keyword w_i.

For OR semantics, the ObjectRank of v is the probability that, at a given point in time, *at least one* of the m random surfers will reach v. Hence, for two keywords w_1 and w_2 it is

$$r_{OR}^{w_1,w_2}(v) = r^{w_1}(v) + r^{w_2}(v) - r^{w_1}(v)r^{w_2}(v) \quad (8)$$

and for more than two, it is defined accordingly. Notice that [19] also sums the topic-sensitive PageRanks to calculate the PageRank of a page.

In [6] we discuss how we handle the difference in the distribution of ObjectRank values of frequent and infrequent keywords. We also explain why the HITS [25] approach, where the base set consists of all objects with at least one of the keywords, can be viewed as a special case of ObjectRank's semantics.

4 Architecture

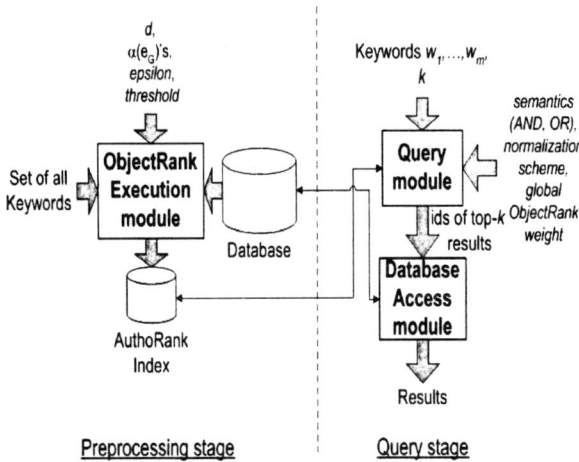

Figure 6: System Architecture.

Figure 6 shows the architecture of the ObjectRank system, which is divided into two stages. The preprocessing stage consists of the *ObjectRank Execution module*, which inputs the database to be indexed, the set of all keywords that will be indexed, and a set of parameters (the rest of the adjusting parameters are input during the query stage). In particular these parameters are: (i) the damping factor d, (ii) the authority transfer rates $\alpha(e_G)$'s of the authority transfer schema graph G^A, (iii) the convergence constant $epsilon$ which determines when the ObjectRank algorithm converges, and (iv) the $threshold$ value which determines the minimum ObjectRank that an object must have to be stored in the ObjectRank Index.

The ObjectRank Execution module creates the *ObjectRank Index*, which is an inverted index, indexed by the keywords. For each keyword w, it stores a list of $\langle id(u), r^w(u)\rangle$ pairs for each object u that has $r^w(u) \geq threshold$. The pairs are sorted by descending $r^w(u)$ to facilitate an efficient querying method as we describe below. The ObjectRank Index has been implemented as an index-based table, where the lists are stored in a CLOB attribute. A hash-index is built on top of each list to allow for random access, which is required by the Query module.

The *Query module* inputs a set of sorted $\langle id(u), r^w(u)\rangle$ pairs lists $L_1, \ldots, L_m$ and a set of adjusting parameters, and outputs the top-k objects according to the combining function (Equation 7 or 8). In particular, these parameters are: (i) the semantics to be used (AND or OR), (ii) the normalization scheme, i.e., the exponents to use, and (iii) the global ObjectRank weight. The naive approach would be to make one pass of all lists to calculate the final ObjectRank values for each object and then sort this list by final ObjectRank. Instead, we use the *Threshold Algorithm* [14] which is guaranteed to read the minimum prefix of each list. Notice that the Threshold Algorithm is applicable since both combining functions (Equations 7 and 8) are monotone, and random access is possible on the stored lists.

Finally, the *Database Access module* inputs the result ids and queries the database to get the suitable information to present the objects to the user. This information is stored into an id-indexed table, that contains a CLOB attribute value for each object id. For example, a paper object CLOB would contain the paper title, the authors' names, and the conference name and year.

5 ObjectRank Index creation

This section presents algorithms to create the ObjectRank index. Section 5.1 presents an algorithm for the case of arbitrary authority transfer data graphs D^A. Sections 5.2 and 5.3 show how we can do better when D^A is a directed acyclic graph (DAG) and "almost" a DAG respectively (the latter property is explained in Section 5.3). Section 5.4 presents optimization opportunities based on manipulating the initial values of the iterative algorithm. Finally, in [6], we present optimizations when the authority transfer graph has a small vertex cover, or is a DAG of subgraphs.

5.1 General algorithm

Figure 7 shows the algorithm that creates the ObjectRank Index. The algorithm accesses the authority transfer data graph D^A many times, which may lead to a too long execution time if D^A is very large. Notice that this is usually not a problem, since D^A only stores object ids and a set of edges which is small enough to fit into main memory for most databases. Notice that lines 2-4 correspond to the original PageRank calculation [9] modulo the authority transfer rates information.

```
CreateIndex(keywordsList, epsilon, threshold, α(.), d){
01. For each keyword w in keywordsList do {
02.   While not converged do
03.   /*i.e., ∃v, |r^(k+1)(v) − r^(k)(v)| > epsilon*/
04.     MakeOnePass(w,α(.), d);
05.   StoreObjectRanks();
06. }
}
MakeOnePass(w,α(.), d) {
07. Evaluate Equation 6 using the r from
    the previous iteration on the right side;
}
StoreObjectRanks() {
08. Sort the ⟨id(i), r(v_i)⟩ pairs list by r(v_i) and
    store it in inverted index, after removing pairs with
    r(v_i) < threshold;
}
```

Figure 7: Algorithm to create ObjectRank Index

5.2 DAG algorithm

There are many applications where the authority transfer data graph is a DAG. For example a database of papers and their citations (ignoring author and conference objects), where each paper only cites previously published papers, is a DAG. Figure 8 shows an improved algorithm, which makes a single pass of the graph D^A and computes the actual ObjectRank values. Notice that there is no need for *epsilon* any more since we derive the precise solution of Equation 6, in contrast to the algorithm of Figure 7 which calculates approximate values. The intuition is that ObjectRank is only transferred in the direction of the topological ordering, so a single pass suffices. Notice that topologically sorting a graph $G(V, E)$ takes time $\Theta(V + E)$ [12] in the general case. In many cases the semantics of the database can lead to a better algorithm. For example, in the papers database, we can efficiently topologically sort the papers by first sorting the conferences by date. This method is applicable for databases where a temporal or other kind of ordering is implied by the link structure.

CreateIndexDAG(keywordsList, $threshold$, $\alpha(.)$, d){
01. Topologically sort nodes in graph D^A;
02. /*Consecutive accesses to D'^A are in topological order.*/
03. For each keyword w in keywordsList do {
04.   MakeOnePass(w,$\alpha(.)$, d);
05.   StoreObjectRanks();
06. }
}

Figure 8: Algorithm to create ObjectRank Index for DAGs

In the above example, the DAG property was implied by the semantics. However, in some cases we can infer this property by the structure of the authority transfer schema graph G^A, as the following theorem shows.

Theorem 5.1 *The authority transfer data graph D^A is a DAG if and only if*

- *the authority transfer schema graph G^A is a DAG, or*
- *for every cycle c in G^A, the subgraph D'^A of D^A consisting of the nodes (and the edges connecting them), whose type is one of the schema nodes of c, is a DAG.*

5.3 Almost-DAG algorithm

The most practically interesting case is when the authority transfer data graph D^A is *almost* a DAG, that is, there is a "small" set U of *backedges*, and if these edges are removed, D^A becomes a DAG. Notice that the set U is not unique, that is, there can be many *minimal* (i.e., no edge can be removed from U) sets of backedges. Instead of working with the set of backedges U, we work with the set L of *backnodes*, that is, nodes from which the backedges start. This reduces the number of needed variables as we show below, since $|L| \leq |U|$.

In the papers database example (when author and conference objects are ignored), L is the set of papers citing a paper that was not published previously. Similarly, in the complaints database (Figure 14), most complaints reference previous complaints. Identifying the minimum set of backnodes is NP-complete[5] in the general case. However, the semantics of the database can lead to efficient algorithms. For example, for the databases we discuss in this paper (i.e, the papers and the complaints databases), a backnode is simply an object referencing an object with a newer timestamp.

The intuition of the algorithm (Figure 9) is as follows: the ObjectRank of each node can be split to the DAG-ObjectRank which is calculated ignoring the backedges, and the backedges-ObjectRank which is due to the backedges.

To calculate backedges-ObjectRank we assign a variable c_i to each backnode c_i (for brevity, we use the same symbol to denote a backnode and its ObjectRank), denoting its ObjectRank. Before doing any keyword-specific calculation, we calculate how c_i's are propagated to the rest of the graph D^A (line 5), and store this information in **C**. Hence C_{ij} is the coefficient with which to multiply c_j when calculating the ObjectRank of node v_i. To calculate **C** (lines 13-15) we assume that the backedges are the only source of ObjectRank, and make one pass of the DAG in topological order.

CreateIndexAlmostDAG(keywordsList, $threshold$, $\alpha(.)$, d){
01. **c**: vector of ObjectRanks of backnodes;
02. Identify backnodes, and topologically sort
    the DAG (D^A without the backedges) D'^A;
03. /*Consecutive accesses to D'^A are in topological order.*/
04. /*Backedges are considered in D'^A for $\alpha(.)$.*/
05. **C**=BuildCoefficientsTable();
06. For each keyword w in keywordsList do {
07.   Calculate ObjectRanks vector **r**' for D'^A executing
      MakeOnePass(w,$\alpha(.)$, d);
08.   Solve $\mathbf{c} = \overline{\mathbf{C}} \cdot \mathbf{c} + \overline{\mathbf{r}'}$;
09.   /*$\overline{\mathbf{D}}$ denotes keeping only the lines of **D**
      corresponding to backnodes.*/
10. $\mathbf{r} = \mathbf{C} \cdot \mathbf{c} + \mathbf{r}'$
11.   StoreObjectRanks();
12. }
}
BuildCoefficientsTable(){
13. For each node v_j do
14. $r(v_j) = d \cdot \sum_{backnode\ c_i\ points\ at\ v_j}(\alpha(c_i \to v_j) \cdot c_i) +$
      $d \cdot \sum_{non-backnode\ v_l\ points\ at\ v_j}(\alpha(v_l \to v_j) \cdot r(v_l));$
15. Return **C**, such that $\mathbf{r} = \mathbf{C} \cdot \mathbf{c}$
}

Figure 9: Algorithm to create ObjectRank Index for *almost* DAGs

Then, for each keyword-specific base set: (a) we calculate the DAG-ObjectRanks **r**' (line 7) ignoring the backedges (but taking them into account when calculating the outgoing degrees), (b) calculate c_i's solving a linear system (line 8), and (c) calculate the total ObjectRanks (line 10) by adding the backedge-ObjectRank ($\mathbf{C} \cdot \mathbf{c}$) and the DAG-ObjectRank(**r**'). Each line of the system of line 8 corresponds to a backnode $c_i \equiv v_j$ (i.e., the ith backnode is the jth node of the topologically sorted authority transfer data graph D'^A), whose ObjectRank c_i is the sum of the backedge-ObjectRank ($\mathbf{C}_j \cdot \mathbf{c}$) and the DAG-ObjectRank ($\mathbf{r}'_j$). The overline notation on the matrices of this equation selects the L lines from each table that correspond to

---

[5]Proven by reducing Vertex Cover to it.

the backnodes. We further explain the algorithm using an example.

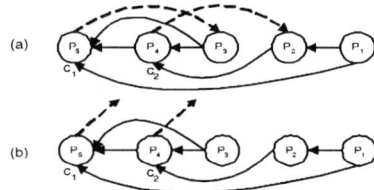

Figure 10: Almost DAG.

Example 1 *The graph D^A is shown in Figure 10 (a). Assume $d = 0.5$ and all edges are of the same type t with authority transfer rate $\alpha(t) = 1$. First we topologically sort the graph and identify the backnodes $c_1 \equiv P_5, c_2 \equiv P_4$. Then we create the coefficients table C (line 5), as follows:*

$$\begin{aligned}
r(P_1) &= 0 \\
r(P_2) &= 0.5 \cdot 0.5 \cdot c_2 = 0.25 \cdot c_2 \\
r(P_3) &= 0.5 \cdot c_1 \\
r(P_4) &= 0.5 \cdot r(P_2) + 0.5 \cdot 0.5 \cdot r(P_3) = \\
&\quad 0.125 \cdot c_1 + 0.125 \cdot c_2 \\
r(P_5) &= 0.5 \cdot 0.5 \cdot r(P_3) + 0.5 \cdot 0.5 \cdot r(P_4) = \\
&\quad 0.156 \cdot c_1 + 0.031 \cdot c_2
\end{aligned}$$

$$\mathbf{C} = \begin{bmatrix} 0 & 0 \\ 0 & 0.25 \\ 0.5 & 0 \\ 0.125 & 0.125 \\ 0.156 & 0.031 \end{bmatrix}$$

Assume we build the index for one keyword w contained in nodes P_1, P_3. We calculate (line 7) ObjectRanks for D'^A (taken by removing the backedges (dotted lines) from D^A).

$$\begin{aligned}
r(P_1) &= 0.5 \\
r(P_2) &= 0.5 \cdot 0.5 \cdot r(P_1) = 0.125 \\
r(P_3) &= 0.5 \\
r(P_4) &= 0.5 \cdot 0.5 \cdot r(P_3) + 0.5 \cdot r(P_2) = \\
&\quad 0.188 \\
r(P_5) &= 0.5 \cdot 0.5 \cdot r(P_4) + 0.5 \cdot 0.5 \cdot r(P_3) + \\
&\quad 0.5 \cdot 0.5 \cdot r(P_1) = 0.297
\end{aligned}$$

$\mathbf{r}' = [0.5\ 0.125\ 0.5\ 0.188\ 0.297]^T$

Solving the equation of line 8:

$$\begin{bmatrix} c_1 \\ c_2 \end{bmatrix} = \begin{bmatrix} 0.156 & 0.031 \\ 0.125 & 0.125 \end{bmatrix} \begin{bmatrix} c_1 \\ c_2 \end{bmatrix} + \begin{bmatrix} 0.297 \\ 0.188 \end{bmatrix}$$

we get: $\mathbf{c} = [\overline{0.361}\ \overline{0.263}]^T$, *where the overline-notation selects from the matrices the 5-th and the 4-th lines, which correspond to the backnodes c_1 and c_2 respectively. The final ObjectRanks are (line 10):* $\mathbf{r} = [0.5\ 0.190\ 0.680\ 0.266\ 0.361]^T$.

This algorithm can be viewed as a way to reduce the $n \times n$ ObjectRank calculation system of Equation 6, where n is the size of the graph, to the much smaller $|L| \times |L|$ equations system of line 8 of Figure 9. Interestingly, the two equations systems have the same format $\mathbf{r} = \mathbf{Ar} + \mathbf{b}$, only with different coefficient tables $\mathbf{A}, \mathbf{b}$. The degree of reduction achieved is inversely proportional to the number of backnodes.

The linear, first-degree equations system of line 8 can be solved using any of the well-studied arithmetic methods like Jacobi and Gauss-Seidel [15], or even using the PageRank iterative approach which is simpler because we do not have to solve each equation with respect to a variable. The latter is shown to perform better in Section 7.

5.4 Manipulating Initial ObjectRank values

All algorithms so far assume that we do a fresh execution of the algorithm for every keyword. However, intuitively we expect nodes with high global ObjectRank to also have high ObjectRank with respect to many keywords. We exploit this observation by assigning the global ObjectRanks as initial values for each keyword specific calculation.

Furthermore, we investigate a space vs. time tradeoff. In particular, assume we have limitations on the index size. Then we only store a prefix (the first p nodes) of the nodes' list (recall that the lists are ordered by ObjectRank) for each keyword. During the query stage, we use these values as initial values for the p nodes and a constant (we experimentally found 0.03 to be the most efficient for our datasets) for the rest[6]. Both ideas are experimentally evaluated in Section 7.1.

6 Relevance Feedback Survey

To evaluate the quality of the results of ObjectRank, we conducted two surveys. The first was performed on the DBLP database, with eight professors and Ph.D. students from the UC, San Diego database lab, who were not involved with the project. The second survey used the publications database of the IEEE Communications Society (COMSOC)[7] and involved five senior Ph.D. students from the Electrical Engineering Department.

Each participant was asked to compare and rank two to five lists of top-10 results for a set of keyword queries, assigning a score of 1 to 10, according to the relevance of the results list to the query. Each result list was generated by a different variation of the ObjectRank algorithm. One of the results lists in each set was generated by the "default" ObjectRank configuration which used the authority transfer schema graph of Figure 4 and $d = 0.85$. The users knew nothing about the algorithms that produced each result list. The survey was designed to investigate the quality of ObjectRank when compared to other approaches or when changing the adjusting parameters.

Effect of keyword-specific ranking. First, we assess the basic principle of ObjectRank, which is the keyword-specific scores. In particular, we compared the default (that is, with the parameters set to the values discussed in Section 1) ObjectRank with the global ranking algorithm that

---

[6]Notice that, as we experimentally found, using the global ObjectRanks instead of a constant for the rest nodes is less efficient. The reason is that if a node u is not in the top-p nodes for keyword k, u probably has a very small ObjectRank with respect to k. However u may have a great global ObjectRank.

[7]http://www.comsoc.org

sorts objects that contain the keywords according to their global ObjectRank (where the base-set contains all nodes). Notice that this is equivalent to what Google used to[8] do for Web pages, modulo some minor difference on the calculation of the relevance score by Google. The DBLP survey included results for two keyword queries: "OLAP" and "XML". The score was 7:1 and 5:3 in favor of the keyword-specific ObjectRank for the first and second keyword query respectively. The COMSOC survey used the keywords "CDMA" and "UWB (ultra wideband)" and the scores were 4:1 and 5:0 in favor of the keyword-specific approach respectively.

Effect of authority transfer rates. We compared results of the default ObjectRank with a simpler version of the algorithm that did not use different authority transfer rates for different edge types, i.e., all edge types were treated equally. In the DBLP survey, for both keyword queries, "OLAP" and "XML", the default ObjectRank won with scores 5:3 and 6.5:1.5 (the half point means that a user thought that both rankings were equally good) respectively. In the COMSOC survey, the scores for "CDMA" and "UWB" were 3.5:1.5 and 5:0 respectively.

Effect of the damping factor d. We tested three different values of the damping factor d: 0.1, 0.85, and 0.99, for the keyword queries "XML" and "XML AND Index" on the DBLP dataset. Two points were given to the first choice of a user and one point to the second. The scores were 2.5 : 8 : 13.5 and 10.5 : 11.5 : 2 (the sum is 24 since there are 8 users times 3 points per query) respectively for the three d values. We see that higher d values are preferred for the "XML", because "XML" is a very large area. In contrast, small d are preferable for "XML AND Index", because few papers are closely related to both keywords, and these papers typically contain both of them. The results were also mixed in the COMSOC survey. In particular, the damping factors 0.1, 0.85, and 0.99 received scores of 5:6:4 and 4.5:3.5:7 for the queries "CDMA" and "UWB" respectively.

Effect of changing the weights of the keywords. We compared the combining functions for AND semantics of Equations 7 with the weighted combining method described in [6] for the two-keyword queries "XML AND Index" and "XML AND Query", in the DBLP survey. The use of the normalizing exponents proposed in Section 3.3 was preferred over the simple product function with ratios of 6:2 and 6.5:1.5 respectively. In the COMSOC survey, the same experiment was repeated for the keyword query "diversity combining". The use of normalizing exponents was preferred at a ratio of 3.5:1.5.

7 Experiments

In this section we experimentally evaluate the system and show that calculating the ObjectRank is feasible, both in the preprocessing and in the query execution stage. For the evaluation we use two real and a set of synthetic datasets: COMSOC is the dataset of the publications of the IEEE Communications Society [9], which consists of 55,000 nodes and 165,000 edges. DBLPreal is a subset of the DBLP dataset, consisting of the publications in twelve database conferences. This dataset contains 13,700 nodes and 101,500 edges. However, these datasets are too small to evaluate the index creation algorithms. Hence, we also created a set of artificial datasets shown in Table 2, using the words of the DBLP dataset. The outgoing edges are distributed uniformly among papers, that is, each paper cites on average 10 other papers. The incoming edges are assigned by a non-uniform random function, similar to the one used in the TPC-C benchmark [10], such that the top-10% of the most cited papers receive 70% of all the citations.

name	#nodes	#edges
DBLP30	3,000	30,000
DBLP100	10,000	100,000
DBLP300	30,000	300,000
DBLP1000	100,000	1,000,000
DBLP3000	300,000	3,000,000

Table 2: Synthetic Datasets.

To store the databases in a RDBMS, we decomposed them into relations according to the relational schema shown in Figure 11. Y is an instance of a conference in a particular year. PP is a relation that describes each paper $pid2$ cited by a paper $pid1$, while PA lists the authors aid of each paper pid. Notice that the two arrows from P to PP denote primary-to-foreign-key connections from pid to $pid1$ and from pid to $pid2$. We ran our experiments using the Oracle 9i RDBMS on a Xeon 2.2-GHz PC with 1 GB of RAM. We implemented the preprocessing and query-processing algorithms in Java, and connect to the RDBMS through JDBC.

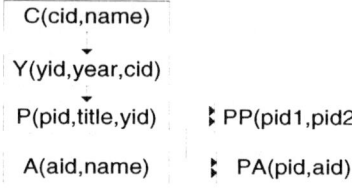

Figure 11: Relational schema.

The experiments are divided into two classes. First, we measure how fast the ObjectRank Execution module (Figure 6) calculates the ObjectRanks for all keywords and stores them into the ObjectRank Index, using the *CreateIndex* algorithm of Figure 7. The size of the ObjectRank Index is also measured. This experiment is repeated for various values of *epsilon* and *threshold*, and various dataset sizes. Furthermore, the General ObjectRank algorithm is compared to the almost-DAG algorithm, and the effect of using various initial ObjectRank values is evaluated. Second, in [6][11] the Query module (Figure 6) is evaluated. In

---
[8]Google's current ranking algorithm is not disclosed.

[9]http://www.comsoc.org
[10]http://www.tpc.org/tpcc/
[11]We moved these experiments to [6] because the Query stage is less

particular, we measure the execution times of the combining algorithm (Section 4) to produce the top-k results, for various values of k, various numbers of keywords m, and OR and AND semantics.

7.1 Preprocessing stage

threshold	time (sec)	nodes/keyword	size (MB)
0.3	3702	84	2.20
0.5	3702	67	1.77
1.0	3702	46	1.26

Table 3: Index Creation for DBLPreal for $epsilon = 0.1$

threshold	time (sec)	nodes/keyword	size (MB)
0.05	80829	9.4	1.17
0.07	80829	8.3	1.08
0.1	80829	7.7	1.03

Table 4: Index Creation for COMSOC for $epsilon = 0.05$

epsilon	time (sec)	nodes/keyword	size (MB)
0.05	3875	67	1.77
0.1	3702	67	1.77
0.3	3517	67	1.77

Table 5: Index Creation for DBLPreal for $threshold = 0.5$

epsilon	time (sec)	nodes/keyword	size (MB)
0.05	80829	7.7	1.03
0.07	77056	7.7	1.03
0.1	74337	7.7	1.03

Table 6: Index Creation for COMSOC for $threshold = 0.1$

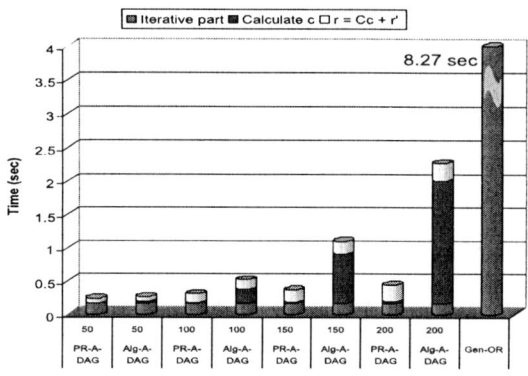

Figure 12: Evaluate almost-DAG algorithm.

General ObjectRank algorithm. Tables 3 and 4 show how the storage space for the ObjectRank index decreases as the ObjectRank *threshold* of the stored objects increases, for the real datasets. Notice that DBLPreal and COMSOC have 12,341 and 40,577 keywords respectively. Also notice that much fewer nodes per keyword have ObjectRank above the *threshold* in COMSOC, since this dataset is more sparse and has more keywords. The time to create the index does not change with *threshold* since *threshold* is not used during the main execution loop of the CreateIndex algorithm. Tables 5 and 6 show how the index build time decreases as *epsilon* increases. The reason is that fewer iterations are needed for the algorithm to converge, on the cost of lower accuracy of the calculated ObjectRanks. Notice that the storage space does not change with *epsilon*, as long as $epsilon < threshold$.

Table 7 shows how the execution times and the storage requirements for the ObjectRank index scale with the database size for the DBLP synthetic datasets for $epsilon = 0.05$ and $threshold = 0.1$. Notice that the average number of nodes having ObjectRank higher than the *threshold* increases considerably with the dataset size, because the same keywords appear multiple times.

General ObjectRank vs. almost-DAG algorithm. Figure 12 compares the index creation time of the General ObjectRank algorithm (*Gen-OR*) and two versions of the almost-DAG algorithm, on the DBLP1000 dataset, for various number of backnodes. The *algebraic* version (*Alg-A-DAG*) precisely solves the $c = \overline{C} \cdot c + \overline{r'}$ system using an off the self algebraic solver. The *PageRank* version (*PR-A-DAG*) solves this system using the PageRank [9] iterative method. The measured times are the average processing time for a single keyword and do not include the time to retrieve the base-set from the inverted text index, which is common to all methods. Also, the time to calculate $\mathbf{C}$ is omitted, since it $\mathbf{C}$ is calculated once for all keywords, and it requires a single pass over the graph. The *Iterative part* of the execution times corresponds to the one pass we perform on the DAG subgraph to calculate $\mathbf{r'}$ for almost-DAG algorithms, and to the multiple passes which consist the whole computation for the General ObjectRank algorithm.

Also, notice that $epsilon = 0.1$ for this experiment (the *threshold* value is irrelevant since it does not affect the processing time, but only the storage space). The time to do the topological sorting is about 20 sec which is negligible compared to the time to calculate the ObjectRanks for all keywords.

Initial ObjectRanks. This experiment shows how the convergence of the General ObjectRank algorithm is accelerated when various values are set as initial ObjectRanks. In particular, we compare the naive approach, where we assign an equal initial ObjectRank to all nodes, to the global-as-initial approach, where the global ObjectRanks are used as initial values for the keyword-specific ObjectRank calculations. We found that on DBLPreal (COMSOC), for $epsilon = 0.1$, the naive and global-as-initial approaches take 16.3 (15.8) and 12.8 (13.7) iterations respectively.

dataset	time (sec)	nodes/keyword	size (MB)
DBLP30	2933	6	0.3
DBLP100	11513	21	0.7
DBLP300	45764	65	1.7
DBLP1000	206034	316	7.9
DBLP3000	6398043	1763	43.6

Table 7: Index Creation for Synthetic Datasets.

challenging than the Preprocessing stage

(a) DBLPreal

List length p	iterations
13700	1
13000	1.2
8000	1.8
2500	3
800	8.7
100	13.3
0	16.3

(b) COMSOC

List length p	iterations
55000	1
54000	2.9
30000	5.3
13000	6.5
1600	7.8
400	10.7
25	13
0	15.8

Figure 13: Number of iterations for various lengths of precomputed lists

Furthermore, we evaluate the space vs. time tradeoff described in Section 5.4. Figure 13 shows the average number of iterations for $epsilon = 0.1$ on DBLPreal and COMSOC for various values of the precomputed list length p.

8 Related Work

We first present how state-of-the-art works rank the results of a keyword query, using traditional IR techniques and exploiting the link structure of the data graph. Then we discuss about related work on the performance of link-based algorithms.

Traditional IR ranking. Currently, all major database vendors offer tools [2, 3, 1] for keyword search in single attributes of the database. That is, they assign a score to an attribute value according to its relevance to the keyword query. The score is calculated using well known ranking functions from the IR community [28], although their precise formula is not disclosed. Recent works [7, 20, 21, 5] on keyword search on databases, where the result is a tree of objects, either use similar IR techniques [7], or use the simpler boolean semantics [20, 21, 5], where the score of an attribute is 1 (0) if it contains (does not contain) the keywords.

The first shortcoming of these semantics is that they miss objects that are very related to the keywords, although they do not contain them (Section 1). The second shortcoming is that the traditional IR semantics are unable to meaningfully sort the resulting objects according to their relevance to the keywords. For example, for the query "XML", the paper [16] on Quality of Service that uses an XML-based language, would be ranked as high as a classic book on XML [4]. Again, the relevance information is hidden in the link structure of the data graph.

Link-based semantics. To the best of our knowledge, Savoy [29] was the first to use the link-structure of the Web to discover relevant pages. This idea became more popular with PageRank [9], where a global score is assigned to each Web page as we explain in Section 2. However, directly applying the PageRank approach in our problem is not suitable as we explain in Section 1. HITS [25] employs mutually dependant computation of two values for each web page: hub value and authority. In contrast to PageRank, it is able to find relevant pages that do not contain the keyword, if they are directly pointed by pages that do. However, HITS does not consider domain-specific link semantics and does not make use of schema information. The relevance between two nodes in a data graph can also be viewed as the resistance between them in the corresponding electrical network, where a resistor is added on each edge. This approach is equivalent to the random walk model [13].

Richardson et al. [27] propose an improvement to PageRank, where the random surfer takes into account the relevance of each page to the query when navigating from one page to the other. However, they require that every result contains the keyword, and ignore the case of multiple keywords. Haveliwala [19] proposes a topic-sensitive PageRank, where the topic-specific PageRanks for each page are precomputed and the PageRank value of the most relevant topic is used for each query. Both works apply to the Web and do not address the unique characteristics of structured databases, as we discuss in Section 1. Furthermore, they offer no adjusting parameters to calibrate the system according to the specifics of an application.

Recently, the idea of PageRank has been applied to structured databases [17, 22]. XRANK [17] proposes a way to rank XML elements using the link structure of the database. Furthermore, they introduce a notion similar to our ObjectRank transfer edge bounds, to distinguish between containment and IDREF edges. Huang et al. [22] propose a way to rank the tuples of a relational database using PageRank, where connections are determined dynamically by the query workload and not statically by the schema. However, none of these works exploits the link structure to provide keyword-specific ranking. Furthermore, they ignore the schema semantics when computing the scores.

Performance. A set of works [18, 11, 23, 24] have tackled the problem of improving the performance of the original PageRank algorithm. [18, 11] present algorithms to improve the calculation of a global PageRank. Jeh and Widom [23] present a method to efficiently calculate the PageRank values for multiple base sets, by precomputing a set of *partial vectors* which are used in runtime to calculate the PageRanks. The key idea is to precompute in a compact way the PageRank values for a set of hub pages, through which most of the random walks pass. Then using these hub PageRanks, calculate in runtime the PageRanks for any base set consisting of nodes in the hub set. However, in our case it is not possible to define a set of hub nodes, since any node of the database can be part of a base set.

9 Conclusion and Future Work

We presented an adjustable framework to answer keyword queries using the authority transfer paradigm, which we believe is applicable to a significant number of domains (though obviously not meaningful for every database). We showed that our framework is efficient and semantically meaningful, with an experimental evaluation and user surveys respectively.

We investigated how this framework can be applied with small modifications to applications other than biblio-

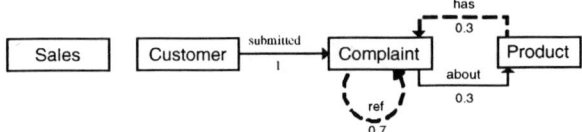

Figure 14: Authority transfer schema graph for Complaints database.

graphic, where the authority transfer intuition is applicable. For example, consider a complaints database (Figure 14), which stores the complaint reports of customers regarding products of the company. Assume we wish to rank the complaint reports according to their urgency, given that the goal of the company is to keep the "good" customers satisfied, and the "goodness" of a customer is the total sales associated with him/her. Then, the base set for the computation of the global ObjectRank is the set of customers, and each customer is given a base ObjectRank proportional to his/her total sales amount. A reasonable assignment of authority transfer rates is shown in Figure 14.

10 Acknowledgements

We thank Michael Sirivianos for creating the Web interface of the ObjectRank demo. We also thank the reviewers for their useful comments.

References

[1] http://msdn.microsoft.com/library/. 2001.

[2] http://technet.oracle.com/products/text/content.html. 2001.

[3] http://www.ibm.com/software/data/db2/extenders/textinformation/index.html. 2001.

[4] S. Abiteboul, D. Suciu, and P. Buneman. Data on the Web : From Relations to Semistructured Data and Xml. *Morgan Kaufmann Series in Data Management Systems*, 2000.

[5] S. Agrawal, S. Chaudhuri, and G. Das. DBXplorer: A System For Keyword-Based Search Over Relational Databases. *ICDE*, 2002.

[6] A. Balmin, V. Hristidis, and Y. Papakonstantinou. ObjectRank: Authority-Based Keyword Search in Databases (extended version). *UCSD Technical Report*, 2004.

[7] G. Bhalotia, C. Nakhey, A. Hulgeri, S. Chakrabarti, and S. Sudarshan. Keyword Searching and Browsing in Databases using BANKS. *ICDE*, 2002.

[8] K. Bharat and M. R. Henzinger. Improved algorithms for topic distillation in a hyperlinked environment. *SIGIR*, 1998.

[9] S. Brin and L. Page. The Anatomy of a Large-Scale Hypertextual Web Search Engine. *WWW Conference*, 1998.

[10] S. Chakrabarti, B. Dom, D. Gibson, J. Kleinberg, P. Raghavan, and S. Rajagopalan. Automatic resource compilation by analyzing hyperlink structure and associated text. *WWW Conference*, 1998.

[11] Y. Chen, Q. Gan, and T. Suel. I/O-efficient techniques for computing PageRank. *CIKM*, 2002.

[12] T. Cormen, C. Leiserson, and R. Rivest. Introduction to Algorithms. *MIT Press*, 1989.

[13] P. G. Doyle and J. L. Snell. Random Walks and Electric Networks. *Mathematical Association of America, Washington, D. C.*, 1984.

[14] R. Fagin, A. Lotem, and M. Naor. Optimal Aggregation Algorithms for Middleware. *ACM PODS*, 2001.

[15] G. H. Golub and C. F. Loan. Matrix Computations. *Johns Hopkins*, 1996.

[16] X. Gu, K. Nahrstedt, W. Yuan, D. Wichadakul, and D. Xu. An XML-based Quality of Service Enabling Language for the Web. *Journal of Visual Languages and Computing 13(1): 61-95*, 2002.

[17] L. Guo, F. Shao, C. Botev, and J. Shanmugasundaram. XRANK: Ranked Keyword Search over XML Documents. *ACM SIGMOD*, 2003.

[18] T. Haveliwala. Efficient computation of PageRank. *Technical report, Stanford University (http://www.stanford.edu/ taherh/papers/efficient-pr.pdf)*, 1999.

[19] T. Haveliwala. Topic-Sensitive PageRank. *WWW Conference*, 2002.

[20] V. Hristidis and Y. Papakonstantinou. DISCOVER: Keyword Search in Relational Databases. *VLDB*, 2002.

[21] V. Hristidis, Y. Papakonstantinou, and A. Balmin. Keyword Proximity Search on XML Graphs. *ICDE*, 2003.

[22] A. Huang, Q. Xue, and J. Yang. TupleRank and Implicit Relationship Discovery in Relational Databases. *WAIM*, 2003.

[23] G. Jeh and J. Widom. Scaling Personalized Web Search. *WWW Conference*, 2003.

[24] S. Kamvar, T. Haveliwala, C. Manning, and G. Golub. Extrapolation Methods for Accelerating PageRank Computations. *WWW Conference*, 2003.

[25] J. M. Kleinberg. Authoritative sources in a hyperlinked environment. *Journal of the ACM 46*, 1999.

[26] R. Motwani and P. Raghavan. Randomized Algorithms. *Cambridge University Press, United Kingdom*, 1995.

[27] M. Richardson and P. Domingos. The Intelligent Surfer: Probabilistic Combination of Link and Content Information in PageRank. *Advances in Neural Information Processing Systems 14, MIT Press*, 2002.

[28] G. Salton. Automatic Text Processing: The Transformation, Analysis, and Retrieval of Information by Computer. *Addison Wesley*, 1989.

[29] J. Savoy. Bayesian inference networks and spreading activation in hypertext systems. *Information Processing and Management*, 28(3):389–406, 1992.

Combating Web Spam with TrustRank

Zoltán Gyöngyi
Stanford University
Computer Science Department
Stanford, CA 94305
zoltan@cs.stanford.edu

Hector Garcia-Molina
Stanford University
Computer Science Department
Stanford, CA 94305
hector@cs.stanford.edu

Jan Pedersen
Yahoo! Inc.
701 First Avenue
Sunnyvale, CA 94089
jpederse@yahoo-inc.com

Abstract

Web spam pages use various techniques to achieve higher-than-deserved rankings in a search engine's results. While human experts can identify spam, it is too expensive to manually evaluate a large number of pages. Instead, we propose techniques to semi-automatically separate reputable, good pages from spam. We first select a small set of seed pages to be evaluated by an expert. Once we manually identify the reputable seed pages, we use the link structure of the web to discover other pages that are likely to be good. In this paper we discuss possible ways to implement the seed selection and the discovery of good pages. We present results of experiments run on the World Wide Web indexed by AltaVista and evaluate the performance of our techniques. Our results show that we can effectively filter out spam from a significant fraction of the web, based on a good seed set of less than 200 sites.

1 Introduction

The term *web spam* refers to hyperlinked pages on the World Wide Web that are created with the intention of misleading search engines. For example, a pornography site may spam the web by adding thousands of keywords to its home page, often making the text invisible to humans through ingenious use of color schemes. A search engine will then index the extra keywords, and return the pornography page as an answer to queries that contain some of the keywords. As the added keywords are typically not of strictly adult nature, people searching for other topics will be led to the page. Another web spamming technique is the

Permission to copy without fee all or part of this material is granted provided that the copies are not made or distributed for direct commercial advantage, the VLDB copyright notice and the title of the publication and its date appear, and notice is given that copying is by permission of the Very Large Data Base Endowment. To copy otherwise, or to republish, requires a fee and/or special permission from the Endowment.

**Proceedings of the 30th VLDB Conference,
Toronto, Canada, 2004**

creation of a large number of bogus web pages, all pointing to a single target page. Since many search engines take into account the number of incoming links in ranking pages, the rank of the target page is likely to increase, and appear earlier in query result sets.

Just as with email spam, determining if a page or group of pages is spam is subjective. For instance, consider a cluster of web sites that link to each other's pages repeatedly. These links may represent useful relationships between the sites, or they may have been created with the express intention of boosting the rank of each other's pages. In general, it is hard to distinguish between these two scenarios.

However, just as with email spam, most people can easily identify the blatant and brazen instances of web spam. For example, most would agree that if much of the text on a page is made invisible to humans (as noted above), and is irrelevant to the main topic of the page, then it was added with the intention to mislead. Similarly, if one finds a page with thousands of URLs referring to hosts like

buy-canon-rebel-300d-lens-case.camerasx.com,
buy-nikon-d100-d70-lens-case.camerasx.com,
...,

and notices that all host names map to the same IP address, then one would conclude that the page was created to mislead search engines. (The motivation behind URL spamming is that many search engines pay special attention to words in host names and give these words a higher weight than if they had occurred in plain text.)

While most humans would agree on the blatant web spam cases, this does not mean that it is easy for a computer to detect such instances. Search engine companies typically employ staff members who specialize in the detection of web spam, constantly scanning the web looking for offenders. When a spam page is identified, a search engine stops crawling it, and its content is no longer indexed. This spam detection process is very expensive and slow, but is critical to the success of search engines: without the removal of the blatant offenders, the quality of search results would degrade significantly.

Our research goal is to assist the human experts who detect web spam. In particular, we want to identify pages

Figure 1: A simple web graph.

and sites that are likely to be spam or that are likely to be reputable. The methods that we present in this paper could be used in two ways: (1) either as helpers in an initial screening process, suggesting pages that should be examined more closely by an expert, or (2) as a counter-bias to be applied when results are ranked, in order to discount possible boosts achieved by spam.

Since the algorithmic identification of spam is very difficult, our schemes do not operate entirely without human assistance. As we will see, the main algorithm we propose receives human assistance as follows. The algorithm first selects a small *seed* set of pages whose "spam status" needs to be determined. A human expert then examines the seed pages, and tells the algorithm if they are spam (*bad* pages) or not (*good* pages). Finally, the algorithm identifies other pages that are likely to be good based on their connectivity with the good seed pages.

In summary, the contributions of this paper are:

1. We formalize the problem of web spam and spam detection algorithms.
2. We define metrics for assessing the efficacy of detection algorithms.
3. We present schemes for selecting seed sets of pages to be manually evaluated.
4. We introduce the TrustRank algorithm for determining the likelihood that pages are reputable.
5. We discuss the results of an extensive evaluation, based on 31 million sites crawled by the AltaVista search engine, and a manual examination of over 2,000 sites. We provide some interesting statistics on the type and frequency of encountered web contents, and we use our data for evaluating the proposed algorithms.

2 Preliminaries

2.1 Web Model

We model the web as a graph $\mathcal{G} = (\mathcal{V}, \mathcal{E})$ consisting of a set $\mathcal{V}$ of N pages (vertices) and a set $\mathcal{E}$ of directed links (edges) that connect pages. In practice, a web page p may have multiple HTML hyperlinks to some other page q. In this case we collapse these multiple hyperlinks into a single link $(p,q) \in \mathcal{E}$. We also remove self hyperlinks. Figure 1 presents a very simple web graph of four pages and four links. (For our experiments in Section 6, we will deal with web sites, as opposed to individual web pages. However, our model and algorithms carry through to the case where graph vertices are entire sites.)

Each page has some incoming links, or *inlinks*, and some outgoing links, or *outlinks*. The number of inlinks of a page p is its *indegree* $\iota(p)$, whereas the number of outlinks is its *outdegree* $\omega(p)$. For instance, the indegree of page 3 in Figure 1 is one, while its outdegree is two.

Pages that have no inlinks are called *unreferenced pages*. Pages without outlinks are referred to as *non-referencing pages*. Pages that are both unreferenced and non-referencing at the same time are *isolated pages*. Page 1 in Figure 1 is an unreferenced page, while page 4 is non-referencing.

We introduce two matrix representations of a web graph, which will have important roles in the following sections. One of them is the *transition matrix* $\mathbf{T}$:

$$\mathbf{T}(p,q) = \begin{cases} 0 & \text{if } (q,p) \notin \mathcal{E}, \\ 1/\omega(q) & \text{if } (q,p) \in \mathcal{E}. \end{cases}$$

The transition matrix corresponding to the graph in Figure 1 is:

$$\mathbf{T} = \begin{pmatrix} 0 & 0 & 0 & 0 \\ 1 & 0 & \frac{1}{2} & 0 \\ 0 & 1 & 0 & 0 \\ 0 & 0 & \frac{1}{2} & 0 \end{pmatrix}.$$

We also define the *inverse transition matrix* $\mathbf{U}$:

$$\mathbf{U}(p,q) = \begin{cases} 0 & \text{if } (p,q) \notin \mathcal{E}, \\ 1/\iota(q) & \text{if } (p,q) \in \mathcal{E}. \end{cases}$$

Note that $\mathbf{U} \neq \mathbf{T}^T$. For the example in Figure 1 the inverse transition matrix is:

$$\mathbf{U} = \begin{pmatrix} 0 & \frac{1}{2} & 0 & 0 \\ 0 & 0 & 1 & 0 \\ 0 & \frac{1}{2} & 0 & 1 \\ 0 & 0 & 0 & 0 \end{pmatrix}.$$

2.2 PageRank

PageRank is a well known algorithm that uses link information to assign global importance scores to all pages on the web. Because our proposed algorithms rely on PageRank, this section offers a short overview.

The intuition behind PageRank is that a web page is important if several other important web pages point to it. Correspondingly, PageRank is based on a mutual reinforcement between pages: the importance of a certain page *influences* and is *being influenced* by the importance of some other pages.

The PageRank score $\mathbf{r}(p)$ of a page p is defined as:

$$\mathbf{r}(p) = \alpha \cdot \sum_{q:(q,p) \in \mathcal{E}} \frac{\mathbf{r}(q)}{\omega(q)} + (1-\alpha) \cdot \frac{1}{N},$$

where α is a decay factor.[1] The equivalent matrix equation

---

[1] Note that there are a number of equivalent definitions of PageRank [12] that might slightly differ in mathematical formulation and numerical properties, but yield the same relative ordering between any two web pages.

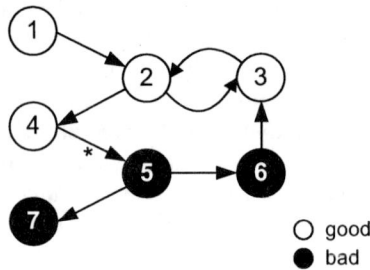

Figure 2: A web of good (white) and bad (black) nodes.

form is:
$$\mathbf{r} = \alpha \cdot \mathbf{T} \cdot \mathbf{r} + (1-\alpha) \cdot \frac{1}{N} \cdot \mathbf{1}_N.$$

Hence, the score of some page p is a sum of two components: one part of the score comes from pages that point to p, and the other (*static*) part of the score is equal for all web pages.

PageRank scores can be computed iteratively, for instance, by applying the Jacobi method [3]. While in a strict mathematical sense, iterations should be run to convergence, it is more common to use only a fixed number of M iterations in practice.

It is important to note that while the regular PageRank algorithm assigns the same static score to each page, a *biased PageRank* version may break this rule. In the matrix equation
$$\mathbf{r} = \alpha \cdot \mathbf{T} \cdot \mathbf{r} + (1-\alpha) \cdot \mathbf{d},$$
vector **d** is a *static score distribution vector* of arbitrary, non-negative entries summing up to one. Vector **d** can be used to assign a non-zero static score to a set of special pages only; the score of such special pages is then spread during the iterations to the pages they point to.

3 Assessing Trust

3.1 Oracle and Trust Functions

As discussed in Section 1, determining if a page is spam is subjective and requires human evaluation. We formalize the notion of a human checking a page for spam by a binary *oracle function* O over all pages $p \in \mathcal{V}$:

$$\mathrm{O}(p) = \begin{cases} 0 & \text{if } p \text{ is bad,} \\ 1 & \text{if } p \text{ is good.} \end{cases}$$

Figure 2 represents a small seven-page web where good pages are shown as white, and bad pages as black. For this example, calling the oracle on pages 1 through 4 would yield the return value of 1.

Oracle invocations are expensive and time consuming. Thus, we obviously do not want to call the oracle function for all pages. Instead, our objective is to be selective, i.e., to ask a human expert to evaluate only some of the web pages.

To discover good pages without invoking the oracle function on the entire web, we will rely on an important empirical observation we call the *approximate isolation* of the good set: good pages seldom point to bad ones. This notion is fairly intuitive—bad pages are built to mislead search engines, not to provide useful information. Therefore, people creating good pages have little reason to point to bad pages.

However, the creators of good pages can sometimes be "tricked," so we do find some good-to-bad links on the web. (In Figure 2 we show one such good-to-bad link, from page 4 to page 5, marked with an asterisk.) Consider the following example. Given a good, but unmoderated message board, spammers may include URLs to their spam pages as part of the seemingly innocent messages they post. Consequently, good pages of the message board would link to bad pages. Also, sometimes spam sites offer what is called a *honey pot*: a set of pages that provide some useful resource (e.g., copies of some Unix documentation pages), but that also have hidden links to their spam pages. The honey pot then attracts people to point to it, boosting the ranking of the spam pages.

Note that the converse to approximate isolation does not necessarily hold: spam pages can, and in fact often do, link to good pages. For instance, creators of spam pages point to important good pages either to create a honey pot, or hoping that many good outlinks would boost their hub-score-based ranking [10].

To evaluate pages without relying on O, we will estimate the likelihood that a given page p is good. More formally, we define a *trust function* T that yields a range of values between 0 (bad) and 1 (good). Ideally, for any page p, T(p) should give us the probability that p is good:

Ideal Trust Property
$$\mathsf{T}(p) = \Pr[\mathsf{O}(p) = 1].$$

To illustrate, let us consider a set of 100 pages and say that the trust score of each of these pages happens to be 0.7. Let us suppose that we also evaluate all the 100 pages with the oracle function. Then, if T works properly, for 70 of the pages the oracle score should be 1, and for the remaining 30 pages the oracle score should be 0.

In practice, it is very hard to come up with a function T with the previous property. However, even if T does not accurately measure the likelihood that a page is good, it would still be useful if the function could at least help us order pages by their likelihood of being good. That is, if we are given a pair of pages p and q, and p has a lower trust score than q, then this should indicate that p is less likely to be good than q. Such a function would at least be useful in ordering search results, giving preference to pages more likely to be good. More formally, then, a desirable property for the trust function is:

Ordered Trust Property

$$T(p) < T(q) \Leftrightarrow \Pr[O(p) = 1] < \Pr[O(q) = 1],$$
$$T(p) = T(q) \Leftrightarrow \Pr[O(p) = 1] = \Pr[O(q) = 1].$$

Another way to relax the requirements for T is to introduce a threshold value δ:

Threshold Trust Property

$$T(p) > \delta \Leftrightarrow O(p) = 1.$$

That is, if a page p receives a score above δ, we know that it is good. Otherwise, we cannot tell anything about p. Such a function T would at least be capable of telling us that some subset of pages with a trust score above δ is good. Note that a function T with the threshold property does not necessarily provide an ordering of pages based on their likelihood of being good.

3.2 Evaluation Metrics

This section introduces three metrics that help us evaluate whether a particular function T has some of the desired properties.

We assume that we have a sample set $\mathcal{X}$ of web pages for which we can invoke both T and O. Then, we can evaluate how well a desired property is achieved for this set. In Section 6 we discuss how a meaningful sample set $\mathcal{X}$ can be selected, but for now, we can simply assume that $\mathcal{X}$ is a set of random web pages.

Our first metric, *pairwise orderedness*, is related to the ordered trust property. We introduce a binary function $I(T, O, p, q)$ to signal if a bad page received an equal or higher trust score than a good page (a violation of the ordered trust property):

$$I(T, O, p, q) = \begin{cases} 1 & \text{if } T(p) \geq T(q) \text{ and } O(p) < O(q), \\ 1 & \text{if } T(p) \leq T(q) \text{ and } O(p) > O(q), \\ 0 & \text{otherwise.} \end{cases}$$

Next, we generate from our sample $\mathcal{X}$ a set $\mathcal{P}$ of ordered pairs of pages (p, q), $p \neq q$, and we compute the fraction of the pairs for which T did not make a mistake:

Pairwise Orderedness

$$\text{pairord}(T, O, \mathcal{P}) = \frac{|\mathcal{P}| - \sum_{(p,q) \in \mathcal{P}} I(T, O, p, q)}{|\mathcal{P}|}.$$

Hence, if pairord equals 1, there are no cases when T misrated a pair. Conversely, if pairord equals zero, then T misrated all the pairs. In Section 6 we discuss how to select a set $\mathcal{P}$ of sample page pairs for evaluation.

Our next two metrics are related to the threshold trust property. It is natural to think of the performance of function T in terms of the commonly used *precision* and *recall* metrics [1] for a certain threshold value δ. We define precision as the fraction of good among all pages in $\mathcal{X}$ that have a trust score above δ:

Precision

$$\text{prec}(T, O) = \frac{|\{p \in \mathcal{X} | T(p) > \delta \text{ and } O(p) = 1\}|}{|\{q \in \mathcal{X} | T(q) > \delta\}|}.$$

Similarly, we define recall as the ratio between the number of good pages with a trust score above δ and the total number of good pages in $\mathcal{X}$:

Recall

$$\text{rec}(T, O) = \frac{|\{p \in \mathcal{X} | T(p) > \delta \text{ and } O(p) = 1\}|}{|\{q \in \mathcal{X} | O(q) = 1\}|}.$$

4 Computing Trust

Let us begin our quest for a proper trust function by starting with some simple approaches. We will then combine the gathered observations and construct the TrustRank algorithm in Section 4.3.

Given a limited budget L of O-invocations, it is straightforward to select at random a *seed set* $\mathcal{S}$ of L pages and call the oracle on its elements. (In Section 5 we discuss how to select a better seed set.) We denote the subsets of good and bad seed pages by $\mathcal{S}^+$ and $\mathcal{S}^-$, respectively. Since the remaining pages are not checked by the human expert, we assign them a trust score of $1/2$ to signal our lack of information. Therefore, we call this scheme the *ignorant* trust function T_0, defined for any $p \in \mathcal{V}$ as follows:

Ignorant Trust Function

$$T_0(p) = \begin{cases} O(p) & \text{if } p \in \mathcal{S}, \\ 1/2 & \text{otherwise.} \end{cases}$$

For example, we can set L to 3 and apply our method to the example in Figure 2. A randomly selected seed set could then be $\mathcal{S} = \{1, 3, 6\}$. Let **o** and $\mathbf{t}_0$ denote the vectors of oracle and trust scores for each page, respectively. In this case,

$$\mathbf{o} = [1, \ 1, \ 1, \ 1, \ 0, \ 0, \ 0],$$
$$\mathbf{t}_0 = [1, \ \tfrac{1}{2}, \ 1, \ \tfrac{1}{2}, \ \tfrac{1}{2}, \ 0, \ \tfrac{1}{2}].$$

To evaluate the performance of the ignorant trust function, let us suppose that our sample $\mathcal{X}$ consists of all 7 pages, and that we consider all possible $7 \cdot 6 = 42$ ordered pairs. Then, the pairwise orderedness score of T_0 is $17/21$. Similarly, for a threshold $\delta = 1/2$, the precision is 1 while the recall is $1/2$.

4.1 Trust Propagation

As a next step in computing trust scores, we take advantage of the approximate isolation of good pages. We still select at random the set $\mathcal{S}$ of L pages that we invoke the oracle on. Then, expecting that good pages point to other good pages only, we assign a score of 1 to all pages that are reachable from a page in $\mathcal{S}^+$ in M or fewer steps. The appropriate trust function T_M is defined as:

M	pairord	prec	rec
1	19/21	1	3/4
2	1	1	1
3	17/21	4/5	1

Table 1: Performance of the M-step trust function T_M for $M \in \{1, 2, 3\}$.

M-Step Trust Function

$$T_M(p) = \begin{cases} O(p) & \text{if } p \in \mathcal{S}, \\ 1 & \text{if } p \notin \mathcal{S} \text{ and } \exists q \in \mathcal{S}^+ : q \rightsquigarrow_M p, \\ 1/2 & \text{otherwise,} \end{cases}$$

where $q \rightsquigarrow_M p$ denotes the existence of a path of a maximum length of M from page q to page p. Such a path must not include bad seed pages.

Using the example in Figure 2 and the seed set $\mathcal{S} = \{1, 3, 6\}$, we present the trust score assignments for three different values of M:

$M = 1$: $\mathbf{t}_1 = [1, 1, 1, \frac{1}{2}, \frac{1}{2}, 0, \frac{1}{2}]$,
$M = 2$: $\mathbf{t}_2 = [1, 1, 1, 1, \frac{1}{2}, 0, \frac{1}{2}]$,
$M = 3$: $\mathbf{t}_3 = [1, 1, 1, 1, 1, 0, \frac{1}{2}]$.

We would expect that T_M performs better than T_0 with respect to some of our metrics. Indeed, Table 1 shows that for $M = 1$ and $M = 2$, both pairwise orderedness and recall increase, and precision remains 1. However, there is a drop in performance when we go to $M = 3$. The reason is that page 5 receives a score of 1 due to the link from good page 4 to bad page 5 (marked with an asterisk on Figure 2).

As we saw in the previous example, the problem with M-step trust is that we are not absolutely sure that pages reachable from good seeds are indeed good. As a matter of fact, the further away we are from good seed pages, the less certain we are that a page is good. For instance, in Figure 2 there are 2 pages (namely, pages 2 and 4) that are at most 2 links away from the good seed pages. As both of them are good, the probability that we reach a good page in at most 2 steps is 1. Similarly, the number of pages reachable from the good seed in at most 3 steps is 3. Only two of these (pages 2 and 4) are good, while page 5 is bad. Thus, the probability of finding a good page drops to 2/3.

4.2 Trust Attenuation

These observations suggest that we reduce trust as we move further and further away from the good seed pages. There are many ways to achieve this attenuation of trust. Here we describe two possible schemes.

Figure 3 illustrates the first idea, which we call *trust dampening*. Since page 2 is one link away from the good seed page 1, we assign it a dampened trust score of β, where $\beta < 1$. Since page 3 is reachable in one step from page 2 with score β, it gets a dampened score of $\beta \cdot \beta$.

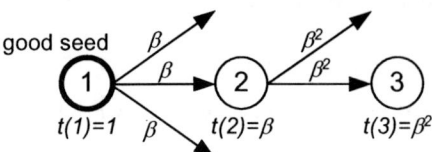

Figure 3: Trust dampening.

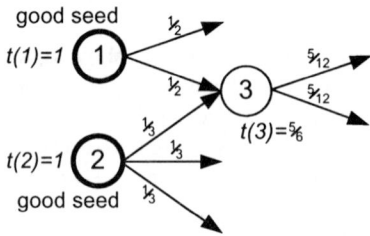

Figure 4: Trust splitting.

We also need to decide how to assign trust to pages with multiple inlinks. For instance, in Figure 3, assume page 1 also links to page 3. We could assign page 3 the maximum trust score, in this case β, or the average score, in this case $(\beta + \beta \cdot \beta)/2$.

The second technique for trust attenuation, which we call *trust splitting*, is based on the following observation: the care with which people add links to their pages is often inversely proportional to the number of links on the page. That is, if a good page has only a handful of outlinks, then it is likely that the pointed pages are also good. However, if a good page has hundreds of outlinks, it is more probable that some of them will point to bad pages.

This observation leads us to splitting trust as it propagates to other pages: if page p has a trust score of $T(p)$ and it points to $\omega(p)$ pages, each of the $\omega(p)$ pages will receive a score fraction $T(p)/\omega(p)$ from p. In this case, the actual score of a page will be the sum of the score fractions received through its inlinks. Intuitively, the more "credit" a page accumulates from some other pages, the more probable that it is good. (We can normalize summed scores to our standard range of $[0, 1]$.)

Figure 4 illustrates trust splitting. Good seed page 1 has two outlinks, so it distributes half of its score of 1 to both pages it points to. Similarly, good seed page 2 has three outlinks, so each page it points to receives one third of its score. The score of page 3 will then be $1/2 + 1/3 = 5/6$.

Notice that we can also combine trust splitting with dampening. In Figure 4, for instance, page 3 could receive a score of $\beta \cdot (1/2 + 1/3)$.

There are multiple ways of implementing trust dampening and/or splitting. In the next section we present one implementation that shares the same mathematical formulation with a biased PageRank computation in M steps. This feature means that we can rely on PageRank code (with minor changes) to compute trust scores. The resulting advan-

```
function TrustRank
input
        T       transition matrix
        N       number of pages
        L       limit of oracle invocations
        α_B     decay factor for biased PageRank
        M_B     number of biased PageRank iterations
output
        t*      TrustRank scores
begin
        // evaluate seed-desirability of pages
(1)     s = SelectSeed(...)
        // generate corresponding ordering
(2)     σ = Rank({1,...,N},s)
        // select good seeds
(3)     d = 0_N
        for i = 1 to L do
            if O(σ(i)) == 1 then
                d(σ(i)) = 1
        // normalize static score distribution vector
(4)     d = d/|d|
        // compute TrustRank scores
(5)     t* = d
        for i = 1 to M_B do
            t* = α_B · T · t* + (1 − α_B) · d
        return t*
end
```

Figure 5: The TrustRank algorithm.

tage is important since substantial effort has been spent on making PakeRank computations efficient with very large data sets (for instance, see [5, 8]).

4.3 The TrustRank Algorithm

Function TrustRank, shown in Figure 5, computes trust scores for a web graph. We explain the algorithm by walking through its execution on Figure 2.

The input to the algorithm is the graph (the transition matrix **T** and the number N of web pages) and parameters that control execution (L, M_B, $α_B$, see below).

As a first step, the algorithm calls function SelectSeed, which returns a vector **s**. The entry $s(p)$ in this vector gives the "desirability" of page p as a seed page. (Please refer to Section 5 for details.) As we will see in Section 5.1, one version of SelectSeed returns the following vector on the example of Figure 2:

$$\mathbf{s} = [0.08, \ 0.13, \ 0.08, \ 0.10, \ 0.09, \ 0.06, \ 0.02].$$

In step (2) function Rank(**x**,**s**) generates a permutation **x**′ of the vector **x**, with elements **x**′(i) in decreasing order of $s(\mathbf{x}'(i))$. In other words, Rank reorders the elements of **x** in decreasing order of their **s**-scores. For our example, we get:

$$σ = [2, \ 4, \ 5, \ 1, \ 3, \ 6, \ 7].$$

That is, page 2 is the most desirable seed page, followed by page 4, and so on.

Step (3) invokes the oracle function on the L most desirable seed pages. The entries of the static score distribution vector **d** that correspond to good seed pages are set to 1.

Step (4) normalizes vector **d** so that its entries sum up to 1. Assuming that $L = 3$, the seed set is $\{2,4,5\}$. Pages 2 and 4 are the good seeds, and we get the following static score distribution vector for our example:

$$\mathbf{d} = [0, \ \tfrac{1}{2}, \ 0, \ \tfrac{1}{2}, \ 0, \ 0, \ 0],$$

Finally, step (5) evaluates TrustRank scores using a biased PageRank computation with **d** replacing the uniform distribution. Note that step (5) implements a particular version of trust dampening and splitting: in each iteration, the trust score of a node is split among its neighbors and dampened by a factor $α_B$.

Assuming that $α_B = 0.85$ and $M_B = 20$, the algorithm computes the following result:

$$\mathbf{t}^* = [0, \ 0.18, \ 0.12, \ 0.15, \ 0.13, \ 0.05, \ 0.05].$$

Notice that because of the way we iteratively propagate trust scores, the good seed pages (namely, 2 and 4) no longer have a score of 1. However, they still have the highest scores. Also notice that good seed page 4 has a lower score than good seed page 2. This is due to the link structure in this example: page 2 has an inlink from a high scoring page (page 3), while page 4 does not. Thus, our TrustRank algorithm "refines" the original scores given by the oracle, determining that there is even more evidence that page 2 is good as compared to 4. If desired, one can normalize the resulting vector by dividing all scores by the highest score (making the score of page 2 equal to one), but this operation does not change the relative ordering of the pages.

We see in this example that the TrustRank algorithm usually gives good pages a higher score. In particular, three of the four good pages (namely, pages 2, 3, and 4) got high scores and two of the three bad pages (pages 6 and 7) got low scores. However, the algorithm failed to assign pages 1 and 5 adequate scores. Page 1 was not among the seeds, and it did not have any inlinks through which to accumulate score, so its score remained at 0. All good unreferenced web pages receive a similar treatment, unless they are selected as seeds. Bad page 5 received a high score because it is the direct target of one of the rare good-to-bad links. As we will see in Section 6, in spite of errors like these, on a real web graph the TrustRank algorithm is still able to correctly identify a significant number of good pages.

5 Selecting Seeds

The goal of function SelectSeed is to identify desirable pages for the seed set. That is, we would like to find pages

```
function SelectSeed
input
    U       inverse transition matrix
    N       number of pages
    α_I     decay factor
    M_I     number of iterations
output
    s       inverse PageRank scores
begin
    s = 1_N
    for i = 1 to M do
        s = α · U · s + (1 − α) · (1/N) · 1_N
    return s
end
```

Figure 6: The inverse PageRank algorithm.

that will be the most useful in identifying additional good pages. At the same time, we want to keep the seed set reasonably small to limit the number of oracle invocations. In this section we discuss two strategies for SelectSeed, in addition to the random selection strategy that was mentioned earlier.

5.1 Inverse PageRank

Since trust flows out of the good seed pages, one approach is to give preference to pages from which we can reach many other pages. In particular, we could select seed pages based on the number of outlinks. For instance, considering our example in Figure 2, the appropriate seed set of $L = 2$ pages would be $\mathcal{S} = \{2, 5\}$, since pages 2 and 5 have the largest number of outlinks (namely two).

Following a similar reasoning, the coverage can be improved even further. We can build the seed set from those pages that point to many pages that in turn point to many pages and so on. Interestingly, this approach leads us to a scheme closely related PageRank—the difference is that in our case the importance of a page depends on its outlinks, not its inlinks. Therefore, to compute the desirability of a page, we perform a PageRank computation on the graph $\mathcal{G}' = (\mathcal{V}, \mathcal{E}')$, where

$$(p, q) \in \mathcal{E}' \Leftrightarrow (q, p) \in \mathcal{E}.$$

Since we inverted the links, we call our algorithm *inverse PageRank*.

Figure 6 shows a SelectSeed algorithm that performs the inverse PageRank computation. Note that the decay factor $α_I$ and the number of iterations M_I can be different from the values $α_B$ and M_B used by the TrustRank algorithm. The computation is identical to that in the traditional PageRank algorithm (Section 2.2), except that the inverse transition matrix **U** is used instead of the regular transition matrix **T**.

For our example from Figure 2, the inverse PageRank algorithm ($α_I = 0.85, M_I = 20$) yields the following scores

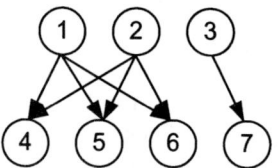

Figure 7: A graph for which inverse PageRank does not yield maximum coverage.

(already shown in Section 4.3):

$$\mathbf{s} = [0.08, \quad 0.13, \quad 0.08, \quad 0.10, \quad 0.09, \quad 0.06, \quad 0.02].$$

For a value of $L = 3$, the seed set is $\mathcal{S} = \{2, 4, 5\}$. Correspondingly, the good seed set is $\mathcal{S}^+ = \{2, 4\}$, so pages 2 and 4 are used as starting points for score distribution.

It is important to note that inverse PageRank is a heuristic (that works well in practice, as we will see in Section 6). First, inverse PageRank does not guarantee maximum coverage. For instance, in the example in Figure 7 and for $L = 2$, maximum coverage is achieved through the seed set $\{1, 3\}$ or $\{2, 3\}$. However, the inverse PageRank computation yields the score vector:

$$\mathbf{s} = [0.05, \quad 0.05, \quad 0.04, \quad 0.02, \quad 0.02, \quad 0.02, \quad 0.02],$$

which leads to the seed set $\mathcal{S} = \{1, 2\}$.

Nevertheless, inverse PageRank is appealing because its execution time is polynomial in the number of pages, while determining the maximum coverage is an $\mathcal{NP}$-complete problem.[2]

A second reason why inverse PageRank is a heuristic is that maximizing coverage may not always be the best strategy. To illustrate, let us propagate trust via splitting, without any dampening. Returning to Figure 7, say we only select page 2 as seed and it turns out to be good. Then pages 4, 5, and 6 each receive a score of $1/3$. Now, assume we only select page 3 as seed and it also happens to be good. Then page 7 gets a score of 1. Depending on our ultimate goal, it may be preferable to use page 3, since we can be more certain about the page it identifies, even if the set is smaller. However, if we are only using trusts scores for comparing against other trust scores, it may still be better to learn about more pages, even if with less absolute accuracy.

5.2 High PageRank

So far we have assumed that the value of identifying a page as good or bad is the same for all web pages. Yet, it may be

---

[2] The general problem of identifying the minimal set of pages that yields maximum coverage is equivalent to the independent set problem [7] on directed graphs as shown next. The web graph can be transformed in a directed graph $\mathcal{G}'' = (\mathcal{V}, \mathcal{E}'')$, where an edge $(p, q) \in \mathcal{E}''$ signals that page q can be reached from page p. We argue that such transformation does not change the complexity class of the algorithm, since it involves breadth-first search that has polynomial execution time. Then, finding a minimal set that provides maximum coverage is the same as finding the maximum independent set for $\mathcal{G}''$, which is an $\mathcal{NP}$-complete problem.

more important to ascertain the goodness of pages that will appear high in query result sets. For example, say we have four pages p, q, r, and s, whose contents match a given set of query terms equally well. If the search engine uses PageRank to order the results, the page with highest rank, say p, will be displayed first, followed by the page with next highest rank, say q, and so on. Since it is more likely the user will be interested in pages p and q, as opposed to pages r and s (pages r and s may even appear on later result pages and may not even be seen by the user), it seems more useful to obtain accurate trust scores for pages p and q rather than for r and s. For instance, if page p turns out to be spam, the user may rather visit page q instead.

Thus, a second heuristic for selecting a seed set is to give preference to pages with high PageRank. Since high-PageRank pages are likely to point to other high-PageRank pages, then good trust scores will also be propagated to pages that are likely to be at the top of result sets. Thus, with PageRank selection of seeds, we may identify the goodness of fewer pages (as compared to inverse PageRank), but they may be more important pages to know about.

6 Experiments

6.1 Data Set

To evaluate our algorithms, we performed experiments using the complete set of pages crawled and indexed by the AltaVista search engine as of August 2003.

In order to reduce computational demands, we decided to work at the level of web sites instead of individual pages. (Note that all presented methods work equally well for either pages or sites.) We grouped the several billion pages into 31,003,946 sites, using a proprietary algorithm that is part of the AltaVista engine. Although the algorithm relies on several heuristics to fine-tune its decisions, roughly speaking, all individual pages that share a common fully qualified host name[3] become part of the same site. Once we decided on the sites, we added a single link from site a to site b if in the original web graph there were one or more links from pages of site a pointing to pages of site b.

One interesting fact that we have noticed from the very beginning was that more than one third of the sites (13,197,046) were unreferenced. Trust propagation algorithms rely on inlink information, so are unable to differentiate among these sites without inlinks. Fortunately, the unreferenced sites are ranked low in query results (receive an identical, minimal static PageRank score), so it is not critical to separate good and bad sites among them.

For our evaluations, the first author of this paper played the role of the oracle, examining pages of various sites, determining if they are spam, and performing additional classification, as we will see. Of course, using an author as an evaluator raises the issue of bias in the results. However, this was our only choice. Our manual evaluations took weeks: checking a site involves looking at many of its pages and also the linked sites to determine if there is an intention to deceive search engines. Finding an expert working at one of the very competitive search engine companies who was knowledgeable enough and had time for this work was next to impossible. Instead, the first author spent time looking over the shoulder of the experts, learning how they identified spam sites. Then, he made every effort to be unbiased and to apply the experts' spam detection techniques.

6.2 Seed Set

As a first step, we conducted experiments to compare the inverse PageRank and the high PageRank seed selection schemes described in Sections 5.1 and 5.2, respectively. In order to be able to perform the comparison quickly, we ran our experiments on synthetic web graphs that capture the essential spam-related features of the web. We describe these experiments in [4]. Due to space limitations, here we just note that inverse PageRank turned out to be slightly better at identifying useful seed sets. Thus, for the rest of our experiments on the full, real web, we relied on the inverse PageRank method.

In implementing seed selection using inverse PageRank, we fine-tuned the process in order to streamline the oracle evaluations. First, we performed a full inverse PageRank computation on the site-level web graph, using parameters $\alpha_I = 0.85$ and $M_I = 20$. (The decay factor of 0.85 was first reported in [12] and has been regarded as the standard in PageRank literature ever since. Our tests showed that 20 iterations were enough to achieve convergence on the relative ordering of the sites.)

After ordering the sites based on their inverse PageRank scores (step (2) in Figure 5), we focused our attention on the top 25,000. Instead of a full oracle evaluation of these sites, we first did a cursory evaluation to eliminate some problematic ones. In particular, we noticed that sites with highest inverse PageRank scores showed a heavy bias toward spam, due to the presence of *Open Directory clones*: some spammers duplicate the entire content of the DMOZ Open Directory either in the hope of increasing their hub score [10] or with the intention of creating honey pots, as discussed in Section 3.1. In order to get rid of the spam quickly, we removed from our list of 25,000 sites all that were not listed in any of the major web directories, reducing the initial set to roughly 7,900. By sampling the sites that were filtered out, we found that insignificantly few reputable ones were removed by the process.

Out of the remaining 7,900 sites, we manually evaluated the top 1,250 (seed set $\mathcal{S}$) and selected 178 sites to be used as good seeds. This procedure corresponded to step (3) in Figure 5. The relatively small size of the good seed set $\mathcal{S}^+$ is due to the extremely rigorous selection criteria that we adopted: not only did we make sure that the sites were not

---

[3]The *fully qualified host name* is the portion of the URL between the http:// prefix, called the *scheme*, and the first slash character that usually follows the top level domain, such as .com, or the server's TCP port number. For instance, the fully qualified host name for the URL http://www-db.stanford.edu/db_pages/members.html is www-db.stanford.edu.

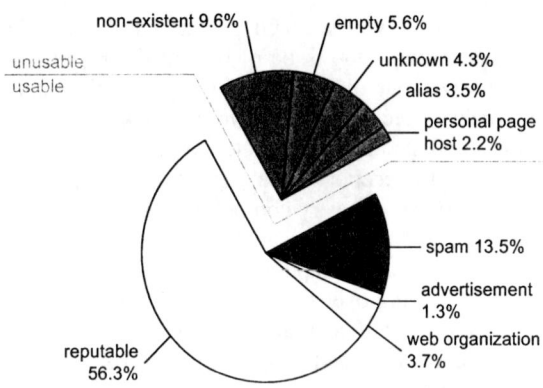

Figure 8: Composition of the evaluation sample.

spam, but we also applied a second filter—we only selected sites with a clearly identifiable authority (such as a governmental or educational institution or company) that controlled the contents of the site. The extra filter was added to guarantee the longevity of the good seed set, since the presence of physical authorities decreases the chance that the sites would degrade in the short run.

6.3 Evaluation Sample

In order to evaluate the metrics presented in Section 3.2, we needed a set $\mathcal{X}$ of sample sites with known oracle scores. (Note that this is different from the seed set and it is only used for assessing the performance of our algorithms.) We settled on a sample of 1000 sites, a number that gave us enough data points, and was still manageable in terms of oracle evaluation time.

We decided *not* to select the 1000 sample sites of $\mathcal{X}$ at random. With a random sample, a great number of the sites would be very small (with few pages) and/or have very low PageRank. (Both size and PageRank follow power-law distributions, with many sites at the tail end of the distribution.) As we discussed in Section 5.2, it is more important for us to correctly detect spam in high PageRank sites, since they will more often appear high in query result sets. Furthermore, it is hard for the oracle to evaluate small sites due to the reduced body of evidence, so it also does not make sense to consider many small sites in our sample.

In order to assure diversity, we adopted the following sampling method. We generated the list of sites in decreasing order of their PageRank scores, and we segmented it into 20 buckets. Each of the buckets contained a different number of sites, with scores summing up to 5 percent of the total PageRank score. Therefore, the first bucket contained the 86 sites with the highest PageRank scores, bucket 2 the next 665, while the 20th bucket contained 5 million sites that were assigned the lowest PageRank scores.

We constructed our sample set of 1000 sites by selecting 50 sites at random from each bucket. Then, we performed a manual (oracle) evaluation of the sample sites, determining if they were spam or not. The outcome of the evaluation process is presented in Figure 8, a pie-chart that shows the way our sample breaks down to various types of sites. We found that we could use 748 of the sample sites to evaluate TrustRank:

- *Reputable.* 563 sites featured quality contents with zero or a statistically insignificant number of links pointing to spam sites.

- *Web organization.* 37 sites belonged to organizations that either have a role in the maintenance of the World Wide Web or perform business related to Internet services. While all of them were good sites, most of their links were automatic (e.g., "Site hosted by Provider X"). Therefore, we decided to give them a distinct label to be able to follow their features separately.

- *Advertisement.* 13 of the sites were ones acting as targets for banner ads. These sites lack real useful content and their high PageRank scores are due exclusively to the large number of automatic links that they receive. Nevertheless, they still qualify as good sites without any sign of spamming activity.

- *Spam.* 135 sites featured various forms of spam. We considered these sites as bad ones.

These 748 sites formed our sample set $\mathcal{X}$. The remaining 252 sites were deemed unusable for the evaluation of TrustRank for various reasons:

- *Personal page host.* 22 of the sites hosted personal web pages. The large, uncontrolled body of editors contributing to the wide variety of contents for each of these sites made it impossible to categorize them as either bad or good. Note that this issue would not appear in a page-level evaluation.

- *Alias.* 35 sites were simple aliases of sites better known under a different name. We decided to drop these aliases because the importance of the alias could not reflect the importance of the original site appropriately.

- *Empty.* 56 sites were empty, consisting of a single page that provided no useful information.

- *Non-existent.* 96 sites were non-existent—either the DNS lookup failed, or our systems were not able to establish a TCP/IP connection with the corresponding computers.

- *Unknown.* We were unable to properly evaluate 43 sites based on the available information. These sites were mainly East Asian ones, which represented a challenge because of the lack of English translation.

6.4 Results

In Section 4 we described a number of strategies for propagating trust from a set of good seeds. In this section we focus on three of the alternatives, TrustRank and two baseline strategies, and evaluate their performance using our sample $\mathcal{X}$:

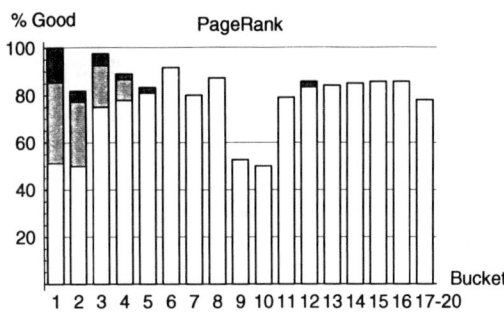
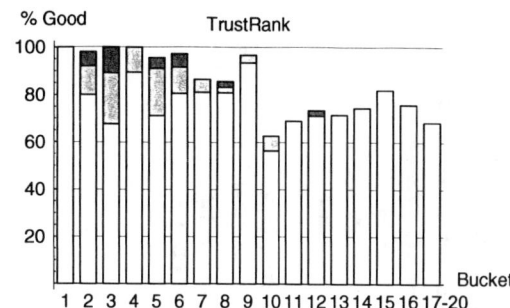

Figure 9: Good sites in PageRank and TrustRank buckets.

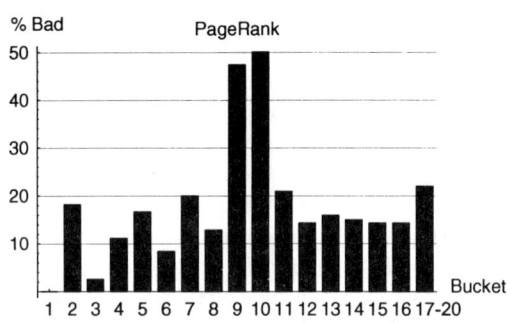
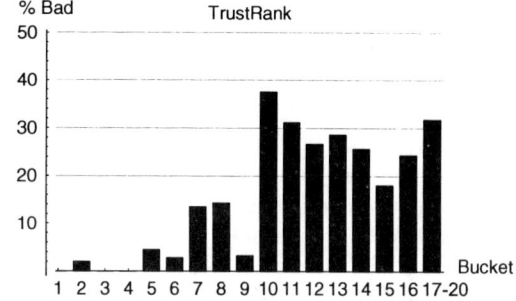

Figure 10: Bad sites in PageRank and TrustRank buckets.

1. *TrustRank*. We used the algorithm in Figure 5 ($M_B = 20$ iterations and decay factor of $\alpha_B = 0.85$) and our selected 178 good seeds.

2. *PageRank*. PageRank was originally considered highly resilient to spamming because it measures global importance (limited, local changes to the link structure have low impact on the scores). Thus, it is natural to ask how well PageRank can cope with spam in today's world. Thus, for this alternative we simply used the PageRank of site a as the value of $T(a)$. We again performed $M = 20$ iterations, with a decay factor of $\alpha = 0.85$.

3. *Ignorant Trust*. As another baseline, we generated the ignorant trust scores of sites. All sites were assigned an ignorant trust score of $1/2$, except for the 1250 seeds, which received scores of 0 or 1.

6.4.1 PageRank versus TrustRank

Let us discuss the difference between PageRank and TrustRank first. Remember, the PageRank algorithm does not incorporate any knowledge about the quality of a site, nor does it explicitly penalize badness. In fact, we will see that it is not very uncommon that some site created by a skilled spammer receives high PageRank score. In contrast, our TrustRank is meant to differentiate good and bad sites: we expect that spam sites were not assigned high TrustRank scores.

Figures 9 and 10 provide a side-by-side comparison of PageRank and TrustRank with respect to the ratio of good and bad sites in each bucket. PageRank buckets were introduced in Section 6.3; we defined TrustRank buckets as containing the same number of sites as PageRank buckets. Note that we merged buckets 17 through 20 both for PageRank and TrustRank. (These last 4 buckets contained the more than 13 million sites that were unreferenced. All such sites received the same minimal static PageRank score and a zero TrustRank score, making it impossible to set up an ordering among them.)

The horizontal axes of Figures 9 and 10 mark the PageRank and TrustRank bucket numbers, respectively. The vertical axis of the first figure corresponds to the percentage of good within a specific bucket, i.e., the number of good sample sites divided by the total number of sample sites in that bucket. Note that reputable, advertisement, and web organization sites all qualify as good ones; their relative contributions are shown by white, middle gray, and dark gray segments, respectively. The vertical axis of the second figure corresponds to the percentage of bad within a specific bucket. For instance, we can derive from Figure 10 that 31% of the usable sample sites in TrustRank bucket 11 are bad ones.

From these figures we see that TrustRank is a reasonable spam detection tool. In particular, note that there is virtually no spam in the top 5 TrustRank buckets, while there is a marked increase in spam concentration in the lower buckets. At the same time, it is surprising that almost 20% of the second PageRank bucket is bad. For PageRank, the proportion of bad sites peaks in buckets 9 and 10 (50% spam), indicating that probably this is as high as average spammers

585

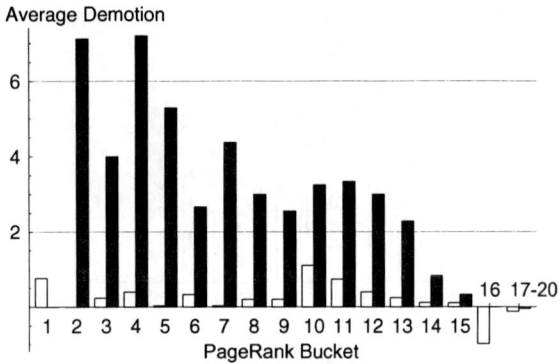

Figure 11: Bucket-level demotion in TrustRank.

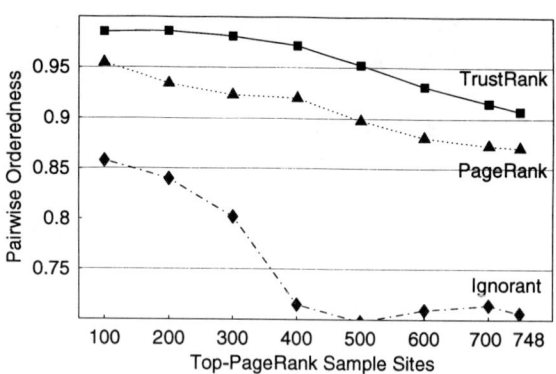

Figure 12: Pairwise orderedness.

could push their sites.

Figure 11 offers another view on the relationship between PageRank and TrustRank. It introduces the notion of *demotion*, the phenomenon that a certain site from a higher PageRank bucket appears in a lower TrustRank bucket. Negative demotion is *promotion*, the case when a site from a lower PageRank bucket shows up in a higher TrustRank bucket. The average demotion of bad sites is an important way to evaluate TrustRank as it shows its success (or lack thereof) to cut the importance of bad sites.

The horizontal axis of Figure 11 stands for PageRank buckets. The vertical axis shows the number of buckets by which sites from a specific PageRank bucket got demoted in TrustRank on average. White bars represent the reputable sites, while black ones denote spam. (Note that we do not show advertisement and web organization sites in the figure.)

As an illustration, we can derive from Figure 11 that spam sites in PageRank bucket 2 got demoted seven buckets on average, thus landing somewhere around TrustRank bucket 9. An example of promotion can be seen in PageRank bucket 16, where good sites appear on average one bucket higher in the TrustRank ordering.

This figure again shows well that TrustRank effectively removes most of the spam from among the top-scored sites. Furthermore, it also reveals that good sites retain their original bucket position in most of the cases. Consequently, we argue that (opposed to PageRank) TrustRank guarantees that top-scored sites are good ones. We also assert that TrustRank is unable to effectively separate low-scored good sites from bad ones, due to the lack of distinguishing features (inlinks) of the sites.

6.4.2 Pairwise Orderedness

We used the pairwise orderedness metric presented in Section 3.2 to evaluate TrustRank with respect to the ordered trust property. For this experiment, we built the set $\mathcal{P}$ of all possible pairs of sites for several subsets of our evaluation sample $\mathcal{X}$. We started by using the subset of $\mathcal{X}$ of the 100 sites with highest PageRank scores, in order to check TrustRank for the most important sites. Then, we gradually added more and more sites to our subset, in their decreasing order of PageRank scores. Finally, we used all pairs of all the 748 sample sites to compute the pairwise orderedness score.

Figure 12 displays the results of this experiment. The horizontal axis shows the number of sample sites used for evaluation, while the vertical axis represents the pairwise orderedness scores for the specific sample sizes. For instance, we can conclude that for the 500 top-PageRank sample sites TrustRank receives a pairwise orderedness score of about 0.95.

Figure 12 also shows the pairwise orderedness scores for the ignorant trust function and PageRank. The overlap between our seed set $\mathcal{S}$ and sample set $\mathcal{X}$ is of 5 good sites, so all but five sample sites received a score of $1/2$ from the ignorant trust function. Hence, the pairwise orderedness scores for the ignorant function represent the case when we have almost no information about the quality of the sites. Similarly, pairwise orderedness scores for PageRank illustrate how much the knowledge of importance can help in distinguishing good and bad. As we can see, TrustRank constantly outperforms both the ignorant function and PageRank.

6.4.3 Precision and Recall

Our last set of experimental results, shown in Figure 13, present the performance of TrustRank with respect to the metrics of precision and recall. We used as threshold values δ the borderline TrustRank scores that separated the 17 TrustRank buckets, discussed in Section 6.4.1. The lowest buckets corresponding to each threshold value are presented on the horizontal axis of the figure; we display the precision and recall scores on the vertical. For instance, if the threshold δ is set so that all and only sample sites in TrustRank buckets 1 through 10 are above it, then precision is 0.86 and recall is 0.55.

TrustRank assigned the highest scores to good sites, and the proportion of bad increases gradually as we move to lower scores. Hence, precision and recall manifest an almost linear decrease and increase, respectively. Note the high (0.82) precision score for the whole sample set: such a value would be very uncommon for traditional informa-

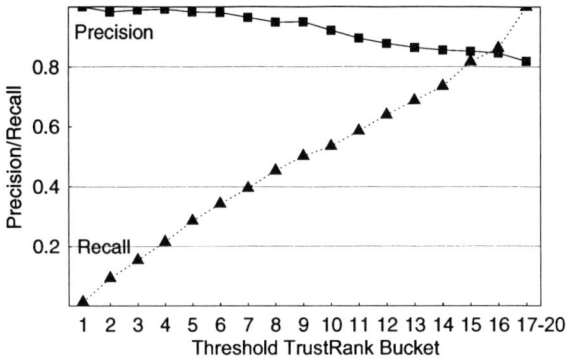

Figure 13: Precision and recall.

tion retrieval problems, where it is usual to have a large corpus of documents, with only a few of those documents being relevant for a specific query. In contrast, our sample set consists most of good documents, all of which are "relevant." This is why the baseline precision score for the sample $\mathcal{X}$ is $613/(613+135) = 0.82$.

7 Related Work

Our work builds on existing PageRank research. The idea of biasing PageRank to combat spam was introduced in [12]. The use of custom static score distribution vectors has been studied in the context of topic-sensitive PageRank [6]. Recent analyses of (biased) PageRank are provided by [2, 11].

The problem of trust has also been addressed in the context of peer-to-peer systems. For instance, [9] presents an algorithm similar to PageRank for computing the reputation or dependability of a node in a peer-to-peer network.

The data mining and machine learning communities also explored the topic of web and email spam detection (for instance, see [13]). However, this research is oriented toward the analysis of individual documents. The analysis typically looks for telltale signs of spamming techniques based on statistics derived from examples.

8 Conclusions

As the web grows in size and value, search engines play an increasingly critical role, allowing users to find information of interest. However, today's search engines are seriously threatened by malicious web spam that attempts to subvert the unbiased searching and ranking services provided by the engines. Search engines are today combating web spam with a variety of ad hoc, often proprietary techniques. We believe that our work is a first attempt at formalizing the problem and at introducing a comprehensive solution to assist in the detection of web spam. Our experimental results show that we can effectively identify a significant number of strongly reputable (non-spam) pages. In a search engine, TrustRank can be used either separately to filter the index, or in combination with PageRank and other metrics to rank search results.

We believe that there are still a number of interesting experiments that need to be carried out. For instance, it would be desirable to further explore the interplay between dampening and splitting for trust propagation. In addition, there are a number of ways to refine our methods. For example, instead of selecting the entire seed set at once, one could think of an iterative process: after the oracle has evaluated some pages, we could reconsider what pages it should evaluate next, based on the previous outcome. Such issues are a challenge for future research.

Acknowledgement

The authors would like to thank David Cossock and Farzin Maghoul for the inspiring discussions and valuable comments.

References

[1] R. Baeza-Yates and B. Ribeiro-Neto. *Modern Information Retrieval*. Addison-Wesley, 1999.

[2] M. Bianchini, M. Gori, and F. Scarselli. Inside PageRank. Tech. rep., University of Siena, 2003.

[3] G. Golub and C. Van Loan. *Matrix Computations*. The Johns Hopkins University Press, 1996.

[4] Z. Gyöngyi and H. Garcia-Molina. Seed selection in TrustRank. Tech. rep., Stanford University, 2004.

[5] T. Haveliwala. Efficient computation of PageRank. Tech. rep., Stanford University, 1999.

[6] T. Haveliwala. Topic-sensitive PageRank. In *Proceedings of the Eleventh International Conference on World Wide Web*, 2002.

[7] J. Hopcroft, R. Motwani, and J. Ullman. *Introduction to Automata Theory, Languages, and Computation*. Addison-Wesley, 2001.

[8] S. Kamvar, T. Haveliwala, C. Manning, and G. Golub. Extrapolation methods for accelerating PageRank computations. In *Proceedings of the Twelfth International Conference on World Wide Web*, 2003.

[9] S. Kamvar, M. Schlosser, and H. Garcia-Molina. The EigenTrust algorithm for reputation management in P2P networks. In *Proceedings of the Twelfth International Conference on World Wide Web*, 2003.

[10] J. M. Kleinberg. Authoritative sources in a hyperlinked environment. *Journal of the ACM*, 46(5):604–632, 1999.

[11] A. Langville and C. Meyer. Deeper inside PageRank. Tech. rep., North Carolina State University, 2003.

[12] L. Page, S. Brin, R. Motwani, and T. Winograd. The PageRank citation ranking: Bringing order to the web. Tech. rep., Stanford University, 1998.

[13] M. Sahami, S. Dumais, D. Heckerman, and E. Horvitz. A Bayesian approach to filtering junk e-mail. In *Learning for Text Categorization: Papers from the 1998 Workshop*, 1998.

Model-Driven Data Acquisition in Sensor Networks[*]

Amol Deshpande[†]   Carlos Guestrin[‡]   Samuel R. Madden[§ ‡]
Joseph M. Hellerstein[† ‡]   Wei Hong[‡]

[†] UC Berkeley   [‡] Intel Research Berkeley   [§] MIT
{amol,jmh}@cs.berkeley.edu   {guestrin,whong}@intel-research.net   madden@csail.mit.edu

Abstract

Declarative queries are proving to be an attractive paradigm for interacting with networks of wireless sensors. The metaphor that "the sensornet is a database" is problematic, however, because sensors do not exhaustively represent the data in the real world. In order to map the raw sensor readings onto physical reality, a *model* of that reality is required to complement the readings. In this paper, we enrich interactive sensor querying with statistical modeling techniques. We demonstrate that such models can help provide answers that are both more meaningful, and, by introducing approximations with probabilistic confidences, significantly more efficient to compute in both time and energy. Utilizing the combination of a model and live data acquisition raises the challenging optimization problem of selecting the best sensor readings to acquire, balancing the increase in the confidence of our answer against the communication and data acquisition costs in the network. We describe an exponential time algorithm for finding the optimal solution to this optimization problem, and a polynomial-time heuristic for identifying solutions that perform well in practice. We evaluate our approach on several real-world sensor-network data sets, taking into account the real measured data and communication quality, demonstrating that our model-based approach provides a high-fidelity representation of the real phenomena and leads to significant performance gains versus traditional data acquisition techniques.

1 Introduction

Database technologies are beginning to have a significant impact in the emerging area of wireless sensor networks (sensornets). The sensornet community has embraced declarative queries as a key programming paradigm for large sets of sensors. This is seen in academia in the calls for papers for leading conferences and workshops in the sensornet area [2, 1], and in a number of prior research publications ([21],[30],[17], etc). In the emerging industrial arena, one of the leading vendors (Crossbow) is bundling a query processor with their devices, and providing query processor training as part of their customer support. The area of sensornet querying represents an unusual opportunity for database researchers to apply their expertise in a new area of computer systems.

[*]This work was supported by Intel Corporation, and by NSF under the grant IIS-0205647.

Permission to copy without fee all or part of this material is granted provided that the copies are not made or distributed for direct commercial advantage, the VLDB copyright notice and the title of the publication and its date appear, and notice is given that copying is by permission of the Very Large Data Base Endowment. To copy otherwise, or to republish, requires a fee and/or special permission from the Endowment.

**Proceedings of the 30th VLDB Conference,
Toronto, Canada, 2004**

Declarative querying has proved powerful in allowing programmers to "task" an entire network of sensor nodes, rather than requiring them to worry about programming individual nodes. However, the metaphor that "the sensornet is a database" has proven misleading. Databases are typically treated as complete, authoritative sources of information; the job of a database query engine has traditionally been to answer a query "correctly" based upon all the available data. Applying this mindset to sensornets results in two problems:

1. **Misrepresentations of data:** In the sensornet environment, it is impossible to gather *all* the relevant data. The physically observable world consists of a set of continuous phenomena in both time and space, so the set of relevant data is in principle infinite. Sensing technologies acquire *samples* of physical phenomena at discrete points in time and space, but the data acquired by the sensornet is unlikely to be a random (i.i.d.) sample of physical processes, for a number of reasons (non-uniform placement of sensors in space, faulty sensors, high packet loss rates, etc). So a straightforward interpretation of the sensornet readings as a "database" may not be a reliable representation of the real world.

2. **Inefficient approximate queries:** Since a sensornet cannot acquire all possible data, any readings from a sensornet are "approximate", in the sense that they only represent the true state of the world at the discrete instants and locations where samples were acquired. However, the leading approaches to query processing in sensornets [30, 21] follow a completist's approach, acquiring as much data as possible from the environment at a given point in time, even when *most of that data provides little benefit in approximate answer quality*. We show examples where query execution cost – in both time and power consumption – can be orders of magnitude more than is appropriate for a reasonably reliable answer.

1.1 Our contribution

In this paper, we propose to compensate for both of these deficiencies by incorporating statistical *models* of real-world processes into a sensornet query processing architecture. Models can help provide more robust interpretations of sensor readings: for example, they can account for biases in spatial sampling, can help identify sensors that are providing faulty data, and can extrapolate the values of missing sensors or sensor readings at geographic locations where sensors are no longer operational. Furthermore, models provide a framework for optimizing the acquisition of sensor readings: sensors should be used to acquire data only when the model itself is not sufficiently rich to answer the query with acceptable confidence.

Underneath this architectural shift in sensornet querying, we define and address a key optimization problem: given a query and a model, choose a data acquisition plan for the sensornet to best refine the query answer. This optimization problem is complicated by two forms of dependencies: one in the statistical *benefits* of acquiring a reading, the other in the system *costs* associated with wireless sensor systems.

First, any non-trivial statistical model will capture correlations among sensors: for example, the temperatures of geographically proximate sensors are likely to be correlated. Given such a model, the benefit of a single sensor reading can be used to improve estimates of other readings: the temperature at one sensor node is likely to improve the confidence of model-driven estimates for nearby nodes.

The second form of dependency hinges on the connectivity of the wireless sensor network. If a sensor node far is not within radio range of the query source, then one cannot acquire a reading from far without forwarding the request/result pair through another node $near$. This presents not only a non-uniform cost model for acquiring readings, but one with dependencies: due to multi-hop networking, the acquisition cost for $near$ will be much lower if one has already chosen to acquire data from far by routing through $near$.

To explore the benefits of the model-based querying approach we propose, we are building a prototype called BBQ[1] that uses a specific model based on time-varying multivariate Gaussians. We describe how our generic model-based architecture and querying techniques are specifically applied in BBQ. We also present encouraging results on real-world sensornet trace data, demonstrating the advantages that models offer for queries over sensor networks.

2 Overview of approach

In this section, we provide an overview of our basic architecture and approach, as well as a summary of BBQ. Our architecture consists of a declarative query processing engine that uses a probabilistic model to answer questions about the current state of the sensor network. We denote a model as a *probability density function* (pdf), $p(X_1, X_2, \ldots, X_n)$, assigning a probability for each possible assignment to the attributes $X_1, \ldots, X_n$, where each X_i is an attribute at a particular sensor (*e.g.*, temperature on sensing node 5, voltage on sensing node 12). Typically, there is one such attribute per sensor type per sensing node. This model can also incorporate *hidden variables* (*i.e.*, variables that are not directly observable) that indicate, for example, whether a sensor is giving faulty values. Such models can be learned from historical data using standard algorithms (*e.g.*, [23]).

Users query for information about the values of particular attributes or in certain regions of the network, much as they would in a traditional SQL database. Unlike database queries, however, sensornet queries request real-time information about the environment, rather than information about a stored collection of data. The model is used to estimate sensor readings in the current time period; these estimates form the answer the query. In the process of generating these

[1] BBQ is short for Barbie-Q: A Tiny-Model Query System

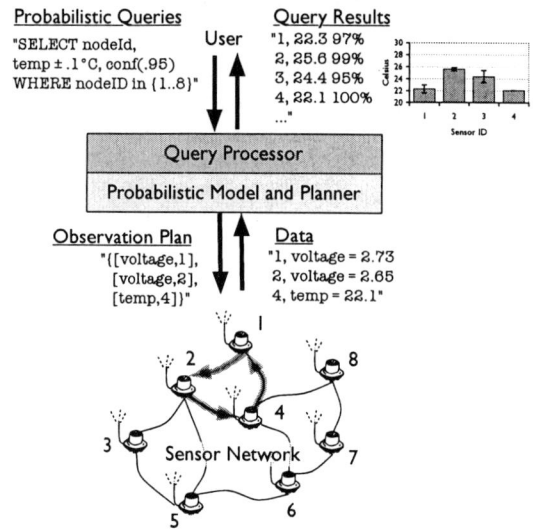

Figure 1: Our architecture for model-based querying in sensor networks.

estimates, the model may interrogate the sensor network for updated readings that will help to refine estimates for which its uncertainty is high. As time passes, the model may also update its estimates of sensor values, to reflect expected temporal changes in the data.

In BBQ, we use a specific model based on time-varying multivariate Gaussians; we describe this model below. We emphasize, however, that our approach is general with respect to the model, and that more or less complex models can be used instead. New models require no changes to the query processor and can reuse code that interfaces with and acquires particular readings from the sensor network. The main difference occurs in the algorithms required to solve the probabilistic inference tasks described in Section 3. These algorithms have been widely developed for many practical models (*e.g.*, [23]).

Figure 1 illustrates our basic architecture through an example. Users submit SQL queries to the database, which are translated into probabilistic computations over the model (Section 3). The queries include error tolerances and target confidence bounds that specify how much uncertainty the user is willing to tolerate. Such bounds will be intuitive to many scientific and technical users, as they are the same as the confidence bounds used for reporting results in most scientific fields (c.f., the graph-representation shown in the upper right of Figure 1). In this example, the user is interested in estimates of the value of sensor readings for nodes numbered 1 through 8, within .1 degrees C of the actual temperature reading with 95% confidence. Based on the model, the system decides that the most efficient way to answer the query with the requested confidence is to read battery voltage from sensors 1 and 2 and temperature from sensor 4. Based on knowledge of the sensor network topology, it generates an *observation plan* that acquires samples in this order, and sends the plan into the network, where the appropriate readings are collected. These readings are used to update the model, which can then be used to generate query answers with specified confidence intervals.

Notice that the model in this example chooses to observe the voltage at some nodes despite the fact that the user's query

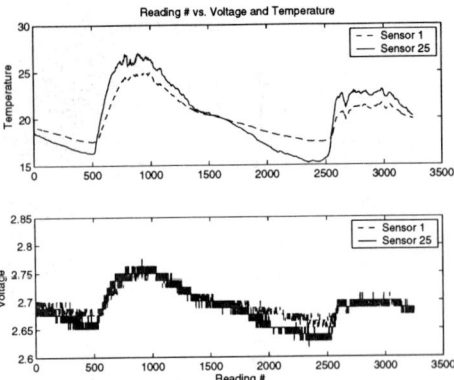

Figure 2: Trace of voltage and temperature readings over a two day period from a single mote-based sensor. Notice the close correlation between the two attributes.

was over temperature. This happens for two reasons:

1. **Correlations in Value:** Temperature and voltage are highly correlated, as illustrated by Figure 2 which shows the temperature and voltage readings for two days of sensor readings from a pair of Berkeley Mica2 Motes [6] that we deployed in the Intel Research Lab in Berkeley, California. Note how voltage tracks temperature, and how temperature variations across motes, even though of noticeably different magnitudes, are very similar. The relationship between temperature and voltage is due to the fact that, for many types of batteries, as they heat or cool, their voltages vary significantly (by as much as 1% per degree). The voltages may also decrease as the sensor nodes consume energy from the batteries, but the time scale at which that happens is much larger than the time scale of temperature variations, and so the model can use voltage changes to infer temperature changes.

2. **Cost Differential:** Depending on the specific type of temperature sensor used, it may be much cheaper to sample the voltage than to read the temperature. For example, on sensor boards from Crossbow Corporation for Berkeley Motes [6], the temperature sensor requires several orders of magnitude more energy to sample as simply reading battery voltage (see Table 1).

One of the important properties of many probabilistic models (including the one used in BBQ) is that they can capture correlations between different attributes. We will see how we can exploit such correlations during optimization to generate efficient query plans in Section 4.

2.1 Confidence intervals and correlation models

The user in Figure 1 could have requested 100% confidence and no error tolerance, in which case the model would have required us to interrogate every sensor. The returned result could still include some uncertainty, as the model may not have readings from particular sensors or locations at some points in time (due to sensor or communications failures, or lack of sensor instrumentation at a particular location). These confidence intervals computed from our probabilistic model provide considerably more information than traditional sensor network systems like TinyDB and Cougar provide in this setting. With those systems, the user would simply get no data regarding those missing times and locations.

Conversely, the user could have requested very wide confidence bounds, in which case the model may have been able to answer the query without acquiring any additional data from the network. In fact, in our experiments with BBQ on several real-world data sets, we see a number of cases where strong correlations between sensors during certain times of the day mean that even queries with relatively tight confidence bounds can be answered with a very small number of sensor observations. In many cases, these tight confidences can be provided *despite the fact that sensor readings have changed significantly.* This is because known correlations between sensors make it possible to predict these changes: for example, in Figure 2, it is clear that the temperature on the two sensors is correlated given the time of day. During the daytime (e.g., readings 600-1200 and 2600-3400), sensor 25, which is placed near a window, is consistently hotter than sensor 1, which is in the center of our lab. A good model will be able to infer, with high confidence that, during daytime hours, sensor readings on sensor 25 are 1-2 degrees hotter than those at sensor 1 without actually observing sensor 25. Again, this is in contrast to existing sensor network querying systems, where sensors are continuously sampled and readings are always reported whenever small absolute changes happen.

Typically in probabilistic modeling, we pick a class of models, and use learning techniques to pick the best model in the class. The problem of selecting the right model class has been widely studied (*e.g.*, [23]), but can be difficult in some applications. Before presenting the specific model class used in BBQ, we note that, in general, a probabilistic model is only as good at prediction as the data used to train it. Thus, it may be the case that the temperature between sensors 1 and 25 would not show the same relationship during a different season of the year, or in a different climate – in fact, one might expect that when the outside temperature is very cold, sensor 25 will read less than sensor 1 during the day, just as it does during the night time. Thus, for models to perform accurate predictions they must be trained in the kind of environment where they will be used. That does not mean, however, that well-trained models cannot deal with changing relationships over time; in fact, the model we use in BBQ uses different correlation data depending on time of day. Extending it to handle seasonal variations, for example is a straightforward extension of the techniques we use for handling variations across hours of the day.

2.2 BBQ

In BBQ, we use a specific probabilistic model based on time-varying multivariate Gaussians. A multivariate Gaussian (hereafter, just Gaussian) is the natural extension of the familiar unidimensional normal probability density function (pdf), known as the "bell curve". Just as with its 1-dimensional counterpart, a Gaussian pdf over d attributes, $X_1, \ldots, X_d$ can be expressed as a function of two parameters: a length-d vector of means, μ, and a $d \times d$ matrix of covariances, Σ. Figure 3(A) shows a three-dimensional rendering of a Gaussian over two attributes, X_1 and X_2; the z axis represents the *joint density* that $X_2 = x$ and $X_1 = y$. Figure 3(B) shows a contour plot representation of the same Gaussian, where each circle represents a probability density contour (corresponding to the height of the plot in (A)).

Intuitively, μ is the point at the center of this probability distribution, and Σ represents the spread of the distribution. The ith element along the diagonal of Σ is simply the variance of X_i. Each off-diagonal element $\Sigma[i, j], i \neq j$ represents the covariance between attributes X_i and X_j. Covariance is a measure of correlation between a pair of attributes. A high absolute covariance means that the attributes are strongly correlated: knowledge of one closely constrains the value of the other. The Gaussians shown in Figure 3(A) and (B) have a high covariance between X_1 and X_2. Notice that the contours are elliptical such that knowledge of one variable constrains the value of the other to a narrow probability band.

In BBQ, we use historical data to construct the initial representation of this pdf p. In the implementation described in this paper, we obtained such data using TinyDB (a traditional sensor network querying system)[2]. Once our initial p is constructed, we can answer queries using the model, updating it as new observations are obtained from the sensor network, and as time passes. We explain the details of how updates are done in Section 3.2, but illustrate it graphically with our 2-dimensional Gaussian in Figures 3(B) - 3(D). Suppose that we have an initial Gaussian shown in Figure 3(B) and we choose to observe the variable X_1; given the resulting single value of $X_1 = x$, the points along the line $\{(x, X_2) \mid \forall X_2 \in [-\infty, \infty]\}$ conveniently form an (unnormalized) one-dimensional Gaussian. After re-normalizing these points (to make the area under the curve equal 1.0), we can derive a new pdf representing $p(X_2 \mid X_1 = x)$, which is shown in 3(C). Note that the mean of X_2 given the value of X_1 is not the same as the prior mean of X_2 in 3(B). Then, after some time has passed, our belief about X_1's value will be "spread out", and we will again have a Gaussian over two attributes, although both the mean and variance may have shifted from their initial values, as shown in Figure 3(D).

2.3 Supported queries

Answering queries probabilistically based on a distribution (*e.g.*, the Gaussian representation described above) is conceptually straightforward. Suppose, for example, that a query asks for an ϵ approximation to the value of a set of attributes, with confidence at least $1 - \delta$. We can use our pdf to compute the expected value, μ_i, of each attribute in the query. These will be our reported values. We can the use the pdf again to compute the probability that X_i is within ϵ from the mean, $P(X_i \in [\mu_i - \epsilon, \mu_i + \epsilon])$. If all of these probabilities meet or exceed user specified confidence threshold, then the requested readings can be directly reported as the means μ_i. If the model's confidence is too low, then the we require additional readings before answering the query.

Choosing which readings to observe at this point is an optimization problem: the goal is to pick the best set of attributes to observe, minimizing the cost of observation required to bring the model's confidence up to the user specified threshold for all of the query predicates. We discuss this optimization problem in more detail in Section 4.

In Section 3, we show how our query and optimization engine are used in BBQ to answer a number of SQL queries,

---

[2]Though these initial observations do consume some energy up-front, we will show that the long-run energy savings obtained from using a model will be much more significant.

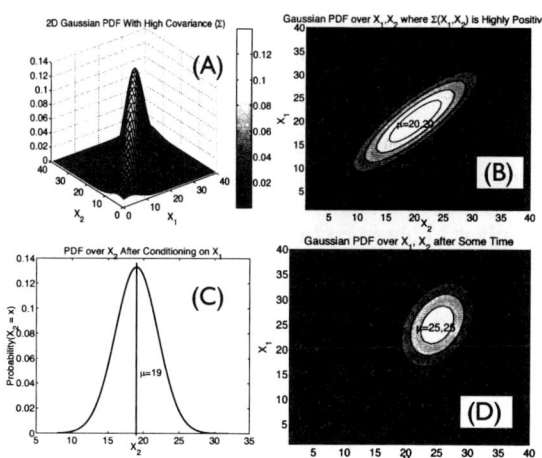

Figure 3: Example of Gaussians: (a) 3D plot of a 2D Gaussian with high covariance; (b) the same Gaussian viewed as a contour plot; (c) the resulting Gaussian over X_2 after a particular value of X_1 has been observed; finally, (d) shows how, as uncertainty about X_1 increases from the time we last observed it, we again have a 2D Gaussian with a lower variance and shifted mean.

including (i) simple selection queries requesting the value of one or more sensors, or the value of all sensors in a given geographic region, (ii) whether or not a predicate over one or more sensor readings is true, and (iii) grouped aggregates such as AVERAGE.

For the purposes of this paper, we focus on multiple one-shot queries over the current state of the network, rather than continuous queries. We can provide simple continuous query functionality by issuing a one-shot query at regular time intervals. In our experimental section, we compare this approach to existing continuous query systems for sensor networks (like TinyDB). We also discuss how knowledge of a standing, continuous query could be used to further optimize our performance in Section 6.

In this paper, there are certain types of queries which we do not address. For example, BBQ is not designed for outlier detection – that is, it will not immediately detect when a single sensor is reading something that is very far from its expected value or from the value of neighbors it has been correlated with in the past. We suggest ways in which our approach can be amended to handle outliers in Section 6.

2.4 Networking model and observation plan format

Our initial implementation of BBQ focuses on static sensor networks, such as those deployed for building and habitat monitoring. For this reason, we assume that network topologies change relatively slowly. We capture network topology information when collecting data by including, for each sensor, a vector of link quality estimates for neighboring sensor nodes. We use this topology information when constructing query plans by assuming that nodes that were previously connected will still be in the near future. When executing a plan, if we observe that a particular link is not available (*e.g.*, because one of the sensors has failed), we update our topology model accordingly. We can continue to collect new topology information as we query the network, so that new links will also become available. This approach will be effective if the topology is relatively stable; highly dynamic topologies will need more sophisticated techniques, which is a problem we briefly discuss in Section 6.

In BBQ, observation plans consist of a list of sensor nodes to visit, and, at each of these nodes, a (possibly empty) list of attributes that need to be observed at that node. The possibility of visiting a node but observing nothing is included to allow plans to observe portions of the network that are separated by multiple radio hops. We require that plans begin and end at sensor id 0 (the *root*), which we assume to be the node that interfaces the query processor to the sensor network.

2.5 Cost model

During plan generation and optimization, we need to be able to compare the relative costs of executing different plans in the network. As energy is the primary concern in battery-powered sensornets [15, 26], our goal is to pick plans of minimum energy cost. The primary contributors to energy cost are communication and data acquisition from sensors (CPU overheads beyond what is required when acquiring and sending data are small, as there is no significant processing done on the nodes in our setting).

Our cost model uses numbers obtained from the data sheets of sensors and the radio used on Mica2 motes with a Crossbow MTS400 [6] environmental sensor board. For the purposes of our model, we assume that the sender and receiver are well synchronized, so that a listening sensor turns on its radio just as a sending node begins transmitting[3]. On current generation motes, the time required to send a packet is about 27 ms. The ChipCon CC1000 radio on motes uses about 15 mW of energy in both send and receive modes, meaning that both sender and receiver consume about .4 mJ of energy. Table 1 summarizes the energy costs of acquiring readings from various sensors available for motes. In this paper, we primarily focus on temperature readings, though we briefly discuss other attributes as well in Section 5. Assuming we are acquiring temperature readings (which cost .5 J per sample), we compute the cost of a plan that visits s nodes and acquires a readings to be $(.4 \times 2) \times s + .5 \times a$ if there are no lost packets. In Section 4.1, we generalize this idea, and consider lossy communication. Note that this cost treats the entire network as a shared resource in which power needs to be conserved equivalently on each mote. More sophisticated cost models that take into account the relative importance of nodes close to the root could be used, but an exploration of such cost models is not needed to demonstrate the utility of our approach.

3 Model-based querying

As described above, the central element in our approach is the use of a probabilistic model to answer queries about the attributes in a sensor network. This section focuses on a few specific queries: range predicates, attribute-value estimates,

---

[3]In practice, this is done by having the receiver periodically sample the radio, listening for a preamble signal that indicates a sender is about to begin transmission; when this preamble is heard, it begins listening continuously. Though this periodic radio sampling uses some energy, it is small, because the sampling duty cycle can be 1% or less (and is an overhead paid by any application that uses the radio).

Sensor	Energy Per Sample (@3V), mJ
Solar Radiation [29]	.525
Barometric Pressure [16]	0.003
Humidity and Temperature[28]	0.5
Voltage	0.00009

Table 1: Summary of Power Requirements of Crossbow MTS400 Sensorboard (From [20]). Certain sensors, such as solar radiation and humidity (which includes a temperature sensor) require about a second per sample, explaining their high per-sample energy cost.

and standard aggregates. We provide a review of the standard methodology required to use a probabilistic model to answer these queries. This probabilistic model can answer many other significantly more complex queries as well; we outline some of these directions in Section 6.

3.1 Probabilistic queries

A *probability density function* (pdf), or *prior density*, $p(X_1, \ldots, X_n)$ assigns a probability for each joint value $x_1, \ldots, x_n$ for the attributes $X_1, \ldots, X_n$.

Range queries: We begin by considering range queries that ask if an attribute X_i is in the range $[a_i, b_i]$. Typically, we would need to query the sensor network to obtain the value of the attribute and then test whether the query is true or false. Using a probabilistic model, we can compute the probability $P(X_i \in [a_i, b_i])$. If this probability is very high, we are confident that the predicate $X_i \in [a_i, b_i]$ is true. Analogously, if the probability is very low, we are confident that the predicate is false. Otherwise, we may not have enough information to answer this query with sufficient confidence and may need to acquire more data from the sensor network. The probability $P(X_i \in [a_i, b_i])$ can be computed in two steps: First, we *marginalize*, or project, the pdf $p(X_1, \ldots, X_n)$ to a density over only attribute X_i:

$$p(x_i) = \int p(x_1, \ldots, x_n) dx_1 \ldots dx_{i-1} dx_{i+1} \ldots dx_n.$$

Marginalization gives us the pdf over only X_i. We can then compute $P(X_i \in [a_i, b_i])$ simply by:

$$P(X_i \in [a_i, b_i]) = \int_{a_i}^{b_i} p(x_i) dx_i. \quad (1)$$

Range queries over multiple attributes can be answered by marginalizing the joint pdf to that set of attributes. Thus, we can use the joint probability density $p(X_1, \ldots, X_n)$ to provide probabilistic answers to any range query. If the user specifies a confidence level $1-\delta$, for $\delta \in [0, 1]$, we can answer the query if this confidence is either $P(X_i \in [a_i, b_i]) > 1-\delta$ or $P(X_i \in [a_i, b_i]) < \delta$. However, in some cases, the computed confidences may be low compared to the ones required by the query, and we need to make new observations, that is, to acquire new sensor readings.

Suppose that we observe the value of attribute X_j to be x_j, we can now use Bayes' rule to *condition* our joint pdf

$p(X_1, \ldots, X_n)$ on this value[4], obtaining:

$$p(X_1, \ldots, X_{j-1}, X_{j+1}, \ldots, X_n \mid x_j) = \frac{p(X_1, \ldots, X_{j-1}, x_j, X_{j+1}, \ldots, X_n)}{p(x_j)}.$$

The *conditional probability density function* $p(X_1, \ldots, X_{j-1}, X_{j+1}, \ldots, X_n \mid x_j)$, also referred as the *posterior density* given the observation x_j, will usually lead to a more confident estimate of the probability ranges. Using marginalization, we can compute $P(X_i \in [a_i, b_i] \mid x_j)$, which is often more certain than the prior probability $P(X_i \in [a_i, b_i])$. In general, we will make a set of observations $\mathbf{o}$, and, after conditioning on these observations, obtain $p(\mathbf{X} \mid \mathbf{o})$, the posterior probability of our set of attributes $\mathbf{X}$ given $\mathbf{o}$.

Example 3.1 *In BBQ, the pdf is represented by a multivariate Gaussian with mean vector μ and covariance matrix Σ. In Gaussians, marginalization is very simple. If we want to marginalize the pdf to a subset $\mathbf{Y}$ of the attributes, we simply select the entries in μ and Σ corresponding to these attributes, and drop the other entries obtaining a lower dimensional mean vector $\mu_{\mathbf{Y}}$ and covariance matrix $\Sigma_{\mathbf{YY}}$. For a Gaussian, there is no closed-form solution for Equation (1). However, this integration problem is very well understood, called the* error function *(erf), with many well-known, simple approximations.*

Interestingly, if we condition a Gaussian on the value of some attributes, the resulting pdf is also a Gaussian. The mean and covariance matrix of this new Gaussian can be computed by simple matrix operations. Suppose that we observe value $\mathbf{o}$ for attributes $\mathcal{O}$, the mean $\mu_{\mathbf{Y}|\mathbf{o}}$ and covariance matrix $\Sigma_{\mathbf{Y}|\mathbf{o}}$ of the pdf $p(\mathbf{Y} \mid \mathbf{o})$ over the remaining attributes are given by:

$$\begin{aligned} \mu_{\mathbf{Y}|\mathbf{o}} &= \mu_{\mathbf{Y}} + \Sigma_{\mathbf{Y}\mathcal{O}} \Sigma_{\mathcal{O}\mathcal{O}}^{-1}(\mathbf{o} - \mu_{\mathcal{O}}), \\ \Sigma_{\mathbf{Y}|\mathbf{o}} &= \Sigma_{\mathbf{YY}} - \Sigma_{\mathbf{Y}\mathcal{O}} \Sigma_{\mathcal{O}\mathcal{O}}^{-1} \Sigma_{\mathcal{O}\mathbf{Y}}, \end{aligned} \quad (2)$$

where $\Sigma_{\mathbf{Y}\mathcal{O}}$ denotes the matrix formed by selecting the rows $\mathbf{Y}$ and the columns $\mathcal{O}$ from the original covariance matrix Σ. Note that the posterior covariance matrix $\Sigma_{\mathbf{Y}|\mathbf{o}}$ does not depend on the actual observed value $\mathbf{o}$. We thus denote this matrix by $\Sigma_{\mathbf{Y}|\mathcal{O}}$. In BBQ, by using Gaussians, we can thus compute all of the operations required to answer our queries by performing only basic matrix operations. □

Value queries: In addition to range queries, a probability density function can, of course, be used to answer many other query types. For example, if the user is interested in the value of a particular attribute X_i, we can answer this query by using the posterior pdf to compute the mean $\bar{x}_i$ value of X_i, given the observations $\mathbf{o}$:

$$\bar{x}_i = \int x_i \, p(x_i \mid \mathbf{o}) dx_i.$$

---

[4]The expression $p(x|y)$ is read "the probability of x given y", and represents the pdf of variable x given a particular value of y. Bayes' rule allows conditional probabilities to be computed in scenarios where we only have data on the inverse conditional probability: $p(x|y) = \frac{p(y|x)p(x)}{p(y)}$.

We can additionally provide confidence intervals on this estimate of the value of the attribute: for a given error bound $\varepsilon > 0$, the confidence is simply given by $P(X_i \in [\bar{x}_i - \varepsilon, \bar{x}_i + \varepsilon] \mid \mathbf{o})$, which can be computed as in the range queries in Equation (1). If this confidence is greater than the user specified value $1 - \delta$, then we can provide a probably approximately correct value for the attribute, without observing it.

AVERAGE aggregates: Average queries can be answered in a similar fashion, by defining an appropriate pdf. Suppose that we are interested in the average value of a set of attributes $\mathcal{A}$. For example, if we are interested in the average temperature in a spatial region, we can define $\mathcal{A}$ to be the set of sensors in this region. We can now define a random variable Y to represent this average by $Y = (\sum_{i \in \mathcal{A}} X_i)/|\mathcal{A}|$. The pdf for Y is simply given by appropriate marginalization of the joint pdf over the attributes in $\mathcal{A}$:

$$p(Y = y \mid \mathbf{o}) = \int p(x_1, \ldots, x_n \mid \mathbf{o}) \, \mathbb{1}\left[\left(\sum_{i \in \mathcal{A}} x_i/|\mathcal{A}|\right) = y\right] dx_1 \ldots dx_n,$$

where $\mathbb{1}[\cdot]$ is the indicator function.[5] Once $p(Y = y \mid \mathbf{o})$ is defined, we can answer an average query by simply defining a value query for the new random variable Y as above. We can also compute probabilistic answers to more complex aggregation queries. For example, if the user wants the average value of the attributes in $\mathcal{A}$ that have value greater than t, we can define a random variable Z:

$$Z = \frac{\sum_{i \in \mathcal{A}} X_i \mathbb{1}(X_i > c)}{\sum_{i \in \mathcal{A}} \mathbb{1}(X_i > c)},$$

where $\frac{0}{0}$ is defined to be 0. The pdf of Z is given by:

$$p(Z = z \mid \mathbf{o}) = \int p(x_1, \ldots, x_n \mid \mathbf{o}) \, \mathbb{1}\left[\left(\frac{\sum_{i \in \mathcal{A}, x_i > c} x_i}{\sum_{i \in \mathcal{A}, x_i > c} 1}\right) = y\right] dx_1 \ldots dx_n.$$

In general, this inference problem, *i.e.*, computing these integrals, does not have a closed-form solution, and numerical integration techniques may be required.

Example 3.2 *BBQ focuses on Gaussians. In this case, each posterior mean $\bar{x}_i$ can be obtained directly from our mean vector by using the conditioning rule described in Example 3.1. Interestingly, the sum of Gaussian random variables is also Gaussian. Thus, if we define an AVERAGE query $Y = (\sum_{i \in \mathcal{A}} X_i)/|\mathcal{A}|$, then the pdf for Y is a Gaussian. All we need now is the variance of Y, which can be computed in closed-form from those of each X_i by:*

$$\begin{aligned} E[(Y - \mu_Y)^2] &= E[(\sum_{i \in \mathcal{A}} X_i - \mu_i)^2 / |\mathcal{A}|^2], \\ &= \tfrac{1}{|\mathcal{A}|^2} \Big(\sum_{i \in \mathcal{A}} E[(X_i - \mu_i)^2] \\ &\quad + 2 \sum_{i \in \mathcal{A}} \sum_{j \in \mathcal{A}, j \neq i} \\ &\quad E[(X_i - \mu_i)(X_j - \mu_j)] \Big). \end{aligned}$$

Thus, the variance of Y is given by a weighted sum of the

---

[5]The indicator function translates a Boolean predicate into the arithmetic value 1 (if the predicate is true) and 0 (if false).

variances of each X_i, plus the covariances between X_i and X_j, all of which can be directly read off the covariance matrix Σ. Therefore, we can answer an AVERAGE query over a subset of the attributes $\mathcal{A}$ in closed-form, using the same procedure as value queries. For the more general queries that depend on the actual value of the attributes, even with Gaussians, we require a numerical integration procedure. □

3.2 Dynamic models

Thus far, we have focused on a single static probability density function over the attributes. This distribution represents *spatial* correlation in our sensor network deployment. However, many real-world systems include attributes that evolve over time. In our deployment, the temperatures have both temporal and spatial correlations. Thus, the temperature values observed earlier in time should help us estimate the temperature later in time. A *dynamic probabilistic model* can represent such temporal correlations.

In particular, for each (discrete) time index t, we should estimate a pdf $p(X_1^t, \ldots, X_n^t \mid \mathbf{o}^{1\ldots t})$ that assigns a probability for each joint assignment to the attributes at time t, given $\mathbf{o}^{1\ldots t}$, all observations made up to time t. A dynamic model describes the evolution of this system over time, telling us how to compute $p(X_1^{t+1}, \ldots, X_n^{t+1} \mid \mathbf{o}^{1\ldots t})$ from $p(X_1^t, \ldots, X_n^t \mid \mathbf{o}^{1\ldots t})$. Thus, we can use all measurements made up to time t to improve our estimate of the pdf at time $t+1$.

For simplicity, we restrict our presentation to *Markovian* models, where given the value of *all* attributes at time t, the value of the attributes at time $t+1$ are independent of those for any time earlier than t. This assumption leads to a very simple, yet often effective, model for representing a stochastic dynamical system. Here, the dynamics are summarized by a conditional density called the *transition model*:

$$p(X_1^{t+1}, \ldots, X_n^{t+1} \mid X_1^t, \ldots, X_n^t).$$

Using this transition model, we can compute $p(X_1^{t+1}, \ldots, X_n^{t+1} \mid \mathbf{o}^{1\ldots t})$ using a simple marginalization operation:

$$p(x_1^{t+1}, \ldots, x_n^{t+1} \mid \mathbf{o}^{1\ldots t}) = \int p(x_1^{t+1}, \ldots, x_n^{t+1} \mid x_1^t, \ldots, x_n^t) p(x_1^t, \ldots, x_n^t \mid \mathbf{o}^{1\ldots t}) dx_1^t \ldots dx_n^t.$$

This formula assumes that the transition model $p(\mathbf{X}^{t+1} \mid \mathbf{X}^t)$ is the same for all times t. In our deployment, for example, in the mornings the temperatures tend to increase, while at night they tend to decrease. This suggests that the transition model should be different at different times of the day. In our experimental results in Section 5, we address this problem by simply learning a different transition model $p^i(\mathbf{X}^{t+1} \mid \mathbf{X}^t)$ for each hour i of the day. At a particular time t, we simply use the transition model $mod(t, 24)$. This idea can, of course, be generalized to other cyclic variations.

Once we have obtained $p(X_1^{t+1}, \ldots, X_n^{t+1} \mid \mathbf{o}^{1\ldots t})$, the prior pdf for time $t+1$, we can again incorporate the measurements $\mathbf{o}^{t+1}$ made at time $t+1$, as in Section 3.1, obtaining $p(X_1^{t+1}, \ldots, X_n^{t+1} \mid \mathbf{o}^{1\ldots t+1})$, the posterior distribution at time $t+1$ given all measurements made up to time $t+1$.

This process is then repeated for time $t+2$, and so on. The pdf for the initial time $t=0$, $p(X_1^0, \ldots, X_n^0)$, is initialized with the prior distribution for attributes $X_1, \ldots, X_n$. This process of pushing our estimate for the density at time t through the transition model and then conditioning on the measurements at time $t+1$ is often called *filtering*. In contrast to the static model described in the previous section, filtering allows us to condition our estimate on the complete history of observations, which, as we will see in Section 5, can significantly reduce the number of observations required for obtaining confident approximate answers to our queries.

Example 3.3 *In BBQ, we focus on Gaussian distributions; for these distributions the filtering process is called a Kalman filter. The transition model $p(X_1^{t+1}, \ldots, X_n^{t+1} \mid X_1^t, \ldots, X_n^t)$ can be learned from data with two simple steps: First, we learn a mean and covariance matrix for the joint density $p(X_1^{t+1}, \ldots, X_n^{t+1}, X_1^t, \ldots, X_n^t)$. That is, we form tuples $\langle X_1^{t+1}, \ldots, X_n^{t+1}, X_1^t, \ldots, X_n^t \rangle$ for our attributes at every consecutive times t and $t+1$, and use these tuples to compute the joint mean vector and covariance matrix. Then, we use the conditioning rule described in Example 3.1 to compute the transition model:*

$$p(\mathbf{X}^{t+1} \mid \mathbf{X}^t) = \frac{p(\mathbf{X}^{t+1}, \mathbf{X}^t)}{p(\mathbf{X}^t)}.$$

Once we have obtained this transition model, we can answer our queries in a similar fashion as described in Examples 3.1 and 3.2. □

4 Choosing an observation plan

In the previous section, we showed that our pdfs can be conditioned on the value $\mathbf{o}$ of the set of observed attributes to obtain a more confident answer to our query. Of course, the choice of attributes that we observe will crucially affect the resulting posterior density. In this section, we focus on selecting the attributes that are expected to increase the confidences in the answer to our particular query at minimal cost. We first formalize the notion of cost of observing a particular set of attributes. Then, we describe the expected improvement in our answer from observing this set. Finally, we discuss the problem of optimizing the choice of attributes.

4.1 Cost of observations

Let us denote a set of observations by $\mathcal{O} \subseteq \{1, \ldots, n\}$. The expected cost $C(\mathcal{O})$ of observing attributes $\mathcal{O}$ is divided additively into two parts: the data acquisition cost $C_a(\mathcal{O})$, representing the cost of sensing these attributes, and the expected data transmission cost $C_t(\mathcal{O})$, measuring the communication cost required to download this data.

The acquisition cost $C_a(\mathcal{O})$ is deterministically given by the sum of the energy required to observe the attributes $\mathcal{O}$, as discussed in Section 2.5:

$$C_a(\mathcal{O}) = \sum_{i \in \mathcal{O}} C_a(i),$$

where $C_a(i)$ is the cost of observing attribute X_i.

The definition of the transmission cost $C_t(\mathcal{O})$ is somewhat trickier, as it depends on the particular data collection mechanism used to collect these observations from the network, and on the network topology. Furthermore, if the topology is unknown or changes over time, or if the communication links between nodes are unreliable, as in most sensor networks, this cost function becomes stochastic. For simplicity, we focus on networks with known topologies, but with unreliable communication. We address this reliability issue by introducing acknowledgment messages and retransmissions.

More specifically, we define our network graph by a set of edges $\mathcal{E}$, where each edge e_{ij} is associated two link quality estimates, p_{ij} and p_{ji}, indicating the probability that a packet from i will reach j and vice versa. With the simplifying assumption that these probabilities are independent, the expected number of transmission and acknowledgment messages required to guarantee a successful transmission between i and j is $\frac{1}{p_{ij}p_{ji}}$. We can now use these simple values to estimate the expected transmission cost.

There are many possible mechanisms for traversing the network and collecting this data. We focus on simply choosing a single path through the network that visits all sensors that observe attributes in $\mathcal{O}$ and returns to the base station. Clearly, choosing the best such path is an instance of the *traveling salesman problem*, where the graph is given by the edges $\mathcal{E}$ with weights $\frac{1}{p_{ij}p_{ji}}$. Although this problem is NP-complete, we can use well-known heuristics, such as k-OPT [19], that are known to perform very well in practice. We thus define $C_t(\mathcal{O})$ to be the expected cost of this (suboptimal) path, and our expected total cost for observing $\mathcal{O}$ can now be obtained by $C(\mathcal{O}) = C_a(\mathcal{O}) + C_t(\mathcal{O})$.

4.2 Improvement in confidence

Observing attributes $\mathcal{O}$ should improve the confidence of our posterior density. That is, after observing these attributes, we should be able to answer our query with more certainty[6]. For a particular value $\mathbf{o}$ of our observations $\mathcal{O}$, we can compute the posterior density $p(X_1, \ldots, X_n \mid \mathbf{o})$ and estimate our confidence as described in Section 3.1.

More specifically, suppose that we have a range query $X_i \in [a_i, b_i]$, we can compute the benefit $R_i(\mathbf{o})$ of observing the specific value $\mathbf{o}$ by:

$$R_i(\mathbf{o}) = \max\left[P(X_i \in [a_i, b_i] \mid \mathbf{o}), 1 - P(X_i \in [a_i, b_i] \mid \mathbf{o})\right],$$

that is, for a range query, $R_i(\mathbf{o})$ simply measures our confidence after observing $\mathbf{o}$. For value and average queries, we define the benefit by $R_i(\mathbf{o}) = P(X_i \in [\bar{x}_i - \varepsilon, \bar{x}_i + \varepsilon] \mid \mathbf{o})$, where $\bar{x}_i$ in this formula is the posterior mean of X_i given the observations $\mathbf{o}$.

However, the specific value $\mathbf{o}$ of the attributes $\mathcal{O}$ is not known *a priori*. We must thus compute the *expected benefit* $R_i(\mathcal{O})$:

$$R_i(\mathcal{O}) = \int p(\mathbf{o}) R_i(\mathbf{o}) d\mathbf{o}. \qquad (3)$$

This integral may be difficult to compute in closed-form, and we may need to estimate $R_i(\mathcal{O})$ using numerical integration.

---
[6]This is not true in all cases; for range predicates, the confidence in the answer may *decrease* after an observation, depending on the observed value.

Example 4.1 *The descriptions in Examples 3.1-3.3 describe how the benefits $R_i(\mathbf{o})$ can be computed for a particular observed value $\mathbf{o}$ in the Gaussian models used in BBQ. For general range queries, even with Gaussians, we need to use numerical integration techniques to estimate the expected reward $R_i(\mathcal{O})$ in Equation (3).*

However, for value and AVERAGE queries we can compute this expression in closed-form, by exploiting the fact described in Example 3.1 that the posterior covariance $\Sigma_{\mathbf{Y}|\mathcal{O}}$ does not depend on the observed value $\mathbf{o}$. Note that for these queries, we are computing the probability that the true value deviates by more than ϵ from the posterior mean value. This probability is equal to the probability that a zero mean Gaussian, with covariance $\Sigma_{\mathbf{Y}|\mathcal{O}}$, deviates by more than ϵ from 0. This probability can be computed using the error function (erf) and the covariance matrix $\Sigma_{\mathbf{Y}|\mathcal{O}}$. Thus, for value and AVERAGE queries $R_i(\mathcal{O}) = R_i(\mathbf{o}), \forall \mathbf{o}$, allowing us to compute Equation (3) in closed-form. □

More generally, we may have range or value queries over multiple attributes. Semantically, we define this type of query as trying to achieve a particular marginal confidence over each attribute. We must thus decide how to trade off confidences between different attributes. For a query over attributes $\mathcal{Q} \subseteq \{1, \ldots, n\}$, we can, for instance, define the total benefit $R(\mathbf{o})$ of observing value $\mathbf{o}$ as either the minimum benefit over all attributes, $R(\mathbf{o}) = \min_{i \in \mathcal{Q}} R_i(\mathbf{o})$, or the average, $R(\mathbf{o}) = \frac{1}{|\mathcal{Q}|} \sum_{i \in \mathcal{Q}} R_i(\mathbf{o})$. In this paper, we focus on minimizing the total number of mistakes made by the query processor, and use the average benefit to decide when to stop observing new attributes.

4.3 Optimization

In the previous sections, we defined the expected benefit $R(\mathcal{O})$ and cost $C(\mathcal{O})$ of observing attributes $\mathcal{O}$. Of course, different sets of observed attributes will lead to different benefit and cost levels. Our user will define a desired confidence level $1 - \delta$. We would like to pick the set of attributes $\mathcal{O}$ that meet this confidence at a minimum cost:

$$\begin{array}{ll} \text{minimize}_{\mathcal{O} \subseteq \{1,\ldots,n\}} & C(\mathcal{O}), \\ \text{such that} & R(\mathcal{O}) \geq 1 - \delta. \end{array}$$

This general optimization problem is known to be NP-hard. Thus, efficient and exact optimization algorithms are unlikely to exist (unless P=NP).

We have developed two algorithms for solving this optimization problem. The first algorithm exhaustively searches over the possible subsets of possible observations, $\mathcal{O} \subseteq \{1, \ldots, n\}$. This algorithm can thus find the optimal subset of attributes to observe, but has an exponential running time.

The second algorithm uses a greedy incremental heuristic. We initialize the search with an empty set of attributes, $\mathcal{O} = \emptyset$. At each iteration, for each attribute X_i that is not in our set ($i \notin \mathcal{O}$), we compute the new expect benefit $R(\mathcal{O} \cup i)$ and cost $C(\mathcal{O} \cup i)$. If some set of attributes $\mathcal{G}$ reach the desired confidence, (*i.e.*, for $j \in \mathcal{G}$, $R(\mathcal{O} \cup j) \geq 1 - \delta$), then, among the attributes in $\mathcal{G}$, we pick the one with lowest total cost $C(\mathcal{O} \cup j)$, and terminate the search returning $\mathcal{O} \cup j$. Otherwise, if $\mathcal{G} = \emptyset$, we have not reached our desired confidence, and we simply add the attribute with the highest benefit over cost ratio to our set of attributes:

$$\mathcal{O} = \mathcal{O} \cup \left(\arg\max_{j \notin \mathcal{O}} \frac{R(\mathcal{O} \cup j)}{C(\mathcal{O} \cup j)} \right).$$

This process is then repeated until the desired confidence is reached.

5 Experimental results

In this section, we measure the performance of BBQ on several real world data sets. Our goal is to demonstrate that BBQ provides the ability to efficiently execute approximate queries with user-specifiable confidences.

5.1 Data sets

Our results are based on running experiments over two real-world data sets that we have collected during the past few months using TinyDB. The first data set, *garden*, is a one month trace of 83,000 readings from 11 sensors in a single redwood tree at the UC Botanical Garden in Berkeley. In this case, sensors were placed at 4 different altitudes in the tree, where they collected collected light, humidity, temperature, and voltage readings once every 5 minutes. We split this data set into non-overlapping training and test data sets (with 2/3 used for training), and build the model on the training data.

The second data set, *lab*, is a trace of readings from 54 sensors in the Intel Research, Berkeley lab. These sensors collected light, humidity, temperature and voltage readings, as well as network connectivity information that makes it possible to reconstruct the network topology. Currently, the data consists of 8 days of readings; we use the first 6 days for training, and the last 2 for generating test traces.

5.2 Query workload

We report results for two sets of query workloads:

Value Queries: The main type of queries that we anticipate users would run on a such a system are queries asking to report the sensor readings at all the sensors, within a specified error bound ϵ with a specified confidence δ, indicating that no more than a fraction $1 - \delta$ of the readings should deviate from their true value by ϵ. As an example, a typical query may ask for temperatures at all the sensors within 0.5 degrees with 95% confidence.

Predicate Queries: The second set of queries that we use are selection queries over the sensor readings where the user asks for all sensors that satisfy a certain predicate, and once again specifies a desired confidence δ.

We also looked at *average queries* asking for averages over the sensor readings. Due to space constraints, we do not present results for these queries.

5.3 Comparison systems

We compare the effectiveness of BBQ against two simple strategies for answering such queries :

TinyDB-style Querying: In this model, the query is disseminated into the sensor network using an overlay tree structure [22], and at each mote, the sensor reading is observed. The results are reported back to the base station using the same tree, and are combined along the way back to minimize communication cost.

Approximate-Caching: The base-station maintains a view of the sensor readings at all motes that is guaranteed to be within a certain interval of the actual sensor readings by requiring the motes to report a sensor reading to the base-station if the value of the sensor falls outside this interval. Note that, though this model saves communication cost by not reporting readings if they do not change much, it does not save acquisition costs as the motes are required to observe the sensor values at every time step. This approach is inspired by work by Olston *et al.* [24].

5.4 Methodology

BBQ is used to build a model of the training data. This model includes a transition model for each hour of the day, based on Kalman filters described in Example 3.3 above. We generate traces from the test data by taking one reading randomly from each hour. We issue one query against the model per hour. The model computes the *a priori* probabilities for each predicate (or ϵ bound) being satisfied, and chooses one or more additional sensor readings to observe if the confidence bounds are not met. After executing the generated observation plan over the network (at some cost), BBQ updates the model with the observed values from the test data and compares predicted values for non-observed readings to the test data from that hour.

To measure the accuracy of our prediction with value queries, we compute the average number of mistakes (per hour) that BBQ made, *i.e.*, how many of the reported values are further away from the actual values than the specified error bound. To measure the accuracy for predicate queries, we compute the number of predicates whose truth value was incorrectly approximated.

For TinyDB, all queries are answered "correctly" (as we are not modeling loss). Similarly, for approximate caching, a value from the test data is reported when it deviates by more than ϵ from the last reported value from that sensor, and as such, this approach does not make mistakes either

We compute a cost for each observation plan as described above; this includes both the attribute acquisition cost and the communications cost. For most of our experiments, we measure the accuracy of our model at predicting temperature.

5.5 Garden dataset: Value-based queries

We begin by analyzing the performance of value queries on the *garden* data set in detail to demonstrate the effectiveness of our architecture. The query we use for this experiment requires the system to report the temperatures at all motes to within a specified epsilon, which we vary. In these experiments we keep confidence constant at 95%, so we expect to see no more than 5% errors. Figure 4 shows the relative cost and number of errors made for each of the three systems. We varied epsilon from between 0 and 1 degrees Celsius; as expected, the cost of BBQ (on the left of the figure) falls rapidly as epsilon increases, and the percentage of errors (shown on the right) stays well below the specified confidence threshold of 5% (shown as the horizontal line). Notice that for reasonable values of epsilon, BBQ uses significantly less communication than approximate caching or TinyDB, sometimes by an order of magnitude. In this case, approximate caching always reports the value to within epsilon, so it does not make

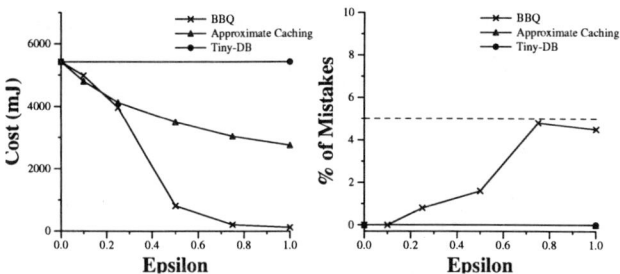
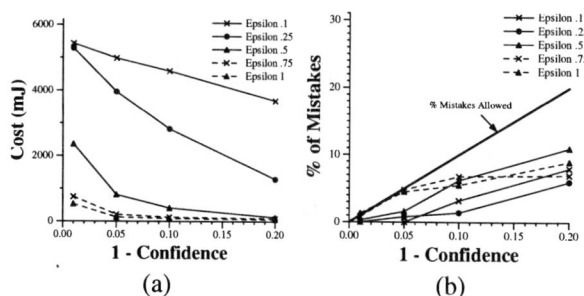

Figure 4: Figure illustrating the relative costs of BBQ versus TinyDB and Approximate Queries, with varying epsilons and a confidence interval of 95%.

Figure 6: Energy per query (a) and percentage of errors (b) versus confidence interval size and epsilon.

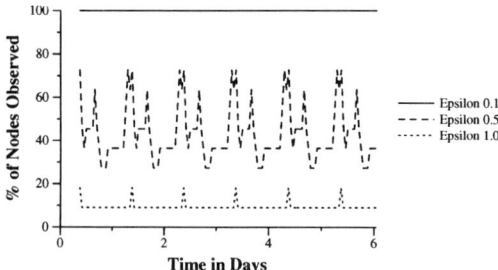

Figure 5: Figure showing the number of sensors observed over time for varying epsilons.

We also ran experiments comparing (1) the performance of the greedy algorithm vs. the optimal algorithm, and (2) the performance of the dynamic (Kalman Filter) model that we use vs. a static model that does not incorporate observations made in the previous time steps into the model. As expected, the greedy algorithm performs slightly worse that the optimal algorithm, whereas using dynamic models results in less observations than using static models. Due to space constraints, we omit those experiments from this paper.

"mistakes", although the average observation error in approximate caching is close to BBQ (for example, in this experiment, with epsilon=.5, approximate caching has a root-mean-squared error of .46, whereas BBQ this error is .12; in other cases the relative performance is reversed).

5.7 Garden Dataset: Range queries

We ran a number of experiments with range queries (also over the *garden* data set). Figure 7 summarizes the average number of observations required for a 95% confidence with three different range queries (temperature in [17,18], temperature in [19,20], and temperature in [20,21]). In all three cases, the actual error rates were all at or below 5% (ranging from 1.5-5%). Notice that different range queries require observations at different times – for example, during the set of readings just before hour 50, the three queries make observations during three disjoint time periods: early in the morning and late at night, the model must make lots of observations to determine whether the temperature is in the range 16-17, whereas during mid-day, it is continually making observations for the range 20-21, but never for other ranges (because it can be sure the temperature is above 20 degrees, but not 21!)

Figure 5 shows the percentage of sensors that BBQ observes by hour, with varying epsilon, for the same set of garden experiments. As epsilon gets small (less than .1 degrees), it is necessary to observe all nodes on every query, as the variance between nodes is high enough that it cannot infer the value of one sensor from other sensor's readings with such accuracy. On the other hand, for epsilons 1 or larger, very few observations are needed, as the changes in one sensor closely predict the values of other sensors. For intermediate epsilons, more observations are needed, especially during times when sensor readings change dramatically. The spikes in this case correspond to morning and evening, when temperature changes relatively quickly as the sun comes up or goes down (hour 0 in this case is midnight).

5.6 Garden Dataset: Cost vs. Confidence

For our next set of experiments, we again look at the garden data set, this time comparing the cost of plan execution with confidence intervals ranging from 99% to 80%, with epsilon again varying between 0.1 and 1.0. The results are shown in Figure 6(a) and (b). Figure 6(a) shows that decreasing confidence intervals substantially reduces the energy per query, as does decreasing epsilon. Note that for a confidence of 95%, with errors of just .5 degrees C, we can reduce expected per-query energy costs from 5.4 J to less than 150 mJ – a factor of 40 reduction. Figure 6(b) shows that we meet or exceed our confidence interval in almost all cases (except 99% confidence). It is not surprising that we occasionally fail to satisfy these bounds by a small amount, as variances in our training data are somewhat different than variances in our test data.

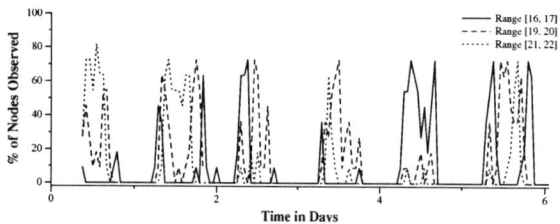

Figure 7: Graph showing BBQ's performance on three different range queries, for the garden data set with confidence set to 95%.

5.8 *Lab* dataset

We also ran similar experiments on the *lab* dataset, which because of the higher number of attributes in it, is a more interesting dataset. Contrary to our initial expectation, temperatures in the lab are actually harder to predict compared to the outdoors; human intervention (in particular, turning the air conditioning on and off) introduces a lot of randomness in this data. We report one set of experiments for this dataset, but defer a more detailed study to future work.

597

Figure 8(a) shows the cost incurred in answering a value query on this dataset, as the confidence bound is varied. For comparative purposes, we also plot the cost of answering the query using TinyDB. Once again, we see that the as the required confidence in answer drops, BBQ is able to answer the query more efficiently, and is significantly more cost-efficient than TinyDB for larger error bounds. Figure 8(b) shows that BBQ was able to achieve the specified confidence bounds in almost all the cases.

Figure 9 shows an example traversal generated by executing a value based query with confidence of 99% and epsilon of .5 degrees C over the *lab* data. The two paths shown are amongst the longer paths generated – one is the initial set of observations needed to improve the model's confidence, and the other is a traversal at 8am just as the day is starting to warm up.

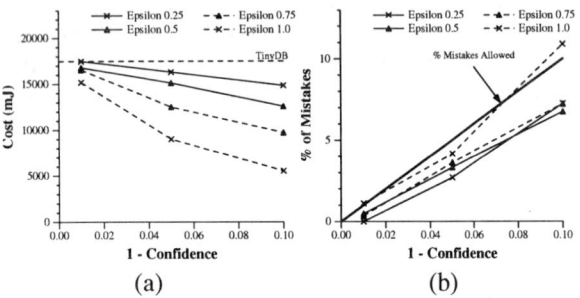

(a)   (b)

Figure 8: Energy per query (a) and percentage of errors (b) versus confidence interval size and epsilon for the Lab Data.

6 Extensions and future directions

In this paper, we focused on the core architecture for unifying probabilistic models with declarative queries. In this section we outline several possible extensions.

Conditional plans: In our current prototype, once an observation plan has been submitted to the sensor network, it is executed to completion. A simple alternative would be to generate plans that include early stopping conditions; a more sophisticated approach would be to generate conditional plans that explore different parts of the network depending on the values of observed attributes. We have begun exploring such conditional plans in a related project [8].

More complex models: In particular, we are interested in building models that can detect faulty sensors, both to answer fault detection queries, and to give correct answers to general queries in the presence of faults. This is an active research topic in the machine learning community (*e.g.*, [18]), and we expect that these techniques can be extended to our domain.

Outliers: Our current approach does not work well for outlier detection. To a first approximation, the only way to detect outliers is to continuously sample sensors, as outliers are fundamentally uncorrelated events. Thus, any outlier detection scheme is likely to have a high sensing cost, but we expect that our probabilistic techniques can still be used to avoid excessive communication during times of normal operation, as with the fault detection case.

Support for dynamic networks: Our current approach of re-evaluating plans when the network topology changes will not work well in highly dynamic networks. As a part

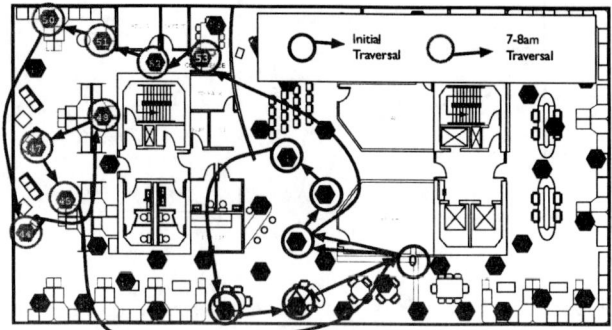

Figure 9: Two traversals of the lab network. An observation is made at every circle. The query was a value-query over all 54 sensors with $\epsilon = .1$ and $\delta = .99$. These paths correspond to times when the model's variance is high – e.g., when the system is first started, and at around 8am when the sun begins to heat the lab, so many observations are needed. For other hours, very few observations are needed.

of our instrumentation of our lab space, we are beginning a systematic study of how network topologies change over time and as new sensors are added or existing sensors move. We plan to use this information to extend our exploration plans with simple topology change recovery strategies that can be used to find alternate routes through the network.

Continuous queries: Our current approach re-executes an exploration plan that begins at the network root on every query. For continuous queries that repeatedly request data about the same sensors, it may be possible to install code in the network that causes devices to periodically push readings during times of high change (*e.g.*, every morning at 8 am).

7 Related work

There has been substantial work on approximate query processing in the database community, often using model-like *synopses* for query answering much as we rely on probabilistic models. For example, the AQUA project [12, 10, 11] proposes a number of sampling-based synopses that can provide approximate answers to a variety of queries using a fraction of the total data in a database. As with BBQ, such answers typically include tight bounds on the correctness of answers. AQUA, however, is designed to work in an environment where it is possible to generate an independent random sample of data (something that is quite tricky to do in sensor networks, as losses are correlated and communicating random samples may require the participation of a large part of the network). AQUA also does not exploit correlations, which means that it lacks the *predictive* power of representations based on probabilistic models. [7, 9] propose exploiting data correlations through use of graphical model techniques for approximate query processing, but neither provide any guarantees in the answers returned. Recently, Considine *et al.* have shown that sketch based approximation techniques can be applied in sensor networks [17].

Work on approximate caching by Olston *et al.*, is also related [25, 24], in the sense that it provides a bounded approximation of the values of a number of cached objects (sensors, in our case) at some server (the root of the sensor network). The basic idea is that the server stores cached values along with absolute bounds for the deviation of those values; when objects notice that their values have gone outside the bounds known to be stored at the server, they send an update of our value. Unlike our approach, this work requires the cached objects to continuously monitor their values, which makes the energy overhead of this approach considerable. It does, however, enable queries that detect outliers, something BBQ currently cannot do.

There has been some recent work on approximate, probabilistic querying in sensor networks and moving object databases [3]. This work builds on the work by Olston *et al.* in that objects update cached values when they exceed some boundary condition, except that a pdf over the range defined by the boundaries is also maintained to allow queries that estimate the most likely value of a cached object as well as an confidence on that uncertainty. As with other approximation work, the notion of correlated values is not exploited, and the requirement that readings be continuously monitored introduces a high sampling overhead.

Information Driven Sensor Querying (IDSQ) from Chu *et al.* [4] uses probabilistic models for estimation of target position in a tracking application. In IDSQ, sensors are tasked in order according to maximally reduce the positional uncertainty of a target, as measured, for example, by the reduction in the principal components of a 2D Gaussian.

Our prior work presented the notion of *acquisitional query processing*(ACQP) [21] – that is, query processing in environments like sensor networks where it is necessary to be sensitive to the costs of acquiring data. The main goal of an ACQP system is to avoid unnecessary data acquisition. The techniques we present are very much in that spirit, though the original work did not attempt to use probabilistic techniques to avoid acquisition, and thus cannot directly exploit correlations or provide confidence bounds.

BBQ is also inspired by prior work on Online Aggregation [14] and other aspects of the CONTROL project [13]. The basic idea in CONTROL is to provide an interface that allows users to see partially complete answers with confidence bounds for long running aggregate queries. CONTROL did not attempt to capture correlations between the different attributes, such that observing one attribute had no effect on the systems confidence on any of the other predicates.

The probabilistic querying techniques described here are built on standard results in machine learning and statistics (*e.g.*, [27, 23, 5]). The optimization problem we address is a generalization of the *value of information* problem [27]. This paper, however, proposes and evaluates the first general architecture that combines model-based approximate query answering with optimizing the data gathered in a sensornet.

8 Conclusions

In this paper, we proposed a novel architecture for integrating a database system with a correlation-aware probabilistic model. Rather than directly querying the sensor network, we build a model from stored and current readings, and answer SQL queries by consulting the model. In a sensor network, this provides a number of advantages, including shielding the user from faulty sensors and reducing the number of expensive sensor readings and radio transmissions that the network must perform. Beyond the encouraging, order-of-magnitude reductions in sampling and communication cost offered by BBQ, we see our general architecture as the proper platform for answering queries and interpreting data from real world environments like sensornets, as conventional database technology is poorly equipped to deal with lossiness, noise, and non-uniformity inherent in such environments.

References

[1] IPSN 2004 Call for Papers. http://ipsn04.cs.uiuc.edu/call_for_papers.html.

[2] SenSys 2004 Call for Papers. http://www.cis.ohio-state.edu/sensys04/.

[3] R. Cheng, D. V. Kalashnikov, and S. Prabhakar. Evaluating probabilistic queries over imprecise data. In *SIGMOD*, 2003.

[4] M. Chu, H. Haussecker, and F. Zhao. Scalable information-driven sensor querying and routing for ad hoc heterogeneous sensor networks. In *Journal of High Performance Computing Applications.*, 2002.

[5] R. Cowell, P. Dawid, S. Lauritzen, and D. Spiegelhalter. *Probabilistic Networks and Expert Systems.* Spinger, New York, 1999.

[6] Crossbow, Inc. Wireless sensor networks. http://www.xbow.com/Products/Wireless_Sensor_Networks.htm.

[7] A. Deshpande, M. Garofalakis, and R. Rastogi. Independence is Good: Dependency-Based Histogram Synopses for High-Dimensional Data. In *SIGMOD*, May 2001.

[8] A. Desphande, C. Guestrin, W. Hong, and S. Madden. Exploiting correlated attributes in acquisitional query processing. Technical report, Intel-Research, Berkeley, 2004.

[9] L. Getoor, B. Taskar, and D. Koller. Selectivity estimation using probabilistic models. In *SIGMOD*, May 2001.

[10] P. B. Gibbons. Distinct sampling for highly-accurate answers to distinct values queries and event reports. In *Proc. of VLDB*, Sept 2001.

[11] P. B. Gibbons and M. Garofalakis. Approximate query processing: Taming the terabytes (tutorial), September 2001.

[12] P. B. Gibbons and Y. Matias. New sampling-based summary statistics for improving approximate query answers. In *SIGMOD*, 1998.

[13] J. M. Hellerstein, R. Avnur, A. Chou, C. Hidber, C. Olston, V. Raman, T. Roth, and P. J. Haas. Interactive data analysis with CONTROL. *IEEE Computer*, 32(8), August 1999.

[14] J. M. Hellerstein, P. J. Haas, and H. Wang. Online aggregation. In *SIGMOD*, pages 171–182, Tucson, AZ, May 1997.

[15] C. Intanagonwiwat, R. Govindan, and D. Estrin. Directed diffusion: A scalable and robust communication paradigm for sensor networks. In *MobiCOM*, Boston, MA, August 2000.

[16] Intersema. Ms5534a barometer module. Technical report, October 2002. http://www.intersema.com/pro/module/file/da5534.pdf.

[17] G. Kollios, J. Considine, F. Li, and J. Byers. Approximate aggregation techniques for sensor databases. In *ICDE*, 2004.

[18] U. Lerner, B. Moses, M. Scott, S. McIlraith, and D. Koller. Monitoring a complex physical system using a hybrid dynamic bayes net. In *UAI*, 2002.

[19] S. Lin and B. Kernighan. An effective heuristic algorithm for the tsp. *Operations Research*, 21:498–516, 1971.

[20] S. Madden. The design and evaluation of a query processing architecture for sensor networks. Master's thesis, UC Berkeley, 2003.

[21] S. Madden, M. J. Franklin, J. M. Hellerstein, and W. Hong. The design of an acquisitional query processor for sensor networks. In *ACM SIGMOD*, 2003.

[22] S. Madden, W. Hong, J. M. Hellerstein, and M. Franklin. TinyDB web page. http://telegraph.cs.berkeley.edu/tinydb.

[23] T. Mitchell. *Machine Learning*. McGraw Hill, 1997.

[24] C. Olston and J.Widom. Best effort cache sychronization with source cooperation. *SIGMOD*, 2002.

[25] C. Olston, B. T. Loo, and J. Widom. Adaptive precision setting for cached approximate values. In *ACM SIGMOD*, May 2001.

[26] G. Pottie and W. Kaiser. Wireless integrated network sensors. *Communications of the ACM*, 43(5):51 – 58, May 2000.

[27] S. Russell and P. Norvig. *Artificial Intelligence: A Modern Approach.* Prentice Hall, 1994.

[28] Sensirion. Sht11/15 relative humidity sensor. Technical report, June 2002. http://www.sensirion.com/en/pdf/Datasheet_SHT1x_SHT7x_0206.pdf.

[29] TAOS, Inc. Tsl2550 ambient light sensor. Technical report, September 2002. http://www.taosinc.com/pdf/tsl2550-E39.pdf.

[30] Y. Yao and J. Gehrke. Query processing in sensor networks. In *Conference on Innovative Data Systems Research (CIDR)*, 2003.

GridDB: A Data-Centric Overlay for Scientific Grids

David T. Liu   Michael J. Franklin

UC Berkeley, EECS Dept.
Berkeley, CA 94720, USA
{dtliu,franklin}@cs.berkeley.edu

Abstract

We present GridDB, a data-centric overlay for scientific grid data analysis. In contrast to currently deployed process-centric middleware, GridDB manages data entities rather than processes. GridDB provides a suite of services important to data analysis: a declarative interface, type-checking, interactive query processing, and memoization. We discuss several elements of GridDB: workflow/data model, query language, software architecture and query processing; and a prototype implementation. We validate GridDB by showing its modeling of real-world physics and astronomy analyses, and measurements on our prototype.

1 Introduction

Scientists in fields including high-energy physics, astronomy, and biology continue to push the envelope in terms of computational demands and data creation. For example, the ATLAS and CMS high-energy physics experiments are both collecting and analyzing one petabyte (10^{15} bytes) of particle collision data per year [13]. Furthermore, continuing advances in such "big science" fields increasingly requires long-term, globe-spanning collaborations involving hundreds or even thousands of researchers. Given such large-scale demands, these fields have embraced *grid computing* [25] as the platform for the creation, processing, and management of their experimental data.

1.1 From Process-Centric to Data-Centric

Grid computing derives primarily from two research domains: cluster-based metacomputing [31, 15] and distributed cluster federation [22]. As such, it has inherited a *process-centric* approach, where the software infrastructure is focused on the management of program invocations (or *processes*). Process-centric grid middleware enables users to submit and monitor jobs (i.e., processes). Modern grid software (e.g., Globus[24] and Condor [31]) also provides additional services such as batching, resource allocation, process migration, etc. These systems, however, provide a fairly low-level, OS-like interface involving imperative programs and files.

Permission to copy without fee all or part of this material is granted provided that the copies are not made or distributed for direct commercial advantage, the VLDB copyright notice and the title of the publication and its date appear, and notice is given that copying is by permission of the Very Large Data Base Endowment. To copy otherwise, or to republish, requires a fee and/or special permission from the Endowment.

Proceedings of the 30th VLDB Conference,
Toronto, Canada, 2004

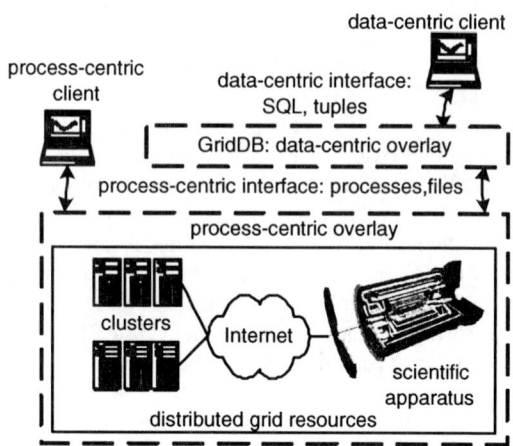

Figure 1: Grid Access Overview

The process-centric approach is a direct extension of the techniques used by scientists in the past. But, with the increasing complexity, scope, and longevity of collaborations and the continuing growth in the scale of the scientific endeavour, it has become apparent that new tools and paradigms are needed. Furthermore, the widespread popularity of interactive processing in many domains has led to a desire among scientists for more interactive access to grid resources. As a result, a number of large, multi-disciplinary efforts have been started by scientists to define the next generation of grid models, tools and infrastructure. These include the Grid Physics Network (GriPhyN) [28], the International Virtual Data Grid Observatory [14], the Particle Physics Data Grid [34], and the European Union DataGrid [47].

GriPhyN, in particular, is built around the notion of "Virtual Data" [51], which aims to put the concept of "data" on an equal footing with that of "process" in grid computing. Our GridDB project, which is being done in the context of GriPhyN, elevates the importance of data one step further, by proposing a *data-centric* view of the grid.

As illustrated in Figure 1, GridDB provides a veneer, or *overlay*, on top of existing process-centric grid services that enables clients to create, manage, and interactively access the results of grid computations using a query language interface to manipulate tables of input parameters and results. The benefits of GridDB include:

- **Declarative Interface**: Scientific computing is a data-intensive task. The benefits of declarative interfaces for such tasks are well-known in the database field, and include: ease of programming, resilience to change, and support for transparent, system-directed optimization.

- **Type Checking**: In contrast to process-centric approaches, which have little or no knowledge of data types, GridDB provides a language for describing data types and function signatures that enables a number of features including more timely error reporting, and support for code sharing [19, 36].

- **Interactive Query Processing**: Scientific computing jobs are often long running. The batch-oriented mode of interaction supported by existing process-centric middleware severely limits scientists' ability to observe and steer computations based on partial results [35, 18]. GridDB's data-centric interface directly supports *computational steering*, giving scientists more effective control over the use of grid resources.

- **Memoization Support**: A key feature advocated by many current grid efforts is the minimization of resources wasted due to the recomputation of previously generated data products [28]. GridDB's data-centric approach provides the necessary infrastructure for supporting such *memoization* [30].

- **Data Provenance**: Because grid data production will entail promiscuous, anonymous, and transparent resource sharing, scientists must have the ability to retroactively check information on how a data product was created [51, 28]. GridDB's model of function-based data processing lends itself well towards tracking the lineage, or *provenance*, of individual data products.

- **Co-existence**: Perhaps most importantly, GridDB provides these benefits by working *on top* of process-centric middleware, rather than replacing it. This allows users to continue to employ their existing (or even new), imperative data processing codes while selectively choosing which aspects of such processing to make visible to GridDB. This approach also enables incremental migration of scientific workflows into the GridDB framework.

1.2 Contributions and Overview

In this paper, we describe the design, implementation and evaluation of GridDB, a data-centric overlay for scientific grid computing. GridDB is based on two core principles: First, scientific analysis programs can be abstracted as typed functions, and program invocations as typed function calls. Second, while most scientific analysis data is not relational in nature (and therefore not directly amenable to relational database management), a key subset, including the inputs and outputs of scientific workflows, have relational characteristics. This data can be manipulated with SQL and can serve as an interface to the full data set. We use this principle to provide users with a SQL-like interface to grid analysis along with the benefits of data-centric processing listed previously.

Following these two principles, we have developed a grid computing workflow and data model, the Functional Data Model with Relational Covers (FDM/RC), and a schema definition language for creating FDM/RC models. We then developed GridDB, a software overlay that models grid analyses in the FDM/RC. GridDB exploits the FDM/RC's modeling of both workflow and data to provide new services previously unavailable to scientists. We demonstrate its usefulness with two example data analysis workflows taken from a High Energy Physics experiment and an Astronomy survey, and report on experiments that examine the benefits of GridDB's memoization and computational steering features.

2 High-Energy Physics Example

In this section we introduce a simplified workflow obtained from the ATLAS High-Energy Physics experiment [18, 21]. We refer to this workflow as HepEx (High Energy Physics Example) and use it as a running example[1].

The ATLAS team wants to supplement a slow, but trusted detector simulation with a faster, less precise one. To guarantee the soundness of the fast simulation, however, the team must compare the response of the new and old simulations for various physics events. A workflow achieving these comparisons is shown in Fig. 2(a). It consists of three programs: an event generator, gen; the fast simulation, atlfast; and the original, slower simulation, atlsim. gen is called with an integer parameter, $pmas$, and creates a file, $\langle pmas \rangle$.evts that digitally describes a particle's decay into subparticles. $\langle pmas \rangle$.evts is then fed into both atlfast and atlsim, each simulating a detector's reaction to the event, and creating a file which contains a value, $imas$. For atlfast to be sound, the difference between $pmas$ and $imas$ must be roughly the same in both simulations across a range of $pmas$ values [2]. All three programs are long-running, and compute-bound, thus requiring grid processing.

Before describing GridDB, it is useful to examine how HepEx would be deployed in a process-centric system. We identify three types of users who would contribute to such a deployment: *coders*, who write programs; *modelers*, who compose these programs into analysis workflows; and *analysts*, who execute workflows and perform data analysis.

To deploy HepEx, *coders* write the three programs gen, atlfast, and atlsim, in an imperative language, and publish them on the web. A *modeler* then composes the programs into an *abstract workflow*, or AWF. Logically, the AWF, is a DAG of programs to be executed in a partial order. Physically, the AWF is encoded as a script, in perl or some other procedural language[1]. Each program execution is represented by a *process specification* (proc-spec) file, which contains a program, a command-line to execute the program, and a set of input files [2, 5]. The AWF script creates these proc-spec files along with a *precendence specification* (prec-spec) file that encodes the dependencies among the programs.

The *analyst* carries out the third and final step: *data procurement*. Existing middleware systems are extremely effective in presenting a single-machine interface to the grid. Thus, the *analyst* works as if he/she is submitting jobs on a single (very powerful) machine and the grid middleware handles the execution and management of the jobs across the distributed grid resources. The *analyst* creates a *grid job* by executing another script that invokes the AWF script mul-

---

[1] The GridDB implementation of a more complex scientific workflow is described in Section 6.

[2] The physics can be described as follows: $pmas$ is the mass of a particle, while $imas$ is the sum of subparticles after the particle's decay. $pmas - imas$ is a loss of mass after decay, which should be the same between the two simulations.

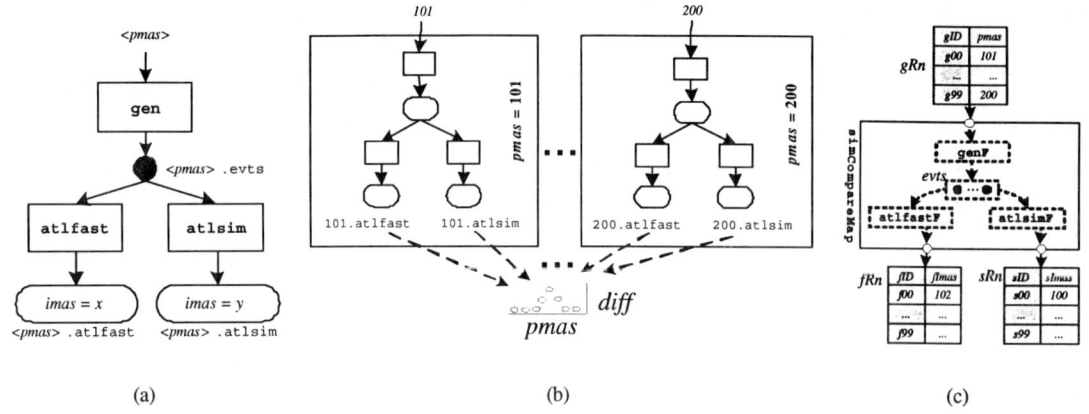

Figure 2: (a) `HepEx` abstract workflow, (b) `HepEx` grid job, (c) GridDB's `simCompareMap` replaces(a) and (b)

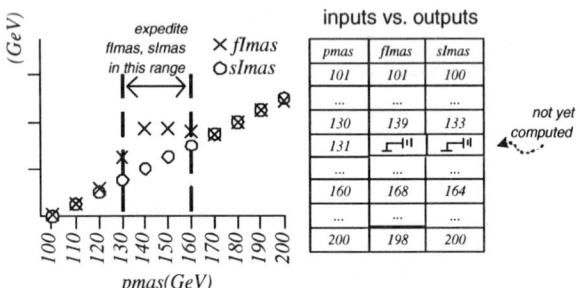

Figure 3: Interactive Query Processing

tiple times. For example, to run `HepEx` for all $pmas$ values from 101 to 200, the AWF script would be invoked 100 times. Each invocation results in three processes being submitted and scheduled. Fig. 2(b) shows the `HepEx` grid job consisting of these invocations.

3 Data Analysis With GridDB

In the previous section, we identified three roles involved in the deployment of grid applications. With GridDB, the job of the *coder* is not changed significantly; rather than publishing to the web, the coder publishes programs into a GridDB code repository available to grid users. In contrast, the *modeler* sees a major change: instead of encoding the AWF in a procedural script, he encodes it with a schema definition language, conveying workflow and data structure information to GridDB, thus empowering GridDB to provide data-centric services. The *analyst*'s interaction with the grid is also changed dramatically.

We describe the workflow and data model and schema definition language used by the *modeler* in detail in Section 4. Here, we focus on the *analyst*'s interactions using GridDB's data manipulation language (DML).

3.1 Motivating Example: IQP

To illustrate the benefits of data-centric grid analysis, we describe how Interactive Query Processing (IQP) can provide increased flexibility and power to the data analysis process.

Recall from Section 1 that GridDB provides a relational interface for data analysis; for example, the table on the right-side of Fig. 3. This table shows, for each value of an input $pmas$, the output $imas$ values from two simulations ($fImas$ and $sImas$). On the left-side of the figure, we show streaming partial results in the table's corresponding scatter plot, which has been populated with 20 out of 200 data points.

The scatter plot indicates discrepancies between $fImas$ and $sImas$ in the range where $pmas$ is between 130 and 160, a phenomenom that needs investigation. Using IQP, an analyst can prioritize data in this range simply by selecting the relevant portion of the x-axis (between the dashed lines) and prioritizing it with a GUI command. GridDB is capable of expediting the minimal set of computations that materialize the points of interest. Through this graphical, data-centric interface, the user drives grid process execution. In contrast, users of process-centric middleware usually run jobs in batch (consider the term "batch" scheduler used to describe many process-centric middlewares).

GridDB's workflow and data model enables it to provide such data-centric services, which are unavailable in process-centric middleware.

3.2 GridDB Modeling Principles

Before walking through an analyst's interaction with GridDB, we describe GridDB's modeling principles and provide a conceptual model for `HepEx`. The GridDB model rests on two main principles: (1) programs and workflows can be represented as *functions*, and (2) an important subset of the data in a workflow can be represented as relations. We refer to this subset as the *relational cover*.

Representing programs and workflows as typed functions provides GridDB with the knowledge necessary to perform type checking of program inputs and outputs and enables a functional representation for AWFs — composite functions. Note, however, that this does not require a change to the programs themselves, but rather, consists of wrapping programs with functional definitions, as we describe in Section 4. In contrast, the process-centered approach uses opaque command-line strings, thereby depriving the middleware of any knowledge of data types for type checking.

In terms of data, while most scientific data is not relational in nature, the inputs and outputs to workflows can typically be represented as tables. For *input* data, consider data pro-

```
1  gRn:set(g); fRn:set(f); sRn:set(s);
2  (fRn,sRn) = simCompareMap(gRn);
3  INSERT INTO gRn VALUES pmas = {101,...,200};
4  SELECT * FROM autoview(gRn,fRn,sRn);
```

Listing 1: DML for analysis in HepEx

curement, as described in Section 2: a scientist typically uses nested-loops in a script to enumerate a set of points within a multidimensional parameter space and invoke an AWF for each point. Each point in the input set can be represented as a tuple whose attributes are the point's dimensional values, a well-known technique in OLAP systems [49]. Therefore, an input set can be represented as a tuple set, or relation.

The relational nature of *outputs* is observed through a different line of reasoning. Scientists commonly manipulate workflow output with interactive analysis tools such as *fv* in astronomy[4] and *root* or *paw* in high energy physics[16, 6]. Within these tools, scientists manipulate — with operations like *projection* and *selection* — workflow data to generate multidimensional, multivariate graphs [48]. Such graphs — including scatter plots, time-series plots, histograms, and bar-charts — are fundamentally visualizations of relations.

Figure 2(c) shows a HepEx model using these two principles[3]. In the figure, the HepEx workflow is a represented as a function, simCompareMap, which is a composition including three functions representing the workflow programs: genF, atlfastF, and atlsimF. The input data is represented as a relation of tuples containing *pmas* values and the outputs are represented similarly.

3.3 Data Manipulation Language

Having described the main modeling principles, we now describe the data manipulation language for *analyst* interaction. With GridDB, analysts first create their own computational "sandbox", in which to perform their analyses. This sandbox consists of private copies of relations to be populated and manipulated by GridDB. Next, the analyst specifies the analysis workflow he/she wishes to execute by connecting sandboxed relations to the inputs and outputs of a GridDB-specified workflow function.

The DML required for setting up HepEx is shown in Listing 1. Line 1 declares the sandbox relations. For example, gRn is declared with a type of set(g). The next statement (Line 2) assigns the two-relation output of simCompareMap, applied to gRn, to the output relations fRn and sRn. The modeler, at this point, has already declared simCompareMap, with the signature: set(g) → set(f) × set(s), an action we show in Section 4.3.2.

With a sandbox and workflow established, data procurement proceeds as a simple INSERT statement into the workflow's input relation, gRn, as shown in Line 3. Insertion of values into the input relation triggers the submission of proc-specs for grid execution. This is conceptually similar to the execution represented by Fig. 2(b). A readily apparent benefit of GridDB's data procurement is that INSERT's are type-checked; for example, inserting a non-integral value, such as 110.5, would result in an immediate exception.

[3]This model is created by schema definition commands written by the modeler, as we describe in Section 4

Analysts commonly seek to discover relationships between different physical quantities. To support this analysis task, GridDB automatically creates relational views that map between inputs and outputs of functions. We call such views *automatic views*. For example, GridDB can show the relationships between tuples of gRn, fRn, and sRn in a view called autoview(gRn, fRn, sRn) (Line 4). Using this view, the *analyst* can see, for each value of *pmas*, what values of *flmas* resulted. The implementation of autoviews is described in Section 5.1.2. The autoview mechanism also plays in an important role in the provision of IQP, as is discussed in Section 7.1.

3.4 Summary

To summarize, GridDB provides a SQL-like DML that allows users to initiate grid analysis tasks by creating private copies of relations, mapping some of those relations to workflow inputs and then inserting tuples containing input parameters into those relations. The outputs of the workflow can also be manipulated using the relational DML. The system can maintain *automatic views* that record the mappings between inputs and outputs; these "autoviews" also play an important role in supporting Interactive Query Processing. By understanding both workflow and data, GridDB provides data-centric services unavailable in process-centric middleware.

4 Data Model: FDM/RC

The previous section illustrated the benefits of GridDB data analysis provided that the modeler has specified a workflow and data schema to GridDB. In this section, we describe a model and data definition language for these schemas. The model is called the Functional Data Model with Relational Covers(FDM/RC) and has two main constructs: *entities* and *functions*. Functions, which map from entities to entities, and can be composed together and iterated over, are used to model workflows. Data entities may be modeled opaquely as blobs, or transparently as tuples, providing the modeling power of the relational model. By modeling both workflows and their data (as tuples), the FDM/RC enables GridDB to provide not only services found in either workflow and database systems, but also services not found in either.

4.1 Core Design Concepts

We begin our discussion with two concepts: (1) the inclusion of *transparent* and *opaque* data and (2) the need for *fold/unfold* operations.

4.1.1 Opaque and Transparent Data

The FDM/RC models *entities* in three ways: *transparent*, *opaque* and *transparent-opaque*.

One major distinction of GridDB, compared with process-centric middleware, is that it understands detailed semantics for some data, which it treats as relations. Within the data model, these are *transparent* entities, as GridDB interacts with their contents. By providing more information about data, transparent modeling enables GridDB to provide richer services. For example, the input, *pmas*, to program gen in Fig. 2(a) is modeled as a transparent entity: it can be modeled as a tuple with one integer attribute, *pmas*. Knowing the contents of this data, that the input is a tuple with an integer attribute, GridDB can perform type-checking on gen's inputs. Other services enabled by transparent data are a declarative SQL interface and IQP based on the declarative interface.

On the other hand, there are times when a modeler wants GridDB to catalog a file, but has neither the need for enhanced services, nor the resources to describe data semantics. GridDB allows lighter weight modeling of these entities as *opaque* objects. As an example, consider an output file of gen, x.evt. The entity is used to execute programs atlfast and atlsim. GridDB must catalog and retrieve the file for later use, but the modeler does not need extra services.

Finally, there is *opaque-transparent* data, file data that is generated by programs, and therefore needs to be stored in its opaque form for later usage, but also needs to be understood by GridDB to gain data-centric services. An example is the output of atlfast; it is a file that needs to be stored, possibly for later use (although not in this workflow), but it can also be represented as a single-attribute tuple (attribute *fImas* of type int). As part of data analysis, the user may want to execute SQL over a set of these entities.

4.1.2 Unfold/Fold

To provide a well-defined interface for grid programs, GridDB allows a modeler to wrap programs behind typed function interfaces. The *unfold* and *fold* operations define the "glue" between a program and its dual function.

For this abstraction to be sound, function evaluations must be defined by a program execution, a matter of two translations: (1) The function input arguments must map to program inputs and (2) the programs outputs files, upon termination, must map to the functions return values. These two mappings are defined by the *fold* and *unfold* operations, respectively.

In Section 4.3.2, we describe *atomic* functions, which encapsulate imperative programs and employ fold and unfold operations. In Section 4.3.3, we elucidate the operations with an example.

4.2 Definition

Having described the core concepts of our grid data model, we now define it:

The FDM/RC has two constructs: *entities* and *functions*. An FDM schema consists of a set *entity*-sets, T, and a set of functions, F, such that each function, $F_i \in F$, is a mapping from entities to entities: $F_i : X_1 \times \ldots \times X_m \to Y_1 \times \ldots \times Y_n$, $X_i, Y_i \in T$, and can be the composition of other functions. Each *non-set* type, $\tau = [\tau_t, \tau_o] \in T$, can have a *transparent* component, τ_t, an *opaque* component τ_o, or both[4]. τ_t is a tuple of scalar entities. Set-types, $set(\tau)$, can be constructed from any type τ. The *relational cover* is the subset, R, of types, T, that are of type $set(\tau)$, where τ has a transparent component. An FDM/RC schema (T, R, F) consists of a type set, T; a relational cover, R; and a function set, F.

4.3 Data Definition Language

An FDM/RC schema, as we have just described, is defined by a data definition language (DDL). The DDL is divided

---

[4]one of τ_t and τ_o can be null, but not both

---

into type and function definition constructs. In this section, we describe the constructs, and illustrate them with HepEx's data definition, when possible. Its DDL is shown in Listing 2.

4.3.1 Types

As suggested in Section 4.1.1, modelers can define three *kinds* of types: *transparent*, *opaque* and *transparent-opaque*. All types, regardless of their kind, are defined with the type keyword. We show declarations for all three HepEx types below.

Transparent type declarations include a set of typed attributes and are prefixed with the keyword transparent. As an example, the following statement defines a transparent type g, with an integer attribute *pmas*:

```
transparent type g = (pmas:int);
```
Opaque types do not specify attributes and therefore are easier to declare. *Opaque* type declarations are prefixed with the keyword opaque. For example, the following statement declares an opaque type *evt*:

```
opaque type evt;
```
Suppose an entity e is of an opaque type. It's opaque component is accessed as e.opq.

transparent-opaque type declarations are *not* prefixed, *and* contain a list of attributes; for example, this statement declares a transparent-opaque type f, which has one integer attribute *imas*:

```
type f = (imas:int);
```
A variable of type f also has an opaque component.

Finally, users can construct set types from any type. For example, this statement creates a set of g entities:

```
type setG = set(g);
```
Because setG has type set(g), and g has a transparent component, setG belongs in the relational cover.

4.3.2 Functions

There are four kinds of functions that can be defined in DDL: *atomic*, *composite*, *map* and *SQL*. Function interfaces, regardless of kind, are defined as typed lists of input and output entities. The definition header of atomic function genF is:

```
atomic fun genF (params:g):(out:evt)
```
This header declares genF as a function with an input params, output out, and type signature $g \to evt$. We proceed by describing body definitions for each kind of function.

As mentioned in Section 4.1.2, *atomic functions* embody grid programs, and therefore determine GridDB's interaction with process-centric middleware. The body of atomic function definitions describe these interactions. Three items need to be specified: (1) the program (using a unique program ID) that defines this function. (2) The *unfold* operation for tranforming GridDB entities into program inputs and (3) the *fold* operation for transforming program outputs to function output entities. Three examples of atomic functions are genF, atlfastF, and atlsimF(function headers in Listing 2, at Lines 12-14). Because the body of an atomic function definition is quite involved, we defer its discussion to Section 4.3.3.

Composite functions are used to express complex analyses, and then abstract it — analogous to the encoding of abstract workflows in scripts. As an example, a composite function simCompare composes the three atomic functions we have just described. It is defined with:

```
fun simCompare(in:g):(fOut:f,sOut:s) =
(atlfastF(genF(in)), atlsimF(genF(in));
```

This statement says that the first output, fOut, is the result of function atlfastF applied to the result of function genF applied to input in. sOut, the second return-value, is defined similarly. The larger function, simCompare, now represents a workflow of programs. The composition is type-checked and can be reused in other compositions.

Map functions, or *maps*, provide a declarative form of finite iteration. Given a set of inputs, the map function repeatedly applies a particular function to each input, creating a set of outputs. For a function, F, with a signature $X_1 \times \ldots \times X_m \to Y_1 \times \ldots \times Y_n$, a map, $FMap$, with a signature: $set(X_1) \times \ldots \times set(X_m) \to set(Y_1) \times \ldots \times set(Y_n)$, can be created, which executes F for each combination of its inputs, creating a combination of outputs.

As an example, consider the following statement, which creates a map function simCompareMap with the type signature $set(g) \to set(f) \times set(s)$, given that SimCompare has a signature $g \to f \times s$:

```
fun simCompareMap = map(simCompare);
```

We call SimCompare the *body* of simCompareMap. Maps serve as the front-line for data procurement — analysts submit their input sets to a map, and receive their output sets, being completely abstracted from grid machinery.

The benefit of transparent, relational data is that GridDB can now support *SQL* functions within workflows. As an example, a workflow function which joins two relations, holding transparent entities of r and s, with attributes a and b, and returns only r tuples, can be defined as:

```
sql fun (R:set(r), S:set(s)):(ROut:set(r)) =
sql(SELECT R.* FROM R,S WHERE R.A = S.B);
```

In Section 6, we will show an SQL workflow function that simplifies a spatial computation with a spatial "overlaps" query, as used in an actual astronomy analysis.

4.3.3 Fold/Unfold Revisited

Finally, we return to defining atomic functions and their *fold* and *unfold* operations. Recall from Section 4.1.2 that the fold and unfold operations define how data moves between GridDB and process-centric middleware.

Consider the body of function atlfastF, which translates into the execution of the program atlfast:

```
atomic fun atlfastF(inEvt:evt):(outTuple:f) =
exec(
''atlfast'',
[(''events'',inEvt)],
[(/.atlfast$/, outTuple, ''adapterX'')]
)
```

The body is a call to a system-defined exec function, which submits a process execution to process-centric middleware. exec has three arguments, the first of which specifies the program (with a unique program ID) which this function maps to. The second and third arguments are lists that specify the *unfold* and *fold* operations for each input or output

```
1  //opaque-only type definitions
2  opaque type evt;
3
4  //transparent-only type declarations
5  transparent type g = (pmas:int);
6
7  //both opaque and transparent types
8  type f = (fImas:int);
9  type s = (sImas:int);
10
11 //headers of atomic function definitions for
      genF, atlfastF, atlsimF
12 atomic fun genF(params:g):(out:evt) = ...;
13 atomic fun atlsim(evtsIn:evt):(outTuple:s)
      = ...;
14 atomic fun atlfastF(inEvt:evt):(outTuple:f) =
15   exec(''atlfast'',
16        [(''events'',inEvt)],
17        [(/.atlfast$/, outTuple, ''adapterX'')]);
18
19 //composite function simCompare definition
20 fun simCompare(in:g):(fOut:f,sOut:s) =
21   ( atlfast(gen(in)), atlsim(gen(in)) );
22
23 //a map function for simCompare
24 fun simCompareMap = map(simCompare);
```

Listing 2: Abridged HepEx DDL

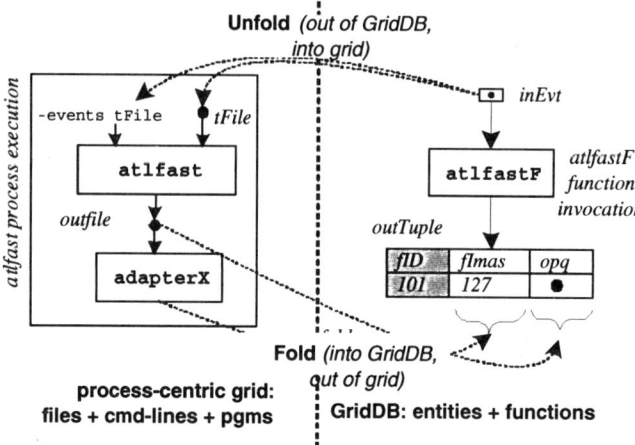

Figure 4: Unfold/Fold in *atomic* functions

entity.

The second argument is a list of pairs (only one here) which specifies how arguments are unfolded. In this case, because evtsIn is an opaque entity, the file it represents is copied into the process' working directory before execution, and the name of the newly created file is appended to the command-line, with the tag events. For example, atlfast would be called with the command-line atlfast -events tFile, where tFile is the name of the temporary file (top of Fig. 4).

The last argument to exec is also a list, this time of triples (only one here), which specify fold operations for each output entity (bottom of Fig. 4). In this case, the first list item instructs GridDB to look in the working directory after process termination, for a file that ends with .atlfast (or matches the regular expression /.atlfast$/). The second item says that the opq component of the output, outTuple, resolves to the newly created file. The third item specifies an adapter program — a program that extracts the attributes

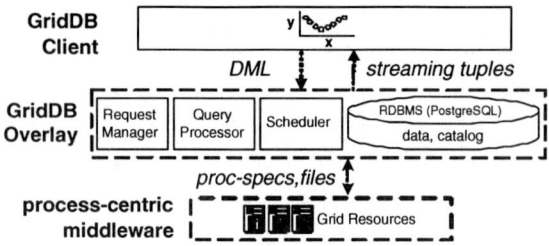

Figure 5: GridDB's Architecture

of outTuple's transparent component into a format understandable by GridDB; for example, comma-separated-value format. GridDB ingests the contents (in this case, *flmas*) into the transparent component. The adapter program is also registered by the *coder* and assigned a unique program ID.

Object-to-file mappings have previously been studied in the ZOO project [10].

5 Design and Implementation

In this section, we discuss the design of GridDB, focusing on the query processing of *analyst* actions, as embodied in DML statements.

GridDB's software architecture is shown in Fig. 5. The GridDB overlay mediates interaction between a GridDB Client and process-centric middleware. Four main modules implement GridDB logic: the Request Manager receives and initializes queries; the Query Processor manages query execution; the Scheduler dispatches processes to process-centric middleware; and an RDBMS (we use PostgreSQL [44]) stores and manipulates data, as well as the system catalog.

In the rest of this section, we describe how GridDB processes DML statements. We do not discuss the processing of schema definition statements, as they are straightforward updates to the system catalog (similar to data definition statements of relational databases).

5.1 Data Representation and Query Processing

Our general implementation strategy is to translate DML statements into SQL, re-using a pre-existing relational query processor for most processing. One consequence of this strategy is that our main data structures must be stored in tables. In this section, we take a bottom-up approach, first describing the tabular data structures, and then describing the query translation process.

5.1.1 Tabular Data Structures

GridDB uses three kinds of tables: two for entities and function mappings and the last for process state. We describe these three in turn.

Entity Tables: Recall from Section ?? that non-set entities may have two components: a transparent component, τ_t, which is a tuple of scalar values; and an opaque component, τ_o, which is a bitstream. Each entity also has a unique system-assigned ID. Thus, an entity of type τ having an m-attribute transparent component (τ_t) and an opaque component (τ_o) is represented as the following tuple: $(\tau ID, \tau_t.attr_1, \ldots, \tau_t.attr_m, \tau_o)$. Entity-sets are represented as tables of these tuples.

Function Memo Tables: Given an instance of its input entities, a function call returns an instance of output entities. Function evaluations establish these mappings, and can be remembered in function *memo tables* [30]. We describe the table of a function with one input and one output, $F : X \rightarrow Y$, as the description easily extends to functions with multiple inputs and outputs. F has an associated memo table, $FMemo$, with the schema (FID, XID, YID). Each mapping tuple has an ID, FID, which is used for process book-keeping (see below); and IDs for its domain and range entities (XID and YID, respectively). Each domain entity can only map to one range entity, stipulating that XID is a candidate key.

Process Table: As described in Section 4.3.3, function evaluations are resolved through process process invocation. Process invocations are stored in a table with the following attributes: $(PID, FID, funcName, priority, status)$. PID is a unique process ID; FID is a foreign key to the memo table of function $funcName$, representing the process' associated function evaluation; *priority* is the process' priority, used for computational steering; and *status* is one of *done*, *running*, *ready*, or *pending*.

5.1.2 DML Query Processing: Translation to SQL

Having represented entities, functions and processes in RDBMS tables, query processing can proceed by translating the DML to standard SQL.

In this section, we describe how each *analyst* action is processed and show, as an example, query processing for the HepEx analysis. The internal data structures for HepEx are shown in Fig. 6. The diagram is an enhanced version of the analyst's view of Fig. 2(c).

Recall the three basic analyst actions from Section 3: *workflow setup* creates sandbox entity-sets and connects them as inputs and outputs of a map; *data procurement* is the submission of inputs to the workflow, triggering function evaluations to create output entities. Finally, streaming partial results can be perused with *automatic views*. We repeat the listing for convenience:

```
1:   gRn:set(g); fRn:set(f); sRn:set(s);
2:   (fRn,sRn) = simCompareMap(gRn);
3:   INSERT INTO gRn VALUES pmas = {101,...,200};
4:   SELECT * FROM autoview(gRn,fRn);
```

Workflow Setup

During workflow setup, tables are created for the entity-sets and workflow functions. At this step, GridDB also stores a *workflow DAG* for the analysis. In the example, workflow setup (Lines 1-2) creates a table for each of the four entity-sets (gRn, fRn, sRn, evts), as well as each of the three functions ($genFMemo, atlfastFMemo, atlsimMemo$). An internal data structure stores the workflow DAG, represented by the solid arrows between tables.

Data procurement and Process Execution

Data procurement is performed with an INSERT statement into a map's input entity-set variables. In GridDB, an INSERT into an entity table connected to a function triggers evaluations of that function. Function outputs are ap-

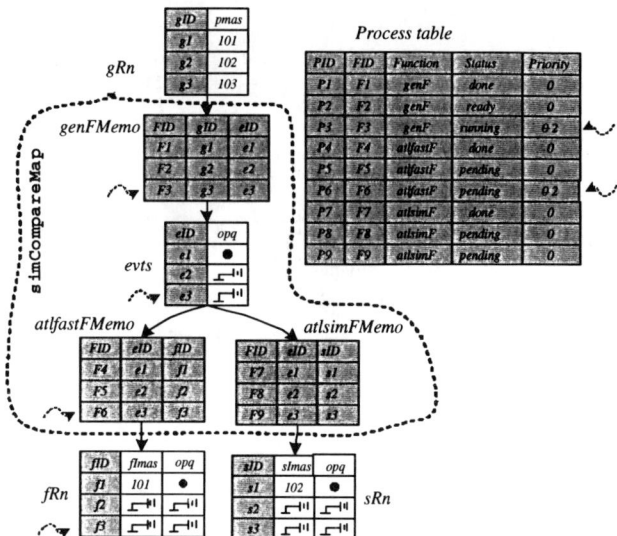

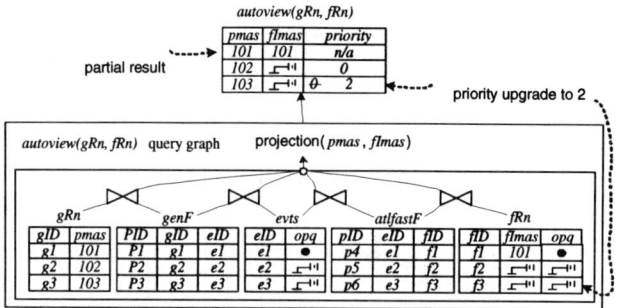

Figure 6: Internal data structures representing `HepEx` functions, entities, and processes. Shaded fields are system-managed. Dashed arrows indicate interesting tuples in our IQP discussion (Sec. 7.1)

pended to output entity tables. If these tables feed into another function, function calls are recursively triggered. Calls can be resolved in two ways: a function can be evaluated, or a memoized result can be retrieved. Evaluation requires *process execution*.

Process execution is a three step procedure that uses the fold and unfold operations described in Section 4.3.3. To summarize: first, the function's input entities are converted to files and a command-line string using the *unfold* operation; second, the process (defined by program, input files and command-line) is executed on the grid; and third, the *fold* operations ingest the process' output files into GridDB entities.

In the example, a data procurement `INSERT` into `gRn` has cascaded into 9 function calls ($F1$-$F9$ in the three function tables) and the insert of tuple stubs (placeholders for results) for the purpose of partial results. We assume an absence of memoized results, so each function call requires evaluation through a process ($P1$-$P9$ in the process table).

The process table snapshot of Fig. 6 indicates the completion of three processes ($P1$, $P4$, $P7$), whose results have been folded back into entity tables (entities $e1$, $f1$, $s1$, respectively).

Automatic Views (Autoviews)

A user may peruse data by querying an autoview. Because each edge in a workflow graph is always associated with a foreign key-primary key relationship, autoviews can be constructed from workflow graphs. As long as a path exists between two entity-sets, an automatic view between them can be created by joining all function- and entity-tables on the path.

In Fig. 7, we show `autoview(gRn, fRn)`, which is automatically constructed by joining all tables on the path from `gRn` to `fRn` and projecting out non-system, non-opaque attributes.

Figure 7: `autoview(gRn, fRn)`

6 ClustFind: A Complex Example

Up until this point, we have demonstrated GridDB concepts using `HepEx`, a rather simple analysis. In this section, we describe how GridDB handles a complex astronomy application. First, we describe the application science. Next, we describe how the analysis can be modeled as an FDM/RC schema. Finally, we describe how `ClustFind` is enhanced by memoization and data-centric computational steering.

6.1 The Science: Finding Clusters of Galaxies

The Sloan Digital Sky Survey (SDSS) [7] is a 12 TB digital imaging survey mapping 250,000,000 celestial objects with two orders of magnitudes greater sensitivity than previous large sky surveys. `ClustFind` is a computationally-intense SDSS analysis that detects galaxy clusters, the largest gravitation-bound objects in the universe. The analysis uses the MaxBCG cluster finding algorithm [11], requiring 7000 CPU hours on a 500 MHz computer [12].

In this analysis, all survey objects are characterized by two spatial coordinates, *ra* and *dec*. All objects fit within a two-dimensional mesh of fields such that each field holds objects in a particular square of (ra, dec)-space (Fig. 8(a)). The goal is to find, in each field, all cluster *cores*, each of which is the center-of-gravitation for a cluster. To find the cores in a *target* field (e.g., F_{33}, annotated with a ⋆ in Fig. 8(a)), the algorithm first finds all core *candidates* in the target, and all candidates in the target's "buffer," or set of neighboring fields (in Fig. 8(a), each field in the buffer of F_{33} is annotated with a •). Finally, the algorithm applies a core selection algorithm, which selects cores from the target candidates based on interactions with buffer candidates and other core candidates.

6.2 An FDM/RC Schema for ClustFind

In this section, we describe the top-level `ClustFind` workflow as an FDM/RC function, `getCores`. Given a target field entity, `getCores` returns the target's set of cores. `getCores` is shown as the outermost function of Fig. 8(b). The analysis would actually build a map function using `getCores` as its body, in order to find cores for a set of targets.

`getCores` is a composite of five functions: `getCands`, on the right-side of the diagram, creates A, a file of target candidates. The three left-most functions — `sqlBuffer`, `getCandsMap`, and `catCands`— create D, a file of buffer candidates. Finally, `bcgCoalesce` is the core selection algorithm; it takes in both buffer candidates, D, and target candidates, A, returning a file of target cores, `cores`. During

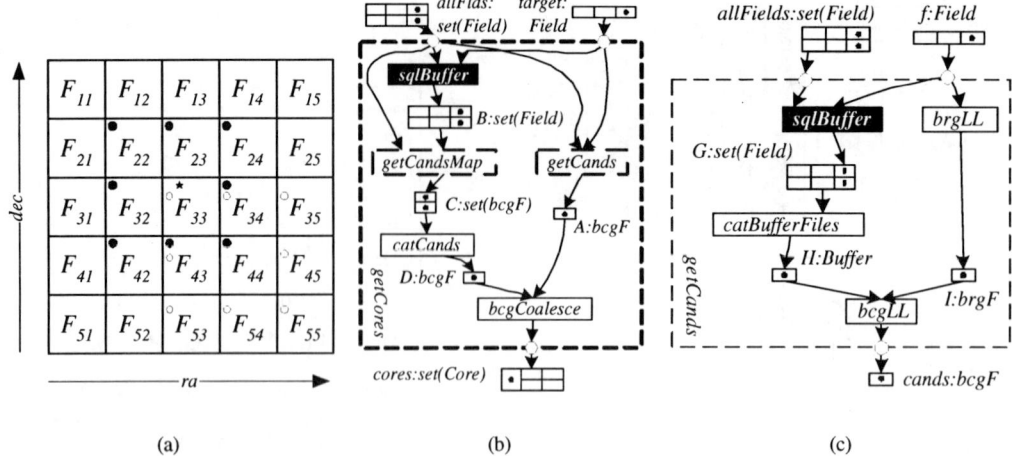

Figure 8: (a) ClustFind divides sky objects into a square mesh of buckets in (ra, dec) space. (b) getCores, the body of the top-level ClustFind map function. (c) getCands, a composite subfunction used in getCores.

the fold operation, cores is ingested as a set of Core entities (shown at the bottom of Fig. 8(b)).

ClustFind analysis is carried out with a map based on the getCores function we have just described, mapping each target field to a set of cores.

This use-case illustrates three notable features not encountered in HepEx: (1) it uses an SQL function, sqlBuffer. Given a target field (target) and the set of all fields (allFields), sqlBuffer uses a spatial overlap query to compute the target's buffer fields, B. (2) it uses a nested map, getCandsMap, which iterates over a dynamically created set of entities. This means that materialization of B will create a new set of processes, each executing the contents of getCands to map an element of B to an element of C. (3) getCores, as a whole, creates a set of Core objects from one target, having a signature of the form $\alpha \rightarrow set(\beta)$. This pattern, where one entity maps to a *set* of entities, is actually quite common and suggests the use of a *nested relational model and query language*[39]. We have decided that even though such a model provides sophisticated support for set types, its added complexity is not justified in the system.

In Fig. 8(c), we show getCands, a function used in getCores, standalone and also as the body of getCandsMap. Given a target field, f, getCands returns a set of core candidates, cands. It is interesting to note that, like getCores, a buffer calculation is needed to compute a field's candidates — resulting in the reuse of sqlBuffer in getCands. As an example, in computing the candidates for F_{44}, we compute its buffer, or the set of fields annotated with a ○ in Fig. 8(a). Note that the bcgLL function within getCands is the most expensive function to evaluate [12], making getCands the bottleneck in getCores.

The analysis touches upon 2 kinds of entity types (examples in parentheses): opaque (A), and transparent-opaque (target); set types (C); and all four kinds of functions: atomic (bcgCoalesce), composite (getCands), sql (sqlBuffer), map (getCandsMap). The atomic functions, which cause grid process executions, are the solid boxes.

6.3 Memoization & IQP in ClustFind

Embedded in our description is this fact: getCands is called ten times per field. getCands is called twice in computing the field's cores and once each for computing the cores of its eight neighbors. By modeling this workflow in a GridDB schema, an astronomer automatically gains the performance of memoization, without needing to implement it himself.

Finally, it is common for astronomers to point to a spot on an image map — for instance, the using SkyServer interface[7] — and query for results from those coordinates. These requests translate to (ra, dec) coordinates, and are accomodated by GridDB's data-driven prioritization of interesting computations.

7 Performance Enhancements

Previous sections have shown how GridDB provides basic services. In this section, we show that GridDB's model serves as a foundation for two other performance-enhancing services: Interactive Query Processing and Memoization. We describe these two services and validate their benefits using a prototype GridDB implementation.

7.1 Interactive Query Processing

Due to the conflict between the long-running nature of grid jobs and the iterative nature of data analysis, scientists have expressed a need for data-centric computational steering (IQP) [18, 35].

In this section, we describe how the FDM/RC enables IQP through a relational interface. We introduce IQP with an example. Consider the autoview at the top of Fig. 7. The view presents the relation between *pmas* and *flmas* values. The user has received one partial result, where pmas= 101. At this point, the user may upgrade the priority of a particular tuple (with pmas= 103) using an SQL UPDATE statement:

```
UPDATE autoview(gRn, fRn) SET PRIORITY = 2
WHERE pmas = 103
```

By defining a relational cover, GridDB allows prioritization of data, rather than processes. In GridDB, the `UPDATE` statement is enhanced; one can update a special `PRIORITY` attribute of any view. This scheme is expressive: a set of views can express, and therefore one may prioritize, any combination of cells in a relational schema (the relational cover).

Next, we turn to how such a request affects query processing and process scheduling, where GridDB borrows an technique from functional languages, that of lazy evaluation [30]. Any view tuple can always be traced back to entities of the relational cover, using basic data lineage techniques [50]. Each entity also has a functional expression, which encodes its computational recipe. Since function evaluations are associated with process execution, GridDB can prioritize only the minimal process executions, delaying the computation of other, irrelevant computations.

As an example, consider the processing of the prioritization request in Fig. 7. The only missing uncomputed attribute is *flmas*, which is derived from from relational cover tuple *f*3. Fig. 6 (see dashed arrows) shows that *f*3 is a result of function evaluation *F*6, which depends on the result function of evaluation *F*3. The two processes for these evaluations are *P*3 and *P*6, which are prioritized. Such lineage allows lazy evaluation of other irrelevant, possibly function evaluation, such as any involving `atlsimF`.

In summary, the FDM/RC, with its functional representation of workflows and relational cover, have provided a data-centric interface for computational steering.

7.2 Memoization

Recall from Section 5.1.1 that function evaluations are stored in memo tables. Using these tables, memoization is simple: if a function call with the same entities has been previously evaluated and memoized, we can return the memoized entities, rather than re-evaluating. This is possible if function calls, and the programs which implement them, are deterministic. Scientific analysis programs are often deterministic, as repeatibility is paramount to computational science [8]. However, if required, our our modeling language could be extended to allow the declaration of non-deterministic functions, which may not be memoized, as is done with the `VARIANT` function modifier of PostgreSQL.

7.3 Implementation

We have implemented a java-based prototype of GridDB, consisting of almost 19K lines of code. Modular line counts are in Table. 1. The large size of the client is explained by its graphical interface, which we implemented for a demonstration of the system during SIGMOD 2003 [32]. Currently, the system uses condor [31] as its process-centric middleware; therefore, it allows access to a cluster of machines. In the future, we plan to use Globus, in order for the system to leverage distributively-owned computing resources. The change should not be conceptually different, as both provide the same process-centric interface.

7.4 Validation

To demonstrate the effectiveness of IQP and memoization, we conducted validation experiments with our prototype implementation and the cluster testbed of Fig. 9. Measurements

Module(s)	LOC	Module(s)	LOC
Rqst Mgr. & Q.P.	1495	Catalog Routines	756
Scheduler	529	Data Structures	7207
Client	7471	Utility Routines	1400
Total	18858		

Table 1: LOCs for a java-based GridDB prototype.

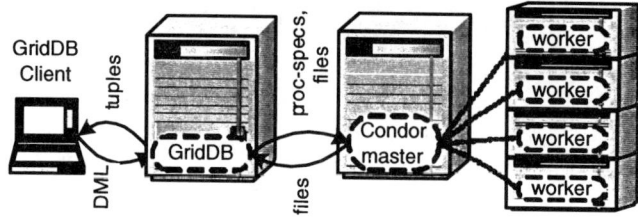

Figure 9: Experimental setup.

were conducted on a miniature "grid" consisting of six nodes (Fig. 9). The GridDB client issued results from a laptop while the GridDB overlay, a "Condor Master" batch scheduler [31] and 4 worker nodes each resided on one of 6 cluster nodes. All machines, with the exception of the client, were Pentium 4, 1.3 GHz machines with 512 MB RAM, running Redhat Linux 7.3. The client was run on an IBM Thinkpad Mobile Pentium 4, 1.7 GHz with 512 MB RAM. The machines were connected by a 100 Mbps network.

7.4.1 Validation 1: IQP

In the first validation experiment, we show the benefits of IQP by comparing GridDB's *dynamic* scheduler, which modifies its scheduling decisions based on interactive data prioritizations, against two static schedulers: *batch* and *pipelined*.

In this experiment, an analyst performs the data procurement of Section 3, inserting 100 values of *pmas* into `simCompareMap`. 200 hundred seconds after submission, we inject a IQP request, prioritizing 25 as yet uncomputed f tuples:

```
UPDATE autoview(gRn, fRn) SET PRIORITY = 2
WHERE 131 ≤pmas≤ 150
```

The *batch* scheduler evaluates all instances of each function consecutively, applying `genF` to all *pmas* inputs, and then to `atlsimF`, and then `atlfastF`. The *pipelined* scheduler processes one input at a time, starting with *pmas*=1, and applying all three functions to it. Neither changes its schedule based on priority updates. In contrast, the GridDB *dynamic* scheduler does change its computation order as a user updates preferences.

In Fig. 10, we plot *Number of Prioritized Data Points* returned vs. *time*. In the plot, GridDB(dynamic) has delivered all 20 interesting results. The figure shows that *dynamic* has delivered all 20 interesting results within 1047s. The static pipelined and batch schedulers require 2608s and 3677s, respectively. In this instance, GridDB cut time-to-interesting-result by 60% and 72%, respectively.

The performance gains are due to the *lazy evaluation* of the expensive function, `atlsimF`, as well as the prioritization of interesting input points, two effects explained in Section 7.1.

609

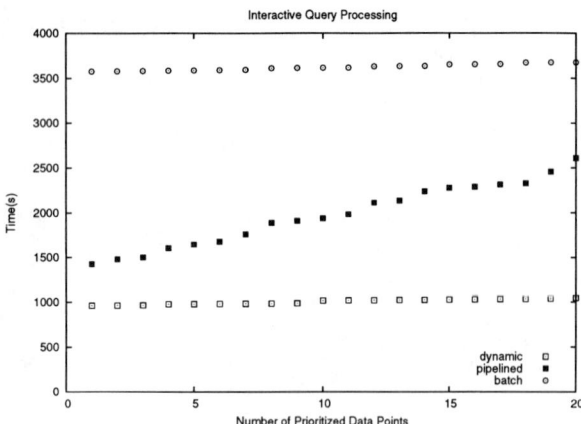

Figure 10: Validation 1, IQP for `HepEx`

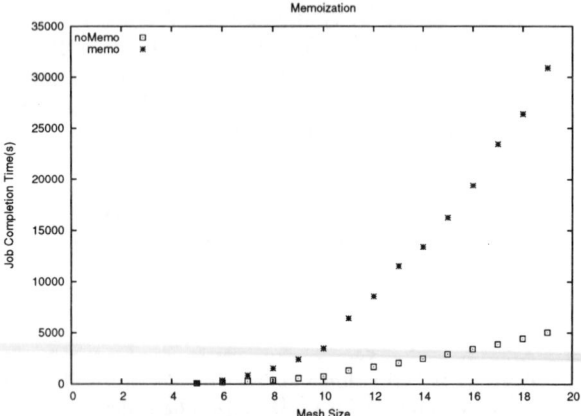

Figure 11: Validation 2, Memoization in `ClustFind`

7.4.2 Validation 2: Memoization Speedup

We validated the GridDB memoization implementation by testing how well it exploits `ClustFind` memoization opportunities (from Section 6). We observed that when memoization is used, system throughput speeds up by 6.13 relative to when it is absent. Note that process-centric middleware typically does not provide a memoization service.

In these experiments, we used GridDB to drive cluster core search for square meshes of varying size. The smallest, of size 5, is shown in Fig. 8(a). Each field was of length 0.1×0.1 degrees. Recall from Section 6.3 that the GridDB modeling of `ClustFind` analysis presents a prime opportunity for memoization, as the most expensive functions are also repeated many times.

As shown in Fig. 11, an analysis using memoization (memo) out-performs an analysis without memoization (noMemo) for meshes from sizes 6 to 19. Meshes of size 5 have no memoization opportunities; we can only calculate one target (each target requires a 5 by 5 buffer around it for computation). At mesh size 19 (361 fields), a memoized analysis requires 5041 seconds while one without memoization requires 30894 seconds — a speedup of 6.13. Analysis using Amdahl's law dictates an upper bound of 7, when exploiting memoization.

To precisely understand these performance gains, we profiled the `ClustFind` analysis, recording the amount of time spent in the four main modules of Fig. 8(b): `sqlBuffer`, `getCands`(and `getCandsMap`), `catCands`, and `bcgCoalesce`. We discovered 95% of the execution time was spent in `getCands`. Our profiling showed that memoization reduced the time calling `getCands` by up to 86%, where 90% is optimal (each call is made a maximum of 10 times, so a 10 to 1 reduction is optimal).

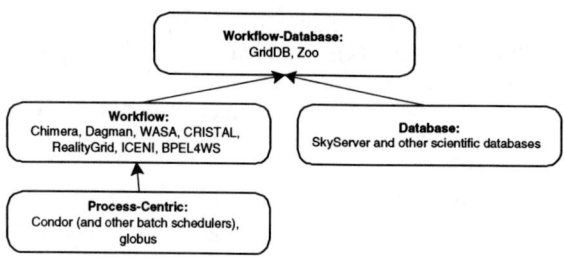

Figure 12: A categorization of related systems.

8 Related Work

We classify related systems into four categories: *Process-Centric*, *Workflow*, *Database* and *Workflow-Database*. In this section, we summarize the salient features of each category, deferring discussions of individual systems to [33]. Using this classification, we argue that by combining the models of both *Workflow* and *Database* systems, GridDB not only provides the feature-sets of both systems, but also provides features absent from both categories.

The four categories are related in Figure 12, where an arrow from category A to category B indicates that B derives from A. *Process-centric* systems such as Condor [31] and Globus [24] provide an OS-like process submission interface. *Workflow* systems, such as WASA [45], CRISTAL [20], chimera [12, 51] and DAGMan [3], focus on the management of processes that create data, but typically do not exploit the structure of the data created by their workflows. Naturally, *Workflow* systems build on top of process-centric systems. On the other hand, *Database* systems used for scientific computing, such as SQL Server (used to build SkyServer [42, 43]), model and manipulate data, the final product of workflows, but do not provide workflow management facilities.

Finally, *Workflow-Database* systems model both workflows and their data. GridDB, along with ZOO [29, 9], fit into this category. To our knowledge, ZOO is the first, and only other system to incorporate workflow and data modeling into a scientific analysis framework. GridDB and ZOO share many similarities; for example, ZOO also provides a data model and query language [46], and maps between files and objects [10].

However, we have identified three main differences: (1) GridDB is focused on the grid environment rather than the desktop environment, (2) GridDB uses the simpler relational model, which we argue is sufficient for input and output modeling (Section 3), and (3) GridDB exploits synergy between workflow and data modeling, providing features unavailable in ZOO, such as IQP.

An alternative parallel programming model is represented by MPI [23] and MPI-based libraries, such as Master-

Worker[26]. These programming models can increase the execution speed of an individual process by running it on multiple machines, but stipulate a lower-level programming model when compared to any of the *Workflow*, *Database*, or *Workflow-Database* systems described above.

Finally, GridDB builds upon the Functional Data Model (FDM) [40, 41, 17] and relational Interactive Query Processing (IQP) [37, 38, 27]. We expand the use of the FDM to model grid workflows and extend previous IQP systems by steering grid computation, rather than the relational queries of previous work.

9 Conclusion

In this paper, we have presented GridDB, a software overlay that provides data-centric services for scientific grid computing. We exploit two key principles: first, imperative programs can be modeled as typed-functions and second, that a key subset of data, the relational cover, can be modeled as relations, and used as a relational interface to the full data set. As such, we have built a workflow and data model (FDM/RC) and query language for representing workflows and accessing their data through a relational interface. Additionally, GridDB exploits the synergy between workflow and data modeling to provide previously unavailable data-centric grid services. Finally, we have demonstrated the use of GridDB in modeling High Energy Physics and Astronomy analyses and have validated our ideas by measuring a prototype implementation.

10 Acknowledgements

We thank many collaborators from the GriPhyN, ATLAS and SDSS projects and other members of the UC Berkeley Database Group. This work was funded in part by the NSF under ITR grants SCI-0086044 and SI-0122599, by the IBM Faculty Partnership Award program, and by research funds from Intel, Microsoft, and the UC MICRO program.

References

[1] Condor-G and DAGMan Hands-On Lab. http://www.cs.wisc.edu/condor/tutorials/miron-condor-g-dagman-tutorial.%html.

[2] Condor Manual. Chapter 2.6: Submitting a Job to Condor. Available at http://www.cs.wisc.edu/condor/manual/.

[3] Dagman home page. http://www.cs.wisc.edu/condor/dagman/. Accessed 10/25/03.

[4] fv: The Interactive FITS File Editor. http://heasarc.gsfc.nasa.gov/docs/software/ftools/fv/. Accessed 10/28/03.

[5] globus-job-submit man page. http://www.globus.org/v1.1/programs/globus-job-submit.html. Accessed 11/19/03.

[6] PAW: Physics Analysis Workstation. http://wwwasd.web.cern.ch/wwwasd/paw/. Accessed 10/28/03.

[7] Sloan digital sky survey. http://www.sdss.org/.

[8] *Handbook of Mathematics and Computational Science*. Springer Verlag, 1998.

[9] A. Ailamaki, *et al.*. Scientific workflow management by database management. In *Statistical and Scientific Database Management*, pp. 190–199. 1998.

[10] V. Anjur, *et al.*. FROG and TURTLE: Visual bridges between files and object-oriented data. In *Proceedings of the Eighth International Conference on Scientific and Statistical Database Management*, pp. 76–85. IEEE, Stockholm, Sweden, 18–20 1996.

[11] Annis, *et al.*. MaxBCG Technique for Finding Galaxy Clusters in SDSS Data . In *AAS 195th Meeting*. 2000.

[12] J. Annis, *et al.*. Applying chimera virtual data concepts to cluster finding in the sloan sky survey. In *Supercomputing*. 2002.

[13] Grid Physics Network High-Energy Particle Physics Description. http://www.griphyn.org/projinfo/physics/highenergy.php. Accessed 11/19/03.

[14] P. Avery. iVDGL ITR proposal: An International Virtual-Data Grid Laboratory for Data Intensive Science. http://www.phys.ufl.edu/~avery/ivdgl/itr2001/proposal_all.pdf, 2001.

[15] A. Bayucash, *et al.*. Portable Batch System: External Reference Specification. Technical report, MRJ Technology Solutions, November 1999.

[16] R. Brun, *et al.*. ROOT - An Interactive Object Oriented Framework and its application to NA49 data analysis. In *Proceedings of Computing in High Energy Physics*. May 1997.

[17] P. Buneman *et al.*. FQL–A Functional Query Language. In *ACM SIGMOD International Conference on Management of Data*. May 1979.

[18] Carminati, F., et al. HEPCAL II: Common Use Cases for a HEP Common Application Layer for Analysis. Technical report, LHC Grid Computing Project, 2003.

[19] Charles W. Krueger. Software Reuse. *ACM Comput. Surv.*, 24(2):131–183, 1992.

[20] Concurrent Repository Information. CRISTAL. URL citeseer.ist.psu.edu/417078.html.

[21] 2003. Personal communication with Craig Tull.

[22] K. Czajkowski, *et al.*. A resource management architecture for metacomputing systems. *LNCS*, 1459, 1998.

[23] M. P. I. Forum. MPI: A message-passing interface standard. Technical Report UT-CS-94-230, 1994.

[24] I. Foster *et al.*. Globus: A metacomputing infrastructure toolkit. *The International Journal of Supercomputer Applications and High Performance Computing*, 11(2):115–128, Summer 1997.

[25] I. Foster, *et al.*. The anatomy of the grid. In *International Journal of Supercomputer Applications*. 2001.

[26] J.-P. Goux, *et al.*. An Enabling Framework for Master-Worker Applications on the Computational Grid. In *HPDC*, pp. 43–50. 2000.

[27] J. M. Hellerstein, *et al.*. Informix under control: Online query processing. In *Data Mining and Knowledge Discovery 4(4)*, pp. 281–314. 2000.

[28] Ian Foster *et al.*. Grid Physics Network (GriPhyN) White Paper, 2003. http://www.griphyn.org/.

[29] Y. E. Ioannidis, *et al.*. Zoo: a desktop experiment management environment. In *Proceedings of the 22 nd Conference on Very Large Data Bases (VLDB), 1996*, pp. 580–583. 1997.

[30] John Hughes. Lazy memo-functions. *Functional Programming Languages and Computer Architecture*, (201):129–146, September 1985.

[31] M. Litzkow, *et al.*. Condor - a hunter of idle workstations. In *Proceedings of the 8th International Conference of Distributed Computing Systems*. 1988.

[32] D. T. Liu, *et al.*. Demo. GridDB: A Relational Interface to the Grid. In *SIGMOD*. 2003.

[33] D. T. Liu *et al.*. GridDB: Data-Centric Services in Scientific Grids. Technical report, UC Berkeley, EECS Department, March 2004. UCB//CSD-04-1311. Available at http://www.cs.berkeley.edu/~dtliu/pubs/griddb_tr.pdf.

[34] M. Livny, *et al.*. Particle physics data grid collaboratory pilot. http://www.ppdg.net/docs/SciDAC/PPDG_overview.pdf, September 2001.

[35] D. Olson *et al.*. PPDG-19: Grid Service Requirements for Interactive Analysis. http://www.ppdg.net/pa/ppdg-pa/idat/papers/analysis_use-cases-grid-reqs%.pdf. Access 11/21/03.

[36] L. Prechelt *et al.*. An experiment to assess the benefits of intermodule type checking, 1996.

[37] V. Raman, *et al.*. Online dynamic reordering for interactive data processing. In *The VLDB Journal*, pp. 709–720. 1999.

[38] V. Raman *et al.*. Partial results for online query processing. In *SIGMOD Conference*, pp. 275–286. 2002.

[39] Serge Abiteboul, *et al.*. *Foundations of Databases: The Logical Level*, chapter Chapter 20: Complex Values. Addison-Wesley Longman Publishing Co., Inc., 1995. ISBN 0201537710.

[40] D. W. Shipman. The functional data model and the data language daplex. *ACM Transactions on Database Systems (TODS)*, 6(1):140–173, 1981.

[41] E. H. Sibley, *et al.*. Data architecture and data model considerations. In *In Proceedings of the AFIPS National Computer Conference, Dallas, Texas*. American Federation of Information Processing Societies, june 1977.

[42] A. S. Szalay, *et al.*. Designing and mining multi-terabyte astronomy archives: the Sloan Digital Sky Survey. pp. 451–462. 2000.

[43] A. S. Szalay, *et al.*. The SDSS skyserver: Public Access to the Sloan Digital Sky Server Data. In *SIGMOD*, pp. 570–581. 2002.

[44] T. P. D. Team. The PostgreSQL Development Team. PostgreSQL User's Guide, 1999.

[45] M. Weske, *et al.*. Wasa: A workflow-based architecture to support scientific database applications. In *DEXA*. 1995.

[46] J. L. Wiener *et al.*. A moose and a fox can aid scientists with data management problems. In *Workshop on Database Programming Languages*, pp. 376–398. 1993.

[47] Wolfgang Hoschek *et al.*. Data Management in an International Data Grid Project. In *IEEE/ACM International Workshop on Grid Computing Grid*. 2000.

[48] P. Wong. 30 years of multidimensional multivariate visualization, 1997.

[49] Yihong Zhao and Prasad M. Deshpande and Jeffrey F. Naughton. An array-based algorithm for simultaneous multidimensional aggregates. In *1997 ACM SIGMOD*, pp. 159–170. 1997.

[50] Yingwei Cui, *et al.*. Tracing the lineage of view data in a warehousing envirolnment. *ACM Transactions on Database Systems*, 25(2):179–227, 2000.

[51] Y. Zhao, *et al.*. Chimera: A virtual data system for representing, querying, and automating data derivation. In *14th Conference on Scientific and Statistical Data Management*. 2002.

Towards an Internet-Scale XML Dissemination Service

Yanlei Diao, Shariq Rizvi, Michael J. Franklin

University of California, Berkeley

{diaoyl, rizvi, franklin}@cs.berkeley.edu

Abstract

Publish/subscribe systems have demonstrated the ability to scale to large numbers of users and high data rates when providing content-based data dissemination services on the Internet. However, their services are limited by the data semantics and query expressiveness that they support. On the other hand, the recent work on selective dissemination of XML data has made significant progress in moving from XML filtering to the richer functionality of transformation for result customization, but in general has ignored the challenges of deploying such XML-based services on an Internet-scale. In this paper, we address these challenges in the context of incorporating the rich functionality of XML data dissemination in a highly scalable system. We present the architectural design of ONYX, a system based on an overlay network. We identify the salient technical challenges in supporting XML filtering and transformation in this environment and propose techniques for solving them.

1 Introduction

A large number of emerging applications, such as mobile services, stock tickers, sports tickers, personalized newspaper generation, network monitoring, traffic monitoring, and electronic auctions, has fuelled an increasing interest in *Content-Based Data Dissemination* (CBDD). CBDD is a service that delivers information to users (equivalently, applications or organizations) based on the correspondence between the content of the information and the user data interests. Figure 1 shows the context in which a data dissemination system providing this service operates. Users subscribe to the service by providing *profiles* expressing their data interests. Data sources publish their data by pushing messages to the system. The system delivers to each user the messages that match her

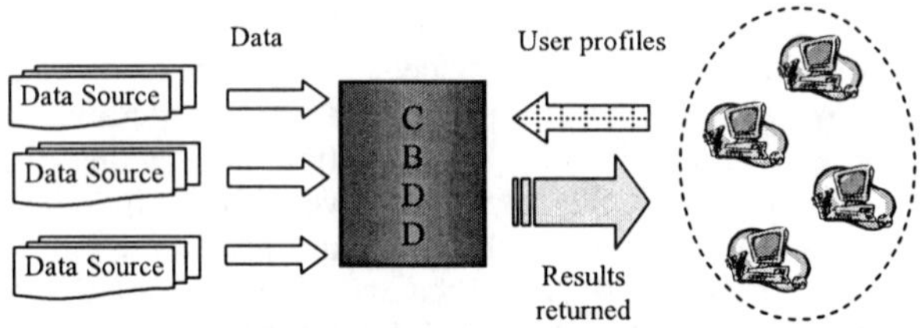

This work was funded in part by the NSF under ITR grants IIS-0086057 and SI-0122599, by the IBM Faculty Partnership Award program, and by research funds from Intel, Microsoft, and the UC MICRO program.

Permission to copy without fee all or part of this material is granted provided that the copies are not made or distributed for direct commercial advantage, the VLDB copyright notice and the title of the publication and its date appear, and notice is given that copying is by permission of the Very Large Data Base Endowment. To copy otherwise, or to republish, requires a fee and/or special permission from the Endowment.
**Proceedings of the 30th VLDB Conference,
Toronto, Canada, 2004**

Fig. 1. Overview of content-based data dissemination

data interests; these messages are presented in the format required by the user.

Over the past few years, XML has rapidly gained popularity as the standard for data exchange in enterprise intranets and on the Internet. The ability to augment data with semantic and structural information using XML-based encoding raises the potential for more accurate and useful delivery of data. In the context of XML-based data dissemination, user profiles can involve constraints over both the structure and value of XML fragments, resulting in potentially more precise filtering of XML messages. In many emerging applications, the relevant XML messages also need to be transformed for data and application integration, personalization, and adaptation to wireless devices.

While XML filtering and transformation has aroused significant interest in the database community [2][8][12][16][20][22][26], little attention has been paid to deploying such XML-based dissemination services on an Internet-scale. In the latter scenario, services are faced with high data rates, large profile population, variable query life span, and tremendous result volume. Distributed publish/subscribe systems developed in the networking community [1][4][9][10][29] have demonstrated their scalability in applications such as sports tickers at the Olympics [21]. Integrating XML processing into such distributed environments appears to be a natural approach to supporting large-scale XML dissemination.

1.1 Challenges

Distributed pub/sub systems partition the profile population to multiple nodes and direct the message flow to the nodes hosting profiles based on the content of messages (referred to as *content-driven routing*). Integrating XML into content-driven routing, however, brings the following key challenges.

- As XML mixes structural and value-based information, content-driven routing needs to support constraints over both. The inherent repetition and recursion of element names in XML data also defeats well-known routing techniques (e.g., the counting algorithms [10][19]) designed for simpler data models. New techniques for XML-based content-driven routing are needed.

- When XML transformation is introduced to a distributed system, the best venue to perform such transformation is another issue to address.
- The criteria used to partition user profiles have an impact on the effectiveness of content-driven routing. The mixture of structure and value-based constraints in profiles and the repetition of element names in XML data complicate the profile partitioning problem.
- As the verbosity of XML results in large messages and these large messages need to be parsed at each routing step, alternative formats should be considered for efficient XML transmission.

A number of XML query processors are available for providing XML processing in this environment. Among them, YFilter [16][17], a multi-query processor that we built previously, represents a set of profiles using an operator network on top of a *Non-Deterministic Finite Automaton* (NFA) to share processing among those profiles. Using YFilter for distributed XML dissemination raises the issues of distributing the NFA-based operator network, and efficient scheduling of the operators for both profile processing and content-driven routing.

1.2 Contributions

In this paper, we present the initial design of ONYX (*Operator Network using YFilter for XML dissemination*), a large-scale dissemination system that delivers XML messages based on user specifications for filtering and transformation. The contributions of our work include the following.

- We leverage the YFilter processor for content-driven routing. In particular, we use the NFA-based operator network to represent routing tables, and provide an initial solution to constructing the routing tables from the distributed profile population.
- We address the issue of how to perform incremental message transformation in the course of routing.
- In order to boost the effectiveness of routing, we provide an algorithm that partitions the profile population based on exclusiveness of data interests.
- We develop holistic message processing for sharing the work among various processing tasks at a node (i.e., content-driven routing, incremental transformation and user profile processing. Dependency-aware priority scheduling is used to support such sharing while providing a fast path for routing.
- We investigate various formats for efficient XML transmission.
- Last but not least, we provide an architectural design of the system and mechanisms for building such a system.

The paper proceeds as follows. Section 2 details the requirements and motivation. Section 3 describes our system model. Core techniques addressing the various challenges are presented in Section 4, followed by a detailed broker architecture design in Section 5. Section 6 includes extended related work. Section 7 concludes the paper.

2 Requirements and Motivation

In this section, we present the requirements for large-scale XML dissemination, and provide a brief survey of existing solutions, which motivates our work presented in this paper.

2.1 Expressiveness

A starting point for our requirements is the use of XML as the data model and a subset of XQuery [7] as the profile model. User profiles can contain constraints over both structure (using path expressions) and value (using value-based predicates) of XML fragments. For example, if a user is interested in stock information distributed in San Francisco and under the subject "Stock", she can express her interest using the query below (based on the NITF DTD [23]). It specifies that the root element *nitf* must (1) have a child element *head* that in turn contains a child element *pubdata* whose attribute *edition.area* has the value "SF", and (2) have a descendant element *tobject.subject* whose attribute *tobject.subject.type* has the value "Stock".

$msg/nitf [head/pubdata[@edition.area = "SF"]]
    [.//tobject.subject[@tobject.subject.type = "Stock"]]

User profiles can also contain specifications for result customization. For example, a user can use the query below to specify that for each NITF article that matches the *for* and *where* clauses (which are equivalent to the query above), transform it to a new article with the root element *stock_news* containing elements selected from the original article using path expressions "*body/body.head/hedline*", and "*body/body.content*".

for $n in $msg/nitf
where $n/head/pubdata/ @edition.area = "SF"
  and $n//tobject.subject/ @tobject.subject.type = "Stock"
return <stock_news>
        {$n/body/body.head/hedline}
        {$n/body/body.content}
  </stock_news>

As the profile model is based on the XQuery language, in the sequel, we use the terms profile and query interchangeably.

2.2 Scalability

The second dimension of requirements is scalability. More specifically, the service must scale along the following dimensions.

Data volume. The data volume is determined by the number of messages per second arriving at the system and the message size. Depending on the application, the number of messages per second ranges from several to thousands. For example, *NASDAQ* real-time data feeds include 3,000 to 6,000 messages per second in the pre-market hours [43]; Network and application monitoring systems such as *NetLogger* can also receive up to a thousand messages per second [44]. The message size can vary from 1 KB (e.g., XML encoded stock quote updates) to 20 KB (e.g., XML news articles).

Query population. The query population in a dissemination system can also span a wide range, reaching millions of queries for applications such as personalized newspaper generation and mobile operators providing stock quote updates.

Frequency of query updates. A third scalability issue is the frequency with which users update their data interests. While in some applications queries change on a daily basis, in some others they can change much more frequently.

Result Volume. When result customization is supported, the volume of results to be delivered can be tremendous. This is because for each message, point-to-point delivery is needed for every query matched by the message. Take, for example, a stock quote update service. Suppose that the peak message rate from a data source is 5000 per second, each message is 1 KB, the user population is 10 million, and the average query selectivity is as low as 0.001%. A back-of-the-envelope calculation gives an estimation of the result volume as 4 Gb per second. Disseminating this volume of data from a central server can be prohibitively expensive.

Having outlined the problem of large-scale XML-based data dissemination, we next present the position of our work within the large body of related work.

2.3 Related Systems

Publish/subscribe systems such as TIBCO Rendezvous [29], Gryphon [1][4], and Siena [9][10] provide distributed subject/content-based data dissemination. Distributed processing spreads the processing load and has the potential of scaling up for both service inputs and outputs. These systems, however, support limited expressiveness in message filtering. Earlier Publish/subscribe systems are subject-based [29]. In such systems, publishers label each message with a subject from a pre-defined set, and users subscribe to all the messages in a specific subject. The expressiveness of this service is restricted by the opaqueness of the message content in its data model. More recent publish/subscribe systems model messages as attribute-value pairs, and allow user profiles to contain a set of predicates over the values of those attributes [1][9][10][19][30]. The expressiveness of these systems amounts to filtering tuple-like messages based on the constituent attributes. Combining low expressiveness and high scalability, distributed pub/sub systems are represented by the upper left corner of the matrix shown in Figure 2.

More recently, a large number of XML filtering approaches have been developed [2][8][12][16][20][22][26][38]. These approaches typically support a subset of XPath 1.0 [15]. XML filtering provides more expressiveness in specifying data interests, resulting in more accurate filtering of messages. YFilter [17], a multi-query processor that we built previously, also supports result customization using a subset of XQuery. Although these XML filtering and transformation systems provide higher levels of expressiveness, their centralized style of processing limits their scalability. Revisiting Figure 2, today's XML filtering and transformation systems can be best described by the lower right corner of the matrix combining lower scalability and higher expressiveness.

Our work on content-based data dissemination adopts the paradigm of distributed processing to exploit aggregated bandwidth and processing power. As indicated in Figure 2, our system ONYX incorporates the high level of expressive-

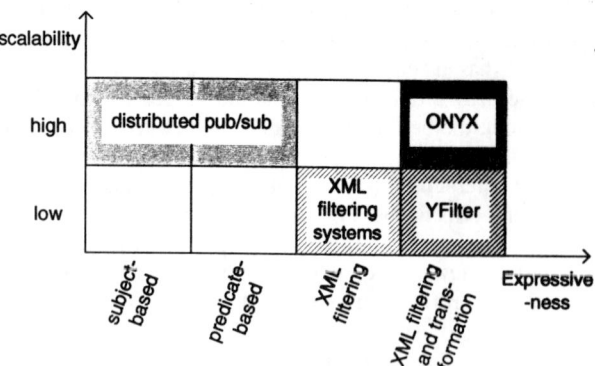

Fig. 2. Combining expressiveness and scalability

ness of XML filtering and transformation into a distributed data dissemination service.

3 System Model

In this section, we present the operational features of ONYX. ONYX provides content-based many-to-many data dissemination from publishers to end users. It consists of an overlay network of nodes. Most of the nodes serve as information brokers (or brokers, for short) that handle messages and user queries, while a few of them collaborate to provide a registration service. The overview is illustrated in Figure 3.

3.1 Service Interface

The service interface provided by ONYX consists of several methods (some of which are similar to those in [3]):

Register a data source: A data source registers with ONYX by contacting the registration service and providing information about its location, the schema used, the expected message rate and message size, etc. (as illustrated by message 1 in Figure 3). The registration service assigns an ID to the data source, and chooses a broker as the *root broker* for the data source. The choice of the root broker is based on its topological distance to the data source, the bandwidth available, and the data volume expected from that source. After the service forwards the information about the new data source to the root broker (message 2), it returns the assigned ID and the address of the root broker to the data source (message 3).

Publish data: After registration, a data source publishes its data by attaching its ID to each message and pushing the message to its root broker (message 4).

Register a data interest: To subscribe, the user contacts the registration service, and provides his profile and network address (message 5). The registration service assigns an ID to this profile, and chooses a broker as the *host broker* for this profile based on the user's location and/or the content of the profile. At the end of the registration, the service forwards the profile and related information to the host broker (message 6), and returns the profile ID and host broker address to the user (message 7). Thereafter, the host broker will deal with all the user requests concerning that profile.

Update a data interest: Subsequent changes to a profile (including updates and deletion) are sent directly to the host broker (message 8).

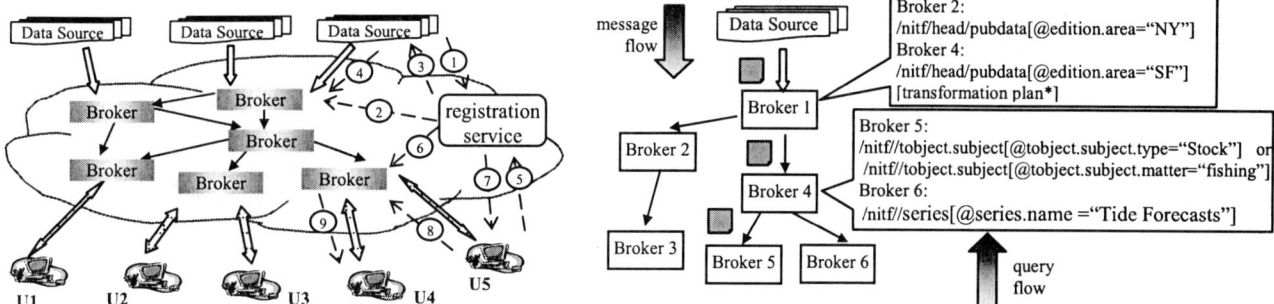

Fig. 3. Architecture of ONYX

Fig. 4. Message routing based on content

Note that users do not need a method to retrieve the messages matching their interests, because those messages are pushed to them from the system (e.g., message 9). Additional methods are provided for data sources to update the schema and other information sent previously.

Fault-tolerance can be achieved by having backup nodes for the registration service and the brokers or using other techniques. That discussion is beyond the scope of this paper.

3.2 Two Planes of Content-Based Processing

ONYX is an application-level overlay network. It consists of two layers of functionality. The lower layer, called the *control plane*, deals with application-level broadcast trees and gives each broker a broadcast tree rooted at that broker that reaches all other brokers in the network. Figure 4 shows such a tree in a network consisting of six brokers. Algorithms for constructing broadcast trees have been provided elsewhere (e.g., [14]).

In this section, we focus on the higher layer of functionality in ONYX – *content-based processing,* which is the primary concern of this paper. We decompose the operations in this layer into two planes of processing - the *data plane* and the *query plane*. The data plane captures the flow of messages in the system while the query plane captures the flow of queries and query-related updates in the system. As we will see, the duality of data and query is a pervasive feature of ONYX. We now discuss the three tasks performed in this layer – content-driven routing, incremental transformation, and user query processing.

Content-driven routing is necessary to avoid the flooding of messages to all brokers in the network. It builds on top of the broadcast tree described above. The routing is *content-driven* because instead of forwarding a message to all the children in the broadcast tree, a broker sends it to only the subset that is "interested" in the message. This routing scheme, which matches a message's content with routing table entries (or *routing queries*) representing the interests of child brokers, is in sharp contrast to the address-based IP routing scheme.

Figure 4 shows an example of routing a message based on its content. The routing tables for Broker 1 and 4 are shown conceptually. The table at Broker 1 specifies a routing query "*/nitf/head/pubdata[@edition.area= "NY"]*" for Broker 2, and a similar one "*/nitf/head/pubdata[@edition.area= "SF"]*" for Broker 4. The matching of a new message arriving at Broker 1 with either routing query results in routing the message to the corresponding child. The building of such routing tables by summarizing the queries of downstream brokers is a subtask in the query plane. The matching of messages against routing queries occurs in the data plane.

Incremental transformation is the second task in the content-based processing layer. Interesting cases of transforming messages during routing include (1) early projection, i.e., removal of data, and (2) early restructuring. An example of early projection is as follows. A data source publishes messages containing multiple news articles. If all the user queries downstream of a link are interested only in a subset of the articles (e.g., those distributed in the area "SF"), messages can be projected onto the articles of interest before they are forwarded along that link using the following query:

```
<batched-nitf>
{ for $n    in     $msg/batched-nitf/nitf
  where          $n/head/pubdata/@edition.area ="SF"
  return         $n
}
</batched-nitf>
```

An example of restructuring is message transcoding based on the profiles of wireless users, say, when all users downstream of a link require images and comments to be removed and tables to be converted to lists. Incremental transformation helps reduce message sizes and avoids repeated work at multiple brokers.

We enable incremental transformation by attaching transformation queries to the output links of brokers on the path of routing. User queries downstream of a link are aggregated and the commonality in their transformation requirements is extracted to form the transformation query. These subtasks happen in the query plane. The corresponding subtask in the data plane consists of transforming messages using these queries, before the messages are sent to the output links.

User query processing is the task of matching and transforming messages against individual user queries at their host brokers. For the user queries resident at a particular broker, this is the last step of message processing (although the arriving messages may be routed and transformed for other downstream user queries). The subtask in the query plane consists of issues such as indexing of user queries for which the broker is a host broker, and the subtask in the data plane consists of matching messages against these indexes.

Table 1 summarizes the content-based processing tasks in ONYX and their subtasks over the query and data planes.

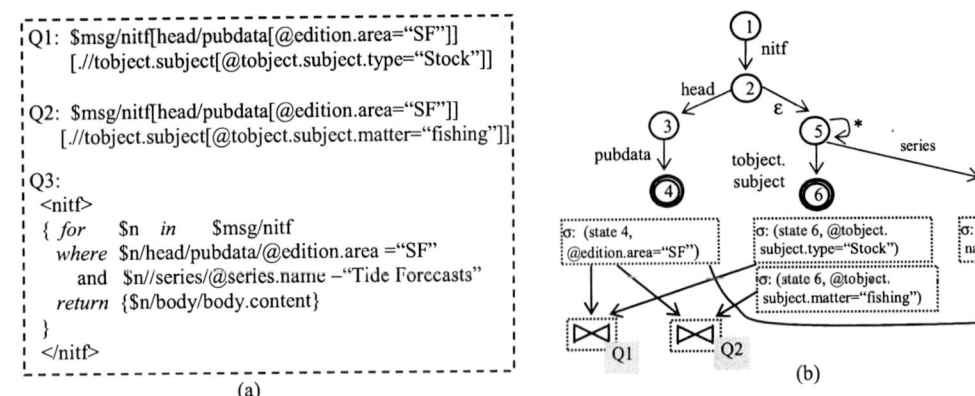

Fig. 5. Example queries and their representation in YFilter

System Task	Query Plane	Data Plane
Content-driven routing	build routing tables	lookup in routing tables
Incremental transformation	build transformation plans	execute transformation plans
User query processing	build query plans	execute query plans

Table 1: System tasks over the two planes of processing

4 Core Techniques

In this section, we describe three key aspects of ONYX, the query plane, the data plane, and the query partitioning strategy. YFilter serves as a basis for these components, so we first present some YFilter basics.

4.1 YFilter Basics

YFilter [16][17] is an XML filtering and transformation engine that processes multiple queries in a shared fashion. In the core of YFilter, a *Non-Deterministic Finite Automaton* (NFA) is used to represent a set of simple linear paths and support prefix sharing among those paths. YFilter provides a fast algorithm for running the NFA on an input message to match the contained paths simultaneously, and an incremental approach for maintaining the NFA when some of the paths change.

While the structural components of path expressions are handled by the NFA, for the remaining portions of the queries, YFilter builds a network of operators starting from the accepting states of the NFA. Each operator performs a specific task, such as evaluation of value-based predicates, evaluation of nested paths, or transformation. The operators residing at an accepting state of the NFA can be executed when that accepting state is reached. Downstream operators in the network are activated when all their preceding operators are finished. In addition, some accepting states and operators are annotated with query identifiers. These identifiers specify that if an annotated accepting state is reached or an annotated operator is successfully evaluated, the queries corresponding to the identifiers are satisfied.

Figure 5 shows three example queries and their representation in YFilter. Take Q1 for example. It contains a root element "/nitf" with two nested paths applied to it. YFilter decomposes the query into two linear paths "/nitf/head/pubdata[@edition.area="SF"]", and "/nitf//tobject.subject[@tobject.subject.type="Stock"]". The structural part of these paths is represented using the NFA (see Figure 5(b)), with the common prefix "/nitf" shared between the two paths. The accepting states of these paths are state 4 and state 6, where the network of operators (represented as boxes) for the remainder of Q1 starts. At the bottom of the network, there is a selection (σ) operator below each accepting state to handle the value-based predicate in the corresponding path. For example, the box below state 4 specifies that the predicate on the attribute *edition.area* should be evaluated against the element that drove the transition to state 4. To handle the correlation between the two paths (e.g., the requirement that it should be the same *nitf* element that makes these two paths evaluate to true), YFilter applies a join (⋈) operator after the two selections. This operator realizes the correct semantics of the nested paths. In Figure 5(b), the left most join operator is annotated with the query identifier Q1. This means that if the join is successfully evaluated, then Q1 is satisfied.

The representation of Q2 follows the same two paths in the NFA as Q1 and uses the same selection at state 4 to process the common predicate with Q1, but it contains a separate selection at state 6 to evaluate the different predicate in the second path. A distinct join operator is built on these two selections. The representation of Q3 is similar to that of Q1 and Q2 for the *for* and *where* clauses, but contains an additional box for transformation using the *return* clause. For more details on YFilter, the interested reader is referred to [16][17].

4.2 Query Plane

In this subsection, we focus on two issues on the query plane: routing table construction and the generation of incremental transformation plans. Our solutions are based on an extension of the YFilter processor. Note that we do not discuss user query processing, as it is completely handled by YFilter.

4.2.1 Routing Table Construction

As stated previously, a routing table conceptually consists of routing query-output link pairs, where each routing query is aggregated from user queries downstream of the corresponding output link. In our work, we decided to implement routing tables using YFilter for three reasons: (1) fast structure matching of path expressions using the NFA, (2) the small maintenance cost of an NFA for query updates (e.g., com-

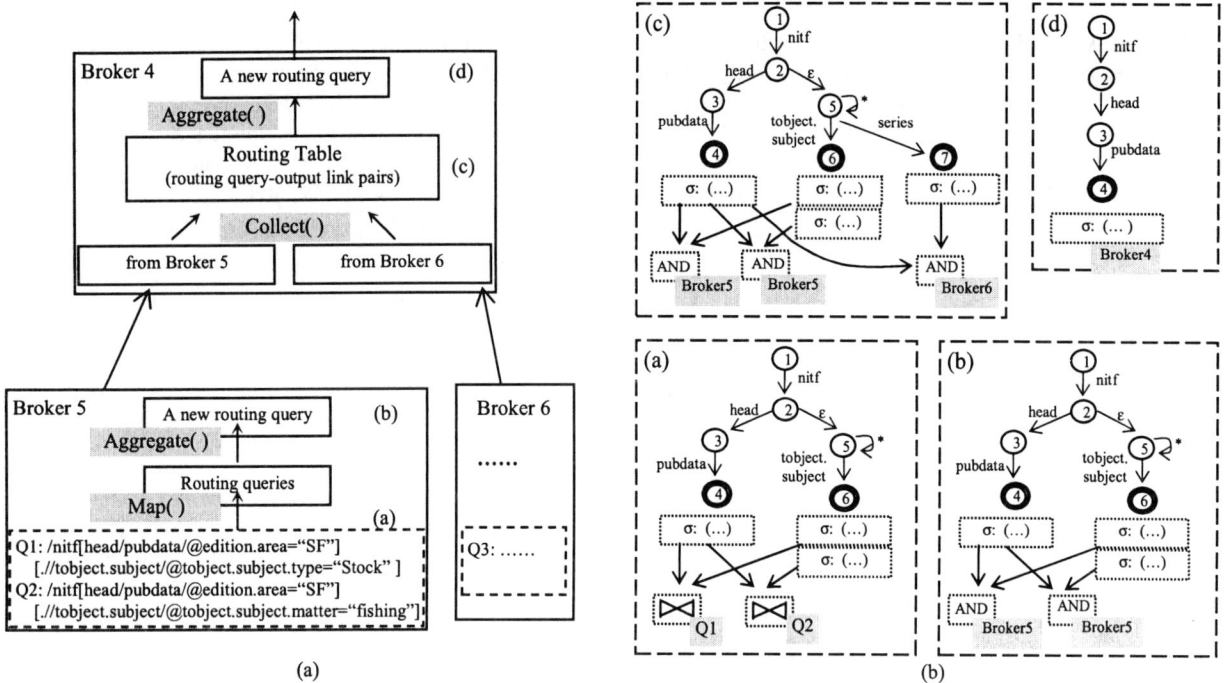

Fig. 6. Examples of constructing routing tables using a disjunctive normal form

pared to deterministic automata), and (3) extensibility for supporting new operations using operator networks. Here, we present the representation of routing tables and mechanisms to construct them. For the purpose of routing, we only consider the matching part of a query, i.e., the *for* and *where* clauses of a query written in XQuery. This part can be converted to a single path expression with equivalent semantics, which we refer to as the *matching path* of a query.

In our current design, routing queries are represented using a *Disjunctive Normal Form* (DNF) of absolute linear path expressions. If a matching path contains n nested paths, it is decomposed into $n+1$ absolute linear paths (possibly with value-based predicates). The routing query constructed for this matching path is the conjunction of the resulting $n+1$ paths. Multiple routing queries can be connected using *or* operators to create a new routing query. Note that an alternative could be to allow any matching path to be a routing query and use *or* operators to connect them. In comparison, DNF relaxes the semantics of nested paths. The motivation of using DNF is that join operators used to evaluate nested paths are relatively expensive, whereas logical *and* operators between path expressions can be evaluated much more efficiently. Investigation of alternative forms is one direction of our future work.

Routing table construction from a distributed query population consists of applying three functions, *Map*( ), *Collect*( ), and *Aggregate*( ), to create routing queries in the chosen form.

- *Map*( ) maps the matching path of a user query to the canonical form of a routing query;
- *Collect*( ) gathers routing queries sent from the child brokers into the routing table of a broker;
- *Aggregate*( ) merges the routing queries in the routing table of a broker with those mapped from the user queries at the broker, and generates a new routing query to represent the broker in its parent broker.

These three functions are illustrated for Brokers 4 and 5 in Figure 6(a). Broker 5 is a host broker with matching paths Q1 and Q2. It uses function *Map*( ) to create a routing query for each of them. Then it applies *Aggregate*( ) to those routing queries to generate a new one that will represent it in its parent (Broker 4). Note that as a leaf, Broker 5 does not contain a routing table. Broker 4 has child brokers Broker 5 and Broker 6, but no user queries. It uses function *Collect*( ) to merge the routing queries sent from the child brokers into a routing table, and then applies *Aggregate*( ) to the routing table to generate a routing query that will represent it in its parent.

Construction operations. Next we present the implementation of the three functions using YFilter.

Map( ) takes as input a YFilter operator network representing a set of matching paths. To create the DNF representations of their routing queries, *Map*( ) simply replaces each join operator in the operator network with an *and* operator.

Collect( ) merges routing queries sent from downstream brokers into a routing table of a parent broker. This operation simply merges the YFilter operator networks that represent those routing queries.

Aggregate( ) performs re-labeling on a YFilter operator network. It changes all the identifier annotations (for queries or brokers) to the identifier of this broker, so that the annotated places become marks for routing to this broker. It essentially adds "*or*" semantics to those annotated places, as encountering any one of them can cause routing of messages to this broker. YFilter treats broker identifiers the same as query identifiers, so these identifiers are simply called "targets" in the sequel.

An example is shown in Figure 6(b). Box (a) in this figure shows the YFilter operator network built for queries Q1

617

and Q2 from Broker 5. Box (b) represents the routing query created for Broker 5 after applying *Map*( ) and *Aggregate*( ) to box (a). Box (c) depicts the result of merging box (b) with the routing query sent from Broker 6 (assumed to be the routing query created for query Q3 in Figure 5(a)). Box (d), the result of applying *Aggregate*( ) to box (c), will be explained shortly below.

Sharing among routing queries. It is important to note the difference between the conceptual representation of a routing table (i.e., routing query-output link pairs) and our implementation of it. Instead of creating a separate operator network for each routing query, we represent all the routing queries in a routing table using a single combined operator network. As a result, the common portions of the routing queries will be processed only once. As an example, box (c) in Figure 6(b) shows that the path leading to accepting state 4 and the selection operator attached to that state can be shared between the routing query for Broker 5 and that for Broker 6. When the commonality among routing queries is significant, the benefit of sharing can be tremendous.

The *or* semantics introduced to routing queries, however, complicates the issue of sharing. When using separate operator networks for routing queries, a short-cut evaluation strategy can be applied in the evaluation of each routing query. Consider box (b) in Figure 6(b) as an operator network created for the routing query for Broker 5. If during execution, one of the two targets labeled as Broker 5 is encountered, the processing for this routing query can stop immediately. In contrast, when using the combined operator network shown in box (c), after a target for Broker 5 is encountered, the processing of the combined operator network has to continue as the target for Broker 6 has not been reached. If care is not taken, some future work may be performed which only leads to the targets for Broker 5. In other words, naïve ways of executing a combined operator network for shared processing may perform wasteful work.

To solve this problem, our solution is to have a runtime mechanism that instructs YFilter to ignore the processing for duplicate targets but not the processing for different targets. This mechanism is based on a dynamic analysis of the operator network which reports the portions of the combined operator network that will only lead to the targets that have already been reached.

Content generalization. Another issue to address in routing table construction is the size of routing tables (i.e., the size of their operator network representation). Larger routing tables can incur high overhead for routing table lookup, thus slowing the critical path of message routing. They may also cause memory problems in environments with scarce memory. For these reasons, we introduce *content generalization* as an additional step that can be performed in *Collect*( ) or *Aggregate*( ). Generalizing the routing table essentially trades the filtering power of the routing table for processing or space efficiency.

We propose an initial set of methods for content generalization. Some of methods generalize individual path expressions with respect to their structural or value-based constraints. Some other methods generalize all the disjuncts in a routing query. For instance, one such method preserves only the path expressions common to all the disjuncts in the new routing query. Consider the routing table shown in box (c) in Figure 6(b). When applying *Aggregate*( ) to this routing table, calling this method after re-labelling the identifiers will result in an operator network containing a single path, as shown in box (d). This generalized operator network will be used to represent Broker 4 in its parent.

4.2.2 Incremental Message Transformation

Incremental transformation happens in the course of routing. As mentioned in Section 3, it can be an early projection or an early restructuring. In this subsection, we briefly describe the extraction of incremental transformation queries from user queries and the placement of these transformation queries.

A transformation query for early projection can be attached to an output link at a broker, if (1) its *for* clause is shared by all the user queries downstream of the link, (2) its *where* clause generalises the *where* clauses of all those queries, and (3) the binding of its *for* clause provides all the information that the *return* clauses of those queries require. The last requirement implies that the *return* clauses of the user queries downstream cannot contain absolute paths or the backward axis ".." to navigate outside the binding.

Similarly, a transformation query for early restructuring can be applied to an output link, if conditions (1) and (2) above are satisfied, and (3) the *return* clauses of the downstream queries all contain a series of transformation steps (e.g., removing images and then converting tables to lists), and the first few steps are shared among all those queries. This transformation query will carry out the common transformation steps on matching messages earlier at this broker.

When opportunities for early transformation are identified at host brokers based on the above conditions, incremental transformation queries representing them are generated and propagated to the parent broker. At the parent, these transformation queries are compared and the commonality among them is extracted to create a new transformation query for its own parent and a set of "remainder queries" for its output links. A remainder query is one that combined with the new transformation query constitutes the original transformation query. Each remainder query is attached to the output link where the corresponding original transformation query came from. The new transformation query is propagated up, and the above process repeats.

A final remark is that although our algorithms for routing table construction and incremental transformation plan construction as presented consider all the user queries in a batch, they can also be applied for incremental maintenance of routing tables or transformation plans. In that case, "delta" routing/transformation queries are constructed and propagated, instead. Details are omitted here due to space constraints.

4.3 Data Plane

Having described the query plane, we now turn to the data plane that handles the XML message flow. In the following, we describe two aspects of this plane, holistic message processing for various tasks and efficient XML transmission.

4.3.1 Holistic Message Processing

In ONYX, a single YFilter instance is used at each broker to build a shared, "holistic" execution plan for the routing table, incremental transformation queries, and local user queries (by holistic, we mean that all these processing tasks are considered as a whole in the data plane). Processing of an XML message using this shared plan is sketched in this section.

The execution algorithm for holistic message processing is an extension of the push-based YFilter execution algorithm [17]. As in that previous work, elements from an XML message are used to drive the execution of NFA. At an accepting state of the NFA, path tuples are created and passed to the operators associated with the state. The network of operators is executed from such operators (i.e., right below accepting states) to their downstream operators. In YFilter, the order of operator execution is based on a FCFS policy among the operators whose upstream operators have all been completed.

In contrast to earlier work, however, the holistic plan contains multiple types of queries, i.e., routing queries, incremental transformation queries, and local user queries. The first two types are on the critical path of message routing. They should not be delayed by the processing for local queries. Moreover, incremental transformation is useful only if the routing query for the corresponding link can be satisfied, which implies the dependency of transformation queries on the routing queries in execution. For these reasons, we propose a dependency-aware priority scheduling algorithm to support shared holistic message processing.

Dependency-aware priority scheduling. In this algorithm, operators that contribute to routing queries are assigned high priority; among other operators, those that contribute to incremental transformation queries have medium priority; and the rest of the operators have low priority. The second priority class, however, is declared to be dependent on the first class with the following condition: an operator in the second class is executed only if at least one incremental transformation query that it contributes to has been necessitated by the successful evaluation of the corresponding routing query. In our implementation, an FCFS queue is assigned to each priority class. In addition, a wait queue is assigned to the dependent class. Priority scheduling works as in a typical OS, except that operators in the dependent class are first placed in the wait queue, and then moved to the FCFS queue when their dependency conditions have been satisfied.

4.3.2 Efficient XML Transmission

Low cost transmission of XML messages is also a paramount concern in a multi-hop distributed dissemination system. XML raises two challenges in this context. First, the verbose nature of XML can cause many redundant bytes in the messages. Second, XML messages need to be parsed at each broker, which can be expensive [16][36]. In this section, we address these two challenges.

The inherent verbosity of XML has led to compression algorithms such as XMill [27]. Compression, however, solves only the first of the above challenges but not the parsing problem. A promising approach that we explored to counter this problem, is using an *element stream* format for XML transmission. This format is an in-memory binary representation of XML messages that can be input to the YFilter processor without any pre-processing or parsing. The binary format is also more space-efficient than raw XML because the latter has white spaces and delimiters. The "wire size" of an XML message can be further reduced by compressing this binary representation.

We also explore schema-aware representation of XML for transmission. Given that the control plane can be used to broadcast the schema of a publishing source to all the brokers in the network, we can perform schema-aware XML encoding of messages for transmission between brokers. In particular, we use a dictionary encoding scheme that maps XML element and attribute names from the schema to a more space-efficient key space. As future work, we would like to explore more advanced schema-aware optimizations, such as avoiding storing parent-child relationships in the binary format, as they can be recovered from the schema.

We experimented with six XML transmission formats: text, binary (i.e., the element stream format), binary with dictionary encoding, and their corresponding compressed versions. Messages were generated using the YFilter XML Generator [16] based on the NITF DTD. The two parameters - *DocDepth* (that bounds the depth of element nesting in the message) and *MaxRepeats* (that determines the number of times an element can repeat in its parent element) allow us to vary the complexity of messages. All our compression was performed using ZLIB, gzip's library, because it outperforms XMill for the relatively small-sized messages (like ours), as reported in [27].

Figure 7 summarizes the performance of different XML formats over our first metric, the *wire size*, for messages of different complexities. Although the element stream format does not remarkably outperform the text format, dictionary encoding gives promising results. Compression helps reduce the wire size for all formats significantly.

Figure 8 presents the evaluation of these XML formats on the complementary metric of *message processing delay*. While uncompressed formats require only serializing messages at the sender and deserializing them at the receiver, the raw format additionally requires parsing and thus proves to be expensive. Compressed formats have significant costs of compression at the sender and decompression at the receiver.

The choice of XML format for transmission must weigh both the wire size and processing delay metrics to get a combined metric. This decision will invariably be influenced by implementation details like the transport protocol used. For example, in the distributed PlanetLab testbed [31], all the message sizes involved in our experiments gave the same transmission delay using TCP. This was attributed to the connection establishment time dominating in TCP for small message sizes. Thus, the message processing delay turned out to be a more important concern than the message size, making compression rather undesirable. On the other hand, if the DCP protocol [36] that sends data in redundant streams over UDP can be employed, compression may be useful.

4.4 Query Population Partitioning

Previous work on distributed publish/subscribe [1][4][10] assumes that queries naturally reside on their nearest brokers, without considering alternative schemes for partitioning the query population. In this subsection, we address the effect of query partitioning on the filtering power of content-driven routing, which is captured by the fraction of query partitions that a message can match.

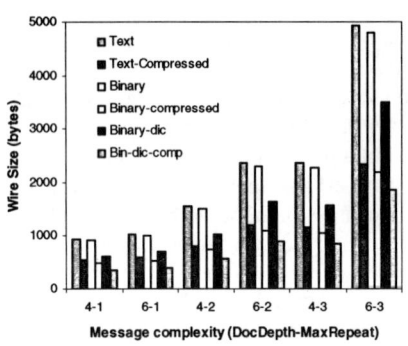 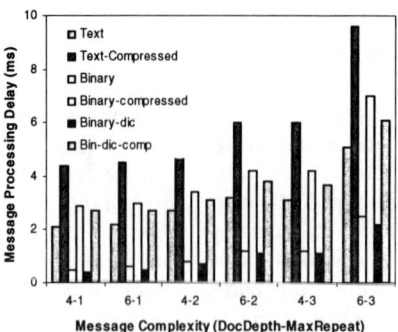 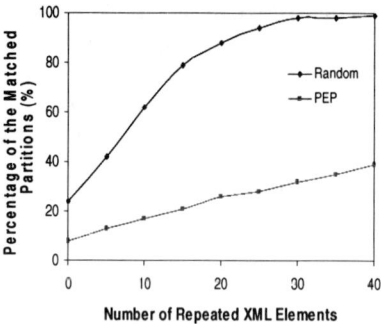

Fig. 7. Wire size of XML messages   Fig. 8. Processing delay for XML transmission   Fig. 9. Random query partitioning vs. PEP

We start with an investigation of the properties of query partitioning and their effect on content-driven routing. Query similarity within a partition seems to be an intuitive property, but is not effective in filtering. For example, in the ideal case that all the queries in one partition are "/a/b" and all the queries in the other partition are "/a/c", a message can still match both partitions by containing the two required elements. Dissimilarity between partitions is another candidate. Consider one partition with two queries "//a" and "//b", and the other partition with "//c" and "//d". Though these two partitions have little in common, it is still quite likely that a message matches both partitions. Mutual exclusiveness turns out to be a desired property. For example, if one partition requires "/a/b[@id=1]" and the other requests "/a/b[@id=2]", the chance that a message satisfies both can be low. The message surely cannot satisfy both if it contains only one "b" element.

The next question is what path expressions can establish such mutual exclusiveness among query partitions. In this regard, we make three key observations. The first is that structural constraints alone are not enough (see the first two examples above). This is because the schema never specifies that two paths are mutually exclusive in a message. In fact, path expressions exhibit potential exclusiveness if they involve the same structure, and contain value-based predicates that address the same target (e.g., an attribute or the data of a specific element), use the "=" operator, but contain different values (see the third example above). We call the common part of these paths an *exclusiveness pattern*. The second observation is that repetition of element names in XML messages limits the exclusiveness of such patterns. Thus, the best choice of an exclusiveness pattern would be one that can appear at most once in any message, as dictated by the schema. The third observation is that in general the coverage of an exclusiveness pattern in the query population could be rather limited, due to the diversity of user data interests. Thus, using a single exclusiveness pattern for query partitioning could cause the majority of queries to be placed in a partition called "don't care". In that case, a set of exclusiveness patterns should be used.

Partitioning based on Exclusiveness Patterns. To achieve exclusiveness of data interests among query partitions, we propose a query partitioning scheme, called *Partitioning based on Exclusiveness Patterns* (PEP). Due to space constraints, we only briefly describe the two steps of this scheme, assuming for now that this algorithm can be run over the entire query population in a centralized fashion. (1) *Identifying a set of exclusiveness patterns*. PEP first searches the YFilter representation of the entire query population, and aggregates the predicates contained in the selection operators at each accepting state to exclusiveness patterns. These patterns are sorted by their coverage of the query population (i.e., the number of queries involving them). Then PEP uses a greedy algorithm to choose a set of patterns such that every query involves at least one pattern from the set. Heuristics can be used to perturb this set with other unselected patterns so that more patterns included in the set can appear at most once in a message, but the coverage of the query population is not sacrificed. (2) *Partition creation*. In the second step, K query partitions are created using the M patterns selected in the first step. To do so, the value range of each exclusiveness pattern is partitioned into K buckets, numbering 1, 2, ..., K. Then queries are assigned to the $K*M$ buckets based on their values in the contained exclusiveness patterns. As a query must involve at least one of those patterns, it must belong to at least one bucket. If the query involves multiple patterns, it is randomly assigned to one of the matching buckets. Finally, K query partitions are created by assigning the queries in the ith bucket of any pattern to query partition i.

In the ideal case, where each exclusiveness pattern appears at most once in a message, a message can match at most M query partitions, i.e., one bucket per pattern. Thus the filtering power of content-driven routing, i.e., the fraction of query partitions that a message can match, can achieve M/K (e.g., 10 patterns, 100 partitions, and filtering power ≈ 1/10). If some patterns can appear multiple times in a message, their repetition degrades the filtering power (in many cases linearly).

To study the potential benefit of our PEP scheme, we compared its performance with the random query partitioning scheme that randomly assigns queries to partitions. We considered assigning a population of 1 million queries to 200 partitions. Every query contained two patterns, each chosen uniformly from a set of 10 exclusiveness patterns. PEP exploited these 10 patterns for partitioning. Figure 9 shows how the percentage of the partitions that a random message matches varies with the amount of repetition of element names in the XML message. Clearly, the random partitioning scheme ends up matching almost all partitions with messages even with a small amount of repetition of element names. In contrast, PEP leads to many fewer partition matches. Unless user interests are influenced by geography, a system that assigns user queries to the closest brokers will end up doing

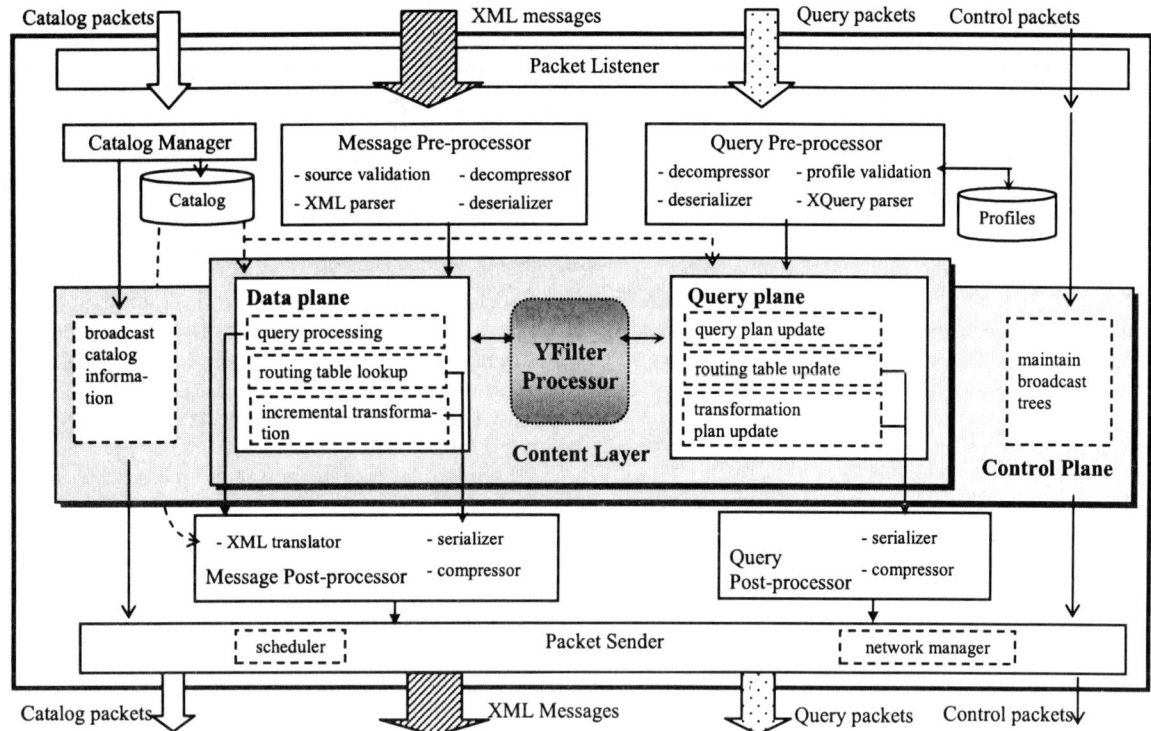

Fig. 10. Broker Architecture

random partitioning of queries, leading to many messages being exchanged between the brokers of the system.

An important remark is that in ONYX, PEP is a core algorithm for query placement used by the registration service. In addition to PEP, query placement also involves the decision of mapping query partitions to brokers, and the use of distributed protocols to perform the initial query partitioning and to maintain the partitions as user queries change over time. These issues will be addressed in our future work.

5 Broker Architecture

Having described the broker functionality in the query and data planes, we now turn to a discussion of the broker architecture that implements this functionality. This architecture is shown in Figure 10. It contains the following components.

Packet Listener. This component listens to each packet arriving at the broker and based on the header, assigns the packet to one of the four flows: catalog packets, XML messages, query packets, and network control packets.

Catalog manager. Catalog packets contain information about a data source. They may originate from the registration service concerning a new data source or from a registered data source to update information sent previously. The catalog manager parses these packets, and stores the information in the local catalog. If the packet is for a new data source, a new entry is added to the catalog including the ID of the data source, information on the data rate, the schema used, etc. If the information relates to a known data source, the existing entry in the catalog describing this data source is updated by the new information. The catalog will be used in other components for message validation, XML formatting, query processing, etc.

Message pre-processor. XML messages can come from data sources as well as other brokers in the system. The messages from a data source carry the source ID and are in the text format. On receiving such a message, the root broker of the data source validates the source ID attached to the message using its catalog. It also parses the message to an in-memory representation for later routing and query processing. If the message comes from an internal broker, source validation is skipped. Depending on the internal representation of XML, the message can be in one of several formats that we discussed earlier, and will need suitable pre-processing (like decompression, deserialization, etc.).

Query pre-processor. This is analogous to the message pre-processor in functionality, except that it also maintains a database of the profiles for which it is the host broker.

Control plane: Taking the control messages, the control plane maintains the broadcast tree for each root broker in the system. Specifically, it records the parent node and the child nodes of a broker on a particular root broker's broadcast tree. It provides two methods for use of the content layer, one for forwarding messages along a broadcast tree, the other for reverse forwarding of queries. The control plane is also responsible for disseminating catalog information for the purposes of optimizing content-based processing. For example, the schema information can be used to optimize query processing and support schema-aware XML encoding.

Data plane. The broker performs three tasks in the data plane, when receiving an XML message. First, it takes a sequence of steps to route the message: (a) if the broker is the root broker for the message, it attaches its broker identifier to the message; (b) it retrieves its output links in the broadcast tree that is specified by the root broker identifier attached to the message; and (c) it looks up in the content-based routing table to filter those output links. Second, for each output link selected, the broker transforms the message, if a transformation plan is attached to that link. Last, the broker processes the message on local queries to generate results. These three tasks are all realized by the YFilter processor.

Query plane. The query plane exhibits duality with the data plane. If an arriving query is from a user, the local query processing plan is updated. If the query comes from another broker to update the routing table (i.e., it is a routing query) or the incremental transformation plan (i.e., it is an incremental transformation query), the modification of the routing table or the transformation plan will cause a new query to be generated for delivery to its parent broker.

YFilter Processor. YFilter has been described in Section 4.1. In this work, it is leveraged to build a holistic processing plan for all the processing tasks, so that the shared processing among the tasks is maximized. For the query plane, it is extended to support the routing table construction operations (as described in Section 4.2.1). For the data plane, its scheduler is augmented to prioritize the processing for different types of queries while exploiting the sharing among them (see Section 4.3.1).

Message and query Post-processor. The results from the data plane are passed to the message post-processor. Results of local query processing are translated into XML messages for delivery to end users, while results of routing and incremental transformation are serialized (and possibly compressed). Queries generated from the query plane also follow the path of serialization and compression.

Packet Sender. This component attaches a header to each packet, specifying the type of flow, the identifier of the root broker (if the packet is an XML message), and the format used. Then it multiplexes the four types of flows into the output channel, through a scheduler and a network manager that sends packets through TCP, UDP, etc.

6 Related Work

Our work is related to a large body of research work in both database and networking communities. Some areas like XML filtering have been described in detail already; we now present a brief overview of other related work.

Multicast. Multicast allows a source to send the same content to multiple receivers. Though bandwidth-efficient, IP multicast [24] is not flexible because of being a network layer paradigm. This has led to application-layer solutions such as *Overcast* [25] and *i3* [37]. Proposals for augmenting IP multicast with content-based routing features have been presented in [35][30]. However, none of this work gives the user fine-grained ways of specifying their interests, like a powerful query language over XML.

Content Distribution Networks (CDN). CDNs provide an infrastructure that delivers static or dynamic Web objects to clients from nearby Web caches or data replicas [13][40], thus offloading the main website. Recent work has focused on allowing the user to specify coherence requirements over data [1][34]. This differs from our approach as it does not give the user a powerful query language to specify her interests. Also, we are dealing with streams of XML messages rather than Web objects.

Publish/Subscribe systems. Publish/Subscribe systems are event-based and provide many-to-many communication between event publishers and subscribers. The SIFT system [41] provided support for matching keyword queries over large sets of documents and some ideas for building a distributed filtering system. Many recent systems [1][9][10][19][30] model an event as a conjunction of (attribute, value) pairs and support relational predicates in subscriptions specifying event interests. We are addressing a more challenging problem as support for rich XML messages and queries leads to increased complexity of query processing, data forwarding and routing table construction.

XML-based overlay networks. A mesh-based overlay network has been proposed in [36] with support for simple XML queries. However, the authors do not address XML query processing issues. The query aggregation scheme given in [11] has been used to perform content-based routing in [13]. However, they do not support powerful query language features like customized transformations.

Transcoding. The transformation functionality in our system is closely related to the transcoding of Web content to suit the profiles of heterogeneous end users, like the users of mobile phones and hand-held computers [42]. However, such a profile usually does not provide expressiveness in querying content as much as the subset of XQuery we support.

7 Status and Future Work

In this paper, we presented our initial design of ONYX, a distributed system providing large-scale XML dissemination. In particular, we provided a detailed architectural design of the system, and addressed the various challenges in distributed XML dissemination in the context of leveraging YFilter, a state-of-the-art XML processor. While we view this work as an initial step towards Internet-scale XML dissemination services, the proposed architecture and solutions to critical issues such as routing table construction and query population partitioning lay the foundation for offering high expressiveness and scalability in such services in massively distributed environments.

As of June 2004, we have implemented the components for message/query pre-processing and post-processing. A collaboration with the Berkeley networking group to build the networking related components, such as the control plane, is underway. We expect to fully implement the data and query planes using YFilter over the course of the summer, and deploy our system on PlanetLab [31] in the fall.

We also plan to extend our research work in the following directions. We will explore alternative forms of routing query representation in addition to DNF and other content generalization algorithms. Typical workloads of XML routing will be collected to evaluate these alternative forms and algorithms to gain insights into the various tradeoffs. We will also exploit the schema for optimization in routing table construction. Furthermore, we plan to extend the notion of data/query duality in the context of multi-source routing; analogous to placing routing queries to filter and direct the message flow, we can place data source descriptions in the network to prune and forward the query flow from host brokers to root brokers. Last, we will address the networking issues that occur when using PEP to move queries away from their closest brokers, and provide distributed protocols to carry out PEP and to maintain the quality of query partitioning as user queries change over time.

8 References

[1] Aguilera, M.K., Strom, R.E., Sturman, D.C., Astley, M., and Chandra, T.D. Matching Events in a Content-Based Subscription System. In *Proc. of Principles of Distributed Computing (PODC'99)*, May 1999.

[2] Altinel, M., and Franklin, M.J. Efficient Filtering of XML Documents for Selective Dissemination of Information. In *VLDB 2000*, 53-64, Sep. 2000.

[3] Altinel, M., Aksoy, D., Baby, T., Franklin, M.J., Shapiro, W., and Zdonik, S.B. DBIS-Toolkit: Adaptable Middleware for Large Scale Data Delivery. In *SIGMOD 1999*, 544-546, 1999.

[4] Banavar, G., Chandra, T. D., Mukherjee, B., Nagarajarao, J., Strom, R. E., and Sturman, D. C. An Efficient Multicast Protocol for Content-Based Publish-Subscribe Systems. In *Proc. of the IEEE International Conference on Distributed Computing Systems* (ICDCS), 262-272, May 1999.

[5] Bell, T.C., Cleary, J.G., and Witten, I.H. *Text Compression*. Prentice Hall, Englewood Cliffs, New Jersey, 1990.

[6] Bhide, M., Deolasse, P., Katker, A., Panchgupte, A., Ramamritham, K., and Shenoy, P. Adaptive Push Pull: Disseminating Dynamic Web Data. *IEEE Transactions on Computers*, 51(6), 652-668, May 2002.

[7] Boag, S., Chamberlin, D., Fernández, M.F., Florescu, D., Robie, J., and Siméon, J. XQuery 1.0: An XML Query Language. W3C Working Draft, Nov. 2003. http://www.w3.org/TR/xquery/.

[8] Bruno, N., Gravano, L., Doudas, N., and Srivastava, D., 2003. Navigation- vs. Index-based XML Multi-query processing. In *ICDE 2003*, 139-150, Mar. 2003.

[9] Carzaniga, A., Rutherford, M.J., and Wolf, A.L. A Routing Scheme for Content-Based Networking. In *Proc. of IEEE INFOCOM 2004*, Mar. 2004.

[10] Carzaniga, A., and Wolf, A.L. Forwarding in a Content-Based Network. In *SIGCOMM 2003*, 163-174, Aug. 2003.

[11] Chan, C.Y., Fan, W., Felber, P., Garofalakis, M.N., and Rastogi, R. Tree Pattern Aggregation for Scalable XML Data Dissemination. In *VLDB 2002*, Aug. 2002.

[12] Chan, C., Felber, P., Garofalakis, M., and Rastogi, R. Efficient Filtering of XML Documents with XPath Expressions. In *ICDE 2002*, 235-244, Feb. 2002.

[13] Chand, R., and Felber, P. A Scalable Protocol for Content-Based Routing in Overlay Networks. In *Proc. of the IEEE International Symposium on Network Computing and Applications* (NCA'03), Apr. 2003.

[14] Chu, Y. Rao, S.G., and Zhang, H. A Case for End System Multicast. In *Proc. of the 2000 ACM SIGMETRICS International Conference on Measurement and Modeling of Computer Systems*, 1-12, Jun. 2000.

[15] Clark, J., and DeRose, S. XML Path Language (XPath) - Version 1.0. Online at http://www.w3.org/TR/xpath.

[16] Diao, Y., Altinel, M., Zhang, H., Franklin, M.J., and Fischer, P.M. Path Sharing and Predicate Evaluation for High-Performance XML Filtering. *TODS*, 28(4), 467-516, Dec. 2003.

[17] Diao, Y., and Franklin, M.J. Query Processing for High-Volume XML Message Brokering. In *VLDB 2003*, 261-272, Sep. 2003.

[18] Dilley, J., Maggs, B., Parikh, J., Prokop, H., Sitaraman, R., and Weihl, B. Globally Distributed Content Delivery. *IEEE Internet Computing*, 50-58, Sep.-Oct. 2002.

[19] Fabret, F., Jacobsen, H.A., Llirbat, F., Pereira, J., Ross, K.A., and Shasha, D. Filtering Algorithms and Implementation for Very Fast Publish/Subscribe Systems. In *SIGMOD 2001*, 2001.

[20] Green, T. J., Miklau, G., Onizuka, M., Suciu, D. Processing XML Streams with Deterministic Automata. In *Proc. of Int'l Conf. on Database Theory (ICDT'03)*, 173-189, Jan. 2003.

[21] Gryphon. http://www.research.ibm.com/gryphon/index.html.

[22] Gupta, A. K., and Suciu, D. Streaming processing of XPath queries with predicates. In *SIGMOD 2003*, Jun. 2003.

[23] Internal Press Telecommunications Council. News Industry Text Format. 2004. http://www.nitf.org/.

[24] Internet Protocol (IP) Multicast. *http://www.cisco.com/univercd/cc/ td/doc/cisintwk/ito_doc/ipmulti.htm.*

[25] Jannotti, J., Gifford, D.K., Johnson, K.L., Kaashoek, M.F., and O'Toole, J.W.Jr. Overcast: Reliable Multicasting with an Overlay Network. In *Proc. of the 4th Symposium on Operating System Design and Implementation (OSDI'00)*, Oct. 2000.

[26] Lakshmanan, L.V.S., and Sailaja, P. On Efficient Matching of Streaming XML Documents and Queries. In *EDBT 2002*, 142-160, Mar. 2002.

[27] Liefke, H., and Suciu, D. XMILL: An Efficient Compressor for XML Data. In *SIGMOD 2000*, 153-164, May, 2000.

[28] McCanne, S., Jacobson, V., Vetterli, M. Receiver0Driven Layered Multicast. In *SIGCOMM 1996*, 117-130, Aug. 2003.

[29] Oki, B., Pfleugl, M., Siegel, A., and Skeen, D. The Information Bus: an Architecture for Extensible Distributed System. In *SOSP 1993*, 58-68, Dec. 1993.

[30] Opyrchal, L., Astley, M., Auerbach, J., Banavar, G., Strom, R., and Sturman, D. Exploiting IP Multicast in Content-Based Publish-Subscribe Systems. In *Proc. of IFIP/ACM Int'l Conference on Distributed Systems Platforms*, 185-207, 2000.

[31] PlanetLab. http:// www.planet-lab.org.

[32] Rodriguez, P., Ross, K.W., and Biersack, E.W. Improving the WWW: Caching or Multicast? *Computer Networks and ISDN Systems*, 30(22-23,25), 2223-2243, Nov. 1998.

[33] Segall, B., Arnold, D., Boot, J., Henderson, M., and Phelps, T. Content Based Routing with Elvin4. In *Proc. of AUUG2K*, Canberra, Australia, Jun. 2000.

[34] Shah, S., Dharmarajan, S., and Ramamritham, K. An Efficient and resilient Approach to Filtering and Disseminating Streaming Data. In *VLDB 2003*, 57-68, Sep. 2003.

[35] Shah, R., Jain, R., and Anjum, R. Efficient Dissemination of Personalized Information Using Content-Based Multicast. In *Proc. of IEEE INFOCOM 2002*, Jun. 2002.

[36] Snoeren, A.C., Conley, K., and Gifford, D.K. Mesh-Based Content Routing using XML. In *SOSP 2001*, Oct. 2001.

[37] Stoica, I., Adkins, D., Zhuang, S., Shenker, S., and Surana, S. Internet Indirection Infrastructure. In *SIGCOMM 2002*, 73-88, Aug. 2002.

[38] Tian, F., DeWitt, D., Pirahesh, H., Reinwald, B., Mayr, T., and Myllymaki, J. Implementing a Scalable XML Publish / Subscribe System Using a Relational Database System. In *Proc. of SIGMOD 2004*, Jun. 2004.

[39] Tolani, P.M., and Haritsa, J.R. XGRIND: A Query-Friendly XML Compressor. In *ICDE 2002*, 225-234, Mar. 2002.

[40] WebSphere Application Server Network Deployment. http://www-306.ibm.com/software/webservers/appserv/was/network/edge.html.

[41] Yan, T. W., and Garcia-Molina, H. The SIFT Information Dissemination System. *TODS*, 24(4), 529-565, Dec. 1999.

[42] WebSphere Transcoding Publisher. http://www-306.ibm.com/software/pervasive/transcoding_publisher.

[43] NASDAQ Pre-Market Volume. http://dynamic.nasdaq.com/dynamic/premarket5dayvolume.stm.

[44] The NetLogger Toolkit. http://www-didc.lbl.gov/NetLogger/.

Efficiency-Quality Tradeoffs for Vector Score Aggregation

Pavan Kumar C. Singitham

Stanford University
Stanford
USA
pavan@cs.stanford.edu

Mahathi S. Mahabhashyam

Stanford University
Stanford
USA
mmahathi@cs.stanford.edu

Prabhakar Raghavan

Verity Inc.
Sunnyvale
USA
pragh@verity.com

Abstract

Finding the ℓ nearest neighbors to a query in a vector space is an important primitive in text and image retrieval. Here we study an extension of this problem with applications to XML and image retrieval: we have multiple vector spaces, and the query places a weight on each space. Match scores from the spaces are weighted by these weights to determine the overall match between each record and the query; this is a case of *score aggregation*. We study approximation algorithms that use a small fraction of the computation of exhaustive search through all records, while returning nearly the best matches. We focus on the tradeoff between the computation and the quality of the results. We develop two approaches to retrieval from such multiple vector spaces. The first is inspired by resource allocation. The second, inspired by computational geometry, combines the multiple vector spaces together with all possible query weights into a single larger space. While mathematically elegant, this abstraction is intractable for implementation. We therefore devise an approximation of this combined space. Experiments show that all our approaches (to varying extents) enable retrieval quality comparable to exhaustive search, while avoiding its heavy computational cost.

Permission to copy without fee all or part of this material is granted provided that the copies are not made or distributed for direct commercial advantage, the VLDB copyright notice and the title of the publication and its date appear, and notice is given that copying is by permission of the Very Large Data Base Endowment. To copy otherwise, or to republish, requires a fee and/or special permission from the Endowment.

**Proceedings of the 30th VLDB Conference,
Toronto, Canada, 2004**

1 Overview: score aggregation

We have n records $E = \{e_1, e_2, \ldots, e_n\}$ and s sources of evidence. For $1 \leq i \leq s$, we have a *source score* $\sigma_i(e_j)$ from source i for record e_j. Additionally, we have a positive real weight w_i for each of the s sources. For a specified positive integer ℓ, we seek the ℓ records of highest *aggregate score* defined as

$$S(e_j) = \sum_{i=1}^{s} w_i \sigma_i(e_j).$$

In the absence of further structure to exploit, no better algorithm is known than to compute all the $\sigma_i(e_j)$'s and then compute all the $S(e_j)$'s in identifying the top ℓ records. Can we perhaps determine ℓ records almost as good as the ℓ best without such exhaustive search? Note that the ℓ-nearest neighbors problem is a special case of this general setting, in which $s = 1$ and the source score is a geometric proximity measure between a query and the records (represented as points). We focus on an important case of score aggregation, motivated below.

1.1 Motivation

A series of papers motivated by the GARLIC [7] and QBIC [19] systems led to work on *score aggregation* [16, 17]. Recent work on the special case of *rank aggregation* [8, 11, 14, 18] focuses on merging lists of documents ranked by multiple search engines. We detail two motivating applications:

1. In applications like Query By Image Content (QBIC) [19], a user specifies the relative contributions of score components such as color, texture, etc. Each component assigns a score to each record (image) with respect to the query at hand.

2. In semi-structured retrieval for text and XML, it is important to be able to weight the contributions of various elements to an overall score. This can range from simply weighting keywords in text search [15, 27] to weighting fields in a semi-structured document ("retrieve *and rank* books

with `Aho` in the **author** and `algorithm` in the **title**, with the **author** score being twice as important as the **title** score": the notion is that the **author** and **title** fields each contribute a nonnegative score that is weighted and summed for the overall score). Already a component of enterprise information retrieval platforms, such functionality becomes even more critical in content-oriented XML retrieval.

1.2 Vector score aggregation

No better algorithm is known for general score aggregation short of an exhaustive search. We focus here on an important case raised by the two examples above. Suppose that record e_j is represented by an s-tuple of vectors $V_{j,i}, 1 \leq i \leq s$, in s vector spaces. For example if each record is a semi-structured document, we would have one vector space for **author**, one for **title**, etc. Each vector space is built from the terms in that field, as in classic information retrieval [30].

Definition 1 *A composite vector query is a pair* $\mathbf{Q} = (\mathbf{q}, \mathbf{w})$ *where* $\mathbf{q}$ *is an s-tuple of query vectors* $(q_1, \ldots, q_s)$ *in the corresponding vector spaces, while* $\mathbf{w}$ *is an s-vector of non-negative real weights* $w_1, \ldots w_s$.

The weight w_i represents the importance assigned by the user to ith field; without loss of generality, we henceforth assume that $\sum_{i=1}^{s} w_i = 1$. We further assume (as is typical in these applications) that the query and record vectors are all normalized within their respective fields, i.e., $||q_i||_2 = ||V_{j,i}||_2 = 1$.

Definition 2 *The* match score *between query* $\mathbf{Q} = (\mathbf{q}, \mathbf{w})$ *and record* $e_j = (V_{j,i})$ *is given by*

$$Match(\mathbf{Q}, e_j) = \sum_{i=1}^{s} w_i (q_i \cdot V_{j,i}), \quad (1)$$

where $q_i \cdot V_{j,i}$ represents the dot product (a.k.a. cosine similarity) between the query and record vector $V_{j,i}$ in the ith field.

Our problem then becomes: given a composite vector query, can we retrieve the ℓ records of highest match score? In other words, how can we exploit the fact that the s source scores are vector cosine similarities? Note that for $s = 1$, this becomes the traditional ℓ-nearest-neighbor problem. Even for this special case of computing the ℓ nearest neighbors in arbitrary dimensions, there appears to be no algorithm that in the worst case avoids exhaustively computing the similarity of the query to every record [1, 10, 23, 25]. This prompts the question: can we find ℓ records that are "almost as good" as the exact ℓ nearest neighbors, while paying significantly less than exhaustive similarity computation? In application settings, an approximation is generally acceptable provided the quality is high enough. For instance, a document or image scoring 0.83 is not likely to be much worse than one scoring (say) 0.87; there is already a (perhaps bigger) approximation in using cosine similarity as a proxy for the user's perception of quality.

We therefore study *efficiency-quality tradeoffs:* suppose that an algorithm $\mathcal{A}$ outputs a candidate set $C = \mathcal{A}_\ell(\mathbf{Q}, E)$ of ℓ records[1]. Can we trade off the computational effort of $\mathcal{A}$ against the quality of C?

To study this question, we must first pinpoint the answers to two questions: (1) how do we quantify the computational effort of $\mathcal{A}$ in a principled manner independent of the scheme $\mathcal{A}$? (2) how do we measure the goodness of a candidate set $C = \mathcal{A}_\ell(\mathbf{Q}, E)$ computed by $\mathcal{A}$? Once we address these questions, we have a basis for comparing various algorithms.

1.3 Metrics

Computational cost: We seek a measure of computational effort that is independent of a particular runtime environment. For any algorithm $\mathcal{A}$, a basic operation is the query-to-record score computation in equation (1) – specifically, this involves s inner product computations. We therefore adopt the number of such query-record score computations by $\mathcal{A}$ as the fundamental measure of work; we denote it by $\mathcal{CC}_\ell(\mathcal{A}, \mathbf{Q}, E)$. We can thus speak of the work done by $\mathcal{A}$ on a query, a query suite, etc. For exhaustive search, $\mathcal{CC}_\ell(Exhaustive, \mathbf{Q}, E)$ is always n. Our interest is in algorithms $\mathcal{A}$ for which $\mathcal{CC}_\ell(\mathcal{A}, \mathbf{Q}, E) \ll n$, while delivering candidate sets of high quality.

Quality of results: To evaluate the performance of an approximate retrieval scheme $\mathcal{A}$ on a given dataset E and query suite $\mathbf{Q}_1, \ldots, \mathbf{Q}_m$, we use a benchmark called the *ground truth*. For each query $\mathbf{Q}$, let the true set of ℓ highest scoring records be $GT_\ell(\mathbf{Q}, E)$. We compare the quality of a candidate set of ℓ records output by an algorithm $\mathcal{A}$ against $GT_\ell(\mathbf{Q}, E)$. To this end, we employ two measures of quality. (For our experiments in Section 4 we use exhaustive search to compute $GT_\ell(\mathbf{Q}, E)$.)

1. The *aggregate goodness* measure

$$AG_\ell(\mathcal{A}, \mathbf{Q}, E) = \sum_{e \in \mathcal{A}_\ell(\mathbf{Q}, E)} Match(\mathbf{Q}, e).$$

Simply put, this is adding up the match scores of the ℓ records returned by $\mathcal{A}$. The idea is that if this net is suitably high, then the user has been given a set of images/documents almost as good as the ground truth. By itself, AG_ℓ does not tell the whole story; for instance, $\mathbf{Q}$ may be a query for which the ground truth does not contain good matches. Rather, we will typically compare

---

[1] Any algorithm $\mathcal{A}$ in fact implies an ordering of the n records in E with respect to the query $\mathbf{Q}$; thus, $C = \mathcal{A}_\ell(\mathbf{Q}, E)$ consists of the first ℓ in this ordering.

AG with the aggregate goodness of the ground truth, measured by $\sum_{e \in GT_\ell(\mathbf{Q},E)} Match(\mathbf{Q}, e)$; in fact our experiments will compare these quantities averaged over a query ensemble rather than on a single query.

2. The *competitive recall* of the top ℓ results

$$CR_\ell(\mathcal{A}, \mathbf{Q}, E) = |\mathcal{A}_\ell(\mathbf{Q}, E) \cap GT_\ell(\mathbf{Q}, E)|.$$

This computes the fraction of the ground truth included in $\mathcal{A}$'s candidate list of ℓ best records. It is more stringent than aggregate goodness in that it gives no credit for a document that may be almost as good as those in $GT_\ell(\mathbf{Q}, E)$. Note that it hinges on comparison with the ℓ best records for each ℓ, rather on the Boolean notion of relevance commonplace in defining precision and recall in information retrieval. In this sense, our notion of competitive recall is related to the competitive analysis of algorithms [29] and is also related to measures used in [20, 32].

All of the above definitions can be extended to an average over a query suite in the natural way.

2 Summary of contributions

We begin by summarizing related prior work in two broad areas: score aggregation and nearest neighbors. We do this in some depth (Section 2.1.1) for a particular approach to nearest neighbors in vector spaces, that we call *cluster pruning*. We do so because cluster pruning is basic building block for the subsequent development of our approaches.

2.1 Related prior work

A series of papers [14, 16, 17] have looked at the problem of retrieving the ℓ best records from combining source scores. They consider the general (not vector) score aggregation problem and insist on finding the ℓ best results rather than ℓ good results as we do. Their focus is on comparing, for a given instance (records, score function and query) the computational cost of an algorithm in comparison to that of the best algorithm, *on that instance*. This in the worst case could mean a computational cost of n; we instead seek ways of spending far less computation and getting good matches. Rank aggregation – the special case in which each source orders the records without assigning scores – owes its roots to voting theory, but has enjoyed a modern renaissance with the advent of metasearch engines [11, 18].

Nearest neighbor problems in vector spaces are the special case $s = 1$ of vector score aggregation. A series of index structures have been developed for this problem in various settings [2, 3, 21, 24, 26, 34]. These studies use the CPU and disk I/O times during query processing as a measure of speed, in contrast to our higher-level measure of the number of cosine computations. ClusterTree [35] creates an index over the data set that is a hierarchy of clusters and subclusters. The nearest neighbors to a given query are obtained by performing a depth first search in this hierarchy. This approach effectively prunes the search space. They examine the number of such clusters to be probed in order to find all the ℓ nearest neighbors – this can be viewed as one extreme in our tradeoff space (with no approximate near-neighbors). This experimental approach is instructive but may be hard to use directly – in practice we do not have a "stopping condition" that informs us the instant we have found the correct ℓ nearest neighbors. In theoretical work related to approximate nearest neighbors, [23, 25] reduce the problem to point location in equal balls and suggest bucketing and locality sensitive hashing algorithms.

More recently [20] show how simple k-means clustering can do well at approximate nearest neighbor retrieval in multimedia databases. They evaluate quality by metrics that are the complement of competitive recall, and by a matching distance measure. They focus on "progressive processing" of approximate nearest neighbor searching: the user looks at the results for a query, one page at a time. They use approximation techniques with exact nearest-neighbor algorithms to progressively improve results quality as the user keeps looking at more results.

2.1.1 Cluster pruning

We build on a class of schemes for the ℓ-nearest neighbors problem that make use of clustering (the special case of our problem where $s = 1$). The goal is to avoid paying a cost of n cosine similarity computations, while still retrieving ℓ "reasonably near" neighbors for any query. The generic idea is to first cluster the vectors in the dataset E, in the process appointing a *representative* for each of the K clusters [5, 22, 32]. Given a query, we first find the $m \ll K$ centroids nearest to the query and then compute cosine similarities from the query *only* to the records in the clusters represented by these m centroids. All records in all other clusters are ignored. The hope (with no absolute guarantee of course) is that many of the near neighbors are in these m clusters. Thus we get near neighbors while avoiding similarity computations with the majority of the vectors in the dataset.

The clean nature of cluster pruning raises hope that it can be extended to $s > 1$; while this is the idea underlying our approaches, some interesting challenges and design decisions arise.

2.2 Contributions of this paper

- *Concrete, usable metrics for cost-quality tradeoffs that do not demand human relevance judgements as in the TREC evaluations [36].* The idea of quantifying the cost-quality tradeoff for scoring has not been systematically studied, even for the traditional ℓ-nearest neighbor problem. All our metrics can be applied to the general setting at the beginning of Section 1.

- *Two broad approaches to vector score aggregation:* one inspired by resource allocation (Section 3.1) and the other by ideas from computational geometry [12] (Section 3.2).

- *Experiments with two variants of our scheme based on resource allocation (Section 4), as well as with the scheme inspired by geometry.* We find that all the schemes attain close to the quality of results in the ground truth, at a computational cost dramatically lower than exhaustive search.

- *A comparison of the two families of schemes.* While the geometric indexes are larger than those from resource allocation, they offer better retrieval quality for a given amount of computation on a query.

3 Two approaches

3.1 Resource allocation schemes

The technical development of our schemes inspired by resource allocation is cleaner if we think in terms of a fixed budget B of the computational effort (number of cosine similarities) that we can use to answer a query. We can then ask how well we perform on the quality of retrieved results for the given budget. We begin with the general idea.

Consider again s vector spaces, one for each field. In seeking a candidate set of ℓ records for a composite vector query $\mathbf{Q} = (\mathbf{q}, \mathbf{w})$ we instead retrieve a set C_i of candidate records from the ith field, for each $i \in [1, s]$. Finally, we return the ℓ best matches from the records in $\cup_{i=1}^{s} C_i$.

These retrievals C_i for each i use the cluster pruning scheme in Section 2.1.1; the precise implementation details and parameter choices are deferred for now. Essentially, we first retrieve nearly best matches from each field, then pick the ℓ best matches from among these candidates. An important question arises: given our budget of B for computational effort, how do we invest this budget across the s vector spaces? This is a resource allocation problem and we study two natural schemes for this investment. For example, consider a simple allocation between two fields **author** and **title**. Suppose that a query places a high weight on the **author** field and relatively little weight on the **title** field. We could on the one hand spread our budget equally in the **author** and **title** vector spaces. On the other hand, we could invest more of our budget into retrieving candidates from the **author** space rather from the **title** space, as this might give us better score-aggregated quality.

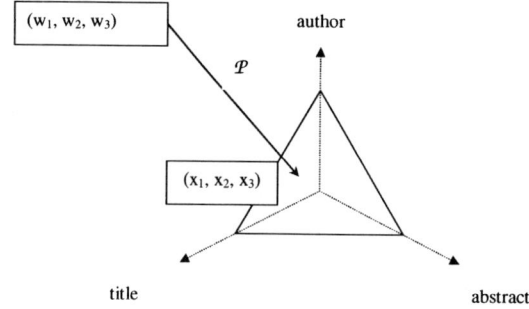

Figure 1: Mapping from query weights to points in the simplex: resource allocation.

Note that at query time we could make use of the weights in **w** to determine this allocation. Interesting questions arise: should we? If so, how do the weights govern the allocation? This question may be viewed at a slightly higher level (for conceptual development only; eventually we will use the number of cosine similarities as the measure of computational effort). Rather than a budget B of cosine similarities, imagine a budget P of the number of *probes*: a probe is a decision to evaluate the query against all the records in any single cluster in any of the s spaces. This view reflects the working of our algorithms built on cluster pruning: the query is always evaluated against all vectors in a cluster, or none.

A weight vector **w** in a query can naturally be viewed as a point on the s-dimensional simplex $\sum_{i=1}^{s} w_i = 1$. Further, any point $\mathbf{x} = (x_1, \ldots, x_i, \ldots, x_s)$ on this simplex represents an allocation as follows: given a budget of P probes, we dispatch $x_i P$ probes into field i. Figure 1 shows this idea for $s = 3$ where the fields are **author**, **title** and **abstract**.

Definition 3 *A probe resource allocation is a mapping $\mathcal{P}$ from the simplex onto itself, $\mathcal{P} : \mathbf{w} \to \mathbf{x}$.*

What properties should hold for an allocation function $\mathcal{P}$? We propose these below; of these the first two should clearly hold for all $\mathcal{P}$, while the remainder are plausible but (as we detail in Section 5) may not hold in all situations.

1. *$\mathcal{P}$ should map each vertex of the simplex into itself.* This simply says that a query that places all its weight into one field demands that all the probes go into that vector space index.

2. *$\mathcal{P}$ should map each edge (in general, lower-dimensional simplex) of the simplex into itself.* This says that if a field gets no weight in the query,

Algorithm 1 *Uniform.*
1: number of cluster probes available = P; Query Q;
2: SearchSet = ∅;
3: **for** $i \leftarrow 1, 2, \ldots, s$ **do**
4:     NSet= set of P/s nearest clusters to Q taken from field i;
5:     SearchSet = SearchSet union records in NSet;
6: **end for**
7: **for all** *record* $\in$ SearchSet **do**
8:     compute Match(Q,record)
9: **end for**
10: Rank SearchSet based on Match

Algorithm 2 *Transparent.*
1: number of cluster probes available = P; Query Q;
2: SearchSet = ∅;
3: **for** $i \leftarrow 1, 2, \ldots, s$ **do**
4:     NSet= set of w_i*P nearest neighbor clusters to Q from field i;
5:     SearchSet = SearchSet union records in NSet;
6: **end for**
7: **for all** *record* $\in$ SearchSet **do**
8:     compute Match(Q,record)
9: **end for**
10: Rank SearchSet based on Match

its vector space should not be probed. This is a more stringent requirement than (1) above.

3. $\mathcal{P}$ *should map the center of the simplex into itself.* In other words, if the query calls for a uniform weighting on the fields, the investment should be uniform; this should recursively hold for any lower-dimensional simplex. In Figure 1, the recursive requirement means that the mid-point of each side of the triangle maps into itself.

4. $\mathcal{P}$ *should act as the identity mapping on each edge (lower-dimensional simplex) of the simplex.* This demands that if any field gets zero weight, the investment in the other fields is *directly proportional* to their weights. In Figure 1 this implies the identity mapping for the perimeter of the triangle.

The third and fourth properties raise the question: can $\mathcal{P}$ be the identity mapping itself? This is the second of our two allocations, detailed below in Section 3.1.2.

3.1.1 Uniform allocation

In this scheme, we allocate the budget of cluster probes uniformly across the vector spaces. Thus the query weighting **w** is ignored for probe allocation purposes (but of course remains in use for the score computations and quality measures). *Uniform* is described in Algorithm 1.

3.1.2 Transparent allocation

Here $\mathcal{P}$ is the identity mapping; thus each field receives an allocation of probes in proportion to the query weight for that field. *Transparent* is described in Algorithm 2.

3.2 Cell decomposition indexes

An alternate approach to having separate vector spaces for each field is to combine them all into a single gigantic vector space. This is inspired by ideas from combinatorial geometry which we now review; these are elegant but not pragmatic at the dimensionality we are discussing. Accordingly we will first develop the approach, then coarsen it to make it practical.

Consider first the standard ℓ-nearest neighbors problem, i.e., $s = 1$. The *Voronoi decomposition* [12] partitions space into n polyhedral cells, one for each record e_i. The crucial property: for any query point within e_i's cell, the nearest neighbor is e_i.[2] Given a query, the nearest-neighbor problem reduces to locating which cell the query lies in. Tight bounds exist on the total number of facets in Voronoi decompositions as a function of n and the number of dimensions d; these bounds are exponential in d. Consequently, the computational costs of building the decomposition and for point location are high when d is large; but for $d \leq 3$ this approach leads to pragmatic nearest neighbor retrieval.

The notion of a Voronoi decomposition has been generalized [12] for ℓ-nearest neighbors. Instead of one cell per record e_i, we now have one cell for every subset of ℓ records that is a valid answer to *some* query. The cell decomposition now has the following property: the same set of ℓ records constitute the ℓ nearest neighbors for any query point within a given cell. Thus identifying the ℓ nearest neighbors again reduces to identifying the cell containing the query. Here too the cells are known to be polyhedra (for cosine similarities between unit vectors) and bounds are known for the facet complexities. Despite its impracticality in high dimensions, we nevertheless pursue this view a little further, as it leads to our eventual index structure.

Let us extend the above notions to composite vector retrieval: denote by $D_1, \ldots, D_s$ the s vector spaces and $d_1, \ldots, d_s$ the corresponding dimensionalities. Note additionally that the set of *all possible* query weightings **w** can be viewed as a vector space W in s dimensions (in fact since $\sum_{i=1}^{s} w_i = 1$, a simplex). Consider a new vector space $U = W \cup_{i=1}^{s} D_i$, having $u = s + \sum_{i=1}^{s} d_i$ dimensions. Any query $\mathbf{Q} = (\mathbf{q}, \mathbf{w})$ can be represented as a single point in U; note however that a record is *not* a single point in U. Nevertheless, U can still be partitioned into cells such that for any query (point in U), the set of ℓ nearest records is invariant. In this cell structure, it suffices to locate the

---
[2] In fact, the shapes of the cells depend on the distance metric; for cosine similarities between unit vectors, we have unbounded polyhedral cones whose apices are at the origin.

query point then read off the ℓ nearest neighbors for any query in that cell. Besides the immense number of cell boundaries due to the high dimensionality, there is an added difficulty here: the cell boundaries are no longer polyhedral, but rather described by (nonlinear) algebraic functions. Point location thus becomes highly non-trivial.

We give two generic ideas to overcome these difficulties, leading to experimentation with a very basic implementation of these ideas in Section 5.4.

1. We can group together cells in the decomposition that are "close together", coarsening the decomposition into a small number of *coarse cells* with similar (rather than the same) answers. In the process, we may project U down to a low-dimensional space.

2. We can approximate the cell boundaries by linear functions.

For any such coarse approximation U' of U, we now have to address (1) point location in a coarse cell of U'; (2) for each coarse cell, an index tuned to efficiently retrieve ℓ high-quality records for that cell. This is necessary since there is no longer a unique set of ℓ answers within a coarse cells.

Example 1 *We begin with an extremely simple manifestation of the above ideas. Suppose we have three vector spaces* **author**, **title** *and* **abstract** *as in Figure 1. Each query has three weights* w_{author}, w_{title} *and* $w_{abstract}$, *together with corresponding query vectors* q_{author}, q_{title} *and* $q_{abstract}$. *For any query in which* $w_{author} \geq 0.34$, *we simply find the* ℓ *nearest neighbors to* q_{author} *in the* **author** *vector space alone, ignoring the other fields. Similar rules can be invoked for the* **title** *and* **abstract** *fields.*

The intuition of this simplistic scheme: if the query places the greatest weight in a field, we run a vector-space query for that field alone and ignore the rest of the query. Notice that this can be viewed as a projection of the huge vector space developed above down to a simplex in three dimensions, a coarsening of this simplex into three regions, and finally an efficient (if not perhaps high-quality) retrieval scheme for all queries falling in each one of these regions. Just as we did for allocation maps $\mathcal{P}$ in Section 3.1, we can enumerate basic symmetry requirements for any version of this scheme; we omit these for brevity here. In Section 5.4 we experiment with a slightly more sophisticated version of this scheme. The generic cell decomposition retrieval algorithm is given in Algorithm 3 *CellDec*.

3.3 Comparing the schemes

In this section we compare the resource usages of the resource allocation and cell decomposition schemes. For the allocation schemes, we would need to maintain

---

Algorithm 3 *CellDec.*
1: number of cluster probes available = P;
2: Query Q = (q,w);
3: Identify the cell decomposition index of the coarse cell i based on the query template.
4: NSet = set of P nearest clusters to Q from index of coarse cell i;
5: SearchSet = Union of records in NSet;
6: **for all** *record* ∈SearchSet **do**
7:    compute Match(Q,record)
8: **end for**
9: Rank SearchSet based on Match

---

s separate indexes, one for each of the s vector spaces. For *CellDec* the number of indexes maintained, r, is the number of *coarse cells* used in the decomposition. In our running examples with three fields (**author**, **title** and **abstract**), we use 3 indexes for the allocation schemes but r indexes for *CellDec*. In Example 1, $r = 3$; in the version we experiment with in Section 5.4, $r = 4$. The index size is arguably larger for *CellDec*, since we are looking at a combined vector space representing all features spaces and their dimensions. On the other hand, there is a trade-off involved in the computational cost at query-time; we study this now. The computational cost(number of cosine similarity computations) stems from two sources in all schemes derived from cluster pruning (including all ours): cosine computations for

- (query,cluster centroid) pairs and
- (query,records in the set SearchSet from the algorithms above). This measure is an invariant in the number of scalar multiplications, across all the three algorithms above, because the *Match* computation is over the entire record irrespective of the higher level indexing scheme used.

For the allocation schemes, the total computation cost is

$$s \cdot K + |\text{SearchSet}| \quad (2)$$

where K is the number of clusters in each of the s fields. For *CellDec*, with each index having K clusters each as well, the cost is

$$K + |\text{SearchSet}|$$

since we are exploring only one *coarse cell* index for a query. In both cases, if n is the total number of records in the data set,

$$E[|\text{SearchSet}|] = O(Pn/K)$$

where $E[]$ denotes the expectation of a random variable. Thus with *CellDec* we gain an advantage of nearly $(s-1)K$ cosine computations at query time, by investing all the P probes into one *coarse cell* index. A point to keep in mind though is that the advantage is not exactly $(s-1)K$, because of the potential difference in centroid lengths of the two schemes.

4 Experimental setup

We now describe the data used in our experiments, followed by the query suite. In Section 5 we describe our findings on the computation-quality tradeoff.

4.1 Data set and preparation

We perform our experiments on a data set obtained from crawling citeseer [37]. This data consists of 480,000 documents; for each document, we have three fields – **author**, **title** and **abstract**. This data is processed by stemming and stop-word elimination (standard data preparation steps in information retrieval [30]) and inserted into three *base tables* in a mySQL database. For each of the fields, the frequency of each term (tf) is computed and normalized; thus, within each field for each document, the squares of the frequencies of various terms add up to one. At this point we have three vectors for each document, one for each field.

Thus if a vector has m features with term frequencies $\{tf_1, ..., tf_m\}$, the weight w_i of the ith term is

$$tf_i / \sqrt{(\sum_{j=1}^{m} tf_j^2)}.$$

4.2 Query suite

Our query suite consists of two sets each having 250 *query prototypes*, each of which is a triplet of vectors corresponding to an instance of **q** in Section 1.2. The first, Set A, is meant to model typical user queries from researchers searching a corpus such as citeseer using composite queries on the three fields. Set B is meant to explore the tradeoffs by systematically neutralizing certain inherent asymmetries in three fields with rather different term distributions (e.g., the **author** field in most documents has fewer than three terms (author names); but few abstract fields have fewer than 30 distinct terms). We motivate Set B further in Section 5.

4.2.1 Query prototypes

For Set A we pick the 250 most popular co-author pairs. From the pool of titles and abstracts of documents authored by each pair, we randomly select words from the 100 most frequent words. This gives us queries of the form ($author_1$, $author_2$, $titleword_1$, $titleword_2$, $abstractword_1$, $abstractword_2$). Thus our query prototypes will not pair (say) authors `Garcia-Molina` (a database researcher) and `Micali` (a cryptographer); because they have not co-authored a paper, it is unlikely that a user is searching for documents co-authored by the pair. Extending the same principle to conditioning the generation of $titleword_1$, $titleword_2$, $abstractword_1$ and $abstractword_2$, we ensure that the query prototypes of Set A are likely to correspond to documents that a user might actually search for. This also ensures that there are likely to be at least some documents in the corpus that are high-quality matches for each query.

T#	w_{author}	w_{title}	$w_{abstract}$
1	0.33	0.33	0.34
2	0.4	0.4	0.2
3	0.4	0.2	0.4
4	0.2	0.4	0.4
5	0.6	0.2	0.2
6	0.2	0.6	0.2
7	0.2	0.2	0.6

Table 1: Weight templates.

For Set B, we use a set of 250 randomly generated queries on a new *synthetic* data set. This new data set has three fields f_1, f_2 and f_3 that are all generated from the **title** field of our original data set. Each *synthetic* document is composed of 3 random *original* document titles, each title forming a field f_i. Given $title_i, i \in 1, 2, ..., n$ of documents $OriginalDoc_i$ in the original collection, the documents $SyntheticDoc_j, j \in 1, 2, ..., n/3$ in the synthetic data set are

$$f_1 = title_j, f_2 = title_{n/3+j}, f_3 = title_{2n/3+j}$$

In this data set the document vector lengths in the three field spaces become comparable. Each query in Set B consists of two terms from each field, generated uniformly at random.

4.2.2 Weight templates

For each query prototype we apply seven weight templates, each a triplet of weights. The weights in a template sum to one and model skewed user weighting. The templates are given in the Table 1.

Note that templates 2-4 are rotations (around the fields) of each other; likewise for templates 5-7. The first template is meant to model an unbiased query (the user does not emphasize any field); note that for such queries an alternative approach would be to treat the entire document (with all its fields) as one "bag of words" (a single vector) and treat the user query terms also as a single vector. Templates 2-4 model situations where the user emphasizes two fields but is less certain or demanding about the third. Similarly, templates 5-7 model situations where the user emphasizes a single field at the expense of the other two. These broad situations clearly span the gamut of symmetric user needs. The rotations are meant to elicit the effects of asymmetries between the three fields. Templates 5, 6 and 7 are especially useful to study: they can be viewed as a "basis" using which an arbitrary **w** can be expressed as a linear combination; thus results on allocation on these templates can be combined to devise allocations for arbitrary weight vectors.

n= 50K	128	256	512
AG	91.54	93.57	91.80
CR	68.37	71.47	67.09

Table 2: Performance for different values of K for collection size 50,000.

n=100K	128	256	512
AG	87.57	92.53	89.80
CR	64.97	66.82	65.27

Table 3: Performance for different values of K for collection size 100,000.

5 Results and analysis

We implement the traditional K-means algorithm in clustering each of the 3 fields. To represent a centroid of the cluster, we use the mean of the document vectors within a cluster. Each cluster centroid is implemented as a hashtable of terms and the term weights, so that the lookup is much faster while performing a similarity computation between the query and the centroid. In order to nullify the difference in size of the index between the cell decomposition and allocation schemes we do the following:

- Use the same number of clusters K for both kinds of indexes.

- Store only the top 1000 highest weight terms of the mean of all document vectors, in the centroid.

This ensures that centroid lengths and index sizes for both the schemes are the same and we can invoke Section 3.3 to determine $CC_\ell(\mathcal{A}, \mathbf{Q}, E)$ and $CC_\ell(CellDec, \mathbf{Q}, E)$; here $\mathcal{A}$ represents either allocation algorithm.

5.1 Choosing the right value of K

Theoretically, the optimal value of K can be estimated as follows. From Equation 2 the computational effort involved for one cluster probe $CC_\ell(Uniform, \mathbf{Q}, E)$ with 3 vector spaces, is given by $3K + n/K$. This is minimized when $K = \sqrt{n/3}$. For our corpus size of 480K documents, the value of $\sqrt{(n/3)}$ is 400. To further validate this estimate for K, we conduct some experiments. For this, we measure the performance of Uniform against the ground truth for different values of K. We experiment with subsets of our document set with 50,000 and 100,000 documents, and cluster them using various values of K. In each case we fix the computational cost at roughly 2500 (there is some variation because when we decide to probe a set of clusters, their sizes may not add up to exactly 2500). The results (for both metrics) are shown in Tables 2 and 3.

We see that the quality peaks around $K = 256$ for both the sample corpora. For $n = 50,000$, the value

n=480K	300	350	400	450	500
AG	96.69	96.85	97.28	97.38	95.54
CR	80.55	80.88	83.67	83.98	75.12

Table 4: Performance for different values of K for collection size 480,000.

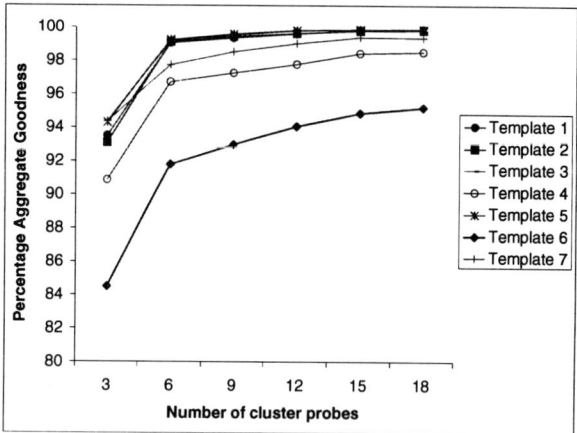

Figure 2: Uniform vs. the ground truth – aggregate goodness.

of $\sqrt{n/3}$ is 128 (approximately) and for $n = 100,000$, this value is 182.

For the collection size $n = 480,000$, we perform the experiments with different values of K. The results are shown in table 4. We choose $K = 450$ as the number of clusters for further experiments on the full data set.

5.2 Uniform vs. the ground truth

We explore the performance of Uniform in further detail. Figures 2 and 3 show its performance for each weight template against the ground truth, for the queries in Set A. The figures illustrate the fundamental tradeoff between computational effort and quality: at low effort the quality (by either measure) is quite modest. By the point where we invest three probes in each field index, we begin to see a significant (but tailing off) improvement. Other key conclusions:

- Cluster pruning even with Uniform performs very well in returning high-quality results with a minuscule fraction of the clusters probed (3 out of 450, which means our computational effort is only 0.67% of exhaustive search).

- The y-axis in Figure 2 is the percentage of the aggregate goodness of the ground truth, averaged over the queries. Note that unlike the (more stringent) competitive recall measure, we quickly get close to 100% by this metric. Thus users get documents essentially as good as (if not the same as) the ground truth.

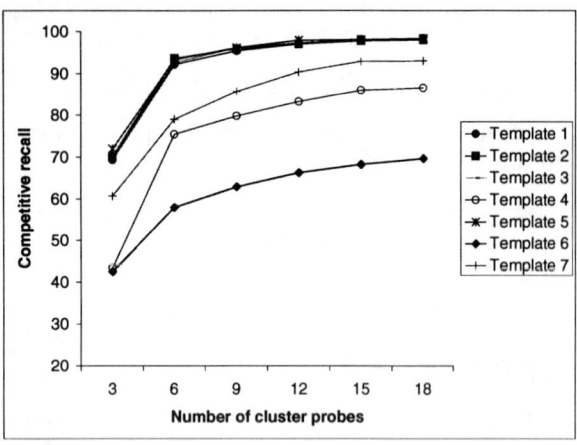

Figure 3: Uniform vs. the ground truth – competitive recall.

We observe that for templates with high weight on the **author** field (Templates 2 and 5), the retrieval quality is much higher than the other templates.

This happens because of two biases:

- The asymmetry of the fields: Each document is represented by fewer nonzero vector components in the **author** field than (for instance) the **abstract** field. Consequently, any match on authors tends to dominate the similarity score more than a similar match on abstracts.

- The query generation scheme for Set A is conditioned by an author pair chosen from the **author** field. The significance is not that our query generation is skewed or misleading. Rather, an application using resource allocation should bias the mapping $\mathcal{P}$ towards the dominant mode by which users think of query tasks (e.g., if they begin by thinking of titles as the primary driver of their queries, $\mathcal{P}$ should invest disproportionately additional work in the **title** index).

5.3 Uniform vs. Transparent

Transparent gives only marginal improvements over *Uniform* on Set A. This stems from our mode of generation of the queries in Set A; so we studied Set B instead to see if a different class of queries would highlight the differences between *Uniform* and *Transparent*. The results are shown in Figures 4 and 5. For these comparisons we show the number of cluster probes P invested on the x-axis (since the computational costs of both the allocation schemes are linear in and proportional to the number of probes invested). We observe that *Transparent* performs consistently better than *Uniform*, for all the templates. In particular, it is interesting to note that it beats *Uniform* especially on highly skewed templates. This suggests that when user needs come from a more homogeneous setting such as Set B, non-uniform allocation

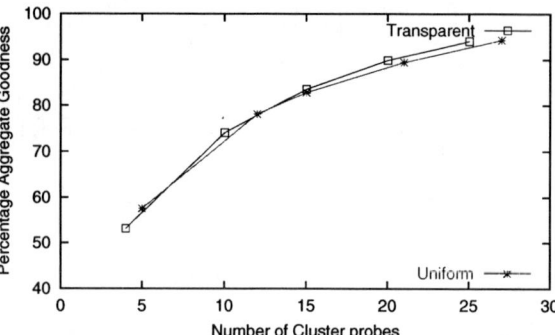

Figure 4: Transparent vs. Uniform - Aggregate Goodness.

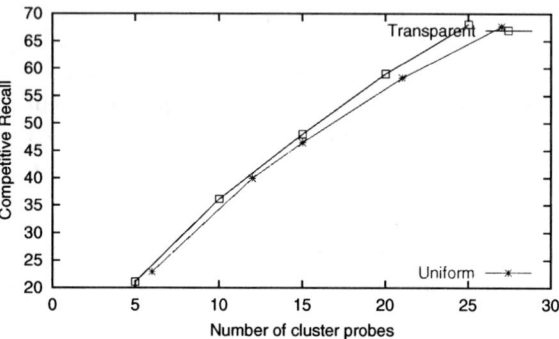

Figure 5: Transparent vs Uniform - Competitive recall.

makes a difference. An interesting area that now opens up: can more sophisticated allocation than *Transparent* make a bigger difference? How do we design the optimal policy $\mathcal{P}$?

5.4 Cell decomposition indexes

We now describe experiments with a slightly more sophisticated cell-decomposition than the simple scheme of Example 1 in Section 3.2. Consider the unit simplex of query weights for each of the three fields, Figure 6. This simplex is partitioned into four cells labeled 1, 2, 3 and 4. Each cell corresponds to a range of weights that a query can take. We maintain one optimized index for each cell; whenever the weights in a query fall into cell $i, 1 \leq i \leq 4$, we use index i. Recall Table 1 listing the weight templates for our experiments; we thus note that Templates 1–4 fall in region 2, with templates 5, 6 and 7 falling respectively in regions 2, 3 and 4.

Next, we describe the index for each region:

- Region 1: For $1 \leq j \leq n$ and $1 \leq i \leq 3$, let $V_{j,i}$ and denote the vector for record j in field i. For each record j we compute a composite vector

$$V_j = \sum_{i=1}^{3} V_{j,i}.$$

We now build an index based on cluster pruning on the *single* vector space spanned by the

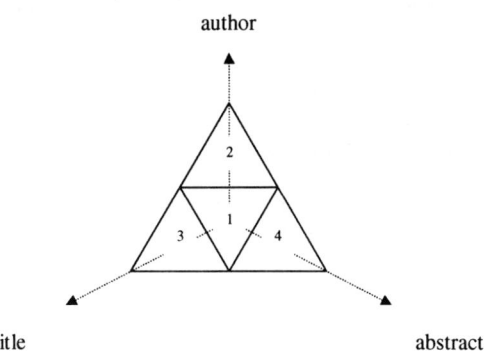

Figure 6: Regions of the triangular simplex covered by each index.

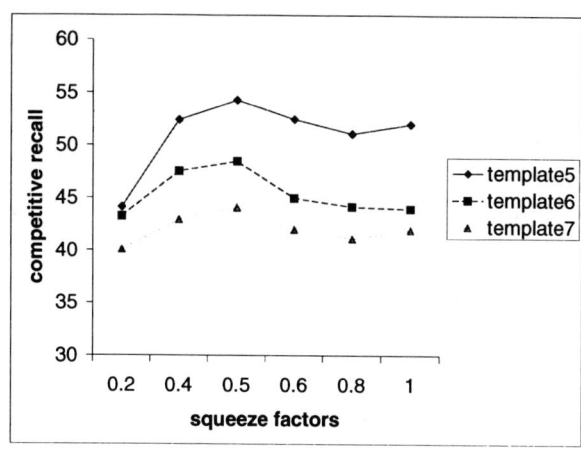

Figure 7: Performance for different squeeze factors.

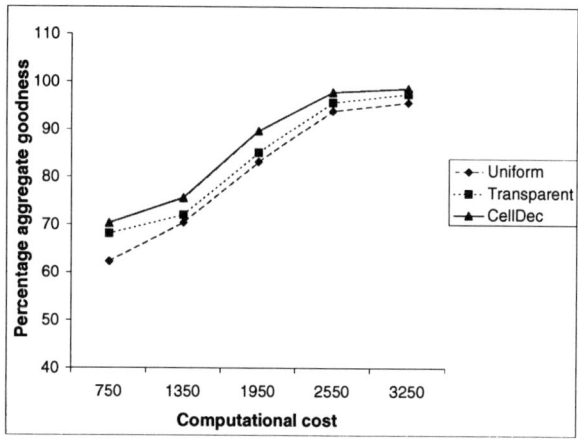

Figure 8: Aggregate goodness vs. Computational cost.

V_j's. Intuitively: in region 1 the query weights are "roughly the same" so we simply treat all the contents of a record – authors, title, abstract – as one bag of words and use cluster pruning on the resulting vectors.

- The index for region 2 is created by a linear combination of the author vector and the vectors from the other two fields – titles and abstracts – the latter each multiplied by a *squeeze factor*, θ. Thus

$$V_j = V_1 + \theta * V_2 + \theta * V_3.$$

  The indices for 3 and 4 are also created similarly by squeezing a different pair of axes. Intuitively, we are attenuating the vectors from fields that are de-emphasized in the queries using the particular region.

Note that these indexes are created up front; when a query specifies a particular weight vector **w**, it is sent to the index that is likely to yield the best *quality* results for that weight vector.

While creating the clusters for cluster pruning, we do K-means clustering of the vectors thus obtained, just as in our earlier schemes. The only difference comes in the computation of the centroid for each cluster. While calculating the mean of the documents within a cluster, we do an L_2-normalization within the terms of each field in a document, before calculating the centroid. This ensures that fields with very few dimensions are not under-represented.

To estimate a good value for the squeeze factor θ, we use a sampled subset of the documents containing 10000 random documents and values of $\theta \in [0.1, 1]$. The results are shown in Figure 7. We observe that for $\theta = 0.5$, queries from all the three templates do the best. Hence we now choose this as our squeeze factor to compare the performance of the cell decomposition scheme with respect to both the uniform and transparent allocation schemes, using the same data set of 10000 documents. The results are shown in Figures 8 and 9.

We observe that even our simple cell decomposition scheme consistently outperforms both *Uniform* and *Transparent*, whether for a fixed cost or for a fixed quality.

6 Conclusions and further work

Our work (particularly with the aggregate goodness measure) suggests that we can find high quality results for vector score aggregation at a small fraction of the computation of exhaustive search. Our experiments raise the pursuit of more sophisticated allocation schemes. This becomes especially intriguing with recursive cluster pruning schemes, where the allocation at higher levels can depend on what is deeper in each sub-tree. The second area for further work is on more sophisticated cell decomposition schemes: given an application, how do we determine the best cell decomposition scheme based on system parameters? How (for either class of schemes) should the algorithm parameters be data-dependent? Empirically studying cost-quality tradeoffs in more general settings [13, 6]

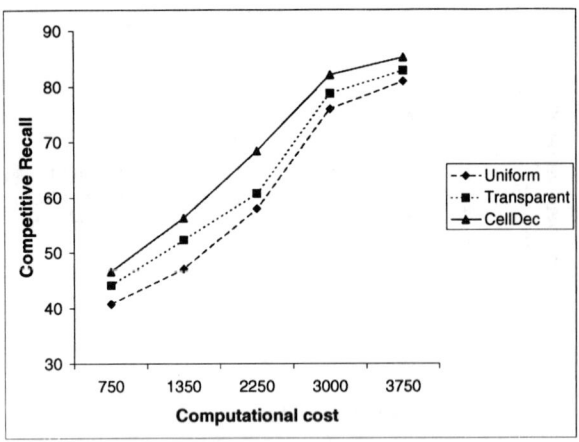

Figure 9: Competitive recall vs. Computational cost.

is an exciting direction.

References

[1] P.K. Agarwal, J. Erickson. Geometric Range Searching and Its Relatives. In *CRC Handbook of Computational Geometry*, 1997.

[2] N. Beckmann, H.-P. Kriegel, R. Schneider, and B. Seeger. The R*-tree: An efficient and robust access method for points and rectangles. *Proceedings of ACM SIGMOD*, 322–331, 1990.

[3] S. Berchtold, D. A. Keim, and H.-P.Kriegel. The x-tree: An index structure for high-dimensional data. *Proc. of the 22th VLDB Conference*, 1996.

[4] M. W. Berry, S. Dumais, G. W. O'Brien. Using Linear Algebra for Intelligent Information Retrieval. *SIAM Review* 37:4 (1995).

[5] S. Bhatia, J. Deogun. Cluster characterization in Information retrieval. *ACM-SAC 1993 Indiana USA, 721-727*.

[6] M. Charikar, R. Fagin, V. Guruswami, J. Kleinberg, P. Raghavan and A. Sahai. Query strategies for priced information. *Journal of Computer and System Sciences* 64(4):785-819, 2002.

[7] W. Cody, L. Haas, W. Niblack, M. Arya, M. Carey, M. Flickner, D. Lee, D. Petkovic, P. Schwarz, J. Thomas, M. Tork Roth, J. Williams, R. Fagin and E. Wimmers. Querying multimedia data from multiple repositories by content: the Garlic project. *IFIP 2.6 3rd Working Conference on Visual Database Systems (VDB-3)*, 1995.

[8] M.-J. Condorcet. Essai sur l'application de l'analyse a la probabilite des decisions rendues a la pluralite des voix, 1785.

[9] T. Cover, P. Hart. Nearest Neighbor pattern classification. *IEEE Transactions on Information Theory*, 13 (1967), 21–27.

[10] D. Dobkin, R. Lipton. Multidimensional Search Problems. *SIAM Journal of Computing*, 5 (1976), 181–186.

[11] C. Dwork, R. Kumar, M. Naor and D. Sivakumar. Rank aggregation methods for the web. *Proceedings of WWW10*, 2001.

[12] H. Edelsbrunner. Algorithms in Combinatorial Geometry. Springer-Verlag, 1987.

[13] O. Etzioni, S. Hanks, T. Jiang, R.M. Karp, O. Madani and O. Waarts. Efficient Information Gathering on the Internet, *37th Annual Symposium on Foundations of Computer Science*, 1996.

[14] R. Fagin. Combining Fuzzy information from multiple systems. *Journal of Computer and System Sciences*, **58**(1):83–99, 1999.

[15] R. Fagin and Y. Maarek. Allowing users to weight search terms, *RIAO (Recherche d'Informations Assistee par Ordinateur)*, 682–700 (2000).

[16] R. Fagin and E. Wimmers. A formula for incorporating weights into scoring rules. *Theoretical Computer Science* **239**, 2000.

[17] R. Fagin, A. Lotem and M. Naor. Optimal aggregation algorithms for middleware. *J. Computer and System Sciences* **66**, 2003.

[18] R. Fagin, R. Kumar, D. Sivakumar. Efficient similarity search and classification via rank aggregation *Proceedings of ACM SIGMOD*, 2003.

[19] C. Faloutsos, W. Equitz, M. Flickner, W. Niblack, D. Petkovic and R. Barber. Efficient and Effective Querying by Image Content. *Journal of Intelligent Information Systems*, 1994.

[20] H. Ferhatosmanoglu, E. Tuncel, D. Agrawal and A.E. Abbadi. Approximate Nearest Neighbor Searching in Multimedia Databases. *Technical Report TRCS00-24*, Comp. Sci. Dept., UC Santa Barbara, 2000.

[21] A. Guttman. R-trees: a dynamic index structure for spatial searching. *Proceedings of ACM SIGMOD*, 47–57, 1984.

[22] J. Hafner, N. Megiddo and E. Upfal. US Patent 5848404: Fast query search in large dimension database, 1998.

[23] P. Indyk and R. Motwani. Approximate Nearest Neighbors: Towards Removing the Curse of Dimensionality. In Proc. of 30th STOC, 604–613, 1998.

[24] N. Katayama and S. Satoh. The SR-tree: An Index Structure for High-Dimensional Nearest Neighbor Queries. *Proceedings of ACM SIGMOD*, 1997.

[25] J. Kleinberg. Two algorithms for nearest-neighbor search in high dimensions. *Proc. 29th ACM Symposium on Theory of Computing*, 1997.

[26] K.-I. Lin, H. V. Jagadish and C. Faloutsos. The TV-tree: An Index Structure for High Dimensional Data. *VLDB Journal*, **3**(4):517–542, 1992.

[27] X. Long and T. Suel. Optimized Query Execution in Large Search Engines with Global Page Ordering. *Proceedings of VLDB*, 2003.

[28] D.G. Luenberger. Investment Science. Oxford Press, 1997.

[29] On-line Problems. *Journal of Algorithms*, 11:208-230, 1990.

[30] G. Salton. The SMART Retrieval System – Experiments in automatic document processing. Prentice Hall Inc., Englewood Cliffs, 1971.

[31] T. Sellis, N. Roussopoulos and C. Faloutsos. The R+-Tree: A Dynamic Index For Multi-Dimensional Objects. *VLDB Journal*, 1987.

[32] S. Sitarama, U. Mahadevan, M. Abrol. Efficient cluster representation in similar document search. *Proceedings of WWW conference*, 2004.

[33] I.H. Witten, A. Moffat, T.C. Bell, Managing Gigabytes: Compressing and Indexing Documents and Images, 1994.

[34] D.A. White and R. Jain. Similarity Indexing with the SS-tree. *In Proceeding s of the 12th Intl. Conf. on Data Engineering*, 1996.

[35] D. Yu, A. Zhang. ClusterTree: Integration of Cluster Representation and Nearest Neighbor Search for Large Datasets with High Dimensionality. *IEEE Internati onal Conference on Multimedia and Expo*, 2000

[36] http://trec.nist.gov/ : Text Retrieval Conference series.

[37] http://citeseer.nj.nec.com : Citeseer Scientific Digital Library.

Merging the Results of Approximate Match Operations

Sudipto Guha
U of Pennsylvania
sudipto@central.cis.upenn.edu

Nick Koudas Amit Marathe Divesh Srivastava
AT&T Labs–Research
{koudas,marathe,divesh}@research.att.com

Abstract

Data Cleaning is an important process that has been at the center of research interest in recent years. An important end goal of effective data cleaning is to identify the relational tuple or tuples that are "most related" to a given query tuple. Various techniques have been proposed in the literature for efficiently identifying approximate matches to a query string against a single attribute of a relation. In addition to constructing a ranking (i.e., ordering) of these matches, the techniques often associate, with each match, scores that quantify the extent of the match. Since multiple attributes could exist in the query tuple, issuing approximate match operations for each of them separately will effectively create a number of ranked lists of the relation tuples. Merging these lists to identify a final ranking and scoring, and returning the top-K tuples, is a challenging task.

In this paper, we adapt the well-known footrule distance (for merging ranked lists) to effectively deal with scores. We study efficient algorithms to merge rankings, and produce the top-K tuples, in a declarative way. Since techniques for approximately matching a query string against a single attribute in a relation are typically best deployed in a database, we introduce and describe two novel algorithms for this problem and we provide SQL specifications for them. Our experimental case study, using real application data along with a realization of our proposed techniques on a commercial data base system, highlights the benefits of the proposed algorithms and attests to the overall effectiveness and practicality of our approach.

1 Introduction

The efficiency of every information processing infrastructure is greatly affected by the quality of the data residing in its databases (see, e.g., [9]). Poor data quality is a result of a variety of reasons, including data entry errors, poor integrity constraints or lack of standards for recording values in database fields (e.g., addresses). Data of poor quality could instigate a multitude of business problems,

Permission to copy without fee all or part of this material is granted provided that the copies are not made or distributed for direct commercial advantage, the VLDB copyright notice and the title of the publication and its date appear, and notice is given that copying is by permission of the Very Large Data Base Endowment. To copy otherwise, or to republish, requires a fee and/or special permission from the Endowment.

**Proceedings of the 30th VLDB Conference,
Toronto, Canada, 2004**

for example inefficient customer relationship management (inability to retrieve customer information during a service call), billing errors (sending a bill to a wrong address) and distribution delays (erroneous delivery of goods) impacting the overall effectiveness of a business. Recognizing the importance of this problem, a variety of commercial products (see, e.g., [1]) and research prototypes (see, e.g., [21]) target the space of data cleaning, offering an array of techniques to identify and correct data quality problems. At a high level, data cleaning solutions can be classified into two broad categories: (a) those that operate on top of an RDBMS using an SQL interface to express and realize data cleaning tasks [16, 17, 18, 7] and (b) those that extract the relevant data out of a database and operate on them using proprietary techniques and interfaces [1].

The majority of cleaning techniques focus on the identification of problems on attribute values of string type (e.g., customer names, addresses, product names, etc.) which abound in customer related databases. These include techniques for indexed retrieval of strings based on notions of approximate string match [7], correlating string attributes using string similarity predicates (e.g., cosine similarity, edit distance and variants thereof) [17, 18, 6, 5] and deploying algorithms and/or rule engines for automatically correcting/transforming strings into canonical forms [1, 3, 22]. These techniques will successfully match a query string (or a collection of strings) approximately (for suitably defined notions of approximate match) against the values of an attribute in a relation R. For a given query string, such techniques can tag each matching attribute value with a score quantifying the degree of similarity (closeness) of the query string to the attribute value string. As a result, they can effectively return a scored ranking of the attribute values (and hence the tuples) in R with respect to the query string. It is then up to the user, to observe the highest scoring attribute values and identify the one(s) that should be declared as good approximate matches.

Although such techniques are effective in identifying approximate matches between a string and the values of a relational attribute, it is often the case that *multiple* attributes should be involved in the approximate match operation. Consider for example a relation $R(custname, address, location)$, recording the name of a customer, the customer address, and the geographical coordinates (latitude, longitude) of the customer address. Given a tuple of query strings, Q (possibly obtained from a different database), we wish to obtain approximate matches

Relation R

tuple id	custname	address	location
t_1	John Smith	800 Mountain Av Springfield	5,5
t_2	Josh Smith	100 Mount Av Springfield	8,8
t_3	Nicolas Smith	800 Spring Av Union	11,11
t_4	Joseph Smith	555 Mt Road Springfield	9,9
t_5	Jack Smith	100 Springhill Lake Park	6,6

Query

$Q_{custname}$	$Q_{address}$	$Q_{location}$
John Smith	100 Mount Rd Springfield	5.1,5.1

Scored Rankings

custname	address	location
t_1 (1.0)	t_2 (0.95)	t_1 (0.95)
t_2 (0.8)	t_1 (0.8)	t_5 (0.9)
t_5 (0.7)	t_4 (0.75)	t_2 (0.7)
t_4 (0.6)	t_3 (0.3)	t_4 (0.6)
t_3 (0.4)	t_5 (0.1)	t_3 (0.3)

Figure 1: Example

with tuples of R. Let $Q_{custname}$, $Q_{address}$, $Q_{location}$ be the values specified in Q. For each of these values assume there is an agreed upon methodology to generate approximate matches with tuples of R. The specific methodology used for each attribute is orthogonal to our discussion; any of the known techniques could be applied. For example, for $Q_{custname}$ one could utilize the technique of [17] deploying string edit distance to generate approximate matches with attribute values from attribute *custname* of R. This effectively creates an ordering (ranking) of relation R based on non-decreasing values of the edit distance (possibly thresholded) between $Q_{custname}$ and R(custname). For $Q_{address}$ one could decide to utilize the techniques of [18, 7] and generate a list of approximate matches using the *address* attribute of R. A ranking of R will be obtained in this case as well, based on tf-idf and cosine similarity of $Q_{address}$ and R(address). Finally, for $Q_{location}$ we could choose spatial closeness (in terms of some spatial norm, e.g., Euclidean distance between $Q_{location}$ and R(location) and generate a corresponding list of matches (and, hence, ranking of R). Figure 1 presents an example of such (scored) rankings. Notice that the resulting rankings and scores heavily depend on the specific methodology applied to derive them.

Although in principle one could use the information conveyed by only one ranking to form an answer, this is not necessarily a good choice. For example, tuple t_5 ranks second (with a score of 0.9) in the ranking on location but ranks poorly on the other query attributes. Evidently, a more conclusive answer could be obtained by merging the positions and/or scores of the tuples in all rankings. This can be accomplished with the use of *merging functions* operating on the tuples of the various rankings. For purposes of exposition, consider a merging function that sums the scores of the tuples in the various rankings. In this case notice that tuple t_1 achieves a better value (2.75) in that sum than any other tuple in R. Intuitively, this is a better approach, as it is obtained by examination of all the query attributes and the results of all the induced rankings. It is evident that, in the presence of different rankings, principled techniques are required to derive a final ranking by taking into account information conveyed by all rankings. Such principled techniques can be realized as merging functions operating on the tuples of rankings. The derivation of a final ranking can then be cast as an optimization problem over the values of such merging functions.

Given that a variety of approximate match techniques are fully expressible in a declarative way, and best deployed in a database, rankings can be easily generated by directly operating on R using SQL. Thus, they can be readily materialized as relations as an input to the merging. The result of the merging itself may be used as an input to other queries/operations in the database. As a result, it is desirable to express methodologies that merge the information conveyed by the rankings in a declarative way as well.

In this paper, we study efficient techniques to merge rankings produced as a result of approximate match operations, and their declarative expression. In particular, we consider the top-k *selection* problem, and propose efficient algorithms for this problem. This is defined as the task of deriving an optimal final ranking (for suitably defined notions of optimality) of user-specified length k when individual rankings to be merged are generated with respect to a single query tuple. We make the following contributions:

- We study the top-k selection problem in the context of merging results of approximate match operations and show how it can be modeled as an instance of the minimum cost perfect matching problem.

- We show how the preferred solution to the minimum cost perfect matching problem, namely the *Hungarian Algorithm* (H A), can be adapted in the context of the top-k selection problem.

- We propose a modification of H A tailored to the top-k selection problem, called M H A, analytically show its superiority over H A, and provide its full SQL specification.

- We propose a new algorithm, called S S P, specifically for the top-k selection problem, and fully specify the algorithm in SQL as well.

- We present a thorough performance evaluation of all the applicable algorithms using real data sets on a commercial database system, identifying their relative performance and applicability.

In section 2, we introduce background material, and formally define the problem of interest on ranked lists. Section 3 presents our proposed techniques, including complete SQL specification of our proposed solutions. Section 4 details a performance evaluation of our proposals. In section 5, we discuss the enhancements of our basic techniques to deal with scores. In section 6 we review work related to the problems of interest in this paper. Finally, section 7 concludes the paper by discussing additional problems of interest in this important area.

2 Background and Definitions

Let R be a relation of cardinality n consisting of m attributes and let $t_1, \ldots, t_n$ denote the tuples of R. A ranking of R is an ordered list = {x_1 x_2 ... x_n}, where

$x_i \in R$ and $\le$ is some ordering relation on R. Such a ranking can be obtained by applying a suitable approximate match operation between a query value and the values of an attribute of R. Without loss of generality, we assume that rankings of R are complete in the sense that every $t_i \in R$ belongs to the ranking. If this is not the case (for example if the approximate match predicate is thresholded) and the ranking contains $S \subset R$ tuples, we obtain a complete ranking by padding the partial ranking at the end (with the same rank value) with all the "missing" $R \setminus S$ tuples. Semantically, this declares that we are indifferent about the relative ordering of the missing tuples and are all equivalently placed at the end of the ranking obtained. For a ranking σ, we use the notation $\sigma(t_i)$ to refer to the position of tuple t_i in the ranking (a highly ranked tuple has a low numbered position). At times an approximate match operation used to generate a ranking provides an approximate match score (see, e.g., [18, 17, 7]).

Given a query tuple t_q with m values, let $\sigma_1, \ldots \sigma_m$ denote the resulting rankings of R after applying approximate match operations on corresponding values of t_q and attributes of R. We will deploy *merging functions* to synthesize new rankings of R out of $\sigma_1, \ldots, \sigma_m$. A variety of such functions have been proposed in the literature [10, 8, 20]. The bulk of our discussion equally applies to metric merging functions [13]. To ease presentation, we adopt for the bulk of the paper one instance of such a function, namely the *footrule distance*. We stress however that our methodologies are orthogonal to the choice of a metric merging function.

Definition 1 (Footrule Distance) *Let σ and τ be two rankings of R. The footrule distance between the two rankings is defined as $F(\sigma, \tau) = \sum_{i=1}^{n} |\sigma(t_i) - \tau(t_i)|$.*

Thus, the footrule distance is the sum of the absolute differences of the positions of tuples of R in the two rankings. Notice that $F(\sigma, \tau)$ can be divided by $\frac{n^2}{2}$ if n is even or $\frac{n^2-1}{2}$ if n is odd (this maximum value is attained when rankings are ordered in opposite ways) and a normalized value between 0 and 1 can be obtained. It is evident that $F(\sigma, \tau)$ can be defined over the approximate match scores of the corresponding rankings as well. For simplicity of exposition, we adopt definition 1 for the bulk of the paper. Such a measure generalizes in a natural way to account for multiple rankings. The footrule distance between rankings σ and $\sigma_1, \ldots, \sigma_m$ is defined as

$$F(\sigma, \sigma_1, \ldots, \sigma_m) = \sum_{i=1}^{m} F(\sigma, \sigma_i)$$

To a large extent, any interpretation of results obtained will be in terms of this distance measure. While such a measure seems natural we will not delve into the discussion of it's goodness. We refer the reader to the vast bibliography [10, 20, 8] discussing and analyzing the relative goodness and applicability of the various distance measures.

We are now ready to define formally the main problem of interest in this paper:

Problem 1 (top-k selection problem) *Given a query tuple t_q specifying m attribute values, let $\sigma_i, 1 \le i \le m$ be the rankings obtained as a result of approximate match operations on R. The top-k selection problem aims to efficiently identify the first k (for a user specified parameter k) tuples of the ranking σ of R that minimizes the footrule distance $F(\sigma, \sigma_1, \ldots, \sigma_m)$.*

The first k tuples of the ranking σ of R are derived as a result of the minimization of $F(\sigma, \sigma_1, \ldots, \sigma_m)$. Each tuple t_i in σ is tagged with a cost, referred to as the *ranking cost* as the result of this minimization. A tuple t_i at position $j, 1 \le j \le k$, in σ has a ranking cost $^r(t_i, j) = \sum_{l=1}^{m} |\sigma_l(t_i) - j|$. The answer to the top-$k$ selection problem is a set (of cardinality k) of triples $(t_i, j, {}^r(t_i, j))$, where j is the rank (position) of t_i in the result σ, such that among all possible mappings of the tuples t_i to positions $j, 1 \le j \le k$, $\sum_{j=1}^{k} {}^r(t_i, j)$ is minimized.

The bulk of this paper deals with merging ranked lists. In section 5, we discuss how our techniques can be extended to effectively deal with approximate match scores.

3 Top-k Selections

In this section we develop our proposed solutions to the top-k selection problem. We first show that the problem can be modeled as a modification of a well-studied problem, namely the *minimum cost perfect matching* [2] problem and show how such an instance can be obtained given our setting. We start from an existing technique to solve the minimum cost perfect matching problem, namely the *Hungarian algorithm* (HA), and show how this algorithm can be adapted to obtain a solution to our top-k problem. We then propose a *Modified Hungarian Algorithm* (MHA) that takes advantage of the special structure of the top-k selection problem, resulting in improved performance. We also design a new solution for the top-k selection problem, the *Successive Shortest Paths* algorithm (SSP), and provide its declarative specification. In section 4, we present a comparative evaluation of the three algorithms.

Given an edge-labeled bipartite graph $G = (N_1 \cup N_2, E)$, let $c_{ij}, i \in N_1, j \in N_2$ be the edge cost associated with each edge in E. A minimum cost perfect matching in G is the set of edges $E' \subseteq E$ of minimum cumulative cost, such that each $i \in N_1$ is incident to exactly one $j \in N_2$ in E' and vice versa. The solution to the minimum cost perfect matching can be reached by solving a linear program minimizing the overall sum of edge costs [2].

Given rankings $\sigma_i, 1 \le i \le m$, provided as a result of approximate match queries on R, we construct a bipartite graph G as follows. Assume that each ranking σ_i is a complete ranking of R (thus contains n tuples). We instantiate n nodes corresponding to each tuple $t_1, \ldots, t_n$ of R and n nodes corresponding to the positions 1 through n of the target ranking σ. For each of the n^2 pairs of tuples t_i and positions j with $1 \le i, j \le n$ we introduce the edge (t_i, j) with a ranking cost $^r(t_i, j) = \sum_{l=1}^{m} |\sigma_l(t_i) - j|$. This will instantiate a full bipartite graph G. A solution of the minimum cost perfect matching problem on G would produce a minimum cost assignment of each of the n tuples to exactly

	1	2	3
t_1	5	3	20
t_2	6	2	3
t_3	1	3	20

Figure 2: Example matrix for graph G

one of the n positions, such that no two tuples are assigned to the same position.

The top-k selection problem is a modification of the minimum cost perfect matching problem, in which we restrict our interest in identifying only the k tuples of R matching the first k positions of having minimum sum of ranking costs. Notice that a solution to the minimum cost perfect matching problem on G, restricted to the first k positions, does not necessarily yield a solution to the top-k selection problem; the cumulative cost might be sub-optimal. To illustrate this point consider the following example. Let G consist of three tuple vertex nodes and three position nodes. The matrix representation of G with each entry expressing the cost associated with the corresponding edge is shown in figure 2. A solution to the top-2 problem for this graph is $\{t_3, t_2\}$ (with a cost of 3) but the minimum cost perfect matching solution is $\{t_3, t_1, t_2\}$ (with a cost of 4, restricted to the first two positions).

3.1 The Hungarian Algorithm (H A)

Let S be the n × n matrix, corresponding to the matrix representation of the bipartite graph G, with elements $r(t_i, j), 1 \leq i, j \leq n$. The Hungarian algorithm solves the minimum cost perfect matching problem by providing a solution to the corresponding linear problem established on S. We start by briefly reviewing this method below; we refer the interested reader to the bibliography on the subject for further details [2]. We then show how such an algorithm can provide a solution to the top-k selection problem as well.

We refer to a row or column of a matrix as a *line*. A set of elements of a matrix is independent if no two of the elements lie on the same line. If a letter c is written next to a row or column of a matrix, we say that the corresponding line is *covered*.

Theorem 1 (Konig's Theorem) *For a square matrix A, the maximum number of independent zeros of A is equal to the minimum number of lines required to cover all the zeros in A.* ∎

This theorem forms the basis for the Hungarian method. The algorithm operates as follows:

1. Subtract the smallest element in each column of S from every element in the column yielding matrix S_1.

2. Subtract the smallest element in each row of S_1 from each element in the row yielding matrix A. A contains at least one zero in every row and column and it is said to be in *standard form*.

3. Find k_m the maximum number of independent zeros of A. Using Konig's theorem, this is the minimum number of lines required to cover all the zeros in A. If $k_m = n$ then there are n independent zeros in A and the row and column position of these zero elements provide a solution to the minimum cost perfect matching problem.

4. If $k_m < n$, let N denote the matrix of non covered elements of A and let h be the smallest element in N. Add h to each twice covered element of A and subtract h from each non covered element of A. Let the resulting matrix be A. Repeat step 3 using matrix A instead of A.

This procedure is guaranteed to terminate after a finite number of steps, due to the reduction at each step of the sum of the elements in the resulting matrices (A, A, etc). It remains to specify the procedure to identify the maximum number of independent zeros k_m.

Identifying maximum number of independent zeros:

The procedure starts by searching each column of A until a column with no entry marked with the special marker 0 is found (if every entry contains a 0, then $k_m = n$ and the problem is solved). This column is referred to as *pivotal* and it is searched for all its zeros. The rows in which these zeros appear are searched for 0 in turn until a row containing no 0 is found. The zero in this row and the pivotal column is marked with the special marker 0. If each 0 in the pivotal column has a 0 in its row, then these row numbers are listed in any order: $i_1, \ldots, i_t$. Further terms are added as follows: Consider the 0 in row i_1 and all zeros in its column; add to the sequence the row numbers of these zeros in any order (avoiding duplication). Continue with the 0's in rows $i_2, \ldots, i_t$ as well as with the terms of the sequence after i_t. There are two possibilities, either a row i_s is reached which does not contain a 0 or every row whose number is after i_t contains a 0. In the former case a transfer of a 0 happens as follows: row number i_s was added to the sequence because row i_s contained a 0 in the column of a 0 belonging to some row i_r. This 0 in the row i_r is transferred to the zero in row i_s thus staying in the same column. Further transfers may happen until the 0 is transferred from a zero in a row in the initial sequence $i_1, \ldots, i_t$. Then the zero in this row and in the pivotal column can be marked by a 0. In the latter case, let v be the rows in the sequence. These rows contain a 0. The v columns containing these 0's along with the pivotal column contains 0's only in the v rows represented in the sequence. It follows that these v rows along with the remaining n − v − 1 columns contain all the zeros in A. Thus the matrix can be replaced by A (as dictated in step 4) and the algorithm can proceed to step 3.

Figure 3 presents an example operation of H A on the data obtained from example 1. Due to space limitations, we do not provide the full SQL specification of algorithm H A.

Our top-k selection problem cannot be solved by a direct application of this procedure, since an answer to the minimum cost perfect matching problem restricted to the first k positions is not necessarily an answer to the top-k selection problem. We observe, however, that it is possible

```
   1  2  5  8 11              0  0  3  7 10
   3  2  3  6  9              2  0  1  5  8
  11  8  5  2  1             10  6  3  1  0
   8  5  2  1  4              7  3  0  0  3
   7  4  3  4  5              5  1  0  2  3
(a) Initial matrix from example 1   (b) After step 2

   0  0  3  7 10  c           0  0  3  7 10
   2  0  1  5  8  c           2  0  1  5  8
  10  6  3  1  0  c          10  6  3  1  0
   7  3  0  0  3  c           7  3  0  0  3
   5  1  0  2  3              5  1  0  2  3
(c) Conflict in row 4 columns 4,3   (d) Final result
```

Figure 3: (a) Initial Matrix (b) after step 2 (c) Conflict in row 4 and columns 4,3, the covered rows are shown at that point. The 0 in row 4 column 3 is moved to row 5 column 3. A 0 can now be placed at row 4 column 4 and the algorithm proceeds by placing the final 0 at row 3 column 5 (d) final result, t_1, t_2, t_5, t_4, t_3

to modify this procedure in a way that deriving a solution to the top-k selection problem becomes possible.

In the top-k selection problem one is only interested in the first k positions of the ranking. Thus, when realizing matrix A for a supplied k value, we only need to compute the elements $r(t_i, j), 1 \leq i \leq n, 1 \leq j \leq k$ of A. Algorithm H A however, requires a square matrix (of size $O(n^2)$) to operate correctly since it solves an n × n matching problem (otherwise the corresponding program will be under specified).

We observe that we can still utilize algorithm H A for the top-k selection problem by inserting a large positive constant[1] for each of the remaining n(n − k) elements. This serves two purposes: (a) it creates a square A matrix as required by algorithm H A and (b) it guarantees that the solution extracted from the solution of the corresponding minimum cost perfect matching on A is a correct solution to the top-k selection problem. By inserting a large positive constant in the corresponding positions of A we essentially add edges of very high cost in the corresponding bipartite graph. Since such edges are of high cost they can never participate in an assignment concerning the first k positions.

A natural question arises regarding the necessity of those n(n − k) additional elements for the algorithm's correctness. The basic form of execution of algorithm H A for the top-k selection problem requires inserting and maintaining these additional n(n − k) values. To see this consider the following: at any iteration of the algorithm, when searching for the maximum number of independent zeros it is possible that step 4 of the algorithm executes. Let i be the column that instigates the execution of step 4. Notice that during the execution of step 4 the contents of any of the elements of A might change but the contents of column i do not. As a result, the contents of column i (for any i) are always required, since they might be affected in later iterations. Consequently, all columns have to be maintained during the entire execution of the algorithm, bringing the total space requirement to $O(n^2)$.

From a performance standpoint, such an adaptation of

---

[1] Greater than the maximum value among $r(t_i, j), 1 \leq i \leq n, 1 \leq j \leq k$

H A for the top-k selection problem only reduces the initial overhead of constructing matrix A. Subsequent operations however, will be on the entire matrix A of n^2 elements. The running time of this procedure is $O(n^3)$ since each of the n columns will be considered and, in the worst case, the algorithm will have to examine $O(n^2)$ elements in A for each column considered.

3.2 Algorithm M H A

In this section, we propose a modification of the basic H A algorithm for the top-k selection problem, which operates in space $O(nk)$, with worst case running time $O(nk^2)$.

One observation regarding the operation of algorithm H A is that since the algorithm provides a solution to a linear program, the optimal solution is not affected by a rearrangement of the columns of matrix A. Thus, consider populating matrix A as follows: insert a large positive constant to positions (i, j) of A with $1 \leq i \leq n, 1 \leq j \leq n - k$ and populate the remaining positions with nk ranking costs $r(t_i, j), 1 \leq i \leq n, 1 \leq j \leq k$ at matrix positions (i, n − k + j). Denote the resulting matrix as A. Algorithm M H A operates similarly to H A on matrix A. Now consider the operation of H A on this modified matrix. While searching for the maximum independent number of zeros in the first n − k columns the algorithm can place 0 in positions (l, l), $1 \leq l \leq n - k$ of A immediately. The reason is that once A is in standard form positions $1 \leq i \leq n, 1 \leq j \leq n - k$ of the matrix are all zero. The final solution is now represented by the position of the 0's in columns n − k + 1 . . . n. The following invariant holds at any point in the execution of the algorithm:

Invariant 1 *All columns from 1 to n − k are identical, differing only in the positions of their 0's. Moreover, for any row containing no 0, the corresponding entry for this row and any column j, $1 \leq j \leq n - k$ is 0.* ∎

As a result of this invariant, it is evident that it is no longer required to explicitly materialize the entire n × (n − k) sub matrix of A with large positive values. It is sufficient to only maintain $O(n)$ values representing the state of all the 0 elements of the A matrix in the first n − k columns. This has the potential for improved efficiency and performance as algorithm M H A has to operate on a matrix of size $O(nk)$ as opposed to one of size $O(n^2)$ as H A does. The running time of this procedure is $O(nk^2)$ since only k columns will be considered and, in the worst case, the algorithm will have to examine $O(nk)$ elements in A for each column considered.

Figure 4 presents an example operation of algorithm M H A on the data of figure 1. For purposes of exposition we show the entries of the entire matrix during the execution presented in figure 4. Notice that for this top-2 example, only 15 (3*n) entries are required to be explicitly maintained.

3.2.1 SQL Specification of M H A

Complete SQL specification in procedural SQL of algorithm M H A is provided in figures 5 and 6. Such forms of

```
  1  2  M  M  M          M  M  M   1  2
  3  2  M  M  M          M  M  M   3  2
 11  8  M  M  M          M  M  M  11  8
  8  5  M  M  M          M  M  M   8  5
  7  4  M  M  M          M  M  M   7  4
 (a) Initial matrix for top-2     (b) After rearrangement

  0  0  0  0  0          0  0  0  0  0
  0  0  0  2  0          0  0  0  2  0
  0  0  0 10  6          0  0  0 10  6
  0  0  0  7  3          0  0  0  7  3
  0  0  0  6  2          0  0  0  6  2
 (c) Conflict in row 1 column 4    (d) Final result.
```

Figure 4: (a) Initial Matrix suitable for top-2 problem (b) after rearrangement of columns (c) Conflict in row 1 columns 1,4. The 0 in column 1 row 1 is moved to column 1 row 4 and the 0 is placed at row 1 column 4. In the next iteration another conflict appears between row 2 columns 5,2. The 0 in column 2 row 2 is moved to row 5 column 2 and a 0 is placed at column 5 row 2. (d) final solution is, t_1, t_2

procedural SQL are offered by all major RDBMS systems. Figure 5 contains variable declarations and initializations required by the main procedure body shown in figure 6. The schema associated with this procedure is not provided due to space limitations; it can be easily derived from the procedure body, however.

Block 1 initializes the Top relation by placing a 0 in each of the last n − k columns. We then iterate over each remaining column. Within every iteration, block 2 tries to place a 0 directly in the current column. If that is not possible, block 3 determines whether a 0 can be placed in the current column by carrying out a series of transfers, as described in section 3.1. If possible, block 4 performs these transfers. Block 5 handles the final case when we find a set of $k_m < n$ lines which cover all the zeroes of the matrix.

3.3 Algorithm SSP

In this section we propose an alternate solution to the top-k selection problem which we refer to as *Successive Shortest Paths* (SSP). We first provide the intuition behind this algorithm with the example shown in figure 7.

The figure presents an example of a top-k selection problem represented as an instance of a minimum cost perfect matching problem. With a database consisting of five tuples the corresponding full bipartite graph G is constructed. An edge between a node t_i and a position j in figure 7 is assumed to have a ranking cost of $^r(t_i, j)$. We refer to the nodes in G corresponding to tuples (t_1 to t_5) as tuple vertices and to the nodes corresponding to positions (1 through 5) as position vertices (or simply positions). Let's observe, in an inductive way, issues arising when, having constructed a top-i answer, we wish to extend it and construct a top-$(i+1)$ answer.

First, constructing a top-1 answer given the graph of figure 7 is an easy task. We just select the edge with minimum ranking cost incident to position 1. The corresponding tuple (say tuple t_3 in figure 7) is the top-1 answer. Assume that through some mechanism we have identified the top-i answers (e.g., i = 3 in figure 7 and the answer is indicated by the highlighted edges). Using the top-i solution

```
DECLARE COMMONCOL integer DEFAULT -1;
DECLARE pivot INTEGER;
DECLARE rcount INTEGER;
DECLARE rowmin FLOAT;
DECLARE colmin FLOAT;
DECLARE elemposmin FLOAT;
DECLARE r integer;
DECLARE c integer;
DECLARE cold integer;
DECLARE cnew integer;
DECLARE found integer;

SET c = 1;
WHILE (c ≤ K) DO
    select min(cost) into colmin
        from Graph
        where pos = c;
    update Graph
        set cost = cost - colmin
        where pos = c;
SET c = c + 1;
END WHILE;
IF (K < N) THEN
    update GTail
    set cost = 0
    where pos = COMMONCOL;
ELSE
SET r = 1;
WHILE (r ≤ N) DO
    select min(cost) into rowmin
        from Graph
        where elem = r;
    update Graph
        set cost = cost - rowmin
        where elem = r;
SET r = r + 1;
END WHILE;
END IF;
    delete from Top;
```

Figure 5: Initialization for M H A

to construct the top-$(i+1)$ solution two cases of interest arise; we will use i = 3 in figure 7 to illustrate these cases. Assume that the top-3 solution $(t_i, j), 1 \leq j \leq 3$ identified is $S_{top-3} = \{(t_2, 1), (t_3, 2), (t_1, 3)\}$. Thus the associated total cost of the top-3 solution is $C_{top-3} = {}^r(t_2, 1) + {}^r(t_2, 2) + {}^r(t_1, 3)$. Constructing the top-4 solution involves including a new tuple in the solution.

The first case arises when following a direct edge from position 4 (position $(i+1)$) to a tuple which is currently un-matched (i.e., not present in the top-3 solution). In this case a *candidate solution* can be constructed by adding the new tuple, say, $(t_4, 4)$ to the current top-3 set. A top-4 candidate solution is obtained as a direct extension of the current top-3 solution. If the total cost of the top-3 solution plus the ranking cost of the new tuple (say tuple t_4 in figure 7) assigned at position 4 in minimum (among all possible four-tuple sets assigned to positions 1 through 4), then this is the top-4 solution. A second case arises when we follow a path from position 4 via some other tuple vertex (or vertices) currently in S_{top-3} in the bipartite graph, to a tuple which is currently un-matched. Consider for example the path from position 4 to tuple vertex t_3 to position 2 and back to tuple t_4 (which is currently un-matched). This path defines a new candidate solution which can be obtained by modification of S_{top-3} by removing $(t_3, 2)$ and adding $(t_3, 4), (t_4, 2)$ with a total cost $C_{top-3} + {}^r(t_3, 4) + {}^r(t_4, 2) - {}^r(t_3, 2)$.

```
CREATE PROCEDURE M H A (IN K integer, IN N integer)
LANGUAGE SQL
BEGIN

    -- Initialization for MHA
1.  SET pivot = N;
    WHILE (pivot > K) DO
      insert into Top values(pivot, pivot);
    SET pivot = pivot - 1;
    END WHILE;

    SET pivot = K;
    pivotiter:

    WHILE (pivot ≥ 1) DO
2     delete from SimpleAugment;
      insert into SimpleAugment
        select Graph.elem, pivot
        from Graph
        where pos = pivot and cost = 0
          and elem not in (select elem from Top)
          fetch first 1 rows only;
      select count(*) into rcount from SimpleAugment;

    IF (rcount > 0) THEN
      insert into Top
      select elem, pos
      from SimpleAugment;
      set pivot = pivot - 1;
    iterate pivotiter;
    END IF;

3.  delete from Reach4;
    insert into Reach4(elem, parent)
      select Graph.elem, N+1
      from Graph
      where pos = pivot and cost = 0;
    SET cold = -1;
    SET found = 0;
      select count(*) into cnew from Reach4;

    WHILE (found = 0 AND cnew > cold) DO
    SET cold = cnew;
      insert into Reach4(elem, parent)
        select Graph.elem, min(Reach4.elem)
        from Reach4, Top, Graph
        where Top.elem = Reach4.elem
          and Top.pos ≤ K
          and Graph.pos = Top.pos and Graph.cost = 0
          and Graph.elem not in (select elem from Reach4)
          group by Graph.elem;
      insert into Reach4(elem, parent)
        select GTail.elem, min(Reach4.elem)
        from Reach4, Top, GTail
        where Top.elem = Reach4.elem
          and Top.pos > K
          and GTail.pos = COMMONCOL and GTail.cost = 0
          and GTail.elem not in (select elem from Reach4)
          group by GTail.elem;

      select count(*) into cnew from Reach4;
      select count(*) into found
        from Reach4
        where Reach4.elem not in (select elem from Top);
    END WHILE;

4.  delete from Augment;
    insert into Augment
      select Reach4.elem
      from Reach4
      where Reach4.elem not in (select elem from Top)
      fetch first 1 rows only;
    select count(*) into rcount from Augment;

    IF (rcount > 0) THEN
      delete from AugmentingPath1;
      insert into AugmentingPath1
      with AugmentingPath(elem, parent, level) as (
        select Reach4.elem, Reach4.parent, 0
        from Reach4, Augment
        where Reach4.elem = Augment.elem
        UNION
        select Reach4.elem, Reach4.parent,
               AugmentingPath.level+1
        from Reach4, AugmentingPath
        where Reach4.elem = AugmentingPath.parent
          and AugmentingPath.level < N)
      select elem, parent
      from AugmentingPath;
      insert into Top values(N+1, pivot);

      delete from TempTop;
      insert into TempTop
      select AugmentingPath1.elem, Top.pos
      from Top, AugmentingPath1
      where Top.elem = AugmentingPath1.parent;

      delete from Top
      where elem in
        (select parent from AugmentingPath1);
      insert into Top
      select * from TempTop;

    SET pivot = pivot - 1;
    iterate pivotiter;
    END IF;

5.  select min(cost) into elemposmin
    from Graph
    where elem not in
      (select elem from Reach4) and (
        pos = pivot or pos in (
        select Top.pos from Top, Reach4
        where Top.elem = Reach4.elem))
      and pos ≤ K;

    update Graph
    set cost = cost - elemposmin
      where elem not in (select elem from Reach4) and (
        pos = pivot or pos in
          (select Top.pos from Top, Reach4
          where Top.elem = Reach4.elem))
        and pos ≤ K;

    update Graph
    set cost = cost + elemposmin
      where elem in (select elem from Reach4) and (
        pos != pivot and pos not in (
        select Top.pos from Top, Reach4
        where Top.elem = Reach4.elem))
        and pos ≤ K;

    update GTail
    set cost = cost + elemposmin
        where elem in (select elem from Reach4);
    END WHILE;
      delete from Top
        where pos > K;
END
```

Figure 6: M H A in Procedural SQL

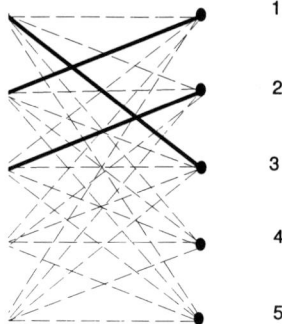

Figure 7: Example Matching

Notice that if more than one already matched vertices in $S_{top\text{-}3}$ are present in the path a similar expression for the total cost can be obtained by adding to $C_{top\text{-}3}$ the ranking costs associated with the edges that are not present in $S_{top\text{-}3}$ and subtracting the ranking costs associated with the edges present in $S_{top\text{-}3}$. The top-4 solution can be derived by identifying the path with the lowest cost, among all possible paths from position 4 to an un-matched tuple vertex and making the suitable modifications to $S_{top\text{-}3}$ in order to derive $S_{top\text{-}4}$.

One observation from the above discussion is that during the construction of the top-i solution the entire graph G is not required. The computation can be correctly performed by manipulating G_i, the bipartite subgraph of G corresponding to the first i positions. Paths involving positions greater than i will be considered at later steps, incrementally towards k.

The above example leads to a natural procedure, the *successive shortest paths* (SSP) algorithm to incrementally evaluate the answer to a top-k selection problem. The algorithm is presented in pseudo-code in figure 8. Starting from a new position i the algorithm obtains the subgraph G_i of interest at this iteration, identifies the transitive closure to un-matched tuple vertices in graph G_i and maintains the one with the cheapest cost, accounting for positive edge costs when the edge is not present in solution S_{i-1} and negative edge costs when it is present. Finally, it adjusts solution S_{i-1} to obtain the new top-i solution, incrementally up to the desired value of k.

The incremental construction of the top-k answer provided by algorithm SSP in figure 8 can be optimized. We introduce an optimization of this basic scheme that can significantly reduce the computation involved. We refer to this optimization as *Early Stopping* (ES). It provides a criterion for terminating the search for the least cost path early on in the search and subsequently avoiding the computation of the transitive closure.

Early Stopping:

During the incremental construction of the top-k answer, algorithm SSP considers positions successively. When a new position is considered the paths to all un-matched tuples are computed. It is easy to show that if at iteration $i+1$ of the algorithm the edge of minimum ranking cost incident to position $i+1$ is also incident to an un-matched vertex tuple, then this edge belongs to the top-$(i+1)$ answer:

```
Algorithm SSP (k) {
   for (i = 1 to k) {
      obtain subgraph G_i of G
      if (i == 1) {
         let t_i the tuple vertex incident to the cheapest
         edge at position 1; add (t_i,1) to S_1
      }
      else {
         1) Starting from position i compute the
            transitive closure to all currently
            un-matched vertex nodes in G_i

         2) Compute the cost of each path in the
            closure accounting for the negative edge
            cost when traversing an edge in S_{i-1} and
            positive edge cost when the edge is not in S_{i-1}

         3) Identify all edges in the cheapest path e_1,...e_m
            and modify S_{i-1} (add/remove edges) accordingly to
            obtain S_i
            S_i = S_{i-1}
            for (j = 1 to m) {
               if e_j   S_{i-1} then S_i = S_i / e_j
               else S_i = S_i   e_j
            }
      }
   }
}
```

Figure 8: SSP pseudo code

Optimization 1 (Early Stopping) *At iteration $i+1$, if the cheapest edge out of the $(i+1)$st position is unmatched then the top-$(i+1)$ answer contains this edge.* ∎

This optimization enables us to terminate the search process for the top-$(i+1)$ answer immediately, without having to evaluate the transitive closure from the $(i+1)$-th position. In this case the top-$(i+1)$ answer can be obtained by extending the top-i answer by the edge of smaller cost out of position $i+1$ to an un-matched tuple vertex.

3.3.1 SQL Statements for SSP

Figure 9 presents the SSP algorithm in procedural SQL (without any optimization introduced). The schema required by this procedure is omitted due to space constraints; it can be easily derived from the procedure body. Block 1 initializes the Top relation to the cheapest edge out of position 1. We then iterate over all positions from 2 to k. Within each iteration, block 2 computes the transitive closure from the current position to all unmatched positions. Block 3 picks an unmatched tuple with the smallest distance from the current position and block 4 computes the path from the current position to this unmatched tuple. Finally, block 5 updates the old solution using this path to obtain the new solution which includes the current position.

Early stopping can be also incorporated by inserting the statements of figure 10 in the sequence of the statements of figure 9 immediately after the first *WHILE* loop. The statements in figure 10 identify whether the least cost tuple vertex which is a target of the current position, is in the current solution. If not, then they augment the current solution and start a new iteration.

```
CREATE PROCEDURE ssp(IN k integer, IN N integer)      delete from Reach4
LANGUAGE SQL                                              where elem in (select elem from R41);
BEGIN                                                     insert into Reach4(elem, parent, cost)
DECLARE index INTEGER DEFAULT 1;                              select RR.elem, min(RR.parent), RR.cost
DECLARE iter INTEGER DEFAULT 1;                               from RR, R41
DECLARE rcount INTEGER;                                       where RR.elem = R41.elem
DECLARE matchsum FLOAT DEFAULT 0;                             and RR.cost = R41.cost
                                                              group by RR.elem, RR.cost;
1. delete from Top;
   insert into Top(elem, pos)                          SET iter = iter+1;
       select min(elem), pos                           END WHILE;
       from graph                                      3. delete from Augment;
       where pos = 1 and cost =                           insert into Augment
           (select min(cost)                               select elem
           from graph where pos = 1)                       from Reach4
           group by pos;                                   where elem not in
                                                               (select elem from Top)
SET index = 2;                                              order by cost
start:                                                      fetch first 1 rows only;
WHILE (index ≤ k) DO
2. delete from R1;                                    4. delete from AugmentingPath1;
   insert into R1(selem, delem, cost)                    insert into AugmentingPath1
       select Top.elem, G2.elem, G2.cost - G1.cost        with AugmentingPath(elem, parent, level) as (
       from Top, Graph G1, Graph G2                       select Reach4.elem, Reach4.parent, 0
       where Top.elem = G1.elem and Top.pos = G1.pos      from Reach4, Augment
       and Top.pos = G2.pos;                              where Reach4.elem = Augment.elem
                                                          UNION
   delete from Reach4;                                    select Reach4.elem, Reach4.parent,
   insert into Reach4(elem, parent, cost)                 AugmentingPath.level+1
       select elem, N+1, cost                             from Reach4, AugmentingPath
       from Graph                                         where Reach4.elem = AugmentingPath.parent
       where pos = index;                                 and AugmentingPath.level < N)
                                                          select elem, parent
SET iter = 1;                                             from AugmentingPath;
WHILE (iter ≤ index) DO
   delete from RR;                                    5. insert into Top values(N+1, index);
   insert into RR(elem, parent, cost)                    delete from TempTop;
       select Y.elem, X.elem, X.cost + R1.cost            insert into TempTop
       from Reach4 X, R1, Reach4 Y                            select AugmentingPath1.elem, Top.pos
       where X.elem = R1.selem and Y.elem = R1.delem       from Top, AugmentingPath1
       and X.cost + R1.cost < Y.cost;                      where Top.elem = AugmentingPath1.parent;
                                                       delete from Top
   delete from R41;                                        where elem in
   insert into R41(elem, cost)                                 (select parent from AugmentingPath1);
       select elem, min(cost)                          insert into Top
       from RR                                             select * from TempTop;
       group by elem;                                 SET index = index+1;
                                                      END WHILE;
                                                      END
```

Figure 9: SSP in Procedural SQL

4 Experimental Evaluation

In this section, we present the results of an experimental case study of the proposed algorithms in a real application scenario, varying various parameters of interest in order to understand the algorithms' comparative performance.

4.1 Implementation

We first provide implementation details on the realization of the algorithms in an RDBMS and some observations on the performance of various SQL constructs and then we detail our experimental case study. Our experiments were conducted on DB2 V8.1 Personal Edition running on a Dell PowerEdge server P2600 with two Intel Xeon processors having 3GB of memory and 400 GB of disk. We maintained the default configuration parameters DB2 ships with, only increasing the transaction log size to 524 MB.

The procedural SQL statements of figures 6 and 9 use recursive SQL statements with UNION semantics as specified in the SQL3 standard. However, no major RDBMS up to date supports an efficient implementation of this construct. In particular, DB2 V8.1 supports this construct only with UNION ALL semantics. As a result, since no duplicate elimination takes place at various stages of the recursion, the number of intermediate tuples generated is very large, and performance is affected. In order to alleviate this problem, we simulated the effects of recursion as follows: instead of using the recursive statement directly, we embedded the join clauses in an iterative statement, issuing duplicate elimination statements after each iteration. This resulted in great performance benefits for all the approaches discussed in this paper. We note that as RDBMSs start implementing recursion with SQL3 semantics, the need for such workarounds will decrease.

```
delete from CheapElem;
    insert into CheapElem(elem)
       select elem
       from graph
       where pos = index
       and cost = (select min(cost)
          from graph where pos = index)
       and elem not in
          (select elem from Top)
       fetch first row only;

select count(*) into rcount from CheapElem;
IF (rcount > 0) THEN
    insert into Top(elem, pos)
       select graph.elem, graph.pos
       from graph, CheapElem
       where graph.elem = CheapElem.elem
       and graph.pos = index;
SET index = index+1;
iterate start;
END IF;
```

Figure 10: Enabling Early Stopping in SSP

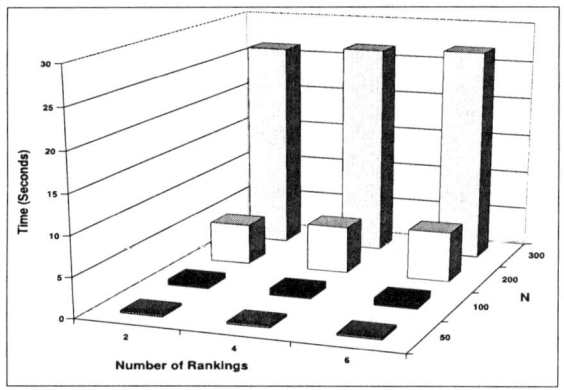

Figure 11: Construction Time for Graph G as a function of n and the number of rankings

4.2 Experimental Case Study

We implemented all three algorithms as outlined using a commercial RDBMS and we conducted experiments to evaluate their performance. In our experiments we used a database containing real customer data with various associated attributes. We utilized the technique of Gravano et al. [18] on various attributes to obtain approximate matches. On a table containing seven million rows it required, in our implementation, approximately 20 seconds to perform an approximate match on an attribute with average length 17 characters and approximately 25 seconds on an attribute with average length 28 characters.

In our first experiment, we seek to quantify the time required to construct the bipartite graph G on which the various techniques operate to provide answers to top-k selection problems. Figure 11 presents this time for different number of rankings and different ranking sizes. The construction time appears more sensitive to the size of the rankings as opposed to the number of rankings used. Notice that, once such a graph is constructed for some value of n (size of the rankings) it can be utilized to answer top-k selection queries for any $k \leq n$.

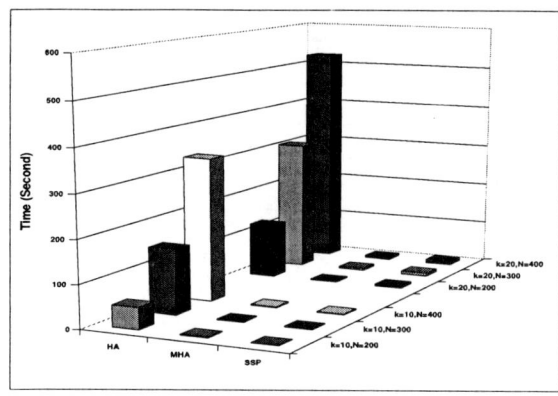

Figure 12: Performance of HA, MHA, SSP as a function of n and k

Our second experiment compares the performance of the three algorithms. Figure 12 presents their performance, as the size of the rankings increases for two distinct values of k. It is evident that the overhead of algorithm HA is prohibitive and its scalability is limited. We chose to keep the scale of this experiment small, as the performance of HA quickly deteriorated. Algorithm MHA and SSP, in contrast, appear much faster.

This prompted us to conduct a more detailed experiment, comparing the performance of MHA and SSP. The result of this experiment is presented in figure 13, for varying values of k and n (the x-axis in figure 13 presents pairs of k, n values). In particular, we vary n from 200 to 1800 and for each value of n we present performance results for four values of k (10,20,30,40). A main observation from this experiment is that there exists a crossover point in the performance of the algorithms which depends on the relative size of k to n. For example, for small values of n (up to 600 in figure 13) SSP offers performance advantages over MHA for values of k up to 10. In that range, SSP is more than 50% faster than MHA. For values of k above 10, MHA is faster than SSP, especially as k increases. As the value of n increases (beyond 600 in figure 13) this crossover point is experienced at a value of k between 20 and 30. In these cases, when k is below 20, SSP is up to three times faster than MHA, especially for large n. For values of k greater than 30, MHA is clearly the algorithm of choice.

These observations lead us to the conclusion that for small values of k comparative to n SSP is the algorithm of choice. As the value of k increases, compared to n, MHA offers great performance advantages. Overall, if only the first few top ranking results are required then algorithm SSP appears the algorithm of choice. For larger values of k, algorithm MHA should be used.

5 Dealing With Scores

Up until now, for simplicity of exposition, we have presented techniques to merge ranked lists, where the list tuples did not have associated scores. Approximate matching techniques used in data cleaning, however, typically associate values matching a query string with a score quantifying the degree of similarity (closeness) of the query string

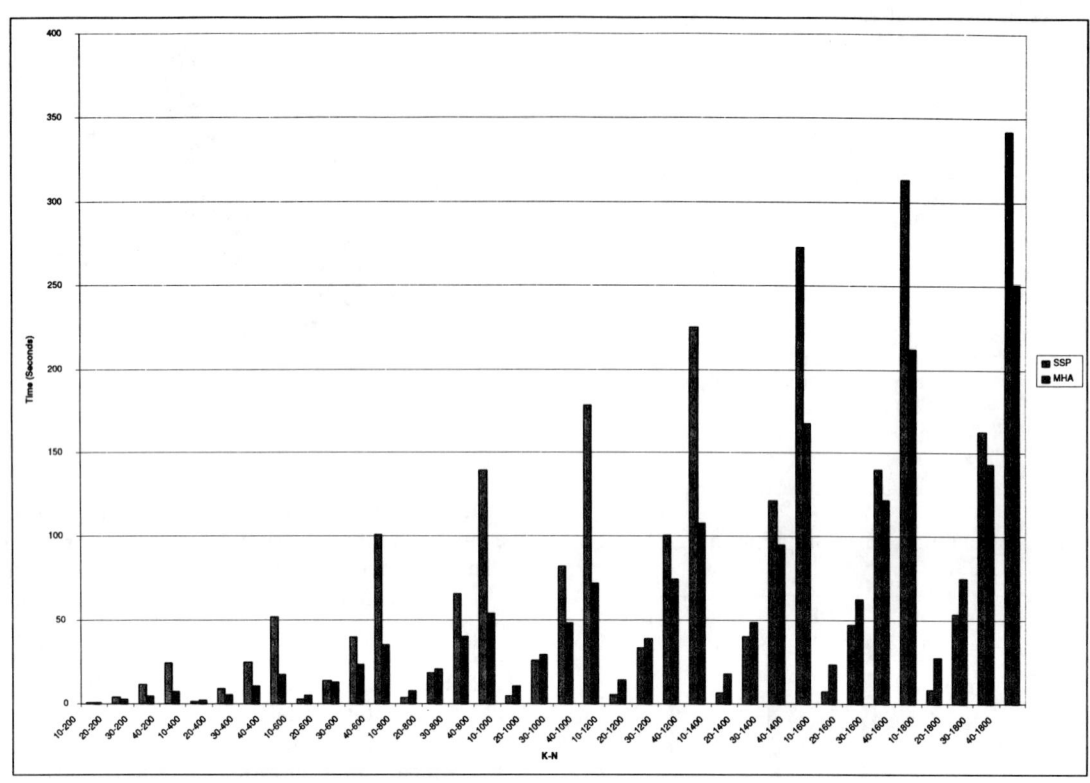

Figure 13: Comparative Performance of MHA and SSP as a function of n and k

to the attribute value string. These scores thus carry more information than the positions of tuples in the ranked lists. In such situations, it would be desirable for (a) the merging technique to use the scores (and not just the rankings) of the tuples in each of the lists to determine the tuple ranks in the merged list, and (b) the tuples in the merged list to be associated with scores, to preserve the closure property. We discuss both these issues in this section.

5.1 Merging Scored Rankings

Essentially, the basis for merging ranked lists discussed in previous sections was to minimize the overall discrepancy in rank positions of the individual tuples, as quantified by the total ranking cost, where the ranking cost of tuple t_i wrt position j was given by $r(t_i, j) = \sum_{\ell=1}^{m} |\ell(t_i) - j|$. This ranking cost was used as the edge cost between tuple t_i and position j in the bipartite graph, as described in section 3, and the solution to our top-k selection problem was based on the minimum cost perfect matching problem over this bipartite graph.

Carrying this analogy to use the scores associated with each of the tuples in the input ranked lists, we define the *scored ranking cost* of tuple t_i wrt position j as

$$s(t_i, j) = \sum_{\ell=1}^{m} |s_\ell(t_i) - s_\ell(j)|$$

where $s_\ell(t_i)$ is the score associated with tuple t_i in the scored ranked list ℓ, and $s_\ell(j)$ is the score associated with the tuple in the jth rank position in list ℓ. The bipartite graph can now be defined as before, except that the edge costs are given by the scored ranking costs $s(t_i, j)$, instead of the ranking costs $r(t_i, j)$. Of course, for the absolute score differences to be meaningfully comparable across lists, the scores in each of the lists would need to be normalized to, say, be a value in $[0,1]$. This was done in the example of figure 1.

Our techniques, MHA and SSP, can now be used *unchanged* on the resulting bipartite graph to identify solutions to the top-k selection problem, taking scores into account. The rankings in the merged list obtained by using scores may be different from those obtained by simply using the input rankings. It is, however, noteworthy that if the scores associated with the tuples in the input ranked lists were *uniformly* distributed in accordance with their rank positions (for example, the tuple in rank position j had a score of $(n - j + 1)/n$), the final rankings in the merged list would be identical.

5.2 Computing Scores in the Merged Ranking

Just as scores are useful when provided by the approximate matching techniques used in data cleaning, they can be useful in the result of the merging. However, the scores that are associated with the tuples in the merged list need to satisfy some robustness properties. First, the scores need to be consistent with the rankings, i.e., there should not be any inversions between the rank order and the score order. Second, the merged scoring should be idempotent, i.e., if two identical scored ranked lists were merged, the score of each tuple in the merged list should be identical to its scores in the input lists.[2] Third, the score of a tuple in the jth position of the merged list can be no larger than the average score of the tuples in the j'th positions of the m input lists. These robustness properties eliminate some obvious candidates, such as computing the score of a tuple in the merged list as the average of its scores in the m input lists.

We describe next an intuitive scoring function that preserves the above robustness properties. Let $sa(j), 1 \leq j \leq k$, be the average score of the tuples in the j'th positions of the m input lists. Let $dsa(j) = sa(j) - sa(j-1), 2 \leq j \leq k$; this is the difference in the average scores between consecutive positions in the input. Next if, in the merged ranking, tuple t_i is at position j, let $srca(j) = {}^s(t_i,j)/m$; this is the average (over the m input lists) of the score differences used in the scored ranking costs in the solution to the top-k problem. Then, the scores of the tuples at rank positions j in the merged list are computed as follows:

$$score(j) = sa(j) - srca(j), j = 1$$

$$score(j) = score(j-1) - \max(dsa(j), srca(j)), j > 1$$

It is easy to verify that the scores computed as described above satisfy the above robustness properties. A more detailed discussion on this merged-scoring function is outside the scope of this paper.

6 Related Work

Data cleaning has attracted lots of research attention in recent years [16, 21, 17, 18, 4, 19, 7]. Most of the recent works [19, 4, 7] deal with various aspects of the classic record linkage problem [15], while others aim to offer a declarative framework for cleaning and approximate matching tasks [16, 17, 18]. Various string distance metrics have been proposed for quantifying approximate string matches including string edit distance, cosine similarity [17, 18, 4] and combinations and extensions thereof [6, 5].

Various functions for merging ranked data have been proposed and studied in the statistical literature [10, 8, 20], including the *Spearman's footrule* and *Kendall's tau*. Such functions have been utilized in the problem of merging the results of various search engines [11]. Variants of such measures have also been considered for similarity search and classification [14]. The metric properties for a large class of functions merging ranked lists have also been studied [13]. We are not aware of any work addressing issues of realization of such merging functions in SQL. A different approach to merging scored lists is to use a combining rule, such as min or average, that combines individual scores to obtain an overall score; this approach has been well investigated in recent years (see, e.g., [12] and references therein).

7 Conclusions

We have considered the problem of merging rankings produced as a result of approximate match operations in relational databases, with the objective of identifying a consensus ranking (under specific metric merging functions) and identifying a few top ranking results. In this context, we introduced the top-k selection problem for which we have identified and proposed applicable algorithms providing their full declarative specification. Our experimental case study using real application data, identified the cases under which two of the proposed algorithms, namely M H A and SSP, are beneficial.

Such problems are of profound interest in practical data cleaning scenarios and we believe research in this direction is well warranted. Future work could investigate incorporation of approximations (e.g., in the spirit of [14]) in a declarative (SQL) framework and quality/performance issues arising in this setting. Moreover, being able to efficiently perform such merging operations in bulk, when a set of queries is provided, is an interesting open question.

References

[1] MindBox Inc. www.mindbox.com.

[2] R. K. Ahuja, T. Magnanti, and J. Orlin. *Network flows*. Prentice Hall, 1992.

[3] V. Borkar, K. Deshmukh, and S. Sarawagi. Automatic segmentation of text into structured records. *Proceedings of SIGMOD*, 2001.

[4] W. Cohen. Integration of heterogeneous databases without common domains using queries based on textual similarity. *Proceedings of SIGMOD*, 1998.

[5] W. Cohen, P. Ravikumar, and S. Fienberg. A comparison of string distance metrics for name-matching tasks. *Proceedings of IIWeb Workshop*, Aug 2003.

[6] W. Cohen, P. Ravikumar, and S. Fienberg. A comparison of string metrics for matching names and records. *Proceedings of KDD Data Cleaning Workshop*, Aug 2003.

[7] S. Chaudhuri, K. Ganjam, V. Ganti, and R. Motwani. Robust and efficient fuzzy match for online data cleaning. *Proceedings of SIGMOD*, 2003.

[8] D. Critchlow. *Metric methods for analyzing partially ranked data*. LNS, Springer-Verlag, 1985.

[9] T. Dasu and T. Johnson. *Exploratory data mining and data cleaning*. John Wiley, 2003.

[10] P. Diaconis and R. Graham. Spearman's footrule as a measure of disarray. *J. of the Royal Statistical Society, 39(2)*, pages 262–268, 1997.

[11] C. Dwork, R. Kumar, M. Naor, and D. Shivakumar. Rank aggregation methods for the web. *Proceedings of WWW10*, 2001.

[12] R. Fagin, A. Lotem, and M. Naor. Optimal aggregation algorithms for middleware. *Proceedings of PODS*, 2001.

[13] R. Fagin, R. Kumar, and D. Shivakumar. Comparing top-k lists. *Proceedings of SODA*, 2003.

[14] R. Fagin, R. Kumar, and D. Shivakumar. Efficient similarity search and classification via rank aggregation. *Proceedings of SIGMOD*, 2003.

[15] I. P. Fellegi and A. B. Sunter. A theory for record linkage. *Journal of the American Statistical Association, 64(328)*, pages 1183–1210, Dec. 1969.

[16] H. Galhardas, D. Florescu, D. Shasha, E. Simon, and E. Saita. Declarative data cleaning. *Proceedings of VLDB*, 2001.

[17] L. Gravano, P. Ipeirotis, H. Jagadish, N. Koudas, S. Muthukrishnan, and D. Srivastava. Approximate string joins in a database (almost) for free. *Proceedings of VLDB*, 2001.

[18] L. Gravano, P. Ipeirotis, N. Koudas, and D. Srivastava. Text joins in an RDBMS for web data integration. *Proceedings of WWW*, 2003.

[19] M. Hernandez and S. Stolfo. The merge purge problem for large databases. *Proceedings of SIGMOD*, 1995.

[20] J. Marden. *Analyzing and modeling rank data*. Chapman Hall, 1995.

[21] S. Sarawagi. Special issue on data cleaning. *IEEE Data Engineering Bulletin, 23(4)*, 2000.

[22] S. Sarawagi and A. Bhamidipaty. Interactive deduplication using active learning. *Proceedings of KDD*, 2002.

---

[2]Note that rank merging satisfies this idempotence property.

Top-k Query Evaluation with Probabilistic Guarantees

Martin Theobald, Gerhard Weikum, Ralf Schenkel

Max-Planck Institute of Computer Science
D-66123 Saarbruecken, Germany
{mtb, weikum, schenkel}@mpi-sb.mpg.de

Abstract

Top-k queries based on ranking elements of multidimensional datasets are a fundamental building block for many kinds of information discovery. The best known general-purpose algorithm for evaluating top-k queries is Fagin's threshold algorithm (TA). Since the user's goal behind top-k queries is to identify one or a few relevant and novel data items, it is intriguing to use approximate variants of TA to reduce run-time costs. This paper introduces a family of approximate top-k algorithms based on probabilistic arguments. When scanning index lists of the underlying multidimensional data space in descending order of local scores, various forms of convolution and derived bounds are employed to predict when it is safe, with high probability, to drop candidate items and to prune the index scans. The precision and the efficiency of the developed methods are experimentally evaluated based on a large Web corpus and a structured data collection.

1. Introduction
1.1 Motivation

Top-k queries on multidimensional datasets compute the k most relevant or interesting results to a partial-match query, based on similarity scores of attribute values with regard to elementary query conditions and a score aggregation function such as weighted summation. This fundamental building block for information discovery arises in many important application classes such as 1) Web and intranet search engines with scores based on word-occurrence statistics and possibly combining criteria like text-based relevance, link-based authority, and recency, 2) multimedia similarity search on feature vectors of images, music, or video, or 3) preference queries over structured and semistructured data such as product catalogs or customer support data (the latter having a major text component as well).

The best known general-purpose method for top-k queries is *Fagin's threshold algorithm*, also known as *TA* [19], which has been independently proposed also by Nepal et al. [33] and Güntzer et al. [22]. This method assumes that each attribute of the multidimensional data space has an index list by which one can access the data items in descending order of the "local" score for the given attribute with regard to an elementary query condition (e.g., tf*idf-based score for a text keyword condition "Trumpet", ontological similarity for categorical attribute conditions such as Genre=Jazz, or absolute distance for numerical attribute conditions such as Year=1970).

The TA method is conservative in that it stops scanning index lists only when it is certain that no more top-k results can be found. We believe that this is overly conservative given that the concept of a top-k query is heuristic anyway. Hardly any end-user would be interested in looking at exactly the k best matches to a similarity query. Rather the rationale of top-k ranking is that users typically find one or a few relevant and novel data items among the top 10 or 20 results. So there is an inherent and unavoidable risk of missing the truly best results (in the subjective judgment of the user) anyway. This in turn justifies relaxing the concept of a top-k query into an *approximate* notion such that the query processor can occasionally tolerate errors: false positives or false negatives with regard to the top k.

The idea of approximate top-k queries has been around in the literature (see, e.g., [3,5,13,17,19]). However, in terms of analyzing how much is lost by the relaxation the prior work either introduced control parameters that are difficult to tune or are based on homogeneity assumptions for multidimensional data distributions. The main focus of the earlier work was image similarity search over color, texture, and contour feature spaces, where the assumptions may indeed be justified. Furthermore, the relaxation control parameters (e.g., a distance slack factor) of these models were difficult to translate into user-perceived guarantees. In contrast, this paper presents a principled approach to approximate top-k queries with *probabilistic guarantees* about the error relative to "exactly top-k" queries, translatable into guarantees about query-result precision and recall. Our approach can cope with heterogeneous distributions where the score variability may radically differ among different text terms or attributes of a semistructured dataset.

We concentrate on algorithms that process index lists by *sorted access only*, as we are aiming at high-dimensional data spaces such as Web or XML documents where queries need to access a potentially large number of very long index lists and random accesses would be very expensive. Our approach allows much more aggressive index list pruning, compared to the original TA method

---

Permission to copy without fee all or part of this material is granted provided that the copies are not made or distributed for direct commercial advantage, the VLDB copyright notice and the title of the publication and its date appear, and notice is given that copying is by permission of the Very Large Data Base Endowment. To copy otherwise, or to republish, requires a fee and/or special permission from the Endowment
Proceedings of the 30th VLDB Conference,
Toronto, Canada, 2004

with sorted access. The paper presents comprehensive experimental results that demonstrate the performance gains.

1.2 Related Work

The state of the art on top-k queries has been defined by the seminal work on the threshold algorithm (TA) [18,19, 22,23,33]. TA scans all query-relevant index lists in an interleaved manner, and aims to compute "global" scores for the encountered data items by means of a monotonic score aggregation function such as (weighted) sum, max, etc. The algorithm maintains the worst score among the current top-k results and the best possible score for all other candidates and items not yet encountered. The latter serves as a threshold for stopping the index scans when no candidate can exceed the score of the kth ranked result. The algorithm comes in two variants. *TA-random* eagerly looks up all local scores of each encountered item and thus knows the full score immediately when it first encounters the item. Since random accesses may be expensive and, depending on the application setting, sometimes infeasible, the alternative *TA-sorted* method (coined NRA in [19] and Stream-Combine in [23]) maintains worst-score and best-score bounds for data items based on partially computed global scores, and its stopping test compares the worst-score of the kth ranked result with the best-score of all other candidates. Obviously, TA-random is more effective in pruning the index scans, but TA-sorted avoids expensive random accesses.

Variants of TA have been studied for multimedia similarity search [12,31], ranking query results from structured databases [1], and distributed preference queries over heterogeneous Internet sources such as digital libraries, restaurant reviews, street finders, etc. [11,29,38]. Marian et al. [29] have particularly investigated how to deal with restrictive sources that do not allow sorted access to their index lists and with widely varying access costs. To this end, heuristic scheduling approaches have been developed, but the threshold condition for stopping the algorithm is a conservative TA-style test. Other top-k query algorithms in the literature include nearest-neighbor search methods based on an R-tree-like multidimensional index [3,6,14,24,25] and mapping techniques onto multidimensional range queries [8] evaluated on traditional database indexes. In this context, probabilistic estimators for selection cutoff values have been developed by [13,17,36] and applied to multidimensional nearest-neighbor queries.

Most of the above TA-centric work has studied the TA-random variant. TA-sorted, on the other hand, has been regarded as the less attractive variant to which one would resort only under specific circumstances. However, with a large number of potentially very long index lists TA-sorted should actually be the method of choice. A small number of papers have considered how to minimize random-access costs in TA-random when data sources vary in speed and selectivity [11,29,38]. To this end simple, histogram-based, probabilistic estimators have been developed for making scheduling decisions (i.e., deciding on which source (i.e., dimension) the next random access should be made). None of this prior work has attempted a principled approach to probabilistic score prediction and result guarantees.

Efficient processing of index lists for ranked retrieval is an old topic in information retrieval (IR) research [30]. In this context sorted-access only is the rule of the game. The pruning techniques considered here (see also [4,10, 21]) are heuristic in nature in that they trade off some loss in result quality (effectiveness in IR jargon) for speed without being able to predict and control the resulting effects (other than by experimentation). For the special but important case where the global score is a weighted sum of tf*idf-based text relevance and link-based, and thus query-independent, authority, additional pruning heuristics have been developed in [7,28].

1.3 Contribution

Our approach is based on predicting the total score of a candidate item for which we know a partial score (e.g., the sum of local scores for one or more elementary conditions, but not the total score for all conditions). In doing this we avoid the overly conservative best-score/worst-score bounds of the original TA-sorted method by calculating the probability that the total score exceeds a threshold that would make the item interesting for the top-k result. If this probability is sufficiently low, we drop the data item from the candidate list. The probabilistic prediction involves computing the convolution of the score distributions of different index lists. To this end, we explore a variety of techniques including histograms, efficiently evaluable Poisson estimations, and convolutions based on moment-generating functions with generalized Chernoff-Hoeffding bounds [32,35] for the resulting tail probabilities. As the overhead of these techniques is crucial, the details of our bookkeeping and candidate testing strategies are all but straightforward; we explore a range of strategies based on different setups of priority queues.

To the best of our knowledge, this is the first paper that presents a method for probabilistic top-k queries. Note that our probabilistic guarantees are not about query run-times but about query result quality; run-time bounds that hold with high probability have been derived in [18]. Also, our approach should not be confused with probabilistic methods for deriving local and global scores, e.g., probabilistic IR techniques [16]; we can handle a wide variety of scoring functions as building blocks but our notion of probabilistic guarantees refers to the approximation of the top k ranks in a completely scored and exactly ranked result set.

2. Computational Model

Consider a *Cartesian product space* $D_1 \times ... \times D_m$ over domains $D_1, ..., D_m$, and a dataset $D \subseteq D_1 \times ... \times D_m$ of m-dimensional data points. The data points could be *records* over structured domains (e.g., product catalog entries) or text *documents* when the domains capture weights of text terms in a high-dimensional IR feature space. In the latter case $D \subseteq \Re^m$ or $D \subseteq [0,1]^m$.

Queries on such a dataset are *partial-match queries* in the form of m-tuples $(q_1, ..., q_m)$ where $q_i \in D_i$ or $q_i = *$ meaning that we do not care about the ith dimension value. In the text-document IR case, usually a few q_i values are set to 1 (the query keywords) and all others set to 0 (but there are other approaches as well). The results $d \in D$ to a query $q = (q_1, ..., q_m)$ do not necessarily have to match all non-zero q_i values or have non-zero components d_i; rather we would like to retrieve *approximate matches* to this condition according to some similarity measures. We assume that for each domain D_i there is a *similarity function* $s_i: D_i \times D_i \to [0,1]$. For numerical domains such as year or price, the similarity function could simply be the absolute difference; for categorical domains such as model (of cars) or genre (of movies or books) the similarity function needs to be explicitly defined for all value pairs.

The domain-specific similarity functions are *aggregated* into a *global similarity* function $s: (D_1 \times ... \times D_m) \times (D_1 \times ... \times D_m) \to [0,1]$, with $s(x,y) = aggr\{s_i(x_i,y_i) | i=1..m\}$ where *aggr* is an aggregation function from $[0,1]^m$ to $[0,1]$. A widely used aggregation function for this purpose would be summation, yielding $s(x,y) = \sum_{i=1}^{m} s_i(x_i, y_i)$; popular alternatives include weighted summation, product (with a probabilistic interpretation), or maximum. The result of a top-k query q then is given by the k data points d for which sim(q,d) is among the k highest values of all similarities between q and any data points.

Our framework for processing top-k queries is based on *sorted access* to the data in descending order of similarity scores for each dimension. Especially for processing IR index lists, where the lists for frequent text terms may be very long, random lookups into these lists would incur extra disk IOs which are orders of magnitudes more expensive than a sorted-access step in memory (with occasional asynchronous and sequential disk reads). TA-sorted operates on *lists L_i*, i=1..m, which, for a given query value q_i, return data values y_i in descending order of $s_i(q_i,y_i)$. The implementation uses B-tree indexes and scans the inverted index lists in sorted order of scores for individual keys, or looks up keys that exactly match a condition and then merges the results of a forward and a backward scan for neighboring keys (e.g., numerical attribute values with small absolute distance to the query value).

In this computational model, the TA-sorted algorithm, which will be our baseline, can be written in the compact pseudocode form shown in Figure 1. Note that, unlike TA-random, the algorithm requires remembering all non-discarded candidates in memory. We will come back to these implementation details in Section 4; neither the original work [19,23] nor the follow-up research [1,9,29] discuss concrete bookkeeping data structures despite their strong performance impact.

When given a query q with specified values $q_1, ..., q_m$, we assume, without loss of generality, that all dimensions are specified or, equivalently, consider only the subspace of dimensions for which the query specifies values. We maintain for each index list L_i the following: a current scan position pos_i and a current score $high_i := s_i(q_i, d)$ for the document d at the current scan position in L_i. We maintain for each record or document d that was already encountered in at least one of the L_i: a set $E(d)$ of dimensions for which we already computed a score s_i, and a partial score $worstscore(q,d) := aggr\{s_i(q_i,d) | i \in E(d)\}$ (e.g., $\sum_{i \in E(d)} s_i(q_i,d)$ with summation as *aggr*).

```
TA-sorted:
top-k := {dummy_1, ..., dummy_k}; // with s(dummy_v)=0
min-k := 0;
candidates := ∅;
scan all lists L_i (i = 1..m) in parallel:
// e.g., round-robin or merged in descending order of s_i values
   consider item d at position pos_i in L_i;
   if d ∉ candidates then
      candidates := candidates ∪ {d};
      E(d) := {i};
   high_i := s_i(q_i,d); // current score in L_i
   E(d) := E(d) ∪ {i};
   bestscore(d):=aggr{aggr{s_v(q_v,d)|v∈E(d)},
                     aggr{high_v|v∉E(d)}};
   worstscore(d) := aggr{s_v(q_v,d)|v∈E(d)};
   if worstscore(d) > min-k then
      if d ∉ top-k then
         remove argmin_d'{worstscore(d')|d'∈top-k} from top-k;
         candidates := candidates ∪ {d'};
         add d to top-k
      min-k := min{worstscore(d') | d' ∈ top-k};
   if bestscore(d) ≤ min-k then candidates := candidates - {d};
   threshold := max {bestscore(d') | d' ∈ candidates};
   if threshold ≤ min-k then exit;
```

Figure 1: Pseudocode for TA-sorted algorithm

All algorithms are based on the invariant
$worstscore(q,d) \leq s(q,d) \leq bestscore(q,d)$ with
$bestscore(q,d) := aggr\{worstscore(q,d), aggr\{high_i | i \notin E(d)\}\}$
For the case of sum as the aggregation function this becomes $\sum_{i \in E(d)} s_i(q_i,d) \leq s(q,d) \leq \sum_{i \in E(d)} s_i(q_i,d) + \sum_{i \notin E(d)} high_i$.

Suppose we already have k items T that are currently the top k results of a given query q, and let $min_k = min\{s(q,d) | d \in T\}$ or, in the case that the items in T have not been fully evaluated, $min_k = min\{worstscore(q,d) | d \in T\}$. Then we can prune documents and remainders of index lists for documents whose upper bound cannot exceed the value min_k, i.e., a document d can be dismissed from the candidate set if

$aggr\{worstscore(q,d), aggr\{high_i | i \notin E(d)\}\} < min_k$

In this case we say that the *threshold test* fails. This consideration is often unnecessarily conservative, because the expected remainder score of a document is much lower than the sum of the $high_i$ bounds. Of course, using expectations for pruning would not give us any guarantees for not missing any of the true top-k results. But we would expect that the sum of the s_i scores in the remainder set

{1...m} − E(d) is lower than the sum of the $high_i$ bounds with very high probability. So we are interested in estimating the probability that a document d that we encounter at position pos_i in the index list L_i and for which $E(d)=\varnothing$ holds qualifies for the top k results:

$$P\left[aggr\{worstscore(q,d), aggr\{s_i(q_i,d) \mid i \notin E(d)\}\} > \min_k\right]$$

If this probability is below some threshold ε (e.g., between 1 and 10 percent) then we may decide to disregard d, without computing its full score. When we choose summation as aggregation function, the above expression becomes

$$p(d) := P\left[\sum\{s_i \mid i \in E(d)\} + \sum\{s_i \mid i \notin E(d)\} > \min_k\right]$$

or equivalently, with $\delta(d) := \min_k - \sum\{s_i \mid i \in E(d)\}$:

$$p(d) = P\left[\sum\{s_i \mid i \notin E(d)\} > \delta(d)\right] .$$ We refer to this condition as the *probabilistic threshold test*. When we compute p(d) during query execution we know upper bounds $high_i$ for the unknown scores. So more precisely, the equation for p(d) should read as

$$p(d) = P\left[\sum\{s_i \mid i \notin E(d)\} > \delta(d) \mid s_i \leq high_i \text{ for } i \notin E(d)\right]$$

3. Probabilistic Score Prediction

In this section we develop the details for estimating the probability p(d) that a document d with non-empty remainder set {1..m} −E(d) may qualify for the top-k results. How we estimate p(d) depends on the assumptions that we make about the distribution of the unknown scores s_i that d would obtain. The following subsections discuss various cases that are of interest from both a fundamental-insight and application viewpoint. We will concentrate on the most important case of using summation for score aggregation, and will discuss generalizations at the end of this section. Note that summation is the standard choice in IR keyword query processing, with tf*idf-style weights being precomputed and stored in the index lists.

3.1 Guarantees with Uniform Distributions

In the absence of any other information, Occam's razor suggests that the simplest assumption about the distribution of unknown partial scores is a *uniform* distribution. More specifically, we assume that for document d and dimension $i \in \{1..m\} - E(d)$ that has not yet been evaluated, the score $s_i(d)$ is uniformly distributed between $high_i$, the currently known upper bound for the true score, and 0, the assumed lower bound. Instead of 0 we may also use the lowest value that occurs in L_i, provided we have stored this information in the index metadata (i.e., without having to scan L_i to its end). We use continuous distributions rather than discrete ones, as this simplifies the subsequent calculations. We assume that all random variables S_i are independent; this will be reconsidered later.

Treating each unknown s_i value as a random variable S_i we thus have to predict $P\left[\sum_i S_i > \delta\right]$. For two random variables S_1 and S_2 with densities $f_1(x)=1/high_1$ and $f_2(x)=1/high_2$ this requires computing the convolution $f(x) = \int_0^x f_1(z) f_2(x-z) dz$. Taking into account the fact that each factor is non-zero only within certain intervals, namely, $0 \leq z \leq high_1$ and $0 \leq x-z \leq high_2$, or equivalently $\max(0, x - high_2) \leq z \leq \min(x, high_1)$, solving the integral leads to the following three cases, assuming $high_1 \leq high_2$ (without loss of generality):

$$f(x) = \begin{cases} x/(high_1 \cdot high_2) & \text{for } 0 \leq x \leq high_1 \\ 1/high_2 & \text{for } high_1 < x \leq high_2 \\ 1/high_1 + 1/high_2 - x/(high_1 \cdot high_2) & \\ & \text{for } high_2 < x \leq high_1 + high_2 \end{cases}$$

and a corresponding cumulative distribution in efficiently evaluable closed form.

Unfortunately, for three and more heterogeneous uniform distributions, this kind of computation, albeit still simple in principle, leads to a rapidly increasing number of cases regarding integration boundaries that are fairly awkward to handle. Therefore, we rather treat the convolution in terms of moment-generating functions $M_i(s) = \int_0^\infty e^{sx} f_i(x) dx = E\left[e^{sS_i}\right]$ for random variables S_i with densities $f_i(x)$. With independent variables, the convolution has the moment-generating function $M(s) = \prod_i M_i(s)$ [32]. With uniform distributions $f_i(x)$ plugged in, this yields a function from which we cannot easily infer the density of the convolution. Instead, we apply Chernoff-Hoeffding bounds to the tail probability of the convolution [32,35]: $P\left[\sum_i S_i > \delta\right] \leq \inf_{s \geq 0}\{e^{-s\delta} M(s)\}$ where the infimum on the right-hand side is either the minimum of the Chernoff bound function, computed by finding the roots of the first derivative, or a limit (e.g., for s approaching 0). This computation can be automated using computer algebra tools like Maple and its programming interface OpenMaple.

A great advantage of this approach is that it can be generalized to incorporate distributions other than uniform ones. Moreover, it can easily handle heterogeneous distributions with say some scores S_i being uniformly distributed and others following, for example, hyperexponential or Zipf distributions. Finally, using results from [35] we can even handle dependent random variables, although the corresponding generalized Chernoff-Hoeffding bounds may not be as strong as in the standard case. Assume that $S_1, ..., S_m$ are our random variables of interest. We construct a set of independent random variables $T_1, ..., T_m$ such that T_i has the same distribution as the marginal distribution S_i. For a partitioning $\delta = \delta_1 + ... + \delta_m$ for the tail quantile of interest consider the Chernoff bounds ε_i with $P[T_i > \delta_i] \leq \varepsilon_i$. [35] have shown that $P\left[\sum_i S_i > \delta\right] \leq \inf_{\delta_1+...+\delta_m=\delta}\{\max\{\varepsilon_i \mid i = 1..m\}\}$. While it is difficult to determine the best choice of the partitioning values δ_i, a good heuristic choice (that is guaranteed to yield correct bounds) is to set $\delta_i := \delta \cdot high_i / \sum_i high_i$ (i.e., choose the δ_i values in proportion to the $high_i$ values of the index lists). Computing these generalized bounds can be programmed as OpenMaple procedures.

3.2 Guarantees with Poisson Distributions

As the computation of convolutions and their bounds using OpenMaple incurs non-negligible overhead, we are also interested in approximations that are computationally cheaper. A form of distribution that has nice theoretical properties, can be efficiently evaluated, and is a reasonable fit for realistic score distributions (e.g., the tf*idf-based score distributions for terms in large Web corpora) is the Poisson distribution. For the fitting to the real distribution we assume that S_i is a discrete random variable with n_i equidistant values $v_j = 1 - j \cdot high_i / n_i$ ($j=0..n_i-1$) where n_i is the number of object ids in the index list L_i. Then the probability for an object having local score v_k is

$$P[S_i = v_k] = e^{-\alpha_i} \frac{\alpha_i^k}{k!}.$$ Here α_i is the parameter that we fit to the actual distribution.

The particularity of the Poisson distribution is that the convolution of m such distributions with parameters $\alpha_1, \ldots, \alpha_m$ is again a Poisson distribution with parameter $\alpha = \alpha_1 + \ldots + \alpha_m$, and it is the only distribution with this convenient property [2].

As the $high_i$ values change during the index scans we actually need to predict $P[\sum_{i \notin E(d)} S_i > v \mid S_i \leq high_i \text{ for } i \notin E(d)]$ where v is the largest value smaller than the relevant δ in the virtual value discretization. We lower-bound this probability as follows:

$$P\left[\sum_{i \notin E(d)} S_i > v \mid S_i \leq high_i \text{ for } i \notin E(d)\right]$$
$$= 1 - P\left[\sum_{i \notin E(d)} S_i \leq v \mid S_i \leq high_i \text{ for } i \notin E(d)\right]$$
$$= 1 - \frac{P\left[\sum_{i \notin E(d)} S_i \leq v \wedge (S_i \leq high_i \text{ for } i \notin E(d))\right]}{P[S_i \leq high_i \text{ for } i \notin E(d)]}$$
$$\geq 1 - \frac{P\left[\sum_{i \notin E(d)} S_i \leq v\right]}{\prod_{i \notin E(d)} P[S_i \leq high_i]}$$

For computing the values of the cumulative distribution, we use the efficient numerical method given in [34] based on the Incomplete Gamma Function.

3.3 Guarantees with Histograms

Real score distributions may sometimes be impossible to capture with basic distribution functions and parameter fitting. In such cases the only remaining method is to explicitly track the distribution in the form of a compact histogram. Since histogram construction is not exactly inexpensive, we precompute a histogram for the score distribution of each index list. At query time we first compute the convolution of the query-relevant histograms (and possibly of subsets of them). For simplicity we consider only equi-width histograms, but our approach could be easily generalized to more sophisticated histogram variants [26] (at higher run-time costs, however). For conservative probabilistic predictions we further assume that all values within one histogram cell coincide with the upper bound of the cell.

We choose the same number n of cells (e.g., between 10 and 100) for each basic histogram covering the score range (0.0, 1.0], and we use $t \cdot n$ cells for the convolution histogram over t basic histograms, with the same width $1/n$ as the basic histograms covering the range $(0.0, t]$. Cell i (for $i=0..n-1$ or $i=0..tn-1$) covers the interval $(lb[i], ub[i]]$ with $lb[i]=i/n$ and $ub[i]=(i+1)/n$. Each cell stores the frequency $freq[i]$ and the cumulative frequency $cum[i]$ of scores that fall into its interval. The convolution H of basic histograms $H_1, \ldots, H_t$ is computed by

$$H.freq[i] = \sum_{(i_1,\ldots,i_t) \text{ with } i_1+\ldots+i_t=i} H_1.freq[i_1] \cdot \ldots \cdot H_t.freq[i_t]$$
$$H.cum[i] = \sum_{j=0..i} H.freq[i]$$

The convolution histograms that we compute for a given query capture the complete distribution of possible global scores ($t=m$) and partial scores over unevaluated dimensions (here, we compute the convolution of the basic histograms for the $t=|\{1..m\}-E(d)|$ unevaluated dimensions).

As the index scans proceed, we are actually interested in the conditional probabilities of the form $P\left[\sum_{i \notin E(d)} S_i > \delta \mid S_i \leq high_i \text{ for } i \notin E(d)\right]$ where the $high_i$ values reflect the current positions in the index scans. Obviously dynamically rebuilding the histograms after every sorted access is out of the question. We have three ways of addressing this point. The first option is to conservatively bound the conditional probability, analogously to the Poisson approximation model:

$$P\left[\sum_{i \notin E(d)} S_i > \delta \mid S_i \leq high_i \text{ for } i \notin E(d)\right] \geq$$

$$1 - \frac{P\left[\sum_{i \notin E(d)} S_i \leq \delta\right]}{\prod_{i \notin E(d)} P[S_i \leq high_i]}$$ which can be directly looked up in the precomputed histograms.

The second option is to start with the full convolution histograms and dynamically "undo" the terms that contribute to $H.freq[i]$ as the $high_i$ values change during query execution. Suppose that $high_j$ changes from some value $ub[k]$ to $ub[k-1]$. Then we modify all $H.freq[i]$ values with $v_i \leq \sum_i high_i$ as follows: $H.freq[i] =$

$$H.freq[i] - \sum_{\substack{(i_1,\ldots,i_t) \\ \text{with } i_1+\ldots+i_t=i \\ \text{and } i_j=k}} H_1.freq[i_1] \cdot \ldots \cdot H_t.freq[i_t].$$

The subtrahend is also precomputed and additionally stored in cell k of the histogram for index list L_j. The computational overhead for the dynamic maintenance is $O(tn)$ whenever one of the index scans crosses a histogram cell boundary, but the, less critical, precomputation cost and the space for each histogram increase considerably ($O(t^2n^2)$ space instead of $O(tn)$).

Finally, the third way is to periodically recompute the histograms, after every r sorted accesses with r being in the order of a few hundred. Each time a convolution histogram is rebuilt from the precomputed basic histograms, the current $high_i$ values are taken into account; so the recomputation becomes cheaper and the histogram smaller as the index scans proceed towards lower local scores.

3.4 Extensions and Generalizations

Our framework for probabilistic predictions could be extended in three ways: 1) further classes of score distributions, 2) correlated local scores, and 3) more general score aggregation functions other than summations.

As for score distributions, we can accommodate a wide variety of distributions into the Chernoff-Hoeffding bound approach discussed in Subsection 3.1. For example, it would be straightforward to incorporate Zipf distributed scores where $P[S_i = v_k]$ for equidistant values v_k is proportional to $1/k$ and the cumulative distribution corresponds to the harmonic series, and we can also easily handle heterogeneous mixes of different distributions, say uniform for some index lists but Zipf for some highly skewed ones. For the histogram approach of Subsection 3.3, more general distributions are a non-issue, because histograms are approximations of arbitrary distributions.

As for correlations between the local scores from different index lists, the generalized Chernoff-Hoeffding bounds already provide an approach. The histogram approach, on the other hand, would have to use multidimensional histograms to capture joint distributions. We are not convinced that this is practically viable except for specialized settings. Multidimensional histograms over all index lists may be very space-consuming or sparse or inaccurate, and the subspace that is relevant for a given query is known only at query time when histogram building would already be part of the user-perceived response time. Fitting a parameterized multidimensional distribution, e.g., a multivariate Normal distribution, to the data seems more promising, but the decision for a particular type of distribution function would have to be carefully justified.

Finally, using monotonous score aggregation functions beyond simple sums is already supported, to a large extent, within our framework. A large class of aggregation options can simply be cast into the precomputation of local scores, so that the actual aggregation step again becomes a simple summation. For example, with weighted summation the weights for each dimension can be factored into the local scores; IR-style tf*idf-based scores are of this type for idf values can be viewed as dimension weights. Also note that cosine similarity in IR is usually reduced to summation (i.e., scalar products between document and query vectors) by pre-normalizing (L_2 norm) vector lengths to 1. Using maximum for score aggregation is even simpler than summation; instead of computing the convolution of several S_i distributions, we merely compute $P[\max_i S_i > \delta] = 1 - \prod_i P[S_i \leq \delta]$.

4. Query Evaluation Algorithms

Our query processing algorithms use the probabilistic models as predictors for the global scores of data objects that have not been fully evaluated or not seen at all in the index scans so far. Based on this central building block we have developed several algorithms that differ a) in their selection of candidates to which they apply the probabilistic predictions and b) in their actions that they take when a threshold test for a candidate fails (i.e., the candidate is unlikely to be able to qualify for the top-k result). All algorithms maintain the set of current top-k objects and the set of candidates organized as a hash table based on object ids.

4.1 Conservative Algorithm

A naive algorithm would simply predict the scores of all candidate objects in every step of the index scans and drop all candidates whose probabilities of qualifying for the top-k result are sufficiently low. This would incur very high overhead for probabilistic threshold tests; moreover, the score prediction for an object d would have to be recomputed whenever one of the $high_i$ values in the set $\{1..m\} - E(d)$ changes. A better way is to group the candidates by their $E(d)$ values, placing all objects with the same set of evaluated dimensions into one partition using their *bestscore* as priority. Then, it suffices to test the best object per group, i.e., the one with the highest predicted score. This object dominates all other candidates in the same group in terms of the probability of qualifying for the top-k result. Across groups, however, the top objects are not directly comparable.

Based on this observation, the *conservative algorithm* maintains a priority queue for each $E(d)$ group, up to $2^m - 1$ queues for a query with m specified conditions. Note that m is often much smaller than the dimensionality of the data space (e.g., for keyword queries over a text document space). The priority queues merely contain pointers to the hash-table entries of the candidate objects.

As an item d is evaluated at the current scan position pos_i in index list L_i, the conservative algorithm deletes d from its obsolete $E(d)$ queue and, if its *worstscore* still fails the threshold *min-k*, inserts it into the $E(d) \cup \{i\}$ queue using its updated *bestscore* as priority; the insertion is possible with cost $O(\log n)$ using a binomial heap or amortized cost $O(1)$ using a Fibonacci heap [15]. If $E(d) \cup \{i\} = \{1..m\}$, i.e., d is completely evaluated, d is dropped from the candidate list.

For periodic index pruning, e.g., after every r = 200 index-scanning steps, the top elements of all queues are probabilistically tested against the current threshold min-k; when a top element fails the test, then all elements of that queue are *dropped* from the candidate list. The algorithm proceeds with fewer candidates and eventually stops when all queues have become empty. Note that there is also one queue for $E(d) = \emptyset$ with a single *virtual element*, capturing the predicted score for an object that has not been seen at all so far.

Advancing the scan pointer in one index list may affect the priorities of other candidates, too, namely by possibly reducing the $high_i$ value of one dimension. But within one queue, this change affects all elements in the same way; so we can simply track $\sum\{high_i \mid i \notin E(d)\}$ per queue in space and time O(1).

4.2 Aggressive Algorithm

The *aggressive algorithm* is the extreme opposite of the conservative algorithm. It considers one candidate object for probabilistic testing, namely, a *virtual element* d with $E(d)=\emptyset$ at the current scan positions. If the score prediction for this object falls below the threshold *min-k*, the algorithm *stops* immediately. The prediction for this unknown object is based on the high scores at the current scan positions only. This item's *bestscore* yields an upper bound for all yet unseen documents, i.e., even without probabilistic pruning this algorithm typically stops before the truly best candidate would fail the *min-k* threshold and, thus, yields an approximate result only. The strength of the aggressive algorithm is its minimal overhead, but we do not expect it to perform well in terms of result precision.

4.3 Progressive Algorithm

In between the overly eager behavior of the aggressive algorithm and the substantial overhead of the conservative algorithm is the *progressive algorithm* that maintains a single priority queue for all candidate objects. Again, the queue elements are ordered by their *bestscore* values. In each step the priority of the current candidate, i.e., the one fetched from the index list, is updated and the queue is accordingly maintained.

The algorithm is conservative for it does not immediately track the *bestscore* changes that result from reduced $high_i$ values in each step, but leaves the *bestscore* values higher than they actually are. Otherwise all queue elements would have to be updated, which would amount to rebuilding the entire queue. An additional implementation trick that we employ is that the queue is periodically traversed, e.g., again after every *r=200* index-scanning steps, and we tentatively compute the up-to-date bestscore values of each queue element based on the current $high_i$ values. All elements that do no longer pass the threshold test are dropped from the queue. The priorities of the "surviving" elements are not updated to avoid a massive batch of queue operations. So this periodic removal of unneeded queue elements can be seen as a kind of *garbage collection* without having to rebuild the entire queue.

In conjunction with the periodic garbage collection, the progressive algorithm invokes the probabilistic predictor for each element of the queue using its up-to-date *bestscore*. All objects that fail this probabilistic threshold test are dropped from the queue. The algorithm stops when its queue becomes empty or the top element's *bestscore* falls below the threshold *min-k*.

4.4 Smart Algorithm

The progressive algorithm could stop earlier if it reconsidered all elements in the priority queue with the changing $high_i$ values reflected in each step. In the *smart algorithm* we periodically rebuild the entire priority queue of current candidates with the currently known $high_i$ values taken into consideration. By default the queue is rebuilt every *r=200* steps. The rebuilding has amortized cost O(n) for n queue elements, using a Fibonacci heap, or O(n log n) with a binomial heap [15]. For an online algorithm operating on very large index lists this cost may still be out of the question. Therefore, the smart algorithm maintains only a *bounded priority queue*. Whenever it is rebuilt only the best *b* elements are kept, with *b* being in the order of a few hundred. Newly encountered data objects are admitted to enlarge the queue until the next rebuild; so the maximum size is actually *b + r* but every rebuild truncates the size back to *b*.

As the priority queue is fully up-to-date after every rebuild, the smart algorithm can take more aggressive actions than the progressive method with regard to candidate pruning. If the top element of the rebuilt queue does not pass the probabilistic threshold test, the smart algorithm immediately *stops* all index scans and terminates.

4.5 Common Framework

All four algorithms share the same algorithmic skeleton illustrated by the pseudocode of Figure 2. We refer to this code as the *Prob-sorted family of algorithms*. Note that, in addition to the probabilistic predictions and corresponding probabilistic threshold tests, all algorithms also include the original Fagin test to compare the maximum *bestscore* of all candidates against the *worstscore* of the current top-k objects. If this test fails all index scans can be stopped immediately, and this extra test is so light-weight that we can always include it.

Prob-sorted (RebuildPeriod r, QueueBound b):
...
scan all lists L_i (i=1..m) in parallel:
   ...same code as TA-sorted...
   // queue management
   for all priority queues q for which d is relevant do
      insert d into q with priority bestscore(d);
// periodic clean-up
if step-number mod r = 0 then
      // dropping of queues; multiple unbounded queues
      if strategy = Conservative then
         for all priority queues q do
            if prob[top(q) can qualify for top-k] < ε then
               drop all elements of q;
      // garbage collection; single unbounded queue
      if strategy = Progressive then
         for all queue elements e in q do
            best(e) := bestscore of e with current $high_i$ values;
            if best(e) < min-k then drop e from q;
            if prob[e can qualify for top-k]<ε then drop e from q;
      // rebuild; single bounded queue
      if strategy = Smart then
         for all queue elements e in q do
            update bestscore(e) with current $high_i$ values;
         rebuild bounded queue with best b elements;
         if prob[top(q) can qualify for top-k] < ε then exit;
      // no queues; greedy threshold approximation
      if strategy = Aggressive then
         if prob[virtual-element qualifies for top-k] < ε then exit;
if all queues are empty then exit;

Fig. 2: Pseudocode for Prob-sorted family of algorithms

Let us finally comment on our implementation of the *TA-sorted* baseline algorithm. The original papers on TA do not specify any concrete data structures for the candidate set and how to determine the best candidate in each step. We decided to implement these aspects analogously to the progressive Prob-sorted algorithm, by maintaining a single priority queue with *bestscore* values as priorities. Like before, we do not update all queue elements when one of the $high_i$ values changes, but only update the element currently encountered in the index scan and perform periodic garbage collection with tentative updates.

5. Guarantees for Top-k Results

The probabilistic predictions in our query processing strategies immediately lead to probabilistic *guarantees* from a user viewpoint if we restrict the action upon a failed threshold test to *dropping candidates* but stop the entire algorithm only if we run out of candidates. This is the situation given in the conservative and progressive algorithms. In this case the probability of missing an object that should be in the true top-k result is the same as erroneously dropping a candidate, and this error, call it p_{miss}, is bounded by the probability ε that we use in the probabilistic predictor when assessing a candidate. For the recall of the top-k result, i.e., the fraction of truly top-k objects that the approximate method returns, this means that $P[recall = r/k] = P[precision = r/k] =$

$$\binom{k}{r}(1-p_{miss})^r p_{miss}^{(k-r)} \leq \binom{k}{r}(1-\varepsilon)^r \varepsilon^{(k-r)}$$

with r denoting the number of correct results in the approximate top k. We can then efficiently compute Chernoff-Hoeffding bounds for this binomial distribution. Note that the very same probabilistic guarantee holds for the precision of the returned top-k result, simply because recall and precision use the same denominator k. The predicted expected precision then is

$E[precision] = \sum_{r=0..k} P[precision = r/k] \cdot r/k = (1-\varepsilon)$.

For the strategies that test top elements of priority queues and, upon a failed probabilistic threshold test, *stop* the entire algorithm, carrying over the candidate-error probability ε to an argument about recall and precision guarantees would be more sophisticated.

6. Experiments

6.1 Setup

All strategies of our framework are implemented in a comprehensive testbed, using Java and Oracle9i. We performed experiments on a 3 GHz dual Pentium PC with 2 GB of memory. Index lists were stored in the Oracle database, but were fetched in large blocks and cached in the Java program. We used two different datasets with three different workloads in the experiments.

The *Gov setting* uses the data of the TREC-12 Web Track which uses the .Gov Data Collection. It consists of about 1.25 million documents (mostly HTML and PDF) from a large crawl of the .gov Internet domain. We used the original 50 queries from the Web Track's topic distillation task, which are keyword queries with up to 5 keywords. Examples are "legalization marijuana", "Lewis Clark expedition", "airbag injuries death". For systematic experimentation we studied three variations of the local scores in the index lists: a) the *original* scores computed by $tf * log\ idf$, with tf and idf normalized by the maximum tf value of each document and the maximum idf value in the corpus, respectively, b) randomly assigned scores with a (0,1] *uniform* distribution, c) randomly assigned scores with a *Zipf* distribution starting from low scores, so that low scores are much more frequent

In the *expanded Gov (XGov) setting* we wanted to study the impact of the number of query-relevant index lists and modified the queries by adding synonyms and other strongly related terms to the keywords of a query. These additional terms were taken from the synonym entries and descriptions of the WordNet thesaurus [20], where we manually identified for each original keyword the relevant word sense. This query expansion typically doubled the number of keywords per query; the longest query contained 20 keywords ("legalization marijuana cannabis euphoric drug abuse pot smoke ...").

The *Imdb setting* used the data of the Internet Movie Database (http://www.imdb.com) to study our methods' performance on a combination of text and structured attributes. The data contains about 375,000 movies and more than 1,200,000 persons (actors, etc.), and we prepared it into a four-attribute object-relational table with the schema Movies (Title, Genre, Actors, Description) where Title and Description are text attributes and Genre and Actors are set-valued categorical attributes. Genre typically contains 2 or 3 genres, and actors were limited to those that appeared in at least 5 different movies. For similarity scores among Genre values and among actors we precomputed the Dice coefficient for each pair of Genre values and for each pair of actors that appeared together in at least 5 movies. So the similarity for genres or actors x and y is set to $\frac{2(\#movies\ containing\ x\ and\ y)}{\#movies\ with\ x\ +\ \#movies\ with\ y}$, and the index list for x contains entries for similar values y, too. A typical query is Title $\supseteq$ {Space} $\wedge$ Genre $\supseteq$ {SciFi} $\wedge$ Actors $\supseteq$ {Harrison Ford} $\wedge$ Description $\supseteq$ {Robot, War}. We compiled 20 queries of this kind by asking colleagues. Note that our similarity scoring does not require a match to satisfy all conditions.

The algorithms compared in the experiments are the four Prob-sorted methods presented in Section 4:
- *Prob-con:* the conservative algorithm,
- *Prob-agg:* the aggressive algorithm,
- *Prob-pro:* the progressive algorithm, and
- *Prob-smart:* the smart algorithm.

For each of them we considered different options for probabilistic prediction. The baseline against which we compare our methods is:

- *TA-sorted*: the threshold algorithm with sorted access only, in the implementation discussed in Section 4.5.

All algorithms access index lists in round-robin manner and cache large index blocks in memory.

6.2 Evaluation Metrics

For efficiency comparison we collected the following measures:

- *accesses*: # sorted access to all index lists altogether,
- *time*: the wall-clock elapsed time,
- *memory*: the peak level of working memory for priority queues.

For assessing the quality of the approximate top-k query results we collected the following measures:

- *precision*: the fraction of top-k results in an approximate result that belongs to the true top-k result,
- *recall*: the fraction of top-k results in the true result that were returned by the approximate top-k query,
- *rank distance*: the footrule distance [27] between the ranks of the approximate top-k results and their true ranks in the exact top-k result, i.e., $\frac{1}{k}\sum_{i=1..k}|i-truerank(i)|$. We did not use Spearman's rank correlation as we wanted to assess only the top k ranks of the approximate result rather than all ranks, but the Spearman measure requires comparing two permutations of the same sets of possible ranks.
- *score error*: the absolute error for approximate vs. exact top-k scores: $\frac{1}{k}\sum_{i=1..k}|score_i^{(approx)} - score_i^{(exact)}|$.

Note that precision and recall have identical values in our setup, because they have the same denominator k. The baseline for precision and recall is the top-k result of the exact TA-sorted algorithm.

6.3 Results

6.3.1 Baseline Experiment

In the baseline experiment all probabilistic predictors use histograms with cell width 0.01 (i.e., n=100 bins for each basic histogram). Convolution histograms were precomputed at query initiation time, and the impact of changing $high_i$ values was taken into consideration by periodically (i.e., every 200 sorted-access steps) rebuilding the remaining parts of the convolution histograms.

We set the probabilistic prediction confidence level to 90 percent, that is, ε is set to 0.1. For the smart strategy with a bounded priority queue the queue size was set to b=200 entries. We measured top-k queries with k=20.

Figures 3 and 4 show the performance results for the five algorithms under comparison for the Gov and the Imdb settings, respectively. For Gov the chart is based on the original, tf*idf-derived, scores. We present the three efficiency metrics in terms of benchmark totals over all queries, and the three result-quality metrics as macro-averages over all queries. For the Gov setting micro-averaged values are heavily biased by a few long-running queries; for these queries the performance gains of Prob-sorted over TA-sorted are even significantly higher than the macro-averaged values indicate. Figure 5 shows the corresponding results for the XGov setting, which posed a stress test to the queue management.

	# sorted accesses	elapsed time [s]	max queue size	precision	rank distance	score error
TA-sorted	2263652	148.7	10849	1	0	0
Prob-con	993414	25.6	29207	0.87	16.9	0.007
Prob-agg	20435	0.6	0	0.42	75.1	0.089
Prob-pro	1659706	44.2	6551	0.87	16.8	0.006
Prob-smart	527980	15.9	400	0.69	39.5	0.031

Fig.3: Performance of Prob-sorted vs. TA-sorted for Gov

	# sorted accesses	elapsed time [s]	max queue size	precision	rank distance	score error
TA-sorted	1003650	201.9	12628	1	0	0
Prob-con	463562	17.8	14990	0.71	119.9	0.18
Prob-agg	41821	0.7	0	0.18	171.5	0.39
Prob-pro	490041	69.0	9173	0.75	122.5	0.14
Prob-smart	403981	12.7	400	0.54	126.7	0.25

Fig.4: Performance of Prob-sorted vs. TA-sorted for Imdb

	# sorted accesses	elapsed time [s]	max queue size	precision	rank distance	score error
TA-sorted	22403490	7908	70896	1	0	0
Prob-con	10165677	6448	51893	0.90	10.9	0.038
Prob-agg	133745	2	0	0.35	80.7	0.182
Prob-pro	20006283	1791	12435	0.95	9.3	0.031
Prob-smart	18287636	1066	400	0.88	14.5	0.035

Fig.5: Prob-sorted vs. TA-sorted for XGov

Efficiency. The results demonstrate the significant cost savings that the Prob-sorted family of algorithms can achieve compared to TA-sorted. In terms of the number of sorted accesses the conservative algorithm Prob-con gains more than a factor of two, and the smart algorithm Prob-smart achieves even a factor of four for Gov. In terms of run-times, the two probabilistic algorithms even reduce the cost by an order of magnitude. Note that the run-time is not simply a linear function of the sorted accesses but reflects also cache and queue management costs. For the Gov and Imdb settings Prob-con temporarily even created a larger queue than the TA-sorted baseline using periodic garbage collection, but Prob-con dropped this large queue quickly after initialization and then distributed the remaining candidate items to multiple small queues. Interestingly, the progressive algorithm Prob-pro did not do as well as expected; its capabilities for early pruning are limited and its queue management, which required many insert and delete operations, is a significant cost factor. The aggressive method Prob-agg outperformed all competitors, but as expected, its result quality was rather poor; so we would not really consider it a winner.

For individual queries, especially those that involve very long index lists, the savings are even more impressive. For example, for the Gov query "weather hazard extremes" Prob-con and Prob-smart needed 25802 and 19401 sorted accesses with run-times 0.59 and 0.68 seconds, whereas TA-sorted required 160002 accesses and ran in 55.60 seconds (for k=20, at precision 0.9 and 0.75, resp.). In the Imdb setting, the reductions of sorted accesses were not as high as for Gov but the run-time reductions reached a factor of about 10 at a high macro-averaged precision of 0.71 to 0.75. A typical query like "Genre ⊇ {Western} ∧ Actor ⊇ {John Wayne, Katherine Hepburn} ∧ Description ⊇ {sheriff, marshall}" required 10802 sorted accesses for both Prob-con and Prob-smart with run-times 0.41 and 0.51 seconds, whereas TA-sorted performed 26402 accesses in time 4.92 seconds (for k=20, both at precision 0.7).

Finally, for XGov queries with more keywords per query the overhead for queue management and probabilistic predictions became a truly decisive issue. Among the methods with acceptable to very good precision, Prob-con performed best in terms of sorted-access savings, but the run-time gains were only modest because of the overhead of maintaining up to 2^m-1 queues. Prob-pro and Prob-smart were the clear winners in terms of run-time, with acceleration factors up to 8 compared to TA-sorted. Interestingly, these methods did not save that many sorted accesses but benefited greatly from their efficient queue management.

Result Quality. The measurements of result quality show very good results for Prob-con and Prob-pro and still acceptable results for Prob-smart. Prob-con and Prob-pro achieved nearly 90 percent precision (and the same recall) for the Gov setting. For the Imdb setting, the precision figures were worse, one reason being that Genre scores had a major influence on the overall ranking and the small number of different values led to a fairly discontinuous score distribution with big gaps and many ties, causing some inaccuracy of probabilistic predictions. We will discuss the influence of the various predictors in Subsection 6.3.2.

The other two result-quality metrics show that the user-perceived "loss" of an approximate result actually seems well tolerable. The average rank distance for Prob-con and Prob-pro was only around 16. For *k=20* or higher this seems acceptable, in particular, when we consider that the average rank distance is dominated by a few outliers with very high rank distance. In terms of score error, the loss even seems negligible. So by and large, the objects that are returned by the Prob-sorted algorithms are nearly as good as the exact top-k results.

Again, the results for the Imdb setting were not quite as good as for Gov. We manually inspected a fair number of the results and found that in most cases the results would be considered as good matches by a human user. For example, the query "Genre ⊇ {Thriller} ∧ Actor ⊇ {Arnold Schwarzenegger} ∧ Description ⊇ {robot}" returned top results Terminator3, The 6th Day, Total Recall, Die Hard 2, Star Wars IV, etc. (recall that top-k results do not necessarily have to satisfy all query conditions).

For XGov, Prob-con, Pro-pro, and Prob-smart showed very good precision, rank distance, and score error values.

6.3.2 Sensitivity Studies

We studied the influence of several parameters on the performance of our four *Prob-sorted* algorithms: the probabilistic prediction confidence level 1−ε, the result size k for top-k queries, the number n of bins per basic histogram, and the maximum size b of a bounded priority queue for the smart algorithm.

Figure 6 shows the results for varying the ε parameter (the vertical dashed line is the baseline setting). The curves show that for ε below 5 percent the progressive and smart algorithms achieve only marginal savings. For ε between 5 and 20 percent, on the other hand, these two methods offer excellent benefit/cost ratios. The conservative method performs best according to the theory of probabilistic guarantees. Already small ε values like 1 percent lead to significant cost savings, and even ε values as large as 50 percent, which results in sorted-access savings of more than a factor of 4, still yield 70 percent precision. The aggressive method always exhibits great cost savings, but this is at the expense of precision values of 40 to 50 percent only. Still, this may possibly be the preferred method in applications with tight response time demands.

We also compared the measured precision with the expected precision that we predict as a function of ε according to the formulas of Section 5. For Prob-con and Prob-pro the prediction model is fairly accurate. The absolute difference between predicted and measured precision is only one or two percent for ε values of 0.2 or less; it increases for larger ε but the prediction is conservative in that it lower-bounds the measured precision.

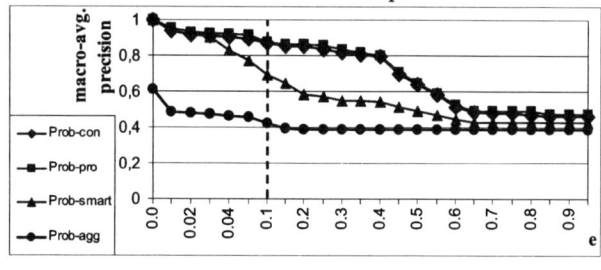

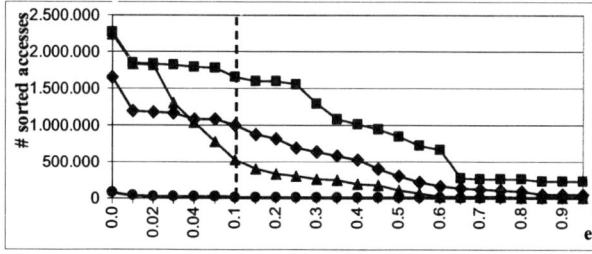

Figure 6: Performance as a function of ε

For space limitation we do not include the charts for the sensitivity studies regarding the k, n, and b parameters and briefly discuss only the main insights. With increasing k which was varied between 1 and 200, all methods exhibit linearly increasing sorted-access costs but with different gradients. For large k, the gains of Prob-con, Prob-pro, and Prob-smart compared to TA-sorted are even higher than in the baseline setting; at the same time the precision of the approximate top-k results becomes even better for high k. The performance for different numbers n of histogram bins is fairly stable over a wide range of settings. Between 50 and 1000 bins the relative performance of the different algorithms does not change much; below 50 bins the Prob-smart method does not work that well anymore but Prob-con and Prob-prog remain more robust and show consistently good performance even with down to 25 bins per histogram. Similarly, we found that the maximum queue size parameter b for the Prob-smart algorithm is largely uncritical. Queue size limits as low as b=100 still worked very well for k=20.

6.3.3 Impact of Probabilistic Predictions

Finally, we compared our different approaches for probabilistic prediction: histograms vs. Poisson approximations vs. Chernoff bounds based on the assumption of uniform distributions vs. Chernoff bounds considering term correlations. We limit the presentation to results for the Prob-con algorithm with k=20, ε=0.1, n=100, and the Gov setting. Due to the high overhead of computing Chernoff bounds with OpenMaple, we removed the three most expensive queries from the Web Tracks's topic distillation task which consumed about 40 percent of the overall run time with 50 queries.

Figure 7 shows the performance comparisons for the original tf*idf scores. The dashed line is the predicted precision (for Prob-con this is simply 1–ε). Similar experiments have been run for the artificially generated Uniform- and Zipf-distributed scores on the Gov index lists.

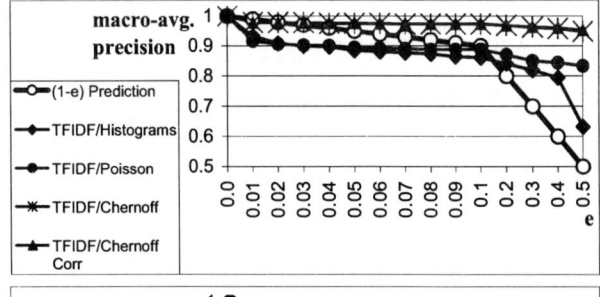

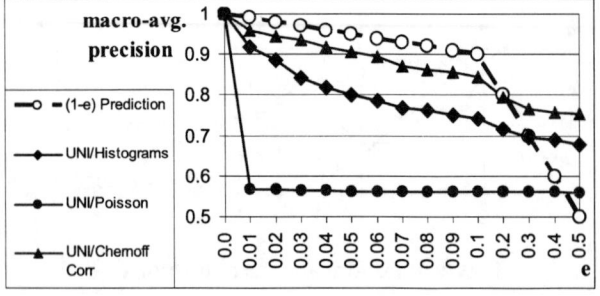

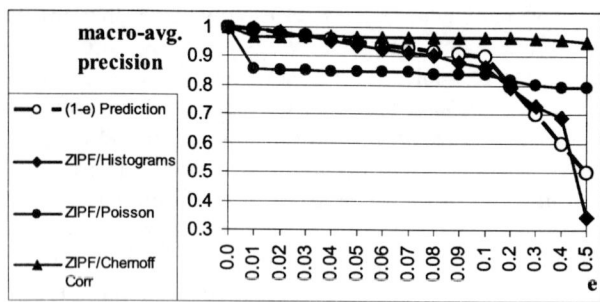

Figure 7: Precision of probabilistic predictors for tf*idf, Uniform-, and Zipf-distributed scores

The charts show that histograms provide the most accurate score predictions. A comparison with the Uniform- and Zipf-distributed scores shows that they are a flexible solution to capture different score distributions already for n as low as 50 to 100 buckets in (0,1]. Both the Poisson estimator and, particularly, the Chernoff-bound method (the latter assuming Uniform-distributed scores) are overly conservative and overestimate score probabilities for the tf*idf and the Zipf case. The difference between the Chernoff-bound methods with and without independence assumption is not really significant for the Gov data, but this could be different in other settings. For Uniform-distributed scores the Chernoff-bounds are fairly accurate over a wide range of ε, whereas, as expected, Poisson estimators do not work for the Uniform case, because they underestimate the tail probability. The Zipf distribution is closer to the original tf*idf score distribution, but has a longer tail of low scores, for which the Poisson estimator works better, but, again, the Chernoff-bounds behave overly conservative.

The advantage of the Poisson approximation method is its very little overhead, whereas the overhead of the histogram method increases with dimensionality. But note that even with the higher-dimensional XGov workload the algorithms still achieved major run-time gains using histograms with dynamic convolutions. The Chernoff-bound predictors are largely independent of the dimensionality, but they suffer from huge startup costs for invoking OpenMaple. For a practically viable solution one would have to hand-code the Maple computations (which involve differentiation and finding roots numerically) in C or C++.

Finally, our model for precision guarantees developed in Section 5 works very well for the Prob-con algorithm. The Prob-pro and Prob-smart algorithms deviate from this basic statistical model, because they merge all candidates into a single queue and Prob-smart even bounds this queue and heuristically stops after testing the top item, only. Here the predictions were reasonably accurate for small ε but degraded and became overly conservative for ε higher than 5 percent. Improving this is subject of future work.

6.4 Discussion

Our comprehensive experiments have shown that Prob-sorted algorithms can achieve major performance gains, in terms of both sorted accesses and actual run-time, and at the same time provide probabilistic guarantees for result precision and recall. Among the four competing algorithms, Prob-con and Prob-smart turned out to be the most interesting ones. Prob-con is closest to the theory of probabilistic guarantees and does best in terms of result quality; Prob-smart offers the best benefit/cost ratio. Both methods achieve run-time gains by an order of magnitude compared to TA-sorted. All four Prob-sorted methods are fairly robust with regard to parameter settings; there is no need for sophisticated tuning. For score predictions, we believe that histograms are the best choice from an engineering viewpoint, but the other two methods showed good results and certainly deserve further studies, too.

7. Concluding Remarks

The novel Prob-sorted family of algorithms that we introduced in this paper are based on two major cornerstones: 1) probabilistic score predictions for trading off a small amount of top-k result quality for a drastic reduction of sorted accesses, and 2) intelligent management of priority queues for efficient implementation. We believe that our experiments have convincingly demonstrated the significant benefits of our approach. We plan to continue the studies of efficient memory management for top-k algorithms, and our future work also includes applying these techniques to ranked retrieval of XML data and integrating them into our XXL search engine [37].

References

[1] S. Agrawal, S. Chaudhuri, G. Das, A. Gionis: Automated Ranking of Database Query Results. CIDR 2003

[2] A.O. Allen: Probability, Statistics, and Queueing Theory with Computer Science Applications. Academic Press, 1990

[3] G. Amato et al.: Region proximity in metric spaces and its use for approximate similarity search. TOIS 21(2), 2003

[4] V.N. Anh, O. de Kretser, A. Moffat: Vector-Space Ranking with Effective Early Termination. SIGIR 2001

[5] K.S. Beyer et al.: When Is "Nearest Neighbor" Meaningful? ICDT 1999

[6] C. Böhm et al.: Searching in high-dimensional spaces: Index structures for improving the performance of multimedia databases. ACM Comput. Surv. 33(3), 2001

[7] S. Brin, L. Page: The Anatomy of a Large-Scale Hypertextual Web Search Engine. WWW Conf. 1998

[8] N. Bruno, S. Chaudhuri, L. Gravano: Top-k selection queries over relational databases: Mapping strategies and performance evaluation. TODS 27(2), 2002

[9] N. Bruno, L. Gravano, A. Marian: Evaluating Top-k Queries over Web-Accessible Databases. ICDE 2002

[10] D. Carmel et al.: Static Index Pruning for Information Retrieval Systems. SIGIR 2001

[11] K.C.-C. Chang, S.-W. Hwang: Minimal probing: supporting expensive predicates for top-k queries. SIGMOD 2002

[12] S. Chaudhuri, L. Gravano, A. Marian: Optimizing Top-K Selection Queries over Multimedia Repositories, to appear in TKDE 2004.

[13] P. Ciaccia, M. Patella: PAC Nearest Neighbor Queries: Approximate and Controlled Search in High-Dimensional and Metric Spaces. ICDE 2000

[14] P. Ciaccia, M. Patella: Searching in metric spaces with user-defined and approximate distances. TODS 27 (4), 2002

[15] T.H. Cormen, C.E. Leiserson, R.L. Rivest, C. Stein: Introduction to Algorithms. MIT Press, 2001

[16] W.B. Croft, J. Lafferty: Language Modeling for Information Retrieval. Kluwer, 2003

[17] D. Donjerkovic, R. Ramakrishnan: Probabilistic Optimization of Top N Queries, VLDB 1999

[18] R. Fagin: Combining Fuzzy Information from Multiple Systems, J. Comput. Syst. Sci. 58(1), 1999

[19] R. Fagin et al.: Optimal aggregation algorithms for middleware. J. Comput. Syst. Sci. 66(4), 2003.

[20] C. Fellbaum (Editor): WordNet: An Electronic Lexical Database, MIT Press, 1998

[21] N. Fuhr, N. Gövert, M. Abolhassani: Retrieval Quality vs. Effectiveness of Relevance-oriented Search in XML Documents. TR, Univ. Duisburg, 2003

[22] U. Güntzer et al.: Optimizing Multi-Feature Queries for Image Databases. VLDB 2000

[23] U. Güntzer et al.: Towards Efficient Multi-Feature Queries in Heterogeneous Environments. ITCC 2001.

[24] G. R. Hjaltason, H. Samet: Distance Browsing in Spatial Databases. TODS 24 (2), 1999

[25] G.R. Hjaltason, H. Samet: Index-driven similarity search in metric spaces. TODS 28(4), 2003.

[26] Y.E. Ioannidis: The History of Histograms (Abridged). VLDB 2003

[27] M. Kendall, J.D. Gibbons: Rank Correlation Methods. Oxford University Press, 1990

[28] X. Long, T. Suel: Optimized Query Execution in Large Search Engines with Global Page Ordering. VLDB 2003

[29] A. Marian et al.: Evaluating Top-k Queries over Web-Accessible Databases. TODS 29(2), 2004

[30] A. Moffat, J. Zobel: Self-Indexing Inverted Files for Fast Text Retrieval. TOIS 14(4), 1996

[31] A. Natsev et al.: Supporting Incremental Join Queries on Ranked Inputs. VLDB 2001

[32] R. Nelson: Probability, Stochastic Processes, and Queueing Theory, Springer, 1995

[33] S. Nepal, M. V. Ramakrishna: Query Processing Issues in Image (Multimedia) Databases. ICDE 1999

[34] W.H. Press et al.: Numerical Recipes in C. Cambridge Univ.Press, 1992

[35] A. Siegel: Towards a Usable Theory of Chernoff Bounds for Heterogeneous and Partially Dependent Random Variables. TR1995-685, Courant Inst., New York Univ., 1995

[36] Y. Tao, C. Faloutsos, D. Papadias: The Power-Method: A Comprehensive Estimation Technique for Multi-Dimensional Queries. CIKM 2003

[37] A. Theobald, G. Weikum: The Index-Based XXL Search Engine for Querying XML Data with Relevance Ranking. EDBT 2002

[38] C.T. Yu et al.: Database selection for processing k nearest neighbors queries in distributed environments. JCDL 2001

STEPS Towards Cache-Resident Transaction Processing

Stavros Harizopoulos

Carnegie Mellon University
stavros@cs.cmu.edu

Anastassia Ailamaki

Carnegie Mellon University
natassa@cs.cmu.edu

Abstract

Online transaction processing (OLTP) is a multi-billion dollar industry with high-end database servers employing state-of-the-art processors to maximize performance. Unfortunately, recent studies show that CPUs are far from realizing their maximum intended throughput because of delays in the processor caches. When running OLTP, instruction-related delays in the memory subsystem account for 25 to 40% of the total execution time. In contrast to data, instruction misses cannot be overlapped with out-of-order execution, and instruction caches cannot grow as the slower access time directly affects the processor speed. The challenge is to alleviate the instruction-related delays without increasing the cache size.

We propose *Steps*, a technique that minimizes instruction cache misses in OLTP workloads by multiplexing concurrent transactions and exploiting common code paths. One transaction paves the cache with instructions, while close followers enjoy a nearly miss-free execution. *Steps* yields up to 96.7% reduction in instruction cache misses for each additional concurrent transaction, and at the same time eliminates up to 64% of mispredicted branches by loading a repeating execution pattern into the CPU. This paper (a) describes the design and implementation of *Steps*, (b) analyzes *Steps* using microbenchmarks, and (c) shows *Steps* performance when running TPC-C on top of the Shore storage manager.

1 Prologue

In the past decade, research has proposed techniques to identify and reduce CPU performance bottlenecks in database workloads. As memory access times improve much slower than processor speed, performance is bound by instruction and data cache misses that cause expensive main-memory accesses. Research [AD+99][LB+98][SBG02] shows that decision-support (DSS) applications are predominantly delayed by *data cache misses*, whereas OLTP is bounded by *instruction cache misses*. Although several techniques can reduce data cache misses (larger caches, out-of-order execution, better data placement), none of these can effectively address instruction caches.

1.1 Instruction cache behavior in OLTP

To maximize first-level instruction cache (L1-I cache) utilization and minimize stalls, application code should have few branches (exhibiting high *spatial locality*), a repeating pattern when deciding whether to follow a branch (yielding low *branch misprediction rate*), and most importantly, the "working set" code footprint should fit in the L1-I cache. Unfortunately, OLTP workloads exhibit the exact opposite behavior [KP+98]. A study on Oracle reports a 556KB OLTP code footprint [LB+98]. With modern CPUs having 16-64KB L1-I cache sizes, OLTP code paths are too long to achieve cache-residency. Moreover, the importance of L1-I cache stalls increases with larger L2 caches (Fig. 1a, stalls shown as non-overlapping components; I-cache stalls are actually 41% of the total execution time [KP+98]). As a large L1-I cache may adversely impact the CPU's clock frequency, chip designers cannot increase L1-I sizes despite the growth in secondary caches (Fig. 1b). The increasing gap between cache levels makes L1-I cache misses the most important CPU stall factor in OLTP.

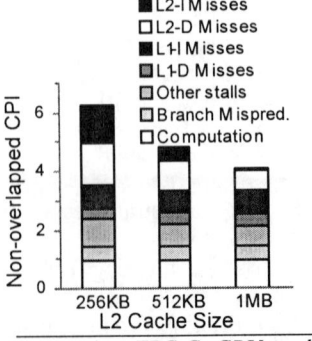

Figure 1a. *TPC-C CPU stall breakdown on PentiumPro. With larger L2 cache size L1-I misses become the dominant stall factor (3rd box from top).* [KP+98]

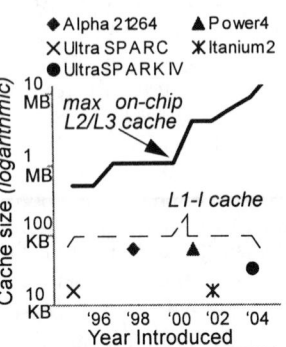

Figure 1b. *A decade-spanning trend shows that L1-I caches do not grow, while secondary, on-chip caches become increasingly larger.*

Permission to copy without fee all or part of this material is granted provided that the copies are not made or distributed for direct commercial advantage, the VLDB copyright notice and the title of the publication and its date appear, and notice is given that copying is by permission of the Very Large Data Base Endowment. To copy otherwise, or to republish, requires a fee and/or special permission from the Endowment.

**Proceedings of the 30th VLDB Conference,
Toronto, Canada, 2004**

1.2 Related research

The full spectrum of approaches to improve instruction cache performance includes the following three areas:

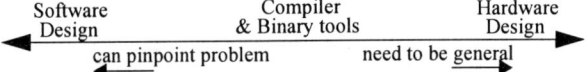

At the hardware end, chip designers study database workload behavior and respond with higher-performance caches, but they are bound by design restrictions on the L1-I cache size [HP96]. Hardware enhancements apply to all workloads, and thus cannot effectively target a specific weakness of database workloads. At the binary representation level, compilers optimize DBMS code for a given set of hardware architectures [RV+97]. This area studies instruction traces and focuses on increasing the cache hit rate by reorganizing the binary code [RB+01]. Compilers still cannot "see" the root of the problem and thus, can partially alleviate L1-I cache misses only for statically trained workload instances.

A software designer has the best insight as to why the program incurs cache misses. For example, studying data cache access patterns and changing the memory page layout proved to be a key factor for reducing data cache misses [AD+01]. While the payoff in software approaches may be larger, improving instruction cache behavior for the entire code (typically millions of lines) is a great challenge. To our knowledge, this paper is the first to address instruction cache misses in transaction processing by proposing small changes in the DBMS code.

1.3 *Steps* to cache-resident code

We propose to exploit the high degree of concurrency that characterizes transaction processing workloads to maximize instruction sharing in the cache across different transactions. Consider, for instance, a hundred concurrent transactions executing the same high-level operation, e.g., record lookup using a B-tree index. Since the code working set typically overwhelms the L1-I cache and context switching occurs at random points, each transaction execution incurs new instruction misses.

To alleviate the problem, we propose a technique called *Synchronized Transactions through Explicit Processor Scheduling*, or *Steps*. *Steps* allows *only one* transaction to incur the *compulsory* instruction misses, while the rest of the transactions can piggyback in order to always find the instructions they need in the cache. To achieve this, *Steps* identifies the points in the code the cache fills up and performs a quick context-switch so that other transactions can execute the cache-resident code. We implemented *Steps* inside the Shore storage manager [Ca+94]. Figure 2a shows that, when running a group of transactions performing an indexed selection on a real machine with 64KB instruction cache, L1-I cache misses are reduced by 96.7% for each additional concurrent thread.

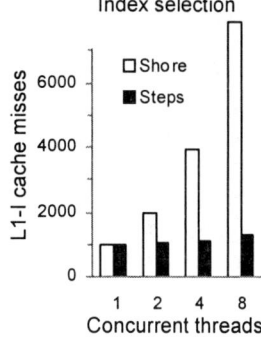
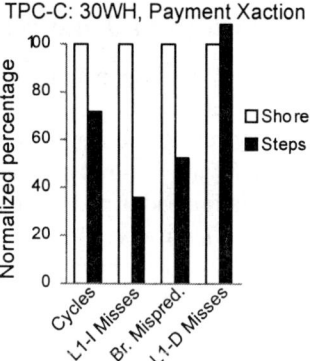

Figure 2a. *For a group of threads performing a tuple retrieval on a similar index,* Steps *practically eliminates additional L1-I misses.*

Figure 2b. *When 300 users run the TPC-C Payment transaction on a dataset of 30 Warehouses,* Steps *outperforms Shore on all of the time-critical events.*

A real transactional workload, however, includes different types of transactions and indices, involves mechanisms for logging and deadlock detection, and its execution is unpredictable due to frequent I/O and lock requests. *Steps* is designed to work with any OLTP workload; we illustrate our results using the widely accepted transactional benchmark TPC-C [Gra93]. Figure 2b shows that *Steps* running the Payment transaction in a 30-Warehouse configuration reduces instruction misses by 65% and mispredicted branches by 48%, while at the same time produces a 39% speedup on a real machine with 64KB L1-I cache. *Steps* incurs a 8% increase in the number of first-level data cache (L1-D) misses, which does not affect performance because the total number of L1-D cache misses is low and the penalty is easily hidden by instruction-level parallelism and out-of-order execution [AD+99].

1.4 Contributions and paper organization

This paper proposes a software technique to minimize instruction-related stalls for transactional database workloads. We demonstrate the validity and usefulness of *Steps* using the TPC-C benchmark running on Shore, a prototype state-of-the-art storage manager with similar behavior to commercial database systems [AD+01]. We use both real hardware (two different processors) and a full-system simulator. We focus on performance metrics that are not affected by the specifics of our system, and most importantly, we report *aggregate* (full-system) results for the execution time and cache usage statistics[1].

The paper is organized as follows. Section 2 provides background on processor caches and related work. Section 3 explains the implementation of *Steps* and demonstrates the benefits using microbenchmarks. Section 4 graduates *Steps* to the real world, removing all assumptions and running a full-fledged OLTP benchmark (TPC-C). We also describe how to apply *Steps* on any DBMS architecture.

---

1. Full-system evaluation is crucial: results on isolated algorithms rarely reflect equal benefits when run inside a DBMS.

2 Background and related work

To bridge the CPU/memory performance gap, today's processors employ a hierarchy of caches that maintain recently referenced instructions and data close to the processor. Figure 3 shows an example of an instruction cache organization and explains the difference between *capacity* and *conflict* cache misses. Recent processors — e.g., IBM's Power4 — have up to three cache levels. At each hierarchy level, the corresponding cache trades off lookup speed for size. For example, level-one (L1) caches at the highest level are small (e.g., 16KB-64KB), but operate at processor speed. In contrast, lookup in level-two (L2) caches typically incurs up to an order of magnitude longer time because they are several times larger than the L1 caches (e.g., 512K-8MB). L2 lookup, however, is still several orders of magnitude faster than memory accesses (typically 300-400 cycles). Therefore, the effectiveness of cache hierarchy is extremely important for performance.

In contrast to data cache, instruction cache accesses are serialized and cannot be overlapped. Instruction cache misses prevent the flow of instructions through the processor and directly affect performance. Current trends towards improving process performance are leading to (i) increased on-chip L2 cache sizes (Figure 1b), and to (ii) increased degree of instruction-level parallelism through increasingly wider superscalar pipelines. In future processors, the combined effect of these two trends will result in significantly reduced cache data stalls (because multiple data cache accesses can be overlapped in parallel) making instruction cache stalls the key performance bottleneck.

2.1 Database workloads on modern processors

Prior research [MDO94] indicates that adverse memory access patterns in database workloads result in poor cache locality and overall performance. Recent studies of OLTP workloads and DBMS performance on modern processors [AD+99][KP+98] narrow the primary memory-related bottlenecks to L1 instruction and L2 data cache misses. More specifically, Keeton et al measure an instruction-related stall component of 41% of the total execution time for Informix running TPC-C on a PentiumPro [KP+98]. When running transactional (TPC-B and TPC-C) and decision-support (TPC-H) benchmarks on top of Oracle on Alpha processors, instruction stalls account for 45% and 30% of the execution time, respectively [BGB98][SBG02]. A recent study of DB2 7.2 running TPC-C on Pentium III [SA04] attributes 22% of the execution time to instruction stalls.

Unfortunately, unlike DSS workloads, transaction processing involves a large code footprint and exhibits irregular data access patterns due to the long and complex code paths of transaction execution. In addition, concurrent request reduces the effectiveness of single-query optimizations [JK99]. Finally, OLTP instruction streams have strong data dependencies that limit instruction-level paral-

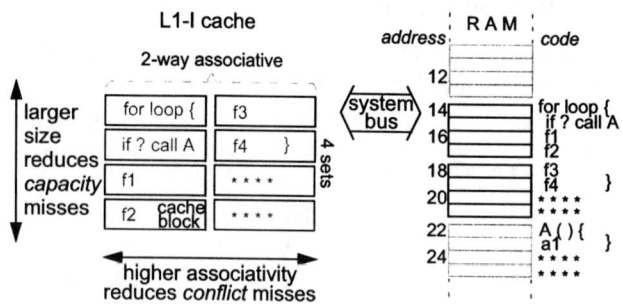

Figure 3. *Example of a 2-way set associative, 4-set (8 cache blocks) L1-I cache. Code stored in RAM maps to one set of cache blocks and is stored to any of the two blocks in that set. For simplicity we omit L2/L3 caches. In this example, the for-loop code fits in the cache only if procedure A is never called. In that case, repeated executions of the code will always hit in the L1-I cache. Larger code (more than eight blocks) would result in capacity misses. On the other hand, frequent calls to A would result to conflict misses because A's code would replace code lines f3 and f4 needed in the next iteration.*

lelism opportunity, and irregular program control flow that undermines built-in pipeline branch prediction mechanisms and increases instruction stall time.

2.2 Techniques to address L1-I cache stalls

In the last decade, research on *cache-conscious* database systems has primarily addressed data cache performance [SKN94][CGM01][GL01][AD+01]. L1-I cache misses, however, and misses occurring when concurrent threads replace each other's working sets [RB+95], have received little attention by the database community. A recent study [PM+01][ZR04] proposes increasing the number of tuples processed by each relational operator, improving instruction locality when running single-query-at-a-time DSS workloads. Unfortunately, similar techniques cannot apply to OLTP workloads because transactions typically do not form long pipelines of database operators.

Instruction locality can be improved by altering the binary code layout so that run-time code paths are as conflict-free and stored as contiguously as possible [RV+97][RB+01]. In the example of Figure 3 one such optimization would be to place procedure A's code on address 20, so that it does not conflict with the for-loop code. Such compiler optimizations are based on static profile data collected when executing a certain targeted workload, therefore, they may hurt performance when executing other workloads. Moreover, such techniques cannot satisfy all conflicting code paths from all different execution threads.

A complementary approach is instruction prefetching in the hardware [CLM97]. Call graph prefetching [APD03] collects information about the sequence of database functions calls and prefetches the function most likely to be called next. The success of such a scheme depends on the predictability of function call sequences. Unfortunately, OLTP workloads exhibit highly unpredictable instruction streams that challenge even the most sophisticated prediction mechanisms (the evaluation of call graph prefetching is done through relatively simple DSS queries [APD03]).

3 *Steps*: Introducing cache-resident code

All OLTP transactions, regardless of the specific actions they perform, execute common database mechanisms (i.e., index traversing, buffer pool manager, lock manager, logging). In addition, OLTP typically processes hundreds of requests concurrently (the top performing system in the TPC-C benchmark suite supports over one million users and handles hundreds of concurrent client connections [TPC04]). High-performance disk subsystems and high-concurrency locking protocols ensure that, at any time, there are multiple threads in the CPU ready-to-run queue.

We propose to exploit the characteristics of OLTP code by reusing instructions in the cache across a group of transactions, effectively turning an arbitrarily large OLTP code footprint into nearly cache-resident code. We synchronize transaction groups executing common code fragments, improving performance by exploiting the high degree of OLTP concurrency. The rest of this section describes the design and implementation of *Steps*, and details its behavior using transactional microbenchmarks.

3.1 Basic implementation of *Steps*

Transactions typically invoke a basic set of operations: *begin, commit, index fetch, scan, update, insert,* and *delete*. Each of those operations involves several DBMS functions and can easily overwhelm the L1-I cache of modern processors. Experimenting with the Shore database storage manager [Ca+94] on a CPU with 64KB L1-I cache, we find that even repeated execution of a single operation always incurs additional L1-I misses. Suppose that N transactions, each being carried out by a thread, perform an *index fetch* (traverse a B-tree, lock a record, and read it). For now, we assume that transactions execute uninterrupted (all pages are in main memory and locks are granted immediately). A DBMS would execute one *index fetch* after another, incurring more L1-I cache misses with each transaction execution. We propose to reuse the instructions one transaction brings in the cache, thereby eliminating misses for the remaining N-1 transactions.

As the code path is almost the same for all N transactions (except for minor, key-value processing), *Steps* follows the code execution for one transaction and finds the point at which the L1-I cache starts evicting previously-fetched instructions. At that point *Steps* context-switches the CPU to another thread. Once that thread reaches the same point in the code as the first, we switch to the next. The Nth thread switches back to the first one, which fills the cache with new instructions. Since the last N-1 threads execute the same instructions as the first, they incur significantly fewer L1-I misses (*conflict* misses, since each code fragment's footprint is smaller than the L1-I cache).

Figures 4a and 4b illustrate the scenario mentioned above for two threads. Using *Steps*, one transaction paves the L1-I cache, incurring all compulsory misses. A second,

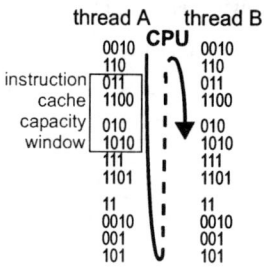
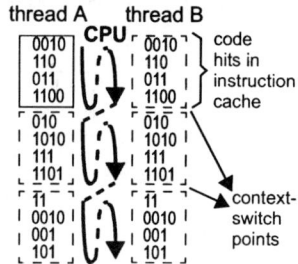

Figure 4a. *As the instruction cache cannot fit the entire code, when the CPU switches (dotted line) to thread B it will incur the same number of misses.*

Figure 4b. *If we "break" the code into three pieces that fit in the cache, and switch execution back and forth between the two threads, thread B will find all instructions in the cache.*

similar transaction follows closely, finding all the instructions it needs in the cache. Next, we describe (a) how to minimize the context-switch code size, and, (b) where to insert the context-switch calls in the DBMS source code.

3.1.1 Fast, efficient context-switching

Switching execution from one thread (or process) to another involves updating OS and DBMS software structures, as well as updating CPU registers. Thread switching is less costly than process switching (depending on the implementation). Most commercial DBMS involve a light-weight mechanism to pass on CPU control (Shore uses user-level threads). Typical context-switching mechanisms, however, occupy a significant portion of the L1-I cache and take hundreds of processor cycles to run. Shore's context-switch, for instance, occupies half of Pentium III's 16KB L1-I cache.

To minimize the overhead of context-switch we apply a universal design guideline: *make the common case fast*. The common case here is switching between transactions executing the same operation. *Steps* executes only the *core* context-switch code and updates only CPU state, ignoring thread-specific software structures such as the ready queue, until they must be updated. The minimum code needed to perform a context-switch on a IA-32 architecture — save/restore CPU registers and switch the base and stack pointers — is 48 bytes (76 in our implementation). Therefore, it only takes three 32-byte (or two 64-byte) cache blocks to store the context-switch code. One optimization that several commercial thread packages (e.g., Linux threads) make is to skip updating the floating point registers until they are actually used. For a subset of the microbenchmarks we apply a similar optimization using a flag in the core context-switch code.

3.1.2 Finding context-switching points in Shore

Given a basic set of transactional operations, we find appropriate places in the code to insert a call to *CTX (next)* (the context-switch function), where *next* is a pointer to the next thread to run. *Steps* tests candidate points in the code by executing the DBMS operations (on simple, synthetic tables) and by inserting *CTX (next)* calls before or

TABLE 1: Processors used in microbenchmarks

CPU	Cache characteristics	
AMD AthlonXP	L1 I + D cache size associativity / block size	64KB + 64KB 2-way / 64 bytes
	L2 cache size	256KB
Pentium III	L1 I + D cache size associativity / block size	16KB + 16KB 4-way / 32 bytes
	L2 cache size	256KB
Simulated IA-32 (SIMFLEX)	L1 I + D cache size associativity	[16, 32, 64KB] [direct, 2, 4, 8, full]

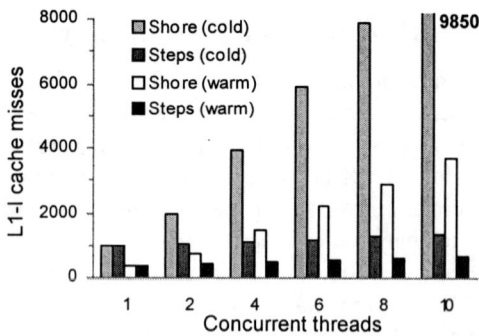

Figure 5. *Proof of concept:* Steps *reduces significantly instruction-cache misses as the group of concurrent threads increases, both with cold and with warm caches.*

after major function calls. Using hardware counters (available on almost all processors [INT04]), we measure the L1-I cache misses for executing various code fragments. Starting from the beginning of a DBMS operation and gradually moving towards its end, *Steps* compares the number of L1-I misses the execution of a code fragment incurs alone with the total number of misses when executing the same fragment twice (using the fast CTX call). A CTX point is inserted as soon as *Steps* detects a knee in the curve of the number of L1-I cache misses. *Steps* continues this search until it covers the entire high-level code path of a DBMS operation, for all operations.

The method of placing CTX calls described above does not depend on any assumptions about the code behavior or the cache architecture. Rather, it dynamically inspects code paths and chooses every code fragment to reside in the L1-I cache as long as possible across a group of interested transactions. If a code path is self-conflicting (given the associativity of the cache), then our method will place CTX calls around a code fragment that may have a significantly smaller footprint than the cache size, but will have fewer conflict misses when repeatedly executed. Likewise, this method also explicitly includes the context-switching code itself when deciding switching points.

The rest of this section evaluates *Steps* using microbenchmarks, whereas the complete implementation for OLTP workloads is described in Section 4. In all experiments we refer as "Shore" to the original unmodified system and as "Steps" to our system built on top of Shore.

3.2 *Steps* in practice: microbenchmarks

We conduct experiments on the processors shown in Table 1. Most experiments run on the AthlonXP, which features a large, 64KB L1-I cache. High-end installations typically run OLTP workloads on server processors (such as the ones shown in Figure 1b). In our work, however, we are primarily interested in the number of L1-cache misses. From the hardware perspective, this metric depends on the L1-I cache characteristics: size, associativity, and block size (and not on clock frequency, or the L2 cache). Moreover, L1-I cache misses are measured accurately using processor counters, whereas time-related metrics (cycles, time spent on a miss) can only be estimated and depend on

the entire system configuration. Instruction misses, however, translate directly to stall time since they cannot be overlapped with out-of-order execution.

Shore runs under Linux 2.4.20. We use PAPI [MB+99] and the `perfctr` library to access the AthlonXP and PIII counters. The results are based on running *index fetch* on various tables consisting of 25 `int` attributes and 100,000 rows each. The code footprint of *index fetch* without searching for the index itself (which is already loaded) is 45KB, as measured by a cache simulator (described in Section 3.2.4). Repeatedly running *index fetch* would incur no additional misses in a 45K *fully-associative* cache, but may incur conflict misses in lower-associativity caches, as explained in Figure 3. We report results averaged over 10 threads, each running *index fetch* 100 times.

3.2.1 Instruction misses and thread group size

We measure L1-I cache misses for *index fetch*, for various thread group sizes. Both *Steps* and Shore execute the fast CTX call, but *Steps* multiplexes thread execution, while Shore executes the threads serially. We first start with a cold cache and flush it between successive *index fetch* calls, and then repeat the experiment starting with a warm cache. Figure 5 shows the results on the AthlonXP.

Steps only incurs 33 misses for every additional thread, with both a cold and a warm cache. Under Shore, each additional thread adds to the total exactly the same number of misses: 985 for a cold cache (capacity misses) and 373 for a warm cache (all conflict misses since the working set of *index fetch* is 45KB). The numbers show that Shore could potentially benefit from immediately repeating the execution of the same operation across different threads. In practice, this does not happen because: (a) DBMS threads suspend and resume execution at different places of the code (performing different operations), and, (b) even if somehow two threads did synchronize, the regular context-switch code would itself conflict with the DBMS code. If the same thread, however, executes the same operation immediately, it will enjoy a warm cache. For the rest of the experiments we always warm up Shore with the same operation, and use the fast CTX call, therefore reporting worst-case lower bounds.

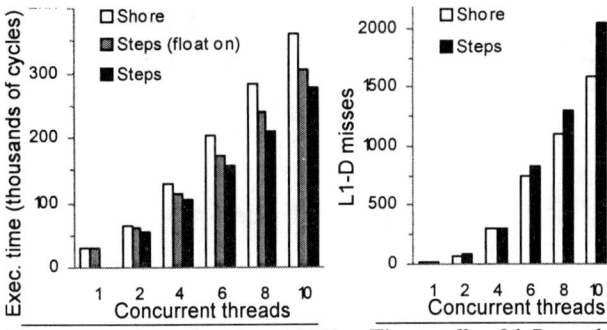

Figure 6a. *Execution time (CPU cycles) for one to ten concurrent threads.* Steps *with* float on *always updates floating point registers.*

Figure 6b. *L1-D cache misses for one to ten concurrent threads.*

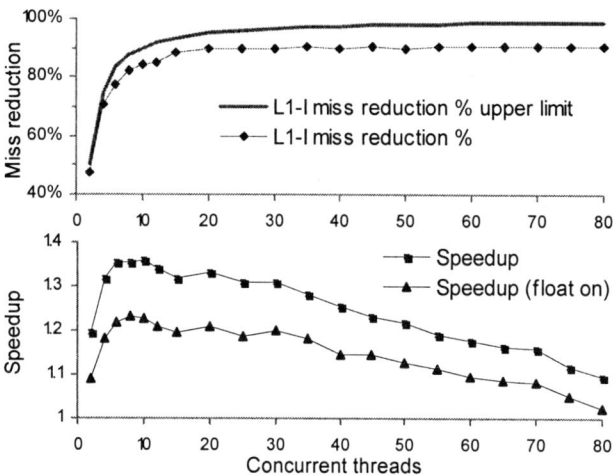

Figure 7. *Lower bounds for speedup using a warm cache for* Shore *(bottom graph) and percentage of reduction in L1-I cache misses (top graph) of* Steps *over Shore, for 2-80 concurrent threads. The top line shows the maximum possible reduction.*

The following brief analysis derives a formula for the L1-I cache miss reduction bounds as a function of the thread group size (for similarly structured operations with no exceptional events). Suppose executing an operation P once, with cold cache, yields m_P misses. Executing P, N times, flushing the cache in-between, yields $N \cdot m_P$ misses. A warm cache yields $N \cdot a \cdot m_P$, $0 < a \leq 1$ misses because of fewer capacity misses. In *Steps*, all threads except the first incur $N \cdot \beta \cdot m_P$ misses, where $0 < \beta < 1$. For a group size of N, the total number of misses is $m_P + (N-1) \cdot \beta \cdot m_P$. For an already warmed-up cache this is: $a \cdot m_P + (N-1) \cdot \beta \cdot m_P$. When comparing *Steps* to Shore, we express the miss reduction percentage as: $(1 - \#\text{misses after}/\#\text{misses before}) \cdot 100\%$. Therefore, the bounds for computing the L1-I cache miss reduction are:

$$\frac{(N-1)}{N} \cdot (1-\beta) \cdot 100\% \qquad \frac{N-1}{N} \cdot \left(1 - \frac{\beta}{a}\right) \cdot 100\%$$

for cold cache   for warm cache

N: group size

For *index fetch*, we measure $a = 0.373$, $\beta = 0.033$, giving a range of 82% - 87% of overall reduction in L1-I cache misses for 10 threads, and 90% - 96% for 100 threads. For the *tuple update* code in Shore, the corresponding parameters are: $a = 0.35$ and $\beta = 0.044$.

The next microbenchmarks examine how the savings in L1-I cache misses translate into execution time and how *Steps* affects other performance metrics.

3.2.2 Speedup and level-one data cache misses

Keeping the same setup as in 3.2.1 and providing Shore with a warmed-up cache we measure the execution time in CPU cycles and the number of level-one data (L1-D) cache misses on the AthlonXP. Figure 6a shows that *Steps* speedup increases with the number of concurrent threads. We plot both *Steps* performance with a CTX function that always updates floating point registers (float on) and with a function that skips updates. The speedup for 10 threads is 31% while for a cold cache it is 40.7% (not shown).

While a larger group promotes instruction reuse it also increases the *collective data working set*. Each thread operates on a set of private variables, buffer pool pages, and metadata which form the thread's data working set. Multiplexing thread execution at the granularity *Steps* does, results in a larger collective working set which can overwhelm the L1-D cache (when compared to Shore). Figure 6b shows that *Steps* incurs increasingly more L1-D cache misses as the thread group size increases. For up to four threads, however, the collective working set has comparable performance to single-thread execution.

Fortunately, L1-D cache misses have minimal effect on execution time (as also seen by the *Steps* speedup). The reason is that L1-D cache misses that hit in the L2 cache (i.e., are serviced within 5-10 cycles) can be easily overlapped by out-of-order execution [AD+99]. Moreover, in the context of Simultaneous Multithreaded Processors (SMT), it has been shown that for 8 threads executing simultaneously an OLTP workload and sharing the CPU caches, additional L1-D misses can be eliminated [LB+98].

On the other hand, there is no real incentive in increasing the group size beyond 10-20 threads, as the upper limit in the reduction of L1-I cache misses is already 90-95%. Figure 7 plots the *Steps* speedup (both with float on/off) and the percentage of L1-I cache misses reduction for 2-80 concurrent threads. The reason that the speedup deteriorates for groups larger than 10 threads is because of the AMD's small, 256KB unified L2 cache. In contrast to L1-D cache misses, L2-D misses cannot be overlapped by out-of-order execution. *Steps* always splits large groups (discussed in Section 4) to avoid the speedup degradation.

3.2.3 Detailed behavior on two different processors

The next experiment examines a wide range of changes in hardware behavior between *Steps* and Shore for *index fetch* with 10 threads. We experiment with both the Athlon XP and the Pentium III, using the same code and a CTX function that updates all registers (float optimization is off). The Pentium III features a smaller, 16KB L1-I and L1-D cache (see also table 1 for processor characteristics). Since the CTX points in Shore were chosen when running

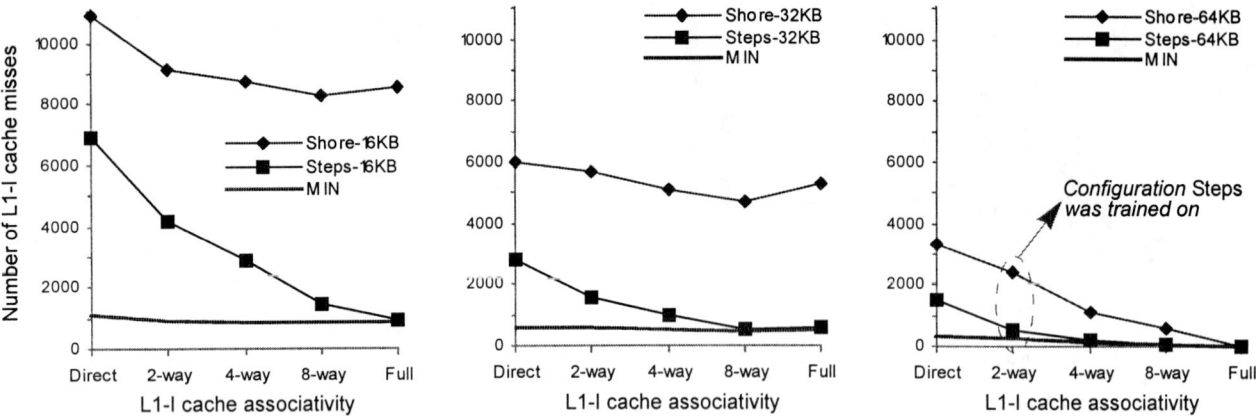

Figure 9a, 9b, 9c. *Simulation results for* index fetch *with 10 threads. We use a L1-I cache with a 64-byte cache block, varying associativity (direct, 2-, 4-, 8-way, full) and size (16KB, 32KB, 64KB).* Steps *eliminates all capacity misses and achieves up to 89% overall reduction (out of 90% max possible) in L1-I misses (max performance is for the 8-way 32KB and 64KB caches).*

on the AthlonXP (64KB L1-I cache), we expect that this version of *Steps* on the Pentium III will not be as effective in reducing L1-I cache misses as on the AthlonXP. The results are in Figure 8. Our observations for each event counted, in the order they appear in the graph, follow.

Execution time and L1-I cache misses. *Steps* is also effective on the Pentium III despite its small cache, reducing L1-I cache misses to a third (66% out of a maximum possible 90% reduction). Moreover, the speedup on the Pentium is higher than the AthlonXP, mainly because the absolute number of misses saved is higher (absolute numbers for *Steps* are on top of each bar in Figure 8). The last bar in Figure 8 shows the reduction in the cycles the processor is stalled due to lack of instructions in the cache (event only available on the Pentium III). The reduction percentage matches the L1-I cache miss reduction.

Level-one data cache. *Steps* incurs significantly more L1-D cache misses on the Pentium's small L1-D cache (109% more misses). However, the CPU can cope well by overlapping misses and perform 24% faster.

Level-two cache. L2 cache performance does not have an effect on the specific microbenchmark since almost all data and instructions can be found there. We report L2 cache performance in the next section, when running a full OLTP workload.

Instructions and branches retired. As expected, *Steps* executes slightly more instructions (1.7%) and branches (1.3%) due to the extra context-switch code.

Mispredicted branches. *Steps* reduces mispredicted branches to almost a third on both CPUs (it eliminates 64% of Shore's mispredicted branches). This is an important result coming from *Steps*' ability to provide the CPU with frequently repeating execution patterns. We verify this observation via an event available to Pentium III (second to last bar in Figure 8), that shows a reduction in the number of branches missing the Branch Target Buffer (BTB), a small cache for recently executed branches.

3.2.4 Varying L1-I cache characteristics

The last microbenchmark varies L1-I cache characteristics using SIMFLEX [HS+04], a Simics-based [MC+02], full-system simulation framework developed at the Computer Architecture Lab of Carnegie Mellon. We use Simics/SIMFLEX to emulate a x86 processor (Pentium III) and associated peripheral devices (using the same setup as in the real Pentium). Simics boots and runs the exact same binary code of Linux and the Shore/*Steps* microbenchmark, as in the real machines. Using SIMFLEX's cache component we modify the L1-I cache characteristics (size, associativity, block size) and run the 10-thread *index fetch* benchmark. The reported L1-I cache misses are exactly the same as in a real machine with the same cache characteristics. Metrics in simulation involving timing are subject to assumptions made by programmers and cannot possibly match real execution times. Figures 9a, 9b, and 9c show the results for a fixed 64-byte cache block size, varying associativity for a 16KB, 32KB, and 64KB L1-I cache.

As expected, increasing the associativity reduces instruction conflict misses (except for a slight increase for fully-associative 16KB and 32KB caches, due to the LRU replacement policy resulting in more capacity misses).

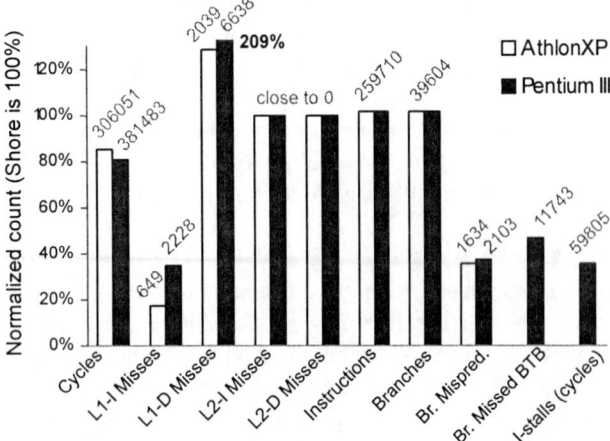

Figure 8. *Relative performance of* Steps *compared to Shore, for* index fetch *with 10 concurrent threads, on both the AthlonXP and the Pentium III. The two last bars are events exclusively available on the Pentium.*

The conflict miss reduction for *Steps* is more dramatic in a small cache (16KB). The reason is that with a 45KB working set for *index fetch* even a few CTX calls can eliminate all capacity misses for the small caches. Since *Steps* is trained on a 2-way 64KB cache, smaller caches with the same associativity incur more conflict misses. As the associativity increases those additional L1-I misses disappear. Despite a fixed training on a large cache, *Steps* performs very well across a wide range of cache architectures, achieving a 89% overall reduction in L1-I misses — out of 90% max possible — for the 8-way 32KB and 64KB caches. Experiments with different cache block sizes (not shown here) find that larger blocks further reduce L1-I misses, in agreement with the results in [RG+98].

4 Applying *Steps* to OLTP workloads

So far we saw how to efficiently multiplex the execution of concurrent threads running the same transactional DBMS operation when (a) those threads run uninterrupted, and (b) the DBMS does not schedule any other threads. This section removes all previous assumptions and describes how *Steps* works in full-system operation. The design goal is to take advantage of the fast CTX calls and maintain high concurrency for similarly structured operations in the presence of locking, latching (which provides exclusive access to DBMS structures), disk I/O, aborts and roll-backs, and other concurrent system operations (e.g., deadlock detection, buffer pool page flushing).

The rest of this section describes the full *Steps* implementation (Section 4.1), presents the experimentation setup (4.2) and the TPC-C results (4.3), and briefly discusses applicability in commercial DBMS (4.4).

4.1 Full *Steps* implementation

Steps employs a two-level transaction synchronization mechanism. At the higher level, all transactions about to perform a single DBMS operation form execution teams. We call S-threads all threads participating in an execution team (excluding system-specific threads or processes and threads which are blocked for any reason). Once all S-threads belong to a team, the CPU proceeds with the lower-level transaction synchronization scheme within a single team, following a similar execution schedule as in the previous section. Next, we detail synchronization mechanisms (Section 4.1.1), different code paths (Section 4.1.2), and threads leaving their teams (Section 4.1.3). Section 4.1.4 summarizes the changes to Shore code.

4.1.1 Forming and scheduling execution teams

To facilitate a flexible assignment of threads to execution teams and construct an efficient CPU schedule during the per-team synchronization phase, each DBMS operation is associated with a double-linked list (Figure 10). S-threads are part of such a list (depending on which operation they

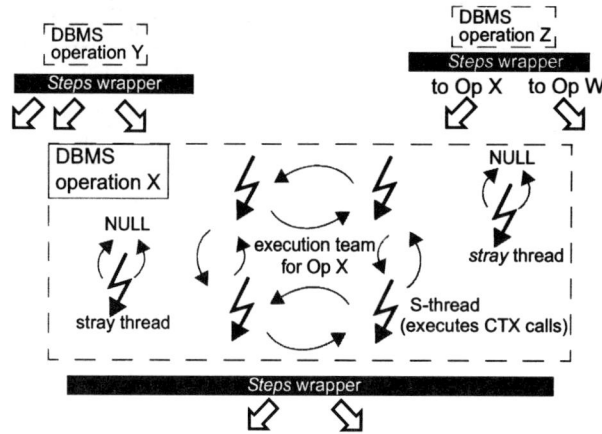

Figure 10. *Additions to the DBMS code: Threads are associated with list nodes and form per-operation lists, during the* Steps *setup code at the end of each DBMS operation.*

are currently executing), while all other threads have the `prev` and `next` pointers set to zero. The list for each execution team guides the CPU scheduling decisions. At each CTX point the CPU simply switches to the next thread in the list. S-threads may leave a team (disconnect) for several reasons. Transactions give up (yield) the CPU when they (a) block trying to acquire an exclusive lock (or access an exclusive resource), or on an I/O request, and, (b) when they voluntarily yield control as part of the code logic. We call *stray* the threads that leave a team.

The code responsible for team formation is a thin wrapper that runs every time a transaction finishes a single DBMS operation ("*Steps* wrapper" in Figure 10). It disconnects the S-thread from the current list (if not stray) and connects it to the next list, according to the transaction code logic. If a list reaches the maximum number of threads allowed for a team (a user-defined variable), then the transaction will join a new team after the current team finishes execution. Before choosing the next team to run, all stray threads are given a chance to join their respective teams (next DBMS operation on their associated transaction's code logic). Finally, the *Steps* wrapper updates internal statistics, checks with the system scheduler if other tasks need to run, and picks the next team to run[2].

Within each execution team *Steps* works in a "best-effort" mode. Every time a transaction (or any thread) encounters a CTX point in the code, it first checks if it is an S-thread and then passes the CPU to the next thread in the list. All S-threads in the list eventually complete the current DBMS operation, executing in a round-robin fash-

---

2. Different per-team scheduling policies may apply at this point. In our experiments, picking the next operation that the last member of a list (or the last stray thread) is interested, worked well in practice since the system scheduler makes sure that every thread makes progress.

TABLE 2: Operation classification for overlapped code

DBMS operation	cross-transaction code overlap		
	always	same tables	same tables + split Op
begin / commit	✓		
fetch		✓	
insert			✓
delete			✓
update	✓		
scan	✓		

ion, the same way as in Section 3. This approach does not explicitly provide any guarantees that all threads will remain synchronized for the duration of the DBMS operation. It provides, however, a very fast context-switching mechanism during full-system operation (the same list-based mechanism was used in all microbenchmarks). If all threads execute the same code path without blocking, then *Steps* will achieve the same L1-I cache miss reduction as in the previous section. Significantly different code paths across transactions executing the same operation or exceptional events that cause threads to become stray may lead to reduced benefits in the L1-I cache performance. Fortunately, we can reduce the effect of different code paths (Section 4.1.2) and exceptional events (4.1.3).

4.1.2 Maximizing code overlap across transactions

If an S-thread follows a significantly different code path than other threads in its team (e.g., traverse a B-tree with fewer levels), the assumed synchronization breaks down. That thread will keep evicting useful instructions with code that no one else needs. If a thread, however, exits the current operation prematurely (e.g., a key was not found), the only effect will be a reduced team size, since the thread will wait to join another team. To minimize the effect of different code paths we follow the next two guidelines:

1. Have a separate list for each operation that manipulates a different index (i.e., *index fetch (table1)*, *index fetch (table2)*, and so on).

2. If the workload does not yield high concurrency for similarly structured operations, we consider defining finer-grain operations. For example, instead of an *insert* operation, we can maintain a different list for creating a record and a different one for updating an index.

Table 2 shows all transactional operations along with their degree of cross-transaction overlapped code. *Begin, commit, scan,* and *update* are independent of the database structure and use a single list each. *Index fetch* code follows different branches depending on the B-tree depth, therefore a separate list per index maximizes code overlap. Lastly, *insert* and *delete* code paths may differ across transactions even for same indices, therefore it may be necessary to define finer-grain operations. While experi-

menting with TPC-C we find that following only the first guideline (declaring lists per index) is sufficient. Small variations in the code path are unavoidable (e.g., utilizing a different attribute set or manipulating different strings) but the main function calls to the DBMS engine are generally the same across different transactions. For workloads with an excessive number of indices, we can use statistics collected by *Steps* on the average execution team size per index, and consolidate teams from different indices. This way *Steps* trades code overlap for an increased team size.

4.1.3 Dealing with stray transactions

S-threads turn into stray when they block or voluntarily yield the CPU. In *preemptive* thread packages the CPU scheduler may also preempt a thread after its time quantum has elapsed. The latter is a rare event for *Steps* since it performs switches at orders of magnitude faster times than the quantum length. In our implementation on Shore we modify the thread package and intercept the entrance of `block` and `yield` to perform the following actions:

1. Disconnect the S-thread from the current list.
2. Turn the thread into stray, by setting pointers `prev` and `next` to zero. Stray threads bypass subsequent CTX calls and fall under the authority of the regular scheduler. They remain stray until they join the next list.
3. Update all thread package structures that were not updated during the fast CTX calls. In Shore these are the current running thread, and the ready queue status.
4. Pass a hint to the regular scheduler that the next thread to run should be the next in the current list (unless a system or a higher priority thread needs to run first).
5. Give up the CPU using regular context-switching.

Except for I/O requests and non-granted locks, transactions may go astray because of mutually exclusive code paths. Frequently, a database programmer protects accesses or modifications to a shared data structure by using a mutex (or a latch). If an S-thread calls CTX while still holding the mutex, all other threads in the same team will go astray as they will not be able to access the protected data. If the current operation's remaining code (after the mutex release) can still be shared, it may be preferable to skip the badly placed CTX call. This way *Steps* only suffers momentarily the extra misses associated with executing a small, self-evicting piece of code.

Erasing CTX calls is not a good idea since the specific CTX call may also be accessed from different code paths (for example, through other operations) which do not necessarily go through acquiring a mutex. *Steps* associates with every thread a counter that increases every time the thread acquires a mutex and decreases when releasing it. Each CTX call tests if the counter is non-zero in which case it lets the current thread continue running without giving up the CPU. In Shore, there were only two places in the code that the counter would be non-zero.

TABLE 3: System configuration

CPU	AthlonXP, 2GB RAM, Linux 2.4.20
Storage	one 120GB main disk, one 30GB log disk
Buffer pool size	Up to 2GB
Page size	8192 Bytes
Shore locking hierarchy	Record, page, table, entire database
Shore locking protocol	Two phase locking

4.1.4 Summary of changes to the DBMS code

The list of additions and modifications to the Shore code base is the following. We added the wrapper code to synchronize threads between calls to DBMS operations (*Steps* wrapper, 150 lines of C++), the code to perform fast context-switching (20 lines of inline assembly), and we also added global variables for the list pointers representing each DBMS operation. We modified the thread package code to update the list nodes properly and thread status whenever blocking, yielding, or changing thread priorities (added/changed 140 lines of code). Finally, we inserted calls to our custom CTX function into the source code (as those were found during the microbenchmarking phase). Next, we describe the experimentation testbed.

4.2 Experimentation setup

We experiment with the TPC-C benchmark which models a wholesale parts supplier operating out of a number of warehouses and their associated sales districts [TPC04]. It involves a mix of five different types of transactions. The two most frequently executed transactions (88% of the time) are the New Order and the Payment transactions. TPC-C transactions operate on nine tables and they are all based on the DBMS operations listed in Table 2.

The TPC-C toolkit for Shore is written at CMU. Table 3 shows the basic configuration characteristics of our system. To ensure high concurrency and reduce the I/O bottleneck in our two-disk system we cache the database in the buffer pool and allow transactions to commit without waiting for the log to be flushed on disk (the log is flushed asynchronously). A reduced buffer pool size would cause I/O contention allowing only very few threads to be runnable at any time. High-end installations can hide the I/O latency by parallelizing requests on multiple disks. To mimic a high-end system's CPU utilization, we set user thinking time to zero and keep the standard TPC-C scaling factor (10 users per Warehouse), essentially having as many concurrent threads as the number of users. We found that, when comparing *Steps* with Shore running New Order, *Steps* was more efficient in inserting multiple subsequent records on behalf of a transaction (because of a slot allocation mechanism that was avoiding overheads when inserts were spread across many transactions). We modified slightly New Order by removing one insert from inside a for-loop (but kept the remaining inserts).

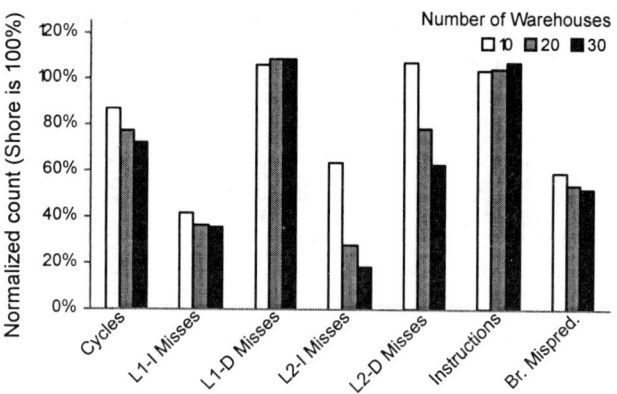

Figure 10. *Transaction mix includes only the Payment transaction, for 10-30 Warehouses (100-300 threads).*

For all experiments we warm up the buffer pool and measure CPU events in full-system operation, including background I/O processes that are not optimized using *Steps*. Measurement periods range from 10sec - 1min depending on the time needed to complete a pre-specified number of transactions. All reported numbers are consistent across different runs, since the aggregation period is large in terms of CPU time. Our primary metric is the number of L1-I cache misses as it is not affected by the AthlonXP's small L2 cache (when compared to server processors shown in Figure 1b).

***Steps* setup:** We keep the same CTX calls used in the microbenchmarks but without using floating point optimizations, and without re-training *Steps* on TPC-C indexes or tables. Furthermore, we refrain from using *Steps* on the TPC-C application code. Our goal is to show that *Steps* is workload-independent and report lower bounds for performance metrics by not using optimized CTX calls. We assign a separate thread list to each *index fetch, insert,* and *delete* operating on different tables while keeping one list for each of the rest operations. Restricting execution team sizes has no effect since in our configuration the number of runnable threads is low. For larger setups, *Steps* can be configured to restrict team sizes, essentially creating multiple independent teams per DBMS operation.

4.3 TPC-C results

Initially we run all TPC-C transaction types by themselves varying the database size (and number of users). Figure 10 shows the relative performance of *Steps* over Shore when running the Payment transaction with standard TPC-C scaling for 10, 20, and 30 warehouses. The measured events are: execution time in CPU cycles, cache misses for both L1 and L2 caches, the number of instructions executed, and the number of mispredicted branches. Results for other transaction types were similar. *Steps* outperforms Shore, achieving a 60-65% reduction in L1-I cache misses, a 41-45% reduction in mispredicted branches, and a 16-39% speedup (with no floating point optimizations). The benefits increase as the database size (and number of

TABLE 4: Team sizes per DBMS operation in Payment

Warehouses →	10		20		30	
Operation (table) ↓	in	out	in	out	in	out
index fetch (C)	8.6	8.6	16	16	25.2	24.7
index fetch (D)	8.9	1.7	16.2	2.6	31.7	5.3
index fetch (W)	8.9	0.5	16.6	1	30	1.9
scan (C)	9.4	8.2	16	14.3	26.2	23.7
insert (H)	7.9	7.8	14.9	14.6	24	23.2
update (C, D, W)	7.5	7.2	14	12.3	21.6	19
average team size	8.6	6.9	15.9	12.3	26.4	20.4
# of ready threads	15		28		48.4	

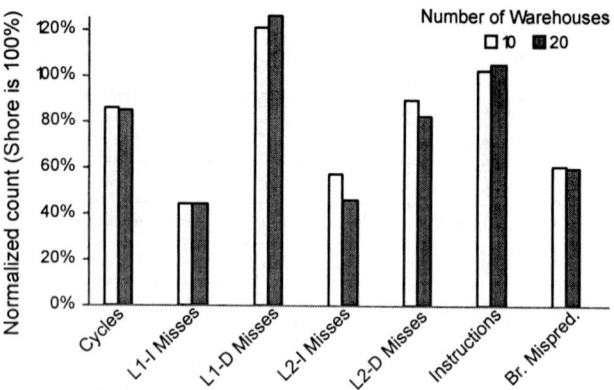

Figure 11. *Transaction mix includes all transactions except the non-interactive Delivery transaction, for 10-20 Warehouses.*

users) scale up. The increase in L1-D cache misses is marginal. *Steps* speedup is also fueled by fewer L2-I and L2-D misses as the database size increases. *Steps* makes better utilization of AMD's small L2 cache as fewer L1-I cache misses also translate into more usable space in L2 for data.

Table 4 shows for each configuration (10, 20, and 30 warehouses running Payment) how many threads on average enter an execution team for a DBMS operation and exit without being strays, along with how many threads are ready to run at any time and the average team size. The single capital letters in every operation correspond to the TPC-C tables/indices used (Customer, District, Warehouse, and History). *Steps* is able to group on average half of the available threads. Most of the operations yield a low rate for producing strays, except for *index fetch* on District and Warehouse. In small TPC-C configurations, exclusive locks on those tables restrict concurrency.

Next, we run the standard TPC-C mix, excluding the non-interactive Delivery transaction (TPC-C specifies up to 80sec queueing delay before executing Delivery). Figure 11 shows that the four-transaction mix follows the general behavior of the Payment mix, with the reduction in instruction cache misses (both L1 and L2) being slightly worse. Statistics for the team sizes reveal that this configuration forces a smaller average team size due to the increased number of unique operations. For the 10-warehouse configuration, there are 14 ready threads, and on average, 4.3 threads exit from a list without being stray. Still, this means a theoretical bound of a 77% reduction in L1-I cache misses, and *Steps* achieves a 56% reduction while handling a full TPC-C workload and without being optimized for it specifically. Results for different mixes of TPC-C transactions were similar.

4.4 Applicability

Steps has the following two attractive features that simplify integration in a commercial DBMS: (a) its application is incremental as it can target specific operations and co-exist with other workloads, (e.g., DSS, which can simply bypass CTX calls), and (b) the required code modifications are restricted to a very specific small subset of the code, the thread package. Most commercial thread packages implement preemptive threads. As a result, DBMS code is *thread safe*, meaning that programmers develop DBMS code anticipating random context-switches that can occur at any time. This is also true for DBMS using processes instead of threads (such as Oracle on Linux). Thread safe code ensures that any placement of CTX calls throughout the code will not break any assumptions.

To apply *Steps* to any thread-based DBMS the programming team needs to augment the thread package to support fast context-switching. Process-based systems may require changes to a larger subset of the underlying OS code. In general, a *Steps* CTX call should bypass the OS scheduler and update only the absolute minimum state needed by a different thread/process for code execution that does not give up CPU control. Whenever a thread gives up CPU control through a mechanism different than fast CTX, all state needed before invoking a regular context-switch should be updated accordingly. The next phase is to add the *Steps* wrapper in each major DBMS operation. This thin wrapper provides the high-level, per-operation transaction synchronization used in *Steps*.

The final phase is to place CTX calls in the code depending on the underlying cache architecture. Readily available binary tools can automate CTX call placement (using either trace-based cache simulation or CPU hardware counters). For example, `valgrind/cachegrind` is a cache profiling tool which can be used to track all instruction cache misses during the execution of a sample operation. It can be easily configured to output the code lines where CTX calls should be placed using a simple cache simulator. Next, a binary modification tool [SE94] can be used to insert the CTX calls to the DBMS binary, while a race-detection binary tool [SB+97] can be used to pinpoint badly placed CTX calls which may cause races or force S-threads to go astray. Moreover, a compiler can "color" the L1-I cache blocks containing the CTX code to make them permanently reside in the cache, thereby reducing conflict misses. The only workload-specific tuning required is the creation of per-index execution teams, which can be done once the database schema is known.

Epilogue

This paper demonstrates that the key to optimal performance for OLTP workloads on modern processors is within the DBMS design. Computer architects have already pushed next-generation processor designs to the market and are now working on proactive memory systems to eliminate data cache misses. Instruction cache stalls are a major barrier towards bringing OLTP performance on par with scientific and engineering workload performance. Software vendors have the best insight of how and where to affect software behavior. *Steps*, our proposed technique, is orthogonal to compiler techniques and its benefits are always additional to any binary-optimized configuration. In this paper we show that *Steps* minimizes both capacity and conflict instruction cache misses of OLTP with arbitrary long code paths, without increasing the size or the associativity of the instruction cache.

Acknowledgements

We thank Babak Falsafi, James Hamilton, Bruce Lindsay, Ken Ross, Michael Stonebraker, and the reviewers for their comments. We also thank Nikos Hardavellas and Tom Wenisch for SIMFLEX, and Mengzhi Wang for the Shore TPC-C toolkit. This work is supported in part by an IBM faculty partnership award and by NSF grants CCR-0113660, IIS-0133686, and CCR-0205544.

References

[AD+01] A. Ailamaki, D. J. DeWitt, M. D. Hill, and M. Skounakis. "Weaving Relations for Cache Performance." In *Proc. VLDB*, 2001.

[AD+99] A. Ailamaki, D. J. DeWitt, at al. "DBMSs on a modern processor: Where does time go?" In *Proc. VLDB*, 1999.

[APD03] M. Annavaram, J. M. Patel, and E. S. Davidson. "Call graph prefetching for database applications." In *ACM Transactions on Computer Systems*, 21(4):412-444, November 2003.

[BGB98] L. A. Barroso, K. Gharachorloo, and E. Bugnion. "Memory System Characterization of Commercial Workloads." In *Proc. ISCA*, 1998.

[Ca+94] M. Carey et al. "Shoring Up Persistent Applications." In *Proc. SIGMOD*, 1994.

[CLM97] I-C. Chen, C-C. Lee, and T. Mudge. "Instruction prefetching using branch predition information." In *Proc. International Conference on Computer Design* 1997.

[CGM01] S. Chen, P. B. Gibbons, and T. C. Mowry. "Improving Index Performance through Prefetching." In *Proc. SIGMOD*, 2001.

[GL01] G. Graefe and P. Larson. "B-Tree Indexes and CPU Caches." In *Proc. ICDE*, 2001.

[Gra93] J. Gray. "The benchmark handbook for transaction processing systems." 2nd ed., Morgan-Kaufmann, 1993.

[HP96] J. L. Hennessy and D. A. Patterson. "Computer Architecture: A Quantitative Approach." 2nd ed, Morgan-Kaufmann, 1996.

[HS+04] N. Hardavellas, S. Somogyi, et al. "SIMFLEX: a Fast, Accurate, Flexible Full-System Simulation Framework for Performance Evaluation of Server Architecture." *SIGMETRICS Performance Evaluation Review, Vol. 31, No. 4, pp. 31-35,* April 2004.

[JK99] J. Jayasimha and A. Kumar. "Thread-based Cache Analysis of a Modified TPC-C Workload." In *2nd CAECW Workshop*, 1999.

[INT04] Intel Corporation. "IA-32 Intel® Architecture Software Developer's Manual, Volume 3: System Programming Guide." (*Order Number 253668*).

[KP+98] K. Keeton, D. A. Patterson, Y. Q. He, R. C. Raphael, and W. E. Baker. "Performance Characterization of a Quad Pentium Pro SMP Using OLTP Workloads." In *Proc. ISCA-25*, 1998.

[LB+98] J. Lo, L. A. Barroso, S. Eggers, et al. "An Analysis of Database Workload Performance on Simultaneous Multithreaded Processors." In *Proc. ISCA-25*, 1998.

[MC+02] P. S. Magnusson, et al. "Simics: A Full System Simulation Platform." In *IEEE Computer*, 35(2):50–58, February 2002.

[MDO94] A. M. G. Maynard, C. M. Donelly, and B. R. Olszewski. "Contrasting Characteristics and Cache Performance of Technical and Multi-user Commercial Workloads." In *Proc. ASPLOS-6*, 1994.

[MB+99] P. J. Mucci, S. Browne, et al. "PAPI: A Portable Interface to Hardware Performance Counters." In *Proc. Dept. of Defense HPCMP Users Group Conference*, Monterey, CA, June 7-10, 1999.

[PM+01] S. Padmanabhan, T. Malkemus, R. Agarwal, A. Jhingran. "Block Oriented Processing of Relational Database Operations in Modern Computer Architectures." In *Proc. ICDE*, 2001.

[RB+01] A. Ramirez, L. A. Barroso, et al. "Code Layout Optimizations for Transaction Processing Workloads." In *ISCA-28*, 2001.

[RG+98] P. Ranganathan, K. Gharachorloo, S. V. Adve, and L. A. Barroso. "Performance of database workloads on shared-memory systems with out-of-order processors." In *Proc. ASPLOS*, 1998.

[RV+97] T. Romer, G. Voelker, et al. "Instrumentation and Optimization of Win32/Intel Executables Using Etch." In *Proc. Usenix NT Workshop*, 1997.

[RB+95] M. Rosenblum, E. Bugnion, S. A. Herrod, E. Witchel, and A. Gupta. "The Impact of Architectural Trends on Operating System Performance." In *Proc. SOSP-15*, pp.285-298, 1995.

[SB+97] S. Savage, M. Burrows, et al. "Eraser: A Dynamic Data Race Detector for Multithreaded Programs." In *ACM TOCS, vol. 15, no. 4, pp. 391-411,* November 1997.

[SA04] M. Shao and A. Ailamaki. "DBmbench: Fast and Accurate Database Workload Representation on Modern Microarchitecture." *In submission. Available as Technical Report CMU-CS-03-161.*

[SKN94] A. Shatdal, C. Kant, and J. Naughton. "Cache Conscious Algorithms for Relational Query Processing." In *Proc. VLDB*, 1994.

[SE94] A. Srivastava and A. Eustace. "ATOM: A system for building customized program analysis tools." In *Proc. SIGPLAN*, 1994.

[SBG02] R. Stets, L. A. Barroso, and K. Gharachorloo. "Detailed Comparison of Two Transaction Processing Workloads," In *Proc. 5th CAECW Workshop*, 2002.

[TPC04] Transaction Processing Performance Council. http://www.tpc.org

[ZR04] J. Zhou and K. A. Ross. "Buffering Database Operations for Enhanced Instruction Cache Performance." In *SIGMOD*, 2004.

Write-Optimized B-Trees

Goetz Graefe
Microsoft

Abstract

Large writes are beneficial both on individual disks and on disk arrays, e.g., RAID-5. The presented design enables large writes of internal B-tree nodes and leaves. It supports both in-place updates and large append-only ("log-structured") write operations within the same storage volume, within the same B-tree, and even at the same time. The essence of the proposal is to make page migration inexpensive, to migrate pages while writing them, and to make such migration optional rather than mandatory as in log-structured file systems. The inexpensive page migration also aids traditional defragmentation as well as consolidation of free space needed for future large writes. These advantages are achieved with a very limited modification to conventional B-trees that also simplifies other B-tree operations, e.g., key range locking and compression.

Prior proposals and prototypes implemented transacted B-tree on top of log-structured file systems and added transaction support to log-structured file systems. Instead, the presented design adds techniques and performance characteristics of log-structured file systems to traditional B-trees and their standard transaction support, notably without adding a layer of indirection for locating B-tree nodes on disk. The result retains fine-granularity locking, full transactional ACID guarantees, fast search performance, etc. expected of a modern B-tree implementation, yet adds efficient transacted page relocation and large, high-bandwidth writes.

1 Introduction

In a typical transaction-processing environment, the dominant I/O patterns are reads of individual pages based on index look-ups and writes of updated versions of those pages. As memory sizes grow ever larger, the fraction of write operations among all I/O operations increases. While "90% reads, 10% writes" was a reasonable rule of thumb 15 or 20 years ago, "33% writes" is more realistic today once a database server and its applications have reached steady state production. In a future with 64-bit addressing in practically all servers and even most workstations, we may expect ever larger fractions of write operations among all I/O. In some scenarios, writes already dominate reads. For example, in a recent result of the SAP SD benchmark (designed for performance analysis and capacity planning of sales and distribution applications), simulating 47,528 users required 75 MB disk reads per second and 8,300 MB disk writes per second [LM 03]. In other words, in this environment with ample main memory, write volume exceeded read volume by a factor of more than 100.

In write-intensive environments, improving the performance of write operations is very important. Both on single disks and in disk arrays, large write operations provide much higher bandwidth than small ones, often by an order or magnitude or even more. In RAID-5 and similar disk arrays, large writes avoid the "small write penalty," which is due to maintenance of parity information. Log-structured file systems have been invented to enable and exploit large writes, but have not caught on in transaction processing and in database management systems. We believe this failed to happen for two principal reasons. First, log-structured file systems introduce overhead for finding the current physical location of a logical page, i.e., a mapping layer that maps a page identifier to the page's current location in the log-structured file system. Typically, this overhead implies additional I/O, locking, latching, search, etc., even if a very efficient mapping mechanism is employed. Second, log-structured file systems optimize write performance to the detriment of scan performance, which is also important in many databases, at least for some tables and indexes. Therefore, even if optimizing write performance is highly desirable for some tables in a database, it might not improve overall system performance if it applies indiscriminately to all data in the database.

The techniques proposed here are designed to overcome these concerns. First, the overhead of finding a single page is equal to that in a traditional B-tree index; retrieving a B-tree node does not require a layer of indirection for locating a page on disk. Second, if scan performance is important for some tables or indexes within a database, our design permits that those can be updated in-place, i.e., without any adverse effect on scan perform-

---

Permission to copy without fee all or part of this material is granted provided that the copies are not made or distributed for direct commercial advantage, the VLDB copyright notice and the title of the publication and its date appear, and notice is given that copying is by permission of the Very Large Data Base Endowment. To copy otherwise, or to republish, requires a fee and/or special permission from the Endowment.
Proceedings of the 30th VLDB Conference, Toronto, Canada, 2004.

ance. Specifically, any individual write operation can be in-place ("read-optimized") or part of a large write ("write-optimized"), and the choice can be independent of the choices taken for other pages. In other words, our design provides the mechanisms for write-optimized operation, but it does not imply or prescribe policies and it does not force a single policy for all data and for all time.

Many policies are possible. For example, "hot" tables and indexes may be permanently present in the I/O buffer, which suggests write-optimized I/O when required, e.g., during checkpoints. Alternatively, B-tree leaf pages may be updated in-place (read-optimized) whereas upper index layers are presumed permanently buffered, and any required write operations bundled into large, efficient writes. Another possible policy writes in-place during ordinary buffer replacement but minimizes checkpoint duration by using write-optimized I/O.

The two extreme policies are updating everything in-place, which is equivalent to a traditional (read-optimized) database, or bundling all write operations into large, append-only writes, which is equivalent to a log-structured (write-optimized) file system. The value of the proposed design is that it permits many mixed policies, and that it applies specifically to B-tree indexes and thus database management systems rather than file systems. Therefore, if policies are set appropriately, our mechanisms will perform as well as or better than a traditional file system for applications in which a traditional file system out-performs a log-structured file system, and they will perform as well as or better than a log-structured file system for applications in which a log-structured file system out-performs a traditional file system.

In the following sections, we review related work including prior efforts to employ log-structured file systems for transaction processing, introduce our data structures and algorithms, consider defragmentation and the space reclamation effort required in a log-structured file system, describe the mechanisms that enable write-optimized B-tree indexes, review the performance of our mechanisms, and finally offer our conclusions from this research.

2   Related work

Our design requires limited modifications to traditional B-trees, and many of the techniques used here have already been employed elsewhere. In this section, we review B-trees, multi-level transactions, log-structured file systems, and prior attempts to use log-structured file systems in transaction processing.

Mentioned here briefly for the sake completeness, the proposed use of B-trees is entirely orthogonal to the data collection being indexed. The proposed technique applies to relational databases as well as other data models and other storage techniques that support associative search, both primary (clustered) and secondary (non-clustered) indexes. Moreover, it applies to indexes on traditional columns as well as on computed columns, including B-trees on hash values, Z-values (as in "universal B-trees" [RMF 00]), and on user-defined functions. Similarly, it applies to indexes on views (materialized and maintained results of queries) just as much as to indexes on traditional tables.

2.1   B-tree indexes

B-tree indexes are, of course, well known [BC 72, C 79], so we review only a few relevant topics. Following common practice, we assume here that traditional B-tree implementations are actually B$^+$-trees, i.e., they keep all records in the leaf nodes and they chain nodes at the leaf level or at each level using "sibling" pointers. These are used for a variety of purposes, e.g., ascending and descending cursors.

For high concurrency, key range locking and equivalent techniques [L 93, M 90] are used in commercial database systems. Unfortunately, when inserting a new key larger than any existing key in a given leaf, the next-larger key must be located on the next B-tree leaf, which is an expensive operation even if all B-tree leaves are chained together. Such "crawling" can be particularly expensive (and complex to code correctly, and even more complex to test reliably as the software evolves) if B-tree leaves can be empty, depending on the policy when to merge and deallocate empty or near-empty leaf pages. Our B-tree modifications avoid all crawling for key range locking as a desirable-but-not-essential by-product.

A common B-tree technique is the use of "pseudo-deleted" or "ghost" records [JS 89, M90b]. Rather than erasing a record from a leaf page, a user's delete operation simply marks a record as invalid and leaves the actual removal to a future insert operation or to an asynchronous clean-up activity. Such ghost records simplify locking, transaction rollback, and cursor navigation after an update through the cursor. Ghost records can be locked and indeed the deleting user transaction retains a lock until it commits or aborts. Subsequent transactions also need to respect the ghost record and its key as defining a range in key range locking, until the ghost record is truly erased from the leaf page. Alternatively, a ghost record can turn into a valid record due to a user inserting a new row with the same index key. Interestingly, an insert operation realized by a conversion from a ghost record into a valid record does not require a key range lock; a key value lock is sufficient.

In most B-tree indexes, internal nodes have hundreds of child pointers, in particular if prefix and suffix truncation [BU 77] are employed. Thus, 99% and more of a B-tree's pages are leaf pages, making it realistic that all or most internal nodes remain in the I/O buffer at nearly all times. This is valuable both for random probes (e.g., driven by an index nested loops join) and for large scans, because efficient large scans on modern disk systems and disk arrays require tens or hundreds of concurrent read-ahead hints, which can only be supplied by scanning the "parent" and "grandparent" level, not by relying on the chain of B-tree leaves.

2.2 Multi-level transactions and system transactions

Modern transaction processing systems separate a database's logical contents from the database's physical representation. This is well known as physical data independence when designing tables, views, and constraints versus indexes and storage spaces. However, this distinction is also found in the implementation of query optimization, where logical query expressions with abstract operations such as join are mapped to physical query evaluation plans with concrete algorithms and access paths such as index nested loops join, and in the implementation of transaction semantics. Modification of physical representation, e.g., splitting a B-tree node or removing a ghost record, is often executed separately as a "nested top-level action" [MHL 92] or as a "system transaction." System transactions may change physical structures but never database contents, and thus differ from user transaction in a fundamental way. System transactions may commit and release their locks independently of the invoking user transaction, yet they may be lock-compatible with the invoking user transaction if that transaction pauses until the system transaction completes. Moreover, system transactions can be committed very inexpensively, i.e., without forcing the recovery log to stable storage, because durability of their effects is needed only if and when a subsequent user transaction and its log records rely on the system transaction's effects. If a user relies on the effects of a committed user transaction, that user transaction will have forced the log, which of course also forces any prior log records to stable storage, including those of any prior system transaction.

2.3 Log-structured file systems

The purpose of log-structured file systems is to increase write performance by replacing multiple small writes with a single large write [RO 92]. Reducing the number of seek operations is the principal gain; in disk arrays with redundancy, writing an entire "array page" at a time also eliminates the "small write penalty," which is due to adjusting parity pages after updates. While the actual parity calculations may be simple and inexpensive "exclusive or" computations, the more important cost is the need to fetch and then overwrite the parity page within an array page each time one of the data pages is updated. Thus, writing a single page may cost as much as 4 I/O operations in a RAID-4 or RAID-5 array, and even more in a RAID-6 or RAID-15 array.

Turning multiple small writes into a much more efficient single large write requires the flexibility to write dirty pages to entire new locations, which entails two new costs. First, there is a distinction between page identifier and page location – most of the file system links pages by page identifier, and page identifiers must be mapped to their current locations on disk. Updates to the structure that maintains this mapping must be logged carefully yet efficiently, quite comparable to the locking, latching, and logging required when splitting a B-tree page in a traditional multi-user multi-threaded database system. The main difference is that updates to the mapping information are initiated when the buffer manager evicts a dirty page, i.e., during write operations, rather than in the usual course of database updates.

Second, as pages are updated and their new images are written to new locations, the old images become obsolete and their disk space should be reclaimed. Unfortunately, disk pages will be freed in individual pages, not in entire array pages at a time, whereas only entire free array pages lend themselves to future fast write operations. The simple solution is to keep track of array pages with few remaining valid pages, and reclaim those disk pages by artificially updating them to their current contents – the update operation forces a future write operation, which of course will migrate the page contents to a new location convenient for the current large write operation at that time. Depending on the overall disk utilization, a noticeable fraction of disk activity might need to be dedicated to space reclamation. Fortunately, disk space is relatively inexpensive and many database servers run with less-than-full disks, because this is the only way to achieve the desired I/O rates. In fact, recent and current trends in disk technology increase storage capacity must faster than bandwidth, which motivates our research into bandwidth improvements through large write operations as well as justifies our belief that disks typically will be less than full and thus permit efficient reclamation and defragmentation of free space.

2.4 Transaction processing and log-structured file systems

A tempting but erroneous interpretation of the term "log-structured" assumes that a log-structured file system can support transactions without a recovery log. This is not the case, however. If a database system supports a locking granularity smaller than pages, concurrent transactions might update a single page; yet if one of the transactions commits and the other one rolls back, no page image reflects the correct outcome. In other words, it is important to realize that log-structured file systems are a software technique that enables fast writes; it is not an appropriate technique to implement atomicity or durability. Interestingly, techniques using shadow pages, which are similar to log-structured file systems as they also allocate new on-disk locations as part of write operations, have been found to suffer from a very similar restriction [CAB 81]. Consequently, shadow page techniques have been abandoned because they do not truly assist in the implementation of ACID transaction semantics, i.e., atomicity, consistency, isolation, and durability [G 81].

Seltzer's attempts of integrating transaction support into log-structured file systems [S 92, S 93, SS 90] did not materialize the expected gains in performance and simplicity, and apparently were abandoned. Rather than integrating transaction support into a file system, whether read-optimized or write-optimized, our approach is to integrate log-structured write operation into a traditional database management system with B-tree indexes, multi-level transactions, etc. It turns out that rather simple mechanisms suffice to achieve this purpose, and that these mechanisms largely exist but are not exploited for write-optimized database operation.

Lomet observed that the mapping information can be considered a database in its own right, and should be maintained using storage and transaction techniques similar to database systems [L 95], as in the Spiralog file system [WBW 96]. Our design follows this direction and keeps track of B-tree nodes and their current on-disk locations using traditional B-trees and database transactions, but it does not force all updates and all writes to migrate as log-structured file systems do.

If the mapping information can be searched efficiently as well as maintained efficiently and reliably, it is even conceivable to build a log-structured storage system that writes and logs not pages but individual records and other small objects, as in the Vagabond system [NB 97]. In contrast, our design leaves it to traditional mechanisms to manage records and objects in B-tree indexes and instead focuses on B-tree nodes stored as disk pages.

3 Proposed data structures and algorithms

In this section, we introduce our proposed changes to B-tree pages on disk and consider some of the effects of these changes. Further new opportunities enabled by these changes are discussed in detail in the subsequent sections.

Our proposed change is designed to solve the following problem. When a leaf page migrates to a new location, three pointers to that page (parent and two siblings) require updating. If a leaf page moves as part of a write operation, which is the essential mechanism of log-structured file systems whose advantageous effects we aim to replicate, not only its parent but also both of its siblings are updated and thus remain as dirty pages in the buffer pool. When those dirty pages are written, they too will migrate, and then force updates, writes, and migration of their respective siblings. In other words, updates and write operations ripple forward, backward, and back among the leaf pages.

3.1 Data structures

Our proposed change in data structures is very limited. It affects the forward and backward pointers that make up the chain of B^+-tree leaves (and may also exist in higher levels of a B^+-tree). Instead of pointing to neighboring pages using page identifiers, we propose to retain in each page a lower and upper "fence" key that define the range of keys that may be inserted in the future into that page. One of the fences is an inclusive bound, the other an exclusive bound, depending on the decision to be taken when a separator key in a parent node is precisely equal to a search key.

In the initial, empty B-tree with one node that is both root and leaf, negative and positive infinity are represented with special fence values. If the B-tree is a partitioned B-tree [G 03], special values in the partition identifier (the artificial leading key column) can represent these two fence values. In principle, the fences are exact copies of separator keys in the parent page. When a B-tree node (a leaf or an internal node) overflows and is split, the key that is installed in the parent node is also retained in the two pages resulting from the split as upper and lower fences.

A fence may be a valid B-tree record but it does not have to be. Specifically, the fence key that is an inclusive bound can be a valid data record at times, but the other fence key (the exclusive bound) is always invalid. If a valid record serving as a fence is deleted, its key must be retained as ghost record in that leaf page. In fact, ghost records are the implementation technique of choice for fences except that, unlike traditional ghost records, fences cannot be removed by a record insertion requiring free space within a leaf or by an asynchronous clean-up utility. A ghost record serving as inclusive fence can, however, be turned into a valid record again when a new record is inserted with precisely equal key.

The desirable effect of the proposed change is that splitting a node into two or merging two nodes into one is simpler and faster with fences than with physical pointers, because there is no need to update the nodes neighboring the node being split or merged. In fact, there is only a single physical pointer (with page identifier, etc.) to each node in a B-tree, which is the traditional, essential parent-to-child pointer. The lack of a physical page chain differs from traditional B-tree implementations and thus raises some concerns, which we address next. The benefits of this change will be considered in subsequent sections.

3.2 Concerns and issues

Before considering the effects of having only a single pointer to a B-tree node, from its parent, the most obvious issue to consider is the additional space requirement due to the fences. After all, the fences are keys, and keys can be lengthy strings values. Fortunately, however, these effects can be alleviated by suffix truncation [BU 77]. Rather than propagating an entire key to the parent node during a leaf split, only the minimal prefix of the key is propagated. Note that it is not required to split a full leaf precisely in the middle; it is possible to split near the middle if that increases the effectiveness of suffix truncation, and it is reasonable to do so because the shorter separator key in the parent will make future B-tree searches a little bit faster. Since the fences are literal copies of the separator key, truncating the separator immediately reduces not only the space required in the parent node but also the overhead due to fences.

While suffix truncation aids compressing the fences, the fences aid compressing B-tree entries because they simplify prefix truncation. The fences define the absolutely lowest and highest keys that might ever be in a page (until a future node split or merge); thus, if prefix truncation within each page is guided by the fences, there is no danger that a newly inserted key reduces the length of the prefix common to all keys in a page and requires reformatting all records within that page. Note that prefix truncation thus simplified can be employed both in leaves and in all internal B-tree nodes. If both prefix and suffix truncation is applied, then the remaining fences retained in a page may not be much larger than the traditional forward and backward pointers (page identifiers) they replace.

The exclusive fence record can simplify implementation of database compression in yet another way. Specifically, this record could store in each non-key field the most frequent value within its B-tree leaf (or the largest duplicate value), such that all data records with duplicate values can avoid storing copies of those values. This is a further simplification of the compression technique implemented in Oracle's database management system [PP 03].

Maybe the lack of forward pointers and its effect on cursors and on large (range or index-order) scans are a more substantial concern. Row-by-row cursors, upon reaching the low or high edge of a leaf node, must extract the fence key and search the B-tree from root to leaf with an appropriate "<", "≤", "≥", or ">" predicate, and the B-tree code must guide this search to the appropriate node, just as it does today when it processes "<" and ">" predicates.

For large scans, note that disk striping and disk arrays require deep read-ahead of more than one page. In a modern data warehouse server with 1 GB/s read bandwidth, 8 KB B-tree nodes, and 8 ms I/O time, 1,000 pages must be read concurrently (1 GB/s × 8 ms / 8 KB/page = 1,000 pages). Thus, a truly efficient range scan in today's multi-disk server architectures must be guided by the B-tree's interior nodes rather than based on the forward pointers, and in fact the page chain is useless today already for high-performance query processing.

Another important use of the page chain today is consistency checking – the ability of commercial database management systems to verify that the on-disk database has not been corrupted by hardware or software errors. In fact, write-optimized B-trees can be implemented without fence keys, but the reduced on-disk redundancy might substantially increase the effort required for detection of hardware and software errors. Thus, write-optimized B-trees without fence keys might not be viable for commercial database management systems. Fortunately, because the fences are precise copies of each other as well as the separator key in the parent node, they can serve the same purpose as the traditional page chain represented by page identifiers. Thus, our proposed change imposes no differences in functionality, performance, or reliability of consistency checks.

Key range locking, on the other hand, is affected by our change. Specifically, a key value captured in the fences is a resource that can be locked. Note that it is the key value (and a gap below or above that key) that is locked, not a specific copy of that key, and that it is therefore meaningless to distinguish between locking the upper fence of a leaf or the lower fence of that leaf's successor page. Because any leaf contains at least two fences, there never is a truly empty leaf page, and crawling through an empty leaf page to the next key is never required. More fundamentally, because a gap between existing keys never goes beyond a fence value (as the fence value separates ranges for the purpose of key range locking), crawling from one leaf to another in order to find the right key to lock is eliminated entirely. Thus, key range locking is substantially simplified by the presence of fences, eliminating both some complex code (that requires complex regression tests) and a run-time cost that occurs at unpredictable times. In fact, this benefit has been observed previously [ELS 97] but not, as in our design, exploited for additional purposes such as defragmentation, free space reclamation, and write-optimized B-trees.

4 Defragmentation and space reclamation

Large range queries as well as order-dependent query execution algorithms such as merge join require efficient index-order scans. Index updates, specifically split and merge operations on B-tree nodes, may damage contiguity on disk and thus reduce scan efficiency. Therefore, many vendors of database management systems recommend periodic defragmentation of B-tree indexes used in decision support.

During index defragmentation, the essential basic operation is to move individual or multiple pages allocated to the index. Pages are usually moved in index order and the move target is chosen in close proximity to the preceding correctly placed index node.

Reclaiming and consolidating free space as needed in log-structured file systems is quite similar. Again, the essential basic operation is to move pages with valid data to a new location. Pages to move are chosen based on their current location, and the move target is either a gap in the current allocation map or an area to which many such pages are moved. Not surprisingly, defragmentation utilities attempt to combine these two purposes, i.e., they attempt to defragment one or more indexes and concurrently consolidate free space in a single pass over the database.

4.1 B-tree maintenance during page migration

Moving a node in a traditional B-tree structure is quite expensive, for several reasons. First, the page contents might be copied from one page frame within the buffer pool to another. While the cost of doing so is moderate, it is probably faster to "rename" a buffer page, i.e., to allocate and latch buffer descriptors for both the old and new locations and then to transfer the page frame from one descriptor to the other. Thus, the page should migrate within the buffer pool "by reference" rather than "by value." If each page contains its intended disk location to aid database consistency checks, this field must be updated at this point. If it is possible that a deallocated page lingers in the buffer pool, e.g., after a temporary table has been created, written, read, and dropped, this optimized buffer operation must first remove from the buffer's hash table any prior page with the new page identifier. Alternatively, the two buffer descriptors can simply swap their two page frames.

Second, moving a page can be expensive because each B-tree node participates in a web of pointers. When moving a leaf page, the parent as well as both the preceding leaf and the succeeding leaf must be updated. Thus, all three surrounding pages must be present in the buffer pool, their changes recorded in the recovery log, and the modified pages written to disk before or during the next checkpoint. It is often advantageous to move multiple leaf pages at the same time, such that each leaf is read and written only once. Nonetheless, each single-page move operation can be a single system transaction, such that locks can be released frequently both for the allocation information (e.g., an allocation bitmap) and for the index being reorganized.

If B-tree nodes within each level form a chain not by physical page identifiers but instead by lower and upper fences, page migration and therefore defragmentation are considerably less expensive. Specifically, only the parent of a B-tree node requires updating when a page moves. Neither its siblings nor its children are affected; they are not required in memory during a page migration, they do not require I/O or changes or log records, etc. In fact, this is the motivation of our proposed change in the representation of B-tree nodes.

4.2 Logging and recovery of page migrations

The third reason why page migration can be quite expensive is logging, i.e., the amount of information written to the recovery log. The standard, "fully logged" method to log a page migration during defragmentation is to log the page contents as part of allocating and formatting a new page. Recovery from a system crash or from media failure unconditionally copies the page contents from the log record to the page on disk, as it does for all other page allocations.

Logging the entire page contents is only one of several means to make the migration durable, however. A second, "forced write" approach is to log the migration itself with a small log record that contains the old and new page locations but not the page contents, and to force the data page to disk at the new location prior committing the page migration. Forcing updated data pages to disk prior to transaction commit is well established in the theory and practice of logging and recovery [HR 83]. A recovery from a system crash can safely assume that a committed migration is reflected on disk. Media recovery, on the other hand, must repeat the page migration, and is able to do so because the old page location still contains the correct contents at this point during log-driven redo. The same applies to log shipping and database mirroring, i.e., techniques to keep a second (often remote) database ready for instant failover by continuously shipping the recovery log from the primary site and running continuous *redo* recovery on the secondary site.

A unique aspect of writing the page contents to its new location is that write-ahead logging is not required, i.e., the migration transaction may write the data page to the new location prior to writing any of its log records to stable storage. This is not true for the changes in the global allocation information; it only applies to the newly allocated location. The reason is that any recovery considers the new location random disk contents until the allocation is committed and the commit record is captured in the log. Two practically important implications are that a migration transaction with forced data write does not require any synchronous log writes, and that a single log record can capture the entire migration transaction, including transaction begin, allocation changes, page migration, and transaction commit. Thus, logging overhead for a forced-write page migration is truly minimal, at the expense of forcing the page contents to the new location before the page migration can commit. Note, however, that the page at the new location must include a log sequence number (LSN), requiring careful sequencing of the individual actions that make up the migration transaction if a single log record captures the entire transaction. The forced-write migration transaction will be the most important one in subsequent sections.

The most ambitious and efficient defragmentation method neither logs the page contents nor forces it to disk at the new location. Instead, this "non-logged" page migration relies on the old page location to preserve a page image upon which recovery can be based. During system recovery, the old page location is inspected. If it contains a log sequence number lower than the migration log record, the migration must be repeated, i.e., after the old page has been recovered to the time of the migration, the page must again be renamed in the buffer pool, and then additional log records can be applied to the new page. To guarantee the ability to recover from a failure, it is necessary to preserve the old page image at the old location until a new image is written to the new location. Even if, after the migration transaction commits, a separate transaction allocates the old location for a new purpose, the old location must not be overwritten on disk until the migrated page has been written successfully to the new location. Thus, if system recovery finds a newer log sequence number in the old page location, it may safely assume that the migrated page contents are available at the new location, and no further recovery action is required.

Some methods for recoverable B-tree maintenance already employ this kind of write dependency between data pages in the buffer pool, in addition to the well-known write dependency of write-ahead logging. To implement this dependency using the standard technique, both the old and new page must be represented in the buffer manager. Differently than in the usual cases of write dependencies, the old location may be marked clean by the migration transaction, i.e., it is not required to write anything back to the old location on disk. Note that redo recovery of a migration transaction must re-create this write dependency, e.g., in media recovery and in log shipping.

The potential weakness of this third method are backup and restore operations, specifically if the backup is "online," i.e., taken while the system is actively processing user transactions, and the backup contains not the entire database but only pages currently allocated to some table or index. Moreover, the detail actions of backup process and page migration must interleave in a particularly unfortunate way. In this case, a backup might not include the page image at the old location, because it is already deallocated. Thus, when backing up the log to complement the online database backup, migration transactions must be complemented by the new page image. In effect, in an online database backup and its corresponding restore operation, the logging and recovery behavior is changed in effect from a non-logged page migration to a fully logged page migration. Applying this log during a restore operation must retrieve the page contents added to the migration log record and write it to its new location. If the page also reflects subsequent changes that happened after the page migration, recovery will process those changes correctly due to the log sequence number on the page. Again, this is quite similar to existing mechanisms, in this case the backup and recovery of "non-logged" index creation supported by some commercial database management systems.

While a migration transaction needs to lock a page and its old and new locations, it is acceptable for a user transaction to hold a lock on a key with the B-tree node. It is necessary, however, that any such user transaction must search for the B-tree node again, with a new search pass from B-tree root to leaf, in order to obtain the new page identifier and to log further contents changes, if any, correctly. This is very similar to split and merge operations of B-tree nodes, which also invalidate knowledge of page identifiers that user transactions may temporarily retain. Finally, if a user transaction must roll back, it must compensate its actions at the new location, again very similarly to compensating a user transaction after a different transaction has split or merged B-tree nodes.

4.3 System transactions for page migration

While one may assume that database management systems already include defragmentation and a system transaction to migrate a page, our design is substantially more efficient than prior designs yet ensures the ability of media and system recovery. The most important advantage of the presented design over traditional page migration are the minimal log volume and the avoidance of ripple effects along the page chain. To summarize details of the redesigned page migration, as they may be helpful in later discussions:

- Since page migration does not modify database contents but only its representation on disk, it can be implemented as a system transaction.
- A system transaction can be committed very inexpensively without writing the commit record to stable storage.
- A page migration changes only one value in one B-tree node, i.e., the pointer from a parent node to one of its children, plus global allocation information.
- A migration transaction can force the page contents to its new location, log the page contents, or log only the migration without flushing.
- For system or media recovery after minimal logging, the page contents must be preserved in the old location, i.e., the old page location must not be overwritten, until the first write to the new location.
- The page migration operation must accept as parameters both the old and the new locations.
- When a B-tree node migrates from one disk location to another, it is required that the page itself is in memory in order to write the contents to the new location, and that its parent node is in memory and available for update in order to keep the B-tree structure consistent and up-to-date.
- The buffer pool manager can contribute to the efficiency of page migration by providing mechanisms to rename a page frame in the buffer pool.

We now employ this system transaction in our design for write-optimized B-trees.

5 Write-optimized B-trees

Assuming an efficient implementation of a system transaction to migrate a page from one location to another, the essence of our design is to invoke this system transaction in preparation of a write operation from the buffer pool to the disk. If the buffer pool needs to write multiple dirty pages to disk that do not require update-in-place for efficient large scans in the future, the buffer manager invokes the system transaction for page migration for each of these pages and then writes them to their new location in a single large write. In other words, the unusual and novel aspect of our design is that the buffer manager initiates and invokes a system transaction, in this case a page migration for each page chosen to participate in a large write.

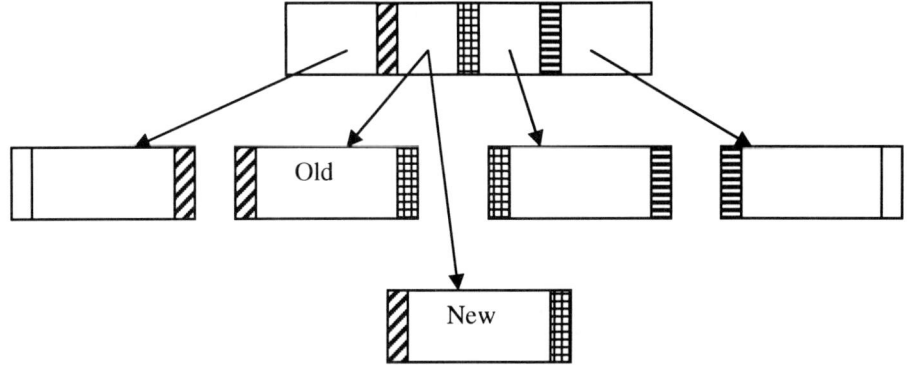

Figure 1. Page migration in a B-tree with fence keys.

Figure 1 illustrates the main concept enabling write-optimized B-trees, and also demonstrates the difference from B-trees implemented on top of log-structured file systems. When a page migrates to a new location as part of large write operation, its current location and thus the migration are tracked not in a separate indirection layer but within the B-tree itself. There is no need to adjust sibling pointers because those have become logical pointers, i.e., when a leaf is split, the separator key propagated to the parent node is retained in both leaves as lower and upper fence keys.

In many ways, recording a page's new location in a parent node is very comparable to recording the new location of a page in a log-structured file system. In fact, all the operations required in our system transaction are also required in a log-structured file system. The main difference is that our design keeps track of page migrations within the B-tree structures already present in practically all database management systems rather than imposing a separate mapping from logical page identifier to physical page location.

5.1 Accessing the parent node

It is essential for efficient page migration that access to the parent node is very inexpensive. We offer three approaches to this concern, with the third approach representing the preferred solution.

First, it is possible to search the B-tree from the root and simply abandon the page migration if the parent node cannot be found without I/O – recall that our design does not require page migration as part of every write as a traditional log-structured file system does.

Second, given that a B-tree node can only be located from its parent node, it is extremely probable that the parent is still available in the buffer pool, suggesting that it is reasonable to require that for each B-tree node in the buffer pool, its parent (and transitively the entire path to the root) be present in the buffer pool. Incidentally, cursor operations can also benefit from the parent's guaranteed presence in the buffer pool. This requirement can be implemented efficiently by linking the buffer descriptor of any B-tree node to the buffer descriptor of its parent node. Since multiple children can link to a single parent, reference counting is required. The most complex and expensive operation is splitting a parent node, since this requires probing the buffer pool for each of the child nodes that, if present, must link to the newly allocated parent node. Note that this operation requires no I/O; only the buffer pool's internal hash tables are probed. To assess the overhead, it may be useful to consider that some commercial database management systems today approximate the effect of write-only disk caches [SO 90] by probing prior to each I/O the buffer manager's hash table for neighboring disk pages that are dirty and could be written without an additional disk seek.

Third, in order to avoid a hard requirement that the parent node be in the buffer for each B-tree node in the buffer, the buffer manager simply avoids page migrations for pages without a link to a parent node. Thus, when evicting an internal B-tree node, all links from child nodes also in the buffer must be removed first, which requires multiple probes into the buffer pool's hash tables but no I/O. If a parent is reloaded into the buffer pool, the buffer manager may again search whether any child nodes are in the buffer, or a child-parent link may be re-established the next time a B-tree search navigates from the parent to a particular child node.

5.2 B-tree root nodes

B-tree root nodes have no parent node, of course, and their locations are recorded in the database catalogs. For root nodes, two alternatives suggest themselves.

679

First, given that page migration must be possible for defragmentation, there probably exists a system transaction to migrate a root page and correctly update the database catalogs. If root pages are appropriately marked in their buffer descriptors, this system transaction could be invoked by the buffer manager.

Second, B-tree root pages are always updated in place, i.e., they do not migrate as part of large write operations. Either the root pages are specially marked in their buffer descriptors or the absence of a link to the buffer descriptor of the parent page is interpreted precisely as for other B-tree nodes whose parent nodes have been evicted from the buffer pool, as discussed above.

5.3 Storage structures other than B-trees

If the database contains data structures other than B-trees, those structures can be treated similar to B-tree root nodes. In other words, they can be updated in place or specialize migration transactions could be invoked by the buffer manager. However, since the focus of this research is on write-optimized B-trees, we do not pursue the topic further. It may be worth to point out, however, that prior research has suggested employing B-tree structures even for somewhat surprising purposes, e.g., for run files in external merge sort [G 03].

5.4 Allocation and deallocation of disk pages

Keeping track of free space is a concern common to all log-structured file systems. Typically, a bitmap with a bit per page on the disk is divided into page-sized sections, these pages kept in the buffer pool for fast access, and dirty pages written to disk during database checkpoints. Some database systems, however, also maintain a bitmap per index. These bitmaps can guide fast disk-order index scans, provide added redundancy during consistency checks, and speed the search for a "lost" page identified in a consistency check. In a write-optimized environment, however, redundancy and update costs should be kept to a minimum, i.e., per-index bitmaps should be avoided. Instead, consistency checks and large scans should exploit the upper B-tree levels. Given that file systems rely entirely on tree structures for both purposes, and given that database management systems often use files in a file system to store data and logs, it is reasonable to conclude that database management systems also do not need this extra form of redundancy.

If a page is newly allocated for an index, e.g., due to a node split, it does not seem optimal to allocate a disk location for the new node if it will migrate as part of writing it to disk for the first time. For those cases, we suggest simulating a virtual disk device. Its main purpose is to dispense unique page identifiers that are used only while a newly allocated page remains in the buffer pool. In fact, the location of the buffer frame within the buffer pool could serve this purpose. When a new page is required, a page identifier on this virtual device is allocated and recorded in the node's parent. More importantly, this page identifier is used in log records whenever a page identifier is required. When the page is written to disk, it migrates from its virtual disk location to a genuine disk location, using the system transaction for page migration defined earlier. This technique avoids the cost of allocating a free disk page when splitting a B-tree node. Its expense, however, is additional complexity should the buffer manager attempt to evict the parent node prior to writing such a newly allocated page.

A very similar technique also applies to deallocation of pages. While multiple newly allocated pages require different virtual page identifiers, deallocated pages can probably all migrate to a single "trash bin" location.

5.5 Benefits

Having considered our design for write-optimized B-trees in some details, let us now review some benefits and advantages of the design, comparing it both to traditional read-optimized B-trees and to log-structured file systems.

An important benefit relative to log-structured file systems is that page migration is tracked and recorded within the B-tree structure. Thus, probing a B-tree for individual nodes, e.g., in an index nested loops join operation, is just as efficient as in read-optimized B-trees, without the complexity and run-time overhead associated with a log-structured file system. Thus, we believe that this design is attractive for online transaction processing environments, whereas prior designs based on log-structured file systems were not.

An important benefit relative to read-optimized B-trees is that write operations can be much larger than individual B-tree nodes. It is well known that disk access time is largely seek and rotation time except for very large transfers, and that random disk writes are not as fast as strictly sequential log writes. In fact, our design enables enormously flexible write logic. Dirty pages can be written in-place as in traditional database management systems, they can use the append-only logic of log-structured file systems in order to make previously random data writes as fast as sequential log writes, or they can be written very opportunistically at a location that is currently particularly convenient. For example, the NetApp file system [HM 00] uses "write anywhere" capabilities to write in any free location near the current location of the disk access mechanism. Using the same rationale, a database management system can write a dirty page to any free location near a currently active read request, as an alternative to write-only disk caches [SO 90].

In disk arrays, the ability to convert multiple small write requests into a single large write operation provides continuous load balancing and it circumvents the "small write penalty" [PGK 88]. In RAID-4, -5, -6, and -15 arrays [CLG 94], modifying a single data page requires reading, modifying, and updating one or more pages with parity data, and possibly even logging them for recovery purposes. Write-optimized B-trees and their large write operations are therefore a perfect complement to such disk arrays.

Finally, B-trees can benefit from a particularly simple and efficient form of compression. Recall that B-tree pages are utilized only about 70 % in most realistic scenarios [JS 89]. Thus, if multiple B-tree pages are written sequentially, multiple B-tree nodes can be compressed without any encoding effort. Unfortunately, data from an individual B-tree node may straddle multiple pages, and whether or not this form of compaction is an overall performance gain remains a topic for future research.

5.6 Space reclamation overhead

Write-optimized B-trees migrate individual pages from their current on-disk location to a new location, very similar to log-structured file systems, and must reclaim the fragmented free space left behind by page migrations. The required mechanisms must identify which areas of disk space to reclaim and then initiate a page migration of the valid pages not yet migrated from the area being reclaimed. It might very well be advantageous to distinguish multiple target areas depending on the predicted future lifetime of the data, e.g., using generation scavenging [OF 89, U 84] or a scheme based on segments like Sprite LFS [RO 92]. Our design makes no novel contributions for space reclamation policies, and we propose to adopt mechanisms developed for log-structured file systems, including space reclamation that also achieves defragmentation within each file or B-tree as a side benefit.

There is, however, an additional technique that is compatible with write-optimized B-trees but has not been employed in log-structured file systems. If disk utilization is very high and space reclamation is urgent, frequent, and thus expensive, the techniques explored in this research permit switching to read-optimized operation at any time. Thus, write-optimized B-trees can gracefully degrade to traditional read-optimized operation, with performance no worse than today's high performance database management systems. Moreover, as space contention eases and free space is readily available again, write-optimized B-trees can switch back to large, high-bandwidth writes at any time.

6 Performance

In migration transactions, each page write requires an update in the page's parent page as well as a log record due to that update. In this section, we analyze how these increases in write volume affect overall performance.

Large write operations increase the write bandwidth of a single disk or of a disk array by an order of magnitude or more. If the increase in write volume is substantially lower than the increase in write bandwidth, the increased write volume will diminish but not negate the I/O advantage of write-optimized B-trees.

If migration transactions happen frequently, it seems worthwhile to optimize their logging behavior. We expect the log volume due to a migration transaction to be between 160 and 400 bytes. If a data page and therefore a B-tree node are as large as 8 KB, and if every single write operation initiates a migration transaction, the logging overhead will remain at 2-5%. Assuming the log writes are always sequential and always fast, the additional logging volume should be small compared to the time savings in data writes.

More importantly, writing a page might dirty a parent page that had been previously clean. If so, this parent page must also be written before or during the next checkpoint. If the parent migrates at that time, the grandparent needs to be written in the subsequent checkpoint, etc., all the way to the B-tree root. Thus, write-optimized B-trees increase the volume of write operations in a database.

Clearly, the B-tree root should be written only once during each checkpoint, no matter how many of its child nodes, leaf pages, and pages in intermediate B-tree layers have been migrated during the last checkpoint period. Thus, in order to estimate the increase in write volume, it is important to estimate at which level sharing begins on a path from a leaf to the root.

Assuming that each B-tree node has 100 children (a conservative value for nodes of 8 KB, in particular if prefix and suffix truncation are employed) and assuming that updates and write operations are distributed uniformly over all leaves, sharing can be estimated from the fraction of updated leaves during each interval between two checkpoints. If 1% of all leaves are updated, each parent node will see one migrated leaf per checkpoint interval, whereas grandparent nodes will see many migrations of parent nodes during each checkpoint interval, i.e., no effective sharing at the parent level but lots of sharing at the level of grandparent nodes. Thus, the volume of write operations is increased by a factor marginally larger than 2. If the fan-out of B-tree nodes is 400 instead of 100, for example because nodes are larger or because prefix and suffix truncation are employed, sharing happens after 2 levels if as little as 0.25% of leaves are updated in each checkpoint interval. If 1% of 1% of all leaf pages (or 1 page in 10,000; or 1 in 160,000 assuming the larger fan-out of 400) are updated during each interval between checkpoints, sharing occurs after two levels. In those cases, the write volume is increased by as much as a factor of 3. If write bandwidth due to large writes increases by a factor of 10, the increased write volume diminishes but does not erase the advantage of large writes.

The situation changes dramatically if updates are not distributed uniformly across all leaves, but instead concentrated in a small section of the B-tree. For example, if a B-tree is partitioned, e.g., using an artificial leading key column [G 03], the most active keys and records can be assigned to a single "hot" partition. Leaf pages in that partition will be updated frequently, whereas all other leaf pages will be very stable. For a data collection where 80% of all updates affect 20% of rows, this design can be quite attractive, not only but in particular when the storage is organized as a partitioned and write-optimized B-tree. Alternatively, a pair of partitions can operate similar to a differential file [SL 76], i.e., one partition is not updated at all and the other one contains all recent changes.

7   Summary, future work, and conclusions

In summary, the design presented here advances database index management in two ways: it improves the performance of B-tree defragmentation and reorganization, and it can be used to implement write-optimized B-trees.

For defragmentation, it substantially reduces the logging effort and the log volume without much added complexity in buffer management or in the recovery from system and media failures. In fact, the reduction in log volume may reverse today's advantage of rebuilding an entire index over defragmentation of the existing index. Incremental online defragmentation, one page and one page migration transactions at a time, is preferable due to better database and application availability, and can now be achieved with competitive logging volume and effort.

Incidentally, efficient primitives for page movement within a B-tree also enable a promising optimization that seems to have been largely overlooked. O'Neil's SB-trees are ordinary B-tree indexes that allocate disk space in moderately large contiguous regions [O 92]. A slight modification of that proposal is a B-tree of super-nodes, each consisting of multiple traditional single-page B-tree nodes (this is reminiscent of proposals to interpret a single-page B-tree node as a B-tree of cache lines, e.g., [CGM 02]). When a super-node fills up, it is split and half its pages moved to a newly allocated super-node. The implied page movement is very similar to that in B-tree defragmentation, and it could be implemented very efficiently using our techniques for defragmentation.

For write-optimized B-trees, the design overcomes the two obstacles that have prevented success in prior efforts to combine ideas from log-structured file systems with online transaction processing. First, page access performance is equal to that of traditional (read-optimized, update-in-place) B-trees, with no additional overhead due to write-optimized operation and page migration. Second, the presented design permits an arbitrary mixture of read-optimized and write-optimized operation, allowing a wide variety of policies that can range from traditional update-in-place to a pure log-structured file system.

Alternatively, the presented design for write-optimized B-trees could be employed in a traditional log-structured file system to manage and maintain the mapping from logical page identifiers to their physical locations. Database researchers have recommended maintaining this mapping and its underlying index structure with strict and reliable transaction techniques, including shared and exclusive locks, transaction commits, checkpoints, durability through log-based recovery, etc. [L 95]. However, to the best of our knowledge, this recommendation has not yet been pursued by operating system or file system researchers.

The essential insights that enable the presented design are that the pointers inherent in B-trees can keep track of a node's current location on disk, and that page migrations in log-structured file systems are quite similar to defragmentation. Exploiting the pointers inherent in B-trees eliminates the indirection layer of log-structured file systems. The similarity to defragmentation permits exploiting traditional techniques for concurrency control, recovery, checkpoints, etc. Thus, the principal remaining problem was equivalent to making defragmentation very efficient. This problem was solved by representing the chain of neighboring B-tree nodes not with physical pointers as in traditional B$^+$-trees but with fence keys, which are copies of the separator key posted to the parent node when a B-tree node is split. Migrating a page from one location to another, both during defragmentation or while assembling multiple dirty buffer pages into a large write operation, requires only a single update in the node's parent. This change can be implemented reliably and efficiently using a system transaction that does not require forcing its commit record to stable storage and also does not require logging or writing the page contents.

In addition to enabling fast defragmentation and write-optimized operation, the design also simplifies splitting and merging nodes as well as prefix truncation within a node. It even substantially simplifies key range locking, because it entirely eliminate the code complexity and run-time overhead of crawling to neighboring pages in search of a key to lock. Thus, lower and upper fence keys instead of sibling pointers may be a worthwhile modification of traditional B$^+$-trees even disregarding defragmentation and write-optimized larger I/O.

As the required mechanisms are simple, robust, and quite similar to existing data structures and algorithms, we expect that they can be implemented with moderate development and test effort. A thorough and truly meaningful performance analysis of alternative policies for page migration and space reclamation will be possible only with a working prototype implementation within a complete database management system supporting real applications. This future investigation must consider policies for choosing between in-place updates and append-only writes, for logging during page migration, for buffer management, for space reclamation, and for incremental defragmentation using the mechanisms described earlier.

Acknowledgements

Discussions with Phil Bernstein, David Campbell, Jim Gray, David Lomet, Steve Lindell, Paul Randal, Leonard

Shapiro, and Mike Zwilling have been stimulating, helpful and highly appreciated. Barb Peters' suggestions have improved the presentation of the material.

References

[BC 72] Rudolf Bayer, Edward M. McCreight: Organization and Maintenance of Large Ordered Indices. Acta Inf. 1: 173-189 (1972).

[BU 77] Rudolf Bayer, Karl Unterauer: Prefix B-Trees. ACM Trans. Database Syst. 2(1): 11-26 (1977).

[C 79] Douglas Comer: The Ubiquitous B-Tree. ACM Comput. Surv. 11(2): 121-137 (1979).

[CAB 81] Donald D. Chamberlin, Morton M. Astrahan, Mike W. Blasgen, Jim Gray, W. Frank King III, Bruce G. Lindsay, Raymond A. Lorie, James W. Mehl, Thomas G. Price, Gianfranco R. Putzolu, Patricia G. Selinger, Mario Schkolnick, Donald R. Slutz, Irving L. Traiger, Bradford W. Wade, Robert A. Yost: A History and Evaluation of System R. Commun. ACM 24(10): 632-646 (1981).

[CGM 02] Shimin Chen, Phillip B. Gibbons, Todd C. Mowry, Gary Valentin: Fractal prefetching B^+-Trees: optimizing both cache and disk performance. SIGMOD Conf. 2002: 157-168.

[CLG 94] Peter M. Chen, Edward L. Lee, Garth A. Gibson, Randy H. Katz, David A. Patterson: RAID: High-Performance, Reliable Secondary Storage. ACM Comput. Surv. 26(2): 145-185 (1994).

[ELS 97] Georgios Evangelidis, David B. Lomet, Betty Salzberg: The hB-Pi-Tree: A Multi-Attribute Index Supporting Concurrency, Recovery and Node Consolidation. VLDB J. 6(1): 1-25 (1997).

[G 81] Jim Gray: The Transaction Concept: Virtues and Limitations (Invited Paper). VLDB Conf. 1981: 144-154.

[G 03] Goetz Graefe: Sorting and indexing with partitioned B-trees. Conf. on Innovative Data Systems Research, Asilomar, CA, January 2003.

[HM 00] Dave Hitz, Michael Marchi: A Storage Networking Appliance. Network Appliance, Inc., TR3001, updated 10/2000, http://www.netapp.com/tech_library/3001.html.

[HR 83] Theo Härder, Andreas Reuter: Principles of Transaction-Oriented Database Recovery. ACM Comput. Surv. 15(4): 287-317 (1983).

[JS 89] Theodore Johnson, Dennis Shasha: Utilization of B-trees with Inserts, Deletes and Modifies. PODS Conf. 1989: 235-246.

[L 93] David B. Lomet: Key Range Locking Strategies for Improved Concurrency. VLDB Conf. 1993: 655-664.

[L 95] David B. Lomet: The Case for Log Structuring in Database Systems. HPTS, October 1995. Also at http://www.research.microsoft.com/~lomet.

[LM 03] Bernd Lober, Ulrich Marquard: Anwendungs- und Datenbank-Benchmarking im Hochleistungsbereich von ERP-Systemen and Beispiel von SAP. Datenbank-Spektrum 7: 6-12 (2003). See also http://www.sap.com/benchmark.

[M 90] C. Mohan: ARIES/KVL: A Key-Value Locking Method for Concurrency Control of Multiaction Transactions Operating on B-Tree Indexes. VLDB Conf. 1990: 392-405.

[MHL 92] C. Mohan, Donald J. Haderle, Bruce G. Lindsay, Hamid Pirahesh, Peter M. Schwarz: ARIES: A Transaction Recovery Method Supporting Fine-Granularity Locking and Partial Rollbacks Using Write-Ahead Logging. ACM Trans. Database Syst. 17(1): 94-162 (1992).

[NB 97] Kjetil Nørvåg, Kjell Bratbergsengen: Write Optimized Object-Oriented Database Systems. Conf. of the Chilean Computer Science Society, Valparaiso, Chile, November 1997: 164-173.

[O 92] Patrick E. O'Neil: The SB-Tree: An Index-Sequential Structure for High-Performance Sequential Access. Acta Inf. 29(3): 241-265 (1992).

[OF 89] John K. Ousterhout, Fred Douglis: Beating the I/O Bottleneck: A Case for Log-Structured File Systems. Operating Systems Review 23(1): 11-28 (1989).

[PGK 88] David A. Patterson, Garth A. Gibson, Randy H. Katz: A Case for Redundant Arrays of Inexpensive Disks (RAID). SIGMOD Conf. 1988: 109-116.

[PP 03] Meikel Pöss, Dmitry Potapov: Data Compression in Oracle. VLDB Conf. 2003: 937-947.

[RO 92] Mendel Rosenblum, John K. Ousterhout: The Design and Implementation of a Log-Structured File System. ACM Trans. Computer Syst. 10(1): 26-52 (1992).

[S 92] Margo I. Seltzer: File System Performance and Transaction Support. Ph.D. thesis, Univ. of California, Berkeley, 1992.

[S 93] Margo I. Seltzer: Transaction Support in a Log-Structured File System. ICDE 1993: 503-510.

[SL 76] Dennis G. Severance, Guy M. Lohman: Differential Files: Their Application to the Maintenance of Large Databases. ACM Trans. Database Syst. 1(3): 256-267 (1976).

[SO 90] Jon A. Solworth, Cyril U. Orji: Write-Only Disk Caches. SIGMOD Conf. 1990: 123-132.

[SS 90] Margo I. Seltzer, Michael Stonebraker: Transaction Support in Read Optimizied and Write Optimized File Systems. VLDB Conf. 1990: 174-185.

[U 84] D. Unger: Generation Scavenging: A Non-Disruptive High Performance Storage Reclamation Algorithm. ACM SIGSOFT/SIGPLAN Software Eng. Symp. on Practical Software Development Environments, Pittsburgh, April 1984.

[WBW 96] Christopher Whitaker, J. Stuart Bayley, Rod D. W. Widdowson: Design of the Server for the Spiralog File System. Digital Technical Journal 8(2): 15-31 (1996).

Cache-Conscious Radix-Decluster Projections

Stefan Manegold   Peter Boncz   Niels Nes   Martin Kersten

CWI, Kruislaan 413, 1098 SJ Amsterdam, The Netherlands

{Stefan.Manegold,Peter.Boncz,Niels.Nes,Martin.Kersten}@cwi.nl

Abstract

As CPUs become more powerful with Moore's law and memory latencies stay constant, the impact of the memory access performance bottleneck continues to grow on relational operators like join, which can exhibit random access on a memory region larger than the hardware caches. While cache-conscious variants for various relational algorithms have been described, previous work has mostly ignored (the cost of) projection columns. However, real-life joins almost always come with projections, such that proper projection column manipulation should be an integral part of any generic join algorithm. In this paper, we analyze cache-conscious hash-join algorithms including projections on two storage schemes: N-ary Storage Model (NSM) and Decomposition Storage Model (DSM). It turns out, that the strategy of first executing the join and only afterwards dealing with the projection columns (i.e., post-projection) on DSM, in combination with a new finely tunable algorithm called Radix-Decluster, *outperforms all previously reported projection strategies. To make this result generally applicable, we also outline how DSM Radix-Decluster can be integrated in a NSM-based RDBMS using projection indices.*

1 Introduction

Random memory access outside the CPU cache(s) has become very expensive over the past decade and will remain so in the future. As such, the bottleneck for low-level database data access is shifting from I/O to memory access [2, 9, 3]. While the performance penalty for inefficient usage can be dramatic, the database field need not despair. Several decades of progress in database technology has already produced a host of techniques for processing data volumes stored on large but slow memories (i.e., disks) by making efficient use of a smaller but faster memory (RAM). The recent research into *cache-conscious query processing* focuses on transforming these techniques to work one level higher up the memory hierarchy (optimize memory access by making efficient use of the CPU caches) and/or to devise new techniques. We build on recent work into making the join operator cache-conscious, among others by introducing a *Partitioned Hash-Join* [18] that can be paired with a fine-grained partitioning operator called *Radix-Cluster* [6] to partition huge relations into a large number of small clusters that each fit a CPU cache with just a few tens of KBs.

A limitation of these previous efforts is that so far they only considered joins on thin relations consisting solely of the join keys and producing only a table of matching oid pairs (i.e., a join-index [20]). However, any real-life RDBMS join query goes accompanied by some projection of non-join columns into the result. The cost of handling such projection columns depends on their number, type(s) and the relation cardinalities (both inputs and result). The actual cost impact can vary from zero (in the not-so-realistic case where there are no projections at all), to totally dominating (e.g., imagine a join with thousands of projection columns to propagate feature vectors in a multimedia application). In our performance evaluation, we find that queries may spend more than 90% of their time in projection. Therefore, efficient handling of projections should be part of any cache-conscious join technique.

1.1 Problem Statement

This paper describes optimization of CPU- and memory-resources of generic equi-join *including* projections:

```
SELECT  larger.a1, .., larger.aY,
        smaller.b1, .., smaller.bZ
FROM    larger, smaller
WHERE   larger.key = smaller.key
```

The focal point of our analysis is the performance impact of the amount of projection columns $a1..aY$ respectively $b1..bZ$, given various relation and join result sizes. Handling projections efficiently only becomes hard when *both* the smaller and larger table have many tuples, such that their individual columns do not fit the cache. Our *Radix-Decluster* algorithm addresses this situation.

Permission to copy without fee all or part of this material is granted provided that the copies are not made or distributed for direct commercial advantage, the VLDB copyright notice and the title of the publication and its date appear, and notice is given that copying is by permission of the Very Large Data Base Endowment. To copy otherwise, or to republish, requires a fee and/or special permission from the Endowment.

**Proceedings of the 30th VLDB Conference,
Toronto, Canada, 2004**

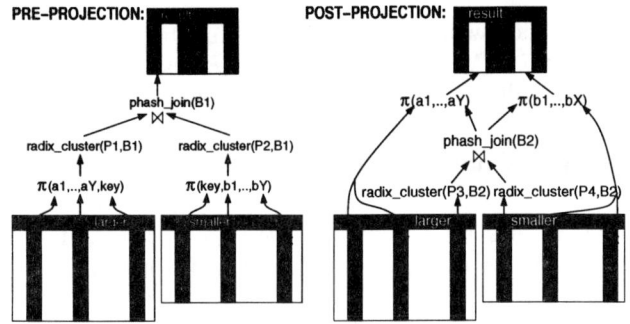

Figure 1. Pre- vs. Post-Projection

The commonly applied projection strategy in a RDBMS is *pre-projection* (see Figure 1), where the projection columns are fetched in the table scans preceding the join, and where the projection column values travel as 'extra luggage' together with the join keys through the join pipeline. In contrast, Radix-Decluster is a *post-projection* method, i.e., one where first the join result is computed, creating a (partial) join-index, and only afterwards the full query result is produced by computing the projection columns. Though we focus the experiments on one particular join algorithm (Partitioned Hash-Join), the Radix-Decluster algorithm is independent of the join method chosen.

1.1.1 RAM vs. Disk Optimization

Since we have already mentioned the analogy between optimizing CPU cache-access and optimizing disk access, it is instructive to point out the main similarities and differences. As for similarities, both disk and RAM have to contend with a high random access latency, that relative to CPU speed is increasing exponentially over time. Also just like disk, RAM is a block device (block=cache line), and sequential data access has now become much faster than random access, even when random access makes use of *all* data in the block (we call this "optimal" random access). This effect is caused by a new feature in memory subsystems called *data prefetching*: the CPU or in some cases the memory chipset automatically detect sequential access patterns and schedule data loads in advance for these [10, 8]. This is complemented by advances in DRAM technology, which keeps banks of recently accessed locations open, such that adjacent locations can be more quickly available. On our experimentation platform, sequential access – as obtained by STREAM [15] – is almost 10 times faster than "optimal" random access: 3.2GB/s vs. 360MB/s (a 178ns latency for getting a cache-line of 64 bytes makes for 360MB/s).

An important difference between disk and RAM is that the disk can be controlled using an OS interface, allowing traditional DBMS systems full control over their buffer cache. In contrast, RAM is cached implicitly in hardware, (most often) using an LRU mechanism with limited associativity. Thus, the only way that query processing algorithms can now influence RAM caching is indirectly by controlling data placement and access pattern. A second difference is the small granularity of the CPU caches. There is a "15 year gap" between CPU cache and RAM sizes: problem sizes of 2004 must now be crammed in caches having the RAM sizes of 1989. This means that e.g., partitioning to fit something large into the CPU cache must create *many* more small partitions than classical partitioning to fit something on disk into RAM ever had to. Having to manage (tens of) thousands of partitions rather than a handful can expose bottlenecks that remained unnoticed in the disk case, as we will see in our discussion of the Radix-Cluster algorithm.

1.1.2 Experimentation Platform

The work reported here partly builds upon the research into cache-conscious query processing in the MonetDB project. MonetDB[1] is a main-memory database system targeted at query-intensive applications [5] that uses a vertically fragmented storage scheme called the Decomposition Storage Model (DSM) [7]. In DSM, each tuple gets a unique system-generated oid that is typically densely ascending (0,1,2,...), and for each column a DSM table is created that holds [oid,value] pairs. Comparable to what RowIds are in Oracle, the MonetDB system has support for *implicit* columns – also dubbed void columns ("virtual-oids") – to represent such densely ascending oid columns on the logical level without taking any physical storage. Thus in MonetDB, each relational column is stored in a separate [void,value] table. Most DSM systems [19, 17] do away with the extra storage for the oids, such that the DSM data layout boils down to a single array for each column. DSM is cache-friendly when (OLAP) queries need only a subset of all table columns (i.e., in case of low *projectivity*). In the commonly used NSM storage scheme (i.e., a layout with each tuple contiguously stored), this means that parts of the cache line will not be used. In DSM, each cache line only contains values from the same column, and only relevant columns are loaded, achieving optimal cache line usage.

A second characteristic of MonetDB is its column-wise query processing model, which allowed for an implementation of its query processing algebra without need for an interpreter to evaluate expressions (each operation performs a simple, hard-coded, operation on large arrays of values, producing a new column as result). This goes in conjunction with the absence of low-level record/attribute lookup and data movement functionality, as columns are accessible by position as arrays of a homogeneous type. The experiments performed confirm these factors give MonetDB a significant advantage in terms of raw CPU efficiency that is strongly linked to this query execution model.

The third main characteristic of MonetDB is cache-conscious query processing. MonetDB has been the birth ground for a number of novel cache-conscious algorithms [6]. *Radix-Decluster* – the contribution of this paper – is a crucial addition to this collection.

---

[1] Available at http://www.sourceforge.net/projects/monetdb

1.1.3 Related Work

Though our experimentation platform is MonetDB, which is a DSM system, we compare our approach with its more common counterpart NSM, and in particular with pre-projection in NSM (which is used in almost all commercial database systems). However, there has recently also been some research into NSM post-projection, in particular the Slam- and Jive-Join algorithms [11]. While these algorithms work under the assumption that the join-index is already computed and available (hence pre-projection is not an option), and they are designed mainly for an I/O setting, we also include them in our NSM comparison with Radix-Decluster to evaluate their usefulness from the perspective of cache-conscious query processing.

An interesting alternative storage scheme is PAX[1], which basically does DSM within an NSM disk page. Thus, PAX cache-line usage can be as efficient as DSM under low projectivity, but PAX still wastes I/O bandwidth on such queries, which easily can cause a performance bottleneck. Though we will make our case that Radix-Decluster on DSM can be scaled to a disk-based RDBMS that runs on a high bandwidth I/O subsystem (e.g., using a well-sized RAID array of SCSI disks controlled through PCI-X), our experimentation is limited to main-memory execution, by lack of such an (expensive) setup. As in main-memory the difference between PAX and DSM is small, we limit ourselves here to the two extremes NSM and DSM.

Finally, we build here on previous work on detailed performance modeling of hierarchical memory access cost [12, 13] using hardware-independent formulas that are parametrized by all relevant architectural characteristics. These parameters can be derived automatically at run-time with the Calibrator utility [2], which is also integrated in MonetDB. The cost formulas are easy-to-define as they consist of a combination of a number of basic patterns (with known formulas) that can be combined automatically with composition functions. In all, these cost models allow us to quickly analyze the behavior of the various algorithms, and to draw conclusions on their optimal parameter settings.

1.2 Outline

In Section 2, we give a short re-cap on cache-conscious Partitioned Hash-Join and Radix-Cluster, which are basic building blocks in this research. In Section 3, we show how Radix-Cluster can be used to optimize memory access of post-projections to one of the join relations. In order to optimize cache usage for projections on *both* join relations, we then introduce our new *Radix-Decluster* algorithm. In Section 4, we perform exhaustive experiments with pre- and post-projection strategies both for the DSM and NSM storage schemes, and compare non cache-optimized strategies with our Radix algorithms, as well as with Jive-Join. In Section 5 we make our case why and how DSM post-projection with Radix-Decluster should be integrated in standard RDBMS technology, before we present our conclusions and discuss directions for future work in Section 6.

2 Cache-Conscious Join

We give a short re-cap on cache-conscious join, using *Partitioned Hash-Join* in conjunction with *Radix-Cluster* [6]. In [14], we give cost model descriptions for these algorithms, and show how these correctly predict their performance (see resp. Figures 9a and 9b).

2.1 Partitioned Hash-Join

In the Hash-Join algorithm considered in this paper, the outer relation is scanned sequentially, while a hash-table is used to probe the inner relation. The very nature of the hashing algorithm implies that the access pattern to the inner relation (plus hash-table) is random. Therefore, *Partitioned Hash-Join* first scans both relations, and partitions them according to a hashing criterion, making each inner partition smaller than the cache size, such that the subsequent Hash-Joins on the corresponding partitions all have good cache behavior [18]. The "cursors" in the output partitions where the partitioning operator inserts tuples as it scans its input, all need to be in a cache-line in order to achieve good performance during partitioning. As the number of available cache lines is limited (especially in systems that have a slow TLB cache, with usually only 64 entries) and the number of cursors grows with the size of the relation (a bigger relation leads to more partitions of a given size), the simple single-pass partitioning is limited in its scalability: above a certain relation size, the partitioning operation itself becomes a performance problem due to cache thrashing, as not all cursors can be kept in cache anymore.

2.2 Radix-Cluster

The *Radix-Cluster* algorithm, which uses incremental multi-pass partitioning, has been shown to solve the operand partitioning problem. It provides efficient partitionings needed for large joins in two or even more passes [6]. Briefly, radix_cluster(B,P) uses the lower B *Radix-Bits* of the integer hash-value of the join attribute to cluster a relation into $H = 2^B$ partitions. By performing P sequential passes, each of which use B_p bits, starting from the left ($\sum_1^P B_p = B$), Radix-Cluster limits the number of partitions created per pass to $H_p = 2^{B_p}$ ($\prod_1^p H_p = H$). Figure 2 sketches a Partitioned Hash-Join of two relations L and R. First, both relations are clustered into 8 partitions (3 bits) using 2 passes. The first pass uses the 2 left-most of the lower 3 bits to create 4 partitions. In the second pass, each of these partitions is sub-divided into 2 partitions using the remaining bit. Once both relations are clustered, a hash-join is performed on all matching partitions. For ease of

---
[2]Calibrator is available from http://monetdb.cwi.nl/Calibrator

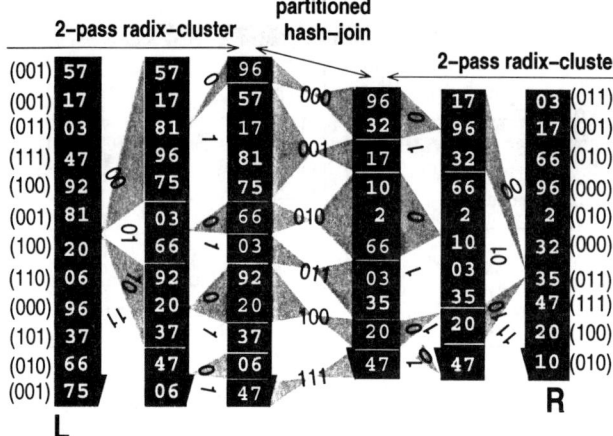

black tuples hit (lowest 3-bits of values in parenthesis)

Figure 2. Partitioned Hash-join

presentation, we did not apply a hash-function in Figure 2. In practice, though, a hash function should even be used on integer values to ensure that all bits of the join attribute play a role in the lower B bits used for clustering.

3 DSM Post-Projection

The DSM post-projection strategy has two phases:

1. *Make a join-index.* First we access only the DSM tables storing the key columns, and join these together to find matching pairs of tuples: a join-index [20].

2. *Do column projections.* One-by-one, we construct the columns of the result relation, each in a separate DSM table, by using the join-index to fetch values from one input column (also stored in a DSM table).

The join-index consists of [oid,oid] combinations of pointers into both "smaller" and "larger" input relations. These oids are not necessarily implemented as pointers, but may also be integer record numbers, byte offsets or RowIds (combinations of disk-block numbers and byte offsets). The projection operations are Pointer-Based Joins or *Positional-Joins*, with negligible CPU cost. In MonetDB, columns are stored in [void,value] tables, which are implement as arrays [3]. Thus, an oid is a simple integer (starting at 0 for the first entry), and Positional-Join equals array lookup.

One should note that the DSM post-projection join strategy *materializes* the join result. This is inevitable for the so-called "hard" join cases, where we must join two relations that do not fit the small-but-fast memory (i.e., the CPU cache). This is similar to scalable I/O-based join algorithms such as Sort-Merge-Join or Hybrid Hash-Join, that must be applied when the inner relation exceeds the RAM buffer size and pipelining is not possible.

---
[3]Columns of variable-sized types like string use an extra – separate – memory buffer, where the array simply contains integer offsets into.

In MonetDB, a join only is "hard" if the *individual* columns - rather than the entire "smaller" relation - exceed the CPU cache. In the other, so-called "easy" cases, we can use e.g., simple non-partitioned Hash-Join, by building a hash-table on the "smaller" relation to generate the join-index. The join-index will then contain the oids of the "larger" relation in ascending order, such that the Positional-Joins for projecting the input columns into the result exhibit a sequential RAM access pattern. As discussed in Section 1.1.1, sequential RAM access is well-supported by modern hardware. In contrast, the Positional-Joins for the projections from the "smaller" relation will have a random access pattern. Luckily, these columns fit the CPU cache in the "easy" cases, so the cache-lines where the input columns are stored will stay cached in the CPU after the first access, such that subsequent (adjacent) data fetches can be serviced from the cache.

In this paper, we attack the problem of executing "hard" joins in a cache-conscious manner. With CPU caches limited to a couple of MBs, and assuming an average column-width of 4 bytes, this currently translates into joins between (intermediate) relations that *both* have 500K or more tuples, which is a common and thus relevant problem.

3.1 Partial Radix-Cluster

We use Partitioned Hash-join, as described in Section 2, to join two relations that both exceed the CPU cache in a cache-conscious manner. Due to the nature of Partitioned Hash-Join, neither the oids of the "larger" nor those of the "smaller" relation appear in ascending order in the resulting join-index. A (standard) improvement is therefore to sort the join-index, in the order of the oids of the "larger" relation. In MonetDB, we re-use the Radix-Cluster algorithm as a fast *Radix-Sort*, by exploiting the property that oids stem from dense domains $[0..N\rangle$ (where N is the size of some relation). For all types but oid, Radix-Cluster transforms each value with a hash function, both to obtain integer bits and to combat skew. For oids, hashing is not applied as oids are integers already and not skewed. This also means that a Radix-Cluster on all *significant* bits (i.e., the lowermost $log_2(N)$ bits) is equivalent to Radix-Sort. Radix-Sort can be compared with traditional run-generating sort algorithms, as it also partitions the data on a sequential pass, and then (iteratively) further processes each partition.

Fully sorting the join-index, however, is overkill as a *partial ordering* can achieve the same effect. If the join-index consists of clusters that each contain oids of only a certain (disjoint) range, a Positional-Join into a projection column sequentially processes each cluster one by one, and while processing each individual cluster, accesses only a limited region in the projection column. If this region is small enough (such that it fits the cache), the algorithm will approach optimal cache (re-)usage. To make partial clustering possible, we added the possibility to indicate to Radix-Cluster to stop early and ignore a certain number of lower

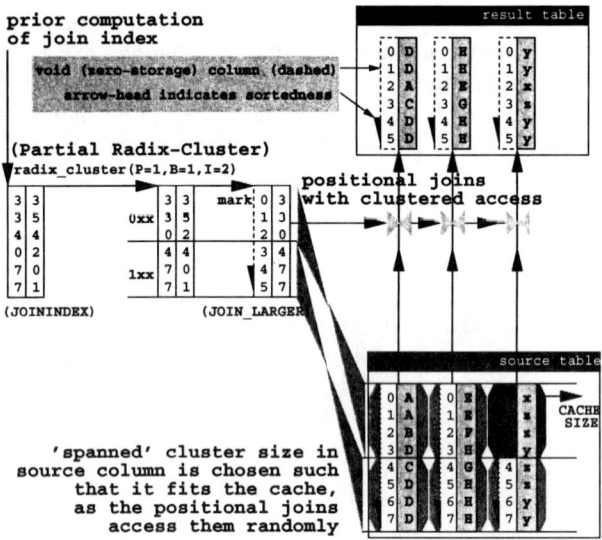

Figure 3. Projection Joins Using Partial Radix-Cluster

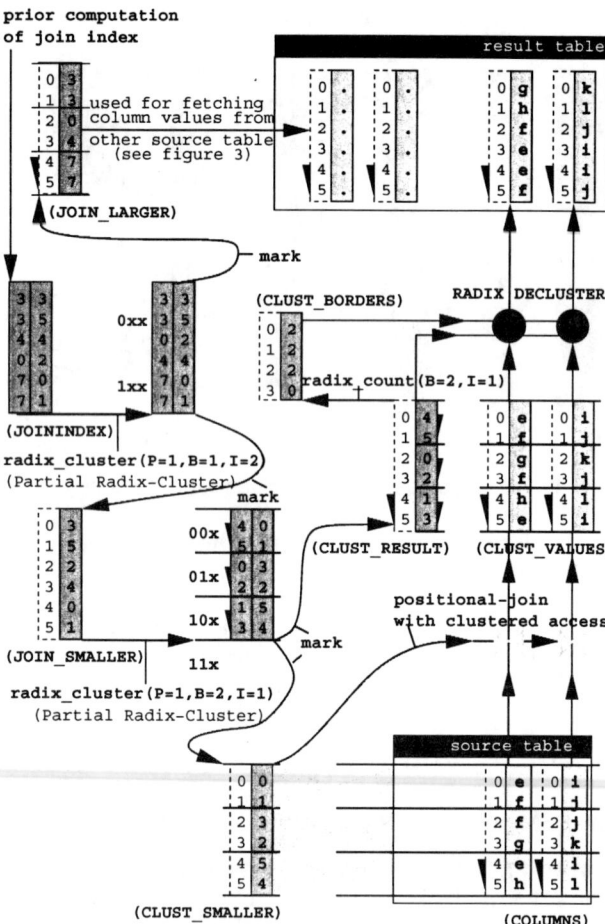

Figure 4. Optimized DSM Post-Projection Using Radix-Decluster

Radix-Bits. Stopping early leaves the relation unsorted on the lowermost bits (i.e., partially ordered). The benefit of this "partial-cluster" strategy is that it has the potential to optimize memory performance of the column projections using Positional-Joins just as well as a full Radix-Sort, but at a clustering cost that is much less.

Figure 3 shows that we first Partially Radix-Cluster JOININDEX in one pass ($P = 1$), using one Radix-Bit ($B = 1$) and stopping early at the first ($I = 1$), lowermost, Radix-Bit. On the resulting [oid,oid] table, we create a [void,oid] view JOIN_LARGER (using the mark() operator [5]). The right column of JOIN_LARGER contains the clustered oid column, and the left column consist of a new densely ascending oid sequence that represents the join result. Subsequent Positional-Joins between this JOIN_LARGER view and the input columns have a nice sequential access pattern, eliminating the cache problem. We compute the optimal number of Radix-Bits B and Ignore-Bits I as follows:

$$B = 1 + log_2(|COLUMN|) - log_2(C / \overline{COLUMN})$$
$$I = log_2(|JOININDEX|) - B$$

where $|R|$ denotes the number of tuples in a table R, $\overline{R}$ denotes the byte-width of these tuples, C is the size of the cache in bytes (see [12, 13]). For example, if we have a CPU cache of 64KB and we have values that are 4 bytes wide, then a cluster of 16,384 tuples would just fit. If the source table from where the projections come has 10M tuples, we would create $2^{10} = 1024$ clusters to arrive at a mean cluster size of 10,000 (which would be the largest cluster size $< 16,384$). Such clusters can be created with a partial Radix-Cluster on the highest significant 10 bits (i.e., bits 24-15, as $log_2(10M) = 24$), allowing Radix-Sort to ignore the lowermost 14 bits.

3.2 Radix-Decluster

Even when using Partial Radix-Cluster to optimize projections into the "larger" relation, cache problems still occur for the projections from the "smaller" relation. It is clear that the join-index (and thus the join result) cannot simultaneously be clustered in *both* oid orders. Figure 4 shows that after performing the projections into the "larger" relation, we re-cluster the view JOIN_SMALLER (that similar to JOIN_LARGER consists of fresh densely ascending oids left, paired with the right column of the clustered join-index). This yields a temporary [oid,oid] table. We then create two [void,oid] views CLUST_RESULT and CLUST_SMALLER from this table using the mark() operator. The left column of these views is a fresh "void" column of new ascending oids. The right column of CLUST_SMALLER holds the oids of the join-index that point into the "smaller" table in a nice clustered order, while the corresponding values of the right column of CLUST_RESULT hold the correct position of those join-tuples in the final result. The next step in the process is to use CLUST_SMALLER to perform the projections with cache-

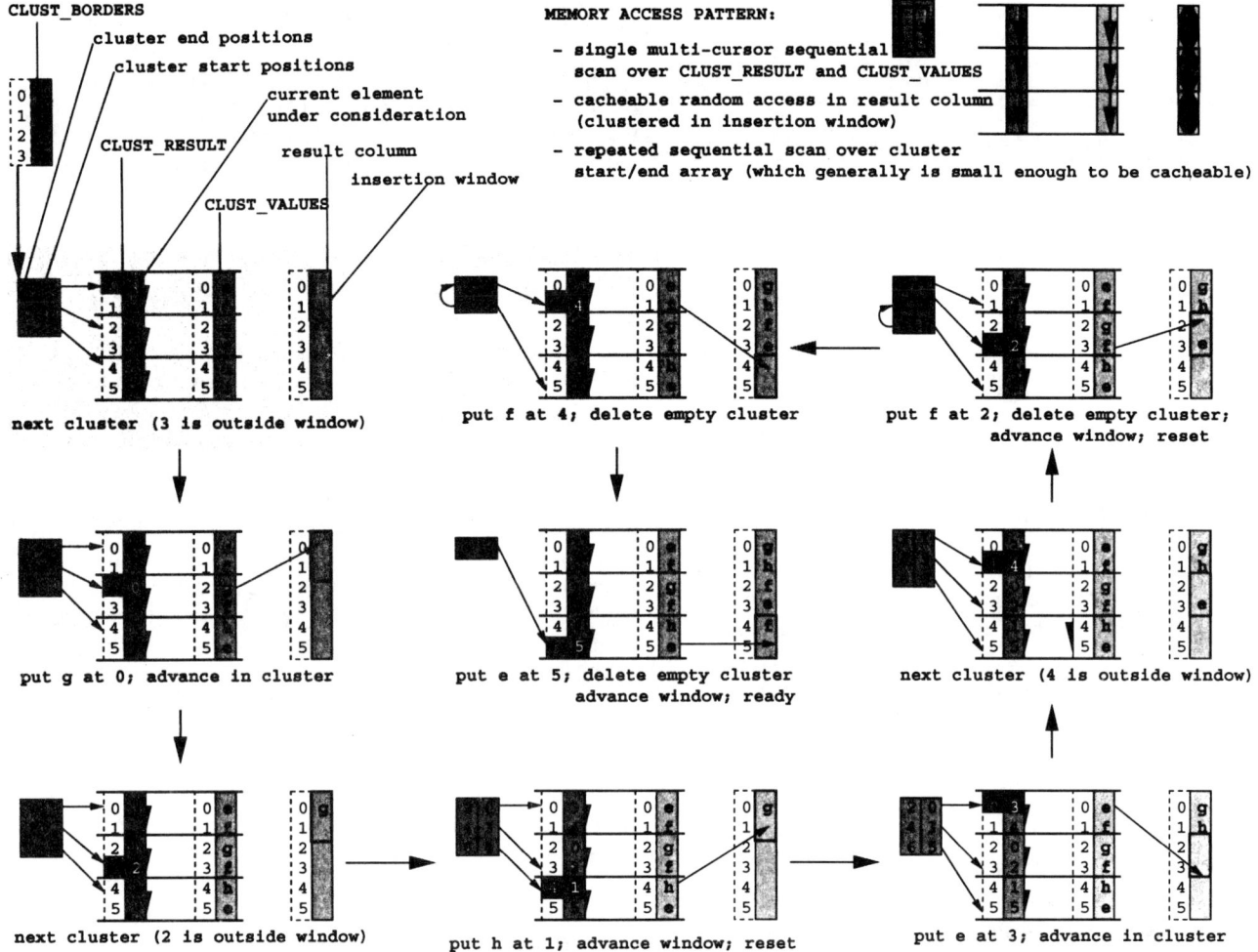

Figure 5. The Memory Access Pattern Of Radix-Decluster

efficient Positional-Joins. This, however, produces projection columns (denoted CLUST_VALUES) which are not yet in the correct order. The *Radix-Decluster* algorithm – depicted in detail in Figure 5 – performs the task of putting them in the correct final result order in a cache-friendly manner.

Radix-Decluster exploits the following two properties of the right column of CLUST_RESULT, which was created by Radix-Clustering a left void column on the order of its right column: (1) as Radix-Cluster neither adds nor deletes any values, this column would again form a dense sequence $(0, 1, ..N-1)$ when sorted. (2) within each cluster, the oids are still sorted. This happens because Radix-Cluster scans its input sequentially, and appends values to their respective output cluster, thus locally respecting the input order.

Property (2) implies that this right column can be sorted by **merging** all sorted clusters. However, the CPU cost of a merge of N tuples partitioned over $H = 2^B$ sorted clusters is at least $O(log(H)N)$. Alternatively, using Property (1) we could just insert the values from CLUST_VALUES in the result array using the oids from CLUST_RESULT as array index, with CPU cost $O(N)$. However, these insertions would constitute a random access pattern larger than the CPU cache.

We obtain the best of both approaches, by restricting the random access to an *insertion-window* W (cf., Figure 5). Each iteration of the algorithm processes each cluster once, advancing a cursor in it while the oids still fit in the window, inserting the values at this oid position. Property (1) tells that after processing each cluster once, *all* positions in the insertion window will have been filled (it is a dense oid sequence). Then, the window is shifted $|W|$ positions and the process repeats until all cursors have reached the end of their cluster. The window size $|W|$ is preferably much larger than the number of clusters, such that per iteration in each cluster multiple tuples fall into the window. These multiple tuples are accessed sequentially in both CLUST_RESULT and CLUST_VALUES. This memory access pattern is crucial, as the sequential access fully uses the cache lines that store both columns. The only restriction is that $|W|$ must fit the memory cache (i.e., $||W|| \leq C$), as it is filled in random order.

Pseudo-code of the algorithm is in Figure 6. The

```
<Type>[]
radix_decluster<Type>(
    int                        cardinality, nclusters,
    Type                       values[cardinality],
    oid                        IDs[cardinality],
    struct { int start, end } cluster[nclusters])
{
    <Type> result_column[] = malloc(cardinality*sizeof(<Type>));
    int windowLimit, windowSize = CACHESIZE / 2*sizeof(<Type>);

    for(windowLimit-windowSize; nclusters>0; windowLimit+=windowSize) {
      for(int i=0; i < nclusters; i++) {
        while (IDs[cluster[i].start] < windowLimit) {
          result_column[IDs[cluster[i].start]] = values[cluster[i].start];
          if (++cluster[i].start >= cluster[i].end) {
            cluster[i] = cluster[--nclusters]; // delete empty cluster
            if (i >= nclusters) break;
          }
        } // while more cluster elements in window
      } // while more clusters to merge
    } // while more insertion windows to fill result
    return result_column;
}
```

Figure 6. The Radix-Decluster Algorithm

`radix_count` previously mentioned in Figure 4, analyzes a (partially) Radix-Clustered column and returns the actual sizes of the clusters. These sizes are used in the Radix-Decluster to initialize the cluster border structure.

The Radix-Decluster projection strategy is more expensive than the partial-cluster strategy discussed earlier. Both strategies feature one initial Radix-Cluster, and for each projection column a Positional-Join, but the former adds an extra Radix-Decluster operation for each projection column. Hence, it will only be used for getting projection columns from the table with cheaper projections. Which input relation in the join has the cheapest projection phase depends on the number of projection columns in both relations, the data types in these projection columns, and the number of tuples in both input relations.

4 Performance Evaluation

In this section, we present experiments done on a 2.2GHz Pentium 4 machine, with a 64-entry TLB with miss latency of 50 cycles, a 16KB L1 cache with 32-byte cache lines and a miss latency of 28 cycles, a 512KB L2 cache with 128-byte lines and a miss latency of 350 cycles (i.e, the latency of the 2GB PC800 RDRAM main memory is 178ns).[4] Our experimentation platform is MonetDB, also in the NSM experiments, where NSM is "simulated" by introducing new atomic types that hold 1, 4, 16, 64, and 256 integer column values, and which are copied and projected from using a NSM projection routine that iterates over such a "record" and copies selected values out of it.

In our experiments, we executed our example project-join SQL query using various DSM and NSM query processing strategies described in the following. We use relations of equal size N ranging from 15K to 16M tuples,

---

[4]The early work on cache-conscious query processing [18] reported a 30 cycle latency, thus we observe a 12-fold increase in 9 years.

consisting of $\omega \in \{1,4,16,64\}$ all-integer (4-byte) columns. We vary the join hit rates $h \in \{3,1,0.3\}$, and project $\pi \in \{1,4,16,64 | \pi \leq \omega\}$ columns from both relations into the result. Finally, we also present experiments where one of the join relations is a selection on a base-table that selected a fraction $s \in \{1, 0.1, 0.01\}$, such that we get *sparse* projections. In all experiments, all processing happens in main-memory (no I/O or page faults).

4.1 DSM Post-Projection Experiments

We first analyze the performance behavior of Radix-Decluster in isolation. Figure 7a shows the relationship between size of the insertion window (cf., Section 3.2 and Figure 5) and performance. We used hardware performance counters [8] to obtain detailed information on the amount of L1, L2 and TLB misses. This data enabled us to formulate and validate the performance model described in [14]. In this formula, $\#w = |X'|/|W|$ denotes the total number of insertion windows used. Our models can predict and accurately explain what is happening, as is seen by the fact that the dots (values obtained by experiments) and lines (the cost model) in Figures 7a, 7b and 9d nicely coincide.

If we look in detail at Figure 7, we see Radix-Decluster become faster as the insertion window becomes larger, which is explained by the fact that a larger insertion window leads to higher average number of tuples w processed per cluster in each iteration, improving sequential memory bandwidth usage in CLUST_RESULT and CLUST_VALUES. However, the insertion window sustains a random access pattern, such that when $||W||$ becomes bigger than the cache size C (our L2 has 512KB), performance drops sharply, due to an increase in L2 misses. A less important threshold is when $||W||$ becomes bigger than the number of pages that fit the TLB, after which TLB misses will start to occur during the inserts. Both these thresholds are drawn in Figure 7a. Another cause for TLB misses is the number of input clusters: if it is bigger than the number of TLB entries (and it is, in the depicted case of 8 Radix-Bits = 256 clusters), each Radix-Decluster iteration will cause two TLB misses when starting to process a new cluster, both in CLUST_RESULT and CLUST_VALUES. However, this happens only every one in w tuples, such that its impact diminishes quickly with increasing window size. Our analysis showed that choosing $w = 32$ is sufficient to achieve good memory bandwidth usage, and this is the value we use in Figure 9d to confirm the accuracy of our model on multiple cardinalities and Radix-Bits.

We then turn our attention to the interplay between Radix-Cluster, Positional-Join and Radix-Decluster in our Radix-Decluster DSM post-projection strategy, as depicted in Figure 7b. In Section 3.1, we already gave a formula for computing a good number of bits for Radix-Clustering the join-index, such that the subsequent Positional-Joins run well. Figure 9c confirms the accuracy of our predictive model for Positional-Joins between relations of multiple cardinalities (hit-rate 1), clustered with varying granu-

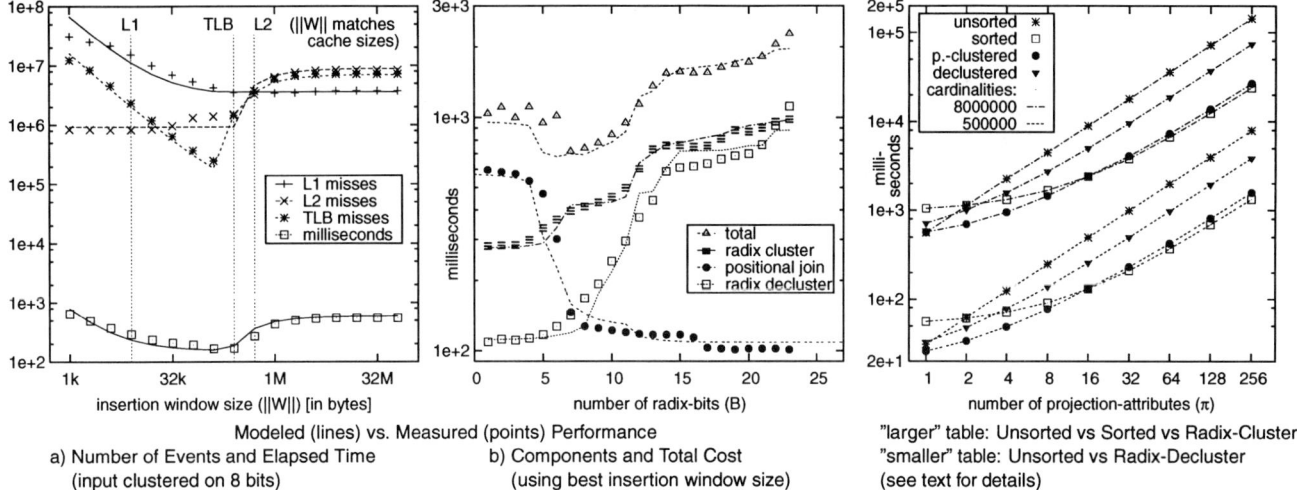

Figure 7. Radix-Decluster ($N = 8M$, $\pi = 1$)

Figure 8. DSM Post-Projection

larity (Radix-Bits). In the setting of Figure 7b we can indeed verify that $|R| = 8M$, $\overline{R} = 4$ leads to $B = 8$, which is the lowest number of Radix-Bits for which Positional-Join runs optimally (it then achieves minimal L2 misses). This is usually the optimal point overall, as Radix-Decluster cost only increases with more Radix-Bits. It sometimes is better to use even fewer Radix-Bits. The performance hit taken on Positional-Join, might then be compensated by a cheaper Radix-Cluster. As Radix-Cluster is executed only once, but Positional-Join for every projection column, this usually happens only if the number of projection columns π is very low. To perform well, that is, without running into cache or TLB problems, Radix-Decluster is limited by two factors. First, we need to process a sufficiently high w tuples from each input cluster to exploit the sequential memory bandwidth. We saw above, that $w = 32$ is the value to choose. Second, the insertion window size must not exceed the cache size C. From this, we can conclude that Radix-Decluster can handle relations of sizes up to $|R| = C^2/(32 * \overline{W}^2)$ efficiently. This formula resembles a similar bound as given in [11] for Jive-Join.

We finally analyze which DSM post-projection strategy for our generic join query works best and under which circumstances. Note that for DSM systems only π matters, not the actual number of columns in the table ω (as they are fragmented vertically in distinct columns - and the unused columns stay untouched). Therefore, a DSM experiment for a certain π holds for all ω. We consider four strategies, each identified with a one-letter code:

- u *Unsorted:* one Positional-Join from the join-index into each projection column.

- s *Sorted:* first Radix-Sort the join-index, then execute the Positional-Joins.

- c *partial-Cluster:* first partially cluster the join-index. We take the number of Radix-Bits that works best (on our platform, this leads to 256KB clusters).

- d *radix-Decluster:* like the previous, but each Positional-Join is followed by Radix-Decluster.

Figure 8 summarizes the performance of the various DSM post-projection strategies, depending on the amount of projection columns π and cardinality N. For small cardinalities ($N \leq 125K$), all strategies that do any kind of reordering lose to simple unsorted processing of the Positional-Joins, since the columns are so small that they fit the cache anyway. For larger cardinalities, however, the unsorted approach always loses by a big margin (e.g., by almost a factor 10 at $N = 8M$ and $\pi = 256$). With small π, partial-clustered processing beats sorted processing. The gap shrinks with growing π, and with $\pi > 16$, sorted processing wins. Finally, we see that the Radix-Decluster strategy always loses from the partial-cluster strategy, but is actually quite competitive, beating unsorted processing by a large margin. As explained, Radix-Decluster is to be used only for the second (smaller) projection table, with unsorted processing as the only alternative, as sorting or partial-cluster is only applicable to the first projection table.

4.2 Comparison of Overall Join Strategies

Figure 10 shows a comparison of DSM Post-Projection using Radix-Decluster with NSM Pre-Projection, DSM Pre-Projection, and two NSM Post-Projection variants: our own Radix-Decluster and Jive-Join [11]. All these variants use the cache-conscious Partitioned Hash-Join; they vary only in the projection strategy. To show the overall effect of all cache optimizations, we also include NSM Pre-Projection with naive non-partitioned Hash-Join ("NSM-pre-hash").

To analyze the impact of all parameters (π, N, h), Figure 10 depicts three plots, each varying one parameter while keeping the others fixed. We observed similar behavior in experiments with different values for the fixed parameters.

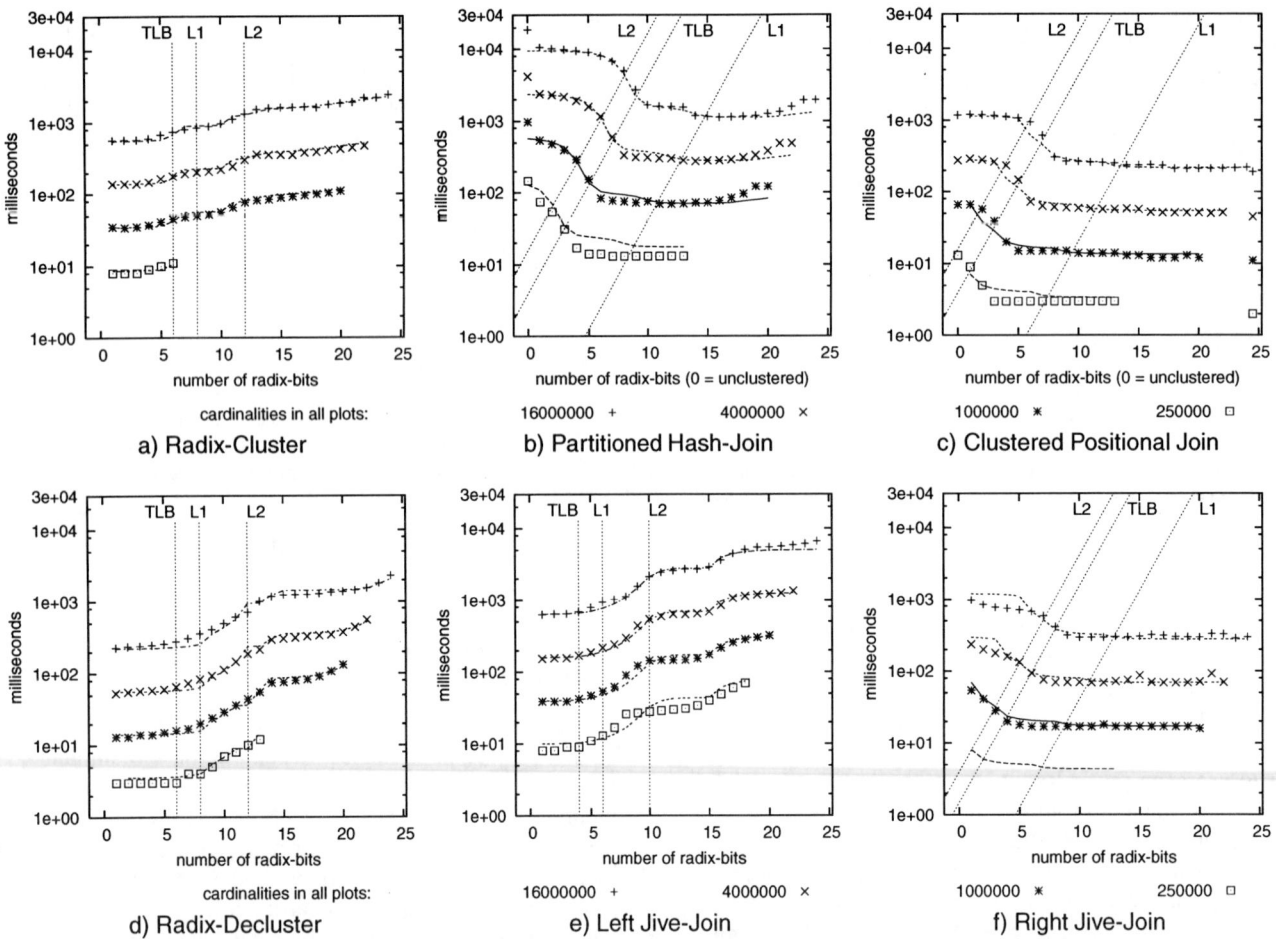

Figure 9. Modeled (lines) vs. Measured (points) Performance of various Join-Phases (DSM, $\pi = 1$)

Figure 10b shows that with decreased hit-rate, all strategies become cheaper (due to the smaller join result) but DSM Post-Projection even more, which is explained by the decreased overall impact of the projection phase (with the relatively expensive Radix-Decluster), with respect to the cost for creating the join-index with Partitioned Hash-Join.

Figure 10c shows that all strategies scale linearly with cardinality. The steeper increase of DSM Post-Projection ("DSM-post-decluster") in the lower range of π occurs because on small cardinalities, individual columns fit in the cache, such that the relatively expensive Radix-Decluster is not necessary, as indicated by the point types that identify the projection method used for both the left and the right table (with the one-letter codes defined in Section 4.1).

4.2.1 Pre-Projection Alternatives

Most systems other than MonetDB that use DSM or other forms of vertical fragmentation, such as transposed files [4] or projection indices [16], use a scan operator that scans all columns simultaneously (called Assemble() in [17]).

One factor to consider in all our comparisons is that DSM Post-Projection has a CPU efficiency advantage over all other alternatives. Due to the column-at-a-time execution in MonetDB, its operators have "zero degree of freedom", such that in their implementation a hard-coded operation on a hard-coded type is executed in a tight inner loop that iterates over large arrays. Modern compilers can handle such code well, achieving high IPC by e.g., loop pipelining. The other strategies handle all projection columns simultaneously (tuple-at-a-time), and have to deal with some degree of freedom, namely a list of projection columns, which is passed at run-time (additionally, the NSM strategies have to extract column values from a NSM record by looking at record offsets stored in a table header). Such code not only has to perform some more work (CPU overhead) but the additional complexity and dependencies in the inner loops are bound to hinder the compiler in getting a good IPC.

The main difference in Figure 10a between DSM Pre-Projection ("DSM-pre-phash") and DSM Post-Projection is this very CPU advantage of the latter. A second smaller difference is that as Pre-Projection handles all projections at the same time (during the join), less tuples fit in the clusters created by Radix-Cluster, such that it more quickly needs multiple passes. This is again compounded by the CPU

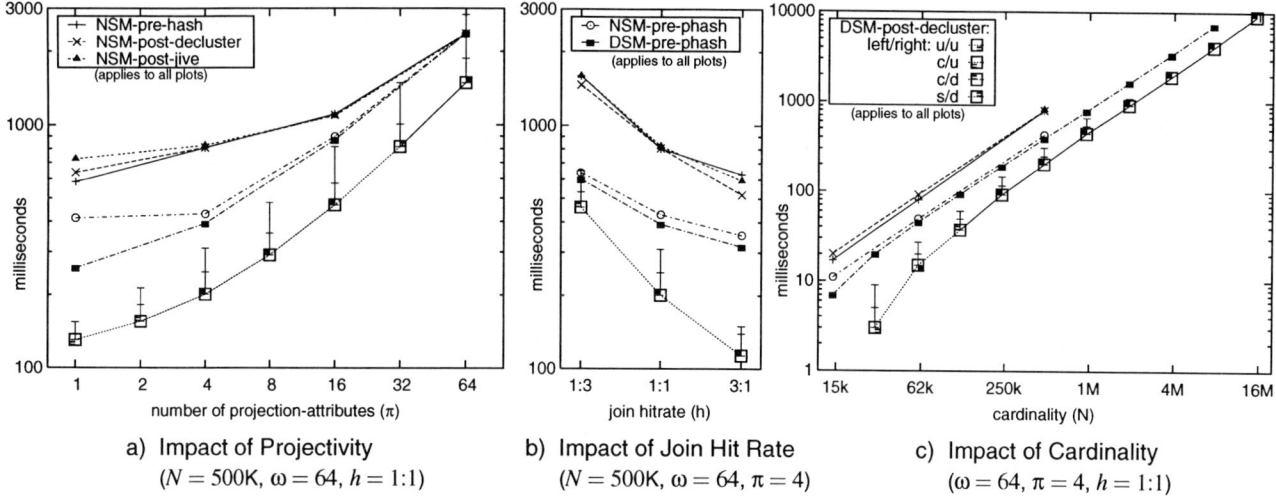

Figure 10. Overall Join Performance

disadvantage, allowing it to trade less extra CPU for better memory access (e.g., two-pass Radix-Cluster for creating many clusters almost never wins, leaving the strategy with a bad memory access pattern).

The difference between DSM Pre-Projection and NSM Pre-Projection ("NSM-pre-phash") is mainly in the better cache-line usage of DSM. On the positive side, the projections done by the Radix-Clustering of the NSM relations access the input relation sequentially. Thus, even if cache-lines are used sparsely, the pain will be reduced somewhat by automatic memory prefetching on modern hardware (it is "only" a bandwidth problem). As can be seen in Figure 10a, this impact is only considerable at low π.

Finally, the big difference in NSM Pre-Projection between non-partitioned and Partitioned Hash-Join is explained by the performance hit taken by uncachable random memory access. As the projectivity π increases, naive Hash-Join uses its cache lines relatively better, and it approaches Partitioned Hash-Join (but on no occasion surpasses it).

4.2.2 NSM Post-Projection Alternatives

The performance of NSM Pre-Projection at $\pi = 1$ in Figure 10a roughly corresponds to the first phase (the creation of the join-index) in the NSM Post-Projection strategies. This cost is considerable, giving both Radix-Decluster on NSM ("NSM-post-decluster") and Jive-Join ("NSM-post-jive") a hard time competing with the other strategies, as creating the join-index is only their first step. Subsequently, they need to access the wide NSM base tables one more time for performing the projections. This would of course have been very different had we assumed the (clustered) join-index to be already present as an accelerator structure. As we concentrate on large ad-hoc joins, however, the join-index cannot have been precomputed.

Jive-Join first sorts the join-index, and then carries out a special Positional-Join ("Left Jive-Join") with the one join input, that directly re-sorts its output on the oids of the other table. It generates two separate outputs, in the same order (which is the final result order), one containing the clustered oids, the other containing all projection columns from the first join input. In the second phase, a second special Positional-Join ("Right Jive-Join") is done between each cluster of oids (that is first sorted for better access) and the second table, where the results are written back in the order of the result (the order of the oids before re-sorting) [11].

As the detailed performance results on Left and Right Jive-Join in Figures 9e and 9f show, the Left Jive-Join phase may suffer from a too high cluster fanout in much the same way single-pass Radix-Cluster does, while the Right Jive-Join may suffer from too few (=big) clusters, much like Partitioned Hash-Join does. However, the strategy of creating not too many cluster in the first phase, then refining them with Radix-Cluster in order not to have too big clusters in the Right Jive-Join, does not work as then the reordering in Right Jive-Join has random access to a too large cluster.

The scalability of both Radix-Decluster as well as Jive-Join is limited to $O(C^2/T^2)$, where T is the tuple width. Therefore, on large cardinalities, wide NSM tuples can quickly get these algorithms into cache problems, limiting their applicability for cache-conscious join.

4.2.3 Sparse Projections

Sparse projections occur when a join relation is a selection on a base table. Figure 11 shows that the performance of Positional-Join suffers significantly with a decreasing selection percentage. This is more of an issue for DSM than for NSM, as in DSM cache-lines hold values of multiple consecutive tuples, and if only a small percentage is used,

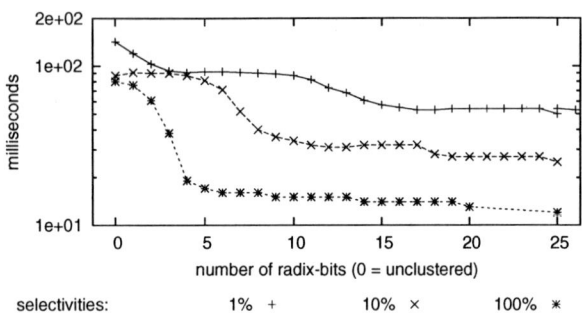

Figure 11. Impact of Selectivity: Sparse Clustered Positional Join ($N = 1M$)

sequential RAM bandwidth utilization decreases. In NSM, cache-lines typically hold only values of a single tuple, and bandwidth efficiency mainly depends on *projectivity*, not on selectivity. Still, this need not be a show-stopper, as sequential RAM bandwidth is in rather generous supply and unlike latency shows steady progress as hardware evolves.

The effect of sparse projections on DSM Post-Projection is also shown in all Figures 10a,b,c using error bars. The smallest error bar shows performance with 10% selectivity (i.e., cardinality of the underlying base-table is $10N$) and the second corresponds to 1% selectivity (cardinality is $100N$). While we see that DSM Post-Projection performance decreases with a lower selectivity percentage, it clearly stays the better strategy overall.

We should note that this comparison is worst-case for DSM Post-Projection. First, for brevity we omitted the sparse access data for NSM, which is also affected by sparse access, only to a much lesser degree. Second, if the selectivity is low, such as 1% or less, then in many cases the intermediate relation would become small, making the join an "easy" instead of a "hard" case (see Section 3). For "easy" joins, DSM Post-Projection could use an u/u strategy, thus significantly improving its performance.

5 DSM Radix-Decluster in a NSM DBMS

Our results strongly suggest that RDBMS performance can be enhanced by introducing vertical fragmentation as an accelerator structure, i.e., projection indices [16]. Such a "DSM-subsystem" would profit in OLAP queries that touch many tuples but few columns, and would preferably use CPU-efficient MonetDB-like hard-coded operators that manipulate columns at-a-time, such as Positional-Join, Radix-Cluster and Radix-Decluster. The very purpose of MonetDB's cache-conscious query processing algorithms is to restrict all random access to very small ranges that fit the CPU caches. Thus, the only I/O access to the DSM fragments are sequential bulk reads and writes. On our evaluation platform, our algorithms caused read and write rates between 200MB/s and 500MB/s, which can be supported

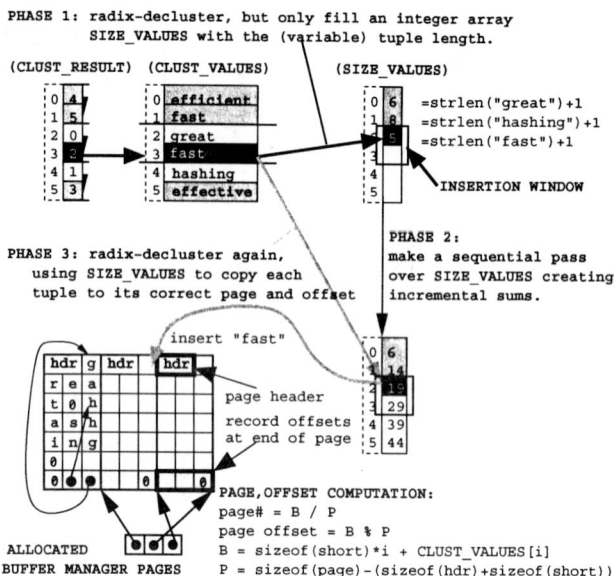

Figure 12. Handling Non-Continuous Addressing and Variable-sized Data

using a PCI-X RAID consisting of 12 SCSI disks.[5]

A case for a DBMS with mixed DSM-NSM storage is made in [17], which also describes how updates could be accommodated efficiently using differential files to the DSM file images. In such an architecture, a buffer manager would still be used as an efficient means of well-controlled (asynchronous) I/O. In MonetDB, however, columns are contiguous arrays, while in an RDBMS the columns would be stored in pages at various locations of the buffer pool. Therefore, the Radix-Decluster technique of inserting "by position" in the insertion window would not apply directly. Finding the correct page and offset would be especially difficult if we were to handle variable-sized values such as strings. Figure 12 shows how both problems are solved in a buffer manager that uses NSM-like pages for storing sequences of variable-size values. Output space has been allocated in a number of buffer pages, whose start addresses are stored in an index array. First, the Radix-Decluster is executed, but it does not insert any values, but just records the lengths of the variable-size values in an extra integer array. This temporary array is, of course, addressable by position. In a second phase, the lengths are summed to calculate locations. In a third phase, the Radix-Decluster operation is re-executed to copy values into the result, and this time the correct page and offset for each value can be calculated, using the computed location accessible by position in the array. Note that for fixed-size values, the extra passes are not even necessary, and page and offset can be determined from the oid, which is the result tuple sequence number.

---

[5] Preliminary experiments with lightweight data (de-)compression indicate that a negligible CPU investment can more than half the needed I/O bandwidth on problems like TPC-H. As I/O bandwidth is precious, this looks a worthwhile approach to help scale DSM to disk-based scenarios.

6 Conclusion

We have investigated the problem of performing large equi-joins with projections in a cache-conscious manner. As can be seen in the left graph of Figure 10, performance may vary by more than an order of magnitude with different relation projectivity, thus proving that projection cost can have a strong impact on overall join efficiency.

Our main contribution, the Radix-Decluster algorithm, is the crucial tool of MonetDB to process (i.e., join, but also re-order) huge tables with a good access pattern, both in terms of CPU cache access as well as I/O access (through virtual memory).

In our experiments, we tested various cache-conscious join (projection) strategies both on the NSM and DSM storage schemes. One important conclusion from these experiments is that Partitioned Hash-Join significantly improves performance not only for MonetDB and DSM, but also for the NSM pre-projection strategy, as is used by all standard RDBMS products (compare in Figure 10 the non-cache-friendly "NSM pre-hash" with "NSM pre-phash"), proving that this algorithm carries generic merit.

The performance evaluation further shows that Radix-Decluster is pivotal in making DSM post-projection the most efficient overall strategy. We should note, that unlike Radix-Cluster, Radix-Decluster is a single-pass algorithm, and thus has a scalability limit imposed by a maximum number of clusters and thus tuples. This limit depends on the CPU cache size and is quite generous (assuming four-byte column values, the 512KB cache of a Pentium4 Xeon allows to project relations of up to half a billion tuples) and scales quadratically with the cache size (so the 6MB Itanium2 cache allows for 72 billion tuples).

This limitation also explains why Radix-Decluster is less successful in NSM post-projection, as its scalability is also inversely quadratically related to the tuple width. Rephrased positively, vertical fragmentation (DSM) and column-wise execution reduce tuple width, fit more tuples in the CPU cache and quadratically improve scalability. For NSM, however, we find the "traditional" pre-projection technique to work best, also outperforming the alternative NSM post-projection strategy of Jive-Join, which was not intended as a generic join method, but rather for exploiting precomputed join-indices.

As for the prospects of applying DSM Radix-Decluster in off-the-shelf RDBMS products, we support the case made in [17] for systems that combine DSM and NSM natively, or that simply add DSM to the normal NSM representation as *projection indices* [16], and show how such disk-based systems could use our Radix-Algorithms through their buffer manager.

References

[1] A. Ailamaki, D. DeWitt, M. Hill, and M. Skounakis. Weaving Relations for Cache Performance. In *Proc. VLDB Conf.*, pages 169–180, Roma, Italy, Sept. 2001.

[2] A. Ailamaki, D. DeWitt, M. Hill, and D. Wood. DBMSs on modern processors: Where does time go? In *Proc. VLDB Conf.*, pages 266–277, Edinburgh, Scotland, UK, Sept. 1999.

[3] L. Barroso, K. Gharachorloo, and E. Bugnion. Memory System Characterization Of Commercial Workloads. In *Proc. ISCA*, Barcelona, Spain, June 1998.

[4] D. Batory. On Searching Transposed Files. *TODS*, 4(4):531–544, 1979.

[5] P. Boncz. *Monet: A Next-Generation DBMS Kernel For Query-Intensive Applications*. PhD thesis, UVA, Amsterdam, The Netherlands, May 2002.

[6] P. Boncz, S. Manegold, and M. Kersten. Database Architecture Optimized for the New Bottleneck: Memory Access. In *Proc. VLDB Conf.*, pages 54–65, Edinburgh, Scotland, UK, Sept. 1999.

[7] G. Copeland and S. Khoshafian. A Decomposition Storage Model. In *Proc. SIGMOD Conf.*, pages 268–279, Austin, TX, USA, May 1985.

[8] G. Hinton, D. Sager, M. Upton, D. Boggs, D. Carmean, A. Kyker, and P. Roussel. The Microarchitecture of the Pentium 4 Processor. In *Intel Technology Journal*, http://developer.intel.com/technology/itj/, Feb. 2001.

[9] K. Keeton, D. Patterson, Y. He, A. Raphael, and W. Baker. Performance Characterization of a quad Pentium Pro SMP using OLTP workloads. In *Proc. ISCA*, pages 15–26, Barcelona, Spain, June 1998.

[10] G. Lauterbach and T. Horel. UltraSparc-III: designing 3rd generation 64bit platforms. *IEEE Micro*, 19(3):56–66, 1999.

[11] Z. Li and K. Ross. Fast Joins Using Join Indices. *The VLDB Journal*, 8(1):1–24, 1999.

[12] S. Manegold. *Understanding, Modeling, and Improving Main-Memory Database Performance*. PhD thesis, UVA, Amsterdam, The Netherlands, Dec. 2002.

[13] S. Manegold, P. Boncz, and M. Kersten. Generic Database Cost Models for Hierarchical Memory Systems. In *Proc. VLDB Conf.*, pages 191–202, Hong Kong, China, Aug. 2002.

[14] S. Manegold, P. Boncz, N. Nes, and M. Kersten. Cache-Conscious Radix-Decluster Projections. Technical Report INS-E0406, CWI, Amsterdam, The Netherlands, June 2004. Available via http://www.cwi.nl/htbin/ins1/publications.

[15] A. McCalpin. Memory Bandwidth and Machine Balance in Current High Performance Computers. *IEEE Technical Committee on Computer Architecture newsletter*, Dec. 1995.

[16] P. O'Neil and D. Quass. Improved Query Performance with Variant Indexes. In *Proc. SIGMOD Conf.*, pages 38–49, Tucson, AZ, USA, May 1997.

[17] R. Ramamurthy, D. DeWitt, and Q. Su. A Case for Fractured Mirrors. In *Proc. VLDB Conf.*, pages 430–441, Hong Kong, China, Aug. 2002.

[18] A. Shatdahl, C. Kant, and J. Naughton. Cache Conscious Algorithms for Relational Query Processing. In *Proc. VLDB Conf.*, pages 510–512, Santiago, Chile, Sept. 1994.

[19] Sybase Corp. Whitepaper. *Adaptive Server IQ*, July 1996. http://www.sybase.com/content/1008840/iq_wp_l00899.pdf.

[20] P. Valduriez. Join Indices. *ACM Trans. on Database Systems*, 12(2):218–246, June 1987.

Clotho: Decoupling Memory Page Layout from Storage Organization

Minglong Shao Jiri Schindler* Steven W. Schlosser[†] Anastassia Ailamaki Gregory R. Ganger

Carnegie Mellon University

Abstract

As database application performance depends on the utilization of the memory hierarchy, smart data placement plays a central role in increasing locality and in improving memory utilization. Existing techniques, however, do not optimize accesses to all levels of the memory hierarchy and for all the different workloads, because each storage level uses different technology (cache, memory, disks) and each application accesses data using different patterns. *Clotho* is a new buffer pool and storage management architecture that decouples in-memory page layout from data organization on non-volatile storage devices to enable independent data layout design at each level of the storage hierarchy. *Clotho* can maximize cache and memory utilization by (a) transparently using appropriate data layouts in memory and non-volatile storage, and (b) dynamically synthesizing data pages to follow application access patterns at each level as needed. *Clotho* creates in-memory pages individually tailored for compound and dynamically changing workloads, and enables efficient use of different storage technologies (e.g., disk arrays or MEMS-based storage devices). This paper describes the *Clotho* design and prototype implementation and evaluates its performance under a variety of workloads using both disk arrays and simulated MEMS-based storage devices.

1 Introduction

Page structure and storage organization have been the subject of numerous studies [1, 3, 6, 9, 10], because they play a central role in database system performance. Research continues as no single data organization serves all needs within all systems. In particular, the access patterns resulting from queries posed by different workloads can vary significantly. One query, for instance, might access all the attributes in a table (*full-record access*), while another accesses only a subset of them (*partial-record access*). Full-record accesses are typical in transactional (OLTP) applications where insert and delete statements require the entire record to be read or written, whereas partial-record accesses are often met in decision-support system (DSS) queries. Moreover, when executing compound workloads, one query may access records sequentially while others access the same records "randomly" (e.g., via non-clustered index). Currently, database storage managers implement a single page layout and storage organization scheme, which is utilized by all applications running thereafter. As a result, in an environment with a variety of workloads, only a subset of query types can be serviced well.

Several data page layout techniques have been proposed in the literature, each targeting different query type. Notably, the N-ary Storage Model (*NSM*) [13] stores records consecutively, optimizing for full-record accesses, while penalizing partial-record sequential scans. By contrast, the Decomposition Storage Model (*DSM*) [7] stores values of each attribute in a separate table, optimizing for partial-record accesses, while penalizing queries that need the entire record. More recently, *PAX* [1] optimizes cache performance, but not memory utilization. Fractured mirrors [14] reduce *DSM*'s record reconstruction cost by using an optimized structure and scan operators, but need to keep an *NSM*-organized copy of the database as well to support full-record access queries. None of the previously proposed schemes provides a universally efficient solution, however, because they all make a fundamental assumption that the pages used in main memory must have the same contents as those stored on disk.

This paper proposes *Clotho*, a buffer pool and storage management architecture that decouples the memory page layout from the non-volatile storage data organization. This decoupling allows memory page contents to be determined dynamically according to queries being served and offers two significant advantages. First, it optimizes storage access and memory utilization by requesting only the data accessed by a given query. Second, it allows new two-dimensional storage mechanisms to be exploited to mitigate the trade-off between the *NSM* and *DSM* storage models. *Clotho* chooses data layouts at each level of the memory hierarchy to match *NSM* where it performs best, *DSM* where it performs best, and outperforms both for query mixes and access types in between. It leverages the *Atropos* logical volume manager [16] to efficiently access two

---

*Now with EMC Corporation
[†] Now with Intel Corporation

Permission to copy without fee all or part of this material is granted provided that the copies are not made or distributed for direct commercial advantage, the VLDB copyright notice and the title of the publication and its date appear, and notice is given that copying is by permission of the Very Large Data Base Endowment. To copy otherwise, or to republish, requires a fee and/or special permission from the Endowment.

**Proceedings of the 30th VLDB Conference,
Toronto, Canada, 2004**

dimensional data structures stored both in disk arrays and in MEMS-based storage devices (MEMStores) [19, 22].

This paper also describes and evaluates a prototype implementation of *Clotho* within the Shore database storage manager [4]. Experiments with disk arrays show that, with only a single storage organization, performance of DSS and OLTP workloads is comparable to the page layouts best suited for the respective workload (i.e., *DSM* and *PAX*, respectively). Experiments with a simulated MEMStore confirm that similar benefits will be realized with these future devices as well.

The remainder of this paper is organized as follows. Section 2 gives background and related work. Section 3 describes the architecture of a database system that enables decoupling of the in-memory and storage layouts. Section 4 describes the design of a buffer pool manager that supports query-specific in-memory page layout. Section 5 describes the design of a volume manager that allows efficient access when an arbitrary subset of table attributes are needed by a query. Section 6 describes our initial implementation, and Section 7 evaluates this implementation for several database workloads using both a disk array logical volume and a simulated MEMStore.

2 Background and related work

Conventional relational database systems store data in fixed-size pages (typically 4 to 64 KB). To access individual records of a relation (table) requested by a query, a scan operator of a database system accesses main memory. Before accessing data, a page must first be fetched from non-volatile storage (e.g., a logical volume of a disk array) into main memory. Hence, a page is the basic allocation and access unit for non-volatile storage. A database storage manager facilitates this access and sends requests to a storage device to fetch the necessary blocks.

A single page contains a header describing what records are contained within and how they are laid out. In order to retrieve data requested by a query, a scan operator must understand the page layout, (a.k.a. storage model). Since the page layout determines what records and which attributes of a relation are stored in a single page, the storage model employed by a database system has far reaching implications on the performance of a particular workload [2].

The page layout prevalent in commercial database systems, called N-ary storage model (*NSM*), is optimized for queries with full-record access common in an on-line transaction processing (OLTP) workload. *NSM* stores all attributes of a relation in a single page [13] and full records are stored within a page one after another. Accessing a full record is accomplished by accessing a particular record from consecutive memory locations. Using an unwritten rule that access to consecutive logical blocks (*LBN*s) in the storage device is more efficient than random access, a storage manager maps single page to consecutive *LBN*s. Thus, an entire page can be accessed by a single I/O request.

An alternative page layout, called the Decomposition Storage Model (*DSM*) [7], is optimized for decision sup-

Data Organization	Cache–Memory		Memory–Storage	
	OLTP	DSS	OLTP	DSS
NSM	√	×	√	×
DSM	×	√	×	√
PAX	√	√	√	×

Table 1: **Summary of performance with current page layouts.**

port systems (DSS) workloads. Since DSS queries typically access a small number of attributes and most of the data in the page is not touched in memory by the scan operator, *DSM* stores only one attribute per page. To ensure efficient storage device access, a storage manager maps *DSM* pages with consecutive records containing the same attribute into extents of contiguous *LBN*s. In anticipation of a sequential scan through records stored in multiple pages, a storage manager can prefetch all pages in one extent with a single large I/O, which is more efficient than accessing each page individually by a separate I/O.

A page layout optimized for CPU cache performance, called *PAX* [1], offers good CPU-memory performance for both individual attribute scans of DSS queries and full-record accesses in OLTP workloads. The *PAX* layout partitions data across into separate minipages. A single minipage contains data of only one attribute and occupies consecutive memory locations. Collectively, a single page contains all attributes for a given set of records. Scanning individual attributes in *PAX* accesses consecutive memory locations and thus can take advantage of cache-line prefetch logic. With proper alignment to cache-line sizes, a single cache miss can effectively prefetch data for several records, amortizing the high latency of memory access compared to cache access. However, *PAX* does not address memory-storage performance.

All of the described storage models share the same characteristics. They (i) are highly optimized for one workload type, (ii) focus predominantly on one level of the memory hierarchy, (iii) use a static data layout that is determined *a priori* when the relation is created, and (iv) apply the same layout across all levels of the memory hierarchy, even though each level has unique (and very different) characteristics. As a consequence, there are inherent performance trade-offs for each layout that arise when a workload changes. For example, *NSM* or *PAX* layouts waste memory capacity and storage device bandwidth for DSS workloads, since most data within a page is never touched. Similarly, a *DSM* layout is inefficient for OLTP queries accessing random full records. To reconstruct a full record with n attributes, n pages must be fetched and $n - 1$ joins on record identifiers performed to assemble the full record. In addition to wasting memory capacity and storage bandwidth, this access is inefficient at the storage device level; accessing these pages results in random one-page I/Os. In summary, each page layout exhibits good performance for a specific type of access at a specific level of memory hierarchy, as shown in Table 1.

Several researchers have proposed solutions to address these performance trade offs. Ramamurthy et al. proposed fractured mirrors that store data in both *NSM* and *DSM* layouts [14] to eliminate the need to reload and reorganize data when access patterns change. Based on the workload type, a database system can choose the appropriate data organization. Unfortunately, this approach doubles the required storage space and complicates data management; two physically different layouts must be maintained in synchrony to preserve data integrity. Hankins and Patel [9] proposed data morphing as a technique to reorganize data within individual pages based on the needs of workloads that change over time. Since morphing takes place within memory pages that are then stored in that format on the storage device, these fine-grained changes cannot address the trade-offs involved in accessing non-volatile storage. The multi-resolution block storage model (MBSM) [23] groups *DSM* table pages together into superpages, improving *DSM* performance when running decision-support systems. The *Lachesis* database storage manager [15] exploits unique disk drive characteristics to improve performance of DSS workloads and compound workloads that consist of DSS and OLTP queries competing for the same storage device. It matches page allocation and access policies to leverage these characteristics, but the storage model itself is not different; *Lachesis* transparently stores the in-memory *NSM* pages in the storage device's logical blocks.

MEMStores [5] are a promising new type of storage device that has the potential to provide efficient accesses to two-dimensional data. Schlosser et al. proposed data layout for MEMStores that exploits their inherent access parallelism [19]. Yu et al. devised an efficient mapping of database tables to this layout that takes advantage of the unique characteristics of MEMStores [22] to improve query performance. Similarly, Schindler et al. [16] proposed data organization for two-dimensional access to database tables mapped to logical volumes composed of several disk drives. However, these initial works did not explore the implications of this new data organization on in-memory access performance.

In summary, these solutions either address only some of the performance trade-offs or are applicable to only one level of the memory hierarchy. *Clotho* builds on the previous work and uses a decoupled data layout that can adapt to dynamic changes in workloads without the need to maintain multiple copies of data, reorganize data layout, or to compromise between memory and I/O access efficiency.

3 Decoupling data layouts

From the discussion in the previous section, it is clear that designing a static scheme for data placement in memory and on non-volatile storage that performs well across different workloads and different device types and technologies is difficult. Instead of accepting the trade-offs inherent to a particular page layout that affects all levels of the memory hierarchy, we propose a new approach.

As each level of the memory hierarchy have vastly different performance characteristics, the data organization at each level should be different. Therefore, *Clotho* decou-

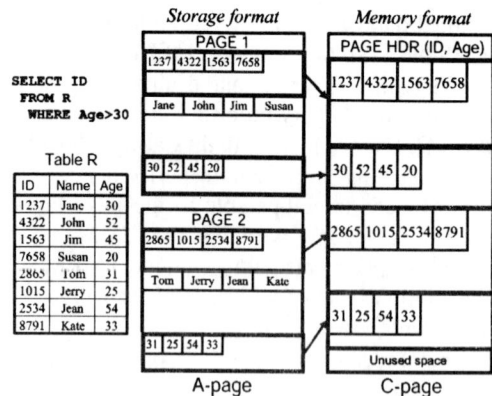

Figure 1: **Decoupled storage device and in-memory layouts.**

ples the in-memory data layout from the storage organization and implements different data layouts tailored to each level, without compromising performance at the other levels. The challenge is to ensure that this decoupling works seamlessly within current database systems. This section introduces the different data organizations and describes the key components of the *Clotho* architecture.

3.1 Data organization in *Clotho*

Clotho allows for decoupled data layouts and different representations of the same table at the memory and storage levels. Figure 1 depicts an example table, *R*, with three attributes: ID, Name, and Age. At the storage level, the data is organized into A-pages. An A-page contains all attributes of the records; only one A-page needs to be fetched to retrieve a full record. Exploiting the idea used in *PAX* [1], an A-page organizes data into minipages that group values from the same attribute for efficient predicate evaluation, while the rest of the attributes are in the same A-page. To ensure that the record reconstruction cost is minimized regardless of the size of the A-page, *Clotho* allows the device to use optimized methods for placing the contents of the A-page onto the storage medium. Therefore, not only does *Clotho* fully exploit sequential scan for evaluating predicates, but it also places A-pages carefully on the device to ensure near-sequential (or semi-sequential [16]) access when reconstructing a record. The placement of A-pages on the disk is further explained in Section 5.1.

The rightmost part of Figure 1 depicts a C-page, which is the in-memory representation of a page. The page frame is sized by the buffer pool manager and is on the order of 8 KB. A C-page is similar to an A-page in that it also contains attribute values grouped in minipages, to maximize processor cache performance. Unlike an A-page, however, a C-page *only* contains values for the attributes the query accesses. Since, the query in the example only uses the ID and Age, the C-page only includes these two attributes, maximizing memory utilization. Note that the C-page uses data from two A-pages to fill up the space "saved" from omitting Name. In the rest of this paper, we refer to the C-page layout as the *Clotho* storage model (*CSM*).

3.2 System architecture

The difficulty in building a database system that can decouple in-memory page layout from storage organization lies in implementing the necessary changes without undue increase in system and code complexity. To allow decoupled data layouts, *Clotho* changes parts of two database system components, namely the buffer pool manager and the storage manager. The changes span limited areas in these components and do not alter the query processing interface. *Clotho* also takes advantages of the *Atropos* logical volume manager (LVM) that allows efficient access to two dimensional structures in both dimensions.

Figure 2 shows the relevant components of a database system to highlight the interplay between *Clotho* and other components. Each component can independently take advantage of enabling hardware/OS technologies at each level of the memory hierarchy, while hiding the details from the rest of the system. This section outlines the role of each component. The changes to the components are further explained in Sections 4 and 5.1 while details specific to our prototype implementation are provided in Section 6.

The operators are essentially predicated scan and store procedures that access data from in-memory pages stored in a common buffer pool. They take advantage of the query-specific page layout of C-pages that leverages the L1/L2 CPU cache characteristics and cache prefetch logic for efficient access to data.

The buffer pool manager manages C-pages in the buffer pool and enables sharing across different queries that need the same data. In traditional buffer pool managers, a buffer page is assumed to have the same schema and contents as the corresponding relation. In *Clotho*, however, this page may contain a subset of the table schema attributes. To ensure sharing, correctness during updates, and high memory utilization, the *Clotho* buffer pool manager maintains a page-specific schema that denotes which attributes are stored within each buffered page (i.e., the page schema). The challenge of this approach is to ensure minimal I/O by determining sharing and partial overlapping across concurrent queries with minimal book-keeping overhead. Section 4 details the buffer pool manager operation in detail.

The storage manager maps A-pages to specific logical volume's logical blocks, called *LBN*s. Since the A-page format is different from the in-memory layout, the storage manager rearranges A-page data on-the-fly into C-pages using the query-specific *CSM* layout. Unlike traditional storage managers where pages are also the smallest access units, the *Clotho* storage manager selectively retrieves a portion of a single A-page. With scatter/gather I/O and direct memory access (DMA), the pieces of individual A-pages can be delivered directly into the proper memory frame(s) in the buffer pool as they arrive from the logical volume. The storage manager simply sets up the appropriate I/O vectors with the destination address ranges for the requested *LBN*s. The data is placed directly to its destinations without the storage manager's involvement or the need for data shuffling and extraneous memory copies.

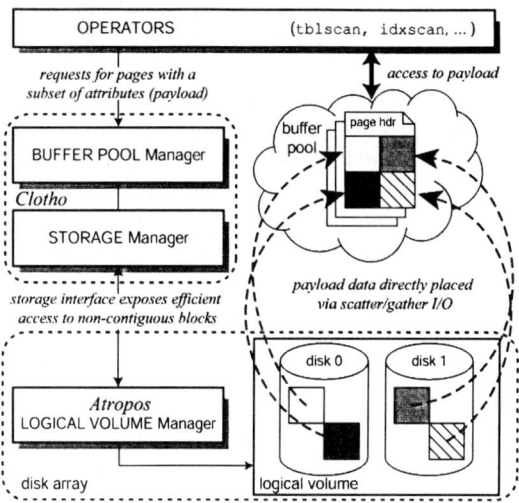

Figure 2: **Interaction of Clotho with other components.**

To efficiently access data for a variety of access patterns, the storage manager relies on explicit hints provided by the logical volume manager. These hints convey which *LBN*s can be accessed together efficiently and *Clotho* uses them for allocating A-pages.

The logical volume manager (LVM) maps volume *LBN*s to the physical blocks of the underlying storage device(s). It is independent of the database system and is typically implemented with the storage system (e.g., disk array). The *Atropos* LVM leverages device-specific characteristics to create mappings that yield efficient access to a collection of *LBN*s. In particular, the *Atropos* storage interface exports two functions that establish explicit relationships between individual *LBN*s of the logical volume and enable the *Clotho* storage manager to effectively map A-pages to individual *LBN*s. One function returns the set of consecutive *LBN*s that yield efficient access (e.g., all blocks mapped onto one disk or MEMStore track). *Clotho* maps minipages containing the same attribute to these *LBN*s for efficient scans of a subset of attributes. Another function returns a set of non-contiguous *LBN*s that can be efficiently accessed together (e.g., parallel-accessible *LBN*s mapped to different MEMStore tips or disks of logical volume). *Clotho* maps a single A-page to these *LBN*s. The *Atropos* LVM is briefly described in Section 5.1 and detailed elsewhere [16, 19]. *Clotho* need not rely on *Atropos* LVM to create query-specific C-pages. With conventional LVMs, it can map a full A-page to a contiguous run of *LBN*s with each minipage mapped to one or more discrete *LBN*s. However, with these conventional LVMs, access only along one dimension will be efficient.

3.3 Benefits of decoupled data layouts

The concept of decoupling data layouts at different levels of the memory hierarchy offers several benefits.

Leveraging unique device characteristics. At the volatile

699

(main memory) level, *Clotho* uses *CSM*, a data layout that maximizes processor cache utilization by minimizing unnecessary accesses to memory. *CSM* organizes data in C-pages and also groups attribute values to ensure that only useful information is brought into the processor caches [1, 9]. At the storage-device level, the granularity of accesses is naturally much coarser. The objective is to maximize memory utilization for all types of queries by only bringing into the buffer pool data that the query needs.
Query-specific memory layout. With memory organization decoupled from storage layout, *Clotho* can decide what data is needed by a particular query, request only the needed data from a storage device, and arrange the data on-the-fly to an organization that is best suited for the particular query needs. This fine-grained control over what data is fetched and stored also puts less pressure on buffer pool and storage system resources. By not requesting data that will not be needed, a storage device can devote more time to servicing requests for other queries executing concurrently and hence speed up their execution.
Dynamic adaptation to changing workloads. A system with flexible data organization does not experience performance degradation when query access patterns change over time. Unlike systems with static page layouts, where the binding of data representation to workload occurs during table creation, this binding is done in *Clotho* only during query execution. Thus, a system with decoupled data organizations can easily adapt to changing workloads and also fine-tune the use of available resources when they are under contention.

4 Buffer pool manager

The *Clotho* buffer pool manager organizes relational table data in C-pages using the *CSM* data layout. *CSM* is a query-optimized in-memory page layout that stores only the subset of attributes needed by a query. Consequently, a C-page can contain a single attribute (similar to *DSM*), a few attributes, or all attributes of a given set of records (similar to *NSM* and *PAX*) depending on query needs. This section describes how the buffer pool manager constructs and maintains C-pages and ensures data sharing and consistency in the buffer pool.

4.1 In-memory C-page layout

Figure 3 depicts two examples of C-pages for a table with four attributes of different sizes. In our design, C-pages only contain fixed-size attributes. Variable-size attributes are stored separately in other page layouts (see Section 6.2). A C-page contains a page header and a set of minipages, each containing data for one attribute and collectively holding all attributes needed by queries. In a minipage, a single attribute's values are stored in consecutive memory locations to maximize processor cache performance. The current number of records and presence bits are distributed across the minipages. Because the C-page only handles fixed-size attributes, the size of each minipage is determined at the time of table creation.

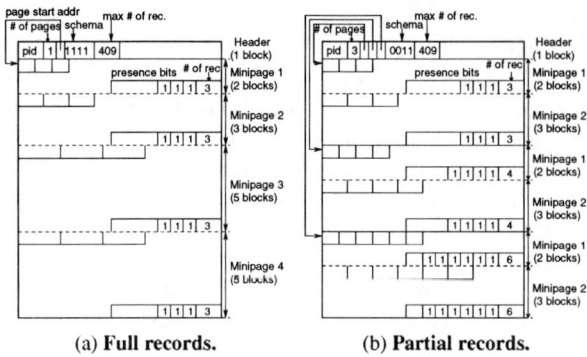

Figure 3: C-page layout.

The page header stores the following information: page id of the first A-page, the number of partial A-pages contained, the starting address of each A-page, a bit vector indicating the schema of the C-page's contents, and the maximal number of records that can fit in an A-page.

Figure 3(a) and Figure 3(b) depict C-pages with complete and partial records, respectively. The leftmost C-page is created for queries that access full records, whereas the rightmost C-page is customized for queries touching only the first two attributes. The space for minipages 3 and 4 on the left are used to store more partial records from additional A-pages on the right. In this example, a single C-page can hold the requested attributes from three A-pages, increasing memory utilization by a factor of three.

On the right side of the C-page we list the number of storage device blocks each minipage occupies. In our example each block is 512 bytes. Depending on the relative attribute sizes, as we fill up the C-page using data from more A-pages there may be some unused space. Instead of performing costly operations to fill up that space, we choose to leave it unused. Our experiments show that, with the right page size and aggressive prefetching, this unused space does not cause a detectable performance deterioration (details about space utilization are in Section 7.6).

4.2 Data sharing in buffer pool

Concurrent queries do not necessarily access the same sets of attributes; concurrent sets of accessed attributes may be disjoint, inclusive, or otherwise overlapping. The *Clotho* buffer pool manager must (a) maximize sharing, ensuring memory space efficiency, (b) minimize book-keeping to keep the buffer pool operations light-weight, and (c) maintain consistency in the presence of updates.

As an example, query Q1 asks for attributes a_1 and a_2 while query Q2 asks for attributes a_2 and a_3. Using a simple approach, the buffer manager could create two separate C-pages tailored to each query. This approach ignores the sharing possibilities in case these queries scan the table concurrently. To achieve better memory utilization, the buffer manager can instead dynamically reorganize the minipages of a_1 and a_2 inside the two C-pages, fetching only the needed values and keeping track of the progress of each query, dynamically creating new C-pages for Q1 and

```
if read-only query then
    if ∃p_sch ⊇ q_sch then
        Do nothing
    else if q_sch ∩ allp_sch = ∅ then
        Add q_sch to the schema list
    else
        New p_sch = ∪(q_sch, {p_sch | p_sch ∩ q_sch ≠ ∅})
        Add the new p_sch to the list
    end if
else if it is a write query (update/delete/insert) then
    Use full schema as the q_sch
    Modify the list: only one full p_sch now
end if
```

Figure 4: **Buffer pool manager algorithm.**

Q2. However, this approach incurs too much book-keeping overhead, and is inefficient in practice.

The *Clotho* buffer pool manager balances memory utilization and management complexity. Each frame in the buffer pool stores a C-page which conforms to a *page schema*, a bitvector that describes which attributes the C-page holds. For each active table, we keep a list of the different page schemas for C-pages that belong to the table and are currently in the buffer pool. Finally, each active query keeps a *query schema*, a bitvector that describes which attributes the query needs for each accessed table.

Whenever a query starts executing, the buffer pool manager notes the query schema and inspects the other, already active, page schemas. If the new query schema accesses a disjoint set of attributes from the over active queries, if any, the buffer pool manager creates a new C-page. Otherwise, it merges the new schema with the most-efficient overlapping one already in memory. The algorithm in Figure 4 modifies the page schema list (p_sch), which is initially empty, based on the query schema (q_sch). Once the query is complete, the system removes the corresponding query schema from the list and adjusts the page schema list accordingly using the currently active query schemas.

During query execution the page schema list dynamically adapts to changing workloads depending on the concurrency degree and the overlaps among attribute sets accessed by queries. This list ensures that queries having common attributes can share data in the buffer pool while queries with disjoint attributes will not affect each other. In the above example, Q1 first comes along, the buffer pool manager creates C-pages with a_1 and a_2. When Q2 arrives, the buffer pool manager will create a C-page with a_1, a_2, and a_3 for these two queries. After Q1 finishes, C-pages with only a_2 and a_3 will be created for Q2.

4.3 Maintaining data consistency

With the algorithm in Figure 4, the buffer pool may contain multiple copies of the same minipage. To ensure data consistency when a transaction modifies a C-page, *Clotho* uses the the mechanisms described below to fetch the latest copy of the data to other queries.

When looking for a record, a traditional database buffer manager looks for the corresponding page id in the page table, and determines whether the record is in memory. To support record lookup in the query-specific C-page in *Clotho*, the page table of the buffer pool manager contains the page ids of all the A-pages used to construct the active C-pages, and is augmented with the page schema bitvectors. To perform a record lookup, *Clotho* uses a key consisting of the page id and the page schema requested. A hit means that the page id matches one of the A-page page ids, and the schema of the C-page subsumes the schema of the requested record as described in the key.

In the case of insertions, deletions, and updates, *Clotho* uses full-schema C-pages. Insertions and deletions need full-record access and modify all respective minipages, whereas full-schema pages for updates help keep buffer pool data consistent at no additional cost. Queries asking for updated records automatically obtain the correct dirty page from the buffer pool. Since deletion of records always operates on full C-pages, CSM can work with any existing deletion algorithms, such as "pseudo deletion" [11].

When a write query is looking up a C-page, it invalidates all of the other buffered C-pages that contain minipages from one A-page. Thus, there is only one valid copy of the modified data. Since the C-page with updated data has a full schema, the updated page will serve all other queries asking for records in this page until it is flushed to the disk. *Clotho* does not affect locking policies because page data organization is transparent to the lock manager.

5 Logical volume manager

This section briefly describes the storage device-specific data organization and the mechanisms exploited by the LVM in creating logical volumes that consist of either disk drives or a single MEMStore. Much of this work builds upon our previous work on *Atropos* disk array logical volume manager [16] and MEMStore [19]. This section describes the high-level points for each device type.

5.1 Atropos disk array LVM

The standard interface of disk drives and disk arrays uses a simple linear abstraction, meaning that any two dimensional data structure that is to be stored on disk needs to be serialized. For example, *NSM* serializes along full records (row-major) and *DSM* serializes along single attributes (column-major). Once the table is stored, access along the dimension of serialization is sequential and efficient. However, access along the other dimension is random and inefficient. *Atropos* uses the same linear abstraction as before, but solves this problem by using a new internal data organization and exposing a few abstractions to the higher-level software.

By exposing enough information about its data organization, the database's storage manager can achieve efficient access along either dimension. *Atropos* exploits the request scheduler built into the disk's firmware and automatically-extracted knowledge of track switch delays to support semi-sequential access: diagonal access to ranges of blocks (one range per track) across multiple adjacent disk tracks. This second dimension of access enables two dimensional data structures to be accessed efficiently. To support efficient sequential access, *Atropos* exploits automatically-extracted knowledge of disk track boundaries, using them as its stripe unit boundaries for achieving efficient sequential access. By also exposing these boundaries explicitly, it allows the *Clotho* storage manager to use previously proposed "track-aligned extents" (*traxtents*), which provide substantial benefits for streaming patterns interleaved with other I/O activity [17, 15]. Finally, as with other logical volume managers, it delivers aggregate bandwidth of all disks in the volume and offers the same reliability/performance tradeoffs of traditional RAID schemes [12].

5.2 Semi-sequential access

To understand semi-sequential access, imagine sending two requests to a disk: one request for the first *LBN* on the first track, and one for the second *LBN* on the second track. These two adjacent tracks are typically in the same cylinder, but different heads are used to access them. First, the disk will seek to the cylinder, then there will be some initial rotational latency before the first *LBN* is read. Next, the disk will switch to the next track, which takes some fixed amount of time (typically around 1 ms), and access the second *LBN*. With properly chosen *LBN*s, the second *LBN* is accessible right after a track switch, with no additional seek or rotational latency incurred. Requesting more *LBN*s laid out in this fashion on successive tracks allows further semi-sequential access.

Naturally, the sustained bandwidth of semi-sequential access is less than that of sequential access. However, semi-sequential access is more efficient than reading randomly chosen *LBN*s spread across adjacent tracks, as would be the case when accessing data in *CSM* along the secondary dimension of a table without *Atropos*. Accessing random *LBN*s would incur an additional rotational latency equal to half a revolution, on average.

5.3 Efficient database organization

With *Atropos*, *Clotho* storage manager can lay out A-pages such that access in one dimension of the table is sequential, and access to the other dimension is semi-sequential. Figure 5 shows the mapping of a simple table with 12 attributes and 1008 records to A-pages stored on an *Atropos* logical volume with four disks. A single A-page includes 63 records and maps to the diagonal semi-sequential *LBN*s, with each minipage mapped to a single *LBN*. When accessing one attribute from all records, *Atropos* can use four track-sized, track-aligned reads. For example, a sequential scan of attribute A1 results in a access of *LBN* 0 through *LBN* 15 Accessing a full A-page) results in three semi-sequential accesses, one to each disk. For example, fetching attributes A1 through A12 for record 0 results in

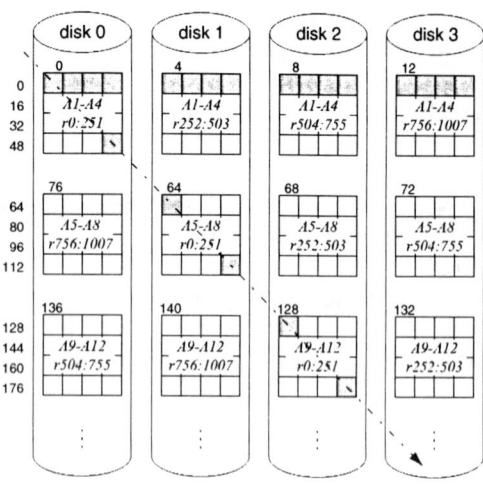

Figure 5: **Mapping of a database table with 12 attributes onto *Atropos* logical volume with 4 disks.** The numbers to the left of disk 0 are the *LBN*s mapped to the gray disk locations connected by the arrow and not the first block of each row. The arrow illustrates efficient semi-sequential access fetching single A-page with 63 records. A single sequential I/O for 16 *LBN*s can efficiently fetch one attribute from 1008 records striped across four disks.

three semi-sequential accesses, each proceeding in parallel on different disks, starting at *LBN*s 0, 64, and 128.

5.4 MEMS-based storage devices

Two groups have evaluated the use of internal access parallelism in MEMStores to efficiently access database tables [19, 22]. *Clotho* shows the benefit of using these techniques in the context of a complete database management system. As these devices are not yet available, we simulate their behavior using the DiskSim simulator combined with the *Atropos* logical volume manager.

Most MEMStore designs [5, 21] consist of a media sled and an array of several thousand probe tips. Actuators position the spring-mounted media sled in the X-Y plane, and the stationary probe tips access data as the sled is moved in the Y dimension. Each read/write tip accesses its own small portion of the media, which naturally divides the media into *squares* and reduces the range of motion required of the media sled.

When a seek occurs, the media is positioned to a specific offset relative to the entire read/write tip array. As a result, at any point in time, all of the tips access the same locations within their squares. An example of this is shown in Figure 6 in which *LBN*s at the same location within each square are identified with ovals. Realistic MEMStores are expected to have enough read/write tips to potentially access 100 *LBN*s in parallel. However, because of power and shared-component constraints, only about 10 to 20 of those *LBN*s could be *actually* accessed in parallel.

Given the simple device in Figure 6, if one third of the read/write tips can be active in parallel, a system could access together up to 3 *LBN*s out of the 9 shown with ovals. The three *LBN*s chosen could be sequential (e.g., 33, 34, and 35), or could be disjoint (e.g., 33, 36, and 51). In each case, all of those *LBN*s would be transferred to or from the

0 ㉝ 54 3 30 57 6 27 60	1 ㉞ 55 4 31 58 7 28 61	2 ㉟ 56 5 32 59 8 29 62
15 ㊱ 69 12 39 66 9 42 63	16 ㊲ 70 13 40 67 10 43 64	17 ㊳ 71 14 41 68 11 44 65
18 (51) 72 21 48 75 24 45 78	19 (52) 73 22 49 76 25 46 79	20 (53) 74 23 50 77 26 47 80

Figure 6: **Data layout with parallel-accessible *LBN*s highlighted.** The *LBN*s marked with ovals are at the same location within each square and, thus, comprise an equivalence class. That is, they can potentially be accessed in parallel.

media in parallel with the same efficiency. A-pages are arranged onto the rows and columns of read/write tips, much as they are across sequential and semi-sequential *LBN*s on a disk drive. By activating the appropriate read/write tips, parallel access to either the rows or columns of the table is possible. In contrast to disk drives, in which access to one dimension is less efficient than access to the other (semi-sequential vs. sequential), the access along the rows and along the columns are equally efficient.

6 Clotho implementation

Clotho is implemented within the Shore database storage manager [4]. This section describes the implementation of C-pages, scan operators, and the LVM. The implementation does not modify the layout of index pages.

6.1 Creating and scanning C-pages

We implemented *CSM* as a new page layout in Shore, according to the format described in Section 4.1. The only significant change in the internal Shore page structure is that the page header is aligned to occupy one block (512 B in our experiments). As described in Section 4, the original buffer pool manager is augmented with schema management information to control and reuse C-page contents. These modifications were minor and limited to the buffer pool module. To access a set of records, a scan operator issues a request to the buffer pool manager to return a pointer to the the C-page with the (first of the) records requested. This pointer consists of the first A-page id in the C-page plus the page schema id.

If there is no appropriate C-page in the buffer pool to serve the request, the buffer pool manager allocates a new frame for the requested page. It then fills the page header with schema information that allows the storage manager to determine which data (i.e., minipages) is needed. This decision depends on the number of attributes in the query payload and on their relative sizes. Once the storage manager determines from the header information what minipages to request, it constructs an I/O vector with memory locations for individual minipages and issues a batch of I/O requests to fetch them. Upon completion of the individual I/Os, the requested blocks with minipages are "scattered" to their appropriate locations.

We implemented two scan operators: S-scan is similar to a scan operator on *NSM* pages, with the only difference that it only scans the attributes accessed by the query. (in the predicate and in the payload). *Clotho* invokes S-scan to read tuples containing the attributes in the predicate and those in the payload, reads the predicate attributes, and if the condition is true returns the payload. The second scan operator, SI-scan, works similarly to an index scan. SI-scan first fetches and evaluates only the attributes in the predicates, then makes a list of the qualifying record ids, and finally retrieves the projected attribute values directly. Section 7.2.1 evaluates these two operators. To implement the above changes, we wrote about 2000 lines of C++ code.

6.2 Storing variable-sized attributes

Our current implementation stores fixed-sized and variable-sized attributes in separate A-pages. Fixed-sized attributes are stored in A-pages as described in Section 3.1. Each variable-sized attribute is stored in a separate A-page whose format is similar to a *DSM* page. To fetch the full record of a table with variable-sized attributes, the storage manager issues one (batch) I/O to fetch the A-page containing all of the fixed-size attributes and an additional I/O for each variable-sized attribute in the table. As future work, we plan to design storage of variable-sized attributes in the same A-pages with fixed-sized attributes using attribute size estimations [1] and overflow pages whenever needed.

6.3 Logical volume manager

The *Atropos* logical volume manager is implemented as a standalone C++ application. It communicates with Shore through a socket (control path) and shared memory (data path) to avoid data copies between the two user-level processes. *Atropos* determines how I/O requests are broken into individual disk I/Os and issues them directly to the attached SCSI disks using the `/dev/sg` Linux raw SCSI device. With an SMP host, the process runs on a separate CPU with minimal impact on Shore execution.

Since real MEMStores do not exist yet, the *Atropos* MEMStore LVM implementation relies on simulation. It uses an existing model of MEMS-based storage devices [18] integrated into the DiskSim storage subsystem simulator [8]. The LVM process runs the I/O timings through DiskSim and uses main memory for storing data.

7 Evaluation

This section evaluates the benefits of decoupling in-memory data layout from storage device organization using our *Clotho* prototype. The evaluation is presented in two parts. The first part uses representative microbenchmarks [20] to perform a sensitivity analysis by varying several parameters such as the query payload (projectivity) and the selectivity in the predicate. The second part of the section presents experimental results from running

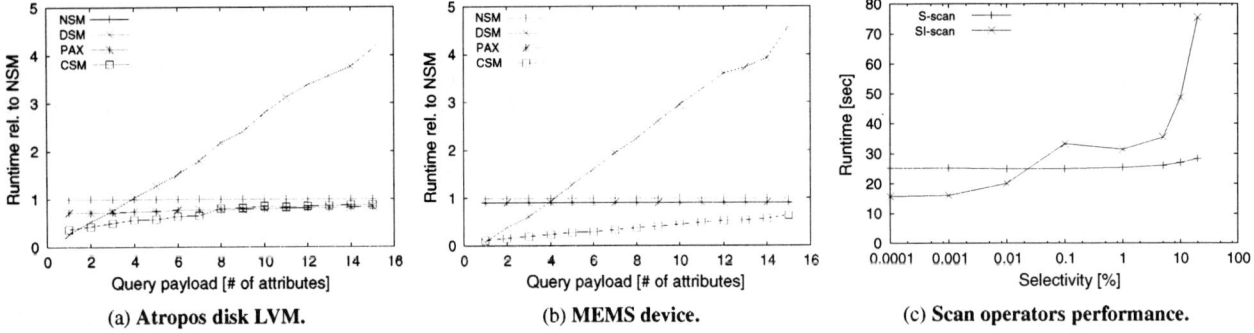

Figure 7: **Microbenchmark performance for different layouts.** The graphs show the total microbenchmark query run time relative to *NSM*. The performance of S-scan and SI-scan is shown for CSM layout running on *Atropos* disk array.

DSS and OLTP workloads, demonstrating the efficiency of *Clotho* when running these workloads with only one common storage organization. The microbenchmarks include queries with sequential and random access, point updates, and bulk insert operations and evaluate the performance of the worst- and best-case scenarios.

7.1 Experimental setup

The experiments are conducted on a two-way 1.7 GHz Pentium 4 Xeon workstation running Linux kernel v. 2.4.24 and RedHat 7.1 distribution. The machine for the disk array experiment has 1024 MB memory and is equipped with two Adaptec Ultra160 Wide SCSI adapters, each controlling two 36 GB Seagate Cheetah 36ES disks (ST336706LC). The *Atropos* LVM exports a single 35 GB logical volume created from the four disks in the experimental setup and maps it to the blocks on the disks' outermost zone.

An identical machine configuration is used for the MEMStore experiments; it has 2 GB of memory, with half used as data store. The emulated MEMStore parameters are based on the G2 MEMStore [18] that includes 6400 probe tips that can simultaneously access 16 *LBN*s, each of size 512 bytes; the total capacity is 3.46 GB.

All experiments compare *CSM* to the *NSM*, *DSM*, and *PAX* implementations in Shore. *NSM* and *PAX* are implemented as described in [1], whereas *DSM* is implemented in a tight, space-efficient form using the tuple-at-a-time reconstruction algorithm [14]. For *CSM*, the *Atropos* LVM uses its default configuration [16]. The *NSM*, *DSM*, or *PAX* page layouts don't take advantage of the semi-sequential access that *Atropos* provides. However, they still run over the logical volume which is effectively a conventional striped logical volume with the stripe unit size equal to individual disks' track size to ensure efficient sequential access. Unless otherwise stated, the buffer pool size in all experiments is set to 128 MB and page sizes for *NSM*, *PAX* and *DSM* are 8 KB. For *CSM*, both the A-page and C-page sizes are also set to 8 KB. The TPC-H queries used in our experiments (Q1, Q6, Q12, Q14) do not reference variable-sized attributes. TPC-C new-order transaction has one query asking for a variable-size attribute, C_DATA, which is stored separately as described in Section 6.2.

7.2 Microbenchmark performance

To establish *Clotho* baseline performance, we first run a range query of the form SELECT AVG(a1), AVG(a2), ... FROM R WHERE Lo < a2 < Hi. *R* has 15 attributes of type FLOAT, and is populated with 8 million records (roughly 1 GB of data). All attribute values are uniformly distributed. We show the results of varying the query's payload by increasing the number of attributes in the select clause from one up to the entire record, and the selectivity by changing the values of *Lo* and *Hi*. We first run the query using sequential scan, and then using a non-clustered index to simulate random access. The order of the attributes accessed does not affect the performance results, because *Atropos* uses track-aligned extents [17] to fetch each attribute for sequential scans.

7.2.1 Queries using sequential scan

Varying query payload. Figure 7 compares the performance of the microbenchmark query with varying projectivity for the four data layouts. *CSM* uses the S-scan operator. The data are shown for a query with 10% selectivity; using 100% selectivity exhibits the same trends.

Clotho shows the best performance at both low and high projectivities. At low projectivity, *CSM* achieves comparable performance to *DSM*, which is the best page layout when accessing a small fraction of the record. The slightly lower runtime of *DSM* for the one attribute value in Figure 7(a) is caused by a limitation of the Linux operating system that prevents us from using DMA-supported scatter/gather I/O for large transfers[1]. As a result, it must read all data into a contiguous memory region and do an extra memory copy to "scatter" data to their final destinations. *DSM* does not experience this extra memory copy; its pages can be put verbatim to the proper memory frames. Like *DSM*, *CSM* effectively pushes the project to the I/O level. Attributes not involved in the query will not be fetched from the storage, saving I/O bandwidth, memory space, and accelerating query execution.

With increasing projectivity, *CSM* performance is better than or equal to the best case at the other end of the spectrum, i.e., *NSM* and *PAX*, when selecting the full record.

---
[1] The size of an I/O vector for scatter/gather I/O in Linux is limited to 16 elements, while commercial UNIX-es support up to 1024 elements.

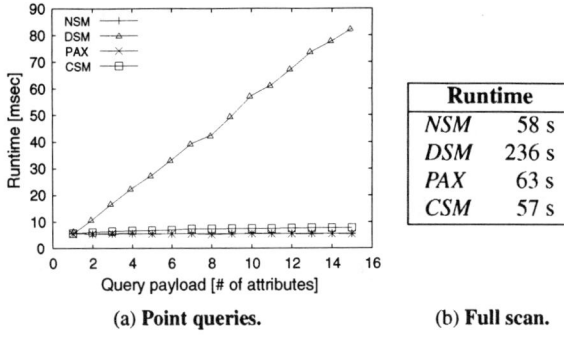

(a) Point queries. (b) Full scan.

Figure 8: **Microbenchmark performance for** *Atropos* **LVM.**

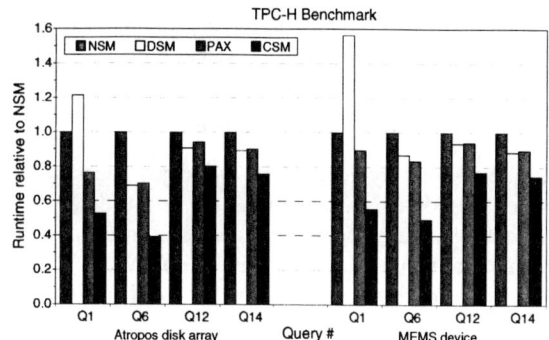

Figure 9: **TPC-H performance for different layouts.** The performance is shown relative to *NSM*.

DSM's suboptimal performance at high projectivities is due to the additional joins needed between the table fragments spread out across the logical volume. *Clotho*, on the other hand, fetches the requested data in lock-step from the disk and places it in memory using *CSM*, maximizing spatial locality and eliminating the need for a join. *Clotho* performs a full-record scan over 3× faster when compared to *DSM*. As shown in Figure 7(b), the MEMStore performance shows the same results.

Comparison of S-scan and SI-scan. Figure 7(c) compares the performance of the above query for the S-scan and SI-scan operators. We vary selectivity from 0.0001% to 20% and use a payload of four attributes (the trend continues for higher selectivities). As expected, SI-scan exhibits better performance at low selectivities, whereas S-scan wins as the selectivity increases. The performance gain comes from the fact that only pages containing qualified records are processed. The performance deterioration of SI-scan with increasing selectivity is due to two factors. First, SI-scan must process a higher number of pages than S-scan. At selectivity equal to 1.6%, all pages will have qualifying records, because of uniform data distribution. Second, for each qualifying record, SI-scan must first locate the page, then calculate the record address, while S-scan uses a much simpler same-page record locator. The optimizer can use SI-scan or S-scan depending on which one will perform best given the estimated selectivity.

7.2.2 Point queries using random access

The worst-case scenario for *Clotho* data placement schemes is random point tuple access (access to a single record in the relation through a non-clustered index). As only a single record is accessed, sequential scan is never used; on the contrary, as the payload increases *CSM* is penalized more by the semi-sequential scan through the disk to obtain all the attributes in the record. Figure 8(a) shows that, when the payload is only a few attributes, *CSM* performs closely to *NSM* and *PAX*. As the payload increases the *CSM* performance becomes slightly worse, although it deteriorates much less that *DSM* performance.

7.2.3 Updates

Bulk updates (i.e., updates to multiple records using sequential scan) exhibit similar performance to queries using sequential scan, when varying either selectivity or payload.

Similarly, point updates (i.e., updates to a single record) exhibit comparable performance across all data placement methods as point queries. *Clotho* updates single records using full-schema C-pages, therefore its performance is always 22% worse than *NSM*, regardless of payload. To alleviate this behavior, we are currently investigating efficient ways to use partial-record C-pages for updates as we do for queries. As with point queries, the performance of *DSM* deteriorates much faster.

7.2.4 Full table scans and bulk inserts

When scanning the full table (full-record, 100% selectivity) or when populating tables through bulk insertions, *Clotho* exhibits comparable performance to *NSM* and *PAX*, whereas *DSM* performance is much worse, which corroborates previous results [1]. Figure 8(b) shows the total runtime when scanning table *R* and accessing full records. The results are similar when doing bulk inserts. Our optimized algorithm issues track-aligned I/O requests and uses aggressive prefetching for all data placement methods. Because bulk loading is an I/O intensive operation, space efficiency is the only factor that will affect the relative bulk-loading performance across different layouts. The experiment is designed so that each layout is as space-efficient as possible (i.e., table occupies the minimum number of pages possible). *CSM* exhibits similar space efficiency and the same performance as *NSM* and *PAX*.

7.3 DSS workload performance

To quantify the benefits of decoupled layout for database workloads, we run the TPC-H decision support benchmark on our Shore prototype. The TPC-H dataset is 1 GB and the buffer pool size is 128 MB.

Figure 9 shows execution times relative to *NSM* for four representative TPC-H queries (two sequential scans and two joins). The leftmost group of bars represents TPC-H execution on *Atropos*, whereas the rightmost group represents queries run on a simulated MEMStore. *NSM* and *PAX* perform the worst by a factor of 1.24× − 2.0× (except for *DSM* in Q1) because they must access all attributes. The performance of *DSM* is better for all queries except Q1 because of the benchmark's projectivity. *CSM* performs best because it benefits from projectivity and avoids the cost of

705

the joins that *DSM* must do to reconstruct records. Again, results on MEMStore exhibit the same trends.

7.4 OLTP workload performance

The queries in a typical OLTP workload access a small number of records spread across the entire database. In addition, OLTP applications have several insert and delete statements as well as point updates. With *NSM* or *PAX* page layouts, the entire record can be retrieved by a single-page random I/O, because these layouts map a single page to consecutive *LBN*s. *Clotho* spreads a single A-page across non-consecutive *LBN*s of the logical volume, enabling efficient sequential access when scanning a single attribute across multiple records and less efficient semi-sequential scan when accessing full records.

The TPC-C benchmark approximates an OLTP workload on our Shore prototype with all four data layouts using 8 KB page size. TPC-C is configured with 10 warehouses, 100 users, no think time, and 60 s warm-up time. The buffer pool size if 128 MB, so it only caches 10% of the database. The completed transactions per minute (TpmC) throughput is repeatedly measured over a period of 120 s.

Table 2 shows the results of running the TPC-C benchmark. As expected, *NSM* and *PAX* have comparable performance, while *DSM* yields much lower throughput. Despite the less efficient semi-sequential access, *CSM* achieves only 6% lower throughput than *NSM* and *PAX* by taking advantage of the decoupled layouts to construct C-pages that are shared by the queries accessing only partial records. On the other hand, the frequent point updates penalize *CSM*'s performance: the semi-sequential access to retrieve full records. This penalty is in part compensated by the buffer pool manager's ability to create and share pages containing only the needed data.

7.5 Compound OLTP/DSS workload

Benchmarks involving compound workloads are important in order to measure the impact on performance when different queries access the same logical volume concurrently. With *Clotho*, the performance degradation may be potentially worse than with other page layouts. The originally efficient semi-sequential access to disjoint *LBN*s (i.e., for OLTP queries) could be disrupted by competing I/Os from the other workload creating inefficient access. This does not occur for other layouts that map the entire page to consecutive *LBN*s that can be fetched in one media access.

We simulate a compound workload with a single-user DSS (TPC-H) workload running concurrently with a multi-user OLTP workload (TPC-C) against our *Atropos* disk LVM and measure the differences in performance relative to the isolated workloads. The respective TPC workloads are configured as described earlier. In previous work [15], we demonstrated the effectiveness of track-aligned disk accesses on compound workloads; here, we compare all of the page layouts using these efficient I/Os to achieve comparable results for TPC-H.

Layout	NSM	DSM	PAX	CSM
TpmC	1115	141	1113	1051

Table 2: **TPC-C benchmark results with *Atropos* disk array LVM.**

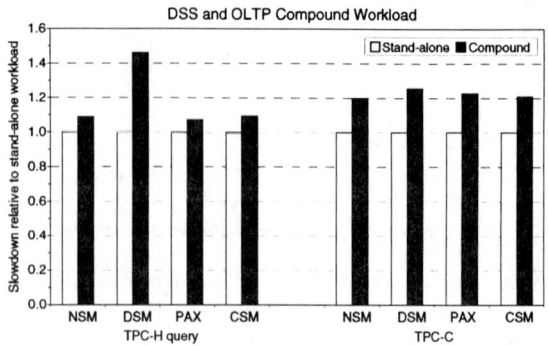

Figure 10: **Compound workload performance for different layouts.** This figure shows the slowdown off TPC-H query 1 runtime when run with TPC-C benchmark relative to the case when runs in isolation and the impact on TPC-C performance.

As shown in Figure 10, undue performance degradation does not occur: *CSM* exhibits the same or lesser relative performance degradation than the other three layouts. The figure shows indicative performance results for TPC-H query 1 (others exhibit similar behavior) and for TPC-C, relative to the base case when OLTP and DSS queries run separately. The larger performance impact of compound workloads on DSS with *DSM* shows that small random I/O traffic aggravates the impact of seeks necessary to reconstruct a *DSM* page. Comparing *CSM* and *PAX*, the 1% lesser impact of *PAX* on TPC-H query is offset by 2% bigger impact on the TPC-C benchmark performance.

7.6 Space utilization

Since the *CSM* A-page partitions attributes into minipages whose minimal size is equal to the size of a single *LBN*, *CSM* is more susceptible to the negative effects of internal fragmentation than *NSM* or *PAX*. Consequently, a significant amount of space may potentially be wasted, resulting in diminished access efficiency. With *PAX*, minipage boundaries can be aligned on word boundaries (i.e., 32 or 64 bits) to easily accommodate schemas with high variance in attribute sizes. In that case, *Clotho* may use large A-page sizes to accommodate all the attributes without undue loss in access efficiency due to internal fragmentation.

To measure the space efficiency of the *CSM* A-page, we compare the space efficiency of *NSM* and *CSM* layouts for the TPC-C and TPC-H schemas. *NSM* exhibits the best possible efficiency among all four page layouts. Figure 11 shows the space efficiency of *CSM* relative to *NSM* for all tables of TPC-C and TPC-H as a function of total page size. Space efficiency is defined as the ratio between the maximum number of records that can be packed into a *CSM* page and the number of records that fit into an *NSM* page.

A 16 KB A-page suffices to achieve over 90% space utilization for all but the customer and stock tables of the

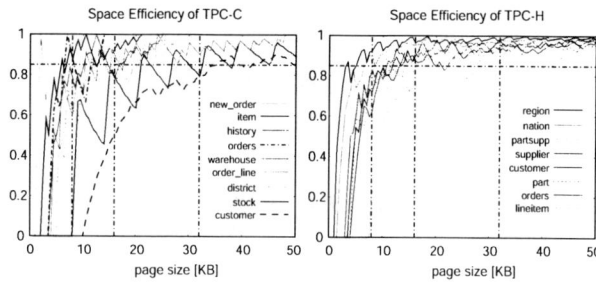

Figure 11: **Space efficiencies with *CSM* page layout.**

TPC-C benchmark. A 32 KB A-page size achieves over 90% space efficiency for the remaining two tables. Both customer and stock tables include an attribute that is much larger than all other attributes. The customer table includes a 500 byte long C_DATA attribute containing "miscellaneous information", while the next largest attribute has a size of 20 bytes. The stock table includes a 50 byte S_DATA attribute, while the next largest attribute is 24 bytes. Both of these attributes are rarely used in the TPC-C benchmark.

8 Conclusions

Clotho decouples in-memory page layout from in-storage data organization, enabling independent data layout design at each level of the storage hierarchy. Doing so allows *Clotho* to optimize I/O performance and memory utilization by only fetching the data desired for queries that access partial records, while mitigating the trade-off between *NSM* and *DSM*. Experiments with our *Clotho* implementation show substantial performance improvements across a spectrum of query types, for both a real disk array and future MEMS-based storage devices.

Acknowledgements

We thank the anonymous referees for their detailed and insightful comments and the members and companies of the PDL Consortium (including EMC, Hewlett-Packard, Hitachi, IBM, Intel, LSI Logic, Microsoft, Network Appliance, Oracle, Panasas, Seagate, Sun, and Veritas) for their interest, insights, feedback, and support. This work is sponsored in part by NSF grants CCR-0113660, IIS-0133686, CCR-0205544, and BES-0329549.

References

[1] A. Ailamaki, D. J. DeWitt, M. D. Hill, and M. Skounakis. Weaving relations for cache performance. International Conference on Very Large Databases, pages 169–180. Morgan Kaufmann Publishing, Inc., 2001.

[2] A. Ailamaki, D. J. DeWitt, M. D. Hill, and D. A. Wood. DBMSs on a modern processor: where does time go? International Conference on Very Large Databases, pages 266–277. Morgan Kaufmann Publishing, Inc., 1999.

[3] P. A. Boncz, S. Manegold, and M. L. Kersten. Database architecture optimized for the new bottleneck: memory access. International Conference on Very Large Databases, pages 54–65. Morgan Kaufmann Publishers, Inc., 1999.

[4] M. J. Carey et al. Shoring up persistent applications. ACM SIGMOD International Conference on Management of Data. 1994.

[5] L. R. Carley et al. Single-chip computers with microelectromechanical systems-based magnetic memory. *Journal of Applied Physics*, 87(9):6680–6685, 1 May 2000.

[6] X. Chen and X. Zhang. Coordinated data prefetching by utilizing reference information at both proxy and web servers. *Performance Evaluation Review*, 29(2):32–38. ACM, September 2001.

[7] G. P. Copeland and S. Khoshafian. A decomposition storage model. ACM SIGMOD International Conference on Management of Data, pages 268–279. ACM Press, 1985.

[8] The DiskSim Simulation Environment (Version 3.0). http://www.pdl.cmu.edu/DiskSim/index.html.

[9] R. A. Hankins and J. M. Patel. Data morphing: an adaptive, cache-conscious storage technique. International Conference on Very Large Databases, pages 1–12. VLDB, 2003.

[10] S. Manegold, P. A. Boncz, and M. L. Kersten. Generic database cost models for hierarchical memory systems. International Conference on Very Large Databases, pages 191–202. Morgan Kaufmann Publishers, Inc., 2002.

[11] C. Mohan et al. ARIES: a transaction recovery method supporting fine-granularity locking and partial rollbacks using write-ahead logging. *ACM Transactions on Database Systems*, 17(1):94–162, March 1992.

[12] D. A. Patterson, G. Gibson, and R. H. Katz. A case for redundant arrays of inexpensive disks (RAID). ACM SIGMOD International Conference on Management of Data, pages 109–116, 1–3 June 1988.

[13] R. Ramakrishnan and J. Gehrke. *Database management systems*, number 3rd edition. McGraw-Hill, 2003.

[14] R. Ramamurthy, D. J. DeWitt, and Q. Su. A case for fractured mirrors. International Conference on Very Large Databases, pages 430–441. Morgan Kaufmann Publishers, Inc., 2002.

[15] J. Schindler, A. Ailamaki, and G. R. Ganger. Lachesis: robust database storage management based on device-specific performance characteristics. International Conference on Very Large Databases, pages 706–717. Morgan Kaufmann Publishing, Inc., 2003.

[16] J. Schindler et al. Atropos: a disk array volume manager for orchestrated use of disks. Conference on File and Storage Technologies, pages 159–172. USENIX Association, 2004.

[17] J. Schindler, J. L. Griffin, C. R. Lumb, and G. R. Ganger. Track-aligned extents: matching access patterns to disk drive characteristics. Conference on File and Storage Technologies, pages 259–274. USENIX Association, 2002.

[18] S. W. Schlosser, J. L. Griffin, D. F. Nagle, and G. R. Ganger. Designing computer systems with MEMS-based storage. Architectural Support for Programming Languages and Operating Systems. 2000.

[19] S. W. Schlosser, J. Schindler, A. Ailamaki, and G. R. Ganger. *Exposing and exploiting internal parallelism in MEMS-based storage*. Technical Report CMU–CS–03–125. Carnegie-Mellon University, Pittsburgh, PA, March 2003.

[20] M. Shao and A. Ailamaki. *DBMbench: Microbenchmarking database systems in a small, yet real world*. Technical Report CMU–CS–03–161. Carnegie-Mellon University, Pittsburgh, PA, October 2003.

[21] P. Vettiger et al. The "Millipede" – more than one thousand tips for future AFM data storage. *IBM Journal of Research and Development*, 44(3):323–340, 2000.

[22] H. Yu, D. Agrawal, and A. E. Abbadi. Tabular placement of relational data on MEMS-based storage devices. International Conference on Very Large Databases, pages 680–693, 2003.

[23] J. Zhou and K. A. Ross. A Multi-resolution Block Storage Model for Database Design. International Database Engineering & Applications Symposium, 2003.

Vision Paper: Enabling Privacy for the Paranoids

G. Aggarwal, M. Bawa, P. Ganesan, H. Garcia-Molina, K. Kenthapadi,
N. Mishra, R. Motwani, U. Srivastava, D. Thomas, J. Widom, Y. Xu

Stanford University
Stanford, CA 94305
{*gagan,bawa,pganesan,hector,kngk,nmishra,rajeev,usriv,dilys,widom,xuying*}@*cs.stanford.edu*

Abstract

P3P [23, 24] is a set of standards that allow corporations to declare their privacy policies. Hippocratic Databases [6] have been proposed to implement such policies within a corporation's datastore. From an end-user individual's point of view, both of these rest on an uncomfortable philosophy of trusting corporations to protect his/her privacy. Recent history chronicles several episodes when such trust has been willingly or accidentally violated by corporations facing bankruptcy courts, civil subpoenas or lucrative mergers. We contend that data management solutions for information privacy must restore controls in the individual's hands. We suggest that enabling such control will require a radical re-think on modeling, release, and management of personal data.

1 Introduction

Information Privacy is concerned with imposing limits on collection and handling of personal information such as credit and medical records by state and private organizations. These are early days for Information Privacy, and norms and laws that impose restrictions on the use of personal information collected by organizations are being worked out as a solution. Technology is being devised to assist the implementation of such laws.

Status The Platform for Privacy Preferences (P3P) [23, 24] is a set of standards that allow organizations to declare their privacy policies. Recently, Hippocratic Databases [6] were envisioned to provide support for an organization's privacy policies within the organization's datastore. In this framework, an organization would post its privacy policies, using agreed-upon language, and an individual would only conduct business with that organization if the published policies were consistent with the individual's expectations.

Example Consider an individual, Alice, who wants to sign up for a DealsRus service on the web. DealsRus requires Alice's email address to inform her of upcoming deals. DealsRus recognizes the privacy concerns of its clients and has placed its P3P policies on their web-site. Alice is privacy-savvy and is using a browser which is P3P enabled. Alice's browser would fetch the P3P policy from the DealsRus web-site. For instance, DealsRus may state that email addresses will only be used for current purpose ("completion and support of the recurring subscription activity") and the recipients of such data will be restricted to ours ("DealsRus and/or entities acting as their agents or entities for whom DealsRus are acting as an agent") but not unrelated third parties. If Alice is happy with this policy, then she can give DealsRus her email address.

Critique With the P3P framework, thus, Alice has to trust that (a) the organization has clearly stated its policies, that (b) the organization will actually adhere to the policies, and that (c) the organization has the means to implement the policies in transit and storage. All three aspects raise troubling issues: Even though DealsRus has used legal language vetted by P3P, the end user may feel inundated with legalese whose exact practicality is open to interpretation [30, 35, 38, 46]. For instance, what exactly does current purpose mean? Perhaps it is within the ambit of current purpose for DealsRus to spam their customer's mailboxes? And what does it mean not to give email addresses to third parties but restrict recipients to ours? Perhaps DealsRus has many wholly-owned subsidiaries which can use the addresses? Does DealsRus provide adequate protection for personal data to prevent easy access to data by intruders? And what would happen if DealsRus declares bankruptcy, or changes management, or changes it policies, or its records are subpoenaed by a court?

Acknowledgements We have benefited from the many pertinent and constructive comments of our anonymous VLDB reviewers and Dennis Shasha. This research was supported in part by NSF Grants ITR-0331640 and EIA-0137761, and a grant from SNRC.

Permission to copy without fee all or part of this material is granted provided that the copies are not made or distributed for direct commercial advantage, the VLDB copyright notice and the title of the publication and its date appear, and notice is given that copying is by permission of the Very Large Data Base Endowment. To copy otherwise, or to republish, requires a fee and/or special permission from the Endowment.

Proceedings of the 30th VLDB Conference,
Toronto, Canada, 2004

Inherency P3P and Hippocratic Databases put the onus of safeguarding privacy in the hands of organizations that are often themselves guilty of trespass or sloppiness. Indeed, recent history chronicles several episodes where organizations have violated, either deliberately or accidentally, their customer's trust when they faced mergers, bankruptcy, courts or hackers [1, 28, 33, 42]. Even if the underlying datastore at DealsRus follows Hippocratic principles, if the rules the datastore is told to follow by DealsRus management are not "ethical" (as far as Alice is concerned), then the Hippocratic guarantees will be of little use to Alice.

Thesis We contend that there is a better way to approach privacy, and that is to enable individuals to retain "control" over their information. At all times, the individual should be able to "choose freely under what circumstances and to what extent they will expose themselves, their attitudes, and their behavior, to others" [54]. The desired "level of control" may vary: for instance, in some cases, the individual may only want that misuse of her information be auditable. In other cases, she may want to prevent access to information to certain organizations or for particular tasks. In any case, however, it should be the individual who pro-actively decides what the level of control is.

We believe that a case can also be made to organizations to leave control in the hands of individuals. In particular, governments are passing new legislation (e.g., California law SB1386) that forces organizations to inform individuals whenever there has been a privacy breach, and makes organizations liable for improper use of information. Given the high overhead of securing data, and potentially high liability costs, organizations could be persuaded to leave control to owners of the information.

Plan How can an individual retain control at the appropriate level given that organizations must have access to her information to conduct business? We contend that control can be retained if the individual can release information to organizations such that *the released information is unusable for illegitimate tasks*. In this paper, we illustrate through examples a series of scenarios where such control can be enabled (Section 2). We claim that these examples are representative of a small set of "information types", and that for each such type, one can devise a general purpose set of mechanisms to retain control (Section 3). We then propose to gather the set of mechanisms that cover all information types in one framework which we call *P4P: Paranoid Platform for Privacy Preferences* (Section 4).

We call this framework "paranoid" because individuals that use it are less trusting of organizations than individuals who use the P3P framework. We caution that our framework is still in its formative stages, and many of our concepts are still not well-defined. Thus, at this point, we are only presenting the *vision* of our framework, with the hopes that others in the community will help us refine it, formalize it, and debug it.

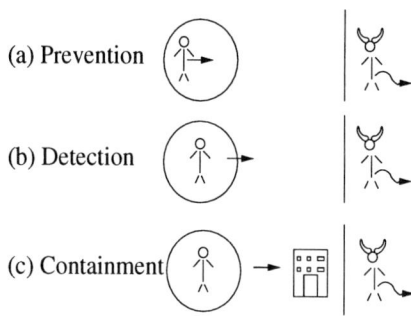

Figure 1: *Privacy has traditionally been assured against adversaries by (a) preventing illegitimate access to personal information or (b) detecting and curtailing release of personal information. In contrast, (c) the P4P framework seeks to contain illegitimate use of personal information that has already been released to an external (possibly adversarial) entity.*

The P4P Framework Figure 1 informally contrasts our P4P framework against prior work on privacy/security of data. We comment on additional related work in Section 5.

Figure 1 depicts an individual, Alice (on the left), who seeks to guard her personal information (the arrow in the figure) from an adversary, shown on the right. A perimeter around Alice represents her personal space over which she can exercise direct control. Generally speaking, there are three ways in which Alice can protect her information from the adversary, illustrated as Figures 1(a), (b) and (c).

Traditionally, Alice secures her information by placing access-control restrictions to *prevent* the adversary from accessing her information (Figure 1). In addition, Alice can place safeguards at her perimeter (e.g., firewalls, query auditing, etc.) to *detect and curtail* release of her information to the adversary (Figure 1(b)). Again, notice that such safeguards can be successfully imposed only while Alice's information resides within her perimeter of direct control *and* requests for information are directed to Alice.

In her daily interactions, Alice has to release her personal information to organizations (e.g., to a bank for obtaining a loan, to an online merchant for a book purchase, etc.). Once her information leaves her perimeter, Alice has no control over its subsequent use. The organization that receives her information may, either deliberately or accidentally, release Alice's information to the adversary, leading to a breach of Alice's privacy. Unfortunately, prevention and/or detection mechanisms discussed above are of little help to Alice now.

The P4P framework (Figure 1(c)) seeks to enable Alice to retain control over her personal information *even after its release to an organization*. Using the P4P framework, Alice can *contain* illegitimate use of remote copies of her information. We note that the P4P framework *complements*, and does not replace, the prevention and detection mechanisms for data privacy. As we investigate in this paper, enabling such control of remote copies requires a radical re-think on modeling and release of information.

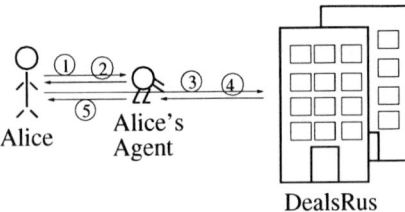

Figure 2: *Alice interacts with DealsRus through her agent. Alice (1) requests and (2) obtains a temporary email address from her agent, which is (3) released to DealsRus. Henceforth, DealsRus can only (4) send messages to the agent at the released email address which are (5) forwarded to Alice after checking for specified restrictions.*

2 Retaining Control – Initial Examples

We claim that it is possible for individuals to retain control over remote copies of their personal information by exploiting the *semantics* of the information. Let us illustrate what we mean using a couple of examples: email addresses and credit card numbers. We note that all of the techniques we will exploit in these two examples are well-known; indeed, solutions based on these techniques have already been deployed today. Our goal here is to illustrate the feasibility of individual control, leading the reader towards Section 3 where general mechanisms are synthesized out of the well-known individual techniques.

2.1 Email Address

To retain control over her email address, Alice constructs a trusted software *agent* that manages her email address. (See Figure 2.) Only the agent is given Alice's true email address, say aly@aliceHost. When Alice wishes to give her email address to DealsRus, the agent generates a new address, say aly1@agentHost, where agentHost is the computer where the agent runs. When DealsRus receives aly1@agentHost (either from Alice or from the agent), it uses that address for communication with Alice. That is, an email to aly1@agentHost is received by the agent, and will be forwarded to aly@aliceHost depending on what restrictions Alice specified when the email was created. These restrictions give Alice some control over how aly1@agentHost can be used. For example:

1. *Timeout:* The email aly1@agentHost is only valid for a period of time. After that time, the agent will refuse to forward messages to Alice.
2. *Limited Use:* The agent will only forward some maximum number of messages.
3. *Restricted Source:* The agent will only forward a message if it comes from a pre-specified source.
4. *Invalidation:* Alice can at any time explicitly instruct the agent to stop forwarding messages.
5. *Isolation:* The email aly1@agentHost is only released to DealsRus. Other organizations will get different email addresses.

How does Alice gain by trusting an agent? Alice now has to trust only *one* entity, as opposed to *every* organization that receives her address under the P3P framework. Furthermore, if the agent code is public and run on a trusted platform [41], Alice (or her auditor) can know precisely what actions the trusted agent will take under different circumstances. This operational description of the agent's "privacy policy" will be much more precise than any legal/natural-language description that an organization provides under P3P. Furthermore, organizations do not have to change their procedures; they handle email just as they did before.

The semantics of email addresses enable Alice to specify restrictions that provide a very useful level of control for Alice. In particular:

A DealsRus can distribute copies of aly1@agentHost to other organizations, but a restricted-source limitation can prevent the other organizations from getting through to Alice.

B If DealsRus gives aly1@agentHost to other organizations, the agent will have proof of this action, since the address aly1@agentHost was only given to DealsRus.

C If the intended use of the address spans a limited time or number of interactions (e.g., perhaps Alice is simply trying to find deals that are available this week), then by implementing a timeout or a limited-use restriction Alice can ensure her address is not used for other tasks later in time or for tasks that require more interactions.

D If DealsRus wishes to use Alice's address in some new way, it is likely that it will have to request permission from Alice (or her agent), as aly1@agentHost is likely to be invalid.

E If Alice uses different email addresses for each organization she interacts with, DealsRus will be unable to use Alice's address as an integration key to obtain more information about her from third-party organizations.

Adoption Notice that the agent can be implemented in a variety of ways. The agent could be part of Alice's desktop email software [26], or it could be a trusted third party that provides the temporary email address generation and email forwarding service. Indeed, www.mailshell.com and www.spamgourmet.com provide such a facility today enabling Alice to specify *Timeout* and *Limited Use* restrictions respectively.

2.2 Credit Card Number

The above ideas can be extended to the handling of credit card numbers as well. An agent can ensure control of an individual, say Bob, over the use of his credit card. However, since credit is extended to Bob by his bank, we need to place the agent either at Bob's bank or between the bank and the organizations that use Bob's credit card number. If the agent is not at the bank, it would have to appear to the organizations as a bank that can handle charges, which may be difficult to achieve. Thus, let us assume that the bank plays the role of trusted agent for Bob.

The interaction between Bob and an organization, say ShopsRus, is analogous to that between Alice and DealsRus. Neither Bob nor his agent gives out Bob's true credit card number. Instead, ShopsRus receives a unique, temporary credit card number, which we will call a *pseudonum*. The agent manages the mapping between this pseudonum and Bob's credit card number. Bob can instruct his agent to restrict the use of pseudonums in a variety of ways:

1. *Timeout:* The pseudonum is only valid for a fixed period of time, or for a fixed number of charges;
2. *Limited Use:* The pseudonum can only be charged upto a fixed amount;
3. *Restricted Source:* The pseudonum can only be charged from specific sites, or for specific types of purchases;
4. *Invalidation:* Bob can at any time explicitly instruct his bank to stop honoring charges on the pseudonum.
5. *Isolation:* A unique pseudonum is released to ShopsRus. Other organizations get different pseudonums.

As with his email, Bob retains some level of control as to how his credit card is used.

A. ShopsRus can distribute copies of the pseudonum to other organizations, but a restricted-source limitation prevents other organizations from charging Bob's credit.
B. If ShopsRus gives the pseudonum to other organizations, the agent has proof of this action, since the pseudonum was only given to ShopsRus.
C. If the intended use of the address spans a limited time or credit, then with an appropriate restriction Bob ensures that his credit is not used for other tasks later.
D. If ShopsRus wishes to charge Bob's credit for a new deal, it is likely that it will have to request permission from Bob (or his agent), as the original pseudonum is likely to be invalid.
E. If Bob uses different pseudonums for each organization he interacts with, ShopsRus will be unable to use Bob's credit card number as an integration key to obtain more information about him from third-party organizations.

Adoption Some credit card companies have begun offering a subset of the above functionalities (e.g., one-time use credit card numbers [8, 31]). The technology was hailed as a "landmark event by the industry" and promptly adopted by online merchants who have to bear the brunt of credit-card fraud, unlike offline merchants in which case the liability is assumed by the bank that issued the card. For example, the travel-site www.expedia.com recorded a fiscal third-quarter charge of 6 million US dollars in 2000 to cover the cost of fraudulent transactions! The above anecdotes suggest that organizations will indeed be willing to leave control in the hands of individuals if appropriate technology is devised.

3 Retaining Control – Generalizing to "Information Types"

Can we generalize these concepts, so that an individual can retain control over other "types" of information? It turns out that email addresses and credit cards are the easiest to control as they represent a "service handle" for a workflow path that terminates at the individual. An agent can be easily placed in this path to provide limited control on how the service is invoked. Indeed, this is why we already have deployments that exercise control in ways described earlier.

In this section, we consider four types of personal information that are ubiquitous today: (a) Local Identifiers, (b) Foreign-Key Identifiers, (c) Value Predicates, and (d) Multi-Source Value Predicates. We will see that it will be harder to retain the same degree of control as with service handles, and organizations may have to dramatically change the way they handle personal information. Nevertheless, we are cautiously optimistic that a collection of techniques can be devised that may lead to the synthesis of a general framework.

3.1 Local Identifiers

In many cases, organizations demand from its users identification numbers like social security numbers (SSN) in the United States, or national identification numbers in other countries. For instance, the first thing that many mail-order or on-line stores ask for is a telephone number, since that is how they locate their customer's records. In many cases, these numbers are *only* used as keys in the local database.

Simple Protocol It is easy for an agent to hide the true identity of an individual, say Carol. The agent generates a unique, private identifier for Carol, which could be for example, a random 256 bit string. The organization, DealsRus receives this private identifier, and uses it as a primary key for Carol. The agent of course remembers all of Carol's identifiers, so whenever Carol needs to contact DealsRus, the proper identifier can be issued. And as in our previous examples, Carol retains control over her identity: DealsRus does not know Carol's true phone number or SSN, so any abuses of the private identifier are limited in scope.

Challenges There are a few practical issues that must be considered for such indirect identifiers to work with today's deployed systems. DealsRus may only be willing to accept identifiers that look like SSNs or phone numbers. In such a case, Carol's agent must map the random identifier into one that conforms to what DealsRus expects.

There is a chance that some other individual will generate the same private identifier as Carol. Organizations may already have procedures in place for duplicate identifiers. For example, two family members who share a phone may be buying goods at the same mail-order store. Even SSNs are known not to be really unique identifiers, and conflicts do happen. The bottom line is that organizations need to be prepared to deal with duplicate user-generated identifiers, and should have a protocol in place to ask the user for a different one. Such protocols are already common at websites where users select their ID: if the ID is taken, the sites prompts the user for a different ID.

A potential scheme to generate good identifiers is the following. Carol can provide her agent with a particular (unique and secret) data item, say her SSN. The agent will then generate all identifiers for Carol based on this data

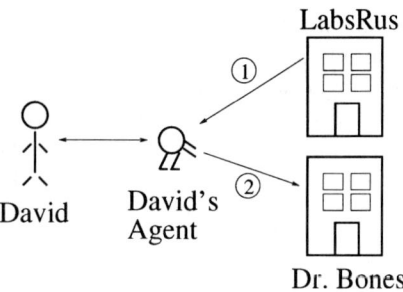

Figure 3: *LabsRus interacts with Dr. Bones through David's agent. (1) LabsRus sends David's reports to his agent, which then (2) forwards the reports to Dr. Bones.*

item and the organization's name, e.g., by using a one-way hash function like SHA-1 [22]. The identifiers that are generated can be shown to have good cryptographic properties: uniqueness, independence and non-invertibility.

Real identifiers such as phone numbers have the advantage that they are more readily remembered by users. Thus, when Carol personally phones the DealsRus help line, it will be a lot easier for her to remember her phone number rather than the randomly generated identifier. Or perhaps Carol has allowed her phone to automatically provide her number to the callee (a feature known as caller-id in the United States), in which case DealsRus will immediately know who is calling. This example illustrates a classic privacy-convenience trade-off which cannot be avoided: If Carol wants privacy, then she is better off giving out agent-generated identifiers, and always relying on the agent for interactions with outside entities. If Carol wants convenience, then she can give out her personal identifiers, and hope that organizations do not do anything bad with them.

Summary Local identifiers can be handled by enabling an individual E to provide organizations $O_1, O_2, \ldots, O_n$ with respective identifiers $i_1, i_2, \ldots, i_n$ that are:

1 *Unique:* no other individual will have the same respective identifiers,
2 *Opaque:* an adversary cannot use the identifier to discover a private attribute of E,
3 *Private:* an adversary cannot discover E's identifiers,
4 *Independent:* identifiers i_j and i_k at organizations O_j and O_k have a small probability of belonging to the same individual.

3.2 Foreign-Key Identifiers

In some cases, an individual's identifiers are used for purposes other than just as local identifiers. The organization may need to use them as foreign-keys to allow a legitimate (individual approved) integration or retrieval of records from other organizations.

To illustrate, say David is a patient at Dr. Bones' clinic, and had some tests done at LabsRus. (See Figure 3.) The patient information system that Dr. Bones uses identifies David by i_1, a local identifier generated by David's agent. Similarly, LabsRus identifies David by i_2, a different local identifier. When David gets a blood test at LabsRus, he requests that the results be sent to Dr. Bones' clinic. Thus, LabsRus needs a way to send records for i_2 that are received as records for i_1 at Dr. Bones' clinic.

Naive Protocol LabsRus asks David's agent for David's identity with Dr. Bones. David's agent provides LabsRus with i_1 after which LabsRus can communicate directly with Dr. Bones to integrate David's records. Although this scheme provides the opt-in property, the privacy and opt-out properties are lost. LabsRus now knows that David is being treated at Dr. Bones' clinic; Dr. Bones now learns that David has his tests done at LabsRus. LabsRus now knows David's identity with Dr. Bones, and David would not know of any future sharing of information between LabsRus and Dr. Bones. David has hence lost control of his personal information.

Simple Protocol LabsRus can route the blood test results to Dr. Bones through David's agent. One way to do this is as follows: David instructs his agent to anticipate blood test results from LabsRus that are to be routed to Dr. Bones. When LabsRus has the results, it sends a message to David's agent which includes:

1 David's local identifier i_2;
2 David's blood test results;
3 A signature that can be used to prove that only LabsRus could have generated the given test results;

At this point, David's agent removes the i_2 identifier and the signature of LabsRus from the message. The agent logs the signature as proof of the authenticity of the report, if needed later. The agent then adds the i_1 identifier and forwards the results to Dr. Bones.

Notice that in this scheme, LabsRus remains unaware of David's doctor who receives the reports. Dr. Bones is unaware of the place where the tests were performed. Thus, David again retains some control over his information. Anytime an organization wants to contact another organization to share David's information, it must go through David's agent.

Challenges In this scenario, it is clear that organizations will have to change the way they operate. That is, they need to be aware that following foreign keys needs to be done though agents, and not directly as they do today. We also observe that the above is still a sketch and a rigorous protocol needs to be defined that will allow such foreign-key mappings to be used via a trusted agent without leaking any personal information. For example, how can David's agent be assured that LabsRus is not hiding information within the test reports that reveals David's and its identity? How can Dr. Bones be assured that the test reports are from a valid laboratory?

Summary Foreign-key identifiers can be handled by enabling an individual E to allow organizations O_1 and O_2 to integrate E's records such that:

1 *Opt-in:* the integration cannot occur without the explicit approval of E,

2. *Opaque:* after integration, an adversarial organization (O_1, O_2 or both) cannot discover a private attribute of E that is not in the records at O_1 and O_2, and
3. *Opt-out:* when the explicit approval of E is withdrawn, the integration cannot occur unless the integrated record has enough information to identify E.

3.3 Value Predicates

In our next example, say Ellen is purchasing a cruise from ShipsRus, and the site asks her for her age. Let us assume that ShipsRus has a legitimate need for Ellen's age y. Perhaps ShipsRus offers a senior citizen discount to individuals with an age over 60 years who take the cruise. We can model this situation by saying that ShipsRus needs to compute a predicate $p := (y > 60)$? true : false. Thus, ShipsRus does not need to know y itself but the value $p(y)$. How can ShipsRus obtain $p(y)$ while Ellen retains control over her age attribute y?

Naive Protocol We can proceed as follows. ShipsRus sends the predicate p to Ellen's agent. (The query will run in a sandbox-ed environment so that it does not have undesired side effects.) Ellen gives y to her agent, which then computes $p(y)$ and sends the result to ShipsRus. In this way, Ellen retains control over her age information, and only gives ShipsRus the *minimal legitimate* information ($p(y)$) it needs to have to provide service to Ellen.

There are, of course, two shortcomings in the naive protocol as stated. First, the organization can "cheat" by using predicates that are easy to invert. For example, ShipsRus may give the trusted agent a series of predicates that serve to identify Ellen's age y uniquely (e.g., $p_1 : (y == 58)$? true : false, $p_2 : (y == 59)$? true : false, etc.) The only way to avoid this problem is to have DealsRus disclose the nature of the predicates by making the source SQL code visible to scrutiny. The source SQL code may be checked for privacy breaches in one of two ways. (1) Ellen and her agent can understand the nature of the information that is being given to ShipsRus. For example, if p is the predicate given earlier that checks if age is greater than 60, Ellen will know that she is disclosing the fact that she is or is not a senior citizen to ShipsRus. (2) Query restriction algorithms may be used to prevent privacy breaches by auditing trails of predicates evaluated.

Second, Ellen may cheat and not give her true age to her agent. Of course, cheating may have later repercussions for Ellen. For example, she may run into trouble when she shows up for the cruise with a senior discount ticket and looking like a teenager! We note that Ellen could cheat by giving a false age even if ShipsRus were to ask Ellen for her age directly.

Notary Protocol Is there anything that could be done to prevent cheating by Ellen? For instance, say ShipsRus does not trust Ellen, but does trust some other organization (e.g., Dr. Bones) that can act as a *notary* and vouch for Ellen's age. Can we enable Ellen to compute a ShipsRus predicate, whose result is vouched for by Dr. Bones?

We present a weak version of the notary protocol that requires Ellen to trust Dr. Bones not to divulge her information. With this protocol, the P3P guarantees are the best we can hope for. Let us say that Ellen discloses her age to Dr. Bones, e.g., by having a medical examination or by showing her birth certificate. There is no way Bones will vouch for Ellen's age without knowing the age, so we cannot avoid disclosing the information.

Ellen's agent must also disclose the mapping between the identifier Ellen used at DealsRus, i_1 and the identifier Ellen uses with Dr. Bones, i_2. Without the $i_1 : i_2$ mapping, Dr. Bones cannot really say whose age he is vouching for. Ellen's agent also provides a signature for the $i_1 : i_2$ mapping, so that if a dispute arises in the future, Dr. Bones can prove that Ellen's agent claimed that i_1 and i_2 were the same person. In summary, the request for Ellen's age proceeds as follows:

1. DealsRus asks Dr. Bones to evaluate $p(y)$ for the person DealsRus calls i_1 and who uses Ellen's agent.
2. Dr. Bones asks Ellen's agent for Ellen's id at DealsRus. If the agent approves, it sends the $i_1 : i_2$ mapping, appropriately signed.
3. Bones then looks up i_2's age, y and computes $p(y)$. The result is returned to DealsRus.

Challenges The weaker protocol we presented requires Ellen to reveal her DealsRus id to Dr. Bones. The notarizing organization (Dr. Bones) could thus gradually get to know Ellen's identity at various organizations.

Of concern to DealsRus is the fact that it has to reveal its predicate p to Dr. Bones. If the predicate p is proprietary, DealsRus may insist on keeping p private. Cryptographers have studied secure multi-party [55] (e.g., 3-party) computation that computes a function $f(a, b, c)$ with inputs a, b and c at three different parties, such that the three parties learn only $f(a, b, c)$ and nothing else.

Ellen, DealsRus and Dr. Bones can engage in a secure multi-party computation with copies of y at Ellen and Dr. Bones, and an encoding of p at DealsRus as the respective secret inputs. However, such schemes incur an excessive communication overhead. Is it possible to devise an *efficient* protocol for a restricted set of predicates? On the other hand, if DealsRus presents the predicate p as a secret input to the above computation, Ellen will be unable to audit p and curtail its computation. Is it possible to achieve the privacy of both Ellen and DealsRus simultaneously?

Trusted Third Party In the above protocol, Ellen's agent could cheat and provide a false mapping since only it knows the relationship between Ellen's two personas. An improvement would be to run agents at sites that could be trusted by both Ellen and the organizations she deals with. In such a scenario, a trusted organization, which we can call the *agency* can run privacy agents for a variety of individuals. The agency somehow gathers evidence that a particular individual is who they say they are (perhaps they have to show up in person and identify themselves with a photo identification), and then runs an agent on their behalf. The code used for the agent can be public so that customers gain trust in the provided services. Even if the agency is trusted, individuals can still cheat in various ways, but at least organizations are able to go to the agency for help in resolving conflicts that may arise.

As far as Ellen is concerned, her agent is a part of the agency. Thus the mappings of its personas are known only to the agency, and need not be revealed to Dr. Bones. DealsRus still has to reveal its predicate p to the agency. All parties now have to trust only *one* organization.

Summary Value Predicates can be handled by enabling an individual E to evaluate a predicate p specified by an organization O_1 such that:

1 *Opaque:* O_1 learns only the result of evaluation of p; the evaluation must not reveal to O_1 information that cannot be computed using the output of the evaluation.
2 *Verifiable:* O_1 can ascertain that the predicate was computed over the correct value of E's attribute.

3.4 Multi-Source Value Predicates

The need for parties trusted by individuals and organizations becomes more evident if we consider more complex scenarios where predicates need values from different sources. To illustrate, consider a bank, EasyLoan, that needs Fred's age and salary in order to determine if it can give him a loan. All that EasyLoan needs is the output of a predicate $p(y, s)$, where y is Fred's age, and s is his salary. Fred does not want to disclose his attributes to EasyLoan; EasyLoan does not trust Fred to compute $p(y, s)$. Fortunately, EasyLoan does trust Fred's employer, Acme, to provide the salary, and Fred's doctor, Dr. Bones, to provide the age needed by the computation. How can EasyLoan obtain $p(y, s)$ from values provided by Acme and Dr. Bones while Fred retains control over his age and salary attributes?

Trusted Third Party As for value predicates, a secure multi-party computation can be used to evaluate multi-source value predicates. A simpler solution is to use an agency that is trusted by all parties. The protocol is then as follows: EasyLoan asks the agency to compute $p(y, s)$ for the person it knows as i_1 and who uses a particular agent. By this point, Fred has already disclosed to EasyLoan who may provide the age and salary, so the request from EasyLoan also includes the identities of Acme and Dr. Bones. The agency then asks Fred's agent for Fred's identities at Acme and Bones, and asks these organizations for the required data. Finally, the agency computes $p(y, s)$ and returns the value to EasyLoan. The agency keeps a record of the computation in case of future disputes.

Summary Multi-source value predicates can be handled by enabling an individual E to evaluate a predicate p specified by organizations $O_1, O_2, \ldots, O_n$ such that:

1 *Opaque:* O_i learns only the result of evaluation of p; the evaluation must not reveal to O_i information that cannot be computed using the output of the evaluation.

2 *Verifiable:* the organizations can ascertain that p was computed over the correct value of E's attributes.

4 P4P: Paranoid Platform for Privacy Preferences

We have illustrated through examples a set of information types where an individual can retain control over his information. We claim that for each such information type, one can devise a general-purpose set of mechanisms to retain control. We propose to gather these set of mechanisms into one framework, which we call *P4P: Paranoid Platform for Privacy Preferences*.

We believe that private information can be classified along three dimensions: (a) ownership, (b) type, and (c) desired level of control. In this section, we illustrate the dimensions and glean principles that can underly the framework. We caution that our framework is still in its formative stages, and many concepts are still not well defined.

For our illustration, we need to refer to a data model, and here we chose a simple entity-attributes model, although of course other models are possible.

- *Attributes* represent the basic building blocks of information, and let us say they are (label, value) pairs. For example, (name:"Alice") and (address:"123 Main St.") are attributes. For ease of notation, we will remove the quotation marks from string values.
- *Entity* has a set of related attributes. We are especially interested in entities that represent individuals or organizations. For ease of notation, we will use the term "entity" to refer to both (a) an individual/organization E in the real world, and (b) the representation of E in our framework as a set of related attributes. For instance, Alice is an entity that may be represented by the following set of attributes: [Name:Alice, Address: 123 Main St., Phone: 555-1234].

Note that in our world, attributes by themselves are usually not sensitive, e.g., nobody will care if someone knows the attribute phone: 555-1234. It is only the *association* of phone: 555-1234 and name: Alice with the entity Alice that is sensitive information. Thus, associations of attributes with an entity will be considered sensitive.

Each entity has a datastore whose contents can be classified by the information's ownership, type and desired level of control. Each entity also associates a trust level for other entities it deals with, and uses those trust levels to determine how to interact with them. Each interaction involves exchange of data between the participant entities that reveals attributes of one entity to others.

Example [*Entity Interaction*] Suppose Alice buys *bread* and *butter* at AllMart using her credit card. Figure 4 shows the interaction between Alice and AllMart as seen in our framework. Alice is an entity with attributes address, credit card information and a grocery list. Similarly, AllMart is an entity with attributes address, inventory and prices of goods. Alice's interaction with AllMart reveals information about one entity to the other. Thus, Alice must

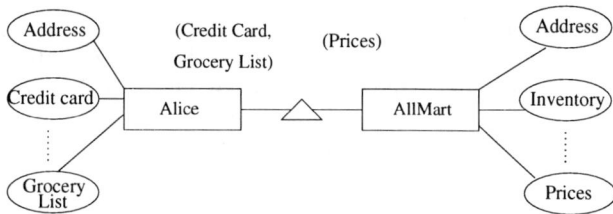

Figure 4: *Rectangles represent entities. Ovals are attributes of, and Triangles are interactions between, entities.*

share her credit card information and grocery list with AllMart. AllMart must reveal its prices of goods to Alice.

Ownership Consider the interaction between two entities, an individual Alice and an organization AllMart. The participant entities share data with each other. The data that is shared can be owned by Alice or by AllMart.

- *By Individual:* This covers data generated by Alice, i.e., her personal data (e.g., address) and preferences (e.g., grocery list). The fact that Alice owns this data means that Alice should retain full control over it, deciding when and how it can be revealed to others.
- *By Organization:* This covers data generated by AllMart. For instance, say Alice buys a particular book there. The fact that someone purchased a book may be represented by a tuple <invoiceNo:123, bookTitle: War and Peace>. This tuple is owned by AllMart, not Alice. Even though it was a purchase by Alice, Alice cannot control the information. Similarly, the tuple: <invoiceNo: 123, identifier: 89> that links this purchase to Alice's local identifier is owned by AllMart.

Information Type In order to control information, one needs to know what semantics it has in interactions between entities. Information can be of the following types, as illustrated by our examples in Section 3. Note that the same information can be of multiple types, depending on how it is used in an interaction. For instance, an email address could be a service handle, and it could also be an identifier.

- *Identifier:* An identifier is an attribute (or a set of attributes) that is used to identify an entity in a datastore. For example, if Alice gives her phone number to AllMart, then AllMart may use that number to refer to Alice in its interactions with Alice (or her agent).
- *Service Handle:* A handle is an attribute that provides a path to a service that some other entity provides on behalf of Alice. Email addresses and credit card numbers are examples of service handles.
- *Input to Predicate:* An attribute is of this type if it can be used as an input to predicates other entities wish to evaluate. In our examples, age and salary were attributes of this type.
- *Copy:* Attributes can be copied to another entity's datastore. In such cases, it is critical to track which of the copies is the *primary* copy (at the site that owns the information) and which are the *secondary* copies.

Desired Level of Control This level specifies how the owner wants the information managed. The level may vary by entity, that is, one level may be desired for one entity, and a different level for another, probably depending on the trust level placed on the entities (see below). We remark that a level of control (except *Sharable*) provides an *operational* description of privacy to individuals which is much more precise than the P3P policies that are descriptions of *intent*.

- *Complete Privacy:* The information should not be revealed at all.
- *Limited Time/Use:* The information can be used for a limited time, or a limited number of times, or for a particular task, as in our email example.
- *No Predicate Input:* The information cannot be used as input to predicates. We may disallow either single-source or multi-source value predicates.
- *No Integration:* The information is given to an entity, but that entity should not be able to integrate that information to other subsets we have given other entities. To enforce this restriction, we need to control the foreign keys we give out.
- *Accountable:* The information is given to an entity, but in a watermarked form such that the entity can be held responsible for a misuse of its copy of the information.
- *Anonymous:* The information is given to an entity, but in a distorted form such that the entity is unable to deduce the true value with a high degree of certainty.
- *Sharable:* As we have argued, there are cases where we must give information to an entity and hope the entity will protect our data. For this type of sharable data, we may specify what guarantees we may want from the entity, as in the P3P framework. For instance, we may only share information with an entity if it promises not to divulge it to third parties, or if it promises to only use it for computing statistics.

Trust As mentioned earlier, in our framework, an entity also needs to specify the trust it has in other entities. There are many ways to specify and manage trust that have been discussed in literature [14, 56]. Given our focus on controlling access to information, one option is to simply specify policies stating the level of control desired on information released to a target entity. For example, if an entity is trusted to enforce no-integration, then we believe it will not attempt to integrate the information we give it with what is available at other entities. If we trust an entity in this fashion, then we do not have to implement precautions with the identifiers we give it.

Adversary In order to build mechanisms, one needs to know what adversaries must be guarded against during interactions between entities. Adversaries can be of the following types:

- *Passive adversary* is an eavesdropper who observes interactions involving a particular individual, say Alice. Such an adversary may have either a *global* view (observes all interactions by Alice) or a *local* view (ob-

715

I. Attribute	II. Information Type	III. Level of Control
Image	Copy	Accountable
Email	Service Handle	Limited Use
Email	Identifier	No Integration
Age	Input to Predicate	No Input

Table 1: *Alice's P4P policy for interactions with DatesRus.*

serves all interactions by Alice with AllMart).
- *Active adversary* acts with deliberate intent to gather information, apart from observing interactions involving Alice. Such an adversary (e.g., a misbehaving AllMart) can issue specific queries, record and correlate answers, or even release information it gathers about Alice to other colluding entities.
- *Open-world adversary* has access to information about Alice gained through channels outside the P4P framework (e.g., a misbehaving AllMart may have access to survey results indicating the buying habits of residents of Alice's zipcode).

Properties of Interaction An unconstrained exchange of information in interactions can reveal an entity's private attribute values to others. We propose that information that is exchanged during an interaction be carefully "trimmed" to ensure information privacy. For example, let Alice participate in successive interactions $I_1, I_2, I_3, \ldots$ with DealsRus. To ensure Alice's privacy, we require the following, which we call the *TRIM* properties, on each interaction:
- *Traceability*: The data that is exchanged during an interaction I_j cannot be used by DealsRus for an interaction with another entity, without Alice having proof of DealsRus' involvement.
- *Revocability*: Alice can "sever" associations with a particular interaction in the future (e.g., on expiry of a subscription; the attribute values that was shared in such an interaction cannot be associated with Alice anymore.
- *Isolation*: Data provided in two interactions I_j and I_k ($j \neq k$) cannot be associated with the same entity Alice.
- *Minimality*: Alice ensures that the data that is exchanged in an interaction is the minimal to successfully achieve its goals.

To illustrate our proposed taxonomy, let us return to our sample entity for Alice [Name:Alice, Age: 23, Email: alice@public.org, Image: myPic.jpg]. Let us assume that Alice wants to sign up with an online dating service called DatesRus, but does not trust DatesRus with her personal information. Alice may define P4P policies as shown in Table 1 to govern her interactions with DatesRus. Each row in the table illustrates a policy that enables Alice to retain control over her personal information vis-a-vis DatesRus. Column I lists examples of attributes over which Alice desires control, Column II specifies the attribute's type, for which Column III specifies the level of control desired. We consider each row in more detail next.

Example [*Image ↦ Copy ↦ Accountable*] Alice wants to upload her image at the DatesRus site. However, she is worried about abuses: e.g., DatesRus may sell her image to advertisers without her permission. Since she needs to make a copy of the image which will be shared with DatesRus, she deems her attribute image: myPic.jpg to have type: copy and level of control: accountable. Therefore, Alice's agent must ensure that the image provided satisfies property: traceable so that Alice will (eventually) obtain proof of DatesRus' misuse. Alice's agent may watermark [34] the image to ensure traceability.

Example [*Email ↦ Service Handle ↦ Limited Use*] Alice wants to provide an email address for DatesRus to inform her of possible interests. However, Alice does not foresee herself using DatesRus for more than an year. She does not want DatesRus to contact her once she ends her membership. So she deems her attribute email: alice@public.org to have type: service handle and level of control: limited use. Therefore, Alice's agent must ensure that the released email address satisfies property: revocable. Alice's agent may provide a temporary email address that can be invalidated by Alice at will.

Example [*Email ↦ Identifier ↦ No Integration*] Alice wants to interact with various organizations (e.g., DatesRus, DealsRus, ShipsRus) each of which wants her email address. Alice realizes that her email address is unique to her, and could be used as her identifier by the organizations. She does not want (a subset of) these organizations to get together and integrate their datasets without her knowledge. So she deems her attribute email: alice@public.org to have type: identifier and level of control: no integration. Therefore, Alice's agent must ensure that the released email address satisfies property: isolation as well. Alice's agent may create distinct temporary email addresses, one each for each organization to ensure isolation.

Example [*Age ↦ Input to Predicate ↦ No Input*] DatesRus has promotional offers from local clubs that provides free entry to DatesRus clients under the age of 25. Alice does not want to reveal her age and has decided to decline any offer that requires her to reveal her age. So she deems her attribute age: 23 to have type: input to predicate and level of control: no input. Therefore, Alice's agent must ensure that optional age-based predicates from DatesRus are not evaluated.

In summary, in our P4P framework, it is important to understand who controls (owns) data, how the data is being used (type), what control is desired, and what agents can be trusted. For each attribute (a point in the ownership, type, control space), our goal is then to provide one or more mechanisms that enforce the desired privacy.

In the P4P framework, trusted agencies play a central role. As illustrated in our examples, they provide agent and predicate evaluator services, so that entities can effectively control and at the same time share their information. Each individual would contract with one or more agencies to provide services, and perhaps to store some of their data too. As the individual interacts with organizations, instead of giving out information directly, it asks its agent to provide appropriate attributes, whether they be private email addresses or private identifiers. When an organization needs additional information about an individual, it can contact its agent or a trusted agency to obtain the data.

5 Analysis of Current Privacy Technologies

Entities (organizations/individuals) have legitimate access to certain information. Privacy is assured by preventing illegitimate use of this information by adversaries. In this section, we discuss proposed privacy solutions and their limits in assuring information privacy.

Secure Databases Research here has focused on enabling storage and query of sensitive information to detect and prevent unauthorized disclosure, alteration, or destruction of data [16, 43]. The work in this area in the context of databases can be broadly classified into role-based access-control and multi-level security. In role-based access-control, accesses to data are allowed or prohibited based on the role in which an entity is acting [44, 51]. Such access-control is usually offered on a per-table granularity. In multi-level security, both data and entities are assigned security levels drawn from a security hierarchy [32]. A "no read up, no write down" policy [11] is imposed: an entity can only read from a level below (and including) their own in the hierarchy, an entity can only write to a level above (and including) their own in the hierarchy. The P4P framework complements this work for securing local copies of data by building mechanisms that seek to contain illegitimate use of released data.

Trust Management Systems generalize the access-control mechanisms described above by operating in distributed systems. They define languages for expressing authorizations and access-control policies [13, 25] that can work under the assumption that all of the parties may not be known when policies are expressed. Recently, researchers have explored automated trust negotiations between two entities participating in an interaction [56]. When an entity E_r requests data from another entity E_s, trust is negotiated between E_r and E_s on the fly by iteratively disclosing their credentials and access policies. The access is permitted only if E_r can establish to E_s that it has the necessary authorization. The trust component in the P4P framework will benefit from the work in this area.

Statistical Databases Research here has focused on enabling queries on aggregate information (e.g., sum, count, average, median, etc.) from a database without revealing individual records [2]. The work in this area can be broadly classified into data perturbation and query restriction. Data perturbation involves either altering the input database [40, 52], or altering query results returned [10, 19]. Query restriction includes schemes that check for possible privacy breaches by keeping audit trails [18] and controlling overlap [21] of successive aggregate queries. While we expect some of these techniques to find applications in our framework (e.g., data perturbation to enable an anonymous level of control, query restriction to audit value predicates), new mechanisms will be needed to perturb the richer P4P information types and audit the richer P4P queries.

Anonymous Networks Deployed systems have often preferred to achieve privacy for an entity participating in an interaction by making its identity anonymous. Application-specific schemes have been designed to enable anonymous messaging (Onion Routing [50]), anonymous emails (Mix Nets [17]), anonymous web browsing (Crowds [45]), anonymous publishing (FreeHaven [20]), and anonymous indexing (Privacy Preserving Indexes [9]). The P4P framework allows an individual to declare the level of control she desires over specific information. We expect some of these techniques to find applications when an individual opts to share her information anonymously.

Cryptography Primitives are used to protect information in transit and storage from adversaries. There is extensive literature on cryptographic tools [48] that will be of use in the P4P framework: e.g., symmetric and public key encryption for secure transit and storage, signatures to establish ownership of information, certificates to establish legitimate access to information, watermarking to trace the origins of data, etc.

Given the new design goals envisioned by our P4P framework, it is not surprising that some of the tools fall short in meeting the challenges posed. For example, the communication overhead of secure multi-party computation [27, 55] makes its application infeasible for "multi-source value predicate": organizations may need to participate in thousands of interactions per minute with their customers. We believe that efficient protocols will need to be designed for specific functions that arise in the P4P framework, much like the recently invented specialized protocols for finding medians [4] and intersections [5] of private values at multiple entities.

6 Challenges

We have sketched our vision for an information processing world where individuals can retain control over their information. Organizations can also benefit by not getting control, and the accompanying liability, of information they do not own. This information processing model will require that organizations and individuals operate with information in different ways. Of course, the challenges to achieve this vision are huge, and in closing we mention a few.

6.1 Interfaces for Entities, Agents and Humans

Adequate programmatic interfaces need to be defined for entities, agents, agencies, predicate evaluators and notaries. Agent interfaces for dealing with information types will have generic and application dependent parts. For example, an agent may be asked to create a service handle that is limited for one day (a generic restriction) or a handle that only allows charges of up to 100 dollars (application specific for money-related handles). Traceable copies of data may require embedding of application-dependent fingerprints [34]. It will be important to explore application-specific controls and services that would be useful.

Human interfaces must be invented that enable people to describe their privacy goals and select appropriate policies for their agents. The interface must also educate people about risks of their options. The recent work on privacy interfaces for ubiquitous computing will be useful here. Research there has highlighted that individuals tend to release information subjectively while weighing in factors like information function, information sensitivity, and trust in recipient [3, 37] which mirror our *owner - type - level of control* dimensions.

There has recently been an interest in exploring the nature of privacy as a value determined by market forces [36, 53]. Instead of a declarative policy, individuals in this model may be willing to relax their level of control in return for a fair compensation. How can such schemes be incorporated in the interface, and indeed, the framework?

6.2 Reasoning about Information Privacy

While we have presented a few useful points in the *ownership - type - level of control* spectrum, it is important to specify information workflows for a variety of interactions and formally reason about privacy guarantees as an aggregate of an entity's interactions.

In our strawman design, we postulated that each entity will log *all* interactions it has participated in with other entities. The agent will use an entity's log to pre-process (or even abort) current interactions to prevent violation of the entity's privacy policies. An entity can query its logs to deduce the personal information that has been released to a particular entity. However, such logs will quickly grow to be quite large. Efficient log management, analysis and summarizing algorithms will need to be invented to allow online entity interactions to be fast. Can we design interactions with properties (e.g., TRIM) that reduce the size of logs? Analysis of logs and auditing of P4P queries will require extending statistical databases techniques for audit of aggregate queries in new directions. Furthermore, how would such an audit scheme work against an open-world adversary with its knowledge of auxiliary datasets that may not be currently known to the individual's agent?

6.3 Architecture of a Privacy Agent/Agency

We touched upon challenges in designing privacy preserving protocols in Section 3. Perhaps the recent advances [15] in designing efficient group signatures [47] for anonymous authentication can be used to devise a Notary Protocol? A group signature scheme allows a member M of a group G to sign messages on behalf of G such that the resulting signature does not reveal M's identity. Thus, in the examples of Section 3, we could place Acme in a group of employers and Dr. Bones in a group of doctors. Acme and Dr. Bones would vouch for Fred's salary and age using their respective group signatures. EasyLoan can verify the signatures, and still not know the identity of Acme or Dr. Bones.

The examples in Section 3 assumed a cryptographic definition of privacy. Can efficient agents be designed when individuals desire an "anonymous" level of control? Such schemes should allow the individual to increase the level of anonymity of interactional data by using various information hiding schemes (e.g., k-anonymity [49], perturbation [7]). The infrastructure should, however, provide statistics to indicate the level of anonymity achieved. How can such statistics be maintained?

6.4 Trust Management

It will be important to understand the interactions between the P3P privacy policies and our privacy control mechanisms. The P3P framework still plays an important role in describing how trusted organizations will manage data they own or have a copy of. Perhaps the agency can play a role in managing trust for the entities it represents. For example, the agency can track privacy breaches (e.g., misuse of limited-use emails or pseudonums) by organizations and assign them "trust ratings". Such trust ratings can be used by individuals to determine policies for their interactions with an organization.

6.5 Secure Society

Individual privacy and societal security are sometimes at logger heads with each other. For example, the "no integration" level of control precludes, among other things, the construction of credit reports and profiling of criminals. Such integration of information without the individual's intervention is essential for a smooth functioning of society. The moral dilemma here is akin to the one faced by designers of mechanisms to ensure communication privacy: the technology is of as much use to drug traffickers, terrorists and subversive elements as to law abiding citizens. Can the P4P framework be designed with sufficient "hooks" to allow law-enforcement agencies to monitor interactions that hamper societal security?

7 Final Thoughts

We contend that technology must be devised to allow individuals to retain control over their information. While other commentators have also stressed the need and suggested legal avenues [12, 39], we have sought to devise an information processing framework to enable such control.

For instance, cryptologists have provided primitives (e.g., Public Key Infrastructure [29]) to individuals to achieve communication privacy. We remark that while communication privacy could have been ensured by legislating that organizations (e.g., email servers, ISPs, etc.) respect individual privacy, PKI primitives have put the right to communication privacy firmly into the individual's hands. Can we, in the database community, build an analogous infrastructure that ensures information privacy?

References

[1] Acxiom opts out of opt-out. http://www.wired.com, 11/17/2003.

[2] N. R. Adam and J. C. Wortman. Security-control methods for statistical databases. *ACM Computing Surveys*, 21(4), 1989.

[3] A. Adams and M. A. Sasse. Taming the wolf in sheep's clothing: Privacy in multimedia communications. In *Proc. of ACM Multimedia*, 1999.

[4] G. Aggarwal, N. Mishra, and B. Pinkas. Secure computation of the k-th ranked element. In *Proc. of the IACR Conf. on Eurocrypt*, 2004.

[5] R. Agrawal, A. Evfimievski, and R. Srikant. Information sharing across private databases. In *Proc. of the ACM SIGMOD*, 2003.

[6] R. Agrawal, J. Kiernan, R. Srikant, and Y. Xu. Hippocratic databases. In *Proc. of the VLDB*, 2002.

[7] R. Agrawal and R. Srikant. Privacy preserving data mining. In *Proc. of the ACM SIGMOD*, 2000.

[8] American express offers disposable credit card numbers for online shopping. http://www.computerworld.com, 9/7/2000.

[9] M. Bawa, R. J. Bayardo Jr., and R. Agrawal. Privacy-preserving indexing of documents on the network. In *Proc. of the VLDB*, 2003.

[10] I. I. Beck. A security mechanism for statistical databases. *ACM TODS*, 5(3), 1980.

[11] D. E. Bell and L. J. LaPadula. Secure computer systems: mathematical foundations and model. Technical report, MITRE, 1974.

[12] J. Berman and D. Mulligan. Privacy in the digital age: Work in progress. *Nova Law Review*, 23(2), 1999.

[13] M. Blaze, J. Feigenbaum, J. Ioannidis, and A. D. Keromytis. The KeyNote trust-management system (Version 2). *RFC 2704*, 1999.

[14] M. Blaze, J. Feigenbaum, and J. Lacy. Decentralized trust management. In *Proc. of the IEEE Symp. on Security and Privacy*, 1996.

[15] D. Boneh. A new life for group signatures. Plenary Talk at RSA Conf., 2004.

[16] S. Castano, M. G. Fugini, G. Martella, and P. Samarati. *Database Security*. Addison-Wesley and ACM Press, 1995.

[17] D. L. Chaum. Untraceable electronic mail, return addresses, and digital pseudonyms. *CACM*, 24(2), 1981.

[18] F. Chin and G. Ozsoyoglu. Auditing and inference control in statistical databases. *IEEE TSE*, 8(6), 1982.

[19] D. Denning. Secure statistical databases with random sample queries. *ACM TODS*, 5(3), 1980.

[20] R. Dingledine, M. J. Freedman, and D. Molnar. The Free Haven project: Distributed anonymous storage service. In *Workshop on Design Issues in Anonymity and Unobservability*, 2000.

[21] D. Dobkin, A. Jones, and R. Lipton. Secure databases: Protection against user influence. *ACM TODS*, 4(1), 1979.

[22] D. Eastlake and P. Jones. US Secure Hash Algorithm 1 (SHA1). *Network Working Group*, RFC 3174, 2001.

[23] M. Langheinrich (Ed.). *A P3P Preference Exchange Language 1.0 (APPEL1.0)*. W3C Working Draft, 2001.

[24] M. Marchiori (Ed.). *The Platform for Privacy Preferences 1.0 (P3P1.0) Specification*. W3C Proposed Recommendation, 2002.

[25] C. M. Ellison, B. Frantz, B. Lampson, R. L. Rivest, B. M. Thomas, and T. Ylonen. SPKI certificate theory. *RFC 2693*, 1999.

[26] E. Gabber, P. Gibbons, Y. Matias, and A. Mayer. How to make personalized web browsing simple, secure and anonymous. In *Proc. of the Conf. on Financial Cryptography*, 1997.

[27] O. Goldreich, S. Micali, and A. Wigderson. How to play any mental game – a completeness theorem for protocols with a honest majority. In *Proc. of the ACM STOC*, 1987.

[28] Hacker accessed customer information, Acxiom reports (08/07/2003). http://www.siliconvalley.com.

[29] R. Housley, W. Polk, W. Ford, and D. Solo. Internet X.509 Public Key Infrastructure certificate and Certificate Revocation List (CRL) profile. *RFC 3280*, 2002.

[30] C. D. Hunter. Recoding the architecture of cyberspace privacy: Why self-regulation and technology are not enough. http://www.asc.upenn.edu/usr/chunter/p3p.html, 2000.

[31] iPrivacy's Internet Identity Protection Service. http://www.iPrivacy.com.

[32] S. Jajodia and R. Sandhu. Toward a multilevel secure relational data model. In *Proc. of the ACM SIGMOD*, 1991.

[33] Jetblue shared passenger data. http://www.wired.com, 09/18/2003.

[34] S. Katzenbeisser and F. A. Petitcolas (Eds.). *Information Hiding Techniques for Steganography and Digital Watermarking*. Artech House, 2000.

[35] J. Kaufman, S. Edlund, D. Ford, and C. Powers. The social contract core. In *Proc. of the WWW*, 2002.

[36] J. Kleinberg, C. H. Papadimitriou, and P. Raghavan. On the value of private information. In *Proc. of the Conf. on Theoretical Aspects of Rationality and Knowledge*, 2001.

[37] S. Lederer, J. Mankoff, and A. K. Dey. Towards a deconstruction of the privacy space. In *Proc. Workshop on Ubicomp Communities: Privacy as Boundary Negotiation*, 2003.

[38] K. Lee and G. Speyer. Platform for Privacy Preferences (P3P) and Citibank. http://www.w3.org/P3P/Lee_Speyer.html, 1998.

[39] Lawrence Lessig. Architecture of privacy. http://cyber.law.harvard.edu/works/lessig/architecture_priv.pdf, 1998.

[40] C. K. Liew, U. J. Choi, and C. J. Liew. A data distortion by probability distribution. *ACM TODS*, 10(3), 1985.

[41] Microsoft next-generation secure-computing base. http://www.microsoft.com/Technet/security/news/NGSCG.asp.

[42] Northwest airlines faces privacy suits. http://www.washingtonpost.com, 01/22/2004.

[43] R. Oppliger. Internet security: Firewalls and beyond. *CACM*, 40(5), 1997.

[44] F. Rabitti, E. Bertino, W. Kim, and D. Woelk. A model of authorization for next-generation database systems. *ACM TODS*, 16(1), 1991.

[45] M. K. Reiter and A. D. Rubin. Crowds: Anonymity for Web transactions. *ACM TISSEC*, 1(1), 1998.

[46] M. Rotenberg. What Larry does'nt get: Fair information practices and the architecture of privacy. *Stanford Technology Law Review*, 1, 2001.

[47] D. Schaum and E. van Heyst. Group signatures. In *Proc. of the EuroCrypt Conf.*, 1991.

[48] Douglas R. Stinson. *Cryptography: Theory and Practice*. CRC Press, 2nd edition, 2002.

[49] L. Sweeney. k-anonymity: A model for protecting privacy. *Journal on Uncertainty, Fuzziness and Knowledge-based Systems*, 10(5), 2002.

[50] P. Syverson, D. M. Coldsehlag, and M. C. Reed. Anonymous connections and onion routing. In *Proc. of the IEEE Symp. on Security and Privacy*, 1997.

[51] T. Ting, S. Demurjian, and M. Hu. A specification methodology for user-role based security in an object-oriented design model. In *Proc. of IFIP Workshop on Database Security*, 1992.

[52] J. Traub, Y. Yemini, and H. Woznaikowski. The statistical security of a statistical database. *ACM TODS*, 9(4), 1984.

[53] H. R. Varian. Economic aspects of personal privacy. *Privacy and Self-Regulation in the Information Age*, NTIA, 1997.

[54] A. Westin. *Privacy and Freedom*. Atheneum, 1967.

[55] A. C. Yao. How to generate and exchange secrets. In *Proc. of the ACM FOCS*, 1986.

[56] T. Yu, M. Winslett, and K. E. Seamons. Automated trust negotiation over the internet. In *Proc. of Multiconference on Systemics, Cybernetics and Informatics*, 2002.

A Privacy-Preserving Index for Range Queries

Bijit Hore, Sharad Mehrotra, Gene Tsudik

University of California, Irvine
Irvine, CA 92697
{bhore,sharad,gts}@ics.uci.edu

Abstract

Database outsourcing is an emerging data management paradigm which has the potential to transform the IT operations of corporations. In this paper we address privacy threats in database outsourcing scenarios where trust in the service provider is limited. Specifically, we analyze the data partitioning (bucketization) technique and algorithmically develop this technique to build privacy-preserving indices on sensitive attributes of a relational table. Such indices enable an untrusted server to evaluate obfuscated range queries with minimal information leakage. We analyze the worst-case scenario of *inference attacks* that can potentially lead to breach of privacy (e.g., estimating the value of a data element within a small error margin) and identify statistical measures of data privacy in the context of these attacks. We also investigate precise privacy guarantees of data partitioning which form the basic building blocks of our index. We then develop a model for the fundamental *privacy-utility* tradeoff and design a novel algorithm for achieving the desired balance between privacy and utility (accuracy of range query evaluation) of the index.

1 Introduction

The recent explosive increase in the Internet usage, coupled with advances in software and networking, has resulted in organizations being able to easily share data for a variety of purposes. This has given rise to a set of new and interesting computing paradigms. In the database context, one such paradigm is *Database-as-a-Service* (DAS)[4, 6, 7] in which organizations outsource data management to a service provider.

In the DAS model, since data is stored at the service provider (that may not be fully trusted) many new security and privacy challenges arise. Most approaches to DAS define a notion of a *security perimeter* around the data owner. The environment within the perimeter is trusted whereas the environment outside the perimeter is not. For instance, in [4], the client (which is also the data owner) is trusted, while the server (service provider) is not. In [6], a smart card solution is considered in which owners access data using a client terminal supporting smart card devices. The client's smart-card devices and terminals are within the security perimeter, whereas the large data store is considered to be outside. [7] considers a DAS architecture in which a secure co-processor resides alongside the server. The secure co-processor is within the perimeter, while the server which supports a large scale storage is considered to be outside the perimeter.

Query processing in the DAS model: In each of the DAS models considered above, data is stored in an encrypted form outside the security perimeter but accessed from within. Usually, data is accessed through a client query Q. A direct way to support Q is to transfer data from the untrusted servers to the trusted environment within the security perimeter. Once within the security perimeter, data can be decrypted and the query predicates evaluated. Such an approach, however, mitigates many of the primary advantages of DAS where we are interested in outsourcing not just the storage but also database operations. The alternative approach is to split the query Q into two components: $Q_{sec} + Q_{insec}$, where Q_{insec} executes at the server on the encrypted representation to compute a (superset of) results for Q and Q_{sec} executes within the security perimeter to filter out the false positives. The objective is to push as much work as possible for evaluating Q to the service provider.

Techniques to split query processing between the client and server in the context of DAS has been explored for various classes of queries. For example, *bucketization* (data partitioning) technique [4] to support

---

Permission to copy without fee all or part of this material is granted provided that the copies are not made or distributed for direct commercial advantage, the VLDB copyright notice and the title of the publication and its date appear, and notice is given that copying is by permission of the Very Large Data Base Endowment. To copy otherwise, or to republish, requires a fee and/or special permission from the Endowment.

**Proceedings of the 30th VLDB Conference,
Toronto, Canada, 2004**

range queries, *deterministic encryption* [4, 6] for join queries, as well as, several other methods [5, 1] have been proposed. The objective of these are to push as much work as possible for evaluating the queries to the service provider.

While techniques to support various types of queries in the DAS model have been developed, much of this work is *ad-hoc* in nature. For instance, it lacks an in-depth analysis of the level of privacy afforded under various attack scenarios. This is challenging, specially given that there is no agreed upon definition or established way to reason about privacy. Privacy, in general, depends upon the user specification, nature of data and the application context. Existing research also lacks analysis of the privacy-utility trade-offs inherent to any privacy-preserving data processing system.

In this paper, we focus on range queries and a bucketization based approach proposed in [4] to support them in the DAS model. In the bucketization approach, an attribute domain is partitioned into a set of buckets each of which is identified by a tag. These bucket tags are maintained as an index (referred to as **crypto-index**) and are utilized by the server to process the queries. Our goal in this paper is to characterize the privacy threats arising from the creation of bucketization-based indices to support range queries. Furthermore, we aim to design algorithms to explore privacy-efficiency trade-offs for the bucketization schemes. Specifically, this paper makes the following contributions:

1. Design of an optimal (that maximizes the accuracy of range queries) solution for data bucketization.

2. Identification of privacy measures most relevant in the DAS model and analysis of privacy levels achieved for any instance of bucketized data[1].

3. Development of a novel privacy-preserving re-bucketization technique that yields bounded overhead (due to commensurately reduced accuracy) while maximizing the defined notions of privacy.

The rest of this paper is organized as follows. Section 2 briefly discusses range queries in [4] and addresses relevant privacy issues. Section 3 develops an optimal data bucketization algorithm which maximizes efficiency of crypto-indices. Section 4 identifies statistical metrics of privacy relevant to the context. Next, section 5 introduces our new re-bucketization technique and section 6 discusses privacy issues for the multi-attribute case. Experimental results are reported in section 7 and related work is over viewed in section 8. The paper concludes in Section 9 and 10 with the summary and future work issues.

[1] In fact, we offer a worst-case analysis where the adversary is assumed to know the entire bucketization scheme.

2 Preliminaries

We begin with the brief overview of the DAS model from [4]. This setting involves clients (data owners) and servers (database service providers). Clients to do not trust servers with data contents and encrypt the outsourced data before storing it at the server. Specifically, each data tuple (record or row) of a relational table is stored at the server as an encrypted unit, the so-called *etuple*.

However, since virtually no useful database operations can be performed over encrypted data, the DAS model involves creation of crypto-indices over sensitive attributes[2] which are expected to appear in queries. Multiple crypto-indices may be created over each attribute to support different kinds of SQL queries. The objective is to maximize the amount of query processing done by the server (without, of course, decrypting any etuples) while minimizing work for the client. At query execution time, instead of the actual cleartext attribute values, crypto indices are used for filtering out tuples for query predicates that involve sensitive attributes.

We focus on crypto-indices designed to support range queries. The technique in [4] involves partitioning (*bucketizing*) each attribute domain into a finite number of regions (in an equi-depth or equi-width manner) and assigning each region a unique random *tag* (bucket-id). Subsequently, the cleartext of sensitive attributes of each tuple is essentially suppressed and only identified by its corresponding bucket-id, for each crypto-index built upon that attribute. If the original table was R, this results in a new server-side table R^S, containing etuples and corresponding bucket-ids. An example is given below:

Example 1: Consider the tables in figure 1, where the left side is the original table and the right is its encrypted version. For each sensitive attribute: X, Y and Z, a separate crypto-index is created. The client

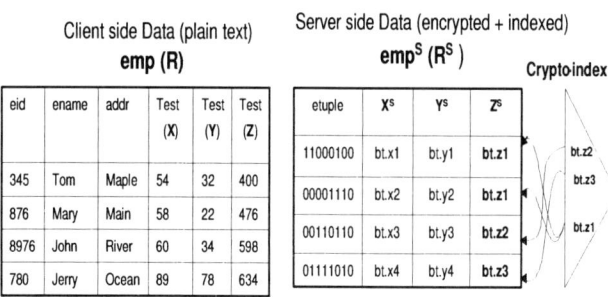

Figure 1: Representation of table on the server

uses *meta-data* (stored within the secure perimeter) to translate normal database queries into server-side queries. The latter can only use indexing information

[2] Crypto-indices corresponding to non-sensitive attributes are the same as in any normal index data structure.

in R^S (i.e., the columns X^S, Y^S, Z^S). For example, an SQL query:

> **Select** *ename, addr* from R **where** $R.Z \geq 450$
> is translated into:
> **Select** *etuple* from R^S **where** $R^S.Z^S =$ bt.z1 $\vee$ bt.z2 $\vee$ bt.z3

where bt.z1, bt.z2 and bt.z3 refer to **bucket-tags** of the buckets created on attribute Z. $\diamond$

It is evident that this approach often results in the query reply containing a superset of records desired by the client. To filter out superfluous data, the client needs to post-process the reply: decrypt each etuple and apply the original query criteria to the cleartext. It is easy to make the following observation:

Observation 1 *Allocating a large number of buckets to crypto-indices increases query precision but reduces privacy. On the other hand, a small number of buckets increases privacy but adversely affects performance.*

The goal of the client is thus twofold:
1) Server Efficiency: maximize the server-side accuracy of range query evaluation. Higher efficiency results in lower server-client communication overhead and lower post-processing costs for the client.
2) Maximum Privacy: minimize the information revealed to the server through the crypto-indices. In other words, maximize data privacy. (What constitutes "information" in this context is clarified in Section 4) below).

We now turn to the problem of optimal bucketization of an attribute domain.

3 Optimal Buckets for Range Queries

As noted in the previous section, the problem of optimal bucketization of attribute domains was not addressed in [4]. In this section we develop such an algorithm.

For simplicity of analysis, we will restrict our attention to building crypto-indices over numeric attributes from a discrete domain like **Z** (set of non-negative integers). But the algorithm applies to the real domain as well. Also we should point out here, that the method by which crypto-indices are actually implemented, is immaterial to us. In reality, any simple data structure that can swiftly retrieve all tuples belonging to any bucket, will suffice. The notion of efficiency that we are concerned with, is only dictated by how the data is partitioned into these buckets.

3.1 Problem Statement

We start by defining the optimal bucketization problem. (Refer to the table 1 for notations.)

Problem: 3.1 *Given an input relation $R = (V, F)$ (where V is the set of distinct numeric values appearing at least once in the column and F is the set of corresponding frequencies), a query distribution P (defined*

V_{min}	minimum possible value for a given attribute
V_{max}	maximum possible value for a given attribute
N	number of possible distinct attribute values; $N = V_{max} - V_{min} + 1$
R	relation (in cleartext), $R = (V, F)$
$|R|$	number of tuples in R (i.e. size of table)
V	ordered set (increasing order) of all values from the interval $[V_{min}, V_{max}]$ that occur at least once in R; $V = \{v_i \mid 1 \leq i \leq n\}$
F	set of corresponding frequencies (non-zero); $F = \{0 < f_n \leq |R| \mid 1 \leq i \leq n\}$ therefore we have $|R| = \sum_{i=1}^{n} f_i$
n	$n = |V| = |F|$ (Note: $n \leq N$)
R^S	encrypted and bucketized relation, on server
M	maximum number of buckets
Q	set of all "legal" range queries over R
q	a random range query drawn from Q; $q = [l, h]$ where $l \leq h$ and $h, l \in [V_{min}, V_{max}]$
Q'	set of all bucket-level queries
q'	random bucket-level query drawn from Q'; basically q' is a sequence of at least one and at most M bucket identifiers
$T(q)$	translation function (on the client side) which, on input of $q \in Q$, returns $q' \in Q'$
R_q	set of tuples in R satisfying query q
$R^S_{q'}$	set of tuples in R^S satisfying query q'
W	query workload, induces probability dist on Q

Table 1: Notations for Buckets

on the set of all range queries, Q) and the maximum number of buckets M, partition R into at most M buckets such that the total number of false positives *over all possible range queries (weighted by their respective probabilities) is minimized.*

Note that for an ordered domain with N distinct values, there are $N(N+1)/2$ possible range queries in the query set Q. Before presenting our algorithm, we would like to point out a couple of things regarding our query model (i.e. the various query distributions that we consider). The problem of histogram construction for summarizing large data, has similarities to the present problem. Optimal histogram algorithms either optimize their buckets i) independent of the workload, by just looking at the data distribution [31] or ii) with respect to a given workload [32, 33]. In the first approach, the query distribution is implicitly assumed to be uniform (i.e. all possible range queries are equi-probable). We address both the cases, where in the query distribution is one of the following:

1) Uniform: All queries are equi-probable. Therefore probability of any query is $= \frac{2}{N(N+1)}$.

2) Workload-induced: There is a probability distribution P induced over the set of possible queries Q, where the probability of a query q is given by the fraction of times it occurs in the workload W (W is a bag of queries from Q).

We analyze the case of uniform query-distribution in detail here. We omit the discussion on how the general distribution (workload induced) case can be tackled due to space restrictions. The interested reader can refer to [11] for the algorithm.

3.2 Uniform query distribution

The total number of false positives (TFP), where all queries are equiprobable can be expressed as:

$$\text{TFP} = \sum_{\forall q \in Q} (\,|R^S_{T(q)}| - |R_q|\,)$$

The average query precision (AQP) can be expressed as (see notation in table 1):

$$\text{AQP} = \frac{\sum_{q \in Q} |R_q|}{\sum_{q \in Q} |R^S_{T(q)}|} = 1 - \frac{\text{TFP}}{\sum_{q' \in Q'} |R^S_{q'}|}$$

where $q' = T(q)$.

Therefore minimizing the total number of false positives is equivalent to maximizing *average precision* of all queries.

As before, consider a single attribute of a relation from a totally ordered discrete domain, such as the set of non-negative integers. For a bucket B, there are $N_B = (H_B - L_B + 1)$ distinct values where L_B and H_B denote the low and high bucket boundary, respectively. Let V_B denote the set of all values falling in range B and let $F_B = \{f^B_1, \ldots, f^B_{N_B}\}$ denote the set of corresponding value frequencies. Recall that Q is the set of all range queries over the given attribute. We need to consider all queries that involve at least one value in B and compute the total overhead (false positives) as follows:

Let the set of all queries of size k be denoted by Q_k and $q_k = [l, h]$ denote a random query from Q_k where $h - l + 1 = k$. Then, the total number of queries from Q_k that overlap with one or more points in bucket B can be expressed as: $N_B + k - 1$. Of these, the number of queries that overlap with a single point v_i within the bucket is equal to k. The case for $k = 2$ is illustrated in figure 2. Therefore, for the remaining $N_B - 1$ queries, v_i contributes f_i false positives to the returned set (since the complete bucket needs to be returned). Therefore, for all $N_B + k - 1$ queries of size k that overlap with B, the total number of false positives returned can be written as:

$$\sum_{v_i \in B} (N_B - 1) * f_i = (N_B - 1) * \sum_{v_i \in B} f_i$$

$$= (N_B - 1) * F_B \approx N_B * F_B$$

where F_B is the total number of elements that fall in the bucket (i.e., the sum of the frequencies of the values that fall in B). We make the following important observation here:-

Observation 2 *For the uniform query distribution, the total number of false positives contributed by a bucket B, for set of all queries of size k, is independent of k. In effect the total number of false positives contributed by a bucket (over all query sizes) depends only on the width of the bucket (i.e. minimum and maximum values) and sum of their frequencies.*

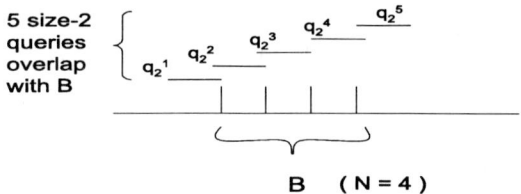

Figure 2: Queries overlapping with bucket

In light of the above observation, we conclude that minimizing the expression $N_B * F_B$ for all buckets would minimize the total number of false-positives for all values of k (the complete set of $\frac{N(N+1)}{2}$ range queries).

3.3 The Query-Optimal-Bucketization Algorithm (uniform distribution case)

As follows from the preceding discussion, our goal is to minimize the objective function: $\sum_{B_i} N_{B_i} * F_{B_i}$. Let $QOB(1, n, M)$ (*Query Optimal Bucketization*) refer to the problem of optimally bucketizing the set of values $V = \{v_1, \ldots, v_n\}$, using at most M buckets (Note that $v_1 < \ldots < v_n$, each occurring at least once in the table). We make the following two key observations:

1) Optimal substructure property: The problem has the optimal substructure property [34], therefore allowing one to express the optimum solution of the original problem as the combination of optimum solutions of two smaller sub-problems such that one contains the leftmost $M - 1$ buckets covering the $(n - i)$ smallest points from V and the other contains the extreme right single bucket covering the remaining largest i points from V:

$$QOB(1, n, M) = Min_i[QOB(1, n - i, M - 1) + BC(n - i + 1, n)]$$

$$\text{where } BC(i, j) = (v_j - v_i + 1) * \sum_{i \leq t \leq j} f_t$$

($BC(i, j)$ is cost of a single bucket covering $[v_i, v_j]$)

2) Bucket boundary property: It can be intuitively seen that for an optimal solution, the bucket boundaries will always coincide with some value from the set V (i.e. values with non-zero frequency). Therefore in our solution space, we need to consider only buckets whose end points coincide with values in V, irrespective of the total size of the domain.

The algorithm solves the problem bottom-up by solving and storing solutions to the smaller sub-problems first and using their optimal solutions to solve the larger problems. All intermediate solutions are stored in the 2-dimensional matrix H. The rows of H are indexed from $1, \ldots, n$ denoting the number of leftmost values from V that are covered by the buckets for the given sub-problem and the columns are indexed by the number of maximum allowed buckets (from $1, \ldots, M$). Also note that the cost of any single bucket covering a consecutive set of values from

```
Algorithm: QOB(D, M)
Input: Data set D = (V, F) and max # buckets M
   (where |V| = |F| = n)
Output: Cost of optimal bucketization & matrix H
Initialize
   (i) matrix H[n][M] to 0
   (ii) matrix OPP[n][M] to 0
   (iii) compute EndSum(j) = EndSum(j + 1) + f_j
       for j = 1 ... n
For k = 1 ... n  // For sub-problems with max 2 buckets
   H[k][2] = Min_{2≤i≤k-1}(BC(1, i) + BC(i + 1, K))
   Store optimal-partition-point i_best in OPP[k][2]
For l = 3 ... M  // For the max of 3 up to M buckets
   For k = l ... n
       H[k][l] = Min_{l-1≤i≤k-1}(H[i][l - 1] + BC(i + 1, k))
       Store optimal-partition-point i_best in OPP[k][l]
Output  "Min Cost of Bucketization = H[n][M]"
end
```

Figure 3: Algorithm to compute query optimal buckets

V can be computed in constant time by storing the cumulative sum of frequencies from the right end of the domain, call them $EndSum$ (i.e. $EndSum_n = f_n, EndSum_{n-1} = f_{n-1} + f_n \ldots$). Storing this information uses $O(n)$ space. We also store along with the optimum cost of a bucketization, the lower end point of its last bucket in the $n \times M$ matrix OPP (Optimal Partition Point) for each sub-problem solved. It is easy to see that the matrix OPP can be used to reconstruct the exact bucket boundaries of the optimal partition computed by the algorithm in $O(M)$ time. The dynamic programming algorithm is shown in figure 3[3] and an illustrative example is given below.

Example 2: Assume the input to QOB algorithm is the following set of (data-value, frequency) pairs:
$D = \{(1, 4), (2, 4), (3, 4), (4, 10), (5, 10), (6, 4), (7, 6), (8, 2), (9, 4), (10, 2)\}$ and say the maximum number of buckets allowed is 4, then (figure 4) displays the optimal histogram that minimizes the cost function. The resulting partition is $\{1, 2, 3\}, \{4, 5\}, \{6, 7\}, \{8, 9, 10\}$. Note that this histogram is not equidepth (i.e all bucket need not have the same number of elements). The minimum value of the cost function comes out to be = 120. In comparison the approximately equi-depth partition $\{1, 2, 3\}, \{4\}, \{5, 6\}, \{7, 8, 9, 10\}$ has a cost = 130. ◊

3.3.1 Computation and Space Complexity

The complexity of the algorithm is $O(n^2 * M)$ which is dominated by the nested loop step, where the outer loop runs M times, inner loop runs $O(n)$ times and computing the minima over i takes another $O(n)$ computations. Computing cost of each bucket, the procedure $BC(i, j)$ can be done in $O(1)$ time if the sequence of numbers $EndSum$ is precomputed, which

[3]in the workload-induced case, only the $EndSum$ computation is done differently, the rest of the algorithms remains the same

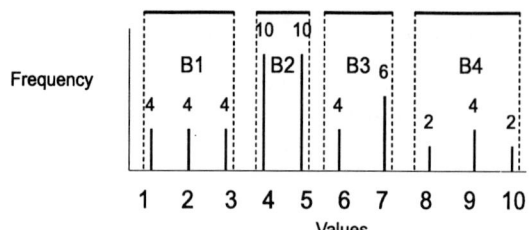

Figure 4: Optimum buckets for uniform query distribution

again takes $O(n)$ time. The space complexity of the algorithm is clearly $O(n * M)$ due to the two matrices H and OPP. Due to lack of space, experimental observations for the running times of the algorithm is omitted in this paper and reported only in [11].

Before ending this section, we would like to point out that our techniques can be utilized to solve multi-attribute range queries as well. This can be done in a relatively straightforward manner, by utilizing the crypto-indices built on each of the query attributes and then returning the common set of tuples which satisfy the range constraints for each dimension. We present some more discussion on multi-attribute range queries in section 6.

4 Privacy Measures

Here we propose two data-level privacy measures relevant to data bucketization and argue their utility.

4.1 Adversary's goal

The pillar of the DAS model is the untrusted server. In the context of our discussion, the adversary (denoted as A) collectively represents the server as well as any other malicious entities in the systems.

While A's possible goals are difficult to enumerate, we focus on the context of the current application. In particular, we make the following two assumptions about A's goals:

Individual-centric information: A is interested in determining the precise values of sensitive attributes of some (all) individuals (records) with high degree of confidence. Eg: *What is the value of salary field for a specific record*. We refer to A's ability to estimate a value as **Value-Estimation-Power (VEP)** of A.

Query-centric information: A is interested in identifying the exact set of etuples that satisfy any (cleartext) query $q \in Q$ with the highest possible *precision* and *recall* [4]. Eg: *Which are the records of people who get salary between 100K and 150K*. We denote A's ability to identify a set of etuples satisfying a query as **Set-Estimation-Power (SEP)**.

We point out an important distinction between the meaning of "precision" for A and for the data owner (client): We assume that the underlying row-level encryption employed by the client is to the table, is *un-*

[4]Precisions and recall refer to accuracy and completeness, respectively, of a set of etuples with respect to a given query

breakable (eg. some non-deterministic encryption algorithm). Therefore A never obtains the plaintext value of a sensitive attribute. Given an etuple, the best A can do is obtain a probabilistic estimate of the true value with high degree of confidence. Similarly, given a cleartext query q and a set S of bucketized etuples, A can assign a certain probability to whether any etuple in S satisfies q. On the other hand, there is no notion of uncertainty involved for the client. After receiving a set of etuples, he decrypts them and finds out exactly which tuples satisfy the query q. The overhead or imprecision for the client is only in terms of the extra false-positives that need to be decrypted and filtered out.

The above discussion makes it clear that A has to reconstruct the whole table by estimating/inferring the correct values of sensitive attributes. A can only achieve this by first *breaking* the bucketization scheme and using this knowledge to form *statistical estimates* of the set (range) of values that the attribute(s) of a tuple can take. We also assume that A employ statistical techniques that maximize its *degree of confidence* and minimize the cardinality (size) of set (range) of possible values (i.e., maximize his VEP and SEP).

To simplify the analysis, we make the following assumption, which allows us to perform the **worst-case breach of privacy** analysis:

Assumption 4.1 *A knows the entire bucketization scheme and the exact probability distribution of the values within each bucket.*

For example, given that bucket B has 10 elements, we assume A knows that: 3 of them have value 85, 3 have value 87 and 4 have value 95, say. However, since the elements within each bucket are indistinguishable, this does not allow A to map values to elements with absolute certainty. We now propose the two measures of privacy.

4.2 Variance

We propose the **Variance** of the distribution of values within a bucket B as its measure of "Individual-Centric-Privacy guarantee". We base our choice of variance on the theorem (see below), however, we first define the term *Average Squared Error of Estimation (ASEE)* as follows:

Definition 4.1 ASEE: *Assume a random variable X_B follows the same distribution as the elements of bucket B and let P_B denote its probability distribution. For the case of a discrete (continuous) random variable, we can derive the corresponding probability mass (density) function denoted by p_B. Then, the goal of the adversary is to **estimate** the true value of a random element chosen from this bucket. We assume that A employs a statistical estimator for this purpose which is, itself a random variable, X'_B with probability distribution P'_B.*

In other words, A guesses that the value of X'_B is x_i, with probability $p'_B(x_i)$. If there are N values in the domain of B, then we define **Average Squared Error of Estimation (ASEE)** as:

$$ASEE(X_B, X'_B) = \sum_{j=1}^{N} \sum_{i=1}^{N} p'_B(x_i) * p_B(x_j) * (x_i - x_j)^2$$

Theorem 4.2 $\mathbf{ASEE(X, X') = Var(X) + Var(X') + (E(X) - E(X'))^2}$ *where X and X' are random variables with probability mass (density) functions p and p', respectively. Also $Var(X)$ and $E(X)$ denote variance and expectation of X respectively.*

Proof: See appendix A

It is easy to see that A can minimize $ASEE(X_B, X'_B)$ for a bucket B in two ways: 1) by reducing $Var(X'_B)$ and 2) by reducing the absolute value of the difference $E(X_B) - E(X'_B)$. Therefore, the best estimator of the value of an element from bucket B that A can get, is the constant estimator equal to the mean of the distribution of the elements in B (i.e., $E(X_B)$). For the *constant estimator* X'_B, $Var(X'_B) = 0$. Also, as follows from basic sampling theory, the "mean value of the sample-means is a good estimator of the population (true) mean". Thus, A can minimize the last term in the above expression by drawing increasing number of samples or, equivalently, obtaining a large sample of *plaintext* values from B. However, note that the one factor that A cannot control (irrespective of the estimator he uses) is the true variance of the bucket values, $Var(X_B)$. Therefore, even in the best case scenario (i.e., $E(X'_B) = E(X_B)$ and $Var(X'_B) = 0$), A still cannot reduce the ASEE below $Var(X_B)$, which, therefore, forms the lower bound of the accuracy achievable by A. Hence, we conclude that the data owner (client) should try to bucketize data in order to **maximize the variance** of the distribution of values within each bucket.

4.3 Entropy

A higher value of variance tends to increase the average error of estimation for the adversary therefore increasing the individual centric privacy guarantee. Nonetheless, variance does not seem to be the appropriate measure of "query centric privacy guarantee" of a bucket. We then turn for help to information theory. As noted above, A's knowledge of the bucket contents are limited by the probability distribution, in the worst case (best case for the A, when he has learnt the complete bucketization). It is well-known that **entropy** of a random variable X is a measure of its uncertainty [17]. Entropy of a random variable X taking values $x_i = 1, \ldots, n$ with corresponding probabilities $p_i, i = 1, \ldots, n$ is given by:

$$Entropy(X) = H(X) = -\sum_{i=1}^{n} p_i \times log_2(p_i)$$

We propose that the measure of "query-centric privacy guarantee" given by a bucket B be the **entropy** of B's probability distribution (i.e., the distribution of values within B, as known to A, which happens to be the true distribution in the worst case scenario). We argue that entropy is an appropriate measure of query-centric privacy, by providing a simple example below. In the same example, we also show that variance and entropy are un-related, i.e., they are important and independent measures of privacy. A more formal argument for choosing entropy as the measure for query-centric privacy is provided in [11].

Example 3: Consider the following data set: $T = \{(2,1), (4,1), (6,1), (8,1)\}$ where each value occurs with frequency 1.

A) There are 10 distinct range queries (classified by their solution sets) possible on this attribute. Consider the case when there are 4 buckets, each containing a single value. The bucket entropy is 0 if A knows the contents of the bucket, since A can identify the exact set of solution tuples for each of the 10 queries. Now consider only 2 buckets, e.g., as in row 1 of table 2. Each bucket in this case have entropy = 1. A can retrieve the precise set of tuples for only 3 of the 10 queries. For the remaining 7 queries, A can only specify the solution set with some probability. Therefore, we make the following observation:

Observation 3 *Increasing bucket entropy reduces the adversary's ability to identify tuples satisfying a query.*

B) To distribute the elements of T into two non-empty buckets, we have the following distinct partitions to consider (where σ^2 denotes variance and H denotes entropy for the respective buckets):

Partition	$\sigma^2_{B_1}$	$\sigma^2_{B_2}$	H_{B_1}	H_{B_2}
1) $B_1 = \{2,4\}; B_2 = \{6,8\}$	1	1	1	1
2) $B_1 = \{2,6\}; B_2 = \{4,8\}$	4	4	1	1
3) $B_1 = \{2,8\}; B_2 = \{4,6\}$	9	1	1	1
4) $B_1 = \{4,6,8\}; B_2 = \{2\}$	2.67	0	1.585	0
5) $B_1 = \{2,6,8\}; B_2 = \{4\}$	6.22	0	1.585	0
6) $B_1 = \{2,4,8\}; B_2 = \{6\}$	6.22	0	1.585	0
7) $B_1 = \{2,4,6\}; B_2 = \{8\}$	2.67	0	1.585	0

Table 2: Variance and Entropy of buckets

Obviously, case 2 represents the most desirable bucketization since it seems to balance variance as well as entropy. We note that the entropies of the buckets do not seem to be correlated with the respective variances.◇

Therefore, as suggested earlier, we treat variance and entropy of each bucket, as two independent measures of privacy and try to achieve a partition that maximizes both simultaneously for every bucket.

5 The Privacy-Performance Trade-off

This section studies the privacy-performance trade-off. Our goal is to develop a bucketization strategy that allows for this exploration to be carried out in a controlled manner. Section 3 gave the QOB-algorithm that computes, for a given number of buckets, the optimum bucketization of data leading to best performance (i.e. minimize false positives). Of course the optimal buckets also offer some level of privacy, but in many cases that might not be good enough (that is buckets might not have a large enough variance and/or entropy). What we now explore is how to re-bucketize the data, starting with the optimal buckets and allowing a bounded amount of performance degradation, in order to maximize the two privacy measures (**entropy** and **variance**) simultaneously. We formalize the problem being addressed below:

Trade-off Problem: Given a dataset $D = (V, F)$ and an optimal set of M buckets on the data $\{B_1, B_2, \ldots, B_M\}$, re-bucketize the data into M new buckets, $\{CB_1, CB_2, \ldots, CB_M\}$ such that no more than a factor K of performance degradation is introduced and the **minimum variance** and **minimum entropy** amongst the M random variables $X_1, \ldots, X_M$ are simultaneously **maximized**, where the random variable X_i follows the distribution of values within the ith bucket.

Solution approach: The above mentioned problem can be viewed as a multi-objective constrained optimization problem [19], where the entities *minimum entropy* and *minimum variance* amongst the set of buckets are the two objective functions and the constraint is the *maximum allowed performance degradation factor K* (we will call it the *Quality of Service* or the *QoS* constraint). Such problems are combinatorial in nature and the most popular solution techniques seem to revolve around the *Genetic Algorithm* (GA) framework [20], [21]. GA's are iterative algorithms and cannot guarantee termination in polynomial time. Further their efficiency degrades rapidly with the increasing size of the data set. Therefore instead of trying to attain optimality at the cost of efficiency, we design a novel algorithm which we call the *controlled diffusion algorithm* (CDf-algorithm). The CDf-algorithm increases the privacy of buckets substantially while ensuring that the performance constraint is not violated.

5.1 Controlled Diffusion

We can compute the optimal bucketization for a given data set using the QOB-algorithm presented in figure 3 of section 3, let us call the resulting optimal buckets B'_is for $i = 1, \ldots, M$. The controlled diffusion process creates a new set of M approximately equidepth buckets which we call *composite buckets* (denoted by $CB_j, j = 1, \ldots, M$) by *diffusing* (i.e. re-distributing) elements from the B_i's into the CB_j's. The diffusion process is carried out in a controlled manner by restricting the number of distinct CB's that the elements from a particular B_i get diffused into. This resulting set of composite buckets, the $\{CB_1, \ldots, CB_M\}$ form the final bucketized representation of the client data.

The M composite buckets need to be approximately equal in size in order to ensure the QoS constraint, as will become clear below. The equidepth constraint sets the target size of each CB to be a constant $= f_{CB} = |D|/M$ where $|D|$ is size of the dataset (i.e. rows in the table). (We do not implement the equidepth constraint rigidly but as our experiments demonstrate, the error is still quite small). Let us see how the QoS constraint is actually enforced: If the maximum allowed performance degradation $= K$, then for an optimal bucket B_i of size $|B_i|$, we ensure that its elements are diffused into no more than $d_i = \frac{K*|B_i|}{f_{CB}}$ composite buckets (as mentioned above $f_{CB} = |D|/M$). We round-off the diffusion factor d_i to the closest integer. Assume that in response to a range query q, the server using the set of optimal buckets $\{B_1, \ldots, B_M\}$, retrieves a total of t buckets containing T elements in all. Then in response to the same query q our scheme guarantees that the server would extract no more than $K*T$ elements at most, using the set $\{CB_1, \ldots, CB_M\}$ instead of $\{B_1, \ldots, B_M\}$. For example, if the optimal buckets retrieved in response to a query q were B_1 and B_2 (here $t = 2$ and $T = |B_1| + |B_2|$), then to evaluate q using the CB_j's, the server won't retrieve any more than $K*|B_1| + K*|B_2|$ elements, hence ensuring that precision of the retrieved set does not reduce by a factor greater than K. An added advantage of the diffusion method lies in the fact that it guarantees the QoS lower bound is met not just for the average precision of queries but for each and every individual query. The important point to note is that the domains of the composite buckets overlap where as in the case of the optimal buckets, they do not. Elements with the same value can end up going to multiple CB's as a result of this diffusion procedure. This is the key characteristic that allows us to tweak the privacy measure while being able to control the performance degradation, in other words this scheme lets us explore the "privacy-performance trade-off curve". The controlled diffusion algorithm is given in figure 5. Though our method does not provably maximize the privacy measures, it is found to perform very well in practice. We illustrate the diffusion process by an example below.

Example 4: Let us take the example 3.3 from section 3 and see how it works when we allow a performance degradation of up to 2 times the optimal ($K = 2$). Figure 6 illustrates the procedure. In the figure, the vertical arrows show which of the composite buckets, the elements of an optimal bucket gets assigned to (i.e. diffused to). The final resulting buckets are shown in the bottom right hand-side of the figure and we can see that all the 4 CB's roughly have the same number size (between 11 and 14). The average entropy of a bucket increases from 1.264 to 2.052 and standard deviation increases from 0.628 to 1.875 as one goes from the B's to CB's. In this example the entropy increases since the number of distinct elements in the $CB's$ are more

---

Algorithm : Controlled-Diffusion(D, M, K)
Input : Data set $D = (V, F)$,
$\quad M = \#$ of $CB's$ (usually same as # opt buckets)
$\quad K = $ maximum performance-degradation factor
Output : An M-Partition of the dataset (i.e. M buckets)

Compute optimal buckets $\{B_i, \ldots, B_M\}$ using QOB algo
Initialize M empty composite buckets $CB_1 \ldots, CB_M$
For each B_i
$\quad$ Select $d_i = \frac{K*|B_i|}{f_{CB}}$ distinct CB's randomly, $f_{CB} = \frac{|D|}{M}$
$\quad$ Assign elements of B_i **equiprobably** to the d_i $CB's$
$\quad$ (roughly $|B_i|/d_i$ elements of B_i go into each CB)
end For
Return the set buckets $\{CB_j | j = 1, \ldots, M\}$.
end

Figure 5: Controlled diffusion algorithm

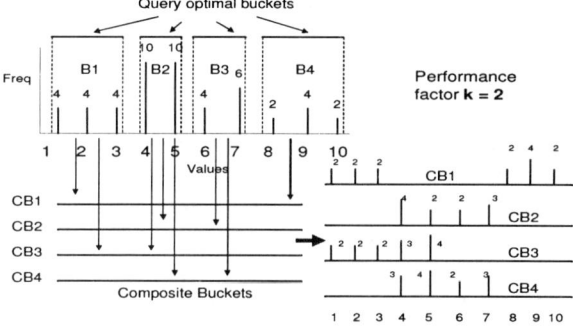

Figure 6: controlled diffusion (adhoc version)

than those in the B's. The variance of the CB's is also higher on an average than that of the B's since the domain (or spread) of each bucket has increased. We can also guarantee that the average precision of the queries does not fall below a factor of 2 from the optimal, for instance take the range query $q = [2, 4]$, it would have retrieved the buckets B_1 and B_2 had we used the optimal buckets resulting in a precision of $18/32 = 0.5625$. Now evaluating the same query using the composite buckets, we would end up retrieving all the buckets CB_1 through CB_4 with the reduced precision as $18/50 \approx 0.36 > \frac{1}{2} * 0.5625$. (Note: Due to the small error margin allowed in the size of the composite buckets (i.e. they need not be exactly equal in size), the precision of few of the queries might reduce by a factor slightly greater than K). ◇

In the next section we address the case of multiple attribute range queries and then go on to discuss our experimental results in the subsequent section.

6 Multi-Attribute Range Queries

We have so far discussed the privacy performance trade-off in range queries in context of a single partitionable attribute. In reality, range queries might refer more than one attribute. A straightforward approach is to apply the privacy enhanced bucketization strategy proposed earlier to each attribute individually. But in multi-attribute case another problem arises: that of *exposure via associations*. In such cases, the unique combination of bucket-tags corresponding to the different attributes in a single tuple might be used to disclose the identity of the owner or perhaps narrow down the space of possible values for critical fields. We first address the issue of *identity disclosure* of the owner of a tuple.

In multi-attribute datasets k-anonymity has been proposed as a measure of privacy [14]. k-anonymity is defined as follows:

Definition 6.1 *k-anonymity is said to hold, when encoding of attribute values in a table are such that for any row r, we can find at least $k-1$ other rows with the same encodings of the corresponding columns. That is for any row, there are at least $k-1$ other indistinguishable rows.*

A goal of adversary A might be to identify the record corresponding to a certain individual I. If A is able to learn the encodings for a few of the attributes for $I's$ record (i.e. the bucket-tags) such that these encoding, together distinguish $I's$ row from any other row, then disclosure is said to have occurred. Therefore it becomes critical to ensure a minimum k level of anonymity for any row of the given table where k is the desired privacy measure. Obviously a higher level of anonymity will reduce the chances of disclosure of any record of interest.

Ensuring k-anonymity in multi-attribute tables can generally tend to get more difficult with the increasing number of attributes that have to be indexed and it has been shown to be NP-Hard in [15]. For tables where only a single attribute needs to be indexed, the *level of anonymity* achieved for any tuple is of course the size of the bucket it is assigned to. The case where multiple attributes have to be indexed, is a more complicated one. Let us consider the special case where there is no correlation between the values of the various attributes and let $N_{A_1 B_1}$ tuples have bucket-id B_1 for the attribute A_1. Then we might expect **on an average** to be able to find $P - 1$ other tuples for a given tuple that are indistinguishable from it, where $P = \frac{N_{A_1 B_1}}{k_2 * k_3 * ... * k_M}$ and attribute A_2 is partitioned into k_2 buckets, A_3 into k_3 buckets and so on to all M attributes. That is we can expect P-anonymity in general where P is defined as above. The value of P rapidly decreases with both, the increasing number of indexed attributes as well as the number of buckets allowed for each of these attribute domains.

Another attack that is a possibility in presence of multiple crypto-indices, is that of *prediction through association*. For instance when the adversary A knows about correlations between different attributes A_i and A_j say, he might be able to predict with high probability the value of attribute A_j of a tuple if he knows the bucketization of the A_i field. Such attack scenarios have been analyzed previously in [3].

Recently authors in [3] have explored the issue of exposure and quantified it in a different setting where hashing has been used instead of bucketization. Based on their work, one could possibly develop the framework to explore exposure in the bucketization case as well. However, a novel strategy proposed in [8] overcomes this problem in a different manner, instead of bucketizing attributes individually, it is done as a multidimensional partitioning. The authors show that the problem of exposure disappears when multidimensional partitioning is used. We feel our proposed diffusion based approach can be adapted to work in the case of multi-dimensional partitioning as well. But any such discussion is out of scope of this paper and will addressed in future work.

7 Experiments

We start by introducing the datasets we used and our experimental setup.

7.1 Datasets and experimental setup

The following two dataset and query set were used:
1) *Synthetic Data Set*: consists of 10^5 integer values generated uniformly at random from the domain $[0, 999]$.
2) *Real Data Set*: consisted of 10^4 data points taken from one of the columns of the "Co-occurrence Texture" table of the "Corel Image" dataset in UCI-KDD archive [18]. The readings correspond to the *angular momentum component* of some colored images. The values came from a real domain (roughly $(-0.800000, 8.000000)$). The frequency of most values was equal to 1 (i.e. unique) or some small integer c.
3) *Benchmark Query Set*: We generated two different set of queries corresponding to the synthetic and real datasets, Q_{syn} and Q_{real} respectively. Each were of size 10000 and were generated uniformly at random from the same ranges as the datasets themselves[5].

We carried out all our experiments on a 1G Hz pentium machine, with 512MB RAM.

7.2 Experiments

We carried out four sets of experiments that measured the following:
1) Decrease in Precision: of evaluating the benchmark queries using optimal buckets (QOB-buckets) and composite buckets (CB's). Figure 7 (a) plots the ratio of the **average precision** using optimal buckets to that using the composite buckets for the benchmark query set Q_{syn} as a function of **# of buckets**. Plots are shown for multiple values of the maximum allowed *performance degradation factor* $K = 2, 4, 6, 8, 10$.

---
[5]though real life datasets and queries rarely come from an uniform distribution, we feel the results reported here still give a good indication of the usefulness of our algorithms

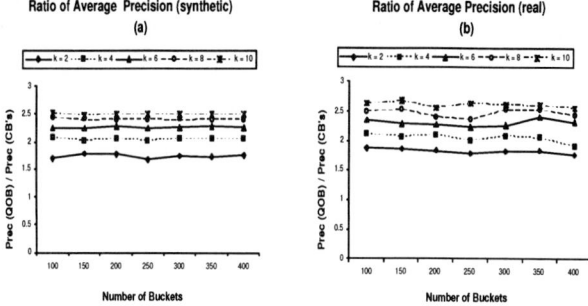
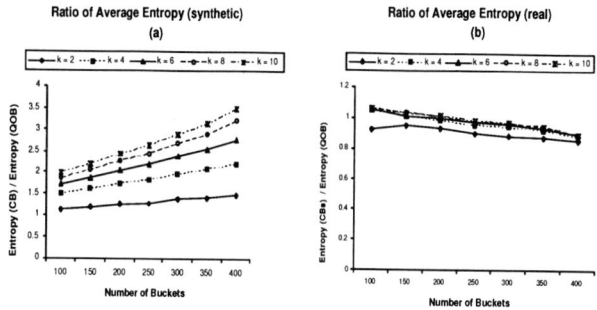

Figure 7: Decrease in Precision a)Synthetic b) Real data

Figure 9: Change in Entropy a)Synthetic b) Real data

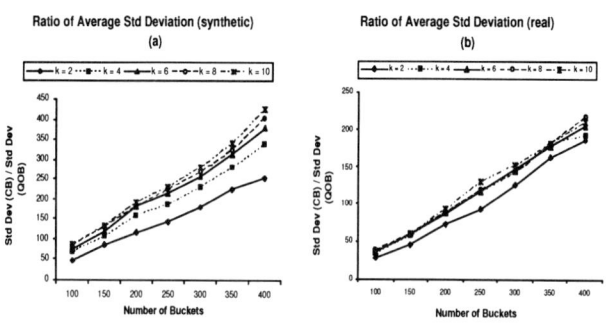
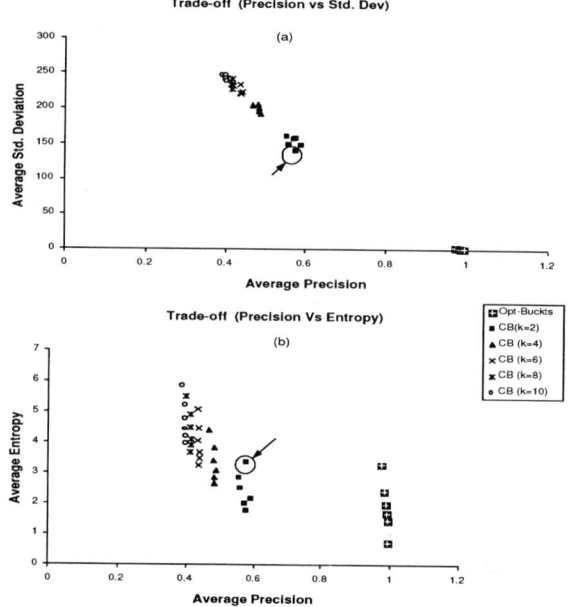

Figure 8: Increase in Std Dev a)Synthetic b) Real data

Figure 7 (b) shows the corresponding plot for the real dataset on query set Q_{real}.

2) Privacy Measure: We plot the ratio of **average standard deviation** of the CB's to that of the QOB-buckets as a function of **# of buckets** in figure 8 (a) for the synthetic dataset and in figure 8 (b) for the real dataset (for values of $K = 2, 4, 6, 8, 10$). Figure 9 (a) plots the ratio of **average entropy** for the two sets of buckets, on the synthetic dataset and figures 9 (b) display the corresponding ratio for the real dataset.

3) Performance-Privacy trade-off: Figure 10 (a) displays the trade-off between **average standard deviation** of buckets and **average precision**. We fix 6 values of M, the # of buckets $M = 100, 150, \ldots, 350$) and for each M, we plot the average standard deviation of the optimal set of buckets (QOB's) as well as the average standard deviation for the 5 sets of composite buckets (CB's) obtained from the QOB's by applying the controlled-diffusion algorithm by setting the degradation factor $K = 2, 4, 6, 8, 10$. In effect we plot 6 different points for each value of M. Similar plots of **entropy-precision trade-off** for the same sets of buckets are plotted in figure 10 (b).

4) Time taken: to compute the optimal buckets by the QOB validates the $O(N^2 M)$ complexity of the QOB algorithm. But the figures are excluded from this paper due to lack of space. The interested reader can refer to [11] for the plots.

Figure 10: Privacy-Performance trade-off a)Std Dev vs Precision b) Entropy vs Precision

7.3 Results

The empirical results on both datasets for the benchmark queries are quite positive in most of our experimental runs: the relative precision measurements for instance show that for most cases, the degradation in average precision is actually much smaller than the allowed maximum of K. In both the datasets, even when the maximum degradation factor allowed is 10, the observed decrease in query precision was less than 3. This is obviously because the controlled-diffusion algorithm leads to some degree of overlap in $range^6$. This results in a much smaller drop in the precision than K, for a majority of the range queries.

Amongst the privacy measures, standard deviation increases by a large factor in most cases even for a small value of K. Whereas entropy, being a logarithmic measure, grows more slowly. Though for some values of K

---
[6]where $range(B)$ is the set of CB's that the elements of B are diffused into

for the real data, average entropy of buckets decreased slightly as a result of diffusion.

Finally the plots in the performance-privacy trade-off space display all the **design points** available to the data-owner. These plots provide a good estimate of the degree of privacy available if one is willing to sacrifice efficiency by a given amount. For e.g, by looking at the plots of figures 10 (a) and 10(b), the data owner might choose a bucketizaton scheme that uses 100 buckets and sets $K = 2$ since it provides a high value for average entropy as well as a sufficiently high value of standard deviation of the buckets for a small loss in efficiency (the design-point is circled in both the figures). One can also use non-integral values of K and explore more points in the trade-off space that might meet one's requirements). The trade-off plots could be made more accurate by choosing an appropriate set of benchmark queries for a given application.

8 Related Work

Privacy and security in databases have been a core area of research for a few decades now. Privacy related problems spring up in many sub-areas of database research, for e.g., access control [26], inference control [29],[28], statistical disclosure control [16], statistical databases [22], etc. More recently quite a bit of research has been done in areas such as privacy preserving data mining [9] [10], DAS oriented work (which we have reviewed earlier) and privacy-preserving information retrieval [30]. We give a brief summary of the research in few of the areas other than DAS.

Privacy Preserving Data mining: There does not seem to be any universally acceptable definition of privacy and the general trend is to define a notion of privacy that is best suited to the application at hand. Authors previously have suggested different measures for various application: Agrawal and Srikant [9] address the classification problem and propose the size l of the interval to which the value of a variable can be restricted with a confidence c to be the measure of privacy at c-confidence level. Agrawal and Aggarwal [10] study distribution reconstruction from randomized data for which they propose measures based on entropy and *mutual information* of random variables. Association rule mining in privacy-preserving manner has been addressed in [2]. [12, 13] take a cryptographic approach to compute decision trees and do EM-clustering for a distributed setting, in a privacy-preserving manner.

Statistical Database Protection and Disclosure Control: The central problem addressed in statistical databases and disclosure control is that of releasing datasets in a manner such that an individual interested in learning aggregate level measures (mean, median, frequency) is able to do so with minimum error and at the same time the data owner is able to secure the values of records from being *disclosed* [22], [23], [24], [25]. Data-perturbation by statistical noise addition is an important method of enhancing privacy [22], [24]. The idea is to perturb the true value by a small amount ϵ where ϵ is a random variable with a mean $= 0$ and a small variance $= \sigma^2$. Statistical disclosure control techniques consist of *generalization, suppression and data swapping* amongst others [16]. Another important privacy-measure, that of k-anonymity [14] has been introduced earlier in section 6. The literature in the area is vast and we refer the interested readers to [23] and [16] for a thorough survey of the field.

Inference Control: The inference problem in databases occurs when sensitive information can be disclosed from non-sensitive data and meta-data. A vast amount of research exists in this area as well [27]. An inference analysis based on variance of estimators has been carried out by the authors in [24] for randomization. Specifically of interest to us are the issues of inference control in i) general purpose databases, ii)statistical databases, iii)data mining and iv)web-based inferencing. Detection of inference channels in above scenarios is an important problem and has been addressed by many researchers. Due to lack of space, we refer the interested reader to [27],[28] and [29] for a detailed exposition and pointers to further literature in the area.

9 Conclusions

In this paper, we investigated "data bucketization" as a privacy-enhancing technique and highlighted the fundamental tradeoff between privacy and performance. We presented some inferencing and disclosure scenarios (that an adversary, primarily the untrusted server, might be interested in) and proposed two useful measures of privacy. We also derived an optimal algorithm for data partitioning that provably minimizes performance overhead in query processing. We presented the *controlled diffusion* algorithm that lets the data owner fine-tune bucketization to achieve the desired level of data privacy by sacrificing the accuracy (of query evaluation) by a small measured amount. The effectiveness of our proposed algorithms is validated by our experiments that show promising results on both synthetic and real datasets.

10 Future Work

In the future, we intend to assess the privacy loss in the case when the adversary has partial information about buckets (which is a more realistic scenario) instead of the worst case scenario where the adversary has complete information as considered here. Also, analyzing disclosure risk and privacy guarantee in case of multi-attribute data is an important goal of our research. Furthermore, we intend to explore/develop optimal partitioning algorithms that **provably maximize** privacy within performance constraints set by the data owner.

We recognize that many other research challenges would arise if we were to incorporate and deploy a bucketization strategy (such as the one proposed in this paper) in real systems. For example, in this paper we assumed a static database. Over time, as the database changes, the bucketization might not remain optimal and will have to be adapted. One approach is to construct a new bucketization periodically (on the fly) and replace the old index with a new one. To make the scheme more attractive for the on-line setting, it is interesting to explore incremental construction and migration schemes. Such incremental schemes have been developed for B-tree or other indices and some of these ideas might apply in our context as well.

Finally, we note that our focus has been on range queries and we showed how bucket content diffusion as a strategy can offer higher privacy with bounded overhead. Approaches involving the privacy/performance tradeoff in the context of other kinds of queries (such as join queries) remain part of our future work.

References

[1] Domingo-Ferrer, J., Castillo, R., X., S. An implementable scheme for Secure Delegation of Computing and Data. *ICICS, 1997*, pp. 445-451.

[2] Evfimievski, A., Srikant, R., Agrawal, A., Gehrke, J. Privacy reserving mining of association rules. SIGKDD, 2002.

[3] Damiani, E., Vimercati, S.D.C., Jajodia, S., Paraboschi, S., Samarati, P. Balancing Confidentiality and efficiency in untrusted relational DBMSs. In *10th ACM CCS, 2003*

[4] Hacigumus, H., Iyer, B., Li, C., Mehrotra, S. Executing SQL over Encrypted Data in the Database Service Provider Model, *SIGMOD 2002*, June 4-6, Madison, Wisconsin, USA.

[5] Hacigumus, H., Iyer, B., Mehrotra, S. Efficient Execution of Aggregation Queries over Encrypted Relational Databases, In *DASFAA, 2004*, pp. 125-136.

[6] Bouganim, L., Pucheral, L. Chip-Secured Data Access: Confidential Data on Untrusted Servers, In *Proc. of the 28th VLDB Conference, 2002*.

[7] Maheshwari, U., Vingralek, R., Shapiro, W. How to build a Trusted Database System on Unstrusted Storage *OSDI 2000*

[8] Jammalamadaka, R., Mehrotra, S. Querying Encrypted XML document *technical report TR-DB-04-03*, www-db.ics.uci.edu/pages/publications/index.shtml

[9] Agrawal, R., Srikant, R. Privacy-Preserving Data Mining. *ACM SIGMOD 2000*

[10] Agrawal, D., Aggarwal, C., C. On the Design and Quantification of Privacy Preserving Data Mining Algorithms. *PODS, 2001*

[11] Hore, B., Mehrotra, S., Tsudik, G. A Privacy-Preserving Index for Range Queries *technical report TR-DB-04-04*, www-db.ics.uci.edu/pages/publications/index.shtml

[12] Lindell, Y., Pinkas, B. Privacy Preserving Data mining. In Advances in Cryptology-CRYPTO 2000, pp. 36-54.

[13] Lin, x., Clifton, C. Distributed EM clustering without sharing local information. Journal of Information sciences, Feb 2003.

[14] Samarati, P., Sweeney, L. Protecting Privacy when Disclosing Information: k-Anonymity and Its Enforcement through Generalization and Suppression. Technical Report, SRI International 1998.

[15] Meyerson, A., Williams R. General k-anonymization is Hard. Tech-report CMU-CS-03-113.

[16] Willenborg, L., De Waal, T. Statistical Disclosure control in Practice. Springer-Verlag, 1996.

[17] Cover, T., M., Thomas, J, A. Elements of Information Theory. John Wiley & Sons, Inc., 1991.

[18] Corel Image Features database, UCI-KDD Archive.

[19] Steuer, R., E. Multiple Criteria Optimization - Theory, Computation and Application, Wiley, 1986.

[20] Goldberg D., E. Genetic Algorithms in Search, Optimization, and Machine Learning, Addison-Wesley, Reading, Massachusetts, 1988.

[21] Jones, D.R. and Beltramo, M.A. Solving Partitioning Problems with Genetic Algorithms, *Proc. of the 4th international conference on Genetic Algorithms*, 1991.

[22] Traub, J., F., Yemini, T., and Wozniakowski, H. The Statistical Security of a Statistical Database. TODS 1984, 672-679.

[23] Shoshani, A. Statistical Databases: Characteristics, Problems, and some Solutions. VLDB 1982, pp.208-222.

[24] Muralidhar, K., Sarathy, R. Security of Random Data Perturbation Methods. TODS 2000, 487-493.

[25] Yu, C., T., Chin, F., Y. A study in protection of statistical databases. SIGMOD 1977, pp. 169-181.

[26] Lunt, T. Access control policies for database systems. In Database Security II:Status and prospects, pp.41-52.

[27] Farkas, C., Jajodia, S. The Inference Problem: A Survey. SIGKDD Explorations, Newsletter, Vol 4, 6-11.

[28] Catalytic inference analysis:Detecting inference threats due to knowledge discovery. In the IEEE Symposium on security and Privacy, 1997, pp.188-199

[29] Thuraisingham, B. The use of conceptual structures for handling the inference problem. In Database Security V, pp.333-362

[30] Chor, B., Goldreich, O., Kushilevitz, E., Sudan, M. Private Information Retrieval. Proc of 36th FOCS (1995), pp.41-50.

[31] Gilbert, A., C., Kotidis, Y., Muthukrishnan, S., Strauss, M.,J. Optimal and Approximate Computation of Summary Statistics for Range Aggregates *PODS, 2001* pp. 227-236.

[32] Gunopulos, D., Kollios, G., Tsotras, V., J. Approximating Multi-dimensional Aggregate Range Queries over Real Attributes *ACM-SIMOD, 2000*, pp. 463-474.

[33] Bruno, N., Chaudhuri, S., Gravano, L. STHoles: a multi-dimensional workload aware histogram *ACM SIGMOD 2001*, pp. 211-222.

[34] Cormen, T., H., Leiserson, C., E., Rivest, R., L. Introdcution to Algorithms, MIT Press.

A Average Squared Error

Proof: We have from definition 4.1, $ASEE(X, X')$ as

$$= \sum_{i=1}^{N}\sum_{j=1}^{N} p'(x_i)p(x_j)(x_i - x_j)^2$$

$$= \sum_{i=1}^{N} p'(x_i) \sum_{j=1}^{N} p(x_j)(x_i - x_j)^2$$

$$= \sum_{i=1}^{N} p'(x_i) \sum_{j=1}^{N} p(x_j)(x_i^2 + x_j^2 - 2x_i x_j)$$

$$= \sum_{i=1}^{N} p'(x_i)[\sum_{j=1}^{N} p(x_j)x_i^2 + \sum_{j=1}^{N} p(x_j)x_j^2 - 2\sum_{j=1}^{N} p(x_j)x_i x_j]$$

Using $Var(X) = \sigma^2 = E(X^2) - \mu^2$ we get

$$= \sum_{i=1}^{N} p'(x_i)[1.x_i^2 + (\sigma^2 + \mu^2) - 2\mu x_i]$$

$$= \sum_{i=1}^{N} p'(x_i)x_i^2 + (\sigma^2 + \mu^2)\sum_{i=1}^{N} p'(x_i) - 2\mu \sum_{i=1}^{N} p'(x_i)x_i$$

$$= (\sigma'^2 + \mu'^2) + (\sigma^2 + \mu^2) - 2\mu\mu'$$

$$= \sigma^2 + \sigma'^2 + (\mu - \mu')^2$$

$$= Var(X) + Var(X') + (E(X) - E(X'))^2$$

Resilient Rights Protection for Sensor Streams [*]

Radu Sion, Mikhail Atallah, Sunil Prabhakar
Computer Sciences, Purdue University
{sion, mja, sunil}@cs.purdue.edu

Abstract

Today's world of increasingly dynamic computing environments naturally results in more and more data being available as fast streams. Applications such as stock market analysis, environmental sensing, web clicks and intrusion detection are just a few of the examples where valuable data is streamed. Often, streaming information is offered on the basis of a non-exclusive, single-use customer license. One major concern, especially given the digital nature of the valuable stream, is the ability to easily record and potentially "re-play" parts of it in the future. If there is value associated with such future re-plays, it could constitute enough incentive for a malicious customer (Mallory) to duplicate segments of such recorded data, subsequently re-selling them for profit. Being able to protect against such infringements becomes a necessity.

In this paper we introduce the issue of rights protection for discrete streaming data through watermarking. This is a novel problem with many associated challenges including: operating in a finite window, single-pass, (possibly) high-speed streaming model, surviving natural domain specific transforms and attacks (e.g.extreme sparse sampling and summarizations), while at the same time keeping data alterations within allowable bounds. We propose a solution and analyze its resilience to various types of attacks as well as some of the important expected domain-specific transforms, such as sampling and summarization. We implement a proof of concept software (wms.*) and perform experiments on real sensor data from the NASA Infrared Telescope Facility at the University of Hawaii, to assess encoding resilience levels in practice. Our solution proves to be well suited for this new domain. For example, we can recover an over 97% confidence watermark from a highly down-sampled (e.g. less than 8%) stream or survive stream summarization (e.g. 20%) and random alteration attacks with very high confidence levels, often above 99%.

1 Introduction

Protecting rights over outsourced digital content becomes essential when considering areas where the data is sensitive and valuable. One example is the outsourcing of data for data mining. In this scenario data is produced/collected by a data collector and then sold to parties specialized in mining it. Different rights protection avenues are available, each with its advantages and drawbacks. Enforcement by legal means is usually ineffective, unless augmented by a digital counter-part such as Information Hiding. Digital Watermarking deploys Information Hiding as a method of Rights Protection to conceal an indelible "rights witness" (watermark) within the digital Work to be protected. The soundness of such a method relies on the assumption that altering the Work in the process of hiding the mark does not destroy the value of the Work, and that it is difficult for a malicious adversary ("Mallory") to remove or alter the mark beyond detection without destroying the value of the Work. The ability to resist attacks from such an adversary (mostly aiming at removing the embedded watermark) is one of the major concerns in the design of a sound solution.

A considerable amount of effort has been invested in the problem of watermarking multimedia data (images, video and audio). More recently, the focus of watermarking for digital rights protection is shifting

---

[*] Portions of this work were supported by Grants EIA-9903545, IIS-0325345, IIS-0219560, IIS-0312357, IIS-9985019 and IIS-0242421 from the National Science Foundation, Contract N00014-02-1-0364 from the Office of Naval Research, by sponsors of the Purdue Center for Education and Research in Information Assurance and Security, and by Purdue Discovery Park's e-enterprise Center.

Permission to copy without fee all or part of this material is granted provided that the copies are not made or distributed for direct commercial advantage, the VLDB copyright notice and the title of the publication and its date appear, and notice is given that copying is by permission of the Very Large Data Base Endowment. To copy otherwise, or to republish, requires a fee and/or special permission from the Endowment.

**Proceedings of the 30th VLDB Conference,
Toronto, Canada, 2004**

toward other data domains such as natural language text [2], software, algorithms [7] [15] and relational data [11] [18] [19]. Since these data domains often have very well defined restrictive semantics (as compared to those of images, video, or music) and may be designed for machine ingestion, the identification of the available "bandwidth" for watermarking is as important a challenge as the algorithms for inserting the watermarks themselves.

In this paper we introduce and study the problem of watermarking sensor streams data, which to the best of our knowledge, has not been addressed. Streaming data sources represent an important class of emerging applications [3] [4]. These applications produce a virtually endless stream of data that is too large to be stored directly. Examples include output from environmental sensors such as temperature, pressure, brightness readings, stock prices etc. Recent efforts in the broader area of streaming data deal with the database challenges of its management [5] [9] [10] [13].

Existing work on itemized data types [11] [18] [19] relies upon the availability of the entire dataset during the watermarking process. While this is generally a reasonable assumption, it does not hold true for the case of streaming data [3]; since the streamed data is typically available as soon as it is generated, it is desirable that the watermarking process be applied immediately on subsets of the data. Additionally, the attack and transformation models in existing research does not apply here. For example a process of summarization would defeat any of the above schemes. Yet another difference from previous research is the lack of a "primary key" reference data set, an essential, required, part in both [11] and [19]. Due to these differences, earlier work on watermarking relational data sets is not applicable to streams.

But why is watermarking streaming data important? Couldn't we simply watermark the data once it is stored? This surely would work and enable rights protection for the stored result. But it would not deter a malicious customer (Mallory), with direct stream access, to duplicate segments of the stream and re-sell them or simply re-stream the data for profit. The main rights protection scenario here (see Figure 1) is to prevent exactly such leaks from a licensed customer.

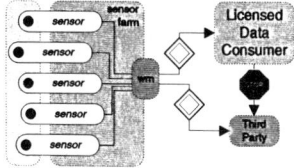

Figure 1: Sensor Streams Watermarking Scenario.

Our contributions include (i) the proposal and definition of the problem of watermarking sensor streams, (ii) the discovery and analysis of new watermark embedding channels for such data, (iii) the design of novel associated encoding algorithms, (iv) a proof of concept implementation of the algorithms and (v) their experimental evaluation. The algorithms introduced here prove to be resilient to important domain-specific classes of attacks, including stream re-sampling, summarization (replacing a stream portion by its average value) and random changes. For example, sampling the data stream down to less than 8% still yields a court-time confidence of watermark embedding of over 97%. Summarization (e.g. 20%) and random data alterations are also survived very well, often with a false-positive detection probability of under 1%.

The paper is structured as follows. Section 2 outlines the major challenges in this new domain. It proposes an appropriate data and transform model, discusses associated attacks and overviews related work. In Section 3 an initial solution is provided. Further resilience-enhancing improvements and attack handling capabilities are gradually introduced in Section 4. Section 5 analyzes the ability to convince in court to survive attacks and natural domain transformations. Section 6 presents **wms.***, a proof-of-concept java implementation of our solution; our experimental setup and results are introduced. Section 7 concludes.

2 Challenges

2.1 The Adversary

As outlined above, the nature of most "fast" time-series data applications imposes a set of strict requirements on any on-the-fly data processing method, such as watermarking. For one, it has to be able to keep up with the incoming data rate and, the fact that only a finite window of memory (e.g. of size ϖ, see below) is available for processing makes certain history-dependent computations difficult or simply impossible. At the same time, metrics of quality can only be handled within this space; any preservation constraints can be formulated only in terms of the current available data window. Including any history information will come at the expense of being unable to store as much new incoming data.

Moreover, the effectiveness of any rights protection method is directly related to its ability to deal with normal domain specific transformations as well as malicious attacks. There are several transforms relevant in a streaming scenario, including the following (or a combination thereof): (A1) summarization, (A2) sampling, (A3) segmentation (we would like to be able to recover a watermark from a finite segment of data drawn from the stream), (A4) linear changes [1] (there might be value in actual *data trends*, that Mallory [2] could still exploit, by scaling the initial values), (A5) addition of stream values and (A6) random alterations.

---
[1] Taken care of by the initial normalization step.
[2] The traditional name of *the* maliciously acting party.

While we discuss most of these (and gradually introduce other attacks of concern) in the next sections, let us note here that with respect to (A5), Mallory is bound to add only a limited amount of data (in order to preserve the value in the original stream) and these new values are to be drawn from a similar data distribution, lest they become easy to identify in the detection process as not conforming to the known original distribution. Also (A6) can be naturally modeled by a combination of (A2) and (A5).

2.2 Model

For the purpose of simplicity let us define a simple data stream as an (almost) infinite timed sequence of $(x[t])$ values "produced" by a set of data sources of a particular type (e.g. temperature sensors, stock market data). $x[t]$ is a notation for the value yielded by our source(s) at time t. Unless specified otherwise, lets denote a stream as $(x[], \varsigma)$ where ς is the number of incoming data values per time unit (*data rate*) [3].

Note: While a time-stamp t can be assigned naturally to each and every data value when produced by a data source, it often becomes irrelevant after such domain-specific transformations as sampling and summarization which destroy the exact association between the value $x[t]$ and the time it was initially generated, t. Thus, the notation $x[t]$ is merely used to distinguish separate values in the stream and is not intended for suggesting the preservation of the time-stamp-value in the resulting stream (which is ultimately just a sequence of values).

Any stream processing is necessarily both time and space bound. The time bounds derive from the fact that it has to keep up with incoming data. We are going to model the space bound by the concept of a window of size ϖ. At each given point in time, no more than ϖ of the stream $(x[t])$ values (or equivalent amounts of arbitrary data) can be stored locally, at the processing point. Unless specified otherwise, as more incoming data becomes available, the default behavior of the window model is to "push" older items out (i.e. to be transmitted further, out of the processing facility) and "shift" the entire window (e.g. to the right) to free up space for new entries.

For simplicity, without sacrificing generality, for the remainder of the paper we are going to assume the stream values being normalized in the interval $(-0.5, +0.5)$. This assumption does not need to hold in general but instead just simplifies the task of understanding the algorithms.

For the purpose of the current framework, we define the *uniform random sampling* of degree χ of a stream $(x[], \varsigma)$ as another stream $(x'[], \varsigma')$ with $\varsigma' = \frac{\varsigma}{\chi}$ such that for each sample data item $x'[t]$, there exists a contiguous subset of $(x[])$, $(x[t_1], x[t_2])$ such that $x'[t] \in (x[t_1], x[t_2])$, $\{x'[t-1], x'[t+1]\} \not\subseteq (x[t_1], x[t_2])$, and t is uniformly distributed in (t_1, t_2). In other words, it is constructed by randomly choosing one value out of every χ values in the original. A subtle variation of *uniform random sampling* is the case when $x'[t]$ is not randomly chosen but rather always the first element in it's corresponding χ sized subset (e.g. $t - t_1$). We call this *fixed random sampling* of degree χ.

We define the *summarization* of degree ν of a stream $(x[], \varsigma)$ as another stream $(x'[], \varsigma')$ with $\varsigma' = \frac{\varsigma}{\nu}$ such that for each two adjacent sample data items $x'_1[t], x'_2[t+\nu]$, there exist two contiguous, adjacent, non-overlapping ν-sized subsets of $(x[])$, $(x[t-\nu+1], x[t-\nu+2], ..., x[t])$, $(x[t+1], x[t+2], ..., x[t+\nu])$ such that $x'_1[t] = \frac{\sum_{i \in (1,\nu)} x[t-\nu+i]}{\nu}$ and $x'_2[t+\nu] = \frac{\sum_{i \in (1,\nu)} x[t+i]}{\nu}$. In other words, for a continuous chunk of ν elements from the original stream summarization outputs its average.

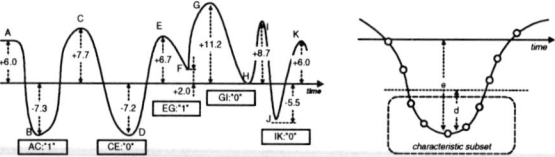

Figure 2: (a) A sample stream. If all the extremes are considered to be major, then the resulting label bits for K are shown (for $\varrho = 2$, Section 4.1) (b) δ-Radius characteristic subset of extreme η.

We define an *extreme* η in a stream simply as either a local minimum or local maximum value. We define the extreme's *characteristic subset of radius* δ, noted $\Xi(\eta, \delta)$ (see Figure 2 (b)), as the subset of stream items forming complete "chunks", immediately adjacent to η and conforming to the following criteria: item i, with value $v_i \in \Xi(\eta, \delta)$ iff $|\eta - v_i| < \delta$ and all the items "between" i and the extreme η, also belong to $\Xi(\eta, \delta)$.

A *major extreme* of degree χ and radius δ is defined as an extreme η such that at least one item in $\Xi(\eta, \delta)$ can be found in *any* uniform random sampling of degree χ of $(x[])$ (i.e. some items in $\Xi(\eta, \delta)$ "survive" sampling of χ degree). For example, in Figure 2 (a), intuitively, it seems likely that extremes such as F,I and J have a smaller chance of surviving sampling than C,E or G. This is so because of the temporal shape of the stream's evolution. C,E,G seem to yield characteristic subsets much "fatter" than F,I,J. Intuitively, δ needs to be chosen such that the characteristic subsets are going to be of an average size greater than χ, to handle sampling of degree χ.

To model the "fluctuating" nature of a stream, let $\varepsilon(\chi, \delta)$ be the average number of stream data items encountered/read per *major extreme* (i.e. before encountering a major extreme) of degree χ and radius

---

[3] The proposed solution does not rely on any characteristic of the actual stream data rate. For space and simplicity purposes in this paper we are discussing streams with fixed data rates.

δ. $\frac{1}{\varepsilon(\chi,\delta)}$ defines the average "frequency of major extremes" in terms of the number of observed data items.

For any numeric value x let $b(x)$ be the number of bits required for its accurate representation and $msb(x,b)$ its most significant b bits. If $b(x) < b$ we left-pad x with $(b - b(x))$ zeroes to form a b-bit result. Similarly, $lsb(x,b)$ is used to denote the least significant b bits of x. Let wm be a watermark to be embedded, $wm[i]$ the i-th bit of wm.

In our solution we leverage the one-way cryptographic hash, a special de-facto secure construct. If $crypto\_hash()$ is a cryptographic secure one-way hash, of interest are two of its properties: (i) it is computationally infeasible, for a given value V' to find a V such that $crypto\_hash(V) = V'$ (one-wayness), and (ii) changing even one bit of the hash input causes random changes to the output bits (i.e. roughly half of them change even if one bit of the input is flipped). Examples of potential candidates for $crypto\_hash()$ are the MD5 (used in the proof of concept implementation) or SHA hash. For more details on cryptographic hashes consult [17]. Let $H(V,k) = crypto\_hash(k;V;k)$ (where ";" denotes concatenation).

2.3 Related Work

Could existing work in non-media data sets watermarking such as relational data [11] [18] [19] be adapted to the new domain? Our work in [19] requires access to the entire data set in an almost random access model, which is certainly not possible here at embedding time. Also, these efforts seem to make extensive use of the existence of a primary key (or an additional attribute, in [18]), thus rendering a direct adaptation impossible. Moreover, the expected attacks and transformations are different. For example a process of summarization would defeat any of the above schemes. Nevertheless it might be worth noting that, if a primary key is assumed to exist, e.g. if there is a guarantee that the time-stamp information for each stream value is going to be preserved in the result, then both the bit alteration method proposed by Kiernan et al in [11] (for numeric types) and the solution in [18] (for discrete data) could be adapted to work on a single attribute, namely the stream value. The result would likely be resilient to (time-stamp preserving) sampling, but fail with respect to any other attack or transformation.

But what about multimedia watermarking? Given the "streaming" nature of our data, would it not be possible to simply adapt an existing audio (or media) watermarking algorithm [6] [8] [12] [16] [20] since audio data is also an example of a data stream? In other words, why is our problem different? While there seem to be similarities between watermarking audio and sensor data for example, at a closer inspection these similarities prove to be just appearances. A multitude of differences are to be found between the two frameworks mainly deriving from different data models, associated semantic scopes and the discrete nature of our sensor stream data.

In theory, a sensor stream could be viewed as an audio signal for example and processed as such. However, for all practical purposes such an approach would not suit reality and/or often yield undesired results. For example, while in sensor data streams, summarization and sampling are routinely expected natural operations, audio streams are not to be summarized, and sampling in the audio domain entails an entirely different semantic. Summarization for example would not be survived by any of the existing [8] efforts. Moreover, data quality to be preserved in audio streaming is usually related to the human auditory system and its limitations. Any watermark-related alteration can be induced as long as the stream still "sounds" good. In the case of sensor streams (e.g. temperature) on the other hand, many scenarios involve widely different quality metrics, that often need to also consider overall stream characteristics [4].

A more in-depth comparison is out of scope here. In summary, while experiences in the multi-media domain are valuable, due to the nature of this new application domain, a solution for watermarking sensor streams needs to naturally handle attacks and transformations such as the ones outlined in Section 2.1.

3 An Initial Solution

This Section outlines the main solution and then gradually improves it to a more robust and resilient version, by identifying and fixing potential flaws.

3.1 Overview

At an overview level, watermark embedding proceeds as follows: (a) first a set of "major" extremes (actual stream items) are identified in the data stream, extremes that feature the property that they (or a majority thereof) can be recovered after a suite of considered alterations (possibly attacks) such as (random) sampling and summarization. Next, (b) a certain criterion is used to select some of these extremes as recipients for parts of the watermark. Finally (c), the selected ones are used to define subsets of items considered for 1-bit watermark embedding of bits of the global watermark. The fact that these extremes can be recovered ensures a consistent overlap (or even complete identity) between the recovered subsets and the original ones (in the un-altered data). In the watermark detection process (d) *all* the extremes in the stream are identified and the selection criteria in step (b) above is used once again to identify potential watermark recipients. For each selected extreme, (e) its corresponding 1-bit watermark is extracted and ultimately the global watermark is gradually re-constructed, by possibly also using error correction (e.g. majority voting).

---
[4]e.g. the total alteration introduced per data item should not exceed a certain threshold.

Thus, one of the main insights behind our solution is the use of extreme values in the stream's evolution as watermark bit-carriers. The intuition here lies in the fact that much of the stream value lies in exactly its fluctuating behavior and the associated extremes, likely to be largely preserved in value-preserving, domain-specific transforms.

3.2 Embedding

Using the notation in Section 2.2, let $\alpha, \beta \in \mathbb{Z}$ such that $\alpha + \beta \leq b(x[])$, where $b(x[])$ is the bit-size of the values in the considered stream $(x[])$. Let χ be a secret integer and $\delta \in (0,1)$ chosen such that $\delta < 2^{(b(x[])-\alpha)}$ (i.e. all elements within a characteristic subset $\Xi(\eta, \delta)$ have the same most significant α bits). $\alpha, \beta, \delta, \chi$ are secret. We use the term "advance the window" to denote reading in more new data items while discarding old ones from the current data window.

---

wm_embed($\delta, \alpha, \beta, wm, k_1, \phi$)
    while (*true*) **do**
        $\eta \leftarrow$ first major extreme in win[]
        compute $\Xi(\eta, \delta)$
        $i \leftarrow H(msb(\eta, \alpha), k_1) \bmod \phi$
        if $i \leq b(wm)$ **then**
            $bit \leftarrow H(msb(\eta, \alpha), k_1) \bmod \beta$
            foreach $v \in \Xi(\eta, \delta)$ **do**
                $v[bit - 1] \leftarrow false$
                $v[bit] \leftarrow wm[i]$
                $v[bit + 1] \leftarrow false$
        advance win[] past η

Figure 3: Initial Embedding Algorithm

In the **initial step** of our embedding algorithm we first identify the first major extreme of degree χ and radius δ in the current window. The assumption here is that there exists a major extreme in the current window. If this is not the case, we can simply advance the window until we find one. Its "majority" can be easily evaluated by comparing the size of the characteristic subset $\Xi(\eta, \delta)$ with the sampling degree χ. The characteristic subset containing at least χ elements guarantees that in a random sampling of degree χ, at least one of those elements is going to survive. If no major extremes can be found for given δ and χ values, one could consider instead extremes with characteristic subsets smaller than χ that guarantee an acceptable chance (e.g. 70%) of survival in case of sampling (i.e. $\frac{subset\_size}{\chi} > 70\%?$).

Once a major extreme (η) is identified in the current window, in the **second step**, a *selection criterion* is used to determine whether η is going to be used in the embedding process or not: if $H(msb(\eta, \alpha), k_1) \bmod \phi = i$ and $i \leq b(wm)$, then η is considered for embedding bit i of the watermark, $wm[i]$. $\phi \in (b(wm), b(wm) + k_2)$ ($k_2 > 0$) is a secret unsigned integer fixed at embedding time, ensuring that only a limited number (a ratio of $\frac{b(wm)}{\phi}$) of these major extremes are going to be selected for embedding. We used a similar "fitness" selection criteria in [18]. Its power derives strength from both the one-wayness and randomness properties of the deployed one-way cryptographic hash, forcing Mallory into a "guessing" position with respect to watermark encoding location. The reason behind the use of the most significant bits of η in the above formula, is resilience to minor alterations and errors due to sampling. As discussed above, the assumption is that for any value $x \in \Xi(\eta, \delta)$, $msb(x, \alpha) = msb(\eta, \alpha)$.

If η is the result of the previous selection step, in the **third step** we embed bit $wm[i]$ into $\Xi(\eta)$. This is done by first, selecting a certain bit position $bit = H(msb(\eta, \alpha), k_1) \bmod \beta$ for embedding. Next, for each value $v \in \Xi(\eta, \delta)$ and in η itself, that bit position is set to $wm[i]$ and the adjacent bits are set to false (to prevent overflow in case of summarization). In other words $v[bit-1] = false$, $v[bit] = wm[i]$ and $v[bit+1] = false$. The reasoning behind modifying an entire subset of items ($\Xi(\eta, \delta)$) is to survive summarizations. This is the case if the bit encoding is such that the average of any combination of ($\nu < |\Xi(\eta)|$ or less) items in $\Xi(\eta, \delta)$, would preserve the embedded bit. It is easy to show that this is indeed the case. Finally, the window is advanced past η and the process re-starts.

3.3 Detection

In the detection process the watermark is gradually reconstructed as more and more of the stream data is processed. The reconstruction process relies on an array of majority voting "buckets" as follows. For each bit $wm[i]$ in the original watermark wm, let $wm[i]^T$ and $wm[i]^F$ be "buckets" (unsigned integers) which are incremented accordingly each time we recover a corresponding true/false bit $wm^{det}[i]$ from the stream. In other words, if the detection process yields at some point $wm^{det}[i] = false$, then the $wm[i]^F$ value is incremented. Similarly, for $wm^{det}[i] = true$, $wm[i]^T$ is incremented. In the end, the actual $wm[i]$ will be estimated by the difference between $wm[i]^T$ and $wm[i]^F$, i.e. if $wm[i]^T - wm[i]^F > \upsilon$ then the estimated value for this particular bit becomes $wm^{est}[i] = true$ and conversely if $wm[i]^F - wm[i]^T > \upsilon$ then $wm^{est}[i] = false$, where $\upsilon > 0$. If detection would be applied on random, un-watermarked data, the probability of detecting $wm^{det}[i] = false$ would equal the probability of $wm^{det}[i] = true$, thus yielding virtually identical (υ is used to distinguish this exact case) values for $wm[i]^T$ and $wm[i]^F$. In this case, $wm^{est}[i]$ would be un-defined, thus the data considered un-watermarked. The watermark effectively lies in a statistical bias in the *true/false* distribution for each bit encoding.

Detection starts by identifying the first extreme η in the current window. The selection criteria deployed in the embedding phase is tested on η. If $H(msb(\eta, \alpha), k_1) \bmod \phi = i$ and $i \leq b(wm)$, then η was likely used in embedding bit i of the watermark, $wm[i]$. This bit is then extracted from bit-position

```
wm_detect(δ,α,β,wm,k₁,φ)
  while (true) do
    η ← first extreme in win[]
    i ← H(msb(η, α), k₁)mod φ
    if i ≤ b(wm) then
      bit ← H(msb(η, α), k₁)mod β
      if (η[bit]==true) then
        wm[i]ᵀ ← wm[i]ᵀ + 1
      else
        wm[i]ᶠ ← wm[i]ᶠ + 1
    advance win[] past η

wm_construct(wm[]ᵀ,wm[]ᶠ,v)
  for (i ← 0; i < b(wm); i ← i + 1)
    if (wm[i]ᵀ − wm[i]ᶠ > v) then
      wm[i] ← true
    else
      if (wm[i]ᶠ − wm[i]ᵀ > v) then
        wm[i] ← false
      else
        wm[i] ← undefined
  return wm[]
```

Figure 4: Initial Detection Algorithm

$H(msb(\eta, \alpha), k_1) \bmod \beta$ and depending on its value, the corresponding bucket $wm[i]^T$ or $wm[i]^F$ is incremented. Finally, the window is advanced past η and the process re-starts. It is to be noted that, because of the infinite nature of the stream, detection is a continuous process. This is why it is enclosed in a **while** loop. At the same time it shares the $wm[]$ array with the watermark reconstruction process (**wm_construct()**).

4 Improvements

Given the initial solution introduced above, we devised a set of improvements aimed at boosting its resilience level including: the ability to handle correlation detection attacks, handling repeated labels, label reconstruction after attacks, introducing a certain hysteresis in the label reconstruction scheme, aimed at defeating targeted extreme values altering attacks, alternative encodings, handling ability of offline multi-pass detection, multi-layer marks aiming to better handle summarization. Due to space constraints we now discuss some of the more important ones.

4.1 Defeating Correlation Detection

One particular issue of concern in the above solution is the fact that because there exists a correlation between the watermarking alteration (the $wm[i]$ bit) and its actual location (determined by $H(msb(\eta, \alpha), k_1))$), Mallory can mount a special attack with the undesirable result of revealing the mark embedding locations. The attack proceeds by first realizing that, despite the one-wayness of the deployed hash function $H()$, in fact, η is the only variable that determines *both* the bit embedding location as well as its value. Mallory can now simply build a set of "hash buckets" for each separate value of $msb(\eta, \alpha)$ (if α is secret the job becomes harder but not impossible) and count, for each extreme η encountered, which of the lower β bits of η is set (resp. reset) more often. For each η for which a bias in a bit position is discovered, that particular bit position is considered mark-carrying and randomized.

Thus, the problem lies here in the correlation between the actual bit location and the bit value, correlation induced by the fact that a single variable (η) determines both of these. A fix could possibly rely on a separate source of information to determine the location of the embedded bit, independently of the bit value. Also, this source of information would need to be consistently recoverable at detection time. For example, if time-stamp information would be assumed available, i.e. if all the processing and the attacks on the data stream could be assumed to preserve the time-stamp to value association, then the actual time-stamp would present an ideal candidate, effectively labeling each and every stream extreme uniquely while at the same time not being correlated (directly) to their values. This unique label could then be used in computing the bit position for embedding. In the selection of the bit embedding location, instead of using $bit = H(msb(\eta, \alpha), k_1) \bmod \beta$ which yields a result correlated to the actual embedded bit value ($wm[i]$, where $i = H(msb(\eta, \alpha), k_1) \bmod \phi$) we propose to use $bit = H(msb(label(\eta), \alpha), k_1) \bmod \beta$ where $label(\eta)$ is the (virtually) unique label of extreme η. A labeling scheme like this would make "bucket counting" attacks impossible. In our model however, timestamps are not assumed to be preserved. Can we envision a different labeling scheme (at least) for extremes, that would survive the attacks and transformations outlined in Section 2.1? We propose to build it from scratch.

One of the challenging aspects of such a labeling scheme becomes clear when one considers data segmentation. To support segmentation, it needs to function based solely on information available close (in terms of stream location) to the considered to-be-labeled extreme. Also, labels computed at detection time from potential segments of sampled and/or summarized data, need to (at least) converge to the original ones, as more and more watermarked data is available. Let λ be the (secret) bit length of the labels resulting in our labeling scheme. Let $\varrho > 1$ be a (secret) unsigned integer. We propose the following labeling scheme: given two extremes i and a subsequent $i + \varrho$, we define $label\_bit(i, i + \varrho) = true$ iff $msb(abs(val(i)), \alpha) < msb(abs(val(i + \varrho)), \alpha)$ and $false$ otherwise. We then define the label for extreme $i + \lambda$, $label(val(i + \lambda))$ as the bit string composed of the concatenation of "1" (binary true) followed by each and every $label\_bit(j, j + \varrho)$ in ascending order of $j \in (i - \varrho, i + \lambda - \varrho)$. In other words, an extreme is labeled by a certain differential interpretation of some of the preceding extreme values, e.g. in Figure 2 (a), the label for extreme **K** becomes "110100" ($\varrho = 2$).

Before going any further, let us analyze what happens if an important extreme is "lost", e.g. if one extreme i is altered so much that its α most significant bits flip the $msb(abs(val(i)), \alpha) < msb(abs(val(i+\varrho)), \alpha)$ inequality, corrupting its corresponding label bit. What happens is in fact not too damaging: labels that were constructed using this particular extreme will be corrupted, until the detection process encounters again a continuous sequence of extremes not altered beyond recognition. But Mallory cannot afford altering extremes to such extents, and the secrecy of ϱ makes a random alteration attack the only choice.

In summary, the main purpose of such a labeling scheme is to ensure that Mallory cannot mount the "bucket counting" type of statistical analysis attack as outlined above. Different labels for adjacent extremes together with the use of one-way hashing completely defeat such an attack. The labeling scheme provides an independent, un-correlated source of information for determining the bit position to be altered.

4.2 Reconstructing Labels

Labeling, while providing a defense for the correlation attack, introduces the requirement to be able to identify major extremes at detection times, possibly in a summarized and/or sampled stream. This becomes a challenge as the definition of "major" does not make sense anymore in the context of a sampled version of the original stream. We propose the following solution. In a first stage, the degree of the transformation performed is determined. In a second stage, the definition of majority of an extreme is updated to reflect the fact that the considered stream is already transformed. A major extreme of degree χ and radius δ in the original stream $(x[], \varsigma)$, becomes a major extreme of degree $\frac{\chi}{\gamma}$ and radius δ in the transformed stream $(x'[], \frac{\varsigma}{\gamma})$, where γ is the degree of the transformation (e.g. summarization, sampling) applied to $(x[], \varsigma)$. Once we know γ identifying major extremes in the transformed stream is simply a matter of considering this updated definition. In a dynamic stream, with consistent stream data rates, γ can be determined by simply dividing the original stream rate to the current (transformed) stream rate, $\gamma = \frac{\varsigma}{\varsigma'}$. The more challenging scenario is to determine the value of γ corresponding to a (possibly transformed) stream $(x'[], \varsigma')$ for which only a segment is available. A reasonable assumption that can be made is that the transform was applied uniformly to the entire stream. In this case, one solution would start by preserving some information about the initial stream, namely the average size of the characteristic subsets of extremes, for a given δ. Then, in the transformed segment, extremes are identified and their average characteristic subset size for the same δ is computed. It is to be expected (arguably) that in a transformed (sampled and/or summarized) stream these sizes would shrink according to the actual transform degree. Dividing the original average characteristic subset size by the sampled stream average would thus yield an estimate of the transform degree γ. In our proof of concept implementation this method is used successfully. Space considerations prevent further elaboration.

4.3 Defeating Bias Detection

But what prevents Mallory from identifying all the major extremes for which there exists a majority of (possibly all) items in the characteristic subset with a certain bit position set to the same identical value? These extremes would then be (rightfully so) considered watermark carrying and Mallory could mount a simple attack of randomizing those bit positions. We propose a new approach that survives summarization and results in alterations effectively appearing random to the eyes of an attacker. Let $\Xi(\eta, \delta) = \{x_1, x_2, ..., x_a\}$. For each $i \leq j \in [1, a]$, let $m_{ij} = \frac{\sum_{u \in [i,j]} x_u}{|j-i+1|}$. Then we define the *characteristic subset bit encoding convention* as follows: (i) we say that a bit value of "true" is embedded in $\Xi(\eta, \delta)$ iff $\forall j, i$ we have $lsb(H(lsb(m_{ij}, \beta), label(\eta)), \zeta) = 2^\zeta - 1$; similarly, (ii) we say that "false" is embedded iff $\forall j, i$ we have $lsb(H(lsb(m_{ij}, \beta), label(\eta)), \zeta) = 0$, where $\zeta > 0$ is a secret fixed at embedding time. The embedding method simply alters the least significant β bits in the values in $\Xi(\eta, \delta)$ until the criteria is satisfied for the desired to-be-embedded $wm[i]$ bit value. It is to be noted that these alterations should aim to minimize the Euclidean distance (or possibly any other desired distance metric) from the starting point defined by $\{x_1, x_2, ..., x_a\}$. We call this a "multi-hash encoding".

The use of m_{ij} ensures survival to summarization, while the cryptographic hash provides the appearance of randomness. But is it feasible to assume that one could find such a point in the a-dimensional space defined by the items in $\Xi(\eta, \delta)$? How many computations are required to at least find one? There are $\frac{a(a+1)}{2}$ possible m_{ij} averages (including all $m_{ii} = x_i$ values). For each we consider the last ζ bits of its hash, effectively getting an output space of $\zeta \frac{a(a+1)}{2}$ bits. The probability that a desired pattern occurs in this space is then $2^{-\zeta \frac{a(a+1)}{2}}$. Thus, on average, the expected number of configurations in the input space that would need to be tested in an exhaustive search before yielding one that results in the desired output, is $2^{\zeta \frac{a(a+1)}{2}}$. For example if $\zeta = 1$ and $a = 5$ we have 2^{15}, that is, approx. 32,000 computations would need to be performed (for each considered major extreme in the window). See Section 6.4 for an experimental analysis.

Given the exponential nature of the increase in required computations for an increasing number of items in the characteristic subset, it is probably not likely to be able to exhaustively handle subsets with more than $8 - 10$ items efficiently. While out of the scope of the current paper, the design and use of efficient pruned-space algorithms would be required to significantly reduce these requirements. Alternately, we could deploy a computation-reducing technique that limits the number of m_{ij} averages for which (i) or (ii) needs to hold in the subset bit encoding convention above. In other words, the search process (in the $\{x_1, x_2, ..., x_a\}$ space) will be stopped once a certain number of the m_{ij} averages feature the desired encoding convention ((i) or (ii)). We call these m_{ij} values "active". The resulting decrease in required computation time comes at the expense of decreased resilience to transforms.

Also, an (arguably) fast(er) encoding than the use of cryptographic hashes above could be adapted from [1]. The method works by altering the β least significant bits until every one of the longest k pre-fixes of the whole value (most significant bits included), when treated as an integer, becomes a quadratic residue modulo a secret large prime, for embedding a 'true' value and a quadratic non-residue modulo the secret prime for embedding a 'false' value.

5 Analysis

In this Section we analyze the ability of our method to convince in court, survive attacks and transforms.

Court-convinceability can be naturally expressed as follows: given a one bit (e.g. true) watermark, what is the probability of false positives (P_{fp}) for the watermark encoding? In other words, we ask: *What is the probability of a one-bit (true) watermark to be detected in another (possibly random) data stream?* If this probability is low enough, then a positive detection would constitute a strong proof of rights, with a "confidence" of $1 - P_{fp}$. Here we define confidence as the probability that a given detected watermark was indeed purposefully embedded in the data by the rights owner.

Using the notation in Section 4.3, for each considered extreme η, the occurrence probability of a "good" corresponding m_{ij} (i.e. encoding "true" with respect to the bit encoding convention) in a random stream is naturally $\frac{1}{2}$, because of the cryptographic hash used in the encoding. There are $\frac{a(a+1)}{2}$ possible m_{ij} averages (including all $m_{ii} = x_i$ values). Because for each we consider the last ζ bits of its hash, we effectively have an output space of $\zeta \frac{a(a+1)}{2}$ bits. Thus the probability of the bit "true" being encoded consistently by all of these becomes $2^{-\zeta \frac{a(a+1)}{2}}$ (per extreme). Now, for each $\varepsilon(\chi,\delta)$ items there is a potential major extreme recipient of a one-bit encoding. Out of these how many are actually selected for encoding? As discussed in Section 3.2 only a fraction of $\frac{1}{\phi}$ (because now b(wm)=1) of them are actually selected for embedding. Thus if ς is the stream data rate, we can determine the relationship between the time elapsed since we started reading the incoming stream (t) and the reached level of persuasiveness, as follows.

If $\varepsilon(\chi,\delta)$ models the average number of items that need to be read before a major extreme is encountered, then $\frac{\varepsilon(\chi,\delta)}{\varsigma}$ represents the average time-interval "between" major extremes. But only $\frac{1}{\phi}$ of the major extremes are selected for embedding, and so the time-interval between two major extremes that encode the watermark is $\frac{\phi\varepsilon(\chi,\delta)}{\varsigma}$. In a time interval of t we are thus likely to see $\frac{t\varsigma}{\phi\varepsilon(\chi,\delta)}$ extremes.

As discussed above, each major extreme has an associated probability of false positives of $2^{-\zeta \frac{a(a+1)}{2}}$, thus if we discover a consistent pattern of embedding in a time interval t, the probability of a false-positive becomes $P_{fp}(t) = (2^{-\zeta \frac{a(a+1)}{2}})^{\frac{t\varsigma}{\phi\varepsilon(\chi,\delta)}}$. For example if $\zeta = 1$, $a = 5$, $\varsigma = 100Hz$, $\phi = 20\%$, $\varepsilon(\chi,\delta) = 50$, after detecting a bit "true" for only $t = 2$ seconds we have $P_{fp}(2) = (2^{-15})^{20} \approx 0$ and an associated proof of rights, with a confidence of close to 100%. Even, at the limit, when due to transforms such as sampling and summarization, for each extreme, only one single m_{ij} average survives and the probability of false positives for each extreme becomes only $\frac{1}{2}$, $P_{fp}(2)$ becomes roughly only "one in a million". Thus, the persuasion power of our method quickly converges to a comfortable level. In Section 6 we provide experimental results for watermark resilience to various transforms, including random attacks.

Next we explore a theoretical analysis of the vulnerability of our scheme under the following attack model: Mallory starts to modify randomly every a_1-th ($a_1 > 1$) extreme (η) in such a way as to alter a ratio of $a_2 \in (0,1)$ of the items in the extreme's characteristic subset of radius a_3, $\Xi(\eta, a_3)$. (Thus, on average, Mallory alters only one in every $a'_1 = a_1\phi$ bit-carrying extremes).

The assumption here is that these alterations do not impact the associated labeling scheme, in other words, they don't change the "greater than" relationship between extremes used in the labeling process. An extension considering this case is out of the current limited-space scope. Due to space constraints we are going to focus directly on a more challenging, "informed", Mallory, aware of the characteristic subset radius used at encoding time. This will strengthen our derived bounds. In other words, we assume that $a_3 = \delta$ is known to Mallory, see Section 3.2.

We propose two ways to analyze the vulnerability of the proposed solution: (i) looking at how much an attack "weakens" the encoding, i.e. how many of the active m_{ij} values are actually destroyed divided by the total number of active ones (making it thus proportionally harder to detect a watermark in court) and (ii) what is the probability that *all* of the active ones are obliterated? It is easy to see that, for a given extreme η, for which $\Xi(\eta, a_3) = \{x_1, x_2, ..., x_a\}$ the number of corresponding m_{ij} values altered is $c_m = \frac{1}{2}aa_2(2a - aa_2 + 1)$.

Now, for (i) the "weakening" of the encoding can be defined as $c_m \times \frac{2}{a(a+1)}$, the ratio of m_{ij} values that are altered from the total number of potential active ones for each altered extreme. Because one in every $a_1' = a_1\phi$ bit-carrying extremes gets impacted, the overall "weakening" factor can be defined as $a_1 \times c_m \times \frac{2}{a(a+1)}$. To answer (ii) we first model this scenario by a sampling experiment without replacement. In this experiment, $x + t, t > 0$ balls are randomly removed from a bowl with a total of y balls. The question answered is: if the bowl contained exactly x black balls what is the probability that the $x + t$ removals emptied the bowl of all of them. It can be shown that this is $P(x+t,x,y) = \frac{\binom{y-x}{t}}{\binom{y}{x+t}}$. In our model $(x + t) = c_m$, $y = a(a+1)\frac{1}{2}$ and if $x = a_4 y$ (a_4 is the ratio of active m_{ij} values) we can compute the probability that *all* of them are altered.

Thus, for each attacked extreme we have a non-zero probability of altering all active m_{ij} values and removing the corresponding watermark bit. Next we ask, how do these alterations impact our ability to convince in court and detect a watermark bias in the resulting data? Because the alteration is necessarily random (the randomness of the one-way hashes in the encoding in Section 4.3 guarantee this) we can model the attack as essentially a random noise addition attack. Evaluating the resilience of any watermark bias becomes now a matter of asking how many of the embeddings actually survive until detection time. Are there enough of them to actually convincingly reconstruct the multi-bit watermark after error correction? At the beginning of the section we looked at how the watermark bias becomes more convincing in time (and seen data). Loosing a fraction of the mark bit encoding extremes can be in fact seen as a reduction of the ϕ value (see Section 3.2). If, for each of the $a_1' = a_1\phi$ bit carrying extremes that are altered by Mallory, the attack success probability is given by $P(x+t,x,y)$, we can perform a similar reasoning with a new $\phi' = \phi + a_1' \times P(x+t,x,y)$. What now happens is that the persuasiveness (court-time convince-ability) converges proportionally slower. In other words, we need to see $a_1 \times P(x+t,x,y)$ more stream data to be able to provide an equally convincing proof in court.

For example, for $a_1 = 5$, $a = 6$, $a_4 = 50\%$, $a_2 = 50\%$ we get the average probability $P(15,10,21) \approx 0.85\%$ of a complete alteration of all the active m_{ij} values at each extreme. This effectively translates in the need to see only an average of $a_1 \times P(x+t,x,y) \approx 4.25\%$ more data to be equally convincing at detection.

But how does our encoding handle transforms? By construction it certainly survives sampling (A2) up to a degree of $\chi_{max} = |\Xi(\eta,\delta)|$. Indeed this is so if at least one element in the characteristic subset of η is to be found in a sampling of degree χ_{max}. This element can be used in the detection process to recover the corresponding watermark bit for η. Higher degrees of sampling are also quite likely to be survived as there is a non-zero probability of elements in $\Xi(\eta,\delta)$ to be in the sampled stream even for $\chi > \chi_{max}$. Due to space constraints we do not elaborate further. This is experimentally analyzed in Section 6.

Summarization (A1) up to a degree of $\nu_{max} = |\Xi(\eta,\delta)|$ is also handled well by design, for example due to the use of m_{ij} in the bit-encoding procedure illustrated in Section 4.3. Any summarization of a degree $\nu \leq \nu_{max}$ naturally results in at least one of the m_{ij} averages being in the summarized stream. Even in the initial algorithm, the bit encoding pattern used on the elements in the characteristic subset ensured survival of the pattern in the process of averaging (thus surviving summarization) within the subset. Summarization is experimentally analyzed in Section 6.

But how well is segmentation (A3) survived? More specifically, what is the minimum size of a stream segment from which we are able to recover the watermark? For simplicity let us assume a one-bit watermark, i.e. $b(wm) = 1$. In the following we are trying to determine the minimum required size of a contiguous watermarked stream segment that would enable a proof more "convincing" than a coin-flip stating that a watermark is embedded in the data. This proof would be obtained if we can correctly detect at least two consistent bits (equal to $wm[0]$) from two different extremes found in the segment. In that case, the probability of a false-positive becomes lower than a random coin-flip. But what is the minimum amount of data we need to see to be able to decode two bits? In the best case, the two extremes are adjacent and we need to see enough data to build correct labels for those two extremes. To build the labels correctly, we need to have seen all the previous $\lambda\varrho$ major extremes correctly. Further qualitative analysis must be data dependent, for example if the fluctuating nature of the stream features a major extreme of degree χ and radius δ for every $\varepsilon(\chi,\delta)$ data items, then the minimum required size of a segment enabling watermark detection is $\varepsilon(\chi,\delta)\lambda\varrho$.

6 Experimental Results

We implemented **wms.*** a Java proof-of-concept of the watermarking solution. Our experimental setup included one 1.8GHz CPU Linux box with Sun JDK 1.4 and 384MB RAM.

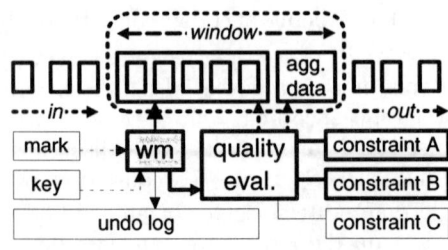

Figure 5: Overview of proof of concept implementation.

We implemented also a temperature sensor synthetic data stream generator with controllable parameters, including the ability to adjust the data stream distribution, fluctuating behavior (e.g. $\varepsilon(\chi,\delta)$) and rate (ς). This sensor was used in the initial design phase of some of our experiments because of the ability to produce various fine-tuned data inputs impacting specific strengths of the encoding.

We explored experiment scenarios modeling both the behavior of sub-systems such as the on-the-fly labeling module as well as the overall watermark resilience. Synthetic (temperature sensor model) and real-world data was used in our evaluation.

Because, as discussed in Section 3.3, watermark encoding relics on altering a certain secret statistical bias within the data, when we present resilience results we refer to the ability to detect and reconstruct this bias as an overall measure of encoding performance. In this case, the notion of a "watermark bias" refers to the number of instances of *active* extremes for which the characteristic subset bit encoding (see Section 4.3), survives with a positive true-bit embedding bias [5].

Unless specified otherwise, the experimental results presented here refer to an underlying normalized stream with values distributed normally with a mean of 0 and a standard deviation of 0.5. The fluctuating behavior of the stream was determined by an average $\varepsilon(\chi,\delta) = 100$ (100 items per each major extreme) and $\varsigma = 100Hz$ (100 items per second). Other parameters include: $\phi = 3$, $\alpha = 16$, $\beta = 16$, $v = 2$, k_1 was chosen by a random number generator. Whenever exact quantitative results are shown, they refer to a data set drawn from about 50 seconds of stream data (i.e. roughly 5000 data values). Additionally, when experiments were performed on real-life test data this is specified in the figure captions. The real life data sets [14] were obtained from the environmental monitors of the NASA Infrared Telescope on the summit of Mauna Kea, at the University of Hawaii. They represent multiple sets of once-every-two-minutes environmental sensor (i.e. temperature) readings at various telescope site locations. The reference data set used refers to 30 days worth of data from the month of September 2003, totaling a number of 21630 temperature readings (with values on the Celsius scale roughly between 0 and 35 degrees).

6.1 Random Alterations

In [19] we defined the *epsilon-attack* in the relational data framework, a transformation that modifies a percentage τ of the input data values within certain bounds defined by two variables ϵ (amplitude of alteration) and μ (mean of alteration). Epsilon-attacks can model any uninformed, random alteration – often the only available attack alternative. A *uniform altering* epsilon-attack (as defined in [19]) modifies τ percent of the input tuples by multiplication with a

---

[5] With respect to court-time confidence, for example, a detected watermark bias of 10 yields a false-positive probability of $\frac{1}{2^{10}}$, and an associated proof of rights with a confidence of roughly 99.9%, as discussed in Section 5.

uniformly distributed value in the $(1-\epsilon+\mu, 1+\epsilon+\mu)$ interval. We believe this attack closely resembles (A6), a very likely combination of (A5) and (A2). In Fig-

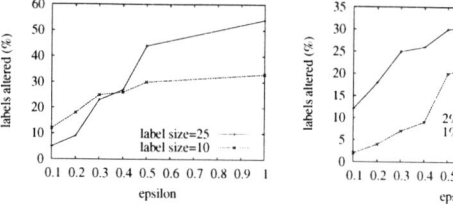

Figure 6: Label alteration for increasingly aggressive uniform altering epsilon attacks. (a) Different label bit sizes shown. A smaller label size seems to survive better. (b) Different altered data percentages shown.

ures 6 and 7 ($\mu = 0$) we analyze the sensitivity of both our labeling module and overall watermarking scheme to such randomly occurring changes, as direct measures for encoding resilience. In Figure 6 (a), label alteration increases with an increasing degree of data change. Smaller label bit sizes seem to better survive such an attack. In Figure 6 (b), as the percentage of altered data items increases, the labeling scheme naturally degrades.

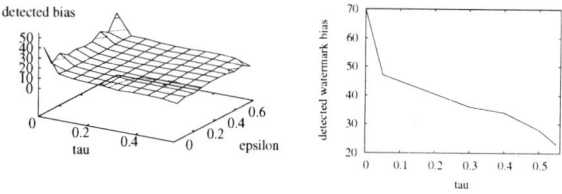

Figure 7: Watermark survival to epsilon-attacks. (a) Naturally, increasing τ and ϵ values result in a decreasing watermark bias. (b) Same shown for $\epsilon = 10\%$. **(real data)**

In Figure 7, an embedded watermark (bias) is detected in a randomly altered stream. Naturally, an increasing distortion results in a decreasing bias detection. Nevertheless, it is to be noted that the encoding scheme proves to be quite resilient by design, for example for $\tau = 50\%$ of the data altered within $\epsilon = 10\%$ (Figure 7 (b)), the detected bias is still above 25, yielding a false-positive rate of less than "one in thirty million".

6.2 Sampling and Summarization

The ability to survive summarization (A1) and sampling (A2) is of extreme importance as both are expected attacks. In Figure 8 the labeling algorithm is evaluated with respect to (a) sampling and (b) summarization. Intuitively, a higher label bit-size results in increased fragility to sampling (shown is a sampling degree of 3). Summarization seems to be naturally survived by our design. For example, a summarization of the data down to 5% ($\nu = 20$) still preserves over 20% of the original label values, thus conferring a strong back-bone to watermark embedding.

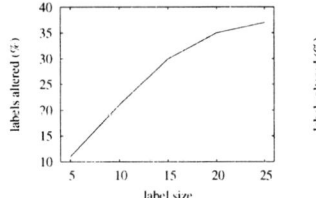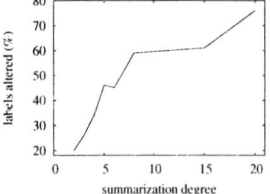

Figure 8: (a) Label resilience under sampling conditions. A higher label bit-size naturally yields an increased fragility to sampling. (b) Label alteration for summarization of increasing degree.

The behavior of the watermark encoding algorithm to sampling and summarization is outlined in Figure 9. The natural strength of the bit encoding convention is clearly illustrated here. Both transformations are survived extremely well.

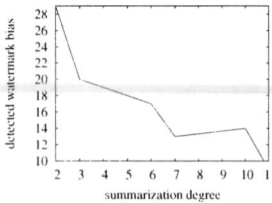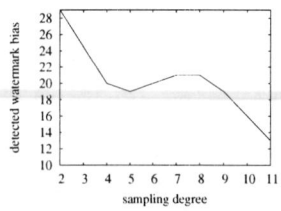

Figure 9: (a) Watermark survival to summarization. An increasing summarization degree results in a decreasing detected watermark bias. (b) Watermark survival to sampling. A bias of 10 ensures a true-positive probability of 99.999%. **(real data)**

6.3 Segmentation. Combinations

In Section 5 we theoretically assessed the ability of our scheme to survive segmentation (A3), by answering the question: what is the minimum size of a stream segment from which we are able to recover the watermark? In Figure 10 (a) we analyze the impact of actual recovered segment size on the detected watermark bias. From a segment of only 2000 stream values we can detect a watermark bias of 10, corresponding to a very convincing low false positive rate of roughly 0.001. In Figure 10 (b) we outline the impact of a *combined* transformation (sampling and summarization) on the watermark embedding. Because of the nature of both transformations and of the resilience featured in each case, the combination seems to be survived equally well. For example, a 25% sampling, followed by a 25% summarization process still yields a watermark bias of up to 20, corresponding to a low false-positive rate of "one in a million".

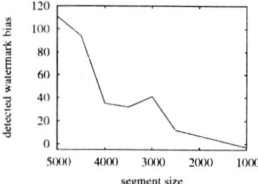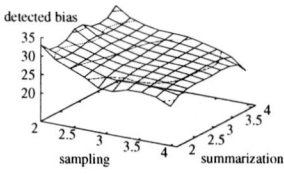

Figure 10: (a) Watermark survival to segmentation. (b) Watermark survival to combined sampling and summarization. **(real data)**

6.4 Overhead and Impact on Data Quality

The proposed watermarking solution is highly adaptive to both speed and space constraints. By far the most computationally intensive operation is the one-bit encoding operation which alters the characteristic subset data to conform to the bit encoding convention defined in Section 4.3. At the expense of embedding resilience, this operation can be sped up significantly by both pruning of the search space or, more importantly, deployment of a computation-reducing technique as described in Section 4.3. Depending on the actual stream rate, these speed-ups can be gradually deployed to be able to keep up with the incoming data. Additionally, the average amount of computation to be performed per window-load of data is defined also by the actual fraction of extremes "selected" to be bit-carriers. This fraction is determined by $\frac{b(wm)}{\phi}$. If the incoming data rate is too high, ϕ can be increased to reduce the workload.

We performed experiments aimed at evaluating the introduced watermarking computation overhead. Unless specified otherwise, we used the multi-hash encoding discussed in Section 4.3 and parameters set such that the resulting watermark survives 100% any combined sampling and summarization up to a degree of 6. First, we compared the computing times required by the watermarking process with the times spent in a simple read and copy model in which each stream item is read and copied to an output port (with fixed writing time-cost). We obtained consistent value classes clearly identifying each of the separate encoding methods presented. It became clear that, as expected, the majority of time is spent in the actual bit encoding convention routine (and not as much in the labeling module). Not surprising, the encoding convention introduced in Section 3.2 performed fastest with an average of only 5.7% increase in processing times per stream item. The poorest performer was the more complex multi-hash routine in Section 4.3 with an average increase of over 1000%, as expected decreasing almost perfectly exponential with the decrease of the guaranteed resilience (see Figure 11 (a)).

There are two lessons to be learned here. First, different encodings should be used for different scenarios with associated value models. For example for a temperature stream with a likely average reading rate of under 1Hz, deploying the multi-hash encoding routine for high resilience would be best suited whereas in a very fast streaming scenario the encoding in Section 3.2 would perform much better. Additionally, subject to future research is the issue of better pruning algorithms as discussed in Section 4.3.

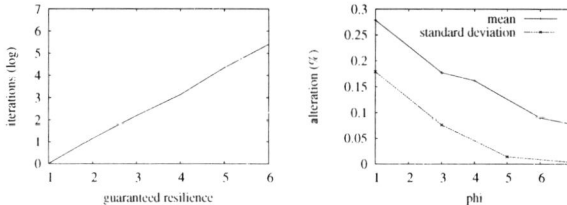

Figure 11: (a) Computation overhead (iterations) in multi-hash encoding increases with increasing guaranteed resilience (e.g. sampling degree) levels (logarithmic scale). (b) Decreasing the number of considered bit-encoding extremes (increasing ϕ) decreases the impact on mean and standard deviation in the watermarked data.

We also performed experiments evaluating the impact of our encoding on data quality. More specifically we analyzed the alterations incurred by the mean and standard deviation of the stream data. For the above parameter settings, over a large number (12000+) of runs over the real (and synthetic) data sets, the value of the mean of the watermarked stream varied less than a mere 0.21% average from the original. The alteration to the standard deviation also maintained itself nicely within 0.27% of the original data. There exists a tunable trade-off between attack/transformation resilience and the incurred alterations. A lower level of resilience would definitely require less modifications to the data and have a lower impact on global statistics. In Figure 11 (b) we show how decreasing the number of considered bit-encoding major extremes decreases the impact on the average and standard deviation in the result.

7 Conclusions

In the present paper we introduced the issue of rights protection for sensor streams. We proposed a watermarking solution, based on novel ideas such as on-the-fly labeling and watermark encoding, resilient to important domain-specific transforms. We implemented a proof of concept of the proposed solution and evaluated it experimentally on real data. The method proves to be extremely resilient to all considered transforms, including sampling, summarization, random alterations and combined transforms. In upcoming research we propose to analyze streams of categorical data, to investigate other aggregates (instead of averages) in the summarization process (e.g. min, max, most likely value) and to experiment with alternative resilient and fast(er) bit-encodings.

References

[1] M. J. Atallah and S. S. Wagstaff Jr. Watermarking with quadratic residues. In *Proc. of IS-T/SPIE Conf. on Security and Watermarking of Multimedia Contents, SPIE Vol. 3657, pp. 283–288.*, 1999.

[2] M.J. Atallah, V. Raskin, C. F. Hempelmann, M. Karahan, R. Sion, K. E. Triezenberg, and U. Topkara. Natural language watermarking and tamperproofing. In *Lecture Notes in Computer Science, Proc. 5th International Information Hiding Workshop 2002*. Springer Verlag, 2002.

[3] B. Babcock, S. Babu, M. Datar, and Motwani R. Models and issues in data stream systems. In *Proc. ACM Symp. on Principles of Database Systems (PODS)*, pages 1–16, 2002.

[4] D. Carney, U. Cetintemel, M. Cherniack, C. Convey, S. Lee, G. Seidman, N. Stonebraker, M.and Tatbul, and S. Zdonik. Monitoring streams – a new class of data management applications. In *Proceedings of the Int. Conf. on Very Large Data Bases (VLDB)*, 2002.

[5] S. Chandrasekaran and M. J. Franklin. Streaming queries over streaming data. In *Proceedings of the Int. Conf. on Very Large Data Bases (VLDB)*, pages 203–214, 2002.

[6] B. Chen and G. W. Wornell. Quantization index modulation: A class of provably good methods for digital watermarking and information embedding. *IEEE Transactions on Information Theory*, 47(4), 2001.

[7] Christian Collberg and Clark Thomborson. On the limits of software watermarking, August 1998.

[8] I. Cox, J. Bloom, and M. Miller. Digital watermarking. In *Digital Watermarking*. Morgan Kaufmann, 2001.

[9] M. Datar, A. Gionis, P. Indyk, and R. Motwani. Maintaining stream statistics over sliding windows. In *Proceedings of the ACM-SIAM Symposium on Discrete Algorithms*, pages 635–644, 2002.

[10] J. Kang, J. F. Naughton, and S. D. Viglas. Evaluating window joins over unbounded streams. In *Proceedings of ICDE*, 2003.

[11] J. Kiernan and R. Agrawal. Watermarking relational databases. In *Proceedings of the 28th International Conference on Very Large Databases VLDB*, 2002.

[12] D. Kirovski and H.S. Malvar. Spread-spectrum watermarking of audio signals. *IEEE Transactions on Signal Processing*, 51(4), 2003.

[13] F. Korn, S. Muthukrishnan, and D. Srivastava. Reverse nearest neighbor aggregates over streams. In *Proceedings of the Int. Conf. on Very Large Data Bases (VLDB)*, 2002.

[14] NASA. The Hawaii University Infrared Telescope Facility (http://irtfweb.ifa.hawaii.edu/).

[15] J. Palsberg, S. Krishnaswamy, M. Kwon, D. Ma, Q. Shao, and Y. Zhang. Experience with software watermarking. In *Proceedings of ACSAC, 16th Annual Computer Security Applications Conference*, pages 308–316, 2000.

[16] F. A. P. Petitcolas, R. J. Anderson, and M. G. Kuhn. Attacks on copyright marking systems. In David Aucsmith, editor, *Information Hiding: Second International Workshop*, volume 1525 of *Lecture Notes in Computer Science*, pages 218–238, Portland, 1998. Springer-Verlag.

[17] Bruce Schneier. Applied cryptography: Protocols, algorithms and source code in c. In *Applied Cryptography*. John Wiley and Sons, 1996.

[18] Radu Sion. Proving ownership over categorical data. In *Proceedings of the IEEE International Conference on Data Engineering ICDE*, 2004.

[19] Radu Sion, Mikhail Atallah, and Sunil Prabhakar. Rights protection for relational data. In *Proceedings of ACM SIGMOD*, 2003.

[20] M. D. Swanson, B. Zhu, and A. H. Tewfik. Audio watermarking and data embedding – current state of the art, challenges and future directions. In J. Dittmann, P. Wohlmacher, P. Horster, and R. Steinmetz, editors, *Multimedia and Security Workshop at ACM Multimedia*, volume 41 of *GMD*, Bristol, United Kingdom, September 1998. ACM.

Reverse *k*NN Search in Arbitrary Dimensionality

Yufei Tao[§]
[§]Department of Computer Science
City University of Hong Kong
Tat Chee Avenue, Hong Kong
taoyf@cs.cityu.edu.hk

Dimitris Papadias[†]

Xiang Lian[†]
[†]Department of Computer Science
Hong Kong University of Science and Technology
Clear Water Bay, Hong Kong
{*dimitris, xlian*}*@cs.ust.hk*

Abstract

Given a point q, a *reverse k nearest neighbor* (R*k*NN) query retrieves all the data points that have q as one of their k nearest neighbors. Existing methods for processing such queries have at least one of the following deficiencies: (i) they do not support arbitrary values of k (ii) they cannot deal efficiently with database updates, (iii) they are applicable only to 2D data (but not to higher dimensionality), and (iv) they retrieve only approximate results. Motivated by these shortcomings, we develop algorithms for *exact* processing of R*k*NN with *arbitrary* values of k on *dynamic multidimensional* datasets. Our methods utilize a conventional data-partitioning index on the dataset and do not require any pre-computation. In addition to their flexibility, we experimentally verify that the proposed algorithms outperform the existing ones even in their restricted focus.

1. INTRODUCTION

Given a multi-dimensional dataset P and a point q, a *reverse nearest neighbor* (RNN) query retrieves all the points $p \in P$ that have q as their nearest neighbor. Formally, RNN(q) = {$p \in P$ | $\neg \exists p' \in P$ such that $dist(p,p') < dist(p,q)$}, where *dist* is a distance metric (in this paper we assume Euclidean distance). Although the problem was proposed recently [KM00], it has already received considerable attention due to its importance in several applications involving decision support, resource allocation, profile-based marketing, etc. Other versions of the problem include (i) *continuous* RNN [BJKS02], where P contains linearly moving objects with fixed velocities, and the goal is to retrieve all RNNs of q for a future interval; (ii) *bichromatic* RNN [SRAA01] where, given a set Q of queries, the goal is to find the objects $p \in P$ that are closer to some $q \in Q$ than any other point of Q; (iii) *stream* RNN [KMS02], where data arrive in the form of streams, and the goal is to report aggregate results over the RNNs of a set of query points.

This paper focuses on conventional (i.e., *monochromatic*) reverse nearest neighbor queries. In addition to single RNN search, we deal with *reverse k nearest neighbor* (R*k*NN) queries, which retrieve all the points $p \in P$ that have q as one of their k nearest neighbors. Specifically, R*k*NN(q) = {$p \in P$ | $dist(p,q) \le dist(p,p_k)$}, where p_k is the k-th farthest NN of p}. Figure 1.1 shows four 2D points, where each point p is associated with a circle covering its two nearest neighbors For example, the two NNs of p_4 (p_2, p_3) are in the circle centered at p_4. Accordingly, $p_4 \in$ R2NN(p_2) and $p_4 \in$ R2NN(p_3). Let *k*NN(p) be the set of k nearest neighbors of point p. It is important to note that $p \in k$NN(q) does not necessarily imply $p \in$ R*k*NN(q) and vice versa. For instance, 2NN(p_4)={p_2,p_3}, while R2NN(p_4)=∅ (i.e., p_4 is not contained in the circles of p_1, p_2, or p_3).

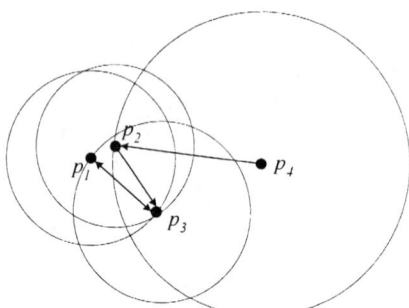

Figure 1.1: 2NN and R2NN examples

As discussed in Section 2.2, all the previous methods for RNN search have at least one of the following deficiencies: (i) they do not support arbitrary values of k (ii) they cannot deal efficiently with database updates, (iii) they are applicable only to 2D data (but not to higher dimensionality), and (iv) they retrieve only approximate results (i.e., potentially incurring false misses). In other words, these methods address restricted versions of the problem without providing a general solution. Motivated by this, we develop algorithms for *exact* processing of R*k*NN queries with *arbitrary* values of k on *dynamic multidimensional* datasets.

Our methods do not require any pre-processing besides a data-partitioning index (e.g., R-tree [BKSS90], X-tree [BKK96]). Similar to the existing algorithms for

---

Permission to copy without fee all or part of this material is granted provided that the copies are not made or distributed for direct commercial advantage, the VLDB copyright notice and the title of the publication and its date appear, and notice is given that copying is by permission of the Very Large Data Base Endowment. To copy otherwise, or to republish, requires a fee and/or special permission from the Endowment

Proceedings of the 30th VLDB Conference, Toronto, Canada, 2004

dynamic data, we follow a filter-refinement framework. Specifically, the filter step retrieves a set of candidate results that is guaranteed to include all the actual reverse nearest neighbors; the subsequent refinement step eliminates the false hits. The two steps are integrated in a seamless way that eliminates multiple accesses to the same index node (i.e., each node is visited at most once). Our experimental comparison verifies that the proposed techniques outperform the previous ones, even in their restricted focus.

The rest of the paper is organized as follows. Section 2 surveys related work on NN and RNN search. Section 3 presents some interesting problem characteristics, and proposes a new algorithm for single RNN (k=1) retrieval. Section 4 extends the solution to arbitrary values of k. Section 5 experimentally evaluates the proposed methods, and Section 6 concludes the paper with directions for future work.

2. BACKGROUND

Although the proposed algorithms can be used with various indexes, in the sequel, we assume that the dataset P is indexed by an R-tree due to the popularity of this structure in the literature. Section 2.1 briefly overviews the R-tree and algorithms for nearest neighbor search. Section 2.2 describes previous work on monochromatic RNN queries.

2.1 Algorithms for NN search using R-trees

The R-tree [G84] and its variants (most notably the R*-tree [BKSS90]) can be thought of as extensions of B-trees in multi-dimensional spaces. Figure 2.1 shows a 2D point set $P=\{p_1,p_2,...,p_{12}\}$ indexed by an R-tree assuming a capacity of three entries per node. Points that are close in space (e.g., p_1, p_2, p_3) are clustered in the same leaf node (N_3). Nodes are then recursively grouped together with the same principle until the top level, which consists of a single root. An intermediate index entry contains the minimum bounding rectangle (MBR) of its child node, together with a pointer to the page where the node is stored. A leaf entry stores the coordinates of a data point and (optionally) a pointer to the corresponding record.

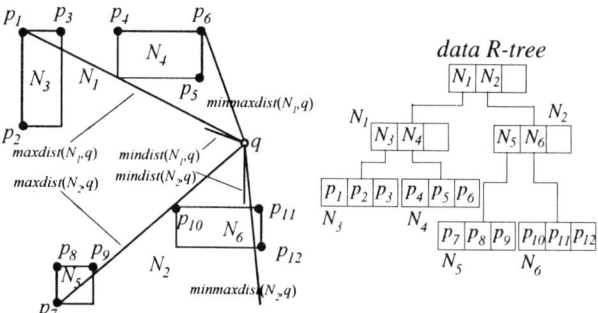

(a) Points and node extents   (b) The R-tree
Figure 2.1: Example of an R-tree and a NN query

Given a d-dimensional set P and a point q, a nearest neighbor query retrieves the point $p \in P$ that is closest to q. The algorithms for NN queries on R-trees utilize some bounds to prune the search space: (i) $mindist(N,q)$, which corresponds to the minimum possible distance between q and any point in the subtree of node N, (ii) $maxdist(N,q)$, which denotes the maximum possible distance between q and any point in the subtree of N, and (iii) $minmaxdist(N,q)$, which gives an upper bound of the distance between q and its closest point in N. In particular, the derivation of $minmaxdist(N,q)$ is based on the fact that each edge of the MBR of N contains at least one data point. Hence, $minmaxdist(N,q)$ equals the smallest of the maximum distances between all edges (of N) and q. Figure 2.1a shows these pruning bounds between point q and nodes N_1, N_2.

Existing NN methods follow either depth-first (DF), or best-first (BF) traversal. DF algorithms [RKV95, CF98] start from the root and visit recursively the node with the smallest $mindist$ from q. In Figure 2.1, for instance, the first 3 nodes accessed are (in this order) root, N_1 and N_4, where the first potential nearest neighbor is found (p_5). During backtracking to the upper levels, DF only visits entries whose minimum distances are smaller than the distance of the NN already retrieved. For example, after discovering p_5, DF backtracks to the root level (without visiting N_3 because $mindist(N_3,q) > dist(p_5,q)$), and then follows the path N_2, N_6 where the actual NN p_{11} is found.

Best-first (BF) algorithms [H94, HS99] maintain a heap H with the entries visited so far, sorted by their $mindist$. As with DF, BF starts from the root, and inserts all its entries into H (together with their $mindist$), e.g., in Figure 2.1, $H=\{<N_1, mindist(N_1,q)>, <N_2, mindist(N_2,q)>\}$. Then, at each step, BF visits the node in H with the smallest $mindist$. Continuing the example, the algorithm retrieves the content of N_1 and inserts all its entries in H, after which $H=\{<N_2, mindist(N_2,q)>, <N_4, mindist(N_4,q)>, <N_3, mindist(N_3,q)>\}$. Similarly, the next two nodes accessed are N_2 and N_6 (inserted in H after visiting N_2), in which p_{11} is discovered as the current NN. At this time, the algorithm terminates (with p_{11} as the final result) since the next entry (N_4) in H is farther (from q) than p_{11}. Both DF and BF can be easily extended for the retrieval of $k>1$ nearest neighbors. $Maxdist$ and $minmaxdist$ can be applied to speed up the search process. Furthermore, BF is $incremental$, i.e., it reports the nearest neighbors in ascending order of their distance to the query, so that k does not have to be known in advance.

2.2 RNN Algorithms

Algorithms for RNN processing can be classified in two categories depending on whether they require pre-processing, or not. For simplicity, we describe all methods for single RNN retrieval in 2D space. At the end of the section we discuss their applicability to arbitrary values of k and dimensionality.

The original RNN method [KM00] pre-computes for each data point p its nearest neighbor NN(p). Then, it represents p as a *vicinity circle* (p, *dist*(p,NN(p))) centered at p with radius equal to the Euclidean distance between p and its NN. The MBRs of all circles are indexed by an R-tree, called the RNN-tree. Using the RNN-tree, the reverse nearest neighbors of q can be efficiently retrieved by a point location query, which returns all circles that contain q. Figure 2.2a illustrates the concept using four data points, each associated with a vicinity circle. Since q falls in the circles of p_3 and p_4, the result of the query is RNN(q) = $\{p_3, p_4\}$.

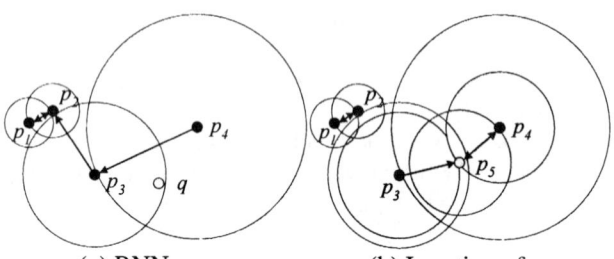

(a) RNN query (b) Insertion of p_5
Figure 2.2: Illustration of KM[1]

Because the RNN-tree is optimized for RNN, but not NN search, Korn and Muthukrishnan [KM00] use an additional (conventional) R-tree on the data points for nearest neighbors and other spatial queries. In order to avoid the maintenance of two separate structures, Yang and Lin [YL01] combine the two indexes in the RdNN-tree. Similar to the RNN-tree, a leaf node of the RdNN-tree contains vicinity circles of data points. On the other hand, an intermediate node contains the MBR of the underlying points (not their vicinity circles), together with the maximum distance from every point in the sub-tree to its nearest neighbor. As shown in the experiments of [YL01], the RdNN-tree is efficient for both RNN and NN queries because, intuitively, it contains the same information as the RNN-tree and has the same structure (for node MBRs) as a conventional R-tree. Another solution based on pre-computation is proposed in [MVZ02]. The methodology, however, is applicable only to 2D spaces and focuses on asymptotical worst case bounds (rather than experimental comparison with other approaches).

The problem of KM, YL, MVZ, and all techniques that rely on pre-processing, is that they cannot deal efficiently with updates. This is because each insertion or deletion may affect the vicinity circles of several points. Consider Figure 2.2b, where we want to insert a new point p_5 in the database. First, we have to perform a RNN query to find all objects (in this case p_3 and p_4) that have p_5 as their new nearest neighbors. Then, we update the vicinity circles of these objects in the index. Finally, we compute the NN of p_5 (i.e., p_4) and insert the corresponding circle. Similarly, each deletion must update the vicinity circles of the affected objects. In order to alleviate the problem, Lin et al. [LNY03] propose a method for bulk insertions in the RdNN-tree.

Stanoi et al. [SAA00] eliminate the need for pre-computing all NNs by utilizing some interesting properties of RNN retrieval. Consider Figure 2.3, which divides the space around a query q into six equal regions S_1 to S_6. Let p be the NN of q in some region S_i; it can be proven that (i) either $p \in$ RNN(q) or (ii) there is no RNN of q in S_i. For instance, in Figure 2.3 the NN of q in S_1 is point p_2. However, the NN of p_2 is p_1. Consequently, there is no RNN of q in S_1 and we do not need to search further in this region. The same is true for S_2 (no data points), S_3, S_4 (p_4, p_5 are NNs of each other) and S_6 (the NN of p_3 is p_1). The actual result is RNN(q) = $\{p_6\}$. Based on the above property SAA adopts a two-step processing method. First, six constrained NN queries [FSAA01] retrieve the nearest neighbors of q in regions S_1 to S_6. These points constitute the *candidate* result. Then, at a second step, a NN query is applied to find the NN p' of each candidate p. If *dist*(p,q)< *dist*(p,p'), p belongs to the actual result; otherwise, it is a false hit and discarded.

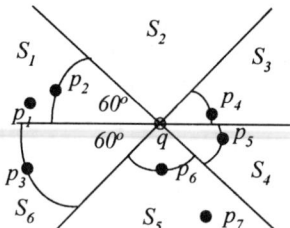

Figure 2.3: Illustration of SAA

The number of regions to be searched for candidate results increases exponentially with the dimensionality[2], rendering SAA inefficient even for three dimensions. Motivated by this, Singh et al. [SFT03] propose a multi-step algorithm that: (i) finds (using an R-tree) the K NNs of the query q, which constitute the initial candidates; (ii) it eliminates the points that are closer to some other candidate than q; (iii) it applies *boolean range queries* on the remaining candidates to determine the actual RNNs. Consider, for instance, the query of Figure 2.4 assuming that K (a system parameter) is 4. The algorithm first retrieves the 4 NNs of q: p_6, p_5, p_4 and p_2. The second step discards p_4 and p_5 since they are closer to each other than q. The third step uses the circles (p_2,*dist*(p_2,q)) and (p_6,*dist*(p_6,q)) to perform two boolean ranges on the data R-tree. The difference with respect to conventional range queries is that a boolean range terminates immediately when (i) the first data point is found, or (ii) the entire side of a node MBR lies within the circle. For instance, *minmaxdist*(N_1,p_2) $\leq$ *dist*(p_2,q), meaning that N_1 contains at least a point within the range (i.e.,). Thus, p_2 is a false

---

[1] We refer to the algorithms according to the author initials.

[2] Determining the number of space partitions in SAA is analogous to the *sphere packing* and the *kissing number* problems. For a discussion see [SFT03].

hit and SFT returns p_6 as the only RNN of q. The major shortcoming of the method is that it may incur false misses. In Figure 2.4, although p_3 is a RNN of q, it does not belong to the 4 NNs of the query and will not be retrieved.

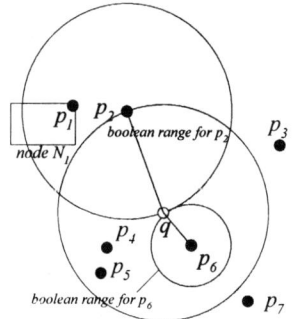

Figure 2.4: Illustration of SFT

Table 2.1 summarizes the properties of each algorithm. As discussed before, pre-computation methods cannot efficiently handle updates. MVZ is suitable only to 2D spaces, while SAA is practically inapplicable for 3 or more dimensions. SFT incurs false misses, the number of which depends on the parameter K: a large value of K decreases the false misses but increases significantly the processing cost.

	dynamic data	arbitrary dimensionality	exact result
KM,YL	No	Yes	Yes
MVZ	No	No	Yes
SAA	Yes	No	Yes
SFT	Yes	Yes	No

Table 2.1: Summary of algorithm properties

Regarding the applicability of the existing algorithms to arbitrary values of k, pre-computation methods only support a specific value (typically equal to 1), used to determine the vicinity circles. SFT can be adapted for retrieval of RkNN by setting a large value of K ($\gg k$) and replacing the boolean with *count* queries (that return the number of objects in the query range instead of their actual ids). The extension of SAA to arbitrary k has not been studied before, but we will discuss it in Section 4.3. In the rest of the paper, we propose algorithms that return the exact results for dynamic datasets of any dimensionality. We start with single (i.e., $k=1$) RNN queries in Section 3, before proceeding to arbitrary values of k in Section 4.

3. SINGLE RNN PROCESSING

Section 3.1 illustrates some problem characteristics that permit the development of efficient algorithms presented in Section 3.2. Section 3.3 analyzes the performance of the proposed techniques with respect to existing methods.

3.1 Problem Characteristics

Consider the perpendicular bisector $\perp(p,q)$ between the query q and an arbitrary data point p as shown in Figure 3.1a. The bisector divides the data space into two half-planes: $PL_q(p,q)$ that contains q, and $PL_p(p,q)$ that contains p. Any point (e.g., p') in $PL_p(p,q)$ cannot be a RNN of q because it is closer to p than q. Similarly, a node MBR (e.g., N_1) that falls completely in $PL_p(p,q)$ cannot contain any candidate. In some cases, the pruning of an MBR requires multiple half-planes. For example, in Figure 3.1b, although N_2 does not fall completely in $PL_{p_1}(p_1,q)$ or $PL_{p_2}(p_2,q)$, it can still be pruned since it lies entirely in the *union* of the two half-planes.

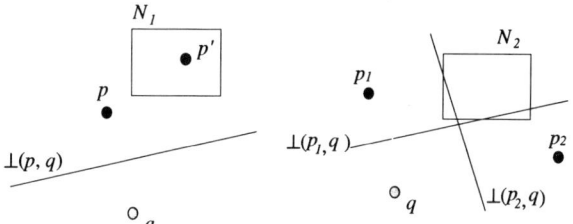

(a) Pruning with one point (b) Pruning with two points
Figure 3.1: Illustration of half-plane pruning

In general, if $p_1, p_2, ..., p_{n_c}$ are n_c data points, then any node whose MBR falls inside $\cup_{i=1 \sim n_c} PL_{p_i}(p_i,q)$ cannot contain any RNN result. Let the *residual region* N^{res} be the area of node N outside $\cup_{i=1 \sim n_c} PL_{p_i}(p_i,q)$ (i.e., the part of the MBR that may contain candidate RNNs of q). Then, N can be pruned if and only if $N^{res}=\varnothing$. Typically, N^{res} is a convex polygon bounded by the edges of N and the bisectors $\perp(p_i,q)$ ($1 \le i \le n_c$). Consider Figure 3.2a that contains $n_c=3$ data points p_1, p_2, p_3. We can compute the residual region N^{res} by *trimming* N with each bisector in turn. Specifically, initially we set $N^{res}=N$ and use $\perp(p_1,q)$, after which N^{res} becomes the shaded trapezoid. In general, trimming with $\perp(p_i,q)$ reduces the *previous* N^{res} to the region inside the half-plane $PL_q(p_i,q)$. Figure 3.2b shows the final N^{res} after processing all bisectors. Given p_1, p_2 and p_3, N^{res} is the only part of the node MBR N that may contain RNNs of q.

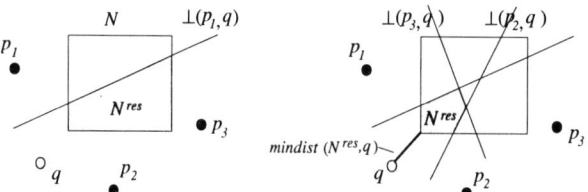

(a) After processing $\perp(q,p_1)$ (b) The final polygon
Figure 3.2: Computing the residual region

The above computation of N^{res} has two problems. First, in the worst case, each bisector may introduce an additional vertex to N^{res}. Consequently, the trimming of the i-th ($1 \le i \le n_c$) bisector takes $O(i)$ time because it may need to examine all edges in the previous N^{res}. Thus, the total processing cost is $O(n_c^2)$, i.e., quadratic to the number of half-planes. Second, this method does not scale with the dimensionality because computing the intersection of a

747

half-space and a hyper-polyhedron becomes increasingly complex [BKOS97]. Motivated by this, we propose a simpler alternative that requires only $O(n_c)$ time. The idea is to bound N^{res} by a *residual MBR* N^{resM}. Figure 3.3 illustrates the residual MBR computation using the example in Figure 3.2. Initially N^{resM} is set to N and then it is trimmed incrementally by each bisector. Figure 3.3a shows trimming with $\perp(p_1,q)$, where, instead of keeping the exact shape of N^{res}, we compute N^{resM} (i.e., the shaded rectangle). In general, bisector $\perp(p_i,q)$ updates N^{resM} to the MBR of the region in the previous N^{resM} that is in $PL_q(p_i,q)$. Figures 3.3b, 3.3c illustrate the residual MBRs after trimming with $\perp(p_2,q)$, $\perp(p_3,q)$, respectively. Note that the final N^{resM} is not necessarily the MBR of the final N^{res} (compare Figure 3.3c and Figure 3.2b). Trimmed MBRs can be efficiently computed (in arbitrary dimensionality) using the *clipping* algorithm of [GRSY97].

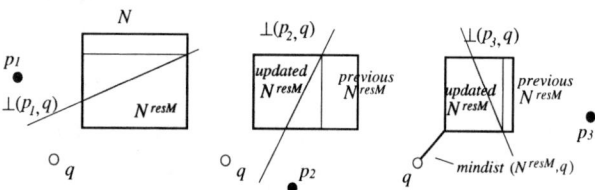

(a) After $\perp(p_1,q)$ (b) After $\perp(p_2,q)$ (c) After $\perp(p_3,q)$

Figure 3.3: Computing the residual MBR

Figure 3.4 presents the pseudo-code for the above approximate trimming algorithm. If N^{resM} exists, *trim* returns the minimum distance between q and N^{resM}; otherwise, it returns ∞. Since N^{resM} always encloses N^{res}, $N^{resM} = \emptyset$ necessarily implies that $N^{res} = \emptyset$. This property guarantees that *pruning is "safe"*, meaning that *trim* never eliminates a node that may contain candidates. The algorithm also captures points as MBRs with zero extents. In this case it will return the actual distance between the point and the query (if the point falls in the half-space of the query), or ∞ otherwise.

Algorithm trim $(q, \{p_1, p_2, ..., pn_c\}, N)$
/* q is the query point, $p_1, p_2, ..., pn_c$ are arbitrary data points, and N is a rectangle being trimmed*/
1. $N^{resM} = N$
2. for $i=1$ to n_c // consider each data point in turn
3. $\quad N^{resM} = clipping(N^{resM}, PL_q(p_i,q))$ //algorithm of [GRSY97]
4. $\quad$ if $N^{resM} = \emptyset$ then return ∞
5. return $mindist(N^{resM}, q)$
End trim

Figure 3.4: The *trim* algorithm

An interesting question is: if $N^{resM} \neq \emptyset$, can N^{res} be $\emptyset$? (i.e., *trim* fails to prune an MBR that can be discarded). Interestingly, it turns out that the answer is negative in the 2D space, as illustrated in the next lemma (which proves an even stronger result):

Lemma 1: Given a 2D query q, an arbitrary number of half-planes and a node N, the residual MBR N^{resM} of N returned by *trim* exists if and only if N^{res} exists. Furthermore, if $N^{resM} \neq \emptyset$, $mindist(N^{res},q) = mindist(N^{resM},q)$, where N^{res} is the residual region of N.

In other words, the residual MBR N^{resM} preserves the minimum distance between N^{res} and q (compare $mindist(N^{res},q)$ and $mindist(N^{resM},q)$ in Figures 3.2b and 3.3c, respectively). It is worth mentioning that the lemma does not hold for arbitrary half-planes (the half-planes in RNN are constrained to contain q). Further, the lemma does not apply to arbitrary dimensionality. However, as mentioned earlier, we can still use *trim* to safely eliminate MBRs that do not contain candidates.

3.2 The TPL Algorithm

Based on the above discussion, we adopt a two-step framework that retrieves a set of candidate RNNs (*filtering step*) and then removes the false misses (*refinement step*). As opposed to SAA and SFT that require multiple queries for each step, the filtering and refinement processes are combined into a single traversal of the R-tree. In particular, our algorithm (hereafter, called TPL) traverses the R-tree in a best-first manner (see Section 2.1), retrieving potential candidates in ascending order of their distance to the query point q because the RNNs are likely to be near q. The concept of half-planes (half-spaces in high dimensions) is used to prune node MBRs (data points) that cannot contain (be) candidates. Each pruned entry is inserted in a *refinement set* S_{rfn}. In the refinement step, the entries of S_{rfn} are used to eliminate false hits. Next we discuss TPL using the example of Figure 3.5, which shows a set of data points (numbered in ascending order of their distance from the query) and the corresponding R-tree (the content of some nodes is omitted for clarity). The query result contains only point p_5.

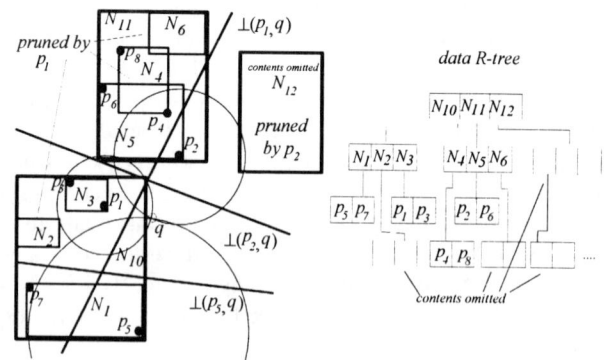

Figure 3.5: Filtering example

Initially, the algorithm visits the root of the R-tree and inserts its entries N_{10}, N_{11}, N_{12} into a heap H sorted on their *mindist* from q. Then it de-heaps N_{10}, visits its child node and inserts into H the corresponding entries: $H = \{N_3, N_{11}, N_2, N_1, N_{12}\}$. The next node accessed is N_3, where the first point p_1 (i.e., the one closest to q) has $dist(p_1,q) < dist(N_{11},q)$ (N_{11} is at the top of the heap) and is added to the candidate set S_{cnd}. The second point p_3 in N_3

lies in $PL_{p_1}(p_1,q)$ (i.e., it cannot be a RNN of q) and is inserted into the refinement set S_{rfn}. In general, any point or node examined during the filter step is not discarded because it may influence (i.e., be a NN of) some candidate. In this example, p_3 will invalidate p_1 (during the refinement step) because $dist(p_1,p_3) < dist(p_1,q)$.

The next de-heaped entry is N_{11}. Trim checks if N_{11} can be pruned. Since part of N_{11} lies in $PL_q(p_1,q)$, it has to be visited. Its child nodes N_4 and N_6 fall completely out of $PL_q(p_1,q)$. Therefore, they cannot contain any candidates and are added to S_{rfn}. On the other hand, N_5 falls partially in $PL_q(p_1,q)$, i.e., trim will return a $mindist(N_5^{resM},q)$ that is different from ∞. Thus, N_5 is inserted into H together with its $mindist(N_5^{resM},q)$. The rationale of this choice, instead of $mindist(N_5,q)$, is that since our aim is to discover candidates according to their proximity to q, the node visiting order should not take into account the part of the node that cannot contain candidates. Assuming that $mindist(N_5^{resM},q) < mindist(N_2,q)$, N_5 is at the top of H and immediately de-heaped. Inside N_5, point p_2 is added to $S_{cnd}=\{p_1,p_2\}$ and p_6 to $S_{rfn}=\{p_3,N_4,N_6,p_6\}$. The next heap entry N_2 lies in $PL_{p_1}(p_1,q)$ and is added to S_{rfn}, without being visited. On the other hand, part of N_1 lies in $PL_q(p_1,q)$ and is accessed, leading to $S_{cnd}=\{p_1,p_2,p_5\}$ and $S_{rfn}=\{p_3,N_4,N_6,N_2,p_6,p_7\}$. Finally, N_1 is also inserted into S_{rfn} as it lies completely in $PL_{p_2}(p_2,q)$. The filtering step terminates when $H=\emptyset$.

The contents of the heap at each phase of the filtering process are shown in Table 3.1. Although omitted in the table, the heap entry for N also contains $mindist(N^{resM},q)$, if N has been trimmed, or $mindist(N,q)$, otherwise. In addition, the heap may include (non-pruned) data points (for simplicity, in the example we assumed that such points were processed immediately).

Action	Heap	S_{cnd}	S_{rfn}
visit root	$\{N_{10},N_{11},N_{12}\}$	$\emptyset$	$\emptyset$
visit N_{10}	$\{N_3,N_{11},N_2,N_1,N_{12}\}$	$\emptyset$	$\emptyset$
visit N_3	$\{N_{11},N_2,N_1,N_{12}\}$	$\{p_1\}$	$\{p_3\}$
visit N_{11}	$\{N_5,N_2,N_1,N_{12}\}$	$\{p_1\}$	$\{p_3,N_4,N_6\}$
visit N_5	$\{N_2,N_1,N_{12}\}$	$\{p_1,p_2\}$	$\{p_3,N_4,N_6,p_6\}$
process N_2	$\{N_1,N_{12}\}$	$\{p_1,p_2\}$	$\{p_3,N_4,N_6,p_6,N_2\}$
visit N_1	$\{N_{12}\}$	$\{p_1,p_2,p_5\}$	$\{p_3,N_4,N_6,p_6,N_2,p_7\}$
visit N_{12}	$\emptyset$	$\{p_1,p_2,p_5\}$	$\{p_3,N_4,N_6,p_6,N_2,p_7,N_{12}\}$

Table 3.1: Heap contents during filtering

Figure 3.6 illustrates the pseudo-code for the filtering step. Note that *trim* is applied twice for each node N; when N is inserted into the heap and when it is de-heaped. The second test is necessary, because N may be pruned by some candidate that was discovered after N's insertion into H. Similarly, when a leaf node is visited, its non-pruned points are inserted into H (instead of S_{cnd}) and processed in ascending order of their distance to q. Although this may increase the heap size (and the CPU cost of heap operations), it maximizes the chance that some points will be subsequently pruned by not-yet discovered candidates that are closer to the query, hence reducing the size of S_{cnd} (and the cost of the subsequent refinement step).

Algorithm TPL-filter(q) /* q is the query point */
1. initialize a min-heap H accepting entries of the form (e, key)
2. initialize sets $S_{cnd}=\emptyset$, $S_{rfn}=\emptyset$
3. insert (R-tree root, 0) to H
4. while H is not empty
5. (e, key)=de-heap H
6.   if (**trim**(q, S_{cnd}, e)=∞) then $S_{rfn}=S_{rfn}\cup\{e\}$
7.   else // entry may be or contain a candidate
8.   if e is data point p
9. $S_{cnd}=S_{cnd}\cup\{p\}$
10.   else if e points to a leaf node N
11.   for each point p in N (sorted on $dist(p,q)$)
12.   if (**trim**(q,S_{cand},p)$\neq\infty$) then insert $(p,dist(p,q))$ in H
13.   else $S_{rfn}=S_{rfn}\cup\{p\}$
14.   else // e points to an intermediate node N
15.   for each entry N_i in N
16. $mindist(N_i^{resM}, q)$=**trim**(q, S_{cnd}, N_i)
17.   if ($mindist(N_i^{resM}, q)=\infty$) then $S_{rfn}=S_{rfn}\cup\{N_i\}$
18.   else insert $(N_i, mindist(N_i^{resM}, q))$ in H
End TPL-filter

Figure 3.6: TPL filtering algorithm

After the termination of the filter step we have a set S_{cnd} of candidates and a set S_{rfn} of node MBRs or data points. Let $P_{rfn}\subseteq S_{rfn}$ be the set of points and $N_{rfn}\subseteq S_{rfn}$ be the set of MBRs in S_{rfn}. The refinement step is performed in *rounds*. Figure 3.7 shows the pseudo-code for each round, where we eliminate the maximum number of candidates from S_{cnd} without visiting additional nodes. Intuitively, a point $p \in S_{cnd}$ can be discarded as a false hit, if (i) there is a point $p' \in P_{rfn}$ such that $dist(p,p') < dist(p,q)$, or (ii) there is an node MBR $N \in N_{rfn}$ such that $minmaxdist(p,N) < dist(p,q)$ (i.e., N is guaranteed to contain a point p' such that $dist(p,p') < dist(p,q)$). For instance, in Figure 3.5, the first condition prunes p_1 because $p_3 \in P_{rfn}$ and $dist(p_1,p_3) < dist(p_1,q)$. Lines 2-9 prune false hits according to the above observations.

Algorithm refinement_round(q, S_{cnd}, P_{rfn}, N_{rfn})
1. for each point p in S_{cnd}
2.   for each point p' in P_{rfn}
3.   if $dist(p,p') < dist(p,q)$
4. $S_{cnd}= S_{cnd} -\{p\}$ //false hit
5.   goto 1 //test next candidate
6.   for each node MBR N in N_{rfn}
7.   if $minmaxdist(p,N) < dist(p,q)$
8. $S_{cnd}= S_{cnd} -\{p\}$ //false hit
9.   goto 1 //test next candidate
10.   for each node MBR N in N_{rfn}
11.   if $mindist(p,N) < dist(p,q)$ add N in $toVisit(p)$
12.   if ($toVisit(p)=\emptyset$)
13. $S_{cnd}= S_{cnd} -\{p\}$ and report p // actual result
End refinement_round

Figure 3.7: The *refinement_round* algorithm

On the other hand, a point $p \in S_{cnd}$ can be reported as an actual result without any extra node accesses, if (i) there is no point $p' \in P_{rfn}$ such that $dist(p,p') < dist(p,q)$ and (ii)

749

for every node $N \in N_{rfn}$: $mindist(p,N) \geq dist(p,q)$. In Figure 3.5, candidate p_5 satisfies these conditions and is removed from S_{cnd}. Each remaining point p in S_{cnd} (e.g., p_2) must undergo additional refinement rounds because there may exist points (p_4) in some not-yet visited nodes (N_4) that invalidate it. In this case, p requires accessing some nodes N such that $mindist(p,N) < dist(p,q)$, which are inserted in $toVisit(p)$, i.e., $toVisit(p)$ is the set of nodes that need to be visited before verifying p as a result.

Our next goal is to access the nodes of $toVisit(p)$ (for $p \in S_{cnd}$) in an order that achieves quick elimination of the remaining candidates. Continuing the running example, after the first round $S_{cnd} = \{p_2\}$ and the nodes that may contain NNs of p_2 are $toVisit(p_2)=\{N_4, N_{12}\}$. We choose to access a lowest level node first (in this case N_4), because it can achieve better pruning since it either encloses data points or MBRs with small extents (therefore the *minmaxdist* pruning is more effective). In case of a tie (i.e., multiple nodes of the same low level), we access the one that may prune the largest number of candidates.

If the node N to be visited is a leaf, then P_{rfn} contains only the data points in N, and N_{rfn} is set to $\emptyset$. Otherwise (N is an intermediate node), N_{rfn} contains only the child nodes of N, and P_{rfn} is $\emptyset$. In our example, the parameters for the second round are $S_{cnd} = \{p_2\}$, $P_{rfn} = \{$points of $N_4\}$ and $N_{rfn} = \emptyset$. Inside N_4, point p_4 eliminates p_2 and the algorithm terminates. Figure 3.8 shows the pseudo-code of the TPL refinement step. Lines 2-4 eliminate candidates that are closer to each other than the query point (i.e., similar to the second step of SFT). This test is required only once and therefore, is not included in *refinement_round* in order to avoid repeating it for every round.

Algorithm TPL-refinement (q, S_{cnd}, P_{rfn}, N_{rfn})
1. for each point p in S_{cnd}
2.   for each other point $p' \neq p$ in S_{cnd}
3.   if $dist(p,p') < dist(p,q)$
4. $S_{cnd} = S_{cnd} - \{p\}$; goto 1
5.   if p is not eliminated initialize $toVisit(p)=\emptyset$
6. repeat
7.   **refinement_round**(q, S_{cnd}, P_{rfn}, N_{rfn})
8.   if ($S_{cnd}=\emptyset$) return // terminate
9. $P_{rfn}=N_{rfn}=\emptyset$ //initialization of next round
10.   Let N be the lowest level node that appears in the largest number of sets $toVisit(p)$, where $p \in S_{cnd}$
11.   remove N from all $toVisit(p)$ and access N
12.   if N is a leaf node
13. $P_{rfn}=\{p/p \in N\}$ //P_{rfn} contains only the points of N
14.   if N is an intermediate node
15. $N_{rfn}=\{N'/ N' \in N\}$//N_{rfn} contains the child nodes of N
End TPL-refinement

Figure 3.8: TPL refinement algorithm

In order to verify the correctness of TPL, observe that the filter step always retrieves a superset of the actual result (i.e., it does not incur false misses), since *trim* only prunes node MBRs (data points) that cannot contain (be) RNNs.

Every false hit p is subsequently eliminated during the refinement step by comparing it with each data point retrieved during the filter step and each MBR that may potentially contain NNs of p. Hence, the algorithm returns the exact set of RNNs.

3.3 Discussion

TPL and the existing techniques that do not require pre-processing (SAA, SFT) are based on the filter-refinement framework. Interestingly, the two steps are independent in the sense that the filtering algorithms of one technique can be combined with the refinement mechanisms of another. For instance, the concept of boolean ranges of SFT can replace the conventional NN queries in the second step of SAA and vice versa. In this section we show that, in addition to being more general, TPL is more effective than SAA and SFT in terms of both filtering and refinement, i.e., it retrieves fewer candidates and eliminates false hits with lower cost.

In order to compare the efficiency of our filtering step with respect to SAA, we first present an improvement of that method. Consider the space partitioning of SAA in Figure 3.9a and the corresponding NNs in each partition (points are numbered according to their distance from q). Since the angle between p_1 and p_2 is smaller than 60 degrees and p_2 is farther than p_1, point p_2 cannot be a RNN of q. In fact, the discovery of p_1 (i.e., the first NN of the query) can prune all the points lying in the region $\nabla(p_1)$ extending 60 degrees on both sides of line segment qp_1 (upper shaded region in Figure 3.9a). Based on this observation, we only need to search for other candidates outside $\nabla(p_1)$. Let p_3 be the next NN of q in the constrained region of the data space (i.e., not including $\nabla(p_1)$). Similar to p_1, p_3 prunes all the points in $\nabla(p_3)$. The algorithm terminates when the entire data space is pruned. Although the maximum number of candidates is still six (e.g., if all candidates lie on the boundaries of the 6 space partitions), in practice it is smaller (in this example, the number is 3, i.e., p_1, p_3 and p_6).

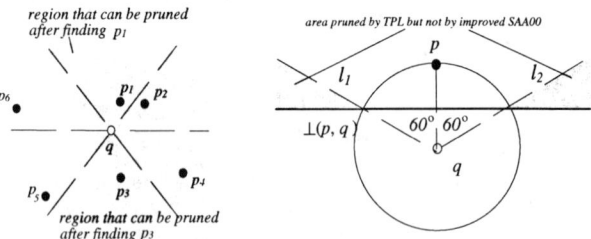

(a) Improved SAA   (b) Pruning comparison
Figure 3.9: Superiority of TPL over SAA

Going one step further, the filter step of TPL is even more efficient than that of the improved SAA. Consider Figure 3.9b where p is the NN of q. The improved SAA prunes the region $\nabla(p)$ bounded by rays l_1 and l_2. On the other hand, our algorithm prunes the entire half-plane $PL_p(p,q)$, which *includes* $\nabla(p_1)$ except for the part below $\perp(p,q)$.

750

Consider the circle centered at q with radius $dist(p,q)$. It can be easily shown that the circle crosses the intersection point of $\perp(p,q)$ and l_1 (l_2). Note that all the nodes intersecting this circle have already been visited in order to find p (a property of our filter step and all BF NN algorithms in general). In other words, *all the non-visited nodes that can be pruned by $\nabla(p)$ can also be pruned by $PL_p(p,q)$*. As a corollary, the maximum number of candidates retrieved by TPL is also bounded by the dimensionality (i.e., $|S_{cnd}|\leq 6$ is 2D space). Further, TPL supports arbitrary dimensionality in a natural way, since it does not make any assumption about the number or the shape of space partitions (as opposed to SAA).

The comparison with the filtering step of SFT depends on the value of K, i.e., the number of NNs of q that constitute the candidate set. Assume that in Figure 3.5 we know in advance that the actual RNNs of the query (in this case p_5) are among the K=5 NNs of q. SFT would perform a 5NN query and insert all the retrieved points p_1, ..., p_5 to S_{cnd}, whereas TPL inserts only the non-pruned points $S_{cnd} = \{p_1,p_2,p_5\}$. Furthermore, the number of candidates in TPL is bounded by the dimensionality, while the choice of K in SFT is arbitrary and does not provide any guarantees about the quality of the result. Consider, for instance, the (skewed) dataset and query point of Figure 3.10. A high value of K will lead to the retrieval of numerous false hits (e.g., data points in partition S_1), but no actual reverse nearest neighbors of q. The problem becomes more serious in higher dimensionality.

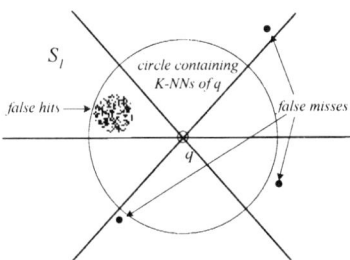

Figure 3.10: False hits and misses of SFT

One point worth mentioning is that although TPL is expected to retrieve fewer candidates than SAA and SFT, this does not necessarily imply that it incurs fewer node accesses during the filter step. For instance, assume that the query point q lies within the boundary of a leaf node N (in fact, q can be a data point) and all six candidates of SAA are in N. Then, as suggested in [SAA00] the NN queries can be combined in a single tree traversal, which can potentially find all these candidates by following a single path from the root to N. A similar situation may occur with SFT if all K NNs of q are contained in the same leaf node. On the other hand, the node accesses of TPL depend on the relative position of the candidates and the resulting half-planes. Nevertheless, the small size of the candidate set reduces the cost of the refinement step since each candidate must be verified.

Regarding the refinement step, it suffices to compare TPL with SFT, since boolean ranges are more efficient than the conventional NN queries of SAA. Although Singh et al. [SFT03] propose some optimization techniques for minimizing the number of node accesses, a boolean range may still access a node that has already been visited during the filter step or by a previous boolean query. On the other hand, the seamless integration of the filtering and refinement steps in TPL (i) re-uses information about the nodes visited during the filter step, and (ii) eliminates multiple accesses to the same node. In other words, a node is visited at most once. This integrated mechanism can also be applied to the methodologies of SAA and SFT. In particular, all the nodes and points eliminated by the filter step (constrained NN queries in SAA, a KNN query in SFT) are inserted in S_{rfn} and our refinement algorithm is performed directly (instead of NN queries or boolean ranges).

4. RkNN PROCESSING

Section 4.1 presents properties that permit pruning of the search space for arbitrary values of k and Section 4.2 extends our methods for this problem. Finally, 4.3 discusses the application of previous techniques.

4.1 Problem Characteristics

The half-plane pruning strategy of Section 3.1 extends to arbitrary values of k. Figure 4.1a shows an example with k=2, where the shaded region corresponds to the intersection $PL_{p_1}(p_1,q) \cap PL_{p_2}(p_2,q)$. Point p is not a R2NN of q, since both p_1 and p_2 are closer to it than q. Similarly, a node MBR inside the shaded area cannot contain any candidate (i.e., N_1 can be pruned at the filter step). In some cases, several half-plane intersections are needed to prune a node. Assume the R2NN query q and the three data points of Figure 4.1b. Each pair of points generates an intersection of half-planes: (i) $PL_{p_1}(p_1,q) \cap PL_{p_2}(p_2,q)$ (i.e., polygon *IECB*), (ii) $PL_{p_1}(p_1,q) \cap PL_{p_3}(p_3,q)$ (*ADCB*) and (iii) $PL_{p_2}(p_1,q) \cap PL_{p_3}(p_3,q)$ (*IFGHB*). The shaded region is the *union* of these 3 intersections (i.e., *IECB* ∪ *ADCB* ∪ *IFGHB*). A node MBR (e.g., N_2) inside this region can be pruned, although it is not totally covered by any individual intersection area.

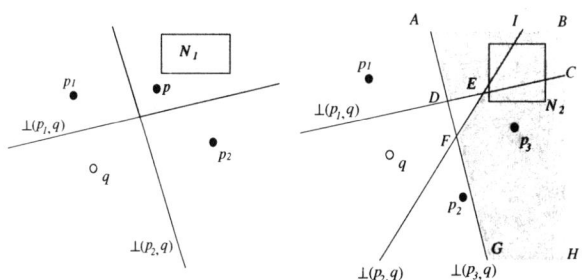

(a) $PL_{p_1}(p_1,q) \cap PL_{p_2}(p_2,q)$ (b) All intersection pairs

Figure 4.1: Examples of R2NN queries

In the general case, assume a RkNN query and $n_c \geq k$ data points $p_1, p_2, ..., p_{n_c}$ (e.g., in Figure 4.1b $n_c=3$ and $k=2$). Let $\{\sigma_1, \sigma_2, ..., \sigma_k\}$ be a subset of $\{p_1, p_2, ..., p_{n_c}\}$. Each subset prunes the intersection area $\cap_{i=1-k} PL\sigma_i(\sigma_i,q)$. The entire region that can be eliminated corresponds to the union of all $\binom{n_c}{k}$ intersections. Given a node N under consideration, the k-trim algorithm (Figure 4.2) computes, for each subset (in turn), the residual MBR N^{resM} of N. If at some point N^{resM} becomes $\varnothing$, it prunes N and terminates. Otherwise ($N^{resM} \neq \varnothing$), it continues with the next subset, by setting $N=N^{resM}$. Similar to trim, for qualifying nodes k-trim returns the minimum distance between q and N^{resM}; for the eliminated ones it returns ∞. The only complication concerns the computation of $\cap_{i=1-k} PL\sigma_i(\sigma_i,q)$ in line 3. For this, we use a variant of [GRSY97], which returns a conservative approximation of the intersection region for each subset.

Algorithm k-trim $(q, k, \{p_1, p_2, ..., p_{n_c}\}, N)$
/* $p_1, p_2, ..., p_{n_c}$ are candidate data points, $n_c \geq k$ */
1. $N^{resM} = N$
2. for $i=1$ to $\binom{n_c}{k}$ //consider each subset in turn
    //assume the subset is $\{\sigma_1, \sigma_2, ..., \sigma_k\}$
3. $\quad N^{resM} = clipping(N^{resM}, \cap_{i=1-k} PL\sigma_i(\sigma_i,q))$
4. $\quad$ if $N^{resM} = \varnothing$ then return ∞
5. return $mindist(N^{resM}, q)$
End k-trim

Figure 4.2: The k-trim algorithm

Examining all $\binom{n_c}{k}$ subsets is prohibitive for large k and S_{cnd}. In order to reduce the cost, we can restrict the number of inspected subsets using the following heuristic. We sort all the candidates in S_{cnd} according to their Hilbert values. Let the sorted order be $\{p_1, p_2, ..., p_{n_c}\}$. Then, k-trim examines only the n_c subsets $\{p_1, ..., p_k\}$, $\{p_2, ..., p_{k+1}\}$, ..., $\{p_{n_c}, ..., p_{k-1}\}$. The rationale of this choice is that points close to each other tend to produce intersections with large areas. The trade-off is that this method may increase the number of candidates, since it fails to prune nodes that can be pruned by some non-inspected subset. In any case, as with trim, pruning with k-trim is always safe, meaning that it will never eliminate nodes that potentially contain candidates.

4.2 The k-TPL Algorithm

The filtering step of k-TPL follows exactly that of the TPL algorithm in Figure 3.6. Specifically, at the beginning, k-TPL uses BF traversal to locate a set of candidates close to the query q. After the size of S_{cnd} reaches k, k-trim prunes nodes (data points) that cannot contain (be) candidates. The pruned nodes and points are kept in S_{rfn}. The refinement step is more complex because a candidate p can only be pruned if we find k points within distance $dist(p,q)$ from p. Thus, we associate p with a counter (initially set to k), and decrease it every time we find such a point. We can eliminate p as a false hit, when its counter becomes 0. The minmaxdist pruning cannot be applied in this case, because even if $minmaxdist(p,N) < dist(p,q)$, we do not know how many points in N are within distance $dist(p,q)$ from N, unless we visit the node. Instead, we use the maxdist and the minimum cardinality of N, i.e., the smallest possible number of points in N, given the minimum node utilization (typically, 40% for R-trees) and the level of N. In particular, a candidate p can be pruned if $maxdist(p,N) < dist(p,q)$ and $min\_card(N) \geq counter(p)$. Figure 4.3 shows the pseudo-code for refinement_round in the case of RkNN. The main refinement algorithm is similar to the one shown in Figure 3.7 and omitted.

Algorithm k-refinement_round$(q, S_{cnd}, P_{rfn}, N_{rfn})$
1. for each point p in S_{cnd}
2. $\quad$ for each point p' in P_{rfn}
3. $\quad\quad$ if $dist(p,p') < dist(p,q)$
4. $\quad\quad\quad$ counter(p)--
5. $\quad\quad\quad$ if counter(p)=0
6. $\quad\quad\quad\quad$ $S_{cnd} = S_{cnd} - \{p\}$ //false hit
7. $\quad\quad\quad\quad$ goto 1 //test next candidate
8. $\quad$ for each node MBR N in N_{rfn}
9. $\quad\quad$ if $maxdist(p,N) < dist(p,q)$ and $min\_card(N) \geq counter(p)$
10. $\quad\quad\quad$ $S_{cnd} = S_{cnd} - \{p\}$; goto 1 //test next candidate
11. $\quad$ for each node MBR N in N_{rfn}
12. $\quad\quad$ if $mindist(p,N) < dist(p,q)$ add N in set $toVisit(p)$
13. $\quad$ if ($toVisit(p) = \varnothing$)
14. $\quad\quad$ $S_{cnd} = S_{cnd} - \{p\}$ and report p // actual result
End k-refinement_round

Figure 4.3: The k-refinement_round algorithm

4.3 Discussion

Although SAA was originally proposed for single RNN retrieval, it can be extended to arbitrary values of k based on the following lemma:

Lemma 2: Given a 2D RkNN query q, divide the space around q into 6 equal partitions using 6 rays emanating from q, such that each partition is bounded by two rays. Then, the k NNs of q in each partition are the only possible results of q. Further, in the worst case, all these points may be the actual results.

As a corollary, the maximum number of reverse k NNs of q in 2D space equals $6k$. Figure 4.4 illustrates the lemma using an example with $k=2$. The candidates of q include $\{p_1, p_2, p_4, p_5, p_6\}$; p_3 (i.e., the 3rd NN in S_2) cannot be a candidate, since p_1 and p_2 are both closer to it than q. Based on Lemma 2, the filtering step of SAA executes 6 constrained kNN queries in each partition. Then, the refinement step verifies or eliminates each of the $6k$ candidates by performing a kNN query. This approach, however, has the same problem as the original SAA, i.e. the number of partitions to be searched increases exponentially with the dimensionality.

As mentioned in Section 2, SFT can be adapted for RkNN by setting a large value of K ($\gg k$). Nevertheless, the concept of boolean ranges cannot be applied for arbitrary values of k for the same reason that *minmaxdist* pruning cannot be applied in our *k-refinement_round* algorithm. Thus, Singh et al. [SFT03] suggest performing the *count* query, which decides if there are at least *k* points inside the query range. Similar to boolean range queries, count queries may also access the same node multiple times, which is avoided in *k*-TPL.

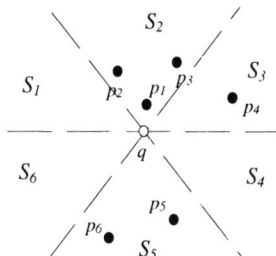

Figure 4.4: Example of Lemma 2

5. EXPERIMENTS

Our evaluation is performed using both real and synthetic data. In particular, we deploy the five real datasets summarized in Table 5.1. *LB*, *NA* and *LA* contain spatial data[3] corresponding to geometric locations in the Long Beach county, North America, and Los Angeles, respectively. *Wave*[4] is obtained from the measurements of wave directions at the National Buoy Center. *Color* includes data from the color histograms of 65k images. The synthetic data follow uniform and Zipf distributions. Their cardinalities range from 128k to 2048k (i.e., over 2 million points), and their dimensionalities vary from 2 to 5.

	LB	NA	LA	Wave	Color
dimensionality	2	2	2	3	4
cardinality	123k	569k	1314k	60k	65k

Table 5.1: Statistics of the real datasets used

Each dataset is indexed by an R*-tree [BKSS00] with node (disk page) size of 1k bytes. The capacity (i.e., the maximum number of entries in a node) equals 50, 36, 28 and 23 entries, for 2, 3, 4, and 5 dimensions, respectively. TPL is compared with SAA (for 2D data) and SFT, since as discussed in Section 2.2, these are the only methods applicable to dynamic data. For SAA, we implemented the optimization of [SAA00] that performs the six constraint NN queries (i.e., the filter step) with a single traversal of the R-tree. The filter step of SFT requires a *K*NN query, where *K* should be significantly larger than the number *k* of requested RNNs to avoid false misses[5]. In our experiments, we set *K* to $10 \cdot d \cdot k$, where *d* is the dimensionality of the dataset being examined, e.g., for single RNN in 2D space *K*=20.

The experiments investigate the effect of the following

---

[3] http://www.census.gov/geo/www/tiger/
[4] http://www.ndbc.noaa.gov/historical_data.shtml
[5] Singh et al. [SFT03], in their evaluation, used *K*=50 for single RNN retrieval.

parameters: (i) data distribution, (ii) dataset cardinality, (iii) dimensionality *d*, and (iv) *k* (for R*k*NN). The reported results represent the average cost per query for a workload of 200 queries with the same parameters. The locations of the queries are uniformly generated in the data space. The cost includes both the I/O overhead (by charging 10ms for each node access) and CPU time. All the experiments are executed on a Pentium IV CPU at 2.4GHz with 512 Mbytes memory. Section 5.1 presents the results for single RNN retrieval, and Section 5.2 discusses R*k*NN.

5.1 Results of Single RNN Search

Figure 5.1 compares the performance of TPL, SAA and SFT using real datasets. The cost of each method is divided in two parts, corresponding to the filter and refinement steps. The number above each column indicates the average percentage of I/O time in the total query cost. For TPL, we also demonstrate (in brackets) the average number of candidates retrieved by the filter step. These numbers are fixed for SAA (6) and SFT ($10 \cdot d$) and omitted. SAA is not performed on *Wave* and *Color*, because the datasets have 3 and 4 dimensions, respectively.

Clearly, TPL is the best algorithm for all datasets. The similar performance of the filter steps is due to the fact that SAA and SFT perform a 6NN or 10*d*NN query, which, in general, visits a limited number of R-tree nodes around the query point. Similarly, the pruning of TPL is very effective in low dimensional spaces. On the other hand, the refinement step of TPL is much faster than that of the other algorithms. Recall that TPL integrates the filter and refinement steps to avoid accessing the same node twice. Further, due to the small number (at most 6.2) of candidates retrieved (by the filter step), the refinement is usually accomplished with only 1 or 2 node accesses. The refinement step of SAA performs 6 NN queries, which traverse the tree multiple times, thus incurring high overhead. The boolean ranges of SFT achieve better performance (than SAA) but are less effective than the refinement step of TPL. All the algorithms are I/O bounded.

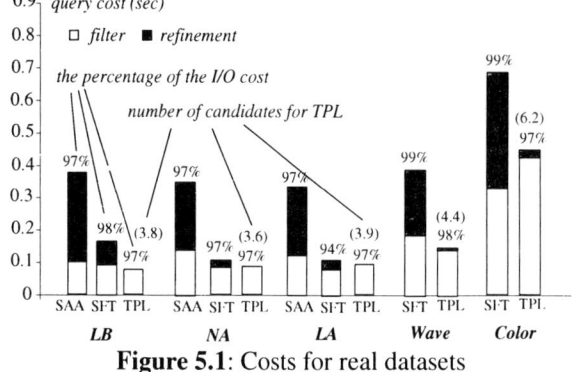

Figure 5.1: Costs for real datasets

Figure 5.2 shows the total cost of TPL and SFT as a function of the dimensionality for synthetic datasets with cardinality 512k. The performance of both algorithms degrades because, in general, R-trees become less efficient as the dimensionality grows [TS96] (due to the large overlap among the node MBRs). In addition, the number of potential candidates for TPL increases (see parenthesis on top of the TPL column), leading to higher cost, especially for the filter step. The data distribution does not have a significant effect on the performance; this observation is confirmed by all experiments (including the real data) despite the different settings.

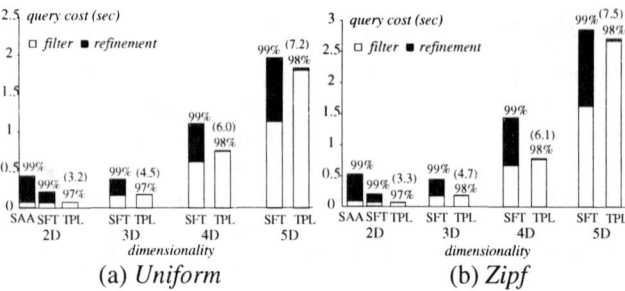

Figure 5.2: Cost vs. dimensionality (512k)

Figure 5.3 fixes the dimensionality to 3, and shows the query cost as a function of the dataset cardinality. TPL incurs around half the cost of SFT in all cases. The stepwise growth corresponds to an increase of the tree height. Specifically, for uniform data, the step occurs at 1024k, whereas for Zipf data at cardinality 2048k. The height increase has a similar effect on both algorithms.

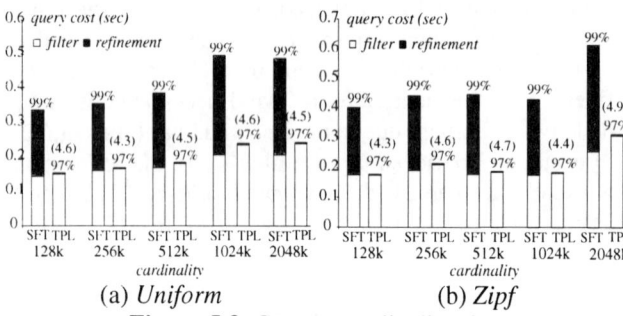

Figure 5.3: Cost vs. cardinality (3D)

5.2 Results of R*k*NN Search

Having confirmed the superiority of TPL for single RNN retrieval, we proceed to evaluate its performance for R*k*NN queries. Our implementation of TPL applies the Hilbert heuristic discussed in Section 4.1 to reduce the number of inspected subsets. Figure 5.4 illustrates the performance of alternative algorithms as a function of k (in the range [1,16]) for real datasets. SAA here refers to the R*k*NN extension discussed in Section 4.3. Similar to the diagrams in the previous section, we also demonstrate the percentage of I/O costs, and the number of candidates for TPL. As expected, the overhead of each algorithm grows with k, due to the significant increase in CPU time (observe that the I/O percentage decreases with k). TPL again outperforms its competitors, and the difference

increases with k. Note that for the 2D datasets, the average number of candidates retrieved by TPL is smaller than 4 for k=1 and increases almost linearly with k.

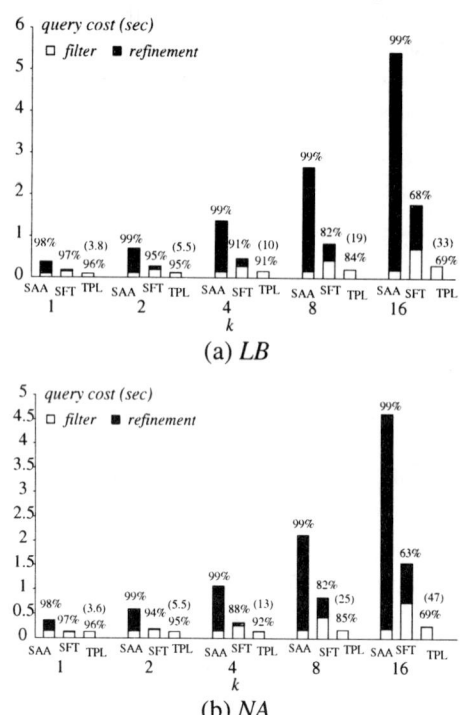

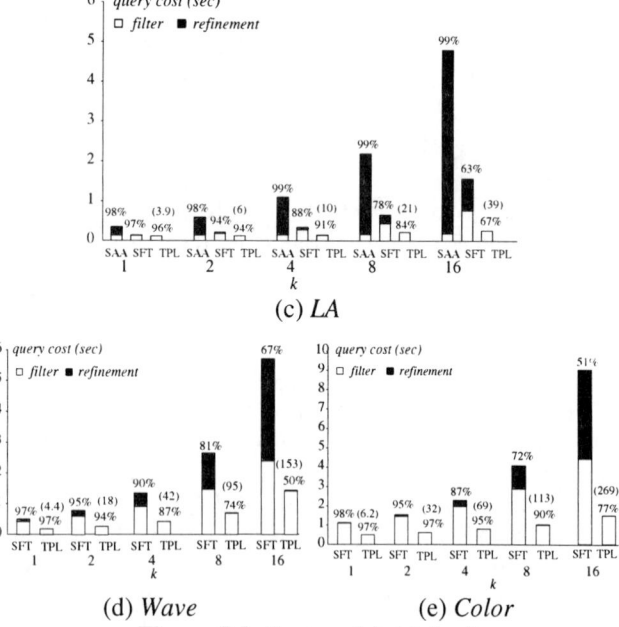

Figure 5.4: Cost vs. k (real data)

Next we explore the effects of dimensionality and cardinality using synthetic data. In the following experiments, k is fixed to its median value 4. Figure 5.5 shows the performance as a function of dimensionality for uniform (Figure 5.5a) and Zipf (Figure 5.5b) distributions, respectively (the cardinality is set to 512k). The diagrams and their explanations are similar to those in Figure 5.2.

The last set of experiments (Figure 5.6) illustrates the query overhead as a function of cardinality (the dimensionality equals 3), confirming the observations of Figure 5.3.

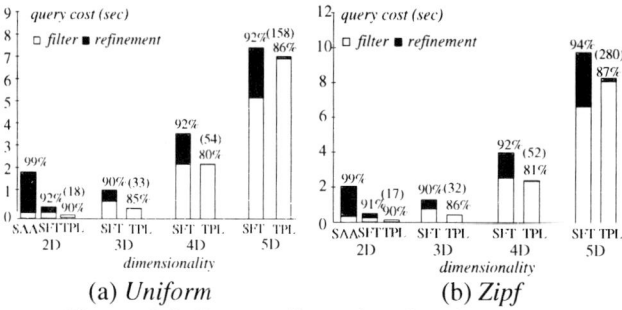

(a) *Uniform* (b) *Zipf*
Figure 5.5: Cost vs. dimensionality (*k*=4, 512k)

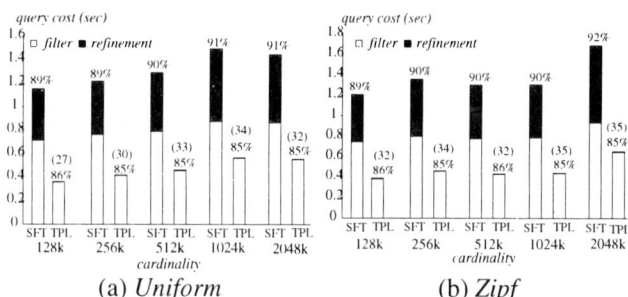

(a) *Uniform* (b) *Zipf*
Figure 5.6: Cost vs. cardinality (*k*=4, 3D)

6. CONCLUSIONS

The existing algorithms for RNN search are applicable only in restricted scenarios. This paper develops the first general methodology for retrieval of an arbitrary number of reverse nearest neighbors in multiple dimensions. In addition to its applicability and flexibility, our solution is better than the previous approaches also in terms of efficiency and scalability. An interesting direction for future work is to adapt the proposed methodology to other variations of RNN problems. Further, currently there does not exist any cost model for estimating the execution time of RNN techniques. The development of such a model will not only facilitate query optimization, but may also reveal new problem characteristics that could lead to even faster algorithms.

ACKNOWLEDGMENTS

This work was supported by grant HKUST 6180/03E from Hong Kong RGC. We would like to thank Kyriakos Mouratidis for proof-reading the paper.

REFERENCES

[BJKS02] Benetis, R., Jensen, C., Karciauskas, G., Saltenis, S. Nearest Neighbor and Reverse Nearest Neighbor Queries for Moving Objects. *IDEAS*, 2002.

[BKK96] Berchtold, S., Keim, D., Kriegel, H. The X-tree: An Index Structure for High-Dimensional Data. *VLDB*, 1996.

[BKOS97] Berg, M., Kreveld, M., Overmars, M., Schwarzkopf, O. Computational Geometry: Algorithms and Applications. ISBN 3-540-65620-0. *Springer*, 1997

[BKSS90] Beckmann, N., Kriegel, H.P., Schneider, R., Seeger, B. The R*-tree: An Efficient and Robust Access Method for Points and Rectangles. *SIGMOD*, 1990.

[CF98] Cheung, K., Fu, A. Enhanced Nearest Neighbour Search on the R-tree. *SIGMOD Record* 27(3): 16-21, 1998.

[FSAA01] Ferhatosmanoglu, H., Stanoi, I., Agrawal, D., Abbadi, A. Constrained Nearest Neighbor Queries. *SSTD*, 2001.

[G84] Guttman, A. R-trees: A Dynamic Index Structure for Spatial Searching. *SIGMOD*, 1984.

[GRSY97] Goldstein, J., Ramakrishnan, R., Shaft, U., Yu, J. Processing Queries By Linear Constraints. *PODS*, 1997.

[H94] Henrich, A. A Distance Scan Algorithm for Spatial Access Structures. *ACM GIS*, 1994.

[HS99] Hjaltason, G., Samet, H. Distance Browsing in Spatial Databases. *TODS*, 24(2), 265-318, 1999.

[KM00] Korn, F., Muthukrishnan, S. Influence Sets Based on Reverse Nearest Neighbor Queries. *SIGMOD*, 2000.

[KMS02] Korn, F., Muthukrishnan, S. Srivastava, D. Reverse Nearest Neighbor Aggregates Over Data Streams. *VLDB*, 2002.

[LNY03] Lin, K., Nolen, M., Yang, C. Applying Bulk Insertion Techniques for Dynamic Reverse Nearest Neighbor Problems. *IDEAS*, 2003.

[MVZ02] Maheshwari, A., Vahrenhold, J., Zeh, N. On Reverse Nearest Neighbor Queries. *CCCG*, 2002.

[RKV95] Roussopoulos, N., Kelly, S., Vincent, F. Nearest Neighbor Queries. *SIGMOD*, 1995.

[SAA00] Stanoi, I., Agrawal, D., Abbadi, A., Reverse Nearest Neighbor Queries for Dynamic Databases. *SIGMOD* Workshop on Research Issues in Data Mining and Knowledge Discovery, 2000.

[SFT03] Singh, A., Ferhatosmanoglu, H., Tosun, A. High Dimensional Reverse Nearest Neighbor Queries. *CIKM*, 2003.

[SRAA01] Stanoi, I., Riedewald, M., Agrawal, D., Abbadi, A. Discovery of Influence Sets in Frequently Updated Databases. *VLDB*, 2001.

[TS96] Theodoridis, Y., Sellis, T. A Model for the Prediction of R-tree Performance. *PODS*, 1996.

[YL01] Yang, C., Lin, K. An Index Structure for Efficient Reverse Nearest Neighbor Queries. *ICDE*, 2001.

GORDER: An Efficient Method for KNN Join Processing

Chenyi Xia[1]　　Hongjun Lu[2]　　Beng Chin Ooi[1]　　Jing Hu[1]

[1] Department of Computer Science, National University of Singapore, {xiacheny, ooibc, hujing}@comp.nus.edu.sg
[2] Department of Computer Science, Hong Kong University of Science and Technology, luhj@cs.ust.hk

Abstract

An important but very expensive primitive operation of high-dimensional databases is the K-Nearest Neighbor (KNN) similarity join. The operation combines each point of one dataset with its KNNs in the other dataset and it provides more meaningful query results than the range similarity join. Such an operation is useful for data mining and similarity search.

In this paper, we propose a novel KNN-join algorithm, called the *Gorder* (or the G-ordering KNN) join method. *Gorder* is a block nested loop join method that exploits sorting, join scheduling and distance computation filtering and reduction to reduce both I/O and CPU costs. It sorts input datasets into the *G-order* and applied the *scheduled block nested loop join* on the G-ordered data. The distance computation reduction is employed to further reduce CPU cost. It is simple and yet efficient, and handles high-dimensional data efficiently. Extensive experiments on both synthetic cluster and real life datasets were conducted, and the results illustrate that Gorder is an efficient KNN-join method and outperforms existing methods by a wide margin.

1 Introduction

K-nearest neighbor join (KNN-join) is a new operation proposed recently [5]. The operation combines each point of one dataset with its K-nearest neighbors in another dataset. With its set-a-time nature, KNN-join can be used to efficiently support various applications where multidimensional data is involved.

In particular, it is identified that many standard algorithms in almost all stages of knowledge discovery process can be accelerated by including KNN-join as a primitive operation. For examples,

- In each iteration of the well-known k-means clustering process, the nearest cluster centroid is computed for each data point. A data point is assigned to its new nearest cluster if the previously assigned cluster centroid is different from the currently computed one. A KNN-join with $k = 1$ between the data points and the cluster centroids can thus be applied to find all the nearest centroid for all data points in one operation.

- In the first step of LOF [7] (a density-based outlier detection method), the K-nearest neighbors for every point in the input dataset are materialized. This can be achieved by a single self KNN-join of the dataset.

- In the hierarchical clustering method called Chameleon [18], a KNN-graph (a graph linking each point of a dataset to its K-nearest neighbors) is constructed before the partitioning algorithm is applied to generate clusters. The KNN-join can also be used to generate the KNN-graph.

Compared to the traditional point-at-a-time approach that computes the K-nearest neighbors for all data points one by one, the set oriented KNN-join can accelerate the computation dramatically[4].

In this paper, we study the efficient processing of the KNN-join. To the best of our knowledge, the MuX KNN-join [5, 4] is the only up-to-date algorithm specifically designed for KNN-join. MuX [6] is essentially an R-tree based method designed to satisfy the conflicting optimization requirements of CPU and I/O cost. It employs large-sized pages (the hosting page) to optimize I/O time and uses the secondary structure, the buckets which are MBRs (minimum bounding boxes) of much smaller size, to partition the data with finer granularity so that CPU cost can be reduced.

MuX iterates over the R pages, and for R page in the memory, potential KNN-joinable pages in S are retrieved through MuX index on S and searched for K-nearest neighbors. Since MuX makes use of an index to reduce the number of data pages retrieved, it suffers as an R-tree based join algorithm. First, like the R-tree, its performance is expected to degenerate with the increase of data dimensionality. Second, the memory overhead of the MuX index

Permission to copy without fee all or part of this material is granted provided that the copies are not made or distributed for direct commercial advantage, the VLDB copyright notice and the title of the publication and its date appear, and notice is given that copying is by permission of the Very Large Data Base Endowment. To copy otherwise, or to republish, requires a fee and/or special permission from the Endowment.

**Proceedings of the 30th VLDB Conference,
Toronto, Canada, 2004**

structure is high for large high-dimensional data due to the space requirement of high-dimensional minimum bounding boxes. Both constraints restrict the scalability of the MuX KNN-join method in terms of dimensionality and data size.

In this paper, we propose a novel KNN-join algorithm, the *Gorder* (or the G-ordering KNN) join method. *Gorder* is a block nested loop join method which achieves its efficiency by sorting data based on an ordering that enables effective join pruning, data blocks scheduling and distance computation filtering and reduction. It first sorts input datasets into the *G-order* (an order based on grid), so that the the dataset can be partitioned into blocks that are amenable for efficient scheduling for join processing. Then, it applies the *scheduled block nested loop join* to find the K-nearest neighbors for each block of R data points. Gorder is efficient due to the following factors: (1) It inherits the strength of the block nested loop join in being able to reduce random reads. (2) It prunes away unpromising data blocks from probing to save both I/O and similarity computation costs by exploiting the property of the G-ordered data. (3) It utilizes a *two-tiers partitioning strategy* to optimize I/O and CPU time separately. (4) It reduces distance computational cost by pruning redundant computation based the distance of fewer dimensions.

Our contributions can be summarized as follows.

- We developed a novel algorithm *Gorder* for an important operation KNN-join, that requires no index for the source data sets.

- A comprehensive performance study was conducted experimentally that indicates the efficiency, scalability and robustness of the proposed algorithm.

Note that it is widely recognized that most high-dimensional indexes do not scale up well, and in fact, many perform worse than sequential scan when the dimensionality is high. KNN join further escalates the complexity and search cost of a high-dimensional index. We therefore developed the join method based on the block nested loop join, however, enhanced it with sorting, data scheduling, and distance computation filtering and reduction to attain good KNN-join performance.

The remainder of the paper is organized as follows. Section 2 defines the KNN-join problem and investigates its properties and reviews some related work. Section 3 presents the algorithm Gorder, including its data scheduling and distance computation pruning and reduction techniques to optimize the both I/O and CPU time. A cost analysis is also given. Section 4 describes a performance study and presents the experimental results. Finally, Section 5 concludes the paper.

2 Preliminary

2.1 KNN Join

In this section, we define the KNN-join problem formally and identify its properties.

Definition 2.1 (KNN-join) *Given two data sets R and S, an integer K and the similarity metric $dist()$, the KNN-join of R and S, denoted as $R \ltimes_{KNN} S$, returns pairs of points (p_i, q_j) such that p_i is from the outer dataset R and q_j from the inner dataset S, and q_j is one of the K-nearest neighbors of p_i.*

Essentially, the KNN-join combines each point of the outer dataset R with its K-nearest neighbors from the inner dataset S. A data point in our study is a multi-dimensional feature vector corresponding to a complex object such as an image. The distance metric in our consideration is the L_ρ metric, where

$$dist(p,q) = \left(\sum_{i=1}^{d} |p.x_i - q.x_i|^\rho\right)^{1/\rho}, \quad 1 \leq \rho \leq \infty$$

For demonstration purposes, we shall use the most commonly used metric, the square of L_2 (the Euclidean distance). The proposed technique can be adapted to other L_ρ metrics such as the Manhattan distance (L_1) and the maximum distance (L_∞) straightforwardly. In the rest of the paper, we use R to symbolize the outer dataset and S the inner dataset.

KNN-join has following properties:

1. It is asymmetric, that is, $(R \ltimes_{KNN} S \not\Leftrightarrow S \ltimes_{KNN} R)$. The reason is that the K-nearest neighbor is asymmetric.

2. The cardinality of the answer set of a KNN-join is predictable, since a KNN-join returns K-nearest neighbors for each point of R.

3. The distance from each point in R to its nearest neighbors is unknown apriori.

Property 2 makes KNN-join more useful than another similarity join – the range-join in situations where a good range ε cannot be determined easily. The range-join returns pairs of points from two data sets with their similarity distance not exceeding a given value. One of the difficulties to use similarity range-join in real application is that the distribution of data points are often unknown and giving an appropriate similarity distance threshold between points is rather difficult, if not impossible. As such the results of similarity range-join are somehow unpredictable that requires applications run on trial-and-error basis.

Property 3 inherits the difficulty of the nearest neighbor query. In order to filter unnecessary distance computation, popular algorithms based on an index such as the R-tree [12] (the RKV [14, 23] and the HS [23]) compute the MinDist (minimum distance between the query point and a node of the R-tree) and choose to traverse the node with the minimum MinDist first. The MinDist is also compared with the pruning distance (the distance between the query point and its Kth nearest neighbor candidate). Nodes with MinDist greater than the pruning distance is pruned away.

Nearest neighbor search, which is I/O bound, has been well studied. KNN-join raises new challenges, just as join to selection in relational databases. We have two starting points as the devising of the KNN-join algorithm.

1) indexed-based multiple KNN query (index nested loop join)

2) block sequential search (block nested loop join).

Both have its strength and weakness. The index-based multiple KNN query is optimized for the CPU cost, however, introduces tremendous I/O time because of large number of random accesses[5]. In addition, as a well-known fact, the index often fails in high-dimensional space, where it performs worse off than sequential scan. On the contrary, the block sequential search is optimized for I/O time. However, without any distance computation pruning, the CPU cost is enormous and the number of distance computation is $|R| \cdot |S|$. Gorder optimizes the block nested loop join with efficient data scheduling and distance computation filtering.

For ease of discussion, in the following, we assume that the data space is a unit hypercube $[0..1]^d$.

2.2 Related Work

Apart from the MuX join method introduced in the introduction, we shall briefly review existing work on similarity join. Most existing techniques have been proposed to support the similarity *range-join* (also known as the distance join[13]). They can be broadly classified into three categories. In the first category, the join methods utilize indexing structures, and examples include the R-tree Spatial Join (RSJ) [8], the breadth first R-tree join [15], the incremental distance join [13] and the MuX range-join [6]. These methods traverse the indexes of R and S synchronously and form joining pairs according to the lower bounding property of the minimum bounding rectangle (MBR). The second category of techniques are hash-based. Examples include the Spatial Hash Join [20] and the Partition-based Spatial Merge Join [21] which partition the data space into buckets and perform the join on pairs of buckets in a recursive manner. The major drawback of such techniques is that the data replication rate grows quickly as dimensionality increases. The third category of techniques are sort-based. The Multi-dimensional Spatial Join (MSJ) [19], GESS [10], and the Epsilon Grid Order (EGO)[3] all belong to this category. [13] introduced the method to use the incremental distance join to support the distance semi-join (similar to the KNN-join) directly by discarding pairs reported by the distance join. However, due to the difficulty in pre-determining the search radius in the KNN-join, the direct application of range-join algorithms to the KNN-join or the implementation of KNN-join as iterative range join is inefficient and I/O expensive.

3 Gorder

We now introduce Gorder KNN-join, a simple yet efficient KNN-join algorithm based on ordering according to grid

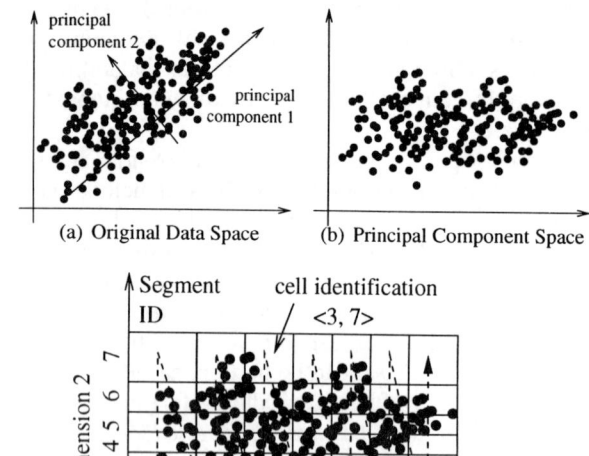

Figure 1: Illustration of G-ordering.

– the *G-ordering*. It is a block nested loop method which achieves its efficiency by exploiting sorting, data scheduling and distance computation reduction. As shown in Algorithm 1, it consists two phases. In the first phase (line 1), it sorts the input datasets R and S based on the *G-ordering*. In the second phase (line 2), it performs the *scheduled block nested loop join* on the G-ordered data and outputs the join results. We describe the algorithm in detail in this section.

Algorithm 1 Gorder_KNN(R, S)
Input:
   R and S are two data sets.
Description:
1: G_Ordering R and S;
2: Join_Grid_Ordered_Data(R, S);

3.1 G-ordering

In relational databases, sorting is used not only to arrange the tuples according to an order, but to group tuples with the same value on the joining attribute together to facilitate processing based on partitions. Similarly in Gorder, we design an ordering based on grid called the *G-ordering* to group nearby data points together, so that in the *scheduled block nested loop join* phase we can identify the partition of a block of G-ordered data and schedule it for join.

As illustrated in Figure 1, the G-ordering has two steps – the PCA (principal component analysis) transformation and the *Grid Order* sorting.

The first step of G-ordering performs the principal component analysis [17] on the input datasets R and S together and transform the original data into the principal component space. PCA captures the variance in the dataset and determines the directions along which the data exhibit high variance. After PCA processing, most of the information in the original space is condenses into the first few dimensions along which the variances in the data distribution are the largest. The first principal component (or dimension) accounts for as much of the variability in the data as possible, and each succeeding component accounts for as much of the remaining variability as possible.

The secondary step of G-ordering sorts R and S into the *Grid Order*. The Grid Order applies a grid onto the data space and partitions it into l^d rectangular cells, where l is the number of segments per dimension of the grid. Figure 1 (c) is an illustration of a two-dimensional space partitioned by a 7x7 grid. Cell length of the grid can be equal or variable. In the following discussions, we assume the cells are of same length $\frac{1}{l}$ for the simplicity of presentation, while the methods can be easily generalized to the grid with variable cell length.

We define the *identification vector* of cell as a d-dimensional vector $\nu = <s_1, ..., s_d>$, where s_i is the segment number to which the cell belongs on the ith dimension. Based on the identification vector of the cell, the cells can be ordered lexicographically as illustrated in Figure 1.

The *Grid Order* is defined as below.

Definition 3.1 (Grid order $\prec_g$) *Given a grid which partitions the d-dimensional data space into l^d rectangular cells, points $p_m \prec_g p_n$ if and only $\nu_m \prec \nu_n$, where ν_m (ν_n) is the cell surrounding point p_m.*

$\nu_m \prec \nu_n$ if and only if a dimension k exists that, $\nu_m.s_k < \nu_n.s_k$ and $\nu_m.s_j = \nu_n.s_j$, for $\forall j < k$.

Essentially, the grid order is to sort the data points according to the cell surrounding the point, so after the second phase of G-ordering, points within the same cell are grouped together.

The G-ordered data exhibit two interesting properties:

1. Suppose we have two points p and q in the dataset in the original d-dimensional space. Let $p_k(q_k)$ denote the projection of the point p (q) on the first k dimensions after G-ordering. Because the first few dimensions are most important, $dist(p_k, q_k)$ can be very near to the actual distance between p and q [9].

2. Given a block of G-ordered data B containing m points $p_1,...,p_m$, we can calculate a *bounding box* which covers all points in that block by examining the first point p_1 and last point p_m of the ordered data.

To compute the *bounding box*, we first calculate the *active dimension* [3] of the G-ordered data.

Definition 3.2 (Active Dimension of the G-order Data) *Assume ν_1 (ν_m) is the identification vector of the cell surrounding $p_1(p_m)$, dimension α is the* active dimension *of the G-ordered data B, if*

(1) $\nu_1.s_\alpha < \nu_m.s_\alpha$
(2) $\nu_1.s_j = \nu_m.s_j \quad \forall j < \alpha$.

Literally, α is the first dimension that $\nu_1.s_j < \nu_m.s_j$ ($1 \leq j \leq d$).

The bounding box of B is represented by the low-left point E = $<e_1, ..., e_d>$ and high-right point T = $<t_1, ..., t_d>$.

$$e_k = \begin{cases} (\nu_1.s_k - 1) \cdot \frac{1}{l} & if \quad 1 \leq k \leq \alpha \\ 0 & if \quad k > \alpha \end{cases}$$

$$t_k = \begin{cases} \nu_m.s_k \cdot \frac{1}{l} & if \quad 1 \leq k \leq \alpha \\ 1 & if \quad k > \alpha \end{cases}$$

The properties of the G-ordered data are used effectively in Gorder for join scheduling and distance computation reduction. Property 1 implicates that the partial distance of the first k dimensions between two points can approximate the real distance effectively and Property 2 will be used to measure the similarity of two blocks of G-ordered data and schedule the data for joining.

3.2 Scheduled Block Nested Loop Join

In the second phase of Gorder, G-ordered data of R and S are examined for joining. The join stage of Gorder is characterized by two properties. First, Gorder employs the *two-tier partitioning strategy* to optimize the I/O time and CPU time separately. Secondarily, it schedules the data for joining in order to optimize the KNN processing.

The *first-tier partitioning* is optimized for I/O time. Gorder partitions the G-ordered input datasets into blocks consisting of several physical pages. Suppose we allocate n_r and n_s buffer pages for the data of R and S, we partition R and S into blocks of the allocated buffer sizes. The blocks of R are loaded into memory sequentially and iteratively one block at a time and the S blocks are loaded into memory in the sequence scheduled based on their similarity to the R data in buffer. This loading of multiple pages at a time is efficient in terms of I/O time as it significantly reduces seek overhead. In addition, in order to optimize the KNN processing, it schedules the S blocks so that the S blocks that are most likely to yield K nearest neighbors can be loaded into memory and joined with R data in buffer early.

The large block size reduces disk seek time, however, as a side effect, it may introduce additional CPU cost due to redundant pair-wise checking of tuples for KNN-join. To overcome such a problem, we introduce the second-tier partitioning in memory. The *second-tier partitioning* segments the R and S data in memory into blocks of much smaller size (the sub-blocks). The optimized size of the sub-block is 20–50 data points according to our experiment results. Again, similarity of two blocks data of R and S is used to schedule the join sequence and filter distance computation between blocks of data.

We measure the similarity of two blocks of G-ordered data by the distance between their *bounding boxes*. As presented in Section 3.1, the *bounding box* of a block of G-ordered data can be computed by examining the first and last points of the G-ordered data.

Definition 3.3 (MinDist of G-ordered Data) *The minimum distance of two blocks of G-ordered data B_r and B_s, denoted as MinDist(B_r, B_s) is defined as the minimum distance between their bounding boxes.*

$$MinDist(B_r, B_s) = \sum_{k=1}^{d} d_k^2$$

$$d_k = max(b_k - u_k, 0) \quad (1)$$

$$b_k = max(B_r.e_k, B_s.e_k); \quad u_k = min(B_r.t_k, B_s.t_k)$$

For blocks with same MinDist, they are sorted by the MaxDist.

Definition 3.4 (MaxDist of G-ordered Data) *The maximum distance of two blocks of G-ordered data B_r and B_s, denoted as MaxDist(B_r, B_s) is defined as the maximum distance between their bounding boxes.*

$$MaxDist(B_r, B_s) = \sum_{k=1}^{d} (u_k - b_k)^2$$

$$b_k = min(B_r.e_k, B_s.e_k); \quad u_k = max(B_r.t_k, B_s.t_k)$$

A direct observation is that MinDist is a lower bound to the distance of any two points from blocks of R and S respectively. The following corollary follows this observation directly.

Corollary 3.1 *For point p_r in block B_r and point p_s in block B_s, $MinDist(B_r, B_s)$ is a lower bound to the distance between p_r and p_s, that is,*

$$\forall p_r \in B_r, p_s \in B_s, \quad MinDist(B_r, B_s) \leq dist(p_r, p_s)$$

Based on Corollary 3.1, we have following pruning strategies:

1. If $MinDist(B_r, B_s)$ > pruning distance of p, B_s does not contain any points belonging to the k-nearest neighbors of the point p, and therefore the distance computation between p and points in B_s can be filtered. Pruning distance of a point p is the distance between p and its Kth nearest neighbor candidate. Initially, it is ∞.

2. If $MinDist(B_r, B_s)$ > pruning distance of B_r, B_s does not contain any points belonging to the k-nearest neighbors of any points in B_r, and hence the join of B_r and B_s can be pruned away. The pruning distance of an R block is the maximum pruning distance of the R points inside.

Algorithm 2 Join_Grid_Ordered_Data(R, S)
Input:
　R and S are two G-ordered data sets that have been partitioned into blocks.
Description:
1:　**for** each block $B_r \in R$ **do**
2:　　ReadBlock(B_r);
3:　　SortBlocks(S, B_r);
4:　　**for** each $B_s \in$ NotPruned(S, B_r) **do**
5:　　　ReadBlock(B_s);
6:　　　MemoryJoin(B_r, B_s);
7:　　OutputKNN(B_r);

Algorithm 2 outlines the scheduled block nested loop join algorithm of Gorder. It loads blocks of R into memory sequentially (lines 1-2). For the R block in memory B_r, S blocks are sorted in the increasing order of their distance to B_r (line 3).[1] At the same time, blocks with $MinDist(B_r, B_s)$ greater than the pruning distance of B_r are pruned (pruning strategy 2). That is, only the remaining blocks are loaded into memory one by one (lines 4-5). With each pair of R and S block, we join them in memory by calling function $MemoryJoin$ (line 6). After all unpruned S blocks are processed with B_r, the KNN candidate sets for points in B_r are output as the join results (line 7).

Algorithm 3 MemoryJoin(B_r, B_s)
Input:
　B_r and B_s are two blocks from R and S respectively.
Description:
1:　Divide B_r, B_s into sub-blocks;
2:　**for** each sub-block $B'_r \in B_r$ **do**
3:　　SortBlocks(B_s, B'_r);
4:　　**for** each sub-block $B'_s \in$ NotPruned(B_s, B'_r) **do**
5:　　　**for** each point $p_r \in B'_r$ **do**
6:　　　　**if** MinDist(B'_r, B'_s) $\leq$ PrunDist(p_r) **then**
7:　　　　　**for** each point $p_s \in B'_s$ **do**
8:　　　　　　ComputeDist(p_s, p_r, d_α^2);

The memory join algorithm is shown in Algorithm 3. Both R-block and S-block are divided into sub-blocks (line 1). For each R sub-block B'_r, the S sub-blocks are arranged according to their distance to B'_r. Pruning strategy 2 is again used to pruning those S sub-blocks with MinDist(B'_r, B'_s) greater than the pruning distance of B'_r. Those unpruned S sub-blocks participate the join with R sub-blocks one by one (lines 4-5). To join R and S sub-block B'_r and B'_s, each data point p_r in B'_r is compared with B'_s. For each point p_r in B'_r, we examine whether MinDist(B'_r, B'_s) is greater than the pruning distance of p_r. If true, by pruning strategy 1, B'_s cannot contain any points

---

[1] Note that after the G-ordering, the bounding box for each block of S is kept in in memory, so the sorting doesn't require any disk accesses. The memory for recording the bounding boxes is very limited as there are only a small number of blocks.

that are K-nearest neighbors of p_r and so the B'_s can be skipped (lines 6-7). Otherwise, function *Compute_Dist* is called for p_r and each data point p_s in B'_s (line 8). Function *Compute_Dist*, as described in the following subsection, inserts those p_s with $dist(p_r, p_s)$ smaller than the pruning distance of p_r into the KNN candidate set of p_r. d_α^2 is the distance between the bounding boxes of B'_r and B'_s on the α-th dimension,[2] where $\alpha = min(B'_r.\alpha, B'_s.\alpha)$.

3.3 Distance Computation

Distance computation reduction is important for optimization of CPU time because of the complexity of the distance metric and the high-dimensional data.

The bounding boxes of the G-ordered data has some special properties which we can utilize for distance computation reduction.

Property 3.1 *The edge of the bounding box of a block G-ordered data B extends the full domain from 0 to 1 on dimension j ($j > B.\alpha$), where $B.\alpha$ is the active dimension of B.*

This property is directly observable from the computation of *bounding box*. Therefore, when we compute the similarity of two blocks of G-ordered data, we only need to take the first α dimensions into account, where $\alpha=min(B_1.\alpha, B_2.\alpha)$ and $B_1.\alpha$ ($B_2.\alpha$) is the active dimension B_1 (B_2). As a result, the computation of MinDist and MaxDist are reduced to:

$$MinDist(B_1, B_2) = MinDist(B_{1,\alpha}, B_{2,\alpha})$$
$$MaxDist(B_1, B_2) = MaxDist(B_{1,\alpha}, B_{2,\alpha}) + d - \alpha$$

$B_{1,\alpha}$ ($B_{2,\alpha}$) is the projection of B_1 (B_2) on the first α dimensions.

The next important property of the *bounding box* is as follows:

Property 3.2 *The projection of the bounding box of a block of G-ordered data B containing m points $p_1,...,p_m$ on the first $B.\alpha - 1$ dimensions is corresponding to a grid cell in the first $B.\alpha - 1$ dimensions.*

The reason is, according to the definition of *Grid Order*, $p_1 \prec_g ... \prec_g p_m \Leftrightarrow \nu_1 \prec ... \prec \nu_m$, where ν_k is the cell surrounding point p_k. Based on the definition of *active dimension*, $\nu_1.s_j = \nu_m.s_j$ ($\forall j < B.\alpha$), so we have $\nu_1.s_j = ... = \nu_m.s_j$ ($\forall j < B.\alpha$).

This property indicates that the projection of all points in a block of G-ordered data B on the first $B.\alpha - 1$ dimensions are within one grid cell in the first $B.\alpha - 1$ dimensions. Hence, for any points p and q from B_1 and B_2 respectively, $MinDist(B_{1,\alpha-1}, B_{2,\alpha-1})$ can be used to approximate the distance between the projection of p and q on the first $\alpha - 1$ dimensions when the grid is of fine granularity. The approximated distance is the low bound of the real distance. That is,

[2] Refer to Equation 1 in Definition 3.3.

$MinDist(B_{1,\alpha-1}, B_{2,\alpha-1}) \approx dist(p_{\alpha-1}, q_{\alpha-1})$. $p_{\alpha-1}$ ($q_{\alpha-1}$) is the projection of p (q) on the first $\alpha - 1$ dimensions.

Based on the above two properties, we now are able to define the pruning strategy based on the approximate distance as formalized by the following corollary.

Corollary 3.2 *For any point p and q from the G-ordered blocks B_r and B_s respectively, if $MinDist(B_{r,\alpha-1}, B_{s,\alpha-1}) + dist(p_{\{\alpha,k\}}, q_{\{\alpha,k\}})(\alpha \leq k \leq d)$ is greater than the pruning distance of p, q cannot be a K-nearest neighbor candidate of p, where $\alpha = min(B_r.\alpha, B_s.\alpha)$ and $p_{\{i,j\}}$ ($q_{\{i,j\}}$) is the projection of p (q) on the dimensions from i to j.*

Algorithm 4 Compute_Dist (p, q, d_α^2)

Input:

  p, q are two data points from B_r and B_s respectively. d_α^2 is the distance between the bounding boxes of B_r and B_s on the α-th dimension.[2]

Description:

1: $pdist := MinDist(B_r, B_s) - d_\alpha^2$;
2: **for** $k := \alpha$ to d **do**
3:    pdist :=pdist+ $(p.x_k - q.x_k)^2$;
4:    **if** $pdist >$ pruning distance of p **then**
5:      Prune q;
6: $pdist := pdist - (MinDist(B_r, B_s) - d_\alpha^2)$;
7: **for** k:=1 to α-1 **do**
8:    pdist :=pdist+ $(p.x_k - q.x_k)^2$;
9:    **if** $pdist >$ pruning distance of p **then**
10:      Prune q;
11: Insert q into the KNN candidate set of p;

Algorithm 4 outlines the algorithm in reducing distance computation. It calculates $MinDist(B_{r,\alpha-1}, B_{s,\alpha-1})$ from $MinDist(B_r, B_s)$ first (line 1). Then, it accumulates the distance between p and q from dimension α, where $\alpha=min(B_r.\alpha, B_s.\alpha)$ (lines 2-5). Whenever $pdist$ is greater than the pruning distance of p, q cannot be one of the K-nearest neighbors of p and can be pruned away (lines 4-5). If q cannot be pruned by the approximation distance, we remove the approximation factor (line 6) and calculate their real distance (lines 7-10). If $dist(p,q)$ is smaller than the pruning distance of p, q is inserted into the KNN candidate set of p.

3.4 Analysis of Gorder

The Gorder algorithm produces KNN-join results correctly. Firstly, the MinDist of two blocks of G-ordered data is the low bound to the distance of any two points from these two blocks respectively (Corollary 3.1). Secondly, Gorder only skips the S blocks (sub-blocks) whose MinDist from the R block (sub-blocks) is greater than the pruning distance of R block (sub-blocks). Finally, the reduced distance computation only prunes away S data points that are not one of the K-nearest neighbors of a R point (Corollary 3.2). Hence,

761

for all blocks of R data, Gorder finds the correct K-nearest neighbors.

Now we analyse the I/O and CPU cost of Gorder. Suppose the number of R (S) data pages is N_r (N_s). In the G-ordering phase, the PCA transformation needs to perform the sequential scan of R and S twice. The cost is $2(N_r + N_s)$. Suppose that there are B buffer pages available in memory, the sorting step of the G-ordering requires

$$2N_r \left(\left\lceil log_{B-1} \frac{N_r}{B} \right\rceil + 1 \right) + 2N_s \left(\left\lceil log_{B-1} \frac{N_s}{B} \right\rceil + 1 \right)$$

page accesses using the external merge sort algorithm [22].

In the *scheduled block nested loop join* phase, suppose we allocate n_r buffer pages to R data and n_s buffer pages to S data. The I/O cost is

$$N_r + \frac{N_r}{n_r} \cdot N_s \cdot \gamma_1$$

where γ_1 is the selectivity of the S blocks. Consequently, the total I/O cost in terms of the number of page accesses is:

$$2(N_r + N_s) + + N_r + \frac{N_r}{n_r} \cdot N_s \cdot \gamma_1$$
$$+ 2N_r \left(\left\lceil log_{B-1} \frac{N_r}{B} \right\rceil + 1 \right) + 2N_s \left(\left\lceil log_{B-1} \frac{N_s}{B} \right\rceil + 1 \right)$$

The major CPU cost of Gorder is the distance computation in the *scheduled block nested loop join* phase. The number of distance computation is:

$$P_r \cdot P_s \cdot \gamma_2$$

where P_r (P_s) is the number of points of R (S), γ_2 is the selectivity of distance computation. The PCA processing of G-ordering performs $(N_r + N_s) \cdot d^2$ multiply [11]. However, the multiply and comparison operations incurred in the G-ordering phase are comparatively much less significant.

We estimate the selectivity ratio γ_1 and γ_2 using the Minkowski Sum model proposed in [2] and [6] which has been shown to be effective in high-dimensional data.

$$\gamma = \sum_{k=0}^{d} \left(\sum_{\{i_1...i_k \in 2^{\{0...d-1\}}\}} \left(\prod_{j=1}^{k} a_{i_j} \right) \right) \cdot V_{sphere}^{d-k}(\varepsilon) \quad (2)$$

$$V_{sphere}^{d-k}(\varepsilon) = \frac{\sqrt{\pi^{d-k}}}{\Gamma\left(\frac{d-k}{2} + 1\right)} \cdot \varepsilon^{d-k} \quad (3)$$

$$\varepsilon = \sqrt[d]{\frac{K \cdot \Gamma(d/2 + 1)}{N_S}} \cdot \frac{1}{\sqrt{\pi}} \quad (4)$$

where, $\Gamma(x+1) = x\Gamma(x)$, $\Gamma(1) = 1$, $\Gamma(1/2) = \sqrt{\pi}$.

Following the analysis in [2], we simplify Equation 2 by approximating the *bounding boxes* with the hypercube. Therefore,

Parameter	Default Setting
number of nearest neighbors (K)	10
buffer size	around 10% of total size of R and S
size of R data in buffer	around 20% of buffer
number of segments per dimension	32
buffer page size	8192

Table 1: Default parameter values.

$$\gamma = \sum_{k=0}^{d} \binom{d}{k} \left(\sqrt[d]{\frac{M_r}{P_r}} + \sqrt[d]{\frac{M_s}{P_s}} \right)^k \cdot V_{sphere}^{d-k}(\varepsilon) \quad (5)$$

where M_r (M_s) is the number of points in the block of R (S) data. When we replace M_r and M_s with the number of points in the block (or sub-block) of data R and S, we get γ_1 (or γ_2).

4 Performance Evaluation

We conducted extensive experimental study to evaluate the performance of Gorder and present the results in this section. In the study, we used both synthetic cluster datasets and real life datasets. The synthetic cluster datasets were generated using the method described in [16], and the real life datasets are from UCI KDD data repository [1]. We used the Corel dataset which contains 64 dimensional feature vectors of 30K images, and the Forest FCoverType dataset which contains 580K records. The original Forest FCoverType dataset has 54 attributes(10 real, 44 binary) and we used the 10 attributes of real value in the experiments.

We compared Gorder with MuX and simple block nested loop join (NLJ). The MuX join [6, 5] is the current state-of-art method for the KNN-join processing, which has been shown to be optimized for both CPU and I/O time and that it outperforms the join algorithm based on the R-tree (RSJ) significantly.

The experiments were conducted on a Sunfire 4800 server with 750MHz Ultra Sparc III CPU and connected with 2 Sun T3 Disk Array. The buffer allocated for all methods is around 10% of the datasets of R and S. Extra memory was allocated to MuX for storing the internal nodes. The number of nearest neighbor (K) is 10 by default. The default settings of Gorder are summarized in Table 1.

Performance is presented in terms of the elapsed time (which includes I/O and CPU time), the I/O time and the distance computation selectivity. The elapsed time and I/O time of Gorder includes the time for both G-ordering and joining phases. Time of MuX does not include the index building time. Distance computation selectivity is calculated by the following equation:

$$\frac{number\ of\ point\ distance\ computations}{|R| \cdot |S|}.$$

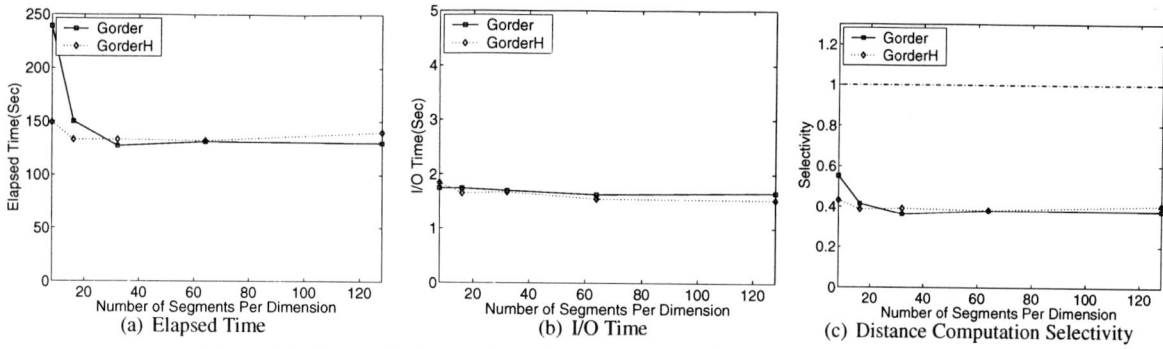

Figure 2: Effect of the number of segments per dimension (Corel dataset)

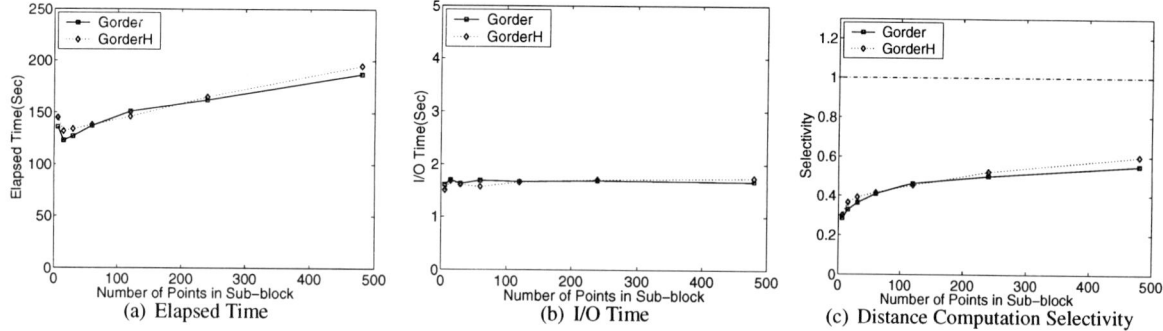

Figure 3: Effect of sub-block size (Corel dataset)

4.1 Evaluation Using Real Datasets

In this set of experiments, we study the performance of Gorder using the real life KDD dataset.

4.1.1 Study of Parameters of Gorder

The first set of experiments evaluates the effect of various parameters on the performance of Gorder. With the expectation that the real life dataset is usually skewed, we implemented the GorderH for comparison purposes. GorderH applies a grid with variable cell length onto the data space during the G-ordering phase. We compute a equi-width histogram for each dimension in the PCA transformation stage and partition each dimension into segments with equal number of points inside. We performed the self KNN-join on the datasets. The presented time for GorderH includes the time for histogram processing.

Effect of grid granularity We first evaluate the effect of the granularity of the grid by varying the number of segments per dimension of the grid from 8 to 128. Figure 2 presents the results of on the Corel dataset. From the results, we observe that when we increase the number of segments from 8 to 32, the performance of Gorder improves noticeably with a speed-up factor of 0.88. The speed-up factor of GorderH is 0.12. The reason is that with finer granularity grid, the *bounding box* bounds the data points more tightly. Hence, the MinDist low bound becomes more accurate and more effective in pruning. An interesting observation is that when we further increase the number of segments per dimension, Gorder (which uses the equilength grid) becomes as efficient as and even better than the GorderH (which uses the variable length grid based on histogram). This indicates the fine-granularity grid makes Gorder adaptive to the data distribution and eliminates the need to maintain the histogram.

Comparing the I/O time with the total elapsed time, we notice that the I/O time is much less significant than the CPU time (only around 1% of the total response time), which confirms the benefit of using the block accessing and that the KNN-join is CPU critical due to the large number and the complexity of the distance computations.

Effect of sub-block size Figure 3 summarizes the effect of the size of the sub-block on KNN-join processing. In this experiment, the size of the sub-block is varied from 6 to 480 and we conducted the experiment on the Coral dataset. As can be observed, the selectivity of distance computation degrades when the number of points in the sub-block grows. The volume of the sub-block increases when there are more points in it, and consequently, its pruning ability become ineffective. This is consistent with the cost analysis. However, on the other hand, smaller sub-blocks do not necessarily lead to better elapsed time. We observed that when the size of the sub-block increases from 6 to 15, the performance of Gorder in terms of the elapsed time improves around 10% despite the slight degeneration of the distance computation selectivity. The reason is that decrease of sub-block size increases the number of sub-blocks

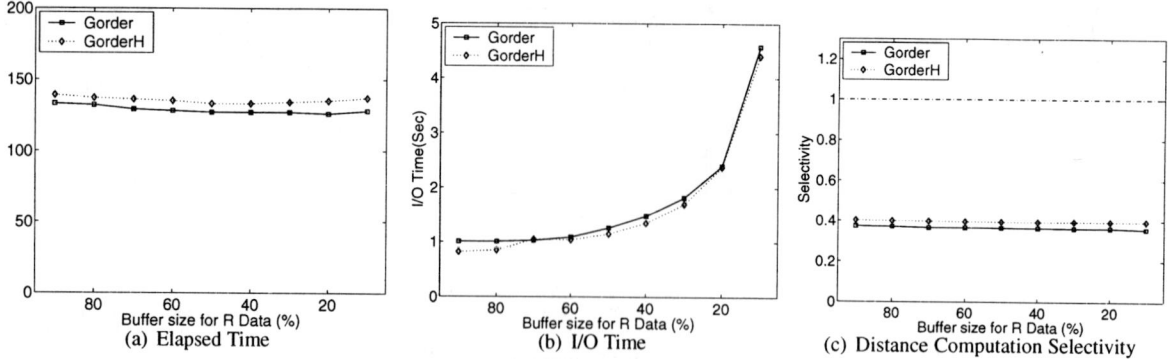

Figure 4: Effect of buffer size for R data (Corel dataset)

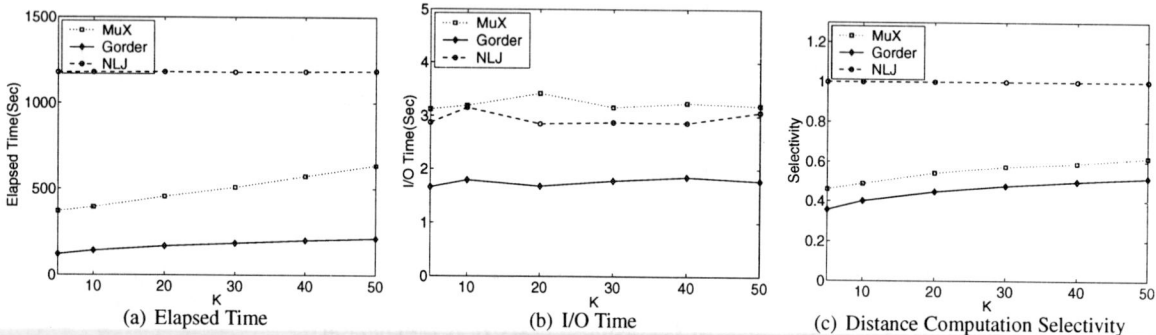

Figure 5: Effect of K (Corel dataset)

and therefore, introduces more MinDist computations. So there is a trade-off between the MinDist computation and the point distance computation. The results indicate that the best setting of the size of sub-block is between 20–50.

Effect of buffer size for R data Next we study the effect of buffer size allocated to R data and present our study in Figure 4. We fixed the buffer size at around 10% of input data set and decreased the number of buffer pages for R from 90% of buffer to 10% of buffer. Size of sub-block is 30. Figure 4 shows that as we reduce the buffer size for R, the I/O time increases quickly with the drop of the number of R buffer pages because the reduction in R buffer size causes the loading time of the S blocks to increase. However, the overall performance of Gorder with regard to the elapsed time hasn't been influenced a lot. The reason is when R buffer size shrinks, more S data can be loaded in buffer and hence, the R data in memory are more likely to join with the S data that yield real K-nearest neighbors first and the selectivity is improved. Therefore, the increase of the I/O time is absorbed by the decrease of CPU time.

4.1.2 Effect of K

We now study the effect of K and compare the performance of Gorder with MuX and NLJ. Figure 5 presents the results on the Corel dataset when we varied the number of nearest neighbors K form 5 to 50.

From the results, we observe that with the increase of number of nearest neighbors, the elapsed time of Gorder increases moderately, while MuX is more affected by K. The gap of the elapsed time between MuX and Gorder widens with the increasing K. On average, Gorder outperforms MuX with the speed-up factor of around 2 with regard to the elapsed time. In terms of distance computation selectivity, Gorder is better than MuX by the average factor of 1.22. Note that the speed-up of the elapsed time is more significant than the improvement of selectivity. This is due to the distance computation reduction technique Gorder employs. Gorder uses a subset of dimensions for block similarity computation and the block similarity is also used to reduce point distance computation; hence the speed-up in terms of elapsed time is even better than the reduction of selectivity. Figure 5(b) presents the I/O time incurred by different methods. Memory allocation of NLJ is the same as Gorder. That is, around 20% for R data and 80% for S data. Gorder outperforms MuX due to its one time accessing one block of data so that the expensive disk seeking time is saved. Gorder is also more efficient than NLJ because with the pruning strategy it filters out S blocks that will not yield KNNs.

Figure 6 presents the results on the Forest dataset. Costs of NLJ are not shown on the graphs because its elapsed time is more than 10,000 seconds. Again, Gorder outperforms MuX significantly with the speed-up factor of 2.45 in terms of elapsed time.

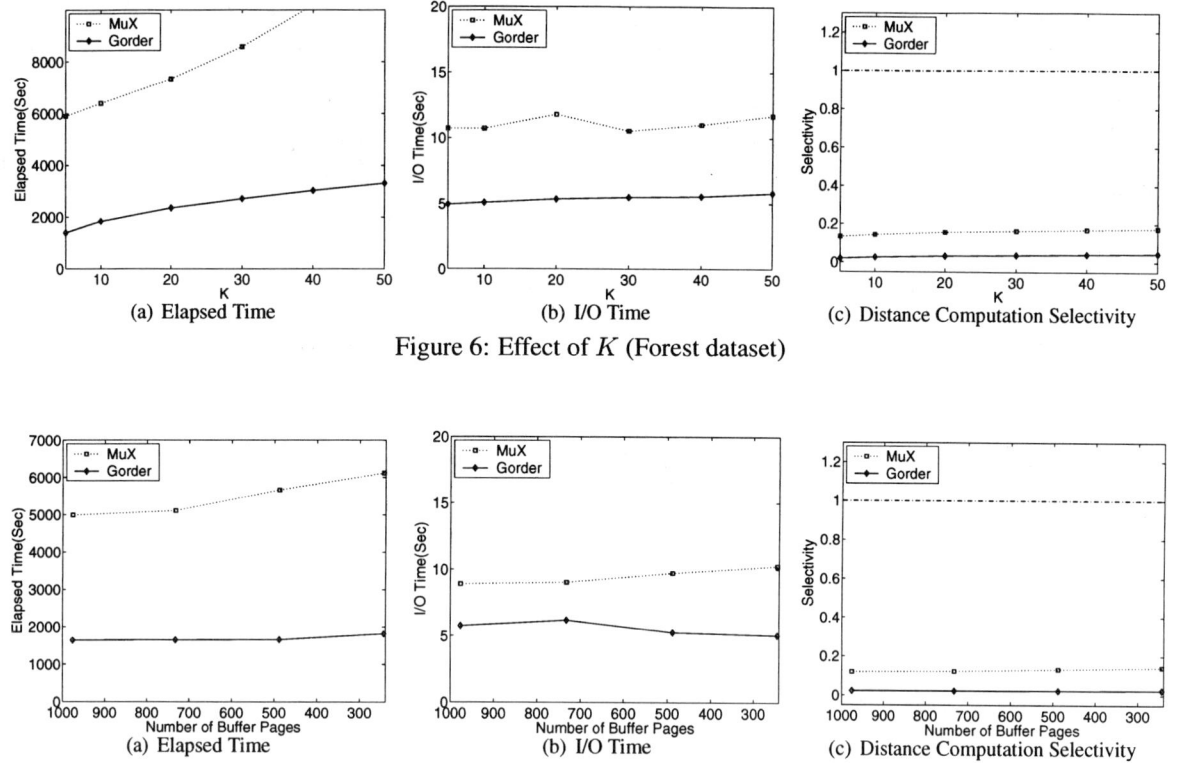

Figure 6: Effect of K (Forest dataset)

Figure 7: Effect of buffer size (Forest dataset)

4.1.3 Effect of Buffer Size

In dealing with large datasets, the KNN-join algorithm must be efficient in utilizing the limited buffer space. In this experiment, we study the behavior of the join methods with respect to buffer sizes.

The study is performed on the Forest dataset and we reduced the buffer size from around 1000 pages (40% of the dataset size) to around 250 pages (10% of the dataset size). The buffer size for R was kept at 25 pages. In Figure 7, we compare the performance of Gorder and MuX. The result shows that MuX is more sensitive to the decrease of buffer size and its elapsed time increases by 23% when the buffer size decreases from 1000 pages to 250 pages. In comparison, performance of Gorder is more stable and degenerates by only 10% for the same amount of reduction. Gorder is therefore more efficient with respect to buffer space.

We observe that the reduction in buffer space does not affected the I/O performance much. The reduction in buffer size reduces the volume of the bounding box and consequently, leads to the improved effectiveness of the filtering of S blocks. However, the smaller block size of S introduces more disk seeking time. As a balance, the I/O time of Gorder is not much affected by the buffer size.

4.2 Evaluation Using Synthetic Datasets

We study the scalability of Gorder on the synthetic datasets of various sizes and dimensionalities. Since real life data set are often clustered and correlated, we utilized method in [16] to generate clustered datasets containing 10 clusters.

4.2.1 Effect of Dimensionality

In this experiment, we shall evaluate the effect of data dimensionality on the join performance by varying the number of dimensions from 8 to 64. Figure 8 presents the results on the 100K clustered datasets. We observe that the efficiency of MuX deteriorates with the increasing dimensionality. The reason is that MuX, like the R-tree, its performance degenerates with the increase of data dimensionality. Figure 8(c) shows the degeneration of distance computation selectivity of MuX with the increase of the number of dimensions. In addition, the cost of similarity computation of MuX also goes up linearly with the data dimensionality.

The deterioration of distance computation selectivity with the increasing dimensionality is not obvious for Gorder. In addition, Gorder employs the distance computation reduction technique to alleviate the distance computation cost for high dimensional data. Therefore, Gorder is more scalable to high-dimensional data and its performance gain over MuX widens as the dimensionality grows. The speed-up factor of Gorder over MuX increases from 0.68 at dimensionality of 8 to 2.9 at dimensionality of 64.

4.2.2 Effect of Size of Dataset

In the second experiment, we study the performance behavior with varying size of datasets. We performed the self

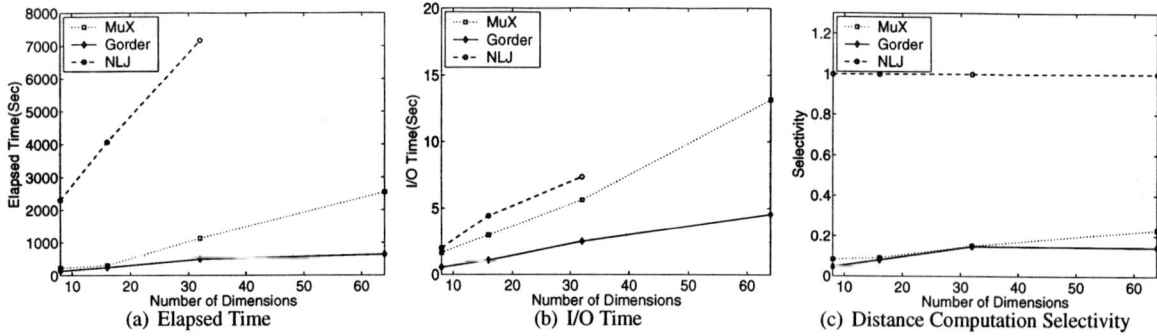

Figure 8: Effect of dimensionality (100k clustered dataset)

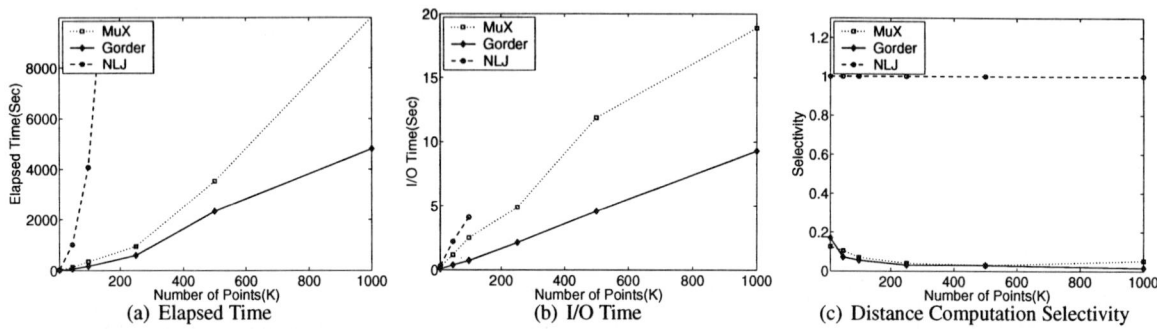

Figure 9: Effect of data size (16-dimensional clustered datasets)

KNN-join of the clustered data in the 16-dimensional space and varied the dataset size from 10,000 to 1,000,000 objects. The results are summarized in Figure 9. From the result, Gorder is noted to be the most efficient method for datasets of various sizes. With the increase of dataset size, the elapsed time of MuX grows faster than Gorder. The speed-up factor of Gorder over MuX ranges from 0.51 to 2.6. Note that even for small datasets where the distance computation selectivity of Gorder is higher than MuX, the elapsed time of Gorder is still lower than MuX due to the use of distance computation reduction technique.

From Figure 9 (c), we observe that the distance computation selectivity improves when the number of data points grows. The reason is that the increase of the number of data points densifies the clusters and reduces the distance between a point and its K nearest neighbors. Therefore, more points can be filtered from distance computation. The study demonstrates that Gorder is scalable to large size of data and has even better performance than MuX for large datsets.

4.2.3 Effect of Relative Size of Dataset

In the last set of experiments, we joined two datasets of different sizes and studied the effect of the relative sizes on the performance of the join algorithms. To study such an effect, we fixed the size of R at 100K points and varied the size of S from 10K to 1,000K so that the relative size of R:S is changed from 10:1 to 1:10. Figure 10 shows the results.

Both the elapsed time and I/O time of Gorder increase moderately with the increase in S data size. The cost of MuX goes up comparatively faster, which leads to the wider performance gap between Gorder and MuX as S dataset size increases. Furthermore, note that even at S size of 10K and 50k, where the selectivity of MuX is better than Gorder, Gorder is still much faster. With regard to the elapsed time, the average speed-up factor of Gorder over MuX is 0.59, which confirms the scalability of Gorder with respect to the data size again.

5 Conclusion

In this paper, we have investigated the KNN-join problem. The K-nearest neighbor (KNN) similarity join is an operation that combines each point of one data set with its KNNs in the other data set, and it can be used to facilitate data mining tasks such as clustering, classification and outlier detection. It is also capable of providing more meaningful query results than just the range similarity join. We proposed *Gorder*, an efficient KNN-join processing algorithm that exploits sorting, data page scheduling and distance computation filtering and reduction to reduce both I/O and CPU costs. We presented our performance study on both synthetic cluster and real life datasets and the results confirm that Gorder is efficient and scalable with regard to both data dimensionality and size, and that it outperforms existing methods by a significant margin. Our future work is to design the KNN-join algorithm based on [24].

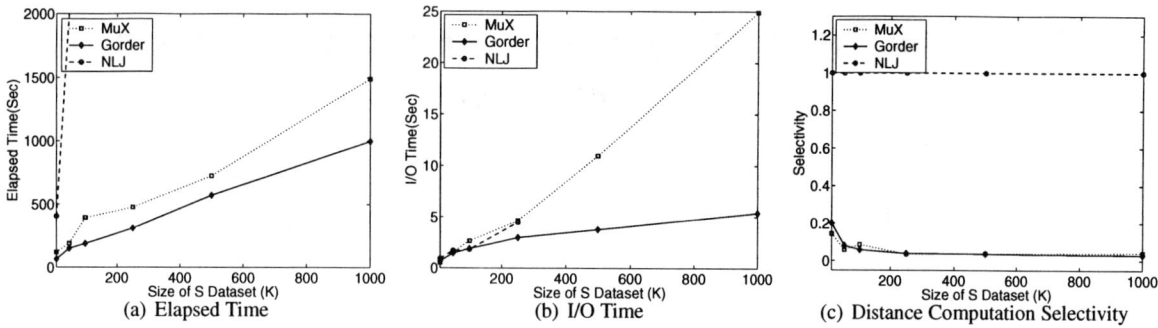

Figure 10: Effect of relative size of datasets (16-dimensional clustered datasets).

Acknowledgment: The authors would like to thank Christian Böhm for providing the code of MuX similarity join.

References

[1] http://kdd.ics.uci.edu/.

[2] C. Böhm. A cost model for query processing in high dimensional data spaces. *ACM TODS*, 25(2):129–178, 2000.

[3] C. Böhm, B. Braunmueller, F. Krebs, and H.-P. Kriegel. Epsilon grid order: An algorithm for the similarity join on massive high-dimensional data. In *Proc. of ACM SIGMOD*, pages 379–388, 2001.

[4] C. Bohm and F. Krebs. Supporting kdd applications by the k-nearest neighbor join. In *Proc. of DEXA*, pages 504–516, 2003.

[5] C. Böhm and F. Krebs. The k-nearest neighbor join: Turbo charging the kdd process. *Knowledge and Information Systems (KAIS)*, 2004.

[6] C. Böhm and H.-P. Kriegel. A cost model and index architecture for the similarity join. In *Proc. of ICDE*, pages 411–420, 2001.

[7] M. M. Breunig, H.-P. Kriegel, R. T. Ng, and J. Sander. Lof: identifying density-based local outliers. In *Proc. of ACM SIGMOD*, pages 93–104, 2000.

[8] T. Brinkhoff, H.-P. Kriegel, and B. Seeger. Efficient processing of spatial joins using r-trees. In *Proc. of ACM SIGMOD*, pages 237–246, 1993.

[9] K. Chakrabarti and S. Mehrotra. Local dimensionality reduction: a new approach to indexing high dimensional spaces. In *Proc. of VLDB*, pages 89–100, 2000.

[10] J. Dirtrich and B. Seeger. Gess: a scalable similarity-join algorithm for mining large data sets in high dimensional spaces. In *Proc. of ACM SIGKDD*, pages 47–56, 2001.

[11] G. H. Golub and C. F. V. Loan. *Matrix Computations*. The Johns Hopkins University Press, 1989.

[12] A. Guttman. R-trees: A dynamic index structure for spatial searching. In *Proc. of ACM SIGMOD*, pages 47–57. 1984.

[13] G. Hjaltason and H. Samet. Incremental distance join algorithm for spatial databases. In *Proc. of ACM SIGMOD*, pages 237–258, 1998.

[14] G. Hjaltason and H. Samet. Distance browsing in spatial databases. *ACM TODS*, 24(2):265–318, 1999.

[15] Y. Huang, N. Jing, and E. A. Rundensteiner. Spatial joins using r-trees: Breadth-first traversal with global optimizations. In *Proc. of VLDB*, pages 396–405, 1997.

[16] H. Jin, B. C. Ooi, H. T. Shen, C. Yu, and A. Y. Zhou. An adaptive and efficient dimensionality reduction algorithm for high-dimensional indexing. In *Proc. of ICDE*, pages 87–98, 2003.

[17] I. T. Jolliffe. *Principal Component Analysis*. Springer-Verlag, 1986.

[18] G. Karypis, E.-H. Han, and V. Kumar. Chameleon: Hierarchical clustering using dynamic modeling. *Computer*, 32(8):68–75, 1999.

[19] N. Koudas and K. Sevcik. High dimensional similarity joins: algorithms and performance evaluation. *IEEE TKDE*, 12(1):3–8, 2000.

[20] M.-L. Lo and C. Ravishankar. Spatial hash-joins. In *Proc. of ACM SIGMOD*, pages 247–258, 1996.

[21] J. Patel and D. DeWitt. Partition based spatial-merge join. In *Proc. of ACM SIGMOD*, pages 259–270, 1996.

[22] R. Ramakrishnan and J. Gehrke. *Database Management Systems (2nd Edition)*. McGraw-Hill, 1999.

[23] N. Roussopoulos, S. Kelley, and F. Vincent. Nearest neighbor queries. In *Proc. of ACM SIGMOD*, pages 71–79, 1995.

[24] C. Yu, B. C. Ooi, K. L. Tan, and H. Jagadish. Indexing the distance: an efficient method to knn processing. In *Proc. of VLDB*, 2001.

Query and Update Efficient B[+]-Tree Based Indexing of Moving Objects

Christian S. Jensen[1]   Dan Lin[2]   Beng Chin Ooi[2]

[1]Department of Computer Science
Aalborg University, Denmark
csj@cs.auc.dk

[2]School of Computing
National University of Singapore, Singapore
{lindan, ooibc}@comp.nus.edu.sg

Abstract

A number of emerging applications of data management technology involve the monitoring and querying of large quantities of continuous variables, e.g., the positions of mobile service users, termed moving objects. In such applications, large quantities of state samples obtained via sensors are streamed to a database. Indexes for moving objects must support queries efficiently, but must also support frequent updates. Indexes based on minimum bounding regions (MBRs) such as the R-tree exhibit high concurrency overheads during node splitting, and each individual update is known to be quite costly. This motivates the design of a solution that enables the B[+]-tree to manage moving objects. We represent moving-object locations as vectors that are timestamped based on their update time. By applying a novel linearization technique to these values, it is possible to index the resulting values using a single B[+]-tree that partitions values according to their timestamp and otherwise preserves spatial proximity. We develop algorithms for range and k nearest neighbor queries, as well as continuous queries. The proposal can be grafted into existing database systems cost effectively. An extensive experimental study explores the performance characteristics of the proposal and also shows that it is capable of substantially outperforming the R-tree based TPR-tree for both single and concurrent access scenarios.

Permission to copy without fee all or part of this material is granted provided that the copies are not made or distributed for direct commercial advantage, the VLDB copyright notice and the title of the publication and its date appear, and notice is given that copying is by permission of the Very Large Data Base Endowment. To copy otherwise, or to republish, requires a fee and/or special permission from the Endowment.
**Proceedings of the 30th VLDB Conference,
Toronto, Canada, 2004**

1 Introduction

An infrastructure is emerging that enables data management applications that rely on the tracking of the locations of moving objects such as vehicles, users of wireless devices, and goods. Further, a wide range of other applications, beyond those to do with moving objects, rely on the sampling of continuous, multidimensional variables. The provisioning of high performance and scalable data management support for such applications presents new challenges. One key challenge derives from the need to accommodate frequent updates while simultaneously allowing for efficient query processing [6, 13].

This combination of desired functionality is particularly troublesome in the context of indexing of multidimensional data. The dominant indexing technique for multidimensional data with low dimensionality, the R-tree [5] (and its descendants such as the R*-tree [1]), was conceived for largely static data sets and exhibits poor update performance. The Time-Parameterized R-tree (TPR-tree) [19] (as well as several of its recent descendants [11]) models object locations as linear functions of time and supports queries on the current and anticipated near-future positions of moving objects. While the use of linear rather than constant functions may reduce the need for updates by a factor of three [3], update performance remains a problem.

Individual updates tend to be costly, and the problem is exacerbated by the concurrency control algorithms of the R-trees, such as the Rlink-tree [8], not being able to adequately handling a high degree of concurrent accesses that involve updates. Notably, frequent tree ascents caused by node splitting and propagation of MBR updates lead to costly lock conflicts. This problem is inherent in many multi-dimensional indexes. Another problem with existing solutions to moving-object indexing is that they are not easily integrated into existing database systems.

This paper proposes a novel way of indexing moving objects using the classical B[+]-tree without compromising on query and storage efficiency. The motivation for using the B[+]-tree is threefold. First, the B[+]-tree is used widely in commercial database systems and has proven to be very efficient with respect to queries as well as updates, robust with respect to varying workloads, and scalable. Second, being a one-dimensional index, it does not exhibit the update performance problems associated with MBR-based multi-dimensional indexes. Third, it is typically appropriate to model moving-object extents as points. This enables linearization and subsequent B^+-tree indexing.

To use the B^+-tree, we must be able to linearize the representation of the locations of the moving objects. This is done by means of a space-filling curve, which enumerates every point in a discrete, multi-dimensional space. Attractive space-filling curves such as the Peano curve (or Z-curve) and the Hilbert curve, which we use in this paper, preserve proximity, meaning that points close in multidimensional space tend to be close in the one-dimensional space obtained by the curve [12].

A B^+-tree with the above space-filling curves works very well for static databases. A naive way to accommodate moving points is to update each object in the database at each time interval. To avoid an excessive update overhead, we propose a novel indexing method, termed the B^x-tree, where "x" indicates the flexibility of the proposed method in employing a specific ("x") space-filling curve as part of the linearization function.

First, we model moving objects as linear functions of time. Thus, the data to be indexed in the B^x-tree are not points (constant functions), but linear functions coupled with the times they were updated. Intuitively, an update occurs when the position predicted by an existing function is deemed inaccurate [3]. Second, we effectively "partition" the index, placing entries in partitions based on their update time. More specifically, we first partition the time axis into intervals where the duration of an interval is an approximation of the maximum duration in-between two updates of any object location. We then partition each such interval into n equal-length sub-intervals, termed *phases*, where n is determined based on minimum time duration within which each object issues an update of its position. Each phase is assigned the time point it ends as a *label timestamp*, and a label timestamp is mapped to a partition. An update is placed in the partition given by the label timestamp of the phase during which it occurs. For an object, the value indexed by the B^x-tree is the concatenation of its partition number and the result of applying the underlying space-filling method to the position of the object as of the label timestamp of its phase.

This mapping scheme overcomes the limitation of the B^+-tree, which is able to only keep the snapshot of all the objects at the same time point. This scheme reduces the update frequency, it preserves spatial proximity within each partition, and it facilitates queries on anticipated near-future positions.

Based on the above, we propose efficient algorithms for range and k nearest neighbor queries, as well as for continuous queries. The algorithms are general and can be applied to indexes that use sampling techniques to model moving objects. Like any new indexing method built on top of the B^+-tree, the paper's proposal can be grafted into existing database systems cost effectively.

The paper reports on an extensive experimental study, which includes a comparison with the TPR-tree. The results show that the B^x-tree is efficient with respect to storage space and range and k nearest neighbor queries. Indeed, the B^x-tree is capable of outperforming the TPR-tree by a wide margin in single and concurrent access environments.

The rest of the paper is organized as follows. Section 2 reviews related work. Section 3, describes the structure of the proposed B^x-tree, and it presents the associated query and update operations. Section 4 covers comprehensive performance experiments. Finally, Section 5 concludes.

2 Related Work

Traditional indexes for multi-dimensional databases, such as the R-tree [5] and its variants (e.g., [1]) were, implicitly or explicitly, designed with the main objective of supporting efficient query processing as opposed to enabling efficient update. This works well in applications where queries are relatively much more frequent than updates. However, applications involving the indexing of moving objects exhibit workloads characterized by heavy loads of updates, in addition to frequent queries.

Several new index structures have been proposed for moving-object indexing, and recent surveys exist that cover different aspects of these [11, 13]. One may distinguish between indexing of the past positions versus indexing of the current and near-future positions of spatial objects. Our approach belongs to the latter category.

Past positions of moving objects are typically approximated by polylines composed of line segments. It is possible to index line segments by R-trees, but the trajectory memberships of segments are not taken into account. In contrast to this, the Spatio-Temporal R-tree [15] attempts to also group segments according to their trajectory memberships, while also taking spatial locations into account. The Trajectory-Bundle tree [15] aims only for trajectory preservation, leaving other spatial properties aside.

The representations of the current and near-future positions of moving objects are quite different, as are the indexing challenges and solutions. Positions are represented as points (constant functions) or functions of time, typically linear functions. The Lazy Update R-tree [9] aims to reduce update cost by handling updates of objects that do not move outside their leaf-level MBRs specially, and a generalized approach to bottom-up update in R-trees has recently been examined [10].

Tayeb et al. [24] use PMR-Quadtrees [20] for indexing the future linear trajectories of one-dimensional moving points as line segments in (x,t)-space. The segments span the time interval that starts at the current time and extends some time into the future, after which time, a new tree must be built. Kollis et al. [7] employ dual transformation techniques which represent the position of an object moving in a d-dimensional space as a point in a $2d$-dimensional space. Their work is largely theoretical in nature. Based on a similar technique, Patel et al. [14] have most recently developed a practical indexing method, termed STRIPES, that supports efficient updates and queries at the cost of higher space requirements.

Finally, we cover the Time-Parameterized R-tree (TPR-tree) [19] in some detail, as we use this tree for comparison in our performance study. An extension to the R*-tree, the TPR-tree indexes linear functions of time. The current location of a moving point is found simply by applying the function representing its location to the current time. MBRs are also functions of time. Specifically, in each dimension, the lower bound of an MBR is set to move with the maximum downward speed of all enclosed objects, while the upper bound is set to move with the maximum upward speed of all enclosed objects. As enclosed objects may be both moving points and moving rectangles, this ensures that the bounding rectangles are indeed bounding at all times considered. Frequent updates are needed to ensure that moving objects that are currently close are assigned to the same bounding rectangles. Further, bounding rectangles never shrink and are generally larger than strictly needed. To counter this phenomenon, the so-called "tightening" is applied to bounding rectangles when they are accessed.

Algorithms for nearest neighbor and reverse nearest neighbor queries on moving objects have been proposed based on the TPR-tree [2]. Next, two notable proposals exist that build on the ideas of the TPR-tree. Procopiuc et al. [16] propose the STAR-tree. This index seems to be best suited for workloads with infrequent updates. Tao et al. [22] adopt assumptions about the query workload that differ slightly from those underlying the TPR-tree. This leads to a different grouping of objects into index tree nodes.

To the best of the authors' knowledge, no proposals for the indexing of moving objects exist that use a combination of temporal partitioning and space-filling curves. However, our work adopts a design philosophy similar to that of iDistance [25], where application of a mapping function that uses reference points and metric distances with respect to the reference points enables B^+-tree indexing of high-dimensional points for the purpose of nearest neighbor search.

3 Structure and Algorithms

We first describe the structure of the B^x-tree. We then cover algorithms for range and kNN queries and continuous queries. Finally, update, insertion, and deletion are covered.

3.1 Index Structure

The base structure of the B^x-tree is that of the B^+-tree. Thus, the internal nodes serve as a directory. In order to support B-link concurrency control [21], each internal node contains a pointer to its right sibling (the pointer is non-null if one exists). The leaf nodes contain the moving-object locations being indexed and corresponding index time. We proceed to describe how object locations are mapped to single-dimensional values.

Specifically, we use a space-filling curve for this purpose. Such a curve is a continuous path which visits every point in a discrete, multi-dimensional space exactly once and never crosses itself.

We consider versions of the B^x-tree that use the Peano curve (or Z-curve) and the Hilbert curve (see Figure 1). Although other curves may be used, these two are expected to be particularly good. Analytical and empirical studies [4, 12] show that for the two-dimensional space we consider, these curves are effective in preserving proximity, meaning that points close in multidimensional space tend to be close in the one-dimensional space obtained by the curve. The Hilbert curve is expected to be (slightly) better than the Peano curve [4].

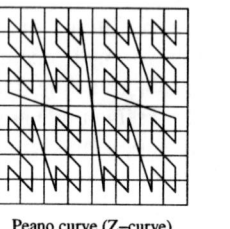

Peano curve (Z-curve)   Hilbert curve (H-curve)

Figure 1: Space-Filling Curves

In what follows, we term the value obtained from the space-filling curve the x_value; and for brevity, we use the Peano curve in most discussions.

To reduce this load, we model point values as linear functions of time, rather than simply as static points, i.e., constant functions. A recent study of GPS logs obtained from two dozen cars traveling in a semi-urban environment measures the number of updates needed to ensure that the values recorded in the database do not differ by more than some threshold from the real values. For realistic thresholds, the use of linear functions reduces the amount of updates to one third in comparison to constant functions [3].

An object location is thus given by $O = (\vec{x}, \vec{v})$, a position and a velocity, and an update time, or timestamp, t_u, where these values are valid.

In a leaf-node entry, an object O updated at t_u is represented by a value $B^x value(O, t_u)$:

$$B^x value(O, t_u) = [index\_partition]_2 \oplus [x\_rep]_2 \quad (1)$$

where $index\_partition$ is an index partition determined by the update time, x_rep is obtained using a space-filling curve, $[x]_2$ denotes the binary value of x, and $\oplus$ denotes concatenation. We proceed to detail this definition.

If we index the timestamped object locations without differentiating them based on their timestamps, we not only lose the proximity preserving property of the space-filling curve; the index will also be ineffective in locating an object based on its x_value. To overcome such problems, we effectively "partition" the index, placing entries in partitions based on their update time. More specifically, we denote by Δt_{mu} the time duration that is the maximum duration in-between two updates of any object location. We then partition the time axis into intervals of duration Δt_{mu}, and we sub-partition each such interval into n equal-length sub-intervals, termed *phases*.

By mapping the update times in the same phase to the same so-called *label timestamp* and by using the label timestamps as prefixes of the representations of the object locations, we obtain index partitions, and the update times of updates determine the partitions they go to. In particular, an update with timestamp t_u is assigned a label timestamp $t_{lab} = \lceil t_u + \Delta t_{mu}/n \rceil_l$, where operation $\lceil x \rceil_l$ returns the nearest future label timestamp of x.

For example, Figure 2 shows a B^x-tree with $n = 2$. Objects with timestamp $t_u = 0$ obtain label timestamp $t_{lab} = \frac{1}{2}\Delta t_{mu}$; objects with $0 < t_u \leq \frac{1}{2}\Delta t_{mu}$ obtain label timestamp $t_{lab} = \Delta t_{mu}$; and so on.

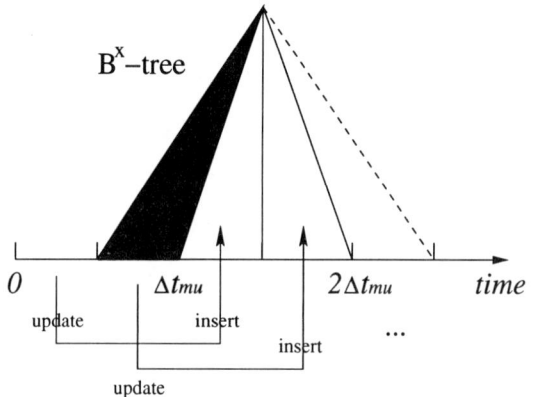

Figure 2: The B^x-Tree

Next, for an object with label timestamp t_{lab}, we compute its position at t_{lab} according to its position and velocity at t_u. We then apply the space-filling curve to this (future) position to obtain the second component of Equation 1.

This mapping has two main advantages. First, it enables the tree to index object positions valid at different times, overcoming the limitation of the B^+-tree, which is only able to index a snapshot of all positions at the same time. Second, it reduces the update frequency compared to having to update the positions of all objects at each timestamp when only some of them need to be updated. The two components of the mapping function in Equation 1 are consequently defined as follows:

$$index\_partition = (t_{lab}/(\Delta t_{mu}/n) - 1) \bmod (n+1)$$
$$x\_rep = x\_value(\vec{x} + \vec{v} \cdot (t_{lab} - t_u))$$

With the transformation, the B^x-tree will contain data belonging to $n + 1$ phases, each given by a *label timestamp* and corresponding to a time interval. Within each of these, we apply a space-filling curve to an object position.

The choice of the value of n affects query performance and storage space. A large n results in smaller enlargements of query windows (covered in Section 3.2), but also results in more partitions and therefore a looser relationship among object locations. In addition, a large n yields a higher space overhead due to more internal nodes. When n is larger than 2, the storage space is a little more than that of the TPR-tree. When n is 1, query windows must be enlarged more than the enlargements of MBRs in the TPR-tree (enlargement details are covered in Section 3.2.1). Therefore, we choose $n = 2$.

To exemplify, let $n = 2$, $\Delta t_{mu} = 120$, and assume a Peano curve of order 3 (i.e., the space domain is 8×8). Object positions $O_1 = ((7, 2), (-0.1, 0.05))$, $O_2 = ((0, 6), (0.2, -0.3))$, and $O_3 = ((1, 2), (0.1, 0.1))$ are inserted at times 0, 10, and 100, respectively. We calculate the B^x *value* for each as follows.

Step 1: Calculate label timestamps and index partitions.
$t_{lab}^1 = \lceil (0 + 120/2) \rceil_l = 60$, $index\_partition^1 = 0 = (00)_2$
$t_{lab}^2 = \lceil (10 + 120/2) \rceil_l = 120$, $index\_partition^2 = 1$
$\quad = (01)_2$
$t_{lab}^3 = \lceil (100 + 120/2) \rceil_l = 180$, $index\_partition^3 = 2$
$\quad = (10)_2$

Step 2: Calculate positions x_1, x_2 and x_3 at t_{lab}^1, t_{lab}^2, and t_{lab}^3, respectively.
$x_1' = (1, 5), x_2' = (2, 3), x_3' = (4, 1)$.

Step 3: Calculate Z-values.
$[Z\_value(x_1')]_2 = (010011)_2$
$[Z\_value(x_2')]_2 = (001101)_2$
$[Z\_value(x_3')]_2 = (100001)_2$

Step 4: Calculate B^x *value*.
$B^x value(O_1, 0) = (00010011)_2 = 19$
$B^x value(O_2, 10) = (01001101)_2 = 77$
$B^x value(O_3, 100) = (10100001)_2 = 161$

It is worth noting that *at most three* ranges exist at a single point in time. As time passes, repeatedly the first range expires (shaded area), and a new range is appended (dashed line). This use of rolling ranges enables the B^x-tree to handle time effectively.

3.2 Querying

In the following, we outline the search strategies for the B^x-tree.

3.2.1 Range Query

A range query retrieves all objects whose location falls within the rectangular range $q = ([qx_1^l, qx_1^u], [qx_2^l, qx_2^u])$ at time t_q not prior to the current time ("l" denotes lower bound, and "u" denotes upper bound).

A key challenge is to support predictive queries, i.e., queries that concern future times. Traditionally, indexes that use linear functions handle predictive queries by means of MBR enlargement (e.g., the TPR-tree); to the best of our knowledge, no algorithm for the predictive queries has been proposed for indexes that use snapshots of moving objects (e.g., the LUR-tree). We present a generic approach to processing such queries that is not constrained by the base structure. Figure 6 outlines the range query algorithm, which we proceed to explain.

To handle queries on the anticipated near future positions of objects, the B^x-tree uses query-window enlargement instead of MBR enlargement. This is done through the TimeParameterizedRegion function call in the algorithm. Because the B^x-tree stores an object's location as of some time after its update time, the enlargement involves two cases: a location must either be brought back to an earlier time or forward to a later time.

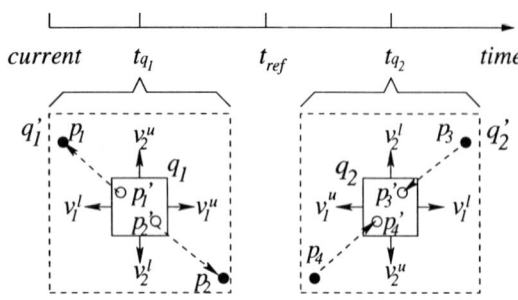

Figure 3: Query Window Enlargement

Consider the example in Figure 3, where t_{ref} denotes the time when the locations of four moving objects are updated to their current value index, and where predictive queries q_1 and q_2 (solid rectangles) have time parameters t_{q_1} and t_{q_2}, respectively. The figure shows the stored positions as solid dots and positions of the two first objects at t_{q_1} and the positions of the two last at t_{q_2} as circles. The two positions for each object are connected by an arrow.

The relationship between the two positions for each object is $p'_i = p_i + \vec{v} \cdot (t_q - t_{ref})$. The first two of the four objects thus are in the result of the first query, and the last two objects are in the result of the second query. To obtain this result, query rectangle q_1 needs to be enlarged to q'_1 (dashed). This is achieved by attaching maximum speeds to the sides of q_1: v^l_1, v^l_2, v^u_1, and v^u_2. For example, v^u_1 is obtained as the largest projection onto the x-axis of a velocity of an object in q'_1. (As we do not yet know q'_1, a conservative approximation is used; more on this shortly.)

For q_2, the enlargement speeds are computed similarly. For example, v^u_2 is obtained by projecting all velocities of objects in q'_2 onto the y-axis; v^u_2 is then set to the largest speed multiplied by -1.

The enlargement of query $q = ([qx^l_1, qx^u_1], [qx^l_2, qx^u_2])$ is given by query $q' = ([eqx^l_1, eqx^u_1], [eqx^l_2, eqx^u_2])$:

$$eqx^l_i = \begin{cases} qx^l_i + v^l_i \cdot (t_{ref} - t_q) & \text{if } t_q < t_{ref} \\ qx^l_i + v^u_i \cdot (t_q - t_{ref}) & \text{otherwise} \end{cases} \quad (2)$$

$$eqx^u_i = \begin{cases} qx^u_i + v^u_i \cdot (t_{ref} - t_q) & \text{if } t_q < t_{ref} \\ qx^u_i + v^l_i \cdot (t_q - t_{ref}) & \text{otherwise} \end{cases} \quad (3)$$

The implementation of the computation of enlargement speeds proceeds in two steps. We first set them according to the maximum speeds of all objects, thus obtaining a preliminary q'. Then, with the aid of a two-dimensional histogram (e.g., a grid) that captures the maximum and minimum projections of velocities onto the axes of objects in each cell, we obtain the final enlargement speed in the area where the query window resides. Such a histogram can easily be maintained in main memory.

The time argument of a query exceeds the reference time of any object by at most Δt_{mu}. This is reasonable, as it is of little use to query so far into the future that all the values on which the result is based will have been updated before that time is reached. Considering the example in Figure 4, suppose a query is issued between $\frac{1}{2}\Delta t_{mu}$ and Δt_{mu} and that T_0, T_1, and T_2 are the partitions corresponding to the label timestamps $\frac{1}{2}\Delta t_{mu}$, Δt_{mu}, and $\frac{3}{2}\Delta t_{mu}$, respectively. Partition (or subtree) T_0 may need to be extended to Δt_{mu}

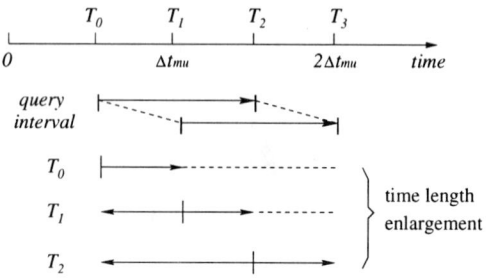

Figure 4: Time Length Enlargement

at most, and after that, T_0 expires; the T_1 may be extended backward to $\frac{1}{2}\Delta t_{mu}$ and forward to Δt_{mu}; T_2 may be extended backward to $\frac{1}{2}\Delta t_{mu}$ and forward to $\frac{3}{2}\Delta t_{mu}$. For either subtree, we can see that the maximum enlargement length is Δt_{mu}.

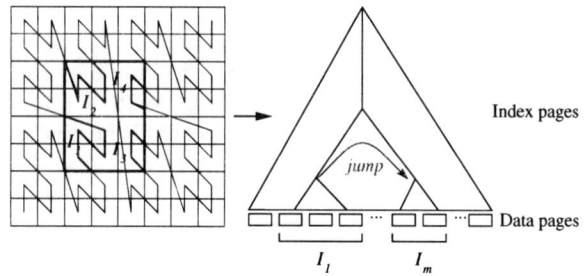

Figure 5: "Jump" in the Index

Next, we traverse the partitions of the B^x-tree with label timestamp no less than $\lceil t_q - \Delta t_{mu} \cdot (n-1)/n \rceil$ (i.e., they should be valid at t_q) to find objects falling in the enlarged query window q'. For example, if $\Delta t_{mu} < t_q \leq \frac{3}{2}\Delta t_{mu}$, Partition T_0 needs not be searched. In each partition, the use of a space-filling curve means that a range query in the native, two-dimensional space becomes a set of range queries in the transformed, one-dimensional space—see Figure 5. Hence multiple traversals of the index result. We optimize these traversals by calculating the start and end points of the one-dimensional ranges and traverse the intervals by "jumping" in the index (as in [17]).

Let us step through the entire algorithm in detail. For each partition of the B^x-tree, we check whether it is valid at the query time t_q according to its label timestamp (lines 1–2). If it is valid, we enlarge query window q to q' by function TimeParameterizedRegion (line 3) and calculate all start and end points $i_1, i_2, \ldots, i_{2m-1}, i_{2m}$ in ascending order of their x_values, where m is the number of intervals (line 4). The pair of points (i_{2j-1}, i_{2j}) start and end interval I_j $(1 \leq j \leq m)$.

We locate the leaf node containing the first point i_1, then traverse its right siblings using the B-link sibling pointers until we reach the next point i_2, where interval I_1 ends (lines 5–10).

To find i_3, the start point of interval I_2, we backtrack to a higher level where one "jumping" occurs, upon which we proceed to retrieve the objects with positions in interval I_2. This takes place in line 6 of the algorithm, where traversal from the root is avoided as much as possible. When all the intervals have been checked in this manner, we have obtained the set of all objects that may possibly belong to the result of range query q. For each object, we compute its position at t and return only those objects whose positions are actually in the query window q (lines 11–14).

Algorithm Range_query(q, t_q)
Input: q is the query range and t_q is the query time
1. **for** $j \leftarrow 0$ **to** n
2.   **if** partition T_j of the B^x-tree is valid at t_q **then**
3. $q' \leftarrow$ TimeParameterizedRegion(q, t_q)
4.   calculate start and end points $i_1, \ldots, i_{2m}$ for q'
5.   **for** $k \leftarrow 1$ **to** m **do**
6.   locate leaf node containing point i_{2k-1}
7.   **repeat**
8.   store candidate objects in L
9.   follow the right pointer to the sibling node
10.   **until** node with point i_{2k} is reached
11. **for** each object in L **do**
12.   **if** the object's position at t_q is inside q **then**
13.   add the object to the result_set
14. **return** result_set

Figure 6: Range Query Algorithm

3.2.2 k Nearest Neighbor Query

Assuming a set of $N > k$ objects and given a query object with position $q = (qx_1, qx_2)$, the k nearest neighbor query (kNN query) retrieves k objects for which no other objects are nearer to the query object at time t_q not prior to the current time.

We compute this query by iteratively performing range queries with an incrementally enlarged search region until k answers are obtained. The algorithm is outlined in Figure 7. We first construct a range R_{q1} centered at q and with extension $r_q = D_k/k$, where D_k is the estimated distance between the query object and its k'th nearest neighbor; D_k can be estimated by the equation [23]:

$$D_k = \frac{2}{\sqrt{\pi}}\left[1 - \sqrt{1 - \left(\frac{k}{N}\right)^{\frac{1}{2}}}\right]$$

We compute the range query with range R_{q1} at time t_q

by enlarging it to a range R'_{q1} and proceeding as described in the previous section. If at least k objects are currently covered by R'_{q1} and are enclosed in the inscribed circle of R_{q1} at time t_q, the kNN algorithm returns the k nearest objects and then stops. It is safe to stop because we have considered all the objects that can possibly be in the result.

Otherwise, we extend R_{q1} by r_q to obtain R_{q2} and an enlarged window R'_{q2}. This time, we search the region $R'_{q2} - R'_{q1}$ and adjust the neighbor list accordingly. This process is repeated until we obtain an R_{qi} so that there are k objects within its inscribed circle.

Algorithm kNN_query$(q(qx_1, qx_2), k, t_q)$
Input: a query point $q(qx_1, qx_2)$, a number k of neighbors, and a query time t_q
1. construct range R_{q1} with q as center and extension r_q
2. $R'_{q1} \leftarrow$ TimeParameterizedRegion(R_{q1}, t_q)
3. $flag \leftarrow$ true   // not enough objects
4. $i \leftarrow 1$ // first query region is being searched
5. **while** $flag$
6.   **if** $i = 1$ **then**
7.   find all objects in region R'_{q1}
8.   **else**
9.   find all objects in region $R'_{qi} - R'_{qi-1}$
10.   **if** k objects exist in inscribed circle of R_{qi} **then**
11. $flag \leftarrow$ false
12.   **else**
13. $i \leftarrow i + 1$
14. $R_{qi} \leftarrow$ Enlarge(R_{qi-1}, r_q)
15. $R'_{qi} \leftarrow$ TimeParameterizedRegion(R_{qi}, t_q)
16. **return** k NNs with respect to q

Figure 7: kNN Query Algorithm

In some B$^+$-tree implementations, leaf nodes are not only chained left to right, but also right to left. The kNN search algorithm can exploit right to left sibling pointers to avoid always having to traverse the tree from the root when an interval is extended for a next iterative range search. This reduces the search cost but increases the update cost.

3.2.3 Continuous Queries

The queries considered so far in this section may be considered as one-time queries: they run once and complete when a result has been returned. Intuitively, a continuous query is a one-time query that is run at each point in time during a time interval. Further, a continuous query takes a now-relative time $now + \Delta t_q$ as a parameter instead of the fixed time t_q we have used so far. The query then maintains the result of the corresponding one-time query at time $now + \Delta t_q$ from when the query is issued at time t_{issue} and until it is deactivated.

Such a query can be supported by a query q_l with time interval $[t_{issue} + \Delta t_q, t_{issue} + \Delta t_q + l]$ ("l" is a time interval) [2]. Query q_l can be computed by the algorithms we have presented previously, with relatively minor modifications: (i) we use the end time of the time interval to perform forward enlargements, and we use the start time of the time interval for backward enlargements; (ii) we store the answer sets during the time interval. Then, from time t_{issue} to $t_{issue} + l$, the answer to q_l is maintained during update operations. At $t_{issue} + l$, a new query with time interval $[t_{issue} + \Delta t_q + l, t_{issue} + \Delta t_q + 2l]$ is computed.

To maintain a continuous range query during updates, we simply add or remove the object from the answer set if the inserted or deleted object resides in the query window. Such operations only introduce CPU cost.

The maintenance of continuous kNN queries is somewhat more complex. Insertions also only introduce CPU cost: an inserted object is compared with the current answer set. Deletions of objects not in the answer set does not affect the query. However, if a deleted object is in the current answer set, the answer set is no longer valid. In this case, we issue a new query with a time interval of length l at the time of the deletion. If the deletion time is t_{del}, a query with time interval $[t_{del} + \Delta t_q, t_{del} + \Delta t_q + l]$ is triggered at t_{del}, and the answer set is maintained from t_{del} to $t_{del} + l$.

The choice of the "optimal" l value involves a trade-off between the cost of the computation of the query with the time interval and the cost of maintaining its result. On the one hand, we want to avoid a small l as this entails frequent recomputations of queries, which involves a substantial I/O cost. On the other hand, a large l introduces a substantial cost: Although computing one or a few queries is cost effective in itself, we must also take into account the cost of maintaining the larger answer set, which may generate additional I/Os on each update.

We note that maintenance of continuous range queries incur only CPU cost. Thus, we compute a range query with a relatively large l such that l is bounded by $\Delta t_{mu} - \Delta t_q$ since the answer set obtained at t_{issue} is no longer valid at $t_{issue} + \Delta t_{mu}$. For the continuous kNN queries, we examine the effect of l further in the experiments.

3.3 Update, Insertion, and Deletion

The insertion algorithm is straightforward. Given a new object, we calculate its index key according to Equation 1, and then insert it into the B^x-tree as in the B^+-tree. To delete an object, we assume that the positional information for the object used at its last insertion and the last insertion time are known. Then we calculate its index key and employ the same deletion algorithm as in the B^+-tree. Therefore, the B^x-tree directly inherits the good properties of the B^+-tree, and we expect efficient update performance.

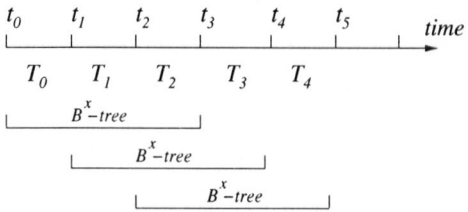

Figure 8: B^x-Tree Evolution

However, one should note that update in the B^x-tree does differ with respect to update in the B^+-tree. The B^x-tree only updates objects when their moving functions have been changed. This is realized by clustering updates during a certain period to one time point and maintaining several corresponding sub-trees. For example (see Figure 8), objects updated between t_0 and t_1 are stored in partition T_0; objects updated between t_1 and t_2 are stored in T_2; etc. T_0, T_1, and T_2 co-exist before t_3. From t_3 to t_4, T_1, T_2, and T_3 co-exist, and T_0 has expired. The total size of the three sub-trees is equal to that of one tree indexing all the objects.

In some applications, there may be some object positions that are updated relatively rarely. For example, most objects may be updated at least each 10 minutes, but a few objects are updated once a day. Instead of letting outliers force a large maximum update interval, we use a "maximum update interval" within which a high percentage of objects have been updated.

Object positions that are not updated within this interval are "flushed" to a new partition using their positions at the label timestamp of the new partition. In the example shown in Figure 8, suppose that some object positions in T_0 are not updated at the time when T_0 expires. At this time, we move these objects to T_2. Although this introduces additional update cost, the (controllable) amortized cost is expected to be very small since outliers are rare.

The forced movement of an object's position to a new partition does not cause any problem with respect to locating the object, since the new partition can be calculated based on the original update time. Likewise, the query efficiency is not affected.

4 Performance Studies

4.1 Experimental Settings

Two versions of the B^x-tree were implemented: B^x(Z-curve) and B^x(H-curve), denoting the B^x-tree using the Peano and the Hilbert curve, respectively. Both B^x-trees and the TPR-tree were implemented in C, and all the experiments were conducted on a 2.6G PentiumIV Personal Computer with 1 Gbyte of memory.

We use synthetic datasets of moving objects with positions in the space domain of 1000×1000. In most experiments, we use uniform data, where object positions are chosen randomly, where the objects move in a randomly chosen direction, and where a speed ranging from 0 to 3 is chosen at random. One may think of the unit of space being kilometer and the unit of speed being kilometer per minute.

Other datasets were generated using an existing data generator, where objects move in a network of two-way routes that connect a given number of uniformly distributed destinations [19]. Objects start at random positions on routes and are assigned at random to one of three groups of objects with maximum speeds of 0.75, 1.5, and 3. Whenever an object reaches one of the destinations, it chooses the next target destination at random. Objects accelerate as they leave a destination, and they decelerate as they approach a destination.

For each dataset, we constructed the index at time 0, and measured the average query cost after the index ran for 10 time units. The parameters used are summarized in Table 1, where values in bold denote default values used.

Parameter	Setting
Page size	4K
Node capacity	200
Max update interval	120
Max predictive interval	60, **120**
Query window size	10, ..., 50, ..., 100
k (kNN query)	10, **20**, 30, 40, 50
Number of queries	200
Dataset size	100K, ..., **500K**, ..., 1M
Space-filling curve	Z, H
Dataset	Uniform, Network-based

Table 1: Parameters and Their Settings

4.2 Storage Requirement

Storage requirement is an important issue in moving object databases since some applications may choose to cache the whole index in main memory to improve performance. Figure 9 shows the storage requirement of both indexes, in which the B^x-trees require less storage space than the TPR-tree. The TPR-tree requires slightly more storage space as its fanout is slightly less than that of the B^x-tree.

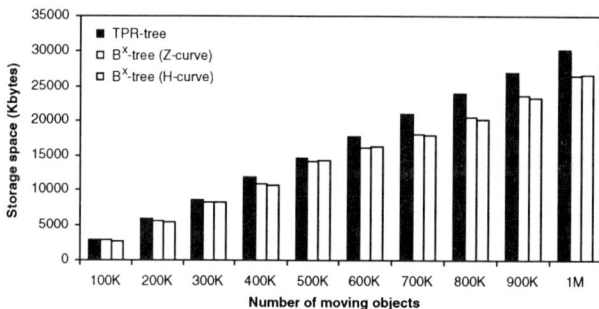

Figure 9: Storage Requirement

4.3 Range Query

4.3.1 Effect of Data Sizes

In the first set of experiments, we study the range query performance of the TPR-tree and the B^x-trees while varying the number of uniformly distributed moving objects from 100K to 1M. Figure 10 shows the average number of I/O operations and the CPU time per range query for each index.

We observe that both B^x-tree variants scale very well and maintain consistent performance, while the TPR-tree degrades linearly with the increase of the dataset size. When the dataset reaches 1M objects, the B^x-trees are nearly 5 times better than the TPR-tree. This behavior may be explained as follows. In the B^x-trees, every object has a linear order, which is determined by the space domain and

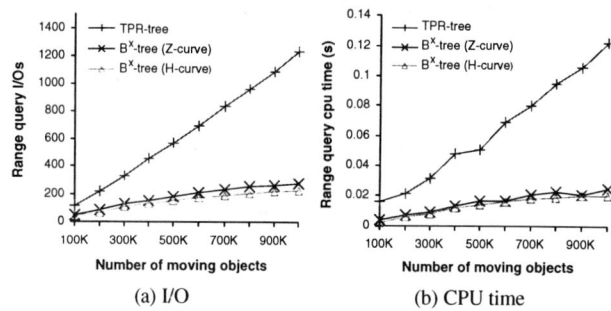

Figure 10: Effect of Data Sizes on Range Query Performance

is relatively independent of the number of moving objects. As the dataset grows, the range query cost of the B^x-trees increases mainly due to the increase of the number of objects inside the range. However, the structure of the TPR-tree is affected more by the dataset size. When the number of objects increases, the MBRs in the TPR-tree have higher probabilities of overlapping; this is consistent with earlier findings for the R-tree [18].

The B^x-tree(H-curve) achieves better performance than the B^x-tree(Z-curve) because the Hilbert curve generates a better distance-preserving mapping than the Peano curve, and hence yields fewer search intervals on the B^x-tree, i.e., less disk access.

4.3.2 Effect of Data Distribution

This experiment uses the road network dataset to study the effect of data distribution on the indexes. The dataset contains 500K data points. Figure 11 shows the range query cost when the number of destinations in the simulated network of routes is varied. The term "uniform" in the figure indicates the case where the objects can choose their moving directions freely.

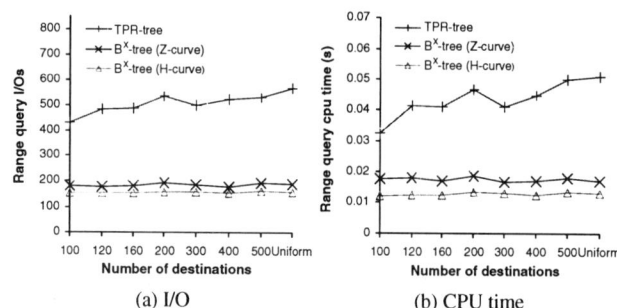

Figure 11: Effect of Data Distribution on Range Query Performance

Observe that the query cost in the TPR-tree increases slightly with the number of destinations, i.e., as the datasets becomes increasingly "uniform." This is consistent with previous results [19]. In contrast, the performance of the B^x-trees is not affected by the data skew because objects are stored using space-filling curves, meaning that the density has less of an effect on the index.

4.3.3 Effect of Speed Distribution

Figure 12 shows the effect of speed of moving objects on the TPR-tree and the B^x-trees, by varying the θ value of the Zipf distribution from 0 (uniform distribution) to 2 (skewed, 80% objects have speed lower than 20% of the maximum speed). All the indexes yield better performance when the number of fast moving objects decreases because MBRs in the TPR-tree obtain smaller expanding speeds and because the enlargements made to query windows for the B^x-trees also become smaller. The results for kNN queries exhibit similar performance trends, so we omit the results due to space constraints.

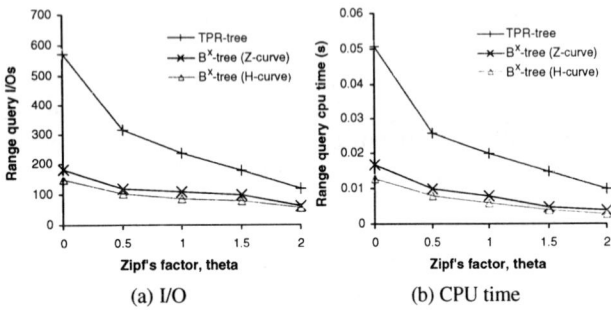

Figure 12: Effect of Speed on Range Query Performance

4.3.4 Effect of Query Window Sizes

We next study the effect of the query window size, varying the window length from 10 to 100 for a dataset of size 500K. As expected, the result in Figure 13 shows that the query cost increases with the query window size. Larger windows contain more objects and therefore lead to more node accesses, and the effect is slightly more obvious on the TPR-tree.

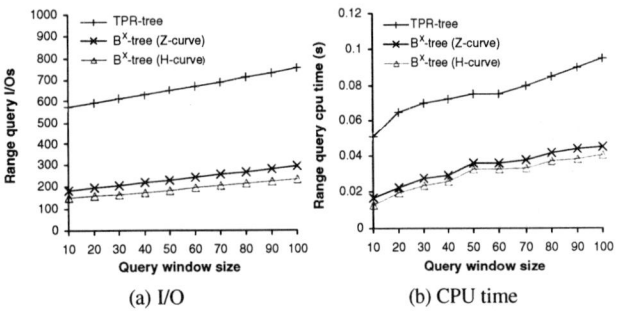

Figure 13: Effect of Query Window Sizes on Range Query Performance

4.3.5 Effect of Time

To study the search performance of the indexes with the passage of time and updates, we compute the query cost using the same 200 range queries with query window size 50, but after every 50K updates in a 500K dataset. Figure 14 summarizes the results, showing that the TPR-tree degrades considerably faster than the B^x-trees due to continuous enlargements of the MBRs which are not updated

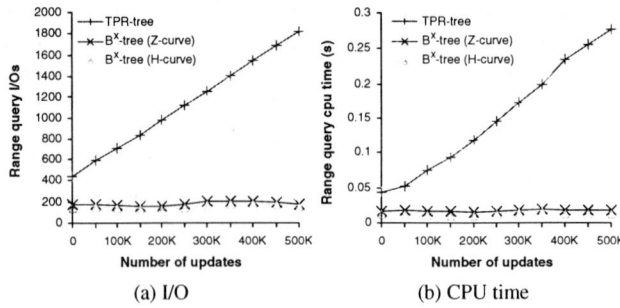

Figure 14: Effect of Time Elapsed on Range Query Performance

as time passes. In contrast, the B^x-tree structure is not affected as much by the updates. In fact, the B^x-trees are almost time independent.

4.4 kNN Query

We proceed to evaluate the efficiency of kNN queries using the same settings as for range queries. Figures 15–17 show in turn the effect of dataset size, data distribution, and time passed on kNN query performance. The performance difference between the TPR-tree and the B^x-tree of the kNN queries exhibits a behavior similar to that of range queries. The B^x-tree's kNN search algorithm is essentially an incremental range query algorithm; hence, the results exhibit similar patterns as the results for range queries.

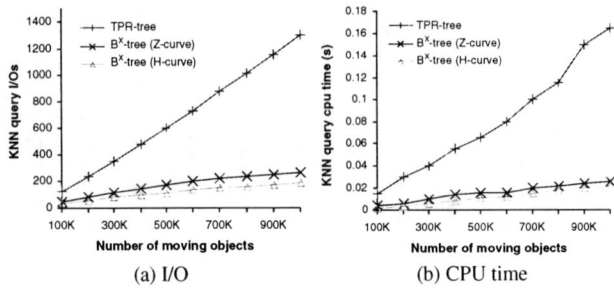

Figure 15: Effect of Data Sizes on kNN Query Performance

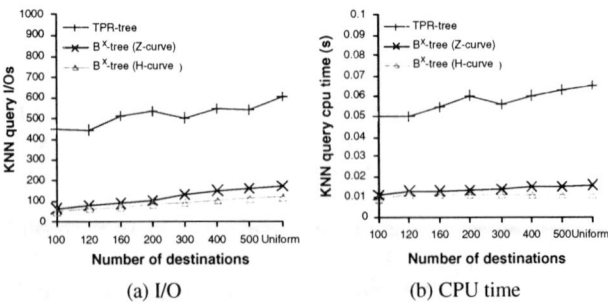

Figure 16: Effect of Data Distribution on kNN Query Performance

Figure 18 shows the effect on performance of the number k of required nearest neighbors. As k increases, the search and CPU costs increase slightly for both indexes.

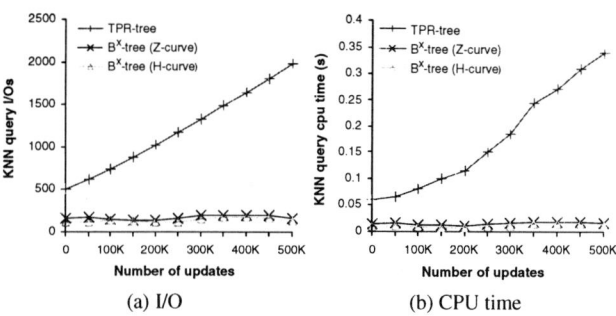

(a) I/O (b) CPU time

Figure 17: Effect of Time Elapsed on kNN Query Performance

Due to the data size and side effect of the query and MBR enlargement, the effect of k is not significant.

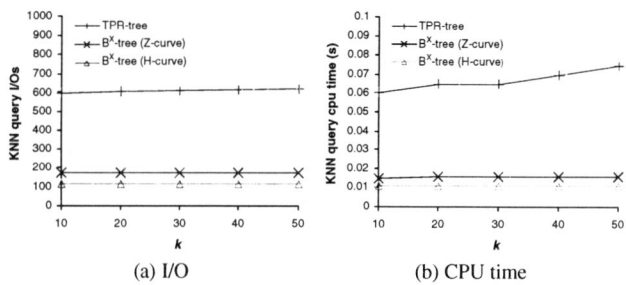

(a) I/O (b) CPU time

Figure 18: Effect of k on kNN Query Performance

4.5 Continuous Range and kNN Queries

In moving object database applications, continuous queries are expected to be common, and hence efficient support for such queries is important. To investigate the maintenance cost of continuous queries, we perform a series of experiments where we vary the length of the query recomputation interval l. We evaluate the amortized cost per single update operation (insertion or deletion) in maintaining one continuous query. Indexes were created at time 0, and after running 10 time units, 200 queries (with maximum predictive interval 60) were issued. Then the workload was run for another 120 time units while maintaining the result set of the queries.

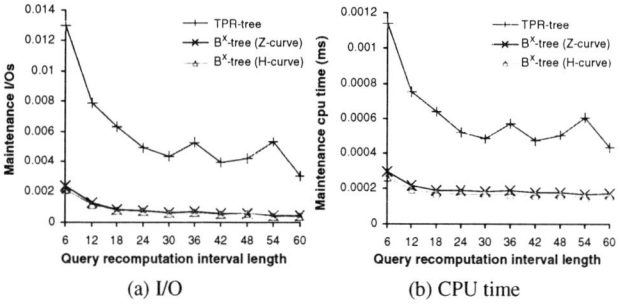

(a) I/O (b) CPU time

Figure 19: Maintenance Cost of Continuous Range Query

Figure 19 shows the continuous range query performance. Since the maximum predictive length is 60 and the

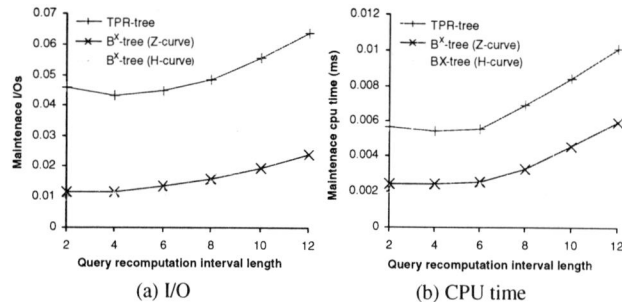

(a) I/O (b) CPU time

Figure 20: Maintenance Cost of Continuous kNN Query

maximum update interval is 120, the maximum recomputation interval tested is $120 - 60 = 60$. As can be observed, the maintenance cost decreases with the increase of the recomputation length in all indexes. This is because the cost to maintain the answer set under continuous updates is very small, and the recomputation cost constitutes the major I/O cost. The smaller the recomputation interval l, the more number of recomputations.

Figure 20 shows the performance of the continuous kNN query. We observe that, for all the indexes, the maintenance cost first decreases until a point before it increases again. The best l is approximately 4 for the TPR-tree and approximately 3 for the B^x-trees. As the l becomes larger, the number of recomputation decreases, however, the possibility to remove objects from the results increases, and consequently, additional recomputations result.

4.6 Update

We compare the average update cost (amortized over insertion and deletion) of the B^x-trees against the TPR-tree. Note that for each update, one deletion and one insertion are issued, leaving the size of the tree unchanged.

4.6.1 Effect of Data Sizes

First we examine the update performance with respect to dataset size. We compute the average update cost after the maximum update interval of 120 time units. From Figure 21, we can see that the B^x-trees achieve significant improvement over the TPR-tree. In most cases, one update

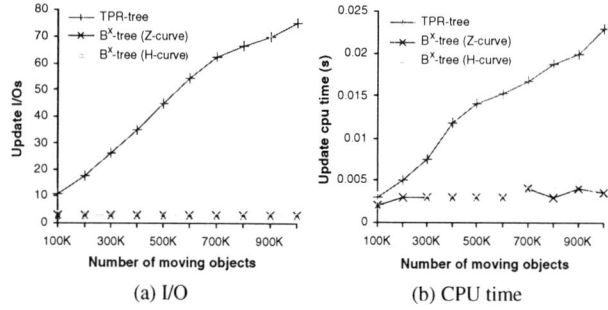

(a) I/O (b) CPU time

Figure 21: Effect of Data Sizes on Update Cost

in the B^x-tree only incurs several I/O operations. However, the update cost in the TPR-tree increases significantly as the dataset grows in size. This is because in the B^x-trees, given the key, an insertion and a deletion needs to traverse only one path, no matter how large the dataset is. Thus, the cost of update in the B^x-tree is only related to the height of the tree.

In this experiment, the performance of the B^x-tree(Z-curve) and the B^x-tree(H-curve) are comparable, since the update efficiency is independent of the spatial proximity preservation. However, in the TPR-tree, traversal of multiple paths is inevitable due to the overlaps among MBRs. As the density of values increases due to the increase in data size, more overlap and hence higher update cost results.

4.6.2 Effect of Time

Next, we investigate performance degradation across time. We measure the performance of the TPR-tree and the B^x-trees after every 50K updates. Figure 22 shows the update cost as a function of the number of updates. As before, the

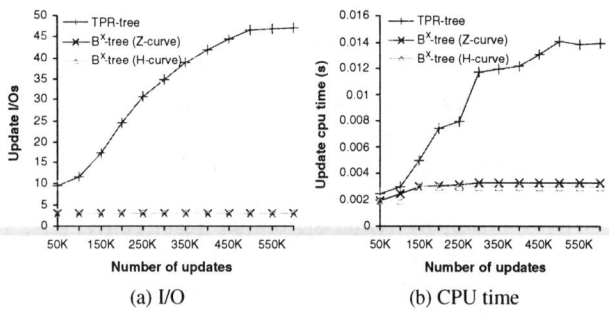

(a) I/O (b) CPU time

Figure 22: Effect of the Number of Updates on Update Cost

B^x-trees are not affected by time, which again illustrates the efficiency and feasibility of the B^+-tree. We observe that the gap between the TPR-tree and the B^x-trees widens as time passes. At the point when the TPR-tree stabilizes after 500K updates, the cost of the TPR-tree is nearly 10 times that of the B^x-trees. The reason for the degeneration of the TPR-tree is that each deletion entails a search to retrieve the object to be removed, and the cost of this search increases with the number of updates.

We note that this cost can be reduced by maintaining a hash-table for quickly locating the object and then performing a bottom-up update [10]. However, such an auxiliary structure incurs additional storage overhead and increases complexity.

4.6.3 Effect of Update Interval Length

In this experiment, we investigate the effect of maximum update interval length on the indexes, by varying the maximum update interval from 60 to 240. Figure 23 shows the average update cost after the indexes run for one maximum update interval. We observe that the performance of the TPR-tree degrades fairly quickly as the maximum update interval increases, whereas the B^x-trees are not affected. The main reason is that, as the update interval increases, the overlap among MBRs becomes more severe and thus

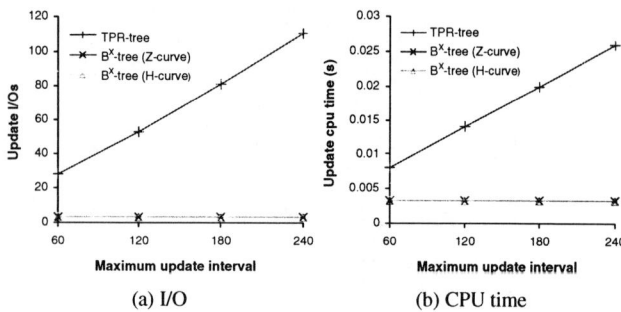

(a) I/O (b) CPU time

Figure 23: Effect of Maximum Update Interval

affects the performance of the TPR-tree significantly. In contrast, the update operation in the B^x-tree depends only on the key value which does not change over time.

4.7 Effect of Concurrent Accesses and Buffer Space

In this section, we compare the concurrent performance of the TPR-tree and the B^x-tree. We implemented the R-link technique [8] for the TPR-tree and the B-link technique [21] for the B^x-tree.

We used multi-thread programs to simulate multi-user environments. The number of threads varies from 1 to 8. Workloads contain an equal number of queries and updates. We investigated the throughput and response time of search and update operations. Throughput is the rate at which operations could be served by the system. Response time is the time interval between issuing an operation and getting the response from the system when the task was successfully completed.

Figure 24 shows throughput and response time for the three indexes. The throughputs of the B^x-trees are much

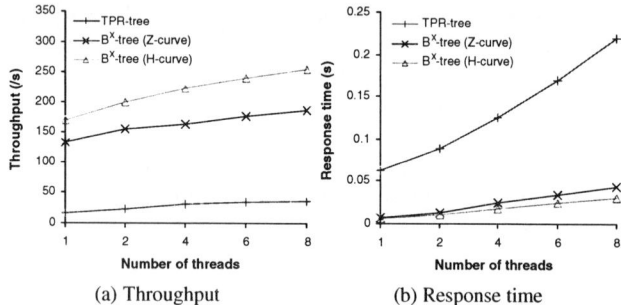

(a) Throughput (b) Response time

Figure 24: Effect of Concurrent Operations

higher than that of the TPR-tree, and the response times of the B^x-trees are always less than those of the TPR-tree. The main reason is that the B^x-trees seldom lock internal nodes. Recall that, in the query processing, we will first travel down to the leaf level, then retrieve the leaf nodes for the answers by following the left-to-right sibling links. We may occasionally ascend to an internal node for a "jump," but this often happens at the lower levels of the index. For the TPR-tree, a query triggers searching of multiple paths, which introduces locks on the internal nodes that reduce the parallelism of concurrent operations.

We also included an LRU buffer and studied the effects of different buffer sizes. As with other indexes, both indexes experience reduced I/O's as the buffer size increases. Since the B^x-tree incurs less page reads originally, the effect of an increasing buffer size on the index is consequently less pronounced than for the TPR-tree. We also examined the effects of the density of objects over the data space. The results are as may be expected; due to space constraints, we do not include the graphs here.

5 Conclusion and Research Directions

Database applications that entail the storage of samples of continuous, multi-dimensional variables pose new challenges to database technology. This paper addresses the challenge of providing support for indexing that is efficient for querying as well as update.

We proposed a new indexing scheme, the B^x-tree, which is based on the B^+-tree. This scheme uses a new linearization technique that exploits the volatility of the data values, i.e., moving-object locations, being indexed. Algorithms are provided for range and kNN queries on the current or near-future positions of the indexed objects, as well as for so-called continuous counterparts of these types of queries. Queries that reach into the future are handled via query region enlargement, as opposed to the MBR enlargement used in TPR-trees.

Extensive performance studies were conducted that indicate that the B^x-tree is both efficient and robust. In fact, it is capable of outperforming the TPR-tree by factors of as much as 10. Further, being a B^+-tree index, the B^x-tree may be grafted into existing database systems cost effectively.

Several promising directions for future work exist, one being to consider the use of the B^x-tree for the processing of new kinds of queries. Another is the use of the B^x-tree for other continuous variables than the positions of mobile service users. Yet another direction is to apply the linearization technique to other index structures.

Acknowledgements

The work of D. Lin and B. C. Ooi was in part funded by an A*STAR project on spatial-temporal databases. In addition to his primary affiliation with Aalborg University, C. S. Jensen is an adjunct professor in Department of Technology, Agder University College, Norway. His work was funded in part by grants 216 and 333 from the Danish National Center for IT Research.

References

[1] N. Beckmann, H. Kriegel, R. Schneider, and B. Seeger. The R*-Tree: An Efficient and Robust Access Method for Points and Rectangles. In *Proc. ACM SIGMOD*, pp. 322–331, 1990.

[2] R. Benetis, C. S. Jensen, G. Karciauskas, and S. Saltenis. Nearest Neighbor and Reverse Nearest Neighbor Queries for Moving Objects. In *Proc. IDEAS*, pp. 44–53, 2002.

[3] A. Civilis, C. S. Jensen, J. Nenortaite, and S. Pakalnis. Efficient Tracking of Moving Objects with Precision Guarantees. In *Proc. MobiQuitous*, 2004, 10 pages, to appear.

[4] C. Faloutsos and S. Roseman. Fractals for Secondary Key Retrieval. In *Proc. PODS*, pp. 247–252, 1989.

[5] A. Guttman. R-trees: A Dynamic Index Structure for Spatial Searching. In *Proc. ACM SIGMOD*, pp. 47–57, 1984.

[6] C. S. Jensen and S. Saltenis. Towards Increasingly Update Efficient Moving-Object Indexing. *IEEE Data Eng. Bull.*, 25(2): 35–40, 2002.

[7] G. Kollios, D. Gunopulos, V. J. Tsotras. On Indexing Mobile Objects. In *Proc. PODS*, pp. 261–272, 1999.

[8] M. Kornacker and D. Banks. High-Concurrency Locking in R-Trees. In *Proc. VLDB*, pp. 134–145, 1995.

[9] D. Kwon, S. Lee, and S. Lee. Indexing the Current Positions of Moving Objects Using the Lazy Update R-Tree. In *Proc. MDM*, pp. 113–120, 2002.

[10] M. L. Lee, W. Hsu, C. S. Jensen, B. Cui, and K. L. Teo. Supporting Frequent Updates in R-Trees: A Bottom-Up Approach. In *Proc. VLDB*, pp. 608–619, 2003.

[11] M. F. Mokbel, T. M. Ghanem, and W. G. Aref. Spatio-Temporal Access Methods. *IEEE Data Eng. Bull.*, 26(2): 40–49, 2003.

[12] B. Moon, H. V. Jagadish, C. Faloutsos, and J. H. Saltz. Analysis of the Clustering Properties of the Hilbert Space-Filling Curve. *IEEE TKDE*, 13(1): 124–141, 2001.

[13] B. C. Ooi, K. L. Tan, and C. Yu. Fast Update and Efficient Retrieval: an Oxymoron on Moving Object Indexes. In *Proc. of Int. Web GIS Workshop, Keynote*, 2002.

[14] J. M. Patel, Y. Chen and V. P. Chakka. STRIPES: An Efficient Index for Predicted Trajectories. In *Proc. ACM SIGMOD*, 2004, to appear.

[15] D. Pfoser, C. S. Jensen, and Y. Theodoridis. Novel Approaches in Query Processing for Moving Objects. In *Proc. VLDB*, pp. 395–406, 2000.

[16] C. M. Procopiuc, P. K. Agarwal, and S. Har-Peled. Star-Tree: An Efficient Self-Adjusting Index for Moving Objects. In *Proc. ALENEX*, pp. 178–193, 2002.

[17] F. Ramsak, V. Markl, R. Fenk, M. Zirkel, K. Elhardt, and R. Bayer. Integrating the UB-Tree Into a Database System Kernel. In *Proc. VLDB*, pp. 263–272, 2000.

[18] N. Roussopoulos and D. Leifker. Direct Spatial Search on Pictorial Databases Using Packed R-Trees. In *Proc. ACM SIGMOD*, pp. 17–31, 1985.

[19] S. Saltenis, C. S. Jensen, S. T. Leutenegger, and M. A. Lopez. Indexing the Positions of Continuously Moving Objects. In *Proc. ACM SIGMOD*, pp. 331–342, 2000.

[20] H. Samet. The Quadtree and Related Hierarchical Data Structures. *ACM Comp. Surv.*, 16(2): 187–260, 1984.

[21] V. Srinivasan and M. J. Carey. Performance of B-Tree Concurrency Control Algorithms. In *the Proc. ACM SIGMOD*, pp. 416–425, 1991.

[22] Y. Tao, D. Papadias, and J. Sun. The TPR*-Tree: An Optimized Spatio-Temporal Access Method for Predictive Queries. In *Proc. VLDB*, pp. 790–801, 2003.

[23] Y. Tao, J. Zhang, D. Papadias, and N. Mamoulis. An Efficient Cost Model for Optimization of Nearest Neighbor Search in Low and Medium Dimensional Spaces. *IEEE TKDE*, to appear.

[24] J. Tayeb, O. Ulusoy, and O. Wolfson. A Quadtree Based Dynamic Attribute Indexing Method. *The Computer Journal*, 41(3): 185–200, 1998.

[25] C. Yu, B. C. Ooi, K. L. Tan and H. V. Jagadish. Indexing the Distance: An Efficient Method to KNN Processing. In *Proc. VLDB*, pp. 421–430, 2001.

Indexing Large Human-Motion Databases

Eamonn Keogh* Themistoklis Palpanas Victor B. Zordan Dimitrios Gunopulos
Department of Computer Science
University of California, Riverside
{eamonn, themis, vbz, dg}@cs.ucr.edu

Marc Cardle
Computer Laboratory
University of Cambridge
mpc33@cl.cam.ac.uk

ABSTRACT
Data-driven animation has become the industry standard for computer games and many animated movies and special effects. In particular, motion capture data recorded from live actors, is the most promising approach offered thus far for animating realistic human characters. However, the manipulation of such data for general use and re-use is not yet a solved problem. Many of the existing techniques dealing with editing motion rely on indexing for annotation, segmentation, and re-ordering of the data. Euclidean distance is inappropriate for solving these indexing problems because of the inherent variability found in human motion. The limitations of Euclidean distance stems from the fact that it is very sensitive to distortions in the time axis. A partial solution to this problem, Dynamic Time Warping (DTW), aligns the time axis before calculating the Euclidean distance. However, DTW can only address the problem of *local* scaling. As we demonstrate in this paper, *global* or *uniform scaling* is just as important in the indexing of human motion. We propose a novel technique to speed up similarity search under uniform scaling, based on bounding envelopes. Our technique is intuitive and simple to implement. We describe algorithms that make use of this technique, we perform an experimental analysis with real datasets, and we evaluate it in the context of a motion capture processing system. The results demonstrate the utility of our approach, and show that we can achieve orders of magnitude of speedup over the brute force approach, the only alternative solution currently available.

Keywords
Motion Capture, Animation, Time Series, Indexing

1. INTRODUCTION
Data-driven animation has now become the industry standard for the production of computer games and many animated movies and special effects. The most promising and widely applied approach so far is the use of motion capture data. These are motion data recorded from live actors, which can subsequently be used for animating realistic human characters. Nevertheless, the manipulation of such data for general use and re-use is still an open problem. Among the issues at hand, the semi-automatic annotation [3][6] and re-ordering of motion data [4][22][23][25] are appearing in animation research conferences and slowly trickling their way into games where realism, interactivity, and speed drive innovation.

Motion capture data, in its rawest form, is recorded with a few technologies, the most popular of which appears to be optical (see Vicon [38] and Motion Analysis [39] products) in which digital cameras record small reflective markers fixed to the human actor as he/she moves. Through multiple cameras and triangulation, three dimensional position traces for the markers are resolved faithfully. The markers can then be identified (as outer left knee, for example) and filtered. Motion capture allows the animation of a 3D model, where the data is mapped to the skeleton of the desired character and body orientations are determined (Figure 1).

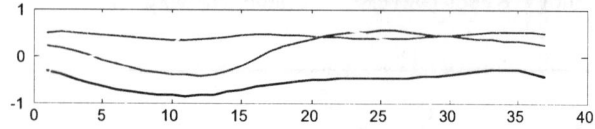

Figure 1: (*Top Left*) An actor being recorded using an Ascension magnetic system while playing table tennis. In post-processing, the data recorded from the actor's motion is manually segmented into motion time series (*Bottom*) and placed in a library that is later used to animate the simulated player shown (*Top Right*).

In practical applications, most motion capture data is stored in segmented sequences in a motion library, for example a modern sports game may contain thousands of

---

* Dr. Keogh is supported by NSF Career Award IIS-0237918.

Permission to copy without fee all or part of this material is granted provided that the copies are not made or distributed for direct commercial advantage, the VLDB copyright notice and the title of the publication and its date appear, and notice is given that copying is by permission of the Very Large Data Base Endowment. To copy otherwise, or to republish, requires a fee and/or special permission from the Endowment.
**Proceedings of the 30th VLDB Conference,
Toronto, Canada, 2004**

motion data "clips". The system, i.e. game engine in this case, selects and plays motions from the database [37]. Our approach aids in the creation and manipulation of such libraries by quickly finding instances of a given motion segment in the complete raw-data repository, e.g., *kicks* or *punches* in the case of a hand-to-hand combat game. In addition to speeding up brute force searches, our main contribution is finding examples independent of the speed in which the actor performed these behaviors.

A major difficulty in indexing and matching motion streams (hereafter used interchangeably with "*time series*") is the variability in the speed of human motion. For example, an actor may perform a fast or slow punch. Such variability can manifest itself as *uniform scaling*, a global stretching or shrinking of the time series (i.e., with respect to the time axis). In this work we introduce the first indexing technique to support uniform scaling. Our contributions can be summarized as follows.

- We motivate the need for similarity search under uniform scaling, and differentiate it from Dynamic Time Warping (DTW). Although the superiority of DTW over Euclidean distance is becoming increasing apparent [1][9][18][35], the need for similarity search which is invariant to uniform scaling is not well understood.
- We introduce the first known lower bounding technique for uniform scaling. This technique allows us to index the time series in order to achieve fast similarity search under uniform scaling.
- We demonstrate the efficiency and effectiveness of our techniques with a comprehensive empirical evaluation on real datasets. We also evaluate our techniques using a motion capture processing system. These experiments validate the utility of the approach we propose.

The rest of this paper is organized as follows. In Section 2 we motivate the need to index motion streams under uniform scaling. Section 3 considers related work on indexing time series. We introduce the problem at hand formally in Section 4, before introducing our solution in Section 5. In Section 6 we describe algorithms that solve the problem in secondary storage. Section 7 offers a comprehensive empirical evaluation of our technique, and we conclude in Section 8.

2. MOTIVATING THE NEED FOR UNIFORM SCALING

In addition to the classic Euclidean and Dynamic Time Warping distance measures, the last decade has seen the introduction of dozens of new similarity measures for time series. Recent empirical studies, however, suggest that the majority of these measures are of dubious utility for real world problems [21]. We will therefore take the time to motivate the need for uniform scaling in our domain.

An important task in motion editing is the concatenation of short motion clips into a longer, plausible motion

[30][37]. For clarity let us consider a concrete example. Imagine we have a motion sequence that contains several distinct motions, and then ends with a particular action, the drawing and aiming of a gun. We would like to append to this action sequence another sequence where the actor falls to the ground. While we have a library of perhaps thousands of sequences labeled "falling", we must decide to which of these we should append our current sequence. The challenge in this case is to make sure that the transition is as smooth and natural as possible. For example, we do not want the character's left arm to instantaneously move from his/her side to above his/her head.

A simple way to guarantee natural plausible motion is to ensure that the suffix of the first motion, lets say the last *n* data points, is an approximate match to the prefix of the candidate sequence, the first *n* data points. This way, instead of concatenating the two sequences end to end, they are allowed to overlap by *n* data points. Averaging or time warping can be used to smooth out any slight inconsistencies within the *n* overlapping data points. Figure 2 illustrates the basic idea with a simple problem, taken from a video segment. Although this example considers a one-dimensional time series, it can easily be extended to multi-dimensional time series, by combining the results for each degree of freedom, possibly weighted by their perceptual importance (i.e., arm motion may be more important than leg motion in some situations).

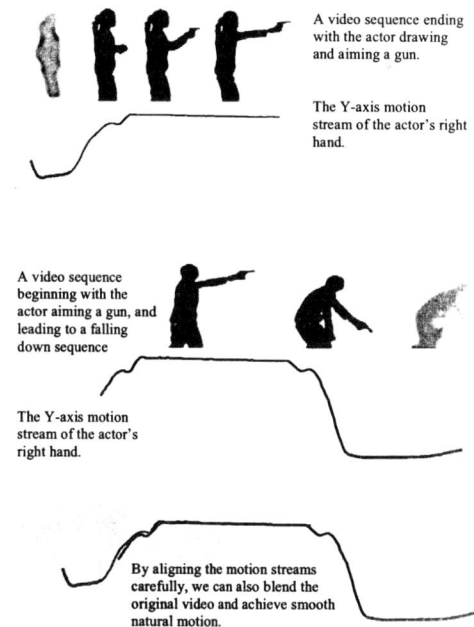

Figure 2: We can create a smooth transition between two video clips (*Top* and *Center*), by ensuring the prefix of one approximately matches the suffix of the other (*Bottom*).

In Figure 2, our contrived example happens to have a closely matching prefix/suffix pair. More generally however, the motion streams may occur at different speeds.

Although the animator can trivially recognize this when he/she see it, human inspection does not scale to large databases. The importance of (time) scale invariance stems from the fact that small differences in scaling can greatly confuse distance calculations. This problem arises in the motion capture domain, and has also been observed in other similar domains. For example, in music retrieval has been reported [9]: *"To achieve tempo invariance, the targets are stretched by 19 different scaling factors from 0.5 to 2.0."* Similar remarks can be found in the literature of gait analysis [14], handwritten archive indexing [28], bioinformatics [1] and data mining [8].

We can reiterate here the utility of uniform scaling with a simple experiment. We created 3 pairs of time series, where each pair was created using one of 3 functions, sine wave, sawtooth I, and sawtooth II. Within each pair, the only difference between the time series is that we allow their length to vary in the range 256 ± 16. We clustered them using two different distance measures, the classic Euclidean distance [6][12][16][19][20][24], and using uniform scaling, where we search over the best possible scaling, truncating off any unmatched suffix (see Section 4 for more formal details). The results are shown in Figure 3.

If these synthetic time series had been, examples of an actor's gait, then using the Euclidean distance, a video clip corresponding to sequence 2 would be concatenated to its closest match, sequence 5. This would be a very abrupt and noticeable transition. In contrast, under uniform scaling, sequence 2 would be concatenated to sequence 1. In this case, the only difference in the resulting animation would be a slight change of pace (if we chose not to permanently rescale one of the sequences). This is why automatic matching of motion capture data *must* consider uniform scaling.

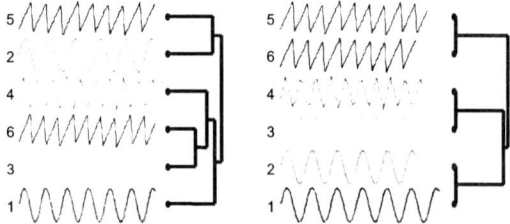

Figure 3: (*Left*) A clustering of 6 synthetic time series using Euclidean distance, and (*Right*) uniform scaling. Subjectively and objectively, the clustering on the right is correct.

Note that the generally useful tool of DTW is *not* the answer to this problem [13][18][35]. On the dataset above DTW is about 200 times slower than uniform scaling, and returns a dendrogram (i.e., a visual representation of the result of a hierarchical clustering, like the ones shown in Figure 3) of ((2,((4,(6,3)),5)),1), which is no better than the Euclidean distance dendrogram. The problem is that DTW is designed to consider only local adjustments of the time axis, whereas it is global adjustments that are required to solve our problem.

To further demonstrate the difference between DTW and uniform scaling, we perform the following experiment. We record twice a one second snippet of an individual's electrocardiogram. On the first occasion, the time series captures two heartbeats, while on the second (during exercise), captures three heartbeats. When we use DTW to measure the similarity of the two sequences, we get meaningless results, because DTW must match every point, and there is simply no sensible way to map two heartbeats to three (Figure 4(left)). In contrast, uniform scaling can stretch the faster heartbeat until finding a near perfect alignment (Figure 4(right)). As mentioned above, DTW can be useful to remove subtle local differences *after* uniform scaling has located the best global match [9].

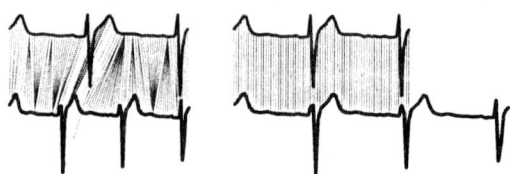

Figure 4: A visual contrast of DTW (*left*) and Uniform Scaling (*right*). Using DTW we cannot achieve an intuitive alignment between 2 heartbeats and 3 heartbeats, even if the sequences happen to be the same length. However uniform scaling, by stretching the bottom sequence can achieve a meaningful alignment.

3. RELATED WORK

The problem of indexing large time series databases has attracted great interest in the database community, and, at least for the Euclidean distance measure, may now be regarded as a solved problem [6][12][16][19][20][29]. However, in recent years, there has been an increasing awareness that Euclidean distance is inappropriate for many real world applications [1][9][35]. The limitations of Euclidean distance stems from the fact that it is very sensitive to distortions in the time axis. A partial solution to this problem, DTW, essentially aligns the time axis before calculating the Euclidean distance [18]. However DTW can only address the problem of *local* scaling, and as we demonstrated above, uniform scaling is just as important in the motion capture editing domain. Similar observations hold for the Longest Common SubSequence measure [10][32].

The utility of uniform scaling has been noted before [1][2][8][27]. However, all previous work has focused on speeding up similarity search, when the scaling factor is *known* [8][17][26]. The feature that differentiates our work from all the rest is that we allow a user to issue a single query, and find the best match at *any* scaling.

Note that although we don't generally know the scaling factor in advance, we may know upper and lower limits on the scaling factor, based on limitations of human biomechanics. For example, most people can only speed up their natural walk about 20% before changing their gait into a run [14].

There is exactly one other technique in the literature that allows similarity search under uniform scaling, while guaranteeing no false dismissals, the "*CD-criterion*" technique of [2]. While pioneering, we do not see this work as a complete solution to our problem for the following reasons. The algorithm can only test if sequences are within a user-supplied epsilon, and thus cannot be used for ranking, classification or clustering. The algorithm requires a parameter to be set; this parameter does not affect the accuracy, but it can affect the speedup. Finally the real weakness of the approach is that is only speeds up main memory search, and cannot be indexed. In fact, the authors suggest that indexing of uniform scaling "*appears infeasible*" [2], although this is exactly the contribution of this work. In spite of these limitations, we empirically compare this work to our approach in Section 7.1.

4. THE UNIFORM SCALING PROBLEM

We begin by formally defining the uniform scaling problem. Suppose we have two time series, a query Q, and a candidate match C, of length *n* and *m* respectively, where:

$$Q = q_1, q_2, \ldots, q_i, \ldots, q_n \tag{1}$$

$$C = c_1, c_2, \ldots, c_j, \ldots, c_m \tag{2}$$

For clarity of presentation we will assume that $n \leq m$, that is, C is always longer than or equal to Q. Thus, we are only interested in stretching the query to match some prefix of C. This assumption is only to simplify notation and does not preclude matching a time series by shrinking. For example, if the user wishes to perform a query of length 100, with the flexibility to shrink or stretch by 10%, the system simply interpolates the data down to 90 data points, and then searches for matches *stretched* by up to 22%.

If we wish to compare the two time series, and it happens that $n = m$, we can use the ubiquitous Euclidean distance [6][12][16][20]:

$$D(Q,C) \equiv \sqrt{\sum_{i=1}^{n}(q_i - c_i)^2} \tag{3}$$

Since the square root function is monotonic and concave, we can remove the square root step to get the squared Euclidean distance which gives identical rankings, clustering and classifications [21].

$$D(Q,C) \equiv \sum_{i=1}^{n}(q_i - c_i)^2 \tag{4}$$

In addition to the utility of slightly speeding up the calculations, working with this distance measure makes other optimizations possible, as well [21].

If *n* is smaller than *m*, then the distance measures introduced above are not defined. To compare the two time series in this case, we have several choices; we can truncate C, and compare Q to $[c_1, c_2, \ldots, c_n]$, we can *stretch* Q to be of length *m*, or more generally, we can *stretch* Q to be of length *p*, ($n \leq p \leq m$), truncate off the last *m-p* values of C, and then use the squared Euclidean distance. The informal idea behind *stretching* can be captured in the more formal definition of scaling. In order to scale time series Q to produce a new time series QP of length *p*, we use the formula:

$$QP_j = Q_{\lceil j*n/p \rceil}, \ 1 \leq j \leq p \tag{5}$$

Note that we can quickly obtain any scaling in O(*p*) time. We call the ratio *p/n* the *scaling factor* or *sf*. Similarly, we use sf_{max} to denote the ratio *m/n*, which can be thought of as the *maximum* scaling factor. Figure 5 visually summarizes the above definitions.

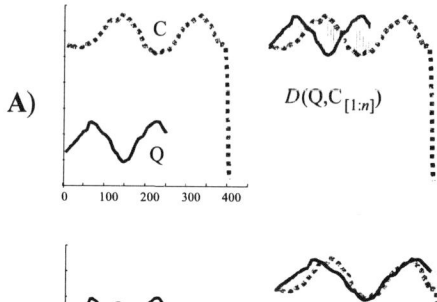

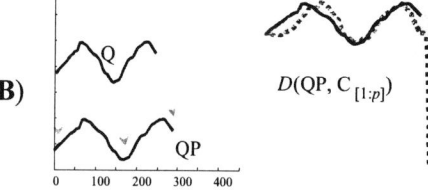

Figure 5. A visual summary of the notation introduced in this section. A) From (*left*) to (*right*) A candidate time series C, and a shorter query Q. The squared Euclidean distance between Q and the first *n* datapoints in C can be visualized as the sum of the squared lengths of the gray hatch lines. B) From (*left*) to (*right*) The query Q can be stretched to length *p*, producing a new time series QP. In this case, QP is a good match to the first *p* datapoints in C.

If we wish to find the best scaled match between Q and C, we can simply test all possible scalings, as illustrated in Table 1.

The algorithm takes O(*p**(*m-n*)) time and seems unworthy of any optimization effort. However, for real world datasets, rather than having a single candidate time series C, we are typically confronted with massive collections of possible candidate time series, which will denote as **D**. In order to find the best scaled match to a query Q in database **D**, we can use a brute force algorithm as shown in Table 2.

Note that the time complexity for this algorithm is O(|**D**|*(m-n)), which is simply untenable for large datasets.

Table 1. An algorithm to find the best scaled match between two time series

```
procedure TestAllScalings(Q,C)
    BestMatchVal     = inf;
    BestScalingFactor = null;
    for p = n to m
        QP = rescale(Q,p);
        Distance = SquaredEuclideanDistance(QP, C[1..p]);
        if distance < BestMatchVal
            BestMatchVal = distance;
            BestScalingFactor = p/n;

    return(BestMatchVal, BestScalingFactor)
```

Table 2. An algorithm to find the best scaled match to query from a set of possible matches.

```
procedure SearchDatabaseforScaledMatch(Q)
    OverallBestTimeSeries = null;
    OverallBestMatchVal   = inf;
    OverallBestScaling    = null;
    for i = 1 to number of time series in (D)
        [dist, scale] = TestAllScalings(Q,C_i)
        if dist < OverallBestMatchVal
            OverallBestTimeSeries = i;
            OverallBestMatchVal   = dist;
            OverallBestScaling    = scale;

    return(OverallBestTimeSeries, OverallBestMatchVal, OverallBestScaling)
```

4.1 Speeding up Search with Lower Bounding

To speed up matching under uniform scaling we will rely on the classic idea of lower bounding. The intuition is the following. Given some technique for quickly calculating the minimum possible distance between the query and a candidate sequence at any possible scaling, we can prune off many calculations. Before calling the subroutine *TestAllScalings()*, we first perform the quick lower bounding test. If the lower bound distance between the candidate and the query is greater than the distance of the best-scaled match already seen, we can simply discard the candidate from consideration. There are two important properties that a lower bounding measure should have.

- It must be fast to compute. A measure that takes as long to compute as *TestAllScalings()* is of little use. We would like the time complexity to be at most linear in the length of the time series.

- It must be a relatively tight lower bound. A lower bound that is not tight, will not prune enough of the search space.

The idea of speeding up search using lower bounding is not new. In fact, it is the cornerstone of virtually every time series similarity search algorithm. However, while dozens of lower bounding measures are known for Euclidean distance [6][12][16][19][20][29], and three lower bounding measures are known for DTW [18][35], only one, recently introduced measure, the *CD-criterion*, is known for uniform scaling [2]. As we mentioned above, the original authors believe this technique is non-indexable, and in any case, as we will show in Section 7, the bounds are quite weak. Therefore, we propose a novel, indexable, and tight lower bounding measure for uniform scaling.

It is important to note here that the lower bounding technique and all the algorithms we describe in this study for the efficient solution of the uniform scaling problem are exact. This means that we are guaranteed to find all the solutions we are looking for, with no false dismissals. The essence of the techniques we propose is that they can effectively prune the search space, by excluding candidate time series that cannot be part of the solution. The result is considerable savings in computation time, since we do not have to perform the expensive distance calculations for every time series in the database.

5. OUR SOLUTION

We will begin by showing how we can lower bound sequences of arbitrary lengths in main memory. Since indexing structures degrade with dimensionality, we will further show how we can lower bound the dimensionality-reduced representations of the time series.

5.1 Lower Bounding in Main Memory

In order to create a lower bounding distance measure for uniform scaling, we will generate a bounding envelope. Bounding envelopes were introduced in [18] to lower bound DTW, and since then they have sparked a flurry of research activity [13][24][28][32][35]. While the principle is the same here, the definitions of the envelope are *very* different. In particular, we create two sequences U and L, such that:

$$U_i = \max(c_{\lfloor (i-1)*m/n \rfloor +1}, \ldots, c_{\lfloor i*m/n \rfloor}) \quad (6)$$

$$L_i = \min(c_{\lfloor (i-1)*m/n \rfloor +1}, \ldots, c_{\lfloor i*m/n \rfloor}) \quad (7)$$

These sequences can be visualized as bounding the first n points of the time series C. Figure 6 shows some examples.

Having defined U and L, we can now introduce the lower bounding function, *LB_Keogh*, which lower bounds the distance between Q and C for any scaling factor sf, $1 < sf \leq sf_{max}$.

$$LB\_Keogh(Q,C) = \sum_{i=1}^{n} \begin{cases} (q_i - U_i)^2 & \text{if } q_i > U_i \\ (q_i - L_i)^2 & \text{if } q_i < L_i \\ 0 & \text{otherwise} \end{cases} \quad (8)$$

This function can be visualized as the squared Euclidean distance between any part of the query time series not falling within the envelope and the nearest (orthogonal) corresponding section of the envelope. Figure 7 illustrates this idea.

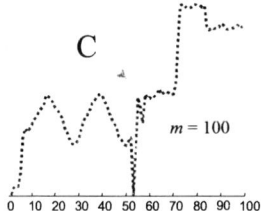

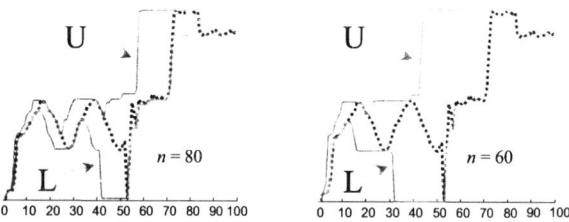

Figure 6. (*Top*) A time series C of length 100. (*Bottom Left*) The time series shrouded by upper and lower envelopes U and L with lengths 80. (*Bottom Right*) The same time series shrouded by upper and lower envelopes U and L with lengths 60.

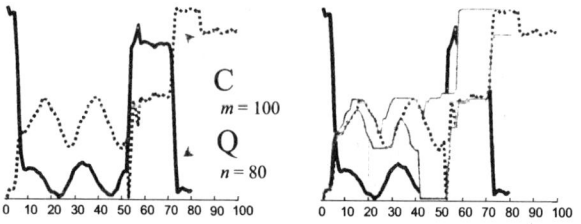

Figure 7. (*Left*) A time series C and a shorter query Q. (*Right*) A visualization of the lower-bounding function *LB_Keogh*(Q,C). Note that any part of query time series Q that falls inside the bounding envelope is ignored. Otherwise the distance corresponds to the sum of the squared straight line distances from the query to the nearest point in the envelope (the gray hatch lines).

We can now prove that *LB_Keogh*(Q,C) is a lower bound for the distance between Q and C under uniform scaling (the proof is in the full version of this paper).

Lemma 1 The distance *LB_Keogh*(Q,C) lower bounds the squared Euclidean distance between any scaling of Q, and the appropriate prefix of C.

5.2 Lower Bounding in Index Space

As noted in Section 4.1, if we have a distance measure that is expensive in terms of CPU time, we can dramatically speed up similarity search using a tight lower bound. However, if the majority of the data exists on secondary storage, the CPU costs may be dwarfed by the disk (or tape) access time. The solution is to *index* the data. Having defined the bounding envelopes, we proceed in a manner similar to previous work [13][18][24][28][32][35].

We have previously denoted a time series as $Q = q_1, \ldots, q_n$. Let N be the dimensionality of the space we wish to index ($1 \leq N \leq n$). For convenience, we assume that N is a factor of n.

A time series Q of length n can be represented in N dimensional space by a vector $\overline{Q} = \overline{q}_1, \ldots, \overline{q}_N$. The ith element of $\overline{Q}$ is calculated using the following equation:

$$\overline{q}_i = \frac{N}{n} \sum_{j=\frac{n}{N}(i-1)+1}^{\frac{n}{N}i} q_j \quad (9)$$

In Section 5.1, we discussed the lowering bounding function *LB_Keogh*. However, calculating this function requires n values. Since n may be in the order of hundreds for realistic human motion, and multi-dimensional index structures begin to degrade rapidly somewhere above 16 dimensions, we need a way to create a lower, N-dimensional version of the function, where N is a number that can be reasonably handled by a multi-dimensional index structure. We also need this lower dimension version of the function to lower bound *LB_Keogh* (and therefore, by transitivity, uniform scaling).

We begin by creating special *Piecewise Constant Approximations (PAAs)* [19] of U and L, which we will denote as $\hat{U}$ and $\hat{L}$. Although they are piecewise constant approximations, the definitions of $\hat{U}$ and $\hat{L}$ differ from those we have seen in Eq. 6 and 7. In particular, we have

$$\hat{U}_i = \max\left(U_{\frac{n}{N}(i-1)+1}, \ldots, U_{\frac{n}{N}(i)}\right) \quad (10)$$

$$\hat{L}_i = \min\left(L_{\frac{n}{N}(i-1)+1}, \ldots, L_{\frac{n}{N}(i)}\right) \quad (11)$$

We can visualize $\hat{U}$ and $\hat{L}$ as the piecewise constant functions which bound, without intersecting, U and L, respectively. Figure 8 illustrates this intuition.

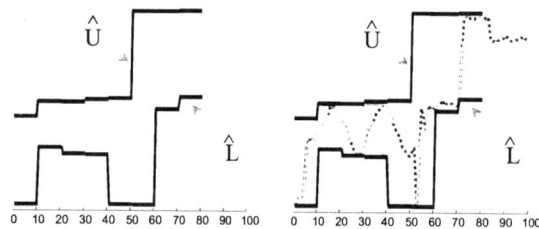

Figure 8. We can readily visualize $\hat{U}$ and $\hat{L}$ as the piecewise constant functions which bound, without intersecting, U and L, respectively. (*Left*) The $\hat{U}$ and $\hat{L}$ for the time series shown in Figure 5. (*Right*) The $\hat{U}$ and $\hat{L}$ shown overlaid on top of the generating time series.

We are now able to define the low dimension, lower bounding function, which we denote as *MINDIST()*. Given a query sequence Q, transformed to $\overline{Q}$ by Eq. 9, and a candidate sequence C, with its companion PAA functions $\hat{R} = \{\hat{U}, \hat{L}\}$, the following function lower bounds *LB_Keogh*

$$MINDIST(\overline{Q}, \hat{R}) = \sqrt{\sum_{i=1}^{N} \frac{n}{N} \begin{cases} (\overline{q}_i - \hat{U}_i)^2 & \text{if } \overline{q}_i > \hat{U}_i \\ (\overline{q}_i - \hat{L}_i)^2 & \text{if } \overline{q}_i < \hat{L}_i \\ 0 & \text{otherwise} \end{cases}} \quad (12)$$

This function is visualized in Figure 9.

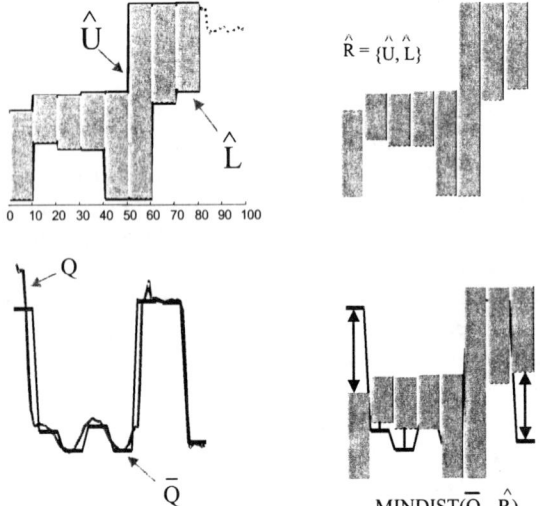

Figure 9. (*Top Left*) The time series C, and its bounding envelopes. (*Top Right*) The set of bounding envelopes $\hat{R}=\{\hat{U}, \hat{L}\}$. (*Bottom Left*) The query Q, and its approximation $\overline{Q}$. (*Bottom Right*) Illustration of the $MINDIST(\overline{Q}, \hat{R})$ function.

Similarly to $MINDIST(\overline{Q}, \hat{R})$, we can also define $MAXDIST(\overline{Q}, \hat{R})$ (illustrated in Figure 10), which serves as an upper bound for the distance between a query Q and $\hat{R}$.

$$MAXDIST(\overline{Q}, \hat{R}) = \sqrt{\sum_{i=1}^{N} \frac{n}{N} \begin{cases} (\overline{q}_i - \hat{U}_i)^2, & \text{if } (\overline{q}_i < \hat{L}_i) or (\overline{q}_i - \hat{L}_i < \hat{U}_i - \overline{q}_i) \\ (\overline{q}_i - \hat{L}_i)^2, & \text{if } (\overline{q}_i > \hat{U}_i) or (\hat{U}_i - \overline{q}_i < \overline{q}_i - \hat{L}_i) \end{cases}} \quad (13)$$

The use of this upper bound will become apparent in Section 6, when we discuss algorithms for fast similarity search under uniform scaling.

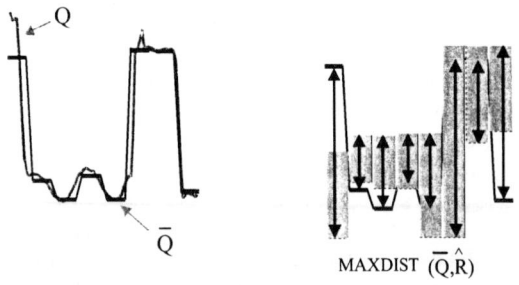

Figure 10. (*Left*) The query Q, and its approximation $\overline{Q}$. (*Right*) Illustration of the $MAXDIST(\overline{Q}, \hat{R})$ function.

Note that there is no inherent restriction in our framework that would prevent us from incorporating into it DTW indexing, as well. DTW can be used in conjunction with uniform scaling to allow small local adjustments to the time axis after uniform scaling has found the best global scaling. In this case, we simply have to compute the upper and lower bounding envelopes for the DTW transform, and then, apply the techniques described in this study on these envelopes. Since this is a straightforward extension, we do not pursue it any further in this work.

6. ALGORITHMS FOR SECONDARY STORAGE

Based on the discussion of the previous section, we can now present algorithms that solve the time series similarity problem under uniform scaling, when the time series database does not fit in main memory. In the following discussion, as well as in the experiments, we assume that all the time series data and their bounding envelopes are disk resident. For ease of exposition, we also make the simplifying assumption that we are only interested in the single best match to our query. The extensions to more general cases are straightforward, and we omit them for brevity. The interested reader can find additional considerations, techniques, and references elsewhere [33].

The pseudocode for all the algorithms presented in this section can be found in the full version of this paper.

6.1 Linear Scan of the Time Series

Linear scan is a brute force approach, where we do not make use of our lower bounding technique. This algorithm sequentially reads each time series C from the disk, and computes its minimum distance to the query series by trying all possible rescalings. The only optimization we can apply in this case, is to stop the computation of the Euclidean distance function as soon as it becomes larger than the currently minimum distance[1]. We call the above algorithm *LinearScan*, and we present it only as a baseline against which we compare our proposed algorithms.

In order to improve the performance of *LinearScan*, we incorporate the use of the bounding envelopes as follows. Along with each time series C, we also store on disk its corresponding envelopes R. As before, we keep track of the minimum distance between the query and a candidate time series in variable *OverallBestMatchVal*. The algorithm starts by reading the envelopes $\hat{R}$ of some time series C and computing the lower bound $MINDIST(\overline{Q}, \hat{R})$. If this lower bound is less than *OverallBestMatchVal*, then we have to call *TestAllScalings()*. Otherwise, we know that C cannot have a distance to Q less than *OverallBestMatchVal*, and we can simply discard C. We refer to this algorithm as *LinearScanLB* (Linear Scan Lower Bound), and we expect it to run faster than *LinearScan*, since it avoids using *TestAllScalings()* for all the time series in the database.

---

[1] We apply the same optimization to all the algorithms we present in this paper. However, the performance benefits are in all cases minimal.

The rest of the algorithms we describe make a more informed use of the bounding envelopes. The premise is that these algorithms will more effectively prune the search space, and result in superior performance.

6.2 Linear Scan of the Bounding Envelopes

The intuition behind our next algorithm, *FastScan*, is the following. Instead of retrieving a time series from disk every time that the lower bound distance is less than *OverallBestMatchVal*, start by retrieving from disk the time series in increasing order of their lower bound value. If the lower bounds we compute are tight enough, then best match to the query time series will be among the first time series to be retrieved.

The *FastScan* algorithm (which is similar in nature to the VA-file method [34]) computes the solution in two phases. First, it performs a linear disk scan of the bounding envelopes of all the time series in the database **D**, and builds a minimum priority queue on the lower bound of the distance between the corresponding candidate time series and the query. Note that this process is relatively fast, since the size of the bounding envelopes is much smaller than the size of the time series themselves. During the second phase, the algorithm dequeues elements from the priority queue, reads from the disk the relevant candidate time series, and calls *TestAllScalings()* to determine the best match. The algorithm stops when the lower bound value for the dequeued element is larger than *OverallBestMatchVal*, or when the priority queue empties. It is easy to see that *FastScan* performs less work than *LinearScanLB*, and only in the worst case does it perform an equal amount of work.

The *FastScan* algorithm requires inserting in the priority queue as many values as there are time series in the database. However, this is not a concern, even though it is a main memory data structure. For example, a heap would require 20 bytes[2] per entry, a small amount even for databases with one million objects. The processing time required for the heap, $O(\log|D|)$, is not of concern either, since it is insignificant compared to the time required for disk I/O and for computing the distances between time series. Note that we can incorporate in the algorithm the use of the upper bound (*MAXDIST*) as well, which can help maintain the size of the priority queue small: usually less than 15% of the original size. However, this comes at a cost in time. In the version of *FastScan* we used in the experiments, we did not take into account this optimization.

6.3 Algorithms based on R-trees

Having the bounding envelopes $\hat{R}$ in a sufficiently low dimensionality allows us to use an R-tree [5][15] for indexing them. The goal is to avoid reading all the bounding envelopes, which is what *FastScan* does.

The use of the R-tree is straightforward. We associate each bounding envelope $\hat{R}=\{\hat{U},\hat{L}\}$ to a Minimum Bounding Rectangle MBR(*l,h*) as follows: *l*=($\hat{L}_1,\hat{L}_2,...,\hat{L}_N$), and *h*=($\hat{U}_1,\hat{U}_2,...,\hat{U}_N$). This allows to compute the lower bound distance $MINDIST(\overline{Q},\hat{R})$ as usual. Along with each MBR that represents a set of bounding envelopes $\hat{R}$, we also store a pointer to the corresponding time series C in the file system. Then, we build the R-tree using one of the traditional construction algorithms [5][15].

The R-tree search algorithm starts by reading an MBR *r*, and computing the lower bound $MINDIST(\overline{Q},r)$. If this lower bound is less than *OverallBestMatchVal*, and *r* is an inner node, then we process *r* recursively. If *r* is a leaf node, that is, it refers to bounding envelopes $\hat{R}$ of candidate time series C, then we have to read C from disk, call *TestAllScalings()* to compute the best match for all possible rescalings, and update *OverallBestMatchVal*. If the lower bound is larger than *OverallBestMatchVal*, then we simply disregard *r*. We refer to this algorithm as *RtreeBF (R-tree Brute Force)*.

An optimization that we can apply to the above algorithm is to use the R-tree index to get a small number of candidate time series with the lowest lower bound values, and then test each of these candidates to determine the true best match. This is the same idea that *FastScan* uses.

Now, the R-tree search algorithm needs to maintain a minimum priority queue on the lower bound values. However, unlike *FastScan*, we can also make use of the upper bound distance between the query and an MBR, $MAXDIST(\overline{Q},r)$, in order to further prune the search space (this optimization is not applicable to *RtreeBF* that only needs to compare the lower bound to *OverallBestMatchVal*).

For each MBR *r*, we compute the lower and upper bounds, and maintain the lowest value for the upper bounds in variable *LowestUpper*. We recursively search the R-tree, following only the MBR nodes whose lower bound is less than *LowestUpper*. If this condition is true for a leaf MBR, then we insert an entry for the corresponding candidate time series in the priority queue. When we have finished processing the R-tree, we start calling *TestAllScalings()* to determine the best match among all the candidates stored in the priority queue. This processing follows the order specified by the queue. We call this algorithm *RtreeProbe*.

7. EXPERIMENTAL RESULTS

In this section we will empirically evaluate our approach. Although we are particularly interested in motion capture data, as we noted above, our algorithm may have utility in domains as diverse as music retrieval [7] and space

---

[2] The elements we need to store are the lower bound value (8 bytes), a pointer to the time series in the file system (4 bytes), and two pointers to the children nodes (8 bytes).

telemetry [8]. We will therefore perform all experiments on the following two datasets.

- **Motion Capture**: This dataset was distilled from several hours of recording with Vicon (an optical motion capture system), using 124 sensors. The data for our experiments are drawn uniformly at random from a pool of 250,000 subsequences.
- **Mixed Bag**: This dataset was created by concatenating 10 diverse datasets from the UCR time series archive. The 10 datasets are foetal ecg, steam generator, space shuttle, Photon Burst, Standard and Poor 500, ocean, power demand, leleccum, Koski ECG, and infrasound_beamd. The subsequences we use for our experiments are drawn at random from this pool, making sure that all 10 seed time series contribute equally.

In both cases, the queries are random subsequences not present in the database of candidate time series.

7.1 Main Memory Experiments

In the first set of experiments, we evaluate the effectiveness of our lower bounding technique when the datasets fit in main memory. We use the main memory version of algorithm *LinearScanLB*, which we call *LB_Keogh*. We compare only to the brute force search algorithm defined in Table 2, and to the recently introduced *CD-criterion* technique [2], because there are no other techniques in existence that support uniform scaling queries. To eliminate the possibility of implementation bias [18], and because *CD-criterion* does not support indexing, we consider the speedup obtained in main memory. To compare the three competing techniques we report the *Pruning Power*, i.e., the fraction of times that each approach must call the squared Euclidean distance function.

$$Pruning\ Power = \frac{Number\ of\ calls\ to\ distance\ function\ by\ proposed\ approach}{Number\ of\ calls\ to\ distance\ function\ by\ brute\ force\ search} \quad (13)$$

This measure depends only on the tightness of the lower bounds, and is independent of language, platform, caching or any other implementation details. As an additional sanity check we also measured the CPU time. However, since it is almost perfectly correlated with the *Pruning Power*, we omit it for brevity. Note that by definition, the pruning power of brute force is always 1.

As noted earlier, the *CD-criterion* algorithm can only test whether the distance of two sequences is within a user-supplied epsilon. In order to allow direct comparison with the two other approaches, we supply to the algorithm the exact epsilon that will return the single nearest neighbor.

Since the speed-up obtained for our approach clearly depends on the range of scaling factors and the length of the time series, we test our approach for the cross product of maximum scaling factors $sf_{max} = \{1.05, 1.10, 1.20\}$ and candidate time series lengths of $\{64, 128, 256\}$. These represent realistic parameters in our motion capture domain,

and seem representative of other domains as well [9][14][35].

We conduct our experiments as follows. We randomly remove a subsequence of the appropriate length from the data to use as a query, and randomly choose 10,000 other subsequences to act as the database. We then search for the best scaled match. We repeated this 500 times for every combination of scaling factors and candidate lengths. Figure 11 shows the results.

The results are quite impressive for the proposed approach, which essentially needs to perform an order of magnitude less work than *CD-criterion*, over all parameter settings on both datasets. In addition, our approach is two to three orders of magnitude more efficient than the brute force algorithm. The above experiments demonstrate that our technique can effectively reduce the amount of required effort by avoiding a considerable number of unnecessary computations.

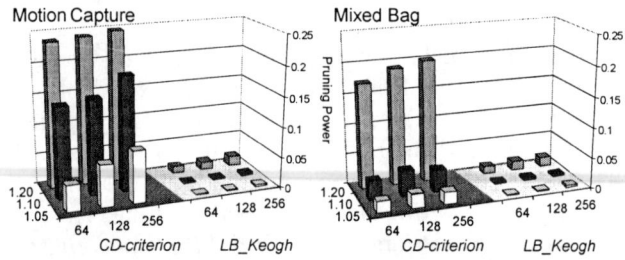

Figure 11. The pruning power of *CD-criterion* and *LB_Keogh* algorithm on two datasets, over a range of scaling factors and candidate lengths.

7.2 Secondary Storage Experiments

In this section, we evaluate the performance of our techniques when the time series database **D** does not fit in main memory. The experiments were performed on an Athlon 1.6GHz Linux machine, with 1GB of main memory. All the data were stored on its local disk. In the interest of space, we only report the results for the motion capture dataset; the results for the mixed bag dataset exhibit similar trends.

In all the following experiments, we measure the time (in seconds) it takes each algorithm to process a single query. We repeated each experiment 500 times, and report the average time. Note that we only need to compare the algorithms in terms of their running-time performance. Since all algorithms are exact, they return in every case the same (correct, based on the distance definition) answer.

7.2.1 Exploring the Properties of the Algorithm

In the first set of experiments, we compare the performance of the algorithms *LinearScan*, *LinearScanLB*, *FastScan*, *RtreeBF*, and *RtreeProbe*, for the cross product of maximum scaling factors $sf_{max} = \{1.05, 1.10, 1.20\}$ and candidate time series lengths of $\{64, 128, 256\}$ (Figure 12). The dimensionality of the approximated bounding envelopes is fixed to 16, and the number of candidate time series to 10,000.

The results clearly show that *LinearScan* cannot compete with the other alternatives, which can actually offer interactive response times, a crucial factor for the real-life applications we have in mind. Note that all the other algorithms outperform *LinearScan* by up to more than an order of magnitude, exactly because they make use of the techniques we introduce in this paper. For the rest of the discussion, we will disregard *LinearScan*, and focus on the comparison among the other algorithms.

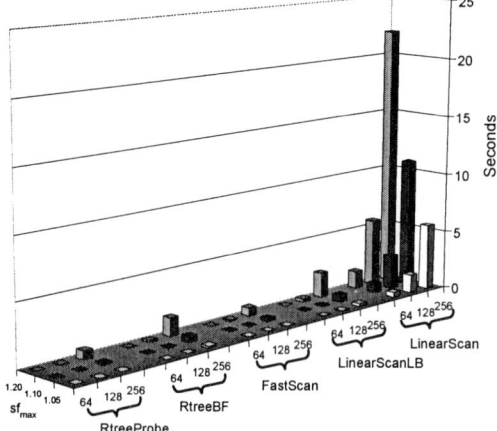

Figure 12. Average time to answer a query for algorithms *LinearScan, LinearScanLB, FastScan, RtreeBF,* and *RtreeProbe*, over a range of scaling factors and candidate lengths.

In Figure 13, we zoom in on the results of the four algorithms that use our proposed technique. As expected, the trends are that the query response time increases with both the length of the candidate time series and the scaling factor. Out of the two, the latter seems to be the dominant factor. All four algorithms exhibit similar trends.

In terms of absolute numbers, *FastScan* and *RtreeProbe* perform better than the other two algorithms, executing up to 3.5 times faster. Note that these two are the algorithms that first determine the most promising order in which to access the candidate time series, and only then start accessing them.

7.2.2 Scalability Experiments

We now turn our attention to the scalability issues, and examine the behavior of the algorithms when we vary the size of the time series database. The default values we use are, unless otherwise noted, 10,000 for the number of candidate time series, 128 for their length, and 16 for the dimensionality of the approximated representations of the bounding envelopes.

In the first set of experiments we vary the number of candidate time series from 5,000 to 80,000. The results are shown in Figure 14. We observe that the query response time for *FastScan* is better than *RtreeBF* for the small database sizes, but then deteriorates faster as the database size increases. This is due to the fact that it still needs to read from disk the bounding envelopes for all the series in the database. *RtreeBF* can effectively prune the search space. Yet, for the smaller database sizes, it pays the price of not determining in advance the most promising order in which to test the candidate time series. The performance of *RtreeProbe* is consistently the best among the proposed approaches (2 to 9 times faster), combining the advantages of both *FastScan* and *RtreeBF*.

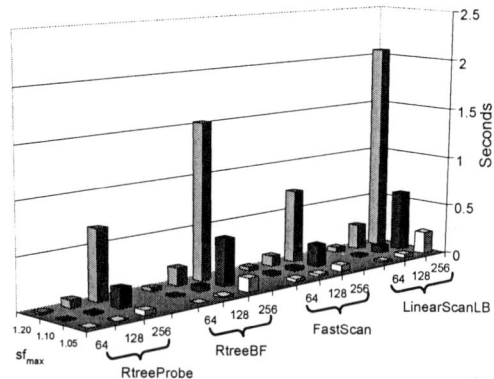

Figure 13. Average time to answer a query for algorithms *LinearScanLB, FastScan, RtreeBF,* and *RtreeProbe*, over a range of scaling factors and candidate lengths.

Figure 15 depicts the results of the experiments where we varied the length of the candidate time series (from 64 to 1024). At the high end of the length spectrum, with the exception of *RtreeProbe*, all the algorithms tend to behave the same. The experimental results indicate that the algorithms fail to prune a significant amount of the candidate time series. On the other hand, *RtreeProbe* manages to do a slightly better job in this respect, which results in significant savings in terms of time. Its performance is 2.5 to 4 times better than the best alternative.

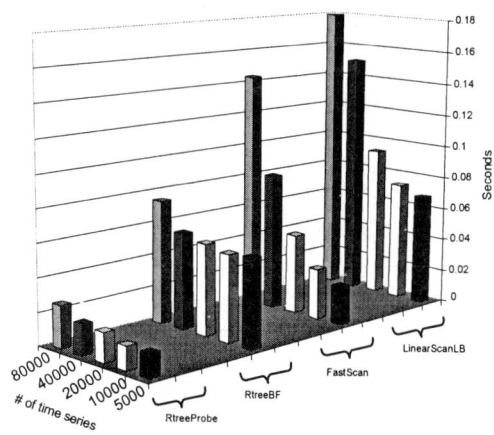

Figure 14. Average time to answer a query for algorithms *LinearScanLB, FastScan, RtreeBF,* and *RtreeProbe*, when varying the number of candidate time series.

In the last set of experiments (Figure 16), we evaluate the effect of the dimensionality of the approximated bounding envelopes on the performance of the algorithms. An increase in the dimensionality results in more accurate representations, and consequently, in more precise lower and upper bounds. The experiments show that this is, in general, beneficial for all the algorithms. However, the benefits are diminishing as the dimensionality increases. In fact, we may also get the reverse effect, as is the case with *RtreeBF* for dimensionality 16. In this case, the bounding envelopes of the candidate time series do not form tight clusters in the high-dimensional R-tree, and consequently, lead to poor performance. *RtreeProbe* avoids the cost of this problem, because it postpones the expensive *TestAllScalings()* operation till the end.

The experimental evaluation indicates that it is beneficial to first identify the most promising candidates entirely in the reduced dimensionality space (i.e., using only $\hat{R}$), and then test the query against the candidate time series, despite the fact that these calculations are not as precise. Though, the above may not be true for large databases (see Figure 14). It is also interesting to note that the behavior of the R-tree algorithms is not always predictable. Consider, for example, the non-intuitive *RtreeBF* results for database sizes 5,000 and 10,000 (Figure 14), and dimensionalities of 12 and 16 (Figure 16). In both cases, the results worsen when the parameters become seemingly more favorable. Nevertheless, one of the R-tree-based algorithms, *RtreeProbe*, exhibits a consistently superior performance across all experiments, outperforming the best alternative by up to 4 times. As a last remark, we should note that *FastScan*, which does not require the use of any indexing structures, performs in many cases competitively to *RtreeProbe*. This makes *FastScan* an attractive alternative for the case where we cannot afford to build an index on the time series in the database.

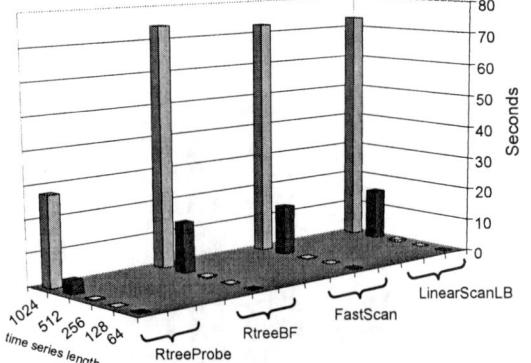

Figure 15. Average time to answer a query for algorithms *LinearScanLB*, *FastScan*, *RtreeBF*, and *RtreeProbe*, when varying the length of the candidate time series.

7.3 Case Study

In addition to the comprehensive experiments on the efficiency of indexing discussed above, we also used a motion capture processing system to evaluate our techniques. We conducted numerous experiments to test the quality of matches obtained by uniform scaling, allowing both stretching and shrinking.

The experimental setup was as follows. We randomly selected a query motion from our motion capture database (sitting up, stretching arms, etc.), and searched the database for the closest (non-self) match. We evaluated the returned sequences in two ways. Objectively, by measuring the Euclidean distance of the sequences (which express the orientations of the joints in the body), and subjectively, by creating and reviewing animations based on the matched sequences. These animations show the query sequence and its best matches superimposed on each other.

The results of the experiments validate the utility and effectiveness of our approach, and also demonstrate that uniform scaling produces better results than DTW. Since such experiments do not lend themselves to a text and graphic exposition, we have created a website with full video examples [40], and only present here a single figure to give the flavor of these experiments.

In Figure 17, we show the best match under uniform scaling (top) and the best match under DTW (bottom) for a query involving a motion of the arms. In the figures and graphs, we have superimposed the query with each of the best match sequences. It is obvious that when we allow uniform scaling we are able to find a match that is much closer to the query sequence (Euclidean distance 51.83) than when we use DTW (Euclidean distance 154.16).

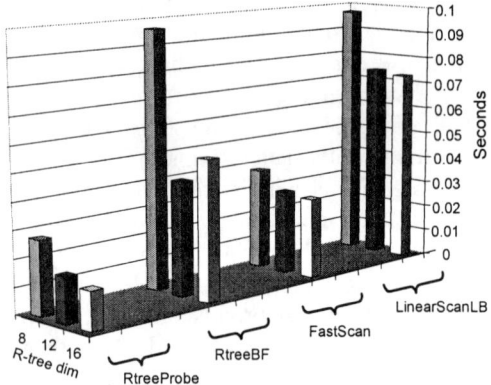

Figure 16. Average time to answer a query for algorithms *LinearScanLB*, *FastScan*, *RtreeBF*, and *RtreeProbe*, when varying the dimensionality of the approximated representations.

8. CONCLUSIONS

In this work, we motivated the need for uniform scaling similarity matching, which has applications in several domains where human variability necessitates this type of matching flexibility (e.g., motion libraries, music retrieval, and historical handwritten archives). We introduced the first technique for indexing time series with invariance to uniform scaling, based on bounding envelopes. This technique enables fast similarity searching in large time series databases. We presented several algorithms that make use of the above technique, and evaluated our proposed approaches with a comprehensive set of experiments on real data, over realistic parameter choices suggested by domain experts. The experimental results demonstrate the significant advantages of our indexing technique, and evaluate the relative benefits of the different alternatives. Finally, we describe the application of our method in a motion capture processing system, and illustrate its usefulness and the superiority of the results it returns when compared to other alternatives.

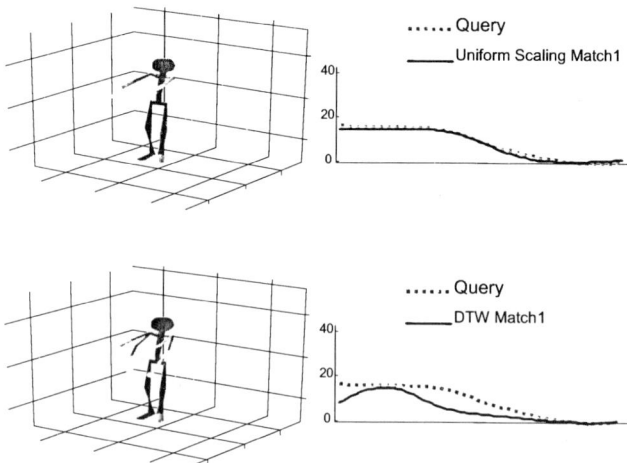

Figure 17: Sample results from a motion-capture similarity search experiment. A query motion (upper body only) was submitted to a motion capture database. (*Top Left*) The stick figure is a superposition of both the query and the best matching sequence under uniform scaling. Since both figures are so similar (after scaling the match back to the query length) we can only see a single figure. (*Bottom Left*) The superposition of the query and the best DTW match show considerable mismatch. (*Right*) The corresponding time series (only the Z-axis is shown) illustrates the source of the difference.

9. REFERENCES

[1] Aach, J. and Church, G. (2001). Aligning gene expression time series with time warping algorithms. Bioinformatics. Volume 17, pp 495-508.

[2] Argyros, T & Ermopoulos, C. (2003). Efficient subsequence matching in time series databases under time and amplitude transformations. IEEE ICDM pp 481-484.

[3] Arikan, O., Forsyth, D. & O'Brien, J. (2003). Motion synthesis from annotations. ACM Transactions on Graphics. V22(3). pp. 402-408.

[4] Arikan, O, &. Forsyth, D. (2002). Synthesizing constrained motions from examples. *ACM Transactions on Graphics*, 21(3):483-490. ISSN 0730-0301.

[5] Beckmann, N., Kriegel, H.-P., Schneider, R., & Seeger, B. (1990). The R*-tree: an efficient and robust access method for points and rectangles. In *Proc of ACM SIGMOD*, pp. 220-231.

[6] Cardle, M., Vlachos, M., Brooks, S., Keogh, E., Gunopulos, D. (2003). Fast Motion Capture Matching with Replicated Motion Editing. In *Proc ACM SIGGRAPH Sketches and Applications*.

[7] Chan, K. & Fu, A. W. (1999). Efficient time series matching by wavelets. In *proceedings of the 15th IEEE Int'l Conference on Data Engineering*. Sydney, Australia. pp 126-133.

[8] Chu, K., Lam., S. & Wong, M. (1998). An efficient hash-based algorithm for sequence data searching. The Computer Journal 41 (6): 402-415.

[9] Dannenberg, R., Birmingham, W., Tzanetakis, G., Meek, C., Hu, N., and Pardo, B. (2003). The MUSART testbed for query-by-humming evaluation. ISMIR 2003, 4th International Conference on Music Information Retrieval Baltimore, Maryland.

[10] Das, G., Gunopulos, D., Mannila, H. (1997). Finding similar time series. In Proc. of the *First PKDD Symp*, pp. 88-100.

[11] DeCoste, D. and Levine, M (2000). Automated event detection in space instruments: a case study using IPEX-2 data and support vector machines. *SPIE Conference Astronomical Telescopes and Instrumentation*.

[12] Faloutsos, C., Ranganathan, M., & Manolopoulos, Y. (1994). Fast subsequence matching in time-series databases. *In Proc. ACM SIGMOD Conf.*, Minneapolis. pp. 419-429.

[13] Fung,. W & Wong., M. (2003). Efficient subsequence matching for sequences databases under time warping. The 7th International Database Engineering and Application Symposium.

[14] Gavrila, D. M. & Davis, L. S.(1995). Towards 3-d model-based tracking and recognition of human movement: a multi-view approach. In *International Workshop on Automatic Face- and Gesture-Recognition*.

[15] Guttman, A. (1984). R-trees: A dynamic index structure for spatial searching. In Proceedings ACM SIGMOD Conference. pp 47-57.

[16] Hetland, M. (2003). A survey of recent methods for efficient retrieval of similar time sequences. To appear in an Edited Volume, *Data Mining in Time Series Databases*. Published by the World Scientific Publishing Company.

[17] Kahveci, T. & Singh, A. (2001). Variable length queries for time series data. In *proceedings of the 17th Int'l Conference on Data Engineering*. Heidelberg, Germany, pp 273-282.

[18] Keogh, E. (2002). Exact indexing of dynamic time warping. In 28th *International Conference on Very Large Data Bases*. Hong Kong. pp 406-417.

[19] Keogh, E,.Chakrabarti, K,. Pazzani, M. & Mehrotra (2000). Dimensionality reduction for fast similarity search in large time series databases. Journal of Knowledge and Information Systems. pp 263-286.

[20] Keogh, E,.Chakrabarti, K,. Pazzani, M. & Mehrotra (2001). Locally adaptive dimensionality reduction for indexing large time series databases. In *Proc of ACM SIGMOD Conference on Management of Data*. pp 151-162.

[21] Keogh, E. and Kasetty, S. (2002). On the need for time series data mining benchmarks: a survey and empirical demonstration. In *the 8th ACM SIGKDD International Conference on Knowledge Discovery and Data Mining*. Edmonton, Canada. pp 102-111.

[22] Kovar, L., Gleicher, M., & Pighin. F (2002). Motion graphs. *Proceedings of ACM SIGGRAPH*.

[23] Lee, J., J. Chai, P.S.A. Reitsma, J. K. Hodgins, & N. S. Pollard. (2002). Interactive control of avatars animated with human motion data. ACM Transactions on Graphics. V21(3) pp. 491-500.

[24] Li, Q., Lopez, I, & Moon, B. (2004). Skyline index for time series data. To appear in TKDE.

[25] Li, Y., Wang, T. & Shum. H.-Y. (2002). Motion texture: a two level statistical model for character motion synthesis. ACM Transactions on Graphics, 21(3):465-472.

[26] Park, S., Chu, W. W., Yoon, J. & Hsu, C. (2000). Efficient searches for similar subsequences of different lengths in sequence databases. In *proceedings of the 16th Int'l Conference on Data Engineering*. San Diego, CA, pp 23-32.

[27] Perng, C., Wang, H., Zhang, S., & Parker, S. (2000). Landmarks: a new model for similarity-based pattern querying in time series databases. In *proceedings of 16th International Conference on Data Engineering*. pp 33-42.

[28] Rath, T. & Manmatha, R. (2002). Lower-bounding of dynamic time warping distances for multivariate time Series. Tech Report MM-40, University of Massachusetts Amherst.

[29] Roddick, J. F. and Spiliopoulou, M. (2001). A survey of temporal knowledge discovery paradigms and methods. *IEEE Tran's on Knowledge and Data Engineering*. pp. 750-767.

[30] Rose, C., Guenter, B., Bodenheimer, B., & Cohen, M.F. (1996). Efficient generation of motion transitions using spacetime constraints. In *Proc of ACM SIGGRAPH*, New Orleans, USA, pp. 147-154.

[31] Vlachos, M., Kollios, G., & Gunopulos, G. (2002). Discovering similar multidimensional trajectories. In *Proc 18th International Conference on Data Engineering*.

[32] Vlachos, M., Hadjieleftheriou, M., Gunopulos, D., & Keogh, E. (2003). Indexing multi-dimensional time-series with support for multiple distance measures. In Proc *ACM SIGKDD*, Washington DC, USA.

[33] Vries, A. P. de, Mamoulis, N., Nes, N., Kersten, M. (2002). Efficient k-NN Search on Vertically Decomposed Data. In *Proc of ACM SIGMOD*, pp. 322-333.

[34] Weber, R., Schek, H & Blott S. (1998) A quantitative analysis and performance study for similarity-search methods in high-dimensional spaces. VLDB pp. 194-205.

[35] Yi, B.-K., Faloutsos, C. (2000). Fast Time Sequence for Arbitrary Lp Norms. VLDB.

[36] Zhu, Y. & Shasha, D. (2003). Query by humming: a time series database approach. *SIGMOD 2003*.

[37] Zordan, V. B., Hodgins, J. K., (2002). Motion capture-driven simulations that hit and react, *ACM SIGGRAPH Symposium on Computer Animation*.

[38] Vicon, http://www.vicon.com

[39] Motion Analysis, http://www.motionanalysis.com

[40] Videos from Case Study, available at:
http://www.cs.ucr.edu/~eamonn/VLDB2004_VLDB.htm

On The Marriage of Lp-norms and Edit Distance

Lei Chen
School of Computer Science
University of Waterloo
l6chen@uwaterloo.ca

Raymond Ng
Department of Computer Science
University of British Columbia
rng@cs.ubc.ca

Abstract

Existing studies on time series are based on two categories of distance functions. The first category consists of the Lp-norms. They are metric distance functions but cannot support local time shifting. The second category consists of distance functions which are capable of handling local time shifting but are non-metric. The first contribution of this paper is the proposal of a new distance function, which we call ERP ("Edit distance with Real Penalty"). Representing a marriage of L1-norm and the edit distance, ERP can support local time shifting, and is a metric.

The second contribution of the paper is the development of pruning strategies for large time series databases. Given that ERP is a metric, one way to prune is to apply the triangle inequality. Another way to prune is to develop a lower bound on the ERP distance. We propose such a lower bound, which has the nice computational property that it can be efficiently indexed with a standard B+-tree. Moreover, we show that these two ways of pruning can be used simultaneously for ERP distances. Specifically, the false positives obtained from the B+-tree can be further minimized by applying the triangle inequality. Based on extensive experimentation with existing benchmarks and techniques, we show that this combination delivers superb pruning power and search time performance, and dominates all existing strategies.

Permission to copy without fee all or part of this material is granted provided that the copies are not made or distributed for direct commercial advantage, the VLDB copyright notice and the title of the publication and its date appear, and notice is given that copying is by permission of the Very Large Data Base Endowment. To copy otherwise, or to republish, requires a fee and/or special permission from the Endowment.

**Proceedings of the 30th VLDB Conference,
Toronto, Canada, 2004**

1 Introduction

Many applications require the retrieval of similar time series. Examples include financial data analysis and market prediction [1, 2, 10], moving object trajectory determination [6] and music retrieval [31]. Studies in this area revolve around two key issues: the choice of a distance function (similarity model), and the mechanism to improve retrieval efficiency.

Concerning the first issue, many distance functions have been considered, including Lp-norms [1, 10], dynamic time wraping (DTW) [30, 18, 14], longest common subsequence (LCSS) [4, 25] and edit distance on real sequence (EDR) [6]. Lp-norms are easy to compute. However, they cannot handle local time shifting, which is essential for time series similarity matching. DTW, LCSS and EDR have been proposed to exactly deal with local time shifting. However, they are non-metric distance functions.

This leads to the second issue of improving retrieval efficiency. Specifically, non-metric distance functions complicate matters, as the violation of the triangle inequality renders most indexing structures inapplicable. To this end, studies on this topic propose various lower bounds on the actual distance to guarantee no false dismissals [30, 18, 14, 31]. However, those lower bounds can admit a high percentage of false positives.

In this paper, we consider both issues and explore the following questions.

- *Is there a way to combine Lp-norms and the other distance functions so that we can get the best of both worlds* – namely being able to support local time shifting and being a metric distance function?

- With such a metric distance function, we can apply the triangle inequality for pruning, but *can we develop a lower bound for the distance function?* If so, is lower bounding more efficient than applying the triangle inequality? Or, is it possible to do both?

Our contributions are as follows:

- We propose in Section 3 a distance function which we call *Edit distance with Real Penalty* (ERP). It can be viewed as a variant of L1-norm, except that it can support local time shifting. It can also be viewed as a variant of EDR and DTW, except that it is a metric distance function. We present benchmark results showing that this distance function is natural for time series data.

- We propose in Section 4 a new lower bound for ERP, which can be efficiently indexed with a standard B+-tree. Given that ERP is a metric distance function, we can also apply the triangle inequality. We present benchmark results in Section 5 comparing the efficiency of lower bounding versus applying the triangle inequality.

- Last but not least, we develop in Section 4 a k-nearest neighbor (k-NN) algorithm that applies both lowering bounding and the triangle inequality. We give extensive experimental results in Section 5 showing that this algorithm gets the best of both paradigms, delivers superb retrieval efficiency and dominates all existing strategies.

2 Related Work

Many studies on similarity-based retrieval of time series were conducted in the past decade. The pioneering work by Agrawal et al. [1] used Euclidean distance to measure similarity. Discrete Fourier Transform (DFT) was used as a dimensionality reduction technique for time series data, and an R-tree was used as the index structure. Faloutsos et al. [10] extended this work to allow subsequence matching and proposed the GEMINI framework for indexing time series. The key is the use of a lower bound on the true distance to guarantee no false dismissals when the index is used as a filter.

Subsequent work have focused on two main aspects: new dimensionality reduction techniques (assuming that the Euclidean distance is the similarity measure); and new approaches for measuring the similarity between two time series. Examples of dimensionality reduction techniques include Single Value Decomposition [19], Discrete Wavelet Transform [20, 22], Piecewise Aggregate Approximation [15, 29], and Adaptive Piecewise Constant Approximation [14].

The motivation for seeking new similarity measures is that the Euclidean distance is very weak on handling noise and local time shifting. Berndt and Clifford [3] introduced DTW to allow a time series to be "stretched" to provide a better match with another time series. Das et al. [9] and Vlachos et al. [25] applied the LCSS measure to time series matching. Chen et al. [6] applied EDR to trajectory data retrieval and proposed a dimensionality reduction technique via a symbolic representation of trajectories. However, none of DTW, LCSS and EDR is a metric distance function for time series.

Most of the approaches on indexing time series follow the GEMINI framework. However, if the distance measure is a metric, then existing indexing structures

Symbols	Meaning
S	a time series $[s_1, \ldots, s_n]$
$Rest(S)$	$[s_2, \ldots, s_n]$
$dist(s_i, r_i)$	the distance between two elements
$\tilde{S}$	S after aligned with another series
DLB	a lower bound of the distance

Figure 1: Meanings of Symbols Used

proposed for metrics may be applicable. Examples include the MVP-tree [5], the M-tree [8], the Sa-tree [21], and the OMNI-family of access methods [11]. A survey of metric space indexing is given in [7]. In our experiments, we pick M-trees and OMNI-sequential as the strawman structures for comparison; MVP-trees and Sa-trees are not compared because they are main memory resident structures. The other access methods of OMNI-family are not used because the dimensionality of OMNI-coordinates is high (e.g., ≥ 20), which may lead to dimensionality curse [28]. In general, a common strategy to apply the triangle inequality for pruning is to use a set of reference points (time series in this case). Different studies propose different ways to choose the reference points. In our experiments, we compare our strategies in selecting reference points with the HF algorithm of the OMNI-family.

3 Edit Distance With Real Penalty

3.1 Reviewing Existing Distance Functions

A *time series* S is defined as a sequence of real values, with each value s_i sampled at a specific time, i.e., $S = [s_1, s_2, \ldots, s_n]$. The *length* of S is n, and the n values are referred to as the n *elements*. This sequence is called the *raw representation* of the time series. Given S, we can normalize it using its mean (μ) and standard deviation (σ) [13]: $Norm(S) = [\frac{s_1-\mu}{\sigma}, \frac{s_2-\mu}{\sigma}, \ldots, \frac{s_n-\mu}{\sigma}]$. Normalization is recommended so that the distance between two time series is invariant to amplitude scaling and (global) shifting of the time series. Throughout this paper, we use S to denote $Norm(S)$ for simplicity, even though all the results developed below apply to the raw representation as well. Figure 1 summarizes the main symbols used in this paper.

Given two time series R and S of the same length n, the L1-norm distance between R and S is: $\sum_{i=1}^{n} dist(r_i, s_i) = \sum_{i=1}^{n} |r_i - s_i|$. This distance function satisfies the triangle inequality and is a metric. The problem in using L1-norm for time series is that it requires the time series to be of the same length and does not support local time shifting.

To cope with local time shifting, one can borrow ideas from the domain of strings. A string is a sequence of elements, each of which is a symbol in an alphabet. Two strings, possibly of different lengths, are aligned so that they become identical with the smallest number of added, deleted or changed symbols. Among these three operations, deletion can be treated as adding a symbol in the other string. Hereafter, we refer to an added symbol as a *gap* element. This distance is called the *string edit distance*. The cost/distance of introducing a gap element is set to 1.

$$dist(r_i, s_i) = \begin{cases} 0 & \text{if } r_i = s_i \\ 1 & \text{if } r_i \text{ or } s_i \text{ is a gap} \\ 1 & \text{otherwise} \end{cases} \quad (1)$$

In the above formula, we highlight the second case to indicate that if a gap is introduced in the alignment, the cost is 1. String edit distance satisfies the triangle inequality and is a metric [27].

To generalize from strings to time series, the complication is that the elements r_i and s_i are not symbols, but real values. For most applications, strict equality would not make sense as, for instance, the pair $r_i = 1, s_i = 2$ should be considered more similar than the pair $r_i = 1, s_i = 10000$. To take the real values into account, one way is to relax equality to be within a certain tolerance δ:

$$dist_{edr}(r_i, s_i) = \begin{cases} 0 & \text{if } |r_i - s_i| \leq \delta \\ 1 & \text{if } r_i \text{ or } s_i \text{ is a gap} \\ 1 & \text{otherwise} \end{cases} \quad (2)$$

This is a simple generalization of Formula (1). Based on Formula (2) on individual elements and gaps, the *edit distance* between two time sequences R and S of length m and n respectively is defined in [6] as Formula (3) in Figure 2. r_1 and $Rest(R)$ denote the first element and the remaining sequence of R respectively. Notice that given Formula (2), the last case in Formula (3) can be simplified to: $\min\{EDR(Rest(R), Rest(S)) + 1, EDR(Rest(R), S) + 1, EDR(R, Rest(S)) + 1\}$. Local time shifting is essentially implemented by a dynamic-programming style minimization of the above three possibilities.

While EDR can handle local time shifting, it no longer satisfies the triangle inequality. The problem arises precisely from relaxing equality, i.e., $|r_i - s_i| \leq \delta$. More specifically, for three elements q_i, r_i, s_i, we can have $|q_i - r_i| \leq \delta$, $|r_i - s_i| \leq \delta$, but $|q_i - s_i| > \delta$.

To illustrate, let us consider a very simple example of three time series: $Q = [0], R = [1, 2]$ and $S = [2, 3, 3]$. Let $\delta = 1$. To best match R, Q is aligned to be $\widetilde{Q} = [0, -]$, where the symbol "-" denotes a gap. (There may exist many alternative ways to align sequences to get their best match. We only show one of the possible alignments for simplicity.) Thus, $EDR(Q, R) = 0 + 1 = 1$. Similarly, to best match S, R is aligned to be $\widetilde{R} = [1, 2, -]$, giving rise to $EDR(R, S) = 1$. Finally, to best match S, Q is aligned to be $\widetilde{Q} = [0, -, -]$, leading to $EDR(Q, S) = 3 > EDR(Q, R) + EDR(R, S) = 1 + 1 = 2!$

DTW differs from EDR in two key ways, summarized in the following formula:

$$dist_{dtw}(r_i, s_i) = \begin{cases} |r_i - s_i| & \text{if } r_i, s_i \text{ not gaps} \\ |r_i - s_{i-1}| & \text{if } s_i \text{ is a gap} \\ |s_i - r_{i-1}| & \text{if } r_i \text{ is a gap} \end{cases} \quad (6)$$

First, unlike EDR, DTW does not use a δ threshold to relax equality, the actual L1-norm is used. Second, unlike EDR, there is no explicit gap concept being introduced in its original definition [3]. We treat the replicated elements during the process of aligning two sequences as gaps of DTW. Therefore, the cost of a gap is not set to 1 as EDR does; it amounts to replicating the previous element, based on which the L1-norm is computed. Based on the above formula, the dynamic warping distance between two time series, denoted as $DTW(R, S)$, is defined formally as Formula (4) in Figure 2. The last case in the formula deals with the possibilities of replicating either s_{i-1} or r_{i-1}.

Let us repeat the previous example with DTW: $Q = [0], R = [1, 2]$ and $S = [2, 3, 3]$. To best match R, Q is aligned to be $\widetilde{Q} = [0, -] = [0, 0]$. Thus, $DTW(Q, R) = 1 + 2 = 3$. Similarly, to best match S, R is aligned to be $\widetilde{R} = [1, 2, -] = [1, 2, 2]$, giving rise to $DTW(R, S) = 3$. Finally, to best match S, Q is aligned to be $\widetilde{Q} = [0, -, -] = [0, 0, 0]$, leading to $DTW(Q, S) = 8 > DTW(Q, R) + DTW(R, S) = 3 + 3 = 6$.

It has been shown in [24] that for speech applications, DTW "loosely" satisfies the triangle inequality. We verified this observation with the 24 benchmark data sets used in [14, 31]. It appears that this observation is not true in general, as on average nearly 30% of all the triplets do not satisfy the triangle inequality.

3.2 ERP and its Properties

The key reason why DTW does not satisfy the triangle inequality is that, when a gap needs to be added, it replicates the previous element. Thus, as shown in the second and third cases of Formula (6), the difference between an element and a gap varies according to r_{i-1} or s_{i-1}. Contrast this situation with EDR, which makes every difference to be a constant 1 (second case in Formula (2)). On the other hand, the problem for EDR lies in its use of a δ tolerance. DTW does not have this problem because it uses the L1-norm between two non-gap elements.

We propose ERP such that it uses real penalty between two non-gap elements, but a constant value for computing the distance for gaps. Thus, ERP uses the following distance formula:

$$dist_{erp}(r_i, s_i) = \begin{cases} |r_i - s_i| & \text{if } r_i, s_i \text{ not gaps} \\ |r_i - g| & \text{if } s_i \text{ is a gap} \\ |s_i - g| & \text{if } r_i \text{ is a gap} \end{cases} \quad (7)$$

where g is a constant value. Based on Formula (7), we define the ERP distance between two time series,

$$EDR(R,S) = \begin{cases} n & \text{if } m=0 \\ m & \text{if } n=0 \\ EDR(Rest(R), Rest(S)) & \text{if } dist_{edr}(r_1,s_1)=0 \\ min\{EDR(Rest(R), Rest(S)) + dist_{edr}(r_1,s_1), & \text{otherwise} \\ EDR(Rest(R), S) + dist_{edr}(r_1, gap), EDR(R, Rest(S)) + dist_{edr}(gap, s_1)\} \end{cases} \quad (3)$$

$$DTW(R,S) = \begin{cases} 0 & \text{if } m=n=0 \\ \infty & \text{if } m=0 \text{ or } n=0 \\ dist_{dtw}(r_1,s_1) + min\{DTW(Rest(R), Rest(S)), & \text{otherwise} \\ DTW(Rest(R), S), DTW(R, Rest(S))\} \end{cases} \quad (4)$$

$$ERP(R,S) = \begin{cases} \sum_1^n |s_i - g| & \text{if } m=0 \\ \sum_1^n |r_i - g| & \text{if } n=0 \\ min\{ERP(Rest(R), Rest(S)) + dist_{erp}(r_1,s_1), & \text{otherwise} \\ ERP(Rest(R), S) + dist_{erp}(r_1, gap), ERP(R, Rest(S)) + dist_{erp}(s_1, gap)\} \end{cases} \quad (5)$$

Figure 2: Comparing the Distance Functions

denoted as $ERP(R,S)$, as Formula (5) in Figure 2. A careful comparison of the formulas reveals that ERP can be seen as a combination of L1-norm and EDR. ERP differs from EDR in avoiding the δ tolerance. On the other hand, ERP differs from DTW in not replicating the previous elements. The following lemma shows that for any fixed constant g, the triangle inequality is satisfied.

Lemma 1 For any three elements q_i, r_i, s_i, any of which can be a gap element, it is necessary that $dist(q_i, s_i) \leq dist(q_i, r_i) + dist(r_i, s_i)$ based on Formula (7).

Theorem 1 Let Q, R, S be three time series of arbitrary length. Then it is necessary that $ERP(Q,S) \leq ERP(Q,R) + ERP(R,S)$.

The proof of this theorem is a consequence of Lemma 1 and the proof of the result by Waterman et al. [27] on string edit distance. The Waterman proof essentially shows that defining the distance between two strings based on their best alignment in a dynamic programming style preserves the triangle inequality, as long as the underlying distance function also satisfies the triangle inequality. The latter requirement is guaranteed by Lemma 1. Due to lack of space, we omit a detailed proof.

3.2.1 Picking a Value for g

A natural question to ask here is: *what is an appropriate value of g?* The above lemma says that any value of g, as long as it is fixed, satisfies the triangle inequality. We pick $g=0$ for two reasons. First, $g=0$ admits an intuitive geometric interpretation. Consider plotting the time series with the x-axis representing (equally-spaced) time points and the y-axis representing the values of the elements. In this case, the x-axis corresponds to $g=0$. Thus, the distance between two time series R, S corresponds to the difference between the area under R and the area under S.

Second, to best match R, S is aligned to form $\widetilde{S}$ with the addition of gap elements. However, since the gap elements are of value $g=0$, it is easy to see that $\sum \widetilde{s}_i = \sum s_j$, making the area under S and that under $\widetilde{S}$ the same. The following lemma states this property. In the next section, we will see the computational significance of this lemma.

Lemma 2 Let R, S be two time series. By setting $g=0$ in Formula (7), $\sum \widetilde{s}_i = \sum s_j$, where S is aligned to form $\widetilde{S}$ to match R.

Let us repeat the previous example with ERP: $Q = [0], R = [1,2]$ and $S = [2,3,3]$. To best match R, Q is aligned to be $\widetilde{Q} = [0,0]$. Thus, $ERP(Q,R) = 1+2 = 3$. Similarly, to best match S, R is aligned to be $\widetilde{R} = [1,2,0]$, giving rise to $ERP(R,S) = 5$. Finally, to best match S, Q is aligned to be $\widetilde{Q} = [0,0,0]$, leading to $ERP(Q,S) = 8 \leq ERP(Q,R) + ERP(R,S) = 3+5 = 8$, satisfying the triangle inequality.

To see how local time shifting works for ERP, let us change $Q = [3]$ instead. Then $ERP(Q,R) = 1+1 = 2$, as $\widetilde{Q} = [0,3]$. Similarly, $ERP(Q,S) = 2+3 = 5$, as $\widetilde{Q} = [0,3,0]$. The triangle inequality is satisfied as expected.

Notice that none of the results in this section are restricted to L1-norm. That is, if we use another Lp-norm to replace L1-norm in Formula (7), the lemma and the theorem remain valid. For the rest of the paper, we continue with L1-norm for simplicity.

3.3 On the Naturalness of ERP

Even though ERP is a metric distance function, it is a valid question to ask whether ERP is "natural" for time series. In general, whether a distance function is natural mainly depends on the application semantics. Nonetheless, we show two experiments below suggesting that ERP appears to be at least as natural as the existing distance functions.

The first experiment is a simple sanity check. We first generated a simple time series Q shown in Figure 3. Then we generated 5 other time series (T_1-T_5) by adding time shifting or noise data on one or two positions of Q as shown in Figure 3. For example, T_1 was generated by shifting the sequence values of Q to the left starting from position 4, and T_2 was derived from Q by introducing noise in position 4. Finally, we used L1-norm, DTW, EDR, ERP and LCSS to rank the five time series relative to Q. The rankings are listed left to right, with the leftmost being the most similar to Q. The rankings are as follow:

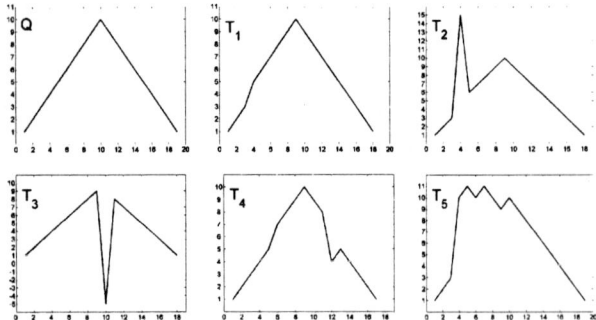

Figure 3: Subjective Evaluation of Distance Functions

L1-norm: T_1, T_4, T_5, T_3, T_2
LCSS: $T_1, \{T_2, T_3, T_4\}, T_5$
EDR: $T_1, \{T_2, T_3\}, T_4, T_5$
DTW: T_1, T_4, T_3, T_5, T_2
ERP: T_1, T_2, T_4, T_5, T_3

As shown from the above results, L1-norm is sensitive to noise, as T_2 is considered the worst match. LCSS focuses only on the matched parts and ignores all the unmatched portions. As such, it gives T_2, T_3, T_4 the same rank, and considers T_5 the worst match. EDR gives T_2, T_3 the same rank, higher than T_4. DTW gives T_3 a higher rank than T_5. Finally, ERP gives a ranked list different from all the others. Notice that the point here is *not* that ERP is the most natural. Rather, the point is that ERP appears to be no worse, if not better, than the existing distance functions.

In the second experiment, we turn to a more objective evaluation. Recently, Keogh et al. [17] have proposed using classification on labelled data to evaluate the efficacy of a distance function on time series. Specifically, each time series is assigned a class label. Then the "leave one out" prediction mechanism is applied to each time series in turn. That is, the class label of the chosen time series is predicted to be the class label of its nearest neighbour, defined based on the given distance function. If the prediction is correct, then it is a hit; otherwise, it is a miss. The classification error rate is defined as the ratio of the number of misses to the total number of the time series. In the table below, we show the average classification error rate using three benchmarks: the Cylinder-Bell-Funnel (CBFtr) data [12, 14], the ASL data [25] and the "cameramouse" (CM) data [25]. (All can be downloaded from *http://db.uwaterloo.ca/~l6chen/testdata*). Compared to the standard CBF data [17], temporal shifting is introduced in the CBFtr data set. The CBFtr data set is a 3-class problem. The ASL data set from UCI KDD archive consists of of signs from the Australian Sign Language. The ASL data set is a 10-class problem; The "cameramouse" data set contains 15 trajectories of 5 classes (words) (3 for each word). As shown in the table below, for three data sets, ERP performs (one of) the best, showing that it is not dominated by other well known alternatives.

Avg. Error Rate	L1	DTW	LCSS	EDR	ERP
CBFtr	0.03	0.01	0.01	0.01	0.01
ASL	0.16	0.10	0.11	0.11	0.09
CM	0.4	0.00	0.06	0.00	0.00

4 Indexing for ERP

Recall from Figure 2 that ERP can be seen as a variant of EDR and DTW. In particular, they share the same computational behavior. Thus, like EDR and DTW, it takes $O(mn)$ time to compute $ERP(Q, S)$ for time series Q, S of length m, n respectively. For large time series databases, it is important that for a given query Q, we try to minimize the computation of the true distance between Q and S for all series S in the database. The topic explored here is indexing for k-NN queries. An extension to range queries is rather straightforward; we omit details for brevity.

Given that ERP is a metric distance function, one obvious way to prune is to apply the triangle inequality. In Section 4.1, we present an algorithm to do just that. Metric or not, another common way to prune is to apply the GEMINI framework – that is, using lower bounds to guarantee no false negatives. Specifically, even though DTW is not a metric, three lower bounds have been proposed [30, 18, 14]. In Section 4.2.1, we show how to adapt these lower bounds for ERP. In Section 4.2.2, we propose a new lower bound for ERP. The beauty of this lower bound is that it can be indexed by a simple B+-tree.

4.1 Pruning by the Triangle Inequality

The procedure TrianglePruning shown in Figure 4 shows a skeleton of how the Triangle inequality is applied. The array *procArray* stores the true ERP distances computed so far. That is, if $\{R_1, \ldots, R_u\}$ is the set of time series for which $ERP(Q, R_i)$ has been computed, the distance $ERP(Q, R_i)$ is recorded in *procArray*. Thus, for time series S currently being evaluated, the triangle inequality ensures that $ERP(Q, S) \geq ERP(Q, R_i) - ERP(R_i, S)$, for all $1 \leq i \leq u$. Thus, it is necessary that $ERP(Q, S) \geq (max_{1 \leq i \leq u}\{ERP(Q, R_i) - ERP(R_i, S)\})$. This is implemented in lines 2 to 4. If this distance *maxPruneDist* is already worse than the current k-NN distance stored in *result*, then S can be skipped entirely. Otherwise, the true distance $ERP(Q, S)$ is computed, and *procArray* is updated to include S. Finally, the *result* array is updated, if necessary, to reflect the current k-NN neighbours and distances in sorted order.

The algorithm given in Figure 5 shows how the *result* and *procArray* should be initialized when the procedure TrianglePruning is called repeatedly in line 4. Line 3 of the algorithm represents a simple sequential scan of all the time series in the database. Note that we are *not* saying that a sequential scan should be used. We include it for two reasons. The first reason is to show how the procedure TrianglePruning can be

```
Procedure TrianglePruning(S, procArray, pmatrix, result, Q, k) {
/* S ≡ the current time series; procArray ≡ the array of
time series with computed true distance to Q; pmatrix ≡
precomputed pairwise distance matrix; result ≡ the k-NN
time series */
(1)  maxPruneDist = 0
(2)  for each time series R in procArray {
(3)    if ( (procArray[R].dist − pmatrix[R, S]) > maxPruneDist)
(4)      maxPruneDist = procArray[R].dist − pmatrix[R, S]
     } /* end-for, line 2 */
(5)  bestSoFar = result[k].dist /* the k-NN distance so far */
(6)  if (maxPruneDist ≤ bestSoFar) { /* cannot be pruned */
(7)    realDist = ERP(Q, S) /* compute true distance */
(8)    insert S and realDist into procArray
(9)    if (realDist < bestSoFar) /* update result */
(10)     insert S and realDist into result,
           sorted in ascending order of ERP distance
     } /* end-if, line 6 */
}
```

Figure 4: Algorithm for Applying the Triangle Inequality

```
Procedure SequentialScan(Q, k, pmatrix) {
/* Q ≡ the query time series; pmatrix ≡
precomputed pairwise distance matrix */
(1)  initialize result so that result[k].dist = ∞
(2)  initialize procArray to empty
(3)  for each time series S in the database
(4)    TrianglePruning(S, procArray, pmatrix, result, Q, k)
(5)  return result
}
```

Figure 5: Sequential Scan Applying the Triangle Inequality

invoked. The second reason is that a sequential scan algorithm can be used to illustrate the *pure* pruning power of the triangle inequality, independent of the indexing structure. This issue will be discussed later when the inequality is used in conjunction with index structures. Moreover, the triangle inequality need not be applied only in the manner shown in Figure 4. It can be applied directly with existing metric space index structures such as M-trees or OMNI-family access methods. Again the issue of comparison will be addressed in Section 5.

Finally, for large databases, the procedure TrianglePruning makes two assumptions. The first assumption is that the matrix *pmatrix* is small enough to be contained in main memory. For every pair of time series R, S in the database, $pmatrix[R, S]$ records the distance $ERP(R, S)$. For large databases, *pmatrix* may be too large. The second assumption is that the size of *procArray* is small enough. The size is left unspecified because procedure TrianglePruning works regardless of the actual size of the array. The larger the size, the more time series can be used for pruning. These two assumptions will be addressed in Section 4.3.

4.2 Pruning by Lower Bounding

For non-metric distance functions, like DTW, the main pruning strategy is lower bounding. However, lower bounding is not restricted only to non-metric distance functions. Below we develop lower bounds for ERP.

4.2.1 Adapting Existing Lower Bounds

Given the similarities between ERP and DTW, as shown in Figure 2, we first adapt existing lower bounds for DTW to become lower bounds for ERP. Specifically, we consider the lower bounds proposed by Yi et al. [30], Kim et al. [18], and Keogh et al. [14].

The lower bound proposed by Yi et al., denoted as $DLB_{yi}(Q, S)$, is based on the area covered by Q that is greater than $max(S)$ and the area of Q that is less than $min(S)$, where $max(S)$ and $min(S)$ denote the maximum and minimum elements of S. Adapting to ERP is rather straightforward. Because ERP uses a constant gap element $g = 0$, we need to compare the original minimum and maximum elements with 0, i.e., $newmin(S) = min\{min(S), 0\}$ and $newmax(S) = max\{max(S), 0\}$. With this modification, we have the following result. The proof is omitted because it is a simple extension of the original proof of $DLB_{yi}(Q, S) \leq DTW(Q, S)$ given in [30].

Lemma 3 Let Q, S be two time series. It is necessary that $DLB_{yi}(Q, S) \leq ERP(Q, S)$.

Instead of just using $min(S)$ and $max(S)$, the lower bound proposed by Kim et al., denoted as $DLB_{kim}(Q, S)$, uses the first and last elements of Q and S as well, i.e., q_1, q_m and s_1, s_n. The lower bound is the maximum of: $|max(Q) − max(S)|$, $|min(Q) − min(S)|$, $|q_1 − s_1|$ and $|q_m − s_n|$. To adapt this lower bound for ERP, we need to take into account that for the aligned time series, the first or the last element may be a gap. With this simple change, we have the following result, which extends $DLB_{kim}(Q, S) \leq DTW(Q, S)$ shown in [18].

Lemma 4 Let Q, S be two time series. It is necessary that $DLB_{kim}(Q, S) \leq ERP(Q, S)$.

Finally, Keogh et al. introduced the concept of a bounding envelop for a time series Q, which is of the form: $Env(Q) = [(Min_1, Max_1), \ldots (Min_n, Max_n)]$. Min_i and Max_i represent the minimum and maximum value of the warping range of an element. The warping range of an element is the maximum number of times the element can be duplicated in local time shifting. To adapt the envelope to ERP, Min_i and Max_i are adjusted with the gap, exactly like in $DLB_{yi}(Q, S)$. The following extends: $DLB_{keogh}(Q, S) \leq DTW(Q, S)$ shown in [14].

Lemma 5 Let Q, S be two time series. It is necessary that $DLB_{keogh}(Q, S) \leq ERP(Q, S)$.

The effectiveness of the three adapted lower bounds will be empirically evaluated in the next section. The focus will be on the pruning power of these lower bounds. Notice that the lower bound DLB_{keogh} is not directly indexable. Thus, in [31], Shasha et al. proposed a lower bound for DLB_{keogh}. We do not include this technique in our experimentation because we will make comparison with DLB_{keogh} directly. As a preview, we will show that our proposed technique dominates DLB_{keogh}, which translates to a superiority over the Shasha's lower bound of DLB_{keogh}.

Finally, as the comparisons are based on pruning power, we consider a sequential scan strategy for exploiting these lower bounds. This can be achieved by modifying procedure TrianglePruning in Figure 4 as follows:

- Delete lines 2 to 4 and line 8, as there is no longer necessary to keep procArray.
- Change line 1 to: $maxPruneDist = DLB_{yi}(Q,S), DLB_{kim}(Q,S)$ or $DLB_{keogh}(Q,S)$.

4.2.2 A New Lower Bound for ERP

Below we develop a new lower bound specifically for ERP. Given a time series S of length n, we use the notation $sum(S)$ to denote $\sum_{i=1}^{n} s_i$. Then we define the distance $DLB_{erp}(Q,S)$ between Q of length m and S of length n as:

$$DLB_{erp}(Q,S) = |sum(Q) - sum(S)| \quad (8)$$

A key result here is the following theorem stating that this is indeed a lower bound for ERP.

Theorem 2 Let Q, S be two time series. It is necessary that $DLB_{erp}(Q,S) \leq ERP(Q,S)$.

Before we present a proof sketch of the theorem, we need the following results from the literature on a convex function. A function $f(x)$ is convex on an interval $[a, b]$ if for any two points x_1 and x_2 in $[a, b]$, $f[\frac{1}{2}(x_1 + x_2)] \leq \frac{1}{2}[f(x_1) + f(x_2)]$.

Lemma 6 [23] Let $\lambda_1, \ldots, \lambda_K$ be non-negative real values such that $\sum_{i=1}^{K} \lambda_i = 1$. If f is a convex function on reals, then $f(\lambda_1 x_1 + \ldots + \lambda_K x_K) \leq \lambda_1 f(x_1) + \ldots + \lambda_K f(x_K)$, where $x_1, \ldots, x_K$ are real values.

As shown in [29], the following corollary can be established for Lp-norms which are convex functions on reals.

Corollary 1 For any sequence $S = [s_1, \ldots, s_K]$, and $1 \leq p < \infty$, we have: $K \cdot |mean(S)|^p \leq \sum_{i=1}^{K} |s_i|^p$.
Proof of corollary: Take $f(x) = |x|^p$, and $\lambda_i = 1/K$. Then $f(\sum_{i=1}^{K} \lambda_i s_i) = f((\sum_{i=1}^{K} s_i)/K) = |mean(S)|^p$. Thus, the inequality follows.

With the above corollary and Lemma 2, we can now establish Theorem 2.

Proof of Theorem 2: Given Q of length m and S of length n, let the aligned sequences, to give the best local time shifting outcome, be $\widetilde{Q}$ and $\widetilde{S}$ respectively. Both $\widetilde{Q}$ and $\widetilde{S}$ are of the same length, say K.

$$\begin{aligned}
ERP(Q,S) &= \sum_{i=1}^{K} |\widetilde{s}_i - \widetilde{q}_i| & \text{(Formula 7)} \\
&\geq K \cdot |mean(\widetilde{S} - \widetilde{Q})| & \text{(Corollary 1, } p=1\text{)} \\
&= K \cdot |\frac{\sum_{i=1}^{K} \widetilde{s}_i - \sum_{i=1}^{K} \widetilde{q}_i}{K}| \\
&= |\sum_{i=1}^{K} \widetilde{s}_i - \sum_{i=1}^{K} \widetilde{q}_i| \\
&= |\sum_{i=1}^{n} s_i - \sum_{j=1}^{m} q_j| & \text{(Lemma 2)} \\
&= DLB_{erp}(Q,S)
\end{aligned}$$

There are two points worth mentioning from the above theorem. The first point concerns the application of Lemma 2, i.e., $\sum_{i=1}^{K} \widetilde{s}_i = \sum_{i=1}^{n} s_i$. This is due to the fact that the gap element is $g = 0$. The beauty of this equality is that regardless of $\widetilde{S}$, which depends on Q, the quantity $sum(S)$ is unchanged and can be inserted into an index for lower bounding purposes for any future query Q. This leads to the second point – $sum(S)$ is a single value. Thus, only a 1-dimensional B+-tree is sufficient.

Figure 6 shows a skeleton of the algorithm for using the B+-tree for lower bounding with $sum(S)$. It first conducts a standard search for the value $sum(Q)$. This results in a leaf node I. The first k time series pointed to by I are used to initialize the result array. Then the leaf nodes of the tree are traversed using the pointer connecting a leaf node to its siblings. All the data values bigger than $sum(Q)$ are visited in ascending order. Similarly, all the data values smaller than $sum(Q)$ are visited in descending order. In both cases, if the lower bound distance $DLB_{erp}(Q,S)$ is smaller than the best k-NN distance so far, the true distance $ERP(Q,S)$ is computed and updates are made if necessary. Otherwise, the remaining data values can be skipped entirely.

4.3 Combining the Two Pruning Methods

For a non-metric distance function like DTW, lower bounding can be used, but pruning by the triangle inequality cannot. ERP is of course different. It is possible to combine both methods – use the triangle inequality to save the computation of the true distance $ERP(Q,S)$ after lower bounding. A skeleton is shown in Figure 7.

Recall from Figure 4 that in applying the TrianglePruning procedure, there are two unresolved issues: (i) the size of the pairwise distance matrix $pmatrix$; and (ii) the size of $procArray$, i.e., the maximum number of time series whose true ERP distances are

```
Procedure DLBerpk-NN(Q, k, Tree, result) {
/* Tree ≡ a B+-tree storing sum(S) for all S in database */
(1)   sumQ = sum(Q)
(2)   conduct a standard B+-tree search on Tree using sumQ
      and let I be the leaf node the search ends up with
(3)   pick the first k time series pointed to by I and
      initialize result with the k true (sorted) ERP distances
(4)   let v_1,...,v_h be the data values in all the leaf nodes
      larger than the data values visited in line 3. v_1,...,v_h
      are sorted in ascending order.
(5)   for each v_i {
(6)      bestSoFar = result[k].dist /* the k-NN distance so far */
(7)      if ((v_i - sumQ) ≤ bestSoFar) /* need to check */
(8)         for each S pointed to by the pointer with v_i {
(9)            realDist = ERP(Q, S) /* compute true distance */
(10)           if (realDist < bestSoFar) { /* update result */
(11)              insert S and realDist into result,
                  sorted in ascending order of ERP distance
(12)              bestSoFar = result[k].dist
               } /* end-if, line 10 */
            } /* end-for, line 8 */
(13)     else break /* else, line 7, skip the rest */
      } /* end-for, line 5 */
(14)  repeat line 4 to 13 this time to the values w_1,...,w_j
      in all the leaf nodes which are smaller than the data values
      visited in line 3. w_1,...,w_j are sorted in descending
      order. Line 7 is modified to: if ((sumQ - w_i) ≤ bestSoFar)
(15)  return result
}
```

Figure 6: Algorithm for Applying DLB_{erp}

```
Procedure ERPCombineK-NN(Q, k, Tree, result) {
   Identical to Procedure DLBerpk-NN except:
   line 8 to 12 is replaced with:
(8')  for each S pointed to by the pointer with v_i
(9')     invoke procedure TrianglePruning() in Figure 4
}
```

Figure 7: Algorithm for Applying first DLB_{erp} followed by the Triangle Inequality

kept for triangle inequality pruning. Below we resolve these issues to make procedure ERPCombineK-NN in Figure 7 practical for large databases and for limited buffer space situations.

Let $maxTriangle$ denote the maximum number of time series whose true ERP distances are kept for triangle inequality pruning. This value should be determined at query time by the query engine. Hereafter we call these time series the *reference series*. There are two ways to pick these reference series:

- *static*: these reference series are randomly picked *a priori*. For that matter, they may not even be series contained in the database.

- *dynamic*: these reference series are picked as procedure ERPCombineK-NN runs. The choices are thus query dependent. In our implementation, we simply pick the first $maxTriangle$ time series that fill up the fixed-size $procArray$.

For the static reference series strategies, the entire $pmatrix$ is not needed. We only need the pairwise ERP distance matrix for each pair of reference series and data series. Thus, if N is the number of time series in the database, then the size of the this matrix is $N * maxTriangle$. For the dynamic reference series strategy, again the entire $pmatrix$ is not needed. As the reference series are picked and kept, the appropriate column of the matrix is read into the buffer space. The buffer space requirement is $maxTriangle$ columns, each of size N. Thus, the total buffer space required is again $N * maxTriangle$.

While the buffer space requirement is the same, there are tradeoffs between the two strategies. For the dynamic strategy, the advantage is that the reference series are chosen based on previously compared time series. Thus, there is no extra cost involved. The disadvantage is that at the beginning of running ERPCombineK-NN, there may not be enough reference series for the triangle inequality to be effective. It takes at least $maxTriangle$ iterations to fill up $procArray$. In contrast, for the static strategy, all $maxTriangle$ reference time series are available right at the beginning of running ERPCombineK-NN. The disadvantage is that the ERP distance must be computed between the query and each reference time series, which represents additional overhead. In the next section, we will present experimental results to compare these two strategies.

In closing, note that ERPCombineK-NN can be generalized to apply to any metric distance function – representing an extension to the GEMINI framework. That is, within the GEMINI framework, once lower bounding has been applied, we can add an additional step to apply the triangle inequality to eliminate more false positives, as long as the underlying distance function is a metric. Thus, in this paper, not only do we find a good marriage between distance functions, but we also develop a framework for combining two popular pruning strategies.

5 Experimental Evaluation

5.1 Experimental Setup

In this section, we present experimental results based on the 24 benchmark data sets used in [31, 14], the stock data set used in [26], and the random walk data set tested in [16, 14, 31]. All experiments were run on a Sun-Blade-1000 workstation with 1G memory under Solaris 2.8. All the algorithms listed in previous sections were implemented in C. The various lower bound strategies for DTW [30, 18, 14], OMNI-sequential and the HF algorithm for selecting reference series [11], were also implemented. We obtained the M-tree code from *http://www-db.deis.unibo.it/Mtree/*.

Our experiments measure either total time or pruning power. Total time includes both CPU and I/O, and is measured in seconds. Given a k-NN query Q, the pruning power is defined to be the fraction of the time series S in the data set for which the true distance $ERP(Q, S)$ is not computed (without introducing false negatives). Following [14, 31], we measure pruning power (P) because this is an indicator free of implementation bias (e.g., page size, thresholds). Moreover, we vary k from 1 to 5, 20, etc.

5.2 Lower Bounding vs Triangle Inequality

The first experiment addressed the issue of lower bounding versus the triangle inequality. To make the comparisons fair, sequential scans were used. Figure 8 shows the pruning power of $DLB_{yi}, DLB_{kim}, DLB_{keogh}, DLB_{erp}$ and the triangle inequality (denoted as TR) on the 24 benchmark data sets for $k = 1, 5, 20$. The pruning power shown is the average over 50 random queries. Each data set contains 200 time series with length 256. As a concrete example, we pick an arbitrary data set among the 24 and show the detailed pruning power figures below for $k = 20$. The third data set is picked and it contains the spot prices (foreign currency in dollars) over 10 years (10/9/86 to 8/9/96).

DLB_{kim}	DLB_{yi}	DLB_{keogh}	DLB_{erp}	TR
0.0	0.28	0.44	0.54	0.63

From the results shown in the above table and Figure 8, it is obvious that among the three previously proposed lower bounds, DLB_{keogh} performs uniformly the best. However, it is dominated by DLB_{erp} proposed in this paper. Furthermore, the triangle inequality (TR) consistently outperforms all the lower bounds. The larger the value of k, the larger is the difference. This shows the value of having a metric distance function.

5.3 Combining DLB_{erp} with Triangle Inequality

From Figure 8, the triangle inequality (TR) performs the best in pruning power. In Figure 9, TR is compared further with:

- M-tree (page size 16K). Compared to other metric space indexing structures, such as MVP-tree and Sa-tree, M-tree is designed to minimize both I/O cost and distance computations.
- OMNI-sequential (OMNI-seq). OMNI-seq is tested with different number of reference points that ranges from 5 to 100.
- B+-tree (page size 1K). This implements DLB_{erp} with an index structure (i.e., Algorithm 6).
- B+-tree incorporating both the triangle inequality and DLB_{erp} (i.e., Algorithm 7). Both the static and dynamic versions are included.

In the experiment, we found that the pruning power of OMNI-seq with 100 reference points behaves very similar to that of TR. This is because they use the same strategies to remove false alarms; the only difference is the number of reference points that they use. Therefore, we do not include the results of OMNI-seq in Figure 9.

From the figure, the first observation is that all the methods do well when $k = 1$. But with $k = 20$, the separation is clear. M-tree is by far the worst, even dominated by the triangle inequality based on sequential scan. This is because with M-tree, the algorithm uses the distance information below each scanned node, rather than on all the true distances previously computed. This restricts the effectiveness of the pruning.

The second observation is that while TR (based on sequential scan) outperforms DLB_{erp} with sequential scan, the reverse is true when DLB_{erp} is used with a B+-tree. This shows the effectiveness of the B+-tree index in facilitating lower bound pruning.

The third observation is that the combination approaches B+TR(static) and B+TR(dynamic) are the best – better than B+-tree alone or the triangle inequality alone. This shows the beauty of combining both lower bounding and pruning by the triangle inequality. For both the static and dynamic combination approaches, the number of reference series varies from 5 to 100. The graph only shows the result with 100 reference series. The following table is included to show the pruning power in greater details on the third data set with $k = 20$.

M-tree	TR	B+tree	B+TR(static)		
			20	50	100
0.59	0.63	0.72	0.76	0.80	0.82

B+TR(dynamic)			B+HF	OMNI-seq
20	50	100	(100)	(100)
0.74	0.76	0.77	0.76	0.63

For both the static and dynamic combination approaches, increasing the number of reference series improves the pruning power as expected. And the static approach appears to perform better than the dynamic approach. However, as will be shown in later experiments, this perspective on pruning power is not yet the complete picture.

Note that in the above table, we also include the pruning power results using the HF algorithm to select the reference series and the OMNI-sequential with 100 reference points [11]. Both are dominated by the static and dynamic approaches we developed.

5.4 Total Time Comparisons

So far we have presented the pruning power results. However, these results do not represent the complete picture because higher pruning power may require additional time spent on pre-processing. Figure 10 shows the total time spent on answering the k-NN queries. This time includes the pre-processing time and the query processing time (both CPU and I/O included). The time taken by TR (the triangle inequality alone) is not shown in the figure because it takes much longer than the others. We also found that the time cost of OMNI-seq is very similar to that of B+TR(static)), because both of them spend the same amount of time on computing the distance between query time series and the reference time series. Thus, we did not include the results of OMNI-seq in Figure 10. Again,

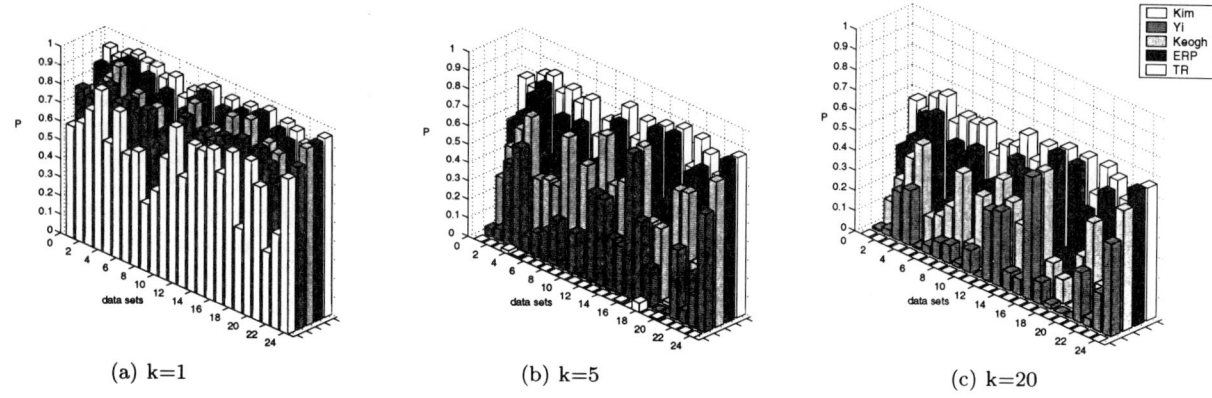

(a) k=1   (b) k=5   (c) k=20

Figure 8: Lower Bounding vs the Triangle Inequality: Pruning Power

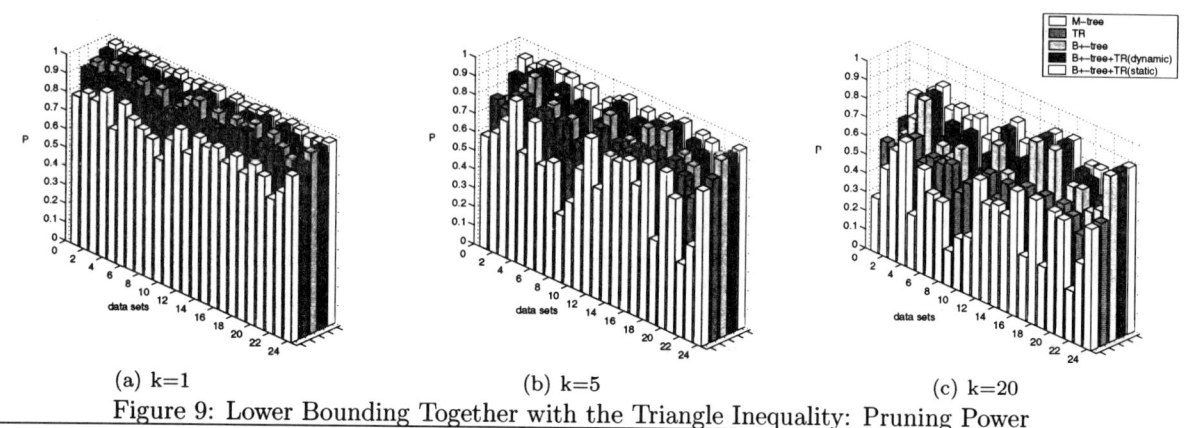

(a) k=1   (b) k=5   (c) k=20

Figure 9: Lower Bounding Together with the Triangle Inequality: Pruning Power

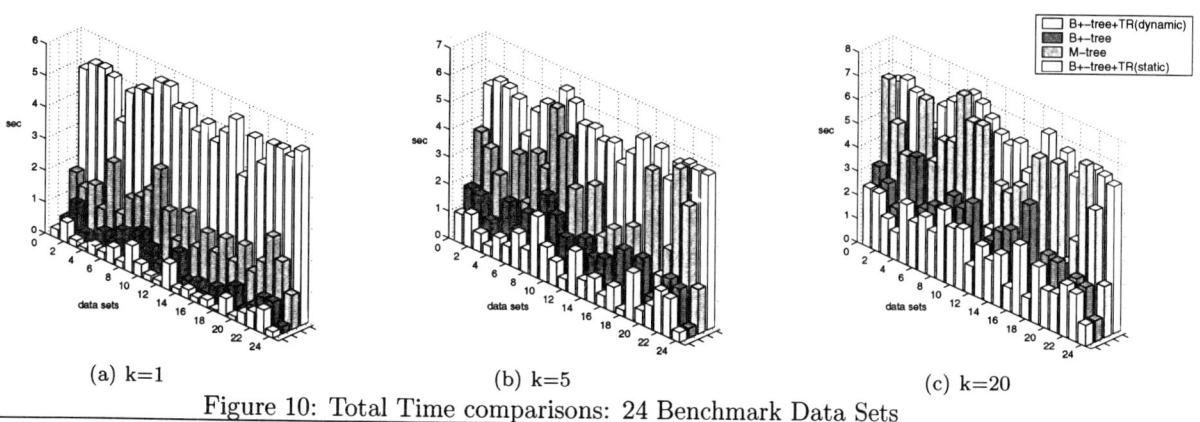

(a) k=1   (b) k=5   (c) k=20

Figure 10: Total Time comparisons: 24 Benchmark Data Sets

the graphs only show the results of combined methods with 100 reference sequences. The detailed run time (in seconds) on the third data set with $k = 20$ and 100 reference series is shown below.

M-tree	B+tree	B+TR (static)	B+TR (dynamic)	OMNI-seq
3.89	1.84	6.36	1.58	5.68

Among the approaches shown in the figure and table, the static combination approach (i.e., B+TR(static)) takes the most time, followed by OMNI-seq, M-tree and the B+-tree alone. The dynamic combination approach appears to be the best, in delivering very good pruning power but not at the expense of sacrificing pre-processing time.

However, it would be a mistake to conclude at this point that the dynamic combination approach is the clear winner. The main reason is that the 24 benchmarks are all small data sets, none of which contains more than 200 time series. We use them because they have been widely used as benchmarks, and represent a wide spectrum of applications and data characteristics. However, to address the size issue, the following set of results is based on much larger data sets.

5.5 Scalability Tests

We used two data sets. The first data set was a real stock data set from [26], which contains daily stock prices from 4622 American companies. Each time series contains 1024 daily closing prices, starting from March 1995 to March 1999. To make the data set bigger, we segmented each time series into 4 disjoint series with length 256 each. Thus, the total number of time series is 18,488. The other data set was the random walk data set used in [16, 14, 31]. We generated 65,536 and 100,000 random walk time series, each of length 256.

Figure 11 shows the total time taken to answer k-NN queries. The time taken for five methods are included: M-tree, B+-tree alone, B+TR(static,400), B+TR(dynamic,400) and OMNI-sequential(400), where 400 refers to the number of reference time series. It is clear that the static and dynamic approaches perform the best. In fact, the static approach manages to catch up with the dynamic approach, and in some cases, it even outperforms. The reason is that when the data set is large and selectivity is high ($k > 1$), the pre-processing represents a small overhead relative to the search. The improvement in pruning power can then compensate for the overhead. We also ran the experiments to confirm the pruning power on these large data sets. Same conclusions can be drawn as for the 24 benchmarks.

6 Conclusions and Future Work

In this paper, we present the ERP distance function for time series similarity retrieval. ERP can be viewed as a perfect marriage between L1-norm and edit distance. It resembles L1-norm in being a metric distance function, and it resembles edit distance in being able to handle local time shifting. We show that this new distance function is as natural for time series as existing distance functions such as DTW and LCSS.

Because ERP is a metric distance function, the triangle inequality can be used for pruning for k-NN queries. Furthermore, we develop a new lower bound for ERP distance. Unlike existing lower bounds which require indexing with a multi-dimensional index, the proposed lower bound is 1-dimensional and can simply be implemented in a B+-tree, which reduces the storage requirement and save the possible I/O cost in consequence. Because pruning by the triangle inequality and by lower bounds are orthogonal, we combine the two strategies. This combination can be considered as an extension of GEMINI framework for indexing time series data with a metric.

We conducted extensive experimentation using 24 benchmarks and other large data sets. Consistently, our new lower bound dominates existing strategies. More importantly, the combination approaches which incorporate both lower bounding and pruning by the triangle inequality deliver superb pruning power as well as wall clock time performance. Among the two combination approaches, both the static and the dynamic approach are viable alternatives depending on k and the size of the database.

A direct extension of the similarity-based time series retrieval is the search of trajectories of moving objects in multimedia databases. Unlike the time series data that we used in this paper, trajectories of moving objects are multi-dimensional and contain possible noises, which brings new challenges. Our future research directions will include the work in this direction.

Acknowledgements: Thanks to Eamonn Keogh, Michalis Vlachos, X. Sean Wang for providing data sets.

References

[1] R. Agrawal, C. Faloutsos, and A. N. Swami. Efficient similarity search in sequence databases. In *Proc. 4th Int. Conf. of Foundations of Data Organization and Algorithms*, pages 69–84, 1993.

[2] R. Agrawal, G. Psaila, E. L. Wimmers, and M. Zaït. Querying shapes of histories. In *Proc. 21th Int. Conf. on Very Large Data Bases*, pages 502–514, 1995.

[3] D. J. Berndt and J. Clifford. Finding patterns in time series: A dynamic programming approach. In *Advances in Knowledge Discovery and Data Mining*, pages 229–248, 1996.

[4] J. S. Boreczky and L. A. Rowe. Comparison of video shot boundary detection techniques. In *Proc. 8th Int. Symp. on Storage and Retrieval for Image and Video Databases*, pages 170–179, 1996.

[5] T. Bozkaya and M. Ozsoyoglu. Indexing large metric spaces for similarity search queries. *ACM Trans. Database Sys.*, 24(3):361–404, 1999.

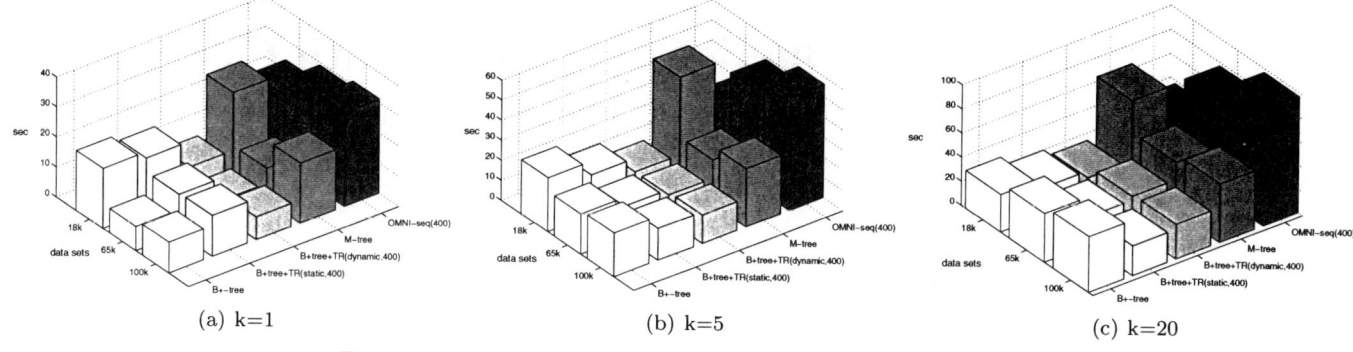

(a) k=1 (b) k=5 (c) k=20

Figure 11: Total Time Comparisons: Large Data Sets

[6] L. Chen, M. T. Özsu, and V. Oria. Robust and efficient similarity search for moving object trajectories. In *CS Tech. Report. CS-2003-30, School of Computer Science, University of Waterloo*.

[7] E. Chvéz, G. Navarro, R. Baeza-Yates, and J. L. Marroquń. Searching in metric spaces. *ACM Comput. Surv.*, 33(3):273–321, 2001.

[8] P. Ciaccia, M. Patella, and P. Zezula. M-tree: An efficient access method for similarity search in metric spaces. In *Proc. 23th Int. Conf. on Very Large Data Bases*, pages 426–435, 1997.

[9] G. Das, D. Gunopulos, and H. Mannila. Finding similar time series. In *Proc. 1st European Symp. on Principles of Data Mining and Knowledge Discovery*, pages 88–100, 1997.

[10] C. Faloutsos, M. Ranganathan, and Y. Manolopoulos. Fast subsequence matching in time-series databases. In *Proc. ACM SIGMOD Int. Conf. on Management of Data*, pages 419–429, 1994.

[11] R. F. S. Filho, A. J. M. Traina, C. Traina Jr., and C. Faloutsos. Similarity search without tears: The OMNI family of all-purpose access methods. In *Proc. 17th Int. Conf. on Data Engineering*, pages 623–630, 2001.

[12] P. Geurts. Pattern extraction for time series classification. In *Proc. 5th Int. Conf. on Principles and Practice of Knowledge Discovery in Databases*, pages 115–127, 2001.

[13] D.Q. Goldin and P.C. Kanellakis. On similarity queries for time series data: Constraint specification and implementation. In *Proc. of the Int. Conf. on Principles and Pratice of Constraint Programming*, pages 23–35, 1995.

[14] E. Keogh. Exact indexing of dynamic time warping. In *Proc. 28th Int. Conf. on Very Large Data Bases*, pages 406–417, 2002.

[15] E. Keogh, K. Chakrabarti, M. Pazzani, and S. Mehrotra. Dimensionality reduction for fast similarity search in large time series databases. *Knowledge and Information Systems*, 3(3):263–286, 2000.

[16] E. Keogh, K. Chakrabarti, M. Pazzani, and S. Mehrotra. Locally adaptive dimensionality reduction for indexing large time series databases. In *Proc. ACM SIGMOD Int. Conf. on Management of Data*, pages 151–162, 2001.

[17] E. Keogh and S. Kasetty. On the need for time series data mining benchmarks: a survey and empirical demonstration. In *Proc. 8th ACM SIGKDD Int. Conf. on Knowledge Discovery and Data Mining*, pages 102–111, 2002.

[18] S Kim, S. Park, and W. Chu. An indexed-based approach for similarity search supporting time warping in large sequence databases. In *Proc. 17th Int. Conf. on Data Engineering*, pages 607–614, 2001.

[19] F. Korn, H. Jagadish, and C. Faloutsos. Efficiently supporting ad hoc queries in large datasets of time sequences. In *Proc. ACM SIGMOD Int. Conf. on Management of Data*, pages 289–300, 1997.

[20] K.P.Chan and A.W-C Fu. Efficient time series matching by wavelets. In *Proc. 15th Int. Conf. on Data Engineering*, pages 126–133, 1999.

[21] G. Navarro. Searching in metric spaces by spatial approximation. *The VLDB Journal*, 11:28–46, 2002.

[22] I. Popivanov and R. J. Miller. Similarity search over time series data using wavelets. In *Proc. 17th Int. Conf. on Data Engineering*, pages 212–221, 2001.

[23] M. H. Protter and C. B. Morrey. *A First Course in Real Analysis*. Sprinter-Verlag, 1977.

[24] E. Vidal and F. Casacuberta. On the verification of triangle inequality by dynamic time-warping dissimilarity measures. *Speech Commun.*, 7(1):67–79, 1988.

[25] M. Vlachos, G. Kollios, and D. Gunopulos. Discovering similar multidimensional trajectories. In *Proc. 18th Int. Conf. on Data Engineering*, pages 673–684, 2002.

[26] C.Z. Wang and X. Wang. Supporting content-based searches on time series via approximation. In *Proc. 12th Int. Conf. on Scientific and Statistical Database Management*, pages 69–81, 2000.

[27] M. S. Waterman, T. F. Smith, and W. A. Beyer. Some biological sequence metrics. advances in mathematics. *Advances in Mathematics*, (20):367–387, 1976.

[28] R. Weber, H.-J Schek, and S. Blott. A quantitative analysis and performance study for similarity-search methods in high-dimensional spaces. In *Proc. 24th Int. Conf. on Very Large Data Bases*, pages 194–205, 1998.

[29] B-K Yi and C. Faloutsos. Fast time sequence indexing for arbitrary Lp norms. In *Proc. 26th Int. Conf. on Very Large Data Bases*, pages 385–394, 2000.

[30] B-K Yi, H. Jagadish, and C. Faloutsos. Efficient retrieval of similar time sequences under time warping. In *Proc. 14th Int. Conf. on Data Engineering*, pages 23–27, 1998.

[31] Y. Zhu and D. Shasha. Warping indexes with envelope transforms for query by humming. In *Proc. ACM SIGMOD Int. Conf. on Management of Data*, pages 181–192, 2003.

Approximate NN Queries on Streams with Guaranteed Error/performance Bounds

Nick Koudas
AT&T Labs-Research
koudas@research.att.com

Beng Chin Ooi   Kian-Lee Tan   Rui Zhang
National University of Singapore, Singapore
{ooibc, tankl, zhangru1}@comp.nus.edu.sg

Abstract

In data stream applications, data arrive continuously and can only be scanned once as the query processor has very limited memory (relative to the size of the stream) to work with. Hence, queries on data streams do not have access to the entire data set and query answers are typically approximate. While there have been many studies on the k Nearest Neighbors (kNN) problem in conventional multi-dimensional databases, the solutions cannot be directly applied to data streams for the above reasons. In this paper, we investigate the kNN problem over data streams. We first introduce the e-approximate kNN (ekNN) problem that finds the approximate kNN answers of a query point Q such that the absolute error of the k-th nearest neighbor distance is bounded by e. To support ekNN queries over streams, we propose a technique called DISC (aDaptive Indexing on Streams by space-filling Curves). DISC can adapt to different data distributions to either (a) optimize memory utilization to answer ekNN queries under certain accuracy requirements or (b) achieve the best accuracy under a given memory constraint. At the same time, DISC provide efficient updates and query processing which are important requirements in data stream applications. Extensive experiments were conducted using both synthetic and real data sets and the results confirm the effectiveness and efficiency of DISC.

Permission to copy without fee all or part of this material is granted provided that the copies are not made or distributed for direct commercial advantage, the VLDB copyright notice and the title of the publication and its date appear, and notice is given that copying is by permission of the Very Large Data Base Endowment. To copy otherwise, or to republish, requires a fee and/or special permission from the Endowment.

Proceedings of the 30th VLDB Conference, Toronto, Canada, 2004

1 Introduction

In many applications, including geographic information systems, content-based retrieval and data mining, finding the k Nearest Neighbors (kNN) to a query object is one of the most frequent operations. The database research community has in recent years provided several novel solutions to efficient kNN processing [22, 6, 21]. The kNN problem can be defined as follows: Given a set of points $S = \{P_0, P_1, ..., P_n\}$ in a d-dimensional space V, and a query point $Q \in V$, find a set kNN which contains k points in S such that, for any $P \in kNN$ and for any $P' \in S - kNN$, $dist(Q, P) \leq dist(Q, P')$.

To further improve performance, the $(1 + \epsilon)$-approximate nearest neighbors problem [1, 17] has been introduced which is defined as follows: Find a point $P \in V$ that is an $(1 + \epsilon)$-approximate nearest neighbor of the query point Q, so that for any point $P' \in S$, $dist(P, Q) \leq (1 + \epsilon)dist(P', Q)$. The k $(1 + \epsilon)$-approximate nearest neighbors problem can be similarly defined [2]. Here ϵ is in fact a bound for the relative error of the k-th nearest neighbor distance, which is specified by the users before the query.

KNN queries over multi-dimensional data streams is a pressing concern when mining streams for unknown patterns. For example, in computer aided manufacturing (CAM) systems, sensors are used to monitor the position, shape[1], size, surface characterization, material properties, etc, of parts passing through on a production line. The data are collected and sent to a control system. The control system analyzes the feedback information and then adjusts the parameters of the production line so as to control the quality of the parts. Often, we tend to identify parts with similar shape to a given part in order to discover patterns of other features. In highway traffic monitoring, sensors are embedded on highways to observe the passing vehicles. Estimates of vehicle speed and length can be obtained and utilized to provide useful traffic related information. Similarly in network traffic monitoring, network

---
[1]Even parts on a same production line have slightly different shapes and sizes due to manufacturing errors.

traffic streams (IP traffic) are usually logged using special programs, such as CISCO's netflow. The network management system will monitor the network packet header information to obtain information on traffic flow patterns [3], which involves finding packets similar to a given packet.

In addition, data stream applications typically operate in an environment where memory is limited (relative to the size of the stream) so that it is not feasible to work with the entire data set in memory. For this reason, one has to resort to approximate kNN answers in the case of continuously evolving data streams. All previous proposals for approximate kNN queries require the user to specify a relative error bound (ϵ) beforehand. However, in certain applications, absolute error bounds are more critical and preferable. In the CAM example, a query typically specifies absolute errors: "Identify 10 parts that are most similar in size to a given part A. The query specifies that as long as a part's resultant error (that is, the root-sum-square of the errors in width and length) to those of the 10 most similar parts is not more than 0.1mm the answer is acceptable." In the highway traffic monitoring example, it may also be more intuitive to specify errors by absolute bounds: "Find the 20 vehicles that are close to position A. An answer is acceptable as long as its distance to A is not larger than say 10 meters than that of the 20 closest vehicles." Similar examples can be drawn from the field of network monitoring and other engineering applications, in which users have good knowledge of the absolute errors acceptable.

Motivated by such applications, we introduce a new type of approximate nearest neighbors problem, called the *e*-**approximate kNN (ekNN) problem**, in which the answers are bounded by absolute value instead of relative one. Formally, we define it as following:

Definition 1 (ekNN) *Given a data set S and a query point Q, find a set ekNN which contains k points in S such that for any $P \in ekNN$ and for any $P' \in kNN$ (the actual kNN set of Q), $dist(Q, P) \leq dist(Q, P') + e$, where e is a bound for the absolute error of the k-th nearest neighbor distance.*

Subsequently, we define the *e*-**approximate kNN problem over Data Streams** as follows:

Definition 2 (ekNN over data streams) *Let X be a sequence of points $(P_0, P_1, P_2, ...)$ (in this paper, we view data records with multiple attributes as multi-dimensional points). X can be either finite or infinite. Each element $P_i (i = 0, 1, 2, ...)$ of X is a point in d-dimensional space and is allowed to be read for at most once in the order of the sequence. Let S_t be the set of points of X that have been read at time t. At any time t and for any query point Q, find the ekNN of Q from the elements of S_t.*

In particular, we identify and provide solutions to the following ekNN problems on data streams:

1. **memory optimization for a given error bound**: given an error bound *e*, use as little memory as possible to answer ekNN queries.

2. **error minimization for a given memory size**: given a fixed amount of memory, achieve the best accuracy for ekNN queries.

We propose a general scheme which aims to reduce the amount of information to be stored while guaranteeing a provable error bound. Specifically, we partition the underlying space into equal square-shaped cells, and then we prove that in each cell we only need to store at most K (for a user specified value K) points to guarantee some error bound. We will prove that the error bound is guaranteed for any ekNN query where $k \leq K$. Next, to facilitate efficient maintenance of K points in each cell, we propose a technique called DISC (aDaptive Indexing on Streams by space-filling Curves), in which points are stored in the leaf nodes of the B*-tree with the Z-values [19] of their cells as keys. DISC has two important properties: first, it only allocates memory for those points that are necessary to guarantee the error bound; second, by merging cells, DISC can adjust the structure to meet the memory constraint. These two properties make it adaptive to different data distributions. In addition, being a B*-tree based indexing structure, DISC provides fast access to a given cell. This facilitates efficient updates and query processing. Overall, DISC can achieve our goals of minimizing memory usage for a given error bound or obtaining best accuracy for a given memory constraint while retaining efficient updates and query processing. We present the ekNN search algorithm based on DISC and also show how to modify DISC to support sliding window ekNN queries. Extensive performance studies using synthetic and real data sets were conducted, and the results demonstrate that DISC is both query and memory efficient. Note that since DISC is essentially a B*-tree based technique, it can also be used as a disk-based structure.

The rest of the paper is organized as follows: Section 2 reviews related work. In Section 3, we propose a general scheme to reduce information while still answering the ekNN problem with some error bound. A brute-force method based on this framework is also presented in this section. Then we present DISC and the algorithms in Section 4. Section 5 reports the results of our experimental studies. Section 6 concludes the paper.

2 Related Work

Various multi-dimensional indexing structures [5, 14, 7, 23] and kNN query processing strategies have been proposed in the literature [12, 21, 22]. These methods assume that the data are disk-resident and can be scanned multiple times. As such, they are not suitable for processing data streams that typically require one-pass algorithms as the data are not stored on disk and are too large to fit into memory. Moreover, it is unclear how these schemes can provide any guarantee on approximate answers to kNN queries.

A structure based on quadtrees for answering kNN queries approximately was proposed in [8]. The relative error is dependent on the dimensionality d so that the larger the value of d, the greater the relative error will be. Then the $(1+\epsilon)$-approximate nearest neighbors problem was studied [1, 2, 17], in which the relative error ϵ is a constant specified by the user. An algorithm requiring exponential time in d and linear space was proposed in [1] and follow-up studies improved its time/space requirements [13, 17, 18]. These studies share the common feature of a relative error bound. The ND P-sphere tree [11] also accelerates kNN search by providing non-exact answers. The algorithm guarantees that for a user specified percentage of time, the returned answers are correct, but it cannot distinguish between the correct and incorrect answers. To our knowledge, there have been no studies on approximate kNN search specifying absolute error bounds. In addition, none of the above studies address the approximate kNN problem in the data stream model, where data can only be scanned once.

The management and processing of data streams has attracted lots of research interest recently. A survey can be found in [3]. In [10] the authors use the Fast Fourier Transform to solve the problem of pattern similarity search. The paper also studies the nearest neighbors problem over streams, but uses values from the incoming stream (time series) as queries to identify the nearest neighbors from an existing pattern database. In our setting, queries are specified by users on demand and we seek to locate nearest neighbors in the streaming data. [10] uses prediction to take advantage of batch processing. When the actual time series arrives, prediction error lower bounds and upper bounds are calculated and used together with the predicted distances to filter candidate patterns. In [9], hamming norms are used to measure the similarity between two streams, and in [20], a regression-based algorithm is proposed to mine frequent temporal patterns for data streams. Reverse nearest neighbor aggregate queries over streams have also been investigated in [16].

3 Analysis of the problem

In this section, we propose a scheme towards solving the ekNN problem with a guaranteed error bound. As we shall see, this scheme provides possibility to reduce the information to be stored, however, the scheme in itself does not guarantee achieving the goal of memory optimization or error minimization. The data structure used to implement it is also critical to achieve these two optimizations. Therefore we will first present the scheme, followed by analysis on adopting the most suitable structure to realize it.

Our overall approach consists of segmenting the underlying space into a number of cells and identifying dynamically a number of points to be stored in each cell (called the *footprints* of the data) as data stream by. We observe that, in order to guarantee the error bound e, which is the largest distance between two points in a cell, for kNN queries, we only need to maintain at most k points in each cell. In the case of data streams, the number of data is very large so that usually exceeds k in many cells. Therefore, by maintaining only k points, we can reduce the data to be stored. In the following, our scheme based on this observation is formally presented.

3.1 Capturing the Footprints

We consider the problem in a d-dimensional metric space V, which is a set of points with an associated distance function *dist*. The distance function *dist* has the following properties:
1. $dist(P_1,P_2)=dist(P_2,P_1)$
2. $dist(P_1,P_2)>0$ $(P_1{\neq}P_2)$ and $dist(P_1,P_2)=0$ $(P_1{=}P_2)$
3. $dist(P_1,P_2)\leq dist(P_1,P_3)+dist(P_2,P_3)$

We divide the data space into a number of square-shaped cells and maintain at most K (K is a user specified constant) points in each cell. Specifically, as data stream by, each data point is placed in the cell it belongs to. If a cell already contains K points, there would be $K+1$ points including the new one. Then, we discard a point according to some discarding policy. The discarding policy is clearly application dependent. For example, if the most recent information is of interest we will always delete the oldest point. When processing ekNN queries, we invoke an exact kNN query on the set of points maintained, that is, the *footprints* of the stream data. Contrasting the kNN answers obtained from the footprints of the data set and on the original data set, we prove that the difference of their k-th nearest neighbor distance is within e, which equals the largest distance between two points in a cell. So the kNN on the footprints is an approximate answer for the kNN query on the original data set with error bound e. We start by defining some functions necessary for the derivations that follow and formalize the scheme for capturing the footprints. Some commonly used symbols in this paper are summarized in Table 1.

We assume that the data space is normalized to a unit hypercube. Each of the d dimensions of X is divided equally into u segments (therefore X is divided into u^d cells). Let S be a set of points in X and c a cell in X. Define $S(c)$ as $\{P \in S | P \in c\}$, that is, the subset of S that is in the cell c.

Let T be a mapping on S which is defined as follows: for each cell c of X, if $|S(c)| > K$, image of $S(c)$ is the set of any K points in $S(c)$; if $|S(c)| \leq K$, image of $S(c)$ is $S(c)$.

Let S' be the image set of S under mapping T. For any query point $Q \in X$, kNN is the set of k nearest neighbors of Q in S and kNN' is the set of k nearest

Table 1: Symbols

Symbol	Meaning
c	A cell
d	Dimensionality
$dist(P_1, P_2)$	Function that returns the distance between the two points P_1 and P_2
e	The error bound of the k-th nearest neighbor distance
$far(S, P)$	Function that returns the farthest point in set S to point P
kNN	The set of the k nearest neighbors
$ekNN$	The set of the e-approximate k nearest neighbors
m	The order of the Z-curve
P	A data record, which is viewed as a multi-dimensional point
p_i	The i-th coordinate of point P
Q	A query point
S	A set of points
t	Current time
T	Some period of time
u	The number of segments a dimension is divided to
V	A metric data space
W	A query window
W_s	The smallest query window that contains $ekNN$

neighbors of Q in S'. Let $far(S, Q)$ be the function returning the point in S, which is of largest distance to Q among all the points of S.

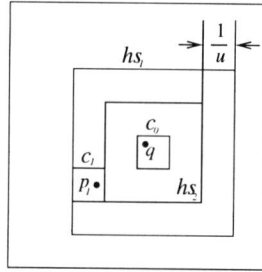

Figure 1: Diagram to explain Theorem 1

Theorem 1
For any positive integer $k \leq K$,
$dist(far(kNN', Q), Q) \leq dist(far(kNN, Q), Q) + d_M$,
where d_M is the maximum distance of two points within a cell.

Proof Suppose query point Q is in cell c_0 as Figure 1 shows. We have two cases to consider:
Case 1. $|S'(c_0)| \geq k$.
In this case, $far(kNN', Q)$ is within cell c_0. $|S(c_0)| \geq |S'(c_0)|$, so $|S(c_0)| \geq k$ and $far(kNN, Q)$ is also within cell c_0. The largest distance between two points within a cell is d_M. So

$$dist(far(kNN', Q), Q) \leq d_M$$

and therefore,

$$dist(far(kNN', Q), Q) \leq dist(far(kNN, Q), Q) + d_M.$$

Case 2. $|S'(c_0)| < k$.
Suppose hs_1 is the smallest hyper-square centered at c_0 and contains at least k points of S', hs_2 is the largest hyper-square centered at c_0 and contains at most $k - 1$ points of S'. Then side length of hs_1 minus side length of hs_2 must be $2/u$. Otherwise, either hs_1 can be smaller or hs_2 can be larger. Suppose there are k_1 points of S' in hs_2, there must be also k_1 points of S in hs_2 according to the definition of S'. Denote these k_1 points as $S(hs_2)$. Then $kNN - S(hs_2)$ and $kNN' - S(hs_2)$ are both in $hs_1 - hs_2$.

If all points in $kNN - S(hs_2)$ are in S', then $kNN' - S(hs_2) = kNN - S(hs_2)$, so $far(kNN', Q) = far(kNN, Q)$ and

$$dist(far(kNN', Q), Q) \leq dist(far(kNN, Q), Q) + d_M$$

holds.

If any point in $kNN - S(hs_2)$ is not in S', say $P_1 \in kNN - S(hs_2)$ and $P_1 \notin S'$. Suppose $P_1 \in c_1$. $P_1 \notin S'$ means $|S(c_1)| > K$, and then S' must have K points in c_1. Let $P_2 = far(S'(c_1), Q)$. Then

$$dist(far(kNN', Q), Q) < dist(P_2, Q) \quad (1)$$

According to the triangle inequality

$$dist(P_2, Q) < dist(P_1, Q) + dist(P_1, P_2) \quad (2)$$

P_2 and P_1 are in the same cell, so

$$dist(P_1, P_2) < d_M \quad (3)$$

$P_1 \in kNN - S(hs_2)$, so $P_1 \in kNN$, therefore

$$dist(P_1, Q) < dist(far(kNN, Q), Q) \quad (4)$$

And from inequalities 1, 2, 3 and 4, we hence get
$dist(far(kNN', Q), Q) \leq dist(far(kNN, Q), Q) + d_M$
□

According to the theorem, if we divide the data space into u^d equal cells and use the above scheme to process the ekNN problem, $e = d_M$. In addition, if the maximum number of points maintained in a cell is K, for any ekNN query where $k \leq K$, the above error bound is guaranteed. For example, if we maintain at most 5 points in a cell, then we can also search for 2NN with an error bounded by $e = d_M$. Note that d_M is determined by the distance function. Without loss of generality, we use the Euclidean distance function in the following discussions and our experimental studies. For the Euclidean metric, $d_M = \sqrt{d}/u$, and therefore the error bound is $e = \sqrt{d}/u$.

3.2 An Array-Based Method

A first method to implement this general scheme would be to organize the data in memory as a big d-dimensional array. Each element of the array represents a cell in the space. We may store at most K

points in each cell, so each array element is a structure consisting of K d-dimensional points. Stream data elements are placed in cells on demand as data stream by. If there are already K points, we discard one of them based on the discarding policy. Processing of ekNN queries using the array is straightforward. We just need to calculate the borders of the square which encloses the ekNN query sphere and check all the elements within the borders. In what follows, we refer to this method as the *array-based method*.

For the array-based method, we can calculate the memory size needed by the following equation:

$$Mem_{array} = u^d \cdot K \cdot d \cdot sizeof(attribute) \quad (5)$$

The array-based method is straightforward, and its processing is simple and fast in terms of memory accesses (reads/writes) and processor time, but the memory required is exponential to u. This static memory allocation strategy can cause excessive memory usage, especially for small error bounds, which implies a large value of u. Real data are often skewed and may be sparse; most cells contain much fewer than K points or even none at all, resulting in poor utilization of the statically allocated memory space. It is obvious that a structure capable of adapting to different data distributions is more desirable.

4 The DISC Method

To better utilize memory, cells that do not contain data points should not be explicitly maintained as opposed to the array-based method. Even within one cell, the number of points may be different, so space usage is different. This calls for a smart strategy to allocate space to each cell.

Besides the central objective of minimizing memory usage, the method should also provide fast updates and query processing. For the error minimization problem, the method may need some self-adjusting mechanism to achieve smallest error.

As discussed in the previous section, the array-based method needs too much memory despite its fast updates and query processing. Or we can organize the cells by a linked list and dynamically allocate only necessary space for each cell. The memory size problem is solved largely (we still have some extra cost due to the links), but the number of node accesses for update and query processing is linear to the number of points. Averagely, half the size of the linked list is accessed to locate a point. This is prohibiting for data stream applications.

A third way is to use a dynamic indexing structure such as an R-tree or a B-tree. On one hand, it dynamically allocates space in the unit of a leaf node so as to avoid excessive memory overheads as in the array-based method. On the other hand, the index provides fast access to the entries in the nodes. It is not as fast as the array-based method, but typically several node accesses are enough, which is much more efficient than linked lists in terms of updates and query processing. A dynamic index is in fact a compromise of the above two, and therefore it avoids the deficiency of either one.

A straightforward structure for multi-dimensional data is the R-tree or some of its variants. A point is stored as a leaf node entry. Since we need to differentiate between points from different cells, an identifier, id, is stored along with each point.

An alternative approach, which we adopt in this paper, is to employ a B*-tree[2] [15] together with a space-filling curve mechanism. Space-filling curves have been used to linearize multi-dimensional data spaces. Various types of space-filling curves exist in the literature; without loss of generality we adopt the Z-curve [19]. Efficient algorithms to compute Z-values can be found in [19]. Each cell corresponds to a Z-value. Footprints of the data stream are stored in the leaf nodes of a B*-tree using their corresponding cell Z-values as keys. Such an approach is expected to be more efficient than the R-tree scheme for the following reasons. Although a point is the unit of storage, a cell is the unit most of our operations deal with as we will see later in the algorithms. To locate a cell by the Z-value in a B*-tree, for each level of the tree, we only need to compare the search key with one value, since there is no overlap in the Z-values. In an R-tree, we need to compare the coordinates of the cell with $2d$ values (lower bound and upper bound for each dimension) for each level of the tree and there is overlap between the MBRs of the R-tree, which translates to more node accesses to update and search the R-tree. In addition, since the R-tree stores more information as keys, the fan-out of the R-tree nodes becomes lower and the height larger.

Another advantage of organizing the footprints in the Z-order is that cells can be arranged in a total order while maintaining cell proximity. The R-tree also keeps the points belonging to the same cell spatially close, but it still happens that they scatter in nearby MBRs. In DISC, points in the same cell are always consecutively stored in the leaf nodes. This property facilitates accesses on the cell level and make possible a very fast *merge-cells* operation, which is required for the error minimization problem and described in Section 4.2. We will also compare DISC to the R-tree in our experimental study. Since several points may belong to the same cell and have the same key in DISC, our B*-tree is designed to accommodate entries with equal keys. For the R-tree method, we have used the R*-tree [5] variant, which has a higher node utilization (about 73%). Moreover, we have also used the Z-values as the id's of cells for the R*-tree method.

Since we are utilizing space-filling curves, each dimension of the data space is partitioned into a number of intervals equal to an integral power of 2, the same for

---

[2] We employ the B*-tree for indexing (instead of B⁺-tree) as its node utilization is about 85% or higher.

all dimensions. Let m denote the order of the Z-curve, then $u = 2^m$.

4.1 Index Creation

We begin by considering the first problem, namely the memory optimization problem for a given error bound e. To guarantee that this error bound is met by our query answers, we calculate the order of the Z-curve m_e according to Theorem 1 as follows.

$$\sqrt{d}/2^{m_e} \leq e$$

Then

$$m_e \geq \log_2(\sqrt{d}/e) \quad (6)$$

The larger the value of m_e, the more memory is required; we let m_e be the smallest integer that can satisfy inequality 6.

$$m_e = \lceil \log_2(\sqrt{d}/e) \rceil \quad (7)$$

Algorithm **Build Index**, shown in Figure 3, describes how the index is constructed. In the algorithm, we initialize the value of m to m_e.

Before we discuss the algorithm, let us consider the second optimization problem, namely error minimization given a specific memory size constraint. The basic idea of the algorithm is to adjust the order of the Z-curve, m, to achieve the best accuracy while satisfying the constraint. Our aim is to minimize the error bound e in the ekNN search. Since the larger the value of m, the smaller the error bound e, and the data distribution is not known apriori, we start with a sufficiently large value for m; the exact value depending on the arithmetic precision we are working with. A value of 16 should suffice for most applications. As data arrive, it may turn out that m is too large and hence memory is exhausted; in this case, we merge small cells into a larger one, discard some points and still maintain at most K points in the larger cell. As a result some memory is freed, and processing of the stream continues. The Z-curve properties enable us to merge cells efficiently. In particular, a Z-value for a cell can be mapped efficiently (using simple bitwise operations) to Z-values corresponding to a curve of different order. For brevity, we omit the details which can be found in [19]. Related properties hold for other curves as well. Each time we need to perform cell merging, we will combine 2^d adjacent small cells into a larger cell as shown in Figure 2, in which cells c_0, c_1, c_2, c_3 are combined to form cell c'_0. The larger cell is still square-shaped. After merging the cells, the order of the Z-curve becomes $m - 1$. The index construction algorithm for this case is similar to that for the memory minimization problem; the difference lies in the merging phase. For brevity, we include this phase in the description of algorithm **Build Index**.

We are now ready to look at algorithm **Build Index** (see Figure 3). In line 1, we let $m = m_e$ for the

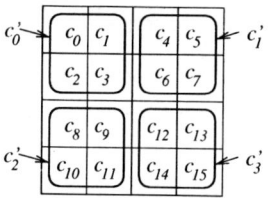

Figure 2: Cell Merging

Algorithm **Build Index**
1 Initialize m
2 Read data from the stream, denote the point read in as P, calculate the Z-value of P, and we know which cell it belongs to, denote it as c
3 Search the B*-tree and obtain the number of points that also belong to cell c, denote the number as N_c
4 If $N_c < K$
    Insert P to the B*-tree
5 Else
    Among P and the K points in c, discard 1 and keep the other K points in the B*-tree
6 If memory runs out /*This only happens for the error minimization problem*/
    Merge cells and let $m = m - 1$.
    /* The merge cells algorithm is presented in the next subsection. */
7 Go to 2
End Build Index

Figure 3: Algorithm **Build Index**

memory optimization problem and let m be a large enough integer for the error minimization problem. In line 5, we should determine which point to discard according to the discarding policy. In our realization of the algorithm, we simply discard the new point P.

In the analysis of Section 3.1 we have assumed the data space is normalized to a unit hypercube. This may have difficulty when the maximum and minimum of the data are unknown. In DISC, we would set the maximum/minimum to safely large/small values. For example, we can use 10 times (suppose the data are positive) the observed maximum value in the history as the maximum value of the data space. This may result in most of the data gathered at the center of the data space. It will not cause a problem for DISC, because no memory would be wasted for the empty space. And this just shows the advantage of DISC's adaptation to the data distribution.

4.2 Algorithms to Merge Cells

For the error minimization problem, we adopted an adaptive approach that consists of merging 2^d adjacent cells to form a larger one in order to meet the memory constraint. Figure 2 shows a 2-dimensional example where the order of the Z-curve m equals 2 before merging. c_0 to c_{15} are the cells before merging. c'_0 to c'_3 are the cells after merging. The subscripts are the Z-values of the cells. Let us denote the larger cell as $M(c)$ if it contains c before merging, then

```
Algorithm General Merge-Cells (GMC)
1   For i from 0 to 2^{m-1} - 1
2       Search the index and obtain the number of points
        in the new cell c'_i, denote the number as N_{c'_i}
3       If N_{c'_i} > K
            Discard N_{c'_i} - K points according to the
            discarding policy
End General Merge-Cells
```

Figure 4: Algorithm **GMC**

$M(c_0) = M(c_1) = M(c_2) = M(c_3) = c'_0$. In general,

$$M(c_{zv}) = c'_{\lfloor zv/2^d \rfloor} \quad (8)$$

where zv is the Z-value of the cell. Let S be a point set. We refer to the cells before merging as *old cells* and to the larger cells after merging as *new cells*. We present two algorithms to merge cells. The first cell merging algorithm applies to any index structure (including DISC and R-tree) that adopts our general scheme, that is, to maintain at most K points in each cell. The second cell merging algorithm is specially designed to exploit DISC's special property that the points are ordered according to the value of the Z-curve (versus the R-tree where points have no ordering). The latter scheme, referred to as the *bulk cell merging* scheme, scans all the leaf nodes once, and hence is expected to be more efficient than the former *general cell merging* algorithm.

In the first algorithm **General Merge-Cells** (GMC), we examine each new cell in the order of the Z-curve. For each new cell, we search the index and find all points belonging to this cell. If there are at most K points in the cell, we will leave them in the index; otherwise, we delete some of them according to the discarding policy and retain only K points. Algorithm **GMC** is presented in Figure 4. While the GMC algorithm is straightforward and applies to any structure, it is quite expensive since it searches the index 2^{m-1} times.

The second algorithm **Bulk Merge-Cells** (BMC), utilizes the property that the points in the leaf nodes of the B*-tree are ordered according to the Z-values. The 2^d adjacent points which will form a larger cell are adjacent in the leaf nodes, so we only need to scan all the leaf nodes once and merge the points in adjacent 2^d old cells into a new cell. In difference to an R-tree, the entries with close keys in the B*-tree are adjacent to each other, therefore in addition to deleting extra points in a new cell, we also need to move the remaining K points into the same cell. We use a *write cursor* pointing to the place where we would store the next points. Algorithm **BMC** is presented in Figure 5.

In line 16 of BMC (Figure 5), rebuilding internal nodes based on existing leaf nodes is very similar to bulk loading of a B+-tree. We do not discuss the details here for brevity.

Comparing the two merging algorithms, we note that BMC scans the leaf nodes only once, while GMC

```
Algorithm Bulk Merge-Cells (BMC)
1   Free all the internal nodes
2   Let ln be the first leaf node. Set write cursor at
    the beginning of ln. Let point set S be empty.
3   While (ln) //when ln is not NULL
4       For each point P in ln
5           If this is the first point in the first leaf node
6               c' = M(c), where c is the cell P belongs to
                S = S ∪ P
7           Else if P ⊂ c'
                S = S ∪ P
8           Else if P ⊄ c'  //We entered the next cell
9               If |S| > K
                    Discard |S| - K points from S
10              Write the points in S to the position of
                write cursor and move the write cursor
                forward accordingly
11              Let S = ∅
12              S = S ∪ P
13              c' = M(c), where c is the cell P belongs to
14      ln = right neighbor of ln
15  Free all the leaf nodes after the write cursor
16  Rebuild internal nodes of the B*-tree based on the
    leaf nodes
End Bulk Merge-Cells
```

Figure 5: Algorithm **BMC**

entails many searches and updates for each new cell. So BMC is expected to be faster than GMC. We will compare them in the experiments.

We note that the merge-cells operation is expensive compared to other operations, especially when the memory is large. As it may take a while to reduce the order of the curve by 1, stream processing may be disrupted. Fortunately, it is not necessary to finish merging all cells at once. Cell merging can be performed incrementally. When the system load is heavy, say, there is a burst of incoming data or many queries, we stop the merge operation at the current new cell we are working on and record this stop position. If the update or the query accesses the points before that stop position, we process them assuming the order of the Z-curve to be $m-1$; if data belonging to cells after the stop position are required, we process them assuming the order of the Z-curve to be m. If the search involves more than one cell, some of which may be old and some are new, query processing is performed assuming the order of the Z-curve in the new cells, $m-1$. Old cells that are accessed in the search are temporarily combined to form larger new cells, but they are in fact merged later as cell merging resumes. The error bound returned with the query results in this case, is the one associated with the order $m-1$. Both GMC and BMC can be performed incrementally. However, it is important to complete the operation fast.

4.3 Query Processing

As analyzed in Section 3.1, an ekNN query in the original data set, is a kNN query in footprints of the data.

```
Algorithm KNN Search
1   S = ∅
2   For i from 1 to d
        wl_i = q'_i - 1/(2u);  wh_i = q'_i + 1/(2u)
3   WindowQuery(W). From the points in W, get the k
    nearest points to Q and put them in S; if there are
    less than k points in W, put all of them in S.
4   if |S| < k or near(W,Q) < far(S,Q)
5       for i from 1 to d
            wl_i = wl_i - 1/u;  wh_i = wh_i + 1/u
6       Go to 3
7   return S
End KNN Search
```

Figure 6: Algorithm **KNN Search**

Let Q be the query point and c_Q be the cell Q belongs to. Denote as Q' the center point of c_Q and as W a query window which is a d-dimensional interval $[wl_1, wh_1], [wl_2, wh_2], ..., [wl_d, wh_d]$. First, we initiate a square-shaped window query centered at Q' with an initial side length of $1/u$ and then increase it gradually. We maintain a k candidate answer set which always contains the nearest k points to Q within the current query window. The function $near(W, Q)$ returns the distance between Q and W's nearest side to Q. The algorithm terminates when $near(W, Q)$ is larger than or equal to the k-th farthest point in the candidate answer set. All the points outside the query window are farther from Q than $near(W, Q)$. So when the algorithm terminates, the farthest point in the candidate set is the k-th nearest point to Q among all the points inside and outside the query window. To avoid searching cells which are already visited in the previous iteration, we maintain a list of addresses of the B*-tree leaf nodes visited. WindowQuery(W) is a function to retrieve all the points in window query W. In DISC, each leaf nodes of the B*-tree corresponds to a continuous segment of the Z-curve. An efficient window query algorithm proposed in [4] accesses only those nodes with their corresponding Z-curve segments intersecting the query window. We use this algorithm for our WindowQuery() function. Figure 6 shows the algorithmic description of the **KNN search**.

For continuous ekNN queries, we maintain the $ekNN$ set as follows. Let W_s be the smallest window centered at Q' that contains all the points in $ekNN$. When a new data point P comes and $P \in W_s$, we may need to discard some points according to the discarding policy (for example, in the sliding window query discussed in the next subsection, points older than T_{sw} are discarded). If a point in $ekNN$ is discarded, the $ekNN$ set would have fewer than k points at the moment. After discarding, there are 3 cases to consider: 1) *There are still k points in $ekNN$*. If P is nearer to Q than the farthest point in $ekNN$, then P will replace the farthest point; otherwise $ekNN$ is kept unchanged. 2) *There are fewer than k points in $ekNN$ and P is nearer to Q than the farthest point in $ekNN$ before discarding*. We add P to $ekNN$ and start kNN search as in the one-time search algorithm, but we set the initial search window as W_s. 3) *There are fewer than k points in $ekNN$ and P is not nearer to Q than the farthest point in $ekNN$ before discarding*. We just start kNN search as in the one-time search algorithm with the initial search window W_s. The proof of the above algorithm is straightforward and we omit it here due to the limitation of space.

4.4 Sliding Window ekNN Queries

In certain applications, recent stream data are of greater interest as opposed to data associated with the entire stream. This gives rise to the sliding window data stream model [3]. The ekNN problem can be expressed in this model as well. Formally, we wish to identify the $ekNN$ of a query point Q among all data stream elements arriving in the last T_{sw} time units.

DISC is capable of supporting such sliding window ekNN queries by simply employing a time-based discarding policy. Let t be the current time. Assume that each arriving stream element is tagged with a timestamp signifying its arrival time. Algorithm **Build Index** can be modified for the sliding window model as follows: When inserting a point P to a cell c, we first check the timestamp of existing points in c. We then delete the stale points, that is, the points that arrived earlier than $t - T_{sw}$. Finally, we insert P. For algorithm **KNN Search**, we only place points arriving later than $t - T_{sw}$ to the candidate answer set S. At any time, if we encounter stale points (during index building or kNN searching), we delete them immediately. Such modifications enable DISC to answer sliding window ekNN queries correctly. However, if there are data in the index that are older than $t - T_{sw}$, but no incoming stream data is added to the cells they belong to, such stale data will remain in the index, occupy space and affect space utilization. To avoid this, we need an operation to eliminate such stale data. This can be accomplished by scanning all the points and deleting stale data from the index. However, such an operation is expected to be time consuming. Again, like the cell merging process, this stale data elimination process can be done incrementally. There exists a tradeoff between memory utilization and processing capability. To achieve best accuracy when addressing the error minimization optimization problem in the sliding window model, we eliminate stale data before each call to the **Merge-Cell** operations. This way, some additional space becomes available and it may be possible to avoid cell merging.

We should take care when processing continuous ekNN queries over sliding windows. Even no new points come in W_s, there still could be stale data due to time. Therefore, in this case we need to check whether the set contains stale data in each time unit to guarantee the correctness of the $ekNN$ set. Or if the $ekNN$

answers are not requested all the time, we can check for stale data when we retrieve answers from the maintained ekNN set. If there were stale data, we discard them and invoke the kNN search on the footprints with the initial search window W_s. This is still much faster than invoking the search from scratch.

5 Experiments

In this section, we present the results of an extensive experimental study using DISC. While we have implemented and worked with an in-memory version of DISC, DISC is also applicable for secondary storage. The experiments are performed on a desktop computer with Pentium IV, 2.6G CPU and 1G RAM. In our study we employed both synthetic and real data sets. We generated exponentially and normally distributed data sets of varying dimensionality. Figure 7 shows 2-dimensional images of the two data distributions. The real data set contains 2-dimensional records

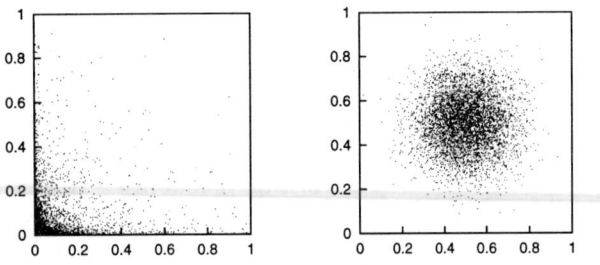

(a)Exponential distribution (b) Normal distribution

Figure 7: Data distributions

extracted from netflow IP data logs. Such logs were aggregated temporally and ekNN queries were issued using the total number of bytes and associated packet rate attributes. All the data are normalized in the range of [0,1]. By default, we let K equal 20 and we set the order of the Z-curve as 10, which implies an error bound of 0.00138 in a 2-dimensional space. For the in-memory B*-tree, we used a default node size of 1024 bytes. First, we focus our experiments on a 2-dimensional space examining DISC's memory usage and accuracy and compare the two cell merging algorithms. Then we examine the behavior of DISC on higher dimensions.

5.1 Memory Usage of DISC

In a first series of experiments, we study the memory usage of DISC as data stream by. No existing structures or algorithms were proposed to process (approximate) kNN queries over streams as discussed in the related work. Therefore we would compare DISC with the R*-tree [5] indexing under our general scheme to see which one is more efficient. Figures 8(a), (b) and (c) present the memory used by DISC and the R*-tree as a function of the observed data stream size (in number of points) on 2-dimensional exponentially distributed

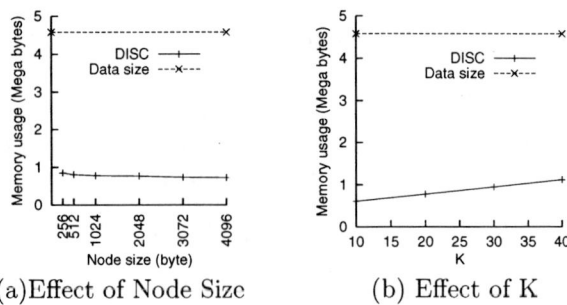

(a)Effect of Node Size (b) Effect of K

Figure 9: Effect of node size and K

and normally distributed data sets and the real data set.

As the data continually arrive and their cumulative size increases, the memory usage of DISC increases also at first, but the increase slows down soon as more data arrive. At first, all the cells are empty and therefore all of the data are stored as footprints. But as more data come in, more and more cells become full (having contains K points) so that memory usage almost keeps constant. When 600K data points have arrived, the memory used by DISC is 10~25% of the size of the data. Using Equation 5, we calculate, for this setting that the amount of memory needed for the array based method is 41943040 bytes, which is more than 8 times the data size. These results show that DISC does adapt to different data distributions because it only stores necessary cells and in each cell, necessary points to guarantee the error bound, while the array-based method suffer from the static memory allocation greatly. The huge space cost of the array-based method make it not applicable in stream applications. In all the following experiments, the array-based method always needs at least several times the space of the original data to operate, therefore we will not compare DISC with it again. We also observe that the memory usage of the R*-tree is always a little higher than DISC. This is because while the R*-tree also allocates space only to the points requiring explicit storage, the leaf node utilization rate of the R*-tree (about 73%) is lower than that of the B*-tree (about 85%).

To see how how some parameters such as the node size and K affect the memory usage of DISC, we varied the node size and K respectively while keep other parameters constant. The memory usage for different node sizes when 600K netflow data points have arrived is presented in Figure 9 (a). The memory usage decreases as the node size increases. This is because for larger nodes, higher node utilization rate can be achieved. However, the effect of node size is small compared to the total data size. In other experiments, we used 1024 as the default node size.

Figure 9 (b) presents memory usage as a function of K for netflow data. Memory usage increases as K increases in an almost linear fashion, according to expectation. This demonstrates that DISC handles the allocation of the available memory in a space efficient fashion. Experiments over the synthetic data sets show

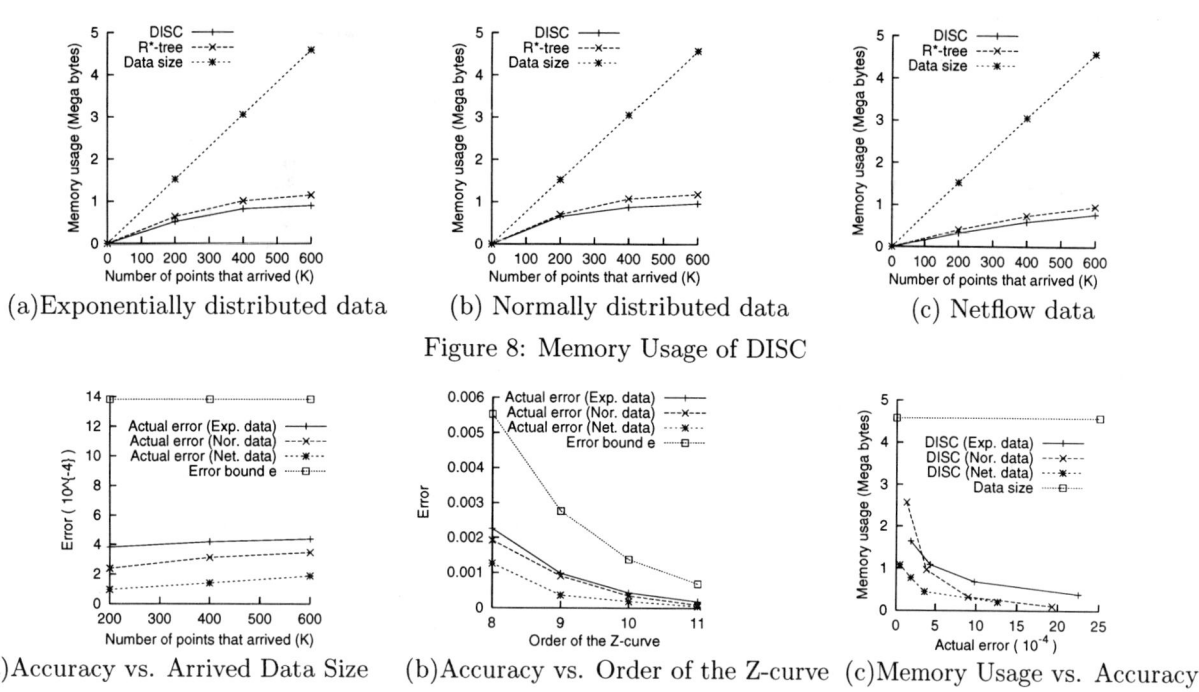

(a) Exponentially distributed data (b) Normally distributed data (c) Netflow data

Figure 8: Memory Usage of DISC

(a) Accuracy vs. Arrived Data Size (b) Accuracy vs. Order of the Z-curve (c) Memory Usage vs. Accuracy

Figure 10: Accuracy of DISC

similar behavior. It is expected that the memory usage of DISC would reach the size of the stream data if K is too large, but it will not be too much beyond the stream size. In the worst case that K is infinite, all the stream data are maintained. The memory usage of DISC would be a little more than the stream size considering the space utilization of the B*-tree, but it will not grow excessively as the array-based method, which may use many times the size of the stream. In many applications, tens of nearest neighbors are enough and K can be determined from domain knowledge or query history. In these cases, DISC is still quite useful. In other experiments, we have used 20 as the default value of K, which is a reasonable number used in data mining applications.

5.2 Accuracy of DISC

While DISC can guarantee a theoretical error bound of e, we run experiments to assess the actual errors. We generated 200 queries following the same distribution as the data. We scan the original data to find the exact kNN to each query and also employ DISC to identify the $ekNN$. We then compare the exact kNN distance and the ekNN distance to obtain the actual error. The results are presented as averages over the 200 queries in Figure 10 (a). The figure shows the comparison between the error bound e and the actual error for the (exponentially distributed, normally distributed and netflow) data streams as the data arrive. We observe that the average actual errors are less than one third of the theoretical error bound. These results demonstrate the accuracy of DISC. In all our experiments, we have also observed that the maximum actual errors are smaller than the theoretical error bounds, which further confirms the effectiveness of DISC.

In our next experiment we evaluate the impact of the order of the space-filling curve on our scheme. We vary the order of the Z-curve from 8 to 11 and see how it affects the actual errors. The error bound and actual errors for different orders of the Z-curve are shown in Figure 10 (b). As the Z-curve order increases, the error bound e and the actual errors also decrease, while the actual errors are always much smaller than e.

To see the relationship between the memory usage and the accuracy, we present for different error bounds, their corresponding memory usage versus the corresponding actual errors when 600K data points have arrived in Figure 10 (c). The memory usage increases as actual errors decrease. This shows that DISC can easily trade error for memory space by suitably setting the order of the Z-curve.

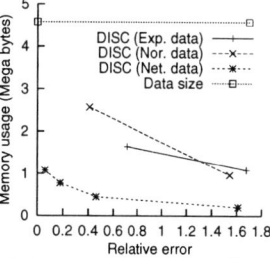

Figure 11: Memory Usage vs. Relative Error

To show that the above absolute errors are reasonably small, we also present the relative kNN distance errors they correspond to in Figure 11. For the netflow data, $ekNN$ has a relative error of 5% when the memory usage is about 1MB, which is less than 1/4 of

813

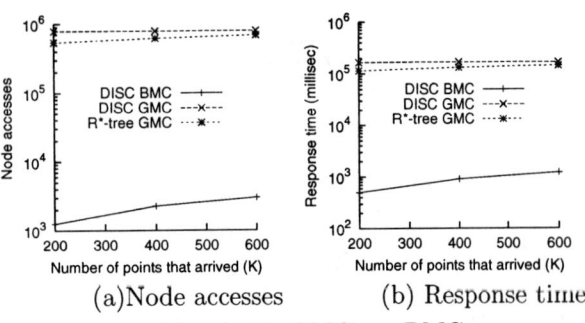

(a) Node accesses (b) Response time

Figure 12: GMC vs. BMC

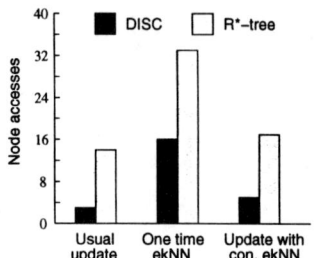

Figure 13: Update and Query Cost

the original data size. Even when the memory usage is only 200KB, which is less than 5% of the original data size, $ekNN$ has a relative error of 1.6. For the exponentially and normally distributed data sets, $ekNN$ also has small relative errors while use much less memory size than the data size.

5.3 GMC vs. BMC

In this experiment, we evaluate the two merge-cell algorithms. We have implemented the GMC algorithm for both DISC and the R*-tree. We also implemented the BMC algorithm, which only applies to DISC. We trigger the Merge-cell operation when 200K, 400K and 600K data points have arrived. (In fact, the merge-cell operation should be invoked in the case of the error minimization problem only when available memory runs out. Here we call it explicitly to observe its behavior under varying data size.) We calculate the number of node accesses and response time as measures of their performance. The results for the real data set are shown in Figure 12. We can see that under the DISC scheme, GMC needs much more node accesses than BMC (about 300 to 600 times). This is because in GMC, we need to traverse the tree for each new cell. To support a reasonably small error bound, usually the order of the Z-curve is large, which is 10 in our experiments. So we have to traverse the tree $2^{9\times 2} = 262144$ times, and each traversal incurs several node accesses (descend the tree and locate the points to the new cell). While in BMC, we only scan all the leaf nodes once (which ranges from hundreds to a few thousand in our experiments). GMC for the R*-tree turns out to be marginally better than its DISC counterpart. This is because in the R*-tree, when some points are discarded from a cell, we are not required to move the remaining points together while in the B*-tree this is necessary. The response time has similar trend. In the experiments, the GMC algorithm takes several minutes to finish while the BMC algorithm takes only 1 or 2 seconds. So clearly, only the BMC algorithm is applicable in practice. This is an additional reason that makes DISC preferable over other approaches. Despite its efficiency, we can still perform incremental cell merging with BMC as described in Section 4.2 in case the memory is very large and the system load is heavy.

5.4 Updates and Query Processing

To evaluate the update and query processing performance of DISC, we measured the number of node accesses of updates, one-time ekNN query and continuous ekNN query processing for DISC and the R*-tree. The cost of a continuous ekNN query consists of the cost of the initial one-time ekNN query and the cost of maintaining the $ekNN$ set continuously. The maintenance cost is the possible search cost when a point in W_s arrives as described in the continuous ekNN algorithm. Specifically, maintaining the $ekNN$ set involves possible kNN search during the insertion of new points. Therefore, the update cost with continuous ekNN queries running is expected to be higher than the usual update cost.

In our experiments, the query costs of the one-time ekNN queries are averaged from 200 queries which follow the same distribution as the real data set. For continuous ekNN queries, we use the same queries but run 10 continuous queries simultaneously each time. The update costs are averaged from the 600K points inserted. K is still set as 20. The results on the netflow data set are shown in Figure 13. First we observe that for all the operations, DISC has much lower node access cost than the R*-tree. The reason is that in DISC we only store the Z-value as the key, but in the R*-tree we need to store $2d$ values as keys so the fan-out of the tree is lower and hence the height of the tree larger. In addition, there are overlaps between the MBRs of the R*-tree, which also incurs more node accesses. We also notice that the query processing cost is not large in terms of node accesses. This is largely due to the Z-order keeping the proximity of the spatial points and the efficient WindowQuery() algorithm. In addition, in two-dimensional space, the points are dense. For skewed data, most points are clustered at a relatively small region and so do the queries. So for most queries, after locating the cell the query belongs to, we need only a few number of node accesses to retrieve near points. The cost of the continuous ekNN is mainly expressed in the additional part of the update cost. We can see that, update with continuous ekNN queries running costs a little more than the usual update, but the increase is not great. Therefore, the continuous ekNN query processing is still quite efficient.

5.5 DISC on Data Sets of Other Dimensions

We study the behavior of DISC when the number of underlying streams increases (and as a result the dimensionality of stream elements increases as well). Due to the limitation of space, we only present the results on 3-dimensional synthetic data sets. Figure 14 (a) shows the memory usage of DISC as 3-dimensional synthetic data stream by. We still set K as 20 and the order of the Z-curve as 10, which corresponds to an error bound of 0.00169 in 3-dimensional space. The results are sim-

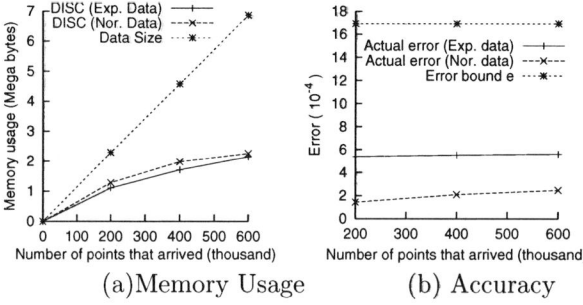

(a) Memory Usage   (b) Accuracy

Figure 14: DISC on 3D data sets

ilar to those of 2-dimensional data (compare with Figures 8 (a) and 8 (b)). DISC uses much less memory compared to the original data size and its memory usage does not increase significantly as the number of arriving data elements increases. As dimensionality increases, DISC tends to occupy more memory than in the 2-dimensional case; this is expected as in higher dimensions, points become relatively sparse and therefore distributed in more cells, which have to be maintained. Similar to the experiments on 2-dimensional data, the average actual errors are much lower than the error bounds as shown in Figure 14 (b).

6 Conclusion

We investigated the k nearest neighbors problem in the data stream model. We introduced the e-approximate k nearest neighbors (ekNN) problem and presented a structure called DISC to address it over data streams. DISC achieves the goals of memory optimization given an error bound or adjusts itself to achieve the best accuracy to answer ekNN queries when a memory constraint is given. At the same time, DISC retains efficient update and query processing which is a common requirement for data stream applications. Extensive studies on both synthetic and real data showed that the memory usage of DISC is small and the actual errors are much lower than the theoretical error bounds that the structure guarantees.

References

[1] S. Arya, D. Mount, N. Netanyahu, R. Silverman, and A. Wu. An optimal algorithm for approximate nearest neighbor searching. In *SODA*, 1994.

[2] S. Arya, D. Mount, N. Netanyahu, R. Silverman, and A. Wu. An optimal algorithm for approximate nearest neighbor searching fixed dimensions. *JACM*, 45(6):891–923, 1998.

[3] B. Babcock, S. Babu, M. Datar, R. Motwani, and J. Widom. Models and issues in data stream systems. In *PODS*, 2002.

[4] R. Bayer. The universal B-tree for multidimensional indexing: General concepts. *World-Wide Computing and Its Applications 97*, pages 10–11, 1997.

[5] N. Beckmann, H.-P. Kriegel, R. Schneider, and B. Seeger. The R*-tree: An efficient and robust access method for points and rectangles. In *SIGMOD*, 1990.

[6] S. Berchtold, C. Böhm, H. Jagadish, H.-P. Kriegel, and J. Sander. Independent quantization: An index compression technique for high-dimensional data spaces. In *ICDE*, 2000.

[7] S. Berchtold, D. Keim, and H.-P. Kriegel. The x-tree: An index structure for high-dimensional data. In *VLDB*, 1996.

[8] M. Bern. Approximate closest-point queries in high dimensions. *Information Processing Letters*, 45(2):95–99, 1993.

[9] G. Cormode, M. Datar, P. Indyk, and S. Muthukrishnan. Comparing data streams using hamming norms (how to zero in). In *VLDB*, 2002.

[10] L. Gao and X. S. Wang. Continually evaluating similarity-based pattern queries on a streaming time series. In *SIGMOD*, 2002.

[11] J. Goldstein and R. Ramakrishnan. Contrast plots and p-sphere trees: Space vs. time in nearest neighbour searches. In *VLDB*, 2000.

[12] G. Hjaltason and H. Samet. Ranking in spatial databases. In *SSD*, 1995.

[13] P. Indyk and R. Motwani. Approximate nearest neighbors: Towards removing the curse of dimensionality. In *STOC*, 1998.

[14] N. Katayama and S. Satoh. The sr-tree: an index structure for high-dimensional nearest neighbor queries. In *SIGMOD*, 1997.

[15] D. E. Knuth. *The Art of Computer Programming, Volume 3*. Addison Wesley, 2002.

[16] F. Korn, S. Muthukrishnan, and D. Srivastava. Reverse nearest neighbor aggregates over data streams. In *VLDB*, 2002.

[17] E. Kushilevitz, R. Ostrovsky, and Y. Rabani. Efficient search for approximate nearest neighbor in high dimensional spaces. In *STOC*, 1998.

[18] C. Li, E. Y. Chang, H. Garcia-Molina, and G. Wiederhold. Clustering for approximate similarity search in high-dimensional spaces. *TKDE*, 14(4):792–808, 2002.

[19] J. A. Orenstein and T. H. Merrett. A class of data structures for associative searching. In *PODS*, 1984.

[20] W.-G. Teng, M.-S. Chen, and P. Yu. A regression-based temporal pattern mining scheme for data streams. In *VLDB*, 2003.

[21] R. Weber, H.-J. Schek, and S. Blott. A quantitative analysis and performance study for similarity-search methods in high-dimensional spaces. In *VLDB*, 1998.

[22] C. Yu, B. Ooi, K.-L. Tan, and H. V. Jagadish. Indexing the distance: An efficient method to knn processing. In *VLDB*, 2001.

[23] R. Zhang, B. C. Ooi, and K. L. Tan. Making the pyramid technique robust to query types and workload. In *ICDE*, 2004.

Object Fusion in Geographic Information Systems

Catriel Beeri   Yaron Kanza   Eliyahu Safra   Yehoshua Sagiv

The Selim and Rachel Benin School of Engineering and Computer Science
The Hebrew University
Jerusalem, 91904
{beeri, yarok, safra, sagiv}@cs.huji.ac.il

Abstract

Given two geographic databases, a fusion algorithm should produce all pairs of corresponding objects (i.e., objects that represent the same real-world entity). Four fusion algorithms, which only use locations of objects, are described and their performance is measured in terms of recall and precision. These algorithms are designed to work even when locations are imprecise and each database represents only some of the real-world entities. Results of extensive experimentation are presented and discussed. The tests show that the performance depends on the density of the data sources and the degree of overlap among them. All four algorithms are much better than the current state of the art (i.e., the one-sided nearest-neighbor join). One of these four algorithms is best in all cases, at a cost of a small increase in the running time compared to the other algorithms.

1 Introduction

When integrating data from two heterogeneous sources, one is faced with the task of fusing distinct objects that represent the same real-world entity. This is known as the *object-fusion* problem. Most of the research on this problem has considered either structured (i.e., relational) or semistructured (notably XML) data (e.g., [1, 10]). In both cases, objects have identifiers (e.g., keys). Object fusion is easier when global identifiers are used; that is, when objects representing the same entity are guaranteed to have the same identifier. When integrating data from heterogeneous sources, however, the object-fusion problem is much harder, due to the lack of global identifiers.

When integrating geographic databases, spatial (and non-spatial) properties should be used in lieu of global identifiers. Since location is the only property that is always available for spatial objects, we investigate location-based fusion for the case of two geographic databases. We assume that each database has at most one object per real-world entity and locations are given as points. Thus, the fusion is *one-to-one*.

Location-based fusion may seem to be an easy task, since locations could be construed as global identifiers. This is not so, however, for several reasons. First, measurements introduce errors, and the errors in different databases are independent of each other. Second, each organization has its own approach and requirements, and hence uses different measurement techniques and may record spatial properties of entities using a different scale or a different structure. For example, one organization might represent buildings as points, while another could use polygonal shapes for the same purpose. While an estimated point location can be derived from a polygonal shape, it may not agree with a point-based location in another database. A third reason could be displacements that are caused by cartographic generalizations.

The motivation for this work was hands-on experience on integrating data sources about hotels in Tel-Aviv. Two of the sources were organizations that obtained their data by different and independent means. Moreover, one organization represented buildings as points while the other—as polygons. It turned out that, in obvious cases, corresponding objects were close to each other, but did not always have identical locations. When locations were not sufficiently close, hotel names could be used to determine some of the corresponding pairs. However, there were also pairs with similar, yet not identical names; and so, some cases remained unresolved.

The current state of the art is the *one-sided nearest-neighbor join* [9] that fuses an object from one dataset with its closest neighbor in the other dataset. The ra-

---

Permission to copy without fee all or part of this material is granted provided that the copies are not made or distributed for direct commercial advantage, the VLDB copyright notice and the title of the publication and its date appear, and notice is given that copying is by permission of the Very Large Data Base Endowment. To copy otherwise, or to republish, requires a fee and/or special permission from the Endowment.

Proceedings of the 30th VLDB Conference, Toronto, Canada, 2004

tionale is that even in the presence of measurement errors, different objects that represent the same entity should have close locations. However, in the one-sided nearest-neighbor join, every object from one of the two datasets is matched with some object from the other dataset, even if each dataset has objects that should not be matched with any object from the other dataset. Thus, the performance is poor when the overlap between the two dataset is small.

Another source of difficulty is due to the fact that in the presence of errors, in a dense dataset, the right match is not always the nearest neighbor. Consequently, one also has to consider objects that are further away. Moreover, there are mutual influences: If an object a is matched with an object b, then both cease to be candidates for possible matches with other objects, thereby increasing the likelihood of other matches between the other objects.

In this paper, we consider the problem of finding one-to-one correspondences among objects that have point locations and belong to two geographic databases. We present several location-based algorithms, with an increasing level of sophistication, for finding corresponding objects that should be fused. We also present the results of extensive tests that illustrate the weaknesses and strengths of these algorithms, under varying assumptions about the error bounds, the density of each spatial database and the degree of overlap between these databases.

The main contribution of our work is in showing that point locations can be effectively used to find corresponding objects. Since locations are always available for spatial objects and since a point is the simplest form of representing a location, additional information (e.g., names or polygonal locations) can only enhance the strength of our location-based algorithms.

The outline of this paper is as follows. In Section 2, we introduce the framework and formally define the problem. Section 3 describes how to measure the quality of the result of a fusion algorithm. In that section, we also discuss the factors that may influence the performance of such an algorithm. Section 4 describes the fusion algorithms that we propose. The tests and their results are discussed in Section 5. In Section 6, we consider further improvements. Section 7 describes how to choose an optimal threshold value. Related work is described in Section 8, and we conclude in Section 9.

2 Object Fusion

A *geographic database* stores *spatial objects*, or *objects* for short. Each object represents a single real-world *geographic entity*. We view a geographic databases as a *dataset* of objects, with at most one object for each real-world entity. An object has associated spatial and non-spatial attributes. Spatial attributes describe the location, height, shape and topology of an entity. Examples of non-spatial attributes are name, address, number of rooms in a hotel, etc.

We assume that locations of objects are recorded as points. This is the simplest form of representing locations. More complex forms of recording locations (e.g, polygons) can be approximated by points (e.g., by computing the center of mass). The *distance* between two objects is the Euclidean distance between their point locations.

When two geographic databases are integrated, the main task is to identify pairs of objects, one from each dataset, that represent the same entity; the objects in each pair should be fused into a single object. In general, a *fusion algorithm* may process more than two datasets and it generates *fusion sets* with at most one object from each dataset. A fusion set is *sound* if all its objects represent the same entity (but it does not necessarily contain all the objects that represent that entity). A fusion set is *complete* if it contains all the objects that represent some entity (but it may also contain other objects). A fusion set is *correct* if it is both sound and complete.

In this paper, we consider the case of two datasets and investigate the problem of finding the correct fusion sets, under the following assumptions. First, in each dataset, distinct objects represent distinct real-world entities. This is a realistic assumption, since a database represents a real-world entity as a single object. Second, only locations of objects are used to find the fusion sets. This is a practical assumption, since spatial objects always have information about their locations. As explained earlier, location-based fusion is not easy, since locations are not accurate.

We denote the two datasets as $A = \{a_1, \ldots, a_m\}$ and $B = \{b_1, \ldots, b_n\}$. Two objects $a \in A$ and $b \in B$ are *corresponding objects* if they represent the same entity. A fusion set that is generated from A and B is either a *singleton* (i.e., contains a single object) or has two objects, one from each dataset. A fusion set $\{a, b\}$ is correct if a and b are corresponding objects. A singleton fusion set $\{a\}$ is correct if a does not have a corresponding object in the other dataset.

In the absence of any global key, it is not always possible to find all the correct fusions sets. We will present novel algorithms that only use locations and yet are able to find the correct fusion sets with a high degree of success. We will discuss the factors that effect the performance of these algorithms and show results of testing them.

3 Quality of Results

3.1 Measuring the Quality

Similarly to information retrieval, we measure the quality of a fusion algorithm in terms of *recall* and *precision*. Recall is the percentage of correct fusion sets that actually appear in the result (e.g., 91% of all the correct fusion sets appear in the result). Precision is the percentage of correct fusion sets out of all the fusion sets in the result (e.g., 80% of the sets in the result are correct).

Formally, let the result of a fusion algorithm have s^r fusion sets and let s_c^r sets out those be correct. Let e denote the total number of real-world entities that are represented in at least one of the two datasets. Then the precision is s_c^r/s^r and the recall is s_c^r/e.

Note that applying the above definitions requires full knowledge of whether two objects represent the same entity or not. Clearly, this knowledge was available for the datasets that we used in the tests.

A similar definition of recall and precision was used in [13]. However, they considered a somewhat different problem, where the correct fusion sets are always of size two and the fusion algorithm only produces fusion sets of size two. Our definition is more general in that it takes into account the possibility that a fusion algorithm produces correct as well as incorrect singleton fusion sets.

Recall and precision could also be defined in a different way, by counting object occurrences instead of fusion sets and entities. When there are only two datasets (as in our case), there is no substantial difference between the two definitions. However, when fusion sets may have more than two objects, counting object occurrences seems to be a more suitable approach. The details of the alternative definitions are beyond the scope of this paper.

3.2 Factors Affecting Recall and Precision

One factor that influences the recall and precision is the *error interval* of each dataset. The error interval is a bound on the distance between an object in the dataset and the entity it represents. The *density* of a dataset is the number of objects per unit of area. The *choice factor* is the number of objects in a circle with a radius that is equal to the error interval (note that the choice factor is the product of the density and the area of that circle). Intuitively, for a given entity, the choice factor is an estimate of the number of objects in the dataset that could possibly represent that entity. It is more difficult to achieve high recall and precision when the choice factor is large. Generally, we consider a choice factor as large if it is greater than 1; otherwise, it is small. Note that the above factors need not be uniform in the geographic area that is represented by a given dataset. In the general case, these factors may have different values for different subareas.

Suppose that the datasets A and B have m and n objects, respectively. Let c be the number of corresponding objects, i.e., the number of objects in all the correct fusion sets of size 2. Note that the number of distinct entities that are represented in the two datasets is $m + n - (c/2)$. The *overlap* between A and B is $c/(m+n)$. The overlap is a measure of the fraction of objects that have a corresponding object in the other set. One of the challenges we faced was to develop an algorithm that has high recall and precision for all degrees of overlap. Note that when the two sets represent exactly the same set of entities, then the overlap is maximal, i.e., 1. Another special case is when one dataset *covers* the second dataset, i.e., all the entities represented in the second dataset are also represented in the first dataset. We tested the performance of the algorithms on datasets with varying degrees of overlap.

4 Finding Fusion Sets

In this section, we present methods for computing the fusion sets of two datasets, $A = \{a_1, \ldots, a_m\}$ and $B = \{b_1, \ldots, b_n\}$. The methods are based on the intuition that two corresponding objects are more likely to be close to each other than two non-corresponding objects. The recall and precision of each method depend on specific characteristics of the given datasets, e.g., the choice factors of the datasets, the degree of overlap, etc. The methods are compared in Section 5.

4.1 The One-Sided Nearest-Neighbor Join

We start by describing an existing method, the *one-sided nearest-neighbor join*, which is commonly used in commercial geographic-information systems [9]. Given an object $a \in A$, we say that an object $b \in B$ is the *nearest B-neighbor* of a if b is the closest object to a among all the objects in B. The one-sided nearest-neighbor join of a dataset B with a dataset A produces all fusion sets $\{a, b\}$, such that $a \in A$ and $b \in B$ is the nearest B-neighbor of a. Note that every $a \in A$ is in one of the fusion sets, while objects of B may appear in zero, one or more fusion sets. Thus, the one-sided nearest-neighbor join is not symmetric, i.e., the result of joining B with A is not necessarily equal to the result of joining A with B.

We modify the above definition by adding to the result the singleton set $\{b\}$ for every $b \in B$ that is not the nearest neighbor of some $a \in A$. We do that to boost up the recall of this method; otherwise, the recall could be very low.

We say that a dataset A is *covered* by a dataset B if every real-world entity that is represented in A is also represented in B. Recall that the one-sided nearest-neighbor join produces singleton fusion sets just for one of the two datasets, even if neither dataset covers the other one. Thus, the result will include wrong pairs and the precision will be low.

In conclusion, the one-sided nearest-neighbor join is likely to produce good approximations only when one dataset is covered by the other and the choice factors of the datasets are not large.

4.2 New Methods

In the following subsections, we present three novel methods for computing fusion sets. Each method computes a *confidence* value for every fusion set. The confidence value indicates the likelihood that the fusion set is correct.

The final result in each method is produced by choosing the fusion sets that have a confidence value that is above a given *threshold value*. The threshold τ ($0 \leq \tau \leq 1$) is chosen by the user. Typically, increasing the threshold value will increase the precision and lower the recall, while decreasing the threshold value will increase the recall and decrease the precision. Controlling the recall and precision by means of a threshold value is especially useful when the datasets have large choice factors.

4.3 The Mutually-Nearest Method

Two objects, $a \in A$ and $b \in B$, are *mutually nearest* if a is the nearest A-neighbor of b and b is the nearest B-neighbor of a. The intuition behind the mutually-nearest method is that corresponding objects are likely to be mutually nearest. Note that some objects of A are not in any pair of mutually-nearest objects (and, similarly, for some objects of B). It happens when the nearest B-neighbor of $a \in A$ is some $b \in B$, but the nearest A-neighbor of b is different from a.

In the mutually-nearest method, a two-element fusion set is created for each pair of mutually-nearest objects. A singleton fusion set is created for each object that is not in any pair of mutually-nearest objects.

Consider an object $a \in A$ and let b be the nearest B-neighbor of a. The *second-nearest B-neighbor* of A is the object $b' \in B$, such that b' is the closest object to a among all the object in $B - \{b\}$.

We will now define the confidence values of fusion sets. First, consider a pair of mutually-nearest objects $a \in A$ and $b \in B$. Let a' be the second-nearest A-neighbor of b, and let b' be the second-nearest B-neighbor of a. The confidence of the fusion set $\{a, b\}$ is defined as follows.

$$confidence(\{a,b\}) = 1 - \frac{distance(a,b)}{\min\{distance(a,b'), distance(a',b)\}}$$

That is, the confidence is the complement to one of the ratio of the distance between the two objects to the minimum among the distances between each object and its second-nearest neighbor.

Now consider a fusion set with one element $a \in A$, i.e., a is not in any pair of of mutually-nearest objects. Let b be the nearest B-neighbor of a and let a' be the nearest A-neighbor of b. The confidence of the fusion set $\{a\}$ is defined as follows.

$$confidence(\{a\}) = 1 - \frac{distance(a',b)}{distance(a,b)}$$

That is, the complement to one of the ratio of the distance between a' and b to the distance between a and b. Note that the confidence cannot be negative, since it would imply that a, rather than a', is the nearest A-neighbor of b. The confidence of a fusion set with a single element from $b \in B$ is defined similarly.

The above formulas are used to compute the confidence value, except when the *distance upper bound* β rules out the possibility that a has a corresponding object in the other set. The parameter β should be equal to the sum of all possible errors in the locations of objects. Thus, if for all $b \in B$, it holds that $distance(a,b) > \beta$, then we define $confidence(\{a\}) = 1$ whereas for all $b \in B$, we define $confidence(\{a,b\}) = 0$.

A threshold can be used to increase the precision of the result by choosing only those fusion sets that have a confidence value above the threshold. Consequently, some objects from the given datasets may not be in the result. A less restrictive approach is to discard two-element fusion sets with a confidence value below the threshold, but to add their elements as singletons.

The main advantage of the mutually-nearest method over the traditional one-sided nearest-neighbor join is lower sensitivity to the degree of overlap between the two datasets. In particular, it may perform well even when neither datasets is covered by the other one. However, it does not perform well when the choice factors are large, since it only takes into account the nearest neighbor and the second-nearest neighbor, while ignoring other neighbors that might be almost as close. In situations characterized by large choice factors, it is likely that an object a will not be the nearest neighbor of its corresponding object b. If this is indeed the case, the pair a and b will not be in the result even if the distance between a and b is only slightly greater than the distance between b and its nearest neighbor.

4.4 The Probabilistic Method

The probabilistic method was devised to perform well when the choice factors are large. In such situations, it is not enough to consider only the nearest and second-nearest B-neighbors of an object $a \in A$, since there could be several objects in B that are close to a.

In the probabilistic method, the confidence of a fusion set $\{a,b\}$ depends on the probability that b is the object that corresponds to a, and that probability depends inversely on the distance between a and b.

Consider two datasets $A = \{a_1, \ldots, a_m\}$ and $B = \{b_1, \ldots, b_n\}$. For each object $a \in A$, we will define the function $P_a : B \to [0,1]$ that gives the probability that a chooses $b \in B$. Similarly, for each $b \in B$, we will define the probability function $P_b : A \to [0,1]$.

Formally, the probability function P_{a_i} is defined, as shown below, in terms of the distance, the *distance decay factor* $\alpha > 0$ and the distance upper bound β.

$$P_{a_i}(b_j) = \frac{distance(a_i, b_j)^{-\alpha}}{\sum_{k=1}^{m} distance(a_i, b_k)^{-\alpha}} \quad (1)$$

The probability function P_{b_j} is defined similarly.

Although β is not shown explicitly in the above formula, it has the following effect. If $distance(a_i, b_j) > \beta$, then $distance(a_i, b_j)$ is taken to be infinity, i.e., $distance(a_i, b_j)^{-\alpha} = 0$. Recall that the distance upper bound should be equal to the sum of all possible errors in the locations of objects. Thus, if $distance(a_i, b_j) > \beta$, then a_i and b_j are not likely to be corresponding objects and setting $distance(a_i, b_j)^{-\alpha}$ to 0 is justified. Note that the denominator of Formula (1) is 0 if the distance between a_i and every object of B is greater than β. In this case, $P_{a_i}(b_j)$ is defined to be 0.

Due to the numerator in the above formula (and the fact that $\alpha > 0$), the probability that a_i chooses b_j increases when the distance between a_i and b_j decreases. Thus, a_i chooses its nearest B-neighbor with the highest probability. The parameter α determines the rate of decrease in the probability as the distance increases. We performed tests with different values for α and the best results were obtained for $\alpha = 2$. Due to the denominator in the above formula, the probability that a_i chooses one of the b_j's is 1, since $\sum_{j=1}^{m} P_{a_i}(b_j) = 1$ (unless a_i does not choose any b_j, which happens when the distance between a_i and every $b_j \in B$ is greater than β and hence $P_{a_i}(b_j) = 0$ for every $b_j \in B$).

The confidence of the fusion set $\{a_i, b_j\}$ is defined as follows.

$$confidence(\{a_i, b_j\}) = \sqrt{P_{a_i}(b_j) \cdot P_{b_j}(a_i)}$$

Note that $P_{a_i}(b_j) \cdot P_{b_j}(a_i)$ is the probability that a_i chooses b_j and b_j chooses a_i, i.e., the probability that a and b are corresponding objects. The confidence is defined as the square root of that probability in order that it will not be too small.

The confidence of a fusion set that includes a single object a_i is defined as follows.

$$confidence(\{a_i\}) = 1 - \sum_{k=1}^{m} \left(\sqrt{P_{a_i}(b_k) \cdot P_{b_k}(a_i)} \right)$$

The rationale for this formula is that the sum of confidences over all fusion sets that contain a_i should be equal to 1. Note that the singleton $\{a_i\}$ is given a confidence value of 1 if the distance between a_i and every object of B is greater than the distance upper bound β. Also note that in some rare cases the above formula may give a value that is less than 0 and, in such cases, we define $confidence(\{a_i\}) = 0$.

The result of the probabilistic method consists of all fusion sets that have confidence values above the threshold τ.

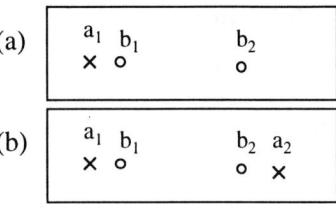

Figure 1: Adding a new object to a dataset.

When the choice factors are large, the probabilistic method performs better than either the mutually-nearest method or the one-sided nearest-neighbor join. The reason for that is that the probabilistic method assigns a confidence value to every pair of objects. Another advantage of the probabilistic methods is the ability to increase the recall by lowering the threshold. Doing so, however, may cause an object to be in more than one fusion set.

In the probabilistic method, the recall is low when the overlap between the two datasets is small. In such a situation, most of the singleton fusion sets, both the correct ones and the incorrect ones, get similar confidence values. Thus, lowering the threshold would introduce into the result many incorrect singletons, while at the same time many correct ones would still remain below the threshold (unless the threshold becomes very low). If the threshold is high, it is likely that many correct singletons would be missing from the result. In conclusion, when the overlap is small, the probabilistic method does not handle correctly objects that should be in singletons. Therefore, this method should only be used when the overlap between the datasets is large.

4.5 The Normalized-Weights Method

The normalized-weights method is a variation of the probabilistic method and it performs better when the overlap is small or medium. As in the probabilistic method, weights (i.e., confidence values) are given to each (correct or incorrect) fusion set, based on the same probability functions P_a and P_b that were defined in the previous section (see Equation 1). The initial weights are normalized by an iterative algorithm that will be described in this section. This algorithm has an effect of mutual influence between pairs of objects, as illustrated in the next example.

Example 4.1 Consider the objects a_1, b_1 and b_2 in Figure 1(a). We assume that a_1 is an object in the dataset A while b_1 and b_2 are objects in the dataset B. Let the distance between a_1 and b_1 be 1 and let the distance between a_1 and b_2 be 5. In the probabilistic method, assuming a distance decay factor of 1 (i.e., $\alpha = 1$), the probability that b_1 will choose a_1 is 1, since a_1 is the only object of A. For a_1, the probabilities to choose b_1 and b_2 are $\frac{5}{6}$ and $\frac{1}{6}$, respectively.

Thus, the confidence value that is given to the fusion set $\{a_1, b_1\}$ is $\sqrt{P_{a_1}(b_1) \cdot P_{b_1}(a_1)} = \sqrt{\frac{5}{6}}$.

In Figure 1(b), the object a_2 is added to the dataset A. The distance between a_2 and b_2 is 1 and the distance between a_2 and b_1 is 5. In the probabilistic method, after adding a_2, the confidence of the set $\{a_1, b_1\}$ is $\sqrt{P_{a_1}(b_1) \cdot P_{b_1}(a_1)} = \sqrt{\frac{5}{6} \cdot \frac{5}{6}} = \frac{5}{6} < \sqrt{\frac{5}{6}}$.

Thus, the addition of a_2 has reduced the confidence of the fusion set $\{a_1, b_1\}$. This reduction is caused by the fact that after the addition of a_2, object b_1 could potentially be the corresponding object of either a_1 or a_2, whereas before the addition of a_2, only the correspondence between b_1 and a_1 was possible. But the addition of a_2 also has an effect of increasing the likelihood of a correspondence between b_1 and a_1, because b_2 is now more likely to correspond to a_2 than to a_1 and, hence, the confidence of the fusion set $\{a_1, b_1\}$ should increase relatively to the confidence of the fusion set $\{a_1, b_2\}$. In summary, the addition of a_2 has two opposite effects: one is an increase in the confidence of the fusion set $\{a_1, b_1\}$ and the other is a decrease of that confidence. The probabilistic method is only capable of capturing the second effect, whereas the normalized-weights method captures both.

Next, we will describe the normalized-weights method. Consider two datasets $A = \{a_1, \ldots, a_m\}$ and $B = \{b_1, \ldots, b_n\}$. The probability functions $P_{a_i}(b_j)$ and $P_{b_j}(a_i)$ are defined as in Section 4.4. The *matchings matrix* M is an $(m + 1) \times (n + 1)$ matrix, such that the element in row i and column j, denoted μ_{ij}, is defined as follows.

$$\mu_{ij} = \begin{cases} P_{a_i}(b_j) \cdot P_{b_j}(a_i) & : 1 \leq i \leq m, 1 \leq j \leq n \\ \prod_{k=1}^{n}(1 - P_{b_k}(a_i)) & : 1 \leq i \leq m, j = n+1 \\ \prod_{k=1}^{m}(1 - P_{a_k}(b_j)) & : i = m+1, 1 \leq j \leq n \\ 0 & : i = m+1, j = n+1 \end{cases}$$

Note that in the first case (i.e., the top line) of the above definition, μ_{ij} is assigned the probability that a_i and b_j mutually choose each other. In each row i, the element in the last column ($j = n + 1$) gives the probability that a_i is not chosen by any $b \in B$. Similarly, in each column j, the element in the last row ($i = m + 1$) gives the probability that b_j is not chosen by any $a \in A$.

A row (or a column) r is *normalized* if $s = 1$, where s is the sum of all the elements of r. We can always normalize r by dividing each element by s (since $s > 0$). The *normalization algorithm* is a sequence of iterations over M, such that in each iteration, the first m rows and the first n columns are normalized one by one in some order. Note that the elements of the last column are changed when the rows are normalized, but the last column itself is not normalized; similarly for the last row.

Let $M^{(0)}$ denote the matrix M, as it was defined above, and let $M^{(k)}$ denote the matrix after k iterations. It was shown by Sinkhorn [14, 15] that the normalization algorithm converges and the result does not depend upon the order of normalizing rows and columns in each iteration. We terminate the normalization algorithm when the sum of each row and each column, except for the last row and the last column, is different from 1 by no more than some very small $\epsilon > 0$ (in the tests, ϵ was equal to 0.001).

Let $M^{(t)}$ denote the matrix upon termination of the iteration algorithms. The confidence of the fusion set $\{a_i, b_j\}$ is the value in row i and column j of $M^{(t)}$. The confidence of the fusion set $\{a_i\}$ is the value in row i and column $n + 1$ of $M^{(t)}$. The confidence of the fusion set $\{b_j\}$ is the value in column j and row $m + 1$ of $M^{(t)}$. Given a threshold τ, the result of the normalized-weights method consists of all the fusion sets with confidence values above the threshold τ.

The normalized-weights method gives good results when the overlap between the datasets is medium or small. However, the results are not as good as those of the probabilistic method when the overlap is large, because the weights that are assigned to singletons (i.e., the weights in the last row and in the last column) are not normalized. Consequently, these weights remain rather large even when they should be almost zero (i.e., when the overlap is large). In Section 6, we discuss how to improve this method by normalizing all the rows and columns of M.

4.6 Tuning the Methods

The performance of the three new methods, which were introduced in the previous sections, can be tuned by choosing appropriate values for the threshold, the distance decay factor and the distance upper bound.

The threshold τ controls the precision and recall. Increasing the threshold increases the precision while decreasing the threshold increases the recall.

The distance decay factor α controls the effect of distant neighbors in either the probabilistic method or the normalized-weights method. In either method, the probability that an object a chooses some object from the other set is split among all the objects of the other set. This probability might be split among many objects, including far away objects that are really no more than "background noise." By choosing $\alpha > 1$, the effect of far away objects decreases exponentially. Thus, increasing α eliminates background noise. However, increasing α too much can cause these methods to act like the mutually-nearest method, i.e., pairs of objects that are not mutually nearest will be ignored.

The distance upper bound β determines which two-element fusion sets $\{a_i, b_j\}$ are a priori deemed incorrect, because the distance between a_i and b_j is too far. In practice, the value of β should be an upper-bound

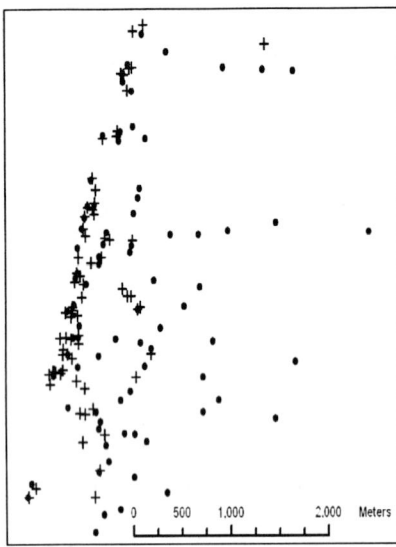

Figure 2: Hotels and tourist attractions in Tel-Aviv (the objects of MUNI are depicted by + and the objects of MAPA are depicted by •).

estimate for the sum of all possible errors in the locations of objects.

5 Testing and Comparing the Methods

We tested the different methods using real-world datasets as well as randomly-generated datasets. The two real-world datasets describe hotels and other tourist attractions in Tel-Aviv. One dataset, called MUNI, was extracted from a digital map that was made by the City of Tel-Aviv. The second dataset, called MAPA, was extracted from a digital map that was made by the Mapa Corp. The randomly-generated datasets were created using a random-dataset generator that we implemented.

5.1 Results for Real-World Datasets

In the MUNI and MAPA datasets, each object has a name, although in MUNI the names are in English and in MAPA the names are in Hebrew. The correctness of the results was checked using the specified names of the objects. However, only locations were used for computing the fusion sets.

The MAPA dataset has 86 objects and the MUNI dataset has 73 objects. A total of 137 real-world entities are represented in these datasets and 22 entities appear in both datasets. The mutually-nearest method was tested with a threshold $\tau = 0$. The probabilistic and the normalized-weights methods were tested with an optimal threshold value (see Section 7). The distance upper bound β was 150 meters and the distance decay factor α was 2. There were 40 objects in MAPA and 6 objects in MUNI without any neighbor in the other dataset at a distance of β or less.

The two datasets are depicted in Figure 2. The performance results are given in Table 1. Note that the table describes both the one-sided nearest-neighbor join of MUNI with MAPA (first column) and the one-sided nearest-neighbor join of MAPA with MUNI (second column). The one-sided nearest-neighbor join performed much worse than the other methods, while the normalized-weights method had the best performance.

5.2 Random-Dataset Generator

There are not sufficiently many real-world datasets to test our algorithms under varying degrees of density and overlap. Moreover, in real-world datasets, it is not always possible to determine accurately the correspondence between objects and real-world entities. Thus, we implemented a random-dataset generator, which is a two-step process. First, the real-world entities are randomly generated. Second, the objects in each dataset are randomly generated, independently of the objects in the other dataset.

For the first step, the user specifies the coordinates of a square area, the number of entities in that area and the minimal distance between entities. The generator randomly chooses locations for the entities, according to a uniform distribution. The generator verifies that entities are not too close to each other, i.e., the distance between entities is greater than the minimal distance specified by the user. This is done to enforce realistic constraints; for example, the distance between two buildings cannot be just a few centimeters.

For the second step, the user specifies the number of objects in the datasets and the error interval. The creation of a random object has two aspects. First, the object is randomly associated with one of the real-world entities that were created in the first step (at most one object, in each dataset, corresponds to any given entity). Second, the location of the object is randomly chosen, according to the normal distribution, in a circle with a center that is equal to the location of the corresponding entity and a radius that is equal to the error interval.

Note that the two datasets have an equal number of objects. However, in each dataset, the association of objects with entities and the locations of objects are chosen randomly and independently of the other dataset. By changing the number of objects, it is easy to control the overlap between the two randomly generated datasets. For example, if each dataset has 500 objects while the number of entities is 500, then there is a complete overlap. However, if there are 50,000 entities, then the overlap between the two datasets is very small, with a very high probability.

5.3 Results for Random Datasets

We have experimented with many randomly-generated datasets, but in this section we only describe a few tests that demonstrate the main conclusions about the

	Joining MAPA objects with nearest neighbors from MUNI	Joining MUNI objects with nearest neighbors from MAPA	Mutually Nearest	Probabilistic	Normalized Weights
Result Size	120	119	124	137	129
Recall	0.38	0.48	0.77	0.80	0.85
Precision	0.43	0.56	0.85	0.80	0.90

Table 1: Performance of the fusion algorithms for datasets of hotels and tourist attractions in Tel-Aviv.

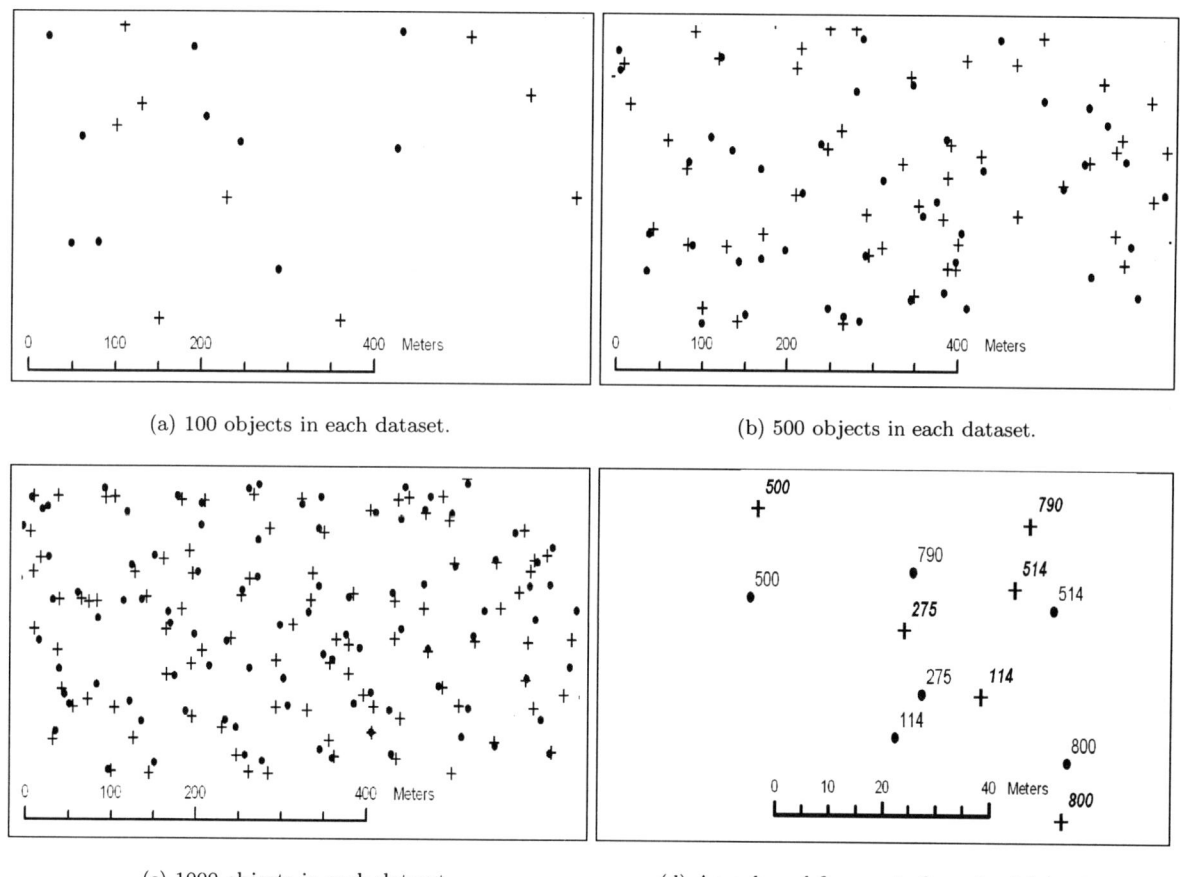

(a) 100 objects in each dataset.

(b) 500 objects in each dataset.

(c) 1000 objects in each dataset.

(d) An enlarged fragment of a pair of datasets.

Figure 3: A visual view of the random pairs of datasets, with 100, 500 and 1000 objects.

performance of each method. The following parameters were given to the random-dataset generator. A square area of $1,350 \times 1,350$ meters, 1,000 entities, a minimal distance of 15 meters between entities, and an error interval of 30 meters for each datasets. The above parameters imply that if a dataset represents all 1,000 entities, then the choice factor is 1.55 and each entity occupies, on the average, an area of 1,822 sq m.

In the tests described below, the 1,000 real-world entities were created once and then three pairs of datasets were randomly generated (see Figure 3). The three pairs had 100, 500 and 1,000 objects in each dataset, respectively. Thus, each pairs had a different degree of overlap and density (1,000 objects in each dataset means a complete overlap). To get a sense of the difficulty in finding the correct fusion sets, an enlarged fragment of the pair of datasets from Figure 3(c) is depicted in Figure 3(d), where an entity identifier is attached to each object.

The recall and precision of each method were measured for every pair of datasets. In all the methods, the distance upper bound β was 60 meters and the error interval was 30 meters. In the mutually-nearest method, the threshold τ was 0, since it gave the highest or close to the highest recall. For the datasets with 100 objects, the recall and the precision were 0.68 and 0.81, respectively; for 500 objects, they were 0.72 and 0.77, respectively; and for 1,000 objects, they were 0.74 and 0.63, respectively.

For the probabilistic method and the normalized-

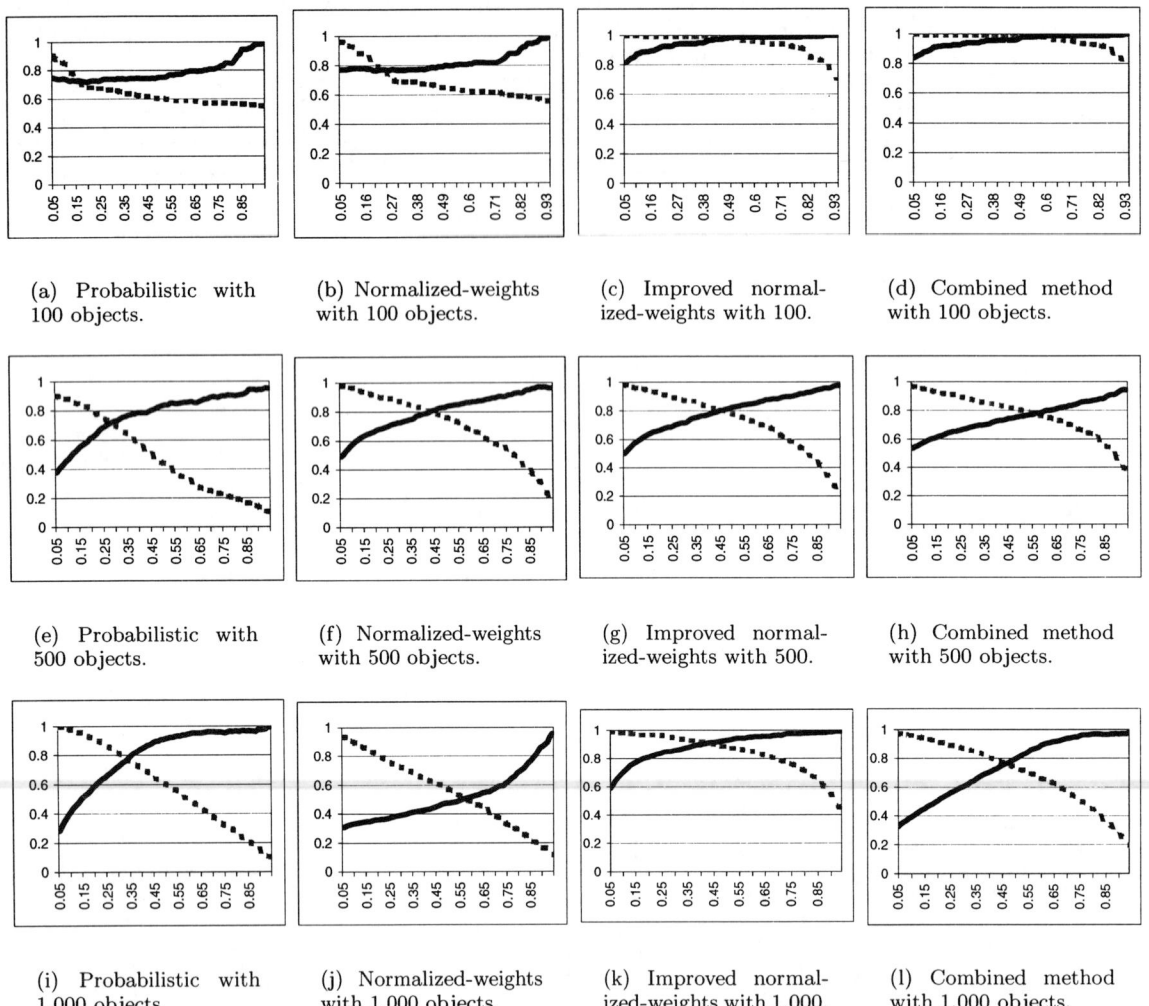

Figure 4: Recall (dotted line) and precision (solid line) as a function of the threshold value.

weights method (as well as for two additional methods that are explained in Section 6), Figure 4 presents the recall and the precision as a function of the threshold. Tests were made with different values for the distance decay factor (i.e., $\alpha = 0.5, 1, 2, 3$). We only show the results for $\alpha = 2$, since this choice was the best for both methods under all circumstances.

The main conclusions from the tests are as follows. When the overlap between the datasets is small, the mutually-nearest and the normalized-weights methods give good results. The probabilistic method does not perform well in this case, because it does not find the correct singletons and instead creates incorrect pairs. For a medium overlap, the best results are given by the normalized-weights method. This is demonstrated in the case of 500 objects in each dataset. When the overlap is large, the best results are given by the probabilistic method. The normalized-weights method does not perform well in this case, because singletons get weights (i.e., confidence values) that are too large.

We will now give a detailed analysis of the graphs in Figure 4. Essentially, a method performs well if it assigns low confidence values to incorrect fusion sets and high confidence values to correct ones. Most of the graphs in Figure 4, except for 4(a), 4(b) and 4(j), exhibit this phenomenon. In the low range of threshold values, a small increase of the threshold value eliminates many incorrect fusion sets and only a few correct ones. Thus, the precision rises sharply while the recall declines slowly. In the high range of threshold values, a small increase of the threshold value eliminates many correct fusion sets and only a few incorrect ones. Thus, the precision rises slowly while the recall declines sharply. Also note that the precision and the recall change more sharply as the overlap grows. A bigger overlap means a bigger density, which causes more pairs to get confidence values that are close to each other.

Figures 4(a) and 4(b) show the performance of the probabilistic and the normalized-weights methods in the case of a small overlap. In that case, many correct singletons get low confidence values while many incorrect pairs get high confidence values. Thus, when a low threshold value is increased, many correct singletons are eliminated and the recall declines sharply. The precision remains about the same, since many incorrect fusion sets are also eliminated. In the high range of threshold values, a small increase of the threshold value eliminates many incorrect pairs and the precision rises sharply while the recall remains about the same. In the medium range of threshold values, there is very little change in the recall and the precision, because the confidence values are either very low or very high, as a result of the low density (i.e., an object has only a few close neighbors in the other dataset).

Figure 4(j) shows the performance of the normalized-weights method in the case of a complete overlap (i.e., there are no correct singletons). In that method, the last row and the last column of the matching matrix are not normalized and, consequently, many incorrect singletons get high confidence values, regardless of the degree of overlap. Thus, the precision rises sharply only in the high range of threshold values.

6 Complete Normalization

In this section, we will show how knowledge about the degree of overlap between the datasets can improve the normalized-weights method.

6.1 The Normalization Value

Ideally, the normalized-weights method should give to singletons high confidence values when the overlap is large and low confidence values when the overlap is small. However, since the last row and the last column of the matching matrix are not normalized, the confidence values of singletons tend to remain high in any case. Recall that each entry in those row and column gives the probability that some object does not have a corresponding object in the other set. Thus, those row and column should not be normalized to 1.

Suppose that the datasets A and B have m and n objects, respectively, and c is the number of real-world entities that are represented in both datasets. Thus, $m - c$ objects of A and $n - c$ objects of B should be in singleton fusion sets. Ideally, an entry in either the last row or the last column should be 1 if its corresponding object is in a correct singleton, and should be 0 otherwise. Consequently, we improve the normalization algorithm by normalizing the last row to $n - c$ and the last column to $m - c$. Note that if $n - c = 0$ (or $m - c = 0$), then we just set all the elements in the last row (or last column) to 0 and need not normalize this row (or column) anymore.

The improved normalized-weights method always performs better than all the other methods, as shown in Figures 4(c), 4(g) and 4(k). Note that in these three tests, the correct value of c was used.

6.2 Estimating the Overlap

The improved normalized-weights method requires a good estimate for the number c of correct pairs of corresponding objects. If the association of objects with entities in each dataset is independent of the other dataset, then an approximation of c is given by

$$c \approx \frac{m}{e} \cdot \frac{n}{e} \cdot e$$

where e is the number of real-world entities and the two datasets have m and n objects, respectively. If e is not known, then a less accurate approximation of c can be obtained by replacing e with the number of pairs that are produced by the mutually-nearest method.

We conducted a series of tests with the following parameters. The number of entities ranged from 500 to 1,000 in increments of 100. The size of the datasets ranged from 50 to 500 in increments of 50. The minimal distance between entities was either 15, 25 or 35 meters. The conclusion from these tests is that c can be approximated by

$$c \approx 1.2p - \frac{e}{10}$$

where p is the number of pairs that are produced by the mutually-nearest method and e is the number of entities. In particular, when p is approximately $\frac{e}{2}$, then c is also approximately $\frac{e}{2}$.

The above formula suggests that p is a good estimate for c. Thus, we also tested the *combined method* that applies the improved normalized-weights method with p as the estimate for c. The results for the random datasets of Section 5.3 are shown in Figures 4(d), 4(h) and 4(l). These results are almost as good as the results for the improved normalized-weights method, using the correct value of c.

7 Choosing the Threshold Value

For the mutually-nearest neighbor, a threshold value of zero will give the highest recall with a good precision. For the other methods, choosing a good threshold value is more complicated. A threshold value of 0.5 is a reasonable choice, since it usually gives results with good recall and precision, and without duplicates (i.e., each object appears in at most one fusion set). Note that if the threshold is just above 0.5, then there cannot be duplicates. An *optimal* threshold gives the best combination of recall and precision. Formally, an optimal threshold can be defined as the one that gives the largest geometric average of the recall and the precision. In Figure 4, this is usually the threshold at the intersection of the graphs of the recall and the precision.

We will now describe how to estimate the optimal threshold without a priori knowledge of the correct fusion sets. The idea is to minimize two types of errors.

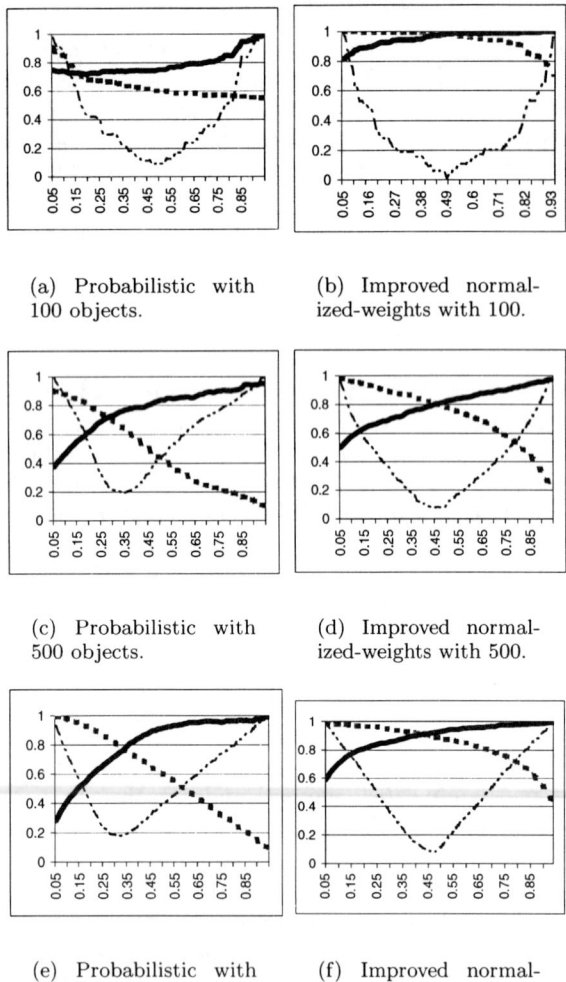

(a) Probabilistic with 100 objects.

(b) Improved normalized-weights with 100.

(c) Probabilistic with 500 objects.

(d) Improved normalized-weights with 500.

(e) Probabilistic with 1,000 objects.

(f) Improved normalized-weights with 1,000.

Figure 5: The error count (shown by a dashed line), recall and precision as a function of the threshold.

A *missing object* is an object that does not appear in any fusion set. A *duplicate object* is an object that appears in more than one fusion set. The *error count* is the number of missing objects plus the number of duplicate occurrences of objects (if an object appears in k fusions sets, then it is counted $k-1$ times). The threshold value should be chosen so that the error count is minimal. Figure 5 shows the error count as a function of the threshold for two methods, using the random datasets of Section 5.3 (the graphs for the other two methods are similar). It can be seen that a threshold value that minimizes the error count is close to the optimal threshold. This was also confirmed for the real-world datasets, MUNI and MAPA. For the probabilistic method, the optimal threshold was 0.31 and the threshold that minimized the error count was 0.4. For these two threshold values, there was only a small difference (0.796 vs. 0.784) between the geometric averages of the recall and the precision. For the normalized-weights method, the optimal threshold was 0.43 and the threshold that minimized the error count was 0.45, while the geometric averages were about the same (0.873 and 0.868). Thus, for a real pair of datasets, the threshold value can be chosen by trying several different values and choosing the one that minimizes the error count.

8 Related Work

Map conflation is the process of producing a new map by integrating two existing digital maps, and it has been studied extensively in the last twenty years. Map conflation starts by choosing some *anchors,* i.e., pairs of points that represent the same location. A triangular planar subdivision of the datasets with respect to the anchors (using Delaunay triangulation) is performed and a rubber-sheeting transformation is applied to each subdivision [4, 5, 6, 11, 12].

Map conflation cannot be applied without initially finding some anchors. Thus, our methods can be used as part of this process. Unlike map conflation, which is a complicated process, our algorithms are most suitable for the task of online integration of geographic databases using mediators (e.g., [2, 17]).

A feature-based approach to conflation, which is similar to object fusion, has been studied in [13]. Their approach is different from ours in that they find corresponding objects based on both topological similarity and textual similarity in non-spatial attributes. Once some corresponding objects have been found, they construct some graphs and use graph similarity to find more corresponding objects.

In [3], topological similarity is used to find corresponding objects, while in [7, 8, 16] ontologies are used for that purpose.

The problem of how to fuse objects, rather than how to find fusion sets, was studied in [10]. Thus, their work complements ours.

9 Conclusion and Future Work

The novelty of our approach is in developing efficient algorithms that find fusion sets with high recall and precision, using only locations of objects. The mutually-nearest method is an improvement of the existing one-sided nearest-neighbor join and it achieves substantially better results.

We also developed a completely new approach, based on a probabilistic model. We presented several algorithms that use this model. The improved normalized-weights method achieves the best results under all circumstances. This method combines the probabilistic model with a normalization algorithm and information about the overlap between the datasets. We showed that the mutually-nearest method provides a good estimate for the degree of overlap. We also showed how to tune the methods and how to choose an optimal threshold value.

Several interesting problems remain for future work. One problem is to deal with situations in which an object from one set could correspond to many objects in the other set. This may happen, for example, when one dataset represents shopping malls while the other dataset represents shops.

A second problem is to develop fusion algorithms for more than two datasets. This problem is similar to the previous one in that both require finding fusion sets that have several, rather than just 2 objects. In principle, this problem can be solved by a sequence of steps, such that only two datasets are involved in each step (where one of those two datasets is the result of the previous step). However, it is not clear whether a long sequence can still give good recall and precision.

A third problem is how to utilize locations that are given as polygons or lines, rather than just points.

A fourth research direction is to combine our approach with other approaches, such as the feature-based approach of [13], topological similarity (e.g., [3]) or ontologies (e.g., [7, 8, 16]).

Acknowledgments

We thank Michael Ben-Or for pointing out to us the work of Sinkhorn [14, 15]. We also thank the anonymous referees for helpful suggestions. This research was supported in part by a grant from the Israel Ministry of Science and by the Israel Science Foundation (Grant No. 96/01).

References

[1] B. Amann, C. Beeri, I. Fundulaki, and M. Scholl. Ontology-based integration of XML Web resources. In *Proceedings of the First International Semantic Web Conference*, pages 117–131, Sardinia (Italy), 2002.

[2] O. Boucelma, M. Essid, and Z. Lacroix. A WFS-based mediation system for GIS interoperability. In *Proceedings of the 10th ACM International Symposium on Advances in Geographic Information Systems*, pages 23–28, 2002.

[3] T. Bruns and M. Egenhofer. Similarity of spatial scenes. In *Proceedings of the 7th International Symposium on Spatial Data Handling*, pages 31–42, Delft (Netherlands), 1996.

[4] M. A. Cobb, M. J. Chung, H. Foley, F. E. Petry, and K. B. Show. A rule-based approach for conflation of attribute vector data. *GioInformatica*, 2(1):7–33, 1998.

[5] Y. Doytsher and S. Filin. The detection of of corresponding objects in a linear-based map conflation. *Surveying and Land Information Systems*, 60(2):117–128, 2000.

[6] Y. Doytsher, S. Filin, and E. Ezra. Transformation of datasets in a linear-based map conflation framework. *Surveying and Land Information Systems*, 61(3):159–169, 2001.

[7] F. T. Fonseca and M. J. Egenhofer. Ontology-driven geographic information systems. In *Proceedings of the 7th ACM International Symposium on Advances in Geographic Information Systems*, pages 14–19, Kansas City (Missouri, US), 1999.

[8] F. T. Fonseca, M. J. Egenhofer, and P. Agouris. Using ontologies for integrated geographic information systems. *Transactions in GIS*, 6(3), 2002.

[9] M. Minami. *Using ArcMap*. Environmental Systems Research Institute, Inc., 2000.

[10] Y. Papakonstantinou, S. Abiteboul, and H. Garcia-Molina. Object fusion in mediator systems. In *Proceedings of the 22nd International Conference on Very Large Databases*, pages 413–424, 1996.

[11] B. Rosen and A. Saalfeld. Match criteria for automatic alignment. In *Proceedings of 7th International Symposium on Computer-Assisted Cartography (Auto-Carto 7)*, pages 1–20, 1985.

[12] A. Saalfeld. Conflation-automated map compilation. *International Journal of Geographical Information Systems*, 2(3):217–228, 1988.

[13] A. Samal, S. Seth, and K. Cueto. A feature based approach to conflation of geospatial sources. *International Journal of Geographical Information Science*, 18(00):1–31, 2004.

[14] R. Sinkhorn. A relationship between arbitrary positive matrices and doubly stochastic matrices. *The Annals of Mathematical Statistics*, 35(2):876–879, 1964.

[15] R. Sinkhorn. Diagonal equivalence to matrices with perscribed row and column sums. *The American Mathematical Monthly*, 74(4):402–405, 1967.

[16] H. Uitermark, P. V. Oosterom, N. Mars, and M. Molenaar. Ontology-based geographic data set integration. In *Proceedings of Workshop on Spatio-Temporal Database Management*, pages 60–79, Edinburgh (Scotland), 1999.

[17] G. Wiederhold. Mediation to deal with heterogeneous data sources. In *Introperating Geographic Information Systems*, pages 1–16, 1999.

Maintenance of Spatial Semijoin Queries on Moving Points

Glenn S. Iwerks [‡†] Hanan Samet [‡*] Kenneth P. Smith [⁊†]

‡Computer Science Department,
Center for Automation Research, and
Institute for Advanced Computer Studies
University of Maryland at College Park
{iwerks,hjs}@umiacs.umd.edu

⁊The MITRE Corporation
7515 Colshire Dr.
McLean, Virginia 22102
{iwerks,kps}@mitre.org

Abstract

In this paper, we address the maintenance of spatial semijoin queries over continuously moving points, where points are modeled as linear functions of time. This is analogous to the maintenance of a materialized view except, as time advances, the query result may change independently of updates. As in a materialized view, we assume there is no prior knowledge of updates before they occur. We present a new approach, *continuous fuzzy sets* (CFS), to maintain continuous spatial semijoins efficiently. CFS is compared experimentally to a simple scaling of previous work. The result is significantly better performance of CFS compared to previous work by up to an order of magnitude in some cases.

1 Introduction

We consider the following queries. For each moving firetruck, keep track of the nearest mobile police unit. For each airplane, keep track of the nearest airport. For each cell phone, keep track of the nearest airborne relay station. For each tank, keep track of the nearest target. For each robot explorer in a swarm of robots, keep track of the nearest maintenance robot. For each unmanned air vehicle, keep track of the nearest observation objective. For each ship, keep track of the nearest sonar tracking station.

These are all examples of spatial semijoin queries on moving objects. Many are examples where all the objects are moving simultaneously and continuously. All must update the query result as the objects move in real time. None know how the object will move ahead of time.

In this paper, we address the maintenance of spatial semijoin queries over continuously moving points. Given two sets of moving points Q and D, we define semijoin $Q \ltimes_k D$ as all the pairs $\langle q, p \rangle$, $q \in Q \land p \in D$, that are in Cartesian product $Q \times D$, and p is one of the k nearest neighbors of q. Set Q is the set of query points, and D is the set of data points. This amounts to a massive scaling of a continuous nearest neighbor query for all query points. Traditionally, a semijoin returns tuples from only one join relation. However, we relax this constraint to make the result meaningful in light of the examples above.

Data sets Q, and D are updated through insertions and deletions to the sets. There is no prior knowledge of what the updates will be in advance of each update occurrence. This is analogous to the maintenance of a materialized view [5], with the difference being that the query result may change as a result of the motion of points represented in the database as well as updates to the database.

Points are modeled as linear functions of time, as opposed to samples of an objects location that are updated as an object moves. Therefore, as time advances, the query result may change independently of updates. Access methods and operators for this data type have been studied extensively including indexing methods [17, 21], ad-hoc queries [17, 19], and continuous queries such as window [17, 19], and within [10, 20], and finding the k nearest neighbors [2, 10, 15, 20] (k-nn) to an object.

To our knowledge there has been no previous work to perform continuous spatial semijoin queries on moving objects so that any of the examples queries given in the first paragraph above for data sets of significant size can be answered. Some work on scaling k-nn queries on point data represented as samples (e.g., [14]) has been done, but not on the scale needed to perform semijoins.

In this paper, we present a new approach, termed *con-*

---

*This work was supported in part by the National Science Foundation under grants EIA-99-00268, IIS-00-86162, and EIA-00-91474.

†This work was supported in part by the National Institute for Mental Health and the National Science Foundation under NIH grant R01-MH64417-01.

Permission to copy without fee all or part of this material is granted provided that the copies are not made or distributed for direct commercial advantage, the VLDB copyright notice and the title of the publication and its date appear, and notice is given that copying is by permission of the Very Large Data Base Endowment. To copy otherwise, or to republish, requires a fee and/or special permission from the Endowment.

**Proceedings of the 30th VLDB Conference,
Toronto, Canada, 2004**

tinuous fuzzy sets (CFS), to perform spatial semijoins. This approach is most similar to a continuous window k-nn algorithm presented in [10]. However, CFS is not just a simple scaling of this previous work. As we will show, previous work (e.g., [10, 20]) does not scale well. CFS is compared experimentally to a simple scaling of the time-parameterized k-nn algorithm presented in [20]. The result is a significant better performance of CFS compared to this previous work by up to an order of magnitude in some cases.

The rest of this paper is organized as follows. Section 2 reviews previous work and the background necessary to understand this paper. Our CFS algorithm is presented in Section 3. Section 4 discusses some performance issues. Experimental results are described in Section 5. Section 6 contains some concluding remarks.

2 Background and Previous Work

Some of the most widely researched queries on static spatial data include within, window, spatial join, k-nearest neighbor (k-nn), and spatial semijoin. A *within* [18] query returns all objects within a given distance $d \geq 0$ from a query object. A *window* query can be thought of as a special case of a within query where the query object is a hyper-rectangle and the distance is zero. A *spatial join* [8] returns all pairs of objects in the Cartesian product of two relations that are within a given distance $d \geq 0$ of each other. A k-nn query [16] returns the closest $k > 0$ spatial objects to a given query object. A *spatial semijoin* [8] is a subset of a spatial join $A \bowtie B$ where a tuple in the result $\langle a, *\rangle$ appears only once for any given $a \in A$, denoted $A \ltimes B$. An additional constraint is imposed in the spatial context of semijoins which stipulates for any tuple $\langle a, b \rangle$ in the result that $b \in B$ is the closest neighbor to a out of all objects in B. Another way to define this form of spatial semijoin is for every object $a \in A$, to find the nearest neighbor $b \in B$ and report $\langle a, b \rangle$. Using this definition, we can relax the 1-nn constraint and find the k nearest neighbors for every object $a \in A$, denoted $A \ltimes_k B$.

The *incremental distance query* [9] returns all the objects within a given distance d of a query object q, one at a time, in increasing order of distance from q. The incremental distance query algorithm can be used for both within queries, and k-nn queries. Retrieving all the objects from q within distance $d < \infty$ is a within query. Retrieving the first k objects and then stopping, with $d = \infty$, is a k-nn query. The incremental distance query algorithm assumes a spatial tree index where, as in the case of the R-tree [6] spatial index, the internal nodes have bounding boxes (BB) that spatially contain all objects in the subtree. It makes use of a priority queue of objects sorted by distance from q. The queue is initialized with the root BB of the index. Objects are successively removed from the queue. Data objects are reported as they are dequeued. Internal nodes are expanded when they are dequeued by inserting each element in the node into the queue. This process continues until a maximum number of elements are reported, a maximum distance is reached, or there are no more elements in the queue.

Motion of a spatial object can be represented in several ways. The most common is samples, or discretely moving points [12]. For example, the motion of an aircraft can be represented by sampling its location using radar every 6 seconds. The problem with this representation is that the costs of updating every aircraft's location in a database every 6 seconds, and maintaining queries between updates, are prohibitive.

A *kinematic*[1] representation is an alternative to sampling. Kinematics represents the extent and location of an object as a function of time. In particular, a moving point can be represented by the linear function $p(t) = \vec{x_0} + (t - t_0)\vec{v}$, where $\vec{x_0}$ is the start location, t_0 is the start time, and $\vec{v}$ its velocity vector. The coefficients of this function are stored in the database for each point. When the speed or direction of an object changes, the database is updated. For example, if an aircraft moving east at 500 miles per hour turns to head south, then the the function describing its motion is updated with a new velocity vector to reflect the new direction of travel. Errors that may arise due to discrepancies between the kinematic model of the objects motion, and the actual location of an object are beyond the scope of this paper. Kinematic data types have been studied in other domains such as simulation [13] (i.e, dead reckoning) to reduce network traffic in distributed simulations, and computational geometry [1] (i.e., kinematics). Kinematic data types, along with an event-driven query processing algorithm are discussed further in [10].

Spatial indexes are used to support spatial queries. They help aggregate objects and prune the search space by organizing objects either in an object hierarchy, such as the R-tree [6], or a spatial decomposition, such as the quadtree [18]. More recently, the indexing of moving objects has also been addressed [17, 21].

The *TPR-tree* [17] indexes moving objects described as a function of time. It is a disk-based object hierarchy R-tree variant. In the R-tree, each node is stored in one disk page. Each node has an associated minimum bounding box (MBB). Leaf nodes contain the MBBs for the indexed objects themselves. Each internal node has an MBB for each subtree spatially bounding the objects in the subtree. In the TPR-tree, a bounding box (BB) is a moving hyper-rectangle specified by two moving points defining opposite corners of the BB. The corner points are chosen so that the BB will always spatially contain the moving objects within it. The BBs in the TPR-tree rarely stay minimal, tending to grow faster than what would be the minimum bounding box at any given time. This is partly compensated for

---

[1]Kinematics is the branch of mechanics that studies the motion of a body or a system of bodies without giving any consideration to its mass or the forces acting on it.

by the TPR-tree update algorithms. As an update occurs, the BB is adjusted to be minimal at the update time. Another compensatory action is that the tpr-tree insertion algorithm tries to insert objects moving in a similar manner (e.g., speed, direction), or to a similar destination, into the same leaf node.

Event-driven query processing is used to maintain queries on kinematic data types. This is similar to event-driven simulation [4], but instead of maintaining a simulation state, events are used to maintain query results as time advances. Events are processed in turn to keep query results consistent as objects move.

In [10], two basic types of events are defined. One basic type, the *within event* (w-event) occurs when two objects move to be at a given distance d to a query object. For a linear point kinematic data type, the time of a within event is based on solving the Euclidean distance equation $|p(time), q(time)| = d$ for *time*, where p and q are two moving points. This results in a closed form quadratic equation. See [15, 20] for more details on the computation of events between pairs of moving spatial objects. The other basic type of event is the *order change event* (oc-event). The oc-event occurs when two objects change order with respect to their distance to a query object. For query point q, and two other points p_1 and p_2, the time of their oc-events is based on solving the equation $|p_1(time), q(time)| = |p_2(time), q(time)|$ for *time* (see [15, 20] for details). A special case of an oc-event is a *nearest neighbor event* (nn-event). Given a query object and its current k^{th} neighbor, the nn-event is the soonest oc-event to occur in the future out of all possible future oc-events among the objects in the data set. For example, suppose that q is a query point, p_k is its current k^{th} neighbor, and S is a set of kinematic data points $S = \{s_1...s_n\}$. For each point $s_i \in S$, if s_i is closer to q than p_k, then the next oc-event e_i of point s_i occurs the next time when s_i moves to become farther from q than p_k. If s_i is farther from q than p_k, then the next oc-event e_i of point s_i occurs the next time when s_i moves to become closer to q than p_k. The next nn-event for q, p_k, and S is the soonest oc-event e_i of all future oc-events $\{e_1...e_n\}$. The time of the next nn-event is the next time in the future the kth neighbor of q will change.

An *incremental within event query* is similar to an incremental distance query, except that an event time metric is used instead of a distance metric [20]. An incremental within event query returns all the objects and the time at which they will enter the region within a given distance d around a query object q, one at a time, in increasing order of event time. If the distance $d = 0$ then the event time will be the time the objects will intersect, or cease to intersect one another. The algorithm assumes an object hierarchy tree index on the moving objects (e.g., the tpr tree) for which internal nodes have bounding boxes (BB) that continually contain all the moving objects in each subtree. The algorithm is identical to the incremental distance query [9] (see above), except that the priority queue is sorted by within event time instead of by the distance from q. The within event time for an internal node BB will always be less than or equal to the within event times of the objects it contains.

A *next nearest neighbor event query* finds the next nearest neighbor given a query object and its current nearest neighbor. In [20], Tao and Papadias describe a method for finding the next nn-event given a query object, the current k^{th} neighbor, and a set of data points indexed in a tpr tree. To find the next event, the bounding box (BB) of each node is examined and the node is placed on a global priority queue sorted by the oc-event time of its BB. Processing starts with the root node of the tpr tree. The first object on the queue is dequeued and expanded, repeating the process recursively. When the first leaf node is examined, the object in the leaf with the soonest oc-event time is saved along with its event as the candidate nn-event. If the next BB on the queue has an oc-event sooner than the candidate nn-event, then it is expanded. And objects in a subsequent leaf node with an oc-event sooner than the candidate nn-event replaces the candidate. When the oc-event time of the next node on the queue is later than the candidate, then the candidate oc-event is returned as the next nn-event and processing stops.

The next nn-event query supports the time parameterized k-NN algorithm (TP KNN) presented in [20]. This computes a k-nn query on kinematic objects, and then finds the next nn-event that will change the result. An even more efficient continuous k-nn algorithm is presented in [20] for finding many subsequent nn-events. Neither of these algorithms support updates.

The *continuous windowing* (CW) k-nn algorithm presented in [10] uses the w-event and oc-event types, the incremental within event query [20], along with an event-driven query processing algorithm to maintain k-nn queries. The idea is to filter the points from the data set with a circular window query centered at a moving query point, and then maintain the k nearest neighbors from the filtered result. At least k points must be selected in the filtering step. The window query is maintained by processing within events to keep a running set of points W that are within a given distance d of the query point. The k neighbors and next nn-event are computed from the points in W. The motivation for this approach is that within events are much cheaper than nn-events to process. This is because, an nn-event changes the kth neighbor rendering all previous oc-events involving the old k^{th} neighbor obsolete. Within events, on the other hand, are independent of the query result.

3 Approach

The *continuous fuzzy set* (CFS) semijoin algorithm maintains a semijoin query result $Q \ltimes_k D$ on the sets of kinematic points Q and D as time advances and updates occur.

The main algorithm is a simple event-driven query processing algorithm that supports updates similar to the one presented in [10]. Events are placed on a priority queue sorted by time and dequeued one at a time for processing. There is one and only one nn-event or underflow event (described below) on the event queue for each query point in Q. Updates (insertions and deletions) are also processed as they occur. The assumption on updates is that there is no priori knowledge of updates, such as is the case in a real-time system.

The *fuzzy set* of a query point $q \in Q$ consists of all the points $S = \{s_1...s_n\}$, where $s_i \subset D$, that are now or will be within some given distance of q sometime in the near future. This maintains a cloud of points around each query point. The next nn-event for any given point $q \in Q$ is computed from q's fuzzy set.

A fuzzy set is determined by a circle (or hypersphere for higher dimensional data) centered at q and with radius r known as the *query circle*. Radius r is chosen so that there are at least k points within distance r of q. The points in the circle, along with points that will enter the circle sometime in the near future, make up the fuzzy set of q. Scalar value r is generally a different value for each query point $q \in Q$. This region around the query point is denoted circle(q, r).

Time is divided up into uniform segments of time called fuzzy-set-intervals. The *fuzzy-set-interval* determines which points entering circle(q, r) belong to the fuzzy set. Only points that enter circle(q, r) during the current fuzzy-set-interval are in q's fuzzy set. At the start of each new fuzzy-set-interval, each query point's fuzzy set is updated (see Update_Fuzzy_Set() below).

Figure 1 illustrates an example fuzzy set for a single query point q in set Q, and data points $\{$**a,b,c,d,e,f,g,h,i**$\}$ $\in D$. Assume for this example, that the length of the arrows in the figure indicate how far each point will travel in one minute. In this example, the query point is not moving for simplicity. Also, assume for this example, that the current fuzzy-set-interval will end in one minute. In this example, all the points in circle(**q**, r), and all the points that will enter circle(**q**, r) within the next minute (up to the end of the current fuzzy-set-interval), are in the fuzzy set of point **q**. The length of each fuzzy-set-interval is a system parameter. Points $\{$**a,b,c,f,g,i**$\}$ are in the fuzzy set of query point **q**. Note that point **d** is closer to the circle than point **c**, but it is moving slower and will not enter the circle during the next minute.

An *underflow event* occurs when the kth neighbor of some query point q leaves circle(q, r). When this happens, r has to be increased to encompass more data points in circle(q, r). Underflow events are denoted by uf(q, p_k, t), where $q \in Q$ is the query point, $p_k \in D$ is the current k^{th} neighbor of q, and t is the underflow event time. For example, suppose that the query for Figure 1 is $Q \ltimes_3 D$, that is, for each point in Q find the 3 nearest neighbors in D. Point **g** is currently the 3rd nearest neighbor from

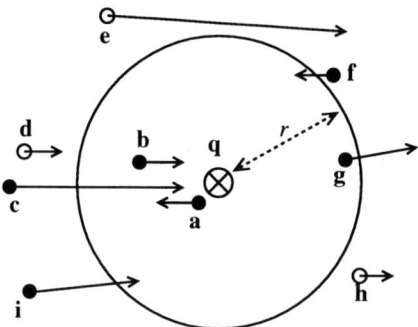

Figure 1: Example fuzzy set, where $\otimes$ is the query point **q**, • indicate points in **q**'s fuzzy set, and ○ indicate points not in the fuzzy set.

point **q**. Recall from Section 1, the subscript k for a semi-join $Q \ltimes_k D$ denotes the number of nearest neighbors in D to be found for every point in Q. Suppose that point **g** will leave circle(**q**, r) at time $t_\mathbf{g}$, then the underflow event is uf(**q**, **g**, $t_\mathbf{g}$). The component members of an underflow event are denoted by query_pt(uf(q, p_k, t)) = q, kth_pt(uf(q, p_k, t)) = p_k, and time(uf(q, p_k, t)) = t. For the sake of consistency with nn-event notation (described below) we define other_pt(uf(q, p_k, t)) = p_k.

An nn-event is denoted by nn(q, r, p_k, o, t), where q is the query point, r is the radius of circle(q, r), p_k is the kth neighbor of q, o is the other data point that will become the new k^{th} neighbor at event time t. For example, suppose that the query for Figure 1 is $Q \ltimes_1 D$, that is, for each point in Q find the nearest neighbor in D. Point **a** is currently the nearest neighbor of point **q**. Let the time for the next oc-event between points **a**, **c**, and **q** be time $t_{\mathbf{a},\mathbf{c}}$. Also, suppose that this is the next oc-event out of all the oc-events among the points in **q**'s fuzzy set. In this case, the nn-event for point **q** is nn(**q**, r, **a**, **c**, $t_{\mathbf{a},\mathbf{c}}$). To support fuzzy sets, the radius of the query circle is stored with the nn-event. The radius is not part of the definition of the nn-event itself, but it will be needed when the nn-event is processed. The component members of an nn-event are denoted by query_pt(nn(q, r, p_k, o, t)) = q, radius(nn(q, r, p_k, o, t)) = r, kth_pt(nn(q, r, p_k, o, t)) = p_k, other_pt(nn(q, r, p_k, o, t)) = o, and time(nn(q, r, p_k, o, t)) = t.

3.1 Data Structures

The event queue E-queue is a priority queue of events (underflow and nn-events) sorted by time. It is made up of three data structures. The first is a B+-tree variant called the *nearest neighbor event B-tree* (NN-B-tree). Every point p is assumed to have an associated unique id denoted id(p). The NN-B-tree B+-tree is sorted on the key id(query_pt(e)) and yields the event values e (i.e., id(query_pt(e)) $\rightarrow e$). In addition to implementing a range tree on id(query_pt(e)), the B+-tree is augmented to implement a heap in the event times. In particular, in addition to the minimum and maximum keys, the minimum event time for a subtree in the NN-B-tree is propagated up to the root. Thus the result is a variant of a priority search tree [11]. Figure 2 shows an example NN-B-tree. The next event time is found by examining the root node, and returning the minimum event time in the root. To obtain the next event, the tree is traversed from its root to the leaf by following the minimum event time down the branches of the tree. The NN-B-tree allows efficient updates based on the id of query points from Q. However, in order to efficiently perform updates using a data point id as a key, additional data structures are needed. The K-B-tree is a standard B+-tree sorted by key $id(kth\_pt(e))$ yielding the value $id(query\_pt(e))$ (i.e., $id(kth\_pt(e)) \rightarrow id(query\_pt(e))$). The O-B-tree is a standard B+-tree sorted by key $id(other\_pt(e))$ yielding the value $id(query\_pt(e))$ (i.e., $id(other\_pt(e)) \rightarrow id(query\_pt(e))$).

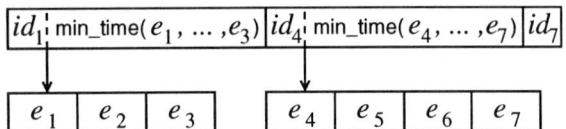

Figure 2: Example NN-B-tree with one root node, and two leaf nodes, where $id_i = id(query\_pt(e_i))$.

Together, these three data structures NN-B-tree, K-B-tree, O-B-tree and their algorithms form the event queue E-queue. The algorithm to insert an event e is given in Figure 3. The algorithm to delete an event, given a query point q, is given in Figure 4. These are straight-forward since there is one and only one event for each query point in Q. The algorithm to delete all events involving a given data point p is more complicated since there may be many events involving p in the queue. The algorithm is given in Figure 5. First, all query points q for which p is the kth neighbor are considered (line 1). The event for each q is found (line 2), then all the entries involving q are removed from the three B+-trees; O-B-tree, NN-B-tree, K-B-tree (lines 3–5). Since $id(q)$ is unique, there is only one entry for a given q in each B+-tree. Second, all query points q are considered where p is the other point involved in q's event (line 7). Likewise, each entry for each of these query points are deleted from the three B+-trees (lines 8–11).

procedure E-queue_Insert(e)
1. Insert $id(query\_pt(e)) \rightarrow e$ into NN-B-tree.
2. Insert $id(kth\_pt(e)) \rightarrow id(query\_pt(e))$ into K-B-tree.
3. Insert $id(other\_pt(e)) \rightarrow id(query\_pt(e))$ into O-B-tree.

Figure 3: E-queue_Insert()

procedure E-queue_Delete_QueryPt(q)
1. Find entry $id(q) \rightarrow e$ in NN-B-tree.
2. Delete entry $id(kth\_pt(e)) \rightarrow id(q)$ from K-B-tree.
3. Delete entry $id(other\_pt(e)) \rightarrow id(q)$ from O-B-tree.
4. Delete entry $id(q) \rightarrow e$ from NN-B-tree.

Figure 4: E-queue_Delete_QueryPt()

To manage fuzzy sets, another set of data structures is

procedure E-queue_Delete_All_DataPt(p)
1. **foreach** $id(p) \rightarrow id(q)$ in K-B-tree **do**
2.   Find entry $id(q) \rightarrow e$ in NN-B-tree.
3.   Delete $id(other\_pt(e)) \rightarrow id(q)$ from O-B-tree.
4.   Delete entry $id(q) \rightarrow e$ from NN-B-tree.
5.   Delete entry $id(p) \rightarrow id(q)$ from K-B-tree.
6. **end foreach**
7. **foreach** $id(p) \rightarrow id(q)$ in O-B-tree **do**
8.   Find entry $id(q) \rightarrow e$ in NN-B-tree.
9.   Delete entry $id(kth\_pt(e)) \rightarrow id(q)$ from K-B-tree.
10.   Delete entry $id(q) \rightarrow e$ from NN-B-tree.
11.   Delete entry $id(p) \rightarrow id(q)$ from O-B-tree.
12. **end foreach**

Figure 5: E-queue_Delete_All_DataPt()

used. The fuzzy set index (FS-index) keeps track of points in fuzzy sets, and the time the points will expire from each fuzzy set. The FS-index utilizes two B+-trees. The first B+-tree is the FS-B-tree. It is sorted by $id(q)$ yielding the value $\{q, p, t\}$ (i.e., $id(q) \rightarrow \{q, p, t\}$), where $q \in Q$, $p \in D$, and t is the *expiration time* for p. The expiration time is the time when p leaves $circle(q, r)$ and is no longer part of q's fuzzy set.

The other B+-tree used by the FS-index is the ID-B-tree. It is sorted by $id(p)$ yielding $id(q)$ (i.e., $id(p) \rightarrow id(q)$). It serves a similar purpose as the K-B-tree or O-B-tree for the E-queue to support deletions of data points. Together, the FS-B-tree and the ID-B-tree form the FS-index. The algorithms to insert and delete objects in the FS-index are similar to those for the E-queue, but simpler since there are only two B+-trees involved.

Two tpr indexes [17] are used by the CFS algorithm. One index is on the query circles $circle(q, r)$ rather than the query points in set Q. A second tpr index used by CFS is on the set of data points D.

3.2 CFS Algorithms

The *main loop* of the event-driven algorithm processes events and updates as they occur to maintain the query result over the moving points. The main loop invokes procedures Process_Event(), Update_Fuzzy_Set(), Insert_Data_Point(), Delete_Data_Point(), Insert_Query_Point(), and Delete_Query_Point() as needed (see below). Updates are not known in advance of their occurrence as we are assuming a real-time system. Processing continues indefinitely.

When an event on the E-queue comes due, it is dequeued and passed to Process_Event() (Figure 6). Every query point has either an nn-event, or an underflow event associated with it in the event queue, E-queue, even if the event time is ∞. This is done so that every query point and its kth neighbor can be found simply by examining the queue. For an nn-event (line 2), if $other\_pt(e)$ was not previously part of the k-neighbor-set for q (line 3), then it pushes the current k^{th} neighbor out of the set and $other\_pt(e)$ becomes the new k^{th} neighbor. This necessitates an update to the query result. The query re-

procedure Process_Event(e)
1. Point $q \leftarrow$ query_pt(e)
2. **if** e is an nn-event **then**
3.   **if** kth_pt(e) is becoming $k+1$ neighbor of q **then**
4.   update the query result
5.   Get all entries for q from FS-index, and remove expired points to get fuzzy set S.
6.   **if** count of expired points > *expired_threshold* **then**
7.   remove all expired entries for q from FS-index
8.   Enqueue_Event(S, q, radius(e), kth_pt(e))
9. **else if** e is an underflow event **then**
10.   Handle_Underflow(q)

Figure 6: Process_Event()

sult is updated by reporting ⟨kth_pt(e), q⟩ deleted, and ⟨other_pt(e), q⟩ inserted (line 4). For example, suppose that the query for Figure 1 is $Q \ltimes_1 D$, that is, for each point in Q find the nearest neighbor in D. Point **a** is currently the nearest neighbor of point **q**. The event on the queue for point **q** is nn(**q**, r, **a**, **c**, $t_{\mathbf{a},\mathbf{c}}$), where time $t_{\mathbf{a},\mathbf{c}}$ is the time points **a** and point **c** will be equidistant from point **q**. When this event comes due and is processed, point **c** pushes point **a** out of the k-neighbor-set (in this case the 1-neighbor-set) of point **q**, and becomes the new nearest neighbor.

If, on the other hand, other_pt(e) was already part of the k-neighbor-set, then it simply becomes the new k^{th} neighbor, and the current k^{th} neighbor becomes the $k-1$ neighbor. For example, suppose that the query for Figure 1 is $Q \ltimes_2 D$, that is, for each point in Q find the 2 nearest neighbors in D. Point **b** is currently the 2nd nearest neighbor from point **q**. In this example, the nn-event for point **q** is nn(**q**, r, **b**, **a**, $t_{\mathbf{b},\mathbf{a}}$), because point **a** will be the first to be equidistant with point **b** from point **q** before any other point in point **q**'s fuzzy set. When nn(**q**, r, **b**, **a**, $t_{\mathbf{b},\mathbf{a}}$) comes due at time $t_{\mathbf{b},\mathbf{a}}$, point **a** becomes the new k^{th} neighbor (2nd neighbor), but point **b** stays in the 2-neighbor-set of point **q**, so the query result does not change. However, since the 2nd neighbor changed, a new nn-event for point **q** must be calculated and enqueued.

The new nn-event is calculated from q's fuzzy set. The fuzzy set S for q is stored in the FS-index. All points in the FS-index that have not expired are in q's current fuzzy set (line 5). A point expires from the fuzzy set when it leaves the circle around q. If the number of expired points exceeds a certain threshold, then all expired points for q are removed from the FS-index (line 6) This keeps down the number of expired entries in the FS-index. The fuzzy set S is used to compute the next event for q (line 8) (see description of Enqueue_Event() below). An *underflow event* occurs when circle(q, r) contains less than k points (line 9). When underflow occurs, the fuzzy set must be expanded (line 10) (see description of Handle_Underflow() below).

Enqueue_Event() (Figure 7), called from line 8 of Figure 6, computes the next event for a query point from its fuzzy set. The current k^{th} neighbor is removed from the fuzzy set S (line 1). The remaining points in fuzzy set S are each considered for the next nn-event by computing each of

procedure Enqueue_Event(S, q, r, p_k)
1. $S \leftarrow (S - p_k)$
2.   Find the next nn-event e from among the points in S.
3.   **if** kth_pt(e) will expire before e occurs **then**
4.   enqueue an underflow event for q in E-queue.
5.   **else** enqueue e in E-queue.

Figure 7: Enqueue_Event()

their next occurring order change events (oc-events) in turn (line 2). Recall from Section 2 that an oc-event for a data point p occurs when p moves to be at the same distance to q as its current k^{th} neighbor. The soonest oc-event becomes the next nn-event (line 5), unless circle(q, r) underflows sooner. In that case, an underflow event is enqueued instead (line 4).

procedure Handle_Underflow(q)
1.   Remove all entries for q from FS-index.
2. $n \leftarrow \lceil k*circle\_factor \rceil$
3.   Get new set S of $n+1$ neighbors around q.
4. $r \leftarrow (\|q, s_n\| + \|q, s_{n+1}\|)/2$, where $s_n, s_{n+1} \in S$
5.   Remove s_{n+1} from S.
6.   Add points to S that will enter circle(q, r) during the current fuzzy-set-interval.
7.   Insert points S, and their expiration times into FS-index.
8.   Enqueue_Event(S, q, r, s_k), where $s_k \in S$ is the kth neighbor of q.
9.   Remove old circle centered at q from query point tpr tree, and insert circle(q, r).

Figure 8: Handle_Underflow()

Handle_Underflow() (Figure 8), called from line 10 of Figure 6, resizes the fuzzy set for a query point. The old fuzzy set needs to be removed from the FS-index, since the radius defining the expiration times for the points in the old fuzzy set will change (line 1). The circle around q is calculated to initially contain some multiple of k points. The global constant *circle_factor* > 1 is used to determine how many points to start with in a circle (line 2). An incremental distance algorithm [9] (see Section 2) is used to get the $n+1$ neighbors of q using the tpr index on the data points (line 3). The $n+1$ neighbor, s_{n+1}, is used to determine the radius of the new circle. The new radius is the average of the distances from q to the nth neighbor, s_n, and q to s_{n+1} (line 4). Note that the Euclidean distance at the current time between two kinematic points q and p is denoted $\|q, p\|$. This technique for finding the radius helps to avoid the situation where points instantly leave the circle after it is resized. Once the radius is computed, s_{n+1} is discarded from the set S because it is outside the circle (line 5). The rest of the fuzzy set is found using an incremental within event algorithm [20] (see Section 2) on the tpr index on the data points (line 6). At this point S contains all the points in q's new fuzzy set. The points in fuzzy set S are inserted into the FS-index along with their expiration times (line 7). The next nn-event is computed from the points in S and enqueued (line 8). Finally, the tpr index on the query circles is updated (line 9).

For example, suppose that the query for Figure 1 is

$Q \bowtie_1 D$, that is, for each point in Q find the nearest neighbor in D. Point **a** is currently the nearest neighbor of point **q**. Also suppose that the radius of the circle is not r as in the figure, but is smaller, and suppose that an underflow event has just occurred. In other words, the radius of the circle is at the distance from point **q** that point **a** is at right now, say r_{old}. Suppose also that *circle_factor* = 3. When Handle_Underflow() is invoked, we get $n = 1 * 3 = 3$ (line 2). We then find the $n + 1$, or 4 nearest neighbors to point **q** (line 3). Set S now contains points {**a, b, g, f**}. The new distance r (the large circle in Figure 1) is calculated to be halfway between point **g** and point **f** from point **q** (line 4). Once r is computed, the 4th neighbor of q is removed from S leaving {**a, b, g**} (line 5). Suppose that the end of the current fuzzy-set-interval is one minute in the future. All the points that will enter circle(**q**, r) before the end of the current fuzzy-set-interval (e.g., within the next minute) are added to set S to give {**a,b,c,f,g,i**} (line 6). In this case, point **f** ends up back in set S, but it would not if it were moving away from the circle. The points {**a,b,c,f,g,i**}, along with their expiration times are inserted into the FS-index (line 7). They are also used to find the next nn-event (line 8). The old circle circle(**q**, r_{old}) is removed from the circle tpr tree and the new circle circle(**q**, r) is inserted (line 9).

procedure Update_Fuzzy_Set()
1. **foreach** circle(q, r) in the query circle tpr tree **do**
2.   Add new points to q's fuzzy set S that will enter circle(q, r) during the current fuzzy-set-interval.
3.   Find the next nn-event e from among the points in S.
4.   **if** e occurs before the currently enqueued event for q
5.   **then** replace currently enqueued event with e.
6. **end foreach**

Figure 9: Update_Fuzzy_Set()

Update_Fuzzy_Set() (Figure 9) is invoked at the start of each new fuzzy-set-interval to update the fuzzy set for each query point. This finds all the data points that will enter query circles during the new fuzzy-set-interval segment of time. The tpr index on the query circles is scanned to get all the query circle circle(q, r) (line 1). The fuzzy set S for each q is updated by finding all the new data points entering circle(q, r) using an incremental within event algorithm [20] (see Section 2) on the data point tpr index (line 2). The current k^{th} neighbor $s_k \in S$ is found, and then the nn-event e from the rest of the points in S is computed (line 3). This is done by considering each point $s_i \in S, i \neq k$ for the next nn-event by computing each s_i's next oc-event with respect to s_k and q. The soonest oc-event out of all is the next nn-event e. If e occurs before the event that is currently in the event queue E-queue for q, then e replaces the one on the queue for point q (line 5).

Insert_Data_Point() (Figure 10) is invoked when a new point p is added to the set of data points D in the semi-join query $Q \bowtie_k D$. The query circle tpr index is used to find all circle(q, r)'s that currently contain, or will contain

procedure Insert_Data_Point(p)
1. **foreach** circle(q, r) with p in q's fuzzy set **do**
2.   **if** p is in the k-neighbor-set of q **then**
3.   Update the query result.
4.   Remove q's event from the E-queue.
5.   Get all entries for q from FS-index, and remove expired points to get fuzzy set S.
6.   Enqueue_Event(S, q, r, s_k), where $s_k \in S$ is the kth neighbor of q.
7.   **else if** p introduces a sooner nn-event for q **then**
8.   Replace the nn-event for q in E-queue.
9.   **end if-else-if**
10. **end foreach**
11. Insert p into the data point tpr index.

Figure 10: Insert_Data_Point()

p between now and the end of the current fuzzy-set-interval (line 1). In particular, this entails the performance of two operations using the query circle tpr index. The first finds all the circles that currently contain point p using a within distance $d = 0$ query [9]. The second uses an incremental within event algorithm [20] (see Section 2) to find all the circles that will contain p before the end of the fuzzy-set-interval. Each query circle circle(q, r) is processed in turn. If p is closer to a given q than the kth neighbor of q, then it is in the k-neighbor-set of q (line 2). Point q's entry in the event queue can be used to find the kth neighbor of q since both nn-events and underflow events keep track of the kth neighbor. When p is in the k-neighbor-set of q, then the current k^{th} neighbor becomes the $k + 1$ neighbor. The entry involving the old k^{th} neighbor $\langle k^{th}, q \rangle$ is removed from the query result and the new entry $\langle p, q \rangle$ is added (line 3). When the kth neighbor changes, the nn-event or underflow event changes as well, so the old event needs to be removed from E-queue (line 4). The new event is calculated from the fuzzy set of q (lines 5–6). If p is not in the k-neighbor-set, then it may still affect the next nn-event. If p's next oc-event occurs before the current nn-event for q, then the oc-event becomes the new nn-event, and replaces the old nn-event on the queue (lines 7–8). After all circles have been processed, the tpr index on the data points is updated (line 11).

Delete_Data_Point() (Figure 11) is invoked when a data point p is deleted from the set of data points D in the semi-join query $Q \bowtie_k D$. First, p is removed from the data point tpr index (line 1), and FS-index (line 2). All the circles that contain p, or would contain p during the current fuzzy-set-interval are processed in turn (line 3). These circles are found by applying an incremental distance [9], and incremental event algorithm [20] (see Section 2) on the data point tpr index. If p is the current k^{th} neighbor, or closer to a given q than its kth neighbor, then the events and query result change (line 4). The current $k + 1$ neighbor becomes the kth neighbor. After the old event for q is removed from the event queue (line 5), the fuzzy set S is found (line 6), and checked for underflow (line 7). Underflow results in a resizing of the fuzzy set, and a new nn-event is enqueued (line 8). If the fuzzy set does not underflow, then a new

procedure Delete_Data_Point(p)
1. Remove p from the data point tpr index.
2. Remove all entries involving p from FS-index.
3. **foreach** circle(q, r) with p in q's fuzzy set **do**
4.   **if** p is in the k-neighbor-set of q **then**
5.   Remove q's event from the E-queue.
6.   Get all entries for q from FS-index, and remove expired points to get fuzzy set S.
7.   **if** number of data points in circle(q, r) $< k$ **then**
8.   Handle_Underflow(q)
9.   **else**
10.   Enqueue_Event(S, q, r, s_k),
            where $s_k \in S$ is the new k^{th} neighbor of q.
11.   Update query result.
12.   **else if** p is involved in q's enqueued event **then**
13.   Remove q's event from the E-queue.
14.   Get all entries for q from FS-index, and remove expired points to get fuzzy set S.
15.   Enqueue_Event(S, q, r, s_k),
         where $s_k \in S$ is the new k^{th} neighbor of q.
16.   **end if-else-if**
17. **end foreach**

Figure 11: Delete_Data_Point()

nn-event is enqueued given the new k^{th} neighbor (line 10). The result is updated by deleting the old k^{th} neighbor and inserting the new one (line 11). When p is not in the k-neighbor-set, but is involved in the nn-event for q (line 12), then the nn-event changes. In particular, the new nn-event is found from the points in q's fuzzy set S, replacing the old nn-event in the queue (lines 13–15).

procedure Insert_Query_Point(q)
1. $n \leftarrow \lceil k * circle\_factor \rceil$
2. Get new set S of $n + 1$ neighbors around q.
3. $r \leftarrow (\|q, s_n\| + \|q, s_{n+1}\|)/2$, where $s_n, s_{n+1} \in S$
4. Remove s_{n+1} from S.
5. Add points to S that will enter circle(q, r) during the current fuzzy-set-interval.
6. Insert points S, and their expiration times into FS-index.
7. Enqueue_Event(S, q, r, s_k),
   where $s_k \in S$ is the kth neighbor of q.
8. Report $\langle s_i, q \rangle$ inserted to result for the closest k points $s_i \in S$ to q.
9. Insert circle(q, r) into query circle tpr index.

Figure 12: Insert_Query_Point()

Insert_Query_Point() (Figure 12) is invoked when a query point is inserted into Q in the semijoin query $Q \ltimes_k D$. This procedure is similar to Handle_Underflow() except that there are no previous entries for q in FS-index or the query circle tpr index to remove. Lines 1–7 are identical to lines 2–8 of Figure 8. Before finishing, the k neighbors of q are added to the query result (line 8), and the query circle is indexed (line 9).

procedure Delete_Query_Point(q)
1. Delete the current k neighbors to q from query result.
2. Remove any entries for q from FS-index, E-queue, and the query point tpr index.

Figure 13: Delete_Query_Point()

Delete_Query_Point() (Figure 13) is invoked when a query point is deleted. It first updates the query result (line 1). This is done by applying an incremental distance algorithm [9] (see Section 2) on the data point tpr tree with q as the query point to determine what entries to delete. It then removes any entires involving the query point q from all the data structures (line 2).

4 CFS vs. CW

The CFS algorithm somewhat resembles the CW k-nn algorithm for one query point presented in [10]. However, there are significant differences. The similarity is that both approaches maintain a circular region around a query point with the constraint that it contain at least k points at all times. This filters the data points for candidates from which to select the k nearest neighbors.

The differences are in the other ways in which the circles are used. In the CW algorithm, the nn-event is computed from only those points found inside the query circle. In the CFS algorithm, points entering the circle in the near future are also considered for the next nn-event. This reduces the number of "false" nn-events that need to be changed before they occur when new candidates enter the widow of the CW algorithm. The CFS algorithm introduces the notion of fuzzy-set-intervals to limit which points are considered for the nn-event. Points entering the window in the distant future are not likely to be involved in the next nn-event. In the CW algorithm, within events are used to process points entering the window of a single query point. The CFS algorithm does not process within events as they occur. Instead, it only processes nn-events and underflow events for each query point. Within events are used in the CFS algorithm to determine when fuzzy set elements will expire.

To scale the CW algorithm to handle many query points at the same time, additional data structures would be needed to keep track of nn-events, the contents of each query circle, the size of each query circle, and underflow. This, in addition to the sheer number of within events that would need to be queued and processed makes scaling the CW algorithm an inferior solution to the CFS algorithm.

5 Experiments

For the purpose of evaluating our algorithm, we scale up an existing k-nn algorithm to perform semijoin queries. We then compare the simple scaling of the previous work to the CFS algorithm.

In [10], the TP k-nn algorithm [20] was extended to support updates (presented as the ETP algorithm in [10]). Here, we scale up the ETP algorithm to do semijoins in addition to updates. We call the extension to perform semijoins the TP-semijoin (TPS) algorithm. To scale the ETP algorithm to perform semijoins, an event queue containing an nn-event for each query point is added. If for some query point q, no such event exists, then a pseudo event nn(q, p_k, p_k, ∞) is added to keep track of the current k^{th} neighbor p_k. When an update occurs, the event queue is scanned to determine what part of the query result, and which events need to be modified. If the set of k neighbors changes due to an update, then new neighbors and events are found using a tpr index on the data points similar to what was done in the ETP algorithm in [10]. No tpr index for the query points is needed since all the query points are in the event queue.

As discussed above (Section 4), the CW algorithm also presented in [10] would not scale well because there would be too many within events to process. Note that a straightforward scaling of the CW algorithm given in [10] can be achieved by adding an nn-event queue in addition to the within event queue. In preliminary results, scaling of the CW algorithm was found to be significantly less efficient than the TPS algorithm.

5.1 Data Sets

We used both real aircraft flight data and synthetic uniformly-distributed data in our experiments. Data sets consist of an initial set of moving points described as a linear function of time ($p(t) = \vec{x_0} + (t-t_0)\vec{v}$), and updates to the function coefficients ($\vec{x_0}, t_0, \vec{v}$) over time. A data set is characterized by the mean and standard deviation in the number of moving points (cardinality) at any given time, the period of time covered by the data set, and the average update interval. The average update interval (UI) is the average length of time between updates for any given point.

All synthetic uniformly-distributed data sets are generated using a data generation tool developed by Saltenis et. al. [17]. The synthetic moving points are uniformly distributed over a 1000x1000 coordinate space. The speed of each point is uniformly distributed between 0 and $3/60 = 0.05$ coordinate distance units per time unit. All synthetic moving points are inserted at the start time of the dataset. Updates change the speed, but not the current location of each point. No new points are introduced after the start time, nor are any removed. The average update interval (UI) for our synthetic data is 600 time units. Each synthetic data set covers 3600 time units. The UI and speed relative to the size of the coordinate space of the synthetic data were chosen to be similar to the aircraft flight data for comparability.

Real commercial aircraft flight data was acquired as location data sampled at one minute intervals. Figure 14 shows an example snapshot in time to see how the data is clustered. The latitude-longitude of sampled locations were converted to linear functions describing aircraft motion by first applying the Douglas-Peucker line simplification algorithm [3] to the 2D latitude-longitude points forming a polyline from earliest to latest sampled location in time.[2] In our application of the Douglas-Peucker algorithm, we used a maximum error bound of $0.0\overline{6}$ degrees.

---

[2]Although experiments were conducted on 2-dimensional data, the al-

Distortions introduced by the latitude-longitude projection onto the Earth's surface was ignored. The resulting vertices serve as the start locations for each update. Each vertex has an associated time stamp. The line segment to the next vertex divided by the time difference between their time stamps gives the velocity vector for each update. The result was an average update interval of 700–735 seconds. The aircraft data sets cover a window [20°, 60°] latitude by [−135°, −60°] longitude. Since only about 5000 aircraft are in the air at any one time, larger data sets are generated by combining flights on different days during the same time period. Each aircraft data set covers a time period of two hours.

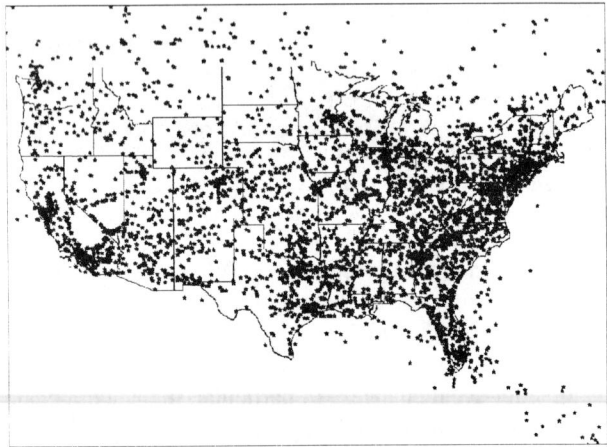

Figure 14: Snapshot of aircraft flight data.

One significant difference between the real and synthetic data is in the size of the data set at any given time. The number of points for the synthetic data stays constant, but the real flight data changes in the number of aircraft as flights land and take off. Figure 15 shows the mean and standard deviation in the size of the data sets used over the entire 2 hour time interval covered by each data set. The figure also shows the average update interval (UI) for each aircraft data set.

μ	4453	9021	12690	17106
σ	330.8	680.8	962.4	1293
UI	700.7	712.8	725.1	734.6

Figure 15: Each column corresponds to a different aircraft data set. Each row is a statistic on the data sets. Row 1 is the mean number of flights at any given time (μ). Row 2 is the standard deviation in the number of flights (σ). Row 3 is the average update interval (UI) in seconds.

To make full use of the real data sets available, each data set was divided into 12 subsets starting at evenly spaced start times over the duration of the data set. For example, for a data set covering a time period of 900 units, the subset start times are 0, 75, 150, etc. If the duration of the experiment is longer than the time between subsets, then

gorithms presented in this paper are applicable to higher dimensions.

the subsets overlaped. If needed, the spacing between start times was adjusted so the experiments didn't run past the time covered by the subset. For our 900 time unit example above, if the experiment duration is 100 time units, then the time between start times might be only 72 time units. The time domains of each subset were then transformed to start at time 0.

Each query was performed on combinations of these subsets, not including self semijoins. Pairs of subsets were chosen at random without replacement from all possible combinations for a total of 100 joins per query. Only subsets taken from the same original data set are used in a query, so the semijoin sets are approximately the same size for each query. In other words, the number of query points is about the same as the number of data points in each semijoin query. This technique was used on both the synthetic and real data sets for comparability.

5.2 Results

Experiments were conducted in a simulation of a real-time system in which semijoin queries are maintained over time as updates occur. The experiments measured the total number of disk accesses over the duration of a query. Since we are concerned primarily with the maintenance portion of the query, the number of disk accesses used to compute the initial join result are not included. The number of disk accesses over 100 trials was averaged to yield the experiment results for a given query.

The implementation of the event queue used the generalized search tree (GiST) [7] version 0.9beta1 code. The code was compiled using gcc 2.96. The experiments were run on several VLSI 80686 CPU based machines running Linux.

The primary independent variables for comparison are the mean data set size (μ), and number of neighbors (k) to find for each query point. For experiments where these do not vary, the defaults are $\mu = 9021$ for real aircraft data, $\mu = 10000$ for synthetic uniform data, and $k = 1$. Other general parameters, unless otherwise specified, are query duration of 130 seconds, disk page size of 4096 bytes, and disk cache size of 8 pages for each disk-based data structure.

Every cache page uses a least recently used (LRU) replacement policy except for the event queues. The event queues use a *Greatest Next Event* (GNE) replacement policy. GNE removes the page whose minimum next event time is the furthest in the future out of all pages in the cache. GNE worked better than LRU for small pages (e.g., 1024 bytes) and large caches (e.g., 32 pages). However, when the cache size was reduced, and the page size increased, we found nearly no difference between the LRU and GNE policies. Therefore, LRU can be used with nearly the same results as GNE.

Parameters specific to the CFS algorithm, unless otherwise specified, are *circle_factor* = 2, *expired_threshold* = 25 events, and fuzzy-set-interval duration of 128 time units to ensure that at least one call is made to Update_Fuzzy_Set() per each 130 second query. We found these particular settings for the CFS algorithm to be nearly optimal in our experiments.

The purpose of the first experiment is to determine which algorithm, TPS or CFS, performs better in terms of disk accesses for different data sets sizes. Figure 16 shows the results for (a) real aircraft flight data, and (b) uniform synthetic data. Parameter k is 1. The x-axis is the average data set size (see row 1 in Figure 15), and the y-axis is the number of disk accesses in millions (M). The points indicated by $\triangle$ symbols are the number of disk accesses for the CFS algorithm, while the $\diamond$ symbol indicates the number of disk accesses for the TPS algorithm. For the aircraft data, the CFS algorithm has 5 times fewer disk accesses than the TPS algorithm for the largest data sets tested. For the uniform synthetic data, the CFS algorithm has 10 times fewer disk accesses than the TPS algorithm for the largest data sets tested.

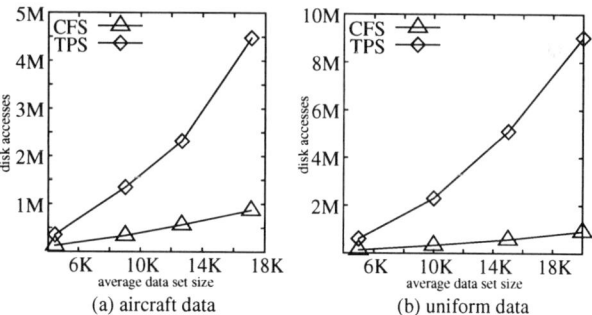

Figure 16: Disk accesses with respect to data set size.

The purpose of the second experiment is to determine the relative performance of the CFS algorithm to the TPS algorithm when k is varied. Figure 17 shows the results for (a) real aircraft flight data (data set size $\mu = 9021$), and (b) uniform synthetic data (data set size $\mu = 10000$). The x-axis is k, and the y-axis is the number of disk accesses in millions (M). The points indicated by $\triangle$ symbols are the number of disk accesses for the CFS algorithm, while the $\diamond$ symbol indicates the number of disk accesses for the TPS algorithm. The CFS algorithm has fewer accesses than the TPS algorithm, but the number of disk accesses for the CFS algorithm increases faster as the value of k is increased.

The purpose of the third experiment is to study the effect of *circle_factor* on the performance of the CFS algorithm. Figure 18a shows the results for real aircraft flight data (data set size $\mu = 4453$), and $k = 1$. The x-axis is the *circle_factor*, and the y-axis is the number of disk accesses in thousands (K). The points indicated by $\triangle$ symbols are the number of disk accesses for the CFS algorithm. Although the TPS algorithm is not affected by *circle_factor*, for comparison purposes, we show the number of disk accesses ($\diamond$ symbol) for this data. From Figure 18a it can be seen that a *circle_factor* value of 2 yields the best perfor-

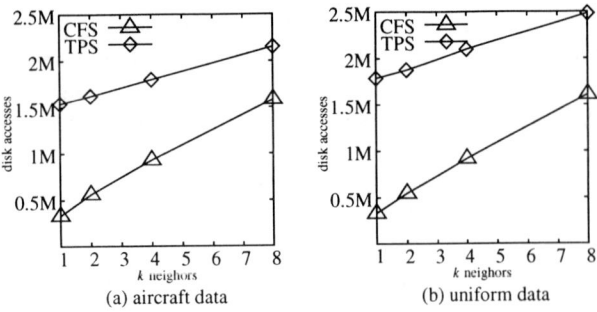

Figure 17: Disk accesses with respect to k with *circle_factor* = 2.

mance for the CFS algorithm with $k = 1$. A *circle_factor* < 2 for $k = 1$ is not meaningful since there needs to be at least $k + 1$ points inside a query circle when it is resized. As we see, larger *circle_factor* values do lead to more disk accesses for the CFS algorithm but this is still much lower than the number of disk accesses for the TPS algorithm.

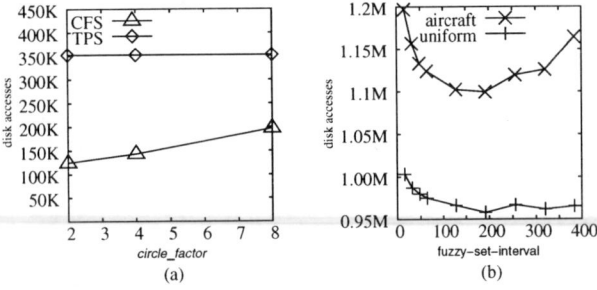

Figure 18: CW algorithm parameters. (a) Disk accesses vs. *circle_factor*. (b) Disk accesses vs. fuzzy-set-interval.

Figure 18b shows disk accesses (y-axis) versus different values for the CFS fuzzy-set-interval parameter (x-axis) for aircraft data ($\mu = 9021$), and $k = 1$. The $\times$ symbols indicate disk accesses for aircraft data, and the $+$ symbol indicates disk accesses for uniform data. Each point is an average over 50 trials. Small values (< 128) show increased disk activity due to more frequent calls to Update_Fuzzy_Set(). Larger values (> 192) show increased disk activity due to larger fuzzy sets for each point for the uniform data set. The reason why aircraft data does not exhibit the same performance characteristics as for uniform data for larger values of fuzzy-set-interval is unclear, and should be a topic for future research.

Data structure size: The implementation resulted in the following entry sizes. The tpr index entries were 32 bytes for internal node and leaf node entries. The NN-B-tree leaf node entries were 115 bytes, and internal node entries were 9 bytes. The FS-B-tree leaf node entries were 73 bytes, and internal node entries were 4 bytes. The K-B-tree, O-B-tree, and ID-B-tree leaf node entries were 8 bytes, and internal node entries were 4 bytes.

Given these numbers, we can estimate the size of the data structures under certain assumptions. Assume for query of $k = 1$ on data sets of size 20k, and page size of 4096 bytes, that 70% space utilization is achived. For each of the 20k query points, there is one event in the E-queue data structure. This gives $\lceil 20000/((4096*0.7)/115) \rceil = 803$ pages of leaf nodes in the NN-B-tree of the E-queue. and $\lceil 803/((4096*0.7)/9) \rceil = 3$ pages of internal nodes. This gives a total size of $(803 + 3) * 4069 = 3301376$ bytes on disk total for the NN-B-tree. For the K-B-tree and the O-B-tree we get $\lceil 20000/((4096*0.7)/8) \rceil = 56$ leaf node pages and 1 internal node page for a total of $(56 + 1) * 4096 = 233472$ bytes on disk for each. The total space taken by the NN-B-tree for this example is $3301376 + 262144 + 262144 = 3768320$ bytes.

To examine the FS-index, lets assume an average of 3 elements in each fuzzy set. This give $(20000*3) = 60000$ entries in the FS-index. For the FS-B-tree, this results in $\lceil 60000/((4096*0.7)/73) \rceil = 1528$ pages of leaf nodes, and $\lceil 1528/((4096*0.7)/4) \rceil = 3$ pages of internal nodes. This gives a total of $(1528 + 3) * 4096 = 6270976$ bytes on disk. For the ID-B-tree, we get $\lceil 60000/((4096*0.7)/8) \rceil = 168$ leaf node pages and 1 internal node page for a total of $(168 + 1) * 4096 = 692224$ bytes on disk. The total space take by FS-index for this example is $6270976 + 692224 = 6963200$ bytes.

Finally, for the tpr indexes, we get $\lceil 20000/((4096*0.7/32) \rceil = 224$ pages of leaf nodes, and $\lceil 224/((4096*0.7)/32) \rceil = 3$ pages of internal nodes. This gives a total $(224 + 3) * 4096 = 929792$ bytes on disk per tpr index.

The total disk space used for the E-queue, FS-index, and two tpr tree indices is $3768320 + 6963200 + (2 * 929792) = 12591104$ bytes in this example.

6 Concluding Remarks

Even with the improved performance over previous work, the number of disk accesses is still too high for the relatively small data sets to be practical. As can be seen in the example at the end of the last section, the size of the data structures is relatively small, yet the disk accesses are in the millions for small data sets over a short time interval. The main cost arises from updates to the data structures. In order to scale these algorithms up to large data sets (i.e., in the order of millions of objects) future work must focus on update efficient disk based data structures for indexing moving objects, event queues, and range trees.

In spite of these shortcomings, our experiments in Figure 16 show that the CFS algorithm clearly outperforms the TPS algorithm. In some cases, the difference can be as much as an order of magnitude (Figure 16b). The CFS algorithm is the first algorithm of its kind to maintain spatial semijoin results on kinematic data types, over an indefinite period of time, and with no prior knowledge of the updates that will be made.

References

[1] J. Basch, L. J. Guibas, and J. Hershberger. Data structures for mobile data. In *8th Annual ACM-SIAM Symposium on Discrete Algorithms*, pages 747–756, New Orleans, LA, January 1997.

[2] R. Benetis, C. Jensen, G. Karciauskas, and S. Saltenis. Nearest neighbor and reverse nearest neighbor queries for moving objects. In *International Database Engineering and Applications Symposium (IDEAS)*, pages 44–53, Edmonton, Canada, July 2002.

[3] D. Douglas and T. Peucker. Algorithms for the reduction of the number of points required to represent a digitized line or its caricature. *The Canadian Cartographer*, 10(2):112–122, 1973.

[4] R. M. Fujimoto. Parallel discrete event simulation. *Communications of the ACM*, 33(10):30–53, October 1990.

[5] A. Gupta, I. S. Mumick, and V. S. Subrahmanian. Maintaining views incrementally. In *Proceedings of the ACM SIGMOD Conference*, pages 157–166, Washington, D.C., May 1993.

[6] A. Guttman. R-trees: a dynamic index structure for spatial searching. In *Proceedings of the ACM SIGMOD Conference*, pages 47–57, Boston, MA, June 1984.

[7] J. M. Hellerstein, J. F. Naughton, and A. Pfeffer. Generalized search trees for database systems. In U. Dayal, P. M. D. Gray, and S. Nishio, editors, *Proceedings of the 21st International Conference on Very Large Data Bases*, pages 562–573, Zurich, Switzerland, September 1995.

[8] G. R. Hjaltason and H. Samet. Incremental distance join algorithms for spatial databases. In *Proceedings of the ACM SIGMOD Conference*, pages 237–248, Seattle, WA, June 1998.

[9] G. R. Hjaltason and H. Samet. Distance browsing in spatial databases. *ACM Transactions on Database Systems*, 24(2):265–318, June 1999. (Also University of Maryland Computer Science TR–3919).

[10] G. S. Iwerks, H. Samet, and K. Smith. Continuous k-nearest neighbor queries for continuously moving points with updates. In *Proceedings of the 29th International Conference on Very Large Data Bases*, pages 512–523, Berlin, Germany, September 2003.

[11] E. M. McCreight. Priority search trees. *SIAM Journal on Computing*, 14(2):257–276, May 1985.

[12] M. A. Nascimento, R. Silva, and Y. Theodoridis. Evaluation of access structures for discretely moving points. In *Proceedings of the International Workshop on Spatio-Temporal Database Management*, pages 171–188, Edinburgh, UK, September 1999.

[13] Standards Committee on Interactive Simulation (SCIS). *IEEE Std 1278.1-1995*. IEEE Computer Society, USA, March 1996.

[14] S. Prabhakar, Y. Xia, D. V. Kalashnikov, W. G. Aref, and S. E. Hambrusch. Query indexing and velocity constrained indexing: Scalable techniques for continuous queries on moving objects. *IEEE Transactions on Computers*, 51(10):1124–1140, October 2002.

[15] K. Raptopoulou, A. N. Papadopoulos, and Y. Manolopoulos. Fast nearest-neighbor query processing in moving-object databases. *GeoInformatica*, 7(2):113–137, 2003.

[16] N. Roussopoulos, S. Kelley, and F. Vincent. Nearest neighbor queries. In *Proceedings of the ACM SIGMOD Conference*, pages 71–79, San Jose, CA, May 1995.

[17] S. Saltenis, C. S. Jensen, S. T. Leutenegger, and M. A. Lopez. Indexing the positions of continuously moving objects. In *Proceedings of the ACM SIGMOD Conference*, pages 331–342, Dallas, TX, May 2000.

[18] H. Samet. *The Design and Analysis of Spatial Data Structures*. Addison-Wesley, Reading, MA, 1990.

[19] A. P. Sistla, O. Wolfson, S. Chamberlain, and S. Dao. Modeling and querying moving objects. In *Proceedings of the 13th IEEE Conference on Data Engineering (ICDE)*, pages 422–432, Birmingham, U.K., April 1997.

[20] Y. Tao and D. Papadias. Spatial queries in dynamic environments. *ACM Transactions on Databases Systems (TODS)*, 28(2):101–139, June 2003.

[21] J. Tayeb, Ö. Ulusoy, and O. Wolfson. A quadtree-based dynamic attribute indexing method. *The Computer Journal*, 41(3):185–200, 1998.

Voronoi-Based K Nearest Neighbor Search for Spatial Network Databases

Mohammad Kolahdouzan and Cyrus Shahabi

Department of Computer Science
University of Southern California
Los Angeles, CA, 90089, USA
[kolahdoz,shahabi]@usc.edu

Abstract

A frequent type of query in spatial networks (e.g., road networks) is to find the K nearest neighbors (KNN) of a given query object. With these networks, the distances between objects depend on their network connectivity and it is computationally expensive to compute the distances (e.g., shortest paths) between objects. In this paper, we propose a novel approach to efficiently and accurately evaluate KNN queries in spatial network databases using first order Voronoi diagram. This approach is based on partitioning a large network to small Voronoi regions, and then pre-computing distances both within and across the regions. By localizing the pre-computation within the regions, we save on both storage and computation and by performing across-the-network computation for only the border points of the neighboring regions, we avoid global pre-computation between every node-pair. Our empirical experiments with several real-world data sets show that our proposed solution outperforms approaches that are based on on-line distance computation by up to one order of magnitude, and provides a factor of four improvement in the selectivity of the filter step as compared to the index-based approaches.

Permission to copy without fee all or part of this material is granted provided that the copies are not made or distributed for direct commercial advantage, the VLDB copyright notice and the title of the publication and its date appear, and notice is given that copying is by permission of the Very Large Data Base Endowment. To copy otherwise, or to republish, requires a fee and/or special permission from the Endowment.

**Proceedings of the 30th VLDB Conference,
Toronto, Canada, 2004**

1 Introduction

Many researchers have focused on the problem of K nearest neighbor (KNN) queries in spatial databases. This type of query is frequently used in Geographical Information Systems and is defined as: given a set of spatial objects (or points of interest), and a query point, find the K closest objects to the query. An example of KNN query is a query initiated by a GPS device in a vehicle to find the 5 closest restaurants to the vehicle. With spatial network databases (SNDB), objects are restricted to move on pre-defined paths (e.g., roads) that are specified by an underlying network. This means that the shortest network distance (e.g., shortest path, shortest time) between objects (e.g., the vehicle and the restaurants) depend on the connectivity of the network rather than the objects' locations.

The majority of the existing work on KNN queries are based on either computing the distance between a query and the objects on-line, or utilizing index structures. The solution proposed by the first group is based on the fact that the current algorithms (e.g., Dijkstra) for computing the distance between a query object q and an object O in a network will automatically result in the computation of the distance between q and the objects that are (relatively) closer to q than O. These approaches apply an optimized network expansion algorithm (e.g., [9]) with the advantage that the network expansion only explores the objects that are closer to q and computes their distances to q during expansion. However, the main disadvantage of these approaches is that they perform poorly when the objects are not densely distributed in the network because then they require to retrieve a large portion of the network for distance computation. The second group of approaches is designed and optimized for metric or vector spatial index structures (e.g., m-tree and r-tree, respectively). These approaches require pre-computations of the distances between objects and object groups based on their distances to some reference nodes (this is more intelligent as compared to a naive approach that pre-computes and stores distances between all the node-pairs in the network). These solutions filter a small subset of possibly large number of objects as the candidates for the closest neighbors of q, and require a refinement step to compute the actual distances between q and the candidates to find the actual nearest neighbors of q. The main drawback of applying these approaches on SNDB is that they do not offer any solution as how to efficiently compute the distances between q and the candidates. Moreover, applying an approach similar to the first group to perform the refinement step in order to compute the distances between q and the candidates will render these approaches, which traverse index structures to provide a candidate set, redundant since the network expansion approach does not require any candidate set to start with. In addition to this drawback, approaches that are based on vector index structures are only appropriate for spaces where the distance between objects is only a function of their spatial attributes (e.g., Euclidean distance) and cannot properly approximate the distances in a network (see [12]).

A comprehensive solution for spatial queries in SNDB must fulfill these real-world requirements: 1) be able to incorporate the network connectivity to provide exact distances between objects, 2) efficiently answer the queries in real-time in order to support KNN queries for moving objects, 3) be scalable in order to be applicable to usually very large networks, 4) be independent of the density and distribution of the points of interest, 5) be adaptive to efficiently cope with database updates where nodes, links, and points of interest are added/deleted, and 6) be extendible to consider query constraints such as direction or range.

In this paper, we propose a novel approach that fulfills the above requirements by reducing the problem of distance computation in a very large network, in to the problem of distance computation in a number of much smaller networks plus some additional table lookups. The main idea behind our approach, termed Voronoi-based Network Nearest Neighbor (VN^3), is to first partition a large network in to smaller/more manageable regions. We achieve this by generating a first-order *network* Voronoi diagram over the points of interest. Each cell of this Voronoi diagram is centered by one object (e.g., a restaurant) and contains the nodes that are closest to that object in *network* distance (and not the Euclidian distance). Next, we pre-compute the intra and inter distances for each cell. That is, for each cell, we pre-compute the distances between all the edges (or *border* points) of the cell to its center. We also pre-compute distances only across the border points of the *adjacent* cells. This will reduce the pre-computation time and space by localizing the computation to cells and handful of neighbor-cell node-pairs. Now, to find the k nearest-neighbors of a query object q, we first find the first nearest neighbor by simply locating the Voronoi cell that contains q. This can be easily achieved by utilizing a spatial index (e.g., R-tree) that is generated for the Voronoi cells. We prove that the next nearest neighbors of q are within the adjacent cells of the previously explored ones (see Section 4.1), which can be efficiently retrieved from a lookup table. We then utilize the intra-cell pre-computed distances to find the distance from q to the borders of the Voronoi cell of each candidate, and finally the inter-cell pre-computed distances to compute the actual network distance from q to each candidate (see Section 4.2). The local pre-computation nature of VN^3 also results in low complexity of updates when the network is modified.

Note that the application of the Voronoi diagrams to KNN queries have been extensively studied in computation geometry. The solution is based on calculating the K-th order Voronoi diagrams of a network. This solution is impractical for real-world scenarios since it requires that the value of K be predetermined. Moreover, K-th order Voronoi cells have complex shapes and the corresponding algorithms have a very high complexity. However, our proposed VN^3 approach utilizes only the first order Voronoi diagrams to only answer the *first* NN queries. The other $(k-1)$ neighbors are found efficiently by utilizing our proven properties and the pre-computed distances.

To the best of our knowledge, the Incremental Network Expansion (INE) approach presented in [9] is the only other approach that efficiently supports the exact KNN queries on spatial network databases. However, this approach suffers from poor performance when the objects (e.g., restaurants) are not densely distributed in the network. Our empirical experiments with real-world data sets (presented in Section 5) show that VN^3 outperforms INE in query processing time by a factor of 1.5 to 12 depending on the density of the points of interest. Moreover, we show that the size of the candidate set generated by the filter step of VN^3 has lower variance and is up to four times smaller than that generated by the traditional approaches optimized for vector index structures. Also, we show that VN^3's performance is independent of the density and distribution of the points of interest, and the location of the query object. Finally, we show that the required computation and space for the pre-computation component of VN^3 is three orders of magnitude less than that of the naive solution that pre-computes all the node-pair distances.

The remainder of this paper is organized as follows. We review the related work on K nearest neighbor queries in Section 2. We then provide a review of the Voronoi diagrams, the basis of our proposed VN^3 approach, in Section 3. In Section 4, we discuss our proposed VN^3 approach and its extensions. Finally, we discuss our experimental results and conclusions in Sections 5 and 6, respectively.

2 Related Work

Numerous algorithms for k-nearest neighbor queries are proposed. This type of queries is extensively used in geographical information systems, shape similarity in image databases, pattern recognition, etc. A majority of the algorithms are aimed at m-dimensional objects and are based on utilizing one of the variations of multidimensional vector or metric index structures. There are also other algorithms that are based on pre-calculation of the solution space or the computation of the distance from a query object to its nearest neighbors on-line and per query. In this section, we consider each group in turn.

The algorithms that are based on index structures usually perform in two filter and refinement steps and their performance depend on their selectivity in the filter step. These approaches can be divided in two group: vector and metric index structures.

Vector Index structures: Roussopoulos et al. in [10] present a branch-and-bound R-tree traversal algorithm to find nearest neighbors of a query point. The main disadvantage of this approach is the depth-first traversal of the index that incurs unnecessary disk accesses. Korn et al. in [7] present a multi-step k-nearest neighbor search algorithm. The disadvantage of this approach is that the number of candidates obtained in the filter step is usually much more than necessary, making the refinement step very expensive. Seidl et al. in [11] propose an optimal version of this multi-step algorithm by incrementally ranking queries on the index structure. Hjaltason et al. in [4] propose an incremental nearest neighbor algorithm that is based on utilizing an index structure and a priority queue. All of these approaches are designed to utilize spatial index structures and aimed to minimize number of candidates, index nodes and disk accesses required to obtain candidates. There are two major shortages with these approaches that render them impractical for networks. first, networks are metric space, i.e., the distance between two objects depends on the connectivity of the objects and not their spatial attributes; however, the filter step of these approaches is based on Minkowski distance metrics (e.g., Euclidean distance). Hence, the filter step of these approaches cannot be used for, or properly approximate exact distances in networks. Second, these approaches do not propose any method to calculate the exact network distance between objects and the query in their refinement step, rather they assume that the distance function can be easily calculated.

Metric Index structures: These approaches are also based on a filter and refinement process, but as opposed to the vector index structures, they index and filter the objects considering their metric distance. Chiueh in [2] proposes Vantage Point (VP) tree structure for image indexing. This algorithm partitions a data set according to the distances between the objects and a reference (vantage) point. The median value of the distances is used to separate the objects into balanced subsets and a recursive algorithm is applied on each subset. This approach builds the tree based on a top-down recursive process, which does not guarantee a balanced tree. Ciaccia et al in [3] propose M-tree, a balanced tree that partitions objects based on their relative distances and stores these objects into fixed-sized nodes. The main disadvantage of these approaches is that they do not offer any solution on how to efficiently compute the distances between the query and the candidates (i.e., the same as the second shortage of the approaches based on vector index) which is required by the refinement step.

Berchtold et al. in [1] suggest precalculating, approximating and indexing the solution space for the nearest neighbor problem in m dimensional spaces. Precalculating the solution space means determining the Voronoi diagram of the data points. The exact Voronoi cells in m dimensional space are usually very complex, hence the authors propose indexing approximation of the Voronoi cells. This approach is only appropriate for the first nearest neighbor problem in high-dimensional spaces. Jung et al. in [6] propose an algorithm to find the shortest distance between any two points in a network. Their approach is based on partitioning a large graph into layers of smaller subgraphs and pushing up the pre-computed shortest paths between the borders of the subgraphs in a hierarchical manner to find the shortest path between two points. This approach can potentially be used in conjunction with one of the approaches that are based on metric index; however, the main disadvantage of this approach is its poor performance when multiple shortest path queries from different sources are issued at the same time.

Jensen et al. in [5] propose a data model and definition of abstract functionality required for NN queries in SNDB. They use algorithms similar to Dijkstra to calculate the shortest distance from a query to an object on-line. Finally, Papadias et al. in [9] propose a solution for nearest neighbor queries in network databases by introducing an architecture that integrates network and Euclidean information and captures pragmatic constraints. Their approach is based on generating a search region for the query point that expands from the query. The advantages of this approach are: 1) it offers a method that finds the exact distance in networks, and 2) the architecture can support other spatial queries like range search and closest pairs. Since the number of links and nodes that need to be retrieved and examined are inversely proportional to cardinality ratio of entities and number of nodes in the network, the main disadvantage of this approach is a dramatic degradation in performance when the above cardinality ratio is (far) less than 10%, which is the usual case for real world scenarios (e.g., the real data sets representing the road network and different types of entities in the State of California show that the above cardinality ratio is usually between 0.04% and 3%). This is because spatial databases are usually very large and small values for the above cardinality ratio will lead to large portions of the database to be retrieved. This problem also happens for large values of K (see Section 5 for a thorough comparison).

3 Background: Voronoi Diagram

Our proposed approach to address the nearest neighbor queries is based on the *Voronoi diagram*. A Voronoi diagram divides a space into disjoint polygons where the nearest neighbor of any point inside a polygon is the generator of the polygon. In this section, we review the principles of the Voronoi diagrams. We start with the Voronoi diagram for *2-dimensional* Euclidean space and present only the properties that are used in our approach. We then discuss the *network Voronoi diagram* where the distance between two objects in space is their shortest path in the network rather than their Euclidean distance and hence can be used for spatial networks. A thorough discussion on regular and network Voronoi diagrams is presented in [8].

3.1 Definition

Consider a set of limited number of points, called *generator points*, in the Euclidean plane (in general, generators can be any type of spatial object). We associate all locations in the plane to their closest generator(s). The set of locations assigned to each generator forms a region called *Voronoi polygon* or *Voronoi cell*, of that generator. The set of Voronoi polygons associated with all the generators is called the Voronoi diagram with respect to the generators set. The Voronoi polygons of a Voronoi diagram are collectively exhaustive because every location in the plane is associated with at least one generator. The polygons are also mutually exclusive except for their boundaries. The boundaries of the polygons, called *Voronoi edges*, are the set of locations that can be assigned to more than one generator. The Voronoi polygons that share the same edges are called *adjacent polygons* and their generators are called *adjacent generators*. The Voronoi polygon and Voronoi diagram can be formally defined as: Assume a set of generators $P = \{p_1, ..., p_n\} \subset \Re^2$, where $2 < n < \infty$ and $p_i \neq p_j$ for $i \neq j, i, j \in I_n = \{1, ..., n\}$. The region given by:

$$VP(p_i) = \{p \mid d(p, p_i) \leq d(p, p_j)\} \text{ for } j \neq i, j \in I_n$$

where $d(p, p_i)$ specifies the minimum distance between p and p_i (e.g., length of the straight line connecting p and p_i in Euclidean space), is called the *Voronoi Polygon* associated with p_i, and the set given by:

$$VD(P) = \{VP(p_1), ..., VP(p_n)\}$$

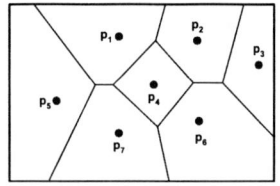 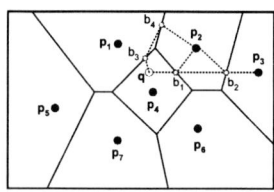

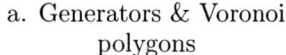

a. Generators & Voronoi polygons   b. Proof of Properties 5 & 7

Figure 1: Example of a Voronoi diagram

is called the *Voronoi Diagram* generated by P. Figure 1a shows an example of a Voronoi diagram, its polygons and generators.

3.2 Properties

We review four of the basic geometric properties of the Voronoi diagrams. The proofs for these properties are presented in [8]. These properties are the basis for the extended properties we introduce in Section 4.

Property 1: The Voronoi diagram of a point set P, $VD(P)$, is unique.

Property 2: The nearest generator point of p_i (e.g., p_j) is among the generator points whose Voronoi polygons share similar Voronoi edges with $VP(p_i)$.

Property 3: Let n and n_e be the number of generator points and Voronoi edges, respectively, then $n_e \leq 3n - 6$.

Property 4: From property 3, and the fact that every Voronoi edge is shared by exactly two Voronoi polygons, we notice that the average number of Voronoi edges per Voronoi polygon is at most 6, i.e., $2(3n-6)/n = 6 - 12/n \leq 6$. This means that on average, each generator has 6 adjacent generators. We use this property to derive the complexity of our algorithm.

3.3 Network Voronoi Diagram

A network Voronoi diagram ([8]), termed *NVD*, is defined for graphs and is a specialization of Voronoi diagrams where the location of objects is restricted to the links that connect the nodes of the graph and distance between objects is defined as the length of the shortest distance (e.g., shortest path or shortest time) in the network rather than their Euclidean distance. Spatial networks (e.g., road networks) can be modeled as weighted graphs where the intersections are represented by nodes of the graph and roads are represented by the links connecting the nodes. The weights can be the distances of the nodes or they can be the time it takes to travel between the nodes (representing shortest times).

Assume a weighted graph $G(N, L)$ that consists of a set of nodes $N = \{p_1, ..., p_n, p_{n+1}, ..., p_o\}$, where the first n elements (i.e., $P = \{p_1, ..., p_n\}$) are the generators (e.g., points of interest in a road network), and a set of links $L = \{l_1, ..., l_k\}$ that connects the nodes. Also assume that the network distance from a point

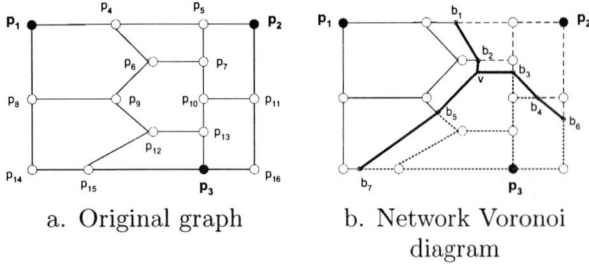

a. Original graph   b. Network Voronoi diagram

Figure 2: Example of a network Voronoi diagram (NVD)

p on a link in L to p_i in N, $d_n(p, p_i)$, is defined as the shortest network distance from p to p_i. For all $j \in I_n \setminus \{i\}$, we define:

$$Dom(p_i, p_j) = \{p | p \in \bigcup_{o=1}^{k} l_o, d_n(p, p_i) \leq d_n(p, p_j)\}$$

$$b(p_i, p_j) = \{p | p \in \bigcup_{o=1}^{k} l_o, d_n(p, p_i) = d_n(p, p_j)\}$$

The set $Dom(p_i, p_j)$, called the *dominance region* of p_i over p_j on links in L, specifies all points in all links in L that are closer to p_i or of equal distance to p_j. The set $b(p_i, p_j)$, called *bisector* or *border points* between p_i and p_j, specifies all points in all links in L that are equally distanced from p_i and p_j. Consequently, the *Voronoi link set* associated with p_i and *network Voronoi diagram* are defined as following, respectively:

$$V_{link}(p_i) = \bigcap_{j \in I_n \setminus \{i\}} Dom(p_i, p_j)$$
$$NVD(P) = \{V_{link}(p_1), ..., V_{link}(p_n)\}$$

where $V_{link}(p_i)$ specifies all the points in all the links in L that are closer to p_i than any other generator point in N. Similar to VD defined in Section 3.1, elements of NVD are also collectively exhaustive and mutually exclusive except for their border points. Note that b is a set of points which unlike Voronoi diagram in Euclidean space, cannot directly generate polygons. However, by properly connecting adjacent border points of a generator g to each other without crossing any of the links, we can generate a bounding polygon, called *network Voronoi polygon*, we term $NVP(g)$, for that generator. Note that generation of $NVP(g)$ only requires local network information, i.e., the links and nodes that are in the area between g and its adjacent generators are used to generate $NVP(g)$.

An example of NVD is shown in Figure 2. Figure 2a depicts the original graph where p_1, p_2 and p_3 are the generators. We can assume that the set of generators is the set of *points of interest* (e.g., hotels, restaurants,...) and p_4 to p_{16} are the intersections of a road network that are connected to each other by the set of streets L. Figure 2b shows the NVD of the graph where each line style corresponds to a Voronoi link set of a generator. As shown in the figure, some links are completely contained in V_{link} of a generator (e.g., the link connecting p_6 and p_9 is completely inside $V_{link}(p_1)$), while others are partially contained in different V_{link}'s (e.g., the link connecting p_4 and p_5 is divided between and contained in $V_{link}(p_1)$ and $V_{link}(p_2)$). The figure also shows how adjacent border points should be connected to each other: if two adjacent border points are between two similar generators (e.g., b_5 and b_7 are between p_1 and p_3), they can be connected with an arbitrary line that does not cross any of the members of L. Three or more adjacent border points (e.g., b_2, b_3 and b_5) can be connected to each other through an arbitrary auxiliary point (e.g., v in the figure). By using arbitrary lines and auxiliary points, NVPs will become non-unique. However, since objects in a graph can only be located on links, different NVPs will contain exactly identical Voronoi link sets and hence are unique in this respect. Moreover, as shown in the figure and unlike Voronoi polygons in the Euclidean space, common edges between two NVPs may contain more than two border points and are not necessarily straight lines. Despite this, properties 3 and 4 of Section 3.2 are still valid for NVPs as shown in [8].

4 Voronoi-Based Network Nearest Neighbor: VN³

In this section, we describe VN³ as our proposed approach to evaluate the nearest neighbor queries in spatial networks. VN³ is based on the properties of the Network Voronoi diagrams and also *localized* pre-computation of the network distances for a very small percentage of neighboring nodes in the network. The intuition is that the NVPs of an NVD can directly be used to find the first nearest neighbor of a query object q. Subsequently, NVPs' adjacency information can be utilized to provide a candidate set for other nearest neighbors of q. Finally, the pre-computed distances can be used to compute the actual network distances from q to the generators in the candidate set and consequently refine the set. The filter/refinement process in VN³ is iterative: at each step, first a new set of candidates is generated from the NVPs of the generators that are already selected as the nearest neighbors of q, then the pre-computed distances are used to select "only the next" nearest neighbor of q. Hence, the filter/refinement step must be invoked k times to find the first k nearest neighbors of q. Note that this is different from the usual filter/refinement process where the two steps are invoked consecutively. VN³ consists of the following components:

1. Pre-calculation of the solution space: As a major component of the VN³ filter step, the NVD for the points of interest (e.g., hotels, restaurants,...) in a network must be calculated and its corresponding NVPs must be stored in a table. Note that sep-

arate NVDs and set of NVPs must be generated for different types of points of interest.

2. Utilization of an index structure: In the first stage of the filter step, the first nearest neighbor of q is found by locating the NVP that contains q (e.g., using *Contain(q)* function in spatial databases). This stage can be expedited by using a spatial index structure generated on the NVPs. Note that although an NVD is based on the network distance metric, its NVPs are regular polygons and can be indexed using index structures that are designed for the Euclidean distance metric (e.g., R-tree). This means that the *Contain(q)* function invoked on an R-tree index structure on NVPs will return the NVP whose generator has the minimum network distance to q.

3. Pre-computation of the exact distances for a very small portion of data: The refinement step discussed in Section 4.2 requires that for each NVP, the network distances between its border points be pre-computed and stored. These pre-computed distances are used to find the network distances across NVPs, and from the query object to the candidate set generated by the filter step.

4.1 VN³ Filter Step

Our proposed approach to generate the candidate set for nearest neighbors of a query point is based on the first two components of VN³ discussed in Section 4. This requires the pre-calculation of NVD and generation of a spatial index structure for NVPs of the NVD. We first introduce the following properties that can be concluded from properties 1 to 4 in Section 3.2. These two properties help the filter step to constrain its search space to only the adjacent Voronoi polygons.

Property 5: Property 2 suggests that the second nearest generator to *"any location"* inside a Voronoi polygon $V(p_i)$ is among the adjacent generators of p_i.
Proof: This property can be proved by contradiction. Consider Figure 1b where the first nearest neighbor of an arbitrary point q is p_4 (i.e., q is inside $V(p_4)$). Now suppose that the second nearest neighbor of q is $p_3 \notin$ {adjacent generators of p_4}. This requires that the shortest path between q and p_3, $L(q,p_3)$, intersects with at least one of the adjacent polygons of $V(p_4)$ ($L(q,p_3)$ in Figure 1b intersects $V(p_2)$ at points b_1 and b_2). Note that in case of NVD, $L(q,p_3)$ may not be a straight line as shown in the figure. From the definition of the Voronoi polygons we know that $d_n(b_2,p_3) = d_n(b_2,p_2)$. We also know that the shortest path in networks and Euclidean distance functions obey triangular inequality, meaning that $d_n(b_1,b_2) + d_n(b_2,p_2) \geq d_n(b_1,p_2)$. We can conclude that $d_n(b_1,b_2) + d_n(b_2,p_3) \geq d_n(b_1,p_2)$, and by adding $d_n(q,b_1)$ to both sides of the inequality, we can ultimately conclude that $d_n(q,p_3) \geq d_n(q,p_2)$. This means that p_2 is a closer generator to q than p_3, or

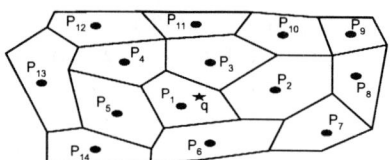

Figure 3: Sample network Voronoi diagram

at least has the same distance, which contradicts our initial assumption.

Property 6: Let $G = \{g_1, ..., g_k\} \in P$ be the set of the first k nearest generators of a location q inside $V(g_1)$, then g_k is among the adjacent generators of $\{G \setminus g_k\}$. This property is in fact the generalization of Property 5.
Proof: The proof of this property by contradiction is similar to the proof of the previous property. We know that the shortest path from q to g_k, $L(q,g_k)$, must intersect with one of the edges of $V(g_k)$, e.g., E_k. Suppose $L(q,g_k)$ intersects E_k at point b_k, and E_k is a common edge between $V(g_k)$ and $V(x)$ where the contradiction of this property requires that $x \notin \{G \setminus g_k\}$. It is clear that $L(q,g_k)$ must also intersect with $V(x)$ at at least another point like b_x. By comparison with Property 5, we can conclude that $d_n(b_x,x) \leq d_n(b_x,b_k) + d_n(b_k,g_k)$, suggesting that x is closer to q than g_k and hence $x \in \{G \setminus g_k\}$. This contradicts our initial assumption.

Using a hypothetical NVD shown in Figure 3, we can now easily describe our filtering approach to generate the candidate set, C, for nearest neighbors of a query point q. The definition of NVD requires that the first nearest neighbor of q be P_1 since $V(P_1)$ contains q, hence P_1 can be found by issuing the *Contain(q)* function on an index structure generated for the NVPs of the NVD. Property 5 suggests that the second nearest neighbor of q is among the adjacent generators of P_1, i.e., $C = \{P_2, P_3, P_4, P_5, P_6\}$. Note that during the generation of NVD, the adjacent generators/NVPs are determined. We store the adjacency information of the NVPs in a lookup table. Hence, finding adjacent NVPs does not require any spatial operation, rather, they can easily be found from a lookup table by one disk block access. At this stage, we need to invoke the refinement step (see Section 4.2) to compute the exact distances between q and all the generators in C to find the second nearest neighbor. Let us assume that the second nearest neighbor of q is P_3. Property 6 requires that the third nearest neighbor of q be among the adjacent generators of $\{P_1, P_3\}$, i.e., $C = \{P_2, P_4, P_5, P_6, P_{10}, P_{11}, P_{12}\}$. Note that P_{12} is adjacent to P_3 as their polygons share the same vertex. Consecutive nearest neighbors of q can then be found using the same iterative approach.

4.1.1 Analysis

In this section, we analyze the complexity of the filter step of VN³ with respect to the size of the candidate set as well as the number of disk block accesses.

Size of the Candidate Set: As described in Section 4.1, the first neighbor is found by applying the *contain()* function on an R-tree index that is generated for NVPs, and hence does not require any distance computation. Property 4 in Section 3.2 suggests that on average, 6 generators have to be examined to explore the second nearest neighbor. Property 6 suggests that at least one of the adjacent generators of any newly found neighbor must have already been explored as a nearest neighbor. Hence, from the second nearest neighbor on, exploration of a new nearest neighbor will lead to only 5 (on average) new generators that must be examined to find the next nearest neighbor. This will lead to a candidate set with an average size of $(5K+1)$, equal to complexity of $O(K)$. This is a conservative bound as our experimental results (Section 5) show that the average size of the candidate set is usually much smaller than $(5K+1)$, and becomes very close to K as the value of K increases.

Disk Block Accesses: Usage of the *Contain()* function on the R-tree index to find the first nearest neighbor incurs a complexity of $O(log(n))$, where n is the number of generators of the network. We also showed that $O(K)$ generators have to be examined and hence retrieved from the database. Hence, the complexity of the number of disk block accesses required by the filter step becomes $O(K + log(n))$.

4.2 VN³ Refinement Step

As we discussed in Section 4.1, once a nearest neighbor of a query point q is found and the candidate set C is updated, the distances from q to all the elements of C must be computed in order to find the next nearest neighbor. In this section, we discuss alternative approaches that are based on properties of NVPs to find the distances between q and the elements of C.

The intuition behind all the proposed approaches is that in an NVD, all possible paths that can connect an object from outside an NVP to a node inside it, including the polygon's generator, must pass through the border points of the polygon. In the sequel we use $BoP(e)$ to specify the set of border points of an entity e. During the generation of the NVPs (described in [8]), the shortest distance between the border points of a Voronoi polygon to the polygon's generator is determined and stored in a lookup table. Hence, if we calculate the distance from the outside object to the border points of a Voronoi polygon, we can find the minimum distance from the object to the generator of the polygon. As an example, consider the NVD shown in Figure 4 where $N = \{P_1, ..., P_{14}\}$ are the generators of the NVD, e.g., points of interest in a road network. Note that only the nodes and links inside $NVP(P_1)$ are drawn. In the figure, $B = \{b_1, ..., b_{40}\}$ specify the border points of the NVPs. An example that describes the intuition is the distance computation between q and P_9. The values of $d_n(P_9, b_{34})$,

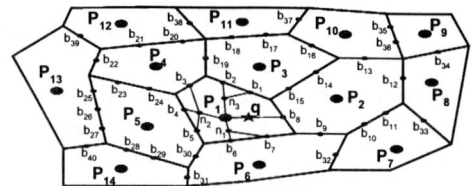

Figure 4: Sample network Voronoi diagram

$d_n(P_9, b_{35})$ and $d_n(P_9, b_{36})$ are determined during the generation of $NVP(P_9)$. Hence, we can compute the distance between q and P_9 as:
$$d_n(q, P_9) = min(d_n(q, b_{34}) + d_n(b_{34}, P_9),$$
$$d_n(q, b_{35}) + d_n(b_{35}, P_9),$$
$$d_n(q, b_{36}) + d_n(b_{36}, P_9))$$

Trivially, we need to have the distance from q to b_{34}, b_{35}, and b_{36} in order to find $d_n(q, P_9)$. As stated above, q can only be connected to $\{b_{34}, b_{35}, b_{36}\}$ through $\{b_1, ..., b_8\}$, which are the border points of the NVP that contains q, $BoP(NVP(q))$. This means that:
$$d_n(q, b_{34}) = min(d_n(q, b_1) + d_n(b_1, b_{34}), ..., d_n(q, b_8) + d_n(b_8, b_{34}))$$

As shown above, finding the network distance from q to P_9, or in general to all the elements of C, requires: 1) Query to border computation: computing the network distances from q to $BoP(NVP(q))$ and 2) Border to border computation: for the set of generators that are candidates for the next nearest neighbor, g, computing the network distances from $BoP(NVP(q))$ to the border points of the NVPs of g, $BoP(NVPs(g))$. We address these two requirements in the following sections.

4.2.1 Query to Border Computation

We propose two alternative approaches to compute the distances from a query point q to the border points of its surrounding NVP, $BoP(NVP(q))$.

1. On-line Progressive Expansion, OPE: With this approach, we use a method similar to what proposed in [9] to find the distance between q and $BoP(NVP(q))$. The average number of disk block accesses required by this approach is $\frac{n}{mb}$ (m points of interest, n nodes in the network, b connected nodes on one disk block) which grows rapidly for large networks with small number of points of interest (see Section 5. Due to lack of space and because our chosen approach in the experiments is OPC, we do not include the discussion for this approach. See the full-paper or [9] for details.

2. Off-line Precalculation, OPC: This approach suggests that in addition to the third component of VN³ discussed in Section 4, the distances from each border point to all the nodes inside the polygons that contain the border point be pre-computed in an off-line process. For example, for the NVD shown in Figure 4, this approach suggests that in addition to the distances from $(b_1, ..., b_8)$ to each other and to P_1, their distances to (n_1, n_2, n_3) be pre-computed. Note that unlike the figure, number of border points of an NVP in a real world scenario is much less than the number of nodes inside the NVP (see results in Section 5). Also note that each border point is shared by at least two NVPs and hence its distances to all the nodes in these NVPs have to be computed, e.g., the distances from (b_6, b_7) to the nodes inside $NVP(P_6)$ should also be computed.

The main advantage of this approach is a significant boost in performance since it eliminates the need for both the execution of complex algorithms (e.g., Dijkstra in OPE) and retrieving large amount of data for distance computations. Rather, the distance from q to $BoP(NVP(q))$ can be retrieved from a lookup table in one disk block access. The disadvantage of this approach is the requirement for an off-line process to pre-calculate and store the above network distances. However, we believe that this approach has a low overall computation and space complexity (similar to the discussion in Section 4.2.2). Our experimental results in Section 5 confirm this intuition, where they show that the network distances for only less than 0.5% of the network (as compared to pre-computing the distances between all the nodes in the network) must be calculated and stored.

4.2.2 Border to Border Computations

To find the network distances from $BoP(NVP(q))$ to the border points of the NVP of any generator, $BoP(NVP(g))$, we propose pre-computing the point-to-point network distances between the border points of each NVP "separately" (the third component of VN^3 discussed in Section 4). For example, this approach suggests that for the NVD shown in Figure 4, the point-to-point network distances among $\{b_1, ..., b_8\}$ (corresponding to $NVP(P_1)$) be pre-computed. It also suggests that the point-to-point network distances among $\{b_1, b_2, b_{14}, ..., b_{19}\}$ (corresponding to $NVP(P_3)$) be pre-computed. Note that each border point (e.g., b_1) belongs to at least two NVPs (e.g., $NVP(P_1)$ and $NVP(P_3)$) and hence, its distances to all the border points of two NVPs must be pre-computed. The intuition for this approach is that once the point-to-point network distances among the border points of "each" NVP is computed, these distances can be used to find the network distances between the border points of "any" two NVPs. The other intuition is that this approach has low complexity with respect to both space and computation. The reasons are: 1) The pre-computation is only performed for the border points of each NVP separately, and in real world scenarios (as opposed to the example shown in Figure 4), the ratio of the total number of the border points to the total number of the nodes in the network is small (see Section 5), and 2) the pre-computation is performed for each NVP separately and not across all NVPs, and the border points of each NVP are fairly close to each other.

The first stage to find the network distances from $BoP(NVP(q))$ to $BoP(NVP(g))$ is to find those NVPs through which the shortest path from q to g will pass. In order to find these NVPs, we introduce the following properties that can be concluded from properties 5 and 6 in Section 4.1.

Property 7: In a Voronoi diagram, if (g_1, g_2) is the set of first two nearest generators of q, then the shortest path from q to g_2 can only go through $\{V(g_1), V(g_2)\}$ and hence, through the common edge of $\{V(g_1), V(g_2)\}$.

Proof: The proof of this property is by contradiction. If the shortest path from q to g_2 crosses a Voronoi polygon $V(g_k)$ where $g_k \notin \{g_1, g_2\}$, then the portion of the shortest path that is inside $V(g_k)$ is closer to g_k than g_2 and consequently, q will become closer to g_k than g_2. This contradicts our assumption that g_2, after g_1, is the nearest generator to q. As an example, consider Figure 1b and suppose that $\{p_4, p_2\}$ is the set of first two nearest generators of q. Suppose that the shortest path from q to p_2 is the line $L = <q, b_3, b_4, p_2>$, which crosses $NVP(p_1)$ at points b_3 and b_4. Since any point on the line segment $<b_3, b_4>$ is closer to p_1 than p_2, this requires that p_1 must be a closer generator to q than p_2, contradicting our assumption about the set of first two nearest generators of q. Note that in network Voronoi Diagrams, the shortest network path from q to g_2 can only cross the common edge of $V(g_1)$ and $V(g_2)$ at one of their common border points.

Property 8: In a Voronoi diagram, if $(g_1, ..., g_k)$ is the set of first k nearest generators of q, then the shortest path from a location q to g_k can only go through a combination of $\{V(g_1), ..., V(g_k)\}$ and hence, through a combination of the common edges of $\{V(g_1), ..., V(g_k)\}$.

Proof: This property is the generalization of Property 7 and its proof is similar to the proof of Property 7.

Property 9: In a Voronoi diagram, if the shortest path from q to a generator g_k passes through $NVP(g_i)$, then g_i is closer to q than g_k.

Proof: Property 8 suggests that the shortest path from q to g_k can only pass through a combination of $\{V(g_1), ..., V(g_{k-1})\}$. Hence, g_i must be a member of $\{V(g_1), ..., V(g_{k-1})\}$ and subsequently, it is closer to q than g_k.

Using the hypothetical NVD shown in Figure 4, we now describe our progressive approach to find the distances from q to $BoP(NVPs(CG))$ (CG are candidates for the next nearest generator of q). As shown in the figure, the first nearest generator of q is p_1 since $NVP(p_1)$ contains q. Property 7 suggests that the shortest path from q to its second nearest generator, say p_i, can only go through the common edges between $NVP(p_1)$ and the $NVP(p_i)$. Hence, to find the second nearest generator of q, we first compute the *minimum possible network distances*, d_{mpn}, from q to $(p_2, ..., p_6)$ through each of the generators' shared border points

with p_1:
$$d_{mpn}(q, p_2) = d_n(q, b_8) + d_n(b_8, p_2)$$
$$d_{mpn}(q, p_3) = min[\ d_n(q, b_1) + d_n(b_1, p_3)\ ,$$
$$d_n(q, b_2) + d_n(b_2, p_3)\ ]$$
...
$$d_{mpn}(q, p_6) = min[\ d_n(q, b_6) + d_n(b_6, p_6)\ ,$$
$$d_n(q, b_7) + d_n(b_7, p_6)\ ]$$

Formally, the minimum possible network distance from q to p_i, $d_{mpn}(q, p_i)$, is the minimum distance from q to p_i for a path that only passes through any of the NVPs whose generators are already selected as the nearest generators of q. Hence, the path can only crosses the common edges between those NVPs. Note that all of the above d_n's are either pre-computed (as we proposed in Section 4.2.2) or calculated using one of the approaches discussed in Section 4.2.1. The generator with the shortest d_{mpn} is then selected as the second nearest generator of q. Note that because of the triangular inequality property, $d_{mpn}(q, p_i) \geq d_n(q, p_i)$. However, Property 7 (and 8) require that $d_{mpn}(q, p_i) = d_n(q, p_i)$ when p_i is the next nearest generator of q. Let us now assume that p_2 is the second nearest generator of q. Property 8 suggests that the shortest path from q to the third nearest neighbor, $p_i \in (p_3, p_4, p_5, p_6, p_7, p_8, p_{10})$, can only go through one of the $\{\ BoP(\{NVP(p_1) \cup NVP(p_2)\}) \cap BoP(NVP(p_i))\ \}$. For example, the property requires that at this stage, the path from q to p_6 can only go through b_6, b_7, or b_9:
$$d_{mpn}(q, p_6) = min[\ d_n(q, b_6) + d_n(b_6, p_6)\ ,$$
$$d_n(q, b_7) + d_n(b_7, p_6)\ ,$$
$$d_n(q, b_8) + d_n(b_8, b_9) + d_n(b_9, p_6)\ ]$$

Note that the actual shortest path from q to b_9 may pass through a different point set than (b_8) (e.g., $SP(q, b_9)$ may pass through (b_1, b_{15})). However, at this stage, where only p_1 and p_2 are found as the nearest generators of q, Property 8 suggests if $SP(q, p_6)$ does indeed go through b_9, then $SP(q, b_9)$ must go through b_8. In other words, the "only possible" path from q to b_9 at this stage is through b_8 and hence, only the length of this path must be computed for $d_{mpn}(q, p_6)$. This significantly simplifies our approach by replacing the need to compute the "actual shortest" network distances from q to $BoP(NVPs(CG))$, with the need to only compute their "minimum possible" network distances. If we assume that p_3 is the third nearest generator of q, then Property 8 suggests that the minimum possible shortest path from q to b_9, in addition to going through b_8, can pass through a combination of (b_1, b_2) and (b_{14}, b_{15}) as well.

We now propose two alternative approaches to find d_{mpn} from a query point to $BoP(NVPs(CG))$. The intuition for both of the approaches is that at each step k, we find the d_{mpn} from q to $BoP(p)$, where $P = \{NVP(g_1) \cup NVP(g_2) \cup ... \cup NVP(g_{k-1})\}$ and $\{g_1, ..., g_{k-1}\}$ is the set of the $(k-1)$-st nearest generators of q.

1. NVP Expansion, NVP-E: This approach works as follows. For the NVD shown in Figure 4, first we generate an auxiliary network, AN_1, containing nodes $N = \{b_1, ..., b_8, q\}$ (i.e., $BoP(NVP(p_1))$ and the query object). Note that all of the elements of AN_1 are connected to each other and their distances are equal to their network distances in the original network that are either pre-computed as part of the third component of VN[3] (Section 4), or are calculated by one of the approaches discussed in Section 4.2.1. We use the distances from q to $\{b_1, ..., b_8\}$ to find the second nearest generator (assume P_2 is the second nearest generator). We then generate a new auxiliary network, AN_2, containing nodes $N = \{b_8, ..., b_{15}\}$ (i.e., $BoP(NVP(P_2))$). Note that based on Property 6, the NVP of the k-th nearest generator must have at least one common edge/border point with the NVPs of the first $(k-1)$-st nearest generators. Hence, we generate a new network from AN_1 and AN_2, $AN = \{AN_1 \cup AN_2\}$, and using Dijkstra's algorithm, compute the distances from q to the nodes in the new network AN. Note that computing the network distances between all the nodes in AN is not necessary. At this stage, we have the minimum possible network distances from q to the nodes in AN, i.e., $BoP(\{NVP(p_1) \cup NVP(p_2)\})$. Consequently, the minimum possible network distances for the k-th step can be found by generating $AN = \{AN_1 \cup ... \cup AN_{k-1}\}$. The intuition here is that the average number of border points for each NVP is small (our experimental results in Section 5 confirms this), and hence, this approach can be efficiently executed in memory.

2. Distance Computing Optimization, DCO: The use of the Dijkstra's algorithm in NVP-E requires that the distances from q to all the nodes in AN be recalculated every time a new nearest generator is explored. This is unnecessary because once a new nearest generator of q is found and its NVP is added to AN, d_{mpn} from q to only a very small number of borders in AN must be reexamined. The distance d_{mpn} from q to the border points of an NVP may "only" change if the distance from q to at least one of the border points of that NVP is changed. Consequently, DCO works as follows: suppose $\{g_1, ..., g_{n-1}\}$ is the set of the first $(n-1)$-st nearest generators of q and d_{mpn}'s from q to all the $BoP(\mathcal{V} = \{NVP(g_1) \cup ... \cup NVP(g_{n-1})\})$ are computed. When the next nearest generator, g_n, is explored, first the length of the minimum possible paths from q to $BoP(NVP(g_n))$ are computed. These paths can only pass through $BoP(\{NVP(g_n) \cap \mathcal{V}\})$. Next, only d_{mpn} for the NVPs whose border point(s) have a new smaller value of d_{mpn} are re-examined. This will reduce the computation complexity by eliminating unnecessary distance computations.

4.3 VN[3] Storage Schema

Figure 5 shows an example of a simple schema needed for the NVD of Figure 4. The proposed schema consists of a spatial component (NVPs component in the figure) that is used to find the first NN of a query, and

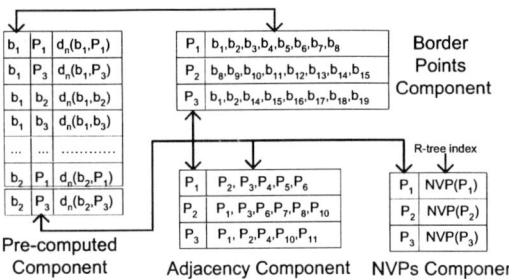

Figure 5: Example of VN^3 data structures

three look up tables: an adjacency component that is used for the filter step of VN^3, a pre-computed component that is used for the refinement step, and a border point component.

4.4 VN^3 Updates

The intuition for updates in VN^3 is that the modification of the original network may require changes in the original NVPs or may require some of the network distances to be recomputed. Due to "local pre-computation" nature of VN^3, an update in the network does not result in updating the entire network Voronoi diagram; rather, it only affects the NVPs in a local scope.

a. Adding/Removing Links/Nodes: Suppose a link L or a node N is added to or removed from a network. If L/N is contained in one NVP, the distances from the border points of that NVP to each other is recomputed. If these distances stay the same as before, then the NVP's shape will remain the same; otherwise, the NVP must be recomputed. Subsequently, if the distances from the border points of adjacent NVPs are also changed, those NVPs are re-examined. If L is contained in a set of NVPs, $\mathcal{N}$, then the adjacent NVPs of $\mathcal{N}$ may change and hence must be regenerated.

b. Adding/Removing Points of Interest: Suppose a point of interest P is added to, or removed from the network. Then only the $NVP(P)$ and (some of) its adjacent NVPs will change (i.e., become smaller/larger). For example, for the NVD shown in Figure 5, if a new point of interest P located in $NVP(p_1)$ is added to the network, then $NVP(p_1)$ and some of the $\{NVP(p_2), ..., NVP(p_6)\}$ will change. Similarly, if p_1 is removed, then the area covered by $NVP(p_1)$ will be covered by $\{NVP(p_2), ..., NVP(p_6)\}$.

5 Performance Evaluation

We conducted several experiments to: 1) compare the performance of VN^3 with its only competitor, the INE approach presented in [9], 2) evaluate the overhead of the pre-computations proposed in Sections 4 and 4.2.1, and 3) compare the performance of the filter step of VN^3 with that of the traditional approaches optimized for spatial index structures. We used two real-world data sets. The first data set is obtained from NavTech Inc., used for navigation systems with GPS devices installed in cars, and represents a network of approximately 110,000 links and 79,800 nodes of the road system in the downtown Los Angeles. The second data set is obtained from USGS and consists of a set of points representing hospitals, major buildings, and churches in the US containing approximately 5200, 14000 and 126000 objects, respectively. The experiments were performed on an IBM ZPro with dual Pentium III processors, 512MB of RAM, and Oracle 9.2 as the database server. We present the average results of 1000 runs of K nearest neighbor queries where K varied from 1 to 500.

1. Overall Performance of VN^3:

Our experiments show that the total query response time of VN^3 is up to one order of magnitude less than that of INE. Table 1 shows the results of comparing query response time between VN^3 and the INE approach proposed in [9]. The first and second columns specify the entities (or points of interest) and their population and cardinality ratio (i.e., the number of entities over the number of links in the network), respectively. Note that for the given data set, restaurants and hospitals represent the entities with the maximum and minimum cardinality ratios. As shown in the table, when $K = 1$, and regardless of the density of the entities, VN^3 generates the result set almost instantly. This is because a simple $contain()$ function is enough to find the first NN. However, depending on the density of the entities, INE approach requires between 0.49 to 12.4 seconds to provide the first NN. Also, both approaches have almost similar CPU processing times (values inside "()"), with VN^3's CPU time tend to be more than INE's for larger values of K. This is because the major computation component in INE is maintaining a sorted queue which grows for larger values of K (e.g., for auto services, the queue size is 50 for $K = 5$ and 6600 for $K = 250$). However, VN^3 has a more complex computation requirement as it requires computation of the distances from the query to the borders of a newly found neighbor every time a new neighbor is explored. However, as shown in the table, the time required by the database to retrieve the links from network is the dominant factor and the CPU times are almost negligible. Depending on the density of the entities, the time incurred by INE to retrieve the network from the database is between 1.5 (for high densities and larger Ks) and 12 (for low densities and higher values of K) times more than that incurred by VN^3. This is because for lower densities of entities, INE requires larger portion of the network to be retrieved. For example, while there are only 340 links retrieved from the database to find the 10 closest restaurants to a query, 17900 links (equal to 16% of the network) need to be retrieved to find the 10

849

Entities	Qty (density)	Query Processing Time (Sec.)										
		K=1		K=5		K=10		K=25		K=50		K=100	
		VN³ (cpu) disk	INE (cpu) disk	VN³ (cpu) disk	INE (cpu) disk	VN³ (cpu) disk	INE (cpu) disk	VN³ (cpu) disk	INE (cpu) disk	VN³ (cpu) disk	INE (cpu) disk	VN³ (cpu) disk	INE (cpu) disk
Hospital	46 (0.0004)	(0) 0.018	(0.3) 12.4	(1.5) 6.5	(1.7) 78.3	(4.5) 14.0	(3.8) 165.1	(15.3) 35.1	(10.1) 430.2	-	-	-	-
Shopping Centers	173 (0.0016)	(0) 0.020	(0.09) 3.6	(0.45) 3.3	(0.5) 21.1	(1.3) 6.9	(1.1) 44.0	(3.4) 18.1	(3.1) 118.0	-	-	-	-
Parks	561 (0.0053)	(0) 0.021	(0.03) 1.4	(0.15) 1.5	(0.2) 8.2	(0.37) 2.8	(0.3) 15.3	(1.4) 6.4	(0.8) 36.4	(2.5) 13.3	(1.6) 71.1	-	-
Schools	1230 (0.0115)	(0) 0.027	(0.015) 0.6	(0.06) 0.75	(0.07) 3.5	(0.18) 1.46	(0.14) 6.6	(0.7) 3.9	(0.36) 15.6	(1.9) 7.5	(0.7) 32.2	-	-
Auto Services	2093 (0.0326)	(0) 0.030	(0.013) 0.57	(0.01) 0.65	(0.05) 2.43	(0.09) 1.4	(0.09) 4.3	(0.58) 2.95	(0.23) 10.0	(1.65) 6.68	(0.44) 19.4	(2.78) 13.1	(0.87) 38.00
Restaurants	2944 (0.0580)	(0) 0.032	(0.01) 0.49	(0.01) 0.57	(0.03) 1.34	(0.04) 1.48	(0.06) 2.7	(0.26) 2.8	(0.15) 6.8	(0.8) 6.1	(0.3) 13.3	(1.85) 12.8	(0.6) 26.0

Table 1: Query processing time of VN³ vs. INE

closets hospital to the same query object. Note that INE does not retrieve the required links in one step, rather, only a small number of links are retrieved from the database at each step. Note that VN³ also requires pre-computed values to be retrieved from the database, and the number of required pre-computed values increases for lower densities of the entities and larger values of K. However VN³ retrieves the required data in only one step, resulting in much faster data retrieval time.

Table 2 shows the overhead incurred by the pre-computations proposed as the third component of VN³. As shown in the table, for entities with higher densities (e.g., restaurants) which generate smaller and more number of NVPs, the average number of nodes inside each NVP and number of border points per NVP are less. This will lead to faster pre-computation process since the pre-computations are performed in smaller size local areas. The third column of the table shows the total number of border-to-border pre-computations, which is almost constant for entities with different densities. This is because when there are more number of NVPs (e.g., restaurants), the average number of border points are smaller and when there are less number of NVPs (e.g., hospital), the average number of border points are larger. Finally, the suggested pre-computations for off-line precalculation method (Section 4.2.1), fourth column in the table, increases for entities with smaller densities. This is because the average number of nodes inside each NVP grows rapidly. Note that a naive approach that pre-computes all the pair node distances in the given network requires 3.2 billion pre-computations. However, in VN³, the highest number of pre-computations required by OPC method is still three order of magnitude less than that of the naive approach.

2. Performance of the VN³ Filter Step: Figure 6 depicts the performance of the VN³ filter step with respect to the size of the candidate set when KNN queries are performed for the second data set. For each value of K (x-axis) we performed 1000 queries where the location of the query point is randomly selected, and we averaged the results. Two observations can

Entities	Points inside each NVP	Average BPs per NVP	Number of Pre-comp. Bor-Bor	Number of Pre-comp. OPC
Hospital	1698	52	232,000	8,781,000
Shopping	458	25	225,600	4,653,000
Parks	142	14	239,500	2,630,000
Schools	64	10	246,000	1,787,000
Auto Svc.	38	7	239,900	1,611,000
Restaurants	27	6	243,600	1,348,000

Table 2: Overhead of pre-computations

be made from the figure. First, the ratio of the size of the candidate set (we term SKS) over K decreases as K increases. For example, while 13 candidates are selected when K=3 (4.3 times the value of K), only 25 candidates are selected when K=10 (2.5 times the value of K). The figure also shows that for large values of K, the size of the candidate sets become very close to K. The reason for this is that as K increases, once a generator g is explored as the K-th nearest neighbor of a query object q, the possibility that some of its adjacent generators have already been explored as the $(K-1)$-st nearest neighbors and no longer need to be examined increases. This is a very important feature of VN³'s filter step since for large values of K, the average number of points of interest that must be examined significantly decreases. The second observation is that the VN³ filter step behaves independently from the density of the points of interest and their distribution in the network. For example, while Churches have a cardinality ratio of almost 24 times the Hospitals, the difference between the corresponding generated candidate sets is only 1.5% (for K=1000) to 11% (for K=3). This means that whether the points of interest are very dense or sparsely scattered in the network, the performance of the VN³ filter step does not change. This is because the average number of adjacent generators specified in Property 4 is "independent" of the density of the points of interest, their distribution, and the underlying network.

We also performed KNN queries on the second data set using the approaches proposed in [11] and [4]. Figure 7 compares the minimum and maximum values of $\frac{SKS}{K}$ for VN³ with those of [11] and [4], which are represented in the figure by "Seidl" and "Hjaltason", respectively. As shown in the figure, there is a significant

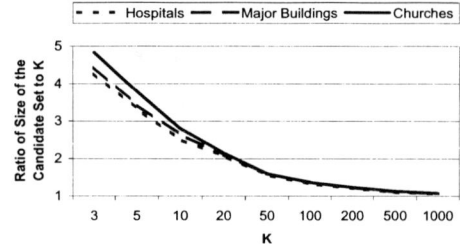

Figure 6: Performance of the filter step of VN^3

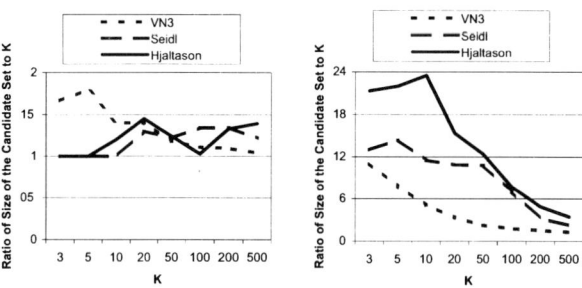

a. Minimum size of the candidate set
b. Maximum size of the candidate set

Figure 7: VN^3 filter step vs. Seidl & Hjaltason

difference between the minimum and maximum values of $\frac{SKS}{K}$, e.g., while the minimum sizes of the candidate sets generated by Seidl and Hjaltason are equal to K when K=5, their maximum sizes are 15 and 22 times larger than K, respectively. The average size of the candidate set generated by these approaches are up to 4 times larger than that of VN^3. We conclude that VN^3 filter step outperforms approaches optimized for index structures by providing better average values and a lower variance on the size of the candidate set, resulting in a more deterministic query response time.

6 Conclusion

In this paper we presented a novel approach for K nearest neighbor queries in spatial network databases. Our approach, VN^3, is based on precalculating the network Voronoi polygons (NVP) and pre-computing some network distances. We showed that since NVPs preserve network distances, they can immediately be used to find the first nearest neighbor of a query object. We also introduced new properties of NVPs that prove the nearest neighbors of the query object are within the adjacent NVPs of the previously explored nearest neighbors. Subsequently, we proposed alternative approaches that utilize the pre-computation component of VN^3 to compute the exact network distances from the query object to its potential nearest neighbors. We finally discussed how VN^3 can cope with database updates. The main features of VN^3 are as follow.

- VN^3 outperforms INE in query response time by a factor of 1.5 to 12 depending on the value of K and density of the points of interest.

- The VN3's filter step results in up to 4 times less number of candidates as compared to that of the traditional approaches. In addition, the size of VN3's candidate set has less variance across different locations of the query points and densities of the points of interest, resulting in more deterministic query response time.

- Although VN^3 is built on complex properties to prove its correctness, but it is a straightforward approach to implement by utilizing simple data structures such as R-tree and lookup tables.

- The pre-computation required by VN^3 has low computation and space complexities due to performing the pre-computations in local areas as opposed to across the entire network. This also results in reasonable update costs.

We plan to extend VN^3 to address similar KNN queries such as group and continuous KNN.

7 Acknowledgement

This research has been funded in part by NSF grants EEC-9529152 (IMSC ERC), IIS-0238560 (CAREER), IIS-0324955 (ITR), unrestricted cash gift from the Microsoft Corporation, and in part by grant 03CRSA0631 from the US Geological Survey (USGS).

References

[1] S. Berchtold, B. Ertl, D. A. Keim, H.-P. Kriegel, and T. Scidl. "Fast Nearest Neighbor Search in High-Dimensional Space". In *ICDE 1998, Orlando, Florida, USA*.

[2] T. Chiueh. "Content-Based Image Indexing". In *VLDB 1994, Santiago de Chile, Chile*.

[3] P. Ciaccia, M. Patella, and P. Zezula. "M-tree: An Efficient Access Method for Similarity Search in Metric Spaces". In *The VLDB Journal*, pages 426–435, 1997.

[4] G. R. Hjaltason and H. Samet. "Distance Browsing in Spatial Databases". *TODS*, 24(2):265–318, 1999.

[5] C. S. Jensen, J. Kolarvr, T. B. Pedersen, and I. Timko. "Nearest Neighbor Queries in Road Networks". In *ACMGIS 2003, New Orleans, Louisiana, USA*.

[6] S. Jung and S. Pramanik. "An Efficient Path Computation Model for Hierarchically Structured Topological Road Maps". In *IEEE Transaction on Knowledge and Data Engineering*, 2002.

[7] F. Korn, N. Sidiropoulos, C. Faloutsos, E. Siegel, and Z. Protopapas. "Fast Nearest Neighbor Search in Medical Image Databases". In *VLDB 1996, Mumbai (Bombay), India*.

[8] A. Okabe, B. Boots, K. Sugihara, and S. N. Chiu. "Spatial Tessellations, Concepts and Applications of Voronoi Diagrams". John Wiley and Sons Ltd., 2nd edition, 2000.

[9] D. Papadias, J. Zhang, N. Mamoulis, and Y. Tao. "Query Processing in Spatial Network Databases". In *VLDB 2003, Berlin, Germany*.

[10] N. Roussopoulos, S. Kelley, and F. Vincent. "'Nearest Neighbor Queries". In *SIGMOD 1995, San Jose, California*.

[11] T. Seidl and H.-P. Kriegel. "Optimal Multi-Step k-Nearest Neighbor Search". In *SIGMOD 1998, Seattle, Washington, USA*.

[12] C. Shahabi, M. R. Kolahdouzan, and M. Sharifzadeh. "A Road Network Embedding Technique for k-Nearest Neighbor Search in Moving Object Databases". In *ACMGIS 2002, McLean, VA, USA*.

A Framework for Projected Clustering of High Dimensional Data Streams

Charu C. Aggarwal
T. J. Watson Resch. Ctr.
charu@us.ibm.com

Jiawei Han[*], Jianyong Wang[†]
UIUC
{ hanj, wangj }@cs.uiuc.edu

Philip S. Yu
T. J. Watson Resch. Ctr.
psyu@us.ibm.com

Abstract

The data stream problem has been studied extensively in recent years, because of the great ease in collection of stream data. The nature of stream data makes it essential to use algorithms which require only one pass over the data. Recently, single-scan, stream analysis methods have been proposed in this context. However, a lot of stream data is high-dimensional in nature. High-dimensional data is inherently more complex in clustering, classification, and similarity search. Recent research discusses methods for projected clustering over high-dimensional data sets. This method is however difficult to generalize to data streams because of the complexity of the method and the large volume of the data streams.

In this paper, we propose a new, high-dimensional, projected data stream clustering method, called **HPStream**. The method incorporates a *fading cluster structure*, and the *projection based clustering* methodology. It is incrementally updatable and is highly scalable on both the number of dimensions and the size of the data streams, and it achieves better clustering quality in comparison with the previous stream clustering methods. Our performance study with both real and synthetic data sets demonstrates the efficiency and effectiveness of our proposed framework and implementation methods.

---

[*]The second author was supported in part by the U.S. National Science Foundation Grant IIS-03-08215 and an IBM Faculty Award.

[†]Current Address: University of Minnesota at Twin-Cities, Minneapolis, MN 55345, Email: jianyong@cs.umn.edu

Permission to copy without fee all or part of this material is granted provided that the copies are not made or distributed for direct commercial advantage, the VLDB copyright notice and the title of the publication and its date appear, and notice is given that copying is by permission of the Very Large Data Base Endowment. To copy otherwise, or to republish, requires a fee and/or special permission from the Endowment.

**Proceedings of the 30th VLDB Conference,
Toronto, Canada, 2004**

1 Introduction

The problem of data streams has gained importance in recent years because of advances in hardware technology. These advances have made it easy to store and record numerous transactions and activities in everyday life in an automated way. The ubiquitous presence of data streams in a number of practical domains has generated a lot of research in this area [8, 10, 12, 13, 17]. One of the important problems which has recently been explored in the data stream domain is that of clustering [17]. The clustering problem is especially interesting for the data stream domain because of its application to data summarization and outlier detection.

The clustering problem is defined as follows: *for a given set of data points, we wish to partition them into one or more groups of similar objects, where the notion of similarity is defined by a distance function*. There have been a lot of research work devoted to scalable cluster analysis in recent years [2, 6, 14, 15, 16, 18]. In the data stream domain, the clustering problem requires a process which can continuously determine the dominant clusters in the data without being dominated by the previous history of the stream.

The high-dimensional case presents a special challenge to clustering algorithms even in the traditional domain of static data sets. This is because of the sparsity of the data in the high-dimensional case. In high-dimensional space, all pairs of points tend to be almost equidistant from one another. As a result, it is often unrealistic to define distance-based clusters in a meaningful way. Some recent work on high-dimensional data uses techniques for *projected clustering* which can determine clusters for a specific subset of dimensions [2, 6]. In these methods, the definitions of the clusters are such that each cluster is specific to a particular group of dimensions. This alleviates the sparsity problem in high-dimensional space to some extent. Even though a cluster may not be meaningfully defined on all the dimensions because of the sparsity of the data, some subset of the dimensions can always be found on which particular subsets of points form high quality and meaningful clusters. Of course, these subsets of dimensions may vary over the different clusters. Such clusters are referred to as *projected clusters* [2].

The concept of a projected cluster is formally defined as follows. Assume that k is the number of clusters to be found. In addition, the algorithm will take as input the dimensionality l of the subspace in which each cluster is reported. The output of the algorithm will be twofold:

- A $(k+1)$-way partition $\{C_1, ..., C_k, \mathcal{O}\}$ of the data, such that the points in each partition element except the last form a cluster, whereas the points in the last partition element are the *outliers*, which by definition do not cluster well.
- A possibly different set $\mathcal{E}_i$ of dimensions for each cluster C_i, $1 \leq i \leq k$, such that the points in C_i cluster well in the subspace defined by these vectors. (The vectors for the outlier set $\mathcal{O}$ can be assumed to be the empty set.) For each cluster C_i, the cardinality of the corresponding set $\mathcal{E}_i$ is equal to the user-defined parameter l.

In the context of a data stream, the problem of finding projected clusters becomes even more challenging. This is because the additional problem of *finding the relevant set of dimensions for each cluster* makes the problem significantly more computationally intensive in the data stream environment. While the problem of clustering has recently been studied in the data stream environment [3, 8, 11], these methods are for the case of full dimensional clustering. In this paper, we will work on the significantly more difficult problem of clustering high-dimensional data stream by exploring projected clustering methods. We note that existing projected clustering methods such as those discussed in [2] cannot be easily generalized to the data stream problem because they typically require multiple passes over the data. Furthermore, the algorithms in [2] are too computationally intensive to be used for the data stream problem. In addition, data streams quickly evolve over time [4, 5] because of which it is essential to design methods which are designed to effectively adjust with the progression of the stream.

In this paper, we will develop an algorithm for high-dimensional projected stream clustering by continuous refinement of the set of projected dimensions and data points during the progression of the stream. We will refer to this algorithm as HPStream, since it describes the High-dimensional Projected Stream clustering method. The updating of the set of dimensions associated with each cluster is performed in such a way that the points and dimensions associated with each cluster can effectively evolve over time. In order to achieve this goal, we utilize a condensed representation of the statistics of the points inside the clusters. These condensed representations are chosen in such a way that they can be updated effectively in a fast data stream. At the same time, a sufficient amount of statistics is stored so that important measures about the cluster in a given projection can be quickly computed. In the next section, we will discuss the *fading cluster structure* which is useful for such book-keeping. This structure is also capable of performing the updates in such a way that outdated data is temporally discounted. This ensures that in an evolving data stream, the past history is gradually discounted from the computation.

In comparison with the previous literature, we have made substantial progress in the following aspects:

1. HPStream introduces the concept of *projected clustering* to data streams. Since a lot of stream data is high-dimensional in nature, it is necessary to perform high quality high-dimensional clustering. However, the previous stream clustering methods, such as STREAM and CluStream, cannot handle such data well, due to their clustering of data in all the relevant dimensions. Moreover, PROCLUS, though exploring *projected clustering*, cannot handle data streams due to its requirement of multiple scans of the data.

2. HPStream explores a linear update philosophy in projected clustering, achieving both high scalability and high clustering quality. This philosophy was first proposed in BIRCH. CluStream introduces this idea to stream clustering, however, it does not show good quality with high dimensional data. With projected clustering, HPStream can reach consistently high clustering quality due to its adaptability to the nature of real data set, where data shows its tight clustering behavior only at different subsets of dimension combinations.

Besides the above major progress, HPStream has proposed and explored several other innovative ideas. For example, the *fading cluster structure*, nicely integrates historical and current data with a user-specified or user-tunable fading factor. Also, using bit-vector for registration and dynamic update of relevant dimensions, and using minimal radius for clustering quality enhancement have improved the clustering efficiency and accuracy.

The remaining of the paper is organized as follows. In Section 2, we will discuss the basic concepts that are necessary for developing the algorithm. In Section 3, we will introduce the HPStream algorithm of this paper. Section 4 reports our performance study on real and synthetic data sets. We will compare the HPStream algorithm to the full dimensional CluStream algorithm. A brief discussion of the possible extensions of this work is included in Section 5. The conclusions and summary are discussed in Section 6.

2 The Fading Cluster Structure: Motivation and Concepts

The data stream consists of a set of multi-dimensional records $\overline{X_1} \ldots \overline{X_k} \ldots$ arriving at time stamps $T_1 \ldots T_k \ldots$. Each data point $\overline{X_i}$ is a multi-dimensional record containing d dimensions, denoted by $\overline{X_i} = (x_i^1 \ldots x_i^d)$. Since the stream clustering process should provide a greater level of importance to recent data points, we introduce the concept of a *fading data structure* which is able to adjust for the recency of the clusters in a flexible way. It is assumed that each data point has a weight defined by a function $f(t)$ to the time t. The function $f(t)$ is also referred to as the *fading function*. The value of the fading function lies in the range $(0, 1)$. It is also assumed that the fading function is a monotonic decreasing function which decays uniformly with time t. In particular, we choose an exponential form for the fading function. The exponentially fading function is widely used in temporal applications in which it is desirable to gradually discount the history of past behavior. In order to formalize the concept of the fading function, we will define the *half-life* of a point in the data stream.

Definition 2.1 *The half life t_0 of a point is defined as the time at which $f(t_0) = (1/2) f(0)$.*

Conceptually, the aim of defining a half life is to define the rate of decay of the weight assigned to each data point in the stream. Correspondingly, the *decay-rate* is defined as the inverse of the half life of the data stream. We denote the decay rate by $\lambda = 1/t_0$. In order for the half-life property to hold, we define the *weight* of each point in the data stream by $f(t) = 2^{-\lambda \cdot t}$. From the perspective of the clustering process, the weight of each data point is $f(t)$. It is easy to see that this decay function creates a half life of $1/\lambda$. It is also evident that by changing the value of λ, it is possible to change the rate at which the importance of the historical information in the data stream decays. The higher the value of λ, the lower the importance of the historical information compared to more recent data.

We will now define the *fading cluster structure*, a data structure which is designed to capture key statistical characteristics of the clusters generated during the course of a data stream. The aim of the fading cluster structure is to capture a sufficient number of the underlying statistics so that it is possible to compute key characteristics of the underlying clusters.

Definition 2.2 *A fading cluster structure at time t for a set of d-dimensional points $\mathcal{C} = \{X_{i_1} \ldots X_{i_n}\}$ with time stamps $T_{i_1} \ldots T_{i_n}$ is defined as the $(2 \cdot d + 1)$ tuple $\mathcal{FC}(\mathcal{C}, t) = (\overline{FC2^x(\mathcal{C}, t)}, \overline{FC1^x(\mathcal{C}, t)}, W(t))$. The vectors $\overline{FC2^x(\mathcal{C}, t)}$ and $\overline{FC1^x(\mathcal{C}, t)}$ each contain d entries. We will now explain the significance of each of these sets of entries:*

1. *For each dimension j, the jth entry of $\overline{FC2^x(\mathcal{C}, t)}$ is given by the weighted sum of the squares of the corresponding data values in that dimension. The weight of each data point is defined by its level of staleness since its arrival in the data stream. Thus, $\overline{FC2^x(\mathcal{C}, t)}$ contains d values. The j-th entry of $\overline{FC2^x(\mathcal{C}, t)}$ is equal to $\sum_{k=1}^{n} f(t - T_{i_k}) \cdot (x_{i_k}^j)^2$.*

2. *For each dimension j, the jth entry of $\overline{FC1^x(\mathcal{C}, t)}$ is given by the weighted sum of the corresponding data values. The weight of each data point is defined by its level of staleness since its arrival in the data stream. Thus, $\overline{FC1^x(\mathcal{C}, t)}$ contains d values. The j-th entry of $\overline{FC1^x(\mathcal{C}, t)}$ is equal to $\sum_{k=1}^{n} f(t - T_{i_k}) \cdot (x_{i_k}^j)$.*

3. *We also maintain a single entry $W(t)$ containing the sum of all the weights of the data points at time t. Thus, this entry is equal to $W(t) = \sum_{k=1}^{n} f(t - T_{i_k})$.*

The clustering structure discussed above satisfies a number of interesting properties. These properties are referred to as *additivity* and *temporal multiplicity*. The additivity property is defined as follows:

Observation 2.1 *Let $\mathcal{C}_1$ and $\mathcal{C}_2$ be two clusters with cluster structures $\mathcal{FC}(\mathcal{C}_1, t)$ and $\mathcal{FC}(\mathcal{C}_2, t)$ respectively. Then, the cluster structure of $\mathcal{C}_1 \cup \mathcal{C}_2$ is given by $\mathcal{FC}(\mathcal{C}_1 \cup \mathcal{C}_2, t) = \mathcal{FC}(\mathcal{C}_1, t) + \mathcal{FC}(\mathcal{C}_2, t)$.*

The additivity property follows from the fact that each cluster can be expressed as a sum of its individual components. The temporal multiplicity property is defined as follows:

Observation 2.2 *Consider the cluster structure at the time $\mathcal{FC}(\mathcal{C}, t)$. If no points are added to $\mathcal{C}$ in the time interval $(t, t + \delta t)$, then $\mathcal{FC}(\mathcal{C}, t + \delta t) = e^{-\lambda \delta t} \cdot \mathcal{FC}(\mathcal{C}, t)$.*

We note that this property holds because of the exponential decay of each component of the cluster structure.

Since the algorithm in this paper is designed for projected clustering of data streams, a set of dimensions is associated with each cluster. Therefore, with each cluster $\mathcal{C}$, we associate a d-dimensional bit vector $\mathcal{B}(\mathcal{C})$ which corresponds to the relevant set of dimensions in $\mathcal{C}$. Each element in this d-dimensional vector has a 1-0 value corresponding to whether or not a given dimension is included in that cluster. This bit vector is required for the book-keeping needed in the assignment of incoming points to the appropriate cluster. As the algorithm progresses, this bit vector varies in order to reflect the changing set of dimensions. In the next section, we will discuss the clustering algorithm along with the various procedures which are used for cluster maintenance.

3 The High Dimensional Projected Clustering Algorithm

In this section, we will discuss how the individual clusters are maintained in an online fashion. The algorithm for high-dimensional clustering utilizes an iterative approach which continuously determines new cluster structures while re-defining the set of dimensions included in each cluster.

At the beginning of the clustering process, we run a *normalization process* in order to weigh different dimensions correctly. This is because the clustering algorithm needs to pick the dimensions which are specific to each cluster by comparing the radii along different dimensions. We note that different dimensions may

Algorithm HPStream (Data Stream Point: $\overline{X}$, Cluster Structures: $\mathcal{FCS}$,
  Dimensionality Vector Sets: $\mathcal{BS}$, MaxClusters: k, Dimensionality: l);
begin
  { Assume that $\mathcal{FCS}$ contains the relevant cluster structures denoted by $\mathcal{FCS} = \{\mathcal{FC}^x(\mathcal{C}_1, t) \ldots \mathcal{FC}^x(\mathcal{C}_r, t) \ldots\}$ }
  { Assume that $\mathcal{BS}$ contains the relevant cluster dimensions denoted by $\mathcal{BS} = \{\mathcal{B}(\mathcal{C}_1) \ldots \mathcal{B}(\mathcal{C}_r) \ldots\}$ }
  Receive the next data point $\overline{X}$ at current time t from stream $\mathcal{DS}$;
  $\mathcal{BS} = ComputeDimensions(\mathcal{FCS}, l, \overline{X})$;
  for $r = 1$ to $|\mathcal{FCS}|$ **do**
    $ds(r) = FindProjectedDist(FC^x(\mathcal{C}_r, t), \mathcal{B}(\mathcal{C}_r, \overline{X}))$;
  $index = \text{argmax}_i \{ds(i)\}$;
  $s = FindLimitingRadius(FC^x(\mathcal{C}_{index}, t,), \mathcal{B}(\mathcal{C}_{index}))$;
  if $ds(index) > s$
  then set $index = |\mathcal{FCS}| + 1$ and add new fading cluster structure $\mathcal{C}_{|\mathcal{FCS}|+1}$ with a solitary data point to $\mathcal{FCS}$;
  else add $\overline{X}$ to $FC^x(\mathcal{C}_{index}, t)$;
  Remove those clusters from $\mathcal{FCS}$ which have zero dimensions assigned to them;
  if $|\mathcal{FCS}| > k$
  then delete the least recently added cluster in $\mathcal{FCS}$;
end;

Figure 1: Basic Algorithm for Clustering High-dimensional Data Streams

Algorithm $FindProjectedDist(FadedClusterStructure : FC^x(\mathcal{C}_r, t), Bitvector : \mathcal{B}(\mathcal{C}_r, Datapoint : \overline{X})$;
begin
  { This procedure finds Manhattan Segmental Distance along the projected dimensions }
  for each dimension with bit value of 1 in $\mathcal{B}(\mathcal{C}_r)$
    find the distance between $\overline{X}$ and the centroid of $\mathcal{B}(\mathcal{C}_r)$;
  return average distance along the included dimensions;
end

Figure 2: Finding the Projected Distance

Algorithm $ComputeDimensions$(Faded Cluster Structures:$\mathcal{FCS}$, NumberofDimensions: l, Incoming Point: $\overline{X}$);
begin
  Create $|\mathcal{FCS}|$ (tentative) fading cluster structures by adding $\overline{X}$ to each of the existing clusters;
  Compute the $|\mathcal{FCS}| * d$ radii of each of the $|\mathcal{FCS}|$ (tentative) clusters along each of the d dimensions;
  Pick the $|\mathcal{FCS} * l|$ dimensions with the least radii;
  Create a bitvector $\mathcal{B}(\mathcal{C}_r)$ for each cluster $\mathcal{C}_r$ reflecting its projected dimensions;
end;

Figure 3: Computing the Projected Dimensions

Algorithm $FindLimitingRadius$(Faded Cluster Structure: $FC^x(\mathcal{C}_{index}, t)$, Bitvector: $\mathcal{B}(\mathcal{C}_{index})$)
begin
  { Find the radius r' of the cluster using only the dimensions contained in $\mathcal{B}(\mathcal{C}_{index})$;}
  $r_j^2 = \overline{FC2^x(\mathcal{C}, t)}_j / W(t) - \overline{FC1^x(\mathcal{C}, t)}_j * \overline{FC1^x(\mathcal{C}, t)}_j / W(t)^2$;
  $R = \sum_{j \in \mathcal{B}(\mathcal{C})} r_j^2$;
  Let d' be the number of bits in $\mathcal{B}(\mathcal{C})$ with value of 1;
  $R = \sqrt{R/d'}$;
  return$(R * \tau;)$
end

Figure 4: Finding the Limiting Radius of the Cluster

refer to different scales of reference such as age, salary or other attributes which have vastly different ranges and variances. Therefore, it is not possible to compare the dimensions in a meaningful way using the original data. In order to be able to compare different dimensions meaningfully, we perform a normalization process. The aim is to equalize the standard deviation along each dimension. We use an initial sample of the data points to calculate the standard deviation σ_i of each dimension i. Subsequently, the value of dimension i for each data point is divided by σ_i. We note that since the data stream may evolve over time, the values of σ_i may change as well. Therefore, the normalization factor is recomputed on a periodic basis. Specifically, this process is repeated at an interval of every N' points. However, whenever the value of σ_i changes, the corresponding fading cluster statistics may also need to be changed. Let us assume that the standard deviation of dimension i changes from σ_i to σ'_i during a normalization phase. Then, the cluster statistics $\mathcal{FC}(\mathcal{C}, t) = (\overline{FC2^x(\mathcal{C}, t)}, \overline{FC1^x(\mathcal{C}, t)}, W(t))$ for each cluster $\mathcal{C}$ needs to be correspondingly modified. Specifically, the ith entry in $(\overline{FC2^x(\mathcal{C}, t)})$ needs to be multiplied by σ_i^2/σ'^2_i, whereas the ith entry in $\overline{FC1^x(\mathcal{C}, t)}$ needs to be multiplied by σ_i/σ'_i.

In Figure 1, we have illustrated the basic (incremental) algorithm for clustering high-dimensional data streams. Thus, the incremental pseudo-code shows the steps associated with adding one point to the data stream. The input to the algorithm includes the current cluster structure $\mathcal{FCS}$, and the sets of dimensions associated with each cluster. These cluster structures and sets of dimensions are dynamically updated as the algorithm progresses. The set of dimensions $\mathcal{BS}$ associated with each cluster includes a d-dimensional bit vector $\mathcal{B}(\mathcal{C}_i)$ for each cluster structure in $\mathcal{FCS}$. This bit vector contains a 1 bit for each dimension which is included in cluster $\mathcal{C}_i$. In addition, the maximum number of clusters k and the average cluster dimensionality l is used as an input parameter. The average cluster dimensionality l represents the average number of dimensions used in the cluster projection.

The data stream clustering algorithm utilizes an iterative approach by assigning data points to the closest cluster structure at each step of the algorithm. The closest cluster structure is determined by using a *projected distance measure*. For each cluster, only those dimensions which are relevant to that cluster are utilized in the distance computation. At the same time, we continue to re-define the set of projected dimensions associated with each cluster. The re-definition of the projected dimensions aims to keep the radii of the clusters over the projected dimensions as low as possible. Thus, *the clustering process requires a simultaneous maintenance of the clusters as well as the set of dimensions associated with each cluster.*

We will now proceed to systematically describe the steps of the high-dimensional clustering algorithm. A pseudo-code of the algorithm is described in Figure 1.

- The set of dimensions associated with each cluster are updated using the procedure *ComputeDimensions*. This procedure determines the dimensions in such a way that the spread along the chosen dimensions is as small as possible. We note that many of the clusters may contain only a few points. This makes it difficult to compute the dimensions in a statistically robust way. In the extreme case, a cluster may contain only one point. In this degenerate case, the computation of the dimensions is not possible since the radii along different dimensions cannot be distinguished. In order to deal with such degenerate cases, we need to use the incoming data point $\overline{X}$ during the determination of the dimensions for each cluster. It is desirable to pick the dimensions in such a way that $\overline{X}$ fits the selected cluster well even after the projected dimensions are selected. Specifically, the data point $\overline{X}$ is temporarily added to each possible cluster during the process of determination of dimensions. This makes significant difference to the chosen dimensions for clusters which contain very few data points. Once these selected dimensions have been chosen, the corresponding bits are stored in $\mathcal{BS}$.

- The next step is the determination of the closest cluster structure to the incoming data point $\overline{X}$. In order to do so, we compute the distance of $\overline{X}$ to each cluster centroid using only the set of projected dimensions for the corresponding cluster. This data in $\mathcal{BS}$ is used as a book-keeping mechanism to determine the set of projected dimensions for each cluster during the distance computation. The corresponding procedure is referred to as *FindProjectedDist*. We will discuss more details about this procedure slightly later.

- Once it is decided which cluster the data point $\overline{X}$ should be assigned to, we determine the natural *limiting radius* of the corresponding cluster. The limiting radius is considered a natural boundary of the cluster. Data points which lie outside this natural boundary are not added to the cluster. Instead such points create new clusters of their own. The procedure for determination of the limiting radius is denoted by *FindLimitingRadius*.

- If the incoming data point lies inside the limiting radius, it is added to the cluster. Otherwise, a new cluster needs to be constructed containing the solitary data point $\overline{X}$. We note that if the new data point is noise, the newly created cluster will subsequently have few points added to it. As explained below, this will ultimately lead to the deletion of that cluster.

- In the event that a new cluster is created, the total number of cluster structures in $\mathcal{FCS}$ may increase. Therefore, one cluster needs to be deleted in order to make room for the incoming cluster. In that case, the cluster structure to which the least recent updating was performed is deleted. Thus rule ensures that only stale and outdated clusters are removed by the update process.

In order to determine the closest cluster to the incoming data point, we use the procedure for determining the projected distance of $\overline{X}$ from each cluster $\mathcal{C}_r$. The method for finding this distance is discussed in the procedure *FindProjectedDist*, and is illustrated in Figure 2. In order to find the projected distance, the distance along each dimension with bit value of 1 in $\mathcal{B}(\mathcal{C}_r)$ is determined. The average distance along these dimensions (also known as the *Manhattan Segmental Distance* [2]) is reported as the projected distance. We note that it is not necessary to normalize the distance measurements at this point, since the entire stream has already been normalized at this point. This distance value is computed for each cluster, and the data point $\overline{X}$ is added to the cluster with the least distance value.

The procedure for finding the limiting radius is illustrated in Figure 4. The motivation for finding the limiting radius is to determine the natural boundary of the clusters. Incoming data points which do not lie within this limiting radius of their closest cluster must be assigned a cluster of their own. This is because these data points do not naturally fit inside any of the existing clusters. The limiting radius is defined as a certain factor τ of the average radius of the data points in the cluster. This radius can be computed using the statistics in the fading cluster structure.

We note that the fading cluster structure contains the first and second order moments of the data points inside the clusters. The average square radius along the dimension j is given by:

$$r_j^2 = \overline{FC2^x(\mathcal{C},t)}_j/W(t) - \overline{FC1^x(\mathcal{C},t)}_j * \overline{FC1^x(\mathcal{C},t)}_j/W(t)^2. \quad (1)$$

The square radius over the dimensions included in $\mathcal{B}(\mathcal{C})$ is averaged in order to find the total square radius of the included dimensions. The square root of this value is the relevant radius of the cluster along the projected set of dimensions. Thus, we find $R = \sqrt{\sum_{j \in \mathcal{B}(\mathcal{C})} r_j^2 / d'}$. Here d' is the number of dimensions included in that projected cluster. This value is scaled by a boundary factor τ in order to decide the final value of the limiting radius. Thus, any incoming data point which lies outside a factor τ of the average radius along the projected dimensions of its closest cluster needs to create a new cluster containing a solitary data point.

In Figure 3, we have illustrated the process of computation of the projected dimensions. This is accomplished by calculating the spread along each dimension for each cluster in $\mathcal{FCS}$. Thus, a total of $|\mathcal{FCS}| * d$ values are computed and ranked in increasing order. We select the $|\mathcal{FCS}| * l$ dimensions with the least radii as the projected dimensions for that cluster. The incoming data point $\overline{X}$ is included in each cluster for the purpose of computation of dimensions. This ensures that if the incoming data point is added to that cluster, the corresponding set of projected dimensions reflect the included data point $\overline{X}$. This helps in a more stable computation of the projected dimensionality when the cluster contains a small number of data points.

We note that whenever a data point is assigned to a cluster, it needs to be added to the statistics of the corresponding cluster. For this purpose, we need to use the additive and temporal multiplicity properties. The temporal multiplicity is applied in a lazy way at specific instants when a new data point is added to a cluster. Thus, the temporal component of the cluster statistics may remain stale in many cases. However, this does not affect the execution of the overall algorithm. This is because the computation of other measures such as finding the projected distance or computing the dimensions is not affected by the temporal decay factor. The first step in assigning a data point to a cluster is to update the temporal decay function for each cluster. Let t be the current time and t^{up} be the last update time for that cluster. Then, each item in the fading cluster structure is multiplied by the factor $e^{-\lambda \cdot (t - t^{up})}$. At this point, the statistics for the incoming data point are added to the corresponding fading cluster structure statistics. The additivity property ensures that the updated cluster is represented by these statistics.

At the beginning of the data stream clustering process, it is necessary to perform an additional initialization process by which the original clusters are created. For this purpose, a certain initial portion (containing *InitNumber* points) is utilized. An offline process is used in order to create the initial clusters. This process is implemented as a K-means algorithm on an initial sample of the data points. First, a full dimensional K-means algorithm is applied to the data points so as to create the initial set of clusters. Then, the *ComputeDimensions* procedure is applied in order to determine the most relevant dimensions for each cluster. The set of dimensions associated with each cluster is used to compute a new set of assignments of data points to the corresponding centroids. We note that this new assignment is different from the full dimensional assignments, since the set of projected dimensions are used in order to calculate the closest centroid to each data point. These new assignments are utilized to create a new set of K centers. The process of recomputing the dimensions and the centroids is repeated iteratively until the procedure converges to a final set of clusters. These clusters are used to create the fading cluster structures at the beginning of the data stream computation.

We observe that the number of projected dimensions l is used as an input parameter. The *ComputeDimensions* procedure uses this input parameter in picking the $|\mathcal{FCS} * l|$ dimensions with the least radii. Instead of using a fixed number of projected dimensions based on the radius rank, we can use a threshold on the radii of the different dimensions. This would allow the number of projected dimensions to vary over the course of the execution of the data stream clustering process. The use of such a threshold can often be more intuitively appealing over a wide variety of data sets. Since the data normalization ensures that the standard deviation along each dimension is one unit, the threshold can be chosen in terms of the number of standard deviations per dimension. While there may be some variation across data sets in picking this value, this choice has better statistical interpretation.

4 Empirical Results

In this section we present our thorough experimental study in evaluating the various aspects of HPStream algorithm. All the experiments were performed on a Intel Pentium IV processor computer with 256MB memory and running on Windows XP professional. In [3], the authors proposed the CluStream algorithm, which has shown better clustering quality than the previously designed STREAM clustering algorithm [17]. In testing the clustering accuracy and efficiency, we compared our HPStream algorithm with CluStream. We implemented both algorithms in Microsoft Visual C++.

In the experiments, HPStream maintained the same number of the *fading cluster structures* as that of *micro-clusters* used by CluStream. The algorithm parameters for CluStream were chosen the same as those adopted in [3]. Unless otherwise mentioned, the parameters for HPStream were set as follows: decay-rate $\lambda = 0.5$, spread radius factor $\tau = 2$, $InitNumber = 2000$. Both real and synthetic data sets were used in evaluating HPStream's clustering quality, stream processing rate, scalability, and sensitivity.

Real data sets. Many previously proposed stream clustering algorithms [17, 3] chose the sum of square distance (or SSQ for short) to evaluate the clustering quality. The SSQ at current time T_c with a given horizon H (denoted as $SSQ(T_c, H)$) is computed as follows. For each point p_i, we find the centroid C_{p_i} of its closest cluster structure, and compute $d(p_i, C_{p_i})$, the distance between p_i and C_{p_i}. Then $SSQ(T_c, H)$ is equal to the sum of $d^2(p_i, C_{p_i})$ for all the points within the previous horizon H. However, SSQ is not a good measure in evaluating projected clustering because full dimensional measures are not very useful for measuring the quality of a projected clustering algorithm. For this purpose, we will try to find some large real data sets which contain class labels for the data points, although we do not use the class labels in the clustering process. Instead of using SSQ, we will use the *cluster purity* to assess the clustering accuracy. As in [1], the cluster purity is defined as the average percentage of the dominant class label in each cluster. Only those subset of points which arrive within a pre-defined window of time from the current instant were used to compute the cluster purity. Our empirical results showed that the qualitative results were generally not very sensitive to this choice of window or *horizon*.

The first real data set used was the KDD-CUP'99 *Network Intrusion Detection* stream data set which has been used to evaluate the clustering accuracy for several stream clustering algorithms [17, 3]. This data set corresponds to the important problem of automatic and real-time detection of cyber attacks and consists of a series of TCP connection records from two weeks of LAN network traffic managed by MIT Lincoln Labs. Each record can either correspond to a normal connection, or an intrusion which can be classified into one of 22 types. Most of the connections in this data set are *normal*, but occasionally there could be a burst of attacks at certain times. Also, this data set contains totally 494020 connection records, and each connection record has 42 attributes. As in [17, 3], all 34 continuous attributes will be used for clustering and one outlier point has been removed.

The second real data set we tested is the *Forest CoverType* data set and was obtained from the UCI machine learning repository website (i.e., http://www.ics.uci.edu/~mlearn). This data set contains totally 581012 observations and each observation consists of 54 attributes, including 10 quantitative variables, 4 binary wilderness areas and 40 binary soil type variables. In our testing, we used all the 10 quantitative variables. There are seven forest cover type classes.

Synthetic datasets. We also generated several synthetic data sets to test the clustering quality, efficiency and scalability. Because we know the true cluster distribution *a priori*, we can compare the clusters found with the true clusters and compute the cluster purity. The synthetic data set generator takes four parameters as input: the number of data points N, the number of natural clusters K, the number of dimensions d, and the average number of projected dimensions l (we required $l > \lfloor \frac{d}{2} \rfloor$). The number of projected dimensions in each cluster is uniformly distributed and drawn from $[l-x, l+x]$, where $1 \leq x \leq \lfloor \frac{d}{2} \rfloor$ and $(l-x) \geq 2$. The projected dimensions for each cluster were chosen randomly. The data points of each cluster are normally distributed with the mean for each cluster uniformly chosen from $[0, K)$. The standard deviation was defined as $\sqrt{v}$ for each projected dimension of any cluster, and $y \times \sqrt{v}$ where $(y > 1)$ for each of the other dimensions, where v was always randomly chosen from $[0.5, 2.5]$ for any dimension. In our experiments, we set parameters x and y at 2 and 3, respectively.

The data points for different clusters were generated at different times according to a pre-defined probability distribution. In order to reflect the evolution of the stream data over time, we randomly re-computed the probability of the appearance of a certain cluster periodically. We also assume the projected dimensions will evolve a little over time. In order to capture this kind of evolution, we randomly dropped one of the projected dimensions in one of the clusters and replaced it by a new dimension in a (possibly different) cluster. In addition, we will use the following notations in naming the synthetic data sets: 'B' indicates the base size, i.e., the number of data points in the data set, whereas 'C', 'D', and 'L' indicate the number of natural clusters, the dimensionality of each point, and the average number of projected dimensions, respectively. For example, *B100kC10D50L30* means the data set contains in total 100K data points of 50-dimensions, belonging to 10 different clusters, and on average, the number of projected dimensions is 30.

4.1 Clustering Evaluation

Here we present and analyze our experimental results on clustering quality (accuracy) and the efficiency of the comparing algorithms. An important discovery is that SSQ is no longer a good measure of clustering quality. Instead, cluster purity is taken as the measure of the clustering quality.

Accuracy comparison. We evaluated the clustering quality of the HPStream algorithm in comparison with the CluStream algorithm using both real and synthetic data sets.

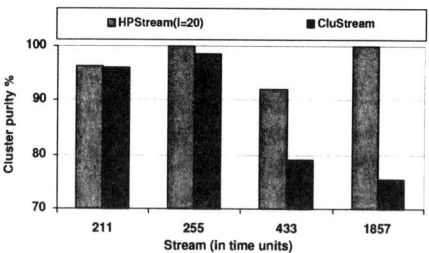

Figure 5: Quality comparison (Network Intrusion data set, horizon = 1, stream_speed = 200)

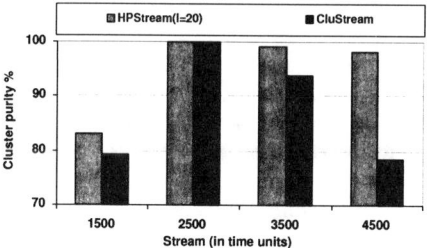

Figure 6: Quality comparison (Network Intrusion data set, horizon = 10, stream_speed = 100)

Figure 5 and Figure 6 show the clustering quality comparison results for the Network Intrusion Detection data set. In the experiments CluStream used all the 34 dimensions, while we set the average number of projected dimensions at 20 (i.e., $l = 20$) for HPStream, which means on average HPStream used 20 projected dimensions. In Figure 5, the stream speed is set at 200 points per time unit and horizon $H = 1$. We chose a series of time points when there were some kind of attack connections happened. For example, at time $T = 211$ there were 1 "*phf*" connection, 23 "*portsweep*" connections, and 176 "*normal*" connections during the past 1 horizon, while at time $T = 1857$, there were totally 79 "*smurf*", 99 "*teardrop*", and 22 "*pod*" attack connections for the last horizon. From Figure 5, we can see that HPStream has a very good clustering quality: its clustering purity is always higher than 90% and better than CluStream. For example, at time $T = 1857$, HPStream grouped different attack connections into different clusters, while CluStream grouped all kinds of attacks into one cluster, this is why HPStream's cluster purity is more than 20% higher than that of CluStream. We also set the stream speed at 100 points per time unit and horizon H at 10 to test the clustering quality, Figure 6 shows the results. Except at time $T = 2500$, HPStream always has a much higher cluster purity than CluStream. We checked the original class labels for the connections in the last ten horizons from the current time 2500 and found all the connections belong to one attack type, "*smurf*". As a result, no matter what clustering algorithms we used, they would always have a 100% cluster purity and this does not mean CluStream can do good job in this case.

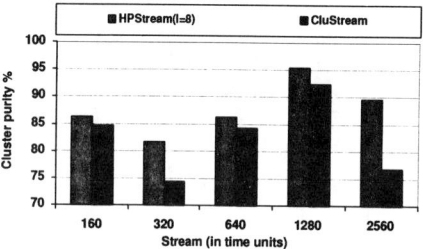

Figure 7: Quality comparison (Forest CoverType data set, horizon=1, stream_speed=200)

We also tested the clustering quality of HPStream for another real data set, *Forest CoverType*. For this data set, we set the average number of projected dimensions at 8 (i.e., $l = 8$). Figure 7 and Figure 8 show the clustering quality comparison results. In Figure 7, we set the stream speed at 200 points per time unit and compute the cluster purity at different time for the last one horizon (i.e., $H = 1$). Figure 7 shows that HPStream always has higher cluster purity than CluStream, even for such a data set with a not very high dimensionality (here $d = 10$). We then changed the stream speed to 100 points per time unit and horizon H to 10 and compare the cluster quality for the two algorithms. Figure 8 shows the similar picture: HPStream always has higher cluster purity than CluStream.

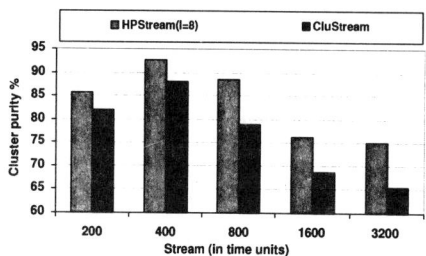

Figure 8: Quality comparison (Forest CoverType data set, horizon = 10, stream_speed = 100)

We generated one synthetic data set,

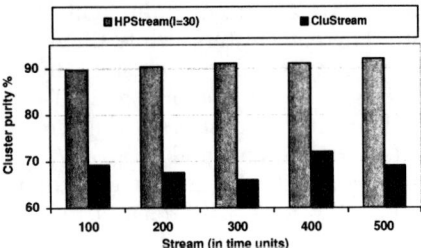

Figure 9: Quality comparison (Synthetic data set B100kC10D50L30, horizon = 1, stream_speed = 200)

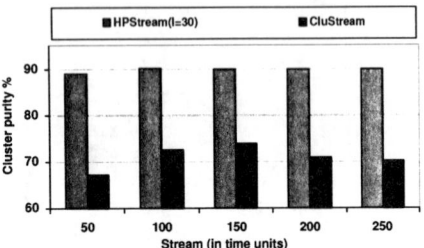

Figure 10: Quality comparison (Synthetic data set B100kC10D50L30, horizon = 10, stream_speed = 400)

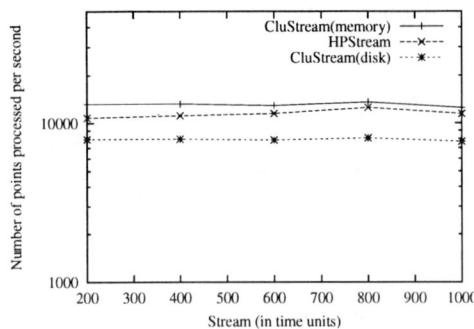

Figure 11: Stream Processing Rate (Network Intrusion data set, stream_speed = 200)

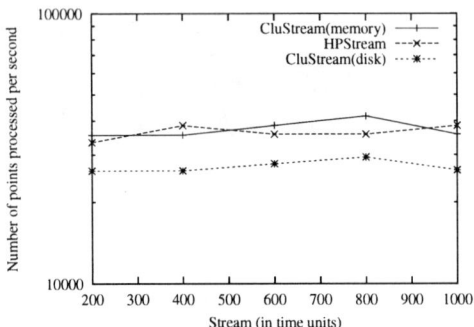

Figure 12: Stream Processing Rate (Forest CoverType data set, stream_speed = 200)

$B100kC10D50L30$, to test the clustering quality. This data set contains 100,000 points that has a total dimensionality of 50 and an average number of projected dimensions 30. The data points belong to 10 different clusters. In the experiments, we set l at 30 for HPStream. As Figure 9 shows when we set the stream speed at 200 points per time unit and horizon at 1, HPStream consistently has much better clustering quality than CluStream: On average, the cluster purity of HPStream is about 20% higher than that of CluStream. We then changed the stream speed to 400 points per time unit and used a lager horizon, $H = 10$, to test the clustering quality. Figure 10 shows that the cluster purity of the HPStream algorithm is always over 15% higher than that of CluStream.

Efficiency test. We used both the *Network Intrusion Detection* and *Forest CoverType* data sets to test the efficiency of HPStream against CluStream. Because the CluStream algorithm needs to periodically store away the current snapshot of *micro-clusters* under the *Pyramidal Time Framework*, we implemented two versions of the CluStream algorithm: One uses disk to maintain the snapshots of *micro-clusters*, and the other stores the snapshots of *micro-clusters* in memory. The algorithm efficiency is measured by the stream processing rate versus progression of the stream, which is defined as the inverse of the time required to process the last 1000 points (The unit is in points/second). In the experiments, we fixed the stream speed at 200 points per second.

Figure 11 shows the stream processing rate for Network Intrusion data set, from which we can see that HPStream is more efficient than the disk-based CluStream algorithm and is only marginally slower than the memory-based CluStream algorithm. However, as we know, the memory-based CluStream algorithm will consume much more memory than HPStream. In addition, for this data set, the processing rate of HPStream is very stable and is around 11,000 points/second, which means HPStream can support a high stream speed at 10,000 points/second. Figure 12 shows the stream processing rate for the *Forest CoverType* data set. Because this data set has a smaller dimensionality than the Network Intrusion data set, all these algorithms have a higher stream processing rate. For example, both HPStream and the memory-based CluStream algorithms have a stream processing speed around 35,000 points/second. Similarly, HPStream has a higher processing speed than the disk-based CluStream algorithm while consumes less memory than the memory-based CluStream algorithm.

4.2 Sensitivity Analysis

In sensitivity analysis, we show how sensitive the clustering quality is in relevance to the average projected dimensionality, the radius threshold, and the decay rate.

Choice of the average projected dimensionality l. The average projected dimensionality l plays an important role in choosing a proper set of projected dimensions that are used by HPStream to do clustering, we want to know how sensitive it is in affecting the clustering quality. Because we know the true average projected dimensionality in advance for synthetic data sets, we will use the synthetic data set *B100kC10D50L30* to test the clustering quality by choosing different average projected dimensionality l.

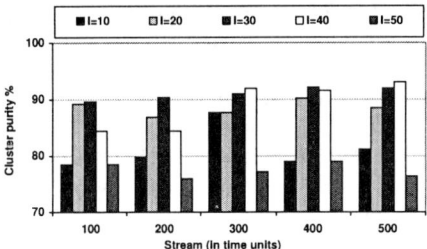

Figure 13: Choice of l (Synthetic data set B100kC10D50L30, horizon = 5, stream_speed = 200)

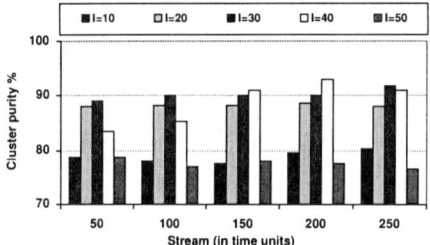

Figure 14: Choice of l (Synthetic data set B100kC10D50L30, horizon = 10, stream_speed = 400)

B100kC10D50L30 was generated with an average projected dimensionality $l = 30$, in our experiments we used a series of different l's, i.e., {10, 20, 30, 40, 50}, to test the clustering quality. We first fixed the stream speed at 200 points per time unit and horizon at 5. Figure 13 shows the result. As we can see, overall $l = 30$ can lead to the best cluster purity, and a too small l at 10 or a too large l at 50 will generate very poor clustering quality. In addition, the cluster purity for $l = 20$ or $l = 40$ is very similar to that for $l = 30$, which suggests as long as we choose a value for l in the range from 20 to 40, HPStream will have a very good clustering quality.

We then set the stream speed at 400 points per time unit and horizon H at 10, and did the same set of tests. Figure 14 shows the result, which is very similar to that in Figure 13. In addition, under the same settings and with the same data set, from Figure 10 we know CluStream never generated a cluster purity higher than 80%, as a result, no matter what value we choose for l from 20, 30, or 40, HPStream always has much better cluster purity than CluStream

The above experiments about the sensitivity of the average projected dimensionality l demonstrate that as long as we choose for l a value not too deviated from the true average projected dimensionality, HPStream will have a high clustering quality. We also did some further tests using the Network Intrusion Detection data set and found HPStream always generated similar clustering solution if we chose for l a value in the range from 20 to 30.

Choice of the radius threshold. Although the average projected dimensionality l provides a very flexible and natural way for HPStream to pick the set of well correlated dimensions for clustering high-dimensional data, however, in some cases a radius threshold may be more intuitively chosen as an alternative in selecting the set of projected dimensions. This quality-controlled parameter would allow the number of projected dimensions evolve over the stream. For example, among the 34 dimensions for Network Intrusion Detection data set, most of them have a deviation 0 for a certain type of connections. If the user has this knowledge in advance, he may choose a radius threshold which is very close to 0 in defining the set of projected dimensions.

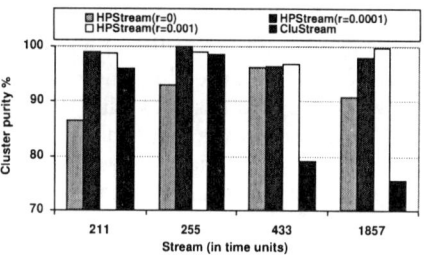

Figure 15: Quality comparison based on the radius threshold (Network Intrusion data set, horizon = 1, stream_speed = 200)

Figure 15 shows the test result for the Network Intrusion data set by setting the stream speed at 200 points per time unit and horizon H at 1. In the experiments, we test against CluStream the clustering quality of HPStream with varying radius threshold as an input parameter. The result shows that if we set the radius threshold at 0.001 or 0.0001, HPStream always has much better clustering quality than CluStream. For example, at time $T = 1857$, the cluster purity of HPStream is more than 20% higher than that of CluStream. This suggests a radius threshold in the range [0.0001, 0.001] could make HPStream generate very good clustering solutions for the Network Intrusion data set.

Choice of the decay rate λ. Another important parameter for HPStream is the decay rate λ, which defines the importance of the historical data. In section 4.1, we set λ at a moderate value, 0.5, with which HPStream showed much better clustering quality than CluStream. We also did several experiments to isolate the effect of decay rate λ by changing λ from a small value to a large one. We used the synthetic data set *B100kC10D50L30* and set the stream speed at 200 points per time unit and average projected dimensionality $l = 30$ to test the cluster purity of HPStream at

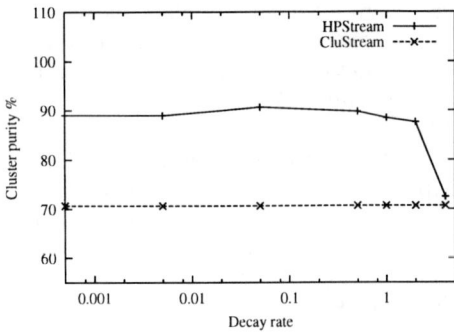

Figure 16: Choice of decay rate λ (Synthetic data set B100kC10D50L30, stream_speed = 200, H = 10, time units = 100, l = 30)

time $T = 100$ with horizon 10. Figure 16 shows the results corresponding to a series of decay rates, 0.0005, 0.005, 0.05, 0.5, 1, 2, and 4. If $0.0005 \leq \lambda \leq 2$, HPStream has a relatively stable cluster purity which is much better than that of CluStream. However, when we use a very high value for λ like 4, HPStream's quality deteriorates quickly, but still is a little better than that of CluStream. We note that the choice of $\lambda = 4$ represents a pathological case in which the clusters are determined based on only a small number of recently arriving data points. In such cases, both algorithms tends to show relatively similar behavior.

4.3 Scalability Test

The scalability tests presented below show that HPStream is linearly scalable with both dimensionality and the number of clusters. We have already shown that HPStream has very stable stream processing speed along with the progression of the stream for the two real data sets. High scalability in terms of dimensionality and the number of clusters is also very critical to the success of a high-dimensional clustering algorithm. We generated a series of synthetic data sets to test the scalability of HPStream.

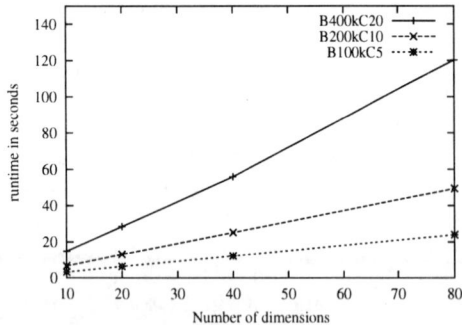

Figure 17: Scalability with dimensionality (stream_speed = 100, $l = 0.8 \times d$)

We first generated 3 data sets with varying number of dimensions to test the scalability against dimensionality. B100kC5 contains 100K points and 5 natural clusters, B200kC10 contains 200K points and 10 clusters, and B400kC20 contains 400K points and 20 clusters. For each series of data sets, we generated 4 data sets with dimensionality d set at 10, 20, 40, and 80, respectively. The average number of projected dimensions for each data set is set at $0.8 \times d$ and the stream speed is set at 100 points per time unit. Figure 17 shows that when we varied the dimensionality from 10 to 80, HPStream has linear increase in runtime for data sets with different number of points and different number of clusters. For example, for data set series B200kC10, the runtime increases from 6.579 seconds to 49.401 seconds when the dimensionality is changed from 10 to 80.

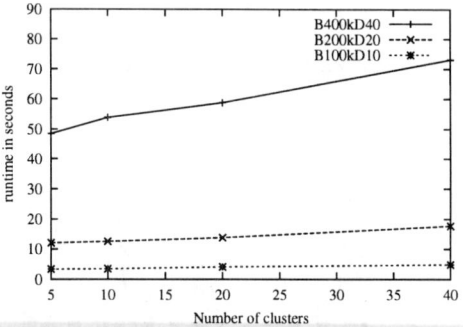

Figure 18: Scalability with number of clusters (stream_speed=100, $l = 0.6 \times d$)

To test the scalability against the number of natural clusters, we generated another 3 series of data sets with varying number of clusters. B100kD10 contains 100K 10-dimensional data points, B200kD20 has 200K 20-d data points, and B400kD40 has 400K 40-d data points. For each series of data sets, we generated 4 data sets with the number of natural clusters set at 5, 10, 20, and 40, respectively. The average number of projected dimensions for each data set is set at $0.6 \times d$ and the stream speed at 100 points per time unit. Figure 18 shows that the runtime of HPStream has very good scalability in terms of the number of clusters for data sets with different number of points and dimensionality. The high scalability of HPStream in terms of the number of clusters stems from both the algorithm design and implementation. Among the three most costly functions in HPStream algorithm, the computation of *FindLimitingRadius* has nothing to do with the number of clusters, *FindProjectedDist* is linearly scalable to the the number of clusters, whereas for *ComputeDimensions*, we can exploit the temporal locality to improve its efficiency: At a certain period, the points usually only belong to a small number of clusters, and only the dimensions of these clusters will be changed during the past period with the necessity to re-compute their radii.

5 Discussion

Our experiments have shown that the HPStream framework leads to accurate and efficient high-dimensional stream clustering. This framework can be extended in many ways to assist stream data mining.

First, some methodologies, such as the cluster structure and micro-clustering ideas, though designed for projected stream clustering, can be applied to projected clustering of non-stream data as well. Moreover, the method worked out here for high-dimensional projected stream clustering represents a general methodology, independent of particular evaluation measures and implementation techniques. For example, one can change the distance measure from Euclidean distance to other measures, or change detailed clustering algorithm, such as k-means, to other methods, the general methodology should still be applicable. However, it is interesting to work out the detail implementation techniques for particular applications.

Second, one extension of the framework is to use tilted time windows to store data at different time granularity. This may take somewhat more space in cluster structure, however, it may give user more flexibility to dynamically assign or modify fading ratio, as well as to discover clusters at more flexibly specified windows or time periods to facilitate the discovery of cluster evolution regularity.

Finally, this study may promote the development of new streaming data mining functions, such as stream classification and similarity analysis based on dynamically discovered projected clusters.

6 Conclusions

We have presented a new framework, HPStream, for high-dimensional projected clustering of data streams. It finds projected clusters in particular subsets of the dimensions by maintaining condensed representations of the clusters over time. The algorithm provides better quality clusters than full dimensional data stream clustering algorithms. We tested the algorithm on a number of real and synthetic data sets. In each case, we found that the HPStream algorithm was more effective than the full dimensional CluStream algorithm.

High-dimensional projected clustering of data streams opens a new direction for exploration of stream data mining. With this methodology, one can treat projected clustering as a preprocessing step, which may promote more effective methods for stream classification, similarity, evolution and outlier analysis.

References

[1] C. C. Aggarwal. A Human-Computer Interactive Method for Projected Clustering. *IEEE Transactions on Knowledge and Data Engineering*, 16(4), 448–460, 2004.

[2] C. C. Aggarwal, C. Procopiuc, J. Wolf, P. S. Yu, J.-S. Park. Fast algorithms for projected clustering. *ACM SIGMOD Conference, 1999.*

[3] C. C. Aggarwal, J. Han, J. Wang, P. Yu. A Framework for Clustering Evolving Data Streams. *VLDB Conference, 2003.*

[4] C. C. Aggarwal. An Intuitive Framework for Understanding Changes in Evolving Data Streams. *ICDE Conference*, 2002.

[5] C. C. Aggarwal. A Framework for Diagnosing Changes in Evolving Data Streams. *ACM SIGMOD Conference*, pp. 575–586, 2003.

[6] R. Agrawal, J. Gehrke, D. Gunopulos, P. Raghavan. Automatic Subspace Clustering of High Dimensional Data for Data Mining Applications. *ACM SIGMOD Conference, 1998.*

[7] M. Ankerst, M. Breunig, H.-P. Kriegel, J. Sander. OPTICS: Ordering Points To Identify the Clustering Structure. *ACM SIGMOD Conference*, 1999.

[8] B. Babcock, S. Babu, M. Datar, R. Motwani, J. Widom. Models and Issues in Data Stream Systems, *ACM PODS Conference*, 2002.

[9] C. Cortes, K. Fisher, D. Pregibon, A. Rogers, F. Smith. Hancock: A Language for Extracting Signatures from Data Streams. *ACM SIGKDD Conference*, 2000.

[10] P. Domingos, G. Hulten. Mining High-Speed Data Streams. *ACM SIGKDD Conference*, 2000.

[11] F. Farnstrom, J. Lewis, C. Elkan. Scalability for Clustering Algorithms Revisited. *SIGKDD Explorations*, 2(1):51-57, 2000.

[12] J. Feigenbaum et al. Testing and spot-checking of data streams. *ACM SODA Conference*, 2000.

[13] S. Guha, N. Mishra, R. Motwani, L. O'Callaghan. Clustering Data Streams. *IEEE FOCS Conference*, 2000.

[14] S. Guha, R. Rastogi, K. Shim. CURE: An Efficient Clustering Algorithm for Large Databases. *ACM SIGMOD Conference, 1998.*

[15] A. Jain, R. Dubes. Algorithms for Clustering Data, *Prentice Hall,* New Jersey, 1998.

[16] R. Ng, J. Han. Efficient and Effective Clustering Methods for Spatial Data Mining. *Very Large Data Bases Conference*, 1994.

[17] L. O'Callaghan, N. Mishra, A. Meyerson, S. Guha, R. Motwani. Streaming-Data Algorithms For High-Quality Clustering. *ICDE Conference*, 2002.

[18] T. Zhang, R. Ramakrishnan, M. Livny. BIRCH: An Efficient Data Clustering Method for Very Large Databases. *ACM SIGMOD Conference*, 1996.

Efficient Query Evaluation on Probabilistic Databases

Nilesh Dalvi   Dan Suciu

{nilesh,suciu}@cs.washington.edu
University of Washington, Seattle, WA, USA

Abstract

We describe a system that supports arbitrarily complex SQL queries on probabilistic databases. The query semantics is based on a probabilistic model and the results are ranked, much like in Information Retrieval. Our main focus is efficient query evaluation, a problem that has not received attention in the past. We describe an optimization algorithm that can compute efficiently most queries. We show, however, that the data complexity of some queries is #P-complete, which implies that these queries do not admit any efficient evaluation methods. For these queries we describe both an approximation algorithm and a Monte-Carlo simulation algorithm.

1 Introduction

Databases and Information Retrieval [5] have taken two philosophically different approaches to queries. In databases SQL queries have a rich structure and a precise semantics. This makes it possible for users to formulate complex queries and for systems to apply complex optimizations, but users need to have a pretty detailed knowledge of the database in order to formulate queries. For example, a single misspelling of a constant in the WHERE clause leads to an empty set of answers, frustrating casual users. By contrast, a query in Information Retrieval (IR) is just a set of keywords and is easy for casual users to formulate. IR queries offer two important features that are missing in databases: the results are *ranked* and the matches may be *uncertain*, i.e. the answer may include documents that do not match all the keywords in the query[1]. While several proposals exist for extending SQL with uncertain matches and ranked results [3, 19, 16], they are either restricted to a single table, or, when they handle join queries, adopt an ad-hoc semantics.

To illustrate the point consider the following structurally rich query, asking for an actor whose name is like 'Kevin' and whose first 'successful' movie appeared in 1995:

```
SELECT   *
FROM     Actor A
WHERE    A.name ≈ 'Kevin'
and      1995 =
    SELECT   MIN(F.year)
    FROM     Film F, Casts C
    WHERE    C.filmid = F.filmid
    and      C.actorid = A.actorid
    and      F.rating ≈ "high"
```

The two ≈ operators indicate which predicates we intend as uncertain matches. Techniques like edit distances, ontology-based distances [15], IDF-similarity and QF-similarity [3] can be applied to a *single* table: to rank all Actor tuples (according to how well they match the first uncertain predicate), and to rank all Film tuples. But it is unclear how to rank the *entire* query. To date, no system combines structurally rich SQL queries with uncertain predicates and ranked results.

In this paper we propose such a system. We introduce a new semantics for database queries that supports uncertain matches and ranked results, by combining the probabilistic relational algebra [13] and models for belief [4]. Given a SQL query with uncertain predicates, we start by assigning a probability to each tuple in the input database according to how well it matches the uncertain predicates. Then we derive a probability for each tuple in the answer, and this determines the output ranking.

An important characteristic of our approach is that *any* query under set-semantics has a meaning, in-

---

Permission to copy without fee all or part of this material is granted provided that the copies are not made or distributed for direct commercial advantage, the VLDB copyright notice and the title of the publication and its date appear, and notice is given that copying is by permission of the Very Large Data Base Endowment. To copy otherwise, or to republish, requires a fee and/or special permission from the Endowment.

**Proceedings of the 30th VLDB Conference,
Toronto, Canada, 2004**

---

[1]Some IR systems only return documents that contain all keywords, but this is a feature specific to those systems, and not of the underlying vector model used in IR.

cluding queries with joins, nested sub-queries, aggregates, group-by, and existential/universal quantifiers[2]. Queries have now a probabilistic semantics, which is simple and easy to understand by both users and implementors.

The main problem is query evaluation, and this is the focus of our paper. Our approach is to represent SQL queries in an algebra, and modify the operators to compute the probabilities of each output tuple. This is called *extensional semantics* in [13], and is quite efficient. While this sounds simple, the problem is that it doesn't work: extensional evaluation ignores the complex correlations present in the probabilities of the intermediate results and the probabilities computed this way are wrong in most cases, and lead to incorrect ranking. In [13], the workaround is to use an *intensional semantics* [3], which is much more complex and, as we show here, impractical. Our approach is different: we rewrite the query plans, searching for one where the extensional evaluation is correct. We show however that certain queries have a #P-complete data complexity under probabilistic semantics, and hence do not admit a correct extensional plan. However, many queries that occur in practice do have a correct extensional plan (8 out of the 10 TPC/H queries fall in this category). For others, we describe two techniques for evaluation: a heuristics to choose a plan that avoids large errors, and a Monte-Carlo simulation algorithm, which is more expensive but can guarantee arbitrarily small errors.

Outline We give motivating examples in Sec. 2, define the problem in Sec. 3, and describe our techniques in Sec. 4-8. Sec. 9 reports experiments and Sec. 10 describes related work. We conclude in Sec. 11.

2 Examples

We illustrate the main concepts and techniques of this paper with two simple examples.

Probabilistic Database In a probabilistic database each tuple has a certain probability of belonging to the database. Figure 1 shows a probabilistic database D^p with two tables, S^p and T^p: the tuples in S^p have probabilities 0.8 and 0.5, and the unique tuple in T^p has probability 0.6. We use the superscript p to emphasize that a table or a database is probabilistic. We assume in this example that the tuples are independent probabilistic events, in which case the database is called *extensional* [13].

The meaning of a probabilistic database is a probability distribution on all database instances, which we call *possible worlds*, and denote $pwd(D^p)$. Fig. 2 (a) shows the eight possible instances with non-zero probabilities, which are computed by simply multiplying

---

[2] In this paper we restrict our discussion to SQL queries whose normal semantics is a set, not a bag or an ordered list.
[3] We define extensional and intensional semantics formally in Sec. 4.

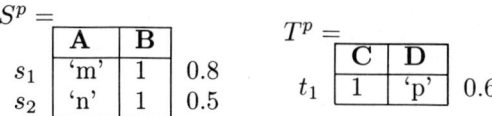

Figure 1: A probabilistic database D^p

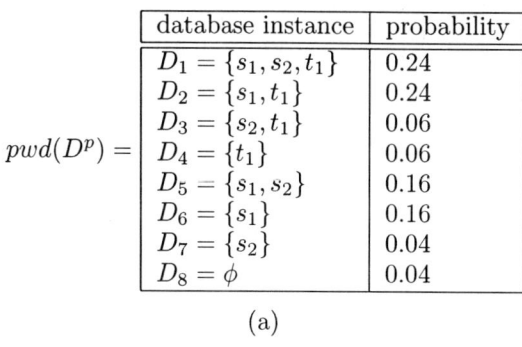

(a)

$$q(u) :- S^p(x,y), T^p(z,u), y = z$$

(b)

$$q^{pwd}(D^p) = \begin{array}{|c|c|} \hline \text{answer} & \text{probability} \\ \hline \{'p'\} & 0.54 \\ \emptyset & 0.46 \\ \hline \end{array}$$

(c)

Figure 2: (a) The possible worlds for D^p in Figure 1, (b) a query q, and (c) its possible answers.

the tuple probabilities, as we have assumed them to be independent. For example, the probability of D_2 is $0.8 * (1 - 0.5) * 0.6 = 0.24$, since the instance contains the tuples s_1 and t_1 and does not contain s_2.

We now illustrate query evaluation on probabilistic databases. Consider the conjunctive query q in Fig. 2 (b). Its meaning on D^p is a set of possible answers, shown in Fig. 2 (c). It is obtained by applying q to each deterministic database in $pwd(D^p)$, and adding the probabilities of all instances that return the same answer. In our example we have $q(D_1) = q(D_2) = q(D_3) = \{'p'\}$, and $q(D_4) = \ldots = q(D_8) = \emptyset$. Thus, the probability of the answer being $\{'p'\}$ is $0.24+0.24+0.06 = 0.54$, while that of the answer $\emptyset$ is 0.46. This defines the set of possible answers, denoted $q^{pwd}(D^p)$. Notice that we have never used the structure of the query explicitly, but only applied it to deterministic databases taken from $pwd(D^p)$. Thus, one can give a similar semantics to *any* query q, no matter how complex, because we only need to know its meaning on deterministic databases.

The set of possible answers $q^{pwd}(D^p)$ may be very large, and it is impractical to return it to the user. Instead, we compute for each possible tuple t a *probability rank* that t belongs to any answer, and return tuples sorted by this rank. We denote this $q^{rank}(D^p)$. In our example this is:

$$q^{rank}(D^p) = \begin{array}{|c|c|} \hline \text{D} & \text{Rank} \\ \hline \text{'p'} & 0.54 \\ \hline \end{array}$$

865

A	B	C	D	prob
'm'	1	1	'p'	0.8*0.6 = 0.48
'n'	1	1	'p'	0.5*0.6 = 0.30

(a) $S^p \bowtie_{B=C} T^p$

D	prob
'p'	(1 - (1 - 0.48)(1 - 0.3)) = 0.636

(b) $\Pi_D(S^p \bowtie_{B=C} T^p)$

Figure 3: Evaluation of $\Pi_D(S^p \bowtie_{B=C} T^p)$

In this simple example $q^{rank}(D^p)$ contains a single tuple and the distinction between q^{pwd} and q^{rank} is blurred. To see this distinction clearer, consider another query, $q_1(x) :- S^p(x,y), T^p(z,y), y = z$. Here q_1^{pwd} and q_1^{rank} are given by:

$q_1^{pwd}(D^p) =$

answer	probability
{'m','n'}	0.24
{'m'}	0.24
{'n'}	0.06
∅	0.46

$q_1^{rank}(D^p) =$

D	Rank
'm'	0.48
'n'	0.30

For example, the rank probability of $'m'$ is obtained as $Pr(\{'m','n'\}) + Pr(\{'m'\})$. In general, $q^{pwd}(D^p)$ may be exponentially large, while $q^{rank}(D^p)$ is simply a set of tuples, which are sorted by **Rank**. The problem in this paper is now to compute $q^{rank}(D^p)$ efficiently.

Extensional Query Semantics A natural attempt to compute $q^{rank}(D^p)$ is to represent q as a query plan then compute the probabilities of all tuples in all intermediate results. For the query q in Fig. 2 (b), such a plan is $p = \Pi_D(S^p \bowtie_{B=C} T^p)$, and the corresponding probabilities are shown in Fig. 3. The formulas for the probabilities assume tuple independence, are taken from [13] and are rather straightforward (we review them in Sec. 4). For example the probability of a joined tuple $s \bowtie t$ is the product of the probabilities of s and t. Clearly, this approach is much more efficient than computing the possible worlds $q^{pwd}(D^p)$ and then computing $q^{rank}(D^p)$, but it is wrong ! It's answer is 0.636, while it should be 0.54. The reason is that the two tuples in $S^p \bowtie_{B=C} T^p$ are not independent events, hence the formula used in Π_D is wrong.

However, let us consider an alternative plan, $p' = \Pi_D((\Pi_B(S^p)) \bowtie_{B=D} T^p)$. The extensional evaluation of this expression is shown in Figure 4, and this time we do get the correct answer. As we will show later, this plan will always compute the correct answer to q, on any probabilistic tables S^p, T^p. In this paper we show how to find automatically a plan whose extensional evaluation returns the correct answer to a query q. Finding such a plan requires pushing projec-

B	prob
1	(1 - (1 - 0.8)(1 - 0.5)) = 0.9

(a) $\Pi_B(S^p)$

B	C	D	prob
1	1	'p'	0.9 * 0.6 = 0.54

(b) $\Pi_B(S^p) \bowtie_{B=C} T^p$

D	prob
'p'	0.54

(c) $\Pi_D(\Pi_B(S^p) \bowtie_{B=C} T^p)$

Figure 4: Evaluation of $\Pi_D(\Pi_B(S^p) \bowtie_{B=C} T^p)$

tions early (as shown in this example), join reordering, and other kinds of rewritings.

Queries with uncertain matches While query evaluation on probabilistic databases is an important problem in itself, our motivation comes from answering SQL queries with uncertain matches, and ranking their results. We illustrate here with a simple example on the Stanford movie database[1].

```
SELECT   DISTINCT F.title, F.year
FROM     Director D, Films F
WHERE    D.did = F.did
  and    D.name ≈ 'Copolla'
  and    F.title ≈ 'rain man'
  and    F.year ≈ 1995
```

The predicates on the director name and the movie title and year are here *uncertain*.

Our approach is to translate the query into a regular query over a probabilistic databases. Each tuple in the table Films is assigned a probability based on how well it matches the predicates title ≈ 'rain man' and year ≈ 1995. Several techniques for doing this exist already, and in this paper we will adopt existing ones: see Sec. 8. In all cases, the result is a probabilistic table, denoted Films^p. Similarly, the uncertain predicate on Director generates a probabilistic table Director^p. Then, we evaluate the following query:

```
SELECT   DISTINCT F.title, F.year
FROM     Director^p D, Films^p F
WHERE    D.did = F.did
```

This is similar to the query q considered earlier (Figure 2 (b)), and the same extensional plan can be used to evaluate it. Our system returns:

title	year	rank
The Rainmaker (by Coppola)	1997	0.110
The Rain People (by Coppola)	1969	0.089
Rain Man (by Levinson)	1988	0.077
Finian's Rainbow (by Coppola)	1968	0.069
Tucker, Man and Dream (Coppola)	1989	0.061
Rain or Shine (by Capra)	1931	0.059
...	...	...

3 Problem Definition

We review here the basic definitions in probabilistic databases, based on [13, 4], and state our problem.

Basic Notations We write R for a relation name, $Attr(R)$ for its attributes, and $r \subseteq U^k$ for a relation instance where k is $arity(R)$ and U is a fixed, finite universe. $\bar{R} = R_1, \ldots, R_n$ is a database schema and D denotes a database instance. We write $\Gamma \models D$ when D satisfies the functional dependencies in Γ.

Probabilistic Events Let AE be a set of symbols and $Pr : AE \to [0,1]$ a probability function. Each element of AE is called a *basic event*, and we assume that all basic events are independent. The event $\bot \in AE$ denotes the impossible event and $Pr(\bot) = 0$. A *complex event* is an expression constructed from atomic events using the operators $\wedge, \vee, \neg$. E denotes the set of all complex events. For each complex event e, let $Pr(e)$ be its probability.

Example 3.1 Consider $e = (s_1 \wedge t_1) \vee (s_2 \wedge t_1)$, and assume $Pr(s_1) = 0.8$, $Pr(s_2) = 0.5$, $Pr(t_1) = 0.6$. To compute $Pr(e)$ we construct the truth table for $e(s_1, s_2, t_1)$ and identify the entries where e is true, namely $(1,0,1), (0,1,1), (1,1,1)$. The three entries have probabilities $Pr(s_1)(1 - Pr(s_2))Pr(t_1) = 0.8 \times 0.5 \times 0.6 = 0.24$, $(1 - Pr(s_1))Pr(s_2)Pr(t_1) = 0.06$ and $Pr(s_1)Pr(s_2)Pr(t_1) = 0.24$ respectively. Then $Pr(e)$ is their sum, 0.54.

This method generalizes to any complex event $e(s_1, \ldots, s_k)$, but it is important to notice that this algorithm is exponential in k. This cannot be avoided: it is known that computing $Pr(e)$ is #P-complete [26] even for complex events without negation.

Probabilistic Databases A *probabilistic relation* is a relation with a distinguished *event attribute* E, whose value is a complex event. We add the superscript p to mean "probabilistic", i.e. write $R^p, r^p, \bar{R}^p, \Gamma^p$. Given R^p, we write R for its "deterministic" part, obtained by removing the event attribute: $Attr(R) = Attr(R^p) - \{E\}$. Users "see" only R, but the system needs to access the event attribute $R^p.E$. The set of functional dependencies Γ^p always contains

$$Attr(R) \to R^p.E$$

for every relation R^p, i.e. $Attr(R)$ functionally determines $R^p.E$. This ensures that we don't associate two different events e_1 and e_2 to the same tuple t (instead, we may want to associate $e_1 \vee e_2$ to t).

In addition to this *tabular* representation of a probabilistic relation, we consider a *functional* representation, where a probabilistic instance r^p, of type R^p, is described by the following function $e_R : U^k \to E$, where $k = arity(R)$. When t occurs in r^p together with some event e, then $e_R(t) = e$, otherwise $e_R(t) = \bot$. Conversely, one can recover r^p from the function e_R by collecting all tuples for which $e_R(t) \neq \bot$.

The input probabilistic databases we consider have only atomic events: complex events are introduced only by query evaluation. A probabilistic relation with atomic events which satisfies the FD $R^p.E \to Attr(R)$ is called *extensional*. Otherwise, it is called *intensional*. For example, the database in Fig. 1 is an extensional probabilistic database, where the atomic events are s_1, s_2, t_1 respectively.

Semantics of a probabilistic database We give a simple and intuitive meaning to a probabilistic relation based on possible worlds. The meaning of a probabilistic relation r^p of type R^p is a probability distribution on deterministic relations r of type R, which we call the *possible worlds*, and denote $pwd(r^p)$. Let $e_R : U^k \to E$ be the functional representation of r^p. Given $r \subseteq U^k$, $Pr(r)$ is defined to be $Pr(\bigwedge_{t \in r} e_R(t)) \wedge (\bigwedge_{t \notin r} \neg e_R(t))$. Intuitively, this is the probability that exactly the tuples in r are "in" and all the others are "out". One can check that $\sum_{r \subseteq U^k} Pr(r) = 1$.

Similarly, the meaning of a probabilistic database D^p is a probability distribution on all deterministic databases D, denoted $pwd(D^p)$.

Query semantics Let q be a query of arity k over a deterministic schema $\bar{R}$. We define a very simple and intuitive semantics for the query. Users think of q as normal query on a deterministic database, but the database is given by a probability distribution rather than being fixed. As a result, the query's answer is also a probability distribution. Formally, given a query q and a probabilistic database D^p: $q^{pwd}(D^p)$ is the following probability distribution on all possible answers, $Pr_q : \mathcal{P}(U^k) \to [0, 1]$:

$$\forall S \subseteq U^k, Pr_q(S) = \sum_{D | q(D) = S} Pr(D)$$

We call this the *possible worlds semantics*. This definition makes sense for every query q that has a well defined semantics on all deterministic databases.

It is impossible to return $q^{pwd}(D^p)$ to the user. Instead, we compute a *probabilistic ranking* on all tuples $t \in U^k$, defined by the function: $rank_q(t) = \sum_S \{Pr_q(S) \mid S \subseteq U^k, t \in S\}$, for every tuple $t \in U^k$. We denote with $q^{rank}(D^p)$ a tabular representation of the function $rank_q$: this is a table with $k+1$ attributes, where the first k represent a tuple in the query's answer while the last attribute, called **Rank** is a real number in [0, 1] representing its probability.

The Query Evaluation Problem This paper addresses the following problem: given schema $\bar{R}^p, \Gamma^p$, a probabilistic database D^p and a query q over schema $\bar{R}$, compute the probabilistic rankings $q^{rank}(D^p)$.

Application to queries with uncertain predicates Consider now a deterministic database D and a query $q^\approx$ that explicitly mentions some uncertain predicates over base tables. We convert this problem into evaluating a deterministic query q, obtained by removing all uncertain predicates from $q^\approx$, on a probabilistic database, obtained by associating a probability $Pr(t)$ to each tuple t based on how well t satisfies the uncertain predicates in the query.

4 Query Evaluation

We turn now to the central problem, evaluating $q^{rank}(D^p)$ for a query q, and a probabilistic database D^p. Applying the definition directly is infeasible, since it involves iterating over a large set of database instances. Instead, we will first review the intensional evaluation of [13] then describe our approach.

We restrict our discussion first to conjunctive queries, which alternatively can be expressed as select(distinct)-project-join queries. This helps us better understand the query evaluation problem and its complexity, and will consider more complex query expressions in Sec. 7. We use either datalog notation for our queries q, or plans p in the select/project/product algebra[4]: $\sigma, \Pi, \times$.

4.1 Intensional Query Evaluation

One method for evaluating queries on probabilistic databases is to use complex events, and was introduced in [13]. We review it here and discuss its limitations. Start by expressing q as a query plan, using the operators $\sigma, \Pi, \times$. Then modify each operator to compute the event attribute E in each intermediate result: denote $\sigma^i, \Pi^i, \times^i$ the modified operators. It is more convenient to introduce them in the functional representation, by defining the complex event $e_p(t)$ for each tuple t, inductively on the query plan p:

$$
\begin{aligned}
e_{\sigma_c^i(p)}(t) &= \begin{cases} e_p(t) & \text{if } c(t) \text{ is true} \\ \bot & \text{if } c(t) \text{ is false} \end{cases} \\
e_{\Pi_{\bar{A}}^i(p)}(t) &= \bigvee_{t': \Pi_{\bar{A}}(t')=t} e_p(t') \quad (1) \\
e_{p \times^i p'}(t, t') &= e_p(t) \wedge e_{p'}(t')
\end{aligned}
$$

The tabular definitions for $\sigma^i, \Pi^i, \times^i$ follow easily: σ^i acts like σ then copies the complex events from the input tuples to the output tuples; Π^i associates to a tuple t the complex event $e_1 \vee \ldots \vee e_n$ obtained from

[4]Notice that Π also does duplicate elimination

A	B	C	D	E
'm'	1	1	'p'	$s_1 \wedge t_1$
'n'	1	1	'p'	$s_2 \wedge t_1$

(a) $S^p \bowtie_{B=C}^i T^p$

D	E
'p'	$(s_1 \wedge t_1) \vee (s_2 \wedge t_1)$

(b) $\Pi_D^i(S^p \bowtie_{B=C}^i T^p)$

D	Rank
'p'	$Pr((s_1 \wedge t_1) \vee (s_2 \wedge t_1)) = 0.54$

(c) $q^{rank}(D^p) = Pr(\Pi_D^i(S^p \bowtie_{B=C}^i T^p))$

Figure 5: Intensional Evaluation of $\Pi_D(S^p \bowtie_{B=C} T^p)$

the complex events of all input tuples $t_1, \ldots, t_n$ that project into t; and $\times^i$ simply associates to a product tuple (t, t') the complex event $e \wedge e'$.

Example 4.1 Let us consider the database D^p described in Figure 1. Consider the query plan, $p = \Pi_D(S^p \bowtie_{B=C} T^p)$. Figure 5 shows the intensional evaluation of the query (we used the tuple names as atomic events). $p^i(D^p)$ contains a single tuple $'p'$ with the event $(s_1 \wedge t_1) \vee (s_2 \wedge t_1)$.

Thus, $p^i(D^p)$ denotes an intensional probabilistic relation. It can be shown that this is independent on the particular choice of plan p, and we denote $q^i(D^p)$ the value $p^i(D^p)$ for any plan p for q, and call it the *intensional semantics*[5] of q on the probabilistic database D^p. We prove now that it is equivalent to the possible worlds semantics, $q^{pwd}(D^p)$.

Theorem 4.2. *The intensional semantics and the possible worlds semantics on probabilistic databases coincide for conjunctive queries. More precisely, $pwd(q^i(D^p)) = q^{pwd}(D^p)$ for every intensional probabilistic database D^p and conjunctive query q.*

(All proofs in this paper are available in our technical report [10].) Theorem 4.2 allows us to compute $q^{rank}(D^p)$, as follows. First compute $q^i(D^p)$, then compute the probability $Pr(e)$ for each complex event. Then $q^{rank}(D^p) = Pr(q^i(D^p))$.

Example 4.3 Fig. 5(c) shows $p^{rank}(D^p)$ for Ex. 4.1. $Pr((s_1 \wedge t_1) \vee (s_2 \wedge t_1))$ was shown in Ex. 3.1.

It is very impractical to use the intensional semantics to compute the rank probabilities, for two reasons. First, the event expressions in $q^i(D^p)$ can become very large. In the worst case the size of such an expression can become of the same order of magnitude as the database. For instance, if a projection on a table

[5]In [13] this is the only query semantics considered.

produces a single output tuple, its event expression is the disjunction of all the events in the table. This increases the complexity of the query operators significantly, and makes the task of an optimizer much harder, because now the cost per tuple is no longer a constant. Second, for each tuple t one has to compute $Pr(e)$ for its event e, which is a #P-complete problem.

4.2 Extensional Query Evaluation

We now modify the query operators to compute probabilities rather than complex events: we denote $\sigma^e, \Pi^e, \times^e$ the modified operators. This is much more efficient, since it involves manipulating real numbers rather than event expressions. We define a number $Pr_p(t) \in [0,1]$ for each tuple t, by induction on the structure of the query plan p. The inductive definitions below should be compared with those in Equations (1).

$$Pr_{\sigma_c^e(p)}(t) = \begin{cases} Pr_p(t) & \text{if } c(t) \text{ is true} \\ 0 & \text{if } c(t) \text{ is false} \end{cases}$$

$$Pr_{\Pi_{\bar{A}}^e(p)}(t) = 1 - \prod_{t':\Pi_{\bar{A}}(t')=t}(1 - Pr_p(t'))$$

$$Pr_{p \times^e p'}(t,t') = Pr_p(t) \times Pr_{p'}(t')$$

Again, the tabular definitions of $\sigma^e, \Pi^e, \times^e$ follow easily: σ^e acts like σ then propagates the tuples' probabilities from the input to the output, Π^e computes the probability of a tuples t as $1-(1-p_1)(1-p_2)\ldots(1-p_n)$ where $p_1,\ldots,p_n$ are the probabilities of all input tuples that project to t, while $\times$ computes the probability of each tuple (t,t') as $p \times p'$.

Thus, $p^e(D^p)$ is an extensional probabilistic relation, which we call the *extensional semantics* of the plan p. If we know $p^e(D^p) = q^{rank}(D^p)$, then we simply execute the plan under the extensional semantics. But, unfortunately, this is not always the case, as we saw in Sec. 2. Moreover, $p^e(D^p)$ depends on the particular plan p chosen for q. Our goal is to find a plan for which the extensional semantics is correct.

Definition 4.4. *Given a schema $\bar{R}^p, \Gamma^p$, a plan p for a query q is* safe *if $p^e(D^p) = q^{rank}(D^p)$ for all D^p of that schema.*

We show next how to find a safe plan.

4.3 The Safe-Plan Optimization Algorithm

We use the following notations for conjunctive queries:

- $Rels(q) = \{R_1,\ldots,R_k\}$ all relation names occurring in q. We assume that each relation name occurs at most once in the query (more on this in Sec. 7).

- $PRels(q)$ = the probabilistic relation names in q, $PRels(q) \subseteq Rels(q)$.

- $Attr(q)$ = all attributes in all relations in q. To disambiguate, we denote attributes as $R_i.A$.

- $Head(q)$ = attributes in the result of q, $Head(q) \subseteq Attr(q)$.

Let q be a conjunctive query. We define the *induced* functional dependencies $\Gamma^p(q)$ on $Attr(q)$:

- Every FD in Γ^p is also in $\Gamma^p(q)$.

- For every join predicate $R_i.A = R_j.B$, both $R_i.A \rightarrow R_j.B$ and $R_j.B \rightarrow R_i.A$ are in $\Gamma^p(q)$.

- For every selection predicate $R_i.A = c$, $\emptyset \rightarrow R_i.A$ is in $\Gamma^p(q)$.

We seek a safe plan p, i.e. one that computes the probabilities correctly. For that each operator in p must be safe, i.e. compute correct probabilities: we define this formally next.

Let q_1, q_2 be two queries, and let $op \in \{\sigma, \Pi, \times\}$ be a relational operator. Consider the new query $op(q_1, q_2)$ (or just $op(q_1)$ when op is unary). We say that op^e is *safe* if $op^e(Pr(q_1^i(D^p)), Pr(q_2^i(D^p))) = Pr(op^i(q_1^i(D^p)), q_2^i(D^p))$ (and similarly for unary operators), $\forall D^p$ s.t. $\Gamma^p \models D^p$. In other words, op is safe if, when given correct probabilities for its inputs op^e computes correct probabilities for the output tuples.

Theorem 4.5. *Let q, q' be conjunctive queries.*

1. *σ_c^e is always safe in $\sigma_c(q)$.*

2. *$\times^e$ is always safe in $q \times q'$.*

3. *$\Pi_{A_1,\ldots,A_k}^e$ is safe in $\Pi_{A_1,\ldots,A_k}(q)$ iff for every $R^p \in PRels(q)$ the following can be inferred from $\Gamma^p(q)$:*

$$A_1,\ldots,A_k, R^p.E \rightarrow Head(q) \qquad (2)$$

A plan p is safe iff all operators are safe.

We explain the Theorem with an example below. A formal proof can be found in our technical report [10].

Example 4.6 Continuing the example in Sec. 2, assume that both S^p and T^p are extensional probabilistic relations, hence Γ^p is:

$$S^p.A, S^p.B \rightarrow S^p.E$$
$$T^p.C, T^p.D \rightarrow T^p.E$$
$$S^p.E \rightarrow S^p.A, S^p.B$$
$$T^p.E \rightarrow T^p.C, T^p.D$$

The last two dependencies hold because the relations are extensional. Consider the plan $\Pi_D(S^p \bowtie_{B=C} T^p)$. We have shown in Fig. 3 that, when evaluated extensionally, this plan is incorrect. We explain here the reason: the operator Π_D^e is not safe. An intuitive justification can be seen immediately by inspecting the intensional relation $S^p \bowtie^i_{B=C} T^p$ in Fig. 5 (a). The two complex events share the common atomic event t_1, hence they are correlated probabilistic events. But the formula for Π^e_D only works when these events are independent. We show how to detect formally that Π^e_D is unsafe. We need to check:

$$T^p.D, S^p.E \rightarrow S^p.A, S^p.B, T^p.C, T^p.D$$
$$T^p.D, T^p.E \rightarrow S^p.A, S^p.B, T^p.C, T^p.D$$

The first follows from Γ^p and from the join condition $B = C$, which adds $S^p.B \rightarrow T^p.C$ and $T^p.C \rightarrow S^p.B$. But the second fails: $T^p.D, T^p.E \not\rightarrow S^p.A$.

Example 4.7 Continuing the example, consider now the plan $\Pi_D(\Pi_B(S^p) \bowtie_{B=C} T^p)$. We will prove that Π^e_D is safe. For that we have to check:

$$T^p.D, S^p.E \rightarrow S^p.B, T^p.C, T^p.D$$
$$T^p.D, T^p.E \rightarrow S^p.B, T^p.C, T^p.D$$

Both hold, hence Π^e_D is safe. Similarly, Π^e_B is safe in $\Pi_B(S^p)$, which means that the entire plan is safe.

Algorithm 1 is our optimization algorithm for finding a safe plan. It proceeds top-down, as follows. First, it tries to do all safe projections late in the query plan. When no more late safe projections are possible for a query q, then it tries to perform a join $\bowtie_c$ instead, by splitting q into $q_1 \bowtie_c q_2$. Since $\bowtie_c$ is the last operation in the query plan, all attributes in c must be in $Head(q)$.

Splitting q into $q_1 \bowtie_c q_2$ is done as follows. Construct a graph G whose nodes are $Rels(q)$ and whose edges are all pairs (R_i, R_j) s.t. q contains some join condition $R_i.A = R_j.B$ with both[6] $R_i.A$ and $R_j.B$ in $Head(q)$. Find the connected components of G, and choose q_1 and q_2 to be any partition of these connected components: this defines $Rels(q_i)$ and $Attr(q_i)$ for $i = 1, 2$. Define $Head(q_i) = Head(q) \cap Attr(q_i)$, for $i = 1, 2$. If G is a connected graph, then the query has no safe plans (more on this below). If G has multiple connected components, then we have several choices for splitting q, and we can deploy any standard cost based optimizations algorithm that works in top-down fashion[7].

Finally, the algorithm terminates when no more projections are needed. The remaining join and/or selection operators can be done in any order.

---

[6] One can show that, if $R_i.A$ is in $Head(q)$, then so is $R_j.B$. Indeed, assume $R_j.B \notin Head(q)$. Then $\Pi_{Head(q)}(q_{R_j.B})$ is safe, so we should have performed it first. Then, both $R_i.A$ and $R_j.B$ are in $Head(q_{R_j.B})$.

[7] It is also possible to adapt our algorithm to work with a bottom-up optimizer.

Algorithm 1 SAFE-PLAN(q)

if $Head(q) = Attr(q)$ then
    return any plan p for q
    (p is projection-free, hence safe)
end if
for $A \in (Attr(q) - Head(q))$ do
    let q_A be the query obtained from q
    by adding A to the head variables
    if $\Pi_{Head(q)}(q_A)$ is a safe operator then
        return $\Pi_{Head(q)}$(SAFE-PLAN(q_A))
    end if
end for
Split q into $q_1 \bowtie_c q_2$ (see text)
if no such split exists then
    return error("No safe plans exist")
end if
return SAFE-PLAN(q_1) $\bowtie_c$ SAFE-PLAN(q_2)

Example 4.8 Continuing the example in Sec. 2, consider the original query in Fig. 2 (b), which we rewrite now as:

$$q(D) :- S^p(A, B), T^p(C, D), B = C$$

Here $Attr(q) = \{A, B, C, D\}$ and $Head(q) = \{D\}$ (we write D instead of $T^p.D$, etc, since all attributes are distinct). The algorithm first considers the three attributes A, B, C in $Attr(q) - Head(q)$, trying to see if they can be projected out late in the plan. A cannot be projected out. Indeed, the corresponding q_A is:

$$q_A(A, D) :- S^p(A, B), T^p(C, D), B = C$$

and Π^e_D is unsafe in $\Pi_D(q_A)$ because $T^p.D, T^p.E \not\rightarrow S^p.A$, as we saw in Example 4.6. However, the other two attributes can be projected out, hence the plan for q is $\Pi_D(q_{BC})$, where:

$$q_{BC}(B, C, D) :- S^p(A, B), T^p(C, D), B = C$$

Now we optimize q_{BC}, where $Attr(q_{BC}) = \{A, B, C, D\}$, $Head(q_{BC}) = \{B, C, D\}$. No projection is possible, but we can split the query into $q_1 \bowtie_{B=C} q_2$ where q_1, q_2 are:

$$q_1(B) :- S^p(A, B)$$
$$q_2(C, D) :- T^p(C, D)$$

The split $q_{BC} = q_1 \bowtie_{B=C} q_2$ is indeed possible since both B and C belong to $Head(q_{BC})$. Continuing with q_1, q_2, we are done in q_2, while in q_1 we still need to project out A, $q_1 = \Pi_B(S^p)$, which is safe since $B, S^p.E \rightarrow A$. Putting everything together gives us the following safe plan: $p' = \Pi_D(\Pi_B(S^p) \bowtie_{B=C} T^p)$.

We state now the soundness of our algorithm: the proof follows easily from the fact that all projection operators are safe. We prove in the next section that the algorithm is also complete.

Proposition 4.9. *The* SAFE-PLAN *optimization algorithm is sound, i.e. any plan it returns is safe.*

5 Theoretical Analysis

We show here a fundamental result on the complexity of query evaluation on probabilistic databases. It forms a sharp separation of conjunctive queries into queries with low and high data complexity, and shows that our optimization algorithm is complete.

The data complexity of a query q is the complexity of evaluating $q^{rank}(D^p)$ as a function of the size of D^p. If q has a safe plan p, then its data complexity is in PTIME, because all extensional operators are in PTIME. We start by showing that, for certain queries, the data complexity is #P-complete. #P is the complexity class of some hard counting problems. Given a boolean formula φ, counting the number of satisfying assignments, denote it $\#\varphi$, is #P-complete [26]. (Checking satisfiability, $\#\varphi > 0$, is NP-complete.) The data complexity of any conjunctive query is #P, since $q^{rank}(D^p) = Pr(q^i(D^p))$. The following is a variant of a result on query reliability by Gradel et al. [14]. The proof is novel and is of independent interest in our setting.

Theorem 5.1. *Consider the following conjunctive query on three probabilistic tables:*

$$q() := L^p(x), J(x,y), R^p(y)$$

Here L^p, R^p are extensional probabilistic tables and J is deterministic[8]. The data complexity for q is #P-hard.

Proof. (Sketch) Provan and Ball [22] showed that computing $\#\varphi$ is #P-complete even for *bipartite monotone 2-DNF* boolean formulas φ, i.e. when the propositional variables can be partitioned into $X = \{x_1, \ldots, x_m\}$ and $Y = \{y_1, \ldots, y_n\}$ s.t. $\varphi = C_1 \vee \ldots \vee C_k$ where each clause C_i has the form $x_j \wedge y_k$, $x_j \in X, y_k \in Y$. (The satisfiability problem, $\#\varphi > 0$, is trivially true.). Given φ, construct the instance D^p where L^p is X, R^p is Y and J is the set of pairs (x_j, y_k) that occur in some clause C_i. Assign independent probability events to tuples in L^p, R^p, with probabilities $1/2$. Then $q^{rank}(D^p)$ returns a single tuple, with probability $\#\varphi/2^{m+n}$. Thus, computing $q^{rank}(D^p)$ is at least as hard as computing $\#\varphi$. □

We state now the main theoretical result in this paper. We consider it to be a fundamental property of query evaluation on probabilistic databases.

Theorem 5.2 (Fundamental Theorem of Queries on Probabilistic DBs). *Consider a schema $\bar{R}^p, \Gamma^p$ where all relations are probabilistic and Γ^p has only the trivial FDs[9] $Attrs(R) \to R^p.E$, $R^p.E \to Attrs(R)$, for every R^p. Let q be a conjunctive query s.t. each relation occurs at most once. Assuming #P≠PTIME the following statements are equivalent:*

1. *The query q contains three subgoals of the form:*
   $$L^p(x, \ldots), J^p(x, y, \ldots), R^p(y, \ldots)$$
   where $x, y \notin Head(q)$.
2. *The data complexity of q is #P-complete.*
3. *The SAFE-PLAN optimization algorithm fails to return a plan.*

Proof. (Sketch) (1) ⇒ (2) is a simple extension of Th. 5.1. (2) ⇒ (3) is obvious, since any safe plan has data complexity in PTIME. The proof of (3) ⇒ (1) is based on a detailed analysis of what happens when SAFE-PLAN fails: the details are in [10]. □

Theorem 5.2 provides a sharp separation of feasible and infeasible queries on probabilistic databases. It can be extended to mixed probabilistic/deterministic databases and richer functional dependencies [10].

6 Unsafe Plans

When a query's data complexity is #P-complete, then SAFE-PLAN fails to return a plan. Since this can indeed happen in practice, we address it and propose two solutions.

6.1 Least Unsafe Plans

Here we attempt to pick a plan that is less unsafe than others, i.e. minimizes the error in computing the probabilities. Recall from Eq.(2) that $\Pi^e_{A_1,\ldots,A_k}$ is safe in $\Pi^e_{A_1,\ldots,A_k}(q)$ iff $A_1, \ldots, A_k, R^p.E \to Head(q)$ for every R^p. Let $\bar{B} = \{A_1, \ldots, A_k, R^p.E\} \cap Attr(R^p)$ (hence $R^p.E \in \bar{B}$) and $\bar{C} = Head(q) \cap Attr(R^p)$. Define R^p_{fanout} to be the expected number of distinct values of $\bar{C}$ for a fixed value of the attributes $\bar{B}$. In a relational database system, it is possible to estimate this value using statistics on the table R^p. Define the degree of unsafety of $\Pi^e_{A_1,\ldots,A_k}$ to be $max_{R^p \in PREL(Q)}(R^p_{fanout} - 1)$. Thus, a safe project has degree of unsafety 0. Also, the higher the degree of unsafety, the higher is the expected error that would result from using the extensional semantics for that project operator.

We modify Algorithm 1 to cope with unsafe queries. Recall that the algorithm tries to split a query q into two subqueries q_1, q_2 s.t. all their join attributes are in $Head(q)$. Now we relax this: we allow joins between q_1 and q_2 on attributes not in $Head(q)$, then project out these attributes. These projections will be unsafe, hence we want to minimize their degree of unsafety. To do that, we pick q_1, q_2 to be a minimum cut of the graph, where each edge representing a join condition is labeled with the degree of unsafety of the corresponding project operation[10]. The problem of finding

---

[8] Allowing J to be deterministic strengthens the result. The theorem remains true if J is probabilistic.

[9] Hence, the probabilistic instances are extensional.

[10] The estimator of R^p_{fanout} should make sure that the estimated value is 0 only when the FD holds, otherwise the algorithm may favor 'expected' safe plans over truly safe plans.

minimum cut is polynomial time solvable as a series of network flow problems or using the algorithm of Stoer and Wagner [23].

6.2 Monte-Carlo Approximations

As an alternative, we present an algorithm based on Monte-Carlo simulation, which can guarantee arbitrarily low errors in the probabilities of output tuples.

Given a conjunctive query q over probabilistic relations $R_1^p, R_2^p \cdots R_k^p$, let q' be its body, i.e. $Head(q') = Attr(q') = Attr(q)$ and $q = \Pi_{Head(q)}(q')$. Modify q' to also return all event attributes $\bar{E} = R_1^p.E, \ldots, R_k^p.E$. Evaluate q' over the probabilistic database, and group of tuples in the answer based on the values of their attributes $Head(q)$. Consider one such group, and assume it has n tuples $t_1, \ldots, t_n$. The group defines the following complex event expression: $\bigvee_{i=1}^n C_i$, where each C_i has the form $e_1 \wedge \ldots \wedge e_k$. We need to compute its probability, since this will be the probability of one tuple in $q^{rank}(D^p)$. For that we use the Monte Carlo algorithm described by Karp [17]: when run for $N \geq \frac{4n}{\epsilon^2} \ln \frac{2}{\delta}$ iterations, the algorithm guarantees that the probability of the error being greater that ϵ is less than δ.

7 Extensions

Additional operators So far, we have limited our discussion to conjunctive queries, or, equivalently to the algebra consisting of $\sigma, \Pi, \times$. We show now how to extend these techniques to $\cup, -, \gamma$ (union, difference, groupby-aggregate [11]. A large fragment of SQL, including queries with nested sub-queries, aggregates, group-by and existential/universal quantifiers can be expressed in this logical algebra [25]. (We omit δ (duplicate elimination) since we only consider queries with set semantics, i.e. δ is implicit after every projection and union.) We define the extensional semantics for these operators, using the functional notation.

$$Pr_{p \cup^e p'}(t) = 1 - (1 - Pr_p(t)) \times (1 - Pr_{p'}(t))$$
$$Pr_{p -^e p'}(t) = Pr_p(t) \times (1 - Pr_{p'}(t))$$
$$Pr_{\gamma_{\bar{A},\min(B)}^e}(t) = Pr_p(t) \prod_{\substack{s \,:\, s.\bar{A} = t.\bar{A} \\ \wedge s.B < t.B}} (1 - Pr_p(s))$$

$$Pr_{\gamma_{\bar{A},\max(B)}^e}(t) = Pr_p(t) \prod_{\substack{s \,:\, s.\bar{A} = t.\bar{A} \\ \wedge s.B > t.B}} (1 - Pr_p(s))$$

For example, to compute the groupby-min operator $\gamma_{A,\min(B)}(R^p)$ one considers each tuple (a,b) in R^p: the

---
[11]Following discussion assumes that a groupby-aggregate operator does not perform any projections, i.e. every attribute in the input to the operator belongs to either the groupby or the aggregate clause.

probability that (a,b) is in the output relation is $p(1 - p_1)\ldots(1-p_n)$ where p is the probability of the tuple (a,b), while $p_1, \ldots, p_n$ are the probabilities of all other tuples (a,b') s.t. $b' < b$. In the case of SUM, the aggregated attribute may take values that are not in the input table. To compute the probabilities correctly one needs to iterate over exponentially many possible sums. Instead, we simply compute the expected value of the sum (details omitted). This is meaningful to the user if SUM appears in the SELECT clause, less so if it occurs in a HAVING clause. We treat COUNT similarly.

We now give sufficient conditions for these operators to be safe.

Theorem 7.1. *Let q, q' be conjunctive queries.*

1. *$\cup^e$ is safe in $q \cup^e q'$ if $PRels(q) \cap PRels(q') = \phi$.*
2. *$-^e$ is safe in $q \cap^e q'$ if $PRels(q) \cap PRels(q') = \phi$.*
3. *$\gamma_{\bar{A},agg(B)}^e$ is safe in $\gamma_{\bar{A},agg(B)}^e(q)$ if $\Pi_{\bar{A}}(q)$ is safe, where agg is min or max.*

Self-joins Self-joins on probabilistic relations may be a cause of #P-complete data complexity [14]. However, a query $q^\approx$ with uncertain predicate rarely results in self-join. Even if the same table R occurs twice in $q^\approx$, the different uncertain predicates on the two occurrences generate distinct events, hence the system makes two probabilistic "copies": R_1^p, R_2^p. Of course, the Monte-Carlo algorithm works fine even in the presence of self-joins.

Extending the optimization algorithm SAFE-PLAN is extended to handle each block of conjunctive queries separately. As an example, the query in Section 1, asking for an actor whose name is like 'Kevin' and whose first 'successful' movie appeared in 1995, has a safe plan as shown below:

$\Pi_{name}(A \bowtie_{actorid}$
    $(\sigma_{year=1995}(\gamma_{actorid,\min(year)}(\Pi_{actorid,year}C))))$

8 Atomic Predicates

Our main motivation is executing a query with uncertain predicates $q^\approx$ on a deterministic database D. As we saw, our approach is to apply the uncertain predicates first, and generate a probabilistic database D^p, then evaluate q (without the uncertain predicates). We discuss here briefly some choices for the uncertain predicates proposed in the literature. All proposals depend on a notion of closeness between two data values. This is domain dependent and can be classified into three categories:

Syntactic closeness This applies to domains with proper nouns, like people's names. Edit distances, q-grams and phonetic similarity can be employed. The excellent surveys on string matching techniques by Zobel and Dart [27] and Navarro [20] describe more than 40 techniques and compare them experimentally. Navarro also has a discussion on the probability of string matching. In our system, we used the 3-gram distance between words, which is the number of triplets of consecutive words common to both words.

Semantic closeness This applies to domains that have a semantic meaning, like film categories. A user query for the category 'musical' should match films of category 'opera'. Semantic distance can be calculated by using TF/IDF or with ontologies like Wordnet [2]. We do not have semantic distances in our system currently.

Numeric closeness This applies to domains like *price* and *age*. A distance can be just the difference of the values.

Once distances are defined between attributes, using any of the above methods, they need to be meaningfully converted into probabilities. We fitted a Gaussian curve on the distances as follows: the curve was centered around the distance 0 where it took value 1. The variance of the Gaussian curve is an indication of the importance of match on that attribute. Its correct value depends on the domain and user preferences. In our experiments, we used fixed, query independent values, for the variances.

Finally, one issue is when to generate new probability events. For example consider the uncertain predicate Product.category $\approx \ldots$ and assume there are two products with the same category. Should they result in two independent probabilistic events with the same probabilities, or in the same probabilistic events? Both choices are possible in our system. In the first case the functional dependency is $Product^p.key \to Product^p.E$ while in the second the FD is $Product^p.category \to Product^p.E$. In the latter case, $\Pi_{category}$ becomes unsafe. This can be taken care of by normalizing the resulting database to 3NF, i.e. creating a separate category table that contains the events for categories.

9 Experiments

We performed some preliminary evaluation of our probabilistic query evaluation framework, addressing four questions. How often does the SAFE-PLAN optimization algorithm fail to find a plan? What is the performance of safe plans, when they exists? Are naive approaches to query evaluation perhaps almost as good as a safe plan? And how effectively can we handle queries that do not have safe plans?

We did not modify the relational engine, but instead implemented a middleware. SQL queries with approximate predicates were reformulated into "extensional" SQL queries, using the techniques described in this paper, and calls to a TSQL function computing 3-gram distances. These queries were then executed by the relational engine and returned both tuples and probabilities. We used Microsoft SQL Server.

We used the TPC-H benchmark, with a database of 0.1GB. We modified all queries by replacing all the predicates in the WHERE clause with uncertain matches. The constants in the queries were either misspelled or made vague. For instance, a condition like part.container = 'PROMO PLATED GREEN' was replace with part.container $\approx$ 'GREEN PLATE'. When executed exactly, all modified queries returned empty answers.

1. Frequency of unsafe queries In our first experiment, we wanted to see how many queries do not have safe plans. Out of the 10 TPC-H queries, 8 turned out to have safe plans. Q_7 and Q_8 were the only query that were unsafe. These also become safe if not all of their predicates

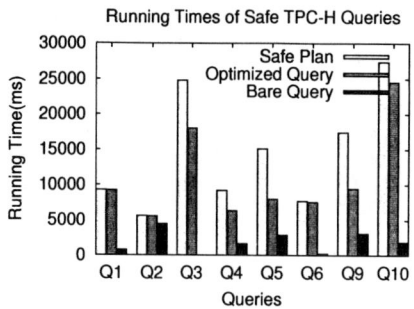

Figure 6: TPC-H Query Running Times

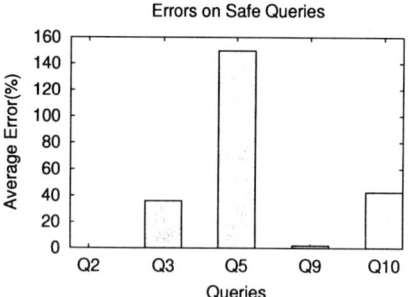

Figure 7: Errors on Safe TPC Queries

are uncertain.

2. Performance Next, we measured the running times for the eight queries that have safe plans, shown in Figure 6. All times are wall-clock. The first column is the running time of the safe plan. The second column represents an optimization where at each intermediate stage, tuples with zero probability are discarded. This optimization does not affect the final answer and as we can see from the graph, it brings about considerable savings for some queries. This also suggests the use of other optimizations like an early removal of tuples with low probabilities if the user is only interested in tuples with high probability. The third column in the graph shows the time for running safe queries without taking into account the computation time for the uncertain predicate, which, in our case, is the 3-gram distance. The graphs show that most of the time is spent in computing the uncertain predicates. (For Q_3 the the running time was almost negligible.) This graph suggests that important improvements would be achieved if the predicates were implemented in the engine.

3. Naive Approaches In the next experiment we calculated the error produced by a naive extensional plan. We considered the naive plan that leaves all project operators (and the associated duplicate elimination) at the end of the plan, which are typical plans produced by database optimizers. Figure 7 shows the percentage relative error of naive plans. We only considered the 8 queries that have safe plans. The naive plans for Q_1, Q_4, Q_6 were already safe, hence had no errors (and SAFE-PLAN indeed returned the same plan): these queries are not shown. Queries Q_3, Q_5 and Q_{10} had large errors with Q_5 showing an average error of 150% in the tuple probabilities. Queries Q_2 and Q_9 had negligible errors. Thus, while some naive plans were bad, others were reasonable. But, in general, naive plans

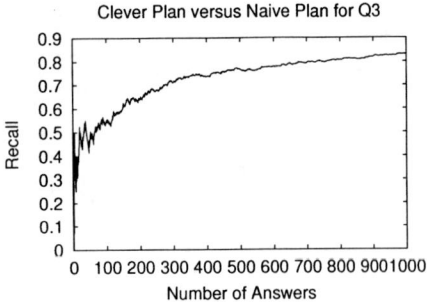

Figure 8: Recall Plot for Q_3

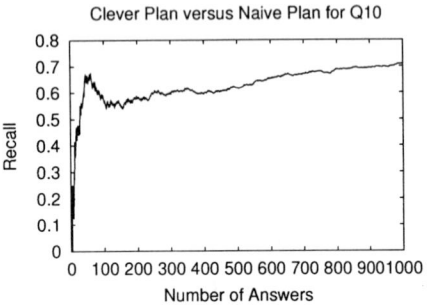

Figure 9: Recall Plot for Q_{10}

can be arbitrarily bad. However, we argue that the low extra complexity of searching for a safe plan is a price worth paying in order to avoid the (admittedly rare) possibility of arbitrarily large errors.

However, since we are only interested in *ranking* the results, not in the actual probabilities, it is worth asking whether high errors in the probabilities translate into high ranking results. We plotted the recall graphs for queries Q_3 and Q_{10} (for which the naive plan produced only medium errors). We defined recall as the fraction of answers ranked among top N by the naive plan that should actually have been in top N. We plotted this as a function of N. Figures 8 and 9 show the recall graphs. By definition, the recall approaches to 1 when N approaches the total number of possible tuples in the answer. However, as the graphs show, the recall was bad for small values of N. A user looking for top 50 or 100 answers to Q_3 would miss half of the relevant tuples. For smaller values of N (say, 10) the naive approach misses 80% of the relevant tuples.

4. Unsafe Queries Finally, we tested our approach to handle queries with no safe plans on Q_7 and Q_8. We ran the Monte Carlo simulation to compute their answer probabilities and used them as baseline. Figure 10 shows the errors in evaluating them with a naive plan and the least unsafe plan (using min-cut, Sec. 6). The graphs show that the plan chosen by the optimizer was better, or significantly better than a naive one. Still, from two data points it is hard to judge the improvement over a naive plan. To see a third data point we wrote a new unsafe query, QQ, where the relation lineitem is joined with orders and suppliers. Here the fanout is larger, and the difference between the naive plan and the optimal break is more pronounced.

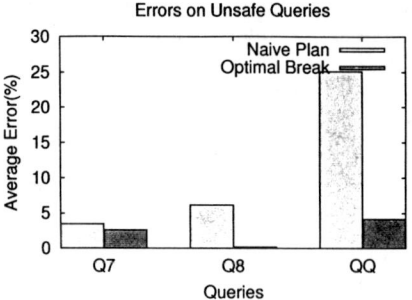

Figure 10: Errors on Unsafe Queries

10 Related Work

The possible worlds semantics, originally put forward by Kripke for modal logics, is commonly used for representing knowledge with uncertainties. Halpern, Baccus et al [11, 4] have showed the use of possible worlds semantics to assign degrees of beliefs to statements based of the probabilities in the knowledge base.

Though there has been extensive work on probabilities in AI, relatively little work has been done on probabilistic databases. There are probabilistic frameworks [7, 6, 13, 18] proposed for databases, but each makes simplifying assumptions for getting around the problem of high query evaluation complexity that lessens their applicability.

Fuhr and Rolleke [13] define probabilistic NF2 relations and introduce the intensional semantics for query evaluation. As we saw, this is correct, but impractical.

Many of these works specialize on logic programming in deductive databases. Ng and Subrahmaniam [21] extend deductive databases with probabilities and give fixed point semantics to logic programs annotated with probabilities, but they use absolute ignorance to combine event probabilities.

Non-probabilistic approaches to imprecise queries have also been considered. Keyword searches in databases are discussed in [16, 8, 15]. Fagin [12] gives an algorithm to rank objects based on its scores from multiple sources: this applies only to a single table. The VAGUE system [19] supports queries with vague predicates, but the query semantics are ad hoc, and apply only to a limited SQL fragments. Surajit et al. [3] consider ranking query results automatically: this also applies to a single table. The WHIRL system [9] computes ranked results of queries with similarity joins, but uses an extensional semantics. Theobald and Weikum [24] describe a query language for XML that supports approximate matches with relevance ranking based on ontologies and semantic similarity.

11 Conclusions

In this paper, we introduce a query semantics on probabilistic databases based on *possible worlds*. Under this semantics, every query that is well defined over a deterministic databases has a meaning on a probabilistic database. We describe how to evaluate queries efficiently under this new semantics. Our theoretical results capture fundamental properties of queries on probabilistic databases, and lead to efficient evaluation techniques. We showed how this approach can be used to evaluate arbitrarily complex

SQL queries with uncertain predicates.

References

[1] Movie database: Uci kdd archive. *http://kdd.ics.uci.edu/databases/movies/movies.html*.

[2] Wordnet 2.0: A lexical database for the english language: *http://www.cogsci.princeton.edu/ wn/*, Jul. 2003.

[3] S. Agrawal, S. Chaudhuri, G. Das, and A. Gionis. Automated ranking of database query results. In *Proceedings of the First Biennial Conf. on Innovative Data Systems Research*, 2003.

[4] Fahiem Bacchus, Adam J. Grove, Joseph Y. Halpern, and Daphne Koller. From statistical knowledge bases to degrees of belief. *Artificial Intelligence*, 87(1-2):75–143, 1996.

[5] R. Baeza-Yates and B. Ribeiro-Neto. *Modern Information Retrieval*. Addison-Wesley, 1999.

[6] Daniel Barbará, Hector Garcia-Molina, and Daryl Porter. The management of probabilistic data. *IEEE Trans. Knowl. Data Eng.*, 4(5):487–502, 1992.

[7] Roger Cavallo and Michael Pittarelli. The theory of probabilistic databases. In *VLDB'87, Proceedings of 13th Int. Conf. on Very Large Data Bases, September 1-4, 1987, Brighton, England*, pages 71–81, 1987.

[8] S. Chaudhuri, G. Das, and V. Narasayya. Dbexplorer: A system for keyword search over relational databases. In *Proceedings of the 18th Int. Conf. on Data Engineering, San Jose, USA*, 2002.

[9] William W. Cohen. Integration of heterogeneous databases without common domains using queries based on textual similarity. In *Proceedings of the 1998 ACM SIGMOD Int. Conf. on Management of data*, pages 201–212. ACM Press, 1998.

[10] Nilesh Dalvi and Dan Suciu. Efficient query evaluation on probabilistic databases. University of Washington Technical Report (TR 04-03-04), January 2004. http://www.cs.washington.edu/research/tr/techreports.html.

[11] Ronald Fagin and Joseph Y. Halpern. Reasoning about knowledge and probability. In *Proceedings of the Second Conf. on Theoretical Aspects of Reasoning about Knowledge*, pages 277–293, San Francisco, 1988.

[12] Ronald Fagin, Amnon Lotem, and Moni Naor. Optimal aggregation algorithms for middleware. In *Proceedings of the twentieth ACM SIGMOD-SIGACT-SIGART symposium on Principles of database systems*, pages 102–113, 2001.

[13] Norbert Fuhr and Thomas Rolleke. A probabilistic relational algebra for the integration of information retrieval and database systems. *ACM Trans. Inf. Syst.*, 15(1):32–66, 1997.

[14] Erich Gradel, Yuri Gurevich, and Colin Hirch. The complexity of query reliability. In *Symposium on Principles of Database Systems*, pages 227–234, 1998.

[15] Lin Guo, Feng Shao, Chavdar Botev, and Jayavel Shanmugasundaram. Xrank: Ranked keyword search over xml documents. In *Proceedings of the 2003 ACM SIGMOD Int. Conf. on Management of Data, San Diego, California, USA, June 9-12, 2003*, pages 16–27, 2003.

[16] V. Hristidis and Y. Papakonstantinou. Discover: Keyword search in relational databases. In *Proc. 28th Int. Conf. Very Large Data Bases, VLDB*, 2002.

[17] Richard Karp and Michael Luby. Monte-carlo algorithms for enumeration and reliability problems. In *Proceedings of the annual ACM symposium on Theory of computing*, 1983.

[18] Laks V. S. Lakshmanan, Nicola Leone, Robert Ross, and V. S. Subrahmanian. Probview: a flexible probabilistic database system. *ACM Trans. Database Syst.*, 22(3):419–469, 1997.

[19] Amihai Motro. Vague: a user interface to relational databases that permits vague queries. *ACM Trans. Inf. Syst.*, 6(3):187–214, 1988.

[20] Gonzalo Navarro. A guided tour to approximate string matching. *ACM Computing Surveys*, 33(1):31–88, 2001.

[21] Raymond T. Ng and V. S. Subrahmanian. Probabilistic logic programming. *Information and Computation*, 101(2):150–201, 1992.

[22] J. S. Provan and M. O. Ball. The complexity of counting cuts and of computing the probability that a graph is connected. *SIAM J. Comput.*, 12(4):777–788, 1983.

[23] M. Stoer and F. Wagner. A simple min cut algorithm. *Algorithms–ESA '94*, pages 141–147, 1994.

[24] Anja Theobald and Gerhard Weikum. The xxl search engine: ranked retrieval of xml data using indexes and ontologies. In *Proceedings of the 2002 ACM SIGMOD Int. Conf. on Management of data*, pages 615–615, 2002.

[25] Jeffrey D. Ullman and Jennifer Widom. *First Course in Database Systems, 2nd ed.* Prentice Hall, 1997.

[26] L. Valiant. The complexity of enumeration and reliability problems. *SIAM J. Comput.*, 8:410–421, 1979.

[27] J. Zobel and P. W. Dart. Phonetic string matching: Lessons from information retrieval. In *Proceedings of the 19th Int. Conf. on Research and Development in Information Retrieval*, pages 166–172, Zurich, Switzerland, 1996. ACM Press.

Efficient Indexing Methods for Probabilistic Threshold Queries over Uncertain Data

Reynold Cheng   Yuni Xia   Sunil Prabhakar   Rahul Shah   Jeffrey Scott Vitter

Department of Computer Sciences, Purdue University
West Lafayette
IN 47907-1398, USA
{ckcheng,xia,sunil,rahul,jsv}@cs.purdue.edu

Abstract

It is infeasible for a sensor database to contain the exact value of each sensor at all points in time. This uncertainty is inherent in these systems due to measurement and sampling errors, and resource limitations. In order to avoid drawing erroneous conclusions based upon stale data, the use of uncertainty intervals that model each data item as a range and associated probability density function (pdf) rather than a single value has recently been proposed. Querying these uncertain data introduces imprecision into answers, in the form of probability values that specify the likeliness the answer satisfies the query. These queries are more expensive to evaluate than their traditional counterparts but are guaranteed to be correct and more informative due to the probabilities accompanying the answers. Although the answer probabilities are useful, for many applications, it is only necessary to know whether the probability exceeds a given threshold – we term these *Probabilistic Threshold Queries* (PTQ). In this paper we address the efficient computation of these types of queries.

In particular, we develop two index structures and associated algorithms to efficiently answer PTQs. The first index scheme is based on the idea of augmenting uncertainty information to an R-tree. We establish the difficulty of this problem by mapping one-dimensional intervals to a two-dimensional space, and show that the problem of interval indexing with probabilities is significantly harder than interval indexing which is considered a well-studied problem. To overcome the limitations of this R-tree based structure, we apply a technique we call *variance-based clustering*, where data points with similar degrees of uncertainty are clustered together. Our extensive index structure can answer the queries for various kinds of uncertainty pdfs, in an almost optimal sense. We conduct experiments to validate the superior performance of both indexing schemes.

1 Introduction

Uncertainty is a common problem faced by sensor databases that interact with external environments. Consider a database system which stores and monitors current pressure, with pressure sensors being deployed in the venue being investigated. Due to resource limitations such as battery power of sensors and network bandwidth, it is often infeasible for a sensor database to contain the exact value of each sensor at all points in time. In particular, since pressure is a continuously changing entity, the system only receives old samples of pressure values. The situation is not helped by the fact that sensor data may not arrive at the system on time, and may even be lost due to network problems. The measurement error incurred by the sensor while measuring the value further aggravates the problem.

In general, uncertainty occurs in any database that attempts to model and capture the state of the physical world, where entities being monitored such as pressure, temperature, locations of moving objects, are constantly changing. As pointed out in [7], if the received (stale) sensor value is directly used to answer queries, erroneous answers may result. In order to alleviate this problem, the idea of incorporating uncertainty information into the sensor data has been pro-

Permission to copy without fee all or part of this material is granted provided that the copies are not made or distributed for direct commercial advantage, the VLDB copyright notice and the title of the publication and its date appear, and notice is given that copying is by permission of the Very Large Data Base Endowment. To copy otherwise, or to republish, requires a fee and/or special permission from the Endowment.

**Proceedings of the 30th VLDB Conference,
Toronto, Canada, 2004**

posed recently. Instead of storing single values, each item is modeled as a range of possible values, associated with a probability density function (pdf) [7].

With the notion of uncertainty, querying on data generates imprecise, rather than exact answers. In these *probabilistic queries*, answers are augmented with probability values that specify the likelihood that they satisfy the query. As an example, suppose there are ten sensors, namely $s_1, s_2, \ldots, s_{10}$ that monitor the temperature values in different offices of a building. Without considering uncertainty, a query that inquires which sensor has a temperature value over 30^oF may yield the answer $\{s_1, s_3, s_9\}$. On the other hand, its probabilistic counterpart can generate $\{(s_1, 0.9), (s_3, 0.7), (s_8, 0.6), (s_9, 0.1)\}$ as an imprecise answer. Here we can observe that sensor s_1 has a very high probability of producing a temperature value over 30^oF, while s_9 only has a marginal chance of satisfying the query. A probabilistic query thus allows us to see the difference in the likelihood of each answer satisfying a query. We can also see that s_8 is a new member of the answer to the probabilistic query, which is *not* in the answer set of the query that does not consider data uncertainty. This is probably because the perceived value of s_8 received by the database is less than 30^oF, but in fact its current actual value can be higher than 30^oF with a non-trivial chance (0.6). A probabilistic query is thus able to produce a more accurate and informative answer than a traditional query.

Despite these advantages over their traditional counterparts, probabilistic queries suffer from a serious problem: they are much more expensive to evaluate. While traditional queries require only exact and single data inputs, probabilistic queries must manage uncertainty information, including intervals and pdfs. In particular, probability values augmented to query answers can be obtained only after costly integration operations are performed. However, it should be noted that although answer probabilities are useful, in practice for many queries, it is only necessary to know whether the probability of answer exceeds a given threshold – we term these *Probabilistic Threshold Queries* (PTQ). A PTQ version for the previous example can be "return the ids of the sensors that have values over 30^oF with a probability of greater than or equal to 0.7", in which case the answer $\{s_1, s_3\}$ is produced.

By exploiting the probability threshold requirement on a probabilistic query, we propose efficient searching techniques. We investigate how an index data structure and its associated algorithms are developed for imprecise data. Two index structures are developed to answer PTQs efficiently. The first index scheme is based on the novel idea of augmenting uncertainty information to an R-tree, where the number of I/Os and integration operations are reduced significantly while the index is still being visited. Although this idea is simple to implement, it is far from being optimal. We then change our focus to study the theoretical complexity of indexing uncertainty, and argue that there is no formerly known optimal solution that is applicable to this problem. By mapping one-dimensional intervals to a two-dimensional space, we illustrate that the problem of indexing uncertainty with probabilities is significantly harder than interval indexing, which is considered a well-studied problem.

Based on the interpretation of theoretical studies, we develop a technique called *variance-based clustering*, in order to overcome the limitations of the uncertainty-information-augmented R-tree structure. In this indexing scheme, data points with similar degrees of uncertainty (e.g., mean and standard deviation) are clustered together. The final extensive index is an R-tree based index, augmented with uncertainty information, and enhanced with the variance-based-clustering technique. This index can answer the queries for various kinds of uncertainty pdfs, in an almost optimal sense. The results are verified by an extensive experimental evaluation.

As a summary of our contributions, we propose two structures to index uncertain data for PTQs. The first index, called *PTI*, augments uncertain information to internal nodes so that more search paths can be pruned while the index is being visited. This index forms the basis of a more extensive scheme, where intervals with similar variance values are clustered together. We also show that with a fixed probability threshold, querying uncertainty intervals with uniform pdf can be answered in optimal time, and establish a theoretical foundation of the problem. We also perform extensive experiments to compare our proposed schemes with an R-tree.

The rest of this paper is organized as follows. In Section 2 we formally define the uncertainty model and probabilistic threshold queries. Section 3 presents a simple index with uncertainty information augmented to evaluate a PTQ. We further establish the theoretical difficulty of the problem in 4. An extensive framework for evaluating PTQ is presented in 5. We present our experimental results in 6. Section 7 discusses related work and Section 8 concludes the paper.

2 Data Uncertainty and Probabilistic Queries

In [7][9], a data representation scheme known as *probabilistic uncertainty model* was proposed. The model requires that at the time of query execution, the range of possible values of the attribute of interest, and their distributions, are known. For notational convenience, we assume that a real-valued attribute a of a set of database objects T is queried. The ith object of T is named T_i, and the value of a for T_i is called $T_i.a$ ($i = 1, \ldots, |T|$), where $T_i.a$ is treated as a continuous random variable. The *probabilistic uncertainty* of $T_i.a$

consists of two components:

Definition 1 *An* **uncertainty interval** *of $T_i.a$, denoted by U_i, is an interval $[L_i, R_i]$ where $L_i, R_i \in \Re$, and the conditions $R_i \geq L_i$ and $T_i.a \in U_i$ always hold.*

Definition 2 *An* **uncertainty pdf** *of $T_i.a$, denoted by $f_i(x)$, is a pdf of $T_i.a$, such that $f_i(x)=0$ if $x \notin U_i$.*

This simple model provides flexibility where the exact model of uncertainty is determined by application-dependent assumptions. A simple example is the modeling of sensor measurement uncertainty, where each U_i is an error range containing the mean value, and $f_i(x)$ is a normal distribution. Another example is the modeling of one-dimensional moving objects based on [20], where at any point in time, the actual location is within a certain bound, d, of its last reported location value. If the actual location changes further than d, then the sensor reports its new location value to the database and possibly changes d. In this case, U_i contains all the values within a distance of d from its last reported value. For $f_i(x)$, one may assume that $T_i.a$ is uniformly distributed, i.e., $f_i(x) = 1/[R_i - L_i]$ for $T_i.a \in U_i$. Treating $f_i(x)$ as a uniform pdf models the scenario where $T_i.a$ has an *equal* chance of locating anywhere in U_i. Due to its simplicity, a uniform distribution facilitates ease of analysis and efficient index design, as illustrated in subsequent sections.

Alternatively, one may perform an estimation of the pdf based on time-series analysis, the discussion of which is beyond the scope of this paper. Interested readers are referred to [5] for details. Also notice that we limit our discussion of uncertainty to interval data. A comprehensive discussion of different types of uncertainty can be found in [21].

A *probabilistic threshold query* (PTQ), proposed in [9], is a variant of probabilistic query, where only answers with probability values over a certain threshold p are returned. The PTQ that we study specifically in this paper is defined formally below.

Definition 3 Probabilistic Threshold Query (PTQ) *Given a closed interval $[a, b]$, where $a, b \in \Re$ and $a \leq b$, a PTQ returns a set of tuples T_i, such that the probability $T_i.a$ is inside $[a, b]$, denoted by p_i, is greater than or equal to p, where $0 < p \leq 1$.*

Simply speaking, a PTQ can be treated as a range query, operating on probabilistic uncertainty information, and returns items whose probabilities of satisfying the query exceed p.

3 A Simple Uncertainty Index

A naive method to evaluate a PTQ is to first retrieve all T_i's, whose uncertainty intervals have some overlapping with $[a, b]$, into a set S. Each T_i in S is then evaluated for their probability of satisfying the PTQ with the following operation:

$$p_i = \int_{OI} f_i(x)dx \quad (1)$$

where p_i is the probability that T_i satisfies the PTQ, and OI is the interval of overlap between $[a, b]$ and U_i. The answer only includes T_i's whose p_i's are larger than p.

Two problems can be seen from this approach. First, how can we find the elements of S i.e., U_i's that overlap with $[a, b]$? It can be very inefficient if each item T_i is retrieved from a large database and tested against $[a, b]$. A typical solution is to build an index structure over U_i's (which are intervals) and apply a range search of $[a, b]$ over the index. This problem is known as the interval indexing problem, and has been well studied [17][15].

The second problem is that the probability of each element in S needs to be evaluated with Equation 1. This can be a computationally expensive operation. Notice that the bottleneck incurred in this step is independent of whether we use an interval index or not. In particular, the interval index does not help much if many items overlap with $[a, b]$, but most have probability less than p. In this situation, we still need to spend a lot of time to compute the probability values for a vast number of items, only to find that they do not satisfy the PTQ after all.

3.1 Probability Threshold Indexing

The above problems illustrate the inefficiency of using an interval index to answer a PTQ. While the range search is being performed in the interval index, only uncertainty intervals are used for pruning out intervals which do not intersect $[a, b]$. Another piece of important uncertainty information, namely the uncertainty pdf, has not been utilized at all in this searching-and-pruning process. As a result, a large number of items may overlap with $[a, b]$, while in fact only a small fraction of them contribute to the results of PTQ.

Our goal is to redesign index structures so that probabilistic uncertainty information is fully utilized during an index search. This structure, called *Probability Threshold Indexing* (PTI), is based on the modification of a one-dimensional R-tree, where probability information is augmented to its internal nodes to facilitate pruning. To illustrate our idea, let us review briefly how a range query is performed on an R-tree. Starting from the root node, the query interval $[a, b]$ is compared with the maximum bounding rectangle (MBR) of each child in the node. Only children with MBRs that overlap with $[a, b]$ are further followed. We thus save the effort of retrieving nodes whose MBRs do not overlap $[a, b]$. We can generalize this idea by constructing *tighter* bounds (that we call x-bounds) than

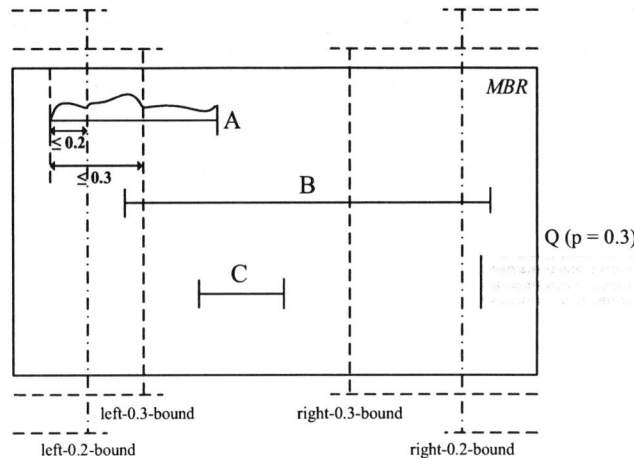

Figure 1: Inside an MBR M_j, with a 0.2-bound and 0.3-bound. A PTQ named Q is shown as an interval.

the MBR in each node, by using uncertainty information of intervals, so as to further reduce the chance of examining the children of the node. Let M_j denote the MBR/uncertainty interval represented by the jth node of an R-tree, ordered by a pre-order traversal. Then the x-bound of M_j is defined as follows.

Definition 4 *An **x-bound** of an MBR/uncertainty interval M_j is a pair of lines, namely left-x-bound (denoted by $M_j.lb(x)$) and right-x-bound (denoted by $M_j.rb(x)$). Every item $T_i.a$ contained in M_j can only have a probability of at most x (where $0 \leq x \leq 1$) both on the left of the left-x-bound and on the right of the right-x-bound. That is to say, if $L_i \leq M_j.lb(x)$ and $R_i \geq M_j.rb(x)$, then the following must hold: $\int_{L_i}^{M_j.lb(x)} f_i(y)dy \leq x$ and $\int_{M_j.rb(x)}^{R_i} f_i(y)dy \leq x$.*

Using the definition of an x-bound, the MBR of an internal node can be viewed as a 0-bound, since it guarantees all intervals in the node are contained in it with probability one i.e., no interval lies beyond the 0-bound. Figure 1 illustrates three children MBRs (A,B,C), in the form of one-dimensional intervals, contained in a larger MBR M_j. A 0.2-bound and a 0.3-bound for M_j are also shown.

As Figure 1 shows, an x-bound is a pair of lines where at most a fraction of x of each interval in the MBR cross either of them. The uncertainty pdf of A is shown, where we can see that $\int_{L_A}^{M_j.lb(0.2)} f_i(x)dx \leq 0.2$, and $\int_{L_A}^{M_j.lb(0.3)} f_i(x)dx \leq 0.3$. For interval B, the constraint on the right-0.3-bound is $\int_{M_j.rb(0.3)}^{R_B} f_i(x)dx \leq 0.3$. Interval C does not cross either the 0.2-bound and the 0.3-bound, so it satisfies the constraints of both x-bounds. Furthermore, we require an x-bound to be unique, where the left-x-bound and right-x-bound are pushed towards the center of the MBR as much as possible, without violating their definitions.

The whole purpose of storing the information of the x-bound in an R-tree node is to avoid investigating the contents of a node. If we can avoid this probing, a considerable amount of I/Os can be saved. Furthermore, we do not need to compute the probability values of those intervals, which cannot satisfy the query anyway. To illustrate how this idea works, let us look at Figure 1 again. Here a range query Q, represented as an interval, is tested against the internal node. Without the aid of the x-bound, Q has to (i) examine which MBR (i.e., A, B, or C) overlaps with Q's interval, (ii) for the qualified MBRs (B in this example), further retrieve the node pointed by B until the leaf level is reached, and (iii) compute the probability of the interval in the leaf level.

The presence of the x-bound allows us to decide with ease whether an internal node contains any qualifying MBRs, without further probing into the subtrees of this node. In this example, we first test Q's range against the left-0.2-bound and the right-0.2-bound. As shown in Figure 1, it intersects none of these bounds. In particular, although Q overlaps the MBR, its overlapping region is somewhere between the right-0.2-bound and the right boundary of M_j's MBR. Recall that a 0.2-bound allows at most an accumulated pdf of 0.2 of any interval in an MBR. This implies that the portion of the intervals (interval B) that passes through the 0.2-bound cannot exceed a probability of 0.2. Therefore, the probability of intervals in the MBR that overlap the range of Q cannot be larger than 0.2. Assume Q has a probability threshold of 0.3 i.e., Q only accepts intervals with an overlapping probability of at least 0.3. Then we can be certain that *none* of the intervals in the MBR satisfies Q, without further probing the subtrees of this node. Compared with the case where no x-bounds are implanted, this represents a significant saving in terms of the number of I/Os and computation time.

In general, given an x-bound of a MBR M_j, and a PTQ with interval $[a,b]$ and probability threshold p, we can eliminate M_j from further examination if the following two conditions hold:

1. $[a,b]$ does not intersect left-x-bound or right-x-bound of M_j i.e., either $b < M_j.lb(x)$ or $a > M_j.rb(x)$ is true, and

2. $p \geq x$

If no x-bound in M_j satisfies these two conditions, the checking of intersections with M_j is resumed, where the contents of the node represented by M_j are loaded, and the range searching process is done in the same manner as for an R-tree.

3.2 Implementation of PTI

Figure 2 illustrates an implementation of PTI. Its framework is the same as R-tree, where each internal

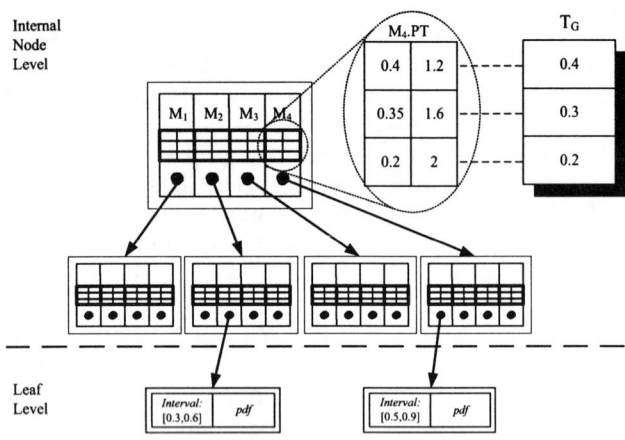

Figure 2: Structure of PTI

node consists of children MBRs and their corresponding pointers. In addition, each child M_j consists of a table, $M_j.PT$, that contains information of its x-bounds. Each entry of $M_j.PT$ is a tuple of the form <left-x-bound, right-x-bound>. Further, a global table called T_G is defined, which contains the values of x for x-bounds. The i-th entry of $M_j.PT$ contains the x-bound whose value of x is stored in the i-th entry of T_G. The data items being indexed are essentially uncertainty intervals and pdfs.

To insert $T_i.a$, we first compute its x-bounds, corresponding to the values of x in T_G. Then we insert $T_i.a$ to the PTI, using a similar procedure as inserting an interval to an R-tree. The main difference is that the x-bounds of the intermediate nodes being traversed during insertion need to be expanded appropriately. In particular, the left-x-bound of an internal node needs to be replaced by the corresponding left-x-bound of $T_i.a$ if the former value is larger than the latter. The right-x-bounds are expanded analogously. Finally, the x-bound information computed for $T_i.a$ is copied to PT of the node that directly points to $T_i.a$.

Removing an object follows a similar procedure of the R-tree. Again, we need to take care of the update issues of x-bounds. We observe that if an MBR M_j is to be deleted, then the left-x-bound of the parent node that points to M_j has to be shrinked to the minimum of left-x-bound of all MBRs in the same node as M_j. The right-x-bound of the parent node is adjusted in a similar manner. We therefore need to keep parent pointers in each node. To update the x-bounds, beginning from the leaf node that contains the interval of interest, the changes to x-bounds are propagated until the root is reached.

Although the fan-out of a PTI node is lower than an R-tree node because each node contains less space to store MBRs (assume the node size is fixed), the fan-out only logarithmically affects the height of the tree. Hence, in most cases this results in an increase in height by an additive constant, which only has a minor effect on PTI's performance. Indeed, its performance illustrates significant improvements over R-tree, as observed in our experimental results (Section 6).

However, PTI by itself is not an optimal solution, because it cannot avoid the problem that an R-tree faces – if the data source consists of both large and small intervals, a lot of smaller intervals will reside in the same leaf node as the large intervals. The search time is increased unnecessarily, because a range search may have to go through many large MBRs consisting of large intervals. The major cause of this problem is that the insertion mechanism of the R-tree does not differentiate between large and small intervals. We investigate this problem in subsequent sections, and develop an extensive framework to tackle this shortcoming. The framework employs the idea of PTI as well. In some cases, the framework is even able to eliminate the extra overhead of PTI altogether, by computing the probability threshold information "on the fly".

4 Theoretical Implications

Any index is considered theoretically efficient if it achieves provably logarithmic update and query times while using a linear amount of space. We will discuss the difficulty of the PTQ problem as compared with other known problems in computational geometry. Interval indexing [14, 3, 2] is considered a well-studied problem and theoretically efficient indexes exist. However, we show here that interval indexing coupled with pdfs is significantly more complex than interval indexing. On the other hand, theoretically efficient index structures for PTQ are possible only when the threshold p is apriori fixed constant for all the queries.

In this section, we will mainly focus on PTQ assuming the pdf in each interval is uniform. That is, if a query specifies 80% threshold, then any interval satisfying this query has at least 80% of its length within the query range. We call this the PTQU problem. In this section, we want to show that PTQ is a hard problem to be provably solved even with uniform pdfs. However, good heuristics can be used for PTQU and they can be extended to PTQs when pdfs are arbitrary using the idea of PTI in the previous section. As a side note, we also show that a provably good index for PTQU can exist if the threshold of probability p is a fixed constant.

4.1 2D mapping of intervals

We first explore PTQUs when the intervals are indexed as points in two dimensional space [14, 3]. Here, each interval $[x, y]$ is mapped to a point (x, y) in 2D. Note that, for all intervals, $x < y$ and hence these points all lie in the region above (and to the left of) the line $x = y$. Figure 3(a) gives the illustration. A stabbing query is a particular kind of query associated with the notion of intervals. Given a point c, a stabbing query reports all the intervals containing point c. A stabbing query [3] for point c is converted to a two-sided orthogonal

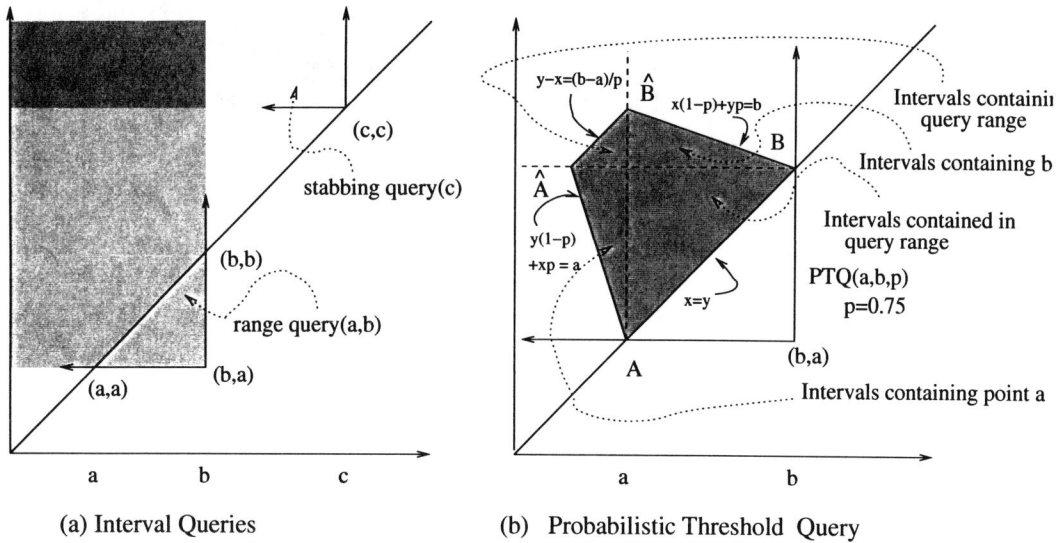

Figure 3: Probabilistic Threshold Queries with Uniform pdf

query originating at point (c,c) in this mapping. A range query (a,b) is just a union of the stabbing queries for all the points from a to b. This is same as a two-sided orthogonal query originating at point (b,a).

A PTQU (a,b,p) where $0 < p \leq 1$ now becomes a 3-sided trapezoidal query as shown in Figure 3(b). To see this, consider any point (x,y) (i.e. interval $[x,y]$) that satisfies PTQU. There are four cases:

$x \leq a < b \leq y$: In this case the query lies within the interval. All we require is that the query covers a sufficient length of the interval. That is $b - a \geq p(y-x)$. That means point (x,y) is in the region below the line $y - x = (b-a)/p$. This line has slope 1.

$x \leq a < y \leq b$: In this case the query region is on the right of the interval. The amount of overlap is given by $y - a$. This condition translates to $y(1-p) + xp \geq a$. That is the region above the line $y(1-p) + xp = a$ which has slope $-p/(1-p)$.

$a \leq x < b \leq y$: In this case is the query region is on the left of the interval. This is given by the region $x(1-p) + yp \leq b$. The separating line has slope $-(1-p)/p$.

$a < x < y < b$: In this case, the entire interval lies within the query and hence it satisfies the PTQU for any p.

Thus, the query satisfying region is given by the intersection of the three regions (first three) above. This becomes an isosceles trapezoid region. The fourth side of the region given by line $x = y$ can be essentially considered redundant since there are no points below (or to the right) of this line. We will call this as an open side of the trapezoid. Thus, PTQU becomes a 3-sided trapezoidal query.

As p approaches 0, this becomes a range intersection query i.e. the slopes of the lines in the second and third cases become zero and infinity respectively. The first constraint becomes redundant. This is the same as a two-sided orthogonal query. At $p = 1$, the trapezoid becomes a right-angled triangle and the query becomes a containment query. At $p = 0.5$ the trapezoid becomes a square. For $p < 0.5$ the close side (as given by first constraint) of the trapezoid is bigger than the open side (on line $x = y$) and for $p > 0.5$ the closed side is smaller than the open side. See Figure 5.

4.2 Relation of PTQU to other well known problems

To establish the difficulty of the problem we will relate PTQU to two well known problems, namely simplex queries in 2D and half-space queries in 2D. First we define these problems and then show that PTQU lies between these two problems in terms of its hardness. This indicates that a provably good indexing may not be possible for PTQU. On the other hand we shall show in the next subsection that if the threshold for PTQU is fixed for all the queries, then provably good query times can be achieved.

Problem 1 Half-space queries in 2D (HQ2D): *Given a dynamic set of points in 2D, report the set of points which satisfy a query given by a linear constraint $ax + by \geq c$ where a, b, c are real numbers.*

Problem 2 Simplex queries in 2D (SQ2D): *Given a dynamic set of points in 2D, report the set of points which satisfy a query given by a constant number of linear constraints $a_i x + b_i y \geq c_i$ where i goes from 1 to a constant j and a_i, b_i, c_i are real numbers.*

It is easy to see that PTQU is a special case of Simplex queries. Also, we can establish that PTQU

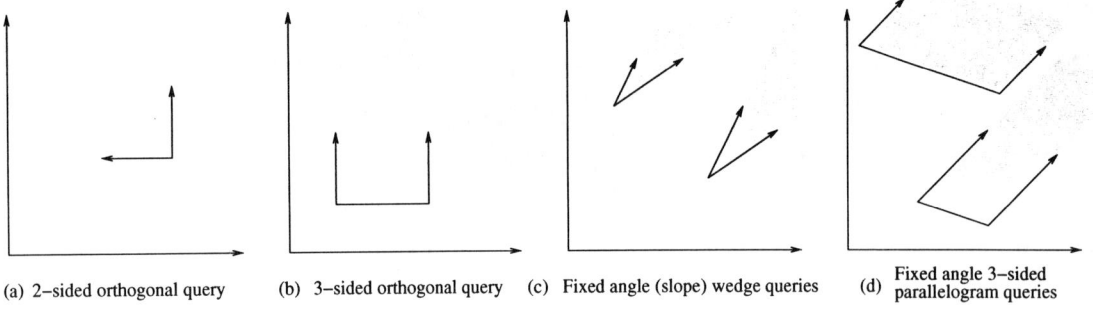

(a) 2-sided orthogonal query (b) 3-sided orthogonal query (c) Fixed angle (slope) wedge queries (d) Fixed angle 3-sided parallelogram queries

Figure 4: Wedge queries and parallelogram queries with fixed slopes

is at least as hard as half-space queries. Let n be the number of points and k be the number of points satisfying a query. We state the following lemma. The proof is skipped for conciseness.

Lemma 1 *If PTQU for n intervals can be answered in time t with update times u and using space s, then HQ2D can be answered in $O(t)$ time, with update time $O(u)$ and in $O(s)$ space.*

□

Here, we consider problems (HQ2D and SQ2D) which report all the points satisfying the query. These are called reporting versions of the problem. Lower bounds exist for these problems in the algebraic model [12, 6]. Data structures which use a linear amount of storage for HQ2D require at least $\Omega(n^{1/3})$ for query and update operations on average[12, 4]. For SQ2D, this lower bound is $\Omega(\sqrt{n})$ [6]. The best known data structures can answer SQ2D queries in $\sqrt{n} \log n$, which is considered almost tight against the lower bound. Half-space range searching, is one of the exceptions in the class of geometric range searching problems where lower bounds from algebraic models do not apply to the reporting version of the problem (i.e. HQ2D as we have defined). See the surveys on Geometric range searching by [18, 11] for more details. However, the best known data structure for HQ2D can answer reporting queries in time $O(n^\epsilon + k)$ using linear storage [1]. If the storage is allowed to be superlinear i.e. $O(n^{1+\epsilon})$, then optimal reporting time of $O(\log n + k)$ can be achieved [10]. Note that ϵ can be made arbitrarily small but this increases the constants hidden in the big-O notation. This implies that we can not hope for a linear space index which gives provably good query times (i.e. $O(\log n + k)$).

However, the above bounds are for the worst case performance of the data structure. In general, when points in 2D are uniformly distributed (and not pathologically arranged to force the worst case), any space partitioning data structure like R-tree gives reasonably good query times for polygonal queries (i.e. SQ2D). Goldstein et al. [13] use R-trees to answer SQ2D queries. Although worst case bounds can not be proven, practically the index works fairly well.

Motivated by [13], we use R-tree in 2D to answer PTQU. For a general pdf (not necessarily uniform) we develop a heuristic based on this idea to answer PTQ. More details are provided in Section 5.

4.3 PTQU with fixed threshold

Here we show that PTQU can be answered provably efficiently when the threshold value p is fixed for all queries and p is not close to 0. However, we wish to note that these results are for theoretical interest only. We can use the data structures which handle 2-sided and 3-sided orthogonal queries [2] (see Figure 4(a,b)). First we establish the following lemma when 2-sided or 3-sided queries are not orthogonal but consist of line segments with fixed slopes (see Figure 4(c,d)). Also, in external memory where the cost model is number of I/Os, with block size B, a 2-sided angular query (also called wedge queries) is a query specified by an angle (i.e. two rays) and it reports all the points in the interior of the angle. A 3-sided parallelogram query is a generalization of 3-sided orthogonal queries, where there are two parallel sides and one closed side, and each of these can be at an arbitrary inclination (not just orthogonal).

Lemma 2 *For n points in two dimensional space, 2-sided wedge queries where the slopes of both the sides are fixed for all queries and 3-sided parallelogram queries where two independent slopes involved are fixed for all queries can be answered in $O(\log n + k)$ time. Also, in external memory where block size for I/Os is B, these queries can be answered in $O(\log_B n + k/B)$ I/Os.*

Proof : (sketch) Since the slopes of lines involved are fixed for all the queries, we use a linear transformation to align the directions of the axes along these slopes. Now, these queries simply become 2-sided and 3-sided orthogonal queries. Known structures from [2] can be used to answer them. □

Theorem 1 *PTQU with fixed threshold p can be answered within $O(\log_B n + k/B)$ I/Os using $O(n)$ space when $p \geq 0.5$ and can be answered in $O(((1-$*

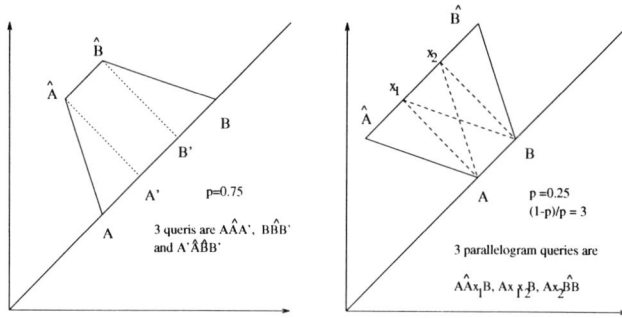

Figure 5: Probabilistic Threshold Queries with fixed Threshold

$p)/p)(\log_B n + k/B)$ *I/Os using* $O((1-p)n/p)$ *space when* $p < 0.5$.

Proof : Figure 5 shows the trapezoidal query regions for $p \geq 0.5$ and $p < 0.5$. When $p \geq 0.5$ the query can be answered by answering two wedge queries $A\hat{A}A'$, $B'\hat{B}B$ and a 3-sided parallelogram query $A'\hat{A}\hat{B}B'$. Recall that side AB is an open side since there are no points on the other side of AB. Hence, the open side for all these queries are along the side AB. Since the slopes of these lines only depend on p and p is fixed, all the slopes involved are fixed. Hence, the answer is the union of these 3 queries. Note that this requires maintaining three separate structures, one for each query.

When $p < 0.5$, the ratio of lengths of $\hat{A}\hat{B}$ and AB is $(1-p)/p$. The query can be answered using $(1-p)/p$ 3-sided parallelogram queries ($\hat{A}\hat{B}$ can be partitioned into $(1-p)/p$ segments which have the same length as AB and each segment forms a separate parallelogram query). The answer is the union of answers of these queries. This requires $(1-p)/p$ simultaneous structures and hence the space and time bounds. □

While these kind of bounds (provable data structures) do not exist when p is not fixed, we can still use 2D R-tree as in [13] to answer the trapezoidal queries. This forms the basis of our index in the next section.

5 An Extensive Uncertainty Index

In the previous section, we observed that if the uncertainty pdfs are uniform over each interval, then PTQ can be answered by indexing intervals as 2D objects and performing polygonal search queries over this index. However, this approach works only for uniform pdfs. When pdfs are allowed to be arbitrary, we cannot always obtain a boundary which separates intervals that satisfy the query from the intervals that do not. However, the pruning approach of Section 3 can be helpful. Here we explore how to combine both ideas to build an extensive index capable of handling arbitrary pdfs.

As discussed in the Section 3, a possible drawback of the simple R-tree based approach is that the MBR of an R-tree can have a small interval as well as a large interval. Suppose a large MBR contains an interval much shorter than the length of the MBR, placed near the right boundary of the MBR. If the result of a PTQ contains the small interval, this implies the PTQ has to visit the large MBR just for the sake of the small interval. This can result in a larger search cost, particularly when the small interval in that MBR is all that the PTQ answer requires, but the large amount of space on the left of the small interval may have to be visited unnecessarily. Although, heuristics for R-tree (e.g., minArea) attempt to avoid such cases they cannot always acheive it.

For uniform pdfs, as we will see in the experiments, 2D indexing supporting trapezoidal queries shows improvement over PTI. Now consider the mapping of intervals to a 2D plane with interval $[x, y]$ mapped to the point (x, y). By rotating this mapping by 45 degrees clockwise and scaling it upwards by a factor of $\sqrt{2}$, the transformation represents the mean points of intervals along x axis, and the lengths of the intervals along the y axis. For uniform pdfs, the length of the interval is directly proportional to the standard deviation (which is one-third of the length). Thus, the 2D mapping when indexed using R-tree not only tends to put the intervals with close proximity (similar mean values) in the same MBR, but also ensures that all intervals in the same MBR have similar standard deviation values (or more generally, variances). We call this property of 2D indexing where intervals with similar variance values are grouped together as *variance-based clustering*. Let us have a closer look at how this property can be extended to handle general cases of pdfs.

Definition 5 *An x-deviation of a node N (either interval or an MBR) in a PTI is defined as $(N.rb(x) - N.lb(x))/2$. It is denoted by $N.dev(x)$.*

Note that $N.dev(x)$ decreases as x increases. Also, $N.dev(x)$ can be negative, if $x > 0.5$. In particular, when N is an interval (and not an MBR), $N.dev(x)$ is necessarily negative, if $x > 0.5$, in which case its left-x-bound and right-x-bound "swap" their positions.

Definition 6 *A set T of data items is variance-monotonic if for any two items T_i and T_j, their uncertainty pdfs f_i and f_j are such that for any values $x, y \in (0, 1]$ if $|T_i.dev(x)| \geq |T_j.dev(x)|$ then $|T_i.dev(y)| \geq |T_j.dev(y)|$.*

Definition 7 *A variance monotonic set T is variance-monotonic smooth if $T_i.dev(x)/T_i.dev(y) = T_j.dev(x)/T_j.dev(y)$ for any i, j, x, y.*

Definition 8 *A set T of data items is symmetric if its pdf is symmetric around the midpoint of the interval.*

Definition 9 *A set T of data items is regular if it is both symmetric and smooth variance-monotonic.*

Many standard pdfs like Gaussian[1] or uniform have the smooth variance-monotonic property. For example, consider two intervals $T_i = [9, 19]$ and $T_j = [35, 55]$ with uniform pdfs. Let us pick two arbitrary values for x and y, say 0.2 and 0.4. Then, $T_i.dev(x) = 6, T_i.dev(y) = 2, T_j.dev(x) = 12$ and $T_j.dev(y) = 4$. Thus, the ratio $T_i.dev(x)/T_i.dev(y) = T_i.dev(x)/T_i.dev(y) = 3$. Thus, for a smooth variance-monotonic set, this ratio only depends on x and y and is same for all the objects in the set when x and y are fixed. A set of data items which consists of all objects with Gaussian pdfs (each object can have different μ, σ) is smooth variance-monotonic. This is true also for a set of all the objects with uniform pdfs. However, if a set of objects has both kinds of pdfs uniform as well as Gaussian simultaneously, then it is no longer smooth variance-monotonic.

Given an interval with a pdf, we first determine its *representative deviation* $T_i.rdev$, defined in the following manner: Select some values $x_1, x_2, x_3, ..., x_j \in (0, 1]$. Then, for each i, $T_i.rdev$ is an aggregate function of $|T_i.dev(x_1)|, ..., |T_i.dev(x_j)|$. In this paper, we will simply take the aggregate function to be the average of these values. The values of $x_1, x_2, .., x_j$ are selected as some of the most relevant thresholds for the index. Note that for smooth variance monotonic data set just one value of x can give the representative deviation. We also calculate an entity called $T_i.mean$ which is the point in the interval such that there is 50% probability on either side of the point (i.e. mean value of the interval according to the pdf).

5.1 Uncertainty Indexing for Regular Sets

As noted earlier, both Gaussian and uniform pdfs are symmetric and smooth variance-monotonic. Thus a set consisting of all Gaussian pdfs is a regular set. For indexing a regular set, we can use a 2D R-tree. First a representative threshold value x is selected (say 30%). Then we calculate $T_i.mean$ and $T_i.rdev$ for all items in T. For different values of $y \in (0, 1]$, a table of ratios of $r(y) = T_i.dev(y)/T_i.dev(x)$ is also calculated. This table is called the *ratio table* and is kept in the main memory. Note that this ratio is the same for each object in T. We index each item by its 2D coordinates $(T_i.mean, T_i.rdev)$, and construct a 2D R-tree on this representation.

To process a query (a, b, p), we first check the query against MBRs of the nodes in this tree. A node N is pruned when it is guaranteed that no item in the subtree rooted at N can satisfy (a, b, p). Let μ_1, μ_2 be the lowest and highest values of $T_i.mean$ over all objects in the subtree of N and let σ_1, σ_2 be the lowest

and highest values of $T_i.rdev$ over all the objects in the subtree. Note that the MBR for N is $[(\mu_1, \sigma_1) : (\mu_2, \sigma_2)]$.[2] Let $\hat{p} \leq p$ be the value where the ratio $r(\hat{p})$ is pre-calculated in the ratio table. We calculate two values L, R such that $L \leq N.lb(\hat{p}) \leq N.lb(p)$ and $R \geq N.rb(\hat{p}) \geq N.rb(p)$. Note that L may be greater than R, when $\hat{p} \geq 0.5$. If $\hat{p} < 0.5$ then, $L = \mu_1 - r(\hat{p})\sigma_2$ and $R = \mu_2 + r(\hat{p})\sigma_2$. If $\hat{p} \geq 0.5$ then, $L = \mu_1 + r(\hat{p})\sigma_1$ and $R = \mu_2 - r(\hat{p})\sigma_1$. In the case where $L \leq R$, if the range of the query $[a, b]$ does not overlap with $[L, R]$ then we can safely prune N. If $L > R$ then the range of the query $[a, b]$ must contain $[R, L]$ to not prune N. If it does not contain, then N is pruned. The following theorem proves the correctness of the method.

Theorem 2 *If a node N with MBR $[(\mu_1, \sigma_1) : (\mu_2, \sigma_2)]$ is pruned by the query (a, b, p) where the set of data items T is regular, then there is no data item in the subtree of N which satisfies the query (a, b, p).*

Proof: Consider the case when $p < 0.5$ and N is pruned. Here, $L \leq R$ and $[a, b]$ does not overlap with $[L, R]$. Without loss of generality, we assume that $b < L$. We prove our claim by contradiction. Assume that there is an object T_i in the subtree of N satisfying the query. Now, $T_i.mean \geq \mu_1$ and $T_i.rdev \leq \sigma_2$. Let $L' = T_i.mean - T_i.dev(\hat{p})$. Thus, by symmetry and the definition of $T_i.dev$, $L' = T_i.lb(\hat{p})$. Since $r(\hat{p}) = T_i.dev(\hat{p})/T_i.rdev$, $L' \geq L$. Also, $\hat{p} < p$ implies T_i satisfies the query $(a, b, \hat{p})$, This means $L' \leq b$ implies $L \leq b$, which is a contradiction. Hence, such an object T_i cannot exist. The proofs for all other cases are exactly the same with appropriate parameters changed, which we skip due to limitation of space. □

Compared with PTI, this scheme has an advantage in terms of space. Recall that PTI requires extra space to store probability threshold information. With this scheme, we exploit the fact that the data set is smooth variance-monotonic and symmetric, and compute the probability threshold information "on the fly". Thus overhead required by PTI can be avoided.

5.2 Uncertainty Indexing for Arbitrary pdfs

For arbitrary pdfs (not necessarily variance monotonic), the correctness of the above approach cannot be guaranteed. We need to revert to the PTI structure of Section 3. Hence, apart from the MBR boundaries we also maintain the boundaries from certain fixed values of probability threshold. We can build an index based on 2D R-tree, with operations like insert, delete and split. For this we index each item by $(T_i.mean, T_i.rdev)$. Here, $T_i.rdev$ is calculated as an average of $T_i.dev(x)$ for some predetermined values of x.

---

[1] When we assume Gaussian pdf the length of the interval may be considered as infinite. Alternatively we may use an approximation of Gaussian distribution by trimming away the portion of the interval beyond which the probability is below a certain threshold and normalizing the pdf inside the interval.

[2] We use $(lx, ly) : (rx, ry)$ to represent a rectangle where (lx, ly) and (rx, ry) are the coordinates of the lower and upper bounds respectively.

However, this structure does not guarantee query correctness and does not allow pruning if we do not include PTI information. Hence, for query processing, we consider each node N's MBR as a one-dimensional object. In PTI structure, we first include $N.lb(0)$ and $N.rb(0)$. This forms the MBR of T_j when it is considered as a one-dimensional entity. Then we also include $N.lb(x)$ and $N.rb(x)$ for various predetermined values of x depending upon likely query thresholds. Then query pruning is done based on this PTI structure given in Section 3. Thus this structure is constructed as a 2D R-tree, but its query processing is treated as a 1D R-tree operation. The main difference between this structure and the one in Section 3 is that this structure attempts directly to cluster the data items with similar variance values. We will see in Section 6 that the variance-clustered R-tree improves the query performance.

6 Experimental Results

In this section we present the performance results of an extensive simulation for the index structures we proposed. We implemented a one-dimensional R-tree without uncertain information augmented (hereby referred to as *R-tree*), a PTI, as well as the extensive uncertainty scheme (referred to as *extensive*), where both the ideas of PTI and two-dimensional variance-based-clustering techniques applied. We will discuss our simulation model followed by experimental results.

6.1 Simulation Model

We generated two sets of data. The first set of data are uncertain data, with their lengths uniformly distributed in $[U_{min}, U_{max}]$, with a uniform uncertainty pdf. The second set of data are the properties of probabilistic threshold queries. Similar to the uncertain data, the length of each query range is also normally distributed with U_{mean} and U_{dev}, with a uniform uncertainty pdf. Their probability thresholds are uniformly distributed between 0.1 and 1. Table 1 presents the parameters for uncertain data and PTQ.

The total insertion and query I/O performance of the indexes is measured. Each disk page contains S_{page} bytes, with N_{entry} entries per page. By default, a PTI node contains five tuples of x-bounds, where $x \in \{0.1, 0.3, 0.5, 0.7, 0.9\}$.

6.2 Results

6.2.1 Scalability of Uncertainty Indexes

In the first experiment, we examine the scalability of the three indexes. Figure 6 shows their I/O performance as the number of items are increased from 25K to 100K. We can see that the total number of I/Os for updates and queries for all three indexes increase linearly with the data set size. This is because all the lengths of queries are normally distributed with μ 100

Param	Default	Meaning
\multicolumn{3}{c}{Uncertain Data}
N_{int}	$100K$	# of intervals
L_{min}	0	Min value of L_i
R_{max}	10,000	Max value of U_i
U_{min}	10	Min value of $U_i - L_i$
U_{max}	1,000	Max value of $U_i - L_i$
$f_i(x)$	$1/(U_i - L_i)$	Uncertainty pdf
\multicolumn{3}{c}{Probabilistic Threshold Queries}
N_{int}	$10K$	# of range queries
a_{min}	0	Min of lower bound(a)
b_{max}	10,000	Max of upper bound(b)
I_{mean}	100	Mean of interval length
I_{dev}	10	Deviation of interval length
p	$[0.1, 1]$	Prob. threshold (uniform)
\multicolumn{3}{c}{Tree parameters}
S_{page}	4096	Size of a page (bytes)
N_{entry}	20	# of entries (per page)

Table 1: Parameters and baseline values.

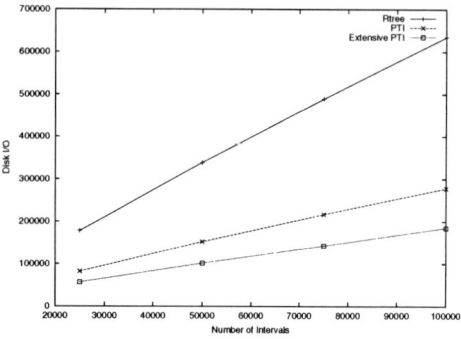

Figure 6: Total I/O vs. Number of Intervals

and σ 10 throughout the experiment while the data size increases. As a result, the number of items that satisfy the queries increases linearly with number of items.

A more interesting observation is that both PTI and *extensive* perform much better than the R-tree. Indeed, PTI almost spent about 50% of the I/Os required for R-tree, while *extensive* needs only about 30% of R-tree's effort. The reason is simply because R-tree does not use uncertainty pdf while the index is being accessed. As a result, many items that do not satisfy the probability thresholds of queries are not pruned. This results in a large set of intervals being needed to be examined. On the other hand, both PTI and *extensive* are designed to be sensitive to uncertainty pdf information during the searching-and-pruning process. Thus, they are able to prune much more items away than R-tree. Notice that although here we only show the number of I/Os, answering PTQ with an R-tree may even suffer more in terms of computation time, because more items are obtained after the index is searched, and the time required for the integration op-

885

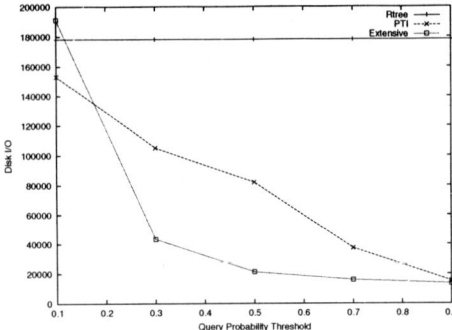

Figure 7: Total I/Os vs. Query Probability Threshold

eration to evaluate the probability will be significantly increased.

We can also see that *extensive* requires about 50% less I/Os than PTI. This is because *extensive* applies the variance-based clustering techniques, while PTI does not. In a PTI node, it is possible for a small interval to be stored in a relatively large MBR. Thus, if that small interval satisfies a PTQ (which is easy because of its small size), the large MBR has to be visited, and the query may need to spend time on the space in the large MBR, which can be avoided in the *extensive* scheme.

6.2.2 Effect of Query Probability Threshold

In the second experiment, we study the effect of probability thresholds (p) of queries on I/O performance. To obtain a data point, the threshold value of each query is made the same in (0,1]. The results are shown in Figure 7, which illustrates the three indexes' performance under different values of p. We can observe that as p increases, the number of I/Os requried for both PTI and *extensive* decreases. This is simply due to the reduction in the number of qualified intervals for the queries with more stringent probability threshold requirements. Nonetheless, R-tree does not take advantage of this at all, since it only prunes away items that do not overlap the queries, regardless of their threshold requirements.

The performance of PTI improves as p increases. Consider a query with some amount of overlap with an MBR. When its threshold increases, it has more chance to use an x-bound. For *extensive*, the size of the trapezoidal region is inversely proportional to p and hence its performance also improves. The advantages of *extensive* over PTI are more pronounced when p is betwen 0.3 and 0.7. When p is 0.5, *extensive* requires four times fewer I/Os than PTI. At the extreme values of p, the advantages of *extensive* are not as pronouced, becasue the query either becomes a containment query or an overlap query. Hence, both PTI and *extensive* perform similarly.

7 Related Work

The probabilistic uncertainty model for sensor data studied here is a modified version of the one discussed in [9]. While we assume the bounds of uncertain intervals are constant, in that paper the uncertain intervals are time-varying functions. That paper also presents a taxonomy of different representations of data uncertainty in terms of intervals. The probabilistic uncertainty model for two-dimensional moving objects is discussed in [8]. Yazici et al. [21] discusses uncertainty in different data types, such as sets, intervals and fuzzy data.

In [7], a general classification, evaluation and quality of different types of probabilistic queries for sensor data are presented. Probabilistic queries in moving object databases are studied in [20] and [8], where range query and nearest-neighbor query algorithms respectively are presented. The probabilistic threshold query for sensor data is proposed in [9], where efficient computation strategies of probability values by exploiting probability thresholds are discussed. However, it does not address indexing of imprecise data.

There are numerous works in the field of interval indexing. In [14][3], the idea of mapping intervals as points in two-dimensional space is discussed. They also talk about the transform of one-dimensional stabbing queries and range queries to two-sided orthogonal queries in two-dimensional space. Manolopoulos et al. [17] propose an efficient interval tree to facilitate the execution of intersection queries over intervals. Kriegel et al. [15] discusses an implementation of interval trees, which is conveniently built on top of relational tables, and algorithms are expressed as SQL queries.

Different types of range queries in two dimensional space have been well studied. For half-space queries, lower bounds are discussed in [12][4], and optimal data structures are presented in [1][10]. The lower bounds of simplex queries are derived by Chazelle [6]. Goldstein et al. [13] modifies the R-tree to answer simplex queries, which works well in practice. Optimal data structures for answering 2-sided and 3-sided queries, which have fixed slopes but not necessarily orthogonal, are discussed in [2]. A comprehensive survey on geometric range searching can be found in [18][11].

Although a rich vein of work exists in interval indexing, the issue of indexing uncertain data that involves probability computation has not been well addressed. A recent paper by Lin et al. [16] discusses an extension of the TPR-tree [19] to index trajectories of moving objects, where each point in the trajectory has a rectangular uncertain bound. We study the indexing of general sensor data, and establish a theoretical foundation of the problem. We also propose novel indexing techniques for fixed/variable probability thresholds, and different kinds of pdfs. To our best knowledge, these questions have not been answered previously.

8 Conclusions

Uncertainty is an important emerging topic in sensor databases. In this paper we investigated the problem of indexing uncertain data. We showed that this problem is theoretically difficult, by showing how it can be transformed to a polygonal range query in two-dimensional space. However, heuristics do exist to handle the problem efficiently in practice. In particular, we proposed the ideas of augmenting probability threshold bounds to an index, as well as clustering intervals based on their statistical information. Our extensive experiments showed that these two ideas, when used together, can significantly improve the performance of probabilistic threshold queries.

There are numerous avenues for future work. We will study the uncertainty indexing problem for other kinds of queries. The indexing of other types of uncertain data, such as sets and fuzzy data, are also worth investigating. We are also interested in the issue of efficient indexing of uncertain intervals with time-dependent bounds.

References

[1] Pankaj K. Agarwal, David Eppstein, and Jirí Matousek. Dynamic half-space reporting, geometric optimization, and minimum spanning trees. In *FOCS*, pages 80–89, 1992.

[2] L. Arge, V. Samoladas, and J. S. Vitter. On two-dimensional indexability and optimal range search indexing. In *PODS*, pages 346–357, 1999.

[3] L. Arge and J. S. Vitter. Optimal dynamic interval management in external memory (extended abstract). In *FOCS*, pages 560–569, 1996.

[4] H. Brönnimann, B. Chazelle, and J. Pach. How hard is half-space range searching. *Discrete and Computational Geometry*, 10:143–155, 1993.

[5] C. Chatfield. *The analysis of time series an introduction*. Chapman and Hall, 1989.

[6] Bernard Chazelle. Lower bounds on the complexity of polytope range searching. *Journal of American Mathematical Society*, 2:637–666, 1989.

[7] R. Cheng, D. Kalashnikov, and S. Prabhakar. Evaluating probabilistic queries over imprecise data. In *Proc. of the ACM SIGMOD Intl. Conf. on Management of Data*, June 2003.

[8] R. Cheng, D. V. Kalashnikov, and S. Prabhakar. Querying imprecise data in moving object environments. *IEEE Transactions on Knowledge and Data Engineering (To appear)*, 2004.

[9] R. Cheng and S. Prabhakar. Managing uncertainty in sensor databases. In *SIGMOD Record issue on Sensor Technology*, December 2003.

[10] Kenneth L. Clarkson. New applications of random sampling in computational geometry. *Discrete and Computational Geometry*, 2:195–222, 1987.

[11] Jeff Erickson and Pankaj K. Agarwal. Geometric range searching and its relatives. *Advances in Discrete and Computational Geometry*, Contemporary Mathematics 223:1–56, 1999.

[12] Michael L. Fredman. Lower bounds on the complexity of some optimal data structures. *SIAM J. Comput.*, 10(1):1–10, 1981.

[13] Jonathan Goldstein, Raghu Ramakrishnan, Uri Shaft, and Jie-Bing Yu. Processing queries by linear constraints. In *PODS*, pages 257–267, 1997.

[14] Paris C. Kanellakis, Sridhar Ramaswamy, Darren Erik Vengroff, and Jeffrey Scott Vitter. Indexing for data models with constraints and classes. *J. Comput. Syst. Sci*, 52(3):589–612, 1996.

[15] H. Kriegel, M. Potke, and T. Seidl. Managing intervals efficiently in object-relational databases. In *Proc. of the 26th Intl. Conf. on VLDB*, Cairo, Egypt, 2000.

[16] B. Lin, H. Mokhtar, R. Pelaez-Aguilera, and J. Su. Querying moving objects with uncertainty. In *Proceedings of IEEE Semiannual Vehicular Technology Conference*, 2003.

[17] Y. Manolopoulos, Y. Theodoridis, and V.J. Tsotras. Chapter 4: Access methods for intervals. In *Advanced Database Indexing*. Kluwer, 2000.

[18] Jirí Matousek. Geometric range searching. *ACM Comput. Surv.*, 26(4):421–461, 1994.

[19] S. Saltenis, C. Jensen, S. Leutenegger, and M. Lopez. Indexing the position of continuously moving objects. *Proc. of ACM SIGMOD*, 2000.

[20] O. Wolfson, P. Sistla, S. Chamberlain, and Y. Yesha. Updating and querying databases that track mobile units. *Distributed and Parallel Databases*, 7(3), 1999.

[21] A. Yazici, A. Soysal, B.P. Buckles, and F.E. Petry. Uncertainty in a nested relational database model. *Elsevier Data and Knowledge Engineering*, 30(1999), 1999.

Probabilistic Ranking of Database Query Results

Surajit Chaudhuri   Gautam Das

Microsoft Research
One Microsoft Way
Redmond, WA 98053
USA
{surajitc, gautamd}@microsoft.com

Vagelis Hristidis

School of Comp. Sci.
Florida Intl. University
Miami, FL 33199
USA
vagelis@cs.fiu.edu

Gerhard Weikum

MPI Informatik
Stuhlsatzenhausweg 85
D-66123 Saarbruecken
Germany
weikum@mpi-sb.mpg.de

Abstract

We investigate the problem of ranking answers to a database query when many tuples are returned. We adapt and apply principles of probabilistic models from Information Retrieval for structured data. Our proposed solution is domain independent. It leverages data and workload statistics and correlations. Our ranking functions can be further customized for different applications. We present results of preliminary experiments which demonstrate the efficiency as well as the quality of our ranking system.

1. Introduction

Database systems support a simple Boolean query retrieval model, where a selection query on a SQL database returns all tuples that satisfy the conditions in the query. This often leads to the *Many-Answers Problem*: when the query is not very selective, too many tuples may be in the answer. We use the following running example throughout the paper:

Example: *Consider a realtor database consisting of a single table with attributes such as (TID, Price, City, Bedrooms, Bathrooms, LivingArea, SchoolDistrict, View, Pool, Garage, BoatDock ...). Each tuple represents a home for sale in the US.*

Consider a potential home buyer searching for homes in this database. A query with a not very selective condition such as "City=Seattle and View=Waterfront" may result in too many tuples in the answer, since there are many homes with waterfront views in Seattle.

The Many-Answers Problem has been investigated outside the database area, especially in Information Retrieval (IR), where many documents often satisfy a given keyword-based query. Approaches to overcome this problem range from *query reformulation* techniques (e.g., the user is prompted to refine the query to make it more selective), to *automatic ranking* of the query results by their degree of "relevance" to the query (though the user may not have explicitly specified how) and returning only the top-K subset.

It is evident that automated ranking can have compelling applications in the database context. For instance, in the earlier example of a homebuyer searching for homes in Seattle with waterfront views, it may be preferable to first return homes that have other desirable attributes, such as good school districts, boat docks, etc. In general, customers browsing product catalogs will find such functionality attractive.

In this paper we propose an automated ranking approach for the Many-Answers Problem for database queries. Our solution is principled, comprehensive, and efficient. We summarize our contributions below.

Any ranking function for the Many-Answers Problem has to look beyond the attributes specified in the query, because all answer tuples satisfy the specified conditions[1]. However, investigating unspecified attributes is particularly tricky since we need to determine what the user's preferences for these unspecified attributes are. In this paper we propose that the ranking function of a tuple depends on two factors: (a) a *global score* which captures the global importance of unspecified attribute values, and

---

Permission to copy without fee all or part of this material is granted provided that the copies are not made or distributed for direct commercial advantage, the VLDB copyright notice and the title of the publication and its date appear, and notice is given that copying is by permission of the Very Large Data Base Endowment. To copy otherwise, or to republish, requires a fee and/or special permission from the Endowment
**Proceedings of the 30th VLDB Conference,
Toronto, Canada, 2004**

---

[1] In the case of document retrieval, ranking functions are often based on the frequency of occurrence of query values in documents (*term frequency*, or TF). However, in the database context, especially in the case of categorical data, TF is irrelevant as tuples either contain or do not contain a query value. Hence ranking functions need to also consider values of unspecified attributes.

(b) a *conditional score* which captures the strengths of dependencies (or correlations) between specified and unspecified attribute values. For example, for the query "City = Seattle and View = Waterfront", a home that is also located in a "SchoolDistrict = Excellent" gets high rank because good school districts are globally desirable. A home with also "BoatDock = Yes" gets high rank because people desiring a waterfront are likely to want a boat dock. While these scores may be estimated by the help of domain expertise or through user feedback, we propose an automatic estimation of these scores via *workload as well as data* analysis. For example, past workload may reveal that a large fraction of users seeking homes with a waterfront view have also requested for boat docks.

The next challenge is how do we translate these basic intuitions into principled and quantitatively describable ranking functions? To achieve this, we develop ranking functions that are based on *Probabilistic Information Retrieval (PIR)* ranking models. We chose PIR models because we could extend them to model data dependencies and correlations (the critical ingredients of our approach) in a more principled manner than if we had worked with alternate IR ranking models such as the Vector-Space model. We note that correlations are often ignored in IR because they are very difficult to capture in the very high-dimensional and sparsely populated feature spaces of text data, whereas there are often strong correlations between attribute values in relational data (with functional dependencies being extreme cases), which is a much lower-dimensional, more explicitly structured and densely populated space that our ranking functions can effectively work on.

The architecture of our ranking has a pre-processing component that collects database as well as workload statistics to determine the appropriate ranking function. The extracted ranking function is materialized in an *intermediate knowledge representation layer*, to be used later by a query processing component for ranking the results of queries. The ranking functions are encoded in the intermediate layer via intuitive, easy-to-understand "atomic" numerical quantities that describe (a) the global importance of a data value in the ranking process, and (b) the strengths of correlations between pairs of values (e.g., "if a user requests tuples containing value y of attribute Y, how likely is she to be also interested in value x of attribute X?"). Although our ranking approach derives these quantities automatically, our architecture allows users and/or domain experts to tune these quantities further, thereby customizing the ranking functions for different applications.

We report on a comprehensive set of experimental results. We first demonstrate through user studies on real datasets that our rankings are superior in quality to previous efforts on this problem. We also demonstrate the efficiency of our ranking system. Our implementation is especially tricky because our ranking functions are relatively complex, involving dependencies/correlations between data values. We use novel pre-computation techniques which reduce this complex problem to a problem efficiently solvable using Top-K algorithms.

The rest of this paper is organized as follows. In Section 2 we discuss related work. In Section 3 we define the problem and outline the architecture of our solution. In Section 4 we discuss our approach to ranking based on probabilistic models from information retrieval. In Section 5 we describe an efficient implementation of our ranking system. In Section 6 we discuss the results of our experiments, and we conclude in Section 7.

2. Related Work

Extracting ranking functions has been extensively investigated in areas outside database research such as Information Retrieval. The vector space model as well as probabilistic information retrieval (PIR) models [4, 28, 29] and statistical language models [14] are very successful in practice. While our approach has been inspired by PIR models, we have adapted and extended them in ways unique to our situation, e.g., by leveraging the structure as well as correlations present in the structured data and the database workload.

In database research, there has been some work on ranked retrieval from a database. The early work of [23] considered vague/imprecise similarity-based querying of databases. The problem of integrating databases and information retrieval systems has been attempted in several works [12, 13, 17, 18]. Information retrieval based approaches have been extended to XML retrieval (e.g., see [8]). The papers [11, 26, 27, 32] employ relevance-feedback techniques for learning similarity in multimedia and relational databases. Keyword-query based retrieval systems over databases have been proposed in [1, 5, 20]. In [21, 24] the authors propose SQL extensions in which users can specify ranking functions via soft constraints in the form of preferences. The distinguishing aspect of our work from the above is that we espouse automatic extraction of PIR-based ranking functions through data and workload statistics.

The work most closely related to our paper is [2] which briefly considered the Many-Answers Problem (although its main focus was on the *Empty-Answers Problem*, which occurs when a query is too selective, resulting in an empty answer set). It too proposed automatic ranking methods that rely on workload as well as data analysis. In contrast, however, the current paper has the following novel strengths: (a) we use more principled probabilistic PIR techniques rather than ad-hoc techniques "loosely based" on the vector-space model, and (b) we take into account dependencies and correlations between data values, whereas [2] only proposed a form of global score for ranking.

Ranking is also an important component in collaborative filtering research [7]. These methods require training data using queries as well as their ranked results. In contrast, we require workloads containing queries only.

A major concern of this paper is the query processing techniques for supporting ranking. Several techniques have been previously developed in database research for the Top-K problem [8, 9, 15, 16, 31]. We adopt the Threshold Algorithm of [16, 19, 25] for our purposes, and show how novel pre-computation techniques can be used to produce a very efficient implementation of the Many-Answers Problem. In contrast, an efficient implementation for the Many-Answers Problem was left open in [2].

3. Problem Definition and Architecture

In this section, we formally define the Many-Answers Problem in ranking database query results, and also outline a general architecture of our solution.

3.1 Problem Definition

We start by defining the simplest problem instance. Consider a database table D with n tuples $\{t_1, ..., t_n\}$ over a set of m categorical attributes $A = \{A_1, ..., A_m\}$. Consider a "SELECT * FROM D" query Q with a conjunctive selection condition of the form "WHERE $X_1=x_1$ AND ... AND $X_s=x_s$", where each X_i is an attribute from A and x_i is a value in its domain. The set of attributes $X = \{X_1, ..., X_s\} \subseteq A$ is known as the set of attributes *specified* by the query, while the set $Y = A - X$ is known as the set of *unspecified* attributes. Let $S \subseteq \{t_1, ..., t_n\}$ be the answer set of Q. The *Many-Answers Problem* occurs when the query is not too selective, resulting in a large S.

The above scenario only represents the simplest problem instance. For example, the type of queries described above are fairly restrictive; we refer to them as *point queries* because they specify single-valued equality conditions on each of the specified attributes. In a more general setting, queries may contain range/IN conditions, and/or Boolean operators other than conjunctions. Likewise, databases may be multi-tabled, may contain a mix of categorical and numeric data, as well as missing or NULL values. While our techniques extend to all these generalizations, in the interest of clarity (and due to lack of space), the main focus of this paper is on ranking the results of conjunctive point queries on a single categorical table (without NULL values).

3.2 General Architecture of our Approach

Figure 1 shows the architecture of our proposed system for enabling ranking of database query results. As mentioned in the introduction, the main components are the preprocessing component, an intermediate knowledge representation layer in which the ranking functions are encoded and materialized, and a query processing component. The modular and generic nature of our system allows for easy customization of the ranking functions for different applications.

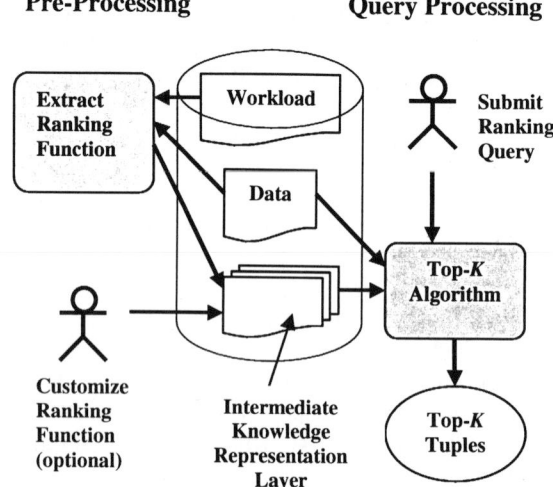

Figure 1: Architecture of Ranking System

In the next section we discuss PIR-based ranking functions for structured data.

4. Ranking Functions: Adaptation of PIR Models for Structured Data

In this section we discuss PIR-based ranking functions, and then show how they can be adapted for structured data. We discuss the semantics of the atomic building blocks that are used to encode these ranking functions in the intermediate layer. We also show how these atomic numerical quantities can be estimated from a variety of knowledge sources, such as data and workload statistics, as well as domain knowledge.

4.1 Review of Probabilistic Information Retrieval

Much of the material of this subsection can be found in textbooks on Information Retrieval, such as [4] (see also [28, 29]). We will need the following basic formulas from probability theory:

Bayes' Rule: $\quad p(a|b) = \dfrac{p(b|a)p(a)}{p(b)}$

Product Rule: $\quad p(a,b|c) = p(a|c)p(b|a,c)$

Consider a document collection D. For a (fixed) query Q, let R represent the set of *relevant* documents, and $\overline{R} = D - R$ be the set of *irrelevant* documents. In order to rank any document t in D, we need to find the probability of the relevance of t for the query given the text features of t (e.g., the word/term frequencies in t), i.e., $p(R|t)$. More formally, in probabilistic information retrieval, documents are ranked by decreasing order of their odds of relevance, defined as the following *score*:

$$Score(t) = \frac{p(R|t)}{p(\overline{R}|t)} = \frac{\frac{p(t|R)p(R)}{p(t)}}{\frac{p(t|\overline{R})p(\overline{R})}{p(t)}} \propto \frac{p(t|R)}{p(t|\overline{R})}$$

The main issue is, how are these probabilities computed, given that R and $\overline{R}$ are unknown at query time? The usual techniques in IR are to make some simplifying assumptions, such as estimating R through user feedback, approximating $\overline{R}$ as D (since R is usually small compared to D), and assuming some form of independence between query terms (e.g., the *Binary Independence Model*).

In the next subsection we show how we adapt PIR models for structured databases, in particular for conjunctive queries over a single categorical table. Our approach is more powerful than the Binary Independence Model as we also leverage data dependencies.

4.2 Adaptation of PIR Models for Structured Data

In our adaptation of PIR models for structured databases, each tuple in a single database table D is effectively treated as a "document". For a (fixed) query Q, our objective is to derive $Score(t)$ for any tuple t, and use this score to rank the tuples. Since we focus on the Many-Answers problem, we only need to concern ourselves with tuples that satisfy the query conditions. Recall the notation from Section 3.1, where X is the set of attributes specified in the query, and Y is the remaining set of unspecified attributes. We denote any tuple t as partitioned into two parts, $t(X)$ and $t(Y)$, where $t(X)$ is the subset of values corresponding to the attributes in X, and $t(Y)$ is the remaining subset of values corresponding to the attributes in Y. Often, when the tuple t is clear from the context, we overload notation and simply write t as consisting of two parts, X and Y (in this context, X and Y are thus sets of values rather than sets of attributes).

Replacing t with X and Y (and $\overline{R}$ as D as mentioned in Section 4.1 is commonly done in IR), we get

$$Score(t) \propto \frac{p(t|R)}{p(t|D)} = \frac{p(X,Y|R)}{p(X,Y|D)}$$
$$\propto \frac{p(X|R)\ p(Y|X,R)}{p(X|D)\ p(Y|X,D)}$$

Since for the Many-Answers problem we are only interested in ranking tuples that satisfy the query conditions, and all such tuples have the same X values, we can treat any quantity not involving Y as a constant. We thus get

$$Score(t) \propto \frac{p(Y|X,R)}{p(Y|X,D)}$$

Furthermore, the relevant set R for the Many-Answers problem is a subset of all tuples that satisfy the query conditions. One way to understand this is to imagine that R is the "ideal" set of tuples the user had in mind, but who only managed to partially specify it when preparing the query. Consequently the numerator $p(Y|X,R)$ may be replaced by $p(Y|R)$. We thus get

$$Score(t) \propto \frac{p(Y|R)}{p(Y|X,D)} \qquad (1)$$

We are not quite finished with our derivation of $Score(t)$ yet, but let us illustrate Equation 1 with an example. Consider a query with condition "City=Kirkland and Price=High" (Kirkland is an upper class suburb of Seattle close to a lake). Such buyers may also ideally desire homes with waterfront or greenbelt views, but homes with views looking out into streets may be somewhat less desirable. Thus, p(View=Greenbelt | R) and p(View=Waterfront | R) may both be high, but p(View=Street | R) may be relatively low. Furthermore, if in general there is an abundance of selected homes with greenbelt views as compared to waterfront views, (i.e., the denominator p(View=Greenbelt | City=Kirkland, Price=High, D) is larger than p(View=Waterfront | City=Kirkland, Price=High, D)), our final rankings would be homes with waterfront views, followed by homes with greenbelt views, followed by homes with street views. Note that for simplicity, we have ignored the remaining unspecified attributes in this example.

4.2.1 Limited Independence Assumptions

One possible way of continuing the derivation of $Score(t)$ would be to make independence assumptions between values of different attributes, like in the Binary Independence Model in IR. However, while this is reasonable with text data (because estimating model parameters like the conditional probabilities $p(Y|X)$ poses major accuracy and efficiency problems with sparse and high-dimensional data such as text), we have earlier argued that with structured data, dependencies between data values can be better captured and would more significantly impact the result ranking. An extreme alternative to making sweeping independence assumptions would be to construct comprehensive dependency models of the data (e.g. probabilistic graphical models such as Markov Random Fields or Bayesian Networks [30]), and derive ranking functions based on these models. However, our preliminary investigations suggested that such approaches, particularly for large datasets, have unacceptable pre-processing and query processing costs.

Consequently, in this paper we espouse an approach that strikes a middle ground. We only make limited forms of independence assumptions – *given a query Q and a tuple t, the X (and Y) values within themselves are assumed to be independent, though dependencies between the X and Y values are allowed.* More precisely, we assume limited conditional independence, i.e., $p(X|C)$ (resp. $p(Y|C)$) may be written as $\prod_{x \in X} p(x|C)$ (resp. $\prod_{y \in Y} p(y|C)$) where C is any condition that only involves Y values (resp. X values), R, or D.

While this assumption is patently false in many cases (for instance, in the example in Section 4.2 this assumes that there is no dependency between homes in Kirkland and high-priced homes), nevertheless the remaining dependencies that we do leverage, i.e., between the specified and unspecified values, prove to be significant for ranking. Moreover, as we shall show in Section 5, the resulting simplified functional form of the ranking function enables the efficient adaptation of known Top-K algorithms through novel data structuring techniques.

We continue the derivation of the score of a tuple under the above assumptions:

$$Score(t) \propto \prod_{y \in Y} \frac{p(y|R)}{p(y|X,D)} = \prod_{y \in Y} \frac{p(y|R)}{\frac{p(X,D|y)p(y)}{p(X,D)}}$$

$$\propto \prod_{y \in Y} \frac{p(y|R)}{p(X,D|y)p(y)}$$

$$= \prod_{y \in Y} \frac{p(y|R)}{p(D|y)p(X|y,D)p(y)}$$

$$= \prod_{y \in Y} \frac{p(y|R)}{p(D|y)p(y)} \prod_{y \in Y} \prod_{x \in X} \frac{1}{p(x|y,D)}$$

$$\propto \prod_{y \in Y} \frac{p(y|R)}{\frac{p(D|y)p(y)}{p(D)}} \prod_{y \in Y} \prod_{x \in X} \frac{1}{p(x|y,D)}$$

This simplifies to

$$Score(t) \propto \prod_{y \in Y} \frac{p(y|R)}{p(y|D)} \prod_{y \in Y} \prod_{x \in X} \frac{1}{p(x|y,D)} \quad (2)$$

Although Equation 2 represents a simplification over Equation 1, it is still not directly computable, as R is unknown. We discuss how to estimate the quantities $p(y|R)$ next.

4.2.2 Workload-Based Estimation of $p(y|R)$

Estimating the quantities $p(y|R)$ requires knowledge of R, which is unknown at query time. The usual technique for estimating R in IR is through user feedback (relevance feedback) at query time, or through other forms of training. In our case, we provide an automated approach that leverages available *workload information* for estimating $p(y|R)$.

We assume that we have at our disposal a workload W, i.e., a collection of ranking queries that have been executed on our system in the past. We first provide some intuition of how we intend to use the workload in ranking. Consider the example in Section 4.2 where a user has requested for high-priced homes in Kirkland. The workload may perhaps reveal that, in the past a large fraction of users that had requested for high-priced homes in Kirkland *had also requested for waterfront views*. Thus for such users, it is desirable to rank homes with waterfront views over homes without such views.

We note that this dependency information may not be derivable from the data alone, as a majority of such homes may not have waterfront views (i.e., data dependencies do not indicate user preferences as workload dependencies do). Of course, the other option is for a domain expert (or even the user) to provide this information (and in fact, as we shall discuss later, our ranking architecture is generic enough to allow further customization by human experts).

More generally, the workload W is represented as a set of "tuples", where each tuple represents a query and is a vector containing the corresponding values of the specified attributes. Consider an incoming query Q which specifies a set X of attribute values. *We approximate R as all query "tuples" in W that also request for X.* This approximation is novel to this paper, i.e., that all properties of the set of relevant tuples R can be obtained by only examining the subset of the workload that contains queries that also request for X. So for a query such as "City=Kirkland and Price=High", we look at the workload in determining what such users have also requested for often in the past.

We can thus write, for query Q, with specified attribute set X, $p(y|R)$ as $p(y|X,W)$. Making this substitution in Equation 2, we get

$$Score(t) \propto \prod_{y \in Y} \frac{p(y|X,W)}{p(y|D)} \prod_{y \in Y} \prod_{x \in X} \frac{1}{p(x|y,D)}$$

$$= \prod_{y \in Y} \frac{\frac{p(X,W|y)p(y)}{p(X,W)}}{p(y|D)} \prod_{y \in Y} \prod_{x \in X} \frac{1}{p(x|y,D)}$$

$$\propto \prod_{y \in Y} \frac{p(X,W|y)p(y)}{p(y|D)} \prod_{y \in Y} \prod_{x \in X} \frac{1}{p(x|y,D)}$$

$$= \prod_{y \in Y} \frac{p(W|y)p(X|W,y)p(y)}{p(y|D)} \prod_{y \in Y} \prod_{x \in X} \frac{1}{p(x|y,D)}$$

$$\propto \prod_{y \in Y} \frac{p(y|W)\prod_{x \in X} p(x|y,W)}{p(y|D)} \prod_{y \in Y} \prod_{x \in X} \frac{1}{p(x|y,D)}$$

892

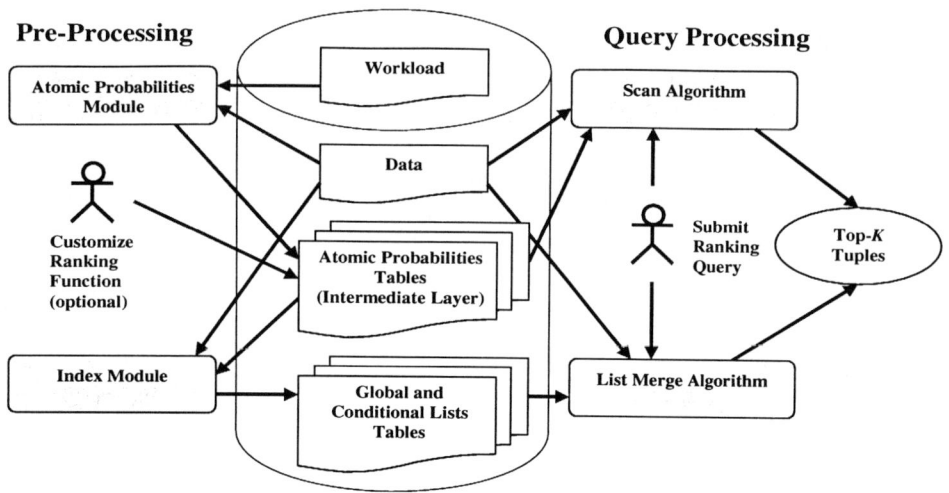

Figure 2: Detailed Architecture of Ranking System

This can be finally rewritten as:

$$Score(t) \propto \prod_{y \in Y} \frac{p(y|W)}{p(y|D)} \prod_{y \in Y} \prod_{x \in X} \frac{p(x|y,W)}{p(x|y,D)} \quad (3)$$

Equation 3 is the final ranking formula that we use in the rest of this paper. Note that unlike Equation 2, we have effectively eliminated R from the formula, and are only left with having to compute quantities such as $p(y|W)$, $p(x|y,W)$, $p(y|D)$, and $p(x|y,D)$. In fact, these are the "atomic" numerical quantities referred to at various places earlier in the paper.

Also note that the score in Equation 3 is composed of two large factors. The first factor may be considered as the *global* part of the score, while the second factor may be considered as the *conditional* part of the score. Thus, in the example in Section 4.2, the first part measures the global importance of unspecified values such as waterfront, greenbelt and street views, while the second part measures the dependencies between these values and specified values "City=Kirkland" and "Price=High".

4.3 Computing the Atomic Probabilities

Our strategy is to pre-compute each of the atomic quantities for all distinct values in the database. The quantities $p(y|W)$ and $p(y|D)$ are simply the relative frequencies of each distinct value y in the workload and database, respectively (the latter is similar to IDF, or the *inverse document frequency* concept in IR), while the quantities $p(x|y,W)$ and $p(x|y,D)$ may be estimated by computing the confidences of pair-wise *association rules* [3] in the workload and database, respectively. Once this pre-computation has been completed, we store these quantities as auxiliary tables in

the intermediate knowledge representation layer. At query time, the necessary quantities may be retrieved and appropriately composed for performing the rankings. Further details of the implementation are discussed in Section 5.

While the above is an automated approach based on workload analysis, it is possible that sometimes the workload may be insufficient and/or unreliable. In such instances, it may be necessary for domain experts to be able to tune the ranking function to make it more suitable for the application at hand.

5. Implementation

In this section we discuss the implementation of our database ranking system. Figure 2 shows the detailed architecture, including the pre-processing and query processing components as well as their sub-modules. We discuss several novel data structures and algorithms that were necessary for good performance of our system.

5.1 Pre-Processing

This component is divided into several modules. First, the *Atomic Probabilities Module* computes the quantities $p(y|W)$, $p(y|D)$, $p(x|y,W)$, and $p(x|y,D)$ for all distinct values x and y. These quantities are computed by scanning the workload and data, respectively (while the latter two quantities can be computed by running a general association rule mining algorithm such as [3] on the workload and data, we instead chose to directly compute all pair-wise co-occurrence frequencies by a single scan of the workload and data respectively). The observed probabilities are then smoothened using the Bayesian *m-estimate* method [10].

These atomic probabilities are stored as database tables in the intermediate knowledge representation layer, with appropriate indexes to enable easy retrieval. In particular, $p(y|W)$ and $p(y|D)$ are respectively stored in two tables, each with columns {AttName, AttVal, Prob} and with a composite B+ tree index on (AttName, AttVal), while $p(x|y,W)$ and $p(x|y,D)$ respectively are stored in two tables, each with columns {AttNameLeft, AttValLeft, AttNameRight, AttValRight, Prob} and with a composite B+ tree index on (AttNameLeft, AttValLeft, AttNameRight, AttValRight). These atomic quantities can be further customized by human experts if necessary.

This intermediate layer now contains enough information for computing the ranking function, and a naïve query processing algorithm (henceforth referred to as the *Scan* algorithm) can indeed be designed, which, for any query, first selects the tuples that satisfy the query condition, then scans and computes the score for each such tuple using the information in this intermediate layer, and finally returns the Top-K tuples. However, such an approach can be inefficient for the Many-Answers problem, since the number of tuples satisfying the query condition can be very large. At the other extreme, we could pre-compute the Top-K tuples *for all possible queries* (i.e., for all possible sets of values X), and at query time, simply return the appropriate result set. Of course, due to the combinatorial explosion, this is infeasible in practice. We thus pose the question: how can we appropriately trade off between pre-processing and query processing, i.e., what additional yet reasonable pre-computations are possible that can enable faster query-processing algorithms than Scan?

The high-level intuition behind our approach to the above problem is as follows. Instead of pre-computing the Top-K tuples for all possible queries, we pre-compute ranked lists of the tuples for all possible "atomic" queries - each distinct value x in the table defines an atomic query Qx that specifies the single value $\{x\}$. Then at query time, given an actual query that specifies a set of values X, we "merge" the ranked lists corresponding to each x in X to compute the final Top-K tuples.

Of course, for this high-level idea to work, the main challenge is to be able to perform the merging without having to scan any of the ranked lists in its entirety. One idea would be to try and adapt well-known Top-K algorithms such as the *Threshold Algorithm* (*TA*) and its derivatives [9, 15, 16, 19, 25] for this problem. However, it is not immediately obvious how a feasible adaptation can be easily accomplished. For example, it is especially critical to keep the number of *sorted streams* (an access mechanism required by TA) small, as it is well-known that TA's performance rapidly deteriorates as this number increases. Upon examination of our ranking function in Equation 3 (which involves *all* attribute values of the tuple, and not just the specified values), the number of sorted streams in any naïve adaptation of TA would depend on the total number of attributes in the database, which would cause major performance problems.

In what follows, we show how to pre-compute data structures that indeed enable us to *efficiently* adapt TA for our problem. At query time we do a TA-like merging of several ranked lists (i.e. sorted streams). However, the required number of sorted streams depends only on s and not on m (s is the number of specified attribute values in the query while m is the total number of attributes in the database, see Section 3.1). We emphasize that such a merge operation is only made possible due to the specific functional form of our ranking function resulting from our limited independence assumptions as discussed in Section 4.2.1. It is unlikely that TA can be adapted, at least in a feasible manner, for ranking functions that rely on more comprehensive dependency models of the data.

We next give the details of these data structures. They are pre-computed by the *Index Module* of the pre-processing component. This module (see Figure 3 for the algorithm) takes as inputs the association rules and the database, and for every distinct value x, creates two lists C_x and G_x, each containing the tuple-ids of all data tuples that contain x, ordered in specific ways. These two lists are defined as follows:

1. **Conditional List C_x:** This list consists of pairs of the form <TID, CondScore>, ordered by descending CondScore, where TID is the tuple-id of a tuple t that contains x and

$$CondScore = \prod_{z \in t} \frac{p(x|z,W)}{p(x|z,D)}$$

where z ranges over all attribute values of t.

2. **Global List G_x:** This list consists of pairs of the form <TID, GlobScore>, ordered by descending GlobScore, where TID is the tuple-id of a tuple t that contains x and

$$GlobScore = \prod_{z \in t} \frac{p(z|W)}{p(z|D)}$$

These lists enable efficient computation of the score of a tuple t for any query as follows: given query Q specifying conditions for a set of attribute values, say $X = \{x_1,...,x_s\}$, at query time we retrieve and multiply the scores of t in the lists $C_{x1},...,C_{xs}$ and in one of $G_{x1},...,G_{xs}$. This requires only $s+1$ multiplications and results in a score[2] that is proportional to the actual score. Clearly this is more efficient than computing the score "from scratch" by retrieving the relevant atomic probabilities from the intermediate layer and composing them appropriately.

We need to enable two kinds of access operations efficiently on these lists. First, given a value x, it should be possible to perform a GetNextTID operation on lists C_x and G_x in constant time, i.e., the tuple-ids in the lists

---

[2] This score is proportional, but not equal, to the actual score because it contains extra factors of the form $p(x|z,W)/p(x|z,D)$ where $z \in X$. However, these extra factors are common to all selected tuples, hence the rank order is unchanged.

should be efficiently retrievable one-by-one in order of decreasing score. This corresponds to the sorted stream access of TA. Second, it should be possible to perform random access on the lists, i.e., given a TID, the corresponding score (CondScore or GlobScore) should be retrievable in constant time. To enable these operations efficiently, we materialize these lists as database tables – all the conditional lists are maintained in one table called *CondList* (with columns {AttName, AttVal, TID, CondScore}) while all the global lists are maintained in another table called *GlobList* (with columns {AttName, AttVal, TID, GlobScore}). The table have composite B+ tree indices on (AttName, AttVal, CondScore) and (AttName, AttVal, GlobScore) respectively. This enables efficient performance of both access operations. Further details of how these data structures and their access methods are used in query processing are discussed in Section 5.2.

Index Module
Input: Data table, atomic probabilities tables
Output: Conditional and global lists

FOR EACH distinct value x of database DO
$C_x = G_x = \{\}$
 FOR EACH tuple t containing x with tuple-id = TID DO
$$CondScore = \prod_{z \in t} \frac{p(x \mid z, W)}{p(x \mid z, D)}$$
  Add <TID, CondScore> to C_x
$$GlobScore = \prod_{z \in t} \frac{p(z \mid W)}{p(z \mid D)}$$
  Add <TID, GlobScore> to G_x
 END FOR
 Sort C_x and G_x by decreasing *CondScore* and *GlobScore* resp.
END FOR

Figure 3: The Index Module

5.2 Query Procesing Component

In this subsection we describe the query processing component. The naïve *Scan* algorithm has already been described in Section 5.1, so our focus here is on the alternate *List Merge* algorithm (see Figure 4). This is an adaptation of TA, whose efficiency crucially depends on the data structures pre-computed by the Index Module.

The *List Merge* algorithm operates as follows. Given a query Q specifying conditions for a set $X = \{x_1,...,x_s\}$ of attributes, we execute TA on the following $s+1$ lists: $C_{x1},...,C_{xs}$, and G_{xb}, where G_{xb} is the shortest list among $G_{x1},...,G_{xs}$ (in principle, any list from $G_{x1},...,G_{xs}$ would do, but the shortest list is likely to be more efficient). During each iteration, the TID with the next largest score is retrieved from each list using sorted access. Its score in every other list is retrieved via random access, and all these retrieved scores are multiplied together, resulting in the final score of the tuple (which, as mentioned in Section 5.1, is proportional to the actual score derived in Equation 3). The termination criterion guarantees that no more GetNextTID operations will be needed on any of the lists. This is accomplished by maintaining an array T which contains the last scores read from all the lists at any point in time by GetNextTID operations. The product of the scores in T represents the score of the very best tuple we can hope to find in the data that is yet to be seen. If this value is no more than the tuple in the Top-K buffer with the smallest score, the algorithm successfully terminates.

List Merge Algorithm
Input: Query, data table, global and conditional lists
Output: Top-K tuples

Let G_{xb} be the shortest list among $G_{x1},...,G_{xs}$
Let $B = \{\}$ be a buffer that can hold K tuples ordered by score
Let T be an array of size $s+1$ storing the last score from each list
Initialize B to empty
REPEAT
 FOR EACH list L in $C_{x1},...,C_{xs}$, and G_{xb} DO
  TID = GetNextTID(L)
  Update T with score of TID in L
  Get score of TID from other lists via random access
  IF all lists contain TID THEN
   Compute *Score*(TID) by multiplying retrieved scores
   Insert <TID, *Score*(TID)> in the correct position in B
  END IF
 END FOR
UNTIL $B[K].Score \geq \prod_{i=1}^{s+1} T[i]$
RETURN B

Figure 4: The List Merge Algorithm

5.2.1 Limited Available Space

So far we have assumed that there is enough space available to build the conditional and global lists. A simple analysis indicates that the space consumed by these lists is O(mn) bytes (m is the number of attributes and n the number of tuples of the database table). However, there may be applications where space is an expensive resource (e.g., when lists should preferably be held in memory and compete for that space or even for space in the processor cache hierarchy). We show that in such cases, we can store only a subset of the lists at pre-processing time, at the expense of an increase in the query processing time.

Determining which lists to retain/omit at pre-processing time may be accomplished by analyzing the workload. A simple solution is to store the conditional lists C_x and the corresponding global lists G_x only for those attribute values x that occur most frequently in the workload. At query time, since the lists of some of the specified attributes may be missing, the intuitive idea is to probe the intermediate knowledge representation layer (where the "relatively raw" data is maintained, i.e., the atomic probabilities) and directly compute the missing information. More specifically, we use a modification of TA described in [9], where not all sources have sorted stream access.

6. Experiments

In this section we report on the results of an experimental evaluation of our ranking method as well as some of the competitors. We evaluated both the *quality* of the rankings obtained, as well as the *performance* of the various approaches. We mention at the outset that preparing an experimental setup for testing ranking quality was extremely challenging, as unlike IR, there are no standard benchmarks available, and we had to conduct user studies to evaluate the rankings produced by the various algorithms.

For our evaluation, we use real datasets from two different domains. The first domain was the MSN HomeAdvisor database (http://houseandhome.msn.com/), from which we prepared a table of homes for sale in the US, with attributes such as Price, Year, City, Bedrooms, Bathrooms, Sqft, Garage, etc. (we converted numerical attributes into categorical ones by discretizing them into meaningful ranges). The original database table also had a text column called Remarks, which contained descriptive information about the home. From this column, we extracted additional Boolean attributes such as Fireplace, View, Pool, etc. To evaluate the role of the size of the database, we also performed experiments on a subset of the HomeAdvisor database, consisting only of homes sold in the Seattle area.

The second domain was the Internet Movie Database (http://www.imdb.com), from which we prepared a table of movies, with attributes such as Title, Year, Genre, Director, FirstActor, SecondActor, Certificate, Sound, Color, etc. (we discretized numerical attributes such as Year into meaningful ranges). We first selected a set of movies by the 30 most prolific actors for our experiments. From this we removed the 250 most well-known movies, as we did not wish our users to be biased with information they already might know about these movies, especially information that is not captured by the attributes that we had selected for our experiments.

The sizes of the various (single-table) datasets used in our experiments are shown in Figure 5. The quality experiments were conducted on the Seattle Homes and Movies tables, while the performance experiments were conducted on the Seattle Homes and the US Homes tables – we omitted performance experiments on the Movies table on account of its small size. We used Microsoft SQL Server 2000 RDBMS on a P4 2.8-GHz PC with 1 GB of RAM for our experiments. We implemented all algorithms in C#, and connected to the RDBMS through DAO. We created single-attribute indices on all table attributes, to be used during the selection phase of the Scan algorithm. Note that these indices are not used by the List Merge algorithm.

Table	NumTuples	Database Size (MB)
Seattle Homes	17463	1.936
US Homes	1380762	140.432
Movies	1446	Less than 1

Figure 5: Sizes of Datasets

6.1 Quality Experiments

We evaluated the quality of two different ranking methods: (a) our ranking method, henceforth referred to as *Conditional* (b) the ranking method described in [2], henceforth known as *Global*. This evaluation was accomplished using surveys involving 14 employees of Microsoft Research.

For the Seattle Homes table, we first created several different profiles of home buyers, e.g., young dual-income couples, singles, middle-class family who like to live in the suburbs, rich retirees, etc. Then, we collected a workload from our users by requesting them to behave like these home buyers and post conjunctive queries against the database - e.g., a middle-class homebuyer with children looking for a suburban home would post a typical query such as "Bedrooms=4 and Price=Moderate and SchoolDistrict=Excellent". We collected several hundred queries by this process, each typically specifying 2-4 attributes. We then trained our ranking algorithm on this workload.

We prepared a similar experimental setup for the Movies table. We first created several different profiles of moviegoers, e.g., teenage males wishing to see action thrillers, people interested in comedies from the 80s, etc. We disallowed users from specifying the movie title in the queries, as the title is a key of the table. As with homes, here too we collected several hundred workload queries, and trained our ranking algorithm on this workload.

We first describe a few sample results informally, and then present a more formal evaluation of our rankings.

6.1.1 Examples of Ranking Results

For the Seattle Homes dataset, both Conditional as well as Global produced rankings that were intuitive and reasonable. There were interesting examples where Conditional produced rankings that were superior to Global. For example, for a query with condition "City=Seattle and Bedroom=1", Conditional ranked condos with garages the highest. Intuitively, this is because private parking in downtown is usually very scarce, and condos with garages are highly sought after. However, Global was unable to recognize the importance of garages for this class of homebuyers, because most users (i.e., over the entire workload) do not explicitly request for garages since most homes have garages. As another example, for a query such as "Bedrooms=4 and City=Kirkland and Price=Expensive", Conditional ranked homes with waterfront views the highest, whereas Global ranked homes in good school districts the highest. This is as expected, because for very rich homebuyers a waterfront view is perhaps a more desirable feature than a good school district, even though the latter may be globally more popular across all homebuyers.

Likewise, for the Movies dataset, Conditional often produced rankings that were superior to Global. For example, for a query such as "Year=1980s and Genre=Thriller", Conditional ranked movies such as "Indiana Jones and the Temple of Doom" higher than "Commando", because the workload indicated that Harrison Ford was a better known actor than Arnold Schwarzenegger during that era, although the latter actor was globally more popular over the entire workload.

6.1.2 Ranking Evaluation

We now present a more formal evaluation of the ranking quality produced by the ranking algorithms. We conducted two surveys; the first compared the rankings against user rankings using standard precision/recall metrics, while the second was a simpler survey that asked users to rate which algorithm's rankings they preferred.

Average Precision: Since requiring users to rank the entire database for each query would have been extremely tedious, we used the following strategy. For each dataset, we generate 5 test queries. For each test query Q_i we generated a set H_i of 30 tuples likely to contain a good mix of relevant and irrelevant tuples to the query. We did this by mixing the Top-10 results of both the Conditional and Global ranking algorithms, removing ties, and adding a few randomly selected tuples. Finally, we presented the queries along with their corresponding H_i's (with tuples randomly permuted) to each user in our study. Each user's responsibility was to mark 10 tuples in H_i as most relevant to the query Q_i. We then measured how closely the 10 tuples marked as relevant by the user (i.e., the "ground truth") matched the 10 tuples returned by each algorithm.

	Seattle Homes		Movies	
	COND	**GLOB**	**COND**	**GLOB**
Q1	0.70	0.26	0.48	0.35
Q2	0.76	0.62	0.53	0.43
Q3	0.90	0.54	0.58	0.20
Q4	0.84	0.32	0.45	0.48
Q5	0.44	0.48	0.43	0.40

Figure 6: Average Precision

We used the formal Precision/Recall metrics to measure this overlap. Precision is the ratio of the number of retrieved tuples that are relevant, to the total number of retrieved tuples, while Recall is the fraction of the number of retrieved tuples that are relevant, to the total number of relevant tuples (see [4]). In our case, the total number of relevant tuples is 10, so Precision and Recall are equal. The average precision of the ranking methods for each dataset are shown in Figure 6 (the queries are, of course, different for each dataset). As can be seen, the quality of Conditional's ranking was usually superior to Global's, more so for the Seattle Homes dataset.

User Preference of Rankings: In this experiment, for the Seattle Homes as well as the Movies dataset, users were given the Top-5 results of the two ranking methods for 5 queries (different from the previous survey), and were asked to choose which rankings they preferred. Figures 7 and 8 show, for each query and each algorithm, the fraction of users that preferred the rankings of the algorithm. The results of the above experiments show that Conditional generally produces rankings of higher quality compared to Global, especially for the Seattle Homes dataset. While these experiments indicate that our ranking approach has promise, we caution that much larger-scale user studies are necessary to conclusively establish findings of this nature.

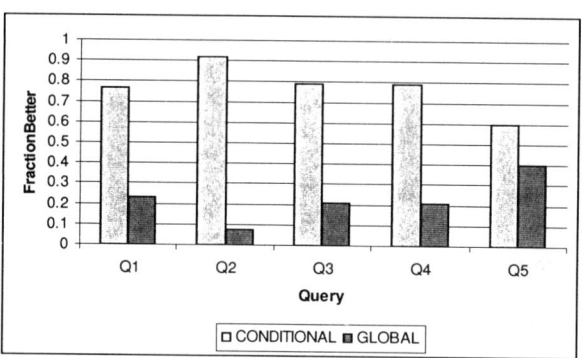

Figure 7: Fraction of Users Preferring Each Algorithm for Seattle Homes Dataset

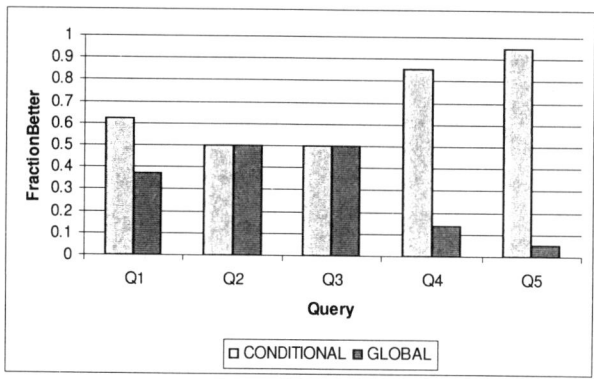

Figure 8: Fraction of Users Preferring Each Algorithm for Movies Dataset

6.2 Performance Experiments

In this subsection we report on experiments that compared the performance of the various implementations of the Conditional algorithm: List Merge, its space-saving variants, and Scan. We do not report on the corresponding implementations of Global as they had similar performance. We used the Seattle Homes and US Homes datasets for these experiments.

Preprocessing Time and Space: Since the preprocessing performance of the List Merge algorithm is dominated by the Index Module, we omit reporting results for the Atomic Probabilities Module. Figure 9 shows the space and time required to build *all* the conditional and global lists. The time and space scale linearly with table size, which is expected. Notice that the space consumed by the lists is three times the size of the data table. While this may seemingly appear excessive, note that a fair comparison would be against a Scan algorithm that has B+ tree indices built on *all* attributes (so that all kinds of selections can be performed efficiently). In such a case, the total space consumed by these B+ tree indices would rival the space consumed by these lists.

Datasets	Lists Building Time	Lists Size
Seattle Homes	1500 msec	7.8 MB
US Homes	80000 msec	457.6 MB

Figure 9: Time and Space Consumed by Index Module

If space is a critical issue, we can adopt the space saving variation of the List Merge algorithm as discussed in Section 5.2.1. We report on this next.

Space Saving Variations: In this experiment we show how the performance of the algorithms changes when only a subset of the set of global and conditional lists are stored. Recall from Section 5.2.1 that we only retain lists for the values of the frequently occurring attributes in the workload. For this experiment we consider Top-10 queries with selection conditions that specify two attributes (queries generated by randomly picking a pair of attributes and a domain value for each attribute), and measure their execution times. The compared algorithms are:

- LM: List Merge with all lists available
- LMM: List Merge where lists for one of the two specified attributes are missing, halving space
- Scan

Figure 10 shows the execution times of the queries over the Seattle Homes database as a function of the total number of tuples that satisfy the selection condition. The times are averaged over 10 queries.

We first note that LM is extremely fast when compared to the other algorithms (its times are less than one second for each run, consequently its graph is almost along the *x*-axis). This is to be expected as most of the computations have been accomplished at pre-processing time. The performance of Scan degrades when the total number of selected tuples increases, because the scores of more tuples need to be calculated at runtime. In contrast, the performance of LM and LMM actually improves slightly. This interesting phenomenon occurs because if more tuples satisfy the selection condition, smaller prefixes of the lists need to be read and merged before the stopping condition is reached.

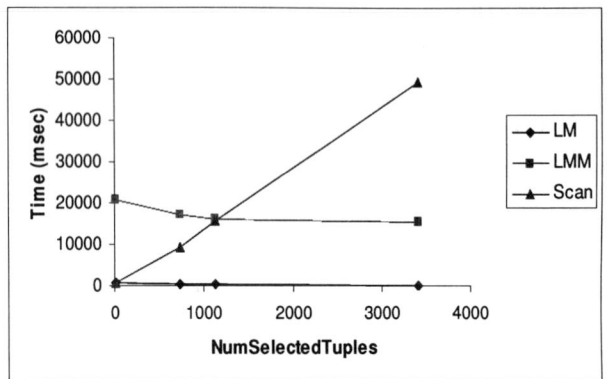

Figure 10: Execution Times of Different Variations of List Merge and Scan for Seattle Homes Dataset

Thus, List Merge and its variations are preferable if the number of tuples satisfying the query condition is large (which is exactly the situation we are interested in, i.e., the Many-Answers problem). This conclusion was reconfirmed when we repeated the experiment with LM and Scan on the much larger US Homes dataset with queries satisfying many more tuples (see Figure 11).

NumSelected Tuples	LM Time (msec)	Scan Time (msec)
350	800	6515
2000	700	39234
5000	600	115282
30000	550	566516
80000	500	3806531

Figure 11: Execution Times of List Merge and Scan for US Homes Dataset

Varying Number of Specified Attributes: Figure 12 shows how the query processing performance of the algorithms varies with the number of attributes specified in the selection conditions of the queries over the US Homes database (the results for the other databases are similar). The times are averaged over 10 Top-10 queries. Note that the times increase sharply for both algorithms with the number of specified attributes. The LM algorithm becomes slower because more lists need to be merged, which delays the termination condition. The Scan algorithm becomes slower because the selection time increases with the number of specified attributes. This experiment demonstrates the criticality of keeping the number of sorted streams small in our adaptation of TA.

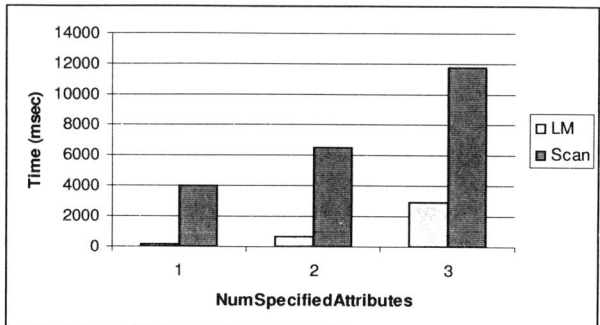

Figure 12: Varying Number of Specified Attributes for US Homes Dataset

7. Conclusions

We proposed a completely automated approach for the Many-Answers Problem which leverages data and workload statistics and correlations. Our ranking functions are based upon the probabilistic IR models, judiciously adapted for structured data. We presented results of preliminary experiments which demonstrate the efficiency as well as the quality of our ranking system.

Our work brings forth several intriguing open problems. For example, many relational databases contain text columns in addition to numeric and categorical columns. It would be interesting to see whether correlations between text and non-text data can be leveraged in a meaningful way for ranking. Finally, comprehensive quality benchmarks for database ranking need to be established. This would provide future researchers with a more unified and systematic basis for evaluating their retrieval algorithms.

References

[1] S. Agrawal, S. Chaudhuri G. Das. DBXplorer: A System for Keyword Based Search over Relational Databases. ICDE 2002.
[2] S. Agrawal, S. Chaudhuri, G. Das and A. Gionis. Automated Ranking of Database Query Results. CIDR, 2003.
[3] R. Agrawal, H. Mannila, R. Srikant, H. Toivonen and A. I. Verkamo. Fast Discovery of Association Rules. Advances in Knowledge Discovery and Data Mining, 1995.
[4] R. Baeza-Yates and B. Ribeiro-Neto. Modern Information Retrieval. ACM Press, 1999.
[5] G. Bhalotia, C. Nakhe, A. Hulgeri, S. Chakrabarti and S. Sudarshan. Keyword Searching and Browsing in Databases using BANKS. ICDE 2002.
[6] H. M. Blanken, T. Grabs, H.-J. Schek, R. Schenkel, G. Weikum (Eds.): Intelligent Search on XML Data: Applications, Languages, Models, Implementations, and Benchmarks. LNCS 2818 Springer 2003.
[7] J. Breese, D. Heckerman and C. Kadie. Empirical Analysis of Predictive Algorithms for Collaborative Filtering. 14th Conference on Uncertainty in Artificial Intelligence, 1998.

[8] N. Bruno, L. Gravano, and S. Chaudhuri.Top-K Selection Queries over Relational Databases: Mapping Strategies and Performance Evaluation. ACM TODS, 2002.
[9] N. Bruno, L. Gravano, A. Marian. Evaluating Top-K Queries over Web-Accessible Databases. ICDE 2002.
10] B. Cestnik. Estimating Probabilities: A Crucial Task in Machine Learning, European Conf. in AI, 1990.
[11] K. Chakrabarti, K. Porkaew and S. Mehrotra. Efficient Query Ref. in Multimedia Databases. ICDE 2000.
[12] W. Cohen. Integration of Heterogeneous Databases Without Common Domains Using Queries Based on Textual Similarity. SIGMOD, 1998.
[13] W. Cohen. Providing Database-like Access to the Web Using Queries Based on Textual Similarity. SIGMOD 1998.
[14] W.B. Croft, J. Lafferty. Language Modeling for Information Retrieval. Kluwer 2003.
[15] R. Fagin. Fuzzy Queries in Multimedia Database Systems. PODS 1998.
[16] R. Fagin, A. Lotem and M. Naor. Optimal Aggregation Algorithms for Middleware. PODS 2001.
[17] N. Fuhr. A Probabilistic Framework for Vague Queries and Imprecise Information in Databases. VLDB 1990.
[18] N. Fuhr. A Probabilistic Relational Model for the Integration of IR and Databases. ACM SIGIR Conference on Research and Development in Information Retrieval, 1993.
[19] U. Güntzer, W.-T. Balke, W. Kießling: Optimizing Multi-Feature Queries for Image Databases. VLDB 2000.
[20] V. Hristidis,Y. Papakonstantinou. DISCOVER: Keyword Search in Relational Databases. VLDB 2002.
[21] W. Kießling. Foundations of Preferences in Database Systems. VLDB 2002.
[22] D. Kossmann, F. Ramsak, S. Rost: Shooting Stars in the Sky: An Online Algorithm for Skyline Queries. VLDB 2002.
[23] A. Motro. VAGUE: A User Interface to Relational Databases that Permits Vague Queries. TOIS 1988, 187-214.
[24] Z. Nazeri, E. Bloedorn and P. Ostwald. Experiences in Mining Aviation Safety Data. SIGMOD 2001.
[25] S. Nepal, M. V. Ramakrishna: Query Processing Issues in Image (Multimedia) Databases. ICDE 1999.
[26] M. Ortega-Binderberger, K. Chakrabarti and S. Mehrotra. An Approach to Integrating Query Refinement in SQL, EDBT 2002, 15-33.
[27] Y. Rui, T. S. Huang and S. Merhotra. Content-Based Image Retrieval with Relevance Feedback in MARS. IEEE Conf. on Image Processing, 1997.
[28] K. Sparck Jones, S. Walker, S. E. Robertson: A Probabilistic Model of Information Retrieval: Development and Comparative Experiments - Part 1. Inf. Process. Manage. 36(6): 779-808, 2000.
[29] K. Sparck Jones, S. Walker, S. E. Robertson: A Probabilistic Model of Information Retrieval: Development and Comparative Experiments - Part 2. Inf. Process. Manage. 36(6): 809-840, 2000.
[30] J. Whittaker. Graphical Models in Applied Multivariate Statistics. Wiley, 1990.
[31] L. Wimmers, L. M. Haas , M T. Roth and C. Braendli. Using Fagin's Algorithm for Merging Ranked Results in Multimedia Middleware. CoopIS 1999.
[32] L. Wu, C. Faloutsos, K. Sycara and T. Payne. FALCON: Feedback Adaptive Loop for Content-Based Retrieval. VLDB 2000.

An Annotation Management System for Relational Databases

Deepavali Bhagwat   Laura Chiticariu   Wang-Chiew Tan*   Gaurav Vijayvargiya

University of California, Santa Cruz
Email: {dbhagwat, laura, wctan, gaurav}@cs.ucsc.edu

Abstract

We present an annotation management system for relational databases. In this system, every piece of data in a relation is assumed to have zero or more annotations associated with it and annotations are propagated along, from the source to the output, as data is being transformed through a query. Such an annotation management system is important for understanding the provenance and quality of data, especially in applications that deal with integration of scientific and biological data.

We present an extension, pSQL, of a fragment of SQL that has three different types of annotation propagation schemes, each useful for different purposes. The *default* scheme propagates annotations according to where data is copied from. The *default-all* scheme propagates annotations according to where data is copied from among *all* equivalent formulations of a given query. The *custom* scheme allows a user to specify how annotations should propagate. We present a storage scheme for the annotations and describe algorithms for translating a pSQL query under each propagation scheme into one or more SQL queries that would correctly retrieve the relevant annotations according to the specified propagation scheme. For the default-all scheme, we also show how we generate *finitely* many queries that can simulate the annotation propagation behavior of the set of all equivalent queries, which is possibly infinite. The algorithms are implemented and the feasibility of the system is demonstrated by a set of experiments that we have conducted.

1 Introduction

For many scientific domains, new databases are often created to support the data analysis needs of domain-specific scientists. Some examples of such databases from biology include UniProt [2] and SWISS-PROT [3]. Data that is collected from other sources is often cleansed and reformatted before it is compiled into the new database. Very often, the newly created database will also contain new analysis or results that are derived by scientists. By associating old and new data together in the new database, an integrated perspective is provided to scientists and this is critical for further analysis and scientific discovery. With the proliferation of many such inter-dependent databases[1], it is natural to ask what is the provenance of a piece of data (i.e., where that piece of data is copied or created from) in a database. Understanding the provenance of data is important towards understanding the quality of data which may help, for example, a scientist to decide on the amount of trust to place on a piece of information that she encounters in a database. We use the term *annotations* to mean information about data such as provenance, comments, or other types of metadata.

We describe an annotation management system for relational databases where annotations may be attached to a piece of data and are transparently carried along as data is being transformed. One immediate application is to use annotations to systematically trace the provenance and flow of data: if we attach to every piece of source data an annotation that describes its address (i.e., origins), then the annotations of a piece of data in the output of a transformation describe its provenance. Even if the data had undergone several transformation steps, we can easily determine the origins (or the flow of data for that matter) through the transformation steps by examining the annotations. Another use of annotations is to describe information about data that would otherwise have not been kept in a database. For example, an error report or remarks about a piece of data may be attached and propagated along to other databases, thus notifying other users of the error or additional information. The quality or security level of a piece of data can also be described in annotations. Since annotations are propagated along as a query is executed, the annotations on the result of a query can be aggregated to determine the quality or degree of sensitivity of the resulting output. This idea of using annotations to describe the security level of various data items or to specify fine-grained access control policies is not new and can be found in various forms in existing literature [11, 13, 19].

We describe three propagation schemes for propagating

---

*Supported in part by an NSF CAREER Award IIS-0347065.

Permission to copy without fee all or part of this material is granted provided that the copies are not made or distributed for direct commercial advantage, the VLDB copyright notice and the title of the publication and its date appear, and notice is given that copying is by permission of the Very Large Data Base Endowment. To copy otherwise, or to republish, requires a fee and/or special permission from the Endowment.

**Proceedings of the 30th VLDB Conference,
Toronto, Canada, 2004**

[1] See [10] for a catalog of biology databases.

annotations that are motivated by different needs. They correspond to the default, default-all, and custom propagation schemes. The *default* scheme uses provenance as the basis for propagating annotations. If an output piece of data d' is copied from an input piece of data d, then the annotations associated with d are propagated to d'. A piece of output data d' is *copied from* an input piece of data d if d' is created from d according to the syntax and evaluation of the query. Although this natural definition corresponds intuitively to how people reason about provenance, the way annotations are propagated is dependent on the way a query is written. As shown in [24], two equivalent queries may propagate annotations differently. While this behavior may seem disturbing at first, in many applications including those described above, such an automatic provenance-based annotation propagation scheme which allows one to trace where data is copied from or copied to based on a given query is still very desirable. Indeed, similar ideas were proposed before in [18, 26]. An alternative method of propagating annotations, called the *default-all* scheme, is to propagate annotations according to where data is copied from in *all* equivalent formulations of the given query since one may be interested in obtaining all relevant annotations of a piece of data in the output regardless of how a query may have been written. Unlike the default scheme, two equivalent queries will always propagate annotations in the same way under this scheme. In some cases, a user may only be interested in annotations provided by a certain trusted data source. Hence we also have a third propagation scheme, the *custom* propagation scheme, where the user is free to specify how annotations should be propagated.

Summary of results We have implemented all three propagation schemes in our annotation management system by extending a fragment of SQL. We call this extension pSQL. A pSQL query is essentially an SQL query extended with a PROPAGATE clause that would propagate annotations according to one of the schemes described above as data is transformed. In our implementation, we assume that there is an "additional column" that stores the annotations for every attribute of every relation. A translation algorithm translates a given pSQL query into one or more SPJ queries against these underlying relations and these SPJ queries will retrieve the relevant annotations according to the specified propagation scheme. In the default-all scheme, we are required to propagate annotations according to every possible equivalent reformulations of a given query. At first sight, the default-all scheme seems impossible to implement as there are infinitely many equivalent reformulations of a given query. We show, however, that it is always possible to find a finite set of equivalent queries whose annotation propagation behavior is "representative" of all equivalent queries. Hence, by running every query in this finite set and taking the union of resulting tuples and annotations, we are able to obtain the annotated output of the given query under the default-all scheme. We have conducted experiments to evaluate the feasibility of such an annotation management system. Our experimental results indicate that the execution time of a query under any propagation scheme increases only slightly when the number of annotations in a database is doubled. Our results also show that for the queries we executed, the performance of a query under the default-all scheme can be at worst eight times slower than the performance of the same query under the default or no propagation scheme (i.e., SQL query). At best, it runs about twice as slow. For the default scheme, however, the execution times of pSQL queries are comparable to those of SQL queries. On the average, the pSQL queries with default scheme that we experimented with on a 100MB database took around 40% more time to execute than their corresponding SQL queries. For larger databases (500MB and 1GB), the pSQL queries with default scheme took only about 18% more time to execute than their corresponding SQL queries on the average.

Related Work The problem of computing data provenance is not new. Cui, Widom, and Wiener [9] first approached the problem of tracing the provenance of data that is the result of a query applied on a relational database. The solution proposed in [9] was to first generate a "reverse" query Q^r when asked to compute the provenance of an output tuple t in the result of a query Q applied on a database D (i.e., $Q(D)$). The result of applying Q^r on D consists of all combinations of source tuples in D such that each combination of source tuples and Q explain *why* t is in the output of $Q(D)$. The type of provenance studied by [9] is called *why-provenance* according to Buneman, Khanna, and Tan [6]. Additionally, we may also be interested in knowing *where* the values of a tuple t in the result of $Q(D)$ are copied from in D. The latter type of provenance is called *where-provenance* in [6] and it is this type of provenance that we use for determining where annotations are propagated from. In both works [6, 9], a "reverse" query is generated in order to answer provenance. While the reverse query approach works well in general, it requires a reverse query to be generated and evaluated every time the provenance of an output tuple is sought for. Hence if the provenance of a large number of output tuples is required, this may not be the optimal way to compute provenance.

The reverse query approach is what we call the *lazy* approach for computing provenance; a query is generated and executed to compute the provenance only when needed. In this paper, we propose to trade space for time and carry along the provenance of data as data is being transformed. Hence, in this approach, the provenance of data is *eagerly* computed and immediately available in the output. The idea of eagerly computing provenance by forwarding annotations along data transformations is also not new and has been proposed in various forms in existing literature [4, 18, 26]. In fact, our annotation propagation rules which propagate annotations based on where-provenance are similar to those proposed in [26]. In [26], however, only information about which source relations a value is copied from is propagated along. In contrast, our system is flexible in the amount of information that is carried along to the result (i.e., it could be the source relations, or the exact location within the source locations, or a comment on the data).

Numerous annotation systems have been built to support and manage annotations on text and HTML documents [14, 17, 21, 23, 25]. Recently, annotation systems for genomic sequences [5, 12, 16] have also been built. Laliberte and Braverman [17] discussed how to use the HTTP protocol to design a scalable annotation system for HTML pages. Schickler, Mazer, and Brooks [23] discussed the use of a specialized proxy module that would merge annotations from an annotation store onto a Web page that is being retrieved before sending it to the client browser. Annotea [14, 25] is a W3C effort to support annotations on any Web document. Annotations are also stored on annotation servers and XPointer is used for pinpointing locations on a Web document. A specialized client browser that can understand, communicate, and merge annotations residing in the annotation servers with Web documents is used. Phelps and Wilensky [20, 21, 22] also discussed the use of annotations with certain desirable properties on multivalent documents [22] which support documents of different media types, such as images, postscript, or HTML. DAS or Biodas [5, 12] and the Human Genome Browser [16] are specialized annotation systems for genomic sequence data. In almost all of these systems, the design includes multiple distributed annotation servers for storing annotations and data is merged from various sources to display it graphically to an end user. The research of these systems has been focussed on the scalability of design, distributed support for annotations, or other added features.

We designed and implemented an annotation management system for relational databases where annotations can be made on relational data. This idea was first proposed in [7, 24]. Unlike Web pages, the rigid structure of relations makes it easy to describe the exact position where an annotation is attached. Web pages, however, are often retrieved in part or as a whole. Hence, the issue of what annotations to propagate along when a web page is retrieved is straightforward. In contrast, an annotated relation in our system may undergo a complex transformation as a result of executing a query. We are thus concerned with how annotations should propagate when such complex transformations occur. To the best of our knowledge, this is the first implementation of an annotation management system for relational databases that would allow a user to specify how annotations should propagate.

In Section 2, we describe pSQL and the three different propagation schemes. In Section 3, we describe the algorithm for generating a finite set of queries that can simulate the annotation propagation behavior of all equivalent queries of a given pSQL query. In Section 4, we describe the architecture of our system and a storage scheme for annotations as well as our translation algorithm that rewrites a pSQL query into an SQL query against the underlying storage scheme. In Section 5, we describe our experimental results and in Sections 6 and 7, we conclude with some possible future extensions to our system.

2 pSQL

In our subsequent discussions, we focus on a fragment of SQL that corresponds to conjunctive queries with union [1] (also known as the Select-Project-Join-Union fragment of SQL). We extend this fragment of SQL with a PROPAGATE clause to allow users to specify how annotations should propagate.

Definition 2.1 A *pSQL query* is a query of the form Q_1 UNION ... UNION Q_k, $k > 0$, where each $Q_i, i \in [1, k]$, is a *pSQL query fragment* of the form shown below:

```
SELECT DISTINCT    selectlist
FROM               fromlist
WHERE              wherelist
PROPAGATE          DEFAULT | DEFAULT-ALL |
                   r_1.A_1 TO B_1, ..., r_n.A_n TO B_n
```

The *fromlist* of a pSQL query fragment is of the form "$R_1\,r_1, ..., R_k\,r_k$" where r_i is a tuple variable of the corresponding relation R_i. The *selectlist* of a pSQL query fragment is of the form "$r_1.C_1$ AS D_1, ..., $r_m.C_m$ AS D_m" where r_i is a tuple variable defined in *fromlist*, C_i is an attribute of the relation that corresponds to r_i, and D_i is an attribute name of the output relation. The WHERE clause is optional and the *wherelist* is a conjunction of one or more equalities between attributes of relations or between attributes of relations and constants. The PROPAGATE clause can be defined with DEFAULT, DEFAULT-ALL, or a list of clauses of the form "$r.A$ TO B" definitions where $r.A$ denotes an attribute A of the tuple that is bound to r and B is an attribute among the D_js. ∎

The *SQL query that corresponds to a pSQL query Q* is the SQL query that results when all PROPAGATE clauses in Q have been removed. The meaning of a pSQL query is similar to that of its corresponding SQL query except that annotations are also propagated to each emitted tuple according to the specification given in the PROPAGATE clauses.

Example 2.1 Consider three databases SWISS-PROT (a protein database), PIR (another protein database), and Genbank (a gene database). Each of these databases is modeled as a relation. The schemas and an instance of each relation are shown in Figure 1 (ignore the rest of the relations in the figure). An annotation, shown in braces, is placed on every column of every tuple. Each annotation can be interpreted as the address of the value in the corresponding column of the tuple. An example of a pSQL query with the default propagation scheme is shown below.

```
Q_1 =   SELECT DISTINCT s.ID AS ID, s.Desc AS Desc
        FROM SWISS-PROT s
        WHERE s.ID = 'q229'
        PROPAGATE DEFAULT
```

Intuitively, the default scheme specified in Q_1 propagates annotations of data according to where data is copied from. The result of Q_1 executed against the relation SWISS-PROT is shown in Figure 1. The annotation a_3 is attached to the value q229 in the output since q229 is copied from the ID attribute of the second tuple in SWISS-PROT. Likewise, a_4 in the output is propagated from the

SWISS-PROT	
ID	Desc
z131 $\{a_1\}$	AB $\{a_2\}$
q229 $\{a_3\}$	CC $\{a_4\}$
q939 $\{a_5\}$	ED $\{a_6\}$

PIR	
ID	Name
p332 $\{a_7\}$	AB $\{a_8\}$
p916 $\{a_9\}$	AB $\{a_{10}\}$

Genbank	
ID	Desc
g231 $\{a_{11}\}$	AB $\{a_{12}\}$
g756 $\{a_{13}\}$	CC $\{a_{14}\}$

Result of Q_1:	
ID	Desc
q229 $\{a_3\}$	CC $\{a_4\}$

Mapping_Table			
entryid	swissprot	pir	genbank
1 $\{a_{15}\}$	z131 $\{a_{16}\}$	p332 $\{a_{17}\}$	g231 $\{a_{18}\}$
2 $\{a_{19}\}$	q229 $\{a_{20}\}$	p916 $\{a_{21}\}$	g756 $\{a_{22}\}$
3 $\{a_{23}\}$	q939 $\{a_{24}\}$	p677 $\{a_{25}\}$	g635 $\{a_{26}\}$

Result of Q_2:	
ID	Name
p332 $\{a_7\}$	AB $\{a_8, a_{10}\}$
p916 $\{a_9\}$	AB $\{a_8, a_{10}\}$

Result of Q_3:	
ID	Desc
g231 $\{a_{11}, a_{12}\}$	AB
g756 $\{a_{13}, a_{14}\}$	CC

Figure 1: Three protein databases, a mapping table, and three annotated outputs.

annotation of the Desc attribute of the second tuple in SWISS-PROT. ∎

While the default scheme is a natural scheme for propagating annotations, this scheme is not "robust" in that two equivalent queries that return the same output may not propagate the same annotations to the output.

Example 2.2 Consider two equivalent SQL queries Q' and Q'' (two queries are equivalent if they produce the same result on every database).

$Q' =$ SELECT DISTINCT p.ID AS ID, p.Name AS Name
FROM PIR p, Mapping_Table m
WHERE p.ID = m.pir

$Q'' =$ SELECT DISTINCT m.pir AS ID, p.Name AS Name
FROM PIR p, Mapping_Table m
WHERE p.ID = m.pir

The results of running Q' and Q'' under the default propagation scheme are shown below.

Result of Q':
ID	Name
p332 $\{a_7\}$	AB $\{a_8\}$
p916 $\{a_9\}$	AB $\{a_{10}\}$

Result of Q'':
ID	Name
p332 $\{a_{17}\}$	AB $\{a_8\}$
p916 $\{a_{21}\}$	AB $\{a_{10}\}$

For Q', the annotations for the ID column are from the PIR table while for Q'', the annotations for the ID column are from the Mapping_Table. ∎

While it is likely that a user will realise that Q' will generate a different annotated outcome from Q'' in general, the situation is not so straightforward for more complex queries. The above example motivates the need for a propagation scheme that is invariant under equivalent queries. One should be able to retrieve all relevant annotations about a piece of output data regardless of how the query is written, if desired. The default-all propagation scheme propagates annotations according to where data is copied from among all equivalent formulations of the given query. Hence the annotated outcome is the same for equivalent queries under this scheme. In case a user prefers to retrieve annotations from one source over another, the user is also free to specify how annotations should propagate in the custom scheme.

Example 2.3 The queries Q_2 and Q_3 are examples of pSQL queries with the default-all and custom propagation schemes respectively.

$Q_2 =$ SELECT DISTINCT p.ID AS ID, p.Name AS Name
FROM PIR p
PROPAGATE DEFAULT-ALL

$Q_3 =$ SELECT DISTINCT g.ID AS ID, g.Desc AS Desc
FROM Genbank g
PROPAGATE g.ID TO ID, g.Desc TO ID

The results of Q_2 and Q_3 are shown in Figure 1. The query Q_2 retrieves all tuples from the PIR table under the default-all propagation scheme. The annotations we get in the result are the combined annotations of results from all equivalent queries. In the custom scheme of Q_3, annotations are propagated according to the given user specification (i.e., g.ID TO ID, g.Desc TO ID). A clause "g.ID TO ID" states that the annotations associated with the value of the ID attribute of the tuple that is currently bound to g should propagate to the ID attribute of the output tuple. Similarly, the annotations associated to the value of the Desc attribute of the tuple that is currently bound to g should propagate to the ID attribute of the output tuple. ∎

Some Terminology A *cell* (or *location*) is a triple (r, t, i) which denotes the ith column of the tuple t in relation r. We sometimes use the attribute name at position i instead of the position i. We also write a cell simply as a pair (t, i) in the context where the relation r is clear. Each cell contains a value of some type. We use $v(c)$ to denote the value at cell c ($v(c)$ is called *a piece of data*). Let $\mathcal{L}$ denote the set of all strings. Each cell c in a database is *associated with* a set of annotations $\{a_1, ..., a_k\}$ where each a_i, $i \in [1, k]$, is an element in $\mathcal{L}$. We also say each a_i, $i \in [1, k]$, is an annotation attached to c. We use the notation $\mathcal{A}(c)$ to denote the set of all annotations attached to cell c.

Containment vs. Annotation-Containment. Two pSQL queries Q and Q' are equivalent, denoted as $Q = Q'$, if for every database D, $Q(D) = Q'(D)$. The query Q is contained in Q', denoted as $Q \subseteq Q'$, for every database D, $Q(D) \subseteq Q'(D)$. Two pSQL queries Q and Q' are *annotation-equivalent*, denoted as $Q =_a Q'$, if Q and Q' produce the same annotated output on all databases. More precisely, this means that for every database D, $Q(D)$ is equal to $Q'(D)$ and the set of annotations $\mathcal{A}((Q(D), t, i))$ is identical to $\mathcal{A}((Q'(D), t, i))$ for every output location (t, i) in $Q(D)$. A pSQL query Q is *annotation-contained* in Q', denoted as $Q \subseteq_a Q'$, if for every database D, $Q(D) \subseteq Q'(D)$ and for every output location (t, i) in $Q(D)$, $\mathcal{A}((Q(D), t, i)) \subseteq \mathcal{A}((Q'(D), t, i))$.

Example 2.4 Figure 1 shows several examples of annotated relations. The value z131 in SWISS-PROT is the value at cell (SWISS-PROT, (z131, AB), ID) which denotes the ID column of tuple (z131, AB) in the SWISS-PROT relation. Note that the attribute names in the tuple (z131, AB) have been omitted. The annotation $\{a_1\}$ is the set of annotations associated with this cell. Hence, $\mathcal{A}((\text{SWISS-PROT}, (z131, AB), ID))$ is $\{a_1\}$. In the result of Q_2, $\mathcal{A}(((p332, AB), \text{Name}))$ is $\{a_8, a_{10}\}$. ∎

2.1 The Custom Propagation Scheme

We allow the user the flexibility to specify custom propagation schemes using a PROPAGATE clause of the form "$r_1.A_1$ TO B_1, ..., $r_n.A_n$ TO B_n". The semantics of a pSQL query fragment Q with custom propagation scheme is as follows. For every binding μ of tuple variables to tuples in the respective relations according to the *fromlist* of Q such that the conditions in the *wherelist* are satisfied, emit an output tuple t according to the *selectlist*. For every clause "$r_i.A_i$ TO B_i" specified in the PROPAGATE clause, we add the set of annotations at the location (r_i, A_i) to the set of annotations (initially empty) at the output location (t, B_i). Finally, duplicate output tuples are merged. Suppose $t_1, ..., t_k$ are the emitted tuples and $s_1, ..., s_m$ are the tuples that result when duplicate output tuples have been merged. Then, for every output location (s, B), $\mathcal{A}((s, B)) = \bigcup_{t_j = s, j \in [1,k]} \mathcal{A}((t_j, B))$. The query Q_3 of Example 2.3 is an example of a pSQL query fragment with a custom propagation scheme; every tuple in Genbank is emitted in such a way that the set of annotations that is associated with the ID column of an output tuple is the union of annotations associated with the ID column and Desc column of the corresponding tuple in Genbank.

2.2 The Default Propagation Scheme

If PROPAGATE DEFAULT is used in a pSQL query fragment, the set of annotations of a piece of output data consists of all the annotations associated with where that piece of data is copied from in the source.

The semantics of a pSQL query fragment Q with the default propagation scheme is as follows. For every binding of tuple variables to tuples in the respective relations according to the *fromlist* of Q such that the conditions in the *wherelist* are satisfied, emit an output tuple t according to the *selectlist* as well as the corresponding sets of annotations for every cell in t. Since every value of an output cell c' in t is generated from some value of an input cell c according to the current bindings, the set of annotations attached to c is also attached to c'. Finally, duplicate output tuples are merged together. Suppose $t_1, ..., t_k$ are the emitted tuples and $s_1, ..., s_m$ are the tuples that result when duplicate output tuples have been merged. Then, for every output location (s, B), $\mathcal{A}((s, B)) = \bigcup_{t_j = s, j \in [1,k]} \mathcal{A}((t_j, B))$.

Example 2.5 Suppose we have the following pSQL query where each fragment uses the default propagation scheme.

```
SELECT      Desc AS Desc
FROM        SWISS-PROT
PROPAGATE   DEFAULT
UNION
SELECT      Desc AS Desc
FROM        Genbank
PROPAGATE   DEFAULT
```

Result:

Desc
AB $\{a_2, a_{12}\}$
CC $\{a_4, a_{14}\}$
ED $\{a_6\}$

The first subquery emits an output tuple "AB" with annotations $\{a_2\}$ and the second subquery emits the same output tuple "AB" but with annotations $\{a_{12}\}$. The merged result of these two tuples is a single output tuple "AB" with annotations $\{a_2, a_{12}\}$. This explains the first output tuple in the result. A similar reasoning applies to the rest of the output tuples. ∎

It is easy to see that a pSQL query fragment with default propagation scheme can be translated into a pSQL query fragment with custom propagation scheme. For example, the query Q_1 of Example 2.1 can be rewritten into a pSQL query with custom scheme where the propagate clause is replaced by "PROPAGATE s.ID TO ID, s.Desc TO Desc" since the ID value and Desc value of an output tuple are copied from s.ID and s.Desc, respectively.

2.3 The Default-All Propagation Scheme

A pSQL query with the default propagation scheme is, essentially, an SQL query with annotations propagated based on where a value is retrieved according to the syntax of the query. We have already seen an example of two pSQL queries under the default propagation scheme (Example 2.2) which are equivalent but not *annotation-equivalent*.

This motivates us to define a third propagation scheme, called the default-all scheme, where the annotation propagation behavior of a pSQL query is invariant to the syntax of the query. A pSQL query Q with default-all propagation scheme propagates annotations according to the default propagation behavior of all equivalent formulations of Q. The resulting tuples that are generated by all equivalent queries of Q according to the default scheme are then merged together. Despite the fact that there are infinitely many equivalent formulations of Q, we describe a method that would compute the desired result by examining only a *finite* number of pSQL queries. We call such a finite set of queries a *query-basis of Q*.

Definition 2.2 Let Q denote a pSQL query with default-all propagation scheme. Let $S(Q)$ denote the SQL query that corresponds to Q and let $\mathcal{E}(S(Q))$ denote the set of all pSQL queries Q' under the default propagation scheme such that $S(Q')$ is equivalent to $S(Q)$. A *query basis of Q*, denoted as $\mathcal{B}(Q)$, is a finite set of pSQL queries with default propagation scheme such that $\bigcup_{q \in \mathcal{B}(Q)} q =_a \bigcup_{q \in \mathcal{E}(S(Q))} q$.

We describe next an algorithm that finds a query basis for a pSQL query with default-all propagation scheme. The size of the query basis that the algorithm returns is always polynomial in the size of Q.

3 Generating a Query Basis

The algorithm for computing a query basis for a pSQL query with default-all propagation scheme proceeds by first generating a *representative* query of Q, called Q_0. Intuitively, a *representative* query of Q is a query that is equivalent to Q and for every attribute A that is equal or transitively equal to an attribute B in the *selectlist* of Q, the annotations of A are propagated to B. From Q_0, a finite number of *auxiliary* queries are also generated and these queries, together with Q_0, form a query basis of Q. Each auxiliary query is equivalent to Q but may propagate additional annotations to the output that are not propagated by Q_0. Intuitively, only a finite number of auxiliary queries are needed because only one auxiliary query needs to be generated for each attribute of a relation that "contributes annotations" to the output. In the rest of the discussion, we restrict our language to be pSQL query fragments. We present an algorithm for generating a query basis of a pSQL query fragment with default-all propagation scheme. The algorithm can be extended to handle pSQL queries in general and the details are omitted.

Algorithm Generate-Query-Basis
Input: A pSQL query fragment Q with default-all propagation scheme.
Output: A query basis of Q, $\mathcal{B}(Q)$.

Let Q be a pSQL query fragment of the form shown in Definition 2.1 with PROPAGATE DEFAULT-ALL clause.

1. *Generate Q_0, the representative query of Q.*
   Generate a query Q_0 that is identical to Q except that the propagation scheme of Q is replaced with the following propagation scheme:
   For every attribute "$r.A$ AS C" in the *selectlist*, add "$r.A$ TO C" in the PROPAGATE clause.
   For every attribute "$r.A$ AS C" in the *selectlist* and every attribute $s.B$ that is equal to $r.A$ or transitively equal to $r.A$ according to the *wherelist*: add "$s.B$ TO C" in the PROPAGATE clause.
   (The effect is that all attributes that are equal to an attribute C in the *selectlist* have their annotations propagated to C.)

2. *Generate auxiliary queries of Q_0.*
   Initialize $\mathcal{B}(Q)$ to the empty set. Add Q_0 to $\mathcal{B}(Q)$. For every attribute "$r.A$ AS C" in the *selectlist* of Q_0 and every "$s.B$ TO C" in the PROPAGATE clause of Q_0, do the following:
   Create a query Q' that is identical to Q_0. Suppose s is a tuple variable of relation S according to the *fromlist* of Q_0. Add "$S\ s'$" to the *fromlist* of Q' where s' is a tuple variable that does not occur in Q'. Add "$s'.B = s.B$" to the *wherelist* of Q' and "$s'.B$ TO C" to the PROPAGATE clause of Q'. Add Q' to $\mathcal{B}(Q)$.
   (The auxiliary query Q' is equivalent to Q but may carry additional annotations to the output.)

3. *Return $\mathcal{B}(Q)$.*

Example 3.1 Consider the three databases, SWISS-PROT, PIR, and Genbank along with a Mapping_table that contains the correspondences between identifiers of genes and proteins in the three databases in Figure 1. Such mapping tables commonly occur in integrating many sources with overlapping information [15]. Suppose we have the following query Q that integrates information from SWISS-PROT and PIR.

SELECT DISTINCT t.swissprot AS ID,
$\quad\quad\quad\quad$ p.Name AS Name, s.Desc AS Desc
FROM Mapping_Table t, SWISS-PROT s, PIR p
WHERE t.swissprot $= s$.ID AND t.pir $= p$.ID
PROPAGATE DEFAULT-ALL

After Step 1 of the above algorithm, we obtain the following representative query Q_0:

SELECT DISTINCT t.swissprot AS ID,
$\quad\quad\quad\quad$ p.Name AS Name, s.Desc AS Desc
FROM Mapping_Table t, SWISS-PROT s, PIR p
WHERE t.swissprot $= s$.ID AND t.pir $= p$.ID
PROPAGATE t.swissprot TO ID, s.ID TO ID,
$\quad\quad\quad\quad$ p.Name TO Name, s.Desc TO Desc

Note that the annotations of t.swissprot and s.ID will propagate to the output ID column according to Q_0. The second step of the algorithm generates four auxiliary queries. The first query is shown below and the rest are shown in Figure 2.

$Q_1 =$
SELECT DISTINCT t.swissprot AS ID,
$\quad\quad\quad\quad$ p.Name AS Name, s.Desc AS Desc
FROM Mapping_Table t, SWISS-PROT s, PIR p, **Mapping_Table t'**
WHERE t.swissprot $= s$.ID AND t.pir $= p$.ID,
$\quad\quad\quad\quad$ **t'.swissprot $= t$.swissprot**
PROPAGATE t.swissprot TO ID, s.ID TO ID,
$\quad\quad\quad\quad$ p.Name TO Name, s.Desc TO Desc,
$\quad\quad\quad\quad$ **t'.swissprot TO ID**

The query Q_1 is different from Q_0 only in the additional highlighted terms shown in Q_1. There is an extra relation, condition, and propagation in the FROM, WHERE, and PROPAGATE clauses respectively. It is easy to verify that the SQL queries of Q_0 and Q_1 are equivalent. There is a homomorphism h from the tuple variables of Q_1 to those of Q_0 such that h maps the *fromlist* of Q_1 to a subset of the *fromlist* of Q_0 and the conditions in the *wherelist* of Q_0 imply the conditions in the *wherelist* of Q_1 under h. Furthermore, h maps the *selectlist* of Q_1 to the *selectlist* of Q_0. There is also a homomorphism in the reverse direction. Similarly, Q_2, Q_3, and Q_4 of Figure 2 are each equivalent to Q_0. ∎

Intuitively, the representative query Q_0 propagates annotations according to where data is copied from and also where data could have been equivalently copied from. The reason why Q_0 is generated becomes clearer if we represent Q using conjunctive query-like notation

$$A(\mathbf{x}) :- S_1(\mathbf{y_1}), ..., S_n(\mathbf{y_n}), equalities.$$

where $\mathbf{x}, \mathbf{y_i}, i \in [1, n]$, denote vectors of variables and every variable in $\mathbf{x}$ occurs in $\mathbf{y_i}$ for some $i \in [1, n]$ and *equalities* is a list of zero of more $y = y'$ clauses where y is a variable that occurs amongst $\mathbf{y_i}$s and y' is a constant. The variables in $\mathbf{x}$ are called *distinguished variables*. Each subgoal corresponds to a relation in the *fromlist* of Q. The

$Q_2 =$
SELECT DISTINCT
    t.swissprot AS ID,
    p.Name AS Name,
    s.Desc AS Desc
FROM Mapping_Table t, SWISS-PROT s,
    PIR p, **SWISS-PROT** s'
WHERE t.swissprot = s.ID AND
    t.pir = p.ID AND s'.**ID** = s.**ID**
PROPAGATE t.swissprot TO ID,
    s.ID TO ID, p.Name TO Name,
    s.Desc TO Desc, s'.**ID** TO **ID**

$Q_3 =$
SELECT DISTINCT
    t.swissprot AS ID,
    p.Name AS Name,
    s.Desc AS Desc
FROM Mapping_Table t, SWISS-PROT s,
    PIR p, **SWISS-PROT** s'
WHERE t.swissprot = s.ID AND
    t.pir = p.ID, s'.**Desc** = s.**Desc**
PROPAGATE t.swissprot TO ID,
    s.ID TO ID, p.Name TO Name,
    s.Desc TO Desc, s'.**Desc** TO **Desc**

$Q_4 =$
SELECT DISTINCT
    t.swissprot AS ID,
    p.Name AS Name,
    s.Desc AS Desc
FROM Mapping_Table t, SWISS-PROT s,
    PIR p, **PIR** p'
WHERE t.swissprot = s.ID AND
    t.pir = p.ID, p'.**Name** = p.**Name**
PROPAGATE t.swissprot TO ID,
    s.ID TO ID, p.Name TO Name,
    s.Desc TO Desc, p'.**Name** TO **Name**

Figure 2: Some of the auxiliary queries generated by Step 2 of Generate-Query-Basis on Example 3.1.

equalities between attributes in the *wherelist* of Q are represented by using the same variable in the respective positions of relations in the conjunctive query-like representation of Q. An equality between an attribute and constant is written out as *equalities*. The head of the query $A(\mathbf{x})$ represents the *selectlist* of Q. We use $C(Q)$ to denote the conjunctive query-like representation of the SQL query that corresponds to Q. For example, $C(Q)$ of Example 3.1 can be written as

$A_0(x, y, z)$:- Mapping_Table(w, x, u, v), SWISS-PROT(x, z), PIR(u, y).

Similar to the semantics of pSQL queries with the default propagation scheme, annotations are propagated according to where data is copied from for such queries [24] by tracing the occurrence of distinguished variables in the query. For example, by tracing the occurrence of the variable x in the query A_0, we can conclude that the annotations in the first column of an output tuple t is obtained from the annotations of the second column of a tuple in Mapping_Table and the first column of a tuple in SWISS-PROT that created t. A similar argument applies to the variables y and z in A_0. Hence, the representative query Q_0 of Example 3.1 is annotation-equivalent to A_0.

Proposition 3.1 *The representative query Q_0 that is generated by Generate-Query-Basis(Q) is annotation-equivalent to $C(Q_0)$.*

In Step 2 the algorithm generates one query for every position in the body where a distinguished variable occurs in A_0. For example, the following four auxiliary queries, in conjunctive query notation, are generated based on A_0. They are annotation-equivalent to the pSQL query fragments $Q_1, ..., Q_4$ shown in Example 3.1 and Figure 2, respectively.

$A_1(x, y, z)$:- Mapping_Table(w, x, u, v), SWISS-PROT(x, z), PIR(u, y), **Mapping_Table**(w_1, x, w_2, w_3).

$A_2(x, y, z)$:- Mapping_Table(w, x, u, v), SWISS-PROT(x, z), PIR(u, y), **SWISS-PROT**(x, w_1).

$A_3(x, y, z)$:- Mapping_Table(w, x, u, v), SWISS-PROT(x, z), PIR(u, y), **SWISS-PROT**(w_1, z).

$A_4(x, y, z)$:- Mapping_Table(w, x, u, v), SWISS-PROT(x, z), PIR(u, y), **PIR**(w_1, y).

Proposition 3.2 *For every query Q' in the result of Generate-Query-Basis(Q) (denoted as $\mathcal{B}(Q)$), $C(Q')$ is annotation-contained in $\bigcup_{q \in \mathcal{B}(Q)} q$.*

Each auxiliary query carries annotations to the output that may have been missed by the representative query of Q. We shall show next that the set of pSQL query fragments in $\mathcal{B}(Q)$ generated by the algorithm is a query basis for Q. We first prove the following lemma.

Lemma 3.1 *Let $\mathcal{B}(Q)$ denote the result of Generate-Query-Basis(Q) where Q is a pSQL query fragment and let Q' denote a pSQL query fragment under the default propagation scheme. If Q' is equivalent to Q, then Q' is annotation-contained in $\bigcup_{q \in \mathcal{B}(Q)} q$.*

Proof. We know from Proposition 3.1 that the representative query Q_0 that is generated at Step 1 of the algorithm is annotation-equivalent to the conjunctive query representation of the SQL query that corresponds to Q, $C(Q)$. We can also easily verify that $Q' \subseteq_a C(Q')$. Since $C(Q)$ and $C(Q')$ are equivalent queries, the minimal queries of $C(Q)$ and $C(Q')$ are identical up to variable renaming. For convenience, we shall assume that the minimal queries are identical in the form shown below. We also assume that there are no equalities between variables and constants, for convenience.

$C(Q)$: $H(\mathbf{x})$:- *minpart, rest1*.

$C(Q')$: $H(\mathbf{x})$:- *minpart, rest2*.

The subgoals denoted by *minpart* are the subgoals in the minimal query of $C(Q)$ or $C(Q')$ and *rest1* and *rest2* denote the rest of the subgoals in $C(Q)$ and $C(Q')$, respectively. Our proof makes use of an earlier result in [24] extended for unions of conjunctive queries. Given a conjunctive query Q, we use the notation $Q[0]$ to denote the head of Q, the notation $Q[i]$, $i > 0$, to denote the ith subgoal of Q, and var$(Q[i])$ to denote the list of variables of the ith subgoal of Q.

Fact 1 ([24]) *Given two unions of conjunctive queries $Q = \bigcup_{i=1}^{m} Q_i$ and $Q' = \bigcup_{j=1}^{n} Q'_j$, $Q \subseteq_a Q'$ if and only if for every Q_r, $r \in [1, m]$, and every variable x that occurs at both the ith position of var$(Q_r[0])$ and the jth position of var$(Q_r[p])$ for some p, there exists a homomorphism h from Q'_s (for some $s \in [1, n]$) to Q_r such that*

1. *h maps the body of Q'_s into the body of Q_r and the head of Q'_s to the head of Q_r, and*

2. *the variable that occurs at the jth position of the qth subgoal of Q'_s (i.e., var$(Q'_s[q])[j]$) is identical to the*

variable at the ith position of the head of Q'_s (i.e., $\text{var}(Q'_s[0])[i]$), where $Q'_s[q]$ is a pre-image of $Q_r[p]$ under h. That is, for some subgoal q, $\text{var}(Q'_s[q])[j] = \text{var}(Q'_s[0])[i]$ and $h(Q'_s[q]) = Q_r[p]$.

We shall show that for every distinguished variable x at the ith position in the head of $C(Q')$ and its occurrence at the jth position of the pth subgoal $S(\mathbf{u})$ (i.e., the jth variable of $\mathbf{u}$ is x) in the body of $C(Q')$, there is a generated query Q_g in $\mathcal{B}(Q)$ and a homomorphism $h : C(Q_g) \to C(Q')$ that satisfies the conditions (1) and (2) stated in the fact. Then by the above fact, we have $C(Q') \subseteq_a C(Q_g)$. We know that $C(Q_g) \subseteq_a \bigcup_{q \in \mathcal{B}(Q)} q$ from Proposition 3.2. Therefore $C(Q') \subseteq_a \bigcup_{q \in \mathcal{B}(Q)} q$. Since $Q' \subseteq_a C(Q')$ and $C(Q') \subseteq_a \bigcup_{q \in \mathcal{B}(Q)} q$, we have $Q' \subseteq_a \bigcup_{q \in \mathcal{B}(Q)} q$.

Let x be a distinguished variable at the ith position in the head of $C(Q')$ and suppose x occurs at the jth position of the pth subgoal $S(\mathbf{u})$ of $C(Q')$. If $S(\mathbf{u})$ is among the subgoals in the *minpart* of $C(Q')$, then it must also be among the subgoals in the *minpart* of $C(Q)$. Hence the algorithm Generate-Query-Basis would have generated one or more queries whose combined effect is the query $C(Q_g)$, shown below,

$H(\mathbf{x}) :\text{-} \textit{minpart}, \textit{rest1}, S(\mathbf{w_1}, x, \mathbf{w_2}).$

(The variable x occurs at the jth position in the subgoal $S(\mathbf{w_1}, x, \mathbf{w_2})$ and $\mathbf{w_1}$ and $\mathbf{w_2}$ are vectors of distinct variables that do not occur in $C(Q)$.) This corresponds to Step 2 of the algorithm where a new relation S is added to the FROM clause and clauses of the form "B TO A" are added to the PROPAGATE clause to simulate the effect of x propagating annotations to the output. We assume that x occurs under the attribute A in the output and B is the attribute name of x in S in the named perspective. If x occurs under another attribute D in the output of $C(Q_g)$, there will be another query generated by Step 2 of the algorithm that propagates the annotations of B to D. Hence, there is possible more than one pSQL query whose combined annotation propagation effect equals that of $C(Q_g)$.

It is easy to see that there is a homomorphism from $C(Q_g)$ to $C(Q')$ with the desired properties required by the fact shown above. The homomorphism is obtained by extending the homomorphism $h' : C(Q) \to C(Q')$ which we know exists since $C(Q) = C(Q')$. The homomorphism h' is extended to h'' by mapping the ith variable in $\mathbf{w_1}$ to the corresponding ith variable in $\mathbf{u}$ and the ith variable in $\mathbf{w_2}$ to the $(j + i)$th variable in $\mathbf{u}$ (this is possible since $\mathbf{w_1}$ and $\mathbf{w_2}$ are distinct variables). Clearly, h'' satisfies the conditions required by the above fact. If $S(\mathbf{u})$ are among the subgoals in *rest2* of $C(Q')$, we first claim that a subgoal $S(\mathbf{u}')$, where the jth variable of u' is x, must also occur among subgoals in the *minpart* of Q'. With this, a similar argument presented before shows that there must be a homomorphism from a query $C(Q_g)$ to $C(Q')$ with the desired conditions required by the above fact and hence, $C(Q') \subseteq_a C(Q_g)$. Since the annotation propagation behavior of $C(Q_g)$ is equal to the combined annotation propagation effect of one or more queries in $\bigcup_{q \in \mathcal{B}(Q)} q$, we have $C(Q_g) \subseteq_a \bigcup_{q \in \mathcal{B}(Q)} q$.

Figure 3: Architecture of our system.

We show next that if $S(\mathbf{u})$ are among the subgoals in *rest2* of $C(Q')$, there must exist such a subgoal $S(\mathbf{u}')$ among the *minpart* of $C(Q')$. Since there is a homomorphism g from $C(Q')$ to the minimal query of $C(Q')$ and $g(x) = x$ (since x is a distinguished variable), this implies that there must be a subgoal $S(...x...)$ among the subgoals in the *minpart* of $C(Q')$ such that x occurs at the jth position of this subgoal. We therefore conclude that $S(\mathbf{u}')$ exists. ∎

Theorem 3.2 *Let Q be a pSQL query fragment with default-all propagation scheme. The algorithm Generate-Query-Basis(Q) returns a query basis of Q.*

Proof. Let $\mathcal{E}(Q)$ denote the set of pSQL query fragments q under the default propagation scheme such that the SQL query that corresponds to q is equivalent to that of Q (i.e., $S(q) = S(Q)$). Let $\mathcal{B}(Q)$ denote the result of running the algorithm Generate-Query-Basis on Q. By Lemma 3.1, $\bigcup_{q \in \mathcal{E}(Q)} q \subseteq_a \bigcup_{q \in \mathcal{B}(Q)} q$. Since $\mathcal{B}(Q) \subseteq \mathcal{E}(Q)$, we immediately have $\bigcup_{q \in \mathcal{B}(Q)} q \subseteq_a \bigcup_{q \in \mathcal{E}(Q)} q$ and hence the result. ∎

Proposition 3.3 *Given a pSQL query fragment Q with the default-all propagation scheme, the number of queries returned by Generate-Query-Basis(Q) is polynomial in the size of Q. Furthermore, each query in Generate-Query-Basis(Q) is polynomial in the size of Q.*

An optmization Observe that the auxiliary pSQL queries overlap significantly in the PROPAGATE clauses (e.g., see Figure 2); they differ only in the last (highlighted) propagation. In fact, we show that the non-highlighted propagations in the auxiliary queries are unnecessary (the details are omitted). Intuitively, they are unnecessary because these propagations are identical to the propagations of the representative query Q_0. Hence, in our *optimized* implementation of Generate-Query-Basis, these non-highlighted propagations are not generated in the auxiliary queries. We refer to our original implementation of algorithm Generate-Query-Basis as the *unoptimized* implementation.

4 System Architecture

The architecture of our Annotation Management System is illustrated in Figure 3. We have two main modules: the translator module and the postprocessor module. The translator module takes as input a pSQL query and returns as output an SQL query (i.e., a union of SPJ queries) which is sent to the RDBMS. The SQL query is then executed by the RDBMS. The tuples that are returned by the RDBMS are sorted in a certain order and sent to the postprocessor module which merges annotations of identical cells of duplicate tuples together in one pass through the returned tuples.

4.1 A Naive Storage Scheme

At present, we store our annotations using a naive storage scheme: we assume that every attribute A of a relation scheme R has an extra column A_a that will be used to store annotations. We denote this new relation with extra columns as R'. For example, a relation $R(A, B)$ will be represented as $R'(A, A_a, B, B_a)$ in the naive storage scheme. Given a tuple t in a relation of R, if $\{a_1, ..., a_k\}$ are the annotations associated with the location (t, A), then there will be k tuples $t_1, ..., t_k$ in R' such that $t_i.A_a = a_i$ for $i \in [1, k]$ and $t_i.R = t$, $i \in [1, k]$ where $t_i.R$ denotes the projection of t_i on the attributes of R. For convenience, we sometimes use the relation name R to refer to R'. As an example, the two instances of R shown below are both valid representations of the tuple (a $\{a_1, a_2\}$, b $\{b_1\}$).

A	A_a	B	B_a
a	a_1	b	b_1
a	a_2	b	—

A	A_a	B	B_a
a	a_1	b	—
a	a_2	b	—
a	a_2	b	b_1

Observe that a query returns the same result regardless of the underlying storage instance used. In the case where every cell has a distinct annotation that denotes its address, then one could define R as a view definition of R using the internal row identifier used in many database systems such as Oracle and Postgres.

4.2 The Translator

The translator module takes as input a pSQL query Q and translates Q to an SQL query Q' against the naive storage scheme. A pSQL query with default or default-all propagation scheme is first reformulated into one with a custom propagation scheme. A pSQL query with the custom propagation scheme is reformulated into an SQL query (i.e., a union of SPJ queries). The algorithm for reformulating a pSQL query fragment with default propagation scheme into a pSQL fragment with custom propagation scheme is described briefly at the end of Section 2.2. The algorithm for reformulating a pSQL query fragment with default-all propagation scheme into a pSQL query fragment with custom propagation scheme is described by the Generate-Query-Basis algorithm in Section 2.3. We describe next the algorithm for reformulating a pSQL query with custom propagation scheme into an SQL query.

Algorithm Custom-pSQL-To-SQL

Input: A pSQL query fragment Q with custom propagation scheme.
Output: An SQL query Q_s written against the naive schema.

Let Q be a pSQL query fragment of the form shown in Definition 2.1 with a *custom-propagatelist*.

1. *Generate intermediate SQL queries.* Each intermediate SQL query retrieves annotations (as much as possible) from the naive schema according to the given query Q.

   Let Q_0 be a query that is identical to Q except that it does not have the PROPAGATE clause of Q.

   For each output attribute C of Q, create an empty bin for C. Denote this bin as bin(C). For each propagate clause "$s.B$ TO C" in the *custom-propagatelist* of Q, add "$s.B_a$ AS C_a" to bin(C).

   Let $\mathcal{Q}$ be the empty set of SQL queries. Repeat until all bins are empty:

   Let Q' be a query that is identical to Q_0. For each output attribute C of Q, if bin(C) is nonempty, remove a clause "$s.B_a$ AS C_a" from bin(C) and add it to the *selectlist* of Q'. If bin(C) is empty, we add 'NULL AS C_a" to the *selectlist* of Q'. Add Q' to $\mathcal{Q}$.

2. *Generate a wrapper SQL query Q_s for $\mathcal{Q}$*.
   SELECT DISTINCT *
   FROM   (Q_1 UNION $\cdots$ UNION Q_n)
   ORDER BY   orderbylist

   where $\mathcal{Q} = \{Q_1, ..., Q_n\}$ and *orderbylist* is the list of all output attributes in the *selectlist* of Q. The *orderbylist* is required so that the Postprocessor can merge annotations of identical tuples together with one pass over the result of Q_s.

3. *Return Q_s*.

Example 4.1 Consider the SWISS-PROT relation of Figure 1 and assume that there is an extra attribute Size. Suppose we have the following pSQL query Q with custom propagation scheme written against SWISS-PROT:

SELECT s.ID AS ID, s.Desc AS Desc, s.Size AS Size,
FROM   SWISS-PROT s
PROPAGATE s.ID TO Desc, s.Desc TO Desc,
           s.Size TO Size,

Observe that every tuple in SWISS-PROT will be emitted in such a way that the set of annotations associated with the Desc column of a tuple in the output is the union of annotations associated with both ID and Desc of the corresponding tuple in SWISS-PROT. Furthermore, the annotations associated with the Size column of a tuple are the same annotations associated with the Size column of the corresponding tuple in SWISS-PROT and the column ID of every tuple in the output does not carry any annotations.

In step 1 of algorithm Custom-pSQL-To-SQL, the following two intermediate SQL queries are generated since bin(ID) is empty, bin(Desc) = { s.ID$_a$ AS Desc$_a$, s.Desc$_a$ AS Desc$_a$} and bin(Size) = { s.Size$_a$ AS Size$_a$ }.

$Q_1 =$ SELECT s.ID AS ID, NULL AS ID$_a$
                 s.Desc AS Desc, s.ID$_a$ AS Desc$_a$,
                 s.Size AS Size, s.Size$_a$ AS Size$_a$,
         FROM   SWISS-PROT s

$Q_2 =$ SELECT s.ID AS ID, NULL AS ID$_a$
                 s.Desc AS Desc, s.Desc$_a$ AS Desc$_a$,
                 s.Size AS Size, NULL AS Size$_a$,
         FROM   SWISS-PROT s

In step 2, the algorithm generates the following wrapper SQL query:

$Q_s =$ SELECT DISTINCT *
         FROM   (Q_1 UNION Q_2)
         ORDER BY   ID, Desc, Size

Observe that Q_1 and Q_2 are unioned and the result is sorted according to the attributes in the *selectlist* of Q. The tuples are sorted according to the *selectlist* of Q so that the Postprocessor can merge annotations associated with identical cells in the output of Q in one pass over the result

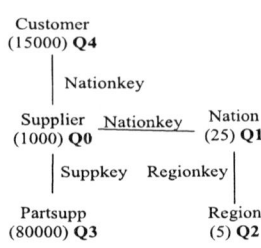
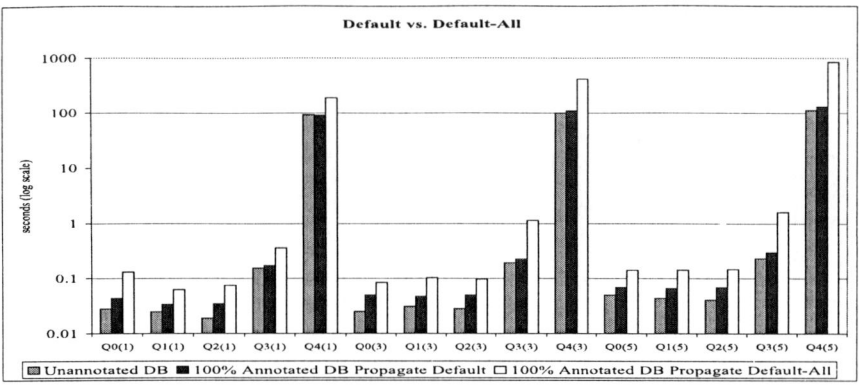

Figure 4: Queries used in our experiments and comparison in performance for 100MB, 100% annotated TPCH database.

of Q_s. Observe also that the number of SQL queries in Q is equal to the maximum bin size. ∎

4.3 The Postprocessor

The Postprocessor scans the set of tuples returned by the RDBMS and unions together the annotations from duplicate tuples for proper display. This operation is done in linear time in the number and size of tuples retrieved, provided that the set of emitted tuples is already sorted. For example, if the postprocessor receives the first table of Section 4.1 as input, it returns { (a $\{a_1, a_2\}$, b $\{b_1\}$) }.

5 Experimental Evaluation

We conducted several experiments to evaluate the feasibility of our annotation management system. Our main goal is to compare the performance of queries under different propagation schemes (default, default-all, or no propagation scheme (i.e., SQL queries)) and to compare the performance of queries when the number of annotations in a database is varied.

Setup We have implemented our system on top of Oracle 9i Enterprise Edition. For our experiments we used 100MB TPCH database (and subsequently 500MB and 1GB TPCH databases), which we call unannotated database. We have also modified TPCH schema to conform to our naive storage scheme by adding an additional attribute for every attribute of every relation in the TPCH schema. We have created three different instances of the modified TPCH database schema corresponding to 30%, 60% and 100% annotated databases. A 30% annotated database means 30% of the total number of cells in every relation instance of the database will contain one annotation. We ran queries of increasing join sizes to determine how well our system scales for this type of queries. (We did not use TPCH queries in our experiments because they include aggregates and nested queries.) The queries $Q_0, ..., Q_4$ denote queries with zero to four joins, respectively, and are shown on the left of Figure 4. For example, Q_2 denotes the query Supplier ⋈ Nation ⋈ Region with two joins, on the attributes Nationkey and Regionkey respectively. The cardinality of each relation is shown in brackets. Our experiments are conducted on a Pentium 4, 2.8GHz machine with 1GB RAM.

Experiments We first measure the performance of our system for queries under the default and default-all propagation scheme on the 100% annotated database. We have implemented and tested both optimized as well as unoptimized versions of our Generate-Query-Basis algorithm. For space reasons we present only our results obtained with the optimized version, as we observed that it consistently and significantly outperforms the unoptimized version. We executed queries $Q_i(1), Q_i(3), Q_i(5), i \in [0, 4]$, which denote queries with i joins and one, three, and five output attributes, respectively. We also executed the SQL query that corresponds to each of these queries on the unannotated database. The results are shown in Figure 4.

Figure 4 illustrates the execution time (the total time taken by the translator, RDBMS, and postprocessor to emit all tuples in the result) of each query for the default and default-all propagation schemes for the 100MB and 100% annotated TPCH database. As expected, the execution time of each query under the default scheme (respectively, default-all scheme) increases slightly as more output attributes are emitted (see, for instance, $Q_0(1)$, $Q_0(3)$, and $Q_0(5)$). The increase in time is due to longer execution time taken by Oracle as well as additional overhead incurred in postprocessing, as more attributes of different tuples need to be compared. Additionally, for the default-all scheme, the number of SPJ queries that are sent to Oracle increases (2, 4, and 6 SPJ queries, respectively) as the number of output attributes increases. Table 1 provides the exact execution times of each query for 100% annotated database and the number of SPJ queries that are generated for the default all-scheme. We note that in the worst case, a query such as $Q_4(5)$ may run about 8 times slower than both the query with default scheme and the actual SQL query. This is not unexpected, however, as there are 6 SPJ queries, each with four joins, that are generated and sent to Oracle for $Q_4(5)$, instead of 1. In the best case (see $Q_4(1)$), a query with default-all scheme runs about twice as slow than the same query with default scheme. We note however that for the default scheme, the execution times of pSQL queries are comparable to those of SQL queries. On

Query	Unannotated	30% Def	30% Def-All	60% Def	60% Def-All	100% Def	100% Def-All	#pSQL	#SPJ
$Q_0(1)$	0.0282	0.0374	0.1316	0.0408	0.125	0.0438	0.1308	2	2
$Q_1(1)$	0.025	0.0344	0.0658	0.034	0.072	0.034	0.0624	2	2
$Q_2(1)$	0.019	0.0312	0.0722	0.0342	0.0748	0.0346	0.075	2	2
$Q_3(1)$	0.1532	0.1752	0.3622	0.1688	0.3594	0.1718	0.356	2	2
$Q_4(1)$	92.4604	92.2198	190.7312	91.7214	190.826	91.2248	190.3552	2	2
$Q_0(3)$	0.0252	0.0468	0.0848	0.0468	0.084	0.05	0.084	4	4
$Q_1(3)$	0.0312	0.0502	0.0968	0.0374	0.0968	0.047	0.103	4	4
$Q_2(3)$	0.0284	0.0502	0.1002	0.0562	0.0998	0.05	0.0968	4	4
$Q_3(3)$	0.191	0.219	1.1186	0.2216	1.1188	0.225	1.1314	4	4
$Q_4(3)$	100.0106	113.4292	422.6232	108.2372	424.6066	109.012	419.5722	4	4
$Q_0(5)$	0.0502	0.069	0.1372	0.072	0.1438	0.069	0.1404	6	6
$Q_1(5)$	0.0438	0.0654	0.138	0.0718	0.1312	0.0658	0.1412	6	6
$Q_2(5)$	0.0406	0.0662	0.1498	0.0658	0.1468	0.0688	0.1466	6	6
$Q_3(5)$	0.231	0.287	1.6128	0.2908	1.6096	0.2968	1.6064	6	6
$Q_4(5)$	111.8918	131.3138	858.8238	130.5282	836.5362	130.6594	850.6284	6	6

Table 1: The execution times of each query for each database and propagation scheme. The columns "#pSQL" and "#SPJ" denote the size of the query basis and number of SPJ queries that are generated, respectively, for the default-all scheme.

the average, the pSQL queries with default scheme that we experimented with took around 40% more time to execute than their corresponding SQL queries, and at best the execution time of a pSQL query with default scheme is the same as the execution time of its corresponding SQL query (e.g., $Q_4(1)$). For larger databases (500MB and 1GB), the pSQL queries with default scheme took only about 18% more time to execute than their corresponding SQL queries on the average (these results are not shown).

Subsequently, we also conducted the same experiments on 30% and 60% 100MB annotated databases. The results are tabulated in Table 1. We observe that the execution time of each query increases only slightly across different databases. For example, the execution time of each query for both default and default-all scheme increases marginally when the number of annotations in the database is doubled from 30% annotations to 60%. We also remark that for the default-all scheme there is no increase in the number of pSQL and SPJ queries that are generated when the number of joins increases because the attributes that are selected do not participate in the joins. The number of pSQL and SPJ queries that are generated increases when the number of output attributes increases and they increase linearly. The execution times of $Q_1(j)$, $j \in [1,3,5]$, decreases slightly when compared with $Q_0(j)$ because a join on a small relation has been made.

We also ran the same set of experiments (results are not shown) on 500Mb and 1GB TPCH databases with 30%, 60% and 100% annotations and we observed the same trend as in Figure 4. All our results indicate that the time required to translate the queries is insignificant when compared to the execution time of the queries and the postprocessing time of the queries is proportional to the number and size of emitted tuples. Also, the execution times of default queries are comparable to the performance of SQL queries since only one SPJ is generated.

6 Discussion

So far, our pSQL queries do not allow aggregates and bag semantics (i.e., the DISTINCT keyword must be present).

We discuss briefly next how we might extend pSQL to handle aggregates and bag queries as well.

Aggregates For the default propagation scheme, if a pSQL query contains aggregates such as count, sum, and average, we assume the semantics that no annotations are associated with the result of these aggregates, since these aggregate values are not copied from any source values. However, for aggregates such as $\min(a)$ and $\max(a)$, where a is an attribute name, our semantics is that the annotations associated with the location of the resulting min (or max) value are the union of all annotations of the corresponding a-values whose value equals to the min (or max) value. It remains to investigate whether the default-all propagation scheme for pSQL queries with aggregates can be achieved.

Bag semantics It is known from [8] that two conjunctive queries are equivalent under bag semantics if and only if they are isomorphic. This result of [8] implies that to propagate annotations for a pSQL query under the default-all propagation scheme and bag semantics, it suffices to generate only the representative query of that pSQL query in Algorithm Generate-Query-Basis. To handle bag queries, however, the naive storage scheme can no longer be used since the multiplicity of a tuple in this storage scheme depends on the number of annotations that are associated with that tuple. An alternative storage scheme that does not modify the original relation is needed (e.g., store every annotation and its location in a separate relation). To propagate annotations under the default-all propagation scheme and bag semantics for unions of conjunctive queries, however, it remains to first provide a characterization of bag equivalence for unions of conjunctive queries.

7 Conclusion and Future Work

We have described an implementation of an annotation management system where different propagation schemes can be used. Insofar, our system only supports annotations on attributes of tuples. We would like to extend our system to handle annotations on tuples or relations and, in general, to handle annotations on hierarchical data, such as XML. In our current system, annotations are propagated based on where-provenance. In addition, we would like to extend our system to propagate annotations based on why-provenance, which will provide reasons to why a tuple is in the output. The default-all propagation scheme returns the union of all annotations of an output location returned by all equivalent queries. Conceivably, there could be a complementary propagation scheme that returns the set of all annotations in an output location if it occurs in the same output location in the results of all equivalent queries. It remains to be investigated whether a query basis can be generated for such propagation scheme. The performance of our annotation management system on other storage schemes also needs to be investigated. It would also be interesting to investigate opportunities for optimizations on the generated SQL queries.

Acknowledgements We thank Xinyu Hua for her help during the initial implementation of this system and Ariel Fuxman for helpful suggestions.

References

[1] S. Abiteboul, R. Hull, and V. Vianu. *Foundations of Databases*. Addison Wesley Publishing Co, 1995.

[2] R. Apweiler, A. Bairoch, C. Wu, W. Barker, B. Boeckmann, S. Ferro, E. Gasteiger, H. Huang, R. Lopez, M. Magrane, M. Martin, D. Natale, C. O'Donovan, N. Redaschi, and L. Yeh. Uniprot: the universal protein knowledgebase. *Nucleic Acids Research*, 32:D115–D119, 2004.

[3] A. Bairoch and R. Apweiler. The SWISS-PROT protein sequence database and its supplement TrEMBL. *Nucleic Acids Research*, 28:45–48, 2000.

[4] P. Bernstein and T. Bergstraesser. Meta-Data Support for Data Transformations Using Microsoft Repository. *IEEE Data Engineering Bulletin*, 22(1):9–14, 1999.

[5] biodas.org. http://biodas.org.

[6] P. Buneman, S. Khanna, and W. Tan. Why and Where: A Characterization of Data Provenance. In *Proceedings of the International Conference on Database Theory (ICDT)*, pages 316–330, London, United Kingdom, 2001.

[7] P. Buneman, S. Khanna, and W. Tan. On Propagation of Deletions and Annotations Through Views. In *Proceedings of the ACM Symposium on Principles of Database Systems (PODS)*, pages 150–158, Wisconsin, Madison, 2002.

[8] S. Chaudhuri and M. Y. Vardi. Optimization of *real* conjunctive queries. In *Proceedings of the ACM Symposium on Principles of Database Systems (PODS)*, pages 59–70, Washington, DC, 1993.

[9] Y. Cui, J. Widom, and J. Wiener. Tracing the Lineage of View Data in a Warehousing Environment. *ACM Transactions on Database Systems (TODS)*, 25(2):179–227, 2000.

[10] DBCAT, The Public Catalog of Databases. http://www.infobiogen.fr/services/dbcat/, cited 5 June 2000.

[11] D. E. Denning, T. F. Lunt, R. R. Schell, W. R. Shockley, and M. Heckman. The SeaView Security Model. In *IEEE Symposium on Security and Privacy*, pages 218–233, Washington, DC, 1988.

[12] R. Dowell. A Distributed Annotation System. Technical report, Department of Computer Science, Washington University in St. Louis, 2001.

[13] S. Jajodia and R. S. Sandhu. Polyinstantiation integrity in multilevel relations. In *IEEE Symposium on Security and Privacy*, pages 104–115, Oakland, California, 1990.

[14] J. Kahan, M. Koivunen, E. Prud'Hommeaux, and R. Swick. Annotea: An open rdf infrastructure for shared web annotations. In *Proceedings of the International World Wide Web Conference(WWW10)*, pages 623–632, Hong Kong, China, 2001.

[15] A. Kementseitsidis, M. Arenas, and R. J. Miller. Mapping Data in Peer-to-Peer Systems: Semantics and Algorithmic Issues. In *Proceedings of the ACM SIGMOD International Conference on Management of Data (SIGMOD)*, pages 325–336, San Diego, CA, 2003.

[16] W. J. Kent, C. W. Sugnet, T. S. Furey, K. M. Roskin, T. H. Pringle, A. M. Zahler, and D. Haussler. The Human Genome Browser at UCSC. *Genome Research*, 12(5):996–1006, 2002.

[17] D. LaLiberte and A. Braverman. A Protocol for Scalable Group and Public Annotations. In *Proceedings of the International World Wide Web Conference(WWW3)*, Darmstadt, Germany, 1995.

[18] T. Lee, S. Bressan, and S. Madnick. Source Attribution for Querying Against Semi-structured Documents. In *Workshop on Web Information and Data Management (WIDM)*, Washington, DC, 1998.

[19] A. C. Myers and B. Liskov. A decentralized model for information control. In *Proceedings of the ACM Symposium on Operating Systems Principles (SOSP)*, pages 129–142, Saint-Malo, France, 1997.

[20] T. A. Phelps and R. Wilensky. Multivalent Annotations. In *Proceedings of the First European Conference on Research and Advanced Technology for Digital Libraries*, pages 287–303, Pisa, Italy, 1997.

[21] T. A. Phelps and R. Wilensky. Multivalent documents. *Proceedings of the Communications of the Association for Computing Machinery (CACM)*, 43(6):82–90, 2000.

[22] T. A. Phelps and R. Wilensky. Robust intra-document locations. In *Proceedings of the International World Wide Web Conference(WWW9)*, pages 105–118, Amsterdam, Netherlands, 2000.

[23] M. A. Schickler, M. S. Mazer, and C. Brooks. Pan-Browser Support for Annotations and Other Meta-Information on the World Wide Web. In *Proceedings of the International World Wide Web Conference(WWW5)*, Paris, France, 1996.

[24] W. Tan. Containment of relational queries with annotation propagation. In *Proceedings of the International Workshop on Database and Programming Languages (DBPL)*, Potsdam, Germany, 2003.

[25] W3C. Annotea Project. http://www.w3.org/2001/Annotea.

[26] Y. R. Wang and S. E. Madnick. A Polygon Model for Heterogeneous Database Systems: The Source Tagging Perspective. In *Proceedings of the International Conference on Very Large Data Bases (VLDB)*, pages 519–538, Brisbane, Queensland, Australia, 1990.

Symmetric Relations and Cardinality-Bounded Multisets in Database Systems

Kenneth A. Ross   Julia Stoyanovich

Columbia University*
kar@cs.columbia.edu, jds1@cs.columbia.edu

Abstract

In a binary symmetric relationship, A is related to B if and only if B is related to A. Symmetric relationships between k participating entities can be represented as multisets of cardinality k. Cardinality-bounded multisets are natural in several real-world applications. Conventional representations in relational databases suffer from several consistency and performance problems. We argue that the database system itself should provide native support for cardinality-bounded multisets. We provide techniques to be implemented by the database engine that avoid the drawbacks, and allow a schema designer to simply declare a table to be symmetric in certain attributes. We describe a compact data structure, and update methods for the structure. We describe an algebraic symmetric closure operator, and show how it can be moved around in a query plan during query optimization in order to improve performance. We describe indexing methods that allow efficient lookups on the symmetric columns. We show how to perform database normalization in the presence of symmetric relations. We provide techniques for inferring that a view is symmetric. We also describe a syntactic SQL extension that allows the succinct formulation of queries over symmetric relations.

---

*This research was supported by NSF grants IIS-0120939 and IIS-0121239.

Permission to copy without fee all or part of this material is granted provided that the copies are not made or distributed for direct commercial advantage, the VLDB copyright notice and the title of the publication and its date appear, and notice is given that copying is by permission of the Very Large Data Base Endowment. To copy otherwise, or to republish, requires a fee and/or special permission from the Endowment.

**Proceedings of the 30th VLDB Conference,
Toronto, Canada, 2004**

1 Introduction

A relation R is *symmetric* in its first two attributes if $R(x_1, x_2, \ldots, x_n)$ holds if and only if $R(x_2, x_1, \ldots, x_n)$ holds. We call $R(x_2, x_1, \ldots, x_n)$ the *symmetric complement* of $R(x_1, x_2, \ldots, x_n)$. Symmetric relations come up naturally in several contexts when the real-world relationship being modeled is itself symmetric.

Example 1.1 *In a law-enforcement database recording meetings between pairs of individuals under investigation, the "meets" relationship is symmetric.* □

Example 1.2 *Consider a database of web pages. The relationship "X is linked to Y" (by either a forward or backward link) between pairs of web pages is symmetric. This relationship is neither reflexive nor antireflexive, i.e., "X is linked to X" is neither universally true nor universally false. While an underlying relation representing the direction of the links would normally be maintained, a view defining the "is linked to" relation would be useful, allowing the succinct specification of queries involving a sequence of undirected links.* □

Example 1.3 *Views that relate entities sharing a common property, such as pairs of people living in the same city, will generally define a symmetric relation between those entities.* □

Example 1.4 *Example 1.1 can be generalized to allow meetings of up to k people. The k-ary meeting relationship would be symmetric in the sense that if $P = (p_1, \ldots, p_k)$ is in the relationship, then so is any column-permutation of P.* □

Example 1.5 *Consider a database recording what television channel various viewers watch most during the 24 hourly timeslots of the day.[1] For performance reasons,[2] the database uses a table*

---

[1] This example is based on a real-world application developed by one of the authors, in which there were actually 96 fifteen-minute slots.

[2] A conventional representation as a set of slots would require a 24-way join to reconstruct V.

$V(ID, ViewDate, C_1, \ldots, C_{24})$ to record the viewer (identified by ID), the date, and the twenty-four channels most watched, one channel for each hour of the day. This table V is not symmetric, because C_i is not interchangeable with C_j: C_i reflects what the viewer was watching at timeslot number i. Nevertheless, there are interesting queries that could be posed for which this semantic difference is unimportant. An example might be "Find viewers who have watched channels 2 and 4, but not channel 5." For these queries, it could be beneficial to treat V as a symmetric relation in order to have access to query plans that are specialized to symmetric relations. □

There is a natural isomorphism between symmetric relationships among k entities, and k-element multisets.[3] We phrase our results in terms of "symmetric relations" to emphasize the column-oriented nature of the data representation in which columns are interchangeable. Nevertheless, our results are equally valid if expressed in terms of "bounded-cardinality multisets".

Sets and multisets have a wide range of uses for representing information in databases. Bounded cardinality multisets would be useful for applications in which there is a natural limit to the size of multisets. This limit could be implicit in the application (e.g., the number of players in a baseball team), or defined as a conservative bound (e.g., the number of children belonging to a parent). We will demonstrate performance advantages for bounded-element multisets compared with conventional relational representations of (unbounded) multisets.

Storing a symmetric relation in a conventional database system can be done in a number of possible ways. Storing the full symmetric relation induces some redundancy in the database: more space is required (up to a factor of $k!$ for k-ary relationships), and integrity constraints need to be enforced to ensure consistency of updates. Updates need to be aware of the symmetry of the table, and to add the various column permutations to all insertions and deletions. Queries need to perform I/O for tuples and their permutations, increasing the time needed for query processing.

Alternatively, a database schema designer could recognize that the relation was symmetric and code database procedures to store only one representative tuple for each group of permuted tuples. A view can then be defined to present the symmetric closure of the stored relation for query processing. The update problem remains, because updates through this view would be ambiguous. Updates to the underlying table would need to be aware of the symmetry, to avoid storing multiple permutations of a tuple, and to perform a deletion correctly. For symmetric relations over k columns, just defining the view (using standard SQL) requires a query of length proportional to $k(k!)$.

[3] A multiset is a set except that duplicates are allowed.

For both of the above proposals, indexed access to an underlying symmetric relationship would require multiple index lookups, one for each symmetric column.

A third alternative is to model a symmetric relation as a set [3] or multiset. Instead of recording both $R(a, b, c, d, e)$ and $R(b, a, c, d, e)$, one could record $R'(q, c, d, e)$, $S(a, q)$, and $S(b, q)$, where q is a new surrogate identifier, and R' and S are new tables. The intuition here is that q represents a multiset, of which a and b are members according to table S. Distinct members of the multiset can be substituted for the first two arguments of R. To represent tuples that are their own symmetric complement, such as $R(a, a, c, d, e)$, one inserts $S(a, q)$ twice. This representation uses slightly more space than the previous proposal, while not resolving the issue of keeping the representation consistent under updates. Further, reconstructing the original symmetric relation requires joins.

We argue that none of these solutions is ideal, and that the database system should be responsible for providing a "symmetric" table type. There are numerous advantages to such a scheme:

1. The database system could choose a compact representation (such as storing one member of each pair of symmetric tuples) and take advantage of this compactness in reducing the amount of I/O required. This representation can be used both for base tables that are identified as symmetric, and for materialized views that can be proven to be symmetric.

2. The database system could go even further, and add a symmetric-closure operator to the query algebra. A query plan over a symmetric relation could then be manipulated using algebraic identities so that the symmetric closure is applied as late as possible. That way, intermediate results will be smaller, and queries will be processed more efficiently.

3. Integrity would be checked by the database system. Single-row updates would be automatically propagated to the other column permutations if necessary. Inconsistencies would be avoided, and schema designers would not have to re-implement special functionality for each symmetric table in the database.

4. The database system could index the multiple columns of a symmetric relation in a single index structure. As a result, only one index traversal is necessary to locate tuples with a given value for some symmetric column.

In this paper, we propose techniques to enable such a "symmetric relation" table type. We provide:

- An underlying abstract data type to store the *kernel* of a symmetric relation, i.e., a particular nonredundant subset of the relation. We show how updates on this data type would be handled by the database system. We describe how relational normalization techniques should take account of symmetric relations during database design. Both normalization and the proposed representation of symmetric relations aim to remove redundancy, so combining these two approaches should be beneficial.

- An extension of the relational algebra with a symmetric closure operator γ. We show how to translate a query over a symmetric relation into a query involving γ applied to the kernel of the relation. We provide algebraic equivalences that allow the rewriting of queries so that work can be saved by applying γ as late as possible.

- A method for inferring when a view is guaranteed to be symmetric. By using this method, the database system has the flexibility to store a materialized view using the more compact representation.

- A syntactic extension to SQL that allows the succinct expression of queries over symmetric relations.

Related Work

Surprisingly, there has been little past work on specialized implementations of symmetric relations (or bounded-cardinality set/multisets) within the database system. The only literature we are aware of that addresses this problem is [3], where database-level implementation is advocated, but specific implementation techniques are not described.

An object-relational database system can provide explicit structures for representing set-valued attributes that are physically embedded in a stored tuple, and can be manipulated directly [6, 7, 8]. For example, Oracle provides an object-relational collection type called a VARRAY [1]. VARRAYs allow the embedded representation of arrays having a fixed cardinality bound. A database schema designer could use this kind of system to implement the set-based representation of symmetric relations mentioned above, without the need for joins to reconstruct the symmetric relation. Nevertheless, one must give up first normal form and/or use an extended relational database system. Further, the encapsulation of these collection types means that the full set has to be dereferenced for accesses and element updates. For example, it is not possible to index the elements of a VARRAY, and so finding rows with VARRAYs containing a particular element must be performed using a full table scan.

The expressive power of cardinality-bounded sets has been previously studied in the context of an object-based data model [4, 5].

2 The Kernel

Definition 2.1 $\gamma_{XY}(R)$ denotes the symmetric closure operator over symmetric attributes X and Y of relation $R(X, Y, Z_1, \ldots, Z_n)$.[4] $(x, y, z_1, \ldots, z_n) \in \gamma_{XY}(R)$ if and only if either $(x, y, z_1, \ldots, z_n) \in R$ or $(y, x, z_1, \ldots, z_n) \in R$. □

If R is symmetric with respect to X and Y, then we aim to determine a minimal relation M such that $R = \gamma_{XY}(M)$. By choosing a minimal M, we can represent R compactly. Several minimal relations M satisfy this constraint. Each such M chooses a particular element from each pair of complementary tuples.

While the choice of minimal relation M does not matter in terms of space consumption, we shall see that certain algebraic equivalences (such as Lemma 3.4 below) hold only if there is a consistent single choice of M for all tables. Thus, we impose a total order (which may be arbitrary) on the domain of X and Y, and insist that the representative tuple chosen has $X \leq Y$ according to this order. The resulting relation is unique, and is denoted by $ker_{XY}(R)$, or just $ker(R)$ when X and Y are clear from context. $ker_{XY}(R) = \sigma_{X \leq Y}(R)$.

We propose that the database stores $ker(R)$ as the internal representation of R. Assuming a set semantics (as opposed to a multiset or bag semantics) for symmetric relations, updates are handled as follows:

```
Insert ( R(X,Y,Z1,...,Zn) )
{
  If (Y<X) then swap(X,Y);
  If (X,Y,Z1,...,Zn) is not in ker(R) then
    append (X,Y,Z1,...,Zn) to ker(R);
}

Delete ( R(X,Y,Z1,...,Zn) )
{
  If (Y<X) then swap(X,Y);
  If (X,Y,Z1,...,Zn) is in ker(R) then
    remove (X,Y,Z1,...,Zn) from ker(R);
}
```

An update is just a delete followed by an insert, assuming the deletion was successful.

A symmetric table implementation should also address systems issues such as how locking and logging are performed on rows of such tables. These issues depend on the locking and logging protocols used, and are beyond the scope of this paper.

---

[4]In general, X and Y are *vectors* (of equal length) of type-compatible attributes. For clarity of presentation, we shall omit vector notation, and employ examples in which X and Y are single attributes.

The formalism above allows multiple disjoint pairs of symmetric attributes. Thus, if R is symmetric in X, Y and also symmetric in V, W, it makes sense to talk about $ker_{XY}(R)$, $ker_{VW}(R)$, and $ker_{XY}(ker_{VW}(R)) = ker_{VW}(ker_{XY}(R))$. We can also generalize symmetry to more than two attributes.

Definition 2.2 *A relation $R(Z_1, \ldots, Z_n)$ is symmetric in $Z_1, \ldots, Z_k$ when $R(Z_1, \ldots, Z_n)$ holds if and only if for every permutation P of $Z_1, \ldots, Z_k$, $R(P(Z_1), \ldots, P(Z_k), Z_{k+1}, \ldots, Z_n)$ holds. Each such $R(P(Z_1), \ldots, P(Z_k), Z_{k+1}, \ldots, Z_n)$ is a symmetric complement of $R(Z_1, \ldots, Z_n)$. We define $ker_{Z_1, \ldots, Z_k}(R)$ to include only those tuples from R with $Z_1 \leq \ldots \leq Z_k$.* □

Indexing

Indexing of all symmetric attributes in $ker(R)$ should be done in a single index structure, so that a single index lookup suffices to find tuples with some symmetric attribute equal to a given probe value.

2.1 Normalization

Database normalization and the proposed kernel representation both aim to remove redundancy. However, normalization may be hampered by the presence of symmetry in the data.

Example 2.1 *Consider a database describing meetings of pairs of people that take place in certain locations at certain times, as in Example 1.1. Suppose that the initial database design has the schema $U(P_1, P_2, L, D, T, A)$, where P_1 and P_2 are the parties, L is the location, D is the date, and T is the time. A is a law-enforcement agent assigned to monitor the meeting, and multiple agents can be assigned to a single meeting. The schema designer is aware that the database system provides facilities for symmetric relations, and wishes to take advantage of these facilities by declaring U to be symmetric in P_1, P_2.*

Suppose that there can be only one meeting that takes place in a given location on a given date and time. The symmetric redundancy prevents the expression of functional dependencies having LDT on the left hand side. As a result, the "obvious" normalization of the table into the meets *relation $M(P_1, P_2, L, D, T)$ and the* monitors *relation $S(L, D, T, A)$ is missed.* □

The solution to the problem identified in Example 2.1 is to apply the kernel first, and then try to normalize the result using standard normalization techniques. In Example 2.1, it is possible to identify the functional dependency $LDT \to P_1 P_2$ in $ker_{P_1 P_2}(U)$. This functional dependency allows the normalization of $ker_{P_1 P_2}(U)$ into $ker_{P_1 P_2}(M)$ and S; M is represented as a symmetric relation.

2.2 Implementation

It is straightforward to implement the γ operator. For each input tuple output that tuple in addition to tuples formed by permuting the symmetric attributes (but don't output a tuple twice if two permutations generate the same tuple). However, in a practical database system, the mapping from algebraic operators to implementations is not necessarily a direct one. For example, it is common to implement a scan operator with predicates, so that the `getnext` function returns the next row satisfying the predicates. This choice allows the scan operator to choose an appropriate access structure, such as an index if one exists.

In a similar way, the natural implementation of symmetric closure should also incorporate predicates on the symmetric attributes. The predicates allow for the efficient use of available access methods, and may avoid the generation of permutations that will be immediately filtered out. The predicates may come from selection operators or from join operators.

Example 2.2 *Consider again the M table from Example 2.1, in which the P_i attributes store the identifiers of persons involved in a pairwise meeting. Suppose that $\sigma_{P_2=456}(M)$ is a subexpression of a query to be evaluated. Let $K = ker(M)$ be stored by the database, so that the subexpression can be evaluated as $\sigma_{P_2=456}(\gamma_{P_1 P_2}(K))$. Suppose also that we store a single index structure for the columns P_1 and P_2. For simplicity of presentation, assume that the database knows that for all rows of M, $P_1 \neq P_2$.*

Then by implementing an operator for the combined selection and symmetric closure, we can directly look up tuples in K having 456 for either of the symmetric attributes, and for each match return the permutation with $P_2 = 456$. The alternative permutation is never generated.

If we implemented symmetric closure as a stand-alone operator, then the best we could do would be to rewrite $\sigma_{P_2=456}(\gamma_{P_1 P_2}(K))$ as $\sigma_{P_2=456}(\gamma_{P_1 P_2}(\sigma_{P_1=456 \vee P_2=456}(K)))$. (See Lemma 3.2 below.) The pushed selection conditions allow the use of the index on K. However, both permutations of each matching row in K are generated, one of which will be filtered by the outer selection condition. □

In the general case for Example 2.2, it is possible that $P_1 = P_2$. A limited form of duplicate elimination would then be needed to avoid generating an output row twice from a single input row. Also observe that the problems highlighted by Example 2.2 become worse for symmetric relations over more than two attributes.

For a fixed number of symmetric columns, the symmetric closure operator can be expressed in relational algebra in terms of the union and attribute-renaming operators. Thus neither γ nor the kernel operator add to the expressive power of relational algebra. Nevertheless, by abstracting the γ operator one can derive implementations directly for γ (or γ together with selection). The situation is analogous to the join operation which, though expressible in terms of selection and cartesian product, is best implemented directly.

3 Query Optimization

Given a query that mentions a symmetric relation R, we assume that we have physically stored just $K = ker(R)$. In an algebraic expression for a query that accesses R, we use $\gamma(K)$ in place of R.

In order to minimize the size of intermediate results, it would be beneficial to push other operators inside the symmetric closure operator γ, where possible. To support such an endeavor, we now describe algebraic equivalences that can form the basis of such rewriting rules. For simplicity of presentation, we phrase these rules for binary symmetric relations. Generalizations to higher symmetric arity are possible.

For the following results, we assume that S_1 and S_2 are arbitrary relations with attributes including X and Y, such that all rows satisfy $X \leq Y$. T represents an arbitrary relation that does not have attributes X or Y. Except for Lemma 3.6, the equivalences hold under both a set semantics and a multiset semantics (in which duplicate rows are permitted) for relations.

Definition 3.1 *Let θ be a condition on X and Y, and (possibly) other attributes. Let θ' be formed from θ by substituting X for Y and vice versa. We say that θ is a symmetric condition on X and Y if $\theta \equiv \theta'$. Given a nonsymmetric condition θ, we call the condition $\theta \lor \theta'$ the symmetric closure of θ, which we denote by $\hat{\theta}$ when the attributes X and Y are clear from context.* □

Example 3.1 *Symmetric selection conditions on X and Y include $X = Y$, $X^2 + Y^2 = 1$, and any condition that mentions neither X nor Y. Symmetric join conditions on $R.X$ and $R.Y$ include $R.X = S.A \land R.Y = S.A$, $R.X^2 + R.Y^2 = S.A^2$, and conditions that do not mention $R.X$ or $R.Y$. The condition $R.X - R.Y > 7$ is not symmetric; its symmetric closure is $R.X - R.Y > 7 \lor R.Y - R.X > 7$.* □

Symmetric conditions can be pushed below the symmetric closure.

Lemma 3.1 *If θ is a symmetric condition, then*

- $\sigma_\theta(\gamma_{XY}(S_1)) = \gamma_{XY}(\sigma_\theta(S_1))$
- $\gamma_{XY}(S_1) \bowtie_\theta T = \gamma_{XY}(S_1 \bowtie_\theta T)$

□

Because the symmetric closure of a condition is always symmetric, Lemma 3.1 implies the following result, which allows us to push down partial information from selections on the symmetric attributes.

Lemma 3.2 *For an arbitrary condition θ,*

- $\sigma_\theta(\gamma_{XY}(S_1)) = \sigma_\theta(\gamma_{XY}(\sigma_{\hat{\theta}}(S_1)))$
- $\gamma_{XY}(S_1) \bowtie_\theta T = \sigma_\theta(\gamma_{XY}(S_1 \bowtie_{\hat{\theta}} T))$

□

Lemma 3.3 *Suppose θ is a condition that implies $X \leq Y$. Then $\sigma_\theta(\gamma_{XY}(S_1)) = \sigma_\theta(S_1)$.* □

Lemma 3.4

- $\gamma_{XY}(S_1) \cup \gamma_{XY}(S_2) = \gamma_{XY}(S_1 \cup S_2)$
- $\gamma_{XY}(S_1) \cap \gamma_{XY}(S_2) = \gamma_{XY}(S_1 \cap S_2)$
- $\gamma_{XY}(S_1) - \gamma_{XY}(S_2) = \gamma_{XY}(S_1 - S_2)$
- $\gamma_{XY}(S_1) \times T = \gamma_{XY}(S_1 \times T)$

□

Lemma 3.5 *If attribute list G includes both X and Y, then $\pi_G(\gamma_{XY}(S_1)) = \gamma_{XY}(\pi_G(S_1))$.* □

Lemma 3.6 *Under a set semantics: (a) If attribute list G includes neither X nor Y, then $\pi_G(\gamma_{XY}(S_1)) = \pi_G(S_1)$. (b) If attribute list G includes X but not Y, and if G' is the same as G except that X is replaced by Y, then $\pi_G(\gamma_{XY}(S_1)) = \pi_G(S_1) \cup \pi_{G'}(S_1)$.* □

Definition 3.2 *Let $\mathcal{A}_G^{\vec{f}}(R)$ denote the aggregate of relation R, grouped by the columns in the list G, computing the aggregate functions $\vec{f}$.* □

Lemma 3.7 *If grouping attributes G include both X and Y, then $\mathcal{A}_G^{\vec{f}}(\gamma_{XY}(S_1)) = \gamma_{XY}(\mathcal{A}_G^{\vec{f}}(S_1))$* □

Aggregates grouping by X alone or Y alone can use Lemma 3.7 to first compute the aggregate grouped by X and Y. Assuming that the aggregate functions are incrementally computable, the coarser aggregates can then be computed in a subsequent operation.

Lemma 3.8 *Let G be grouping attributes other than X and Y, and let $\vec{f}$ contain just idempotent aggregates such as* `min` *and* `max`*. Then $\mathcal{A}_G^{\vec{f}}(\gamma_{XY}(S_1)) = \mathcal{A}_G^{\vec{f}}(S_1)$.* □

It is tempting to think of analogous equivalences to those of Lemma 3.8 for other aggregates. However, a row in the kernel maps to either one or two rows in the symmetric closure, depending on whether the symmetric attributes have equal values. To take account of this difference, one can split the kernel into two fragments.

Lemma 3.9 *Let G be grouping attributes other than X and Y, and let $\vec{f}$ contain just linear aggregates such as* `sum` *and* `count`*. Let $2\vec{f}$ denote the aggregate that computes double the aggregate functions $\vec{f}$. Then*

- $\mathcal{A}_G^{\vec{f}}(\gamma_{XY}(\sigma_{X<Y}(S_1))) = \mathcal{A}_G^{2\vec{f}}(\sigma_{X<Y}(S_1))$
- $\mathcal{A}_G^{\vec{f}}(\gamma_{XY}(\sigma_{X=Y}(S_1))) = \mathcal{A}_G^{\vec{f}}(\sigma_{X=Y}(S_1))$

□

For incremental aggregate functions, one can compute $\mathcal{A}_G^{\vec{f}}(\gamma(S_1))$ by partitioning S_1 into two pieces, using Lemma 3.9.

To be able to compose the various lemmas above, we need to verify that in each case the subexpression created by pulling γ up one level retains the property that $X \leq Y$. This verification is straightforward, and is omitted here.

Example 3.2 *Consider again the "meets" relation $M(P_1, P_2, L, D, T)$ from the law-enforcement database of Example 2.1. Let $S(V, \ldots)$ be another relation indicating that person V is a suspect. Let $R(W, \ldots)$ be a relation indicating that W is a location being monitored. The law-enforcement user poses the query*

$$S \bowtie_{V=P_1} M \bowtie_{W=L} R$$

to find meetings involving suspects at monitored locations. Suppose M is stored in the database as $K = ker_{P_1 P_2}(M)$. Using Lemmas 3.1 and 3.2, the query can be rewritten so that it has the following tree form:

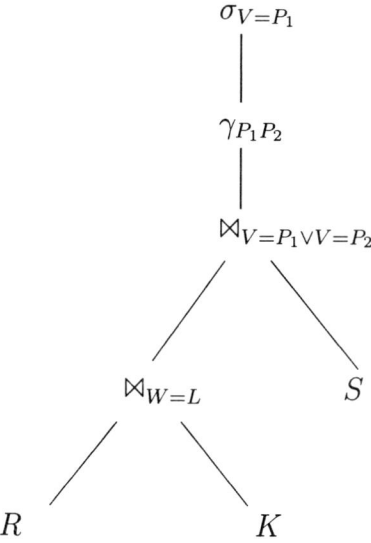

The joins are pushed below the γ operator, one fully and the other partially. When the joins are selective, the rewritten plan is more efficient than one in which γ is applied directly to K, because (a) the symmetric closure is applied to fewer tuples, and (b) the operators below γ are applied to fewer tuples. □

Example 3.3 *Suppose that in Example 2.1 we simply wish to list all records in the meets relation, without redundancy. The user writes the query as*

$$\sigma_{P_1 \leq P_2} M.$$

If $K = ker_{P_1 P_2}(M)$, then the query can be rewritten as $\sigma_{P_1 \leq P_2}(\gamma_{P_1 P_2} K)$. By Lemma 3.3, this expression is equivalent to $\sigma_{P_1 \leq P_2} K$. One can even use semantic query optimization to observe that $P_1 \leq P_2$ is an integrity constraint on K, which allows further simplification of the query to simply K. Thus, even if the user does not query the kernel, appropriately formulated queries over the symmetric closure can achieve the performance that would have been available by querying the kernel directly. □

3.1 Conditions Revisited

Consider again the "meets" relation M, and suppose that we wish to identify pairs of meetings that share one (or more) members. Assume there is no index available on M. Using subscripts to distinguish two instances of M, we might write this query as

$$M_1 \bowtie_{M_1.P_1 = M_2.P_1} M_2 \quad (Q1)$$

This query cannot be effectively optimized, because all permutations of tuples in the two instances of M need to be generated to test the condition on P_1.

Now imagine we defined a function $overlap_{R,S}$, where R and S are symmetric relations on $X_1, \ldots, X_n$ and $Y_1, \ldots, Y_m$ respectively. Suppose that r and s represent rows of R and S respectively. Applied to (r, s), $overlap_{R,S}$ returns the cardinality of the multiset intersection of $\{r.X_1, \ldots, r.X_n\}$ and $\{s.Y_1, \ldots, s.Y_m\}$. In other words, $overlap_{R,S}$ returns the number of common values among the symmetric attributes of the two rows. The $overlap$ function can be implemented efficiently, even for symmetric relations of high arity, by sorting the symmetric attributes from each tuple and then scanning through each list.

Given this $overlap$ function, we can rephrase the query above as

$$\sigma_\theta(M_1 \bowtie_{overlap_{M_1,M_2} \geq 1} M_2) \quad (Q2)$$

Here θ is the condition $M_1.P_1 \leq M_1.P_2 \wedge M_2.P_1 \leq M_2.P_2$; like in Example 3.3, the outer selection removes redundant copies of qualifying rows. This query *can* be optimized, because the join condition is symmetric. After several transformations, the query becomes

$$K_1 \bowtie_{overlap_{K_1,K_2} \geq 1} K_2$$

where $K = ker_{P_1,P_2}(M)$. The $overlap$ function can be implemented particularly efficiently on kernels, because the symmetric attributes are already in order.

There is a difference between formulations Q1 and Q2 of the query: Q1 requires the first symmetric attribute of each component row to be the common member, while Q2 does not.[5] Thus, if the user doesn't

---
[5] Also, Q1 will output two rows for pairs of meetings between the same two people, while Q2 outputs one.

need a special way of identifying the common member, then it pays (in terms of query execution time) to use the formulation Q2. The trick is to formulate the query using properties of the *set* of symmetric attributes where possible, because such conditions are always symmetric and can be better optimized.

Finally, note that the $overlap_{R,S} \geq 1$ test can be expressed alternatively as $r.X_1 = s.Y_1 \vee r.X_1 = s.Y_2 \vee r.X_2 = s.Y_1 \vee r.X_2 = s.Y_2$. Nevertheless, we advocate the use of a specialized *overlap* function, because (a) it simplifies the job of identifying symmetric conditions for the query compiler, (b) for symmetric relations of higher arity the equivalent logical expressions become unwieldy, and (c) the *overlap* function can be used to test other kinds of set-oriented relationships, such as disjointness and subset relationships.

The arguments in favor of a special *overlap* function for join conditions extend also to selection conditions. Definition 3.1 (the symmetric closure of a condition) can be extended to k-ary conditions by taking the disjunction of all expressions formed by permuting the symmetric columns. Thus, in a symmetric relation of arity k with symmetric columns $P_1, \ldots, P_k$, the closure of $P_1 = 123$ is $P_1 = 123 \vee \cdots \vee P_k = 123$. The closure of $P_1 = 123 \wedge P_2 = 456$ has $k(k-1)$ disjuncts. These expressions are unwieldy, and are likely to hide optimization alternatives from a realistic query optimizer. Instead, we propose to represent the symmetric closure of $P_1 = 123$ as "$\{123\}$ Among $\{P_1, \ldots, P_k\}$" and the closure of $P_1 = 123 \wedge P_2 = 456$ as "$\{123, 456\}$ Among $\{P_1, \ldots, P_k\}$". This representation is compact, and can represent the closure of common conditions that equate an attribute with a constant. It also allows for easier recognition of efficient plans, such as using a common index on $\{P_1, \ldots, P_k\}$, by the query compiler.

4 Inferring Symmetry

Being able to infer that a subexpression is symmetric enables additional options for query optimization. Also, if we can infer that a materialized view is guaranteed to be symmetric, then we can choose to store it in the more compact form, saving space and query processing time.

To formulate the inference problem, we use the notion of a conjunctive query [9] to represent a view. An *ordinary* subgoal employs a table predicate, while a *built-in* subgoal employs an interpreted predicate, such as equality or "<". An ordinary subgoal is *symmetric* if its predicate is a table that is marked as symmetric in the database schema. For ease of presentation we shall assume that we are dealing with binary symmetric relations whose symmetric attributes are the leftmost attributes as written.

Definition 4.1 Let

$$Q(X, Y, \vec{Z}) : -B(X, Y, \vec{Z}, \vec{W})$$

be a conjunctive query, where B is a conjunction of subgoals. $Q^T(X, Y, \vec{Z})$ is the conjunctive query defined by

$$Q^T(X, Y, \vec{Z}) : -B(Y, X, \vec{Z}, \vec{W})$$

with X and Y interchanged in B. □

Note that $(Q^T)^T = Q$, and that containment mappings from Q to Q^T are isomorphic to containment mappings from Q^T to Q.

Lemma 4.1 *Let Q be a conjunctive query containing nonsymmetric ordinary subgoals, and no built-in subgoals. Q is symmetric if and only if there exists a containment mapping from Q to Q^T.* □

Example 4.1 *Let $E(K, M)$ represent an employee relation, where K is the unique key of the employee, and M is the employee's manager. Let Q be the conjunctive query*

$$Q(K_1, K_2) : -E(K_1, M), E(K_2, M).$$

Q^T is then

$$Q^T(K_1, K_2) : -E(K_2, M), E(K_1, M)$$

and the identity mapping is a containment mapping from Q to Q^T. We therefore conclude that Q is symmetric in K_1 and K_2. □

When subgoals may themselves be symmetric, a simple containment mapping is not sufficient, as illustrated by the following example.

Example 4.2 *Consider again table E from Example 4.1. Let S be a symmetric relation; think of $S(M_1, M_2)$ as meaning that M_1 and M_2 are siblings. Let Q be the conjunctive query*

$$Q(K_1, K_2) : -E(K_1, M_1), S(M_1, M_2), E(K_2, M_2).$$

Q is indeed symmetric. However, Q^T is

$$Q^T(K_1, K_2) : -E(K_2, M_1), S(M_1, M_2), E(K_1, M_2)$$

and the identity mapping is not a containment mapping from Q to Q^T. The mapping that interchanges M_1 and M_2 is not a containment mapping, because $S(M_1, M_2)$ in Q maps to $S(M_2, M_1)$ in Q^T. □

Definition 4.2 *Let h be a symbol mapping from a conjunctive query $Q : -B$ to a conjunctive query $Q' : -B'$. We say that h is a symmetric containment mapping from Q to Q' if $h(Q) = Q'$, and for every subgoal S in B, either (a) $h(S)$ appears in B', or (b) S is symmetric and the symmetric complement of $h(S)$ appears in B', or (c) S is a built-in subgoal, and $h(S)$ is equivalent to a subgoal of B'.* □

Unlike parts (a) and (b), part (c) of Definition 4.2 is not syntactic identity; it depends on the proof system available to demonstrate equivalence. Part (c) allows us to identify symmetric conditions (Definition 3.1) in a logic-based formalism.

Lemma 4.2 *Let Q and Q' be conjunctive queries with ordinary subgoals that may be symmetric, and no built-in subgoals. Q is contained in Q' if and only if there exists a symmetric containment mapping from Q' to Q.* □

Lemma 4.3 *Let Q be a conjunctive query containing ordinary subgoals that may be symmetric, and no built-in subgoals. Q is symmetric if and only if there exists a symmetric containment mapping from Q to Q^T.* □

Lemma 4.3 resolves the difficulty of Example 4.2, because the mapping that interchanges M_1 and M_2 is a symmetric containment mapping. As in the nonsymmetric case [9], when built-in subgoals are allowed we lose the "only-if" part of Lemma 4.3.

Lemma 4.4 *Let Q be a conjunctive query containing ordinary subgoals that may be symmetric, and built-in subgoals. Q is symmetric if there exists a symmetric containment mapping from Q to Q^T.* □

4.1 Optimization using Inference

Suppose we can infer that a query subexpression is guaranteed to be symmetric. Then we can deliberately insert a "kernelization" operation paired with a symmetric closure operation, and move the predicates around to minimize the size of intermediate results. Thus we can benefit from the proposed query optimization techniques of Section 3 even if we do not have any stored kernels in the database.

Example 4.3 *Consider again table E from Example 4.1. We write E_1 and E_2 to distinguish two instances of E in a single query, and we similarly subscript the attributes of E. Consider a query*

$$(E_1 \bowtie_{M_1=M_2} E_2) \bowtie_{\theta_1} R_1 \ldots \bowtie_{\theta_m} R_m.$$

Suppose that none of the θ_i conditions mention K_1 or K_2. We begin by inferring that the subexpression $(E_1 \bowtie_{M_1=M_2} E_2)$ is symmetric in K_1 and K_2; see Example 4.1. We can therefore rewrite the query as

$$\gamma_{K_1,K_2}(\sigma_{K_1 \leq K_2}(E_1 \bowtie_{M_1=M_2} E_2)) \bowtie_{\theta_1} R_1 \ldots \bowtie_{\theta_m} R_m.$$

By repeatedly applying Lemma 3.1, this is equivalent to

$$\gamma_{K_1,K_2}(\sigma_{K_1 \leq K_2}(E_1 \bowtie_{M_1=M_2} E_2) \bowtie_{\theta_1} R_1 \ldots \bowtie_{\theta_m} R_m)$$

which is more efficient than the original expression because the intermediate joins are smaller. □

5 Extending SQL

In this section, we extend SQL with features that allow the expression of bounded-cardinality multisets as database columns. Our extended SQL can be translated into the algebra described previously. The proposed syntactic constructs enable the succinct expression of queries that manipulate bounded multisets. Further, specialized syntax for commonly used operations can help the database system choose efficient query processing algorithms to execute the query [2, 11].

When creating a table, one may declare k columns of the same type to be a named *multiset*. This declaration serves two purposes. It provides a name for the group of attributes that can be used in writing queries. It also gives a hint to the database system to create an index on the union of all columns in the group. The multiset may optionally be declared to be symmetric, in which case the database system is free to permute the columns (e.g., to store the kernel) to make integrity constraint checking and query processing more efficient.

Example 5.1 *In Example 1.4, a multiset* Persons *would be declared for the columns containing the (integer) identifiers of persons participating in the meeting, and* Persons *would be declared symmetric.*

```
Create Table M (
    Meeting-id integer,
    Symmetric Multiset Persons
      { P1, ..., Pk } integer,
    ... )
```

In Example 1.5, a multiset Slots *would be declared for the columns C_1 through C_{24}.* Slots *would not be declared symmetric.*

```
Create Table V (
    ID integer,
    ViewDate date,
    Multiset Slots
      { C1, ..., C24 } integer,
    ... )
```

In these examples, users may query the attributes Pi *and* Ci *directly as regular attributes, using standard SQL syntax.* □

We introduce new "column variables" that are allowed to take values from any one of a set of columns. The original columns of a table are not permuted. This choice allows us to access a symmetric base table T directly in the conventional way, without forcing the query "Select * from T" to have $k!$ copies of each tuple representing a k-element multiset. The scope of a column variable is defined using the **Among** keyword in the **Where** clause.[6]

---
[6]The occurrences of column variables must be *safe* in the sense of [10].

Example 5.2 *Consider Example 1.5 together with the sample query "Find all individuals who, on the given date, have watched channels 2 and 4, but not channel 5." We would write this query as*

```
Select ID, ViewDate
From V
Where {X1,X2} Among Slots and X1=2 and X2=4
   and not ({5} Among Slots)
```

There is one row per `ID` *and* `ViewDate` *in the output, even though there may be many possible combinations of slots satisfying the conditions in the* `Where` *clause.* □

When we write `{X1,X2} Among Slots` it is implicit that X1 and X2 correspond to different columns within `Slots`. If X is a column variable, we use the syntax `X.name` to denote the column name of the column actually bound to X in the query. One can use the `Among` keyword for groups not explicitly defined as multisets by explicitly listing the columns, as in "`{X1,X2} Among {Jan,Feb,Mar,Apr}`".

Example 5.3 *Continuing Example 5.2, suppose that we include a column variable in the* `Select` *clause.*

```
Select ID, ViewDate, X1.name, X1
From V
Where {X1,X2} Among Slots and X1=2 and X2=4
   and not ({5} Among Slots)
```

Unlike before, there are multiple rows per `ID`/`ViewDate` *in the output, one for each binding of* `X1` *to a column whose value (together with some* `X2` *value) satisfies the conditions of the* `Where` *clause. The column-variables in the select clause implicitly control duplicate elimination. Since only* `X1` *is mentioned in the select clause, there is one value output for each* `X1` *column binding, irrespective of how many valid* `X2` *values are present.* □

Example 5.3 shows how to "unpivot" a k-element multiset from a column-based representation into a more traditional row-based representation. One could use variants of Example 5.3 to define views over which traditional SQL methods of set manipulation can be expressed. As a result, none of SQL's expressive power for set manipulation has been lost by using a column-wise representation. We emphasize that since the unpivoted table is just a view, queries over the unpivoted table could be translated into queries over the original (pivoted) table, which may be more efficient because joins are not required.

Example 5.4 *Consider Example 1.4 in which we have a meeting table M with k attributes $P_1, \ldots, P_k$ grouped into a multiset called* `Persons`*. We wish to find all pairs of people X and Y at three degrees of separation. In other words, we need three meetings* M_1, M_2, M_3 *such that X attended* M_1*, Y attended* M_3*, M_1 and M_2 have overlapping membership, and M_2 and M_3 have overlapping membership. We can write this query as*

```
Select X, Y
From M M1, M M2, M M3
Where {X} Among M1.Persons
   and {W} Among M1.Persons
   and {W} Among M2.Persons
   and {Z} Among M2.Persons
   and {Z} Among M3.Persons
   and {Y} Among M3.Persons
```

`{W} Among M2.Persons` *and* `{Z} Among M2.Persons` *are written separately, meaning that* W *and* Z *may bind to the same column. Had we written* `{W,Z} Among M2.Persons`*, they would have to be different columns. One could also formulate the query succinctly using an "overlap" method, as discussed in Section 3.1:*

```
Select X, Y
From M M1, M M2, M M3
Where {X} Among M1.Persons
   and Overlap(M1.Persons,M2.Persons) >= 1
   and Overlap(M2.Persons,M3.Persons) >= 1
   and {Y} Among M3.Persons
```

□

Without the `Among` syntax, there would be no way to output values from multiple columns in a single select statement. One would need to form the union of k^2 select statements to express Example 5.4.

A conventional set representation would require a six-way join to express Example 5.4.

When a symmetric multiset has fewer elements than the cardinality bound, the remaining columns are padded with NULLs. Column-variables cannot be bound to NULL values.

We also advocate additional syntactic elements for directly expressing multisets formed as the intersection or difference of other multisets. (Note that union of two k-bounded multisets is not necessarily a k-bounded multiset.)

The translation of the extended SQL into the extended algebra is relatively straightforward. When symmetric attributes are referenced using the `Among` keyword, the underlying relation has its symmetric columns copied into new columns. Some of these new columns correspond to the column variables. The symmetric closure operator is applied to the new columns to find combinations of values satisfying the conditions on column variables in the `Where` clause. An algebraic duplicate-elimination step is also needed, as is special handling for NULL values. After the query has been translated, it can be optimized and executed as outlined in Sections 2.2 and 3.

6 Experimental Evaluation

In this section we describe an experimental evaluation of various representations of multisets on a state-of-the-art commercial database system. We wish to demonstrate the qualitative performance characteristics of various representations. A comprehensive performance evaluation is beyond the scope of this paper.

We consider a database of randomly generated 3-element multisets, where each element is a string chosen uniformly from a set of about 8,000 English words. The schema of the kernel table K is (X_1, X_2, X_3, Y) where X_1, X_2, X_3 are the set elements. We construct K so that $X_1 \leq X_2 \leq X_3$, and create an index on X_1, an index on X_2, and an index on X_3. We store 500,000 such sets in the database.

We define a view V over K as the union of all six permutations (each expressed using a select statement) of X_1, X_2, X_3 from K.

We also store a conventional set-based representation of the same data in which a new set-identifier attribute ID is defined. We create one table $S(ID, Y)$, and another $M(ID, X)$ containing the unpivoted sets. An index on X in M is created.

We consider four variants of a query that finds sets with all three members specified by constants. In the first variant Q_1, we query K for some combination of attributes.[7]

```
Select X1,X2,X3,Y
From K
Where (X1='foo' and X2='bar' and X3='baz')
   or (X1='foo' and X3='bar' and X2='baz')
   or (X2='foo' and X1='bar' and X3='baz')
   or (X2='foo' and X3='bar' and X1='baz')
   or (X3='foo' and X1='bar' and X2='baz')
   or (X3='foo' and X2='bar' and X1='baz')
```

In the second variant Q_2 of the query, we write the query in terms of V.

```
Select X1,X2,X3,Y
From V
Where (X1='foo' and X2='bar' and X3='baz')
```

In the third variant Q_3, we query the conventional set-based representation.

```
Select M1.X, M2.X, M3.X, S.Y
From S, M M1, M M2, M M3
Where (M1.X='foo' and M2.X='bar'
       and M3.X='baz') and
  M1.ID=S.ID and M2.ID=S.ID and M3.ID=S.ID
```

Our extended syntax for the query would be

```
Select X1,X2,X3,Y
From K
Where {'foo','bar','baz'} Among {X1,X2,X3}
```

Our proposed access plan (use a combined index on all set columns) is not directly supported by the database system. Thus, the best we can do is to construct a query Q_4 whose performance is likely to be comparable to our intended query plan. (We need to verify that the chosen plan for Q_4 is similar to our intended plan.) Q_4 is

```
Select X1,X2,X3,Y
From K
Where (X1='bar' and X2='baz' and X3='foo')
```

in which the constants are selected in alphabetical order.

We ran each of these queries using a commercial database system on a 1.4GHz Intel Centrino machine under Windows XP. We record the optimization time and execution time as reported by the database system. These are elapsed-time measurements. Each query was run on a cold database that had just been started. The numbers below reflect the average of five runs for each query. In each run a different combination of constants was used, and the combinations were chosen so that there was always a match in the database. The database system also reported the plan chosen to execute each query.

The plan chosen for Q_4 uses the indexes on X1, X2 and X3 to find matching row identifiers, intersects the set of identifiers, and finds rows from K for the matching identifiers. Our intended plan would do the same operations, but using a single common index for X1, X2 and X3. While the number of row identifiers being intersected may be higher with our proposed method, the performance of Q_4 should roughly approximate the performance of our proposed method.

The plans chosen for Q_1 and Q_2 are similar to each other, consisting of the union of 6 subplans of the form mentioned for Q_4, one subplan per permutation of the attributes.

The plan chosen for Q_3 was a tree of three index-nested-loops joins. The innermost (i.e., leftmost) table is M accessed using an index lookup based on the X column. The other three index lookups are on the ID attributes of M (twice) and S.

Figure 1 shows the actual execution time for each of the four queries as reported by the database system. Figure 1 does not include the query optimization time, which is shown separately in Figure 2.

Figure 1 shows that the execution cost of Q_4 is smallest, with Q_1 and Q_2 having comparable execution cost. The cost of Q_3 is about 35 times higher than Q_4.

Figure 2 shows that the optimization cost of all three queries is comparable, although Q_2 has a noticeably lower optimization cost. This lower optimization

---

[7] In general we cannot take advantage of the order of constants mentioned in the query since the constants we're looking for may be bound at query time, and since we may be querying on just a subset of the available columns.

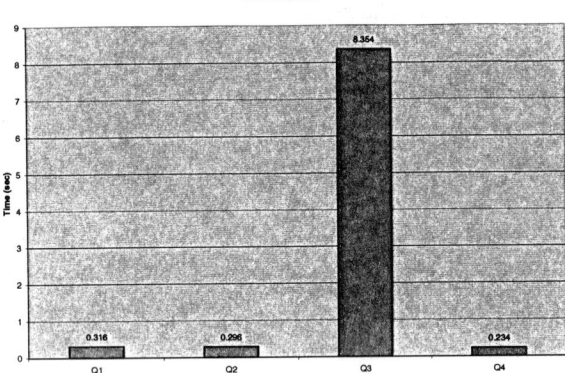

Figure 1: Execution time of the four queries.

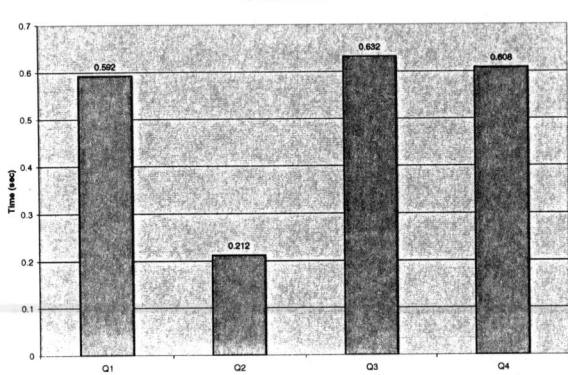

Figure 2: Optimization time of the four queries.

cost is probably just an artifact of a smaller search space of plans within the query optimizer, and not something intrinsic to the query itself. (Note the importance of separating the optimization time from the execution time in interpreting these results. Had we just reported the total elapsed time, Q_2 would have been the winner.)

Of the four solutions (Q_1, Q_2, Q_3, and our proposed method), only our method scales with the number of attributes. Q_3 does not scale because it requires a k-way join for multisets containing k elements. As one can see in Figure 1, even for $k = 3$ the performance of Q_3 is more than an order of magnitude worse than competing approaches.

Suppose that writing a basic condition (of the form `table.attribute=value`) takes 10 bytes of memory. If we try to generalize Q_1 and Q_2 to k-element multisets, then they require either a query or view definition whose size is approximately $10k(k!)$ bytes. The impact of this rate of growth is shown in Figure 3; note the logarithmic vertical scale. Q_1 and Q_2 quickly become impractical: with $k = 11$ the space for the query/view definition alone is four gigabytes.

In contrast, our query specification has size linear in k, and it can be evaluated without joins.

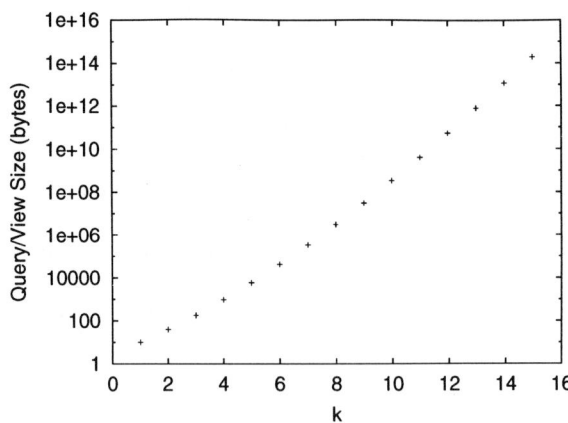

Figure 3: Growth of Q_1 and Q_2 with the multiset cardinality k.

7 Conclusions

We provide techniques that enable a database engine to support a symmetric table type. The techniques include

- A nonredundant data structure with update methods and specialized indexes.

- Methods for normalization in the presence of symmetric tables.

- An algebraic symmetric closure operator, together with algebraic equivalences useful for query optimization.

- Inference methods to determine when a query/view is guaranteed to be symmetric.

- A syntactic SQL extension to enable compact query expression.

A symmetric table type allows database schema designers to model symmetric relationships without having to worry about integrity, redundancy, consistency of updates, query efficiency, or suboptimal physical design.

One could go even further and implement different kinds of symmetric table. For example, the class of *antireflexive* symmetric relations (i.e., k-element sets rather than multisets) satisfies simpler algebraic rules, and some duplicate elimination steps can be omitted in the implementation of the γ operator (see Example 2.2).

We have argued that our approach is applicable when there is a natural cardinality bound in the application. One could extend our approach to general multisets by using a combined structure, i.e., a bounded cardinality multiset for an initial subset of elements, and a conventional set representation for additional elements.[8] An appropriate syntax could hide this di-

---

[8]This idea was suggested to us by Wisam Dakka.

vision from the user, presenting a single multiset abstraction. When small sets are typical, such an approach would have performance benefits, even in the absence of a strict cardinality bound.

References

[1] *Oracle Database Application Developer's Guide — Object-Relational Features*, 2004. 10g Release 1 (10.1), Part Number B10799-01.

[2] D. Chatziantoniou and K. A. Ross. Querying multiple features of groups in relational databases. In *Proceedings of the International Conference on Very Large Databases*, pages 295–306, 1996.

[3] C. J. Date. On various types of relations. *Database Debunkings*, April 20, 2003. Available at http://www.dbdebunk.com/.

[4] Jan Van den Bussche and Dirk Van Gucht. A hierarchy of faithful set creation in pure OODB's. In Joachim Biskup and Richard Hull, editors, *Database Theory - ICDT'92, 4th International Conference, Berlin, Germany, October 14-16, 1992, Proceedings*, volume 646 of *Lecture Notes in Computer Science*, pages 326–340. Springer, 1992.

[5] Jan Van den Bussche and Dirk Van Gucht. The expressive power of cardinality-bounded set values in object-based data models. *Theoretical Computer Science*, 149(1):49–66, 1995.

[6] Sven Helmer and Guido Moerkotte. Evaluation of main memory join algorithms for joins with set comparison join predicates. In *International Conference on Very Large Databases*, pages 386–395, 1997.

[7] N. Mamoulis. Efficient processing of joins on set-valued attributes. In *Proceedings of the ACM Conference on Management of Data (SIGMOD)*, pages 157–168, 2003.

[8] Karthikeyan Ramasamy, Jignesh M Patel, Raghav Kaushik, and Jeffrey F Naughton. Set containment joins: The good, the bad and the ugly. In *International Conference on Very Large Databases*, pages 351–362, 2000.

[9] D. Jeffrey Ullman. *Principles of Database and Knowledge-Base Systems*, volume 2. Computer Science Press, 1989.

[10] Allen Van Gelder and Rodney W. Topor. Safety and translation of relational calculus. *ACM Trans. Database Syst.*, 16(2):235–278, 1991.

[11] Andrew Witkowski, Srikanth Bellamkonda, Tolga Bozkaya, Gregory Dorman, Nathan Folkert, Abhinav Gupta, Lei Shen, and Sankar Subramanian. Spreadsheets in RDBMS for OLAP. In *Proceedings of the 2003 ACM SIGMOD international conference on on Management of data*, pages 52–63. ACM Press, 2003.

Algebraic Manipulation of Scientific Datasets

Bill Howe
OGI School of Science & Engineering at
Oregon Health & Science University
Beaverton, Oregon
bill@cse.ogi.edu

David Maier
OGI School of Science & Engineering at
Oregon Health & Science University
Beaverton, Oregon
maier@cse.ogi.edu

Abstract

We investigate algebraic processing strategies for large numeric datasets equipped with a possibly irregular *grid* structure. Such datasets arise, for example, in computational simulations, observation networks, medical imaging, and 2-D and 3-D rendering. Existing approaches for manipulating these datasets are incomplete: The performance of SQL queries for manipulating large numeric datasets is not competitive with specialized tools. Database extensions for processing multidimensional discrete data can only model regular, rectilinear grids. Visualization software libraries are designed to process gridded datasets efficiently, but no algebra has been developed to simplify their use and afford optimization. Further, these libraries are data dependent – physical changes to data representation or organization break user programs. In this paper, we present an algebra of *gridfields* for manipulating both regular and irregular gridded datasets, algebraic optimization techniques, and an implementation backed by experimental results. We compare our techniques to those of spatial databases and visualization software libraries, using real examples from an Environmental Observation and Forecasting System. We find that our approach can express optimized plans inaccessible to other techniques, resulting in improved performance with reduced programming effort.

Permission to copy without fee all or part of this material is granted provided that the copies are not made or distributed for direct commercial advantage, the VLDB copyright notice and the title of the publication and its date appear, and notice is given that copying is by permission of the Very Large Data Base Endowment. To copy otherwise, or to republish, requires a fee and/or special permission from the Endowment.

**Proceedings of the 30th VLDB Conference,
Toronto, Canada, 2004**

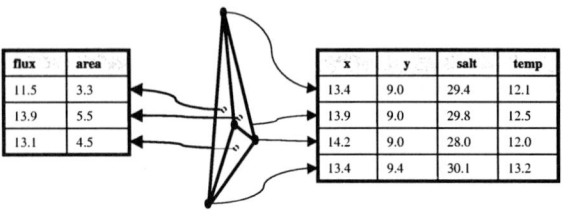

Figure 1: Datasets bound to the nodes and polygons of a 2-D grid.

1 Introduction

Many scientific datasets can be characterized by the topological structure, or *grid*, over which they are defined. For example, a timeseries might be defined over a 1-dimensional (1-D) grid, while the solution to a partial differential equation using a finite-element method might be defined over a 3-dimensional (3-D) grid.

These datasets consist of data tuples bound to the *cells* of a grid. A grid may possess cells of many dimensions; data can be associated with the nodes (0-cells), edges (1-cells), polygons (2-cells), and so on. Figure 1 shows a 2-D irregular (non-rectilinear) grid with two datasets bound to it. Geometric coordinates x and y are associated with the nodes of the grid, as are salinity and temperature values. Area and flux values are associated with each polygon. The grid structure consists of topological information only – generic cells, and incidence and adjacency relationships between cells that are invariant with respect to a particular geometric embedding. A geometric embedding in this example is captured by associating coordinate pairs with the nodes. As these datasets are manipulated and transformed, both the grid and the associated data must be updated in tandem; new grid-aware operators are required. Such operators must handle both regular grids encoded as multidimensional arrays and irregular grids that explicitly enumerate their cells. Since these datasets tend to be large, efficiency is paramount.

Gridded datasets are especially common in scientific and engineering domains. The context for our interest in gridded data is CORIE [1], an Environmental

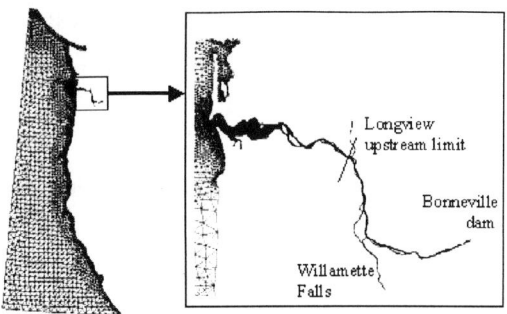

Figure 2: The CORIE grid, extending from the Baja peninsula to Alaska.

Observation and Forecasting System designed to support scientific and industrial interests in the Columbia River estuary. The CORIE system both measures and simulates the physical properties of the estuary, generating 5GB of data and thousands of *data products* for each simulation run, including visualizations, aggregated results and derived datasets. The data products are consumed for many purposes, including salmon habitability studies and environmental impact assessments. Figure 2 shows the CORIE domain. The horizontal irregular grid extends from the Baja peninsula up to Alaska to capture the large-scale influences of the Columbia River. The Columbia River estuary and the ocean waters around the mouth of the river (inset) have a very high density of grid elements, to also capture local hydrodynamic processes. Using a vertical grid to discretize the depth of the river along with this large horizontal grid, a 3-D grid can be generated. Time represents a fourth dimension.

Traditional Approaches. Database languages for processing multidimensional arrays have been proposed [2, 13], but multidimensional arrays cannot directly model irregular grids, such as those used in the CORIE system. A facility to manipulate both regular (rectilinear) grids and irregular (non-rectilinear) grids is missing. Additionally, representing different datasets bound to the nodes, edges, and faces of the same grid is difficult with multidimensional arrays. Raster GIS are similarly unable to model irregular grids precisely.

Relational databases extended with spatial types can model irregular grids, but have several weaknesses. Explicit foreign keys and redundant geometric coordinates[1] can more than double database size. With 5-20GB generated each day, even relatively inexpensive disk space is at a premium. Transfer times into and out of the database are excessive. Using the bulk load facility of Postgres [23], loading one timestep of one variable (about 800,000 floats) takes over one minute. With six primary variables and 96 timesteps per day, the load time approaches the time to generate the data in the first place on a similar platform. Retrieving data from the database involves copying tuples to fast, memory-resident structures such as arrays. When retrieving numeric datasets from a relational database, tuples are usually converted to arrays at the client, incurring an "impedance mismatch" penalty. The scale of scientific datasets makes the performance issues associated with impedance mismatch more pronounced [24]. In Section 3.5, we review modeling challenges stemming from storing gridded datasets in relational databases.

Visualization libraries such as the Visualization Toolkit (VTK) [19] provide efficient grid processing, but the routines are highly data dependent and therefore quite brittle. The library functions also exhibit complex semantics, making algebraic properties difficult to derive if they exist. We discuss these issues in more detail in Section 3.5.

Our Approach. These issues led us to seek a technology that 1) efficiently generates relevant data products, 2) reduces programming effort to design and implement new data products by allowing manipulation of grid structures directly, 3) integrates neatly with client tools, especially rendering tools for visualization, and 4) manages topology considerations for both regular and irregular grids transparently.

Our approach has been to devise and implement an algebra specially suited for manipulating gridded datasets, extending previous work [9]. Our algebra consists of grids, *gridfields*, and operators over these structures. A gridfield represents the association of a dataset with a grid. Several gridfields may share the same grid; indeed this eventuality allows algebraic identities important for optimization (see Section 6). Our data model distinguishes topological information from geometric information, handling geometry as ordinary data attributes. The separation of topology and geometry allows multiple geometric embeddings to be handled simultaneously, unlike other data models proposed, e.g., for scientific visualization [5, 8, 15]. Some of our operators are analogous to those of relational algebra, but extended to correctly handle the grid structure. Other operators are specific to gridfields.

Contributions. We extend previous efforts at devising scientific data models [3, 5, 8, 9, 18] by developing algebraic optimizations at both the logical and physical levels. We contribute a data model and implementation that satisfies the goals above. Specifically:

1. The data model captures regular and irregular grids uniformly.

2. The operators manipulate grid structures directly, avoiding the complexity associated with encoding grids as assemblies of arrays.

3. The design is well-aligned with client visualization and analysis tools.

---

[1] Coordinates of a node are repeated everywhere the node is referenced.

4. Our operators admit algebraic identities and consequent optimization techniques unique to gridfields.

5. We have tested our data model and implementation on real applications; we present results from the CORIE simulation system.

In this paper, we discuss the gridfield model, then describe data representation, operator implementation, and algebraic optimization of gridfield *recipes*, a form of query plan. Results are validated via experimental comparisons with existing approaches.

2 Related Work

The database community has given multidimensional discrete data (MDD) significant attention over the past decade. OLAP systems have been extended with visualization capabilities [21], but modeling and querying irregular grids in a relational system is difficult, as we demonstrate. Query languages and processing techniques based on multidimensional arrays [6, 12, 13, 26] have been developed, but arrays are not the correct abstraction for general grid manipulations.

Multidimensional arrays capture only rectilinear grids. If, as in the CORIE system, cells in a particular grid may be triangles, quadrilaterals, or a mix of cell types, the grid structure is awkward to encode using arrays. The interpretation of an assembly of arrays as an irregular grid is left to the application, undermining data independence. Further, we encounter multiple datasets bound to the same grid, but perhaps to cells of different dimension. Using arrays, the relationship between these datasets is lost; each must use its own distinct "spatial domain" [2]. Finally, the topology suggested by these grids is always implicit, making it difficult to separate geometry from topology. This capability is required when attempting to support two geometric embeddings of the same grid simultaneously, e.g., into different coordinate systems.

Several higher-level data models for scientific data have been proposed that capture both regular and irregular grids, and some separate topology from geometry [3, 5, 8]. However, algebraic manipulation of grid structures is not supported and experimental results are not reported.

Others have demonstrated that relational databases do not scale up to handle large scientific datasets [16, 22]. One proposed solution is to treat scientific datasets as external data sources, and access them using the SQL standard for management of external data (SQL-MED) [14]. Papiani et al. [17] report some success applying the standard to manage turbulence simulations.

Designers of spatial database systems are becoming aware that topological "connection" information can be as important as geometry for modeling and query processing. ESRI's ArcGIS version 8.3 [7] includes topology information modeled as integrity rules.

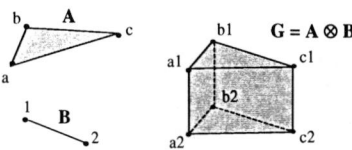

Figure 3: The cross product of two simple grids.

Users can express the rule that every polygon representing a building must be explicitly connected to a line segment representing a road. ESRI's product also supports raster data manipulation using a Map Algebra, but irregular grids are difficult to model precisely as raster data. Laser-Scan has produced a topology-enabled GIS extension for Oracle called Radius [25]. They allow nodes to be snapped together to express topological relationships independently of geometric embeddings. However, there is no notion of a manipulable gridded dataset, and therefore, our Goals 2 and 3 are not met.

3 The Gridfield Algebra

Grids are constructed from sets of k-dimensional *cells*. We refer to a cell of dimension k as a k-cell, following the topology literature [3]. Intuitively, a 0-cell is a point, a 1-cell is a line segment (or poly-line), a 2-cell is a polygon, and so on. These geometric interpretations of cells guide intuition, but a grid does not explicitly indicate its cells' geometry.

Nodes and Cells. We will refer to a 0-cell as a *node*. A node is named, but is otherwise featureless. A k-cell c is a set of nodes $(c_0, c_1, \ldots, c_n)$, where $k < n$. The order of the nodes allows interpretation of cells as visual shapes, but is not strictly necessary in the model. For example, a 1-cell must refer to at least two nodes, but can refer to more. Let $N(c)$ be the nodes of a cell c viewed as a set. We say a cell c is *incident* to a cell d if $N(c) \subseteq N(d)$. The dimension k of a k-cell c is written $\dim(c)$.

Node sets and the incidence relationship are sufficient to encode some topological relationships. Two cells are *adjacent* if they share nodes but neither is incident to the other. Two cells are *connected* if they appear in the transitive closure of the adjacency relationship. A topological *distance* measure can be defined by counting the number of cells traversed through the adjacency relationship to reach another cell. Note that containment and overlap are geometric relationships, since they depend on a particular geometric embedding.

Namespaces. Nodes are referenced with respect to a *namespace*. For example, nodes can be named by their physical position within an array. Let L be a set of labels and C be a set of nodes. A namespace is a 1-1 function $h : C \rightarrow L$. Cell equality is only defined with respect to a particular namespace. Cells in different namespaces are assumed to be unequal.

3.1 Grids

A grid is a sequence of sets of cells, $[G_0, G_1, G_2, \ldots, G_d]$, where each set G_i contains cells of dimension i. A non-empty grid must have a non-empty set of 0-cells (nodes). The dimension of a grid G is the greatest i such that G_i is non-empty. A grid's dimension is written $\dim(G)$. In Figure 1, the grid has four 0-cells, six 1-cells, and three 2-cells, and it therefore has dimension 2. Note that a d-dimensional grid G must have a non-empty component G_d, but may have an empty component G_i for $0 < i < d$.

This definition is very general; a grid may be a collection of unconnected polygons for GIS data, a set of scattered points for values of a random variable, or a well-connected graph modeling the truss structure of a bridge. The grids in our application are used to discretize the Columbia River estuary, for solving the 3-D transport equations via a finite-element method.

We can define set-like operations on grids with respect to a namespace to test cell equality. The intersection of two grids G and F is the componentwise intersection of the sets G_i and F_i. That is, $G \cap F = [G_0 \cap F_0, G_1 \cap F_1, \ldots]$. Union and difference can be defined similarly.

Grids must be *well-formed*; no cell in G_i may reference a node not in G_0, for $0 < i \leq \dim(G)$. Operations on grids must preserve well-formedness. If nodes are removed from a grid, then cells that reference those nodes must also be removed.

Cross Product. The cross product of two grids generates a higher-dimensional grid based on cross products of their constituent sets. The *node product* of two 0-cells a and b is written ab. The result is a 0-cell x in a new namespace. The *cell product* of a cell $c = (c_1, c_2, \ldots, c_n)$ and a cell $d = (d_1, d_2, \ldots, d_m)$, written $c \times d$, is a cell e with $\dim(e) = \dim(c) + \dim(d)$ such that $e = (c_1 d_1, c_1 d_2, \ldots, c_1 d_m, c_2 d_1, c_2 d_2, \ldots, c_2 d_m, \ldots, c_n d_1, c_n d_2, \ldots, c_n d_m)$.

Figure 3 shows an example of the cross product. The cross product of grids A and B contains six 0-cells, nine 1-cells, five 2-cells, and one 3-cell. The 3-cell is the interior of the prism, the 2-cells are the three rectangular faces and the two triangular bases, the 1-cells are the edges, and the 0-cells are the vertices.

We capture all these cases using the set-theoretic cross product of the components of the grids A and B. For example, the 3-cell prism in G is generated by sweeping the triangle of A through a third dimension defined by the line segment of B. This construction can be expressed as the cross product of the 2-cells of grid A (A_2) and the 1-cells of grid B (B_1). The rectangular faces are generated by sweeping the 1-cells of A through the space defined by the 1-cell of B. Again, the construction is expressed as the cross product of A_1 and B_1. More precisely, the cells of G are given by

$$G_0 = A_0 \times B_0$$
$$G_1 = (A_1 \times B_0) \cup (A_0 \times B_1)$$
$$G_2 = (A_2 \times B_0) \cup (A_1 \times B_1)$$
$$G_3 = A_2 \times B_1$$

Evaluating these expressions, we obtain

$G_0 = \{a1, b1, c1, a2, b2, c2\}$
$G_1 = \{(a1, b1), (b1, c1), (c1, a1), (a2, b2),$
$\qquad (b2, c2), (c2, a2), (a1, a2), (b1, b2), (c1, c2)\}$
$G_2 = \{(a1, b1, c1), (a2, b2, c2),$
$\qquad (a1, a2, b1, b2), (b1, b2, c1, c2), (c1, c2, a1, a2)\}$
$G_3 = \{(a1, a2, b1, b2, c1, c2)\}$

In general, let $A = [A_0, A_1, \ldots, A_a]$ and $B = [B_0, B_1, \ldots, B_b]$ be grids. The *cross product* of A and B, written $A \otimes B$, is a grid $[G_0, G_1, \ldots, G_d]$ such that $G_k = \bigcup_{j=0}^{k} A_j \times B_{k-j}$ for $0 \leq k \leq a + b$.

We have used the cross product operator frequently in expressing the data products of the CORIE system. The 3-D CORIE grid is the cross product of a 2-D horizontal grid and a 1-D vertical grid. The time dimension can be incorporated with another cross product. Note that simpler rectilinear grids can be modeled as the cross product of two 1-D grids. By commuting other operations through the cross product, we can reduce its complexity or remove it altogether. Tools that do not provide an explicit cross product operator do not have access to these optimizations, as we shall see.

3.2 Gridfields

When data is bound to a grid, the grid becomes a gridfield. Formally, a *gridfield* **G** is a triple (G, k, f), where G is a grid, k is a non-negative integer, and f is a function $G_k \to \tau$ for some type τ. The integer k is called the *rank* and can be extracted from a gridfield **G** by writing $\text{rank}(\mathbf{G})$. The *type* of a gridfield is the return type τ of its function component f, written $\mathbf{G} : \tau$. We will generally use only primitive numeric types and tuples of primitive numeric types as return types.

Earlier we used a trussed bridge as an example of a grid. Gridfields defined over such a grid might return the net force at each node, or the linear force along each truss. Gridfields capture both cases naturally by binding data to 0-cells or 1-cells, respectively. Images can be viewed naturally as a gridfield defined over 2-cells of a rectilinear grid. We can also model unstructured sets as a gridfield over a grid consisting solely of 0-cells.

To support multiple geometric embeddings, geometric information is modeled as ordinary data values bound to the cells of a grid. A simple example is a

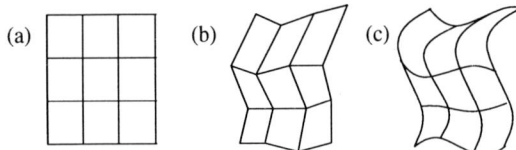

Figure 4: Three different geometric realizations of the same topological grid.

2-D grid with a gridfield binding (x,y) pairs to the nodes, which embeds the grid in Euclidean space. Additional coordinate systems can be captured through additional attributes. Many models [3, 8, 19] distinguish geometric attributes from other data, consequently requiring two versions of common operations: one for geometric attributes and one for ordinary attributes. Non-standard geometries that are not anticipated by the system designer are left unsupported. For example, the curvilinear grid shown in Figure 4 requires interpolation functions to be associated with each k-cell to specify how the cell curves in a geometric space. Our model can express such an embedding. Further, our model captures the topological equivalence between all three grids in Figure 4. Systems commonly use geometry as the identifying feature of a grid, thereby obscuring this equivalence.

3.3 Operators

The operators for manipulating gridfields must correctly handle both the grid and the bound data values. Some operators we define are analogous to relational operators, but grid-enabled. For example, our restrict operator filters a gridfield by removing cells whose bound data values do not satisfy a predicate. However, restrict also ensures the output grid is well-formed, and that cells of all dimensions are passed along. Other operators are novel, such as aggregate. The aggregate operator maps data from one grid onto another and then aggregates the values.

Bind. The bind operator constructs a gridfield from a grid G, an integer k, and a function $f : G_k \rightarrow \tau$. Bind allows us to perform operations on grids prior to associating data. We can therefore construct a topologically regular grid via cross product, but then bind irregular geometry functions to it, as in Figure 4b. The bind operator is rather simple at the logical layer, but at the physical layer, the bind operator is important for correct and efficient processing (see Section 6).

Restrict. The restrict operator behaves like a relational select, except that the output must be defined on a well-formed grid. If $\text{rank}(\mathbf{G}) = 0$, then cells that reference deleted nodes must themselves be deleted. Note that if $\text{rank}(\mathbf{G}) = k > 0$, then only the k-cells need to be removed; the grid is guaranteed to be well-formed. Formally, let $\mathbf{A} = (A, k, f)$ be a gridfield, with $f : A_k \rightarrow \tau$. Let p be a predicate over data values of type τ. Then $restrict(p, \mathbf{A})$ is a gridfield (G, k, f). For the case $k > 0$, $G = [G_0, G_1, \ldots, G_n]$, where $G_k = \{c \mid c \in A_k, \ p \circ f(c) = \text{true}\}$ and $G_i = A_i$ for all $i \neq k$ and $i \leq \dim(A)$. The predicate p is used to filter out some cells of dimension k, but all other cells are included in G. For the case $k = 0$, G_k is defined as before but we must remove any cells that reference deleted nodes. Thus, $G_i = \{c \mid c \in A_i, \ \forall v \in N(c).p \circ f(c) = \text{true}\}$

Merge. The merge operator computes the intersection of two grids and retains data values defined over this intersection. If the input gridfields are of different ranks, then the data values of the second argument are discarded and the rank of the result is the rank of the first argument. In this case, merge is not commutative. Formally, let $\mathbf{A} = (A, i, f)$ and $\mathbf{B} = (B, j, g)$ be gridfields. Then $merge(\mathbf{A}, \mathbf{B})$ produces a gridfield $\mathbf{G} = (A \cap B, i, h)$. For the case $i = j$, $h(e) = \langle f(e), g(e) \rangle$. For the case $i \neq j$, $h(e) = f(e)$.

Cross Product. The cross product operator for gridfields builds on the cross product operator on grids. Let $\mathbf{A} = (A, i, f)$ and $\mathbf{B} = (B, j, g)$ be gridfields. The cross product of $\mathbf{A}$ and $\mathbf{B}$, written $\mathbf{A} \otimes \mathbf{B}$, is a gridfield $\mathbf{G} = (A \otimes B, i + j, h)$, where $h(c) = \langle g(c), f(c) \rangle$.

This definition can result in a gridfield with a partial function if there are multiple ways to form cells of intermediate dimension in the cross product. To avoid this complication in the current implementation, we force the function h to be total by requiring that either $\text{rank}(\mathbf{A}) = \text{rank}(\mathbf{B}) = 0$, or that $\text{rank}(\mathbf{A}) = \dim(A)$ and $\text{rank}(\mathbf{B}) = \dim(B)$.

Aggregate The aggregate operator maps a *source* gridfield's cells onto a *target* gridfield's cells, and then aggregates the data values bound to the mapped cells. The behavior of aggregate is controlled by two functions, an *assignment* function and an *aggregation* function. The assignment function associates each cell in the target grid with a set of cells in the source grid. To perform the assignment, the function may use topological information only (e.g., a "neighbors" function that identifies incident cells), or it may use the attributes of the two gridfields (e.g., an "overlaps" function that uses geometry data).

To illustrate a simple use of aggregate, consider a timeseries of temperature values for a particular point in the river. We discretize the time dimension using a 1-D source grid S, as shown in Figure 5a. One use of the aggregate operator is to perform a "chunking" operation to coarsen the resolution of the grid. The assignment function maps each node in the target grid T to a set of n nodes, the chunk, in the source grid S (Figure 5b). The aggregation function can then, say, average the n nodes to obtain a single value (Figure 5c).

We could also pass a "window" function as the assignment function to perform a smoothing operation. The target grid and the source grid are the same in that case. For target node i, the window function as-

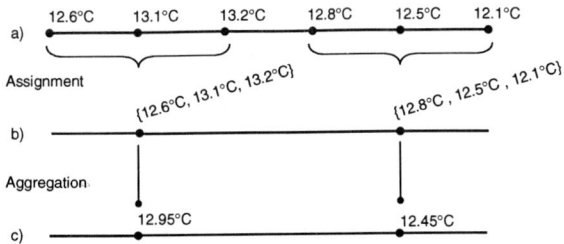

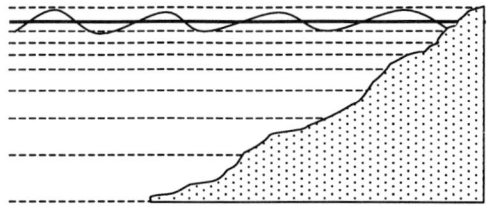

Figure 5: (a) A 1-D gridfield returning temperatures. (b) Assignment to the target grid T. (c) Aggregation using arithmetic mean.

Figure 6: The vertical grid and the river's bathymetry in the CORIE domain.

signs source nodes $[i-k, i-k+1, \ldots, i, i+1, \ldots, i+k]$. The aggregation function could be anything, but for smoothing, an arithmetic or weighted mean seems appropriate. We have used a 1-D example for illustration, but multidimensional window and chunking functions are common.

Formally, let $\mathbf{T} = (T, k, f)$ and $\mathbf{S} = (S, j, g)$ be gridfields, where $f : T_k \to \alpha$ and $g : S_j \to \beta$. Let m be a function $m : T_k \to \mathcal{P}(S_j)$. Let $a : \mathcal{P}(\beta) \to \gamma$ be a function for some type γ. Then $aggregate(\mathbf{T}, m, a, \mathbf{S})$ produces a gridfield $\mathbf{G} = (T, k, h)$ where $h(c) = a(\{g(e) \mid e \in m(c)\})$.

3.4 Benefits

We summarize the benefits of our data model:

- Grids are first-class and of arbitrary dimension.
- Grids can be shared between datasets.
- Geometry is modeled as data, exposing topological equivalences between geometric interpretations; e.g., different coordinate systems.
- Data can be associated with cells of any dimension, avoiding ambiguities arising from associating, for example, cell areas with nodes.
- The data model captures irregular grids directly, but the cross product operator expresses the regularity of rectilinear grids.
- The aggregate operator is extensible, allowing application-specific assignment and aggregation functions.
- The operators obey algebraic identities enabling optimization (see Section 6).
- Client programs can process grids without intricate array manipulations.

3.5 Detailed Example

Many of the CORIE datasets are defined over a 3-D grid constructed as the cross product of a 2-D irregular grid and a 1-D grid. The 2-D grid H describes the domain parallel to the earth's surface, a *horizontal* orientation. The 1-D grid V extends in a *vertical* direction perpendicular to the earth's surface. These grids are illustrated in Figures 2 and 6, respectively.

Although the simulation code operates over the grid formed from the cross product of H and V, the output datasets are produced on a reduced grid. To see why, consider Figure 6. The shaded region illustrates the bathymetry of the river. The horizontal grid is defined to cover the entire surface of the water. Below the surface, some nodes in the full 3-D cross product grid are positioned underground! The simulation code outputs only valid, "wet," data values to conserve disk space. Therefore, we must define this "wet" grid to obtain an adequate description of the topology of the data. The bathymetry data can be modeled as a gridfield over the horizontal grid H, associating a depth with each node. To filter out nodes in the product grid G that are deeper than the river bottom, we need to compare the node's depth (bound to V) with the bottom depth (bound to H). In the following, we will refer to a rank 0 gridfield $\mathbf{H}$ constructed from the 2-D horizontal grid H and attributes x, y, b. The attribute b captures the river's bathymetry at a particular location. We will also refer to a rank 0 gridfield $\mathbf{V}$ constructed from the 1-D vertical grid V and an attribute z.

The task is to construct the grid over which the simulation outputs are defined, bind a dataset to it, and visualize the results. The recipe for this task is shown in Figure 7. Each gray oval is an operator in our algebra. The unfilled oval at the right represents a client task: render the grid as an image. The recipe begins at left with the $\mathbf{H}$ and $\mathbf{V}$ gridfields. The cross product operator produces a different, 3-D gridfield. After using restrict to filter out the river bottom, we have our "wetgrid" (at the point labelled in Figure 7). After binding a salinity dataset to the wetgrid, we restrict the grid to a user-supplied region. The term "region" is shorthand for a bounding-box condition involving $x, y,$ and z.

Using a Relational Database. Our initial attempt to manage the CORIE datasets was to load them into a relational table and manipulate them using SQL. The first task is to devise a schema that captures both the grid and the data. One method is to store each logical gridfield as a separate relation: one attribute stores the cells to which the data is bound, while the other attributes store the bound data. A problem with this approach is that each scalar dataset bound to a grid is modeled as an attribute of a relation. New datasets are generated daily. To capture each new dataset, we can either extend the existing table with an additional attribute or add the new dataset

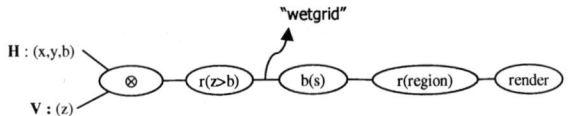

Figure 7: A recipe for visualizing a 3-D CORIE dataset.

as a separate table. Either way, we are changing the database schema daily, making robust queries difficult to write.

A better strategy for modeling grids and gridfields using an RDBMS is to allow any number of datasets to be bound to the same grid. The relation grid stores metadata about the grid. Each grid is associated with a number of cells of varying dimension, stored in the relation kcell. Tuples in the values relation are bound to cells using foreign keys, perhaps integers. Now no schema changes are required to insert new datasets, but binding a particular dataset to its grid involves a join between the kcells relation and the values relation using the ordinal. Including the bound cell's definition itself in the value relation seems to avoid the join. However, working with multiple bound datasets simultaneously requires a self-join on the cell column for each dataset. Computing joins on these complex columns is more expensive than computing joins on an integer column.

To associate cells with data values, we already must have computed the appropriate grid. However, it is valuable at times to store grids intensionally; that is, *decomposed*. For example, a frequently used CORIE grid is the cross product of the horizontal grid H and the vertical grid V. Although a relational approach allows us to express the cross product as a query, we cannot declare that the tuples in a physical table have a foreign key to a query result. An alternative is to use a 2-part foreign key, where the first part references a cell in the grid H, and the second part references a cell in the grid V. Now the space required is higher, and datasets bound to cross-product grids are accessed differently from other datasets. Precomputing and storing an intensional grid consumes space and obscures the relationship between the composed grid and its base grids.

Using Visualization Software. Another approach, which sacrifices data management capabilities for a richer toolset, is to use a visualization library specifically designed to work with gridded datasets. Such libraries are usually oriented toward working with a single dataset at a time, and therefore provide little support for reasoning about the relationships between datasets. Unfortunately, recognizing and exploiting relationships between datasets is a great source of optimization opportunities, as we show later. Further, the programmer is under a significant burden in making use of the library, as each tool has complicated and nuanced semantics.

Software libraries provide functions (or objects) for each specific task. The programmer is often asked to choose between two similar functions that differ only in the type of data on which they operate or the particular algorithm they implement. For example, in the Visualization Toolkit [19], to extract a subset of a grid, there are a variety of functions to choose from. The operation vtkExtractUnstructuredGrid accepts internal ids of points and cells, or a function over the geometry of the points. The operation vtkExtractGrid works only on structured grids and accepts i, j, and k index ranges that define a structured subgrid. The operation vtkExtractGeometry works on a wider range of datasets, but accepts only geometric functions rather than topological ids. A more efficient version is available for polygonal data, vtkExtractPolyDataGeometry. Another operator, vtkThreshold filters grids based on non-geometric attributes.

The physical concerns of representations and algorithms are intermingled with semantic concerns such as which data is used to filter the grid. All of the operations above can be implemented using the restrict operator, possibly with the aggregate operator to evaluate complex geometric functions. The distinction between filtering geometric data and other bound data is removed in our model.

As we gained experience with VTK and another visualization library [10], we found that simple concepts we used to describe our data products often did not have counterparts in these libraries. Below we list some specific concepts we found weak or missing.

- Cross Product Grids.
- Shared Grids.
- Combinatorial algorithms. Berti observes that combinatorial algorithms for grid manipulation are superior to geometric algorithms [3].
- Aggregation. Both libraries we reviewed implement particular instances of aggregation, but do not provide a general aggregation abstraction.
- Time. We found it useful to reason about time similarly to other dimensions.
- Irregular Grids. Manipulating regular grids is easier than manipulating unstructured grids. Since CORIE involves both kinds of grids, we sought a unifying model.

4 Gridfield Representations

A goal of this work is to support and exploit multiple representations of gridfields, for two reasons: First, supporting a variety of representations can promote interoperability with existing systems. Second, no one representation is efficient for all recipes.

We have identified four major patterns of gridfield representation used in practice. The *tabular* representation forms $\langle cell, value \rangle$ tuples, making it easy to

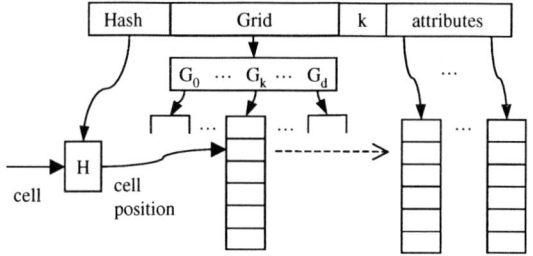

Figure 8: Internal representation of a gridfield in our current implementation.

pipeline data from one operator to another, but difficult to separate grid from data.

The *parallel* representation uses a separate array for each attribute, all aligned positionally with another array for the cells to which the attributes are bound. With this representation, binding in new attributes and projecting out unneeded ones are trivial operations.

The *decomposed* representation stores gridfields intensionally, requiring the client program to assemble the gridfield as needed. Cross product grids are often decomposed in order to save space.

The *nested* representation involves gridfield attributes that can themselves be gridfields. A 4-D timespace gridfield may be a timeseries (the outer grid) and a 3-D spatial grid (the inner, nested grid).

Our Representation. Figure 8 illustrates the representation we use in our current implementation. The gridfield at top stores an integer rank k, and pointers to the grid and each attribute. An attribute is an array of data values, and a grid is a sequence of arrays of cells. Cells of dimension k are aligned positionally with the attributes; we use the parallel representation described above. We began with the parallel representation because it exhibits good performance characteristics (see Section 8) and is used frequently in client software [10, 19] and standard file formats (cf. [11]).

A hash index (H in Figure 8) maps cell definitions to their ordinal position. This index allows the function semantics prescribed by the model to be evaluated in constant time on average. A cell definition is mapped to an array index, which is then used to lookup a data value in each of the attribute arrays. The hash function used maps each cell to its first node, exploiting the fact that seldom do more than 4 or 5 cells touch any one node. Our tests show that this hash function generates very few collisions while offering fast evaluation time.

Another index (not shown in Figure 8) speeds up navigation of the incidence relationship. Each node in the grid is mapped to the cells to which it is incident. The aggregate operator frequently uses this index.

5 Operator Implementation

Our operators are implemented in C++, with in-memory indices implemented using the Standard Template Library (STL) [20]. Physical recipes are currently constructed by hand, though we are designing a declarative query language as an interface to the physical operators.

The parallel representation improves performance in some cases. Binding a new attribute to a grid is inexpensive, as is projecting out attributes. We need not iterate of the arrays; we can simply make a copy of the gridfield header structure (see Figure 8) containing pointers to the information we want.

The merge operator might compute the intersection of two grids during evaluation, and is therefore potentially expensive. However, if the two argument gridfields are defined over the same grid, merge can be evaluated in constant time. Since gridfields may share grids via pointers, checking for grid equivalence is essentially free.

The aggregate operator admits specialized implementations for syntactic convenience and to exploit efficient algorithms. The *apply* specialization uses identical source and target grids, but applies an arithmetic expression to the data values. The *project* specialization also uses identical source and target grids, but simply removes attributes from each logical tuple. The *affix* operator changes the rank of a gridfield by transferring the data values to cells of a different dimension and averaging. The *unify* operator aggregates all of the values in a grid, binding the result to the *unit* grid consisting of a single node.

Cross product is usually the most expensive operator in the algebra. In the next section, we investigate algebraic rewrites to reduce its cost or remove it altogether. We can also improve its implementation in some cases. The cross product of a grid with nodes, edges, and polygons and a grid with nodes and edges produces nodes, edges, polygons, and polyhedra. However, for visualization purposes, we may only need the polyhedra and the nodes; cells of intermediate dimensions need not be computed. However, to use such a "prune" implementation, we must be able to determine which dimension cells will be consumed downstream.

Another implementation of the cross product operator (applicable to Figure 7) exploits the fact that it is followed immediately by a restrict. In relational algebra, a join is semantically equivalent to a cross product followed by a restrict. We can create an analogous "join" operator that evaluates the restrict as the cross product is computed, computing fewer cells overall.

6 Optimization

Having described our data representation and operator implementation, we now present optimization techniques enabled by our algebra for improving the per-

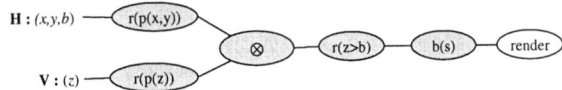

Figure 9: An optimized recipe for visualizing a 3-D CORIE dataset.

formance of recipes. Our examples are actual CORIE data products, though the techniques we use generalize to any domain involving irregular grids, cross product grids, or selected sub-regions.

Forward Binding. The recipe in Figure 7 computes a 3-D salinity gridfield, then restricts the result to a user-specified region. The logical model allows us to freely commute the restrict operator with the bind, and then with the cross product [9], to significantly reduce the size of the intermediate results. However, the physical implementation materializes functions as arrays, so special handling is required. The array we wish to bind can only be correctly interpreted using the ordinal positions of the wetgrid. If we push the restrict earlier, we will produce a grid smaller than the wetgrid, and the bound array will be misaligned. To solve this problem, we can pre-compute the ordinal positions of cells in the wetgrid and record these values in an attribute. This attribute can then be passed to the bind operator and used as offsets into the array on disk.

Our goal is to push the restrict on "region" before the cross product, but there are two obstacles. One is the cross product itself, and the other is another restrict involving attributes b and z from **H** and **V**, respectively[2]. A cell's ordinal position in a cross product grid can be derived from the ordinal positions of the cells used to construct it. However, the grid we want is not just a cross product of two grids, but the restriction of a cross product. Therefore, the ordinals of the cells of the wetgrid are dependent on the condition used to filter out the "dry" cells.

In the general case, the 1000th cell in the grid prior to a restrict could be the 1st cell or the 1000th cell in the restricted grid. However, we know a *physical property* of the gridfield **V**: It is sorted on the attribute z. We can therefore compute the positions of the wetgrid's cells without actually materializing the grid itself.

Recall the attribute b of the gridfield **H** stores bathymetry information for the river. Specifically, b is an index into the gridfield **V**. Since **V** is sorted on z, we can use b to determine the number of cells in each vertical column of water. With these cell counts, we can compute an offset into the array to be bound to the wetgrid.

The result of these transformations is the optimized recipe shown in Figure 9. The potentially highly selective restricts on x, y and z are evaluated prior to

[2]This restrict compares attributes from both **H** and **V** and does therefore not commute with the cross product.

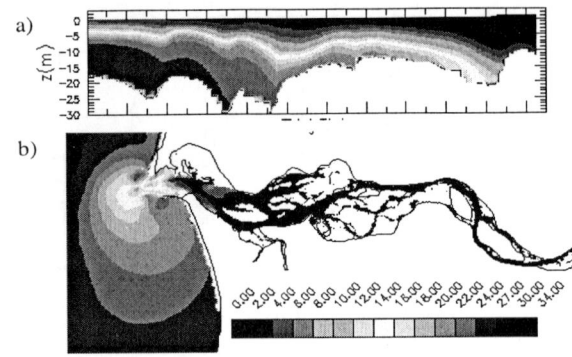

Figure 10: (a) A vertical slice data product. (b) A horizontal slice data product.

the cross product.

Lowering Dimensionality Two common 2-D CORIE data products are horizontal and vertical "slices." Examples of these data products for the salinity variable are shown in Figure 10. One way to express the horizontal slice data product is to use the same recipe as in Figure 7, but restrict the z dimension to a single node. As before, we could push the restricts through the cross product. This time, though, we observe that restricting **V** to a single node produces the unit grid. The unit grid is the identity for the cross product operator, up to namespace isomorphism. We can therefore remove the cross product operator altogether.

This optimization is unavailable to systems that cannot reason about grids algebraically. We have not only produced a faster recipe, but we have also naturally expressed a critical correctness criteria: The output grid is 2-D. Although the wetgrid is constructed from prism-shaped cells, this data product is defined over triangles. (We have assumed that the depth at which a slice is to be taken corresponds to one of the depths in the vertical grid V. We could relax this assumption by using an aggregate operator equipped with an interpolation function.)

Computing a vertical slice is more difficult. The horizontal grid H has an irregular topology consisting of triangles. To take a vertical slice, we must still project the 3-D grid down to two dimensions, but the target is a new grid not appearing elsewhere in the recipe. Consider a user who wants to view a vertical profile of the salinity intrusion along a deep channel near the mouth of the estuary. To specify "along a deep channel" to the system, the user selects a sequence of points in the xy plane, as shown in Figure 11a. We can connect these points to form a 1-D grid, P. A cross product with the vertical grid gives us a 2-D slice, $P \otimes V$ (Figure 11b).

Using VTK, we must manually construct the grid $P \otimes V$ producing points in 3-D space. For each point, we must search in the 3-D wetgrid for the cell that contains the point, then perform a 3-D interpolation

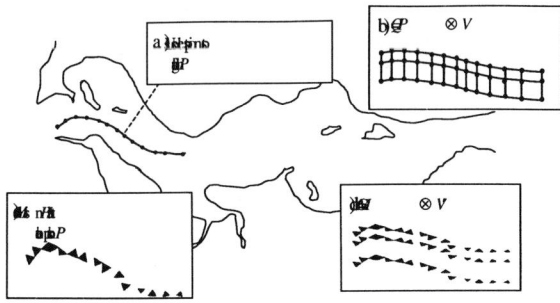

Figure 11: Four intermediate steps in an efficient "vertical slice" recipe.

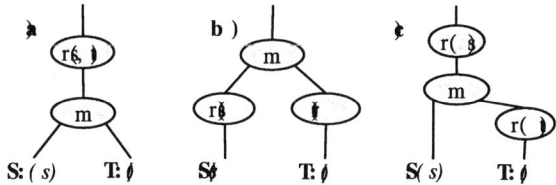

Figure 12: Three equivalent sub-recipes. (a) Restrict operations are combined into one. (b) The restrict operators are pushed through a merge, resulting in a *less* efficient plan. (c) Evaluating one restrict at a time might require less memory.

of salinity values.

With the gridfield algebra, we can do the work in two dimensions for considerable savings. Each point in P can be positioned in a triangle in the horizontal grid H. We can restrict H to only those cells that contain one or more points in P using the aggregate operator followed by a restrict, producing a grid M (Figure 11c).

Since the grid M is a restriction of the grid H, we can use forward binding (as we did previously) to construct a 3-D grid (not shown in Figure 11) and bind the appropriate salinity values to it. We can now perform the same search-and-interpolate operation required by VTK, but using a much smaller 3-D grid.

An additional optimization is possible. Instead of considering V as a 1-D grid, we prune the 1-cells, leaving only the nodes. Call this grid V'. The grid $M \otimes V'$ consists of "stacks" of 2-D triangles (Figure 11d), rather than a connected set of 3-D prisms. Interpolation using triangles is much cheaper than interpolation using prisms, further reducing the cost.

By working primarily in two dimensions, we were able to produce a less expensive recipe. Lowering the dimension of the intermediate results saves time since a) higher dimensional gridfields tend to have more cells, and b) algorithms for manipulating 3-D cells are more expensive than their 2-D counterparts.

Merging Related Grids The *plume* is the region of water beyond the mouth of the river with a salt content below a given threshold. The recipe to compute the plume extends the recipe to bind salinity to the wetgrid in Section 6. We encode the definition of the plume as conditions passed to the restrict operator.

Consider a recipe to find the portion of the plume above a certain temperature. Assume temperature data has been bound, separately, to another instance of the wetgrid, and we now need to merge this data with the salinity gridfield.

We need to evaluate two restrict operators (r) and one merge operator (m) to obtain the correct gridfield. Three versions of the relevant fragment of this new recipe are shown in Figure 12. Figure 12a shows the two restricts evaluated after the merge. Previously, we improved performance by evaluating restricts early, as in Figure 12b. In this case the merge operator must compute the intersection of two grids – an $O(nm)$ algorithm, where n and m are the number of cells in **S** and **T**, respectively. But observe that in Figure 12a, both arguments are defined over the same grid. This knowledge allows the merge to be evaluated trivially. The recipe in Figure 12c may also be a good choice. Since the grid T is known to be a subset of the grid S, we can still evaluate the merge in constant time. We can also evict the attribute t from memory right after we have evaluated the first restrict, possibly lowering the memory footprint of the overall recipe.

7 Experimental Results

We performed experiments to 1) validate our design choices in the physical implementation and 2) to determine whether algebraic optimization techniques could improve performance over more traditional solutions.

The experiments were run on a dual 2.4 GHz processor with 4GB of RAM. This machine is nearly identical to one node of the cluster on which the CORIE simulations are executed. Each experiment involved 5 trials, and three experiments were done at different times. The samples produced a variance of less than 1% of the mean, demonstrating stability.

The CORIE horizontal grid consists of 29,602 nodes and 55,081 2-cells. The vertical grid has 62 nodes and 61 1-cells. The wetgrid has 829,852 nodes, and therefore each timestep of each dataset has 829,852 values.

Our first experiment compared physical implementations of the cross product operator. The "prune" implementation avoids extra work by computing only the nodes and polyhedra of the 3-D cross product. The "join" implementation composes the cross product and subsequent restrict. Figure 13 shows results for the original cross product implementation ("no opt"), the "prune" implementation ("prune") and with both improvements ("both"). If C_w and C_r are the cardinalities of the wetgrid and the result gridfield, respectively, then the selectivity (x-axis) is $1 - \frac{C_r}{C_w}$.

Times reflect overall execution time of the 3-D scalar data product described in Section 3.5, highlighting the cross product operator's significant cost relative to the other operators in the recipe. The graph shows that avoiding cell materialization does indeed

933

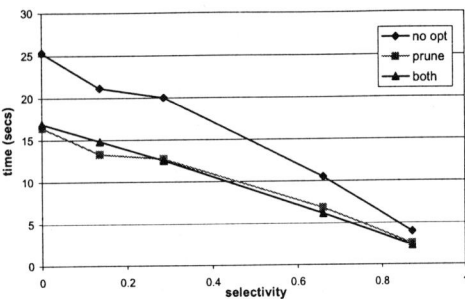

Figure 13: Comparing implementations of the cross product operator.

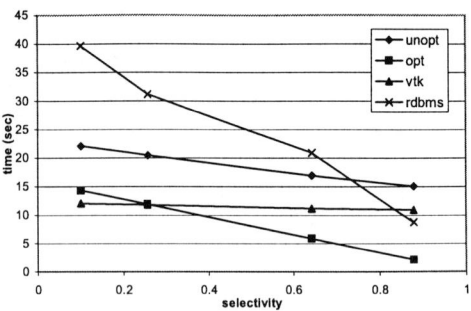

Figure 14: Optimized and unoptimized recipes compared with two traditional approaches.

improve performance. On average, the prune implementation results in 35% faster times than computing the full cross product. The join implementation does not provide a consistent improvement. With the standard cross product implementation, we can predict precisely the space requirements of the output. With the join implementation, we must estimate the selectivity of the join condition and dynamically resize arrays when we are wrong. Although the join implementation produces no unnecessary cells, the extra complexity of memory management washes out the performance gain.

The second experiment compares our algebraically optimized recipe in Figure 9 with the unoptimized recipe in Figure 7, as well as with two more traditional approaches. First, we used a relational database extended with spatial data types to represent the cells. Second, we used VTK along with custom code that handles those operations inexpressible in VTK.

The relational approach uses SQL to join data with cells and select the "wet" values. Our test DBMS was Postgres [23], configured appropriately for the large main memory of our experiment platform.

The times for the relational approach are artificially low, as we did not include the time to extract the results to the client. Instead, the results were simply loaded into a temporary table on the server. We felt that the diversity of potential client interfaces muddles the results, and a query-only experiment represents a conservative lower bound. For our own approach, we did include the time required to convert our gridfield representation into a form suitable for rendering by a third party library, but not the rendering time itself.

The implementation in VTK required a custom reader for our file formats. Restrictions were implemented using the VTKThreshold object. The cross product and bind operators were implemented in a custom reader since these tools were not available in VTK. Unlike our general operators, we were free to design the reader for specific tasks: reading in a CORIE dataset, computing the wetgrid, and building a VTK object. This focused goal afforded a very efficient design. Indeed, the reader was not the bottleneck despite representing the majority of work.

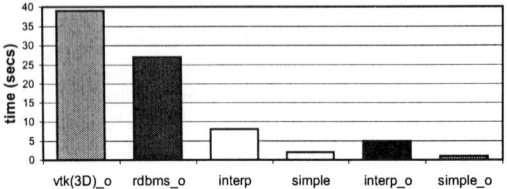

Figure 15: Experimental results for the vertical slice data product.

Figure 14 shows test results for various size regions, which translate to various selectivities of the full wetgrid. Observe that our unoptimized recipe is slower than the VTK implementation, even though they implement similar recipes. The specialized reader, implementing the cross product, restrict, and bind operations constitutes only about 15% of the total execution time. In our program, these operations constitute about 30% of the total. The specialized reader is indeed more efficient than the generic operators.

The optimized recipe performs better in all but the lowest selectivities. The advantage of reducing dataset size as early as possible is apparent here just as it is in relational processing. Note that VTK's times are effectively the same for all selectivities, as would be expected given the recipe of Figure 7a. Regardless of the region being displayed, the entire 3-D grid is generated and iterated through. The relational approach is far behind in all but the highest selectivities. Although the optimizer produces query plans that behave like our optimized recipe, the overhead of processing gridded datasets using joins dwarfs the effect.

The third experiment compares the optimized vertical slice recipe against a VTK program and an SQL query (Figure 15). The bar labelled "interp" uses interpolation as described above. The bar labelled "simple" approximates interpolation and improves performance by taking the value of a random node in the cell. The bars labelled with the 'o' suffix make use of a semantic optimization: We restrict the grid to the relevant region before searching for cells that contain points. Note that even our recipes that do *not* exploit this optimization outperform the optimized VTK program and the optimized SQL query.

8 Future Work and Conclusions

Our primary goal is a data server that can accept gridfield recipes expressed in a declarative query language and produce gridded dataset answers in a flexible yet efficient manner. As a first step, we have derived an algebra that captures procedural recipes. We are building prototype applications that will generate recipes in this algebra.

We are modeling the taxonomy of gridfield representations more precisely, so as to include representations in our space of optimization techniques. Nested gridfields seem especially flexible, as they are key to modeling and processing multi-resolution grids. Nested gridfields also provide a mechanism by which we may segment a large grid for parallel processing or for secondary storage management.

The recipes we have used in this paper have involved only a few gridfields. In reality, there are terabytes of gridded datasets one might wish to manipulate. Finding and retrieving these gridded datasets requires a form of catalog, for which relational or object-relational databases are quite appropriate. Technology such as IBM's Datalinks [4] for managing files external to the database may be useful.

We are studying additional grid properties and deriving versions of the operators to preserve them. For example, notions of grid *quality* are used by grid generation packages.

We have presented an implementation of an algebra for manipulating scientific datasets and shown that this approach offers benefits in both expression and performance. In summary, our contributions are:

- A design and implementation of a gridfield algebra.
- Algebraic optimization techniques for improving performance of gridfield recipes.
- Application to real data products.
- Experimental evidence that such processing strategies result in superior performance.

References

[1] A. Baptista, M. Wilkin, P. Pearson, P. Turner, M. C., and P. Barrett. Coastal and estuarine forecast systems: A multi-purpose infrastructure for the columbia river. *Earth System Monitor, NOAA*, 9(3), 1999.

[2] P. Baumann. A database array algebra for spatio-temporal data and beyond. In *Next Generation Information Technologies and Systems*, pages 76–93, 1999.

[3] G. Berti. *Generic software components for Scientific Computing*. PhD thesis, BTU Cottbus, Germany, 2000.

[4] S. Bhattacharya, C. Mohan, K. W. Brannon, I. Narang, H.-I. Hsiao, and M. Subramanian. Coordinating backup/recovery and data consistency between database and file systems. In *SIGMOD*, pages 500–511, 2002.

[5] D. M. Butler and S. Bryson. Vector-bundle classes form powerful tool for scientific visualization. *Computers in Physics*, 6(6):576–584, 1992.

[6] D. J. DeWitt, N. Kabra, J. Luo, J. M. Patel, and J.-B. Yu. Client-Server Paradise. In *VLDB*, pages 558–569, Santiago, Chile, 1994.

[7] ESRI Corporation. ArcGIS: Working with geodatabase topology. Technical report, ESRI, 2003.

[8] R. Haber, B. Lucas, and N. Collins. A data model for scientific visualization with provision for regular and irregular grids. In *Visualization*. IEEE Computer Society Press, 1991.

[9] B. Howe, D. Maier, and A. Baptista. A language for spatial data manipulation. *Journal of Environmental Informatics*, 2(2), December 2003.

[10] IBM Corporation. *IBM Visualization Data Explorer User Guide*, 4th edition, 1993.

[11] H. L. Jenter and R. P. Signell. Netcdf: A public-domain-software solution to data-access problems for numerical modelers. Unidata, 1992.

[12] L. Libkin, R. Machlin, and L. Wong. A query language for multidimensional arrays: design, implementation, and optimization techniques. In *SIGMOD*, pages 228–239, 1996.

[13] A. P. Marathe and K. Salem. A language for manipulating arrays. In *VLDB*, pages 46–55, 1997.

[14] J. Melton, J.-E. Michels, V. Josifovski, K. Kulkarni, P. Schwarz, and K. Zeidenstein. SQL and management of external data. *SIGMOD Record*, 30(1):70–77, 2001.

[15] P. Moran. Field model: An object-oriented data model for fields. Technical report, NASA Ames Research Center, 2001.

[16] R. Musick and T. Critchlow. Practical lessons in supporting large-scale computational science. *SIGMOD Record*, 28(4):49–57, 1999.

[17] M. Papiani, J. Wason, and D. A. Nicole. An architecture for management of large, distributed, scientific data using SQL/MED and XML. In *EDBT*, pages 447–461, 2000.

[18] P. J. Rhodes, R. D. Bergeron, and T. M. Sparr. Database support for multisource multiresolution scientific data. In *SOFSEM*, pages 94 – 114, 2002.

[19] W. J. Schroeder, K. M. Martin, and W. E. Lorensen. The design and implementation of an object-oriented toolkit for 3D graphics and visualization. In *IEEE Visualization*, pages 93–100, 1996.

[20] A. A. Stepanov and M. Lee. The Standard Template Library. Technical Report X3J16/94-0095, WG21/N0482, 1994.

[21] C. Stolte, D. Tang, and P. Hanrahan. Query, analysis, and visualization of multidimensional relational databases. In *SIGKDD*, pages 112–122, 2002.

[22] E. Stolte and G. Alonso. Efficient exploration of large scientific databases. In *VLDB*, pages 622–633, 2002.

[23] M. Stonebraker, L. A. Rowe, and M. Hirohama. The implementation of postgres. *TKDE*, 2(1):125–142, 1990.

[24] A. Thakar, P. Kunszt, A. Szalay, and J. Gray. The sdss science archive: Object vs relational implementations of a multi-tb astronomical database. *Computers in Science and Engineering*, 2002.

[25] P. Watson. Topology and ORDBMS technology. Technical report, Laser-Scan, 2002.

[26] N. Widmann and P. Baumann. Efficient execution of operations in a dbms for multidimensional arrays. In *SSDBM*, pages 155–165, 1998.

Multi-objective Query Processing for Database Systems

Wolf-Tilo Balke
Computer Science Department
University of California
Berkeley, CA, USA
balke@eecs.berkeley.edu

Ulrich Güntzer
Institut für Informatik
University of Tübingen
Tübingen, Germany
guentzer@informatik.uni-tuebingen.de

Abstract

Query processing in database systems has developed beyond mere exact matching of attribute values. Scoring database objects and retrieving only the top k matches or Pareto-optimal result sets (skyline queries) are already common for a variety of applications. Specialized algorithms using either paradigm can avoid naïve linear database scans and thus improve scalability. However, these paradigms are only two extreme cases of exploring viable compromises for each user's objectives. To find the correct result set for arbitrary cases of multi-objective query processing in databases we will present a novel algorithm for computing sets of objects that are non-dominated with respect to a set of monotonic objective functions. Naturally containing top k and skyline retrieval paradigms as special cases, this algorithm maintains scalability also for all cases in between. Moreover, we will show the algorithm's correctness and instance-optimality in terms of necessary object accesses and how the response behavior can be improved by progressively producing result objects as quickly as possible, while the algorithm is still running.

1. Introduction

Optimizing parameters under multiple constraints and negotiating compromises between different objectives has a long history in economic problems. Though simplifying approaches often reduce business decisions to 'maximize profits', common problems often deal with non-monetary intangibles like product quality, public image, tradition, corporate identity or ethics like environmental concerns or safety features. But apart from mere business problems multi-objective optimization also plays a role in many areas of computer science:

- Multi-objective agents negotiate compromises on behalf of different users or interest groups
- Decision support systems try to integrate various interests to recommend strategic decisions
- Trade-offs in e-commerce environments e.g. between price, efficiency and quality of certain products have to be assessed
- Personal preferences of users requesting a Web service for a complex task have to be evaluated to select most appropriate services

Also in the field of databases and query optimization such optimization problems often occur like in [22] for the choice of query plans given different execution costs and latencies or in [19] for choosing data sources with optimized information quality. Let us mathematically formulate the problem of multi-objective optimization in database retrieval and then consider typical sample applications for information systems:

Multi-objective Retrieval: Given a database containing N objects $O := \{o_1,...,o_N\}$, n characteristics $s_k(o)$ ($1 \leq k \leq n$) to describe the objects (e.g. scoring functions for low-level features, aggregations of attribute values, etc.) and m monotonic functions f_i ($1 \leq i \leq m$) aggregating subsets of the characteristics by objective functions, the problem is how to find the overall best database objects with respect to all m scoring functions.

For the scope of the paper we will assume that the characteristics s_k are scoring functions to evaluate certain characteristics of database objects assigning normalized scores in [0,1], i.e. we use a numerical domain for retrieval. Other approaches relying on more general characteristics like projections on the attributes themselves are more powerful in that they can also handle attribute-valued data with partial preference orders. However, all algorithms presented so far for this problem, are of quadratic complexity, whereas those assuming numerical scoring functions can use algorithms of essentially improved complexity, see e.g. [15]. To abstract from attribute-valued domains, we thus might need to derive suitable metrics for each dimension like shown in [18] to always enable numerical scoring of database objects.

Let us now consider a common use case scenario in database applications. A database usually stores a large number of values characterizing certain real world objects. Database applications usually rely on these characteristics, but provide an added value by selecting and aggregating the data along either domain-specific or user-provided functions or algorithms. From a retrieval point of view the derived measures in case of very simple arithmetical functions (avg, max, etc.) can be directly integrated into SQL statements, but for more complex functions user defined functions (UDFs) or stored procedures become necessary. The naïve way of addressing the problem of getting best values is to calculate the UDF for *every* database object and then order the objects by the derived scores. Consider the following example:

Example 1: Real Estate Information
When considering to buy a house, a database of real estate information on available objects may be particularly helpful. Generally the database can provide a variety of basic data like a house's size, its price or its location. But in buying a convenient place to live users often consider other measures derived from these initial data. For instance a user can put a constraint on the maximum budget and minimum size, but then might be interested in bargains with a good price per square-meter, thus aggregating the basic price and size information. On the other hand a user might be interested to find a good location and thus use a function on the location information in terms of rating the neighborhood or ranking houses according to the relative distance from the user's workplace.

As we can see this example poses a multi-objective problem because ranking schemes in price and size simply will not do, but a complex function reordering the database objects is called for (Note that neither the top-ranked houses according to price nor the top-ranked houses according to size have to be top-ranked with respect to our price/size function). And the bargains offered of course do not affect their respective location, thus this gives the user an independent ranked list to choose from in a skylining fashion. The problem becomes even harder, if personal preferences come into the aggregation. Consider the following example:

Example 2: Web Information Services
Imagine a personalized route planning system like [3] where different characteristics of each route are mapped onto a numerical domain. Such characteristics may be the length of each route relative to the shortest one s_1, the probable delay by traffic jams s_2 (e.g. measured by aggregating the number, length and grade of congestion of current jams on a route) or the weather conditions s_3 aggregating visibility (rain, fog) or the danger of black ice. Retrieving the 'best' route for every driver now, however, poses a severe problem: whereas it is natural to aggregate some characteristics others might again be considered incomparable.

For instance users will generally be willing to drive a slightly longer route, if it is not congested. Hence the trade-off between relative length and congestion can usually be determined by taking the average pain/gain ratio. The length of a route and its estimated delay by traffic jams can thus be aggregated using a suitably weighted average as compensation function for economy (e.g. in terms of shortest expected travel times) and our two basic scores as input, i.e. f_{eco} (s_1, s_2). Unlike length and traffic density the weather conditions will generally not be aggregated as easily, because the relative gain through 'better' weather is quite subjective. A motorcyclist may insist on better weather routes whereas a car driver might care less and anyway the respective compensation function lacks intuition. What does it mean, if good weather is said to be e.g. 0.63 times more important than economy?

A good solution here is exploring the skyline recommending very economic routes with possibly bad weather conditions, less economic routes with fair conditions and some possible compromises in between. Depending on the personal preferences a user then might decide for one of these possibilities. Thus our multi-objective problem in route planning has three score functions (length, congestion and weather) that are mapped onto a two-dimensional objective space (economy, weather). The objective functions used are the compensation function for economy and the trivial projection for the weather scores, i.e. for each route x we consider $F(x) := (f_{eco}(s_1(x), s_2(x)), s_3(x))$. In the following we will revisit this sample problem and present a single optimal algorithm to solve it efficiently.

The rest of the paper is organized as follows: section 2 will investigate the nature of multi-objective retrieval and revisit basic approaches of top k retrieval and skylining as special cases in database retrieval. Section 3 will present our unifying multi-objective retrieval algorithm and prove its basic properties and instance-optimality. We show the possibility and optimality of progressive delivery of result objects in section 4 and focus on practical scenarios and their impact on the result complexity in section 5.

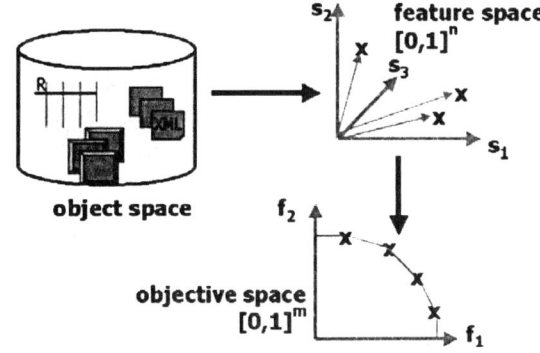

Fig. 1: Multi-objective retrieval

2. Towards Multi-objective Retrieval

In the problem definition and the use case scenario we have gained insight into the basic problem. Characteristics of database objects (like table data, images, XML documents, etc.) are numerically evaluated in the feature space and these scores are aggregated by means of user-specific objective functions (cf. fig. 1). To get a further understanding of the multi-objective optimization problem we now have to determine what 'overall best' means in this instance. For each database object o we get an m-dimensional vector containing the aggregated scores $(f_1(s_1(o),...,s_n(o)),..., f_m(s_1(o),..., s_n(o)))$ for each objective f_i. The problem of picking best vectors among these is one of the central problems addressed in operations research, e.g. [9], [4]. Operations research literature basically distinguishes between returning all non-dominated solutions (also known as 'efficient frontier' or 'Pareto optimal' solutions) among all m-dimensional vectors, or using specific qualitative ordering techniques (usually complex functions, the so-called 'utilities') that allow to order vectors by further aggregating their score values and then returning only the best-ranked objects [12].

2.1. Utility-based Retrieval Models

In utility-based approaches doing worse in some features can be compensated by doing better in others. A utility function then aggregates each vector to a scalar overall utility. Often even the existence of a *single* global utility function is implicitly or explicitly assumed. This global aggregation of objective scores can be processed by **top k retrieval** algorithms. Often besides the scoring functions also some fixed a priori constraints on the values for each vector component are given, so-called bottleneck conditions. Before returning the result set to the user these constraints can discard solutions that violate essential constraints. However, top k retrieval cannot work with multiple objectives, i.e. incomparable utilities or goals.

Among the non-aggregated definitions of overall best objects, the notion of **Pareto optimality** (often referred to as skyline queries in database literature) is the broadest, because only objects are discarded from the final result set that are in all components of their describing vectors worse or equal (with a strict 'worse' in at least one component) than another object of the database, i.e. $o < w$, iff $(s_i(o) \leq s_i(w))$ $(1 \leq i \leq n) \land \exists q \in [1,...,n] : s_q(o) < s_q(w)$. Thus best objects with respect to any monotonic optimization function can be found among the Pareto set (and so can the optimal objects with respect to multiple objectives). This good behavior in recall is, however, generally affecting the precision and the size of Pareto sets has been shown to increase exponentially with growing dimensions of the vectors, i.e. numbers of data characteristics [4].

Besides Pareto optimality, there are other qualitative definitions of the term 'overall best' in the formulation of our problem. For example **lexicographic optimization**, where objective vectors are compared lexicographically, i.e. given a certain order of indexes from 1 to n: $x < y$ iff $s_k(x) < s_k(y)$, where k is the smallest index such that $s_i(x) = s_i(y)$ for all i $(1 \leq i < k \leq n)$. This can be done with respect to one (user-specified), or even all permutations of scoring functions. Operating on numerical domains, this behavior can be realized using top k retrieval, if the order of characteristics is enforced with high weightings in a compensation function such that more important characteristics are assigned weightings that cannot be compensated by less important characteristics, see e.g. [17].

For the use in personalization in database retrieval and engineering of user preferences recent research in [7] and [13] has shown that these three operators (score aggregation, Pareto accumulation and lexicographic ordering) are the most common and essential constructors to build complex user preferences into queries allowing arbitrary combinations. Besides, also the closure of preference construction with these operators is shown for general partial orders. However, up to now for query processing only the naïve algorithm accessing and pairwise comparing all database objects has been proposed.

2.2. Basic Object Access Model

Our work in multi-objective database retrieval aims at using a minimum number of object accesses before delivering the final result set. Unlike statistical approaches we will always guarantee a correct result set. There have been a number of approaches for top k or skyline algorithms (see sections 2.3 and 2.4) that show advantages in different architectures or for different data distributions. For the scope of this paper we will abstract from the underlying system architecture and just rely on some very basic access functions common in query processing literature. We will assume (several) ranked lists for each feature of the query in which database objects are ranked in descending order according to their score values with respect to a single feature. A *sorted access* iterates these lists and accesses objects rank by rank. A *random access* on the other hand can be posed to a data source retrieving the score values of a specific object with respect to a single feature.

Owing to this abstraction our approach can be applied in both middleware architectures and over central multi-dimensional indexes. Obviously the use of central indexes will essentially speed up the retrieval, but e.g. in Web information systems using various subsystems and assembling the information on the fly it is not always possible to operate on such a central index structure. The main difference is that in distributed systems the iteration over sorted lists for each characteristic (possibly provided by different subsystems) is stopped, if a certain condition becomes true and all unseen objects may be discarded, whereas using multidimensional indexes like R*-trees whole subtrees can instantaneously be pruned, if the upper/lower bounds for their maximum/minimum objects meet the necessary condition. Examples for this are e.g. the middleware top k retrieval in [11] and the central index top k retrieval in [8] or the distributed skylining in [1] and the central index skylining in [23]. However, in all these cases basic algorithms are similar. We will revisit their basic traits in brief within the following sections.

2.3. Top k Retrieval (m = 1)

Top k retrieval states the basic idea that a *single* monotonic compensation function can be used to aggregate a certain number of characteristics of database objects into a single score providing the final order of the all objects among which k best objects are to be singled out. For weighting the relative importance of each single characteristic and thus determining the degree of compensation, users are generally allowed to specify weights, e.g. in a weighted average as compensation function. This approach often occurs e.g. in information retrieval, where weighted averages for the keyword occurrences are calculated or in content-based retrieval over Multimedia databases. Please note, that in this case all database objects are ranked into a (non-strict) total ordering. Besides central index approaches like k-nearest-neighbor searches, the algorithm using a threshold condition has been proved to be most efficient for applications [20], [11], [21], [6], [2] and has even been shown to be instance-optimal [10]. To be self-contained we present the basic algorithm below.

Basic Top k Retrieval:
1. Get an object by sorted access on one of the lists
2. For new objects perform random accesses on the other lists and aggregate the object's total score using the compensation function
3. Aggregate a threshold using the current minimum scores in each list as input for the compensation function
4. If there are k objects having a higher or equal score than the current threshold, discard all unseen objects, otherwise return to step 1
5. Output the k objects with highest score as top k objects

Please note that top k algorithms generally will neither retrieve all, nor only strictly the optimal objects with respect to the compensation function. They will output some k best objects and stop, even if some of these k objects are already dominated or there are more than k objects having the optimal score. The choice of a suitable value of k for each application is therefore difficult. If all objects with the optimal score should be retrieved ('all top objects'), the condition in step 4 has to be altered to 'strictly higher (>)' instead of 'higher or equal ($\geq$)'.

2.4. Skyline Queries and Pareto Optimality (m = n, $(f_1,...,f_n) = (id_{S1},...,id_{Sn})$)

A skyline query describes the case when *all* characteristics are considered to be incomparable and the objective functions are just the projections on the respective scores (i.e. $f_i(s_1,...,s_n) = s_i$). Since no compensation between characteristics is possible, the query result (the so-called skyline) consists of all objects that are not dominated in all aspects by any other object in the sense of Pareto optimality. Efficient algorithms have been heavily researched in recent years; see e.g. [5], [24], [14], [23]. Also in this case the algorithms differ in a variety of heuristics and techniques used, but again we will present the basic optimal algorithm only using the abstract access methods over sorted lists for each aspect as given in [1].

Basic Skylining:
1. Get an object by sorted access on one of the lists
2. For new objects perform random accesses on the other lists
3. If an object has already occurred in all of the lists, retrieve all additional objects that have the same score as the current minimum in each list and discard all unseen objects, otherwise return to step 1
4. Compare objects pairwise and output all non-dominated objects as the skyline

3. An Multi-objective Retrieval Algorithm

Having revisited the special algorithms we are ready to present an efficient unifying algorithm that allows to handle *all* cases of multi-objective retrieval. Given sorted lists for each characteristic and using the two basic access techniques of sorted and random access all retrieval algorithms will start iterating over the lists (since wild guesses cannot be sensible). The naïve approach would just iterate completely over the lists, get the score values for each database object and then start the aggregation with the objective functions and compare the objects pairwise for domination. Obviously this algorithm accesses all database objects and is of quadratic complexity $O(N^2)$ in terms of pairwise comparisons. Thus it definitely cannot scale with large database sizes. To improve this behavior the important issue is to know when the iteration over the sorted lists can be stopped at the earliest time and the rest of database objects can be discarded. We will show the important result that our algorithm only uses an **instance-optimal** number of expensive object accesses.

But first we need some basic properties of the objective functions and then we are ready to present an algorithm introducing a virtual object. Throughout this paper we will assume that all objective scores are given by a set of monotonic functions. We will also assume the objective functions not to be constant on the set of all objects (constant functions could simply be omitted, because they do not influence the result). And we will denote the objective scores of an object o as $F(o) := (f_1(s_1(o),...,s_n(o)),..., f_m(s_1(o),...,s_n(o)))$ and the domination in the sense of Pareto optimality as $F(x) > F(y)$.

Basic Multi-objective Retrieval:
0. Given *n* lists ranking *N* database objects, each sorted descending by score and *m* monotonic functions $f_1,...,f_m$
1. Get an object *o* by sorted access from any list in a round robin fashion
2. For new objects perform random accesses on the other lists and calculate the object's objective scores $F(o)$

3. Create a virtual database object p characterized by the minimum score values that have occurred in each list, as its score values (i.e. $s_i(p)$ is the current minimum score in the i-th list) and calculate its objective scores $F(p)$

4. If some object w has already been seen for which holds $F(w) > F(p)$, i.e. its objective scores are better or equal, but in at least one dimension strictly better than the virtual object's, discard all unseen objects, else return to step 1

5. Compare all seen objects pairwise and output all non-dominated objects as the result set of non-dominated objects.

Let us now consider our traffic information example (example 2) and see, how the algorithm works. We got three ranked lists of which the first two (distance and congestion) can be compensated say using a weighted average $f_{eco}(o) := ½ (s_1(o) + s_2(o))$ and consider the third score (weather) under the notion of Pareto optimality. Please note that this is just a simple case of two objectives that could be realized by first running a top k algorithm on list s1 and s2 and then run a skyline algorithm on the materialized list f_{eco} and s3, however resulting in linear database scans accessing all database objects. Consider the following three lists s1, s2 and s3 containing database objects o_i and their scores in descending order. Table 1 shows the first few top ranked objects of each list.

We will start with sorted accesses in a round robin fashion on all three lists (shown bold) in table 2 (step 1). After each sorted access we do the necessary random accesses to calculate the object's objective scores (step 2). The first part of the objective score is then calculated using the function f_{eco}, whereas the second part here is simply the projection on s_3. Then we calculate the virtual object with scores using the minimum values in each list as input (step 3). After retrieving object o_7 however, we can according to step 4 of our algorithm already stop object accesses and discard all unseen objects, because object o_4 now dominates the virtual object. After comparing all seen object pairwise for domination (step 5) we will find that in our small example only o_2, o_3 and o_4 are non-dominated by other objects and can be output as optimal results (o_1, o_5, o_6 and o_7 are all dominated by o_4). Thus, even though in this case a implementation by top k/skylining algorithms would be possible, we are able to provide a definitive output already after the first few object accesses instead of needing a linear database scan.

Before we further refine the algorithm let us state its correctness and compare it to the basic algorithms in the special cases in 2.3 and 2.4.

Theorem 1: *Correctness of Multi-objective Retrieval*
The basic algorithm for multi-objective retrieval always terminates and delivers all non-dominated and only the non-dominated objects with respect to the given set of monotonic objective functions F.

Proof:
If all objects are non-dominated, the algorithm obviously will terminate after one of the lists has been entirely processed and all objects have been seen and correctly output. However, generally not all objects will be non-dominated with respect to the objective functions F. Thus, if we have seen any two objects x and y with $F(x) > F(y)$, i.e. y is dominated by x, termination is obviously guaranteed at the latest when y has already occurred in all lists, due to $F(x) > F(y) \geq F(p)$.

Now we have to prove that by discarding all unseen objects after $F(x) > F(p)$ holds for any seen object x we will never discard a relevant, i.e. non-dominated, object. Let U be the set of still unseen (and thus in step 4 discarded) objects after termination and Q the set of all seen objects. Let's assume that until termination we have iterated all i lists down to values p_i ($1 \leq i \leq n$) and have also retrieved in step 4 at least one object q dominating the virtual object. Since the objects in U have not been seen, we can conclude that their score is smaller or equal in all lists than the score of the virtual object p with $s_i(p) := p_i$. Due to the set of objective functions being monotonic we get: $\exists q \in Q \, \forall u \in U : F(u) \leq F(p) < F(q)$.

Thus q dominates all the unseen objects and since in step 5 we check all seen objects pairwise for domination, we can neither leave out relevant objects nor return dominated objects. ∎

	s_1 distance		s_2 jam free		s_3 weather	
rank	oid	score	Oid	score	oid	Score
1	o_1	0.98	o_2	0.92	o_3	0.9
2	o_4	0.94	o_5	0.84	o_6	0.8
3	o_7	0.9	o_8	0.82	o_9	0.8
4	o_{10}	0.87	o_{11}	0.81	o_{12}	0.8
...	...	...	...	...	...	...

Table 1: Sample values for three lists

Oid	score s_1	score s_2	Score s_3	Objective scores	scores of the virtual object at access time
o_1	**0.98**	0.62	0.3	(0.8, 0.3)	(0.99, 1.0)
o_2	0.88	**0.92**	0.1	(0.9, 0.1)	(0.95, 1.0)
o_3	0.5	0.5	**0.9**	(0.5, 0.9)	(0.95, 0.9)
o_4	**0.94**	0.82	0.8	(0.88, 0.8)	(0.93, 0.9)
o_5	0.56	**0.84**	0.2	(0.7, 0.2)	(0.89, 0.9)
o_6	0.6	0.4	**0.8**	(0.5, 0.8)	(0.89, 0.8)
o_7	**0.9**	0.5	0.7	(0.7, 0.7)	(0.87, 0.8)

Table 2: Object accesses using the new algorithm

Additionally, we will now show that our algorithm's I/O costs (i.e. total number of object accesses) are instance-optimal. The concept of instance optimality was defined by [10] over abstract classes of algorithms and database instances. If an algorithm's complexity over any possible instance of databases (i.e. any number of objects and any distribution of scores) is optimal among all algorithms in a certain class, it is said to be instance-optimal for this class of algorithms. Or more formally, consider our algorithm X as an element of the class A of all algorithms, which are capable of delivering correct multi-objective retrieval results for monotonic objective functions, and D as a specific instance of all possible database instances D, which are sorted lists of database objects with score values assigned. Since we want to focus on I/O costs we have to consider the necessary number of object accesses, denoted as *accesses*(A). Then X is instance-optimal over A and D, if for every algorithm $A \in A$ and every database instance $D \in D$ holds: *accesses*(X, D) = O(*accesses*(A,D)), i.e. for any chosen algorithm A of class A we can state *accesses*(X,D) ≤ C *accesses* (A,D) + C' with some positive constants C ('optimality ratio') and C'. The following theorem shows the instance-optimality of our approach:

Theorem 2: *Instance-optimality of object accesses*
Let D be the class of all possible database instances in the form of n lists of database objects ranked by score, and A the class of all possible algorithms that use only sorted and random accesses and correctly retrieve all optimal objects from these lists for any set of m monotonic objective functions. The preceding multi-objective retrieval algorithm is instance-optimal over A and D, i.e. accesses an optimal number of objects up to a constant factor.

Proof:
At our algorithm's termination (and thus the end of object accesses) the first object has been accessed, whose scores are better or equal than the virtual object's and strictly better in at least one dimension. We will show that for any algorithm that will not do sorted accesses up to that point there can be an object that is non-dominated with respect to the objective functions and thus a relevant object would have been missed by the algorithm. Hence the expansion of lists (and thus the number of objects accessed) for our multi-objective retrieval algorithm is instance-optimal.

Since random accesses can be performed only on objects that have been previously seen by sorted accesses and excluding 'wild guesses' on the database content, an algorithm can only access formerly unknown objects by sorted access. For the sake of contradiction let us now assume there would exist a correct algorithm A of class A that could stop object accesses before at least one seen object o fulfills $F(o) > F(p)$, i.e. there is no object that has better or equal objective scores dominating the virtual object. We will show that now we can construct a database instance of D containing at least one object still unseen by A, but nevertheless optimal with respect to the objective functions F, and therefore we get a contradiction to algorithm A's correctness and hence its existence.

Let p be a (virtual) object, whose scores are given by the minimum seen by sorted access in each list. Assume that algorithm A has terminated over database instance $D \in D$ having performed sorted accesses up to scores $p_1, ..., p_n$ in the n lists, however without having accessed at least one object with larger objective scores than the virtual object's (otherwise our algorithm would also already have terminated). We will now construct a database instance $D' \in D$ that is exactly like instance D up to the object p's scores $p_1, ..., p_n$, but immediately behind the last object that A has accessed by sorted access in each list on D, in D' we will insert a new object w having also score values $p_1, ..., p_n$. Obviously D' is a valid instance of class D. Due to construction algorithm A will terminate over D' exactly at the point it terminated over D and since no object o with $F(o) > F(p)$ in D has been accessed, also no object with $F(o) > F(p)$ will be accessed in D'.

Let us now take a closer look at object w. Since it has not been accessed by algorithm A before termination, it cannot have been output in the result set of non-dominated objects. Thus either it must be dominated or algorithm A is not correct. We will now show that w cannot be dominated by any object in D' and therefore is optimal with respect to the objective functions. According to theorem 1 w cannot be dominated by any unseen object, because every unseen object has score values lesser or at most equal $p_1, ..., p_n$, i.e. due to the objective functions being monotonic, an unseen object cannot have a strictly better score in any dimension, which however is necessary for domination. Thus w would have to be dominated with respect to the objective functions by an object o already seen by algorithm A. But by dominating w the object o would also dominate the virtual object p and we would have an object that fulfills $F(o) > F(w) = F(p)$ in contradiction to our assumption. Though having proved that the termination condition is necessary, there still could be an algorithm using a more sophisticated strategy to choose lists for the next access than round robin (cf. section 5.2). However, let a be this number of accesses, then a round robin strategy will at the latest stop after $n*a$ accesses. Thus the instance optimality still holds with an optimality ratio C = n. Please note, that we did not make any assumptions on the distribution of scores or the nature of the objective functions (except being monotonic). Thus our basic algorithm is instance-optimal over all multi-objective retrieval algorithms for all possible database instances. ∎

We will now state that both basic algorithms for top k retrieval and skylining are just special cases of our multi-objective retrieval algorithm. Please note that the respective algorithms were proven to be optimal in [10] and [1].

Observation 1: *Relationship of multi-objective retrieval to top k queries and skylining*
Top k retrieval and skylining are special cases of multi-objective retrieval and in either case the basic multi-objective retrieval algorithm will behave like the given basic algorithms for top k retrieval and skylining.

Proof:
The basic behavior in iterating the sorted lists and doing random accesses to get all score values is the same in all three algorithms. In the special case of top k retrieval (m = 1) the termination condition for multi-objective retrieval is $F(o) := f_1(s_1(o),...,s_n(o)) > f_1(p_1,...,p_n)$. Thus the complete number of objects having the top score is retrieved, i.e. all non-dominated objects being strictly better than the threshold. Generally we will get more than one object, but we will really get *all* top objects (the progressive algorithm in section 4 outputs objects with the respective top score one by one at the earliest possible point in time like progressive top k algorithms). To derive the top k objects, we can return any arbitrary subset of cardinality k out of the top objects or return all top objects and then run the algorithm again with these objects removed, if k is larger than the number of maximal elements.

In the case of skylining we have $n = m$ and $(f_1,...,f_n) := id$. Thus our termination condition becomes:
$$F(o) := (id)(s_1(o),...,s_n(o)) = (s_1(o),...,s_n(o)) > (p_1,...,p_n) = (id)(p_1,...,p_n) =: F(p)$$
which means that $\forall\ 1 \leq i \leq n : s_i(o) \geq p_i$ with at least one dimension in which it is strictly better. Thus also in this case we are not allowed to terminate before $F(o) > F(p)$ holds, because otherwise we could miss optimal objects. If an object o has occurred in all lists and we retrieve all objects with minimum scores like in the skylining algorithm (step 3), obviously this object also dominates the virtual object and thus our algorithm would terminate at the same time and would deliver exactly the same correct result set. On the other hand, if $F(o) > F(p)$ holds and $f_i(s_i(o)) := s_i(o)$, then we must have accessed all lists down to $s_i(o) \geq s_i(p_i)$ and thus seen o in all lists. ∎

4. Progressive Output of Result Sets

We have seen our algorithm in both special cases to behave like the known optimal algorithms and to handle any arbitrary number and all instances of monotonic objective functions with instance-optimal complexity. Now we enable our algorithm to output result objects not only in a single batch after termination, but *on the fly* as soon as they are found and have been proved to be Pareto-optimal. This successive output of objects essentially reduces the psychological response time. To allow for outputting a result object at the earliest possible point in time, we now investigate which objects could possibly dominate it.

Lemma 1: *Finding dominated objects*
Let f be any monotonic objective function defined over a subset S_f of the n ranked score lists. At any point in time an object o that is accessed in one of the lists of S_f can only be dominated with respect to f by an object w having a strictly better score than o in at least one list in S_f.

Proof:
To be dominated with respect to a single objective function means that $f(w) = f(s_h(w),...,s_l(w)) > f(s_h(o),...,s_l(o)) = f(o)$ with $s_h,...,s_l$ being the score lists of S_f. Since f is monotonic, it follows directly that there has to be a list s_i such that $s_i(w) > s_i(o)$. ∎

Lemma 2: *Distinguishing objects by objectives*
Assume that all objects seen by sorted access, are divided into some m sets $K_1,...,K_m$ according to the lists in which they were seen and the objective function that uses these lists as input, i.e. if an object o is accessed by sorted access in list s_i ($1 \leq i \leq n$) and objective function f_k uses this set as (one of its) input(s), it is added to set K_k. Now let f_k be defined over the score lists $S_{fk} := \{s_h,...,s_r\}$ and let $p_h,...,p_r$ be the minimum scores accessed by sorted access in the lists of S_{fk}. Any object o, for which $f_k(s_h(o),...,s_r(o)) > f_k(p_h,...,p_r)$ holds, can only be dominated by any database object w that is already in the same set K_k.

Proof:
Let o be an object assigned to set K_k and let o be dominated by some object w. Let us further assume that $f_k(s_h(o),...,s_r(o)) > f_k(p_h,...,p_r)$ holds with s_i and p_i defined above, i.e. o dominates object p with score values $p_h,...,p_r$ wrt. objective function f_k. If w would not be in set K_k, it cannot have been accessed by sorted access in any of the lists in S_{fk} yet. Since the score lists in S_{fk} have been accessed down to scores $p_h,...,p_r$, it follows that $s_h(w) \leq p_h,...,s_r(w) \leq p_r$. Due to lemma 1 w therefore cannot dominate the virtual object p. However, we know w to dominate object o, which in turn dominates the virtual object p, leading to a contradiction. Hence w must be part of K_k. ∎

Theorem 3: *Correctness of the progressive output*
Let $f_1,...,f_m$ be m monotonic objective functions, $K_1,...,K_m$ be defined like in lemma 2 and add all objects that have been accessed by sorted access in a certain score list, to each set K_k of all objective functions f_k that are defined over this score list. Then:

a) If in any set K_k there is an object o for which holds $f_k(s_h(o),...,s_r(o)) > f_k(p_h,...,p_r)$ (with $s_h,...,s_r$ and $p_h,...,p_r$ as in lemma 2) and this object o is not dominated by any other member of K_k having a higher or equal score with respect to f_k, we can immediately output o as correct result with respect to our multi-objective retrieval problem.

b) If there is no object w for which holds $F(w) > F(p)$, all objects, also all seen objects z with $F(z) = F(p)$ can immediately be output.

Proof:
a) Accessing an object by sorted access means that due to the sorting of the score lists, we have already seen all objects having better scores in the list. Since each score list only contributes to objective scores if the respective objective function is also defined over that list, after each sorted access we can focus on the respective subset of sets K_k. This way we keep each set K_k as small as possible. Lemma 2 shows that for each single set K_k the condition $f_k(s_h(o),...,s_r(o)) > f_k(p_h,...,p_r)$ is sufficient for object o to be dominated with respect to f_k only by objects in the same set K_k. We thus only have to show that if o is not dominated in any *single* set K_k, it also cannot be dominated with respect to *all* objective functions $F := (f_1,...,f_m)$ and therefore can be correctly output.

For the sake of contradiction let us assume that we have found an object o in any set K_k with the above characteristics and let us further assume that though o is not dominated by any object in K_k, it is dominated by another object $x \notin K_k$ with respect to F. Being dominated with respect to F means $F(x) > F(o)$, i.e. $f_i(s_1(x),...,s_n(x)) \geq f_i(s_1(o),...,s_n(o))$ for all $1 \leq i \leq m$ (with a strictly better for at least one i). Thus we also have $f_k(s_1(x),...,s_n(x)) \geq f_k(s_1(o),...,s_n(o))$. Since $f_k(s_h(o),...,s_r(o)) > f_k(p_h,...,p_r)$ and f_k is only defined over score lists $s_h,..., s_r$, we can conclude: $f_k(s_h(x),...,s_r(x)) \geq f_k(s_h(o),...,s_r(o)) > f_k(p_h,...,p_r)$.

Therefore using lemma 1 we know that there must be at least one score $s_i(x) > p_i$ among all score lists over which f_k is defined. Since they have been accessed down to $p_h,...,p_r$ we must already have accessed x by sorted access in one of the lists and thus x would be an element of K_k in contradicting our assumption. Hence o is optimal with respect to F, if o it is not dominated in any K_k.

b) The second statement is obvious, since if any object z with $F(z) = F(p)$ would be dominated by some seen object w, this object w would also satisfy $F(w) > F(z) = F(p)$. On the other hand z cannot be dominated by any unseen object x, since $F(z) = F(p) \geq F(x)$. ∎

Observation 2: *Earliest possible progressive output*
The conditions a) $f_k(s_h(o),...,s_r(o)) > f_k(p_h,...,p_r)$ in any set K_k, and b) $F(o) = F(p)$, while there is no w with $F(w) > F(p)$, for successive output of results given in theorem 3 a) and b) lead to the earliest possible output of result objects with guaranteed correctness. That means for arbitrary database instances, all monotonic objective functions and any result object o our algorithm needs no more accesses (up to an universal multiplicative constant) to correctly return o as any other algorithm.

Proof:
For brevity we will just sketch the proof of observation 2; it works along the lines of the proof for theorem 2: If some algorithm A would deliver object o before either condition a) holds in some K_k, or condition b) holds, we can construct an object q hitherto *unseen* by algorithm A that has exactly the minimum scores $p_1,...,p_n$ (if A had seen q it would have accessed objects at least in one score list with sorted accesses down to the respective score of p and then it would *not* be better than the round robin strategy of our algorithm up to a multiplicative constant). Since neither a) holds for any k, we get $f_k(s_h(o),...,s_r(o)) \leq f_k(p_h,...,p_r) = f_k(s_h(q),...,s_r(q))$ for all k, nor b) holds, we get that there is a k with $f_k(s_h(o),...,s_r(o)) < f_k(p_h,...,p_r) = f_k(s_h(q),...,s_r(q))$. Thus q dominates o and o would have been output incorrectly by A. Hence either A is incorrect or needs the same number of object accesses to output o than our algorithm (up to a multiplicative constant). ∎

Let us now consider how the progressive output scheme works together with our basic multi-objective retrieval algorithm. The next theorem shows that when our termination condition becomes true, we have *already* progressively output *all* correct result objects and thus can immediately discard all other objects.

Theorem 4: *Completeness of output result objects*
At the first point in time that any seen object o dominates the minimum scores in each list with respect to all objective functions, i.e. $F(o) > F(p)$, and objects have been output successively like stated in theorem 3, the *entire* correct multi-objective result set has already been output

Proof:
Theorem 3 shows that all objects w are output, immediately after the condition $f_k(s_1(w),...,s_n(w)) > f_k(p_1,...,p_n)$ has become true in some set K_k. So we have to show that no object, which has not yet been output, can be optimal with respect to F after $F(o) > F(p)$ has become true for some object o. Let p_i be the minimum scores seen by sorted access in each score list. Since we have output all non-dominated objects w with $f_i(s_1(w),...,s_n(w)) > f_i(p_1,...,p_n)$ for all i, $1 \leq i \leq m$, we have to check that no object q with $f_i(s_1(q),...,s_n(q)) \leq f_i(p_1,...,p_n)$ for *all* i can be optimal with respect to F. However, since we have seen an object o dominating the virtual object p, for all $1 \leq i \leq m$ we know $f_i(s_1(q),...,s_n(q)) \leq f_i(p_1,...,p_n) \leq f_i(s_1(o),...,s_n(o))$ and due to the definition of domination there is an index j for which $f_j(s_1(q),...,s_n(q)) \leq f_j(p_1,...,p_n) < f_j(s_1(o),...,s_n(o))$. Thus object q is always dominated by object o and can not be in the non-dominated result set. ∎

Now we are ready to formulate the improved algorithm and demonstrate its output behavior with a short example. We will further adopt the sets K_i to be sorted lists, where every new object is inserted in the right place according to its score with respect to f_i. This does not alter the algorithm's complexity in terms of accesses, but makes the necessary object comparisons easier. We will also use two variables a_i and b_i with each list K_i, such that all objects in K_i having larger scores than a_i with respect to f_i have already been output or discarded as dominated and b_i is the current value of f_i using the lowest scores seen so far as input. That means in every K_i we are done with objects having higher or equal values of f_i than a_i, and we have to consider objects for output having values between a_i and b_i and cannot yet output all objects with values up to b_i (for a detailed discussion of a_i and b_i see [1]). Furthermore we will use two sets R and X containing the output optimal result objects and the discarded dominated objects respectively. Thus we will never scrutinize already output objects or those known to be dominated.

Progressive Multi-objective Retrieval:
0. Given n lists of database objects sorted descending by score, m monotonic functions $f_1,...,f_m$, two empty lists R (returned objects) and X (dominated objects) and m empty sorted lists $K_1,...,K_m$ with variables $a_1, b_1,..., a_m, b_m := 1$.
1. Get an object o by sorted access from any list s_i in a round robin fashion
2. For new objects perform random accesses on the other lists and calculate the object's objective scores $F(o)$
3. Create a virtual object p assuming the minimum score values that have occurred in each list to be its score values (i.e. $s_i(p)$ is the current minimum score in the i-th list) and calculate its objective scores $F(p)$

4. For all functions f_k that are defined over s_i do
   4.1. Insert o into K_k, if o is not in set X
   4.2. $a_k := b_k$, $b_k := f_k(s_1(p),...,s_n(p))$
   4.3. Compare all objects $q \in K_k$ that are not in set R and for which $b_k < f_k(s_1(q),...,s_n(q)) \leq a_k$ holds, pairwise for domination. If any object is dominated, delete it from the list K_k and add it to set X.
   4.4. Compare the remaining objects q that are not in set R for domination with all objects $y \in K_k$ with $a_k < f_k(s_1(y),...,s_n(y))$. If q is dominated by any object y delete it from K_k and add it to set X, else output q and add it to set R.
5. If an object w has already been seen for which holds $F(w) > F(p)$, i.e. its objective scores are better or equal, but in at least one dimension strictly better than the virtual object's, discard all objects that have not yet been output, and terminate the algorithm.
6. Consider all objects z in any of the sets K_k ($1 \leq k \leq m$) for which $f_k(s_1(z),...,s_n(z)) = b_k$ holds for all k. Output those objects z and add them to set R.
7. Proceed with step 1

Before we will give an example that the output behavior of our progressive algorithm effectively enhances the basic version, we will state a short observation on the new algorithm's correctness and instance-optimality.

Observation 3: *Correctness and optimality for the progressive multi-objective retrieval algorithm*
The multi-objective retrieval algorithm with progressive output of result objects is correct and instance-optimal with respect to the object accesses needed and the response time till the delivery of the first result object.

Proof:
Theorem 3 a) + b) and 4 show that the progressive multi-objective retrieval algorithm only delivers correct result objects and does not miss any relevant objects. Since we have not altered the termination condition in step 5, also the instance-optimality of the number of necessary object accesses like shown in theorem 2 still holds. Thus our progressive algorithm is correct and instance-optimal. The last statement follows directly from observation 2. ∎

Let us now focus on our example to show how the algorithm works. Again we will use the simple three list traffic information scenario given by example 2 (table 1). Like before we will aggregate the first two lists with an average and just project the third list into objective space. The algorithm runs as before, but now assigns objects accessed in lists s_1 and s_2 to set K_1 and objects accessed in list s_3 to set K_2. Table 2 shows our object accesses (sorted accesses shown bold) whereas table 3 shows our two sets K_1 and K_2. First we make a sorted access on s_1 and add the object o_1 to set K_1, the same happens for o_2 in list s_2. Object o_3 is added to K_2, because s_3 only contributes to f_2, whereas s_1 and s_2 only contribute to f_1 (=f_{eco}). Please note that processing more complex objectives may involve several or even all sets K_k for each object, but our algorithm keeps the K_k as small as possible to reduce necessary comparisons within the K_k for progressive output.

After we have accessed o_5 by sorted access in s_2, we can safely output o_2, because the minimum scores of s_1 and s_2 lead to the threshold $b_1 := f_1(0.94, 0.84) = 0.89$ for the first time being strictly smaller than o_2's score of 0.9 with respect to f_1 and o_2 is not dominated by any other object in K_1 (all objects in K_1 have strictly lower scores with respect to f_1). For the same reasons we can safely output o_3 in K_2 after we have accessed o_6. And after accessing o_7 we can output o_4 from K_1 (because it could only be dominated by o_2 in K_1. However o_4's score with respect to f_2 is strictly higher than o_2's; thus it is not dominated by o_2). Like before, o_4 is also the first element dominating the virtual object and thus the algorithm terminates having successively output all optimal objects with respect to our multi-objective query. Table 3 shows the final state with counters $b_1 = 0.87$ and $b_2 = 0.8$. All objects with higher scores have been output.

K_1			K_2			prog. Output	
oid	score		Oid	score		oid	Score
o_2	0.9		o_3	0.9		o_2	(0.9, 0.1)
o_4	0.88	←b_1	o_6	0.8	← b_2	o_3	(0.5, 0.9)
o_1	0.8					o_4	(0.88, 0.8)
o_5	0.7						
o_7	0.7						

Table 3: Lists K_1 and K_2 and progressive output

5. Experiences in Practical Applications

As we have discussed in section 2 the only ways to handle multiple objectives today are given by complex preference frameworks like given in [7] or [13], since the top k (compensating *all* score lists) and skyline (compensating *no* score lists) approaches only accommodate the extreme cases. However, the actual algorithms given for evaluating complex preference queries up to now always create views containing the non dominated objects by accessing all database objects and compare pairwise for domination. Our algorithm can do essentially better. Consider for instance our running example: using basic constructors, we would have three preferences P_1 (shortest route), P_2 (least congestion) and P_3 (best weather) given by our basic score lists s_1, s_2, s_3. Then we would have to evaluate a complex expression averaging the first two preferences and merging this new list with the third list s_3 in a Pareto optimal fashion. Since our algorithm has transparent access to score lists, it does not have to calculate a complex view over the base relations accessing all the database objects. It focuses on the *necessary* accesses only, using $F(o) = ((s_1(o)+s_2(o))/2, s_3(o))$ and with an instance optimal number of object accesses nevertheless always delivers the correct result set. In the following we will focus on the complexity of the result sets and the connection with the objective functions used.

5.1. Bounding of Multi-objective Result Complexity

When using the multi-objective algorithm for practical applications in information systems, queries can quickly involve a rather high number of objectives, i.e. dimensions. However, Pareto optimal sets tend to grow exponentially with increasing numbers of dimensions [4] (often referred to as 'curse of dimensionality'). Thus, we will have to investigate this relevant problem also for multi-objective retrieval and see how multiple objectives affect the size of the subsequently retrieved result set.

Let us first assume that all objective functions are defined over a *disjoint* set of score lists, e.g. f_1 is defined over $s_1,\ldots,s_k$, f_2 is defined over $s_{k+1},\ldots,s_r$, and so on. Then the complexity of the result set is always reduced from growing with the number of score lists n to only growing with the smaller number of objective functions m. The importance of this can be seen in our practical experiments in figure 2. Assuming statistically independent uniform score distributions, figure 2 shows the actual size of average result sets in our tests for different numbers of dimensions (3, 5, 10) and different database sizes. As we can see the result sets have manageable sizes only in case of low dimensionality, but in cases of only ten dimensions, we e.g. already have to return up to 50% of all database objects in the result set for 10,000 objects. This behavior is due to Pareto optimality being a rather weak concept and producing lots of incomparable result objects with growing numbers of dimensions.

A dimensionality reduction with suitable objective functions is therefore needed. Moreover, the strong assumption that all objective functions work on a disjunctive set of score lists generally does not hold leading to a certain degree of correlation in the results of the objective functions, which in practical experiments has been shown to further reduce results sizes, see e.g. [5]. So if the number of objective functions m is smaller than the number of score lists n, we can always assume the result size to be reasonably small. But what if a user adds objectives over a certain number of score lists? Assuming a sensible characteristic of the set of objective functions, in the following observations we will show that in this case not only does the result set does not grow exponentially with the number of objectives, but is always limited by the size of the basic Pareto set over the score lists. Let us therefore state the following definition:

Definition 1: *Strict monotonic set of functions*
As set of n objective functions $F := (f_1,\ldots,f_n)$ is called strict monotonic, if $(o < w) \Rightarrow (\forall\ 1 \leq i \leq n : f_i(o) \leq f_i(w)$ $\wedge\ \exists\ 1 \leq k \leq n : f_k(o) < f_k(w))$.

Examples for basic strict monotonic functions include e.g. the large group of weighted sums like the average, geometrical means, etc. To obtain a set of strict monotonic functions it is sufficient that only a subset of the functions is strict monotonic. However, the subset then already has to be defined over all of the score lists s_i. Using that, let us now state a helpful bounding property.

Observation 4: *Bounding of multi-objective results*
The size of the multi-objective result set R for a strictly monotonic set F of m objective functions $f_1,\ldots,f_m$ over n ranked score lists $s_1,\ldots,s_n$ is always upper bounded by the size of the set of Pareto-optimal objects P over the ranked score lists $s_1,\ldots,s_n$.

Proof:
We will show the set inclusion $R \subseteq P$ and therefore the size of P is always an upper bound for the size of R. Assume for the sake of contradiction there would exist an object o in R, which is not in P. Since $o \notin P$, we have to conclude that there is some object $w \in P$ with $s_i(o) \leq s_i(w)$ ($1 \leq i \leq n$) and there is a $1 \leq k \leq n$ for which $s_k(o) < s_k(w)$. Since the objective functions $f_1,\ldots,f_m$ are all monotonic we get $f_i(s_1(o),\ldots,s_n(o)) \leq f_i(s_1(w),\ldots,s_n(w))$ ($1 \leq i \leq m$) and thus due to the set F being strictly monotonic w would also dominate o with respect to $f_1,\ldots f_m$. ∎

Theorem 5: *Result set size and object accesses*
The cardinality of result sets for multi-objective retrieval over $F = (f_1,\ldots,f_m)$ grows only with increasing $\min(n, m)$. Moreover, computing the multi-objective result set never needs more object accesses than computing the respective skyline (i.e. the Pareto-optimal set).

Proof:
For the growth of the result sets cardinality, we have to distinguish two cases. If $m < n$ and all score lists are used by at least one objective function, there has to be at least one f_i that is defined over more than one score list, i.e. aggregating some score lists into a single one. Thus the Pareto-optimal set's cardinality over $f_1,\ldots,f_m$ can only be influenced by m score lists and thus grows with m. If $m \geq n$ observation 4 shows that the set of optimal result objects always is a subset of the basic set of all Pareto-optimal objects over n score lists, growing only with n.

For the optimality of object accesses we know from observation 1 that computing skylines is a special case of multi-objective retrieval and thus at the latest if the skyline computation terminates by accessing some object o

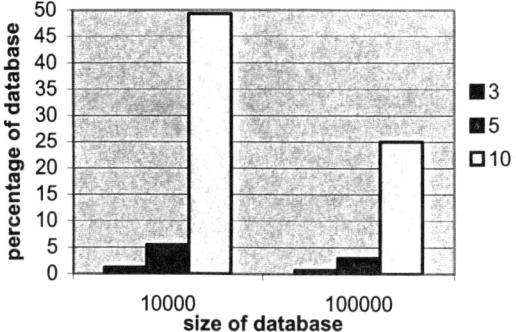

Fig. 2: Result sizes for different numbers of lists

with $(s_1(o),...,s_n(o)) > (p_1,...,p_n)$, due to F being strict monotonic also $F(o) > F(p)$ holds and also our multi-objective retrieval algorithm would have terminated. ■

Though expensive Pareto set computations can be avoided in most practical cases, still high dimensional problems without suitable aggregation functions will exist. Also in these cases our algorithm returns the correct result set with an instance-optimal number of accesses.

5.2. Heuristics to Speed Up the Average Runtime

Though we have shown our algorithm to be instance-optimal in terms of object accesses especially in cases of skewed data distributions the average runtime can be improved up to a factor of n (cf. theorem 2) by an advanced control flow deciding which score list to access next by sorted access (which can easily be integrated into step 1 of the algorithm). Moreover, by ascertaining that once in a while *every* list will be accessed (e.g. after at most x accesses) we can even make sure that a greedy control flow will still guarantee an instance-optimal algorithm (however with a somewhat higher optimality ratio, cf. [10]).

Adopting a better control flow than round robin strategy relies on making the necessary condition $F(o) > F(p)$ hold more quickly for some object o and virtual object p. Since the virtual object's score values are given by the minimum in each list, a virtual object with lower objective scores improves the chances that one of the already accessed objects is able to dominate it. Thus we will focus on fostering a quick decrease in the virtual object's objective scores. Assuming that all objective functions are partially differentiable, we will have to assess the influence that a sorted access on any list will have on the virtual object's objective scores. Let us assume that a sorted access on the i-th list will decrease the minimum score seen in that list by d_i. Then the objective scores of p will in each objective function f_k decrease by $(\partial f_k / \partial s_i) d_i$ ($1 \leq k \leq m$). Since we want to decrease p's objective scores most quickly, we choose the list for the next sorted access that maximizes the sum of decreases in all f_k. There may be lists and objective functions discriminating well between objects and show rapidly declining score distributions, whereas other characteristics may not discriminate too well and the scores in the respective lists may change only slowly or even remain constant. For rapid decreases in the virtual object's scores and thus quick termination, we are interested in accessing highly discriminating lists first.

Since we cannot know how much scores in the *next* access on each list will decrease before we make an actual access on this list, we need another heuristic to estimate d_i. A similar approach in [11] assumes that the recent development in each list gives a sufficient estimation what will happen next. If we use the difference between the current minimum and a score that has been accessed before h accesses in that list, we will usually get a good estimation how scores in the list will decline. Let q be an (virtual) object that is given by the scores occurring h

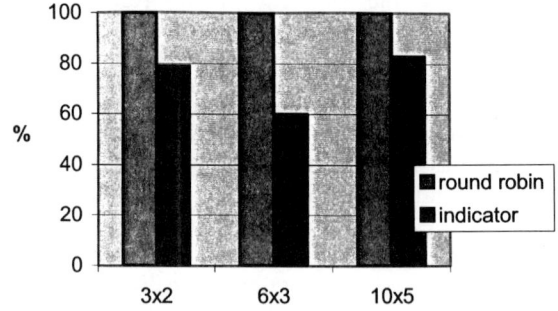

Fig. 3: Improved number of object accesses

accesses before the current minimum in each list. We will estimate d_i by $d_i := 1/h (s_i(q) - s_i(p))$. With these simple heuristics we will define an indicator Δ_i for each list that represents the expected gain by accessing this list:

$$\Delta_i := 1/h \, \Sigma (\partial f_k / \partial s_i) (s_i(q) - s_i(p)) \qquad (1 \leq k \leq m)$$

We have run practical experiments on statistical averages of run times for different score lists with skewed data distributions and the average of arbitrary subsets of these score lists as objective functions. We basically have compared the round robin strategy in our basic algorithm against the use of our indicator technique in step 1 for choosing lists. We then measured the average numbers of object accesses (in %) in a database with 10000 objects for three different scenarios over a database with 10% skew in the score distributions. The different scenarios focus on 3 lists with two objective functions (3x2), 6 lists with 3 objective functions (6x3) and 10 lists with 5 objective functions (10x5). Figure 3 shows the respective improvement factors for these scenarios for the basic and improved algorithm. Depending on the scenario improvement factors even for these simple examples range between 20% and 40% and grow with more skew, less objective functions and more score lists to combine.

6. Summary and Outlook

This paper addresses the problem of multi-objective retrieval in database query processing. We have in deep discussed applications for this retrieval paradigm and the meaning of 'overall best' objects from a database perspective. Multi-objective retrieval is especially useful for personalization problems, where multiple user preferences have to be taken into account, and one has to compromise between certain desired characteristics of database objects to deliver high quality results. However, up to now only for two extreme cases of such retrieval, namely top k retrieval and skyline queries, efficient algorithms have been investigated. Handling cases involving several distinct objectives, still needs to access and compare all database objects. We have presented a novel multi-objective retrieval algorithm and proved that it always retrieves a correct result set and uses only an instance-optimal number of object accesses. Moreover, it contains the respective optimal algorithms for top k retrieval and skylining as special cases. We have subsequently enhanced it by allowing for a successive output of result objects at the earliest possible time while the algorithm is still running.

Finally we have addressed preliminary practical experiences with applications of our algorithm. Our algorithm can be easily integrated into practical personalization frameworks or relational query processing. Concerning the manageability of query results, we have also shown that the cardinality of the multi-objective result set is bounded by the size of Pareto-optimal sets over the minimum of the number of score lists and objective function limiting down the set's cardinality in most practical cases. Implementing an advanced control flow we then addressed how to save additional object accesses in the case of skewed data distribution by focusing on the most prominent objects at an early time. Based on the practical experiences gained with our algorithm our future work will focus on the problem of high dimensional multi-objective sets, where the quality even between optimal objects has to be assessed. Sophisticated sampling strategies (cf. e.g. [1]) that give users an overview of the expected result set, and subsequent refinement of the query may be techniques employed to tackle this problem.

7. References

[1] W.-T. Balke, U. Güntzer, J. Zheng. Efficient Distributed Skylining for Web Information Systems. In *Proc of the Int. Conf. on Extending Database Technology (EDBT'04)*, Heraklion, Crete, Greece, 2004.

[2] W.-T. Balke, U. Güntzer, W. Kießling. On Real-time Top k Querying for Mobile Services, In *Proc. of the Int. Conf. on Cooperative Information Systems (CoopIS'02)*, Irvine, USA, 2002.

[3] W.-T. Balke, W. Kießling, C. Unbehend. Personalized Services for Mobile Route Planning: A Demonstration. In *Proceedings of the Int. Conf. on Data Engineering (ICDE 2003)*, Bangalore, India, 2003.

[4] J. Bentley, H. Kung, M. Schkolnick, C. Thompson. On the Average Number of Maxima in a Set of Vectors and Applications. In *Journal of the ACM (JACM)*, vol. 25(4) ACM, 1978.

[5] S. Börzsönyi, D. Kossmann, K. Stocker. The Skyline Operator. In *Proc. of the Int. Conf. on Data Engineering (ICDE'01)*, Heidelberg, Germany, 2001.

[6] N. Bruno, L. Gravano, A. Marian. Evaluating Top-k Queries over Web-Accessible Databases. In *Proc. of the Int. Conf. on Data Engineering (ICDE'02)*, San Jose, USA, 2002.

[7] J. Chomicki. Querying with intrinsic preferences. In *Proc. of the Int. Conf. on Extending Database Technology (EDBT'02)*, Prague, Czech Republic, 2002.

[8] P. Ciaccia, M. Patella. The M2-tree: Processing Complex Multi-Feature Queries with Just One Index. In *Proc. of the Int. DELOS Workshop on Querying Digital Libraries*, Zurich Switzerland, 2000

[9] K. Deb. Multi-Objective Optimization Using Evolutionary Algorithms. J. Wiley & Sons, London, 2001

[10] R. Fagin, A. Lotem, M. Naor. Optimal Aggregation Algorithms for Middleware. *ACM Symp. on Principles of Database Systems (PODS'01)*, Santa Barbara, USA, 2001.

[11] U. Güntzer, W.-T. Balke, W. Kießling. Optimizing Multi-Feature Queries for Image Databases. In *Proc. of the Int. Conf. on Very Large Databases (VLDB'00)*, Cairo, Egypt, 2000

[12] R. Keeney, H. Raiffa. Decisions with Multiple Objectives: Preferences and Value Tradeoffs. Wiley, 1976

[13] W. Kießling. Foundations of Preferences in Database Systems. In *Proc. of the Int. Conf. on Very Large Databases (VLDB'02)*, Hong Kong, China, 2002

[14] D. Kossmann, F. Ramsak, S. Rost. Shooting Stars in the Sky: An Online Algorithm for Skyline Queries. In *Proc. of Conf. on Very Large Data Bases (VLDB'02)*, Hong Kong, China, 2002

[15] H. Kung, F. Luccio, F. Preparata. On Finding the Maxima of a Set of Vectors. *Journal of the ACM*, vol. 22(4), ACM, 1975

[16] M. Lacroix, P. Lavency. Preferences: Putting more Knowledge into Queries. In *Proc. of the Int. Conf. on Very Large Databases (VLDB'87)*, Brighton, UK, 1987

[17] A. Leubner, W. Kießling. Personalized Keyword Search with Partial-Order Preferences. In *Proc. of Brazilian Symp. on Databases (SBBD'02)*, Gramado, Brazil, 2002.

[18] A. Motro. VAGUE: A User Interface to Relational Databases that Permits Vague Queries. In *ACM Transactions on Office Information Systems (TOIS)* 6(3), 1988

[19] F. Naumann, U. Leser, J. Freytag. Quality-driven Integration of Heterogenous Information Systems. In *Proc. of Conf. on Very Large Data Bases (VLDB'99)*, Edinburgh, UK, 1999

[20] S. Nepal and M. Ramakrishna. Query processing issues in image (multimedia) databases. In *Proc. of Int. Conf. on Data Engineering (ICDE'99)*, Sydney, Australia, 1999

[21] M. Ortega, Y. Rui, K. Chakrabarti, et al. Supporting ranked boolean similarity queries in MARS. *IEEE Transactions on Knowledge and Data Engineering (TKDE)*, Vol. 10 (6), 1998

[22] C. Papadimitriou, M. Yannakakis. Multiobjective Query Optimization. In *Proc. of the ACM Symp. on Principles of Database Systems (PODS'01)*, Santa Barbera, USA, 2001

[23] D. Papadias, Y. Tao, G. Fu, B. Seeger. *An Optimal and Progressive Algorithm for Skyline Queries.* In *Proc. of the Int. ACM SIGMOD Conf. (SIGMOD'03)*, San Diego, USA, 2003.

[24] K. Tan, P. Eng, B. Ooi. Efficient Progressive Skyline Computation. In Proc. *of Conf. on Very Large Data Bases (VLDB'01)*, Rome, Italy, 2001.

Lifting the Burden of History from Adaptive Query Processing[*]

Amol Deshpande[†] and Joseph M. Hellerstein[†][‡]

[†]University of California, Berkeley and [‡]Intel Research, Berkeley
{amol, jmh}@cs.berkeley.edu

Abstract

Adaptive query processing schemes attempt to re-optimize query plans during the course of query execution. A variety of techniques for adaptive query processing have been proposed, varying in the granularity at which they can make decisions [8]. The eddy [1] is the most aggressive of these techniques, with the flexibility to choose tuple-by-tuple how to order the application of operators. In this paper we identify and address a fundamental limitation of the original eddies proposal: the *burden of history* in routing. We observe that routing decisions have long-term effects on the state of operators in the query, and can severely constrain the ability of the eddy to adapt over time. We then propose a mechanism we call STAIRs that allows the query engine to manipulate the state stored inside the operators and undo the effects of past routing decisions. We demonstrate that eddies with STAIRs achieve both high adaptivity and good performance in the face of uncertainty, outperforming prior eddy proposals by orders of magnitude.

1 Introduction

"Stair above stair the eddying waters rose
circling immeasurably fast..."
– Percy Bysshe Shelley

In many scenarios, it is difficult or impossible at compile time to translate a declarative query into an efficient static execution plan. This problem has been highlighted in querying remote data sources [11, 1], in querying data streams [14, 3, 15], and even in traditional centralized databases [9, 4, 12]. To address this problem, a variety of adaptive query processing techniques have been proposed [8]. Among these, the eddy [1] is the most flexible and aggressive mechanism. An eddy is a tuple router that is placed at the center of a dataflow, intercepting all incoming and outgoing tuples between operators in the flow. By sitting at the center of the flow, the eddy can both observe the rates of all the operators, and make decisions about the order in which tuples will visit the operators. Eddies are intended to merge the statistics-collection and operator ordering facilities of a query optimizer into a query engine's runtime system.

In principle, eddies are able to choose different operator orderings for each tuple during query processing, subject only to the constraints of whether an operator is able to process a tuple (for example, a selection operator on table S can only process tuples from that table). But, as we observe in this paper, the *query execution plans* that eddies can effect for multi-join queries are limited not only by the semantic properties of the operators, but also by the *burden of routing history*: routing decisions made early in query's execution limit the eddy's routing options later on. These limitations can remove much of the adaptive power of eddies. The crux of the problem is the state accumulated by joins: once routed, a tuple that resides in the state of a join can effectively determine the order of execution for subsequently arriving tuples from other tables. To illustrate, we review an example from the original eddies paper [1]:

Example: Consider the query $R \bowtie_a S \bowtie_b T$, using two pipelining hash join operators (Figure 1). At the beginning of query processing, the data source for R is stalled, and no R tuples arrive. Hence the $R \bowtie_a S$ operator never produces a match, which makes it an attractive destination for routing S tuples: it efficiently removes work from the query engine. The result is that the eddy emulates a static query plan of the form $(R \bowtie S) \bowtie T$. Some time later, R tuples arrive in great quantity and it becomes apparent that the best plan would have been $(S \bowtie T) \bowtie R$. The eddy can switch the routing policy so that subsequent S tuples are routed to $S \bowtie_b T$ first. Unfortunately, this change is "too little too late": all the previously-seen S tuples are still stored in the internal state of the $R \bowtie_a S$ operator. As R tuples arrive, they *must* join with these S tuples before the S tuples are joined with T tuples. As a result, the eddy effectively continues to emulate the suboptimal plan $(R \bowtie S) \bowtie T$, even after its routing decision for S has

---

[*]This work was supported by NSF under grants 0208588 and 0205647, and by an IBM Fellowship.

Permission to copy without fee all or part of this material is granted provided that the copies are not made or distributed for direct commercial advantage, the VLDB copyright notice and the title of the publication and its date appear, and notice is given that copying is by permission of the Very Large Data Base Endowment. To copy otherwise, or to republish, requires a fee and/or special permission from the Endowment.

**Proceedings of the 30th VLDB Conference,
Toronto, Canada, 2004**

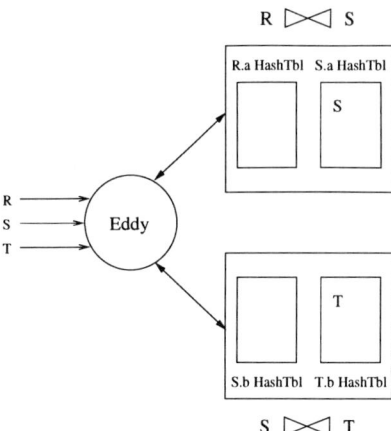

Figure 1: If the data from relation R is delayed, the eddy may route all of S to $R \bowtie_a S$, resulting in accumulation of state as shown.

changed.

This example illustrates both how easy it is to make incorrect routing decisions, and how these decisions can have permanent effects on the query plan achieved by an eddy – even when routing policies are changed. As we discuss in Section 2.3, the state accumulation inside the operators also makes it impossible for the eddy to perform aggressive adaptations such as changing the join spanning tree used for cyclic queries, or to perform *query scrambling* [18] in presence of delayed data sources.

In this paper we introduce a modified eddy architecture that makes use of a query operator called a STAIR (Storage, Transformation and Access for Intermediate Results), which holds the state traditionally encapsulated in joins. STAIRs address the problems illustrated above by allowing query state to be modified and migrated across STAIRs during query execution. The ability to modify and migrate state lifts the burden of history described above, enabling this architecture to undo the effects of prior routing decisions. In essence, STAIRs complete the picture begun with eddies: they allow a query executor to achieve the full effect of adapting the operator ordering at any point during runtime. As we discuss in Section 3.3, the flexibility in state management provides a number of additional novel optimization opportunities as well for trading off computation and storage during query execution.

We have implemented our architecture in the PostgreSQL 7.3 database management system in the context of the Telegraph project [2], and we present experimental results showing that eddies with STAIRs achieve both high adaptivity and good performance in the face of uncertainty, outperforming prior eddy proposals by orders of magnitude.

2 Eddies: Review and Pitfalls

We begin with a description of the eddy mechanism, and illustrate how state accumulation through bad routing choices can restrict eddy's ability to adapt. We then briefly review the SteMs architecture [16] that also provides a so-lution to this problem, and discuss why that solution is unsatisfactory. To make this discussion concrete, we focus on a common usage scenario for adaptive query processing [1, 10, 16, 18, 11], where the query processor is asked to evaluate a declarative select-project-join query over a set of finite relations that are being *streamed into* the query processor (from disk or from network). We ignore selection predicates, and restrict the choice of join operators to pipelining symmetric hash join operators. The discussion in this section, however, can be easily extended to other kinds of join operators as well (*e.g.*, index join operators, traditional non-pipelining join operators *etc.*).

2.1 Eddies

Traditional database systems execute queries by choosing a query plan a priori, and adhering to it throughout the query execution. The basic idea behind eddies is to treat query execution as a process of *routing* tuples through operators, and to allow changing the order in which tuples are routed on a per-tuple basis. A special *eddy* operator is used to route tuples between the query operators, and follows a simple procedure:

- Choose a tuple to process next; this could either be a new tuple from a base relation, or it could be the result of processing an earlier tuple.
- Among the operators that are *valid* routing destinations for this tuple, choose one, route the tuple to it, and store the resulting tuples in the eddy's internal buffer. Valid routing destinations for a tuple are determined by the semantic properties of the operators. For example, a tuple can be routed to a *join operator* only if the tuple contains a component from exactly one of the relations in the join.

Notation

Before going on, we define the notation we use in this paper. We use capitalized italics to denote base relations (*e.g.*, R, S), and small italics to denote base tuples belonging to those relations (*e.g.*, r, s). We use boldface letters to denote sets of relations (*e.g.*, $\mathbf{Q} = \{R, S\}$). Given a set of relations $\mathbf{Q}$ such that the relations in the set can be joined without use of cartesian products, we denote the resulting join relation by $\bowtie \mathbf{Q}$, or simply as the concatenation of the relations in $\mathbf{Q}$ (*e.g.* RS denotes the result relation obtained by joining R and S). We use small boldface letters to denote *intermediate* tuples belonging to such joined relations (e.g., $\mathbf{q}$ is a tuple in $\mathbf{Q}$.) Finally, we denote by R_τ all the tuples of R that have been processed by the eddy at time τ.

Definition 2.1 *[16] Consider a tuple* $\mathbf{q}$ *that belongs to the join of k base-tables $T_1, \ldots, T_k$. The tuples of these base-tables that participate in the generation of this tuple $\mathbf{q}$ are called* base-table components *of $\mathbf{q}$, and are denoted by* $q_{T_1}, \ldots, q_{T_k}$ *respectively. We denote $\mathbf{q}$ by* $q_{T_1} q_{T_2} \ldots q_{T_k}$.

Definition 2.2 *A tuple* $\mathbf{q}' \in \mathbf{Q}'$ *is called a* sub-tuple *of a tuple* $\mathbf{q} \in \mathbf{Q}$, *if* $\mathbf{Q}' \subseteq \mathbf{Q}$ *and all base-table components of $\mathbf{q}'$ are also present in $\mathbf{q}$. We call $\mathbf{q}$ a* super-tuple *of $\mathbf{q}'$*.

Given this background, Figure 2 shows the eddy instantiated for a three-relation join query $R \bowtie S \bowtie T$ (we will use

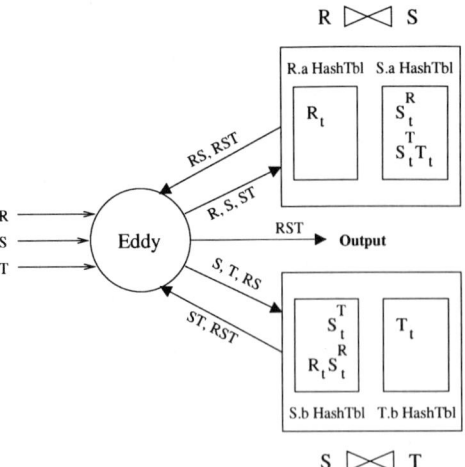

Figure 2: An eddy instantiated for $R \bowtie S \bowtie T$. Valid options for routing are labeled on the edges. The state materialized inside the join operators at time τ is shown, where S_τ^R and S_τ^T denote the parts of S_τ that were routed to $R \bowtie S$ and $S \bowtie T$ respectively.

this query as the running example throughout this paper), and the valid routing choices for various types of tuples. For example, the only valid routing choice for R tuples is the $R \bowtie S$ operator, whereas S tuples can be routed to either of the two join operators.

2.2 Uncertainties in Routing

The key to achieving good performance with eddies is making intelligent routing decisions. Unfortunately, the eddy can never have complete information about the data, or about the environment, and has to make decisions in presence of incomplete information. Continuing with our example query, let us say that the eddy was able to compute the selectivities of the two joins $R \bowtie S$ and $S \bowtie T$ accurately over the data it has seen. The eddy now could use these selectivities to make routing choices, under the assumption that these selectivities will remain constant in the future. But, there are many reasons why such extrapolation may turn out to be wrong.

- **Delays in arrival of data:** If there are delays in arrival of data from some relations, the eddy may have a very small sample of the data, leading to incorrect estimation of selectivities, and possibly of the sizes of the relations. To be able to estimate join selectivities accurately, both these factors need to be correctly estimated.

- **Order-dependent selectivities:** Selectivities are often correlated with the order of arrival of data. For example, if the data is ordered by *age*, then the selectivity of a predicate on *salary* changes as the tuples stream in.

- **Unpredictable data rates:** Unpredictable data rates can result in incorrect estimation of table sizes, and consequently of selectivities of joins involving those relations.

2.3 Burden of Routing History

Given the unpredictable nature of the data, there is not much the eddy can do to avoid making routing mistakes, and the penalties for such wrong decisions must be incurred to some degree during execution. Unfortunately, because of the state that gets materialized in the operators, especially the join operators, the effects of such mistakes can be long-lived. Figure 2 shows the state materialized in the joins at time τ. As we can see, the routing choices made for S determine what gets stored in the joins (S_τ^R was routed toward $R \bowtie S$, and S_τ^T toward $S \bowtie T$ resulting in those two parts of S getting stored in those join operators respectively). This results in several problems in query execution later. We discuss them in turn.

Constraints on Future Adaptation

The join state can significantly constrain the adaptation opportunities that the eddy has in future. Though the eddy can choose how to route a tuple when it first processes it, the choice made at that time constrains subsequent operator orderings for future results that involve this tuple. Coming back to our example, when a tuple $s \in S_\tau^R$ arrived at the eddy, the eddy could have chosen to route it to either of the joins. But once this choice has been made (in this case, $R \bowtie S$ operator), the query plan used for generating *any* result tuple that contains s (even one that may be generated in future), is constrained to be $(R \bowtie S) \bowtie T$. This is because any R tuples that come in later will be routed to $R \bowtie S$ and thus will join with s. As such, even if the eddy, in future, deduces that joining s with R is sub-optimal, it is prevented from doing any adaptation. This can result in significantly sub-optimal performance in many cases, as we will see in Section 5.

Cyclic Queries

A join query can be represented as a query graph, with vertices denoting the relations and edges denoting join predicates between relations. Cyclic queries are those in which the query graph has cycles. For example, the query $\sigma_{R.a=S.a \wedge S.b=T.b \wedge R.c=T.c}(R \times S \times T)$, is a cyclic query. As in traditional database systems, eddies choose a spanning tree of the query graph a priori, and are not able to change the spanning tree mid-execution. This is because the tuples that get routed to a join operator are "lost" if a spanning tree without that join operator is used later on. As an example, if we routed according to the spanning tree containing $R \bowtie S$ and $S \bowtie T$ in the example above, resulting in state as shown in Figure 2 at time τ, switching to the spanning tree consisting of $R \bowtie T$ and $S \bowtie T$ is not possible, because R_τ is stored inside $R \bowtie S$ and will not be available to the new spanning tree.

Pre-computation in presence of delays

If data from remote data sources is delayed, it might be attractive to perform other useful work while waiting for that data to arrive. Such pre-computation can be useful to produce partial results [17] that may contain missing attribute values, or to join the data that has already arrived as much as possible [18]. The eddy is prevented from performing such adaptations because of the accumulation of state inside the operators, and the eddy's inability to change rout-

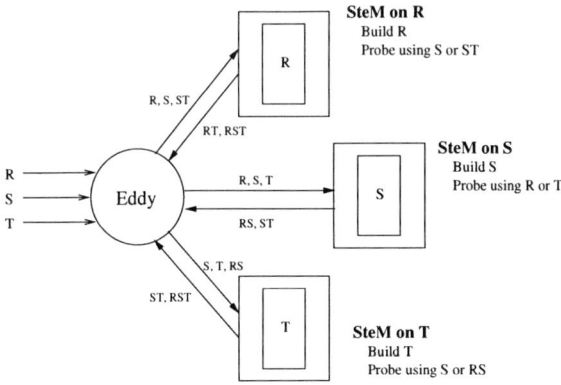

Figure 3: SteMs architecture for the query $R \bowtie S \bowtie T$; annotations on the edges show the types of tuples that are exchanged.

ing decisions once they are made. In fact, the inability to produce partial results aggressively was one of the main reasons the SteMs architecture that we describe below was developed.

2.4 SteMs: A Preliminary Solution

The State Modules (SteMs) architecture [16] is an extension of the eddy architecture, and inoculates eddies from these problems by ensuring that the state stored in the operators is entirely independent of the routing history. The main operator in this architecture is a *SteM*, which is instantiated for each relation in the query as shown in Figure 3. This operator stores all the tuples from that relation, and also handles all the probes involving that relation. The query is once again executed by routing tuples through these operators. As an example, when a new R tuple comes into the system, it is (1) inserted into the R SteM, (2) probed into the S SteM to find matching S tuples corresponding to the join $R \bowtie S$, and (3) the resulting RS tuples are probed into the T SteM to find matching T tuples in order to generate RST results. The intermediate RS tuples are not stored anywhere, and are thrown away as soon as results are produced.

As a result of not storing any intermediate tuples, the state accumulated inside the SteMs is independent of the routing history. This addressed some of the challenges mentioned above, but it is also the cause of two significant drawbacks:

- **Re-computation of intermediate tuples:** Since intermediate tuples generated during the execution are not stored for future use, they have to be recomputed each time they are needed.

- **Constrained plan choices:** More importantly, the query plans that can be executed for any new tuple are significantly constrained. For example, any new R tuple, r, that comes in at time τ must join with S_τ (the tuples for S that have already arrived) first, and then with T_τ. This effectively restricts the query plans that the eddy can use for this tuple to be $(r \bowtie S_\tau) \bowtie T_\tau$, even if the eddy *knows* that that plan is sub-optimal.

As we will see in Section 5, these inherent flaws with the basic design of the mechanism result in significantly worse performance than the original eddy architecture in most cases.

3 STAIRs

As we argued in the preceding section, and as we will further demonstrate in Section 5, routing mistakes are quite common in adaptive query processing, and the resulting burden of history can have long-lasting effects on the query execution. These effects can be attributed to the state that gets stored in the operators during execution. This observation naturally leads us to the basic idea behind our proposed modifications to the eddy architecture: *expose the state stored in the operators to the eddy, and allow the eddy to manipulate this state.* We do this by introducing an operator we call a *STAIR*, which holds the state traditionally encapsulated in joins, and provides the eddy with primitives to manipulate this state.

3.1 STAIR Operator

A STAIR operator encapsulates the state typically stored inside the join operators. More formally, a STAIR on relation R and an attribute a, denoted by $\mathcal{R}.a$, holds (possibly intermediate) tuples that contain a base-table component from relation R, and supports the following two basic operations[1]:

insert($\mathcal{R}.a$, t)
Given a tuple **t** that contains a base-table component from relation R, store the tuple inside the STAIR.

probe($\mathcal{R}.a$, val)
Given a value **val** from the domain of the attribute $R.a$, return all tuples r stored inside $\mathcal{R}.a$ such that $r.a$ = **val**.

Figure 4 shows the STAIRs instantiated for our example 3-relation query. In essence, for each join operator that would have been instantiated in the original *EddyJoins*[2] approach of [1], we instead use two STAIRs that interact with the eddy directly. We will call the pair of STAIRs corresponding to a single join *duals* of each other. Note that even if both the joins were on the same attribute, we would have two STAIRs on relation S and attribute $a(= b)$. These two STAIRs are treated as separate operators, as they participate in different joins.

The query execution using STAIRs is similar to query execution using join operators. Instead of routing a tuple to a join operator as in EddyJoins, the eddy itself performs an *insert* on one STAIR, and a *probe* into its dual. In fact, in this paper, we will assume that the following property is always obeyed during query execution:

---

[1] To capture join predicates such as $R.a = S.a$ AND $R.b = S.b$, a STAIR can be more generally defined on a *list* of attributes from the schema of R. For ease of exposition we assume a single join attribute in our discussion; the extension to multi-attribute predicates is straightforward.

[2] We will refer to the original eddy architecture that uses explicit join operators by EddyJoins, to distinguish it from the other eddy-based architectures that we discuss in this paper.

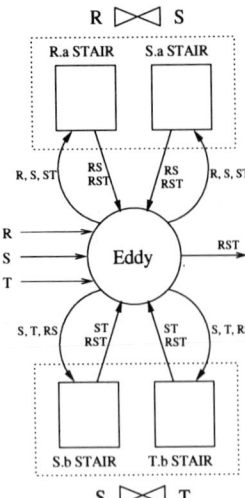

Figure 4: Executing $R \bowtie S \bowtie T$ using an eddy and STAIRs.

Dual Routing Property: *Whenever a tuple is routed to a STAIR for probing into it, it must be simultaneously inserted into the dual STAIR.*

This property is analogous to the BuildFirst constraint described in [16], and is also obeyed by the symmetric join operator. The Dual Routing Property can be relaxed by using timestamps in a similar fashion to the one described in [16], so that the probe must follow the insert in time but need not be atomically combined with the insert.

For brevity, we will use the phrase *routed to $R \bowtie_a S$ operator* to mean performing the two operations outlined above on the two STAIRs, $\mathcal{R}.a$ and $\mathcal{S}.a$, corresponding to the join.

3.1.1 State Management Primitives

Other than the two basic operations described above, STAIRs also support two state management primitives:

Demotion($\mathcal{R}.a$, t, t')
Intuitively, the *demotion* operation involves reducing an intermediate tuple stored in a STAIR to a sub-tuple of that tuple, by removing some of the base tuple components that it contains.

The following pre-conditions must be satisfied by the arguments to this function:
- t must be a tuple stored in $\mathcal{R}.a$,
- t' must be a sub-tuple of t,
- t' must contain the base-table component of t corresponding to the relation R.

Given that these pre-conditions are satisfied, the demotion operation simply replaces t by t' in $\mathcal{R}.a$.

This operation can be thought of as *undoing* some work that was done earlier during execution, and this work may have to be redone if the tuple is required again in future. Figure 5 shows the result of applying $demotion(\mathcal{S}.b, r_1 s_1, s_1)$ to an example initial state. As we can see, after applying this operation, the tuple $r_1 s_1$ in $\mathcal{S}.b$ gets replaced by the tuple s_1.

Promotion($\mathcal{R}.a$, t, $\mathcal{S}.b$)
The *promotion* operation replaces a tuple in a STAIR with *super*-tuples of that tuple that are generated using another join in the query.

The following conditions must be satisfied by the input to this operation:
- t must be stored in $\mathcal{R}.a$.
- t must contain the base-table component corresponding to relation S (note that S and R may be identical).
- Let the dual STAIR of $\mathcal{S}.b$ be $\mathcal{T}.b$. Then, t must not contain the base-table component corresponding to relation T.

Intuitively, the point of promotion is to use the join $S \bowtie T$ to generate super-tuples of t; the last two conditions simply make sure that this is a valid operation.

Given this, the promotion operation performs the following steps:
1. Remove t from $\mathcal{R}.a$,
2. Insert t into $\mathcal{S}.b$,
3. Probe $\mathcal{T}.b$ using the tuple t, and
4. Insert the resulting matches (that are super-tuples of t), if any, back into $\mathcal{R}.a$.

Figure 5 shows the result of applying $promotion(\mathcal{S}.b, s_3, \mathcal{S}.a)$, to an example initial state. As a result of this, the s_3 tuple in $\mathcal{S}.b$ gets replaced by $r_1 s_3$ and $r_2 s_3$, whereas s_3 itself gets stored in $\mathcal{S}.a$.

3.1.2 Duplicates

Both these state management operations, as described above, can result in a state configuration that allows spurious duplicate results to be generated in future. Such duplicates may be acceptable in some scenarios, but can also optionally be removed by maintaining the following local invariant on the STAIRs.

Invariant: *A STAIR never contains two tuples $t_1 \in T_1$ and $t_2 \in T_2$, such that t_1 and t_2 match on all base-table components corresponding to the relations in $T_1 \cap T_2$.*

In Appendix A we discuss techniques to maintain this invariant during query execution, and also how it guarantees duplicate-free execution.

3.2 Lifting the Burden of History using STAIRs

As we discussed in Section 2.2, storing intermediate result tuples generated during query execution can have a significant impact on future query processing. In this section we show an example of how STAIRs can be used to manipulate the state stored within the join operators so that such prior decisions can, in effect, be reversed.

Figure 6 shows the state maintained inside the join operators at time τ for our example query. Let us say that, at this time, we have better knowledge of the future and we know that routing S_τ^R toward $R \bowtie S$ was a mistake, and will lead to sub-optimal query execution in future (say

952

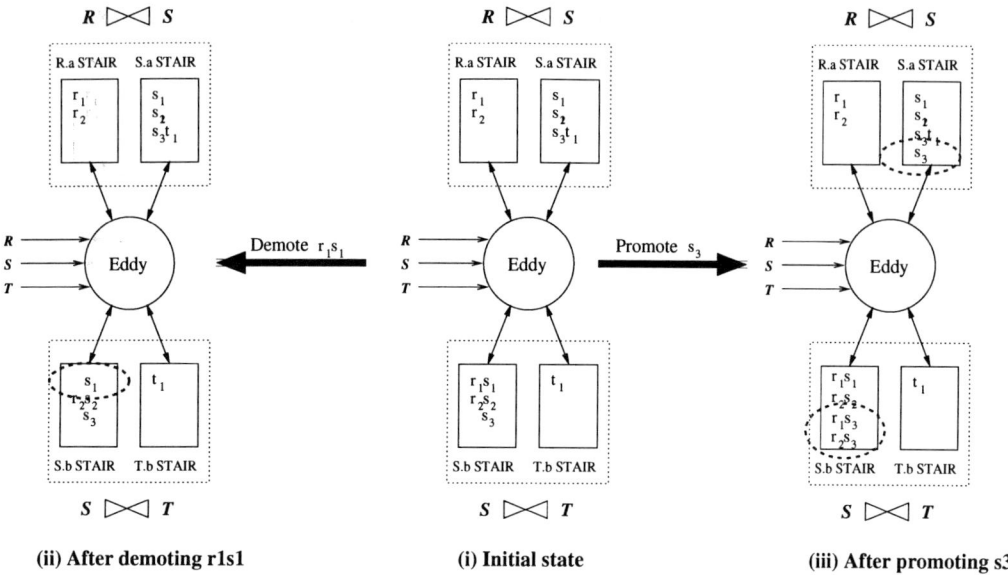

Figure 5: **Examples of promotion and demotion.** The middle plan (i) shows the state of the system after the eddy has received six tuples, $r_1, r_2, s_1, s_2, s_3, t_1$, and has chosen to route s_1 and s_2 to $R \bowtie S$, and s_3 to $S \bowtie T$. The left-hand plan (ii) shows the state after $r_1 s_1$ has been demoted to s_1 in $\mathcal{S}.b$. The right-hand plan (iii) shows the effect, starting from the initial state, of promoting s_3 using $\mathcal{S}.a$.

because $R \bowtie S_T^R$ has high selectivity). This prior routing decision can be reversed as follows (Figure 6):

- Demote the $S_T^R \bowtie R_T$ tuples in $\mathcal{S}.b$ to S_T^R.
- Promote the S_T^R tuples from $\mathcal{S}.a$ to $S_T^R \bowtie T_T$.

Figure 6 shows the result of these operations. As we can see, the state now reflects what it would have been if S_T^R had previously been routed to the $\mathcal{S}.b$ and $\mathcal{T}.b$ STAIRs, instead of $\mathcal{R}.a$ and $\mathcal{S}.a$ STAIRs. As a result, future R tuples will not be forced to join with S_T^R.

We will refer to this process of moving state from one join operator to another as *state migration*.

3.3 Further motivating adaptive state management

Executing queries using STAIRs allows the eddy to adapt for reasons other than removing the burden of history. In this section, we will briefly discuss how this can be done.

Cyclic queries

Like the original eddy architecture, the base STAIRs architecture only works naturally with acyclic queries; as such, a spanning tree of cyclic query graphs must be chosen at the query initialization. However, unlike the EddyJoins architecture, the state management features provided by the STAIRs can be used to switch the spanning tree used for execution mid-way through query processing. Briefly, this is done by manipulating the state inside the operators to reflect query execution using the new spanning tree. In the interest of brevity we omit the details in this paper. We do note here that this process can involve fair amount of state movement, and if we expect to change the spanning tree used frequently, the SteMs architecture is an attractive alternative since it can change the spanning trees more easily.

Partial Results, Query Scrambling

When a data source in the query is relatively slow or even stalled, it is often desirable to ameliorate the delay by either producing partial results, or by aggressively joining together previously-received tuples (query scrambling). Both of these ideas involve a form of pre-computation of results. The *promotion* primitive provided by STAIRs can be used to perform such pre-computation as required. As an example, if the data from a relation R is delayed and the query engine wants to join data from relation S that is waiting for data from R (and hence, was routed to $R \bowtie S$ operator) with data from relation T, the eddy can use the promotion operation to move T tuples to $S \bowtie T$ operator, and thus perform useful work while waiting for data from R. The original query scrambling proposal [18] only addressed *initial* delays; the ability of STAIRs to allow precomputation even after some data from R generalizes that approach.

Flexible Storage and Reuse of Intermediate Results

The SteMs architecture demonstrated that it is possible to do query processing without storing any intermediate results at all. The state management primitives provided STAIRs enable the eddy to take this idea even further by providing flexibility in choosing the intermediate result tuples to be stored for further reuse. As an example, the eddy could choose to store only base-table tuples in the STAIRs by instantly demoting inserted tuples. This can be used to reduce the memory footprint of the query processor down to the memory footprint of the SteMs architecture (though the actual query execution will not be identical to using SteMs).

Another instance where such flexibility could be useful is when we are executing sliding window queries over streaming data [14, 3, 2, 7, 19]. Storing and reusing intermediate results is problematic in such a setting, because when a window on a base relation slides, some base-table

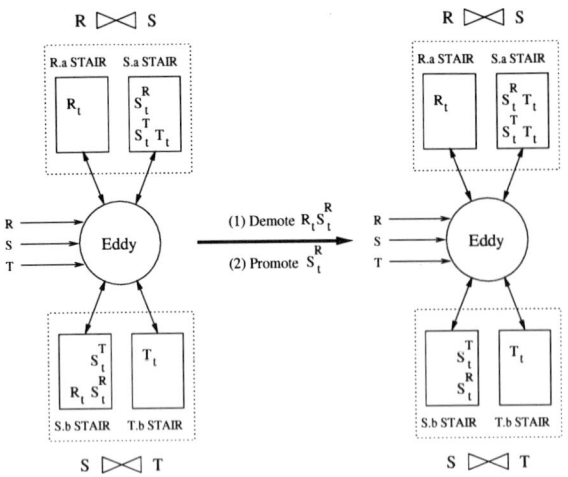

Figure 6: State Migration: Reversing prior decisions using STAIRs

tuples are dropped from the window, and all intermediate tuples that contain those base-table tuples must be removed from the engine. The cost of deletion can be quite significant, and many of these architectures choose to discard intermediate result tuples (e.g. CACQ [14]). STAIRs can be used to store only long-living intermediate tuples, thus enabling selective caching of intermediate tuples.

3.4 Correctness of Operation

Given the generality of the operations that can be performed on STAIRs, it is not clear that the eddy will always produce correct query result when using STAIRs. In Appendix A we prove the following:

Theorem 3.1 *An eddy with STAIRs always produces the correct query result in spite of arbitrary applications of the promotion and demotion operations.*

4 Implementation Details

We have implemented this architecture in the PostgreSQL 7.3 database management system in the context of the Telegraph project [2]. In this section, we will briefly discuss our implementation (please see [5] for the full details of the implementation). We have added two main new operators to the PostgreSQL code base:

Eddy: An eddy operator handles a single select-project-join query block that may contain arbitrary selections, joins and projections, but no aggregates, groupbys or subqueries. The latter constructs are handled by existing PostgreSQL operators that interact with the eddy operator using the traditional *iterator* interface. To be able to support such an interface, the eddy operator is implemented as a finite state machine that internally keeps track of its computational state. The eddy instantiates a set of operators (STAIRs, joins, SteMs *etc.*) as required, and executes the query by fetching tuples from the source modules (with which it interacts using the iterator interface as well) and by routing the tuples among the operators. The eddy also maintains statistics about the data, and uses them to make routing choices, and state migration decisions.

We developed the routing mechanism carefully to minimize the overheads of routing. The main idea behind these optimizations is to perform mini-batch routing instead of per-tuple routing. As we show in [5], the cost of making routing decisions can be effectively amortized over very few tuples, resulting in very low routing mechanism overheads with significant flexibility.

STAIR: We currently implement a STAIR as an in-memory hash table built on the tuples that have been inserted into the STAIR. It supports the four basic operations described above (*insert, probe, demote*, and *promote*), and also supports the iterator interface allowing it to be used in traditional query plans without eddies.

The STAIR operator is also used to implement two other operators:

- **Symmetric Hash Join:** As discussed previously, a symmetric hash join operator is simply two STAIRs used together.
- **SteM:** There are two main differences between SteMs and STAIRs: (1) SteMs only store base tuples, (2) a single SteM manages all inserts and probes on the base tuples corresponding to a single relation. We emulate this architecture by (1) inserting each base tuple into all the STAIRs on the corresponding relation, (2) never inserting an intermediate tuple into any of the STAIRs, and (3) routing a probe on a relation to the appropriate STAIR on that relation. It might seem that we pay a penalty relative to SteMs for maintaining multiple STAIRs on the same relation. However, as described in [16], a SteM actually maintains multiple internal hash-indexes, one corresponding to each probing attribute, and as such, the overheads of the two architectures are identical.

4.1 Routing Policy

The routing policy we use for the experiments in this paper is based on the rank ordering technique [13] for ordering selections. The eddy maintains two sets of statistics on the data: (1) the selectivities of the predicates on the base relations, and (2) the domain sizes of the join attributes corresponding to the joins, which are used to compute the join selectivities periodically. For SteMs, a greedy routing policy of routing a tuple such that it joins with the relation with the lowest join selectivity is used; this policy produces the minimal number of intermediate tuples in response to a new base tuple, and hence is optimal under that metric for SteMs (assuming that the selectivity estimates are accurate).

The same policy is however not optimal for EddyJoins or STAIR; the state accumulation through making locally optimal routing choices can result in sub-optimal overall performance. For these two techniques, we use the following routing policy to route a given tuple:

1. For each join (or corresponding STAIRs) that the tuple could be routed to, compute *cumulative* selectivity of joining it with the tuples from all relations that the

tuple is connected to through this join (e.g., while considering a R tuple and the $R \bowtie S$ join in our example query, cumulative selectivity is the result of joining this R tuple with $S_T \bowtie T_T$).

2. Route the tuple to the join with the lowest cumulative selectivity.

Note that, the computation of these selectivities is amortized using the mini-batch routing optimizations as we describe in detail in [5], and is not done per-tuple.

4.2 State Migration Policy

We currently use a greedy state migration policy that eagerly migrates state when routing decisions are changed. This approach ignores the cost of state migration, and could potentially result in sub-optimal performance for two reasons: the eddy might thrash by performing too many migrations in response to fluctuating selectivities, and the eddy might perform a large state migration at the end of query execution, with no subsequent payoff. As our experimental results demonstrate, these scenarios may be infrequent in practice. We are planning to address these shortcomings of the state migration policy by instituting a back-off mechanism to avoid thrashing, and by migrating state in stages to avoid large migrations at the end of a query.

5 Experimental Study

In this section, we present an experimental study that validates our approach. We begin by studying in detail an illustrative query on the TPC-H benchmark schema, to analyze the effect of state on the eddy architecture. We demonstrate the advantages of our architecture for both a completion-time metric, and an online delay metric that looks at the output times of tuples. We then present a more extensive set of experiments on an synthetic database modeled after the Wisconsin benchmark [6]. We use a set of randomly generated queries on this benchmark, and focus on the completion time metric to demonstrate the advantages of such adaptive query processing.

5.1 Setup

We ran the experiments on two machines, a 2GHz Pentium IV machine and a 1.4 GHz Pentium III machine with 512MB of memory each, running RedHat Linux. We present experiments comparing four query processing techniques: *Symmetric Hash Joins (SHJ)*, which uses traditional static query plans with symmetric hash join operators, and our three adaptive schemes: *EddyJoins*, *SteMs*, and *STAIRs*. Each experiment compared all four schemes on the same machine. The data was read off of local disks, and for the adaptive query processing techniques, the data was presented to the eddy through a module that controlled the input rates, and introduced delays as required by the setup. The "mini-batch" size for the eddy was set so that it could change routing decisions every 1000 tuples.

5.2 An Illustrative TPC-H Query

We begin with an illustrative query to validate the need for state management in adaptive query processing, and to understand the trade-offs involved in the state migration process. We use the following query on the TPC-H Benchmark schema that asks for *lineitem's* in a specified period and corresponding to a specified set of customers.

```
select *
from customer c, orders o, lineitem l
where c.custkey = o.custkey and
      o.orderkey = l.orderkey and
      c.nationkey = 1 and
      c.acctbal > 9000 and
      l.shipdate > date '1996-01-01'
```

The data from relation *lineitem* arrives at the query engine sorted in ascending order by *shipdate*. Early on in the query, the selectivity of the predicate on *lineitem* appears much lower than that of *customer*, so the eddy makes routing mistakes in the beginning by routing the tuples from the *orders* to the join with relation *lineitem*. Figure 7(i) shows the execution times of the various query processing techniques for this query in the scenario, where data rates are proportional to the sizes of the relations. This, *in effect*, gives the eddy correct estimates of the sizes of the relations, in spite of which, EddyJoins performs significantly worse than STAIRs because of the initial routing mistake of routing *orders* tuples to *lineitem* $\bowtie$ *orders*. On the other hand, STAIRs is able to correct this routing mistake by migrating the *orders* tuples to the second join when it gets more information, performing almost as well as having routed correctly from the beginning. This *switch* happens when the eddy has seen about 55% of the tuples from *orders*, and the corresponding state migration operation migrates all those tuples to the second join at that time.

Even though reuse of intermediate tuples is quite minimal in this query, SteMs perform poorly compared to the other techniques because there is no way to avoid joining the later-arriving *lineitem* tuples with *orders*; intermediate results from *customer* $\bowtie$ *orders* must be materialized to avoid this expense.

To better understand the trade-offs involved in state migration, we change the setup so that the eddy is not allowed to either change its routing decisions or perform state migrations until it has seen a certain number of *orders* tuples. Figure 7(ii) shows the results of this experiment. Since the change in the selectivities happens at about 55%, the execution times of these techniques are unaffected until that time. As we can see, the state migration cost up to this point is about 7% of the total execution cost with STAIRs. As we increase the number of *orders* tuples that need to be migrated, the cost of state migration increases, and its benefit goes down. Even then, the cost of state migration is low enough that STAIRs outperform EddyJoins, except at the very end when STAIRs migrate the entire *orders* relation without any benefit to doing so since the query execution is over.

Finally, we take a brief look at an interactive metric, namely, the rate at which output tuples are produced by these techniques. Figure 7(iii) shows the output rates for these four techniques (for SHJ, we show the output rates two plans, the best static plan and the worst static plan) for the above TPC-H query. As we can see, STAIRs pro-

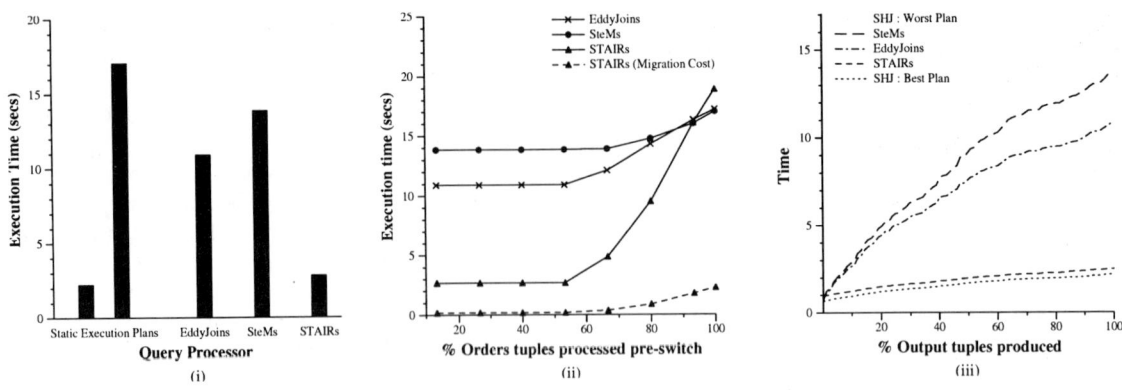

Figure 7: An illustrative TPC-H query: (i) The execution costs of the query processing techniques assuming data is streamed at rates proportional to the sizes of the relations (for SHJ, we show the costs for *two* static query execution plans, the best plan and the worst plan), (ii) Micro-benchmarking the state migration cost, (iii) Rates at which tuples are produced.

duce results at a much better rate except when the *best* static execution plan is used for SHJ, and even in that case, the performance of STAIRs is very close.

5.3 Synthetic Query Workload

To get a sense of benefits in a variety of different scenarios, and for different queries, we present results from a set of experiments over a synthetic dataset modeled after the Wisconsin Benchmark [6] using a randomly generated query workload. We populate the database with a total of 20 tables, five each of sizes 1k, 10k, 50k and 100k. Queries were generated randomly by first choosing a query graph shape from among four choices (path-shaped queries with 4 or 5 relations each, and star-shaped queries with 4 or 5 relations each), choosing the relations participating in the query randomly among the 20 tables above, choosing selection predicates with randomly chosen selectivities, and finally, choosing the selectivities of the joins randomly between 0 and 10. The initial plan for the all techniques was also chosen randomly among all the query plans for the query. Finally, we randomly varied the rates at which data from various relations was streamed, and also introduced random delays in the beginning.

We ran these experiments for 475 such setups, and measured the execution costs of the four techniques (SHJ, SteMs, EddyJoins, and STAIRs). In Figure 8 we present three graphs, comparing the relative performance of STAIRs with each of the other three techniques. In each data point, we plot the *ratio of the slower runtime to the faster*; when STAIRs is faster, the plot is *dark gray*. The x axis orders the experiments in ascending order of the benefit of STAIRs.

As we can see in Figure 8, STAIRs perform better than either SHJ or SteMs in almost all cases, with orders of magnitude difference in many cases. While comparing EddyJoins and STAIRs, we observe that, in about 66% of the cases, the execution costs of the two techniques differed by less than 10%, whereas out of the remaining 33% cases, STAIRs outperform EddyJoins in most cases, once by a factor of almost 10. In spite of using a greedy state migration policy which can result in late migrations and/or thrashing, STAIRs perform worse than EddyJoins in a very few cases, and at worst by a factor of 2.25. In future, we plan to address both these remaining problems with better migration policies as sketched in Section 4.2.

5.4 Adaptivity Benefits in a Traditional Setting

We close this section with an example over locally stored relations. The example illustrates the potential for "mixtures" of query plans to improve query performance even in traditional database scenarios, a direction we hope to pursue more deeply in future.

We use a 3-relation join query, $R \bowtie S \bowtie T$, over a synthetic dataset. The tables contains 50000 100-byte tuples each, and the selectivities of the two joins were set up such that, over the first 25000 tuples of the tables (ordered by the primary key of the table), the selectivity of $R \bowtie S$ was high (each S tuple joins with 5 R tuples), and the selectivity of $S \bowtie T$ was zero, whereas over the last 25000 tuples, the selectivities were reversed. Figure 9 shows the results of running this query for the variety of query processing architectures (including *Base*, the vanilla PostgreSQL query processor with its full range of join algorithms). We use a variation of the routing policy described in Section 4.1 for the adaptive query processing techniques, where the routing and state migration decisions are made based on the selectivities observed over a small window in the past. As we can see, both EddyJoins and STAIRs execute the query much faster than the best static plan for the query, with STAIRs performing slightly better because of the initial delay in adapting, during which the eddy makes bad routing choices.

The fundamental reason behind this is that the table S is naturally divided into two *partitions*, which exhibit very different join characteristics. Choosing the same query plan for both of them results in sub-optimal performance. Both EddyJoins and STAIRs, on the other hand, are able to identify and exploit this horizontal partitioning by routing part of the table through one query plan, and part of the table through another query plan. This example is simplified by

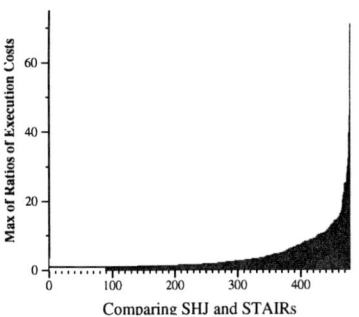 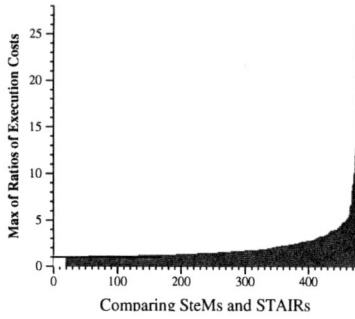 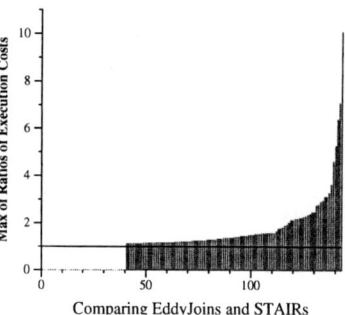

Figure 8: Comparing the execution costs of SHJ, SteMs and EddyJoins with STAIRs over 475 runs. The plots show the distribution of the ratios of execution costs, with gray bars on the left showing cases where STAIRs perform worse than the alternative technique. For the comparison of EddyJoins and STAIRs, we only plot results for the experiments where the execution costs differed by more than 10% (about 33% runs).

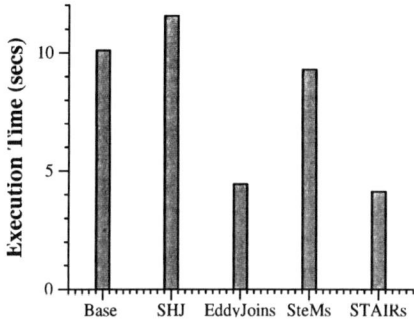

Figure 9: An experiment illustrating that the eddy architecture can perform much better than the *best* static plan when the data has natural *horizontal partitioning*.

the ordering of the relations. In future work we intend to explore techniques to learn content-sensitive routing strategies that can identify such partitions via tuple attributes rather than arrival order.

6 Related Work

There has been much work on adapting join and selection ordering during query execution. Due to lack of space, we will briefly discuss only the most relevant work here - for a detailed survey, please see [8].

Kabra and DeWitt [12] propose mid-query reoptimization, where a running query is reoptimized after every blocking point in the query plan. Tukwila [11] uses a similar technique, where in the absence of enough information about the data, only partially-complete plans are built in the beginning. Query scrambling [18] reacts to delays in the arrival of sources by rescheduling operators mid-flight, and in some cases, by reoptimizing the query to enable other operators. Most of these techniques, however, can not change the order of in-flight joins. Convergent query processing [10] proposes changing the query execution plan (and the join order) in-flight in response to changing runtime conditions. The times at which the query plans were changed divide the query execution in *phases*, and the *inter-phase* query results are generated at the end of the query execution, using the optimal plan for the query. In contrast, the eddy architecture produces all query results as soon as they are available. However, in absence of *state migration*, eddies can result in sub-optimal performance because of the query plans it is forced to use as a result of accumulated state.

Our work builds on the earlier work on eddies [1] and SteMs [16]. The eddy architecture has since been extended to execute continuous queries over streaming data [14, 3, 2]. These continuous query engines are based primarily on the SteMs architecture, and hence, do not reuse intermediate results generated during query processing. We believe that reusing intermediate results using STAIRs can result in better performance in data-stream environments as well, and we plan to work on this in future.

7 Conclusions

In this paper, we focused on the effect of the *burden on history* on the effectiveness of eddies, a highly adaptive query processing technique. Despite the ability to make mid-flight corrections to the query plan chosen to execute a query, the state that gets accumulated in the query operators can significantly constrain the ability of an eddy to adapt, resulting in sub-optimal performance in many cases. To alleviate this problem, we propose STAIRs, a modified eddy architecture that exposes the state accumulated inside the operators to the eddy, and provides state management primitives to manipulate this state. Our implementation of this architecture in a full-function database management system (PostgreSQL 7.3) demonstrates the viability of our architecture, even in traditional query processing applications.

References

[1] Ron Avnur and Joe Hellerstein. Eddies: Continuously adaptive query processing. In *SIGMOD*, 2000.

[2] Sirish Chandrasekaran *et al*. TelegraphCQ: Continuous dataflow processing for an uncertain world. In *CIDR*, 2003.

[3] Sirish Chandrasekaran and Michael J. Franklin. Streaming queries over streaming data. In *VLDB*, 2002.

[4] Richard Cole. A decision theoretic cost model for dynamic plans. *IEEE Data Engineering Bulletin*, 2000.

[5] Amol Deshpande. An initial study of overheads of eddies. *SIGMOD Record*, March 2004.

[6] David J. DeWitt. The Wisconsin Benchmark: Past, present, and future. In *The Benchmark Handbook Database and Transaction Systems (2nd Edition)*. 1993.

[7] Lukasz Golab and M. Tamer Ozsu. Processing sliding window multi-joins in continuous queries over data streams. In *VLDB*, 2003.

[8] Joe Hellerstein et al. Adaptive query processing: Technology in evolution. *IEEE Database Engineering Bulletin*, June 2000.

[9] Yannis Ioannidis and Younkyung Cha Kang. Randomized algorithms for optimizing large join queries. In *SIGMOD*, 1990.

[10] Zachary Ives. *Efficient query processing for data integration*. PhD thesis, University of Washington, Seattle, 2002.

[11] Zachary G. Ives et al. An adaptive query execution system for data integration. In *SIGMOD*, 1999.

[12] Navin Kabra and David J. DeWitt. Efficient mid-query re-optimization of sub-optimal query execution plans. In *SIGMOD*, 1998.

[13] Ravi Krishnamurthy, Haran Boral, and Carlo Zaniolo. Optimization of nonrecursive queries. In *VLDB*, 1986.

[14] Sam Madden, Mehul Shah, Joe Hellerstein, and Vijayshankar Raman. Continously adaptive continous queries over streams. In *SIGMOD*, 2002.

[15] Rajeev Motwani et al. Query processing, approximation, and resource management in a data stream management system. In *CIDR*, 2003.

[16] Vijayshankar Raman, Amol Deshpande, and Joe Hellerstein. Using state modules for adaptive query processing. In *ICDE*, 2003.

[17] Vijayshankar Raman and Joe Hellerstein. Partial results for online query processing. In *SIGMOD*, 2002.

[18] Tolga Urhan, Michael J. Franklin, and Laurent Amsaleg. Cost based query scrambling for initial delays. In *SIGMOD*, 1998.

[19] Stratis Viglas, Jeffrey F. Naughton, and Josef Burger. Maximizing the output rate of multi-way join queries over streaming information sources. In *VLDB*, 2003.

A Proof of Correctness

Given the generality of the operations that can be performed on STAIRs, it is not clear that the eddy will produce the correct query result in all cases. In this section, we give a rigorous proof of correctness of this architecture. For simplicity, we will assume that when the eddy receives a new base tuple s from a relation S, it completely finishes processing s as well as all the intermediate tuples that result from joining s with existing tuples, before starting to process a new base tuple. We will also assume that the promotion and demotion operations are only applied at such times, also called *points of stasis*.

We begin with an invariant on the state maintained in the STAIRs operators at points of stases.

Let $\mathbf{C}$ be a connected subgraph of the query graph. As the query graph is acyclic, $\mathbf{C}$ induces a cut on the query graph as shown in Figure 10 (i). Let $X_i \bowtie Y_i$ denote the edge between $\mathbf{C}$ and $\mathbf{D}_i$. Furthermore, let $\mathbf{C}_\tau$ denote the result of joining the data for the relations in $\mathbf{C}$ that has arrived before time τ.

Invariant A: *At any point of stasis τ, for any connected subgraph $\mathbf{C}$ of the query graph, the state maintained in the STAIR operators satisfies the following property: for every tuple $\mathbf{c} \in \mathbf{C}_\tau$, a sub-tuple of $\mathbf{c}$, $\mathbf{c}'$, is contained in some $X_i \bowtie Y_i$ (ie., $\mathbf{c}$ has been built into a STAIR on some X_i).*

We say that $\mathbf{c}$ is present as $\mathbf{c}'$ in join $X_i \bowtie Y_i$.

Intuitively, if this were not true, then if there were to exist a final result tuple $\mathbf{q}$ such that (1) $\mathbf{c}$ is a sub-tuple of $\mathbf{q}$, and (2) the final base component of $\mathbf{q}$ that arrives in the system is from a relation outside $\mathbf{C}$, then this final base component will not be able to join with $\mathbf{c}$ to produce $\mathbf{q}$ at all.

The invariant is clearly true in the beginning of the query (at $\tau = 0$), when $\mathbf{C}_\tau = \mathbf{C}_0$ is empty for all $\mathbf{X}$.

Lemma A.1 *If the invariant is true before applying the demotion operation, the invariant remains true after application of the operation.*

Proof: If $\mathbf{c} \in \mathbf{C}_\tau$ was present in a join $X_i \bowtie Y_i$ as $\mathbf{c}'$, and if we replace $\mathbf{c}'$ by a sub-tuple $\mathbf{c}''$, $\mathbf{c}$ is still present in $X_i \bowtie Y_i$.

Lemma A.2 *If the invariant is true before applying the promotion operation, the invariant remains true after application of the operation.*

Proof: Let $\mathbf{c} \in \mathbf{C}_\tau$ be present in $X_1 \bowtie Y_1$ as a sub-tuple $\mathbf{c}_1 \in (\mathbf{C}_1)_\tau$, where $\mathbf{C}_1 \subseteq \mathbf{C}$. $\mathbf{C}_1$, which itself is a connected subgraph, induces a cut on $\mathbf{C}$ as shown in Figure 10 (ii).

We will prove that promoting tuple $\mathbf{c}_1$ does not change the invariant for $\mathbf{c}$.

As $\mathbf{c}_1 \in (\mathbf{C}_1)_\tau$, the pair of STAIRs used for promoting $\mathbf{c}_1$ must correspond to a join that includes one relation from $\mathbf{c}_1$. There are two such sets of STAIRs.

- STAIRs corresponding to a join that includes a relation outside $\mathbf{C}$, and a relation inside $\mathbf{C}_1$. Say we use the STAIRs on the join $X_2 \bowtie Y_2$, where $X_2 \in \mathbf{C}_1$. In that case, during Step 2 of the promotion operation (cf. 3.1.1), $\mathbf{c}_1$ will be built into the STAIR on X_2 and the invariant remains true for $\mathbf{c}$, as $\mathbf{c}$ will now be present in $X_2 \bowtie Y_2$ as $\mathbf{c}_1$.

- STAIRs corresponding to a join on two relations in $\mathbf{C}$. Let us say we use the join between Z_1 and Z_2 for this purpose, where $Z_1 \in \mathbf{C}_1$ and $Z_2 \in \mathbf{C}_3$. Let $\mathbf{c}_3 \in (\mathbf{C}_3)_\tau$ be the projection of $\mathbf{c}$ on the relations in $\mathbf{C}_3$. Applying the invariant to $\mathbf{c}_3$, a sub-tuple of it (say $\mathbf{c}_3'$) must:

  - *Either* be built into the join between Z_1 and Z_2: in that case, when $\mathbf{c}_1$ is promoted using that join, the result $\mathbf{c}_1 \mathbf{c}_3'$ will be built back into $X_1 \bowtie Y_1$ (Step 4, Section 3.1.1), and the invariant will remain true for $\mathbf{c}$, as $\mathbf{c}_1 \mathbf{c}_3'$ is a sub-tuple of $\mathbf{c}$.

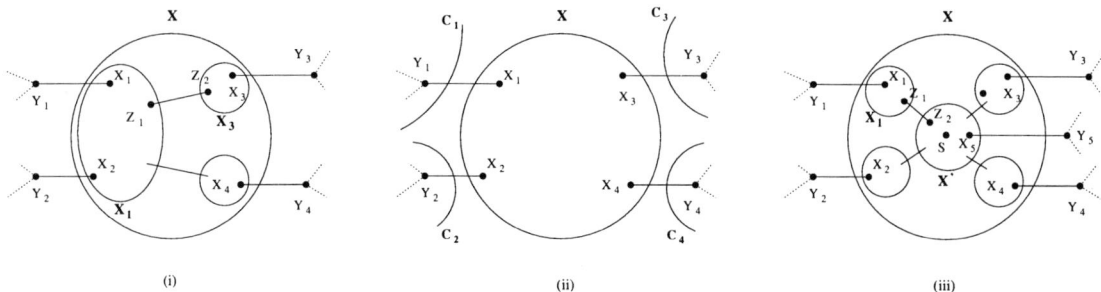

Figure 10: Proof of correctness figures

- *Or* be built into the join between some relation in C_3 and some relation outside C: in that case, the invariant will still be satisfied for c, as c'_3 is a sub-tuple of c built into a join that goes outside C.

Lemma A.3 *If a new base tuple $s \in S$ arrives in the system at time τ, and if the invariant is true at time τ, then the invariant remains true after the eddy has finished processing s and all the intermediate tuples that it generates (at time τ').*

Proof: The invariant may only be affected for connected subgraphs of the query graph that contain S, and furthermore, only for those intermediate tuples that have the new tuple s as a base-table component. Let C be such a connected subgraph and let $c \in C_\tau$ be a tuple for which the invariant is not satisfied after the eddy has finished processing s. We have that s is sub-tuple of c.

Let c' be the largest sub-tuple of c that was generated by the eddy when it processed s.

Clearly, $c' \neq c$. The only valid routing choices for c, if it was generated during processing, are $X_i \bowtie Y_i$ operators, and it would have been built into one such join when the eddy routed it. Let $c' \in C'_\tau$, where $C' \subset C$. Once again, C' induces a cut on C as shown in Figure 10 (iii). Now, the valid routing choices for c' are:

- $X_5 \bowtie Y_5, X_5 \in C', Y_5 \notin C$ (Figure 10 (iii)): If routed to this join, c', which is a sub-tuple of c, would have been built into that join, satisfying the invariant for c. As such, c' could not have been routed to such a join.

- $Z_1 \bowtie Z_2, Z_1 \in C', Z_2 \in C - C'$: Now, let $c_1 \in (C_1)_\tau$ be the intermediate tuple that contains base-table components of c corresponding to relations in C_1. Note that, c_1 does not contain s and as such, the invariant is true for this tuple. Hence, we get that, a sub-tuple c_1, say c'_1 (which is also a sub-tuple of c), is:

  - *either* present in join $X_i \bowtie Y_i, X_i \in C_1, Y_i \notin C$: this is not possible as the invariant would have been satisfied for c in that case.

  - *or* present in the join $Z_1 \bowtie Z_2$: in that case, when the eddy routed c' to $Z_1 \bowtie Z_2$, it would have joined with c'_1 to produce $c'c'_1$, which would have been returned to the eddy. This contradicts our assumption that c' was the largest sub-tuple of c processed by the eddy, as $c'c'_1$ is also a sub-tuple of c.

Lemma A.4 *If a new base tuple $s \in S$ arrives in the system at time τ, and if the invariant is true at time τ, then the eddy produces the result of joining that tuple with all the tuples of the other relations that have already arrived, ie., the eddy produces $s \bowtie (T_1)_\tau \bowtie \ldots \bowtie (T_l)_\tau$, where $T_1, \ldots, T_l$ denote the rest of the relations in the query.*

Proof: This follows from the above proof, by letting C be the entire query graph, and observing that, in that case, the only join c'_1 can be present in, is $Z_1 \bowtie Z_2$, and thus contradicting the assumption that the largest sub-tuple of the result tuple c that was generated, was a strict sub-tuple of c. ∎

From Lemmas A.1, A.2, A.3, and A.4, it follows that:

Theorem A.1 *The eddy always produces all the result tuples for acyclic queries inspite of arbitrary applications of the promotion and demotion operations.*

A.1 Duplicates

Though the above proof guarantees that all results for a query will be produced, it does not guarantee that every result will be produced exactly once. We avoid generating duplicate results by maintaining the following local invariant on the STAIRs at all times.

Invariant B: *A STAIR never contains two tuples $t_1 \in T_1$ and $t_2 \in T_2$, such that, t_1 and t_2 agree on all base-table components corresponding to the relations in $T_1 \cap T_2$.*

As an example, at time τ, $S.a$ is not allowed to contain both $sab, s \in S_\tau, a \in A_\tau, b \in B_\tau$ and $sac, s \in S_\tau, a \in A_\tau, E \in E_\tau$, as the two tuples agree on the common base-table components s and a.

Due to lack of space, we will state the following theorem without proof:

Theorem A.2 *If the above invariant is true when a new tuple enters the system, no duplicate results will be generated, and the invariant will remain true after processing that tuple to completion.*

As the duplicate avoidance invariant remains true after processing a new tuple, we only need to explicitly enforce it after a state management operation (which we do explicitly using a sorting-based algorithm). The following theorem completes our proof of correctness:

Theorem A.3 *If **Invariant A** is true and the eddy manipulates the state to enforce **Invariant B**, **Invariant A** will remain true after the operation.*

A Combined Framework for Grouping and Order Optimization

Thomas Neumann, Guido Moerkotte
tneumann|moerkotte@informatik.uni-mannheim.de

Fakultät für Mathematik und Informatik,
University of Mannheim, Germany

Abstract

Since the introduction of cost-based query optimization by Selinger et al. in their seminal paper, the performance-critical role of interesting orders has been recognized. Some algebraic operators change interesting orders (e.g. sort and select), while others exploit them (e.g. merge join). Likewise, Wang and Cherniack (VLDB 2003) showed that existing groupings should be exploited to avoid redundant grouping operations. Ideally, the reasoning about interesting orderings and groupings should be integrated into one framework.

So far, no complete, correct, and efficient algorithm for ordering and grouping inference has been proposed. We fill this gap by proposing a general two-phase approach that efficiently integrates the reasoning about orderings and groupings. Our experimental results show that with a modest increase of the time and space requirements of the preprocessing phase both orderings and groupings can be handled at the same time. More importantly, there is no additional cost for the second phase during which the plan generator changes and exploits orderings and groupings by adding operators to subplans.

1 Introduction

The most expensive operations (e.g. join, grouping, duplicate elimination) during query evaluation can be performed more efficiently if the input is ordered or grouped in a certain way. Therefore, it is crucial for query optimization to recognize cases where the input of an operator satisfies the ordering or grouping requirements needed for a more efficient evaluation. Since a plan generator typically considers millions of different plans – and, hence, operators –, this recognition easily becomes performance critical for query optimization, often leading to heuristic solutions.

The importance of exploiting available orderings has been recognized in the seminal work of Selinger et al [4]. They presented the concept of interesting orderings and showed how redundant sort operations could be avoided by reusing available orderings, rendering sort-based operators like sort-merge join much more interesting.

Along these lines it is beneficial to reuse available grouping properties, usually for hash-based operators. While heuristic techniques to avoid redundant group-by operators have been given [1], groupings have not been treated as thoroughly as orderings. One reason might be that while orderings and groupings are related (every ordering is also a grouping), groupings behave somewhat differently. For example, a tuple stream grouped on the attributes $\{a,b\}$ need not be grouped on the attribute $\{a\}$. This is different from orderings, where a tuple stream ordered on the attributes (a,b) is also ordered on the attribute (a). Since no simple prefix (or subset) test exists for groupings, optimizing groupings even in a heuristic way is much more difficult than optimizing orderings. Still it is desirable to combine order optimization and the optimization of groupings, as the problems are related and treated similarly during plan generation. Recently, some work in this direction has been published [7]. However, this only covers a special case of grouping, as we will discuss in some detail in Section 3.

Experimental results have shown that the costs for order optimization can have a large impact on the total costs of query optimization [3]. Therefore, some care is needed when adding groupings to order optimization, as a slowdown of plan generation would be unacceptable. In this paper, we integrate groupings by con-

---

Permission to copy without fee all or part of this material is granted provided that the copies are not made or distributed for direct commercial advantage, the VLDB copyright notice and the title of the publication and its date appear, and notice is given that copying is by permission of the Very Large Data Base Endowment. To copy otherwise, or to republish, requires a fee and/or special permission from the Endowment.

**Proceedings of the 30th VLDB Conference,
Toronto, Canada, 2004**

structing a state machine for groupings and combining it with a state machine for orderings. Experimental results show that this efficiently handles orderings and groupings at the same time, with no additional costs during plan generation and only modest one time costs. Actually the operation needed for grouping optimization during plan generation can be performed in $O(1)$, basically allowing to exploit groupings for free.

The rest of the paper is organized as follows. In Section 2, we introduce some notations and formalize the problems of order optimization and grouping optimization. Section 3 describes related work. This is followed by a rough sketch of our approach in Section 4. The detailed algorithm is described in Section 5. Finally, an experimental evaluation of our algorithm is presented in Section 6. Conclusions are drawn in Section 7.

2 Problem Definition

The described framework combines order optimization and the handling of grouping in one consistent set of algorithms and data structures. In this section, we give a more formal definition of the problem and the scope of the framework. First, we define the operations of ordering and grouping (Sections 2.1 and 2.2). Then we briefly discuss functional dependencies (Section 2.3) and how they interact with algebraic operators (Section 2.4) and finally we explain how the framework can be used for plan generation (Section 2.5).

2.1 Ordering

During plan generation, many operators require or produce certain orderings. To avoid redundant sorting it is required to keep track of the orderings a certain plan satisfies. The orderings that are relevant for query optimization are called *interesting orders* [4]. The set of *interesting orders* for a given query consists of

1. all orderings required by an operator of the physical algebra that may be used in a query execution plan for the given query, and

2. all orderings produced by an operator of the physical algebra that may be used in a query execution plan for the given query.

This includes the final ordering requested by the given query, if this is specified.

The interesting orders are *logical orderings*. This means that they specify a condition a tuple stream must meet to satisfy the given ordering. In contrast, the *physical ordering* of a tuple stream is the actual succession of tuples in the stream. Note that while a tuple stream has only one physical ordering, it can satisfy multiple logical orderings. For example, the stream of tuples $((1, 1), (2, 2))$ with schema (a, b) has one physical ordering (the actual stream), but satisfies the logical orderings a, b, ab and ba.

Some operators, like sort, actually influence the physical ordering of a tuple stream. Others, like select, only influence the logical ordering. For example, a sort[a] produces a tuple stream satisfying the ordering (a) by actually changing the physical order of tuples. After applying select[a=b] to this tuple stream, the result satisfies the logical orderings $(a), (b), (a, b), (b, a)$, although the physical ordering did not change. Deduction of logical orderings can be described by using the well-known notion of *functional dependencies* (FD) [5]. In general, the influence of a given algebraic operator on a set of logical orderings can be described by a set of functional dependencies.

We now formalize the problem. Let $R = (t_1, \ldots, t_r)$ be a stream (ordered sequence) of tuples in attributes $A_1, \ldots, A_n$. Then R *satisfies the logical ordering* $o = (A_{o_1}, \ldots, A_{o_m})$ $(1 \leq o_i \leq n)$ if and only if for all $1 \leq i < j \leq r$ the following condition holds:

$$(t_i.A_{o_1} \leq t_j.A_{o_1})$$
$$\wedge \quad \forall 1 < k \leq m \quad (\exists 1 \leq l < k(t_i.A_{o_l} < t_j.A_{o_l})) \vee$$
$$((t_i.A_{o_{k-1}} = t_j.A_{o_{k-1}}) \wedge$$
$$(t_i.A_{o_k} \leq t_j.A_{o_k})).$$

Next, we need to define the inference mechanism. Given a logical ordering $o = (A_{o_1}, \ldots, A_{o_m})$ of a tuple stream R, then R obviously satisfies any logical ordering that is a prefix of o including o itself.

Let R be a tuple stream satisfying both the logical ordering $o = (A_1, \ldots, A_n)$ and the functional dependency $f = B_1, \ldots, B_k \rightarrow B_{k+1}$[1] with $B_i \in \{A_1 \ldots A_n\}$. Then R also satisfies any logical ordering derived from o as follows: add B_{k+1} to o at any position such that all of $B_1, \ldots, B_k$ occurred before this position in o. For example consider a tuple stream satisfying the ordering (a, b); after inducing the functional dependency $a, b \rightarrow c$ the tuple stream also satisfies the ordering (a, b, c), but not the ordering (a, c, b). Let O' be the set of all logical orderings that can be constructed this way from o and f after prefix closure. Then we use the following notation: $o \vdash_f O'$. Let e be the equation $A_i = A_j$. Then $o \vdash_e O'$ where O' is the prefix closure of the union of the following three sets. The first set is O_1 defined as $o \vdash_{A_i \rightarrow A_j} O_1$, the second is O_2 defined as $o \vdash_{A_j \rightarrow A_i} O_2$, and the third is the set of logical orderings derived from o where a possible occurrence of A_i is replaced by A_j or vice versa. For example, consider a tuple stream satisfying the ordering (a); after inducing the equation $a = b$ the tuple stream also satisfies the orderings $(a, b), (b)$ and (b, a). Let e be an equation of the form $A = const$. Then O' ($o \vdash_e O'$) is derived from o by inserting A at any position in o. This is equivalent to $o \vdash_{\emptyset \rightarrow A} O'$. For example, consider a tuple stream satisfying the ordering (a, b); after inducing the equation $c = const$ the tuple

---
[1] Any functional dependency which is not in this form can be normalized into a set of FDs of this form.

stream also satisfies the orderings $(c,a,b), (a,c,b)$ and (a,b,c).

Let O be a set of logical orderings and F a set of functional dependencies (and possibly equations). We define the sets of inferred logical orderings $\Omega_i(O, F)$ as follows:

$$\begin{aligned} \Omega_0(O, F) &:= O \\ \Omega_i(O, F) &:= \Omega_{i-1}(O, F) \cup \bigcup_{f \in F, o \in \Omega_{i-1}(O,F)} O' \text{ with } o \vdash_f O' \end{aligned}$$

Let $\Omega(O, F)$ be the prefix closure of $\bigcup_{i=0}^{\infty} \Omega_i(O, F)$. We write $o \vdash_F o'$ if and only if $o' \in \Omega(O, F)$.

2.2 Grouping

It was shown in [7] that similar to order optimization, it is beneficial to keep track of the groupings satisfied by a certain plan. Traditionally, group-by operators are either applied after the rest of the query has been processed or are scheduled using some heuristics [1]. However, the plan generator could take advantage of grouping properties produced e.g. by avoiding re-hashing if such information was easily available.

Analogous to order optimization we call this *grouping optimization* and define that the set of *interesting groupings* for a given query consists of

1. all groupings required by an operator of the physical algebra that may be used in a query execution plan for the given query

2. all groupings produced by an operator of the physical algebra that may be used in a query execution plan for the given query.

This includes the grouping specified by the group by clause of the query, if any exists.

These groupings are similar to logical orderings, as they specify a condition a tuple stream must meet to satisfy a given grouping. Likewise functional dependencies can be used to infer new groupings.

More formally, a tuple stream $R = (t_1, \ldots, t_r)$ in attributes $A_1, \ldots, A_n$ satisfied the grouping $g = \{A_{g_1} \ldots, A_{g_m}\}$ $(1 \leq g_i \leq n)$ if and only if for all $1 \leq i < j < k \leq r$ the following condition holds:

$$\begin{aligned} \forall 1 \leq l \leq m \quad t_i.A_{g_l} &= t_k.A_{g_l} \\ \Rightarrow \forall 1 \leq l \leq m \quad t_i.A_{g_l} &= t_j.A_{g_l} \end{aligned}$$

Two remarks are in order here. First, note that a grouping is a set of attributes and not – as orderings – a sequence of attributes. Second, note that given two groupings g and $g' \subset g$ and a tuple stream R satisfying the grouping g, R need not satisfy the grouping g'. For example the tuple stream $((1, 2), (2, 3), (1, 4))$ with the schema (a, b) is grouped by $\{a, b\}$, but not by $\{a\}$. This is different from orderings, where a tuple stream satisfying a ordering o also satisfies all orderings that are a prefix of o.

New groupings can be inferred by functional dependencies as follows: Let R be a tuple stream satisfying both the grouping $g = \{A_1, \ldots, A_n\}$ and the functional dependency $f = B_1, \ldots, B_k \to B_{k+1}$ with $\{B_1, \ldots, B_k\} \subseteq \{A_1, \ldots, A_n\}$. Then R also satisfies the grouping $g' = \{A_1, \ldots, A_n\} \cup \{B_{k+1}\}$. Let G' be the set of all groupings that can be constructed this way from g and f. Then we use the following notation: $g \vdash_f G'$. For example $\{a, b\} \vdash_{a,b \to c} \{a, b, c\}$. Let e be the equation $A_i = A_j$. Then $g \vdash_e G'$ where G' is the union of the following three sets. The first set is G_1 defined as $g \vdash_{A_i \to A_j} G_1$, the second is G_2 defined as $g \vdash_{A_j \to A_i} G_2$, and the third is the set of groupings derived from g where a possible occurrence of A_i is replaced by A_j or vice versa. For example $\{a, b\} \vdash_{b=c} \{a, c\}$. Let e be an equation of the form $A = const$. Then $g \vdash_e G'$ is defined as $g \vdash_{\emptyset \to A} G'$. For example $\{a, b\} \vdash_{c=const} \{a, b, c\}$.

Let G be a set of groupings and F be a set of functional dependencies (and possibly equations). We define the set of inferred groupings $\Omega_i(G, F)$ as follows:

$$\begin{aligned} \Omega_0(G, F) &:= G \\ \Omega_i(G, F) &:= \Omega_{i-1}(G, F) \cup \bigcup_{f \in F, g \in \Omega_{i-1}(G,F)} G' \text{ with } g \vdash_f G' \end{aligned}$$

Let $\Omega(G, F)$ be $\bigcup_{i=0}^{\infty} \Omega_i(G, F)$. We write $g \vdash_F g'$ if and only if $g' \in \Omega(G, F)$.

2.3 Functional Dependencies

The reasoning about orderings and groupings assumes that the set of functional dependencies is known. The process of gathering the relevant functional dependencies is described in detail in [5], predominantly there are three sources of functional dependencies:

1. key constraints
2. join predicates
3. filter predicates

However the algorithm makes no assumption about the functional dependencies, if for some reason an operator induces another kind of functional dependency this can be handled the same way.

2.4 Algebraic Operators

To illustrate the propagation of orderings and groupings during query optimization, we give some rules for concrete (physical) operators in Figure 1. Note that these rules somewhat depend on the actual implementation of the operators, e.g. a blockwise nested loop join might actually destroy the ordering if

operator	requires	produces
scan(R)	-	$O(R)$
select($S,a=b$)	-	$\Omega(O(S), a=b)$
bnl-join(S_1,S_2)	-	$O(S_1)$
sort($S,a_1,\ldots,a_n$)	-	$(a_1,\ldots,a_n)$
hash($S,a_1,\ldots,a_n$)	-	$\{a_1,\ldots,a_n\}$
sort-merge($S_1,S_2,a=b$)	$(a) \in O(S_1) \wedge (b) \in O(S_2)$	$\Omega(O(S_1), a=b)$
hash-join($S_1,S_2,a=b$)	$\{a\} \in O(S_1) \wedge \{b\} \in O(S_2)$	$\Omega(O(S_1), a=b)$

Figure 1: Propagation of orderings and groupings

the blocks are stored in hash tables. As a shorthand, we use the following notation:

$O(R)$ set of logical orderings and groupings satisfied by the physical ordering of the relation R

$O(S)$ inferred set of logical orderings and groupings satisfied by the tuple stream S

2.5 Plan Generation

To exploit available logical orderings and groupings, the plan generator needs access to the combined order optimization and grouping component, which we describe as an *abstract data type* (ADT). An instance of this abstract data type OrderingGrouping represents a set of logical orderings and groupings, and wherever necessary, an instance is embedded into a plan note. The main operations the abstract data type OrderingGrouping must provide are

1. a constructor for a given logical ordering or grouping,

2. a membership test (called contains(LogicalOrdering)) which tests whether the set contains the logical ordering given as parameter,

3. a membership test (called contains(Grouping)) which tests whether the set contains the grouping given as parameter, and

4. an inference operation (called infer(set<FD>)). Given a set of functional dependencies and equations, it computes a new set of logical orderings and groupings a tuple stream satisfies.

These operations can be implemented by using the formalism described before: contains(LogicalOrdering) tests for $o \in O$, contains(Grouping) tests for $o \in G$ and infer(F) calculates $\Omega(O, F)$ respectively $\Omega(G, F)$. Note that the intuitive approach to explicitly maintain the set of all logical orderings and groupings is not useful in practice. For example, if a sort operator sorts a tuple stream on (a, b), the result is compatible with logical orderings $\{(a, b), (a)\}$. After a selection operator with selection predicate $x = const$ is applied, the set of logical orderings changes to $\{(x, a, b), (a, x, b),$ $(a, b, x), (x, a), (a, x), (x)\}$. Since the size of the set increases quadratically with every additional selection predicate of the form $v = const$, a naive representation as a set of logical orderings is problematic. This led Simmen et al. to introduce a more concise representation, which is discussed in the next section. As Simmen's technique is not easily applicable to groupings, currently no algorithm exists to efficiently maintain the set of available groupings. We close this gap. Further, our approach avoids these problems by only implicitly representing the set. Before presenting our approach, let us discuss the existing literature in detail.

3 Related Work

Very few papers exist on order optimization. While the problem of optimizing interesting orders was already introduced by Selinger et al.[4], later papers usually concentrated on exploiting, pushing down or combining orders, not on the abstract handling of orders during query optimization.

A more recent paper by Simmen et al.[5] introduced a framework based on functional dependencies for reasoning about orderings. The main idea was that instead of storing the potentially large set of logical orderings for each plan, only the initial ordering and the (usually much smaller) set of all induced functional dependencies is stored. When testing if a plan satisfies a given logical ordering, both the initial and the requested ordering are *reduced* using the available functional dependencies: An attribute is removed from an ordering if it is determined by an earlier attribute. E.g. given the ordering (a, b) and the functional dependency $a \rightarrow b$, the ordering can be reduced to (a), as the attribute b is redundant. After the reduction, two orderings can be compared using a simple prefix test. The main problem with this approach is that it requires a reduction step for each comparison. Although the reduced version of the initial ordering can be cached, the required ordering has to be reduced for every comparison. Since such comparisons are performed millions of times during plan generation, the performance impact is quite severe [3]. Also note that the reduction algorithm is not applicable for groupings (which of course was never intended by Simmen): Given the grouping $\{a, b, c\}$ and the functional dependencies $a \to b$ and $b \to c$, the grouping would be reduced to $\{a,c\}$ or to $\{a\}$, depending on the order in which the reductions are performed. This problem does not occur with orderings, as the attributes are sorted and can be reduced back to front.

In previous work [3] we presented a framework that also used functional dependencies to reason about orderings, but described these orderings as finite state machines. The main idea was that since the interesting orderings and the functional dependencies were already known before starting the plan generation, the possible transitions between orderings could be precomputed and stored as a state machine. Then, during plan generation the orderings could be treated as states in the state machine, allowing very efficient comparisons and inference ($O(1)$ after the preparation step). More details about this approach will be given in Section 4. Experimental results have shown that modeling order optimization as state machines is very efficient and has a very positive influence on the runtime of plan generation.

A recent paper by Wang and Cherniack[7] presented the idea of combining order optimization with the optimization of groupings. Based upon Simmen's framework, they annotated each attribute in an ordering with the information whether it is actually ordered by or grouped by. For a single attribute a they write $O_{a^O}(R)$ to denote that R is ordered by a, $O_{a^G}(R)$ to denote that R is grouped by a and $O_{a^O \to b^G}$ to denote that R is first ordered by a and then grouped by b (within blocks of the same a value). Before checking if a required ordering or grouping is satisfied by a given plan, they use some inference rules to get all orderings and groupings satisfied by the plan. Basically, this is Simmen's reduction algorithm with two extra transformations for groupings. In their paper the check itself is just written as $\in$, however, at least one reduction on the required ordering would be needed for this to work (and even that would not be trivial, as the stated transformations on groupings are ambiguous). The promised details in the cited technical report are currently not available, as the report has not appeared yet. Also note that as explained above, the reduction approach is fundamentally not suited for groupings. In WangÁs and CherniackÁs paper this problem does not occur, as they only look at a very specialized kind of grouping: As stated in their Axiom 3.6, they assume that a grouping $O_{a^G \to b^G}$ is first grouped by a and then (within the block of tuples with the same a value) grouped by b. However, this a very strong condition that is usually not satisfied by a hash-based grouping operator. Therefore, their work is not general enough to capture the full functionality offered by a state-of-the-art query execution engine.

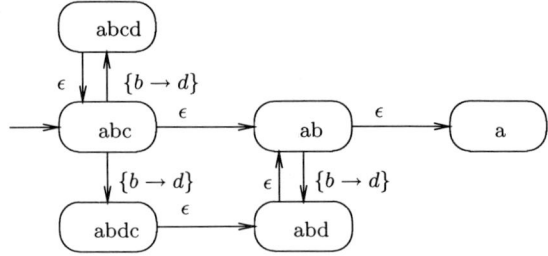

Figure 2: Possible FSM for orderings

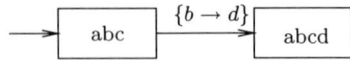

Figure 3: Possible FSM for groupings

4 Idea

As we have seen, explicit maintenance of the set of logical orderings and groupings can be very expensive. However, the ADT OrderingGrouping required for plan generation does not need to offer access to this set: It only allows to test if a given interesting order or grouping is in the set and changes the set according to new functional dependencies. Hence, it is *not* required to explicitly represent this set; an implicit representation is sufficient as long as the ADT operations can be implemented atop of it. In other words, we need not be able to reconstruct the set of logical orderings and groupings from the state of the ADT.

In previous work [3], a framework was presented that provided an implicit representation of the set of logical orderings by using a *finite state machine* (FSM). An example of this is shown in Figure 2. The states are used to represent *physical orderings* and the edges are labeled with functional dependencies. *Logical orderings* are handled by pretending that the physical ordering changes as allowed by the functional dependency. Since one physical ordering can imply multiple logical orderings, ε-edges are used. They also provide a mechanism to compute the prefix closure. As a result, the FSM is a *non-deterministic finite state machine* (NFSM). Before the actual plan generation, the NFSM is converted into a *deterministic FSM* (DFSM), [3] describes some techniques to do this efficiently. It proposes techniques to avoid producing a large DFSM. Representing the set of orderings as FSM is very attractive, since during plan generation only the state of the FSM has to be remembered. Aside from the construction of the FSM this allows for order optimization operations in time $O(1)$.

The idea of our combined framework is to construct a similar FSM for groupings and integrate it into the FSM for orderings, thus handling orderings and groupings at the same time. An example of this is shown in Figure 3. Here, the FSM for the grouping $\{a,b,c\}$ and the functional dependency $b \to c$ is shown. We represent states for orderings as rounded boxes and

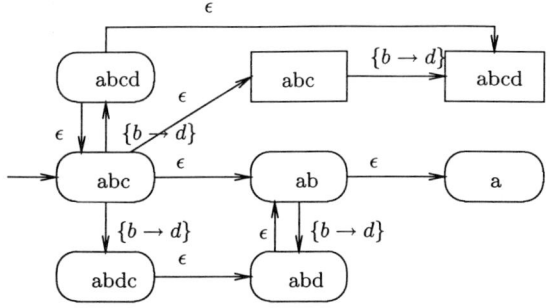

Figure 4: Combined FSM for orderings and groupings

states for groupings as rectangles. Note that although the FSM for groupings has a start node similar to the FSM for orderings, it is much smaller. This is due to the fact that groupings are only compatible with themselves, no nodes for prefixes are required. However, the FSM is still non-deterministic: given the functional dependency $b \to c$, the grouping $\{a, b, c, d\}$ is compatible with $\{a, b, c, d\}$ itself and with $\{a, b, c\}$; therefore, there exists an (implicit) edge from each grouping to itself.

The FSM for groupings is integrated into the FSM for orderings by adding ϵ edges from each ordering to the grouping with the same attributes; this is due to the fact that every ordering is also a grouping. Note that although the ordering (a, b, c, d) also implies the grouping $\{a, b, c\}$, no edge is required for this, since there exists an ϵ edge to (a, b, c) and from there to $\{a, b, c\}$.

After constructing an FSM as described above, the ADT can easily be mapped to the FSM: The state of the ADT is a state of the FSM and testing for a logical ordering or grouping can be performed by checking if the node with the ordering or grouping is reachable from the current state by following ϵ edges (as we will see, this can be precomputed to yield the O(1) time bound for the ADT operations). If the state of the ADT must be changed because of functional dependencies, the state in the FSM is changed by following the edge labeled with the functional dependency. However, the non-determinism of this transition is a problem. Therefore, for practical purposes the NFSM must be converted into a DFSM.

The framework for logical orderings [3] already described an algorithm for the conversion from NFSM to DFSM that can be reused for the combined framework. Some pruning techniques for groupings are described in Section 5 to minimize the NFSM, but the inclusion of groupings is not critical for the conversion, as the grouping part of the NFSM is nearly independent of the ordering part. In Section 6 we look at the size increase due to groupings. The memory consumption usually increases by a factor of two, which is the minimum expected increase, since every ordering is a grouping.

1. Determine the input
   (a) Determine interesting orders
   (b) Determine interesting groupings
   (c) Determine set of functional dependencies
2. Construct the NFSM
   (a) Construct nodes of the NFSM
   (b) Filter functional dependencies
   (c) Build filters for orderings and groupings
   (d) Add edges to the NFSM
   (e) Prune the NFSM
   (f) Add artificial start node and edges
3. Convert the NFSM into a DFSM
4. Precompute values
   (a) Precompute the compatibility matrix
   (b) Precompute the transition table

Figure 5: Preparation steps of the algorithm

5 Detailed Algorithm

5.1 Overview

Our approach consists of two phases. The first phase is the preparation step taking place before the actual plan generation starts. The output of this phase are the precomputed values used to implement the ADT. Then the ADT is used during the second phase where the actual plan generation takes place. The first phase is performed exactly once and is quite involved. Most of this section covers the first phase. Only Section 5.6 deals with the ADT implementation.

Figure 5 gives an overview of the preparation phase. As the pure ordering framework is described in [3], we only briefly describe the general part and concentrate on the changes needed to support groupings. During the discussion, we illustrate the different steps by a simple running example. More complex examples can be found in Section 6.

5.2 Determining the Input

Since the preparation step is performed immediately before plan generation, it is assumed that the query optimizer already has determined which indices are applicable and which algebraic operators can possibly be used to construct the query execution plan.

Before constructing the NFSM, the set of interesting orders, the set of interesting groupings and the sets of functional dependencies for each algebraic operator are determined. We denote the set of sets of functional dependencies by $\mathcal{F}$. It is important for the correctness of our algorithms that we note which of the interesting orders are (1) produced by some algebraic operator or (2) only tested for. Note that the interesting orders which satisfy (1) may additionally be tested for as well. We denote those orderings under (1) by O_P, those under (2) by O_T. The total set of interesting orders is defined as $O_I = O_P \cup O_T$. The orders produced are treated slightly differently in the following steps. For details on determining the set of interesting orders we refer to [4, 5]. The groupings are classified similarly to the orderings: We denote the grouping produced by some algebraic operator by G_P, and those just tested for by G_T. The total set of interesting groupings is defined as $G_I = G_P \cup G_T$. More information on how to extract interesting groupings can be found in [7]. Furthermore, for a sample query the extraction of both interesting orders and groupings is illustrated in Section 6.

To illustrate subsequent steps, we assume that the set of sets of functional dependencies

$$\mathcal{F} = \{\{b \to c\}, \{b \to d\}\},$$

the interesting groupings

$$G_I = \{\{b\}\} \cup \{\{b,c\}\}$$

and the interesting orders

$$O_I = \{(b), (a,b)\} \cup \{(a,b,c)\}$$

have been extracted from the query. We assume that those in $O_T = \{(a,b,c)\}$ and $G_T = \{\{b,c\}\}$ are tested for but not produced by any operator, whereas those in $O_P = \{(b), (a,b)\}$ and $G_P = \{\{b\}\}$ may be produced by some algebraic operators.

5.3 Constructing the NFSM

An NFSM consists of a tuple (Σ, Q, D, q_o), where

- Q is the set of possible states,
- Σ is the input alphabet,
- $D \subseteq Q \times (\Sigma \cup \{\epsilon\}) \times Q$ is the transition relation, and
- q_0 is the initial state.

Coarsely Q consists of the relevant orderings and groupings, Σ of the functional dependencies and D describes how the orderings or groupings change under a given functional dependency. Some refinements are needed to provide efficient ADT operations. The details of the construction are described now.

For the order optimization part the states are partitioned in $Q = Q_I \cup Q_A \cup \{q_0\}$, were q_0 is an artificial node to initialize the ADT, Q_I is the set of nodes corresponding to interesting orderings and Q_A is a set of artificial nodes only required for the algorithm itself.

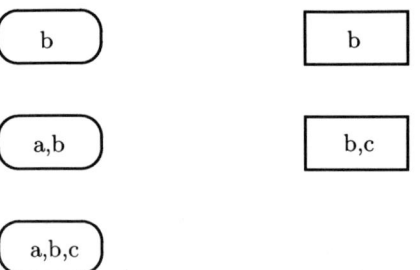

Figure 6: Initial NFSM for sample query

Q_A is described later. Furthermore, the set Q_I is partitioned in Q_I^P and Q_I^T, representing the orderings in O_P and O_T respectively. To support groupings, we add to Q_I^P nodes corresponding to the groupings G_P and to Q_I^T nodes corresponding to the groupings in G_T.

The initial NFSM contains the states Q_I of interesting groupings and orderings. For the example, this initial construction not including the start node q_o is shown in Figure 6. The states representing groupings are drawn as rectangles and the states representing orderings are drawn with rounded corners.

When considering functional dependencies, additional groupings and orderings can occur. These are not directly relevant for the query, but have to be represented by states to handle transitive changes. Since they have no direct connection to the query, these states are called artificial states. Starting with the initial states Q_I, artificial states are constructed by considering functional dependencies

$$Q_A = (\Omega(O_I, \mathcal{F}) \setminus O_I) \cup (\Omega(G_I, \mathcal{F}) \setminus G_I)$$

. In our example this creates the states (b,c) and (a), as (b,c) can be inferred from (b) when considering $\{b \to c\}$ and (a) can be inferred from (a,b), since (a) is a prefix of (a,b). The result is show in Figure 7 (ignore the edges).

Sometimes the ADT has to be explicitly initialized with a certain ordering or grouping (e.g. after a sort). To support this, artificial edges are added later on. These point to the requested ordering or grouping (states in Q_I^P) and are labeled with the state that they lead to. Therefore, the input alphabet Σ consists of the sets of functional dependencies and produced orderings and groupings:

$$\Sigma = \mathcal{F} \cup Q_I^P \cup \{\epsilon\}.$$

In our example $\Sigma = \{\{b \to c\}, \{b \to d\}, (b), (a,b), \{b\}\}$.

Accordingly, the domain of the transition relation D is

$$\begin{aligned}D \subseteq\quad &((Q \setminus \{q_0\}) \times (\mathcal{F} \cup \{\epsilon\}) \times (Q \setminus \{q_0\})) \\ \cup\ &(\{q_o\} \times Q_I^P \times Q_I^P).\end{aligned}$$

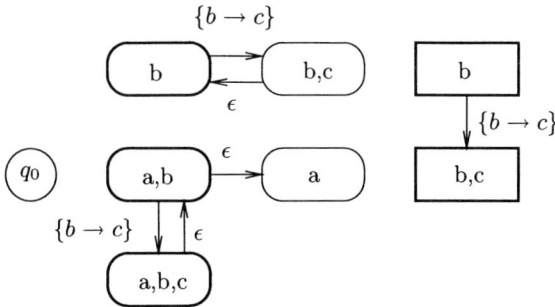

Figure 7: NFSM after adding D_{FD} edges

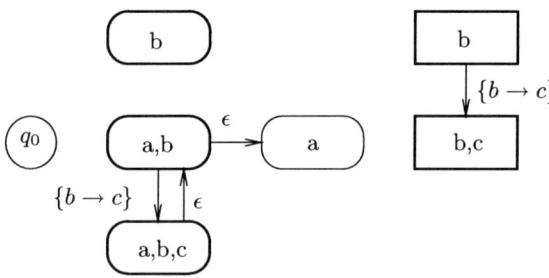

Figure 8: NFSM after pruning artificial nodes

The edges are formed by the functional dependencies and the artificial edges. Furthermore, ϵ edges exist between orderings and the corresponding groupings, as orderings are a special case of grouping:

$$
\begin{aligned}
D_{FD} &= \{(q, f, q') \mid q \in Q, f \in \mathcal{F} \cup \{\epsilon\}, q' \in Q, q \vdash_f q'\} \\
D_A &= \{(q_0, q, q) \mid q \in Q_I^P\} \\
D_{OG} &= \{(o, \epsilon, g) \mid o \in \Omega(O_I, \mathcal{F}), g \in \Omega(G_I, \mathcal{F}), o \equiv g\} \\
D &= D_{FD} \cup D_A \cup D_{OG}
\end{aligned}
$$

First, the edges corresponding to functional dependencies are added (D_{FD}). In our example, this results in the NFSM shown in Figure 7.

Note that the functional dependency $b \to d$ has been pruned, since d does not occur in any interesting order or grouping. The NFSM can be further simplified by pruning the artificial node (b, c) which cannot lead to a new interesting order. The result is shown in Figure 8. A detailed description of these pruning techniques can be found in [3]. Additional pruning techniques relevant for groupings are described in Section 5.7.

The artificial start node q_0 has emanating edges incident to all nodes representing interesting orders in O_I^P and interesting groupings in G_I^P (D_A). Also, the nodes representing orderings have edges to their corresponding grouping nodes (D_{OG}), as every ordering is also a grouping. The final NFSM for the example is shown in Figure 9. Note that the nodes representing (a, b, c) and $\{b, c\}$ are not linked by an artificial edge since it is only tested for, as they are in Q_I^T.

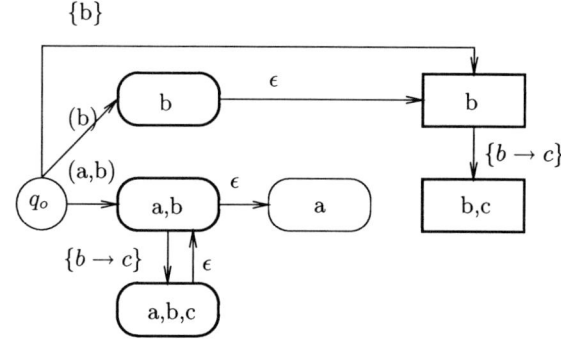

Figure 9: Final NFSM

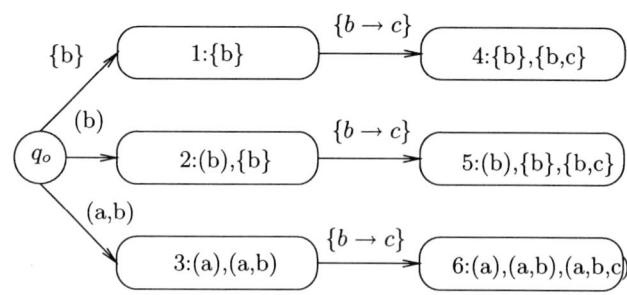

Figure 10: Resulting DFSM

5.4 Constructing the DFSM

The DFSM in constructed as described in [3]. Basically, the the standard power set construction for converting an NFA into a DFA [2]. is used. It is important to note that this construction preserves the start node and the artificial edges, allowing easy initialization of the ADT. The resulting DFSM for the example is shown in Figure 10.

5.5 Precomputing Values

To allow for an efficient precomputation of values, every occurrence of an interesting order, interesting grouping or functional dependency is replaced by integers. This allows comparisons in constant time (equivalent entries are mapped to same integer). Further, the DFSM is represented by an adjacency matrix.

The precomputation step itself computes two matrices. The first matrix denotes whether an NFSM

state	1: (a)	2: (a,b)	3: (a,b,c)	4: (b)	5: {b}	6: {b,c}
1	0	0	0	0	1	0
2	0	0	0	1	1	0
3	1	1	0	0	0	0
4	0	0	0	0	1	1
5	0	0	0	1	1	1
6	1	1	1	0	0	0

Figure 11: *contains* Matrix

state	1: $\{b \to c\}$	2: (a,b)	3: (b)	4: $\{b\}$
q_o	-	3	2	1
1	4	-	-	-
2	5	-	-	-
3	6	-	-	-
4	4	-	-	-
5	5	-	-	-
6	6	-	-	-

Figure 12: *transition* Matrix

node is in Q_I, i.e. an interesting order or an interesting grouping, is contained in a specific DFSM node. This matrix can be represented as a compact bit vector, allowing tests in $O(1)$. For our running example, it is given (in a more readable form) in Figure 11. The second matrix contains the transition table for the DFSM relation D. Using it, edges in the DFSM can be followed in $O(1)$. For the example, the transition matrix is given in Figure 12.

5.6 During Plan Generation

During plan generation, larger plans are constructed by adding algebraic operators to existing (sub-)plans. Each subplan contains the available orderings and groupings in the form of the corresponding DFSM state. Hence, the state of the DFSM, a simple integer, is the state of our ADT OrderingGrouping.

When applying an operator to subplans the ordering and grouping requirements are tested by checking whether the DFSM state of the subplan contains the required ordering or grouping of the operator. This is done by a simple lookup in the *contains* matrix.

If the operator introduces a new set of functional dependencies, the new state of the ADT is computed by following the according edge in the DFSM. This is performed by a quick lookup in the *transition* matrix.

For "atomic" subplans like table or index scans the ordering and grouping is determined explicitly by the operator. The state of the DFSM is determined by a lookup in the transition matrix with start state q_o and the edge annotated by the produced ordering or grouping. For sort and group by operators the state of the DFSM is determined as before by following the artificial edge for the produced ordering or grouping and then reapplying the set of functional dependencies that currently hold.

In the example, a sort on (b) results in a subplan with ordering/grouping state 2 (the node 2 is active in the DFSM), which satisfies the ordering (b) and the grouping $\{b\}$. After applying an operator which induces $b \to c$, the ordering/grouping changes to state 5 which also satisfies $\{b, c\}$.

5.7 Reducing the Size of the NFSM

Reducing the size of the NFSM is very important because it reduces both preparation time by avoiding large DFSMs and the search space for plan generation, as irrelevant orderings can be ignored. Effective techniques for pruning irrelevant ordering states and merging artificial nodes were already presented [3], we now describe how to avoid irrelevant grouping nodes.

First, in Step 2.3 (see Figure 5) the set of attributes occurring in interesting groupings is determined:

$$A_G = \{a \mid \exists g \in G_I : a \in g\}$$

Now, for every attribute a occurring on the right-hand side of a functional dependency the set of potentially reachable relevant attributes is determined:

$$\begin{aligned}
r(a, 0) &= \{a\} \\
r(a, n) &= r(a, n-1) \cup \\
&\quad \{a' \mid \exists (a_1 \ldots a_m \to a') \in \mathcal{F} : \\
&\quad \{a_1 \ldots a_m\} \cap r(a, n-1) \neq \emptyset\} \\
r(a) &= r(a, |\mathcal{F}|) \cap A_G
\end{aligned}$$

This can be used to determine if a functional dependency actually adds useful attributes. Given a functional dependency $a_1 \ldots a_n \to a$ and a grouping g with $\{a_1 \ldots a_n\} \subseteq g$, a should only be added to g if $r(a) \not\subseteq g$, i.e. the attribute might actually lead to a new interesting grouping. For example, given the interesting groupings $\{a\}, \{a, b\}$ and the functional dependencies $a \to c, a \to d, d = b$. When considering the grouping $\{a\}$, the functional dependency $a \to c$ can be ignored, as it can only produce the attribute c, which does not occur in an interesting grouping. However the functional dependency $a \to d$ should be added, since transitively the attribute b can be produced, which does occur in an interesting grouping.

Since there are no ϵ edges between groupings, i.e. groupings are not compatible with each other, a grouping can only be relevant for the query if it is a subset of an interesting ordering (as further attributes could be added by functional dependencies). However a simple subset test is not sufficient, as equations of the form $a = b$ are also supported; these can effectively rename attributes, resulting in a slightly more complicated test:

In Step 2.3 (see Figure 5) the equivalence classes induced by the equations in $\mathcal{F}$ are determined and for each class a representative is chosen:

$$\begin{aligned}
E(a, 0) &= \{a\} \\
E(a, n) &= E(a, n-1) \cup \\
&\quad \{a' \mid ((a = a') \in \mathcal{F}) \vee ((a' = a) \in \mathcal{F})\} \\
E(A) &= E(A, |\mathcal{F}|) \\
e(a) &= \text{rep } E(A) \quad \text{(arbitrary)} \\
e(\{a_1 \ldots a_n\}) &= \{e(a_1) \ldots e(a_n)\}.
\end{aligned}$$

Using these equivalence classes a mapped set of interesting groupings is produced, that will be used to test if a grouping is relevant:

$$G_I^E = \{e(g) \mid g \in G_I\}$$

Now a grouping g can be pruned if $\nexists g' \in G_I^E : e(g) \subseteq g'$. For example, given the interesting grouping $\{a\}$ and the equations $a = b, b = c$, the grouping $\{d\}$ can be pruned, as it will never lead to an interesting grouping; however, the groupings $\{b\}$ and $\{c\}$ have to be kept, as they could change to an interesting grouping later on.

Note that although they appear to test similar conditions, the first pruning technique (using $r(a)$) is not dominated by the second one (using $e(a)$). Consider e.g. the interesting grouping $\{a\}$, the equation $a = b$ and the functional dependency $a \rightarrow b$. Using only the second technique, the grouping $\{a, b\}$ would be created, although it is not relevant.

6 Experimental Results

Integrating groupings in the order optimization framework allows the plan generator to easily exploit groupings and thus produce better plans. However, order optimization itself might become prohibitively expensive by considering groupings. Therefore, we evaluated the costs of including groupings for different queries.

Since adding support for groupings has no effect on the runtime behavior of the plan generator (all operations are still one table lookup), we measured the runtime and the memory consumption of the preparation step both with and without considering groupings. When considering groupings, we treated each interesting ordering also as an interesting grouping, i.e. we assumed that a grouping-based (e.g. hash-based) operator was always available as an alternative. Since this is the worst-case scenario, it should give an upper bound for the additional costs. All experiments were performed on a 2.4 GHz Pentium IV, using the gcc 3.3.1.

To examine the impact for real queries, we choose a more complex query from the well-known TPC-R benchmark ([6], Query 8):

```
select
    o_year,
    sum(case when nation = '[NATION]'
        then volume
        else 0
    end) / sum(volume) as mkt_share
from
    (select
        extract(year from o_orderdate) as o_year,
        l_extendedprice * (1-l_discount) as volume,
        n2.n_name as nation
    from   part,supplier,lineitem,orders,customer,
           nation n1,nation n2,region
    where
        p_partkey = l_partkey and
        s_suppkey = l_suppkey and
        l_orderkey = o_orderkey and
        o_custkey = c_custkey and
        c_nationkey = n1.n_nationkey and
        n1.n_regionkey = r_regionkey and
        r_name = '[REGION]' and
        s_nationkey = n2.n_nationkey and
        o_orderdate between date '1995-01-01' and
            date '1996-12-31' and
        p_type = '[TYPE]'
    ) as all_nations
group by o_year
order by o_year;
```

When considering this query, all attributes used in joins, group-by and order-by clauses are added to the set of interesting orders. Since hash-based solutions are possible, they are also added to the set of interesting groupings. This results in the sets

$$\begin{aligned}
O_I^P &= \{(o\_year), (o\_partkey), (p\_partkey), \\
&\quad (l\_partkey), (l\_suppkey), (l\_orderkey), \\
&\quad (o\_orderkey), (o\_custkey), (c\_custkey), \\
&\quad (c\_nationkey), (n1.n\_nationkey), \\
&\quad (n2.n\_nationkey), (n\_regionkey), \\
&\quad (r\_regionkey), (s\_suppkey), (s\_nationkey)\} \\
O_I^T &= \emptyset \\
G_I^P &= \{\{o\_year\}, \{o\_partkey\}, \{p\_partkey\}, \\
&\quad \{l\_partkey\}, \{l\_suppkey\}, \{l\_orderkey\}, \\
&\quad \{o\_orderkey\}, \{o\_custkey\}, \{c\_custkey\}, \\
&\quad \{c\_nationkey\}, \{n1.n\_nationkey\}, \\
&\quad \{n2.n\_nationkey\}, \{n\_regionkey\}, \\
&\quad \{r\_regionkey\}, \{s\_suppkey\}, \{s\_nationkey\}\} \\
G_I^T &= \emptyset
\end{aligned}$$

Note that here O_I^T and G_I^T are empty, as we assumed that each ordering and grouping would be produced if beneficial. For example, we might assume that it makes no sense to intentionally group by o_year: If a tuple stream is already grouped by o_year it makes sense to exploit this, however instead of just grouping by o_year it could makes sense to sort by o_year, as this is required anyway (although here it only makes sense if the sort operator performs early aggregation). In this case $\{o\_year\}$ would move from G_I^P to G_I^T, as it would be only tested for, but not produced.

The set of functional dependencies (and equations) contains all join conditions and constant conditions:

$$\begin{aligned}
\mathcal{F} = \{\{p\_partkey = l\_partkey\}, \{\emptyset \rightarrow p\_type\}, \\
\{o\_custkey = c\_custkey\}, \{\emptyset \rightarrow r\_name\},
\end{aligned}$$

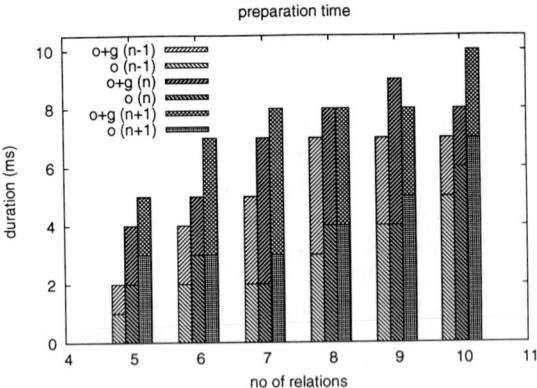
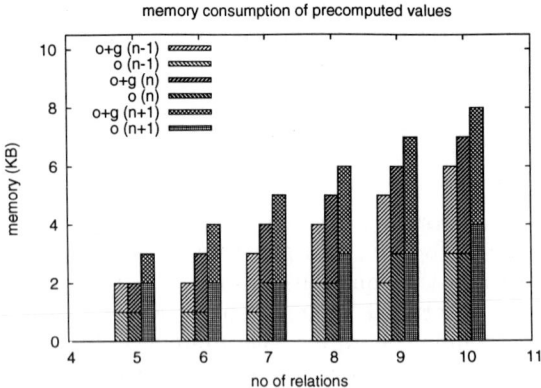

Figure 13: Time requirements for the preparation step

Figure 14: Space requirements for the preparation step

$$\{c\_nationkey = n1.n\_nationkey\},$$
$$\{s\_nationkey = n2.n\_nationkey\},$$
$$\{l\_orderkey = o\_orderkey\},$$
$$\{s\_suppkey = l\_suppkey\},$$
$$\{n1.n\_regionkey = r\_regionkey\}\}$$

To measure the influence of groupings, the preparation step was executed two times: Once with the data as given above and once with $G_I^P = \emptyset$ (i.e. groupings were ignored). The space and time requirements are shown below:

	With Groups	Without Groups
Duration [ms]	0.6ms	0.3ms
DFSM [nodes]	63	32
Memory [KB]	5	2

Here time and space requirements both increase by a factor of two. Since all interesting orderings are also treated as interesting groupings, a factor of about two was expected.

While Query 8 is one of the more complex TPC-R queries, it is not overly complex when looking at order optimization. It contains 16 interesting orderings/groupings and 8 functional dependencies, but they cannot be combined in many reasonable ways, resulting in a comparatively small DFSM. In order to get more difficult examples, we produced randomized queries with 5 – 10 relations and a varying number of join predicates. We always started from a chain query and then randomly added additional edges to the join graph. The results are shown for $n-1$, n and $n+1$ additional edges. In the case of 10 relations that means that the join graph consisted of 18, 19 and 20 edges respectively.

The time and space requirements for the preparation step are shown in Figure 13 and Figure 14, respectively. For each number of relations the requirements for the combined framework (o+g) and the framework ignoring groupings (o) are shown. The numbers in parentheses ($n-1$, n and $n+1$) are the number of additional edges in the join graph.

As with Query 8, the time and space requirements roughly increase by a factor of two when adding groupings. This is a very positive result, given that a factor of two can be estimated as a lower bound (since every interesting ordering is also an interesting grouping here). Furthermore, the absolute time and space requirements are very low (a few ms and a few KB), encouraging the inclusion of groupings in the order optimization framework.

7 Conclusion

The combined framework presented allows a very efficient handling of order optimization and grouping optimization during plan generation. The experimental results showed that with only a modest increase of the one-time costs, groupings can be exploited during plan generation at no additional costs. In summary, using an FSM to keep track of the available orderings and groupings is very efficient and is easily integrated in a plan generator.

One topic for future work is the minimization of the DFSM using the operator structure. Currently, only the NFSM is pruned by detecting irrelevant or redundant nodes. The DFSM could also be pruned by intentionally dropping available logical orderings or groupings when it is clear that the ordering or grouping will never be used (because of operator dependencies). Besides minimizing the DFSM, this technique would also reduce the search space for the plan generator, as more plans could be pruned (since more plans would be dominated by other plans).

References

[1] Surajit Chaudhuri and Kyuseok Shim. Including group-by in query optimization. In Jorge B. Bocca, Matthias Jarke, and Carlo Zaniolo, editors, *VLDB'94, Proceedings of 20th International Conference on Very Large Data Bases, September 12-15, 1994, Santiago de Chile, Chile*, pages 354–366. Morgan Kaufmann, 1994.

[2] H. Lewis and C. Papadimitriou. *Elements of the Theory of Computation.* Prentice Hall, 1981.

[3] Thomas Neumann and Guido Moerkotte. An efficient framework for order optimization. In *Proceedings of the 20th International Conference on Data Engineering, 30 March - 2 April 2004, Boston, MA.* IEEE Computer Society, 2004.

[4] Patricia G. Selinger, Morton M. Astrahan, Donald D. Chamberlin, Raymond A. Lorie, and Thomas G. Price. Access path selection in a relational database management system. In Philip A. Bernstein, editor, *Proceedings of the 1979 ACM SIGMOD International Conference on Management of Data, Boston, Massachusetts, May 30 - June 1*, pages 23–34. ACM, 1979.

[5] David E. Simmen, Eugene J. Shekita, and Timothy Malkemus. Fundamental techniques for order optimization. In H. V. Jagadish and Inderpal Singh Mumick, editors, *Proceedings of the 1996 ACM SIGMOD International Conference on Management of Data, Montreal, Quebec, Canada, June 4-6, 1996*, pages 57–67. ACM Press, 1996.

[6] Transaction Processing Performance Council, 777 N. First Street, Suite 600, San Jose, CA, USA. *TPC Benchmark R*, 1999. Revision 1.2.0. http://www.tpc.org.

[7] Xiaoyu Wang and Mitch Cherniack. Avoiding sorting and grouping in processing queries. In Johann Christoph Freytag, Peter C. Lockemann, Serge Abiteboul, Michael J. Carey, Patricia G. Selinger, and Andreas Heuer, editors, *VLDB 2003, Proceedings of 29th International Conference on Very Large Data Bases, September 9-12, 2003, Berlin, Germany.* Morgan Kaufmann, 2003.

The Case for Precision Sharing *

Sailesh Krishnamurthy[*]   Michael J. Franklin[*]   Joseph M. Hellerstein[*][†]
Garrett Jacobson[*]

[*] Dept of EECS, UC Berkeley   [†] Intel Research, Berkeley

{sailesh,franklin,jmh,garrettj}@cs.berkeley.edu

Abstract

Sharing has emerged as a key idea of static and adaptive stream query processing systems. Inherent in these systems is a tension between *sharing common work* and avoiding *unnecessary work*. Increased sharing has generally led to more unnecessary work.

Our approach of *precision sharing* aims to share aggressively *without* unnecessary work. We show why "adaptive" tuple lineage is more generally applicable and use it for precisely shared static dataflows. We also show how "static" ordering constraints can be used for precision sharing in adaptive systems. Finally, we report an experimental study of precision sharing.

1 Introduction

Data streaming systems support long running continuous queries. Since many queries are concurrently active over common streams, shared processing is very attractive.

Two approaches to shared stream processing have emerged. In systems like NiagaraCQ [6], Aurora [3] and STREAM [14], tuples flow through *static* dataflow networks. In contrast, the idea of *adaptive* query processing has led to approaches like CACQ [12], PSoup [4], TelegraphCQ [5] and "distributed eddies" [18] where tuples are variably routed through an adaptive network.

Sharing in streams, as in classical systems (Sellis [16]) aims "to limit the redundancy due to accessing the same data multiple times in different queries." We illustrate this redundancy with a two query example in Figure 1.

Figure 1: Sharing 2 queries: redundancy and waste

In the example, the queries' result sets overlap. Without sharing, the overlapping tuples are produced twice - a redundancy. In attempting to avoid redundancy, however, current shared schemes produce too much data. In the figure, a shared scheme from the literature (such as NiagaraCQ) would produce the tuples in the entire rectangle, including the "useless tuples" in the two darkly shaded regions. Thus, it would appear that sharing has to balance the inherent tensions of:

- **Repeated work** caused by applying an operation multiple times for a given tuple, or its copies.
- **Wasted work** caused by the production and removal of "useless tuples".

While existing systems have taken this tension for granted, the goal of our paper is to show that this tension is not, in fact, irreconcilable; to design and implement techniques that resolve the tension in static and adaptive dataflows; and to experimentally verify these techniques.

1.1 Precision Sharing

Precision sharing is a way to characterize any shared query processing scheme. We show that when sharing is precise, it is possible to avoid the overheads of repeated work *as well as* that of wasted work. Precision sharing applies to static and adaptive streaming systems, and is orthogonal to query optimization. It can also be used with traditional multiple-query optimization (MQO) schemes.

Static shared dataflows

We first show how NiagaraCQ's static shared plans are imprecise. We then consider tuple lineage, an idea from the adaptive query processing literature. While lineage has

---

*This work was funded in part by the NSF under ITR grants IIS-0086057, SI-0122599, IIS-0205647 and IIS-0208588, by the IBM Faculty Partnership Award program, and by research funds from Intel, Microsoft, and the UC MICRO program.

Permission to copy without fee all or part of this material is granted provided that the copies are not made or distributed for direct commercial advantage, the VLDB copyright notice and the title of the publication and its date appear, and notice is given that copying is by permission of the Very Large Data Base Endowment. To copy otherwise, or to republish, requires a fee and/or special permission from the Endowment.

**Proceedings of the 30th VLDB Conference,
Toronto, Canada, 2004**

been thought of as useful in highly variable environments, our insight is that it is more generally applicable. Specifically, we show how to use tuple lineage to make static shared dataflows precise. We call our approach TULIP, or TUple LIneage in Plans.

Adaptive shared dataflows

Next we show how the CACQ shared adaptive dataflow system is also imprecise. Our strategy toward adaptive precision sharing is to borrow from the static world. We show how we can place constraints on how tuples are routed in an adaptive scheme to ensure that sharing is precise. Our approach is CAR, or Constrained Adaptive Routing.

We implemented both schemes, TULIP and CAR, in the TelegraphCQ system that we are building at Berkeley.

1.2 Contributions

Our contributions in this paper are to:

1. Argue that the tension between avoiding the overheads of repeated work and wasteful work in sharing is not irreconcilable, and define *precision sharing* to show how both overheads can be reduced in tandem.

2. Demonstrate the general utility of tuple lineage beyond adaptive query processing, and show how it can be used to achieve static precision sharing.

3. Show how to implement adaptive precision sharing with proper operator routing.

4. Validate our claims experimentally.

The rest of this paper is organized as follows. We briefly describe relevant work on shared stream processing in Section 2. Next, in Section 3, we define precision sharing and explain pitfalls in prior art. This is followed by a description of TULIP in Section 4 and a study of its performance in Section 5. We then present CAR in Section 6 followed by more experiments in Section 7. We end with a summary of our findings in Section 8.

2 Shared queries on streams

In this section we briefly describe the two major approaches to sharing: static query plans and adaptive dataflows. While sharing has also been studied in the multiple-query optimization (MQO) literature [16], there has been comparatively less work on shared processing of queries over data streams and the related topic of pipelined MQO [8, 17].

As has been well noted[12, 14], pipelined join operators are a natural fit for streaming query processors. For this reason we assume the exclusive use of symmetric join operators for the rest of this paper. This also simplifes the MQO problem by limiting the choice of join operators.

2.1 Static shared plans

The first approach we describe is the logical extension of traditional pipelined query plans to shared data stream processing. Here, a set of continuous queries is processed using a single static query plan that is a dataflow network of relational algebra operators. Figure 2 shows an example of a static dataflow that represents two shared queries.

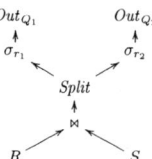

Figure 2: Static shared dataflow example

When new tuples arrive in the system they are driven through the network according to an operator scheduling policy. While different operators may be executed at different times, the *paths* taken by a tuple from a given stream to its various destinations are always the same[1]. Sharing is thus determined entirely by sub-expressions that are common to individual queries. This model has been adopted by NiagaraCQ, Aurora, and STREAM. NiagaraCQ [7, 6] describes ways to form *grouped* plans for multiple queries.

There are in general two approaches to MQO: (a) optimize each individual query and then look for sharing opportunities in the access plans, and (b) globally optimize all the queries to produce a shared access plan.

The first approach is easier to employ and is used in NiagaraCQ to group together plans for queries with similar structure. When new queries enter the system they are attached to an existing group whose *signature* it matches closely. A query that has many signatures is merged into multiple groups in the system.

2.2 Adaptive shared dataflows

The second approach we review is based on the idea of adaptive tuple routing and used in TelegraphCQ [5], CACQ [12] and PSoup [4]. In this approach too, a set of queries are decomposed into a dataflow of relational algebra operators. The major differences are: (a) the dataflow is adaptive and can route tuples in a variety of different ways, (b) tuples are extended to carry their "lineage" consisting of "steering" and "completion" vectors, and (c) the operators are aware of the completion vector of each input tuple - in other words two otherwise identical tuples with different completion vectors may be processed differently. We discuss adaptive dataflow technology in more detail in Section 6.

3 Precision Sharing

In this section we introduce and explain the importance of precision sharing, a way to characterize the overheads of shared query processing. We then show how current systems result in plans that are not precisely shared. We begin by defining precision sharing in terms of all operations performed on tuples in a shared dataflow.

---
[1]Work [10] on dynamism in static plans has generally been limited to one-time *late-binding* based on query parameters.

Precision sharing: A sharing scheme where for all stream inputs, the following properties *both* hold:

PS1 For each tuple processed, any given operation may be applied to it, or any copy of it, at most once.

PS2 No operator shall produce a "zombie" tuple; that is, a tuple whose presence or absence in the dataflow has no effect on the result of any query, irrespective of any other possible input.

A plan that does not satisfy PS1 suffers from redundancy overheads. A plan that does not satisfy PS2 results in the wasteful *production* and subsequent *elimination* of zombies. We say that a given plan is *precisely shared* if it satisfies both the properties PS1 and PS2 for all inputs.

Approaches in the MQO literature [16, 17, 8] have all assumed that reducing redundancy is paramount, without considering its side-effects. This definition of precision sharing lets us characterize the nature of such side-effects, and is essential to limiting unnecessary work for the query processor.

We now consider examples of imprecise sharing of join queries in the presence of selections on individual sources. We build on an example studied in NiagaraCQ [6, 7].

3.1 Imprecise sharing in action

Consider the following scenario involving two queries, Q_1 and Q_2, each of which join the streams R and S and apply a unique selection predicate on R.

- $Q_1 : \sigma_{r_1}(R) \bowtie S$
- $Q_2 : \sigma_{r_2}(R) \bowtie S$

NiagaraCQ suggests the two alternate plans for these queries. The plan in Figure 3(a) uses *selection pull-up* to share the RS join. In Figure 3(b) we see *selection push-down* where tuples in R are split according to the predicates first and then run in separate join groups. In actuality, NiagaraCQ combines the *Split* operator and its immediate downstream filters together, using an index for the filter predicates. We separate them for ease of exposition. Also, we use *Out* to represent a generic output operator that is equivalent to *TriggerAction* in NiagaraCQ.

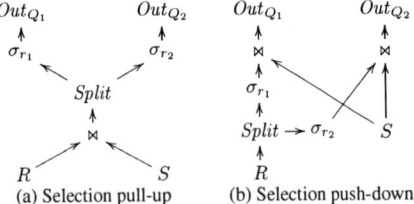

Figure 3: Imprecise sharing of joins with selections

Selection push-down (Figure 3(b)) violates PS1 in two ways. First, a tuple r_x from R that passes both predicates r_1 and r_2 will be processed in both join operators, producing identical join tuples. Second, every tuple from S will be inserted twice in each join operator (assuming symmetric hash joins). Note that in this selection push-down example, PS2 is obeyed as each tuple from each join operator must satisfy at least one query.

Selection pull-up (Figure 3(a)), on the other hand, violates PS2. For example, the output of the join operator can include an (r_x, s_x) tuple where r_x fails both predicates, r_1 and r_2, satisfying neither query. The tuple (r_x, s_x) is an example of a zombie tuple, and shows how increased sharing can cause wasteful work. Note that this plan has only one join operator that produces the common sub-expression $R \bowtie S$ and has no redundancy. Since no operation is applied on any tuple more than once, this satisfies PS1.

We have seen how both pull-up and push-down violate at least one of the properties of precision sharing. A third alternative, however, was proposed in later work on NiagaraCQ [7]. This is a variant of pull-up called *filtered pull-up* which creates and then pushes down predicate disjunctions ahead of the join. In this example, the disjunctive predicate $(r_1 \vee r_2)$ is pushed down between the join and the scan on R. Such a plan is shown in Figure 4.

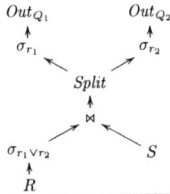

Figure 4: Precisely shared filtered pull-up

Unlike pull-up, the filtered pull-up plan for this example satisfies PS2. This is because every R tuple r_x that reaches the join operator must have passed at least one of the r_1 and r_2 predicates. So every join tuple (r_x, s_x) must also satisfy at least one of the queries Q_1 and Q_2. Filtered pull-up also satisfies PS1 here for the same reasons as selection pull-up.

The filtered pull-up plan for this example satisfies both the properties PS1 and PS2. We now have an example of a sharing scheme that is precise. It is not surprising that the experimental and simulation results in NiagaraCQ [7] generally show this plan as the most efficient. It is reasonable to ask if a filtered pull-up plan will always be precisely shared. It turns out that the answer is no, and we explain why in the next section.

3.2 Why filtered pull-up is not good enough

We now show why a filtered pull-up strategy is not precisely shared in general. We demonstrate this with an example where two queries, Q_3 and Q_4, join the streams R and S and apply unique selection predicates on *both* R and S. Notice that the only differences from the previous example are the selection predicates on S.

- $Q_3 : \sigma_{r_1}(R) \bowtie \sigma_{s_1}(S)$
- $Q_4 : \sigma_{r_2}(R) \bowtie \sigma_{s_2}(S)$

The filtered pull-up technique suggests that we pick the plan in Figure 5. The behavior of this query plan is shown

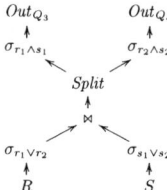

Figure 5: Imprecisely shared filtered pull-up

in Figure 6. In the figure, R_1 and R_2 are respectively defined as $\sigma_{r_1}(R)$ and $\sigma_{r_2}(R)$. Similarly, S_1 and S_2 are respectively defined as $\sigma_{s_1}(S)$ and $\sigma_{s_2}(S)$.

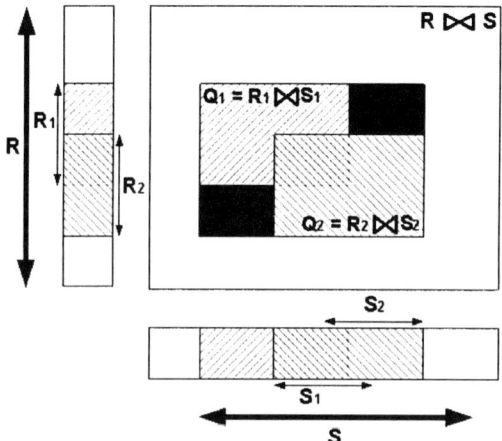

Figure 6: Filtered pull-up and zombies

Observe that the inputs to the join operator are the sets $R_1 \cup R_2$ and $S_1 \cup S_2$, and the join operator produces the set $(R_1 \cup R_2) \bowtie (S_1 \cup S_2)$. Notice that this is a superset of $(Q_1 \cup Q_2)$, our desired result. These extra tuples are zombies and are indicated in the figure as the two darkly shaded areas inside the smaller rectangle.

With two queries, it is easy to see the relationship between result set commonality and waste. When the intersection of Q_1 and Q_2 (result set commonality) is larger, the wasted work is less and vice versa. When more queries are added to the system, however, situations with high commonality and high waste are easily possible. In Figure 7 we show an illustration of such a scenario. The lightly shaded areas represent results of individual queries. The darkly shaded areas denote zombie tuples that are produced for no utility. In such cases, when there is both redundancy and waste, both the push-down and pull-up models are expensive.

The upshot of this example is that in spite of pushing down disjunctions, in the presence of *sharing*, a join can produce unnecessary *zombie* tuples that have to be eliminated later in the dataflow. With many queries this wasted work can increase significantly.

In this example, the worst case overhead of lost precision is the maximal area of the region identified as the output of the shared join operator, i.e., $|R_1 \cup R_2| \times |S_1 \cup S_2|$. With two streams, the overhead is quadratic. As the number of streams increase, the overhead becomes more sig-

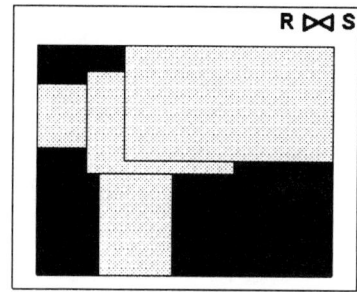

Figure 7: Zombies with many queries

nificant. In fact, it becomes *exponential* in the number of participating streams. We see more examples of this in the next section.

3.3 Disjunctions on intermediate results

We have shown how filtered pull-up can cause the production of zombie tuples, violating property PS2. Now, we will show how zombies cause further inefficiencies when they participate in later join work, producing even more zombies. Consider what happens when the queries in the example from Section 3.2 above also involve a third stream T.

- $Q_5 : \sigma_{r_1}(R) \bowtie \sigma_{s_1}(S) \bowtie \sigma_{t_1}(T)$
- $Q_6 : \sigma_{r_2}(R) \bowtie \sigma_{s_2}(S) \bowtie \sigma_{t_2}(T)$

A solution based on the pull-up strategy is to reuse the shared plan of Q_3 and Q_4 from Figure 5 and attach a join operator with T to each of Out_{Q_3} and Out_{Q_4}. That approach, however, could result in substantial duplicate join processing if there is significant overlap in the result sets of Q_3 and Q_4. This causes the appearance of a PS1 violation, which was not present in either of the pull-up schemes of the previous section. Given that the push-down plan already suffered from a PS2 violation, the resultant plan would be very inefficient.

The alternative is to discard the split from the plan shown in Figure 5 and use its input, complete with zombies, in another shared join with T. This, however, exacerbates the zombie situation as the zombies that are input to the join cause even more zombies to be produced. These tuples will still ultimately be eliminated by the conjuncts evaluated at the top of the plan. Note that in this situation's worst case, the number of zombie tuples, is the product of the cardinality of the filtered sets of each source. With three sources, this overhead is cubic.

This situation, i.e. the effects of zombies, can be ameliorated by pushing a *partial disjunction* down between the RS and ST join operators, assuming a left-deep strategy with an RST join order. In this case, this partial disjunctive predicate will be $(r_1 \wedge s_1) \vee (r_2 \wedge s_2)$. the plan is as shown in Figure 8.

Note that this plan still produces zombies after the RS join operator and still is in violation of PS2. In addition, a careful examination of this plan, reveals that the predicates r_1, r_2, s_1 and s_2 are each applied three times and t_1 and t_2 two times. This is a violation of PS1. With more streams

975

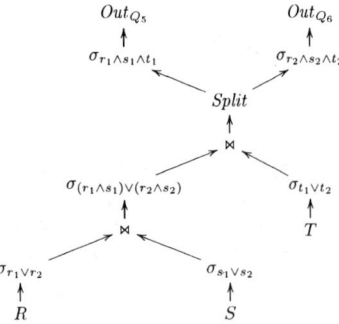

Figure 8: Eliminate zombies through disjunctions

being joined, the disjunction push-down scheme becomes increasingly complicated, suggesting that this approach is not very scalable.

Now suppose further that we are executing the queries Q_5 and Q_6 along with the queries Q_3 and Q_4. In keeping with our stated aim to share aggressively without generating zombies, we need to modify the plan in Figure 8 to produce the plan shown in Figure 9(a). Clearly the plan gets increasingly complicated with a lot of work being spent repeatedly re-evaluating predicates – the predicates on R and S are each potentially evaluated four times for a given tuple.

In addition to these violations of precision sharing, efficient execution of the Split operator is not easy. Recall that in actuality the Split operator is combined with all the predicates that are executed immediately after it. These predicates are built into a query index that the Split consults to route tuples. When the predicates involve more than one attribute, as is the case here, this index will have to be multi-dimensional.

In this section we showed how the standard techniques of shared query processing are not precise. In an attempt to efficiently reuse common work, they can end up producing useless data that can be exponential in the number of streams involved. Not only is the production of such useless tuples wasteful, the work done to eliminate them is an added waste.

4 TULIP: Tuple Lineage in Plans

Based on the observations above, we propose TULIP: TUple LIneage in Plans, an approach that uses tuple lineage in static plans to achieve precision sharing.

4.1 A review of imprecise static sharing

We saw in Section 3.3 why disjunctions on intermediate results can lead to complicated query plans with repeated predicate re-evaluation. Worse, these predicates evaluated on intermediate results are disjuncts of conjuncts – e.g. $(r_1 \wedge s_1) \vee (r_2 \wedge s_2)$ – and more expensive to evaluate than those that are disjuncts of simple predicates on base relations. This is especially the case, when the number of queries is very large. We also saw how the filtered pull-up approaches can cause join operators to produce zombies, however early they can be eliminated. We summarize and then consider in turn each of these problems to guide us to our solution.

1. *PS1 violation in push-down:* When identical tuples reach different upper-level join groups the build and probe operations on the tuples are duplicated.

2. *PS1 violation in filtered pull-up:* The issue is that a predicate evaluation on a tuple, when successful, is likely to be repeated, potentially many times for complex queries.

3. *PS2 violation in pull-up:* In both the filtered pull-up and pull-up strategies, join operators can produce zombie tuples that have to be subsequently processed and eliminated.

With problem (1), the only time we can expect pushdown to be competitive is when a very few upper-level join groups are activated for each base tuple. This observation was also made in NiagaraCQ [7]. The filtered pull-up strategies are the best way to reduce these overheads of repeated work and should be part of our solution.

Problem (2) arises because in static plans we throw away the results of earlier predicate evaluations. This makes sense in classical non-shared systems when predicates are generally conjuncts and the presence of a tuple above a filter is enough to deduce that the tuple passed every conjunct of the filter. Why not *memoize* the effect of each predicate evaluation and reuse it subsequently ?

Problem (3) is again the result of discarding information on predicate evaluation. If, for each tuple, the information on each predicate evaluation is memoized with the tuple, then a smart join operator can easily avoid producing zombie tuples.

With this problem analysis we are ready to describe our solution.

4.2 Tuple Lineage

We now consider the use of "tuple lineage" to accomplish memoization of predicate evaluation. To date, tuple lineage has been used profitably only in adaptive query processing schemes. Our insight is that tuple lineage is more generally applicable, and is in fact useful in static dataflows.

As described in CACQ, all tuples that flow through the system carry lineage information that consists of: (1) a steering vector [1] that describes the operators in the dataflow that have been visited (done) and are to be visited (ready) and (2) a completion vector [12] that describes the queries in the system that are "dead" for this tuple, i.e., those that this tuple cannot satisfy. In CACQ, the distinction between these parts of lineage was blurred while in truth they have two distinct roles. The steering vector is entirely used as a tuple routing mechanism. Apart from the routing infrastructure, such as an Eddy operator, no other operator must use its contents. In contrast, the completion vector is a query sharing mechanism, should be entirely

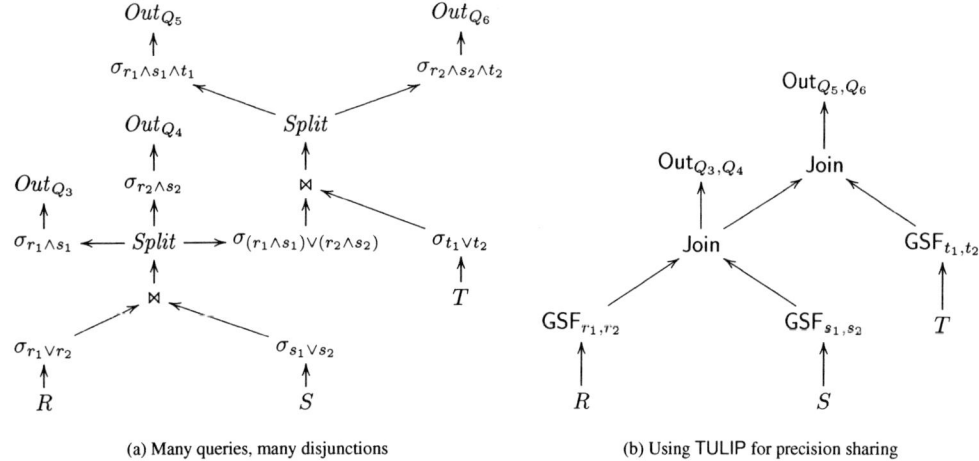

Figure 9: **To precisely share, or not to precisely share**

opaque to the routing fabric (the Eddy) and can be used by the other non-Eddy operators.

The storage and manipulation costs of these vectors represent a major overhead in the tuple routing schemes. The completion vectors are particularly profligate in memory consumption – a bit per tuple per query results in space overhead that is linear in the product of the number of queries and currently active tuples. In contrast, when the queries in question share a lot of their operators, the steering vector size is much smaller.

4.3 The TULIP solution

Having defined the notion of tuple lineage, we are ready to present the TULIP solution. Our main tool is tuple lineage of which, we only need the "completion vector" part. For the rest of this paper, we refer to this portion as the "lineage vector".

The insight for the solution to Problem (2) is from Rete [9], a discrimination network for the many pattern/many match problem, the most time-consuming part of which is the match step. To avoid performing the same tests repeatedly, the Rete algorithm stores the result of the match with working memory as temporary state. The lineage vector that tags along each tuple keeps track of the queries that this tuple has already failed.

Grouped filters: The same idea was also borrowed in CACQ with a GSFilter that evaluates multiple similar predicates. The GSFilter maintains indexes on the conjunctive predicate clauses registered with it. When it receives a new tuple, it efficiently probes the index to identify all registered clauses that it fails. It then records all these failures in the tuple's lineage vector. If, at the end of processing the tuple, there still are any live queries for the tuple (i.e., queries that can still get satisfied) the tuple is sent to the output. The GSFilter implements the disjunction of the predicates and memoizes the results of each clause into the tuple's payload. All predicates are evaluated exactly *once*. Note that the GSFilter is doing *more* than what a simple disjunction would do. Apart from the disjunction it also sets up things so that the clauses of the disjunct need never be re-evaluated. This is not dissimilar to index OR-ing strategies [13] for disjunctive predicates that are used in classical systems.

Zombie-killing symmetric join: To eliminate the zombies of problem (3), we need to (a) ensure that tuples go through grouped filters prior to entering the join and (b) a symmetric join operator that preserves the completion vector of inner tuples when building into an index of the join. When an outer tuple probes the index and finds a matching inner tuple, we compute the union of the completion vectors of the inner and outer. If this union consists of all queries that these operators are used by, then the match is discarded. We call this operator a *zombie-killing* symmetric join.

To summarize, TULIP involves the following components:

1. Any appropriate MQO scheme that results in filtered pull-ups can be chosen to determine join orders.

2. The disjunctions that are pushed down should be replaced with GSFilter operators.

3. Using zombie-killing symmetric join operators.

We now put it all together for our driving example, the scenario that shares queries Q_3, Q_4, Q_5 and Q_6. The static query plan for the TULIP model is shown in Figure 9(b). We use three kinds of lineage sensitive operators. The GSF is a grouped selection filter, the Join is a zombie-killing symmetric join and the Out which is an output operator. The Out is similar to that used with the classic static plans except that it is a single operator that delivers its input tuples to target queries based on their completion vectors. We now consider the precision sharing properties of this approach. First, PS1 is satisfied as this plan does not perform any operation on a given tuple more than once: all predicate evaluations are memoized in the lineage vectors of tuples and since the grouped filters push down disjunctions, no tuple is processed twice as part of a join operator. Next,

PS2 is also satisfied as no join operators produce zombie tuples of any kind.

It is instructive to compare this plan with the equivalent traditional shared plan in Figure 9(a). Not only is the TULIP plan an example of precision sharing, it is easy to see how the plan for many queries looks very similar to a plan for a single query. This makes it easy to use TULIP with multiple queries. In contrast, as we deal with more queries and streams, the filtered pull-up plan gets increasingly complicated.

Our main insight in TULIP is that the use of lineage helps: (a) to memoize predicate evaluation and avoid repetitive computations, à la Rete networks and (b) lineage sensitive operators to recognize and eliminate potential zombie tuples even before they are produced. These uses of tuple lineage ensure that TULIP does not respectively violate properties PS1 and PS2. In fact, TULIP guarantees precision sharing irrespective of optimizer decisions such as join order.

It is important to note that there can be many precisely shared plans, and the optimal plan is not necessarily one of them. When an optimizer estimates the cost of a plan, it uses the number of tuples at each stage of the plan to determine the cost of each operator, in accordance with the cost model. With TULIP, a new set of plans that emit fewer tuples between operators can now be considered during plan enumeration. The estimated cost of each operator is slightly higher because of the overhead of lineage manipulation. The key issue is the expected number of zombies produced at each stage. If this number can be estimated, then the optimizer can choose between TULIP and other plans in its pursuit of an optimal solution.

5 Performance of TULIP

In this section we study the performance of TULIP, our static precision sharing approach and compare the static schemes described in NiagaraCQ. In particular we consider the filtered pull-up and the selection pushdown schemes.

5.1 Experimental setup

Our experiments were performed on a 2.8 GHz Intel Pentium IV processor with 512 MB of main memory. We implemented TULIP in the TelegraphCQ [11, 5] system. Since we have no shared query optimizer, programmatically hook up static plans using the TelegraphCQ operators.

To fairly evaluate the static NiagaraCQ plans, we set up the system so that no lineage information is stored in intermediate tuples and TelegraphCQ's operators do not perform any unnecessary work manipulating lineage. For instance, the disjunctions of filtered pull-up are realized with a GSFilter that does not set lineage. Similarly, the a symmetric join operator ignores lineage. We emphasize here, that the intermediate data structures in the Niagara measurements have *no* space overhead for lineage. The static plans shown in Section 3 have *Split* operators that are separate from the predicate filters that follow them, suggesting that each individual predicate is evaluated separately.

However, in our experiments we follow the NiagaraCQ approach and use a Split operator that probes its input tuples into a predicate index implemented by a GSFilter. This lets Split send tuples only to those plan elements of queries that passed the probe. The top of each plan has one *Output* operator for each query.

In our TULIP implementation, TelegraphCQ's intermediate tuples have lineage turned on. TULIP plans use GS-Filters, zombie-killing symmetric hash joins, and output operators that manipulate lineage.

In both implementations, the output operator makes a tuple available for delivery to a query by queueing it to the process managing the query's connection. The queue is in shared memory, access to which can be expensive. So, for all of these experiments we suppress output production. Even so, output processing is still not trivial. For latency computations, we make a system call to find the current time for each output tuple. This is still, however, cheaper than the actual system overheads of sending the same tuple multiple times through shared memory.

It is important to see where the savings of zombie elimination come from. In TelegraphCQ, where all the operators execute in a *single* thread of execution in one process, the cost of operator invocation is minimal - a function call and a pointer copy. The real savings is the avoidance of unnecessary zombie production and elimination. In other systems where operators are often invoked in different threads, e.g. Aurora, the savings are even more as fewer zombies leads to fewer operator invocations that in turn mean less context switching overheads.

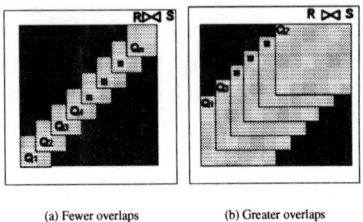

(a) Fewer overlaps   (b) Greater overlaps

Figure 10: Experimental setup: Query result sets

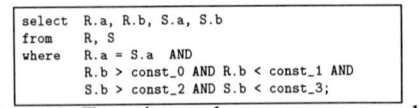

Figure 11: Experimental setup: query template

Our experiments all share a set of queries that are joins on streams R and S with individual predicates on each stream. The queries have identical structure and correspond to queries Q_3 and Q_4 from Section 3.2. The template of these queries is in Figure 11. We generate 256 queries for our experiments by supplying values for the constants in each of the queries in two setups. We show these visually in Figure 10. As before, shaded areas represent results of queries and darkly shaded pieces are zombies that would be generated by selection pull-up. We used TULIP to log the number of zombies actually eliminated. This is shown for both cases in Figure 12.

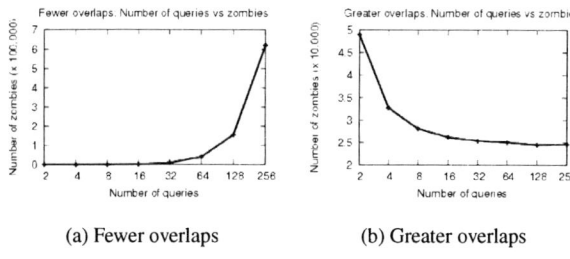

(a) Fewer overlaps (b) Greater overlaps

Figure 12: Experimental setup: Zombies

In the first setup, shown in Figure 10(a), the result set of each query overlaps with few other sets. To be precise, each query's result set overlaps with that of two other queries. In this case, as queries are added in the system, more and more zombies are produced, as shown in Figure 12(a).

Conversely, in the second setup, shown in Figure 10(b), the result set of each query overlaps with many other sets. To achieve this, the first two queries are arranged so that they have almost no overlap (i.e., they are the two queries farthest apart). Subsequently, every query that is added overlaps with one or both of the first two queries. Since each such query contributes no extra zombies, the effect of adding queries is to steadily reduce the number of zombies produced, as shown in Figure 12(b).

In our experiments, we measure the average latency of each of the results of each query. Synthetic data is generated and piped into TelegraphCQ by an external process. Each tuple arriving at the system is timestamped on entry in the TelegraphCQ Wrapper ClearingHouse even before it is read by any scan operator. When a tuple arrives at an output operator, we examine its components and compute the difference between the current time and the time it originally entered the system. This represents the latency of the tuple, and the average latency is what we measured in our experiments.

We consider the 4 static approaches that we studied earlier: (a) selection pull-up (SPU), (b) filtered pull-up (FPU) (Figure 5), (c) selection push-down (SPD) and (d) TULIP. In our graphs, we do not report the SPU case as it is dominated by FPU. Plans for selection pull-up and push-down with predicates on only one source are shown in Figure 3 and the multiple predicate case is just a simple extension.

5.2 Performance results

For each setup, we plot in Figure 13 the average latency of result tuples for each approach against the number of queries being shared. Note that the number of queries is shown in a log_2 scale on the x-axis.

In both setups, the average latency for all plans is very small (under 25ms) for 2 queries and increases steadily as queries are added. In each approach, there is a certain number of queries at which there is a knee in the graph showing each scheme's scalability limits.

The following overheads affect average latencies:

- **PS1 violations:** Repeated work for the same tuples in intersecting result sets:
  (SPD) In the various separate join operators.
  (FPU) In output processing.
- **PS2 violations:** (FPU) Unnecessary work caused by the production of zombies in joins and removal afterward.
- **Other:** (TULIP) CPU instructions for lineage management. The state overhead was negligible in our experiments.

Setup 1 (Fewer overlaps):

As seen in Figure 13(a), for 32 or fewer queries the behavior of all three plans remains similar. Latencies increase steadily from 6ms to 17ms, while zombies produced by SPD increase increases from 14 to 9133.

At 64 queries, the latency for FPU jumps to 72 ms while that of SPD and TULIP stay at 30ms. For twice as many queries, the number of zombies increased four-fold to $\approx$ 39000. FPU's zombie overheads slow it materially and it scales no more for 128 and 256 queries. For these query sets its average latency is 430ms and 43 seconds.

Returning to SPD and TULIP, for more than 64 queries performance of both approaches start degrading. As queries are added, each new query causes more tuples that cannot be easily eliminated before joins. TULIP is, however, slightly more expensive than SPD and at 256 queries its latency is 147ms as opposed to SPD's 125ms.

In general, sharing does not have much advantage when the results of the queries being shared have fewer overlaps. This is exactly what we observe in this case and the minimally shared SPD scheme does better overall. The repeated work overheads in SPD are slightly dominated by that of lineage management in TULIP. Both are comprehensively dwarfed by the zombie overheads of FPU.

Setup 2 (Greater overlaps):

As seen in Figure 13(b), all three plans behave similarly for 4 or fewer queries with latencies $\approx$ 25ms. For 2 queries, FPU is the outright winner as both queries have no overlap.

From 4 to 32 queries, the performance of FPU and SPD both degrade very fast. As queries are added, lots of tuples overlap causing repeated work. One instance of this is in output processing for which SPD and FPU behave similarly. These new tuples, however, also cause: (1) repeated join overheads in SPD and (2) overheads resulting from zombies in FPU. As zombies decrease from $\approx$ 49000 to plateau at $\approx$ 25000 the former overheads increase and the latter decrease. From 32 to 64 queries, both SPD and FPU perform the same. Beyond 64 queries, the join overheads of SPD become much worse, leading to SPD having a latency of 8.02 seconds for 128 queries as opposed to 1.7 seconds for FPU (these are not shown in the graph).

In contrast, the TULIP scheme performs very well, gracefully degrading in performance as the number of queries are added. At 256 queries, the latency of TULIP is 113ms. The FPU and SPD schemes have a comparable overhead of 111ms and 102ms for 16 queries. For the same latency, TULIP scales to 16 times, more than an order of magnitude, as many queries as traditional schemes.

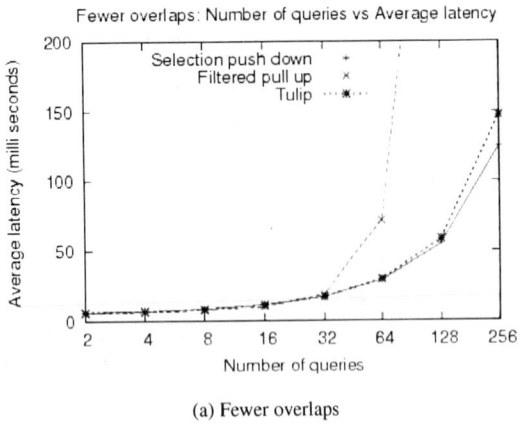
(a) Fewer overlaps

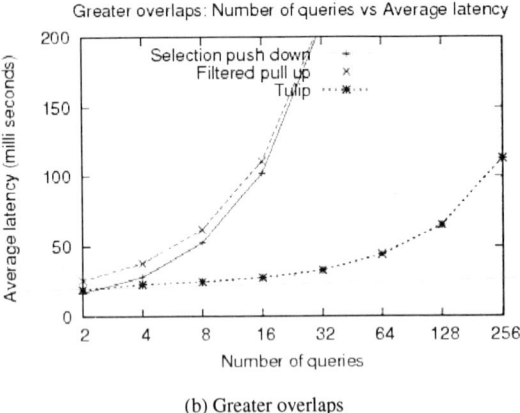
(b) Greater overlaps

Figure 13: Static query plans: average query latencies

Summary: The insights of our performance analysis are as follows:

1. The overheads of both repeated work *and* unnecessary work are significant.
2. Our two setups demonstrate two extreme cases, each favoring one of the two traditional approaches (FPU and SPD).
3. In each extreme case, the TULIP solution of precision sharing performs very well. While in the case of minimal sharing it is competitive with the ideal FPU, in the face of high sharing it is more than an order of magnitude better than either traditional scheme.

Our experiments demonstrate the robustness of TULIP. When sharing is useful, TULIP gives significant improvements over the best known approaches. When, however, there is not much use in sharing, the extra overheads of TULIP are minimal. This suggests that TULIP is capable of giving very good benefits in many cases while staying competitive otherwise.

6 Adaptive Precision Sharing

We begin this section by studying tuple routing in the CACQ adaptive sharing scheme, and then show how it is also susceptible to violations in precision sharing inspite of using lineage. Just as we used ideas from the adaptive approach to make static sharing precise, it turns out that we can use techniques from the static world to remove the precision sharing violations from the adaptive approach.

6.1 Tuple routing in CACQ

Here we explain how tuples are routed in an adaptive dataflow as described in CACQ.

In Figure 14 we show how CACQ will process the queries Q_3 and Q_4 from Section 3.2. Scan modules for R and S are scheduled to bring data in to the system from wrappers [11]. The tuples are fed into the eddy, which adaptively routes the tuples through its slave operators.

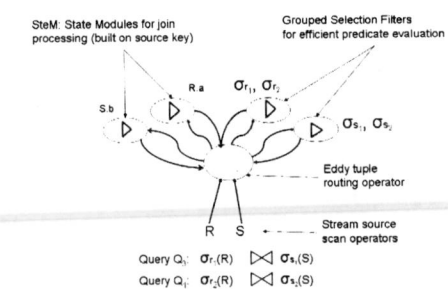

Figure 14: CACQ: Eddy, SteMs and Grouped Filter

There are two GSFilters, one each for all predicates over R and S, and two SteM operators. A SteM is a "state module" [15] that can be conceptualized as one half of a decoupled symmetric join operator. For e.g., a join operator $R \bowtie_a S$ over streams R and S may be decoupled into two SteMs $R.a$ and $S.a$.

In CACQ, a tuple is routed to candidate operators based on its signature - i.e., the set of base tuples that are its constituents. Operators amongst a set of candidates may be chosen in any order, with a routing policy governing this choice. A base tuple from R has a signature r and has to be *built* and *probed* into the R and S SteMs respectively. For correctness reasons, however, both SteMs cannot be used as candidates for tuples with signature r as that will destroy the atomic "build then probe" property of pipelined joins. As described in Section 3.3.1 of CACQ [12], "a singleton tuple must be inserted into all its associated SteMs before it is routed to any of the other SteMs with which it needs to be joined". The system's constraints force tuples to be built directly into their associated SteMs right after they have been scanned.

Thus, in this example, the adaptivity features of CACQ play no role, as there is only one join to be performed. In Figure 15 we show the dataflow of r and s tuples in CACQ for this example. A base tuple goes through Build, GSFil-

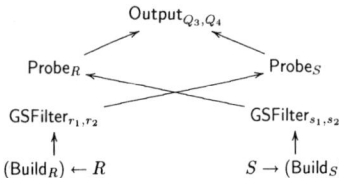

Figure 15: Effective tuple dataflow in CACQ

ter, Probe and Output operators. Note that an r tuple gets respectively built and probed in the R and S SteM. Similarly an s tuple gets respectively built and probed in the S and R SteMs. For simplicity, we assume that the predicates in question are not expensive and so CACQ always orders the GSFilter before a Probe.

Without sharing, in the single query eddy scheme [1] the steering vector of a tuple indicates when its work is done and it can be output to a query. With sharing however, any intermediate tuple in the eddy could satisfy a query, and checking and delivering tuples to query outputs is part of the CACQ eddy's responsibilities.

6.2 Precision sharing violations in CACQ

Now we show how CACQ violates our precision sharing rules. We are concerned only with sharing and do not address any of the considerable benefits that an adaptive system may have in volatile scenarios.

Zombie production (PS2 violation): The tuples that are built into SteMs are the original base tuples and do not contain any record of predicate evaluation, and thus carry no useful lineage. This, however, means that when producing the join tuples, there is no way to combine the lineage of the probe and build to eliminate zombies as described in Section 4. To see why this is so, recall from Section 4.3 our description of a zombie-killing symmetric join. To be able to eliminate matching zombie tuples, the operator needs to perform the union of the lineage vectors of the outer and inner tuples. Since, in CACQ, the inner tuples carry no lineage, the join cannot eliminate any zombies and violates the PS2 property of precision sharing.

Explained in another way, this is a problem of the optimal placement of individual selection predicates in the presence of joins. With a conventional binary join operator there are the two choices explored by NiagaraCQ and discussed in Section 3 - pushing the selections down below the join in "selection push-down" and pulling them above in "filtered pull-up". When, however, the internal build and probe operations of a join are decoupled as shown in Figure 15 there are *three* choices for locating selection predicates (as disjunctions): after the probe, between the build and the probe, and before the build. Since, in CACQ, the build and scan are performed together, there are only two choices - either between the build and probe, or after the probe - with the routing policy deciding which wins in an adaptive fashion. Unfortunately both choices result in the production of zombies.

Repeated output processing (PS1 violation): Output processing in CACQ is done every time a tuple returns to the eddy, i.e., in each major loop. An intermediate tuple's steering vector is compared with the completion requirements of each query. If the tuple satisfies any query it is immediately delivered. Not only is this an expensive operation, especially in the presence of a large number of queries, a given tuple may be processed repeatedly as an output for multiple queries. This is a violation of the PS1 property. As we saw in Section 5, repeated processing of the same tuple in the outputs of multiple queries (PS1 violation) can drastically hurt performance. What we really need is a way to route tuples to output operators *only* when they are finally ready for them.

6.3 CAR: Constrained Adaptive Routing

Here, we propose as an alternative to CACQ, *Constrained Adaptive Routing*, or CAR. We will show that this scheme has almost all the adaptivity benefits of CACQ and still satisfies precision sharing.

As explained in Section 6.2 CACQ violates precision sharing by producing zombies and repeating output processing operations. The former is because of a hidden constraint (*build along with scan*) that causes poor selection placement. The latter is because output processing is performed in an unconstrained *ad hoc* fashion. The root of the problem is that there are multiple constraints that must be satisfied in an adaptive dataflow. Some, such as *build before probe* are for correctness, and others such as *filters before build* and *output only when done* are for performance. In our architecture such constraints can be expressed explicitly and ensure correctness and performance.

In CAR, we introduce the *operator precedence* routing mechanism. In this approach, we record precedence relationships between operators in a *precedence graph*. As with CACQ, this mechanism is used to generate a set of candidate operators to which tuples must be routed. In its simplest form, this is a graph with nodes that are sets of operators (called "candidates") and edges that represent legal transitions from one node to the other. When a tuple is routed through the candidates of a particular node it is subject to a routing policy such as the lottery scheme in CACQ. This ensures that CAR can adaptively respond to changes in selectivity, data rates etc.

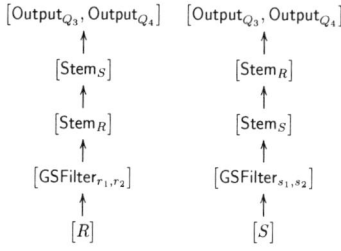

Figure 16: Operator precedence graph for CAR

In Figure 16 we show an operator precedence graph for the queries Q_3 and Q_4. There are 8 nodes in the graph and operators (such as the SteMs and Outputs) appear in more than one node. Clearly, with this scheme tuples are filtered and then built into SteMs. This enables the early recognition and elimination of zombies and preserves the PS2 property. A given tuple is subject to output processing only once - when it is ready. This preserves the PS1 property.

Effects on adaptivity: Note that fixing predicate placement can hurt adaptivity. In order to reduce zombies, GS-Filters ought to be processed before builds. If, however, the filters in question are expensive and cost more than join operations then reducing zombies may be less important. Adaptivity in CACQ allowed for efficient join ordering as well as delayed execution of expensive filters at the cost of zombies. In contrast, with CAR joins are ordered efficiently without zombies at the cost of early evaluation of expensive filters. In the presence of a filter that is known to be expensive, it is easy to fix the CAR precedence graph to revert to CACQ behavior. An interesting question is if it is possible to make this choice *adaptively*. It is not yet clear how to devise such a routing policy. In practice, however, simple filters are very much more common and the heuristic of reverting to CACQ in the presence of expensive predicates should be enough for most applications.

The main insight of this approach is our use of techniques from the static world. A purely adaptive approach makes routing decisions every step of the way. Constraints on the adaptivity makes it possible to ensure that predicate placement is appropriate for precision sharing.

7 Performance of CAR and CACQ

In this section we compare the performance of CACQ with CAR, the constrained adaptive routing technique we described above. Our experimental setup and methodology is identical to that described for static plans in Section 5.

For each of the two setups we report the average latencies of query results for each of CACQ and CAR in Figures 17(a) and 17(b). Note that as before, the number of queries is shown in a log_2 scale on the x-axis.

As in the static case, for both setups, the average latency of CACQ and CAR with 2 queries is small (5-30 ms) and increases steadily with query addition until scalability limits are reached.

The following overheads can affect latencies:

- **PS1 violations:** (CACQ) Repeated output processing of the same tuple in different queries.
- **PS2 violations:** (CACQ) Unnecessary work caused by the production and removal of zombies.
- **Other:** (CAR,CACQ) CPU instructions involving lineage management.

In this experiment, for CACQ the tuples produced by probes into SteMs are immediately ready for output. There are no more filtering steps and so there are, in fact, no PS1 violations causing output processing overheads.

In both setups, the performance of CAR comfortably outstrips that of CACQ. Just like TULIP, the performance of CAR gracefully degrades with the addition of new queries.

In the fewer overlaps case, with 2 queries there are actually no overlaps. In spite of this, the production of 14 zombies is enough to cause CACQ's latency to be 21 ms as opposed to 6ms for CAR. This shows the savings in output processing (PS1 preservation) for CAR. At 256 queries, the latency of CAR is $\approx$ 151 ms. An equivalent latency of CACQ supports only 18 queries. For this latency, CAR supports 14 times (an order of magnitude) more queries than CACQ.

In the greater overlaps case, CACQ scales more gracefully than with fewer overlaps. Note that in this case, the relative overheads of zombies actually drop with more queries. The behavior of CACQ that we observe is really a *damped* version of CAR. With 256 queries CACQ has a latency of 550 ms as opposed to 131 ms of CAR. Note that CACQ can support a latency of 131 ms for only 48 queries, while CAR handles 5 times as many.

The difference in both setups is the number of zombies. With fewer overlaps, the production of zombies cripples CACQ.

In comparison to the static schemes, CAR performs almost as well as TULIP. With 256 queries, the latency of CAR in the greater overlap case is 131 ms as opposed to 113 ms for TULIP. In the fewer overlap case it is 151 ms for CAR as opposed to 147 with TULIP. These results are not surprising as the only difference between CAR and TULIP is cost of adaptivity. Since there are no choices to be made in our experiments, the latency differences we observe lets us reckon the baseline cost of adaptivity.

In summary, our experiments indicate that:

1. The overheads of producing zombies, or unnecessary work, are significant in adaptive dataflows even when relatively fewer zombies are produced.
2. In each scheme, the CAR approach of adaptive precision sharing performs very well.
3. In these scenarios, the baseline costs of adaptivity are not very significant.

8 Conclusions

Shared query processing has focused on reducing the overheads of redundancy. Aggressive reduction of repeated work can, however, cause additional wasted work in post-processing useless data.

Thus far, this inherent tension between repeated work and wasted work has been taken for granted. Our major contributions are: (1) to show that this tension is not irreconcilable and (2) To develop both static and adaptive techniques that balance the tension gracefully.

We defined *precision sharing* as a way to characterize any sharing scheme with neither repeated work, nor wasted work. We then showed how previous work in shared stream processing led to imprecisely shared plans. Armed with these observations we charted a strategy to make static shared plans precise.

Our insight is that *tuple lineage*, an idea from adaptive query processing, is actually more generally applica-

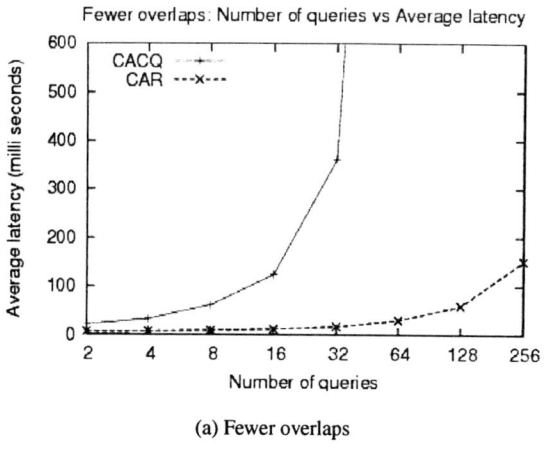
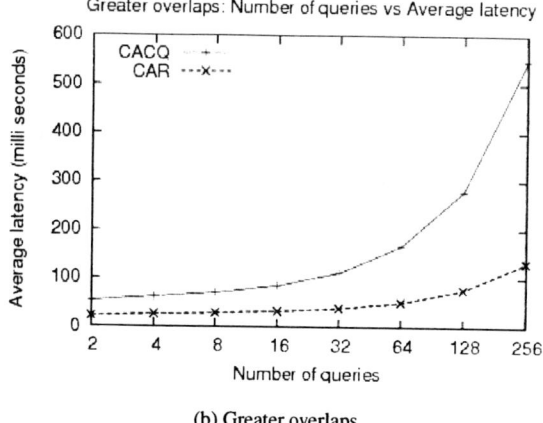

(a) Fewer overlaps
(b) Greater overlaps

Figure 17: Adaptive query plans: average query latencies

ble. We then proposed TULIP, or "TUple LIneage in static Plans", or technique to make static shared plans precise by using tuple lineage.

Our next contribution was to show how shared adaptive query processors also violate precision sharing. Here we reversed our strategy, and adopted the idea of operator ordering in static dataflows. Our new approach CAR, or "Constrained Adaptive Routing", has almost all the benefits of adaptivity without the side-effects of precision sharing.

Finally we reported a performance study of the various schemes: precise and imprecise, static and adaptive. Our experiments show that the precision sharing approaches either significantly outperform, or are competitive with, all the other schemes under different extreme conditions.

References

[1] R. Avnur *et al.*. Eddies: Continuously adaptive query processing. In *SIGMOD*, pp. 261–272. 2000.

[2] B. H. Bloom. Space/time trade-offs in hash coding with allowable errors. *CACM*, 13(7):422–426, 1970.

[3] D. Carney, *et al.*. Monitoring streams - a new class of data management applications. In *VLDB*. 2002.

[4] S. Chandrasekaran *et al.*. Streaming queries over streaming data. In *VLDB*. 2002.

[5] S. Chandrasekaran, *et al.*. TelegraphCQ: Continuous dataflow processing for an uncertain world. In *CIDR*. 2003.

[6] J. Chen, *et al.*. NiagaraCQ: a scalable continuous query system for Internet databases. In *SIGMOD*. 2000.

[7] J. Chen, *et al.*. Design and evaluation of alternative selection placement strategies in optimizing continuous queries. In *ICDE*. 2002.

[8] N. N. Dalvi, *et al.*. Pipelining in multi-query optimization. In *PODS*. 2001.

[9] C. L. Forgy. Rete: A fast algorithm for the many pattern/many object match problem. *Artifical Intelligence*, 19(1):17–37, September 1982.

[10] G. Graefe *et al.*. Dynamic query evaluation plans. In *SIGMOD*, pp. 358–366. 1989.

[11] S. Krishnamurthy, *et al.*. TelegraphCQ: An architectural status report. *IEEE Data Eng. Bull.*, 26(1):11–18, 2003.

[12] S. R. Madden, *et al.*. Continuously adaptive continuous queries over streams. In *SIGMOD*. 2002.

[13] C. Mohan, *et al.*. Single table access using multiple indexes: optimization, execution, and concurrency control techniques. In *EDBT*, pp. 29–43. 1990.

[14] R. Motwani, *et al.*. Query processing, resource management, and approximation in a data stream management system. In *CIDR*. 2003.

[15] V. Raman, *et al.*. Using state modules for adaptive query processing. In *ICDE*. 2003.

[16] T. K. Sellis. Multiple-query optimization. *ACM TODS*, March 1988.

[17] K. Tan *et al.*. Workload scheduling for multiple query processing. *Inf. Proc. Letters*, 55(5):251–257, 1995.

[18] F. Tian *et al.*. Tuple routing strategies for distributed eddies. In *VLDB*, pp. 333–344. 2003.

INDUSTRIAL AND APPLICATIONS PAPERS

Returning Modified Rows – SELECT Statements with Side Effects

Andreas Behm, Serge Rielau, Richard Swagerman

IBM Toronto Lab
8200 Warden Avenue
Markham, ON
Canada
{abehm, srielau, swagrman}@ca.ibm.com

Abstract

SQL in the IBM® DB2® Universal Database™ for Linux®, UNIX®, and Windows® (DB2 UDB) database management product has been extended to support nested INSERT, UPDATE, and DELETE operations in SELECT statements. This allows database applications additional processing on modified rows. Within a single unit of work, applications can retrieve a result set containing the modified rows from a table or view modified by an SQL data-change operation. This eliminates the need to select the row after an INSERT or UPDATE, or before a DELETE statement. As a result, fewer network round trips, less server CPU time, fewer cursors, and less server memory are required. In addition, deadlocks can be avoided. The proposed approach is integrated with the set semantics of SQL, and does not require any procedural logic or modifications on the underlying relational data model. Pipelining multiple update, insert and delete operations using the same source data provides a very efficient way for multi-table data-change statements typically found in ETL (extraction, transformation, load) applications. We demonstrate significant performance benefit with our experiences in the TPC-C benchmark. Experimental results show that the new SQL is more efficient in query execution compared to classic SQL.

1. Introduction

Commercial DBMS vendors constantly extend the SQL query language to address emerging business demands for increasing functionality and improving performance. One aspect of new features is to push more processing into the database engine. While most language extensions apply to data retrieval, extending UPDATE, DELETE, and INSERT statements (henceforth called *data-change statements*) has found less attention.

Prominent language extensions in the context of data-change statements are triggers, MERGE statement, identity columns using sequences, expression-generated columns, and default values. Modern RDBMS can use these features to produce surrogate keys. In doing so it becomes apparent that a way needs to be found to retrieve data back from data-change statements, which traditionally only provide a very limited set of information. The information returned today is usually limited to the number of rows changed.

Another area where performance of data-change statements plays a key role is a data-cleansing environment, where large quantities of data need to be imported into the RDBMS. The data needs to be processed efficiently in several phases, and dispatched into the appropriate tables such as fact and dimension tables in a star-schema scenario.

There are band-aid solutions in the industry today, which allow the return of specific properties. Examples include functions to return the last generated *identity_value* or sequence value to retrieve generated primary keys. Other more general solutions allow for returning data back into the procedural context using temporary tables or set-valued host variables.

We found that the problem of returning data from data-change statements needs to be solved in a more holistic and set-oriented fashion. A general, more relational approach needs to address more complex scenarios such as data cleansing in addition to covering the simple cases described above.

Permission to copy without fee all or part of this material is granted provided that the copies are not made or distributed for direct commercial advantage, the VLDB copyright notice and the title of the publication and its date appear, and notice is given that copying is by permission of the Very Large Data Base Endowment. To copy otherwise, or to republish, requires a fee and/or special permission from the Endowment

**Proceedings of the 30th VLDB Conference,
Toronto, Canada, 2004**

One of the challenges the authors faced was to maintain the spirit of the relational model within the context of standard SQL while allowing for optimal performance through pipelining and parallelization.

In the following sections, we propose a fairly small set of changes SQL, which result in a major extension to the expressive power of SQL. The changes include:

- The exposure of the NEW and OLD transition table as defined for SQL statement triggers in the FROM clause of an SQL SELECT statement.
- A definition of the order of execution for nested queries.
- An extension of the column lists for data-change statements using an include clause.

These three simple changes allow data-change statements to fully integrate with the select statement and hence exploit the expressive power of SQL.

The structure of this paper is as follows. Section 2 introduces our major SQL extensions. In Section 3 we discuss how we approached the implementation of the new statement type. We demonstrate a pipelining mechanism for update, delete and insert operations in Section 4, which leads to significant performance benefit for multi-table data-change statements. In Section 5 we discuss our experiences with the new SQL in the TPC-C benchmark, and the performance benefit of OLTP applications. Related approaches for returning modified data are discussed in Section 6. Section 7 provides a conclusion.

2. SQL Changes

In this section, we introduce the SQL extensions for data-change statements. We show how `insert`, `update`, or `delete` operations can be embedded in the `from` clause of a `select` statement. We enhance common table expressions to provide a way for embedding multiple data-change operations within one SQL statement. Finally, we introduce modifying table functions, which allow more complex scenarios for returning modified data. All language extensions introduced in this chapter are available in DB2 UDB for Linux, UNIX, and Windows Release 8.1.4. The complete new SQL can be found in the SQL Reference [5].

Select From Data-Change Statement

In the simplest form, an SQL data-change statement is characterized as a select statement having an `insert`, `update` or `delete` operation embedded in the `from` clause. The columns of the target object of the specified SQL data-change statement are considered the columns of this intermediate result table and can be referenced by name in the select list of the query.

```
create table orders (
    purchase_date date,
    sales_person varchar(16),
    region varchar(10),
    quantity varchar,
    order_num integer not null
        generated always as identity
        (start with 100, increment by 1))

select * from new table
    (insert into orders
        (pdate, salesp, region, quantity)
    values
        (current date,'Judith','Beijing',6),
        (current date,'Marieke','Medway',5),
        (current date,'Hanneke','Halifax',5))
```

PDATE	SALESP	REGION	QUANT	ONUM
12/22/2003	Judith	Beijing	6	100
12/22/2003	Marieke	Medway	5	101
12/22/2003	Hanneke	Halifax	5	102

Note that the syntax of the `insert` statement is not changed by this approach. The `insert` operation is wrapped in a `from` clause to indicate that the intermediate result table represented by the inserted rows should be returned. A data-change-table-reference can be specified as the only table-reference in the `from` clause of the outer fullselect that is used in a select-statement, a `select into` statement, a common-table expression, or as the only fullselect in an assignment statement. To execute select from data-change statements, the user must have the proper SQL authorization. For example, to perform a select from insert statement on a table ORDERS, the user would have to hold both, select and insert privileges on the ORDERS table.

The contents of the intermediate result table dependend on the qualifier specified in the `from` clause. If `old table` is specified, the rows in the intermediate result table will contain values of the target table rows at the point immediately preceding the execution of before triggers and the SQL data-change operation. For the `new table` qualifier, the rows in the intermediate result table will contain values of the target table rows at the point immediately after the SQL data-change statement has been executed, but before referential integrity evaluation and the firing of any after triggers. The `old table` qualifier applies to `update` and `delete` operations, the `new table` qualifier applies to `update` and `insert` operations.

Include Columns

We introduce the concept of include columns, which allows you to specify additional columns that do not exist in the target table of a select from data-change statement. These additional columns are available for use in the `select` list or `order by` clause of the query containing the SQL data-change statement in the `from` clause, but have no effect on the SQL data-change of the target table. One typical example for using include columns is to provide a way for update statements to return both, the new and the old value of a column. The following select from update statement defines an include column `old_salary`, and assigns the salary value to `old_salary` in the `set` clause of the `update` operation. Additional examples can be found in chapter 4 and the IBM TPC-C disclosure report [9].

```
create table employee (
  ssn char(10), salary integer);
insert into employee values
  ('1234567890', 90000);

select * from new table
    (update employee
      include (old_salary integer)
      set old_salary = salary,
          salary = salary * 1.2);
```

```
ssn          salary    old_salary
----------   -------   ----------
1234567890   108000    90000
```

Views

Special care needs to be taken when the target of a select from data-change statement is a view containing a where clause. A view containing a where clause in its definition is by default non-symmetric. That is, a row modified by an `insert` or `update` operation does not need to remain in the view. In contrast, a symmetric view is defined by specifying the `with cascaded check option` clause during the creation of the view, which indicates that an inserted or updated row has to remain in the view after the modification [4].

Non-symmetric views pose a security issue for select from data-change statements if, for example, a before trigger of an `insert` or `update` operation modifies a value of the row which should not be seen by the user. We concluded that non-symmetric views as the target of a select from data-change statement must satisfy the restrictions of symmetric views, if the qualifier `new table` is used. The following example shows a view containing employees having a salary less than 100.000, and a before trigger modifying the salary if the employee is promoted. The given select from update statement is rejected because the modified row with the updated salary (i.e., 108000) does not remain in the view. No row is updated or returned.

```
create table employee (
  ssn char(10),
  salary integer,
  ranking integer);

insert into employee values
  ('1234567890', 90000, 3);

create trigger promote
before update on employee
referencing old as o new as n for each row
when (n.rank > o.rank)
  set n.salary = n.salary * 1.2;

create view lowemps as
select * from employee
where salary < 100000;

select * from new table (
  update lowemps set rank = rank+1);
```

Common Table Expressions

In addition to simple select from data-change statements, we want to support a way to perform multiple data-change operations within one SQL statement. This is in particular useful for complex data-change scenarios, where the result of one data-change operation is used as input for another one. It allows us to construct better performing plans, since we can see multiple operations together when we rewrite and optimize a statement. Furthermore, it is not necessary to return the result of a select from data-change statement to the client in order to use the data as input for another statement.

We use common table expressions for this purpose, and allow select from data-change statements in the definition of temporary views in a common table expression. The main advantage of using common table expressions for embedding multiple data-change statements is that the syntax specifies an order for temporary views, which determines the semantics of executing a common table expression. All temporary views are executed in the order they occur in the common table expression.

In the following example, we illustrate common table expressions using two tables `Employee` (`EmpNr`, `Name`) and `Project` (`ProjNr`, `Name`, `Lead`). The common table expression replaces an employee 'Old Emp' with a new employee 'New Emp', assigns all projects lead by 'Old Emp' to 'New Emp', and returns the names of the updated projects.

```
with
  NewEmp AS (select EmpNr from new table
                (insert into Employee(name)
                  values ('New Emp'))),
  OldEmp AS (select EmpNr from Employee
                where Name = 'Old Emp'),
  UpProj AS (select Name from new table
                (update Project
                  set Lead = (select EmpNr
                                from NewEmp))),
  DelEmp AS (select EmpNr from new table
                (delete from Employee
                  where EmpNr = (select EmpNr
                                  from OldEmp)))
select Name from UpProj
```

Modifying Table Functions

We introduce modifying table functions as another concept for embedding multiple data-change operations in a single statement. In contrast to common table expressions, two additional tasks can be accomplished. First, the body of a modifying table function can be defined as a compound statement containing a sequence of SQL-procedure-statements [5] including data-change statements. Second, it allows applying a data-change operation multiple times for a collection of input data, as shown in the example below. Both features have been widely used in the implementation of our TPC-C benchmark [9].

A select statement can contain one modifying table in the from clause. To guarantee order of execution in case the from clause contains more than one table reference, the modifying table function has to be the last table reference in the from clause, correlated to all other table references.

The following table function upsal() updates the salary of an employee, records the salary change in an audit table, and returns the salary increase. The subsequent select statement updates the salary using the upsal() function for three employees.

```
create function upsal(upeid int,
                     factor float)
returns table (increase int)
modifies sql data
return
with i1 as (
select eid, old_salary, salary
    from new table
        (update emp
         include (old_salary int)
         set salary = salary * factor,
             old_salary = salary
         where emp.eid=upeid))
select new_salary-old_salary
  from new table (
    insert into audit select
    eid,old_salary,salary from i1);
```

```
select sum (increase)
  from table (values (1, 1.1),
                     (2, 1.2),
                     (3, 1.05))
              as upemp(eid,factor),
       table (upsal(upemp.eid,upemp.factor))
              as upsal;
```

The update effect on the emp and audit table is equivalent to the following sequence of insert and update statements:

```
insert into audit
with i1(eid,factor) as
  (values (1, 1.1),
          (2, 1.2),
          (3, 1.05))
select emp.eid, emp.salary,
       emp.salary * factor
  from emp, i1
  where emp.eid = i1.eid;

update emp set salary = salary * 1.1
       where eid=1;
update emp set salary = salary * 1.2
       where eid=2;
update emp set salary = salary * 1.05
       where eid=3;
```

3. Implementation

In this section, we provide a high-level summary of some of the key design issues we faced during implementation of the new SQL features. The proposed approach mostly takes advantage of existing "tooling" within and around the relational database engine. In the query compiler, we mostly applied "plug-and-play" of existing infrastructure, that is, combining constructs used for representing select statements as well as insert, update and delete statements. The optimizer is already capable handling data-change operations in a complex statement to ensure, for example, that predicates are not pushed down through data-change operations. We did not need to implement any changes for the client infrastructure.

The first interesting problem when executing a select from data-change statement is to get hold on the new and old values of the rows modified by an insert, update or delete operation. Fortunately, this functionality has already been implemented for after statement triggers [3]. An after statement trigger for data-change statements can access the new and old transition table containing all modified rows. The following example shows an after update statement trigger for the emp table. The trigger inserts the content of both, old and new transition table into the audit table.

```
create table emp
(eid int, name varchar(10), salary int);
insert into emp values (1, 'Peter',50000),
                       (2, 'Paul',60000),
                       (3, 'Mary',70000);
create table audit(eid int, salary int);

create trigger audtrig
after update on emp
referencing old_table as old
            new_table as new
for each statement
insert into audit
  select eid,salary from old union all
  select eid,salary from new);

update emp set salary=salary*1.1
where eid<3;

select * from audit;

EID         SALARY
-----------  -----------
          1        55000
          2        66000
          1        50000
          2        60000
```

The data flow for select from data-change statements has to be constructed in a way that either the new or old transition table is returned to the client instead of flowing into a trigger.

A table that has been modified by a data-change operation within a complex statement can be accessed in the same statement through a subquery or another data-change operation. Consequently, all read and write operations on the same data within one statement need to be synchronized. The infrastructure for handling read/write conflicts is already required for standard SQL. For example, a before trigger or an after trigger can contain a subquery over the target table. The same concepts have been extended to ensure correct semantics for select from data-change statements. In the following, some examples for read/write conflicts are shown.

```
select c1, (select sum(salary) from emp)
from new table (insert into emp(eid,salary)
                values (1,50000));

with v1 as (select * from new table
             (update emp
              set salary=salary+1000)),
     v2 as (select * from new table
             (update emp
              set salary=salary*1.1))
select * from emp
```

In the first example, the subquery select sum(salary) from emp includes the salary 50.000 inserted in the nested insert operation. In the second example, the table emp is updated twice. First, the salary is increased by 1000 for each row, the intermediate result is then multiplied by 1.1. The fullselect select * from emp returns the final result in the salary column after executing both update operations.

The most fundamental change in the infrastructure we made was the execution of select from data-change statements at runtime. In general, a select statement returning more than one row is performed using a cursor. The typical execution of a cursor consists of three consecutive tasks: declare, open, and fetch. The statement is compiled when the cursor is declared. In theory, opening the cursor completes the operation and positions the cursor on to the first row of the result set. Each row of the result set can be accessed through the fetch command, which moves the cursor towards the end of the result set. However, in practice we are trying to avoid executing a statement completely at one time, as it requires temporary storing the result.

Instead, we execute the statement as we fetch the rows, such that no temporary storage for the result set needs to be used, unless, for example, the statement contains an order by clause and the statement needs to be completely executed in order to determine the first row.

For select from data-change statements, this strategy does not work. Any insert, update or delete operation is an atomic operation which needs to be driven to completion at one time. Data-change operations cannot be executed on a row-by-row basis. Instead, they are processed as follows: first, the before triggers for all modified rows are performed. Second, all insert, update, and delete operations are applied. Third, constraints for all modified rows are checked. Finally, all after statement triggers are executed.

We have chosen to completely execute select from data-change statements at cursor open time. This allows applications to keep X locks for a minimum amount of time when using cursors specified as with hold, and committing the transaction right after opening the cursor. The following example shows typical use of cursors for select from data-change statements:

```
declare emp_cur cursor with hold for
  select id from new table
    (insert into emp(name)
     values 'Peter', 'Paul', 'Mary');

open emp_cur;
commit;

fetch emp_cur;
...
```

All X locks are acquired at cursor open time, and immediately released at commit. The application can then fetch the result set without blocking other transactions.

We call the execution at cursor open time *do-at-open* semantics. In order to achieve do-at-open semantics, we need to teach the optimizer to include an additional operator at the top of the generated plan, which is called a zero-key sort operator. A zero-key sort is a specialized sort operator where the set of keys is empty. This concept has several advantages. First, it is an elegant way to drive execution of a statement to completion using an existing, slightly modified operator. Second, we are using existing infrastructure in terms of the sort buffer to efficiently store the result set. Note that a zero-key sort does not actually sort any data, it only indicates that runtime has to drive the execution of the statement to completion.

In the following, we illustrate the do-at-open semantics using two interleaving transactions T1 and T2 in isolation level *uncommitted read*. T1 declares a cursor for a select from insert statement modifying a table emp, T2 reads the content of table emp. T2 can see all the rows inserted by T1 as soon as the cursor is opened.

T1	T2
declare emp_cur cursor for select id from new table (insert into emp(name) values 'Peter', 'Paul', 'Mary');	
	select id from emp; 0 rows selected
open emp_cur;	
	select * from emp; 1 2 3 3 rows selected
fetch emp_cur; 1 fetch emp_cur; 2 ...	

Since our approach for returning modified rows makes use of select statements as the data carrier, no change was needed for the client infrastructure. Regardless of which client is used to perform select from data-change statements, the statement is always considered a select statement, and the APIs can be used respectively. Typically, a cursor containing a select from data-change statement can be declared, and after opening the cursor the modified rows are available in the result set for fetch.

4. Pipelining

The fact that multiple data-change operations can be embedded in a single SQL statement gives the compiler a chance to optimize the data flow between operations. In this section, we describe how performance of multi-table data-change statements can be significantly increased when constructing a plan as a pipeline of insert, update, and delete operations.

In the following example, we introduce two tables emp and mgr used as target for insert operations, and a table src containing some source data for both, employees and managers.

```
create table emp (
    eid    int not null primary key,
    salary int);

create table mgr (
    eid    int not null primary key,
    bonus int);

create table src (
    eid    int not null primary key,
    salary int,
    bonus  int,
    ismgr  char(1));
```

We are now looking for an SQL statement which transfers data from the source table to the two target tables. The first example shows a classic SQL solution with two insert statements, embedded in an atomic compound statement. The plan shows that the two insert statements are executed in sequential order, reading the data from the source table twice.

```
begin atomic
insert into emp select eid,salary from src;
insert into mgr select eid,bonus from src
 where ismgr='Y';
end;
```

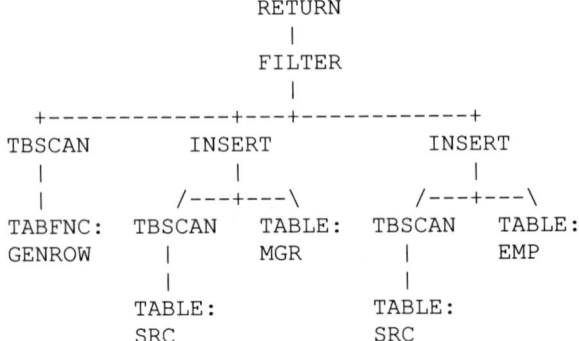

With a common table expression and two nested select from insert operations, the query can be expressed in a way that the result of the first insert operation is used as source for the second one. In the generated plan, the two insert operations are stacked upon each other, which allows pipelining the data flow through both operations.

```
with i1 as (
  select eid,bonus,ismgr
  from new table (
        insert into emp
        include (bonus int, ismgr char(1))
        select eid,salary,bonus,ismgr
        from src))
select count(*) from new table (
  insert into mgr
  select eid,bonus from i1 where ismgr='Y');
```

```
                    RETURN
                      |
                    TBSCAN
                      |
                     SORT
                      |
                    GRPBY
                      |
                    INSERT
                      |
                   /---+---\
              FILTER    TABLE: MGR
                |
              INSERT
                |
             /---+---\
        TBSCAN    TABLE: EMP
          |
      TABLE: SRC
```

With the above approach, the total cost of the query is reduced by 20% and the CPU cost is reduced by 40%, independent of the number of rows in the source table.

The example above has the property that all rows inserted into the mgr table must be inserted into the emp table as well. An insert operator is not able to pass rows not participating in the insert operation to the following operator. Consider a revised example, where the source data is partitioned into employees and manager tables. Rows in the src table are inserted into either emp or mgr table, but not into both.

```
create table emp (
   eid    int not null primary key,
   salary int);

create table mgr (
   eid    int not null primary key,
   salary int,
   bonus  int);
```

In order to solve this problem, we propose an extension of our approach to support the merge statement in the from clause of a select statement. The merge statement is a combination of insert, update, and delete statements, and allows conditional insert, update, and delete operations on a table. We need to extend the merge statement with a set clause, so that rows not participating in any data-change operation can be returned.

The following SQL statement contains nested select from merge and select from insert operations. The merge operation inserts source rows into the emp table where ismgr='N', and includes source rows where ismgr='Y' in the result of the inline view i1. The subsequent insert operation inserts the rows from i1 where ismgr='Y' into the mgr table.

```
with i1 as (
  select eid,salary,bonus from new table (
    merge into emp
    include (bonus int, ismgr char(1))
    using src on (1=0)
    when not matched and ismgr='N' then
      insert (eid,salary)
      values (src.eid,src.salary)
    when not matched and ismgr='Y' then
      set eid      = src.eid,
          salary   = src.salary,
          bonus    = src.bonus,
          ismgr    = src.ismgr)
select count(*) from new table (
  insert into mgr
    select eid,salary,bonus
    from i1 where ismgr='Y')
```

SQL queries such as above are very common in the area of ETL (Extraction, Transformation, Load), for transforming, cleansing and integrating data from operational databases to a data warehouse. With the full support the merge statement in the from clause of a select statement, we are able to provide efficient plans for multi-table insert, update, and delete statements.

5. TPC-C Benchmark

In this section, we describe the impact of the new SQL statement type on the result of the TPC-C benchmark. The TPC-C benchmark [10] represents a typical workload for online transaction processing, based on an order-entry application for a wholesale supplier. The logical database design is composed of 9 relations: Warehouse, District, Customer, Stock, Item, Order, New_Order, Order_Line, and History. A more detailed description of the schema can be found in [7][10].

The application defines five types of short, moderately complex transactions: entering and delivering orders, recording payments, checking the status of orders, and monitoring stock level. Three of these transactions modify data: entering and delivering orders, and recording payments.

In the following sections, we introduce how the three modifying transactions are implemented using classic

SQL statements. We illustrate how we rewrite the statements using the new select from data-change statement type. For better readability, we will use simplified examples out of the three transactions to illustrate the benefit of the new SQL. The complete SQL statements we used for the transactions can be found in the disclosure report [9].

Generally, several assumptions are made for improving performance of OLTP applications. First, the codepath in the database engine for executing transactions should be reduced. Second, network traffic can be reduced through decreasing the number of I/O operations between client and database. Finally, lock contention should be minimized and deadlocks avoided.

New Order Transaction

The New Order transaction places an order for an average 10 items from a warehouse. The following database operations (in a simplified pseudocode) are required: first, the new order ID is retrieved from the District table; for each item, the stock level will be updated; the order is stored in two tables Order and New_Order (containing pending orders), and each item is stored in the table Order_Line. The Stock table is updated 10 times, so in total 17 statements are executed in classic SQL.

1. Select from District
2. Update District
3. Select from Item
4. for each item: Update Stock
5. Insert into Order_Line
6. Insert into Orders
7. Insert into New_Order
8. Select from Warehouse, Customer

Our New Order transaction contains only three SQL statements. The first statement implements the first two operations, select and update the District table. This table contains an ID and an order number, which represents the next order number to be used for a new order in this district. The new order transaction needs to read and increment the next order ID from the DISTRICT table. With classic SQL, two separate statements are required for this task:

```
select d_next_o_id into :new_id
from district
where d_id = :district_id;

update district
set d_next_o_id = d_next_o_id+1
where d_id = :district_id;
```

The approach above has two problems. First, we observe two I/O operations, one for each statement, such that the row in the district table is fetched twice. Second, the fact that we first read the district row and subsequently update the same row, is causing lock conversion. This is a typical scenario for a deadlock, where two transactions concurrently read the same row, and later on attempt to write it, requesting to upgrade a read lock to a write lock [1].

With the new SQL, the scenario can be implemented in one single SQL statement containing a nested update operation. The plan of the statement shows only one table scan for the District table.

```
select d_next_o_id from old table
    (update district
     set d_next_o_id = d_next_o_id+1
     where d_id = :district_id))
```

```
         RETURN
           |
         UPDATE
           |
        /---+--\
    TBSCAN      TABLE:
       |        DISTRICT
    TABLE:
    DISTRICT
```

The second statement implements the operations 3 to 5. A table function is provided which retrieves the price of the item, updates the stock level and inserts a row into the Order_Line table. The following example shows a (simplified) table function, and a select statement referencing the order items and the table function in the from clause.

```
create function new_ol
(i_id int, i_qty int, o_id int, ol_nr int)
returns table (i_price int)
modifies sql data
begin atomic
  declare i_price int;
  set i_price =
    (select i_price from item
     where item.i_id = new_ol.i_id);
  update stock set qty = qty - i_qty
    where s_i_id = new_ol.i_id;
  insert into order_line
    values (o_id, ol_nr, i_id, i_qty,
            (i_price * i_qty));
  return values (i_price * i_qty);
end
```

In the select statement calling the table function, we define a table `ol` containing the new order line items. Then, we join this table with the function `new_ol`, such that every row in `ol` is used as input for `new_ol`. Finally, we return the sum of the total price for each order line.

```
select sum(i_price) into :total_price
from table (values (1, 15, 200),
                   (2, 31, 150),
                   (3, 47, 250))
    as ol(ol_nr, i_id, i_qty),
    table(new_ol(i_id, i_qty, 17, ol_nr))
    as new_ol(i_price);
```

As shown below, the plan of the new SQL statement contains only one update and one insert operation. The subtree below the UNION box represents the table function.

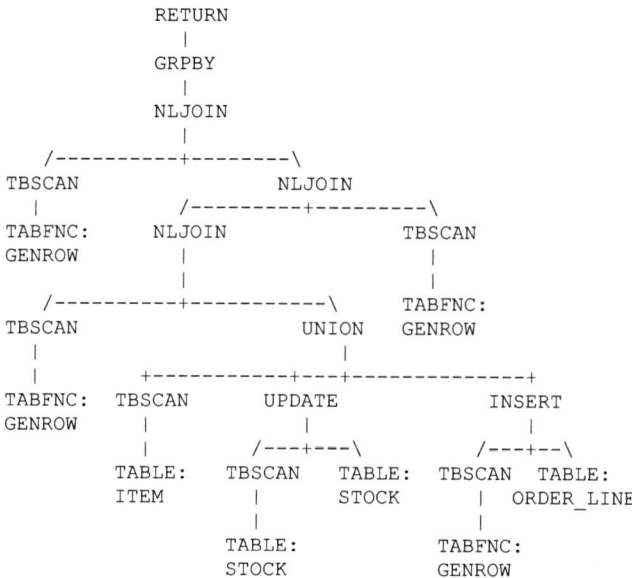

The third statement implements operations 6 to 8 in another table function.

Payment Transaction

The Payment transaction processes a payment for a customer and updates the Warehouse, District and Customer tables. A History table contains the history of payment transactions. Seven statements are executed for the payment transaction in classic SQL.

1. Select from Customer
2. Update Customer
3. Select from District
4. Update District
5. Select from Warehouse
6. Update Warehouse
7. Insert into History

We managed to collapse all 7 operations into one new SQL statement, providing one table function containing a sequence of 4 select from update and insert statements. The benefit is similar to the New Order transaction, avoiding separate select and update statements.

Delivery Transaction

The Delivery transaction processes one order per district. The next order to be processed is identified by the oldest order number in the New_Order table.

1. Select min(order_id) from New_Order
2. Delete from New_Order
3. Update Order
4. Select sum(ol_amount) from Order_Line
5. Update Order_Line
6. Update Customer

The table function we used for the delivery transaction contains one select from delete and three select from update statements. The deletion of a new order shows a select from delete statement with other SQL features like order by and fetch first in subqueries, and fullselect as target of delete statements. In order to deliver a new order, the oldest order of a given district (i.e., the smallest order id), needs to be deleted and returned. All this can be contained in one SQL statement, which we call a *destructive read*. The plan shows that the New_Order table needs to be scanned only once in order to find and delete the oldest order.

```
select no_o_id, ... into :no_o_id, ...
from old table (
    delete from (select * from new_order
                 order by no_o_id
                 fetch first row only));
```

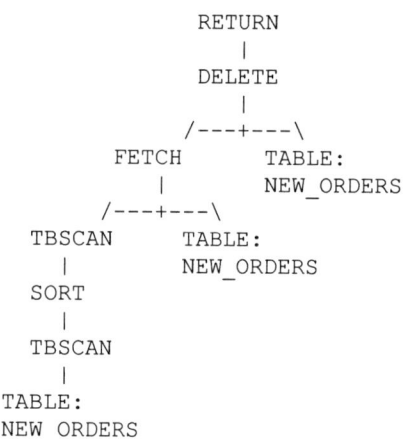

Summary

In our implementation of the TPC-C transactions, all insert, update, and delete operations are embedded in the from clause of a select statement, or in a modifying table function. As a consequence, we have been able to significantly reduce the total number of SQL statements executed for each transaction. In addition, less data has to be bound into and out of the database server. We summarized the result for the three modifying transactions in Fig. 1 and Fig. 2. The first row shows a remote New Order transaction for a remote good customer, the second row shows a Payment transaction for a good customer identified by ID, and the third row shows a Delivery transaction. For the new order transaction we assume 10 order lines associated.

Fig. 1 shows the number of SQL statements that are executed in one transaction for the classic case and for using the new SQL statement type. The last column shows the total codepath reduction of the transaction on the server achieved by having less runtime overhead for executing SQL statements.

	Stmts classic	Stmts new	Codepath reduction
New Order (remote good)	17	3	11%
Payment (by CID)	7	1	16%
Delivery	61	11	3%

Figure 1

Fig. 2 shows the number of rows passed between application and database server. The first two columns denote how many times we bind in rows from client to server for the classic case and for using the new SQL statement type. The last two columns show the same information for rows returned from server to client.

	Bindin classic	Bindin new	Bindout classic	Bindout new
New Order (remote good)	28	4	24	14
Payment (by CID)	8	1	4	1
Delivery	61	11	21	11

Figure 2

6. Related Work

The idea of returning modified rows has already been adopted by the JDBC™ specification and other database vendors. The JDBC 3.0 Specification [6] introduces in chapter 13.6 an interface for retrieving auto-generated columns of insert statements. A method `Statement.getGeneratedKeys()` is provided, which produces a result set containing the generated key values for all inserted rows. The following example inserts a row into an ORDERS table, and returns the generated ORDER_ID value:

```
Statement stmt = conn.createStatement();
int rows = stmt.executeUpdate
          ("INSERT INTO ORDERS " +
           "(ISBN, CUSTOMERID) " +
           "VALUES (966431502, 'SAMP')",
           "ORDER_ID");
ResultSet rs = stmt.getGeneratedKeys();
boolean b = rs.next();
if (b == true) {
    // retrieve the new key value
    ...
}
```

Oracle has introduced a `returning` clause for `insert`, `update` and `delete` statements [8]. The `returning` clause specifies which columns are returned, followed by an `into` clause and a set of host variables in which the values are stored. The approach allows returning more than one row, in which case the host variables need to be declared as arrays. Applications require PL/SQL extensions to access the returned data; they are not returned as a result set to the client. Oracle is using the `returning` clause for `update` and `delete` statements in the Delivery and Payment transactions of the TPC-C benchmark. In contrast to the DB2 approach, an `insert` or `update` statement always returns all modified rows, even if the target is a view with a where clause, and a before trigger modifies a value so that it violates the view predicate. The following is an example of an `insert` with `returning` clause (the bind variables must first be declared).

```
INSERT INTO employees
     (employee_id, last_name, email,
      hire_date, job_id, salary)
  VALUES
  (employees_seq.nextval, 'Doe',
   'john.doe@oracle.com',
    SYSDATE, 'SH_CLERK', 2400)
  RETURNING salary*12, job_id
      INTO :bnd1, :bnd2;
```

7. Conclusions

We have proposed and implemented a clean SQL extension to provide applications a way to return values that have been modified by `insert`, `update`, or `delete` operations. The main contributions of our implementation are as follows.

- We provide a way for applications to find out the value of an automatically generated column when a new value is inserted into a column. Similarly, default values or values changed by a before insert or update trigger can be returned to the application.
- We support `insert`, `update` and `delete` operations embedded in the `from` clause of a `select` statement. For more complex scenarios

996

of data-change operations, modifying table functions can be used.
- The approach is fully embedded in SQL and solves the problem in a set-oriented fashion, using select statements as carrier for returned values, using respective client APIs.
- Common table expressions containing multiple data-change operations provide an efficient way for multi-table `insert`, `update` and `delete` operations using the same source data. The generated plans create a single data flow through all data-change operations, such that source data needs to be read only once.
- Our experiences in the TPC-C benchmark have proven the performance of select from data-change statements. The main reasons are significantly reduced number of SQL statements, generation of better performing plans, less data to be transferred between client and server, and deadlock avoidance.

The idea of returning modified data can be applied to other query languages besides SQL. In particular, the new XQuery language [2] will address update capabilities for XML documents in the future. We expect that update composability and the ability to return updated data will be addressed when designing the language.

References

[1] P. Bernstein and E. Newcomer. *Principles of Transaction Processing*. Morgan Kaufmann, 1997.

[2] Scott Boag, Don Chamberlin, Mary F. Fernandez, Daniela Florescu, Jonathan Robie, Jerome Simeon, and Mugur Stefanescu. XQuery 1.0: An XML Query Language. *World Wide Web Consortium*, Working Draft WD-xquery-2003.

[3] D. Chamberlin. *Using the New DB2*. Morgan Kaufmann, 1996.

[4] R. Cochrane, H. Pirahesh, and N. Mattos. Integrating triggers and declarative constraints in SQL database systems. *In Proc. Inl. Conf. on Very Large Databases*, 1996.

[5] IBM. *DB2 Universal Database$^{(TM)}$ Version 8.1.4*. 2003

[6] John Ellis, Linda Ho, and Maydene Fisher. *JDBC^{TM} 3.0 Specification*, 2001.

[7] Scott T. Leutenegger and Daniel Dias. A Modeling Study of the TPC-C Benchmark. *In Proc. ACM SIGMOD Int. Conf. On Management of Data*, 1993.

[8] Oracle^{TM} Database. *SQL Reference 10g Release 1*.

[9] TPC Benchmark C Full Disclosure Report. *IBM eServer™ pSeries® 690 Model 7040-681 Using AIX® 5L V5.2 and DB2 Universal Database 8.1*, 2004.

[10] Transaction Processing Council. *TPC Benchmark C, Standard Specification*, Rev. 5.2, Dec. 2003.

Trademarks

AIX, DB2, DB2 Universal Database, eServer, IBM, and pSeries are trademarks or registered trademarks of International Business Machines Corporation in the United States, other countries, or both.

Java and all Java-based trademarks are trademarks of Sun Microsystems, Inc. in the United States, other countries, or both.

Linux is a trademark of Linus Torvalds in the United States, other countries, or both.

Windows is a registered trademark of Microsoft Corporation in the United States, other countries, or both.

UNIX is a registered trademark of The Open Group in the United States and other countries.

Other company, product, and service names may be trademarks or service marks of others.

PIVOT and UNPIVOT: Optimization and Execution Strategies in an RDBMS

Conor Cunningham, César A. Galindo-Legaria, Goetz Graefe
Microsoft Corporation
One Microsoft Way
Redmond, WA 98052 USA
{conorc,cesarg,goetzg}@microsoft.com

Abstract

PIVOT and UNPIVOT, two operators on tabular data that exchange rows and columns, enable data transformations useful in data modeling, data analysis, and data presentation. They can quite easily be implemented inside a query processor, much like select, project, and join. Such a design provides opportunities for better performance, both during query optimization and query execution. We discuss query optimization and execution implications of this integrated design and evaluate the performance of this approach using a prototype implementation in Microsoft SQL Server.

1. Introduction

Pivot and Unpivot are complementary data manipulation operators that modify the role of rows and columns in a relational table. Pivot transforms a series of rows into a series of fewer rows with additional columns. Data in one source column is used to determine the new column for a row, and another source column is used as the data for that new column. Unpivot provides the inverse operation, removing a number of columns and creating additional rows that capture the column names and values from the wide form. The wide form can be considered as a matrix of column values, while the narrow form is a natural encoding of a sparse matrix. Figure 1 demonstrates how Pivot and Unpivot can transform data between narrow and wide tables. For certain classes of data, these operators provide powerful capabilities to RDBMS users to structure, manipulate, and report data in useful ways.

Implementations of pivoting functionality already exist for the purpose of data presentation, but these operations are usually performed either outside the RDBMS or as a simple post-processing operation outside of query processing. Microsoft Excel, for example, supports pivoting. Users can perform a traditional SQL query against a data source, import the result into Microsoft Excel, and then perform pivoting operations on the results returned from that data source. Microsoft Access (which uses the Microsoft Jet Database Engine) also provides pivoting functionality. This pivot implementation is a post-processing operation through cursors. While existing implementations are certainly useful, they fail to consider Pivot or Unpivot as first-class RDBMS operations, which is the topic of this paper.

Month	2001	2002	2003
Jan	100	150	300
Feb	110	200	310
Mar	120	250	NULL

Wide Table of Months

Unpivot ↓ ↑ Pivot

Year	Month	Sales
2001	Jan	100
2001	Feb	110
2001	Mar	120
2002	Jan	150
2002	Feb	200
2002	Mar	250
2003	Jan	300
2003	Feb	310

Narrow Table ("SalesTable")

Pivot ↓ ↑ Unpivot

Year	Jan	Feb	Mar
2001	100	110	120
2002	150	200	250
2003	300	310	NULL

Wide Table of Years

Figure 1 Pivot and Unpivot

Permission to copy without fee all or part of this material is granted provided that the copies are not made or distributed for direct commercial advantage, the VLDB copyright notice and the title of the publication and its date appear, and notice is given that copying is by permission of the Very Large Data Base Endowment. To copy otherwise, or to republish, requires a fee and/or special permission from the Endowment
Proceedings of the 30th VLDB Conference,
Toronto, Canada, 2004

Inclusion of Pivot and Unpivot inside the RDBMS enables interesting and useful possibilities for data modeling. Existing modeling techniques must decide both the relationships between tables and the attributes within those tables to persist. The requirement that columns be strongly defined contrasts with the nature of rows, which can be added and removed easily. Pivot and Unpivot, which exchange the role of rows and columns, allow the *a priori* requirement for pre-defined columns to be relaxed. These operators provide a technique to allow rows to become columns dynamically at the time of query compilation and execution. When the set of columns cannot be determined in advance, one common table design scenario employs "property tables", where a table containing (id, propertyname, propertyvalue) is used to store a series of values in rows that would be desirable to represent columns. Users typically use this design to avoid RDBMS implementation restrictions (such as an upper limit for the number of columns in a table or storage overhead associated with many empty columns in a row) or to avoid changing the schema when a new property needs to be added. This design choice has implications on how tables in this form can be used and how well they perform in queries. Property table queries are more difficult to write and maintain, and the complexity of the operation may result in less optimal query execution plans. In general, applications written to handle data stored in property tables can not easily process data in the wide (pivoted) format. Pivot and Unpivot enable property tables to look like regular tables (and vice versa) to a data modeling tool. These operations provide the framework to enable useful extensions to data modeling.

Item Table   Property Table

ItemKey	Item Name
1	2001
2	2002
3	2003

ItemKey	PropName	PropValue
1	Jan	100
1	Feb	110
1	Mar	120
2	Jan	150
2	Feb	200
2	Mar	250

Figure 2 Property Table

Including Pivot and Unpivot explicitly in the query language provides excellent opportunities for query optimization. Properly defined, these operations can be used in arbitrary combinations with existing operations such as filters, joins, and grouping. For example, since Unpivot transposes columns into rows, it is possible to convert a filter (an operation that restricts rows) over unpivot into a projection (an operation that restricts columns) beneath it. Algebraic equivalences between Pivot/Unpivot and existing operators enable consideration of many execution strategies through reordering, with the standard opportunity to improve query performance. Furthermore, new optimization techniques can also be introduced that take advantage of unique properties of these new operators. Consideration of these issues provides powerful techniques for improving existing user scenarios currently performed outside the confines of a query optimizer.

We argue that pivoting operations can be performed more quickly and powerfully inside a RDBMS. By implementing these operations as relational algebra operators within a cost-based optimization framework, superior execution strategies can be considered. This design choice also allows other relational operations to be performed on the results of pivot and unpivot. Considerations of the interactions between pivot/unpivot and other operators yield more efficient orderings of operations over post-processing. The inclusion of these operations within the declarative framework of a SQL statement also allows consideration of additional access paths, such as indexes or materialized views, to more efficiently compute results. Consideration of Pivot and Unpivot within a cost-based optimizer framework provides opportunities for superior performance over existing approaches.

The rest of this paper is organized as follows: Section 2 defines Pivot and Unpivot syntax and semantics as well as useful variations. Algebraic optimizations are covered in Section 3, followed by execution considerations in Section 4. An implementation and evaluation of these operators using Microsoft SQL Server is performed in Section 5. Possible extensions are discussed in Section 6, followed by related work and conclusions.

2. Introducing Pivot and Unpivot

2.1. PIVOT and UNPIVOT in SQL

It is possible to implement pivoting in standard SQL, though the syntax is cumbersome and its performance is generally poor. One method to express pivoting uses scalar subqueries in the projection list. Each pivoted column is created through a separate (but nearly identical) subquery as seen in Figure 3. For database implementations that do not support PIVOT, users could employ this technique to perform pivoting operations. (Note that SalesTable is defined graphically in Figure 1).

```
SELECT
Year,
(SELECT Sales FROM SalesTable AS T2 WHERE Month = 'Jan' AND T2.Year = T1.Year) AS 'Jan'
(SELECT Sales FROM SalesTable AS T2 WHERE Month = 'Feb' AND T2.Year = T1.Year) AS 'Feb'
(SELECT Sales FROM SalesTable AS T2 WHERE Month = 'Mar' AND T2.Year = T1.Year) AS 'Mar'
FROM SalesTable AS T1
GROUP BY Year
```

Figure 3 Possible PIVOT Syntax

Unfortunately, this approach has limitations that restrict the power of pivoting. Each column has repetitive syntax, which is cumbersome as the number of pivoted columns increases. These syntaxes are also potentially harder to optimize. For this syntax, the query optimizer is presented with a number of subqueries, making it more difficult to determine that this whole operation represents a "Pivot" on a single table. In practice, this is not an easy operation, making pivot-specific optimizations very difficult. The common problem is that the *intent* of the query is difficult to infer from the syntax or common relational algebra representation.

Therefore, we propose the following syntax for PIVOT in Figure 4 as an additional option under the <table expression> rule of the ANSI SQL grammar. This syntax is easier to read and better captures the intent of the desired operation. Repetition is eliminated, making queries easier to ready, write, and maintain. Section 3 shows that this approach also enables additional query optimization techniques.

```
SELECT * FROM
(SalesTable PIVOT (Sales for Month IN ('Jan','Feb','Mar'))
```

Figure 4 PIVOT Syntax

PIVOT operates on a table, like other operations, converting from narrow form to wide form. The column 'Sales' in SalesTable provides values for the pivoted columns, while the values of the Month column define the mapping describing in which column the value from Sales belongs. The IN list describes the values of interest from the Month column as well as the names of the new columns to create in PIVOT. The remaining columns from SalesTable, though not listed, implicitly divide the rows of SalesTable into groups. Each group of rows becomes a single output row as a result of PIVOT.

For Unpivot, we propose similar syntax to undo the pivoting operation. The UNPIVOT syntax in Figure 5 contains the same major elements. The set of columns to be removed are listed in the IN list, and the two new columns to create are listed (Sales and Month in this example). While PIVOT collapses similar rows into a single, wider row, UNPIVOT does the opposite. The operation multiplies the number of rows by the number of elements in the IN list while reducing the number of columns.

```
SELECT * FROM
(SalesReport UNPIVOT (Sales for Month IN ('Jan', 'Feb', 'Mar'))
```

Figure 5 UNPIVOT Syntax

2.2. PIVOT and UNPIVOT Semantics

While the conceptual model for PIVOT and UNPIVOT is straightforward, several important details must be further defined to operate well with existing SQL constructs. One problem that must be addressed is how to handle data collisions (two values mapping to the same location). Missing values is the opposite condition, and behavior must also be defined for this case. Finally, the use of PIVOT and UNPIVOT on dynamic (open) schemas must be addressed. Any Pivot and Unpivot definitions must handle these semantic issues.

Data collisions are possible and can be handled in a number of ways. It is possible to error on collisions, though this requires special run-time logic in a query plan to enforce the behavior. It may be useful to pivot data that has duplicate values, and adding a collapsing function (such as an aggregate) enables PIVOT to work in this scenario. In Figure 6, the PIVOT syntax is extended to handle collisions through the SUM() aggregate. Avoidance of collisions is also possible through a special constraint that precludes duplicates from being introduced at all. For example, if the grouping columns and the pivot column (Sales, in this example) together form a unique key, then PIVOT is guaranteed not to have any collisions. Still another strategy could involve nested result sets, where all values are preserved in nested tables in the output of PIVOT. All of these strategies are effective techniques in our implementation to resolve any ambiguity of the PIVOT operation.

```
SELECT * FROM
(SalesTable PIVOT (SUM(Sales) for Month IN ('Jan', 'Feb', 'Mar'))
```

Figure 6 PIVOT Syntax with Aggregation

Missing values as a result of both PIVOT and UNPIVOT is the complimentary condition to data collisions. For PIVOT, it is possible just to use NULL to represent this condition. However, NULLs are also a valid output, leading to the problem of disambiguating which NULLs were introduced by the PIVOT operation. This problem is also seen in operations such as CUBE [4], and can be handled by a special disambiguating function that outputs whether the row was introduced in the operation. Another technique to handle the absence of values exists if a collapsing function (such as an

Let R be the input relation.
Let D be the set of columns from R that define groups.
Let p be a column in R not in D. Its value is the name of the new column to create when pivoting.
Let v be a column in R not in D where p not equal to v.
Let F be a collapsing aggregate function.
R' is a copy of R, with columns D', p', v' corresponding to D, p, and v respectively.
Let X by the set of columns $w_{1..k-1}$ representing the set of pivoted columns.
PIVOT has result columns D plus columns $w_{1..k}$ representing the pivoted values.

Base Case (no pivoted rows):

$$PIVOT(D, v, p \text{ in } \{\}, F) = GroupBy(D)$$

over R = over R

Inductive Case (one or more pivoted value(s) x):

$$PIVOT(D, v, p \text{ in } X + \{x\}, F)$$

over R = LeftOuterJoin($D=D'$) of PIVOT(D, v, p in X, F) over R, and GroupBy(D', $w_i = F(v')$) over $\sigma_{(p' = x)}$

Figure 8 PIVOT Definition

aggregate) is used. In this case, it is possible to treat this as an empty set, returning whatever the empty aggregate result would be. For COUNT(column), this would be zero. UNPIVOT is relatively simple - it transposes the values in columns into their own rows, so no new NULLs are introduced. UNPIVOT can be defined to preserve or eliminate NULL values when generating rows.

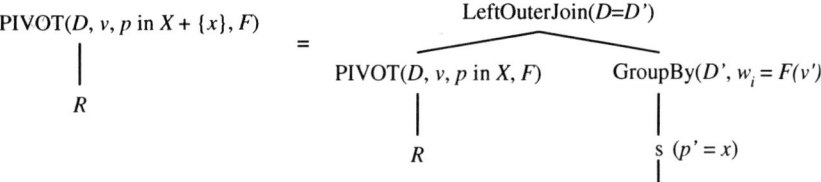

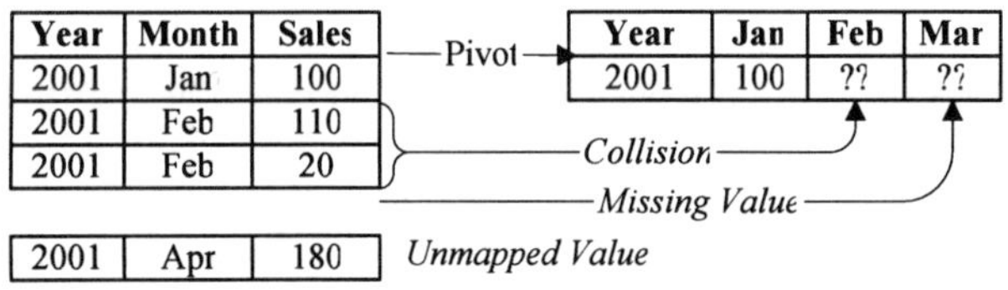

Figure 7 Collisions and Empty Values

PIVOT and UNPIVOT may or may not preserve data, based on how they are defined and used in queries. To fully preserve data, these operations must be defined to avoid collisions and to not introduce empty values (NULLs). Furthermore, "missing" values in the PIVOT IN list are implicitly removed, acting like a projection. PIVOT and UNPIVOT are not inverses if their IN lists do not cover the complete set of data values in the pivot operation, so care is required to preserve data when using PIVOT and UNPIVOT. As a whole, avoiding these restrictions would reduce the flexibility of these operators, so extending PIVOT and UNPIVOT to work on non-invertible data enables broader application to operations beyond inversing data.

While there is no formal database mechanism to enforce that PIVOT and UNPIVOT be used in a data-preserving, invertible fashion, it is possible to get most of this capability through CHECK constraints. By restricting the pivot column to a list of valid values, the query optimizer can infer whether the PIVOT operation is data-preserving if its IN-list matches the constraint. This could be further extended by either limiting PIVOT and UNPIVOT to cases when such constraints exist or through the creation of a stronger class of constraint in the RDBMS.

In the syntax proposed in this paper, the pivot columns are explicitly defined in the query. If PIVOT were to generate output columns at runtime (i.e. late binding), this would introduce problems about how references would be resolved for query operators in a tree. Typically, SQL queries must define the list of columns at compile time to allow the user know the set output columns before running the query. If PIVOT exists below other query operators (as this client syntax allows), it also would cause problems for existing operators that expect a fixed set of columns (i.e. distinct). The actual limitations imposed by this restriction are small, as most database systems support transactions with multiple commands that could be used to build the current list of columns and then pivot on them in separate queries, maintaining the existing strongly bound semantic.

3. Algebraic Optimizations

Queries containing PIVOT and/or UNPIVOT have the opportunity to perform better if interactions with existing operators (filters, projections, join, etc.) are considered. Algebraic rewrites of PIVOT/UNPIVOT and other operators enable cost-based optimizers to consider alternative execution strategies to find more optimal plans. This section covers some basic rewrites related to filters and projections, more complicated transformations converting PIVOT or UNPIVOT into existing operators, using pivoting efficiently in property tables, and the introduction of PIVOT and UNPIVOT into queries that contain neither.

As a note about the terminology used in this section, this paper assumes that duplicates work as in SQL. As a result, Project and Union operations preserve duplicates and are cardinality-preserving. Group By operations are used to distinct values and can also be used to compute aggregate functions.

We formally define PIVOT in Figure 8 by defining PIVOT without any pivoted columns as DISTINCT, and then inductively add pivoted columns to the base definition through a left outer join to calculate the pivoted values.

UNPIVOT is defined using the same variables used in the definition of PIVOT. It is defined as an Apply over the Union of a series of row constructors (one for each column to be unpivoted).

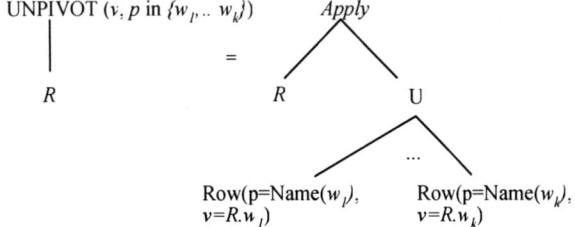

Figure 9 UNPIVOT Definition

3.1. Projections and Filters

Projections and Filters are both restricting operations on different dimensions of relations (one restricts columns, while the other restricts rows). Interestingly, since PIVOT and UNPIVOT exchange rows and columns, this provides an opportunity to transform a projection to and from selections. This section describes different PIVOT/UNPIVOT algebraic rewrites invoking projection and selection.

Projections can be used to simplify PIVOT and avoid unnecessary computation. If a query uses a Project to restrict column(s) introduced by PIVOT, the query can be rewritten to not PIVOT those columns at all. This simplification is possible since each pivoted column is independent from all others.

It might be assumed this class of projection also implies that a filter could be introduced below pivot to restrict the pivot column (Month, in this example) to be limited to 'Jan' or 'Feb'. Unfortunately, this is not true. Semantically, PIVOT produces a row for each group even when input rows exist that do not match the pivot column list. Pushing such a filter would eliminate groups with no pivoted values, and it therefore does not work in the general case. There are situations when filters can be used, and these are described later in this section.

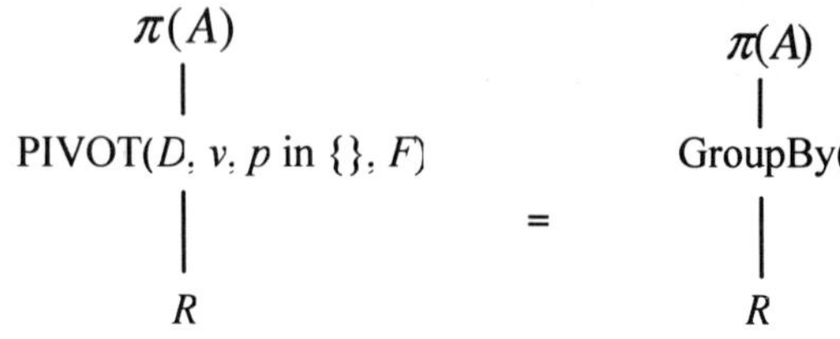

$$\begin{array}{ccc} \pi(A) & & \pi(A) \\ | & & | \\ PIVOT(D, v, p\ in\ \{\}, F) & = & GroupBy(D) \\ | & & | \\ R & & R \end{array}$$

If A is a subset of D (i.e. no pivoted columns)

Figure 10 PIVOT Projection Pushdown Identity

Filters over columns created in PIVOT can be pushed in some cases. If there are guaranteed to be no duplicates (if the grouping columns and the pivot column together comprise a key) and the collapsing function is the identity, it is possible to use the technique described in Figure 11. One scan of the input finds any value matching the filter criteria, and then a join is performed with another instance of the input to gather the remaining columns to complete the PIVOT operation. This technique is most beneficial if indexes are defined that allow efficient searching of these tables.

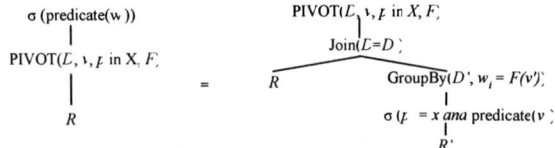

If predicate(w) is NULL-intolerant (i.e. is false or NULL when predicate(w) is NULL), D+{p} is a key of R, and F(v) = v

Figure 11 PIVOT Filter Pushdown

Projections over UNPIVOT are straightforward. Projections limiting grouping columns can be safely applied below the UNPIVOT. A projection removing the value column implies that none of the pivoted columns are actually needed to perform the UNPIVOT. It is still necessary to perform some transformation in this case to generate the correct number of duplicates of each input row to UNPIVOT. However, this transformation could actually performed by UNION ALL instead of UNPIVOT.

Filters interact with UNPIVOT in a similar fashion to how Projects interact with PIVOT. A filter on the columns introduced by UNPIVOT enables a whole column to be removed from the input to UNPIVOT. UNPIVOT does not have the same problem PIVOT faces in preserving groups since it operates on columns. Columns listed for transformation are all transformed, and columns not listed become grouping columns. Thus, data is preserved in all cases and a projection can be safely introduced below the UNPIVOT.

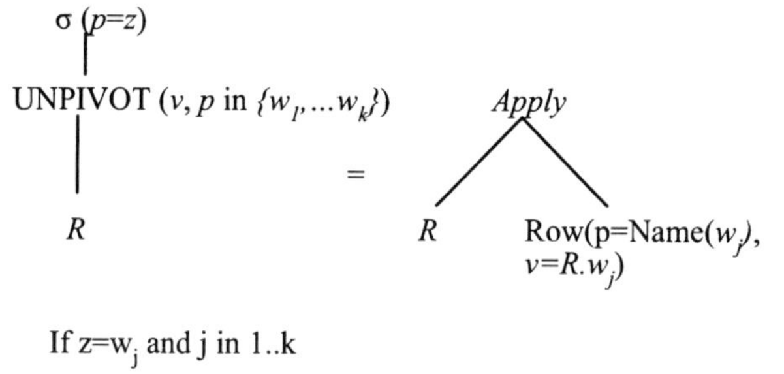

$$\sigma\ (p=z)\ |\ \text{UNPIVOT}\ (v, p\ \text{in}\ \{w_1, ... w_k\})\ |\ R\quad =\quad \text{Apply}\ /\ \backslash\ R\quad \text{Row}(p=\text{Name}(w_j), v=R.w_j)$$

If $z=w_j$ and j in $1..k$

Figure 12 Filters Interact with UNPIVOT

The PIVOT syntax described in Figure 4 contains an IN list describing the set of values used to create new pivoted columns. This limits the set of interesting rows to rows that have a column value in this IN list, as other values would be ignored by PIVOT. While it seems possible to use this IN list to introduce an implied filter under PIVOT, it does not preserve all groups correctly. The following section describes a scenario when an implied filter can be used.

3.2 PIVOT and Property Tables

PIVOT is useful in data modeling because they can hide the physical storage design and provide a consistent "wide" format to the rest of a database. In a typical scenario, two tables are used, storing a list of items in one table and all its properties with their values in the other. In terms of PIVOT, the grouping columns are delivered from one table, while the pivot and value columns are delivered from the other. Property tables contain property name and value columns that represent the sparse matrix of (column, value) pairs of the virtualized table. PIVOT can transform this physical representation into a virtual table containing all the columns (with NULLs in any missing locations). As these tables are typically joined together using a left outer join on a set of key columns (matching the grouping columns in PIVOT), it is possible to perform transformations on this structure to improve plan selection.

While the additional complexity of this design does have some overhead, the overall impact can be minimized through proper plan and index selection. In most cases, creating indexes over the grouping columns on the item table as well as the property and value columns of the property table enable index lookup plans. One observation about query transformations in this design is that pushing projections and filters will not always produce superior plans. Some transformations require additional scans of the input, so they will only be beneficial if the proper indexes exist and predicates are sufficiently selective.

When used against property tables, a projection that removes all pivoted columns can be simplified as in Figure 13. PIVOT becomes a Distinct over the left outer join between the item and property table. However, since no columns are used from the property table, that join can be removed. Furthermore, since the property table design typically has a key over the grouping columns in the item table, the complete pattern can be satisfied with a scan of the item table.

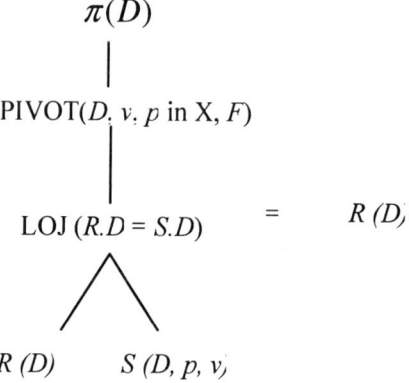

If $D+\{p\}$ is a key of S and D is a key of R

Figure 13 Property Table Projection Reduction

A filter can be implied from the IN-list in PIVOT when used against the property and item tables. Since groups are preserved by the outer join, a filter can be introduced below the join to restrict the property table to only have property names in the set of columns being pivoted. In Figure 13, the grouping columns are delivered by R, while the property table is S. A left outer join between these tables allows all the properties from the groups listed in R to be surfaced above the join. However, it is known that PIVOT will only consume property values (from S) if they are in the IN-list of the

PIVOT. Therefore, properties can be pre-filtered on S before the join.

PIVOT(D, v, p in X, F)   PIVOT(D, v, p in X, F)
        | |
   LOJ (R.D = S.D)   =   LOJ (R.D = S.D)
       / \   / \
   R (D)   S (D, p, v)   R (D)   σ (S.p in X)
                                                    |
                                                 S (D, p, v)

If D+{p} is a key of S and D is a key of R

Figure 14 Implying a Filter from PIVOT

Projections restricting the set of pivoted output columns from PIVOT also can introduce a filter on the property table. Since such a projection is equivalent to not pivoting the extra columns at all, the set of pivoted columns can be reduced, and the introduction of a filter follows from Figure 14.

Filters over PIVOT can be pushed, but only with the introduction of an additional scan of the property table. In Figure 15, a filter on a pivoted column can be rewritten to restrict the item table (R) to only consider items that have qualifying properties. Since this rewrite introduces an additional scan of the property table, this may be appropriate only when certain indexes are defined on the item and property tables.

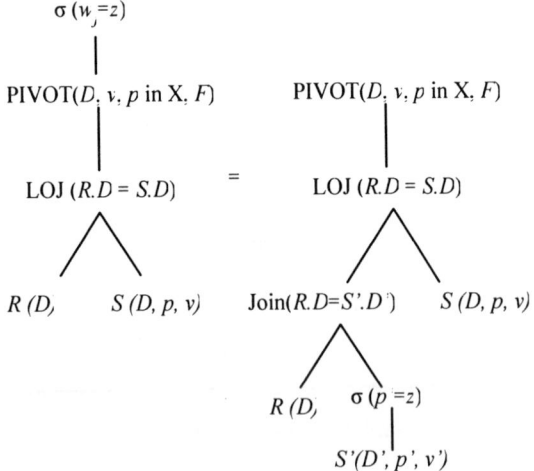

If D+{p} is a key of S, S' is a copy of S, and D is a key of R

Figure 15 Filter Pushdown on Property Tables

3.3 PIVOT as GROUP BY

It is possible to rewrite queries using PIVOT to instead use GROUP BY. Each value in the IN-list uses a copy of the aggregate function listed in the PIVOT definition. Beneath each aggregate, conditional logic is used to pick only the input rows that map to the correct output column. Non-matching rows are changed to NULL instead. Columns not listed in PIVOT become the set of grouping columns for the GROUP BY. The syntax from Figure 6 maps as follows:

MIN(CASE Month WHEN 'Jan' THEN Sales ELSE NULL END) AS 'Jan',
MIN(CASE Month WHEN 'Feb' THEN Sales ELSE NULL END) AS 'Feb',
MIN(CASE Month WHEN 'Mar' THEN Sales ELSE NULL END) AS 'Mar'

PIVOT(D, v, p in X, F)   GroupBy(D', $w_i = F(v')$ i=1..k)
        | = |
        R   R

Figure 16 PIVOT Identity

While the transformation to GROUP BY is straightforward, there are very good reasons to perform this step during the optimization of the query instead of as part of the declarative SQL definition. Queries defined using a series of aggregates in a GROUP BY are typically much harder for optimizers to examine and understand. Using PIVOT, logic is not distributed over a number of aggregate functions and operators with additional non-trivial scalar logic in each. Therefore, it is easier for rule-based optimizers to target with special-purpose transformation logic. Additionally, the syntax suggested in this paper is far simpler than current workarounds using standard SQL.

Mapping PIVOT to GROUP BY requires an assumption that the collapsing (aggregate) function be invariant to additional NULLs. The scalar logic beneath each aggregate substitutes NULL for each row that does not match that pivoted column. Formally speaking, a collapsing function F needs to support the condition that for any set of input values S, F(S) = F(S ∪ {NULL}). Aggregates such as SUM() and MAX() have this property. However, COUNT(*) does not have this property, as it counts each row in its output.

Since PIVOT is a specialization of GROUP BY, RDBMS implementations can leverage this information to easily add PIVOT support without writing new logic throughout every portion of a query processor. Transforming PIVOT into GROUP BY early in query compilation (for example, at or near the start of query optimization or heuristic rewrite) requires relatively few changes on the part of the database implementer. With such an approach, no new execution operators are required, and little new optimization or costing logic is needed. This provides an effective technique to extend existing RDBMS products with little effort.

In addition to implementation simplicity, viewing PIVOT as GROUP BY also yields many interesting optimizations that already apply to GROUP BY. Reusing existing GROUP BY optimization logic can yield an efficient PIVOT implementation without significant changes to existing code. These benefits include:

- Removal of duplicate or grouping columns by other grouping columns, which reduces overall row width
- Filters and semi-joins restricting complete groups can be performed below the GROUP BY.
- Local/Global techniques [7] for pushing grouping optimizations below joins and other operations
- Query logic to perform groupings using parallel threads of execution.

3.4 UNPIVOT as Apply

UNPIVOT can leverage existing implementation code as well. As an operation that takes each row and returns a number of additional rows as output, this is very similar to a correlated join (which we call an *Apply* [1]). If a join is made with a special constant table containing one row for each column to unpivot, then one row for each pivot column will be created in the output. This technique allows database implementations to get good performance characteristics without implementing a full operator in the query processor. While this approach introduces some additional overhead by using multiple iterators, this has not been significant in our implementation. It is not difficult to write a special purpose iterator if needed.

This transformation yields similar performance benefits to implementing PIVOT as GROUP BY. Apply can be reordered easily with other join operators, and it has well-defined interactions with filters, projections, and other query operations. It is also possible to perform these operations in parallel by segmenting the input rows into different groups. None of these problems need to be explicitly considered for UNPIVOT, as they are already solved for the regular join case. This greatly reduces the required implementation effort while still providing excellent performance for the operation.

Figure 9 describes a possible implementation of UNPIVOT using Apply, UNION, and a number of special "Constant Tables". Each UNION branch generates one unpivoted row with two columns. One column contains the name of the original column, and another contains the value associated with that column. The grouping columns are added to this row in the Apply. The Apply needs to be a Left Outer Apply, preserving rows from the input table when the UNPIVOT specifies no matching column names from the relation.

3.5 Join Cardinality Reduction

If PIVOT and UNPIVOT are inverses, a query optimizer can introduce PIVOT and UNPIVOT into a query tree as a technique to reduce cardinality in portions of a query tree around expensive operations, such as joins. If PIVOT can be used to reduce the cardinality of the input in a lossless fashion, joins (or other expensive operations) would be executed far fewer times, followed by an UNPIVOT to expand rows back to their original state. Cost-based optimizers can then pick the cheaper technique for query evaluation. Figure 17 shows an example of this.

The PIVOT and UNPIVOT operations must preserve the rows from the pivoted table as if they were processed by the join to be used in this transformation. Furthermore, if PIVOT uses a collapsing (aggregate) function, then UNPIVOT must be able to invert it in all cases. This could be achieved through nested scalars or other complex data types, invertible aggregate functions, or just avoiding data collisions through constraints on the input relation.

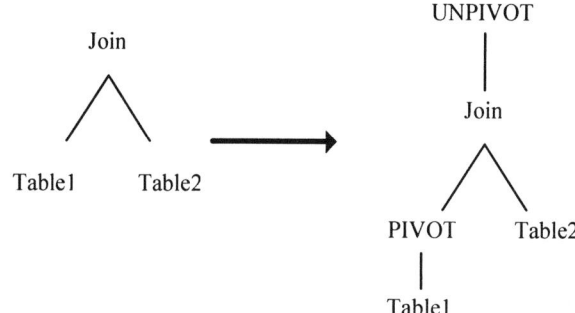

Figure 17 PIVOT-based Join Cardinality Reduction

PIVOT also provides the opportunity to represent a series of scalar subqueries (as seen in Figure 3) in a more semantically useful internal representation. A naive implementation would create a series of subqueries over the same table to compute each column. By converting this series of operations into PIVOT, the poor user representation can be handled with a far fewer number of tables. This allows the database implementer to handle existing work-around queries generated by users before PIVOT existed.

4. Execution Strategies

Defining PIVOT in terms of GROUP BY and Apply provide an excellent opportunity to re-use existing execution operators in new ways. In Section 3.3, we demonstrated that PIVOT can be implemented as GROUP BY. Hash and stream aggregation are available for PIVOT, and have similar execution properties. Parallel query execution can also be supported using these execution strategies as long as the members of each group are processed in the same thread. PIVOT does use a relatively large number of identical aggregates with almost identical scalar logic. One novel execution strategy could group the computation of these aggregates together, either by treating the set of aggregates as a vector computation or by rewriting each individual aggregate computation into a dispatch table (as each column will be looking for a single and likely unique scalar for each input row).

PIVOT can also be implemented through a special-purpose iterator transposing rows into columns. Consuming a sorted (grouping columns and the pivot column) stream, the next row in the current group becomes the source of the value for the next column. If a pivoted column does not have a corresponding row in the input, it returns the empty value for all output columns until the correct location for the current input row is located. Similar to the grouping operators, this technique can be performed simultaneously over values from different groups.

As described in this paper, UNPIVOT can be implemented as a correlated nested loops join (Apply). Each invocation of the Apply can be performed in parallel, leveraging existing parallel techniques available to joins. UNPIVOT can also be implemented using a special purpose execution iterator that consumes one row and returns a number of rows in unpivoted form. Parallelism is slightly easier for UNPIVOT since each input row can be processed independently (instead of groups of rows).

5. Experimentation

We implemented PIVOT and UNPIVOT in Microsoft SQL Server, adding support in the parser and in the query processor for these new operators. The architecture of our query optimizer is based on the Cascades framework [3], which enables defining new relational operators and optimization rules for them. These optimization rules follow from the properties described earlier for PIVOT and UNPIVOT.

In this section we go over a number of scenarios and show the performance obtained in our system. We use the well-known TPCH database, at 1 GB scale, as a basis for our experiments. The experiments were conducted on a dual-processor machine running at 2 Gigahertz, with 1 GB of main memory. We flush data caches before executing queries, so the numbers shown are on a cold cache. Parallel execution is disabled in the results we present, since it does not qualitatively affect our results.

5.1. PIVOT vs. SQL sub-query form

We first compare the performance of our PIVOT operator with that of the equivalent formulation with sub-queries described in Section 2.1. The following query summarizes sales data in the ORDERS table, returning one row per year, and columns for each of the twelve months.

```
SELECT * FROM
(SELECT
    YEAR(O_ORDERDATE),
    MONTH(O_ORDERDATE),
    O_TOTALPRICE
    FROM ORDERS) ORD(YEAR, MONTH, PRICE)
PIVOT (SUM(PRICE)
FOR MONTH IN (1,2,3,4,5,6,7,8,9,10,11,12)) T
```

Figure 18 shows the execution time of the PIVOT query and the equivalent sub-query formulation. For each of the two forms, we change the number of months to PIVOT; only three months of the year, then six months, and finally all twelve months. The performance difference is due to the duplication of work in the sub-query formulation, as each pivoted column is computed separately, because our common sub-expression code does not currently handle this case.

More indices can be used to speed up the computation of the sub-query form, even if the common sub-expression is not detected. Fast lookup of the value from the dimensions columns (e.g. and index on year, month, price in the case above) would make performance comparable to the PIVOT form. However, it remains verbose and repetitive to the application writer.

5.2. Property table access

Earlier, we mentioned the use of PIVOT to support property tables. This allows presenting a view of wide rows to application writers, even if a sparse representation is used to store data internally. For this experiment, we added a property table to store information about the TPCH CUSTOMER table. The property table has the following schema:

CUSTPROPERTY(CP_CUSTKEY, CP_NAME, CP_VALUE)

Columns (CP_CUSTKEY, CP_NAME) make up a key of the property table. A customer property is registered in the database by inserting a new row to CUSTPROPERTY. We also create an index on CP_NAME, CP_VALUE, CP_CUSTKEY, to lookup property values efficiently.

We now create a view that exposes a "wide" customer row, having a column for property in a set of interest. The view uses an outer join to find the registered properties for the set of customers, because we want to retain customers even if no property is defined for them. Say we are only interested in five properties, 'A' through 'E':

```
CREATE VIEW EXTCUSTOMER AS
SELECT *
FROM (
   SELECT *
   FROM CUSTOMER LEFT JOIN CUSTPROPERTY
      ON C_CUSTKEY = CP_CUSTKEY
) CUSTNARROW
   PIVOT (MIN(CP_VALUE)
         FOR CP_NAME IN ('A', 'B', 'C','D','E')
      ) CUSTPIVOTED
```

An application wishing to find customers with a certain property can query the view directly, e.g.

```
SELECT * FROM EXTCUSTOMER
WHERE A IS NOT NULL
```

Figure 19 shows the performance obtained on the abstraction provided by the view. It compares three techniques:

- Store all the information in a single "wide" table that has five columns for the properties above. Have a single-column index of each of the properties.
- Have a separate property table, but do not exploit reordering properties, i.e. execute the view EXTCUSTOMER first and then apply additional operations such as filtering.
- Have a separate property table and enable PIVOT reordering.

To change the selectivity of predicates, we use different distributions for the property values. There are only 10 customers for which property 'A' is defined (i.e. not null in the "wide" row); then there are 100, 1000, 10000, and 100000 customers for which properties 'B' through 'E' are defined, respectively. For this experiment, we scaled up the number of customers from 150,000 to 600,000. Figure 20 shows the execution plan picked for properties 'A' and 'B' in this example, which are both very selective. An index seek is done against the non-clustered index on the CUSTPROPERTY table to determine what customers have this property. Then, another index seek is performed on clustered index of the CUSTOMER table to retrieve all the columns from the base table. Next, an index seek is performed to retrieve the remaining property values for this particular customer. After all the data has been assembled, it is sorted and stream aggregation is used to complete the pivot.

The property table is relatively small compared to the CUSTOMER table, so the performance difference between a separate property table and the "wide" table, when all the data is retrieved, is mostly due to the execution cost of our current PIVOT implementation. When there are predicates, our transformation rules can generate very efficient execution plans that exploit indices to locate qualifying rows quickly, making performance comparable to that obtained if we had a single table.

There is one restriction to point out regarding the benefits that can be obtained through indexing. When modeling directly as a "wide" table, it is possible to create and exploit multi-column indices. A separate property table does not naturally allow setting up such access paths, so the expected behavior is similar to that obtained with single-column indices.

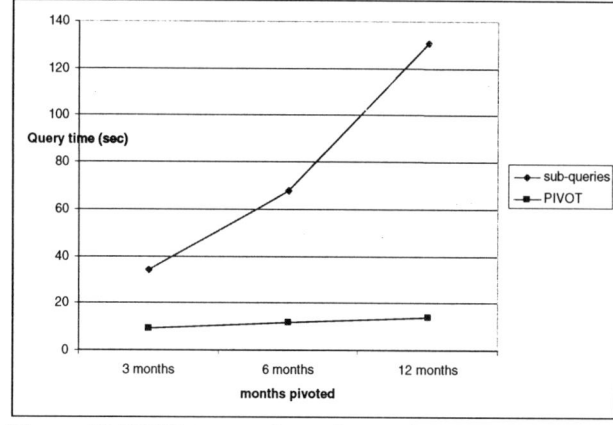

Figure 18 PIVOT vs. scalar sub-queries

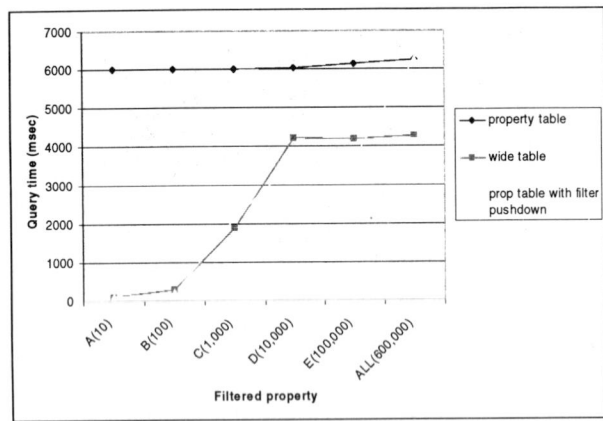

Figure 19 PIVOT Property Table Results

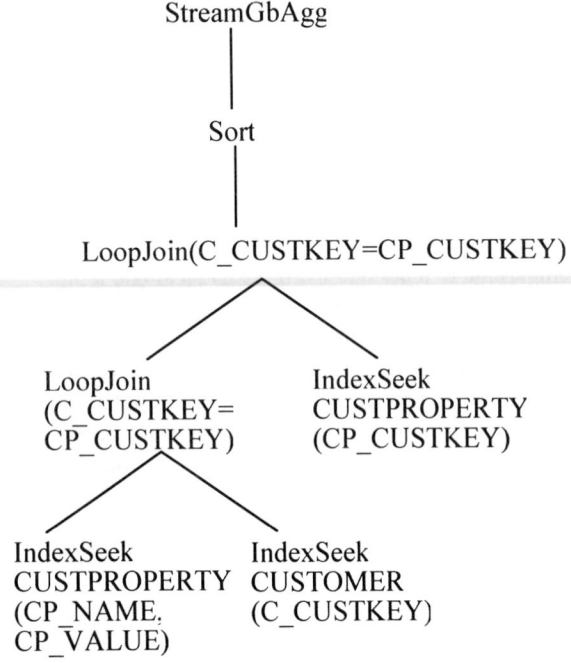

Figure 20 Property Table With Filter Pushdown Plan

6. Extensions

While this paper's PIVOT and UNPIVOT examples show a single value column, it is not difficult to extend this to an arbitrary number of columns. Each value column could be transposed into independent sets of columns in PIVOT, and UNPIVOT can similarly collapse different groups at the same time. Each group could use a different collapsing function (aggregate), and different aggregates could be used over the same column. Alternatively, complex data types could be created to hold multiple values in the same result column for as many values as are desired. None of these extensions

significantly change the possible optimization or implementation techniques presented in this paper.

Extending the collapsing function also increases the utility of these two operators. The collapsing function is described as a single column aggregate function (SUM(), MIN(), etc.). Any RDBMS aggregate function, including user-defined or order-sensitive aggregate functions, could be allowed without affecting the transformations presented in this paper. Even more exotic aggregate functions, such as those that allow multiple input columns and/or produce multiple output columns, also fit nicely with simple extensions to the syntax proposed. Finally, it is possible to consider non-aggregate functions in this context. These could be used to throw an error when a data collision is detected in a cell or to handle data collisions by storing data from multiple rows as a nested relation or some other format that UNPIVOT can reassemble into multiple rows without losing data. These extensions allow a great deal of flexibility beyond traditional aggregation for PIVOT and UNPIVOT.

PIVOT and UNPIVOT are related to OLAP structures such as data cubes. However, OLAP operations do not always fit nicely into the SQL language. If a multi-dimensional structure is accessible through SQL, PIVOT and UNPIVOT could work on a portion of a cube visible as a relation (i.e. a two-dimensional set of rows and columns). Unpivoting a portion of a cube would be analogous to the operations presented for UNPIVOT in this paper.

7. Related Work

The idea behind PIVOT is not new. [4] described a number of extensions to grouping including a "cross-tab" query, though discussion was limited to PIVOT and did not discuss how to efficiently implement it or to expose pivoting below other operators.

SchemaSQL [5] implements transposing operations. The implementation appeared to be outside the RDBMS, however, and there was not significant discussion of query optimization in this context. [6] implements pivoting and unpivoting through unfold and fold operations, respectively. This work also does not attempt to push this capability deeply into the RDBMS.

[8] describes a system to expose spreadsheet-like functionality into a RDBMS, including how queries can be optimized using this approach. This model exposes behavior closer to OLAP than traditional flat relations, though some predicate pushing would be related in these two models.

[8] also describes a model of data n-dimensional array where cells are described through a coordinate system

using names. While similar in capabilities, the paradigm presented to the user differs from traditional SQL operators and may be harder to understand. We feel that our representation is a more natural representation of data rotation in the SQL language.

Both [8] and [4] describe that a relational table is a two-dimensional view of a cube, and this can represent a cross-tabulation of data. However, only [4] discusses how to move between the cross-tabulated and flat (narrow) form of data, and [4] only mentions that this capability exists in Microsoft Access.

Finally, our own prior work [2] exploited the basic design of unpivot operations for a special purpose that would be better served by deep integration into a database query processor.

8. Conclusion

We introduce two new data manipulation operators, Pivot and Unpivot, for use inside the RDBMS. These improve many existing user scenarios and enable several new ones. Furthermore, this paper outlines the basic syntactic, semantic, and implementation issues necessary to add this functionality to an existing RDBMS based on algebraic, cost-based optimization and algebraic data flow execution. Pivot is an extension of Group By with unique restrictions and optimization opportunities, and this makes it very easy to introduce incrementally on top of existing grouping implementations. Finally, we present a number of axioms of algebraic transformations useful in an implementation of Pivot and Unpivot.

8. References

[1] C. A. Galindo-Legaria, M. M. Joshi. Orthogonal Optimization of Subqueries and Aggregation, ACM SIGMOD 2001, May 21-24, 2001, Santa Barbara, California, USA, pages 571-581.

[2] G. Graefe, U. Fayyad, and S. Chaudhuri. On the Efficient Gathering of Sufficient Statistics for Classification from Large SQL Databases, Proceedings of The Fourth International Conference on Knowledge Discovery and Data Mining, 1998, pages 204-208.

[3] G. Graefe. The Cascades Framework for Query Optimization. Data Engineering Bulletin 18 (3) 1995, pages 19-29.

[4] J. Gray, A. Bosworth, A. Layman, H. Pirahesh. Data Cube: A Relational Aggregation Operator Generalizing Group-By, Cross-Tab, and Sub-Totals, Data Mining and Knowledge Discovery, vol. 1, no. 1, 1997.

[5] L. V. S. Lakshmanan, F. Sadri, and S. N. Subramanian. On Efficiently Implementing SchemaSQL on a SQL Database System. In Proceedings of 25th International Conference on Very Large Data Bases, September 7-10, 1999, Edinburgh, Scotland, pages 471-482.

[6] R. Agrawal, A. Somani, Y. Xu. Storage and Querying of E-Commerce Data, In Proceedings of 27th International Conference on Very Large Data Bases, September 11-14, 2001, Roma, Italy, pages 149-158.

[7] M. Jaedicke, B. Mitshcang. On Parallel Processing of Aggregate and Scalar Functions in Object-Relational DBMS. 1998 Proceedings of the ACM SIGMOD International Conference on Management of Data, Seattle, WA, pages 379-389.

[8] A. Witkowski, S. Bellamkonda, T. Bozkaya, G. Dorman, N. Folkert, A. Gupta, L. Shen, S. Subramanian. Spreadsheets in RDBMS for OLAP. 2003 Proceedings of the ACM SIGMOD International Conference on Management of Data, San Diego, CA, pages 52-63.

A Multi-Purpose Implementation of Mandatory Access Control in Relational Database Management Systems

Walid Rjaibi   Paul Bird

IBM Toronto Software Laboratory
8200 Warden Avenue
Markham, Ontario
Canada
{wrjaibi, pbird}@ca.ibm.com

Abstract

Mandatory Access Control (MAC) implementations in Relational Database Management Systems (RDBMS) have focused solely on Multilevel Security (MLS). MLS has posed a number of challenging problems to the database research community, and there has been an abundance of research work to address those problems. Unfortunately, the use of MLS RDBMS has been restricted to a few government organizations where MLS is of paramount importance such as the intelligence community and the Department of Defense. The implication of this is that the investment of building an MLS RDBMS cannot be leveraged to serve the needs of application domains where there is a desire to control access to objects based on the label associated with that object and the label associated with the subject accessing that object, but where the label access rules and the label structure do not necessarily match the MLS two security rules and the MLS label structure. This paper introduces a flexible and generic implementation of MAC in RDBMS that can be used to address the requirements from a variety of application domains, as well as to allow an RDBMS to efficiently take part in an end-to-end MAC enterprise solution. The paper also discusses the extensions made to the SQL compiler component of an RDBMS to incorporate the label access rules in the access plan it generates for an SQL query, and to prevent unauthorized leakage of data that could occur as a result of traditional optimization techniques performed by SQL compilers.

1 Introduction

Mandatory Access Control (MAC) is a means of restricting access to objects based on the sensitivity (as represented by a label) of the information contained in the objects and the formal authorization (i.e., clearance) of subjects to access information of such sensitivity[8]. A well-known implementation of MAC is Multilevel Security (MLS), which, traditionally, has been available mainly on computer and software systems deployed at highly sensitive government organizations such as the intelligence community or the U.S. Department of Defense. The Basic model of MLS was first introduced by Bell and LaPadula[9]. The model is stated in terms of objects and subjects. An object is a passive entity such as a data file, a record, or a field within a record. A subject is an active process that can request access to objects. Every object is assigned a classification, and every subject a clearance. Classifications and clearances are collectively referred to as labels. A label is a piece of information that consists of two components: A hierarchical component and a set of unordered compartments. The hierarchical component specifies the sensitivity of the data. For example, a military organization might define levels Top Secret, Secret, Confidential and Unclassified. The compartments component is nonhierarchical. Compartments are used to identify areas that describe the sensitivity or category of the labeled data. For example, a military organization might define compartments NATO, Nuclear and Army. Labels are partially ordered in a lattice as follows: Given two labels L_1 and L_2, $L_1 >= L_2$ if and only if the hierarchical component of L_1 is greater than or equal to that of L_2, and the

---

Permission to copy without fee all or part of this material is granted provided that the copies are not made or distributed for direct commercial advantage, the VLDB copyright notice and the title of the publication and its date appear, and notice is given that copying is by permission of the Very Large Data Base Endowment. To copy otherwise, or to republish, requires a fee and/or special permission from the Endowment.

**Proceedings of the 30th VLDB Conference,
Toronto, Canada, 2004**

compartment component of L1 includes the compartment component of L_2. L_1 is said to *dominate* L_2. MLS imposes the following two restrictions on all data accesses:

- The Simple Security Property or "No Read Up": A subject is allowed a read access to an object if and only if the subject's label dominates the object's label.

- The *-Property (pronounced the star property) or "No Write Down": A subject is allowed a write access to an object if and only if the object's label dominates the subject's label.

1.1 Problem Statement

MAC implementations in Relational Database Management Systems (RDBMS) have focused solely on MLS. MLS has posed a number of challenging problems to the database research community, and there has been an abundance of research work to address those problems. There has also been three commercial MLS RDBMS offerings, namely, Trusted Oracle[16], Informix OnLine/Secure[17], and Sybase Secure SQL Server[20]. Unfortunately, the use of MLS RDBMS has been restricted to a few government organizations where MLS is of paramount importance such as the intelligence community and the Department of Defense. In fact, very few commercial organizations need such type of security. The implication of this is that the investment of building an MLS RDBMS cannot be leveraged to serve the needs of application domains where there is a desire to control access to objects based on the label associated with that object and the label associated with the subject accessing that object, but where the label access rules and the label structure do not necessarily match the MLS two security rules and the MLS label structure (*i.e.*, a hierarchical component and a set of unordered compartments). The question that begs to be asked is therefore the following: Do such application domains exist and, if so, what are they?

We contend that the answer to that question is an unequivocal yes. Privacy[19] is one example of such application domain. Generally, a privacy policy indicates for which purposes an information is collected, whether or not it will be communicated to others, and for how long that information is retained before it is discarded. For example, a user cannot access a customer record for the purpose of sending that customer marketing information if that customer did not agree to receive such information. Access to privacy-sensitive data can be regarded as analogous to access to MLS data in the sense that in both cases there is a tag associated with the object being accessed and the subject accessing that object. The tag represents a "purpose" in the case of the former and represents a "security label" in the case of the latter. Unfortunately, a MAC implementation in an RDBMS that strictly implements MLS fails to address privacy requirements for the following two main reasons. First, MLS labels include a hierarchical component that is not applicable in the case of privacy. Next, the MLS security properties do not apply in the context of privacy. For example, to read an object in MLS, the subject's compartment component must include that object's compartment component (the simple security property). In privacy, the rule is exactly the opposite. That is, if an object is tagged with the purposes *marketing* and *purchase*, then a user accessing that object for the purpose of sending marketing information must be allowed to access that object.

Another application domain is private banking. In private banking, country laws and regulations often require to limit the amount of data that can be viewed by a bank employee. For example, Swiss banking laws do not allow a Swiss bank employee located in Toronto to access account information for customers based in Switzerland. Typically, banking applications code this fine-grained access control in the application itself, as opposed to delegating this task to the RDBMS. Unfortunately, this *application-aware* approach has made enterprise security policies a laborious and complex task. It also has the drawback of exposing the security policies to the application programmers. If each customer account is tagged with a label indicating the geographical location of the customer and if each bank employee can be assigned a label that also indicates the geographical location of that employee (for example, based on the system security context established when that employee logs on to the database), then an RDBMS that implements a form of MAC where the database administrator could define the label structure and the label access rules could relieve the applications from implementing such fine-grained access control policies.

Moreover, the ever increasing enterprise demands for more security has led to the emergence of label security products that provide the ability to set up and control access based upon labels throughout an entire network from end-to-end. For example, such label security products have the ability to control the network to decide whether or not a particular labeled data row can be transmitted on a particular channel or be delivered to a particular workstation on that network. An important advantage of such label security products is their ability to offer a centrally managed tool for defining label access policies and for assigning access labels to users as well as to other entities on the network. Traditional implementations of MAC in RDBMS (*i.e.*, MLS) do not offer the required flexibility to efficiently integrate with such label security products and to provide pervasive system coverage using a unified and centrally managed label access policy.

Therefore, there is a need for a flexible and generic implementation of MAC in RDBMS that can be used to address the requirements from a variety of application domains, including those of MLS, and to efficiently take part in an end-to-end MAC enterprise solution.

1.2 Contributions

The contributions made in this paper can be summarized as follows:

1. A methodology to define labels and to set up a database table such that access to a row in that table is based upon the label associated with that row and the label associated with the user accessing that row. More specifically, the methodology introduces a number of extensions to SQL that would allow a database administrator to:

   - Define label types
   - Define label access rules and exceptions to them
   - Assign labels and exceptions to database users
   - Attach a label type and a set of label access rules to a database table

2. Extensions to the SQL compiler component of an RDBMS to:

   - Incorporate the label access rules in the access plan it generates for an SQL query
   - Prevent unauthorized leakage of data that could occur as a result of traditional optimization techniques performed by SQL compilers

3. Extensions to the runtime processor component of an RDBMS to enforce label access rules

4. A method to allow an RDBMS to efficiently take part in an end-to-end MAC enterprise solution

1.3 Synopsis

Section 2 gives a brief survey of MAC implementations in RDBMS. Section 3 introduces our methodology for defining labels and for setting up a database table such that access to a row in that table is based upon the label associated with that row and the label associated with the user accessing that row. Section 4 presents our extensions to the SQL compiler component of an RDBMS to incorporate the label access rules in the access plan it generates for an SQL query, and to prevent unauthorized leakage of data that could occur as a result of traditional optimization techniques performed by SQL compilers. Section 5 describes our extensions to the methodology introduced in section 3 in order to allow an RDBMS to efficiently take part in an end-to-end MAC enterprise solution. Lastly, section 6 summarizes our results and discusses future work.

2 Related Work

MAC implementations in Relational Database Management Systems have focused solely on MLS, which is of paramount importance to a few government organizations such as the intelligence community or the Department of Defense. In fact, there has been an abundance of research within the last two decades or so in the area of multilevel secure relational databases. The results of such research can be divided into three broad areas as follows.

2.1 Multilevel Secure Relational Database Models

The Sea View model[1] was the pioneering formal multilevel secure relational database designed to provide mandatory access control. It extended the concept of a database relation to include the security labels. A relation that is extended with the security labels is called a multilevel relation. The Sea View model also coined the concept of *polyinstantiation*, which refers to the simultaneous existence of multiple tuples with the same primary key, where such tuples are distinguished by their security labels. In order to avoid covert channels, subjects with different security labels are allowed to operate on the same database relation through the use of polyinstantiation[1]. The Jajodia-Sandhu model[2] was derived from the Sea View model. It was shown in [3] that the Sea View model can result in the proliferation of tuples on updates and the Jajodia-Sandhu model addresses this drawback. The Smith-Winslett model[4] was the first model to extensively address the semantics of an MLS database. The MLR model[5] is based on the Jajodia-Sandhu model, and also integrates the belief-based semantics of the Smith-Winslett model. It was shown in [7] that all the aforementioned models can present users with some information that is difficult to interpret. The BCMLS model[6] addresses those concerns by including the semantics of an unambiguous interpretation of all data presented to the users.

2.2 Multilevel Secure RDBMS Architectures

Multilevel secure RDBMS architectures schemes can be divided into two general categories: The Trusted Subject architecture and the Woods Hole architectures.

The Trusted Subject architecture[10] is a scheme that contains a trusted RDBMS and a trusted operating system. The RDBMS is custom-developed to include all the required security rules, but uses the associated trusted operating system to make actual disk data accesses. A benefit of this scheme is that the

RDBMS has access to all levels of data at the same time, which minimizes retrieval and update processing. However, this scheme results in a special purpose RDBMS that requires a large amount of trusted code to be developed and verified along with the normal RDBMS features.

The Woods Hole architectures assume that an untrusted off-the-shelf RDBMS is used to access data and that trusted code is developed around that RDBMS to provide an overall secure RDBMS. They can be divided into two main categories: The kernelized architectures and the distributed architectures[10, 11].

The kernelized architecture scheme uses a trusted operating system and multiple copies of the RDBMS, where each copy is associated with some trusted front-end. Each pair (trusted front-end, RDBMS) is associated with a particular security level. The trusted operating system ensures that data at different security levels is stored separately, and that each copy of the RDBMS gets access to data that is authorized for its associated security level. A benefit of this scheme is that data at different security levels is isolated in the database, which allows for higher level assurance. However, this scheme results in an additional overhead as the trusted operating system needs to separate data at different security levels when it is added to the database and might also need to combine data from different security levels when data is retrieved by an RDBMS copy that is associated with a high security level.

The distributed architecture scheme uses multiple copies of the trusted front-end and RDBMS, each associated with its own database storage. In this architecture scheme, an RDBMS at security level l contains a replica of every data item that a subject at level l can access. Thus, when data is retrieved, the RDBMS retrieves it only from its own database. Another benefit of this architecture is that data is physically separated into separate hardware databases. However, this scheme results in an additional overhead when data is updated as the various replicas need to be kept in sync.

2.3 Multilevel Secure Transaction Processing

Although the two MLS security properties described above prevent direct legal flow of information from a security level to another nondominated security level, they are not sufficient to ensure that security is not compromised since it could be possible for leakage of information to occur through indirect means via covert channels. A covert channel can easily be established with conventional concurrency control algorithms such as two-phase locking (2PL) and timestamp ordering (TO). In both 2PL and TO algorithms, whenever there is contention for the same data item by transactions executing at different security levels, a lower level transaction may be either delayed or suspended to ensure correct execution. In such a scenario, two colluding transactions executing at high and low security levels can establish an information flow channel from a high security level to a low security level by accessing the selected data item according to some agreed-upon code[12].

Considerable effort has been devoted to the development of efficient, secure algorithms for the major schemes of RDBMS architectures described above. In [13], Keefe *et al.* present a formal framework for secure concurrency control in multilevel databases. Lamport[14] offers solutions to the secure readers/writers problem. While these solutions are secure, they do not yield serializable schedules when applied to transactions, and they suffer from the problem of starvation, *i.e.*, transactions that are reading data items at a low security level may be delayed indefinitely[18]. In [15], Ammann and Jajodia offer two timestamp-based algorithms that yield serializable schedules, but both suffer from starvation. On the commercial secure RDBMS side, both Trusted Oracle RDBMS[16] and Informix OnLine/Secure RDBMS[17] offer concurrency control solutions that are free from covert channels.

3 Methodology for Setting up MAC in an RDBMS

The methodology we propose allows a database administrator to define labels and to set up a database table such that access to a row in that table is based upon the label associated with that row and the label associated with the user accessing that row. More specifically, the methodology allows the database administrator to:

- Define label types
- Define label access rules and exceptions to them
- Assign labels and exceptions to database users
- Attach a label type and a set of label access rules to a database table

We now introduce our extensions to SQL to implement this methodology. The goal of this exercise is not to describe the blueprint for the implementation. Rather, we will focus on the new SQL concepts that must be implemented to support such methodology. Also, we have chosen not to overload the paper with the details of the exact syntax of the SQL extensions proposed, as we believe that such level of details is more appropriate for a standardization proposal to the SQL standard committee. However, we will illustrate the syntax and the concepts introduced via examples.

3.1 Label Component

A label component is a database entity that can be created, altered and dropped. It is introduced as a building block for labels (*i.e.*, a label is composed of one or more label components). The label component definition specifies the set of valid elements for that label component. This set of elements can be either ordered or unordered (the default). In an ordered set, the order in which the elements appear is important: The rank of the first element is higher than the rank of the second element, the rank of the second element is higher than the rank of the third element, and so on. To allow database administrators to create, alter and drop label components, we introduce the CREATE, ALTER and DROP label component SQL statements. The CREATE LABEL COMPONENT SQL statement creates a label component that can be used to define a label type. The ALTER LABEL COMPONENT SQL statement permits to add or drop an element to/from a label component. The DROP LABEL COMPONENT SQL statement drops a label component.

Example 1

The following SQL statement creates a label component called level and specifies the set of valid values for this label component.

    CREATE LABEL COMPONENT level
    OF TYPE varchar(15)
    USING ORDERED SET
    {"TOP SECRET", "SECRET", "CLASSIFIED"}

The following SQL statement creates a label component called compartments and specifies the set of valid values for this label component. Note that the set specified is unordered.

    CREATE LABEL COMPONENT
    compartments OF TYPE varchar(15)
    USING SET
    {"NATO", "NUCLEAR", "ARMY"}

The following SQL statement adds a new element to the level component and specifies the rank of this new element within the ordered set.

    ALTER LABEL COMPONENT level
    ADD ELEMENT "UNCLASSIFIED"
    AFTER "CLASSIFIED"

The following SQL statement drops the level component.

    DROP LABEL COMPONENT level

3.2 Label Type

The relationship between a label and a label type is analogous to the relationship between a data row and a table schema. As the table schema defines the set of columns that make up a data row, so the label type defines the set of label components that make up a label. To allow database administrators to create, alter and drop label types, we introduce the CREATE, ALTER and DROP label type SQL statements. The CREATE LABEL TYPE creates a label type by specifying the label components that make up such label type. The ALTER LABEL TYPE alters the definition of a label type by adding or dropping a label component to/from that label type. The DROP LABEL TYPE SQL statement drops a label type.

Example 2

The following SQL statement creates a label type called MLS and specifies its label components. Note the keyword MULTIVALUED next to the compartments component. This indicates that the compartments component can have more than a single value at a time. This keyword can only be specified for label components based on an unordered set (section 3.4 explains the reason behind this choice).

    CREATE LABEL TYPE MLS
    COMPONENTS level,
    compartments MULTIVALUED

The following SQL statement drops the level component from label type MLS.

    ALTER LABEL TYPE MLS DROP level

The following SQL statement drops the MLS label type.

    DROP LABEL TYPE MLS

3.3 Access Labels and Row Labels

We distinguish two types of labels: *Access labels* and *row labels*. Access labels are created and assigned to database users, which, in conjunction with the label access rules (section 3.4), determine which labeled rows these users have access to. To allow database administrators to create, drop, grant and revoke access labels, we introduce the CREATE, DROP, GRANT and REVOKE access label SQL statements. The CREATE ACCESS LABEL SQL statement creates an access label based on an existing label type. The GRANT ACCESS LABEL SQL statement grants an access label to a database user. The REVOKE ACCESS LABEL SQL statement revokes an access label from a database user. The DROP ACCESS LABEL SQL statement drops an access label and revokes it from any database user to whom it has been granted.

Example 3

The following SQL statement creates an access label.

    CREATE ACCESS LABEL L_1
    OF LABEL TYPE MLS
    level "SECRET", compartments "NATO"

The following SQL statement grants access label L_1 to database user Joe.

    GRANT ACCESS LABEL L_1
    TO USER Joe

The following SQL statement revokes access label L_1 from database user Joe.

    REVOKE ACCESS LABEL L_1
    FROM USER Joe

The following SQL statement drops access label L_1.

    DROP ACCESS LABEL L_1

A row label labels a data row in a database table. To allow database users to provide a row label when inserting or updating a row in a database table, we introduce the ROWLABEL function. ROWLABEL is a means of providing the label value of a data row.

Example 4

The following INSERT SQL statement shows how the row label can be provided using the ROWLABEL function. The statement inserts a row into a database table called T1 having two columns A and B both of type integer. We assume that rows in table T1 are labeled with a label of label type MLS defined above.

    INSERT INTO T1 VALUES
    (ROWLABEL("SECRET", "NATO"), 1, 2)

The following SQL statement shows how the ROWLABEL function can be used to update the level component of the row label for the row inserted above.

    UPDATE T1 SET
    ROWLABEL(level) = "TOP SECRET"
    WHERE A = 1 AND B = 2

3.4 Label Access Policy

A label access policy defines the label access rules that the RDBMS evaluates to determine whether or not a database user is allowed access to a labeled data row in a database table. Access rules can be divided into two categories: Read access rules and write access rules. Read access rules are applied by the RDBMS when a user attempts to read a labeled data row (e.g., a SELECT statement). The RDBMS applies the write access rules when a user attempts to insert, update or delete a labeled data row. In both cases, an access rule is a predicate that puts together the same component from an access label and a row label and an operator as follows:

    Access Label *component-name*
    <operator>
    Row Label *component-name*

The type of operator allowed depends on the label component. For label components based on an ordered set, the operator can be any of the relational operators $\{=, <=, <, >, >=, !=\}$. For label components based on an unordered set, the operator must be one of the set operators {IN, INTERSECT}. Recall from section 3.2 that a label component based on an unordered set can be multivalued. That is, it can contain more than a single value at a time. Thus, when comparing multivalued label components we are actually comparing data sets. This is the reason why the operators supported are set operators, *i.e.*, inclusion and intersection. Obviously, certain RDBMS could choose to support additional operators but we contend that the ones given above would be the most commonly used. To allow database administrators to create, alter and drop label policies, we introduce the CREATE, ALTER and DROP label policy SQL statements. The CREATE LABEL POLICY SQL statement creates a label access policy for a given label type by specifying one or more read access rules and one or more write access rules. The ALTER LABEL POLICY SQL statement permits the addition or dropping an access rule to/from a label access policy. The DROP LABEL SQL statement drops a label access policy.

Example 5

The following SQL statement creates a label access policy that implements the two MLS properties introduced in section 1 above (*i.e.*, "No Read Up" and "No Write Down").

    CREATE LABEL POLICY mls-policy
    LABEL TYPE MLS
    READ ACCESS RULE rule1
        ACCESS LABEL level >= ROW LABEL level
    READ ACCESS RULE rule2
        ROW LABEL compartments IN
        ACCESS LABEL compartments
    WRITE ACCESS RULE rule1
        ACCESS LABEL level <= ROW LABEL level

WRITE ACCESS RULE rule2
ACCESS LABEL compartments IN
ROW LABEL compartments

The following SQL statement drops read access rule rule2 from label access policy mls-policy.

ALTER LABEL POLICY mls-policy
DROP READ ACCESS RULE rule2

The following SQL statement drops label access policy mls-policy.

DROP LABEL POLICY mls-policy

3.5 Exceptions

Exceptions are introduced to provide the flexibility for some database users to bypass one or more access rules. For example, in an MLS context, it is often the case that some special users are allowed to write information to lower security levels even though this is in contradiction with the *-security property. Thus, exceptions are introduced to allow the database administrator to grant a database user an exception to bypass one or more access rules in a particular label access policy. To allow database administrators to grant and revoke exceptions, we introduce the GRANT and REVOKE exception SQL statements. The GRANT EXCEPTION SQL statement grants a database user an exception to bypass one or more access rules in a label access policy. The REVOKE EXCEPTION SQL statement revokes a previously granted exception from a database user.

Example 6

The following SQL statement grants an exception to database user Joe so that he can bypass the write access rules in label access policy mls-policy.

GRANT EXCEPTION
ON WRITE ACCESS RULE rule1, rule2
FROM LABEL POLICY mls-policy
TO USER Joe

The following SQL statement revokes the above exception from user Joe.

REVOKE EXCEPTION
ON WRITE ACCESS RULE rule1, rule2
FROM LABEL POLICY mls-policy
FROM USER Joe

3.6 Labeled Tables

A labeled table is a database table that contains labeled data rows. When the database administrator creates a labeled table he/she specifies the label type and the label access policy to be used for that table. The label type determines the structure of the label to be used to label the table's data rows and the label access policy determines the access rules to be used for enforcing access to that labeled table. To allow database administrators to create labeled tables, we extend the CREATE TABLE SQL statement by a new optional clause to specify the label type and the label access policy.

Example 7

The following SQL statement creates a database table T1 and specifies the label type and the label access policy. Note that in our examples so far we have used MLS-like label types and label access policies because they are well understood by the database research community. But it is obvious that one can follow the methodology given in this paper to define any label type and any label access policy, and attach them to a database table.

CREATE TABLE T1 (A integer, B integer)
LABEL TYPE MLS
LABEL POLICY mls-policy

When creating such table, the RDBMS internally adds a third column to store the label associated with each row in this table. The choice of the column's type depends on the label type. For example, if the label type is made up of a single component of type, say varchar(15), then the column's type would be varchar(15). If the label type is made up of more than a single column then the column's type must be an Abstract Data Type (ADT). ADTs have been introduced in SQL'99[21] and are supported by most commercial RDBMS. Alternatively, the RDBMS could choose not use an ADT and store the different label components in separate columns.

4 Extensions to the SQL Compiler Component in an RDBMS

When a labeled table is accessed, the RDBMS needs to enforce two levels of access control. The first level is the traditional Discretionary Access Control (DAC) which is implemented by all commercial RDBMS[21]. That is, the RDBMS verifies whether the user attempting to access the table has been granted the required privilege to perform the requested operation on that table. A discussion of this level of access control is beyond the scope of this paper. The second level is MAC. That is, for each data row accessed, the RDBMS verifies whether the user is allowed access to that row based on the label associated with the row and the user's access label.

4.1 Enforcing MAC on Labeled Tables

There are two possible ways that MAC can be enforced when a labeled table is accessed. The first possibility is for the SQL compiler to modify any query that refers to a labeled table in order to incorporate the access rules from the label access policy associated with that table in the form of regular predicates. Next, the SQL compiler compiles the modified query and generates an access plan for the query in the normal fashion. The main advantage of such an approach is its simplicity. However, it has a major drawback: The access plan generated for a query that refers to a labeled table cannot be reused by other users because it is dependent on the access label of the user who issued the query. Note that some commercial RDBMS cache the access plan generated for an SQL query so that it can be reused the next time the SQL query is submitted. This has some performance benefits as it eliminates the need to recompile the query. Another drawback of this approach is that it could result in unauthorized leakage of data if special care is not taken by the SQL compiler. This will be detailed further in section 4.2.

The second possibility is to not modify a query that refers to a labeled table. Rather, the SQL compiler inserts logic into the access plan that implements the access rules from the label access policy associated with any labeled table referred to in the query. Thus, when the access plan is executed, the access rules from the label access policy associated with a labeled table are evaluated for each data row when that labeled table is accessed. The general processing algorithm to be inserted in the access plan for a labeled table is as follows.

Begin
    Fetch the user's access label (e.g., from a
    system catalog table)
    if (SELECT access)
    {
      for each row accessed
      {
        if (read access rules do not permit access)
        {
          Skip row
        }
      }
    }
    else
    {
      // INSERT, UPDATE, or DELETE access
      for each row
      {
        if (INSERT or UPDATE)
        {
          if (the row label provided is not valid with
          respect to the label type associated with
          the labeled table)
            Reject INSERT or UPDATE
        }
        if (write access rules do not permit access)
          Reject INSERT, UPDATE or DELETE
      }
    }
End

This second approach addresses the two shortcomings of the previous approach (i.e., query modification). That is, it allows the cached access plan to be reused because the access label of the user who issued the query is acquired at runtime, and it is more secure as it will be demonstrated in section 4.2.

4.2 Predicates Evaluation Sequence

SQL compilers have traditionally been guided by performance reasons in selecting the order in which the predicates contained in a query are evaluated. For example, more selective predicates are often evaluated first to narrow down the set of rows to be passed on to a subsequent join because join operations are costly. If the method chosen to enforce MAC on a labeled table is based on query modification to incorporate the access rules in the form of regular predicates, then special care must be taken in selecting the order in which the predicates on that table are evaluated to avoid unauthorized leakage of labeled data rows. For example, suppose that a query has a predicate on a labeled table that involves a User-Defined Function (UDF). Further suppose that this UDF takes the whole data row as an input parameter and that the UDF source code makes a copy of the data row outside the database (or sends it as an e-mail to some destination). Now, suppose that some data row R cannot be returned to the user who issued the query because this would violate the access rules from the label access policy associated with this labeled table. If the predicate involving the UDF is evaluated prior to evaluating the predicates that implement the access rules then data row R will be consumed by the UDF and consequently leaked to an unauthorized user.

If the RDBMS chooses the query modification method to enforce MAC on a labeled table, then it must ensure that the predicates that implement the access rules are evaluated before any other predicate so that no labeled row leakage could occur. The alternative approach that is not based on query modification evaluates the access rules immediately after the row is accessed, and before any predicate is evaluated. It is therefore more secure than the query modification approach. It also allows the SQL compiler to continue to select the order in which predicates are evaluated in the usual way.

4.3 Index-Only Access Methods

When selecting an access plan, SQL compilers choose between three methods of accessing the data in a database table: Scanning the entire table sequentially, locating specific table rows by first accessing an index on the table, or accessing just an index on the table if all the required columns are part of the index key. This latter method is known as index-only access. SQL compilers usually rely on the statistics available about the table and the indices to choose between those three access methods. If an index only plan is selected then the label column is not available and therefore the access rules from the label access policy associated with the table cannot be evaluated. MLS RDBMS extended the primary key on an MLS relation with the security label column in order to allow the simultaneous existence of multiple tuples with the same (non extended) primary key (*i.e.*, polyinstantiation)[1]. We borrow this idea from the MLS work to extend every index created on a labeled table (including the primary key) with the row label column(s). This would allow SQL compilers to continue to choose index only access methods when this is appropriate, and for the access rules from the label access policy associated with the table on which the index is created to be evaluated.

5 Methodology for an End-to-end MAC Enterprise Solution

The ever-increasing enterprise demands for more security has led to the emergence of label security products that provide the ability to set up and control access based upon labels throughout an entire network from end to end. For example, such label security products have the ability to control the network to decide whether or not a particular labeled data row can be transmitted on a particular channel or be delivered to a particular workstation on that network. Cryptek[22] is an example of such a label security product. An important advantage of such label security products is their ability to offer a centrally managed tool for defining label access policies and for assigning access labels to users as well as to other entities on the network. We contend that a MAC implementation in RDBMS should offer the flexibility to integrate with a label security product for the following reasons:

1. Eliminate the need for the system administrator to define the label access rules in more than a single location (*i.e.*, both in the RDBMS and in the label security product)

2. Eliminate the need for the system administrator to assign access labels to users in more than a single location

3. Allow the access to a labeled data row in the database to be based on more sophisticated label access rules that a particular implementation of MAC in an RDBMS may not allow to express

We will now show how the methodology described earlier in this paper could be extended to allow an RDBMS to take part in such an end-to-end MAC scheme by providing the flexibility to integrate with a label security product.

5.1 Integration Approach

Recall from section 3.6 that we have extended the CREATE TABLE SQL statement with an optional clause to specify the label type and the label access policy. We further extend this SQL statement such that the LABEL POLICY clause could either specify the name of a label access policy defined within the RDBMS, or a label access policy defined externally to the RDBMS (*i.e.*, within a label security product). The keyword EXTERNAL is introduced to support this latter possibility as shown below.

CREATE TABLE T1 (A integer, B integer)
LABEL TYPE *some-label-type*
LABEL POLICY EXTERNAL

When a data row in such a table is accessed, the RDBMS needs to supply the ID of the user making the access together with the data row label and the table name to the label security product through a well-defined interface. The label security product evaluates the label access rules based on the information received from the RDBMS and returns a response to the RDBMS through that same interface. The response could be a Boolean flag indicating whether or not the access should be allowed.

The SQL compiler will now need to take into account where the label access rules are defined when inserting logic into an access plan to enforce MAC on a labeled table. Thus, a more general description of the algorithm to be inserted in the access plan for a labeled table is as follows.

```
Begin
  if (policy defined within RDBMS)
  {
      Fetch the user's access label (e.g., from a
      system catalog table)
  }
  if (SELECT access)
  {
      for each row accessed
      {
          if (policy defined within RDBMS)
          {
              if (read access rules do not permit access)
              {
                  Skip row
```

```
        }
      }
    else
    {
      response = callLabelSecurityProduct(userid,
                        rowlabel, table-name)
      if (response is No)
      {
         Skip row
      }
    }
  }
}
else
{
  // INSERT, UPDATE, or DELETE access
  for each row
  {
    if (INSERT or UPDATE)
    {
      if (the row label provided is not valid with
          respect to the label type associated with
          the labeled table)
          Reject INSERT or UPDATE
    }
    if (policy defined within RDBMS)
    {
      if (write access rules do not permit access)
          Reject INSERT, UPDATE or DELETE
    }
    else
    {
      response = callLabelSecurityProduct
                    (userid, rowlabel, table-name)
      if (response is No)
      {
         Reject INSERT, UPDATE or DELETE
      }
    }
  }
}
End
```

Clearly, the calls to the label security product, which is external to the RDBMS, would cause a performance degradation. In the next section, we will show how this performance degradation could be minimized.

5.2 Performance Improvement

To minimize the performance degradation that could result from the calls to the label security product, a caching technique could be used. Before making the call to the label security product, the RDBMS would first check the cache to see if a similar call was made earlier, and if so fetches the response directly from the cache. The cache structure could look as follows.

Userid	RowLabel	Table	Access	Resp.
Joe	L	T	Read	Yes
Bob	L'	T	Write	No

Table 1: Label security product responses cache

To ensure that the cache entries are always valid, the label security product must signal to the RDBMS through a well-defined interface any changes to the label access rules associated with a database table, or to the access labels assigned to a database user. When such a signal is received, the RDBMS invalidates the cache entries that are affected by the change in label access rules or user access labels. For example, if the label access rules associated with table T have changed, then all cache entries for table T must be invalidated. Similarly, if the access label for user Joe has changed or has been revoked, then all cache entries for user Joe must be invalidated.

6 Conclusion and Future Directions

This paper has introduced a flexible and generic implementation of MAC in RDBMS that can be used to address the requirements from a variety of application domains, as well as to allow an RDBMS to efficiently take part in an end-to-end MAC enterprise solution. This implementation differs from traditional MAC implementations in RDBMS, which have focused solely on MLS, and thus cannot be leveraged to serve the needs of application domains where there is a desire to control access to objects based on the label associated with that object and the label associated with the subject accessing that object, but where the label access rules and the label structure do not necessarily match the MLS two security rules and the MLS label structure (*i.e.*, a hierarchical component and a set of unordered compartments). Moreover, such implementations do not offer the flexibility to integrate with an external label security product and therefore cannot take part in an end-to-end MAC enterprise solution.

There are a number of additional problems related to implementing a generic MAC solution in an RDBMS that have not been addressed in this paper. These will be the subject of our future work. For example, triggers could cause labeled data rows to flow from a labeled table to a nonlabeled table if the subject of a trigger is a labeled table but the target of that trigger is a nonlabeled table. Without proper flow control measures, triggers could cause unauthorized leakage of information to occur. Also, there needs to be a mechanism to accommodate views based on labeled tables. For example, if a view is based on a join between two labeled tables how would the row label of a join result row be selected. Should the RDBMS make the decision about how to combine labels? or should the RDBMS offer the flexibility that would allow database administrators to provide the rules for combining two labels from the same label type?

Acknowledgements

Some of the ideas expressed in this paper were generated when the first author was a Research Staff Member at the IBM Zurich Research Lab (ZRL). The first author would like to thank Dr. Michael Waidner, manager Network Security & Cryptography, for giving him the opportunity to start up the database security research activity at ZRL. The first author would also like to thank his wife Hue Phan Dam for her valuable comments on an earlier version of this paper and for her help with the examples.

Trademarks

IBM and Informix are registered trademarks of International Business Machines Corporation in the United States, other countries, or both. Other company, product and service names may be trademarks or service marks of others.

Disclaimer

The views expressed in this paper are those of the authors and not necessarily of IBM Canada Ltd. or IBM Corporation.

References

[1] D. E. Denning. The Sea View Security Model. In *Proc. of the IEEE Symposium on Security and Privacy*, Oakland, California, USA, 1988.

[2] S. Jajodia, R. Sandhu. Toward a Multilevel Secure Relational Data Model. In *Proc. of ACM SIGMOD*, Denver, Colorado, USA, 1991.

[3] S. Jajodia, R. Sandhu. Polyinstantiation Integrity in Multilevel Relations. In *Proc. of the IEEE Symposium on Security and Privacy*, Oakland, California, USA, 1988.

[4] K. Smith, M. Winslett. Entity Modeling in the MLS Relational Model. In *Proc. of the 18th VLDB Conference*, Vancouver, BC, Canada, 1992.

[5] R. Sandhu, F. Chen. The Multilevel Relational Data Model. *Transactions on Information and System Security*, Vol. 1, No. 1, 1998.

[6] N. Jukic, S. V. Vrbsky. Asserting Beliefs in MLS Relational Models. *SIGMOD Record*, Vol. 26, No. 3, 1997.

[7] N. Jukic, S. V. Vrbsky, A. Parrish, B. Dixon, B. Jukic. A Belief-Consistent Multilevel Secure Relational Data Model. *Information Systems*, Vol. 24, No. 5, 1999.

[8] Trusted Computer Security Evaluation Criteria, DoD 5200.28-STD. US Department of Defense, 1985.

[9] E. Bell, L. J. LaPadula. Secure computer systems: Unified exposition and multics interpretation. Technical Report MTR-2997, The Mitre Corporation, Burlington Road, Bedford, MA 01730, USA.

[10] M. D. Abrams, S. Jajodia, H. J. Podell. Information Security An Integrated Collection of Essays. *IEEE Computer Society Press*, Los Alamitos, CA, USA, 1995.

[11] S. Castano, et al. Database Security. *ACM Press*, New York, NY, USA, 1995.

[12] V. Atluri, S. Jajodia, T. F. Keefe, C. MaCollum, R. Mukkamal. Multilevel Secure Transaction Processing: Status and Prospects. *Database Security, X: Status and Prospects*, Chapman & Hall 1997, eds. Pierangela Samarati and Ravi Sandhu.

[13] T. F. Keefe, W. T. Tsai, T. F. Keefe, J. Srivastava. Multilevel Secure Database Concurrency Control. In *Proc. IEEE sixth International Conference on Data Engineering*, Los Angeles, CA, USA, 1990.

[14] L. Lamport. Concurrent Reading and Writing. In *Comm. ACM*, Vol. 20, No. 11, 1997.

[15] P. Ammann, S. Jajodia. A Timestamp Ordering Algorithm for Secure, Single-Version, Multilevel Databases. *Database Security, V: Status and Prospects*, C.E. Landweher, ed., Amsterdam, Holland, 1992.

[16] Oracle Corporation. Trusted Oracle Administrator's Guide. Redwood City, CA, USA, 1992.

[17] Informix. Informix OnLine/Secure Administrator's Guide. Menlo Park, CA, USA, 1993.

[18] E. Bertino, S. Jajodia, L. Mancini, I. Ray. Advanced Transaction Processing in Multilevel Secure File Stores. *IEEE Transactions on Knowledge and Data Engineering*, Vol. 10, No. 1, 1998.

[19] R. Agrawal, J. Kiernan, R. Srikant, Y. Xu. Hippocratic Databases. In *Proc. of the 28th International Conference on Very Large Databases*, Hong Kong, China, 2002.

[20] Sybase Inc. Building Applications for Secure SQL Server, Sybase Secure SQL Server Release 10.0. Emeryville, CA, USA, 1993.

[21] ISO/IEC 9075:1999. Information-Technology-Database Languages-SQL-Part 1: Framework (SQL/Framework), 1999 .

[22] Cryptek. www.cryptek.com.

Hardware Acceleration in Commercial Databases: A Case Study of Spatial Operations*

Nagender Bandi[†] Chengyu Sun[‡] Divyakant Agrawal[†] Amr El Abbadi[†]

[†]University of California, Santa Barbara {nagender, agrawal, amr}@cs.ucsb.edu
[‡]California State University, Los Angeles {csun}@cs.calstatela.edu

Abstract

Traditional databases have focused on the issue of reducing I/O cost as it is the bottleneck in many operations. As databases become increasingly accepted in areas such as Geographic Information Systems (GIS) and Bio-informatics, commercial DBMS need to support data types for complex data such as spatial geometries and protein structures. These non-conventional data types and their associated operations present new challenges. In particular, the computational cost of some spatial operations can be orders of magnitude higher than the I/O cost. In order to improve the performance of spatial query processing, innovative solutions for reducing this computational cost are beginning to emerge. Recently, it has been proposed that hardware acceleration of an off-the-shelf graphics card can be used to reduce the computational cost of spatial operations. However, this proposal is preliminary in that it establishes the feasibility of the hardware assisted approach in a stand-alone setting but not in a real-world commercial database. In this paper we present an architecture to show how hardware acceleration of an off-the-shelf graphics card can be integrated into a popular commercial database to speed up spatial queries. Extensive experimentation with real-world datasets shows that significant improvement in the performance of spatial operations can be achieved with this integration. The viability of this approach underscores the significance of a tighter integration of hardware acceleration into commercial databases for spatial applications.

1 Introduction

The cost of a DBMS query consists of two factors: *I/O cost*, the time spent in loading the data from the secondary storage into the main memory, and *computational cost*, the time spent by the DBMS in processing this data and returning the result. Traditionally, database research has focused on reducing I/O cost during query processing as it is the major bottleneck in many operations.

With the increased acceptance of databases in various areas such as Geographic Information Systems (GIS) and Bio-informatics, commercial DBMS, which historically handled simple data types like numbers and alpha-numeric characters, need to support complex data types. These new data types and the associated operations present new challenges for DBMS researchers. One such case is the support for efficient storage and retrieval of spatial data, which typically consists of large complex datasets representing real world GIS and CAD information.

Spatial database queries are typically evaluated in two steps: the *filtering* step and the *refinement* step. In the *filtering* (also referred to as *primary filtering*) step, the Minimum Bounding Rectangles (MBRs) of the objects and spatial indexes such as R-tree [9] are used to quickly determine a set of candidate results. In the *refinement* step (also referred to as *secondary filtering* step), the final results are determined by retrieving the actual geometries of the candidates from the database, and comparing them to either a query geometry or to each other. For complex geometries such as polygons, the cost of the *secondary filtering*

---

*This work is supported by the NSF grants under IIS 02-20152 and EIA 00-80134

Permission to copy without fee all or part of this material is granted provided that the copies are not made or distributed for direct commercial advantage, the VLDB copyright notice and the title of the publication and its date appear, and notice is given that copying is by permission of the Very Large Data Base Endowment. To copy otherwise, or to republish, requires a fee and/or special permission from the Endowment.

Proceedings of the 30th VLDB Conference, Toronto, Canada, 2004

step usually dominates the query cost due to the complexity of the underlying computational geometry algorithms in this step. The ratio of the *computational cost* of comparing the geometries to the *I/O cost* for loading the geometries varies significantly depending on the type of spatial queries and the complexity of the geometries, which can be roughly characterized by the number of vertices of a geometry. Generally speaking, the more complex the data, the higher the *computational cost*. For instance, a recent study on spatial selections [13] shows that for point geometries, the *I/O cost* is the dominant factor, but for polygon geometries, both costs are significant. In the case of a spatial join, the *computational cost* could be several orders of magnitude higher than the I/O cost. This is because once a geometry is loaded, it is buffered in the main memory and compared to many other geometries.

In order to reduce the *computational cost* of the *secondary filtering* step, various *intermediate filtering* techniques have been proposed. For intersection queries, Brinkhoff et al. [4] proposed using simple geometries such as convex hulls, *n*-corners, and maximum enclosing rectangles to approximate complex polygons. These simple geometries serve as an *intermediate filtering* step, in addition to the MBR filtering, and can identify a significant number of false positive hits without performing the costly geometry-geometry comparison. Recent work has proposed several tiling based intermediate filters [24, 2, 13], which approximate polygons with rectangular tiles.

With recent advancements in the graphics hardware technology, several proposals [19, 10, 11, 1, 15, 8] have been made to use commodity Graphics Processor Unit (GPU) to speed up conventionally computation-intensive applications. It is believed that the performance enhancement reported in these works will further improve because the peak performance of graphics processors is increasing at the rate of 2.5 - 3.0 times a year: much higher than the corresponding rate for the central processing units (CPUs) [14].

In the spatial database context, Sun et al. [19] developed a hardware-assisted intersection test as an intermediate filter for spatial database operations. However, this work was preliminary in that it established the feasibility of the approach, referred to as the *hardware filter*, in a stand-alone setting and not in a real-world commercial database where different storage layouts, index structures, query plans and proprietary optimizations may effect the effectiveness of this technique.

In this paper, we show how hardware acceleration of a commodity graphics card can be integrated into a commercial DBMS. We use Oracle 9I as a representative of a commercial DBMS. We present various approaches of integration provided by Oracle's extensibility architecture [7] and discuss their suitability for integration with the hardware filter. We chose to integrate the hardware filter as an external procedure [7] and the hardware filter itself was implemented using OpenGL because OpenGL provides a generic high level interface to any graphics hardware. We built spatial query operators using the integrated hardware filter and Oracle's primary and secondary filters thus providing similar functionality as Oracle's spatial operators [16]. We provide a cost analysis of different query operators and use it for discussing the results of the experimental section where we compare the performance of our spatial query operator against Oracle's corresponding operators. Through a detailed analysis of the experimental results, we not only validate the effectiveness of the hardware filter but also intend to provide feedback which will be helpful to database designers in integration of hardware acceleration.

The main contributions of this paper are:

- We discuss various integration options provided by Oracle and develop a system framework for integrating hardware acceleration into a commercial DBMS.

- Though many techniques have been proposed to use graphics hardware for non-visualization applications, few of them [19, 1] have made the effort to compare hardware-assisted techniques with leading software solutions. To the best of our knowledge, this paper is the first work which implements and evaluates a hardware acceleration technique in a commercial database setting.

- We conducted extensive experimentation using real world datasets, indexed by both R-tree as well as fine-tuned Quadtree indexes. The performance results of spatial selection and join confirm the advantage of the hardware filter [19], even against a preprocessing filter in most cases. The analysis also gives more insights regarding filtering techniques at different stages of spatial processing in a complex commercial database environment.

The rest of the paper is organized as follows. In Section 2, we summarize the hardware-assisted intersection test proposed by Sun et al. [19]. In Section 3, we present the details of Oracle's support for extensibility. In Section 4, we propose our architectures for integration and discuss its details. Section 5 presents the details of the data and query models of *Oracle Spatial*. In Section 6, we analyze the performance of the hardware filter for spatial selection and spatial join queries. Section 7 concludes the paper.

2 Hardware Acceleration of Spatial Operations

In [19], Sun et al. propose using graphics hardware to speed up the refinement step in spatial query operations. The technique is based on the observation that most low-level algorithms used in spatial databases have been well studied by the computational geometry community. Under current computer architectures, it is unlikely that algorithmic advances will significantly reduce the cost of geometry-geometry comparison. On the other hand, the last few years have seen tremendous advances in graphics hardware technologies. Off-the-shelf graphics cards are capable of handling thousands of polygons in real time, and are widely used in computer games, 3D modeling, and virtual reality applications. Since both graphics hardware and spatial databases work on geometries such as points, lines, and polygons, and they both deal with geometric relations such as intersection and containment in a 2D or 3D space, it is only natural to exploit the computational power of graphics hardware to speed up spatial database operations.

The idea is based on the intuitive notion of intersection of two polygons in the digital domain:

1. Render the first polygon with color c_1.

2. Render the second polygon with color c_2 adding the pixel-to-pixel color values of the second polygon to the first polygon.

3. Search for overlapping pixels with color $c_1 + c_2$. If such pixels exist, these two polygons intersect.

Figure 1: Hardware Intersection Test

An example of this strategy is illustrated in Figure 1, where the two polygons are rendered with color *gray*, and the overlapping pixels are *black*. However, it should be noted that a naive implementation of this approach will lead to both false hits and false dismissals due to the limited window resolution of the graphics hardware. So in [19], the hardware intersection test is implemented with a combination of a software point-in-polygon test and the rendering of only the polygon boundaries. Because of the rendering property of the anti-aliased line segments, this hardware test guarantees no false dismissals at any window resolution. However, false hits may exist because two disjoint objects might be mapped to the same pixel. Therefore, the hardware test is used as an intermediate filter as a part of the following 3-step filtering setup:

1. *Primary filtering* where MBR filtering and point-in-polygon tests are performed to determine a candidate set.

2. *Intermediate filtering* with graphics hardware to further reduce the candidate set.

3. *Secondary filtering* where a software intersection test is performed to determine the final results.

In the intermediate filtering step, which we will refer to as *hardware filtering*, the two geometries are rendered using graphics hardware, and the frame buffer is searched for overlapping pixels using the efficient *hardware minmax* test [18]. Using this hardware filter, [19] showed that significant reductions in the computational costs of spatial operations for complex queries resulted. In the experimental setup, the spatial data was stored in flat files and simple MBR comparison was used for primary filtering. In this paper, we evaluate the effectiveness of the hardware filter in a more realistic commercial database setup. In particular, we use Oracle's R-tree and Quadtree in the primary filtering step, and the geometry comparison functions in the refinement step. In the following sections, we first present how to integrate the hardware filter with Oracle Spatial, then report on the experimental setup and results.

3 Database Extensibility

In addition to the efficient and secure management of data specified by the relational model, commercial databases like Oracle and DB2 now provide support for data organized under the object model. Object types and other features such as large objects (LOBs), *external procedures*, extensible indexing and query optimization can be used to build powerful, reusable server-based components called data cartridges by Oracle [7] and Data Blades by DB2 [6]. In this paper, we use a data cartridge to integrate the hardware filter with the Oracle database engine. Through data cartridges, Oracle allows users to capture the business logic and the processes associated with domain-specific data in user-defined data types. It also allows them to build and integrate their own indexing and query optimization techniques into the database. For example, the Oracle extension for spatial data, popularly known as *Oracle Spatial*, is simply a data cartridge consisting of all the relevant spatial data types, as well as the associated indexes, functions, and operators [16].

The data types and operations encapsulated in a data cartridge can be used in user queries written in PL/SQL, which is the query language in Oracle. PL/SQL itself is a powerful programming language, but is not suitable for implementing complex algorithms due to performance reasons. For example, a numerical routine is faster when implemented in C or Java. To support such special-purpose processing, PL/SQL provides an interface for calling routines written in other languages, which makes the strengths and capabilities of third generation languages (3GL) like C and Java available through calls from a database server. Such a 3GL routine, called an *external procedure* or a *stored procedure*, is stored in a shared library, registered with PL/SQL, and called from PL/SQL at runtime to perform special-purpose processing. For instance, suppose we have a database table X with two columns A and B, and a data cartridge Y which provides operation C. A user query selecting information from X can be written as

select /* */ from X where Y.C(A, B) = value;

In the rest of this section, we discuss the details of stored procedures and external procedures, which are later used for integrating the hardware filter into Oracle.

3.1 Stored procedures

Stored procedures are implemented on the server side and are written in an interpreted language such as Java. Oracle provides an area in the database address space for the execution of the stored procedure, called the Java Virtual Machine (JVM). Since a stored procedure implemented in Java runs in the same address space as Oracle, a stored procedure invocation causes a context switch from Oracle's run-time threads to the JVM. Although both PL/SQL and Java are interpreted languages, Java is preferable over PL/SQL for implementing efficient procedures because Java has hundreds of classes, allowing interfaces with diverse functionality. Oracle does not allow C stored procedures for normal developers because unlike Java programs where program failures are handled by the JVM, C program failures can lead to database failure which is not desirable. However, Oracle allows C stored procedures for trusted developers i.e., people who write Oracle's proprietary software.

3.2 External procedures

External procedures are written in compiled languages, such as C and C++, and executed in an external address space separate from the database server. The external address space is managed by a process known as *Listener*. This separation ensures that the database server is insulated from any program failures that might occur in external procedures and, under no circumstances, is an Oracle database corrupted by such failures. But at the same time, the execution of a procedure in a separate address space implies an Inter Process Communication(IPC) overhead between Oracle and the external procedure. So implementing an algorithm as an external procedure is efficient only if the IPC overhead is insignificant with respect to the CPU cost incurred by the algorithm. The architecture of a typical external procedure is given in Figure 2

An important detail in the discussion of external procedure is the mapping of the PL/SQL data types of Oracle to the data types of the external procedure language, e.g., C. While conventional PL/SQL data types like numbers and varchar have corresponding mapping data types in C, complex data types like Large OBjects (LOB) do not have a simple mapping. These LOBs

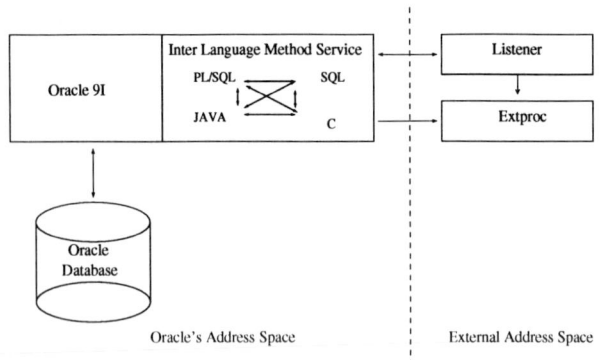

Figure 2: External Procedure - Architecture

are transferred to the external procedure in a complex format and the external procedure needs to map these LOBs into its data structures using the Oracle Call Interface (OCI) [17] data manipulation callbacks. These callbacks are particularly useful for processing LOBs such as the Spatial Data Objects (SDO) [16]. For example, by using callbacks, an external procedure can perform piece-wise reads or writes of the SDOs stored in the database.

3.3 Comparison

The decision of whether to use an external procedure or a stored procedure depends on various factors. Java class procedures are generally slower than a compiled C external procedure because of the interpreted nature of Java which makes external procedures obvious choice if speed is the main concern. If the IPC overhead is more significant than the processing cost, then stored procedures are preferable. One other factor is the amount of library support offered by the programming language. If the user wants to integrate hardware acceleration into the database, he/she would prefer to use a language like C. This is because current state of the art interfaces to access most hardware devices are more widely available in C than in Java. In particular, we use OpenGL for interacting with the graphics hardware. OpenGL provides a high level interface to the developers while hiding driver level details of the graphics hardware. OpenGL is a widely accepted standard and typically every graphics card manufacturer provides an implementation for this interface. Despite the IPC overhead drawback, we chose to integrate the hardware filter as an external procedure because C interfaces to OpenGL are ubiquitous; Java interfaces are not yet standardized and are not widely available.

4 Hardware Filter Integration

Traditional OpenGL programs are designed to run in an infinite loop waiting for interactive events to occur. Typically these event-driven programs consist of a set of *initialization* operations followed by a recurring set of *rendering* operations which handle event occurrences. The hardware filter consists of the following operations in sequential order: data retrieval, MBR filtering, point-in-polygon test, rendering the polygons and doing the minmax test. As the hardware filter requires *rendering* operations for performing the hardware test, *initialization* must be completed before the rendering operations can be performed. Since a typical spatial query would require the *rendering* operations (for the hardware tests) to be performed a number of times, it is not desirable to execute the *initialization* operations every time as these operations are very expensive. In order to avoid this *initialization* overhead, we propose to separate the process of accessing the graphics hardware from the process of data retrieval and software tests. This separation will make the hardware filter efficient because *initialization* is done only once for any query.

We present an architecture, referred to as Dual thread architecture, where we separate the hardware access and implement it as a separate thread within the address space of the external procedure. The external procedure consists of two threads (primary thread and graphics thread) running synchronously to perform the intersection test (Figure 3). The primary thread deals with the data retrieval and the initial filtering tests like the MBR test and the Point in the Polygon test. The graphics thread performs the OpenGL initializations and the hardware test. While the graphics thread is created at the beginning of the query and remains alive as long as the query runs, the primary thread is loaded in a nested manner. The two threads share data using global variables. Synchronization between the threads is done using the system calls provided by the pthread library. We describe the dual thread architecture below.

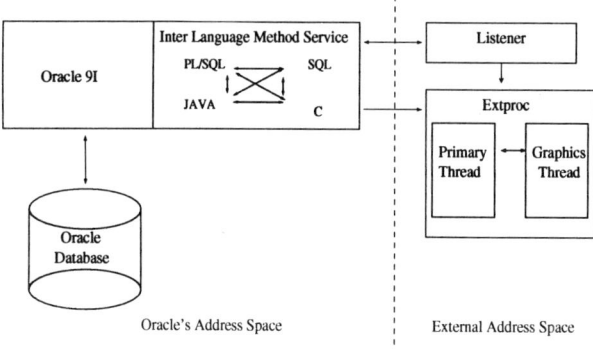

Figure 3: Dual Thread Architecture

The primary thread performs the following operations in sequential order:

1. Retrieve the data corresponding to the Spatial Data Objects (SDO) using Oracle Call Interface (OCI) callbacks into global variables.

2. Test the query polygons for Minimum Bounding Rectangle (MBR) intersection. If this test succeeds, go to step 3 else the two polygons do not intersect.

3. Test the query polygons for the Point in the Polygon condition. If this test succeeds the two polygons intersect, else go to step 4 for the hardware test.

4. Inform the graphics thread, which is waiting for a signal from the primary thread (as will be described below), so that the polygons are rendered.

5. Wait for a signal from the graphics thread. Upon receiving the signal from the graphics thread check the result of the hardware intersection test given by the graphics thread. If the result is true the software intersection test needs to be done. Otherwise the polygons do not intersect.

The graphics thread performs the following operations in sequential order:

1. Wait for the primary thread to generate the required data so that polygons can be rendered for doing the hardware test.

2. Upon receiving the signal from the primary thread, render the polygons and check for the intersection condition using hardware minmax test. Store the result of this test in a global variable and signal the waiting primary thread. Go back to step 1.

5 Oracle Spatial

As described in the previous section, Oracle Spatial [16] is an integrated set of functions and procedures that enables spatial data to be stored, accessed, and analyzed quickly and efficiently in an Oracle database. In this section, we give the details of the data and query models of Oracle Spatial.

5.1 Data Model

Oracle Spatial's data model is a hierarchical structure consisting of elements, geometries, and layers, which correspond to representations of spatial data. An element is the basic building block of a geometry. The supported spatial element types are points, line strings, and polygons. A geometry (or geometry object) is the representation of a spatial feature, modeled as an ordered set of primitive elements. A layer is a collection of geometries having the same attribute set. Each layer's geometries and the associated spatial index are stored in the database in standard tables.

5.2 Indexes and Query Model

Oracle provides support for both linear Quadtree and R-tree indexes. These indexes are implemented using the extensible framework of Oracle [7, 16]. The linear Quadtree (or Quadtree for short) computes tile approximations for the interior and boundary of geometries and uses existing B-tree indexes for performing spatial search and other operations. The R-tree indexing in Oracle is implemented logically as a tree and physically uses tables inside the database. The search involves recursive SQL from the root to the relevant leaves.

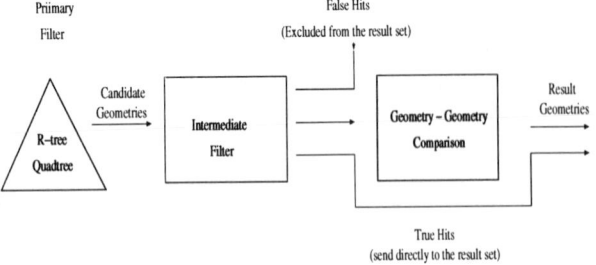

Figure 4: Oracle Spatial Query Model

Oracle Spatial uses a multi-stage query model as shown in Figure 4. In the first stage, referred to as the *primary* filter, the spatial index is used for query filtering. Candidate geometries that may satisfy a given query criterion are first identified in this stage with the help of exterior approximations in the spatial index. In the case of a Quadtree, Quadtree tiles are used as exterior approximation and in the case of an R-tree, minimum bounding rectangles (MBRs) are used. In the *intermediate* stage, candidate geometries from the primary filtering step are compared with the query geometry using a sorted list of interior tiles approximating the interior of the query geometry. This is referred to as the *interior approximation* filter [13] and is used either to accept or reject candidate geometries based on the query criterion. The rest of the geometries whose interaction are not determined in the *intermediate* filter are then passed through to the final stage, referred to as the *secondary* filter, and the exact result set is determined and returned to the user. Whereas the secondary filter uses computational geometry algorithms to determine the interaction between query and candidate geometries, the primary and intermediate filters use the exterior and interior approximations of query and data geometries (from the index).

As described above, during the intermediate filtering stage, Oracle uses the interior approximation filter [13] to reduce the candidate set for the secondary filter. If Quadtree indexing is used then interior approximations of both the query and also the data geometries are used during the interior filtering step. This is because, in the case of Quadtree indexing, the interior approximations of the datasets are calculated statically during index creation and stored inside the index tables. For queries that use R-trees, the interior approximations are calculated during run-time and hence are done only for query geometries. For R-trees, the choice of tiling level for interior approximations is decided by the Oracle run time optimizer.

5.3 Spatial Operators and Functions

In order to define a spatial query in Oracle three parameters must be defined: two for the geometries used in the spatial query, and the third for parameters defining the type of spatial query (selection or join). Given below are two spatial operators and a function provided by Oracle Spatial.

1. **SDO_FILTER** : This operator functions as a primary filter and returns a super-set of the actual query result.

2. **SDO_RELATE** : This operator performs both the primary and the secondary filtering operations and returns the exact query result. In addition to using the indexing for primary filtering, it also performs interior approximation filtering [13] before secondary filtering. This operator has two options specified by the third argument:

   - **WINDOW**: When this option is enabled, it performs a selection of the query geometry (second parameter) over the data geometries.

   - **JOIN**: When this option is enabled, it performs a spatial join of the geometry columns specified by the two parameters. Currently, Oracle allows join queries only when the geometries are indexed using Quadtrees. In the case of R-trees, it performs a nested join in the same way as a selection query. This operator requires the second column to be indexed using the same tiling level as the first column. When both data columns are indexed using Quadtrees, it performs a *hash* join during the primary filtering step followed by a direct application of the secondary filter. If the second column is not indexed, a *nested* join is performed as in the case of selection queries.

3. **SDO_GEOM.RELATE** : This function (not operator) applies exact computational geometry to find out the kind of interaction between two given geometries and is used as the secondary filter in SDO_RELATE.

6 Performance Evaluation

In this section, we evaluate the effectiveness of the hardware filter integrated with an Oracle database, and compare the performance of intersection queries with and without the hardware filter. We build a hardware intersection operator by applying the hardware filter to the result set produced by the primary filter (SDO_FILTER) and then apply the secondary filter (SDO_GEOM.RELATE). We call this the *hardware* operator. We also give a conservative estimate for the performance of the hardware operator, if the hardware filter is implemented right after the *primary filter* as a part of Oracle's Spatial data cartridge and not as an external procedure. This is done by deducting the IPC overhead which occurs because of transferring the data to the external procedure. We refer to the *hardware* operator without the IPC overhead as *hardware-no-ipc* operator. In the rest of this section we discuss the experimental setup, describe a theoretical cost analysis for the *hardware* operator, and analyze the performance of selection and join operations.

6.1 Experimental Setup

The experiments were performed on a desktop PC with an AMD AthlonXP 1800+ CPU and 1GB Double Data Rate (DDR) memory. The graphics card is equipped with an NVIDIA GeForce4 Ti4600 processor and 128MB on-board memory. Experiments are performed on an Oracle database (version 9.2.0.1) running on Linux Operating System. The hardware filter is coded in C++, compiled to a shared library using g++ and integrated with Oracle using the *Dual Thread* architecture.

The experiments are conducted with the following real world datasets:

- **PRISM** [5]. Average annual precipitation in the contiguous United States at 1:2,000,000 scale for the climatological period 1961-1990.

- **HYDRO** [23]. Hydrological unit boundaries for the United States, Puerto Rico and the US Virgin Islands at 1:2,000,000 scale.

- **COUNTY** [22]. The boundaries of the US counties at 1:2,000,000 scale.

- **STATES50** [20]. The boundaries of the main land boundaries of the 50 US states at 1:2,000,000 scale.

- **LSOVER** [21]. The boundaries of Landslide Incidence and Susceptibility distribution in the United States at 1:2,000,000.

Some statistics of the datasets are summarized in Table 1, where N is the number of objects in a dataset.

Dataset	N	Number of Vertices Per Polygon		
		Min	Max	Average
STATES50	50	91	70238	4416
PRISM	6243	4	45854	94
HYDRO	5348	4	12450	218
COUNTY	4933	4	10838	139
LSOVER	2814	4	91752	92

Table 1: Statistics of experimental Datasets

6.2 Operator Cost Analysis

In this subsection, we describe the cost analysis for the hardware operator and Oracle's software operator. Here, the cost refers to the total elapsed time for a spatial query. This cost analysis will provide the details of the various costs which constitute the total cost of hardware and software operators and will be used in later subsections to discuss the results.

6.2.1 Hardware operator

As described before, the hardware operator is built by applying an ordered sequence of filters: primary, hardware and secondary. It should be noted that for the primary and secondary filtering, we use Oracle's SDO_FILTER and SDO_GEOM.RELATE respectively. Since the hardware filter is implemented inside an external procedure, the total cost (t_{total}) of the hardware operator can be expressed as the sum of the costs of the following components:

1. cost of the primary filter ($t_{primary}$).

2. cost of the external procedure.

3. cost of the secondary filter ($t_{secondary}$).

The cost of the primary filtering step ($t_{primary}$) not only includes the cost of loading and using the index tables for calculating a superset of the actual result but also the cost of loading the geometries corresponding to the result set of the primary filter from secondary storage to Oracle's address space.

The cost incurred by the external procedure ($t_{extproc}$) can be partitioned into the following components.

1. cost of transferring data geometries to the address space of the external procedure ($t_{transfer}$).

2. cost of retrieval of the received data into local data structures using OCI function calls ($t_{retrieval}$).

3. cost of hardware filtering test which includes MBR test, Point-in-Polygon test, hardware test and also the thread synchronization overhead ($t_{hardware}$).

The cost of secondary filtering ($t_{secondary}$) comprises of the time for retrieval of data into internal data structures (same as $t_{retrieval}$ mentioned above) and the actual cost of comparing the data geometries using the computational geometry algorithms. It should be noted that both the external procedure and the secondary filter have to make OCI callbacks for retrieving data into local data structures before any processing. This implies that for those geometry pairs which successfully pass through the hardware filter, these OCI callbacks are made twice. This can be avoided if the external procedure is tightly integrated on the Oracle server itself as a part of the Oracle Spatial cartridge instead of being integrated as an external procedure. Since Oracle does not allow normal developers to modify its proprietary data cartridges, this overhead is currently unavoidable. Furthermore, $t_{retrieval}$ can be reduced to a great extent by efficient cache management which can be done once the hardware filter is tightly integrated into Oracle Spatial as a stored procedure. Overall, the cost of the hardware-no-ipc operator described in the beginning of this section gives a conservative estimate of the performance of the hardware operator if integrated into Oracle Spatial.

6.2.2 Software operator

We now describe the cost analysis for Oracle's software operator. The software operator is a sequence of two filters: the primary and the secondary filters and for certain operations, an interior filter in between. The cost of the primary ($t_{primary}$) and secondary ($t_{secondary}$) filters is defined in the same way as for the hardware operator. When the interior filter is used by the software operator, it uses interior approximations to filter out geometry pairs thereby reducing the processing cost of the secondary filter. The cost incurred by the interior filter ($t_{interior}$) is predominantly the time taken for contracting the interior approximations. Although a general breakdown of the total cost into primary filter and the remaining cost can be calculated, Oracle does not provide a breakdown of the remaining cost into interior and secondary filter cost. Since the interior filter is supposed to have insignificant cost [13], we assign the cost of the interior filter ($t_{interior}$) to 0.

We also add the costs of the intermediate (hardware and interior) filter and the secondary filter for both the hardware and software operators respectively and name the total cost as t_{comp}. We use t_{comp} because the total I/O cost which is incurred during the loading of the geometries is included inside the primary filter cost ($t_{primary}$). It should be noted that in the case of the hardware operator, we also add $t_{retrieval}$ to t_{comp} apart from the hardware and secondary filter costs while noting that this cost can be greatly reduced once the hardware filter is tightly integrated into Oracle Spatial. A comparison of t_{comp} for the hardware operator with that of the software operator gives a conservative estimate of the performance enhancement due to the hardware filter over the interior filter. We consider it conservative because in the case of the software operator, the interior filter does not need to retrieve the data geometries (by making OCI callbacks) for calculating the polygonal approximations (MBRs or interior approximations) as these approximations are precomputed and stored in the index structures.

6.3 Spatial Selections

In this subsection, we analyze the performance of spatial selection queries by measuring the time taken for selection queries using the following operators: SDO_RELATE, hardware and hardware-no-ipc. We refer to the selection query with the SDO_RELATE operator as *software selection* when discussing the results in this subsection. We evaluate the performance of these queries using the R-tree and Quadtree indexes. Using the boundaries of STATES50 of the United States, we perform the selection queries over three datasets, PRISM, HYDRO, and LSOVER. Based on the experimental results in [19], we chose a fixed 12x12 window resolution for the hardware filter and use it in all the experiments. In the following subsections we discuss the results for R-tree and Quadtree indexes over these data sets.

6.3.1 R-trees

The results of the R-tree selection for the above queries are shown in Figure 5. A breakdown of various costs incurred during the selection query for the hardware and the software operators are shown in the Tables 2 and 3. A comparison of the costs of primary ($t_{primary}$) and secondary filters ($t_{secondary}$) for the software operator (Table 3) shows that the primary filtering cost is minimal when compared to the secondary filtering cost. This implies that years of research efforts which focused on providing better spatial indexes have been able to reduce the primary filtering cost to the point where the secondary filtering cost becomes the bottleneck.

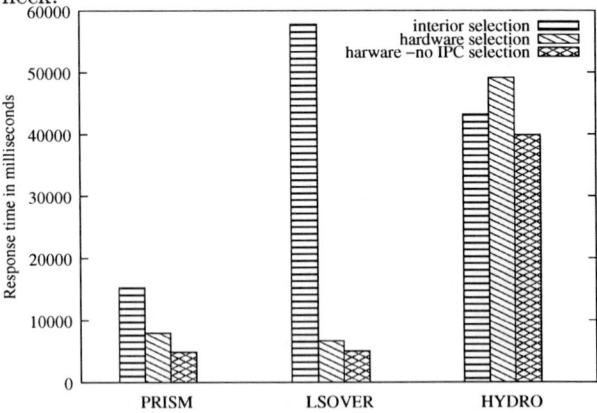

Figure 5: Selection results for R-trees

For the PRISM dataset, the hardware and the hardware-no-ipc selections improve the overall performance of the selection queries by 48.3% and 68.84% respectively. A comparison of computation cost (t_{comp}) values in Tables 2 and 3 shows that the hardware operator improves the performance of the software operator's computation cost for the PRISM dataset by 78.9%. Results for the case of selection over the LSOVER dataset show a computation cost improvement of 93% for the hardware operator over the software operator. These results also confirm the results reported in [19] where similar improvements are reported for the computation cost.

Cost parameter		PRISM	LSOVER	HYDRO
$t_{primary}$		1156	470	3000
$t_{extproc}$	$t_{transfer}$	3137	1627	9294
	$t_{retrieval}$	310	349	156
	$t_{hardware}$	304	160	1019
$t_{secondary}$		2980	3774	36291
Total Cost		7903	6647	49117
t_{comp}		3594	4444	37466

Table 2: Cost breakdown of hardware operator for R-Tree selections (milliseconds)

For the HYDRO dataset, the hardware-no-ipc selection performs marginally better than the software selection. It should be noted that although the hardware filter *can* assert when two polygons intersect by containment and also when two polygons *do not* intersect, it *cannot* assert when two polygons intersect by overlapping. In the case of datasets such as HYDRO where many data polygons have an overlapping intersection with the query polygon, the hardware operator has to go through the secondary filtering step to check for this condition in which case the hardware filter becomes an overhead. However, a close look at Table 2 indicates that in all the experiments, the hardware filtering step ($t_{hardware}$) consumes less than 3% of the total query response time in the worst case (2% for HYDRO). This implies that the hardware filter is a perfect run-time filter which can potentially enhance the performance of spatial queries without incurring any significant overhead.

For the PRISMS dataset, the large difference between hardware and hardware-no-ipc selections shows that IPC overhead ($t_{transfer}$) can account for a significant proportion of the total query cost. In the above result, $t_{transfer}$ accounts for 40% of the overall hardware operator's cost. As discussed before, the sum of the costs of IPC overhead ($t_{transfer}$) and the retrieval time ($t_{retrieval}$) gives an estimate of the amount of cost reduction that can be achieved if the hardware filter is tightly integrated into Oracle as a stored procedure. For the PRISM, HYDRO and LSOVER datasets, this cost accounts for 43%, 19% and 30% respectively of the total cost thus underscoring the need for a tighter integration.

In the current query model of Oracle Spatial, the interior filter is tightly integrated into the database where it has direct access to the polygonal approximations (MBRs) stored inside the index structures. This means that the interior filter incurs very little cost because it directly operates on the MBRs from the index and saves on the I/O and retrieval costs of loading the actual data geometries and calculating the MBRs respectively. We find this tightly integrated interior filter to be complimentary to the hardware filter because the interior filter uses the MBRs stored in the R-tree index, and reduces the I/O cost of retrieving the actual geometries, while the hardware filter operates on the geometries that are already loaded in memory, and thus reduces the computation required for the secondary filtering. So an ideal setup would integrate the hardware filter right after the interior filter inside the Oracle Spatial data cartridge.

Cost parameter	PRISM	LSOVER	HYDRO
$t_{primary}$	1156	470	3000
$t_{secondary}$	14137	57784	40235
t_{comp}	14137	57784	40235

Table 3: Cost breakdown of software operator for R-Tree selections (milliseconds)

6.3.2 Quadtrees

In this subsection, we analyze the performance of selection queries when the data geometries are indexed using Quadtrees. When Quadtrees are used, a $2^n * 2^n$ grid of tiles is used to approximate the interior and boundaries of geometries, where n is a user specified value usually referred to as the Quadtree tiling level. These interior and boundary approximations are calculated during the index creation step and stored in the index tables. Quadtree interior filtering has the advantage of using these preprocessed interior approximations during the filtering process. However, these approximations become very expensive to calculate and consume a lot of disk storage when the tiling levels become high. Timing and storage statistics of Quadtree index structures for the PRISM and HYDRO datasets shown in Figures 6 and 7 suggest an exponential growth for index creation time and disk utilization with increasing tiling levels. These statistics can be compared with the timing and storage details of the corresponding R-tree index structures in Table 4.

Intuitively, queries using Quadtree indexes have better query performance than R-tree indexes because the interior and the boundary tiles provide a better approximation of a geometry than the MBR, hence more results can be identified without accessing the geometries in the database table. However, this advantage of query performance comes at the costs of longer index creation time, larger index storage, as well as degraded update performance. Ideally, it would be desirable to have a filter which has the high performance of a preprocessing filter without incurring any preprocessing overhead.

It should be noted that the R-tree hardware filter (hardware filter using R-tree index for primary filtering) discussed in the previous subsection is absolutely run-time because the required R-tree index can be built very quickly (Table 4) and the hardware filter is inherently run-time. In the rest of this subsection, we analyze the performance of selection queries using the run-time R-tree hardware filter and compare the performance with the preprocessed Quadtree software (interior) filter.

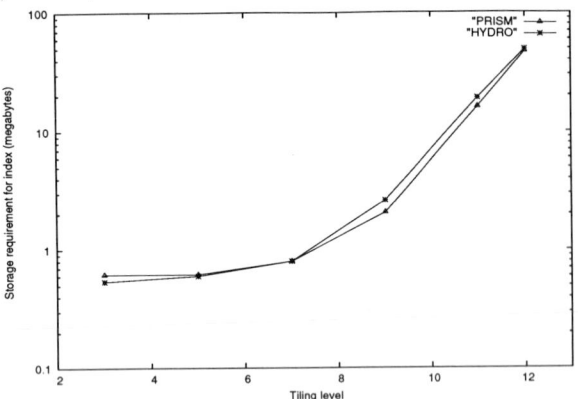

Figure 6: Quadtree index storage for PRISM and HYDRO (in log scale)

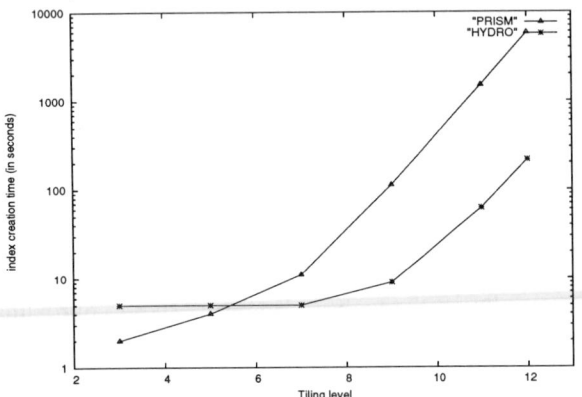

Figure 7: Quadtree index creation time for PRISM and HYDRO (in log scale)

type	PRISM	HYDRO
Index Creation time (seconds)	5	5
Index Storage cost (Megabytes)	0.5625	0.5

Table 4: Index statistics for R-Trees

The Quadtree software selection queries are performed for Quadtree tiling levels between 3 and 11. Results for selection queries over the PRISM dataset are given in the Figure 8. It can be observed that the response time for the software selection query decreases as the tiling level increases. This is because the candidate set returned by the primary filter gets increasingly refined with the increase in tiling level thus requiring less disk I/O during the ensuing filtering steps. As the tiling level is not defined for R-trees, the performance of the R-tree hardware filter appears as a straight line. For lower tiling levels, the hardware and the hardware-no-ipc selections outperform the preprocessed selection query. At higher tiling levels, the difference in the response time of hardware assisted selection queries and the preprocessed selection query decreases. This is because of the increase in effectiveness of the Quadtree interior filter due to improved approximation of interior of data geometries. But at higher tiling levels, the Quadtree indexes in-

cur very high preprocessing cost which is not reflected in the performance cost of the selection query. These results suggest that the hardware filter coupled with the inexpensive R-tree indexing can significantly improve the performance of spatial intersection queries for complex datasets without incurring any preprocessing overhead. Results for the selection query over the LSOVER dataset (can be found in [3]) show that the R-tree hardware filter outperforms the static interior filter for all tiling levels thus supporting our argument that, the R-tree hardware filter is a perfect replacement for the Quadtree interior filter.

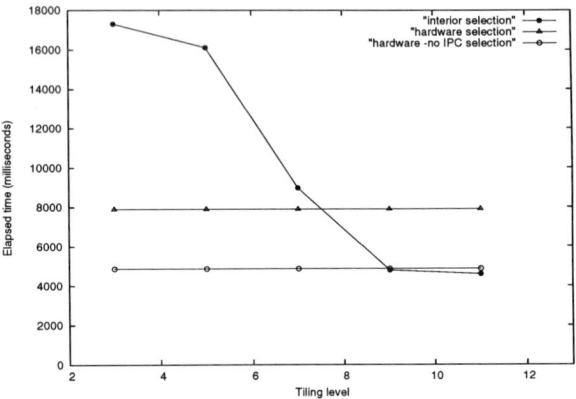

Figure 8: Timing results for selection over PRISM

Results for selection queries over the HYDRO dataset are shown in the Figure 9. As in the case of R-tree selection, the hardware-no-ipc operator performs at par with the Quadtree software operator. A closer look at the performance of the nested indexed join suggests that its query performance tends to converge to an asymptotic value. This supports our earlier argument made for the hardware filter that the intersection of certain pairs of geometries cannot be asserted by the intermediate filter (here the interior filter) and they have to go through the secondary filter, and this asymptotic value is the cost of the secondary filtering step.

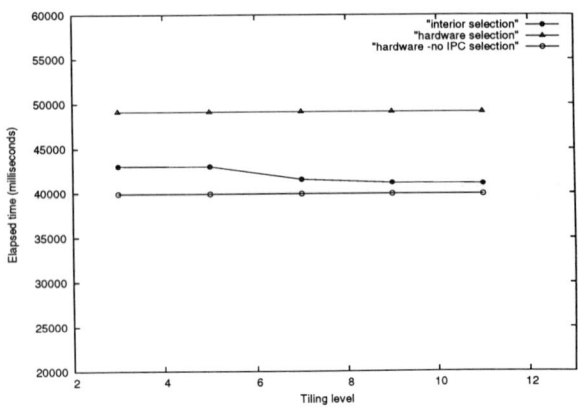

Figure 9: Timing results for selection over HYDRO

6.4 Spatial Joins

In this subsection, we analyze the performance of spatial join operations when assisted by the hardware filter. Here, we compare the performance of the *R-tree hardware join* against software joins of both R-trees and Quadtrees. For R-tree indexed cases, Oracle9i currently supports only a indexed nested join, which we refer to as *R-tree software join*. If both geometry columns are indexed using Quadtree tiles, SDO_RELATE performs a hash join during primary filtering followed by a direct application of the secondary filter. We refer to this join as the *Quadtree hash join*. If only the first column is indexed, then it performs the nested loop join using primary, interior and secondary filters. We call this the *indexed nested join*. In the rest of this subsection, we analyze the performance of a spatial join query by measuring the time taken for the following approaches: hash join, indexed nested join, hardware join and hardware-no-ipc join. We consider the join of the datasets COUNTY and HYDRO, PRISM and HYDRO followed by join on the datasets COUNTY and PRISM.

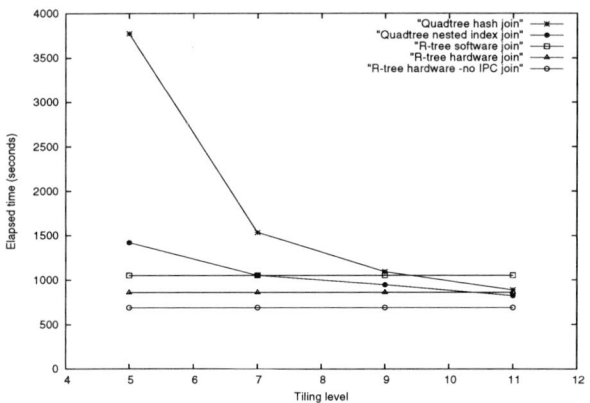

Figure 10: Timing results for join of COUNTY X HYDRO

Figure 10 shows the results of the above spatial join queries over COUNTY and HYDRO with various levels of tiling for the Quadtree indexing. These results show that the R-tree hardware-no-ipc join outperforms the R-tree software join and also both the Quadtree software joins for all the tiling levels. Among the Quadtree software joins, the indexed nested join performs better than the hash join because of the effectiveness of the interior filter which is not used in the latter. Results of the join of the PRISM and HYDRO datasets are given in Figure 11. It can be noted that at higher tiling levels, the indexed nested join performs well because the interior filter uses more accurate preprocessed approximations which identify more positive results, thereby reducing the I/O required for loading the actual geometries. These results show that although the hardware filter significantly improves the performance of Quadtree joins at lower tiling levels, the interior filter can be efficient

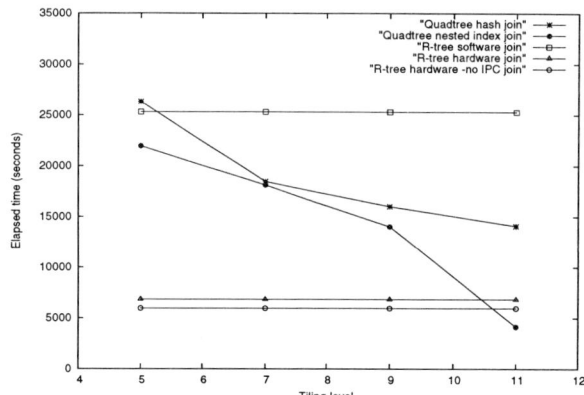

Figure 11: Timing results for join of HYDRO X PRISM

enough at higher tiling levels. However as shown in Figures 6 and 7, higher tiling levels have very expensive preprocessing and storage costs which is the reason why Oracle, in general, recommends using R-trees over Quadtrees [12]. Results for the join of COUNTY and PRISM (shown in [3]) also confirm that the R-tree hardware filter is very effective in improving the performance of joins.

7 Conclusion and Future Work

In this paper, we addressed the problem of integrating hardware acceleration into a commercial databases. We analyzed various approaches of integration provided by Oracle and integrated hardware acceleration for spatial operations as an external procedure. Using the hardware filter and the primary filter of an inexpensive R-tree index, we developed a run-time spatial intersection operator which has similar functionality as Oracle's software intersection operator. We analyzed the performance of this operator for spatial selection and join operations through extensive experimentation over real-world datasets and compared its performance with Oralce's run-time and preprocessed intersection operators. Our experimentation demonstrates that the hardware operator not only can improve the performance of the Oracle's run-time software operator significantly, but also can perform as well if not better than the preprocessed intersection operator without incurring any preprocessing and storage overhead. Since the hardware operator uses an R-tree index which has very low index update, creation and storage costs, we achieve the best of both worlds: low storage requirement and very low processing time. We also suggest that performance improvements can be expected if the hardware filter is integrated after the R-tree interior filter, as part of the DBMS itself. In the near future, we plan to explore the use of hardware filter integration for alternative complex queries.

8 Acknowledgment

We would like to thank Dr. Ravikanth Kothuri from Oracle for providing us necessary information about Oracle Spatial as well as giving valuable feedback on this work.

References

[1] P. Agarwal, S. Krishnan, N. Mustafa, and S. Venkatasubramanian. Streaming geometric optimization using graphics hardware. In *ESA 2003, Proceedings of Annual Meeting, Budapest, Hungary, September 15-20, 2003*.

[2] W. M. Badawy and W. G. Aref. On local heuristics to speed up polygon-polygon intersection tests. In *Proceedings of the 7th International Symposium on Advances in Geographic Information Systems (ACM-GIS '99)*, pages 97–102, 1999.

[3] N. Bandi, C. Sun, D. Agrawal, and A. El Abbadi. Hardware acceleration in commercial databases: A case study of spatial operations. Technical report, Computer Science Department, University of California, Santa Barbara, 2004. http://www.cs.ucsb.edu/research/trcs/docs/2004-15.pdf.

[4] T. Brinkhoff, H.-P. Kriegel, R. Schneider, and B. Seeger. Multi-step processing of spatial joins. In *Proceedings of the ACM SIGMOD International Conference on Management of Data (SIGMOD'94)*, pages 197–208, 1994.

[5] C. Daly and G. Taylor. *United States Average Annual Precipitation, 1961-1990*. Spatial Climate Analysis Service, OSU, 2000.

[6] Data Blades. http://www-3.ibm.com/software/data/informix/blades/, 2002.

[7] Data Cartridges. http://downloadwest.oracle.com/docs/cd/b10501_01/appdev.920/a96595/toc.htm, 2002.

[8] N. Goodnight, C. Woolley, G. Lewin, D. Luebke, and G. Humphreys. A multigrid solver for boundary value problems using programmable graphics hardware. In *Proceedings of the ACM SIGGRAPH/EUROGRAPHICS conference on Graphics hardware (SIGGRAPH'03)*, pages 102–111, 2003.

[9] A. Guttman. R-trees: a dynamic index structure for spatial searching. pages 599–609. Morgan Kaufmann Publishers Inc., 1988.

[10] K. E. Hoff III, T. Culver, J. Keyser, M. C. Lin, and D. Manocha. Fast computation of generalized voronoi diagrams using graphics hardware. In *Proceedings of the Annual Conference on Computer Graphics (SIGGRAPH'99)*, pages 277–286, 1999.

[11] K. E. Hoff III, A. Zaferakis, M. Lin, and D. Manocha. Fast and simple 2d geometric proximity queries using graphics hardware. In *Proceedings of the Symposium on Interactive 3D Graphics*, pages 145–148. ACM Press, 2001.

[12] R. K. Kothuri. Personal commnunications, 2004.

[13] R. K. Kothuri and S. Ravada. Efficient processing of large spatial queries using interior approximation. In *Proceedings of the 7th International Symposium on Advances in Spatial and Temporal Databases (SSTD'01)*, pages 404–421. ACM Press, 2001.

[14] Macedonia, Michael. The gpu enters computing's mainstream. *Computer*, 36(10):106–108, 2003.

[15] K. Moreland and E. Angel. The fft on a gpu. In *Proceedings of the ACM SIGGRAPH/EUROGRAPHICS conference on Graphics hardware (SIGGRAPH'03)*, pages 112–119, 2003.

[16] Oracle Spatial 9.2.0.1. http://download-west.oracle.com/docs/cd/b10501_01/appdev.920/a96630/toc.htm, 2002.

[17] OracleCallInterface. http://download-west.oracle.com/docs/cd/b10501_01/appdev.920/a96584/toc.htm, 2002.

[18] M. Segal and K. Akeley. *The OpenGL Graphics System: A Specification (Version 1.2.1)*. Silicon Graphics, Inc., April 1999.

[19] C. Sun, D. Agrawal, and A. El Abbadi. Hardware acceleration for spatial selections and joins. In *Proceedings of the ACM SIGMOD international conference on on Management of data (SIGMOD'03)*, pages 455–466. ACM Press, 2003.

[20] U. G. Survey. *State Boundaries of the United States*. U.S. Geological Survey, November 1999.

[21] U. G. Survey. *Landslide Incidence and Susceptibility distribution in United States*. U.S. Geological Survey, February 2001.

[22] J. Watermolen. *1:2,000,000-Scale County Boundaries*. U.S. Geological Survey, 2001.

[23] J. Watermolen. *1:2,000,000-Scale Hydrologic Unit Boundaries*. U.S. Geological Survey, 2002.

[24] G. Zimbrao and J. M. de Souza. A raster approximation for processing of spatial joins. In *Proceedings of 24rd International Conference on Very Large Data Bases (VLDB'98)*, pages 558–569. Morgan Kaufmann, August 24-27, 1998.

P*TIME: Highly Scalable OLTP DBMS for Managing Update-Intensive Stream Workload

Sang K. Cha and Changbin Song

Transact In Memory, Inc.
1600 Adams Drive
Menlo Park, CA 94025
USA

Seoul National University
School of Electrical Eng. and Computer Science
Kwanak P.O.Box 34, Seoul 151-600
Korea

{chask, tsangbi}@transactinmemory.com

Abstract

Over the past thirty years since the system R and Ingres projects started to lay the foundation for today's RDBMS implementations, the underlying hardware and software platforms have changed dramatically. However, the fundamental RDBMS architecture, especially, the storage engine architecture, largely remains unchanged. While this conventional architecture may suffices for satisfying most of today's applications, its deliverable performance range is far from meeting the so-called growing "real-time enterprise" demand of acquiring and querying high-volume update data streams cost-effectively.

P*TIME is a new, memory-centric light-weight OLTP RDBMS designed and built from scratch to deliver orders of magnitude higher scalability on commodity SMP hardware than existing RDBMS implementations, not only in search but also in update performance. Its storage engine layer incorporates our previous innovations for exploiting engine-level micro-parallelism such as differential logging and optimistic latch-free index traversal concurrency control protocol. This paper presents the architecture and performance of P*TIME and reports our experience of deploying P*TIME as the stock market database server at one of the largest on-line brokerage firms.

Permission to copy without fee all or part of this material is granted provided that the copies are not made or distributed for direct commercial advantage, the VLDB copyright notice and the title of the publication and its date appear, and notice is given that copying is by permission of the Very Large Data Base Endowment. To copy otherwise, or to republish, requires a fee and/or special permission from the Endowment

Proceedings of the 30th VLDB Conference, Toronto, Canada, 2004

1. Introduction

1.1. Demand for new OLTP DBMS architecture

Thirty years have passed since the system R and Ingres projects started to lay the foundation for today's RDBMS implementations [1]. Over this period, Moore's law has driven CPU processing power and memory capacity to grow million times, or 60% per year, respectively. The underlying software platform also changed significantly. Most operating systems now support virtually infinite address for 64-bit CPUs. The POSIX lightweight thread package enables efficient utilization of high-performance commodity multiprocessor hardware.

However, despite these dramatic underlying changes, the fundamental architecture of a single RDBMS instance largely remains unchanged. Even though data and indexes are cached in large buffer memory, they are managed as disk-resident structures. The heavyweight process architecture, which incurs high context switching overhead among multiple processes involved in executing a transaction, is still dominant [2]. This disk-centric heavyweight RDBMS architecture with the multi-million-line code base evolving over decades is inevitably subject to growing impedance mismatch with the underlying hardware capability. Recent research on L2-cache-conscious database structures and algorithms such as [3][4][5][6][7] addresses a crucial aspect of this mismatch that was not taken into consideration when existing RDBMS implementations, whether disk-centric or in-memory, were architected and implemented.

While the conventional disk-centric RDBMS architecture may suffice to serve search-dominant applications, the number of applications demanding the performance beyond the practical limit of today's RDBMS implementations is growing. Such applications typically deal with update-intensive stream workload, and are often called "real-time enterprise" applications by the business community. Some representative examples are:

- Stock market data stream in financial services.
- Call detail record (CDR) and network monitoring data streams in communication carriers: Especially challenging to cope with is the increasing CDR volume with the support of packet-granularity billing.
- Click streams in large portals.
- Update streams in on-line travel services.
- RFID data streams in supply chain management and retail.
- Traffic data management.

With the update transaction processing capability of typical RDBMS implementations limited to a few hundred TPS (transactions per second) on commodity SMP hardware, many painful hacks are commonly used in practice for handling update-intensive stream workload.

- Use of low-level ISAM files instead of RDBMS at the cost of giving up the high-level declarative SQL and ACID transaction quality.
- Heavy dependence on message queue systems placed in front of OLTP database at the cost of increased latency and capital expenditure.
- Excessive database partitioning and tuning on top of heavy hardware investment.
- Application-level batch processing with the risk of data loss and at the expense of application complexity.

1.2. P*TIME with storage engine innovations

Designed and built from scratch starting in 2000 with about 50 man-year effort, P*TIME is a new, memory-centric lightweight OLTP RDBMS that delivers up to two orders of magnitude higher scalability on commodity SMP hardware than existing RDBMS implementations.

P*TIME manages performance-critical data and indexes in the memory of a single multithreaded process. This architectural framework resulted from our prior experience of developing and benchmarking an in-memory storage engine over several years, which became the basis of multiple in-memory DBMS products in commercial production at Korean telecom and financial institutions [8][9][10]. However, the internal storage engine implementation details and capability fundamentally differ from those of its predecessor and other first-generation in-memory DBMS implementations such as [11] in following ways:

- Highly scalable durable-commit update transaction processing performance up to 140K TPS on a single non-partitioned physical table residing in a commodity 4-way 64-bit PC server.
- Highly scalable fast database recovery: Recovering a database of several gigabytes in memory takes only a little over 1 minute.
- Superior multiprocessor scalability: By eliminating the well-known index locking bottleneck that limits the multiprocessor scalability of the first-generation in-memory or the memory-cached disk-centric database, P*TIME can execute 1.4M concurrent search TPS on a 4-way 64-bit PC server.
- Ability of dealing with time-growing database through transparent management of the aging portion in disks.

From the interview with major telecom and financial institutions that have deployed or attempted to deploy the first-generation in-memory DBMS technology for mission-critical applications, we have learned that the lack of these capabilities has led to the disappointment with the technology and eventually the substantial scale-down of planned deployments or the project cancellation in some cases. As a specific example of the technology disappointment, restarting a 50GB in-memory billing database system at a major Korean wireless carrier takes four hours on HP Super dome machine. This long recovery time is unacceptable even with hot-standby database replication.

Enabling the above differentiated set of P*TIME capabilities are our own storage-engine-level innovations that exploit micro parallelism on today's shared-memory multiprocessor (SMP) hardware with multi-GHz CPUs, large memory, and a number of inexpensive disks. Differential logging, which enables fine-grained parallelism in logging and recovery of memory-centric databases [12], and optimistic latch-free index traversal (OLFIT) concurrency control, which maximizes parallel concurrent access to index nodes on SMP machines [5], are two representative innovations embedded in P*TIME to exploit such micro parallelism.

Differential logging uses bitwise XOR for undo and redo of database changes, each of which is captured as bitwise XOR difference between the after and before images of a fine-grained memory location. It minimizes the log volume to flush to the secondary storage while enabling fully parallel processing of an arbitrary number of differential log record streams independent of serialization order both during run time and recovery time. With each log record stream mapped to a physical disk, this means that the more log disks are added to a P*TIME database system, the shorter becomes the time to recover a database in memory and the higher durable-commit update transaction processing performance can be delivered.

The OLFIT defines an L2-cache-conscious concurrent tree index access protocol focused on minimizing node latch and unlatch operations. In an SMP environment, these operations incur excessive coherence L2 cache misses in reading or writing nodes, especially, upper ones, because the control information of an index node updated by one processor is highly likely to be updated by another

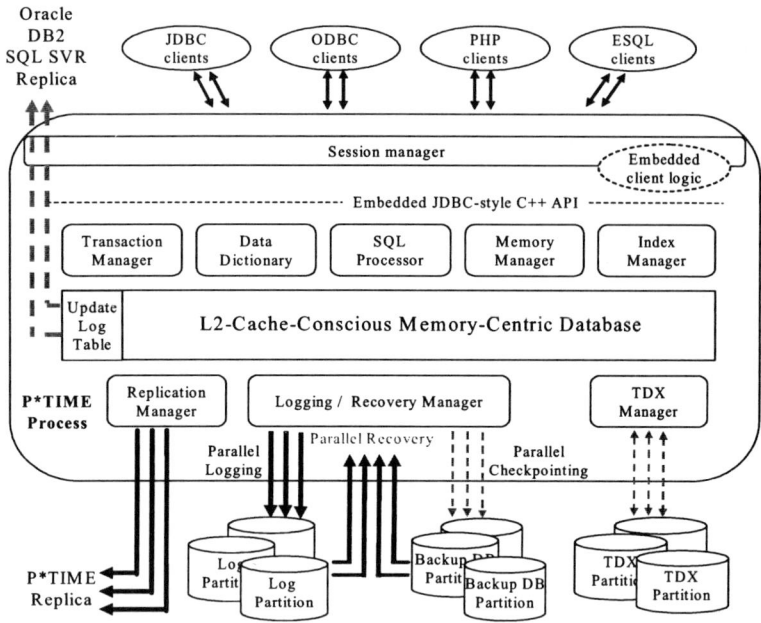

Figure 1. P*TIME Architecture

processor next time [5]. The coherence cache misses caused by index latching and unlatching is known for the major source of limiting the multiprocessor scalability of conventional in-memory or memory-cached disk-centric database systems. P*TIME, embedding the OLFIT protocol, enables multiple processors to access most index nodes concurrently without latching. For this reason, P*TIME shows almost linear multiprocessor scalability for indexed search, comparable to the scalability with no concurrency control. With minimized index node latching, P*TIME shows highly scalable multiprocessor index performance even for 100% update workload.

P*TIME currently supports SQL 92 with some extensions and standard RDBMS APIs such as ODBC/JDBC and a JDBC-style C++ API for building multi-tier and embedded applications, respectively. With its lightweight session management, P*TIME can sustain a thousand concurrent ODBC/JDBC connections without performance degradation.

P*TIME has been successfully in production since November 2002 as the stock market database server at Samsung Securities in Korea, one of the world-largest on-line stock brokerage companies that serves 50K – 60K concurrent on-line traders. P*TIME-based stock market database server processes 4 million trading messages per day with 2.6 million trading messages over the six hour window for the real-time update of the market database through SQL/ODBC API. This real-time database update consumes about 10% of the CPU power of 6-way 450Hz HP server and the rest is available for concurrent processing of up to 20K SQL query transactions per second per machine for the users who query the database through one of the best developed broadband and wireless infrastructures in the world. Our laboratory experiment shows that P*TIME is capable of processing up to eight times as fast as the peak-time arrival rate of real trading messages while reserving 70% of CPU power for concurrent query processing on a 4-way 700MHz PC server.

As another evidence for its industrial strength, porting a major enterprise software vendor's application with about 500 tables took only about a week. P*TIME is also being deployed in communications carriers, government agencies, and RFID-based supply chain management systems as reliable high-performance lightweight OLTP database systems.

1.3. Contribution of this paper

This paper presents the architecture and performance of P*TIME and reports our experience of deploying P*TIME as the stock market database server.

The major contribution of this paper is to show existentially that a new, carefully engineered memory-centric OLTP DBMS with the focus of exploiting engine-level micro parallelism can support the challenging performance requirement of update-intensive stream OLTP workload cost-effectively. Our previous work of differential logging and OLFIT concurrency control protocol plays critical roles in achieving up to two orders of magnitude difference in performance scalability combined with many implementation optimizations to minimize unnecessary overhead.

Our contribution is complimentary to the recent progress in the stream data management research focusing on the same target application domains. While the stream data management research focuses on the incremental, adaptive on-line analysis of stream data through a data flow network of operators, queues, and synopsis [13], our focus is on the high-performance storage and ad hoc query of update data streams addressing the needs of mission-critical enterprise applications that cannot tolerate any loss of data or continuity of service. The new TelegraphCQ implementation approach of starting from PostgresSQL instead of expanding its early Java implementation supports the need for a powerful storage engine for building practical stream data management systems [14].

This paper is organized as follows. Section 2 presents P*TIME architecture and its components. Section 3 presents the performance scalability of P*TIME storage engine with a brief description of the experimental measurement environment. Section 4 describes the challenges and experience of deploying P*TIME as the stock market database server. Section 5 concludes this paper.

2. P*TIME Architecture

P*TIME is a fully functional RDBMS. Figure 1 shows P*TIME architecture. Rounded boxes represent essential DBMS functional modules, and ovals represent applications.

2.1. Overall design goal

Based on our several years of experience of implementing and benchmarking a multithreaded in-memory DBMS since early 1990's [8][9][10], we designed P*TIME architecture with two major goals: maintaining a compact code base structure for the ease of code changes, and maximization of micro parallelism for exploiting the ever-increasing hardware capability.

To meet the first goal, C++ is chosen as the implementation language to structure the P*TIME code base as a collection of C++ classes, and the C++ template feature is used extensively. To meet the second goal, innovations are made to most of DBMS functionality layers, starting from the most fundamental layer of logging and recovery. In addition, the detailed implementation is guided by a derived guideline of avoiding unnecessary L2 cache misses and minimizing context switches, which also incur substantial L2 cache misses.

Our current focus of P*TIME on micro parallelism does not mean that we are excluding the natural extension of P*TIME exploiting macro parallelism on a distributed grid of P*TIME instances. In fact, to exploit the cost advantage of commodity SMP boxes, P*TIME provides the industry standard XA interface for supporting distributed transactions on partitioned databases, and the fast active-active database replication based on asynchronous fine-grained log propagation.

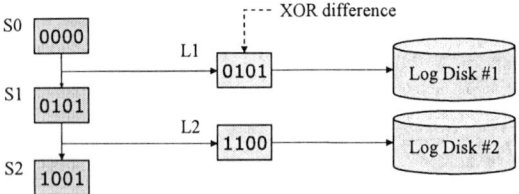

(a) Differential Logging to Multiple Log Partition Disks

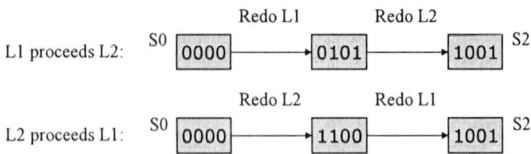

(b) Order-independent Recovery of Database

Figure 2. Inherent Parallelism of Differential Logging

2.2. L2-cache-conscious in-memory database

P*TIME manages performance-critical data and indexes primarily in the memory of a single multithreaded process. For the data, memory is divided into a set of pages, each of which contains multiple homogeneous slots for holding records, large variable-length fields, or pieces of BLOB data. A container is defined to manage a list of homogeneous pages. By default, a table is mapped to a container. Optionally, a table may be mapped to multiple containers, each of which stores a vertical partition of a table for efficient column-wise scan.

In P*TIME, indexes are by default managed as non-persistent structures supporting isolation and rollback and are rebuilt in parallel during the database restart process. P*TIME implements CPU-optimized hash and B+-tree index structures with direct memory addressing. In implementing B+-tree, we optimized the node layout and search and insertion procedures to minimize L2 cache misses. We chose B+-tree instead of CSB+-tree, the well-known cache-conscious B+-tree ([3]), because the optimized version of B+-tree performs better than CSB+-tree in the overall performance for the update-intensive workload.

2.3. Fine-grained parallel differential logging and recovery

P*TIME supports ACID transactions by storing every update log, first in an in-memory log buffer, and eventually in one of log partition disks. To recycle the log disk space and to shorten the database recovery time, P*TIME uses the parallelized version of fuzzy checkpointing. Dirty in-memory database pages are occasionally flushed in parallel to backup partition disks without interrupting transaction processing.

Compared with existing in-memory or disk-centric RDBMS implementations, P*TIME takes a very different architectural approach to logging. Based on the fine-grained differential logging of updates, P*TIME first minimizes log volume for maximal utilization of CPU processing power and memory and IO bandwidth. Dynamic selection of field-level or record-level logging represents the degree of P*TIME optimization for log volume minimization. Even for the same logging granularity, differential logging stores the XOR difference between "before" and "after" images and thus reduces the log volume by almost half compared with the conventional "before/after image" logging such as ARIES [15] [16]. Compared with the block-level "before/after image" logging implementations, the fine-grained differential logging of P*TIME reduces the log volume by an order of magnitude without sacrificing the recovery performance.

Figure 2 illustrates the inherent parallelism of differential logging as two serial transactions change a data item from S0 to S2. When the first transaction T1 changes the data from "0000" to "0101", the log record L1 with the XOR difference "0101" is flushed to the log disk #1 and T1 commits. When the second transaction T2 changes the data from "0101" to "1001", the log record L2 with the XOR difference "1100" is flushed to the log disk #2, and T2 commits. At this point, if the system crashes, the database is restarted by initializing the data item with the backup image S0 ("0000"). Differential logging uses the bit-wise XOR operation as redo and undo. Figure 2 (b) shows that the log records in two log disks can be processed in parallel because the associativity and commutativity of XOR enables the correct recovery of the state S2 can be recovered independent of the order of applying L1 and L2. Note that if the system crashed before the transaction T2 writing the commit record to the disk #2, T2 can be undone by applying L2 to S2 after doing all redo operations. Alternatively, the single pass recovery is possible by scanning the log files backward and applying only log records of committed transactions.

Parallel nature of differential logging further multiplies the gain in logging performance with the number of log partition disks, making it possible for P*TIME to deliver up to two orders of magnitude higher scalability in durable-commit update performance than existing RDBMS implementations. P*TIME supports hot spot updates by allowing a transaction to proceed to access the updates of a proceeding transaction waiting for the commit record to be flushed to log disks.

The scalability of durable-commit update performance is essential for the mission-critical real-time enterprise applications that cannot tolerate any loss of data. For less mission-critical applications, P*TIME also supports the so-called "deferred-commit" update mode, with which the system does not wait for the commit record to be flushed to the log disk to issue the commit signal to applications. In section 3, we shall demonstrate that the engine-internal performance of P*TIME in both durable-commit and deferred-commit modes is superior to the reported deferred-commit update performance of a popular in-memory DBMS implementation on a comparable hardware platform [17].

P*TIME supports high availability first with fine-grained parallel recovery of in-memory database. Breaking the common misconception that parallel logging lengthens database recovery time because of the overhead of sorting multiple log streams by serialization order, which is true for most conventional RDBMS implementations, the inherent parallelism of differential logging enables fast recovery of P*TIME database, scalable with the number of log and backup partition disks. Differential logging even permits simultaneous processing of multiple log partitions and backup database partitions. In addition to fast database recovery, P*TIME supports active-active log-based N-way asynchronous and synchronous replication to meet the high availability requirement of mission-critical applications.

2.4. Concurrency control

Another distinguishing feature of P*TIME is the OLFIT index concurrency control [5], which minimizes expensive coherence L2 cache misses incurred by conventional, latch-based index locking protocols in the SMP environment. The OLFIT scheme, based on the optimistic assumption that the conflict is rare and even if it occurs, can be resolved by retrying the node access, is designed to avoid latching and unlatching operations as much as possible. With OLFIT maximizing hardware-level parallelism in concurrent index node access, P*TIME does not suffer from the well-known index locking bottleneck of existing in-memory or memory-cached disk-centric RDBMS implementations. Since the effectiveness of the OLFIT depends on how well it is implemented, P*TIME uses assembly language to implement its key primitives to make sure that unnecessary L2 cache misses do not occur.

For the concurrency control of base tables, P*TIME implements multi-level locking and supports all four isolation levels of SQL.

2.5. Transparent Disk eXtension

For the time-growing data such as stream data, it is not feasible to keep the entire table in memory. P*TIME TDX (Transparent Disk eXtension) transparently migrates aging or infrequently accessed portion of a table to TDX partitions on disk. Each TDX partition is a self-describing indexed data set which supports compression and direct SQL access. TDX manager pins a TDX partition in memory when it is frequently accessed.

2.6. Application binding

On top of P*TIME core modules lies the SQL processor which includes a cost-based query optimizer and a query plan execution engine. This SQL processor is accessed through the standard programming interfaces such as ODBC, JDBC, ESQL, PHP, and a JDBC-style embedded

C++ API.

To protect the database system from application errors, application processes are completely decoupled from the multithreaded P*TIME database server. This differentiates P*TIME from the more tightly coupled heavyweight process architecture such as TimesTen, where multiple application processes directly access the database and the lock information in the shared memory. While this tightly coupled heavyweight process architecture has the advantage of eliminating client/server communication overhead for the clients running on the same machine with the database, it runs the risk of corrupting the database or blocking legitimate access by other processes because of locks unreleased by hanging applications. Furthermore, the gain in client/server communication disappears for the remote applications.

P*TIME also supports tight coupling of P*TIME with application logic but takes a different approach of providing an embedded C++ API. An application logic of accessing P*TIME database through a collection of JDBC-style C++ classes can be embedded inside a P*TIME server. This is useful for building P*TIME-embedded tools such as LDAP server.

To maximize multi-tier application performance, P*TIME transparently supports transaction group shipping (TGS) between P*TIME server and multi-threaded application servers. This feature reduces the number of interactions by shipping temporally adjacent independent transaction requests or responses in a group between P*TIME server and application servers.

2.7. Heterogeneous database integration interface

To facilitate the integration with heterogeneous RDBMS implementations, P*TIME provides an elegant interface called update log table whose entries representing recent update, insert, or delete on individual records can be accessed and deleted in SQL.

Compared with the common approach of vendor-specific, black-box synchronization functionality, this open-ended API enables application developers to implement arbitrary application-specific update propagation semantics to heterogeneous databases. With this feature, P*TIME can function as the transaction processing front-end to existing RDBMS implementations.

3. Performance Scalability

To measure the internal OLTP performance scalability of P*TIME, we embedded a simple benchmark logic inside the P*TIME server using its JDBC-style embedded C++ API. Workload clients are emulated by embedded connection objects iterated by several worker threads, which carry out actual transaction execution.

The test database consists of a single non-partitioned table of 8 million records that we adopted from a telco database. Since we are interested in measuring the scalability limit, we have intentionally avoided the

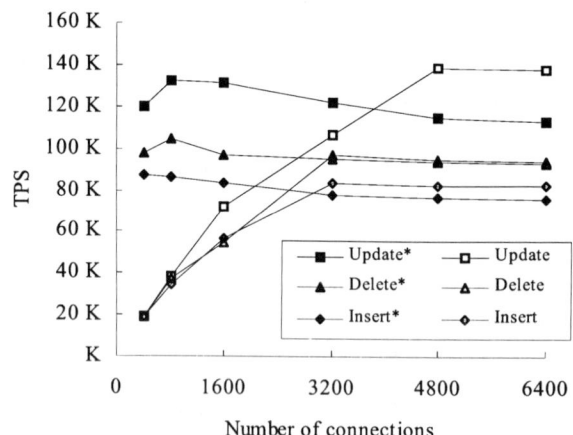

Figure 3. Update/Insert/Delete Performance with Varying Number of Connections
(The symbol * denotes that on-disk write cache is enabled.)

creation of multiple tables or multiple partitions, which may distribute the internal contention pressure. The standard TPC benchmark was not adequate first because it is not intended for the OLTP of high-volume stream data, and secondly because the specification includes preset parameters such as think time that limit the maximum deliverable performance given a database size.

Each record of our test database is 168 bytes long. A hash index is built on its primary key field of BIGINT type. While we created the hash index in this experiment, the result is more or less the same for the B+-tree supporting range queries. The size of the initial database is about 1.4GB, including 100MB for the non-persistent hash index.

Each tested transaction type contains a single operation which is one of the following:

- Search a record with a given primary key and return a BIGINT-type column of the selected record.
- Update a BIGINT-type column of the record matching a given primary key.
- Insert a record.
- Delete a record matching a given primary key.

The experiment was mainly conducted on a Compaq ML 570 server running UNIX, with four 700MHz Xeon CPUs, each with 2MB L2 cache, 100MHz front-side bus, 6GB PC-100 SDRAM, Ultra 160 SCSI card, and several 7200 rpm SCSI disks. Each disk has 300KB of on-disk write cache (WC) for track buffering.

3.1. Update/Insert/Delete performance

From the durability perspective, we have two options in measuring the durable-commit update performance:

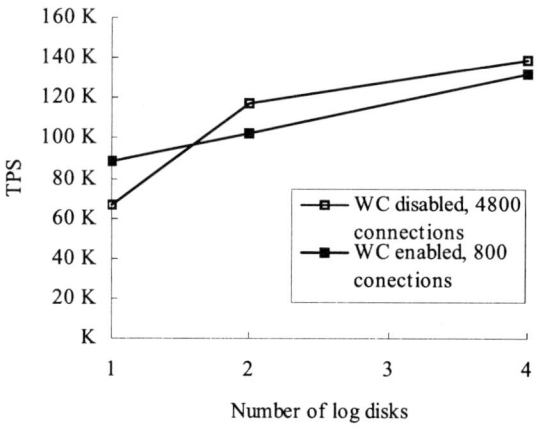

Figure 4. Update Scalability with Varying Number of Log Disks

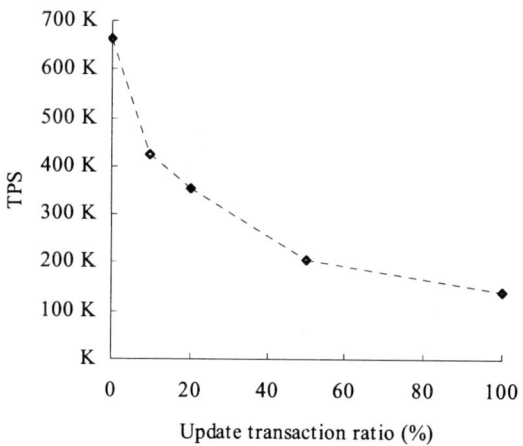

Figure 6. Mixed Workload Performance with Varying Ratio of Updates (WC disabled, 4800 connections)

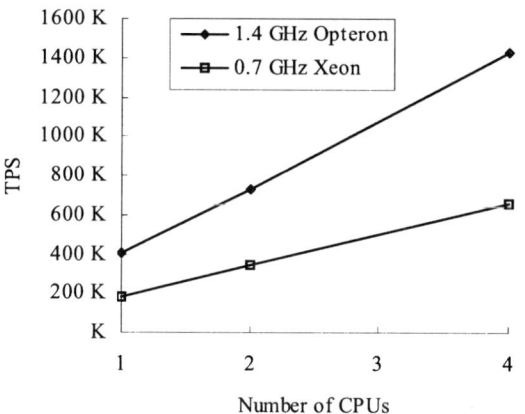

Figure 5. Search Scalability with Varying Number of CPUs

enabling and disabling on-disk write cache. The use of on-disk write cache is acceptable if the power supply to disk drives is securely backed up by UPS to cope with power failure.

Figure 3 shows that P*TIME can process 140K field update transactions per second (TPS) with four log disks used for parallel logging. For pure insert and delete workloads, P*TIME handles 80K and 100K TPS, respectively. The response time with on-disk write cache enabled (1~3 ms) is better than that disabled (9~16 ms). In both cases, the response time improves significantly with the reduced number of connections.

This figure also shows that the performance with on-disk write cache disabled converges to the performance with on-disk cache enabled as the number of connections increases. With the "deferred commit" option, P*TIME can deliver the same peak performance with one log disk with slightly better response time. However, with this option, the durability of updates is not guaranteed in case that the operating system failure occurs.

Figure 4 shows the scalability of P*TIME update performance with the varying number of log disks. As the number of log disks increases, the update throughput also increases until CPU, memory bus or IO channel capacity is saturated by a specific hardware configuration.

3.2. Search performance

Figure 5 shows that P*TIME can process 650K search transactions per second on the 4-way 700MHz Xeon server, and more than 1.4 million transactions per second on a 4-way 1.4GHz AMD Opteron server running RedHat AS 3.0 with 1MB L2 cache. Careful design of P*TIME internal data structures and algorithms minimizing L2 cache misses enables such linear search scalability with the number and the speed of CPUs.

Figure 6 shows the overall throughput when update and search transactions are intermixed, ranging from 100 % search to 100 % update. When the search/update ratio is 90/10, 80/20 and 50/50, the overall throughput is about 430K, 350K and 200K TPS, respectively.

3.3. Multi-tier performance

To evaluate P*TIME performance in a multi-tier application environment, we created a number of multithreaded Java application processes on several machines, which are connected to the P*TIME server process on the 4-way 700MHz Xeon server via gigabit Ethernet. In this environment, P*TIME shows 70,000 TPS for search-only workload and 42,000 TPS for the update-only workload. Transaction group shipping was turned on to utilize the server's communication bandwidth efficiently. When only a single client thread is connected, P*TIME shows 5,800 search TPS with the average response time of 0.17ms or 1,320 update TPS with the

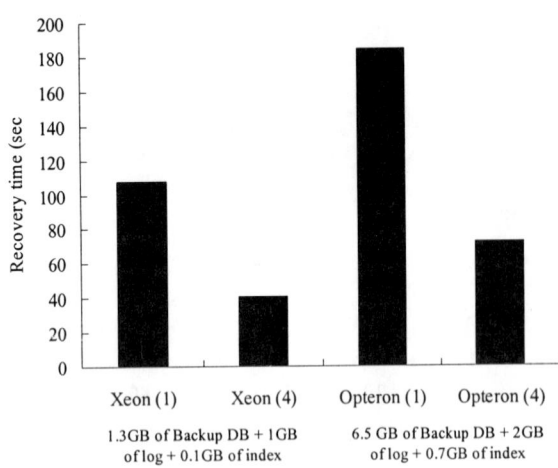

Figure 8. Database Recovery Time (The number in parentheses denotes the number of CPUs and disks.)

average response time of 0.76ms with WC enabled. Although these numbers represent significant drops from the peak engine performance numbers, they correspond to ten times in search and hundred times in update compared with a fully-memory-cached disk-centric database running in the same environment.

3.4. Restart time

To see the impact of P*TIME parallel recovery, we measured the time to recover the whole database from 1.3GB of backup database (8M records), 1GB of log records (10M update transactions), and 0.1GB of non-persistent index. The recovery time is broken down to loading the checkpointed backup database, replaying the log records, and rebuilding non-persistent indexes. The first column in Figure 8 shows that the total recovery time of the sequential recovery based on a single log disk and a single checkpoint backup database is 107 seconds, which is reduced to only 41 seconds by parallelizing all individual recovery steps: loading backup database, replaying log records, and rebuilding indexes. Note that even the sequential recovery time of P*TIME is shorter than that of existing in-memory RDBMS implementations.

To measure the restart time for a larger database, we scaled the database size five times (6.5GB of backup database and 0.7GB of non-persistent index for 40M records) and the log size twice (20M update transactions or 2 GB). Since this database size exceeds the process address limit of the 32 bit Xeon machine, we used the 4-way 1.4GHz 64 bit Opteron server with 16GB DDR memory and several 15000 rpm disks connected through U320 SCSI controller. The fourth column in Figure 8 shows that the recovery time with 4 CPUs and 4 disks is only 72 seconds, while the recovery time with 1 CPU and 1 disk is 184 seconds. This experimental result leads us to conclude that the database recovery performance of P*TIME is scalable with the number of log and checkpoint disks used and the CPU/IO capability of the underlying hardware system.

4. Stock Market Database Case

4.1. Challenges

The stock market database keeps track of the current state and history of individual stock item's bid-and-ask and settled price and volume data. It is critical for this database to minimize the latency in capturing the continuous stream of stock trading messages and

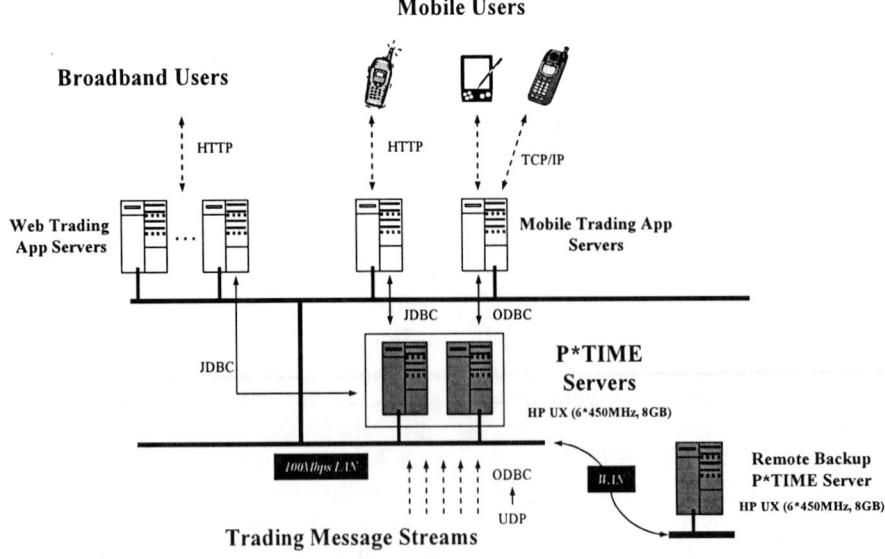

Figure 7. P*TIME-based Stock Market Database Servers

delivering updates to the interested users or responding to ad hoc user queries. Another important requirement is to lower the cost of quality service because of the competition among the stock brokerage firms. Conventional RDBMS implementations observing the ACID transaction quality is not adequate for cost-effective management of stock market data because of the amount of update volume to process.

4.2. Samsung Securities, Inc. case study

Samsung Securities, Inc. is the number 1 brokerage firm in Korea, serving 50K – 60K concurrent users out of 800K registered on-line users. Korean stock market is well known for its volatility and fast adoption of on-line trading because of the well-developed broadband and wireless infrastructures enabling easy access to the market database and the low transaction fee which resulted from the competition among many on-line brokerage firms.

Recognizing that implementing the market database servers with conventional RDMBS technology is cost-prohibitive, Samsung Securities, Inc. maintained a farm of about 50 C-ISAM-based market data servers communicating with the user's fat MS Windows client program in a custom protocol. Each server runs on a SUN Enterprise 3500 or 4500 hardware with six to eight CPUs. There is no clear separation of database and applications in this architecture, and the IT staffs has the burden of maintaining the application code base of manipulating C-ISAM and shared memory with ad hoc concurrency control.

When Samsung Securities, Inc. planned to launch the mobile trading service to mobile phone and PDA users in August 2002, it decided to separate the database server from the application because of the various difficulties that it has experienced in maintaining the C-ISAM-based server. Samsung Securities, Inc. chose P*TIME to manage the market database because its update scalability will lower the long-term capital expenditure and the standard RDBMS interface will lower the application maintenance cost.

Figure 7 shows the architecture of P*TIME-based market database server deployment at Samsung Securities, Inc. For the high availability reason, two copies of P*TIME servers are co-located with a single remote backup server. Since the trading message streams are broadcast via UDP from the stock exchange and the message processing burden is not severe for P*TIME, each P*TIME server is responsible for updating its own database. After a few months of operation, Samsung Securities, Inc. also decided to move the customer's profile of watch list groups from eight LDAP servers to the operational P*TIME servers. For this database, P*TIME servers are configured as active-active replicas. Although the operational systems were not planned to serve web trading services, the IT staffs of Samsung Securities, Inc. also implements the new functionalities to introduce in the web trading service using the operational P*TIME servers because of the ease of manipulating the database with SQL and JDBC.

4.3. Schema and Workload

The stock market database consists of 50+ relations. Figure 9 shows five representative relations. For each relation, the number of columns and the record length in bytes are shown as well as some column names. The primary key columns are printed in bold face.

STOCK_MASTER relation holds the reference information of stock items such as code, name, and trade status. The Korean stock market has 1700+ stock items managed by KSE and KOSDAQ. BIDNASK relation keeps track of ten closest bid and ask prices/volume pairs for each stock item. TRADE relation keeps track of the

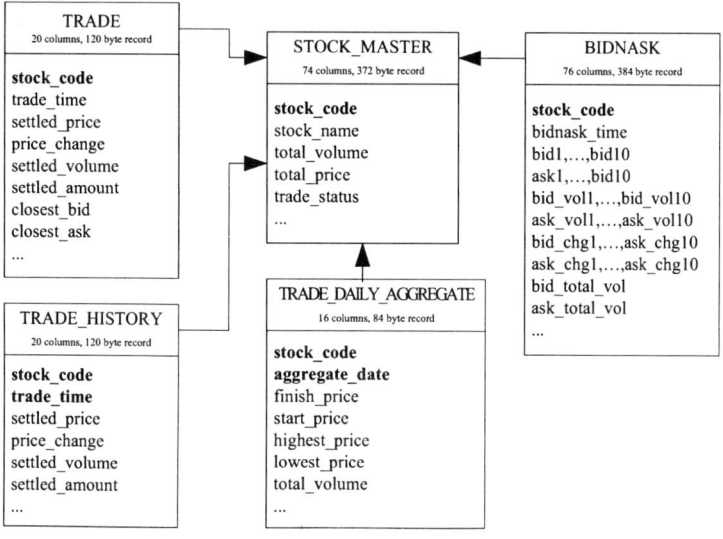

Figure 9. Representative Relations of P*TIME-Based Market Database

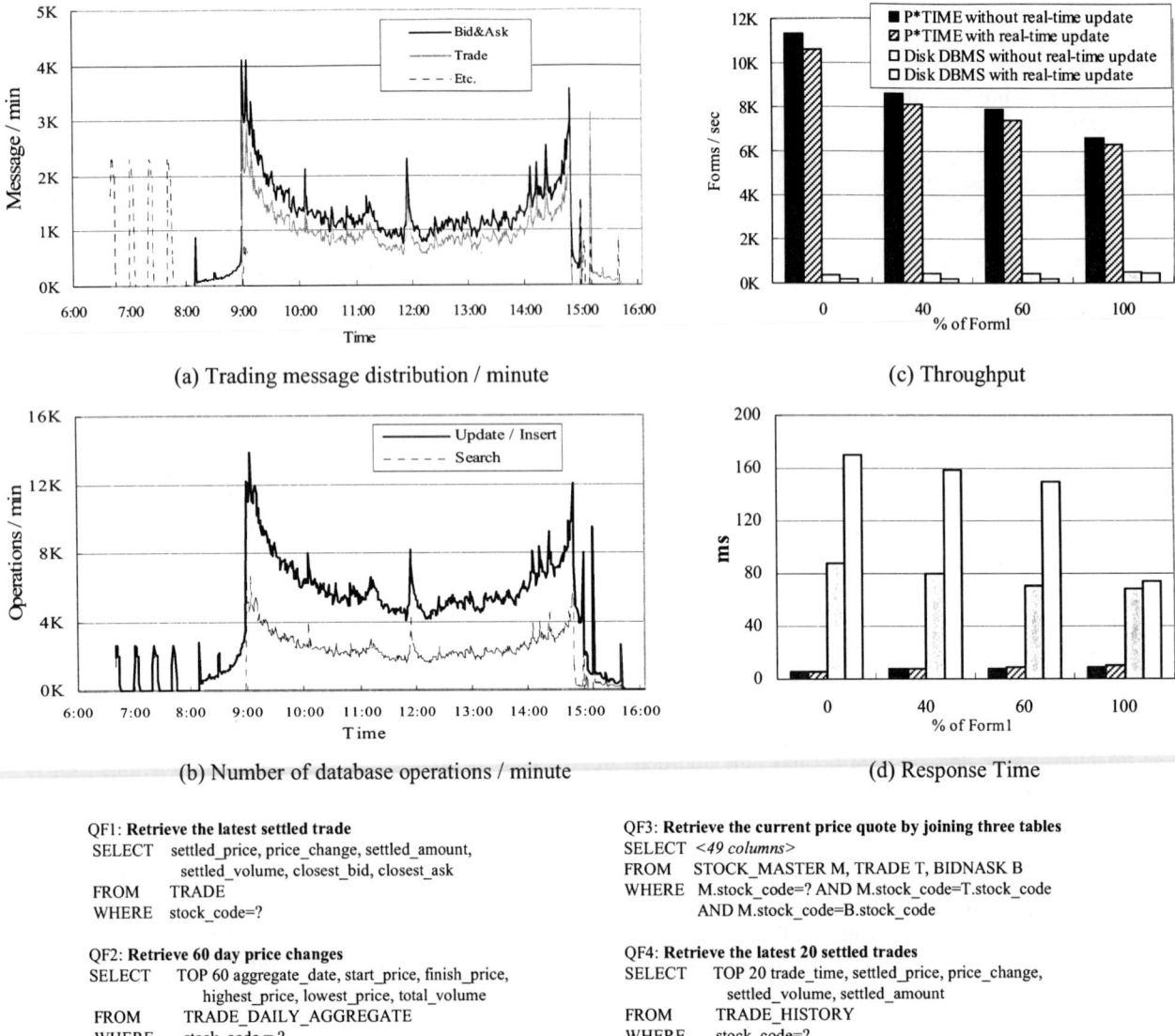

Figure 10. P*TIME-Based Stock Market Database Performance

latest settled trade information of each stock item, such as settled price and volume. In addition, it also keeps track of the closest bid and ask prices and volumes. TRADE_HISTORY relation stores the history of settled trades. TRADE_DAILY_AGGREGATE stores the daily aggregates of stock items such as high and low prices and traded volume. In addition, there are relations, which are not shown in the figure, for keeping track of options, futures, market indexes, and market statistics.

The challenging workload from DBMS perspective is processing the trading message stream from the stock exchange. Figure 10(a) shows the time distribution of one-day volume of real trading messages from Korean stock market. A major portion of this message stream consists of bid-and-asks and settled trades. Figure 10(b) shows the distribution of required update / insert and search queries to process the trading message stream.

For each bid-and-ask message, the following two updates are required.

- Update a row of BIDNASK with new values of bid and ask prices/volumes, etc.
- Update a row of TRADE with new values of the closest bid and ask information.

To process each settled trade message, the following operations are needed.

- Check the trade_status value of STOCK_MASTER.
- If the status is ok, search BIDNASK relation with a

given stock item to get the closest bid-and-ask match (bid1, ask1, bid_vol1, ask_vol1) because this information is not contained in the message.
- Update TRADE with new values of settled price, volume, etc.
- Insert the new trade record into TRADE_HISTORY.

Another type of major workload is query processing. Figure 10 (e) and (f) show two popular query forms. The first one displays the 60-day price changes of a stock item. The second one queries the current price quote of a stock item. Both forms generate two SQL queries in sequence, and each query is processed as a separate transaction.

In addition, there are periodic batch jobs conducted during night time or weekends to compute the daily, weekly, monthly aggregates.

4.4. Comparative P*TIME performance

To measure the comparative gain of using P*TIME over the existing DBMS implementation, we selected one of the easily accessible disk-centric DBMS implementations, and created two databases, one for P*TIME and another for the selected disk-centric DBMS, on the same Compaq ML 570 server that we use to report the experiment result of Section 3. In-memory DBMS implementations were not available for experimental comparison.

We used the real trading message stream of Figure 10 (a) to generate the update stream workload, and two query forms in Figure 10 (e), (f) to measure the concurrent query processing capability.

Figure 10 (c) and (d) shows the throughput and average response time with the varying ratio of two query forms. For each ratio, four values are shown. The first two values represent P*TIME and the remaining two values the disk-centric database. For each DBMS, the first value represents the performance without real-time market database update, and the second represents the performance with real-time market database update. The graphs shows that P*TIME is up to 40 times more scalable than the disk-centric database in throughput while the disk-centric database experiences severe degradation of response time.

4.5. Scalability with respect to stream data volume

To measure the scalability of update stream processing capability of P*TIME, we ran the experiment of accelerating trading message arrival using the one-day real trading message volume set. Figure 11 shows the throughput of concurrent query processing with the varying acceleration of trading message arrival rate. The query form 2, shown in Figure 10 (f), which has more interference with the real-time market database update is used to measure the throughput. In this figure, "No" means that there is no market database update load, 1x means the original speed of the stream, and 8x means that the message arrives at the eight times of the original speed.

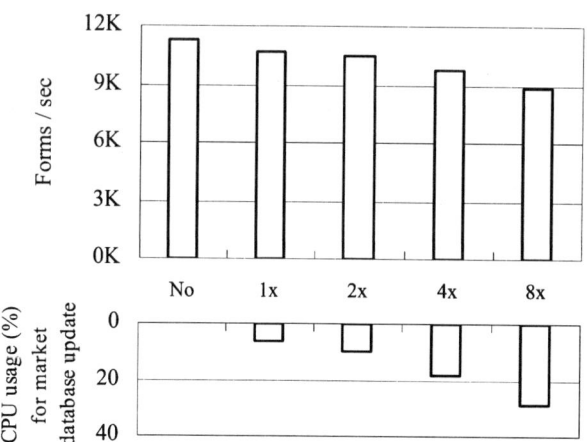

Figure 11. Concurrent Query Processing Throughput with Varying Rate of Trading Message Arrival

At 8x, about 2000 update transactions and 1000 search query transactions are performed per second to update the market database.

From Figure 11 we observe that the concurrent query processing is not much affected even though the rate of arrival changes from 1x to 8x. The minor drop in the concurrent query throughput is roughly proportional to the CPU usage for the real-time market database update.

5. Summary and Related Work

In this paper, we have presented:

- Rationale for the new OLTP DBMS for handling update-intensive stream workload which is frequently found in the so-called real-time enterprise applications.
- Architecture and performance scalability of P*TIME.
- Real-world deployment of P*TIME as the stock market database server.

With the exponentially growing gap between the CPU speed and the memory access speed, there has been much research lately on the L2-cache-conscious index structures ([3][4]), database layout ([6]), index concurrency control ([5]), and query processing ([7]).

Based on our experience of building, benchmarking, and deploying P*TIME in the real world transaction processing environment, we believe that careful implementation of L2-cache-conscious DBMS-internal protocols and algorithms such as the OLFIT and minimizing thread context switches leveraging the lightweight multithread architecture are more crucial than L2 cache-conscious data structures alone, which provide only marginal gain in improving overall throughput. As future work, we expect to formalize this experience further through experiment.

1043

P*TIME architecture design and implementation has benefited from the author's experience of building and benchmarking the first-generation in-memory DBMS over several years [8][9][10], which was motivated by the exposure to the early in-memory query processing project at HP Laboratories [18].

Building P*TIME follows the vision of RISC-style DBMS [19]. Although we have not yet incorporated the self-tuning functionality, our compact code, which uses the C++ template feature extensively, coupled with the inherent simplicity of the memory-centric database performance model compared with the disk-centric one would be make it easier to incorporate the self-tuning capability.

As future work, we plan to extend P*TIME to incorporate the continuous query processing capability, and exploit the macro parallelism using a number of inexpensive SMP blades connected through a high-speed switch fabric. In another direction of research, we plan to refine the stock market database domain further so that it can serve as a benchmark database for the update-intensive stream workload.

Acknowledgement

The authors thank Gio Wiederhold at Stanford University for his invaluable comment on the early version of this paper. They also thank other members of P*TIME development team for their contribution.

REFERENCES

[1] Paul McJones, Ed.. The 1995 SQL Reunion: People, Projects, and Politics. Digital SRC Technical Note. 1997-018. http://www.mcjones.org/System_R/T

[2] Jack L. Lo, Luiz A. Barroso, Sujan J. Eggers, Kourosh Gharachorloo, Henry M. Levy, and Sujay S. Parekh. An Analysis of Database Workload Performance on Simultaneous Multithreaded Processors. In Proceedings of the 25th Annual International Symposium on Computer Architecture, June 1998.

[3] Jun Rao and Kenneth Ross. Making B+-trees Cache Conscious in Main Memory. In Proceedings of ACM SIGMOD Conference, 2000.

[4] Kihong Kim, Sang K. Cha, and Keunjoo Kwon. Optimizing Multidimensional Index Trees for Main Memory Access. In Proceedings of ACM SIGMOD Conference, 2001.

[5] Sang K. Cha, Sangyong Hwang, Kihong Kim, and Keunjoo Kwon. Cache-Conscious Concurrency Control of Main-Memory Indexes on Shared-Memory Multiprocessor Systems. In Proceedings of VLDB Conference, 2001. (Under patent application)

[6] Anastassia Ailamaki, David J. DeWitt, Mark D. Hill, and Marios Skousnakis. Weavering Relations for Cache Performance. In Proceedings of VLDB Conference, 2001.

[7] Peter Boncz, Stefan Manegold, and Martin Kersten. Data Architecture Optimized for the new Bottleneck: Memory Access. In Proceedings of VLDB Conference, 1999.

[8] Sang K. Cha, Jang Ho Park, Sung Jik Lee, Sae Hyeok Song, Byung Dae Park, S. J. Lee, S. Y. Park, and G. B. Kim. Object-Oriented Design of Main-Memory DBMS for Real-Time Applications. In Proceedings of the 2nd International Workshop on Real-Time Computing Systems and Applications, 1995.

[9] Sang K. Cha, Jang Ho Park, Sung Jik Lee, Byung Dae Park, and J. S. Lee. An Extensible Architecture for Main-Memory Real-Time Storage Systems. In Proceedings of the 3rd International Workshop on Real-Time Computing Systems and Applications, 1996.

[10] Jang Ho Park, Yong Sik Kwon, Ki Hong Kim, Sangho Lee, Byoung Dae Park, and Sang K. Cha. Xmas: An Extensible Main-Memory Storage System for High-Performance Applications. Demo in Proceedings of ACM SIGMOD Conference, 1998.

[11] TimesTen Performance Software. http://www.timesten.com

[12] Juchang Lee, Kihong Kim, and Sang K. Cha. Differential Logging: A Commutative and Associative Logging Scheme for Highly Parallel Main Memory Databases. In Proceedings of IEEE ICDE Conference, 2001. (Under patent application)

[13] B. Babcock, S. Babu, M. Datar, R. Motwani, and J. Widom. Models and Issues in Data Stream Systems. In Proceedings of ACM PODS Conference, 2002.

[14] S. Krishnarmurthy, S. Chanrasekaran, O. Cooper, A. Deshpande, M. Franklin, J. Hellerstein, W. Hong, S. Madden, F. Reiss, M. Shah. TelegraphCQ: An Architectural Status Report. IEEE Data Engineering Bulletin, Vol 26(1), March 2003

[15] C. Mohan, Don Haderle, Bruce Lindsay, Hamid Pirahesh, and Peter Schwarz. ARIES: A Transaction Recovery Method Supporting Fine-Granularity Locking and Partial Rollbacks Using Write-Ahead Logging. ACM Transactions on Database Systems, Vol. 17, No. 1, pp. 94-162, 1992.

[16] IBM, ARIES Family of Locking and Recovery Algorithms. http://www.almaden.ibm.com/u/mohan/ARIES_Impact.html

[17] M-A. Neimat, TimesTen Caching Infrastructure and Tools, An Industry Session Presentation, In IEEE ICDE Conference, 2002.

[18] Tore Risch. The Translation of Object-Oriented Queries to Optimized Datalog Programs. HPL-DTD-91-9, Hewlett-Packard Laboratories, 1501 Page Mill Rd., Palo Alto, CA 94303.

[19] Surajit Chaudhuri and Gerhard Weikum. Rethinking Database System Architecture: Towards a Self-Tuning RISC-style Database System. In Proceedings of VLDB Conference, 2000.

Generating Thousand Benchmark Queries in Seconds

Meikel Poess
Oracle Corporation
400 Oracle Parkway
Redwood Shores, CA-94065
650-633-8012

meikel.poess@oracle.com

John M. Stephens, Jr.
Gradient Systems
643 Bair Island Road #103
Redwood City, CA-94063
650-566-9380

jms@gradientsystems.com

ABSTRACT

The combination of an exponential growth in the amount of data managed by a typical business intelligence system and the increased competitiveness of a global economy has propelled decision support systems (DSS) from the role of exploratory tools employed by a few visionary companies to become a core requirement for a competitive enterprise. That same maturation has often resulted in a selection process that requires an ever more critical system evaluation and selection to be completed in an increasingly short period of time. While there have been some advances in the generation of data sets for system evaluation (see [3]), the quantification of query performance has often relied on models and methodologies that were developed for systems that were more simplistic, less dynamic, and less central to a successful business. In this paper we present QGEN, a flexible, high-level query generator optimized for decision support system evaluation. QGEN is able to generate arbitrary query sets, which conform to a selected statistical profile without requiring that the queries be statically defined or disclosed prior to testing. Its novel design links query syntax with abstracted data distributions, enabling users to parameterize their query workload to match an emerging access pattern or data set modification. This results in query sets that retain comparability for system comparisons while reflecting the inherent dynamism of operational systems, and which provide a broad range of syntactic and semantic coverage, while remaining focused on appropriate commonalities within a particular evaluation process or business segment.

1. INTRODUCTION

The number of different queries executed on production systems far exceeds the practical number of queries that can be covered in a benchmark specification. Hence, a major task in designing a data warehouse benchmark is to create a query set that both represents the real world and executes in a reasonable amount of time. TPC-D [7], as the first industry-standard benchmark, defined 17 complex, industry relevant SQL queries. While it relied on some broad simplifying assumptions, it represented a major step forward from the simple, home-grown query workloads that had been used for early characterization efforts. As query functionality improved, its successors, TPC-H and TPC-R [4], added 5 queries to keep pace. TPC's next generation DSS benchmark, TPC-DS [5], is anticipated to employ more than one hundred queries. Due to increased database system functionality (e.g., SQL99 with OLAP extensions), the number of representative SQL query combinations on any particular schema is still very large. With an ever-increasing number of queries comes a need for a fast, reliable, extensible query generator.

DBMS functionality has improved dramatically since the TPC introduced the first industry-standard DSS benchmark in 1995. Today's systems rely heavily on sophisticated cost based query optimizers to generate the most efficient query execution plan. A DSS benchmark that evaluates optimizers must both provide the rich data set details on which they rely (uniform and non-uniform distributions, data sparcity, etc.), and must also test the optimizer's capability to generate the most optimal plan under all circumstances. Functionality to partition a data set and limit IO activity to that portion of the global data set that is of interest to a particular query is now commonplace. Traditional SQL operators have been buttressed by new semantics, which allow business processes to be closely modeled in query syntax (i.e., MDD and OLAP), and novel access patterns that allow the use of data sampling and pre-computation to speed answers to common business questions (i.e., summary tables and join indexes). With increasing sophistication and complexity available in even commodity systems, a successful benchmark must provide a transparent and adaptive architecture that allows meaningful comparisons across different systems, while allowing easy adaptation to emerging technologies.

As DSS have become an increasingly common and important piece of successful IT infrastructure, the focus and sophistication that vendors apply to benchmarks and their tuning has increased significantly. To compare the performance of different systems, it is essential that all systems run the same workload under the exact same execution rules. At the same time, it is important that the person conducting the test be allowed to tune the system appropriately. The challenge is to assure that the benefits that arise from pre-benchmark tuning are appropriate to the environment being evaluated and representative of

---

Permission to copy without fee all or part of this material is granted provided that the copies are not made or distributed for direct commercial advantage, the VLDB copyright notice and the title of the publication and its date appear, and notice is given that copying is by permission of the Very Large Data Base Endowment. To copy otherwise, or to republish, requires a fee and/or special permission from the Endowment

**Proceedings of the 30th VLDB Conference,
Toronto, Canada, 2004**

improvements that can be achieved outside of a benchmark situation (i.e. in a production system).

Finally, the operational environment for query systems has also changed. There is still a significant set of queries that is run in a batch environment, and can appropriately be subjected to highly specialized tuning. Other queries, however, are not known in advance except in broad terms, giving less possibility to optimally tune the system (ad-hoc queries To properly characterize both query approaches, a benchmark needs to acknowledge the different operational assumptions of each methodology. In cases where a batch query environment is being modeled, it is acceptable to provide well known, largely static queries, since it is assumed that the target operational environment would subject the queries to the same level of high-specialized tuning that would inevitably result in a competitive benchmark setting. To model an ad-hoc environment, the amount of fore knowledge of a particular query's phrasing needs to be limited. Regardless of the predominance of static or ad-hoc queries, a benchmark methodology must provide consistent, verifiable, comparable results.

Each of these technologies and enhancements can be exploited to provide an unrealistic vision of system performance, unless benchmarks are careful structured to realistically reflect the enhancement provided, without allowing unreasonable or inappropriate over optimization. QGEN addresses many of these concerns. For instance, if all query substitutions are known prior to benchmark execution, the optimizer can be tuned only for those predicates while ignoring the more general cases. If data access patterns are known prior to benchmark execution, the system under test (SUT) can be tuned for in a non-realistic way and system weaknesses can be easily covered up by, for instance, only creating auxiliary structures for part of the data set. QGEN's linkage to the underlying data generation assures appropriate coverage of the whole data set. Most DSS benchmarks include a multi user test (e.g. TPC-H/ TPC-R) in which multiple concurrent sessions execute queries simultaneously. Executing the same queries across multiple sessions is not desirable because one could easily implement a feature that materializes the result of every new query. Subsequent sessions executing these queries can take advantage by simply displaying the content of the previously materialized data without computing any results themselves. QGEN's ability to dynamically parameterize a query set minimizes these risks. Its ability to create query sets which are extensible and random, but statistically comparable, , makes it possible to construct a query set that retains query characteristics without resorting to blind query repetition. This removes the need for repetition that is not representative of the query environment being modeled.

The remaining sections of this paper review the evolution of query models culminating in a detailed description of the SQL query generator, QGEN, which was developed by the TPC for generating queries in TPC-DS. Before discussing the general concepts behind QGEN we will briefly introduce the data and query models, which motivated its development. Prior to concluding we will show empirically that QGEN generates comparable queries using examples from TPC-DS's query set.

2. RELATED WORK

In [1] Slutz presented RAGS, a system to stochastically generate valid SQL statements. This system has been employed at Microsoft for deterministic testing of SQL statements. For a specific database schema RAGS generates syntactically correct SQL statements by walking a stochastic parse tree. As RAGS can quickly generate and execute millions of statements to increase the coverage of system functionality testing, it is not quite suitable to generate queries to test system's performance. For benchmark purposes it is not desirable to completely randomly generate queries since their execution times cannot be predicted or limited, especially, because of the large query set that needs to be executed to achieve good coverage of performance characteristic.

3. EXISTING QUERY MODELS
3.1 STATIC QUERY MODELS

The simplest approach to benchmarking is to record pre-existing events or behaviors and simply replay them under controlled conditions. Early vendor benchmarks employed a similar approach. Sample queries were captured from a production system (or crafted to match an intended implementation) and executed against potential solutions to provided comparative performance data.

This approach has some obvious and attractive benefits. The testing methodology is easily understood and, since the queries are completely static, comparability between benchmark executions is guaranteed. Unfortunately, the shortcomings of this approach are equally compelling. The functionality coverage provided by the benchmark is limited by the captured queries, the benchmark is unlikely to adapt well for evaluating changes to the schema or workload without significant intervention, and the results produced by a multi-user execution are likely to be misleading, as the limited and static nature of

```
SELECT  sum(l_extendedprice)
FROM    lineitem
WHERE   l_shipdate >= '10-01-03'
AND     l_shipdate < '12-31-03';
```

Figure 1: Static DSS Query

the query makes it easier to pre-compute its result, or to reuse the result that was computed in one user session to speed execution in another (i.e. multi user run).

The simple DSS type query in Figure 1 can be used to illustrate additional drawbacks of a static query model. It aggregates the extended price of all lineitems in the fourth quarter of 2003. A simplified materialized view, only covering the fourth quarter of 2003, turns this IO intensive query into a single row lookup query reducing the elapsed time to sub-second. If there is no other query that benefits from aggregation of lineitem data, there is no need to cover any more data than the fourth quarter of 2003. Similarly, other auxiliary structures such as indexes could only be created on a subset of data, for instance, using local indexes build on a subset of data, for instance by using table partitions. Assuming that the remaining data of 2003 is not accessed in any other query, another possible optimization is to horizontally partition the table into accessed and non-accessed sections. The non-accessed sections can then be moved to cheaper permanent storage, such as tape drives increasing performance and reducing the total cost of the system[1].

3.2 SIMPLE SUBSTITUTIONS

A completely dynamic query model model, in which the query text was created only at the time of query execution and little or none of the text was known to the benchmarker in advance would remove much of the potential for over-optimization, but would be likely to violate the most fundamental requirement for any benchmark: to impose a reproducible stimulus on the system under test. For a decision support benchmark with its focus on query execution, this means that if a query is executed multiple times under the same circumstances, the execution times from run to run do not vary significantly. TPC's original data warehouse benchmarks (TPC-D, TPC-H and TPC-R) fulfilled this requirement by assuming a very simple data model, (e.g., uniform distributions for all columns), and by constraining the scope of possible query-to-query variation. Figure 2 (see below) shows the template of TPC-H's Query 6. It uses three substitution variables, DATE (the first of January of a randomly selected year within [1993 .. 1997]), DISCOUNT (randomly selected within [0.02 .. 0.09]) and QUANTITY (randomly selected within [24 .. 25]).

```
SELECT   SUM (l_extendedprice*l_discount)
FROM     lineitem
WHERE    l_shipdate>=date'[DATE]'
AND      l_shipdate<date'[DATE]'+interval'1'year
AND      l_discount between [DISCOUNT] - 0.01
              and [DISCOUNT] + 0.01
AND      l_quantity < [QUANTITY];
```

Figure 2: TPC-H's Query Template 6

This approach is clearly an improvement over the purely static query model that it replaced. The risk of pre-computation is greatly reduced (controlled largely by the range of possible substitution values), the query set scales to multi-user execution without the risk of result reuse, and the lack of complete predictability provides a meaningful test of query optimizers. Further, by providing a standardized method for the execution and reporting of test results, the TPC benchmarks provided a more robust and trusted basis for system comparison. That the benchmarks were widely published is a testament to their success. They too had problems, however. The inflexible linkage between the query set and the data generator made it difficult to expand or alter the query set as DBMS technology improved, and the limited query breadth imposed by this increased maintenance burden left the benchmark vulnerable to over-optimization through specialized indexes and other data structures. While appropriate constraint of the configuration and execution rules of TPC-H have allowed it to remain viable, it became clear that the benchmark, with it simplified, third-normal data model and proscriptive implementation rules was not sufficient to capture the breadth of modern decision support systems performance.

4. NEW APPROACH TO QUERY MODELING

In an attempt to address some of the shortcomings of the simple substitution models used in the past, and to update its benchmark suite to align with common DSS methodologies, the TPC is developing a new benchmark, TPC-DS. The new benchmark is built around an updated data model, a more sophisticated concept of a decision support user, and a next generation query model, implemented in QGEN, the query generator for the new benchmark.

The examples in this paper use TPC-DS' data model. In line with modern data warehouse systems, QGEN and MUDD employ a variant of a star schema. The schema utilizes the business model of a large retail company having multiple stores located nation-wide. Beyond the brick and mortar stores, the fictitious company sells goods through catalogs and the Internet. Consequently, its operational processes include a store order and return system, a catalog order and return system, and a web order and return system. In addition, it provides an inventory system for all warehouses and a promotion system. Each system is represented in the schema as a snowflake with dimensions shared among all snowflakes. Dimensions such as Date, Store, Item and Promotion are arranged in the classical star constellation around Store Sales. Customer, Customer Address, Customer Demographics, Household Demographics and Income Band are arranged in a snowflake fashion. Apart from their relationships to Store Sales, Customer Address, Customer Demographics and Household Demographics have additional relationships to Customer. This allows the data model to capture both the classification of the customer at the time of the sale (through the links to the Sales fact tables) and at the time of

---

[1] Performance Analysis is often paired with a cost analysis. In every TPC benchmark publication includes a price analysis and in most benchmarks price performance gets reported as a metric.

the query (through the links to other dimensions). The Store Returns system shares all dimensions of Store Sales. Additionally, it introduces a new dimension describing the reason for the return (Reason).

The structure of the Catalog and Internet sales channels are identical to the Store Channel, except that some dimensions are renamed (e.g., store becomes catalog). Rows in the fact table store the numerical measurements of the business modeled. In our case, these are sales, returns (store, catalog and internet), inventory movements and promotions. Each of these subject areas is modeled with one fact table. It contains foreign keys to dimension tables and numerical measures (additive and non-additive).

Dimensions contain numerical surrogate primary keys and descriptive attributes to further describe the dimension. There are static and non-static dimensions. Non-static dimensions are maintained as part of an ETL process. Describing the details of this process exceeds the scope of this paper. Details can be found in [5].

The aforementioned star schema defines three hierarchies to allow for easy browsing of dimension data. Despite the normalization that led to the snowflake schema, each hierarchy is confined to one dimension. Each hierarchy is strict meaning that an entity in the lower level maps to exactly one entity of the higher level. For instance, one city maps to exactly one county, which maps to exactly one state.

The development of QGEN has been driven by the requirements of the TPC-DS query model. The benchmark characterizes the queries submitted to the SUT into one of four query classes, representing different kinds of database activity: reporting, ad-hoc queries, iterative enquiries and data extraction (e.g., data mining activities). In this query model, different degrees of complexity, variability and predictability of the queries submitted to the SUT are captured in the different query classes. Accordingly, the query generator needs to produce an arbitrarily large, random set of queries within the constraints of each class while meeting the reproducibility requirements for the benchmark as a whole.

4.1 QGEN

QGEN is a command-line utility that translates an arbitrary set of query templates into streams of fully-qualified, valid SQL. Based on a LALR(1) grammar that defines the template syntax, QGEN can quickly produce an arbitrarily large query set for any of a number of query classes.

Template-based queries are defined to be sets of one or more pseudo-random, valid SQL statements generated shortly before benchmark execution. Template-based queries are intended to model common, well-understood queries, which are generated in conjunction with periodic reports or common business tasks. It is assumed that the precise values or targets of a given instance of a template-based query is random, but that the general format and syntax for the query is tightly tied to a business process and the syntax is therefore largely predictable and well-known.

To make queries less "known" is to vary SQL predicates. QGEN defines a query template language, which allows for the different types of SQL predicates, found in today's decision support systems:

- single value.
- range,
- in-list, and
- like.

Queries resulting from the same template execute in an equivalent execution time, even though the underlying data set is highly skewed and non-uniform.

4.1.1 MUDD AND QGEN

QGEN depends heavily on the underlying data set. A query generator can only uncover data relationships that exist in its target data population, and a query tool intended for cross-vendor comparisons must rely on the existence of a data set from which it is possible to produce comparable queries. It is the creation and manipulation of the data domains and distributions within the data set that makes the generation of meaningful and comparable query sets.

The data generator that is coupled with QGEN is called MUDD [6]. MUDD and QGEN represent an evolution in query benchmarking, because they have externalized the dependency between a query tool and its data generator into a set of external text files that define the data domains and distributions for both the data generation and query creation. This allows the modification of the data distributions and their use in the queries without requiring the recompilation of the underlying tool set.

The core of the domain and distribution functionality within MUDD and QGEN is the ability to define an arbitrary distribution of values. In addition to defining the values themselves, the tools rely upon the relative frequencies of the values (which may vary when the same value set is used in different ways) along with any related or correlated values. All of this information is contained in an ASCII file, so values and weightings can be altered during experimentation, and fine tuning of the benchmark can occur without requiring changes to the toolset itself.

4.1.2 GENERAL DEFINITION SYNTAX

A query template is divided into two parts. The Substitution Declaration declares the substitution rules. They consist of a list of substitution tags. Each tag is declared as a substitution type (distribution) with specific substitution parameters. The so defined tags can be used in the SQL Text part of the query template, which consists of a SQL query, to specify the substitution values of query predicates. Each occurrence of the substitution tag in the SQL text is substituted according to the substitution type. Multiple occurrences of the same tag are substituted with the same value. However, if a substitution tag is post-fixed with a number, then each occurrences is substituted with a new value. The general syntax for a substitution rule is:

```
DEFINE <tag>=
          <substitution type>
          (<substitution parameters>);
<tag> = string[30];
<substitution type> = <RANDOM | DIST | TEXT>
```

Consider the following example T1 in Figure 3.

```
#SUBSTITUTION DECLARATION
DEFINE
     month = RANDOM (1, 5, UNIFORM);
DEFINE
     high_color=dist("colors",1,high);
#SQL TEXT
SELECT sum(S.salesprice)
FROM   store S, item I, time T
WHERE  T.sold_date between month
                       AND month+2
AND    I.color = high_color
```
Figure 3: Example Query Template T1

In its substitution declaration it defines two substitution tags, *month* and *high_color*. They will be explained more in detail in the following sections. The SQL joins the fact table *stores* with the two dimension tables *item* and *time*. Its sums the sales of all items in a specific time window (first predicate) which are of a specific color (second predicate).

4.1.3 RANDOM SUBSTITUTION

The *Random* substitution type allows templates to use randomly-generated integers in a inclusive range [min,max] using normal or uniform distributions. The specific syntax for the RANDOM substitution rule is:

```
RANDOM(<min>,<max>,<distribution>)
<distribution> = [NORMAL | UNIFORM]
```

The RANDOM substitution is very commonly used in data warehouse queries since it can be used to implement the very common time predicates. Usually decision support queries are time based using month, quarter or year as their window of operation. The designer of a query template must assure that the values picked for *min* and *max* fall within the targeted comparability zone (range in the data domain with a uniform distribution). Figure 4 shows a very simple example of a random substitution. It defines the tag *month*, which uses a uniform distribution between 1 and 5. This tag is then on the predicate on sold_date.

4.1.4 DIST SUBSTITUTION

The *DIST* substitution type allows a template to use one of the arbitrary distributions defined in conjunction with its data generator (MUDD) through their shared distribution files (.dst, .idx), which provide step functions of arbitrary complexity and resolution. The specific syntax for a DIST substitution rule is:

```
DIST (<name>, <value set>, <weight set>)
<name> = name of the distributions as defined in .idx
<value set> = 1-based index for the value to be returned
              from the distribution tuple
<weight set> = 1-based index for the selected weighting
               from the distribution tuple
```

```
DEFINE color = TEXT (
       ("red", 10),
       ("blue", 80),
       ("green", 10);
DEFINE add_predicate = TEXT (
       ("and palette like "[color]%", 30),
       ("", 70)
       );
Select count(*) from products where color != [color]
       [add_predicate];
```
Figure 5: TEXT Substitution Syntax

The DIST substitution does not require the template designer to know the specifics of the data distribution, only the names of the distribution and its weight and value sets (e.g., "colors" or "leap_year_sales").

4.1.5 TEXT SUBSTITUTION

The TEXT substitution replaces a particular tag with one of a weighted set of ASCII strings. In its basic form, this is can be employed in a like clause to produce a wild card predicate such as: `column_name like "<string>%"`, providing a crude form of text searching as demonstrated in the first part of Figure 5.

The real power of the TEXT substitution lies in its ability to include both static text and additional substitution tags. Whenever QGEN employs a TEXT substitution, it traverses the selected text looking for additional substitution tags. These are evaluated in turn, and final static text replaces the TEXT substitution tag in the query template. An example of this behavior can be seen in the second example from Figure 5, where the initial substitution for [add_predicate] can result in an additional occurrence of the *palette* predicate.

4.1.6 DATA POPULATION WITH COMPARABILITY ZONES

Synthetic data generators face an inherent challenge. If the data is too synthetic (e.g., completely uniform distributions), it runs the risk of being rejected for not capturing the "interesting" attributes of a real data set. Conversely, if it employs data that is gathered from transactions or installations ("the real world") it risks being of little or no value to researchers and benchmarks, since it can neither produce comparable workload results nor be scaled to answer interesting hypothetical questions. MUDD attempts to find an appropriate mix of these two endpoints. For a majority of its data, it employs traditional synthetic distributions, yielding uniformly distributed integers, or word selections with a Gaussian distribution. For a number of crucial distributions, however, the data generator relies on data from the real world to produce more realistic data sets.

Given the importance of skew in a data set, and the dominance of this particular skew in this particular data set, omission would clearly be a poor choice. Instead, the data set needs to be "adjusted", introducing zones of comparability – essentially flat spots in the distribution – that can be used to provide both the variability and the comparability that the eventual user of the generated data requires. With MUDD's flexible approach to comparability zones each column domain can define its own comparability zones. They can differ in size within the column domain and in number between column domains. However, in order to allow for a large number of possible substitutions, one needs to adjust the number of comparability zones so that the requirements for parameter substitutions of the application to be tested are met. There should be at least one comparability zone large enough to fit the largest range substitution. Depending on how many different range substitutions the applications calls for this size must be adjusted. The upper bound of any comparability zone is limited by the number of comparability zones that can fit into the column domain.

As an example for a distribution with comparability zones, consider the likelihood of retail sales throughout the calendar year. Census data shows that a dramatic proportion of sales occur during the year-end holiday season, often as much as 30% of annual sales within the last two months of the year (and much of that in the last half of December) [3]. Figure 6 shows the Census data for retail sales by month in th USA.

For date predicates TPC-DS requires range substitutions of at most 90 days (one quarter). Hence to mimic the sales distribution above, in each year we define three comparability zones; 1) January to July; 2) August to October; 3) November to December. The database we are using for the remaining of this paper contains 5 years of data each year following the same distribution. Domain values in the first zone occur with a low likelihood in the data set (low zone), domain values in the second zone occur with a medium likelihood and domain values in the third zone occur with a high likelihood in the dataset. The actual likelihood of occurrences in each zone may vary from domain to domain. However, MUDD guarantees that all domain values in one domain have the same likelihood.

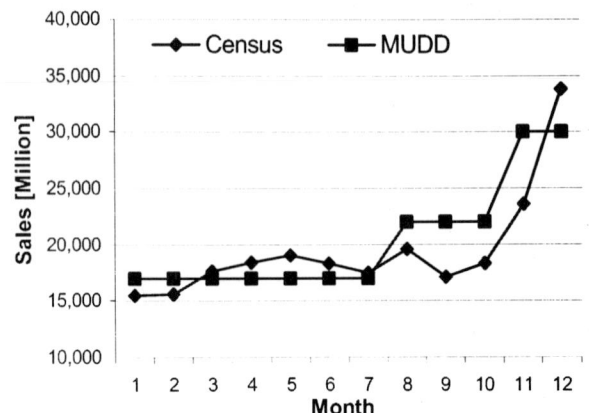

Figure 6: Retail Sales by Month

The fact that there is a correlation between month and sales amount is very imperative to this kind of column domain. If after ordering the domain values of a distribution the graph shows a step functions, that is, neighboring domain values (except for the edges) have the same occurrence likelihood, we define this as a Type A distribution. This characteristic enables the use of range predicates.

Clearly a skew this dramatic constitutes an important feature in the data set, and needs to be captured by the data generator. The use of the data needs to be considered too, however, if the year-end bulge were to be captured precisely, then it is likely that no two days would generate precisely the same sales volume. In our query example, it would then be impossible to assure that queries based on a date in this crucial range (or elsewhere throughout the year, for that matter) generated comparable amounts of load or activity on the system under test. The option left to the dataset/benchmark designer is to either remove queries based on dates in this region from the benchmark, or find some way to assure that they are comparable to one another.

The query designer needs to be aware of the comparability zones and write his queries accordingly. Consider the previous example. The first comparability zone contains 7x30=210 days. Assuming one would like to define predicates covering 90 days in this zone, the valid range for the left end point of all range predicates is 10-90=120 range substitutions of 90 days, the second zone allows for 1 substitutions, while the third zone is too small for any 30 day substitution.

MUDD defines other distributions that are not derived from the real world, and, most importantly, that do not constrain the relationship between domain values and their frequency. We define these as Type B distributions. Because of neighboring domain values not occurring with the same likelihood, range predicates are not allowed on Type B distributions. An example defines the domain of common colors (see Figure 9 and 10). The colors are sorted on their number of occurrences in the dataset. Similarly to the sales distribution, we define three comparability zones: low, medium and high. Colors are arbitrarily chosen to belong to any of the three comparability zones. Colors belonging to the low comparability zone occur less likely in the data set than colors of the medium zone. Colors belonging to the high comparability zone have the highest likelihood to occur in the dataset.

4.1.7 COMPATIBILITY OF SUBSTITUTION TYPES AND QUERY PREDICATES

Due to their characteristics not all types of query predicates are supported by each substitution type with each type of distribution. Table 6 shows which substitution type is compatible with the different types of query predicates. Type A and Type B distributions can be used with the DIST and RANDOM substitution types for single value predicates. Range predicates can be used with Type A distributions and RANDOM. Using DIST range predicates can be used with both Type A and Type B distributions.

		Substitution Type		
		RANDOM	DIST	TEXT
Predicate	single	A & B	A & B	-
	range	A	A & B	-
	in-list	-	A & B	-
	like	-	-	A&B

Figure 7: Substitution Types Compatibility Matrix

4.1.8 IMPLEMENTATION OF COMPARABILITY ZONES IN QGEN

The core of the domain and distribution functionality within MUDD and QGEN is the ability to define an arbitrary distribution of values. In addition to defining the values themselves, the tools rely upon the relative frequencies of the values (which may vary when the same value set is used in different ways) along with any related or correlated values. All of this information is contained in Distribution Configuration (ASCII file), so values and weightings can be altered during experimentation, and fine tuning of the benchmark can occur without requiring changes to the toolset itself.

The format of a distribution definition is summarized in Figure 8 and 9. The result is a step function of arbitrary complexity and resolution. Two examples of common usage are provided. In Figure 7, two weights are provided – one to cover both leap and non-leap year. In Figure 9, common color names are grouped into classes. By selecting the appropriate weight set, it is possible to produce a weighted distribution across the entire color spectrum, or to randomly select a color from within a given class. The distribution example also demonstrates the use of multiple entries within the value set to provide correlated attributes to be selected from the distribution. In this case, the constituent primary colors are available for each listed entry.

```
SALES =
(1, "Jan 1"; 10, 10)
(2, "Jan 2"; 10, 10)
[...]
(59, "Feb 28"; 10, 10)
(60, "Feb 29"; 0, 10)
(61, "Mar 1"; 10, 10)
[...]
(348, "Dec 13"; 30, 30)
(349, "Jan 14"; 50, 50)
(350, "Jan 15"; 50, 50)
```
Figure 8: Sales Distribution

```
COLORS =
("Red", "Red", "None"; 100, 1, 0, 0)
("Blue", "Blue", "None"; 100, 1, 0, 0)
("Yellow", "Yellow", "None"; 100, 1, 0, 0)
("Green", "Blue", "Yellow"; 50, 0, 1, 0)
("Purple", "Red", "Blue"; 50, 0, 1, 0)
("Orange", "Red", "Yellow"; 50, 0, 1, 0)
("Taupe", "Orange", "Green"; 10, 0, 0, 1)
("Mauve", "Purple", "Blue"; 10, 0, 0, 1)
("Pink", "Yellow", "Green"; 10, 0, 0, 1);
```
Figure 9: Color Distribution

4.1.9 PRESERVATION OF COMPARABILITY ZONES

So far we have seen how step functions can be defined on single table column distributions to assure comparable queries in the presence of substitutions. But what happens to comparability zones if predicates are defined on multiple columns or if tables are joined? MUDD prohibits correlation between intra table column distributions and between join columns. That is all comparability zone distributions must be statistically independent. For instance, it is disallowed to define item color and size distributions such that green items are larger than blue items or sales distributions such that red items are more likely to be sold in December than in March. This is very important since comparability zones need to be preserved in the presence of multiple predicates and joins. If indeed there is no correlation between columns, choosing predicates in comparability zones of multiple columns still yields comparable queries. This is true for joins as well if there is no correlation of the join columns.

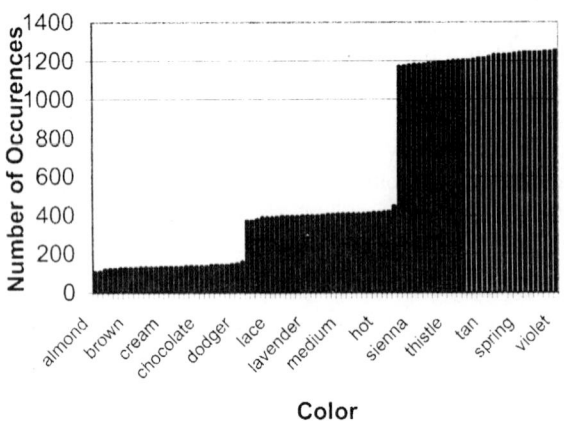

Figure 10: Color Distribution

4.2 EXAMPLE AND EXPERIMENTAL RESULTS

In this section we will present some experimental results of queries executed against a database demonstrating that QGEN indeed generates comparable query sets. We will discuss the example shown in Figure 3 in more detail. First, lets create a variant T1a of T1, which contains only one substitution parameter, high_color (see T1a).

```
#SUBSTITUTION DECLARATION
DEFINE
    high_color=dist("colors",1,high);
#SQL TEXT
SELECT sum(S.salesprice)
FROM   store S, item I, time T
WHERE  I.color = high_color
```

Figure 11: QGEN Query Template T1a

The existing benchmarks TPC-H and TPC-R have already shown that substitution parameters on uniform data distributions yield comparable queries. Since the parameter substitution model of QGEN operates on comparability zones, which have uniformly distributed data, it yields to comparable queries. To demonstrate this, we generate 10000 queries from templates T1a and T1 using QGEN. All queries of template T1a use substitution parameters for colors that are of the high likelihood comparability zone. Then we run these queries sequentially against a TPC-DS database and collect the elapsed times. In addition to the color substitution parameters of T1a, T1 uses a date predicate on sold_date (sold_date between *month* AND *month*+2) of the low season in the sales distribution (January to July). We also generate 10,000 queries using QGEN, execute them sequentially and collect the elapsed times. The y-axis in 11 shows the deviation from the mean of the elapsed time of these queries. The deviations are graphed in sorted order. The label on the x-axis shows the query run number.

Elapsed times for queries generated from the T1a template deviate between –0.5% and 0.5% from the mean. The Coefficient of Deviation for this dataset is 0.00177, well within the requirements. The second graph shows the elapsed time deviation to the mean of queries generated from the T1 template. They differ from about -0.5% to about 1%. This translate into a Coefficient of Deviation is 0.00317, which is also well within the requirements.

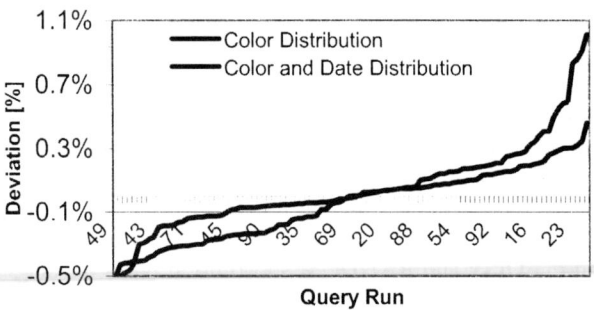

Figure 12: Deviation from Men for Queries generated with T1 ad T1a Query Templates

These two examples show that when multiple substitution parameters, which in isolation yield comparable queries, are combined in one query template the resulting query template yields comparable queries if the distributions of which the predicates are defined, are independent. For our example this means that there must not be a correlation between sales date and item color.

5. FUTURE DIRECTIONS FOR QUERY MODELS

One of the goals of TPC-DS is to generate comparable queries. This is guaranteed by comparability zones and by careful selection of parameter substitutions for selected predicates.

As query modeling embraces an increasingly interactive approach (i.e., OLAP), the requirement for individual query comparability will give way to comparability on final metric level. As business intelligence moves beyond basic SQL (i.e., into cubes or other complex data structures), even complex queries can provide sub-second response time. As a result it becomes possible to execute thousands of queries while keeping the benchmark execution time manageable. Today's QGEN can already quickly generate thousands of queries, and can satisfy the response time demands of a true OLAP workload. To mimic true ad-hoc queries, however, it will be necessary to model iterative, scenario-based query sequences, including changes to the select-list columns, group-by or order-by clauses, as well as function substitutions (min, max, average, etc). These substitutions reduce query-to-query comparability. Preliminary research has confirmed that the increase in queries executed leads to continued stability in the overall metric even with this increased variability.

The next stage of QGEN development will coordinate group-by, order-by and select-list substitutions (using dependency graphs and more complex statistical models such as Hidden Markov Models) to provide the truly random query generation that OLAP benchmarking will require.

6. CONCLUSION
In this paper we introduced QGEN, a flexible, high-level query generator optimized for DSS performance evaluation. QGEN is able to generate arbitrary, comparable query sets, which conform to a selected statistical profile without requiring that the queries be statically defined or disclosed prior to testing. It is currently being tested by the TPC for use in its new DSS benchmark TPC-DS. Its close integration with MUDD, a multi dimensional data generator, combined with its elegant query template language ease query workload development and maintenance.

7. ACKNOWLEDGMENTS
The development of the data generation prototype that this paper discusses has been funded by the TPC, as part of their on-going efforts to define comparable, relevant and timely decision support benchmarks. They, in turn, rely on the dedication and contribution of the representatives that TPC member companies provide to the TPC's benchmark development subcommittees. The authors would like to thank the TPC, and the members of the TPC-DS subcommittee for their contribution to this effort.

8. REFERENCES
[1] Slutz, D. *Massive Stochastic Testing of SQL, Proc.* 24th Int. Conf. Very Large Data Bases, VLDB, 1998

[2] ISO/IEC 9075. *Database Language SQL*. International Standard ISO/IEC 9075:1992, American National Standard X3.135-1992, ANSI, New York, NY 10036, November 1992.

[3] Kimball, R. The Data Warehouse Toolkit: Practical Techniques for Building Dimensional Data Warehouses. John Wiley & Sons, 1996

[4] Poess, M. and Floyd, C., "New TPC Benchmarks for Decision Support and Web Commerce". ACM SIGMOD RECORD, Vol 29, No 4 (Dec 2000)

[5] Poess, M., Smith B., Kollár L., Larson P.: *TPC-DS: Taking Decision Support Benchmarking to the Next Level*. SIGMOD Conference 2002

[6] Stephens, J., Poess, M.: Mudd: A Multi-Dimensional Data Generator, WOSP 2004

[7] Transaction Processing Performance Council (TPC), "TPC Benchmark D (Decision Support)", May 1995 http://www.tpc.org/tpcd/spec/tpcd_current.pdf

[8] Transaction Processing Performance Council (TPC), "TPC-H Specification Version 2.1.0", August 2003 http://www.tpc.org/tpch/spec/tpch2.1.0.pdf

[9] Transaction Processing Performance Council (TPC), "TPC-R Specification Version 2.1.0", August 2003 http://www.tpc.org/tpcr/spec/tpcr_2.1.0.pdf

[10] US Census Bureau, Unadjusted and Adjusted Estimates of Monthly Retail and Food Services Sales by Kinds of Business:2001, Department stores (excl.L.D) 4521. http://www.census.gov/mrts/www/data/html/nsal01.html

Supporting Ontology-based Semantic Matching in RDBMS

Souripriya Das, Eugene Inseok Chong, George Eadon, Jagannathan Srinivasan
Oracle Corporation
One Oracle Drive, Nashua, NH 03062, USA

Abstract

Ontologies are increasingly being used to build applications that utilize domain-specific knowledge. This paper addresses the problem of supporting ontology-based semantic matching in RDBMS. Specifically, 1) A set of SQL operators, namely ONT_RELATED, ONT_EXPAND, ONT_DISTANCE, and ONT_PATH, are introduced to perform ontology-based semantic matching, 2) A new indexing scheme ONT_INDEXTYPE is introduced to speed up ontology-based semantic matching operations, and 3) System-defined tables are provided for storing ontologies specified in OWL. Our approach enables users to reference ontology data directly from SQL using the semantic match operators, thereby opening up possibilities of combining with other operations such as joins as well as making the ontology-driven applications easy to develop and efficient. In contrast, other approaches use RDBMS only for storage of ontologies and querying of ontology data is typically done via APIs. This paper presents the ontology-related functionality including inferencing, discusses how it is implemented on top of Oracle RDBMS, and illustrates the usage with several database applications.

1. Introduction

An ontology is a shared conceptualization of knowledge in a particular domain. It facilitates building applications by separating knowledge about the target domain from the rest of the application code. The key benefits of this approach are: simplification of the application code, possible sharing of knowledge among multiple applications, and the flexibility of evolving the knowledge without requiring changes to the application.

This approach has been used to build applications for various domains (such as clinical applications [3], geographic information system [2], integrated knowledge management [1], and knowledge acquisition system [7]). The same approach can be adopted to build database applications. This paper addresses the problem of supporting ontology-based semantic matching in RDBMS.

To motivate the need for ontology-based semantic matching, consider a restaurant guide application, which recommends restaurants to a user based on her/his preferences. Consider a table served_food that contains the types of cuisines served at restaurants.

Table 1: served_food

R_id	Cuisine
1	American
2	Mexican
2	American
14	Portuguese

In the absence of semantic matching, the application would most likely resort to syntactic matching via the '=' operator as shown below:
```
SELECT * FROM served_food
WHERE cuisine = 'Latin American';
```
This query generates no rows since none of Cuisine values in the table will match 'Latin American'.

In contrast, the user can get more meaningful results by performing semantic matching that consults an ontology (such as the cuisine ontology in Figure 1) for computing the results. Specifically, a user can issue the following query:
```
SELECT * FROM served_food
WHERE ONT_RELATED(cuisine,
                  'IS_A',
                  'Latin American',
                  'Cuisine_ontology')=1;
```
Here the ONT_RELATED operator determines if the two input terms are related by the input relationship type argument by consulting the specified ontology. If they are related, then the operator will return 1, otherwise 0.

Permission to copy without fee all or part of this material is granted provided that the copies are not made or distributed for direct commercial advantage, the VLDB copyright notice and the title of the publication and its date appear, and notice is given that copying is by permission of the Very Large Data Base Endowment. To copy otherwise, or to republish, requires a fee and/or special permission from the Endowment

**Proceedings of the 30th VLDB Conference,
Toronto, Canada, 2004**

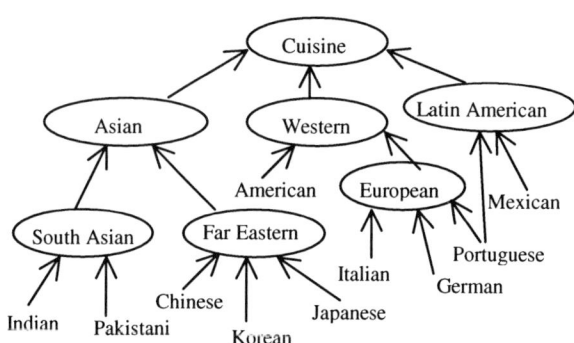

*Figure 1: A Cuisine Ontology
(Each node represents an Individual and each edge represents a* `transitive ObjectProperty 'IS_A'`*)*

The query identifies rows containing cuisines that are related to `'Latin American'` based on `'IS_A'` relationship. The query will generate restaurants 2 and 14 since `'Mexican'` and `'Portuguese'` are related to `'Latin American'` cuisine. Thus, one can incorporate semantics of the particular knowledge domain in SQL queries by introducing ontology-based semantic matching.

Optionally, a user may want to get a measure for the rows filtered by `ONT_RELATED` operator. This can be achieved by using `ONT_DISTANCE` ancillary operator. The `ONT_DISTANCE` operator gives a measure of how closely the terms are related by measuring the distance between the two terms. Continuing with the example, one can get the result sorted on distance measure as follows:

```
SELECT * FROM served_food
WHERE ONT_RELATED (cuisine,
                   'IS_A',
                   'Latin American',
                   'Cuisine_ontology',
                   123) = 1
ORDER BY ONT_DISTANCE (123¹);
```

Similarly, another ancillary operator `ONT_PATH` would be useful, which computes path information between the two terms.

In addition, a user may want to query an ontology independently (without involving user tables). The `ONT_EXPAND` operator can be used for this purpose (see Section 2 for details).

Providing ontology-based semantic matching capability as part of SQL greatly facilitates developing ontology-driven database applications. Applications that can benefit include e-commerce (such as supply chain management, application integration, personalization, and auction). Also, applications that have to work with domain-specific knowledge repositories (such as BioInformatics, Geographical Information Systems, and Healthcare Applications) can take advantage of this capability. These capabilities can be exploited to support semantic web applications (such as web service discovery [8]) as well. A key requirement in these applications is to provide semantic matching between syntactically different terms or sometimes between syntactically same, but semantically different terms [10].

Another category of the semantic matching application is related to knowledge reuse. Neutral Authoring [9] is an application area, where information is represented in a single language and then converted into different languages for multiple target systems. Corporate knowledge bases on which documentation and software development can be based is another big application area of such a capability.

Support for ontology-based semantic matching is achieved by introducing the following:

- Two new SQL operators, `ONT_RELATED` and `ONT_EXPAND` (as described above) are defined to model ontology-based semantic matching operations. For queries involving `ONT_RELATED` operator, two ancillary SQL operators `ONT_DISTANCE` and `ONT_PATH`, are defined that return distance and path respectively for the filtered rows. Additional operators may be introduced for querying purposes, e.g., for finding datatype property values.

- A new indexing scheme `ONT_INDEXTYPE` is defined to speed up ontology-based semantic matching operations.

- A schema has been designed to store information extracted from an ontology. This schema is not directly visible to the user.

The proposed functionality can be implemented by exploiting the database extensibility capabilities (namely, the ability to define user-defined operators, user-defined indexing schemes, and table functions) typically available in an RDBMS.

We support ontologies specified in Web Ontology Language (OWL [19], specifically, OWL Lite and OWL DL) by extracting information from the OWL document and then storing this information in the schema.

Oracle's Extensibility Framework [5] has been used to implement the operators and the new indexing scheme. Specifically, ONT_RELATED, ONT_DISTANCE, and ONT_PATH operators are implemented as user-defined operators. ONT_EXPAND is implemented as a table function. The operator implementation typically requires computing a transitive closure based upon explicit relationships and inferred relationships. This is performed via queries with CONNECT BY clause. The ONT_INDEXTYPE is implemented as a user-defined indexing scheme (See Section 3.3 for details).

---

[1] This argument identifies the filtering operator expression (ONT_RELATED) that computes this ancillary value [11].

1.1 Related Work

Ontologies have been around for sometime and in recent years they have received wider attention in the context of semantic web [4]. Several ontology building tools have been developed (for example, OntoEdit [13], OntoBroker [14], OntologyBuilder and OntologyServer [16], KAON [15]). Most of these tools use a file system to store ontologies. Among these, KAON and VerticalNet products (OntologyBuilder and OntologyServer) as well as the Jena2 Semantic Web Framework [21] allow storing of ontology using RDBMS and they provide an API for access and manipulation of ontologies. However, the key difference is that our approach makes ontology-based semantic matching available as part of SQL.

1.2 Organization of the Paper

Section 2 presents a feature overview of supporting ontology-based semantic matching operations. Section 3 discusses the implementation of the ontology-related changes on top of Oracle RDBMS and its performance results. Section 4 illustrates their usage with several database applications. Section 5 describes our experience and Section 6 concludes with a summary and outlines future work.

2. Supporting Ontology-based Semantic Matching on Oracle RDBMS

Although the feature is described in the context of Oracle RDBMS, it can be supported in any RDBMS that support a few basic extensibility capabilities as outlined in Section 1.

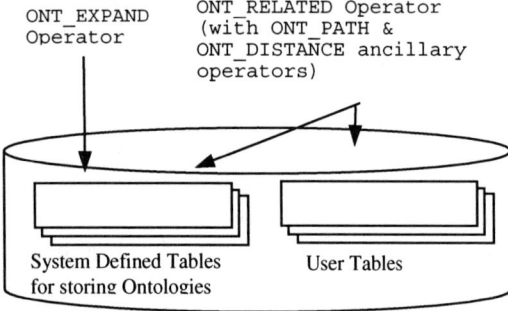

Figure 2: Ontology-related Functionality

2.1 Overview

The ontology-related functionality (see Figure 2) is as follows:

- An RDBMS schema, consisting of several system-defined tables (see Section 2.2 for details), is created for storing information extracted from the ontologies.
- Two operators are provided for querying purposes. The ONT_EXPAND operator can be used to query the ontology independently, whereas ONT_RELATED operator can be used to perform queries on a user table holding ontology terms.
- Optionally, a user can use two (ancillary) operators, ONT_DISTANCE and ONT_PATH, in queries involving the ONT_RELATED operator to get additional measures (distance and path) for the filtered rows.

These are further elaborated below.

2.2 RDBMS Schema for Storing Ontologies

An RDBMS schema has been created for storing ontologies specified in OWL. The tables in this schema include:

```
Ontologies (
  OntologyID, OntologyName, Owner, ...)
```

```
Terms (
  TermID, OntologyID, Term, Type, ...)
Properties (
  OntologyId, PropertyID,
  DomainClassID, RangeClassID,
  Characteristics, ...)
Restrictions (
  OntologyID, NewClassID, PropertyID,
  MinCardinality, MaxCardinality,
  SomeValuesFrom, AllValuesFrom, ...)
```

```
Relationships (
  OntologyID, TermID1, PropertyID,
  TermID2, ...)
PropertyValues (
  OntologyID, TermID, PropertyID,
  Value, ...)
```

- **Ontologies**: Contains basic information about various ontologies.
- **Terms**: Represents classes, individuals, and properties in the ontologies. A term is a lexical representation of a concept within an ontology. TermID value is generated to be unique across all ontologies. This allows representation of references to a term in a different ontology than the one that defines the term. Also, even an OntologyID is handled as a TermID which facilitates storing values for various properties (e.g., Annotation Properties) and other information that applies to an ontology itself. Note that, as a convention, any column in the above schema whose name is of the form "...ID..", would actually contain TermID values (like a foreign key).
- **Properties**: Contains information about the properties. Domain and range of a property are represented with TermID values of the corresponding classes. Characteristics indicate

which of the following properties are true for the property: symmetry, transitivity, functional, inverse functional.
- *Restrictions*: Contains information about property restrictions. Restrictions on a property results in definition of a new class. This new class is not necessarily named (i.e., 'anonymous' class) in OWL. However, internally we create a new (system-defined) class for ease of representation.
- *Relationships*: Contains information about the relationship between two terms.
- *PropertyValues*: Contains <Property, Value> information associated with the terms. In order to handle values of different data types, some combinations of the following may be used: Define separate tables (or separate columns in the same table) for each of the frequently encountered types and use a generic self-describing type (ANYDATA in Oracle RDBMS) to handle any remaining types.

System-defined Classes for Anonymous Classes: We create internal (i.e., not visible to the user) or system-defined classes to handle OWL anonymous classes that arise in various situations such as Property Restrictions, enumerated types (used in DataRange), class definitions expressed as expression involving IntersectionOf, UnionOf, and ComplementOf.

Bootstrap Ontology: The first things that are loaded into the above schema are the basic concepts of OWL itself. In some sense this is like the bootstrap ontology. For example:

- Thing and Nothing are stored as Classes.
- subClassOf is stored as a transitive (meta) property that relates two classes.
- subPropertyOf is stored as a transitive (meta) property that relates two properties.
- disjointWith is stored as a symmetric (meta) property that relates two classes.
- SameAs is stored as a transitive and symmetric property that relates two individuals in Thing class.

Storing these OWL concepts as a bootstrap ontology facilitates inferencing. A simple example would be the following: If C1 is a subclassOf C2 and C2 is a subclassOf C3, then (by transitivity of subClassOf) C1 is a subclassOf C3. Note that the reflexive nature of subClassOf and SubPropertyOf is handled as a special case.

Loading Ontologies: An ontology is loaded into the database by using an API that takes as input an OWL document. Information from the OWL document is extracted and then stored into the system-defined tables in the RDBMS schema described above.

The `Ontologies` table stores some basic information about all the ontologies that are currently stored in the database. A portion (view) of this table is visible to the user.

2.3 Modeling Ontology-based Semantic Matching

To support ontology-based semantic matching in RDBMS several new operators are defined.

2.3.1 ONT_RELATED Operator. This operator models the basic semantic matching operation. It determines if the two input terms are related with respect to the specified `RelType` relationship argument within an ontology. If they are related it returns 1, otherwise it returns 0.

```
ONT_RELATED (Term1, RelType, Term2,
             OntologyName
) RETURNS INTEGER;
```

The `RelType` can specify a single ObjectProperty (for example, 'IS_A', 'EQV', etc.) or it can specify a combination of such properties by using AND, NOT, and OR operators (for example, 'IS_A OR EQV'). Note that both `Term1` and `Term2` need to be simple terms. If `Term2` needs to be complex involving AND, OR, and NOT operators, user can issue query with individual terms and combine them with INTERSECT, UNION, and MINUS operators. See Section 2.3.4 for an example.

`RelType` specified as an expression involving OR and NOT operators (e.g., `FatherOf OR MotherOf`) is treated as a virtual relationship (in this case say `AncestorOf`) that is transitive by nature (also see Section 3.2.5).

2.3.2 ONT_EXPAND Operator. This operator is introduced to query an ontology independently. Similar to ONT_RELATED operator, the `RelType` can specify either a simple relationship or combination of them.

```
CREATE TYPE ONT_TermRelType AS OBJECT (

Term1Name VARCHAR(32),
PropertyName VARCHAR(32),
Term2Name VARCHAR(32),

TermDistance NUMBER,
TermPath VARCHAR(2000)
);

CREATE TYPE ONT_TermRelTableType AS
    TABLE OF ONT_TermRelType;

ONT_EXPAND (Term1, RelType, Term2,
            OntologyName
) RETURNS ONT_TermRelTableType;
```

Typically, non-NULL values for `RelType` and `Term2` are specified as input and then the operator computes all the appropriate <Term1, RelType, Term2> tuples in the closure taking into account the characteristics (transitivity and symmetry) of the specified `RelType`. In addition, it also computes the relationship measures in terms of distance (`TermDistance`) and path (`TermPath`). For cases when a term is related to input term by multiple paths, one row per path is returned. It is also possible that ONT_EXPAND invocation may specify input values for any one or more of the three parameters or even none of the three parameters. In each of these cases, the appropriate set of <Term1, RelType, Term2> tuples is returned.

2.3.3 ONT_DISTANCE and ONT_PATH Ancillary Operators.
These operators compute the distance and path measures respectively for the rows filtered using ONT_RELATED operator.

```
ONT_DISTANCE (NUMBER) RETURNS NUMBER;
ONT_PATH (NUMBER) RETURNS VARCHAR;
```

A single resulting row can be related in more than one way with the input term. For such cases, the above operators return the optimal measure, namely smallest distance or shortest path. For computing all the matches, the following two operators are provided:

```
ONT_DISTANCE_ALL (NUMBER)
  RETURNS TABLE OF NUMBER;
ONT_PATH_ALL (NUMBER)
  RETURNS TABLE OF VARCHAR;
```

2.3.4 A Restaurant Guide Example.
Consider a restaurant guide application that maintains type of cuisine served at various restaurants. It has two tables, 1) `restaurants` containing restaurant information, and 2) `served_food` containing the types of cuisine served at restaurants.

The restaurant guide application takes as input a type of cuisine and returns the list of restaurants serving that cuisine. Obviously, applications would like to take advantage of an available cuisine ontology to provide better match for the user queries. The cuisine ontology describes the relationships between various types of cuisines as shown earlier in Figure 1.

Thus, if a user is interested in restaurants that serve cuisine of type 'Latin American', the database application can generate the following query:

```
SELECT r.name, r.address
FROM served_food sf, restaurant r
WHERE r.id = sf.r_id AND
      ONT_RELATED(sf.cuisine,
                  'IS_A OR EQV',
                  'Latin American',
                  'Cuisine_ontology')=1;
```

To query on 'Latin American' AND 'Western' the application program can obtain rows for each and use the SQL INTERSECT operation to compute the result.

Also, the application can exploit the full SQL expressive power when using ONT_RELATED operator. For example, it can easily combine the above query results with those restaurants that have lower price range.

```
SELECT r.name
FROM served_food sf, restaurant r
WHERE r.id = sf.r_id AND
      ONT_RELATED(sf.cuisine,
                  'IS_A OR EQV',
                  'Latin American',
                  'Cuisine_ontology')=1
AND r.price_range = '$';
```

2.3.5 Discussion.
Note that the queries in section 2.3.4 can also be issued using the ONT_EXPAND operator. For example, the first query in that section can alternatively be expressed using ONT_EXPAND as follows:

```
SELECT r.name, r.address
FROM served_food sf, restaurant r
WHERE r.id = sf.r_id AND
      sf.cuisine IN
      (SELECT Term1Name from TABLE(
         ONT_EXPAND(NULL, 'IS_A OR EQV',
                    'Latin American',
                    'Cuisine_ontology')));
```

The ONT_RELATED operator is provided in addition to ONT_EXPAND operator for the following reasons:

- The ONT_RELATED operator provides a more natural way of expressing semantic matching operations on column holding ontology terms.
- It allows use of an index created on column holding ontology terms to speed up the query execution by taking column data into account.

2.4 Inferencing

Inferencing rules employing the symmetry and transitivity characteristics of properties are used to infer new relationships. This kind of inferencing can be achieved through the use of the operators defined above (see Section 3.2 for details). Note that our support for inferencing is restricted to OWL Lite and OWL DL, both of which are decidable.

To support more complete inferencing using the above operators, an initial phase of inferencing is done after ontology is loaded, and the results of this inferencing are stored persistently and used in subsequent inferencing. Several examples of the initial inferencing follow.

All subPropertyOf relationships are derived and stored during this phase. The transitive aspects of sameAs (e.g., sameAs(x,y) AND sameAs(y,z) IMPLIES sameAs(x,z)) can be handled by the operators defined above. However, the more complex rules which imply sameAs (e.g., p is a functional property AND p(a,x) AND p(b,y) AND sameAs(a,b) IMPLIES sameAs(x,y)) are best handled outside of the operator implementation. We expect these complex sameAs inferences to be done during the initial inferencing phase. To provide the semantics of sameAs during closure computation, the operators will treat an individual 'I' as 'I OR J' for all J where sameAs(I, J).

Furthermore, we are introducing an internal relationship that will be useful for inferencing over complex subPropertyOf and inverseOf interactions: SubPropertyOfInverseOf(f,g) iff f(x,y) IMPLIES g(y,x). Again, we expect that the rules that introduce

SubPropertyOfInverseOf (spiOf, for short) into an ontology (e.g., inverseOf(f,g) IMPLIES spiOf(f,g) AND spiOf(g,f)) will be handled during the initial inferencing phase. However, the transitive aspects of spiOf can be handled as a special case within our operators, according to the following rules:

- subPropertyOf(f,g) AND spiOf(g,h)
  IMPLIES spiOf(f,h)
  (Proof: f(x,y) IMPLIES g(x,y) IMPLIES h(y,x))

- spiOf(f,g) AND subPropertyOf(g,h)
  IMPLIES spiOf(f,h)
  (Proof: f(x,y) IMPLIES g(y,x) IMPLIES h(y,x))

- spiOf(f,g) AND spiOf(g,h)
  IMPLIES SubPropertyOf(f,h)
  (Proof: f(x,y) IMPLIES g(y,x) IMPLIES h(x,y))

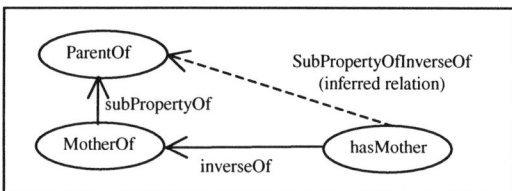

Given the expansion of subPropertyOf and spiOf, we can find all relationship tuples for a given property, including those that are implied through sub-properties and inverse-properties. Consider the following example (see adjoining figure), where non-transitive properties are used for clarity, which expands ParentOf. In this case, if we have subPropertyOf(MotherOf, ParentOf) and inverseOf(MotherOf, hasMother), we will get spiOf(hasMother, ParentOf) based on result of the initial inferencing phase and the above rules. Then hasMother(child, mother) will be sufficient to yield ParentOf(mother, child) in the result set:

```
SELECT r.termID1, 'ParentOf', r.termID2
FROM relationships r, terms t
WHERE r.propertyID = t.termID
  AND t.term IN
  (select term1Name FROM
   TABLE(ONT_EXPAND(NULL,
                    'subPropertyOf',
                    'ParentOf',
                    'Family_ontology')))
UNION
SELECT r.termID2, 'ParentOf', r.termID1
FROM relationships r, terms t
WHERE r.propertyID = t.termID
  AND t.term IN
  (select term1Name FROM
   TABLE(ONT_EXPAND(NULL,
                    'spiOf',
                    'ParentOf',
                    'Family_ontology')))
```

3. Implementation of Ontology Related Functionality on Oracle RDBMS

This section describes how the ontology-related functionality is implemented on top of Oracle RDBMS.

3.1 Operators

The ONT_RELATED operator is defined as a *primary* user-defined operator, with ONT_DISTANCE and ONT_PATH as its *ancillary* operators. The primary operator computes the ancillary value as part of its processing [11]. In this case, ONT_RELATED operator computes the relationship. If ancillary values (the distance and path measure) are required, it computes them as well.

Note that the user-defined operator mechanism in Oracle allows for sharing state across multiple invocations. Thus, the implementation of the ONT_RELATED operator involves building and compiling an SQL query with CONNECT BY clause (as described in Section 3.2) during its first invocation. Each subsequent invocations of the operator simply uses the previously compiled SQL cursor, binds it with the new input value, and executes it to obtain the result.

The ONT_EXPAND operator is defined as a table function as it returns a table of rows, which by default includes the path and distance measures.

3.2 Basic Algorithm

Basic processing for both ONT_RELATED and ONT_EXPAND involves computing transitive closure, namely, traversal of a tree structure by following relationship links given a starting node. Also, as part of transitive closure computation, we need to track the distance and path information for each pair formed by starting node and target node reached via the relationship links.

Oracle supports transitive closure queries with CONNECT BY clause as follows:

```
SELECT ... FROM ... START WITH <condition>
CONNECT BY <condition>;
```

The starting node is selected based on the condition given in START WITH clause, and then nodes are traversed based on the condition given in CONNECT BY clause. The parent node is referred to by the PRIOR operator. For computation of distance and path, the Oracle-provided LEVEL pseudo-column and SYS_CONNECT_BY_PATH function are respectively used in the select list of a query with CONNECT BY clause.

Note that in the system-defined *Relationships* table, a row represents 'TermID1 is related to TermID2 via PropertyID relationship.' For example, if 'A IS_A B', it is represented as the row <1, A, IS_A, B> assuming that the ontologyID is 1.

Note that any cycles encountered during the closure computation will be handled by the CONNECT BY NOCYCLE query implementation available in Oracle 10g (not explicitly shown in the examples below). Also, the proposed index-based implementation (described in

Section 3.3) can handle this case even in Oracle 9i Release 2.

For simplicity, we use a slightly different definition for the `relationships` table where term names are stored instead of termIDs as follows:

```
Relationships (
  OntologyName, Term1, Relation, Term2,
  ...)
```

To illustrate the processing, we use the restaurant guide example. The data for the two tables used are as shown in Table 2 below.

Table 2: Example Restaurant Database

restaurant

Id	Name	price_range	......
1	Mac	$	
2	Chilis	$$	
3	Anthonys	$$$	
4	BK	$	
5	Uno	$$	
6	Wendys	$	
7	Dabin	$$	
8	Cheers	$$	
9	KFC	$	
10	Sizzlers	$$	
11	Rio	$$	
12	Maharaj	$$	
13	Dragon	$$	
14	Niva	$$	

served_food

R_id	cuisine
1	American
2	Mexican
2	American
3	American
4	American
5	American
5	Italian
6	American
7	Korean
7	Japanese
8	American
9	American
10	American
11	Brazilian
12	Mexican
12	Indian
13	Chinese
14	Portuguese

3.2.1 Handling Simple Terms. Consider a query that has simple relation types, i.e., no AND, OR, NOT operators. The first query given in Section 2.3.4 can be converted as follows:

Original Query:
```
SELECT r.name, r.address
 FROM served_food sf, restaurant r
 WHERE r.id = sf.r_id AND
       ONT_RELATED(sf.cuisine, 'IS_A',
'Latin American',
'Cuisine_ontology')=1;
```

Transformed Query:
```
SELECT r.name, r.address
 FROM served_food sf, restaurant r
 WHERE r.id = sf.r_id AND
    sf.cuisine IN
    (SELECT term1 FROM relationships
     START WITH
      term2 = 'Latin American' AND
```
```
      relation = 'IS_A'
     CONNECT BY
      PRIOR term1 = term2 AND
      relation = 'IS_A');
```

The text in boldface above is the portion that has been converted. Basically, the third argument is translated into START WITH clause and the second argument into CONNECT BY clause.

The result for this query is as follows:

NAME	ADDRESS
Chilis	......
Maharaj	......
Niva	......

3.2.2 Handling OR Operator. Consider a case where 'Brazilian' cuisine was not originally included in the ontology and is now inserted under the 'South American' cuisine. Also, to put 'South American' cuisine in the same category as 'Latin American' cuisine, the transitive and symmetric 'EQV' relationship is used as shown in the Figure 3 below:

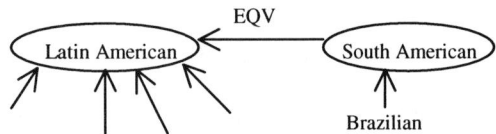

Figure 3: Adding EQV Relationship

Now, to get 'Latin American' cuisine, disjunctive conditions should be used to traverse both relationship links, that is, 'IS_A' and 'EQV'. Such disjunctive conditions can be directly specified in the START WITH and CONNECT BY clauses.

Original Query:
```
SELECT r.name, r.address
 FROM served_food sf, restaurant r
 WHERE r.id = sf.r_id AND
       ONT_RELATED(sf.cuisine,
                   'IS_A OR EQV',
                   'Latin American',
                   'Cuisine_ontology')=1;
```

Transformed Query:

The only differences from the transformed query of the previous example is that the relationships table:

```
FROM relationships
```

is replaced by a sub-query to introduce the implicit symmetric edges into the query:

```
FROM (SELECT term1, relation, term2
      FROM relationships
      UNION
      SELECT term2, relation, term1
      FROM relationships
      WHERE relation = 'EQV')
```

and the occurrence of the following predicate in START WITH and CONNECT BY clauses

```
relation = 'IS_A'
```

is replaced with the following predicate:

```
    (relation = 'IS_A' OR relation =
'EQV')
```

3.2.3 Handling AND operator. Conjunctive conditions between transitive relationship types can be handled by independently computing the transitive closure for each relationship type and then applying set INTERSECT on the resulting sets. For each node in the intersection, a path exists from the start node to this node for each relationship type and hence this is sufficient.

Let us consider another relationship between cuisines, which identifies the spiciest cuisine using the term MOST_SPICY. The ontology can now contain information such as 'South Asian cuisine is MOST_SPICY Asian cuisine' and 'Indian cuisine is MOST_SPICY South Asian cuisine,' etc.

To find very spicy cuisine from the ontology, user can issue a query using conjunctive conditions in the relationships as follows:

Original Query: Find a restaurant that serves very spicy Asian cuisine.
```
SELECT r.name FROM served_food sf,
                    restaurant r
  WHERE r.id = sf.r_id AND
    ONT_RELATED(sf.cuisine,
        'IS_A AND MOST_SPICY'
        'Asian',
        'Cuisine_ontology') = 1;
```
Transformed query:
```
SELECT r.name FROM served_food sf,
                    restaurant r
  WHERE r.id = sf.r_id AND
      sf.cuisine IN
  (
    SELECT term1 FROM relationships
     START WITH
         term2 = 'Asian' AND
         relation = 'IS_A'
     CONNECT BY
         PRIOR term1 = term2 AND
         relation = 'IS_A'

    INTERSECT

    SELECT term1 FROM relationships
     START WITH
         term2 = 'Asian' AND
         relation = 'MOST_SPICY'
     CONNECT BY
         PRIOR term1 = term2 AND
         relation ='MOST_SPICY');
```

3.2.4 Handling NOT operator. A NOT operator specifies which relationships to exclude when finding transitive closure. Therefore, given the start node all relationships except ones specified in NOT operator will be traversed. NOT operators can be directly specified in the START WITH and CONNECT BY clauses.

Original Query: Find all Latin American cuisine, excluding 'EQV' relationship types.
```
SELECT r.name FROM served_food sf,
                    restaurant r
```
```
  WHERE r.id = sf.r_id AND
    ONT_RELATED(sf.cuisine,
        'NOT EQV',
        'Latin American',
        'Cuisine_ontology')=1;
```
Transformed Query: Only difference from the transformed query of the example in Section 3.2.1 is that the occurrence of the following predicate in START WITH and CONNECT BY clauses
```
    relation = 'IS_A'
```
is replaced with the following predicate:
```
    relation != 'EQV'
```
Note that if a user wants to retrieve all cuisines except Latin American cuisine, then the query can be formulated using the operator ONT_RELATED returning 0 as follows:
```
    ......
    ONT_RELATED(sf.cuisine,
        'IS_A',
        'Latin American',
        'Cuisine_ontology')=0;
```

3.2.5 Handling Combination of OR, AND, and NOT. OR and NOT operators are directly specified in the CONNECT BY clause and AND operators are handled by INTERSECT. All conditions are rewritten as conjunctive conditions. For example, 'A OR (B AND C)' will be converted into '(A OR B) AND (A OR C).' Then, '(A OR B)' and '(A OR C)' are specified in the CONNECT BY clause in separate queries that can be combined with INTERSECT operator.

3.3 Speeding up ONT_RELATED and ONT_EXPAND Operations

Finding transitive closure from an ontology can be a time-consuming process especially if the ontology has a large number of terms. In addition, different relationship types can further increase the computation cost. To address this problem, a *transitive closure table* is pre-computed. Note that as part of this computation both distance and path measures are computed as well. For the example cuisine ontology, the transitive closure table will be as shown in Table 3.

Table 3: Transitive Closure Table

RootTerm	RelType	Term	Distance	Path
...				
Latin American	IS_A	Mexican	1	...
Latin American	IS_A	Portuguese	1	...
...				

The data is stored in a key compressed index-organized table [18] (primary B$^+$-tree) with <RootTerm, RelType, Term> as the key. The commonly occurring <RootTerm, RelType> prefixes are compressed. The distance and path are stored as overflow-resident

1061

columns. This allows for basic index-structure to remain compact thereby providing efficient index-lookup.

For a query involving ONT_EXPAND, say with arguments 'Latin American' and 'IS_A' this pre-computed transitive closure table is looked up instead of traversing the ontology to find the transitive closure, and the matching rows are returned. The rows returned include the distance and path measures, which are also available in the Transitive Closure table.

To speed up queries involving ONT_RELATED, a new indexing scheme ONT_INDEXTYPE is implemented using Oracle's Extensible Indexing Framework [5]. Users only need to create an index on the column holding ontology terms using ONT_INDEXTYPE as follows:

```
CREATE INDEX <index_name>
ON <table_name> (<term_column>)
INDEXTYPE is ONT_INDEXTYPE
PARAMETERS('Ontology =
            <ontology_name>');
```

The basic processing of indexing scheme works as follows. Consider the following index creation statement:

```
CREATE INDEX idx1
ON served_food (cuisine)
INDEXTYPE is ONT_INDEXTYPE
PARAMETERS('Ontology=cuisine_ontology');
```

The index creation results in creation of a key-compressed index-organized table with two columns <cuisine, row_id> as shown in Table 4. The row_id column contains the row identifier for the served_food table.

Table 4: Index Table

cuisine	row_id
...	
Mexican	ROWID7
Portuguese	ROWID8
...	

Now, a query involving ONT_RELATED operator say with arguments (sf.cuisine, 'IS_A', 'Latin American', ...), is executed by first searching the transitive closure table using the key ('Latin American', 'IS_A') to find the terms, and then for each term the corresponding row identifier is obtained by doing a lookup into the Index Table.

If a query with ONT_RELATED operator references ONT_DISTANCE and/or ONT_PATH, then the indexed implementation of ONT_RELATED operator retrieves distance and/or path measures from the transitive closure table. These values are simply returned as part of ONT_DISTANCE and ONT_PATH invocations.

The index idx1 created on served_food table behaves likes a regular index, which can be incrementally maintained. That is, if a new row is added to served_food table, the corresponding <cuisine, row_id> values are added to the index table. Similarly, the delete and update operations also result in incremental maintenance of the index.

The transitive closure table is meant for a stable ontology. If the ontology changes, the table needs to be updated. For inserts/deletes/updates into ontology, the transitive closure table can be incrementally maintained. The algorithm is omitted due to lack of space.

3.4 Performance Study using Cancer Ontology

To characterize the performance of ontology-based semantic matching, a part of the National Cancer Institute's Thesaurus and ontology [17] was stored using a prototype implementation built on Oracle RDBMS. Specifically, the following experiments were conducted using Oracle9i Release 2 (9.2.0.3) on a SunOS 5.6, Ultra-60 Sparc Workstation with one 450Mhz CPU and 512 MB of main memory.

The stored ontology consisted of 25,762 terms and 54,387 relationships among them. The resulting transitive closure took 6 minutes to build and contained 186,211 rows.

The following query was executed with the index (transitive closure table) for several different terms. This queries the ontology directly.

```
SELECT count(*) FROM TABLE(
  ONT_EXPAND(NULL, 'IS_A',
       :term,
       'Cancer_Ontology'));
```

Figure 4 illustrates that query runtime increases linearly as the number of rows in the ONT_EXPAND result set increases.

Next a series of database tables, named patients, were created with a varying number of rows, such that 10% of all rows contained a diagnosis term that was one of the 961 subclasses of 'Experimental_Organism_Diagnoses' (EOD).

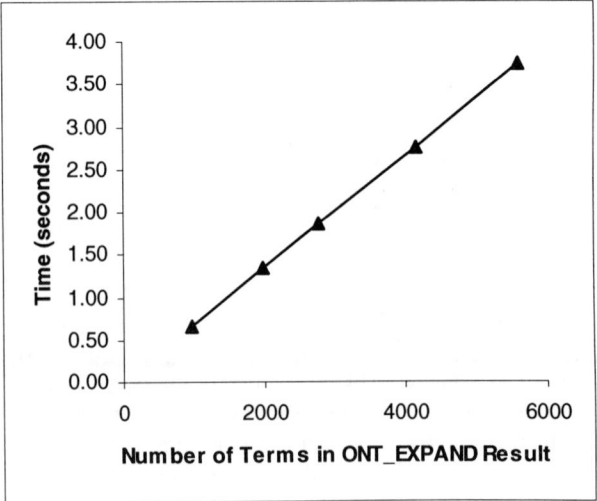

Figure 4: Performance of ONT_EXPAND

Given these `patients` tables, the following query was executed, using all three ONT_RELATED evaluation mechanisms (functional evaluation without an index, functional evaluation with an index, and index evaluation), to count the number of patients whose diagnosis is an EOD:

```
SELECT count(*) FROM patients
WHERE ONT_RELATED(diagnosis,
                  'IS_A',
          'Experimental_Organism_Diagnoses',
                  'Cancer_Ontology') = 1;
```

Figure 5 illustrates how query runtime varies as the number of rows in the `patients` table changes.

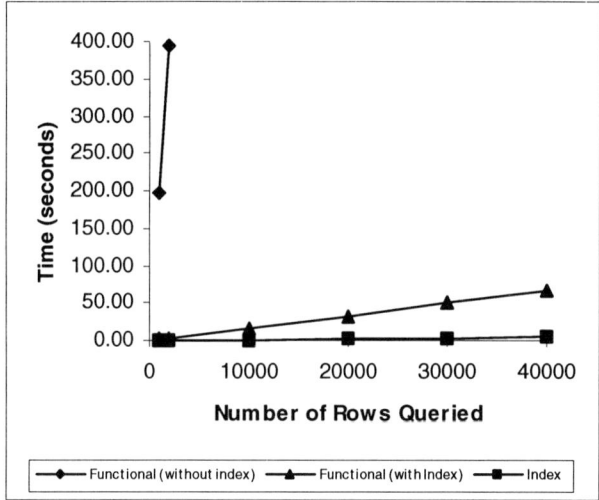

Figure 5: Performance of ONT_RELATED

Functional evaluation without an index computes transitive closure for ONT_RELATED using CONNECT BY clause (without using a pre-computed transitive closure table). Functional evaluation with an index uses the transitive closure table to check if two terms are connected. Index evaluation uses the index table (Table 4) and the transitive closure table to compute the result. Again the query time increases linearly as the result set size increases. The results clearly show that finding transitive closure by traversing the ontology during query processing time is time-consuming and utilizing the pre-computed transitive closure table provides significant performance gains.

4. Ontology-driven Database Applications

This section illustrates the usage of the ontology-related semantic matching operations by considering several database applications.

4.1 A Homeland Security Application

An intelligence analyst for homeland security would be very much interested in an activity that might be related to terrorism. From the example pattern given in [20], where a person rents a truck and another person buys fertilizer, and they reside in the same house, we can formulate an SQL query using ONT_RELATED operator for a given activity table:

Person_name	Address	Activity	Object
John Buck	Addr1	Rent	Ford F-150
Jane Doe	Addr1	Buy	Ammonium Nitrate
...	...	...	...

```
SELECT *
FROM ACTIVITY x, ACTIVITY y
WHERE
  x.Activity = 'Rent' AND
  y.Activity = 'Buy' AND
  ONT_RELATED(x.object,'IS_A','Truck',
              'vehicle_ontology') = 1 AND
  ONT_RELATED(y.object,'IS_A','Fertilizer',
              'chemical_ontology')=1 AND
  x.Address = y.Address;
```

By referring to more than one ontology we can analyze suspicious activities involving a combination of different actions.

4.2 A Supply Chain Application

A supply chain where thousands of products and services are exchanged has a major issue of standardizations of purchase order, bill of material, catalogs, etc. There could be name, language, currency, and unit differences to resolve to name a few. Standardization efforts such as RosettaNet [22], UNSPSC [23] for product category and ebXML [24] to standardize business processes and products are not enough to meet individual vendor/customer needs to resolve semantic differences. Typically, these conflicts have been resolved using some form of mapping mechanisms [6].

These conflicts can be resolved by issuing an SQL query with ONT_RELATED operator using ontologies. Even individually developed ontologies may need the ontology mappings to communicate each other. We can apply ONT_RELATED and ONT_EXPAND operators to the mapping ontology to resolve the conflicts as well.

4.3 A Life Science Application

Life Science domain applications have been using ontologies for representing knowledge as well as the basis of information integration of several heterogeneous sources of life science web databases. Let us consider Gene Ontology (GO)[12], which is primarily used to represent the current knowledge in this domain. It allows user to query using SQL. One sample query is '*Fetching every term that is a transmembrane receptor*'. The GO Graph is stored using the 'term' (=node) and 'term2term' (=arc) tables. It also maintains a table called `graph_path`, which stores all paths between a term and all its ancestors. In GO database the following SQL query can be issued for this purpose:

```
SELECT
  rchild.*
FROM
  term AS rchild, term AS ancestor,
  graph_path
WHERE
  graph_path.term2_id = rchild.id and
  graph_path.term1_id = ancestor.id and
  ancestor.name = 'transmembrane
                    receptor';
```

The following query can be used if the data is stored in Oracle RDBMS:

```
SELECT * FROM TABLE
  (ONT_EXPAND (NULL, 'IS_A',
              'transmembrane receptor',
              'gene_ontology'));
```

The key difference is that the GO database exposes the underlying schema and requires users to formulate queries against those tables, whereas the operator approach attempts to simplify the specification.

4.4 A Web Service Application

Similarly, web service applications can also utilize the ONT_RELATED operator to match two different terms semantically. Consider the web-service matching example described in [8], where user is looking to purchase a sedan. The user requests a web service using the term 'Sedan'. The vehicle ontology contains 'Sedan', 'SUV', and 'Station Wagon' as subclasses of the term 'Car'. The web service can alert the user by using the query with the ONT_RELATED operator as follows:

```
  ......
ONT_RELATED(user_request,
            'IS_A',
            'Car',
            'Vehicle_Ontology') = 1;
```

The degree of match between terms, i.e. how closely the terms are related, as described in [8], can be handled using ONT_DISTANCE and ONT_PATH operators.

5. Experiences

This section summarizes our experience with supporting ontology-related functionality using Oracle RDBMS.

Ontology Access and Manipulation. Instead of providing an API to access and manipulate ontology, we opted for using SQL capabilities. For semantic matching, a set of SQL operators was introduced. The key benefit is that user can fully exploit the expressive power of SQL when performing ontology-based semantic matching.

Ontology Storage. In contrast to system like Gene Ontology Database, where a single domain-specific ontology is handled by a set of tables, we decided to store ontologies in a domain-independent manner. That is, multiple ontologies belonging to different domains are stored in a single set of Oracle tables. The key benefit is that a set of canonical operators can be used for semantic match using any ontology. However, the domain-specific approach can lead to a more efficient implementation.

Transitive Closure Table Computation and Its Maintenance. We decided to pre-compute transitive closure table as is done in Gene Ontology Database as well. Their motivation for this pre-computing was to deal with the non-availability of recursive querying capability in the RDBMS used (which is not the case in Oracle). Our primary motivation for pre-computing the transitive closure table was to speed up queries involving semantic matching. The preliminary performance results (as discussed in Section 3.4) clearly demonstrate the significant performance gains by the use of the transitive closure table. The overhead of storing pre-computed transitive closures can be reduced by storing only those closures that are frequently used. The performance gains far outweigh the space overhead drawback.

6. Conclusions and Future work

With the increasing importance of ontologies in business database application areas, it is important that ontologies are stored in databases for efficient maintenance, sharing, and scalability. Equally important is the capability for ontology-based semantic matching in SQL for performance and ease of application development.

The paper addresses these issues by allowing OWL Lite and OWL DL based ontologies to be stored in Oracle RDBMS and by providing a set of SQL operators for ontology-based semantic matching. The approach was further validated by building a prototype implementation on Oracle RDBMS and conducting performance experiments with National Cancer Institute's Thesaurus and ontology.

In future, we plan to support ontology merging (including semantic matching across ontologies) and ontology evolution. Also, we plan to explore extending the inference engine to support user-defined rules.

Acknowledgments

We thank Jay Banerjee for his comments on an earlier version of this paper.

References

[1] Y. Kalfoglou, J. Domingue, E. Motta, M. Vargas-Vera, and S. Buckingham-Shum, "MyPlanet: an ontology-driven Web-based personalised news service," In *Proceedings IJCAI 2001 workshop on Ontologies and Information Sharing*, Seattle, WA, Aug. 2001.

[2] F. T. Fonseca, M. J. Egenhofer, "Ontology-Driven Geographic Information Systems," In *Proceedings of the 7th ACM Symposium on Advances in Geographic Information Systems*, pp. 14-19, Nov. 1999.

[3] M. Musen, S. Tu, A. Das, and Y. Shahar, "EON: A component-based architecture for automation of protocol-directed therapy," In *Proceedings of 5th Artificial Intelligence in Medicine in Europe*, pp. 3-13, Jun. 1995.

[4] T. Berners-Lee, J, Handler, O Lassila. "The Semantic Web," *Scientific American*, May 2001.

[5] J. Srinivasan, R. Murthy, S. Sundara, N. Agarwal, S. DeFazio, "Extensible Indexing: A Framework for Integrating Domain-Specific Indexing into Oracle8*i*," In *Proceedings of the 16th International Conference on Data Engineering*, pp. 91-100, Feb. 2000.

[6] C. A. Knoblock and S. Minton, "Building Agents for Internet-based Supply Chain Integration," *Proceedings of the Workshop on Agents for Electronic Commerce and Managing the Internet-Enabled Supply Chain*, 1999.

[7] G. van Heijst, A. Th. Schreiber and B. J. Wielinga, "Using Explicit Ontologies for KBS Development," *Int. Journal of Human-Computer Studies*, 46(2-3), pp. 183-292, 1997.

[8] M. Paolucci, T. Kawamura, T. Payne, and K. Sycara, "Semantic Matching of Web Services Capabilities," *Proceedings of Int. Semantic Web Conference*, pp. 333-347, 2002.

[9] M. Uschold and R. Jasper, "A Framework for Understanding and Classifying Ontology Applications," *Proceedings of IJCAI Workshop on Ontologies and Problem-Solving Methods*, Aug. 1999.

[10] L. D. Stein, "Integrating Biological Databases," *Nature Reviews (Genetics)*, Vol. 4, pp. 337-345, May 2003.

[11] R. Murthy, S. Sundara, N. Agarwal, Y. Hu, T. Chorma, J. Srinivasan, "Supporting Ancillary Values from User Defined Functions in Oracle", In *Proceedings of the 19th International Conference on Data Engineering*, pp. 151-162, 2003.

[12] Gene Ontology Consortium, http://www.geneontology.org.

[13] OntoEdit, http://www.ontoknowledge.org/tools/ontoedit.shtml.

[14] OntoBroker, http://ontobroker.semanticweb.org

[15] B. Motik, A. Maedche, and R. Volz, "A Conceptual Modeling Approach for Semantics-Driven Enterprise Applications," In *Proceedings of the 2002 Confederated Int. Conferences DOA/CoopIS/ODBASE*, 2002.

[16] A. Das, W. Wu, and D. McGuinness, "Industrial Strength Ontology Management," *The Emerging Semantic Web*, IOS Press, 2002.

[17] National Cancer Institute Thesaurus, http://www.mindswap.org/2003/CancerOntology.

[18] J. Srinivasan, S. Das, C. Freiwald, E. I. Chong, M. Jagannath, A. Yalamanchi, R. Krishnan, A. Tran, S. DeFazio, J. Banerjee, "Oracle8*i* Index-Organized Table and its Applications to New Domains," In *Proceedings of the 26th Int. Conf. on Very Large Data Bases*, pp. 285-296, Sept. 2000.

[19] OWL Web Ontology Language Reference, http://www.w3.org/TR/owl-ref

[20] T. Coffman, S. Greenblatt, and S. Marcus, "Graph-based Technologies for Intelligence Analysis," *Communications of the ACM*, Vol. 47, No.3, pp. 45-47, Mar. 2004.

[21] Jena2 – A Semantic Web Framework, http://www.hpl.hp.com/scmweb/jena.htm

[22] RosettaNet, http://www.**rosettanet**.org/RosettaNet

[23] UNSPSC, http://www.**unspsc**.org

[24] ebXML – Enabling A Global Electronic Market, http://www.**ebxml**.org/

BioPatentMiner: An Information Retrieval System for BioMedical Patents

Sougata Mukherjea, Bhuvan Bamba

IBM India Research Lab
New Delhi, India
E-mail: {smukherj,bhuvanbh}@in.ibm.com

Abstract

Before undertaking new biomedical research, identifying concepts that have already been patented is essential. Traditional keyword based search on patent databases may not be sufficient to retrieve all the relevant information, especially for the biomedical domain. More sophisticated retrieval techniques are required. This paper presents BioPatentMiner, a system that facilitates information retrieval from biomedical patents. It integrates information from the patents with knowledge from biomedical ontologies to create a Semantic Web. Besides keyword search and queries linking the properties specified by one or more RDF triples, the system can discover Semantic Associations between the resources. The system also determines the importance of the resources to rank the results of a search and prevent information overload while determining the Semantic Associations.

1 Introduction

Before undertaking expensive and time consuming research for Drug Discovery, it is essential to determine what related biomedical concepts have already been patented. Online Patent databases exist for most countries that generally allow traditional keyword based search on various fields of a Patent (like Inventor, Assignee, Abstract, etc.) However, sometimes more complex retrieval techniques need to be supported. For example, a company may need to identify relationships with a competitor based on their assigned patents. For the biomedical domain there are additional complexities. Firstly, many biomedical concepts are known by a variety of names; therefore keyword based search on just a few of the synonyms may not retrieve all the relevant patents. Moreover, sometimes researchers may want to query on a class of biological terms; for example one may wish to retrieve all patents related to genes that have been issued to a competitor. Another complication is that sometimes Pharmaceutical companies patent a group of related molecules or an amino acid sequence. Therefore, discovering semantic relationships between biological concepts and patents, companies and inventors will be very useful. Because of these complexities most Pharmaceutical companies employ several Patent Analysts to manually examine hundreds of patents retrieved by querying the Patent databases.

In this paper we present **BioPatentMiner**, a system that facilitates information retrieval from biomedical patents. The system integrates information from the patents with biomedical ontologies and creates a *Biomedical Semantic Web*. Since the user information requirement will be varied, different views of the underlying information space are utilized. While for keyword based search, the traditional information retrieval model is useful, to answer queries linking the properties specified by one or more *RDF* triples, SQL-type declarative query languages are the most effective. On the other hand, to determine the semantic associations between Semantic Web resources, Graph algorithms are utilized. Since a real-world Biomedical Semantic Web will consist of thousands of resources we have also developed a technique to determine the importance of a resource in a Semantic Web. The importance is used to rank the results of a search and to filter the information space while determining the Semantic Associations between two resources.

The paper is organized as follows. Section 2

Permission to copy without fee all or part of this material is granted provided that the copies are not made or distributed for direct commercial advantage, the VLDB copyright notice and the title of the publication and its date appear, and notice is given that copying is by permission of the Very Large Data Base Endowment. To copy otherwise, or to republish, requires a fee and/or special permission from the Endowment.

**Proceedings of the 30th VLDB Conference,
Toronto, Canada, 2004**

cites related work. Section 3 gives an overview of the system. Section 4 explains our method for determining the importance of the Semantic Web resources. Section 5 describes how we utilize the importance values to determine the Semantic associations between two resources. Section 6 presents some scenarios to show how BioPatentMiner can be used for information retrieval from a collection of biomedical patents. Finally, section 7 concludes the paper.

2 Related Work

2.1 Patent Retrieval Systems

Many countries provide Web interfaces for searching their patent databases (for example, the United States Patent and Trademark Office (USPTO)[22]). Research systems that utilize different techniques for retrieving information from Patent databases have also been developed. [15] introduces a system that integrates a series of shallow natural language processing techniques into a vector based document information retrieval system for searching a subset of US patents. On the other hand [13] uses a probabilistic information retrieval system for searching and classifying US patents. Another related system is described in [14] which tries to use techniques like Correspondence and Cluster analysis for mining patents. A report on a SIGIR Workshop on Patent Retrieval [9] highlights some of the challenges in the domain of Patent Retrieval.

In this paper we are focusing on Biomedical patents whose retrieval involves some unique challenges. An interesting system for querying Protein Patents is Kleisli [7]. Given a protein sequence, it uses Patent and Protein databases as well as Bioinformatics tools to identify whether similar protein sequences have already been patented. Some of these Bioinformatics tools can be utilized to augment our system as well.

2.2 Semantic Web Languages

BioPatentMiner creates a Semantic Web integrating the knowledge from patents and biomedical dictionaries. RDF [16] has become the standard language for representing any Semantic Web. It describes a Semantic Web using *Statements* which are *triples* of the form *(Subject, Property, Object)*. Subjects are *resources* which are uniquely identified by a *Uniform Resource Identifier (URI)*. Objects can be resources or literals. Properties are first class objects in the model that define binary relations between two resources or between a resource and a literal.

RDF Schema (RDFS) [17] makes the model more powerful by allowing new resources to be specializations of already defined resources. RDFS Classes are resources denoting a set of resources, by means of the property *RDF:type* (instances have property RDF:type valued by the class). All resources have by definition the property RDF:type valued by *RDF:Resource*. Moreover, all properties have RDF:type valued by *RDF:Property* and classes are of the type *RDFS:Class*.

Two important properties defined in RDFS are *subClassOf* and *subPropertyOf*. Two other important concepts are *domain* and *range* which apply to properties and must be valued by classes. They restrict the set of resources that may have a given property (the property's *domain*) and the set of valid values for a property (its *range*). A property may have as many values for *domain* as needed, but no more than one value for *range*. For a triple to be valid, the type of the object must be the range class and the type of the subject must be one of the domain classes.

RDFS allows inference of new triples based on several simple rules. Some of the important rules are:

1. $\forall s, p_1, o, p_2$ $(s, p_1, o) \wedge (p_1, \text{RDFS:subPropertyOf}, p_2) => (s, p_2, o)$

2. $\forall r, c_1, c_2$ $(r, \text{RDF:type}, c_1) \wedge (c_1, \text{RDFS:subClassOf}, c_2) => (r, RDF:type, c_2)$

3. $\forall c_1, c_2, c_3$ $(c_1, \text{RDFS:subClassOf}, c_2) \wedge (c_2, \text{RDFS:subClassOf}, c_3) => (c_1, RDFS:subClassOf, c_3)$

2.3 Building and Querying the Semantic Web

In recent times tools like Jena [8] have been developed to facilitate the development of Semantic Web applications. Researchers have also endeavored to represent existing knowledge bases in the Semantic Web languages. For example, [11] describes an effort to represent Unified Medical Language System (UMLS) [21] using Semantic Web languages.

The development of effective information retrieval techniques for the Semantic Web has become an important research problem. There are a number of proposed techniques for querying RDF data including RQL [10] and RDQL [18]. Most of these query languages use a SQL-like declarative syntax to query a Semantic Web as a set of RDF triples. They also incorporate inference as part of query answering. However, these languages are not able to determine complex relationships between two resources. For this purpose, [1] introduced the concept of **Semantic Associations** between Semantic Web resources. However no effective implementation of Semantic Associations was presented. We discuss our implementation of semantic associations in Section 5.

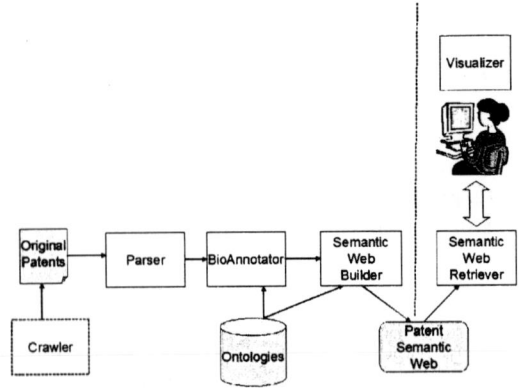

Figure 1: Architecture of BioPatentMiner

2.4 Determining WWW Page Importance

In this paper we introduce a technique to determine the importance of resources in a Semantic Web. This has been influenced by the extensive research in recent years to determine the importance of World-wide Web pages. The most well-known technique is *Page Rank* [4] which has been used very effectively to rank the results in Google Web search engine.

Another technique of finding the important pages in a WWW collection has been developed by Kleinberg [12] who defined two types of scores for Web pages which pertain to a certain topic: **authority** and **hub** scores. Documents with high Authority scores are authorities on a topic and therefore have many links pointing to them. On the other hand, documents with high hub scores are resource lists - they do not directly contain information about the topic, but rather point to many authoritative sites. Transitively, a document that points to many good authorities is an even better hub, and similarly a document pointed to by many good hubs is an even better authority. Kleinberg's algorithm has been refined in CLEVER [6] and Topic Distillation [2]. Both of these algorithms augment Kleinberg's link analysis with textual analysis. A good overview of various link analysis techniques to find hubs and authorities and suggestions for improvements are presented in [3].

3 BioPatentMiner: System Overview

BioPatentMiner is a system to facilitate knowledge discovery from patents related to Biomedicine. Figure 1 shows the overall architecture of the system. The system uses a crawler to download patents from the USPTO site [22] based on a query. The system can be also used on a collection of biomedical patents obtained by other techniques. The Parser parses these patents to extract information like Inventors, Assignees, Title, Abstracts etc. At present the parser assumes that the patents are in the HTML format of the USPTO site. It can be tuned for other formats.

The biological terms in the parsed files are then annotated by the **BioAnnotator** system [19]. BioAnnotator identifies and classifies biological terms in scientific text. It uses publicly available biomedical dictionaries like UMLS for this purpose. BioAnnotator also uses a Rule Engine to identify unknown and new biological terms. The annotated patents are represented in XML.

To facilitate knowledge discovery we want to integrate the information of the patents and biomedical ontologies. We believe that Semantic Web languages enable information from heterogeneous sources to be seamlessly integrated. Moreover one can utilize inference during querying. Therefore, **SemWebBuilder** is utilized to build a Semantic Web based on the annotated patents and biomedical dictionaries using RDF and RDFS. The patents, assignees and inventors of the patents as well as the Biomedical concepts identified by the BioAnnotator are represented as resources in the Semantic Web. Four properties link the resources:

- <*patentA* **refers_to** *patentB*> (patentA refers to patentB)

- <*inventorC* **invented** *patentD*> (inventorC has invented patentD)

- <*assigneeE* **assigned** *patentF*> (patentF is assigned to assigneeE)

- <*patentG* **has_term** *bioTermH*> (patentG has the biological concept bioTermH, as determined by BioAnnotator)

At present Unified Medical Language System (UMLS) [21] is used as the biomedical knowledge source. UMLS is a consolidated repository of medical terms and their relationships, spread across multiple languages and disciplines (chemistry, biology, etc). An essential section of UMLS is a **Semantic Network** which has 135 biomedical semantic classes like *Gene* or *Genome* and *Amino Acid, Peptide, or Protein*. The semantic classes are linked by a set of 54 semantic relationships (like *prevents*, *causes*). In addition there are biological concepts each of which are associated with one or more semantic classes. For example, the concept *blood cancer* has the semantic class *Neoplastic Process*. We created RDFS classes for all the Semantic Network classes and RDF Properties for all Semantic Network relationships except *isa*. A RDF statement is created to represent each relationship among the classes. The *isa* relationship is represented by *RDFS:subClassOf* relationship if it is between classes and *RDFS:subPropertyOf* relationship if it is between properties. The biological concepts are represented as RDF resources. They are named by their UMLS concept ids and the various names associated with the concept are stored as RDFS labels. The property *has_term* links the patents to the UMLS concepts they refer to.

SemWebRetriver is the run-time component of the system running inside a Web Application Server. It facilitates various types of information retrieval from the Semantic Web:

- SemWebRetriever supports keyword search on the annotated patents using the Juru XML search engine [5]. It facilitates retrieval of patents based on various criteria similar to USPTO.

- We develop Semantic Webs using Jena [8] which utilizes RDQL, a query language for RDF in Jena [18]. RDQL uses a declarative SQL-like syntax for querying information contained in one or more RDF triples. Although RDQL is data-oriented and does not support inference, Jena can create certain triples on-demand using inference. For example, if the triples *(c1 RDFS:subClassOf c2)* and *(r1 RDF:type c1)* are present, Jena can automatically infer that *(r1 RDF:type c2)* also exists.

- SemWebRetriever also identifies Semantic Associations between Web resources. This is discussed further in Section 5.

Visualizer is a client side Swing-based Java WebStart application. It allows the visualization of the Semantic Associations.

3.1 Graphical Representation of the Information Space

To fully capture the richness of a Semantic Web, a graphical representation of the information space is required. Let us define a Semantic Web as (C, P, NC) where C are the classes, P are the properties and NC are the normal resources (neither classes nor properties) that are defined for the Semantic Web. For creating the graphs we ignore classes and properties that are not defined in the local namespace (for example *RDF:Resource, RDFS:subClassOf*, etc.) We represent the information space using two graphs: isaGraph and propertyGraph.

3.1.1 isaGraph

The isaGraph is a directed graph whose vertices represent C, the classes of the Semantic Web. For all triples *(c1 RDFS:subClassOf c2)* defined in the Semantic Web, an edge $(c2, c1)$ is created in the isaGraph. Thus, the isaGraph represents the class hierarchy (*subClassOf* relation) of the Semantic Web. We ignore triples formed by inference while creating this graph. Note that the *subClassOf* relation cannot be represented as a tree, since a class can have more than one parent.

3.1.2 propertyGraph

Let P_r be a subset of P, containing only properties whose objects are resources. Let R be a subset of $(C \cup NC)$ satisfying the condition:
$\forall (r \in R) \exists (p_r \in P_r)$ such that r is a subject or object of a triple whose predicate is p_r or r is the domain or range of p_r.
The propertyGraph is a directed graph representing the properties defined in the local namespace. Its vertex set is R, the resources that are related to other resources by local properties. An edge from r_1 to r_2 exists in the propertyGraph if any one of the conditions hold:

- A triple (r_1, p_r, r_2) exists in the Semantic Web for any $(p_r \in P_r)$. In other words, an edge is created between two resources in the propertyGraph if they are the subject and object of a triple.

- $(p_r, RDFS:domain, r_1)$ and $(p_r, RDFS:range, r_2)$ exist in the Semantic Web for any $(p_r \in P_r)$. In other words, an edge is created between two resources (classes) in the property graph if they are the domain and range of a local property (and are thus related).

Note that we ignore triples formed by inference while creating this graph.

4 Semantic Web Resource Importance

SemWebRetriever queries can retrieve patents, assignees, inventors or biological concepts. In many cases many results will be retrieved and effective ways of ranking the results are required. Just ranking using information retrieval techniques like term frequency may not always provide the most intuitive results for the user. As Web search engines have shown, ranking based on the importance of the retrieved Web pages is very useful. Similarly, we can determine the importance of a resource in the Semantic Web to facilitate ranking. In this section we will discuss how we determine the importance of Semantic Web resources.

4.1 Subjectivity and Objectivity scores

A resource that has relationships with many other resources in the Semantic Web can be considered to be important since it is an important aspect of the overall semantics; the meaning of many other resources of the Semantic Web have to be defined with respect to that resource. In the context of the propertyGraph, vertices that have a high in-degree or out-degree should be considered important.

Kleinberg's hub and authority scores give a good indication about the connectivity of nodes in the WWW graph. It not only considers the number of links to and from a node but also the importance of the linked nodes. If a node is pointed to by a node with high hub score, its authority score is increased. Similarly, if a node points to a node with high authority score, its hub score is increased. Therefore, we calculate scores similar to the hub and authority scores of the propertyGraph to get an estimate of the importance of the resources in the Semantic Web. These scores are called **Subjectivity** and **Objectivity** scores corresponding to hub and authority scores. A node with high subjectivity/objectivity score is the subject/object of many RDF triples.

In the WWW all links are similar and can be considered to be equally important while calculating the hub and authority scores. On the other hand in a Semantic Web links in the propertyGraph represent properties; all the properties may not be equally important. For example, consider the property *has_term* in the Patent Semantic Web which links a Patent to the biological term it contains. The importance of the patent should not be dependent on the number of biological terms it contains. However, a biological term's importance should increase if it is referred to in many patents. On the other hand, consider the property *invented* in our Semantic Web which links an Inventor to a patent. The importance of a patent should not increase if it has many inventors. However, the importance of an inventor is obviously dependent on her patents. Therefore for each property we have a predefined subjectivity and objectivity weights which determine the importance of the subject/object of the property. By default these scores are 1.0. Properties like *has_term* will have a lower subjectivity weight while properties like *invented* will have a lower objectivity weight.

Kleinberg's algorithm has been modified to calculate the subjectivity and objectivity scores of Semantic Web resources as follows:

1. Let N be the set of nodes and E be the set of edges in the propertyGraph.

2. For every resource n in N, let $S[n]$ be its subjectivity score and $O[n]$ be its objectivity score

3. Initialize $S[n]$ and $O[n]$ to 1 for all r in R.

4. While the vectors S and O have not converged:

    (a) For all n in N, $O[n] = \sum_{(n1,n) \in E} S[n1] * objWt$ where $objWt$ is the objectivity weight of the property representing the link

    (b) For all n in N, $S[n] = \sum_{(n,n1) \in E} O[n1] * subWt$ where $subWt$ is the subjectivity weight of the property representing the link

    (c) Normalize the S and O vectors

Our modification is that while determining the subjectivity and objectivity scores of a vertex we multiply the scores of the adjacent vertex by the subjectivity/objectivity weights of the corresponding link. This will ensure that the scores of the resources are not influenced by unimportant properties. For example, a low objectivity weight for the *invented* property will ensure that the objectivity scores of patents are not increased by the number of inventors for that patent.

An important observation is that there is no "preferred direction" for a property. For example instead of the *invented* property we can have the *invented_by* property for which a patent is the subject and the inventor is the object. Thus, depending on the schema, a resource could equally well be a subject or an object. That is, the Subjectivity and Objectivity scores will be affected by the schema. However, the combined Subjectivity and Objectivity scores will be independent of the schema.

4.2 Determining Class Importance

The importance of a Semantic Web class is determined by how well it is connected to other classes. Obviously, this will be dependent on its subjectivity and objectivity scores. If c_1 is a subclass of c_2, all the properties of c_2 should be inherited by c_1. Therefore, the importance of a class should also be influenced by its parents. Because of the transitive property of the *subClassOf* relation, the importance of a class should actually be dependent on all its ancestors. However, we believe that a class should only marginally influence a distant descendent much lower in the *isa* hierarchy. Based on these beliefs, we calculate the importance of a class as:

1. Let $parentWt, subWt, objWt$ be predefined constants that determine the importance attached to the parents, subjectivity and objectivity scores while calculating the importance.
$parentWt + subWt + objWt = 1.0$

2. If there are no links between class and non-class resources, filter the propertyGraph to include only

the classes and the links between them. (In other words, we remove all data resources and their related properties from the propertyGraph). If there are links between the schema and data resources the filtering is not necessary.

3. Calculate the Subjectivity and Objectivity scores of the classes from this graph.

4. Let C be the set of nodes and E be the set of edges in the isaGraph. (Obviously C contains the classes of the Semantic Web).

5. For every class c in C, let $S[c]$, $O[c]$, $PI[c]$ and $I[c]$ be its subjectivity, objectivity, parent importance and importance scores respectively.

6. $PI[c] = \frac{\sum_{(c1,c) \in E} I[c1]}{indegree(c)}$

7. $I[c] = PI[c] * parentWt + S[c] * subjWt + O[c] * objWt$

Thus, the importance of a class is determined by its subjectivity and objectivity scores and the importance of its parents. If $(c_1, subClassOf, c_2)$ and $(c_2, subClassOf, c_3)$, then $I(c_2)$ will be influenced by $I(c_3)$. Since $I(c_1)$ is influenced by $I(c_2)$, it is also influenced by $I(c_3)$. However, the influence of an ancestor on a node is inversely proportional to its distance from the node. It should be noted that we ignore RDF and RDFS vocabulary elements like RDF:Resource while calculating the Class Importance because we are only interested in the classes defined in the local namespace.

In many Semantic Webs, there will be no links connecting the schema (Class) and non-class (Data) resources. Thus there will be two separate subgraphs. If one of these subgraphs is more densely connected compared to the other subgraph, the importance scores of the vertices in the sparsely connected subgraph will be insignificant. To prevent this scenario, if there are no links between class and non-class resources, we filter non-class resources from the propertyGraph while calculating the Subjectivity and Objectivity scores of classes.

4.3 Determining Resource Importance

We believe that the importance of a Semantic Web non-class resource should be determined by how well it is connected to other resources. We also believe that it should be influenced by the importance of the classes it belongs to. Therefore we calculate the importance of a non-class resource as follows:

1. Let $classWt$, $subWt$, $objWt$ be predefined constants that determine the importance attached to the classes, subjectivity and objectivity scores while calculating the importance.
$classWt + subWt + objWt = 1.0$

2. If there are no links between class and non-class resources, filter the propertyGraph to only include the non-class resources in the Semantic Web and the links between them. (In other words, we remove all schema resources and their related properties from the propertyGraph).

3. Calculate the Subjectivity and Objectivity scores from this graph.

4. Let NC be the non-class resources in the Semantic Web. For every resource n in NC, let $S[n]$, $O[n]$, $CI[n]$ and $I[n]$ be its subjectivity, objectivity, class importance and importance scores respectively.

5. Let $noClass[n]$ be the number of triples in the Semantic Web where n is the subject and $RDF{:}type$ is the predicate.

6. $CI[n] = \frac{\sum_{(n, RDF:type, c) \in SemanticWeb} I[c]}{noClass[n]}$

7. $I[n] = CI[n] * classWt + S[n] * subWt + O[n] * objWt$

Thus the importance of a resource r is determined by its subjectivity and objectivity scores as well as the importance of all classes for which the triple $(r, RDF{:}type, c)$ is defined explicitly in the Semantic Web. Note that the $subWt$ and $objWt$ constants for calculating the Class and Resource importance are different.

5 Semantic Associations

The RDF query languages like RDQL allow the discovery of all resources that are linked to a particular resource by an ordered set of specific relationships. For example, one can query a Semantic Web to find all resources that are linked to resource r_1 by the properties p_1 followed by p_2. Another option is to determine all the paths between resources r_1 and r_2 that are of length n. However, none of the query languages allow queries like "How are resources r_1 and r_2 related?" without any specification of the type of the properties or the length of the path. It is also not possible to determine relationships specified by undirected paths between two resources. In order to determine any arbitrary relationships among resources, Anyanwu and Sheth introduced the notion of **Semantic associations** based on ρ-queries [1]. In this section we will discuss an efficient implementation of Semantic Associations.

5.1 Definitions

Let us first give some definitions related to Semantic Associations based on the propertyGraph and the isaGraph. For the original definitions one should refer to [1]. For our definitions let Figure 2 represent a propertyGraph. Several resources are shown with the dashed

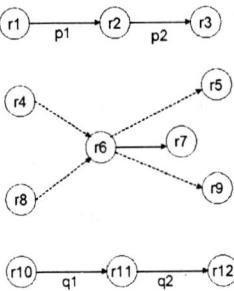

Figure 2: An Example propertyGraph

arrows representing paths between the resources and solid arrows representing edges between the resources.

- Two resources r_1 and r_2 are $\rho - path - associated$ if there is a direct path from r_1 to r_2 or r_2 to r_1 in propertyGraph. For example, in the example graph shown in Figure 2, resources $(r4, r9)$ and $(r5, r8)$ are $\rho - path - associated$.

- Two directed paths in the propertyGraph are said to be *joined* if they have at least one vertex common. The common vertex is the *join node*. For example, the directed paths from $r4$ to $r9$ and $r8$ to $r5$ are joined with the common vertex $r6$. Two resources r_1 and r_2 are $\rho - join - associated$ if there are joined paths p_1 and p_2 and either of these two conditions are satisfied:

    1. r_1 is the origin of p_1 and r_2 is the origin of p_2
    2. r_1 is the terminus of p_1 and r_2 is the terminus of p_2

    Thus in Figure 2 $(r4, r8)$ and $(r5, r9)$ are sets of $\rho - join - associated$ resources.

- Two resources r_1 and r_2 are $\rho - cp - associated$ if r_1 is of type c_1, r_2 is of type c_2 and either of these two conditions are satisfied:

    1. $c_1 = c_2$
    2. In the isaGraph there exists a class c_3 from which directed paths to both c_1 and c_2 exists.

    Thus resources are $\rho - cp - associated$ if they belong to the same class or classes which have a common ancestor. To prevent meaningless associations (like all resources belong to *RDF:Resource*), one can specify a *strong* $\rho - cp - associated$ relation which is true if either of these two conditions are also satisfied:

    1. The maximum path length from c_1 and c_2 to c_3 is below a threshold
    2. c_3 is a subclass of a set of user-specified general classes called the *ceiling*.

- Two directed paths of length n in the propertyGraph P and Q are isomorphic if:

    - They represent the properties $p_1, p_2, \ldots p_n$ and $q_1, q_2, \ldots q_n$ respectively; and
    - $\forall i, 1 \leq i \leq n, (p_i = q_i) \vee (p_i \subset q_i) \vee (q_i \subset p_i)$. Here $\subset$ represents the *subPropertyOf* relation.

    Two resources are $\rho - iso - associated$ if they are the origins of isomorphic paths. For example, in Figure 2 if $p1 \subset q1 \wedge p2 \subset q2$, $r1$ and $r10$ are $\rho - iso - associated$.

Two resources are said to be **semantically associated** if they are either $\rho - path - associated$ or $\rho - join - associated$ or $\rho - cp - associated$ or $\rho - iso - associated$.

5.2 Implementation

5.2.1 $\rho - path - associated$

To determine whether two resources are $\rho - path - associated$, a linear time algorithm can be used to determine whether there is a direct path between the two vertices in the propertyGraph. However, to be really useful, the user also needs to know how the two resources are related, that is, all the paths between the resources need to be determined. Just showing the shortest path may not be enough. Although fast algorithms exist for finding all paths between two vertices [20], for any real-world Semantic Web there will be a large number of paths between most resources. One solution suggested in [1] is to show paths whose length is less than some arbitrary number n. However, for a well connected propertyGraph, there may be a large number of such paths unless n is very small. While very small paths may not be very important, showing all sufficiently large paths may lead to information overload.

We have developed an algorithm that selectively shows the paths between the resources of interest based on the importance of the vertices in the path. The procedure $\rho\_path\_associated(r1, r2, N)$ determines at least the N most important paths between the resources $r1$ and $r2$ in the propertyGraph as follows:

- Let th be the current threshold and n be the number of paths found so far. Initialize th to a fairly large value less than one (≈ 0.5) and n to 0.

- while $(n < N)$ && $(th >= 0)$

    - Filter the property graph to include only $r1$ and $r2$ and resources whose importance is greater than th.
    - Determine the directed paths from $r1$ to $r2$ as well as $r2$ to $r1$ in the filtered graph.

– Increment n by the number of paths found and decrement th by a small value (≈ 0.005)

The procedure can be initially called with a small value of N to identify the most important paths. If more paths are desired it can be subsequently called with a larger value of N. The procedure takes an optional fourth parameter, the initial threshold value; if a large number of paths are desired a smaller initial value of threshold can be specified. Thus the algorithm allows the user to see the important paths between two resources and still avoid information overload.

5.2.2 $\rho - join - associated$

The procedure $\rho\_join\_associated(r1, r2, N)$ determines the N most important join nodes forming join associations between the resources $r1$ and $r2$ in the propertyGraph as follows:

- Let th be the current threshold and n be the number of paths found so far. Initialize th to a fairly large value less than one (≈ 0.5) and n to 0.

- while $(n < N)$ && $(th >= 0)$

  – Filter the property graph to include only $r1$ and $r2$ and resources whose importance is greater than th.

  – Let S_{end} be a set of all pairs of paths from $r1$ and $r2$ which have a common end vertex. Let vector C_{end} contain the common end vertices of these paths.

  – For every pair of paths in S_{end} check the paths from $r1$ to the end node and $r2$ to end node. If both the paths contain a vertex which already belongs to the vector C_{end} then this pair of paths does not lead to a join association and is eliminated from the set S_{end}. (This step will, for example, remove vertices $r5$, $r7$ and $r9$ in Figure 2 while determining the join association between $r4$ and $r8$).

  – Similarly, determine the set S_{start} that contains all pairs of paths to $r1$ and $r2$ from a common start vertex and the vector C_{start} containing the common start vertices of these paths.

  – Increment n by the join nodes found in C_{end} and C_{start}. Decrement th by a small value (≈ 0.005)

The procedure finds paths from/to $r1$ and $r2$ that end/start in a common (join) node. These paths represent the join associations.

5.2.3 $\rho - cp - associated$

The procedure $\rho\_cp\_associated(r1, r2, L, Ceiling)$ determines the $\rho\_cp\_associations$ between the resources $r1$ and $r2$. L and Ceiling are optional parameters to specify strong $\rho\_cp\_associations$. While L is the maximum permissible path length between the classes corresponding to the resources and the common ancestor, Ceiling specifies the most general set of classes that are to be considered. The procedure can be described as follows:

- Determine the set of classes $C1$ and $C2$ that the resources belong to. (If the resources are themselves classes, this step is not necessary).

- The ancestors of $C1$ and $C2$ can be determined from the Jena inference engine. We only consider ancestors that are subclasses of the set of classes specified by the Ceiling. Let the sets $C1_a$ and $C2_a$ contain the classes in $C1$ and $C2$ as well as their ancestors.

- Now a set of classes C_c that belong to both $C1_a$ and $C2_a$ is identified. We remove from C_c those classes whose children also belong to the set. If C_c is empty then $r1$ and $r2$ are not $\rho\_cp\_associated$.

- We check the paths from the common classes in C_c to the classes in $C1$ and $C2$ in the isa-Graph. All paths of length less than L indicate the $\rho\_cp\_associations$ between $r1$ and $r2$. Note that since the number of edges in the isaGraph is quite small, there will not be many such paths.

5.2.4 $\rho - iso - associated$

Let us assume that two resources r_1 and r_2 have outgoing edges representing properties p_1 and p_2 respectively. If p_1 is the same as p_2 or is a $subPropertyOf$ p_2 or vice versa, r_1 and r_2 are $\rho - iso - associated$ (with an isomorphic path of length one). Therefore, determining whether two resources are $\rho - iso - associated$ is trivial. However, determining the longest isomorphic path will require an exponential algorithm. Performance can be improved by applying it to a graph filtered by the importance scores.

5.2.5 Determining Path/Join Associations between a class and a non-class resource

The propertyGraph will generally not have many paths between a class and a non-class resource. This is because in most cases RDF triples are not created between schema and data resources except for triples of the form ($r1\ RDF:type\ c1$) specifying that a resource is of a particular class. Therefore for determining path or join associations between a class and a non-class resource the propertyGraph is not sufficient. There are two alternatives:

- Create a combined graph from propertyGraph and isaGraph containing all the vertices and edges of the graph as well as links from $r1$ to $c1$ for all triples of the form ($r1$ RDF:type $c1$).

- To determine an association between a class $c1$ and a non-class resource $r1$, besides finding paths between them (if any) in the propertyGraph, determine all resources of type $c1$ and find associations between these resources and $r1$. Inference should be utilized to find resources which are of a type which is a subclass of $c1$.

6 Experiments

A formal evaluation of the various techniques of BioPatentMiner is difficult since there is no standard corpus of biomedical patents available for testing. In this section we will present some scenarios where BioPatentMiner can be effectively used for information retrieval and knowledge discovery.

6.1 Experimental Collections

For our experiments we queried the USPTO site with the keyword *glycolysis*. We downloaded the 1346 patents retrieved by the query (in January 2004) and extracted relevant information about them. The title and abstracts of the patents were annotated by BioAnnotator. Then a Semantic Web was created from the patents (both the original 1346 patents and the patents they referred to), the assignees, the inventors and the UMLS biological terms in the patents. In total there were 7299 patents, 2852 inventors or assignees (some inventors are also assignees). The patents refer to 1291 UMLS concepts. The UMLS Semantic Network was also included in the Semantic Web.

6.2 Searching Annotated Documents

BioAnnotator annotates the patents with the baseform and the class of the identified biological terms. Baseform refers to the canonical form of the concept. For example, *caspase-3* has the baseform *CPP32 protein*. A biological concept can be referred to by various synonyms. For example, *caspase 3* is variously referred as *apopain*, *Yama protein*, *CPP32 protein*, etc. A consistent baseform tag allows the recognition of every reference to the biological concept even if it is called by different names. The class feature assigns each biological concept to its correct semantic class. For example, caspase-3 has the class *Amino Acid, Peptide or Protein*.

The annotated patents allow the retrieval of documents that would be missed by traditional keyword search. For example, a query on USPTO with *glycolysis* and *nucleic acid* in title or abstract only retrieved 29 patents. On the other hand, our system retrieved 196 patents for the query *nucleic acid* using the Juru search engine. This is because BioAnnotator identified several biological concepts that belong to the class *Nucleic Acid*. For example, unlike USPTO, BioPatentMiner retrieved the patent 6461611 since it contained *mRNA* which is a Nucleic Acid (UMLS concept C0035696).

6.3 Ranking Search Results

By default, the patents retrieved by a Juru search are ranked based on the date a patent was issued. However, sometimes ranking the patents by the importance of the patents is more useful. For example, if a company wants to determine the impact of its patents ranking by the importance is more appropriate. Similarly for RDQL queries to retrieve assignees, inventors or biological terms based on some criteria, ranking the results by the importance scores will be useful.

Figure 3 shows a search which retrieves all the patents issued to *University of Texas* ranked by the importance of the patents. The patent *5410016* is ranked the highest. This patent seems to have a high impact since it is referred to by 142 other patents. Similarly the second ranked patent is referred to by 36 other patents.

6.4 Semantic Associations

Sometimes a patent analyst will like to discover knowledge that is distributed across multiple patents. For example, a company or an inventor may like to find out all relationships with a competing company or all relationships with a class of biological concepts. Traditional retrieval techniques may not be adequate for the task. Semantic Associations may be useful for this purpose.

Figure 4 shows the Path Associations between inventor *Jeffrey A. Hubbell* and the UMLS class *Chemical*. Note that the Jena inference engine is utilized while determining all concepts of type *Chemical*. (For example, UMLS concept *C0017423* is of type *Biomedical or Dental Material* which is a subclass of *Chemical*). Determining this type of association from traditional retrieval techniques is very difficult.

Figure 5 shows the Join Associations between two assignees *DSM Biotech GmbH* and *Purdue Research Foundation*. It shows that the Assignees are related based on several patents which are the join nodes. For example, *DSM Biotech GmbH* is assigned a patent 6316232 which refers to the patent 5168056 of *Purdue Research Foundation*. This kind of information may be useful for the companies for discovering potential patent infringements. Note that this technique of determining Semantic associations is

Search Results

S.No.	Annotated Document	Relevance	Original Document
1.	Photopolymerizable biodegradable hydrogels as tissue contacting materials and controlled-release carriers	96.15	Patent Number: 5410016
2.	Photopolymerizable biodegradable hydrogels as tissue contacting materials and controlled-release carriers	80.14	Patent Number: 5626863
3.	Photopolymerizable biodegradable hydrogels as tissue contacting materials and controlled-release carriers	75.40	Patent Number: 6060582
4.	Photopolymerizable biodegradable hydrogels as tissue contacting materials and controlled-release carriers	71.13	Patent Number: 6306922
5.	Photopolymerizable biodegradable hydrogels as tissue contacting materials and controlled-release carriers	68.63	Patent Number: 6602975
6.	Gels for encapsulation of biological materials	64.12	Patent Number: 5573934
7.	Multifunctional organic polymers	64.05	Patent Number: 5462990
8.	Gels for encapsulation of biological materials	63.10	Patent Number: 5858746
9.	Coating substrates by polymerizing macromers having free radical-polymerizable substituents	60.07	Patent Number: 6632446
10.	Treating medical conditions by polymerizing macromers to form polymeric materials	57.29	Patent Number: 6465001
11.	Gels for encapsulation of biological materials	50.79	Patent Number: 5843743
12.	Photopolymerizable biodegradable hydrogels as tissue contacting materials and controlled-release carriers	49.00	Patent Number: 5567435
13.	Gels for encapsulation of biological materials	47.91	Patent Number: 5834274
14.	Gels for encapsulation of biological materials	44.58	Patent Number: 5801033
15.	Method of determining sources of acetyl-CoA under nonsteady-state conditions	40.68	Patent Number: 5413917

Figure 3: Results of a search with *University of Texas* as the *Assignee* ranked by the importance score

The following resources of type Chemical and resource hubbell_jeffrey_a.xml are Path associated:

1	C0017243.xml **(gels)**	Details
2	C0600484.xml **(hydrogels)**	Details
3	C0040277.xml **(adhesives, tissue)**	Details
4	C0013227.xml **(medication(s))**	Details
5	C0032521.xml **(polymer)**	Details
6	C0071526.xml **(polycations)**	Details

Figure 4: Path Associations between an inventor and a UMLS class

Join Association between dsm_biotech_gmbh.xml and purdue_research_foundation.xml

Join Node	Path from Vertex dsm_biotech_gmbh.xml	Path from Vertex purdue_research_foundation.xml
P_5168056.xml	dsm_biotech_gmbh.xml->P_6316232.xml->P_5168056.xml	purdue_research_foundation.xml->P_5168056.xml
P_5168056.xml	dsm_biotech_gmbh.xml->P_6316232.xml->P_5168056.xml	purdue_research_foundation.xml->P_5776736.xml->P_5168056.xml
P_4753883.xml	dsm_biotech_gmbh.xml->P_6316232.xml->P_5168056.xml->P_4753883.xml	purdue_research_foundation.xml->P_5776736.xml->P_4753883.xml
P_4681852.xml	dsm_biotech_gmbh.xml->P_6316232.xml->P_5168056.xml->P_4681852.xml	purdue_research_foundation.xml->P_5776736.xml->P_4681852.xml
P_4908312.xml	dsm_biotech_gmbh.xml->P_6316232.xml->P_5168056.xml->P_4908312.xml	purdue_research_foundation.xml->P_5776736.xml->P_4908312.xml
P_3970522.xml	dsm_biotech_gmbh.xml->P_6316232.xml->P_5168056.xml->P_3970522.xml	purdue_research_foundation.xml->P_5776736.xml->P_3970522.xml

Figure 5: Join Associations between two assignees

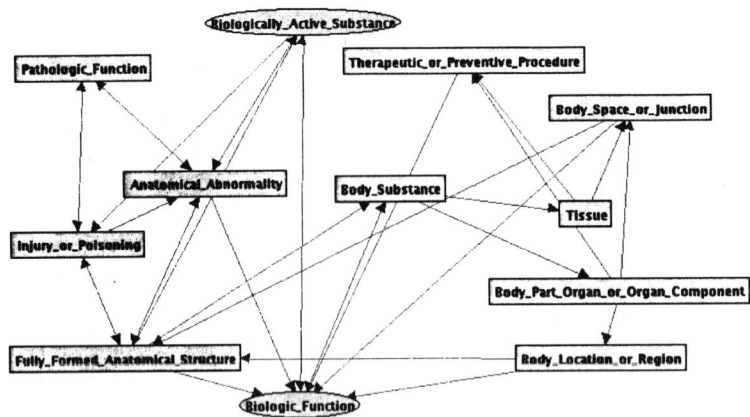

Figure 6: Visualizing the Path Associations between two UMLS Classes

useful for all classes of patents and not restricted to the Biomedical domain.

Besides determining associations between patents, inventors, assignees and UMLS concepts and classes, one can also identify associations within UMLS Semantic Network classes. For example, Table 1 shows the number of paths of different length identified between the resources representing UMLS classes *Biologically_Active_Substance* and *Biologic_Function* in the Semantic Web for different values of threshold. There are 124 paths of length ≤ 5 between the resources *Biologically_Active_Substance* and *Biologic_Function*. Showing all these paths will result in an information overload. Filtering the graph to show the most important paths will be more useful. For example at a threshold of 0.05 there are only 20 paths.

Showing the Semantic Associations textually may not be very intuitive for the users if many paths are retrieved. Therefore one can visualize the different types of associations between Semantic Web resources. For example, Figure 6 is a visualization that shows the $\rho - path - associated$ directed paths of length ≤ 5 between *Biologically_Active_Substance* and *Biologic_Function* for a threshold of 0.05. Note that to prevent clutter, the labels of the edges are only shown by clicking on them. The interface allows the user to change the value of threshold to see a different number of paths.

Path Length	Threshold				
	0.0	0.005	0.01	0.03	0.05
1	2	2	2	2	2
2	3	3	3	3	2
3	6	6	6	4	3
4	20	20	20	12	3
5	93	91	87	68	10

Table 1: Number of paths of different lengths for different values of threshold between *Biologically_Active_Substance* and *Biologic_Function*

7 Conclusion

This paper introduced BioPatentMiner, a system that facilitates information retrieval for biomedical patents. The system identifies and classifies the biologically significant terms in the patents and integrates them with concepts in biomedical dictionaries to create a Semantic Web. The system incorporates a technique to calculate the importance of Semantic Web resources that can be used to rank the results of a query. We have also presented a method to determine the Semantic Associations between resources based on the importance of the resources. Some scenarios have been presented to show the usefulness of the system. Future work is planned along various directions:

- We plan to conduct user studies with domain experts to validate the effectiveness of our techniques to facilitate information retrieval for biomedical patents. We are collaborating with a Pharmaceutical company for this purpose.

- In addition to refining our procedures for determining resource importance and Semantic Associations, we are trying to discover whether other techniques of information retrieval are useful for the Semantic Web. Scalability of the techniques should also be evaluated and improved.

- There are various sources of biomedical knowledge like patents, dictionaries and ontologies. Since it is difficult for researchers to easily gain understanding of a biomedical concept from these different knowledge sources, we believe that a Biomedical Semantic Web is essential. Our vision is that distributed Web servers would store the "meaning" of biological concepts and sets of inference rules will be stored in biomedical ontologies to enable automated reasoning on the concepts. This will enable researchers to perform a single semantic search to retrieve all the relevant information about a biological concept.

References

[1] K. Anyanwu and A. Sheth. ρ-Queries: Enabling Querying for Semantic Associations on the Semantic Web. In *Proceedings of the Twelfth International World-Wide Web Conference*, Budapest, Hungary, May 2003.

[2] K. Bharat and M. Henzinger. Improved Algorithms for Topic Distillation in a Hyperlinked Environment. In *Proceedings of the ACM SIGIR '98 Conference on Research and Development in Information Retrieval*, pages 104–111, Melbourne, Australia, August 1998.

[3] A. Borodin, G. Roberts, J. Rosenthal, and P. Tsaparas. Finding Authorities and Hubs from Link Structures on the World Wide Web. In *Proceedings of the Tenth International World-Wide Web Conference*, pages 415–429, Hong Kong, May 2001.

[4] S. Brin and L. Page. The Anatomy of a Large-scale Hypertextual Web Search Engine. *Computer Networks and ISDN Systems. Special Issue on the Seventh International World-Wide Web Conference, Brisbane, Australia*, 30(1-7):107–117, April 1998.

[5] D. Carmel, E. Amitay, M. Hersovici, Y. Maarek, Y. Petruschka, and A. Soffer. Juru at TREC-10: Experiments with Index Pruning. In *the Proceedings of the 10th Text Retrieval Conference*, pages 228–237, 2001.

[6] S. Chakrabarti, B. Dom, D. Gibson, J. Kleinberg, P. Raghavan, and S. Rajagopalan. Automatic Resource Compilation by Analyzing Hyperlink Structure and Associated Text. *Computer Networks and ISDN Systems. Special Issue on the Seventh International World-Wide Web Conference, Brisbane, Australia*, 30(1-7):65–74, April 1998.

[7] J. Chen, L. Wong, and L. Zhang. A Protein Patent Query System Powered by Klesili. In *the Proceedings of the ACM SIGMOD Conference*, Seattle, WA, 1998.

[8] JENA. http://www.hpl.hp.com/semweb/jena2.htm.

[9] N. Kando and M. Leong. Workshop on Patent Retrieval: SIGIR 2000 Workshop Report. *ACM SIGIR Forum*, 34(1):28–30, April 2000.

[10] S. Karvounarakis, S. Alexaki, V. Christophides, D. Plexousakis, and M. Scholl. RQL: A Declarative Query Language for RDF. In *Proceedings of the Eleventh International World-Wide Web Conference*, Honolulu, Hawaii, May 2002.

[11] V. Kashyap and A. Borgida. Representing the UMLS Semantic Network using OWL (Or "Whats in a Semantic Web Link?"). In *the Proceedings of the Second International Semantic Web Conference*, Sanibel Island, Florida, 2003.

[12] J. Kleinberg. Authorative Sources in a Hyperlinked Environment. In *Proceedings of the 9th ACM-SIAM Symposium on Discrete Algorithms*, May 1998.

[13] L. Larkey. A Patent Search and Classification System. In *the Proceedings of the ACM Digital Library Conference*, Berkeley, CA, 1999.

[14] M. Marinescu, M. Markellou, G. Mayritsakis, K. Perdikuri, S. Sirmakessis, and A. Tsakalidis. Knowledge Discovery in Patent Databases. In *the Proceedings of the ACM Conference on Information and Knowledge Management*, McLean, Virginia, 2002.

[15] M. Osborn, T. Strzalknowski, and M. Marinescu. Evaluating Document Retrieval in Patent Database: a Preliminary Report. In *the Proceedings of the ACM Conference on Information and Knowledge Management*, Las Vegas, Nevada, 1997.

[16] Resource Description Format. http://www.w3.org/1999/02/22-rdf-syntax-ns.

[17] Resource Description Format Schema. http://www.w3.org/2000/01/rdf-schema.

[18] A. Seaborne. RDQL: A Data Oriented Query Language for RDF Models. http://www.hpl.hp.com/semweb/rdql-grammar.html.

[19] L. Subramaniam, S. Mukherjea, P. Kankar, B. Srivastava, V. Batra, P. Kamesam, and R. Kothari. Information Extraction from Biomedical Literature: Methodology, Evaluation and an Application. In *the Proceedings of the ACM Conference on Information and Knowledge Management*, New Orleans, Lousiana, 2003.

[20] R. Tarjan. Fast Algorithms for Solving Path Problems. *Journal of ACM*, 28(3), July 1991.

[21] UMLS. http://umlsks.nlm.nih.gov.

[22] United States Patent and Trademark Office. http://www.uspto.gov/patft/.

Flexible String Matching Against Large Databases in Practice

Nick Koudas   Amit Marathe   Divesh Srivastava

AT&T Labs–Research

{koudas, marathe, divesh}@research.att.com

Abstract

Data Cleaning is an important process that has been at the center of research interest in recent years. Poor data quality is the result of a variety of reasons, including data entry errors and multiple conventions for recording database fields, and has a significant impact on a variety of business issues. Hence, there is a pressing need for technologies that enable flexible (fuzzy) matching of string information in a database. Cosine similarity with tf-idf is a well-established metric for comparing text, and recent proposals have adapted this similarity measure for flexibly matching a query string with values in a single attribute of a relation.

In deploying tf-idf based flexible string matching against real AT&T databases, we observed that this technique needed to be enhanced in many ways. First, along the *functionality* dimension, where there was a need to flexibly match along multiple string-valued attributes, and also take advantage of known semantic equivalences. Second, we identified various *performance enhancements* to speed up the matching process, potentially trading off a small degree of accuracy for substantial performance gains. In this paper, we report on our techniques and experience in dealing with flexible string matching against real AT&T databases.

1 Introduction

The efficiency of every information processing infrastructure is greatly affected by the quality of the data residing in its databases. Poor data quality is the result of a variety of reasons, including data entry errors (e.g., typing mistakes), poor integrity constraints and multiple conventions for recording database fields (e.g., company names, addresses). This has a significant impact on a variety of business issues, such as customer relationship management (e.g., inability to retrieve a customer record during a service call), billing errors and distribution delays. As a result, data cleaning has been at the center of research interest in recent years (see, e.g., [3]).

A key technology in data cleaning is flexible (fuzzy) matching of string information in a database. Such information is prevalent in corporate databases (e.g., customer names, company names, product names, addresses), and effectively matching such attribute values, taking into account the many sources of poor data quality, is a challenge. Consider, for example, the address of AT&T's headquarters in the US: "900 Route 202/206, Bedminster, NJ". Due to multiple conventions in representing such addresses, this address also occurs in various databases as "900 USHwy 202/206, Bedminster, NJ", "900 Rt 202, Bedminster, NJ". Similarly, when considering company names, it is common to see "Microsoft", "Microsoft Inc." and "Microsoft Corporation" being used in different records to represent the same entity. A simple equality or (even) substring comparison on names or addresses will not properly identify them as being the same entity, leading to a variety of potential business problems.

To effectively deal with flexible matching of string values in a database, while accounting for data quality issues, recent techniques [2, 4] have proposed the use of the well-established tf-idf (term frequency, inverse document frequency) metric, commonly used in Information Retrieval for comparing text. Intuitively, tokens (words, q-grams, etc.) are extracted from database strings, and each token is associated with a weight (idf) reflecting its commonality in the database (common tokens are assigned a low weight, uncommon tokens are assigned a high weight). Each database string is then associated with a (normalized) weight vector (incorporating both tf and idf) corresponding to the tokens extracted from it. Similarity between database strings, or between a database string and a query string, is then computed using the cosine similarity (inner product) of the corresponding weight vectors, essentially taking the weights of the common tokens into account.

In deploying such a technique against real AT&T databases, we observed that applications do not want to merely match string values in a single attribute.

- Often, there is a need to flexibly match along multiple string-valued attributes, for example, both company name and (partial) address. As can be expected, this helps to focus the search considerably. While

Permission to copy without fee all or part of this material is granted provided that the copies are not made or distributed for direct commercial advantage, the VLDB copyright notice and the title of the publication and its date appear, and notice is given that copying is by permission of the Very Large Data Base Endowment. To copy otherwise, or to republish, requires a fee and/or special permission from the Endowment.

**Proceedings of the 30th VLDB Conference,
Toronto, Canada, 2004**

there might be many high-similarity flexible matches for both the company name (e.g., "Microsoft") and the partial address ("New York, NY"), individually, the combined query has much fewer high-similarity matches.

- Again, there are semantic relationships that are often known, which are unlikely to be matched using basic flexible string matching techniques. For example, AT&T's headquarters also has the (personalized) address "1 ATT Way, Bedminster, NJ", which is hard to match with (the standard address of) "900 Route 202/206, Bedminster, NJ". Similarly, "Worldcom Corp." and "MCI Inc." refer to the same company, but would not be matched using basic string matching techniques.

Such needs require that the basic string matching technique be enhanced along the *functionality* dimension. In addition, when such flexible string matching is done against large databases (with tens of millions of records), performance becomes a bottleneck, even when the technique is implemented, using SQL, inside the database. This requires the identification of novel *performance enhancements* to speed up the matching process. In talking to users of the tools that we built, we identified that it was acceptable to trade off a small degree of accuracy for substantial performance gains.

In this paper, we address these functionality and performance issues, and report on our experience in using flexible string matching techniques against real AT&T databases. The rest of this paper is structured as follows. In Section 2, we present a detailed description of tf-idf and cosine similarity, along with the SQL that serves as our baseline in this paper. We describe our various functionality enhancements in Section 3, and the performance enhancements in Section 4. In each section, we provide both the conceptual contributions and an experimental evaluation of the impact of these contributions. We identify additional challenges that we faced in practice, both along the functionality and performance dimensions, in Section 5, before concluding in Section 6.

2 Single Attribute TF-IDF Matching

In this section, we present a detailed description of tf-idf (term frequency, inverse document frequency) and cosine similarity for matching against the values in a single relational attribute, along with the SQL that serves as our baseline in this paper. Our description is based on the approach mentioned by Gravano et al. [4]. Our techniques can be adapted to use alternate approaches, such as the one proposed by Chaudhuri et al. [2], as well.

Let Base denote a base table with a string-valued attribute sva against which the flexible matching needs to be performed, and let Search denote the table containing the search strings (this may consist of just a single record with a single attribute value, or may be more complex). Flexible string matching is performed in two stages:

- At *pre-processing time*, the Base table is pre-processed, and tokens (words, q-grams, etc.) are extracted from each database string in Base.sva. A variety of auxiliary tables get created, to compute the idf's of each token, and ultimately to associate each database string with a (normalized) weight vector (incorporating both tf and idf) corresponding to the tokens extracted from it.

- At *query time*, a similar process is first done with respect to the Search table. Then, an SQL query that operates on the auxiliary tables created from Base and Search is executed, which identifies the matching records, along with their similarity score. Essentially, this query computes the cosine similarity (inner product) of the weight vectors of the search string with the weight vectors of the database strings in Base.sva, taking the weights of the common tokens into account.

2.1 Pre-processing Time: Steps

We now describe the SQL of the pre-processing in a step-by-step fashion. Assume that we have extracted the tokens from the string values in Base.sva and stored the result in the term frequency table BaseTF(tid, token, tf), where tid refers to the record identifier in the Base table (and hence uniquely identifies the string in the sva attribute of that table), and tf is the number of occurrences of token in that string. Also, for simplicity, assume that the table BaseSize(size) contains a single one-attribute record containing a count of the number of records in Base. The next sequence of steps is as follows.

First, each token needs to be associated with a weight (idf) that reflects its commonality in the database; common tokens are assigned a low weight, uncommon tokens are assigned a high weight. This is computed into the BaseIDF(token, idf) table below.

```
insert into BaseIDF(token, idf)
  select T.token, LOG(S.size) -
    LOG(COUNT(T.tid))
  from BaseTF T, BaseSize S
  group by T.token
```

Once the idf's have been computed, and the tf's are known from the BaseTF table, the weight vector corresponding to a string can be easily computed by associating the product tf*idf with each token extracted from the string. However, this is an un-normalized weight vector. Before computing this vector, the second step computes this normalization term, for each tid, as the L_2-norm (length in the Euclidean space) of the unnormalized weight vector. This is computed into the BaseLength(tid, len) table below.

```
insert into BaseLength(tid, len)
  select T.tid,
    SQRT(SUM(I.idf*I.idf*T.tf*T.tf))
  from BaseTF T, BaseIDF I
```

```
where T.token = I.token
group by T.tid
```

In the third, and final, pre-processing step, the normalized weight vector, associated with each string, is computed into the `BaseWeights(tid, token, weight)` table below.

```
insert into BaseWeights(tid, token, weight)
  select T.tid, T.token, T.tf*I.idf/L.len
  from BaseTF T, BaseIDF I, BaseLength L
  where T.token = I.token
    and T.tid = L.tid
```

2.2 Query Time: Steps

At query time, given a query string in the `Search(sva)` table, the above sequence of steps are performed to compute the `SearchWeights(tid, token, weight)` table. Note that the `BaseIDF` table is used to obtain the idf's of the tokens extracted from the search string, to ensure that the data in the database table drives the weight vector associated with the search string.

Finally, our baseline query, for computing all matches (along with the scores) whose scores exceed a pre-specified similarity threshold T, is given below.

```
select S.tid, B.tid, SUM(S.weight*B.weight)
from SearchWeights S, BaseWeights B
where S.token = B.token
group by S.tid, B.tid
having SUM(S.weight*B.weight) > T
```

If, instead of being given a single search string to match against a database table, we would like to compute the join of two database tables based on a flexible string match of their columns, the above SQL code works (more or less) unchanged.[1]

2.3 Contributions of the Paper

In the rest of this paper, we describe how the above technique for effectively identifying flexible string matches was extended by us to satisfy the needs of applications against AT&T databases.

- In Section 3, we discuss functionality enhancements. In particular, the ability to flexibly match multiple string-valued attributes (eg., company name and address), and the ability to take advantage of known semantic relationships (e.g., multiple names for the same company, or multiple addresses for the same location).

- In Section 4, we discuss performance enhancements that are necessary when dealing with large databases (tens of millions of records) with string-valued attributes. Most of these result in a small loss of recall

---
[1]The only change would be to use the strings in both tables to compute the idf's.

(i.e., some answers are not returned), for substantial performance gains. However, for the answers that are returned, their scores are computed accurately.

In each section, we provide both the conceptual contributions and an experimental evaluation of the impact of these contributions.

3 Functionality Enhancements

3.1 Multiple attributes

Consider a `Contacts` table containing the name and address for all companies. We can perform flexible string matching on each field individually. But what may be desired is a "combined" search which, given a name-address pair (N,A), returns all tuples from the table that are "close" to the search pair. The problem is to define metrics for the distance between a search pair (N,A) and a tuple pair (N_i,A_i).

These metrics should be efficient to implement and have the same robustness properties as the cosine similarity metric. We also want these metrics to be "data-driven" to the extent possible. In other words, the number of parameters that require user intervention to adjust should be kept to a minimum. The cosine similarity metric can be categorized as "data-driven" because it has a single parameter, the similarity threshold, that has to be varied to change the behavior of the match.

For the sake of illustration, the rest of the discussion is in terms of the `Contacts` table with name and address attributes. But is should be noted that our enhancements work with any table that has multiple string-valued attributes.

3.1.1 Attribute Concatenation

A straightforward approach is to concatenate the name and address attributes into a single string and perform flexible string matching on this concatenation. The disadvantage with this simple metric is that it ignores a lot of statistical information. For example, if "Corporation" is common within the name attribute but rare within the address attribute then all the tokens derived from "Corporation" are assigned a low weight in the combined name-address string. Hence, a search for an address containing "Corporate Drive" won't assign a particularly high score to the relevant tuples, even if the tokens derived from "Corporate" are uncommon among addresses. By concatenating the name and address strings we have lost useful data about the tokens which are common among names but not among addresses (or vice versa).

3.1.2 Using Static Weights

Another metric that comes to mind is combining the similarity scores from individual flexible matches on name and address. That is, if, after running two separate flexible searches, the name attribute value in a tuple has score p and the address attribute value in that tuple has score q then we

sim	name	address
0.75	WORLDCOM	600 s federal st chicago il
0.75	WORLDCOM	400 international pkwy dallas tx
0.75	WORLDCOM	300 renaissance ctr detroit mi
0.75	WORLDCOM	111 8th ave new york ny
0.75	WORLDCOM	165 boulevard se atlanta ga
0.75	WORLDCOM	165 boulevard ne atlanta ga
0.75	WORLDCOM	910 15th st denver co
0.75	WORLDCOM	401 fieldcrest dr greenburgh ny
0.75	WORLDCOM	1102 grand blvd kansas city mo
0.75	WORLDCOM	1102 grand blvd kansas city mo

Figure 1: Static weights: name = 0.75, address = 0.25

sim	name	address
0.5	WORLDCOM	600 s federal st chicago il
0.5	WORLDCOM	400 international pkwy dallas tx
0.5	WORLDCOM	300 renaissance ctr detroit mi
0.5	WORLDCOM	111 8th ave new york ny
0.5	WORLDCOM	165 boulevard se atlanta ga
0.5	WORLDCOM	165 boulevard ne atlanta ga
0.5	WORLDCOM	910 15th st denver co
0.5	WORLDCOM	401 fieldcrest dr greenburgh ny
0.5	WORLDCOM	1102 grand blvd kansas city mo
0.5	WORLDCOM	1102 grand blvd kansas city mo

Figure 2: Static weights: name = 0.50, address = 0.50

sim	name	address
0.568945894389856	TC PAYPHONES	w houston st mar
0.563179091332391	TC PAYPHONES	w 30th st manhat
0.559800387826103	PSI COLOCATE AMTRAK	w 33rd st manhat
0.559800387826103	LIRR	w 33rd st manhat
0.543052687383282	AMERICAN MUSEUM OF N	w 79th st manhat
0.522269095184392	AUDREY ZUCKNER	manhattan ny
0.522269095184392	TUMBLE INTERACTIVE M	manhattan ny
0.522269095184392	AMS TECHNOLOGIES	manhattan ny
0.522269095184392	EASTERN ELECTRONICS CORP	manhattan ny
0.493439926229466	SPRINT SPECTRUM	64th st manhattar

Figure 3: Static weights: name = 0.25, address = 0.75

sim	name	address	tid1	tid2
0.540166767574879	WORLDCO	110 wall st new york ny	1	90213
0.540166767574879	WORLDCO	110 wall st new york ny	1	90740
0.482300726524807	MANHATTAN CENTER FOR	e 116th manhattan ny	1	97312
0.447666521564224	WORLDCOM POP	750 e main st chattanooga tn	1	28302
0.445944986954701	MANHATTAN COMMUNICATION	963 manhattan ave brooklyn ny	1	96276
0.436408539297653	ALS CAGE AT MANHATTA	193 manhattan ave new york ny	1	87652

Figure 4: Attribute concatenation

define the combined score of that tuple to be $rp + (1-r)q$ where r is a real number between 0 and 1. Such metrics have been well studied. It has the advantage of being easy to implement and by varying the value of r we can adjust the relative importance of the name and address attributes in the search. And while it preserves the different distributions of the name and address tokens it has the drawback that we a-priori have to fix the value of r and cannot change the weights assigned to the name and address scores in a dynamic manner. It is also not obvious how to infer a good value for r from the data.

3.1.3 Using Dynamic Weights

The metric we propose avoids these shortcomings by generalizing the normalization step performed during flexible matching. Recall that, in the 1-column flexible matching algorithm the raw tf-idf weights of all tokens in a tuple are divided by the L_2-norm of the weight vector to obtain normalized weights in the range [0, 1]. This normalization step also ensures that the similarity score of any tuple will be between 0 and 1.

In our metric, we run two flexible matches on the name and address attributes. But rather than normalize each weight vector separately, we normalize the disjoint union of the two vectors. Thus, the raw weight vectors from the name and address strings might be $X = (x_1, x_2, \ldots x_k)$ and $Y = (y_1, y_2, \ldots y_l)$. Let $L(X), L(Y)$ be the L_2-norms of these two vectors. Then, rather than dividing each weight in X by $L(X)$ and each weight in Y by $L(Y)$, we define $L(X, Y) = \sqrt{L(X)^2 + L(Y)^2}$ and divide all weights in X and Y by $L(X, Y)$.

Such normalization across attributes results in a dynamic adjustment in the relative importance of the attributes. For example, a search containing a common address like "100 Main St" will tend to give more importance to the name component. Conversely, a search on a common name will tend to place more emphasis on the address component.

3.1.4 Experiments

We now present an experiment comparing our dynamic weighting technique with static weighting. A table containing 100,000 rows of company names and addresses was used for this purpose. Both the name and address columns were indexed for flexible matching. We then ran a series of searches for the name-address pair ("Worldcom", "Wall St Manhattan NY") using static weights. The weights on the name and address columns took on the values (0.25, 0.75), (0.5, 0.5) and (0.75, 0.25). Finally, the same search was performed using attribute concatenation and with our technique.

Figures 1, 2 and 3 show the top results from static weight

1081

sim	name	address
0.568322017929254	WORLDCO	110 wall st new york ny
0.568322017929254	WORLDCO	110 wall st new york ny
0.481778518568938	WORLDCOM	111 8th ave new york ny
0.462023103220271	WORLDCOM	60 hudson st new york ny
0.461736895695425	WORLDCOMM	140 west st new york ny
0.461223519217079	WORLDCOM POP	750 e main st chattanooga t
0.455999984346651	LIRR	w 33rd st manhattan ny
0.433164297375569	WORLDCOM	600 s federal st chicago il
0.425561077229952	TC PAYPHONES	w houston st manhattan ny
0.424860726905206	TC PAYPHONES	w 30th st manhattan ny

Figure 5: Dynamic weights

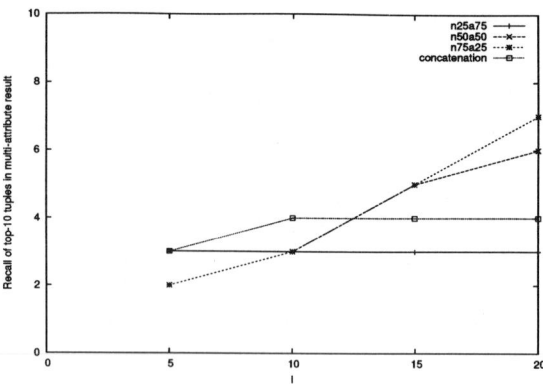

Figure 6: Ordered recall

searches. It is interesting to observe that the results from all the static weight searches are lopsided: figures 1 and 2 have exact matches on the name string but poor matches on the address string, while figure 3 has poor matches on the name component, but better matches on the address component. This is exactly the problem with static weights that we alluded to previously: it is difficult to choose a good distribution of weights among the attributes.

In contrast, the top result in the dynamic weights search ("Worldco", "110 Wall St New York NY"), shown in figure 5, is a very good overall match. This tuple is completely absent from the static weights searches because neither its match on name nor its match on address is high enough to place it at the top of any of those searches.

The attribute concatenation technique, shown in figure 4, does have the same top-2 matches as our dynamic weights technique. However, the latter matches are not as good: there are many tuples for which "Manhattan" appears in the name attribute. This illustrates the drawback inherent in the loss of information resulting from concatenating the two attributes.

The next experiment looks at top-k recall. Typically, we are interested in only the few top matches from a flexible match. Rather than considering the entire result set, we can restrict attention to the top-k matches from dynamic weighting and ask what fraction of those are found in the top- matches from competing techniques for various values of . Figure 6 presents the results of this experiment for k=10 and =5,10,15,20.

The results demonstrate that dynamic weighting is qualitatively different from static weighting or attribute concatenation and cannot be approximated by those techniques. As increases, some of the top-k matches from dynamic weighting are obtained using competing techniques. But even with = 20, the recall numbers of competing techniques are quite low: only 40% for the attribute concatenation approach, and between 30% and 70% for the static weights approach. It is evident that the recall of static weighting is quite sensitive to the actual weights.

We have presented above a comparison of our multi-attribute dynamic weights matching with the attribute concatenation and the static weights techniques, on a specific query. Other queries exhibit a similar behavior in that static weighting tends to miss tuples that don't have a high match on at least one of the attributes. Thus the results of this section are illustrative of the ability of our multi-attribute matching technique to dynamically adjust the attribute weights and thereby return the most relevant tuples.

There may very well be domains in which dynamic weighting performs poorly as compared to other techniques. But the "data-driven" aspects of our multi-attribute matching lead to very desirable results, in all the domains we have encountered. An investigation into the quality of the metrics considered here is left for the future.

3.2 Semantic knowledge

The next enhancement involves incorporating domain specific semantic knowledge into the flexible string matching algorithm. It often happens that the same entity is represented in multiple ways inside the database. For example, the addresses "1 ATT Way Bedminster NJ" and "900 Route 202/206 Bedminster NJ" refer to the same location, AT&T's headquarters. Similarly, the same corporation may appear as "MCI" and as "Worldcom". Observe that the presence of more than one representation is not in itself an error: as these examples show, all the representations may be valid.

If the representations of an entity are sufficiently close in a textual sense then they can be captured using the cosine similarity metric. Thus, a flexible search for "IBM Corp" on a company names database will pick up not only exact matches but also alternate names like "IBM Corporation" and "IBM Inc". But some representations, like the address pair above, can be so far apart as to have few tokens in common. We would like our flexible matching to retrieve not only strings that are close to the search string but also their synonyms. Thus, a search for "900 Route 202 Bedminster NJ" should return "900 Route 202/**206** Bedminster NJ" and also "1 ATT Way Bedminster NJ".

Our proposed solution to this problem assumes that semantic equivalences are explicitly specified in a new relation. Conceptually, this is a symmetric two attribute relation S(A,B). That is, for each equivalence x = x , the tuples (x,x) and (x ,x) would be in relation S. Let T(P)

1082

sim	address	tid1	tid2
Explain sim 0.752483612033064	4001 queens blvd queens ny	6	76542
Explain sim 0.701585125233138	4011 queens blvd queens ny	6	76364
Explain sim 0.692897932355297	queens ny	6	76627
Explain sim 0.692897932355297	queens ny	6	76630
Explain sim 0.692897932355297	queens ny	6	25573
Explain sim 0.692897932355297	queens ny	6	46546

Figure 7: Semantics: search on "4001 Rte 25 Forrest Hills NY"

be the one attribute relation on which we would like to enable this semantic-aware search.

3.2.1 Pre-processing Relation T

The first step involves pre-processing attribute values in relation T. This is done by computing the flexible string join of T and S, using attributes P and A respectively. For every result (p_i, a_i, b_i) in the join with a "high" similarity score, we augment the tokens associated with attribute value p_i in relation T with tokens derived from b_i. This has the effect of associating with each attribute value all the tokens corresponding to its synonyms as per relation S. In our company names example, the strings "MCI" and "Worldcom" will both be associated with the same set of tokens: those derived from the strings "MCI" and "Worldcom".

3.2.2 Processing at Query Time

In the next step, we carry out an analogous procedure on the search string q. The search string q is used in a flexible match operation on relation S. For all high scoring tuples (q, a_j, b_j) in the result, the set of tokens associated with the search string q is extended by the tokens derived from attribute value b_j.

The final step involves running the flexible match algorithm on the pre-processed relation T and the modified search string. Because we augment the set of tokens associated with both the search string and the attribute values in relation T with synonym information, this method is very robust in dealing with errors and multiple conventions in the string attributes of relation T and of synonym relation S.

3.2.3 Experiments

We now present the results from an experiment on using the above algorithm. We used a table of addresses containing 100,000 rows. A synonym table was populated by hand with a few sample equivalences. One of these tuples identified "Route 25 Forrest Hills NY" as a synonym for "Queens Blvd Queen NY". The modified index was built on the addresses as described above with a threshold of 0.5. A relatively low threshold is required because the equivalences in the synonym table specified street aliases rather than complete address synonyms. In other words, none of the equivalences included a street number and hence a low threshold on the similarity score was needed when joining to the address table. The search string was "4001 Rte 25 Forrest Hills NY". This string was joined to the synonym table and a modified index was built using all tuples with a score of 0.6 or higher. The top results from the semantic match are shown in Figure 7.

We note that even in the presence of deliberate errors in both the synonym table (i.e., "Queen NY" instead of "Queens NY") and the search string (i.e., "Forrest Hills" instead of "Forest Hills", and "Rte 25" instead of "Route 25"), our algorithm was able to pick out the exact match and place it at the top of the results. This is a good illustration of the robustness of our technique.

4 Performance Enhancements

Recall that the basic query we run to find approximate matches above a certain similarity threshold T is

```
select S.tid, B.tid,
   sum(S.weight*B.weight)
from SearchWeights S, BaseWeights B
where S.token = B.token
and S.tid = N
group by S.tid, B.tid
having sum(S.weight * B.weight) > T
```

where N is the tuple id of the string we want to search on.

4.1 Indexing the Weights Table

The primary key on the BaseWeights table is (tid, token). In the absence of any other indices the above query has to scan through the BaseWeights table for each token in the search string. The obvious optimization that can be applied at this point is to build an index I1(token) on BaseWeights. Adding this index results in a "nested loops with indexing" execution plan for the above query. The performance improvement is shown below for base tables of different sizes.

Table size	Running time (sec)	
	NonIndexed	Indexed
100000	2	1
7000000	48	22
13000000	105	42

Searches run much faster with the index but, as the figure shows, they can still take a significant amount of time. The reason is that the SQL fragment above computes the dot product of the search vector with every tuple vector with which it shares a common token. For a base table with millions of rows that can be an expensive operation.

4.2 Pre-selecting High Weight Tuples

The next class of optimizations we consider all involve pre-selecting tuples from BaseWeights which are likely to be in the final result. This is done by adding another conjunctive condition to the where clause. This condition takes the following form

```
B.tid in (SubQuery)
```

where SubQuery selects a subset of tids from BaseWeights. Note that any optimization in this class has perfect precision: it may miss some tuples but it won't overestimate or underestimate the similarity score for any tuple. This is in contrast with [4] where the scores themselves are approximated by the performance enhancements. We now consider 4 optimizations in this class.

4.2.1 O1: High Weight Token

Each score in the final result is a sum of terms with each term being the product of the weight of a token in the search string and the weight of that token in the base table. We can conjecture that if this sum of terms exceeds the threshold T then at least one of the base weights exceeds a fixed fraction F of T. This is the basis for our first optimization which is defined by the following SubQuery.

```
select B.tid
from SearchWeights S, BaseWeights B
where S.tid = N
and B.token = S.token
and B.weight > T * F
```

Perusing the query above we observe that another index I2(token, weight) on the BaseWeights table is called for.

4.2.2 O2: High Weight Term

It may be the case that a token has low weight in the base table but high weight in the search string. The above optimization will miss such tuples. To compensate for this deficiency, we can change the last condition in O1's where clause to get the SubQuery below.

```
select B.tid
from SearchWeights S, BaseWeights B
where S.tid = N
and B.token = S.token
and B.weight > T * G / S.Weight
```

where G is a suitable fraction. Here, we cast a wider net in the SubQuery by also considering tokens which may have a low base weight, provided that the product of the search weight and the tuple weight is at least a fixed fraction of threshold T. Note that the index I2 we defined previously on BaseWeights also improves the execution plan for this SubQuery.

4.2.3 O3: Many High Weight Tokens

Both O1 and O2 pre-select tuples that have at least one "promising" token in common with the search string. To further narrow down this set of tuples we can pre-select only those tuples which have at least K (> 1) high weight tokens in common with the search string.

Optimization O3 is obtained by applying this heuristic to O1. The SubQuery in this case is as follows.

```
select B.tid
from SearchWeights S, BaseWeights B
where S.tid = N
and B.token = S.token
and B.weight > T * F
group by B.tid
having count(*) >= K
```

4.2.4 O4: Many High Weight Terms

The SubQuery obtained by applying the above heuristic to optimization O2 is given below.

```
select B.tid
from SearchWeights S, BaseWeights B
where S.tid = N
and B.token = S.token
and B.weight > T * G / S.Weight
group by B.tid
having count(*) >= K
```

4.3 Experiments

We now present some experiments comparing these optimizations. We used a company names table containing 13 million rows for the flexible matching. The similarity threshold was set to 0.4. Parameter F was varied from 0.2 to 0.8 (for optimizations O1 and O3), parameter G was varied from 0.05 to 0.20 (for optimizations O2 and O4) while parameter K was varied from 2 to 4 (for optimizations O3 and O4). These ranges were chosen to illustrate interesting tradeoffs in the various enhancements. In each experiment, we measured the running time and recall of each optimization relative to the naive query presented at the beginning of this section (with the I1 index on BaseWeights).

Figures 8, 9, 10 and 11 show the effect of parameters F, G and K on the recall and running time of these optimizations. We note that recall is inversely proportional to parameters F and G. Low values of these parameters lead to perfect (or near-perfect) recall. As we increase F and G, the number of tuples pre-selected by the SubQuery decreases because fewer tuples are likely to share a high weight token (optimizations O1 and O3) or a high weight term (optimizations O2 and O4) in common with the search string. Also, increasing K means that we insist on more and more high weight tokens or terms in common. Therefore, recall declines as K increases.

Execution time is positively correlated with recall for the same reasons. As we increase F, G and K the subset of tuples pre-selected by the SubQuery decreases in size.

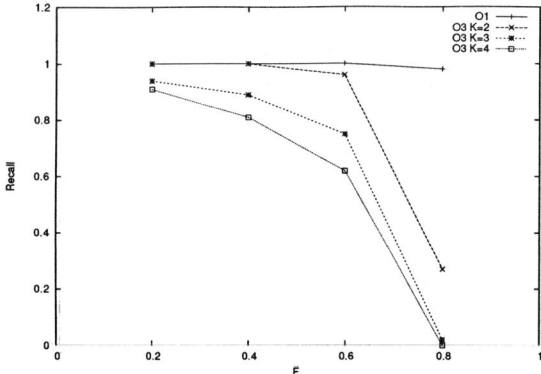

Figure 8: Recall for optimizations O1, O3

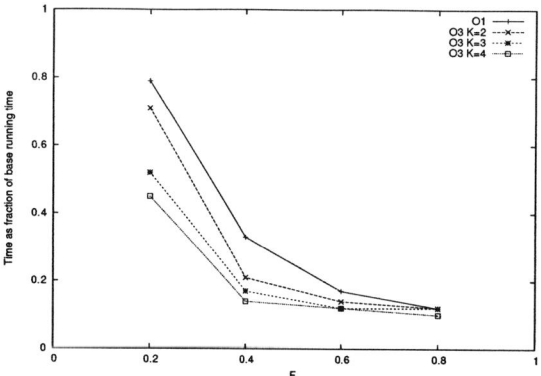

Figure 10: Execution times for optimizations O1, O3

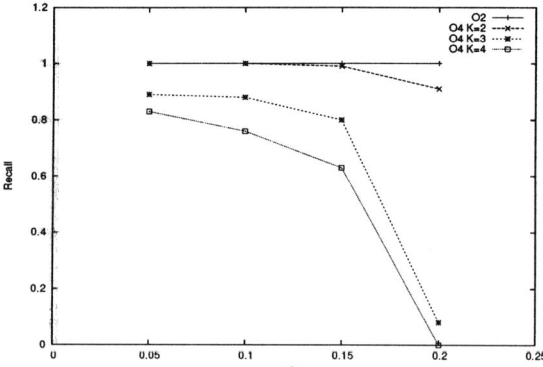

Figure 9: Recall for optimizations O2, O4

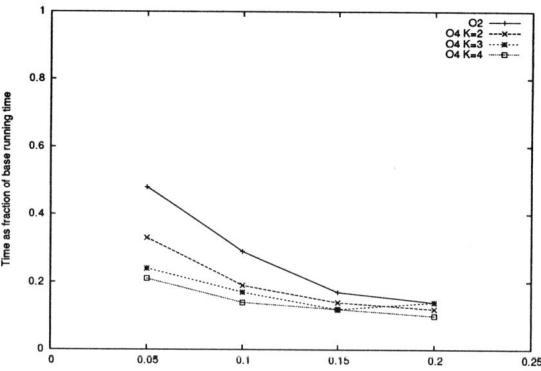

Figure 11: Execution times for optimizations O2, O4

Consequently, there are fewer tuples for which we have to compute the exact cosine similarity score and hence the overall query runs faster.

Since optimizations O3 and O4 have very good running times but low recall, the next two experiments try to understand which tuples from the base result set are absent from the results of these optimizations. We fixed the parameter values at F=0.6 and G=0.15, and measured the ordered recall for the top-50 results in the base result set. Figures 12 and 13 plot the number of these top-50 tuples found in the top-i result sets for optimizations O3 and O4 for i=50, 100, 150, 200.

From the figures we see that K = 4 leads to very bad recall. That is, optimizations O3 and O4 fail to return even 50% of the top-50 tuples with this value of K, even when the range is extended to the first 200 tuples. K = 3 is also not particularly good on recall. Therefore, for applications in which recall in the top tuples is important it is best to stick to lower values of parameters F and G at the cost of increased execution time.

It can be said that the parameters which control the Sub-Query are somewhat arbitrary. An improvement that can be made in that regard is to replace F and G in all SubQueries with (F/L) and (G/L) respectively, where L is the length of the search string. The idea is that when the search string is long there are many tokens/terms which can contribute to the final score and we lower the bar a tuple must meet for pre-selection. This adjustment makes the choice of parameters more robust to a different data set.

5 Open Issues

5.1 Functionality

Multi-column flexible matching is important in many practical applications. Our proposed technique for this problem works on columns within a single table. In general, the columns on which we want to enable flexible matching will belong to different tables, with various join paths between them. Efficiently implementing flexible matching across tables (without having to materialize the join of the base tables beforehand) is a topic for future work.

Another open question is the handling of semantic dissimilarities, a.k.a. antonyms. We have come across this problem very frequently in the context of flexible address matching where the same city name may be present in multiple states, e.g., Manhattan KS = Manhattan NY. In this setting, the algorithm has to somehow filter out the antonyms corresponding to the search string while still assigning a high score to all the synonyms.

An ad-hoc approach would be to create a separate antonym table and query this table before returning the results. Thus a search string of "Manhattan KS" would match

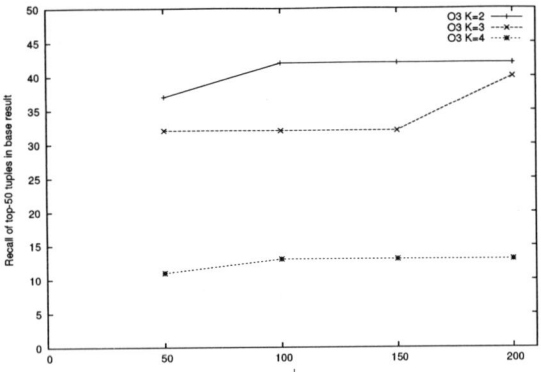

Figure 12: Ordered recall for optimization O3

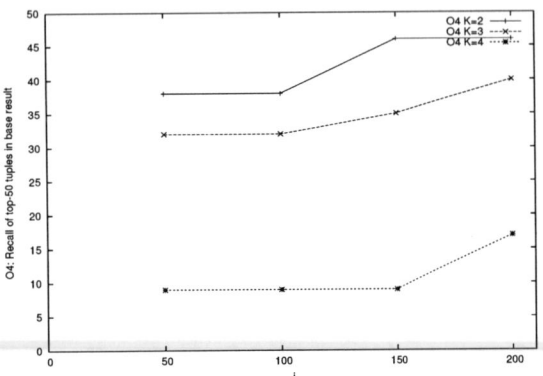

Figure 13: Ordered recall for optimization O4

"Manhattan NY" with a high score but the final step would consult the antonym table and drop that tuple. However, this method is very rigid when it comes to mistakes in the search string and/or the antonym table. Ideally, we would like antonyms to be processed in a robust manner, in much the same way that the cosine similarity metric captures errors in both the search string and the field values. An interesting research problem is the development of principled techniques (as opposed to ad-hoc ones) that can correctly and flexibly process such semantic negations.

So far, we have dealt only with string attributes. However, there are many data types that are commonly encountered in practice. Numeric data is of particular interest. For example, a table might contain an age field of type integer or latitude/longitude fields of type double. The conventional approach of finding fuzzy matches with respect to a given numeric value is to issue a range query against the corresponding field. But this does not take advantage of the data distribution to return a better result. Consider, for example, a database containing the latitude/longitude of all towns in the US. We might want a search on latitude/longitude to have small range in dense population areas like New Jersey and a large range in sparse population areas like Idaho.

Many search engines work with just the string representation of numeric values. This turns out to be inadequate for flexible matching purposes: a google search on "186000" turns up a few pages mentioning the speed of light but a search on "185900" does not find any such pages. Part of the reason is that the string representation of numbers which are very close may not have enough tokens in common. Alternatively, we could define a notion of tf/idf for numbers. The extension of the cosine similarity metric to non-string data types is an intriguing research direction [1].

5.2 Performance

Also of importance is the adaptation of our techniques to a dynamically updated database. So far, we have assumed that the data does not change (or if it does, we can quickly rebuild the flexible string match index). In practice, there are tables that are big enough that rebuilding the index on every change is not feasible. The key difficulty arises with "global" metrics such as tf-idf and cosine similarity. There the weight of a token depends on its inverse document frequency which in turn is a function of the fraction of tuples in which that token appears. Therefore, inserting a new tuple into the table, in principle, changes the weights of all tokens and thereby necessitates an index rebuild. In practice, the token weights will have changed by a non-zero but small amount. Since we are doing flexible matching it is acceptable to not insist on absolute accuracy. The challenge then is to identify criteria for the index rebuilds which work in practice by striking the right balance between accuracy and efficiency.

Index rebuilds can take a long time (a few hours for a table with a few million rows) during which time flexible matching cannot be performed against the table. So once we define a suitable criterion for rebuilding the index we also need to investigate ways to restructure the computation to avoid causing any downtime of the query functionality.

6 Conclusion

In this paper, we related our experiences in deploying flexible string matching on large databases within AT&T. We started with the cosine similarity metric and extended it to handle multi-attribute flexible matching. We enhanced the algorithm to use semantic equivalences that cannot be captured by textual means. We also suggested a number of optimizations that allow the results to be retrieved more quickly. These performance improvements preserve precision and enable a dramatic reduction in the running time while decreasing recall by only a small amount.

References

[1] R. Agrawal and R. Srikant. Searching with numbers. *Proceedings of WWW*, 2002.

[2] S. Chaudhuri, K. Ganjam, V. Ganti, and R. Motwani. Robust and efficient fuzzy match for online data cleaning. *Proceedings of SIGMOD*, 2003.

[3] T. Dasu and T. Johnson. *Exploratory data mining and data cleaning*. John Wiley, 2003.

[4] L. Gravano, P. Ipeirotis, N. Koudas, and D. Srivastava. Text joins in an RDBMS for web data integration. *Proceedings of WWW*, 2003.

DB2 Design Advisor: Integrated Automatic Physical Database Design

Daniel C. Zilio[1], Jun Rao[2], Sam Lightstone[1], Guy Lohman[2]

Adam Storm[1], Christian Garcia-Arellano[1], Scott Fadden[3]

[1]IBM Toronto Laboratory
{zilio,light,ajstorm,cmgarcia}@ca.ibm.com

[2]IBM Almaden Research Center
{junrao,lohman}@almaden.ibm.com

[3]IBM Portland
sfadden@us.ibm.com

Abstract

The DB2 Design Advisor in IBM® DB2® Universal Database™ (DB2 UDB) Version 8.2 for Linux®, UNIX® and Windows® is a tool that, for a given workload, automatically recommends physical design features that are any subset of indexes, materialized query tables (also called materialized views), shared-nothing database partitionings, and multidimensional clustering of tables. Our work is the very first industrial-strength tool that covers the design of as many as four different features, a significant advance to existing tools, which support no more than just indexes and materialized views. Building such a tool is challenging, because of not only the large search space introduced by the interactions among features, but also the extensibility needed by the tool to support additional features in the future. We adopt a novel "hybrid" approach in the Design Advisor that allows us to take important interdependencies into account as well as to encapsulate design features as separate components to lower the reengineering cost. The Design Advisor also features a built-in module that automatically reduces the given workload, and therefore provides great scalability for the tool. Our experimental results demonstrate that our tool can quickly provide good physical design recommendations that satisfy users' requirements.

1 Introduction

Technology advances and competition continue to significantly reduce the cost and increase the capacity of database systems, making large, complex database applications commonplace. For example, popular database applications such as SAP [19] typically contain over 30,000 database objects, which include tables and indexes. Concurrently, the cost of skilled database administrators (DBAs) to manage those increasingly complex systems has relentlessly increased. These economic trends have driven the total cost of ownership of systems today to be dominated by the cost of people, not hardware or software. This new reality has sparked recent interest in developing self-managing, or *autonomic* [18], systems that can relegate many of the DBAs' more mundane and time-consuming tasks to automated tools [6,13].

Perhaps the best candidate to date for such automation is physical database design. DBAs have, for years, systematically tuned applications by time-consuming trial and error – methodically creating each index, collecting statistics on it so that the query optimizer knew its properties, recompiling every query that might benefit, and then evaluating whether the index was, in fact, exploited to improve performance for that workload. Each iteration of this painstaking process could take

---

Permission to copy without fee all or part of this material is granted provided that the copies are not made or distributed for direct commercial advantage, the VLDB copyright notice and the title of the publication and its date appear, and notice is given that copying is by permission of the Very Large Data Base Endowment. To copy otherwise, or to republish, requires a fee and/or special permission from the Endowment

**Proceedings of the 30th VLDB Conference,
Toronto, Canada, 2004**

minutes or even hours on today's terabyte-sized databases, and there was no way to assure convergence to something considered "optimal". Recent research has produced powerful utilities that use the query optimizer as a "What if?" tool to automate this process for indexes, drastically reducing the manual effort while increasing the number of promising solutions [5,21].

New database features to enhance performance -- such as materialized views, parallelism, and different ways to cluster data – have only compounded this task by providing more options that the beleaguered DBA must consider when designing and tuning an application. To make matters worse, these features interact in complex ways. For example, materialized views, being stored tables, themselves require indexes. And one partitioning option is to replicate smaller tables among all nodes, resembling materialized views.

This paper describes the DB2 Design Advisor in DB2 Version 8.2 [9], the first integrated commercial tool to automatically determine all aspects of physical database design, including not only indexes and materialized views (called materialized query tables in DB2 UDB), but also partitioning and multi-dimensional clustering of tables. As in the individual advisors that this tool integrates, the Design Advisor exploits the DB2 Optimizer to recommend promising candidate solutions and to evaluate alternative solutions. We adopt a novel "hybrid" searching approach that not only takes into account important interdependencies among different features, but also makes the tool easy to extend for supporting new features in the future. To improve the scalability of the tool, we add a built-in workload compression module that automatically reduces the workload size while not sacrificing the quality of the design recommendations.

The rest of the paper is organized as follows. Section 2 explains the terminology specific to DB2 UDB. We summarize related work in Section 3. The overview of our design is given in Section 4 and the implementation details are provided in Section 5. Section 6 describes the workload support, including the workload compression module in the Design Advisor. We present our experimental results in Section 7. The future work is discussed in Section 8 and we conclude in Section 9.

2 Terminology

In this section, we define some of the terminology used in DB2 UDB.

A materialized query table (MQT) is a stored and maintained query result, more commonly known in the literature as a materialized view. MQTs were known as Automatic Summary Tables [22] before Version 8.1 of DB2, when support for join-only views was added.

A multi-dimensional clustering (MDC) table [15] organizes a table in a multi-dimensional cube. Each unique combination of dimension attribute values is associated with one or more physical regions called blocks. A block is a basic unit of clustering and typically contains tens of pages. Indexes are created at the block level for fast access. Since data is clustered in an MDC table, range queries (especially with more than one dimension) can be answered much more efficiently than secondary indexes. The design of an MDC table involves choosing the dimensions as well as the granularity (i.e., the number of distinct values) of each dimension.

The DB2 Enterprise Server Edition has a data partitioning feature (DPF) that enables a shared-nothing parallel architecture [3], where independent processors are interconnected via high-speed networks. Each processor stores a horizontally hash-partitioned (referred to simply as partitioning in the rest of the paper) portion of the database locally on its disk. The design of a partitioning includes selecting a set of columns as the partition key, as well as a set of nodes to which the data will be distributed. A good partitioning design minimizes the movement of data by allowing operations such as joins and aggregations to be done at each node locally and thus are much cheaper to execute. In DB2 UDB, an index does not have its own partitioning, but rather shares the partitioning with the table on which it is defined.

3 Related Work in Database Design

The design of many individual physical features has been well studied in the literature. We cannot possibly list all the related references here. Instead, we simply point out that many works on the selection of indexes, materialized views and partitionings are referenced in [5], [1,23], and [17], respectively.

Work in self-managing databases started as early as 1988 [7], in which the authors proposed to use the optimizer to evaluate the goodness of index structures.

Microsoft Research's AutoAdmin project [1,5] has developed wizards that automatically select indexes and materialized views for a given workload. Their tools also exploit the cost model used by the optimizer to estimate the benefit of suggested indexes and materialized views. More recently, their tools have been extended to support both vertical and horizontal partitions in a research prototype [2].

DB2 UDB has had an Index Advisor [21] since Version 6. A tool [17] that recommends the partitionings in a shared-nothing database system has also been prototyped in DB2 UDB. More details on the architecture of these tools is given in Section 1.1.

Other commercial database vendors such as Informix (bought by IBM in 2001) [11] and Oracle 8i [14] have made similar efforts to build such design tools.

However, most of those existing tools only handle the design of one or two features. The only exception is the tool in [2] where as many as four features can be recommended. [2] uses integrated search among all candidates in order to take into consideration the interactions among features. In comparison, we employ a hybrid approach for both the quality of design recommendations and the extensibility of the tool. The Design Advisor also has a built-in workload compression module for scalability. Finally, the DB2 Design Advisor is the first product to recommend a total of four features so far. In the rest of this paper, we address the challenges that we faced when building this tool.

4 Overview

We first formally defined the problem that we were trying to solve: Given a workload W (a set of SQL statements that may include queries, inserts, updates and deletes), a set of selected features F, and a disk space constraint D, find a set of recommendations for F that reduces the total cost of W the most, while using no more space than D. Our Design Advisor currently supports an F that is any subset of {index, MQT, partitioning, MDC}. Notice that while indexes and MQTs are auxiliary data structures, partitionings and MDCs are modifications to existing structures.

It was clear from the beginning that the Design Advisor would face a huge design search space. Suppose that for a given workload, the number of possible indexes, MQTs, partitionings, and MDCs is NI, NM, NP, and NC, respectively. The combined search space could be as large as $2^{NI+NM+NP+NC}$, because different features could potentially interact with one another. Therefore, we needed a novel approach to solving this problem. In Section 4.1, we discuss two potential approaches to this problem, and compare the pros and cons of each. We then discuss in detail the dependencies among the four features in Section 4.2. Finally, in Section 4.3, we introduce a "hybrid" approach that combines the advantages of the two previous ones.

4.1 Iterative vs. Integrated Approach

A relatively straightforward approach to our problem is to use an iterative approach, which selects each feature one at a time. However, the problem with this approach is that it ignores the interactions among different design features. For example, as explained in [1,23], indexes and MQTs are closely dependent on each other. An MQT, like a regular table, normally needs indexes defined on itself in order to be attractive to a query. The selection of an MQT, on the other hand, can also make an index useless, and vice versa. As another example, in a DPF-enabled database, an MQT can be partitioned. The selection of the partitioning can make an MQT more or less useful to a given query. It is such a dependency among features that significantly complicates our problem. The iterative approach does have an advantage, though. It can treat the selection of each feature as a black box, and does not need to know the implementation details inside a feature, which makes future extension much easier. To support a new feature f, we can just plug in a new component implementing the selection of f. It also gives flexibility to the implementation of each feature selection, since a different searching algorithm can be used for each feature.

An alternative to the iterative approach is an integrated one, in which joint searching is performed directly in the combined search space, and heuristic rules are applied to limit the candidate sets being considered. The advantage of the integrated approach is that it can better handle the interdependencies among different features. For example, by jointly enumerating indexes and MQTs together, it is very likely to identify the optimal index and MQT combination. For this particular reason, The Microsoft Tuning Wizard [1,2] uses an integrated approach to recommend indexes and materialized views.

The main drawback of the integrated approach is its extensibility. While it may be suitable for selecting a couple of features, it will not scale with the addition of new features since the search space grows combinatorially with respect to the number of new search points. Also, to support an additional feature, a large portion of the code needs to be changed to support joint searching with the new feature, which makes the reengineering cost high and can lead to a higher cost of ownership for customers. As a result, neither the iterative nor the integrated approach alone solves our problem well.

4.2 Feature Dependency

We recognize that although interdependencies often exist, the degree of interdependencies among different pairs of features is not always the same. We say that feature A "strongly" depends on feature B, if a change in selection of B often results in a change in that of A. Otherwise, we say A "weakly" depends on B. We argue that weak dependencies are likely to exist because a new physical design feature is normally introduced to help the areas where existing features do not apply or do not perform well. It's unlikely for a system to support two features that duplicate each other on functionalities.

We categorize the degree of dependencies among the four features that we currently support in Table 1, where an S represents strong and a W represents weak. We explain how the dependency of each feature pair is decided by sweeping through the table diagonally from the upper left.

A \ B	Index	MQT	Partitioning	MDC
Index		S	W	W
MQT	S		W	S
Partitioning	W	S		W
MDC	W	S	W	

Table 1. Classification of Dependencies of A on B

As we described earlier in Section 4.1, indexes and MQTs mutually depend on each other a lot, and thus it's clear that their interdependencies should be classified as strong. One of the complexities comes from the fact that

MQTs can have indexes which competes with indexes on base tables.

The interaction between indexes and partitionings is different. First of all, indexes for local predicates are relatively insensitive to how data is partitioned. Partitioning keys are usually determined by joins and aggregations. Next, consider those indexes selected for nested loop joins. It is true that changing which indexes are available can possibly change the join methods in the execution plan, and therefore may affect the selection of partitionings. However, good partitionings are more influenced by intermediate result sizes, which depend only on cardinalities and predicate selectivities (independent of the existence of indexes or not). Conversely, although the selection of a table's partitioning can potentially influence the selection of join methods and consequently the selection of indexes, such influence is not as strong as that of predicate selectivities. Consider the following SQL query on a TPC-H[20] database as an example.

```
Q1. SELECT L_ORDERKEY, O_ORDERKEY,
           P_PARTKEY
    FROM LINEITEM, ORDERS, PART
    WHERE L_ORDERKEY = O_ORDERKEY
      AND L_PARTKEY = P_PARTKEY
      AND P_NAME = 'SOME PART'
```

Notice that a good set of indexes for Q1 probably should include I_1=(p_name, p_partkey) on PART, I_2=(l_partkey, l_orderkey) on LINEITEM and I_3 = (o_orderkey) on ORDERS, where I_1 helps the evaluation of the local predicate and I_2 and I_3 can be used in nested loop joins. Such a choice is mostly based on the fact that the local predicate on PART is very selective, not much based on how tables are partitioned. We observe that whether I_2 and I_3 exist or not affects the join methods and thus can affect the partitioning selection. For example, LINEITEM can be chosen to be partitioned on l_orderkey in one case and on l_partkey in another. However, since all intermediate results are small in both cases, the performance difference on two partitioning selections will also be small, if any. Based on the above analysis and the finding in [8] that complex queries tend to use hash joins more often, we classify that indexes and partitionings weakly depend on each other.

A similar argument can be made on the dependencies between MQTs and partitionings. The only difference is that MQTs themselves can have partitionings, which makes partitionings strongly dependent on MQTs, but not vice versa. This is an interesting example where the degree of dependencies is not necessarily symmetric.

We classify the dependencies between indexes and MDCs as weak, which seems somewhat controversial. Indeed, MDC enables and requires a special kind of index. However, MDC was actually developed to serve a different class of queries than traditional indexes serve.

For example, a secondary index is typically useful when the number of matching records is relatively small. On the other hand, an MDC organization is especially beneficial for OLAP types of queries, taking slices of the multi-dimensional cubes, for which there are typically many matches, since the matching records have all been pre-clustered together. There is, in fact, a strong interaction (similarity) between a one-dimensional MDC and a conventional clustered index. We address this issue in Section 5.3.

Finally, we do find that MDCs are very similar to indexes in their relationship to MQTs and partitionings, which means that MDCs and MQTs are strongly coupled while MDCs and partitionings are weakly coupled. Similar to partitioning, an MQT can be further clustered through an MDC organization.

4.3 The Hybrid Approach

We observe that mutual strong dependencies are difficult to break and thus are better handled using an integrated approach. We decouple other dependencies (unilateral strong and weak) and apply the iterative approach. To minimize the impact of doing so, we carefully choose the ordering within an iteration and add special cases within a component whenever necessary. We are now ready to outline our "hybrid" approach.

In general, for a pair of features A and B, if A and B are mutually strongly dependent on each other, we will create a component that jointly searches both A and B. If only B strongly depends on A, we will iteratively search A and B, but make sure that A is searched before B so that B is properly influenced by A. Finally, if A and B are weakly coupled, we will again separate them into different components, but can iterate through them in any order. Furthermore, we try not to lose the weak dependencies completely; we allow each component to optionally implement a quick and simple search of a feature in another component to account for the weak relationship. Our hybrid approach enables us to break the implementation of different features into smaller components while capturing the most important interdependencies among them. Such an approach makes it possible for us to build a tool that can handle the design of all four features and be able to extend in the future. In the next section, we describe in detail how we developed the hybrid approach in the Design Advisor.

5 The Implementation of the Hybrid Approach

We developed the hybrid approach by extending the infrastructure of the existing Index Advisor in DB2 UDB. In Section 1.1, we revisit the architecture of the Index Advisor. We then describe the necessary extensions in Section 5.2. In Section 5.3, we describe the main algorithm used in the Design Advisor. Finally, we discuss some of the issues concerning MQT selection in Section 5.4 and unused structures in Section 5.5.

5.1 Index Advisor Revisited

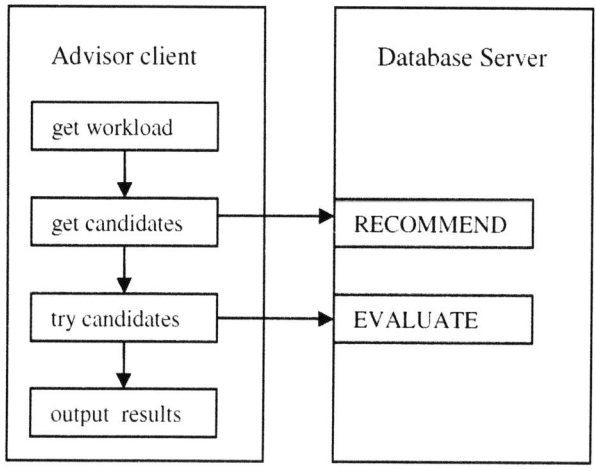

Figure 1. Architecture of an Index Advisor

The DB2 Index Advisor [21] uses an architecture as depicted in Figure 1. The database server is augmented with two special "EXPLAIN" modes—RECOMMEND INDEXES and EVALUATE INDEXES. Under a special explain mode, a given statement is compiled but not executed. In the RECOMMEND mode, the optimizer is extended such that it will generate promising "virtual" indexes for a given statement on the fly. Virtual indexes are then considered during optimization as if they are physically present. Those indexes that are part of the final best execution plan are treated as the best index candidates for the given SQL statement. They are collected by the optimizer and are written to a special advise_index table. In the EVALUATE mode, the optimizer obtains from the advise_index table those candidates marked as "in_use" and generates the corresponding virtual indexes before optimization starts. In other words, the EVALUATE mode causes the virtual indexes in the advise_index table to act as a temporary extension to the DB catalog information. The optimization then continues to compute the best execution plan assuming those virtual indexes are physically present.

The client side of the Index Advisor first collects a workload. It then compiles each statement in the RECOMMEND mode and collects the best index candidates for each. An enumeration algorithm then combines those candidates in various ways, and for each combination compiles the workload in the EVALUATE mode to get a corresponding cost estimation for each statement in the workload. Finally, the combination with the lowest total cost is returned as the best solution for the workload. One of the advantages of this architecture is that it uses the RECOMMEND mode to suggest index candidates. Since the RECOMMEND mode is integrated inside the database engine, it is able to find candidates quicker and more accurately.

5.2 Explain Mode Extension

We extend the methodology used for the Index Advisor to the three other features as well. For each additional feature we intend to support, we add two special EXPLAIN modes, one for recommending the feature and the other for evaluating the feature. We also add a corresponding "advise" table to store the candidates. Most importantly, we extend the EXPLAIN register from a single value to a bit set such that multiple EXPLAIN modes can be set at the same time. Such an extension is very powerful, since it provides the capability of conducting both joint searching and iterative searching. For example, by setting RECOMMEND INDEXES and RECOMMEND MDC together, the optimizer is able to suggest RID index and MDC dimension candidates together. In another example, by setting EVALUATE INDEXES and RECOMMEND PARTITIONINGS mode together, the optimizer can try to generate the best partitionings for a statement while assuming the existence of indexes suggested from a previous iteration. Note that although the infrastructure appears to be the same for each feature, it does not prevent each feature (if in a separate component) from using a different searching method in the try candidates phase. Finally, the bit set representation can easily support additional features in the future.

5.3 The Hybrid Algorithm

We divide the Design Advisor into three components, IM, P, and C, where IM is responsible for index and MQT recommendation, and P and C are responsible for partitionings and MDCs, respectively. Each component F recommends candidates within its own disk constraint D_F. The components are iterated in the order of IM, P, and C. This closely reflects the degree of dependencies as described in Table 1, except for the relationship between MQTs and MDCs. We chose not to integrate the selection of MDCs with indexes and MQTs for several practical reasons. First, we want to limit the search space within a single component. Second, we feel that MQTs are more closely coupled with indexes than with MDCs. Finally, MDCs do not compete for as much space as both indexes do since they use block indexes instead of RID indexes, and we wanted to integrate only the resource-intensive features together.

The implementation of each of the three components has been described in detail in [12,17,23] and is not the focus of this paper. We just want to point out that the searching algorithm used for each component is customized. For example, a knapsack algorithm followed by a random-swapping phase was used for the IM component [23], and a rank-based search was used for the P component [17]. While components are relatively

1091

independent of each other, they are aware of the presence of others whenever needed. For example, we support using sampling in each component to obtain more accurate statistics. When this occurs, components share as much sampling as possible. Each component can be disabled. This is useful when a feature is not available on a particular platform (e.g., partitioning is only available when DPF is enabled) or the user does not select all the features.

```
1.  get the workload information, database and
    system characteristics and the disk constraint D
2.  get initial cost of the workload
3.  while (stop criteria met) {
4.    for each enabled component F of IM,P,C {
5.      invoke F with D_F
6.      (solutions for F now stored in advise_F)
7.      if (current_cost < best_cost)
8.        best_cost = current_cost
9.      else
10.       unmark candidates in advise_F
11.     turn on EVALUATE F in explain register
12.   }
13. }
14. output solutions
```

Figure 2. Main Algorithm

Our main hybrid algorithm used in the Design Advisor is presented in Figure 2. As usual, the advisor first obtains the workload, information on the database (e.g., DB name, user ID, and password) and a disk constraint D. If D is not provided, the Advisor automatically recommends a D based on such information as the amount of available space and used space in a database. Each statement in the workload is then compiled to get an optimizer-estimated initial workload cost. After that, the algorithm starts to iterate through each enabled component. The total disk constraint is divided among all components. More space is given to indexes and MQTs than partitionings and MDCs because the latter two tend to use less space. (The only type of partitioning that takes extra space beyond the base data is replication.) After invoking a component with an allocated constraint D_F, the suggested candidates for F are recorded in the corresponding advise table (with the "in_use" field marked). Note that if a component does not use all the allocated space, unused space is passed to the next component and can be consumed by other features. The current workload cost (with the solutions for F) is used to compare against the best workload cost. If the current cost is smaller, the new solution for F is accepted and the best cost is updated. Otherwise, the new solution is discarded by unmarking the "in_use" field in the advise table. We then turn on the EVALUATE F mode in the special explain register so that the solutions for F become visible by subsequent components. As a special case, we let the C component handle all clustered indexes. If an MDC solution has only one dimension, the C component will decide whether to use an MDC organization or simply create a conventional clustered index.

The main algorithm is capable of iterating through each component F more than once, and therefore solutions for F can change after the design of other features is exposed. Such iterations continue until some stopping criteria are met, which can either be that solutions do not improve the workload any more, or a user-specified time limit is reached. In a prototype we implemented that repeats the iteration between component IM and P, we found that the second invocation of IM (with the solutions for partitioning) does not change the previous index and MQT recommendations significantly. This actually verifies our assumption that indexes and MQTs only weakly depend on partitionings. Therefore, we currently only iterate through each component exactly once.

We add a special support in the IM component to address MQTs' weak dependency on partitionings. Observe that although the influence of partitionings on MQTs is relatively weak, a terrible partitioning key for an MQT can still reduce its potential benefit, especially when maintenance cost needs to be considered. Hence, we extend IM by adding a module that quickly selects a reasonable initial partitioning for each MQT to prevent a good MQT from being pruned. Every incrementally maintainable MQT in DB2 UDB has an implied unique key [22]. For instance, the implied key is the grouping columns for an aggregate MQT. For a join MQT, the implied key is the concatenation of the key on each joined table. We choose an arbitrary column from the implied key to serve the initial partitioning key of the MQT. During incremental maintenance, such a partitioning key (a subset of the implied key) allows the join between the MQT and the "delta" to be performed locally at each node, and thus reduces the maintenance cost. Subsequently, the partitioning of the MQTs will be further tuned by the P component.

5.4 MQT Selection

The goal of the Design Advisor is to allow users to select any subset of the supported features. If a feature is not requested by the user, normally, we can simply bypass the corresponding component during the iteration. However, when the user only asks for MQTs, the semantic is a little bit tricky. If we faithfully follow the request and suggest only MQTs and nothing else, such MQTs may not be usable because they typically need some indexes on them. On the other hand, since the users probably have some confidence in existing indexes, we probably should not voluntarily perform a full index search. As a solution, we decide that if MQT is the only feature requested by the user, the Design Advisor will automatically recommend indexes and partitionings (if DPF is enabled) on suggested

MQTs. We choose not to cluster suggested MQTs using MDC since it is a more advanced feature.

In order to support this, we introduce another EXPLAIN mode VIRTUAL_MQT. When this mode is enabled in the EXPLAIN register bit set, indexes and partitionings are only recommended and evaluated for newly recommended (virtual) MQTs.

5.5 Unused Structures

While the Design Advisor recommends new design structures, would it make sense for it to remove structures that are not used at all? House-cleaning often has lower priority than adding new designs, so it's common to have indexes and MQTs that are out-of-date. However, the danger is that the Design Advisor may not see the complete workload. Although more built-in workload supports have been added to the Design Advisor (Section 6.1 describes the details), infrequent queries are still hard to collect. Therefore, we may delete an index that seems useless but is very important for a CEO query that runs only every quarter. Because of this, the Design Advisor does not recommend any deletion of existing structures. Instead, it reports a list of existing indexes and MQTs that are useful to the given workload. The set of unused indexes and MQTs can be inferred from this list.

6 Workload Support

Since the Design Advisor is a workload-driven tool, we pay a lot of attention to workload-related issues. In Section 6.1, we describe additional ways in the Design Advisor for users to conveniently obtain a workload. In Section 6.2, we introduce the built-in workload compression method for scalability.

6.1 Obtaining a Workload

The DB2 Index Advisor accepts a workload from the command line (a single statement), a file, or an advise_workload table. In the Design Advisor, we add two additional workload sources, one from the dynamic statement cache and the other from the Query Patroller.

The dynamic statement cache stores the plans for all dynamic SQL queries submitted to a database engine to avoid recompilation. As a side effect, each dynamic SQL statement itself is cached, together with the frequency of execution. Therefore, the statement cache serves as a good source for a typical workload. With this new option, users can run their favourite applications for a while and then invoke the Design Advisor, which will then collect the SQL statements and associated frequencies from the cache automatically.

Query Patroller [16] is a powerful query management tool included in DB2 Data Warehouse Enterprise Edition. It provides the capability of classifying queries into classes, prioritizing queries, and tracking runaway queries. We add an option in the Design Advisor so that we can fetch all statements passed through Query Patroller.

6.2 Built-in Workload Compression

A key factor that affects the scalability of the Design Advisor is the size of the workload. Since each statement in the workload needs to be compiled by the optimizer (most likely more than once) in order to obtain the estimated cost, the larger the workload, the longer it takes the advisor to run. As a matter of fact, the time to run design tools such as Microsoft Tuning Wizard and DB2 Index Advisor typically grows exponentially with a linear increase of the workload size (verified through experiments). Thus, workload compression is imperative for the scalability of these design tools.

A simple workload compression technique is to merge statements that are exactly the same, but with different parameter bindings. In fact, for workloads that are obtained from the dynamic package cache, such compression has already been done. One study [4] proposes a more sophisticated workload compression technique that employs mining-like methods to summarize the workload. The authors demonstrate that using the reduced workload, both the Microsoft Tuning Wizard and DB2 Index Advisor can provide design recommendations very close to those based on the full workload. However, to get the reduced workload, the technique requires relatively intensive computation such as calculating the distance between pairs of statements in the original workload.

We see a benefit in adding workload compression as a built-in module for the Design Advisor. The Design Advisor will invoke the workload compression module if it feels that the workload is too large and the analysis cannot finish in a reasonable amount of time. One important requirement for the compression module is efficiency. We want to spend a relatively small fraction of the total amount of time on compression the workload. Therefore, we take an approach that only keeps the top K most expensive queries, whose total cost is no more than X% of the original workload cost. The Design Advisor already compiles each statement in the workload to obtain an estimated cost (line 2 in Figure 2). We then sort the statements in descending cost order and keep selecting statements from the top into a reduced workload until the cost of the reduced workload is less than or equal to X% of the original workload. Our approach, although simple, is quite effective in reducing the workload size, especially when the distribution of statement cost is skewed. The reduced workload includes the most time-consuming statements, which typically need tuning.

We can control the compression ratio by scaling the percentage X. Instead of burdening the users to come up with an appropriate value for X, we expose only three compression levels: low, medium and high, with X set to 60, 25, and 5, respectively. By default, medium compression level will be used. Once compression is done, the hybrid algorithm simply works on the reduced workload and gives recommendations accordingly. It makes one final pass over the original workload at the end to obtain the cost for the whole workload with the recommendations based on the reduced workload. Finally, we allow the user to turn off workload compression completely for more accurate design tuning.

7 Experimental Results

In this section, we select two sets of experiments to present. All experiments were conducted on a regular build for DB2 UDB Version 8.2. In Section 7.1, we test the Design Advisor by selecting all four features. In Section 7.2, we focus on the selection of indexes and MQTs only, and demonstrate the benefit of our built-in workload compression module. We summarize our experimental results in Section 7.3.

7.1 TPCH Results

The first experiment was to demonstrate how well the Design Advisor recommends all design features. This was done using a 1 GB TPCH [20] database stored on an 8 CPU AIX® 5.2 system with 4 logical partitions. The workload contains all the 22 TPCH queries.

We started with a baseline design that stored the tables across all 4 partitions and used the primary key as the partition key for all tables except for LINEITEM, which was partitioned on L_PARTKEY, part of the primary key. The LINEITEM partitioning was chosen based on the fact that L_PARTKEY is used in quite a few of the 22 queries. The rest of the baseline physical DB design is derived from a TPCH benchmark.

Design Feature	Number Recommended
Indexes	20
MDC dimensions	6
Partitioning Changes	4
Materialized Views	2

Table 2. Design Advisor Recommendations for a TPCH 1GB Database

The Design Advisor was able to finish the design of all features in about 10 minutes. Table 2 shows how many recommendations the advisor made for each design feature. For example, we show below one of the MQTs recommended (MQT2) that contains the subquery in Q18 using LINEITEM. In this MQT, the partitioning key was also properly selected on C1, because the MQT sometimes needs to be further joined with the ORDERS table. An index IDX3 was also recommended on MQT2. Notice that the index key is ordered in (C0,C1). This is because the subquery result in Q18 was subsequently filtered though a range predicate on L_QUANTITY.

```
CREATE SUMMARY TABLE MQT2 AS (
    SELECT SUM(L_QUANTITY) AS C0,
        L_ORDERKEY AS C1
    FROM TPCD.LINEITEM
    GROUP BY L_ORDERKEY)
DATA INITIALLY DEFERRED
REFRESH DEFERRED
PARTITIONING KEY (C1)
IN TPCDLDAT

CREATE INDEX IDX3 ON MQT2
(C0 DESC,
 C1 DESC)
ALLOW REVERSE SCANS
```

An MDC recommendation from this experiment is also given below. The recommendation was for the PARTSUPP table to be MDC clustered (as shown by the ORGANIZE BY clause) based on a newly generated column. This column groups the values of PS_PARTKEY such that each group falls into a clustered block of the MDC. In this particular case, a single-dimensional MDC is better than a conventional clustered index because the generated column condenses the value domain.

```
CREATE TABLE TPCD.PARTSUPP (
    PS_PARTKEY INTEGER NOT NULL ,
    PS_SUPPKEY INTEGER NOT NULL ,
    PS_AVAILQTY INTEGER NOT NULL ,
    PS_SUPPLYCOST DOUBLE NOT NULL ,
    PS_COMMENT VARCHAR(199) NOT NULL,
    MDC040303204738000 GENERATED
        ALWAYS AS (
            INT((PS_PARTKEY-11)/(792))) )
PARTITIONING KEY (PS_PARTKEY)
IN TPCDTDAT
ORGANIZE BY (MDC040303204738000 )
```

Finally, we note that besides the partitionings recommended for MQTs, the partitioning key of LINEITEM is also changed from L_PARTKEY to L_ORDERKEY. The latter is useful for fewer, but much more expensive, queries.

The DB2 Design Advisor makes its recommendations based on estimated response times for workloads using the cost model in the optimizer. In this experiment, we obtained an estimated response time improvement over the baseline (without recommendations from the Design Advisor) of 88.01%. We implemented all the recommendations made by the Design Advisor and measured the actual cost of the workload. Figure 3 shows the real performance improvement as 84.54% (the baseline is normalized to 100%), which is very close to the optimizer's estimation.

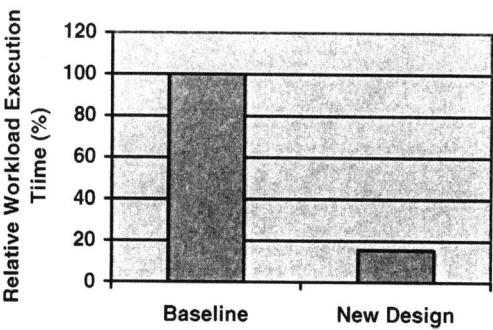

Figure 3. 1 GB TPCH Real Workload Performance Improvement

7.2 MOLAP Results

In the next set of experiments, a DB was set up as a classic MOLAP schema. Both the data and the workload are synthetic, but represent similar characteristics seen in various customer MOLAP schemas. The DB has a fact table with 8 measures, and there are 16 hierarchical dimensions. Table 3 shows the number of levels in each hierarchy and the cardinality of each dimension.

Experiments were run on a Windows® 2000 Server SP4 with four 400 MHz CPUs. We set up the database to have four logical partitions. Note that these experiments only selected indexes and materialized views.

Dimension	Number of Levels in Hierarchy	Cardinality
1	2	4
2	2	3
3	2	2
4	4	52
5	3	3000
6	2	7
7	2	4
8	3	300
9	2	331
10	2	2
11	4	189
12	2	11
13	3	3000
14	4	372
15	2	2
16	2	2

Table 3. MOLAP Schema Characteristics

We demonstrate the usefulness of our workload compression with respect to reducing the Design Advisor execution time. Medium compression was compared to no compression with workloads of varying numbers of queries. All queries include range predicates, join one or two dimensional tables with the fact table, and aggregate at various levels in the hierarchy. Figure 4 shows the results. Note that we only show the 80 to 150 query cases for no compression because that is where the interesting differences occur. The results indicate that as the number of queries increases, the advisor execution time also increases with and without compression. However, under the medium compression, the Design Advisor runs twice as fast when there are 80 and 100 queries in the workload, and an order of magnitude faster when there are 150 queries (note the logarithmic scale on the y-axis). Although not shown here, a higher level of compression provides a more significant reduction of the execution time of the Advisor. There is a slight increase at the 80 query workload mainly because its random-swapping phase was longer than that in the 100 query case. In the 100 query case, the advisor found a very good solution early and thus finished the algorithm earlier. We also compared these results to our competitors' and found that the Design Advisor achieved a more significant reduction in the execution times.

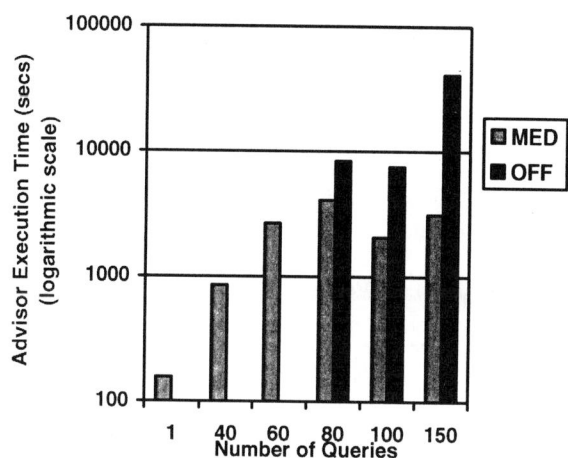

Figure 4. Medium (MED) and no (OFF) workload compression advisor execution time comparison using the MOLAP schema workload

There is a trade-off between workload compression and the quality of the design recommendations. The higher the compression level, the faster the advisor runs, but potentially the lower the quality of the recommendations. In Figure 5, we present the progress made by the Design Advisor with and without workload compression. Each point in the figure represents the workload improvement achieved by the Advisor after running for a certain amount of time. In the end, the advisor ended up with a 77% estimated improvement with the medium compression, and an improvement of 93% with no compression. However, with medium compression, the advisor finished about 4,300 seconds sooner than with no compression. As a result, medium compression provides a good compromise between execution time and design quality. Figure 5 also demonstrates that a large portion of the performance improvement is achieved in a relatively short amount of time by the Design Advisor (both with compression and without). Subsequent searching only further improves the performance marginally. This is very useful for designing the stopping criteria in our main algorithm. It becomes reasonable to stop the Advisor when no improvement has been made after the advisor has executed for a certain number of iterations.

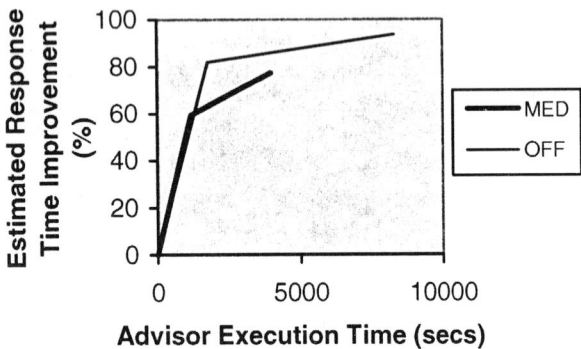

Figure 5. Workload improvement vs. advisor execution time for medium (MED) and no (OFF) workload compression for the 80 query MOLAP schema workload

7.3 Summary

To summarize, our experiments demonstrate that the Design Advisor is capable of recommending a design that includes all the four features, significantly improves the performance of the workload over a benchmark baseline, and completes in a reasonable amount of time. We also validate the effectiveness of our workload compression technique that allows the Design Advisor to scale with the increase of workload size. Our analysis shows that a medium compression level reduces the Advisor execution time considerably without compromising the quality of the recommendations.

8 Future Work

While we categorize the interaction between MQTs and partitionings as weak in Table 1, a novel usage of MQTs can change that. For example, suppose that two queries Q1 and Q2 prefer a table T to be partitioned using P1 and P2 respectively. Normally, we can only choose one of the partitionings for table T. However, it's possible to define an MQT that duplicates T and also carries a different partitioning than T. That way, we can use T to serve one of the queries, say Q1, and use the MQT to serve Q2. When used this way, MQTs become strongly coupled with partitionings. We'd like to investigate an efficient way to support this special case in the future, although we have addressed this issue partially through the replicated partitioning recommendations made by the P component.

The Design Advisor is currently focused on physical database design. In the future, we'd like to investigate the possibility of extending it to support logical designs as well. Logical design is currently done by tools such as Rational® Rose® and XDE™ [10], when database schemas are derived from modelling specifications such as UML. How to integrate the Design Advisor with such tools is an interesting study for the future.

9 Conclusion

The DB2 Design Advisor is the first comprehensive physical database design tool to recommend indexes, materialized views, partitioning, and clustering for multiple dimensions in an integrated and scalable fashion. We have described a framework that permits any combination of recommending some features while holding others fixed to a given solution, as well as a hybrid algorithm that efficiently searches through the enormous space of possible solutions while taking into consideration the interactions of related features. The Design Advisor also has built-in workload compression for reducing the execution time of the Advisor without sacrificing quality in the solution. Initial experimental results verify that solutions selected by the Design Advisor improve by almost 100% the performance of workloads of hundreds of queries after running for under three hours, less time than it would take a human DBA to evaluate a handful of possible solutions, and represents a major advance in automating perhaps the most complex and time-consuming task that DBAs now perform.

References

1. Sanjay Agrawal, Surajit Chaudhuri and Vivek R. Narasayya, Automated Selection of Materialized Views and Indexes in SQL Databases, Proceedings of 26th International Conference on Very Large Data Bases, 2000: 496-505.
2. Sanjay Agrawal, Vivek R. Narasayya, Beverly Yang, Integrating Vertical and Horizontal Partitioning Into Automated Physical Database Design. SIGMOD Conference 2004.
3. Chaitanya K. Baru, Gilles Fecteau, Ambuj Goyal, Hui-I Hsiao, Anant Jhingran, Sriram Padmanabhan, Walter G. Wilson: An Overview of DB2 Parallel Edition. SIGMOD Conference 1995: 460-462
4. Surajit Chaudhuri, Ashish Gupta, Vivek R. Narasayya: Compressing SQL workloads. SIGMOD Conference 2002: 488-499

5. Surajit Chaudhuri and Vivek R. Narasayya, Microsoft Index Tuning Wizard for SQL Server 7.0, Proceedings ACM SIGMOD International Conference on Management of Data, 1998: 553-554.
6. Surajit Chaudhuri and Vivek R. Narasayya, AutoAdmin "What-If" Index Analysis Utility. Proceedings of ACM SIGMOD, Seattle, 1998.
7. S. Finkelstein and M. Schikolnick and P. Tiberio, Physical Database Design for Relational Databases, ACM Transactions of Database Systems, 13(1): 91-128, 1988.
8. Goetz Graefe: The Value of Merge-Join and Hash-Join in SQL Server. VLDB 1999: 250-253
9. http://www.ibm.com/software/ db2/
10. http://www.ibm.com/software/ rational/
11. http://www.ibm.com/software/data/informix/redbrick/
12. Sam Lightstone and Bishwaranjan Bhattacharjee, Automated design of Multi-dimensional Clustering tables for relational databases, VLDB 2004.
13. Guy M. Lohman, Sam Lightstone: SMART: Making DB2 (More) Autonomic. VLDB 2002: 877-879
14. http://www.oracle.com/
15. Sriram Padmanabhan, Bishwaranjan Bhattacharjee, Timothy Malkemus, Leslie Cranston, Matthew Huras: Multi-Dimensional Clustering: A New Data Layout Scheme in DB2. SIGMOD Conference 2003: 637-641
16. Query Patroller, http://www.ibm.com/software/data/db2/querypatroller/.
17. Jun Rao, Chun Zhang, Nimrod Megiddo, Guy M. Lohman: Automating physical database design in a parallel database. SIGMOD Conference 2002: 558-569.
18. http://researchweb.watson.ibm.com/autonomic/manifesto/
19. http://www.sap.com/
20. TPC-H benchmark, http://www.tpc.org/
21. Gary Valentin, Michael Zuliani, Daniel C. Zilio, Guy Lohman and Alan Skelley, DB2 Advisor: An optimizer smart enough to recommend its own indexes, Proceedings of the ICDE Conference, 2000: 101-110.
22. Markos Zaharioudakis, Roberta Cochrane, George Lapis, Hamid Pirahesh, Monica Urata: Answering Complex SQL Queries Using Automatic Summary Tables. SIGMOD Conference 2000: 105-116
23. Daniel C. Zilio, et al, Recommending Materialized Views and Indexes with IBM's DB2 Design Advisor, International Conference on Autonomic Computing 2004.

Trademarks

AIX, DB2, DB2 Universal Database, IBM, and Informix, Rational, Rational Rose, and XDE are trademarks or registered trademarks of International Business Machines Corporation in the United States, other countries, or both.

Windows is a registered trademark of Microsoft Corporation in the United States, other countries, or both.

Other company, product, and service names may be trademarks or service marks of others.

Automatic SQL Tuning in Oracle 10g

Benoit Dageville, Dinesh Das, Karl Dias,

Khaled Yagoub, Mohamed Zait, Mohamed Ziauddin

Oracle Corporation
500 Oracle Parkway
Redwood Shores, CA 94065
U.S.A
{Benoit.Dageville, Dinesh.Das, Karl.Dias, Khaled.Yagoub, Mohamed.Zait, Mohamed.Ziauddin}@oracle.com

Abstract

SQL tuning is a very critical aspect of database performance tuning. It is an inherently complex activity requiring a high level of expertise in several domains: query optimization, to improve the execution plan selected by the query optimizer; access design, to identify missing access structures; and SQL design, to restructure and simplify the text of a badly written SQL statement. Furthermore, SQL tuning is a time consuming task due to the large volume and evolving nature of the SQL workload and its underlying data.

In this paper we present the new Automatic SQL Tuning feature of Oracle 10g. This technology is implemented as a core enhancement of the Oracle query optimizer and offers a comprehensive solution to the SQL tuning challenges mentioned above. Automatic SQL Tuning introduces the concept of SQL profiling to transparently improve execution plans. It also generates SQL tuning recommendations by performing cost-based access path and SQL structure "what-if" analyses.

This feature is exposed to the user through both graphical and command line interfaces. The Automatic SQL Tuning is an integral part of the Oracle's framework for self-managing databases. The superiority of this new technology is demonstrated by comparing the results of Automatic SQL Tuning to manual tuning using a real customer workload.

Permission to copy without fee all or part of this material is granted provided that the copies are not made or distributed for direct commercial advantage, the VLDB copyright notice and the title of the publication and its date appear, and notice is given that copying is by permission of the Very Large Data Base Endowment. To copy otherwise, or to republish, requires a fee and/or special permission from the Endowment

**Proceedings of the 30th VLDB Conference,
Toronto, Canada, 2004**

1. Introduction

Over the past decade two clear trends have emerged: (a) database systems have been deployed in new areas, such as electronic commerce, bringing a new set of database requirements, and, (b) database applications have become increasingly complex with support for very large numbers of concurrent users. As a result, the performance of database systems has become highly visible and thus critical to the success of the businesses running these applications.

One important part of database system performance tuning is the tuning of SQL statements. SQL tuning involves three basic steps:

1. Identify high load or top SQL statements that are responsible for a large share of the application workload and system resources, by looking at the past SQL execution history available in the system;
2. Attempt to find ways to improve execution plans produced by the query optimizer for these statements; and
3. Implement possible corrective actions to generate better execution plans for poorly performing SQL statements.

The three steps outlined above are repeated in that order until the overall system performance reaches a satisfactory level or no more statements can be tuned. The corrective actions include one or more of the following:

1. Enable the query optimizer to find a better plan by:
   a. Gathering or refreshing the data statistics it uses to build an execution plan. For example, by creating a histogram on a column that contains skewed data.
   b. Changing the value of configuration parameters that will affect the optimizer behavior. For

example, by changing the optimization mode for the SQL statement from "all rows" to "first <n> rows" to produce an execution plan minimizing the time to produce the first <n> rows.
   c. Adding optimizer hints to the statement. For example, by using an access path hint to replace a full table scan by an index range scan.
2. Manually rewrite the SQL statement, not necessarily into a semantically equivalent form, to enable more efficient data processing. For example, by replacing UNION operator by UNION ALL.
3. Create or drop a data access structure on a table. For example, by creating an index or a materialized view.

Typically the database administrator (DBA) or an application developer performs the tuning process. However, it is often a challenging task even for a tuning expert. First, it requires a high level of expertise in several complex areas: query optimization, access design, and SQL design. Second, it is a time consuming process because each statement is unique and needs to be tuned individually. Third, it requires an intimate knowledge of the database (i.e., view definitions, indexes, table sizes, etc.) as well as the application (e.g. process flow, system load). Finally, the SQL tuning activity is a continuous task because the SQL workload and the database are always changing.

To help the DBA and the application developer overcome these challenges, several software companies have developed diagnostics tools that help identify SQL performance issues and suggest actions to fix them [3, 4]. However, these tools are not integrated with the query optimizer, the system component that is most responsible for SQL performance. Indeed, these tools interpret the optimization information outside of the database to perform the tuning, so their tuning results are less robust and limited in scope. Moreover, they cannot directly tackle the internal challenges faced by the query optimizer in producing an optimal execution plan. Finally, the recommended actions often require modification of the SQL text in the application source code, making the recommendations hard to implement by the DBA.

In Oracle 10g, the SQL tuning process has been automated by introducing a new manageability feature called **Automatic SQL Tuning**. This feature is designed to work equally well for OLTP and Data Warehouse workloads. Unlike existing tools, Automatic SQL Tuning is performed in the database server by the Oracle query optimizer itself, running in a special mode. When running in this mode, the Oracle query optimizer is referred to as the **Automatic Tuning Optimizer**.

It is important to point out that the Automatic Tuning Optimizer is a natural extension of the Oracle query optimizer. In fact, the goal for both modes of the optimizer (i.e., regular optimization mode and tuning mode) is to find the best possible execution plan for a given SQL statement. The main difference is that the Automatic Tuning Optimizer is allowed to run for a much longer period of time, generally minutes versus a sub-second during the regular optimization mode. The Automatic Tuning Optimizer takes advantage of this extra time to profile the SQL statement and validate the statistics and estimates used in the process of building an execution plan. In addition, the Automatic Tuning Optimizer can also explore execution plans that are outside the search space of the regular optimizer. This is because these execution plans are only valid if some external changes made by the DBA (e.g. create a new index) or by the application developer (e.g. rewrite the SQL statement, possibly into a semantically non-equivalent form) are assumed. The Automatic Tuning Optimizer uses this what-if capability for access path and SQL structure analysis.

Among all the above aspects, SQL profiling is probably the most novel one. The main goal of SQL profiling is to build custom information (a SQL Profile) for a given SQL statement to help the query optimizer produce a better execution plan. SQL profiles are stored persistently in the database and are transparently used every time their associated SQL statements are optimized. This new technology allows tuning SQL statements without altering their text, a key advantage for users of packaged applications. As such, SQL profiling can be considered an integral part of the optimization process. Given that it is a resource-intensive process, we believe it works best when it is limited to a subset of SQL statements, namely those that have the highest impact on the system resources or whose performance is most critical to the database application.

Except for SQL profiling, all other aspects of SQL tuning require interaction with the end user (the DBA or the application developer). As a result, the Automatic SQL Tuning feature is exposed to the end user via an advisor called the **SQL Tuning Advisor**. The SQL Tuning Advisor takes one or more SQL statements, and produces statement-specific tuning advices to help produce well-tuned execution plans. Here, the term "advisor" should not confuse the reader. It is important to remember that the SQL Tuning Advisor is neither a tuning tool nor a utility but rather an Oracle server interface that exposes a comprehensive tuning solution implemented inside the Oracle optimizer.

Finally, the Automatic SQL Tuning feature is fully integrated in the Oracle 10g manageability framework making it an end-to-end solution to the SQL tuning challenges [7].

The rest of the paper is organized as follows. In Section 2, we present the architecture of the Automatic SQL Tuning. In Section 3, we give details about SQL profiling. In Section 4, we describe the access path analysis. Section 5 details SQL structure analysis. The manageability framework is discussed in Section 6.

Section 7 contains a real case study comparing manual to automatic tuning. Related work is summarized in Section 8. Finally, we conclude the paper in Section 9.

2. Automatic SQL Tuning Architecture

The Automatic SQL Tuning is based on an extension of the Oracle query optimizer called the Automatic Tuning Optimizer. The Automatic Tuning Optimizer performs additional tasks such as SQL profiling and what-if tuning analyses while building an execution plan for a SQL statement being tuned. The result of SQL profiling and tuning analyses is a set of tuning recommendations. The tuning output is presented to the user via the SQL Tuning Advisor.

The Automatic Tuning Optimizer and the SQL Tuning Advisor constitute the Automatic SQL Tuning component in Oracle 10g. Figure 1 shows the Automatic SQL Tuning architecture and the functional relationship between its two sub-components.

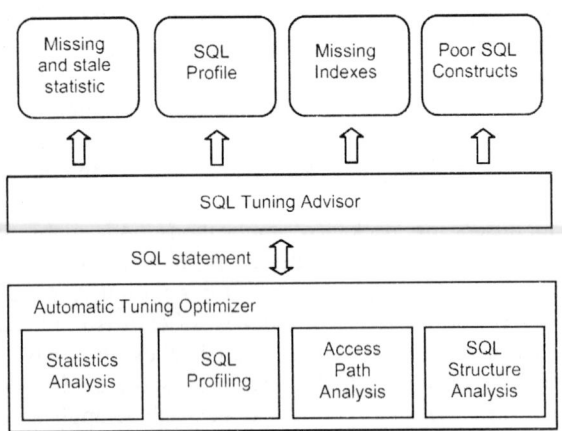

Figure 1. Automatic SQL Tuning Architecture

There are several advantages from using the Oracle query optimizer as the basis for the Automatic SQL Tuning:

- The tuning is done by the same component that is responsible for picking the execution plan, and knows best what additional information help produce a better plan.
- Future enhancements to the query optimizer are automatically taken into account in the tuning process.
- The tuning process uses the execution history of a SQL statement and customizes the optimizer settings for that SQL statement because it knows the effect of a particular setting on the query performance.

The Oracle query optimizer normally has stringent constraints on the amount of time and system resources it can use to find a good execution plan for a given SQL statement. For example, it is allotted an optimization budget in the form of a number of join permutations. Therefore, it uses a combination of cost-based and heuristics-based techniques to reduce the optimization time. Furthermore, it cannot validate the size estimates of intermediate results when standard estimation methods based on data independence assumption are known to cause large errors. Most validation techniques require running part of the query on a sample of the input data, which can be time consuming. As a consequence of these constraints, a sub-optimal plan can be generated.

In contrast, the Automatic Tuning Optimizer is given a larger time budget, e.g., several minutes, to perform necessary investigation and verification steps as part of the tuning process. It uses the extra time mainly to profile the SQL statement, verify data statistics, and perform what-if tuning analyses. The output of SQL profiling and verification gives it a much better chance to generate a well-tuned plan. The Automatic Tuning Optimizer uses dynamic sampling and partial execution (i.e. execute fragments of the SQL statement) techniques to verify its standard estimates of cardinality, cost, etc. It also uses the past execution history of the SQL statement to determine appropriate settings of the optimization parameters.

The SQL Tuning Advisor accepts a SQL statement and passes it to the Automatic Tuning Optimizer along with other input parameters, such as a time limit. The Automatic Tuning Optimizer then performs SQL profiling and what-if tuning analyses while building a query plan, which may produce one or more tuning recommendations as output.

The Automatic Tuning Optimizer results are relayed to the user via the SQL Tuning Advisor in the form of tuning advices. An advice consists of one or more recommendations, each with a rationale and an estimate of the benefit. The user is given an option to accept one or more recommendations, thus completing the tuning of the corresponding SQL statement.

3. SQL Profiling

The query optimizer relies on data and system statistics to function properly. For example, it uses the number of blocks and number of rows to estimate the cost for a full scan of a table. From these base statistics, the query optimizer derives, using probabilistic models, various data size estimates such as the table cardinalities, the join cardinalities, and the distinct cardinalities (e.g., the number of rows resulting from applying aggregate or duplicate elimination operation).

Some of the factors that lead the query optimizer to generate a sub-optimal plan are:

- Missing or stale base statistics. Missing statistics cause the optimizer to apply guesses. For example, the optimizer assumes uniform data distribution

even though the column contains skewed data when there is no histogram.
- Wrong estimation of intermediate result sizes. For example, the predicate (filter or join) is too complex, such as *(a*b)/c > 10*) to apply standard statistical methods to derive the number of rows.
- Inappropriate optimization parameter settings. For example, the user may set a parameter that tells the query optimizer that he intends to fetch the complete query result but actually fetches only few rows. In this case, the query optimizer will favor plans that return the complete result fast, while a better plan would be the one that returns first few rows fast.

To cope with the factors mentioned above, we provide a SQL profiling capability inside the optimizer, to collect auxiliary information specific to a SQL statement. A SQL Profile is built from the auxiliary information generated during 1) statistics analysis (e.g., provide missing statistics for an object), 2) estimates analysis (e.g., validation and correction of intermediate result estimates), and 3) parameters settings analysis. When it is built, the Automatic Tuning Optimizer generates a recommendation for the user to either accept or reject the SQL profile.

In the remainder of this section we provide more details about the three tasks outlined above, and then describe the content of the SQL profile.

3.1 Statistics Analysis

The goal of statistics analysis is to verify that statistics are neither missing nor stale. The query optimizer logs the types of statistics that are actually used or needed during the plan generation process, in preparation for the verification process. For example, when a SQL statement contains an equality predicate, it logs its use of the number of distinct values statistic of predicate column.

Once the statistics logging is complete, the Automatic Tuning Optimizer checks if each of these statistics is available on the associated query object (i.e. table, index or materialized view). If the statistic is available then it samples data from the corresponding query object and compares its result to the stored statistic to check its accuracy (or staleness). However, the sampling result must be sufficiently accurate before it can be used to verify the stored statistic. Iterative sampling with increasing sample size is used to meet this objective.

If a statistic is found to be missing, auxiliary information is generated to supply the missing statistic. If a statistic is available but found to be stale, auxiliary information is generated to compensate for staleness.

Note that the statistics analysis phase produces two kinds of output:

- Recommendations to gather statistics for the objects that are found to have either no statistics or stale statistics,
- Auxiliary information to supply missing statistics or correct stale statistics.

It is preferable to implement the recommendation to gather statistics and re-run the SQL Tuning Advisor. The auxiliary information is used in case the recommendation to gather statistics is not accepted by the user.

3.2 Estimates Analysis

One of the main features of a cost-based query optimizer is its ability to derive the size of intermediate results. For example, the query optimizer estimates the number of rows from applying table filters when deciding which join algorithm to pick. One of the main factors causing the optimizer to generate a sub-optimal plan is the presence of error in its estimates. Wrong estimates can be caused by a combination of the following factors: a) standard statistical methods cannot be used to derive the number of rows because the predicate (filter or join) is too complex, b) assuming uniform data distribution in the absence of a histogram when, in fact, there is skewed data, and c) data in different columns is correlated but the query optimizer is not aware of it, causing it to assume data independence.

During SQL profiling, various standard estimates are validated, and when errors are found, auxiliary information is generated to compensate for errors. The validation process may involve running part of the query on a sample of the input dataset, or on the entire input dataset when efficient access paths are available.

3.3 Parameter Settings Analysis

The Automatic Tuning Optimizer uses the past execution history of a SQL statement to determine the correct optimizer settings. For example, if the execution history shows that the output of a SQL statement is often partially consumed, the appropriate setting is to optimize it to quickly produce the first n rows, where n is derived from this execution history. This constitutes a customized parameter setting for the SQL statement. Note that the past execution statistics for SQL statements are automatically collected and stored in the Automatic Workload Repository (AWR) presented in section 6.

3.4 SQL Profile

The result of the above three analyses is stored in a SQL Profile. It is a collection of customized information for the SQL statement that is being tuned. Thus SQL Profile is to a SQL statement what statistics is to a table or index object. Once a SQL Profile is created, it is used in conjunction with the existing statistics by the Oracle query optimizer to produce a well-tuned plan for the corresponding SQL statement.

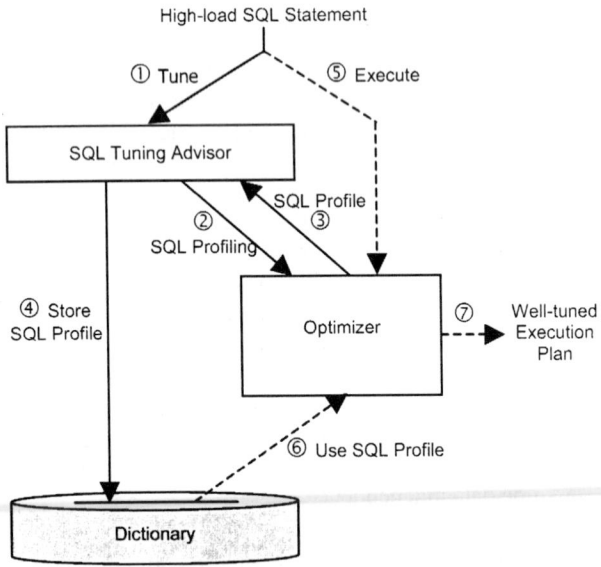

Figure 2. Creation and Use of SQL Profile

Figure 2 shows the process flow of the creation and use of a SQL Profile. The process consists of two separate phases: an Automatic SQL Tuning phase, and a regular optimization phase. In figure 2, the solid arrows are used to show the Automatic SQL Tuning process flow, while the broken arrows are used to show the regular optimization process flow.

During the Automatic SQL Tuning phase, a DBA selects a SQL statement and runs the SQL Tuning Advisor using either the Oracle Enterprise Manager (Oracle's database server GUI), or the command-line interface (step 1). The SQL Tuning Advisor invokes the Automatic Tuning Optimizer to perform SQL profiling and what-if analyses on the SQL statement (step 2). The Automatic Tuning Optimizer generates tuning recommendations possibly with a SQL Profile (step 3). Assuming a SQL Profile is built, it is stored in the data dictionary once it is accepted by the DBA (step 4).

Later, during the regular optimization phase, a user submits the same SQL statement for execution (step 5). The Oracle query optimizer finds the matching SQL Profile from the data dictionary (step 6), and uses it together with other statistics to build a well-tuned execution plan (step 7). The use of SQL Profile remains completely transparent to the user.

It is important to note that the creation and use of a SQL Profile doesn't require changes to the application source code. Therefore, SQL profiling is the only way to tune SQL statements issued from packaged applications, such as Oracle E-Business Suite, where the users have no control over the application source code.

4. Access Path Analysis

Creating suitable indexes is a well-known tuning technique that can significantly improve the performance of SQL statements because the amount of data fetched from an object is typically a small fraction of the data stored on disk. The Automatic Tuning Optimizer recommends the creation of indexes based on what-if analysis of various predicates and clauses present in the SQL statement being tuned. It recommends an index only when the query performance can be improved by a large factor because it is based on tuning of a single statement without knowing the workload characteristics.

The Automatic Tuning Optimizer determines the candidate indexes that could potentially improve the performance of the statement were they to exist. This what-if analysis can result in the discovery of several promising indexes. The following are some examples of the techniques used to identify index candidates:

- Equality predicate on a column, e.g., State='CA'. In this case, an index with *State* as a leading column will help to access only the relevant rows from the table and avoid a full scan,
- Predicates on several columns, e.g., State='CA' AND Age > 33. In this case, a multi-column index on *State* and *Age*, in that order, is considered a candidate,
- The query contains an ORDER BY on a column, and creating an index on that column could eliminate an expensive sort operation.

Once candidate indexes are identified, the next step is to verify their effectiveness. To do that, the Automatic Tuning Optimizer derives statistics for each candidate index based on the statistics of its table and relevant columns. It then optimizes the SQL statement pretending that these indexes actually exist. If the cost of a plan that uses one or more candidate indexes is cheaper by a large factor compared to the cost of best plan using no candidate indexes, then the Automatic Tuning Optimizer alerts the user that these critical indexes are missing, and recommends to add them.

Since Automatic SQL Optimizer does not perform an analysis of how its index recommendations are going to affect the entire SQL workload, it also recommends running the SQL Access Advisor [6] on the SQL statement along with a representative SQL workload. The SQL Access Advisor is a workload-based server-side tuning solution of the Oracle 10g database. The SQL Access Advisor collects tuning advice given on each statement of a SQL workload, and consolidates them into a global advice for the entire SQL workload. The SQL Access Advisor takes into account the level of DML activity on the related objects in its global recommendations. It also recommends other types of access structures like materialized views, as well as indexes on the recommended materialized views.

5. SQL Structure Analysis

Often a SQL statement can be a high load SQL statement simply because it is badly written. This usually happens when there are different, but not semantically equivalent, ways to write a statement to produce same result. Knowing which of these alternate forms is most efficient is a difficult and daunting task for application developers since it requires both a deep knowledge about the properties of data they are querying as well as a very good understanding of the semantics and performance of SQL constructs. Besides, during the development cycle of an application, developers are generally more focused on how to write SQL statements that produce desired results than improving their performance.

It is important to note that the Oracle query optimizer performs extensive query transformations while preserving the semantics of the original query. Some of the transformations are based on heuristics (i.e. internal rules), but many others are based on cost-based selection. Examples of query transformations include subquery unnesting, materialized view (MV) rewrite, simple and complex view merging, rewrite of grouping sets into UNIONs, and other types of transformations. SQL profiling improves the outcome of this process by reducing the errors in various cost estimates, thereby improving the cost-based selection of query transformations.

However, the query optimizer applies a transformation only when the query can be rewritten into a semantically equivalent form. Semantic equivalence can be established when certain conditions are met; for example, a particular column in a table has the non-null property. However, these conditions may not exist in the database but enforced by the application. The Automatic Tuning Optimizer performs what-if analysis to recognize missed query rewrite opportunities and makes recommendations for the user to undertake.

There are various reasons related to the structure of a SQL statement that can cause poor performance. Some reasons are syntax-based, some are semantics-based, and some are purely design issues.

1. **Syntax-based constructs**: Most of these are related to how predicates are specified in a SQL statement. For example, a predicate involving a function or expression (e.g. func(col) = :bnd, col1 + col2 = :bnd) on an indexed column prevents the query optimizer from using an index as an access path. Therefore, rewriting the statement by simplifying such complex predicates can enable index access paths leading to a better execution plan.

2. **Semantic-based constructs**: A SQL construct such as UNION, when replaced by a corresponding but not semantically equivalent UNION-ALL construct can result in a significant performance improvement. However, this replacement is possible only if there is no possibility of duplicate rows (e.g., a unique constraint is maintained in the application), or duplicate rows when produced do not matter to the application. If this is the case, it is better to use UNION-ALL instead thus eliminating an expensive duplicate elimination operation from the execution plan. Another example is the use of NOT IN sub-query while a NOT EXIST sub-query could have produced same result much more efficiently.

3. **Design issues**: An accidental use of a cartesian product, for example, occurs when one of the tables is not joined to any of the other tables in a SQL statement. This can happen especially when the query involves a large number of tables and the application developer is not very careful in checking all join conditions. Another example is the use of an outer-join instead of an inner-join when the referential integrity together with non-null property of the join key is maintained in the application.

The SQL structure what-if analysis is performed by the Automatic Tuning Optimizer to detect poor SQL constructs falling in one or more categories listed above. This analysis is performed in two steps.

In the first step, the Automatic Tuning Optimizer generates internal annotations to remember the reasons why a particular rewrite was not possible. The annotations include the necessary conditions that were not met, as well as various choices that were available at that time. For example, when the Automatic Tuning Optimizer explores the possibility of merging a view, it will check necessary conditions to see if it is logically possible to merge the view. If not possible, it will record the reasons for not merging the view. It will also record other alternatives that were available, such as pushing join predicates inside of the view to make it into a LATERAL view.

The second step of the analysis takes place after the best execution plan has been built. The Automatic Tuning Optimizer examines the annotations associated with costly operators in the execution plan. A costly operator can be defined as one whose individual cost is more than 10% of the total plan cost. Using the annotations associated to expensive plan operators, it produces appropriate recommendations. For example, if it was not possible to merge a view because of *rownum* predicate (i.e., a limit to clause) present in the view, the recommendation would be to move *rownum* predicate outside of the view. With each recommendation, a rationale is given in terms of cost improvement.

Since the implementation of SQL structure recommendations requires rewriting the problematic SQL statements, the SQL structure analysis is much more suited for SQL statements that are being developed but not yet deployed into a production system or packaged application. Another important benefit of the SQL structure recommendations is that it can help educate the developers in writing well-formed SQL.

6. Automatic SQL Tuning in the Oracle10g Self Managing Database

As shown in the previous sections, the main focus of the automatic SQL Tuning feature is to tune a SQL statement by profiling it and by recommending other tuning actions to the end user. However, the scope of SQL tuning goes far beyond tuning a single statement. Indeed, the SQL tuning task usually starts by identifying high-load SQL. High-load SQL typically represents a small subset of SQL statements (generally a small fraction) that are either consuming a large share of system resources (e.g., more than 80 percent) or account for a large portion of the time spent by a database application to perform one of its essential functions.

In Oracle10g, a substantial amount of development effort and focus has been put into making the database self-managing. Automatic SQL Tuning is an integral part of the manageability framework that was developed for this purpose. The goal is to provide an end-to-end solution to the many SQL tuning challenges faced by the database administrators and application developers. Figure 3 represents a typical illustration of the SQL tuning life cycle as it is now performed in Oracle10g. It includes four key manageability components: AWR (Automatic Workload Repository), ADDM (Automatic Database Diagnostic Monitor), STS (SQL Tuning Set), and STB (SQL Tuning Base). These components are described in detail below.

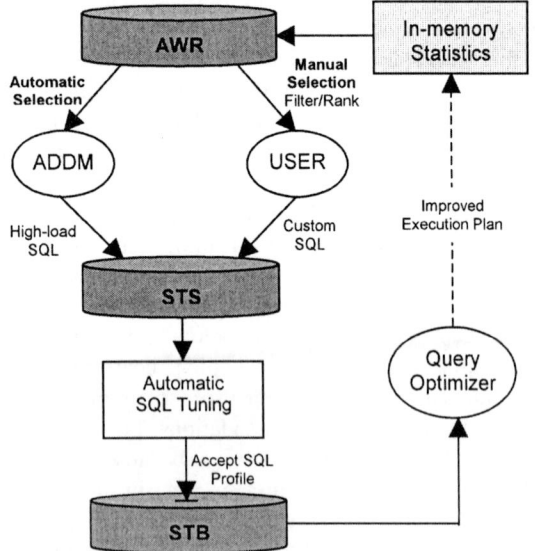

Figure 3. SQL Tuning Life Cycle in Oracle10g

The SQL tuning life cycle follows the three phases of the Oracle10g self-managing loop: **Observe, Diagnose,** and **Resolve**. Each of the components of the self-managing framework (labeled AWR, ADDM, STS and STB in Figure 3) plays a key role in one or more of these three phases.

6.1 Observe Phase

This phase is automatic and continuous in Oracle10g. It provides the data needed for analysis. To enable accurate system performance monitoring and tuning, it is imperative that the system under consideration expose relevant performance measurements. The manageability framework allows for instrumentation of the code to obtain precise timing information, and provides a lightweight comprehensive data collection mechanism to store these measurements for further online or offline analysis.

The chief component of the observe phase is the **Automatic Workload Repository** (AWR). The AWR is a persistent store of performance and system data for Oracle10g. The database collects performance data from in-memory views every hour and stores it in AWR. Each collection is referred to as a snapshot. A snapshot provides a consistent view of the system for its respective time period. For example, among other things, the AWR identifies and captures top SQL statements that are resource intensive in terms of CPU consumption, disk reads, parse calls, memory usage, etc. for each time interval.

AWR is self-managing, and based on internal measurements its overhead is less than 2 percent of the system load. AWR has standard policy for data retention but also accepts user input and, if required, proactively purges data should it encounter space pressure.

6.2 Diagnose Phase

The activities in this phase refer to the analyses of various parts of the database system using the data in AWR or in-memory performance views. Oracle10g introduces a framework for analyzing and optimizing the performance of its respective sub-components, such as the buffer cache, SQL execution, undo management, etc.

At the heart of the diagnose phase is the **Automatic Database Diagnostic Monitor** (ADDM). ADDM is a central database-wide performance diagnostic engine that optimizes for system throughput by taking a holistic view of the entire database system for a given analysis period. It runs automatically and identifies the root causes of the top performance bottlenecks and excessive resource consumption along with the exact impact on the workload in terms of time. It also provides a set of recommendations to alleviate the problems detected.

In the case of SQL statements consuming excessive resources, ADDM will recommend the invocation of the SQL Tuning Advisor for those high-load SQL statements. Besides the automatic selection performed by

ADDM, Oracle10g also provides a user driven mechanism to manually select the set of SQL statements to tune. This manual path (illustrated by downward arrows on the right side of Figure 3 exists because the user - generally the application developer or the DBA - might have to tune the response time of a subset of SQL statements involved in a critical function of the database application, even if that function accounts for a small percentage of the overall load.

The **SQL Tuning Set** (STS) feature is introduced in Oracle10g for the user to create and manage the SQL workload to tune. A SQL Tuning Set is a database object that persistently stores one or more SQL statements along with their execution statistics and execution context. The execution context stored with each SQL statement includes the parsing schema name, application module name, list of bind values, and compilation parameters. This enables the system to replicate the runtime environment under which the SQL statement was detected. The execution statistics include elapsed time, CPU time, disk reads, rows processed, statement fetches, etc.

SQL statements can be loaded into a SQL Tuning Set from different SQL sources. The SQL sources include the Automatic Workload Repository, the statement cache, and custom SQL statements supplied by the user. The capability to specify complex filters and rankings for the SQL statements are provided while loading into or reading data from the STS. For example, the user can create a STS storing the top N SQL statements issued by application module "order entry", where top N is based on the cumulative elapsed time of each statement.

Once created and populated, a SQL Tuning Set becomes the main input of the SQL Tuning Advisor.

6.3 Resolve Phase

The various advisors, after having performed their analyses, provide as output a set of recommendations that need to be implemented or applied to the database. The recommendations may be automatically applied by the database itself or be initiated manually. This is referred to as the Resolve Phase.

In the context of SQL tuning, the action part includes accepting SQL Profiles recommended by the SQL Tuning Advisor. When a SQL Profile is accepted, it is stored in the **SQL Tuning Base** (STB). The SQL Tuning Base is an extension of the Oracle dictionary that stores and manages all the tuning actions targeting specific SQL statements.

Accepting SQL profile recommendations closes an iteration of the SQL tuning loop; SQL Profiles will most likely improve the execution plan of the targeted set of SQL statements, hence reducing their overall performance impact on the system. This will be reflected in the performance measurements being collected. The next tuning cycle can then begin with a different set of high-load SQL statements. The process can be repeated several times until the desired performance level is achieved.

7. Experimental Results

The Automatic SQL Tuning feature was evaluated using a decision support workload obtained from one of Oracle's customers, a market research firm. Even though we do not demonstrate it in this paper, Automatic SQL Tuning can also tune OLTP queries equally well. In fact, we used it successfully on several queries from our internal OLTP systems. It is commonly assumed that OLTP queries are very simple with obvious execution plans, and thus do not offer many optimization opportunities. However, this is generally not true. Some OLTP queries can be very complex, joining more than 20 tables with multiple sub-queries and predicates. In this type of environment, the optimizer can fail to find optimal execution plans. Additionally, most OLTP applications run complex batch and reporting queries. Our SQL tuning methodology can be very effective in tuning OLTP queries.

For this experiment, we chose 73 decision support queries that had the highest impact on the performance of the customer's database system. As a result, the customer and an Oracle consulting team spent a significant amount of time to manually tune each of these queries. Figure 4 shows the response time of all 73 queries prior to tuning. Throughout this section, graphs show response time in ascending order (i.e. from fastest to slowest) using a logarithmic scale to improve readability. One can observe that without tuning, most queries perform very poorly. The worst response time for a query is almost 2 hours (5,751s) with an average response time of 817s and a cumulative response time (time to run the entire workload sequentially) close to 16 hours. This was unacceptable to the customer who had to resort to manual tuning of these SQL statements.

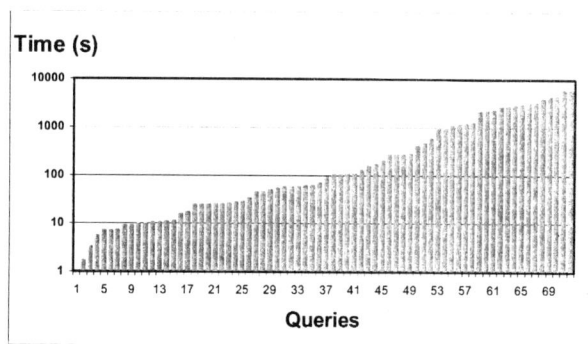

Figure 4. Response Time Without Tuning

Most statements were manually tuned using optimizer hints to improve their execution plans. In this particular instance, the Oracle query optimizer was unable to find the most optimal execution plan because these SQL statements used complex join predicates (e.g. inequality join predicates like "T1.C1 between T2.C1 and T2.C2") and had filters on highly correlated columns originating from different tables being joined (i.e. intertable correlation). The combination of these two factors made it very hard for the Oracle query optimizer to properly estimate the cardinality of some intermediate joins. Hence, the optimizer would sometime fail to produce a good join order, leading to a sub-optimal execution plan and poor query performance.

Figure 5 below graphs the response time after performing manual tuning. As one can see, manual tuning was able to dramatically improve the response time of most queries in the set. The worst response time was reduced to 275s - instead of the initial 5,751s - with an average response time of 30s - instead of the initial 817s - and a cumulative response time of 2131s, instead of the initial 16 hours.

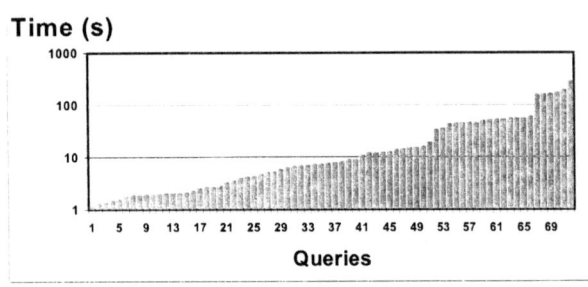

Figure 5. Response Time after Manual Tuning

The initial set of 73 queries was then stored in a SQL Tuning Set, which was then tuned using Oracle 10g Automatic SQL Tuning feature. For the purpose of this particular test, we decided to implement only SQL profile recommendations since our goal was to show how the execution plans for these statements could be improved without performing any SQL rewrite (i.e., altering SQL source code), and without modifying the underlying database schema. Figure 6 presents the new response time after the SQL Profiles recommended by the Automatic SQL Tuning were all accepted.

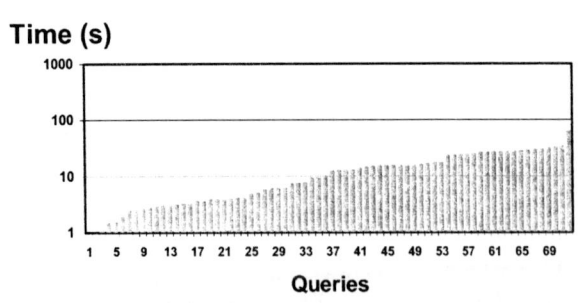

Figure 6. Response Time after Automatic Tuning

Overall, the results show dramatic improvements over manual tuning. The maximum response time was reduced from 275s to 59s. The average response time reduced from 30s to 13s. The cumulative SQL workload response time was less than 15 minutes instead of the 16 hours before tuning or the 35 minutes after manual tuning. Table 1 below summarizes these results.

	Average Response Time	Maximum Response Time	Cumulative Response Time
No Tuning	817s	5,751s	58,821s
Manual Tuning	30s	275s	2131s
Auto Tuning	13s	59s	929s

Table 1. Result Summary

These first results are very encouraging and demonstrate that SQL profiling represents a very effective way to empower the query optimizer in finding better execution plans. Overall, SQL profiling even surpassed manual tuning.

The last aspect of the benchmark is the performance of the Automatic SQL Tuning process itself. Internally, the goal of SQL profiling is to regulate its time such that, at worst, the time spent to tune a query is no more than the response time of that query before tuning. To achieve this goal, a cost-based and bottom-up tuning approach is used to determine which internal optimizer estimates are worth verifying. This, combined with the use of dynamic and iterative sampling techniques, makes Automatic SQL Tuning very efficient.

Figure 7 validates this goal. On average, the time to tune a query ranged from less than a minute to a maximum of less than two minutes. The entire workload was tuned in a little more than an hour (74 minutes) versus 16 hours to run the set of queries before tuning. This should be contrasted with the significant man-hours spent by domain experts to perform the manual tuning task, making Automatic SQL Tuning a very cost-effective solution.

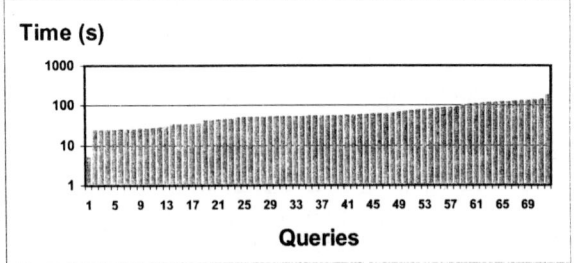

Figure 7. Automatic Tuning Time

8. Related Work

Several research groups, commercial databases and tools vendors have tried to solve the SQL tuning problem. Their solutions have concentrated on one of many areas. These include improving the optimizer itself; providing novel data statistics; rewriting the SQL statements into semantically equivalent forms; and making recommendations for new indexes to improve performance. However, none of the commercially available query optimizers exploit a selective body of knowledge built by a learning component to influence future query plan generation. In Oracle10g, this body of knowledge is encapsulated by SQL profiles built by the Automatic Tuning Optimizer, our learning component.

The LEO (LEarning Optimizer) research project at IBM [1] [2] corrects errors in cardinality estimates made by the query optimizer by comparing them with the actual values measured at each step of the execution plan. The corrections are computed as adjustments to the query optimizer estimates and stored in dictionary tables. When a SQL statement is compiled, the query optimizer first checks whether any adjustments are available as a result of previous executions of a related query and if so, it applies them. The idea of correcting errors in optimizer estimates to produce a better execution plan is similar to SQL Profiling. However, the two approaches differ in several ways:

1. LEO detects cardinality estimate errors only in the final plan selected by the optimizer. In contrast, SQL profiling error detection is performed when the Oracle optimizer is searching for an optimal plan. As a result, SQL profiling guides the optimizer in its plan search algorithm so that the true optimal plan can be found. On the other hand, LEO tries to find an optimal plan through several iterations, each of which requires a new execution of the SQL statement by the application. Several issues with LEO's iterative error correction model are detailed in [2] and outlined here:
   a. Performance of intermediate execution plans is not guaranteed to improve because of partial error corrections. Indeed, during the learning phase, performance can even degrade making this method hard to use in production systems. By contrast, the Automatic Tuning Optimizer produces a SQL profile in a single iteration, without impacting the application.
   b. The process of converging to an optimal plan can extend over a long period of time since a single estimate error can be the source of many other estimate errors. For example, an error in the cardinality estimate of a join between tables A and B, will cascade to every join permutation that includes A and B (e.g., C, A, D, B). Hence, before finding the optimal join permutation, LEO might have to correct many join permutations, each correction requiring a full execution of the SQL statement by the application. This issue does not exist for SQL profiling since all relevant estimates are validated during the plan search process, using partial query execution techniques on data samples.
   c. Finally, there is no guarantee that LEO will be able to find the optimal plan. For example, two errors can cancel each other out, making the real error impossible to detect. Also, it may not be possible to pinpoint the source of an estimate error in a combination of predicates (e.g., C1<10 and C2>50) because the optimizer chose to evaluate them together, e.g. during a full table scan. Identifying the exact source of an error is important since it could enable a different access path (e.g., an index range scan). On the other hand, the Auto Tuning Optimizer judiciously verifies cardinality estimates during the plan search process. In the above example, it will verify in isolation the selectivity of predicates that are access path enablers.

2. Another difference between LEO's approach and our approach is the usage model. SQL Profiling can target a small subset of SQL statements, generally the ones that have the highest impact on the performance of the system. By contrast, LEO will potentially gather corrections for every statement executed in the system and what is learned could impact many other statements. This could be viewed as an advantage for LEO since it could learn even for queries executed only once (e.g. purely ad-hoc queries) while SQL profiling cannot do this. On the other hand, the corrections gathered by LEO can be overwhelming, both in terms of storage requirements and time spent in managing them. SQL Profiling maximizes the benefit/overhead ratio since it can be used in a very selective way to focus on a small subset of important statements, while not disturbing the performance of other statements. In addition, the impact of SQL profiling is easier to understand and evaluate, making this feature probably less risky to deploy in a real world production system.

3. The feedback mechanism used by LEO is defined in very general terms, simply by saying that predicate corrections are stored in the dictionary. In our opinion, this aspect is one of the most challenging. That is, how to represent, store, lookup, and manage feedback information. In LEO's approach, it is not clearly explained how cardinality corrections can be applied in cases other than for single table estimates, e.g., join, aggregate, set operations. By contrast, SQL Profiles allow correction of any type of estimate made by the Oracle optimizer during the plan search process. Also, lookup of a SQL Profile is simply done by computing a signature on the text of the SQL statement, making the feedback retrieval process very efficient.

4. A SQL Profile is a general feedback mechanism to deliver any type of information to the optimizer to influence query plan generation. For instance, in addition to correcting optimizer estimates, we use it to customize the optimization mode of a SQL

statement. As far as we know, LEO has no provision for this.

Microsoft SQL Server offers an Index Wizard [5] to provide recommendations to the DBA on the indexes that can potentially improve the query execution plans. This approach is similar to the DB2 Advisor [10], and SQL Access Advisor [6] component in Oracle 10g manageability framework. However, Index Wizard is limited to access path recommendations and cannot be used to improve the quality of execution plans, unlike what SQL Profiles can do.

There are a number of commercial tools that assist a DBA in some aspects of tuning inefficient SQL statements. None of them, however, provides a complete tuning solution, partly because it is not integrated with the Oracle database server. Quest Software's SQLab Vision [3], provides a mechanism for identifying high load SQL based on several measures of resource utilization. It also can rewrite SQL statements into semantically equivalent, but potentially more efficient, alternative forms and suggests creation of indexes to offer more efficient access path to the data. Since the product resides outside of the Oracle RDBMS, the actual benefit of these recommendations is unknown until they are actually implemented and executed by the user.

LeccoTech's SQLExpert [4] is a toolkit that scans new applications for problematic SQL statements as well as high load SQL statements in the system. It generates alternative execution plans for a SQL statement by rewriting it into all possible semantically equivalent forms. There are three problems with this approach. First, it cannot identify all forms of rewriting a SQL statement (which is normally the domain of a query optimizer). Second, equivalent forms of a SQL statement do not guarantee that the query optimizer will find an efficient execution plan if the bad plan is a result of errors in the optimizer estimates, such as cardinality of intermediate results. Third, all the alternative plans will have to be executed to actually determine which, if any, is superior to the original execution plan found by the optimizer.

9. Conclusion

In this paper, we have described the Automatic SQL Tuning feature introduced in Oracle10g. It is tightly integrated with the Oracle query optimizer, and is an integral part of the manageability framework for self-managing databases introduced in Oracle10g. The Automatic SQL Tuning is based on the Automatic Tuning Optimizer, the new generation Oracle query optimizer. The SQL Tuning Advisor tunes SQL statements and produces a set of comprehensive tuning recommendations including SQL Profiles. The user decides whether to accept the recommendations. Once a SQL Profile is created, the Oracle query optimizer will use it to generate a well-tuned plan for the corresponding SQL statement. A tuning object called the SQL Tuning Set is also introduced that enables a user to create a customized SQL workload, e.g., in order to tune it. The interface to the Automatic SQL Tuning is provided primarily through Oracle Enterprise Manager but is also accessible via a programmatic interface.

Many of the techniques we have described in this paper have been proposed before in different contexts [1], [2], [5], [10], [11]. But SQL Profiling is a novel technique that we have described here. Also, we have shown how these techniques have been combined together in order to offer an innovative end-to-end SQL tuning solution in Oracle 10g.

Finally, we have illustrated the feature using a real customer workload. It works equally well for OLTP and DSS workloads, because it helps the query optimizer cope with query complexity by improving its estimates. Although the feature is in its first production release, initial case studies have demonstrated the superiority of Automatic SQL Tuning over manual tuning. This position is further cemented by the fact that Automatic SQL Tuning results can scale over a large number of queries, and they can evolve over time with changes in the application workload and the underlying data. Automatic SQL Tuning is also far cheaper option than manual tuning. Together, these reasons position Automatic SQL Tuning as an effective and economical alternative to manual tuning.

References

[1] Michael Stillger, Guy M. Lohman, Volker Markl, Mokhtar Kandil: LEO – DB2's Learning Optimizer, *The VLDB Journal*, 2001.

[2] V. Markl, G.M. Lohman, V. Raman: LEO: An autonomic query optimizer for DB2, *IBM Systems Journal, Vol 42, No 1, 2003*.

[3] Quest Software, Quest Central for Oracle: SQLab Vision, http://www.quest.com, 2003.

[4] Leccotech, LECCOTECH Performance Optimization Solutions for Oracle, *White Paper*, http://www.leccotech.com/, 2003.

[5] S. Chaudhuri, V. Narasayya: An Efficient, Cost-driven Index Tuning Wizard for Microsoft SQL Server, *23rd International Conference on Very Large Data Bases*, 1997.

[6] Oracle Corporation: Performance Tuning using the SQL Access Advisor, *Oracle White Paper*, http://otn.oracle.com, 2003.

[7] Oracle Corporation: Database 10g: The Self-Managing Database, *Oracle White Paper*, http://otn.oracle.com, 2003.

[8] Oracle Corporation: The Self-Managing Database: Automatic Performance Diagnosis, *Oracle White Paper*, http://otn.oracle.com, 2003.

[9] Oracle Corporation: The Self-Managing Database: Guided Application and SQL Tuning, *Oracle White Paper*, http://otn.oracle.com, 2003.

[10] Gary Valentin, Michael Zuliani, Daniel Zilio, Guy Lohman, Alan Skelley: DB2 Advisor: An Optimizer Smart Enough to Recommend Its Own Indexes, *16th International Conference on Data Engineering, 2000.*

[11] Hamid Pirahesh, Joseph Hellerstein, Waqar Hasan: Extensible/Rule Based Query Rewrite Optimization in Starburst, *ACM SIGMOD Conference, 1992.*

Database Tuning Advisor for Microsoft SQL Server 2005

Sanjay Agrawal, Surajit Chaudhuri, Lubor Kollar, Arun Marathe, Vivek Narasayya, Manoj Syamala

Microsoft Corporation
One Microsoft Way
Redmond, WA 98052.
USA

{sagrawal,surajitc,lubork,arunma,viveknar,manojsy}@microsoft.com

Abstract

The Database Tuning Advisor (DTA) that is part of Microsoft SQL Server 2005 is an automated physical database design tool that significantly advances the state-of-the-art in several ways. First, DTA is capable to providing an *integrated* physical design recommendation for horizontal partitioning, indexes, and materialized views. Second, unlike today's physical design tools that focus solely on performance, DTA also supports the capability for a database administrator (DBA) to specify manageability requirements while optimizing for performance. Third, DTA is able to scale to large databases and workloads using several novel techniques including: (a) workload compression (b) reduced statistics creation and (c) exploiting test server to reduce load on production server. Finally, DTA greatly enhances scriptability and customization through the use of a public XML schema for input and output. This paper provides an overview of DTA's novel functionality, the rationale for its architecture, and demonstrates DTA's quality and scalability on large customer workloads.

1. Introduction

The performance of an enterprise database system can depend crucially on its physical database design. Automated tools for physical database design can help reduce the total cost of ownership (TCO) of databases by reducing the DBA's burden in determining the appropriate physical design. The past few years have seen an emergence of such automated tools. Indeed, today's major commercial database systems include as part of their product, automated tools such as [2,3,4,6,15,18,21] that analyze a representative *workload* consisting of queries and updates that run against the database, and recommend appropriate changes to physical design for the workload.

1.1 Requirements of a Physical Design Tool

While these state-of-the-art tools represent an important step in the direction of reducing TCO, there are a number of important requirements, described below, in which currently available tools are still lacking that can make it difficult to use in an enterprise environment.

Integrated selection of physical design features: Today's database engines offer a variety of physical design features such as indexes, materialized views and horizontal partitioning, each of which can have a significant impact on the performance of the workload. A physical design tool should ideally provide an integrated "console" where DBAs can tune all physical design features supported by the server. In supporting such a console, it may appear natural (for scalability reasons) to employ a staged solution to the physical design problem, -- for example, first choose partitioning of tables only, then pick indexes, then pick materialized views etc. However, as shown in [3,4] (and discussed in Section 3), due to the strong interaction among these features, such staging can potentially lead to an inferior physical design. Thus, a tool that is capable of making an integrated physical design recommendation that takes into account the interactions among all these features is important since otherwise: (a) Ad-hoc choices need to be made on how to stage physical design selection; and (b) It is difficult to quantify how much performance is compromised for a given database and workload as a result of staging. There are tools that integrate tuning of certain physical design features, e.g., [3,21], but to the best of our knowledge, no tool until now offers a fully integrated approach to tuning indexes, materialized views and horizontal partitioning together.

Incorporating manageability aspects into physical design: The focus of today's physical design tools is on improving performance. However, manageability of physical design is often a key requirement. For example,

---

Permission to copy without fee all or part of this material is granted provided that the copies are not made or distributed for direct commercial advantage, the VLDB copyright notice and the title of the publication and its date appear, and notice is given that copying is by permission of the Very Large Data Base Endowment. To copy otherwise, or to republish, requires a fee and/or special permission from the Endowment

**Proceedings of the 30th VLDB Conference,
Toronto, Canada, 2004**

DBAs often use horizontal range partitioning to ensure easy backup/restore, to add new data or remove old data. In these scenarios, having a table and all of its indexes *aligned*, i.e., partitioned identically makes these tasks easier. On the other hand, the manner in which a table (or an index) is partitioned can have significant impact on the performance of queries against the table (using the index). Therefore, it becomes important for an automated physical design tool to allow DBAs the ability to specify alignment requirements while optimizing for performance.

Scaling to large databases and workloads: Enterprise databases can be large and a typical representative workload can also be large (e.g., number of queries/updates that execute on a server in one day can easily run into hundreds of thousands or more). Thus, to be effective in an enterprise environment, these tools need to be able to scale well, while maintaining good recommendation quality.

Ability to tune a production database with very little overhead: Consider a case where a DBA needs to tune a large workload. Tuning such a workload can incur substantial load on the production server. Therefore, there is a need to tune these databases by imposing very little overhead on production server. Sometimes test servers exist, but it is often infeasible or undesirable to copy the entire database to the test server for tuning. Moreover the test server may have different hardware characteristics, and thus the recommendations of the tool on the test server may not be appropriate for the production server.

Scriptability and customization: As physical design tools become more feature rich, and get increasingly used in enterprises, the ability to script these tools for DBAs and build value added tools on top by developers becomes more important. Moreover different degrees of customization are necessary for different scenarios. At one extreme, the tool should be able to make all physical recommendations on its own. At the other extreme, the DBA should be able to propose a physical design that is simply evaluated the tool. In between, the DBA should be able to specify a physical design partially (e.g., clustering or partitioning of a given table) and the tool should complete the rest of the tuning. Such support is inadequate in today's physical design tools.

1.2 Advancements in DatabaseTuning Advisor

In this paper, we describe **Database Tuning Advisor (DTA)**, an automated physical design tool that is part of Microsoft SQL Server 2005. DTA significantly advances functionality, manageability, scalability, and scriptability relative to the state-of-the-art physical design tools. DTA is the next generation physical design tool that builds upon the Index Tuning Wizard in Microsoft SQL Server 2000. First, DTA can provide *integrated* recommendations for indexes, materialized views as well as single-node horizontal partitioning for a given workload (Section 3). DTA provides the user the ability to specify the requirement that the physical database design should be *aligned*, i.e., a table and its indexes should be partitioned identically (Section 4). DTA scales to large databases and workloads using several novel techniques including: (a) workload compression that helps scaling to large workloads; (b) reduced statistics creation that helps to reduce time for creating statistics for large databases; and (c) exploiting test server to reduce tuning load on production server. These techniques for improving scalability are discussed in Section 5. The input and output to DTA conforms to a public XML schema for physical database design which makes scripting and customization easy, and enables other tools to build value-added functionality on top of DTA. Such usability enhancements in DTA are discussed in Section 6. DTA exposes a novel feature called *user specified configuration* that allows DBAs to specify the desired physical design partially (without actual materialization), while optimizing for performance. This allows for greater customizability. These and other important usability enhancements in DTA are discussed in Section 6. In Section 7 we present results of extensive experiments on several customer workloads and the TPC-H 10GB benchmark workload that evaluates: (a) the quality of DTA's recommendation compared to a hand-tuned physical design and (b) its scalability to large databases and workloads. We summarize related work in Section 8. We begin with an overview of DTA functionality and its internal architecture in Section 2.

2. Overview of Database Tuning Advisor

2.1 Functionality

Figure 1 shows an overview of the Database Tuning Advisor (DTA) for Microsoft SQL Server 2005. DTA is a client physical database design tuning tool. It can be run either from a graphical user interface or using a command-line executable.

Input: DTA takes the following inputs:
- A set of databases on a server. Many applications use more than one database, and therefore, ability to tune multiple databases simultaneously is important.
- A workload to tune. A workload is a set of SQL statements that execute against the database server. A workload can be obtained by using SQL Server Profiler, a tool for logging events that execute on a server. Alternatively, a workload can be a SQL file containing an organization or industry benchmark, for example.

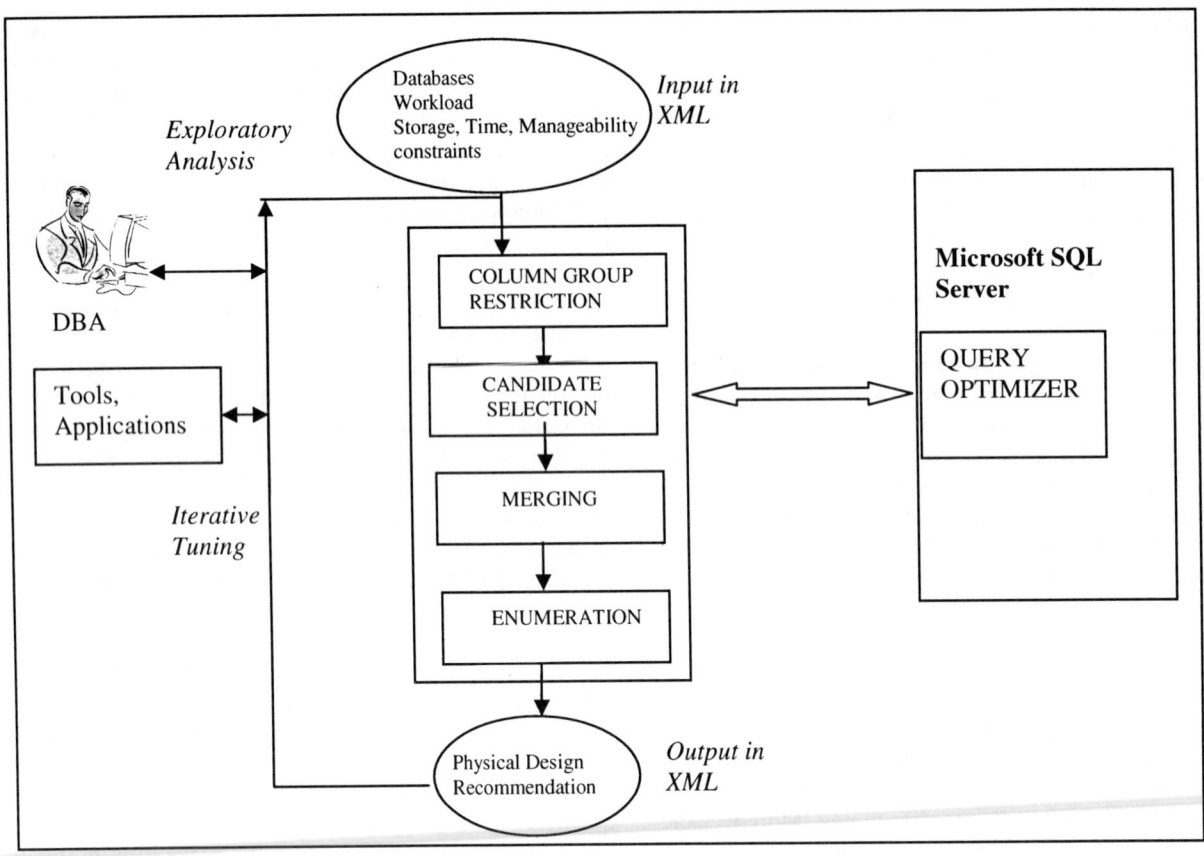

Figure 1. Overview of Database Tuning Advisor

- Feature set to tune. Although DTA is capable of tuning indexes, materialized views, and partitioning together, DBAs may sometimes need to limit tuning to subsets of these features. For example, a DBA of an OLTP system may decide *a priori* to not include any materialized views.
- Optional *alignment* constraint that a table and all its indexes must be partitioned identically (although different tables may be partitioned differently).
- User can specify a partial configuration (e.g., clustered index on a table, partitioning of a table or materialized view), and constrain DTA's recommendation to honor this specification.
- An optional storage constraint: DTA allows specifying a bound on the storage that the physical design it recommends can consume.
- An optional time constraint: an upper bound on the time that DTA is allowed to run. Although DTA's ability to perform tuning within a time bound is an interesting technical problem in itself, in this paper we do not focus on the problem of time-bound tuning or on DTA's specific solution.

Output: The output of DTA is a physical design recommendation (which we refer to as a *configuration*) consisting of indexes, materialized views, and a recommendation on horizontal range partitioning of tables, indexes, and materialized views.

2.2 Architecture

DTA extends the architecture developed in the context of previous work for index and materialized view selection [3] (used by Index Tuning Wizard in Microsoft SQL Server 2000). DTA's architecture is shown in Figure 1. Several properties of this architecture should be noted: (a) It is not specific to a particular physical design feature, and in principle, requires little changes as new physical design features are added; (b) It provides an integrated physical design recommendation; (c) It is in-sync with the query optimizer component of the database server. Below we briefly summarize the salient aspects of this architecture, and highlight extensions made compared to [3], where appropriate.

DTA's Cost Model: The basis of DTA's recommendations is the "what-if" analysis interfaces of Microsoft SQL Server described in [9], which have been extended to also support simulation of horizontally partitioned tables, indexes and materialized views [4] (in addition to non-partitioned indexes and materialized views). Microsoft SQL Server 2005 supports single-column range partitioning. Using these interfaces, for a given query Q and a configuration C, DTA can obtain the optimizer-estimated cost of Q as if configuration C were materialized in the database. Among all the configurations that DTA explores for the given workload, it recommends the one with the lowest optimizer-estimated cost for the workload. There are several advantages of being "in-sync" with the query optimizer: (a) The configuration DTA recommends, if implemented, will in fact be used by the query optimizer; (b) As query optimizer's cost model evolves over time, DTA is able to automatically benefit from improvements to it; (c) DTA takes into account all aspects of performance that the query optimizer can model including the impact of multiple processors, amount of memory on the server, and so on. It is important to note, however, that query optimizers typically do not model all the aspects of query execution (e.g. impact of indexes on locking behavior, impact of data layout etc.). Thus, DTA's estimated improvement may be different from the actual improvement in execution time.

Column-Group Restriction: The space of all physical design structures (indexes, materialized views, partitioning) that need to be considered for a given workload can be very large. The explosion in the number of physical design structures that must be considered is a result of the large number of column-groups (i.e., sets of columns) that are, in principle, relevant for the workload. Column-group restriction a pre-processing step that eliminates from further consideration a large number of column-groups that can at best have only a marginal impact on the quality of the final recommendation (in particular, column-groups that occur only in a small fraction of the workload by cost). The output of this step is a set of "interesting" column-groups for the workload. Indexes and partitioning considered by DTA is limited only to interesting column groups, thereby significantly improving scalability with little impact on quality [4]. For scalability, we construct the interesting column-groups for a workload in a bottom-up manner leveraging the idea of frequent itemsets [5]. This module is an extension of the previous architecture presented in [3].

Candidate Selection: The Candidate Selection step selects for each query in the workload (in particular, one query at a time), a set of very good configurations for that query in a cost-based manner by consulting the query optimizer component of the database system. A physical design structure that is part of the selected configurations of one or more queries in the workload is referred to as a *candidate*. We use a greedy search strategy, called Greedy (m,k) [8] to realize this task. To recap, Greedy (m,k) algorithm guarantees an optimal answer when choosing up to m physical design structures, and subsequently uses a greedy strategy to add more (up to k) structures.

Merging: Since Candidate Selection operates only at the level of an individual query, if we restrict the final choice of physical design to only be a subset of the candidates selected by the Candidate Selection step, we can potentially end up with "over-specialized" physical design structures that are good for individual queries, but not good for the overall workload. Specifically, when storage is limited or workload is update-intensive, this can lead to poor quality of the final solution. The goal of the Merging step is to consider new physical design structures, based on candidates chosen in the Candidate Selection step, which can benefit multiple queries in the workload. The Merging step augments the set of candidates with additional "merged" physical design structures. The idea of merging physical design structures has been studied in the context of un-partitioned indexes [8], and materialized views [3]. Merging becomes a lot harder with the inclusion of partitioning, and requires new algorithmic techniques. Our techniques for merging partitioned indexes and materialized views are described in [4].

Enumeration: This step takes as input the union of the candidates (including candidates from Merging), and produces the final solution: a physical database design. We use Greedy (m,k) search scheme. As shown in [4], with the additional constraint that the physical design for each table should be aligned, introducing new candidates that are required (for alignment) eagerly can be unscalable. In [4], we describe how it is possible to delay the introduction of additional candidates that need to be introduced to satisfy the alignment constraint *lazily*, thereby greatly improving the scalability of the enumeration step.

3. Integrated Physical Design Recommendations

An important challenge in physical design tuning is being able to judiciously deal with the tradeoffs in performance of various physical design *features* available (indexes, materialized views, partitioning etc.). This tradeoff is challenging for the following two reasons. First, for a given query, different features can overlap in their ability to reduce the cost of execution for query.

Example 1. Consider the query: Select A, COUNT(*) FROM T WHERE X < 10 GROUP BY A. For this query several different physical design structures can reduce its execution cost: (i) A clustered index on (X); (ii) Table range partitioned on X; (iii) A non-clustered, "covering" index on (X, A); (iv) A materialized view that matches the query, and so on.

Second, these features can have widely varying storage and update characteristics. Thus in the presence of storage constraints or for a workload containing updates, making a global choice for a workload is difficult. For example, a clustered index on a table and horizontal partitioning of a table are both non-redundant structures (incur negligible additional storage overhead); whereas non-clustered indexes and materialized views can potentially be storage intensive (similarly their update costs can be higher). However, non-clustered indexes (e.g., "covering" indexes) and materialized views can often be much more beneficial than a clustered index or a horizontally partitioned table.

Thus, a physical design tool that can give an integrated physical design recommendation can greatly reduce/eliminate the need for a DBA to make ad-hoc decisions such as: (a) how to stage tuning, e.g., pick partitioning first, then indexes, and finally materialized views; (b) How to divide up the overall storage to allocate for each step in this staged solution, etc. The following example (showing the interaction between indexes and horizontal partitioning) illustrates the pitfalls of a staged solution.

Example 2. Consider the query from Example 1 and suppose that we wish to consider only clustered indexes and horizontal range partitioning of the table. We compare two approaches for the query above. (1) A staged solution that first selects the best clustered index, and in the next step considers horizontal range partitioning of the table. (2) An integrated solution that considers both features together. Observe that both a clustered index on column X or a range partitioning on column X can help reduce the selection cost, whereas a clustered index on column A is likely to be much more beneficial than a horizontal range partitioning on A as far as the grouping is concerned. Thus, if in the first step of the staged solution we recommend a clustered index on X, then we can never expect to find the optimal solution for the query: a clustered index on A and horizontal range partitioning of the table on X. On the other hand, an integrated solution is capable of finding this solution since it considers these features together.

As noted earlier, DTA can recommend indexes, materialized views, and horizontal partitioning in an integrated manner. Although doing so is important for the reasons described above, when all of the physical design features are considered together, the space of configurations that need to be considered for a given workload can become very large. The techniques that DTA uses to reduce the space of configurations that are explored without impacting the quality of recommendations significantly have been summarized in Section 2.2 and are described in greater detail in [4].

Finally, we note that DTA allows DBAs to choose only a subset of the available physical design features should they wish to do so. For example, in certain environments, a DBA may not wish to consider materialized views. In this case, the DBA can specify that DTA should only consider indexes and partitioning as the physical design options.

4. Aligned Partitioning

As discussed earlier, DBAs often require the physical design to be *aligned* (i.e., a table and all of its indexes are partitioned identically) so that it is easy to add, remove, backup, and restore data partitions. Horizontal range partitioning is important for manageability reasons, but it can also have a significant impact on performance of the workload. Therefore, DTA allows users the option of specifying that the physical design should be aligned. Choosing this option implies that the physical design recommended by DTA will satisfy the property of alignment for each table. The impact of specifying the alignment requirement on DTA is that it constrains the overall search space that DTA needs to traverse. The key technical challenge arising out of alignment is that different queries that reference a given table T may benefit from different ways of partitioning T or indexes on T. Thus, efficiently finding a compromise that works well across all queries in the workload is difficult. DTA efficiently incorporates alignment constraints into its search algorithm by exploiting the fact that in many cases, it is sufficient to introduce new candidates for the purposes of satisfying alignment *lazily*. Such lazy introduction of candidates during the Enumeration step (Section 2.2), can significantly improve scalability. The details of this technique are described in [4].

5. Improved Scalablity

5.1 Scaling to Large Workloads

One of the key factors that affect the scalability of physical design tools is the size of the workload, i.e., the number of statements (queries, updates) in the workload. As explained earlier, the workload given to DTA for tuning can be very large. In such cases, a natural question to ask is whether tuning a much smaller subset of the workload would be sufficient to give a recommendation with approximately the same reduction in cost as the recommendation obtained by tuning the entire workload.

Two obvious strategies for determining a subset of the workload to tune have significant drawbacks. The approach of sampling the workload uniformly at random ignores valuable information about queries in the workload (such as cost and structural properties), and thus may end up tuning a lot more queries than necessary. The other strategy of tuning the top k queries by cost, such that at least a pre-defined percentage of the total cost of the workload is covered, suffers from a different problem. Queries in the workload are often *templatized* (e.g., invoked via stored procedures). In such cases, often all queries belonging to one template may have higher cost than any query belonging to another template. Thus, the above strategy can end up tuning a disproportionate number of queries from one template, while never tuning queries from a different template.

The technique of *workload compression* in the context of physical design tuning has been studied in [7]. The idea behind workload compression is to exploit the inherent templatization in workloads by partitioning the workload based on the "signature" of each query, i.e., two queries have same signature if they are identical in all respects except for the constants referenced in the query. The technique picks a subset from each partition using a clustering based method. We have adapted the above technique and integrated it into DTA, which allows us to dramatically reduce the amount of time spent in tuning without significantly compromising the quality of physical design recommendation. We demonstrate the effectiveness of this technique on large workloads in Section 7.4.

5.2 Reduced Statistics Creation

As part of its tuning, DTA needs to consider indexes that may not exist in the current database, i.e., "what-if" indexes [9]. To simulate the presence of such a what-if index to the query optimizer, DTA needs to create the necessary statistics that would have been included in that index had it been actually created. Thus for a given set of indexes, there is a corresponding set of statistics that DTA needs to create. This is achieved using the standard "create statistics" interface available in SQL Server (using the sampling option of create statistics for scalability). The problem is that despite the use of sampling, the naïve strategy of creating all statistics can become very expensive, particularly on large databases,, because each "create statistics" statement incurs I/Os for sampling the pre-defined number of pages from the table, sorting it, and creating the summary statistics.

When SQL Server creates a statistic on columns (A,B,C), it generates a histogram on the leading column only (i.e., column A) and computes *density* information for each leading prefix (i.e., (A), (A,B), (A,B,C)). The density of a set of columns is a single number that captures the average number of duplicates of that set of columns. Since density is defined on a *set* of columns, it is not dependent on the order of the columns, i.e., Density (A,B) = Density (B,A).

Example 3. Suppose that DTA needs to consider indexes on (A), (B), (A,B), (B,A) and (A,B,C). Using the naïve approach, we would need to create all five statistics. However, it is easy to see that if we only create statistics on (A,B,C) and (B), these two statistics contain the same information (histograms and density) as when all five statistics are created.

Thus our problem can be stated more formally as follows:

> Given a set of statistics S = {s_1, ... s_n} where each s_i contains a histogram on its leading column and density information on each leading prefix; find a subset S' of S of smallest cardinality such that it contains the same histogram and density information as S does.

Note that we seek to minimize cardinality of S' rather than to minimize the time to create S'. In reality, this simplification is reasonable since for a large table, the cost of creating a statistic is typically dominated by the I/O cost of sampling the table, which is independent of the specific statistic being created.

DTA's solution to the above problem is outlined below.

Step 1. Using S, create two lists: H-List and D-List. The H-List is a list of columns over which histograms need to be built. The D-List is the set of column groups over which density information needs to be obtained. In essence, the H-List and D-List identify the distinct statistical information that still needs to be created. In Example 3 above, the H-List is {(A), (B)} and the D-List is {(A), (B), (A,B), (A,B,C)}. Note that we do not need (B,A) in the D-List since Density (A,B) = Density (B,A).

Step 2. From the remaining statistics in S, pick the one (say *s*) whose creation "covers" as many elements of H-list and D-List as possible. In the above example, we pick (A,B,C) and create statistics on it.

Step 3. Remove all elements from the H-List and D-List which have been covered by the creation of *s* in Step 2 above. Remove *s* from S. In our example, we would remove (A) from the H-List and (A), (A,B), (B,A) and (A,B,C) from the D-List., and (A, B, C) from S.

Step 4. Repeat 2-3 until both H-List and D-List are empty. In our example, we would end up creating {(A,B,C), (B)}.

The above greedy algorithm works well in practice (see Section 7.5 for an experimental evaluation) since the cost of creating a statistic depends mainly on the table size and not much on how many columns are present in the statistic. Thus it is usually beneficial to pick the largest remaining statistic to create, which contains the most statistical information. A more formal treatment of this problem is an interesting area of future work.

We note that the technique presented above simply reduces redundant statistical information that DTA creates. This is orthogonal to the techniques presented in [10] for determining whether or not a particular statistic actually impacts the plan chosen (or cost of plan chosen) by the query optimizer. Thus both of these techniques can be applied to reduce creation of unnecessary statistics. Finally, we note that the technique presented in this section will need to be modified if the database server uses different statistical information, for example, multi-column histograms.

5.3 Tuning in Production/Test Server Scenario

The process of tuning a large workload can impose significant overhead on the server being tuned since DTA needs to potentially make many "what-if" calls to the query optimizer component. In enterprise databases, it is common for DBAs to use *test servers* in addition to the production server(s). A test server can be used for a variety of purposes including performance tuning, testing changes before they are deployed on the production server and so on. A straightforward way of reducing the impact of tuning on a production server is to use a test server as follows:

- Step 1: Copy the databases one wants to tune from the production server to the test server.
- Step 2: Tune the workload on the test server.
- Step 3: Apply the recommendation that one gets on the test server to the production server.

The advantage of such a simplistic approach is that once the databases are copied out to the test server, then there is no tuning overhead imposed on the production server. However, the approach suffers from many drawbacks that severely limit its applicability. First, the databases can be large (production databases can run into hundreds of gigabytes or more) or changing frequently. In such situations, copying large amounts of data from production to test server for the purposes of tuning can be time consuming and resource intensive. Second, the hardware characteristics of test and production servers can be very different. Production servers tend to be much more powerful than test servers in terms of processors, memory etc. Since the tuning process relies on the optimizer to arrive at a recommendation and that in turn is tied to the underlying hardware, this can lead to vastly different results on the test server.

DTA provides the novel capability of exploiting a test server, if available, to tune a database on a production server *without* copying the data itself. The key observation that enables this functionality is that the query optimizer relies fundamentally on the *metadata* and *statistics* when generating a plan for a query. We leverage this observation to enable tuning on the test server as outlined in Figure 2.

The steps in the tuning process are as follows:

- Step 1: Copy the *metadata* of the databases one wants to tune from the production server to the test server.. We do *not* import the actual data from any tables. Note that this requires not only importing the (empty) tables, and indexes, but also all views, stored procedures, triggers etc. This is necessary since the queries in workload may reference these objects. The metadata can be imported using the scripting capability that is available in today's database systems. This is generally a very fast operation as it requires working with system catalog entries and does not depend on data size.

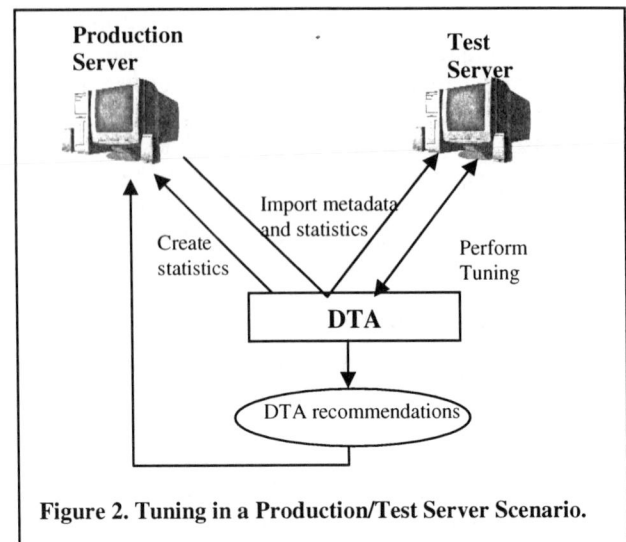

Figure 2. Tuning in a Production/Test Server Scenario.

- Step 2: Tune the workload on the test server. For getting the same plan on the test server as we would have got on the production server, we need two important functionalities from the database server. (1) During the tuning process, DTA may determine that certain statistics may need to be present (on the test server) so that the query optimizer can optimize the query accurately. However the statistics creation requires access to the actual data, and that is present only on production server. When that happens, DTA imports statistics from the production server (creating the statistics on the production server if necessary) and into the test server. (2) The hardware parameters of production server that are modeled by the query optimizer when it generates a query plan need to be appropriately "simulated" on the test server. For example, since query optimizer's cost model considers the number of CPUs and the available memory, these parameters need to be part of the interface that DTA uses to make a "what-if" call to the query optimizer. Microsoft SQL Server 2005 has been extended to provide us with both of these functionalities.
- Step 3: Apply the recommendation that one gets on the test server to the production server.

Note that the only overhead introduced on the production server during tuning is the creation of additional statistics (if any) that are necessary as tuning progresses (Step 2). The rest of the tasks that include simulating what-if interfaces, optimizing queries under different physical designs etc. are all performed on the test server. In

Section 7.3, we present experimental results that quantify the reduction in overhead on the production server as a result of exploiting this feature in DTA.

6. Enhanced Usability

6.1 Scriptabilty

As described in the introduction, tools for automated physical database design have emerged over the past few years and become part of commercial database systems. As such physical database design tools become more widely used, it can be advantageous to define a public XML schema for physical database design that forms the basis of input and output to such tools. First, having a public schema facilitates development of other tools that can program against the schema. Moreover, scriptability of the physical design tool can become much easier once such a schema is available. Second, as physical design tools evolve over time, having an XML schema makes it easy to extend it to meet the changing input/output needs of physical design tools. Finally, an XML schema makes it possible for different users/tools to interchange and communicate physical database design information within and across organization boundaries. We have defined such an XML schema for physical database design that is used by DTA, and that will be made public with the release of Microsoft SQL Server 2005 at [11]. The schema is described using the "XML Schema" schema definition language [19,20]. The schema defines elements to describe the common entities in physical database design, for example, databases (and tables within them), workloads, configurations, and reports.

6.2 Customizability via Partial Specification of Physical Design

In certain cases, DBAs may need to tune workload while being able to specify the physical design partially. Consider the following scenario where the DBA needs to decide whether a large table T (e.g., a fact table) should be range partitioned by month or quarter. Although either form of partitioning may be acceptable from a manageability standpoint, the DBA would prefer the option that results in better performance for the workload.

DTA allows the user to provide as (an optional) input a *user specified configuration*. A user specified configuration is a set of physical design structures that is valid, i.e. all physical design structures specified must be realizable in the database. An example of a physical design that is not valid is when there are more than one ways of clustering specified on the same table as a part of the same user specified configuration. DTA tunes the given workload and provides a recommendation while honoring the constraint that the user specified configuration is included in the recommendation provided by DTA. Thus in the above scenario, the DBA can first invoke DTA with a user specified configuration C_1 in which T is partitioned by month, and have DTA recommend the best physical design while honoring the constraint. The DBA can then run DTA again, this time with a user specified configuration C_2 in which T is partitioned by quarter. Finally, the DBA can compare the two recommendations and pick the one with better overall performance.

Since DTA never needs to physically alter the partitioning of the table, a DBA can try out various physical design alternatives efficiently without interfering with the normal database operations. In the scenario mentioned above, the DBA never needs to physically alter the partitioning of the large table (which can be an expensive operation) while making the decision of which partitioning to pick.

6.3 Exploratory Analysis and Iterative Tuning

A common scenario that DBAs encounter is the need to perform exploratory or "what-if" physical design analysis to get answers to question of the following type: What is the performance impact on a given set of queries and updates if I add a particular index or change the partitioning of a particular table? DTA enables this functionality through the *user specified configuration* mechanism described earlier (see Section 4.2). In particular, the user can specify a configuration, i.e., a valid physical design consisting of existing or hypothetical objects, and request DTA to *evaluate* the configuration for a given workload. DTA exploits the "what-if" interfaces of Microsoft SQL Server [9] to simulate the given configuration, and it evaluates each statement in the workload for the given configuration. DTA returns as output the expected percentage change in the workload cost compared to the existing configuration in the database. In addition, DTA provides a rich set of analysis reports that provides details about changes in cost of individual statements in the workload, usage of indexes and materialized views, and so on.

Another common scenario that DBAs face is the need for iterative tuning and refinement. For example, a DBA obtains a recommendation from DTA for a particular workload, and wishes to modify the recommendation and re-evaluate the modified configuration for the same workload. The DBA may repeat such evaluation until she is satisfied with the performance/impact of the configuration. Once again, such a scenario becomes simple via the user specified configuration feature of DTA. Moreover, given that the DTA input and output conform to an XML schema, it is easy for users or other automated tools to take the output configuration from one run of DTA and feed a modified version of it as input into a subsequent run of DTA.

7. Experiments

In this section, we present results of experiments that evaluate:
- Quality of recommendations by DTA on several customer workloads, by comparing it to a hand-tuned physical design.
- Quality of DTA on TPC-H 10GB benchmark workload.
- Impact on production server overhead because of DTA's ability to exploit a test server for tuning.
- Impact of workload compression technique (Section 5.1) on quality and scalability of DTA.
- Effectiveness of technique for reduced statistics creation (Section 5.2).
- An end-to-end comparison of DTA with Index Tuning Wizard for SQL Server 2000.

7.1 Quality of DTA vs. hand-tuned design on customer workloads

In this experiment, we compare the quality of DTA's physical design recommendation with a manually-tuned physical design. The databases and workloads used in this experiment were obtained from internal customers of Microsoft SQL Server. The methodology we adopt for this experiment is as follows. For each workload, we obtain the optimizer estimated cost of the workload for the current physical design (put in place by the DBA of that database). We refer to this cost as $C_{Current}$. We then drop all physical design structures (except those that enforce referential integrity constraints) and once again obtain the cost of the workload. We refer to this cost as C_{raw}. We then tune the workload using DTA, and obtain the cost of the workload for DTA's recommended configuration. We refer to this cost as C_{DTA}. We define the quality of DTA as $(C_{raw} - C_{DTA})/C_{raw}$ and the quality of the hand-tuned design as $(C_{raw} - C_{Current})/C_{raw}$, i.e., the percentage reduction relative to C_{raw}.

A brief overview of each customer database/workload used in this experiment in shown in Table 1. We note that depending on the type of application, the amount of updates in these workloads varies (higher for CUST3).

Database	Total size (GB)	#DBs	#Tables
CUST1	10.7	31	4374
CUST2	1.4	6	48
CUST3	105.9	23	1624
CUST4	0.06	2	11

Table 1: Overview of customer databases and workloads.

As can be seen from Table 2, in all the customer workloads, the quality of DTA is comparable to the hand-tuned physical design for the CUST 1 workload. DTA is significantly better for CUST2 and CUST4. In CUST4 (which is a small database), the hand-tuned design consisted of only the primary-key and unique indexes, whereas DTA was able to considerably improve upon that design. In CUST3, the hand-tuned design was worse than the raw configuration due to presence of updates. For this workload, DTA correctly recommended no new physical design structures to be created. This experiment demonstrates DTA's ability to effectively tune real-world workloads. Finally, we note that the tuning time of DTA can vary depending on the complexity of queries in the workload. For example, in this experiment DTA tuned anywhere between 134 events/min (CUST4) to about 500 events/min (CUST2).

Workload	Quality of hand-tuned design	Quality of DTA	#events tuned	Tuning time (hr:min)
CUST1	82%	87%	15K	0:35
CUST2	6%	41%	252K	8:21
CUST3	-5%	0%	176K	15:14
CUST4	0%	50%	9K	1:07

Table 2: Quality of DTA vs. hand-tuned design on customer workloads.

7.2 Evaluation on TPC-H 10GB benchmark workload

In this experiment, we evaluate DTA on the TPC-H 10GB benchmark workload [17]. We start with a raw database (i.e., consisting of only indexes that enforce referential integrity constraints), and tune the benchmark workload consisting of 22 queries. The size of the raw database is about 12.8 GB. The expected improvement reported by DTA for this workload is 88% (the total storage space allotted was three times the raw data size). We implemented DTA's recommendations and executed the queries (warm runs). For each query, we conduct 5 warm runs, discard the highest and lowest readings and take the average of the remaining 3 readings. The actual improvement in execution time for the workload is 83%. This experiment shows that (a) DTA is able to achieve significant improvements on a workload containing complex queries; and (b) the query optimizer's estimates are reasonably accurate for this workload.

7.3 Production/Test Server Scenario

The following experiment illustrates the impact of DTA's ability to use a test server for tuning purposes. The database used for this experiment is TPC-H [17], the 1 GB configuration. TPCHQ1-I (and TPCH22-I) denotes the first query (resp. 22 queries) in TPC-H benchmark and only indexes are selected for tuning. TPCHQ1-A (and

TPCH22-A) denotes the first query (resp. all 22 queries) in TPC-H benchmark and both indexes and materialized views are considered during the process of tuning. We use a test server to tune the production server and compare the overhead on the production server to the case where we had no test server. The *overhead* is measured as the total duration (i.e., elapsed time) of all statements that were submitted to the production server by DTA. No other queries were running on the test and production servers during the period of the experiment.

Figure 3 shows that even in the simplest case of single query tuning and only indexes are considered, TPCHQ1-I, during tuning, the overhead on the production server is reduced by about 60%. For TPCH22-A the reduction is significant (90%). Note that as the complexity of tuning increases (e.g., larger workload, or more physical design features to consider) we expect the reduction in overhead to become more significant (as seen in Figure 3). We have observed similar benefits of reduced overhead for several customer workloads as well.

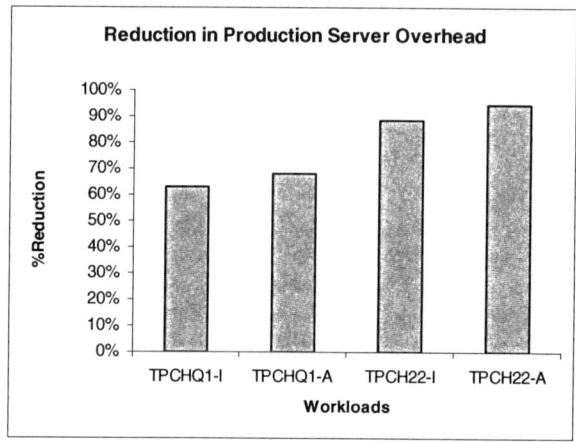

Figure 3. Reducing load on production server by exploiting test server

7.4 Effectiveness of Workload Compression

The following experiment illustrates the impact of workload compression (see Section 5.1) on the quality of DTA's recommendations as well on its running time for a few real and synthetic workloads. We use three database and workloads for this comparing (a) TPCH22 queries on TPC-H 1GB data; (b) PSOFT is a customer database (a PeopleSoft application) where the workload consists of about 6000 queries, inserts, updates and deletes, the database is about .75 GB; and (c) SYNT1 is a synthetic database that conforms to the well known SetQuery benchmark schema, and contains 8000 queries in the workload. The queries are SPJ queries with grouping and aggregation, with approximately 100 distinct "templates." Each query was generated by randomly selecting selection columns, grouping columns, aggregation columns/functions, etc.

Table 3 summarizes the results of this experiment. For TPCH22 (which contains only 22 queries), the queries in the workload are all very different and no workload compression is possible using our technique. The benefits of workload compression are much larger when we have larger workloads and this is reflected in PSOFT and SYNT1. We observe a speed up of more than a factor of 5x for the PSOFT workload and more than 40x for SYNT1. This is because these workloads have many queries but relatively few distinct *templates* (see Section 5.1). For PSOFT, DTA tunes about 10% of the number of queries in the workload, whereas for SYNT1 this was about 2%. Thus, by leveraging the ideas of workload compression, we are able to significantly improve the performance of DTA with almost no adverse impact on the quality of recommendations.

Database and Workloads	% Decrease in Quality compared to no workload compression	Reduction in Running Time of DTA compared to no workload compression
TPCH22	0	-1%
PSOFT	0.5%	5.8x
SYNT1	1%	43x

Table 3: Impact of Workload Compression on Quality and Running Time of DTA.

7.5 Impact of Reduced Statistics Creation

In this experiment we measure the reduction in statistics creation time using techniques described in Section 5.2 for two different workloads, TPC-H 10GB and PSOFT. We measure: (a) reduction in number of statistics created (b) reduction in statistics creation time. The number of statistics created was reduced by 55% for TPC-H and about 24% PSOFT. Similarly, the reduction in statistics creation time was 62% and 31%, respectively. In both of these cases there was no difference in the quality of DTA's recommendation since the above technique only reduces creation of redundant statistical information.

7.6 End-to-End comparision against ITW in SQL Server 2000 (SS2K)

The Index Tuning Wizard (ITW) in Microsoft SQL Server 2000 is one of the currently available physical design tools for Microsoft SQL Server. In this section, we conduct an end-to-end comparison of the quality and running time of DTA compared to ITW in Microsoft SQL Server 2000. We compare the overall quality of the recommendation produced by the tools, and running time of DTA compared to that of Index Tuning Wizard in Microsoft SQL Server 2000. We measure the quality by the percentage improvement in the optimizer estimated cost for the workload.

The experiments below compare the running time and quality. We use the three databases and workloads TPCH22, PSOFT and SYNT1 described in Section 7.4. To ensure a fair comparison, in this experiment, we consider only indexes and materialized views (since ITW is not capable of recommending partitioning). The comparisons were performed by running both the tools against the same server (a Microsoft SQL Server 2000 server). Figures 4 (and 5) compare the quality (resp. running time) of DTA compared to ITW in SQL Server 2000. We observe that for the same database/workload, we get comparable recommendation qualities for TPCH22, PSOFT and SYNT1 (DTA is slightly better in all cases), and DTA is significantly faster for the large workloads.

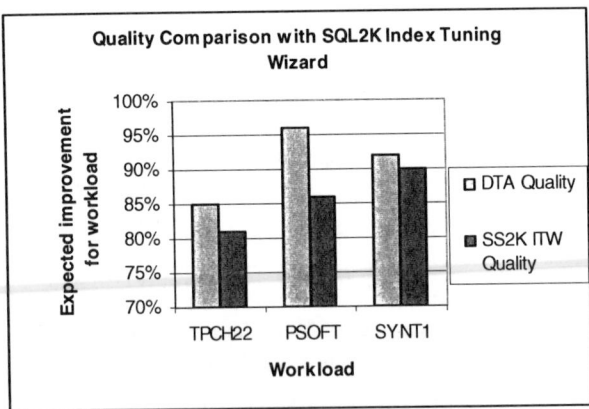

Figure 4. Quality of recommendation of DTA compared to Index Tuning Wizard for Microsoft SQL Server 2000.

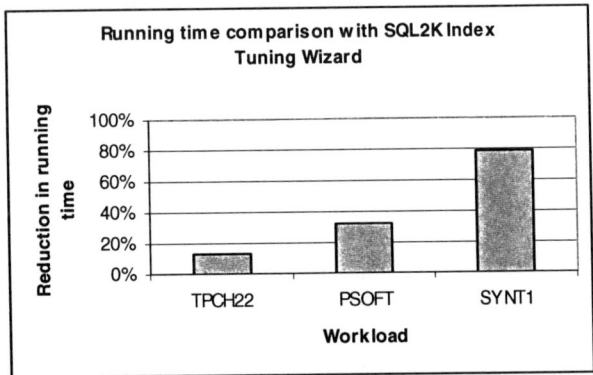

Figure 5. Running time of DTA compared to Index Tuning Wizard for Microsoft SQL Server 2000

8. Related Work

There are currently several automated physical design tools developed by commercial database vendors themselves, and by third-party tool vendors. To the best of our knowledge, the Database Tuning Advisor (DTA) for Microsoft SQL Server 2005 is the first tool with the capability of providing a fully integrated recommendation for indexes, materialized views and horizontal range partitioning, i.e., DBAs do not need to stage the selection of different physical design features.

Today's tools support tuning of different sets of physical design features. Index Tuning Wizard in Microsoft SQL Server 2000 [2] was the first tool to recommend indexes and materialized views in an integrated manner. DTA builds upon the Index Tuning Wizard and significantly advances upon it in several aspects including functionality, scalability and manageability. The algorithmic techniques underlying DTA were developed in the context of the AutoAdmin project [1] at Microsoft, whose goal is to reduce TCO by making database systems more self-tuning and self-managing.

IBM's DB2 Advisor [21] recommends indexes and materialized views, and IBM's Partition Advisor [11] recommends horizontal hash partitioning in a shared-nothing parallel database. Oracle's Index Tuning Wizard [12] and BMC's Index Advisor [6] recommend indexes. Leccotech [13] provides tools for tuning a SQL statement by recommending indexes, and also by suggesting rewritten SQL that can obtain a potentially better execution plan.

The idea of workload compression as a technique to improve scalability of workload based tuning tools was first presented in [7]. We have adapted these ideas and implemented them in the context of DTA, to obtain significant improvement in scalability for large workloads (see Section 5.1). The technique presented in Section 5.2 for reducing the redundant statistical information from a given set of statistics is complementary to the techniques presented in [10] for determining whether or not a particular statistic actually affects the plan chosen (or cost of plan chosen) by the query optimizer. Thus both of these techniques can be applied to reduce creation of unnecessary statistics. The techniques of pruning column-groups based on frequency of occurrence in the workload and cost, and algorithmic techniques for handling alignment requirements inside a physical database design tool as well as merging in the presence of horizontal partitioning were developed in the context of DTA and have been presented in [4].

Finally, there are several aspects of DTA's functionality which are the first for any physical database design tool. These include: (a) the ability to specify an alignment constraint as well as a partially specified configuration; (b) an XML schema for input/output that enhances scriptability and customizability of the tool; and (c) efficient tuning in production/test server scenarios.

9. Conclusion

As tuning tools continue to encompass more features, it is important to keep the usage of these tools simple for DBAs by providing integrated recommendations for various features when possible. Database Tuning Advisor for Microsoft SQL Server 2005 is built around a scalable architecture that makes it easy to incorporate new physical design features, while ensuring integrated recommendations. In the future, we will continue to expand the scope of DTA to include other important aspects of performance tuning.

10. Acknowledgements

We are grateful to Alex Boukouvalas, Campbell Fraser, Florian Waas, and Cesar Galindo-Legaria for helping with necessary extensions to Microsoft SQL Server 2005 for DTA. We thank Djana Milton, Maciek Sarnowicz, and Dima Sonkin who developed the GUI component of DTA.

11. References

[1] The AutoAdmin project. http://research.microsoft.com/dmx/AutoAdmin .
[2] Agrawal S., Chaudhuri S., Kollar L., and Narasayya V. Index Tuning Wizard for Microsoft SQL Server 2000. White paper. http://msdn.microsoft.com/library/techart/itwforsql.htm
[3] Agrawal, S., Chaudhuri, S., and Narasayya, V. Automated Selection of Materialized Views and Indexes for SQL Databases. Proceedings of VLDB 2000.
[4] Agrawal, S., Narasayya, V., and Yang., B. Integrating Vertical and Horizontal Partitioning Into Automated Physical Database Design. In Proceedings of ACM SIGMOD 2004.
[5] Agrawal R., and Ramakrishnan S. Fast Algorithms for Mining Association Rules for Large Databases. Proceedings of VLDB 1994.
[6] BMC Index Advisor. http://www.bmc.com .
[7] Chaudhuri S., Gupta A., and Narasayya V. Workload Compression. Proceedings of ACM SGMOD 2002.
[8] Chaudhuri, S., and Narasayya, V. An Efficient Cost-Driven Index Selection Tool for Microsoft SQL Server. VLDB 1997.
[9] Chaudhuri, S., and Narasayya, V. AutoAdmin "What-If" Index Analysis Utitlity. Proceedings of ACM SIGMOD 1998.
[10] Chaudhuri S., and Narasayya V. Automating Statistics Management for Query Optimizers. Proceedings of ICDE 2000.
[11] http://schemas.microsoft.com/sqlserver/2004/07/dta/ XML schema for physical database design used by DTA.
[12] http://otn.oracle.com/products/oracle9i/index.html.
[13] LeccoTech's Performance Optimization Solutions for Oracle. White Paper. LeccoTech Inc. http://www.leccotech.com
[14] Program for TPC-D data generation with Skew. ftp://ftp.research.microsoft.com/users/viveknar/TPCDSkew .
[15] Rao, J., Zhang, C., Lohman, G., and Megiddo, N. Automating Physical Database Design in a Parallel Database. Proceedings of the ACM SIGMOD 2002.
[16] Stohr T., Martens H.., and Rahm E.. Multi-Dimensional Aware Database Allocation for Parallel Data Warehouses. Proceedings of VLDB 2000.
[17] TPC Benchmark H. Decision Support. http://www.tpc.org
[18] Valentin, G., Zuliani, M., Zilio, D., and Lohman, G. DB2 Advisor: An Optimizer That is Smart Enough to Recommend Its Own Indexes. Proceedings of ICDE 2000.
[19] World Wide Web Consortium. Extensible Markup Language (XML). W3C Recommendation (October 2000). http://www.w3.org/XML/. Web-page, 2003.
[20] World Wide Web Consortium. XML Schema. W3C Recommendation (May 2001). http://www.w3.org/XML/Schema. Web-page, 2003.
[21] Zilio D. et al. Recommending Materialized Views and Indexes with IBM's DB2 Design Advisor. Proceedings of International Conference on Autonomic Computing, 2004.

Query Rewrite for XML in Oracle XML DB

Muralidhar Krishnaprasad, Zhen Hua Liu, Anand Manikutty, James W. Warner, Vikas Arora, Susan Kotsovolos

Oracle Corporation
400, Oracle Parkway
Redwood Shores, CA 94065
USA

{Muralidhar.Krishnaprasad, Zhen.Liu, Anand.Manikutty, Jim.Warner, Vikas.Arora, Susan.Kotsovolos}@oracle.com

Abstract

Oracle XML DB integrates XML storage and querying using the Oracle relational and object relational framework. It has the capability to physically store XML documents by shredding them as relational or object relational data, and creating logical XML documents using SQL/XML publishing functions. However, querying XML in a relational or object relational database poses several challenges. The biggest challenge is to efficiently process queries against XML in a database whose fundamental storage is table-based and whose fundamental query engine is tuple- oriented. In this paper, we present the **'XML Query Rewrite'** technique used in Oracle XML DB. This technique integrates querying XML using XPath embedded inside SQL operators and SQL/XML publishing functions with the object relational and relational algebra. A common set of **algebraic rules** is used to reduce both XML and object queries into their relational equivalent. This enables a large class of XML queries over XML type tables and views to be transformed into their semantically equivalent relational or object relational queries. These queries are then amenable to classical relational optimisations yielding XML query performance comparable to relational. Furthermore, this rewrite technique lays out a foundation to enable rewrite of XQuery [1] over XML.

1. Introduction

XML processing in the Oracle XML DB is based on the XMLType datatype. This is a native datatype introduced in Oracle 8i [4]. Built using the object relational infrastructure, the XMLType is similar to other built-in datatypes such as number and character. Various XML related operations are supported on the XMLType. These are useful for shredding the XML data to relational and object relational data, for traversing the XML content using XPath notation, or for generating XML from relational and object relational data. [2]

In particular, users can create tables of XMLType storing all XML document instances conforming to a particular XMLSchema [11] registered in Oracle XML DB. This is referred to as XMLSchema-based storage where the XMLType instances are stored in a shredded form in object-relational columns. The object relational types and columns are generated when the XML schema is registered [5]. **Collection elements** (elements with maximum occurrences greater than one) can be stored inline as a variable array (VARRAY) of object instances or stored in a separate collection table.

Users can also convert existing relational data into logical XML values using views. Oracle XML DB supports the SQL/XML standard [3,12,13] which allows users to leverage a set of SQL/XML publishing functions, such as *XMLElement, XMLAgg, XMLForest*, and *XMLConcat* to flexibly generate XMLType instances from the relational data. *XMLAgg* is an important aggregate function for concatenating a rowset of XML values through a relational query.

To query XML tables or views, Oracle XML DB provides a set of functions, such as *Extract, ExistsNode*, and *Extractvalue* that use XPath to locate and extract data from XML documents [2]. Users can then use SQL/XML publishing functions to construct new XML nodes. Collection of XML values can be un-nested using the table function, *XMLSequence* that converts a list of XML elements into multiple rows.

A simple approach to querying XML in a database is to first materialize the entire XMLType instance as a DOM and then use an XPath engine to traverse the DOM. However, this solution is very expensive due to the cost of materializing the entire XML, and is foreign for a

---

Permission to copy without fee all or part of this material is granted provided that the copies are not made or distributed for direct commercial advantage, the VLDB copyright notice and the title of the publication and its date appear, and notice is given that copying is by permission of the Very Large Data Base Endowment. To copy otherwise, or to republish, requires a fee and/or special permission from the Endowment
**Proceedings of the 30th VLDB Conference,
Toronto, Canada, 2004**

relational engine, which is designed to process tuple-oriented data instead of tree-oriented XML data.

A key observation is that since the XML is constructed logically through the underlying relational data in Oracle XML DB, it is feasible to rewrite the XPath navigation to select just the underlying data that is needed for the construction of the result. Further, XPath predicates can be transformed to predicates on the underlying relational tables. Thus, the original query over XML can be logically rewritten into an equivalent relational query. This can be then optimized by a standard relational optimizer, for instance, by picking the best join order and index on the underlying tables.

This approach, referred to as **'XML Query Rewrite'**, enables Oracle XML DB to transform XML queries into their equivalent relational queries. The theme of this paper is to show the framework that we use in Oracle XMLDB to perform such rewrites.

The rest of this paper is organized as follows. Section 2 provides examples of querying XML in Oracle XDB. Section 3 gives an overview of XML query rewrite. Section 4 discusses XPath transformation to SQL operators. Section 5 discusses operator tree optimizations with SQL/XML normalization and optimization algebra rules. Section 6 discusses the integration with view merging. Section 7 discusses performance experiments. Section 8 discusses related work. Section 9 discusses future direction and section 10 concludes the paper.

2. XML Query Motivating Examples

2.1 Querying an XML view constructed via SQL/XML function

Oracle XML DB enables users to create a view of XML type instances via SQL/XML publishing functions over relational tables. Consider a classic case of the *dept* and *emp* tables. The *dept* table keeps track of all the departments and *emp* table keeps track of all employees. The *deptno* column of the *emp* table is a foreign key referencing the *deptno* column of the *dept* table. The content of the *dept* and *emp* tables are shown in table 1 and table 2.

Deptno	Dname	loc
10	ACCOUNTING	NEW YORK
40	OPERATIONS	BOSTON

Table 1 - content of dept table

empno	ename	job	sal	deptno
7782	CLARK	MANAGER	2450	10
7839	KING	PRESIDENT	5000	10
7934	MILLER	CLERK	1300	10
7954	SMITH	VP	4900	40

Table 2 - content of emp table

To generate XML from the relational tables *dept* and *emp*, we create a view *dept_xmlview* as shown in table 3:

```
CREATE VIEW dept_xmlview AS
SELECT XMLElement("Department",
        XMLAttributes(deptno as "Deptno"),
    XMLElement("DeptInfo",
       XMLForest(dname as "DepartName", loc as "Location")),
    (SELECT XMLAgg(XMLElement("Employee",
           XMLAttributes(empno as "Empid"),
       XMLForest(ename as "EmpName", job as "Job", sal as "Salary")))
     FROM emp e
     WHERE e.deptno = d.deptno)) AS department
FROM dept d
```

Table 3- SQL/XML constructed XML view dept_xmlview

This view generates two rows of XMLType instances as shown in table 4. For each row in the *dept* table, it uses the SQL/XML standard publishing functions to construct an XMLType instance. The SQL query containing *XMLAgg* is a correlated scalar subquery that aggregates the XML information from the *emp* table. Thus, for each *dept* row, the relevant *emp* rows are retrieved and converted into a collection of *employee* elements.

```
<Department Deptno="10">
 <DeptInfo>
  <DepartName>ACCOUNTING</DepartName>
  <Location>NEW YORK</Location>
 </DeptInfo>
 <Employee Empid="7782">
  <EmpName>CLARK</EmpName>
  <Job>MANAGER</Job>
  <Salary>2450</Salary>
 </Employee>
 <Employee Empid="7839">
  <EmpName>KING</EmpName>
  <Job>PRESIDENT</Job>
  <Salary>5000</Salary>
 </Employee>
 <Employee Empid="7934">
  <EmpName>MILLER</EmpName>
  <Job>CLERK</Job>
  <Salary>1300</Salary>
 </Employee>
</Department>
<Department Deptno="40">
 <DeptInfo>
  <DepartName>OPERATIONS</DepartName>
  <Location>BOSTON</Location>
 </DeptInfo>
 <Employee Empid=7954>
  <EmpName>SMITH</EmpName>
  <Job>VP</Job>
  <Salary>4900</Salary>
 </Employee>
</Department>
```

Table 4 - Two rows of XMLType instances from *dept_xmlview*

Example 1: Consider an XML query shown in table 5 that finds all the rows in *dept_xmlview* where the Deptno attribute is 10. This can be expressed in XPath as '/Department[@Deptno=10]'. The query further extracts the DeptInfo element for each such Department.

```
select Extract(department, '/Department/DeptInfo')
from dept_xmlview v
where ExistsNode(department, '/Department[@Deptno= 10]') = 1
```
Table 5 - Query dept_xmlview example 1

This query uses the *Extract* and *ExistsNode* functions with XPath to query the XML instances from *dept_xmlview*. These are Oracle XMLDB specific SQL functions that allow querying XML instances. *ExistsNode* checks for the existence of the node(s) targeted by the XPath expression and returns 1 or 0 depending on whether the XPath identifies any nodes in the document. The *Extract* function returns an XMLType consisting of the resultant nodes from applying the XPath expression on the source XML instance. It returns NULL if there are no nodes found by the XPath expression. The advantage of *ExistsNode* is that it allows short circuit evaluation if a node is found, whereas the *Extract* function has to find and return all matching nodes. The above query returns one row containing XMLType instance as shown in table 6:

```
<DeptInfo>
  <DepartName>ACCOUNTING</DepartName>
  <Location>NEW YORK</Location>
</DeptInfo>
```
Table 6 - Result from query example 1

A straightforward evaluation of the query first materializes the contents of *dept_xmlview* by constructing the XMLType instances and then evaluates the *ExistsNode* function by evaluating the XPath '/Department[@Deptno=10]'. If the *ExistsNode* returns 1, then it evaluates the *Extract* function by evaluating the XPath '/Department/DeptInfo'. An optimal evaluation plan, however, exploits the fact that the XPath '/Department[@Deptno=10]' maps to a predicate on the underlying *deptno* column of the *dept* table and the XPath '/Department/DeptInfo' maps to the XML node constructed by the function *XMLElement("DeptInfo", ...)*. The query can then be evaluated using a simple relational query shown in table 7. Note that this rewritten query does not contain any XPath functions.

```
select XMLElement(("DeptInfo",
    XMLForest(dname as "DepartName", loc as "Location"))
from dept
where deptno = 10
```
Table 7 - Rewritten query for query example 1

Oracle XML DB uses this optimal evaluation plan by rewriting the query in Example 1 to the query shown in Table 7 using the **XML Query Rewrite** technique. The rewritten query in table 7 is a relational query on the relational table and the standard relational optimizer can select the index on the *deptno* column of the *dept* table to speed up the query. The execution plan for example 1 query is shown below in table 8.

```
>SELECT STATEMENT
 >TABLE ACCESS BY INDEX ROWID (DEPT)
   >INDEX UNIQUE SCAN   (INDEX ON DEPT.DEPTNO)
   >- access("DEPTNO"=10)
```
Table 8 - Execution Plan for query example 1

Example 1 query only involves XPath traversal on non-collection elements. Here we show another rewrite example where the XPath traversal involves a collection element *Employee*.

Example 2: Consider the XML query shown in table 9. It finds all XML instances in *dept_xmlview* where there exists a node satisfying the XPath expression '/Department/Employee[@Empid=7839]'. For such XML instances, it extracts the '/Department/DeptInfo/Location' node and attaches it to a new *Department* element node constructed by the *XMLElement* function.

```
select XMLElement("Department",
    Extract(v.department, '/Department/DeptInfo/Location'))
from dept_xmlview v
where ExistsNode(v.department, '/Department/Employee[@Empid= 7839]') =1
```
Table 9 - Query dept_xmlview example 2

This XML query returns one row containing the XMLType instance shown in table 10:

```
<Department>
  <Location>NEW YORK</Location>
</Department>
```
Table 10 - Result from query example 2

Again, the optimal way to evaluate the query is to map the XPath predicate as a SQL predicate on the *empid* column of the *emp* table and map the XPath '/Department/DeptInfo/Location' to the *XMLForest* node on the *loc* column of the *dept* table. Oracle XMLDB also rewrites this query and evaluates it as a relational query as shown in table 11.

```
select XMLElement("DeptInfo",
    XMLForest(loc as "Location"))
from emp, dept
where empno = 7839 and emp.deptno = dept.deptno
```
Table 11 - Rewritten query for query example 2

We now show how to convert a forest of collection element nodes into a virtual SQL table using the *XMLSequence* table function and how they get rewritten.

Example 3: Here is an XML query to list the department name and the names of the employees that are in that department.

```
select extractValue(v.department, '/Department/DeptInfo/DepartName'),
    extractValue(value(v2), '/Employee/EmpName')
from dept_xmlview v,
```

1124

```
table(XMLSequence(Extract(v.department, '/Department/Employee')))
  v2
```
Table 12 - Query dept_xmlview example 3

This query returns the set of rows shown in table 13.

ACCOUNTING	CLARK
ACCOUTING	KING
ACCOUNTING	MILLER
OPERATIONS	SMITH

Table 13 - Result from example 3 query

The *Extract*value function is similar to **Extract** but returns only scalar values. This is a type aware function and returns the appropriate type (NUMBER, DATE etc.) based on the XMLSchema type information, or the underlying SQL expression information, if available, at query compilation time. In this particular example all the title elements are simple strings, so the result is of type VARCHAR2.

XMLSequence is a SQL function that takes an XMLType containing a forest of XML element nodes and transforms it to a collection of XMLType instances. The TABLE function can then be used to convert the collection of XML into multiple rows. Multiple correlated TABLE functions containing XMLSequence and *Extract* expressions can be used to un-nest the hierarchical information contained in the XML document. The query is optimized into a simple relational query (shown in table 14) over the underlying relational tables contained in the *dept_xmlview*.

```
select dname, ename
from dept d , emp e
where d.deptno = e.deptno
```
Table 14 - Rewritten query for example 3 query

All previous query examples are on an XML view constructed via SQL/XML functions. We now show the examples of XMLType table storing XMLType instances conforming to an XML schema.

2.2 Querying schema based XML table examples

We first define an XML schema '*http://www.oracle.com/dept.xsd*' as shown in table 15 and have registered it with the Oracle XML DB. Then we create an XMLType table *dept_xmltab* containing XMLType instances that conform to the '*http://www.oracle.com/dept.xsd*' schema as shown in table 16. The table *dept_xmltab* table now contains the hidden columns designated as *deptid_hc, deptname_hc, deptloc_hc* for storing the *department id, name, location* values and the collection of employees are stored as a separate storage table *emp_col_tab*. The object relational infrastructure is used to create object types, collection types and subtypes to reflect the various XML Schema constructs. See reference [5] for more details on schema-based storage.

```
<schema xmlns="http://www.w3.org/2001/XMLSchema"
   targetNamespace="http://www.oracle.com/dept.xsd" version="1.0"
   xmlns:xdb="http://xmlns.oracle.com/xdb"
   elementFormDefault="qualified">
  <element name "Department">
   <complexType>
    <sequence>
     <element name = "DeptInfo">
      <complexType>
       <sequence>
        <element name = "DepartName" type = "string"/>
        <element name = "Location" type = "string"/>
       </sequence>
      </complexType>
     </element>
     <element name = "Employee" maxOccurs = "unbounded">
      <complexType>
       <sequence>
        <element name = "EmpName" type = "string"/>
        <element name = "Job" type = "string"/>
        <element name = "Salary" type = "positiveInteger"/>
       </sequence>
       <attribute name="Empid" type="positiveInteger"/>
      </complexType>
     </element>
    </sequence>
    <attribute name="Deptno" type="positiveInteger"/>
   </complexType>
  </element>
</schema>
```
Table 15 - dept.xsd XML schema

```
create table dept_xmltab of xmltype
   xmltype store as object relational
   xmlschema "http://www.oracle.com/dept.xsd" element "Department"
```
Table 16 - dept_xmltab schema based XML table

When XMLType instances are inserted into the *dept_xmltab* table, they are appropriately shredded and the values are inserted into the underlying hidden columns of *dept_xmltab* and *emp_col_tab*. The collection table internally has a hidden column *nested_table_id* to join with the hidden *set_id* column of the parent table *dept_xmltab*.

XML queries on the XMLType table *dept_xmltab* are optimized through the rewrite technique similar to those on *dept_xmlview* view as shown in examples 1, 2 and 3.

Example 4: The equivalent of the query in example 1 on the *dept_xmltab* and its rewritten counterpart are shown in table 17. For the rewritten query, *mkxml* is a SQL primitive operator converting an object type instance constructed by the object constructor (*ocons*) into XML.

```
select Extract(value(t), '/Department/DeptInfo',
  'xmlns="http://www.oracle.com/dept.xsd"')
from dept_xmltab t
where ExistsNode(value(t), '/Department[@Deptno = 10]',
  'xmlns="http://www.oracle.com/dept.xsd"') = 1
select mkxml(ocons('deptInfo', t.deptname_hc, t.deptloc_hc),...)
from dept_xmltab t
```

where t.deptno_hc = 10

Table 17 – Query on dept_xmltab table example 4

Example 5: The equivalent of the query in example 2 on the *dept_xmltab* and its rewritten counterpart are shown in table 18.

select XMLElement("Department",
    Extract(value(t), '/Department/DeptInfo/Location',
      'xmlns="http://www.oracle.com/dept.xsd"'))
from dept_xmltab t
where ExistsNode(value(t), '/Department/Employee[@Empid = 7839]',
    'xmlns="http://www.oracle.com/dept.xsd"') =1

select XMLElement("Department", mkxml(deptloc_hc,...)) from emp_col_tab col, dept_xmltab as t where col. empid = 7839 and col.nested_tabl_id=t.set_id

Table 18 – Query on dept_xmltab table example 5

Example 6:. Equivalent of example 3 query on *dept_xmltab* and its rewritten query are shown in table 19.

select extractValue(value(t), '/Department/DeptInfo/DepartName',
    'xmlns="http://www.oracle.com/dept.xsd"'),
    extractValue(value(t2), '/Employee/EmpName',
    'xmlns="http://www.oracle.com/dept.xsd"')
from dept_xmltab t,
    table(XMLSequence(Extract(value(t),
        '/Department/Employee',
        'xmlns="http://www.oracle.com/dept.xsd"'))) t2

select t.deptname_hc, col.empname from dept_xmltab t, emp_col_tab col where col.nested_table_id = t.set_id

Table 19 – Query on dept_xmltab table example 6

3. XML Query Rewrite Overview

As shown in the previous examples, the XML Query Rewrite technique rewrites XPath operations to XML data, which is physically stored relationally, to directly operate on the underlying data. This enables further optimizations by the classic relational optimizer in terms of optimal index access methods and join-order, and thus avoids the need to physically materialize the XML in memory.

The query rewrite happens at query compilation time. After a query passes through the parser, semantic analyzer and pre-type checking phases, it is internally represented as a query tree composed of query blocks and operator trees. We walk through all the query blocks to identify XPaths in every *Extract, Extractvalue* and *ExistsNode* function and convert them into SQL operator trees with possible subquery blocks. The query tree is then further optimized through view merging and subquery to join conversion and operator tree optimization. The resultant query tree is then given to the relational optimizer, which generates the execution plan for the execution engine. Figure 1 shows the logic flow of rewrite during the query compilation phases.

The key to implementing this query rewrite idea is to develop a new set of primitive SQL operators for XPath navigation and SQL/XML publishing functions. Some of the operators are directly exposed to the user while others are not. We have also developed a new set of algebra rules to optimize those primitive SQL operators. The new operators and their algebra rules are directly integrated with the existing relational and object relational algebra in Oracle. Since the backbone storage of the XML is relational or object relational, this approach leverages the existing relational and object relational algebra framework.

The XML Query rewrite technique consists of the following key modules:
- XML input analysis
- XPath Expansion based on input XML meta-data
- XPath step meta-data annotation
- XPath transformation to the SQL operator tree
- SQL/XML publishing function normalization
- Operator tree optimization based on a new set of XML operator algebra rules.

The technique also integrates with relational algebra rules for view merging, object relational algebra rules for object construction and attribute access, and collection view merging.

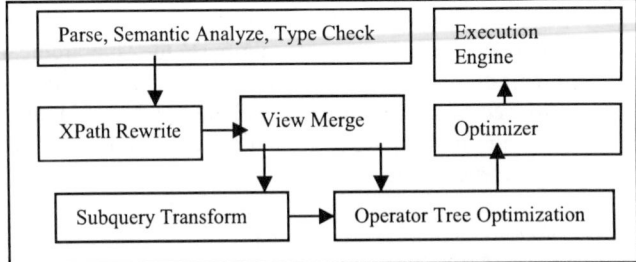

Figure 1 - Query Rewrite Logic Flow

4. XPath Rewrite

4.1 XML Input Analysis

During the compilation of a query, we examine the XML input to each XML Query function, *Extract, ExistsNode* and *Extract*value, and rewrite them if the underlying XML input data satisfies one of the following criteria:
- The input XML is stored in a schema-based XMLType table or column.
- The input XML is generated by an object view using an XML generation function that relies on the default mapping of object-relational data to XML.
- The input XML is generated from standard SQL/XML publishing functions, such as *XMLElement, XMLAgg*, and *XMLForest*.
- The input XML is from a view column, which is constructed on top of the above three cases.

We do not do rewrite if the underlying XML input structure is opaque to the query compiler, such as when the input XML is CLOB based storage or generated from arbitrary user defined functions returning XMLType. The idea is that we need to know the meta-data that describes the structure of the input XML in order to optimize the XPath operation on top of it. The **input XML meta-data** itself, on the other hand, can be very flexible - it can be an XML schema annotated with shredding information of the mapping object meta-data and object relational table, or merely object meta-data descriptor, or an arbitrary SQL/XML operator tree constructing the XML input. For an XML input whose structure is opaque, the user can still use a functional index or a text index to do query optimization. However, the discussion of optimization using a functional or text index is beyond the scope of this paper.

4.2 XPath Expansion based on input XML meta-data

For each XPath that is a compile time constant used in the *Extract*, *ExistsNode* and *Extractvalue* functions, we expand the XPath if it contains wildcard character matching and double slash abbreviation based on the meta-data information of the input XML that we gathered from the input XML analysis . We expand the double slash into its constituents. For example, an XPath *'/a//d'* can be rewritten as *'/a/b/c/d'* if we know from the meta-data that all the possible elements between element *'a'* and element *'d'* is element *'b'* followed by element *'c'*. We also expand wildcard character '*' based on meta-data information. For example, the XPath *'/a/b/*/d'* is rewritten to *'/a/b/c/d'*.

4.3 XPath Step Meta-data Annotation

After the expansion of the XPath, we annotate each step of an XPath with the meta-data from the underlying input XML meta-data. The meta-data of an XPath element may contain the object attribute meta-data to which this element is mapped or a sub-tree of the SQL/XML operator tree from which this element is constructed.

The XPath step meta-data also indicates whether this step is feasible. For example, for an XPath *'a/b'*, if *'b'* is not a possible child element of element *'a'* based on the meta-data, then the element *'b'* step is marked as a not feasible step. A non-feasible step is transformed to the SQL NULL constant in the subsequent 'XPath Transformation to SQL operator tree' section.

We annotate each element step with the element cardinality information. This information can be used by other XPath transform functions to determine if the element is a collection or scalar element. For example, for an XPath step that matches the element *'employee'*, if the maximum occurrences property for that element in the XML schema is more than 1 or it maps to a collection object type, then element *'employee'* is a collection element. With neither an XML schema nor an object descriptor, we can derive this information from the input SQL/XML operator tree. For example, if the *'employee'* element is constructed by applying *XMLAgg* to a set of rows as a query *'select XMLAgg(XMLElement("employee"...)) from emp'* or is constructed from an *XMLConcat* expression, such as *'XMLConcat(XMLElement("employee" ,'Miller'), XMLElement("employee", 'Smith'))'*, then the element is a collection element.

4.4 XPath Transformation to SQL operator tree

After we finish the annotation of meta-data of each XPath step, we transform the entire XPath into a SQL operator tree. The transformation engine walks through the input XPath expression and recursively applies the following rewrite functions depending on the node type of the XPath expression tree. The rewrite functions are

- Rewrite of XPath steps
- Rewrite of XPath predicates
- Rewrite of XPath expressions, such as relation operators, logical operators, arithmetic operators and XPath built-in functions.

4.4.1 Rewrite of XPath Steps

We convert each step of element or attribute extraction into a primitive SQL operator that extracts that node out of the underlying construction XML operator. If the element is a collection element, we further expand the result of the extraction into a subquery block, which represents the selection of a logical table formed by the conversion of collection elements into relational rows. The purpose of transforming XPath steps into a SQL operator tree along with subquery blocks is that when they are applied to the input XML construction SQL operator tree by the operator tree optimization and view merge module, many operators can be cancelled so that an optimal operator tree is derived.

The SQL extraction operators are primitive SQL operators, *XATG* and *OATG*. If the element is constructed from a SQL/XML operator tree, then *XATG* is used. For example, *Extract(XMLElement("foo", 3), './foo'* is transformed into *XATG(XMLElement("foo", 3), '.', 'foo')*, which can be further optimized by the operator tree optimization module into just *XMLElement("foo", 3)*. *XATG* is a primitive SQL operator not exposed to the user. Semantically, *XATG(xmltype, '.', 'A')* is equivalent to *Extract(xmltype,'A')* and *XATG(XATG(xmltype, '.', 'A'), 'A', 'B')* is equivalent to *Extract(xmltype, A/B')*.

If the element is constructed from object relational data, then the *OATG* operator is used. For example,
Extract(MKXML(OCONS('obj', attr1Val, attr2Val)), 'attr2')
is transformed into
(MKXML(OATG(OCONS('obj', attr1Val, attr2Val), 'attr2')).

This can be further optimized by the operator tree optimization module into just *MKXML(attr2Val)*. Here the *OCONS* is an object constructor SQL operator which constructs an object of type 'obj' containing two attributes 'attr1' and 'attr2' and the *MKXML* is a SQL operator which converts an object value instance into an XMLType instance value. Details of these SQL operators, such as *MKXML, OCONS* and *OATG*, are discussed in Section 5.4.

For the extraction of collection elements, we also form a subquery block that represents a selection from a logical table. For schema based XML or XML formed by object relational data, the logical table is either the physical storage table for the collection object if the collection object is stored out of line or constructed via conversion of a collection object type instances into a tuple stream if the collection object is stored inline with the main table. For SQL/XML generated XML, the logical table is mapped to the result of the SQL query that contains the *XMLAgg*. This subquery block can then be view merged into the parent query block recursively through the relational view merge and collection view merge process. Consequently, this logical table does not have to be materialized at run time.

4.4.2 Rewrite of XPath Predicates

XPath predicates are transformed into SQL predicates. In the case of predicates on collection elements, the SQL predicate created is attached to the subquery created corresponding to the collection element. This effectively pushes down the predicate to the source table so that the relational optimizer can do its optimization job.

XPath predicates on scalar elements are transformed into SQL CASE expressions where are further optimized using algebra rules that are applied by the operator tree optimization module.

4.4.3 Rewrite of XPath Expressions

We transform XPath operators, such as logical operators, arithmetic operators, relational operators, etc, into their equivalent SQL operators. We also transform XPath built-in functions into their equivalent SQL functions. Most of these transformations are straightforward. The principle here is that if we do not find an equivalent SQL operator, we can create one that implements the semantics required by the XPath. This is an advantage of rewriting these XML queries inside the database server since we can always extend it with new SQL operators. It also enables us to expose PL/SQL and other SQL functions as XPath functions.

The XPath comparison operators, such as equality, greater-than, lesser-than etc., have existence semantics if either of their arguments are collection elements. From the XPath step meta-data, we know if the step results in a collection element or not. So, for an XPath predicate containing the comparison operator, such as '*[b = c]*', we transform it differently depending on the element cardinality.

- If both element '*b*' and element '*c*' are scalar elements, then this is transformed into the equivalent SQL '=' operator.

- If both element '*b*' and element '*c*' are collection elements, then this is transformed into an EXISTS SQL operator with a subquery block testing the existence relationship. So it is transformed into

  EXISTS (select null from collection_b
     where EXISTS (
      select null from collection_c
      where collection_b.column_value =
       collection_c.column_value).

- If one element is a scalar and the other element is a collection, (say '*b*' is scalar element), then it is transformed into

  EXISTS(select null from collection_c
     where collection_c.column_value = b).

For input to logical operators, such as AND and OR, we again convert the subquery input which represents collection elements into *EXISTS* SQL operator representing existential check.

Rewriting into exists subquery blocks enables further transformation into semi-joins by the regular relational subquery transformations.

After an XPath is transformed into SQL operators for the *Extract* function, the rewrite is done. For *ExistsNode*, we apply a final SQL operator to compute the effective boolean value of the result XML. If the result XML is a collection element node, then we apply EXISTS SQL operator, otherwise, we apply the SQL *CASE* operator. For *ExtractValue*, we apply a final SQL operator that atomizes the node by extracting the text value and cast it into an appropriate SQL type.

We also handle the rewrite of query over XML with XML schema having Choice, substitution groups and inheritance construct by exploiting object type inheritance, SQL CASE and TREAT operators. However, the discussion of such is beyond the scope of this paper.

5. Operator Tree Optimization

Algorithmically, operator tree optimization is an algebraic transformation of the operator tree by applying a set of algebraic rules for each operator node in the tree. We do this recursively, from bottom up, so that an optimal operator tree is derived. Optimization arises from the elimination of unnecessary operator nodes and overall simplification in the operator tree. The extraction and generation operators can be cancelled when the two operators are the inverse of each other. Operator nodes of the XML generation tree that are not selected by the XPath are also eliminated. Consequently, the operator tree is reduced down to a minimal set of operator nodes that are needed to compute the query result.

For each SQL operator, we define a set of algebraic rules to optimize the operator. The algebraic rules fall into the following categories:

- **Nullification rule:** The nullification rule is cost-reductive because it simplifies the operator if any argument to the operator is SQL NULL. The nullification rule usually simplifies the operator by replacing it with NULL, if all the arguments are NULL, or by eliminating any arguments that are NULL.

- **Elimination rule:** This rule is cost-reductive because it eliminates unnecessary intermediate operators.

- **Distribution rule**: This rule applies an operator *f* to another operator *g* by distributing operator *f* to all the children of operator *g*.

- **Cancellation rule:** This rule cancels two operators that are the inverse of each other.

- **Normalization rule:** Normalization does not reduce the number of SQL operators in the operator tree, however it canonicalizes all the syntax exposed to the user to the low-level operators so that fewer algebra rules need to be added into the system. Thus, the operator tree optimization needs to deal with fewer possible cases of input operators. This is especially useful when a language provides a large number of high-level syntactic variations to the users.

5.1 SQL/XML publishing function normalization

We normalize SQL/XML publishing functions into a set of primitive SQL operators that generate XML. Normalization is to transform user-exposed functions, such as a SQL/XML publishing function, into an operator tree composed of primitive SQL operators. The higher-level operators can be viewed effectively as syntactic sugar for the primitive operators.

Consider the SQL/XML function *XMLForest*. *XMLForest* examines each input argument expression, and if the argument expression is not null, then a new *XMLElement* node is formed with the input tag name, otherwise, the result is null. The rest is *XMLConcat* applied on each of the new *XMLElement* nodes. For example, the expression *XMLForest(name as "DeptName", location as "DeptLocation")* generates the following XML fragment if *name* column value is '*Engineering*' but *location* column value is NULL: *<DeptName>Engineering</DeptName>*.

The above *XMLForest* expression can be syntactically transformed into the following equivalent:
```
XMLConcat(
    CASE WHEN name IS NOT NULL, THEN
        XMLElement("DeptName", name) ELSE NULL END,
    CASE WHEN location IS NOT NULL THEN
        XMLElement("DeptLocation", location) ELSE NULL END)
```

5.2 New SQL/XML Algebra Rules

In the examples below, we designate *XE, XC, XAG, CS,* and *INN* to represent the SQL functions *XMLElement, XMLConcat, XMLAgg, CASE WHEN,* and *IS NOT NULL* respectively. We use "*T*" and "*U*" to represent XML element tag name, *e* to represent an expression, and *c* to represent conditional expression. For example, *XMLElement("T", e_1, .., e_n)* is represented as *XE("T", e_1, .., e_n)*. *CASE WHEN c_1 THEN e_1 WHEN c_2 THEN e_2 ELSE e_d END* is represented as *CS(c_1, e_1, c_2, e_2, e_d)*.

Note that the list in this section is not exhaustive – it is a subset, and is meant to provide a flavor of the algebraic rules used in Oracle XML DB.

The second column of the tables of algebraic rules uses the following abbreviations for the classification of algebraic rules: N: Nullification Rule; E: Elimination Rule; D: Distribution Rule; O: Normalization Rule

5.2.2 Algebraic rules for *XMLElement*

XE("T", NULL) = XE(T)	N1	If the input argument to XMLElement is SQL NULL itself, then it merely creates an element with empty content
XE("T", e_1, .., NULL, .. e_n) = XE("T", e_1, ... e_n)	N2	If any of the input argument to XMLElement is NULL, then that argument can be eliminated from the input
XE("T", e_1, .., XC(e_i, .., e_j), . e_n) = XE("T", e_1, .., e_i, .., e_j, .. e_n)	E1	If any input argument to XMLElement is XMLConcat, then all the arguments to XMLConcat can be merged into the parent XMLElement as its argument. The intermediate XMLConcat operator is eliminated.

5.2.3 Algebraic rules for *XMLForest*

XMLFOREST(e_1 as "T_1", .., e_n as "T_n") = XC(CS(INN(e_1), XE("T_1", e_1), NULL), .., CS(INN(e_n), XE("T_n", e_n), NULL))	O1	Normalize XMLForest into XMLConcat of CASE of XMLElement

5.2.4 Algebraic rules for *XMLConcat*

XC(NULL) = NULL	N1	If the input argument t to XMLConcat is SQL NULL itself, then the output is SQL NULL.
XC(e_1, .., NULL, .. e_n) = XC(e_1, .., e_n)	N2	If any of the input arguments to XMLConcat is NULL, then that argument can be eliminated from the input
XC(e_1, .., XC(e_i, .., e_j), .., e_n) = XC(e_1, .., e_i, .., e_j, .., e_n)	E1	If any input argument to XMLConcat is XMLConcat, then all the arguments to XMLConcat can be merged into the parent XMLConcat as its argument. The intermediate XMLConcat function is eliminated.
XC(e) = e	E2	XC with single input argument can be

5.2.5 Algebraic rules for the XATG operator

XATG(NULL, "T", "U") = NULL	N1	If the input argument t to XATG is SQL NULL itself, then the output is SQL NULL.
XATG(XE("T", e), '.', 'T') = XE("T", e)	E1	This rule eliminates the XATG operator.
XATG(XE("T_1", e), 'T_1', 'T_2') = XATG(e, '.', 'T_2')	E2	This rule eliminates the XMLElement function. "e" is assumed to be an XMLType
XATG(XE("T", e), '.', 'T_1') = NULL	E3	This rule eliminates the XATG and XE operators because tag 'T' and 'T_1' does not match
XATG(XC(e_1, .., e_n), 'T', 'U') = XC(XATG(e_1, 'T', 'U'), .., XATG(e_m, 'T', 'U'))	D1	This rule distributes XATG operator to all the arguments to XMLConcat function.
XATG(CS(c_1, e_1, .., c_n, e_n, e_d), 'T', 'U') = CS(c_1, XATG(e_1, 'T', 'U'), .., c_n, XATG(e_m, 'T', 'U'), XATG(e_d, 'T', 'U'))	D2	This rule distributes XATG operator to all the branches of a CASE operator.
XATG(XAGG(e), 'T', 'U') = XAGG(XATG(e, 'T', 'U'))	D3	This rule distributes XATG operator to the argument of XAGG.

5.2.6 Algebraic rules for IS NOT NULL (INN) expression

INN(NULL) = false	N1	If the input argument t to INN is SQL NULL itself, then the output is false.
INN(not_null_e) = true	E2	If the input argument to INN is a not null expression (such as a non-nullable column), then the output is true.

5.2.7 Algebraic rules for CASE expressions (CS)

CS(true, e_1, e_2) = e_1	E1	Eliminates the CS operator when the case value is known to be true.
CS(false, e_1, e_2) = e_2	E2	Eliminates the CS operator when the case value is known to be false.
CS(c, e, e) = e	E3	Eliminates the CS operator when the branched expressions are equivalent.

5.3 Example of operator tree optimization by application of algebraic rules

Assume *colb* is a nullable column and *colc* is a non-nullable column. The following is an example to show how *Extract(XMLElement("a", XMLForest(colb as "b", colc as "c")), './a/c')* is optimized to just *XMLElement("c", colc)* by applying the algebraic rules.

- Applying normalization of *XMLForest* and transformation of XPath into XATG operators yields:
  XATG(XATG(XE("a", XC(CS(INN(colb), XE("b", colb), NULL), CS(INN(colc), XE("c", colc), NULL))), '.', 'a'), 'a', 'c')

- Applying INN-E2 and CS-E1 (note *colc* is not a nullable column) yields:
  XATG(XATG(XE("a", XC(CS(INN(colb), XE("b", colb), NULL), XE("c", colc))), '.', 'a'), 'a', 'c')

- Applying XATG-E1 to eliminate the inner XATG yields:
  XATG(XE("a", XC(CS(INN(colb), XE("b", colb), NULL), XE("c", colc))), 'a', 'c').

- Applying XATG-E2 to eliminate the outer XE yields:
  XATG(XC(CS(INN(colb), XE("b", colb), NULL), XE("c", colc)), '.', 'c')

- Applying XATG distribution rules XATG-D1 and XATG-D2, and XATG-N1 yields:
  XC(CS(INN(colb), XATG(XE("b", colb), '.', 'c'), NULL), XATG(XE("c", colc), '.', 'c'))

- Applying XATG-E3 to eliminate the first XATG and XATG E1 rule to eliminate the second XATG yields:
  XC(CS(INN(colb), NULL, NULL), XE("c", colc))

- Applying CS-E3 yields:
  XC(NULL, XE("c", colc))

- Applying XC-N2 yields the final optimal tree:
  XE("c", colc)

5.4 Integration with Object Relational Algebra Rules

Oracle uses a set of algebraic rules to optimize object operations. These rules can be used seamlessly with the XML algebraic rules to perform XML optimizations in the presence of object operands, and object optimizations in the presence of XML.

Object operators in Oracle include OCONS for object construction, and OATG for attribute access. As an example of object algebraic optimization, consider the following rule :

OATG(OCONS('obj', attr1Val, attr2Val), 'attr2') = attr2Val .

This rule states that to get 'attr2' attribute of an object constructed with *attr1* having value *attr1Val* and *attr2* having value *attr2Val*, the result is just *attr2Val*.

In order to integrate with XML, two new operators *MKXML* and *UMKXML* have been developed. *MKXML* converts an object instance into an XMLType instance and *UMKXML* converts an XMLType instance back into an object instance. *MKXML* and *UMKXML* are the inverses of each other.

Algebraic rules are used to specify the transformation of XPath steps over XML constructed from object instances – this will results in a tree with *OATG* over *OCONS*. Consider the following SQL expression:
extractValue(MKXML(OCONS('obj', attr1Val, attr2Val)), 'attr2'),
This is transformed into an equivalent SQL expression :
OATG(UMKXML(MKXML(OCONS('obj', attr1Val, attr2Val))), 'attr2'),
This is optimized by the operator tree optimization into just the simple *attr2Val* SQL expression..

6. Integration with relational view Merging

Relational view merge merges a query or a view definition in the FROM clause into the main query. For example, the following query *select * from (select * from t)* may be optimized into *select * from t*.

In an object-relational system, an XPath query over a collection column, with or without a predicate, (e.g. *'/Department/Employee[EmpName = 'CLARK']'*)
is converted into a subquery selecting from a logical table:
*select * from table(cast(multiset(
  select * from table where pred) as collectionType))*
Here *tab* is the underlying storage table for the instances of *collectionType*. The predicate *pred* is present only if the XPath query has a predicate. Collection view merge cancels the *table* function with the *cast(multiset(query) as collectionType)* operation, leaving the query as
*select * from (select * from tab where pred)*.
This is then further optimized via relational view merge into the simple query :
*select * from tab where pred*.
Alternatively, in a relational system, collections may be constructed using the *XMLAgg* function to aggregate XMLType values. In this case, the rewritten query for an XPath such as *'/Department/Employee[EmpName='JO']'* is of the form
*select xmlagg(v.column_value)
from table(XMLSequence(
  select xmlagg(XMLElement(..)) from t where pred))) v*
This query can be effectively transformed into the following form:
*select xmlagg(v.column_value)
from table(cast(multiset(select XMLElement(...) from t where pred)
  as xmlsequenceType) v,*
Note that the *XMLSequence* over *XMLAgg* has been transformed into a *cast(multiset())*. Here, *XMLSequenceType* represents an array of XMLType. Collection view merge then optimizes the query to :
select xmlagg(v.column_value) from(select XMLElement(...) from t where pred) v
Relational view merge then optimizes the query to:
select xmlagg(XMLElement(...)) from t where pred.
Through the relational and collection view merge, the query over the underlying storage table or view constructing the collection elements is folded into the parent query. The predicates on the collection elements automatically become the predicates on the underlying collection storage table or view. This effectively pushes the predicate down, and various access methods can be better exploited. No run-time materialization of the collection elements is needed.

7. Performance

To measure the performance of XML query rewrite over SQL/XML viewed over relational data, we create the SQLX-Bucky benchmark based on Bucky[10] benchmark. We use SQL/XML publishing functions to create XMLType views over relational tables. To measure the performance of XML query rewrite over schema based XML table, we use XMark[14]. In both benchmarks, we express the query using *Extract*,

ExistsNode, *ExtractValue*, XMLSequence and SQL/XML publishing functions.

The performance objectives are two-fold. The first is to compare the performance of rewritten XML queries with the performance of the same query without rewrite. Without query rewrite, XML needs to be materialized followed by XPath evaluation. The performance of rewritten queries, however, scales gracefully similar to that of relational queries. Rewritten queries are *orders of magnitude* faster than non-rewritten queries since they can use indexes.

Our second objective is to compare the performance of the XML queries against their semantically equivalent object relational or relational queries combined with SQL/XML publishing functions. We find that the performance of the two is comparable for both XMark and SQLX-Bucky benchmark. Figure 2 and Figure 3 show the ratio of the query performance using query rewrite to the semantically equivalent relational or object relational query written directly over the underlying storage tables. This demonstrates that query over XML combined with rewrite yields performance comparable to that of queries directly on the underlying data.

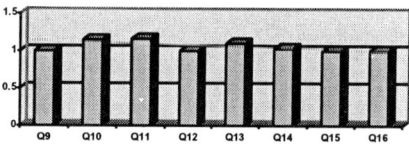

Figure 2 – Query Speed Ratio for SQLX-Bucky

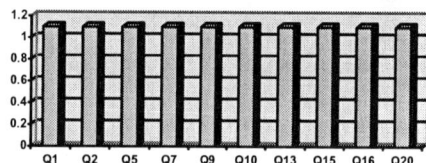

Figure 3 – Query Speed Ratio for XMark

8. Related Work

Many of the concepts presented in this paper have been studied in other contexts. XML algebra [6][7] and optimizing queries of XML views of relational data in the middleware [8][9], in particular, have been the subject of much research.

Our work is unique in the following respects. First, our query optimization rules are based on optimizing XPath expressions over SQL/XML and object relational SQL. Second, query processing is performed inside a popular, commercial database server, as opposed to non-integrated mid-tier solutions. Our solution does not materialize large volumes of XML in the middleware. We primarily optimize queries over XML whose underlying storage is relational and object-relational. Third, our algebraic rules for XML processing and optimization is tightly integrated with existing relational and object-relational rules. This enables optimization involving a mix of relational and XML queries.

Since the majority of business data is stored in relational and object-relational database, Oracle XML DB focuses on a practical subset of XML querying problems that, we believe, are the most useful for customers. We bridge the relational and XML worlds within Oracle XML DB by leveraging the relational and object relational algebra, and its optimization infrastructure.

9. Future Direction

As XQuery [1] becomes the standard to query XML, and the SQL/XML standard embraces XQuery functionality, Oracle XML DB will optimize XQuery over XML data. The XML Query Rewrite techniques presented in this paper has laid out the groundwork to fully optimize XQuery over XML stored object-relationally or generated by SQL/XML functions from relational data. We will discuss this in our future paper

XML data can be recursive. Such XML can be constructed using the Oracle *CONNECT BY* expression and hierarchical XML generation methods. The rewrite of queries over such recursive constructs has scope for future investigation.

10. Conclusion

In this paper, we have focused on a technique of optimizing queries on XML whose underlying storage is relational or object-relational. The idea is to transparently transform the XML query into its equivalent relational or object-relational equivalent through query rewrite techniques at compile time, so that a classic optimizer can further optimize it and a tuple-oriented execution engine can efficiently execute it. We create a set of new SQL operators for XPath navigation, and incorporate a new set of algebra rules for SQL/XML operators with existing relational and object relational algebra rules in the Oracle database server. Our experience has shown that this technique enables customers to leverage their existing relational and object relational systems, and to provide interoperability between XML and their existing data and applications.

Acknowledements

We gratefully acknowledge the contributions of all the members of the Oracle XML DB development and product management teams. We would especially like to thank *Ravi Murthy* and *Muralidhar Subramanian*, who have given us valuable and insightful ideas for query rewrite.

References

[1] World Wide Web Consortium, "XQuery 1.0: An XML Query Language", W3C Working Draft, November 2003.

[2] Oracle XML DB Developer's Guide: Oracle 9iR2. See http://otn.oracle.com/tech/xml/xmldb

[3] Database Languages – SQL - Part 14: XML Related Specifications (SQL/XML) – Aug 2003

[4] Sandeepan Banerjee, Vishu Krishnamurthy, Muralidhar Krishnaprasad, Ravi Murhty: "Oracle 8i – The XML Enabled Data Management System", ICDE 2000.

[5] Ravi Murthy, Sandeepan Banerjee: "XML Schemas in Oracle XML DB". VLDB 2003

[6] Flavius Frasincar, Geert-Jan Houben, Cristian Pau: "XAL: an Algebra for XML Query Optimization". In ADC 2002, Melbourne, Australia, 2002, ACS

[7] H.V. Jagadish, Laks V.S. Lakshmanan, Divesh Srivastava, Keith Thompson: "TAX A Tree Algebra for XML". In DBPL 2001.

[8] Jayavel Shanmugasundaram, Jerry Kiernan, Eugene Shekita, Catalina Fan, John Funderburk: "Querying XML Views of Relational Data". VLDB 2001.

[9] Mary Fernandez, Atsuyuki Morishima, Dan Suciu: "Efficient Evaluation of XML Middleware Queries", SIGMOD Conf., May 2001

[10] Michael J. Carey, David J. DeWitt, Jeffrey F. Naughton, Mohammad Asgarian, Paul Brown, Johannes E. Gehreke, Dhaval N. Shah: "The Bucky Object Relational Benchmark",0 http://www.cs.wisc.edu/~naughton/bucky.html.

[11] The W World Wide Web Consortium, "XML Schema Standard", see http://www.w3.org/XML/Schema

[12] Andrew Eisenberg and Jim Melton: SQL/XML and the SQLX Informal Group of Companies, , ACM SIGMOD Record, Vol. 30 No. 3, Sept. 2001, http://www.acm.org/sigmod/record/issues/0109/standards.pdf

[13] Andrew Eisenberg and Jim Melton: SQL/XML Is Making Good Progress" http://www.acm.org/sigmod/record/issues/0206/standard.pdf

[14] Albrecht Schmidt, Florian Waas, Martin Kersten, Michael J. Carey, Ioanna Manolescu, Ralph Busse: "Xmark: A Benchmark for XML Data Management" http://www.csd.uch.gr/~hy561/Papers/XMark-vldb02.pdf

Appendix Benchmark Query

For reference, we list a sample of XMark queries and SQLX-Bucky queries that we use for our performance experiments.

XMark Benchmark

The XMLdata is stored in a schema based XMLType table *site_tab*, with the XML schema derived from the XMark Internet auction site.

Q1: Return the name of the person with ID 'person0':
```
select extract(value(v), '/person/name')
from site_tab v0,
    table(xmlsequence(extract(value(v0), '/site/people/person'))) v
where extractValue(value(v), '/person/@id') = 'person0'
```

Q5: How many sold items cost more than 40:
```
select count(*)
from (select extract(value(v), '/closed_auction/price')
    from site_tab v0, table(xmlsequence(extract(value(v0),
            '/site/closed_auctions/closed_auction'))) v
where extractValue(value(v), '/closed_auction/price') >=40 )v
```

Q7: How many pieces of prose are in our database ?:
```
select xmlelement("cnt",
    (select count(*)
    from table(xmlsequence(extract(value(v), '/site//description')))) +
    (select count(*)
    from table(xmlsequence(extract(value(v), '/site//annotation')))) +
    (select count(*)
    from table(xmlsequence(extract(value(v), '/site//email')))))
from site_tab v0, table(xmlsequence(extract(value(v0), '/site'))) v
```

Q9: List the names of persons and the names of the items they bought in Europe:
```
select xmlelement("person",
    xmlattributes(extractValue(value(p), '/person/name') as "name"),
    (select xmlagg(xmlelement("item",
        (select xmlagg(extract(value(t2), '/item/name'))
        from site_tab v000,
            table(xmlsequence(extract(value(v000),
                '/site/regions/europe/item'))) t2
        where extractValue(value(t),
            '/closed_auction/itemref/@item')=
                extractValue(value(t2), '/item/@id') )))
    from site_tab v00, table(xmlsequence(extract(value(v00),
            '/site/closed_auctions/closed_auction'))) t
    where extractValue(value(p), '/person/@id' )=
        extractValue(value(t), '/item/buyer/@person') ) )
from site_tab v0,
    table(xmlsequence(extract(value(v0), '/site/people/person'))) p
```

Q13: List the names of items registered in Australia along with their descriptions:
```
select xmlelement("item",
    xmlattributes(extractValue(value(i), '/item/name/text()') as "name"),
    extract(value(i), '/description') )
from site_tab v0, table(xmlsequence(extract(value(v0),
            '/site/regions/australia/item'))) i
```

Q20: Group customers by their income and output the cardinality of each group:
```
select xmlelement("result",
    xmlelement("preferred",
        (select count(*) from site_tab v,
            table(xmlsequence( extract(value(v),
                '/site/people/profile[@income >= 100000]'))))),
    xmlelement("standard",
        (select count(*) from site_tab v,
            table(xmlsequence( extract(value(v),
                '/site/people/profile[@income < 100000
                and @income >= 30000]'))))),
    xmlelement("challenge",
        (select count(*) from site_tab v,
            table(xmlsequence( extract(value(v),
                '/site/people/profile[@income < 30000]'))))),
    xmlelement("na",
        (select count(*) from site_tab v
        where existsNode(value(v), '/site/people/person/@income') = 0
        ))) from dual
```

SQLX-Bucky Benchmark

Relational tables are created to hold base data and SQL/XML views are created on the relational tables.

Q1: Find the address of the staff member with id 6966:
```
select extractvalue(staff, '/ROW/NAME') name,
    extractvalue(staff, '/ROW/ADDRESS/STREET') street,
    extractvalue(staff, '/ROW/ADDRESS/CITY') city,
    extractvalue(staff, '/ROW/ADDRESS/STATE') state,
    extractvalue(staff, '/ROW/ADDRESS/ZIPCODE') zip
from Staff_sqlxv e
where extractvalue(staff, '/ROW/SSN') = 6966;
```

The *Staff_sqlxv* is a SQL/XML view created on top of the *rf_person* table as:
```
Create View Staff_sqlxv AS
    SELECT XmlElement("ROW",
        XmlElement("SSN", id), XmlElement("NAME", name),
        XmlElement("ADDRESS", XmlElement("STREET", street),
            XmlElement("CITY", city), XmlElement("STATE", state),
            XmlElement("ZIPCODE", zipcode)),
        XmlElement("BIRTHDATE", birthdate),
        XmlElement("KIDNAMES",
            (select XMLAgg(XmlElement("CHLDNAME", kidname))
            from rf_Kids k    where k.id = p.id)),
        XmlElement("PICTURE", picture),
        XmlElement("PLACE", XmlElement("LATITUDE", latitude),
            XmlElement("LONGITUDE", longitude)),
        XmlElement("DATEHIRED", DateHired),
        XmlElement("STATUS", status),
        XmlElement("WORKSIN", worksin),
        XmlElement("ANNUALSALARY", annualSalary)) as staff
    FROM rf_PersonFlat p
    WHERE p.type=10;– type code for staff in table rf_person.
```

Q8: Find all staff whose children are named "girl16" and "boy16":
```
select distinct extractvalue(e.staff, '/ROW/NAME') name,
    extractvalue(e.staff, '/ROW/ADDRESS/STREET') street,
    extractvalue(e.staff, '/ROW/ADDRESS/CITY') city,
    extractvalue(e.staff, '/ROW/ADDRESS/STATE') state,
    extractvalue(e.staff, '/ROW/ADDRESS/ZIPCODE') zip
from Staff_sqlxv e,
    TABLE(xmlsequence(extract(e.staff,
        '/ROW/KIDNAMES/CHLDNAME'))) k1,
    TABLE(xmlsequence(extract(e.staff,
        '/ROW/KIDNAMES/CHLDNAME'))) k2
where  extractvalue(value(k1), '/CHLDNAME') = 'girl16'
and extractvalue(value(k2), '/CHLDNAME') = 'boy16'
```

Indexing XML Data Stored in a Relational Database

Shankar Pal, Istvan Cseri, Oliver Seeliger, Gideon Schaller, Leo Giakoumakis, Vasili Zolotov

Microsoft Corporation
One Microsoft Way
Redmond WA 98052
USA
{shankarp, istvanc, oliverse, gideons, leogia, vasilizo}@microsoft.com

Abstract

As XML usage grows for both data-centric and document-centric applications, introducing native support for XML data in relational databases brings significant benefits. It provides a more mature platform for the XML data model and serves as the basis for interoperability between relational and XML data. Whereas query processing on XML data shredded into one or more relational tables is well understood, it provides limited support for the XML data model. XML data can be persisted as a byte sequence (BLOB) in columns of tables to support the XML model more faithfully. This introduces new challenges for query processing such as the ability to index the XML blob for good query performance. This paper reports novel techniques for indexing XML data in the upcoming version of Microsoft® SQL Server™, and how it ties into the relational framework for query processing.

1. Introduction

Introducing XML [3] support in relational databases has been of keen interest in the industry in the past few years. One solution is to generate XML from a set of tables based on an XML schema definition and to decompose XML instances into such tables [2][5][11][16][20]. Once shredded into tables, the full power of the relational engine, such as indexing using B+trees and query capabilities, can be used to manage and query the data.

Permission to copy without fee all or part of this material is granted provided that the copies are not made or distributed for direct commercial advantage, the VLDB copyright notice and the title of the publication and its date appear, and notice is given that copying is by permission of the Very Large Data Base Endowment. To copy otherwise, or to republish, requires a fee and/or special permission from the Endowment
**Proceedings of the 30th VLDB Conference,
Toronto, Canada, 2004**

The shredding approach is suitable for XML data with a well-defined structure. It depends on the existence of a schema describing the XML data and a mapping of XML data between the relational and XML forms.

The XML data model, however, has characteristics that make it very hard if not practically impossible to map to the relational data model in the general case. XML data is hierarchical and may have a recursive structure; relational databases provide weak support for hierarchical data (modeled as foreign key relationships). Document order is an inherent property of XML instances and must be preserved in query results. This is in contrast with relational data, which is unordered, and order must be enforced with additional ordering columns. On the query front, a large number of joins are required to re-assemble the result for realistic schemas. Even with co-located indexes, the reassembly cost of an XML subtree can be prohibitively expensive.

XML is being increasingly used in enterprise applications for modeling semi-structured and unstructured data, and for data whose structure is highly variable or not known *a priori*. This has motivated the need for native XML support within relational databases.

Microsoft SQL Server 2005 introduces a native data type called XML [12]. A user can create a table T with one or more columns of type XML besides relational columns. XML values are stored in the XML column as large binary objects (BLOB). This preserves the XML data model faithfully, and the query processor enforces XML semantics during query execution. The underlying relational infrastructure is used extensively for this purpose. This approach supports interoperability between relational and XML data within the same database making way for more widespread adoption of the XML features.

XQuery expressions [19] embedded within SQL statements are used to query into XML data type values. Query execution processes each XML instance at runtime; this becomes expensive whenever the instance is large in size or the query is evaluated on a large number of rows in the table. Consequently, an indexing mechanism is required to speed up queries on XML blobs.

B+tree index has been used extensively in relational databases and is a natural choice for indexing XML blobs as well. The B+tree index must provide efficient evaluation of queries on XML blobs. Query execution may need to reassemble the XML result from the B+tree index (*XML serialization*) while preserving document order and document structure. Some operators in XPath 2.0 [18] — most notably the descendant-or-self axis // — navigate down an XML tree recursively. Thus, B+tree lookups can be recursive.

In this paper, we discuss the techniques used in Microsoft SQL Server 2005 for indexing XML blobs. A shredded representation conforming to Infoset items [4] of nodes is stored in a B+tree. This is referred to as the *primary XML index*. A novel node labeling scheme called ORDPATH [13] allows us to capture document order and document hierarchy within a single column of the primary XML index. This index is clustered on the ORDPATH value for each XML instance and provides very efficient access to subtrees using a simple range scan. The ORDPATH column is used extensively to determine relative order of nodes within a document and the parent-child and ancestor-descendant relationships between two nodes. The ancestor-descendant relationship check eliminates the need for recursive traversal down the XML tree and is a significant optimization.

Materialization of the Infoset speeds up query processing on XML columns by eliminating runtime shredding costs. Further performance gains can be obtained by creating secondary indexes on the primary XML index for different classes of queries. We identify three important classes of queries (path-based queries, property bag scenarios and value-based queries) that commonly occur in practice and investigate three secondary indexes — PATH, PROPERTY and VALUE — to optimize those classes of queries. Content indexing of XML instances based on the structural information stored in primary XML index is also discussed.

The performance gains using the XML indexes for the well-known XMark benchmark [15] are presented in the paper.

The reminder of the paper is organized as follows. Section 2 gives a background of native XML support in Microsoft SQL Server 2005 and describes the concept of ORDPATH. Section 3 introduces the techniques for indexing XML data, Section 4 provides experimental results, and Section 5 discusses related work. The paper concludes with a summary in Section 6.

2. XML Support in Microsoft SQL Server 2005

This section provides a brief overview of XML support in Microsoft SQL Server 2005.

2.1 XML Data Type

Native support for the XML data model is introduced using a new, first-class data type called "xml". It can be used as the type of a column in a table or view, a variable and a parameter in a function or stored procedure. Thus, a table can be created with an integer column and an XML column as follows:

Create table DOCS (ID int primary key, XDOC xml)

XML values saved in the XDOC column can be trees ("XML document") or fragments ("XML content"). They are stored in an internal, binary representation that is streamable and optimized for query processing. Some compaction occurs, which is incidental rather than the goal of the binary representation.

The supplied XML values are checked for well-formedness and conformity to the XML data model (e.g. end tags match start tags) for storage in the XML column.

The XML column can optionally be typed by a collection of XML schemas that may be related (e.g. by <xs:import>) or unrelated to one another. Each XML instance specifies the XML namespace from the schema collection it conforms to. The database engine validates the instance according to the XML schema before storing it in the XML column.

XML type information is stored in the database's meta-data. It contains the XML schema collections (and their contained XML schemas) and mapping between the primitive XSD and relational type systems. Typed XML instances contain XSD type information in the internal, binary representation. This enables efficient processing for typed XML and allows building domain based value indexes for efficient lookups.

2.2 Node Labeling Using OrdPath

ORDPATH [13] is a mechanism for labelling nodes in an XML tree, which preserves structural fidelity. It allows insertion of nodes anywhere in the XML tree without the need for re-labelling existing nodes. It is independent of XML schemas typing XML instances.

ORDPATH encodes the parent-child relationship by extending the parent's ORDPATH with a labelling component for the child. In the following, we use a string representation for the ORDPATH to illustrate the idea while the internal representation is based a compressed binary form. For example, children of a parent node labelled with the ORDPATH "1.5.3.9" may have the labels "1.5.3.9.1" and "1.5.3.9.7", where the ending "1"and "7" are labelling components for the children. A byte comparison of two ORDPATH labels yields the relative order of the nodes in the XML tree. Thus, the child "1.5.3.9.1" precedes "1.5.3.9.7" in document order.

For the XML instance shown in Figure 1, sample ORDPATH labels are shown for the corresponding XML tree in Figure 2.

```
<BOOK ISBN="1-55860-438-3">
    <SECTION>
        <TITLE>Bad Bugs</TITLE>
        Nobody loves bad bugs.
        <FIGURE CAPTION="Sample bug"/>
    </SECTION>
    <SECTION>
        <TITLE>Tree Frogs</TITLE>
        All right-thinking people
        <BOLD> love </BOLD> tree frogs.
    </SECTION>
</BOOK>
```
Figure 1. Sample XML data

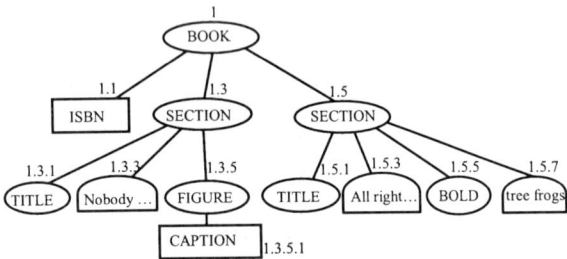

Figure 2. ORDPATH Node Label

In the ORDPATH values shown in Figure 2 (such as "1.3.5.1"), each dot separated component value ("1", "3", "5", "1") reflects a numbered tree edge at successive levels on the path from the root to the labelled node. Only positive odd integers are assigned during an initial load; even-numbered and negative integer component values are reserved for later insertions into an existing tree.

A new node N (possibly the root node of a subtree) can be inserted under any node in an existing tree. It is assigned a label component in between those of its left and right siblings using an even numbered auxiliary position that introduces a new level for N. This preserves the relative order between the siblings and avoids re-labelling the left or right siblings of N. Leftmost and rightmost insertion is supported equally efficiently by extending the range of label components on both ends. Leftmost insertions may generate label components that are negative numbers.

2.3 XML Query Processing

XQuery [19] embedded in SQL is the language supported for querying XML data type. XQuery is a W3C standards-based language in development. It is a very powerful functional language for querying XML data. In particular, it includes XPath 2.0 [18].

Methods are provided on XML data type for querying into XML values. These methods accept XQuery expressions as arguments. The methods are:

- query(): returns XML data type
- value(): extracts scalar values
- exist(): checks conditions on XML nodes
- nodes(): returns a rowset of XML nodes that the XQuery expression evaluates to

As an example, consider the following query that retrieves section titles in the book with a specified ISBN:
```
SELECT ID, XDOC.query('
    for $s in
        /BOOK[@ISBN= "1-55860-438-3"]//SECTION
    return <topic>{data($s/TITLE)} </topic>')
FROM DOCS
```

Query execution is tuple-oriented as in the rest of the relational framework. The SELECT list is evaluated on each row of table DOCS and produces a two-column result. Query compilation proceeds by producing a single query plan for both the relational and the XML parts of the query, and the overall query tree is optimized by the cost-based query optimizer.

The XML data type methods process the XML instances on which they are invoked. Each XML instance can be up to 2GB in storage, so that the runtime shredding cost can be significant for large XML instances.

In the next section, we consider techniques for indexing XML instances to speed up queries.

3. Indexing XML Data

For an XPath expression such as /BOOK[@ISBN = "1-55860-438-3"]//SECTION shown in Section 2.3 and executed on the XDOC column of DOCS table, the XPath expression is evaluated on all rows in the table. This is costly for the following reasons:

- The XDOC column value in each row must be shredded at runtime to evaluate the query.
- We cannot determine which of the XML instances satisfies @ISBN = "1-55860-438-3" without processing the XDOC values in all rows.

We can speed up query processing by saving the parsing cost at runtime. This is achieved by materializing the shredded form of the XML instances in a B$^+$tree that retains structural fidelity of the XML instances in the XDOC column. The query processor decides whether to process rows of the base table before those in the XML index (*top-down execution*) or use targeted seeks or scans on the XML index first followed by a back join with the base table (*bottom-up execution*). (The table in which an XML column is defined is referred to as the *base table*.) Additional secondary XML indexes provide another degree of freedom for the optimizer to choose the execution plan.

This section introduces the notion of a *primary XML index* on an XML column. It is a B$^+$tree that materializes the Infoset content of each XML instance in the XML column. Indexing the Infoset content in additional ways is discussed as *secondary XML indexes*.

In the following discussions, we use table DOCS of Section 2.1 for illustrative purposes.

3.1 Primary XML Indexes

This subsection describes the structure of the primary XML index and discusses query execution using it.

3.1.1 Structure of Primary XML Index

The B$^+$tree containing the shredded form of the XML instances in a column is called the *primary XML index* or the "Infoset" table.

We generate a subset of the fields in the Infoset items of the XML nodes by shredding an XML instance. This is stored in a B$^+$tree in the system. The Infoset contains information such as the tag, value and parent of each node; we add the path from the root of the tree to the node to allow path-based lookups. The B$^+$tree has the following columns amongst others:

ORDPATH	TAG	NODE_TYPE	VALUE	PATH_ID
1	1 (BOOK)	1 (Element)	Null	#1
1.1	2 (ISBN)	2 (Attribute)	'1-55860-438-3'	#2#1
1.3	3 (SECTION)	1 (Element)	Null	#3#1
1.3.1	4 (TITLE)	1 (Element)	'Bad Bugs'	#4#3#1
1.3.3	10 (TEXT)	4 (Value)	'Nobody loves Bad bugs.'	#10#3#1
1.3.5	5 (FIGURE)	1 (Element)	Null	#5#3#1
1.3.5.1	6 (CAPTION)	2 (Attribute)	'Sample bug'	#6#3#1
1.5	3 (SECTION)	1 (Element)	Null	#3#1
1.5.1	4 (TITLE)	1 (Element)	'Tree frogs'	#4#3#1
1.5.3	10 (TEXT)	4 (Value)	'All right-thinking people'	#10#3#1
1.5.5	7 (BOLD)	1 (Element)	'love '	#7#3#1
1.5.7	10 (TEXT)	4 (Value)	'tree frogs'	#10#3#1

Figure 3. XML "Shredded" into relational Infoset table

Figure 3 shows the rows corresponding to the XML tree in Figure 2. The ORDPATH column preserves structural fidelity within a single XML instance; the Infoset table also contains the primary key column ID of the base table (not shown) for *back join*. The primary key of the Infoset table is the combination of the primary key ID of the base table and the ORDPATH column.

The TAG column shows the markups found in the XML instance; it is used here for illustrative purposes only. Instead of storing string values, each markup is mapped to an integer value and the mapped values are used in storage. This mapping is referred to as *tokenization* and yields significant compression.

The NODE_TYPE column stores the type of the node in the Infoset content. For typed XML column, it stores a tokenized type value corresponding to the XSD type of the node.

The VALUE column stores the node's value, if one exists, otherwise it is NULL. It stores typed XML values as SQL Server's native type within a generic variant type.

The PATH_ID column contains a tokenized path value from the root to the node. This column represents all the paths in the tree similar to the dataguide computation [7]. Whereas each node within an XML instance has a distinct ORDPATH value, the PATH_ID value is the same for multiple nodes with the same path. Thus, nodes 1.3.1 and 1.5.1 refer to two different TITLE nodes but the paths leading to these nodes are both expressed as /BOOK/SECTION/TITLE. As such, they have the same PATH_ID value #4#3#1, where #1, #3 and #4 are for BOOK, SECTION and TITLE, respectively.

Nodes of the XML tree are traversed in XML document order and ORDPATH labels are generated during the population of the primary XML index.

The primary XML index contains some redundancy and is larger in size than the textual form of the XML instance; the primary key column of the base table, ID, for example is repeated in all rows for an XML instance. The increased I/O cost, added to the serialization cost of converting shredded rows in the Infoset table to XML form, makes retrieval of the XML blob cheaper from the base table when the whole XML instance is required.

Primary XML index stores values using the SQL type system. Most of the SQL types are compatible with XQuery type system (e.g. integer), and value comparisons on XML index columns suffice. A handful of types (e.g. xs:datetime) are stored in an internal format and processed specially to preserve compatibility with the XQuery type system.

The primary XML index can be optimized in various ways, such as by generating a single row for simple-valued elements (instead of two rows). This in practice significantly reduces on-disk size. Prefix compression [1] reduces the size of the primary XML index significantly. Another optimization is to point back from the VALUE column for large-sized values to the XML blob to avoid redundancy. A more detailed discussion of these and other optimizations are beyond the scope of this paper.

3.1.2 Query Compilation and Execution

An XQuery expression is translated into relational operations on the Infoset table. The result is a set of rows from the Infoset table that must be re-assembled into an XML result.

Consider the evaluation of the path expression /BOOK[@ISBN = "1-55860-438-3"]/SECTION on an XML instance. The following SQL statement expresses the execution logic. PATH_ID (*path*) yields the tokenized path value for the specified *path*. SerializeXML (ID, ORDPATH) assembles the XML subtree rooted at the node (ID, ORDPATH) from the Infoset table. Parent (C-

ORDPATH) returns the parent's ORDPATH as the prefix of C-ORDPATH without the last component for the child.

```
SELECT SerializeXML (N2.ID, N2.ORDPATH)
FROM   infosettab N1
       JOIN infosettab N2 ON (N1.ID = N2.ID)
WHERE N1.PATH_ID = PATH_ID(/BOOK/@ISBN)
AND    N1.VALUE = '1-55860-438-3'
AND    N2.PATH_ID = PATH_ID(
                    BOOK/SECTION)
AND    Parent (N1.ORDPATH) =
       Parent (N2.ORDPATH)
```

When the path expression /BOOK[@ISBN = "1-55860-438-3"]/SECTION is evaluated on the XDOC column of a row in DOCS table, the primary key value ID is used to seek into the Infoset table (N1). Rows for the XML instance in N1 are scanned to locate the ones having the values /BOOK@ISBN and "1-55860-438-3" in the PATH_ID and the VALUE columns, respectively. Using the same primary key value, the execution seeks into the Infoset table a second time (N2), finds rows containing the PATH_ID value for /BOOK/SECTION and determines whether the BOOK elements found in N1 is the parent of the SECTION elements found in N2. The XML fragments corresponding to the qualifying SECTION element are serialized from the Infoset table.

The cost of reassembly may be non-trivial. For queries that retrieve the whole XML instance, it is cheaper to retrieve the XML blob. Similarly, a query containing a simple path expression that must be evaluated on all rows of the base table may be more efficient on the XML blob than on the primary XML index if the re-assembly cost outweighs the cost of parsing the XML blobs. A cost-based decision must be made whether to execute the query by shredding XML blobs at runtime or to operate on XML indexes.

Insertion, deletion and modification of XML values require primary XML index maintenance as is to be expected.

3.2 Secondary XML Indexes

The primary XML index is clustered in document order and each path expression is evaluated by scanning all rows in the primary XML index for a given XML instance. Performance slows down for large XML values.

Secondary indexes can be created on the primary XML index to speed up different classes of queries. While a secondary index can be created on any of the columns in the primary XML index, it is interesting to study the specific indexes that benefit common classes of queries. We introduce four such index types: PATH (and its variation PATH_VALUE), PROPERTY, VALUE and content indexing in the following subsections.

Secondary XML indexes help with bottom-up evaluation. After the qualifying XML nodes have been found in the secondary XML indexes, a back join with the primary XML index enables continuation of query execution with those nodes. This yields significant performance gains.

3.2.1 PATH and PATH_VALUE Indexes

Going back to the SQL rewrite in Section 3.1.2, evaluation of path expressions over an entire XML column benefits from a secondary index built on the PATH_ID column. The path expression is compiled into the tokenized form (e.g. /BOOK/@ISBN ⇒ #2#1 in the example of Figure 3). An index with PATH_ID as the leading key column helps such queries.

The PATH index is built on the columns PATH_ID, ID and ORDPATH, where ID is the primary key of the base table. During query evaluation, the tokenized path value PATH_ID and ID are used to seek into the PATH index and find the corresponding ORDPATH values, thereby saving the cost of primary XML index scans. The index seek is what brings the performance gain, and the cost is relatively independent of the path length. A back join with the primary XML index on ID and ORDPATH pair continues with query execution to check conditions such as the specified value of ISBN, and re-assemble the resulting XML fragments (e.g. the subtrees rooted at the SECTION nodes in our example).

The PATH_ID column stores a "reversed" representation of the path. When a full path such as /BOOK/SECTION/TITLE is specified, it is mapped into the value #4#3#1 for PATH index lookup; the full PATH_ID value is known in this case. However, a wildcard or the descendant-or-self (//) or the descendant axis requires careful handling.

For a path expression containing the //-axis, such as //SECTION/TITLE, only the last two steps in the path expression are known. Storing the forward path in the PATH_ID column is not very useful in this case; the entire PATH index would have to be scanned. With the reverse path, however, prefix match of the PATH_ID column for the value #4#3 yields faster execution. The situation is similar for path expressions containing a wildcard or //-axis in the middle of the path expression, such as /BOOK/*/TITLE or /BOOK/SECTION//TITLE. In the latter case, the exact match for the PATH_ID value for /BOOK/SECTION (i.e. #3#1) and prefix match for TITLE (i.e. #4) yield two sets of nodes. The ancestor-descendant relationship between node pairs from these sets is verified using their ORDPATH values.

For path expressions such as /BOOK/SECTION[TITLE ="Tree Frogs"] that fit the pattern "path=value", a variation of the PATH index is more useful. If the PATH index is built only on the PATH_ID column, this type of query requires a back join with the primary XML index to check the node's value. This back join can be avoided by including the VALUE column in the index to yield a PATH_VALUE index, which is built on the columns (PATH_ID, VALUE, ID and ORDPATH). The path /BOOK/SECTION/TITLE is compiled to the tokenized value #4#3#1 and an index seek is performed on the PATH_VALUE index with the key values (#4#3#1, "Tree Frogs"). For the qualifying TITLE nodes, the parent's key value (ID, Parent (ORDPATH)) is then used to seek into the primary XML index to obtain and re-assemble the SECTION subtrees in the result.

3.2.2 PROPERTY Index

A useful application of XML is to represent an object's properties with the help of XML markup, especially when the number and type of the properties are not known *a priori*, or properties are multi-valued or complex. This allows properties of different types of objects to be stored in the same XML column. The XML schema (if one exists) for this scenario is typically non-recursive.

Common queries have the form "find properties X, Y, Z of object P", where X, Y and Z are path expressions. In our model, this means the ID value is known for the object and the PATH_ID values are know for X, Y and Z. Evaluating this query on the primary XML index requires scanning all rows corresponding to the given ID value.

On the other hand, the rows for each of the paths X, Y and Z from all objects are clustered together in the PATH_VALUE index. Thus, the execution becomes a seek into the PATH_VALUE index for each of the paths, scan of all rows with the same PATH_ID value and a match for the specified ID value.

Clustering all properties of each object together into a PROPERTY index significantly speeds up property lookup for objects. The columns in the PROPERTY index are (ID, PATH_ID, VALUE and ORDPATH). This organization helps retrieve multi-valued properties for an object (same ID and PATH_ID values). Retrieving all properties of an object requires scanning the same number of rows in the primary XML index and the PROPERTY index. However, the higher record density of the PROPERTY index yields faster result, especially when no back join with the primary XML index is required.

To illustrate the point with an example, consider the extractions of the ISBN (i.e. /BOOK/@ISBN) and the title of the first section (i.e. (/BOOK/SECTION/TITLE)[1]) from the XDOC column of table DOCS. The execution logic can be expressed in the following SQL statement:

```
SELECT (SELECT TOP 1 N1.VALUE,
        FROM   infosettab N1
        WHERE  DOCS.ID = N1.ID
        AND    N1.PATH_ID =
               PATH_ID (/BOOK/@ISBN)),
       (SELECT TOP 1 N2.VALUE,
        FROM   infosettab N2
        WHERE  DOCS.ID = N2.ID
        AND    N2.PATH_ID =
               PATH_ID(/BOOK/ SECTION/TITLE))
FROM   DOCS
```

The primary key ID and the PATH_ID values are known, so that seeking into the PROPERTY index permits efficient retrieval of the ISBN and TITLE values.

To retrieve a single property of an object, the PROPERTY index is more suitable than the PATH_VALUE index, since the latter clusters the same path from all objects together. When N properties are to be retrieved, the cost-based optimizer must decide between N seeks into the PROPERTY index (same ID, N different PATH_ID values) or a scan in the PROPERTY index for the N property values of the object.

3.2.3 VALUE Index

Value-based queries of the type /BOOK/SECTION[FIGURE/@* = "Sample Bug"] specify a value and have a wildcard for the path. It requires scanning the primary XML or PROPERTY index for each XML instance while trying to match the specified portion of the path. Using the PATH_VALUE index is worse and a larger part of the index is usually scanned.

For efficiency, an index that locates the specified value first can induce a bottom-up query plan and perform much better. Such an index is the VALUE index built on the columns (VALUE, PATH_ID, ID and ORDPATH). An index lookup occurs using the value "Sample Bug" and, for the qualifying rows, the specified part of the PATH_ID is matched. A back join with the primary XML index is generally needed to re-assemble the result (the ancestor node SECTION in this example). As noted above, the ORDPATH of a parent or ancestor can be computed as a prefix of a descendant's ORDPATH.

If the XML column is typed, then values stored in the index receive appropriate typing. If the XML column is untyped, then values are indexed as strings. Untyped XML is more beneficial for document scenarios than data scenarios.

As an example, consider the evaluation of the path expression /BOOK/SECTION[FIGURE/@* = "Sample Bug"] on an XML instance. The following SQL statement expresses the execution logic:

```
SELECT SerializeXML (N1.ID,
                Parent (N1.ORDPATH))
FROM   infosettab N1 JOIN infosettab N2 ON
       (N1.ID = N2.ID AND
        N1.ORDPATH = Parent(N2.ORDPATH))
WHERE  N1.PATH_ID =
       PATH_ID(/BOOK/SECTION/FIGURE)
AND    N2.NODE_TYPE = Attribute
AND    N2.VALUE = 'Sample Bug'
```

An index seek into the VALUE index with the search value 'Sample Bug' yields (ID, ORDPATH) pairs that are joined with the primary XML index. Each such (ID, ORDPATH) node is checked for attribute type and child relationship to the nodes found for the path

/BOOK/SECTION/FIGURE. The resulting SECTION elements are serialized in the result.

3.2.4 Content Indexing

The origin of the XML standard is in the document community where the most important part of an XML instance is the text (the "content") in the document marked up by the tag structure. Accordingly there has been increasing amount of focus on information retrieval (IR) techniques in the XML space. These range from simply discarding the markup and using traditional inverted word list techniques augmented with tag/path information to include the markup in the full text index and so leverage the IR search even for element and attribute names.

We support two solutions in this space. We can leverage the IR capabilities of the engine by creating a full text index over an XML data type column. The filter in the text indexer discards the markup and creates an inverted word index with full support of our SQL text search sublanguage over the XML data type instances. The text search expressions now can be combined with XQuery expressions in the same SQL statement and the optimizer leverages all existing indexes (relational, XML and full text) in order to evaluate the query efficiently.

This solution works well for traditional IR queries but it is not optimal if we want to combine searching for a certain word within a specific context, for example, in a particular XML element. Here we want to take advantage of the XML indexes we build over the XML infoset but we want to have finer granularity than text nodes since the VALUE index does not help us locate individual words efficiently. In order to achieve this we can extend the full text inverted word index with information from the infoset or we can extend our infoset table with word information. Here we choose the later solution by building what we call the *word break index*.

The word break index has the same structure as the infoset table except that we break up the text nodes into words according to XML whitespace. Now we can take advantage of all the information present in this table and we can do efficient fine granularity searches on XML whitespace boundaries and tag boundaries. This does not replace a fully annotated full text index since it does not have weighting, ranking and relevance-oriented information [9] but it provides a very efficient index structure for most of the full text like searches.

3.3 Evaluating Complex Path Expressions

A complex path expression may require multiple lookups of one or more XML indexes. Rows found in different lookups are joined (on the primary key ID and ORDPATH in the most common cases) as required for evaluating the path expression. (Section 4 discusses several examples.) This is executed using the proper JOIN type (nested loop join, merge join or hash join [17]).

Thus, the overall execution consists of relational operations with special optimizations for ORDPATH properties (order and hierarchy).

A complex path expression is rewritten to use the primary XML index as shown in the previous sections. The choice of PATH, PROPERTY and VALUE indexes are done by the cost-based optimizer using such information as the distributions of PATH_ID, VALUE, primary key and ORDPATH. The query rewrites in the above sections also indicate that the query optimizer may choose to use multiple XML indexes, and evaluate parts of the XPath expression using a post-filter on the output of the index lookups.

The next section presents experimental data on the gain in query performance using various XML indexes.

4. Experimental Results using XMark Benchmark

XMark [15] is an XML query benchmark that models an auction scenario. It specifies 20 queries for exact match, ordered access, regular path expressions, following references, construction of complex results, join on values, search for missing elements, and so on.

This section reports the performance improvements we found with different XML indexes. We explain the reasons for the performance gain for several queries.

4.1 Workload

Sample XML data conforming to the XMark schema was produced using the document generator XMLGEN provided by the authors of XMark. Instead of storing the entire data as a single, large XML instance, it is more natural in a relational database to store the data in tables representing the different entities in the data model. This yields five tables for people, open auctions, closed auctions, items and categories.

Information about bidders is stored in the table PEOPLE, while those about ongoing and closed auctions are stored in the tables OPEN_AUCTIONS and CLOSED_AUCTIONS, respectively. The table ITEMS contains data about the auction items. Lastly, the CATEGORIES table contains information on the classification scheme of items.

Each of these tables contains two columns: an integer id column and an untyped XML column containing the data. The table schema is shown in the appendix. XML indexes of the same type are created on all the XML columns to measure the usefulness of that index type.

Cross references among XML instances is maintained as ordinary attributes instead of IDREF since the reference is across XML instances with our five tables. For example, the bidder of an open auction is stored as a "person" attribute with the person's id as the value in the open auction XML instance.

We manually rewrote the original XMark queries to use joins among our five tables. Some of the query rewrites are shown in the appendix.

We generated data only for the North America region and changed Q9 accordingly to avoid returning an empty result for Europe. Q13 (reconstruction query) does not have an auction item that satisfies the path /site/regions/australia/item used in the query. An optimization in the relational engine knows upfront that no rows will be returned and the path expression is not executed in the indexed case. We changed the query slightly to use "africa" instead of "australia" to return a non-null result.

4.2 Experimental Setup and Results

The XMark database is created for scale factors 0.5 and 30, the latter having sixty times as many rows in each table as the former. The size of the XML data type instances are the same in both cases.

XMLGEN generates a single XML instance whose size is 60 MB for scale 0.5 and 3.35 GB for scale 30. The number of rows in the PEOPLE, OPEN_AUCTIONS, CLOSED_AUCTIONS, ITEMS and CATEGORIES tables are 12750, 6000, 4875, 10875 and 500, respectively, for scale 0.5, and 765000, 360000, 292500, 652500 and 30000, respectively, for scale 30.

The disk space consumption for scale factor 0.5 is 142 MB for the five tables and 345 MB for the primary XML indexes. The secondary XML indexes of each type (PATH, PROPERTY and VALUE) took up another 101 MB. The corresponding sizes for scale factor 30 are 8.3GB, 20GB and 5.9GB, respectively.

The workload is run in single user mode on a 4-way 700 MHz Pentium III machine running Windows Server 2003. It has 2GB RAM and a 3-disk array of 36GB each. The database is a pre-release build of Microsoft SQL Server 2005. The query execution time is measured at the client.

QUERY	PRIMARY	PATH_VALUE	PROPERTY	VALUE
Q1	5.8	28.8	6.7	28.8
Q2	2.8	2.6	3.5	2.0
Q3	2.2	1.8	2.3	2.4
Q4	8.3	8.0	7.8	7.7
Q5	2.9	2.9	2.7	2.9
Q6	1.0	1.1	1.2	1.1
Q7	7.9	43.6	14.7	12.8
Q8	1.7	1.8	1.7	1.7
Q9	0.6	0.6	0.6	0.6
Q10	6.3	6.3	19.7	5.9
Q11	3.7	3.8	3.8	3.7
Q12	2.9	3.0	3.0	1.5
Q13	2.8	3.4	5.4	2.6
Q14	7.0	8.3	7.6	7.3
Q15	7.7	7.5	7.5	6.4
Q16	7.4	19.1	9.6	10.2
Q17	3.0	2.0	1.9	2.0
Q18	6.0	1.0	2.5	0.8
Q19	2.3	5.7	5.5	2.4
Q20	0.8	1.0	0.8	0.8

Table 1 Gain in using XML index for XMark queries (i.e. execution time using XML blob/execution time using XML index) for scale factor 0.5.

We compare the benefits of using the various XML indexes with the blob case. Table 1 shows the "gain" in using XML indexes as measured by the ratio of the execution times using XML blobs (i.e. without any XML indexes) and the execution times with different XML index configurations for scale factor 0.5. For example, the PROPERTY configuration creates the primary and PROPERTY XML indexes on each XML column since a secondary XML index is created on the Infoset table. These measurements are taken with no parallelism in query execution. Parallel plans make the gain higher in some cases. Owing to space limitations, we discuss the measurements for scale factor 30 briefly in Section 4.7.

Execution on XML blobs evaluates simple path expressions without predicates and produces an Infoset work table with rows for the qualifying nodes and their subtrees. The PATH_ID column is not present in this work table. Predicates are applied as a post-filter step. The rest of query execution proceeds as in the indexed case described in Section 3.

Looking at the gains in Table 1 — which gives the factor by which the choice of an XML index speeds up queries relative to the blob case — it is evident that XML indexes benefit the workload significantly. We consider a few of the queries below.

4.3 Primary XML Index

The performance gains are mainly related to parsing XML blob multiple times to evaluate the path expressions in the blob case. For primary XML index, not only is the parsing cost saved but also path expressions of the form "path=value" can be evaluated faster using the PATH_ID and VALUE columns. A case in point is Q4 (ordered access query), where the path expressions /site/open_auctions/open_auction/bidder/personref [@person="person18829"] and (/site/open_auctions/ open_auction/bidder/personref [@person = "person10487"] are evaluated using the primary XML index and yields nodes whose relative positions can be determined by comparing their ORDPATH labels.

Q6 (regular path expression query) performance is the same with and without XML indexes since the query counts the number of rows in the ITEMS table and no XML processing occurs.

One of the queries — Q9 (reference chasing query) — is slower than the execution on XML blob. It scans all rows of the primary XML index and evaluates two joins on values within XML instances. Owing to the larger size of the primary XML index compared to the XML blobs, the index scan cost outweighs the cost of parsing and slows down the query. Query Q20 (aggregation query) has about the same performance as blobs.

4.4 PATH_VALUE Index

The PATH_VALUE index is very effective in speeding up some of the XMark queries, as shown in the PATH_VALUE column in Table 1.

Consider query Q1 (exact match query), which evaluates the two path expressions PE_1 = (/site/people/person/name/text())[1] and PE_2 = /site/people/person/@id[.= "person0"], as shown in the appendix. The path expression /site/people/person/@id is compiled into a PATH_ID value, and "person0" is the required VALUE, which is unique in the XML column in the PEOPLE table. The combination (PATH_ID, VALUE) yields a very selective seek into the PATH_VALUE index. The other path expression PE1 yields a PATH_ID value. Lookup of the PATH_VALUE index with only this value would cause a large number of rows in the index to be scanned. Instead, a primary XML index seek occurs with the ORDPATH of the "person" node (and the same ID value). Scanning down the primary XML index, the rest of the path expression is evaluated using the PATH_ID column. Evaluation of the query on the XML blob is much slower since PE2 is evaluated on all rows in the PEOPLE table. For the qualifying rows, the XML blob is parsed a second time to evaluate PE_1.

The performance gain with Q7 (regular path expression query) is large. The XML blob query has to scan all rows in four of the five tables and evaluate the three path expressions //description, //annotation and //email. On the other hand, these path expressions locate the "description", "annotation" and "email" node clusters within the PATH_VALUE index on each XML column, and eliminate duplicate ID values for each cluster. This yields very efficient evaluation of the query.

Other queries also benefit from the PATH_VALUE index to varying degrees, such as Q16, which evaluates long path expressions.

4.5 PROPERTY Index

Q2 (ordered access query) evaluates the path expression /site/open_auctions/open_auction/bidder[1]/increase/text() on all rows of the OPEN_AUCTIONS table. The primary key value ID is known from this table. Using ID and the PATH_ID value for the path /site/open_auctions/open_auction/bidder (ignoring the ordinal [1]), an index seek into the PROPERTY index finds the first bidder node within the XML instance. A back join with the primary XML index on the (ID, ORDPATH) value for the bidder node and a subtree scan for the remaining part of the path expression (increase/text()) yields the result. As a matter of fact, performing the tree scan on the primary XML index for a given ID value also performs quite well for the given data.

Q10 (construction of complex result query) finds persons with interest (the path expression PE is /site/people/person[profile/interest/@category]) and for each such person retrieves personal attributes. The primary key ID of the PEOPLE table and the compiled PATH_ID value is known. Consequently, PE can be evaluated very efficiently using an index seek on the PROPERTY index. For these persons (ID and ORDPATH values are known), various properties (e.g. gender and age) are retrieved efficiently from the PROPERTY index using ID and PATH_ID values for the different properties (identified by appropriate path expressions). The gain is pronounced compared to the other XML index types. An index seek into the PROPERTY index occurs for each property. In the other indexed cases, an index scan of the rows for each person occurs on the primary XML index to retrieve the properties.

4.6 VALUE Index

Q1 (exact match query) performs very well with the VALUE index. Two path expressions PE_1 = (/site/people/person/name/text())[1] and PE_2 = /site/people/person/@id[.= "person0"] occur in the query, as shown in the appendix. The value "person0" is unique in the XML column of the PEOPLE table, and the PATH_ID value is known at compilation time. Consequently, PE_2 is very selective on the VALUE index. Other queries benefit to different extents. Q9 does not use the VALUE index and uses the primary XML index.

4.7 Results for Scale Factor 30

The gains for scale factor 30 generally are more subdued than scale factor 0.5 since the processing becomes I/O bound. We present only a few of the measurements in Table 2 owing to space limitations.

QUERY	PRIMARY	PATH_VALUE	PROPERTY	VALUE
Q1	2.8	595.3	5.2	602.2
Q5	1.2	1.1	0.8	1.1
Q15	1.8	18.3	6.2	5.9
Q16	1.4	48.2	4.5	5.0

Table 2 Gain in using XML index for XMark queries (i.e. execution time using XML blob/execution time using XML index) for scale factor 30.

Q1 performs extremely well with PATH_VALUE and VALUE indexes since the search predicate is highly selective. Bottom-up evaluation leads to improved gain in Q15 and Q16 as well using the PATH_VALUE index.

In the case of primary XML index, many more rows in the Infoset table are scanned for Q1 to evaluate the predicate, for which the gain is smaller than in the case of scale factor 0.5. Similar effects are seen in the other queries as well, such as Q5.

The PROPERTY index is a little slower in Q1 because a larger number of rows in the PEOPLE table are scanned to find their primary key values that are then used in PROPERTY index lookup.

5. Related Work

Several ideas have been proposed in the literature for decomposing XML data into a fixed database schema. Document order and structure is efficiently captured using a single ORDPATH in our approach as opposed to the EDGE table [6], Monet system [14], XRel [21], XParent [10] and accelerator table [8].

The EDGE table and XParent both use an Ordinal column to store the relative order of siblings in XML instances. They also store parent-child relationships, so that determining ancestor-descendant relationship and serializing XML require transitive closure computation. The XParent approach suggests materializing the ancestor-descendant relationship in an ANCESTOR table with a Level column that can be used for parent-child checks as well, but requires more space than ours.

In both EDGE table and XParent, insertion of subtrees requires incrementing the Ordinal value of the "following-siblings" [18]. The ANCESTOR table requires more maintenance. ORDPATH avoids such relabelling.

The Monet system partitions the XML data into a set of tables corresponding to the different paths. This distributes the children of a node into different tables, and determining the children of a node requires a number of joins. The Monet and XRel systems store the byte range of each XML subtree in the original XML. Serialization of XML is straightforward: the byte range is used to retrieve the corresponding XML fragments, and avoids scanning rows from the primary XML index in our approach. Document order is determined by comparing the starting byte of each node. Ancestor-descendant relationship requires checking for byte range inclusion, and a check for the minimal containing range is needed for parent-child relationship; for ORDPATH, both result in matching prefixes. The byte ranges of the "following" nodes [18] must be changed when a subtree is inserted or deleted, which is an expensive operation. ORDPATH is very flexible for subtree insertion and deletion.

The accelerator table labels XML nodes with their pre-order and post-order ranks in the XML tree, and is otherwise an edge table. Its properties are similar to the byte range approaches. For example, ancestor-descendant relationship requires checking for inclusion of pre- and post-order rank pairs, and subtree insertion updates the pre- and post-order ranks of a large number of nodes.

Path-value based queries require multiple joins to match the path in EDGE and accelerator tables. The Monet system looks up the value in the table corresponding to the path. For wildcard and //-axis queries, it potentially requires a large number of table look ups. The XRel and XParent schemes look up the data table using a mapped value for the path stored in a path directory. Property look ups have similar characteristics.

Value-based lookups benefit from a separate VALUE table in the EDGE table approach, which is similar in spirit to our VALUE index. The Monet system has to search a number of CDATA tables for imprecisely specified path. The specified value is used as a filter on the data table in XRel and XParent, and the accelerator table.

Our notion of secondary XML indexes can be applied to each of these approaches to speed up different query classes. On the other hand, we could introduce a path directory to save space in XML indexes, although it adds a JOIN in case of wildcard and //-axis queries.

6. Conclusions

This paper introduces techniques for indexing XML instances stored in a relational database in an undecomposed form. It introduces a B$^+$tree called primary XML index that encodes the Infoset items of XML nodes. We have avoided the approach of decomposition of XML instances based on their schema since our goal is uniform data representation and query processing with or without XML schemas. Secondary XML indexes improve the performance of common classes of queries: (a) PATH (or PATH_VALUE) index for path-based queries, (b) PROPERTY index for property bag scenarios (c) VALUE index for value-based queries, and (d) work break index for content indexing with structural information. Performance measurements using the XMark benchmark show that these indexing ideas are highly effective for a wide class of queries.

The above indexing ideas can be extended in several ways. Many applications know the expected query workload and will benefit by indexing only the paths occurring in the queries. An expression-based XML index is the solution. Navigational queries, such as opening a folder, go down a hierarchy one level at a time in breadth-first order. If this type of query is prevalent in a workload, it is beneficial to create an index for the parent-child relationship. ID/IDREF sets up linking within an XML instance which is different from document order. Primary XML index is not geared toward efficient traversal of IDREF links. Instead, an index can be created on the IDREF links for efficient traversal of IDREF links.

XML index maintenance can be performed by reconstructing the index rows corresponding to the modified XML instance. Alternatively, it can be done incrementally, and ORDPATH is especially suited to handle such changes. This is an interesting topic for future investigation, as also is an experimental comparison between our indexing scheme and the comparable ones.

Acknowledgment

The authors would like to thank their colleagues Adrian Baras, Denis Churin, Wei Yu, Sameer Verkhedkar, Goetz Graefe and Soner Terek for their invaluable discussions on indexing of XML data; José Blakeley, Goetz Graefe and the anonymous reviewers for their suggestions on improving the content and the presentation of the paper.

References

[1] R. Bayer and K. Unterauer. Prefix B-trees. ACM Transactions on Database Systems, 2(1):11 26, 1977.

[2] P. Bohannon, J. Freire, P. Roy, J. Simeon. From XML Schema to Relations: A Cost-Based Approach to XML Storage. ICDE 2002.

[3] Extensible Markup Language (XML) 1.0. http://www.w3.org/TR/REC-xml.

[4] J. Cowan, R. Tobin, eds. XML Information Set. http://www.w3.org/TR/2001/WD-xml-infoset-20010316.

[5] M. Fernandez, Y. Kadiyska, A. Morishima, D. Suciu, W-C Tan. SilkRoute : a framework for publishing relational data in XML. ACM TODS, vol. 27, no. 4, December, 2002.

[6] D. Florescu and D. Kossmann. Storing and Querying XML Data Using an RDBMS. IEEE Data Engineering Bulletin, 22(3):27-34, 1999.

[7] R. Goldman, J. Widom. DataGuides: Enabling Query Formulation and Optimization in Semistructured Databases. VLDB 1997.

[8] T. Grust. Accelerating XPath Location Steps. SIGMOD 2002.

[9] L. Guo, F. Shao, C. Botev, J. Shanmugasundaram. XRANK: Ranked Keyword Search over XML Documents. SIGMOD 2003.

[10] H. Jiang, H. Lu, W. Wang, J. X., Yu. Path Materialization Revisited: An Efficient Storage Model for XML Data. 2nd Australian Institute of Computer Ethics Conference, 2000.

[11] Microsoft® SQL Server™. http://www.microsoft.com/sql.

[12] S. Pal, M. Fussell, I. Dolobowsky. XML support in Microsoft SQL Server 2005. http://msdn.microsoft.com/xml/default.aspx?pull=/library/en-us/dnsql90/html/sql2k5xml.asp.

[13] P. O'Neil, E. O'Neil, S. Pal, I. Cseri, G. Schaller. ORDPATHs: Insert-Friendly XML Node Labels. SIGMOD 2004.

[14] A. Schmidt, M. Kersten, M. Windhouwer, F. Waas. Efficient Relational Storage and Retrieval of XML Documents. In Proc. of WebDB 2000, pp. 47-52.

[15] A. R. Schmidt, F. Waas, M. L. Kersten, M. J. Carey, I. Manolescu, R. Busse. XMark: A Benchmark for XML Data Management. VLDB 2002.

[16] J. Shanmugasundaram, R. Krishnamurthy, I. Tatarinov. A General Technique for Querying XML Documents using a Relational Database System. SIGMOD 2001.

[17] A. Silberschatz, H. F. Korth, S. Sudarshan. Database System Concepts, 4th edition, McGraw-Hill, 2001.

[18] XML Path Language (XPath) 2.0. http://www.w3.org/TR/2003/WD-xpath20-20031112.

[19] XQuery 1.0: An XML Query Language. http://www.w3c.org/TR/xquery.

[20] I. Tatarinov, E. Viglas, K. Beyer, J. Shanmugasundaram, E. Shekita. Storing and Querying Ordered XML Using a Relational Database System. SIGMOD 2002.

[21] M. Yoshikawa and T. Amagasa. XRel: a path-based approach to storage and retrieval of XML documents using relational databases. ACM Transactions on Internet Technology, vol. 1, August 2001, pp. 110-141.

APPENDIX — XMARK Benchmark

For completeness of the presentation, we present the XMARK queries adapted for our system. The data is contained in the following tables:

Create table PEOPLE (p_id   int IDENTITY PRIMARY
        KEY, p_xmlperson   xml)
Create table ITEMS (i_id   int IDENTITY PRIMARY
        KEY, i_xmlitem   xml)
Create table open_auctions(oa_id   int IDENTITY
        PRIMARY KEY, oa_xmlopen_auction   xml)
Create table closed_auctions(ca_id   int IDENTITY
        PRIMARY KEY, ca_xmlclosed_auction   xml)
Create table categories(c_id   int identity primary key,
        ct_xmlcategory   xml)

Some of the queries described in the XMark benchmark and discussed in this paper are presented below along with their implementation in our system.

Query Q1: Return the name of the person with ID 'person0'
select p_xmlperson.value('(/site/people/person/name
    /text())[1]', 'nvarchar(4000)')
from people
where p_xmlperson.exist('/site/people/person/@id[.=
"person0"]') =1

Query Q2: Return the initial increases of all open auctions.
select oa_xmlopen_auction.query('<increase> {
        /site/open_auctions/open_auction/bidder[1]
            /increase/text() } </increase>')
from open_auctions

Query Q4: List the reserves of those open auctions where a certain person issued a bid before another person
select oa_xmlopen_auction.query('<history>
        {/site/open_auctions/open_auction/reserve/text()}
    </history>')
from open_auctions
where oa_xmlopen_auction.exist('
    (/site/open_auctions/open_auction/bidder/
        personref[@person = "person18829"])[1] <<
    (/site/open_auctions/open_auction/bidder/
        personref[@person = "person10487"])[1]')=1

Query Q6: How many items are listed on all continents?
select count(i_id) from items

Query Q7: How many pieces of prose are in our database?
SELECT SUM(c) as pieces_of_prose
FROM (SELECT COUNT(i_id) AS c FROM items
WHERE i_xmlitem.exist('//description') = 1 UNION all
SELECT COUNT(oa_id) AS c FROM open_auctions
WHERE oa_xmlopen_auction.exist('//description') = 1
UNION all
SELECT COUNT(ca_id) AS c FROM closed_auctions
WHERE ca_xmlclosed_auction.exist('//description') = 1
UNION all
SELECT COUNT(ct_id) AS c FROM categories
WHERE ct_xmlcategory.exist('//description') = 1
UNION all
SELECT COUNT(i_id) AS c FROM items
WHERE i_xmlitem.exist('//annotation') = 1 UNION all
SELECT COUNT(oa_id) AS c FROM open_auctions
WHERE oa_xmlopen_auction.exist('//annotation') = 1
UNION all
SELECT COUNT(ca_id) AS c FROM closed_auctions
WHERE ca_xmlclosed_auction.exist('//annotation') = 1
UNION all
SELECT COUNT(ct_id) AS c FROM categories
WHERE ct_xmlcategory.exist('//annotation') = 1
UNION all
SELECT COUNT(i_id) AS c FROM items
WHERE i_xmlitem.exist('//email') = 1
UNION all
SELECT COUNT(oa_id) AS c FROM open_auctions
WHERE oa_xmlopen_auction.exist('//email') = 1
UNION all
SELECT COUNT(ca_id) AS c FROM closed_auctions
WHERE ca_xmlclosed_auction.exist('//email') = 1
UNION all
SELECT COUNT(ct_id) AS c FROM categories
WHERE ct_xmlcategory.exist('//email') = 1) as i

Query Q9: List the names of persons and the names of the items they bought in Europe.
SELECT t.p_xmlperson.query('
    <person name="{(/site/people/person/name)[1]}">
        {sql:column("i_name")}</person>')
FROM (
    SELECT p_xmlperson, p_id, i_id, i_xmlitem.value('
        (/site/regions/namerica/item/name)[1]',
        'nvarchar(400)') i_name
    FROM people LEFT OUTER JOIN closed_auctions
        ON (p_xmlperson.value('
            (/site/people/person/@id)[1]',
            'nvarchar(400)') =
            ca_xmlclosed_auction.value('
            (/site/closed_auctions/closed_auction/
            buyer/@person)[1]', 'nvarchar(400)')
        LEFT OUTER JOIN items
        ON (ca_xmlclosed_auction.value('
            (/site/closed_auctions/closed_auction/
            itemref/@item)[1]', 'nvarchar(400)') =
            i_xmlitem.value('
            (/site/regions/namerica/item/@id)[1]',
            'nvarchar(400)')) t ORDER BY p_id, i_id

Query Q10: List all persons according to their interest; use French markup in the result.
select person.value('(.)[1]', 'varchar(50)') category,
    cp.p_xmlperson.query(
    '<personne><statistiques>
<sexe>{/site/people/person/gender/text()}</sexe>,
<age>{/site/people/person/age/text()}</age>,
 <education>{/site/people/person/education/text()}
</education>, <revenu>
{/site/people/person/income/text()}</revenu>
</statistiques><coordonnees>
<nom>{/site/people/person/name/text()}</nom>,
<rue>{/site/people/person/address/street/text()}</rue>,
<ville>{/site/people/person/address/city/text()}</ville>,
<pays>{/site/people/person/address/country/text()}
</pays>, <reseau>
<courrier>{/site/people/person/emailaddress/text()}
</courrier>
<pagePerso>{/site/people/person/homepage/text()}
</pagePerso></reseau></coordonnees>
<cartePaiement>{/site/people/person/creditcard/text()}
</cartePaiement></personne>')
from people cp cross apply
cp.p_xmlperson.nodes('/site/people/person/profile/interest
/@category') n(person) ORDER BY category

Query Q16: Return the IDs of those auctions that have one or more keywords in emphasis.
select ca_xmlclosed_auction.query('
    <person id ="{(/site/closed_auctions/
    closed_auction/seller/@person)[1]}"/> ')
from closed_auctions
where ca_xmlclosed_auction.exist('
    /site/closed_auctions/closed_auction/annotation/
    description/parlist/listitem/parlist/listitem/text/
    emph/keyword/text()') =1

Query Q20: Group customers by their income and output the cardinality of each group.
SELECT CAST(('<result>' + '<preferred>' +
    cast(sum(case when income>=100000 then 1
    else 0 end) as nvarchar(10))+ '</preferred>' +
    '<standard>' +   cast(sum(case when
income<100000 and
    income>=30000 then 1 else 0 end) as
    nvarchar(10))+ '</standard>' +
    '<challenge>' +
    cast(sum(case when income<30000 then 1 else 0
    end) as nvarchar(10)) + '</challenge>' +
    '<na>' + cast(sum(case when income is null then 1
        else 0 end) as nvarchar(10))+
    '</na>' + '</result>') AS XML)
FROM (SELECT p_xmlperson.value('
    (/site/people/person/profile/@income)[1]','float')
    as income FROM people) i

Automated Statistics Collection in DB2 UDB

A. Aboulnaga[*] P. Haas[*] M. Kandil[+] S. Lightstone[+] G. Lohman[*] V. Markl[*] I. Popivanov[+] V. Raman[*]

[*]IBM Almaden Research Center
650 Harry Road
San Jose, CA
USA

[+]IBM Toronto Development Lab
8200 Warden Avenue
Markham, ON
Canada

{aashraf, phaas, lohman, marklv, ravijay}@us.ibm.com, {mkandil, light, ivannp}@ca.ibm.com

Abstract

The use of inaccurate or outdated database statistics by the query optimizer in a relational DBMS often results in a poor choice of query execution plans and hence unacceptably long query processing times. Configuration and maintenance of these statistics has traditionally been a time-consuming manual operation, requiring that the database administrator (DBA) continually monitor query performance and data changes in order to determine when to refresh the statistics values and when and how to adjust the set of statistics that the DBMS maintains. In this paper we describe the new Automated Statistics Collection (ASC) component of IBM® DB2® Universal Database™ (DB2 UDB). This autonomic technology frees the DBA from the tedious task of manually supervising the collection and maintenance of database statistics. ASC monitors both the update-delete-insert (UDI) activities on the data as well as query feedback (QF), i.e., the results of the queries that are executed on the data. ASC uses these two sources of information to automatically decide which statistics to collect and when to collect them. This combination of UDI-driven and QF-driven autonomic processes ensures that the system can handle unforeseen queries while also ensuring good performance for frequent and important queries. We present the basic concepts, architecture, and key implementation details of ASC in DB2 UDB, and present a case study showing how the use of ASC can speed up a query workload by orders of magnitude without requiring any DBA intervention.

1. Introduction

Query optimizers employ database statistics to determine the best execution strategy for a query. This metadata usually includes the number of rows in a table, the number of distinct values for a column, the most frequent values in a column, and, for numeric data, the distribution of data values in a column (usually stored as a set of quantiles). The optimizer uses these statistics to compute the *cardinality* (i.e., number of rows processed) at each intermediate step of a query execution plan. Advanced optimizers also use joint statistics on groups of columns within a table in order to deal with possible correlations between column values.

The presence of inaccurate or outdated statistics causes the optimizer to inaccurately estimate the cardinalities and costs of the steps in a query plan, which can result in a poor choice of plan and lead to unacceptably long query processing times. Unfortunately, it is all too easy for the statistics in a DBMS to deteriorate over time. In general, database statistics are not incrementally updated during data manipulations such as insert, update, delete, and load, because such incremental maintenance is too expensive. Statistics for tables with high data change rates are therefore very likely to be out of date. Even if the statistics are refreshed frequently, they may still lead to inaccurate cost estimates if the configuration parameters for the statistics are not set properly. Examples of such parameters include the number of frequent values and the number of quantiles to maintain. These parameters depend heavily on the statistical properties of the data, which can change over time.

Previous commercial database systems have required the DBA to manually configure and schedule the collection and maintenance of statistics, a tedious and time-consuming task. In this paper we describe the new Automated Statistics Collection (ASC) component of DB2 UDB, which has been developed as part of a general effort to incorporate autonomic technology into DB2 UDB products [LLZ02, LSZ03]. The ASC subsystem frees the DBA from the burden of statistics management. ASC monitors update-delete-insert (UDI) activity on the data tables in order to detect outdated statistics. ASC also monitors query feedback (QF), i.e., the results of the queries that are executed on the data, in order to detect

---

Permission to copy without fee all or part of this material is granted provided that the copies are not made or distributed for direct commercial advantage, the VLDB copyright notice and the title of the publication and its date appear, and notice is given that copying is by permission of the Very Large Data Base Endowment. To copy otherwise, or to republish, requires a fee and/or special permission from the Endowment

**Proceedings of the 30th VLDB Conference,
Toronto, Canada, 2004**

and adjust for outdated or improperly configured statistics. Based on this information, ASC decides which statistics to gather, at what level of detail to gather them, and when to gather them, without requiring any DBA intervention.

The novel features of ASC include (1) the simultaneous use of both a "UDI-driven" autonomic process that monitors UDI activity (including load operations) on tables and a "QF-driven" feedback loop that monitors estimated and actual results of query executions, (2) methods for deciding if the data in a table has changed sufficiently to require a refresh of the statistics, (3) methods for deciding which statistics to gather and at what level of detail to gather them based on monitored query results, and (4) methods for scheduling statistics collection that combine and prioritize the recommendations from the UDI-driven and QF-driven analyses.

Neither a UDI-driven nor a QF-driven approach is sufficient by itself. UDI-driven approaches are proactive and therefore can handle unforeseen queries, but may not concentrate enough effort on maintaining statistics that are critical to the users' workload. QF-driven approaches are reactive and require some learning time, but focus on the most critical statistics, and hence use system resources very efficiently. ASC combines the strengths of both approaches, proactively collecting basic statistics on every table periodically so as to be prepared for queries that have not been anticipated, and reactively refining statistics as required by the workload so as to be well prepared for the most important queries.

The remainder of the paper is organized as follows: in Section 2 we describe the overall ASC architecture. Sections 3 and 4 focus respectively on the UDI-driven and QF-driven approaches to detection of outdated and inaccurate statistics. In Section 5 we describe how the ASC scheduler combines and prioritizes the recommendations from both the UDI-driven and the QF-driven autonomic components in order to schedule the actual statistics collection. Section 6 presents a case study using a realistic workload of queries on a database of car-accident records. Section 7 surveys related work. Section 8 presents conclusions and gives an outlook on future work.

2. Automated Statistics Collection

We first review some basic facts about the collection and use of statistics in DB2 UDB. We then describe the modifications to DB2 UDB that comprise the ASC component.

2.1 Statistics in DB2

DB2 UDB stores in the system catalog [IBM04] the statistics pertinent to each table, including overall properties of the table, detailed information about the columns in the table, and information about any indexes on columns of the table. The DB2 UDB optimizer uses

Table Name	Content
tables	number of rows in a table
columns	number of distinct values for that column
indexes	number of distinct index keys, clustering of the table with respect to. the index, physical properties of the index
coldist	quantiles and frequent values of a column
colgroups	distinct number of values for a group of columns

Table 1: DB2 Statistics

the information in the catalog when selecting a query plan. Table 1 summarizes the statistical information used by the optimizer and the names of the tables in the DB2 UDB SYSTAT schema that store the information.

The DB2 RUNSTATS utility collects the statistics and populates the system catalog tables. RUNSTATS is executed on a per table basis, and for any given table the user can specify the specific columns and indexes on which statistics are to be created. For each table in a database schema, the system catalog records the most recent time that RUNSTATS has been executed on the table. The exact configuration parameters for RUNSTATS on each table (i.e., the set of columns on which to gather statistics, the number of quantiles and frequent values to collect for a column, the set of column-group statistics to maintain, etc.) are recorded in a *RUNSTATS profile*. RUNSTATS profiles are stored in the system catalog (in the SYSSTAT.PROFILE table) and can be modified through the RUNSTATS command and queried through SQL.

2.2 ASC Architecture

The ASC component introduces both a UDI-driven and a QF-driven autonomic process into the DB2 UDB system. The first process monitors table activity and recommends execution of RUNSTATS on a table whenever UDI or LOAD statements against this table have changed the data distribution so that the present statistics for that table are substantially outdated. The second process monitors query results on a table. The process modifies the RUNSTATS profile for the table and recommends execution of RUNSTATS whenever it detects either that configuration parameters have been set improperly or that the statistics are outdated. The scheduler component combines the output of these two processes and triggers the execution of RUNSTATS on appropriate sets of tables and at appropriate times. In general, the scheduler causes RUNSTATS to be executed on one or more tables during a *maintenance iteration* that is concentrated within a specified time period called a *maintenance window*. The

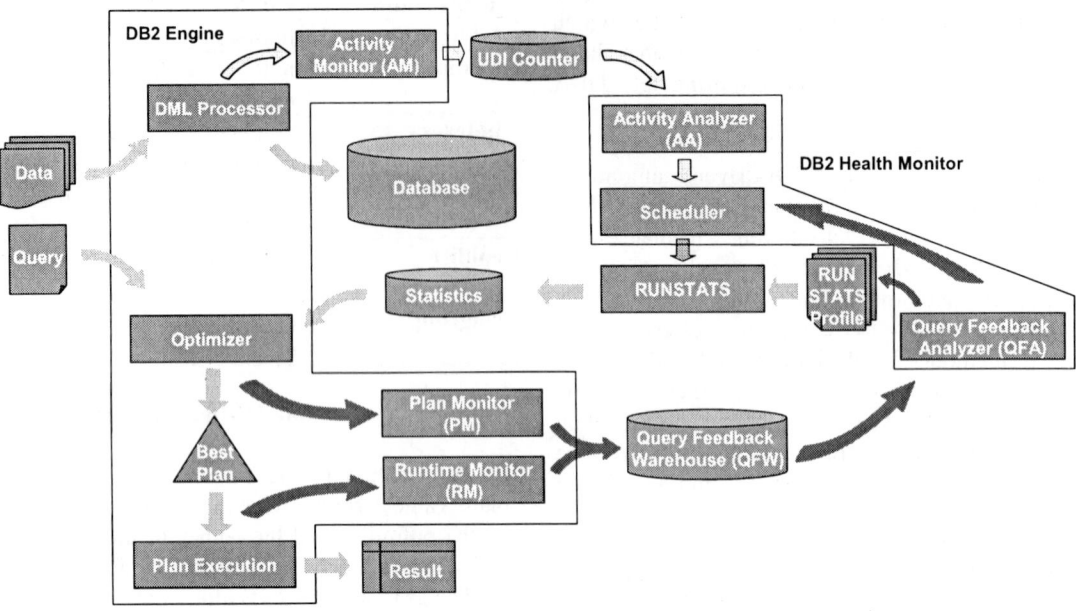

Figure 1: ASC Architecture

frequency and length of maintenance windows can be controlled by the DBA.

Figure 1 depicts the overall architecture of the ASC component. The left side of the figure depicts functionality that is implemented in the DB2 UDB engine, i.e., the query processor with optimizer and plan execution, the data manipulation language (DML) processor, and the monitors that facilitate several of the autonomic capabilities of DB2 UDB. The right side of the figure depicts a pair of analyzers and a scheduler that have been added to the DB2 Health Monitor to realize automated statistics collection. The analyzers periodically investigate the output of the monitors and recommend to the scheduler a set of tables on which to collect statistics.

The upper portion of the figure pertains to the UDI-driven autonomic process. When changing the data in a table according to a UDI or LOAD statement, the DML processor not only modifies the database, but also sends information to an *activity monitor* (AM) that records the number of changes against each table using a UDI-counter. The *activity analyzer* (AA) uses this information to determine whether statistics on an active table have changed enough to justify statistics collection for this table. The AA also estimates the degree to which activity on a table has altered the data distribution; the *scheduler* uses such estimates to prioritize tables for statistics collection. To avoid starvation, "critical" tables that have experienced UDI activity but have been ignored over many past maintenance iterations eventually receive top priority for statistics collection.

The lower portion of the figure pertains to the QF-driven autonomic process. This process observes query activity by using a *plan monitor* (PM), which stores the best plan together with the optimizer's cardinality estimate for each intermediate result. During plan execution, a *run-time monitor* (RM) observes the actual cardinalities. All of this compile-time and run-time information is stored in a *query feedback warehouse* (QFW) in the form of relational tables. A *query feedback analyzer* (QFA) periodically reviews these tables in order to generate modifications to the RUNSTATS profiles. The QFA bases these modifications on the discrepancy between actual and estimated cardinalities. Besides modifying RUNSTATS profiles, QFA communicates to the scheduler its findings about tables with modified RUNSTATS profiles and tables with outdated statistics, so that the scheduler can properly prioritize the automatic execution of RUNSTATS.

The statistics-collection process, like any other background maintenance task, must not significantly impede more important business-critical tasks. Therefore, the scheduler executes each RUNSTATS task as a "throttled" background process in order to guarantee that the user workload is not slowed down by more than a specified amount. During a maintenance window, RUNSTATS tasks are allocated a large portion of the available system resources. If there are tables that still need to be processed when the maintenance window ends, then processing continues, but RUNSTATS is throttled back so that the maximum allowable impact on query performance is limited to a small value (typically around 7%). When it is time to start the next maintenance window, any RUNSTATS tasks that are under way are first allowed to complete. To throttle the maintenance process, the scheduler exploits the general mechanism in DB2 UDB for adaptively tuning resource consumption during process execution [PRH+03a, PRH+03b]. This mechanism, which rests on control-theoretic techniques, is used to manage

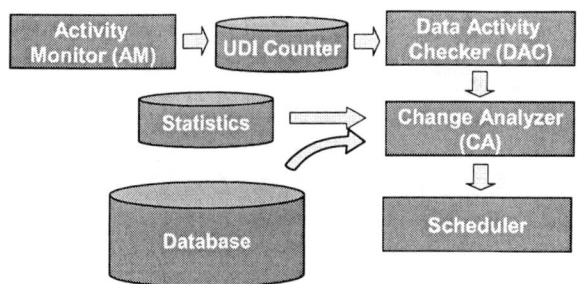

Figure 2: UDI-Driven Autonomic Process

other expensive maintenance processes such as database backup and table reorganization.

3. Detecting Stale Statistics via Data Activity

The UDI-driven autonomic process analyzes both the number of UDI and load operations and the changes in data values to determine whether the statistics on a table T have changed sufficiently so that statistics collection is justified. The process takes as input a list G of tables to be checked, as provided by the scheduler, and its output is a prioritized list of tables D, where D is a subset of G.

Figure 2 illustrates the overall detection process. As can be seen, the activity analyzer comprises two components. The *data activity checker* (DAC) is first executed to ensure that only tables with a reasonably large amount of data activity are considered for statistics collection. Each table in G that is not eliminated by the DAC is inserted into D. The list D is then passed to a *change analyzer* (CA). For each table T in D, the CA estimates for each "analyzable" column in T the degree of change in the data distribution since RUNSTATS was last executed on T; a column is analyzable if quantile statistics for the column are maintained in the system catalog. If no analyzable column in T evidences a significant degree of change, then T is removed from D.

After execution of the CA, the list D contains essentially only those tables having both significant data activity and significant changes in data values in at least one column. This list is then passed to the scheduler. We now describe the various components of the detection process in more detail.

3.1 Activity Monitor

The task of the activity monitor (AM) is to quantify the update activity for each table. It monitors both the loading of data into tables and UDI operations on tables. The AM maintains a UDI-counter for each table. The counter is increased by 1 whenever an existing row is updated or deleted, or a new row is inserted. The counter is set to 0 when the table is created, and is reset to 0 whenever RUNSTATS is executed on the table.

The UDI-counter is stored in the table descriptor together with other internal data structures. It is usually cached in memory and flushed to disk using the same discipline as for the rest of the data structures. Therefore, maintenance of the UDI-counter rarely causes extra I/O operations.

3.2 Data-Activity Checker

The DAC is the first process invoked when searching for outdated statistics because the presence of data activity is necessary in order for statistics to change. Lack of data activity means statistics need not be updated unless the QF-driven process gives a different indication, i.e., unless the QFA modifies the configuration parameters for some statistics or detects outdated statistics. This multi-tier approach significantly reduces the number of maintenance tasks performed over time. Tables with either low data activity or marginal changes to the statistics are ignored, so that system resources can be devoted to maintaining the most important tables.

The DAC first verifies that the table-related data structures are cached in memory. Their absence from the cache means that the table has not been used recently; it follows that the table has low data activity and can be ignored. Otherwise, the table is considered to be a candidate for statistics collection, and the DAC inspects the UDI-counter maintained for that table. If the UDI-counter suggests that at least τ% of the rows have been modified, this table is passed on to the change analyzer to further investigate whether statistics on this table need to be collected. The current implementation of DAC uses a value of $\tau = 10$.

It is possible that in some unusual cases a small number of records in a given table are changed, but the data values in these records are altered so drastically that query performance is affected. In this case, the table may not be detected by the DAC, and hence the AA. If this table is referenced in the query workload, however, then it will be detected by the QFA.

3.3 Change Analyzer

For each table T in its input list D, the CA takes a small sample from T and computes a synopsis data structure $S = S(T)$, where S comprises histograms of the marginal data

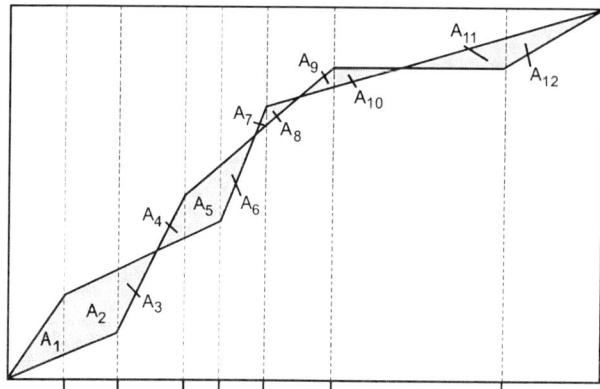

Figure 3: Computing the Change Value

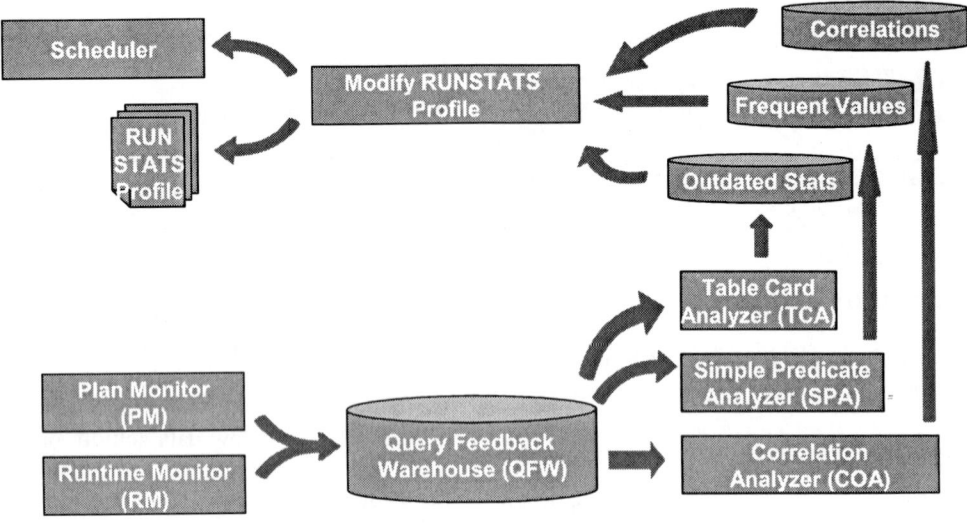

Figure 4: QF-driven Autonomic Process

distribution for each analyzable column. We have found that a sample consisting of about 2000 pages of table data, selected using page-level Bernoulli sampling, provides sufficient statistical precision for our purposes; see [PIHS96, IMHB04]. The CA also obtains an analogous synopsis $R = R(T)$ based on the (possibly outdated) marginal data distributions that are stored in the system catalog. For each analyzable column, the CA then measures the "distance" between the histograms. The CA deletes table T from D, i.e., declares the change in data values to be insignificant, if and only if the distance for each analyzable column lies below a specified threshold. If the change is significant for at least one analyzable column, then the CA leaves table T in D and, as described below, assigns to T a priority that the scheduler can use to determine when to update T relative to other tables.

For a fixed analyzable column $T.C$ (assumed to contain numeric data) the CA uses a normalized L_1 distance to measure the change in the data distribution. Specifically, denote by $e_Y(T.C \leq v)$ the cardinality estimate for the predicate $T.C \leq v$ (i.e., the estimated number of rows in T that satisfy the predicate) based on synopsis Y, and by l and u the smallest and largest bucket boundary points that appear in R and S. Then

$$\text{change}(T.C, R, S) = \frac{1}{|u-l|} \int_l^u |e_R(T.C \leq v) - e_S(T.C \leq v)| dv.$$

Observe that change($T.C,R,S$) can be interpreted as the average absolute discrepancy in cardinality estimates over a family of one-sided inequality predicates.

Suppose that the histogram of $T.C$ values is represented by a set of bucket boundaries (typically quantiles) in both synopses R and S. Then change($T.C,R,S$) can be computed in a simple manner using essentially a "line sweep" algorithm. Specifically, determine the union of the two sets of bucket boundaries, and observe that $e_R(T.C \leq v)$ and $e_S(T.C \leq v)$ are linear and nondecreasing functions of v over each subinterval defined by a pair of successive bucket boundary points. Thus, the integral $\int_l^u |e_R(T.C \leq v) - e_S(T.C \leq v)| dv$ can be represented as the area of the region that lies between two piecewise-linear curves; see, for example, the shaded region in Figure 3, where the dashed lines correspond to the combined bucket boundaries. This area can in turn be expressed as a sum of areas of simple trapezoids and triangles, each of which is quick and easy to compute. Summing these areas and dividing by $l - u$ yields the value of change($T.C, R, S$).

If change($T.C,R,S$) > θ for at least one column, where θ is an empirically determined threshold value, then the CA concludes that data distribution has changed, identifies table T as a candidate for statistics collection, and assigns to T a priority equal to $\max_C$ change($T.C,R,S$).

The CA can also use the foregoing measurement technique to quantify the change in data values as measured by successive sets of catalog statistics. Dividing this change value by the amount of time between the corresponding executions of RUNSTATS yields an estimate of the data change rate. As described in Section 5, the scheduler uses such rate-of-change estimates to project the next time at which a table will be due for statistics maintenance.

4. Detecting Poor Statistics from Queries

The QF-driven autonomic process monitors query execution and records estimation errors in the QFW. The QFA analyzes the data in the QFW to determine which tables have outdated statistics, whether and how the frequent values for columns on a particular table should be reconfigured, and which (intra-table) correlation statistics should be created in order to reduce estimation errors in the future. As shown in Figure 4, the QFA comprises three components. The *table cardinality analyzer* (TCA) detects whether statistics are outdated by comparing the estimated and actual size of a table. The *simple-predicate analyzer* (SPA) uses estimated and actual cardinalities of simple equality predicates to determine the number of frequent values that should be used when creating the statistics for a particular column. The *correlation analyzer* (COA) uses cardinality information about tables, simple equality predicates, and conjunctive predicates to determine the set of column-group statistics to recommend to the scheduler. The output of the QFA is a prioritized list of tables Q that require statistics collection, along with the configuration parameter changes for the statistics of each table. The list Q is sent to the scheduler, and the configuration changes are stored in the RUNSTATS profiles.

4.1 The QFW and Its Maintenance

The QFW (see Figure 5) is populated periodically using the information generated by the PM and the RM. For each query, the PM records, at compile time, the predicates in the query (i.e., the column names, relational operators, and values) along with the optimizer's cardinality estimate for each predicate. The RM records run-time information about each query that includes the actual cardinalities for each table and predicate, as well as the actual values of parameter markers or host variables used in a query.

The data in the QFW is organized into relational tables. The *feedback query table* stores each query in its entirety, along with a skeleton query plan.

The *feedback predicate table* stores detailed predicate information. In our current implementation, the QFW stores information for simple predicates of the form COLUMN $\oplus$ 'literal' (where $\oplus$ is a relational operator such as "=" or "<"), as well as compound predicates that reference a single table and are conjunctions of simple predicates. During the planning and processing of a query containing a compound predicate that comprises $N \geq 1$ "Boolean factors" (i.e., conjuncts), the PM and RM have the opportunity to observe actual and estimated cardinalities for one or more "sub-predicates," each consisting of the conjunction of a subset of the N Boolean factors. Each such sub-predicate generates an entry in the feedback predicate table that includes the table referenced by the sub-predicate, the number of Boolean factors, and the estimated and observed cardinality.

The *feedback column table* contains an entry for each Boolean factor that appears in the feedback predicate table. Each entry includes the column name, relational operator, and literal of the predicate. The literal may come from either PM (in case of hard-coded predicates) or RM (in case of parameter markers or host variables).

The recommendations of the QFA concerning outdated statistics, frequent values, and correlations are also stored in the QFW. The *recommendation column table* contains column information for these recommendations, i.e., the column name and number of frequent values. The *recommendation column-group* table stores similar information but for column groups rather than individual columns.

The QFW is an autonomic component of DB2 UDB in its own right. It automatically purges old data, when necessary, and it never grows beyond a DBA-specified size.

4.2 Operation of the QFA

The QFA processes the query feedback stored in the QFW and generates recommendations for correcting cardinality estimation errors in the future. The QFA proceeds by measuring, classifying, aggregating, and prioritizing the differences between optimizer-based cardinality estimates and actual cardinalities. Cardinalities considered include those for table size, for simple equality predicates of the form COLUMN = 'literal', and for pairwise conjuncts of simple equality predicates. The QFA determines the cause of each estimation error by sequentially executing the table cardinality analyzer, the simple-predicate analyzer, and then the correlation analyzer. The QFA then aggregates the errors for each column and table, prioritizes the tables, and communicates its results to the scheduler and to the RUNSTATS profiles. We describe each of these operational phases in more detail below.

4.2.1 Table Cardinality Analyzer

The TCA simply compares the actual cardinality of each table in the feedback warehouse with the estimated cardinality based on the system catalog statistics. A discrepancy indicates that the statistics for this table are out of date. (This analysis is similar in spirit to the use of the UDI-counter by the DAC.)

4.2.2 Simple-Predicate Analyzer

For each column represented in the QFW, the SPA examines the errors in the simple equality predicates that reference the column to check whether the number of frequent values maintained for the column in the system

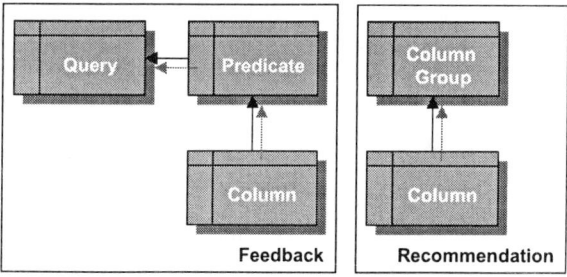

Figure 5: Tables in the QFW

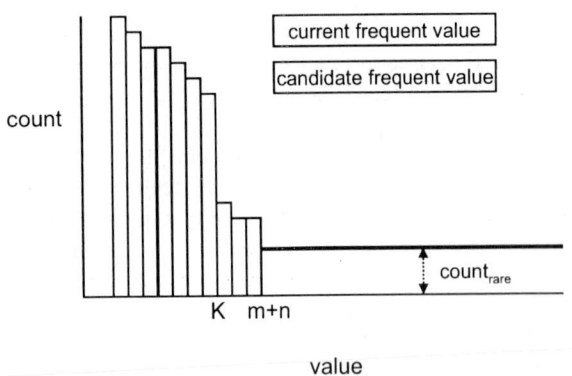

Figure 6: Frequencies Used by SPA

catalog is sufficient. If not, then the SPA automatically recommends an appropriate number of frequent values to maintain. Note that following such a recommendation also results in bringing the frequent-value statistics up to date. Because some of the statistics in the catalog are collected using random-sampling techniques, the QFA considers only those QFW entries where the observed error exceeds the expected error from normal sampling fluctuations.

Use of frequent-value statistics minimizes estimation errors arising from skew in the column-value frequencies. It is difficult, however, for a DBA to manually determine the "right" number of frequent values to track. The automated approach used by the SPA is as follows. First the SPA scans the QFW and the system catalog to compile a list of all "known" value frequencies for the column. These include:

- The frequencies $fv_1 .. fv_n$ of the currently maintained frequent values, as recorded in the system catalog.
- The frequencies $cfv_1 ... cfv_m$ of all values for which there is a relevant error record in the QFW. These values can be considered as candidate frequent values to maintain.
- An average frequency assigned to each of the remaining "rare" (i.e., infrequent) values, computed using a uniformity assumption from the estimated number of rows in the table and the number of distinct values in the column.

When multiple frequency estimates are available for a given column value, the SPA uses the most recent one.

Figure 6 illustrates the frequency list as a bar graph, in descending order of frequency. Suppose that the table has d distinct values in total, and a total cardinality of C. Then the successive bar heights are $f_1, f_2, ... f_{m+n}, count_{rare}, count_{rare}, ... , count_{rare}$ ($d - m - n$ times), where $f_1, f_2, ..., f_{m+n}$ is $\{fv_1, ... fv_n, cfv_1, ... cfv_m\}$ arranged in descending order, and

$$count_{rare} = (C - f_1 - f_2 - \cdots - f_{m+n})/(d - m - n).$$

SPA now determines the number K of frequent values to maintain, where $n \leq K \leq m + n$. If DB2 UDB maintains K

```
// G, P, D, Q, C are lists of tables
// T is a table
G := tables to be checked by AA during the initial
        maintenance iteration
P, D, Q, C := {}
while(true)
{
  // Call the AA on the Tables in G
  D := AA(G);
  // Call the Query Feedback Analyzer
  Q := QFA();
  // prioritize D and Q based on the ranking criteria
  // and merge with list of critical tables C
  P := prioritizeMerge(D, Q, C);
  while (still time in maintenance window)
  {
    T := Pop(P); // T is table in P with highest priority
    execute RUNSTATS on T
            and estimate the data change rate;
  }
  // Construct list for next maintenance interval
  (G, C) := constructDueTables()
  sleep until the next maintenance window;
}
```

Figure 7: Scheduling Algorithm

frequent values, then, when estimating cardinalities, the optimizer uses the exact count for these values and an average count of

$$newcount_{rare} = \left(C - \sum_{i=1}^{K} f_i\right)/(d - K)$$

for each of the remaining values. The total absolute estimation error over all possible simple equality predicates is

$$AbsError(K) = \sum_{i=K+1}^{m+n} |f_i - newcount_{rare}|$$
$$+ (d - m - n)\,|count_{rare} - newcount_{rare}|.$$

The first term represents the contribution due to the $m + n - K$ known frequencies that DB2 UDB chooses not to retain, and the second term is the contribution from the remaining values. Observe that $AbsError(K)$ is decreasing in K. To determine the number of frequent values to maintain, we initially set $K = n$ and then increase the value of K until either $AbsError(K)$ falls below a specified threshold or $K = \min(m + n, \beta)$, where β is a pre-specified upper bound on the number of frequent values to maintain.

4.2.3 Correlation Analyzer

The COA focuses on pairwise correlations between columns in a table, because experiments indicate that the marginal benefit of correcting for higher-order correlations is relatively small; see [IMHB04]. For each pair of columns that appear jointly in a QFW record, the COA compares the actual selectivity of each conjunctive

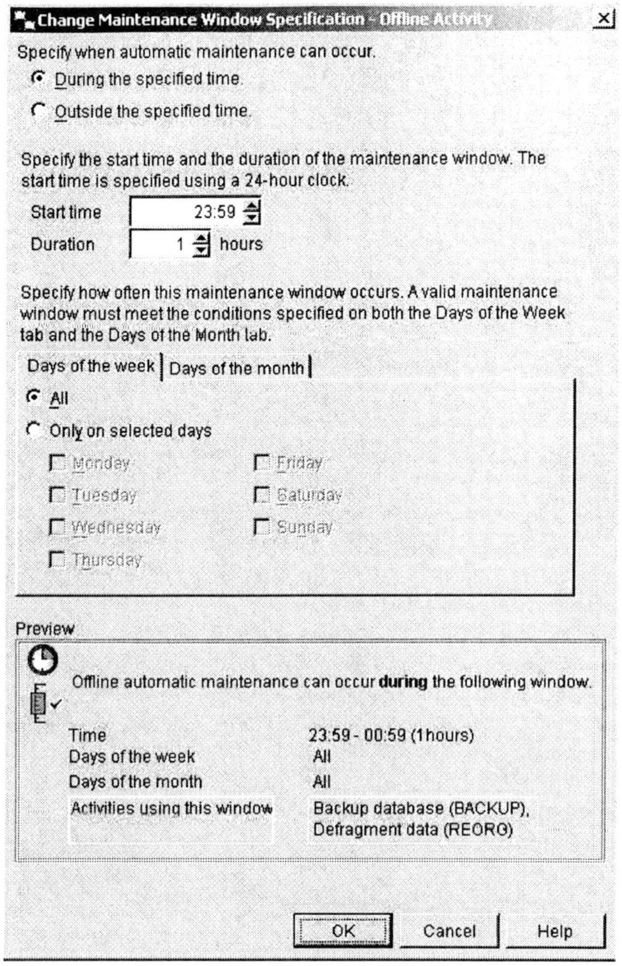

Figure 8: Specifying the Maintenance Window

predicate to the product of the actual selectivity of the Boolean factors of the conjunct, assuming that this information is available. For example, suppose that simple equality predicates p_1 and p_2 are evaluated while processing a query, along with the conjunctive predicate $p_1 \wedge p_2$. Denote by α_1, α_2, and α_{12} cardinalities for these queries that are observed during execution of the query, and denote by m the cardinality of the entire table. Then the COA deems the independence assumption to be valid if and only if

$$1 - \Theta \leq \frac{\alpha_{12} m}{\alpha_1 \alpha_2} \leq 1 + \Theta,$$

where $\Theta \in (0,1)$ is a small pre-specified parameter. Otherwise, the COA declares that a correlation error of absolute magnitude $|\alpha_{12} - (\alpha_1 \alpha_2 / m)|$ has occurred.

The analysis becomes more complicated when one or more of the actual cardinalities are not available, as is often the case in practice. The COA deals with the problem by estimating the missing information and adjusting the error-detection threshold and estimate of the error magnitude accordingly. Details of the complete algorithm will appear in a forthcoming paper.

4.2.4 Synthesizing the Final Outputs

The QFA processes feedback records as described above, grouped either by column name or, for records involving column pairs, by *column-group identifier*, where a column-group identifier comprises the pair of column names enumerated in lexicographic order. The QFA then sums up the absolute errors for each column and column group, and records the column-wise or group-wise error in the appropriate recommendation table. Next, the QFA identifies those columns and column groups that are responsible for the most severe errors. QFA modifies the RUNSTATS profiles so that RUNSTATS will increase the number of frequent-value statistics for each identified column and create joint statistics for each identified column group when it is next executed on the table that contains the column or column group. Finally, the QFA computes the total error for each table by combining the errors for table cardinality, cardinality of simple predicates, and cardinality of pairwise conjunctive predicates, weighing each error by its frequency (number of queries experiencing this error as stored in the QFW). Based on these table-wise errors, the QFA sends to the scheduler a list Q of tables on which to execute RUNSTATS.

5. Scheduling the Collection of Statistics

The scheduler drives the statistics-collection process. During periodic maintenance iterations (with corresponding maintenance windows), the scheduler invokes the AA and QFA, and combines the output D of the AA and the output Q of the QFA to create a combined prioritized list P of tables to be processed. The scheduler also invokes RUNSTATS as a throttled background process to collect statistics on those tables having the highest priority. Figure 7 displays the overall scheduling algorithm. As can be seen from Figure 7, the *prioritizeMerge* and *constructDueTables* procedures form the heart of the scheduling algorithm. We discuss these procedures in the following subsections.

The DBA can control the behavior of autonomic background activities by configuring the scheduler. For example, the DBA can limit the scope of automated statistics collection to certain tables, or can exclude certain tables from automatic maintenance. The DBA can also specify the maintenance window. Finally, the DBA can also control whether the scheduler should invoke QFA, AA, or both, and specify the maximum allowable disk space for the QFW. Figure 8 shows the GUI for specification of the maintenance window.

5.1 Prioritizing Tables for Processing

Prioritizing tables for processing is an important and challenging task. For large databases with potentially

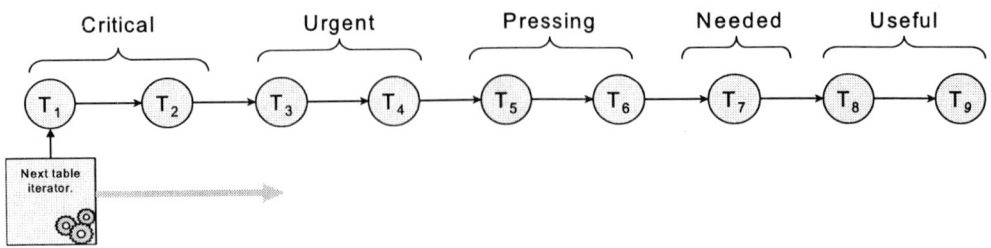

Figure 9: Priority Queue for Scheduler

thousands of tables and terabytes of data, selecting the wrong tables for statistics collection might mean that very needy tables will have to wait an unreasonable length of time, with detrimental effects on query performance.

The scheduler classifies tables into five distinct "urgency" classes. A table is *useful* with respect to statistics refresh if more than 0% but less than 50% of the rows have experienced some data change since the last statistics refresh on the table. A table is *needed* if it has been recommended for processing by the QFA. A *pressing* table has had 50% or more rows experiencing change since the last statistics refresh. An *urgent* table is both needed and either pressing or useful. A *critical* table is a table that has been starved: either the UDI-counter is positive but an excessive number of maintenance iterations have passed since the last statistics refresh, or RUNSTATS has never been executed on the table. Critical tables are always inserted into the list P of tables to be processed in the current maintenance window and are given top priority in this list. If a table falls into multiple classes, then the most urgent of the classes defines the table's final categorization.

The scheduler prioritizes critical tables above urgent tables, urgent tables above pressing tables, and so forth. The tables are then prioritized within each class, resulting in a priority queue that specifies the order in which tables are selected for statistics refresh; see Figure 9.

Useful tables are prioritized within their class by the percentage of rows changed, and similarly for pressing tables. Tables within both the needed and urgent classes are prioritized by a combination of their *frequency count* and *aggregated estimation error*. The frequency count of a table is the number of error records in the QFW that reference the table, and measures a table's relative importance within the workload. Aggregated estimation error is the table-wise error that is computed by the QFA, as described in Section 4.2.4. Finally, critical tables are ranked by their data change rate, as defined in Section 5.2 below; tables with no rate-of-change information (because RUNSTATS has been executed on the table less than two times) receive top priority. This ranking scheme ensures that a single table never appears more than once in the queue.

The rationale for the ranking scheme is as follows. It is useful to refresh statistics on tables that experience low to moderate data change, but which have not been detected by QFA as impacting the workload, in case these tables are accessed by the workload in the future. Such refresh activity should be subject to preemption by more important tasks. Tables that are known to be accessed by the workload and have obsolete statistics clearly need a statistics update. Tables that have experienced massive data change will almost surely cause massive query optimization problems if their statistics are not refreshed, and are also likely to show up in the workload, so that there is a pressing need for a statistics update. If such tables have actually shown up in the workload and generated significant estimation errors, then processing these tables becomes even more urgent. Finally, we allow the scheduler to identify tables as critical in order to avoid starvation problems in which tables experience UDI operations or lack statistics altogether, but are deferred indefinitely.

5.2 Constructing the List of Due Tables

After RUNSTATS has been executed on a table T, the newly collected statistics N for T are stored in the system catalog. The scheduler now invokes the CA to estimate the rate of change of the statistics, using N and the previous set of statistics R for T. (See the discussion at the end of Section 3.3.) Based on this rate of change, the scheduler determines the next maintenance iteration at which T will be due for consideration by AA.

Prior to the first maintenance iteration, the list G of input tables to the AA is initialized to contain all of the tables in the database that are subject to automatic statistics collection. (Recall that the DBA can limit the scope of ASC to a subset of the tables.) At the end of each maintenance window, the *constructDueTables* procedure (see Figure 7) is invoked to create the list G of tables that are due to be checked by AA in the next iteration. This function also constructs the list C of tables that are now critical (as previously defined).

6. A Case Study using a DMV Database

We illustrate the effect of ASC on query processing using a case study on a database that stores information about car accidents in various countries. The statistics maintenance is completely controlled by ASC: no statistics are configured or collected by the DBA at any

time. The study consists of running and timing a typical workload of 11 reporting queries on the database both before and after the execution of the various components of ASC. Specifically, the case study consists of running the workload after each of the following steps:
   A. Initial loading of the database
   B. Execution of ASC (AA only)
   C. Insertion of additional accidents that occurred in Canada
   D. Execution of ASC (AA only)
   E. Execution of ASC (QFA only)

We refer to the set of queries executed after step A as "query-group A," the queries executed after step B as "query-group B," and so forth. We modified the operation of ASC in steps D and E above in order to investigate the benefits of QFA over and above those of AA.

We carried out the case study using a one-CPU 333 Mhz PowerPC 604® system with 512 MB memory, two 8.5 GB disks, running AIX® 4.3.3. ML11. The DMV database has a size of 1.5 GB and consists of four major tables: ACCIDENTS, CAR, OWNERS, and owner DEMO-GRAPHICS. These tables use the following schema:

- *Car* (ID, Make, Model, Color, Year, OwnerID)
- *Owner* (ID, Name, City, State, Country1, Country2, Country3)
- *Demographics* (ID, Age, Salary, Assets, OwnerID)
- *Accident* (ID, Year, SeatBeltOn, With, Driver, Damage, CarID)

Of particular interest are the column pairs (COUNTRY3, CITY) in the owner table and (MAKE, MODEL) in the car table. The columns in each pair are related by a functional dependency, and each pair is referenced in queries 10 and 11 via predicates of the form (MAKE = 'Honda') AND (MODEL = 'Accord') AND (CITY = 'Toronto') AND (COUNTRY3 = 'Canada'). Figure 10 shows the improvement in workload performance after statistics have been generated by ASC. Query-group A was executed using default statistics, whereas query-group B was able to take advantage of detailed distribution statistics on the individual columns. Note that whereas most queries experience a performance benefit, query 10 experiences a major regression. The reason behind this regression is that query 10 contains several predicates that reference correlated columns.

Figure 11 shows query performance after inserting further accidents for Canada into the database. Note that the results in Figure 10 and Figure 11 are not comparable because the queries used to obtain Figure 11 are executed against a larger data set.

Query-group C in Figure 11 uses the outdated statistics collected prior to the insertions. Query-group D uses updated statistics, but with no changes to the previous statistics configuration. Query-group E uses

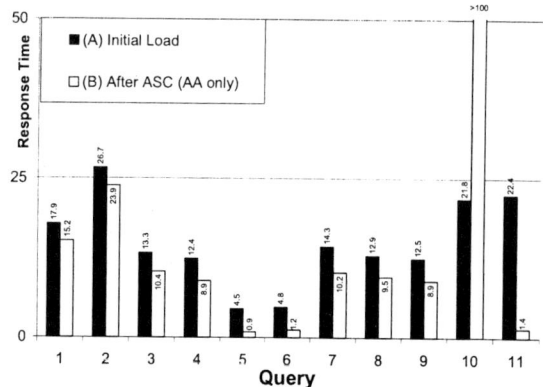

Figure 10: Performance after Loading

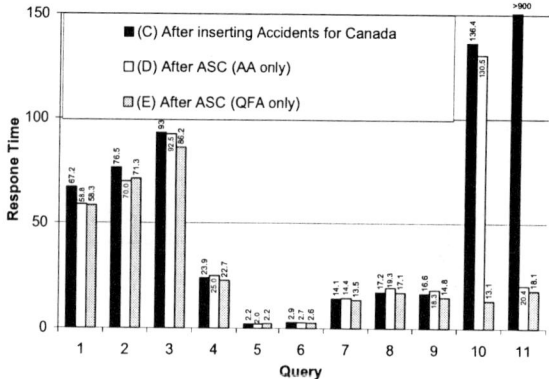

Figure 11: Performance after Inserting Additional Accident Records

statistics that are both updated and reconfigured. The correlations that caused the regression for query 10 in Figure 10 are detected when the QFA is executed at Step E, appropriate column-group statistics are collected, and the performance of query 10 improves dramatically. The performance improvements displayed in Figure 11 for queries 10 and 11 illustrate the strength of combining the UDI-driven and the QF-driven approaches: the orders-of-magnitude speedup of query 10 results primarily from the collection of column-group statistics by the QFA, whereas query 11 benefits mostly from the updating of single-column distribution statistics triggered by the execution of the AA at Step D.

Overall, the case study demonstrates the effectiveness of the autonomic technology in DB2 UDB. The use of ASC resulted in orders-of-magnitude speedups without requiring any intervention by a DBA. Even though autonomic features do not come for free, the overhead of ASC is negligible. In our case study, the use of ASC increased query execution times by 1-2%, primarily because of monitoring overhead. As the analyzers are executed during off-peak times in throttled background processes, their overhead did not really impact the operational DBMS. For example, at a time when the DBMS had previously processed 20,000 queries, the QFA required less than a minute to analyze the QFW and recommend statistics. Both the performance benefit and the ease of use of this autonomic feature thus easily justify this overhead.

7. Related Work

There have been five major approaches toward automating statistics maintenance in database systems: UDI-driven change detection, static query-workload analysis, QF-driven maintenance, mining-type approaches, and piggybacking.

Several industrial products have delivered statistics-refresh automation features based on detection of UDI operations. These include DB2 UDB for the iSeries™ server [IBM02], Microsoft® SQL Server [MICR04], and Oracle 10g [ATLB03]. These products essentially automate statistics refresh on all tables where the percentage of UDI operations exceeds a threshold. Our approach provides three major extensions to this technology. First, we combine UDI measurement with a histogram analysis to reduce maintenance overhead. Secondly, we combine the UDI-driven process with a QF-driven process to provide a solution that is at once both proactive, preparing the system for unforeseen queries, and reactive to problems with the current system workload. Finally, we provide a prioritization scheme to rank tables so that, within a reasonable time interval, multiple tables can have their statistics refreshed, and the maintenance effort is concentrated on the most important tables.

Static query-workload analysis is based solely on the form of the queries and does not exploit run-time feedback. Primary examples of this approach are given by the SQL Server technique described in Chaudhuri and Narasayya [CN01] and the work of Bruno and Chaudhuri on SITS [BC02]. Both of these techniques analyze the query workload in order to select a set of statistics to maintain, such as multidimensional histograms on base data or query expressions. In contrast, our approach exploits run-time feedback and focuses on very simple statistics that are quick and easy to collect, maintain, and exploit. Although our statistics are relatively simple, we can effectively detect and model correlations between columns.

Use of QF-driven techniques in DB2 UDB was originally described in [SLMK01]. The proposed approach compares estimated and actual cardinalities to create adjustment factors that can be applied in the future to improve selectivity estimates. Our current work builds on these ideas by (1) adding the QFW mechanism for aggregating and prioritizing the feedback information, (2) adding the QF-driven methods for modifying the RUNSTATS profiles and recommending tables for processing, thereby improving selectivity estimates in a manner that does not require major modifications to existing query optimizers, and (3) integrating the QF-driven methods with a UDI-driven approach. Other QF-driven methods include the work in [AC99] and [BCG01], where query feedback is used to incrementally build a multidimensional histogram that can be used to estimate the selectivity of conjunctive predicates. Unlike the current work, these algorithms do not discover correlation between columns; the set of columns over which to build the histogram must be specified *a priori*.

Mining-type approaches attempt to discover correlated columns by systematically enumerating sets of potentially correlated columns and statistically analyzing the data. These techniques do not take into account the amount of change activity on the tables, and so are even more proactive than UDI-driven techniques. The CORDS system described in [IMHB04] exemplifies this approach. To make the detection efficient and scalable, CORDS applies candidate-pruning techniques together with random sampling. CORD can detect correlations between columns in the same or in different tables. Other proposed mining algorithms build sophisticated data synopses such as "probabilistic relational models," Markov-network-based histogram models, and Bayesian network models, which are then used to improve selectivity estimates. These latter techniques, as they currently stand, do not appear to scale well to very large databases, however, which limits their potential use in commercial systems; see [IMHB04] for a more detailed discussion. Lim et al. [LWV03] propose a QF-driven variant of the synopsis approach, called SASH, but this technique also suffers from scalability problems. We note that mining-type techniques such as CORDS (as well as static query-workload analysis) can potentially be used in conjunction with the methods described in the current paper.

Piggybacking was proposed as a technique for automated statistics collection by Zhu et al. [ZDS+98]. The idea is to collect statistics based on observing the data that is scanned during normal DML processing. Piggybacking avoids the asynchronous background refresh of table data statistics used by DB2 UDB for iSeries, DB2 UDB, Oracle 10g, and SQL Server. However, this technique suffers from a serious drawback. Although the overhead for any one SQL statement may be small, the cumulative overhead can be significant, and this adverse impact on query processing is present at all times. Our asynchronous approach to statistics refresh avoids these problems.

8. Conclusions

Our novel methodology for automating the collection of database statistics removes from the DBA the burden of manual statistics maintenance. The ASC learns which statistics are needed for good query performance and collects these statistics in background mode and at appropriate times, without requiring any DBA intervention. The two autonomic processes that comprise the ASC subsystem monitor UDI and query activity to determine which statistics to collect and when to collect them, automatically determining the number of frequent values to maintain for each column and the appropriate set of column-group statistics to store in the system catalog. Statistics collection takes place as a throttled background process, ensuring minimal impact on mission-critical queries.

ASC is implemented in DB2 UDB v8.2. Our case study using the ACCIDENTS database has shown ASC to be effective in improving query performance over time, in some cases by orders of magnitude.

In future work, we plan to enhance QFA to also recommend the number of quantiles to maintain for a column, and perhaps to recommend more sophisticated column-group statistics such as limited bivariate histogram information. We are also exploring extensions of our techniques to column groups of order 3 and higher. We are also investigating approaches to directly use the query feedback to alter statistics as opposed to triggering RUNSTATS. Moreover, we are looking at ways of enhancing the UDI-driven and QF-driven techniques with mining-type methods such as CORDS [IMHB04]. A further interesting enhancement of autonomic function would be to automatically determine the maintenance intervals, perhaps by monitoring the number of critical tables in the system. Autonomic techniques for allocating and de-allocating CPU and disk resources would further enhance the technology described in this paper.

References

[AC99] A. Aboulnaga and S. Chaudhuri. Self-tuning histograms: Building histograms without looking at data. *Proc. 1999 ACM SIGMOD*, 181-192, June, 1999.

[ATLB03] M. Ault, M. Tumma, D. Liu, D. Burleson. *Oracle Database 10g New Features: Oracle10g Reference for Advanced Tuning and Administration*. Rampant TechPress, 2003.

[BCG01] N. Bruno, S. Chaudhuri, and L. Gravano. STHoles: a multidimensional workload-aware histogram. *Proc. 2001 ACM SIGMOD*, 211-222, June 2001.

[BC02] N.Bruno, S. Chaudhuri. Exploiting statistics on query expressions for optimization. *Proc. 2002 ACM SIGMOD*, 263-274, June, 2002.

[CN01] S. Chaudhuri, V. Narasayya. Automating statistics management for query optimizers. *IEEE Trans. Knowl. Data Engrg.*, 13(1), 7-20, 2001.

[IBM02] DB2 Universal Database for iSeries - Database Performance and Query Optimization. IBM Corp., 2002.

[IBM04] DB2 v8.2 Performance Guide. IBM Corp., 2004.

[IMHB04] I. F. Ilyas, V. Markl, P. J. Haas, P. G. Brown, A. Aboulnaga. CORDS: Automatic discovery of correlations and soft functional dependencies. *Proc. 2004 ACM SIGMOD*, June 2004. To appear.

[LLZ02] S. Lightstone, G. Lohman, D. Zilio. Toward autonomic computing with DB2 Universal Database. *SIGMOD Record*, 31(3), 2002.

[LSZ03] S. Lightstone, B. Schiefer, D. Zilio. Autonomic computing for relational databases: the ten year vision. *Proc. IEEE Workshop Autonomic Computing Principles and Architectures (AUCOPA '03)*, 2003.

[LWV03] L. Lim, M. Wang, and J. S. Vitter. SASH: A self-adaptive histogram set for dynamically changing workloads. *Proc. 29th VLDB*, 369-380, 2003.

[MICR04] SQL Server 2000 Books Online v8.00.02. Microsoft Corp., 2004.

[PIHS96] V. Poosala, Y. Ioannidis, P. Haas, E. Shekita. Improved histograms for selectivity estimation of range predicates. *Proc. 1996 ACM SIGMOD*, 294-305, June 1996.

[PRH+03a] S. Parekh, K. Rose, J. Hellerstein, S. Lightstone, M. Huras, V. Chang. *Managing the Performance Impact of Administrative Utilities*. IBM Research Report RC22864, IBM Corp., 2003

[PRH+03b] S. Parekh, K. Rose, J. Hellerstein, V. Chang, S. Lightstone, M. Huras. A general approach to policy-based management of the performance impact of administrative utilities. *Proc. 14th IFIP/IEEE Intl. Workshop Distributed Systems: Operations and Management (DSOM '03)*, 20-22, October, 2003.

[SLMK01] M. Stillger, G. M. Lohman, V. Markl, M. Kandil. LEO - DB2's LEarning Optimizer. *Proc. 27th VLDB*, 19-28, 2001.

[ZDS+98] Q. Zhu, B. Dunkel, N. Soparkar, S. Chen, B. Schiefer, T. Lai. A piggyback method to collect statistics for query optimization in database management systems. *Proc. 1998 Conf. Centre for Advanced Studies on Collaborative Research (CASCON '98)*, 25, 1998.

Trademarks

AIX, DB2, DB2 Universal Database, IBM, iSeries, and PowerPC 604 are trademarks or registered trademarks of International Business Machines Corporation in the United States, other countries, or both.

Microsoft is a registered trademark of Microsoft Corporation in the United States, other countries, or both.

Other company, product, and service names may be trademarks or service marks of others.

Further Information

Further up-to-date information about DB2 and IBM Data Management Solutions can be found at: http://www.software.ibm.com/data/

High Performance Index Build Algorithms for Intranet Search Engines

Marcus Fontoura Eugene Shekita Jason Y. Zien Sridhar Rajagopalan Andreas Neumann

IBM Almaden Research Center
650 Harry Road
San Jose, CA 95120
USA
trevi@almaden.ibm.com

Abstract

There has been a substantial amount of research on high-performance algorithms for constructing an inverted text index. However, constructing the inverted index in a intranet search engine is only the final step in a more complicated *index build process*. Among other things, this process requires an analysis of all the data being indexed to compute measures like PageRank. The time to perform this *global analysis* step is significant compared to the time to construct the inverted index, yet it has not received much attention in the research literature. In this paper, we describe how the use of slightly outdated information from global analysis and a fast index construction algorithm based on radix sorting can be combined in a novel way to significantly speed up the index build process without sacrificing search quality.

1 Introduction

Most web and intranet search engines use an inverted text index to execute queries [29]. Because inverted indexes are expensive to update [7, 8, 28], search engines typically reconstruct their index from scratch on a periodic basis. This is simplier and faster than trying to incrementally update the index. The more frequently an index can be reconstructed, the faster updates will be reflected in search results, which in turn improves search quality. Therefore, the time to construct an inverted index is an important issue in search engines.

There has been a substantial amount of research on high-performance algorithms for constructing an inverted text index [1, 17, 22, 29]. However, constructing the inverted index in a intranet search engine is only the final step in a more complicated *index build process*. Before data is indexed, it has to be analyzed as a whole in a *global analysis* (GA) step. Examples of GA computations include static rank [23], duplicate detection [5, 6], anchor text extraction [14, 15], and template detection [2]. The information gleaned from GA is then used as input to construct the inverted text index. For example, static rank can used to put the index in rank order [19]. The time to perform GA is significant compared to the time to construct an inverted index, since all the data being indexed has be analyzed. Moreover, the proportion of time spent in GA is likely to grow as analysis becomes more sophisticated [12].

In this paper, we describe how the use of slightly outdated GA information, that is *lagging GA*, and a fast index construction algorithm based on radix sorting can be combined in a novel way to significantly speed up the index build process without sacrificing search quality. Results from the Trevi search engine are presented. Trevi was developed in IBM Research and is currently used to support all the searches on IBM's global intranet, which runs in 7x24 mode and supports over 350,000 employees. The main contributions of this paper include:

- An index build process that uses lagging GA, allowing Trevi's inverted index to be constructed with just one pass over the data.

- A fast index construction algorithm based on a pipelined radix sort.

- Experimental results showing that lagging GA can speed up the index build process, with only a negligible degradation in precision.

Permission to copy without fee all or part of this material is granted provided that the copies are not made or distributed for direct commercial advantage, the VLDB copyright notice and the title of the publication and its date appear, and notice is given that copying is by permission of the Very Large Data Base Endowment. To copy otherwise, or to republish, requires a fee and/or special permission from the Endowment.

**Proceedings of the 30th VLDB Conference,
Toronto, Canada, 2004**

- Experimental results showing that Trevi's index construction algorithm is significantly faster than alternative approaches described in the research literature.

2 Architecture Overview

Figure 1 shows Trevi's hardware and software architecture for IBM's intranet. As shown, there are four processing nodes in a cluster. Each node is a commodity two-way x86 SMP running Linux, with its own direct-attached RAID for storage. The cluster is connected with a local gigabit Ethernet to ensure ample bandwidth for copying data between nodes.

As shown in Figure 1, each node in the Trevi cluster is assigned a particular task. This partitioning of nodes by task makes it easy to crawl, construct inverted indexes, and execute queries in parallel. The *Crawler* is responsible for crawling data. It stores raw documents (HTML pages, PDF files, XML, etc.) along with associated metadata in a database. Raw documents are copied to the *Index Build* node, which is responsible for periodically running the index build process. Once an index has been constructed, it is copied to the *Query Servers*, which execute end-user searches. Two Query Servers are used for fault-tolerance and load balancing.

The RAID storage on each node is spread over two physical arrays, and data is never updated in-place, much like in a log-structured file system [25]. When a new index is constructed, data is always read from one disk array and written to the other array. This dual-array storage architecture greatly improves the performance of the index build process by making all disk I/O sequential. It also makes it possible to atomically install a new index on a Query Server without taking the server down.

3 Index Build Data Structures

The main focus of this paper is on the index build process, so we do not present further details on the Crawler and Query Servers. This section describes the main data structures used in the index build process, which we subsequently refer to as simply *index build*. The data structures used during index build are the *Store*, the *Index*, the *DeltaStore*, and the *DeltaIndex*. All of these data structures are maintained on the Index Build node and copied to the Query Servers, where they are accessed in read-only mode.

3.1 The Store

The Store is a repository for the tokenized version of each document. Documents read from the Crawler database are parsed, tokenized, and then added to the Store. The reason for storing tokenized content in the Store is performance. Multi-format parsing and multilingual tokenization of a document is extremely CPU

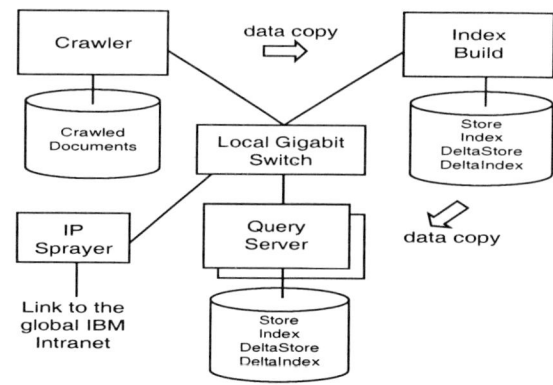

Figure 1: High-level view of Trevi's hardware and software architecture

intensive, on the order of 50 times slower than a random disk I/O. Consequently, we want to do it only once. After the bulk of the documents on the intranet have been crawled, there are typically just small additions to the Store, on the order of 5% to 10% per day. When a document changes it will eventually be recrawled.

Tokenized documents tend to be small, so they are aggregated into *bundles* in the Store to enable big-block I/O for improved performance. Currently, each bundle in Trevi corresponds to a 8 MB file. The Store is scanned sequentially during index build, but an API also exists for randomly accessing documents. This API is used during query processing to generate summaries for results. Each document in the Store has an associated *store locator* that encodes the bundle and offset within that bundle for a document.

Each document in the Store is identified by a 64-bit hash of its URL. We refer to this as the *URL hash* of a document. Auxiliary data structures are kept that make it possible to obtain the store locator of a document given its URL hash.

3.2 The Index

Each token occurrence (posting) in the inverted text index contains a position and an attribute, i.e, *posting=(position, attribute)*. The position encodes the document ID (docID) and the offset within the document in which the token appeared. Positional information is necessary for implementing phrase search and proximity queries. The attribute field encodes ranking and display information about the token occurrence, e.g. if the occurrence was in a title, anchor text, or normal text. This attribute field is similar to the fancy postings used in [4], and is used at query time for ranking purposes. Attributes are typically one byte in size, although we allow arbitrary sizes. The index can be viewed as a collection of posting lists, one for each token. Each posting list is a set of postings ordered by position.

3.3 The DeltaStore and DeltaIndex

In order to make new documents and updates to existing documents appear as soon as possible in search results, Trevi uses a DeltaStore and a DeltaIndex. The DeltaStore is used to accumulate changes to the Store, while the DeltaIndex is an index of the documents in the DeltaStore. The DeltaStore and DeltaIndex basically mirror the structure and functionality of the Store and Index, respectively.

The index construction algorithm used to build the DeltaIndex is similar to the one used to build the Index. In particular, the DeltaIndex is reconstructed from scratch each time. However, one key difference is that GA is not done when the DeltaIndex is constructed, since it would take too long. The result of this is that, although the DeltaIndex enables updates to appear in search results as soon as possible, it does not eliminate the need for a fast index build process that includes GA.

4 Global Analysis

In this section we describe the main computations performed by GA. These are duplicate detection, anchor text processing, and static ranking. All of these have been discussed at length in the literature [5, 6, 14, 15, 23], so we only highlight how they are implemented in Trevi. The main focus of this section is to provide background for the index build algorithm presented in Sections 5 and 6.

4.1 Duplicate Detection

Duplicate detection identifies and discards duplicate documents. During tokenization, each document is annotated with a fingerprint, which is computed by hashing the document's content. This information is put in the *Fingerprint Table*. Duplicate detection uses a union-find algorithm [10] on fingerprints to identify groups of documents with the same (or nearly the same) content.

After identifying groups of similar documents, duplicate detection picks a *master* document for each group. In order to avoid duplicate answers to search queries, only master documents are indexed by Trevi. There are several heuristics that can be used to pick the masters, such giving priority to documents with shorter URLs. The output of duplicate detection is the *Dup Table*, which assigns a master to each document in the Store. Given the URL hash of a document D, the Dup Table can be used to determine if D is a master or a duplicate.

4.2 Anchor Text Processing

We define the anchor text of a document D as the collection of text contained in anchors that point to D from other documents. For example, if a given document points to http://trevi.ibm.com with text "search engine", then "search engine" is part of the anchor text for http://trevi.ibm.com. Several studies have shown that indexing anchor text significantly improves search quality [11, 15]. The intuition is that, very often, anchor text resembles end-user queries [18].

Trevi's anchor text algorithm extracts the links and their surrounding text from all the documents in the Store and puts them in the *Link Table*. The data kept for each link includes the link's source URL hash, its destination URL hash, and its associated anchor tokens. The Link Table is sorted and then aggregated on the destination URL hash to create a virtual anchor document for each destination. These anchor documents are written sequentially to the *AnchorStore*. A separate storage area is created to avoid updating the Store in-place, which would require seeking all over disk.

4.3 Static Ranking

Trevi assigns a static rank to each document in the Store. Currently, the static rank of a document D is simply set to the the number of different hosts that point to D, i.e., the hostcount. The higher the hostcount, the higher the static rank. Although more sophisticated techniques for assigning static rank are available, such as PageRank [23], hostcounts are easy to compute and have produced satisfactory results on IBM's intranet. To compute static ranks, Trevi simply runs a count on the sorted Link Table.

The result of the static rank computation is the *Rank Table*, which is a mapping from the URL hash of a document to its static rank. Given the URL hash of a document D, the Rank Table can be used to determine D's static rank. As in many search engines, docID is synonymous with static rank in Trevi. This effectively puts Trevi's inverted indexes in static rank order, making it possible to terminate top-k queries early [19].

5 The Index Build Algorithm

In this section we first present the index build algorithm at a high level, ignoring GA computations. We then describe a straightforward way to incorporate GA computations, which requires two passes over the data being indexed. Finally, we present an index build algorithm that uses lagging GA, allowing just one pass over the data being indexed.

5.1 The Basic Index Build Algorithm

The basic high-level flow of Trevi's index build algorithm is illustrated in Figure 2(a). The algorithm takes the current version of the Store, that is, $Store_{i+1}$ and merges it with the current version of the DeltaStore to generate the new version of the Store and the new Index, that is, $Store_{i+1}$ and $Index_{i+1}$. The Store and Index always move together in time this way, with

$Index_{i+1}$ over $Store_{i+1}$. By generating a new version of the Store each iteration we get to garbage collect the Store, keeping it sequential on disk and free of old, deleted, or duplicate documents. Since the performance of index build is proportional to the time to scan the Store, this greatly improves performance.

The DeltaStore and the DeltaIndex also move together in time, but at a faster clip than the Store and the Index. As shown in Figure 2(b), $DeltaStore_j$ is merged with newly crawled documents to generate $DeltaStore_{j+1}$ and $DeltaIndex_{j+1}$. Note that newly crawled documents in Figure 2 (b) are analogous to the DeltaStore in Figure 2 (a). Consequently, the underlying algorithm for both figures is effectively the same.

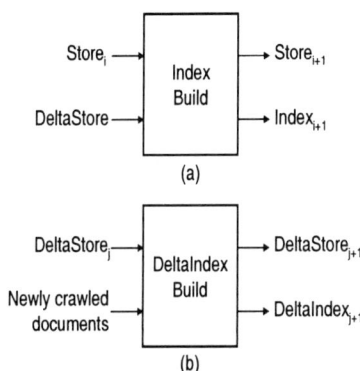

Figure 2: High-level view of (a) index build and (b) DeltaIndex build

It is important to note that the performance of the algorithms for constructing both the Index and the DeltaIndex benefit greatly from Trevi's dual-array storage architecture. For example, while the $Store_i$ and DeltaStore are sequentially read from one disk array, $Store_{i+1}$ and $Index_{i+1}$ can be written in parallel to the other array.

5.2 Incorporating Global Analysis

We now provide a more detailed description of the index build algorithm that incorporates GA. The naive approach to do this is:

1. *Duplicate Elimination*: Scan the Store to generate the Fingerprint Table, which maps URL hashes to fingerprints and is input to duplicate detection. When the Fingerprint Table is ready, duplicate detection is performed, generating the Dup table.

2. *Anchor Text Extraction*: Scan the Store to extract links from each document. Once all links are extracted, they are saved in the Link Table. The anchor text algorithm then generates the AnchorStore from the Link Table.

3. *Static Ranking*: Use the Link table to assign static ranks to documents in the Store and to generate the Rank Table. Note that no sort is needed in this phase since the Link Table was already sorted for anchor text extraction.

4. *Index Construction*: Scan the Store and DeltaStore to construct the Index. The tables generated during the GA phases are needed as input for index construction to remove duplicates, index anchor text, and obtain each document's static rank.

5. *Creation the New Store*: Scan the Store and DeltaStore to create the next generation of the Store. After this step, the DeltaStore and the DeltaIndex are reset.

Clearly, this naive approach is inefficient, requiring four passes over the Store. But we can easily reduce the number of passes to just two. First, observe that a single Store scan can be used to generate the input tables for duplicate elimination and anchor text extraction. Then if we are clever about the way we scan the Store, we can also combine index construction with the creation of the next generation of the Store.

These optimizations are illustrated in Algorithm 1. In the algorithm, a subscript is used with each data structure to denote which version of the Store it reflects. For example, $Rank_{i+1}$ corresponds to the Rank Table for $Store_{i+1}$.

Algorithm 1: Straightforward Index Build

1. Scan $Store_i$ and the $DeltaStore$ to generate $FingerPrint_{i+1}$ and $Link_{i+1}$
2. Dup_{i+1} = duplicate detection($FingerPrint_{i+1}$)
3. $AnchorStore_{i+1}$ = anchor text processing($Link_{i+1}$)
4. $Rank_{i+1}$ = static ranking($Link_{i+1}$)
5. $GA_{i+1} = Dup_{i+1}, AnchorStore_{i+1}$, and $Rank_{i+1}$
6. Scan $Store_i$, the $DeltaStore$, and using GA_{i+1}, generate $Store_{i+1}$ and $Index_{i+1}$

As shown, in step 1, the algorithm scans $Store_i$ and the DeltaStore to generate the inputs for GA, which runs in steps 2-5 and produces GA_{i+1}. In step 6, the algorithm scans the stores again and using GA_{i+1} generates $Store_{i+1}$ and $Index_{i+1}$. After Algorithm 1 finishes, the DeltaIndex build process is resumed. It cycles at its own rate, generating a new DeltaStore and DeltaIndex each cycle.

5.3 Index Build with Lagging Global Analysis

The performance of index build is largely bound by the time to do a disk scan of the Store and to perform GA. Two disk scans of the Store are required in Algorithm 1, one to generate GA_{i+1} and another to generate $Store_{i+1}$ and $Index_{i+1}$. The number of scans can be reduced to just one by using GA_i to generate $Index_{i+1}$ rather than GA_{i+1}, that is, by using *lagging* GA. Lagging GA causes some loss of index precision, but, as we will show, the loss is negligible because information like the static rank of a document does not change drastically from generation i to $i+1$. Index build with lagging GA is illustrated in Algorithm 2.

Algorithm 2: Index Build with Lagging GA

1. Scan $Store_i$, the $DeltaStore$, and using GA_i as input, generate $Store_{i+1}$, $Index_{i+1}$, $FingerPrint_{i+1}$, and $Link_{i+1}$
2. Dup_{i+1} = duplicate detection($FingerPrint_{i+1}$)
3. $AnchorStore_{i+1}$ = anchor text processing($Link_{i+1}$)
4. $Rank_{i+1}$ = static ranking($Link_{i+1}$)
5. $GA_{i+1} = Dup_{i+1}$, $AnchorStore_{i+1}$, and $Rank_{i+1}$

An important point to note in Algorithm 2 is that, in step 1, both $Store_{i+1}$ and $Index_{i+1}$ are generated using the same disk scan of $Store_i$. Another important point to note is that, because GA_i is used in step 1, new documents will have no static rank computed for them when they are indexed. New documents are assigned a low, default static rank, under the assumption they will have few incoming links. The next iteration of index build will fix this if it is not true. Finally, note that $Index_{i+1}$ is ready after step 1, enabling DeltaIndex construction to run in parallel with GA_{i+1}. This in turn reduces the cycle time of index build, as illustrated in Figure 3.

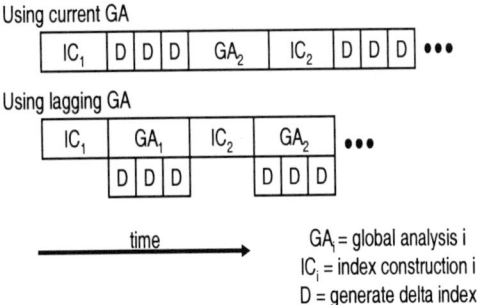

Figure 3: Index build cycle time using the current GA versus lagging GA

Algorithm 2 has to be run twice initially, with the appropriate inputs set to null, to generate $Index_0$. More specifically, bootstrapping begins with $Store_0$ and no GA.

5.4 Creating the Next Generation Store

This section describes how $Store_{i+1}$ is generated in step 1 of Algorithm 2 using $Store_i$, the DeltaStore, and GA_i as input.

The document bundles in $Store_i$ and the DeltaStore are scanned in LIFO order to generate $Store_{i+1}$. In order to index only the most recent version of each document, a Bloom Filter [3] on URL hash is used to filter out older versions of documents. More specifically, if document D in $Store_i$ has been replaced by a newer version of D in the DeltaStore (call it D'), then only D' will appear in $Store_{i+1}$. In addition, Dup_i is used to eliminate duplicates. Surprisingly, eliminating duplicates reduces the size of the Store by 50% on the IBM intranet.

Figure 4 illustrates how $Store_{i+1}$ is generated. In the example shown, documents $D1$ and $D5$ have newer versions, $D1'$ and $D5'$, that appear in the DeltaStore. Therefore, the original versions of these documents are garbage collected and do not appear in $Store_{i+1}$. The DeltaStore is handled similarly. As noted earlier, to improve performance, $Store_i$ and the DeltaStore are read from one disk array, while $Store_{i+1}$ is written to the other array.

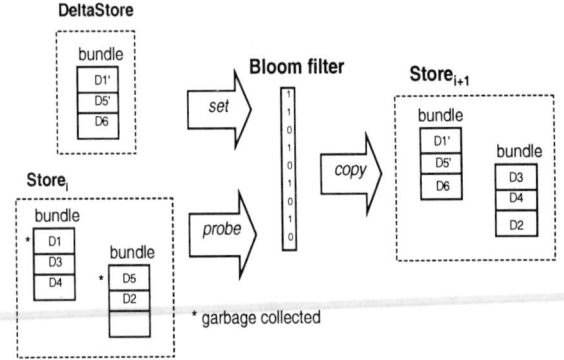

Figure 4: Generating $Store_{i+1}$

6 High-Performance Index Construction

This section describes how $Index_{i+1}$ is constructed in step 1 of Algorithm 2 using $Store_i$, the DeltaStore, and GA_i as input. The index construction algorithm takes the tokenized documents from the Store and DeltaStore as input and produces the inverted index. Recall that the index is basically a collection of posting lists, one list for each token that appears in the corpus. Each posting is a pair *(position, attribute)*, and each position in turn consists of a *(docID, offset)*. To reduce storage and I/O costs, posting lists are compressed using a simple variable-byte scheme based on computing the deltas between positions.

Trevi's index construction is based on sorting. Document tokens are streamed into a sort, which is used to create the posting lists. The primary sort key is on token, the secondary sort key is on docID (static rank), and the tertiary sort key is on offset within a document. By sorting on this compound key, token occurrences are effectively grouped into ordered posting lists.

The well-known sort-merge technique [1, 29] is used for sorting. Sort-merge is particularly suitable for batch index construction, where all of the data is indexed at once, which is true in most search engines. Sort-merge has two main phases in Trevi's index construction:

1. *Sort Phase*: Scan *Store_i* and the DeltaStore, streaming document tokens into a memory buffer. Each time the memory buffer fills, it is sorted and then written to disk in compressed form. This process is repeated until there are no more documents to scan.

2. *Merge Phase*: Create a memory heap to merge the sorted runs. Perform a multi-way merge of the runs to generate the final compressed posting lists.

We made two important optimizations that greatly improved the performance of these phases. First, we used a highly tuned radix sort [10, 26] to generate sorted runs. Second, we used a pipelined software architecture to enable I/O and CPU to be overlapped. We describe each of these optimizations below.

6.1 Using Radix Sort

Radix sort has two important characteristics that Trevi exploits to improve performance: it sorts in linear time and is stable, meaning it preserves the original order of input data when there are ties on the sort key. However, radix sort requires fixed-length keys, whereas text tokens are variable length. Therefore, tokens need to be transformed into fixed-length *tokenIDs*.

Transforming tokens to tokenIDs can be done in a variety of ways – for example, by generating unique sequential IDs or by using a hash function. The disadvantage of generating unique IDs is that a potentially large map of tokens to IDs needs to be kept. Hashing does not suffer from this problem, but there may be collisions when two or more tokens hash to the same tokenID. However, by using enough bits in the hashing function, the probability of a collision can be brought to nearly zero, which is good enough for a search engine. So we opted for hashing in Trevi, using a 64-bit Pearson's hash function [24]. On the IBM intranet, which has over 260 million unique tokens, there were no collisions using this hash function.

Using tokenID's, the fixed-length sort keys for index construction have the form *(tokenID, docID, offset)*, where tokenID is a 64-bit hash value, docID is 32 bits, and offset within a document is 32 bits. The encoding of the sort key is illustrated in Figure 5. As shown, the upper bit in the offset is used to denote the section of a document. This is so a given document can be streamed into the sort in different sections. More will be said about this shortly. Note that, by sorting the full 128-bit key, we are able to simultaneously:

- Group tokens into posting lists.

- Order each posting list by docID, effectively putting it in static rank order.

- After docID, order each posting list by the offset within a document and bring different sections of a document together.

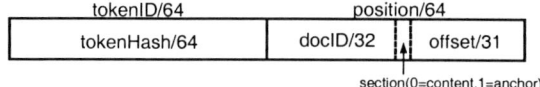

Figure 5: Sort Key

To index anchor text tokens, the AnchorStore is scanned and streamed into the sort after the Store and the DeltaStore are scanned. The section bit of the offset is used to indicate whether a token is for content or anchor text. Anchor text tokens have their section bit set to "1". Consequently, after sorting, the anchor text tokens for a document D follow the content tokens for D. By using more section bits, this approach could be generalized, allowing documents to have multiple sections, with each section stored separately.

Within a document D, tokens are streamed into the sort in the order in which they appear in D, that is, in offset order. Taking advantage of the fact that radix sort is stable, this allows us to use a 96-bit sort key that excludes offset, rather than sorting on the full 128-bit key. Note that if posting lists did not need to be put in static rank order, a 64-bit radix sort on just tokenID would be sufficient.

Trevi's radix sort was implemented using a 16-bit radix, so for the 96-bit sort key, this requires six linear passes through the data to accumulate the radix counters. With a 16-bit radix, we needed radix counter tables that are able to hold 65K 32-bit integer values. Experiments showed that using this large radix was faster than using a smaller one because fewer passes through the data were required.

Note that we can incorporate new sort criteria in Trevi by simply changing its sort key. So by using a key-based radix sort for index construction, we obtain both high performance and flexibility. This is in contrast to an approach based on accumulating postings using a dictionary [17], which would require an additional sort on each posting list to incorporate new sort criteria.

6.2 Pipelining the Merge-Sort

Overlapping I/O and CPU is the key to good sorting performance. This is accomplished by using a software pipeline to create sort runs, as shown in Figure 6. Although it is not shown, we also use a two-stage pipeline for the merge phase, with one stage reading and merging runs from disk, and the other stage compressing and writing the final postings to disk. Our work here follows from [22], except that we replaced a comparison-based sort for each run with a more efficient radix sort. In addition, we used a two-stage pipeline rather than a three-stage pipeline to create sort runs. We found that the flush stage was so fast compared to the other stages that combining it with the radix sort resulted in a more balanced pipeline.

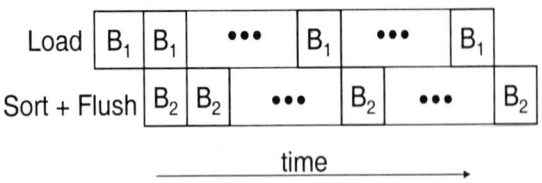

Figure 6: The pipeline for generating sort runs; B_1 and B_2 are the sort buffers

Determining an optimal sort buffer size was a key contribution of [22]. They found that the buffer size should be neither too small nor too large – a balance has to be struck. This is intuitive because, on the one hand, a larger buffer improves I/O efficiency. But on the other hand, comparison-based sorting is nonlinear, which means sorting can become a CPU bottleneck if the sort buffer is too large.

With radix sort, there is no balance that needs to be struck, since the time to sort a run is linear in the buffer size. Moreover, radix sort is so fast that the fraction of time spent in the merge phase becomes larger. The time spent in the merge phase is $O(S \log N)$ where S is the total size of the data and N is the number of runs. These observations imply that we want as large a sort buffer as possible – to maximize I/O efficiency and to minimize N. We ran experiments to verify this, as shown in Figure 7. Note that, for Trevi's two-stage pipeline to work, the sort buffer is actually split into two equal-sized sub-buffers.

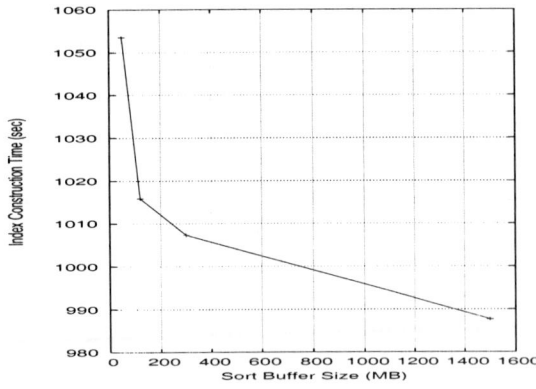

Figure 7: Index construction time with different sort buffer sizes and 600,000 documents

We consciously tried to balance the work in the pipeline stages. For example, instead of accumulating the radix counters as tokens were loaded into the sort buffer, we performed this computation in the Sort+Flush stage because it resulted in a more balanced pipeline.

We can calculate the maximal speedup of the merge-sort from pipeling. First consider the sort phase. Let B_i denote the sort buffer size. The Load stage is linear in the buffer size and takes time λB_i. The Sort+Flush stage is also linear in the buffer size and takes time ϕB_i. Thru experimentation, we found that $\lambda = 1.20$ and $\phi = 1.00$. In other words, the Load stage, which includes a fair bit of per-token processing, was actually more costly than the Sort+Flush stage. Based on our values for λ and ϕ, the theoretical speedup of the sort phase is the serial execution time divided by the pipelined execution time, that is, $(1.20 + 1.00)/1.20$ or 1.83. The merge phase tends to be I/O bound, and intuitively has a speedup of at most 2.0.

The fraction of time spent in the merge phase was found to be 45%. Hence, the maximal speedup of the merge-sort from pipelining is $0.55 \cdot 1.83 + 0.45 \cdot 2.0$ or 1.91. Therefore, we should be able to effectively use two CPUs and no more. Experimentally, we saw a speedup of about 1.30 using two CPUs. Using two CPUs also provides a nice balance with Trevi's dual-array storage architecture.

6.3 Aggregating Token Occurrences

Aggregating all the occurrences of a particular token within a document D just once when D is tokenized and stored can speed up index construction [4]. Although the volume of data to be sorted is not dramatically reduced, fewer individual tokens need to be sorted, which in turn reduces CPU usage. In all of our experiments, unless otherwise noted, we used this approach.

7 Experimental Results

In this section, we present experimental results from the Trevi search engine. Results are provided for Trevi's index build process, showing that lagging GA can improve the performance of index build without sacrificing search quality. Results are also provided for Trevi's index construction algorithm, showing that it is significantly faster than alternative approaches described in the research literature. We ran all our experiments on a two-way SMP with dual 2.4 Ghz Intel Xeon processors running Linux. The disk storage was configured as two physical RAID0 arrays, each with 6 drives. We were able to read from one disk array and write to the other array at a rate of 95MB/s.

7.1 Global Analysis

In these experiments, we constructed several generations of the index, starting from a 3.5 million document Store and adding 500,000 documents each generation.

Our data set was based on a partial crawl of IBM's intranet. The *change interval* of 500,000 was chosen because that is the daily rate of change we see in IBM's intranet. This includes changes to existing documents and newly crawled documents.

In our first set of experiments, we used the Kendall's tau distance for top k lists by Fagin et. al. [16] to measure the *discrepancy* in static rank between different generations of the index, i.e., how static rank changes from $Index_i$ to $Index_j$. Similar experiments were carried out for anchor text. Given two ordered lists, Kendall's tau computes a similarity measure by checking every possible pair $\{i,j\}$ of items in the two lists and applying a penalty whenever the order of items i and j differ in the input lists. We use a normalized version of the measure that scales the values to be between 0 (when the lists are identical) and 1 (when the lists are in the opposite order). This measure has been widely used before in different contexts, such as index pruning [9] and rank aggregation [13].

Figure 8 shows how the discrepancy measure changes for the documents with the top 100,000 static ranks. The bottom curve shows how the ranks vary from generation i to $i+1$, while the top curve one shows how the ranks vary over time, comparing the ranks in generation 1 with the ranks in generation i.

Figure 8 shows that, in the steady state, the top 100,000 static ranks differ by no more than 2% between two consecutive generations, and by up to 18% from the start after 7 generations. This means that by using lagging static ranks we lose less than 2% accuracy on static ranks if a 500,000 change interval is used to trigger the construction of a new index. This graph also shows that the loss of accuracy in the static rank grows linearly with the number of changed documents that accumulate between generations. Another interesting observation is that the difference between the static ranks in two consecutive generations decreases over time, from about 6% to about 1.5%.

One of the reasons for this behavior is that in intranets the crawl date is a very good static rank, as described in [15]. This means that the documents with the highest static rank tend to be crawled first since they are closer to the intranet's "root". After the first few index generations, when most of the "important" documents are already in the Store, the ranks are quite stable.

Another characteristic of the data is the Zipfian distribution of the static ranks. Figure 9 shows the distribution of the ranks on a log-log scale. It is interesting to notice that after 10,000 documents all the static rank values are extremely low and they are 0 after 600,000 (this point is not shown in the graph). This means that after the most important documents have been crawled, the discrepancy in the top static ranks tends to be very low. This also explains why the bottom curve of Figure 8 decays and stabilizes after a few generations.

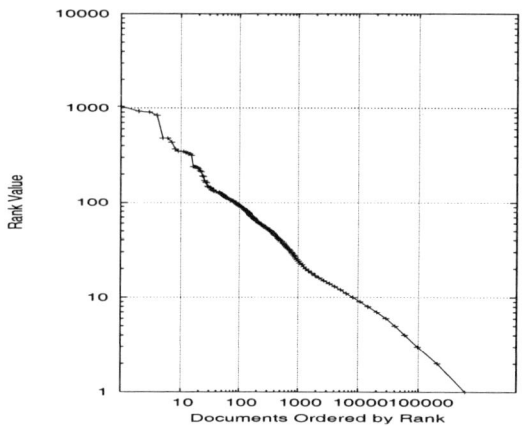

Figure 9: Distribution of the static ranks for the IBM intranet

Figure 10 shows similar discrepancy results for anchor text. We generated lists of the 100,000 most frequent anchor tokens for every index generation and applied the same discrepancy measure as before. The graphs for anchor text and ranks exhibit a similar shape and range of discrepancy values. The difference between consecutive generations is between 2% and 4% and after the 7 generations it is still less than 14%. The main point here is that both static ranks and anchor texts are very stable between consecutive generations for the change interval we considered.

The use of lagging duplicate detection might cause a potential loss of precision. This is due to the fact that, if we use lagging information, all documents added to the Store between generation i and $i+1$ are added to $Index_{i+1}$, even if they are duplicates and should be filtered out. If there are no duplicates among the documents added to the Store in a given generation there is no degradation in quality, since no duplicates are indexed. On the other hand, if there are duplicates

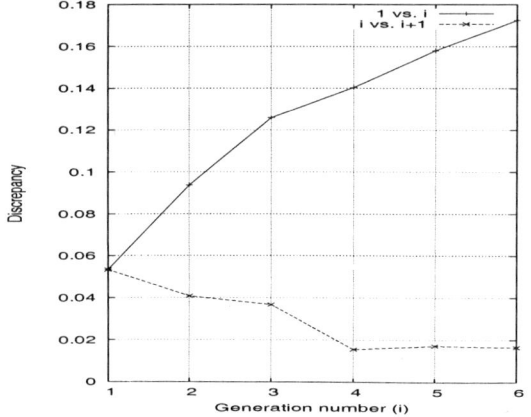

Figure 8: Discrepancy between the top 100,000 static ranks in different index generations

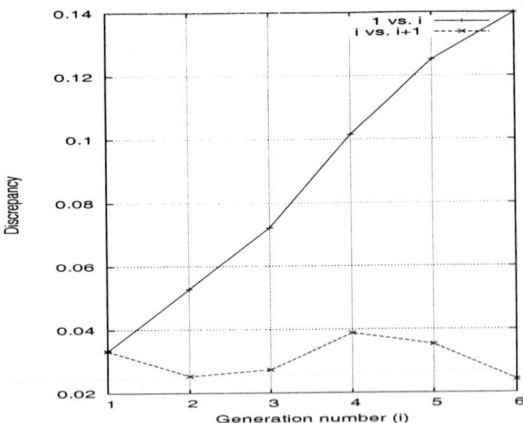

Figure 10: Discrepancy between the top 100,000 anchor text tokens in different index generations

added to the Store there can be a degradation in quality, since there is a chance that the index might return duplicate documents in the results of a query.

We analyze this in Figure 11 by comparing the ratio of duplicate documents added in a generation to the total number of documents. The graph shows that, if we use lagging GA, only 2.6% to 5.1% of the documents added to the Store are incorrectly classified by duplicate detection. Moreover, these are new documents that are assigned a low, default static rank. Consequently, this makes it highly unlikely that duplicate documents will be returned in search results, unless the query is very specific and not enough highly ranked documents appear in the results.

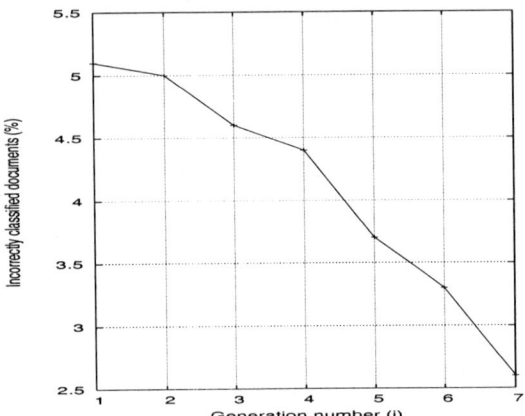

Figure 11: Analysis of the duplicate detection for several index generations

We also ran a quality test by selecting 180 queries from the Trevi query log, manually identifying relevant documents for these queries. We measured the average precision at 1 and at 10 over all the queries for the different index generations. The results were stable, varying less than 2% in both cases over the 7 generations. Precision at 1 varied from 0.639 to 0.650 while precision at 10 varied from 0.215 to 0.219. This shows that no precision is lost over the generations due to the use of lagging GA.

Figure 12 shows the difference in the time to perform index build with and without lagging GA. Note that the time to scan the Store and run GA, which is the difference between the two curves, grows linearly with the number of documents. The improvement in index build from lagging GA depends on the complexity of GA. In Trevi, GA is very simple and yet the performance gains are significant, on the order of 25%. In the extreme case, GA could be orders of magnitude slower than index construction. For that scenario, Trevi's index build algorithm could be modified to let GA lag for two or more generations to reduce its impact. Another advantage of using lagging GA, which is not reflected in Figure 12, is that it allows delta indexes to be built in parallel with GA.

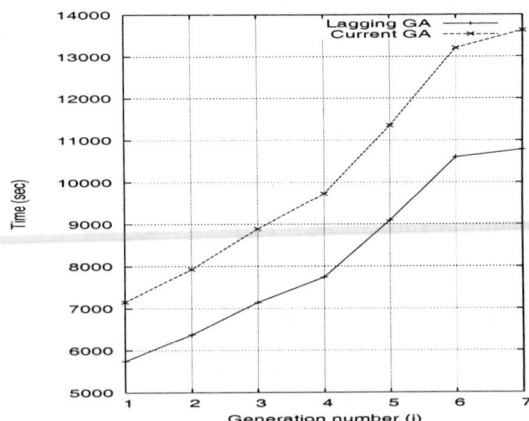

Figure 12: Performance improvement in index build from lagging GA

7.2 The Performance of Index Construction

We begin this section by looking at how Trevi's index construction algorithm scales. In Figure 13, we see that it scales nearly linearly with the index size. Our time complexity is actually $O(S \log N)$ where S is the total size of the data and N is the number of runs, but since we use very large sort buffer sizes (1.5GB by default), N tends to be small.

All the points in Figure 13 correspond to a partial crawl of the IBM intranet except for the last point, which corresponds to a full 10,666,580 document crawl. The crawl included 6,515,728 unique documents after duplicate elimination plus 4,150,852 anchor documents. Only the last point in the graph includes anchor documents, which tend to be smaller than the average document.

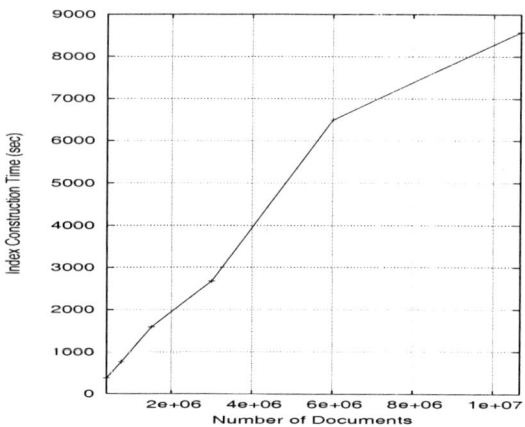

Figure 13: Nearly linear scaling of index construction

7.2.1 Comparison to Other Index Construction Algorithms

It is difficult to compare Trevi's index construction algorithm to alternative approaches described in the research literature. This is because different index features may have been supported, or a different hardware platform was used, or different input data was used, and so on. Nonetheless, we still tried to carry out a comparison in as fair a manner as possible. All of the results shown below are from constructing an index on a partial crawl of IBM's intranet with 2,000,000 documents. The document collection did not include anchor text documents, and was about 23GB. The tokenized documents included stemmed and unstemmed tokens.

- *Trevi with Token Aggregation*: 4,000,000 docs/hour. This was using Trevi's default index construction algorithm, where all the occurrences of a particular token in a document D are aggregated when D is tokenized and stored, as described in Section 6.3. Postings contain full position information, a one-byte attribute, and they are ordered by rank. The final index size was 10.5GB.

- *Trevi without Token Aggregation*: 2,800,000 docs/hour. This was using Trevi's default algorithm but without aggregated token occurances.

- *Trevi without Attributes*: 3,100,000 docs/hour. This is using Trevi's default algorithm but without the one-byte attribute in postings to try and be more comparable with Lucy (see below).

- *Lucy*: 3,000,000 docs/hour This was using Lucy [21] on our hardware and our data set. Lucy is a C-based open source text index from RMIT University. At this time, we know of no papers published describing Lucy, but it does not appear to order postings by rank or support attributes in postings, so it had considerably less work to do than Trevi. Lucy's index was 7.3GB, which was smaller than Trevi's index because it stored much less information per posting. There were 2.7 billion postings in the index, so if a one-byte attribute was added to every posting, Lucy's index size would be have been 10.0GB, which is nearly identical in size to Trevi's index.

- *Melnik et al.*: 1,100,000 docs/hour. This was the result reported in [22]. Experiments were run on a 350-500 Mhz PC with 300-500MB of RAM and multiple IDE disks. Their index does not appear to contain per-token attributes or document offsets, and postings are not ordered by rank. Also, the result reported seems to only include the time to write sorted runs and excludes the time to merge them. When we obtained an executable version of their algorithm and ran it on our hardware and our data set, we obtained 600,000 docs/hour.

- *Long and Suel*: 700,000 docs/hour. This was the result reported in [19]. Experiments were run on a Dell Optiplex 240GX, 1.6Ghz Pentium 4, with 1GB RAM and two 80GB Seagate Barracuda hard disks. Postings are ordered by rank and contain attribute information, and most likely also position information. They actually had a larger data set and ran 16 machines in parallel.

- *Lucene*: 350,000 docs/hour. This was using Lucene [20] on our hardware and our data set. Lucene is an open source Java-based index [20]. Postings do not contain attribute information and are not ordered by rank.

8 Related Work

Although several papers have focused on specific GA algorithms [2, 5, 6, 14, 15, 23], to the best of our knowledge, this is the first paper that describes how to integrate these algorithms into a complete index build process. In [30], the authors describe how to design stable rank algorithms. That work is relevant to this paper since Trevi's index build process relies on the fact that document ranks should be stable across consecutive generations of its index. Another related work [19], describes how to use static rank ordering in an inverted index to improve query performance. However, the authors did not provide any details about how their index is actually construction.

Brin and Page [4] discuss an early version of the Google search engine. The authors describe a system consisting of a crawler, document repository, GA (PageRank), and index construction. However, they do not discuss how frequently GA is computed or how tightly coupled it is in their index build process. Their index construction algorithm is also not described in as much detail has here.

Witten, Moffat, and Bell [29] describe a sort-based index construction algorithm that saves temporary disk space by using an in-place merge algorithm. A table mapping index blocks to their location on disk was maintained, and an extra pass over the blocks is needed to shuffle them into sorted order. The drawback to this scheme is that it generates more I/O, and in particular more random I/O, during index construction to save disk space, which has become an inexpensive commodity. In contrast, Trevi's index construction maximizes performances without worrying about temporary disk space. It tries to do as much sequential I/O as possible, reading from one disk array while writing to the other.

Heinz and Zobel [17] describe an index construction algorithm that uses an in-memory lexicon to accumulate compressed posting lists. When memory is used up, the posting lists are dumped to disk in lexicographic order and the process is repeated. When all the documents have been processed, an in-place merge is used to produce the final results. Their index construction algorithm differs from the one described here in that they use an in-place merge, they do not attempt to order posting lists in rank order, they do not allow documents to be indexed in sections, and they do not include per-posting attribute information.

Sinha and Zobel [27] describe a new index construction algorithm based on dynamic tries. They provide results showing that their algorithm performs better than one based on radix sorting for large collections of strings. However, it is unclear whether their algorithm could be adapted to efficiently build the kind of rank-ordered posting lists described here.

9 Conclusions

The time to construct an inverted index is an important issue in web and intranet search engines [1, 17, 22, 29] But constructing the inverted index is only the final step in a more complicated *index build process*, which includes a global analysis (GA) of all the data being indexed to compute measures like PageRank [23]. In this paper, we showed how the use of slightly outdated GA information, that is *lagging GA*, and a fast index construction algorithm based on radix sorting can be combined in a novel way to speed up the index build process without sacrificing search quality.

We presented experimental results from the Trevi search engine, which is currently used to support all the searches on IBM's global intranet. Results show that the use of lagging GA does not compromise search quality and can reduce the time of the index build process by 25% or more. If the complexity of GA increases, perhaps due to clustering or data mining, the use of lagging GA will result in even greater time savings. Results also showed that index construction using a pipelined radix sort can outperform alternative approaches by 33% or more.

References

[1] Ricardo Baeza-Yates and Berthier Ribeiro-Neto. *Modern Information Retrieval*. Addison Wesley, New York, NY, 1999.

[2] Ziv Bar-Yossef and Sridhar Rajagopalan. Template detection via data mining and its applications. In *Proceedings of the International World Wide Web Conference, WWW2002*, 2002.

[3] Burton Bloom. Space/time trade-offs in hash coding with allowable errors. *Communications of the ACM*, 13(7):422–426, 1970.

[4] Sergey Brin and Lawrence Page. The anatomy of a large-scale hypertextual web search engine. In *WWW7 / Computer Networks 30(1-7)*, pages 107–117, 1998.

[5] Andrei Z. Broder. Identifying and filtering near-duplicate documents. In *Combinatorial Pattern Matching, 11th Annual Symposium*, pages 1–10, 2000.

[6] Andrei Z. Broder, Steven C. Glassman, Mark S. Manasse, and Geoffrey Zweig. Syntactic clustering of the web. In *WWW6 / Computer Networks 29(8-13)*, pages 1157–1166, 1997.

[7] Eric William Brown. Execution performance issues in full-text information retrieval. Technical report, University of Massacusetts, Amherst, MA, February 1996. Ph.D. Thesis.

[8] E.W. Brown, J.P. Callan, and W.B. Croft. Fast incremental indexing for full-text information retrieval. In *Proceedings of the 20th International Conference on Very Large Databases (VLDB)*, pages 192–202, Santiago, Chille, September 1994.

[9] David Carmel, Doron Cohen, Ronald Fagin, Eitan Farch, Michael Herscovici, Yoelle S. Maarek, and Aya Soffer. Static index pruning for information retrieval systems. In *Proceedings of 24th ACM SIGIR Conference on Research and Development in Information Retrieval (SIGIR '01)*, pages 43–50, New Orleans, Louisiana, USA, September 2001.

[10] Thomas H. Cormen, Charles E. Leiserson, Ronald L. Rivest, and Clifford Stein. *Introduction to Algorithms*. The MIT Press, Cambridge, MA, 2003.

[11] Nick Craswell, David Hawking, and Stephen Robertson. Effective site finding using link anchor information. In *Research and Development in Information Retrieval*, pages 250–257, 2001.

[12] Stephen Dill, Nadav Eiron, David Gibson, Daniel Gruhl, R. Guha, Anant Jhingran, Tapas Kanungo, Sridhar Rajagopalan, Andrew Tomkins, John A. Tomlin, and Jason Y. Zien. Semtag and seeker: bootstrapping the semantic web via automated semantic annotation. In *Proceedings of the Twelfth International World Wide Web Conference, WWW2003*, May 2003.

[13] Cynthia Dwork, Ravi Kumar, Moni Naor, and D. Sivakumar. Rank aggregation methods for the web. In *Proceedings of the Tenth International World Wide Web Conference (WWW 10)*, pages 613–622, Hong Kong, China, May 2001.

[14] Nadav Eiron and Kevin S. McCurley. Analysis of anchor text for web search. In *SIGIR Conference*, pages 459–460, 2003.

[15] Ronald Fagin, Ravi Kumar, Kevin S. McCurley, Jasmine Novak, D. Sivakumar, John A. Tomlin, and David P. Williamson. Searching the workplace web. In *Proceedings of the Twelfth International World Wide Web Conference, WWW2003*, May 2003.

[16] Ronald Fagin, Ravi Kumar, and D. Sivakumar. Comparing top k lists. In *Proceedings of ACM-SIAM Symposium on Discrete Algorithms (SODA '03)*, pages 28–36, Baltimore, MD, USA, January 2003.

[17] Steffen Heinz and Justin Zobel. Efficient single-pass index construction for text databases. *JASIST*, 54(8):713–729, 2003.

[18] Reiner Kraft and Jason Zien. Mining anchor text for query refinement. In *Proceedings of the Thirteenth International World Wide Web Conference (WWW 10)*, page (to appear), New York, NY, May 2004.

[19] Xiaohui Long and Torsten Suel. Optimized query execution in large search engines with global page ordering. In *Proceedings of 29th International Conference on Very Large Databases (VLDB 2003)*, pages 129–140, Berlin, Germany, September 2003.

[20] Lucene. http://jakarta.apache.org/lucene/.

[21] Lucy. http://www.seg.rmit.edu.au/lucy.

[22] Sergey Melnik, Sriram Raghavan, Beverly Yang, and Hector Garcia-Molina. Building a distributed full-text index for the web. In *World Wide Web*, pages 396–406, 2001.

[23] Lawrence Page, Sergey Brin, Rajeev Motwani, and Terry Winograd. The pagerank citation ranking: Bringing order to the web. Technical report, Stanford Digital Library Technologies Project, 1998.

[24] Peter K. Pearson. Fast hashing of variable-length text strings. *Communications of the ACM*, 33(6):677–680, June 1990.

[25] Mendel Rosenblum and John K. Ousterhout. The design and implementation of a log-structured file system. *ACM Transactions on Computer Systems*, 10(1):26–52, 1992.

[26] Robert Sedgewick. *Algorithms in C++*. Addison-Wesley Publishing Company, Boston, MA, 1998.

[27] Ranjan Sinha and Justin Zobel. Cache-conscious sorting of large sets of strings. In *Proceedings of the ALENEX Workshop on Algorithm Engineering and Experiments*, pages 93–105, 2003.

[28] Anthony Tomasic, Héctor García-Molina, and Kurt Shoens. Incremental updates of inverted lists for text document retrieval. pages 289–300, 1994.

[29] Ian Witten, Alistair Moffat, and Timoty Bell. *Managing Gigabytes*. Morgan Kaufmann Publishers, Inc., San Francisco, CA, 1999.

[30] Alice X. Zheng, Andrew Y. Ng, and Michael I. Jordan. Stable algorithms for link analysis. In *Proceedings of 24th ACM SIGIR Conference on Research and Development in Information Retrieval (SIGIR '01)*, pages 258–266, New Orleans, Louisiana, USA, September 2001.

Automated design of multidimensional clustering tables for relational databases

Sam S. Lightstone
IBM Toronto Laboratory
Markham, Ontario, Canada
light@ca.ibm.com

Bishwaranjan Bhattacharjee
IBM T. J. Watson Research Center
Hawthorne, New York, USA
bhatta@us.ibm.com

Abstract

The ability to physically cluster a database table on multiple dimensions is a powerful technique that offers significant performance benefits in many OLAP, warehousing, and decision-support systems. An industrial implementation of this technique for the DB2® Universal Database™ (DB2 UDB) product, called multidimensional clustering (MDC), which co-exists with other classical forms of data storage and indexing methods, was described in VLDB 2003. This paper describes the first published model for automating the selection of clustering keys in single-dimensional and multidimensional relational databases that use a cell/block storage structure for MDC. For any significant dimensionality (3 or more), the possible solution space is combinatorially complex. The automated MDC design model is based on what-if query cost modeling, data sampling, and a search algorithm for evaluating a large constellation of possible combinations. The model is effective at trading the benefits of potential combinations of clustering keys against data sparsity and performance. It also effectively selects the granularity at which dimensions should be used for clustering (such as week of year versus month of year). We show results from experiments indicating that the model provides design recommendations of comparable quality to those made by human experts. The model has been implemented in the IBM® DB2 UDB for Linux®, UNIX® and Windows® Version 8.2 release.

Permission to copy without fee all or part of this material is granted provided that the copies are not made or distributed for direct commercial advantage, the VLDB copyright notice and the title of the publication and its date appear, and notice is given that copying is by permission of the Very Large Data Base Endowment. To copy otherwise, or to republish, requires a fee and/or special permission from the Endowment

**Proceedings of the 30th VLDB Conference,
Toronto, Canada, 2004**

1. Introduction

Multidimensional clustering (MDC) techniques have been shown to have very significant performance benefits for complex workloads [4][12][14][15][20]. In fact, the literature on MDC has focused on how to better design database storage structures, rather than on how to select the clustering dimensions. However, for any given storage structure used for MDC, there are complex design trade-offs in the selection of the clustering dimensions. In this paper we present a model for doing so in the form of an MDC Advisor that will select MDC keys (i.e., designs) optimized for a specified combination of workload, schema, and data. We also describe its implementation for the MDC physical layout scheme introduced in DB2 UDB Version 8.1 [2] and report the results of experiments that indicate the model provides design recommendations that are in line with the quality of human expert recommendations. The value of exploiting MDC would be superior system performance, reduced time from test to production system, and reduced skill requirements within an enterprise.

MDC is motivated to a large extent by the spectacular growth of relational data, which has spurred the continual research and development of improved techniques for handling large data sets and complex queries. In particular, online analytical processing (OLAP) and decision-support systems (DSS) have become popular for data mining and business analysis [16]. OLAP and DSS systems are characterized by multidimensional analysis of compiled enterprise data, and typically include transactional queries including group-by, aggregation, (multidimensional) range queries, cube, roll-up and drill-down.

The performance of multidimensional queries, (such as GROUP BY and range queries) is often improved through data clustering, which can significantly reduce I/O costs, and modestly reduce CPU costs. Yet the choice of clustering dimensions and the granularity of the clustering are nontrivial choices and can be difficult to design even for experienced database designers and industry experts.

In recent years, there have been several research and industrial initiatives focused on physical database design. In particular, a number of projects have focused on design automation for indexes, materialized views, and table partitioning [3][5][6][7][8][13][17][18][19].

The recent flurry of papers on index and materialized view selection, and the development of industrial applications in self-managing, or autonomic, systems by leading RDBMS vendors such as Microsoft, IBM and Oracle, all attest to the growing corporate recognition of this important area of investigation.

The rest of the paper is organized as follows: Section 2 gives an overview of relevant design advisor issues, Section 3 describes the approach used with the MDC Advisor, Section 4 describes experiments with the MDC Advisor, and we conclude with Section 5.

2. Background

2.1 DB2 UDB V8.1 MDC implementation

In the MDC implementation in DB2 UDB V8.1 proposed by Padmanabhan et al. [15], each unique combination of dimension values forms a logical cell that is physically organized as blocks of pages, where a block is a set of consecutive pages on disk. Every page of the table is part of exactly one block, and all blocks of the table consist of the same number of pages. The clustering dimensions are individually indexed by B+ indexes, known as dimension block indexes, which have dimension values as keys and block identifiers as key data.

The DB2 UDB implementation was chosen by its designers for its ability to co-exist with other database features such as row-based indexes, table constraints, materialized views, high-speed load, and mass delete.

Figure 1 illustrates these concepts. It depicts an MDC table clustered along the dimensions year(orderDate), region and itemId. The figure shows a simple logical cube with only two values for each dimension attribute. Logical cells are represented by sub-cubes in the figure and blocks by shaded oval, and are numbered according to the logical order of allocated blocks in the table. We show only a few blocks of data for a cell identified by the dimension values <1997,Canada,2>.

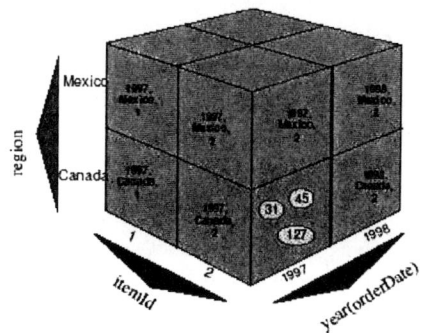

Figure 1: Logical view within an MDC table

2.2 Cost-based evaluation for database advisors

Lohman et al. [13] suggest using cost estimates provided by the database optimizer as part of the evaluation engine of an index advisor that recommends table indexes. In this model, Lohman et al. used a simulation technique to determine access cost impact of potential table indexes. Tthe DBMS is taught to consider "virtual" indexes within its query compiler, resulting in an effective costing of query performance.

The key advance in Lohman's technique is the use of optimizer estimates to evaluate the value of a potential change in the design of a database. The empirical results for this technique were found to be quite good for index selection. A variation of this method was exploited again for another physical database design problem in [18] to design partitioning schemes for shared-nothing massively parallel processing (MPP) databases.

The idea of reusing the database optimizer's cost estimations for evaluating cost benefit of physical design changes in the database is based on the observation that the query optimizer's cost modeling is sensitive to both the logical and physical design of a database. Having the model for workload resource consumption allows us to exploit this model for "what-if" analysis.

In the area of automating MDC dimension selection, there are implementations such as WARLOCK [21], which was limited to parallel warehouses for shared- everything or shared-disk architectures. It used its own cost model instead of using the database engines.

2.3 Estimating the cardinality of distinct values in a set from a data sample

The ability to estimate the cardinality of a set from a sample is an important aspect of MDC design. This topic was surveyed in depth in the 1990s, notably in [9][10].

The known estimators can be divided into two main categories: i) those that evaluate cardinality while examining the frequency data in the sample, and ii) those that generate a result without considering frequency distribution across classes in the sample. The latter type are significant to this paper because they can be calculated easily with only a small set of input variables describing the sample, such as sample frequency, sample size and the cardinality of unique values in the sample. The best of these latter estimators is the First Order Jackknife estimator, which can be described as follows:

When the data set contains no skew the scale-up factor, defined as $Scale = D/E[d]$, is given by

$$Scale = D/E[d] = 1/(1-(1-q)^{(N/d)}) \quad (1.)$$

Here D is the number of distinct values in the set and d is the number of distinct values in the sample. Also, $E[d]$ is the expected number of distinct values in the sample under Bernoulli sampling with rate $q = n/N$, where n is the sample size and N is the set size. $E[d]$ is the theoretical expected value of d, i.e., the average value of d over many repeated samples. The idea behind the "method of moments" estimator is to derive an equation relating $E[d]$ to D, based on theoretical considerations. We solve for D to get a relation of the form:

$$D = f(E[d])$$

for some function f. Our estimator $\hat{D}$ is then obtained by substituting d for $E[d]$ in the above relation:

$$\hat{D} = f(d) \quad (2.)$$

Such a substitution is reasonable if the sample is not too small. $E[d]$ is the "first moment" of d, so we are replacing a moment by an observed value.

2.4 Expression based columns

Some popular RDBMS products available today provide the ability to define expression-based columns as part of a relational table definition. These columns, sometimes called generated columns or virtual columns, are mathematical functions of columns within their record tuple. For example, one might define an expression-based column on an employee table that is a function of each employee's SALARY as follows:
CREATE TABLE EMPLOYEES
(EMPLOYEE_ID INT,
SALARY DECIMAL(10,4),
SALARY_RANGE INT
GENERATED ALWAYS AS
(SALARY/1000))

These expression-based columns based on mathematical and lexical models in many cases have superior clustering potential over one or more base columns. For example, INT(SALARY/1000) is likely to be superior in terms of clustering potential to clustering directly on SALARY.

3. MDC Dimension Selection

MDC requires the allocation of storage blocks to disk for all cells (unique combinations of dimensions) that have at least one tuple. Since in practice all cells will have at least one incompletely filled block, MDC will generally cause some storage expansion. Since storage may be constrained and does impact system performance, it is treated as a constraint on the selection problem. Accordingly, MDC solutions are considered only if they require no more than 10% extra space than a non-MDC implementation. 10% was chosen as a reasonable trade-off to a) constrain increased storage costs and b) constrain any possible negative effect that storage increase may have on queries processing data along access patterns that do not benefit from MDC.

With this constraint in mind, we exploit the SQL query optimizer to model the resource consumption of the workload with and without MDC clustering. Once a set of candidate dimensions,, and their respective benefits to the workload, is identified, we also model how each dimension's benefit will degrade at various coarsifications. Finally, through a search and sample process, the space of possible combinations of dimensions and their coarsifications is examined to find the MDC design for a table that maximizes the combinations of dimensions while satisfying the expansion constraint.

The search space for selecting clustering dimensions is huge. The basic problem of selecting clustering dimensions from a finite set can be modeled easily as a simple combination problem. However, since each dimension has some number of degrees of coarsification, the search space expands exponentially. Assuming an equal number of degrees of coarseness for each dimension, the following equation shows the combinations of n dimensions each with c degrees of coarsification:

$$(\sum_{r=1}^{n-1}((n!)/(r!(n-r)!))c^r) + c^n \quad (3.)$$

This equation takes a standard formula for the combination of n items, and expands based on the fact that, for each iteration of the sum, each tuple has its combinations expanded by a factor of c^r because each part of the tuple has c degrees of coarsification (i.e., c ways in which it can be selected). Similarly, the formula concludes with c^n since the selection space for a selection that includes every dimension, each being selected at one of c degrees, is c^n. In general, not all dimensions have the same number of degrees of coarsification. Even so, equation (3) suggests the complexity of the space.

In Subsection 3.1 we give an overview of the methodology adopted, and in subsequent subsections we expand on some key areas. This methodology expects the following inputs from the user:
1. A workload specification, detailing specific queries and the frequency of execution of each.
2. A sample database including the database tables, indexes, and a sample of data. The more complete this database is, the better the recommendations.

Note that the MDC Advisor was designed as an extension to the DB2 Design Advisor, which supports several techniques for automated workload capture, compression, ranking, and weighting [11][17].

3.1 High-level overview of the MDC selection model

Our approach is based on searching over the constellation of combinations of dimensions at various coarsifications to find a combination that has the highest expected benefit while satisfying the storage expansion constraint.

1) Identify candidate clustering dimensions and their maximal potential workload benefit:
   a) Baseline the expected resource consumption (via SQL optimizer estimates) of each query in the workload with all optimizer clustering statistics simulated to represent poor clustering.
   b) Each query in the workload is reoptimized in a special mode, whereby the SQL optimizer simulates the effect of clustering on all candidate clustering dimensions. The dimensions are selected by their use in predicates, as described in Section 3.2. During this phase the optimizer is essentially modeling a best-case scenario where the data is clustered perfectly along all potentially useful clustering dimensions. Also, during this phase we are modeling the maximum potential benefit of MDC apart from its total storage requirement. The clustering dimensions are modeled within the query compiler/optimizer at the finest level of granularity possible for each dimension as if that dimension was the only clustering dimension used. This granularity is titled the Finest Useful Dimensions Granularity (FUDG, pronounced fudge), and represents an upper bound on the granularity of each dimension that satisfies the storage expansion constraint. At the FUDG coarsification, a single dimension can be reasonably useful as a clustering dimension while still populating most of the storage blocks. The maximum cardinality of cells is deterministic, as described in Section 3.3, and can be used directly in the optimizer virtual simulation.
   c) Contrasting 1a and 1b we can determine which virtual clustering dimensions in 1b resulted in significant positive differences in the access plans and resource consumption of the queries. The relative reduction in query resource consumption (estimated by the query optimizer) provides an estimate of the benefit gained by clustering on each candidate dimension at its FUDG coarsification.

2) Generate a search space of candidate MDC keys:
   a) A list of candidate dimension and their maximal potential contributions was generated in the previous step. We begin the next phase by designing potential coarsifications of each dimension (where supported): for example, SALARY/1000, SALARY/2000, SALARY/4000, etc., described in detail in Sections 3.4, 3.5, 3.6). A sample of data for each table is then collected. This sample includes a small percentage of tuples from the base but covers exclusively the clustering dimensions identified in step 1c above. The sample data also includes generated expressions that define the coarsifications for each dimension.
   b) Statistics are then collected regarding the cardinality of distinct values for each column in the sampled data, and extrapolated by means of the First Order Jackknife estimator to estimate the cardinality of each dimension at the various degrees of coarsification considered.
   c) The maximum potential clustering benefit or each dimension was determined in step 1c but only at the FUDG coarsification. Now for each dimension its potential value will be estimated again at each of the coarsifications considered, with the assumption that benefit generally decreases as coarsification increases. The benefit attenuation is determined by a curve-fitting process, described in Section 3.7. This yields an expected benefit for each coarsification of each dimension.
   d) For each table, a set of candidate clustering keys is then generated, forming a search space, as per Section 3.8. Each key in the set includes a possible final clustering solution for an individual table. The generated keys are produced by a weighted randomized search. With just one or two candidate dimensions, it is possible to perform an exhaustive search, but

with more dimensions the search space can be prohibitive.

This process yields a set of candidate MDC keys (i.e., potential designs) for each table.

3) For each table, test the candidate MDC clustering keys for satisfaction of the storage expansion constraint.
   a) The candidate clustering keys in 2d are sorted by expected benefit. Benefit is assumed to be the sum of the estimated benefits of the parts (i.e., individual dimensions) for the key. This is not entirely accurate, but a sufficient simplification.
   b) For each table, the candidate clustering keys are then evaluated for space constraint. The space consumption for each candidate key is evaluated through a sampling process (Section 3.9.2) and keys that exceed the space expansion constraint are rejected.
   c) Since the candidate keys were first sorted in rank order (by expected benefit), the first candidate key that satisfies the storage expansion constraint is selected as the winner.
   d) This process is repeated for subsequent tables, until all tables identified in 1c have been evaluated.

Note that phase 1 of this analysis (Select dimension candidates) is done across all tables simultaneously by simulating virtual clustering across all referenced tables in the workload. One of the important observations by Lohman et al. is that early algorithms for index selection assumed separability, such that design decisions on one table could be made independently of design decision for another table (specifically in the case of index advisors). However, Lohman et al. [13] observe that this assumption is not always true, as in the case of a nested loop join between relations R and S where an index on one of R or S reduces the need for an index on the other. This is so because as long as one of R and S has an index, the join predicate can be applied to the inner relation. Thus, it appears that, at least in the case of joins between relations, data access patterns are co-dependent, and design decisions should not be made for each table in complete isolation. The same arguments apply to the problem of MDC design, so separability should not be assumed. Our approach is a hybrid in which we modeled dimension interdependency in steps 1 and 2 above, but assumed independence in 3a.

3.2 Identifying candidate columns

Candidate clustering columns are identified during optimization of SQL queries and the simulation of virtual MDC: these include columns that are used for predicates and operators and are likely to benefit from clustering, such as:
- GROUP BY,
- ORDER BY,
- CUBE,
- ROLLUP,
- WHERE predicates for equality, inequality, and ranges.

3.3 Modeling space waste from table conversion to MDC

Figure 2 illustrates several cells each containing a number of storage blocks, with the final blocks in each cell only partially filled. The greater the number of cells there are, the more partially filled blocks, and therefore the more space wasted. An estimate of the space waste can be made by assuming each cell contains a single partially filled block at the end of its block list. The space waste is then:

$$W = \eta_{cells} \cdot P_{\%} \cdot \beta \qquad (4.)$$

where $P_{\%}$ is the average percentage of each storage block left empty per cell, and β is the blocking size. On average, the last block in each cell will be 50% filled, except in cases of largely empty cells (very few tuples in the cell). In the presence of either data skew, or very high cell cardinality, the number of cells with very few tuples may increase, resulting in a high vacancy rate in the final block of some cell. In fact, the choice of $P_{\%}$ is not critical, provided it is larger than 50%, since the goal is to observe gross expansion of space rather than to estimate space use accurately. In our implementation, we have used a conservative estimate for $P_{\%}$ of 65%.

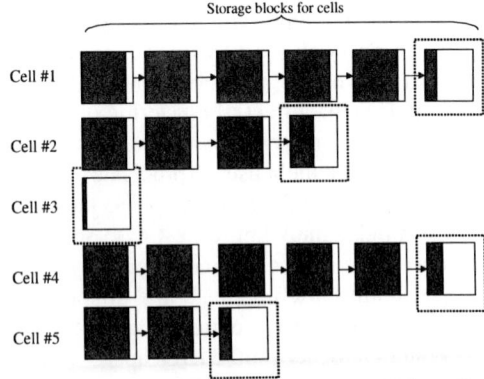

Figure 2: Partially filled blocks within cells

3.4 Coarsification approaches for specific dimension types

For each range dimension, there are specific ways that we can coarsify the clustering, but not an infinite set. In practice, once we have identified FUDG, as illustrated in the following examples, there are approximately 4 to 10 degrees of useful coarsification that we can apply. For example, when coarsifying a date field, we can imagine the following possibilities:

day->month->quarter->year

Similarly, for an INTEGER type, we can coarsify the dimension using division, with a logarithmic scale (i.e., divide by 2, 4, 8, 16, etc).

However, since storage expansion will be proportional to the cardinality of cells in the resulting MDC table, clearly to satisfy the expansion constraint the combinations of dimensions in the final solution must be small enough as per equation (4.). Since the cardinality of cells can only grow as dimensions are taken in combination (e.g., AB will have a cardinality of cells >= A or B individually), therefore, the finest useful granularity that is worth considering in the search space for any single dimension must likewise satisfy this constraint. This granularity is known as the FUDG coarsification, and is described in more detail in the next section. In our selection scheme we begin with the FUDG coarsification, and consider further coarsification of the FUDG coarsification for each clustering dimension showing workload benefit.

3.5 Determining the FUDG coarsification for a candidate clustering dimension

For numeric types, coarsification begins by calculating the FUDG coarsification using the HIGH2KEY statistic (second largest column value) and LOW2KEY statistic (second smallest column value) to define the range of the dimensions, then defining an expression that divides that range into η_{cells_max} ranges (cells). If the base column has cardinality that is below the FUDG cardinality, then the base column defines the FUDG coarsification for that candidate dimension (i.e., this column's FUDG coarsification is simply the base column itself and requires no coarsification).

We define a mathematical function that divides the range between HIGH2KEY and LOW2KEY into a number of ranges, where the number of ranges is the same as the maximum number of cells possible in the table given the space constraint, as shown in Figure 3. HIGH2KEY and LOW2KEY are assumed to represent the reasonable range of values for the dimension.

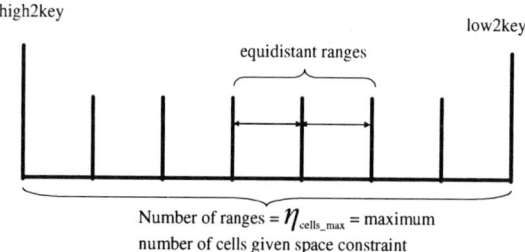

Number of ranges = η_{cells_max} = maximum number of cells given space constraint

Figure 3: Calculating FUDG for numeric types

$D_{FUDG} = (Column - LOW2KEY)/iCoarsifier$ (5.)

where *iCoarsifier* is....

$iCoarsifier = ((HIGH2KEY - LOW2KEY)/iNum\_blocks\_min);$ (6.)

and *iNum_blocks_min* is...

$iNum\_blocks\_min = MAX(1, table\_size/\beta);$ (7.)

In (7) table_size is the size of the table we are evaluating for MDC, and β is the size of the storage blocks in the cell-block model. In order for this process to work, it is necessary that the dimension be converted to integer form (so that the cardinality of the resulting range is discrete). For real types (DECIMAL, FLOAT, DOUBLE) this means ensuring that they have a substantial positive range. To accomplish this, the FUDG coarsification for Real types includes a multiplicative factor that ensures HIGH2KEY is > 1000.

For DATE and TIMESTAMP fields, we coarsify by casting first to INT and BIGINT, respectively, then using integer division to coarsify to week, month, quarter, year. Special assumptions are made when determining the FUDG coarsification for DATE and TIMESTAMP because of the practical concern that the data currently in the database at the time the MDC Advisor is run may only be a time-fragment of the real data (for example one month's worth of data). This is a very significant and realistic situation for database designers. If only a single month of data were provided, the cardinality of cells in the DATE dimension might be limited to 31 distinct values, while in fact the data may only be a one month sample of a seven-year data warehouse. Therefore, to mitigate this risk, in both TIMESTAMP and DATE cases, we assume that WEEK of YEAR is a reasonable estimate of FUDG since it coarsifies the column to a maximum of 52 cells per year. We do not recommend clustering on DATE or TIMESTAMP without coarsification, even when the apparent cardinality of cells in the dimension data is low enough.

3.6 Sampling for cardinality estimates

For each dimension, once the FUDG coarsification has been estimated, further coarsification is designed. The search model requires a reasonable estimate of the cardinality of each dimension at each of the dimension coarsifications (during step 2b of the process described in 3.1 above), as well as the ability to measure the cardinality of combinations of these dimensions (during step 3a in Section 3.1 above). To facilitate a reasonable response time for the MDC Advisor, a sampling approach is used. In this sampling model, data is sampled for each candidate table only once, and stored in a temporary staging table. The sampling is performed using a Bernoulli sampling method. Statistics including cardinality of dimensions, dimension coarsifications and combination of dimensions can be collected over the sampled data rather than the base table, which enables the evaluation of a large number of variants while only sampling the base table once. While the staging table holding the sample may need to be scanned multiple times, significant performance benefit accrues from the fact that the staging table is a small fraction of the size of the base table from which its data came.

Cardinality estimation research [9][10] suggests that the accuracy of statistical cardinality estimators drop off precipitously when sampling rates fall below 1%. Therefore, the staging table constructed here uses the larger of a 1% sample or a sample of 10000 tuples to construct its sample.

The staging table T_{temp}, includes a definition of all the base columns from T_{base} that are candidate clustering dimensions. In addition, T_{temp} includes expression-based columns for all of the coarsification of the base columns the MDC Advisor will consider, starting with the FUDG coarsification level, and increasing from there. For example, if SALARY may have a FUDG coarsification of $SALARY_f$ = SALARY/1000, we may also create generated columns of $SALARY_f$ /4, $SALARY_f$ /16, $SALARY_f$ /64..., etc. The staging table is populated with a 1% sample from the base table. This allows the cardinalities of unique values that are needed in 2c and 3a of Section 3.1 to be counted while only taking the sample once (i.e., sample once, count many).

3.7 Modeling workload benefit consequences of clustering coarsification

One of the key issues is to understand the likely effect of coarsification on the expected benefit in clustering on any given dimension. A brute force approach to solving this problem would be to re-evaluate (simulate) the workload cost with each individual coarsification of each dimension, or perhaps all possible combinations. Such an approach for workloads of any significant dimensionality is impractical. Instead we use a simple model sufficient for the MDC selection process, based on the following two observations

1. When a database table has only one cell, MDC provides no value.
2. Expected benefit at the FUDG coarsification was determined through simulation within the SQL optimizer.

This gives us two points of reference on a performance versus cardinality of distinct values graph, when cardinality is 1 (i.e., zero benefit) and at the cardinality of distinct values at the FUDG coarsification. We also infer that the benefit due to clustering is monotonic and decreasing as coarsification increases.

Although the exact shape of the monotonic curve cannot be easily determined, we have modeled it as a smooth logarithmic relationship, such that the penalty for coarsifying a dimension is initially minor, but increases dramatically at higher coarsification levels. We apply a curve-fitting process to plot a concave polynomial between the two well-known points to derive a benefit-coarsification function, as per **Figure 4**. From this relationship function, we can model the performance benefit of any coarsification level of a dimension given its cardinality of cells at the FUDG coarsification level.

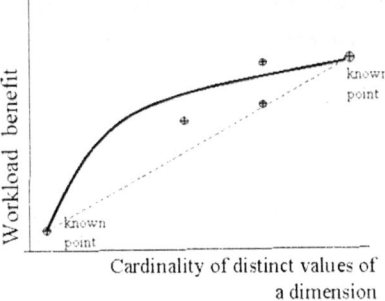

Figure 4: Curve-fitted benefit-coarsification function

The benefit versus cardinality of cells function is then determined as follows in equations (8) and (9).

$$B = m * log(C) \quad (8.)$$
$$m = Bf/(log(Cf)) \quad (9.)$$

B is the performance benefit at a given coarsification level, and **C** is the cardinality of cells at the same coarsification level. **Bf** is the performance benefit at the FUDG coarsification and **Cf** is the cardinality of cells at the FUDG coarsification level for the dimension.

3.8 Search algorithm

To find an optimal combination of dimensions that satisfies our storage expansion constraint, we have used a simple weighted randomized search, which includes some qualities of a genetic algorithm including weighted selection of attributes. After completing steps 1a, 1b, and 1c described in Section 3.1, the algorithm is left with a search problem that must select the best possible MDC design given a list of candidate dimensions with estimated performance benefit at their FUDG coarsification. The search space for this problem is all possible combinations and permutations of all these candidate dimensions at any of their possible coarsifications. The complexity of this search was described in equation (3). Since the evaluation of a candidate clustering key requires some degree of cardinality evaluation (to ensure the storage constraint is not exceeded) the evaluation function requires some sampling and counting. Therefore, the need for cardinality estimation requires a computationally costly evaluation function, and an exhaustive search is not practical.

Using our weighted randomized search, combinations of dimensions at various coarsifications are selected in probabilistic proportion to their relative benefit to the workload. Each such combination forms a candidate solution. The set of generated candidate MDC keys (i.e., solutions) are then sorted by benefit. For simplicity, the benefit of each MDC solution is assumed to be the sum of the workload benefit for each dimension in the solution. Once the candidate clustering keys have been generated and ranked, they are evaluated in rank order using the evaluation function described in the previous section to determine whether they satisfy the storage expansion constraint. Since the candidate clustering keys are sorted in rank order, the first candidate key to pass the test for storage expansion is chosen as the final clustering recommendation for a given table.

To improve the efficiency of the search, when a candidate key is found to have a design that will lead to gross storage expansion (e.g., >5x storage growth), then we reject this key, and also eliminate near neighbours in the search constellation. This near-neighbour reduction has been effective in high dimensionality search spaces in greatly reducing the search cost. On our experiments, the efficiency of the search was improved by 400% in some cases by this addition.

3.9 Evaluation function for candidate keys

3.9.1 Estimating workload benefit

The search method used in this paper will require an evaluation function to assess the fitness (or value) of each search point in the candidate solution space. The value in this context is the potential benefit to the query workload in improving performance. To do this we exploit a variation of the technique used by Lohman et al. [13] where the database optimizer is used to provide a cost estimate of the workload. In this method the optimizer is given a simulation of the table definition and table statistics (and statistics for dependent objects) against which it makes its estimations. In the case of MDC the problem is more complex for these reasons:

- MDC affects the base table: it is not simply an optional attachment, as in the case of an index;
- MDC affects the statistics of the base table, namely table size;
- The MDC search typically includes search points for dimensions at multiple degrees of coarsification.

To deal with the complexities, the optimizer model is extended to model MDC candidates, affecting statistics of the base table as well as cluster ratios on existing indexes. The benefit of the FUDG coarsification of a dimension is then calculated as the aggregate of the resource consumption reduction for each query in the workload that exploits the virtual clustering dimension as compared to the same resource consumption analysis without MDC clustering. However, the cardinality of cells at a given coarsification of a dimension cannot be reliably estimated, and sampling is required to determine this. Once a reasonable estimate of the cardinality of cells is obtained, the attenuated workload benefit due to coarsification of a dimension can be estimated using equation (8) as described in Section 3.7. Therefore, the SQL query optimizer is used to estimate the workload benefit for each dimension at its FUDG coarsification, while sampling, counting, and curve fitting are used to estimate the benefit of the same dimension at increased levels of coarsification.

Once the benefit of each candidate dimension is calculated at its FUDG coarsification, the expected benefit for each dimension at further coarsifications is modeled through the process described in Section 3.7 and the curve-fitting algorithm described there, provided cardinalities or estimates of cardinalities are known for each coarsification of the dimensions we wish to model. These estimates of cardinality for each candidate dimension are similarly detected through the sampling process described in Section 3.6, and extrapolated using the First Order Jackknife Estimator.

Using these methods in combination, we now have a model for:
a) Detecting candidate dimensions.
b) Estimating the workload benefit of a candidate clustering dimension at its FUDG coarsification.

c) Modeling the benefit of each candidate clustering dimension at coarsifications beyond the FUDG coarsification, as a logarithmic function of cardinality reduction.

3.9.2 Evaluating satisfaction of the storage expansion constraint

The remaining problem in the evaluation function is to determine for any given combination of dimensions and coarsifications what the cardinality of resulting cells will be. This measure of cardinality of cells is critical to determine in order to satisfy the storage expansion constraint. Using the same data sample collected above into T_{temp}, we can use SQL to count the cardinality of the unique values of a combination of dimensions that correspond to the dimensions in a MDC solution we being evaluated.

To do this, we use an SQL query such as the following:

**SELECT COUNT(*) FROM (SELECT DISTINCT A,B,C FROM T-TEMP)
AS CELL_CARD;** (10.)

This returns the COUNT of distinct values of the clustering key (ABC). Once the cardinality in T_{temp} of distinct values of the candidate clustering key is determined, we can scale this sampled cardinality using the First Order Jackknife Estimator to estimate the number of cells that would exist in the entire table. This sampling and extrapolation method effectively models correlation between the dimensions in a candidate solution.

Once the cardinality of cells is estimated, it can be tested against equation (4) to determine whether the storage expansion constraint is satisfied.

3.10 Data skew

In a few instances (see 3.6, 3.7 and 3.9.2), the MDC Advisor algorithm requires a statistical estimator to extrapolate the cardinality of unique values in a sample. The First Order Jackknife Estimator was chosen for its simplicity. This estimator is known to be weak in the presence of severe data skew. Though length limitations do not allow for a detailed analysis here, it can be shown that the specific requirements in this algorithm are quite tolerant to estimation inaccuracies, which allow the First Order Jackknife estimator to be adequate in the presence of data skew in most cases. Even so, several other estimators with superior skew handling are described in [9][10], which can be substituted to improve the robustness of the algorithm.

4. Experimental Results

4.1 Test Objectives & Description

The objective of the tests was to compare the quality of the MDC Advisor recommendation when compared to expert human recommendation against a well-known schema and workload. The industry standard TPC-H benchmark was used for the tests [1]. The metric used for comparison is called the TPC-H Composite Query-per-Hour (QphH@Size). For the experiments a 10 GB TPC-H database running on DB2 UDB V8.1 on a pSeries® server with AIX® 5.1, 4 X 375 MHz CPUs and 8 GB RAM was used. Six experimental tests were performed:

1. Baseline: The performance of the benchmark without MDC. Table 1 describes those tradition RID (row) indexes used for the baseline experiment, which had cluster ratio quality of 5% or better, a measure of percentage of data that is well clustered along one dimension.
2. Advisor 1: The performance of the benchmark using the top most MDC design (described in Table 2) of the Advisor.
3. Advisor 2: The performance of the benchmark using the second best MDC design (described in Table 3) for the Advisor.
4. Expert 1: The MDC design used during IBM's most recent 2003 TPC-H publication. This is described in Table 4. According to TPC-H guidelines, the MDC design was constrained to clustering exclusively on base columns (coarsification was not permitted).
5. Expert 2: The top MDC design provided by the DB2 MDC development team described in Table 5.
6. Expert 3: An alternative MDC design provided by the DB2 MDC development team is described in Table 6.

Index name	Base table	Columns (key parts)	Cluster quality (%)
L_OK	LINEITEM	+L_ORDERKEY	100
R_RK	REGION	+R_REGIONKEY	100
S_NK	SUPPLIER	+S_NATIONKEY	36.8
PS_PK_SK	PARTSUPP	+PS_PARTKEY +PS_SUPPKEY	100
S_SK	SUPPLIER	+S_SUPPKEY	100
PS_PK	PARTSUPP	+PS_PARTKEY	100

Table 1: Single dimensional clustering in baseline

Base table	MDC dimensions
CUSTOMER	C_NATIONKEY, C_MKTSEGMENT
LINEITEM	(INT(L_SHIPDATE))/7, L_RETURNFLAG, (INT(L_RECEIPTDATE))/14, L_SHIPINSTRUCT
ORDERS	(INT(O_ORDERDATE))/7, O_ORDERSTATUS
PART	P_SIZE
PARTSUPP	(((PS_PARTKEY)/(((1999999 - 2)/(19956))*(8))))
SUPPLIER	S_NATIONKEY

Table 2: MDC design for "Advisor 1"

Base table	MDC dimensions
CUSTOMER	C_NATIONKEY/2, C_MKTSEGMENT
LINEITEM	(INT(L_SHIPDATE))/14, L_RETURNFLAG, (INT(L_RECEIPTDATE))/7, L_SHIPINSTRUCT
ORDERS	(INT(O_ORDERDATE))/14, O_ORDERSTATUS
PART	P_SIZE/2, P_CONTAINER
PARTSUPP	(((PS_PARTKEY)/(((1999999 - 2)/(19956))*(16))))
SUPPLIER	S_NATIONKEY/2

Table 3: MDC design for "Advisor 2"

Base table	MDC dimensions
LINEITEM	L_SHIPDATE
ORDERS	O_ORDERDATE

Table 4: MDC design for "Expert 1"

Base table	MDC dimensions
CUSTOMER	C_NATIONKEY
LINEITEM	(INT(L_SHIPDATE))/100, L_SHIPMODE, L_SHIPINSTRUCT
ORDERS	O_ORDERDATE
SUPPLIER	S_NATIONKEY

Table 5: MDC design for "Expert 2"

Base table	MDC dimensions
CUSTOMER	C_NATIONKEY, C_MKTSEGMENT
LINEITEM	(INT(L_SHIPDATE))/100, L_SHIPMODE, L_SHIPINSTRUCT, (INT(L_RECEIPTDATE)/10000)
PART	P_SIZE, P_BRAND

Table 6: MDC design for "Expert 3"

The TPC-H workload was run three times for each test; the shortest run for each design is noted here. Execution time variability was found to be quite minimal among the three runs, generally less than 2%. The tests were done with identical database and database manager parameters.

4.2 MDC Advisor search space

A graphical display of search points considered by the MDC Advisor algorithm (Figure 14) for the two largest tables, LINEITEM and ORDERS illustrates some interesting search characteristics. The shaded areas covering the rightmost portions of the space are areas where the search points would have caused severe table storage expansion. As a result, these high expansion candidates are not practical as solutions and are simply rejected from the candidate solution set.

Figure 5 shows the performance benefit versus storage expansion projected for each candidate solution explored in the MDC search. Note that the benefit model assumed < 10% growth, so that candidate solutions resulting in more than 10% growth have bogus benefit. The density of search points that lie along a region in the x domain between 1.0x and 1.1x expansion is quite reasonable, illustrating that the search algorithm is successful in finding many candidate solutions in the acceptable range of expansion. The circled area shows the keys with highest benefit and reasonable data expansion from which the final recommended MDC solution is chosen.

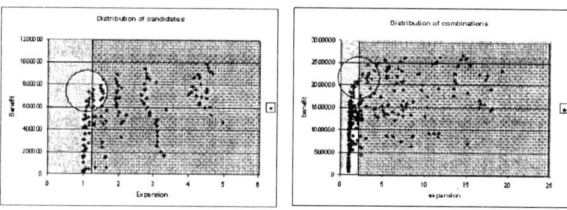

Figure 5: Distribution of search points for TPC-H two largest tables

4.3 MDC table expansion

Table 7 shows the actual table expansion rates for the TPC-H tables for the six clustering designs.

The MDC Advisor logic, was quite effective at selecting MDC designs that were constrained to the space constraint goal of 10% expansion. The largest table expansion was seen in Advisor 1 experiment where LINEITEM table expanded by 11.98%, and 12.76% expansion on PARTSUPP, which is quite good given the 1% sampling rate of the First Order Jackknife estimator.

Table name	No MDC Size (4K)	Expert 1 Growth (%)	Expert 2 Growth (%)	Expert 3 Growth (%)	Advisor 1 Growth (%)	Advisor 2 Growth (%)
LINEITEM	2081040	1.05	4.69	8.42	11.98	11.95
ORDERS	443840	4.08	4.08	0.00	5.23	4.89
PART	76240	0.00	0.63	5.56	0.63	9.99
PARTSUPP	319296	0.00	0.00	0.00	12.76	6.49
CUSTOMER	69168	0.00	0.35	1.50	1.50	3.63
SUPPLIER	4096	0.00	7.81	0.00	7.81	6.25
Total	2993680	1.34	3.90	6.03	10.53	10.07

Table 7: Table expansion with MDC

Also the expert designs by human designers (Expert 1, Expert 2, and Expert 3) were generally more aggressive than the MDC Advisor in constraining space expansion (1.34%, 3.90% and 6.03% total expansion, respectively), a likely reflection of their deep knowledge and many years of experience with the TPC-H workload

4.4 Query performance results

The MDC Advisor completed its design analysis and reported its recommendations in less than an hour.

Figure 6 shows the QphH results for the six clustering designs and they show the performance benefit of MDC and the effectiveness of the MDC Advisor algorithm in selecting MDC designs in comparison to human experts.

In these experiments, all of the MDC designs showed significant benefit over the baseline throughput. The rank ordering of the five MDC designs according to their performance benefit Advisor 2 with 11.12%, Expert 1 with 13.35%, Expert 3 with 14.20%, Advisor 1 with 14.54%, and Expert 2 with 18.08%. Significantly, Advisor 1, which represents the MDC Advisor's best recommendation was measurably superior to to MDC Advisor 2, and both Expert 1 and Expert 3.

Also revealing is a view of the performance by individual queries, as shown in Figure 7. No single clustering design achieved gains across the entire workload, highlighting the complexity of the search problem. Specifically, a successful advisor algorithm must consider the overall benefit of clustering designs across all tables and all queries, which is one of the highlights of the approach described in this paper.

5. Conclusion and future work

5.1 Summary

The MDC Advisor algorithm leverages past work in automated physical database design and statistical modeling, in combination with new ideas on MDC, to provide a method for automating the design problem of MDC. To our knowledge, this is the first published algorithm to tackle this important problem. The algorithm exploits a combination of query optimizer what-if analysis, weighted randomized search, data sampling, and statistical extrapolation. Six experiments were performed using a 10 GB TPC-H database to compare the advisor designs against those of human experts and it was found to provide design recommendations that were in line with the quality of these experts. The advisor was effective at modeling correlation between dimensions through sampling, and was able to limit the database expansion under MDC to a value very close to its design goal of 10%. Based on the value shown through these experiments and the importance of the studied problem, the model described in this paper has been implemented for the V8.2 release of DB2 UDB for Linux, UNIX and Windows.

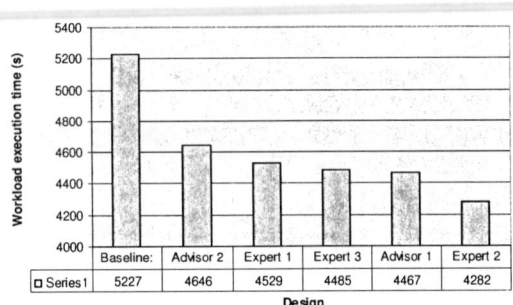

Figure 6: TPC-H overall results

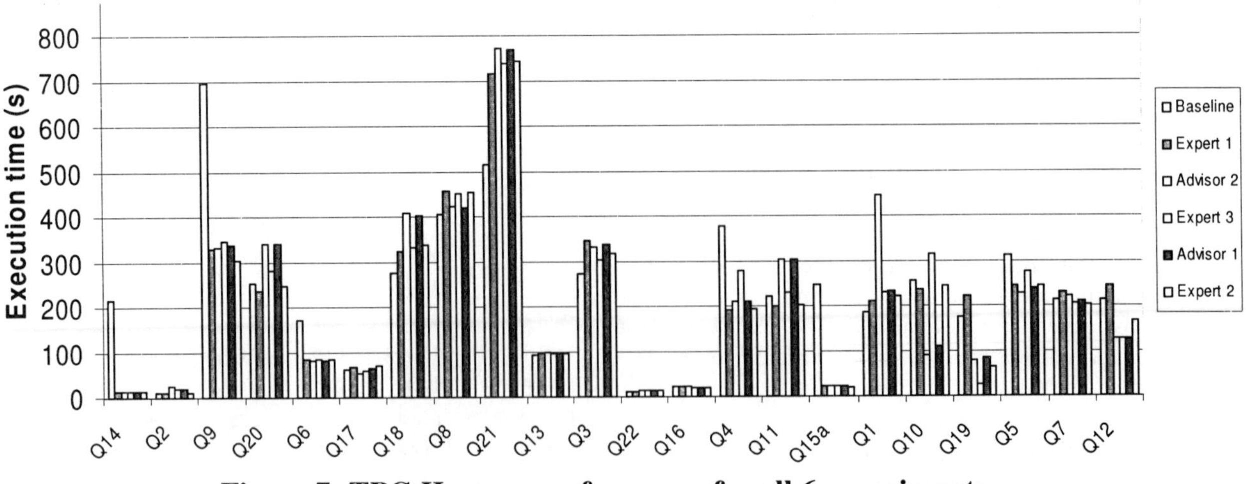

Figure 7: TPC-H query performance for all 6 experiments

5.2 Future work

This work can be enhanced by investigating:
- Hierarchy climbing for dimension coarsification.
- Improving coarsification models and storage estimates in the presence of data skew.
- Efficient table migration (alter) schemes for conversion to MDC.
- Recommendation of block size and adaptive blocking sizes, to better accommodate data skew.
- Improved selection of the storage expansion constraint, including adaptive algorithms.
- Experimentation on larger/varied data sets, schemas, and workloads, in particular including database schemas and workloads from user environments

References

[1] "Transaction Processing Performance Council" http://www.tpc.org/default.asp.

[2] "DB2 Universal Database for Linux, UNIX and Windows" http://www-306.ibm.com/software/data/db2/udb/

[3] S. Agrawal, S. Chaudhuri, V.R. Narasayya, "Automated selection of materialized views and indexes in SQL databases". Proc. VLDB 2000, Cairo, Egypt

[4] B. Bhattacharjee, S. Padmanabhan, T. Malkemus, T. Lai, L. Cranston, M. Huras, "Efficient Query Processing for Multi-Dimensionally Clustered Tables in DB2", Proc. VLDB 2003, Berlin, Germany

[5] S. Chaudhuri, E. Christensen, G. Graefe, V. Narasayya, M. Zwilling, "Self-Tuning Technology in Microsoft SQL Server", IEEE Data Eng. Bul. 22(2), June 1999

[6] S. Chaudhuri, V. Narasayya, "AutoAdmin 'What-if' Index Analysis Utility", Proc. SIGMOD, 1998, Seattle, USA

[7] S. Chaudhuri, V. Narasayya, "Microsoft Index Tuning Wizard for SQL Server 7.0", Proc. SIGMOD, 1998, Seattle, USA

[8] M.R. Frank, E.R. Omiecinski, S.B. Navathe, "Adaptive and Automated Index Selection in RDBMS", Proc. EDBT 1992, Vienna, Austria

[9] P.J. Haas, J.F. Naughton, S. Seshadri, L. Stokes, "Sampling Based Estimation of the Number of Distinct Values of an Attribute", Proc. VLDB 1995, Zurich, Switzerland

[10] P.J. Haas, L. Stokes, "Estimating the number of classes in a finite population", JASA, V. 93, Dec, 1998

[11] S. Lightstone. D. Zilio, C. Zuzarte, G. Lohman, J. Rao, K. Cheung, "DB2 Design Advisor: More than just index selection", IDUG 2004, Orlando, USA.

[12] J.H Liou, S.B. Yao, "Multi-dimensional clustering for database organizations". Information Systems, 2:187--198, 1977.

[13] G. Lohman, G. Valentin, D. Zilio, M. Zuliani, A. Skelly, "DB2 Advisor: An optimizer smart enough to recommend its own indexes", Proc. ICDE 2000, San Diego, USA

[14] V. Markl, F. Ramsak, R. Bayer, "Improving OLAP Performance by Multi-dimensional Hierarchical Clustering", Proc. IDEAS'99, Montreal, Canada

[15] S. Padmanabhan, B. Bhattacharjee, T. Malkemus, L. Cranston, M. Huras, "Multi-Dimensional Clustering: A New Data Layout Scheme in DB2." SIGMOD 2003, San Diego, USA

[16] N. Pendse, R. Creeth, "The OLAP Report", http://www.olapreport.com/.

[17] J. Rao, S. Lightstone, G. Lohman, D. Zilio, A. Storm, C. Garcia-Arellano, S. Fadden "DB2 Design Advisor: integrated automated physical database design", Proc. VLDB 2004, Toronto, Canada.

[18] J. Rao, C. Zhang, N. Megiddo, G. Lohman, "Automating physical database design in a parallel database.", Proc. SIGMOD 2002, Madison, USA

[19] B. Schiefer, G. Valentin, "DB2 Universal Database Performance Tuning", IEEE Data Eng. Bul 22(2), June 1999

[20] T. Stöhr, H. Märtens, E. Rahm, "Multi-Dimensional Database Allocation for Parallel Data Warehouses", Proc. VLDB 2000, Cairo, Egypt

[21] T. Stohr, E. Rahm, "WARLOCK : A Data Allocation Tool for Parallel Warehouses", Proc. VLDB 2001, Rome, Italy (Software Demonstration)

Trademarks

AIX, DB2, DB2 Universal Database, IBM, and pSeries are trademarks or registered trademarks of International Business Machines Corporation in the United States, other countries, or both.

Linux is a trademark of Linus Torvalds in the United States, other countries, or both.

Windows is a registered trademark of Microsoft Corporation in the United States, other countries, or both.

UNIX is a registered trademark of The Open Group in the United States and other countries.

Other company, product, and service names may be trademarks or service marks of others.

Integrating Automatic Data Acquisition with Business Processes Experiences with SAP's Auto-ID Infrastructure

Christof Bornhövd, Tao Lin, Stephan Haller[*], Joachim Schaper

SAP Research Center Palo Alto, LLC, 3475 Deer Creek Road, Palo Alto, CA 94304, USA
[*] SAP Research, CEC Karlsruhe, Vincenz-Priessnitz-Strasse 1, D-76131 Karlsruhe, Germany
Contact email: {christof.bornhoevd, tao.lin, stephan.haller, joachim.schaper}@sap.com

Abstract

Smart item technologies, like RFID and sensor networks, are considered to be the next big step in business process automation [1]. Through automatic and real-time data acquisition, these technologies can benefit a great variety of industries by improving the efficiency of their operations. SAP's Auto-ID infrastructure enables the integration of RFID and sensor technologies with existing business processes. In this paper we give an overview of the existing infrastructure, discuss lessons learned from successful customer pilots, and point out some of the open research issues.

1. Introduction

With RFID mandates from retailers like Wal-Mart, Metro, Tesco, and Target, manufacturers like Procter & Gamble and Kimberly Clark, and even the U.S. Department of Defense, smart item technology has received a lot of attention.

By *smart item* we mean a device that can provide some data about itself or the object it is associated with and that has the ability to communicate this information [7].

For example, a Radio Frequency IDentification (RFID) tag that contains information about the object it is attached to provides a simple form of a smart item [5]. RFID tags typically combine a modest storage capacity with a means of wirelessly communicating stored information like an electronic product code (EPC) [2] to an RFID reader. In a supply chain management context, an object to be tagged is usually a pallet, a case or even a single sales item. Passive RFID tags require no on-board battery and can be read from a distance ranging from a few centimeters to a few meters. Active tags, on the other hand, come with an on-board battery which provides larger read ranges and memory sizes but also higher unit cost and size and a limited lifespan of typically 3-5 years. Another example of a smart item is an environmental sensor, such as a temperature or humidity sensor, which can provide a more complete picture of a tracked object and its physical environment [10].

Through automatic, real-time object tracking, smart item technology can provide companies with more accurate data about their business operations in a more timely fashion, as well as help streamlining and automating the operations themselves. This leads to cost reduction and additional business benefits like increased asset visibility, improved responsiveness and even extended business opportunities. However, bridging the gap between the physical and the digital world requires a flexible and scalable system architecture to integrate automatic data acquisition with existing business processes.

Therefore, we have developed the so-called *Auto-ID Infrastructure* (AII), which integrates data from smart item devices with enterprise applications. The AII converts RFID or sensor data into business process information by associating it with specified mapping rules and metadata. These mapping rules can feed incoming observation data directly to business processes running on either SAP or non-SAP backend systems, execute predefined business logic, or simply record the data in a persistent store for later analysis.

The remainder of this paper is organized as follows. In Section 2 we will outline the system requirements that have shaped the design of our Auto-ID infrastructure. Section 3 will give an overview of the existing system architecture and discuss the key components: the Device Controller and the Auto-ID Node. A discussion of our experiences with the existing Auto-ID Infrastructure is given in Section 4. We will conclude by pointing out some of the main open issues in Sections 5, and summarize the paper in Section 6.

2. Auto-ID System Requirements

Our initial Auto-ID Infrastructure has been architected with the following system requirements in mind.

Permission to copy without fee all or part of this material is granted provided that the copies are not made or distributed for direct commercial advantage, the VLDB copyright notice and the title of the publication and its date appear, and notice is given that copying is by permission of the Very Large Data Base Endowment. To copy otherwise, or to republish, requires a fee and/or special permission from the Endowment

Proceedings of the 30th VLDB Conference, Toronto, Canada, 2004

Scalability. Companies like large retailers are assumed to require throughput rates of about 60 billion items per annum [9]. Assuming 100 distribution centers, each with an average of 5 checking points per item, the system needs to guarantee an average throughput of at least 100 messages per second per distribution center. The size of an observation message can be assumed to be around 200 bytes, and the processing of an incoming observation message usually requires multiple database updates and the execution of business procedures at the backend system.

Open System Architecture. In addition to being hardware-agnostic, the architecture should be based on existing communication protocols like TCP/IP and HTTP, as well as syntax and semantics standards like XML, PML [6] and EPC [2]. This will allow the use of sensors from a wide array of hardware providers, and will support the deployment of Auto-ID solutions across institutional or even country boundaries.

Efficient Event Filtering. The infrastructure needs to provide efficient means to filter out false or redundant readings from RFID or sensor devices. Also, it needs to provide flexible and configurable filtering of events to only pass on relevant information to the appropriate backend processes.

Event Aggregation. The infrastructure needs to support the composition of multiple related events to more complex events for further processing. For example, the system must allow the composition of individual object identification events for multiple individual cases and the corresponding pallet to only one *complete-pallet-detected* event.

Flexibility. The infrastructure needs to be adaptable to different business scenarios. Furthermore, the infrastructure needs to provide flexible means at the business logic layer to respond to abnormal situations, like the missing of expected goods or company-internal re-routing of goods. To avoid redundant implementations of the same business rules in different enterprise applications, the infrastructure needs to offer means to deploy and execute them within the Auto-ID Infrastructure.

Distribution of System Functionality. A real deployment of an Auto-ID solution can be distributed across sites, across companies, or even across countries. This naturally requires a distributed system architecture. As a first step, we require that the Auto-ID Infrastructure supports the distribution of message pre-processing functionality (for example, filtering and aggregation) and, to some degree, business logic across multiple nodes to better map to existing company and cross-company structures.

System Administration and Test Support. The infrastructure must provide support for the testing of individual custom components used in the filtering and aggregation of events, as well as the end-to-end processing of RFID and sensor data. Good administration and testing support is a prerequisite for the deployment of a distributed Auto-ID solution in large-scale applications.

3. System Overview

The architecture of our Auto-ID Infrastructure (AII) is shown in Figure 1. Conceptually, it can be divided into the following four system layers.

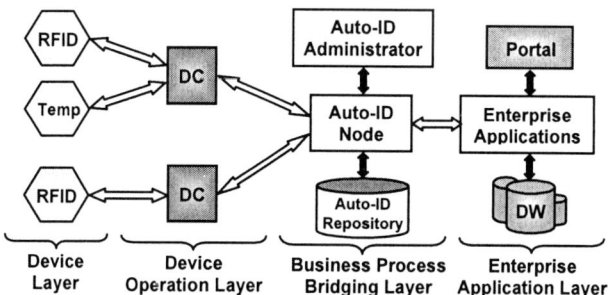

Figure 1: AII System Architecture

At the *Device Layer* different types of sensor devices can be supported via a hardware-independent low-level interface. It consists of the basic operations for reading and writing data and a publish/subscribe interface to report observation events. By implementing this API, different kinds of smart item devices can be deployed within the Auto-ID infrastructure. Besides RFID readers, these devices can include environmental sensors, or PLC devices. The *Device Operation Layer* coordinates multiple devices. It also provides functionality to filter, condense, aggregate, and adjust received sensor data before passing it on to the next layer. This layer is formed by one or more Device Controllers (DC). The *Business Process Bridging Layer* associates incoming observation messages with existing business processes. At this layer status and history information of tracked objects is maintained. This information includes object location, aggregation information, and information about the environment of a tagged object. A so-called Auto-ID Node realizes this functionality. Finally, the *Enterprise Application Layer* supports business processes of enterprise applications such as Supply Chain Management (SCM), Customer Relationship Management (CRM), or Asset Management running on SAP or non-SAP backend systems.

Our Auto-ID Infrastructure provides an infrastructure for realizing a complete Auto-ID solution. Most existing solutions only focus on a portion of such a complete solution, for example a Savant as defined in [3] corresponds to a Device Controller in our infrastructure. Since Auto-ID solutions can span organizations or even countries, standards for the interfaces between the components are essential. Therefore, the AII is compliant with the standards proposed by the EPCglobal consortium.

As part of the infrastructure, a test and workload generator tool is provided that can simulate messages coming from one or more Device Controllers or backend systems to an Auto-ID Node. Also, a scriptable simulator is available that can simulate multiple RFID readers. These tools allow the testing of an Auto-ID deployment without the installation of physical devices.

The following two subsections will explain the two main building blocks of the AII: the Device Controller and the Auto-ID Node.

3.1 Device Controller

A Device Controller (DC) is responsible for coordinating multiple smart item devices and reporting incoming observation messages to one or more Auto-ID Nodes. A DC supports two operation modes. In the *synchronous mode*, the Device Controller receives messages from an Auto-ID Node for direct device operations, such as to read or write a specific data field from/to a tag currently in the range of an RFID reader, or to read the value from a temperature sensor at a given point in time.

In the *asynchronous listening mode*, the DC waits for incoming event messages from the sensor devices. Upon receiving such a message, additional data can be read and event messages can be filtered or aggregated according to the configuration of the DC. Note that when a DC is configured for asynchronous operations, it is still capable of synchronously receiving and executing commands.

Message processing in the DC is based on so-called *Data Processors*. We distinguish six different types of data processors. (1) *Filters* filter out certain messages according to specified criteria. For example, they can be used to filter out all event messages coming from case tags, or clean out false reads ("data smoothing"). (2) *Enrichers* read additional data from a tag's memory or other device and add this data to the event message received. (3) *Aggregators* can be used to compose multiple incoming events into one higher-level event (for example, mapping data from a temperature sensor to a *temperature-increased* event), or for batching purposes. (4) *Writers* are used to write to or change data on a tag or control an actuator. (5) *Buffers* buffer event messages for later processing and/or keep an inventory of tags currently in the reading scope of an RFID reader. (6) *Senders* transform the internal data structure of the messages to some output format and send them to registered recipients. We currently use PML Core [6] as the output format. As new standards are developed, they can be incorporated by simply implementing appropriate new Senders.

The core functions of the Device Controller, in particular the message processing described above, are independent of the hardware used. For reading and writing the data on the tags, we use logical field names to abstract from concrete tag implementations. A field map provides the mapping between memory addresses on the tag and logical data fields.

Since all Data Processors implement the same publish/subscribe interface, they can be arranged into processing chains. Powerful message processing and filtering operations can be achieved by chaining together the right, possibly customized, set of simple data processors. This results in a very flexible framework which allows for the distribution of message processing functionality close to the actual sensor devices to reduce message traffic and improve system scalability.

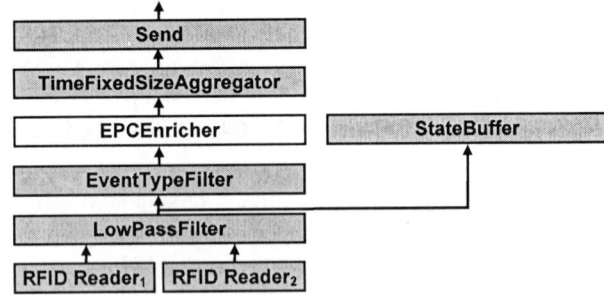

Figure 2: Typical Data Processor Chain

Figure 2 shows an example of a typical processor chain used for dock doors in a supply chain scenario. For full coverage dock doors commonly use more than one reader. This holds especially true for Europe with much stricter radio frequency regulations than in the U.S. RFID readers sometimes generate false event messages. For example, because of physical reasons a tag is not seen during a particular read cycle. To filter out these false *tag-disappeared* messages, a LowPassFilter is applied. Also, every tag that passes the radio field will issue two event messages: a *tag-appeared* and a *tag-disappeared* message. Since in the dock door scenario we are only interested in the fact that an item has passed the door, we can safely filter out *tag-disappeared* messages by using an EventTypeFilter. The EPCEnricher in the example is only needed if non-EPC tags (which are still common today) are used. These tags have a unique ID set by the manufacturer, and the EPC is actually stored in the user memory of the tag. In this case, the EPCEnricher reads the EPC and adds it to the event message. At a dock door, we want to collect all tags that are seen during a certain time window and report them in a single message to the backend system. The TimeFixedSizeAggregator and the Send processor in our example do this. In addition, a StateBuffer keeps track of all tags currently in the reader's scope for auditing and reporting purposes.

3.2 Auto-ID Node

An Auto-ID Infrastructure can contain multiple Auto-ID Nodes. An Auto-ID Node (AIN) is responsible for integrating incoming observation messages from the Device Controllers with the business processes running at the backend systems.

For an AIN, we distinguish between the interactions with Device Controllers (reader events from and control commands to Device Controllers), and interactions with backend enterprise systems (such as receiving master data from a logistics system and returning a confirmation). These interactions with the AIN are treated as either incoming or outgoing messages.

Incoming observation messages are routed to a rule engine which, based on the message type, evaluates a specified list of conditions. The result of the evaluation step is a set of qualifying rules for which one or more actions are executed in a specified order. Such an action can, for example, update the system status of an object in the local repository, communicate with the backend system, or generate and write EPC data to a tag.

Actions of a rule can pass on parameters and can trigger other rules at the Auto-ID Node. Based on the message type, messages can be assigned different processing priorities and can be specified as being persistent in the Auto-ID Node.

An Auto-ID Node provides a local repository which contains information about the current status and history of the objects being processed. This information includes data about the operations that have been applied to an object (e.g, move, pack, or unpack), its movement and current location, and its structure (e.g, packing information). Also, the repository replicates master data from the backend system about products and business partners, or the physical location and type of the RFID readers. The Auto-ID Repository provides the basis for the execution of business logic in the Auto-ID Node.

The use of customizable rules provides a flexible mechanism to specify and execute business logic at the Auto-ID Node. This allows the pre-processing of incoming observation data and the handling of abnormal situations within the Auto-ID Infrastructure, such as discrepancies between a received advanced shipping notification (ASN) and a detected pallet. Which in turn allows the system to offload processing from the backend systems.

Our work to date has focused mainly on Supply Chain Management scenarios, for which a standard set of rules is in place. The deployment of our Auto-ID Infrastructure in a different context simply requires the adoption or extension of the existing rules.

The Auto-ID Administrator provides a graphical tool which supports the reconfiguration of existing or the definition of new rules in an AIN at run-time. In addition, it allows the central configuration, monitoring, and control of the Device Controllers and smart item devices in the system.

4. Case Studies

The following sub-sections discuss two Auto-ID pilot installations based on the research prototype described in Section 3: a real-time retail application, and an adaptive planning application. In section 4.3 we will summarize the lessons learned from these and other real-world experiences.

4.1 A Retail Application

The first pilot was conducted at a large retailer in Europe. Here, the Auto-ID Node was used as a kind of "Auto-ID data hub" to feed business event information from several processes to two backend systems: a data warehouse (SAP Business Information Warehouse) for analytical purposes, and a tracking system (SAP Event Management) to track the status of deliveries. On top of this, the SAP Enterprise Portal was used as the user interface to provide both employees and project partners with a unified view on the entire system.

From the perspective of the retailer, the goal of this project was mainly to evaluate if and how RFID technology can be used in practice. While there is a lot of hype about the technology, only by putting it in a real environment one can learn what works and what does not, and possibly how to get around technical difficulties. In addition to technical issues, another question was how customers would accept the technology.

The main process covered by RFID technology was the tracking of deliveries from the distribution center to one dedicated store, as well as the movement of goods from the store's back room to the shop floor. Tagging was done on case and pallet level. There were four read points in this business process:

1. *Packing Station*: At the distribution center, all cases needed to be tagged and assembled into deliveries. An association between the pallet and the cases loaded onto it was recorded. Once the packing was finished, a message was sent to the Auto-ID Node with information about the pallet and its associated cases.

2. *Goods Issue Gate*: After the deliveries were loaded onto a truck at the distribution center, they passed through a reader that registered what had passed. The reader was mounted in the dock door. The data from the reader was filtered, aggregated and then sent to the Auto-ID Node, which updated its inventory of goods.

3. *Goods Receiving Gate*: Similar to the previous read point, incoming goods were read and recognized as they arrived at the store.

4. *Back room / Shop Floor Gate*: This represents another automatic gate where goods were scanned when they passed through to determine if goods were in the back room or already on the shop floor. Previously, the retailer was not able to make this distinction.

Bulk reading took place at all read points except at point 1. Depending on the nature of the products (metal cans, bottles with soda water, and so on) in the delivery, it was impossible to always read all tags of inner cases. However, since the pallets were not unpacked until they were on the shop floor, it proved to be unnecessary to achieve a read accuracy of 100%. Since the system provided the information about what was packed together from read point 1 (where the operational process guarantees a 100% read accuracy) in principle it was sufficient to only detect a single tag of the whole delivery at the other read points.

The Auto-ID Node was able to deduce the other tags from the packing information.

The Auto-ID Node received observation messages from all read points to update its inventory information in its repository. Information was also sent to a data warehouse to allow for later analysis. The AIN stored information about the deliveries (actual and expected), so whenever it received a message from one of the first three read points, it inferred the delivery number from the EPCs detected. It could then tell the Event Manager System, which was responsible for tracking deliveries overall, about the status change of the delivery, for example, that it had arrived at the shop.

RFID technology was also used on the item level for some distinct goods. For example, processed cheese was tagged in order to track expiration dates using a Smart Shelf. Because of limited space we will not describe these processes in more detail in this paper. This pilot implementation showed that item level tagging is technically feasible, but that the cost of tags themselves, of applying the tags to products, and of the required infrastructure (readers and so on) is currently still too high to make sense economically. Another reason against tagging at the item level is concerns in public regarding privacy.

At the time of the project, EPC tag data standards as now defined by EPCglobal [4] had not been developed. However, user requirements required standard identifiers encoded on the tag. Cases needed to have a GTIN (Global Trade Identification Number) of the product, and pallets either a SSCC (Serial Shipping Container Code) or a GRAI (Global Returnable Asset Identifier). We therefore had to define our own mapping of these standard identifiers to EPCs, adding a serial number in the case of the GTIN mapping. Our mapping was based on [2].

The main benefit provided by RFID technology in this pilot was increased visibility of the goods, which could be used to make better decisions on when to reorder goods, leading to cost reductions because of lower inventory levels and increased sales because of increased on-shelf availability.

The software worked reliably. Because of the size of the pilot, scalability was not an issue and a single Auto-ID Node was sufficient. More daunting were the challenges regarding the hardware, like positioning and tuning the reader antennas to achieve good read accuracy while conforming to regulatory requirements in Europe, tag placement, cabling, and availability of tags, just to name a few. Workplace safety regulations added additional constraints.

4.2 A Real-time Adaptive Planning Application

The second pilot involved a large retailer and a manufacturer in North America. In this pilot, SAP provided the same components as in the pilot described in Section 4.1, plus a supply chain planning component (SAP Advanced Planning and Optimization). This pilot included three sites: a distribution center of the manufacturer, a distribution center of the retailer, and a retail shop. The main operational process consisted of three steps.

First, in the distribution center of the manufacturer, items were packed into cases and shipped to the distribution center of the retailer based on shipment orders. In the second step, the distribution center of the retailer verified the shipment on the case level and then sent a case to the retail shop. Finally, in the retail shop, the case was first placed in the backroom and then moved to the shop floor. The items contained in the case were put on a smart shelf in the shop. The following read points were defined:

1. ***Pack Station at the Manufacturer:*** After packing a case, a message with all the EPCs of the case and the contained items was sent to the Auto-ID Node. The Auto-ID Node forwarded the EPC of the case and associated shipment order to the tracking system (SAP Event Management), where an Event Handler was created with the expected shipment time, a tolerance for the shipping time and rules for exception handling — that is, what to do when a shipment has not arrived in time.

2. ***Goods Receiving Gates at the Retailer***: There were similar gates both at the distribution center and at the shop. When these gates detected a case tag, messages with the detected case tags were sent to the Auto-ID Node. After updating the status of the associated locations and the physical objects, the Auto-ID Node sent a message to the tracking system to update the status of the corresponding Event Handler.

3. ***Back Room / Shop Floor Gate***: These read points were similar to the read points at the receiving gates of the retailer.

4. ***Smart Shelves in the Shop***: When items were added or removed from the smart shelf, messages containing the EPC of the moved objects were sent to the Auto-ID Node with the logical reader ID and the timestamp of when the objects were scanned. The AIN then forwarded the observation message for the first item from a case that appeared on the smart shelf to the tracking system to indicate that the contents of a case had been put onto the shelf and that the tracking process for that case was completed.

In this pilot, a shipment was associated with a single case as only one case was sent from the manufacturer to the retailer at a time. The Auto-ID Node maintained the status and also the history of the objects including cases, items and shipments. The tracking system was used to track all shipments. Therefore, only messages on the case level were sent to the tracking system, which monitored the delivery of shipments and handled possible exceptions in almost real-time.

Through the Auto-ID Node, the manufacturer could get inventory information about its products in the retail shop. Based on the history of sale records, the Auto-ID Node maintained a local prediction model. This model could be used to trigger a request to the SAP Advanced Planning and Optimization to adjust the shipment planning.

SAP Business Information Warehouse was used for analytical operations and reporting, in a similar way as in the pilot discussed in Section 4.1.

4.3 Lessons Learned

Our experiences with the pilots described in the previous sections can be summarized by the following lessons learned.

Cross-Organizational Collaboration. The pilots contained multiple sites, and in the case of the second pilot even multiple companies. The full potential of smart items technology can only be unlocked through collaboration and data sharing across sites and organizations. The hope is that the potential business improvements offered by Auto-ID technology can bring companies to overcome their current reluctance to collaborate in the near future. This reluctance, as well as technical integration challenges, are the main reasons why EDI has not been implemented to the extent initially expected.

Standards. We found that one of the key issues is the use of common standards. To avoid integration nightmares, standards on the hardware layer (readers, tags), the communication layer (HTTP, XML), and also on the syntax and semantics layer (PML, EPC) should be used or must be developed. Deployment of components from different providers becomes feasible at a reasonable cost of ownership only with the right standards in place. We are actively involved in ongoing standardization efforts at EPCglobal and the W3C.

Automatic Identification is Not Just RFID. The main use case of smart items today is the universal unique identification of items. RFID is not the only technology that allows this, for example barcodes can be used as well. Different technologies have different advantages and use cases. Thus, all of these must be easily integratable into one system. Furthermore, in a real working environment RFID readers sometimes need to work with other devices such as traffic lights and light beam sensors. These heterogeneities are the rule not the exception.

100% RFID Reading Accuracy Cannot be Expected. Because of physical reasons, one cannot expect to have a 100% tag reading accuracy. As described in Section 4.1, one way to work around this problem is to keep information about how objects are assembled and have the Auto-ID Infrastructure infer the missing information. For example, detecting the movement of a pallet known in the system will allow the system to infer the movement of all associated cases.

Need to Support Out of Sequence Messages. To an Auto-ID Node, the connected Device Controllers form a distributed environment. In a real-world installation, network latency, different system clocks at the readers, and message batching all can cause the order in which observation messages arrive to be different from the order in which the corresponding events took place in the physical world. Therefore, the Auto-ID Infrastructure needs to be able to reorder incoming event messages based on knowledge about the physical structure and the business processes of a given site.

Device Administration and Management. The deployment of an Auto-ID solution usually includes a large number of RFID and sensor devices. Centralized administration tools to visualize, plan (capacity planning), configure, deploy, test, monitor, and upgrade remote devices is a prerequisite for the deployment of large, highly distributed Auto-ID solutions. Our existing tools are a good a starting point but more powerful tools are needed.

Deploying an Auto-ID Solution is a Long Term Task. The deployment of an Auto-ID solution will change the IT infrastructure, the business processes and the operational processes of an organization. These fundamental changes cannot be done in a few weeks and may result in significant costs up front. It is essential for a company to have a long term migration plan addressing the required changes in the organization. Therefore, it is a good idea to start with a small pilot installation to learn about the required changes in an existing business environment before rolling out an Auto-ID solution on a large scale.

5. Open Issues

Based on our experiences with our existing prototype, we would like to point out the following open issues for future research in the area of smart items technology.

Different Qualities of Service. Different smart items applications require different qualities of service regarding event processing. For example, for high data quality an Auto-ID infrastructure may have to provide end-to-end transaction support to guarantee exactly once semantics for the processing of observation messages. That is, the system needs to guarantee that a predefined reaction to an event is executed exactly once — even in the case of a system or power failure. There is obviously a trade-off between higher degrees of reliability on the one hand and performance on the other. Accordingly, different qualities of service need to be defined and provided for different application classes.

Distributed Smart Items Infrastructure. The nature of smart items applications as well as scalability requirements may force a distributed system architecture. Although our existing Auto-ID Infrastructure allows the distribution of functionality between Device Controllers, Auto-ID Nodes, and backend systems, a full-fledged solution to the distribution problem needs to support the distribution and replication of functionality *and data*, requiring the sharing and synchronization of data across multiple nodes. The evaluation and adaptation of distribution and replication strategies developed in distributed database systems, database caching, distributed event-based systems, and peer-to-peer systems could be a good starting point.

Seamless Integration of Environmental Sensors. Currently, most work in the area of smart items has focused on RFID and Supply Chain Management. To support application scenarios like product life-cycle management (PLM) or transportation, we need to seamlessly integrate other sensors like environmental sensors with RFID technology. From the application perspective, RFID readers and environmental sensors like temperature or light sensors simply provide event sources. From the perspective of the infrastructure, however, they are different. RFID readers are aperiodic event sources, whereas environmental sensors provide a stream of periodic events, that is, discrete readings of the corresponding environmental conditions. Conceptually such a sensor provides a current value for each point in time. The seamless integration of RFID and environmental sensors requires means to represent and resolve this mismatch.

Networked Embedded Systems. Smart items provide small embedded systems capable of independently collecting information from their environment, processing data, and communicating over wireless networks. With advances in memory capacity and processing power, these devices allow the execution of business logic at the periphery of a smart items infrastructure rather than in the middle layers or in a central backend system. Smart items can form entire networks of collaborating devices thereby increasing reliability (through replication), efficiency, and flexibility. In addition to the question for new appropriate system architectures, efficient ways are required to model, generate, deploy, and manage business functions at the devices. Here approaches developed in the area of grid and peer-to-peer computing could be a good starting point for further research.

Privacy. The use of RFID technology, especially in retail, has raised a lot of discussion regarding privacy. The main concerns here are the possible profiling of customer behavior and the potential to track people. Although this discussion is not a purely technical one, on the technical side mechanisms are required that enable the efficient encoding of tag and sensor information, ensure data security, and allow the disabling of tags at predefined stages in a retail chain. The resulting technology needs to be an integral part of a sophisticated smart items infrastructure.

6. Summary

We have described our Auto-ID Infrastructure which was architected with scalability, flexibility, and usability in mind. Device Controllers allow the processing of event messages close to the periphery of the system; Auto-ID Nodes enable the execution of business logic in the infrastructure and integrate incoming observation messages with backend business processes. We have discussed our practical experiences with different pilot projects and summarized the main lessons learned. Smart item technology is very likely to change current business and operational processes, which will require changes in the IT infrastructure of many companies. Challenging issues remain that make this area an interesting topic for both hardware and software research.

Acknowledgements

We would like to thank Brian Mo, Uwe Kubach, Rama Gurram, Peter Ebert, and Hartmut Vogler for their valuable contributions to the Auto-ID Infrastructure project. We also benefited from fruitful discussions with other colleagues in SAP including Bernd Sieren, Bernd Lauterbach, Christoph Lessmoellmann, Ami Heitner, Alexander Renz, and Kai Morisse.

REFERENCES

[1] Alexander, K.; Gillian, T.; Gramling, K.; Kindy, M.; Moogimane, D.; Schultz, M.; Woods, M.: *"IBM Business Consulting Services – Focus on the Supply Chain: Applying Auto-ID within the Distribution Center"*, Auto-ID Center, White paper IBM-AUTOID-BC-002, Sep. 2003

[2] Brock, D.L: *"Integrating the Electronic Product Code (EPC) and the Global Trade Number (GTIN)"*, Auto-ID Center, White Paper MIT-AUTOID-WH-004, Nov. 2001

[3] Clark, S.; Traub, K.; Anarkat, D.; Osinski, T.: *"Auto-ID Savant Specification 1.0"*, Auto-ID Center, White Paper MIT-AUTOID-TM-003, Sep. 2003

[4] EPCGlobal: *"EPC Tag Data Standards Version 1.1 Rev. 1.24"*, EPCGlobal, Standards Specification, Apr. 2004, http://www.epcglobalinc.org

[5] Finkenzeller, K.: *"RFID Handbook: Fundamentals and Applications in Contactless Smart Cards and Identification"*, John Wiley & Sons, 2nd Edition, May 2003

[6] Floerkemeier, C.; Anarkat, D.; Osinski, T.; Harrison, M.: *"PML Core Specification 1.0"*, Auto-ID Center Recommendation, Sep. 2003

[7] Haller, S.; Hodges, S.: *"The Need for a Universal Smart Sensor Network"*, Auto-ID Center, White Paper CAM-AUTOID-WH-007, Nov. 2002

[8] Kubach, U.: *"Integration von Smart Items in Enterprise Software Systeme"*, In: Praxis der Wirtschaftsinformatik, Special Issue on Ubiquitous Computing, 2003

[9] Miles, S.; Brock, D.L.; Engels, D.: *"Web Services WAN SIG: Proposals for Engineering the 'Silk Road of the Internet'"*, Auto-ID Center, White Paper MIT-AUTOID-WH-04, Apr. 2003

[10] Thede, A.; Schmidt, A.; Merz, C: *"Integration of Goods Delivery Supervision into E-Commerce Supply Chains"*, Second International Workshop on Electronic Commerce (WELCOM'01), Heidelberg, Germany, Nov. 2001

Managing RFID Data

(Extended Abstract)[*]

Sudarshan S. Chawathe[*], Venkat Krishnamurthy[†], Sridhar Ramachandran[†], and Sanjay Sarma[‡]

[*]Computer Science Department
University of Maryland
College Park, MD 20742, USA
chaw@cs.umd.edu

[†]OAT Systems
265 Winter Street
Waltham MA 02451, USA
{venkat,sridhar}@oatsystems.com

[‡]Department of Mechanical Engineering
35-010 Massachusetts Inst. of Technology
Cambridge, MA 02139, USA
sesarma@mit.edu

Abstract

Radio-Frequency Identification (RFID) technology enables sensors to efficiently and inexpensively track merchandise and other objects. The vast amount of data resulting from the proliferation of RFID readers and tags poses some interesting challenges for data management. We present a brief introduction to RFID technology and highlight a few of the data management challenges.

1 Introduction

RFID technology has gained significant momentum in the past few years, with several high-profile adoptions (e.g., Walmart.) In addition to applications in retail and distribution, RFID technology holds the promise to simplify aircraft maintenance, baggage handling, laboratory procedures, and other tasks. RFID tags have recently been used to monitor patients in their homes, in order to alert medical workers when abnormal conditions are observed [19]. Standardization efforts such as EPC-IS and PML Core [7] provide the beginnings of a framework for using this technology that spans industries.

Nevertheless, there are some significant challenges that must be overcome before these benefits are realized. Below, we first present an overview of RFID technology, with a focus on major recent applications, such as retail and distribution. We present a high-level system architecture of a distributed RFID system, followed by a discussion of some key data management challenges. We hope to expose some of the issues raised by this technology and to stimulate further work in the area.

The core RFID technology is not new, and its roots can be traced back to World War II where it was used to distinguish between friendly and enemy aircrafts [18]. Technological improvements over the years have led to smaller and cheaper RFID devices. A single-chip design led to the *RFID tag*, a small device composed of a chip, an antenna, and an optional power source, that carries a unique identifier. The 1990s witnessed the use of such tags for card-keys, fuel-station payment systems, and automated toll payment. Such tags were typically specialized for a certain class of applications and cost a few dollars each. The tags typically stored application-specific data and were capable of modest processing on-tag.

Recent years have seen the emergence of a different kind of tag: one that is extremely limited in its abilities and does little more than provide a unique identifier. This approach has two key advantages: First, the simplicity of the tags makes it possible to manufacture them at very low cost. (The target number quoted is 5 cents per tag, a price achievable when the volumes reach the billions.) As a result, it is economically feasible to attach such tags to a large number of objects, even very inexpensive ones (e.g., razors in a retail store). Second, the tags are not application-specific and can be used across application domains. As a result, standards developed for managing RFID data are likely to see a wide cross-industry adoption.

The ability to inexpensively [16] tag and thus monitor a large number of items does raise some serious privacy concerns, especially when the tags are small enough to be unobtrusively attached [20]. Many RFID tags accept a *kill* command that permanently disables the tag. Conceivably, this feature may be used to protect consumers by disabling the tags when the items are purchased at checkout. Another alternative is the

---

[*]This work was partly supported by the National Science Foundation with grants IIS-9984296 and IIS-0081860.

Permission to copy without fee all or part of this material is granted provided that the copies are not made or distributed for direct commercial advantage, the VLDB copyright notice and the title of the publication and its date appear, and notice is given that copying is by permission of the Very Large Data Base Endowment. To copy otherwise, or to republish, requires a fee and/or special permission from the Endowment.

**Proceedings of the 30th VLDB Conference,
Toronto, Canada, 2004**

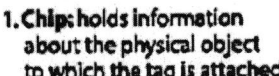
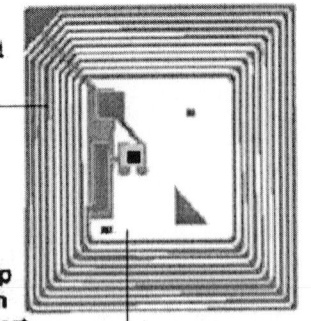
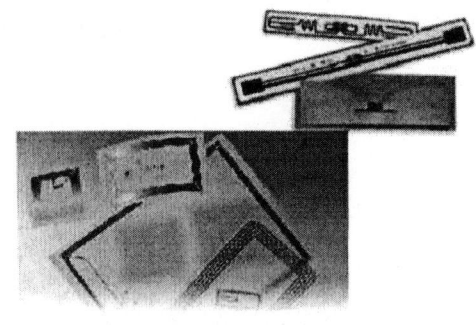

Figure 1: RFID tags

use of techniques such as blocker tags [10].

RFID devices are capable of operating on frequencies ranging from 100 Hz to beyond 2.5 GHz. However, due to regulatory restrictions (typically, country-specific) on use of the radio-frequency spectrum, only a few frequencies are commonly used. The two most common are 13.56 MHz in the HF band and some frequencies around 900 MHz in the UHF band. The HF frequency is usable world-wide, while the UHF frequencies are usable only in the U.S., E.U., and Japan (and vary among them). As in other transmissions, the frequency affects the characteristics of the resulting sensing environment. For example, HF signals propagate more easily through plastic, paper, and moisture than do UHF signals. HF tags are therefore a good choice for applications such as tagging bottles for the pharmaceutical industry. On the other hand, UHF signals have a longer range in the absence of obstructions. Therefore, UHF tags are a better choice for tagging items for the retail industry.

RFID tags may derive the energy to operate either from an on-tag battery or by *scavenging* power from the electromagnetic radiation emitted by tag readers. Further, tags may respond to signals from a reader by either passively reflecting or actively transmitting a signal. The features of tags resulting from different combinations are summarized in Figure 3. (The missing fourth combination is not currently used.)

RFID tags (and readers) have been categorized into five classes based on their capabilities, as summarized by Figure 4. Devices in the higher classes are, in general, larger, more expensive, and more capable than those in lower ones. For example, a class I device scavenges power and provides only a simple identifier using reflective transmission. It may be powered using a class V device, which is essentially a tag reader that can communicate with devices of several other classes. A class II device provides a larger data store than a class I device. In a shipping application, this additional memory may be used to store the electronic packing slip and billing information. (Further details are available elsewhere [6, 17].) An infrastructure for RFID needs methods to cope with such a diversity of devices.

The simplest RFID tag stores only a 96-bit identifier called the EPC. Such tags typically operate on the UHF band and are popular in retail and distribution environments (e.g., Walmart) due to their low cost. Other applications demand tags with enhanced capabilities. For example, the airline industry is using HF tags that can operate in the environmental extremes on an aircraft (including inside the engine) [11, 1]. These tags store not only an EPC but also supplementary data such as a the repair and service history of a part. RFID systems generate data at a high rate. For example, both UPS and FedEx are investigating the use of RFID to further streamline their transportation and delivery systems [8]. Every day, UPS handles 13.6 million packages, amounting to roughly 1.3 Gb/day from this source alone, even assuming the simplest tag (100 bits) and only one read per tag per day. In practice, the data rate is likely to be much higher because a package is scanned at several locations by several sensors.

2 System Architecture

Figure 5 suggests a layered architecture for managing RFID data. The lowest layer consists of RFID tags (located on objects such as cases and pallets). The next

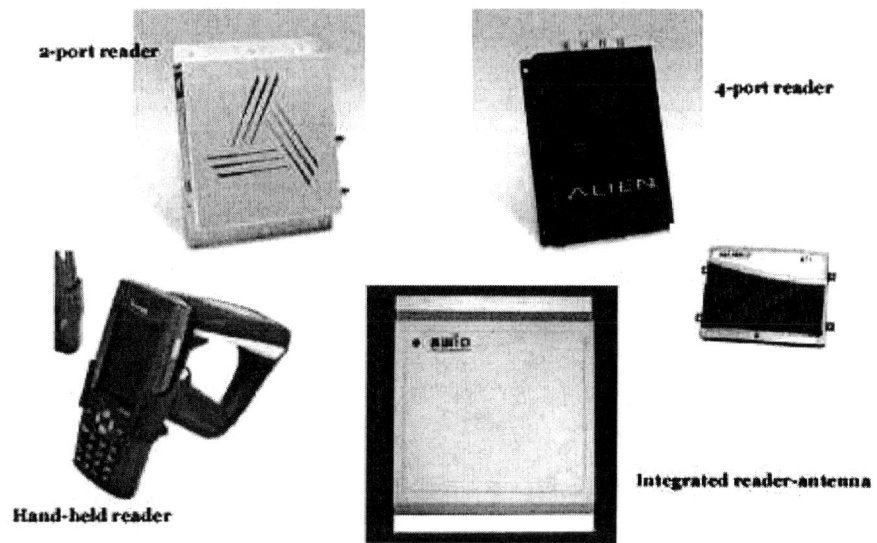

Figure 2: RFID tag readers

Transmission mode	Power source	Name	Range	Life
reflective	scavenging	passive	3 meters	unlimited
reflective	battery	semi-passive	10 meters	5–10 years
active	battery	active	100 meters	1–5 years

Figure 3: RFID tags classified by transmission mode and power source

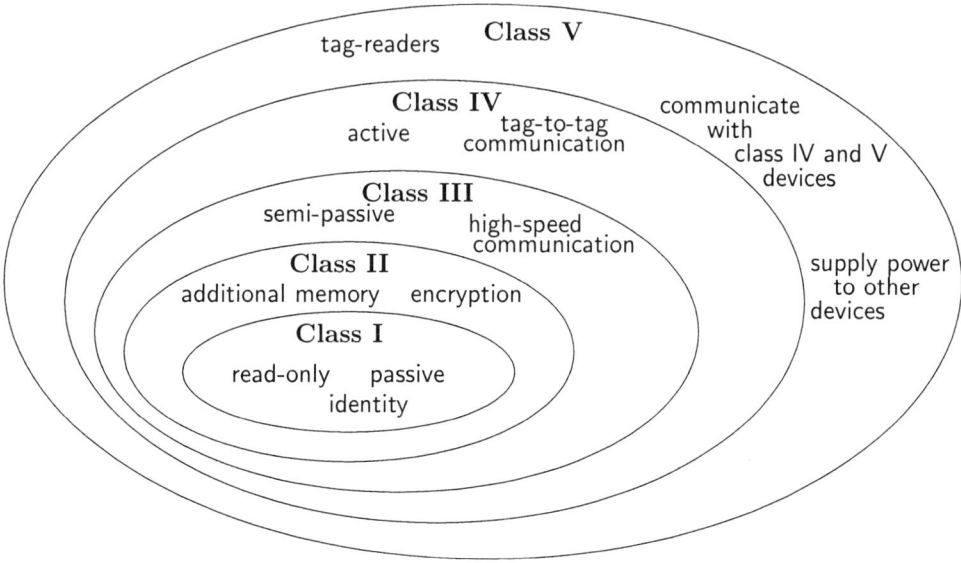

Figure 4: RFID classes

1191

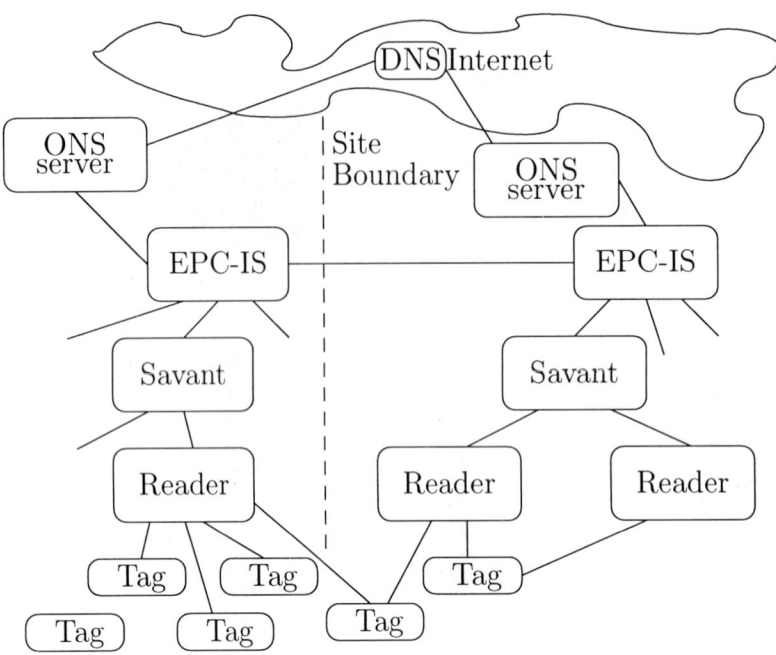

Figure 5: System Architecture

layer consists of tag readers. The interface between these two layers is the so-called *RFID Air Interface* and the RFID protocols for this interface specify the low-level details such as anti-collision techniques (similar to those used by other networking technologies). The focus of this paper is the part of the system that lies above the second layer. The data emerging from the second layer may be regarded as a stream of tuples of the form (r, s, t), denoting that reader r read tag s at time t. Both reader and tag are identified using a global naming scheme called EPC (for Electronic Product Code, by analogy with the UPC standard used for bar-codes). Readers emit such tuples typically in response to some event, such as a timer expiring or a motion-sensor signalling that a new pallet has arrived at a dock door in a warehouse. A reader's mode of operation, and the resulting frequency with which it emits data, is often configurable. A reader may also be capable of filtering the stream of tuples in simple ways.

The third layer of the architecture is responsible for mapping the low-level data stream from readers to a more manageable form that is suitable for application-level interactions. The modules responsible for this mapping were called *Savants* in the original EPC work. Savants may be likened to the wrappers used in data integration systems. In addition to cleaning data and coping with the idiosyncrasies of different kinds of readers, Savants performed further filtering and cleaning of data. Savants were also responsible for setting up the readers (initialization, firmware configurations, etc.). Today, the Savant concept is subject to a standardization effort under the new names "middleware" and "edge systems."

Applications may interact with Savants by issuing simple queries on the state maintained at the Savant (typically, small) as well as by installing standing queries (subscriptions) that result in a stream of matching data. The fourth layer consists of provides higher-level services that are easier for applications to use. For example, this level maps EPC codes to the type of object it represents (individual item, case, pallet) and provides information such as product names and manufacturers. It is also responsible for providing instance-specific information, such as the expiration date of the frozen meat represented by an EPC code.

Perhaps the most interesting and challenging tasks in this layer are those that combine business logic (obtained from other enterprise data systems) with the stream of data emerging from the sensing framework below them. For example, a common task is tracking an item as it travels in the distribution channel (the so-called *track and trace* query). At first glance, this query appears to be nothing more than a simple selection on the tag-ID attribute. However, we need to address problems due to incomplete sensing data and make inferences based on physical axioms or business rules. For example, if a case of razors and a pallet are sensed together in a packing station, a desirable inference is that the case has been packed in the pallet. As a result of such packing, it is possible that readers may fail to sense the tag on the case as the pallet moves through the distribution channel. An implementation of the track-and-trace query must implement such containment scenarios, and must operate correctly when items are unpacked and repackaged in a distribution center.

The final component of the architecture in Figure 5

is part of the *Object Name Service (ONS)*. The ONS is essentially a global lookup service that maps an EPC to a URL that describes the item represented by the EPC.

The design of the ONS service [14] uses the NAPTR facility of the standard Domain Name Service (DNS) [12, 13, 15] to rewrite EPCs into URLs. The mapping may be dynamic. For example, as a case of meat products moves from manufacturer to distributor and further down the supply chain, the ONS mapping changes to reflect the current custodian of the product.

3 Inferences

As noted earlier, the base data emerging from a network of tag readers consists of triples of the form (r, s, t) indicating that reader r read tag s at time t. In order to transform this raw data into a form that enterprise applications such as inventory tracking and resource planning can use, several levels of inference must be made. As a simple example, we may combine join a relation $R_1(r, s, t)$ representing the stream of data from tag-reader R_1 with a relation $L(r, l)$ providing the locations of readers and a relation $N(s, n)$ providing the names of items associated with EPCs to yield a data stream which provides information such as the existence of 27 cases of Gillette razors in aisle 7. However, as noted in Section 2, we also need to make inferences based on containment of items. Further, if a reader (say, reader 5) that has been continually reading the tag of a case of razors (say, case 73) suddenly stops reading it, but if none of the neighboring readers reports any reads for case 73, we may not wish to infer that case 73 has disappeared. Rather, when asked for the location of case 73 (or for an inventory count), we my wish to assume that case 73 is still in the vicinity of reader 5 but is not being detected due to interference, or temporary or permanent malfunction of some component.

We may build a complex web of such inferences, yielding derived data with varying levels of confidence. The methods we use for making, storing, and using such inferences must handle negations of prior assumptions well. (In other words, some level of non-monotonic reasoning is required.) For example, suppose the operation of readers at a shipping center indicates that case c_1 is now contained in pallet p_1. An application may query for c_1's location and the system may respond based on the location of the pallet p_1 on truck t_1. Now if the readers at the receiving center that unpacks pallet p_1 fail to read c_1, we must consider various possible explanations. Readers may have simply missed c_1 at the receiving site, in which case, we continue to infer its location based on p_1. Alternatively, readers at the shipping site may have incorrectly read c_1. (Such false positive reads, while less common than false negatives, do occur.) Another possibility is that c_1 simply fell off the pallet at some location away from readers or was stolen. False positives may also lead to a database state that indicates an item's presence at two incompatible locations.

At a higher level, an application may wish to examine the history of inferences and contradicting tag reads in order to detect problems or improve the inference procedure. For example, if we observe a high correlation between pallets shipped using truck t_1 and those with missing cases, an investigation may be in order.

This problem is closely related to the problems of data provenance and lineage tracing in data warehouses [2, 5, 4]. An interesting difference is that while most data warehouses do not directly control their inputs (which are determined, for example, by customer actions at a cash register), in an RFID scenario, we have the option of probing readers and changing configurations (often electronically, by adjusting sensitivity parameters).

4 Online Warehousing

The task of funneling a stream of data from tag readers to a centralized database (real or virtual) shares many features with the analogous task in data warehousing [9]. We need methods for collecting data, cleaning it, shipping it, installing it at the warehouse, and updating derived data. As with materialized-view maintenance in data warehouses, we must decide which inferences (Section 3) are made eagerly and which are made lazily, at query time, with the usual tradeoffs. However, there are important differences (in addition to the tentative nature of some inferences in an RFID system): Currency of data is typically not a major requirement for data warehouses. To the contrary, it is often desirable that the warehouse be updated only infrequently (daily, weekly) and at predictable times, so that an analyst is guaranteed a consistent working set over the duration of her study, which may last several days. In contrast, currency is very important in a typical RFID deployment. We wish to learn of the arrival of pallets at a distribution center without significant delay so that it may be acted upon (unpacked, repackaged, shipped) and the inventory turned over quickly. Thus, we need online methods for data propagation in the RFID infrastructure.

Another feature that distinguishes an RFID infrastructure from a warehousing infrastructure is the much greater emphasis on station-local activities in the former. In a typical data warehousing setup (e.g., for a department store), it is uncommon for the data to be queried at its source (e.g., the point-of-sale terminal). The emphasis is on aggregating data at a central warehouse, where it can be indexed and queried using grouping and aggregation. In contrast, data generated by the tag readers at a dock door in a distribution center is more likely to be used within the distribution center than away from it. For example, the arrival of pallets as they are unloaded from a truck triggers tag reads that, in turn, trigger the activation of business rules and workflows directing personnel to take action on the new items. Thus, while warehousing systems can use a store-and-forward approach to data generated at point-of-sale terminals and other sources, an RFID system must enable efficient transformation (cleaning, filtering, correlation) and querying of data at the data source (as well as querying from foreign locations). For this purpose, a carefully crafted data replication and migration policy is required: A simple policy is to perform immediate (online) updates to the local database in response to tag-read and other event and to push the data to the central infrastructure (which may be composed of several distributed servers) using persistent queues [3].

5 Configuration Design

The above discussion has implicitly assumed a pre-existing placement and configuration of tag readers and other hardware. In practice, determining number, type, and placement of readers, and the manner in which they are connected to other sensors (e.g., motion detectors) and actuators (e.g., conveyor belt speed controls) is part of a large design problem.

As an example, suppose we wish to use RFID tags to keep track of rare books in a large bookstore. Perhaps the most straightforward design is to assign a reader to each bookshelf in order to determine the books in its vicinity. However, the number of readers required by this design, and the implied size of higher-level infrastructure to support the data rate from them, may not be economically feasible. An alternate design is to assign readers to the points of entry and exit from aisles between bookshelves. In this case, we can infer the current location of a book based on the location of the reader that read its tag most recently. In the former case, tag readers provide state information (book x is at location y) while in the latter case, readers provide change-of-state (event) information (book x just entered aisle z). This design choice at the lower layers of the architecture (Figure 5) affects the amount and nature of data that must be stored at other layers. In the state-based design, if all past sensor readings for book x are somehow lost (perhaps due to a system malfunction) the book can still be very easily located by simply issuing a query for its EPC. In the event-based design, this option may not be available because the current location of x is out of the range of all sensors.

As another example, suppose we wish to monitor the operation of a distribution center that receives shipments of pallets from manufacturers, unpacks them, and repackages their contents into new pallets to be shipped down the distribution channel (thus regrouping items from sender-based groups to receiver-based groups). We may need to use multiple tag reader (perhaps of different classes, Figure 4) to read the tags on the pallets and those on the cases within them. We also need a method to determine when one pallet has been completed and a new one started. A method that relies purely on tag readers would be error-prone. It is preferable to use a more reliable indicator of when a pallet is done (say, an optical sensor that detects its passage beyond a certain point on the conveyor belt). If items move too fast on a conveyor belt, the readers may miss tags or produce erroneous reads. Thus, the system must be coupled with an actuator that controls the speed of the conveyor (which is also subject to other constraints, such as the rate at which a human operator can load or unload items).

While the hardware configuration (placement of readers, interconnections, etc.), is difficult to change on a frequent basis, the software configuration (manner in which readings are interpreted and routed) can be changed without much labor. This possibility provides the opportunity to rapidly incorporate new business processes into the RFID infrastructure. For example, if a batch of oversized items cannot be processed at the warehouse in the usual manner, a different physical workflow may be used (perhaps bypassing narrow hallways and expediting outbound shipping for the oversized items). A corresponding change to the electronic (RFID) workflow must also be made. Such changes affect not only the interpretation of the base data from readers but also higher-level inferences. As an example of the former, a state-based tag read for regular items may need to be interpreted as an event-based tag-read for the oversized items. As an example of the latter, the presence of oversized items in the warehouse may increase the likelihood of errors in reading tags (due to obstruction of signals).

6 Conclusion

We have described the new enterprise applications and architectures emerging as a result of RFID technology and illustrated the nature of data management problems they pose: There is a need for methods that can cope with the large variety of RFID tags and readers and their differing capabilities. An architecture for efficiently cleaning, filtering, and augmenting the raw data generated by tag readers is essential for the data to provide any real value. We discussed specific problems in inferencing, online warehousing, and configuration design.

References

[1] B. Brewin. Delta, boeing to test RFID on engine parts. *Computerworld*, pages 1,61, June 2004.

[2] P. Buneman, S. Khanna, and W.-C. Tan. Why and where: A characterization of data prove-

nance. In *Proceedings of the International Conference on Database Theory*, 2001.

[3] S. Ceri and J. Widom. Managing semantic heterogeneity with production rules and persistent queues. In *Proceedings of the Nineteenth International Conference on Very Large Data Bases*, pages 108–119, Dublin, Ireland, Aug. 1993.

[4] S. Chaudhuri and U. Dayal. An overview of data warehouse and OLAP technology. *ACM SIGMOD Record*, Mar. 1997.

[5] C. Cui and J. Widom. Practical lineage tracing in a data warehouse. In *Proceedings of the International Conference on Data Engineering*, pages 367–378, 2000.

[6] K. Finkenzeller. *RFID Handbook: Radio-Frequency Identification Fundamentals and Applications*. John Wiley and Sons, Jan. 2000.

[7] C. Floerkemeier, D. Anarkat, T. Osinski, and M. Harrison. PML Core specification 1.0. Auto-ID Center Recommendation. http://develop.autoidcenter.org/, Sept. 2003.

[8] G. Gruman. UPS v. FedEx: Head-to-head on wireless. *CIO*, pages 66–71, June 2004.

[9] A. Gupta and I. Mumick. Maintenance of materialized views: Problems, techniques, and applications. *IEEE Data Engineering Bulletin, Special Issue on Materialized Views and Data Warehousing*, 18(2):3–18, June 1995.

[10] A. Juels, R. L. Rivest, and M. Szydlo. The blocker tag: Selective blocking of RFID tags for consumer privacy. In *Proceedings of the ACM Conference on Computer and Communications Security*, Washington, D.C., Oct. 2004.

[11] T. Kontzer. RFID flies high with airplane makers. *Information Week*, page 28, June 2004.

[12] M. Mealling. The naming authority pointer (NAPTR) DNS resource record. IETF Network Working Group Request for Comments 2915, Sept. 2000.

[13] M. Mealling. Dynamic delegation discovery system (DDDS) part one: The comprehensive DDDS. IETF Network Working Group Request for Comments 3401, Oct. 2002.

[14] M. Mealling. Auto-ID Object Name Service (ONS) 1.0. Auto-ID Center Working Draft. http://develop.autoidcenter.org/, Aug. 2003.

[15] P. V. Mockapetris and K. J. Dunlap. Development of the domain name system. In *Proceedings of the ACM SIGCOMM Conference on Applications, Technologies, Architectures, and Protocols for Computer Communication (SIGCOMM)*, pages 123–133. ACM Press, 1988.

[16] S. Sarma. Towards the five-cent tag. Auto-ID Center Technical Report. http://develop.autoidcenter.org/, 2001.

[17] S. Sarma and D. W. Engels. On the future of RFID tags and protocols. Auto-ID Center Technical Report. http://develop.autoidcenter.org/, June 2003.

[18] H. Stockman. Communication by means of reflected power. In *Proceedings of the IRE*, pages 1196–1204, Oct. 1948.

[19] L. Sullivan. Alzheimer's patients get help at home. *Information Week*, page 32, June 2004.

[20] K. Takaragi, M. Usami, R. Imura, R. Itsuki, and T. Satoh. An ultra small individual recognition security chip. *IEEE Micro*, 21(6):43–49, 2001.

Production Database Systems: Making Them Easy is Hard Work

David Campbell

Microsoft Corporation
One Microsoft Way
Redmond, WA
USA
davidc@microsoft.com

Abstract

Enterprise capable database products have evolved into incredibly complex systems, some of which present hundreds of configuration parameters to the system administrator. So, while the processing and storage costs for maintaining large volumes of data have plummeted, the human costs associated with maintaining the data have continued to rise. In this presentation, we discuss the framework and approach used by the team who took Microsoft SQL Server from a state where it had several hundred configuration parameters to a system that can configure itself and respond to changes in workload and environment with little human intervention.

1. Introduction

In order to optimally service requests, database systems must manage available resources such as memory and processing power; understand the distribution of the stored data to make good choices about querying the data; and balance the needs of competing requests into the system. The first generation of database systems forced administrators to make many of these choices, up front, before starting the database through a set of configuration parameters or a configuration file. Changing these parameters typically required that the database system be stopped and then restarted to adopt the new configuration profile. Thus, reconfiguration was very costly in a highly available environment. Furthermore, the skill set required to truly comprehend the meaning of hundreds of configuration parameters and the interaction between them was very high. Many systems in the field performed poorly due to mis-configuration.

In the mid-1990's the complexity of these systems was beginning to exceed the capacity of the existing talent pool to manage them. Commercial database vendors began to recognize that future wide scale adoption of database technology would require more efficient ways to manage these systems. In response to this, several products began introducing features to codify the knowledge required to "set the knobs". These "configurators" let less skilled users configure the system based upon a series of questions or rudimentary workload analysis. Adopting the recommendations of these configurators still required changes to the underlying configuration set and, typically, a restart of the system.

The team that architected Microsoft SQL Server 7.0 took a radically different approach to this problem. Rather than adding features to help "turn the knobs", they took a holistic approach that focused on eliminating the knobs while simultaneously maintaining administrative control where necessary. This approach focused on three major themes:
- Closed loop control
- Intention based design
- Profile guided configuration and tuning

2. Closed loop control

The Microsoft SQL Server team used control theory technologies long known in other engineering disciplines to encode closed loop, feedback based, systems for configuring many elements of the system in near real-time. These technologies are used in SQL Server to control the size of the buffer pool, growing and shrinking

---

Permission to copy without fee all or part of this material is granted provided that the copies are not made or distributed for direct commercial advantage, the VLDB copyright notice and the title of the publication and its date appear, and notice is given that copying is by permission of the Very Large Data Base Endowment. To copy otherwise, or to republish, requires a fee and/or special permission from the Endowment
**Proceedings of the 30th VLDB Conference,
Toronto, Canada, 2004**

the size of the overall memory pool dynamically in response to memory pressure from other processes on the running system. By default, SQL Server is configured to completely control the amount of memory it consumes, however, an administrator can define upper and lower bounds on the amount of memory used and the control algorithm will be constrained to honor those boundaries. This is an example where, by default, the system manages itself, however administrative policy can be enforced if desired. These dynamic control algorithms are also used elsewhere in the system such as automatically configuring the read ahead and write behind depth for prefetch and bulk write operations.

Not only have these closed loop algorithms eliminated a large number of configuration parameters, they also have the advantage of responding to external forces to automatically reconfigure the running system in response to changing conditions resulting in more efficient use of system resources. For example, in many database systems, an administrator must set aside a portion of system memory for various needs such as working memory for sorting, or storing compiled SQL plans. In SQL Server, the system dynamically manages these different memory needs based upon system conditions – only allocating sort working memory when there is a sort operation being performed. Thus, memory is a fungible resource that can be employed wherever it can do the most good at any instant in time.

3. Intention based design

The control surface of most database products evolved as the implementers added new configuration parameters as they added features. As a result, system administrators were forced to wrestle the existing set of knobs into the right form to do their jobs. So, while an administrator might want to ensure that restart recovery completed in less than 60 seconds, he may have to set checkpoint frequency, number of outstanding dirty log blocks and several other parameters to achieve the desired state. Intention based design turns this around by aligning the control inputs of the database product with the specific objectives of the administrator. So, the administrator can specify they want restart recovery to complete in 60 seconds rather than manipulating a number of other controls. Obviously, there may be conflicts between the specified inputs; with intention based design however, it is up to the database product to understand and negotiate these constraints rather than the administrator.

4. Profile guided configuration and tuning

During the process of trying to understand the costs of mis-configured systems, the Microsoft SQL Server team realized that there were a number of administrative tasks such a maintaining table and index statistics or providing an optimal index set for a particular workload that could be automated. As a result, the product development and research teams created features to automatically create and maintain distribution statistics on stored data and to recommend a set of optimal indexes for a specified workload.

Automatic statistics update can create index and column level distribution statistics to improve the cost based query optimization decisions. Since this is done automatically in response to knowledge required to perform effective query optimization, the system actually "learns" as it processes new queries. If a query plan choice could benefit from column level statistics, the system will schedule building the statistics so subsequent query activity can benefit from the knowledge.

The Index Tuning Wizard [1] can process a previously recorded workload and, in cooperation with the query optimizer, propose an optimal set of indexes to process the workload balancing both the query benefit from the indexes and the costs required to maintain the index set. Ultimately, the goal is to eliminate the need for the CREATE INDEX statement and to have the system maintain optimal indexing based upon system needs.

5. Conclusion

A holistic approach to "Ease of Use", coupled with use of well known techniques from other engineering disciplines can be used to build very sophisticated database systems where the intent of the administrator, coupled with workload analysis, can be used to dynamically control the configuration of the system. Use of closed loop control, intention based design, and profile guided tuning can result in a system that is more responsive; resource efficient; and much less prone to mis-configuration Systems build with these techniques require much less direct human input to maintain; freeing administrators to perform tasks that provide much more direct business value.

References

[1] Chaudhuri, S., Narasayya V., "An Efficient, Cost-Driven Index Selection Tool for Microsoft SQL Server." Proceedings of the 23rd VLDB Conference Athens, Greece, 1997, pages 146-155

Managing Data from High-Throughput Genomic Processing: A Case Study

Toby Bloom

Broad Institute of MIT and Harvard

tbloom@broad.mit.edu

Ted Sharpe

Broad Institute of MIT and Harvard

tsharpe@broad.mit.edu

Abstract

Genomic data has become the canonical example of very large, very complex data sets. As such, there has been significant interest in ways to provide targeted database support to address issues that arise in genomic processing. Whether genomic data is truly a special case, or just another application area exhibiting problems common to other domains, is an as yet unanswered question. In this abstract, we explore the structure and processing requirements of a large-scale genome sequencing center, as a case study of the issues that arise in genomic data managements, and as a means to compare those issues with those that arise in other domains.

1. Overview

The Broad Institute high-throughput genome sequencing center currently produces genome sequence at the highest rate in the world. The sequencing laboratory is essentially a large manufacturing facility: it uses DNA samples as raw material and produces digitized sequence where other manufacturing facilities might produce widgets. We produce over 50 billion high-quality nucleotide base calls per year, each of which has multiple pieces of information associated with it. The amounts of data produced by sequencing, as well as the data maintained for tracking the process, and reporting on progress, raise significant challenges for informatics resources. The following sections provide background on the sequencing processes that must be tracked, and the type and size of the data produced. We then discuss the issues that arise in performing those functions, and compare them to data management to problems that arise in other domains.

2. Background : the Genome Sequencing Process

The sequencing process starts with a piece of DNA and produces from it a character string of A's.C's, T's and G's that represent the four nucleotide bases from which DNA is composed. During the sequencing process, an initial DNA sample undergoes a series of laboratory procedures that include steps such as cutting the DNA into many small pieces, replicating each of those pieces many times, and attaching flourescent dyes. In the final step, those dyes are detected by lasers, and a signal trace (a "read") is produced for each of those small pieces. Tracking the samples through the various lab procedures is essential for mapping the millions of sequence reads from the laser sequence detectors back to the original DNA samples. Tracking is also needed to troubleshoot laboratory problems and monitor lab performance.

Once the signal trace is produced, the informatics data acquisition begins. The data is processed through a pipeline that cleans and validates each read. Signal processing software analyzes the binary trace file from the lasers, and produces the string of As, Cs, Ts, and G's denoting the DNA sequence. Since this is a chemical process and not absolutely accurate, we also maintain quality data for the sequence: the intensity of the flourescence for each of the four dyes at regular intervals, and a certainty score for each base (actually four certainty scores are produced.) Each read is typically about 800 to 900 bases long, with about 650 of those bases usable for further processing. The lab tracking data is used to associate each read with its original sample. The sequence is checked to make sure it looks like it came from the correct organism and that it hasn't been confused with or contaminated by other material in the lab process. Numerous metrics are collected for monitoring the process and for maintaining reportable data. The sequence data is then organized for assembly.

Permission to copy without fee all or part of this material is granted provided that the copies are not made or distributed for direct commercial advantage, the VLDB copyright notice and the title of the publication and its date appear, and notice is given that copying is by permission of the Very Large Data Base Endowment. To copy otherwise, or to republish, requires a fee and/or special permission from the Endowment

**Proceedings of the 30th VLDB Conference,
Toronto, Canada, 2004**

Once enough sequence data for a genome has been collected, the assembly process can be started. In assembly, the read sequences are matched against each other, like a giant jigsaw puzzle, to figure out in what order the reads appear in the organism's genome. There can be 40 to 60 million reads or more used in a single assembly, with no a priori structure known among them. The reads cover the genome many times over, to ensure enough data to fit all the pieces together unambiguously, despite the errors present in the detection process and the many nearly identical but distinct sequences that typically occur within a genome. Not all of the reads will fit together, and some will match in multiple places due to repeat structure within the genome.

Following assembly, there is often a process known as finishing, which determines where there are gaps in the assembled sequence, or regions with insufficiently high quality, and orders additional lab work to fill in the holes. Then the cycle repeats. But since other work, like annotation, or SNP detection, or comparative genomics projects will have begun, we have a versioning problem for assemblies – and a corresponding merge problem as well. These introduce yet more data complexity.

3. Challenges in Processing Genome Sequence Data

In this section, we discuss the issues that arise in managing the high-throughput genome sequence data. We then compare these challenges to those found in other domains.

3.1 Data Structure and Data Set Size

There are several categories of data handled in the sequencing informatics process: one is the sequence data itself; a second is the lab process workflow, tracking and process data; yet a third is the operational oversight information; and finally we have tracking of biological samples. In addition, we maintain the structure of the assembled genome, and the finishing data that includes versions and updates of those assemblies.

3.1.1 Sequence Data

The Broad Sequencing Center produces over 50 billion bases a year. Since most processing is performed at the read level, not the base level, in most cases we're dealing with millions, not billions, of entities. However, there are many data points associated with each base: the value of the most probable base (A,C,T,G); four quality scores representing the likelihood of each of the four possible calls at that position; numerous intensity scores – the intensity of the signal for each of the four dye colors—in the vicinity of the intensity peak that marks the presence of a base.

The most probable base and the quality score associated with it are, by far, the most frequently used data, and these attributes are stored as a set of parallel strings, at the read level. Thus, one string contains the called bases. Another contains the certainty score for each of those bases, in order. This significantly reduces the overhead of storing the data. However, that comes at the expense of processing. All queries on that data now need to parse those strings.

The signal traces themselves (which include not only the base calls and quality scores, but the intensity data in four channels for each sample) are maintained in file systems in a hashed directory structure, indexed by the database. This obviously increases complexity of queries on that data, while significantly reducing data size.

The scale is not as large as one might expect. Compression techniques have reduced our storage requirements to only about 5 terabytes per year. Our database is currently only about 1 terabyte. But within that, we maintain multiple tables of hundreds of millions of rows each. The size of our indexes is therefore significant, and query optimization becomes more complex.

Perhaps surprisingly, transaction rates are not problematic. The transactions can be complex, primarily because they involve coordination with external equipment, but the rate is relatively low. The system handles approximately one million lab transactions per day, and another one million data analysis transactions. Most of the data within the sequence acquisition system is write-once, which significantly reduces the complexity of transaction management.

3.1.2 Assembly and Closure Data

One example of the complex structures we maintain is the assembly structure used in the closure and finishing process that follows assembly.

The process starts with the set of contiguous sequences generated from the assembly process. We maintain the map of these "contigs", along with their predicted location on the genome, information about gap sizes between contigs, where known, and the locations of all the reads within those stretches of sequence. We also maintain the map of all large-insert clones that span contiguous regions, but for which we don't yet have full sequence coverage. These templates can be used to generate additional sequence to fill gaps. During the iterative finishing process, we order additional sequencing of these spanners, and maintain the information about pending orders, the primers that were ordered for purchase for each those, and then the results of those new sequencing requests. New sequence generated must be placed on the assembly, thereby generating a new version, with different coordinates for each of the reads and the contigs. In fact, since the new sequence may close gaps, some contigs merge, and so we need to maintain the history of the assembly, so that when other orders come back, or work is performed by a collaborator on an earlier version, it can be mapped to the new assembly. In addition, neighboring contigs must be updated to reflect their new neighbors. All changes tend to propagate through the assembly, with the attendant naming and relationship problems. And this structure may identify thousands of gaps, thousands of spanners, and millions of reads. The relationship management and propagation problems present interesting performance issues.

3.1.3 Taxonomies

One of the issues that arises regularly is the representation of non-uniform hierarchies. We encounter a number of situations in which branches of the tree may be of varying lengths in what should be analogous situations. This makes it difficult to structure the database. Taxonomies are one such situation.

The sequencing center handles large numbers of samples. These need to be categorized with respect to taxonomic classifications, from the genus and species, sometimes down to the individual. We need to know when we're sequencing a single individual vs. samples from multiple different individuals. This hierarchy is not uniform. Genus and species are standard, but the taxonomic levels above them vary among the kingdoms. And below that level, there is also a lack of uniformity: . some organisms are classified as subspecies within that hierarchy; others have breeds, or strains. In some organisms, an isolate is a single individual; in others a colony. The DNA from inbred mice of the same strain might be considered interchangeable in some situations. This means that there is no single hierarchy that represents the taxonomy. A simple organism dimension for categorizing sequencing targets becomes problematic.

3.1.4 Sample Data and Derivations

Another example of a problem in representing hierarchies is the DNA sample tracking in the lab. DNA is sequenced by cutting it into pieces and sequencing the ends of the pieces. The problem arises because any strand of DNA can be cut into a set of smaller strands of DNA, until you get down to a piece you can read in its entirety. (The usual process, however stops far short of this exhaustive recursion, however. We assemble continuous sequence by stitching together overlapping bits of separate samples, rather than exhaustively sequencing a single sample.) However, depending upon the task at hand, different techniques and lengths are used.

Thus, we may take a sample of genomic DNA and create from it sequencing libraries of small clones – hence creating a two-level hierarchy to maintain. Or we may instead create a library of large insert clones. We might sequence the ends of those without further cutting, or we might instead create from each large-insert clone, its own small-insert library. And from small-insert libraries, we might create yet smaller "shatter" libraries. At each level, we can take one DNA entity and create a library of smaller pieces of DNA. Or at any level, we can sequence directly. We therefore have a recursive structure in the sample dimension. We need to maintain the relationship among all those levels – which samples at one level were used to derive sets of samples at another level, so that we can understand how the sequences generated are related. There is no flat, tabular layout that represents these relationships, because the depth can vary, and there are no fixed joins that can find all related samples.

3.2 Querying

Queries again pose an interesting contrast to business applications.

The hierarchical data structures and compression techniques described above will of course add to query complexity. Many of our reports perform the equivalent of tree-walks on very large tables, with large numbers of constraints. Tricks like nested sets help, but are not sufficient [2]. Many of our complex queries require hand optimization. Better automatic parallelization might be a substantial help.

We have not yet addressed lab requests for trending and various other time-series reports. These are likely to present significant challenges as well.

In addition, the databases serve as back ends for complex genome analysis applications. As such, the queries presented often expect result sets numbering in the millions or tens of millions of rows, pulled from tables with hundreds of millions of rows. Rather than expecting aggregated results from the database, these applications require the individual records. Performance in retrieving those results is frequently a problem.

3.3 Impact of a Research Environment

In most respects, the sequencing center is no more than a large, automated flexible manufacturing floor. It happens to generate digitized DNA sequence rather than widgets, but in other ways, it differs little.

However, it should not be forgotten that this is a research environment, and some aspects of that environment are responsible for the complexity of data handling, rather than the complexity being inherent in the data itself.

There is an explicit goal of changing the lab processes and technology every six months, with major upgrades every two years. From an informatics standpoint, that means the number of steps in the process, the lab measures maintained at each step, the kinds of branching and pooling that occur in the workflow must be fully flexible. The process is separated from the basic data acquisition as much as possible, but the schema still changes very frequently. Constraints become very hard to maintain and automated error checking is difficult, because so little information is embedded in the schema. Thus, some of the complexity of our schemas, and the resulting complexity and performance issues in our queries, are a result of designing for flexibility rather than performance.

3.4 Data Integration and Analysis

Thus far, we've described the issues involved in maintaining sequencing data in isolation. But of course, the goal is genetic analysis, not just production of sequence data. Integration problems are the problems most often discussed in bioinformatics. Our center alone collects not only sequence data, but expression analysis data, and genotyping data. We will soon be collecting proteomic data as well. Integrative genomics [5] involves combining results from analysis of multiple kinds of data where any one is insufficient. And of course, there are large numbers of public and proprietary databases available with overlapping but not identical sets of genomic data of various types. Often the naming across them is inconsistent. The formats are certainly inconsistent. And so we bring all of the well known problems of data integration to a domain with many, many terabytes of data, and on-demand integration. This may be a quantitative rather than qualitative difference from other application domains, but it will still be a very significant challenge.

4. Conclusions

This abstract describes many of the problems faced in managing large-scale genomic data. We have addressed issues of data structure, and its impact on transactions and on queries; the unique issues brought on by very large data size, and the complexity of the application space.

All of these issues present serious challenges to maintaining and accessing this type of data. We have illustrated no problems here that do not exist in other domains, in whole or in part. However, the conjunction of these problems, in a domain with such large data volume does present significant challenges. We summarize here the various issues we raised and assess their impact in other application domains.

Traversing complex data structures, and maintaining the complex hierarchical relationships among the data entities, is certainly one of the biggest underlying problems in this space. However, this is the same problem that led to so much work on object databases years ago. It is not new.

The frequently changing structure and the impact on the schema again occur at larger scales here. But that problem underlies the work on metadata repositories as well. These kinds of problems are not unlike those that occur in a flexible manufacturing environment, or in environments such as clinical trials, where there is a basic framework that must be customized for each use. The frequency, as well as the scale, is different here. But the problem is similar. There is a tradeoff between the generality needed to allow for unpredictable changes, and the complexity of querying and data validation in those environments.

Data integration across multiple sources on demand certainly requires significant work to become a reality in genomic analysis. The problems are identical to those faced in other domains: inconsistent naming, inconsistent ranges, differing data formats. The sheer size of the problem may appear to verge on a qualitative difference here, but integration is a major problem everywhere.

Overall, at least from the perspective of sequence data, which is a small subset of genomic data in general, we see many unresolved issues in data management, but none that seem unique to this type of application data.

Acknowledgements

Andrew Zimmer leads the finishing informatics effort and architected the mapping structures to meet the challenges described. J.P.Leger is leading the data warehousing effort and manages the reporting team. Jen Baldwin, Rob Nicol, Chad Nussbaum, Bruce Birren, and Kerstin Linblad-Toh direct the Genome Sequencing and Analysis platform and program. Jill Mesirov is the Chief Informatics Officer of the Broad Institute, and Eric Lander is Founding Director of the Broad Institute. And thanks go to all members of the Production Sequencing Informatics team for building the software that enables the sequencing center to function.

References

[1] S. Batzoglou, et al ARACHNE: A whole-genome shotgun assembler. *Genome Res.* 12: 177-189 (2002).
[2] J. Celko, SQL for Smarties, Academic Press, San Diego, 2000.
[3] International Human Genome Sequencing Consortium, Initial Sequencing and Analysis of the Human Genome, Nature, 409, 860-921, (2001).
[4] D.B. Jaffe, et al. Whole-genome sequence assembly for mammalian genomes: Arachne 2. *Genome Res.* 13: 91_96 (2003).
[5] V.K. Mootha, et. al . Identification of a gene causing human cytochrome c oxidase deficiency by integrative genomics. *Proc Natl Acad Sci USA* 100: 605_610 (2003).

Database Challenges in the Integration of Biomedical Data Sets

Rakesh Nagarajan
Washington University School of Medicine
Department of Pathology & Immunology
660 South Euclid Avenue, Campus Box 8118
Saint Louis, MO, 63110, USA.
rakesh@wustl.edu

Mushtaq Ahmed and Aditya Phatak
Persistent Systems Private Limited
Bhageerath, 402, Senapati Bapat Road
Pune 411016, India
{mushtaq, aditya}@persistent.co.in

Abstract

The clinical and basic science research domains present exciting and difficult data integration issues. Solving these problems is crucial as current research efforts in the field of biomedicine heavily depend upon integrated storage, querying, analysis, and visualization of clinicopathology information, genomic annotation, and large scale functional genomic research data sets. Such large scale experimental analyses are essential to decipher the pathophysiological processes occurring in most human diseases so that they may be effectively treated. In this paper, we discuss the challenges of integration of multiple biomedical data sets not only at the university level but also at the national level and present the data warehousing based solution we have employed at Washington University School of Medicine. We also describe the tools we have developed to store, query, analyze, and visualize these data sets together.

1. Introduction

It is becoming increasingly apparent that the majority of human diseases including tumorigenesis are the product of multi-step pathophysiological processes, and that each of these processes involve the complex interplay of a multitude of genes acting at different levels of the genetic program. Indeed, it is clear that genome-wide detection of genetic alterations, transcriptional profiles, and protein compositions is required to comprehensively describe the complex pathophysiology of polygenic diseases.

Fortunately, in the post-human genome sequencing era, many analyses on the genomic scale are possible. The biggest challenge in interpreting the results of these analyses lies in the data integration problem. The experimental methods employed in genomics and proteomics generate high throughput data, which is stored in different formats at multiple sources. In a university, this data is generated at various core labs and has to be shared across investigators. The data management, integration and analysis needs for this kind of heterogeneous data are enormous.

Typically, groups have utilized three major mechanisms to integrate biological databases. These include:

- Indexed data sources: This approach indexes and links a large number of data sources. Here a user begins a query with one data source, and then follows links (*e.g.* hypertext) to related information in other data sources. For example, the Sequence Retrieval System (SRS) is a popular keyword indexing and search system for biological databases [18].
- Federated databases: In this approach, the information resides in the respective source databases. Federated systems maintain a common data model and rely on schema mapping to translate heterogeneous source database schemas into the target schema for integration. For example, the Kleisli Query System provides a high-level query language, simplified SQL (sSQL), which can be used to express cross-database queries [3]. K2, a successor to Kleisli, is a view integration environment developed by the database group at the University of Pennsylvania [4], and IBM's Discovery Link is another popular integration system based on the federated approach [7].
- Data warehousing: This approach assembles data sources into a centralized system with a global data schema and indexing system for integration and navigation. This approach is dominated by relational database management systems (RDBMS).

For our university setup, the major design considerations included fast querying of data from

---

Permission to copy without fee all or part of this material is granted provided that the copies are not made or distributed for direct commercial advantage, the VLDB copyright notice and the title of the publication and its date appear, and notice is given that copying is by permission of the Very Large Data Base Endowment. To copy otherwise, or to republish, requires a fee and/or special permission from the Endowment
**Proceedings of the 30th VLDB Conference,
Toronto, Canada, 2004**

multiple sources, efficient handling of large amounts of data, allowing users to upload and analyze their data, and access to data via a campus-wide intranet for approximately 100 concurrent users. In addition, while the experimental data generated within the university needed to be accessed in almost real time, the annotation data coming from publicly available databases needed to be up to date only within the past few weeks. Therefore, we chose to use the data warehousing model to store these experimental and annotation data sets. In this paper, we discuss the challenges of integration of these diverse data sets not only at the university level but also at the national level and present the data warehousing based solution we have employed at Washington University School of Medicine.

The rest of the paper is organized as follows. Section 2 provides necessary background. It describes the need for data integration in detail and provides details of various bioinformatics data sets and the technologies that generate this data. In Section 3 we present our data warehouse solution and various tools we have developed to store, query, analyze, and visualize the data. In Section 4, we discuss several ongoing standardization efforts required to store and annotate such data sets in a uniform manner, and we discuss our future work and overall conclusions in Sections 5 and 6 respectively.

2. Background

Foremost among the high throughput technologies in post-genomics era is the ability to monitor the messenger RNA (mRNA) expression of all genes in a particular tissue, cell type, or pathological process [6, 14]. There is great potential in this experimental modality, termed microarray analysis, as evidenced by the recent explosion of publications using this technique to monitor genome-wide expression and to correlate expression changes to biological processes or to disease states.

Some of these modalities of molecular analysis have also been combined with clinically relevant parameters such as patient survival or the existence of metastatic disease in the study of tumorigenesis. However, it is becoming increasingly apparent that it is necessary to *simultaneously* analyze the results derived from different functional genomic experiments such as expression profiling and mutation analysis with clinical and pathological data and gene annotation. This will increase the power of the analysis and will provide complementary confirmation such that meaningful insights into the disease process may be made.

However, most end-users (biologists and clinicians) find the task of performing such integrated *in-silico* analyses daunting in the functional genomic era; the main reason for this being the variety of disparate data sources, different software applications, and varied output formats that exist today. Thus, a flexible data integration framework, which will take care of such complexities and will allow the researcher to focus on the results of analyses, is needed. In the remainder of this section, we describe the different data sets that are used in such integrated analyses.

2.1 Gene Annotation

In 2001, a draft of the entire human genome sequence or the human DNA genetic sequence was deciphered as part of the Human Genome Project [8, 10]. This enormous fund of knowledge along with the requisite annotation describing each gene is represented by a rich and diverse set of data elements. These include a total of 24 chromosomes representing approximately 3×10^9 base pairs of DNA sequence and the position of each of approximately 35,000 genes, 36,000 corresponding

---

GLOSSARY

Allele: One of the variant forms of a gene
Clinicopathology: Of or relating to clinical and/or pathology parameters
Exon: Protein coding portion of a gene
Expression/Transcription: Synthesis of mRNA from a DNA template
Functional genomics: Application of genome-wide experimental approaches to assess gene function
Homolog: Any member of a set of genes whose nucleotide sequences show a high degree of one-to-one correspondence
Intron: Intervening portion of a gene between exons, removed during the transcriptional process and not translated into protein
Metastatic disease: Cancer stage where the tumor has spread to remote tissues

Ortholog: Homologous sequences in different species that arose from a common ancestral gene during speciation
PCR: Polymerase Chain Reaction used to amplify and detect DNA
Polygenic diseases: An inherited disease controlled by several genes at once
Proteomics: The identification, characterization and quantification of all proteins involved in a particular pathway, organelle, cell, tissue, organ, or organism that can be studied in concert to provide accurate and comprehensive data about that system.
Primer: A short synthetic piece of DNA used to initiate a PCR reaction
Transcriptional profiles: mRNA content of tissues
Tumorigenesis: Process of tumor formation

messenger RNAs and proteins, and coding region or exonic and intervening region or intronic coordinates. In addition, the following types of genomic annotation data need to be stored:

- Over 2,000,000 Single Nucleotide Polymorphisms or SNPs: These are sequence variations, which together create a unique DNA pattern in each person.

- Over 20,000 protein domains: These are independent sub-regions of proteins known to have specified functionality

- Annotation describing a gene product's molecular function, cellular compartmentalization, and/or biological process

- Protein-protein interaction and pathway information

Gene annotations reside in multiple publicly available biomedical databases, and acquiring gene annotations from various data sources involves identifying important and reliable data sources, regularly querying these sources, parsing and interpreting the results, and establishing associations between related entities. There are major difficulties at every step of this process. Each data source has custom text formats, and these formats change occasionally. Furthermore, an entire data source may be retired or completely restructured using a new schema. In addition, genomic data sources are usually updated on different schedules, and the size of such data sources may prohibit all versions of a data source from being loaded into a data warehouse. Finally, some data sources are inconsistent at the semantic level, and frequently, there is inadequate use of controlled vocabularies and common data elements to specify the metadata.

The National Center for Biotechnology Information (NCBI) is one major resource that maintains public biomedical annotation databases [17]. It includes nucleotide and protein sequence (GenBank), structure (MMDB), genome (RefSeq), and expression (GEO) databases. The OMIM (Online Mendelian Inheritance in Man) database is a catalog of human genes and genetic disorders [16]. GO (Gene Ontology) is a popular database that contains information about the cellular localization, molecular function, and the biological process in which a gene product is involved [1]. PubMed is a literature database from the National Library of Medicine, which includes over 14 million citations for biomedical articles [16].

Our warehouse fetches and stores annotations for all genes represented in humans and several other model organisms from OMIM, GO, PubMed and the following databases of NCBI: UniGene, dbSNP, RefSeq, HomoloGene, and LocusLink.

2.2 Microarray Profiling

A microarray is designed to detect the mRNA content (Expression Profiling) or the genomic DNA content (Comparative Genomic Hybridization) of thousands of genes in a particular tissue, cell type or pathological process [5, 12, 13]. It is based on the principle of hybridization between targets and probes. In this experimental modality, fluorescent-labeled nucleic acid from a sample of interest is called the target while short DNA fragments attached to a microarray are called probes. Probes on a single microarray represent most genes in the entire genome. Array experiments are typically conducted using one of two experimental formats. In the single channel system, a single sample of biological material is labeled with a fluorescent dye, hybridized to an oligonucleotide array, and the intensity value at each oligonucleotide is determined. In the two-channel system, a pair of samples is labeled with different fluorophores, hybridized to an oligonucleotide or cDNA array, and the intensity value of each fluorophore at each spot is determined.

The measured fluorescent values are meaningful only in the context of sample metadata (e.g. prostate versus breast tumor or benign versus malignant) and the associated genomic annotation of "interesting" probe sequences. Therefore, a gene expression data management system must integrate data from three different data sets: *gene expression measurements, sample metadata, and gene annotations*.

The data generated by a microarray system contains several data types. Typically, it includes

- Raw data consisting of binary image files generated by scanners

- Probe intensity data consisting of numerical values associated with each probe

- Summarized gene expression data estimates generated by combining probes representing the same gene

In a single microarray experiment, a raw image file is approximately 50 MB in size, the probe intensity data file is approximately 12MB, and the summarized gene expression data consists of between 12,000-50,000 values. Typically, a biologist would conduct between 5-100 such chip experiments and would thus have to store, query, analyze, and visualize ~100K-2500K data points.

2.3 Mutation Profiling

Microarray gene expression profiling has identified numerous genes in important pathways whose expression is altered in complex diseases. A complementary experimental modality involves the precise and comprehensive definition of the genetic changes, which are responsible for disease development or susceptibility, at the DNA level [2, 15]. This experimental methodology called mutation profiling is now possible due to the progress made in large scale DNA sequencing. Biomedical researchers may now sequence hundreds of genes in hundreds of tissue samples to identify mutations responsible for the disease phenotype.

This experimental modality also generates a rich set of data types. These include:
- Binary data: Sequencing a gene in one sample generates approximately 12-20 trace files, each of which is ~35 KB. For each gene sequenced in each sample, a binary analysis file (~6 MB) is generated. These are stored as BLOBs.
- DNA base information: The DNA sequence, quality information, and mutation probability are stored for ~500 bases in each of the trace files. This data is a combination of character, string, integer, and float data types.
- Consensus data: A consensus sequence is the overall DNA sequence derived by integrating the sequence information from all the traces of a gene. For each gene sequenced in a sample, the consensus sequence and its alignment to the reference DNA sequence are stored. This data is stored as a large string in a CLOB.

2.4 Proteomics Analysis

This analysis is aimed at high throughput separation and identification of proteins that are differentially expressed in a disease state as compared to the healthy state [9]. 2D PAGE (**2 D**imensional **P**oly**A**crylamide **G**el **E**lectrophoresis) is by far the most commonly used method for protein separation. In this method, a complex mixture of proteins is first separated into bands based on the isoelectric point using Immobilized pH Gradient (IPG) gels. These bands of proteins are further separated into spots after being subjected to mass based separation using Sodium Dodecyl Sulfate (SDS) gels. Every spot on the gel roughly corresponds to one protein. Spot volume ratio comparison in disease state vs. normal state helps in selecting only those protein spots that are significantly different. Mass spectrometry analysis, single (MS) or tandem (MS/MS), after digestion (i.e. fragmentation) of selected spots generates corresponding spectra. These experimental spectra are compared with theoretical spectra of protein sequence digests using various software tools in order to identify the protein at each spot.

The data generated by these experiments consists of the following:
- Images (~50 MB per gel): Depending on the number of samples loaded on a gel, a gel may be scanned at multiple wavelengths to generate several image files.
- Workspaces (~50 MB per gel): Containing image analysis and comparison details
- Metadata: Describing experiments, samples gels, and spots excised from gels.
- Mass spectrometry data (~100 MB per spot)
- Spectral similarity reports

2.5 Clinical Data

Clinical data refers to any information that is contained in a patient's medical record. This information may be acquired from notes derived from a hospital admission or a doctor's visit. This data comes in various forms such as text or numbers (patient identification, demographics, history, laboratory data, etc), analog or digital signals (ECG, EEG, EMG, ENG etc), images (histological, radiological, ultrasound, etc), and videos. Furthermore, clinical studies involve specimen collection from multiple patients. The complete specimen may not be consumed at once and may be preserved in a specimen bank. Therefore, all of this patient-derived clinical and specimen-derived pathology data must be interlinked to research results derived from analyzing DNA, RNA, or protein samples. Further complicating the storage of this data is the fact that because patient identification information cannot be publicly accessible by law (HIPAA) [11], such identifiers must be removed and decoupled from other clinical parameters. Apart from humans, specimen collection and genome-wide profiling experiments may be conducted in other species such as mouse and rat. The major difficulty in storing this type of data is that each disease and species can only be adequately described using greatly different vocabularies and data elements.

3. Our Solution

In this section, we present our data warehouse solution for integrating various biomedical data sets deployed at Washington University School of Medicine. The major goals of this data integration project and the resulting Data Warehouse from the perspective of the university are:

- To develop an informatics center that will allow investigators to collect and manage large amounts of gene expression, gene sequence, proteomics, and coded clinicopathology data generated from various research studies.
- To develop data mining and analysis tools that will allow investigators to generate and validate new hypotheses based on the integration of collected functional genomic and clinicopathology data sets.
- To provide a publicly accessible venue for "publishing" experimental findings and corresponding data sets generated from investigator-based studies.
- To provide authentication, authorization and security such that investigators can give access privileges to other investigators on the data sets owned by them.

The data warehouse integrates data from the following important core facilities:
- Microarray Facility (MAF): Performs microarray experiments for investigators
- Washington University Genome Sequencing Center (GSC): Performs high throughput sequencing for mutation profiling
- Proteomics Facility (PRF): Provides access to proteomics technologies for molecular profiling
- Siteman Clinical Information Portal (SCIP): Collects and stores patient-derived clinical parameters
- Tissue Procurement Facility (TPF): Collects, stores and tracks anonymized patient identifiers, associated tissue specimens, and pathology data; generates DNA, RNA, and protein samples to be analyzed by the GSC, MAF, and PRF (Collectively called the Functional Genomic Cores or FGCs) respectively

Apart from these facilities, data is also integrated from reliable publicly available annotation data sources. The data from the above sources is integrated using the following workflow. Typically, patients are enrolled in a clinical trial, and appropriate clinical parameters depending upon the disease under question are curated from the medical record and stored in SCIP. Anonymized patient identifiers are also entered into the TPF database. As part of the clinical trial, one or more specimens are collected, tracked and stored at the TPF. The TPF processes these specimens to produce DNA, RNA, and/or protein and assigns each of these specimens and samples tracking identifiers. These biomolecular samples are then sent to the appropriate FGC to conduct microarray, mutation, and/or proteomic profiling experiments. After completion of the experiments, these FGCs load experimental data into our data warehouse. Similarly, clinical and pathology data as well as requisite inter-relationships between patient, specimen, and sample identifiers are loaded into our database from SCIP and the TPF. Genes represented in each of the experimental paradigms are annotated by importing data into our warehouse from multiple, publicly available biomedical data sources described in Section 2. Thus, clinical data (from SCIP), specimen, sample, and pathology data and their inter-relationships (from TPF), experimental data (from FGCs), and gene annotation data (from publicly available annotation databases) are loaded into our data warehouse (Figure 1).

Our data warehouse runs on Oracle 9i (version 9.2.0.4- 64 bit) database which is hosted on a Sun Enterprise 420R consisting of 4 X 450 Mhz Ultra Sparc-II processors, 4 GB of internal RAM memory, 36 GB of

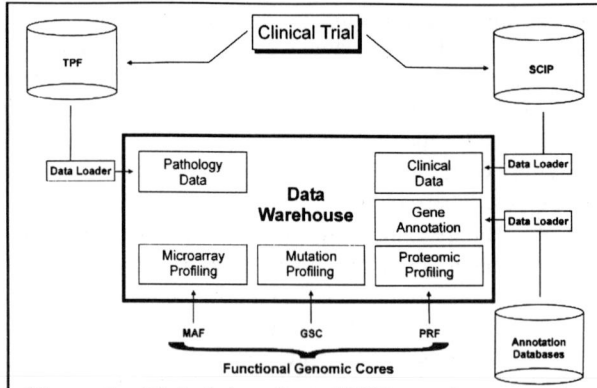

Figure 1. Clinical data (from SCIP), specimen, sample, and pathology data and their inter-relationships (from TPF), experimental data (from FGCs), and gene annotation data (from publicly available annotation databases) are loaded into our data warehouse.

mirrored internal drive space, and two Sun StorEdge A1000 RAID boxes, containing 654 GB of total disk space set up to operate in RAID 5 mode. The warehouse currently has about 150 GB of data.

We have also built analysis tools that let investigators perform integrated analysis and visualization of the various data sets stored in our data warehouse. The following subsections describe our software components that address issues of importing, querying, analyzing, and visualizing the biomedical data sets described in Section 2.

3.1 Function Express Server

Function Express Server, which is written in Java, extracts annotation data from publicly available gene annotation databases, loads it into the warehouse, and links it to genes represented in microarray, sequence, and proteomic data. Integrating these annotations into a data warehouse facilitates better representation of semantics, enhanced query performance, and superior data quality.

Function Express Server includes an Extract-Transform-Load (ETL) tool that downloads various reliable publicly available gene annotation databases, parses the data to extract relevant annotation such as the gene name and chromosomal localization, and loads them into the warehouse. Because annotation sources have custom text formats, parsers are written for each biomedical data source. These parsers are used to load data into our warehouse, and automatic updates to the warehouse are conducted at a user-specified frequency, a necessary feature as the data in the annotation databases is being updated frequently. As most annotation sources do not provide deltas, updates are detected in the ETL process.

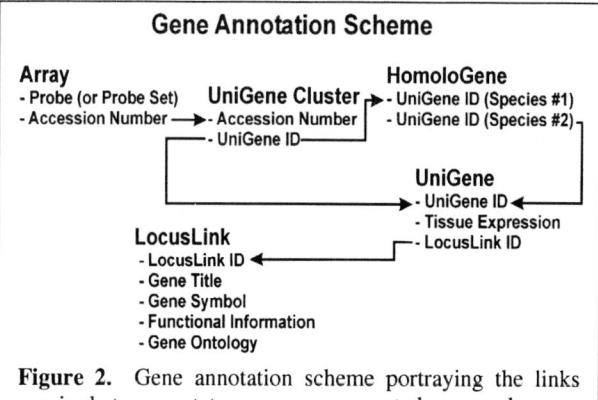

Figure 2. Gene annotation scheme portraying the links required to annotate genes represented as probes on microarrays. Genes are either directly linked via the UniGene cluster and LocusLink ID or indirectly via HomoloGene.

Function Express Server currently fetches annotations for all genes represented in humans as well as other major model organisms from UniGene, LocusLink, HomoloGene, dbSNP, OMIM, Gene Ontology, and PubMed. The linking of these annotations with individual spots or probes on a microarray is conducted as follows (Figure 2). Each probe or probeset on a microarray is linked to an accession number, a unique identifier issued by GenBank to represent a nucleotide sequence. These accession numbers are grouped together into **Uni**que **Gene** (UniGene) clusters by sequence homology. Each cluster is assigned a unique UniGene ID which in turn can be linked to a gene identified during the genome sequencing process. Each of these genes is assigned to or **link**ed to a chromosomal **Locus** (LocusLink) and is assigned a unique LocusLink ID. Individual annotations such as functional categorization (Gene Ontology), chromosomal localization (LocusLink), tissue expression (UniGene), DNA sequence variation (dbSNP), links to disease (OMIM), and gene homologs and orthologs (HomoloGene- see below) may be acquired using the accession number, UniGene ID, or LocusLink ID.

To enrich the annotation for each gene, an additional resource, HomoloGene, provided by the National Center for Biotechnology Information (NCBI) is utilized. Two gene sequences are said to be homologs of each other if they share significant sequence similarity. The HomoloGene database calculates homologs by nucleotide sequence comparisons between genes across organisms (human, mouse, rat, cow, zebrafish, frog, and fly). Using HomoloGene, we can relate functional annotation information for the same gene across species (called orthologs). Thus, while a rat or mouse gene may not be annotated with any functional information in UniGene or LocusLink, its human ortholog may be extensively annotated. The functionality of orthologous genes across species is known to be similar, and this fact is used to infer the functionality of genes that are not annotated. Because we have linked probesets on different microarray platforms (e.g. single versus two channel) to standard identifiers (Accession Number, UniGene ID, and/or LocusLink ID and HomoloGene), our database can automatically link orthologous genes from different array designs of the same or different species. Currently, we provide automated annotation for probe sets from 52 chip types representing human, mouse, and rat genes, which facilitate studies across different species.

Once the base annotation data is loaded, a set of materialized views are created in a format supportive of the queries that would run against the warehouse. In these views, not only is the annotation about each gene saved, but hierarchical trees are also generated for annotation imported from Gene Ontology (functional categorization), UniGene (tissue expression), and LocusLink (chromosomal localization).

Our data integration approach facilitates powerful queries on the annotations from multiple sources. For example, it is feasible to view all genes that are transcription factors (Gene Ontology), all genes expressed in pancreas (UniGene), or all genes located on chromosome 1p31 (LocusLink).

3.2 Chip Import Utility

The Chip Import Utility (CIU), a microarray data loader application which is written in Java, is used at the MAF. Using the CIU, the data generated from this core facility and possibly other future microarray facilities are sent to the data warehouse. The GUI allows the database curator to create and enter metadata about new experiments, investigators, samples and chips. Once this metadata is entered, the data, which includes a raw image file and one or more primary numerical fluorescence intensity files, is uploaded into the data warehouse.

However, prior to importing chip data, information about the array design or array metadata on which the experiment was performed must be provided. Since there can be multiple sources and, thus, multiple vendors for these microarrays, we have formulated a general mechanism by which the information about the arrays may be imported into the database. Namely, the species from which the probes on the array were synthesized needs to be specified (i.e. human for the Affymetrix HG-U95A, mouse for the MG-U74A, etc.). Next, the array must be given a unique name (i.e. HG-U95A, MG-U74A, etc.), and each probe must be given a unique ID (i.e. 1000_at, 1001_at, etc.). Finally, to provide automatic annotation, an accession number, UniGene ID, or LocusLink ID must be provided for each probe. Once the array metadata has been imported, the array is "registered" in the database, and data derived from experiments using this array can be imported.

The importing of chip data is complicated by the fact that the data files may be in various formats. For example, there may be a header prior to the actual data,

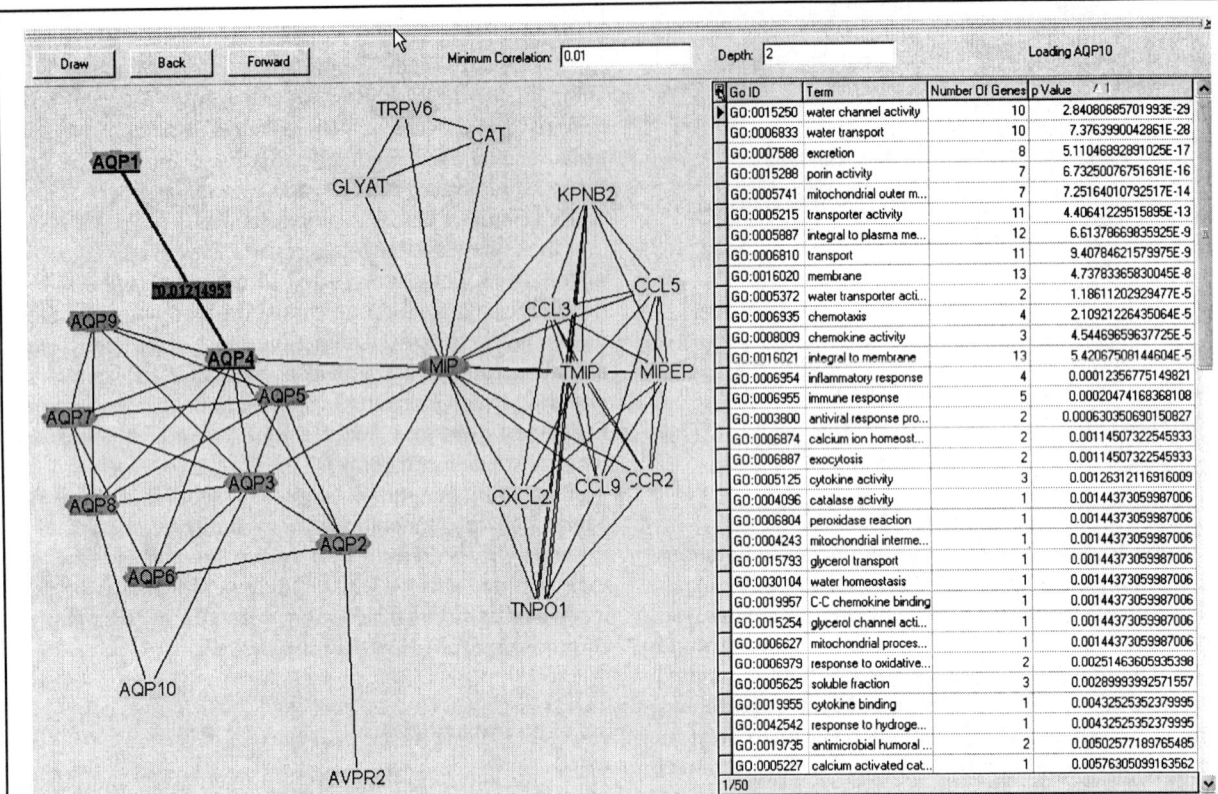

Figure 3. The Literature Gene Network window in the Function Express client displays a gene-gene literature co-citation network, centering around a selected gene (AQP4). The depth of the network (e.g. depth=2 includes all genes linked by two or fewer edges to the selected gene) and the strength of gene interaction (termed Minimum Correlation) are user configurable. The genes in this network are further grouped by Gene Ontology categories and the p value for the overrepresentation of each category in this gene set is given.

only some columns may be important to import, and different characters may delimit columns. While importing the chip data, the user will be required to provide information about these formats. To avoid entering such details again and again, an "Import Template" wizard is provided for each file format where in the user enters information about the format of data files. One can then save this template and use it for subsequent imports.

3.3 Function Express Client

The powerful features of our annotation and microarray data warehouse are leveraged by the data mining and visualization capabilities of the Function Express Client (FE). In FE, which is written in C++ using Borland Builder Enterprise 6.0, gene annotation data is accessed on demand from the database and can be coupled to gene expression data sets that are independently loaded from the MAF. Using FE it is possible to perform complex data queries using both expression and gene annotation data. For example, expression data may be filtered, normalized, and clustered; this facilitates identification of genes which are co-regulated and thus, are inferred to be involved in a particular disease process. Results of such analyses may be visualized in the context of gene annotation data. Examples of this include:

- Visualize expression of all genes that are transcription factors located on chromosome 1p and that are down-regulated in tumor samples relative to non-malignant tissue
- View expression of selected genes across different experiments conducted in same or different species on same or differing array platforms
- Display literature-based gene to gene co-citation networks

To facilitate displaying a literature-based gene network, we link over 12 million abstracts for over 500,000 gene names representing almost 200,000 distinct LocusLink IDs (or genes). The weight of a gene-gene link is calculated based on the number of abstracts where both genes are mentioned (Figure 3).

With the combined data warehouse/FE platform, the ability to access data from multiple sources for *simultaneous* meta-analysis becomes straightforward, thus increasing the analytical power of many of these studies. Through this platform, it is also possible to seamlessly

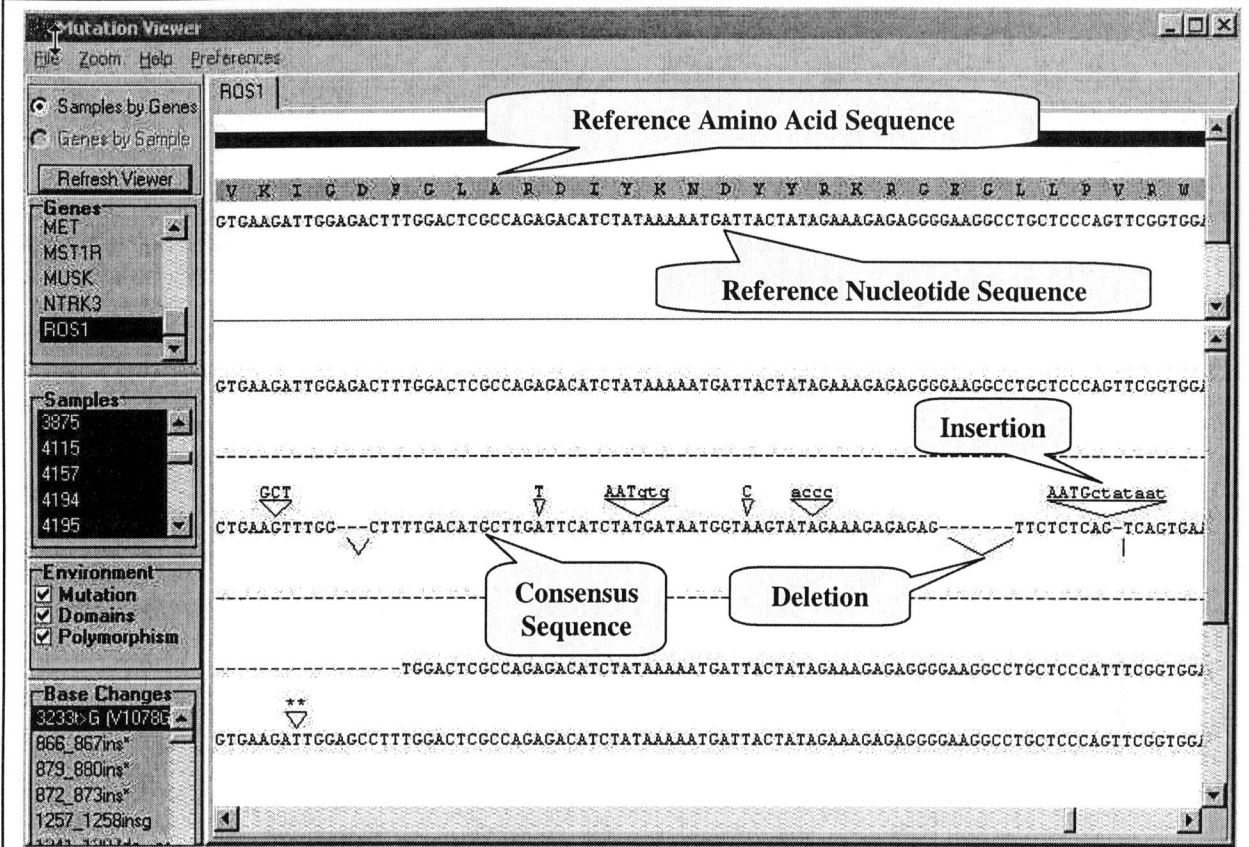

Figure 4. An example of the output from MV is shown. Selected genes, samples, and environmental features (left panel- upper two list boxes and checkbox panel) are drawn in the right two panes. The upper pane contains the reference nucleotide and amino acid sequence for ROS1. In the lower pane, each individual nucleotide sequence represents a consensus sequence from an individual patient sample, and the position of identified mutations (insertions and deletions) is indicated. Identified mutations are automatically named and are present in the lower left listbox.

integrate information from different organisms, thus clues gleaned from mouse models can be easily examined in studies involving human specimens. For instance, genes differentially regulated in a mouse model of cancer can be selected and immediately examined in human data sets to determine whether they are expressed aberrantly in corresponding human tumors. This database and software suite is constructed as an integrated set of modules so that additional genomic information, such as that derived from mutational profiling and proteomics, can also be incorporated and analyzed along with expression profiling data.

3.4 Mutation Viewer Pipeline

We have set up a process and software infrastructure where we have integrated data from the TPF and the GSC with gene annotation so that high throughput mutation profiling of large numbers of genes in hundreds of samples may be conducted. The workflow of this mutation profiling pipeline, which includes three key pieces of software we have developed, is described as follows.

DNA samples from selected specimens are bar coded, and sent to the GSC by the TPF. The design of primers for PCR amplification of selected genes is facilitated by an application, which we wrote using Borland Builder Enterprise 6.0. This software, which is a wrapper around the popular Primer3 software package, automatically designs primers for large numbers of genes in high throughput. These primers are designed using a known normal sequence called the reference sequence, which has been imported into our database by the Function Express Server from RefSeq. This primer information is then transmitted to the GSC where every primer is assigned a unique bar code, thus ensuring accurate tracking of each experiment. At the GSC, selected genes are sequenced in patient DNA samples in high throughput. The sequencing results, which may be visualized as plots for each of the bases present in DNA, need to be analyzed in an automated fashion as a single mutation profiling project may generate thousands of sequence trace files. For example, a project where 100 genes are sequenced in 100 patient samples would generate approximately 160,000 trace files.

To analyze the large number of sequence traces, we have designed and written software in Perl in collaboration with Informax, Inc. This software calculates the probability of a mutation at each base in a trace using a neural net algorithm. Traces of a single gene from an individual patient sample are analyzed together for sequence quality and are grouped together based on sequence homology to generate contigs, regions of overlapping DNA sequences. These contigs are then aligned to the reference sequence, and automated mutation/polymorphism detection is performed. The results of the initial tests with this software appear to be extremely accurate as it was necessary to manually inspect less than 1 per 1000 base calls in pilot projects. This allows us to dramatically reduce the number of traces that need to be inspected manually for potential sequence alterations. This is crucial as most mutations will occur in only a single allele and will therefore show up as 'mixed peaks' on the traces (See Figure 5). Individual trace files, consensus sequences, alignment information with respect to the reference sequence, and mutation confidence scores are imported into our warehouse for each gene-sample combination where it is then interrelated to protein domain and SNP data for each gene.

To visualize this data and to extract the salient information, we have developed a graphical user interface in C++ using Borland Builder Enterprise 6.0. In this application, called Mutation Viewer (MV, Figure 4), protein motifs (e.g. kinase domain) are shown on the DNA schematic, and mutations/polymorphisms are then "painted" onto this scaffold of protein domains, so that alterations in critical domains are easily appreciated. The presence of known SNPs (derived by scanning dbSNP) within each individual DNA are also noted on this viewer, thus commonly occurring polymorphisms can be quickly eliminated from further analysis. Furthermore, the program prioritizes mutations based on their potential functional significance (synonymous vs. non-synonymous substitutions) as well as frequency. It is also possible to zoom-in such that the amino acid and nucleotide sequence for reference and consensus sequences may be seen.

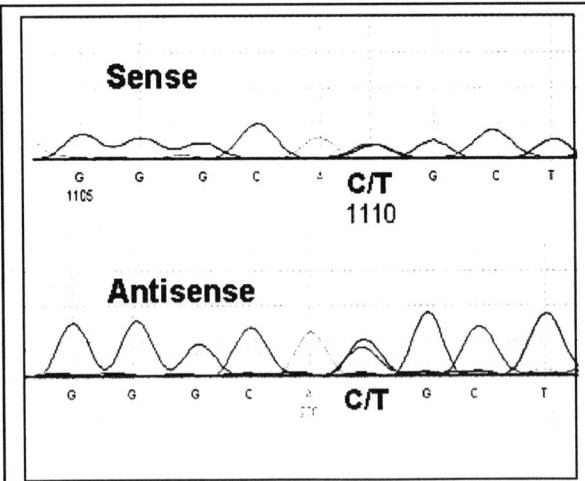

Figure 5. Example of sequence traces demonstrating a mixed peak found in a lung tumor.

Finally, the actual trace files derived from sequencing may be viewed for any consensus sequence, thus allowing the user to verify the computer-based identification of a mutation (Figure 5).

3.5 Proteomics LIMS

Experiments conducted at the PRF are aimed at identifying differentially expressed proteins in two or more patient samples (e.g. tumor versus normal) in high throughput. Protein samples, which are acquired from the TPF, are first separated into "spots" using 2D gel electrophoresis. Mass spectrometry and subsequent database searching then identify the protein at each spot. The complete workflow involves a number of laboratory steps that are sequential in nature. Users are assigned different roles based on what portion of the workflow they perform. Proteomics LIMS, which is written in Java using the Eclipse framework, is designed to automate the information flow among these roles. It also helps users in doing gel related calculations, reporting and visualization. The LIMS allows users to examine the current job queue, metadata information about each lab element, and the status of a particular lab element (tracking). The stages of the laboratory workflow where the LIMS contributes are as follows:

- Sample Procurement and Experiment Design: An investigator logs into the TPF system to request samples from already existing specimens at the TPF or to enter new specimens or samples. Metadata such as specimen source, associated pathology data, and isolation protocol are entered for each new sample. Using these samples, the investigator may design a proteomics experiment in terms of number of gels to be used and sample allocation for each gel. The completed experiment design is then sent electronically to the PRF for execution, and samples are delivered to the PRF by the TPF or the investigator.
- Sample Curation: This role uses LIMS for validating sample metadata and experiment designs.
- Sample Processing: Samples are depleted of unwanted proteins and then are subjected to a protein concentration assay. Protein concentrations are used by the LIMS to calculate the volume of each sample to be loaded on a gel.
- Gel Processing: Fluorescently labeled samples are run on IPG and SDS gels as a part of the 2D-electrophoresis. These gels are then scanned at multiple wavelengths resulting in images files that are generated for each fluorescently labeled sample. Comparative analysis of all the images from one gel or an entire experiment (consisting of multiple gels) is done using third party software to mark differentially expressed protein

spots. The LIMS stores primary image files, comparison results, and the list of differentially expressed spots. The LIMS has also implemented an image manipulation algorithm which maps coordinates of each spot from the original image file to coordinates of a second image file that the robotic picker requires for excising spots from the gel.
- Mass Spectrometry: Excised spots are trypsin (an enzyme) digested and subjected to two types of MS analysis using MALDI and ESI as ion sources. At this step, the LIMS is designed to upload spectral and peak related information for every spot into our data warehouse.

3.6 Proteomics Searching and Reporting Tools

The spectrum of a spot is searched against theoretically digested proteins from a protein sequence database to find matches. Identified proteins are automatically linked to their annotations from LocusLink, GO, UniGene and other available data sources in our data warehouse. To visualize this information, we have developed a reporting tool in Borland Builder Enterprise 6.0 that visually annotates a protein sequence with the MS and the MS/MS hits identified by multiple similarity search algorithms.

3.7 Specimen registration and banking system

Investigators use specimens and samples to carry out multi-modal (genomics, proteomics, and clinical) experiments. These specimens may be shared across experiments, modalities, or even investigators. Thus, it should be possible to analyze the results of shared specimens simultaneously. Also, it should be possible for investigators to identify specimens of interest obtained by others that have not yet been analyzed completely. This is the objective of caTIS (**ca**ncer **TIS**sue repository), the specimen registration and banking system, we are developing for the TPF. For this system to serve its purpose, every investigator must use it as a single point of entry to register their specimens. This system will be the gateway for submitting, obtaining, and querying specimens and biomolecular samples. This tissue banking effort will allow for the correlation of research results from a single specimen across multiple experimental modalities.

3.8 Authorization and Security

Biomedical research is frequently collaborative with researchers at a university sharing experimental data and results of analyses. Thus, we have developed extensive user authorization and security modules for our data warehouse where investigators use a single sign on system. Because different core facilities have varying data objects and differing access control requirements, our system provides role-based as well as object-based security.

In object-based security, privileges can be defined for both the data and metadata. For example, the metadata generated by the MAF is accessible to all users by default, and this allows investigators to query and search for microarray experiments of interest. An investigator can share the data of his experiment in the warehouse with a select set of investigators. Apart from the experimental data, the analysis results (e.g. a collection of 'interesting' genes) can also be shared and published.

In role-based security, roles are assigned to each user, and, each role has certain privileges (e.g. accessing or modifying a type of object). Therefore, a user having a specific role will be able to perform only the set of actions permitted for that role. For example, in the Proteomics LIMS, a user assigned to a particular role, may perform only certain workflows.

4. Emerging Trends

The data warehousing based solution we have implemented has the advantage of having all the data in one place, with the data transformed to match the desired queries. The queries are fast, and there is no dependence on individual data sources. There are, however, several further challenges we face.

First, with the tremendous diversity of data elements present in the biomedical domain, especially in the storage and representation of clinicopathology data such as that found in caTIS and SCIP, flexible and extensible data storage models must be utilized. One such medium for data storage and exchange, XML, is becoming increasingly important within the bioinformatics community. Since XML allows uniform description of data and metadata, it can be efficiently used to specify ontological descriptions of biomedical data. However, XML formats, like flat file formats, can be large, and complex, making data access difficult and inefficient. Better techniques on compression and lazy loading of XML data are required to make XML the universal medium for the storage of biological data.

Second, semantic integration is an important challenge that needs to be addressed. For example, the same protein sequence is known by different names or accession numbers in different biomedical data sources. These nomenclature differences must be resolved in order to integrate these data sources. One of the emerging trends is an effort to define semantics precisely through ontologies that attempt to capture concepts, objects, and their relationships within a biological domain. For example, Gene Ontology is a popular database that contains information about a gene product's cellular localization, molecular function, and biological process [1]. These ontologies encapsulating controlled vocabularies may be utilized in object models with defined data elements to describe and define entities. Additionally, there is a need for data models that efficiently store the objects and data persistently.

Such new standards, vocabularies and common data elements are evolving for different biological data sets. For example, the Microarray Gene Expression Database Group (MGED) has consolidated standardization efforts for microarray data. MGED is a consortium of academic and commercial organizations with the shared goal of defining standard formats that will allow gene expression data repositories to share and exchange data. MGED has recently published the **Minimum Information About a Microarray Experiment (MIAME)** standard, to enable interpretation of the results of an experiment unambiguously, and, potentially to reproduce the experiment. They have also developed a data exchange format, **MicroArray Gene Expression Markup Language (MAGE-ML)** and an object model, **MicroArray Gene Expression Object Model (MAGE-OM)**. Similar to microarray data sets, HUPO (Human Proteome Organization) is developing a standard called **Minimum Information About a Proteomics Experiment (MIAPE)**. Again as with MIAME, this minimum information will be described using an ontology that not only contains vocabulary terms for describing proteomics related concepts but also defines the interrelationship between these terms.

While MIAME and MIAPE provide useful guidelines for organizing gene expression and proteomic data into a database, such adequate standards do not yet exist for the description of clinicopathology data acquired from patients afflicted with most polygenic diseases. One exception is in the field of cancer, where the National Cancer Institute Center of Bioinformatics (NCICB) has made considerable progress in developing such standards. Their Enterprise Vocabulary Service provides a controlled vocabulary for the cancer domain, and their Cancer Data Standards Repository contains a set of standardized data elements used in cancer research. While many other biomedical disease domains may be able to "borrow" essential elements and design principles from these standards, each disease research initiative will ultimately have to develop such controlled vocabularies and data elements in order to facilitate data integration and reliable representation. Third, as we move from a university to a national level, our data warehousing solution may not scale when different annotation, experimental and clinical data is gathered at multiple institutions. Again, in the field of cancer, NCICB has recently started an initiative, the **ca**ncer **B**iomedical **I**nformatics **G**rid (caBIG) that will tackle such issues. This initiative aims to deploy an integrating biomedical informatics infrastructure that will connect all the cancer centers across the United States and worldwide.

5. Future Work

We have developed and deployed a data warehousing based solution for data management, integration and analysis of the biomedical data at Washington University School of Medicine. We have also developed tools to store, query, analyze, and visualize the data sets available from core facilities and publicly available annotation data sources.

Continuing this work, we will add more extensive annotation databases and will implement common data elements and underlying controlled vocabularies. We are also currently in the process of defining XML descriptions for clinical and pathology parameters and for mutation and sequence information. To facilitate this process, Oracle9i has a dedicated XML datatype called XMLTYPE where Oracle internally shreds the XML data and puts it in separate tables. In addition, we are reconfiguring the Function Express data import and export capabilities to be MIAME/MAGEML compliant by using the MAGE-OM, so that data from different types of microarray platforms may be analyzed simultaneously. Additional future work includes making Function Express and Mutation Viewer caBIG interoperable by communicating with caBIG databases, using caBIG common data elements, ontologies and vocabularies, and supporting caBIG-compatible APIs. Finally, we will expose a web services API to deliver the linked annotation from our warehouse to the outside world.

6. Conclusions

Although difficult to achieve, database interoperability is critical to the future of biomedical research. The longer this capability is delayed, the more difficult and costly establishing interconnectivity will become. The community at large should come together and build systems that conform to standards which will support common data interchange formats, dynamic, programmatic access to local and remote data sources, and common application programming interfaces. The major issue in the integration of biomedical data is the large number of distributed, semantically disparate data sources that need to be combined into a useful and usable system for biologists. The challenges are big, but so are the rewards. For the first time many incurable illnesses may be effectively treated and even cured as integrated research becomes feasible.

Acknowledgments

We would like to thank Arvind Hulgeri for all of his effort and advice in critical editing of this paper. Our most sincere gratitude goes to Anand Deshpande for his overall guidance and assistance during the initial conception of this manuscript. Finally, we wish to thank our incredibly intelligent, hard working, and dedicated team of software engineers at Persistent Systems and at Washington University who have developed the software applications described in this paper.

References

[1] M. Ashburner, C. A. Ball, J. A. Blake, et al., "Gene ontology: tool for the unification of biology. The Gene Ontology Consortium," *Nat Genet*, vol. 25, pp. 25-9, 2000.

[2] A. Bardelli, D. W. Parsons, N. Silliman, et al., "Mutational analysis of the tyrosine kinome in colorectal cancers," *Science*, vol. 300, pp. 949, 2003.

[3] S. Y. Chung and L. Wong, "Kleisli: a new tool for data integration in biology," *Trends Biotechnol*, vol. 17, pp. 351-5, 1999.

[4] S. B. Davidson, J. Crabtree, B. P. Brunk, et al., "K2/Kleisli and GUS: Experiments in integrated access to genomic data sources," *IBM Systems Journal*, vol. 40, pp. 512-531, 2001.

[5] F. Forozan, R. Karhu, J. Kononen, et al., "Genome screening by comparative genomic hybridization," *Trends Genet*, vol. 13, pp. 405-9, 1997.

[6] T. R. Golub, D. K. Slonim, P. Tamayo, et al., "Molecular classification of cancer: class discovery and class prediction by gene expression monitoring," *Science*, vol. 286, pp. 531-7, 1999.

[7] L. M. Haas, P. M. Schwarz, P. Kodali, et al., "DiscoveryLink: A system for integrated access to life sciences data sources," *IBM Systems Journal*, vol. 40, pp. 489-511, 2001.

[8] E. S. Lander, L. M. Linton, B. Birren, et al., "Initial sequencing and analysis of the human genome," *Nature*, vol. 409, pp. 860-921, 2001.

[9] K. H. Lee, "Proteomics: a technology-driven and technology-limited discovery science," *Trends Biotechnol*, vol. 19, pp. 217-22, 2001.

[10] M. Olivier, A. Aggarwal, J. Allen, et al., "A high-resolution radiation hybrid map of the human genome draft sequence," *Science*, vol. 291, pp. 1298-302, 2001.

[11] L. H. Prince and A. Carroll-Barefield, "Management implications of the Health Insurance Portability and Accountability Act," *Health Care Manag (Frederick)*, vol. 19, pp. 44-9, 2000.

[12] G. Ramsay, "DNA chips: state-of-the art," *Nat Biotechnol*, vol. 16, pp. 40-4, 1998.

[13] M. Schena, R. A. Heller, T. P. Theriault, et al., "Microarrays: biotechnology's discovery platform for functional genomics," *Trends Biotechnol*, vol. 16, pp. 301-6, 1998.

[14] V. G. Tusher, R. Tibshirani, and G. Chu, "Significance analysis of microarrays applied to the ionizing radiation response," *Proc Natl Acad Sci U S A*, vol. 98, pp. 5116-21, 2001.

[15] Z. Wang, D. Shen, D. W. Parsons, et al., "Mutational analysis of the tyrosine phosphatome in colorectal cancers," *Science*, vol. 304, pp. 1164-6, 2004.

[16] D. L. Wheeler, C. Chappey, A. E. Lash, et al., "Database resources of the National Center for Biotechnology Information," *Nucleic Acids Res*, vol. 28, pp. 10-4, 2000.

[17] R. M. Woodsmall and D. A. Benson, "Information resources at the National Center for Biotechnology Information," *Bull Med Libr Assoc*, vol. 81, pp. 282-4, 1993.

[18] E. M. Zdobnov, R. Lopez, R. Apweiler, et al., "The EBI SRS server-new features," *Bioinformatics*, vol. 18, pp. 1149-50, 2002.

The Bloomba Personal Content Database

Raymie Stata
Stata Labs, Inc., UC Santa Cruz
raymie@{statalabs.com, cs.ucsc.edu}

Patrick Hunt
Stata Labs, Inc.
phunt@statalabs.com

Thiruvalluvan M. G.
iSoftTech, Ltd.
thiru@isofttech.com

Abstract

We believe continued growth in the volume of personal content, together with a shift to a multi-device personal computing environment, will inevitably lead to the development of Personal Content Databases (PCDBs). These databases will make it easier for users to find, use, and replicate large, heterogeneous repositories of personal content.

In this paper, we describe the PCDB used to power Bloomba, a commercial personal information manager in broad use. We highlight areas where the special requirements of personal content and personal platforms have influenced the design and implementation of our PCDB. We also discuss what we have and have not been able to leverage from the database community and suggest a few lines of research that would be useful to builders of PCDBs.

1. Introduction

End users are facing two secular trends we believe will drive the development of a new type of "very large database:"

- **Proliferation of data.** Facing an explosion of email, office documents, IM transcripts, photos, and music, people need to manage an increasing number of digital items (in our view, what matters is the number, not the size, of items). Traditionally, hierarchical folders have been the primary means of managing these items. However, folders don't scale, and for increasing numbers of users, this problem is reaching crisis proportions.

- **Proliferation of devices.** Given multiple desktops (home and office), PDAs, smart phones, the Internet, and even in-dash car computers, the increasing volume of personal content is necessarily being distributed over multiple devices. Currently, movement of personal data among these devices is painful, if possible at all. Over time, this needs to become seamless if users are going to be able to fully utilize their digital content.

Today, users face a hodge podge of software and services for storing this data. Email, for example, is sometimes stored in specialized, local files (e.g., Outlook's .pst files), sometimes on servers, and sometimes replicated on both. Some office documents are stored in the local file system, but a surprisingly large number of them are stored as attachment in one's email repository. Photos are often stored in the file system, possibly indexed by specialized software running beside the file system, and also possibly replicated to a Web server. Contact information, like email, might be stored in a specialized, local file (again, a .pst file) and also synchronized out to a PDA and a phone. These various storage schemes do not interoperate, are all folder based, and are difficult to manage.

We believe this hodge podge of storage systems will be replaced by a single *Personal Content Database,* or PCDB. The PCDB will encompass all of the user's personal data: email, documents, photos, and even Web pages visited by the user. It will use associative retrieval, rather than folders, as the primary means of organizing. The PCDB will transparently move content among a user's multiple devices, and the PCDBs of multiple users will share content with each other based on policies set by the user. PCDBs will initially be small by VLDB standards – say, tens to small hundreds of gigabytes – but current trends suggest that they will grow to terabytes.

With Bloomba [1], we are trying to bring this vision to life. Bloomba is a search-based, desktop email client, with support for RSS, contact, and calendar

---

Permission to copy without fee all or part of this material is granted provided that the copies are not made or distributed for direct commercial advantage, the VLDB copyright notice and the title of the publication and its date appear, and notice is given that copying is by permission of the Very Large Data Base Endowment. To copy otherwise, or to republish, requires a fee and/or special permission from the Endowment

**Proceedings of the 30th VLDB Conference,
Toronto, Canada, 2004**

Table 1. Properties of Web vs. Personal Search

	Web Search	Personal Search
Corpus	Global & Infinite	Local & Finite
Activity	Discovery	Recovery
Computing Environment	Dedicated, Controlled	Borrowed, Hostile
Interface	Single task	Multi task
Dynamics	Batch	Interactive

management, built on a proprietary Personal Content Database. Bloomba is a commercial product, in wide use, primarily in business contexts. It replaces, rather than runs next to, other applications such as Eudora or Outlook. Its advantage is its fast, scalable search, and the productivity that results. As one CEO put it, "I estimate that Bloomba saves me about an hour per day, as a result of faster searching, quicker filing, better spam filtering and the automated organization of the smart groups." A review in Business Week put it more simply: "Bloomba is email that blows the others away."

Bloomba and its PCDB do not yet fulfill our full vision for PCDBs. Most significantly, it doesn't yet support replication. However, the positive response Bloomba has received so far suggests that PCDBs, even in limited forms, bring great value to users and will have an important role to play in the future of personal content management. In the meantime, we chose to focus first on email for a reason. Email is the largest, fastest-growing, and most dynamic collection of documents managed by most users. Also, it is becoming the primary gateway for bringing content into a personal environment, especially in a business setting. In tackling email, we've learned a lot about building PCDBs.

This paper provides an architectural overview of Bloomba's PCDB, with an eye to placing it in the context of the tradition of database work reported at VLDB and elsewhere. In the next section we describe some of the requirements and environmental constraints that shaped the PCDB. Section 3 describes the design of the PCDB. Section 4 provides a bit more design detail on a particularly interesting part of the PCDB, query execution. Section 5 discuses the concepts and technologies from the database community that we have and have not used; it also suggests areas of future research that would be of particular relevance to PCDBs. Finally, Section 6 offers some concluding remarks.

2. Requirements

Today, people are talking about personal search as if it were a simple extension of Web search. On the one hand, the success of Web search has elevated "search," as a User Interface metaphor, to a point where it is almost as widely understood as the venerable "folder" metaphor. This is a significant breakthrough. Even two years ago, the average business user had difficulty grasping Bloomba's search-based UI design. Thanks to the success of Web search, users today can quickly understand Bloomba and other applications that incorporate search as a major UI metaphor.

On the other hand, when we consider search as an application rather than a UI metaphor, Web and personal search are quite different. Further, personal search is hard, but for different reasons than Web. Table 1 summarizes some of these differences. When considering only the corpus, personal search seems much easier. The Web is vast and global; the desktop is local and finite. From a pure scale perspective, the Web is the harder problem. But personal search presents significant challenges in other ways.

Activity. First, it is easier to *discover* information than *recover* it. The simple query "Aaron Burr," for instance, will yield thousands of documents about him on the Web. For the most part, information on the Internet wants to be found; it is intentionally – even aggressively – optimized for search engines results.

But recovery of personal information requires higher precision. There is typically only one right answer, one message or document (or version of the document!) the user is looking for. Making matters worse, people typically adopt a steep discount function on our time. This means they won't invest the time to organize up front – nor should they, with the tsunami of digital information they face – so they invest it on the back end, with the expectation of a quick recovery process. Further, they know they once had the information. So the process of looking for things can quickly feel redundant, frustrating and interminably time-consuming.

Computing Environment. Web search engines are built from thousands to tens of thousands of dedicated machines. These machines are assigned specific tasks – some crawl, some index, some respond to queries. All the resources of a machine are dedicated to its one task.

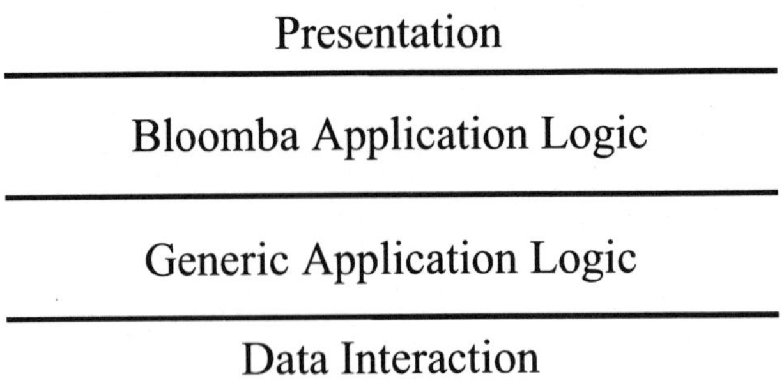

| Presentation |
| Bloomba Application Logic |
| Generic Application Logic |
| Data Interaction |

Figure 1. Architectural layering of Bloomba

On personal machines, resources such as computing cycles, RAM, and I/O transactions are expected to be dedicated primarily to the user's foreground activity. When this expectation is violated, users quickly get impatient. Thus, resources for indexing and disk-structure maintenance must be borrowed from this primary use.

In addition, Web search engines typically house their machines in dedicated host facilities with backup servers, restoration services, and redundant power supplies. Operating systems, memory configurations and hardware configurations are all finely tuned to be application-specific. The desktop is another world entirely. It's hostile. File scanners of various types can lock files for long periods of time, preventing even reads from occurring. Virus detectors and "garbage collectors" feel free to delete files they deem dangerous or redundant. And of course, there are users, who feel free to remove files and even entire directories they (mistakenly) deem to be unnecessary.

Interface. The interface to Web search engines supports a single task: executing queries. PCDBs are embedded in applications that support multiple tasks. In email, for example, finding messages is one of many tasks; users also want to view messages (and, at times, *avoid* reading messages), create them, and even relate them to their on-going projects. Search can support many of these tasks, but only if the UI is redesigned around the search paradigm (rather than being relegated to a "fast find" dialog box).

Dynamics. For the purposes of an individual query, content on the Web is static. Naturally, it changes over time, but the lifetime of a Web query is far shorter than the update cycle of the index.

Personal content, on the other hand, is dynamic, in two directions. First, new information is constantly being added. Emails come in and go out at a dizzying pace. New documents are created and sent and received as attachments. And all sort of content is being downloaded off the Web. Second, the information itself is dynamic over time. Emails change state as they are read, sent, and filed. Plus, capturing different versions of documents is essential to the flow of business. Business contracts, negotiations and agreements all have multiple versions; retrieving the correct version can have broad and deep financial implications.

In a PCDB, the lifetime of queries far exceeds these changes. As a simple example, when you look at the Inbox in a search-based email client, you are looking at the output of a query: as new messages enter the system, this output needs to be updated accordingly.

3. The Bloomba PCDB

As mentioned in the Introduction, Bloomba is a desktop, search-based, email, RSS, contact, and calendar manager, built on a proprietary Personal Content Database. In this section, we summarize the high-level design of Bloomba and its PCDB. We start by describing the layering of the Bloomba application, to provide the overall context in which the PCDB was designed. Next, we provide a brief functional description of the PCDB, summarizing its data model and the operations it supports. Finally, we describe the architecture of the PCDB itself, listing its components and explaining their functions.

3.1 Application Architecture

Even though Bloomba is a desktop system, it is structured like a modern N-tier server-based application. As illustrated in Figure 1, Bloomba is rigorously layered into four layers. Starting from the bottom, these layers have the following responsibilities:

- **Data Interaction.** The data interaction layer is responsible for data access and storage in our system. A central component of this layer is our PCDB, but it also includes other functionality, such as the protocol-specific part of message download, and the foreign-repository parsing part of import.

Rigorously separating data interaction from application logic has served us well. For example, the data access part of import – which we call a DatastoreReader – is responsible for reading foreign data stores and mapping its content in a universal model. Separate DatastoreReaders for Eudora, Mozilla, Outlook, and Outlook Express all map the foreign data to this universal model. Common application logic is used to map this universal model into Bloomba's model. This separation has made it easier to add new importers and also to tweak the details of how we map any data store into Bloomba.

- **Generic Application Logic.** The Generic Application Logic is responsible for that part of the application logic that would be common to any search-based PIM application. It includes document download and insertion, query execution, and the message-rules engine.

- **Bloomba Application Logic.** The Bloomba Application Logic is responsible for that part of the application logic that is specific to Bloomba, including folders, saved-searches, and smart groups. (As this implies, we do not see folders as being inherent to search-based email – a point illustrated by the design of Gmail [5].) In places, the generic application logic uses callback functions to call into the Bloomba Application Logic. For example, between downloading a message an inserting it into the PCDB, the Generic Application Logic calls back into the Bloomba Application Logic to ensure that the message is placed into the Inbox, which exists only at the level of the Bloomba Application Logic.

- **Presentation.** The Presentation Layer is responsible for direct interaction with the user. It's a thin layer which relies on the Bloomba Application Logic to implement the smarts of the program. This would allow us, for example, to build an alternative UI to Bloomba tailored to, say, smaller screens, such as those found on smart phones and PDAs. Also, the API between the Presentation Layer and the Bloomba Application Logic was designed to be friendly to high-latency environments, opening up the possibility of running the core part of Bloomba on one machine and its presentation another machine separated by a LAN or even a WAN.

3.2 PCDB Functionality

The PCDB is the central element of Bloomba's data-interaction layer. It is responsible for storing, searching, and returning documents.

The PCDB supports a simple, document-oriented data model more typical of an Information Retrieval system than a SQL database. In particular, the PCDB stores and retrieves objects we call *documents*. Documents themselves are immutable (although not immortal). However, documents are also associated with a mutable set of *tags*. Thus, when Bloomba receives an email message, it stores it in the PCDB as a single document. Bloomba then uses a tag to mark the message as "unread" and also uses a tag to indicate that the message is being stored in the Inbox. As the user manipulates the message, e.g., by reading it and/or moving it to another folder, the Bloomba Application Logic manipulates this tag set, not the actual message.

The PCDB's document abstraction is slightly richer than a plain sequence of characters. In particular, documents are recognized to have (immutable) fields, e.g., "From" and "Subject" are considered fields of an email message. Further, the PCDB also has a primitive notion of documents having a tree structure, i.e., a notion of compound documents containing other documents. We are considering moving to a more normalized model in which sub-documents are referred to by reference rather than by inclusion, allowing, among other things, space-savings when the same document appears as an attachment in multiple messages.

Documents in the PCDB have two different identifiers. *Document identifiers* are permanent, unique keys for individual documents. *Object identifiers* are non-unique identifiers that are shared by multiple documents that are meant to be versions of one another. For example, when a contact record in Bloomba is updated, a new document is created containing the updated version of the record. This new contact record has a unique document id, but it shares an object id with the previous versions of the record. To date, the Application Logic rarely uses object identifiers, a bit to our surprise. One idea we're considering is to eliminate object identifiers in favor of a "related-to" relationship which can track document precedence more generally than a straight versioning relationship.

In addition to storing documents themselves, the PCDB also stores *summary records* for the documents it is storing. Through a document's summary record, the application has fast access to useful summary information, such as the subject of an email, and also access to the tags associated with the document. Initially, the summary record was used solely for the purpose of quickly displaying a summary-list of large

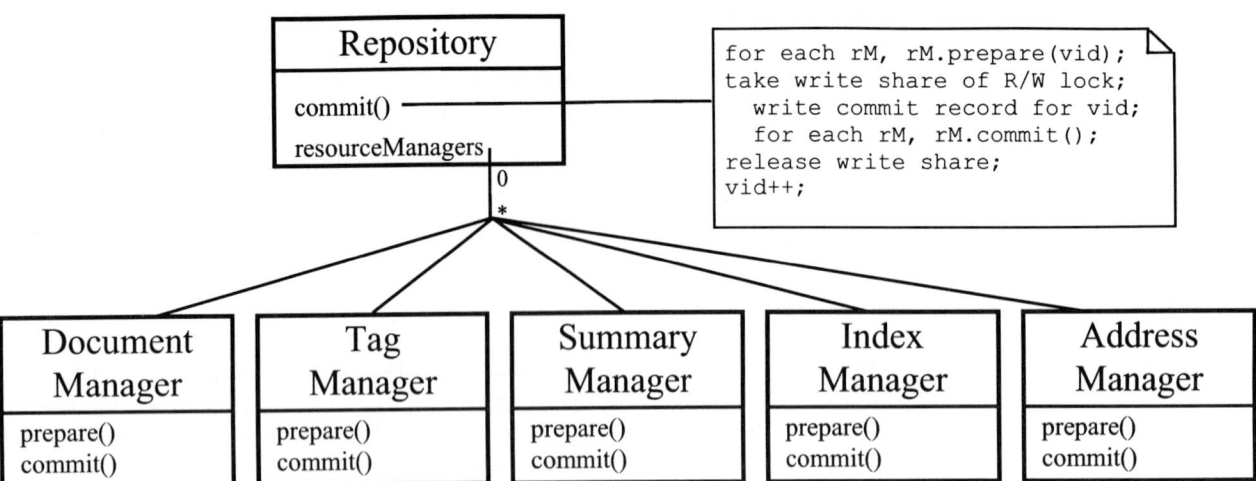

Figure 2. Component Diagram for the PCDB

result sets. However, the summary record turns out to be the only way to retrieve the full tag-set associated with a document. Thus, the summary record has been useful for implementing many pieces of application logic and is even used by the query engine.

Against this data model, the PCDB exports a simple set of operations: creation of documents, retrieval of documents and summary records, modification of tag sets, and retrieval of indexes. In our design, the PCDB is not responsible for query execution but rather for delivering indexes against which the query engine runs. The query engine itself is considered part of the Generic Application Logic.

PCDB operations run within a light-weight transaction system designed largely around ensuring atomicity of updates. Threads in the Application Logic start transactions by calling "beginTransaction" and finish by calling "commit." Writes (e.g., document creation, tag updates) must occur inside a transaction, reads need not. Transactions do not cross thread boundaries. There's no way to abort a transaction other than by crashing the program. Transactions enforce the following weak variation of the ACID properties:

- **Atomicity and durability.** Transactions are, of course, atomic in the traditional sense (all or nothing), and their effects are persistent after a successful commit.

- **Consistency.** The PCDB ensures consistency across its own data (i.e., among the documents, the summary records, the tag collections, and various indexes). In addition, at commit time, the PCDB calls a callback function that allows the application logic to maintain application-level consistency constraints. As already suggested, this callback cannot abort the current transaction; instead, it ensures consistency by modifying the data about to be committed to ensure it satisfies certain (simple) application invariants.

- **Isolation.** We provide a weak form of isolation. The writes to transactional data made by one thread are not seen by other threads until commit time. However, transactions are not serialized. For instance, if a thread T reads transactional data and another thread subsequently commits changes to that same data before T commits, then T can see the new updates in subsequent reads.

3.3 PCDB Architecture

Figure 2 contains a component diagram for our PCDB. The PCDB is decomposed into a Repository object that coordinates the activities of five Resource Managers: the Document Manager, Tag Manager, Summary Manager, Index Manager, and Address Manager.

- **Repository.** The Repository serves two roles. First, it's a "Façade" object a la the Gang-of-Four [3]: a simplified interface to the complicated interactions among the Resource Managers. Thus, for example, a single "newDoc" method in the Repository calls methods on all of the Resource Managers. Second, the Repository is a Transaction Monitor in the classic sense [6], coordinating the transactions across the five Resource Managers.

- **Document Manager.** The Document Manager is responsible for persistent storage of documents. The Document Manager stores document data in a textual format similar to mbox files; this provides an extra-level of assurance to more technical users that they can be recovered. The Document Manager has a "dup detection" feature which prevents multiple copies of the (exact) same document from being inserted more than once.

- **Tag Manager.** The Tag Manager is responsible for persistent storage of tag data. It is also responsible for delivering an inverted form of that data to the query engine. (In fact, the data is actually stored in inverted form, i.e., as a map from tag ids to lists of doc ids.)

- **Summary Manager.** The Summary Manager is responsible for persistent storage of summary records. Because summary records contain mutable tag data as well as immutable document data, the Summary Manager must support record updates.

- **Index Manager.** The Index Manager is responsible for managing the full-text index of the document data. It is the manager most responsible for the signature feature of the Bloomba product: fast, scalable search. We choose to build our own index manager for reasons of cost, functionality, and performance (see Section 5).

- **Address Manager**. The Address Manager supports a PCDB operation not mentioned in the previous subsection: a guesser for address autocomplete. It does this by managing an index of email addresses. Address autocomplete is used during message composition: as the user types a name or address into the "to" or "cc" fields of the message, Bloomba suggests completions based on what has been typed so far. Rather than list completions alphabetically, which does not scale and is also error prone, Bloomba ranks possible completions according to factors such as recency and frequency of use and displays the top-five ranking addresses in rank order. Bloomba performs this ranking over all addresses in all messages rather than just those addresses in the user's address book. The index managed by the Address Manager ensures that this ranking occurs quickly even for a corpus of tens of thousands of addresses.

The Document and Tag managers together manage data we consider *precious data*, data provided by the user that we cannot replace. The other managers store non-precious data, data which can be reconstructed from the Document and Tag managers. In the implementations of the Document and Tag managers, we have striven to emphasize transparency, in an effort to improve reliability, over performance. However, the Tag manager is in the critical path of some performance-sensitive operations, which sometimes stresses our commitment to simplicity.

A desktop-friendly footprint and behavior was an important requirement influencing the design of all these components. This requirement has not influenced our design – the components described above should be familiar to any database implementer – but rather has influenced the design one level deeper. This point is illustrated by the transaction-coordination performed by the Repository. The Repository utilizes the venerable two-phase commit protocol well known to the database community (see pseudocode in Figure 2). Nothing new in the abstract, but we've engineered the details to fulfill our desktop requirements, for example:

- **Hiding latency and deferred work.** Of course, we have pushed almost all disk activity into the "prepare" methods to minimize contention on the reader/writer lock. We go further by deferring disk-intensive work onto (persistent) work queues and perform it in the background. For example, when documents are created, they are parsed, but their tokens are not immediately inserted into the index. Instead, a background thread is created to periodically insert the tokens of multiple documents into the index as a batch.

  Even this much is familiar to the database community, but we go further still. The deferred work performed by the background thread is performed only when the machine is idle (because, as mentioned in Section 2, we are "borrowing resources"). Thus, we've engineered the Resource Managers so that (a) background work can be deferred for long periods without adversely impacting PCDB performance and (b) background tasks can be aborted before completion, which we do when we detect that the user has started using the computer again.

- **Customizing semantics.** As mentioned earlier, our transaction semantics allow at most one document-insertion transaction to run at a time. This limitation allows us to easily stream those documents directly to disk without requiring substantial disk activity in the case of an abort. This reduces buffering requirements and disk activity, leading to a more desktop-friendly footprint.

- **Accommodating hostility.** Desktop file systems are hostile environments: between virus scanners, backup programs, garbage collectors, and rouge user behavior, files can be locked, modified and even deleted in unexpected ways. All of our Resource Managers have evolved to be highly robust to these possibilities. For all file operations other than reading and writing from already-opened files, we assume that failure is common rather than a rare exception. We've designed the Resource Managers to be robust under this assumption. An example of this design-principle in action is the commit record: we've both provided several layers of redundancy for the commit record itself and have actually designed our restart sequence to work in the absence of a commit record.

- **Interactivity.** Users of desktop applications expect programs to be "responsive," which means, among other things, that the user can perform UI actions even when the system is busy with the synchronous parts of updating the database the user can see evidence of progress (e.g., a "spinning disk") for even relatively short (1/2 s) operations, can cancel long-running (>2 s) operations, and receive reasonable error messages when an operation fails (e.g., due to lack of disk space). These requirements have forced us to design a two-way communication channel that connects all layers of our system – Presentation, Application Logic, and Data Interaction. For example, as the data interaction layer is downloading a large message, it sends byte-level progress information back up to the presentation; or, when the user issues a cancellation, a signal must find its way down into the Resource Managers. Achieving interactivity has not only driven many of our detailed design decisions, it has also prevented us from using many off-the-shelf libraries (e.g., parsers) that are designed around a batch versus interactive model.

4. Query Runner

To provide a deeper look into how the requirements of the desktop environment have influenced our design, we present a deeper examination of one part of our system, *Query Runners*.

Query Runners are responsible for returning query results to the user interface. In addition to the usual constraints implied by our desktop environment (e.g., small footprint, few cycles, etc.), the design of our user-interface implied further requirements for our Query Runners:

- **Continuous.** Traditionally, queries are discrete: you start them, a result set is computed and returned, and the query terminates. In Bloomba, queries are used to populate aspects of the user-interface that need to be updated based on changes to the database. For example, when you select the "Inbox" for display in the message list, the message list is populated by a Query Runner executing the query "folder:Inbox". As the user moves messages out of the Inbox and/or new messages arrive in the background, the contents of this message list – and thus the results of this query – need to be updated automatically.

- **Counting.** Bloomba allows users to save an arbitrary number of searches. These "saved searches" are given names and are listed in a convenient location on the left-hand side of the UI (where folders are traditionally displayed). Bloomba displays a count of the messages that match each of these saved searches. These counts are tallied and provided to the UI via a special kind of Query Runner called a *Query Count Runner*.

- **Scalable concurrency.** The Bloomba user-interface runs a large number of these Query Runners in parallel: the main message list is populated by one; a large number are started for displaying message counts; and a few less-obvious ones are run for other purposes (e.g., providing fast access to one's calendar data from within the mail UI). Thus, Query Runners have to be light-weight and run in parallel.

In IR terminology, we have more of a filter engine than a query engine. That is, we're running a stream of new and changing documents against a relatively large set of fixed queries. As we discover that a new or changed document does or does not match one of these fixed queries, we need to update the result-set or count of that query. In the case of a changed document (or, more specifically, a document whose tag-set has changed), this implies knowing whether the old version of the document was or was not part of the old result set. We call this the *delta problem*.

One way to solve the delta problem is to memoize, that is, save in RAM the current result set for each query. However, the size of our result-sets can number in the thousands; multiplied by many outstanding queries, this approach does not scale. An alternative solution is to provide an "old version" and "new version" of the document to our query executive, which can then run the query twice and decide if a change is an "add," "remove," or "update." While this "pair approach" is more complicated than memoization, it scales better. Also, because documents themselves don't change but rather only their tag-sets change, the pair approach is easier to implement than it might first appear.

Given this background, let's look at the design of the Query Runner in a bit more detail. Figure 3 contains an object-diagram of the objects that cooperate to run a query. In this diagram, changes are made by the mutator thread on the right and are communicated to the query-runner thread on the left. The communication channel between these two threads is the "IndexWatcher" object. An IndexWatcher is really a producer-consumer queue of IndexPair objects (the mutator producing, the query-runner consuming).

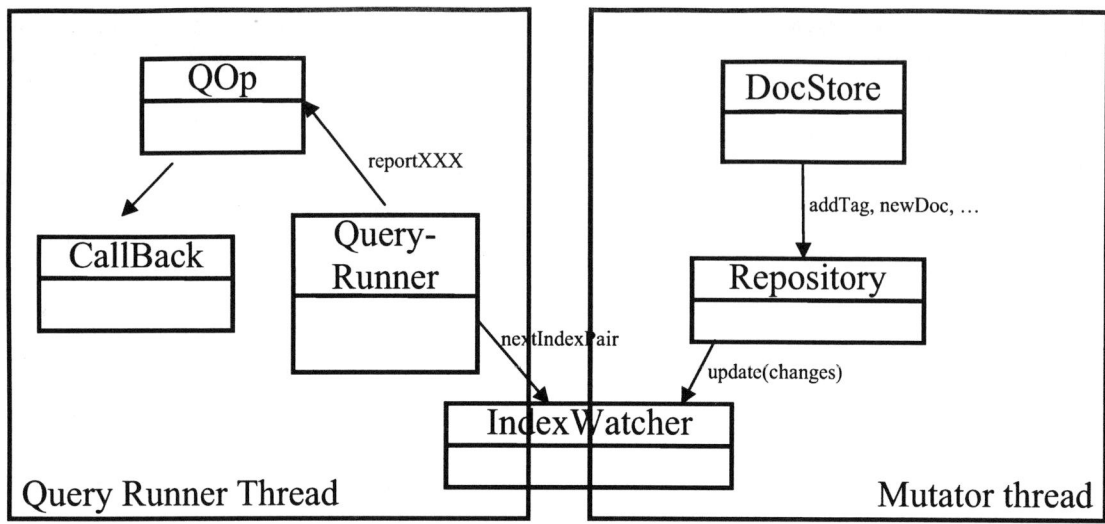

Figure 3. Object diagram for query execution

When the mutator thread commits a transaction, it places into this queue an IndexPair for the transaction. This IndexPair is a pair of Index objects, and "old state" Index and a "new state" Index. An Index object is a traditional inverted file: Given a term, the Index object returns a posting list of documents containing that term. These Index object contain posting lists for both the immutable documents and the mutable tag sets. The old and new Index objects share posting lists for the immutable terms, but have different lists for the mutable tags. The Indexes contained by an IndexPair contain postings for the same universe of documents. This universe is guaranteed to include all new and changed documents (it may include more).

The Query Runner sits in a loop asking the IndexWatcher to return the next pair in the queue. When the queue is empty, this loop blocks waiting for an update. When a new pair is returned, the query is compiled against both the old and new Indexes. From these two results sets, a delta is computed, and results are pushed up to the User Interface via the Callback object (in the lower-left of Figure 3). (As mentioned earlier, the PCDB implements just the IndexWatcher, IndexPair, and Index objects. Query compilation and execution are considered part of the application logic.)

5. The PCDB and the database community

We have been asked to comment on what we have used from the database community, what we have not used, and what we'd like to use (i.e., what database research might be of use to us).

When people from the database community learn of Bloomba they often ask, "Did you build it on a SQL database." The answer is no. When we started, we considered relational databases, XML databases, and also existing full-text indexers. In the end, we decided to build the PCDB from scratch.

As an Independent Software Vendor selling a product priced under $100, our ability to re-use existing software is severely limited by cost considerations. In particular, any commercial database would be cost-prohibitive. Still, there are a number of open-source SQL or XML databases and full-text indexing systems we could have embedded into Bloomba. When we looked at systems such as these, we found they were not suitable for personal content and/or for a desktop environment. For example:

- Early on we realized that the utility of personal data is strongly related to its freshness (i.e., people are much more likely to look for new email messages than old ones) (c.f., [2]). This observation is built into almost all of our Resource Managers: for example, the document and summary managers automatically "age" documents, and posting lists return new documents before old ones. The open-source systems we looked at did not have this same chronological bias.

- As mentioned in previous sections, for long-running operations, desktop programs need to provide feedback on progress; otherwise, users believe the system has hung. Our PCDB was built to provide such information, the open-source systems were not.

- Our PCDB uses a number of techniques to minimize its impact on other activities the user might be performing on the machine (such as editing its document). This includes minimizing the use of RAM by spilling to temporary files, and aborting intensive maintenance operations when we detect user activities. Again, the open-source systems were not written with such sensitivities in mind.

- As mentioned earlier, desktops, and Windows desktops in particular, are quite hostile environments. We were concerned that these open-source systems would not be reliable in the face of virus scanners, garbage collectors, and so forth.

While we built the PCDB from scratch, we have used a many concepts and technologies developed in the database and information retrieval communities. Our bibles have been [6], [4], and [9]. Our challenge has been more to implement existing technologies consistent with the limits and expectations of desktop applications rather than to start from a blank slate.

Looking forward, one part of the database literature we are eager to dig into is the data mining literature. We believe there are many algorithms and techniques in that literature to be effectively leveraged on personal content. As one example of this, consider contact information. In addition to the user's own collection of contact cards, Bloomba has access to email addresses and associated "Display Names" in the headers of emails, plus a plethora of contact information in message bodies themselves. Further, databases of contacts are starting to emerge on the Web [7]. While a lot of data is available, it contains lots of duplicates, contradictions, and holes. Data fusion and cleaning techniques from the world of data mining might turn this raw data into more useful information.

There are a number of areas where we wished we had more support from the database community:

- **Data models.** We do not believe that the relational model is the best model for personal content. First, while personal content is definitely typed – emails, events, and contacts are all distinct types – these data in a PCDB doesn't want to be segregated by type. If personal content wants to be grouped at all, it's into heterogeneous, dynamic groups like "Personal" or "FallRelease." Also, personal content tends to be denormalized, e.g., a contact card contains multiple phone numbers. For these and other reasons, we don't believe the relational model is a good match to personal content.

  To those who disagree and believe that the relational model is appropriate for personal content, a proof point would be nice. For those who agree, this begs the evergreen issue of the database community: If not relational, then what? We leave this question as an exercise to the reader.

- **Incrementality.** Personal Content Databases receive a steady stream of incoming data that the user often expects to be indexed as soon as it arrives. One area where it felt like we were inventing more than we wanted to is in the area of incremental indexing. In this context, "indexing" is not just the full-text indexing but other indexes in our system, e.g., the Address Manager mentioned above, or the index on our lexicon (which we haven't discussed in this paper). Many promising indexing techniques we found in the literature assumed a batch context (or didn't address index-construction at all). Also, the desktop context introduces the requirements to defer intensive work until the machine is idle, and also to minimize the amount of RAM used; incremental indexing techniques in we did find failed to consider these additional requirements.

- **Availability.** It's obvious that a Personal Content Database needs to be highly reliable in that it does not lose data. The database literature is full of techniques for increasing reliability, techniques we've been able to leverage. However, a Personal Content Database also needs to be highly *available*. When a user gets on the phone with an important customer, for example, it is disastrous if personal content crucial to the call suddenly becomes unavailable.

  The standard database approach to availability is replication, typically across multiple machines, which is not applicable in a desktop context. The database literature also makes another, less obvious assumption regarding availability: it's either all or nothing. Our progress on the problem of perceived availability accelerated greatly when we realized that partial availability has high utility for users. For example, in the "important customer on the phone" scenario, let's say the index has become corrupted (e.g., because the user inadvertently deleted a file), requiring a 30-60 minute "rebuild." In this context, if you can let the user access the Inbox (i.e., receive messages into it, read message in it, and reply to message in it), then there's a good chance the user can have the phone call even if fast searching is not available.

  Thus, architectures and algorithms that support partial availability without the user of stand-by machines would be of great value.

- **Specialized indexes.** As we seek to add even more intelligence into Bloomba, we see our selves building more specialized indexes such as the Address Manager. This feels a bit unsatisfying. First, there's a layering problem: the functionality supported by these indexes is fairly specific to Bloomba and thus best fits in the Bloomba Application Logic, yet they also need to be at the

Data Interaction layer to participate in the transaction mechanism. Second, we're concerned that, if too many of these specialized indexes are added, commit latency could suffer – which has significant impact on the user's perception of system performance. Thus, another potential area of research is an extensible, scalable, high-performance system for specialized, applogic indexes.

- **Replication.** We believe that disconnected replication is a crucially important feature for personal content databases. However, in the database literature, replication is most often considered in the context of entire-database replication or strict-subset replication.

  We believe personal content databases need document-level replication as well. To illustrate, imagine a husband and wife with a large, family photo collection. The husband and wife each want their own databases, but they want those databases to share the family photos. In fact, they may want to share those photos (or a subset) with the extended family. As one person updates the metadata on the photos, the others probably want to see those updates. What's needed here is not sharing of entire databases, therefore, but flexible sharing of documents within those repositories.

6. Summary

We believe continued growth in the volume of personal content, together with a shift to multi-device personal computing environment, will inevitably lead to the development of Personal Content Databases (PCDBs). These databases will make it easier to find, use, and replicate a large, heterogeneous repository of personal content.

The database literature already contains many useful concepts and technologies for building PCDBs. However, the requirements of PCDBs imply engineering details that differ from today's typical database systems. These requirements include the need to ensure that the majority of the machine's resources are dedicated to the user's foreground task, the need for interactivity with the user, and the need for robustness within a hostile environment. PCDBs also introduce opportunities for new areas of database research, including research into new data models, incremental indexing, partial availability, specialized indexes, and extended models of replication.

Acknowledgements

Bloomba and its PCDB owe their existence to the entire teams at Stata Labs and Integrated SoftTech Solutions.

References

[1] Bloomba: http://www.statalabs.com

[2] Dumais, Cutrell, Cadiz, Jancke, Sarin, Robbins. Stuff I've Seen: A system for personal information retrieval and re-use. *Proceedings of SIGIR 2003*. Association for Computing Machinery, 2003.

[3] Gamma, Helm, Johnson, Vlissides. *Design Patterns: Elements of Reusable Object-Oriented Software.* Addison-Wesley, 1995.

[4] Garcia-Molina, Ullman, Widom. *Database System Implementation.* Prentice Hall, 1999.

[5] Gmail: http://gmail.google.com

[6] Gray, Reuter. *Transaction Processing: Concepts and Techniques.* Morgan Kaufmann, 1993.

[7] Plaxo: http://www.plaxo/com

[9] Witten, Moffat, Bell. Managing Gigabytes: Compressing and Indexing Documents and Images, 2nd Ed. Morgan Kaufmann, 1999.

Trends in Data Warehousing: A Practitioner's View

William O'Connell

IBM Toronto Lab
boconnel@ca.ibm.com

Abstract

This talk will present emerging data warehousing reference architectures, and focus on trends and directions that are shaping these enterprise installations. Implications will be highlighted, including both of new and old technology. Stack seamless integration is also pivotal to success, which also has significant implications on things such as Metadata.

Trends in Data Warehousing

Industries experience with data warehousing over the last decade has provided important lessons on what works in today's business intelligence (BI) solutions. It is not only these lessons, but also the emerging trends which are also shaping our industry directions in business solutions. As a result, our emerging reference architectures used in building these enterprise data warehouse solutions are changing to meet business demands.

This evolving reference architecture used in building solutions will be overviewed, followed by the implications of these changes. It is these evolving reference architectures that are putting new demands on the databases that are used in warehousing. An important point is that although many of these concepts are not new, databases are being pushed in new ways which are requiring further technology invention.

With the emergence and evolution of the intranet, as well as more businesses exploiting semi-structured data, the more traditional business models are evolving with respect to such things as data accessibility, delivery, and concurrency. Technology such as XML and webservices become more critical as databases integrate with web portals and BI tooling. Moreover, additional demands on more broad decision making within enterprises are causing heavy consolidation and non-traditional mixed workloads (heavily mixing OLTP and DSS) beyond what has been conventional in the past. Service level agreements, as well as normal operational characteristics are not the same (e.g., backups). Moreover, in many cases the consolidation is not an option and or desired. In such latter cases, the business question still needs to be run. As a result, federation augmentation is also very real in enterprise systems. Query management in a federated environment is still a challenging task. A combination of consolidation and federation augmentation is being seen.

In addition to heavy consolidation and federation augmentation, both real-time (right-time) and active data warehousing systems are being built. These systems present interesting challenges to traditional maintenance and extract/transformation/load operational procedures. Specifically, in large multi-terabyte systems which are 24x7x365. Queries in such systems that execute over aggregated data (including materialized views) need to be very close in time to a consolidated operational data store (ODS) in the same enterprise data warehouse. The maintenance challenges are pushing the technology. Finally, the closed loop processing in an enterprise-wide solution, allows warehouses to play an even more crucial role. Not only are operational systems creating events, so are data warehouses; they play a crucial active role in an enterprise. One such example of events produced in a warehouse is measures, which may be key business indicators (KPIs) used in business performance monitoring through portals.

In addition to this talk presenting emerging data warehousing reference architectures, trends and directions shaping these enterprise data warehousing installations will be overviewed. In doing so, some key implications to databases will be highlighted. In addition to the database itself, any warehouse solution consists of a solution stack. Implications on the whole stack will be touched upon, including such things as metadata and interoperability via standard interfaces such as XML.

Permission to copy without fee all or part of this material is granted provided that the copies are not made or distributed for direct commercial advantage, the VLDB copyright notice and the title of the publication and its date appear, and notice is given that copying is by permission of the Very Large Data Base Endowment. To copy otherwise, or to republish, requires a fee and/or special permission from the Endowment

**Proceedings of the 30th VLDB Conference,
Toronto, Canada, 2004**

Technology Challenges in a Data Warehouse

Ramesh Bhashyam

NCR Corporation
Teradata Research and Development
San Diego, California
USA
Bhashyam.ramesh@ncr.com

Abstract

This presentation will discuss several database technology challenges that are faced when building a data warehouse. It will touch on the challenges posed by high capacity drives and the mechanisms in Teradata DBMS to address that. It will consider the features and capabilities required of a database in a mixed application environment of a warehouse and some solutions to address that.

A data warehouse integrates large volumes of detailed and current data across entire organizations and enables different forms of decision making from the same data base. It provides a unified view of operational and historical data. It will often use as a foundation a detailed data model and enable different summaries or views, as appropriate to the business, to be built on top of the detailed model.

The usage of a data warehouse has evolved from reporting and decision support system to mission critical decision-making operational systems. Data warehouses are often used for mining types of applications. These applications read massive volumes of data from within the data warehouse and are demanding of both CPU and IO resources. Data warehouses can also be used for operational decision-making applications, applications which read a small but well-focused set of data from the warehouse, and use few resources. These operational applications are differentiated by short response time requirements, making scalability a challenge. Data warehouses that combine both these types of applications require that the operational data be integrated, current and up to date. The common belief that warehouse data is static is no longer valid.

An emerging requirement is that warehouses should have the ability to detect events and enable actions based on complex analysis. For example, the decision to replenish an item may be based on wider criteria than simply low inventory levels.

In this talk we will examine some of the technology challenges to a successful implementation of a data warehouse.

Various components of a data warehouse hardware platform have seen impressive improvements but these various improvements have not been equally powerful. This has led to imbalances in comparative performances. For example, although the CPU power has followed Amdahl's law and has improved significantly, the ability to supply the processor with data has not improved to the same degree. This imbalance is best observed in the disk subsystem. Disk storage capacities have gone up from few GB a few years ago to hundreds or even thousands of GB now - a factor of several hundred. However, the access rates have gone up by only a factor of three or four. So the challenge is how to adopt the latest high capacity drives while not impacting performance for IO intensive applications. Some of the techniques that Teradata uses in this context will be detailed.

It is well accepted that the only viable solution for large warehouses is a shared nothing MPP platform. But there are challenges to making operational queries demonstrate scalable performance on such platforms. While the optimizer, combined with proper data distribution, are important prerequisites for making complex queries scale, more is needed from the execution engine and the optimizer for making very short queries similarly

Permission to copy without fee all or part of this material is granted provided that the copies are not made or distributed for direct commercial advantage, the VLDB copyright notice and the title of the publication and its date appear, and notice is given that copying is by permission of the Very Large Data Base Endowment. To copy otherwise, or to republish, requires a fee and/or special permission from the Endowment

**Proceedings of the 30th VLDB Conference,
Toronto, Canada, 2004**

scalable. This must be achieved without affecting complex query scalability. Typical solution such as table duplication and storing tables in few nodes are inappropriate for complex queries although they are good for operational queries.

An important area for operational query performance is indexes. Operational queries access a focused set of data. They may access few rows from a number of tables and join them. These queries are not resource intensive but require short response times. Different kinds of secondary indexes that enrich the mechanisms available for accessing base table rows are therefore important. These include both local indexes and global indexes. In addition various forms of materialized views such as Teradata's Join Indexes and aggregate join indexes are important. The join indexes are also appropriate for complex queries besides short operational queries.

Managing a multi-user system with very different application profiles requires sophisticated workload management. Workload management implies maximizing system throughput while meeting widely varying service levels. Management can be broadly classified under two distinct categories - controlling access to the system and managing access once inside the system. While both of these are non-trivial problems, they are even more challenging in a parallel architecture where multiple threads and processes execute on behalf of a query from within a single node and from across multiple nodes.

Finally, integrating a warehouse to the external system and closing the loop by taking action based on analysis is the most recent technology challenge. Most existing technologies allow interaction with a data warehouse using a pull model. In such a model the application or user periodically polls the database for analysis or state changes. However a push model becomes essential for data warehouses that must integrate and provide notifications on actionable events to external systems. In a push model a change in "status" is evaluated and a user or application is asynchronously notified. It is also important to understand what a change means. The definition of a change must evolve from simple state changes such as "inventory below a level" to complex analytics based state changes. Such an environment requires that data ingest be asynchronous with data processing which must be asynchronous with analysis output through events. Simple database triggers therefore are insufficient for this model.

This talk will address some or all of these warehouse technology challenges.

Sybase IQ Multiplex – Designed For Analytics

Roger MacNicol   Blaine French

Sybase Inc
561 Virginia Road
Concord, MA 01742

rdm@sybase.com   blainef@sybase.com

Abstract

The internal design of database systems has traditionally given primacy to the needs of transactional data. A radical re-evaluation of the internal design giving primacy to the needs of complex analytics shows clear benefits in large databases for both single servers and in multi-node shared-disk grid computing. This design supports the trend to keep more years of more finely grained data online by ameliorating the data explosion problem.

1. Background

Historically, databases have been designed around the requirement to support large numbers of small concurrent updates. The primary design criterion has been to minimize the portion of stored data that must be locked for exclusive access and the length of time that locks are held. Consequently, when the writer of data has primacy, the internal design generally adheres to the following rules

1. Data should be stored in rows to enable a single disk i/o to write the modified data out to the table.
2. Data should be stored on small page sizes to minimize the i/o cost and portion of disk locked for exclusive access.
3. The database must support the imperfect notion of isolation levels to enable reports to run in acceptable time while negotiating held locks.
4. Few columns should be indexed because locks on tree structures may deny access to more rows than row-page locks and increase the time locks are held.
5. Data pages should typically not be compressed because of poor amortization of the compression cost. Rows typically do not compress well because of the mix of data types stored adjacently.
6. Adding or dropping a column or index may be expensive since page storage may need to be updated for all rows.
7. Searched update statements may be relatively expensive since the entire row must be read and written for a single column to be updated.

Given these consequences, IQ's designers started by asking one fundamental question "What would a database look like internally if it were designed from the ground up for complex analytics on massive amounts of data"? It was understood that a reader-friendly analytics server must also support many concurrent update streams and, increasingly, it would be an operational data store rather than a store for cleansed and summarized data. But, data update streams in such a server are likely to be well-bounded. Once the primary criterion for the internal design becomes the performance of complex analytics, rather than row-oriented updates, a radical *volte-face* in design becomes self-obvious.

2. Designed for analytics

Typical analytical queries access relatively few columns of the storage-dominating fact tables and may access a notable proportion of the rows stored in the fact tables. While CPU performance and available cache memory has increased dramatically with 64-bit servers and lower memory prices, disk performance has not kept up and, consequently, disk-bound performance is typical for many analytics. So, were design primacy to be given to complex analytics, many of the previous rules are reversed as follows:

Permission to copy without fee all or part of this material is granted provided that the copies are not made or distributed for direct commercial advantage, the VLDB copyright notice and the title of the publication and its date appear, and notice is given that copying is by permission of the Very Large Data Base Endowment. To copy otherwise, or to republish, requires a fee and/or special permission from the Endowment
**Proceedings of the 30th VLDB Conference,
Toronto, Canada, 2004**

1. Data would be stored in columns, not rows, so only the columns required to answer a query need be read – in effect every possible ad-hoc query could have performance akin to a covering index. Since data is only written once but read many times any increase in load time would be more than offset by improved query performance. Column storage would enhance main cache efficiency since commonly used columns would be more likely to be cached.
2. Data would be stored in a large page size so that many cells of a column can be retrieved in a single read and the larger page size plays to technological changes in how physical disk reads are structured. Traditional DBMS cannot use large pages sizes since each read drags along unneeded columns in the row.
3. The database would use page-level snapshot versioning so that data modification happens without interfering with running reports. Consequently, there would be no need for the notion of isolation levels – every query would see an internally consistent database state while navigating a nearly lockless environment.
4. Every column could be indexed: data will be written once and read many times so the cost will be amortized. Column storage at the physical layer greatly simplifies parallel index updates and adding an index requires only that column to be read, not the entire row.
5. Data could be compressed on disk. The compression cost would be well amortized and the homogenous datatype of a stored column would offer optimal compression.
6. Adding or dropping a column or index to reflect changing business requirements would be cheap, as no other data would be accessed.
7. Searched updates would be relatively cheap since only the columns being modified would need to be read and written.

From these design principles, IQ was developed from the ground up to be a 64-bit DBMS using kernel threads giving design primacy to the needs of complex analytics without compromising load performance.

3. Designed for scalability (Multiplex)

Sybase IQ optimizes workloads across multiple servers through Sybase IQ-M, which is a multi-node, shared-storage, parallel database system whose design focus is on large-scale data warehousing workloads. IQ-M offers grid-computing through multiple IQ instances running on multiple server nodes connected to a single shared IQ data store, which can comprise multiple disk arrays. Each node (instance) sees the entire database and has direct physical access to it, unlike the horizontally partitioned databases (such as MPP (massively parallel processors) with shared-nothing architecture). There are two types of IQ-M nodes, writer (one per Multiplex) and reader (all other nodes in the Multiplex).

1. The Writer node owns all database locks, performs DBA tasks, and updates the database. The Writer is tuned for data loading efficiency and speed.
2. Reader nodes have read only access to the shared database and perform tasks such as ad-hoc queries and reporting. The reader access data without the need for acquiring locks or for a distributed lock manager.

There is no node-to-node interference since a single query is limited to a single node. The use of snapshot versioning requires minimal communication between the IQ-M nodes, consequently there is no requirement for an expensive high-speed interconnect between nodes.

The design offers a better approach to analytics scalability. Adding additional applications and users to a database can be solved simply by adding additional cheaper reader nodes. The impact of additional nodes on existing nodes is minimal until the disk array is saturated. The non-traditional storage model offered by IQ's design enables more user requests to be satisfied before for a given disk configuration is saturated than traditional DBMS clusters since each node typically accesses fewer pages to satisfy each query.

4. The role of compression

Vertical storage enables IQ to use a multi-tiered compression strategy:
1. Domains that have less than 65,535 distinct values are stored in enumerated form. A column store can use enumeration directly as the stored form rather than in an data structure.
2. Each column is written to disk using a compression algorithm specifically tailored to the patterns typical of its datatype.
3. Index record lists are stored in compressed form as segmented bitmaps. Bitmap index pages utilize a range of internal representations depending on the density of bits in any given segment.

A consistent emphasis on data compression has advantages. **First**, it requires less disk space and a smaller storage system footprint than other DBMS, reducing both system purchase and administration costs. **Second**, the required disk I/O bandwidth is typically reduced by over 90% allowing better CPU utilization. Sybase IQ systems are typically CPU bound unlike conventional DBMS, which are typically I/O bound. **Third**, as a result of using a large I/O request size, Sybase IQ systems can exploit denser disk configurations using fewer larger disks than other DBMS without sacrificing performance. **Fourth**, because Sybase IQ reads only the columns referenced, it has a smaller memory footprint.

Businesses and government regulations are requiring: more data to be kept online; that it be kept highly available; and for that data to be more finely grained. Increasingly, a DW must keep operational data and not summarized data to meet reporting requirements. A column store enables more operational data to be kept online on a given configuration through the combination of enumerated storage and better compression thus ameliorating the inherent data explosion problem.

5. Query efficiency

The combination of column storage and compression enables every column in a Sybase IQ database to be indexed, often with more than one index type. For a column store, the results of the Where clause needs to be a mask of rows to be projected that can be applied to each column and virtual rows created as cells are read in parallel from each column and combined. This mask takes the form of a bitmap termed the "foundset".

The IQ query engine aims to make maximal use of available indices and push all sensible predicates (including predicates on functions and expressions) into column indexes in parallel. The result of each predicate is a bitmap of rows. The resulting bitmaps are combined through Boolean operators to solve the Where clause. Having bitmap indexes on all columns means that IQ does not need or support "update statistics" – meta-data required by the optimizer is obtained directly from the indexes and, by definition, is never stale.

6. Sizing rules

Sizing rules for IQ: I/O efficiency and comparison with typical RDBMS

DBsize/raw data size:	0.4-0.9 vs 2-8
Storage:	RAID_5_ovhd B vs RAID_1_ovhd
DB page size:	256K-512K vs 2K-32K
IO Bandwidth per CPU:	8 MB/s vs 10-200
Typical io/sec per CPU:	<100 vs >1000
Optimal disk size:	100GB vs 18-36GB

7. Results on Multi-Node system

A recent benchmark on a Sun Fire 6800 (24 750MHz US-III CPUs, 48GB RAM) of the current shipping version of IQ Multiplex showed 64-bit addressing by using 40 GB RAM for the IQ cache. Storage was on Sun StorEdge T3 arrays. 253 million rows were loaded in 1h35min for a loading speed of 2.6 million rows/min or 160 million rows/hour. 79 GB of raw input data was compressed to 33 GB (41% of its raw size).

Several queries were run first on a single domain, and then on four multiplex domains simultaneously against a single IQ-M data store. Each query test consisted of running 10 queries concurrently on one domain. As more domains were added to the Multiplex to run additional query streams, the overall query response times stayed the same (one would have expected degradation in performance as more query streams were being run against the same database on the same shared storage), and demonstrated excellent scalability of the described design. The following table gives time in seconds for a single domain and the range of times for four domains:

Query	Single domain	4 Multiplex domains
1a	2434	2372 - 2419
1b	2705	2660 - 2811
2a	1992	1936 - 1978
2b	2324	2446 - 2305
3a	2853	2806 - 2849
3b	2326	2287 - 2446
4a	731	665 - 693
4b	725	662 – 690
5a	672	797 - 832
5b	692	684 - 778

8. Summary

Sybase IQ-M demonstrates that complex analytics on very large databases benefit from a radical re-evaluation of many aspects of internal database design. By basing the primary design assumptions on the nature of analytic workloads, the combination of column storage, bitmaps, aggressive compression, and shared disk grid-computing through IQ Multiplex offers significant performance benefits for multi-terabyte databases.

PANELS

Biological Data Management: Research, Practice and Opportunities

Thodoros Topaloglou
Senior Vice President, Scientific Computing
MDS Proteomics, Toronto, Canada
ttopaloglou@mdsp.com

1. Panelists

Susan B. Davidson, Professor of Computer and Information Science, and Bioinformatics, UPenn

H. V. Jagadish, Professor of Electrical Engineering and Computer Science, and Bioinformatics, University of Michigan

Victor M. Markowitz, Chief Informatics Officer Joint Genome Institute and Head of Biological Data Management and Technology Center at Lawrence Berkeley National Laboratory

Evan W. Steeg, Independent Bioinformatics Consultant

Mike Tyers, Senior Investigator, Samuel Lunenfeld Research Institute and Professor of Medical Genetics and Microbiology, University of Toronto

2. Introduction

Biological research and drug development are routinely producing terabytes of data that need to be organized, queried and reduced to useful scientific knowledge. Although data management technology can provide solutions to problems, in practice the data needs of biomedical research are not well served. The goal of this panel is to expose the barriers blocking the effective application of advanced data management technology to biological data.

Management of biological data involves acquisition, modeling, storage, integration, analysis and interpretation of diverse data types including analog signals, digital images, sequences, spreadsheets, taxonomies, structured records and unstructured text data. Existing data management technology is often challenged by the lack of stability, evolving nature, diversity and implicit scientific context that characterize biological data.

3. Biological Data Management

Why is biological data management such an important field? Just in the last 10 years we have witnessed the sequencing of the human genome, the genesis and widespread use of gene arrays, the industrialization of Proteomics and an explosion in biological data available in reference public databases and special purpose information products. These advances have profound influence in biology and drug discovery. Biological research has transformed from a purely experimental to an information-driven discovery science. Drug development is moving away from the hit-and-miss model towards rational and information-driven practices. Today, a biology student can get access to all the elements of a biological system (that is, the complete genome sequence and all the genes and proteins encoded by the genome) from (more than one) archival databases, and do hypothesis-driven science or global analyses.

The volume of available data and the pace by which post genomic era technologies generate data creates both risks and challenges that biological data management has to tackle. Is biological data management up to the task? The answer varies depending on who provides it: the database researcher, the bioscience user, and the bioinformatics practitioner in industry and in research. The answer to this question is also a topic that will be addressed by the panelists. Here we will briefly outline the different perspectives and translate them into a list of provocative statements that the panelists will elaborate on.

3. Biological Data Challenges

What do biological data look like and how are they used in research and drug development? Biological data are broad and diverse. Biology encompasses many domains of knowledge (molecular and cell biology, genetics, structural biology, pharmacology, physiology, etc.) each one of which is concerned with overlapping or complementary entity types, and has it is own terminology and data needs. Furthermore, the variety of experimental procedures yield related but not identical data. New bio-analytical procedures and progress in the science add another dimension of instability to biological data types. The data types vary from sequences, to 3-dim structures, images, graph structures, data tables, semi-structured and unstructured text.

Most of the information that the biological research is interested in is available in public reference databases, specialized private data sources, and the over 12 million articles of the scientific research literature, most of which is accessible on the web. It is estimated that 80% of the biological data are in text form, and the rest resides in databases that range from indexed files, to relational and specialized formats. Biological databases may contain primary data i.e., have their own data entry or submission policy, or secondary data i.e., built by integrating data from primary sources in which case their integrity depends on the constituent sources. As many of these data sources are non-standard and not well documented, accessing, integrating and sharing biological data becomes a challenge and an art.

4. Current Practice

Despite the challenges, scientific users have available a wealth of information, and have built specialized applications to access portions of it. The widespread use of the web and Excel spreadsheets, makes the ad-hoc and unsustainable data access practices, unnoticeable to many. To the bioscientist, database development means production of a dataset and not the construction of system that manages data. The separation of the application from the representation is also not recognized as well as the need for a DBMS. Even when a DBMS is used, standard database design principles are not always followed. Just imagine the gains in productivity if all the loss of time due to sub-optimal means of managing and accessing data, were to be replaced with efficient data management solutions.

So, what stands in the way? Education is perhaps the single most significant obstacle. As the biology sounds complicated and distant to the database community, and truly is, similarly data management technology is distant and incomprehensive to the biosciences. Only a small fraction of database professionals has crossed paths with biology compare to financials for instance.

In the biopharmaceutical industry the situation is much better. Due to the size of the data management problem, concerns of productivity and sometimes regulatory requirements, many organizations are taking aggressive steps to establish strong information management practices. Data management technology and database vendors are partners in such endeavors. Oftentimes the state of the art in data management technology may not be able to provide a complete solution and needs to be extended. For example, federated queries against heterogeneous data sources had limited DBMS support a few years ago, support for generic transformations from one representation is still not solved in DBMSs, and workflow management solutions are not there either. Our panelists are invited to describe examples where the biological data management requirements have led to the development of novel solutions that have contributed to the state of the art in database technology.

The scale and scope of the data management problem varies between organizations that generate data and centers that host community databases.

The "data cycle" in an organization that generates data, such as MDS Proteomics or a sequencing laboratory, starts with sample tracking, followed by the laboratory processing that produces vast amount of raw data, followed by analytical processing to translate the signals to measurements, to biological data such as sequence tags or abundance of gene or proteins, and ultimately to conclusions. There are several heterogeneous information systems with distinct data requirements involved in this process. Data and process tracking, data file management, high performance algorithms for data processing, efficient database loading and workflow management are everyday business whether or not optimal technology options exist. Daily production rates are in the order of tens of Gigabytes a fraction of which ultimately makes it into relational databases.

In the community database environments the pressure points are different. The two important functions are data curation / annotation and web publishing. Technology and tools for data curation and annotation has been the focus of bioinformatics research from the early days, and is still an active area of research with a significant data integration and application interoperability challenge as part of it. Fast access to community database data from the web could be served by "off the shelf" technology, however, for historical reasons or due to the specialized data types, specialized indexing schemes and sequence similarity search applications are deployed.

The solutions providers in biological data management vary across the board. Scientific users in academia are supported by bioinformaticians which in some cases, but not always, are linked to the data management community. In research networks such as the NIH, DOE and EMBL, biological data management is well served by groups that have pioneered in the field such as LBL, NCBI, EBI, CBIL and others. In industry, certain companies have built their own centers of excellence and others access the services of specialized vendors. In terms of tools, the field started with its own homegrown solutions such as AceDB and over time migrated to relational technology where the popular choices include MySQL, Oracle and DB2. XML is also popular as a data exchange format and oftentimes is misused as a data management solution but without the management tools support that the database community is active on. Finally, Excel and Perl/CGI contribute to the successes and to the pitfalls in managing biological data as they make users, for a while, independent of professional data management, which ultimately comes in to solve the scalability, performance or integration problems.

5. Open Problems

In recent a workshop organized by NSF[1], scientists from database research and biosciences debated the open problems in biological data management as perceived by both communities and aimed at defining a research agenda for data management technology support of basic and applied research in molecular and cell biology. The participants were asked to contribute an opinion paper based on a list of suggested topics.

---

[1] "Database Management for Life Science Research: Summary Report of the Workshop on Data Management for Molecular an Cell Biology at the National Library of Medicine, Bethesda, Maryland, Feb 2-3, 2003", Jagadish, H.V., and Olken, F. OMICS, Vol. 7, No. 1, 2003.

We reviewed 27 opinion papers grouped in four categories based on the author's background. The categories include database/comp.science (DB/CS) background with academic (AC) or industry (IN) affiliation, and bioinformatics/biology (BFX/BL) background with academic or industry affiliation. The research institution affiliation was counted as academic. The number under each category indicates the category membership. The list of topics is extracted from the papers themselves and is slightly different than the suggested topics. A topic is given a check if it is mentioned as a challenge, open problem or proposed for future work in a paper. The following table summarizes the importance count of each topic.

Topic	DB/CS AC (13)	DB/CS IN (4)	BFX/BL AC (8)	BFX/BL IN (3)	#
hierarchical repr., taxonomies			xx		2
biological data types	xxxx		xxxx		8
heterogenous, complex queries	xx	x	xx		5
schema mgmt, data transformation	x	x			2
data exchange formats	x		x		2
metadata repr. / management	x		xxx		4
ontologies, controlled vocabularies	x	xx	xxxxx	xx	10
interoperability, web services		xx	x	x	4
data quality	x	x	x		3
data provenance	x	xx			3
data modeling / data evolution	x	x	x		3
graph / pathway representation	xxx				3
data integration / semantics	xxxxx	xxx		x	9
workflow management		x	x		2
text mining			xx		2
natural language processing			x		1
understanding scientific requirements	x		xx		3
data life cycle		xx			2
semi-structured data / XML, ANS1	xxx	x			4
usability/ robustness/ performance	x	x			2
visualization	x				1

Ontology development was the top pick with data integration and support for biological data types close behind. The next group of important topics includes support for heterogeneous and complex queries, interoperability and web-services, metadata representation and management, and support for semi-structured data and XML. The low number of industry participants and the exclusion of drug research as an area of focus, leave some open questions that our panelist will have to comment on. For example, one would expect that schema management, workflow management and data provenance are important to technology practitioners while text mining, data quality metrics and visualization are important to the industrial scientist. Nobody besides academic computer scientists selected the graph representation as an important topic, is this really the case?

The fact that ontologies, controlled vocabularies and domain specific terminologies was commented across the board but mostly by the user community, speaks of the importance of domain aware data management. But should the computer scientists embark on developing terminology for biology? Clearly not, but their information management tools should be compatible with such concepts, for instance by allowing attribute domains to be hierarchical terminologies and by providing proper query support for those. Also, repositories of domain terminologies, common schemas components and tools to manage and extend those can shift the paradigm of database development for biosciences as software information repositories impacted software engineering in the past.

Reference to the concepts of semantic web, web services, WSDL, and XML was made mainly by the industrial participants. Clearly these concepts have become popular in industrial bioinformatics and the database community is further ahead, but so far this topic has received little attention in the biological data management literature. Is it an area of promise for follow up research? Good question for our panelists. They are also invited to make the connection with some earlier efforts for creating interoperability and integration infrastructures for bioinformatics, the infamous CORBA/JAVA buzz, which led to some unsatisfying results.

3. Panel Questions

Our panelists are invited to comment on the following questions:

1. Is the current state of biological data management well suited to support the bioinformatics challenges in biological research and drug discovery?
2. Interpret the data of the above table. Do you agree with the top five priorities? Or, what your top five choices would be? Are there any other important topics that should be added?
3. Do the areas above require new or additional research? Or can existing data management tools and methods be adapted for them?
4. Discuss the difference between problems in the above areas and problems in analogous traditional data management areas.
5. Provide examples of biological data management systems that address (some of) the problems in the areas above
6. Comment on adequacy of commercial DBMSs and tools for these problems.
7. Does the database research community need more education with respect to the challenges in biology and drug discovery, and if so, what do you propose

Where is Business Intelligence taking today's Database Systems?

William O'Connell

IBM Toronto Lab
boconnel@ca.ibm.com

Panel Participants

Andy Witkowski
Oracle
andrew.witkowski@oracle.com

Ramesh Bhashyam
NCR-Teradata
RB121990@teradata-ncr.com

Surajit Chauduri
Microsoft Research
surajitc@microsoft.com

1. Introduction

The invention of technology made Business Intelligence (BI) possible over relational engines, but now the experiences of putting them into production has unearthed a new set of problems in need of further invention.

Over a period of few past years, academia has provided very performant and storage efficient technologies for fundamental BI objects: cubes (Dwarf, Quotient Cube), instigated research in stream technologies resulting in renewed interest in continues and temporal queries, supplied further data mining and data exploration algorithms and research query optimizations for complex queries with variety of histograms.

Database industry either incorporated into their SQL engines some of these algorithms (like data mining algorithms, OLAP engines), or tried to integrate better stand alone BI engines like OLAP, or provided their own unique solutions for BI (Spreadsheet in SQL, statistical and window functions in SQL, new join methods for data densification, etc.).

2. The Challenge

Applying these lessons has provided successful solutions to the BI user community over the years. In fact it was the innovation in BI technologies within the database offerings which made business community apply relational engines to their problems. This application provided valuable feedback on performance, functionality, manageability and integration of BI features in RDBMs. Consequently it gave a raise to new trends in BI technologies.

As a result, these new trends and issues are quickly emerging as they are being driven by the continued acceptance of the intranet for business infrastructures. Database core technology needs to adapt, as well as enhance its language bindings.

3. Discussion

This panel will discuss a few of these emerging issues and trends. The intent is not to overview individual products and or solutions, nor to provide a background on BI solutions. But, it is to point out select trends and issues, as well as old issues that are still very real. The panelists will also describe why these issues are important for the research community.

The initial questions posed to the panelists will be twofold. First, is where should the BI community go on extending the SQL Language bindings (such as for data mining, reporting, and data analysis), as well as associated DBMS implications to support new and existing BI extensions. And, Second, what does XML mean to BI, as well as associated DBMS implications.

Permission to copy without fee all or part of this material is granted provided that the copies are not made or distributed for direct commercial advantage, the VLDB copyright notice and the title of the publication and its date appear, and notice is given that copying is by permission of the Very Large Data Base Endowment. To copy otherwise, or to republish, requires a fee and/or special permission from the Endowment

Proceedings of the 30th VLDB Conference,
Toronto, Canada, 2004

TUTORIALS

Database Architectures for New Hardware

Anastassia Ailamaki
Computer Science Department
Carnegie Mellon University
5000 Forbes Avenue
Pittsburgh, PA 15213
U.S.A.
e-mail: natassa@cmu.edu

Abstract

Thirty years ago, DBMS stored data on disks and cached recently used data in main memory buffer pools, while designers worried about improving I/O performance and maximizing main memory utilization. Today, however, databases live in multi-level memory hierarchies that include disks, main memories, and several levels of processor caches. Four (often correlated) factors have shifted the performance bottleneck of data-intensive commercial workloads from I/O to the processor and memory subsystem. First, storage systems are becoming faster and more intelligent (now disks come complete with their own processors and caches). Second, modern database storage managers aggressively improve locality through clustering, hide I/O latencies using prefetching, and parallelize disk accesses using data striping. Third, main memories have become much larger and often hold the application's working set. Finally, the increasing memory/processor speed gap has pronounced the importance of processor caches to database performance.

This tutorial will first survey the computer architecture and database literature on understanding and evaluating database application performance on modern hardware. We will present approaches and methodologies used to produce time breakdowns when executing database workloads on modern processors. We will contrast traditional methods that use system simulation to the more realistic, yet challenging use of hardware event counters. Then, we will survey techniques proposed in the literature to alleviate the problem and their evaluation. We will emphasize the importance and explain the challenges when determining the optimal data placement on all levels of memory hierarchy, and contrast to other approaches such as prefetching data and instructions. Finally, we will discuss open problems and future directions: Is it only the memory subsystem database software architects should worry about? How important are other decisions processors make to database workload behavior? Given the emerging multi-threaded, multi-processor computers with modular, deep cache hierarchies, how feasible is it to create database systems that will adapt to their environment and will automatically take full advantage of the underlying hierarchy?

About the speaker

Anastassia Ailamaki received a B.Sc. degree in Computer Engineering from the Polytechnic School of the University of Patra, Greece, M.Sc. degrees from the Technical University of Crete, Greece and from the University of Rochester, NY, and a Ph.D. degree in Computer Science from the University of Wisconsin-Madison. In 2001, she joined the Computer Science Department at Carnegie Mellon University as an Assistant Professor. Her research interests are in the broad area of database systems and applications, with emphasis on database system behavior on modern processor hardware and disks. Her projects at Carnegie Mellon (including Staged Database Systems, Cache-Resident Data Bases, and the Fates Storage Manager), aim at building systems to strengthen the interaction between the database software and the underlying hardware and I/O devices. Her other research interests include automated database design for scientific databases, storage device modeling, and internet querying. She has received three best-paper awards (VLDB 2001, Performance 2002, and ICDE 2004), an NSF CAREER award (2002), and IBM Faculty Partnership awards in 2001, 2002, and 2003. She is a member of IEEE and ACM.

Permission to copy without fee all or part of this material is granted provided that the copies are not made or distributed for direct commercial advantage, the VLDB copyright notice and the title of the publication and its date appear, and notice is given that copying is by permission of the Very Large Data Base Endowment. To copy otherwise, or to republish, requires a fee and/or special permission from the Endowment

**Proceedings of the 30th VLDB Conference,
Toronto, Canada, 2004**

Security of Shared Data in Large Systems: State of the Art and Research Directions

Arnon Rosenthal
The MITRE Corporation
202 Burlington Road /k308
Bedford MA 01730 USA
arnie@mitre.org

Marianne Winslett
University of Illinois
Dept. of Computer Science, 201 N. Goodwin
Urbana, IL 61820 USA
winslett@cs.uiuc.edu

Abstract

The goals of this tutorial are to enlighten the VLDB research community about the state of the art in data security, especially for enterprise or larger systems, and to engage the community's interest in improving the state of the art. The tutorial includes numerous suggested topics for research and development projects in data security.

1. Introduction

Security is increasingly recognized as a key impediment to sharing data in enterprise systems, virtual enterprises, and the semantic web. Yet the topic has not been a focus for mainstream database research, industrial progress in data security has been slow, and (too) much security enforcement is in application code, or else is coarse grained and insensitive to data contents.

The VLDB community is in an excellent position to make significant improvements in the way people think about security policies, due to the community's experience with declarative and logic-based specifications, automated compilation and physical design, and both semantic and efficiency issues for federated systems. These strengths provide a foundation for improving theory and practice.

This tutorial aims to enlighten the VLDB research community about the state of the art in *data* security, especially for enterprise or larger systems, and to engage the community's interest in improving the state of the art. Thus after a very brief look at security basics, the tutorial focuses on the following questions:

- What is the current state of the art in the real world, with respect to data security?
- What sorts of additional research results are needed to improve the current state of affairs?
- What frameworks can be helpful for architects and researchers tackling these problems?

We will present many open research problems (some grad-student ready, others requiring more formalization) as we move through the sections of the tutorial. For architects, we will suggest unifying concepts and distinctions that they could support, even before the research matures.

Our overall goal for the tutorial is to present material that is not found in any textbook---to show the audience how *they* can help improve the state of the art in data security. Thus the first section of the tutorial, entitled *Basics*, is not intended as a replacement for a security textbook. While a tutorial focused entirely on security basics might be helpful to the SIGMOD community, that is not our goal.

2. About the Presenters

Arnie Rosenthal is a Principal Scientist at MITRE. He has broad interests in problems that arise when data is shared between communities, including a long-term interest in the security issues that arise in data warehouses, federated databases, and enterprise information systems. He has also had a first-hand look at many security problems that arise in large government and military organizations.

Marianne Winslett has been a professor at the University of Illinois since 1987. She started working on database security issues in the early 1990s, focusing on semantic issues in MLS databases. Her interests soon shifted to issues of trust management for data on the web. Trust negotiation is her main current research focus.

Self-Managing Technology in Database Management Systems

Surajit Chaudhuri
Microsoft Research
surajitc@microsoft.com

Benoit Dageville
Oracle Corp.
benoit.dageville@oracle.com

Guy Lohman
IBM Almaden Research Center
lohman@almaden.ibm.com

1. The Problem

We are increasingly dependent on information systems for business as well as for personal usage. However, for information systems to provide value to their customers, we must reduce the complexity associated with their deployment and usage. While the cost of hardware and software in such systems continue to decrease dramatically through technological advances and competition, the total cost of ownership (TCO) of information technology is increasingly dominated by people costs.

2. Self-Managing Technology

All major providers of information technology have acknowledged the importance of the TCO problem and have attempted to rectify it in one way or another by making their systems more self-managing or "autonomic". While the idea of self-managing is easy to articulate, it is extremely challenging to design and build a completely self-managing information system. The range of solutions and techniques that have been developed to improve self-manageability of systems vary, and so does the degree to which they reduce the total cost of ownership. While we have no "magic bullet" as yet, progress is being made on many fronts to improve the manageability of systems through a variety of techniques.

3. Outline of the Tutorial

This tutorial will introduce the motivation of the problem and the core concepts in self-managing technology. It will then focus on providing self-manageability for relational database management systems, and how recent releases of IBM DB2, Microsoft SQL Server, and Oracle have embedded tools and techniques to enhance self-managcability. Finally, it will provide our perspectives on this challenging problem and the research topics that remain to be solved.

4. Intended Audience

The core concepts and examples of self-managing database technology to date, as well as the potential research topics, will be useful for researchers who are interested in contributing to this fruitful area of reducing total cost of ownership for databases. Users of database systems who are not familiar with some of the more advanced self-managing features of these products should also be interested in the details of these systems and the outlook for the future.

Architectures and Algorithms for Internet-Scale (p2p) Data Management

Joseph M. Hellerstein

EECS Computer Science Division, UC Berkeley
Intel Research, Berkeley

The database community prides itself on scalable data management solutions. In recent years, a new set of scalability challenges have arisen in the context of Internet-scale peer-to-peer (p2p) systems, in which the scaling metric is the number of participating computers, rather than the number of bytes stored. This is new and intriguing territory for the design of data management algorithms and systems.

The best-known application of p2p technology to date has been filesharing, which despite its sometimes unsavory use has been a vibrant technology driver. In addition to filesharing, there are compelling new application agendas for p2p systems including Internet monitoring, content distribution, distributed storage, multi-user games and next-generation Internet routing. The energy behind p2p technology has led to an academic renaissance in the distributed algorithms and distributed systems communities, much of which directly addresses issues in massively distributed data management.

Internet-scale systems present numerous unique technical challenges, including steady-state "churn" (nodes joining and leaving), the need to evolve and scale without reconfiguration, an absence of ongoing system administration, and adversarial participants in the processing. These challenges are not unique to what we commonly think of as p2p deployment scenarios. Hence many "p2p" techniques have relevance for any large distributed system in which the scale and distribution of the infrastructure makes traditional administrative models untenable.

In this tutorial we will focus on key data management building blocks including:

- Architectures for popular filesharing systems
- Indirection in time and space
- Structured overlay networks such as Distributed Hash Tables (DHTs), and their relationship to Interconnection Networks in parallel computers
- Embeddings of computations and communication in structured networks
- Persistence models for the Internet, including soft state and stronger guarantees
- Federated resource allocation
- Challenges in security and trust

We will also discuss motivations for the use of p2p technologies in both the popular conception of the term, and in related scenarios.

We will ground the presentation in experiences from deployed systems, including popular filesharing systems (Gnutella, KaZaA, BitTorrent), DHTs (Chord [7], Bamboo [6], Kademlia [5]), storage systems (LOCKSS [4], OceanStore [3]), and general-purpose query engines (PIER [2]). We will also discuss the PlanetLab [1] infrastructure for prototyping and deploying distributed systems.

References

[1] A. Bavier, L. Peterson, M. Wawrzoniak, S. Karlin, T. Spalink, T. Roscoe, D. Culler, B. Chun, and M. Bowman. Operating systems support for planetary-scale network services. In *Proc. 1st Symposium on Networked Systems Design and Implementation (NSDI)*, San Francisco, CA, Mar. 2004.

[2] R. Huebsch, J. M. Hellerstein, N. Lanham, B. T. Loo, S. Shenker, and I. Stoica. Querying the Internet with PIER. In *Proc. 19th VLDB*, Sep 2003.

[3] J. Kubiatowicz, D. Bindel, Y. Chen, S. Czerwinski, P. Eaton, D. Geels, R. Gummadi, S. Rhea, H. Weatherspoon, W. Weimer, C. Wells, and B. Zhao. OceanStore: An Architecture for Global-Scale Persistent Storage. In *Proc. 9th ASPLOS*, Nov. 2000.

[4] P. Maniatis, M. Roussopoulos, T. Giuli, D. S. H. Rosenthal, M. Baker, and Y. Muliadi. Preserving peer replicas by rate-limited sampled voting. In *Proc. 19th ACM SOSP*, Oct. 2003.

[5] P. Maymounkov and D. Mazières. Kademlia: A peer-to-peer information system based on the XOR metric. In *Proc. 1st International Workshop on Peer-to-Peer Systems (IPTPS)*, Mar. 2002.

[6] S. Rhea, D. Geels, T. Roscoe, and J. Kubiatowicz. Handling Churn in a DHT. In *Proc. USENIX*, June 2004.

[7] I. Stoica, R. Morris, D. Karger, M. F. Kaashoek, and H. Balakrishnan. Chord: A Scalable Peer-to-Peer Lookup Service for Internet Applications. In *Proc. ACM SIGCOMM*, 2001.

Permission to copy without fee all or part of this material is granted provided that the copies are not made or distributed for direct commercial advantage, the VLDB copyright notice and the title of the publication and its date appear, and notice is given that copying is by permission of the Very Large Data Base Endowment. To copy otherwise, or to republish, requires a fee and/or special permission from the Endowment.

**Proceedings of the 30th VLDB Conference,
Toronto, Canada, 2004**

The Continued Saga of DB-IR Integration

Ricardo Baeza-Yates

Center for Web Research
Dept. of Computer Science
University of Chile
Blanco Encalada 2120
Santiago, Chile
rbaeza@dcc.uchile.cl

Mariano Consens

Mechanical & Industrial Engineering Dept.
University of Toronto
5 King's College Road
Toronto, Ontario
Canada, M5S 3G8
consens@mie.utoronto.ca

Content

The world of data has been developed from two main points of view: the structured relational data model and the unstructured text model. The two distinct cultures of database and information retrieval now have a natural meeting place in the Web with its semi-structured XML model. As web-style searching becomes an ubiquitous tool, the need for integrating these two viewpoints becomes even more important.

The tutorial will provide an overview of the different issues and approaches put forward by the IR and DB communities and survey the DB-IR integration efforts. Both earlier proposals as well as recent ones (in the context of XML in particular) will be discussed. A variety of application scenarios for DB-IR integration will be covered.

The target audience of this tutorial includes researchers in database systems, as well as developers of Web and database/information retrieval applications. Our goal is that at the end there is a clear view of the main problems and pitfalls that should be avoided.

Short Bios

Ricardo Baeza-Yates is professor and chair of the CS department of the University of Chile. He is also director of the Center for Web Research. As professional volunteer, he is member of the IEEE CS Board of Governors for 2002-04; president of CLEI, a Latin American association of CS departments; and coordinator of the Iberoamerican cooperation program in Electronics and Informatics. His research interests include information retrieval, algorithms, and information visualization. He is co-author of the popular textbook *Modern Information Retrieval*, published in 1999 by Addison-Wesley, as well as co-author or co-editor of other books in algorithms and data structures or information retrieval, in addition to more than 50 publications in journals and over 100 other papers. Ricardo received the BSc in CS in 1983, the MSc in CS and the professional title in EE in 1985, and the MEng in EE in 1986 from the University of Chile. He received his PhD in CS from the U. of Waterloo, Canada, in 1989. He has been the president of the Chilean CS Society for 1992-95 and 1997-98. During 1993, he received the Organization of American States award for young researchers in exact sciences. In 1994 he received the award to the best engineering research from the Institute of Engineers of Chile. In 1997 with two Brazilian colleagues obtained the COMPAQ prize to the best Brazilian research article in CS. In 2002 he was appointed to the Chilean Academy of Sciences, being the first person from CS to achieve this position in Chile.

Mariano Consens research interests are in the areas of Data Management Systems and the Web, with a current focus on XML searching, autonomic systems and pervasive computing. He has over 20 publications and two patents, including journal publications selected from best conference papers. Mariano received his PhD and MSc degrees in Computer Science from the University of Toronto. He also holds a Computer Systems Engineer degree from the Universidad de la Republica, Uruguay. Consens has been a faculty member in Information Engineering at the MIE Department, University of Toronto, since 2003. Before that, he was research faculty at the School of Computer Science, University of Waterloo, from 1994 to 1999. In addition, he has been active in the software industry as a founder and Director of Freedom Intelligence (a query engine provider), as the CTO of Classwave Wireless (a Bluetooth software infrastructure company) and as a technology advisor for Xign (an electronic payment systems supplier), OpenText (an early web search engine turned knowledge management software vendor) and others.

Permission to copy without fee all or part of this material is granted provided that the copies are not made or distributed for direct commercial advantage, the VLDB copyright notice and the title of the publication and its date appear, and notice is given that copying is by permission of the Very Large Data Base Endowment. To copy otherwise, or to republish, requires a fee and/or special permission from the Endowment.

Proceedings of the 30th VLDB Conference, Toronto, Canada, 2004

DEMONSTRATIONS

GPX: Interactive Mining of Gene Expression Data [*]

Daxin Jiang
State University of New York
at Buffalo, USA
djiang3@cse.buffalo.edu

Jian Pei
State University of New York
at Buffalo, USA
Simon Fraser University, Canada
jianpei@cse.buffalo.edu

Aidong Zhang
State University of New York
at Buffalo, USA
azhang@cse.buffalo.edu

Abstract

Discovering co-expressed genes and coherent expression patterns in gene expression data is an important data analysis task in bioinformatics research and biomedical applications. Although various clustering methods have been proposed, two tough challenges still remain on how to integrate the users' domain knowledge and how to handle the high connectivity in the data. Recently, we have systematically studied the problem and proposed an effective approach [3]. In this paper, we describe a demonstration of *GPX* (for **G**ene **P**attern e**X**plorer), an integrated environment for interactive exploration of coherent expression patterns and co-expressed genes in gene expression data. *GPX* integrates several novel techniques, including the *coherent pattern index graph*, a *gene annotation panel*, and a *graphical interface*, to adopt users' domain knowledge and support explorative operations in the clustering procedure. The *GPX* system as well as its techniques will be showcased, and the progress of *GPX* will be exemplified using several real-world gene expression data sets.

1 Motivation

The DNA microarray technology has enabled measuring the expression levels of thousands of genes during important biological processes and across collections of related samples. It is often an important task to identify the co-expressed genes and the coherent expression patterns from the gene expression data. A group of *co-expressed genes* are the ones with similar expression profiles, while a *coherent expression pattern* characterizes the common trend of expression levels for a group of co-expressed genes. In practice, co-expressed genes may belong to the same or similar functional categories and indicate co-regulated families [9]. Coherent expression patterns may characterize important cellular processes and suggest the regulating mechanism in the cells [7].

To find co-expressed genes and discover coherent expression patterns, many gene clustering methods have been proposed, e.g., [9, 8, 1, 4, 5]. Each cluster is considered as a group of co-expressed genes and the coherent expression pattern can be simply the mean (the centroid) of the expression profiles of the genes in that cluster. While the clustering algorithms have been shown useful to identify co-expressed gene groups and discover coherent expression patterns, due to the specific characteristics of gene expression data and the special requirements from the biology domain, several great challenges for clustering gene expression data remained. Two of them are as follows.

Challenge 1: It is hard to integrate the domain- and user-knowledge to properly unfold the hierarchies of co-expressed genes and coherent patterns.

In a gene expression data set, there are usually multiple groups of co-expressed genes as well as the corresponding coherent patterns. Moreover, there is typically a hierarchy of co-expressed genes and coherent patterns in a gene expression data set. At the high levels of the hierarchy, large groups of genes approximately follow some "rough" coherent expression patterns. At the low levels of the hierarchy, the large groups of genes break into smaller subgroups. Those smaller groups of co-expressed genes follow some "fine" coherent expression patterns, which inherit some characteristics from the "rough" patterns, and add some distinct characteristics.

One subtle point here is that *there is no precise definition or objective standard to identify co-expressed gene groups*. The interpretation of co-expression depends on the knowledge from domain experts. For example, a microarray ex-

---

[*] This research is supported in part by NSF grants DBI-0234895, IIS-0308001 and NIH grant 1 P20 GM067650-01A1. All opinions, findings, conclusions and recommendations in this paper are those of the authors and do not necessarily reflect the views of the funding agencies.

Permission to copy without fee all or part of this material is granted provided that the copies are not made or distributed for direct commercial advantage, the VLDB copyright notice and the title of the publication and its date appear, and notice is given that copying is by permission of the Very Large Data Base Endowment. To copy otherwise, or to republish, requires a fee and/or special permission from the Endowment.

**Proceedings of the 30th VLDB Conference,
Toronto, Canada, 2004**

periment typically involves thousands of genes. However, only a small subset (e.g. several hundred) of those genes may play important roles in the biological process under investigation. As an initial examination, biologists may prefer browsing the "rough" patterns in the data set. Then, they may choose the patterns of particular interest and decompose them into "finer" patterns in further analysis. In other words, biologists may have different requirements of "coherence" for different parts of the data set and at different stages of the analysis.

However, many clustering algorithms generate clusters at a single level. It is hard to see the inherent hierarchical relationship among the groups of co-expressed genes as well as the coherent patterns. Although some hierarchical approaches exist, it is usually hard to determine where to cut the resulted hierarchical dendrogram to meet the various clustering requirements for different subsets of genes.

Moreover, most clustering algorithms are "purely" unsupervised approaches. A user often cannot be involved in the clustering procedure. To derive a satisfactory result, a user may have to try different algorithms and/or different parameter values. Apparently, such a make-do-and-mend approach is deficient. Instead, if users can apply their domain knowledge at some critical points during the clustering process, it may become more effective and efficient to get meaningful results. However, how to involve users in the clustering process and integrate the domain knowledge is still an open problem.

Challenge 2: It is hard to handle the high connectivity in the gene expression data sets.

An interesting phenomenon in gene expression data sets is that *groups of co-expressed genes may be highly connected by a large amount of "intermediate" genes.* Technically, two genes g_i and g_j that have very different expression profiles in a data set may be bridged by a series of intermediate genes such that each two consecutive genes on the bridge have similar profiles. Our empirical study has shown that such "bridges" are common in gene expression data sets.

The high connectivity in the gene expression data raises a challenge: *It is often hard to find the (clear) borders among the clusters.* Many existing clustering methods use one of the following two strategies.

On the one hand, the data set is decomposed into numerous small clusters. While some clusters consist of groups of biologically meaningful co-expressed genes, many clusters may consist of only intermediate genes. Since there is no biologically meaningful criteria (e.g., size, compactness) to rank the resulted clusters, it may take a lot of effort to examine which clusters are meaningful groups of co-expressed genes. On the other hand, an algorithm may form several large clusters. Each cluster contains both the co-expressed genes and a large amount of intermediate genes. However, those intermediate genes may mislead the centroids of the clusters into going astray. The centroids then no longer represent the true coherent patterns in the groups of co-expressed genes.

To address the above challenges, we developed *GPX* (for Gene Pattern eXplorer), a research prototype system that supports interactive exploration of co-expressed genes and coherent expression patterns in gene expression data sets.

2 Features of GPX

2.1 Interactive Exploration Operations

A user can explore the co-expressed genes and their coherent patterns by unfolding a hierarchy of genes and patterns. The exploration starts from the root. To help a user to make decision to split the genes and detect the patterns, a *coherent pattern index graph* [3] is used at each node of the tree to illustrate the cluster structure in the corresponding subset of data at the node. Each pulse in the coherent pattern index graph indicates the potential existence of a coherent pattern, and a higher pulse represents a stronger indication. Based on the index graph, GPX supports several exploration operations [6]. Two essential ones are *drill-down* and *roll-up*.

Drill-down. A user can select the pulse(s) in the index graph, and the system will split the genes accordingly. Each split subset of genes becomes a child node of the current node. If the user does not specify any pulse, the system will choose the highest pulse by default and split the genes accordingly.

Roll-up. A user can revoke any drill-down operation. The user can select a node and undo the drill-down operation from this node. All descendants of this node will be deleted. The user can also roll up one node A to its parent P. This equals to skipping the selection of the pulse in P's index graph that corresponds to A, and undoing the drill down operation for P.

2.2 A Robust Model for Clusters and Patterns

Most existing clustering methods try to find the clusters (i.e., groups of co-expressed genes) based on some global criteria, and then derive the coherent patterns as the centroids of the clusters. Such strategies may be sensitive to a large amount of intermediate genes in data sets. Contrast to those methods, *GPX* adopts a novel strategy: it first explores the hierarchy of coherent patterns in the data set and then finds the groups of co-expressed genes according to the coherent expression patterns.

In *GPX*, a cluster of co-expressed genes is modeled as a dense area in the multidimensional gene space. Genes at the "center" of the dense area have relatively high density and present the coherent pattern of the whole cluster. Genes at the periphery of the dense area have relatively low density and will be "attracted" toward the center area level by level.

Through this density-based model, *GPX* can distinguish co-expressed genes from intermediate genes by their relative density. The coherent expression pattern in a dense area is represented by the expression profile of the gene that has the highest local density in the dense area. Other genes in the same dense area can be sorted in a list according to the similarity (from high to low) between their expression profiles and the coherent expression pattern. Since the intermediate genes have low similarity to the coherent pattern, they are at the rear part of the sorted list. Users can set up a similarity threshold and thus cut the intermediate genes from the cluster.

2.3 Graphical Interface and Gene Annotation Panel

A graphical interface provides users a direct impression of the trends of gene expression levels. Users may interpret the underlying biological process and decide whether the co-expressed genes should be further split into finer subgroups. In *GPX*, we use the *parallel coordinate* to illustrate the expression profiles of genes. We also visualize the whole hierarchical structure of the co-expressed genes and coherent patterns. Users can browse the hierarchical tree, select a node and apply the exploration operations (Figure 1(b)).

There exist very rich literatures about the functions and regulation mechanisms of genes. It would be very helpful to integrate such domain knowledge into the system. For example, given a group of co-expressed genes, if the well studied genes in this group are significantly populated in a certain gene function category, biologists may postulate that the functions of the novel genes in the group fall in the same function category. On the other hand, if a group of co-expressed genes scatter into diverse functional categories, biologists may further split this group or roll back to the parent node and choose a different splitting path. To meet this need, we design a *gene annotation panel*. Given a specific node on the hierarchical tree, the panel sorts the genes belonging to the node as we described in Feature 2, and displays the name and the annotation (if any) for each gene (Figure 1(c)). The gene annotations are downloaded from some public databases, such as the Gene Ontology Consortium (http://www.geneontology.org).

3 Major Components of GPX

3.1 Data Preprocessor and Pattern Manager

Usually the original data obtained from microarray experiments contains missing values and variations arising from the experimental procedure. Data pre-processing is indispensable before any cluster analysis can be performed. In *GPX*, we apply the K-nearest neighbor approach described in [10] to estimate the missing values. Then the system performs a logarithmic transformation of each expression level and standardizes each gene expression profile with a mean of zero and a variance of one. Finally the system calculates the pairwise distance between gene expression profiles and stores the pre-processed data and the pairwise distances. Once a data set has been pre-processed, users can explore the coherent patterns in the data set and save/load the coherent patterns through the pattern manager (Figure 1(a)).

3.2 Interactive Exploration Environment

GPX has a *working zone* (Figure 1(b)), which integrates the parallel coordinates, the coherent pattern index graph, and a *tree view*. An example tree view is shown in Figure 2, which illustrates the hierarchical structure of co-expressed genes and coherent expression patterns in the well known Iyer's data set [2]. Users can select a node in the tree view, then the working zone will display the corresponding expression profiles and coherent pattern index graph. Users can click on the coherent pattern index graph to split the node or roll back previous split operations. The tree structure is adjusted dynamically according to the exploration operations.

3.3 Gene Annotation Panel

Once users select a node on the tree structure, the gene annotation panel will sort the genes and display their names and annotations accordingly (Figure 1(c)).

4 About the Demonstration

Our demo consists of three major parts.

First, we present the *techniques* to interactively clustering and analyzing gene expression data. We will analyze the rationale of our designs, as well as their advantages and disadvantages. We will also illustrate the effects of our method using real data sets.

Second, we present a set of *real case studies* on the proposed techniques. The experimental results on several real data sets will be exhibited.

Last, we showcase our *prototype system*, including a data analysis engine and an interactive user interface. The audience is encouraged to play with the prototype system and experience the exciting tour over real data sets.

After the demonstration, the integrated *GPX* system will be available on web for public access.

References

[1] Eisen M.B., Spellman P.T., Brown P.O. and Botstein D. Cluster analysis and display of genome-wide expression patterns. *Proc. Natl. Acad. Sci. USA*, 95(25):14863–14868, December 1998.

[2] Iyer V.R., Eisen M.B., Ross D.T., Schuler G., Moore T., Lee J.C.F., Trent J.M., Staudt L.M., Hudson Jr. J., Boguski M.S., Lashkari D., Shalon D., Botstein D. and Brown P.O. The transcriptional program in the response of human fi broblasts to serum. *Science*, 283:83–87, 1999.

[3] Jiang D., Pei J. and Zhang A. Interactive exploration of coherent patterns in time-series gene expression data. In *Proceedings of the Ninth ACM SIGKDD International Conference on Knowledge Discovery and Data Mining (KDD'03)*, Washington, DC, USA, August 24-27 2003.

[4] Jiang D., Pei J. and Zhang A. Towards interactive exploration of gene expression patterns. *ACM SIGKDD Ex-*

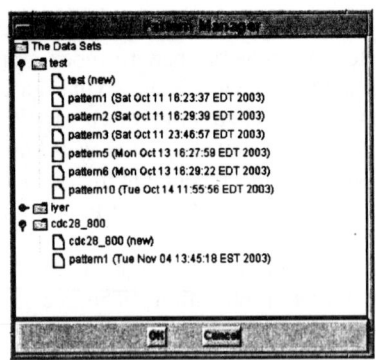 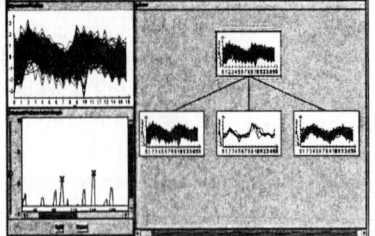 

(a) Pattern manager   (b) Working zone   (c) Gene annotation panel

Figure 1: Screen snapshots of *GPX*

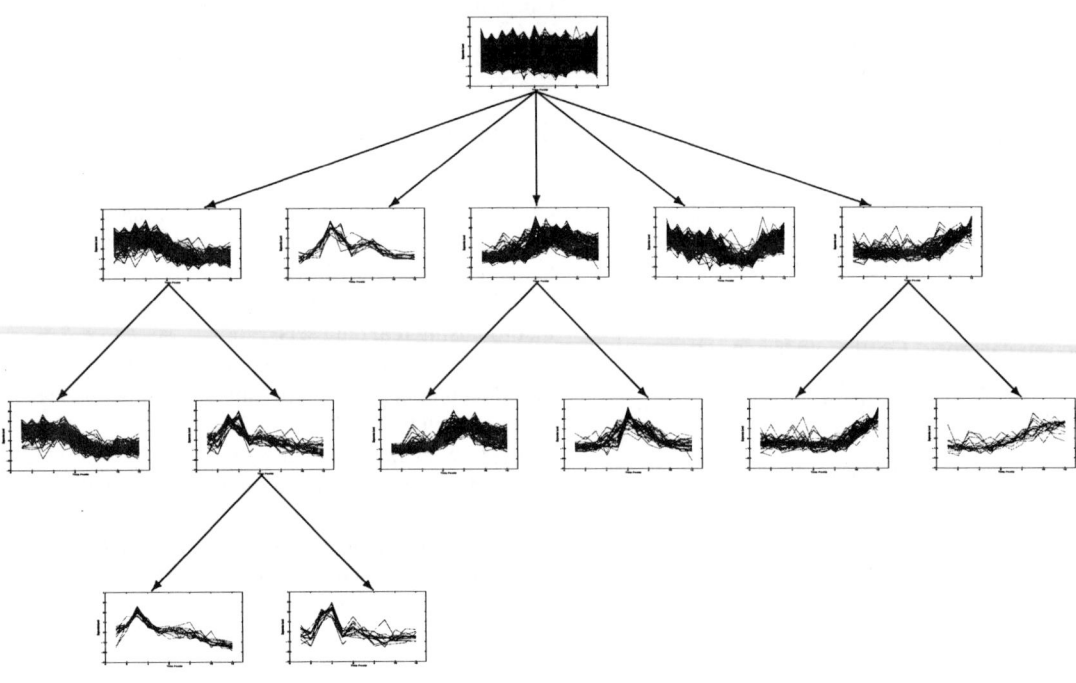

Figure 2: The tree view of co-expressed gene groups on Iyer's data set [2]

plorations (Special Issue on Microarray Data Analysis), 5(2):79–90, 2004.

[5] Jiang D., Pei J., Ramanathan M., Tang C. and Zhang A. Mining coherent gene clusters from three-dimensional microarray data. In *Proceedings of the Tenth ACM SIGKDD International Conference on Knowledge Discovery and Data Mining (KDD'04)*, Seattle, Washington, USA, August 22-25 2004.

[6] Pei, J. A general model for online analytical processing of complex data. In *Proceedings of the 22nd International Conference on Conceptual Modeling (ER'03)*, Chicago, IL, October 13-26 2003.

[7] Spellman P.T., Sherlock G., Zhang M.Q., Iyer V.R., Anders K., Eisen M.B., Brown P.O., Botstein D. and Futcher B. Comprehensive identification of cell cycle-regulated genes of the yeast Saccharomyces cerevisiae by microarray hybridization. *Mol Biol Cell*, 9(12):3273–3297, 1998.

[8] Tamayo P., Solni D., Mesirov J., Zhu Q., Kitareewan S., Dmitrovsky E., Lander E.S. and Golub T.R. Interpreting patterns of gene expression with self-organizing maps: Methods and application to hematopoietic differentiation. *Proc. Natl. Acad. Sci. USA*, Vol. 96(6):2907–2912, March 1999.

[9] Tavazoie S., Hughes D., Campbell M.J., Cho R.J. and Church G.M. Systematic determination of genetic network architecture. *Nature Genet*, pages 281–285, 1999.

[10] Troyanskaya O., Cantor M., Sherlock G., Brown P., Hastie T., Tibshirani R., Botstein D. and Altman R. Missing value estimation methods for dna microarrays. *Bioinformatics*, 17(6):520–525, Jun 2001.

Computing Frequent Itemsets Inside Oracle 10G

Wei Li

Oracle Corporation
500 Oracle Parkway
Redwood Shores, CA 94065
U.S.A

weili@oracle.com

Ari Mozes

Oracle Corporation
10 Van de Graaff
Burlington, MA 01803
U.S.A

ari.mozes@oracle.com

Abstract[1]

Frequent itemset counting is the first step for most association rule algorithms and some classification algorithms. It is the process of counting the number of occurrences of a set of items that happen across many transactions. The goal is to find those items which occur together most often. Expressing this functionality in RDBMS engines is difficult for two reasons. First, it leads to extremely inefficient execution when using existing RDBMS operations since they are not designed to handle this type of workload. Second, it is difficult to express the special output type of itemsets.

In Oracle 10G, we introduce a new SQL table function which encapsulates the work of frequent itemset counting. It accepts the input dataset along with some user-configurable information, and it directly produces the frequent itemset results. We present examples of typical computations with frequent itemset counting inside Oracle 10G. We also describe how Oracle dynamically adapts during frequent itemset execution as a result of changes in the nature of the data as well as changes in the available system resources.

1. Introduction

---

(1) Permission to copy without fee all or part of this material is granted provided that the copies are not made or distributed for direct commercial advantage, the VLDB copyright notice and the title of the publication and its date appear, and notice is given that copying is by permission of the Very Large Data Base Endowment. To copy otherwise, or to republish, requires a fee and/or special permission from the Endowment.

**Proceedings of the 30th VLDB Conference,
Toronto, Canada, 2004.**

Frequent itemset counting operation is a common data mining operations and it is used for several important mining algorithms, such as association rules and large bayes classification.

Frequent itemset counting has been directly used in business-intelligence for many years. The most common application has been in the retail industry in determining which products are most commonly purchased together. For instance, people who buy beer are likely to buy pretzels. This is known as Market Basket Analysis.

In the Market Basket Analysis model, a transaction contains a limited number of items that occur together. Let A be a set of m items: $A = \{A_1, A_2, ... , A_m\}$ and T be a set of n transactions: $T = \{T_1, T_2, ... , T_n\}$. Frequent itemsets are subset of items in A which occur together in T above a predefined support threshold. If the data is stored organized by transaction, where each transaction has a number of items, we define this as a horizontal layout. Otherwise, if the data is stored organized by item, where each item has a number of supporting transactions, we define this as a vertical layout.

R. Agrawal, T. Imielinski, A. Swamy introduced association rules and the Apriori Algorithm in [1]. The Apriori Algorithm, which is based on the horizontal layout, is an iterative algorithm that has two steps in each iteration:

- generating candidate itemsets using Apriori-rule

- reading all the transactions, and for each combination of items within a transaction, incrementing a counter for that combination of items

A. Savasere, E. Omiecinski, S. Navathe introduced a different algorithm that is based on the vertical layout in [6]:

- a list of transactions for each item is created

- an itemset can be counted by simply intersecting all the involved items' transaction lists

Most of the research literature is based on these two categories of algorithms.

Given the nature of the operation, producing frequent itemsets using existing SQL functionality is not trivial. In [4], S. Sarawagi, S. Thomas, R. Agrawal discussed various approaches to integrate the operation into RDBMS systems. We decided to push the functionality into the RDBMS engine for the following reasons:

- We want to provide end-users a simple and flexible interface yielding optimal performance.
- The SQL implementation stays closer to the dataset and avoids huge raw data transfers to and from the RDBMS system.
- We can closely interact with other built-in database functionality such as dynamic memory management and parallel execution.

Because we support frequent itemset counting as an internal database operation, we face several problems that are not considered in the research literature, including:

- output format: an itemset is a set of items, which does not have a corresponding native datatype in a pure RDBMS system
- resource usage: we can not use an arbitrary amount of resources (e.g., memory); we must consider the situation that the operation is running inside complex queries and, at the same time, there may be many other queries running inside the RDBMS system vying for system resources

The rest of this paper is organized as follows. In section 2, we describe our SQL interface. In section 3, we present our general execution ideas, including algorithms and adaptive execution. We give the demo content in section 4.

2. SQL interface - Table Functions

We support the frequent itemset counting operation in the form of a table function in Oracle 10g. We will describe the interface, using a simple example from [7].

Suppose that you are a product manager in Oracle. One of your job responsibilities is to write technical white papers. You have access to simple web reports that show you how many people have downloaded each piece of collateral, so you know which papers are popular.

Assume that you have a *web_log* table with three columns:

- *session_id*: downloading session ID
- *command*: downloaded white papers
- *time_stamp*: session start time

You can use the following simple query to find the six most popular white papers downloaded from the website during a fixed time period:

```
select command,
       rank() over (order by support desc) rnk
from (select command, count(session_id) support
      from web_log
      where time_stamp between '01-APR-2002'
                    and '01-JUN-2002'
      group by command)
where rnk <= 6;
```

And you get the following results:

```
White paper title                                   #
-------------------------------------------------------
Table Compression in Oracle9i                       1
Field Experiences with Large Data Warehouse         2
Key Data Warehouse Features                         3
Materialized Views in Oracle9i                      4
Parallel Execution in Oracle9i                      5
Query Optimization in Oracle9i                      6
```

But now you want to go one step further and find the most common pairs of collateral downloaded in a single session. You can use the frequent itemset table function in Oracle 10g to answer the question:

```
select itemset,
    rank() over (order by support desc) rnk
from
(select cast(itemset as fi_char) itemset,
       support
from
table(dbms_frequent_itemset.fi_transactional(
   cursor(select session_id, command
          from web_log
          where time_stamp between
             '01-APR-2002' and '01-JUN-2002'),
   (60/2600), 2, 2))
where rnk <= 3;
```

The above query uses the *dbms_frequent_itemset* package[2] to find the most frequently downloaded pairs of papers. We use a nested table type to represent the output itemsets. Here, the nested table type is *fi_char*, which is defined as:

```
create type fi_char as table of varchar2(50);
```

The following results yields interesting findings. Although the white paper "Table Compression in Oracle9i" is the most popular individual paper, only one of the top three pairs includes this paper. Neither of the papers in the second most popular pair show up as individual items above.

```
White paper titles                                  #
-------------------------------------------------------
Table Compression in Oracle9i and                   1
Field Experiences with Large Data Warehouse
Data Warehouse Performance Enhancements and         2
Oracle9i Performance and Scalability in DSS
Materialized Views in Oracle9i and                  3
Query Optimization in Oracle9i
```

---

(2) You can reference [8] for the detailed syntax and examples about *dbms_frequent_itemset* package.

3. General Execution

In section 1, we mentioned that there are two categories of frequent itemset counting algorithms: horizontal-layout and vertical-layout based. We implemented versions of both algorithms for the internal operation in Oracle 10g. We were surprised to find that there is no research describing how to execute those algorithms with a limited amount of memory and how changes in available memory can greatly influence the performance of the algorithms.

Horizontal layout algorithms: There are three reasons that this category remains promising:

- In almost all situations, users store their information in this layout. Therefore, horizontal based algorithm can avoid the costly transformation from horizontal layout to vertical layout.

- The algorithm is very efficient for sparse datasets, which is reinforced by the fact that the average number of items per transaction is less than 20.

- The memory requirement is based on the candidate itemsets, not the transaction database. This behavior is desirable in some situations. For example, if we have a huge transaction database and a small set of candidate itemsets, the algorithm can work efficiently with a limited amount of memory.

Vertical layout algorithms: It has been found that vertical layout algorithms([3] [5] [6]) work better than horizontal layout algorithms in many situations.

The general idea of the vertical layout algorithm is to compute lists of transactions for each item and then intersect these lists to compute the number of transactions that have those items in common. There are two possible representations for each item's list of transactions:

- linked list of all the transaction IDs

- bitmaps: each bit represents whether the corresponding transaction contains the item

We chose a bitmap representation for the following reasons:

- In our analysis, an intersection-based algorithm is most efficient when working on dense datasets. Bitmaps are a better representation for dense datasets.

- We can leverage proven Oracle bitmap index technology.

For frequent itemset computation, only the final count for a given itemset is of interest; there is no need to preserve information regarding which transactions contributed to a given itemset. Thus, to enable bitmap index representation, a simple mapping function is designed to map each transaction ID to a unique rowid, which results in each bit position being mapped to an actual transaction. After the mapping, we can utilize existing bitmap index counting and intersection techniques. Figure 1 shows the mapping process.

Figure 1 **transaction IDs -> bitmap Mapping**

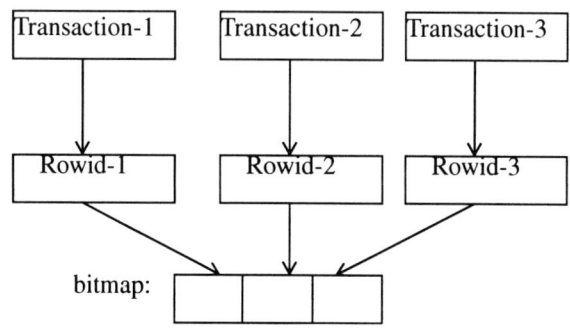

The major drawback of the vertical layout approach for itemset counting comes from its large memory requirement. No matter whether the algorithm uses bitmaps or transaction lists, both of which can be compressed representations, the data is proportional to the original transaction table in size. Considering that the original transaction table may be gigantic, there is no guarantee that we can fit all of this data in memory.

Adaptive Execution: In our study, neither algorithm is clearly better than the other; the actual data, selection criteria, and available system resources will favor one over the other. A complication is that frequent itemsets are usually computed in phases where each successive phase increases the length of the itemset being processed; while one algorithm may be most efficient for one phase, the same algorithm may be quite inefficient for another phase. Due to the varying nature of the system resources and itemset combinations, our implementation adapts during execution, both within an algorithm and across algorithms.

To facilitate choosing the correct algorithm, during the first phase of execution we collect statistics that estimate the run time costs of both approaches. Then, for all of the remaining phases, we execute frequent itemset counting using the following steps to make it a self-tuning operator:

- Generate candidate itemsets using Apriori-rule. Statistics on candidates will also be collected.

- Using the Oracle query optimizer in conjunction with the collected statistics, estimate the IO and CPU costs of both algorithms. Comparing the two final costs, we proceed with the cheaper algorithm. At a very high level, the costs are as follows:

```
- Horizontal Cost = transactions scan cost +
                    counting tree setup cost +
                    recursive counting cost
- Vertical Cost = bitmap scan cost +
                  bitmap intersection cost +
                  bit counting cost +
                  final aggregation cost
```

Adaptation does not cease once an algorithm is chosen for a

particular phase. A phase may take a long time to complete, and available memory in an RDBMS system will always be changing as users connect and disconnect from the database, firing off queries of varying complexity. There is a definite need to adapt within a phase as the utilization of the overall system changes.

To enable this type of intra-algorithm adaptive execution, two things were done in the Oracle implementation. First, the operator was written to take advantage of the ability to grow memory dynamically and to graciously handle the situation where memory usage needs to be reduced. Second, the operator cooperates fully with the Oracle memory manager regarding its memory usage.

As an example of adapting to memory constraints within the vertical layout approach, let us take the following scenario. We have 26 frequent items, item-A to item-Z, and a transaction database of 8 million transactions. Let us further assume that we have 10MB memory and can only fit 10 full items in memory. In general, we can not assume item-A and item-Z are in memory at the same time. One solution is to create a lightweight index on all of the items' bitmaps. Given the candidate itemset (A, B, Z), if only item-A and item-B are in memory, we can search in the index, find the position of item-Z, read the corresponding bitmap into memory (replacing another bitmap), and intersect all of the bitmaps to get the final counts. The cost of random I/O as used in this approach can be prohibitive, so this approach has clear performance issues.

We propose partitioning the bitmaps to address this memory constraint. First, bitmaps are partitioned according to available memory in such a way that the portion of each bitmap corresponding to a single set of transaction IDs fits in memory. Then, we intersect these partitions to produce partial itemset counts for each of the candidate itemsets. To produce complete aggregates, we will add another aggregation operator on top to sum across the partition subtotals. We must take care not to produce very small partitions since such an approach will degrade the good CPU performance of bitmap intersections and will be costly from an I/O perspective due to many small reads and writes.

When working with the Oracle memory manager, we define three types of executions for this partitioned bitmap intersection:

- *cache execution*: all bitmaps fit in memory
- *one-pass execution*: at least one partition of all bitmaps fits in memory
- *multi-pass execution*: even a single partition of bitmaps cannot completely fit in memory, in which case we propose to avoid partitioning and simple perform random access to retrieve a given bitmap from the index

Throughout execution, the frequent itemset counting operator will communicate with the Oracle memory manager [9], providing the memory requirements for its three possible mechanisms for execution, retrieving the memory bound, and deciding which execution method to use. The above example detailing the use of partitioned bitmaps is just one area in which the frequent itemset counting operator interacts with the memory manager to dynamically adjust to available resources.

4. Demo content

The demo will contain experiments for both a real world dataset and a synthetic dataset. We will show the benefit of integrating this functionality within the RDBMS: users can access and post-process results in the relational query environment. In addition, we will show how frequent itemset execution communicates with the Oracle memory manager so as to adapt to the current environment.

References

[1] [RTA93] "Mining association rules between sets of items in large databases", R. Agrawal, T. Imielinski, A. Swamy, ACM SIGMOD Conf. 1993

[2] [RJ96] "Parallel mining of association rules", R. Agrawal, J. Shafer, IEEE Trans. on Knowledge And Data Engineering, 1996

[3] [MJZ97] "New algorithms for fast discovery of association rules", M. J. Zaki, Int'l Conf. on Knowledge Discovery and Data Mining, 1997

[4] [SSR98] "Integrating association rule mining with relational database systems", Alternatives and Implications, S. Sarawagi, S. Thomas, R. Agrawal, ACM SIGMOD Conf. 1998

[5] [PJH00] "Turbo-charging vertical mining of large database", by P. Shenoy, J. Haritsa, S. Sudarshan, ACM SIGMOD Conf. 2000

[6] [AES95] "An efficient algorithm for mining association rules in large databases", A. Savasere, E. Omiecinski, S. Navathe, Proc. 21st Int'l Conf. Very Large Databases, San Francisco, 1995

[7] [FIO03] "Frequent itemsets in Oracle 10g", 2003, www.otn.oracle.com/products/bi/pdf/10gr1_twp_bi_dw_freqitemsets.pdf

[8] [O10G] Oracle 10G PL/SQL Packages and Types Reference

[9] [BM02] SQL Memory Management in Oracle9i, Proc. 28th Int'l Conf. Very Large Databases, Hong Kong, 2002

StreamMiner: A Classifier Ensemble-based Engine to Mine Concept-drifting Data Streams

Wei Fan

IBM T.J.Watson Research
19 Skyline Drive
Hawthorne, NY 10532, USA
weifan@us.ibm.com

Abstract

We demonstrate StreamMiner, a random decision-tree ensemble based engine to mine data streams. A fundamental challenge in data stream mining applications (e.g., credit card transaction authorization, security buy-sell transaction, and phone call records, etc) is concept-drift or the discrepancy between the previously learned model and the true model in the new data. The basic problem is the ability to judiciously select data and adapt the old model to accurately match the changed concept of the data stream. StreamMiner uses several techniques to support mining over data streams with possible concept-drifts. We demonstrate the following two key functionalities of StreamMiner:

1. Detecting possible concept-drift on the fly when the trained streaming model is used to classify incoming data streams *without* knowing the ground truth.

2. Systematic data selection of old data and new data chunks to compute the optimal model that best fits on the changing data streams.

1 Introduction

One of the recent challenges facing traditional data mining methods is to handle real-time production systems that produce large amount of data continuously at unprecedented rate and with evolving patterns. Traditionally, due to limitation of storage and practitioner's ability to mine huge amount of data, it is a common practice to mine a subset of data at preset frequency. However, these solutions have been shown to be ineffective due to possibly over-simplified model as a result of sub-sampling as well as dynamically unpredictable evolving pattern of the production data. Knowledge discovery on data streams has become a research topic of growing interest. Much work has been done on modeling [Babcock et al., 2002], querying [Babu and Widom, 2001, Gao and Wang, 2002, Greenwald and Khanna, 2001], classification [Hulten et al., 2001, Street and Kim, 2001, Wang et al., 2003, Fan et al., 2004, Fan, 2004b], regression analysis [Chen et al., 2002] and clustering [Guha et al., 2000]. The fundamental problem is the following: given an infinite amount of continuous measurements, how do we model them in order to capture possibly time-evolving trends and patterns in the stream, compute the optimal model and make time critical decisions?

2 The Motivation of StreamMiner

The fundamental problem in learning drifting concepts is how to identify in a timely manner those data in the training set that are no longer consistent with the current concepts. These data must be discarded. A straightforward solution, which is used in many current approaches, discards data indiscriminately after they become old, that is, after a fixed period of time T has passed since their arrival. Although this solution is conceptually simple, it tends to complicate the logic of the learning algorithm. More importantly, it creates the following dilemma which makes it vulnerable to unpredictable conceptual changes in the data: if T is large, the training set is likely to contain outdated concepts, which reduces classification accuracy; if T is small, the training set may not have enough data, and as a result, the learned model will likely carry a large

---

Permission to copy without fee all or part of this material is granted provided that the copies are not made or distributed for direct commercial advantage, the VLDB copyright notice and the title of the publication and its date appear, and notice is given that copying is by permission of the Very Large Data Base Endowment. To copy otherwise, or to republish, requires a fee and/or special permission from the Endowment.

**Proceedings of the 30th VLDB Conference,
Toronto, Canada, 2004**

variance due to overfitting.

We use a simple example to illustrate the problem. Assume a stream of 2-dimensional data is partitioned into sequential chunks based on their arrival time. Let S_i be the data that came in between time t_i and t_{i+1}. Figure 1 shows the distribution of the data and the optimum decision boundary during each time interval.

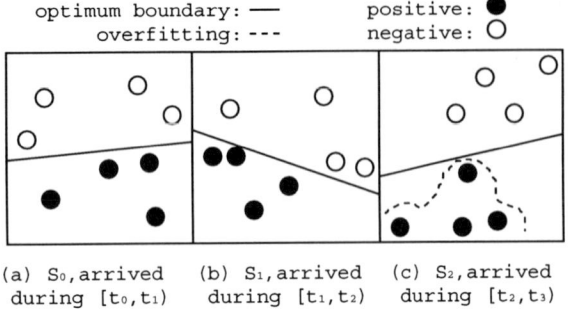

(a) S_0, arrived during $[t_0, t_1)$ (b) S_1, arrived during $[t_1, t_2)$ (c) S_2, arrived during $[t_2, t_3)$

Figure 1: data distributions and optimum boundaries

The problem is: after the arrival of S_2 at time t_3, what part of the training data should still remain influential in the current model so that the data arriving after t_3 can be most accurately classified?

On one hand, in order to reduce the influence of old data that *may* represent a different concept, we shall use nothing but the most recent data in the stream as the training set. For instance, use the training set consisting of S_2 only (i.e., $T = t_3 - t_2$, data S_1, S_0 are discarded). However, as shown in Figure 1(c), the learned model may carry a significant variance since S_2's insufficient amount of data are very likely to be overfitted.

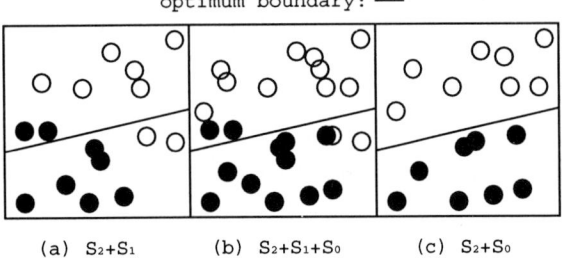

(a) $S_2 + S_1$ (b) $S_2 + S_1 + S_0$ (c) $S_2 + S_0$

Figure 2: Which training dataset to use?

The inclusion of more historical data in training, on the other hand, may also reduce classification accuracy. In Figure 2(a), where $S_2 \cup S_1$ (i.e., $T = t_3 - t_1$) is used as the training set, we can see that the discrepancy between the underlying concepts of S_1 and S_2 becomes the cause of the problem. Using a training set consisting of $S_2 \cup S_1 \cup S_0$ (i.e., $T = t_3 - t_0$) will not solve the problem either. Thus, there may not exists an optimum T to avoid problems arising from overfitting and conflicting concepts.

We should not discard data that may still provide useful information to classify the current test examples. Figure 2(c) shows that the combination of S_2 and S_0 creates a classifier with less overfitting or conflicting-concept concerns. The reason is that S_2 and S_0 have similar class distribution. Thus, instead of discarding data using the criteria based solely on their arrival time, we shall make decisions based on their class distribution. Historical data whose class distributions are similar to that of current data can reduce the variance of the current model and increase classification accuracy. However, it is a non-trivial task to select training examples based on their class distribution.

3 The StreamMiner Solution

There are a large number of possibilities that can happen when mining data streams. Before we go into the details of the main mining engine, we enumerate all situations that we can think of and discuss the best choice in each case and how to find the optimal model. The two main themes of our comparison is on possible data insufficiency and concept drift. We start from simple cases.

- **New data is sufficient by itself *and* there is no concept drift.** The optimal model should be the one trained from the new data itself since new data is sufficient. The older model may also be an optimal model if it is trained from sufficient data. However, the tricky issue is that we do not know and will usually never know if the data is indeed sufficient and the concept indeed remains the same. However, it doesn't hurt to train a new model from the new data, a new model from combined new data and old data, and compare with the original older model to choose the more accurate one if the learning cost is affordable.

- **New data is sufficient by itself *and* there is concept drift.** The optimal model should be the one trained from the new data itself. Similar to the previous situation, we do not know and will never know if the data is indeed sufficient and the concept indeed remains the same. Ideally, we should compare a few sensible choices if the training cost is affordable.

- **New data is insufficient by itself *and* there is no concept drift..** If the previous data is sufficient, the optimal model should be the existing model. Otherwise, we should train a new model from new data plus existing data and choose the one with higher accuracy.

- **New data is insufficient by itself *and* there is concept drift.** Obviously, training a new model from new data only doesn't return the optimal model. However, choosing old data unselectively, as shown previously, will only be misleading. The correct approach is to choose only those examples from previous data chunks that have consistent concept with the new data chunk and combine those examples with the new data

3.1 Computing optimal models

We notice that the optimal model is completely different under different situations. The choice for optimal model completely depends on if the data is indeed sufficient and if there is indeed concept drift. The ideal solution would be to compare a few plausible optimal models statistically, and choose the one with the highest accuracy. To clarify some notation conventions, $FN(\mathbf{x})$ denotes a new model trained from recent data. $FO(\mathbf{x})$ denotes an optimal model finally chosen after some statistical significance tests. i is the sequence number of each sequentially received data chunk.

1. Train a model $FN_i(\mathbf{x})$ from the new data chunk S_i only.

2. Assume that D_{i-1} is the dataset that trained the most recent "optimal" model $FO_{i-1}(\mathbf{x})$. It is important to point out that D_{i-1} may not be the most recent data chunk S_{i-1}. D_{i-1} is collected iteratively throughout the streaming data mining process. The exact way how D_{i-1} is collected will be clear next. We select these examples from D_{i-1} that both the trained new model $FN_i(\mathbf{x})$ and the recent optimal model $FO_{i-1}(\mathbf{x})$ make the correct prediction. We denote these chosen examples as s_{i-1}. In other words, $s_{i-1} = \{\forall (\mathbf{x}, y) \in D_{i-1}, \text{such that}, (FN_i(\mathbf{x}) = y) \wedge (FO_{i-1}(\mathbf{x}) = y)\}$.

3. Train a model $FN_i^+(\mathbf{x})$ from the new data plus the selected data in the last step or $S_i \cup s_{i-1}$.

4. Update the most recent model FO_{i-1} with S_i and call this model $FO_{i-1}^+(\mathbf{x})$. To update a model, we keep the "structure" of the model and update its internal statistics. Using decision tree as an example, every example in S_i is "classified" or sorted to each leaf node. The statistics, i.e., the number of examples belonging to each class label, are updated. Obviously, the training set for $FO_{i-1}^+(\mathbf{x})$ is $D_i \cup S_i$.

5. Compare the accuracy of all four models ($FN_i(\mathbf{x})$, $FO_{i-1}(\mathbf{x})$, $FN_i^+(\mathbf{x})$), and $FO_{i-1}^+(\mathbf{x})$) using "cross-validation" and choose the one that is the most accurate and we name it $FO_i(\mathbf{x})$.

6. D_i is the training set that computes $FO_i(\mathbf{x})$. It is one of S_i, D_{i-1}, $S_i \cup s_{i-1}$, and $S_i \cup D_{i-1}$.

3.2 Main Engine

The main engine of StreamMiner trains a number of random and uncorrelated decision trees. Details of the main engine can be found in [Fan et al., 2003, Fan, 2004a, Fan, 2004b]. Each decision tree is constructed by randomly selecting available features. The structure of the tree is uncorrelated. Their only correlation is on the training data itself. To classify an example, raw posterior probability is required. If there are n_c examples out of n in the leaf node with class label c, the probability that $\mathbf{x}$ is an example of class label c is $P(c|\mathbf{x}) = \frac{n_c}{n}$. Each tree computes a posterior probability for an example and the probability outputs from multiple trees are averaged as the final posterior probability of the ensemble. To make a decision, application specific loss function is required. For a binary problem under 0-1 loss, if $P(y|\mathbf{x}) > 0.5$, the best prediction is y.

Cross-validation is implemented by using the model itself. Assuming that n is the size of the training set, n-fold cross validation leaves one example $\mathbf{x}$ out and uses the remaining $n-1$ examples to train a model and classify on the left-out example $\mathbf{x}$. When we compute the probability for the excluded $\mathbf{x}$ under n-fold cross validation using the original decision tree ensemble, we need to compensate this difference. Assuming that we have two class labels, either fraud or non-fraud, to compute the probability of the excluded $\mathbf{x}$ being fraudulent is simply

$$\begin{cases} \frac{n_{fraud}-1}{n_{fraud}-1+n_{normal}} & \text{if } \mathbf{x} \text{ is indeed a fraud} \\ \frac{n_{fraud}}{n_{fraud}+n_{normal}-1} & \text{if } \mathbf{x} \text{ is a normal transaction} \end{cases}$$

4 About this Demo

Streaming Data Generator

We create synthetic data with drifting concepts based on a moving hyperplane that is commonly used to simulate concept-drifting data streams. A hyperplane in d-dimensional space is denoted by equation: $\sum_{i=1}^{d} a_i x_i = a_0$. We label examples satisfying $\sum_{i=1}^{d} a_i x_i \geq a_0$ as positive, and examples satisfying $\sum_{i=1}^{d} a_i x_i < a_0$ as negative. Hyperplanes have been used to simulate time-changing concepts because the orientation and the position of the hyperplane can be changed in a smooth manner by changing the magnitude of the weights [Hulten et al., 2001]. We generate random examples uniformly distributed in multi dimensional space $[0,1]^d$. Weights a_i ($1 \leq i \leq d$) are initialized randomly in the range of $[0,1]$. We choose the value of a_0 so that the hyperplane cuts the multi-dimensional space in two parts of the same volume, that is, $a_0 = \frac{1}{2} \sum_{i=1}^{d} a_i$. Thus, roughly half of the examples are positive, and the other half negative. Noise is introduced by randomly switching the labels of $p\%$ of the examples. In our experiments, the noise level $p\%$ is set to 5%.

We provide a few parameters that the attendees of our demo can choose to simulate different degrees of concept-drift. Parameter k specifies the total number of dimensions whose weights are changing. Parameter $t \in \mathcal{R}$ specifies the magnitude of the change (every N examples) for weights $a_1, \cdots, a_k$, and $s_i \in \{-1, 1\}$ specifies the direction of change for each weight a_i, $1 \leq i \leq k$. Weights change continuously, i.e., a_i is adjusted by $s_i \cdot t/N$ after each example is generated. Furthermore, there is a possibility of 10% that the change would reverse direction after every N examples are generated, that is, s_i is replaced by $-s_i$ with probability 10%. Also, each time the weights are updated, we recompute $a_0 = \frac{1}{2} \sum_{i=1}^{d} a_i$ so that the class distribution is not disturbed.

Concept Change Illustration

Conceptual change is best illustrated through the change of error rate of models. For every historically trained model, we show its changing error rate on the evolving data stream. Based on the attendee's parameter selection, the trend we will show is that models trained from recent data and systematically selected old data will have a generally lower error rate than the older models.

5 Demonstration Scenario

In our demo, the attendees have the freedom to choose different parameters to simulate a data stream with changing concept and the amount of new data collected until a new model need to be learned. After the attendee chooses these parameters, the stream data generator will produce incoming data streams. StreamMiner collects the data continuously and starts to compute or update an existing model when the number of new examples are above a threshold the attendee chooses. This process can either run continuously continuously or in batch mode, as chosen by the demo attendee.

Acknowledgement

The original synthetic data generator was written by my colleague, Dr. Haixun Wang, as described in a previous paper [Wang et al., 2003]. The original source was modified to generate continuous data streams with drifting concepts.

References

[Babcock et al., 2002] Babcock, B., Babu, S., Datar, M., Motawani, R., and Widom, J. (2002). Models and issues in data stream systems. In *ACM Symposium on Principles of Database Systems (PODS)*.

[Babu and Widom, 2001] Babu, S. and Widom, J. (2001). Continuous queries over data streams. *SIGMOD Record*, 30:109–120.

[Chen et al., 2002] Chen, Y., Dong, G., Han, J., Wah, B. W., and Wang, J. (2002). Multi-dimensional regression analysis of time-series data streams. In *Proc. of Very Large Database (VLDB)*, Hongkong, China.

[Fan, 2004b] Fan, W. (August 2004b). Systematic data selection to mine concept-drifting data streams. In *Proceedings of 2004 ACM SIGKDD International Conference on Knowledge Discovery and Data Mining (KDD'2004)*, Seattle, Washington, USA.

[Fan, 2004a] Fan, W. (July 2004a). On the optimality of probabililty estimation by random decision trees. In *Proceedings of the Nineteenth National Conference on Artificial Intelligence (AAAI'2004)*, San Jose, California, USA.

[Fan et al., 2004] Fan, W., an Huang, Y., Wang, H., and Yu, P. S. (April 2004). Active mining of data streams. In *Proceedings of 2004 SIAM International Conference on Data Mining*, pages 457–461.

[Fan et al., 2003] Fan, W., Wang, H., Yu, P. S., and Ma, S. (2003). Is random model better? on its accuracy and efficiency. In *Proceedings of Third IEEE International Conference on Data Mining (ICDM'2003)*.

[Gao and Wang, 2002] Gao, L. and Wang, X. (2002). Continually evaluating similarity-based pattern queries on a streaming time series. In *Int'l Conf. Management of Data (SIGMOD)*, Madison, Wisconsin.

[Greenwald and Khanna, 2001] Greenwald, M. and Khanna, S. (2001). Space-efficient online computation of quantile summaries. In *Int'l Conf. Management of Data (SIGMOD)*, pages 58–66, Santa Barbara, CA.

[Guha et al., 2000] Guha, S., Milshra, N., Motwani, R., and O'Callaghan, L. (2000). Clustering data streams. In *IEEE Symposium on Foundations of Computer Science (FOCS)*, pages 359–366.

[Hulten et al., 2001] Hulten, G., Spencer, L., and Domingos, P. (2001). Mining time-changing data streams. In *Int'l Conf. on Knowledge Discovery and Data Mining (SIGKDD)*, pages 97–106, San Francisco, CA. ACM Press.

[Street and Kim, 2001] Street, W. N. and Kim, Y. (2001). A streaming ensemble algorithm (SEA) for large-scale classification. In *Int'l Conf. on Knowledge Discovery and Data Mining (SIGKDD)*.

[Wang et al., 2003] Wang, H., Fan, W., Yu, P., and Han, J. (2003). Mining concept-drifting data streams with ensemble classifiers. In *Proceedings of ACM SIGKDD International Conference on knowledge discovery and data mining (SIGKDD2003)*, pages 226–235.

Semantic Mining and Analysis of Gene Expression Data

Xin Xu   Gao Cong   Beng Chin Ooi   Kian-Lee Tan   Anthony K. H. Tung*

School of Computing, National University of Singapore
3 Science Drive 2, Singapore 117543
{xuxin, conggao, ooibc, tankl, atung}@comp.nus.edu.sg
*Contact Author

Abstract

Association rules can reveal biological relevant relationship between genes and environments / categories. However, most existing association rule mining algorithms are rendered impractical on gene expression data, which typically contains thousands or tens of thousands of columns (gene expression levels), but only tens of rows (samples). The main problem is that these algorithms have an exponential dependence on the number of columns. Another shortcoming is evident that too many associations are generated from such kind of data. To this end, we have developed a novel depth-first row-wise algorithm FARMER [2] that is specially designed to efficiently discover and cluster association rules into *interesting rule groups* (*IRGs*) that satisfy user-specified minimum support, confidence and chi-square value thresholds on biological datasets as opposed to finding association rules individually. Based on FARMER, we have developed a prototype system that integrates semantic mining and visual analysis of *IRGs* mined from gene expression data.

1 Introduction

Recent studies have shown that association rules can reveal the relationship between genes and environments / categories. For example, they help identify gene predictors for cancer diagnosis. In addition to their simplicity and ease of interpretation, association rules show much promise in the analysis of gene expression data.

However, gene expression data has a large number of columns which poses a great challenge for existing rule mining algorithms, since their basic approaches are the column-wise enumerations where combinations of columns are tested incrementally to search for frequent occurrences of certain combinations. Column-wise association rule mining algorithms generally have the following three problems on gene expression data:
Problem 1: *Extremely long running time due to the huge column enumeration space,*
Problem 2: *Too many association rules found due to the combinatorial explosion of frequent* itemsets, and
Problem 3: *No support of semantic navigation of the huge number of association rules for biologists.*

To address the first 2 problems, we propose a novel row-wise depth-first algorithm FARMER [2] that mines all the *interesting rule groups* (*IRGs*) satisfying user-specified minimum measure (support, confidence, chi square value) thresholds, instead of finding individual association rules. For the last problem, we introduce visualization technique to effectively interpret and compare the semantics of *IRGs*. The graphic interface enables users to conduct semantic explorations over the *IRGs* and identify the most discriminating *IRGs* rapidly.

In the next section, we will briefly introduce the *IRG* mining process with FARMER. *IRG* visualization techniques will be described in details in Section 3. We will discuss the promising applications of our demo system in Section 4. The description of the demo is given in Section 5. We will conclude our work in Section 6.

2 IRG Mining

To have a rough idea of FARMER [2] and *IRGs*, let's look at a simple example. Suppose there is a two-row discretized dataset, 1:{g_1, g_2, g_3, g_4, g_5, g_6, $Cancer$}, 2: {g_7, g_8, g_9, g_{10}, g_{11}, g_{12}, $\neg Cancer$}, where item g_i (i = 1, 2, ..., 12) is the discretized value of the original gene expression level. We could generate 63

Permission to copy without fee all or part of this material is granted provided that the copies are not made or distributed for direct commercial advantage, the VLDB copyright notice and the title of the publication and its date appear, and notice is given that copying is by permission of the Very Large Data Base Endowment. To copy otherwise, or to republish, requires a fee and/or special permission from the Endowment.
**Proceedings of the 30th VLDB Conference,
Toronto, Canada, 2004**

association rules in the form of "$A \rightarrow Cancer$" from the same row set $\{1\}$, where A is any combination of $g_1, g_2, ..., g_6$, and 63 association rules in the form of "$B \rightarrow \neg Cancer$" from the same row set $\{2\}$, where B is any combination of $g_7, g_8, ..., g_{12}$. Obviously, many of them are redundant.

For the above example, FARMER utilizes the following two core techniques.

- *Mining Interesting Rule Groups*: All the above 126 rules of the running example belong to two **rule groups**. One *rule group* is identified with a unique *antecedent support set* [1] $\{1\}$, a unique *upper bound rule* $g_1g_2g_3g_4g_5g_6 \rightarrow Cancer$, and 6 *lower bound rules* $g_i \rightarrow Cancer$, $i = 1, 2, ..., 6$. The other *rule group* is identified with another *antecedent support set* $\{2\}$, a unique *upper bound rule* $g_7g_8g_9g_{10}g_{11}g_{12} \rightarrow \neg Cancer$, and 6 *lower bound rules* $g_i \rightarrow \neg Cancer$, $i = 7, 8, ..., 12$. The rules between the *upper bound rule* and the *lower bound rules* are the remaining members of the corresponding *rule group*. In this way, we only need to generate 2 *upper bound rules* and 12 *lower bound rules* instead of all the 126 rules. As can be seen, the rules in the same *rule group* share the same *antecedent support set* and the same consequent, thus the same support, confidence and chi square values. From this point of view, the *rule group* is a lossless compression of the association rules. FARMER only outputs **interesting rule groups** (IRGs). For two *rule groups* of the same consequent, rg_1 and rg_2, if $rg_1.upperbound \subset rg_2.upperbound$ and rg_1 has a higher confidence, then FARMER only outputs rg_1, because rg_1 is defined to be more interesting.

- *Row Enumeration Combined with Efficient Pruning Strategies*: As the row enumeration space is orders smaller than the column enumeration space in gene expression data, FARMER performs search by a depth-first traversal of a **row enumeration tree**. Each node corresponds to a certain row enumeration, where a **transposed table** is set up and a new IRG may be identified. For the simple example, the *row enumeration tree* without applying pruning strategies is shown in Figure 1. The traversal starts from the root node $\{\}$, goes through node $\{1\}$ and node $\{1, 2\}$ in sequence, and ends at node $\{2\}$. Figure 2 lists the corresponding three non-empty transposed tables, where $R(g_i)$ represents the complete set of rows that contain item g_i. In this way, the *upper bound rule* $g_1g_2g_3g_4g_5g_6 \rightarrow Cancer$ is discovered at node $\{1\}$, and the *upper bound rule* $g_7g_8g_9g_{10}g_{11}g_{12} \rightarrow \neg Cancer$ is discovered at node $\{2\}$. To avoid redundancy and to comply with the minimum measure thresholds, efficient pruning strategies are applied to further speed up the mining process.

---
[1] The *antecedent support set* of a rule is the complete set of rows that contain the antecedent of the rule

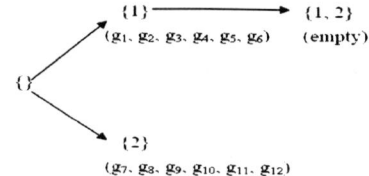

Figure 1: Row Enumeration Tree

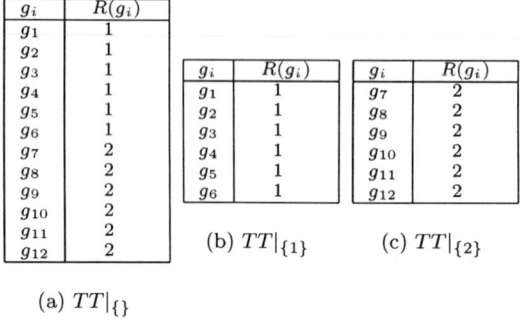

Figure 2: Transposed Tables

According to our experiments, FARMER is orders of magnitude faster than CHARM [4] and Bayardo's algorithm [1], two well-known column-wise mining algorithms on several bench mark gene expression datasets, as shown in [2].

3 IRG Visualization

Figures 3, 4, and 5 show our system interfaces. We ran the system on the Colon Tumor [2] dataset for demonstration purpose here. We split the original dataset to 47 training samples and 15 test samples randomly. The training dataset consists of 47 rows representing the tissue samples of patients and 2000 columns representing the expression levels of various genes.

The IRGs are sorted based on their rank (descending) as evaluated first by confidence (descending), next by support (descending), and last by # item (ascending). The top 5 IRGs ($IRG_1 \prec IRG_2 \prec IRG_3 \prec IRG_4 \prec IRG_5$) are specified as the **IRG subset**. Meanwhile the order of the items in the specified IRG subset and the rows in the dataset are determined based on their memberships in the *itemsets*[3] and *antecedent support sets* of the IRGs respectively. An item i will be ranked higher than an item j if the highest ranked IRG that contain i is above the highest ranked IRG that contain j in the IRG ranking. Likewise, a row r will have a higher rank than a row s if the highest ranked IRG that is matched by r is above the highest

---
[2] http://microarray.princetion.edu/oncology/affydata/index.html
[3] the *itemset* of an IRG is the complete set of items that appear in at least one of the antecedents of the association rules in the IRG

ranked *IRG* that is matched by *s* based on the *IRG* ranking.

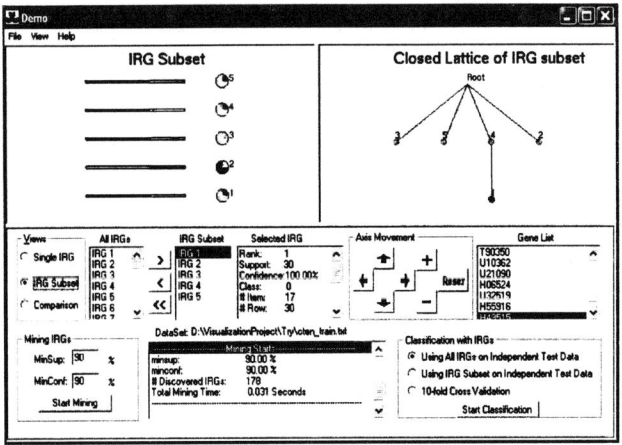

Figure 3: Semantic Visualization of the *IRG* Subset Using the Barcode View and the Flower View

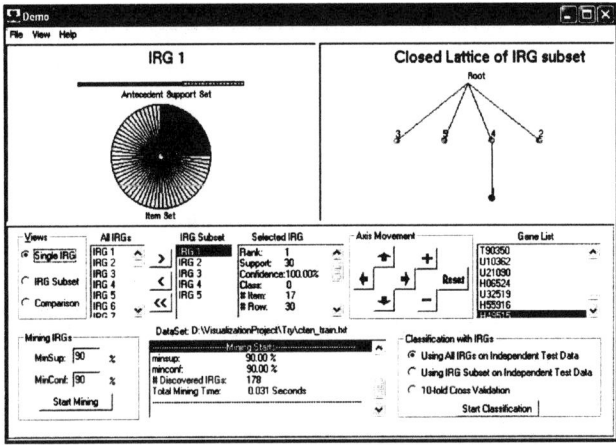

Figure 4: Semantic Visualization of a Single *IRG* Using the Barcode View and the Flower View

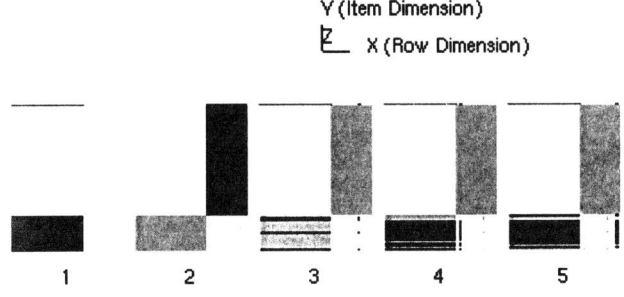

Figure 5: *IRG* Comparisons Using the Matrix View

For each *IRG*, we can visualize its *antecedent support set* and its *itemset* with a "**barcode**" and a "**flower**" separately, or with a "**matrix**" jointly. A "**closed lattice**" graph is also proposed to summarize the *IRGs* in the *IRG* subset based on the subset/superset relationship of their *antecedent support sets*.

• *Antecedent Support Set Visualization*: The "**barcode**" (left hand of Figures 3 and 4) is the identification number of the *IRG*. The "bar" consists of several small grids, each mapping to one ordered row of the dataset. If the mapped row is a member of the IRG's *antecedent support set*, the grid is dyed according to the class label of the row (i.e., red for "negative", blue for "positive"). In this way, the semantics of the *IRG*, like support and confidence, can be obtained by a snapshot. The overall "barcode" view (left hand of Figure 3) suggests that the *antecedent support set* of IRG_1 occupies only the "negative" tissue samples (all red, no blue), while the *antecedent support set* of IRG_2 occupies only the "positive" tissue samples (all blue, no red). They are the only two *IRGs* of confidence 100% in the *IRG* subset. The "**closed lattice**" (right hand of Figures 3 and 4) is another summarization based on the superset/subset relationships of the *antecedent support sets* of *IRGs* in the *IRG* subset. Each node in the lattice except the root node maps to the *antecedent support set* of one *IRG* in the *IRG* subset. The *antecedent support set* of the parent node includes that of the child node. The root node corresponds to the set of all the 47 rows.

• *Itemset Visualization*: We visualize the *itemset* of the *IRG* in the user-specified *IRG* subset as a "**flower**" (left hand of Figures 3 and 4). Each "flower" corresponds to the same set of ordered items that appear in the *IRG* subset and each item is represented by a "petal" of the "flower". The "petal" is dyed if the corresponding item appears in the current *IRG*, otherwise it is left blank.

• *Joined Visualization*: The x-dimension of the "matrix" represents the set of rows in the dataset while the y-dimension of the "matrix" represents the set of items in the *IRG* subset. The items and rows along each dimension are ordered. Given a "matrix" representing a *rule group* IRG_i, a cell valued (x,y) in the "matrix" will be colored red if item y is in the antecedent of the *upper bound rule* for IRG_i and row x matches the *upper bound rule* of IRG_i. Due to the ordering of the items and rows, the red cells in the "matrix" of the highest ranked *IRG* (i.e. IRG_1) will always be clustered at the bottom left corner of the "matrix" as can be seen from Figure 5.

To compare IRG_i against other higher ranked *IRGs*, a cell in the "matrix" for IRG_i will be colored dark grey if it has been colored red in any "matrix" of higher ranked *IRGs*. For example, the dark grey patch in the "matrix" of IRG_2 indicates that these cells have been colored red in the "matrix" of IRG_1. In the case in which the cell also has to be painted red to represent IRG_i, the color of dark red will be used to paint the cell. Finally, the top most cells in each "matrix" are used to represent the class labels of the corresponding rows. By looking at the highest cells in the "matrix" of IRG_1, we can see that IRG_1 has a 100% confidence prediction for a certain class. Overall, we can see that IRG_1 and IRG_2 are the most discriminating $IRGs$ with the largest number of non-overlapped red cells.

4 IRG Application

With the effective visualization techniques in Section 3, we can identify the most discriminating $IRGs$, which can be of great value in understanding the mechanics of disease and identifying new pathways by describing what genes are expressed as a result of certain cellular environments.

One promising application of IRG is disease diagnosis. As an example, 14 out of the 15 colon tumor test samples have been classified correctly using only the *upper bound rules* of IRG_1 and IRG_2. In [2], we made a first try to build a simple classifier by aggregating the discriminating powers of the *upper bound rules* of $IRGs$ on five benchmark gene expression datasets. The simple classifier is competitive with SVM as well as being efficient.

5 Description of the Demo

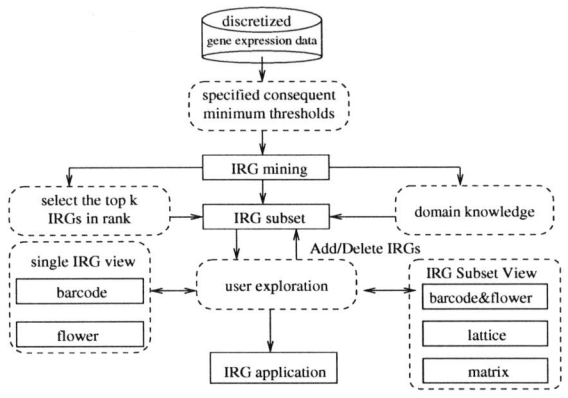

Figure 6: System Framework

In this demo, we will demonstrate an interactive prototype system that specifically involves the following three components (Figure 6).

- *IRG Mining*: For each user-specified consequent, mine IRGs that satisfy user-specified minimum measure (support, confidence and chi square value) thresholds.

- *IRG Exploration*: Users select/adjust the IRG subset of interest, analyze and compare the IRGs in the IRG subset interactively.

- *IRG Application*: Output the most discriminating IRGs for disease diagnosis and so on.

We will showcase (1) how a user can interact with the system with the specified minimum measure thresholds and how the system can find $IRGs$ efficiently with FARMER; (2) how the IRG summarizes the set of association rules effectively; (3) how the semantics and the discriminating powers of the discovered $IRGs$ can be interpreted and compared using our visualization techniques effectively and efficiently; and (4) how the discovered $IRGs$ can be used to build an accurate rule-based classifier.

6 Conclusion

In this paper, we used the concept of IRG so that numerous rules discovered from gene expression data are clustered into limited number of $IRGs$ that encapsulate the complete information about the set of globally significant rules and that we avoid generating billions of redundant rules. From another point of view, $IRGs$ could be considered as clusters of emerging patterns [3], an important concept for discovering significant rules from bio-medical data.

Our prototype system not only finds the discriminating associations completely and efficiently, but also provides an interactive graphic interface to identify the associations of the highest biological meanings. Furthermore, it shows great promise in the clinical application, i.e., disease diagnosis.

References

[1] R. J. Bayardo, R. Agrawal, and D. Gunopulos. Constraint-based rule mining on large, dense data sets. In *Proc. 1999 Int. Conf. Data Engineering (ICDE'99)*.

[2] G. Cong, Anthony K. H. Tung, X. Xu, F. Pan, and J. Yang. Farmer: Finding interesting rule groups in microarray datasets. *In the 23rd ACM SIGMOD International Conference on Management of Data*, 2004.

[3] G. Dong, X. Zhang, L. Wong, and J. Li. Caep: Classification by aggregating emerging patterns. In *Proc. 2nd Int. Conf. Discovery Science (DS'99)*.

[4] M. J. Zaki and C. Hsiao. Charm: An efficient algorithm for closed association rule mining. In *Technical Report 99-10*, Computer Science, Rensselaer Polytechnic Institute, 1999.

HOS-Miner: A System for Detecting Outlying Subspaces of High-dimensional Data

Ji Zhang[1], Meng Lou[1], Tok Wang Ling[2], Hai Wang[1]
[1]Department of Computer Science, University of Toronto,
Email: {jzhang, mlou, hai}@cs.toronto.edu
[2]Department of Computer Science, National University of Singapore
Email: lingtw@comp.nus.edu.sg

Abstract

We identify a new and interesting high-dimensional outlier detection problem in this paper, that is, detecting the subspaces in which given data points are outliers. We call the subspaces in which a data point is an outlier as its Outlying Subspaces. In this paper, we will propose the prototype of a dynamic subspace search system, called HOS-Miner (HOS stands for High-dimensional Outlying Subspaces), that utilizes a sample-based learning process to effectively identify the outlying subspaces of a given point.

1 Introduction

Outlier detection is an important step in data mining that enjoys a wide range of applications such as the detection of credit card frauds, criminal activities and exceptional patterns in databases. Outlier detection problem can typically be formulated as follows: given a set of data points or objects, find a specific number of objects that are considerably dissimilar, exceptional and inconsistent with respect to the remaining data.

To deal with the above definition of outlier detection problem, numerous research works have been proposed. They can broadly be divided into the distance-based methods [5, 6, 8] and the local density-based methods [3, 4, 7]. However, many of these outlier detection algorithms are unable to deal with high-dimensional datasets effectively as many of them only consider outliers in the entire space. This implies that they will miss out on the important information about the subspaces in which these outliers exist. Recently, a new technique in high-dimensional outlier detection uses evolutionary search method [1] where outliers are detected by searching for sparse subspaces. Points in these sparse subspaces are assumed to be the outliers. All the exiting outlier detection techniques, regardless of in low or high dimensional scenario, invariably fall into the framework of detecting outliers in a specific data space, either in the full space or a certain subspace. We term these methods "$space \rightarrow outliers$" techniques. For instance, [1] detects outliers by first finding locally sparse subspaces, and [6] discoveries the so-called Strongest/Weak Outliers by first finding the Strongest Outlying Spaces.

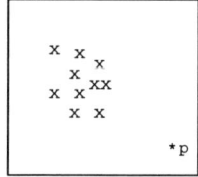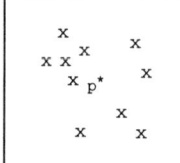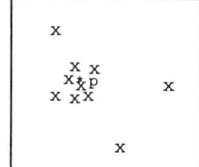

Figure 1: 2-dimensional views of the high-dimensional data

While knowing which data points are the outliers can be useful, in many applications, it is more important to identify the subspaces in which a given point is an outlier, which motivates the proposal of a new technique in this paper to handle this new outlier detection task. First, let us consider the example in Figure 1 where three 2-dimensional views of the high-dimensional data are presented. Note that point p exhibits different outlying degrees in these three views. In the leftmost view, p is clearly an outlier. However, this is not so in the other two views. There are also a number of real-life applications that can benefit from the results of the this new task. In the case of designing a training program for an athlete, it is critical to identify the specific subspace(s) in which an athlete deviates from his or her teammates in the daily training performances. Knowing the specific weakness (subspace) allows a more targeted training program to be designed. In a medical system, it is useful for the Doctors to identify from voluminous medical data the subspaces in which a particular patient is found abnormal and therefore a corresponding medical treatment can be provided in a timely manner.

We will identify this new and interesting high-dimensional outlier detection problem in this paper, that is, detecting the subspaces in which given data points are outliers. We call the subspaces in which a data point is an outlier as its *Outlying Subspaces*. We now formulate this new problem as following: given a data point or object, find the subspaces in which this data is considerably dissimilar, exceptional or inconsistent with respect to the remaining points or objects. This problem can be mathematically stated as: for any given point p, find the set of subspaces S such that for each subspace $s \in S$, we have $OD_s(p) \geq T$, where OD is the distance function used (to be discussed in the sequal). If the answer set is empty for p, we say that p is not an outlier in any subspaces.

In this paper, we will propose the prototype of *a dynamic subspace search system, called HOS-Miner (HOS stands for High-dimensional Outlying Subspaces), that utilizes a sample-based learning process to effectively identify the outlying subspaces of a given point*. In contrast to the so-called "*space $\to$ outliers*" outlier detection techniques, our method can be described as a "*outlier $\to$ spaces*" technique. To our best knowledge, this is the first such work in the literature so far.

The main features of HOS-Miner include: (1) The outlying measure, OD, is based on the sum of distances between a data and its k nearest neighbors. This measure is simple and independent of any underlying statistical and distribution characteristics of the data points. (2) The properties of OD are investigated and incorporated to speed up the search for outlying subspaces. (3) A fast dynamic subspace search algorithm with a sample-based learning process is proposed. (4) A refinement mechanism is incorporated to screen superfluous outlying subspaces in the final result.

2 Outlying Degree Measure and Its Properties

For each point, we define the degree to which the point differs from the majority of the other points in the same space, termed the outlying degree (*OD in short*). OD is defined as the sum of the distances between a point and its k nearest neighbors. Mathematically speaking, the OD of a point p in space s is computed as:

$$OD(p,s) = \sum_{i=1}^{k} Dist(p,p_i) | p_i \in KNNSet(p,s)$$

where $KNNSet(p,s)$ is the set containing the KNNs of p in s.

OD maintains two interesting properties that allow the design of an efficient outlier subspace search algorithm.
Property 1: If a point p is not an outlier in an m-dimensional subspace s, then it cannot be an outlier in any subspace that is a subset of s.
Property 2: If a point p is an outlier in an m-dimensional subspace s, then it will be an outlier in any subspace that is a superset of s.

The above properties are based on the fact that the OD value of a point in a subspace cannot be less than that in its subset space. Mathematically, we have $OD_{s_1}(p) \geq OD_{s_2}(p)$ if $s_1 \supseteq s_2$.

3 HOS-Miner

In the section, we present an overview of HOS-Miner. Figure 2 shows an overview of the system. It mainly consists

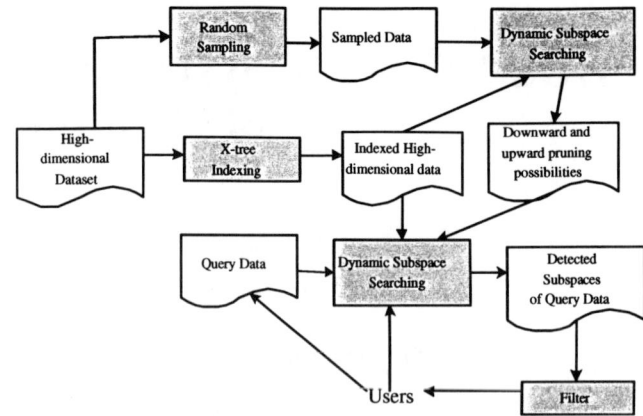

Figure 2: The overview of HOS-Miner

of 4 modules. The X-tree Indexing module performs X-tree [2] indexing of the high-dimensional dataset to facilitate k-NN search in every subspace. Sample-based Learning module randomly samples the dataset and perform dynamic subspace search to estimate the downward and upward pruning probabilities of subspaces from 1 to d dimensions. Subspace Outlier Detection module uses the probabilities obtained in the Learning module to carry out a dynamic subspace search to find all the subspaces in which the given query data point is an outlier and the Filtering Module screen superfluous outlying subspaces in the final result that will be returned to the users.

3.1 Subspace Pruning

To find the outlying subspaces of a given point, we make use of the properties of OD to quickly detect the subspaces in which the point is not an outlier or the subspaces in which the point is definitely an outlier. All these subspaces can be removed from further consideration in the later stage of the search process.

There are two basic pruning strategies: the upward pruning strategy and the downward pruning strategy. In the downward pruning strategy, we make use of Property 1 of OD to quickly prune away those subspaces in which the point cannot be an outlier. This is because if $OD_{s_1}(p) < T$, then $OD_{s_2}(p) < T$, where $s_1 \supseteq s_2$ and T is the distance threshold. In the upward pruning strategy, Property 2 of OD is utilized to detect those subspaces in which the point is definitely an outlier. The reason is that if $OD_{s_2}(p) \geq T$, then $OD_{s_1}(p) \geq T$. Hence, these detected subspaces can be immediately returned in the answer set and excluded from further exploration in the subsequent search.

Next, we will compute the savings obtained by applying the pruning strategies during the search process quantitatively. Before that, let us first give three definitions.
Definition 1: *Downward Saving Factor (DSF) of a Subspace*

The Downward Saving Factor of an m-dimensional subspace s is defined as the savings obtained by pruning all the subspaces that are subsets of s. In other words, the Downward Saving Factor of s, denoted as DSF(s), is computed as:

$$DSF(s) = \sum_{i=1}^{m-1} C_m^i * i$$

where C_m^i denotes the combinatorial number of choosing i items out of m items.

Definition 2: *Upward Saving Factor (USF) of a Subspace*

The Upward Saving Factor of an m-dimensional subspace s, denoted as USF(s), is defined as the savings obtained by pruning all the subspaces that are supersets of s. It is computed as

$$USF(s) = \sum_{i=1}^{d-m} [C_{d-m}^i * (m+i)]$$

e.g. Refer to a 4-dimensional space, $DSF([1,2,3]) = C_3^1 * 1 + C_3^2 * 2 = 9$ and $USF(1,4]) = C_2^1 * (2+1) + C_2^2 * (2+2) = 10$.

Definition 3: *Total Saving Factor (TSF) of a Subspace*

The Total Saving Factor of an m-dimensional subspace, in terms of a query point p, denoted as TSF(m, p), is defined as the combined savings obtained by applying the two pruning strategies during the search process. It is computed as follows:

$$TSF(m,p) = \begin{cases} p_{up}(m,p) * f_{up}(m) * USF(m), & m=1 \\ p_{down}(m,p) * f_{down}(m) * DSF(m) \\ \quad + p_{up}(m,p) * f_{up}(m) * USF(m), & 1<m<d \\ p_{down}(m,p) * f_{down}(m) * DSF(m), & m=d \end{cases}$$

where

(1) $f_{down}(m)$ and $f_{up}(m)$ are the percentages of the remaining subspaces to be searched. specifically,

$$f_{down}(m) = C_{down\_left}(m)/C_{down}(m)$$

and

$$f_{up}(m) = C_{up\_left}(m)/C_{up}(m)$$

Let dim(s) denote the number of dimensions in subspace s. $C_{down\_left}(m)$ and $C_{up\_left}(m)$ are computed as:

$$C_{down\_left}(m) = \sum dim(s)$$

where s is unpruned or unevaluated subspaces and dim(s) < m.

$$C_{up\_left}(m) = \sum dim(s)$$

where s is unpruned or unevaluated subspaces and dim(s) > m.

$C_{down}(m)$ and $C_{up}(m)$ are the total subspace search workload in the subspaces whose dimensions are lower and higher than m, respectively. Intuitively, $f_{down}(m)$ and $f_{up}(m)$ approximate the fraction of DSF and USF of an m-dimensional subspace that are potentially achievable in each step of the search process.

(2) $p_{up}(m,p)$ and $p_{down}(m,p)$ are the probabilities that upward and downward pruning can be performed in the m-dimensional subspace respectively. In other words, $p_{up}(m,p) = Por(OD_s(p) \geq T)$ and $p_{down}(m,p) = Por(OD_s(p) < T)$, where s is an m-dimensional subspace. A difficulty in computing the two prior probabilities, i.e. $p_{up}(m,p)$ and $p_{down}(m,p)$, is that their values cannot be known without any priori knowledge of the dataset. To overcome this difficulty, we first perform a sample-based learning process to obtain some knowledge about the dataset and then apply this knowledge in the later subspace search for each query point.

3.2 Sampling-based Learning Process

To facilitate the computation of $p_{up}(m,p)$ and $p_{down}(m,p)$, we adopt a sample-based learning process to obtain some prior knowledge about the dataset before subspace search of the query points are performed. In this learning process, a small number of points randomly sampled from the dataset are obtained and the subspace searches are performed on each of the sampling points. For each sampling point sp, we set

$$p_{up}(m,sp) = p_{down}(m,sp) = 0.5, 1 < m < d$$
$$p_{up}(m,sp) = 1 \text{ and } p_{down}(m,sp) = 0, m=1$$
$$p_{up}(m,sp) = 0 \text{ and } p_{down}(m,sp) = 1, m=d$$

This implies that we assume there are equal probabilities for upward and downward pruning in the subspaces of any dimension, except 1 and d, for each sampling point. After all the m-dimensional subspaces have been evaluated for sp, the $p_{up}(m,sp)$ and $p_{down}(m,sp)$ are computed as the percentage of m-dimensional subspaces s in which $OD_s(sp) \geq T$ and the percentage of subspaces s in which $OD_s(sp) < T$, respectively. The average p_{up} and p_{down} values of subspaces from 1 to d dimensions can be obtained as follows:

$$\overline{p_{up}(m)} = \sum_{i=1}^{S} p_{up}(m, sp_i)/S$$
$$\overline{p_{down}(m)} = \sum_{i=1}^{S} p_{down}(m, sp_i)/S$$

where S is the number of sampling points, $\overline{p_{down}(1)} = \overline{p_{up}(d)} = 0$.

For each query point p, we set $p_{up}(m,p) = \overline{p_{up}(m)}$ and $p_{down}(m,p) = \overline{p_{down}(m)}$ in the computation of TSF(m, p) of the query point p.

3.3 Dynamic Subspace Search

In HOS-Miner, we use a dynamic subspace search method to find the outlying subspaces of the sampling and query points. The basic idea of the dynamic subspace search method is to commence search on those subspaces with the same dimension that has the highest TSF value. As the search proceeds, the TSF of subspaces with different dimension will be dynamically updated and the set of subspaces with the highest TSF value are selected for exploration in each of subsequent steps. The search process terminates when all the subspaces have been evaluated or pruned. Note that the only difference between the dynamic subspace search method used on the sample points and query points lies in the decision of values of $p_{up}(m,p)$ and $p_{down}(m,p)$: *For sample points, we assume an equal probability of upward and downward pruning (referring to Section 3.2) while for query points we use the averaged probabilities obtained in the learning process.*

3.4 Result Refinement

Given the typically large number of data points in the dataset and outlying subspaces for each data point, which may overwhelm the users, we devise a filter in HOS-Miner to help refine the result returned by HOS-Miner. For each data point, HOS-Miner only returns the outlying subspaces with the lowest possible number of dimensions. This is because the subspaces that are supersets of a known outlying subspaces are also outlying subspaces. This outlying subspaces selection process adopts an upward search strategy which starts with outlying subspaces of the lowest number of dimension. A subspace is discarded if it is found to be a superset of a previously selected subspace. The whole selection process terminates when all the subspaces returned by HOS-Miner have been examined. Now, we will give an example to illustrate such outlying subspaces selection process. Let us suppose that the outlying subspaces of a data point, in a 4-dimensional space, are [1,3], [2,4], [1,2,3], [1,2,4], [1,3,4], [2,3,4] and [1,2,3,4]. The filter will only return [1,3] and [2,4] to the users and ignore all the rest. This is because all of remaining subspaces are supersets of either [1,3] or [2,4] or both.

4 The Plan of Demo

Our demo will consist of the following 4 parts.

First, we will present the new task of detecting the outlying subspaces of high-dimensional data by pictorially showing the different distribution nature of high-dimensional data points in varied subspaces, which motivate our research work. We will also show the audience some real-life applications in which our technique can be potentially applied. These examples will provide the audience with insights into the interesting notion of outlying subspaces for high-dimensional data and the valuable knowledge that can be explored from them.

Second, we will showcase the system architecture of HOS-Miner. Among the focuses of system architecture demostration are the *sampling-based learning module*, the *dynamic subspace search module* and the *filtering module*, the three core modules of HOS-Miner used to perform fast subspaces learning, exploration/pruning and filtering in high-dimensional space.

Third, by using both synthetic and real-life datasets, we will show to the audience the experimental evaluation of HOS-Miner and the comparative study of HOS-Miner and the latest high-dimensional outlier detection technique, i.e. the evolutionary-based searching method, in terms of efficiency and effectiveness under a wide spectrum of settings.

Finally, we will showcase the prototype of HOS-Miner and the audience will be encouraged to play the demo interactively themselves.

References

[1] C. C Aggarwal and P.S. Yu. Outlier Detection in High Dimensional Data. Proc. *ACM SIGMOD'00*, Santa Barbara, California, 2001.

[2] S. Berchtold, D. A. Keim and H. Kriegel. The X-tree: An Index Structure for High-Dimensional Data. Proc. *VLDB'96*, Mumbai, India, 1996.

[3] M. Breuning, H-P, Kriegel, R. Ng, and J. Sander. LOF: Identifying Density-Based Local Outliers. Proc. *ACM SIGMOD'00*, Dallas, Texas, 2000.

[4] W. Jin, A. K. H. Tung, J. Han. Finding Top n Local Outliers in Large Database. Proc. *SIGKDD'01*, San Francisco, CA, August, 2001.

[5] E. M. Knorr and R. T. Ng. Algorithms for Mining Distance-based Outliers in Large Dataset. Proc. *VLDB'98*, pages 392-403, New York, NY, August 1998.

[6] E. M. Knorr and R. T. Ng. Finding Intentional Knowledge of Distance-based Outliers. Proc. *VLDB'99*, pages 211-222, Edinburgh, Scotland, 1999.

[7] S. Papadimitriou, H. Kitagawa, P. B. Gibbons, and C. Faloutsos: LOCI: Fast Outlier Detection Using the Local Correlation Integral. Proc. *ICDE'03*, pages 315, Bangalore, India, 2003.

[8] S. Ramaswamy, R. Rastogi, and S. Kyuseok. Efficient Algorithms for Mining Outliers from Large Data Sets. Proc. *ACM SIGMOD'00*, Dallas, Texas, 2000.

VizTree: a Tool for Visually Mining and Monitoring Massive Time Series Databases

Jessica Lin[a]   Eamonn Keogh[a]   Stefano Lonardi[a]   Jeffrey P. Lankford[b]   Daonna M. Nystrom[b]

[a]Computer Science & Engineering Department
University of California, Riverside
Riverside, CA 92521
{jessica, eamonn, stelo}@cs.ucr.edu

[b]The Aerospace Corporation
El Segundo, CA 90245-4691
{Jeffrey.P.Lankford, Donna.M.Nystrom}@aero.org

Abstract

Moments before the launch of every space vehicle, engineering discipline specialists must make a critical *go/no-go* decision. The cost of a false positive, allowing a launch in spite of a fault, or a false negative, stopping a potentially successful launch, can be measured in the tens of millions of dollars, not including the cost in morale and other more intangible detriments. The Aerospace Corporation is responsible for providing engineering assessments critical to the *go/no-go* decision for every Department of Defense (DoD) launch vehicle. These assessments are made by constantly monitoring streaming telemetry data in the hours before launch. For this demonstration, we will introduce VizTree, a novel time-series visualization tool to aid the Aerospace analysts who must make these engineering assessments. VizTree was developed at the University of California, Riverside and is unique in that the same tool is used for mining archival data and monitoring incoming live telemetry. Unlike other time series visualization tools, VizTree can scale to very large databases, giving it the potential to be a generally useful data mining and database tool.

1. Introduction

One of the crucial responsibilities of The Aerospace Corporation is to provide engineering assessments for the government engineering discipline specialists who make the critical *go/no-go* decision moments before the launch of every DoD space vehicle. The analyst making these engineering assessments has access to data from previous launches and must constantly monitor streaming telemetry from the current mission. Currently, the analysts use electronic strip charts similar to those used to record earthquake shock on paper rolls. However, while these charts illustrate the recent history of each sensor, they do not provide any useful higher-level information that might be valuable to the analyst.

To reduce the possibility of wrong *go/no-go* decisions, The Aerospace Corporation is continually investing in research. There are two major directions of research in this area.

- Producing better techniques to mine the archival launch data from the massive databases collected during previous missions. Finding rules, patterns, and regularities from past data can help us "*know what to expect*" for future missions, and allow more accurate and targeted monitoring, contingency planning, etc [3].
- Producing better techniques to visualize the streaming telemetry data in the hours before launch. This is particularly challenging because analysts may have to monitor dozens of rapidly changing sensors [3].

Although these two tasks are quite distinct, and are usually tackled separately, the contribution of this work is to introduce a single framework that can address both. Having a single tool for both tasks allows knowledge gleaned in the *mining* stage to be represented in the same visual language of the *monitoring* stage, thus allowing a more natural and intuitive transfer of knowledge.

More concretely, we will demonstrate VizTree, a time series pattern discovery and visualization system based on augmenting suffix trees. VizTree simultaneously visually summarizes both the global and local structures of time series data. In addition, it provides novel interactive solutions to many pattern discovery problems, including the discovery of frequently occurring patterns (motif discovery), surprising patterns (anomaly detection), and query by content. The user interactive paradigm allows users to visually explore the time series, and perform real-time hypotheses testing.

2. Our approach: VizTree

Our visualization approach works by transforming the time series into a symbolic representation, and encoding the data in a modified suffix tree in which the frequency and other properties of patterns are mapped onto colors and other visual properties.

In [5], we introduced Symbolic Aggregate approximation (SAX), a novel symbolic representation for time series that transforms a time series into equiprobable symbols. The utility of SAX has been demonstrated in [5], and adaptations or extensions of SAX by other researchers further shows its impact in diverse fields such as medical data mining and video indexing [1, 7]. We refer interested readers to [5] for more details on SAX. Figure 1

---

*Dr. Keogh is supported by NSF Career Award IIS-0237918

Permission to copy without fee all or part of this material is granted provided that the copies are not made or distributed for direct commercial advantage, the VLDB copyright notice and the title of the publication and its date appear, and notice is given that copying is by permission of the Very Large Data Base Endowment. To copy otherwise, or to republish, requires a fee and/or special permission from the Endowment

**Proceedings of the 30th VLDB Conference,
Toronto, Canada, 2004**

shows an example of how a time series of length 1024 is converted to a string of length eight: "*acdcbdba.*" In this example, the number of SAX symbols is eight, and the cardinality of alphabet is four (i.e. *a, b, c,* and *d*).

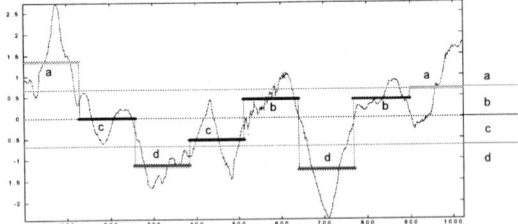

Figure 1: A time series dataset of length 1024 is converted into an eight-symbol string "**acdcbdba.**" Note that the general shape of the time series is preserved, in spite of the massive amount of dimensionality reduction.

To construct a tree representing the input time series, subsequences of specified lengths are extracted from the time series via a sliding window and normalized to have a mean of zero and a standard deviation of one. Applying SAX on these subsequences, we obtain a set of strings, and these strings are inserted into the tree one by one. Each branch/node represents one symbol. The resulting tree is a complete tree with depth equals to the number of SAX symbols. Each node in the tree has α children, where α is the cardinality of alphabet (i.e. if the alphabet size is four, then each node has children denoting *a, b, c,* and *d*, respectively).

Figure 2 shows a simple example of the tree, representing strings of length three with cardinality of two. If we have a string *aba*, then we insert it into the tree, following the top thick path: the first symbol, *a*, is inserted into the first child node, A, of the root; the second symbol, *b*, is inserted into the second child node, AB, of node A; and the last symbol, *a*, is inserted into the first child node, ABA, of node AB. Each time a symbol is inserted, its frequency of occurrence, which is reflected as the thickness of the branch, is updated. The frequently occurring patterns (motifs) "*aba*" and "*bab*" can be easily identified from the tree, since these two paths are thicker compared to the other branches.

We call such trees *subsequence trees*. Differing from a classic suffix tree, a subsequence tree maps all subsequences onto the branches of the tree. Thus, given the same parameters, the trees have the same overall shape for any dataset. This approach makes comparing two arbitrarily long time series easy and, as we shall see, it makes anomaly detection possible.

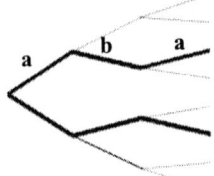

Figure 2: Subsequence tree for strings of length three and cardinality of two. The motifs "aba" and "bab" can be easily identified.

2.1 A first look at VizTree

Figure 3 shows a screen shot of VizTree[1]. When the program is executed, four blank panels and a parameter-setting area are displayed. To load a time series dataset, the user selects the input file using a familiar dropdown menu. The input time series is plotted in the top left-hand panel. Next to the time series plotting window is the parameter setting area; the analyst can enter the sliding window length, the number of SAX segments per window, and select alphabet size from a dropdown menu. Once the parameters are entered, the user can click on the "Show Tree" button to display the subsequence tree on the bottom left panel.

The time series used for this example is an industrial dataset of smog emissions from a motor vehicle. The length of the time series is 2478. The length of the sliding window is arbitrarily set to 53; the number of segments (i.e., the depth of the tree) is four, and the alphabet size (i.e., the number of children for each node) is four.

The mappings of the symbols are consistent with the natural shape of the tree. For example, for any given node, a branch at a higher position denotes segments with higher values. Traversing breadth-first from the top-most branch of any given node, the symbols that represent the branches are *a, b, c,* and *d,* respectively. Each level of the tree represents one segment. To retrieve any string, we simply traverse down the appropriate branches.

The frequency of a pattern is encoded in the thickness of the branch. For clarity, the full tree is drawn. Branches with zero frequency are drawn in light gray, while others are drawn in red with varying thicknesses.

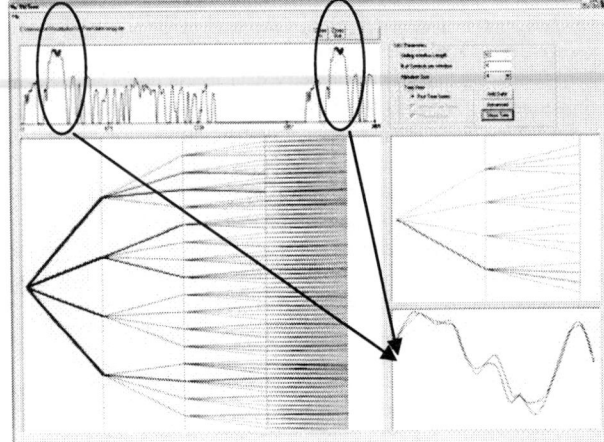

Figure 3: A screenshot of Viztree. The top panel is the input time series. The bottom left panel shows the subsequence tree for the time series. On the right, the very top is the parameter setting area. Next to the subsequence tree panel, the top window shows the zoom-in of the tree, and the bottom window plots the actual subsequences when the analyst clicks on a branch.

On the right hand side of VizTree, there are two panels. The upper one shows the zoom-in of the tree shown in the left panel. This is very useful especially for deep and bushy trees. The user can click on any node (on the subsequence tree window, or recursively, on the zoom-in window) and the sub-tree rooted at this node will be displayed in this upper panel. The sub-tree shown in Figure 3 is rooted at the node representing the string "*abxx*," where the "*xx*" denotes *don't-care* since we are not at the leaf level. If the user clicks on any branch, then the actual subsequences having the string represented by this particular branch will be displayed in the bottom panel and highlighted in the time series plot window. In the figure, subsequences encoded to "*abdb*" are shown.

---

[1] We note that all the figures in this text suffer from their small scale and monochromatic printing. We encourage the interested reader to visit [4] to view high-resolution full-color examples.

2.2 Subsequence matching

Similarity search can be done very efficiently with VizTree. Instead of feeding another time series as query, the user provides the query in an intuitive way. The top branch corresponds to the region with the highest values, and the bottom branch corresponds to the region with the lowest values. Therefore, any path can be easily translated into a general shape and can be used as a query. For example, the top-most branch at depth one (i.e., string "*axxx*") represents all subsequences that start with high values, or more precisely, whose values in the first segment have the mean value that resides in the highest region. In the previous example, the user is interested in finding a concave-down pattern (i.e., a U-shape). This particular pattern, according to the domain experts, corresponds to a change of gears in the motor vehicle during the smog emission test. From the U shape, the user can approximate the query to be something that goes down and comes up, or a string that starts and ends with high branches, with low branches in the middle. As a result, clicking on the branch representing "*abdb*" as shown in the figure uncovers the pattern of interest.

2.3 Motif discovery

A substantial body of literature has been devoted to techniques to discover frequently recurring, overrepresented patterns in time series; however, each work considered a different definition of *pattern*. In previous work, we unified and formalized the problem by defining the concept of "time series motif" [6].

VizTree provides a straightforward way to identify motifs. Since the thickness of a branch denotes the frequency of the subsequences having the same, corresponding strings, we can identify approximate motifs by examining the subsequences represented by thick tree paths. A feature unique to VizTree is that it allows users to visually evaluate and inspect the patterns returned. This interactive feature is important since different strings can also represent similar subsequences, such as those that differ by only one symbol. Figure 4 shows an example.

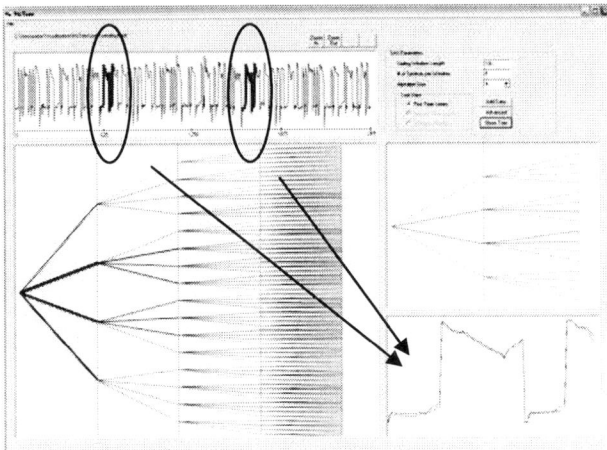

Figure 4: Example of motif discovery on the winding dataset. Two nearly identical subsequences are identified, among the other motifs.

The subsequences retrieved in the lower right panel have the string representation "*dacb*." Examining the motifs in this dataset allowed us to discover an interesting fact: while the dataset was advertised as real, we noted that repeated patterns occur at every 1000 points. For example, in Figure 4, the two nearly identical subsequences retrieved are located at offsets 599 and 1599, exactly 1000 points apart. We checked with the original author and discovered that this is actually a synthetic dataset, composed from parts of a real dataset, a fact that is not obvious from inspection of the original data.

2.4 Simple anomaly detection

The complementary problem of motif discovery is anomaly detection. While frequently occurring patterns can be detected by thick branches in the VizTree, unusually thin branches can signal simple anomalous patterns. Figure 5 demonstrates both motif discovery and simple anomaly detection on an MIT-BIH Noise Stress Test Dataset (ECG recordings) obtained from PhyioBank [2]. Here, motifs can be identified very easily from the thick branches. More remarkably, there is one very thin line straying off on its own (the path that starts with "a"). This line turns out to be an anomalous heartbeat, independently annotated by a cardiologist as a premature ventricular contraction.

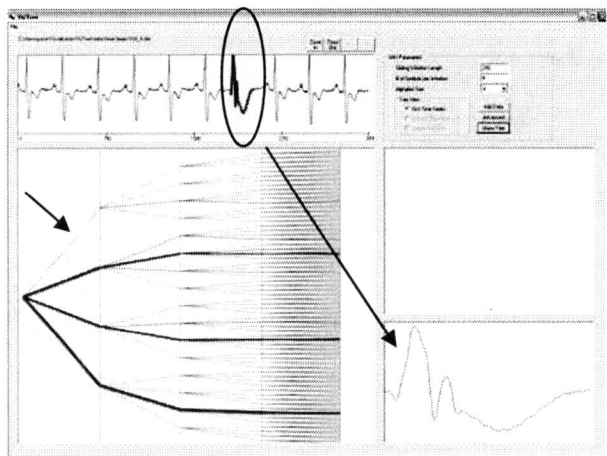

Figure 5: Heartbeat data with anomaly. The thick lines represent the reoccurring normal heartbeat; the thin line pointed to by the short arrow suggests an infrequently occurring pattern, an *anomaly*. Simply by clicking on this line the source of the data is highlighted in the top panel, and a zoom-in is shown in the bottom right panel.

As another motivating example, we used a power demand dataset provided by a Dutch research facility. Electricity consumption is recorded every 15 minutes; therefore, for the year of 1997, there are 35,040 data points. Figure 6 shows the resulting tree with the sliding window length set to 672 (exactly one week of data), and both alphabet size and number of segments to 3. The majority of the weeks follow the regular Monday-Friday, 5-working-day pattern, as shown by the thick branches. The thin branches denote the anomalies. The one circled is from the branch "*bab*." The zoom-in shows the beginning of the three-day week during Christmas (Thursday and Friday off). The other thin branches denote other "anomalies"[2] such as New Year's Day, Good Friday, Queen's Birthday, etc.

While anomalies can be detected this way for trivial cases, in more complex cases, the anomalies are usually detected by comparing the time series against a normal, reference time series. Anything that differs substantially from this reference time series can signal anomalies. This is exactly the objective of the Diff-tree, as described in the next section.

---

[2] "Anomalies" in the sense that the electricity consumption is abnormal given the day of the week.

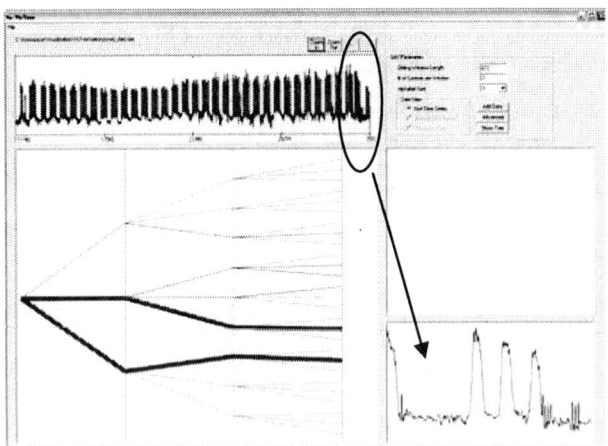

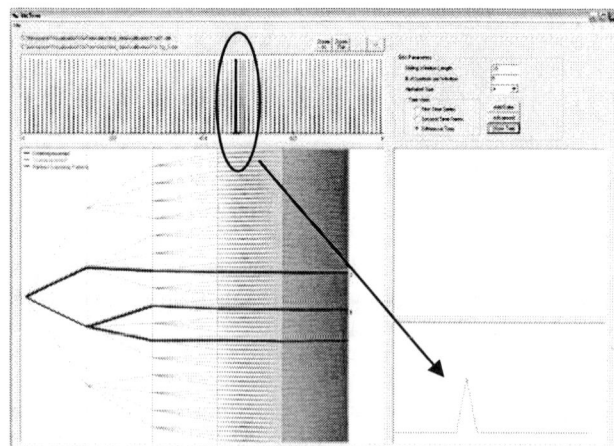

Figure 6: Anomaly detection on power consumption data. The anomaly shown here is a short week during Christmas.

Figure 8: Diff-tree on the datasets shown in the previous figure. The gap is successfully identified.

3. Diff-tree

We have described how global structures, motifs, and simple anomalies can be identified by a subsequence tree. In this section, we extend these ideas to further allow the comparison of two time series by means of a "diff-tree." A diff-tree shows the distinction between two time series. It is constructed by computing the difference in thickness (i.e., frequency of occurrence) for each branch between two subsequence trees. Intuitively, time series data with similar structures can be expected to have similar subsequence trees, and in turn, a sparse diff-tree. In contrast, those with dissimilar structures will result in distinctively different subsequence trees and therefore a relatively dense diff-tree.

3.1 Anomaly detection

The datasets used for anomaly detection, constructed independently of the current authors and provided by The Aerospace Corporation for a sanity check, are shown in Figure 7. The one on the top is the normal time series, and the one below is similar to a normal time series, except it has a gap in the middle as anomaly. Figure 8 shows a screenshot of the anomaly detection by diff-tree. The tree panel shows the diff-tree between the two datasets. The two thick paths denote the beginning and the end of the anomaly, respectively. This is a very trivial example for demonstration purpose. However, the effect is similar for more complex cases.

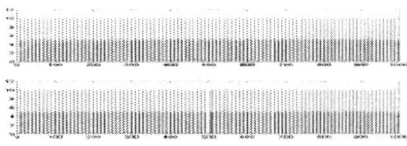

Figure 7: The input files used for anomaly detection by diff-tree. *(Top)* Normal time series. *(Bottom)* Anomaly is introduced as a gap in the middle of the dataset.

3.2 Scalability

The pixel space of the subsequence tree is determined solely by the number of segments and alphabet size. In particular, we note that the pixel size of the tree is *constant* and independent to the length of time series. With a slider on the time series-viewing panel (not shown on the simple examples in this paper), VizTree can accommodate *massive* time series with a constant-size tree. This desirable property makes it easy to view and summarize large time series database on one screen. We have already shown that large amounts of dimensionality reduction do not greatly affect the accuracy of our results (in Section 2.4, the dimensionality is reduced from 672 to 3, a compression ratio of 224-to-1). The size of the database plays a role in memory requirements only for subsequence retrieval purpose, and here we use modified B-trees to allow real time retrieval.

4. References

[1] Chen, L., Ozsu, T. & Oria, V. (2003). Symbolic Representation and Retrieval of Moving Object Trajectories. Univ. of Waterloo. 2003.

[2] Goldberger, A. L., et. al. (2000). PhysioBank, PhysioToolkit, and PhysioNet: Componenets of a New Research Resource for Complex Physiologic Signals. *Circulation*. vol. 101(23), June 13. pp. e215-e220. http://circ.ahajournals.org/cgi/content/full/101/23/e215]

[3] Lankford, J. P. & Quan, A. (2002). Evolution of Knowledge-Based Applications for Launch Support. In *proceedings of Ground System Architecture Workshop*. El Segundo, CA.

[4] Lin, J. VizTree Website. *http://www.cs.ucr.edu/~jessica/VLDB04.htm*

[5] Lin, J., Keogh, E., Lonardi, S. & Chiu, B. (2003). A Symbolic Representation of Time Series, with Implications for Streaming Algorithms. In *Workshop on Research Issues in Data Mining and Knowledge Discovery, the 8th ACM SIGMOD*. San Diego, CA. June 13, 2003.

[6] Lin, J., Keogh, E., Patel, P. & Lonardi, S. (2002). Finding Motifs in Time Series. In *the 2nd Workshop on Temporal Data Mining, the 8th ACM Int'l Conference on Knowledge Discovery and Data Mining*. Edmonton, Alberta, Canada. July 23-26, 2002.

[7] Ohsaki, M., Sato, Y., Yokoi, H. & Yamaguchi, T. (2003). A Rule Discovery Support System for Sequential Medical Data, in the Case Study of a Chronic Hepatitis Dataset. In *Discovery Challenge Workshop, the 14th ECML/the 7th PKDD*. Cavtat-Dubrovnik, Croatia. Sep 22-26, 2003.

An Electronic Patient Record "on Steroids": Distributed, Peer-to-Peer, Secure and Privacy-conscious*

Serge Abiteboul[1]   Bogdan Alexe[2]   Omar Benjelloun[1]   Bogdan Cautis[1]
Irini Fundulaki[2]   Tova Milo[1,3]   Arnaud Sahuguet[2]

[1]:INRIA Futurs, [2]: Bell Labs, Lucent Technologies, [3]: Tel-Aviv University

1 Introduction

Getting sick or injured is never a good idea. You never know when it's going to happen or where. In such situations, it is crucial to be able to gather all the relevant information to make the diagnosis and treatment as effective as possible.

By nature, an electronic patient record (EPR) [9] consists of many pieces owned and managed by different entities: yourself as a patient, your referring doctor, the various specialists you are dealing with (e.g. gynecologist, optometrist, physical therapist), the pharmacist(s) you shop from, the various hospitals you go to for surgery or special examination, the insurance company (private or state-owned) that handles the billing and reimbursement, some wearable devices that monitor your heartbeat or glucose level, etc.

Besides the distribution of the data, one of the main challenges in the management of EPR information is its sensitive nature. Clearly, a patient does not want unauthorized parties to access confidential parts of her medical record. One should note that the issue of managing information that is both highly distributed and partly confidential does not arise only in the EPR context, but is also typical of many other distributed applications, such as the management of user profiles, shared agendas, collaborative workspaces, etc. *The goals of this demo are (1) to propose a unified, peer-to-peer, privacy conscious solution to the management of distributed sensitive information, and (2) illustrate it through an EPR management example scenario.*

So far, most approaches to the management of EPRs considered a setting where the information is highly centralized (e.g. in hospitals), for which centralized approaches – like the one advocated by Hippocratic databases [5] – make perfect sense. As EPR relevant information is more and more distributed, we argue that a centralized approach is not always satisfactory. To handle the inherent distribution of data, we advocate for a peer-to-peer architecture, where EPR data can be seen as a large virtual XML document [12] – one per user – that is being accessed and modified by the numerous players involved. As far as access control on XML data is concerned, existing approaches [6, 8] offer great flexibility in terms of the definition and the enforcement of access rules, but do not provide means to handle highly distributed data. In a peer-to-peer setting, each peer may want to enforce particular access control rules for the data that it owns and for the data that is accessible through it, and possibly delegate to other peers the task of defining/enforcing these rules. These functionalities are precisely the ones provided by the system demonstrated here.

Contribution: We demonstrate a novel solution for the privacy-conscious integration of distributed data, that relies on the combination of two key technologies: Active XML [4], that provides a highly flexible peer-to-peer paradigm for data integration, and GUP^{ster} [14], that unifies the enforcement of access control and source descriptions. While each of these two technologies has been demonstrated separately before [4, 1, 2, 11], we show here that their synergy yields a powerful generic platform that seamlessly handles data integration and privacy enforcement tasks in a highly distributed setting.

Active XML (AXML for short) is a framework to manage XML documents where some of the data is given explicitly, whereas other parts are calls to Web services [16] that generate the "missing" data. Such documents can be viewed as a partially virtual. The AXML platform makes it possible to manage and query these documents, offering rich features such as lazy/distributed query evaluation and typing [13, 3].

GUP^{ster} is a framework for the privacy-conscious management of distributed XML data. Source descrip-

---

* This work was partially supported by EU IST project DB-Globe (IST 2001-32645), and by the French government grant ACI MDP2P.

Permission to copy without fee all or part of this material is granted provided that the copies are not made or distributed for direct commercial advantage, the VLDB copyright notice and the title of the publication and its date appear, and notice is given that copying is by permission of the Very Large Data Base Endowment. To copy otherwise, or to republish, requires a fee and/or special permission from the Endowment.

**Proceedings of the 30th VLDB Conference,
Toronto, Canada, 2004**

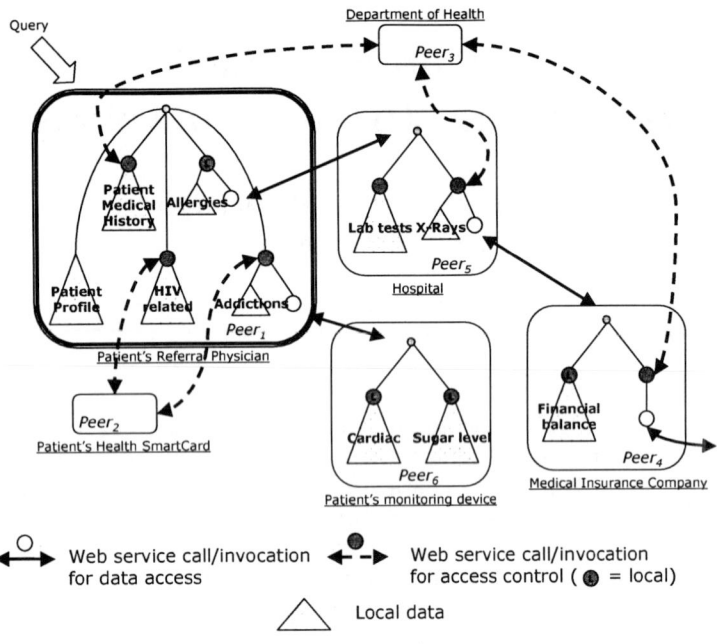

```
<patientData>
  <identity>
    <name>
      <first>Mary</first>
      <last>Smith</last>
    </last>
    <dateOfBirth>19710402</dateOfBirth>
    <ssn>
      <call svc="filterSSN@ssa.org">
        <call svc="getMySSN@local" />
      </call>
    </ssn>
  </identity>
  <address>2200 Broadway, NY, 10023 NY</address>
  <medicalRecord>
    <call svc="filterMR@DeptOfHealth">
      <visit>
        <date>20030102</date>
        <MD>
          <name>John Jones</name>
          <specialty>eyeMD</specialty>
        </MD>
        <prescription>Eye drops</prescription>
        <diagnosis>
          <call svc="diagDescription@DoctorPepper">
            <call svc="getDiagnosis@DoctorPepper">
              <visitID>627692876693</visitID>
            </call>
          </call>
        </diagnosis>
      </visit>
      ...
      <call svc="getVisits@MDVisits">
        <patient>Mary F. Smith</patient>
      </call>
    </call>
  </medicalRecord>
  ...
</patientData>
```

Figure 1: Global architecture

tions (i.e. the queries supported by each source) and user access rights are specified *in a uniform way* using XSquirrel, a specialized XML query language. The nice closure properties of this language for operators such as union and composition allow user queries to be statically *rewritten* into queries that are both *authorized* (from the access control rules) and *compatible* (with the source descriptions).

Together, the two technologies are combined in the architecture of Fig. 1, where peers can act as data sources, integrators, and provide/enforce access control/source descriptions. In this demo, this enables us to (i) represent a user's EPR as a virtual document, distributed among different peers on the network, (ii) enforce fine-grained access control policies over this document, also in a distributed way, and (iii) process queries while enforcing the access control, in a distributed, privacy conscious manner. In Fig. 1, an EPR at a physician's peer has some part on a monitoring device, and some part at the hospital and (recursively) at the insurance company. Access control on this distributed data is partly determined by the patient's preferences (through her SmartCard), partly by the general regulations of the Department of Health, and partly locally at each participating peer.

The rest of this paper is organized as follows. Section 2 overviews AXML and GUP^{ster}. Section 3 explains how their combination supports privacy-conscious data integration. Section 4 outlines a demonstration scenario for the management of electronic patient records.

2 Underlying technologies

In this Section, we briefly introduce Active XML documents and the GUP^{ster} query rewriting mechanism.

Figure 2: An EPR as an AXML document

2.1 Active XML: P2P data integration

AXML is a declarative framework that harnesses Web services for data integration, and is put to work in a peer-to-peer architecture. An AXML document is an XML document where some of the data is given extensionally, as regular XML elements, while some data is given *intensionally*, by means of calls to Web services [16]. These service calls are represented by special `call` elements, that are embedded in the document. The data inside the `call` element is the *parameter* of the service call. When a service is invoked, the call parameter is passed to it, and its result replaces the service call in the document.

For example, consider the document in Fig. 2, that represents an electronic patient record (ignore for now the boxed parts). The document contains the patient's identity information and medical record. Some of the data is given explicitly, e.g. the patient name, and some can be obtained by calling Web services, e.g. her social security number (`ssn`) that is available from `getMySSN@local`, and additional visits information that can be obtained via the `getVisits` service hosted by the `MDVisits` peer.

Lazy query evaluation When a query is evaluated on a document, the service calls whose answer is relevant for the query are invoked [1]. To optimize the computation, when possible, (sub)queries are "pushed" to the service providers, thus reducing the materialization and transfer of data (see [3] for details). When a query is pushed to a service, it is passed to it as an extra parameter. The service, depending on its particular implementation, can either naively perform its normal computation, and then evaluate the pushed query on the result, or have a more optimized strategy.

Note that, since the called services may themselves be defined as queries over AXML documents, the called peers may run a similar computation, thus achieving a P2P ad-hoc style of data mediation.

2.2 GUP^{ster}: Declarative access control

To ensure the privacy of data, one needs a fine grained control over the requests initiated by users. We adopt here the GUP^{ster} approach [11], that unifies access control (AC) and source descriptions, by relying on a single query language to specify both, and a single query rewriting mechanism to enforce them.

The query language used by GUP^{ster} to describe AC rules and source descriptions is XSquirrel, a simple XML *projection* query language. The language uses a syntax similar to that of XPath [7], but has different semantics: rather than returning sets of nodes, like XPath, it returns a projection of the queried document. Intuitively, the result of an XSquirrel query on a document is the sub-document that contains (a) all descendant leaf nodes of the requested nodes and (b) their ancestors up to the root of the initial document.

As a simple example, suppose that we want to restrict the access to the visit elements in Mary's EPR, allowing Dr. Hull to access only the prescription, diagnosis and MD's specialty elements. The corresponding XSquirrel access rule would be:

AC1: Hull, /visit/(MD/specialty ∪ prescription ∪ diagnosis)

Similar rules can be used to describe the access rights of other users, or the queries accepted by data sources (in our case, the embedded Web service calls).

To process a query, GUP^{ster} fetches the relevant AC/source description rules and composes them with the query, yielding a *restricted* query that accesses/returns only allowed information. For instance, suppose that Dr. Hull attempts to retrieve all the data regarding her visits to ophthalmologist by issuing the query: /visit[MD/specialty="eyeMD"]
The restricted query would be:
/visit[MD/specialty="eyeMD"]/(prescription
∪ diagnosis ∪ MD/specialty)
While the result of the composition in this case is very intuitive, the general rewriting technique for more complex queries and rules is more intricate, and relies on XSquirrel's closure properties. See [10] for details.

---
[1] Service calls (and their parameters) represent *virtual* data and are not queriable.

It should be noted that, in the original GUP^{ster} system, AC rules as well as source descriptions are specified with respect to a global schema, and are managed by a centralized mediator, in charge of applying them for all the queries asked on the global schema. The main contribution of the present work is in leveraging GUP^{ster}'s access control mechanism for P2P, schema-free integration of decentralized data.

3 Privacy-conscious P2P integration

We first present filtering services, our basic construct for distributed access control, then explain how they are used to enforce access control, and finally consider some important security aspects.

3.1 Filtering services

GUP^{ster}'s access control functionality is naturally incorporated into AXML documents, by being provided as Web services. We define *filtering services*, that enforce GUP^{ster}-like rules on AXML data. Each of these services can protect some AXML data by filtering the queries that can be evaluated on them, according to a set of access control rules. Note that the protected data does not have to be sent extensionally as a parameter, but can be represented intensionally by a service call, and thus hidden from the filtering service.

In our EPR document, calls to such services are the boxed ones. For instance, filterMR@DeptOfHealth is a filtering service that restricts Dr. Hull's access to Mary's visit information, by using the access control rule AC1 given in Section 2.2.

It should be noted that, like for other Web services, filtering services can be freely used and combined inside AXML documents. Therefore, in the same way that service calls are used to integrate data from various sources, they can also be used to combine access control/source descriptions that are enforced/provided by various parties. For instance, queries targeted at the diagnosis information, that is retrieved from getDiagnosis@DoctorPepper will be both protected by the AC enforced by the call to filterMR@DeptOfHealth and limited by the source description provided by diagDescription@DoctorPepper.

We next explain how access control is enforced while queries are evaluated.

3.2 Query evaluation and access control

To enable the enforcement of access control, we extend Active XML's lazy evaluation and query pushing mechanisms to apply also to filtering services. When a query is evaluated on an AXML document, and a call to a filtering service is met, the corresponding subquery is pushed to the filtering service, which combines it with the access control rules defined for the user asking the query, using GUP^{ster}'s rewriting algorithms.

Then, the filtering service can either (lazily) evaluate the resulting rewritten query on the guarded data and return the result of this evaluation, or let the requester evaluate this query. This choice is controlled by the input/output types specified for the filtering services, using techniques introduced in [13].

Consider our previous GUP^{ster} example. Suppose the peer of Mary's referring MD (RMD) receives a request from Dr. Hull to evaluate, on the document of Fig. 2, the following query:

`/patientData/medicalRecord/visit[MD/specialty="eyeMD"]`

The RMD peer pushes a query about visits to `filterMR@DeptOfHealth`, which composes it with the access control rule AC1, as discussed in Section 2.2. Then, the composed query is evaluated (either at the RMD peer or at the filtering peer `DeptOfHealth`). This will also entail pushing a subquery to `getVisits@MDVisits`, which, recursively, may also invoke calls to filtering services guarding its own data (hence further restricting the pushed query).

3.3 Security aspects

Classical transport-level security mechanisms, based on public-key encryption and digital signatures will be used to enforce properties such as confidentiality, authentication and non-repudiation, at the message level. When a finer level of control is required, XML Encryption and XML Signature standards [15, 17] will be used to encrypt/sign only parts of the exchanged messages.

Basic Web services for handling encryption and signature will be present locally on every peer, and calls to these local services will be used in AXML documents, e.g. to provide means to decrypt some encrypted data, or to verify a signature. The typing mechanisms mentioned above will also be used to enforce constraints such as: queries pushed to `getDiagnosis@DoctorPepper` must be signed by `filterMR@DeptOfHealth`.

4 Demonstration scenario

We will demonstrate how an EPR document can be managed by a number of AXML peers representing hospitals, MD's, insurance companies, Department of Health. These peers will be living on remote servers, laptops and mobile devices. Each of them will provide/integrate information/filtering services, or a combination of these. E.g., a hospital provides information about visits, while an insurance company gives reimbursement reports, and access control on both of them is enforced by both the regulations of the Dept. of Health, and their own respective privacy policies.

We will illustrate how this distributed data can be queried by different users (referring doctor, nurse, insurance company), and how the specified access control rules are enforced along the way. We will in particular show how:

- a patient manages her EPR, by adding or removing sources, and protecting this integrated data, by using external filtering services, or defining her own, using access control rules.
- a doctor can access/query this EPR with some restrictions,
- a nurse can access the EPR in an even more restricted way,
- the insurance company can check the latest prescriptions for future reimbursement.

For all these scenarios, we will demonstrate how the queries are executed efficiently:

- only the relevant/permissible parts of the AXML document are exchanged between peers,
- an AXML peer can fully or partially evaluate a query (similar to LDAP referral mode), by delegating some of the computation to filtering peers or information sources.

References

[1] S. Abiteboul, B. Amann, J. Baumgarten, O. Benjelloun, F. Dang Ngoc, and T. Milo. Schema-driven Customization of Web Services (demo). In *Proc. of VLDB*, Berlin, 2003.

[2] S. Abiteboul, J. Baumgarten, A. Bonifati, G. Cobena, C. Cremarenco, F. .Dragan, I. Manolescu, T. Milo, and N. Preda. Managing Distributed Workspaces with Active XML (demo). In *Proc. of VLDB*, Berlin, 2003.

[3] S. Abiteboul, O. Benjelloun, B. Cautis, I. Manolescu, T. Milo, and N. Preda. Lazy Evaluation for Active XML. In *Proc. of ACM-SIGMOD*, Paris, June 2004.

[4] S. Abiteboul, O. Benjelloun, I. Manolescu, T. Milo, and R. Weber. Active XML: Peer-to-Peer Data and Web Services Integration (demo). In *Proc. of VLDB*, Hong Kong, 2002.

[5] R. Agrawal, J. Kiernan, R. Srikant, and Y. Xu. Hippocratic databases. In *Proc. of VLDB*, Hong Kong, 2002.

[6] E. Bertino and E. Ferrari. Secure and Selective Dissemination of XML Documents. *ACM Trans. on Information and System Security*, 5(3):290–331, 2002.

[7] J. Clark and S. DeRose (eds.). XML Path Language (XPath) Version 1.0. W3C Recommendation, November 1999. http://www.w3c.org/TR/xpath.

[8] E. Damiani, S. De Capitani di Vimercati, S. Paraboschi, and P. Samarati. A Fine-Grained Access Control System for XML Documents. *ACM Trans. on Information and System Security*, 5(2):169–202, May 2002.

[9] Health Level Seven. http://www.hl7.org/.

[10] I. Fundulaki and A. Sahuguet. A language-based approach for distributed user profile data management. Technical Report, November 2003.

[11] I. Fundulaki, A. Sahuguet, D. Lieuwen, N. Onose, G. Giraud, and N. Pombourcq. Share your data, keep your secrets (demo). In *Proc. SIGMOD*, Paris, 2004.

[12] E. Kuikka, A. Eerola, and J. Komulainen. Structuring the electronic patient record. Technical report, University of Kuopio, 2001.

[13] T. Milo, S. Abiteboul, B. Amann, O. Benjelloun, and F. Dang Ngoc. Exchanging Intensional XML Data. In *Proc. of ACM SIGMOD*, San Diego, 2003.

[14] A. Sahuguet, R. Hull, D. Lieuwen, and M. Xiong. Enter Once, Share Everywhere: User Profile Management in Converged Networks. In *Proc. of CIDR*, 2003.

[15] W3C. XML Encryption WG, 2001. http://www.w3.org/Encryption.

[16] W3C. Web Services Activity, 2002. http://www.w3.org/2002/ws.

[17] W3C. XML Signature WG, 2002. http://www.w3.org/Signature.

Queries and Updates in the coDB Peer to Peer Database System

Enrico Franconi[†], Gabriel Kuper[‡], Andrei Lopatenko[†,§], Ilya Zaihrayeu[‡]

[†]Free University of Bozen–Bolzano, Faculty of Computer Science, Italy,
franconi@inf.unibz.it, lopatenko@inf.unibz.it

[‡]University of Trento, DIT, Italy,
kuper@acm.org, ilya@dit.unitn.it

[§]University of Manchester, Department of Computer Science, UK

Abstract

In this short paper we present the coDB P2P DB system. A network of databases, possibly with different schemas, are interconnected by means of GLAV coordination rules, which are inclusions of conjunctive queries, with possibly existential variables in the head; coordination rules may be cyclic. Each node can be queried in its schema for data, which the node can fetch from its neighbours, if a coordination rule is involved.

1 Introduction

In the paper [Franconi *et al.*, 2003] we introduced a general logical and computational characterisation of peer-to-peer (P2P) database systems. We first defined a precise model-theoretic semantics of a P2P system, which allows for local inconsistency handling. We then characterised the general computational properties for the problem of answering queries to such a P2P system. Finally, we devised tight complexity bounds and distributed procedures in few relevant special cases. The basic principles of the characterisation given in [Franconi *et al.*, 2003] are: (a) the role of the coordination formulas between nodes is for data migration (as opposed to the role of logical constraints in classical data integration systems); (b) computation is delegated to single nodes (distributed local computation); (c) the topology of the network may dynamically change; (d) local inconsistency does not propagate; (e) computational complexity can be low.

In the paper [Franconi *et al.*, 2004] we thoroughly analysed a distributed procedure for the problem of local database update in a network of database peers, as defined in [Franconi *et al.*, 2003]. The problem of local database update is different from the problem of query answering. Given a P2P database system, the answer to a local query may involve data that is distributed in the network, thus requiring the participation of all nodes at query time to propagate in the direction of the query node the relevant data for the answer, taking into account the (possibly cyclic) coordination rules bridging the nodes. On the other hand, given a P2P database system, a "batch" update algorithm will be such that all the nodes consistently and optimally propagate all the relevant data to their neighbours, allowing for subsequent local queries to be answered locally within a node, without fetching data from other nodes at query time. The update problem has been considered important by the P2P literature; most notably, recent papers focused on the importance of data exchange and materialisation for a P2P network [Fagin *et al.*, 2003; Daswani *et al.*, 2003].

The coDB P2P DB system we present here implements the above ideas in a very general fashion. A network of databases, possibly with different schemas, can be interconnected by means of GLAV coordination rules, which are inclusions of conjunctive queries, with possibly existential variables in the head. Each node can be queried in its schema for data, which the node can fetch from its neighbours, if a coordination rule is involved. Note that rules can be cyclic, i.e., a fix-point computation may be needed among the nodes in order to get all the data that is needed to answer a query. In the abovementioned papers we have showed the correctness of the procedures we have implemented in the coDB system.

coDB supports *dynamic* networks: even if nodes and coordination rules appear or disappear during the

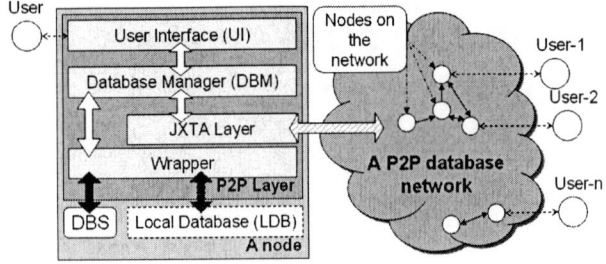

Figure 1: First level architecture

computation, the proposed algorithm will eventually terminate with a sound and complete result (under appropriate definitions of the latter, see [Franconi et al., 2004]).

2 The Architecture

We implement database peers on top of *JXTA* [Project JXTA, 2004]. JXTA specifies a set of protocols which provide implementation of basic, as well as rather sophisticated P2P functionalities. As basic functionalities we can distinguish: definition of a peer on a network; creation of communication links between peers (called pipes); creation of messages, which can envelope arbitrary data (e.g. code, images, queries); sending messages onto pipes, etc. Examples of more sophisticated functionalities provided by JXTA are: creation of peer groups; specification of services and their implementation on peers; advertising of network resources (i.e. peers, pipes, peer groups, services, etc.) and their discovery in a distributed, decentralised environment. JXTA has a number of advantages for developing P2P applications. It provides IP independent naming space to address peers and other resources, it is independent of system platforms (e.g. Microsoft Windows, Macintosh or UNIX) and networking platforms (e.g. Bluetooth, TCP/IP), it can be run on various devices such as PCs or PDAs, and provides support for handling firewalls and NATs. We have chosen JXTA since it already gives practically all basic building blocks for developing P2P applications and thus allow the developer to concentrate on implementation of specific functionalities a given application is required to provide.

The first level logical architecture of a node, inspired by [Bernstein et al., 2002], is presented on Figure 1. A node consists of *P2P Layer*, *Local Database* (LDB) and *Database Schema* (DBS). DBS describes part of LDB, which is shared for other nodes. P2P Layer consists of *User Interface* (UI), *Database Manager* (DBM), *JXTA Layer* and *Wrapper*. Nodes connect to a P2P database network by means of connecting to other peer(s), as it is schematically shown on Figure 1 (see the arrow from JXTA Layer to the network and arrows between nodes in the network).

By means of UI users can commence network queries and updates, browse streaming results, start topology discovery procedures, and so on. Among other things, UI allows to control other modules of P2P Layer. For instance, user can modify the set of coordination rules w.r.t. other nodes, define connection details for Wrapper, etc. DBM processes both user queries and queries coming from the network, as well as global and query-dependent update requests. It is also responsible for processing of query results coming both from LDB and the network, as well as for processing of updates results coming from the network. Finally, DBM manages propagation of queries, update requests, query results and update results on the network. JXTA Layer is responsible for all node's activities on the network, such as discovering of previously unknown nodes, creating pipes with other nodes, sending messages containing queries, update requests, query results, etc. Wrapper manages connections to LDB and executes input database manipulation operations. This is a module which is adjusted depending on the underlying database. For instance, when LDB does not support nested queries, then this is the responsibility of Wrapper to provide this support. Yet another task of Wrapper is retrieval and maintenance of DBS.

The LDB rectangle stands for RDBMS. It has dashed border to mean that local database may be absent. Nevertheless DBS must always be specified in order to allow a node to participate on the network. In this situation a given node acts as a mediator for propagating of requests and data, and all required database operations (as join and project) are executed in Wrapper. The DBS rectangle has rounded corners because it represents a repository, where DBS is stored. Arrows between UI and DBM as well as arrows between JXTA Layer, Wrapper and DBM have the same graphical notation because they represent procedure calls between different execution modules. The arrow between JXTA Layer and the network has another notation because it represents communication supported by JXTA. The arrows connecting Wrapper, DBS and LDB have yet another notation because the communication they denote is LDB dependent.

Nodes may import data from their *acquaintances* using definitions of *coordination rules*. The head of a coordination rule is a conjunctive query which refers to some local relation at a given node, and the body is another conjunctive query (sharing some variables with the head) which refers to relations of an acquaintance. In data integration literature this kind of mapping between two schemas is called *Global-Local-As-View*, or GLAV [Lenzerini, 2002]. The body of a coordination rule may also contain a set of comparison predicates which specify constraints over the domain of particular attributes of the acquaintance's relations. In order to import data from a node's acquaintance using a given coordination rule definition, the acquaintance executes the coordination rule and sends the results back to that node.

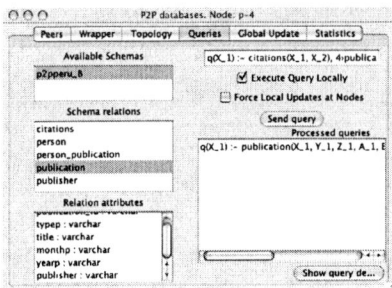

Figure 2: Query interface

A *global update* in a P2P database network is a process of updating nodes' databases using *all* definitions of coordination rules they maintain. A global update is started when some (dedicated) node sends to all its acquaintances global update requests, containing definitions of appropriate coordination rules. These acquaintances executes the queries, respond with the query results, and propagate the global update to their acquaintances, and so on. The global update request propagation is stopped at some node if that node has no acquaintances to propagate the request, or if that node has already received this request message. For the purpose of global update identification, all global update request messages carry the same unique identifier generated at the node which started the global update procedure. We use JXTA to generate global updates identifiers.

3 The Algorithm

Herein we provide a concise description of the global update algorithm [Franconi et al., 2004]. In order to understand how nodes process incoming query results and when results propagation is complete, we introduce some additional notions. We call coordination rules, *incoming links* at some node, if these rules are used by some other (acquainted) nodes for importing data from that given node. We call coordination rules, *outgoing links* at some node, if that node uses these rules in order to import data from its acquaintances. We say that an incoming link is *dependent* on an outgoing link, or that an outgoing link is *relevant* for some incoming link, if the head of the outgoing link reference to a relation, which is referenced by a body subgoal of the incoming link.

Query propagation is being done using extension of "diffusing computation" approach [Lynch, 1996]. When node gets a query request, it answers it using local data immediately, and it forwards it through all outgoing links. Each query request is labelled by a sequence of IDs of nodes it passed through. A node does not propagate a query request, if its ID is contained in the label of query request.

Query results coming from an acquaintance via some outgoing link (say, O) can be seen as an additional, possibly empty set of tuples (say, T) for the relations (R) referenced by the head of this outgoing link. This, in turn, means that re-computing of incoming links, dependent on O, may produce new results for the acquainted nodes. For performance reasons, it is important to avoid duplication in producing and propagating data. Therefore we first remove from T those tuples which are already in R, and get the set of tuples T'. If the conjunctive query in the head of the rule contains existential variables, then fresh new marked null values are used in tuples of T'. Then, T' is added to R. Incoming links, which are dependent on O, are computed by substituting R by T'. The reason for that is avoiding producing query results which might have been already produced for these incoming links. For each incoming link i we get query results R_i. Afterwards, we delete from R_i those tuples which have been already sent to the incoming link, and then send remaining tuples onto i. The receiver node processes these results analogously and may evoke, in turn, further results' propagation. Therefore, incoming data can be seen as a result of *transitive* propagation of query results via a path of nodes, which we call *update propagation path*. At each node in the path, we reconcile and store results sent to corresponding incoming links until global update processing is complete for that node.

The global update processing is finished for some node (we say that after this the node is in the state "closed") if all outgoing links are in the state "closed". Initially, when a node starts a global update propagation or receives a global update request message, it is in the state "open" and all its outgoing links (if any) are in the state "open". An acquaintance closes an incoming link (and, respectively, outgoing link at some acquainted node) if all its outgoing links which are relevant for this incoming link are in the state "closed". A node closes its outgoing link if a) it got query results for all the maximal paths[1] passing through it; b) all query results did not bring any new data to local database. When all outgoing links of a node are in the state "closed", then the node is also in the state "closed". The global update processing is complete, when all nodes are in the state "closed". It is worth saying that our algorithm processes global update properly in the presence of cyclic dependencies and guarantees termination. Under a proper global update processing nodes update their databases with all data that can be retrieved from their acquaintances, taking into account transitive dependencies between incoming and outgoing links. After the termination of the algorithm each node contains a sound and complete set of data (with respect to the semantics given in [Franconi et al., 2003]).

In addition to global updates handling and query answering at a node, coDB supports a topology discov-

---

[1] By *maximal dependency path* for a node I and query Q, we call a dependency path which a) originates in the node initiated Q, b) passes node I; c) is simple; d) can not be extended to any other simple dependency path by adding nodes to the tail.

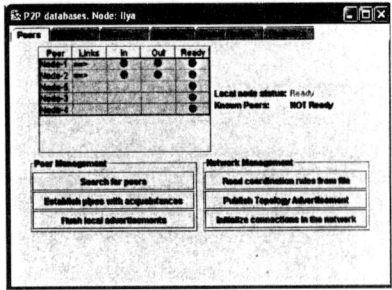

Figure 3: Peer discovery window

ery algorithm. When a node starts, it creates pipes with those nodes, w.r.t. which it has coordination rules, or which have coordination rules w.r.t. the given node. Several coordination rules w.r.t. a given node can use one pipe to send requests and data. If some coordination rules are dropped and a pipe is not assigned any coordination rule, then this pipe is also closed.

4 The Demo

In the demo we will measure the performance of various networks arranged in different topologies: we need to start-up all the nodes, establish coordination rules between pairs of nodes, run a set of experiments and, finally, collect statistical information. In order to facilitate these tasks we provide some peer (called *super-peer*) with some additional functionalities. In particular, that peer can read coordination rules for *all* peers from a file and broadcast this file to all peers on the network. Once received this file, each peer looks for relevant coordination rules and creates necessary pipe connections. If a coordination rules file is received when a peer has already set up coordination rules and pipes, then it drops "old" rules and pipes, and creates new ones, where necessary. Thus, a super-peer can dynamically change the network topology at *runtime*. Each node shows to its user the other nodes it has pipes with, and w.r.t. which nodes it has incoming and outgoing links. It also shows which other nodes (not acquaintances) it has discovered with the help of JXTA (Figure 3).

For the purposes of collecting experimental data, each node has an additional statistical module. This module accumulates various information about global updates such as: total execution time of an update, number of query result messages received per coordination rule and the volume of the data in each message, longest update propagation path, and so on. During the lifetime of a network, each node accumulates this information. A super-peer has the possibility to collect, at any given time, statistical information from *all* nodes on the network. Then, the super-peer processes all incoming statistical messages, aggregates them and creates a final statistical report.

For intermediate nodes, global update processing is done on the background, transparently for the user.

Each node maintains a global update processing report and makes it available for the user on request. The report includes information about starting and finishing times of an update, volume of data transferred, which acquaintances have been queried and to which nodes query results have been sent.

References

[Bernstein et al., 2002] P. Bernstein, F. Giunchiglia, A. Kementsietsidis, J. Mylopoulos, L. Serafini, and I. Zaihrayeu. Data management for peer-to-peer computing: A vision. *Workshop on the Web and Databases, WebDB*, 2002.

[Calvanese et al., 2003] Diego Calvanese, Elio Damaggio, Giuseppe De Giacomo, Maurizio Lenzerini, and Riccardo Rosati. Semantic data integration in p2p systems. In *Proc. of the VLDB International Workshop On Databases, Information Systems and Peer-to-Peer Computing (DBISP2P-2003)*, 2003.

[Calvanese et al., 2004] Diego Calvanese, Giuseppe De Giacomo, Maurizio Lenzerini, and Riccardo Rosati. Logical foundations of peer-to-peer data integration. In *Proc. of the 23rd ACM SIGACT SIGMOD SIGART Sym. on Principles of Database Systems (PODS-2004)*, 2004. To appear.

[Daswani et al., 2003] Neil Daswani, Hector Garcia-Molina, and Beverly Yang. Open problems in data-sharing peer-to-peer systems. In *ICDT 2003*, 2003.

[Fagin et al., 2003] Ronald Fagin, Phokion G. Kolaitis, Renée J. Miller, and Lucian Popa. Data exchange: Semantics and query answering. In *Proceedings of the 9th International Conference on Database Theory*, pages 207–224. Springer-Verlag, 2003.

[Franconi et al., 2003] Enrico Franconi, Gabriel Kuper, Andrei Lopatenko, and Luciano Serafini. A robust logical and computational characterisation of peer-to-peer database systems. In *Proc. of the VLDB International Workshop On Databases, Information Systems and Peer-to-Peer Computing (DBISP2P-2003)*, 2003.

[Franconi et al., 2004] Enrico Franconi, Gabriel Kuper, Andrei Lopatenko, and Ilya Zaihraeu. A distributed algorithm for robust data sharing and updates in p2p database networks. In *Proc. of the EDBT International Workshop on Peer-to-Peer Computing and Databases*, 2004.

[Ghidini and Serafini, 1998] Chiara Ghidini and Luciano Serafini. Distributed first order logics. In Franz Baader and Klaus Ulrich Schulz, editors, *Frontiers of Combining Systems 2*, Berlin, 1998. Research Studies Press.

[Halevy et al., 2003] Alon Y. Halevy, Zachary G. Ives, Dan Suciu, and Igor Tatarinov. Schema mediation in peer data management systems. In *ICDE*, 2003.

[Hellerstein, 2003] Joseph M. Hellerstein. Toward network data independence. *SIGMOD Rec.*, 32(3):34–40, 2003.

[Kementsietsidis et al., 2003] Anastasios Kementsietsidis, Marcelo Arenas, and Renee J. Miller. Mapping data in peer-to-peer systems: Semantics and algorithmic issues. In *Proceedings of the SIGMOD International Conference on Management of Data (SIGMOD'03)*, 2003.

[Lenzerini, 2002] Maurizio Lenzerini. Data integration: A theoretical perspective. In Lucian Popa, editor, *Proceedings of the Twenty-first ACM SIGACT-SIGMOD-SIGART Symposium on Principles of Database Systems*, pages 233–246, 2002.

[Lynch, 1996] Nancy A. Lynch. *Distributed Algorithms*. Morgan Kaufmann Publishers Inc., 1996.

[Project JXTA, 2004] Project JXTA, 2004. See http://www.jxta.org.

[Serafini et al., 2003] Luciano Serafini, Fausto Giunchiglia, John Mylopoulos, and Philip A. Bernstein. Local relational model: A logical formalization of database coordination. In *CONTEXT 2003*, pages 286–299, 2003.

A-ToPSS: A Publish/Subscribe System Supporting Imperfect Information Processing

Haifeng Liu   Hans-Arno Jacobsen

Department of Computer Science & Department of Electrical and Computer Engineering
University of Toronto
hfliu@cs.toronto.edu, jacobsen@eecg.toronto.edu

1 Introduction

A new data processing paradigm – publish/subscribe – is becoming increasingly popular for information dissemination applications. Publish/subscribe systems anonymously interconnect information providers with information consumers in a distributed environment. Information providers publish information in the form of publications and information consumers subscribe their interests in the form of subscriptions. The publish/subscribe system performs the matching task and ensures the timely delivery of published events to all interested subscribers. Publish/subscribe has been well studied and many systems have been developed supporting this paradigm. Existing research prototypes, include, among others, Gryphon, LeSubscribe, and ToPSS; industrial strength systems include various implementations of JMS, the CORBA Notification Service, and TIB/RV. All these systems are based on a crisp data model, which means that neither subscribers nor publishers can express uncertain information in subscriptions and publications, respectively. In this crisp model, subscriptions are either evaluated to be true or to be false, for any given publication.

However, in many situations exact knowledge to crisply specify subscriptions or publications is not available. In these cases, the uncertainty about the state of the world has to be cast into a crisp data model that defines absolute limits. Moreover, for a user of a publish/subscribe system, it may be much simpler to describe the state of the world with vague or uncertain terms. That means in an approximate manner.

In a selective information dissemination context, for instance, users may want to submit subscriptions about an apartment whose constraint on rent is "cheap". On the other hand, information providers may not have exact information for all items published. In a second-hand market, a seller may not know the exact age of a vase so that she can just describe it as an "old" vase, but can not describe it with an exact age. Temperature and humidity information collected by sensors are often not fully precise, but only correct within a certain error interval around the value measured. It would be more precise to publish such imprecise information, rather than a wrong exact value, if such publish/subscribe capabilities were possible.

For these reasons, it is of great advantage to provide a publish/subscribe data model and an approximate matching scheme that allows the expression and processing of uncertainties for both subscriptions and publications. There are five interesting cases according to the different combinations of subscriptions and publications with uncertainties. These are: 1. crisp subscriptions and crisp publications (conventional publish/subscribe), 2. approximate subscriptions and crisp publications, 3. crisp subscriptions and approximate publications, and 4. approximate subscriptions and approximate publications. A fifth case combines crisp and approximate constraints in subscriptions and publications. Models 2 to 5 constitute completely novel publish/subscribe system models not previously investigated. All existing publish/subscribe systems are based on a crisp data model that cannot process uncertainty in either publications or subscriptions. The only exception is A-ToPSS, the Approximate Matching based Toronto Publish/Subscribe System [3, 4], which has introduced a model that can express imperfect information, such as "cheap", "large", and "close to" in subscriptions and publications. In [3], only Case 2 was demonstrated and in [4] we have developed the theory to support all five cases. In this work we aim at demonstrating all the above cases and show approximate matching on real data sets based on an online auction scenario.

Permission to copy without fee all or part of this material is granted provided that the copies are not made or distributed for direct commercial advantage, the VLDB copyright notice and the title of the publication and its date appear, and notice is given that copying is by permission of the Very Large Data Base Endowment. To copy otherwise, or to republish, requires a fee and/or special permission from the Endowment.

**Proceedings of the 30th VLDB Conference,
Toronto, Canada, 2004**

2 Publish/Subscribe Model

In a publish/subscribe system, two types of *imperfect information*, as classified by [5], may arise: *imprecision* and *uncertainty*. Imprecision relates to the content of a statement, which is used to refer to the incomplete information upon which publications or subscriptions may be based. The second type of imperfect information relates to the matching between publications and subscriptions, which we refer to as uncertainty. Uncertainty concerns the state of knowledge about the relationship between the world and the statement about the world. Often, *fuzzy sets* [2] are used to model imprecision and *possibility measures* [1] are used to model uncertainty. Our objective is to model imperfect information in subscriptions and publications and to define an approximate matching semantic for different cases of matching crisp with approximate subscriptions and publications. A detailed discussion of the theoretical framework of our approach can be found in [4]. Below, we summarize the key aspects of this framework to keep the demonstration description self-contained.

2.1 Publication and Subscription Model

Publications describe real world artifacts or states of interest through a set of attribute value pairs. When an exact value for a certain attribute is not available, we use a possibility distribution [1] to express the confidence that the attribute has a given value. As described in detail in [4], a publication is defined as a list of attribute function pairs as follows:

$$p = \{(a_1, \pi_1), (a_2, \pi_2), \cdots, (a_n, \pi_n)\}.$$

For example, a condo advertised for sale, may be described as "(size is $160m^2$) and (price is cheap)". The first attribute is *crisp*; it defines a definite value for size. The second attribute is *approximate*. It is qualified as cheap, which is defined as a function that designates the possibility of each value in the domain of discourse (i.e., all admissible rent values) as being "cheap". More formally, this publication can be represented by a set of attribute function pairs as follows.

$$P = \{(size, \pi_{60}), (price, \pi_{cheap})\}$$

The possibility distribution functions are depicted

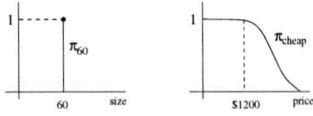

Figure 1: Possibility distributions for publication

graphically in Figure 1. Subscriptions define users' interests and consist of individual predicates linked by (Boolean) operators. To continue our example from above, let us define a subscription for a family who is looking for an apartment with constraints on price, size, and condition. The subscription in natural language that specifies these constraints is as follows:

S: size   is medium   AND
    price   is no more than $1500 AND
    condition is not old.

We use the following membership functions, depicted in Figure 2, to represent the concept of "$\leq$ \$1500", "medium" and "old", respectively. So, the formal subscription language can be represented by

$$S = (size, \mu_{medium}) \wedge (price, \mu_{\leq \$1500}) \wedge (condition, 1 - \mu_{old})$$

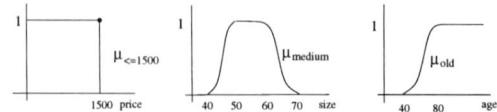

Figure 2: Membership functions for predicates

2.2 Approximate Matching

The semantics of matching subscriptions with publications is to measure the *possibility* and the *necessity* with which the publication satisfies the expectation expressed by a subscription. Based on possibility theory, we use a pair (Π_i, N_i) to denote the evaluation of the possibility and necessity of how a publication satisfies each predicate i (i.e., the match between μ_i and π_i) in a subscription. This measure is done by computing the intersection between μ_i and π_i as follows:

$$\Pi_i = \sup_{x \in D} \min(\mu_i(x), \pi_i(x))$$

$$N_i = \inf_{x \in D} \max(\mu_i(x), 1 - \pi_i(x))$$

Note that sup and inf have been chosen to represent the general case that μ_i and π_i are defined on an infinite domain. For the finite case, sup and inf are equivalent to max and min. The graphical interpretation of these measures is illustrated through a list of figures in Figure 3. With this matching semantic, users may be

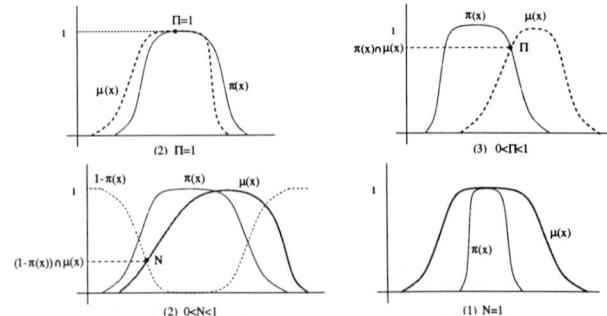

Figure 3: Possibility and necessity measures

overwhelmed with a large number of slightly matching subscriptions, i.e., with a low degree of match. Thus, the approximate matching model introduces two parameters θ_Π and θ_N to control the tolerance of a match on a per-predicate basis for each subscription. These thresholds capture a users' satisfaction with the possibility and the necessity of how their interests are matched. Users' constraints are matched if both the possibility and the necessity degrees are larger than the thresholds θ_Π and θ_N. To illustrate these parameters, we adapt the apartment subscription example from above to:

S: $(size, \mu_{medium}, 0.8, 0)$ $\wedge$
$(price, \mu_{\leq 1500}, 1, 0)$ $\wedge$
$(condition, 1 - \mu_{old}, 1, 0.3)$.

This subscription matches a publication as long as its `size` predicate matches a *medium* value with a degree of more than 0.8, which is the possibility threshold. The necessity threshold is irrelevant in this example (since it is 0). The `price` should be less than $1500, and the age predicate matches a `not-old` value with a possibility threshold of 1 and a necessity threshold of 0.3.

The general representation of a subscription is as follows:

$$S = R((a_1, \mu_1, \theta_{\Pi_1}, \theta_{N_1}), \cdots, (a_n, \mu_n, \theta_{\Pi_n}, \theta_{N_n}))$$

Here, R is the relation that aggregates the truth values of the individual predicates to an overall truth value for the subscription, S (e.g., a conjunction, a disjunction, or a normal form). The approximate matching problem can now be stated as follows. Given a set of subscriptions S and a publication p, the matching problem comes down to identifying all $s \in S$ such that s and p match with degrees greater than the thresholds defined on s by any subscriber.

3 Membership Function Mining

The A-ToPSS model offers its users great flexibility and leaves room for tuning a wide range of default parameters. It is often a challenge to select the right membership function parameterization, the exact number of membership functions to represent one dimension, the appropriate aggregation function or the right thresholds. However, A-ToPSS is used in a context where many subscribers (potentially millions) seek the right information. Consequently, much information about what defines certain concepts in specific domains is readily available, such as an "average understanding" of what constitutes a "cheap" price of a popular electronics gadget available in an online auction. If this information could be exploited, better default parameter choices could be determined for subscribers and publishers of such a system.

In A-ToPSS we experiment with a clustering-based approach that determines default value settings from past data (i.e., from past subscriptions and publications). We demonstrate our approach on real data traces that we have collected from an online auction site. The parameter estimation task is performed by an additional analyzer component on top of the core publish/subscribe system (see Figure 4 for details).

In the clustering analysis we do not differentiate between subscriptions or publications, but mine for default parameterizations of the membership functions underlying both entities. This is possible due to the link of a fuzzy set and a possibility distribution, explained in further detail in [4]. The mined parameterization is then used to provide default values for imperfect concepts. Currently, we focus on estimating the number of concepts that define one dimension and their function representation. For example, the dimension price, could be represented by the concepts "cheap", "fair" and "expensive" or by four concepts, adding, for instance, "luxurious". Each of these concepts is represented by a parameterized membership function, which can be adapted to a specific understanding by modifying its parameters.

4 Demonstration

The main challenge in applying publish/subscribe systems to selective information dissemination lies in the design of efficient algorithms that exhibit good scalability. At Internet-scale, such systems have to be able to process millions of subscriptions and react to thousands of events. The introduction of approximate matching increases the number of possible matches for a subscription, since more events will be matched, but to different degrees of match. To understand how the notion of approximate matching can help to better satisfy users' queries for information, we have taken an experimental approach that demonstrates how the results returned from crisp and approximate matching compare side-by-side. We have built a matching engine that can manage more than ten million subscriptions and process many events per second. We have integrated this with a web-server and an application server. Figure 4 represents the overall system architecture. All components are fully implemented. We will use an online auction application example to

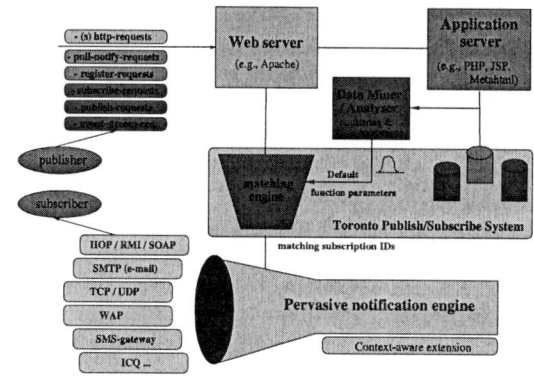

Figure 4: Overall system architecture

demonstrate our approximate matching scheme. Our

software demonstration will look at two aspects. One, an approximate publish/subscribe-based online auction driven by real world data (i.e., traces collected over the web from an auction site, referred to as Scenario 1) and two, an experimental comparison between the traditional publish/subscribe model and our model supporting imperfect information processing and approximate matching (referred to as Scenario 2). The former serves to demonstrate the viability of our model in a real world context and the latter serves to show the difference between crisp and approximate publish/subscribe.

Scenario 1 will demonstrate the flexibility in expressing publications and subscriptions in the approximate model. A subscriber chooses among a family of functions to represent imperfect information. The system will provide default parameters for selected functions based on mining of past data seen (subscriptions and publications). We model past data from the collected trace data. Figure 5 shows a screen shot of the subscription entry panel of our system, where a user can view and adapt the default membership functions representing her subscriptions. The default parameters are set by the analyzer component and will adapt over time. Expressiveness is further demonstrated by

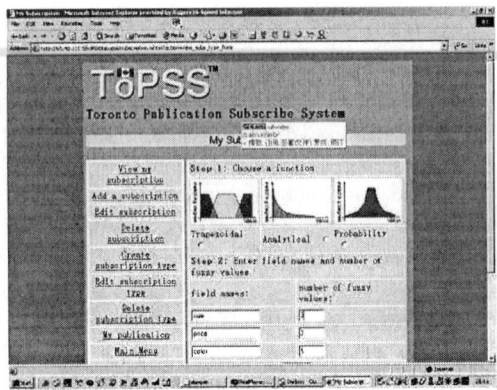

Figure 5: The power user's interface for defining membership functions

allowing subscribers to submit subscriptions in disjunctive or conjunctive normal forms (DNF/CNF), a unique feature of our matching engine. To date, most existing publish/subscribe research focuses on conjunctive subscriptions only. Figure 6 illustrates the panel for a DNF subscription. To demonstrate Scenario 2, a panel to dynamically control publication representations is available, which concentrates on integer interval values, in which case the publication is of the form ($attribute_i, [a, b]$). By changing the range of the interval $[a, b]$, the number of matched subscriptions can be influenced. This effect can be observed in a monitoring panel and compared to crisp matching. Figure 7 illustrates the numbers of matched subscriptions, comparing crisp with approximate match-

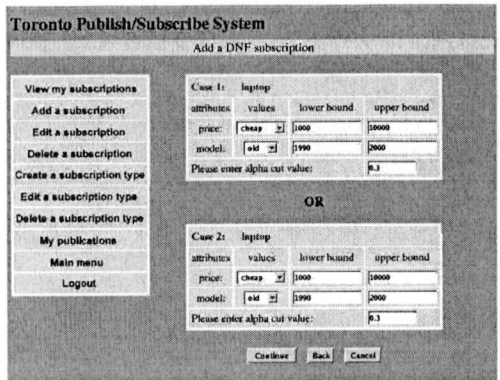

Figure 6: The interface to define a DNF subscription

ing. The intuition is to provide default settings for values, a and b that accommodate pessimistic, optimistic, or indifferent subscribers (i.e., those who have a low tolerance for matches versus those who fear to miss a good match.) Scenario 2 will allow us to also

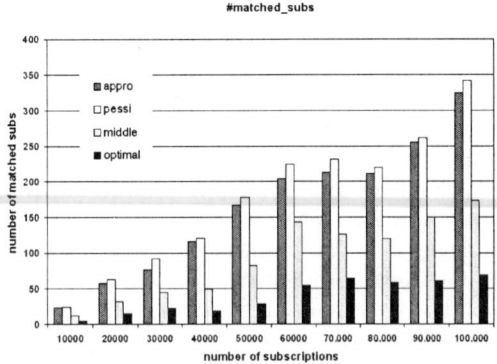

Figure 7: Number of matches for different cases

demonstrate the effects of the representation of membership functions, the influence of different aggregation functions (i.e., min, max, or product in subscription evaluation), and the effects of various thresholds. It is difficult to absolutely quantify subscriber satisfaction, we therefore expect the software demonstration to further illustrate pros and cons of our approach.

References

[1] D. Dubois and H. Prade. *Possibility Theory: An Approach to Computerized Processing of Uncertainty.* Plenum Press, New York, 1988.

[2] G. J. Klir and T. A. Folger. *Fuzzy Sets, Uncertainty, and Information.* Prentice Hall International Editions, 1992.

[3] H. Liu and H.-A. Jacobsen. A-TOPSS – a publish/subscribe system supporting approximate matching. In *28 th International Conference on VLDB*, Hong Kong, China, 2002.

[4] H. Liu and H.-A. Jacobsen. Modeling uncertainties in publish/subscribe system. In *20th International Conference on Data Engineering*, Boston, USA, 2004.

[5] P. Smets. *Imperfect information: Imprecision-Uncertainty, Uncertainty Management in Informaiton Systems: From needs to Solutions.* Kluwer Academic Publisher, 1977.

Efficient Constraint Processing for Highly Personalized Location Based Services

Zhengdao Xu   Hans-Arno Jacobsen

Department of Computer Science and
Department of Electrical and Computer Engineering,
University of Toronto,
zhengdao@cs | jacobsen@eecg{.toronto.edu}

1 Overview

Recently, with the advances in wireless communications and location positioning technology, the potential for tracking, correlating, and filtering information about moving entities (i.e., generally speaking moving objects, such as automobiles, people, packages etc.) has greatly increased. Potential applications range from location-aware, selective information dissemination, personalized route planning, goods tracking, surveillance of group formation to buddy tracking.

The implementation of efficient tracking, correlation, and filtering schemes supporting millions of mobile objects, poses significant challenges. The knowledge of spatial, temporal, and causal relationship between moving objects would allow the support of highly personalized and effective location-based service (LBS) for tracking, correlating, and processing object positions, profiles, and trends. For example, shoppers walking on the street may want the advertisements to be displayed on their PDAs only when they are near a specific store (location-aware m-commerce); a driver only wants traffic information effecting his immediate future surroundings (proximity-based alerts); in a buddy tracking application, two (or more) friends may wish to be notified if they are within a certain distance of each other or within a certain distance of a point of demarcation (location-constraint correlation).

All these applications can be broadly classified as location-aware information dissemination tasks, which, as has been shown, can be well supported by the publish/subscribe paradigm [2]. In a publish/subscribe systems, clients exchange information by publishing events and subscribing to events of interest. The central component of this architecture is the event broker, which maintains all the subscriptions and matches incoming events against all subscriptions. Upon a subscription match, a subscriber is notified.

The above location-aware applications are supported by two communication styles, orthogonal to the coordination mechanism used. These are pull-oriented and push-oriented styles. Pull-oriented LBS works in the request/response manner, which requires the clients to poll the available service from the server who respond by returning the result. In contrast, in the push-oriented style, service initiation (after an initial registration or sign-up phase) is carried out by the server (the service provider.)

The push-oriented style is better suited for LBS, since it puts less strain on the mobile devices and network resources (the network is subjected to less polling.) For example, in the buddy tracking application, two (or more) users may wish to be notified when they are within a certain distance of one another. In this case, each of them needs to subscribe to this event, expressed by a location constraint, stating that they wish to be notified if the distance between them is within a certain range. Once the constraint is in the system, the location information of the moving objects is checked against all location constraints stored in the system. We assume that location position information is available, such as provided by GPS, network-enhanced GPS, ground-based sensors, or other location positioning technology [12]. When the constraint is satisfied, the notification is sent to the corresponding user.

Due to the scalability of publish/subscribe in terms of number of supported clients and event processing speed [4], we believe that this is an extremely promising paradigm for enabling push-oriented LBS. However, we argue that to support location-awareness in such system additional needs must be addressed. Especially, the tracking of moving entities and the efficient correlation of their locations and interests. Typi-

---

Permission to copy without fee all or part of this material is granted provided that the copies are not made or distributed for direct commercial advantage, the VLDB copyright notice and the title of the publication and its date appear, and notice is given that copying is by permission of the Very Large Data Base Endowment. To copy otherwise, or to republish, requires a fee and/or special permission from the Endowment.

**Proceedings of the 30th VLDB Conference,
Toronto, Canada, 2004**

cally in such systems, a vast number of the constraints are expected to be evaluated in a timely manner. The scalability and the efficiency of these algorithms becomes an issue.

L-ToPSS (Location-based Toronto Publish/Subscribe System) is our research prototype that provides LBS in a push-oriented style. In this demonstration, we will focus on demonstrating an algorithm that efficiently evaluates two types of location constraints:

1. n-body constraint: constraints of the form $|p_1, p_2...p_n| \leq d$ that designates whether n moving points $p_1, p_2...p_n$ are in a circle with the given diameter d. p_i $(1 \leq i \leq n)$ is the identifier of the object i; p_i is further translated into the coordinate of object i in the location matching engine at time t. Value d is called alerting distance. Buddy tracking is an example of the n-body constraint problem, with n equals to two.

2. n-body (static) constraint: constraints of the form $|A, p_1, p_2...p_n| \leq d_A$, (where A is the coordinate of some static point) that designates whether n moving points $p_1, p_2...p_n$ are within a given range from the static point A. Here d_A is the alerting distance. The location-aware mobile commerce mentioned earlier represents an example of the n-body (static) constraint problem with the advertising publisher (the store) as a static body.

More formally, the problem we are solving can be stated as follows: *Given a set of constraints $C = \{c_1, c_2...c_m\}$, which designates the desired location constraint relationships among a set of n possibly moving points $P_t = \{p_1, p_2...p_n\}$ in the space at time t, find all constraints c_i in C that are satisfied.*

In the next section we briefly introduce related work. In Section 3, we sketch our algorithm. Section 4 presents the L-ToPSS research prototype. In Section 5, we describe the software demonstration.

2 Related work

Many spatial indexing schemes, like Time-Oblivious indexing in [1], dynamic external memory data structures [7] and R-tree based indexing [9], have been proposed, which can be used to index mobile objects in space. However, they do not solve the above mentioned location constraint matching problem. In the buddy tracking system [10] that is studied by Arnon Amir et al. a centralized 2D quadtree-based algorithm is introduced. However it only solves the 2-body problem. And a quadtree data structure is not straight forward to extend to multi-dimensions, which may be useful for the constraint evaluation for the past and future (e.g, add time as one dimension). They also assume the same alerting distance for every pair of the objects, which is a limitation since different location constraints will have different alerting distances.

Other related work includes spatial database of moving object and query of location dependent data [3, 5].

3 Sketch of the algorithm

Our algorithm for location constraint evaluation uses the Kd-tree indexing, which is usually used to solve the orthogonal range search problem with static objects. Our contribution is that we improved it to efficiently process the location constraints among mobile objects.

To index moving objects in space, the whole space is partitioned into small equally sized partitions. Those partitions are well managed in a Kd-tree data structure. And the whole space can be expressed by the union of the partitions represented by all the nodes in the same level of the tree. After the whole space is partitioned, each object (mobile or static) is associated with a certain leaf node of the tree according to its current position. The distance between the partitions serves as a rough measure of the bounds of the distance between objects, which is lying inside those partitions. This can be further exploited to evaluate the constraints.

As an example of partitioning the space, Figure 1(a) shows how this works in the 2D space, where a 4km×4km square is partitioned into 8 partition and a corresponding tree is also constructed (see Figure 1(b)).

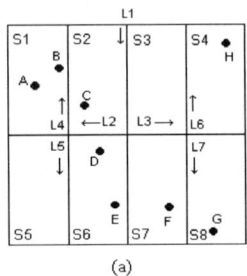
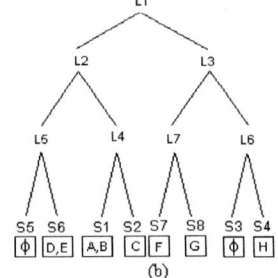

Figure 1: space partition: (a) 2D partition, (b) Kd-tree of the partition

We assume that our system is periodically informed of the position of the mobile objects by GPS or ground based sensors, for example. To keep track of the moving objects, a quick partition update management for those moving objects is very essential. In our system, when the new position of the mobile object is received, a backtracking partition update is performed, which backtracks from the leaf node of the tree up until the node representing the partition accommodates the current mobile object is found, and then the object is inserted from that node down to the appropriate leaf node.

When the constraint is evaluated, the partitions where objects in question are located is determined first; and based on the partitions they are in, we further make decisions for evaluation to reduce the need of distance computation. The technique we use to evaluate the n-body constraint is to use the partitions that are represented at the appropriate level of the tree, such that the distance between two objects is smaller than the alerting distance, if and only if, they are in the same or adjacent partitions. If all n points are in the same or adjacent partitions, the smallest circle that encloses those n points can be computed in $O(n)$ time [11]. For evaluating the n-body static constraint, we use the breadth-first search on the Kd-tree to decide the internal, bounding and external leaf partitions to the region with static object A as the center and d_A as the radius, depending on whether the partition is inside, intersecting with or outside the boundary of the region. Then the distance between the moving object and static object A can be tracked according to the partition the moving object is in. The explicit distance computation is only needed for the moving object inside the bounding partition.

4 System architecture

L-ToPSS is our research prototype. The system architecture is shown in Figure 2. We assume that the matching of the publications against the subscriptions has been done by the filter engine and the identification numbers of the entities are sent to the location matching engine. The main component of our concern is the location matching engine, which stores the location constraints, as well as the link to the subscription and publication it is associated with. Our system

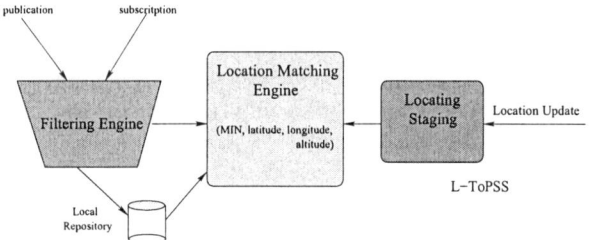

Figure 2: L-ToPSS System Architecture

model is very similar to that used in [2]. Each mobile publisher or subscriber is identified with a unique Mobile Identification Number (MIN). The subscription from some mobile user contains the MIN of the mobile device on which the user wants to receive notifications. Similarly, the publication from some mobile publisher also contains a MIN. For a static publisher or subscriber, its location (latitude, longitude, altitude) is retrieved directly from the local database based on its identifier. The constraint is expressed in the form $(MIN_1, MIN_2, ...MIN_n, d)$ for the n-body constraint or $(id_{static}, MIN_1, MIN_2, ...MIN_n, d_{id_{static}})$ for the n-body (static) constraint; and they can be submitted into the system along with either the publications or the subscriptions.

The system receives the updates of mobile users' location and processes them in the location staging component. When the new update comes into the system, the corresponding location information and its timestamp are updated. The location information is represented as a (MIN_i, current_latitude, current_longitude, current_altitude) tuple. This tuple is forwarded to the location matching engine. All the constraints are managed in the location matching engine and they are evaluated periodically. During the evaluation, the system will first check the timestamps of all the mobile objects in the constraint to make sure that they are not obsolete. If the timestamps of all the objects are still valid, it matches them against the corresponding location constraint. We distinguish two types of constraints (n-body and n-body static) and the evaluation is based on the algorithm introduced the Section 3. Once the constraint is found satisfied, the subscribers associated with the constraint are notified with the publication they have subscribed. Through the demonstration, we show that by reducing the chance of distance computation, our algorithm speeds up the constraint evaluation thus allows the system to accommodate more constraints and serve more location-aware requests from the clients.

We are also aware of the system limitation mentioned in [2]; to avoid updating subscriptions with each location change of the subscriber, our location matching engine is processed independently from the matching between publications and subscriptions. The constraint is put into or retrieved from the system explicitly by the subscriber or the publisher when they subscribes or publishes.

In the next section, we present the demonstration of evaluation of constraints in the location matching Engine.

5 Software demonstration

In this demonstration, we will show the efficiency of our algorithm by evaluating a set of constraints for a given set of mobile objects in space. The constraints are submitted into or removed from the system in batch by the constraint generator. This can also be done for individual constraint through the demo panel.

The software setup for our demonstration is shown in the Figure 3. We use two IBM tools facilitating LBS evaluation: City Simulator [6], and Location Transponder [8]. The City Simulator generates dynamic spatial data simulating the motion of up to 1 million people and produces the trace-files that contain timestamped data records representing coordinate positions of the mobile objects. The Location Transponder takes the trace-files from the City Simulator as input and transmits the data to the location updates information to our system. We also develop a web application for insertion and retrieval of the constraints.

The evaluation is executed periodically, and once some constraint is satisfied, appropriate notification is sent out using different protocols.

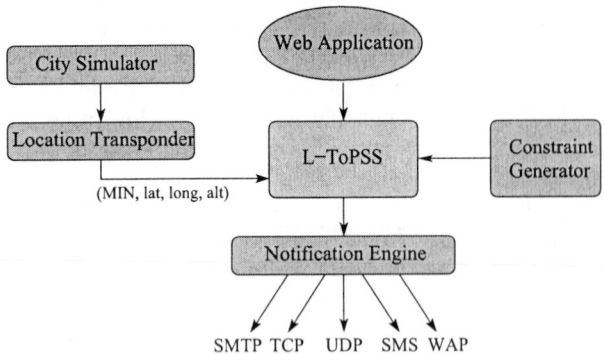

Figure 3: Demonstration Setup

To simulate the activity of a real-life system, our location matching engine stores millions of location constraints (both n-body and n-body static) that are to be evaluated against incoming location data of the mobile objects. To demonstrate the efficiency, we vary the number of objects in the constraints. Through the continuous evaluation, those satisfied constraints are alerted graphically to the users on the demo panel.

The performance of our algorithm is also compared with naive approach where the constraints are evaluated sequentially without the help of Kd-tree indexing. We will visualize the matching time for constraint evaluation, the number of explicit computations of the smallest enclosing disk and the number of partition update of the objects on the Kd-tree. Those statistics are shown on our demo panel when two methods are running as different processes on our pc. We will show through those statistics that even with little overhead for the partition update, our approach using Kd-tree indexing still outperform the naive approach.

We also show that by leveraging the size of the partition, the algorithm can reaches its best performance (least time needed for constraint evaluation and partition updating without sacrifices the accuracy).

References

[1] Pankaj K. Agarwal, Lars Arge, and Jeff Erickson. Indexing moving points. In *Symposium on Principles of Database Systems*, pages 175–186, 2000.

[2] Ioana Burcea and Hans-Arno Jacobsen. L-topss - push-oriented location-based services. In *4th VLDB Workshop on Technologies for E-Services (TES'03)*, 2003.

[3] Susanne Hambrush Dmitri V. Kalashnikov, Sunil Prabhakar and Walid Aref. Efficient evaluation of continuous range queries on moving objects. In *DEXA 2002, Proc. of the 13th International Conference and Workshop on Database and Expert Systems Applications, Aix en Provence, France, September2-6 2002*.

[4] Françoise Fabret, H. Arno Jacobsen, François Llirbat, João Pereira, Kenneth A. Ross, and Dennis Shasha. Filtering algorithms and implementation for very fast publish/subscribe systems. *SIGMOD Record (ACM Special Interest Group on Management of Data)*, 30(2):115–126, 2001.

[5] Dimitris Papadis Yufei Tao Jun Zheng, Manli Zhu and Dik Lun Lee. Location-based spatial queries. *In SIGMOD Conference*, 2003.

[6] James Kaufman Jussi Myllymaki and Jared Jackson. City simulator. ibm alphaworks emerging technologies toolkit, http://www.alphaworks.ibm.com/tech/citysimulator, November 2001.

[7] George Kollios, Dimitrios Gunopulos, and Vassilis J. Tsotras. On indexing mobile objects. In *Proceedings of the Eighteenth ACM SIGACT-SIGMOD-SIGART Symposium on Principles of Database Systems, May 31 - June 2, 1999, Philadelphia, Pennsylvania*, pages 261–272. ACM Press, 1999.

[8] Jussi Myllymaki and James Kaufman. Location transponder. ibm alphaworks emerging technologies toolkit, http://www.alphaworks.ibm.com/tech/transponder, April 2002.

[9] Simonas Saltenis, Christian S. Jensen, Scott T. Leutenegger, and Mario A. Lopez. Indexing the positions of continuously moving objects. In *SIGMOD Conference*, pages 331–342, 2000.

[10] Arnon Amir. Alon Efrat. Jussi Myllymaki. Lingeshwaran Palaniappan. Kevin Wampler. Buddy tracking - efficient proximity detection among mobile friends. In *Infocom 2004*.

[11] Emo Welzl. Smallest enclosing disks (balls and ellipsoids). In H. Maurer, editor, *New Results and New Trends in Computer Science*, LNCS. Springer, 1991.

[12] Y. Zhao. Standardization of mobile phone positioning for 3g systems. *IEEE Communication Magazine, July 2002*.

LH*$_{RS}$: A Highly Available Distributed Data Storage

Witold Litwin   Rim Moussa
CERIA Lab., Université Paris Dauphine
FRANCE
Witold.Litwin@dauphine.fr   Rim.Moussa@dauphine.fr

Thomas J.E. Schwarz, S.J.
Santa Clara University
USA
TSchwarz@scu.edu

Abstract

The ideal storage system is always available and incrementally expandable. Existing storage systems fall far from this ideal. Affordable computers and high-speed networks allow us to investigate storage architectures closer to the ideal. Our demo, present a prototype implementation of LH*$_{RS}$: a highly available scalable and distributed data structure.

1. Introduction

Scalable and Distributed Data Structures [SDDS] are intended for computers over fast networks, usually local networks, i.e. for the *multicomputers*. This new hardware architecture is promising and gaining in popularity. In spite of the advantages given by distributing data, vulnerability to failures remains a problem that grows with the number of machines supporting the SDDS.

Many approaches to build highly available, i.e., fault tolerating, distributed data storage systems have been proposed. They generally use either (*i*) data mirroring or (*ii*) parity calculus [WK02]. The latter approach uses erasure-correcting codes. The simplest codes, e.g. in RAID systems [PGK88], use XOR calculus for the tolerance of a single site failure. Multiple failures need more complex codes. These can be the binary codes [H94] for double or triple failure, or character codes, more generally. Examples of character codes are array codes such as the EVENODD code [BB94], the X-code [XB99] or Reed Solomon codes. The latter appear at present to be the best to deal with multiple failures [R89] [BK95][P97] [LS00] [ML02] [S02] [MS04] [LMS04] [M04].

Below, Section 2 recalls the LH*$_{RS}$ file structure. Section 3 overviews our bucket architecture. Section 4 presents the demonstration outline. Finally, performance results are given in section 5.

2. LH*$_{RS}$ Scheme

LH*$_{RS}$ scheme is described with details in [LS00] and [LMS04]. An LH*$_{RS}$ file is subdivided into groups. Each group is composed of *m* Data Buckets and *k* Parity Buckets. Buckets are basically in distributed RAM, each at a different server node. The data buckets store the data records of the group. These are encoded into the parity records for high availability as follows in the parity buckets. Every data record has a rank *r* in its data bucket. It receives this rank upon insertion.

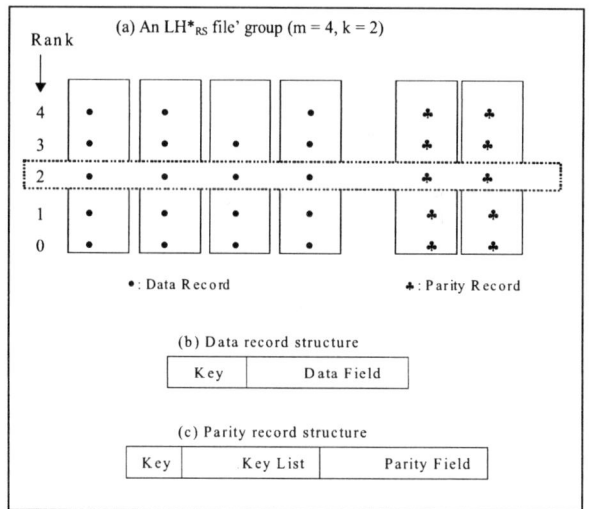

Figure 1: LH*$_{RS}$ file Structure

A *record group* consists of all records with the same rank in a *bucket group*. We construct parity records from data records having the same rank within data buckets forming a bucket group (Fig. 1(a)). The record grouping has an impact on the data structure of a parity record. Fig. 1(b-c) shows the structure of a data record and a parity record. The *key* field of the parity record is its rank; the *key list* keeps track of the data records in the record group. The parity field contains the actual parity symbols for the record group that we calculate using our version of Reed Solomon codes.

Thanks to the coding scheme, we can calculate the contents of all records in a record group if we have access to m out of the $n = m+k$ records. This provides us with k availability. The actually parity calculation proceeds as follows: When a record is updated (and here an insert counts as a modification of a zero record) we calculate its Δ-record, which is the XOR of the old and the new data field. We send this Δ-record to all parity buckets, who update their parity field by XORing the Δ-record multiplied symbol-wise by a given fixed element, contained in a *parity matrix* **P**. The multiplication is done in a Galois field. According to our experiments we achieve the overall best performance with the Galois field with 2^{16} elements. Since we use the logarithmic method to multiply, we actually store directly the logarithms of **P** in a matrix **Q**. Thanks to an optimization of **P**, the first row and the first column of **P** contain only 1's coefficients. In this case, we obviously can do away with the multiplication. In any case, our experiments show that the processing overhead of Reed-Solomon is small. Table 1 below shows our demo matrices **P** and **Q**.

(P)	0001	0001	0001
	0001	eb9b	2284
	0001	2284	9e74
	0001	9e44	d7f1

(Q)	0000	0000	0000
	0000	5ab5	e267
	0000	e267	0dce
	0000	784d	2b66

Table 1: Our demo matrices P and Q for $m = 4$ and $k = 3$.

In order to reconstruct lost records in a record group, we gather the columns of **P** corresponding to available records in a matrix **H**, invert **H** with the Gaussian algorithm, multiply each available record with a coefficient of **H** and XOR the results together to obtain a missing record. Since the inversion is done once for all records to be reconstructed, it does not constitute a significant overhead.

The file starts with one data bucket and $K \geq 1$ parity buckets. The K value, called Intended Availability Level, is a file parameter. It scales up through data buckets splits, as the data buckets get overloaded. Each bucket group has then the availability level k that is K or $K-1$, [LMS04]. Each data bucket contains a maximum number of b records. The value of b is the bucket capacity. When the number of records within a data bucket exceeds b, the bucket alerts the coordinator, a special entity coordinating splits. The latter designates a data bucket to split.

3. System Architecture

The goal of the prototype is to tune and experimentally determine LH*$_{RS}$ performance. Our current LH*$_{RS}$ implementation is described in depth in [M04]. It completes and improves that in [L00][ML02].

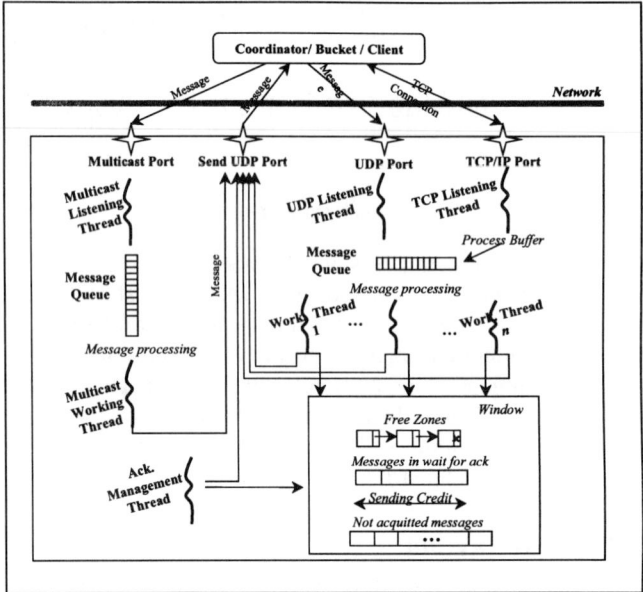

Figure 2: Bucket Architecture.

Figure 2 shows the multithreaded architecture of a bucket. Initially, a bucket is either connected to the *data buckets multicast group* or to the *parity buckets multicast group*. It starts with the multicast listening thread and the multicast working thread. When it receives a multicast group inviting the bucket to be a new or a spare bucket, it instantiates the other threads, responds positively to the coordinator, and waits for the confirmation. A selected bucket, upon receiving the confirmation, disconnects from its multicast group. Non-selected buckets cancel the instantiation process, and can commit to other invitations. Here are the functions of each thread.

- The *Multicast Listening Thread* is a temporary thread that listens to a fixed data or parity multicast port, and queues multicast messages.
- The *Multicast Working Thread* is also a temporary thread that processes queued multicast messages.
- The *UDP Listening Thread* listens to a fixed UDP port, calculated from the bucket number.
- The *Working Threads*, usually four, process queued UDP messages.
- The *TCP Listening Thread* accepts and handles multiple TCP/IP connections.
- The *Acknowledgement Manager Thread*: Each UDP message to be acknowledged is

added to the *messages in wait for the ack. list*, from which it is removed when the acknowledgement is received. This thread scans the list periodically, checks the send time of each message, and resends the message if necessary, provided that the maximum number of resends is not exceeded. In the latter case, it removes the message. Two cases may then happen. Either the sender commits an addressing error or the receiver failed. In both cases, the thread informs the coordinator.

4. Demonstration Outline

We coded our prototype in C. It includes a data and parity storage manager, and a query manager. The demonstration shows the use of LH*$_{RS}$ as a highly available distributed data storage system. The focus is to show how an LH*$_{RS}$ file scales up and how it recovers from a multiple bucket unavailability. We show the following operations.

(a) Creation of a *K*-available LH*$_{RS}$ file. We show how a data bucket is split, and how updates propagate to parity buckets. New data buckets are chosen from data buckets connected to the *data buckets multicast group*.

(b) Increase of the high availability of a group, by adding parity buckets. We show the interactions between the new parity bucket and its data buckets group. Each newly created parity bucket is chosen among the parity buckets connected to *parity buckets multicast group*.

(c) Recovery of *k* buckets in the group, into which we introduce failures.

(d) Key search directed to an unavailable bucket. We show that when search time-out elapses, the client alarms the coordinator. The latter checks if it is an addressing error or if the bucket is unavailable. In the latter case, the coordinator starts the recovery process.

(e) Bucket recovery operation. First, the coordinator designates a parity bucket as a recovery manager. The latter recovers records by *slices* of a given size *s*. It requests *s* successive records from each of the *m* data/parity buckets, and recovers the *s* record groups. Then, it requests the next *s* records from each bucket. While waiting, it sends the recovered slice to the spare(s). We show interaction between the coordinator, the spare data buckets, the recovery manager and the available buckets in the group.

(f) Finally, we issue search queries or display the contents of the recovered buckets, to show the recovery operation.

We also show other functions of the prototype: key search queries in normal mode, update queries, their propagation to parity buckets, record recovery using UDP, bucket recovery through UDP, we display data and parity bucket content, various statistics, etc.

Along the demonstration, we show the actual performance factors. These are basically various execution times proving the rapidity of various manipulations. We now resume those we have measured as the basis, on the original configuration [M03] [LMS04] [M04].

5. Performance Results

The hardware test bed consisted of six machines; each one has 512 MB of RAM, with a 1.8GHz Pentium processor under Windows 2K. All the machines were connected to a regular Ethernet configuration with a max bandwidth of 1 Gbps.

For the experimental set up, the record size was (and is) set to 100 bytes and the group size is set to 4 buckets. Performance results degrade for higher values of record size and group size. The best obtained performance results use Reed Solomon codes over the Galois Field GF(2^{16}). We use this field in our demonstration.

The time to create an LH*$_{RS}$ file of 25000 records was 7.896 sec for k = 0, 9.990 sec for k = 1 and 10.963 sec for k = 2. The related average times per record inserted were, 0.32 ms, 0.41 ms, and 0.44 ms for *k* = 0, 1, 2 respectively.

The average individual and bulk search times were 0.2419 ms and 0.0563 ms respectively.

Table 2 presents creation times for a parity bucket (PB) of 31 250 records.

	Total Time	Processing Time	Communication Time
1PB-XOR	2.062	1.484	0.322
1PB-RS	2.103	1.531	0.322

Table 2: Parity bucket creation times in seconds.

To measure the recovery performance, we simulated the creation of an LH*$_{RS}$ group with 4 data buckets and 1, 2, or 3 parity buckets. The group contained 125 000 = 4 * 31 250 data records. The recovery of a single data bucket (DB) uses the first parity bucket and consequently the XOR decoding only. The first line of Table 3 presents this case. Alternatively, the recovery can use another parity bucket, applying the RS decoding (with XORing and Galois field multiplications). The second line of the table shows the measurements for this case. Our numbers prove the efficiency of the LH*$_{RS}$ bucket recovery mechanism. It takes only 1.555 seconds to recover 9.375 MB of data in three buckets.

	Total Time	Processing Time	Communication Time
1DB-XOR	0.720	0.265	0.414
1DB-RS	0.855	0.380	0.400
2 DBs	1.162	0.600	0.434
3 DBs	1.555	0.911	0.464

Table 3: Data bucket recovery times in seconds.

6. Conclusion

Our demonstration shows the prototype implementation of LH*$_{RS}$: a highly available distributed data structure. We show how it actually functions. The efficient distributed storage system that our prototype constitutes can benefit modern data intensive applications: databases, grids, P2P files… Further work, in progress, concerns various aspects of current implementation, evaluation of other encoding and decoding techniques, and the applications of the prototype.

References

[B00] F. Bennour, *Un Gestionnaire de Structures Distribuées et Scalables pour les multiordinateurs Windows: Fragmentation par Hachage*, PhD thesis in French, Paris Dauphine University, 2000.

[BB94] M. Blaum, J. Brady, J. Bruck & J. Menon, *EVENODD: An Optimal Scheme for Tolerating Double Disk Failures in RAID Architectures*, IEEE 1994.

[BK95] J. Blomer, M. Kalfane, R. Karp, M. Karpinski, M. Luby & D.Zuckerman, *An XOR-Based Erasure-Resilient Coding Scheme*, ICSI Tech. Rep. TR-95-048, 1995.

[H94] L. Hellerstein, G.A. Gibson, R.M. Karp, R.H. Katz & D.A. Patterson, *Coding Techniques for handling Failures in Large Disk Arrays*, Algorithmica, 1994, 12, pp.182-208.

[L00] M. Ljungström, *Implementing LH*$_{RS}$: a Scalable Distributed Highly-Available Data Structure*, Master Thesis, Feb. 2000, CS Dept., U. Linkoping, Suede.

[LS00] W. Litwin & J.E. Schwarz, *LH*$_{RS}$, A High-Availability Scalable Distributed Data Structure using Reed Solomon Codes*, p.237-248, Proceedings of the ACM SIGMOD 2000.

[LMS04] W. Litwin, R. Moussa & J.E. Schwarz, *LH*$_{RS}$ – A Highly-Available Scalable Distributed Data Structure*, CERIA Res. Rep. May 2004.

[ML02] R. Moussa & W. Litwin, *Experimental Performance Management of LH*$_{RS}$ Parity Management*, Distributed Data and Structures, 4, (WDAS02) Carleton Scientific, Waterloo, Ontario, CA. 2003, pp. 87-98.

[M03] R. Moussa, *Experimental Performance Analysis of the new LH*$_{RS}$ Scenarios and Architecture Design*, CERIA Res. Rep., June 2003, http://ceria.dauphine.fr/Rim/comparison0603.pdf.

[M04] R. Moussa, *Contribution à l'étude des Structures de Données Distribuées et Scalables à Haute disponibilité*, PhD thesis in French, Paris Dauphine University, 2004.

[MS04] R. Moussa & J.E. Schwarz, *Design and Implementation of LH*$_{RS}$: a Highly Available Distributed Data Storage System*, Workshop on Distributed Data and Structures (WDAS04).

[P97] J. S. Plank, *A Tutorial on Reed-Solomon Coding for fault-Tolerance in RAID-like Systems*, Software – Practise & Experience, 27(9), Sept. 1997, pp 995- 1012.

[PGK88] D. A. Patterson, G. Gibson & R. H. Katz, *A Case for Redundant Arrays of Inexpensive Disks*, Proc. of ACM SIGMOD Conf, pp.109-106, June 1988.

[R89] M. O. Rabin, *Efficient Dispersal of Information for Security, Load Balancing and Fault Tolerance*, Journal of ACM, Vol. 26, N° 2, April 1989, pp. 335-348.

[S02] T. J.E. Schwarz S.J., *Reed Solomon Codes for Erasure Correction in SDDS*, Distributed Data and Structures, 4, (WDAS02) Carleton Scientific, Waterloo, Ontario, CA. 2003.

[SDDS] http://ceria.dauphine.fr/SDDS-bibliographie.html

[XB99] L. Xu & J. Bruck, *Highly Available Distributed Storage Systems*, Proceedings of workshop on Distributed High Performance Computing, Lecture notes in Control and Information Sciences, Springer Verlag, 1999.

[WK02] H. Weatherspoon & J. D. Kubiatowicz, *Erasure Coding vs. Replication: A quantitative Comparison*, Proceedings of the 1st International Workshop on Peer-to-Peer Systems, March 2002, p.328-338.

Acnowledgements

This work was partly supported by the European Commission project ICONS (*project no. IST-2001-32429*), Microsoft Research, as well as by a scholarship from the Tunisian government.

Semantic Query Optimization in an Automata-Algebra Combined XQuery Engine over XML Streams

Hong Su, Elke A. Rundensteiner and Murali Mani

Department of Computer Science, Worcester Polytechnic Institute, Worcester, MA 01609
{suhong, rundenst, mmani}@cs.wpi.edu

1 Introduction

Our *Raindrop* framework [6, 9] aims at tackling challenges of stream processing that are particular to XML. In contrast to the tuple-based or object-based data streams, XML streams are usually modeled as a sequence of primitive tokens, such as a start tag, an end tag or a PCDATA item. Unlike a *self-contained* tuple or object whose semantics are completely determined by its own values, a token lacks semantics without the *context* provided by other tokens in the stream. This poses specific challenges for query processing over such XML streams.

State-of-the-Art. Since the *automata model* was originally designed for matching patterns over strings, it is a natural paradigm for structural pattern retrieval on XML token streams [7, 8, 4]. However the automata model suffers from not being able to strike a balance between the expressive power of the query it can handle and the manageability of its constructs. It either provides limited "recognizer-like" query capabilities, e.g., [4] gives only boolean answers to XPath expressions rather than constructing the results. Or, it may require a huge number of states, actions and transitions, resulting from the low level description of the patches for providing more query capabilities [8, 7].

In contrast, the *algebraic query processing paradigm* has been proven to be practical for query optimization, because of (1) its modularity of composing a query from individual operators, and (2) its support for iterative and thus manageable optimization decisions at several abstraction levels (e.g., logical and physical plans). However, the data model underlying this paradigm assumes sets of self-contained tuples. XML token streams however do not meet this requirement.

Features of Raindrop. Either paradigm has its own deficiencies. Yet, they complement each other. We therefore propose a novel paradigm for XQuery stream processing, called *Raindrop*, that is the first system to strike a balance between the two paradigms. The novel features of *Raindrop* include:

1. **Uniform Modeling.** *Raindrop* is a layered algebraic framework that uniformly models both the tuple-based and token-based paradigms. This leads to the optimization opportunities not studied in the previous literature [2, 8, 7, 4], namely, the tradeoff between pushing computation into and out of the automata.

2. **Layered Optimization.** The framework supports several abstraction levels of plan refinement, which would not be as easily feasible as . We have developed XML stream-specific optimization techniques for each level.

In this demo, we highlight the schema-based optimization (SQO) on one abstraction level. Schema knowledge is used to rewrite a query into a more efficient one. Most current literature on SQOs in XML focuses on techniques that are either (1) general regardless of persistent or streaming XML sources [1] or (2) specific to persistent XML sources [3]. For example, *query tree minimization* [1] is a general technique. It eliminates a pattern from the query if the pattern is known to always exist. Since the pruned query involves less computation than the original one, it is more efficient to evaluate regardless of the nature of data sources. For another example, the *query rewriting using state extents* [3] technique requires indices on the data. Applications on persistent XML can usually afford the preprocessing of building indices while this is often not the case for XML stream applications due to the on-the-fly arriving nature of their data. Therefore this technique is more suitable for persistent XML. We instead focus on SQOs specific to XML streams. To the best of our knowledge, no previous work has proposed a comprehensive solution for XML stream specific SQO techniques. [4] is the closest to our work. It handles only limited query (i.e., boolean XPath match) with one type of constraint. In con-

Permission to copy without fee all or part of this material is granted provided that the copies are not made or distributed for direct commercial advantage, the VLDB copyright notice and the title of the publication and its date appear, and notice is given that copying is by permission of the Very Large Data Base Endowment. To copy otherwise, or to republish, requires a fee and/or special permission from the Endowment.

**Proceedings of the 30th VLDB Conference,
Toronto, Canada, 2004**

trast, first, we handle more complex query type, i.e., a subset of XQuery; Second, we support most commonly used constraints in XML Schema.

2 Uniform Modeling

To exploit both algebraic and automata paradigms, we choose to extend the algebraic model to accommodate automata for two reasons. First, this allows us to reuse the well-studied algebra-based techniques. Second, algebra provides multiple description levels which allows us to present the details of automata computation at the lower level while presenting the semantics of automata computation at the higher level.

Our *Raindrop* algebraic framework is composed of four levels of abstraction [6, 9]. The highest level, a *semantics-focused plan*, describes the semantics of a query regardless of persistent or stream data sources. We reuse Rainbow [10], an XQuery engine for persistent inputs, for the initial plan construction and general XQuery optimization. Next, the *stream logical plan* extends the first level with new constructs for tokenized stream inputs. The next lower level is the *stream physical plan* describing implementation strategies for each logical operator. The final level, the *stream execution plan*, captures the synchronization and data transfer mechanisms among physical operators (i.e., scheduling). Each level refines the plan at the adjacent higher level with more details.

We here highlight the stream logical plan level since new operators and plan structures are first introduced into this level to model the token-based automata computation as algebraic plans. Also this level is where SQO techniques are applied. Such plans are seamlessly integrated with the tuple-based algebraic plans, providing a uniform view of all computation.

Example 1   FOR $a in Stream("onlinenews")/news
LET $b = $a/source, $c = $a/keyword
WHERE $b = "CNN"
RETURN <CNN>$c</CNN>

Example 1 gives an XQuery which asks for the keywords of online news reported by CNN. Suppose we perform all pattern retrieval in the automata, the previous literature [5, 2] models the whole automata computation as a single operator. This operator (called *x-scan* in [5]) exposes a fixed interface, namely, the bindings to *all* the XPath expressions in the XQuery, to its downstream operators. Such an operator cannot be rewritten in combination with the other non-automata operators due to its coarse granularity and fixed interface. Instead, we propose to model the automata computation as an algebraic plan consisting of operators at finer granularity compared to *x-scan*. The benefit is that this overall algebraic plan can be uniformly understood and optimized even it contains more traditional tuple-based operators and the novel token-based automata operators.

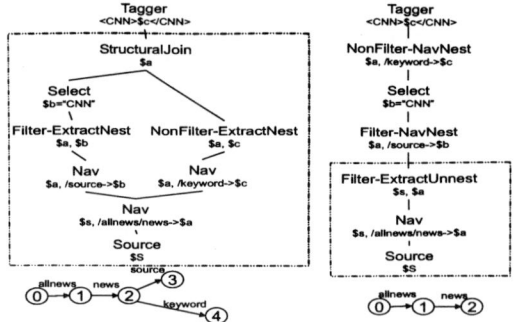

Figure 1: Alternative Stream Logical Plans

The subplan in the dashed box in Figure 1 (a) shows our modeling of the pattern retrieval in Example 1. The intuition behind this modeling is that the retrieval of a tree pattern in the automata can be decomposed into (1) the retrieval of its "linear patterns", and (2) the combination of bindings of individual linear patterns into bindings of tree patterns. For example, see Figure 1 (a). First, $Nav_{\$a,/source \to \$b}$ locates all the tokens that form the elements accessible via */source* from $\$a$ and binds these tokens to variable $\$b$. Second, $Filter\text{-}ExtractNest_{\$a,\$b}$ composes the tokens identified by $Nav_{\$a,/source \to \$b}$ into self-contained elements. The linear pattern $\$a/keyword$ is similarly resolved except that a different composition operator $NonFilter\text{-}ExtractNest_{\$a,\$c}$ is used. The difference between $Filter\text{-}ExtractNest_{\$a,\$b}$ and $NonFilter\text{-}ExtractNest_{\$a,\$c}$ is that: in the former, the absence of $\$b$ (i.e., the *source* elements) within a *news* element filters out this $\$a$ (i.e., the *news* element); while in the latter, the absence of $\$b$ does not filter out $\$a$, e.g., $<CNN></CNN>$ will be returned for a *news* element whose source is CNN but does not contain any keywords. Finally, $StructuralJoin_{\$a}$ joins together the composed *source* and *keyword* elements that are within the same *news* element. The automaton in Figure 1 (a), similar to those used in [5, 2], is one implementation for Nav operators in the plan.

We now show that different amount of computation can be done in the automata for the same semantics-focused plan. Figure 1 (b) shows another stream logical plan for Example 1. This plan only retrieves *news* elements from the token streams. Compared to Figure 1 (a), it has less computation done in the automata[1]. Suppose only a small proportion of *news* are from CNN, then plan (b) may benefit from the early applying of $Sel_{\$b="CNN"}$, because this saves the time of finding those *keyword* elements whose source is not CNN. Figure 2 shows our experimental results of the execution time of two plans for a query similar to Example 1 but with more path expressions and

---

[1] *Filter-NavNest* and *NonFilter-NavNest* [10] are non-automata operators navigating into self-contained tree-like elements (e.g., *news* elements composed by *Filter-ExtractUnnest*$_{\$s,\$a}$) to find the targets.

selections [9]. For data with different selectivities for the select conditions, different plans are optimal. Note that the previous literature [2, 7, 8, 4] simply embraces a *maximal pushdown* strategy (corresponds to the "5 Navs Pushed Down" strategy in Figure 2) which does not ensure the optimality. This illustrates that our framework opens up more optimization opportunities beyond the existing solutions in the literature.

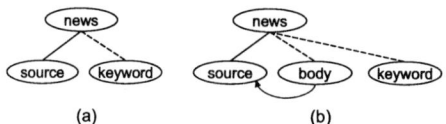

Figure 3: Query Tree for Figure 1 (a)

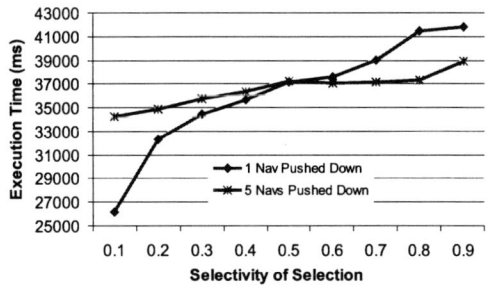

Figure 2: Execution Time of Two Alternative Plans (on a 85M XML Stream)

3 Schema-Based Optimization

At the stream logical plan level, schema knowledge is used to rewrite a query into a more efficient one. We focus on SQO techniques specific to XML streams. The distinguishing feature of pattern retrieval on XML token streams is that it solely relies on the document-order traversal of tokens due to the lack of indices. We observe that the order or occurrence constraints of XML elements can be used to expedite the traversal by avoiding unnecessary pattern retrieval.

Let's consider a query similar to Example 1 but asking for both the *news* and its *keyword* elements. For ease of illustration, we use DTD as the schema description language here (even though we use XML schema in our system). We suppose the element type *news* is described as <!ELEMENT news (source?, body, related, keyword$^+$)>.

Our approach consists of three phases. In the first phase, i.e., the *initiation phase*, we construct query trees describing the structural pattern to be resolved in the automata (there can be multiple query trees when there are multiple data sources). Figure 3 shows the query tree for Figure 1 (a). The relationship between *news* and *source* (represented as solid line) is distinguished from that between *news* and *keyword* (represented as dashed line). As mentioned in Section 2, the absence of *source* subelement in a *news* element would filter out this *news* while the absence of *keyword* would not. Furthermore, we apply type inference [3] on the query trees so that nondeterministic navigation steps such as "//" or "*" are resolved as much as possible.

The second phase is the *reasoning phase*, namely, to apply a set of schema-based rewriting rules on the initialized query trees. An example rewriting rule is *pattern introduction*. For example, a structural pattern /*body* can be introduced to the query tree in Figure 3 (a). Figure 3 (b) shows the rewritten query tree. The arc from *body* to *source* indicates that if *body* has been encountered, the recognition of *source* will then be dropped within the current *news* element. This is because a *source* element, if any, must have appeared before the *body* element. If the recognition of *source* element is dropped without finding any *source* elements, all other pattern retrievals within the current *news*, i.e., composing the *news* element and retrieving *keyword* elements, will also be dropped. This can be a major saving when the *body*, *related* and *keyword* elements are long.

We analyze the relationship among the rewriting rules and derive an application order to ensure the quality of modified query tree. This order ensures two properties, *completeness* and *minimality*. *Completeness* indicates that no beneficial rule application is missed, e.g., the introduction of pattern /*body* will not be missed. *Minimality* means no redundant rule application is introduced. For example, pattern /*related* will not be introduced since the pattern /*body* already serves the purpose for marking the completion of pattern /*source* and bindings of /*body* occur before bindings of /*related* within a binding of *news*.

In the third phase, *plan generation*, we rewrite the original plan to a new plan according to the new query tree. Figure 4 shows the new plan corresponding to the modified query tree in Figure 3 (b). Compared to Figure 1 (b), a new state, i.e., state 5, is added to the automaton. State 5 is associated with the $ExtractNest_{\$a,\$b}$ operator, indicating that if state 5 is activated, this operator is checked. If no outputs within current binding of $\$a$ exist or no outputs satisfy the predicate $\$b = "CNN"$, the transitions from state 2 will be suspended which results in the automaton in the left bottom part in Figure 4.

4 Demonstration

We will use two applications in the demonstration:

1. *Sports news dissemination*. We use the real data set conforming to *SportsML* DTD (www.sportsml.com), the standard for sharing sports data developed by International Press Telecommunications Council.

2. *On-line auction monitoring*. We generate synthetic data conforming to on-line auction DTDs proposed by XMark (www.xml-benchmark.org), an XML benchmark.

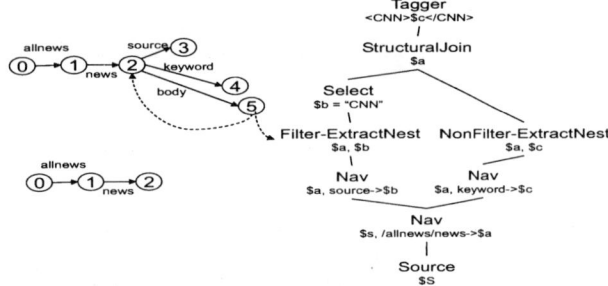

Figure 4: Modified New Plan

Our demonstration is composed of two parts.

Stream Logical Plan.

1. *Generating Alternative Plans.* Given an XQuery, we first show its semantics-focused plan. We generate a set of alternative stream logical plans from the semantics-focused plan, using different computation pushdown strategy. Users can choose a plan from the left panel in Figure 5 and view the plan as well as its automata in the right panel.

2. *Comparing Alternative Plans.* We deploy a stream generator on one machine and send the stream continuously to another machine on which the stream processing engine runs. For comparison of alternative plans, alternative plans run in turn. We provide a "plot all performances" functionality (in the bottom panel) to visually compare their performances. We will change the data characteristics of the stream source, illustrating that under different circumstances, the optimal plan can be different.

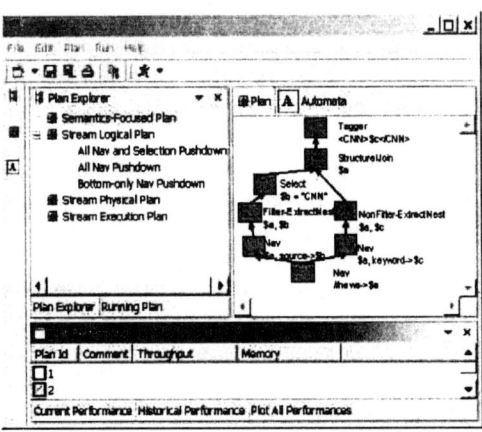

Figure 5: GUI Showing Stream Logical Plans

Schema-Based Optimization.

1. *Showing Static Structures.* We show the required static structures, including (1) query tree; (2) schema (modeled in graphs), and (3) a library of rewriting rules in the upper panel in Figure 6.

2. *Tracing Reasoning Process.* When a rule is applied on a query tree node, the rule in the library, the node and any changes made to the query tree are highlighted in the bottom panel in Figure 6. The history of rule applications can be traced by scrolling the bottom panel.

3. *Comparing Optimized Plans with Original Plans.* We plot the performances comparing an original plan with those optimized ones under various data characteristics of the stream.

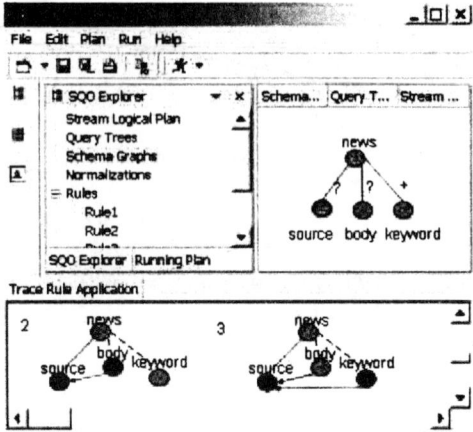

Figure 6: GUI Showing Schema-Based Optimization

References

[1] S. Amer-Yahia, S. Cho, L. V. Lakshmanan, and D. Srivastava. Minimization of Tree Pattern Queries. In *SIGMOD, Santa Barbara, California*, pages 497–508, June 2001.

[2] Y. Diao and M. Franklin. Query Processing for High-Volume XML Message Brokering. In *Proceedings of VLDB*, pages 261–272, 2003.

[3] M. Fernandez and D. Suciu. Optimizing Regular Path Expressions Using Graph Schemas. In *ICDE, Orlando, Florida*, pages 14–23, February 1998.

[4] A. Gupta and D. Suciu. Stream Processing of XPath Queries with Predicates. In *Proceedings of SIGMOD*, pages 419–430, 2003.

[5] Z. Ives, A. Halevy, and D. Weld. An XML Query Engine for Network-Bound Data. *VLDB Journal*, 11 (4): 380–402, 2002.

[6] J. Jian, H. Su, and E. Rundensteiner. Automaton Meets Query Algebra: Towards A Unified Model for XQuery Evaluation over XML Data Streams. In *Proceedings of ER*, 2003.

[7] B. Ludascher, P. Mukhopadhyay, and Y. Papakonstantinou. A Transducer-Based XML Query Processor. In *Proceedings of VLDB*, pages 227–238, 2002.

[8] F. Peng and S. Chawathe. XPath Queries on Streaming Data. In *Proceedings of SIGMOD*, pages 431–442, 2003.

[9] H. Su, J. Jian, and E. A. Rundensteiner. Raindrop: A Uniform and Layered Algebraic Framework for XQueries on XML Streams. In *Proceedings of CIKM*, 2003.

[10] X. Zhang, K. Dimitrova, L. Wang, M. El-Sayed, B. Murphy, B. Pielech, M. Mulchandani, L. Ding, and E. A. Rundensteiner. Rainbow: Multi-XQuery Optimization Using Materialized XML Views. In *SIGMOD Demo*, page 671, 2003.

ShreX: Managing XML Documents in Relational Databases

Fang Du
OGI/OHSU
fangdu@cse.ogi.edu

Sihem Amer-Yahia
AT&T Labs – Research
sihem@research.att.com

Juliana Freire
OGI/OHSU
juliana@cse.ogi.edu

Abstract

We describe *ShreX*, a freely-available system for shredding, loading and querying XML documents in relational databases. *ShreX* supports all mapping strategies proposed in the literature as well as strategies available in commercial RDBMSs. It provides generic (mapping-independent) functions for loading shredded documents into relations and for translating XML queries into SQL. *ShreX* is portable and can be used with any relational database backend.

1 Introduction

As applications manipulate an increasing volume of XML data, there is a growing need for reliable systems to store and provide efficient access to these data. The use of relational database systems for this purpose has attracted considerable interest with a view to leveraging their powerful and reliable data management services.

In order to store an XML document in a relational database, the tree-structure of the XML document must first be mapped into an equivalent, flat, relational schema. XML documents are then shredded and loaded into the mapped tables. Finally, at runtime, XML queries are translated into SQL, submitted to the RDMBS, and the results are then translated into XML.

There is a rich literature addressing the issue of storing XML documents in relational backends. Several mapping strategies (*e.g.*, [3, 5, 6, 10, 9]) and query translation algorithms (see [7] for a survey) have been proposed. In addition, support for XML storage is already available in most commercial RDBMSs. Unfortunately, existing XML-to-relational mapping solutions suffer from several drawbacks. None of these solutions addresses all the storage problems in a single framework. For example, works on mapping strategies often have little or no details about query translation [7]. Although it has been shown that the efficiency of a mapping depends on the data and on the requirements of the applications that use the data [3], many of the available mapping solutions hard-code mapping choices; and whereas some of the solutions proposed by relational vendors do provide flexible mechanisms to define mappings, they are proprietary, *i.e.*, tied to one relational backend, making the shredding and query translation algorithms system- and mapping-dependent.

ShreX (Shredding XML) is a freely available system[1] that addresses many of the limitations of existing mapping systems. To the best of our knowledge, *ShreX* is the first system to provide a comprehensive solution to the relational storage of XML data. In *ShreX*, an XML-to-relational mapping is specified through annotations over an XML Schema, making the mapping easy to define as well as validate. By combining different annotations, a wide range of mappings can be expressed, including all mapping strategies proposed in the literature as well as strategies supported by database vendors. *ShreX* also provides generic (mapping-independent) functions for document shredding and query translation. This is made possible by an API which provides access to the mapping information.

In what follows, we give an overview of the key features of *ShreX*. In Section 2, we describe the architecture of the system including the mapping interface, the shredder and the query translator. The demonstration is described in Section 3. We review related work in Section 4 and conclude in Section 5.

2 The System

The main components of the *ShreX* system are shown in Figure 1. In *ShreX*, a mapping is defined by adding annotations to an XML Schema which indicate how elements and attributes should be stored in a relational database (*e.g.*, as columns, as tables). The *annotation processor* parses an annotated XML Schema, checks the validity of the mapping and creates the corresponding relational schema. In addition, the mapping information is made persistent in the *mapping repository*. The *document shredder* accepts as in-

---

Permission to copy without fee all or part of this material is granted provided that the copies are not made or distributed for direct commercial advantage, the VLDB copyright notice and the title of the publication and its date appear, and notice is given that copying is by permission of the Very Large Data Base Endowment. To copy otherwise, or to republish, requires a fee and/or special permission from the Endowment.

**Proceedings of the 30th VLDB Conference,
Toronto, Canada, 2004**

---

[1] *ShreX* is available at http://www.cse.ogi.edu/~fangdu/shreX.

put a document and uses the mapping API to access the information in the mapping repository to generate the tuples and populate the tables in the relational schema. The mapping repository is also accessed by the *query translator*, which generates SQL queries from XML queries.

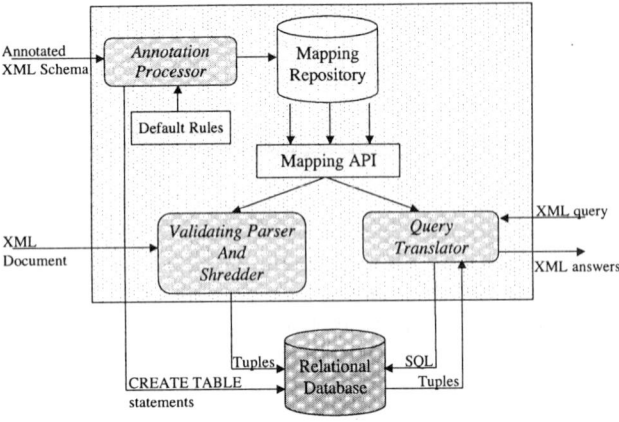

Figure 1: *ShreX* Architecture

Below, we give a brief overview of the mapping definition framework, and of the various modules of *ShreX*. The reader is referred to [1] for more details.

2.1 Mapping Definition Framework

A *ShreX* mapping is expressed by annotating an XML Schema. This not only makes the mapping definition portable, *i.e.*, independent from the underlying relational database, but also expressive and extensible. Mapping specifications also enable useful analyses, for example, to ensure that a mapping is valid (Section 2.2).

Annotations can be associated to attributes, elements and groups in the input XML Schema. Their syntax corresponds to adding attributes from a namespace called **shrex** to a given XML Schema. The attributes supported by *ShreX* are shown in Table 1. Figure 2 illustrates the use of some of the annotations (shown in boldface). The sample schema describes information about shows, where a SHOW has a TITLE, a YEAR, zero or more REVIEWs, and zero or more alternative titles (AKAs).

Mapping document structure. An important aspect of a mapping is how it captures element identity, document structure and order. In *ShreX*, the choice of structure mapping can be specified through the **structurescheme** attribute (see Table 1). For example, in Figure 2, the structure scheme selected for the document is Dewey[2] (see annotation in the root element). Other supported schemes include: key-foreign-key for parent-child relationships and ordinal for siblings ("KFO") [3]; and interval encoding [8]. The ability to define multiple document structure schemes is a feature that is unique to *ShreX*.

Outline, tablename, columnname, sqltype. Annotations are also used to specify how individual elements and attributes in a document are represented in the relational schema. Figure 3 shows the relational configuration for the annotated schema of Figure 2. The annotation **outline="true"** in the element TITLE indicates it should be mapped to a separate table; and the annotation **tablename** specifies that this table should be named **Showtitle**. The element YEAR, on the other hand, has its **outline** attribute set to false, consequently it is inlined in the table corresponding to its parent element, SHOW. The annotations **sqltype** and **columnname** in the YEAR element specify that it should be mapped to a column named **Showyear** and SQL type **NUMBER(4)**. Although not illustrated in the example, an element can also be mapped into a CLOB, using the annotation **maptoclob**.

```
<element name="SHOW">
    shrex:structurescheme="Dewey" />
  <sequence>
    <element name="TITLE" type="string"
        shrex:outline="true"
        shrex:tablename="Showtitle"/>
    <element name="YEAR" type="integer"
        shrex:outline="false"
        shrex:columnname="Showyear"
        shrex:sqltype="NUMBER(4)"/>
    <element name="REVIEW" type="ANYTYPE"
        minOccurs="0" maxOccurs="unbounded"
        shrex:edgemapping="true"/>
    <element name="AKA" type="string"
        minOccurs="0" maxOccurs="unbounded"/>
</element>
```

Figure 2: Annotated movie schema

```
TABLE SHOW( ID VARCHAR(128),
  Showyear NUMBER(4))

TABLE Showtitle( ID VARCHAR(128),
  ParentID VARCHAR(128), TITLE VARCHAR(512))

TABLE REVIEW( ParentID VARCHAR(128),
  source VARCHAR(128),
  ordinal VARCHAR(128),
  attrname VARCHAR(128),
  flag VARCHAR(128),
  value VARCHAR(128))

TABLE AKA( ID VARCHAR(128),
  ParentID VARCHAR(128), AKA VARCHAR(512))
```

Figure 3: Relational configuration for movie schema

Mapping schemaless documents and mixing strategies. The use of annotated schemata in *ShreX* does not preclude the system from expressing generic (schemaless) mappings. For example, in Figure 2, the annotation **edgemapping="true"** in the element REVIEW indicates that REVIEW and its descendants are mapped using Edge mapping [6], *i.e.*, a single table to store all the REVIEW elements and contents. This functionality is specially useful to map elements whose structures are not known in advance, such as for example, elements of type ANYTYPE.

Annotations naturally allow the definition of mappings that combine different mapping strategies. Note that in this example, part of the document is mapped using Edge, and part is mapped using KFO.

---
[2] http://www.oclc.org/dewey/about/about_the_ddc.htm.

Transformation-based mappings. Additional mapping strategies are supported by combining *ShreX* annotations with the schema transformations proposed in [3]. For example, if repetition split is applied to AKA in the original schema, *i.e.*, AKA* → AKA?, AKA*, the first occurrence of AKA could be inlined in the table SHOW:

```
TABLE SHOW( ID VARCHAR(128),
            Showyear NUMBER(4),
            AKA VARCHAR(512))
```

2.2 Annotation Processor

This module is in charge of parsing an annotated XML Schema, checking the validity of a mapping, generating a mapping repository, and producing the CREATE TABLE statements necessary to construct the relational schema. In order to check the validity of a mapping, the annotation processor validates the input (annotated) schema against an XML Schema for annotations [1]. Validity checks include verifying whether annotations are attached to the appropriate elements, and if table names are unique in the mapping definition. Additional checks, such as verifying whether a mapping is lossless, are also possible.

Writing an annotation for every element and attribute definition in an XML Schema can be tedious, especially for large schemata. *ShreX* provides a set of default rules that is used to *complete* mapping specifications. In fact, using these default rules, the system is able to automatically map an XML Schema without any user input. It is worthy of note that users can add to or override these rules.

2.3 Mapping Repository and API

Mapping information is processed and stored in a database. By making this information persistent, *ShreX* avoids the need to re-parse a mapping specification each time a document is loaded into the target database or that a query needs to be translated into SQL. *ShreX* provides an API to the mapping repository that allows access to information such as, how elements and attributes are mapped (**isInlined(ElemName|AttName)**), which mapping is used to capture document structure (**getStructureScheme()**), and which tables are available in the relational schema (**getTableInfo(TableName)**) (see [1] for details). This API allows users to write mapping-independent code which is not tied to specific features of a particular mapping.

The API also contains functions that expose information about the schema being mapped. These functions are useful both during shredding and query translation. For example, in order to translate a descendent step //t, the query translator needs to determine all paths from the root to tag t – in *ShreX*, this can be done through a call to **pathToTag**.

2.4 Document Shredder

The shredder is in charge of generating tuples, field values and CLOBs from an input document. It was designed to be generic and independent from the mapping specification: it uses the mapping API to retrieve information about how a particular element or attribute is mapped. Since mapping annotations are specified using attributes from a different namespace, the document shredder can validate the input XML document against the annotated Schema. Tuples are generated while the document is parsed, using a standard XML parser. In our implementation, we use the SAX interface of Xerces [11], which is both efficient and scalable. For example, *ShreX* is able to shred and load a 1GB document into DB2 in less than 30 minutes. It is worth pointing out that even significantly smaller files cannot be loaded in commercial RDBMSs using their XML extensions. Consistently with what has been reported in [12], we were not able to load documents larger than 10MB using DB2's XML Extender.

Users can set various parameters for the shredder, *e.g.*, target database system, login information, bulk loading option. These parameters can be set either through the command line or through a configuration file.

2.5 Query Translator

In the current implementation, the query translator supports a subset of XPath that includes child and descendant axes; position-based predicates [position()=n]; and simple path predicates, to SQL.[3] Similar to the document shredder, the query translator does not hard-code mapping choices, instead it uses the information provided by the mapping API to dynamically decide how to perform the translation.

3 Demonstration Overview

We will demonstrate the various features of *ShreX* and its utility for building applications that need to store and query XML data in relational databases.

Specifying mappings. We will show how different *storage mapping strategies* can be represented using our mapping specification. Users will be able to define mappings by choosing from a variety of XML schemata or creating their own schema. Using *ShreX*, they will annotate a schema, validate the corresponding mapping, and create the corresponding relational schemata. We will show how this process is simplified by the *ShreX* graphical user interface (GUI), which allows users to browse and select tables and fields in the relational schema and visually see the corresponding XML elements and attributes, and vice versa.

Shredding and loading. After a relational schema is created, users will be able to select a target RDBMS and instruct the system to *shred and load a document* into the target RDBMS. Shredding and loading can be done through the command-line, or from the GUI. Users can load the XML documents directly into the relational tables (*i.e.*, they can be bulk-loaded), or generate loading commands and tuples.

Querying. Users will be able to input XPath queries and see the corresponding (translated) SQL queries as well as have these queries executed against the relational backend.

---

[3] An XQuery translator is currently under development, and will be available in the next version of *ShreX*.

Annotation attributes	Target	Value	Action
outline	attribute or element	true, false	If value is true, a relational table is created for the attribute or element. Otherwise, the attribute or element is mapped to one or multiple columns in its containing table (*i.e.*, inlined).
tablename	attribute, element or group	string	The string is used as the table name.
columnname	attribute or element of simple type	string	The string is used as the column name.
sqltype	attribute or element of simple type	string	The string overrides the SQL type of a column.
structurescheme	root element	KFO, Interval, Dewey	Specifies structure mapping.
edgemapping	element	true, false	If value is true, the element and its descendants are shredded according to Edge mapping [6].
maptoclob	attribute or element	true, false	If value is true, the element or attribute is mapped to a CLOB column.

Table 1: Annotation Attributes. Each row in the table contains an annotation attribute, its target (*i.e.*, element, attribute, and group to which it applies), its possible values and its action depending on its value.

4 Related Work

Bourret et al [4] developed XML-DBMS, a generic tool for loading XML documents into relational tables. Although similar to *ShreX* in motivation, the mappings supported by this tool are limited to the basic, shared, and hybrid techniques described in [10]. In addition, XML-DBMS has no support for query translation.

MXM [2] has been proposed as a declarative mechanism to express XML-to-relational mappings. Our mapping specification shares the flexibility of MXM while having the advantage of using an XML Schema syntax and providing a comprehensive set of tools.

Although XML support in commercial relational engines is improving rapidly, there is a wide variation in the supported features. Some practical problems include proprietary solutions, lack of flexibility and scalability. To define a storage strategy, the IBM DB2 XML Extender requires users to write a Document Access Definition specification; consequently, developers must learn a new language in order to use DB2 (and only DB2) as a backend. The mapping facilities provided by Oracle 9iR2 are not flexible enough to specify many useful strategies, for example, it is not possible to specify that *part* of the data is to be stored using a generic mapping such as Edge [6]. SQLServer's OpenXML requires that documents be compiled into an internal DOM representation, which greatly limits its scalability.

5 Conclusion

To the best of our knowledge, *ShreX* is the first comprehensive system for mapping, loading and querying XML documents. *ShreX* has many novel features including the ability to mix mapping strategies and to specify a document structure scheme. We designed *ShreX* to be modular and extensible. And by making the source code available, we hope *ShreX* will serve as a platform to develop and evaluate new mapping strategies, query translation and optimization algorithms.

Acknowledgments. The National Science Foundation partially supports Juliana Freire under grant EIA-0323604.

References

[1] S. Amer-Yahia, F. Du, and J. Freire. A generic and flexible framework for mapping XML documents into relations. Technical report, OGI/OHSU, 2004.

[2] S. Amer-Yahia and D. Srivastava. A mapping scheme and interface for XML stores. In *Proc. of WIDM*, 2002.

[3] P. Bohannon, J. Freire, P. Roy, and J. Siméon. From XML schema to relations: A cost-based approach to XML storage. In *Proc. of ICDE*, pages 64–75, 2002.

[4] R. Bourret, C. Bornhvd, and A. P. Buchmann. A generic load/extract utility for data transfer between XML documents and relational databases. In *WECWIS*, pages 134–143, 2000.

[5] A. Deutsch, M. Fernandez, and D. Suciu. Storing semistructured data with STORED. In *Proc. of SIGMOD*, pages 431–442, 1999.

[6] D. Florescu and D. Kossman. Storing and querying XML data using an RDMBS. *IEEE Data Engineering Bulletin*, 22(3):27–34, 1999.

[7] R. Krishnamurthy, R. Kaushik, and J. F. Naughton. XML-SQL query translation literature: The state of the art and open problems. In *Proc. XSym*, 2003.

[8] S. Paparizos and et al. Timber: A native system for querying XML. In *Proc. of SIGMOD*, page 672, 2003. Demonstration.

[9] A. Schmidt, M. Kersten, M. Windhouwer, and F. Waas. Efficient relational storage and retrieval of XML documents. In *Proc. of WebDB*, pages 47–52, 2000.

[10] J. Shanmugasundaram, K. Tufte, G. He, C. Zhang, D. DeWitt, and J. Naughton. Relational databases for querying XML documents: Limitations and opportunities. In *Proc. of VLDB*, pages 302–314, 1999.

[11] Xerces Java parser 1.4.3. http://xml.apache.org/xerces-j.

[12] B. B. Yao, M. T. Özsu, and N. Khandelwal. XBench benchmark and performance testing of XML DBMSs. In *Proc. of ICDE*, pages 621–632, 2004.

A Uniform System for Publishing and Maintaining XML Data

Byron Choi
University of Pennsylvania
kkchoi@gradient.cis.upenn.edu

Xibei Jia
University of Edinburgh
x.jia@sms.ed.ac.uk

Wenfei Fan[*]
University of Edinburgh & Bell Laboratories
wenfei@inf.ed.ac.uk

Arek Kasprzyk
European Bioinformatics Institute
arek@ebi.ac.uk

1 Introduction

XML has become the prime standard for data exchange on the Web. To exchange data currently residing in databases, one needs to *publish it in* XML, *i.e.,* to extract data from the database and transform the data into an XML format. In practice, data publishing is often done with a predefined "schema". A community agrees on a certain schema, and subsequently all members of the community exchange their data *w.r.t.* the predefined schema, by ensuring their published (*target*) XML data to conform to the fixed schema. This is called *schema-directed* XML *publishing*. The need for this is particularly evident in biological data exchange and services. However, it is nontrivial to ensure that the target XML data conforms to a given schema. The difficulty is introduced by, among others, recursion in a target schema, which is common in, *e.g.*, biological ontologies [7].

With XML publishing also comes the increasing need for *maintaining* target XML data. The underlying source data often changes and evolves, and the source updates should be reflected in its XML target accurately and efficiently. A naive approach would be to recompute the XML target from scratch in response to source data changes. This is not very realistic in many applications where XML publishing involves voluminous data and may take hours to complete. This suggests that one needs to deal with updates incrementally: propagate the updates from the source data to its XML target with minimal recomputation. While this is reminiscent of traditional database view maintenance, incremental updates are more challenging for hierarchical and possibly recursive XML views constrained by a predefined schema.

In response to the need we proposed a new approach for schema-directed publishing of relational data in XML, based on the novel notion of attribute transformation grammars (ATGs [3]). ATGs provide guidance on how to define views conforming to *target* schemas (DTDs) and better still, they automatically ensure schema conformance. We also developed an incremental algorithm for maintaining XML views produced by ATGs [4], based on new incremental computation techniques that capitalize on the hierarchical structure of XML data and unique features of ATGs.

Recently we have implemented a middleware system that supports both schema-directed XML publishing based on ATGs, and incremental updates of XML views created by ATGs. We have also been deploying and evaluating the system at the European Bioinformatics Institute (EBI). Our experimental results are promising: our system is capable of efficiently publishing real-life biological data (in the order of GigaBytes) and guaranteeing the XML views to conform to predefined (recursive) DTDs; moreover, our incremental update algorithm outperforms the recomputation approach by two orders of magnitude. The system will possibly be adopted by EBI in the near future. To the best of our knowledge, it is the first practical system that supports schema-directed XML publishing and incremental updates.

Taking real-life data from Gene Ontology [7] (GO), this paper demonstrates how this system can efficiently publish the GO data in XML *w.r.t.* a predefined recursive DTD, and how it incrementally updates the target XML data in response to changes to the underlying GO database.

Related work. Although a number of XML publishing systems have been developed (*e.g.,* [5, 8, 6, 9, 10]), none of these systems takes schema-conformance into account. Type-checking approaches to DTD conformance are impractical since type checking of transformations, even for simple DTDs, is computationally intractable for extremely restricted views and undecidable for realistic views [1]. Worse still, type-checking does not provide any guidance on how to repair an XML view that does not typecheck.

The notion of ATGs was proposed in [3] and the incremental update algorithm was developed in [4]. However, the work in this paper is the first effort to fully implement ATGs and incremental updates, combine them in a uniform system, and to verify the effectiveness of the techniques in real-life applications. Furthermore, in our implemen-

---

[*] Supported in part by NSF Career Award IIS-0093168, NSFC 60228006 and EPSRC GR/S63205/01.

Permission to copy without fee all or part of this material is granted provided that the copies are not made or distributed for direct commercial advantage, the VLDB copyright notice and the title of the publication and its date appear, and notice is given that copying is by permission of the Very Large Data Base Endowment. To copy otherwise, or to republish, requires a fee and/or special permission from the Endowment.

Proceedings of the 30th VLDB Conference,
Toronto, Canada, 2004

Source relational schema R:
```
primary_terms(go_id, name, updated)
terms(go_id, name, updated)
ancestors(parent_id, child_id)
main(protein_id, name, source)
protein2go(protein_id, go_id)
```
Target DTD D_0:
```
<!ELEMENT db          (term*)>
<!ELEMENT term        (children, id, tname,
                       updated, proteins)>
<!ELEMENT children    (term*)>
<!ELEMENT proteins    (protein*)>
<!ELEMENT protein     (pname, pid, source)>
/* #PCDATA is omitted here. */
```

Figure 1: Example of a source schema and a target DTD

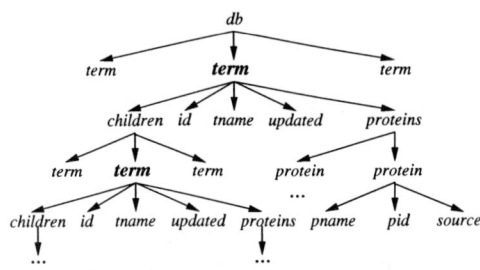

Figure 2: An XML tree conforming to D_0

tation we developed new optimization ideas that were not explored by [3, 4]. Another extension of ATG was proposed in [2] for integration, which is not part of this demo system.

2 Schema-Directed Publishing

The problem of *schema-directed publishing* can be stated as follows: given a DTD D, to define a view σ for relational databases I such that $\sigma(I)$ is an XML document conforming to D. We conduct schema-directed publishing by means of Attribute Transformation Grammars (ATGs [3]).

Given an arbitrary target DTD D, an ATG defines a view as follows: (1) For each element type A in D, it defines a variable $\$A$; intuitively, each A element in an XML tree is to have a variable $\$A$, which contains a single relational tuple as its value. (2) For each element type definition (production) $A \rightarrow \alpha$ in D, where α is a regular expression, it specifies a set of semantic rules such that for each element type B in α, there is a rule for computing the values of $\$B$ via SQL queries; the query is treated as a function that may take $\$A$ as a parameter. Given a relational database I, the ATG is evaluated top-down: starting at the root element type of D, evaluate semantic rules associated with each element type encountered, and create nodes following the DTD to construct the target XML tree. The values of the variable $\$A$ are used to control the construction.

As an example, consider publishing (simplified) GO [7] data in XML. The GO data is stored in a relational database, which, as show in Fig. 1, consists of three relations for GO terms: `primary_term` stores the GO id, name and the date of the last update for each primary term; similarly for other `terms`; as a term may be composed of other terms, the composition hierarchy is given by the `ancestors` relation (keys are underlined). The database has also two relations for proteins: `main` specifies the id, name and source of each protein; and `protein2go` tells how terms and proteins are related.

Now one wants to construct a target XML document T that contains all the primary terms immediately under the root, along with their composition hierarchy and the proteins they are related to. Furthermore, T is required to conform to the DTD D_0 given in Fig. 1. Observe that D_0 is *recursive*: a `term` may have other `terms` as its children; this leads to XML trees of unbounded depths.

An ATG σ_0 specifying the publishing is shown in Fig. 3.

When being evaluated over the GO database, σ_0 produces a target XML tree T as depicted in Fig. 2, as follows.

(1) It first creates the root element, `db`, and then triggers the rules associated with the production `db` $\rightarrow$ `term*`. Observe that the production contains a Kleene star; thus there is no bound on the number of the `term` children of the root. These children are determined by the evaluation of the SQL query Q_1 over the GO database, which returns all the `primary term` tuples. For each t of these tuples, a `term` element is created as a child of the root, carrying t as the value of its variable $\$term$. The operator "$\leftarrow$" in the rule denotes the iteration for generating the `term` children, corresponding to the Kleene star.

(2) At each `term` element t, the XML tree T is expanded by generating the children of t. In contrast to the last case, the production for `term` tells us that t has exactly five children: `children`, `id`, `name`, `updated` and `source`. The variables associated with these children are assigned values extracted from fields of the parent variable $\$term$, e.g., $\$children$ inherits the value $\$term.go\_id$.

(3) At each `children` element c, the target tree T is further expanded as follows. The SQL query Q_2 finds the `go_id`s of all the children terms of c from the `ancestors` relation, by using $\$children.go\_id$ as a constant parameter; it then extracts tuples from the `term` relation using these `go_id`s. For each t' of these tuples, a `term` child of c is created carrying t' as the value of its variable, and the `term` node is in turn processed as described in (2).

(4) Similarly, at each `proteins` child p of `term` t, the SQL query Q_3 extracts all the `protein` tuples related to t from the `main` and `protein2go` relations, by using $\$proteins.go\_id$ as a constant. For each of these tuples a `protein` child of p is generated, whose children are in turn created as described in (2).

Steps (2) and (3) are repeated until the target tree T cannot be further expanded, i.e., when all the `terms` at the leaves of T are no longer composed of other `terms`. At this point the evaluation of the ATG is completed.

ATG has several salient features. First, when the evaluation of an ATG terminates, the target XML tree generated is guaranteed to conform to its embedded DTD. Second, it adopts a *data-driven* semantics: the expansion of an XML tree in the recursive case are determined by the source data. Third, it is easy to use ATGs to specify schema-directed XML publishing. The DTD productions provide a guidance on how to write semantic rules to expand the tree that conforms to the DTD. There is no need to learn a new language: one can write ATGs as long as she/he knows SQL and DTD.

db → term*
Q_1: $term ← select go_id, name, updated from primary_terms
term → children, id, tname, updated, proteins
  $children = $term.go_id, $id = $term.go_id,
  $tname = $term.name, $updated = $term.updated,
  $proteins = $term.go_id,
children → term*
Q_2: $term ← select t.go_id, t.name, t.updated
           from ancestors a, terms t
           where $children = a.parent_id and a.child_id = t.go_id
proteins → protein*
Q_3: $protein ← select m.name, m.protein_id, m.source
              from protein2go p, main m
              where $proteins = p.go_id and
                    p.protein_id = m.protein_id
protein → pname, pid, source
  $pname = $protein.name, $pid = $protein.go_id,
  $source = $protein.source

Figure 3: An example ATG σ_0

3 Incremental Updates

The *incremental update* problem for ATGs can be stated as follows: given an ATG σ, a relational database I, the XML view $T = \sigma(I)$, and changes ΔI to I, to compute XML changes ΔT to T such that $T \oplus \Delta T = \sigma(I \oplus \Delta I)$, where the operator $\oplus$ denotes the application of these updates. In contrast to recomputing the new view from scratch, incremental update of ATGs improves performance by applying only the changes ΔT to the old view T.

Our incremental algorithm [4] is based on a notion of ΔATG. A ΔATG $\Delta\sigma$ is statically derived from an ATG σ by deducing and incrementalizing SQL queries for generating edges of XML views. In response to relational changes ΔI to the source data, $\Delta\sigma$ computes XML changes ΔT via the incrementalized SQL queries, which yield a pair of relations (E^+, E^-), denoting the insertions (*buds*) and deletions (*cuts*) of the edges of the old XML view T, respectively. More specifically this is carried out in three phases: (1) a *bud-cut generation phase* that determines the impact of ΔI on *existing* parent-child (edge) relations in the old XML view T by evaluating a fixed number of incrementalized SQL queries; (2) a *bud completion phase* that iteratively computes newly inserted subtrees top-down by pushing SQL queries to the relational DBMS; and finally, (3) a *garbage collection* process that removes the deleted subtrees. It minimizes unnecessary recomputations via a novel caching strategy such that each new subtree in the XML view is computed at most once no matter how many times it occurs in the XML view, and moreover, it maximally reuses subtrees in the old XML view. The caching strategy is based on the *subtree property* of XML data and ATGs: each subtree in an XML view generated by an ATG is *uniquely determined* by the tuple-value of the variable associated with the subtree root. This allows us to efficiently identify and reuse existing subtrees via a hash table.

As an example, consider changes ΔI to the GO database I that modify the ancestors relations of terms, which can be understood as *group updates* consisting of insertions and deletions of multiple ancestors tuples. Referring to the XML view T of Fig. 2 generated by $\sigma_0(I)$, the corresponding XML changes ΔT are computed as follows. The bud-cut-generation phase generates a set of cuts to the (children, term) edges of T, as well as a set of buds N_{term} consisting of the newly inserted term tuples, in response to ΔI. It then deletes the edge of the cuts, and creates a term node for each tuple in N_{term}, along with edges from the root db or children elements to these terms. Then, the bud-completion phase generates the subtrees for these new terms, maximumly reusing the subtrees that have been computed or are already in T by capitalizing on the subtree property. Finally, after the subtree are constructed, the garbage collection process runs in the background to remove the subtrees deleted by the cuts. Note that the physical deletion is delayed such that the removed subtrees can be reused in the bud-completion phase.

Another salient feature of the incremental algorithm is that it computes ΔT in parallel with the updating process of T with ΔT. More specifically, each iteration in the generation phase computes ΔT to a certain depth below newly added buds, and thus partial results of the new XML view can be returned to the users before the computation of ΔT is completed; this allows *lazy evaluation* that overlaps the view update process with client access.

4 System Architecture

Our middleware supports two evaluation modes: *publishing* and *incremental updates*. See Fig. 4 for its architecture.

In the ATG-based XML publishing mode, the system takes an ATG σ and a source relational database I as input and generates a target XML view $T = \sigma(I)$ that conforms to the DTD embedded in σ. Specifically, it parses σ, generates a query plan for evaluating the SQL queries embedded in σ, and pushes the SQL queries down to the underlying DBMS to extract data from the source I. The system has fully implemented the optimization techniques proposed in [3], including query composition to reduce communication cost between the middleware and the DBMS. The XML view T is stored in a subtree pool with a hash table built on top of it, leveraging the subtree property described early.

In the incremental update mode, the system accepts SQL updates and a handle (name) for an ATG σ (see also Fig. 5(a)); it then conducts the relational updates, derives $\Delta\sigma$, evaluates $\Delta\sigma$ using our incremental algorithm to compute XML changes to the corresponding XML view, and updates the subtree pool and the hash table accordingly, as described in the last section. Alternatively, the system allows the underlying DBMS to function independently and accept updates; an *update monitor* (not explored in [4]) detects source updates, and triggers our incremental algorithm to propagate the changes to XML views automatically.

The user interface of the system is shown in Fig. 5(a). In a window one can select and display a source schema and an ATG; the system also supports an interface for accepting SQL updates, and for the choice of ATG publishing or incremental updates. A graphic tool is provided to facilitate ATG design. Output XML data is browsed by popping up another window (Fig. 5(b)).

1303

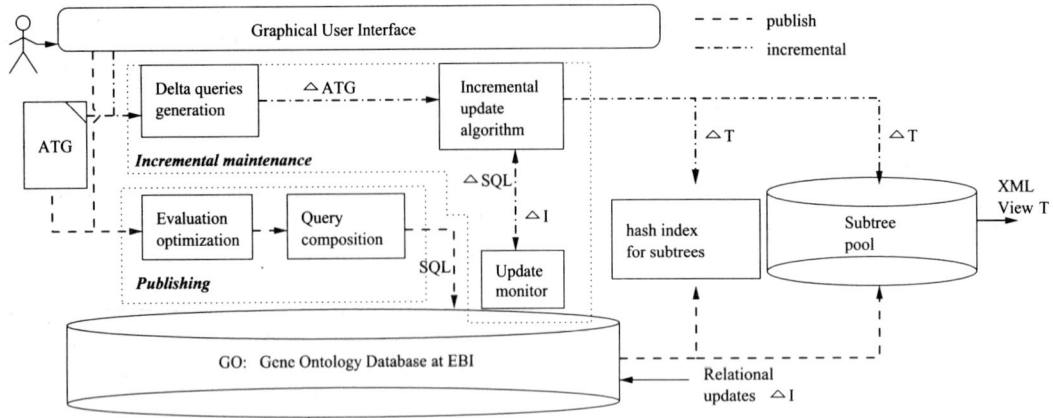

Figure 4: System architecture

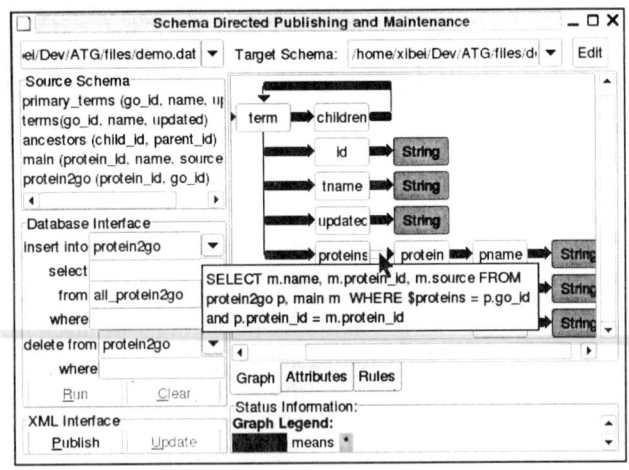

(a) Visual user interface

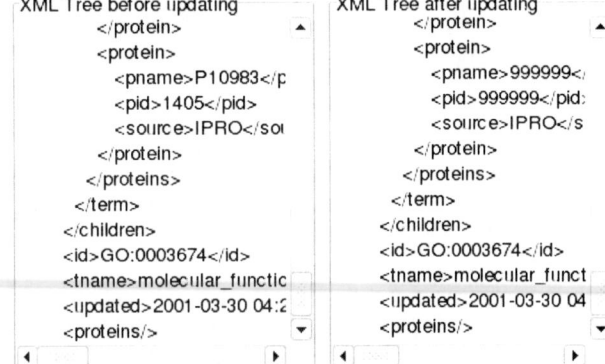

(b) XML data before and after updates

Figure 5: User Interface

5 Demonstration Overview

The demonstration will show the following.

Schema-directed publishing. To illustrate the main aspects of ATG-based XML publishing, we show how to publish Gene Ontology (GO) data in XML w.r.t. predefined recursive DTDs via ATGs. We demonstrate that our system is efficient when dealing with the real-life data.

Incremental updates. To verify the effectiveness of our incremental algorithm, we show how source updates can be efficiently propagated to XML views created by ATGs in contrast to the recomputation approach: the former takes seconds to evaluate while the latter takes minutes.

Aids to ATG specification. We provide a graphic user interface to facilitate ATG design (Fig. 5(a)). An ATG is depicted as a graph, in which each edge represents a parent-child relation in a production in the target DTD. Clicking on the edge, a text window displays the corresponding semantic rule and allows the user to display and edit the rule.

Aids to answer analysis. We also demonstrate graphic tools for viewing the published XML data, and for illustrating update propagation from source to target by comparing XML views before and after updates (Fig. 5(b)).

References

[1] N. Alon, T. Milo, F. Neven, D. Suciu, and V. Vianu. Typechecking XML views of relational databases. In *LICS*, 2001.

[2] M. Benedikt, C. Y. Chan, W. Fan, J. Freire, and R. Rastogi. Capturing both types and constraints in data integration. In *SIGMOD*, 2003.

[3] M. Benedikt, C. Y. Chan, W. Fan, R. Rastogi, S. Zheng, and A. Zhou. DTD-directed publishing with attribute translation grammars. In *VLDB*, 2002.

[4] P. Bohannon, B. Choi, and W. Fan. Incremental evaluation of schema-directed XML publishing. In *SIGMOD*, 2004.

[5] P. Bohannon, S. Ganguly, H. Korth, P. Narayan, and P. Shenoy. Optimizing view queries in ROLEX to support navigable result trees. In *VLDB*, 2002.

[6] M. J. Carey, D. Florescu, Z. G. Ives, Y. Lu, J. Shanmugasundaram, E. J. Shekita, and S. N. Subramanian. XPERANTO: Publishing object-relational data as XML. In *WebDB*, 2000.

[7] EBI. Gene Ontology. http://www.geneontology.org/.

[8] M. F. Fernandez, Y. Kadiyska, D. Suciu, A. Morishima, and W. C. Tan. SilkRoute: A framework for publishing relational data in XML. *TODS*, 27(4):438–493, 2002.

[9] Intelligent Systems Research. XML from databases: ODBC2XML. http://www.intsysr.com/odbc2xml.htm.

[10] Oracle. Using XML in Oracle internet applications. http://technet.oracle.com/tech/xml/.

An Injection with Tree Awareness: Adding Staircase Join to PostgreSQL

Sabine Mayer°   Torsten Grust°   Maurice van Keulen[•]   Jens Teubner°

°University of Konstanz
Department of Computer and Information Science
P.O. Box D 188, 78457 Konstanz, Germany
{mayers,grust,teubner}@inf.uni-konstanz.de

[•]University of Twente
Faculty of EEMCS
P.O. Box 217, 7500 AE Enschede, The Netherlands
m.vankeulen@utwente.nl

1 Introduction

The syntactic wellformedness constraints of XML (opening and closing tags nest properly) imply that XML processors face the challenge to efficiently handle data that takes the shape of *ordered, unranked trees*.

Although RDBMSs have originally been designed to manage table-shaped data, we propose their use as XML and XPath processors. In our setup, the database system employs a relational XML document encoding, the *XPath accelerator* [1], which maps information about the XML node hierarchy to a table, thus making it possible to evaluate XPath expressions on SQL hosts.

Conventional RDBMSs, nevertheless, remain ignorant of many interesting properties of the encoded tree data, and were thus found to make no or poor use of these properties. This is why we devised a new join algorithm, *staircase join* [2], which incorporates the tree-specific knowledge required for an efficient SQL-based evaluation of XPath expressions.

In a sense, this demonstration delivers the promise we have made at VLDB 2003 [2]: a notion of tree awareness can be injected into a conventional disk-based RDBMS kernel in terms of staircase join. The demonstration features a side-by-side comparison of both, an original and a staircase-join enhanced instance of PostgreSQL [4]. The required changes to PostgreSQL were local, the achieved effect, however, is significant: the demonstration proves that this injection of tree awareness turns PostgreSQL into a high-performance XML processor that closely adheres to the XPath semantics.

Permission to copy without fee all or part of this material is granted provided that the copies are not made or distributed for direct commercial advantage, the VLDB copyright notice and the title of the publication and its date appear, and notice is given that copying is by permission of the Very Large Data Base Endowment. To copy otherwise, or to republish, requires a fee and/or special permission from the Endowment.

**Proceedings of the 30th VLDB Conference,
Toronto, Canada, 2004**

2 Staircase Join

2.1 XPath Accelerator and Pre/Post Plane

The *XPath accelerator* [1] encodes the tree structure of an XML document using unique pairs of integer values, the nodes' *preorder* and *postorder* traversal ranks.

If these ranks are used to place the document nodes in the two-dimensional *pre/post plane* (Figure 1), it becomes apparent that the encoding preserves an important property. Any context node v divides the XML document into four disjoint regions, whose union plus v itself covers all nodes of the document. The four regions correspond to the result of the XPath location steps v/preceding, v/ancestor, v/following, and v/descendant, respectively.[1]

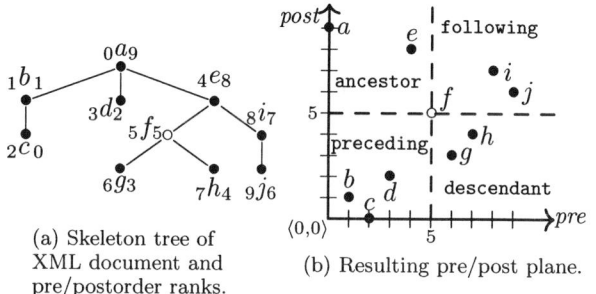

(a) Skeleton tree of XML document and pre/postorder ranks.

(b) Resulting pre/post plane.

Figure 1: The regions associated with the four major XPath axes in the pre/post plane. Context node is f.

The nodes of the plane are maintained in a table $doc = \underline{pre \mid post}$, the *document table*. The document nodes n contained in the respective plane regions may then be defined for any arbitrary context node $v \in doc$ by simple conjunctive range queries:

$n \in v/\text{preceding} \;\;\Leftrightarrow\;\; v.pre > n.pre \wedge v.post > n.post$
$n \in v/\text{following} \;\;\Leftrightarrow\;\; v.pre < n.pre \wedge v.post < n.post$
$n \in v/\text{descendant} \;\;\Leftrightarrow\;\; v.pre < n.pre \wedge v.post > n.post$
$n \in v/\text{ancestor} \;\;\Leftrightarrow\;\; v.pre > n.pre \wedge v.post < n.post$

---
[1] These four axes constitute the focus of our demonstration. We will refer to them as *major XPath axes* in the following. For the treatment of further XPath features, *e.g.*, node and name tests, please refer to [1, 2].

These region queries enable us to translate XPath path expressions into SQL queries. Each location step in a given expression is converted into a join which links the initial context node set *context* or the result of the previous location step to the document table. The join predicates directly correspond to the region queries. Thus, the XPath expression $Q_1 = context/\texttt{following}/\texttt{descendant}$ will be translated into the following SQL query:

```
SELECT DISTINCT n₂.*
  FROM context v, doc n₁, doc n₂
  WHERE v.pre < n₁.pre AND v.post < n₁.post
    AND n₁.pre < n₂.pre AND n₁.post > n₂.post
  ORDER BY n₂.pre;
```

The `DISTINCT` and `ORDER BY` clauses make the result comply with the W3C XPath semantics: nodes are returned in document order with duplicates removed.

2.2 Pruning, Partitioning, and Skipping

In a conventional RDBMS, this evaluation of an XPath location step amounts to query plans in which the computation of the region queries happens on a per-context-node basis, *i.e.*, it will typically involve several rescans of the document table.

In contrast to that, *staircase join* [2] employs three techniques (*pruning*, *partitioning*, and *skipping*) which devise a significantly more efficient way to work with tree-structured data. Most importantly, staircase join makes sure that the evaluation of an XPath location step requires at most one sequential scan of the document table and that the result of each location step is duplicate-free and sorted in document order.

Context pruning reduces the work load by removing redundant nodes from the context set. Figures 2 (a) and (b) show how pruning works for the `descendant` axis. The removal of nodes is based on *inclusion*, which means that the `descendant` region of context node v_3 is completely contained in the `descendant` region of v_1. For the `preceding` and `following` axes, pruning even reduces the context set to a single node.

Partitioning ensures that one sequential scan of the document table is enough to evaluate an XPath axis. Since the node distribution in the pre/post plane is isomorphic to the XML tree structure, certain plane regions are guaranteed to not contain any nodes (∅ in Figure 2 (c)). Staircase join uses this observation to avoid unnecessary rescans of the plane.

Skipping reduces the number of document nodes that must be considered during the evaluation of a partition. Figure 2 (d) shows an example of `descendant` axis skipping. As soon as we come across the first `following` node n of context node v_1, we know, again due to the tree isomorphism, that region Z is necessarily empty and the remaining nodes in the partition may be skipped.

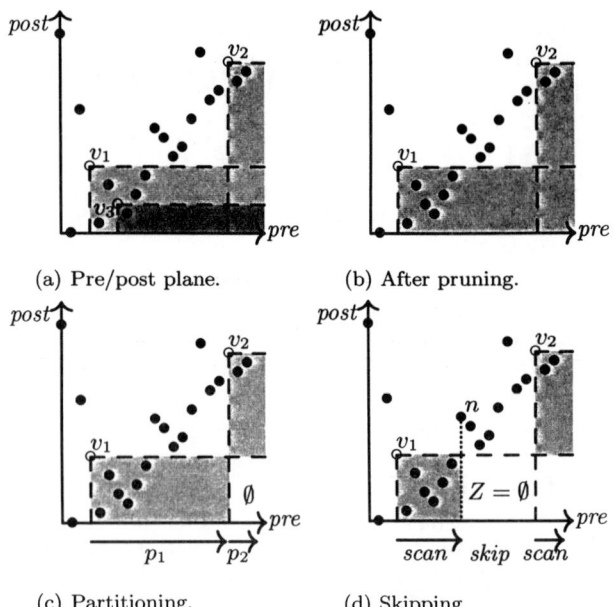

Figure 2: The pre/post plane before (a) and after pruning (b), partitioning (c), and skipping (d) for a `descendant` location step. Context nodes v_1, v_2, v_3.

3 Tree Awareness for PostgreSQL

Completely encapsulated inside staircase join, we injected this awareness of the XML tree structure into PostgreSQL 7.3.3 [4]. The integration mainly affected two query processing stages [3].

3.1 Planning/Optimization

During planning/optimization, we detect the cases in which staircase join is the optimal join method. The decision is based on an examination of the join clauses (region queries): (1) both operands of a *staircase join clause* must be of data type `tree`[2], (2) there must be two such clauses (the *pre* and *post* clause), and (3) their comparison operator combination must specify a valid XPath axis (*e.g.* (<,<) for the `following` axis).

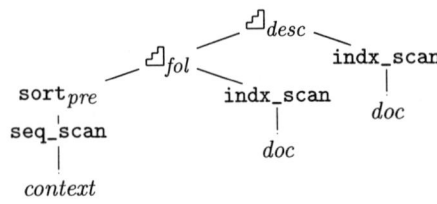

Figure 3: Execution plan for query Q_1 of Section 2.1.

The typical execution plan of an SQL-based XPath query is shown in Figure 3. As staircase join (⋈) produces identical execution cost for both types of linear

---
[2] The data type was newly introduced into PostgreSQL to indicate that a column contains tree-structured data. It is a derivative of the SQL `int` type.

join trees, only the left-deep variant is considered, *i.e.*, the current context set will always be the left (outer) input parameter of the join and the document table the right (inner).

3.2 Execution

Staircase join was adapted to fit into PostgreSQL's execution environment. This involved a local change to the executor, *i.e.*, the introduction of a new execution module which implements pruning, partitioning, and skipping and adapts these phases to the streaming mechanisms of PostgreSQL. In any other respect, the module relies on the already available PostgreSQL internals.

The most important native PostgreSQL data structure for the execution of staircase join is a variant of the B-tree index, the *inner-join index*. As the name implies, it was especially designed to serve as inner relation in a join. Assume a join clause *context.pre* < *doc.pre*, where *context* is the outer and *doc* the inner relation and *doc* has an index on column *pre*. In this case, a preorder rank p of a node in *context* can be used as index search key to trigger an index scan of *doc* which is guaranteed to start directly at the first tuple with *doc.pre* > p. Since we scan *context* in ascending *pre*-order (Figure 3) and due to partitioning as well as pruning, this leads to a progressive forward scan of *doc*. This also blends perfectly with PostgreSQL's page caching behavior (Section 4).

For staircase join, we assume that such an index exists on (at least) the *pre* column of the document table. This feature is also crucial for the efficient implementation of skipping.

The original staircase join algorithms [2] materialize the join result. However, since PostgreSQL strives to avoid materialization, the algorithms had to be modified such that each operator in the execution plan only requests the next input tuple from its subplan if immediately required for processing.

The clearly distinguished execution steps predefined by pipelining and the three staircase join-specific techniques (pruning, partitioning, and skipping) suggested the use of a *finite state automaton* to implement the staircase join execution module. Each of the four major axes was assigned its own automaton.

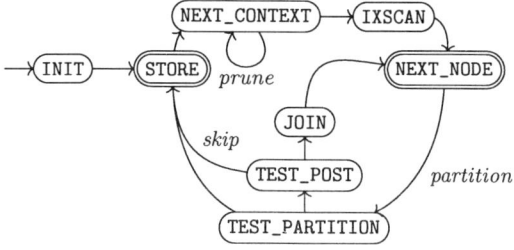

Figure 4: The `descendant` axis state automaton.

The state automaton of the `descendant` axis is outlined in Figure 4. After the first context tuple v_1 has been retrieved from the outer subplan in the INIT state, it is stored as lower boundary of the first partition. To identify the upper boundary of the partition (cf. v_2 in Figure 2), the NEXT_CONTEXT state continues to request context nodes from the outer subplan, until the next one with a higher post value than v_1 is found (pruning). As soon as the first partition is set, the join starts to retrieve the document nodes within the partition. To do so, a scan of the document table index is initiated. It makes sure that all returned document nodes n have a higher pre value than context node v_1 (IXSCAN and NEXT_NODE). The TEST_PARTITION state verifies that the pre value of n does not exceed the upper partition boundary ($v_2.pre$). If the post clause is also satisfied for v_1 and n, the JOIN state can build and return the next result node. If the TEST_PARTITION state encounters the first document node outside the current partition, the executor switches to the next partition (STORE).

The real benefit of the document table index becomes apparent in connection with skipping. In case of the `descendant` axis, this technique was incorporated into the TEST_POST state. If the post clause evaluates to false, we have found the first following node of v_1 (cf. node n in Figure 2 (d)) and may skip the remaining inner tuples in the current partition. The index directly guides us to the first node of the subsequent partition.

The automaton reaches a final state, if either the outer or the inner subplan runs out of tuples.

4 Performance Benefits

To assess the benefits of tree awareness, tests were executed on a 2.2 GHz Dual-Pentium 4 machine with 2 GB RAM. Experiments were run on both, an original and a tree-aware instance of PostgreSQL 7.3.3. The tests examine the buffer-related behavior and the execution times of the example XPath expression $Q_2 = \text{//descendant::}t_1/\text{ancestor::}t_2$ in dependence on the size of the input XML document (XMark instances of size 110 KB up to 1.1 GB). More experiments were conducted in [3].

The original database chooses two index nested-loop joins to answer Q_2 and evaluates all region query clauses in the index. The execution plan chosen by the tree-aware database is similar to the plan of Figure 3. It evaluates the pre and post clause during staircase join, the index is exclusively responsible for skipping.

4.1 Execution Times

Figure 5 compares the execution times obtained in both database instances. It shows that staircase join leads to a performance boost of up to several orders of magnitude. While the execution times of the original DBMS grow quadratically for this two-step XPath query, those of the enhanced DBMS grow linearly with the document size as expected.

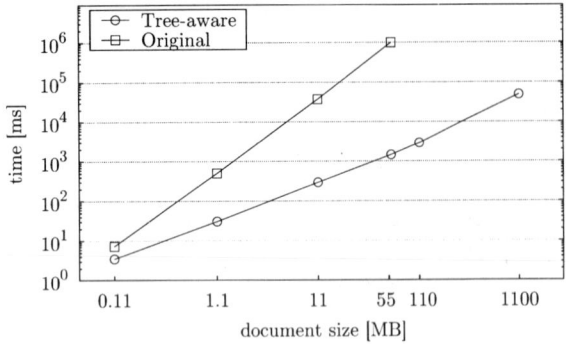

Figure 5: Execution times of Q_2 in the tree-aware and the original PostgreSQL instance.

4.2 Buffer and Cache Behavior

Figure 6 shows the buffer statistics of the document index in both databases. The growth in index page requests almost exactly reflects the tendencies observed in Figure 5. We find a quadratic growth in the original and a linear growth in the tree-aware DBMS. This is due to the fact that staircase join requires exactly one scan of the document table, while the nested-loop join requires $|context|$ scans.

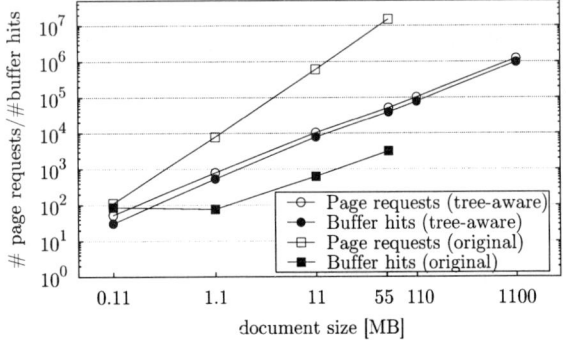

Figure 6: Total number of requested index pages of Q_2 in the tree-aware and the original DBMS ○/□ and buffer hits ●/■ occurred.

The high number of buffer hits in the tree-aware DBMS is caused by partitioning and the interconnected manner in which the location steps of Q_2 are executed. When the ancestor automaton switches to the next partition, the tuples that make up its boundaries are already in the buffer, because their pages were loaded immediately beforehand by the descendant automaton. Thus, when the work on the nodes within the subsequent partition begins, it is very likely that these nodes reside on a disk page already in the buffer.

5 Demonstration Setup

The demonstration features a side-by-side comparison of both, an original and a tree-aware instance of PostgreSQL 7.3.3. Both database systems act as back-ends to a common XPath front-end. This front-end allows for a more complete set of XPath features than has been outlined here (in particular the supported XPath dialect includes all major XPath axes as well as node and name tests).

The front-end compiles an XPath expression into an equivalent SQL query that operates on the *doc* table. This SQL text is then presented to the user as well as shipped to both back-ends for execution.

Since the efficient management of XML documents of *very large* size is one of the core contributions of database technology in XML processing, both databases are supplied with XMark instances whose size ranges between 110 KB and 1.1 GB (or 5,000 to 50 million nodes).

The demonstration makes use of diagnostic features of PostgreSQL to make the preparation as well as the progess of query execution visible for the user. Hooks are installed in both back-ends to generate a graphical presentation of the chosen query plans (much like in Figure 3). Due to its enhanced query planner, the tree-aware instance relies on ⫪ operators to evaluate XPath location steps, while the original instance will fall back to *sort* and index nested-loop join.

During execution, both back-ends record timings, page request and cache statistics to provide a detailed graphical post-query feedback (cf. Figures 5 and 6).

Finally, an XML serialization routine hooked into PostgreSQL displays the nodes/subtrees selected by the input XPath expression.

To provide a further point of reference and to exemplify the promising potential of database-supported XML processing, the demonstration additionally evaluates the input XPath expression via a "conventional" main-memory based XPath processor. In anticipation of the live demonstration, the latter class of processors are no match for an RDBMS that has received an injection of tree awareness.

References

[1] Torsten Grust. Accelerating XPath Location Steps. In *Proc. of the 21st ACM SIGMOD Int'l Conference on Management of Data (SIGMOD)*, pages 109–120. ACM Press, Madison, Wisconsin, USA, June 2002.

[2] Torsten Grust, Maurice van Keulen, and Jens Teubner. Staircase Join: Teach a Relational DBMS to Watch its Axis Steps. In *Proc. of the 29th Int'l Conference on Very Large Databases (VLDB)*, pages 524–535. Berlin, Germany, September 2003.

[3] Sabine Mayer. *Enhancing the Tree Awareness of a Relational DBMS: Adding Staircase Join to PostgreSQL*. Master's thesis, Universität Konstanz, February 2004.

[4] PostgreSQL 7.3.3. http://www.postgresql.com/.

FluXQuery: An Optimizing XQuery Processor for Streaming XML Data

Christoph Koch[†,*]   Stefanie Scherzinger[‡]   Nicole Schweikardt[♮]   Bernhard Stegmaier[♯]

[†]: Technische Universität Wien, Vienna, Austria, Email: koch@dbai.tuwien.ac.at
[‡]: Technische Universität Wien, Vienna, Austria, Email: scherzinger@wit.tuwien.ac.at
[♮]: Humboldt Universität zu Berlin, Berlin, Germany, Email: schweikardt@informatik.hu-berlin.de
[♯]: Technische Universität München, Munich, Germany, Email: bernhard.stegmaier@in.tum.de

1 Introduction and Motivation

XML has established itself as the ubiquitous format for data exchange on the Internet. An imminent development is that of streams of XML data being exchanged and queried. Data management scenarios where XQuery [11] is evaluated on XML streams are becoming increasingly important and realistic, e.g. in e-commerce settings.

Naturally, query engines employed for stream processing are main-memory-based, yet contemporary XQuery engines consume main memory in large multiples of the actual size of the input documents (cf. [10, 8]). This excessive need for buffers has proven to be a serious scalability issue and significant research challenge [10, 9, 5, 3].

So far, the efficient evaluation of XPath on streams has been closely investigated to the point where state-of-the-art techniques use very little main memory [1, 4, 6, 7]. However, corresponding approaches to the effective and economical processing of XQuery on streams are still at a preliminary stage. XQuery, as a *data-transformation* query language, is of an entirely different nature than *node-selecting* XPath. This constitutes the need to develop sophisticated techniques for coping with and reducing main memory buffers during XQuery evaluation.

What is required is a well-principled machinery for processing XQuery which is parsimonious with resources in that it minimizes the amount of buffering necessary. Any such solution should allow for both extensibility and the leverage of a large body of the database community's related earlier work to take effect. Under these considerations, such machinery needs to employ an algebraic view of queries and optimizations.

So far, no principled work exists on algebraic query optimization for *structured data streams* (such as XML, but unlike flat tuple streams, e.g. [2]) which takes into account the special features of stream processing. In particular, we lack an algebra for querying structured data which truly captures the spirit of stream processing and which prepares the ground for optimizing query evaluation using schema information.

In this demonstration, we present the FluXQuery engine as the first optimizing XQuery engine for streams. Optimization in FluXQuery is based on a new internal query language called *FluX* [8] which slightly extends the main structures of XQuery by a construct for event-based query processing. By allowing for the conscious use of main memory buffers, it supports reasoning over the employment of buffers during query evaluation.

2 The FluX Query Language

We consider the following XQuery Q in a bibliography domain, as found among the XML Query Use Cases [12] (XMP Q3):

```
<results>
{ for $b in $ROOT/bib/book return
    <result> { $b/title } { $b/author } </result> }
</results>
```

This query lists the title(s) and authors of each book in the bibliography and groups them inside a "result" element. Note that the XQuery language requires that, within each book, titles are output before all authors. Now the DTD

```
<!ELEMENT bib (book)*>
<!ELEMENT book (title|author)*>
```

[*] Work support by project Z29-N04 of the Austrian Science Fund (FWF).

Permission to copy without fee all or part of this material is granted provided that the copies are not made or distributed for direct commercial advantage, the VLDB copyright notice and the title of the publication and its date appear, and notice is given that copying is by permission of the Very Large Data Base Endowment. To copy otherwise, or to republish, requires a fee and/or special permission from the Endowment.

**Proceedings of the 30th VLDB Conference,
Toronto, Canada, 2004**

allows each `book` node to have several `title` and several `author` children, while imposing no order among these items.

In the course of evaluating this query, we may output the `title` children of a `book` node as soon as they arrive on the stream, while the output of the `author` children must be delayed (using a memory buffer) until we reach the closing tag of the `book` node. Only then we may be sure that no further `title` nodes will be encountered and we may write the contents of the buffer containing `author` nodes to the output and then empty it. Later on, we may refill it with the `author` nodes from the next `book`.

Consequently, we only need to buffer the `author` children of one `book` node at a time, but not the titles. Current main memory query engines do not exploit this fact. Rather, they buffer either the entire book nodes or, as an optimization [10], *all* `title` and *all* `author` nodes of each `book`. Previous frameworks for evaluating or optimizing XQuery do not provide any means of making this seeming subtlety explicit and reasoning about it.

We introduce the FluX query language together with its `process-stream` construct which allows us to express precisely the mode of query execution just described. Given the DTD from above, XQuery Q may be phrased as a FluX query as follows:

```
<results>
{ process-stream $ROOT: on bib as $bib return
  { process-stream $bib: on book as $book return
     <result>
     { process-stream $book:
         on title as $t return {$t};
         on-first past(title,author) return
          { for $a in $book/author return {$a} } }
     </result> } }
</results>
```

A `process-stream $x` expression consists of a number of *handlers* which process the children of the XML tree node bound by variable `$x` from left to right. An "on a" handler fires on each child labeled "a" visited during such a traversal, executing the associated query expression. In the `process-stream $book` expression above, the `on-first past(title,author)` handler fires exactly once, namely as soon as the DTD implies for the first time that no further `author` or `title` node can be encountered among the children of `$book`. (As observed above, in the given, very weak DTD, this is the case only as soon as the last child of `$book` has been seen.) In the query associated with the `on-first past(title,author)` handler, we may safely use paths of the form `$book/author` or `$book/title`, because such paths cannot be encountered anymore. Consequently, we may assume that the query engine has buffered all matches of that path for us. It is a feasible task for the query engine to buffer only those paths that the query actually employs (see also [10]).

```
<!ELEMENT bib  (book)*>
<!ELEMENT book (title,(author+|editor+),
                              publisher,price)>
```

Figure 1: A DTD.

We call a FluX query *safe* for a given DTD if, informally, it is guaranteed that XQuery subexpressions (such as the for-loop in the query above) do not refer to paths that may still be encountered in the stream. The above FluX query is safe: The for-expression employs the `$book/author` path, but is part of an on-first handler that cannot fire before all `author` nodes relative to `$book` have been seen.

If the path `$book/author` in the previous FluX query was replaced by, say, `$book/price` and the DTD production for `book` were

```
<!ELEMENT book ((title|author)*,price)>
```

then the FluX query such modified would not be safe: On the firing of `on-first past(title,author)`, the buffer for `$book/price` items would still be empty and the query result would be incorrect.

Let us now return to XQuery Q. This query can be processed more efficiently with the DTD shown in Figure 1: Here, no buffering is required to execute query Q because the DTD asserts that for each book, the title occurs strictly before the authors (we call this an *order constraint*).

Thus, we may phrase our query in FluX so as to directly copy titles and authors to the output as they arrive on the input stream:

```
<results>
{ process-stream $ROOT: on bib as $bib return
   { process-stream $bib: on book as $book return
      <result>
      { process-stream $book:
          on title  as $t return {$t};
          on author as $a return {$a} }
      </result> } }
</results>
```

3 FluXQuery System Architecture

FluXQuery is, to our knowledge, the first XQuery engine that optimizes query evaluation using schema constraints derived from DTDs[1]. Query optimization is carried out on an algebraic, query-language level (rather than, say, on some form of derived automata). Thus, a main strength of FluXQuery is its extensibility and the ability to benefit from a large body of previous database research on algebraic query optimization.

The main focus of our efforts was to develop a system for automatically rewriting XQueries into FluX queries and thereby optimizing (reducing) the use of main memory buffers. We have developed an algebra for optimizing XQuery on streams using a DTD

---
[1] Note that the static information required for optimization could just as well be derived from XML Schema.

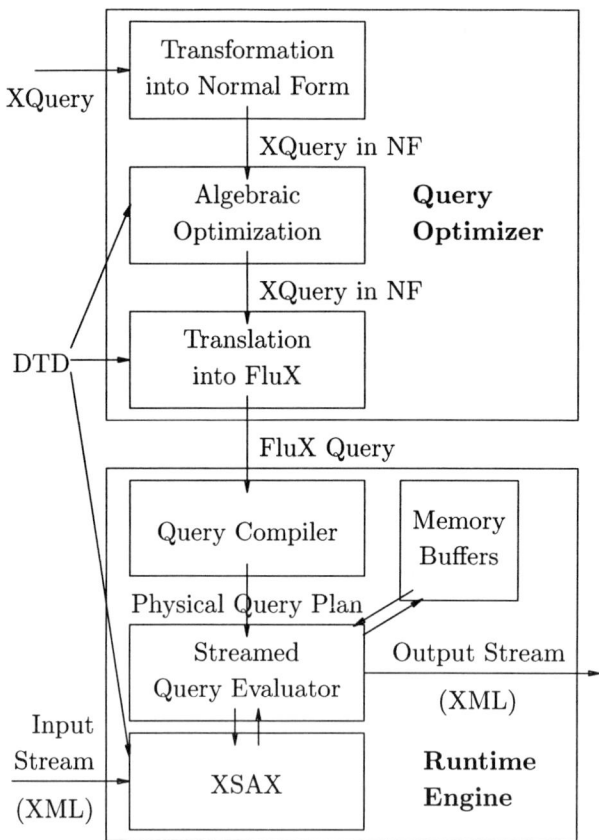

Figure 2: The FluXQuery system architecture.

and an efficient algorithm for DTD-aware scheduling of XQueries as FluX queries [8].

We next discuss the system architecture of FluX-Query, which consists of the *query optimizer* and the *runtime engine*, as depicted in Figure 2.

3.1 The Query Optimizer

Our query optimizer translates user queries written in XQuery into optimized FluX queries. The translation and optimization proceeds in three steps.

First, XQueries are rewritten into a *normal form* which allows us to use a simple set of equivalences as rewrite rules in the subsequent optimization steps.

Next, we statically optimize the normalized XQuery, exploiting schema information gained from the DTD. More precisely, we employ *algebraic optimizations* that are based on *cardinality constraints* and *language constraints* derived from the DTD. As a result, we may generate FluX queries which can be evaluated more efficiently on data streams conforming to the given schema.

For the intuition behind cardinality constraints, consider the following query expression with two subsequent for-loops

```
{ for $x in $book/publisher return α }
{ for $x in $book/publisher return β }
```

where α and β are arbitrary subexpressions. In order to perform two iterations over the same set of publisher nodes, we are automatically forced to buffer all such nodes.

However, if the schema states that a book node has at most one publisher among its children, as does the DTD of Figure 1, then we denote this cardinality constraint by publisher $\in \|_{\text{book}}^{\leq 1}$.

Application of the algebraic optimization rule

$$\frac{\{ \text{ for } \$x \text{ in } \$r/a \text{ return } \alpha \ \} \quad \{ \text{ for } \$x \text{ in } \$r/a \text{ return } \beta \ \}}{\{ \text{ for } \$x \text{ in } \$r/a \text{ return } \alpha \ \beta \ \}} \quad \left(a \in \|_{\$r}^{\leq 1}\right)$$

merges both for-loops into a single and equivalent for-loop:

```
{ for $x in $book/publisher return α β }.
```

Clearly, the second query is preferable, as it requires only one loop over publishers instead of two subsequent iterations. Depending on the nature of subqueries α and β, we may even be able to evaluate the query expression completely on-the-fly.

Based on language constraints derived from the DTD, we can also eliminate unsatisfiable conditional subexpressions. Again, consider the DTD of Figure 1. Then we may eliminate an expression

```
if $book/author = "Goedel"
and $book/editor = "Goedel" then α
```

where α is an arbitrary subexpression, since the DTD does not permit book elements with both author and editor children.

Finally, the pre-optimized XQuery is rewritten into FluX, with process-stream extensions (as briefly described in Section 2) enabling a streaming execution of the query. The key idea here is to exploit *order constraints* defined by the DTD. For instance, the DTD of Figure 1 ensures that all title elements precede all author elements. The rewriting process schedules the execution of query subexpressions with respect to order constraints and therewith generates FluX queries with reduced buffer consumption.

In contrast to existing techniques, our algebraic optimizations aim at minimizing the size of main memory buffers, rather than the execution speed.

A main strength of our approach is its extensibility, and even though our system is currently restricted to a (powerful) *fragment* of XQuery with nested loops and joins, our approach can be generalized to larger XQuery fragments.

3.2 The Runtime Engine

The second part of our FluXQuery system architecture is the runtime engine. It evaluates FluX queries as obtained from XQueries by the query optimizer. The runtime engine is organized as follows.

1311

The *query compiler* transforms an optimized FluX query into a physical query plan. It first computes the *buffer description forest* data structure, BDF for short, which defines those paths of the input document which need to be buffered. Based on the BDF, it schedules query operators, such as the execution of `process-stream` expressions, the streamed execution of for-where-return-statements, and buffer population. Our approach improves on that of [10] in that it allows us to avoid the buffering of the data which can be processed on the fly.

The resulting query can either be compiled into an internal representation, which is interpreted during execution, or directly into executable JAVA code.

Finally, the physical query plan is executed by the *streamed query evaluator*. The latter uses our validating SAX parser, *XSAX*, which is an extension of a standard SAX parser that in addition produces on-first events in addition to customary SAX-events (such as on-begin-element).

Basically, the XSAX parser works as follows. We first register the DTD and all on-first event handlers of the input query with the XSAX parser. Based on this information, the XSAX parser builds a finite state automaton and lookup-tables for validating the input and generating on-first events. While reading the input XML stream, the state of this automaton is checked and the on-first events are properly inserted among the generated stream of conventional SAX events. The streamed query evaluator processes these events and delivers its output in turn as an XML stream.

4 Conclusions

FluXQuery currently supports a fairly powerful XQuery fragment with arbitrarily nested for-loops and joins, but does not yet cover aggregation.

The FluX query language, an algorithm for rewriting XQuery into FluX and thereby scheduling event processors using the DTD, as well as buffer management, are described in detail in [8]. There, the efficiency of our system is also benchmarked against two other XQuery engines. Our experiments show that FluXQuery consumes both far less memory and runtime than other XQuery systems. The difference is particularly clear for main memory consumption, which is of great importance in stream processing and vital to scalability.

Our algebraic optimization techniques will be described in detail in a forthcoming paper.

References

[1] M. Altinel and M. Franklin. "Efficient Filtering of XML Documents for Selective Dissemination of Information". In *Proc. VLDB 2000*, pages 53–64, Cairo, Egypt, 2000.

[2] A. Arasu, B. Babcock, S. Babu, M. Datar, K. Ito, I. Nishizawa, J. Rosenstein, and J. Widom. "STREAM: The Stanford Stream Data Manager". In *Proc. SIGMOD 2003*, page 665, 2003.

[3] P. Buneman, M. Grohe, and C. Koch. "Path Queries on Compressed XML". In *Proc. VLDB 2003*, pages 141–152, 2003.

[4] C. Y. Chan, P. Felber, M. N. Garofalakis, and R. Rastogi. "Efficient Filtering of XML Documents with XPath Expressions". In *Proc. ICDE 2002*, San Jose, California, USA, February 26–March 1 2002.

[5] L. Fegaras, D. Levine, S. Bose, and V. Chaluvadi. "Query Processing of Streamed XML Data". In *Proc. CIKM 2002*, pages 126–133, 2002.

[6] T. J. Green, G. Miklau, M. Onizuka, and D. Suciu. "Processing XML Streams with Deterministic Automata". In *Proc. ICDT'03*, 2003.

[7] A. K. Gupta and D. Suciu. "Stream Processing of XPath Queries with Predicates". In *SIGMOD Conference*, pages 419–430, 2003.

[8] C. Koch, S. Scherzinger, N. Schweikardt, and B. Stegmaier. "Schema-based Scheduling of Event Processors and Buffer Minimization for Queries on Structured Data Streams". In *Proc. VLDB 2004*, 2004.

[9] B. Ludäscher, P. Mukhopadhyay, and Y. Papakonstantinou. "A Transducer-Based XML Query Processor". In *Proc. VLDB 2002*, pages 227–238, 2002.

[10] A. Marian and J. Siméon. "Projecting XML Documents". In *Proc. VLDB 2003*, pages 213–224, 2003.

[11] World Wide Web Consortium. "XQuery 1.0 and XPath 2.0 Formal Semantics. W3C Working Draft (Aug. 16th 2002), 2002. http://www.w3.org/TR/query-algebra/.

[12] "XML Query Use Cases. W3C Working Draft 02 May 2003", 2003. http://www.w3.org/TR/xmlquery-use-cases/.

COMPASS: A Concept-based Web Search Engine for HTML, XML, and Deep Web Data

Jens Graupmann, Michael Biwer, Christian Zimmer, Patrick Zimmer,
Matthias Bender, Martin Theobald, Gerhard Weikum

Max-Planck Institute for Computer Science
66123 Saarbruecken, Germany
{graupman, mbiwer, czimmer, pzimmer, mbender, mtb, weikum}@mpi-sb.mpg.de

1 Introduction

Today's web search engines are still following the paradigm of keyword-based search. Although this is the best choice for large scale search engines in terms of throughput and scalability, it inherently limits the ability to accomplish more meaningful query tasks. XML query engines (e.g., based on XQuery or XPath), on the other hand, have powerful query capabilities; but at the same time their dedication to XML data with a global schema is their weakness, because most web information is still stored in diverse formats and does not conform to common schemas. Typical web formats include static HTML pages or pages that are generated dynamically from underlying database systems, accessible only through portal interfaces.

We have developed an expressive style of concept-based and context-aware querying with relevance ranking that encompasses different, non-schematic data formats and integrates Web Services as well as Deep Web sources. Coined COMPASS (*Context-Oriented Multi-Format Portal-Aware Search System*), our system features this new language that combines the simplicity of web search engines with the expressiveness of (simple forms of) XML query languages ([7]).

2 Features of COMPASS

2.1 Concept-based Search

All web search engines are based on keyword-based search, but this style of query is strongly limited in its expressiveness. For example, neither a search for documents that contain either the keyword or one of its synonyms is possible, nor a search for documents in which one search term describes a concept or concept property while another one describes an instance value or a refinement of the first term.

Also, today's search engines are, for example, not capable of including Deep Web sources because they are unable to assign keywords to matching form fields. XML query languages, on the other hand, can support this feature by interpreting some keywords as element names corresponding to concepts, while interpreting other keywords as element contents corresponding to instance values, but are typically rather obscure to the average user.

As an example, consider a query about the book 'War and Peace' written by Tolstoy. If we can only use keywords to express this query, there is no way to specify any semantic relationship between these terms. In our system, we can express this query as follows: *title='war and peace' AND author=tolstoy*. Thus, we can use the semantic relationships between the terms for query processing purposes.

2.2 Context-aware Search

Another limitation of current web search engines is the fact that all keywords have to be matched on a single page. In reality, however, the desired information is often spread over multiple pages. Consider a query about a book store in our home town selling the book 'War and Peace'. Whereas the address of the book store (in our case 'Saarbrucken') is typically on the book store's home page A, a list of all available titles, including 'War and Peace', might be on a different page B that can be reached via a direct link from A. By following HTML-style href-links as well as XML-style XLinks, our system allows to exploit this link structure in order to find the combination of pages A and B as an appropriate query result.

Permission to copy without fee all or part of this material is granted provided that the copies are not made or distributed for direct commercial advantage, the VLDB copyright notice and the title of the publication and its date appear, and notice is given that copying is by permission of the Very Large Data Base Endowment. To copy otherwise, or to republish, requires a fee and/or special permission from the Endowment.

**Proceedings of the 30th VLDB Conference,
Toronto, Canada, 2004**

2.3 HTML, XML, and Beyond

XML is the desired format for all kinds of semistructured data. If XML were already ubiquitously used, the semantic relationships between query terms would be explicit by the hierarchical tree structure of the document. Thus, we apply heuristics to transform HTML pages and other web formats into semantically annotated XML documents. In most cases, simple heuristics can lead to meaningful XML data with a clearer structure than the original HTML documents. An example for our heuristics is the transformation of HTML structures like `<b>Title:</b>Tolstoy` into the following structure: `<Title>Tolstoy</Title>`.

We have implemented a framework with different modules to convert various data formats into XML. Currently these modules include HTML2XML and PDF2XML. Other modules are under development. These modules are based on heuristic rules, and may be combined with other information extraction approaches such as [1, 8].

2.4 Web Services and the Deep Web

Many information sources are not accessible via crawling. Rather, one needs to fill out a query form for retrieving documents that are dynamically generated from underlying database systems. The key difficulty in automatically generating meaningful queries against such web portals is to assign the appropriate values (which may be given merely as a set of keywords) to the available set of form fields. For this task, our system can analyzes the interface (e.g., the HTML form) to determine the available parameters ([4]). The result of the analysis is stored as meta information in a registry and used to generate wrappers that encapsulate the portal interface as a web service. Thus, each HTML form that we have successfully analyzed is represented by a WSDL interface in our system ([2]) and its information can be exploited when executing a query.

3 The COMPASS Query Language

The internal query language of COMPASS resembles a highly simplified version of mainstream languages like SQL, XPath, or XQuery. Search conditions refer to concepts and values, which correspond to element names and contents in an XML setting and attribute names and values in a SQL setting. Our query language includes the following types of conditions:

Keyword conditions: Keyword search is supported because of its benefits for querying data without a global schema or even an unknown structure (see also [3] for keyword search in an XML context). An example is: `A[keyword]=Tolstoy`.

Concept-value conditions: A concept-value condition has the form *concept=value* and would be the preferred type of searching if all web or intranet data were richly annotated with concepts corresponding to XML tags and values appearing in element or attribute contents. The comparison operator could be generalized to include type-specific comparisons (e.g., on dates). An example for this condition type is `A.title="War and Peace"`.

Similarity conditions: We have added a similarity operator ~ that can be applied to both concepts and values. This operator was first introduced in the XXL query language ([7]). It expands a term in the query with similar terms, supplied by an ontology service that the user can interact with. For example, adding the similarity operator to the concept *author* would not only return matches for the concept *author* but also for *writer* and other highly similar results. An example is `A.~author=Tolstoy`.

Path conditions: To express that different pages should be connected (within a small distance), we use two kinds of path conditions: Reachability through a direct link is expressed by a dot notation combining multiple variables, and reachability through a path of arbitrary length uses the wildcard symbol '#'. These conditions take into consideration hyperlinks, the parent-child relationship within XML documents, and also arbitrary XPointer or XLink references across document boundaries; so we consider connectivity in a global data graph.

For efficiency, COMPASS currently supports only conjunctions of search conditions. We believe that this is sufficient to cover almost all typical queries that users pose. Upon query execution, documents that satisfy one specific search conditions are bound to a variable; by using this variable as a prefix in other conditions one can reference this document in other search conditions. For example, once again consider the query about a book store in our home town that offers the book 'War and Peace' by Tolstoy. In our query language, this query could be expressed as follows:

```
SELECT A,B FROM INDEX
  WHERE A.~address=Saarbrucken
  AND   A[keyword]="book store"
  AND   B.title="War and Peace"
  AND   B.~author=Tolstoy
  AND   A.B
```

In this case, matches for the conditions *address = Saarbrucken* and *bookstore* are bound to the variable A, which can be used to express the path condition *A.B* that additionally requires all matches for A to directly link to a match B for *title="War an Peace"* and ∼*author=Tolstoy*.

4 The Architecture of COMPASS

4.1 System Overview

Figure 1 illustrates the main parts of the COMPASS prototype system. The crawler component collects the

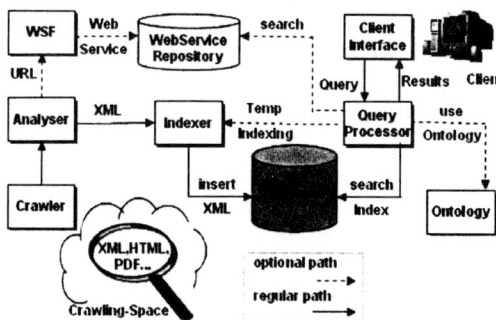

Figure 1: The architecture of COMPASS

data. It offers the functionalities of a Web Crawler combined with a local File Crawler. Depending on the data format, a transformation and semantic annotation into XML is performed by the Analyzer component in a heuristic manner. If applicable, the WSF component (see Section 4.3) creates a Web Service wrapper and saves the resulting WSDL description into a Web Service registry for later use during query processing. Eventually, all transformed data is inserted into the centralized index by the Indexer component.

We provide a graphical user interface that allows users to construct search requests in a visual manner without any knowledge of the COMPASS query language itself. For semantic expansion of similarity conditions, the user can interact with an ontology service. The query processor analyzes the query and can invoke further modules. In order to include Deep Web sources, the query processor interacts with the Web Service registry that attempts to find applicable Deep Web sources and accesses these using Web Services when executing the query. Finally, the results of the query evaluation are scored and returned to the user as a ranked list.

The system is completely implemented in Java running on a Tomcat application server. COMPASS uses Oracle 9.2i as its underlying relational database. The graphical user interface is implemented in the form of a JAVA applet using the JHotDraw library.

4.2 Data Indexer

COMPASS uses a centralized data index for efficent search evaluation. All data and also the relationships between documents are represented in a relational database. All data formats are transformed into XML by using heuristics as well as external annotation tools such as GATE ([6]). The documents' structure and tags are available for efficient evaluation of concept-value conditions, because all documents are inserted preserving their original link structure. This link structure is captured to evaluate path conditions. Moreover, to efficiently probe reachability by arbitrary paths (including paths across documents via XLink, XPointer, or href references), the transitive closure is materialized. Information about dynamically created Web Services is included in the index as well to select appropriate services when a user wishes to include Deep Web portals in her search.

4.3 Web Service Framework

When a crawl discovers a portal candidate (a web page that contains at least one HTML form), the Web Service Framework ([2]) is invoked which applies heuristic rules for generating a WSDL description on the fly. Typically, highlighted text next to form fields will become parameter names, and the type of a form field determines the corresponding parameter type (e.g., an enumeration type in the case of a pull-down menu). The generated WSDL descriptions and additionally generated Java classes are stored in a registry. The main index holds pointers to Web Services for invocation during query processing.

4.4 Query Processing and Ranked Retrieval

Internally, the query processor transforms each submitted query into an operator tree consisting of Java objects. A concept-value condition (see Section 3) is evaluated by first looking up the occurrences of both the concept name and the value in the index and then comparing the relative positions of each occurrence pair. In a good match, the concept is found 'above' the value with regard to the document structure; that is, the value should occur in a child node or a descendant of the node that matches the concept name. The distance between the two matches is reflected in the scoring of a result.

Simple keyword conditions are satisfied if the keyword occurs on a page. If the similarity operator ~ is used and, thus, this query condition is expanded with similiar terms, a page is matched if at least one of these terms is found. The score for this condition depends on the similarity of the matched term compared to the original query term as well as on the term frequency.

Path conditions (i.e., reachability through a single link or arbitrary path) refer to multiple pages bound to different variables. Whenever the query processor has determined candidate matches for local conditions and bound to variables, it tests the path condition using the materialized transitive closure, and discards candidates that are not connected or too far apart. The score of a path condition is based on the path length between the considered pages.

The order in which the conditions are evaluated is determined by a coarse selectivity estimation using simple statistics about term frequencies. Portals are included if the concepts of one or more concept-value conditions can be matched with parameter descriptors of generated Web Services. When portals are included into the search, the corresponding Web Services are invoked during query evaluation and their results are stored and indexed in a temporary table. The query processor treats the page with the query form and a result page returned by the portal as a single logical unit. This way, a result page is bound to the corresponding variable even if some conditions are actually satisfied by the query submission page (e.g., names of concepts appearing as labels in the form and values appearing in the result page).

The overall ranking of a query match is computed based on the partial scores for all conditions, using a simple probabilistic model with independence assumptions.

5 Demo

We demonstrate the search on a large XML data collection, queries on a combined index containing XML and HTML web documents, and finally the additional integration of Deep Web portals.

5.1 Web Encyclopedia Data

We indexed a version of the Wikipedia project ([9]), a free web encyclopedia that is collaboratively created by the internet community. The data collection consists of more than 215000 documents which do not follow a common schema. The documents are highly interconnected, with a total of more than 2 million links to other Wikipedia articles.

For example, consider a query about towns along the river Rhine that have hosted the Olympics. Figure 2 illustrates how this query can be posed using our graphical user interface. The system will search for information units that include the keyword *Olympics* and, at the same time, are connected to an information unit that matches the keyword condition *town* as well as the concept-value condition *river=rhine*.

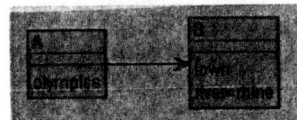

Figure 2: Query: Web Encyclopedia Data

5.2 Extended Bibliographic Data

The DBLP project ([5]) provides bibliographic information on major computer science journals and proceedings with almost 500000 articles. From this data we have created single XML files representing each occuring author, publication, and conference journal respectively; preserving their interconnections by adding more than 4000000 XLinks between the documents. Additionally, we crawled the authors' home pages that were also linked to by DBLP.

For example, consider a query about German professors that published an article in the journal of VLDB'02. This query is difficult because the necessary information is spread over multiple information units: while the authors of VLDB'02 are contained in the respective conference document, the origin of the author can only be found on the author's homepage on the web. COMPASS can exploit the fact that conference journals contain XLinks to the respective authors and all authors' documents contain XLinks to the respective authors' homepages. The resulting COMPASS query is shown in 3.

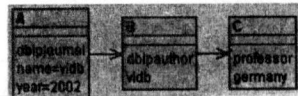

Figure 3: Query: Extended Bibliographic Data

5.3 Deep Web Data

We automatically generated Web Service wrappers for some popular portal sites including *www.amazon.com* and *www.imdb.com*. Thus, we are able to transparently access these portals when executing a query.

For example, consider a query about all conference articles and published books of Michael Stonebraker. This query combines the conference articles matched from Stonebraker's bibliographic data with the results about his other publications returned from Amazon.

References

[1] R. Baumgartner, S. Flesca, and G. Gottlob:. Visual web information extraction with lixto. *VLDB*, 2001.

[2] J. Graupmann and G. Weikum:. The role of web services in information search. *IEEE Data Engineering Bulletin 25(4)*, 2002.

[3] L. Guo, F. Shao, C. Botev, and J. Shanmugasundaram. Xrank: Ranked keyword search over xml documents. *ACM Sigmod Conference*, 2003.

[4] H. He, W. Meng, C. T. Yu, and Z. Wu. Wise-integrator: An automatic integrator of web search interfaces for e-commerce. *28th Conference on Very Large Data Bases (VLDB)*, 2003.

[5] M. Ley. Digital bibliography & library project. http://www.informatik.uni-trier.de/ ley/db/.

[6] U. of Sheffield. GATE – General Architecture for Text Engineering. http://gate.ac.uk/ie/.

[7] A. Theobald and G. Weikum. The index-based xxl search engine for querying xml data with relevance ranking. *EDBT*, 2002.

[8] V.Crescenzi, G. Mecca, and P. Merialdo. Roadrunner: Automatic data extraction from data-intensive web sites. *SIGMOD*, 2002.

[9] Wikipedia project. http://www.wikipedia.org.

Discovering and Ranking Semantic Associations over a Large RDF Metabase

Chris Halaschek, Boanerges Aleman-Meza, I. Budak Arpinar, Amit P. Sheth

Large Scale Distributed Information Systems (LSDIS) Lab
Computer Science Department, University of Georgia
Athens, GA 30602-7404,
USA
{ch, boanerg, budak, amit}@cs.uga.edu

Abstract

Information retrieval over semantic metadata has recently received a great amount of interest in both industry and academia. In particular, discovering complex and meaningful relationships among this data is becoming an active research topic. Just as ranking of documents is a critical component of today's search engines, the ranking of relationships will be essential in tomorrow's semantic analytics engines. Building upon our recent work on specifying these semantic relationships, which we refer to as Semantic Associations, we demonstrate a system where these associations are discovered among a large semantic metabase represented in RDF. Additionally we employ ranking techniques to provide users with the most interesting and relevant results.

1. Introduction

The focus of contemporary data and information retrieval systems has been to provide efficient support for the querying and retrieval of data. Significant academic and industrial research has now transitioned to mainstream search engines, such as Google, Vivisimo, and Teoma. With the increasing move from data to knowledge and the rising popularity of the Semantic Web vision [4], there is also significant interest and ongoing work in automatically extracting and representing metadata as semantic annotations to documents and services on the Web (e.g., [7]).

Given these developments, the stage is now set for the next generation of information systems that will facilitate getting actionable information from massive data sources. Through our NSF funded research project, SemDIS: Discovering Complex Relationships in the Semantic Web[1], we are developing such a system. Automatic metadata extraction resulting in semantically annotated Web entities via RDF[2], allows us to use ontologies and diverse knowledge-bases to "understand" in a limited way what a document is about (i.e. meaning of data). These knowledge-bases can then used for discovering previously unknown and potentially interesting relations between the entities, through a set of relationships between the metadata/annotations of the documents. Arguably, relationships are at the heart of semantics (e.g., [9]), lending meaning to information, making it understandable and actionable and providing new and possibly unexpected insights. One interesting type of complex relationships that we call Semantic Associations is defined next [3].

Definition 1 (ρ–Semantic Association): Two entities e_1 and e_n are ρ–semantically associated if there exists a sequence $e_1, P_1, e_2, P_2, e_3, \ldots e_{n-1}, P_{n-1}, e_n$ in an RDF graph where e_i, $1 \leq i \leq n$, are entities, P_j, $1 \leq j < n$, are properties, and entities e_i and e_{i+1} are in relationship P_i.

Such Semantic Associations are illustrated in Figure 1. Other types of more complex Semantic Associations involve finding similarity patterns and are not discussed here for brevity. For simplicity, in the remaining sections of this document we will refer to ρ–Semantic Associations as Semantic Associations and leave the presentation of other types of associations to further papers.

Permission to copy without fee all or part of this material is granted provided that the copies are not made or distributed for direct commercial advantage, the VLDB copyright notice and the title of the publication and its date appear, and notice is given that copying is by permission of the Very Large Data Base Endowment. To copy otherwise, or to republish, requires a fee and/or special permission from the Endowment

**Proceedings of the 30th VLDB Conference,
Toronto, Canada, 2004**

---

[1] http://lsdis.cs.uga.edu/Projects/SemDis/
[2] http://www.w3.org/TR/REC-rdfsyntax/

In the quest for finding Semantic Associations, users are frequently overwhelmed with too many results. For example, in our current semantic test-bed developed for open access and use by the Semantic Web research community, SWETO[3] (Semantic Web Technology Evaluation Ontology detailed in [2]), there are over 800,000 entities and 1.5 million explicit relationships among them. Simple Semantic Association queries between two entities result in hundreds of results and understanding the relevance of these associations requires comparable intellectual effort to understanding the relevance of a document in response to keyword queries.

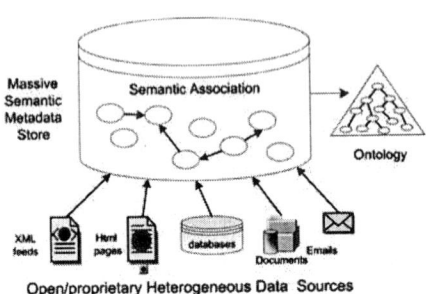

Figure 1: Semantic Associations

Therefore, it is important to locate interesting and meaningful relations and to rank them before presenting them to the user. The main goal of SemDIS is to demonstrate the discovery of Semantic Associations, as well as our ranking formalization presented in [1]. Thus, this shows the system's capabilities for semantic analytics across different sources of data through enabling users to uncover the most interesting associations by discovery and then ranking them in a relevant fashion.

The rest of the paper is organized as follows: Section 2 describes an overview of the ranking criterion; Section 3 presents the system implementation; lastly, Section 4 details the plans for the demonstration.

2. Ranking Criterion Overview

As mentioned earlier, ρ–Semantic Associations are essentially paths connecting two entities that can span across multiple domains and may involve any number of intermediate entities and relations. In this section, we describe various criteria for ranking these associations such that higher ranked associations are more relevant. Our approach defines an association rank as a function of various intermediate ranking components. For brevity, the following descriptions of these criteria exclude in depth examples and actual formulas; however, the details regarding the ranking approach can be found in [1]. We also note here that we are developing additional ranking criteria, which consider the popularity (number of incoming and outgoing edges) of the entities within a resulting association, as well as the frequency occurrence of the entities and relationships in an association.

2.1 Context

An association between two entities can pass through a variety of *regions*. By *regions*, we refer to areas of interest of a user in an ontology with respect to a specific query. For example, a user may be interested in the way two 'Persons' are related to one another in the domain of 'Computer Science Publications'. Taken from the SWETO ontology, the user would be most interested in associations that included concepts such as 'Scientific Publication', 'Computer Science Professor', etc. To capture this, we define the notion of a query *context*. This *context* is made up of various *regions* specified by the user. A context specification (discussed in Section 3.3) is thus used to capture a user's interest in order to provide him/her with the relevant knowledge among the numerous indirect relationships between the entities. Since the types of the entities are described using RDF Schema[4], we can use the associated class and relationship types to restrict our attention to the entities and relations of interest. Thus, by defining regions (or sub-graphs) of the RDF Schema, the areas of interest of the user are captured. Lastly, because a user can be interested in a variety of different regions with differing degrees on interest, we associate a weight with each region specified.

2.2 Subsumption

When considering entities in an ontology, those that are lower in the hierarchy can be thought of as more specialized instances of those further up in the hierarchy [6] (i.e. entities have more specific meaning). For example, in the SWETO ontology, the class 'Computer Science Professor' is a subclass of class 'Professor', which in turn is a subclass of class 'Person'. It is clear that a 'Professor' is a more specific type of 'Person'. Similarly, a 'Computer Science Professor' conveys more meaning than both 'Person' and a 'Professor'. This notion is captured through a criterion we refer to as 'Subsumption'. The intuition is assigning a higher rank to more "specific" entities in Semantic Associations.

2.3 Path Length

In some queries, a user may be interested in the most direct paths (i.e., short paths). This may infer a stronger relationship between two entities. Yet in other cases a user may wish to find possibly hidden, indirect, or discrete paths (i.e., long paths). The latter may be more significant in certain domains, for example, potential terrorist cells remain distant and avoid direct contact with one another in order to defer possible detection [5]. Hence, the user determines which *Path Length* influence, if any, should be used (this is largely domain dependent).

---

[3] http://lsdis.cs.uga.edu/proj/Sweto

[4] http://www.w3.org/TR/rdf-schema/

2.4 Trust

Due to the distributed nature of the data sources in a system of this type, various relationships and entities in a path originate from different sources. Some of these sources may be trusted while others may not. For example, Reuters could be regarded as a more trusted source on international news than some of the other news organizations. Thus, trust values are assigned by the user to relationships depending on the source. With trust values assigned to the knowledge, the system can rank paths coming from more trustworthy sources over those that are less trustworthy.

3. System Implementation

The SemDIS system has been designed so that it can be interacted with and almost entirely administered through a Web interface. The main components of the system are illustrated in Figure 2. The entire system, except for the Knowledge Extraction Module, is Web-accessible, and all code was written in Java. The following sections will detail the main components of the system architecture.

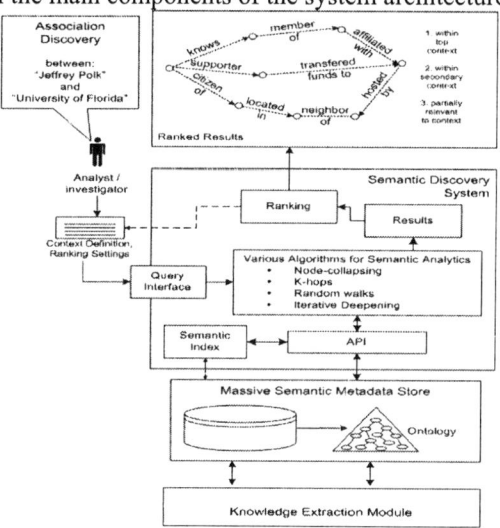

Figure 2: SemDIS System Architecture

3.1 Knowledge Extraction Module

In the SemDIS system, the knowledge extraction module (including the metadata extraction and storage) is implemented using Semagix[5] Freedom, a commercial product which evolved from the LSDIS lab's past research in semantic interoperability and SCORE technology [8]. Using this technology, we have created SWETO, a populated ontology with a large number of instances. It includes organizations, countries, people, researchers, conference, publications, etc., that are related by named relationships. Extractors are created within the Freedom environment, in which regular expressions are written to extract text from standard html, semi-structured (XML), and database-driven Web pages. As the Web pages are 'scraped' and analyzed by the extractors, the extracted entities are disambiguated and stored in the appropriate classes in the ontology. Additionally, provenance information, including source, time and date of extraction, etc., is maintained for all extracted data. We later utilize Freedom's API for exporting both the ontology and its instances in either RDF or OWL[6] syntax.

In order to query the knowledge base, we have implemented a Java API that allows for loading the ontology and its instances into main memory. Thus the system is provided with fast access to the data.

3.2 Knowledge Discovery

The query processing algorithms for discovery of Semantic Associations include adapted ideas based on k-hops, random walks, iterative deepening and node collapsing. The inputs for the query engine are two entities in the dataset. The query engine then finds all Semantic Associations between the entities of interest and forwards the results to the ranking module. We are developing heuristics to prune the search space based on semantics (e.g. through context), as well as index structures in order to reduce the time to perform a search.

3.3 Context Definition Module

As described in Section 2.1, the intuition behind a query context is that a user can specify at a high level the relevant types of data and relationships according to his/her needs; for example the 'Financial' or 'Scientific Publication' domains.

In this system, we utilize a modified version of Touchgraph[7], a Java applet for visual interaction with a graph, to define a query context. Essentially, a user can define regions, with their associated weights, classes, and properties using this interface. Figure 3 shows a screenshot of the context definition interface used within the system.

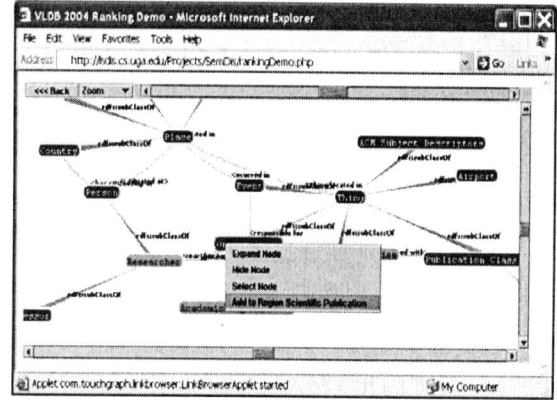

Figure 3: Context Definition Interface

---

[5] http://www.semagix.com

[6] http://www.w3.org/TR/owl-ref/
[7] http://www.touchgraph.com

3.4 Ranking Module

The ranking module is a Java implementation of the previously mentioned ranking approach. Unranked associations are passed from the query processor to the ranking module. The paths are then traversed and ranked according to the ranking criteria defined earlier. In the current implementation of the system, a user can interact with the ranking module so that s/he can specify context, whether to favor long or short paths, and which sources are the trustworthiest. Additionally, the user is also able to assign a weight to each of these individual ranking criteria.

3.5 User Interface

The user interface for the system is entirely Web accessible. The current implementation is servlet based (using Apache Tomcat), thus allowing the user to interact with the various system modules. A snapshot of the ranked results of a query to find Semantic Associations between Amit Sheth (one of the authors of this paper) and University of Georgia (UGA) is provided in Figure 4.

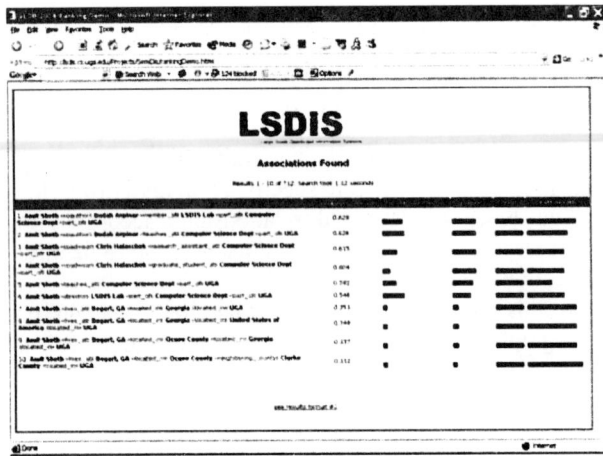

Figure 4: User Interface

4. Plan for Demonstration

The demonstration will be shown using a Web interface (driven by Apache Web server and Tomcat), in which users will be able to specify two entities and the system will return Semantic Associations between them. Additionally, the user will be allowed to define a query context through the Context Definition Interface, as well as customize the additional ranking criteria. Once the query is performed the ranked results will be displayed to the user through the Web interface. Alternatively, the results can be viewed in a random order to provide a comparison with ranked results. Hence, the demonstration will be a seamless integration of these facets of the systems.

5. Acknowledgements

We would like to thank other project members J. Miller, and K. Kochut, for their valuable comments, as well as Semagix, Inc. for providing its Freedom product. Additionally, we would like to acknowledge Meenakshi Nagarajan, Jason Lynes, and William Milnor for their work on the user interface. This project is funded by NSF-ITR-IDM Award # 0325464 titled 'SemDIS: Discovering Complex Relationships in the Semantic Web.'

6. References

[1] B. Aleman-Meza, C. Halaschek, I. B. Arpinar, and A. Sheth, "Context-Aware Semantic Association Ranking", 1st Intl. Workshop on Semantic Web and Databases, Berlin, Germany, September 7-8, 2003; pp. 33-50.

[2] B. Aleman-Meza, C. Halaschek, A. Sheth, I. B. Arpinar, and G. Sannapareddy, "SWETO: Large-Scale Semantic Web Test-bed", Intl. Workshop on Ontology in Action, Banff, Canada, June 20-24, 2004 (submitted).

[3] K. Anyanwu and A. Sheth, "ρ-Queries: Enabling Querying for Semantic Associations on the Semantic Web", 12th Intl. WWW Conference, Budapest, Hungary, 2003.

[4] T. Berners-Lee, J. Hendler, and O. Lassila, "The Semantic Web: A new form of Web content that is meaningful to computers will unleash a revolution of new possibilities", Scientific American, May 2001.

[5] V. Krebs, "Mapping Networks of Terrorist Cells". Connections, 24(3): 43-52, 2002.

[6] M. Rodriguez, and M. Egenhofer, "Determining Semantic Similarity among Entity Classes from Different Ontologies", IEEE Transactions on Knowledge and Data Engineering, 15(2): 442-456. 2003.

[7] U. Shah, T. Finin, A. Joshi, R. S. Cost, and J. Mayfield, "Information Retrieval on the Semantic Web", 10th Intl. Conference on Information and Knowledge Management, November 2002.

[8] A. Sheth, C. Bertram, D. Avant, B. Hammond, K. Kochut, and Y. Warke. (2002). "Managing semantic content for the Web." IEEE Internet Computing, 6(4), 80-87. 2002.

[9] A. Sheth, I. B. Arpinar, and V. Kashyap, "Relationships at the Heart of Semantic Web: Modeling, Discovering, and Exploiting Complex Semantic Relationships," Enhancing the Power of the Internet Studies in Fuzziness and Soft Computing, M. Nikravesh, B. Azvin, R. Yager and L. Zadeh, Springer-Verlag, 2003.

An Automatic Data Grabber for Large Web Sites

Valter Crescenzi [1], Giansalvatore Mecca [2],
Paolo Merialdo [1], Paolo Missier [1]

[1] Università Roma Tre
Roma - Italy
[crescenz,merialdo]@dia.uniroma3.it,
pmissier@acm.org

[2] Università della Basilicata
Potenza - Italy
mecca@unibas.it

Abstract

We demonstrate a system to automatically grab data from data intensive web sites. The system first infers a model that describes at the intensional level the web site as a collection of classes; each class represents a set of structurally homogeneous pages, and it is associated with a small set of representative pages. Based on the model a library of wrappers, one per class, is then inferred, with the help an external wrapper generator. The model, together with the library of wrappers, can thus be used to navigate the site and extract the data.

1 Introduction

This paper presents a system to automatically grab data from the web. The target of our system is that relevant portion of the web consisting of large data intensive web sites. Prominent examples are popular e-commerce web sites, financial web sites, the web sites of relevant scientific institutions, or the web site of events of worldwide interest. These sites represent rich and up-to-date information sources. However, since they mainly deliver data through an intricate hypertext collection of HTML documents, it is not easy to build applications that access to and compute over these sources.

A partial solution to the problem comes from some recent research proposals. Based on the observation that many web sites contain large collections of structurally similar pages, several researchers have developed techniques to automatically infer web wrappers [1, 3, 4, 9], i.e., programs that extract data from HTML pages, and transform them into a machine processable format, typically in XML. These techniques take as input a small set of sample pages exhibiting a common template, and generate as output a wrapper that can be used to extract the data from any page sharing the same structure as the input samples.

These proposals represent an important step towards the automatic extraction of data from web data sources. However, as argued in [1, 4], intriguing issues arise when scaling up from the single collection of pages to whole sites. The main problems, which significantly affect the scalability of the wrapper approach, are how to identify the structured regions of the target site, and how to collect the sample pages to feed the wrapper generation process. Presently, these tasks are done manually.

The subject of our demonstration is a system that addresses these issues, making it feasible to automatically extract data from large data intensive web sites. Our system explores a target web site and automatically infers a model for the site. To reduce the number of visited pages, site exploration is driven by an adaptive approach. The inferred model describes the web site as a directed graph: nodes are classes of structurally homogeneous pages, while arcs represent collections of links among pages that belong to different classes. Each class is associated with a small set of representative pages, that can be used to infer a library of wrappers with the help an external wrapper generator.[1] The model, together with the associated wrappers, can be used to continuously extract data from the target web sites.

2 Related work

To the best of our knowledge the only system that is similar to ours in spirits is that proposed by Kao et

---

[1] We use ROADRUNNER, our wrapper generator module [4, 5].

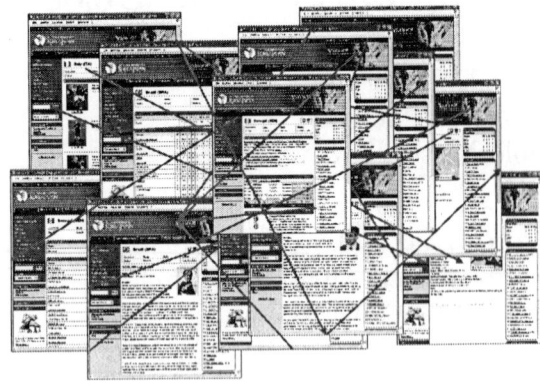
a. Web site

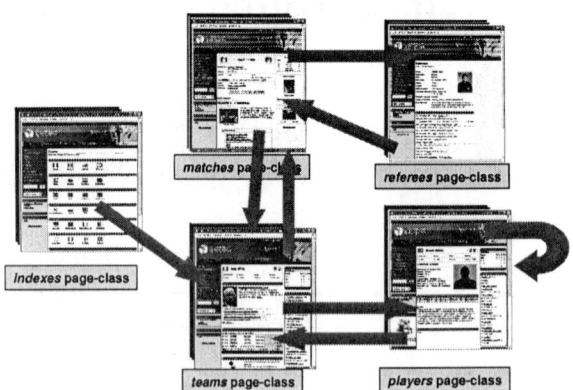
b. Site model

Figure 1: A site model example

al. [6]. They have have developed an entropy based technique for analyzing news web sites. Namely the goal of their proposal is to identify, within a news web site, pages of indexes to news, and pages containing news. Compared to our approach, Kao et al. only distinguish two predefined classes of pages (indexes and content), in a specific domain (news web site). On the contrary we aim at classifying pages according to their structure, without any a priori assumption.

Another field that is somehow related to our research is that of focused-crawling [2]. The goal of a focused crawler is to selectively seek out pages that are relevant to a pre-defined set of topics possibly from many different web sites. Our system can be considered as a crawler focused on recognizing structure (for extraction purposes) rather than looking for topic-relevant pages. However, we conjecture that the intensional description of a web site that we can infer could be profitably combined with approaches that crawl sites by topics.

Finally, it is worth mentioning that our approach does not crawl data behind forms. In order to extract data also from the hidden web, our system could cooperate with specific techniques, such as those proposed in [8, 7].

3 An overview of the system approach

The goal of the system is to infer a model, that describes at the intensional level the overall structure of the site in terms of classes of pages and navigational paths among them. We expect that structurally similar pages are grouped into classes, and that the link between pages can be grouped into classes of links between classes. Also, we aim at generating the model efficiently, i.e. by visiting a small portion of the target site: while building the model, the system adaptively chooses pages to visit in order to infer a complete model for the site.

Figure 2: A player page from `fifaworldcup.com`

Figure 1 shows an example of the approach: given a large web site composed by thousands of interconnected page, the system produces a model, that describes at the intensional level the structure of the site.

We illustrate the intuition behind our approach by means of an example. Consider the official FIFA 2002 world cup web site,[2] whose roughly 20,000 pages contain information about teams, players, matches, and news. Both the contents and the topology of the site are structured in a regular way: there is one page for each player, one page for each team, and so on; the links between pages reflect the semantic relationships between contents: for instance, every team page con-

---
[2] http://fifaworldcup.yahoo.com/02

tains links to the pages of its players.

A key observation in our approach is that in data-intensive web sites links reflect both the internal structure of pages and the topological structure of the site. Whenever two (or more) pages contain links that share the same layout and presentation properties, then it is likely that the two pages share the same structure. This can be more easily observed by grouping the links into (possibly singleton) *collections*: each collection is characterized by uniform layout and presentation properties.[3] Consider for example Figure 2, which shows the web page of a player from Fifaworldcup.com: every player page (they are all generated from the same template) contains the same link collections shown in this page (e.g. one link collection on the right leading to the other player of the same team, and one link collection on the top pointing to other pages about its team, and so on).

In addition, we observe that usually links within the same collection are organized either as a list of link pointing to similar pages, or as a tuple of links leading to pages with different structures. Again from our example, we have that every player page contains one link collection on the right, which is a list of links to other player pages, one link collection on the top pointing to several different kinds of page about a team ("overview", "profile", "stats" ...), etc..

Our approach for inferring a model describing the structure of a web site builds on the above observations. We model pages as objects containing tuples and list of links; a *page class* models sets of pages; links are typed: the type corresponds to the class of the target page. To infer a model, the system considers pages from the target site, and groups them into classes considering several alternative partitions, which are then ranked according to a metrics of quality.

The inference process is performed incrementally. The system starts from a given entry point (e.g. the home page), which becomes the first member of the first class in the model; then, it refines the model by exploring its boundaries to gather new pages. At each iteration, the system selects a link collection from the model outbound and iteratively fetches a page by following one of the link in the collection. In order to reduce the number of pages actually visited, after each download the system makes a guess on the class of remaining pages. If looking at the pages already downloaded there is sufficient evidence that the guess is right, the remaining pages of the collections are assigned to classes without actually fetching them. The process iterates until all the link collections are typed with a known class.

---

[3]The layout and presentation properties of each link collection can be described in terms of their paths on the DOM tree.

4 The Demonstration

During the demonstration we will show the system at work on some real-life web sites. Figure 3 depicts the main components of our system and their interaction.

Our demonstration will focus on the main steps of our approach for grabbing data from large web sites. Taking as input an entry point (e.g. the home page) of a target site, we will demonstrate:

Automatic web site model generation: we will show how the system is able to build a model of the site even visiting a small number of pages. In particular, we will demonstrate how the system adaptively chooses pages to visit in order to create a complete intensional description of the hypertext structure; also, we will demonstrate that large web sites containing thousands of pages can be indeed modelled with a small number of classes;

Wrapper generation: the model generated in the previous step will be used for feeding the automatic wrapper generator. The system builds a library of wrappers for the target web site, taking as input the pages from each class of the model. To perform this step, we use our wrapper generator system [5, 4]; however, other wrapper generators, such as those described in [1, 3, 9], may be used.

Data extraction: the site model, together with the wrappers, will then be used to extract data from the site. We will show that, with the help of the model and of the associated wrappers, the system provides a structured virtual view of the site.

Selective data grabbing: based on the model of the site, the user can select page classes containing data of interest. The system navigates the actual site to reach the target pages, then it applies the associated wrappers and extract the requested data.

References

[1] ARASU, A., AND GARCIA-MOLINA, H. Extracting structured data from web pages. In *ACM SIGMOD International Conf. on Management of Data (SIGMOD 2003), San Diego, California* (2003).

[2] CHAKRABARTI, S., VAN DEN BERG, M., AND DOM, B. Focused crawling: a new approach to topic-specific Web resource discovery. *Computer Networks (Amsterdam, Netherlands) 31*, 11–16 (1999), 1623–1640.

[3] CHANG, C.-H., AND SHAO-CHEN, L. Iepad: Information extraction based on pattern discovery. In *Proceedings of the tenth international conference on World Wide Web* (2001).

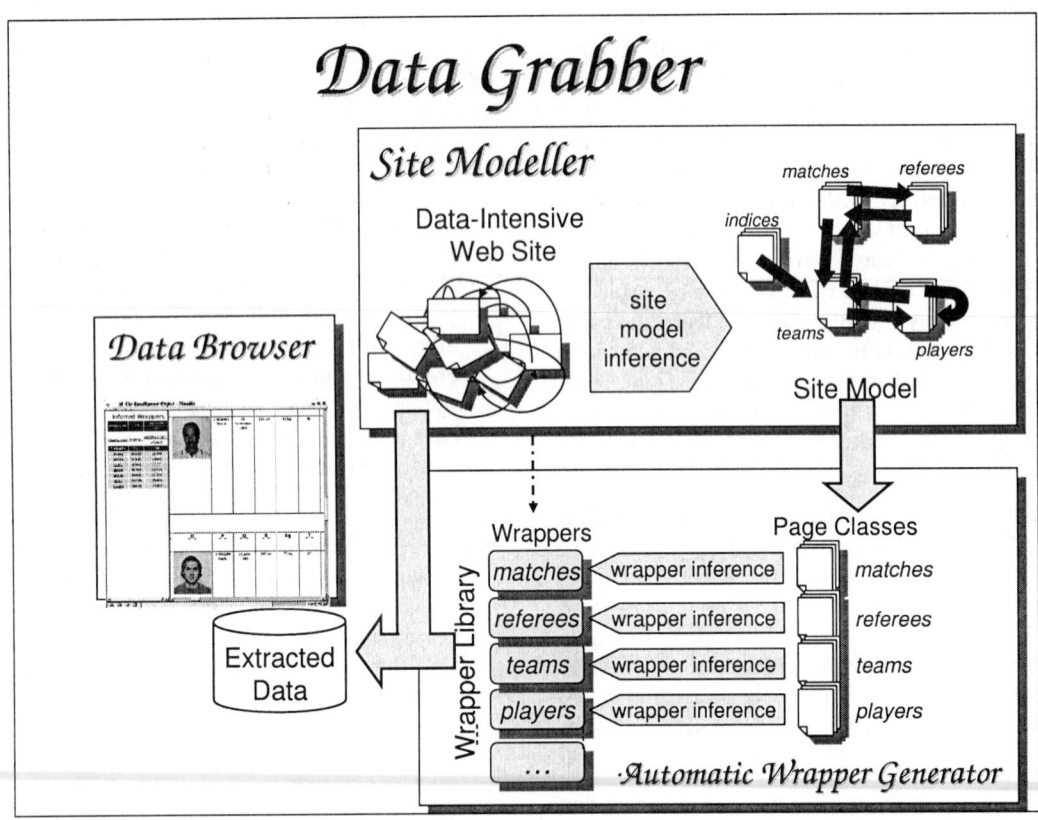

Figure 3: System components and their interaction

[4] CRESCENZI, V., MECCA, G., AND MERIALDO, P. ROADRUNNER: Towards automatic data extraction from large Web sites. In *International Conf. on Very Large Data Bases (VLDB 2001), Roma, Italy, September 11-14* (2001).

[5] CRESCENZI, V., MECCA, G., AND MERIALDO, P. Roadrunner: Automatic data extraction from data-intensive web sites. In *ACM SIGMOD International Conf. on Management of Data (SIGMOD'2002), Madison, Wisconsin* (2002).

[6] KAO, H., LIN, S., HO, J., AND M.-S., C. Mining web informative structures and contents based on entropy analysis. *IEEE Transactions on Knowledge and Data Engineering 16*, 1 (January 2004), 41–44.

[7] PALMIERI, J., DA SILVA, A., GOLGHER, P., AND LAENDER, A. Collecting hidden web pages for data extraction. In *ACM WIDM 2002* (2002).

[8] RAGHAVAN, S., AND GARCIA-MOLINA, H. Crawling the hidden web. In *International Conf. on Very Large Data Bases (VLDB 2001), Roma, Italy, September 11-14* (2001).

[9] WANG, J., AND LOCHOVSKY, F. Data-rich section extraction from html pages. In *Proceedings of the 3rd International Conference on Web Information Systems Engineering (WISE 2002), 12-14 December 2002, Singapore, Proceedings* (2002), IEEE Computer Society, pp. 313–322.

WS-CatalogNet: An Infrastructure for Creating, Peering, and Querying e-Catalog Communities

Karim Baïna[1], Boualem Benatallah[1], Hye-young Paik[1]*, Farouk Toumani[2], Christophe Rey[2], Agnieszka Rutkowska[1], and Bryan Harianto[1]

[1]CSE, University of New South Wales, Sydney, Australia,
[2] Laboratoire LIMOS, ISIMA, Clermont-Ferrand, France
{kbaina,boualem,hpaik,agr225,bryanh}@cse.unsw.edu.au, {ftoumani,rey}@isima.fr

1 Introduction

E-catalog portals, such as Expedia.com and Amazon.com, are becoming more and more prominent feature of the Web. They aim to offer one-stop shopping experience for the users. However, the users still need to access a number of portals separately, or to use search engines in order to get complete information they are looking for. It is clearly useful to provide a unified interface to access multiple e-catalog portals. The issue here is that the technology to create, organise, integrate and search these portals has not kept pace with the rapid growth of the available information space. Most existing approaches for providing access to integrated e-catalogs as a portal are based on (i) creating centralised product data repository collected from participating e-catalog providers, (ii) statically linking manually (ad-hoc) identified e-catalogs to the portal. Surely, these are not scalable approaches. First, we cannot expect the integrators to understand underlying schemas of thousands of online e-catalogs and produce a single schema. Second, considering the dynamic nature of the Web, the underlying schema of any online e-catalog may change any time and change frequently, which has to be reflected to the central schema.

We have developed WS-CatalogNet to address the two issues: (i) scalable integration of e-catalogs, and (ii) flexible query processing technique whereby a portal collaborate with other portals to locate information which is not locally available.

More precisely, in WS-CatalogNet, e-catalogs catering for similar customer needs are grouped together into *e-catalog communities* (communities in short) [2]. Individual e-catalogs *register* themselves to a community as *members*. Also, communities are linked together as *peers* based on inter-ontology relationships (e.g. similarity). Query routing among communities occurs to identify a set of e-catalogs that, when put together, can satisfy all constraints specified in the user query.

WS-CatalogNet is a hybrid of peer-to-peer and web-services technologies. Given the highly dynamic and distributed nature of e-catalogs, a novel approach that involves techniques such as peer-to-peer and Web services will become increasingly attractive in building e-catalog portals.

WS-CatalogNet consists of a set of integrated tools that allow for creating communities, registering e-catalog members, creating peer relationships between communities, querying individual communities and routing queries among communities. It has been implemented using Java and the IBM Web Services Development Kit 5.0 (WSDK) which provides several components for developing Web services. In particular, we used the UDDI Java API (UDDI4J) to access a private UDDI registry (i.e. hosted by the WS-CatalogNet), as well as the WSDL generation tool for creating the WSDL documents and SOAP service descriptors for e-catalog communities and the product e-catalogs.

2 WS-CatalogNet Design Overview

The general architecture of WS-CatalogNet contains three main components (see Figure 1): *Community Manager*, *Member Manager* and *Cooperative Query Manager*. These components are built on a panel of libraries and packages which the authors have either developed or integrated into WS-CatalogNet (e.g. HTML2WS: HTML to Web Service Wrapper, BQR:

---

*The author is now at the School of Information Systems, Queensland University of Technology, Brisbane Australia, h.paik@qut.edu.au

Permission to copy without fee all or part of this material is granted provided that the copies are not made or distributed for direct commercial advantage, the VLDB copyright notice and the title of the publication and its date appear, and notice is given that copying is by permission of the Very Large Data Base Endowment. To copy otherwise, or to republish, requires a fee and/or special permission from the Endowment.

**Proceedings of the 30th VLDB Conference,
Toronto, Canada, 2004**

Best Query Rewriting algorithm and WordNet).

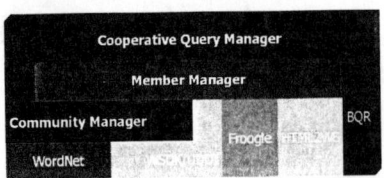

Figure 1: WS-CatalogNet Architecture

2.1 Community Manager

The Community Manager is used to create communities and build peer relationships between communities.

Creating Communities. A community is a *container* of e-catalogs of the same domain (e.g. community of Flights). It provides a description of desired products without referring to actual product providers (e.g. Qantas Airlines). The schema of a community is described in terms of categories and descriptive attributes. For example, the community FlightCenter may have a category Flights, which is described using attributes such as arrival, departure, price, etc. In fact, a community schema can be viewed as an ontology (integrated schema) of its underlying e-catalogs.

To provide formal semantics in describing categories and attributes, necessary for precise characterisation of queries over the e-catalogs, we use a class description language that belongs to the family of description logics[1]. The users do not describe schemas and queries directly using description logic. Instead, a graphical interface is used to automatically generate these descriptions.

A community implements a common interface of service operations which are invoked by end users or peers (e.g. *addCategory()*, *addPeer()* and *queryCommunity()*). After the community schema is defined, the community manager generates the WSDL which contains details of the interface (e.g. signature of the operations) and description of the schema. The newly created community is deployed and registered to a service directory hosted by WS-CatalogNet.

Building Peer Relationships. Communities may create a peer relationship with each other. When building a relationship, any mismatches of the terms used in categories and attributes between communities need to be resolved. Let us consider that the administrator of a community (noted Source) forms a relationship with another community (noted Target). The administrator then defines a mapping description which states how the categories (respectively the attributes) in Source are mapped to Target. For flexibility, we consider three types of mappings: (i) explicit mapping between categories (respectively, attributes) of the corresponding communities (*full mapping*), (ii) explicit mapping between only categories of the corresponding communities (*category mapping*), (iii) no explicit mapping between the corresponding community schemas. When the translation of a query between peers is needed, and explicit mapping description is not available, the Source and Target use synonyms[2] to solve mismatches between the corresponding community schemas.

2.2 Member Manager

The Member Manager supports registering individual e-catalogs into communities. The e-catalogs are either already web services, or converted to web services through the member manager.

When registering an e-catalog, the e-catalog provider first indicates which categories, in the community schema, the e-catalog belongs to (e.g., Qantas Airlines may belong to the category international flights of the community Flights). Then, for each category chosen, the provider specifies what kind of attributes are supported for the selected categories (called *member definition*). Similarly to describing mappings between peer communities, the e-catalog provider must define mappings between the community and e-catalog descriptions.

2.3 Cooperative Query Manager

Since a community does not store product data locally, processing the query requires locating e-catalogs that are capable of answering the query. We propose a cooperative query processing technique that consists of two steps: (i) identify best combinations of members whose query capabilities, when put together, satisfy the constraints expressed in the query, (ii) resolve the query by sending it to the selected combination of members. The name "cooperative" comes from the fact that the first step involves communities forwarding queries to each other to find the members who can resolve the query.

We adapted a query rewriting algorithm developed by the authors [1] – Best Query Rewriting (BQR). This algorithm identifies which part of the query can be answered by local members of the community and which part of the query cannot (hence, needs help of peers). The algorithm takes as input the community schema, member definitions and the query (all expressed in the class description language) then produces the following output:

(a) Q_{local}: the part of the query Q that *can be answered* by the community's local members. It gives the best combinations of the local members that can answer all (or part of) the query.

(b) Q_{rest}: the part of the query that *cannot be answered* by the local members. This part of the query will be forwarded to peer communities. It is

---

[1] http://dl.kr.org/

[2] Synonyms are defined for each categories and attributes in a community.

noted that the expected answers of the forwarding is the combination of the external members (i.e. members of peer communities) that are capable of answering the part of the query.

Each community has a *query forwarding policy* which controls what should be done with Q_{rest}. The forwarding policy can express (i) when the query should be forwarded (e.g. when no local members can answer, when the community is too busy, etc.) (ii) to which peer (e.g. all, top K, random, etc.) the query should be forwarded, and (iii) how far the query should be forwarded (i.e., hop limit).

After forwarding, the community collects the returned results from the peers and chooses the best combination of e-catalog members (local and external) based on the quality of the members' (e.g. reliability) and user preferences. After all necessary members are selected, each of the selected member processes parts of the query that it is capable of processing, and the results are returned to the community.

3 Demonstration Scenario

We have used WS-CatalogNet to deploy an application in the tourism domain. It covers the following 6 communities: FlightCenter - international/domestic flight information, TravelInfo - flights and accommodation information, CarRentals - rent cars information, TouristAttractionInfos - tourist attractions in the world, Accommodations - hotels, youth hostels, B&B information, TravelPortals - travel tips, special deals information.

In the demonstration, we first create a community FlightCenter using Community Manager. We will show how FlightCenter builds a peer relationship with another community TravelInfo. Then we register two e-catalog members STAFlightCenter and Qantas.com through Member Manager. Here, we will demonstrate that we support two kinds of e-catalogs: one that is already a web service, the other that is converted to a web service through our custom developed tool. Finally, we show how the community FlightCenter is queried and Q_{rest} part of a query is forwarded to its peer.

3.1 Creating Community FlightCenter

Figure 2 shows how the administrator of the community FlightCenter creates the hierarchy of the categories using the Community Manager. For example, the Add Category operation lets the user add a category DomesticFlights as sub category of Flights. Using the Add Attribute operation, the user adds attributes such as fromCity and toCity to the category Flights.

Using WordNet. To demonstrate how WordNet assists the user in defining the community schema,

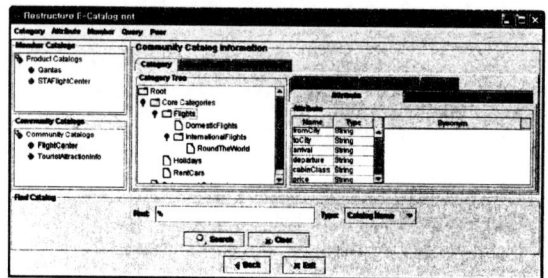

Figure 2: Creating categories

we show the following. After creating the category RentCars, the user uses Add Category with WordNet operation to create a sub category Car under RentCars. WordNet proposes that there are five different *meanings* in the category Car, and for each meaning, it suggests Car's sub categories and their synonyms. The user chooses the one s/he wants and customises the proposed sub categories of the categorie Car (e.g. by removing unwanted sub categories, or editing synonyms, etc.). Figure 3 displays the sub categorise of Car suggested by WordNet (e.g. Convertible, Coupe, Limousine, Sedan, etc.) and its synonyms (e.g. auto, automobile, etc.). After creating the categories, the user uses Add Attributes with WordNet operation to see possible attributes of the categorie Car. WordNet proposes a large list of attributes, and their synonyms (e.g. accelerator, airbag, sunroof, etc.). The user customises the proposed attributes (e.g, by removing unwanted attributes, or adding synonyms, etc.). After editing the community schema is completed, the Community Manager generates corresponding class descriptions for the community.

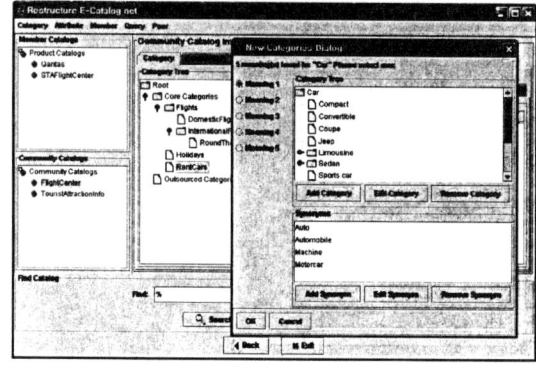

Figure 3: Creating categories using WordNet

3.2 Peering communities

The administrator of the community FlightCenter first searches for other communities in WS-CatalogNet via Community Manager's search functionality. When s/he selects the community TravelInfo, the Community Manager displays categories and attributes

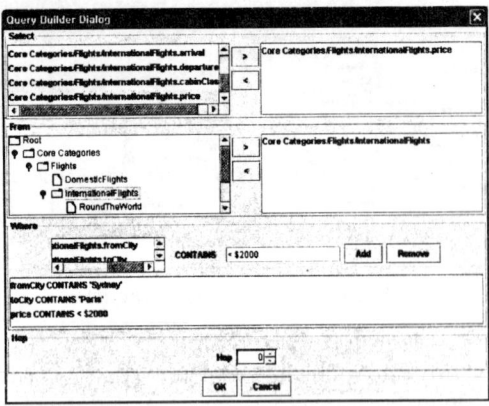

Figure 4: Expressing a query on `FlightCenter`

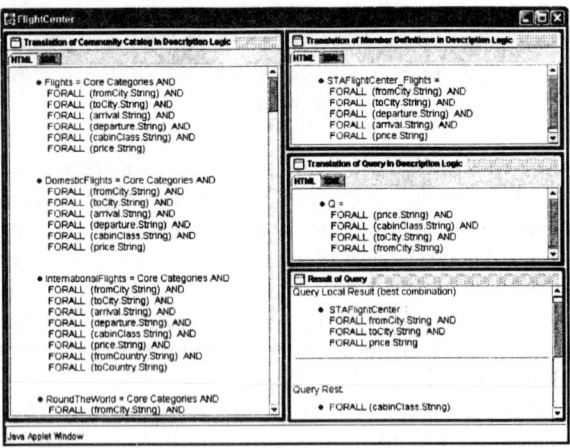

Figure 5: Querying `FlightCenter` using BQR

of `TravelInfo`. To create a peer relationship with category mapping information only, s/he clicks the category `Holidays` of the community `FlightCenter` and drag it to the category `holidaysOffers` of `TravelInfo` community.

3.3 Registering members

The e-catalog `STAFlightCenter` which provides cheap international flight tickets is already implemented as a web service. It has three categories `Airfares`, `Insurance` and `CarHire`. The provider of the e-catalog `STAFlightCenter` uses the `Member Manager` to display the categories of `FlightCenter` community and decides to register its own `Airfares` category with `FlightCenter`'s `Flights` category. To register with this community, the provider points & clicks `FlightCenter`'s categories and attributes that s/he can support (i.e., `Flights` category and its attributes). For each attribute in the category clicked, the provider selects, from his/her own list of attributes, the one that maps to it (e.g., `Flights`'s `price` attribute is mapped to `Airfares`'s `farePrice`)[3]. After mapping information is entered, the member manager generates corresponding class descriptions.

3.4 Querying the community `FlightCenter`

As shown in figure 4, the `Query Manager` displays the community `FlightCenter`'s categories and attributes to the user. The user then formulate a query, mainly by pointing&clicking, "**category**:*InternationalFlights*, **attributes**: *fromCity=Sydney, toCity=Paris, price ≤ 1000, travelInsurance= full* ". The Query Manager generates corresponding class description of the user query. Then it runs the Best Quality Rewriting algorithm to compute Q_{local} and Q_{rest}. In this case, the local member `STAFlightCenter` is selected as a relevant e-catalog (i.e., Q_{local}) to answer the user query (it provides the attributes: `fromCity`, `toCity` and `price`). The

Q_{rest} part of the query contains only the attribute (`travelInsurance`). In this scenario, the community `FlightCenter` uses a predefined query forwarding policy. It specifies that Q_{rest} should be forwarded to all of its peers with hop limit of 3. The Q_{rest} (`travelInsurance`) is forwarded to the communities `TravelInfo` and `WebJetDeal`. After forwarding, both `TravelInfo` and `WebJetDeal` return `SmileTravel` and `BestTravel` as members who can answer `travelInsurance` respectively. The community `FlightCenter` decides to combine the e-catalogs `STAFlightCenter` (local) and `SmileTravel` (external, referred by `TravelInfo`) and send the query to them. Figure 5 shows the first result of running BQR.

Other scenarios of more complex queries will be presented in the demo to illustrate how peer communities collaborate to answer a user query. We show how a query is routed among several communities, where at each community the part of the query that can be answered by the local members is identified and the remaining part of the query is forwarded to other peers according to the community forwarding policy.

References

[1] B. Benatallah, M.-S. Hacid, A. Leger, C. Rey, and F. Toumani. On Automating Web Services Discovery. *To appear in VLDB Journal*, 2004.

[2] H.-Y. Paik, B. Benatallah, and F. Toumani. WS-CatalogNet: Building Peer-to-Peer E-Catalogs. In *FQAS 2004, Lyon, France.*, 2004.

---

[3]Corresponding figure not shown due to space reasons.

Trust-Serv: A Lightweight Trust Negotiation Service

Halvard Skogsrud[1], Boualem Benatallah[1], Fabio Casati[2], Manh Q. Dinh[1]

[1] University of New South Wales
Sydney NSW 2052, Australia
{halvards,boualem,mdinh}@cse.unsw.edu.au

[2] Hewlett-Packard Laboratories
Palo Alto, CA, 94304 USA
fabio.casati@hp.com

1 Introduction

In Web service environments, scalable access control methods are required, as requester populations are often large and dynamic. For this reason, requester identities are often not known in advance, and traditional access control models that rely on identity to determine access do not fit. Other models require requesters to submit *credentials* (i.e., signed assertions describing attributes of the owner) along with service invocations. These models often do not consider credentials to be resources, an assumption that does not hold when credentials may contain sensitive information. *Trust negotiation* addresses these problems by granting access based on the level of trust established in a negotiation between the requester and the provider. During this trust negotiation, credentials are exchanged to gradually build trust.

However, several issues need to be addressed before trust negotiation can become a viable technology. The description of trust negotiation *policies* is mainly characterized by the use of ad hoc methods, such as editing XML-based policy documents. These policies specify which resources (i.e., credentials and service operations) that can be disclosed at a given state of the trust negotiation, and the conditions to disclose them. Since trust negotiation policies may be quite complex, largely ad hoc development can be time-consuming and error prone. Incorrectly specified policies may cause, e.g., confidential information to be revealed to unauthorized parties, and open avenues for loss of data through malicious or ignorant clients or partners.

Another interesting problem that has not been addressed before is the *lifecycle management* of trust negotiation policies [4]. Enterprise policies often change for a variety of reasons, including emerging competitors, new products, mergers and acquisitions, updated business processes, and changes to laws and regulations. For trust negotiation to become a viable security solution for enterprises, there is a need for high-level frameworks and tools to provide support for automating the development, enforcement, and evolution of trust negotiation policies.

Motivated by these concerns, we have developed the Trust-Serv platform for model-driven trust negotiation in Web service environments [4]. One innovative feature of Trust-Serv is the state machine-based model for the specification of trust negotiation policies, which is translated into structures used to automatically control trust negotiations at run-time. Another innovative features is the support for *dynamic policy evolution*, that is, changes to a policy while there are ongoing trust negotiations.

2 Trust-Serv Design Overview

In Trust-Serv, trust negotiation policies are expressed as state machines [4]. States represent the level of trust achieved by the requester so far in the negotiation. By entering a new state, a requester is given access to the resources mapped to that state. However, instead of associating resources directly to states, we use the abstraction of *roles* [1]. Roles are semantic abstractions that describe some function performed by people or processes (e.g., *developer* and *tester*). Trust-Serv maps resources to roles and roles to states. Roles are cumulative, so a requester may be a member of several roles.

Transitions are extended beyond traditional state machines to capture security abstractions necessary for trust negotiation by labeling them with *authorization abstractions*. Authorization abstractions define the conditions that must be met for transitions to be fired. There are two types of authorization abstractions; *explicit* and *implicit*. Explicit transitions are triggered by actions performed by the requester. One type of explicit transition is *credential disclosure*. This type of transition requires the other party to disclose one or more credentials, and it may place constraints

---

Permission to copy without fee all or part of this material is granted provided that the copies are not made or distributed for direct commercial advantage, the VLDB copyright notice and the title of the publication and its date appear, and notice is given that copying is by permission of the Very Large Data Base Endowment. To copy otherwise, or to republish, requires a fee and/or special permission from the Endowment.

**Proceedings of the 30th VLDB Conference,
Toronto, Canada, 2004**

on acceptable values of attributes contained within the credentials. Other explicit transitions include *provisions* and *obligations*. Provisions require actions to be taken before proceeding, while obligations require actions to be taken in the future. We represent provisions as service operations that must be invoked before the trust negotiation can proceed. Obligations are represented as service operations that require the requester to digitally sign a message stating what service operation to invoke, the deadline, and any compensation required if the obligation is not met. Implicit transitions are triggered by the provider. *Timed transitions* are implicit, and they are fired when timeout events occur, usually because the requester did not perform any action for a period of time.

Once trust negotiation policies have been specified, Trust-Serv will take care of enforcing them on behalf of the users, relieving developers from the need of implementing such logic into the service provider's code, as described below.

Enterprise policies often change to adhere to changing business strategies. Lifecycle management of policies is therefore an important issue to be considered in trust negotiation systems. Since trust negotiations may be long-lived, it may be necessary to change a policy while there are ongoing trust negotiations based on this policy. It may not always be possible to let these ongoing negotiations finish according to the old policy, especially if it was found to be in breach of laws and regulations, or if it did not properly protect business assets. In these situations, it is necessary to appropriately *migrate* the trust negotiation instances to the new policy.

Trust-Serv supports several *migration strategies* to handle migration of trust negotiation instances from an old policy to a new policy, details of which may be found in [4]. The use of these strategies is controlled by a *strategy selection policy*, which is a meta-policy specified separately from the trust negotiation policies. This meta-policy is a collection of rules, such as "Requesters who have visited state B are migrated to the new policy". When a trust negotiation policy is updated, a strategy selection policy is defined. Ongoing trust negotiations are then evaluated against this meta-policy, and the outcome of this evaluation determines which strategy to apply to each trust negotiation instance and how to migrate it to follow an appropriate policy.

3 Implementation

The Trust-Serv platform provides environments where (i) service developers may create and manage trust negotiation policies for their Web services, and (ii) both providers and requesters may observe the negotiations, and participate by negotiating manually, if desired. Trust-Serv is implemented as an extension to the Self-Serv platform [3]. Self-Serv supports Web service development based on established standards such as SOAP, WSDL (Web Service Description Language), and UDDI (Universal Description, Discovery, and Integration) [2]. An overview of this architecture is shown in Figure 1. Trust-Serv is implemented in C# using Microsoft Visual Studio .NET 2003, and implementations of security standards are provided by the Web Service Enhancements (WSE) for Microsoft .NET.

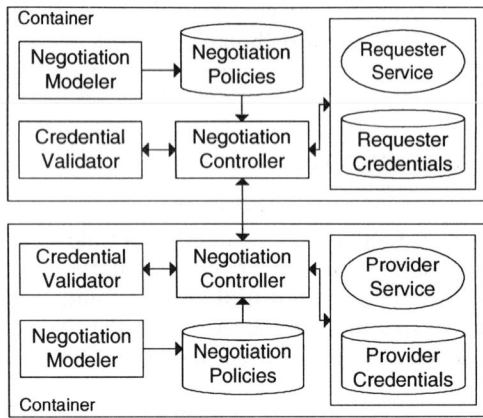

Figure 1: Architecture of Trust-Serv.

The Trust-Serv architecture introduces the notion of Web service *containers*. A container acts as a middleware layer that takes on the chore of enforcing trust negotiation policies, avoiding the need to code this logic into the Web service itself. This means that tasks such as controlling negotiations and verifying credentials are delegated to the container, thereby considerable simplifying service development. The three main components of the Trust-Serv container are the *controller*, the *modeler*, and the *validator*.

The Trust-Serv container features a *trust negotiation controller*, which is implemented as a Web service that provides the capabilities to participate in trust negotiations. The controller is responsible for receiving messages such as service operation invocations and credential disclosures, determining if new trust negotiation instances should be created, and triggering transitions if their conditions are met. Messages are sent between trust negotiation instances and service instances as SOAP request and response messages.

The *trust negotiation modeler* facilitates the specification and management of trust negotiation policies. Trust negotiation policies are edited through a visual interface, as shown in Figure 2. The modeler is also used to automatically generate *control rules*, which are used by the controller to determine actions to be taken in response to events. The control rules are generated from the state machine-based specification of the trust negotiation policy using algorithms presented in [4], and they are represented as XML documents.

The *credential validator* performs the task of validating credentials. Validation includes checking the

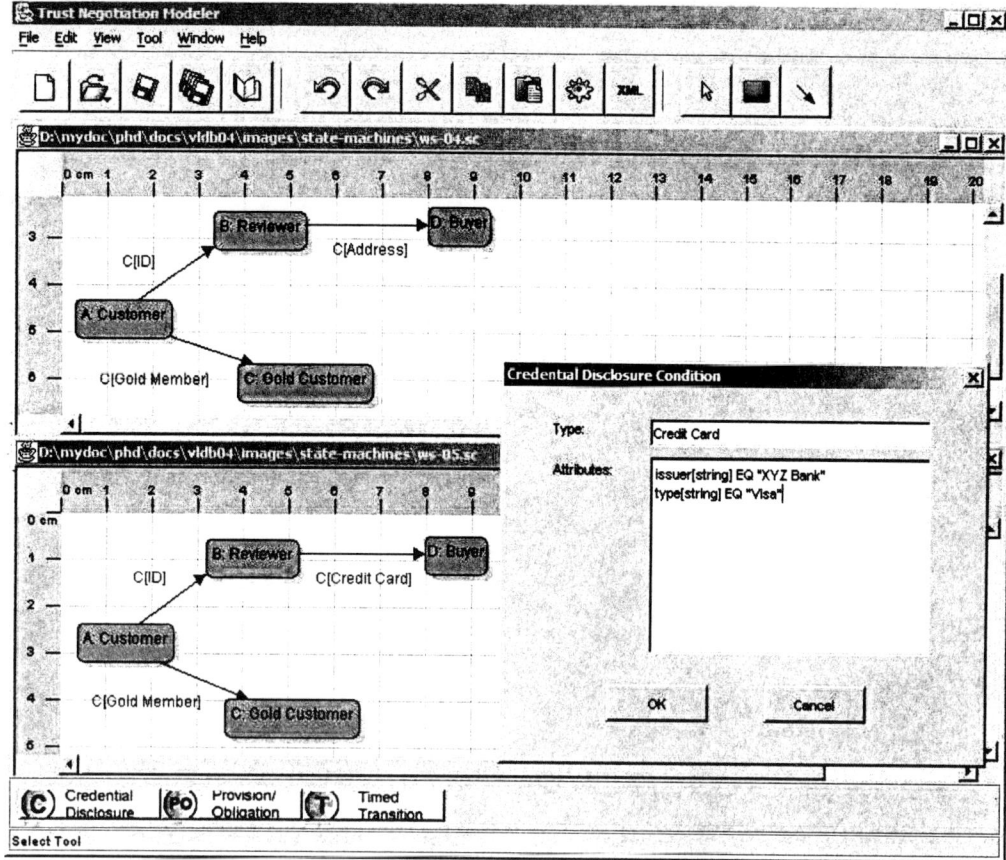

Figure 2: Defining and managing policies in Trust-Serv.

expiry date, verifying the issuer's signature, and ensuring that the credential has not been revoked. Rather than implementing this functionality in the container, we use Security Token Services (STS) as defined in the WS-Trust specification (www-106.ibm.com/developerworks/library/ws-trust). The STS is a trust service that can be used to outsource the complexity of public key infrastructure. The credential validator communicates credentials to the STS, which performs the validation and returns the result.

4 Demo Scenario

A bookshop scenario has been developed using the Trust-Serv platform. The scenario involves an online bookshop and a requester, Alice. The scenario works as follows: Alice invokes an operation of the bookshop service to buy a book. The trust negotiation controller of the bookshop service intercepts the request and initiates a trust negotiation with Alice's trust negotiation controller. Later, the provider deploys a new policy, and the trust negotiation with Alice is migrated to this new policy. We will demonstrate (i) how to define a trust negotiation policy for the bookshop service, (ii) how to perform trust negotiations both automatically and manually, and (iii) how to migrate ongoing trust negotiations to new policies using strategies.

Defining a trust negotiation policy. Firstly, we will demonstrate how to create a trust negotiation policy using the modeler. We will define a policy for the provider service, as shown in Figure 2. However, before the roles may be mapped to the states, the roles must first be created. We will show how this is achieved in the trust negotiation modeler. We will also show how credentials are mapped to roles. By default, the credentials are stored in plain XML files, so there is no need to deploy a DBMS purely for the purpose of supporting trust negotiation. However, support for a DBMS may be configured if desired.

Defining transition conditions based on our authorization abstractions are achieved in separate windows, as shown in the lower right-hand corner of Figure 2. Once the definition of the policy is complete, we will show how it is converted into control rules and how the control rules are deployed to the provider's container.

Performing trust negotiations. Once the provider's container is ready, we will deploy a requester service called Alice. Alice has her own Web service with its own trust negotiation policy and container, and her service will attempt to invoke operations of the provider service.

For the purpose of the demonstration, we have developed *trust negotiation monitors*. These monitors

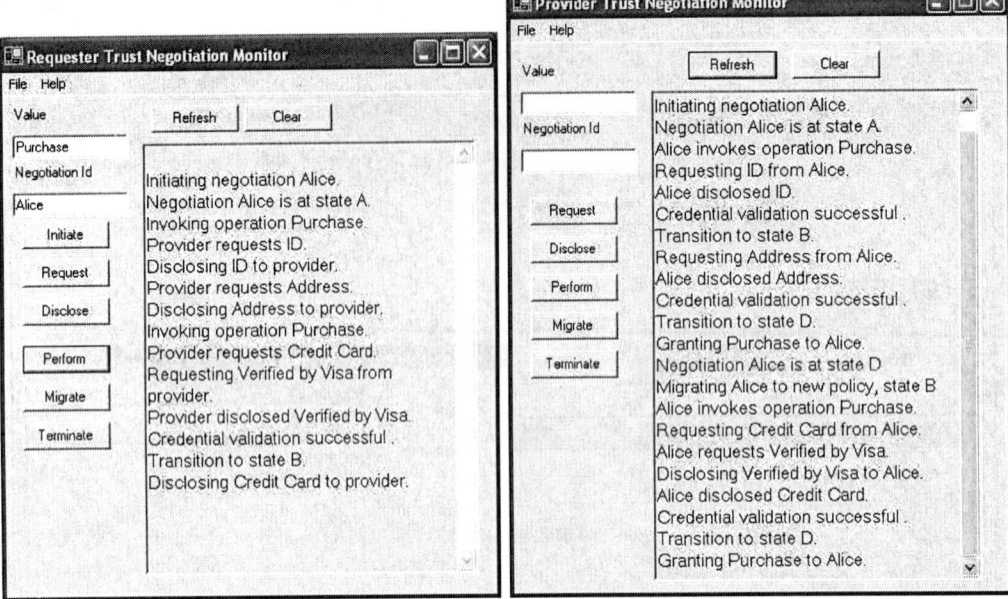

Figure 3: Alice invokes the `Purchase` operation twice, first according to policy *P.I*, then according to *P.F*. The window on the left shows Alice's trust negotiation monitor, while the window on the right is the provider's monitor. Since Alice's trust negotiation was migrated to state B in the new provider policy *P.F* after the first invocation of the `Purchase` operation, she has to disclose her `Credit Card` for the second invocation.

may be deployed by the requesters and the providers, and they show the progress of the negotiation, including all the messages sent between the controllers of the requester and the provider. In addition to monitoring the trust negotiations, the monitors also permit both the requester and the provider to negotiate manually, by invoking trust negotiation operations on each others' controllers. Figure 3 shows both the requester's monitor and the provider's monitor.

Alice starts by invoking the `Purchase` operation of the provider service. When she sends the invocation, her container deploys a trust negotiation controller instance to handle this trust negotiation. Alice's invocation is intercepted by the provider's container, which similarly spawns a controller instance to deal with Alice. The controller instances send requests and responses back and forth according to the policies of both the requester service and the provider service. In the provider's monitor, we can see when the requester service (Alice) enters a new state. Finally, Alice has negotiated sufficient trust, and her invocation of the `Purchase` operation is forwarded to the provider service, which sends its reply (Figure 3).

Migrating trust negotiations. At this point, the provider decides to change its policy from the one shown in the upper window of Figure 2 to the one in the lower window. For Alice, this requires a different credential to be disclosed to invoke the `Purchase` operation, a credential Alice has not yet disclosed. The provider also defines a strategy selection policy to appropriately migrate all existing trust negotiations. As a result of the policy update, Alice's trust negotiation instance is migrated from state D in the old policy to state B in the new policy, and her membership in the `Buyer` role is deactivated (Figure 2).

Alice then attempts to invoke the `Purchase` operation again. However, due to the migration of her trust negotiation instance at the provider, she no longer has access to this operation. Her trust negotiation then resumes, and the provider requests that she discloses her `Credit Card` to continue. Upon disclosing this credential, Alice is again able to invoke the `Purchase` operation (Figure 3).

In a more complex scenario we will deploy multiple requesters and show how a different migration strategy may be applied for each trust negotiation instance.

References

[1] D. Ferraiolo et al. Proposed NIST Standard for Role-Based Access Control. *ACM Trans. Information and System Security*, 4(3), Aug. 2001.

[2] M. P. Papazoglou and D. Georgakopoulos. Service-Oriented Computing. *Comm. ACM*, 46(10), 2003.

[3] Q. Z. Sheng et al. SELF-SERV: A Platform for Rapid Composition of Web Services in a Peer-to-Peer Environment. In *Proc. VLDB*, Aug. 2002.

[4] H. Skogsrud, B. Benatallah, and F. Casati. TrustServ: Model-Driven Lifecycle Management of Trust Negotiation Policies for Web Services. In *Proc. 13th World Wide Web Conf.*, May 2004.

Green Query Optimization: Taming Query Optimization Overheads through Plan Recycling

Parag Sarda Jayant R. Haritsa*

Database Systems Lab, SERC/CSA
Indian Institute of Science, Bangalore 560012, INDIA.

Abstract

PLASTIC [1] is a recently-proposed tool to help query optimizers significantly amortize optimization overheads through a technique of plan recycling. The tool groups similar queries into clusters and uses the optimizer-generated plan for the cluster representative to execute all future queries assigned to the cluster. An earlier demo [2] had presented a basic prototype implementation of PLASTIC. We have now significantly extended the scope, useability, and efficiency of PLASTIC, by incorporating a variety of new features, including an enhanced query feature vector, variable-sized clustering and a decision-tree-based query classifier. The demo of the upgraded PLASTIC tool is shown on commercial database platforms (IBM DB2 and Oracle 9i).

1 Introduction

Query optimization is a computationally intensive process, especially for complex queries. Recently, in [1], we presented a tool called PLASTIC (PLAn Selection Through Incremental Clustering), that can be used by query optimizers to amortize the optimization overheads through a technique of "plan recycling". Specifically, PLASTIC groups similar queries into clusters and uses the optimizer-generated plan for the cluster representative to execute all future queries assigned to the cluster. Queries are characterized by a feature vector that captures both query structures and statistics, and query similarity is evaluated using a distance function on these feature vectors. Experiments with a variety of queries (based on the TPC-H benchmark [5]) on a commercial optimizer showed that PLAS-

TIC predicts the correct plan choice in most cases, thereby providing significantly improved query optimization times. Further, even when errors were made, only marginal additional execution costs were incurred due to the sub-optimal plan choices.

Apart from the obvious advantage of speeding up optimization time, PLASTIC also improves query execution efficiency because optimizers can now always run at their highest optimization level – the cost of such optimization is amortized over all future queries that reuse these plans. Further, the benefits of "plan hints", a common technique for influencing optimizer plan choices for specific queries, automatically percolate to the entire set of queries that are associated with this plan. Lastly, since the assignment of queries to clusters is based on database statistics, the plan choice for a given query is *adaptive* to the current state of the database.

An earlier demo [2] had presented a basic prototype implementation of PLASTIC. We have, in the interim period, significantly extended the scope, useability, and efficiency of PLASTIC, by incorporating a host of new features, including:

- variable-sized clustering to match volatility in plan space;
- integration of a decision tree classifier for fast cluster identification;
- increased scope for query matching across resources and schemas; augmented feature vector to account for table access paths and organizations, as also index types
- computation and incorporation of cost estimations in plan generation;
- automated mechanisms for creating and visualizing integrated "plan-cost diagrams", which enumerate the plans chosen by the optimizer over the query space, and show the associated costs; and
- a plan analyzer module for comparing plan choices within and across database platforms.

In this demo, we present a walk-through of the upgraded PLASTIC tool, and explain how it helps to (a) significantly amortize the overheads of query optimization, and (b) serve

---

*Contact Author: haritsa@dsl.serc.iisc.ernet.in

Permission to copy without fee all or part of this material is granted provided that the copies are not made or distributed for direct commercial advantage, the VLDB copyright notice and the title of the publication and its date appear, and notice is given that copying is by permission of the Very Large Data Base Endowment. To copy otherwise, or to republish, requires a fee and/or special permission from the Endowment.

**Proceedings of the 30th VLDB Conference,
Toronto, Canada, 2004**

as a research, educational and administrative tool for understanding the intricacies of query plan generation. The demo is hosted on commercial database platforms (IBM DB2 and Oracle 9i).

2 Overview of PLASTIC

The well-known inherent costs of query optimization are compounded by the fact that a query submitted to the database system is typically optimized afresh, providing no opportunity to amortize these overheads over prior optimizations. While current commercial query optimizers do provide facilities for reusing execution plans (e.g. "stored outlines" in Oracle 9i [6]), the query matching is extremely restrictive – only if the incoming query has a close *textual resemblance* with one of the stored queries is the associated plan re-used to execute the new query.

Our recently-proposed PLASTIC tool [1] attempts to significantly increase the scope of plan reuse. It is based on the observation that even queries which differ in projection, selection and join predicates, as also in the base tables themselves, may still have identical *plan templates* – that is, they share a common database operator tree, although the specific inputs to these operators could be different. By identifying such similarities in the plan space, we can materially improve the utility of plan cacheing.

PLASTIC captures these similarities by characterizing queries in terms of a feature vector that includes structural attributes such as the number of tables and joins in the query, as well as statistical quantities such as the sizes of the tables participating in the query. Using a distance function defined on these feature vectors, queries are grouped into clusters, which are built incrementally. Each cluster has a representative for whom the template of the optimizer-generated execution plan is persistently stored, and this plan template is used to execute all future queries assigned to the cluster. In short, PLASTIC recycles plan templates based on the expectation that its clustering mechanism is likely to assign an execution plan identical to what the optimizer would have produced on the same query.

A block-level diagram of the PLASTIC architecture is shown in Figure 1. The user query is first processed by the *Feature Vector Extractor* which also accesses the system catalogs and obtains the information required to produce the feature vector. The *SimilarityCheck* module establishes whether this feature vector has a sufficiently close match with any of the cluster representatives in the *Query Cluster Database*. If a match is found (solid lines in Figure 1), the plan template for the matching cluster representative is accessed from the *Plan Template Database*. The plan template is converted into a complete plan by the *Plan Generator* module, which fills in the operator inputs based on the specifics of the current query.

On the other hand, if no matching cluster is found (dashed lines in Figure 1), the Query Optimizer is invoked in the traditional manner and its output plan is used to execute the query. This plan is also passed to the *Plan Template Generator* which converts the plan into its template

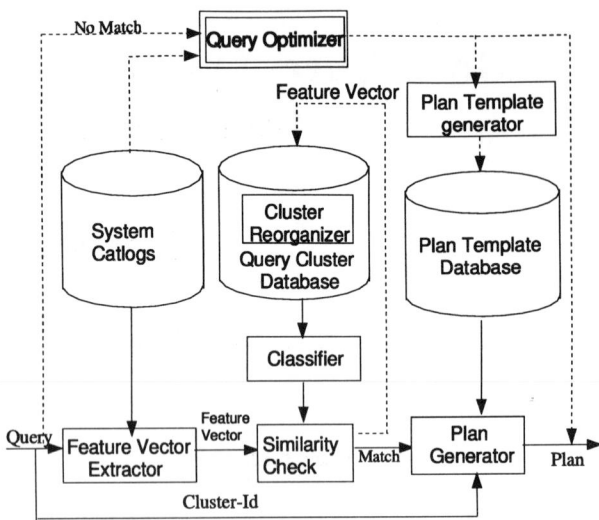

Figure 1: The PLASTIC Architecture

representation for storage in the *Plan Template Database*. Concurrently, the query feature vector is stored in the *Query Cluster Database*, as a new cluster representative.

3 New Features of PLASTIC

A basic prototype implementation of PLASTIC was demonstrated earlier in [2]. In this section, we describe in detail the new features of PLASTIC that are highlighted in the current demo. These new features significantly extend the scope, useability, and efficiency of PLASTIC, as explained below.

Variable-Sized Clustering. PLASTIC originally implemented *fixed-size* clusters, resulting in the twin problems of insufficient clusters in the *high-volatility* (rapid changes in plan choices) regions of the plan space and redundant clusters in the *low-volatility* (gradual changes in plan choices) regions. We have now incorporated *variable-sized* clustering in PLASTIC, providing several small-sized clusters in the high-volatility region and a few large-sized clusters in the low-volatility region. Our scheme is based on the observation that the high-volatility region is typically present in the highly-selective region of the plan space. Therefore, we have modified the distance function, used to compare similarities between queries, such that the cluster size thresholds are small in the highly-selective regions, and large in the less-selective regions – details are available in [3].

A sample output of variable-sized clustering for a TPC-H-based *query template*[1] is shown in Figure 2. Here, the axes represents the selectivities of a pair of the participating relations, namely PART and PARTSUPP, and the dots represent the cluster representatives. Our initial experimental results indicate that variable clustering can reduce plan prediction errors by almost 50 percent [3].

---

[1] A query template represents a query in which some or all of the constants in the where-clause predicates have been replaced by bind variables.

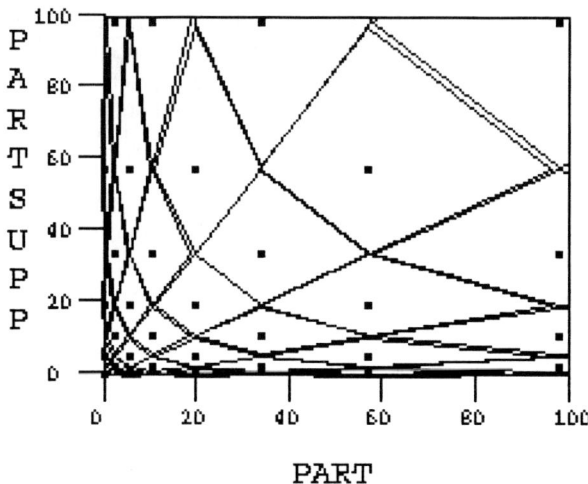

Figure 2: Variable-Sized clustering

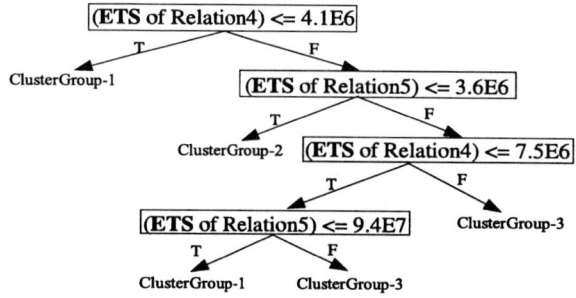

Figure 3: Classifier Module Output

Decision-Tree Classifier. In the original tool, identifying the matching cluster (if any) for the new query, was achieved by comparing the new query with the cluster representatives until either a similar representative was found, or all were found to be dis-similar. This process can become computationally expensive when a large number of clusters are present, as would often be the case. To hasten the process of cluster identification, we have now incorporated a new classifier module into the PLASTIC architecture (see Figure 1), which operates on the clusters in the database, after grouping them based on plan commonality – that is, clusters sharing the same plan are grouped together and a classifier is built on these groups. Specifically, the popular C 5.0 [7] decision-tree classifier has been integrated into our prototype.

To optimize the grouping process, initially the plan template of each query representative is traversed in post-order and an MD5 hash signature of this traversal is computed. Subsequently, these signatures, rather than the plans themselves, are compared to decide plan commonality among clusters. Such grouping significantly reduces the number of class labels in the cluster database, and has twofold advantages: Firstly, it increases the accuracy of the classifier, and secondly, results in a decision tree of lesser height, thereby requiring lesser time for classification. Quantitatively, our experiments show that the cluster identification time reduces by an *order of magnitude*, at only a small cost in the overall matching accuracy [3]. In fact, with the classifier, the identification cost is proportional to the *heterogeneity* of the clusters, whereas in the earlier version, the cost was proportional to the *cardinality* of the clusters.

The decision tree also helps to identify the attributes of the query feature vector that have the most impact on plan choices. We expect that this information will be especially beneficial for both database administrators and query optimization researchers/students. A sample output of the classifier module is shown in Figure 3 (here, ETS refers to Effective Table Size, a query feature vector component [1]).

Increased Scope for Query Matching. Our earlier work was effective only when all the queries were on a common schema. We have now extended the PLASTIC tool to share plan templates even for queries operating on different schemas. An example of the breadth of matching is shown in Figure 4, where Query 2 is correctly identified as having the same plan template as Query 1, which is a cluster representative in the database.

```
SELECT *
FROM EMPLOYEE, EMP_ACT, EMP_PHOTO
WHERE EMPLOYEE.empno = EMP_ACT.empno
   and EMP_ACT.empno = EMP_PHOTO.empno
   and EMPLOYEE.empno > 0
   and EMP_ACT.empno  < 400
   and EMP_PHOTO.empno between 10 and 390
```
Query 1

```
SELECT EMPLOYEE.name, EMPLOYEE.project,
       EMP_RESUME.resume
FROM EMPLOYEE, EMP_ACT, EMP_RESUME
WHERE EMPLOYEE.empno = EMP_ACT.empno
   and EMP_ACT.empno = EMP_RESUME.empno
```
Query 2

Figure 4: Breadth of Matching by PLASTIC

We have also augmented the PLASTIC feature vector to take into account different *table access paths* (table scans and index scans), *table organizations* (clustered and B-tree), and *index types* (unique, cluster, and reverse).

Further, it was earlier conservatively assumed that the presence of an index on a query attribute in the cluster representative meant that it would be used and therefore a new query that lacked an index on its corresponding attribute could not be matched to this representative. The system now checks for the *actual usage* of such resources in the representative and removes it from the representative's feature vector if not used, thereby increasing the scope for query matching and plan sharing.

Including Cost Estimations in Generated Plans. The plans generated by PLASTIC were incomplete in that they did not include the associated *operator costs*, although this is a standard feature of plans generated by the optimizer. Note that the costs of the cluster representative's plan cannot be directly used for this purpose since there can be significant variation in the matched queries, although they share a common plan template. To address this issue, we have included an estimation module in the plan generator that scales and interpolates the costs of the cluster representative to reflect the costs of the new query, and includes this information in the generated plan.

Since the new query and its matched cluster representative may differ on selectivities of multiple relations, a *multivariate* strategy is required to compute the interpolated values. Currently, we have implemented first order multivariate interpolation based on barycentric coordinates [8], which has a low time complexity. Our initial experiments indicate that the interpolation is accurate to within 90 percent [3].

Automated Plan-Cost Diagram Generator. Generating a "plan diagram" [1], which is an enumeration of the plan choices of the optimizer over the query space, is a computationally expensive process since it involves firing of a large number of queries. Earlier, this diagram was constructed from scratch for each query, but we have now added a facility for persistently storing these diagrams directly in the database, from which they can be immediately retrieved at the desired time. We have also mapped these stored plan diagrams with the associated clusters, to provide better visual interfaces for generating, viewing, and reorganizing query clusters. Further, we have augmented the plan diagram, which is a qualitative picture, to include quantitative costs, thereby resulting in a combined *plan-cost* diagram. An example plan-cost diagram[2] corresponding to a TPC-H-based query, is shown in Figure 5. Note that there are eleven plan optimality regions (P1 through P11) spanning the entire selectivity spectrum on the PART and PARTSUPP relations, and the sizes of the dots indicate the relative plan costs.

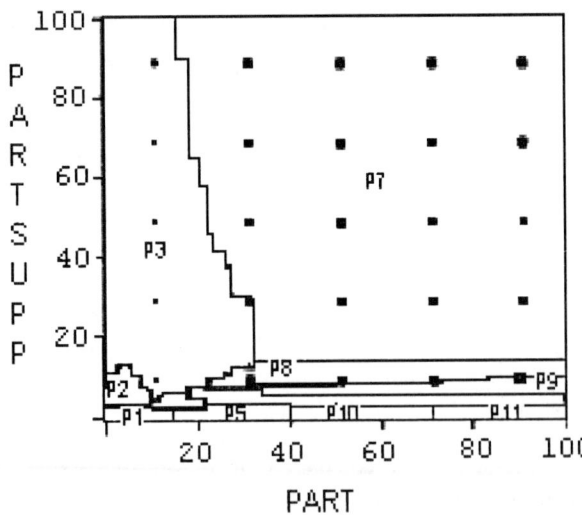

Figure 5: PLASTIC Plan-Cost Diagram

Plan Analyzer Module. A new Plan Analyzer module, intended for analyzing the specific differences between a pair of query execution plans, has been incorporated in the Plastic tool. We expect that this module will be especially beneficial for database administrators and query optimization researchers/students to help understand plan choices made by the optimizer.

The module identifies differences between plans using an adaption of the X-Diff [4] algorithm (which was proposed for computing differences between XML documents). It can be used in two ways: (a) to compare plan choices for different versions of a query on a single platform, or (b) to compare choices for the same query across database platforms. Part of a sample output of the module, showing the differences between Plan 7 and Plan 9 of Figure 5, is shown in Figure 6 (the source plans are omitted because of their complexity and size). From this figure, we can see that these two plans differ only in the access method (*index scan* versus *table scan*) for the PARTSUPP relation.

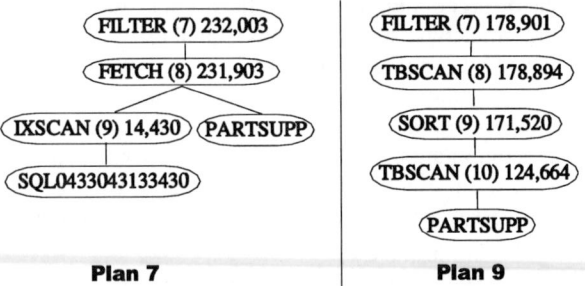

Figure 6: Plan Differences

Acknowledgements. This work was supported in part by a Swarnajayanti Fellowship from the Dept. of Science & Technology, Govt. of India. We thank Vibhuti Sengar for his technical advice.

References

[1] A. Ghosh, J. Parikh, V. Sengar and J. Haritsa, "Plan Selection based on Query Clustering", *Proc. of 28th Intl. Conf. on Very Large Data Bases (VLDB)*, August 2002.

[2] V. Sengar and J. Haritsa, "PLASTIC: Reducing Query Optimization Overheads through Plan Recycling", *Proc. of ACM SIGMOD Intl. Conf. on Management of Data*, June 2003.

[3] P. Sarda, "Green Query Optimization: Taming Query Optimization Overheads through Plan Recycling", *Master's Thesis*, CSA, Indian Institute of Science, July 2004.

[4] Y. Wang, D. DeWitt and J.Cai, "X-Diff: A Fast Change Detection Algorithm for XMLDocuments" *Proc. of 19th IEEE Intl. Conference on Data Engineering*, March 2003.

[5] http://www.tpc.org

[6] http://download-east.oracle.com/otndoc/oracle9i/ 901_doc/server.901/a87503/toc.htm

[7] http://www.rulequest.com/see5-info.html

[8] www.library.uu.nl/digiarchief/dip/diss/2003-1028-125323/appd.pdf

---

[2]The diagram is based on plan selections obtained with the IBM DB2 query optimizer.

Progressive Optimization in Action

Vijayshankar Raman   Volker Markl   David Simmen   Guy Lohman   Hamid Pirahesh

IBM Almaden Research Center
650 Harry Road
San Jose, CA 95120
U.S.A.
{ravijay,marklv,simmen,lohman,pirahesh}@us.ibm.com

Abstract

Progressive Optimization (POP) is a technique to make query plans robust, and minimize need for DBA intervention, by repeatedly re-optimizing a query during runtime if the cardinalities estimated during optimization prove to be significantly incorrect. POP works by carefully calculating validity ranges for each plan operator under which the overall plan can be optimal. POP then instruments the query plan with checkpoints that validate at runtime that cardinalities do lie within validity ranges, and re-optimizes the query otherwise. In this demonstration we showcase POP implemented for a research prototype version of IBM's DB2 DBMS, using a mix of real-world and synthetic benchmark databases and workloads. For selected queries of the workload we display the query plans with validity ranges as well as the placement of the various kinds of CHECK operators using the DB2 graphical plan explain tool. We also execute the queries, showing how and where re-optimization is triggered through the CHECK operators, the new plan generated upon re-optimization, and the extent to which previously computed intermediate results are reused.

1. Introduction

Virtually every commercial query optimizer chooses the best plan for a query using a cost model that relies heavily on accurate cardinality estimation. Cardinality estimation errors can occur due to the use of inaccurate statistics, invalid assumptions about attribute in-dependence, parameter markers, and so on. These errors can lead to substantially sub-optimal plans.

"Progressive query optimization" (POP) is an approach to make query processing more robust, and substantially reduce the need for DBA intervention to debug problem queries. POP makes query plans robust by automatically detecting and recovering from cardinality estimation errors. POP validates cardinality estimates against actual values as measured during query execution. If there is significant disagreement between estimated and actual values, execution might be stopped and re-optimization might occur. Oscillation between optimization and execution steps can occur any number of times. A re-optimization step can exploit both the actual cardinality and partial results, computed during a previous execution step. Checkpoint operators (CHECK) validate the optimizer's cardinality estimates against actual cardinalities. Each CHECK has a condition that indicates the cardinality bounds within which a plan is optimal. We compute this validity range through a sensitivity analysis of query plan operators. If the CHECK condition is violated, CHECK triggers re-optimization. POP places CHECK operators judiciously in query execution plans.

POP is implemented in a research prototype version of IBM's DB2 DBMS, and an experimental evaluation of POP using TPC-H queries as well as a real-world data base and workload showed that POP can provide speedups up to two orders of magnitude for complex OLAP queries [1].

Figure 1 depicts the control flow of POP. Upon compilation of a SQL query, the optimizer generates a variety of alternative query execution plans. Whenever

---

Permission to copy without fee all or part of this material is granted provided that the copies are not made or distributed for direct commercial advantage, the VLDB copyright notice and the title of the publication and its date appear, and notice is given that copying is by permission of the Very Large Data Base Endowment. To copy otherwise, or to republish, requires a fee and/or special permission from the Endowment
**Proceedings of the 30th VLDB Conference,
Toronto, Canada, 2004**

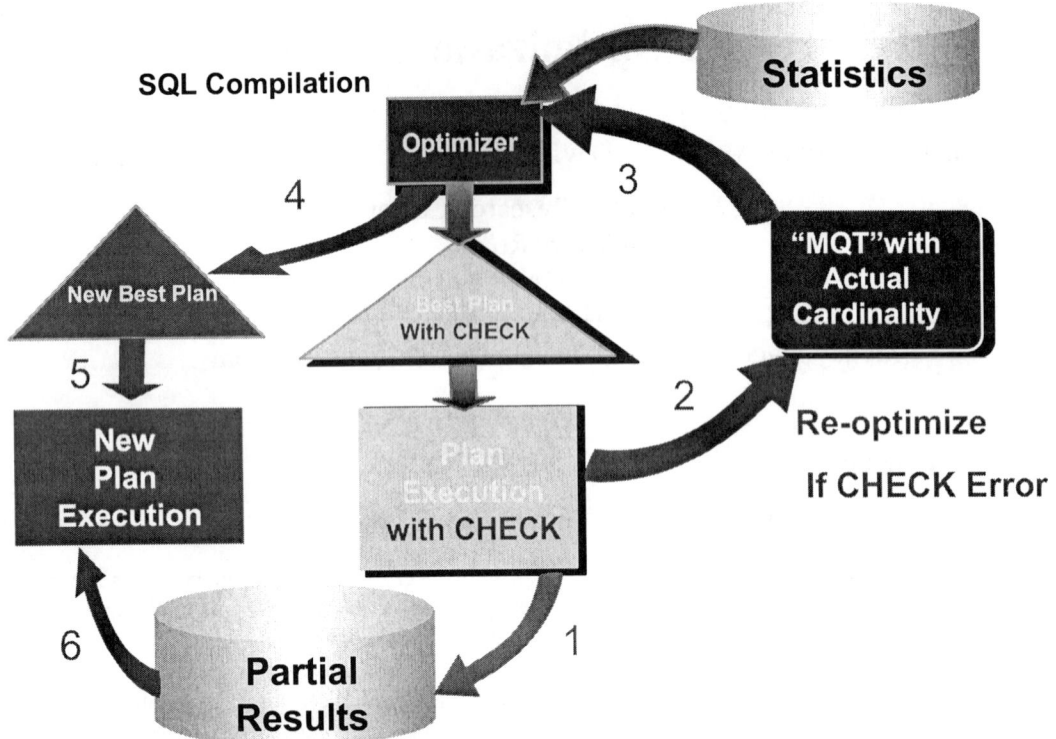

Figure 1: Overview of Progressive Optimization

one plan is pruned by another plan during optimization, POP uses a variant of the Newton-Raphson method to determine the cardinality at which the cost functions of the dominating and the dominated plan intersect. This cross-over cardinality is used to continuously refine the validity range of the optimal plan. Once the optimal plan has been determined, POP adds CHECK operators at selected points in the plan. During query runtime, these CHECKs act as safeguards to ensure that the cardinality of tuples flowing through them is indeed within the validity ranges determined during optimization.

In the Figure, step 1 shows the initial execution of the plan with the check, and the computation of intermediate results. If the validity range for any CHECK operator is violated, re-optimization is triggered (step 2), creating a materialized query table "MQT" for each intermediate result computed by the previous partial execution. The actual cardinalities of these MQTs are fed back into the optimizer (step 3), and the query is optimized again (step 4). The optimizer also generates access plans over the MQTs into its mix of possible plans, and thus has the option to reuse these pre-computed results. This second iteration (steps 5 and 6) can again employ CHECK operators and start the re-optimization cycle again, thus continuously improving the query plan over several iterations.

Further details on POP can be found in [MRS+04], available upon request for the reviewers. Further references and a discussion of related work can also be found in [MRS+04] and are omitted in this proposal in order to describe the demonstration system in more detail.

2. Demonstration

We demonstrate our implementation of POP using a research prototype version of IBM's DB2 DBMS. We show a case study with a workload of queries that are hard to optimize accurately using typical optimizer statistics such as single-column histograms. The databases we are going to use to demonstrate POP are (1) a DMV database storing cars and accidents, as well as (2) a TPC-H database. The DMV database stores tables of car models, makes, owners, accident records, and owner demographics. The main feature of this database is extensive correlation between various columns, both within and between tables. Next to these correlations, other source of error in our workloads for TPC-H and DMV are LIKE predicates and parameter markers. These errors in many cases cause the optimizer to choose a suboptimal plan. POP detects this during runtime, as the validity range for a specific part of a query plan is violated, and triggers re-optimization. In the following we describe the two major components of our demonstration: (1) the validity range computation and CHECK placement, and (2) the re-optimization of an example query.

3.1 Validity ranges and CHECK placement

The first part of our case study is to use our graphical explain tool to demonstrate validity ranges and checkpoint placement. We will use our graphical explain tool to visually navigate the query plan for each of our example queries. The query plan is shown as a tree, and clicking on tree nodes (plan operators) pops up a window with various properties of these operators. One of the properties is the validity range – the range of cardinalities flowing out of this operator under which this plan could be optimal. The span of these validity ranges denotes the robustness of these plans to cardinality errors, independent of whether we re-optimize or not. We will pick a single query, we will force alternative query plans by altering optimizer configurations, and show the validity ranges, to highlight the tradeoff between plan robustness and plan cost.

We will also use these plans to illustrate the different flavors of CHECK operators (see [MRS+04]) and the tradeoff between their risk and opportunity. Looking at the plan below a CHECK helps us gauge how much of the work below the CHECK will have to be redone upon re-optimization, and thus how risky it is. Likewise the distribution of CHECKs in the query plan shows the opportunity provided by each kind of CHECK.

3.2 Re-Optimization of an example query

The second part of our case study is the complete execution of example queries, with POP enabled. The query is initially submitted and optimized. After showing this initial query plan, we let the plan run until a validity range is violated. The execution engine outputs a warning message that cardinality estimates are highly inaccurate. Then the system automatically goes through another round of optimization. In the demo, again using the DB2 graphical explain tool, we show the new plan that has been computed during re-optimization, using the knowledge about actual cardinalities, correlations, parameter marker values, etc. learned from the previous partial execution. Figure 2 shows both the initial plan and the re-optimized plan for a query listing all lineitems for all orders placed in the 1990s against the TPC-H database:

SELECT * FROM ORDERS, LINEITEM
WHERE L_ORDERKEY = O_ORDERKEY
AND O_ORDERDATE LIKE '%199%'

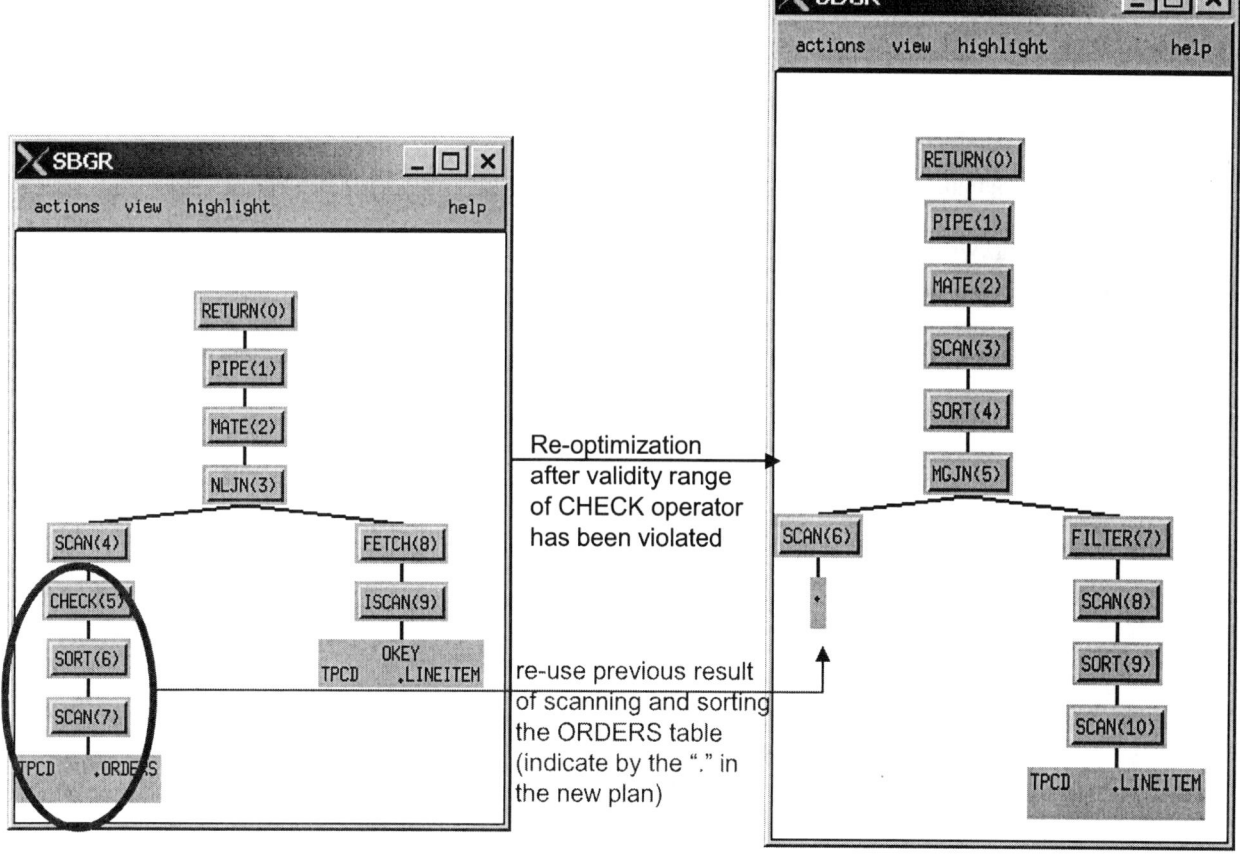

Figure 2: Comparing the Initial Plan with the Plan after Re-optimization

The initial plan for that query located at the left of Figure 2 shows that POP has placed a CHECK operator as operator number 5 into the plan to safeguard the nested-loop join (NLJN, operator 3) by ensuring that the cardinality of the outer leg of the nested loop join is within bounds. Because of the LIKE predicate, the output cardinality for the SCAN and SORT operators is highly underestimated (most of the records in the database are from the 1990s). This causes the CHECK operator to trigger re-optimization, which changes the initial plan to the plan displayed in the right part of Figure 2. Note that this plan has changed the join method from a nested-loop join (NLJN in the Figure) to a merge-join (MGJN in the Figure). Also note that the new plan re-uses the intermediate result generated by the partial execution of the initial plan. This intermediate result (indicated by a "dot" in the new plan in the right part of Figure 2) contains a subset of the ORDERS table after the application of the LIKE predicate and is already sorted by ORDERKEY.

This query runs orders of magnitude faster with POP than it would when continuing along the initial plan, as we also show in our demonstration by running the query both with and without POP enabled.

For the demonstration of POP on the DMV database, most estimation errors are not due to like predicates, but due to correlations within and between tables, parameter markers, and user-defined functions. All of these sources of errors can trigger re-optimization because of a violation of the validity ranges. Our demonstration also includes showing the robustness POP adds to query optimization for these sources of errors.

3. Conclusions

Progressive Optimization (POP) is a major step towards making query optimization a dynamic process, where the DBMS continually adjusts the plan based on a closed feedback loop between the runtime and the optimizer. Our demonstration shows the effectiveness and efficiency of POP.

We illustrate where CHECK operators are placed in query plans in a research prototype version of IBM's DB2 DBMS. We also show the conditions under which re-optimization takes place, using both a real-world DMV database and the TPC-H database. POP makes query plans more robust to estimation errors; and speeds-up query execution by orders of magnitude for some realistic queries.

4. References

MRS+04   V. Markl, V. Raman, D. Simmen, G. Lohman, H. Pirahesh. Progressive Optimization for Robustness in Query Processing. SIGMOD 2004.

This full paper has detailed references to other related work.

CORDS: Automatic Generation of Correlation Statistics in DB2

Ihab F. Ilyas[1] Volker Markl[2] Peter J. Haas[2] Paul G. Brown[2] Ashraf Aboulnaga[2]

[1] University of Waterloo
200 University Avenue
Waterloo, Ontario N2L 3G1, Canada
ilyas@uwaterloo.ca

[2] IBM Almaden Research Center
650 Harry Road, K55/B1
San Jose, CA, 95139
marklv,phaas,pbrown1,aashraf@us.ibm.com

Abstract

When query optimizers erroneously assume that database columns are statistically independent, they can underestimate the selectivities of conjunctive predicates by orders of magnitude. Such underestimation often leads to drastically suboptimal query execution plans. We demonstrate CORDS, an efficient and scalable tool for automatic discovery of correlations and soft functional dependencies between column pairs. We apply CORDS to real, synthetic, and TPC-H benchmark data, and show that CORDS discovers correlations in an efficient and scalable manner. The output of CORDS can be visualized graphically, making CORDS a useful mining and analysis tool for database administrators. CORDS ranks the discovered correlated column pairs and recommends to the optimizer a set of statistics to collect for the "most important" of the pairs. Use of these statistics speeds up processing times by orders of magnitude for a wide range of queries.

1 Introduction

CORDS is a data-driven tool that automatically discovers correlations and soft functional dependencies (FDs) between pairs of columns and, based on these relationships, recommends a set of statistics for the query optimizer to maintain. By *correlations*, we mean general statistical dependencies, not merely approximate linear relationships. By a *soft* FD between columns C_1 and C_2, we mean a generalization of the classical

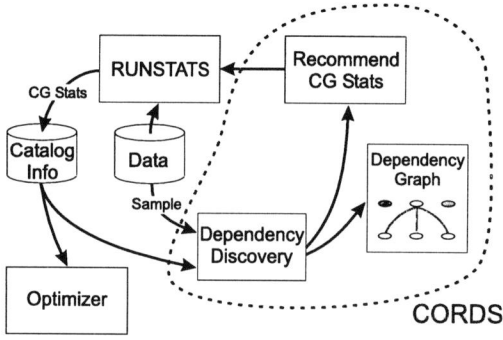

Figure 1: Role of CORDS in query optimization.

notion of a *hard* FD in which the value of C_1 completely determines the value of C_2. In a soft FD (denoted by $C_1 \Rightarrow C_2$), the value of C_1 determines the value of C_2 not with certainty, but merely with high probability. CORDS focuses on column pairs because this greatly simplifies the algorithms, and experiments have shown that the marginal benefit of capturing n-way dependencies for $n > 2$ is relatively small. The column pairs examined by CORDS can be in the same table or different tables. We briefly outline the CORDS system below; details may be found in [1]. In developing CORDS, we have found that algorithmic simplicity and judicious use of sampling can lead to efficient and highly scalable self-management algorithms that are suitable for immediate incorporation into commercial database systems.

2 CORDS Overview

Figure 1 illustrates the role of CORDS in DB2 query optimization. CORDS uses system-catalog statistics that are collected by the DB2 RUNSTATS utility together with samples of the base data to discover dependencies between column pairs. The "most important" column pairs are identified and RUNSTATS is instructed to collect *column group* (CG) statistics on each recommended column pair; these statistics are then stored in the system catalog and available to the query optimizer.

CORDS first searches for column pairs that are likely to be related in an interesting and useful way by systematically enumerating candidate pairs and simultaneously pruning unpromising candidates using a flexible set of heuristics.[1] Pruning rules can include constraints on allowable data types, constraints on statistical properties of the columns, constraints based on schema information, constraints based on workload information, and so forth. CORDS also uses catalog statistics to identify certain "trivial" instances of correlation and, simultaneously, to eliminate certain columns from further consideration. For each surviving candidate, CORDS collects a sample of value-pairs from the columns. CORDS then analyzes the number of distinct values in the sampled columns to test for a soft FD. If no FD is found, CORDS then applies a robust chi-squared analysis to test for statistical dependence. As shown in [1], the required sample size for the chi-squared analysis is essentially independent of the database size, which is why CORDS is scalable to very large databases.

In more detail, CORDS discovers the following properties and relationships:

- *Trivial Cases*: Prior to candidate generation, CORDS examines the system catalog to identify two trivial cases: "soft" keys and "trivial" columns. A *soft* key is "almost" a key w.r.t the number of distinct values. A soft key is trivially statistically correlated with every other column in the table because a value from that column, with high probability, determines the row, and hence the value in any other column. A *trivial* column is a single-valued or NULL column. The value in any row of such a column is trivially "determined" by the values in any other column, leading to spurious correlations.

- *Soft FDs*: The *strength* of a soft FD $C_1 \Rightarrow C_2$ is computed as $|C_1|/|C_1, C_2|$, where $|C_1|$ is the number of distinct values in column C_1 and $|C_1, C_2|$ is the number of distinct value-pairs for columns C_1 and C_2. This strength is always less than or equal to 1, with a strength of 1 indicating a hard functional dependency. CORDS estimates $|C_1|$ and $|C_1, C_2|$, and hence the strength, from the sample and declares the existence of a soft FD if the estimated strength is greater than a prespecified value.

- *Correlations*: Column pairs in this category are those pairs for which CORDS does not detect a soft FD but does detect statistical dependence using the sample-based chi-squared analysis.

The output of CORDS may optionally be displayed as a dependency graph, facilitating database design and data mining. In any case, CORDS recommends to the optimizer sets of CG statistics to maintain. Such recommendations are necessary because, as we show in our demonstration, real-world databases typically contain a very large number of correlations and soft FDs. The overhead of collecting and maintaining statistics for every correlated column pair would outweigh any benefits resulting from a better choice of query plans. The CORDS recommendation algorithm ranks the discovered soft FDs based on their strengths and the discovered correlations on their "benefit" to the query optimizer. A useful measure of benefit is the magnitude of the adjustment factor used by the optimizer to correct selectivity estimates that are based on faulty independence assumptions when CG statistics are available. The larger the adjustment factor, the more serious the estimation error that is corrected. Our demonstration focuses on a simple CG statistic, namely $|C_1, C_2|$ as defined above, and on simple conjunctive predicates of the form "$C_1 = x$ AND $C_2 = y$." A naive estimate of the selectivity for such a predicate, assuming uniform data frequencies and independence between the columns, is $1/|C_1| \cdot 1/|C_2|$, and the adjustment factor that corrects for a faulty independence assumption is $|C_1||C_2|/|C_1, C_2|$. Although this adjustment factor does not correct for a faulty uniformity assumption, we have found in practice that correcting for a faulty independence assumption usually eliminates most of the error.

3 Demonstration

Using synthetic, real-world, and benchmark databases, we demonstrate the application of CORDS and show how CORDS can improve query performance by orders of magnitude. We run CORDS on top of DB2. The scenario of the demonstration for a given database is as follows:

1. We run CORDS using a set of parameters that determine, e.g., the scope of correlation discovery (intra-table or inter-table) and the candidate pruning heuristics.

2. CORDS outputs the discovered correlations and soft FDs in the form of dependency graphs, such as the dependency graphs shown in Figure 2 for the tables in the TPC-H database. Nodes (ovals in Figure 2) correspond to columns and arcs correspond to correlations or soft FDs.[2] The thick-

---

[1] Technically, a candidate consists of a pair of columns (C_1, C_2) along with a *pairing rule* that specifies which particular C_1 values get paired with which particular C_2 values to form the set of potentially correlated value-pairs. When the columns lie in the same table and each C_1 value is paired with the C_2 value in the same row, the pairing rule is trivial; when the columns lie in different tables, the pairing rule corresponds to a join predicate between the tables. Self-joins are also permitted.

[2] The name CORDS was partially inspired by the visual "cords" that connect correlated columns.

ness or color of the arcs can be used to show the strength of the relationships. For example, the thickness of an arc that represents a soft FD can be an increasing function of the estimated strength. Soft keys and trivial columns are indicated by specified node colors.

3. We apply the CORDS statistics-recommendation algorithm that ranks the discovered correlations and soft FDs based on their benefit to the optimizer. For example, Table 1 gives the ranking of the discovered correlations in a synthetic database of car-accident data. Although CORDS discovers a correlation between the two columns ACCIDENTS.Driver and ACCIDENTS.Damage (last row in the table), the corresponding adjustment factor equals 1. CORDS does not recommend collection of statistics for this pair of columns, since the presence of such statistics would not change any optimizer cardinality estimates. On the other hand, collecting statistics on the first pair of columns in Table 1 adjusts optimizer estimates by a factor of roughly 3070.

4. We collect CG statistics based on the CORDS recommendations and we contrast the optimizer estimates for several queries both with and without these statistics. We show the actual query execution plan in each case, augmented by the actual and estimated cardinality for each operator. Figure 3 displays such a pair of execution plans for the following query:

```
SELECT o.Name, a.Driver
FROM OWNER o, CAR c, DEMOGRAPHICS d, ACCIDENTS a
WHERE
   c.OwnerID = o.ID AND o.ID = d.OwnerID AND
   c.ID = a.ID AND c.Make = 'Mazda' AND
   c.Model = '323' AND o.Country3 = 'EG' AND
   o.City = 'Cairo' AND d.Age < 30;
```

In the figure, actual cardinalities (i.e., number of rows processed) are displayed above each query operator and estimated cardinalities are displayed below. E.g., in the original query plan without CG statistics (left side), the upper circled index scan processes 14,222 rows, the number of rows that satisfy the predicate c.make = 'Mazda' AND c.model = '323'. The optimizer underestimates this number by almost a factor of 20 as 753.723. Using the CG statistics recommended by CORDS, the optimizer improves this estimate to roughly within a factor of 2, as can be seen in the modified plan on the right. Similarly, the optimizer originally underestimates the number of rows satisfying the predicate o.country3 = 'EG' AND o.city = 'Cairo' by a factor of almost 500 (see the lower circled index scan on the left). Using CG statistics, the optimizer reduces the error to a factor of about 2 in the modified query plan.

The modified plan that is based on the new statistics is orders of magnitude faster than the original.

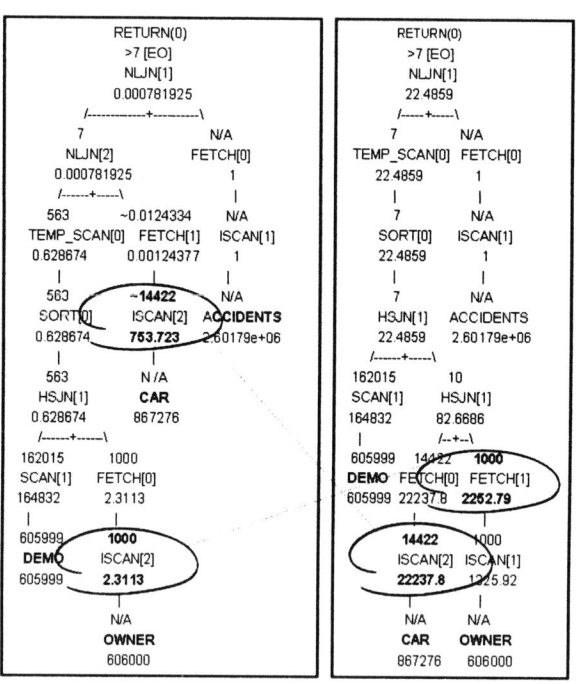

Figure 3: Query execution plans before and after collecting statistics on correlated columns.

The databases that we use are as follows.

- *Synthetic Data*: The *Accidents* database is synthetically generated and represents car-accident records. When generating the database, we created a predetermined set of correlations by manipulating the data distributions. The database also contains a number of natural hard and soft FDs, e.g., Model ⇒ Make in the CAR table.

- *Benchmarking Data*: The *TPC-H* benchmark dataset was not explicitly designed to have specified correlations between different columns. CORDS can discover hidden correlations that may not be known to the database designer or administrator.

- *Real-world Data*: We apply CORDS to several real-world databases. These include a subset of the *Census* database and the *Auto* database, which contains motor vehicle information and comprises over 20 tables and hundreds of columns.

References

[1] I. F. Ilyas, V. Markl, P. J. Haas, P. G. Brown, and A. Aboulnaga. CORDS: Automatic discovery of correlations and soft functional dependencies. In *Proc. 2004 ACM SIGMOD*, 2004.

First Column	Second Column	Adj. Factor
DEMOGRAPHICS.Salary	DEMOGRAPHICS.Assets	3069.69
CAR.Color	CAR.OwnerID	311.25
DEMOGRAPHICS.Assets	DEMOGRAPHICS.Age	77.71
ACCIDENTS.CarID	ACCIDENTS.Year	30.06
CAR.Model	CAR.OwnerID	27.14
CAR.Year	CAR.Color	21.80
CAR.Make	CAR.OwnerID	16.00
CAR.Model	CAR.Color	14.91
CAR.Make	CAR.Color	9.15
CAR.Model	CAR.Year	2.31
CAR.Year	CAR.Make	1.88
ACCIDENTS.Driver	ACCIDENTS.With	1.13
ACCIDENTS.Driver	ACCIDENTS.SeatBeltOn	1.00
ACCIDENTS.Damage	ACCIDENTS.With	1.00
ACCIDENTS.Driver	ACCIDENTS.Damage	1.00

Table 1: Discovered correlations ranked by adjustment factor

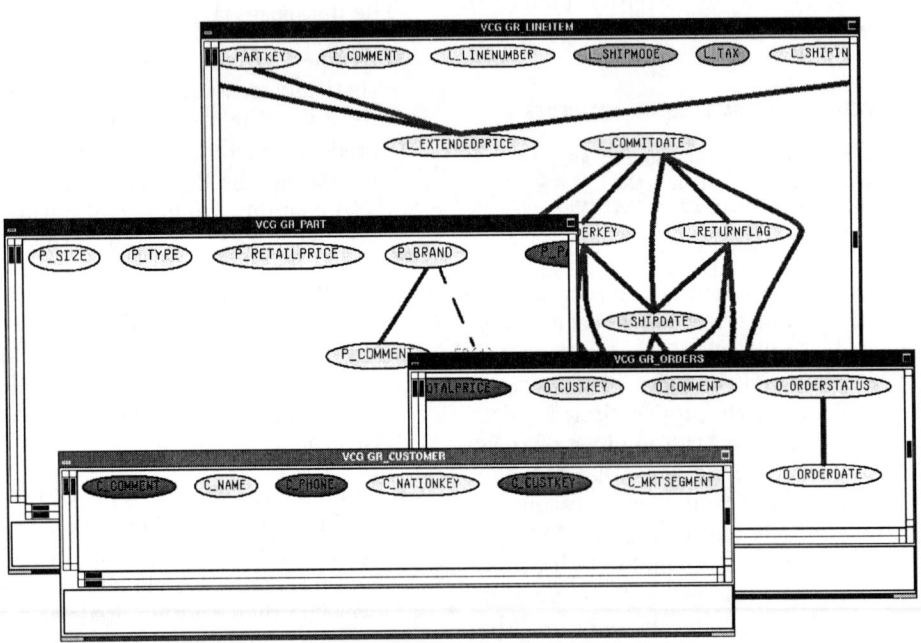

Figure 2: Snapshot of the automatically generated dependency graphs for TPC-H (sample size 10,000 records).

CHICAGO: A Test and Evaluation Environment for Coarse-Grained Optimization

Tobias Kraft

Holger Schwarz

Institute of Parallel and Distributed Systems
University of Stuttgart
Universitätsstraße 38, 70569 Stuttgart, Germany
{Tobias.Kraft, Holger.Schwarz}@informatik.uni-stuttgart.de

Abstract

Relational OLAP tools and other database applications generate sequences of SQL statements that are sent to the database server as result of a single information request issued by a user. Coarse-Grained Optimization is a practical approach for the optimization of such statement sequences based on rewrite rules. In this demonstration we present the CHICAGO test and evaluation environment that allows to assess the effectiveness of rewrite rules and control strategies. It includes a lightweight heuristic optimizer that modifies a given statement sequence using a small and variable set of rewrite rules.

1. Introduction

Many applications, such as information retrieval systems, search engines, and business intelligence tools embed query generators. Some of these applications produce more than one query as a result of an information request that is defined by a user interacting with a graphical user interface. Statement sequences produced by query generators are typically tuned to a certain target database system. However, the response time of such an information request is often far from optimal. One alternative is to rewrite the statement sequence into an equivalent sequence such that the database system consumes far less resources. This is exactly the concept of Coarse-Grained Optimization (CGO). It complements the conventional query optimization phase. The associated rewrite rules exploit the fact that statements of a sequence are correlated. It is possible, e.g., to combine similar statements into a single one, or to move predicates from one statement to a dependent one. An optimizer prototype is introduced in [3].

The CGO approach is not tied to a fixed set of rewrite rules. Several control strategies that determine how these rules are applied to a given statement sequence are possible. Different rulesets and control strategies as well as combinations of them have to be assessed.

Our CGO prototype is based on the results and experience of state-of-the-art optimizer technology as described for example in [2, 5]. Based on few but effective heuristic rewrite rules it produces several SQL statements that are less complex for a single-query optimizer. The ruleset and the control strategies of the CGO optimizer can easily be modified and extended. This allows to flexibly control the optimization process and to identify the appropriate ruleset and control strategy for a given environment.

To further refine the CGO approach, it is crucial to investigate the effectiveness of rewrite rules and control strategies in different settings. The CHICAGO system provides a test and evaluation environment that supports this assessment. The flexibility that is needed is achieved by extending the CGO prototype with additional tools. They allow to define different test scenarios and to measure the effectiveness of several options for combinations of rewrite rules and control strategies in the CGO approach.

In the following section we provide supplementary details regarding the CGO approach. The architecture and the main components of the CHICAGO system are introduced in Section 3. More information on modules that will be demonstrated is provided in Section 4. The paper concludes with remarks on future work.

Permission to copy without fee all or part of this material is granted provided that the copies are not made or distributed for direct commercial advantage, the VLDB copyright notice and the title of the publication and its date appear, and notice is given that copying is by permission of the Very Large Data Base Endowment. To copy otherwise, or to republish, requires a fee and/or special permission from the Endowment

**Proceedings of the 30th VLDB Conference,
Toronto, Canada, 2004**

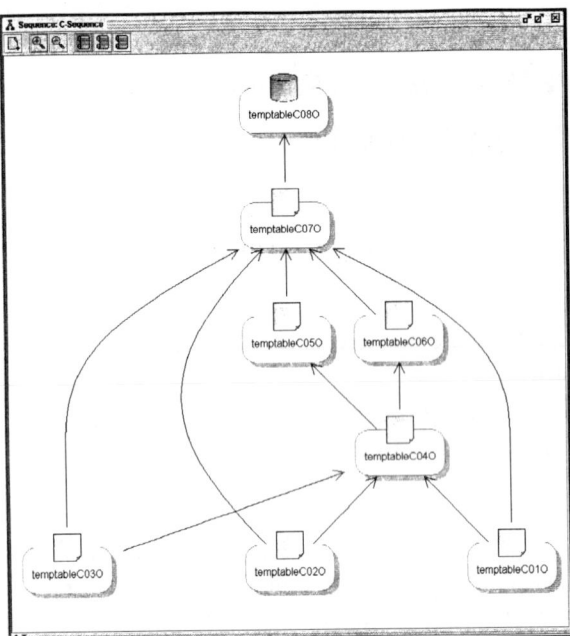

Figure 1: Screenshot of a dependency graph

2. Coarse Grained Optimization

Coarse-grained optimization is a rule-based approach to optimize sequences of SQL statements. The sequences we focus on consist of:

- CREATE TABLE statements that create tables to hold intermediate results or the final result of an information request.
- INSERT statements with a *query* as body that computes an intermediate or the final result by accessing base tables as well as tables storing intermediate results of the sequence. There is exactly one INSERT statement for each table created by a statement sequence.
- DROP TABLE statements that remove tables storing intermediate results.

Such sequences can become very complex. Figure 1 shows a sequence as a dependency graph where each node represents a base table or a statement triple consisting of a CREATE TABLE, INSERT and DROP TABLE statement. This graph shows the direct dependencies and therewith the dataflow between the queries.

We have identified three classes of rewrite rules that can be applied to such statement sequences:

- rules based on similarity among queries,
- rules based on dependencies among queries, and
- rules restricted to a single query.

Figure 2 shows the WhereToGroup rewrite rule being applied to parts of a sample sequence. It belongs to the first class of rewrite rules, because queries *q1* and *q2* only differ in a single predicate of the WHERE clause that compares the same attribute to different constant values. Therefore, these queries can be merged into a new query *q12* that computes and stores the result of both queries. The queries that depend on the result of *q1* and *q2* have to be extended by a predicate that filters out the result of *q1* and *q2*. These optimizations are similar to rewrite rules used in conventional single-query optimization [4] as well as in multi-query optimization [1, 6].

A control strategy is needed to decide on the rewrite rules that should be applied to a given statement sequence. In our prototype we use a priority-based control strategy. The static priority scheme assigns a priority to each rule of the ruleset. The priority assignment is based on experience gained by experiments. If several rules could be applied to the same sequence, the rule of highest priority is picked.

More information on the CGO approach and the optimizer prototype can be found in [3].

```
INSERT INTO q1(a, sum_b)      INSERT INTO q2(a, avg_b)
  SELECT  t.a, SUM(s.b)         SELECT  t.a, AVG(s.b)
  FROM    s, t                  FROM    s, t
  WHERE   t.c = 1               WHERE   t.c = 2
    AND   s.d = t.d               AND   s.d = t.d
  GROUP BY t.a                  GROUP BY t.a

           ↓                             ↓

INSERT INTO q3(a)             INSERT INTO q4(a)
  SELECT  a                     SELECT  a
  FROM    q1                    FROM    q2
  WHERE   sum_b > 100           WHERE   avg_b > 100
```

⇓

```
    INSERT INTO q12(a, c, sum_b, avg_b)
      SELECT  t.a, t.c, SUM(s.b), AVG(s.b)
      FROM    s, t
      WHERE   t.c IN (1, 2)
        AND   s.d = t.d
      GROUP BY t.a, t.c
```

```
          ↙                             ↘

INSERT INTO q3(a)             INSERT INTO q4(a)
  SELECT  a                     SELECT  a
  FROM    q12                   FROM    q12
  WHERE   sum_b > 100           WHERE   avg_b > 100
    AND   c = 1                   AND   c = 2
```

Figure 2: Example of a rule application

3. System Architecture

Figure 3 shows the overall architecture of the CHICAGO system. A brief description of its components and some implementation issues are provided below.

3.1 Control and Presentation Module

The whole process of generating test cases, optimizing statement sequences and running these sequences on a data warehouse database is controlled by means of a Control and Presentation Module (CPM). Hence, it directly interacts with the CGO Optimizer and the

Sequence Execution Engine. The main features of this module are:

Choose statement sequence: Browsing functionality is provided to the user that allows to view all statement sequences stored in the Test Series Database and choose one of them for optimization. Sequences are visualized as dependency graphs showing the direct dependencies, i.e., the data flow between the queries of a sequence, as shown in Figure 1.

Choose optimizer policy: A set of rewrite rules is provided by the CGO Optimizer. The user may decide to use only a subset of these rules for optimization. The control strategy may also be changed, e.g., by altering the priority assigned to each of the rewrite rules. This allows to adjust and evaluate different optimizer policies.

Control optimization process: The user may leave the entire optimization of a statement sequence to the optimizer. In this case, the series of transformations applied to a statement sequence is shown. Optionally, a single-step mode is available. In this approach only one rewrite rule is applied to the statement sequence. This is useful to explore the benefit of a specific rule in different settings.

Execute statement sequence: As soon as the sequence has been executed, each statement is augmented by its runtime and the cardinality of its result set. This allows the user to identify expensive queries as well as rewrite rules that lead to performance improvements or degradations.

3.2 CGO Optimizer

The CGO Optimizer is the core of the CHICAGO system. It allows to optimize SQL statement sequences by applying rewrite rules. Calls to the optimizer include a statement sequence as well as several parameters that define the ruleset and the control strategy the rule engine of the optimizer should activate. The output of the optimizer is an optimized statement sequence and a list of rewrite rules applied to the original sequence. Optionally, the optimizer can be executed in single-step mode, where only one rule is applied. In this case the output consists of the resulting sequence and a list of all possible rule applications for the next step.

3.3 Sequence Execution Engine

The execution of the statement sequences is controlled by the Sequence Execution Engine. Its input is a configuration that consists of the sequence of SQL statements, name and location of the database that stores the base tables, and other parameters that have to be provided to run the sequence. It provides runtime statistics as the output and stores them in the Test Series Database. These statistics include the runtime for each statement and the cardinality of the temporary tables that are produced by the sequence, as well as errors that occur during execution.

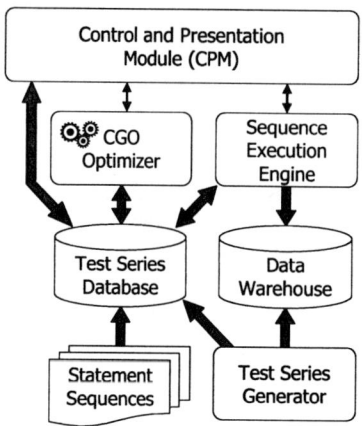

Figure 3: CHICAGO System Architecture

3.4 Test Series Generator

The system offers several options to provide test series. Statement sequences generated by external tools, e.g. commercial OLAP tools, may be provided as well as sequences that are handwritten. Another option is to use the Test Series Generator that is part of the CHICAGO system as well. It provides data sets and statement sequences accessing these data sets. The tool provides a graphical user interface that allows to specify the characteristics of the data sets and the sequence. This serves as a basis for the evaluation of different rewrite strategies with regard to these characteristics.

3.5 Implementation

All components in Figure 3 that are represented as rounded boxes are implemented in Java using Swing for the graphical user interface. Eclipse was chosen as IDE for development of the CHICAGO system.

The SQL statement sequences are parsed and stored as XML documents in the Test Series Database. We use JavaCC as parser generator and DOM to access and manipulate the XML representation of a sequence. XSLT is utilized to retranslate this representation into a SQL statement sequence. The Sequence Execution Engine employs JDBC for access to the data warehouse stored in IBM DB2.

4. Demonstration

The goal of this demonstration is to show the complete evaluation cycle that is supported by the CHICAGO system. This starts with the generation of statement sequences and data sets specifically adjusted to the evaluation purpose. It includes the visualization of the statement sequences as well as the visualization of the optimization process showing how the optimizer works in different settings. Finally, it covers the execution of statement sequences (non-optimized as well as optimized sequences) and shows how the performance gain is related to the characteristics of rewrite rules, sequences and data.

4.1 Provide Test Sequences and Data

The Test Series Generator includes algorithms to create statement sequences and appropriate data sets. The user may choose from a set of predefined statement patterns. Each pattern corresponds to a single rewrite rule. The main purpose is to provide statement sequences, which allow at least one predefined rewrite step. Additional settings may be used to specify further characteristics of the statement sequence and the underlying data. Hence, the patterns define a subset of interesting test cases for each rule and enable the user to produce test cases for the optimizer in an easy and fast way. This allows to assess the effectiveness of a single rule with respect to the characteristics of statements and data.

Pattern-specific settings for the tables, which are generated, include domain restrictions, value distributions, and indexes on certain attributes. Furthermore, the selectivity of pattern-specific predicates may be defined. There are also some general settings, e.g., the number of columns and the number of rows in the table that has to be generated.

A screenshot of the Test Series Generator is presented in Figure 4. It shows the pattern for the WhereToGroup rule with the INSERT statements of the queries that are produced by the settings. In the demonstration the Test Series Generator will be used to produce simple statement sequences that focus on a special rule, similar to the one in Figure 2.

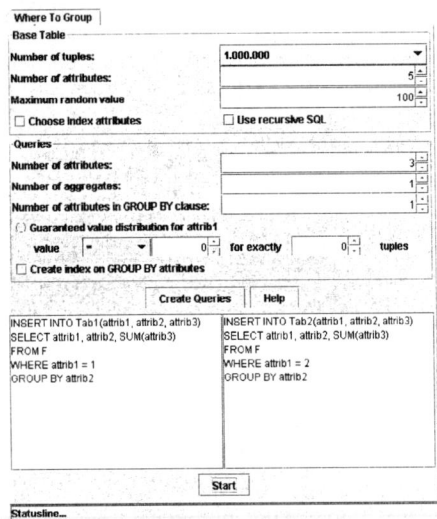

Figure 4: Screenshot of the Test Series Generator

4.2 Load and View Statement Sequences

The Control and Presentation Module offers the basic functionality of loading and viewing statement sequences. It allows to access all sequences in the Test Series Database. This includes statement sequences provided by the Test Series Generator as well as sequences generated by other tools. For each statement sequence that is loaded the corresponding dependency graph is displayed as shown in Figure 1.

4.3 Optimize and Execute Statement Sequences

This part of the demonstration shows how the optimization of statement sequences is managed by the Control and Presentation Module. The single-step optimization mode allows to apply exactly one rewrite rule to the statement sequence, whereas the n-step mode includes several optimization steps according to the control strategy of the CGO Optimizer. For both optimization modes, the set of usable rewrite rules may be restricted.

The Sequence Execution Engine is used to execute statement sequences. In particular, it allows to record the runtime for optimized statement sequences as well as for the corresponding initial sequence.

We will demonstrate the optimization process for a set of statement sequences that includes sequences within a broad complexity range. The effect of different settings will also be demonstrated.

5. Future Work

Planned extensions of the CHICAGO system aim at further exploring and refining the control strategy for CGO. To achieve this, additional control strategies will be provided in the CGO Optimizer. Moreover, the options to control and visualize the optimization process will be enhanced. This includes the navigation in the search space of alternative rewrite processing steps.

References

[1] S. Finkelstein. Common Subexpression Analysis in Database Applications. In Proc. SIGMOD, Orlando, Florida, USA, June 1982.

[2] G. Graefe. The Cascades Framework for Query Optimization. Data Engineering Bulletin, 18(3), 1995.

[3] T. Kraft, H. Schwarz, R. Rantzau, B. Mitschang: Coarse-Grained Optimization: Techniques for Rewriting SQL Statement Sequences. In Proc. VLDB, Berlin, Germany, September 2003.

[4] H. Pirahesh, J. Hellerstein, W. Hasan. Extensible Rule-Based Query Rewrite Optimization in Starburst. In Proc. SIGMOD, San Diego, California, USA, June 1992.

[5] A. Rosenthal, U. Chakravarthy. Anatomy of a Modular Multiple Query Optimizer. In Proc. VLDB, Los Angeles, California, USA, August/September 1988.

[6] T. Sellis. Multiple-Query Optimization. TODS, 13(1), 1988.

SVT: Schema Validation Tool for Microsoft SQL-Server*

Ernest Teniente   Carles Farré   Toni Urpí   Carlos Beltrán   David Gañán

Universitat Politècnica de Catalunya
Jordi Girona 1-3. 08034 – Barcelona. Catalonia (Spain)
teniente@lsi.upc.es

Abstract

We present SVT, a tool for validating database schemas in SQL Server. This is done by means of testing desirable properties that a database schema should satisfy. To our knowledge, no commercial relational DBMS provides yet a tool able to perform such kind of validation.

1. Introduction

Database schema validation is related to check whether a database schema correctly and adequately describes the user intended needs and requirements. The correctness of the data managed by database management systems is vital to the more general aspect of quality of the data and thus of their usage by different applications.

This is an increasingly important problem in database engineering, particularly since database schemas are becoming more complex. Indeed, detecting and removing possible flaws at schema design time will prevent those flaws from materializing as run time errors or other inconveniences at operation time.

As an example, assume we have two tables containing information about categories and employees: *Category* (*name*, salary) and *Employee*(*ssn*, name, catName), where underlined attributes correspond to primary keys and where *catName* is a foreign key for the *Employee* table. We could define those tables as follows:

```
CREATE TABLE Category (
   name   char(10) PRIMARY KEY,
   salary  real   NOT NULL,
   CONSTRAINT chName  CHECK (name <> 'ceo' ),
   CONSTRAINT chMinSal CHECK (salary > 50000),
   CONSTRAINT chMaxSal CHECK (salary < 45000) )
```

*Research partially supported by Microsoft Research, grant 2003-192.
Permission to copy without fee all or part of this material is granted provided that the copies are not made or distributed for direct commercial advantage, the VLDB copyright notice and the title of the publication and its date appear, and notice is given that copying is by permission of the Very Large Data Base Endowment. To copy otherwise, or to republish, requires a fee and/or special permission from the Endowment
**Proceedings of the 30th VLDB Conference,
Toronto, Canada, 2004**

```
CREATE TABLE Employee (
   ssn   int   PRIMARY KEY,
   name   char(30) NOT NULL,
   catName char(10) NOT NULL,
   CONSTRAINT chCatName CHECK (catName <> 'ceo' ),
   CONSTRAINT fkCat FOREIGN KEY ( catName )
            REFERENCES Category(name) )
```

Syntactically, those tables are correctly defined. However, a deeper analysis of the schema allows determining that they may not contain any tuple. The reason is that it is impossible for a category to have a salary lower than 45000 and higher than 50000 as stated by constraints *chMinSal* and *chMaxSal*. Moreover, since employees must belong to categories it is also impossible to insert any employee in the previous database.

We could also realize that the constraint *chCatName* is redundant because it may never be violated. Clearly, employees must belong to categories that may not be named 'ceo' (constraints *fkCat* and *chName*). Then, we do not need to enforce this condition again in the definition of the Employee table by means of *chCatName*.

The designer could fix the previous problems by removing *chCatName* and defining the range of the salary correctly (for instance, by stating that it may range from 45000 to 50000). Now, the database schema could be populated and would allow tuples like *Category(a,30000)* and *Employee(1,john,a)*.

The designer could also be interested to define some views on the new (modified) schema. For instance, a view to retrieve employees' salary (*EmpSalaries*) and another one to retrieve those employees that are not assigned to any category yet (*EmpWithoutCat*):

```
CREATE VIEW EmpSalaries AS (
SELECT ssn, Employee.name, salary
FROM   Employee, Category
WHERE  catName = Category.name )

CREATE VIEW EmpWithoutCat AS (
SELECT ssn, Employee.name
FROM   Employee
WHERE  catName NOT IN(SELECT name FROM Category))
```

Some weaknesses may appear also during view definition. As entailed by *fkCat*, there is no database state where we may find an employee without a category. Therefore, the second view is ill-defined since it may never contain any tuple.

Those are just some examples to illustrate the kind of flaws that may appear during the definition of a database schema. Unfortunately, no relational DBMS provides any tool to perform validations like the ones we have just seen [TG01]. In this demonstration we present a tool, the Schema Validation Tool (SVT), to address this problem.

SVT allows a database designer to perform several tests to check desirable properties of database schemas defined in SQL Server. Among them we have: schema satisfiability, liveliness, integrity constraint redundancy, reachability, etc. SVT is able to check whether a given property is satisfied or not. In the first case, it provides also an example of a database state satisfying the property.

SVT accepts schemas defined by means of a subset of the SQL language provided by SQL Server. It accepts the definition of:
- Primary key, foreign key, boolean check constraints.
- SPJ views, negation, subselects (exists, in), union.
- Data types: integer, real, string.

The current implementation of SVT assumes a set semantics of views and queries and it does not allow null values neither aggregate nor arithmetic functions.

2. Testing Desirable Properties

The goal of this section is to define the set of desirable properties implemented in SVT (inspired on [DTU96]) to validate SQL Server database schemas and to explain the method used by SVT to check them.

2.1 Property Definition

State-satisfiability:

A database schema is state-satisfiable if there is at least one, non-empty, database state where all integrity constraints are satisfied. For instance, the schema containing the initial tables *Category* and *Employee* is not state-satisfiable.

Liveliness:

A table or a view *R* is lively if there is one consistent database state where at least one fact about *R* is true. A state is consistent if no integrity constraint is violated on it.

Hence, tables or views that are not lively correspond to relations that are empty in each consistent state of the database. This may be due to the presence of some integrity constraints, to the view definition itself or to a combination of both.

Such predicates are clearly not useful and possibly ill-specified. For instance, the view *EmpSalaries* of the previous section was lively while *EmpWithoutCat* was not.

Integrity constraint redundancy:

An integrity constraint (or a subset of constraints) is redundant if database consistency does not depend on it. In other words, it is redundant when it is already guaranteed that the database instances that it wants to avoid will never occur.

SVT distinguishes two different types of redundancy. A constraint is absolutely redundant if it may never be violated. A constraint is relatively redundant (wrt a set of constraints) if it may never be violated when none of the constraints in the set is violated.

In our example, *chCatName* is relatively redundant wrt to *fkCat* and *chName*.

Reachability:

A database designer may be interested also in more general properties like checking whether certain desirable states may be satisfied according to the current schema. This is usually known as checking reachability of partially specified states.

SVT provides two different ways to check reachability: wizard and query reachability. In the first case, the designer may specify by means of a wizard a set of tuples that tables and views should contain. Using this facility, he could define questions like: may the database contain Employee(1,maria,sales) and EmpSalaries (2,joan,47000)? Then, SVT would provide a positive answer and an example database, like for instance Employee(1,maria,sales), Employee(2,joan,sales) and Category(sales,47000), that satisfies the previous question.

In the second case, the desired state is specified by means of an SQL query. For instance, SVT would determine that the state defined by the following query is not reachable:

SELECT Employee.name, salary
FROM Employee, Category
WHERE Employee.catName = Category.name and salary > 80000 and salary < 90000

Query containment:

A query Q1 is contained into another query Q2 if the answers that Q1 obtains are always a subset of the answers of Q2, independently of the database state.

2.2 Checking Desirable Properties

SVT uses the CQC Method [FTU03, Far03] to effectively and efficiently check desirable properties of SQL Server database schemas. The main goal of this method is to perform query containment tests, i.e. to check whether the answers that a query obtains are a subset of the answers obtained by another query for every database.

Intuitively, the aim of the CQC Method is to construct a *counterexample* that proves that the query containment relationship being checked does not hold. The method uses different *Variable Instantiation Patterns*, according to the syntactic properties of the queries and the databases considered in each test. The aim is to prune the search of possible counterexamples by generating only the relevant ones but at the same time without diminishing the requirement of completeness.

The CQC Method requires two main inputs. The first one is the definition of the *goal to attain*, which must be achieved on the database that the method will try to obtain by constructing a database state. The second one is the set of constraints to enforce, which must not be violated by the constructed database.

The initial goal to attain may be any conjunction of literals expressing a certain property. Consequently, the CQC Method can check any property that may be formulated in terms of a goal to attain under a set of constraints to enforce. In particular, it is suited to check the database schema validation properties we have previously defined since all of them are aimed to prove that a certain goal is satisfied provided that it does not violate a set of integrity constraints.

The CQC Method is sound and complete in the following terms:

Failure soundness: if the method terminates without building any counterexample, the specified property holds

Finite success soundness: if the method builds a finite counterexample then the property does not hold when queries contain no recursively-defined derived predicates.

Failure completeness: if the property holds between two queries then the method terminates reporting its failure to build a counterexample when queries contain no recursively-defined derived predicates.

Finite success completeness: if there exists a finite counterexample, the method finds it and terminates when either recursively-defined derived predicates are not considered or recursion and negation occurs together in a strict-stratified manner.

Query containment is undecidable for the general case. Therefore in some cases, e.g. in the presence of solutions with infinite elements, it may happen that the CQC Method does not terminate. However, the previous completeness results guarantee that if either there exist one or more finite states for which the property does not hold or there is no state (finite or infinite) satisfying the property, the CQC Method terminates.

3. SVT System Description

In the SVT System we implemented the ideas presented in the previous sections. Its internal architecture consists of several components as it is shown in figure 1.

The GUI component allows using the SVT in an easy and intuitive way. To perform the different tests available in SVT, users go along the following interaction pattern:

1. Select the database schema to be tested.
2. Select one among the available tests: Schema satisfiability, Relation liveliness, Query reachability, Wizard reachability, Integrity Constraint Redundancy, Query Containment. Moreover, users must specify one of the two usual semantics regarding to integrity constraint enforcement: Immediate or Deferred.
3. Fill the required data that the selected test requires.
4. Execute and obtain the test results. To perform the same test with other input data, users may go back to step 3. To perform a different test on the same schema, users should go back to step 2.

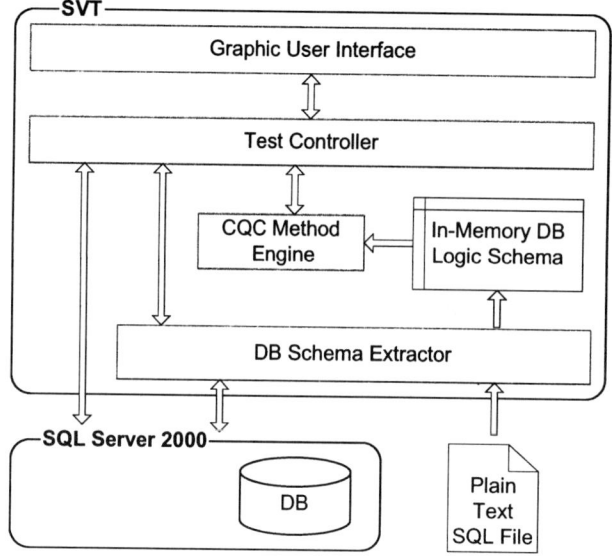

Figure 1. Architecture of SVT System.

The Test Controller component processes the commands and data provided by users through the GUI component and transfers back the obtained results. Among the tasks performed by this component, we highlight the following five ones:

1. To establish the connection with the required local or remote SQL Server running system.
2. To ask the DB Schema Extractor component to load the schema to be tested from either a given SQL Server system or a plain text SQL file.
3. To ask the CQC Method Engine component to perform the required test on the loaded schema.
4. If the CQC Method execution provides a counter-example for a given test by specifying a possible content of the database, the Test Controller generates a SQL script that contains the table insertions that allow recreating such database content. The SQL script can be displayed in the GUI component.

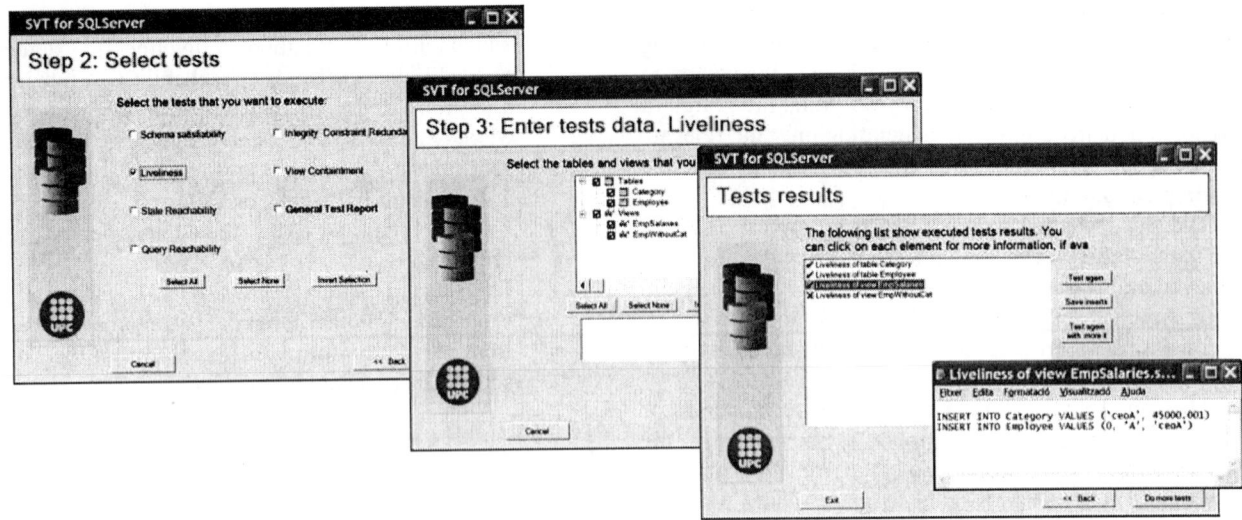

Figure 2. Screenshots of the SVT Demo

5. In any case, then the Test Controller generates also an HTML document describing the execution of the CQC method that lead to such a conclusion.

The main goal of the DB Schema Extractor component is to load an SQL DB schema from a specified source and then transform it to a format that is tractable by the CQC Method Engine. In this way, the DB Schema Extractor generates an in-memory representation of the schema where integrity constraints, views and queries are expressed in terms of deductive rules.

Finally, the CQC Method Engine implements the CQC Method in order to perform the concrete tests asked by the Test Controller component. Such tests must be expressed in terms of the goal to attain the set of constraints to enforce, as explained in previous section.

The whole SVT System has been implemented in the C# language by using Microsoft Visual .NET Studio as a development tool. Our implementation can be executed in any system that features the .NET framework and has access to a local or remote SQL Server system.

4. SVT Demo Description

The demo that we will present is intended to illustrate the main features of the SVT System. The script of the demo is as follows. First, we will define a syntactically correct SQL database schema on a local SQL Server system with the SQL Server Query Analyzer Tool, SQAT for short.

Second, we will start up the SVT system in order to validate the schema previously defined. The first test to perform will be to check whether the schema is satisfiable. In this first test, the obtained result will show that initial schema is unsatisfiable.

Third, we will modify the initial schema with the SQAT in order to make the schema satisfiable. The modification will consist on removing or changing some table constraints.

Four, returning to the SVT, we will test the satisfiability of the modified schema. In this case, the SVT will corroborate such satisfiability.

Five, we will check the liveliness property of the tables and views of the modified schema. We will see examples with or without this property.

Figure 2 shows a sequence of screenshots corresponding to the steps that we would follow if we tested liveliness for the tables and views of the example with which we illustrated Sections 1 and 2. Recall that the two database tables and the view EmpSalaries were lively whereas the view EmpWithouCat was not.

Five, we test the redundancy of the integrity constraints defined in the example. The SVT system will find several cases of redundancy.

Six, we will perform several state reachability test by means of queries or by providing the concrete rows that we want the tables to contain or the views to obtain, with examples of both successful and unsuccessful cases.

Finally, we will perform a variety of query containment tests.

References

[DTU96] H. Decker, E. Teniente, T. Urpí. How to Tackle Schema Validation by View Updating. In *Proceedings of EDBT'96*: 535-549, LNCS 1057, Springer, 1996.

[Far03] C. Farré. *A New Method for Query Containment Checking in Databases*. PhD. Thesis, Universitat Politècnica de Catalunya, 2003

[FTU03] C. Farré, E. Teniente, T. Urpí. Query Containment With Negated IDB Predicates. *Proceedings of ADBIS 2003*, LNCS, Springer, 2003.

[TG01] C. Türker, M. Gertz. Semantic Integrity Support in SQL-99 and Commercial (Object-)Relational Database Management Systems. *VLDB Journal* 10(4): 241-269, 2001.

CAPE: Continuous Query Engine with Heterogeneous-Grained Adaptivity [*]

Elke A. Rundensteiner, Luping Ding, Timothy Sutherland, Yali Zhu, Brad Pielech, Nishant Mehta

Department of Computer Science, Worcester Polytechnic Institute
100 Institute Road, Worcester, MA 01609, U.S.A
{rundenst, lisading, tims, yaliz, winners, nishantm}@cs.wpi.edu

1 Introduction

We present CAPE, our **C**ontinuous **A**daptive Query **P**rocessing **E**ngine, that is designed to efficiently evaluate continuous queries in highly dynamic stream environments with the following characteristics: (1) the input data may stream into the query engine at widely-varying rates; (2) meta knowledge such as punctuations [10] may dynamically be embedded into data streams; (3) as queries are registered into or removed from the query engine, the computing resources available for processing an individual operator may vary greatly over time; (4) different users may impose different quality of service (QoS) requirements.

In view of these uncertainties, no one unique optimization technique can be expected to always succeed. Correspondingly, CAPE employs an optimization framework with heterogeneous-grained adaptivity for effectively coping with such dynamic variations.

In our demonstration, we will focus on the following novel features of the CAPE system:
1. Highly reactive query operators capable of exploiting metadata to reduce resource usage and to improve execution efficiency (*intra-operator adaptivity*).
2. Online query reoptimization and migration between sub-plans to continuously converge to the best possible plan given the current situation (*plan-level adaptivity*).
3. Adaptive operator scheduling and plan distribution among multiple machines (*system-wide adaptivity*).

Our system differs from prior continuous query systems in several ways. The STREAM system [7], focusing on formal continuous query semantics, also applies some adaptation strategies such as runtime modification of the resource allocation and scheduling policy [2]. In addition to this, our system enables finer-grained intra-operator adaptivity [4, 5] and distributes a query plan to run on multiple machines for scaling purposes [9].

TelegraphCQ [3] provides a very fine-grained level of flexibility by continuously routing each tuple individually through its network of operators. However, it only achieves lightweight online query rewriting such as changing the order of query operators. Furthermore, the Eddies approach has the inherent problem of recomputing all delta intermediate results in the case of multiple joins. This may incur a significant overhead given high stream rates and join selectivities. Our system instead takes the more established approach of working with pre-defined optimized query plans, such as query networks in Aurora [1] or STREAM, and then extends this approach with adaptive techniques.

Unlike the Aurora system, we focus on the design of the fine-tuned individual query operators [4, 5], such as the join operator with intra-operator scheduling of various related tasks including state purge and metadata propagation. Moreover, we support online migration of sub-plans not only composed of stateless operators, but also containing stateful operators, to allow for maximal online adjustments in plan execution performance [11].

In summary, CAPE aims to deliver exact query answers by making the best effort through heterogeneous-grained adaptations with the goal to meet users' QoS requirements.

2 Application Example

The applications we will use to demonstrate CAPE are online auction management and web log analysis. Figure 1 shows several streams and a sample query in an online auction application. For each person that has registered to the auction system, this query asks for the count of distinct categories that include the items

---

[*]The research was partly supported by the RDC grant 2003-04 on "On-line Stream Monitoring Systems: Untethered Healthcare, Intrusion Detection, and Beyond."

Permission to copy without fee all or part of this material is granted provided that the copies are not made or distributed for direct commercial advantage, the VLDB copyright notice and the title of the publication and its date appear, and notice is given that copying is by permission of the Very Large Data Base Endowment. To copy otherwise, or to republish, requires a fee and/or special permission from the Endowment.

**Proceedings of the 30th VLDB Conference,
Toronto, Canada, 2004**

this person has bid on within 12 hours of her registration time. Since the exploitation of dynamic metadata, i.e., punctuations, is a novel feature in CAPE, we now explain our techniques for optimizing this query.

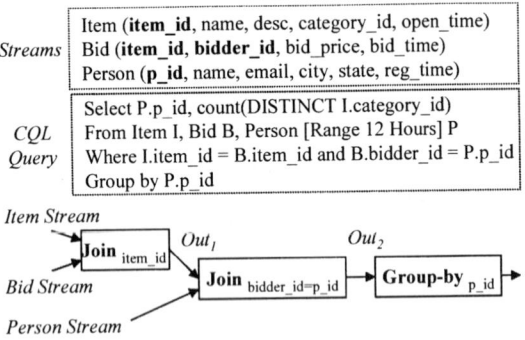

Figure 1: Sample Query in an Online Auction System.

Since the auction system knows the closing time for each auction, it can insert punctuations into the *Bid* stream to mark the end of bids for each specific item. This kind of dynamic metadata along with static metadata such as the unique key and window semantics can help the stateful operators to shrink the runtime state and the blocking operators to emit partial results regularly. Therefore, in the first join (Item ⋈ Bid), when a punctuation is received from the *Bid* stream, the tuple with the same *item_id* from the *Item* stream can be purged. The second join (Out_1 ⋈ Person) is a window join which applies a 12-hour window on *Person.reg_time*. Whenever a Person tuple drops out of the window, no more join results will be generated for that person. Thus, a punctuation for this *p_id* can be produced and placed into the Out_2 stream. This will trigger the *group_by* operator to emit a partial result for this person. Our experimental results [4, 5] show that by exploiting appropriate metadata, the join only requires near-constant memory overhead. The group-by operator is able to produce partial results at the earliest time possibly by exploiting the punctuations propagated by the upstream join.

3 System Overview

CAPE embeds novel adaptation techniques for tuning different levels of query evaluation, including intra-operator execution, operator scheduling, query plan structuring and plan distribution. Each level of adaptation yields maximally optimized performance by working on its own. However, none of them can possibly handle all variations that occur in a stream environment. In addition, the improper use of all levels of adaptations may cause either optimization counteraction or over-optimization. Hence, an important task is to coordinate different levels of adaptations, guiding them to function properly on their own and also to cooperate with each other in a well-regulated manner. CAPE not only incorporates novel adaptation strategies for all aspects of continuous query evaluation, but also employs a well-designed mechanism for coordinating different levels of adaptations.

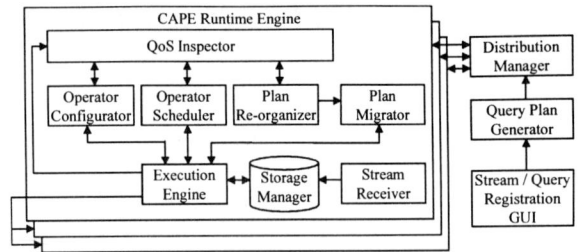

Figure 2: CAPE System Architecture.

In the system architecture shown in Figure 2, the key adaptive components are Operator Configurator, Operator Scheduler, Plan Reorganizer and Distribution Manager. Once the Execution Engine starts executing the query plan, the QoS Inspector will regularly collect statistics within each sampling interval from the Execution Engine. All of the four adaptive components use these statistics along with QoS specifications to determine if they need to adjust their behavior.

To synchronize adaptations at all levels, we have designed a heterogeneous-grained adaptation schema. Since these adaptations deal with dissimilar runtime scenarios and have different overheads, they are invoked in CAPE under different conditions.

The intra-operator adaptation incurs the lowest overhead so that it functions within an operator's execution time slot. Second, the Operator Scheduler adjusts the operator processing order after a run of a single operator or a group of operators, called a scheduling unit. After a scheduling unit finishes its work, the scheduler will check the QoS metrics for the operators and decide which operator to run next or even switch to a better scheduling strategy. This is a novel feature unique to our system. The Plan Reorganizer will wait for the completion of several scheduling units and then check the QoS metrics for the entire query plan residing on its local machine to decide whether to restructure the plan. The Distribution Manager, which likely incurs the highest cost, is assigned the longest decision making time interval. If a particular machine is detected to be overloaded, the Distribution Manager will redistribute one or multiple query plans among a cluster of machines. The Plan Migrator is invoked as necessary by the Plan Reorganizer to migrate from the old plan to the new plan, or by the Distribution Manager to migrate a query from one machine to another machine.

4 Adaptive Techniques in CAPE

4.1 Highly Reactive Query Operators

Our operators are able to adjust their behavior according to changes in the environment. We take our adaptive punctuation-exploiting join operator *PJoin* [4, 5] as an example. PJoin is able to utilize punctuations to remove no-longer-needed data from its join state in a timely manner, thereby reducing the memory overhead and improving the probe efficiency. It can also propagate punctuations to help the blocking operators or stateful operators downstream.

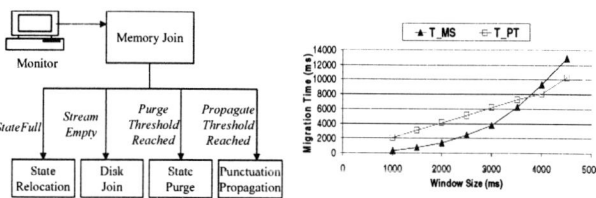
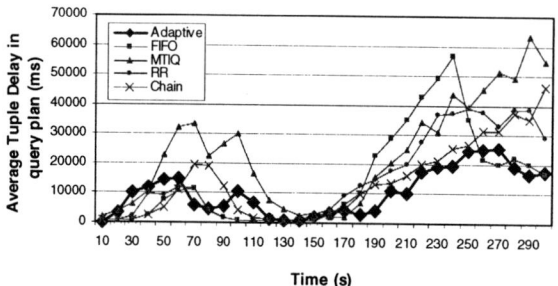

Figure 3: PJoin.   Figure 4: Migration Time.

Figure 5: Improving QoS w/ Adaptive Scheduling.

The PJoin execution logic is composed of several tasks including *join*, *purge* and *propagation*. We have designed various state purge and punctuation propagation strategies, including eager and lazy purge, and active and passive propagation, to achieve different optimization goals. We also employ an event-driven intra-operator scheduling mechanism (Figure 3) to switch among individual tasks driven by the events modeling the punctuation arrivals, the memory threshold reached, etc. The events, listeners and thresholds are configured by the Operator Configurator and can be dynamically adjusted at runtime. This realizes an adaptive execution logic for PJoin.

All stateful operators in CAPE are equipped with a punctuation-exploiting adaptive execution logic. These operators can react to punctuation arrivals, resource (memory) modifications and punctuation requests from downstream operators.

4.2 Adaptive Operator Scheduling

The existing stream systems usually stick to an operator scheduling algorithm once it is determined to be the optimal one from the beginning of the query execution. However, as the stream environment experiences changes, this initially optimal scheduling algorithm may become sub-optimal. In response, in CAPE we employ an *adaptive scheduler-selection framework* [8]. Our Operator Scheduler can take any number of scheduling algorithms and a set of QoS requirements as input, and dynamically select the scheduling algorithm to use based on how well the system is performing. Thus, it leverages the strengths of multiple scheduling strategies and also works even under changing QoS requirements at runtime. No a priori knowledge about the scheduling algorithms in the system is required. Due to the lightweight nature of the framework, the overhead of using an adaptive strategy rather than a static algorithm has been shown experimentally to be minimal. Figure 5 shows how the adaptive framework reduces average tuple delay in the query plan.

CAPE currently incorporates a wide variety of scheduling algorithms, ranging from well established ones like Round Robin and FIFO, to those proposed recently for continuous query processing such as Train [1] and Chain [2].

4.3 Online Plan Migration

When a relatively dramatic change occurs in the stream environment, it may be more effective to optimize the query plan itself to improve the performance. We have developed a set of online plan reoptimization methods and corresponding rewriting rules. Depending on the user QoS requirements, such as output rates, the appropriate optimization method and rewriting rules are dynamically invoked.

Once the Plan Reorganizer has generated new query sub-plans, the existing plans can then be seamlessly migrated to the new ones on-the-fly [11]. This is a feature thus far unique to CAPE. We have developed two lightweight online plan migration strategies [11]: parallel track strategy and moving state strategy. Both strategies take special care to safely migrate the state of stateful operators, such as joins, to prevent any missing or duplicate results.

The *moving state strategy* first drains out tuples inside intermediate queues, and then carefully maps and moves over all relevant tuples in the states of the old query plan to their corresponding location in the new plan. In contrast, the *parallel track strategy* operates in a more gradual fashion by plugging in the new plan and starting to execute both plans in parallel. The old plan can be disconnected once the old tuples inside it are all purged. The cost of the two strategies are determined by several system parameters, such as operator selectivities, window sizes, and data arrival rates. As one of our experiment results on query plans with multiple joins, Figure 4 shows the relation between migration elapsed time and window size for both strategies (MS for moving state and PT for parallel track). The Plan Migrator dynamically evaluates the cost of these two strategies and chooses the more efficient one.

4.4 Self-Adjusting Plan Distribution

CAPE handles query plan distribution with a *Distribution Manager* which manages the tuple queues between machines [9]. A distributed query plan is created by connecting multiple machines over a network connection to distribute operators. There are many distribution plans available for use in CAPE. Newly-developed distribution plans can also be plugged in easily. To maintain the integrity and validity of the data, especially the data in the state of the stateful operators, the Distribution Manager follows a strict set of rules to migrate an operator to another processing machine.

In addition, CAPE has the unique ability to redistribute a workload in both a local (decentralized) and a global (centralized) control mode at runtime. This enables ultimate flexibility in distribution based on the number of processing machines. The distribution is based on a cost model, which considers memory usage, network costs and overall processing costs.

4. **Runtime plan reoptimization and migration.** We will show how the *Plan Reorganizer* locates the sub-plan that needs to be restructured when it detects the performance decline of a query plan exceeds a pre-determined threshold. It then invokes the Plan Migrator to migrate from the old sub-plan to the new one at runtime.

5. **Plan distribution.** We will show that when one machine is overloaded, the *Distribution Manager* redistributes query plans to handle this situation.

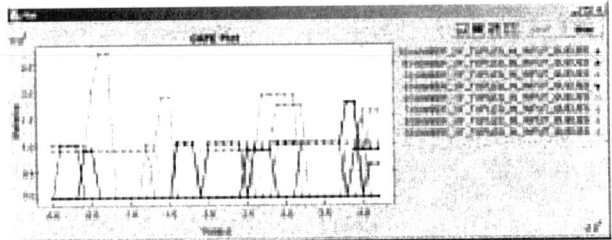

Figure 7: Statistics Monitor.

5 Demonstration

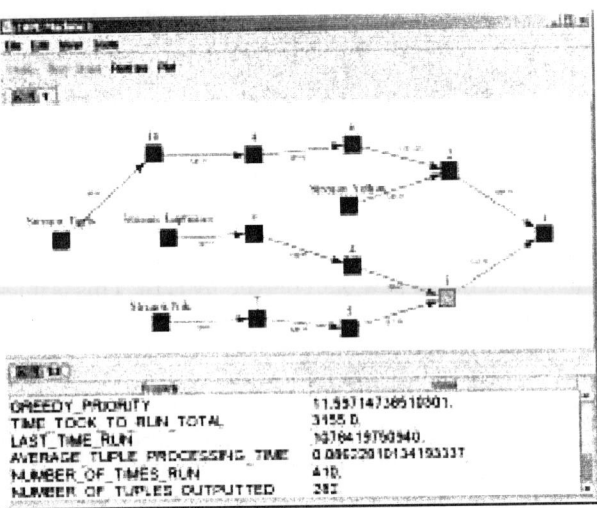

Figure 6: View of Query Plan During Execution.

In the demonstration, we will visually show the six aspects of the CAPE system listed below through a GUI (Figure 6). We employ a *stream feeder* to supply the application data at varying arrival rates, which can be as fast as 400 tuples/sec in our FIFA World Cup 1998 web log analysis application [6].

1. **General system features**. We will show the runtime status of query plan structures, inter-operator queues and storage manager. In particular, we have the ability to monitor the QoS statistics as they are updated at runtime (Figure 7).

2. **Reactive operators**. We will show the PJoin intra-operator scheduling switches from one task to another upon the arrival of punctuations, or when the allocated memory is used up. We will also show how the punctuations delivered by the upstream join operator unblock the downstream group-by operator.

3. **Adaptive operator scheduling.** We will show how the system switches to a different scheduling algorithm to yield better query performance.

6 Acknowledgment

The authors wish to thank Maylene Natasha Waltz for the CAPE GUI development.

References

[1] D. Abadi, D. Carney, U. Cetintemel, M. Cherniack, C. Convey, S. Lee, M. Stonebraker, N. Tatbul, and S. Zdonik. Aurora: A new model and architecture for data stream management. *VLDB Journal*, 12(2):120–139, August 2003.

[2] B. Babcock, S. Babu, R. Motwani, and M. Datar. Chain: operator scheduling for memory minimization in data stream systems. In *ACM SIGMOD*, pages 253–264, 2003.

[3] S. Chandrasekaran, O. Cooper, A. Deshpande, M. Franklin, J. Hellerstein, W. Hong, S. Krishnamurthy, S. Madden, V. Raman, F. Reiss, and M. Shah. TelegraphCQ: Continuous dataflow processing for an uncertain world. In *CIDR*, pages 269–280, 2003.

[4] L. Ding, N. Mehta, E. A. Rundensteiner, and G. T. Heineman. Joining punctuated streams. In *EDBT*, pages 587–604, March 2004.

[5] L. Ding, E. A. Rundensteiner, and G. T. Heineman. MJoin: A metadata-aware stream join operator. In *DEBS*, June 2003.

[6] Internet Traffic Archive. http://www.acm.org/sigcomm/ITA/, 2003.

[7] R. Motwani, J. Widom, A. Arasu, B. Babcock, S. Babu, M. Datar, G. Manku, C. Olston, J. Rosenstein, and R. Varma. Query processing, resource management, and approximation in a data stream management system. In *CIDR*, pages 245–256, Jan 2003.

[8] B. Pielech, T. Sutherland, and E. A. Rundensteiner. Adaptive scheduling framework for a continuous query system. Technical Report WPI-CS-TR-04-16, Worcester Polytechnic Institute, April 2004.

[9] T. Sutherland. D-cape: A self-tuning continuous query plan distribution architecture. WPI, MS Thesis, May 2004.

[10] P. A. Tucker, D. Maier, T. Sheard, and L. Fegaras. Exploiting punctuation semantics in continuous data streams. *TKDE*, 15(3):555–568, May/June 2003.

[11] Y. Zhu, E. A. Rundensteiner, and G. T. Heineman. Dynamic plan migration for continuous queries over data streams. In *ACM SIGMOD*, June 2004, to appear.

HiFi: A Unified Architecture for High Fan-in Systems
(System Demonstration)

Owen Cooper*, Anil Edakkunni*, Michael J. Franklin*, Wei Hong[+], Shawn R. Jeffery*,
Sailesh Krishnamurthy*, Fredrick Reiss*, Shariq Rizvi*, and Eugene Wu*

*EECS Dept., UC Berkeley [+]Intel Research Berkeley

Abstract

Advances in data acquisition and sensor technologies are leading towards the development of "High Fan-in" architectures: widely distributed systems whose edges consist of numerous receptors such as sensor networks and RFID readers and whose interior nodes consist of traditional host computers organized using the principle of successive aggregation. Such architectures pose significant new data management challenges. The *HiFi* system, under development at UC Berkeley, is aimed at addressing these challenges. We demonstrate an initial prototype of *HiFi* that uses data stream query processing to acquire, filter, and aggregate data from multiple devices including sensor motes, RFID readers, and low power gateways organized as a High Fan-in system.

1. Introduction

Emerging wireless sensor networks and RFID technologies are on a fast track to widespread deployment in applications such as environmental monitoring, asset tracking, telemetry-based remote monitoring, and real-time supply chain management. Driven by both technological and market forces, sensor and RFID-based deployments raise the promise of taking computing from its current, user-driven mode, to one of direct and continuous interaction with the physical world.

1.1 High Fan-in Systems

In many cases, sensors and readers will serve as the receptors at the edges of widely distributed systems. For example, in a supply chain management deployment, collections of sensors and RFID readers on individual store shelves (in a retail scenario) or dock doors (in a warehouse/manufacturing scenario) continuously collect readings. These readings include "beeps" from low-function passive RFID tags (indicating the presence of particular tagged objects, such as cases of goods), as well as more content-rich information from smart sensors and higher-function tags (such as temperature readings, shipping histories, etc.).

These "edge" devices produce data that will be aggregated locally with data from other nearby devices. That data will be further aggregated within a larger area, and so on. This arrangement results in a distinctive bowtie topology we refer to as a High Fan-In system (see Figure 1). A sophisticated system such as one supporting a nation-wide supply chain application may consist of vast numbers of widely dispersed receptor devices (i.e., many thousands or more depending on the technology) and many levels of successively wider-scoped aggregation and storage. Such systems will comprise a vast array of heterogeneous resources, including inexpensive tags, wired and wireless sensing devices, low-power compute nodes and PDAs, and computers ranging from laptops to the largest mainframes and clusters.

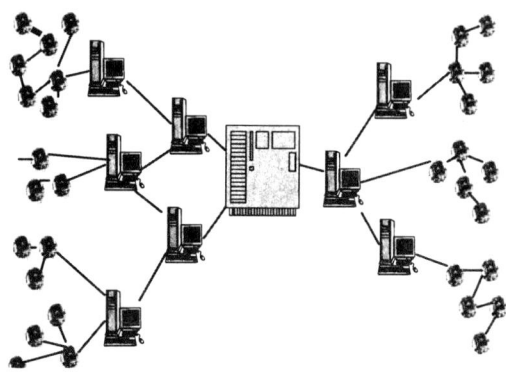

Figure 1 - A High Fan-in Architecture

---

* This work was funded in part by NSF under ITR grants IIS-0086057 and SI-0122599, by the IBM Faculty Partnership Award program, and by research funds from Intel, Microsoft, and the UC MICRO program.

Permission to copy without fee all or part of this material is granted provided that the copies are not made or distributed for direct commercial advantage, the VLDB copyright notice and the title of the publication and its date appear, and notice is given that copying is by permission of the Very Large Data Base Endowment. To copy otherwise, or to republish, requires a fee and/or special permission from the Endowment

**Proceedings of the 30th VLDB Conference,
Toronto, Canada, 2004**

1.2 Query Processing: A Unifying Framework

Traditionally, sensor-based information systems have been deployed using a piecemeal approach — a sensor-specific programming environment is used to task the edge receptors, a separate transport or information bus is used to route the sensor readings, and a database system or other data manager is used to collect and process the sensor readings. As a result, sensor application deployments have tended to be costly, difficult, and inflexible.

In contrast, our work is based on the notion that database techniques in general and data stream query processing in particular have a role to play *at all levels* of large-scale High Fan-in systems. In fact, we propose to use stream query processing and views as a *unifying framework* for data access across an entire High Fan-in environment. Thus, while it is certainly the case that the various types of sensor devices and computing platforms present in such systems all have their own unique characteristics and idiosyncrasies, our design uses stream query processing as the glue that binds these disparate pieces together to become a highly-functional application deployment platform.

Building on earlier work at Berkeley on both adaptive data stream processing (TelegraphCQ [CCDF+03]) and sensor network databases (TinyDB [MFHH03]) we have developed a new multi-level system for continuous and historical data processing in large-scale, sensor-rich applications. Our system, called HiFi, consists of host-centric processing components and device-centric processing components that can interoperate in a seamless manner. As such, HiFi runs across a gamut of platforms, ranging from battery powered wireless sensor motes and RFID readers, to mid-tier Linux-based sensor platforms and PDAs, to plugged-in, diskful servers.

2. HiFi Challenges and Architecture

While building on the growing body of work in the areas of data stream processing, sensor network databases, and data integration, the design of HiFi also addresses a number of challenges that arise from the unique properties of High Fan-in architectures and the applications they support.

2.1 The Challenges of Scale

From a data management perspective, the most challenging new aspect that High Fan-in systems bring to the table is the tremendous range they span in terms of three key characteristics: time, space, and resources.

Time – Timescales of interest in a High Fan-in system can range from seconds or less at the edges, to years in the interior of the system. At the edges of a High Fan-in system are the receptor devices that repeatedly measure some aspect of the physical world (or perhaps the virtual world, say in the case of a network monitor or other logical sensor). These devices are typically concerned with fairly short time scales, perhaps on the order of seconds or less. As one moves away from the edges, the timescales of interest increase.

For example, in a retail RFID scenario, individual readers on shelves may read several times a second, while the manager of a store may be concerned with how sales of particular items are going over the course of a morning, and planners at regional and corporate centers may be more concerned with longer-term sales trends over a season or several seasons.

Space - As with time, the area of geographic interest grows significantly as one moves from the edges of a High Fan-in system to the interior. Again using the retail RFID scenario, individual readers are concerned with a space of a few square meters, aggregation points within the store would be concerned with entire departments or perhaps the store as a whole, and regional and national centers are concerned with those much larger geographical areas.

Resources – Finally, the range of computing resources available at various levels of a High Fan-in system also vary dramatically, from small, cheap sensor motes (e.g., Berkeley Motes, see Figure 2) on the edges up to the largest mainframes in the interior of the system. Communication resources also can range from low power, lossy radios at the edges, to dedicated high-speed fiber in the interior.

Figure 2 - Berkeley Mica Wireless Sensor Mote

The key architectural principle on which the design of HiFi rests is the use of declarative query processing to provide *uniform* data access across all of these various scales. As with other data-intensive environments, the idea is to use the declarative approach to shield application developers from the complexities of the underlying platform, while enabling the system to optimize and efficiently execute data access and processing operations.

2.2 Cascading Stream Processing

HiFi is based on a notion of cascading stream processing, in which data streams collected at the very edges of the network are continually filtered, refined, aggregated and brought in towards the interior of the network. The multi-platform nature of the system enables seamless transitions between sensor-like devices, mid-tier single-board sensor aggregators, and host computers.

Each RFID reader or sensor network access point in a HiFi network is a data stream generation machine at the edge of a large (potentially global) information system. While the volume of data from any single stream is likely to be modest, the low cost and eventual ubiquity of such devices leads to a torrent of data in aggregate.

Furthermore, because these devices are embedded in the physical world, they are geographically proximate to the entities or spaces they are intended to be monitoring. As such, the processing of the data streaming from these devices will exhibit highly-localized patterns at many granularities. For example, an RFID reader on a store shelf sampling several times a second will constantly and repeatedly detect the presence of items on that shelf. While at one level, these "beeps" are indeed a data stream, in general the continued presence of an item on the shelf is not data of interest beyond the scope of that shelf. Rather, it is only when an item is removed or a new item appears that an interesting event worthy of propagation can be said to occur.

Such concerns argue for the ability to place stream processing at or close to the edges of these receptor-based systems, in order to perform highly-local tasks such as data cleaning, filtering, and simple event detection. Another argument for pushing stream query processing out towards the edges of the network is to reduce the communication requirements for battery-powered wireless devices such as Berkeley Motes, as has been demonstrated in our TinyDB work and other sensor network database projects.

On the other hand, much stream processing is likely to be best performed on mid-tier devices such as the Intel Stargate single-board computer (see Figure 3), which is a low-power Linux machine that can run on Li Ion batteries or can be plugged into the wall, and can use 802.11 communication (compared to the lower range/lower power radios used on sensor motes). Processing tasks that involve the correlation of multiple streams and/or the application of more sophisticated filtering and business rules are good candidates for such devices.

Still other stream processing will best be done on host computers. As you move in towards the interior of the network, three factors combine to change the nature of device requirements. First, these nodes serve as aggregation points for ever larger geographic regions, resulting in an increase in the number of streams being monitored and the aggregate data volume to be processed. Secondly, many applications will need to archive streams and provide access to that past data. Thus, diskful systems will be required. Finally, the availability of large volumes of both live and historical stream data will make such systems magnets for queries from throughout the network.

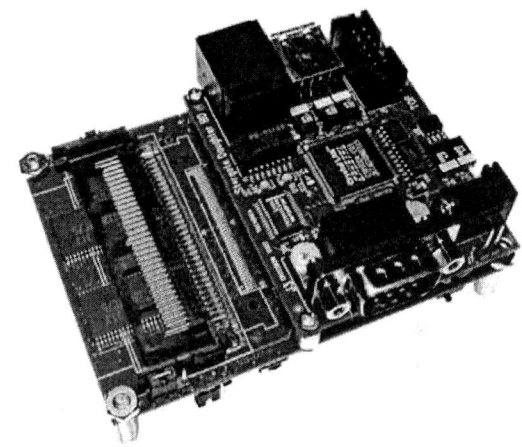

Figure 3 - Stargate Mid-tier Processing Node

The hierarchical nature of a High Fan-in architecture leads naturally to the use of stream query processing for *aggregation*. That is, as data streams flow from the edges towards the interior they can be combined and aggregated in order to produce summaries and reduce data volume. Indeed, aggregation is one of the major uses of stream query processing in HiFi. There are, however, a number of other important tasks for which we believe stream query processing is particularly well suited. These include:

- **Data Cleaning** – Sensors and RFID readers are notoriously noisy devices, and dealing with the poor quality of data they produce is one of the main challenges in a High Fan-in (or any sensor-based) system. We believe that declarative queries can be used to specify cleaning functionality for any single device as well as across groups of devices.

- **Event Monitoring** – One of the main functions of a High Fan-in system is to continuously monitor the edge environment, and to send alerts when events of interest are detected. These events may vary significantly in terms of the timescales and geographic areas over which they are detected. While many commercial systems have developed their own "event languages", we believe that a stream query language (perhaps suitably extended) is the right substrate for such functionality.

- **Stream Correlation** – A further advantage of a query-based approach is that it natively supports the ability to compare and correlate data from multiple streams. Such streams may be homogeneous, as in the case of comparing temperature readings from a group of identical sensors, or heterogeneous, as in the case of combining temperature readings with RFID "beeps".

- **Outlier Detection** – Another form of data reduction provided by a HiFi System is outlier detection. In many monitoring systems, expected events are of less immediate interest than anomalies. Queries can be used to detect and propagate various types of outliers in a streaming environment.

As the above (partial) list indicates, we believe that stream query processing can serve as the basis of a wide range of High Fan-in functionality in a uniform manner. This is a significant departure from the *ad hoc* way in which such systems are currently being constructed. Our initial HiFi prototype has been developed as a proof-of-concept platform, in order to test the viability of our query-based approach.

3. Overview of the Demo

We have built an initial version of HiFi using the TelegraphCQ stream query processor and the TinyDB sensor database system. The goal of this prototype is to examine the feasibility of the uniform query processing model and to derive a better understanding of the core components required for building High Fan-in systems.

In this demo, we will show how to use HiFi to query and correlate data from multiple streaming sources. In particular we intend to implement a simple tracking application using passive RFID tags and sensor motes and showing the power of stream query processing for providing real-time analyses of correlated readings across multiple streams and device types and successive levels of aggregation. In addition to showing some gadgets such as RFID tags/readers and several classes of wireless sensor devices, we will also demonstrate some of the salient features of the architecture, including:

- Integration of multiple platforms including wireless sensor motes, passive RFID tags and readers, mid-tier sensor aggregation points, and host computers.

- Unified and adaptive cross-platform query optimization in this heterogeneous environment.

- In-network query processing both in the interior and at the edges of the network.

- The use of stream queries and views for providing key functionality such as data cleaning, filtering, and event detection.

- Support for continuous multi-level aggregation.

We will show HiFi running on a heterogeneous network consisting of at least the following platforms:

1) Laptop PCs

2) Intel Stargate low-power single-board computer.

3) Berkeley sensor motes capable of sensing light, temperature, and sound.

4) RFID readers with passive, read-only RFID tags.

The demonstration will highlight the various features and underlying technology of the HiFi design and will emphasize the power and flexibility of a uniform stream query model for supporting applications over multiple classes of receptor devices and networks.

REFERENCES

[CCDF+03] S. Chandrasekaran, O. Cooper, A. Deshpande, M. Franklin, J. Hellerstein, W. Hong, S. Krishnamurthy, S. Madden, V. Raman, F. Reiss, and M. Shah, "TelegraphCQ: Continuous Data Flow Processing for an Uncertain World", Proceedings of the 1st Conference on Innovative Data Systems Research (CIDR 2003), Asilomar, CA, January, 2003.

[MFHH03] S. Madden, M. Franklin, J. Hellerstein, and W. Hong, "The Design of an Acquisitional Query Processor for Sensor Networks", Proceedings of the ACM SIGMOD Int'l Conf. on Management of Data (SIGMOD 2003), San Diego, CA, June 2003, pp 491-502.

An Integration Framework for Sensor Networks and Data Stream Management Systems

Daniel J. Abadi
MIT

Wolfgang Lindner
MIT

Samuel Madden
MIT

Jörg Schuler
Tufts University

Computer Science and Artificial Intelligence Lab.
Massachusetts Institute of Technology
{dna, wolfgang, madden}@csail.mit.edu

Dept. of Computer Science
Tufts University
js@cs.tufts.edu

Abstract

This demonstration shows an integrated query processing environment where users can seamlessly query both a data stream management system and a sensor network with one query expression. By integrating the two query processing systems, the optimization goals of the sensor network (primarily power) and server network (primarily latency and quality) can be unified into one quality of service metric. The demo shows various steps of the unified optimization process for a sample query where the effects of each step that the optimizer takes can be directly viewed using a quality of service monitor. Our demo includes sensors deployed in the demo area in a tiny mockup of a factory application.

1 Introduction

Collections of tiny, radio-equipped, battery-powered sensing devices, or *sensornets* promise to collect a significant amount of interesting data about the world around us. Unlike conventional remote (satellite-based) sensing which typically consists of large images, sound files, or scientific data processed by individually developed software, much of the data from sensornets promises to be small, tuple-oriented, and structured. Typical applications include sensors that continuously report the temperature of refrigerated boxes being shipped across the country to detect spoilage or theft, or sensors that report the light and temperature values in various offices in a building as input to an HVAC (Heating, Ventilation, and Air Conditioning) control system. In recent years we have seen the development of sensor network query-processing systems (SNQPs), most notably Cougar [1] and TinyDB [8].

Alone, these systems provide a convenient interface for extracting data from sensornets. Furthermore, query optimization appears to be a promising approach for reducing sensornet power consumption [11, 7, 4], the primary sensor performance metric [6, 10]. Despite the promising advances seen in the research, we believe there is a substantial opportunity to further improve both the power efficiency and utility of SNQPs by their integration with one of several streaming database systems, such as STREAM [9], TelegraphCQ [5], or Aurora [3], commonly referred to as data stream management systems (DSMSs).

This integration offers three major benefits:

- The ability to combine stored or streaming data from the DSMS with data from the sensornet. For example, users may want to compute a join to decide if readings from a motion-detector are correlated with network activity, or if truck locations match the expected locations on the planned route.

- A single, integrated interface for interacting with both the streaming database and the sensor network. TinyDB currently allows users to log query results into a RDBMS table via JDBC, but queries must still be input to TinyDB independently of the RDBMS. By providing a single, seamless system, users are only required to learn to configure and interact with one set of interfaces.

- The ability to optimize between the database system and the sensor network. For example, it may be desirable to push certain filters and aggregates into the sensor network if user queries are interested in only particular subsets or coarse summaries of readings.

Permission to copy without fee all or part of this material is granted provided that the copies are not made or distributed for direct commercial advantage, the VLDB copyright notice and the title of the publication and its date appear, and notice is given that copying is by permission of the Very Large Data Base Endowment. To copy otherwise, or to republish, requires a fee and/or special permission from the Endowment.

**Proceedings of the 30th VLDB Conference,
Toronto, Canada, 2004**

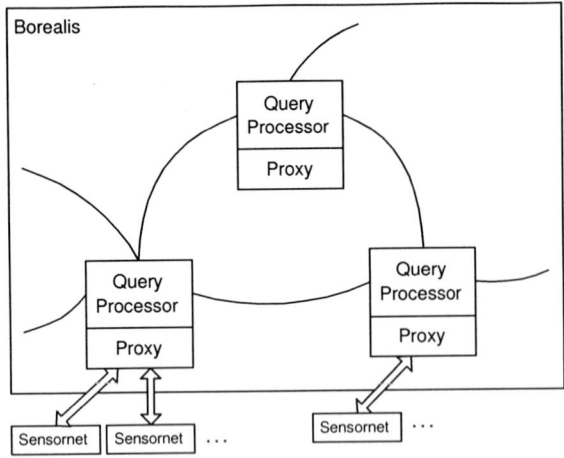

Figure 1: General Architecture

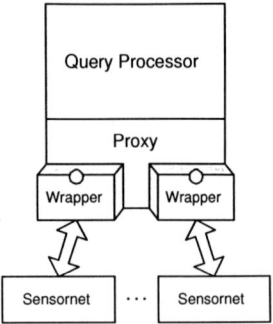

Figure 2: Proxy and Wrapper

We have begun the development of a next generation stream processing system, called Borealis [2], with a team from Brandeis, Brown, and MIT. This demonstration shows one piece of this larger project where the stream processing engine seamlessly queries a SNQP system.

Our demo includes sensors deployed in the demo area in a tiny mockup of a factory application; users can query both Borealis and TinyDB, and see the power consumption and efficiency of execution of their queries. A detailed description of our demonstration is provided in Section 4. Next we describe the general architecture of our system with a description of a few of the technical challenges.

2 Architecture

The architecture allows the sensor network to communicate its processing capabilities and constraints, along with descriptions of the data it can produce to the DSMS. It also provides a translation mechanism so that query operations entered through the DSMS application interface can be performed in the sensornet should the system choose to do so. In addition, it provides a way to resolve contrasting optimization goals of sensor networks and DSMSs. Finally, the architecture is sufficiently general so that future efforts to integrate other forms of data sources (with limited query processing capabilities) with DSMSs (such as xml-streams, web sources or even other DSMSs) can be worked into the same architecture.

Figure 1 shows an overview of our architecture. Here we show a DSMS (in our demonstration, a Borealis prototype) distributed across 3 sites, two of which receive data from sensor networks. The fundamental idea behind the integration architecture is to place a proxy intermediary at each interface between sensor networks and instances of the DSMS. The role of the proxy is to make the sensor network appear to the DSMS instance as if it were another instance running on a different site. The DSMS can then move operators and stored relations across the server/sensor boundary with the same ease as if it were moving across server/server boundaries.

We assume that each sensornet is uniquely connected to just one DSMS instance and that the sensornet is capable of performing some portion of the query plan. The proxy has three primary functions. First, it gathers statistics about constraints of connected subnetworks so that it can reject proposals from the DSMS to move operators or stored relations into the network (or change the parameters of operators already in the sensor network) that the sensor network does not have the processing power, storage, or bandwidth capacity to handle. Second, if it accepts an operator on behalf of the sensor network, it selects the appropriate implementation of the operator. Finally, it works with the DSMS to optimize the query (with respect to application QoS). This third function is described in Section 3. These functions are performed by the proxy for all connected sensor networks. However the proxy needs information about the current state of each connected subnetwork (e.g. how much available bandwidth is being used or how much power is remaining). For this reason, the proxy interacts with its sensornets using a *wrapper* for each network as shown in Figure 2. The wrapper provides a standardized API to integrate the connected sensornets into the optimization process. That includes a set of meta data which describes the related sensornet. All additional data sources to the DSMS are connected through these wrappers.

3 Query Optimization

Query optimization across a DSMS-sensor network integration faces three primary challenges. First, the processing capabilities of the sensor network is much smaller than the capabilities of the DSMS and thus only a subset of potential query plans (mappings of query operators to nodes upon which they will be run and implementations of these operators) can actually be executed.

Second, in contrast to a DSMS, in a sensor network the same operator will be run on multiple nodes (for standard SNQPs such as TinyDB). Thus, the decision is not where to put an operator in the sensor network, but whether to place an operator in the network at all. Such a decision must be made in a centralized manner since the result affects multiple nodes. The proxy architecture described above provides a simple solution to both of these problems in that the proxy serves as a central decision maker that is cognizant of the processing capabilities of the underlying network and can accept or reject query plans and operator movements using knowledge of these capabilities. For example, if the sensor network does not support windowed aggregations, the proxy can reject all query plans that involve the network performing a windowed aggregate operator.

The third challenge is that a DSMS and a sensor network have different and potentially conflicting goals. The DSMS is responsible for maximizing the QoS to end applications, and thus is interested in decreasing latency, increasing throughput, and maximizing the quality of results delivered to these applications. In contrast, a sensor network is primarily concerned with minimizing power consumption in order to extend lifetime and reduce cost. In some cases, these goals conflict. As a case in point consider whether or not to place a join operation (of sensor data with a static table) in a sensor network. Assume that the join predicate is highly selective, but that the static table is large so that the table must be horizontally partitioned and the join performed in parallel on many sensors. Assuming the network has the processing capability for the operator, it is in the sensor network's interest to perform the operation in-network since it reduces the number of transmitted tuples and thus power used. Due to the lossy nature of wireless communication, tuples generated by sensors might not reach nodes storing parts of the static join table, leading to lost join results. This affects the quality of results observed by the end application. While the sensor network might want to perform the join in-network, the DSMS might prefer to have the network just transmit the original data and perform the join once the data reaches the wired interface.

We attempt to solve this problem by aggregating sensor network constraints into one lifetime metric and supplementing DSMS QoS with an additional dimension to optimize. The lifetime of a query is equal to the minimum of the lifetimes of all data sources of this query. Lifetime can be thought of as a fixed amount of service the DSMS has bought from the sensor network. When the service runs out, no data will be produced for the query. This effectively terminates the query as a consequence. The more work the query requires of a sensor network, the faster the fixed amount of service is used. Thus, there is cost observable to the application in making decisions that might improve latency or quality while also increasing power utilization in the

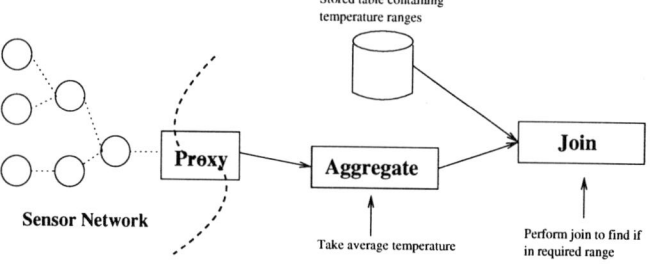

Figure 3: Query Shown as a Workflow Diagram

sensor network. This allows the DSMS to choose in which direction of the power/latency/quality trade-off to optimize using application QoS functions.

4 Demonstration Highlights

This demonstration shows a simulated factory environment with temperature sensitive construction phases. The factory produces a product whose creation requires the temperature to remain in a small, fixed range that varies over time. Should the temperature fall outside this range, the product is in danger of being damaged and action must be taken immediately. A continuous query is thus desired that joins aggregate temperature readings from sensors located at various positions in the factory with a time-indexed relation that encodes the desired temperature range. Should the temperature ever fall outside the required range, an appropriate reaction can be taken (such as to halt production until temperature falls within the required range).

We simulate this factory query with a small factory replica built out of Lego and placing inside it a portable air conditioner and several Mica motes that can sense ambient temperature.

The continuous query demonstrated is (in a derivative of TinySQL [8]):

```
SELECT a.atemp, a.anum
FROM schedule AS s,
     (SELECT AVG(temp) AS atemp,
             COUNT(temp) AS anum
      FROM sensors) AS a
WHERE s.ts > t.tsmin AND
      s.ts < t.tsmax AND
      a.atemp > t.tempmin AND
      a.atemp < t.tempmax
```

This query can be more clearly shown in a workflow diagram as in Figure 3.

As shown, the sensors relay their temperature readings through the proxy to the DSMS which then aggregates these readings and joins them with a stored table. There is clearly an alternative choice for where the aggregation and join can be performed: the sensor network. However, the decision of where to perform these operators has a variety of consequences on the QoS dimensions of power utilization, tuple loss rate, and latency. Further, the system has the option of changing the sensor sample rate to maximize the lifetime-tuple quality trade-off.

The demonstration shows, through a QoS monitor graphical interface, how QoS varies with system optimization decisions of operator movements and sensor sample rates. Other monitors show the results in each individual QoS dimension of these optimization decisions (the user can see the lifetime QoS increase when the aggregate operator moves into the sensor network and the quality dimension increasing at the same time as lifetime decreasing as the sensor sample rate is increased). The effects on latency, loss rate, and lifetime of moving the join operator into the sensor network depend on the size of the static table and the selectivity of the join predicates. We allow the user to send updates to the join table to observe how changing these statistics increases or decreases QoS upon moving the join into the network. We also allow the user to change the temperature of the air conditioned "factory" and to change the parameters of the query to observe the DSMS/sensor network integration successfully run the query.

5 Conclusion

It is clear that the integration of sensor networks and DSMSs is important. Sensor networks serve as a natural data source to DSMSs, and in return DSMSs are capable of executing much more complex operations on the data than nodes in the network, allowing a wider variety of queries to be performed on sensor produced data. Integration of these systems to create a unified query plan that will execute across DSMS/sensor boundaries is not a trivial task because of the different architectures and assumptions of these systems. Sensor networks (using SNQPs such as TinyDB) perform the same operation in parallel across many different nodes in a lossy and power constrained environment. The DSMS performs only one instance of an operation on a server node with fewer power, CPU, and storage constraints. Optimization of this query plan presents further difficulties. We demonstrate a successfully integrated sensor network and DSMS where user queries can be run and optimized across these heterogeneous query processing components.

References

[1] Cougar web page. http://www.cs.cornell.edu/database/cougar/.

[2] Daniel Abadi, Yanif Ahmad, Hari Balakrishnan, Magdalena Balazinska, Ugur Cetintemel, Mitch Cherniack, Jeong-Hyon Hwang, John Jannotti, Wolfgang Lindner, Samuel Madden, Alexander Rasin, Michael Stonebraker, Nesime Tatbul, Ying Xing, and Stan Zdonik. The design of the borealis stream processing engine. (submitted for publication).

[3] Daniel J. Abadi, Don Carney, Uğur Çetintemel, Mitch Cherniack, Christian Convey, Sangdon Lee, Michael Stonebraker, Nesime Tatbul, and Stan Zdonik. Aurora: A new model and architecture for data stream management. *VLDB Journal*, September 2003.

[4] Boris Bonfils and Philippe Bonnet. Adaptive and decentralized operator placement for in-network query processing. In *Proceedings of the First Workshop on Information Processing in Sensor Networks (IPSN)*, April 2003.

[5] S. Chandrasekaran, A. Deshpande, M. Franklin, J. Hellerstein, W. Hong, S. Krishnamurthy, S. Madden, V. Raman, F. Reiss, and M. Shah. TelegraphCQ: Continuous Dataflow Processing for an Uncertain World. January 2003.

[6] Chalermek Intanagonwiwat, Ramesh Govindan, and Deborah Estrin. Directed diffusion: A scalable and robust communication paradigm for sensor networks. In *MobiCOM*, Boston, MA, August 2000.

[7] Samuel Madden, Michael J. Franklin, Joseph M. Hellerstein, and Wei Hong. The design of an acquisitional query processor for sensor networks. In *ACM SIGMOD*, 2003.

[8] Samuel Madden, Wei Hong, Joseph M. Hellerstein, and Michael Franklin. TinyDB web page. http://telegraph.cs.berkeley.edu/tinydb.

[9] R. Motwani, J. Window, A. Arasu, B. Babcock, S.Babu, M. Data, C. Olston, J. Rosenstein, and R. Varma. Query processing, approximation and resource management in a data stream management system. In *CIDR*, 2003.

[10] Greg Pottie and William Kaiser. Wireless integrated network sensors. *Communications of the ACM*, 43(5):51 – 58, May 2000.

[11] Yong Yao and Johannes Gehrke. Query processing in sensor networks. In *Proceedings of the First Biennial Conference on Innovative Data Systems Research (CIDR)*, 2003.

QStream: Deterministic Querying of Data Streams

Sven Schmidt, Henrike Berthold and Wolfgang Lehner

Dresden University of Technology
Database Technology Group
dbgroup@mail.inf.tu-dresden.de

Abstract

Current developments in processing data streams are based on the best-effort principle and therefore not adequate for many application areas. When sensor data is gathered by interface hardware and is used for triggering data-dependent actions, the data has to be queried and processed not only in an efficient but also in a deterministic way. Our streaming system prototype embodies novel data processing techniques. It is based on an operator component model and runs on top of a real-time capable environment. This enables us to provide real Quality-of-Service for data stream queries.

1 Motivation

In recent years, the amount of data delivered by a variety of sensors has grown significantly. There are a lot of examples of sensors being installed to continuously measure physical properties and to send these values to back-end systems for further processing.

Once a sensor data stream is connected to a stream processing system, the continuous/standing queries have to be evaluated on that data. Based on the query results, fast reactions may be necessary. To give an example, think of a meteorological system where acquired data such as temperature, humidity, atmospheric pressure, brightness and rainfall etc. form the basis for statistical analyses on the one hand and for sophisticated forecast and reaction on the other hand. The latter includes the detection of abnormal situations identified by characteristic constellations of the sensor input values.

In industrial application areas, sensors are used in production processes to observe the progress of single manufacturing steps. For example, the positional measures of a complex robotics form a data stream and are used for position tracking. Once the robotics reaches its final destination or is intended to stop immediately in case of an emergency, the data stream processing system has to react within a given time limit. Thus, based on the sensor data, the processes can be controlled and successfully completed.

Within a best-effort streaming system (e.g. [1, 2]), no one can give any guarantees for the exact evaluation of queries and for the amount of time elapsing between a characteristic constellation of input values and the reaction of the system. Within our real-time streaming project (QStream) we

- describe a set of stream operators plus their functional and non-functional properties,
- rely on a model for resource description in streaming environments,
- define Quality-of-Service parameters and enable the user to negotiate them, and
- implement this conceptual work on top of a real-time capable system environment.

The goal of QStream is to evaluate queries on data streams in a deterministic way: Once a query is registered and accepted by the system, it will be successfully completed independently from any system load or data stream load without compromising the negotiated quality constraints. These quality constraints mainly consist of result precision and time delay of the query evaluation system.

2 Operator Component Model

In QStream, after query parsing, a stream query is represented by a network of operators (figure 1). This network deals with a number of sensor originated input streams and produces one single output stream for each registered query.

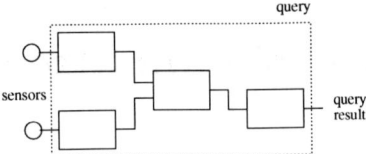

Figure 1: operator network

Thereby an operator is a small work unit which reads tuples from its input buffer, does some processing work, and writes the resulting tuples to an output buffer. The basic work includes *one* data read, *one* data processing and *one* data write. We will call it a *run*. The amount of data such an operator processes within a certain (amount of) time is reflected by the data rate. The initial data rate is determined by the sensor data sources. The relationship between input and output data rate of an operator belongs to the operator description.

Within QStream we do not contribute a new data model or completely new operators. Instead we propose a novel technology for their implementation. For sake of completeness, the operators currently supported are listed below:

- Filter: A filter drops tuples which do not conform to a given predicate. The resulting data rate depends on the input data rate and on the selectivity of the applied predicate, which has to be derived from statistical information, such as value distributions, about the input stream.

- Sample: The sample operator randomly discards tuples with a specified sampling rate. The data rate of the output stream can be calculated from the data rate of the input stream and the sampling rate.

- Aggregation: An aggregation operator is either a summation or the calculation of an average on a specified attribute. The output data rate decreases with a larger aggregation group size.

- Grouping and Aggregation: The grouping-and-aggregation operator performs a grouping on an ordering attribute (such as the minutes of a time attribute with precision of seconds) and an aggregation (SUM or AVG) on another attribute. As with aggregation, the output data rate depends on the input data rate and on the average group size.

- Map: The map operator applies a scalar function locally to a tuple. It calculates for example a new value from two tuple values and adds it to the tuple. The data rates of both streams are identical. Only the tuple size may change.

- Pairing: The pairing operator performs a join operation on an ordered attribute for example on a global time. It consists of two input streams and one output stream. The data rate of the output stream is identical to the data rates of the input streams.

Operator interfaces

One of our basic ideas is to run each operator of the operator network independently within the operating system environment. Thus, an operator has a control and a data exchange interface (figure 2). Through the control interface, each operator is parameterized before the data stream processing starts; it is continuously monitored; and (if necessary) it is adjusted during runtime. The data exchange interface is responsible for transferring the tuples from operator to operator.

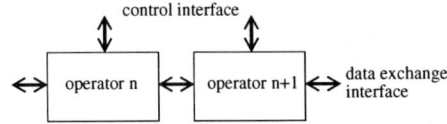

Figure 2: operator interfaces

3 Controlling the Operator Network

The QStream control application first builds an operator network from a stream query. Thereafter, it calculates memory requirements and processing times for each single operator based on the data stream characteristics and on the users negotiated quality constraints. When the network construction and resource calculation process is complete, the control application tries to schedule the values with the operating system's resource manager and, thus, performs an admission control. This implies that the number of accepted stream queries depends on the characteristics of the data stream (data rate, bursts) and on the complexity of the queries, and that it is limited by the overall resources of the QStream system. It is important to notice that once a query has passed the admission control, a successful evaluation of the data streams within the negotiated quality constraints is guaranteed.

Scheduling

Scheduling covers issues about how often and how long an operator is supposed to perform its work. We propose the concept of an 'optimal processing speed' of the operator network: If the operators run too slow (perform a run very rarely), the quality constraints regarding query delay and precision may not be fulfilled. On the other hand it is inadequate to speed up the operator network (perform the runs very frequently) or pass through the sensors high data rates if the user is only interested in approximate values and if a time limit for answering the queries does not exist. This would result in slowing down concurrently running processes.

For the deterministic behavior regarding the processing times we rely on a real-time operating system (RTOS) environment. Firstly, this enables us to schedule precisely, and secondly, we are able to encapsulate the QStream operators from applications with no real-time requirements.

All of the QStream operators are periodic processes. Thus, an operator periodically performs some work. Moreover, the RTOS signals the operator the start of the next run.

Periods

Based on the data rate of the sensors and based on the data rate requirements/quality constraints at the output of the operator network, the period length P_O of each operator is determined. Therefore, the number of tuples which are to be produced during a single run (given by the operator description) is taken into account. The resulting periods are scheduled for the QStream operators. The RTOS has the responsibility to signal each period start to the specific operator. The operator itself has to ensure that it completes its work during the operator processing time t_O, whereas $t_O << P_O$.

The processing time t_O is the time required by a virtually isolated operator for a single operation. The simplest method for obtaining t_O is to measure it on a reference system with only one operator running at a time.

In general, multiple operators $O_1, ..., O_n$ form an operator network and, thus, work in parallel (all in real-time mode). The time needed to run all n operators is the sum of the single operators' processing times. Therefore, the operator processing times t_O have to be normalized ($\hat{t}_O$) to a common period length $\hat{P}_O$ for summation: $T = \sum_{k=1}^{n}(\hat{t}_O)$. The n operations may be considered as 'serialized', even though the RTOS scheduler will break down each t_O into a number of CPU time slices and execute them in an interleaved way.

Thus, for a well-scheduled system we have to ensure that $T < \hat{P}_O$. Otherwise, there would be not enough processing time to let all the operators work in parallel.

Data Exchange Model

Since operators are independently scheduled real-time processes within our prototype, they cannot make blocking function calls to the previous or to the next operator for handing over tuples. Obviously, an intermediate buffer between each pair of consecutive operators is established. One of the operators takes the role of a data producer, the other has the role of a consumer regarding the intermediate buffer (figure 3).

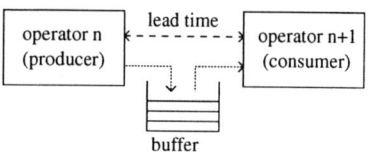

Figure 3: producer-consumer-relationship

Each time the producer completes a run, it puts the output tuples into the intermediate buffer for the consumer to pick them up at the start of its next working period. There are two conditions that must hold for the non-blocking data exchange: The producer must not try to write into a full buffer and the consumer must not try to read from an empty one. Thus, the minimum size of the buffer as well as the starting point of the different operators are of interest. In our prototype, we use the model of jitter-constrained periodic streams (JCP, [4]). This model is applied to a single producer-consumer relationship and allows the calculation of the minimum intermediate buffer size B and the lead time t_{lead} of the consumer. Relying on the model, we have to provide

- the average number of tuples the producer writes during one run

- the number of tuples the consumer reads during one run

- the period lengths P_O of both producer and consumer

- the producers' processing time t_O for one run

Additionally, this model takes into account the effects of jitter within the data stream and within the operators behavior: A size jitter allows the operator to produce a varying number of output tuples (depending on the stream data) per operation and a time jitter reflects the fact that the processing time for a run t_O may jitter in certain constraints. The general observation is: the larger the different jitters are, the higher the resulting intermediate buffer must be.

4 Prototype

We selected the Realtime Application Interface (RTAI, [3]) as operating system environment for QStream because, first, RTAI supports hard real-time as well as soft real-time. Second, real-time code may not only run as a kernel module but also as a user program. And third, a lot of data exchange mechanisms such as FIFOs, mailboxes and shared memory are originally provided by RTAI.

Within RTAI, our operators run in real-time mode while other processes (e.g. other Linux applications) have only non-real-time privileges. Non-real-time processes get the remaining processing time after all operators have finished the work within their periods.

Figure 4 illustrates measured times t_O of a filter operator running as a real-time process and the same operator running as non-real-time. In both scenarios we produce heavy load in the background.

The real-time graph of figure 4 shows that the background load does not significantly influence our periodic filter operator because the background process runs as non-real-time Linux process.

The measured run times for the filter operator in non-real-time mode are permanently higher than in real-time mode because the filter process only gets the same priority as concurrently running Linux processes.

Much more important, the filter's t_O increases by multiples of ten due to the varying load of the background process. Thus, for deterministic operator behavior we *must* rely on a real-time capable environment.

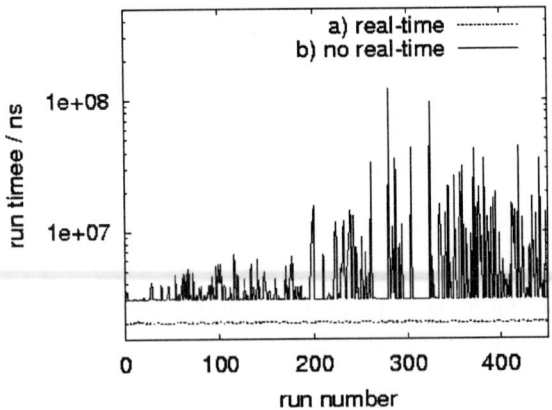

Figure 4: filter operator with background load

Controlling

The control application is executed in five steps. First, the control application traverses the user-given operator network and calculates the data rates between each couple of operators. This is done from the data sources (sensors) down to the data sink (last operator). If the resulting data rate at the data sink is higher than the user requirements (QoS), an initial sample operator is inserted in front of the first operator to reduce the amount of processed data.

Second, the control application calculates the operator period lengths with the operators' input and output data rate in mind. The model of jitter-constrained periodic streams is subsequently applied to each producer-consumer relationship of operators. This provides the intermediate buffer sizes and the lead time of an operator in producer role.

Third, the total memory requirement is obtained as the sum of all buffer sizes plus the static amount of operator memory. The absolute starting points of the single operators are derived from the relative values (lead time).

In a fourth step, the operator processes are initialized with the period length P_O and queued to start exactly at the pre-calculated point in time.

Finally, the operators continuously work and periodically start a new run after the specified period has elapsed.

Data Exchange

We exploit the features of the RTAI FIFOs for data exchange. An arbitrary number of applications is allowed to connect to such a FIFO, either as a FIFO writer (producer) or as a FIFO reader (consumer). In QStream, two FIFOs are established between consecutive operators: one for exchanging the tuples (variable tuple size) and one for handing over the packet control information.

The synchronization of the FIFO access is entirely managed by RTAI. From the operators' point of view, the FIFO is created with a size parameter which is equal to the buffer size B calculated in the control application. Relying on the scheduling and on the deterministic real-time behavior, none of our operators is blocked when reading from or writing to a FIFO.

The QStream demonstration will show how to negotiate QoS parameters for a given operator network and how the QStream operators run on top of the real-time environment.

References

[1] Don Carney, Ugur Çetintemel, Alex Rasin, Stan Zdonik, Mitch Cherniack, and Michael Stonebraker. Operator scheduling in a data stream manager. In *Proc. of 29th International Conference on Very Large Databases, September 9-12, 2003, Berlin, Germany*, pages 838–849, 2003.

[2] Charles D. Cranor, Theodore Johnson, Oliver Spatscheck, and Vladislav Shkapenyuk. Gigascope: A stream database for network applications. In *Proc. of the 2003 ACM SIGMOD International Conference on Management of Data, June 9-12, 2003, San Diego, CA, USA*, pages 647–651, 2003.

[3] Lorenzo Dozio and Paolo Mantegazza. Real time distributed control systems using rtai. In *In Proc. of the 6th IEEE International Symposium on Object-Oriented Real-Time Distributed Computing, May 14-16, 2003, Hakodate, Hokkaido, Japan*, pages 11–18, 2003.

[4] Claude-Joachim Hamann. On the quantitative specification of jitter constrained periodic streams. In *Proc. of the Fifth International Symposium on Modeling, Analysis and Simulation of Computer and Telecommunication Systems, January 12-15, 1997 Haifa, Israel*, pages 171–176, 1997.

AIDA: an Adaptive Immersive Data Analyzer

Mehdi Sharifzadeh, Cyrus Shahabi, Bahareh Navai, Farid Parvini and Albert A. Rizzo

Integrated Media Systems Center & Computer Science Department
University of Southern California
Los Angeles, CA 90089-0781
[sharifza,shahabi,navai,fparvini,arizzo]@usc.edu

Abstract

In this demonstration, we show various querying capabilities of an application called AIDA. AIDA is developed to help the study of attention disorder in kids. In a different study [1], we collected several immresive sensory data streams from kids monitored in an immersive application called *the virtual classroom*. This dataset, termed *immersidata* is used to analyze the behavior of kids in the virtual classroom environment. AIDA's database stores all the geometry of the objects in the virtual classroom environment and their spatio-temporal behavior. In addition, it stores all the immersidata collected from the kids experimenting with the application. AIDA's graphical user interface then supports various spatio-temporal queries on these datasets. Moreover, AIDA replays the immersidata streams as if they are collected in real-time and on which supports various continuous queries. This demonstration is a proof-of-concept prototype of a typical design and development of a domain-specific query and analysis application on the users' interaction data with immersive environments.

1 Introduction

With *Immersive Environments*, a user is immersed into an augmented or virtual reality environment in order to interact with people, objects, places, and databases. Many prototypical applications of these immersive environments already exist (see [3] for a list). In a previous publication [1], we reported on the implementation of an immersive environment, called *the virtual classroom (VC)*, designed to conduct attention testing. In particular, the application focused on the assessment of attention process in children with Attention Deficit Hyperactivity Disorder (ADHD). With VC, we conducted trials with 18 children experiencing a virtual class environment through a Head Mounted Display (HMD). The children were asked to complete a task in the presence of different types of virtual distractions. While they were accomplishing the task, we collected several immersive sensory data streams including their body movements through trackers. This valuable dataset, termed *immersidata*, is a rich source of information by analyzing which we can learn a lot about the kids behavior as well as the application itself. For example, one can issue complex queries on the dataset retrieving high-level behavioral patterns such as *loss of attention* or even differentiate between ADHD-diagnosed and normal kids.

In this demonstration, we present AIDA, a data analyzer for the virtual classroom. We show our schema developed for VC on top of an OR-DBMS. AIDA's database which is built in Oracle 9i stores three different sets of data. The first set includes all the geometry data of the VC's virtual environment such as the shape and location of a blackboard. AIDA uses Oracle Spatial Option to conceptualize this set as spatio-temporal data. The second set is similar to traditional record-based data and includes the personal profile about each kid, her answers to pre and post experiment questionnaires and the mouse clickstreams responses to the VC tasks. Finally, the third set is the streamed data acquired from a kid's interactions with VC. The immersidata mainly includes the position and orientation of a kid's head, legs and hands generated by various trackers on the body parts.

AIDA exploits the schema to support sophisticated and useful queries on the kids' interactions with the application. AIDA's graphical user interface facilitates forming spatial and temporal parameters for various query types on the VC data. Moreover, we have implemented a simulated immersidata generator within

---

Permission to copy without fee all or part of this material is granted provided that the copies are not made or distributed for direct commercial advantage, the VLDB copyright notice and the title of the publication and its date appear, and notice is given that copying is by permission of the Very Large Data Base Endowment. To copy otherwise, or to republish, requires a fee and/or special permission from the Endowment.

**Proceedings of the 30th VLDB Conference,
Toronto, Canada, 2004**

AIDA. This simulator *replays* the kids' interactions with VC and the spatio-temporal behavior of its objects. Subsequently, AIDA supports online continuous queries on the corresponding data streams. The online query component of AIDA can be incorporated in a real-time query interface for VC. Furthermore, the support for online and *continuous* queries in AIDA provides useful inputs for the future *feedback driven* applications [3].

The remainder of the paper is organized as follows. Section 2 describes the virtual classroom application. Section 3 discusses AIDA's components, namely its database schema, queries and GUI. In Section 4, we describe research issues in immersive data query and analysis. Section 6 draws the conclusion.

2 The Virtual Classroom Application

The *Virtual Classroom* is an HMD virtual environment designed to test attention performance in normal children and those diagnosed with ADHD [1]. The objective of the application is to differentiate these two user groups by analyzing their performances within VC. The VC's virtual environment consists of a typical classroom with all common objects (e.g., desks and chairs). A typical VC task consists of alphabetic characters that are sequentially displayed on the blackboard with the child instructed to press a button when a particular letter pattern (e.g., an X preceded by an A) is seen. At the same time, a series of typical classroom distractions are systematically manipulated within VC. In addition to the attention response measures, trackers placed on the head, hands and legs monitor body movements of the child and stream the data continuously.

Upon collecting such immersidata over a series of trials, psychologists would like to be able to ask a variety of queries about the stored dataset. The queries can be as simple as: "Which distraction was present when a particular child missed a target?", to more complex queries such as "Automatically distinguish ADHD children from normal ones". We conducted a clinical trial using VC with 8 physician-referred ADHD and 10 nondiagnosed children and stored their interaction data in AIDA's database.

3 AIDA's Components

In this section, we first conceptualize the VC's data using an object-relational data model. This conceptual database design is included in the Stream Query Repository (SQR)[1], a repository of data stream schema and queries maintained as a resource for researchers in data streams. Then, we briefly discuss different query categories supported in AIDA. Finally, we describe the look and feel of our demonstration.

[1] http://www-db.stanford.edu/stream/sqr.

3.1 Database Schema

We used the general schema proposed in [3] to design the database schema of AIDA. According to [3], the main components of an immersive environment are subject(s), *virtual space*, *actor objects* and a task objective, *mission*. We briefly define each in turn. **Subject** is a human character who performs a task in the environment. During the task performance, she interacts with virtual objects and/or other subjects in the environment. **Virtual space** is a simulation of real world generated using Virtual Reality (VR) techniques or Projected Videos. The space is defined as geometry of some static *scene objects*. These are static objects like chairs, desks and blackboard in the VC application. **Actor objects** are objects whose appearance or disappearance in the space or their changes in position during the system lifetime are main causes of the system events (e.g., characters displayed on the blackboard in VC). **Mission** is the task which a subject is asked to perform while immersed in the environment. Recognizing AX patterns is the main mission of VC.

Different entity types are required in order to describe different datasets generated by and maintained for an immersive environments such as VC. These datasets are categorized into three groups. The first group of entities conceptualizes various traditional datasets within VC. The conventional relational model would suffice to describe these datasets:

- Subjects <sid, age, gender, type> represents the subject(s) monitored within VC.
- OnlineInput$_s$[2] <sid, time, response> includes subject's answers to the VC mission as mouse clickstreams.
- OfflineInput <sid, question, response> specifies subject's answer to off-line questionnaires before or after the VC mission.

The second group describes the spatial and temporal datasets. The object-relational model is used to describe these data types. For implementation purposes, an object-relational database with spatial and temporal extensions can be used. In this demonstration, we have used Oracle 9i with Oracle Spatial Option installed in order to store and query the VC's spatial datasets. Spatial, geometry and temporal aspects of objects are provided accurately by the rendering subsystem. The position attribute in the following entities is implemented as a SDO_GEOMETRY data type in Oracle spatial cartridge:

- SceneObjects <soid, name, position> contains geometry of scene objects that constitute the virtual space (i.e., a classroom in VC).
- ActorObjects <aoid, name, type> are dynamic moving objects in the environment (e.g., a flying paper plane).
- ObjectsTrajectory$_s$ <aoid, time, position> represents *actor_object* movements.

[2] We use the subscript *s* for the entities whose corresponding dataset is a data stream.

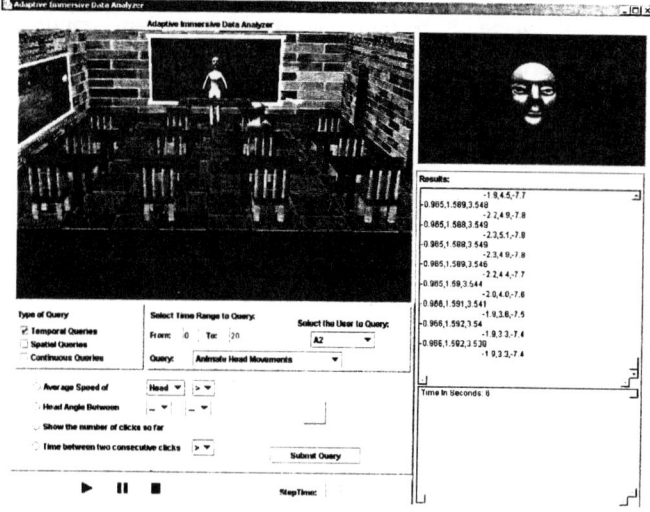

Figure 1: The main interface window of AIDA

The immersidata, conceptualizes data generated as a result of subject(s) interactions VC:

- $BodyPositions_s$ <sid, partId, time, position, rotation> specifies the position of each part of the subject body as well as the rotation of the part with reference to a 3-D coordinate space. This information has been acquired during the mission through the trackers.

3.2 Queries

We have implemented a rich set of queries to extract a subject behavior or search for patterns of interest from the subject's interactions with VC. Although AIDA is a specific data analyzer for the VC application but this interactive system supports various predefined queries which are common across different immersive environments. Below are some examples of the queries:

Subject behavior queries are focused on extracting relationships among her performance during the mission, her body movements and the events occurred in the environment. As an example, *subject attention* is a common behavioral concept that can be identified by analyzing subject's interactions. This concept is useful to evaluate the subject performance after a mission. We define subject attention based on whether she should have been distracted while performing a VC task or not. In our conceptual design for the VC application, appearance of an actor object within a certain distance of subject can potentially result in a distraction. If the subject has moved her head towards the object, a distraction has occurred.

Subject performance queries report the quality of her responses to the corresponding task while she was interacting with the environment components. One simple example is this query: *"Grade the subject based on the number of correct button clicks and missed AX patterns"*.

Spatio-temporal range queries can retrieve components based on their both spatial and temporal dimensions. Different query types are identified in this category based on the definition of spatial or temporal range window. For one class of range queries in the form: *Report all the objects with a distance more than d from the subject in the first 10 seconds of the mission,* the temporal window has a fixed width. A different query is defined when temporal or spatial window size is the result of another query. For example, *"Which actor objects were within a distance d of the subject during the times that she was looking to the left?"*

Spatial/Temporal kNN queries[3] are specified with a temporal range and a kNN predicate on spatial dimensions or vice versa. An example of the implemented kNN queries is *"Identify the 2 closest actor objects to the subject in the recent 20 seconds"*. We use spatial primitive functions provided by spatiotemporal databases for retrieving N nearest objects to a given object.

Spatial aggregate queries deal with abstractions of subject and/or object locations in space. For example, *"What is the average speed of the subject's leg movement during the VC mission?"* or *"For each subject, report the total distance of her head movements"*.

Temporal aggregate queries are specified by aggregating the temporal dimension of entities. For example, *"What is the subject average response time to AX patterns?"* or *"What is the percentage of the times when subject was not looking at the blackboard during the whole mission period?"*

3.3 Continuous Queries

We have built a simulated data stream generator within AIDA that replays the immersidata streams as if they are collected in real-time during the experimentation with the VC application. AIDA's *stream mode* addresses common stream processing challenges to answer continuous queries issued on the *replayed* immersidata streams.

We have implemented continuous version of the queries described in Section 3.2. With the *stream mode*, each query is assigned a sliding window parameter. An example of a continuous spatial aggregate query using a sliding window is *"Continuously report the average speed of the subject's head movements during the recent 10 seconds."*. The result helps to find the subject's specific disorders in the real environment. Likewise, a continuous behavior query helps to monitor the subject in real-time and direct her attention to the task. An example is *"Show a warning when the subject is looking at the window."*.

3.4 Graphical User Interface

AIDA is implemented in Java, using JDBC protocol for connecting to the back-end OR-DBMS. As it is shown in Figure 1, AIDA's user interface consists of several frames. In the upper left window, the immersive classroom as it is seen by the subject is mod-

---
[3] k-nearest neighbor search

elled. This 3-D model has been generated based on the spatial data maintained about the immersive environment. This model displays the general plan of the class, location of the subject, scene objects and distractions (e.g., activities occurring outside the window). In the upper right window, a head model representing the subjects head is displayed based on the immersidata generated by her head tracker. The movements of the subjects head during the mission can be visualized by this model. In the bottom window, the user can choose either spatial or temporal types of queries and specify the appropriate parameters. Different input controls have been provided to specify required temporal ranges for temporal queries as time intervals relative to the total duration of each mission.

In the *static mode*, all the queries are issued against the data stored in the database. Since the received data from the immersive environment can be used to represent the animated model and reconstructing the events, typical media browsing controls (e.g., play and pause) have been provided in the user interface. Using this set of controls, user can easily *replay* the mission for each subject in order to verify the validity of the query results. In the *stream mode*, AIDA provides the user with the ability to perform online and continuous queries on the replayed data streams as if they are being generated from the actual VC environment.

4 Research Issues

In this section, we briefly describe our previous studies in managing immersive datasets. In [1], we reported on how the virtual classroom application is used for the study, assessment, and rehabilitation of human cognitive and functional processes. We reported our initial observations revealed after a clinical trial conducted with 18 normal and ADHD-diagnosed kids.

In [3], we provided a framework towards the modelling data of immersive environments after studying several prototypical immersive environments. We showed the effectiveness of our model by using it in formalization of a wide range of complex queries from knowledge discovery to spatio-temporal queries.

In [2], we introduced *AIMS*, An Immersidata Management System. We discussed the challenges involved in managing the multidimensional sensor data streams generated within immersive environments. We studied the challenges of two main modes of operations on immersidata: off-line and online query and analysis. In addition, we proposed complementary approaches for efficient acquisition and storage of immersidata. The core promising idea behind *AIMS* approaches is a '*database friendly*' utilization of linear algebraic transformations on both datasets and queries to efficiently abstract, aggregate, classify and/or approximate multidimensional data streams.

We studied online stream queries over immersidata in [4]. We focused on recognizing a specific behavior by real-time analysis of immersidata as it becomes available, e.g., recognizing American Sign Language (ASL) sign from a user's hand motion. We viewed this problem as *real-time pattern isolation and recognition over immersive sensor data streams*. We first proposed a distance metric, Weighted-Sum Singular Value Decomposition (WSSVD), suitable for similarity measurement of immersive data sequences. Subsequently, we proposed a mutual information based heuristic for segmentation of the immersidata sequences.

5 Acknowledgement

This research has been funded in part by NSF grants EEC-9529152 (IMSC ERC), IIS-0238560 (CAREER), and IIS-0307908, and unrestricted cash gifts from Microsoft. Any opinions, findings, and conclusions or recommendations expressed in this material are those of the authors and do not necessarily reflect the views of the National Science Foundation.

6 Conclusion

We described AIDA, an application to help the study of attention disorder in children. We implemented AIDA's database using an object-relational database and populated it by data pertaining to the virtual classroom application. Within AIDA, we incorporated a rich set of continuous and static spatio-temporal queries whose answers help in assessment and rehabilitation of ADHD-diagnosed kids. Moreover, AIDA employs animation to replay the real-world experiments, illustrates the kid's behavior, and supports online continuous queries. We believe that AIDA's database schema design and efficient querying capabilities are common for general immersive environments. As a proof of concept for our ongoing research on immersive datasets, AIDA showed the effectiveness of our data model by incorporating different classes of general-purpose and application-specific continuous and static spatio-temporal queries.

References

[1] Albert A. Rizzo, Todd Bowerly, Cyrus Shahabi and J. Galen Buckwalter, Diagnosing Attention Disorders in a Virtual Classroom, *IEEE Computer*, Vol. 37, No 6, June 2004.

[2] Cyrus Shahabi, AIMS: An Immersidata Management System, *CIDR'03: Conference on Innovative Data Systems Research*, January 2003.

[3] Cyrus Shahabi, Mehdi Sharifzadeh and Albert A. Rizzo, Modeling Data of Immersive Environments, *ACM First International Workshop on Immersive Telepresence (ITP 2002)*, Juan Les Pins, France, December 2002.

[4] C. Shahabi and Donghui Yan, Real-Time Pattern Isolation And Recognition Over Immersive Sensor Data Streams, *The 9th International Conference On Multi-Media Modeling*, Taiwan, January 2003.

BilVideo Video Database Management System

Özgür Ulusoy, Uğur Güdükbay, Mehmet Emin Dönderler, Ediz Şaykol and Cemil Alper

Department of Computer Engineering
Bilkent University
06800, Ankara, Turkey

Abstract

A prototype video database management system, which we call BilVideo, is presented. BilVideo provides an integrated support for queries on spatio-temporal, semantic and low-level features (color, shape, and texture) on video data. BilVideo does not target a specific application, and thus, it can be used to support any application with video data. An example application, news archives search system, is presented with some sample queries.

1. Introduction

We present a video database management system (BilVideo), which provides an integrated support for queries on spatio-temporal, semantic and low-level features (color, shape, and texture) on video data. The aspects of BilVideo distinguishing it from the others can be listed as follows:

- BilVideo handles spatio-temporal queries using a knowledge-base, which consists of a fact-base and a comprehensive set of rules implemented in Prolog, while queries on semantic and low-level features are handled by an object-relational database. A spatio-temporal query may contain any combination of directional, topological, 3D-relation, object-appearance, trajectory-projection and similarity-based object-trajectory conditions. The rules in the knowledge-base significantly reduce the number of facts representing the relations that need to be stored for spatio-temporal querying of video data whilst keeping the query response time reasonably short.
- A novel approach is proposed for the segmentation of video clips based on the spatial relationships between salient objects in video data. Video clips are segmented into shots whenever the current set of relations between video salient objects changes.
- The systems proposed so far in the literature associate video features with scenes that are defined to be the smallest logical units of video clips. However, our data model supports a finer granularity for query processing, which is independent of semantic segmentation of video clips: it allows users to retrieve any segment of a video clip, in addition to semantic video units, as a result of a query.
- BilVideo supports any application with spatio-temporal and semantic query requirements on video data; therefore, it is application-independent. However, it can easily be tailored according to specific requirements of such applications through the definition of external predicates supported by its query language without any loss in performance.

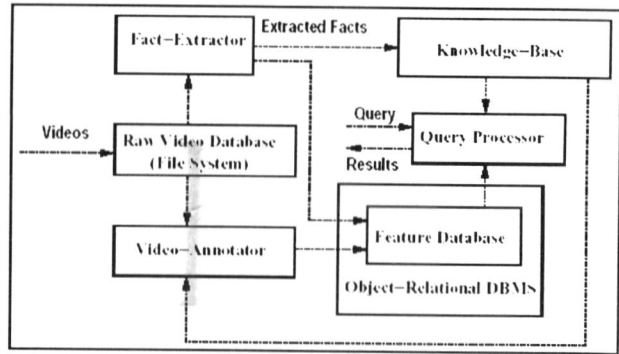

Figure 1: BilVideo System Architecture.

2. BilVideo System Architecture

In BilVideo, a visual query is formed by a collection of objects with some conditions, such as object trajectories with similarity measure, spatio-temporal ordering of objects, annotations and events. Object motion is specified as an arbitrary trajectory and annotations are used for keyword-based search. A text-based SQL-like query language is also available for the users. In the heart of the system lies the query processor (see Fig. 1). The feature database contains semantic properties of videos used for keyword, activity/event and category-based queries. These features are generated by *Video-Annotator*. The knowledge-base is used to support spatio-temporal queries and the facts-base is populated by *Fact-Extractor*.

Permission to copy without fee all or part of this material is granted provided that the copies are not made or distributed for direct commercial advantage, the VLDB copyright notice and the title of the publication and its date appear, and notice is given that copying is by permission of the Very Large Data Base Endowment. To copy otherwise, or to republish, requires a fee and/or special permission from the Endowment

**Proceedings of the 30th VLDB Conference,
Toronto, Canada, 2004**

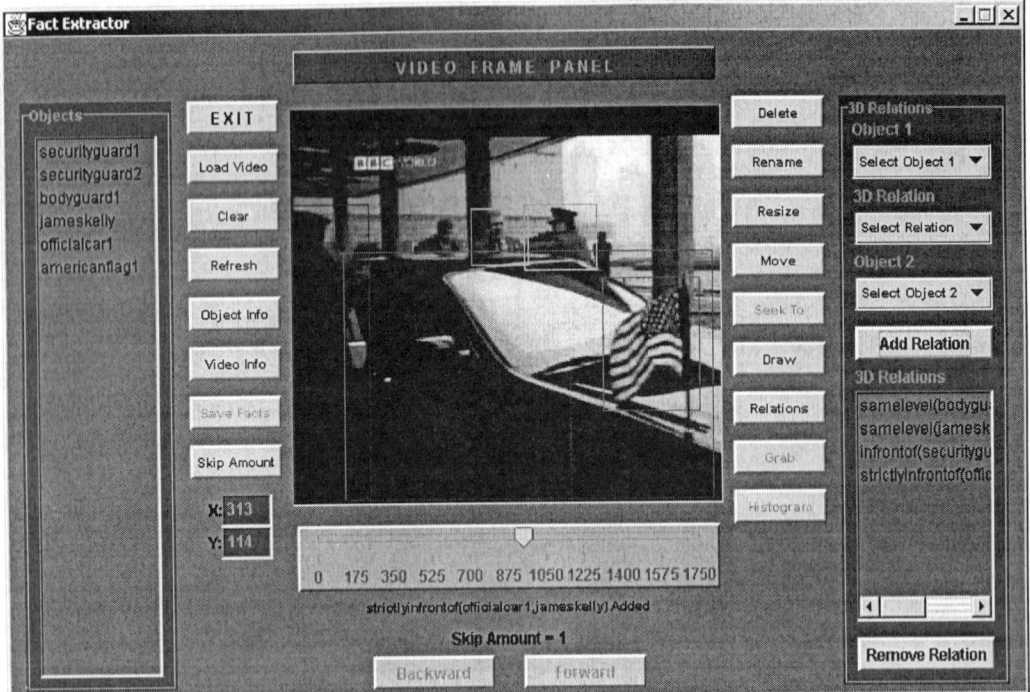

Figure 2: Fact-Extractor

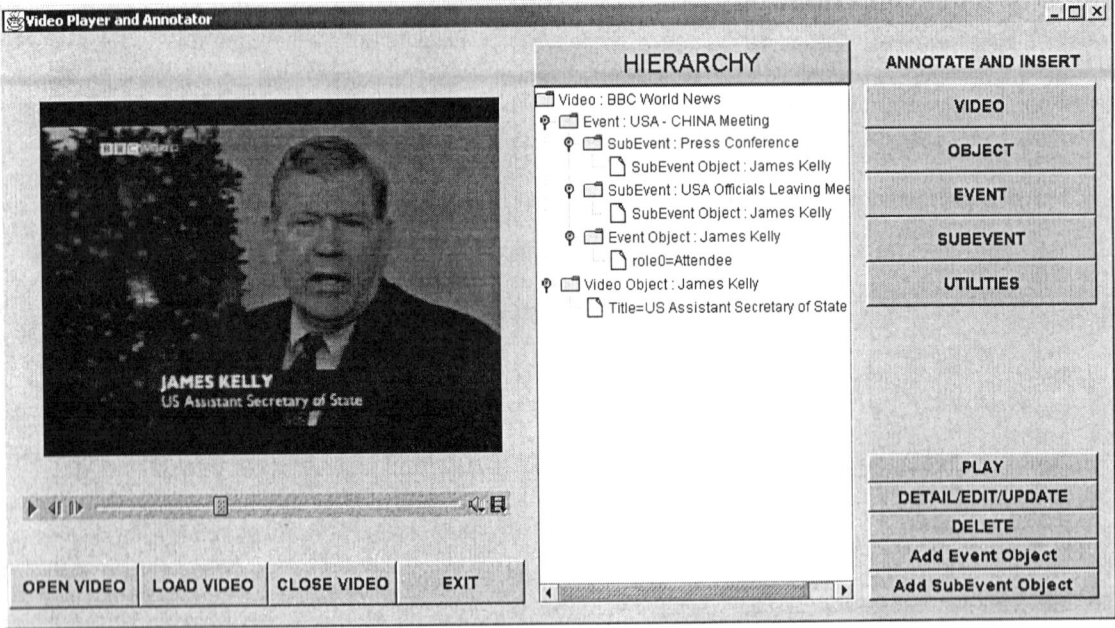

Figure 3: Video Annotator Tool.

2.1 Fact-Extractor

Fact Extractor computes a set of spatio-temporal relations between the salient objects in frames using the objects' minimum bounding rectangles (MBRs). The rules in the knowledge-base are used to eliminate the relations that can be derived using existing ones. Object trajectories and object-appearance relations are also extracted (Fig. 2).

2.2 Video Annotator

The *Video-Annotator* tool is used to extract semantic data from video clips (Fig. 3). Our semantic video hierarchy contains three levels: *video, sequence* and *scene. Videos* consist of *sequences* and *sequences* contain *scenes* that need not be consecutive in time. With this semantic data model, we plan to answer *video, event/activity* and *object* queries. *Video* queries can be based on title, length, producer, production year, category etc. *Event/activity* queries can be used to retrieve videos by specifying events that occur at semantic layer *sequence* because events are associated with sequences. *Object* queries are used to retrieve videos by specifying semantic object features. As videos are annotated, video salient objects are also associated with annotations.

2.3 Web-Based User Interface

BilVideo can handle multiple requests over the Internet through a graphical query interface.

Spatial Query Specification: Spatial content of a keyframe is the relative positioning of its salient objects with respect to each other. This relative positioning consists of *directional*, *topological* and *3D-relations*. In the spatial query specification window (Fig. 4), objects are sketched by rectangles representing MBRs of the objects. Similar to the database population phase, the directional and topological relations between objects are extracted automatically in the query specification phase. Since it is not possible to extract 3D-relations from 2D-data, users are guided to select appropriate 3D-relations.

Trajectory Query Specification: Trajectory of a salient object is described as a path of vertices corresponding to the locations of the object in different video frames. Displacement values and directions between consecutive frames (vertices) are used in defining the *trajectory* fact of an object. In the trajectory query specification window, users can draw trajectories of objects (Fig. 5). Object-trajectory queries are similarity-based; therefore, users specify a similarity value between 0 and 100.

Semantic Query Specification: The semantic query specification interface (Fig. 6) currently supports three types of semantic queries, which are *event*, *object* and *metadata* queries. In an event query, user can specify three item types: the event itself, a sub-event that occurs in this event, and the objects appearing in this event or in a sub-event of it. Object queries are used for specifying the attributes of the objects. A semantic query for the BBC news video that we used is as follows:

Query 1: *"Retrieve all news videos produced in year 2003 that has a `USA - CHINA Meeting' event in which one of the attendees `James Kelly', the US assist. Secr. of state, is giving a press conference behind microphones."*

```
select video
from all
where meta(vtype:news and pyear:2003) and
    etype:`USA - CHINA Meeting' with
        (`James Kelly':role = attendee and
         setype:`Press Conference') and
    odata(`James Kelly' (Title:`US Assistant
         Secretary of State')) and
    behind(`James Kelly',Microphones);
```

Some of the data used for specifying the query are retrieved from the database to guide the user for entering a valid query. Such data include video name and attributes, event and subevent types, and object attributes.

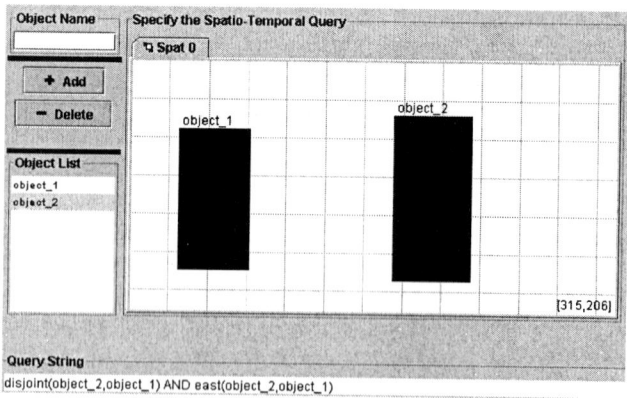

Figure 4: Spatial Query Formulation.

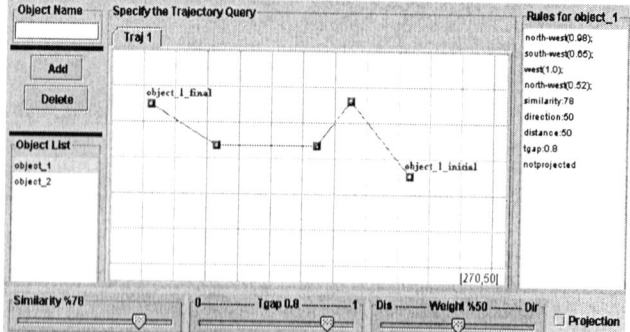

Figure 5: Trajectory Query Specification.

3. Example: News Archives Search System

In this section, we present an application, *news archives search system*, for BilVideo. A news archives search system contains video clips of news broadcasts and is used to retrieve specific news fragments based on some descriptions given as query conditions. The traditional approach for accomplishing this task is to provide some keywords that would describe the semantic content of the news fragments for retrieval. For this, a traditional database system would suffice since news fragments are indexed by some textual data. However, spatio-temporal relations between objects and object trajectories are not considered. BilVideo fills up this gap by providing support for spatio-temporal and semantic video queries. Users may also query news archives by some specific application-dependent external predicates that they define (see Query 2). For Query 2 and 3, we have used two sample news video clip fragments captured from BBC News and Kanal D (a Turkish TV channel).

Query 2: *"Retrieve the segments from the news clips, where James Kelly and his assistant appear together alone (no other object of interest is in the scene) and Kelly is to the right of his assistant."*

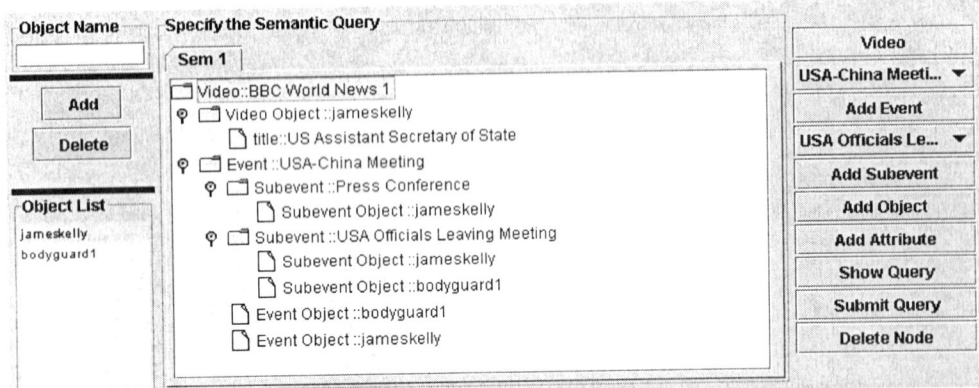

Figure 6: Semantic Query Specification.

```
select segment from vid
where appear_alone(james_kelly, assistant1)
      and right(james_kelly, assistant1);
```

In this query, *appear_alone/2* is an external (application-dependent) predicate. It is used to search for video keyframes, where the only objects appearing are those specified. The predicate *right/2* is a directional predicate. *Vid* is a unique video identifier assigned to a video clip.

Query 3: *"Retrieve the segments from the sample news clip, where James Kelly moves west together with two security guards on his right and left, given a similarity threshold 0.8 and an allowed time gap 1 second."*

```
select segment from vid
where (tr(james_kelly, [[west]]) sthreshold 0.8
       tgap 1) repeat
      and    right(james_kelly, securityguard1)
      and left(james_kelly, securityguard2);
```

In this query, a similarity-based trajectory condition is given, along with directional and topological conditions. The keywords *tgap* and *repeat* are used to specify the trajectory conditions, which ensure that all the segments in the clip satisfying the given conditions are returned.

4. Conclusion

BilVideo does not target a specific application, and thus, it can be used to support any application, where vast amount of video data needs to be searched by spatio-temporal and semantic queries. Moreover, the query language of BilVideo provides a simple way to extend the system's query capabilities through *external predicates*, which makes the system application-independent but yet easily fine-tunable for specific needs of such applications without much effort and any loss in performance at all. This can be achieved by adding to the knowledge-base some application-dependent rules and/or facts that will be used for queries. In this article, we presented an example application of BilVideo; *news archives search system*. Among other applications that may be supported by BilVideo are sports event analysis systems (soccer, basketball, etc.), object movement tracking systems (medical, biological, astrophysical, etc.) and video archive search systems (movie retrieval, digital libraries, etc.).

5. Current Status Of BilVideo

We have already implemented the Query Processor and Web-based User Interface as well as the Fact-Extractor and Video-Annotator tools. We have also developed the knowledge-base of the system. Our work on semantic query execution and query-by-low-level-properties (color, shape, and texture) is ongoing. We are currently working on the integration of the Web-based query interface and the query processor. Tutorial video clips demonstrating the query interface and the tools of BilVideo are available at *http://www.cs.bilkent.edu.tr/~oulusoy/BilVideo/*.

6. Acknowledgements

This work was supported by Scientific and Technical Research Council of Turkey (TUBITAK) under the grant number EEEAG-199E025, and is supported in part by Turkish State Planning Organization (DPT) under grant number 2004K120720, and European Commission 6th Framework Program MUSCLE Network of Excellence Project with grant number FP6-507752.

7. Related Publications

[1]. M.E. Dönderler, E. Şaykol, U. Arslan, Ö. Ulusoy, U. Güdükbay, BilVideo: Design and Implementation of a Video Database Management System, to appear in Multimedia Tools and Applications.

[2]. M.E. Dönderler, E. Şaykol, Ö. Ulusoy, U. Güdükbay, BilVideo: A Video Database Management System, IEEE Multimedia, Vol.10, No.1, pp. 66-70, 2003.

[3]. M.E. Dönderler, Ö. Ulusoy and U. Güdükbay, A rule-based video database system architecture, Info. Sci., Vol. 143, No. 1-4, pp. 13-45, 2002.

[4]. M.E. Dönderler, Ö. Ulusoy and U. Güdükbay, Rule-based spatio-temporal query processing for video databases, VLDB Journal, Vol.13, No.1, pp. 86-103, 2004.

PLACE: A Query Processor for Handling Real-time Spatio-temporal Data Streams*

Mohamed F. Mokbel   Xiaopeng Xiong   Walid G. Aref   Susanne E. Hambrusch
Sunil Prabhakar   Moustafa A. Hammad

Department of Computer Sciences, Purdue University, West Lafayette, IN 47907-1398
{mokbel,xxiong,aref,seh,sunil,mhammad}@cs.purdue.edu

Abstract

The emergence of location-aware services calls for new real-time spatio-temporal query processing algorithms that deal with large numbers of mobile objects and queries. In this demo, we present PLACE (*Pervasive Location-Aware Computing Environments*); a scalable location-aware database server developed at Purdue University. The PLACE server addresses scalability by adopting an *incremental* evaluation mechanism for answering concurrently executing continuous spatio-temporal queries. The PLACE server supports a wide variety of stationery and moving continuous spatio-temporal queries through a set of pipelined spatio-temporal operators. The large numbers of moving objects generate real-time spatio-temporal data streams.

1 Introduction

Combining the functionalities of personal locator technologies, global positioning systems (GPSs), wireless and cellular telephone technologies, and information technologies enables new environments where virtually all objects of interest can determine their locations. These technologies are the foundation for pervasive location-aware environments and services. Such services have the potential to improve the quality of life by adding location-awareness to virtually all objects of interest such as humans, cars, laptops, eyeglasses, canes, desktops, pets, wild animals, bicycles, and buildings.

By enabling an upward link, the data sent from the mobile objects to the servers enables an environment in which objects are aware of the locations of surrounding objects as well as other related information. Applications can range from locating lost or stolen objects, to tracking little children and alerting parents when their children step out of the backyard, and completely automating traffic and vehicle navigation systems.

In this demo, we present the PLACE server, developed at Purdue University [1]. The PLACE server employs special query processing techniques to support scalable and incremental evaluation of a wide variety of continuous spatio-temporal queries. In particular, the PLACE server has the following distinguishing characteristics:

1. **Scalability.** The PLACE server uses a *shared execution* paradigm as a means for achieving scalability in terms of the number of outstanding continuous spatio-temporal queries.

2. **Incremental evaluation.** The PLACE server employs an *incremental* evaluation paradigm by continuously updating the user with any change to the query answer by using the notion of *positive* and *negative* tuples.

3. **New operators.** The PLACE server employs a new set of spatio-temporal incremental operators (e.g., INSIDE and kNN operators) that support scalable and incremental evaluation of continuous queries through SQL.

4. **Wide variety of continuous queries.** By encapsulating the scalable and incremental algorithms into physical pipelined query operators, the PLACE server has the ability to express and evaluate a wide variety of continuous spatio-temporal queries.

---
*This work was supported in part by the National Science Foundation under Grants IIS-0093116, EIA-9972883, IIS-9974255, IIS-0209120, 0010044-CCR, and EIA-9983249.

Permission to copy without fee all or part of this material is granted provided that the copies are not made or distributed for direct commercial advantage, the VLDB copyright notice and the title of the publication and its date appear, and notice is given that copying is by permission of the Very Large Data Base Endowment. To copy otherwise, or to republish, requires a fee and/or special permission from the Endowment.
**Proceedings of the 30th VLDB Conference,
Toronto, Canada, 2004**

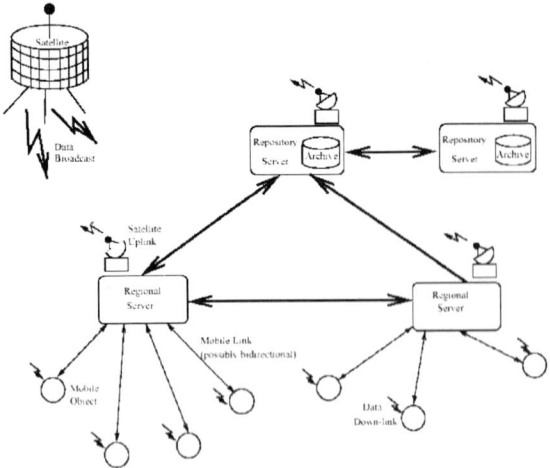

Figure 1: The PLACE Architecture.

5. **Predicate-based Sliding Windows**: We extend the notion of sliding windows beyond time-based and tuple-count windows to accommodate for predicate-based windows (e.g., an object expires from the window when it appears again in the stream).

2 The PLACE Architecture

Figure 1 sketches a hierarchical architecture of the PLACE server. Location detection devices (e.g., GPS devices) provide the objects with their geographic locations. Objects connect directly to regional servers that form the lowest level in this hierarchy. Regional servers handle the incoming data and process time-critical spatio-temporal queries. Regional servers communicate with each other, as well as with the high level servers i.e., the repository servers. Repository servers archive the past locations of moving objects.

The servers are interconnected by high bandwidth links. However, the mobile links between the regional servers and the objects have low bandwidth and a high cost per connection. For data that is being sent from the moving objects to the regional servers (i.e., in the uplink direction), we regulate the amount of data collected and the rate at which data is sent (the *upload frequency*). For query results and other data being sent from the location-aware regional servers to the objects (i.e., the downlink direction), an alternative to the point-to-point mobile links is allowed. Servers can transmit data to a satellite that broadcasts the information over the air to all objects. Broadcasting allows a server to send data to a large number of *listening* objects [4].

3 Shared Execution of Continuous Spatio-temporal Queries

The PLACE server [8, 9, 10, 12] exploits a *shared execution* paradigm as a means for achieving scala-

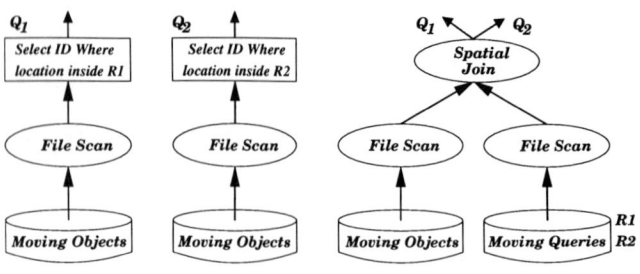

Figure 2: Shared execution of continuous queries.

bility when concurrently executing continuous spatio-temporal queries. The main idea is to group similar queries in a query table. Then, the evaluation of a set of continuous spatio-temporal queries is abstracted as a spatial join between the moving objects and the moving queries. Similar ideas of shared execution have been exploited in the NiagaraCQ [3] for web queries, PSoup [2], and [6] for streaming queries.

Figure 2a gives the execution plans of two simple continuous spatio-temporal queries, Q_1: "Find the objects inside region R_1", and Q_2: "Find the objects inside region R_2". Each query performs a file scan on the moving object table followed by a selection filter. With *shared execution*, we have the execution plan of Figure 2b. The table for moving queries contains the regions of the range queries. Then, a spatial join is performed between the table of objects (points) and the table of queries (regions). The output of the spatial join is split and is sent to the individual queries.

Shared execution for a collection of spatio-temporal range queries can be expressed in the PLACE server by issuing the following continuous query:

SELECT Q.ID, O.ID
FROM QueryTable Q, ObjectTable O
WHERE O.location inside Q.region

The query processor recognizes that both the object and query tables are being updated continuously by the newly incoming objects and queries. Thus, the query is executed continuously.

4 Incremental Execution

The PLACE server employs an *incremental* execution paradigm [8, 10], where only the updates of the previously reported answer are sent to the user. We distinguish between two types of updates, namely *positive* and *negative* updates. Positive/Negative updates indicate that a certain object needs to be added to/removed from the previously reported answer, respectively. By employing *incremental evaluation*, the PLACE server achieves the following goals: (1) Fast query evaluation, since we compute only the update (change) of the answer not the whole answer. (2) In a typical location-aware server query results are sent to the users via satellite servers [4]. Thus, limiting the amount of transmitted data to the positive and negative updates only rather than the whole query answer saves in network bandwidth. (3) When encapsulating incremental algorithms into physical pipelined query operators, limiting the tuples that go through the whole query pipeline to only the *positive* and *negative* updates reduces the flow in the pipeline. Thus, efficient query processing is achieved.

In the demo, we will show how the users and query operators interpret the *positive* and *negative* updates to continuously maintain the query results.

5 Spatio-temporal Pipelined Operators

The PLACE server encapsulates scalable and incremental algorithms into pipelined query operators. Examples of such operators are the *INSIDE* operator for range queries and the *k*NN operator for *k*-nearest-neighbor queries. Such operators can represent both stationary and moving queries. In addition spatio-temporal queries may have a time window that allows querying recent history. A typical continuous query for the PLACE server may have the following form:

```
SELECT select_clause
FROM from_clause
WHERE where_clause
INSIDE inside_clause
kNN knn_clause
WINDOW window_clause
```

The *inside_clause* can represent stationary rectangular range or circular queries by specifying the two corners or the center and radius of the query region, respectively. If the first parameter to the *inside_clause* is M, then the query is moving and the second parameter represents the ID of the *focal* object of the query. Similarly, the *knn_clause* can represent stationary as well as moving *k*-nearest-neighbor queries. The *window_clause* allows having sliding window queries [5].

Incremental pipelined query operators may output *positive* or *negative* tuples. Thus, we furnish the rest of the query operators (e.g., aggregate, distinct, and joins) with special mechanisms to interpret the *negative* tuples.

6 Spatio-temporal Queries

By having the basic spatio-temporal operators, the PLACE server has the ability to evaluate a wide variety of continuous spatio-temporal queries. The following are some examples that are typical in the PLACE server:

Example I: Spatio-temporal aggregates. *Continuously, report the number of distinct cars that are inside a certain area*

```
SELECT COUNT (DISTINCT (M.ID)
FROM MovingVehicles M
WHERE M.type = "Car"
INSIDE 20,20,30,30
```

Example II: Catching speedy moving objects. *Continuously, report any car that passes through area R_2 then area R_1 in less than five minutes. Such query can catch speedy cars that go very fast from area R_2 to area R_1.*

```
SELECT DISTINCT M1.ID
FROM (SELECT ID
      FROM MovingObjects
      INSIDE R_1) M1,
     (SELECT ID
      FROM MovingObjects
      INSIDE R_2
      WINDOW 5) M2
WHERE M1.ID = M2.ID
```

7 Demo Description

The PLACE server is implemented on top of the NILE query processor [7]; an extended version of the PREDATOR database management system [11] to handle stream data. Figures 3 and 4 give snapshots of the client and server graphical user interface (GUI) of PLACE[1].

The PLACE server GUI (Figure 3) is for the purpose of administration at the server side. The main idea is to keep track of the concurrently executing continuous queries from each type. All the processed queries along with their parameters are displayed in the bottom of the screen. In addition, the server GUI contains a regional map showing the movement of objects, and the parameters of the selected queries.

Client GUI (Figure 4) simulates a client end device used by the users. Users can choose the type of query from a list of available query types. The spatial region of the query can be determined using the map of the area of interest (the bold plotted rectangle on the map). Once the query is submitted to the server, the result appears to the query as a drop-down list at the bottom of Figure 4. A client can send multiple queries of different types to the PLACE server.

References

[1] W. G. Aref, S. E. Hambrusch, and S. Prabhakar. Pervasive Location Aware Computing Environments (PLACE). http://www.cs.purdue.edu/place/, 2003.

[2] S. Chandrasekaran and M. J. Franklin. Streaming Queries over Streaming Data. In *VLDB*, 2002.

[3] J. Chen, D. J. DeWitt, F. Tian, and Y. Wang. NiagaraCQ: A Scalable Continuous Query System for Internet Databases. In *SIGMOD*, 2000.

---
[1]The map in Figures 3 and 4 is for the Greater Lafayette area, IN, USA.

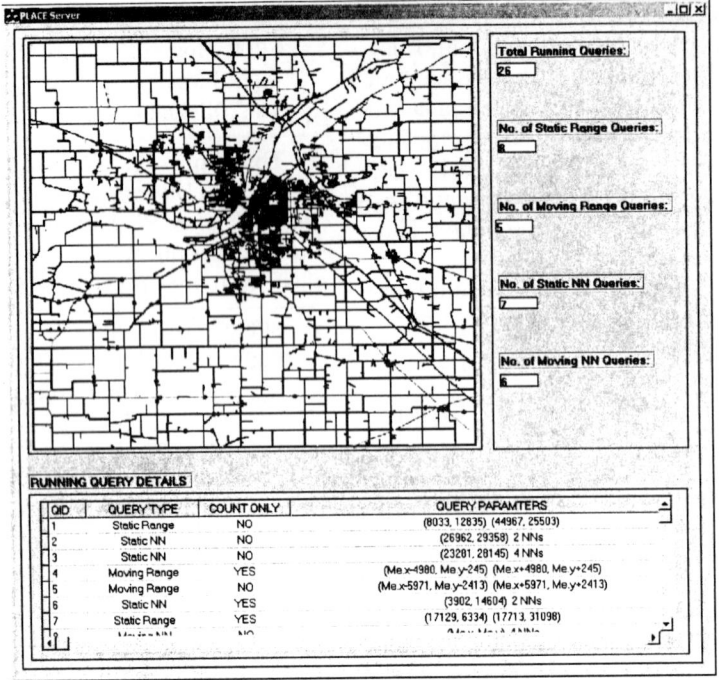

Figure 3: Snapshot of the PLACE server.

[4] S. E. Hambrusch, C.-M. Liu, W. G. Aref, and S. Prabhakar. Query Processing in Broadcasted Spatial Index Trees. In *SSTD*, 2001.

[5] M. A. Hammad, W. G. Aref, M. J. Franklin, M. F. Mokbel, and A. K. Elmagarmid. Efficient execution of sliding-window queries over data streams. Technical Report TR CSD-03-035, Purdue University Department of Computer Sciences, Dec. 2003.

[6] M. A. Hammad, M. J. Franklin, W. G. Aref, and A. K. Elmagarmid. Scheduling for shared window joins over data streams. In *VLDB*, 2003.

[7] M. A. Hammad, M. F. Mokbel, M. H. Ali, W. G. Aref, A. C. Catlin, A. K. Elmagarmid, M. Eltabakh, M. G. Elfeky, T. M. Ghanem, R. Gwadera, I. F. Ilyas, M. Marzouk, and X. Xiong. Nile: A Query Processing Engine for Data Streams. In *ICDE*, 2004.

[8] M. F. Mokbel. Continuous Query Processing in Spatio-temporal Databases. In *Proceedings of the ICDE/EDBT PhD Workshop*, 2004.

[9] M. F. Mokbel, W. G. Aref, S. E. Hambrusch, and S. Prabhakar. Towards Scalable Location-aware Services: Requirements and Research Issues. In *GIS*, 2003.

[10] M. F. Mokbel, X. Xiong, and W. G. Aref. SINA: Scalable Incremental Processing of Continuous Queries in Spatio-temporal Databases. In *SIGMOD*, 2004.

[11] P. Seshadri. Predator: A resource for database research. *SIGMOD Record*, 27(1):16–20, 1998.

[12] X. Xiong, M. F. Mokbel, W. G. Aref, S. Hambrusch, and S. Prabhakar. Scalable Spatio-temporal Continuous Query Processing for Location-aware Services. In *SSDBM*, June 2004.

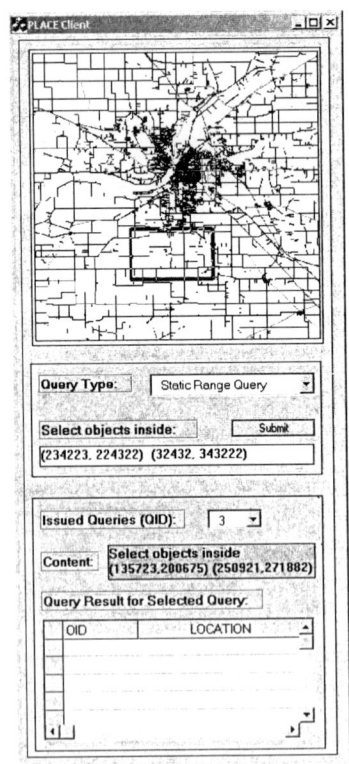

Figure 4: Snapshot of a client of the PLACE server.